THE

PROVINCE OF ONTARIO

GAZETTEER AND DIRECTORY,

CONTAINING

CONCISE DESCRIPTIONS OF

CITIES, TOWNS AND VILLAGES IN THE PROVINCE,

WITH THE

NAMES OF PROFESSIONAL AND BUSINESS MEN

AND PRINCIPAL INHABITANTS,

TOGETHER WITH A FULL LIST OF

MEMBERS OF THE EXECUTIVE GOVERNMENTS, SENATORS, MEMBERS OF THE COMMONS AND LOCAL LEGISLATURES, AND OFFICIALS OF THE DOMINION,

AND A LARGE AMOUNT OF OTHER

GENERAL, VARIED AND USEFUL INFORMATION,

Carefully Compiled from the most recent and Authentic data.

C. E. ANDERSON & CO.,

PROPRIETORS.

H. McEVOY, Editor and Compiler.

TORONTO:

ROBERTSON & COOK, PUBLISHERS,

DAILY TELEGRAPH PRINTING HOUSE (DIRECTORY BRANCH.)

1869.

PREFACE.

The present edition of the Gazetteer and Directory of the Province of Ontario, is presented to the public with the hope that the publishers have been successful in compiling a work which will supply a want long felt by all classes of the community.

The production of a work of this nature necessarily requires an immense amount of labour and research. And the publishers beg to assure their patrons that every exertion on their part has been made to secure accuracy, and to render the work full and complete in all its details. The information is of the latest that could be obtained, and the varied and complete contents of the appendix will doubtless prove of great value.

The publishers have great pleasure in returning their sincere thanks to the numerous friends who have so kindly assisted them by providing information of the greatest value. To the several Postmasters they particularly wish to acknowledge their indebtedness.

THE PUBLISHERS

CONTENTS.

GENERAL INDEX

TO

CITIES, TOWNS, VILLAGES AND POST OFFICES IN ONTARIO.

INDEX TO ADVERTISEMENTS.

N. B.—The Alphabetical Order of places has, in a few instances, been slightly interrupted to avoid the division of a short list of names. A reference, however, to the General Index, will prevent the least delay in finding any place in the work.

PROVINCE OF ONTARIO

GAZETTEER AND DIRECTORY,

1869.

C. E. ANDERSON & CO.,

PUBLISHERS,

DIRECTORY BRANCH OF THE DAILY TELEGRAPH PRINTING HOUSE.

NOTE.—Villages received too late for regular insertion, will be found in the Addenda, at the end of this work.

Aberarder.—A Village on the Grand Trunk Railway and Moffatt's Creek, in the Township of Plympton, County, Lambton. Distant from County Town, 20 miles. Average price of land $10 to $25. Population, 50.

Adams, Robert, cabinet-maker.
Bell, Thos., wagon-maker.
Brown, John, farmer.
Cairns, Helen, dressmaker.
Cairns, James, farmer.
Cairns, Rachel, dressmaker.
Cairns, R., tailor.
Covan, R. S., teacher.
Hamilton, Alexander, carpenter.
Hamilton, John, carpenter.
Harvey, Joseph, farmer.
Jardine, Robert, farmer.
Lowrie, James, farmer.
McBEAN, D., Post master and general merchant.
McKinlay, Donald, farmer.
May, Frederick, butcher.
Moffatt, James, farmer.
Simpson, John, shoemaker.
Smith, Finlay, farmer.
Stirret, George, weaver.
Taylor, Archibald, farmer.
Watson, David, tailor.
Wheelet, Elijah, brick-maker,
Wilkinson, Archibald, farmer.

Aberfoyle.—A village in the Township of Puslinch, County Wellington. Distance from County Town 7 miles, and from Toronto 54 miles. Stages to Guelph and Hamilton. Average price of land $20. Population, 100.

Beattie, Wm., teacher.
Black, John, farmer.
Couzens, C., shoemaker.
FALCONBRIDGE, S., Postmaster.
Fleming, R., prop. Anglo-American Hotel.
Grant, Joseph, farmer.
Hammersley, J., J.P.
Ingram, Thomas, auctioneer.
Johnston, B., prop. Johnston's Hotel.
Little, R., carpenter.
Little, Thos., butcher.
McBeath, Malcolm, farmer.
McDonald, Rev. K., (Presbyterian.)
McIntosh, James, tailor.
McIntyre & McGibbon, wagon makers.
McLaren. Peter, teacher.
McLean, George, miller.
McLeod, R., shoemaker.
Miller, William, cabinet maker.
Smith, A., J.P.
Smith, Joseph, carpenter.
Weir, Andrew, teacher.

Abingdon.—A village in the Township of Caistor, County Lincoln, 28 miles from St. Catherines, and 60 from Toronto. Population, 50.

Asher, James, brickmaker.
Benson, Rev. M., (Methodist.)
Black, David, blacksmith.
Chesney, Rev. Mr., (Baptist).
Cheyne, Rev. George.
Clelland, W. L., wagon maker.
Cobley, James, blacksmith.
Culp & Spence, potters.
Greer, A. M., lumber merchant.
Haney, R. A., M.D.
Harmon, Lawrence, cooper.
Horne, James, hotel.
Hughson, J. L., hotel.
Jackson & Vandusen, carpenters.
Jackson, John, blacksmith.
Johnson, J., general merchant.
McCaster, John.
McIntosh, Colin, attorney.
McIntosh, Jo n, cabinet maker.
Miller, John, general merchant.
Park, James, J.P.
PEARSON, THOMAS, Postmaster.
Smith, Thomas, grist miller.
Waites, John.

Acton.—A station on the Grand Trunk Railway, in the Township of Esquesing, County Halton, containing 2 flour mills, 4 saw mills, 2 shingle factories, 1 planing mill, 1 tannery, 1 foundry, 1 cloth factory, 4 churches, 1 common school, 3 hotels. The principal trade is in grain, lumber, cordwood, leather and hops. Land averages from $28 to $35 per acre. Distant from County Town 11 miles, from Toronto, 30 miles, and from Guelph, 14 miles. Money order office. Daily mail. Population, 700.

Adams, Ransom, broker.
Ahern, John, express agent and station master.
Allan, John, hop grower.
Baird, H. A., dentist.
BEARDMORE, G. L. & CO., tanners.
Bell James, lime manufacturer.
Bell, Wm., prop. Rossin House.
Brown, Alexander.
Brown, James, shingle maker.
Burrows, Jeremiah, shoemaker.
Cameron, Hugh, carpenter.
Cameron, Miss Isabella, teacher.
CAMERON, JAMES.
Cameron, John, carpenter.
Cameron, Rev. Lachlan, (Presbyterian.)
Chapman, J. J., dentist.
CLARK, THOMAS, prop. Royal Exchange Hotel (see adv.)
Coats, F. D., cooper.
Coats, John, cooper.
Collins, Joseph.
Cook, Rev. R. B., (Baptist.)
Cooper, Alexander, painter.
Dempsey, J., tanner.
Dempsey, Mrs., dressmaker.
Dixon, Adam, tailor.
Ebbage, Thomas, painter.
Firstbrook, William, lumber dealer.
Fraser, James, bailiff.
Freeman, A. H. & Co., druggists.
Fulljames, Thomas, carpenter.
Grant, Alexander, shoemaker.
Grant, William, wagon maker.
Hall, Asa.
Hamilton, Richard, carpenter.
Hannah, John, baker.
Hewer, John, tanner.
Hill, Chrles J, general merchant.
Hume, Thomas, councillor.
Jeffers, Rev. Thomas, (Wesleyan Methodist.)
Kennedy, Mrs., hop grower.
LESLIE, GEORGE & CO., general merchants.
Lighthart, John, cooper.
Lindsay, James, councillor.
Little, Robert, teacher.
Livingston, Daniel, carpenter.
Lozier, Oliver plasterer
McBain, John, general merchant.
McEnery, William, councillor.
McGarvin, Nelson, physician.
McGregor, Peter, J. P.
McKee, John, general merchant.
McNaughton, John.
Maloney, David, shoemaker.
Mann, Alexander.
Mann, Hugh, hop grower.
Marshall, Miss, dressmaker.
Marshall, Thomas, shoemaker.
Matthews, Abraham.
Matthews, George, butcher.
MATTHEWS JAMES, Postmaster, Clerk Div. Court, Telegraph Office, Commissioner in B. R., Issuer of Marriage Licenses, Insurance agent, &c.
Milburn, Thomas, & Co., druggists.
Moore Bros., shingle makers.
Morrow, Robert, physician.
Nicklin, B. & E., millers.
O'Haran, John, station master, G. T. R.
Pearin, Rev. James, (Wesleyan Methodist.)
Scott, James, miller.
SECORD, S. A., general merchant.
Sharp, Wm. & Co., lumber dealers.
SLINGERLAND, FRANCIS.
Smith, C. S. & J. H., planing mill.
SMITH, SIDNEY, lumber dealer and hop grower.
Snyder, Eli, carpenter.
Spaight, John, wagon maker.
Spaight, Michael, wagon maker.
Stafford, Sumner, potash manufacturer.
Stauffer, Abraham, lime manufacturer.
Steel, George, carpenter.
Steel, Miss, dressmaker.
Stone, Richard, tanner.
Storey, Wm. H., saddler.
Symon, Charles, J. P.
Symon, C. & J., general merchants & lumber dealers.
Vanallan Charles, tailor.
Ward, James, proprietor California House.
Warren, John, councillor.
Webler, William, miller.
Weiger, Charles, tinsmith.

Adare.—A Village in the Township of McGillivray, County Middlesex. Distant from County Town 23 miles, from Toronto 137 miles. Average price of land $40 to $60. Population 70.

Berryfield, S., carpenter.
Diamond, William, miller.
Elliott, Miss Matilda, teacher.
Fitzgerald, Gerald, saddler.
Hicks, Samuel, teacher.
Kilgallin, P. proprietor Adare House.
LEVETT, MRS. AGNES, Postmistress.
Lewis, Wm., jr.
McGee, J. proprietor Farmer's Rest.
McNamee, J. & W. woolen factors.
McNamee, R. J., shoemaker.
Maguire James, jr., wagon maker.
Maguire, J. carpenter.
Maguire, Wm., carpenter.
Quarry, H. B., general merchant.
Regan, Miss M., teacher.
Thompson, J., carpenter.
Thompson, Miss M., dressmaker.
Thompson, R., carpenter.
Winter, Rev., (Presbyterian.)

Addison.—A Village in the Township of Elizabethtown and County of Leeds. Distant from Brockville the County Town 12 miles, and from Perth 33 miles; daily mail. Population about 200.

LEWIS, COLEMAN, Postmaster and general merchant.

Adelaide.—A Village situated on the Sarnia branch of the Great Western Railway, in the Township of Adelaide, County Middlesex, 25 miles from London and 36 from Sarnia. Population 100. Money order office.

HOARE, JOHN S., Postmaster, and J. P.

Admaston.—A Village in the Township of Admaston, County Renfrew, distant from County Town 30 miles, from Toronto 300 miles, stages to Renfrew and Douglas. Average price of wild land $1 to $4, improved $8. Population 160.

Allen, John, weaver.
Bain, Alexander, weaver.
Bain, James, weaver.
Black, William, wagon maker.
Bolger, Martin, carpenter.
Brown, Alexander, farmer.
Brown, George, sen., carpenter.
Brown, James, cooper.
Burlangett, George, teacher.
Campbell, John, sen., J. P.
Campbell, Peter, sen., shoemaker.
Cardiff, George, farmer.
Cardiff, Richard, farmer.
Cherry, W. H., weaver,
Connolly, Thomas, cooper.
Farquharson, David, carpenter.
Felion, Vital, blacksmith.
Foley, John, carpenter.
Gillan, John, carpenter.
Gorman, John, general merchant.
Gorman, Patrick, J. P.
Gorman, Simon, hotel keeper.
Graham, David, farmer.
Hartnett, John, blacksmith.
Hudson, Charles, proprietor Shamrock hotel.
Lamont, Helen, teacher.
Lyons, Thomas, teacher.
McCormick, William, tailor.
McDougall, Mrs. A., hotel keeper.
McDougall, Mrs. S., hotel keeper.
McDougall, W. & A., grocers.
McGee, James, shoemaker.
PATTERSON, MISS JANE, Postmistress.
Reid, Ephraim, woolen factor.
Reid, Robert, weaver.
Sellar, Alexander, carpenter.
Walker, Rev., F. H., (Wesleyan.)
Wilson, Matthew, shoemaker.

Adolphustown.—A station on the Grand Trunk Railway and shore of Bay of Quinte, in the Township of Adolphustown, County of Lennox. The principal trade is in grain, stock and cordwood. Land averages from $30 to $40 per acre. Distant from County Town 16 miles, and from Kingston 30 miles. Daily mail. Population 100.

Allen, Parker, J. P.
Allison, Joseph B.
Baker, James, butcher.
Bartlett, Francis, architect and builder.
Bogert, M. C., councillor.
Cutlett, C. J., clerk.
Curlett, E. H.
Daverne, R, councillor.
Davis, P. D. councillor.
Dorland, Paul J. auctioneer.
Dorland, Philip
Evans, Dr.
Gibb, Thos. F., P. L. S.
Haight, D., treasurer.
Harding, Rev. R., (Church of England.)
Hart, James, wagon maker.
Hawley, Samuel
Johnston, Samuel, shoemaker.
Loynes, James, carpenter.
Ogden, J. D., teacher.
Outwater, John, J. P.
Penner, Chas., J. P.
Platt, B. & P., farmers.
Poole, A. W., proprietor Adolphustown Hotel.
Ruttan, E., councillor.
Sweetman, Capt. W. H.
Trampour, Paul
Trampour, S. W.
WATSON, J. J., Postmaster and general merchant.

Agincourt.—A post Village in the Township of Scarboro, County York. Distant from Toronto 18 miles, and from Markham 7 miles. Daily mail. Population 40.

Fletcher, Rev. D. H., (Presbyterian.)
Irving, William, teacher.
MILNE, JOHN, Postmaster and general merchant.

Ailsa Craig.—An important Village and Station of the Grand Trunk Railway, situated on the Sauble River, in the Townships of McGillivray and East Williams, County Middlesex, 42 miles from London by rail and 24 by road; from Park Hill 7, Lucan 7 and Carlisle 3. The surrounding country is unsurpassed for its fertility, and an extensive and increasing business is done in the exportation of grain, lumber, stoves, etc. Money order office. Population, 500.

AILSA CRAIG HOTEL, A. Munro, proprietor.
Alexander, Charles, carriage maker.
Armstrong, Robert, shoemaker.
ATKINSON, W. K. & CO., general merchants and manufacturers boots and shoes.
BELCH, ALEXANDER, editor and prop. North Middlesex *Review;* books and stationery.
Blackwell, Thomas, telegraph operator.
Boles, L. C., hotel.
Bruce, Adam, section superintendent G. T. R.
Christopherson, Rev. Hall, (Wesleyan).
Coulter, Andrew, hotel.
Crawford, William, cooper.
Cusick, C., hotel.
ESSERY, CAMPBELL & JOHNSTON, flour mills.
Evans, John, baker.
GOODFELLOW, THOMAS, tinsmith
Harcus, George, builder.
Harrison, James, tailor.
Henderson, Donald, M.D., druggist.
HERSEY, S. C., produce merchant.
Hey, Thomas, drugs and groceries.
Hughes, John, general merchant.
Jamieson, Alexander, blacksmith.
Kinsman, H., dentist.
Long, Joshua, cooper.
Longstaff, J. C., hotel.
McAlpine, Duncan, carpenter.
McAlpine, John, carpenter.
McBRIDE, M., boots and shoes. (See adv.)
McDonald, Roland, general merchant.
McIntosh, William, planing mill.
McKinnon, Angus, M.D.
Martin, J. J., bricklayer.
Mihell, George A., general merchant.
MUMFORD, E. A., station agent.
MUNRO, A., proprietor Ailsa Craig Hotel.
Munro, Hector, carpenter.
NEVILLS, T. G. S., groceries, wines and liquors.
NORTH MIDDLESEX REVIEW, Alex. J. Belch, proprietor.
Prangley, E., wagon maker.
Price, Thomas H., general merchant.
Priestley, John W., produce and lumber.
Priestley, Thomas C., bailiff.
RANTON, JOHN & JAMES, general merchants.
Revington, Joseph, saddler.
Sherwin, William, cabinetmaker.
Shoff, Dennis, general merchant.
Smith, J. S., M.P.P.
Sweeney, John, grocer.
Weber, Albin, merchant tailor.

Ainlayville.—(Dingle P. O.)—A Village situated on the Maitland River, in the Townships of Grey and Morris, County of Huron, 30 miles from Goderich, 95 from Hamilton and 13 from Seaforth Station, G.T.R. Improved land in the neighborhood averages $20 per acre. The river affords excellent manufacturing power. Manufactures of all kinds are required. Population, 600.

Ainlay, Charles, cabinetmaker.
Armstrong, William, hotel.
Beaton, Norman, carpenter.
Bristol, Rev. S., (Wesleyan).
Davidson, J. & J., wagon makers.
Evans, J. R., books and stationery.
Fishleigh & Gerry, cabinetmakers.
Gerry, Benjamin, sash factory.
Graham, A. W., M.D.
Grant, A., carpenter.
Grant, J. R., druggist.
GRANT, WILLIAM, Postmaster.
Hamilton, A., butcher.
Haysett, Rev. S., (Bible Christian).
Holmes, W. G. R., M.D.
Johnson, J. B., dentist.
Jones, Rev. R. S., (Canada Presbyterian).
Kelly Brothers, lime and stone dealers.
Kennedy, J. E. & Co., bakers.
Kerr, Rev. John, (Episcopal).
Kerr, J. W., insurance agent.
Knetchtel, J., leather and findings.
Knetchtel William, saddler.
Knox, T., grocer.
Leckie, John, general merchant.
Leonard, J., hotel.
Livingstone, William, general merchant.
McCormack, John, carpenter.
McLaughlin, James, shoemaker.
McPhail, John, cooper.
Main, A., general merchant.
Morris, S. B., carpenter.
Pearson, S., shoemaker.
Preston, Rev. P., (New Connection Methodist).
Ross, D., tailor.
Smale, S., tailor.
Shelton, James, auctioneer.
Smith, John, R., leather and findings.
Smith Brothers, shingle makers.
Thompson, Peter, carpenter.
Thynne, Alexander, teacher.
Vanstone, William, miller.
West Brothers, general merchants.
Willson, William, wagon maker.
Wright, Charles, butcher.
Wright, G. H., general merchant.

Airey.—(P. O. Aldborough.)—A Village in the Township of Aldborough, County Elgin, 30 miles from St. Thomas. Stages daily to Chatham and St. Thomas. Population, 100.

Beaton, Alexander, shoemaker.
Bolden, John, shoemaker.
Campbell, Duncan, wagon maker.
Campbell, John, carpenter.
CARPENTER, L., Postmaster, estate agent.
Carpenter & McLean, general merchants.
Currie, Rev, Peter, (Presbyterian).
Gray, Angus, tailor.
Groh, Henry, tailor.
Lamont, Dugald, blacksmith.
Lamont, John, blacksmith.
McDiarmid, L., Clerk Division Court.
McIntyre, Duncan, carpenter.
McIntyre, John, carpenter.
McLean, Adam, miller.
Timewell, James, hotel.

Alberton.—A Village in the Township of Ancaster, County Wentworth, 14 miles from Hamilton and 55 from Toronto.

SMITH, S. W., Postmaster.

Albion.—(See Bolton.)—A Post Village on the River Humber, in the Township of Albion, County Peel. Distant from County Town, 16 miles; from Toronto, 28 miles. Money Order office and Savings Bank.

EVANS, GEORGE, Postmaster.

Albury.—A Post Village on the Grand Trunk Railway and shore of Bay of Quinté, in the Township of Ameliasburgh, County of Prince Edward, with a large trade in grain, lumber and cordwood. Land averages from $40 to $50 per acre. Distant from County Town, 24 miles; from Toronto, 106 miles. Population, 150.

Alley, John, cooper.
Alley, Thomas, butcher.
Carrington, William, sash and door manufacturer.
Cunningham, Henry, senr., commission merchant.
Dempsey, Isaac.
Dempsey, Peter, junr., J.P.
Dempsey, P. C., cabinetmaker.
Dempsey, W. R., butcher.
Dempsey, W. T.
Fones, W. A., architect.
Germain, Sarah J., teacher.
Graydon, William, cabinetmaker.
Hunt, Henry B., councillor.
Kemp. N., councillor.
Maxen, Levi, painter.
Onderdonk, John, wagon maker.
Peck, James, senr., shoemaker.
PECK, JAMES H., Postmaster, attorney, insurance agent, nurseryman, etc.
Peck, M. A., dressmaker.
Peck, William, coroner.
Pierson, A.
Pierson, David, broker.
Roblin, George.
Roblin, Philip, councillor.
Sager, Albert, constable.
Sager, George W., saddler.
Sprague, Sylvanus.
Thomson, Rev. James, (Wesleyan).
Vancleaf, Jesse, carpenter.

Aldborough.—(See Airey.)—A Post-office in the Township of Aldborough, County Elgin.

CARPENTER, L., Postmaster.

Aldershott.—(Waterdown Section and Port Flamboro'.)—A Village and Station of the Toronto branch of the Great Western Railway, in the Township of East Flamboro', County Wentworth. 4½ miles from Hamilton and 35 from Toronto.

Baker, Wm., station agent.
Belfour, Peter, wagon maker.
Brown, Alex., J.P., forwarder.
Feeley, Wm., section master.
Hill, A., farmer.
Kenney, James A., hotel.
McMahon, Daniel, blacksmith.
Mosgrove Jared, hotel.
Oliver, Hamilton, Postmaster, hotel.
Orr, Wm., soap maker.
Sinclair, Robt., shoemaker.
Smith, Wm., farmer.
Stock, G., farmer.
Wyatt, H., farmer.

Alderville.—A Post-office in the Township of Alnwick, County Northumberland.

CURTIS, JAMES, Postmaster.

Alexandria.—The Chief Town of the County of Glengary, situated on Loch Garry, in the Township of Lochiel. 293 miles from Toronto. Stages to Lancaster and L'Orignal. Money Order office and Savings Bank. Population, 800.

Chisholm, C. D., clerk 2d Division Court.
Harrison, C., general merchant.
Kerr, C., general merchant.
Kennedy, John, wagon maker.
Le Clair, N. P., M.D.,
McAllister, J. M. prin. grammar school.
McDONALD, A. S., Postmaster, general merchant.
McDonald, Allan, wagon maker.
McDonald, Angus, tailor.
McDonald, D. A., J.P., M.P.P.
McDonald, Duncan, gen. merch't.
McDonald, Hugh, tailor.
McDonald, Mrs., hotel.
McDougall, Alex., tailor.
McGillis, D., hotel.
McKenzie, A., county registrar.
McKenzie, J., hotel.
McKenzie, J. B., auctioneer.
McMaster, John, gen. merchant.
McMillan, Donald, M.D.
McMillan, Mrs. hotel.
McPhee, D. & D., general merchant.
McRae, Donald, wagon maker.
Miller & Campbell, founders.
O'Connor, Rev. J. S., (Roman Catholic).
Simpson, John, general merchant.
Wallis & McPhee, general merchants.

Alfred.—A post Village of the Township of Alfred, County Prescott. Distant 12 miles from L'Orignal.

Brady, Mrs., hotel-keeper.
Brady, Thomas, J.P.
HILL, J., Postmaster and hotel keeper.
Hughes, Humphrey, J.P.
Langlor, L., school teacher.
Lawlor, George, grocer.
McGauveran, Josh, steam saw mill.
Seyers, John, shingle-maker.
Seyers, Oliver, shingle-maker.

Algonquin.—A Post Village situated in the Township of Augusta, County Grenville. Population about 100. WRIGHT, SILAS, Postmaster.

Allanburgh.—A Station on the Welland Railway, and Port on the Welland Canal, in the Township of Thorold, County of Welland. Principal trade, shipping. Average price of land, $30 to $40. Distant from County Town, 7 miles, from Toronto, 85 miles, from Buffalo, N.Y., 30 miles. Daily Mail Population 300.

Allison, John.
Anderson, James, carpenter.
Carr, John, butcher.
Church, Arch.
Dyke, Henry, proprietor Welland House.
Gray, George, butcher.
Harle, George, saddler.
McKenzie, Charles, teacher.
Mussen, Henry, grocer.
Plumsteel, Daniel, carpenter.
RANNIE, JOHN, Postmaster and general merchant.
Smith, Edward, carpenter.
Spencer, Robert, J. P.
Starr, Rev. —, (Wesleyan.)
Taylor, Sylvester, woolen factory.
Tucker, B.
Tucker & Rannie, lumber dealers.
Underhill, Wm., proprietor Black Horse hotel.
Upper, James, proprietor Allanburgh House.
Upper, Joseph, proprietor Upper House.
Upper, Wm., livery stable.
Upper, Willis, carpentar.
Vanalstine, Miles, carpenter.
Vanderburgh, Henry, carpenter.
Wilkerson, Jacob, carpenter.
Williams, James, carpenter.

Allandale Mills.—A Post Village situated on the Indian River, in the Township of Otonabee and County Peterboro', in the neighborhood of Rice Lake. Distant from Peterboro', the County Town, 10 miles. Population about 250.

SHORT, RICHARD J., Postmaster and saw mill proprietor.

Allan Park.—A Post-office Station on the Saugeen River, in the Township of Bentinck, County o Grey, with a good trade in grain and lumber. Land averages $25. Distant from County Town, 34 miles, from Toronto, 90 miles. Daily Mail.

Adlam, George, carpenter.
Bamfud, John, carpenter.
Blakeley, John.
BODDY, THOMAS, Postmaster and gen. merchant.
Brigham, Henry, wagon-maker.
Campbell, Robert.
Chittick, Guy, hotel-keeper.
Cochrane, Alexander.
Collett, Henry.
Cook, Wm.
Devlin, James, carpenter.
Devlin, Thomas, carpenter.
Evans, Rev. W. B., (Episcopal).
Fensom Bros., millers and lumber dealers.
Goodrue, Charles F., general merchant.
Herd, Wm., carpenter.
Hopkins, James.
McDonald, Daniel, councillor,
McKenna, Michael.
Marshall, James.
Stephens, Alex. teacher.
Tyreman, Thomas.
Whiteford. William.
Wilkinson, Robert.

Allendale.—A Village and Station of the Northern Railway, in the Township of Innisfil, County Simcoe, one mile South of Barrie. Money order office. Population, 150.

Boon, John, hotel keeper.
Burns, Edward, mason.
Brooks, Stanley, blacksmith.
Cline, Francis, carpenter.
Culross, Wm., blacksmith.
Durham, John, proprietor saw mill.
Hamlin Ambrose, hotel keeper.
Little, Thomas, hotel keeper.
LITTLE, W. C., M.P.P.
McMahon, James, dry goods.
Milburn, S. J., proprietor of saw mill.
MISCAMPBELL, A., Postmaster.
Myers, Jacob, land agent.
Ross, John, station agent N.R.R.
Sheridan Felix, merchant.
Sheridan, James, merchant.

Allenford.—A Post-office in the Township of Amabel, County Bruce.
SHARP, WM., Postmaster.

Allisonville.—A Village on the Consecon Creek, in the Township of Hillier, County Prince Edward. Distant from the County Town 12 miles, and from Toronto, 100 miles. Average price of land, $30 to $35. Population. 60.

Ainsworth, Henry, farmer.
Ainsworth, Phillip, farmer.
Allison, Cyrus R., proprietor lumber yard.
Benson, David, teacher.
Burr, Wm., farmer.
HICKS, ROYAL C., Postmaster.
McFaul, Nelson, farmer.
Noxon, D., farmer.
Spafford, Samuel, carpenter.
Thomas, A., farmer.
Thorne, Wm., teacher.
Valliere, Peter, farmer.
Vancleny, W. H., carpenter.
William, Daniel J., farmer.

Alliston.—A Village in the Townships of Essa and Tecumseth, County Simcoe, 25 miles from Barri and 60 from Toronto. Stages to Cookstown and Rosemont. Population, 175.

Buyers, Wm., carpenter.
Chaffey, R., M. D.
Crosbie, Aitken & Co., founders.
Dillane, M., wagonmaker.
Drury, T., general merchant.
Edwards, W., hotel.
Fahey P., hotel.
FLETCHER, GEO. P. M., flour mills.
Hands, W., hotel.
Hislop, Rev. J, K., (Canada Presbyterian.)
Keppel, Rev. J. H., (Wesleyan.)
Kinzie, Abel, cabinetmaker.
Madill, John, M. D.
Mawhinney, Wm., saddler.
Rayson, J., general merchant.
Seager, J., general merchant.
Sleightholm & Fletcher, general merchants.
Strachan, John, shoemaker.
Wightman, Adam, blacksmith.

Alloa,—A Post Office in the Township of Chinguacousy, County Peel.
CLARRIDGE, THOMAS, Postmaster.

Alma.—A Post Village situated on the Gravel Road leading to Guelph, at the junction of the Town line of Nichol, Peel, Pilkington, in the County Wellington. Distant from Guelph, the County Town, 18 miles, and from Hamilton 49 miles. Population, 100.

Blakely, Wm.
Cousins, Henry, carpenter.
Cromar, Robert.
Cullum, Crofton, carpenter.
GRAHAM, THOS., Postmaster and gen. merchant.
Johnston, James.
Johnston, Thomas.
McCrae, Robert.
Miller, Henry, cabinetmaker.
Rumble, Henry.
Steele, J. C., hotel proprietor.
Switzer, James.
Tindale, Richard.

Almira.—A Village on the River Rouge, in the Township of Markham, County York, containing 1 flour mill, 1 foundry, 4 churches, 1 common school, &c. The principal trade is in grain, flour, cord-wood, and agricultural implements. Average price of land, $60. Distant from County Town, 24 miles. Daily mail. Population, 75.

Armstrong, E. B., accountant.
Bowman, James, dentist.
BOWMAN, JOHN, Postmaster and miller.
Bruce, John, teacher.
Campbell, Rev. John, (Presbyterian.)
Denison, Thomas.
Doner, John, cooper.
Duncan, Rev. John, (Presbyterian.)
Farmer, Thomas, planing mill.
Gilmour, James, general merchant.
Hayles, Robert, tailor.
Hayles, Robert H., veterinary surgeon.
Hoover, Jacob B., cooper.
McClellan, Rev. John, (Baptist.)
Miller, Elijah, dyer.
Miller, Lyman, woollen factor,
Miller, Mrs. Lyman, dressmaker.
Morrison & Armstrong, iron founders, &c.
Mustard, James.
Mustard, William
Nigh, Jonathan. accountant.
Sinklater, Thos., shoemaker.
Spofford, Alfred.
Spofford, Arthur.
Spofford, William, accountant.
Wideman, Rev. Jacob, (Mennonite.)

Almonte.—A flourishing Village, situated on the Mississippi river, in the Township of Ramsay, County Lanark. Distant from Perth, 26 miles, from Ottawa 35, and from Brockville 35. It is a station of the Brockville and Ottawa Railroad, and possesses first-class water privileges. The woolen goods factory of Messrs. B. & W. Rosamond, are among the most extensive in the Dominion. Money order office and Savings Bank. Population 2,000.

Ackland, Dudley, wagonmaker.
Acton, Nassau, shoemaker.
Aikenhead, David, farmer.
ALMONTE GAZETTE; (weekly) Wm. Templeman.
ALMONTE HOUSE, S. H. Davis, prop. (See adv.)
Bain, Walter, farmer.
Baird, William, farmer.
Barker, William, farmer.
Barrie James, hotel.
Bennett, M.. blacksmith.
Black James, farmer.
Bond, Joseph H., tinsmith.
Braggs & Northrup, (Cyrus Bragg, L. C. Northrup,) woolen factory.
Brown & McArthur (Robert Brown, Peter McArthur) general merchants.
Bruce, James, general merchant.
Burke, Rev. E., (Church of England.)
CANNON, GILBERT, woollen factor (see adv.)
Cannon, John, farmer.
Cole, J. K., innkeeper.
Coulter, John, farmer.
Curry, William, blacksmith.
DAVIS, S. H., prop. Almonte House (see adv.).
Doherty, Francis J., tailor.
Doyle & McLean (Thos. Doyle, Daniel McLean), general merchants.
Drennan, James, farmer.
Drury, Robt., saddler.
Edwards, C., shoemaker.
Emper, Wm., grocer.
Foley, Patrick, farmer.
Forgie, Andrew, storekeeper.
Galbraith, Daniel, M.P.P.
Gilmore, John. farmer.
Gleason, Wm., farmer.
Glossop, Daniel, shoemaker.
Gordon, Rev. John, (Presbyterian.)
Gregg, James, farmer.
Gregg, John, farmer.
Hamlin, —, fanning mill maker.
Henderson, C. E., books, &c.
Hume, John, tinsmith.
Jamieson, Joseph, attorney-at-law.
Johnston, R., storekeeper.
Lawson, Walter, harness maker.
Lindsay, Garvin, farmer.
Lochead & Tomlinson, general store.
Long, George, tailor.
McArthur, Arch., farmer.
McCullough, J. W., tailor.
McDowell, Rev. Henry, (Wesleyan).
McEwan, D., tailor.
McFarlane, David, farmer.
McFarlane, James, farmer.
McFarlane, Matthew, farmer.
McGuire, John, cabinet factory.
McKenzie, Rev. Wm., (Free Church).
McKinnon, John, grocer.
McLean, Alex., grist mill.
McPhee, A. woollen factory.
Marshall, A., farmer,
Medcalf, Hugh, farmer.
Menzies, John, Registrar N. R. Lanark.
Millians, Wm., farmer.
Moore, Gilbert, farmer.
Morrison, Daniel, general store.
Mostyn, Wm., M. D.
Nasmith, Lawrence, farmer.
Nicholson, Edward, farmer.
NORTHGRAVES, G. D., watchmaker and jeweler. (See adv.)
O'Brien, George, farmer.
O'Brien, Richard, builder.
O'Hare, John, carriage maker.
O'MALLEY, REV. ANTHONY E., (Roman Cath.)
O'Reilly, John, general merchant.
O'Reilly, Patrick, hotel.
Paterson, George, general merchant.
Paterson, James, general merchant.
Patterson, James, M.D., druggist.
Patterson, William, farmer.
Paul, John, farmer.
Pueblo, — blacksmith.
Raines, T. W., dentist.
Rea, James and John, farmers.

Reburn & Watson, general merchants.
Reed, J. L., grocer,
Robinson, John, farmer.
Robinson, William, sawmill.
ROSAMOND, B. and W. & Co., manufacturers of woolen goods. (See adv.)
Shaw, Alexander, druggist.
Smith, William, farmer.
Snedden, J. D., farmer.
Stafford, Henry, hotel.
Stafford, John, shoemaker.
Steele, Alexander, farmer.
Steele John, farmer.
Stephens, John, gristmill.
TEMPLEMAN, WM., Editor Almonte Gazetter.
Thompson, George, farmer.
THRULL, J. H., watchmaker. (See adv.)
Turgeon, C., barber.
Wallace, James, farmer.
Ward, David, general merchant.
Whyte, Francis, tailor.
WYLIE, JAMES A., Postmaster, gen. merchant.
Young, Peter, farmer.
Young, Robert, farmer.
Young, Stein, farmer.
Young & Flett, founders.

Alport.—A village on the Muskoka River, in the Township of Monck, County Simcoe. Distant from county town, 60 miles; from Toronto, 120. Government lands 50c. per acre.

ALPORT, A. F. C., Postmaster.
Alport, A. J., J. P.
Browning, A. H., insurance agent.
Chapman, Mrs. E. J., teacher.
Dane, P., farmer.

Alton.—A village in the township of Caledon, County Peel, on the river Credit, 22 miles from Brampton and 45 from Toronto. The river affords unlimited water power for manufacturing purposes. Population, 300.

Allan, Wm., butcher.
Alton Hotel, Mrs. A. Weeks, proprietor.
Alton House, J. McQuire, proprietor.
Boddy, Wm., boot and shoe maker.
Brooks, H., shingle maker.
Bull, George F., cabinet maker.
Bull, G. F., carpenter.
Cameron, Robert, carpenter.
Clark, J., lumber yard.
Collins, W., painter.
Dennison, James, carpenter.
Dodds, George, manufaturer of edge tools.
Dodds, Geo., J. P.
Dodds, Joseph.
Fermers' House, J. Cronkwright prop.
Ford, John, cabinet maker.
Glover, Edwin, wagon maker.
Glover, J., carpenter.
Glover, John, wagon maker.
Hartsett, R., lumber yard.
Harrison, James, general merchant.
Harrison, James, cabinet maker.
Harvey James, flour mills.
Kennedy Emery, dyer and scourer.
Kennedy, G. W., dentist.
Keys, Andrew, blacksmith.
Leeson, M., saw mills.
Leffler, John, carpenter.
Lemon, Justice.
Lemon, W.
Limeber, William.
McClellan, John L., carpenter.
McClellan, L. Laurence, carpenter.
McGinnis, P., dyer and scourer.
McClellan, James.
McGregor, Alexander.
MEEK, MRS. AGNES, Postmistress, hotel keeper.
Meek, Robert, general merchant.
Mullen, Michael, boot and shoemaker.
Pinkeny, John, butcher.
Pinkeny, Joseph, blacksmith.
Riddell, J. R., druggist.
Rowecliffe, E. blacksmith.
Russell, H. C.
Russell, Thomas.
Russell, Thomas, J.P.
Smith, A., livery stables.
Smith, Alfred, general merchant.
Smith, Alfred, boot and shoe dealer.
Smith, Charles, general merchant.
Smith, M., lumber yard.
Smith, James, butcher.
Smith, Robert, lime and stone dealer.
Sinclair, Isaac, carpenter.
Stephens, W. J., lumber yard.
Travellers' End, Joseph Alexander, proprietor.
Unger, Johnstone W., carpenter.
West, S. E., general store.
Wilkinson, R. L., lumber yard.

Altona.—A Village in the Township of Pickering, County Ontario, 20 miles from Whitby, and 30 from Toronto. Stages to Toronto and Stouffville. Population, 200.

Brown, Andrew, hotel.
Brown, Joseph, farmer.
Burkholder, Samuel, cabinet maker.
Cliff, Edward, carder,
Hoover, Jacob
Jones, Abijah, farmer.
Key, M., carpenter.
McKay, Donald, teacher.
MONKHOUSE, JOSEPH, Postmaster.
Monkhouse, Thomas, general merchant.
Morden, George.
Millard, Timothy, farmer.
Neighswander, Martin, farmer.
Neighswander, Samuel, miller.
Robertson, Robert, shoemaker.
Stouffer, Jacob, farmer.

Alvanley.—A Post Village, in the Township of Derby, County Gray, distant from County Town 8 miles, from Toronto 120 miles. Stages to Owen Sound and Saugeen. Average price of land $10 to $20. Population, 50.

Dezell, John.
Griffith, John.
Hart, Thomas.
Marshall, David.
Marshall, John.
Matthews, Gordon M., hotel keeper.
Walker, James T., teacher.
Walker, William.
Webster, A.
WEBSTER, JAMES, Postmaster.
White, Robert.
Wilson. George.
Witherspoon, James.

Alvinston.—A village in the township of Brooke, County Lambton, 38 miles from Sarnia.
BRANNAN, J. W., Postmaster.

Amberley.—A post office in the township of Ashfield, County of Huron.
FRASER, ALEXANDER, Postmaster.

Ameliasburg.—A Village at the outlet of Roblin Lake, in the township of Ameliasburgh, County Prince Edward. The principal trade is in grain, flour and lumber. Average price of land, $30. Distant from County Town, 16 miles, from Toronto, 110 miles. Daily mail. Population, 170.

Brooks, Jacob, shoemaker.
Coleman, David, carpenter.
Cousand, George T., lime manufacturer.
Delong, Henry, tailor.
Drewry, Charles E., millwright.
Duke, Henry, cooper.
Dulmage, Daniel, dentist.
Graham, Wm., carpenter.
Higgins, J. H., shoemaker.
Livella. Peter, cooper.
Meyers, B. W., saddler and innkeeper.
Nash, S. L., physician.
Roblin, George, general merchant.
ROBLIN, OWEN, Postmaster, miller, general merchant, &c.
Roblin, Roger, accountant.
Rothwell, Benjamin, accountant.
Scragham, Darvin, carpenter.
Sprague, James E., wagon maker.
Thompson, Rev. James, (Methodist.)
Thwaite, James, physician.
Vandusen, George E., teacher.

Amherstburg.—The town of Amherstburg is situated on the Detroit River, in the Township of Malden, County Essex, 16 miles from Sandwich, and 18 from Windsor. It was first settled in 1796, many of the houses are built in the French style of a century ago, giving the town a very old fashioned appearance. Fort Malden, formerly occupied as a garrison, is now converted into a Lunatic Asylum. This is a Port of Entry, Money Order office and Post Office savings bank. Population, 2,500.

Allan, Wm., grocer.
ANDERSON, EDMUND, Collector H. M. Customs.
Archer, Mrs. Wm., dry goods and groceries.
ASHDOWN, C. H., teacher.
Askin, Mrs. M.
Atkinson, J., carriage maker.
Baker, James, grocer.
Bastein, Augustin, carpenter.
Bastein, John B., carpenter.
Bastein, Joseph, shoemaker.
Baufford, Daniel, farmer.
Beaufour, Gregory, cooper.
Bell, John, farmer.
Bernard, Antoine, proprietor Dominion House.
Bertrand, Simeon, butcher.
Betrie, Michael, shoemaker.
Bofour, James, harness maker.
Borrowman, James,
Borrowman, J. W., stoves and tinware.
BORROWMAN, WILLIAM (Park & Borrowman.)
Botsford, Alanson, clerk second Division Court.
BOTSFORD, A., (McGee & Botsford).
Brett, John, boots and shoes.
Breault, Marc, proprietor Amherstburg House.
Brisbois, Gilbert, merchant tailor.
Brown, Chas., harness maker.
Brown, Ellis, Western Hotel.
Brown, Henry J., saloon keeper.
Brown, Henry
Brown, George, billiard saloon.
Brown, John, watchmaker.
Bungey, William, carriage and wagon manufacturer.
Burke, J. D., baker.
Bush, Rev. Fountain, Baptist.
Caderat, Edward, carpenter.
Cadaret, Joseph, wagon and carriage manufacturer.
Callam, Alex., prop. steam saw mill.
Campbell, Miss Barbara, milliner.
Call, John, baker.
CONROY, FARRELL, Prince Albert Hotel.
Conroy, John, deputy sheriff.
Conroy, John, constable.

Coté, Horace, clerk.
Coté, Thos., wagon maker.
Cousins, Wm., grocer.
Cousins, Wm., farmer.
Crawford, George, carpenter.
Dall, John D., cabinet maker.
Delisle, Dennis, saddler, boot and shoemaker.
Drouillard, Lambert, cigar manufacturer.
Duff, Wm.
Duling, Rev. R. M., (Baptist.)
DUNBAR, JAMES, livery stable prop. (See adv.)
Dumon, Amable, carpenter.
Dummon, Maxim, gunsmith.
England, James, builder.
Fleming, James, boot and shoemaker.
Fortier, Chas. G., collector of Inland Revenue.
Foster, Levi, livery stable.
Gascon, Luke, grocer.
Gerard, Daniel, carpenter.
Gibb, Andrew, carpenter.
Gordon, Mrs. L. G.
Gott, James, boot and shoe manufacturer.
Green, George, painter.
Greenie, Henry, cooper.
Grenier, John B., carpenter.
Grierner, Lewis, farmer.
Grondin, Frederick, carpenter.
Hackett, F. B.
Hackett, Capt. James.
Hamilton, James, surveyor, H. M. Customs.
Harkin, James, tailor.
Healy, John, merchant.
Healy, John, dealer in glassware and crockery.
Horsley, Robert, boarding house.
Horsman, Wm., White Horse Hotel.
Hutton, John, keeper, Malden Asylum.
Ince, Henry, dry goods, grocer.
Johnston, Alex., laborer.
Johnston, John, farmer.
Jones, Alfred, laborer.
Jones, Alex., stock and money broker.
Jones, James, dealer in groceries and provisions.
Kalchthaler, Theodore M., cigar manufacturer.
Kane, John A., druggist.
Kenan, Wm., laborer.
KEVILL & CO., wharfingers, forwarders, and commission merchants. (See adv.)
KEVILL, ANGUS M. (Kevill & Co.)
KEVILL, JAMES, Postmaster.
King, Ray, carpenter.
Kingsmill, Mrs. Louisa.
KOLFAGE, JOHN G., tannery, general merchant.
LAFFERTY, G., general merchant (see adv.)
Lambert, W., M.D.
LANDOR, HENRY, M.D., Superin't Asylum.
LAURENT, REV. P. D. (Roman Catholic).
Legros, Antoine, manufacturer of boots and shoes.
Lelmay, Victor, blacksmith.
Logan, Peter, blacksmith.
Lowe, John, chemist and druggist.
Lopier, Benjamin.
MACK, REV. FREDERICK, (Church of England.)
Maiville, John B., blacksmith.
Marcott, Patrick F., wagon maker & blacksmith.
Marie, Lewis, pattern maker.
Mavill, John, senr., dealer in groceries & provisions.
Meloche, Cyrille, baker.
Mears, Thomas A.
Menzies, Mrs. J.
MIDDLEDITCH, HENRY & SONS. (Henry, Wm. & George) agricultural implement manufacturers. (See adv.)
Morin, Archibald, clerk.
Morin, Felix, grocer.
Morin, James, mason.
Mullen, Alexander.
McCurdy, Nathan, carpenter,
McDonald, George A., billard room and saloon.
McDonald, George A., railroad contracter.
McGEE & BOTSFORD, dealers in groceries, provision and produce. (See adv.)
McGEE, SAMUEL, (McGee & Botsford.)
McGregor, Miss Ellen, dressmaker.
McGuire, Terence, shoemaker.
McGuire, William.
McLeod, John, prop. of Malden mills and distillery.
McLeod, Gordon, counsellor at law.
McVitty, James, Sexton Church of England.
Netles, A. G., shoemaker.
O'Calligham, William, cattle dealer.
Odette, Levi, moulder.
Pargaton, Mrs., dressmaker.
Park, John R. & Co.
PARK, JOHN R. Jun., (Park & Borrowman.)
PARK & BORROWMAN, (J. R. & W.), sash and door manufacturer. (See adv.)
Park Street Brewery, W. McLean, proprietor.
Paxton, Thomas.
Peto, Henry.
Pierson, Dr. Daniel.
Presston, Press, blacksmith.
Primeau, Francis, blacksmith.
Primeau, Francis F., blacksmith.
Princau, Israel, blacksmith.
Prineau, Frank, blacksmith.
Racicot, Miss Mary, dressmaker.
Reaume, Alex., blacksmith.
Reano, Lewis, blacksmith.
Reneaud, Noah, blacksmith.
Reheau, Nelson, farmer.
REYNOLDS, R. T., M.D.
Roberts, Mrs. Isabella, grocer.
Rose, John, cooper.
SALMONI, M. J., general merchant. (See adv.)
Sammond, Miss Matilda, groceries and provisions.
Skinner, Mrs. C.
Skinner, Miss E. B., teacher.
Smith, David, barber.
Smith, Daniel, baker.
Smith, Mrs. Elizabeth, groceries and provisions.
Sudner, Wm., shoemaker.
Stanton, Dr.
Stephens, Major, farmer.
Stephens, Ezekial, farmer.
Tansey, John, shoemaker.
TEMPLETON, JAMES, solicitor. (See adv.)
THOMAS, CHAS. W. & Co., millers. (See adv.)
Tomlinson, Thomas, blacksmith.
Tomlinson, Mrs. Thomas.
TWOMEY, MICHAEL, grocer. (See adv.)
Valentine, E., shoemaker.
Ward, John, groceries, and eating house.
Webber, Mrs., boarding house.
West, Henry, shoemaker.
Wilkinson, W. T., saddler.
WILSON, GEO., land, ins. and gen. agt. (See adv.)
Young, Asa, grocer.

Amiens.—A Post Office in the Township of Lobo, County Middlesex.
McARTHUR, C. SEN., Postmaster.

Ancaster.—A Village in the Township of Ancaster, County Wentworth, 7 miles from Hamilton, 3 from Dundas station G. W. R., and 47 from Toronto. It is surrounded by an excellent agricultural country, and possesses several extensive manufacturing establishments, the principal of which are as follows:—Mr. E. Thuresson's card clothing manufactory is an entirely new business in this country, 38 machines are constantly at work turning out all sizes of card clothing of the most superior quality. The Ancaster Knitting Company employs over 100 hands in the manufacture of all kinds of knitted goods. Messrs. H. & A. Egleston do an extensive business in the manufacture of agricultural implements, and every description of cotton and woolen machinery, and Mr. A. Egleston has lately erected commodious woolen and cloth mills and employ about 20 hands. Population 500.

Ancaster Knitting Company; Wm. Dewar, Manager.
ANCASTER HOTEL, Chas. Phillipo, proprietor.
Arkell, Arthur, miller.
Ballard, Rev. J. McLean, B.A., (Church of England.)
Brandon, J., M. D.
Bull, John Jones, blacksmith.
Bull, Wm. Jones, hotel keeper.
Bush, Thos., farmer.
Byrns, George, shoemaker.
Campbell, James, farmer.
Carpenter, John, tailor.
Chamberlain, Wm. H., grocer.
Chep, James
Clark, Edwin, baker and grocer.
CRANN, JOHN, prop. Ancaster Hotel. (See adv.)
CROOKS, ARTHUR, bailiff.
Dewar, W., Ancaster Knitting Company,
Donnelly, B. W., druggist.
Dunbar, Thos., farmer.
Egleston, Frank, carpenter,
EGLESTON, H. & A. (Harris & Alonzo Egleston) foundry and machine shop. (See adv.)
Ellis, Robert, woolen manufacturer.
Evans, Lewis, machinist.
Farmer, Wm.
FINDLAY, S. A., general merchant.
Forsyth, Robert, tailor.
Gabel, Francis, tanner.
Gabel, Jacob, tanner.
Guest, George, builder.
Guest, George, jun., blacksmith.
Gurnett, James, general merchant.
GURNETT, L. A., clerk 6th Div. Court & mercht.
Halson, Charles
Hammil, Richard, butcher.
Hinton, George, woollen manufactory,
IRWIN, RICHARD, hotel keeper. (See adv.)
Kelly, Isaac, flour miller.
Kemp, Lewis, carpenter.
Lees, Rev. John, (Presbyterian.)
Liddycott, D., engineer.
Lodor, Wm., farmer.
Lowrey M. S., hotel keeper.
McCrimmon, Wm. builder.
McKAY, MRS., Postmistress,
McMillian, John, blacksmith.
Marr, Adam, cabinet maker.
Marr, Thomas, cabinet maker.
Milne, James, attorney-at-law.
Murdock, Andrew, carpenter.
Murdock, George, carpenter.
Nichols, James, manufacturer.
O'Hara, Richard, farmer.
Orton, Henry, M. D.
PHILLIPO, CHARLES, prop. Ancaster Hotel,
Postan, Richard, general merchant.
Postan, Thomas, farmer.
Raymond, Anson, druggist.
Richardson, Henry, M. D.
Rickard, Daniel, saddler.
Rousseaux, George B.
Sproul, Thomas, blacksmith,
Stone, Samuel, farmer.
Taylor, Jos., wagon maker.
THURESSON, EYRE, J. P., manufacturer of card clothing for cotton and wool machines, and all kinds of machinery. (See adv.)
Thuresson, W. H., manufacturer of agricultural implements.
Tisdale, M. L. D.
Wethey, W. H., principal grammar school.
Williamson, William
WILSON, JAMES, shoemaker.
Yokam, Rev. Mr., (Methodist Episcopal.)

Anderson.—A Post Village on Flat Creek, in the Township of Blanshard, County Perth. Distant from County Town 20 miles; from Toronto 108 miles. Average price of land $30. Population 50.

Holmes, Rev. J., (Wesleyan.)
McCallum, Rev. E., (Wesleyan.)
O'Connor, Rev. R., (Roman Catholic.)
Smith, Rev., (New Connexion.)
WHITE, H., Postmaster.

Angus.—A Village situated in the Township of Essa, County Simcoe, between the Nottawasaga and Pine Rivers, and a station on the Northern Railway, 12 miles from Barrie, the County Town, 22 from Collingwood, and 72 from Toronto. The two rivers supply ample water privileges. Money order office. Daily mail. Population 350.

Bush, Jones T., estate agent,
Bush, John L. T., hotel keeper.
Boyes & Nelson, general merchants.
Cameron D., builder.
Chapin, T. F. station agent.
Clarke Richard, shoemaker.
Cooper, A. & R., general merchants.
Cradock, A. & W., general merchants.
Devlin, S. L., furniture dealer.
Foster, Robert, hotel keeper..
Foster, Samuel, hotel keeper.
Graham, James, hotel keeper.
Hewlett, Wm., blacksmith.
Hislop, Rev. J. P., (Canada Presbyterian.)
Lawrence, D. L., saddler.
McDougall, W, H., hotel keeper.
Mather, John, general merchant.
Price, Chas., shoemaker.
Still, Charles, shoemaker.
Sparling, Edward Adolph, teacher.
Tomlinson, Joseph, painter.
Tucker, Rev. Samuel, (Wesleyan.)
Turton, Wm., tanner.
Vantassel, J. H,, tinsmith.
Wilkinson, Joseph, blacksmith.

Antrim.—A Village in the township of Fitzroy, County Carleton, 31 miles from Ottawa. Population, 50.
T. CAVANAGH, Postmaster.

Appin.—A village and station on the Great Western Railway, 26 miles from London, in the Township of Ekfrid, County Middlesex. Population, 150.

Black, Angus, general merchant.
Black, George, hotel.
Black, Duncan, farmer.
CAMPBELL, ANGUS, Postmaster, insurance agent.
Dewitt, S., cabinet maker.
Jollick, Rev. J., (N. C. Methodist.)
Ford, Henry G.. general merchant.
Holmes, Thos., hotel, lumber merchant.
Henry, Isaac, blacksmith.
Johnston, Robt. A., hotel.
Kimble, Almon, grist and saw mills.
Loton, Joseph, wagon maker.
McKellar, Dugald, M.D.
McIntyre, J. P., farmer.
Monroe, James, shoemaker.
Morrison, Wm., shoemaker,
Pole, James, section master, G. W. R.
Rankin, Hugh, farmer.
Sutton, Chris., blacksmith.
Swaby, C. C., blacksmith.

Appleby.—A village in the Township of Nelson, County Halton. Distant from County Town, 12 miles, from Toronto, 28 miles. Average price of land, $60. Population, 30.

Acrell, J., M.D.
Atkinson, T., J. P.
Blanchard, Wm., farmer.
Breckon, G., agent.
Brown, E., brick and tile manufacturer.
COTTER, JAMES W., Postmaster.
Fisher, Rev. John S., (Wesleyan.)
Fothergill, John, farmer.
Haddow, R., saddler.
Hopkins, Alton, farmer.
McCullough, Rev. William, (Wesleyan.)
Marshall, J., teacher.
Pettit, W. G., accountant.
Railton, E., carpenter.
Tufford, E., proprietor Grove Inn.
Wheeler, W., carpenter.
Young, Lucas, farmer.

Appleton.—A Post Village in the Township of Ramsay. County Lanark. Distant from Perth, the County Town, 25 miles. Money order office. Population, 250.
TESKEY, ALBERT, J.P., Postmaster, lumber and general merchant.

Apsley.—A village on Eels' Creek, in the Township of Anstruther, County Peterborough, Distant from County Town, 40 miles, from Toronto, 130 miles. Stage to Peterborough weekly. Average price of wild land, 50 cents per acre. Population, 50.

Benson, Miss, teacher.
Defries, William, farmer.
Eastland, Henry, general merchant.
Hales, Benjamin, farmer.
HALL, E. S., Postmaster.
Lonsley, Caleb, farmer.
Rendle, A., proprietor Apsley Hotel.
Steen, Joseph, farmer.
Stuart, Thomas, proprietor Stuart's Hotel.
Wilson, William, farmer

Apto.—A village in the Township of Flos, County Simcoe, 11 miles from Barrie. Population, 30.

Bernard, Thomas, farmer.
Casey, Nicholas, farmer.
Coughlin, John, farmer.
Cummings, John, J. P.
Huton, John, tailor.
Johnston, James, farmer.
Long, William, shingle maker.
McEvoy, Thomas, farmer.
McLAUGHLIN, CONSTANTINE, Postmaster, hotel and store.
McLaughlin, John, farmer.
Mabin, William, farmer.
Martin, William, shoemaker.
Murphy, James, blacksmith.
O'Neill, John, hotel.
Richardson, James, farmer.
Robinson, James, farmer.
Shaughnessy, John, farmer.

Arden.—A Post-office in the Township of Kenebec, County Addington.
OSBORNE, D., Postmaster.

Ardoch.—A Post-office in the Township of Clarendon, County Frontenac, 68 miles from Kingston, and 50 from Perth. Improved land in the vicinity averages $10 per acre.

BUCHER, F. W., Postmaster.
Christian, August, farmer.
David, B., carpenter.
Elkington Francis, farmer.
Jacobi, E., farmer,
Jacobi, O. R., farmer.
Leckie, Alex., cooper.
Perry, M., innkeeper.
Playfair, E., miller.
Plotz, Wm., carpenter.
Walker, R., carpenter.
Watkins, Bramwell, farmer.

Ardtrea.—A village in the Township of Orillia, County Simcoe, distant from County Town 34 miles, from Toronto, 95 miles. Stages to and from Muskoka. Average price of land $10 to $20. Population 50.

BLAIR, WILLIAM, Postmaster, and prop. Ardtrea Home.
Dick, Daniel.
Kean, Joseph.
Reynolds, George.
Robinson, Charles, M.D.
Selman, Joseph.
Wood, Lieut. William.

Argyle.—A Post village in the Township of Eldon, County Victoria. Distant from County Town 21 miles, from Toronto 80 miles. Stage to Woodville, Kirkfield and Lindsay. Average price of land $5, improved $25, population, 50.

Bowie, Alexander, tailor.
Campbell, John, farmer.
Gillespie, Dugald, general merchant.
Gunn, John, farmer.
McDougall, Rev. Neil, (Presbyterian).
McEachern, Allan, farmer.
McEachern, Malcolm, farmer.
McFadyn, A., teacher.
McIntyre, Andrew, farmer.
McIntyre, Archibald, farmer.
McKAY, JOHN, Postmaster, general merchant.
McKinnon, D., hotel keeper.
McRea, D., J. P.,
McTavish, Rev. John, (Presbyterian).
Morrison, John, farmer.
Murray, Thomas, shoemaker.
Ross, William, farmer.

Arkell.—A Village in the Township of Puslinch, County Wellington. Distant from County Town five miles; from Toronto fifty-two miles. Stages to and from Wellington Square, Advertised price of land $40. Population, 100.

Arkell, John, woollen factor.
Arkell, Thomas, farmer.
Burgess, James, prop. Farmer's Inn.
Findlow, Rev. Alexander, (Church of England.)
Haines, Henry, farmer.
Haton, John, wagon maker.
Hess, John, senr., farmer.
Hough, Rev. John. (Wesleyan).
Iles, John, junr., farmer.
King, David, constable.
King, David, junr., butcher.
McFarlane, Duncan, J. P.
McLennan, Simon, teacher.
Neville, Miss Elizabeth, dressmaker.
Neville, John, shoemaker.
Nichols George, blacksmith.
Oulton, John, farmer.
Petty, John, farmer.
STONE, F. W., farmer.
Wakefield, George, butcher.
WATSON, WILLIAM, Postmaster and gen. mercht.
Willoughby, Charles, farmer.
Wood, William, woolen factor.

Arkona.—A flourishing Village in the Township of Bosanquet, County Lambton, 35 miles from Sarnia, and 7 from Widder Station, Grand Trunk Railway. Improved land in the vicinity averages $25 per acre. Stage daily to Widder. Money order office and Savings Bank. Population, 500.

Armitage, Mark, baker.
Budham, George, stone and lime dealer.
Boyd, W. M.D.,
Brown, A., general merchant.
Carnoghan, A., farmer.
Carnoghan, D., farmer,
Carton, John, blacksmith.
Champion and Nosworthy, founders,
Connell, B., farmer.
Davidson, Alexander, J. P., insurance agent.
Donnelly, F., butcher.
Douglass, P., tinsmith.
Dunn, Robert, Colonial hotel.
Eastman, C. M., general merchant.
Eastman, T. F., druggist.
Eastman, Z. F., J. P.
Eccles, F. R., M.D.
Everest, G. M., watchmaker.
Everest, George M., druggist.
Ensher, Rev. W., (Episcopal Methodist).
Feather, Rev. Thomas, (Wesleyan.)
Freeman, Rev. B., (Baptist).
Goodfellow, Rev. Peter, (Presbyterian).
Ginn, John, painter.
Hannah, Robert, tinsmith.
Howe, H., cabinet maker.
Jackson, A., shoemaker.
Jackson, J. wagon maker.
Jackson, W, H.
James Joseph, carpenter.
Knicely, John, farmer.
Langle, M. J., tailor.
Learn, Benjamin, general merchant.
Locke, Rev. W., (Church of England)
McHaig, John, nurseryman.
McFarlane, R., teacher.
Melton, Charles P. blacksmith.
Miller, William, carpenter.
Myres, — hotel.
Paisley, James, tanner.
Paisley and Jackson, gen. lumber merchants.
Petler, John, shoemaker.
Rosenberry, P. B., dentist.
Saul, John, flour mills.
SCHOOLEY, MRS. CATHERINE, Postmistress.
Shawley & Vahey, general merchants.
Showler, T. W., tailor.
Stephenson, G. B., insurance agent.
Tremble, Z., wagon maker.
Vahey, William, saddler.
Ward, D., carpenter.
White, M., carpenter.

Arkwright.—A post Village in the Township of Arran, County Bruce. Distant from Owen Sound 21 miles, Southampton, 11 miles. Money order office. Population, 50.

KILBOURNE, G. D., Postmaster.

Arlington.—A Village in the Township of Adjala, County Simcoe. 30 miles from Barrie, 16 from Angus and 22 from Gilford Stations Northern Railway. Stages daily to Cookstown and Gilford. Population, 100.

Brazil, James, accountant.
Brown, George, farmer.
Brown, Thomas, hotel keeper.
Burke, Patrick, farmer.
Cassidy, James, farmer.
Cassidy, Thomas, saddler.
Cassidy, William, farmer.
Connell, Thomas, blacksmith.
Conway, Edward, farmer.
Duff, William, wagon maker.
Donnelly, Hugh, woolen factor.
Ellard, William, shoemaker.
Gallagher, Thomas, J.P.
Hamilton, John, auctioneer.
Hesslip, Samuel, farmer.
Hosier, John, wagon maker.
Hunter, James, farmer.
KIDD, THOMAS, J.P., Postmaster, & gen. merch't
Langley, Patrick, hotel-keeper.
Langley Thomas, veterinary surgeon.
Lemon, Robert, hotel and general store.
Lyons, John, farmer.
McGregor, Malcolm, lumber dealer.
McMulkin, Thomas, general agent.
Moore, John, shoemaker.
Murphy, John, J.P.
Nichol. David, miller.
Rusk, John, woolen factor.
Ryan, W. J., tailor.
Stephens, Thomas, blacksmith.
Wait. Whitney, wagon maker.

Arnott.—A Post-office in the Township of Holland, County Grey, 12 miles south-east of Owen Sound. Population 75.

MURRAY, WILLIAM J., Postmaster.

Arnprior.—An Incorporated Village on the Brockville and Ottawa Railway, at the junction of the Madawaska and Ottawa Rivers, in the Township of McNab, County Renfrew. Distance from County Town, 65 miles, from Ottawa, 40 miles. from Toronto, 260 miles. Stages in winter to and from Ottawa. Average price of land $20 to $40. Money order office and Savings Bank. Population, 2000.

Allan, J., tailor.
Armstrong, —, M.D.
Arthur, J. W., teacher.
Ash, Rev. J. C., (Wesleyan.)
Bates, E. A. attorney.
Bell, James, insurance agent.
Bell, J., grocer.
Bellamy, J., tinsmith.
Blair, Rev. Mr., (Methodist Episcopal.)
Blair, James.
Bouvier, Rev. J., (Roman Catholic.)
Brown, David, tanner.
Brown and Wilson, general merchants.
Butler, John, tinsmith.
Butler, John, auctioneer.
Campbell, Mrs., hotel-keeper.
Caras, Robert.
Caras, William, general merchant.
Caras, W. & Co., planing mill.
Connors & McGill, shoemakers.
Craig, George, baker.
Cranston, —, M.D.
Dashnan, D., cooper.
Dassie, Peter, wagon-maker.
Dean, William.
Dorwin, —, watchmaker.
Dowsell, A. H., J.P.
Dwinell, J. C., grocer.
Lauroche, Rev. C. T., (Episcopal.)
Edey, E., hotel-keeper.
Edey, Henry, wagon-maker.
Elliott, Thomas.
Farmer & Gibb, shoemakers.
Fletcher, R., painter.
Foy, Thomas.
Frazer, J., railway agent.
Frazer, George, bookseller.
Glenn, J. F., grocer.
Goodwin, John,
Hanly, George, painter,
Harrington, E., general merchant.
Harvey, John.
Harvey, William.
Heath, J., tailor.
Hope, Samuel, weaver.
Junkins, John, carpenter.
Kenny, J.
Lang, John, painter.
Lang, W. H., gunsmith.
Laycock, Andrew.
Lindsay, Rev. Peter, (Presbyterian.)
Lyons, R., hotel-keeper.
Lyons, W., shoemaker.
McDermid, James, carpenter.
McDonald, Archibald.
McDonald, W. T., insurance agent.
McDougal, J.
McGuire, H. M., tanner.
McLACHLAN, DANIEL, M.P.P
McLachlan, John.
McLachlan & Bros., millers,
McLachlan & Bros., planing mills.

McNamara, D. hotel-keeper.
McPhee, Miss, teacher.
McPherson, A., carpenter.
Mackay, William.
Marcellas, C., shoemaker.
Marquand, —, tailor.
Maynard, J., saloon keeper.
Miller, William, cooper.
Mitchell, —, telegraph operator.
Mitchell, J. C., fancy goods.
Moore, John, carpenter.
NEILSON, A. G., publisher & prop. *Canadian Times*
Neilson, G. E., general merchant.
Ogden. —, livery stable.
Ogden, —, butcher.
Parker, Andrew, shoemaker.
Pettypiece, Miss, teacher.
Prout, Mrs., hotel keeper.
Ramsay, Daniel, general merchant.
Robertson, Neil.
Rorison & McEwan, iron founders.
RUSSELL, ANDREW, Postmaster.
Russell, Andrew & Son, general merchants.
Schofield, W., carpenter.
Sherlock, —, butcher.
Sack, H. L., teacher.
Sipence, F., marble cutter.
Stewart, Thomas, woolen factor.
Stewart & Tierney, general merchants.
Storie, Thomas, carpenter.
Sutherland, Thomas.
Swan, —, butcher.
Taylor, George, general merchant.
Thompson, John.
Tilley, Arthur.
Wait, J., druggist.
Walker, —, tailor.
Watson, Miss, tailoress.
White, James, wagon maker.
White, James, grocer.
White, John.
Willis, William.
Wilson, J., tanner.
Wilson, William, shoemaker.
Wolf, Jonathan, cabinet maker.
Young, Mrs., general store.

Aros.—A Village on Balsam Lake, in the Township of Bexley, County Victoria. Distant from County Town, 22 miles; from Toronto, 90 miles. Average price of land, $4 to $10. Population, 50.

Butler, Miss Emma, teacher.
Ferguson, Miss T., teacher.
Hardie, Rev., (Wesleyan.)
Hodgins, Charles, prop. Coboconk Hotel.
Kerr, Miss Nancy, teacher.
King, John, carpenter.
McINNIS, CHARLES, Postmaster.
McLean, Miss J., teacher.
McLean, Rev. John, (Presbyterian.)
Reynolds, John.

Arthur.—A flourishing Village in the Township of Arthur, County Wellington, on the Owen Sound road, 12 miles north of Fergus, 25 miles from Guelph and 15 from Mount Forest. The Conestogo river passes through the village. Money order office and Savings Bank. Population, 500.

Ballentine, Adam, general merchant.
Bond, John, blacksmith.
Buschlen, A., blacksmith.
Buschlen, John, miller and wagon maker.
Canton, Adam, farmer.
Cavanagh, Garrett.
Church, George, blacksmith.
Clayton, James, tanner.
Clayton, Samuel L., wagon maker.
Corbett, John, carpenter.
Costello, John.
Cushing, William, township clerk.
Drake, Patrick, shoemaker.
Draper, Joseph, general merchant.
Drummond, William H., shoemaker.
Ebbs, James.
Eden, Francis, farmer.
Frazer, Alexander, pump maker.
Frazer, Hugh, farmer.
Frazer, James W., carpenter.
Gordon, J. H., M.D.
Gourlay, James, plasterer.
Gourlay, Peter, tailor.
GREEN, CARLTON C., prop. Green's Hotel.
Green, William, tinsmith.
Hay, James, potash manufacturer.
Henderson, Robert, druggist.
Henderson, Walter, M.D.
Hewitt, Isaac, miller.
Hewitt, Mark, miller.
Hollinger, J. & J., tanners.
Hughes, William, tailor and grocer.
Lewis, Harry & Co., general merchants.
McIntosh, Duncan, shoemaker.
McPherson, John, groceries, hardware, etc.
Mann, Patrick, carpenter.
Mitchell, Joseph, tailor.
Moore, George, bailiff.
Morris, Rev. F. T. J., (Roman Catholic).
Ostrander, Thomas, J. P.
Peterkin, William.
SMALL, MRS. JOSEPH, Postmistress.
Smith, James, merchant.
Stephenson, Robert, cabinetmaker.

Arva.—(Village St. Johns.)—A post office in the Township of London, County Middlesex, 5½ miles from London. Money order office. Population 250.

Beamish, Henry, shoemaker.
BERNARD, W. B., Postmaster, clerk Division Court
Brough, Rev. C. C., (Episcopal.)
Carson, Silas, cabinet maker.
Elliot, Thomas, Crown hotel.
English, George, blacksmith.
Hawkins, George, miller.
McNab, John, blacksmith.
Martin, H. O., M. D.
Monaghan, George, hotel keeper.
Orr, Robert, auctioneer and bailiff.
Platt, Frederick, blacksmith.
Shea, Daniel, tailor.
Stevenson, Thomas, tinsmith.
Stiles & Kent, general merchants.
Teer, Daniel, saddler.
Willson, Crowell, J. P.
Willson & Bernard, woolen factory.
Zendler, John, shoemaker.

Ashburn.—A Village in the Township of Whitby, County Ontario, distant from County Town 9 miles, from Toronto 40 miles. Stages to Whitby and Uxbridge. Average price of Land $45 to $50. Population 100.

Alexander, A. G., teacher.
Bowler, Daniel, wagon maker.
Brasch, Robert, farmer.
Brunscombe, John, shoemaker.
Burchill, Isaac, tailor.
Creighton, David, general merchant.
Dawson, Rev. Alexander, (Presbyterian.)
Fisher, Timothy, farmer.
Hasty, Miss E., dressmaker.
Herron, William, farmer.
Hubertus, G. J., general merchant.
Lawrence, James, saddler.
Lowerby, John, shoemaker.
Lowerby, J., druggist.
Menah, Alexander, farmer.
Metcalf, George, proprietor Ontario House.
Mitchell, James, farmer.
Nicol, John, farmer.
OLVER, EDWARD, Postmaster.
Olver, W. H., tailor.
Reid, John, carpenter.
Smith, J. W., M. D.
Wakem, Luther, carpenter.
Webster, James, butcher.
Wilson, Alexander, farmer.

Ashburnham.—An incorporated Village, in the Township of Otonabee, County Peterborough, immediately adjoining the County Town, 90 miles from Toronto. Population 1000. (See Peterborough.)

Ainslie, Walter, shoemaker.
Anderson, John, carpenter.
Armstrong, Thomas, hotel.
Bennett, Henry, J. P., cooper.
Brown, George, grocer.
Burnham, Rev. Mark, (Episcopal.)
Beck, Rev. J. W. R., (Episcopal.)
Burnham, George, M. D.
Brook, D., woolen factory.
Cain, George, carpenter.
CALCUTT, HENRY, flax mills and brewer.
Clancy, Edward & Peter, blacksmiths.
Clarke, John, tanner.
Coe, Thomas, butcher.
Connell, James, cooper.
Cope, Alex., turner.
Craigie & Stephenson, planing mills.
Dunlop, Charles A., J. P.
Fisher, Amos J., produce merchant.
Hunter, Alexander, grocer.
Kells, W. H., hotel keeper.
McDonald, Daniel, tailor.
McDougall & Ludgate, lumber merchants.
McDougall, William, (McDougall & Ludgate.)
Ludgate, John, (McDougall & Ludgate.)
McGregor, William, grocer.
Mowry, Aldus, founder.
O'Brien, John, wagon maker.
Orde, G. F., general agent.
Rickey, George, blacksmith.
ROGERS, R. D., Postmaster and flour mill prop.
Rogers, James Z., general merchant.
Sargent, Philip, builder.
Storey, George, axe maker.
Stratton, James, clerk municipality.
Sutherland Donald, produce and commission.
Swanston, William, baker.
Toole & Robertson, planing mills.
Wood, John, teacher
Wright, Stewart, builder.

Ashgrove.—A Village in the Township of Esquesing, County Halton. Average price of land $30 to $40. Distant from County Town 8 miles, from Toronto 38 miles. Mail stage to Milton, fare 20 cents. Population 30.

Flemming, Robert, teacher.
Graham, Richard.
Hood, Wm., blacksmith.
Huffman, H.
Hunter, J., J. P.
HUNTER, SARAH, Postmistress.
Huston, Francis,
Keys, Rev., (New Connexion.)
McColl, J., J. P.
Payne, James, proprietor Ashgrove hotel.
Ruddle, Joseph.
SMYTH, ROBT., deputy Postmaster and grocer.
Taylor, Wm., wagon maker.
Thompson, William.
Weir, Andrew.
Wilson, J.
Wilson, Wm.
Wrigglesworth, George.

Ashton.—A Village on the Jock, in the Township of Goulbourne, County Carleton, containing 1 foundry, 1 tannery, 3 churches, 1 common school, 2 hotels, &c. Land averages from $12 to $20. Population 200.

Argue, George, tanner.
Blair, Archibald, shoemaker.
Brown, Rev. C., (Episcopal.)
Brown, John M., lime manufacturer.
Caswell, Rev. (Presbyterian.)
Church, C., M. D.
Cosier, James, wagon maker.
Cosier & Lindsay, shingle manufacturers.
Coun, James, general merchant.
Fanning, Daniel, hotel keeper.
Ford, Miss, dressmaker.
Gowe, Peter, livery stable.
Hueston, James, shoemaker.
Kennedy, Robt., grocer.
Lammond, John, tailor.
Lindsay, James & Co., wagon makers.
McEwan, Miss Mary, teacher.
McFarlane, Donald, hotel-keeper,
McFarlane, John, iron founder.
McFarlane, Robert liquor dealer.
Mullin, Rev. (Presbyterian.)
MUNRO, JOHN M., editor Ashton Examiner.
Robinson, Hugh, wagon maker.
Shore, John, carpenter.
Stewart, Benjamin, cabinet maker.
Sumner, James, general merchant.
SUMNER, JOHN, Postmaster & general merchant.
Sykes, Hiram, J. P.

Ashworth.—A Post office in the Township of Scott, County Ontario.
MUSTARD, JOHN, Postmaster.

Atha.—A Post Village in the Township of Pickering, in the County of Ontario, 16 miles from Whitby, the County Town, and 28 miles from Toronto. Population, about 50.

BELL, JOHN M., Postmaster.
Bentley, Nathan, farmer.
Dundas, James, general merchant.
Harrison, George, farmer.
Lapp, Andrew, farmer.
Miller, William, farmer.
Spears, Adam, J. P.
Spears, J. & J., lumber manufacturers.
Whitson, James, farmer.

Athens P. O.—Township of Uxbridge, County of Ontario. Distant from County Town, 24 miles, from Toronto, 44 miles.

BRIGHAM, ROBERT, Postmaster and gen. mercht.
CLELAND, REV. W. (Presbyterian)

Atherly.—A village situated on Lake Simcoe, in the Township of Mara, County Ontario, 70 miles from Whitby and 90 from Toronto. Average value of improved land in the vicinity, $25 per acre. Population, 200.

Adam, Andrew, cooper.
Boulton, William, township treasurer,
Burnett, Peter, P. L. S.
Cahill, Timothy, shoemaker.
Campbell, Rev. K. A. (Roman Catholic)
Cramer, Lawrence, carpenter.
DUDENHAFER, A., Postmaster.
Dudenhafer, George, farmer.
Dudenhafer, William, carpenter.
Fo ey, J. P., councillor.
H arahy, John, councillor.
Hewitt, Charles, general merchant.
Kennedy, Alexander, general merchant.
M Donald, Alexander, carpenter.
Malone, Denis, hotel keeper.
Mulvahill, Thomas, blacksmith.
Prettyfoot, Edward, farmer.
McDonald, Angus, carpenter.
McPherson, James, J. P.
McPhee, William, lumber merchant.
Reeve, Arthur, general merchant.
Revell, Henry, farmer.
Smith, Colin, general merchant,
Strathern, George, farmer.
Thompson, Oliver, farmer.
Thompson, Peter, farmer.
Thorne, Amos, general merchant.
Tivnan, Bernard, wagon maker.
Whitney, John, hotel keeper.

Atherton.—A post village in the Township of Windham, County of Norfolk.

Athol.—A Village on Scotch river, in the Township of Kenyon, County Glengary. The principal trade is in Grain, Dairy Produce and Cordwood. Average price of land, $6 to $15. Distant from County Town, 27 miles; from Toronto, 293 miles. Stages tri-weekly to and from Alexandria and Plantagenet. Population, 150.

Aird, Alexander D., carpenter.
Begg, Alexander, general merchant.
BENNETT, HON. THOMAS.
Brodie, William. miller.
Cameron, Angus.
Campbell, Angus M., attorney.
Campbell, Duncan, wagon maker.
Campbell, John, wagon maker.
Campbell, John M,
Fisher, Christy.
Fisher, John, livery stable.
FISHER, M.A., Postmaster and general merchant.
Fisher, Peter A., accountant.
Games, Martin, tanner.
Gordon, Rev. Daniel, (Presbyterian.)
Gray, Rev. —, (Church of Scotland.)
Hunter, Mary, teacher.
Jacob Max, general merchant.
LeClair, Mrs. John, dressmaker.
McArthur, John.
McDiarmid, Donald, M. D.
McDonald, Allan, cooper.
McGregor, Alexander R., weaver.
McGregor, Charles, shoemaker.
McGregor, C., saddler.
McGregor, Duncan.
McGregor, Malcolm.
McGregor, Peter, weaver.
McIntyre, Angus, teacher.
McIntyre, John.
McIntyre, Margaret, teacher.
McKenzie, James, auctioneer.
McKERCHAR, COLIN, teacher.
McKerchar, Donald, teacher.
McLachlan, Angus, wagon maker.
McNaughton. John G., shingle manufacturer.
McPherson, John, shoemaker.
McRae, Alexander, general merchant.
McRae, Finlay, auctioneer.
McRae, Hugh, general agent.
Matheson, Miss Mary, dressmaker.
Peacock, Rev. W. (Congregational)
Sabourin, Charles, carpenter.
Sinclair, Donald, brick manufacturer.
Sinclair, Peter.
Urquhart, A., miller.
Wollette, Gabriel, cabinet maker.

Athlone.—A village in the Township of Adjala, County Cardwell. Distant from County Town, 10 miles, from Toronto, 45 miles. Average price of land, $40 to $60. Money Order office. Population, 75.

Agnew, W. H., dentist.
Barton, James, cabinet maker.
Barton, Robert, farmer.
Colgan, John, cooper.
Connor, John T., farmer.
Dorney, John, shingle manufacturer.
Ellard, Michael, proprietor New Dominion Hotel.
Ethridge, William, gunsmith.
Grogan, Hugh, shoemaker.
Haffey, John, farmer.
Hayder, James, carpenter.
Hislen, Edward, auctioneer.
Kelly, John, farmer.
Kidd, George, farmer.
KIDD, JOHN, Postmaster and general merchant.
Lloyd, Thomas, saddler.
McCabe, James, wagon maker.
McCabe, Peter, carpenter.
McCullough, James, carpenter.
McDermot, Thomas H., teacher.
McGuiness, Sarah, dressmaker.
McLaughlin, John, miller.
McLaughlin & Piggott, tanners.
Segsworth, James, farmer.
Thompson, John, tailor.

Attercliffe.—A village on the Chippawa River, in Township of Caistor, County Lincoln. Distance from County Town, 24 miles, from Toronto, 75. Average price of land, $20 to $30. Population, 100.

Broughton, Amos, shingle manufacturer.
Crowther, James, general merchant.
Davidson, Alexander, hotel keeper.
Fulsom, James, farmer.
Green, Robert, farmer.
Haislip, Abraham, general merchant.
Hodge, Homer, wagon maker.
Hodge, Seth, teacher.
Jones, Adam, farmer.
Jones, Darius, teacher.
Kirk, Jno. L., M.D.
Laidlaw, Andrew, farmer.
Lymburner, Ralph, hotel keeper.
Miller, Robert, farmer.
Montague, Mrs. Jane, dressmaker.
Montague, Robert, shoemaker.
Pitcher, Peter F., farmer.
Sammons, John, farmer.
Sensabaugh, C., farmer.
Sensabaugh, W., shingle manufacturer.
Shirton, Charles, carpenter.
Stollery, Jacob, farmer.
Thompson, Isaac, carpenter.
TISDALE, JAMES, Postmaster.
Tisdale, James K., painter.
Tisdale, John, carpenter.
Tisdale, John W., painter.
Tisdale, Reuben H., general merchant.

Auburn (see Manchester).—A post office in the Townships of Wawanosh and Hullett, County Huron. Distant from County Town, 11 miles, from Toronto, 143.

JAMES SUTHERLAND, Postmaster.

Aultsville.—A Village on the Grand Trunk Railway and River St. Lawrence, in the Township of Osnabruck County Stormont. The principal trade is in lumber and cordwood. Land averages from $40 to $70. Distant from County Town, 18 miles; from Toronto, 250. Money Order office. Daily mail. Population 200.

Anderson, Francis, wagon maker.
Anderson, James, blacksmith.
Andrews, Rev. Wm., (Wesleyan).
Archer, George, blacksmith.
AULT, ISAIAH R., Postmaster, general merchant, lumber dealer, etc.
Ault, J. R. & S., gen. merchants and lumber dealers.
Ault, Samuel, J.P.
Ault, Simeon N.
Ault, William R.
Baker, Joshua, saddler.
Baker, Simeon, general merchant.
Barnhart, Ebenezer, wagon maker.
Barnhart, Miss, dressmaker.
Barnhart, Simeon, painter.
Bennetto, John, teacher.
Brown, Robert, tailor.
Cook, Guy H., hotel keeper.
Croil, John.
Dafoe, Erastus, general merchant.
Dafoe, Richard, shoemaker.
Elliot, John, potter and brick maker.
Elliot, William, potter.
Empey, Ira, blacksmith.
Ferguson, Rev. J., (Methodist Episcopal).
Garrett, Rev. T., (Episcopal).
Gogo, George, shoemaker.
Gove, Nathaniel.
Haines, John, shoemaker.
Hanes, Charles J., blacksmith.
Hanes, H., saddler.
Hume, John.
Hunter, Peter, carpenter.
Jackson, Thomas, tanner.
Loucks, Richard, lumber dealer.
McConnell, Thomas, potter.
Markell, Solomon, M. D.
Morgan, Nelson, shoemaker.
Mullin, Rev. J. B., (Presbyterian.)
Richmin, George, carpenter.
Sampson, George, carpenter.
Sampson, James, carpenter.
Silmsor, Nathaniel, general merchant.
Snyder, John, general merchant.
Summers, David D.
Summers, Jacob,
Wells, George, general merchant.
Whitney, R. L.

Aughrim.—A village on the Sydenham River, in the Township of Brooke, County Lambton. Distant from County Town, 40 miles, from Toronto, 170. Average price of wild land, $6 to $10, improved $20 to $25. Population, 75.

Archer, Joseph, farmer.
Armstrong, W., teacher.
Gunn, Rev. J. (Church of England)
Lovell, James, farmer.
McAlpin, Joseph, farmer.
McCallum, A., blacksmith.
McDorman, W., carpenter.
McKENNA, JOHN, Postmaster.
Murray, B., tailor.
Paterson, Dugald. teacher.
Patterson, John, shoemaker.
Sinclair, J., J. P.
Stafford, Rev. E. A., (Wesleyan)
Wall, Thomas, farmer.

Aurora.—An Incorporated Village and Station of the Northern Railway in the Townships of King and Whitchurch, County York. 30 miles from Toronto. Money Order office and Savings' Bank. Population 1200.

Andrews E., tailor.
Andrews, James & Co., general merchants.
Appleton, S., fire inspector.
Arnold R., brewer.
Ashton, Seth.
Atkinson, John, shoemaker.
AURORA BANNER, (Friday), E. F. Stephenson, editor.
Bacon, H. J., tailor.
Blevins & Severs, attorneys at law.
Bond, John, druggist.
Bosanko, J., butcher.
Boynton, A., blacksmith.
Brodie, A., cooper.
Butcher, Charles, general merchant.
Catcher, C., carpenter.
Campbell, Hugh & Sons, rope and cordage factory.
Campbell, Hugh, farmer.
Clift & Neis, carriage makers.
Connor, Robert, insurance agent.
Denbrook, Henry, boots and shoes.
DOAN, CHARLES, J. P., postmaster and general merchant.
Doan, David, agent Vicker's Express Company.
Earl, George W., general merchant.
Elliott, J., general merchant.
Ellston, Benjamin, hotel keeper.
Field, John, general merchant.
FLEURY, JOSEPH, founder and machinist.
Ford, M.D.
Fry, Stephen, agent N.R.R.
Fryatt, Henry, machinist.
GEIKIE, WALTER B., coroner
Gundy, Rev. S. B., (New Connexion Methodist.)
Harris, Henry, cabinet maker.
Hawthorne, Henry, carpenter.
Hillary, R. W., M.D.
Halladay, J., butcher.
Ireland, William, cabinet maker.
Irwin, Charles & S. P., lumber merchants.
Irwin, M. B., farmer.
Irwin, R.P., J.P., farmer.
Kirsopp, J. W., Railroad Hotel.
Lemon, W., Marbell House.
LEPPER, MATTHEW, general merchant.
Long, Frederick, paper box factory.
McCallum, Rev. James, (Episcopal).
McCarthy, William, watchmaker.
McDonnell, J., blacksmith.
McGaffin, J., merchant.
McNalley, J. E., insurance ag't, Com'r in B. R., etc.
Marritt, John, patent rights agent.
Moore, G. F., general merchant and auctioneer.
Moseley, James, farmer.
Moseley. William, estate agent.
Nichol, J., brick maker.
Ough, William, tinsmith.
Patterson, J. M., auctioneer.
Pearson, Benjamin, J.P., conveyancer.
Pearson, B., furniture.
Pearson, D., painter.
Pease, E., leather dealer.
Peck, N. J., dentist.
RANSOM, T. G.
Reeves, R. D., baker.
Richardson, J., hotel keeper.
Robinson, A. B., dentist.
Rogers, Josiah, farmer.
Rupert, J. W., photographer.
Shaw, Rev. John, (Wesleyan).
Siddons, S. B., grocer.
Snowden, R., tailor.
STEPHENSON, E. F., editor *Banner*
Stevenson, George L., saddler.
Stiles, H. B., auctioneer and general merchant.
Suttle, N. S., grocer.
SUTTLE & HARTMAN, (Fredk. and Isaac), general merchants.
Taylor, William, painter and paper manufacturer.
Thompson, J. R., lumber merchant.
Todd, James, blacksmith.
Todd & Co., carriage makers.
Tracy, John, tailor.
Wallace, A., land agent.
Wells, J. M., dentist.
Whaley, A. T., shingle maker.
Willis, William. saddler.
Willson, J., china and glassware.
Woodsworth, Rev. R. W., (Wesleyan).
York, Charles H., carpenter.

Avon.—A Village in the Township of North Dorchester, County Middlesex, and on the line dividing the County of Elgin. Distant from London, 20 miles, and 11 from Ingersoll. Mails tri-weekly. Population, 100.

Andrews, John, wagon maker.
Barnett, William, blacksmith.
Degroat, Elias, farmer.
Egler, Christian, farmer.
Egler, John, general merchant.
Herron, Henry, carpenter.
Kiltz, Rev. James. (Episcopal Methodist.)
McLochlin, John, farmer.
Pullen, Felix, tailor.
Stover, Jacob, tailor.
SMITH, O. C., Postmaster.

Avening.—A Village in the Township of Nottawasaga, County Simcoe. From Barrie, 22 miles, Sunnidale Station, 6 miles, and from Toronto, 60 miles. Improved lands in the vicinity averages $50 per acre, wild, $10. All kinds of mechanics are required. Population, 300.

Bowman & Pingle, millers and lumber dealers.
Carruthers, G. lumber merchant.
Carruthers, William, sawyer.
Duff, William, general agent.
Gardener, W. C., hotel keeper.
Geyer, Albert, painter.
Graham, R. & Co., general merchants.
Granger, T., livery stables.
Heaney, L., contractor.
Houston, G., auctioneer.
Ingham, Joseph, carpenter.
Island, G., blacksmith.
Jamieson, J., wagon maker.
Kendrick. John, carpenter.
Leslie, A., tailor.
Little, John, weaver.
Lossie, J., tinsmith.
McIntosh, James, accountant.
McManus, J., accountant.
McMahon, J. J., dentist.
Martin, Joseph, builder.
Martin, R., builder.
Matchett, Edward, builder.
Matchett, R., builder.
MORRIS. R., Postmaster and general merchant.
Seroggie, R., insurance agent.
Shepard, G., butcher.
Stonehouse, Thomas, carpenter.
Taylor, G., carpenter.
Weir, H., shoemaker.
Wilson, J., hotel keeper.
Woodruff, E., carpenter.
Woodruff, Kendrick & Co., manufacturers patent window blinds.

Aylmer.—A Village in the Township of Malahide, County Elgin, 12 miles from St. Thomas, 26 from London, 80 from Hamilton, and 130 from Toronto. Catfish Creek, passing through the village, affords good water power. Money Order office and Savings Bank. Population, 800.

Aldrich, R. J., carpenter.
Aldright, R. R., tanner.
Arkell, J. H., general merchant,
Bayes, James E., brickmaker,
Bencroft, Henry, cooper.
Bingham & Sons, general merchants.
Brown, A. C., grocer.
Brown, James.
Brown, M. J., miller.
Calvert, Joseph, teacher.
Caverley, Weisbrod & Thompson, wagon makers.
Campbell, Wm., stove dealer.
Caswell, Asa, tinsmith.
Chester, A., teacher.
Chute, A., teacher.
Chute, Miss, dressmaker.
Clappison, Rev. D. C. (Wesleyan.)
Clark, Geo. F., M. D.
Clark, Chas., M. D.
Clayton, Miss Maggie, teacher.
Clayton, Peter, J. P.
Correy, J. M., saddler.
Cronk, J. H., shoemaker.
Cropp, David, wagon maker.
Darling, Wm., tailor.
Davis, Edwin.
Davis, Loder.
Davidson, Rev. T. L., D. D., (Baptist,)
Dean, John, saddler.
Doty, Joshua, proprietor Union Hotel.
Durkee, M. P., cooper.
Durrant, Thomas, butcher.
Fairchilds, Rev. J. (Episcopal Methodist)
Farthings, John, grocer.
Farthings, R. W., general merchant.
Faulds, William, painter.
Foot, Ezra, M. D.
Freeman, Melinda, teacher.
Gillespie, Robert, miller.
Gillet, John W., J. P.
Glen, Peter, tailor.
Goff, James, carpenter.
Goff, W. & J., sash and door manufacturers.
Goff, William H., carpenter.
Graham, Robert, tailor.
Gregory, Kirby, livery stable.
Gundry, L. J., watchmaker.
Harding, Rev. F. (Church of England)
Herrington, J., painter.
Hicks, J., marble cutter.
HODGKINSON, PHILIP, Postmaster.
Holmes, Rev. E. (New Connexion)
Hughes. William E., dentist.
Jansen, J. E., carpenter.
Kerr, Miss, dressmaker.
Lewis, Amasa, proprietor Commercial Hotel.
Lightfoot, Thomas.
Lobdell, Albert.
Lorings, Harry, miller.
McAdams, James & Son.
McCausland, John A., wagon maker.
McDonald, James E., wagon maker.
McDonald, Robert, wagon maker.
Macklin, Henry, general merchant.
Mann, S. H. & N., iron founders.
Mann, T. T., bookseller.
Martin, Henry, general merchant.
Moore, N. A., saddler.
Murdie, William, auctioneer.
Murray & Furnie, general merchants.
Murray, W. B., commissioner for taking affidavits.
Moseley, Henry.
Nairn, J. B., painter.
Nairn, T. M., general agent.
O'Riley, James, proprietor Exchange Hotel.
Ousterhout, A. H., proprietor National Hotel.
Parks, James, shoemaker.
Price, Aaron, druggist.
Price, Edwin, M. D.
Rushner, William
Secord, Thomas, butcher.
Simonds, Mrs. baker.
Smith, George M., carpenter.
Smith, Rev. N., (Wesleyan.)
Smith, Samuel, cabinet maker.
Stewart, Daniel, general agent.
Teeple, J. A., livery stable.
Thompson, Robert, proprietor British American.
Tozer, C. G. A.
Treadwell, Alexander
Vanpatter. F. D.
Walker, George J. & E., hardware merchants.
Walker, John & Son, cabinet makers.
Ward, Robert, tailor.
Williams, Adolphus, M.D.
Wright, R. C., baker.
York, S. D., tanner.

Avon Bank.—A small Village situated in the Township of Downie, County Perth. Population 50.
MUIR, DAVID, Postmaster.

Avonmore.—A Post-office in the Township of Roxborough, County Stormont.
SHAVER, E. N., Postmaster.

Avonton.—A Village in the Township of Downie, County Perth. 7½ miles from Stratford, the County Town, 4 from Sebringville Station, and 104 from Toronto. Average price of improved lands in the vicinity, $40 per acre.

Armstrong, George, farmer.
Ballantyne, Thomas, cheese factor.
Doak, Rev. William. (Presbyterian.)
Grieve, Adam, farmer.
Inman, Samuel, saw mill proprietor.
McKellar, J., blacksmith.
McNicol, Archibald, carpenter.
Murray, George, farmer.
Murray, Walter, farmer.
SHIELLS, ARCHIBALD, Postmaster and merchant

Ayr.—A Village on the River Nith, in the Township of North Dumfries, County Waterloo. The principal trade is in grain, flour, lumber and agricultural implements. Average price of land $40 to $60. Stage to Paris and Galt. Population, 1,000.

ANDERSON, JOHN McK., teacher.
Anderson, Thomas M., accountant.
AYR HERALD, weekly, James G. Watson, editor and proprietor.
Bain, James, M.D.
Baker, William, general merchant.
Bell, William, M.D.
Bingham, G. W., M.D.
Buckley & Lang, tinsmiths.
Chittenden, George, farmer.
Cunningham, Peter, brewer.
Currie, Eben, general merchant.
Cuthbertson, Hugh, shoemaker.
Dent, John C., attorney.
Ellis, H. & J., hotel keeper
Gillespie, Joseph, painter.
Gillet, Ralph, dentist.
Gladstone, James, cabinet maker.
Goldie, David, miller.
Hall, Robert, carpenter.
Hendershot & Donaldson, general merchants.
Hillborn, Henry C., hotel keeper.
Hood, Thomas, hotel keeper.
Howell, B. O., farmer.
Howie, Rev. J. (Evangelical Union)
Kay, James, cabinet maker.
Kilgour, Joseph, general merchant.
McCrae, James, shoemaker.
McGregor & Bell, wagon makers.
McLean, Miss, teacher.
McLean, Mrs. Sarah, teacher.
McRuar, Rev. D., (Presbyterian).
Marshall, Thomas, insurance agent.
Mathieson, Alexander, carpenter.
Mills, Rev. J., (Wesleyan).
Murray, John, baker.
Piper, James, miller.
Renwick, John, watchmaker.
Robertson, William, livery stable.
Richmond, William, farmer.
Rose, Alexander, bailiff.
Ross, Alexander, butcher.
Scott, Michael, general merchant.
Scott, Thomas C., carpenter.
Senior, Richard.
Stark, Miss, dressmaker.
Souter James, tailor.
Thomson, William, general merchant.
Wallace, Marion, dressmaker.
Ward, George, auctioneer.
WATSON, JAMES G., editor and proprietor *Ayr Herald.*
WATSON, JOHN, J.P., iron founder.
White, Charles, butcher.
White, Henry, gunsmith.
Willison, Walter, tailor.
Wyllie, John, Division Court clerk, bookseller, etc.
WYLLIE, ROBERT, Postmaster, ins. agent, etc.

Ayton.—A Village on the south branch of the Saugeen River, in the Township of Normanby, County Grey. Distant from Owen Sound the County Town, 46 miles; from Toronto, 93 miles. Average price of land, $30 to $40. Population, 200.

Baster, August, proprietor Commercial Hotel.
Bracht, B., saddler.
Card, David, cooper.
Faber, Bernard, cooper.
Fink, John, shoemaker.
Fitzpatrick, Patrick, shoemaker.
Lewis, Robert, carpenter.
Lissamer, Conrad, tinsmith.
Müller, John C., wagon maker.
Nasmith, George, general merchant.
PHILLIPS, JOHN M., Postmaster.
Pinkerton, James, M.D.
Pöerr, Henry, proprietor British Hotel.
Skelly, Patrick, carpenter.
Widmeyer, Barbara, proprietor Ayton Hotel.
Widmeyer, Schröder, general merchant.

Baby's Point.—A Village on the river St. Clair, in the Township of Sombra, County Lambton. Distant from Sarnia the County Town 24 miles, from Toronto 192 miles; stages to Wallaceburg and Chatham steamers to Sarnia and Detroit. Average price of land on river $25 to $50, back from river $4 to $10, improved land $12. Population 100.

Cain, B., proprietor British Hotel.
Calder, Hugh, customs officer.
Carroll, K. butcher.
Crocker, William, baker.
Devlin, Miss Jeannie, teacher.
Hatter, George W., farmer.
Henderson, John M. carpenter.
Kelly, John G., grocer.
Kilroy, Rev. Father, (Roman Catholic.)
McEvoy, Daniel, proprietor American Hotel.
MENTEN, JAMES, sen., Postmaster and Ex. agent.
Menten, William, general merchant.
Stonehouse, R. C., tinsmith.

Baden.—A Village on the Grand Trunk Railway, and Wilmot Creek, in the Township of Wilmot, County Waterloo. The Principal trade is in grain, flax and cattle. Average price of land $40 to $60. Distant from County Town 9 miles, from Toronto 72 miles. Money order office. Daily mail. Stages to and from Wellesley. Population, 500.

Beach, Alexander, teacher.
BECK, JACOB, Postmaster, miller, iron founder, &c.
Boys, Earnest, tailor.
Prodhecker, John, carpenter.
Cohn, Samuel, general merchant.
Cook, Earnest, wagon maker.
Craig, John R., farmer.
Emery, John, farmer.
Emmrich, Charles, saddler.
Erbach, Philip, cooper.
Forde, Henry, express agent.
Gable, Jacob, hotel keeper.
Garbig, George, carpenter.
Geiger, Peter, gunsmith.
Kaufman, Adam, hotel keeper.
Kraus, Christopher, hotel keeper.
Kumpf, Ernest, butcher.
Liersch, Henry, general merchant.
Livingston, J. & J., proprietor flax mill.
McIntyre, G. A., generol merchant.
Menges, Conrad, shoemaker.
Miller, Christian, farmer.
Morley, Michael, planing mill.
Myers, Abram, farmer.
Ross, Jacob, painter.
Rupp, Lorenzo, brewer.
Schmidt, Rev. George, (Lutheran.)
Smalltree, Matthew, cooper.
Smith, Henry, farmer.
Stattelberger, Henry, tinsmith.
Steppler, Adolphus, carpenter.
Sterrit, James, telegraph operator.
Wagler, Christian, farmer.
Weiler, John & Son, cabinet makers.
Witte, Charles, carpenter.
Woodhead, Charles, woollen factor.
Zarnsky, William, cooper.
Zehr, Joseph, farmer.
Zinn, George, carpenter.

Bagot.—A Post office situated in the Township of Bagot, County Renfrew.
HALLIDAY, JOHN, Postmaster.

Baillieboro.—A Village in the Township of Cavan, Co. Durham, 18 miles from Cobourg, 14 from Port Hope, 16 from Peterboro, and 7 from Millbrook Railway Station. Average value of land in the neighborhood, $45 per acre. Money order office. Population 200.

Allen, Rev. T. W. (Church of England)
Armstrong, John, farmer.
Barnard, Joseph, J. P.
Beard, Rev. James (Baptist)
Clemesha, John, druggist.
Cowan, J. J., general merchant.
Dixon, Robert, farmer.
Eakins, James, hotel.
Elliott, G. F., farmer.
Fisher, James, farmer.
FITZGERALD, JOHN, Postmaster, gen. mercht.
Greer, George, carpenter.
Kidd, George, farmer.
King, Richard, M.D.
Lewis, George, tailor.
Moffatt, James, hotel.
Northcote, William, farmer.
Parker, Martin, farmer.
Parker, Richard, saddler.
Phillips, Jeremiah, cabinet maker.
Porter, Samuel, farmer.
Quinn, Thomas, carpenter.
Reed, Alexander, farmer.

Bakersville.—A Village on Grindstone Creek, in the Township of Flamborough, County Wentworth, with a good trade in grain, flour, &c. Land averages $50. Distant from County Town, 8 miles, from Toronto, 40 miles. Stage to Hamilton. Daily mail. Population, 50.

Armstrong, George, carpenter.
BAKER, JOHN, Postmaster, prop. Bakerville Hotel.
Binkley, Peter.
Bremner, John, teacher.
Burns, M.
Burns & Son, millers, &c.
Green, John.
Griffin, B.
McDougall, D.
Mitchell, John.
Pepper, William, wagon maker.
Speck, S.

Balderson.—A Post-office of the Township of Lanark, County Lanark, S. R.
WATSON, SAUNDERS, Postmaster.

Baldwin.—A small village in the Township of Camden, County Addington. Distant from Kingston, 30 miles, and from Toronto, 144 miles. Population, 180.
YORK, GORDON P., Postmaster.

Ballantrae.—A Village in the Township of Whitchurch, County York. Distant from County Town 16 miles, from Toronto 35 miles. Average price of land, $35 to $50. Population, 75.

Gee, Rev. Daniel, (Wesleyan.)
LEPARD, ISAAC, Postmaster.
McCormack, R., J.P.
Markham, Rev. J., (Primitive).
Miller, Elijah, hotel keeper.
Moore, David, carpenter.
Patterson, James, auctioneer.
Pryon, Daniel, general merchant.
Sexsmith, George, general merchant.
Will, Robert, carpenter.
Willson, Henry, teacher.

Ballinafad.—A Village in the Township of Erin, County Wellington. Distant from County Town 20 miles, from Toronto 35 miles. Stage to Erin and Georgetown. Average price of land, $25 to $30. Population, 160.

APPLEBY, J. S., Postmaster.
Bennett, Robert, proprietor Commercial Hotel.
Binnie, Thomas, blacksmith.
Bonesteel, Albert, shingle manufacturer.
Campbell, A., saddler.
Coke, Joseph, farmer.
Czerwinski. L., shoemaker.
Eckart, Adam, pump maker.
Fletcher, A., wagon maker.
Gibbs, George, proprietor British Hotel.
Gibson, David, carpenter.
Grant, Miss A., teacher.
Hamilton, W., farmer.
Hills, Joseph, farmer.
Hunter, Miss, teacher.
Kennedy, John, farmer.
Luke, Rev. C. V., (Episcopal.)
Lellwood, W., brick maker.
McDonald, John, shingle manufacturer.
McEnery, William, farmer.
McKinnon, Miss, teacher.
Russell, John, farmer.
Sayers, George, proprietor livery stable.
Sayers, G. O., blacksmith.
Shortic, John, farmer.
Snider, G. H., general merchant.
Stewart. Mrs., dressmaker.
Webster, H. B., farmer.
Yeaman, Peter, farmer.

Ballycroy.—A Village in the Township of Adjala, County Simcoe, on the River Humber, 39 miles from Barrie and 22 from Bradford. Population 100.

Beatty, Samuel, carding mill.
Campbell, Archibald, blacksmith.
Crisp, John, farmer.
Faulkner, William.
Fletcher, Joseph, saddler.
Hurst, James, shoemaker.
McCLELLAND, JOHN, Postmaster, auctioneer and merchant.
Patton, James, blacksmith.
Reynolds, William, farmer.
Scott, James, shoemaker.
Small, Peter, general merchant.
Small, William E., teacher.
Welsh, John J., teacher.

Ballyduff.—A Village in the Township of Manvers, County Durham, 30 miles from the County Town, 17 from Newcastle, and 7 from Manver's Station, Grand Trunk Railway. Population 150.

Benson, Greg, hotel keeper.
Benson, Thos., J. P., farmer.
Benson, Wm., farmer.
Brown, Lucas, tailor.
Davey, Thos. G., farmer.
Dewell, John, farmer.
Dewell, Matthew, farmer.
McCabe, William, grist mill.
McCullough, George, farmer.
MAXWELL, W. A., Postmaster, and gen. merchant.
Mitchell, John, farmer.
Mordaunt, Robert, blacksmith.
Morrow, Thomas, shoemaker.
Muligan, Robert, farmer.
Porter, David, farmer.
Graham, James, weaver.
Graham, John, farmer.
Holmes, James, farmer.
Holmes, Joseph, farmer.
Jenning, John, saw and shingle mill.
Kellett, Edward, farmer.
Sethbridge, Andrew, farmer.
Porter, Francis, farmer.
Porter, Joseph, farmer.
Porter, William, farmer.
Ream, Reuben, teacher.
Staple, Henry, saw mills.
Ward, Mrs. Joseph, hotel keeper.
Williamson, James P., carpenter.
Windle, Rev. W. C., (Presbyterian.)

Ballymote.—A Post Village in the Township of London, County Middlesex.

O'BRIEN, J. W., Postmaster.

Balmer's Island.—A Village on the Madawaska River, in the Township of McNab, County Renfrew Distant from County Town, 50 miles. Population, 100.

Arnott, William, farmer.
Brown, David, farmer.
Brown, Walter, farmer.
Dickson, James, farmer.
Douglas John, farmer.
Duff, Alexander, general merchant.
Fyfe, Daniel, teacher.
Hamilton, Andrew, farmer.
Hill, William, farmer.
Jailor, Andrew, farmer.
McAllister, Duncan, farmer.
McClearn, hotel keeper.
McIntyre, Daniel, farmer.
McIntyre, John, J.P.
McKenzie, Peter, farmer.
McNab, Duncan, farmer.
Mackie, David, farmer.
Munroe, Donald, prop. Glencairn Inn.
Robertson, James, farmer.
Robertson, Neil, farmer.
Stewart, Alexander, farmer.
STEWART, ALLAN, Postmaster.
Sutherland, Donald, farmer.
Wilson, Alexander, farmer.

Balmoral.—A Village on the Buffalo and Lake Huron Railroad, in the Township of Rainham, County Haldimand. Distant from Cayuga, the County Town, 6 miles, from Toronto, 91 miles. Average price of land $40 per acre. Population, 80.

Anguish, Chapins, wagon maker.
Anguish, Mrs. E., prop. Travellers' Home.
Anguish, William, farmer.
Best, William, J.P.
Boucher, Nicholas.
Brown, Alfred, painter.
Butler, Finley, general merchant.
Campbell, Hugh.
Dougherty, Michael, shoemaker.
Finch, N. P., teacher.
LUNDY, GEORGE B., Postmaster and gen. merch't.
McDonald, Christopher, prop. Ontario House.
Moulin, Walton.
Whelan, Adolphus, cabinet maker.

Balsam.—A post Village in the Township of Pickering County Ontario. Distant from Whitby, the County Town, 14 miles, and from Toronto, 34 miles. Population about 100.

DODDS, ROBERT, Postmaster.

Baltimore.—A Village in the Township of Hamilton, County Northumberland, 5 miles from Cobourg. Population, 400.

Boyd, John, carriage maker.
Burgess, John, tanner.
Burnett, David, M.D.
Burrows, Charles, shoemaker.
Campbell, J. H., cloth factory.
Chapman, N., blacksmith.
Cockburn, George, hotel keeper.
Duncan, John.
GILLBARD, JOHN, Postmaster and gen. merch't.
Haig, Thomas, saddler.
Hogg, G. M., blacksmith.
Kelly, George, machinist.
McDougall, William, miller.
Mann, William, miller.
Pickering, E., hotel keeper.
Turner, John, M.D.
Wimble, F., shoemaker.

Bamberg.—A Village on Kroetsch Creek, in the Township of Wellesley, County Waterloo. Distant from County Town 13 miles, from Toronto 75 miles. Stages to and from St. Agatha. Average price of land $36 to $40. Population 200.

Ball, Joseph, blacksmith.
Ball, Nicolas, shoemaker.
Becker, Martin, cabinet maker.
Bersang, Blasius, teacher.
Bohmer, Jacob, cooper.
Boppre, A., farmer.
Dietrich, Joseph, cabinet maker.
Dietrich, M., farmer.
Forster, Lewis, carpenter.
Held, Adam, farmer.
Herryot, John, farmer.
Kiswetter, J., farmer.
Kroetsch, John, lumber dealer.
Lattrer, C., farmer.
Lorentz, Joseph, farmer.
Metzdorf, Charles, teacher.
Moser, John, farmer.
Reichert, W., farmer.
Rumig, J., farmer.
Rutz, Matthias, farmer.
Schloegel, John, blacksmith.
Snyder, Matthias, farmer.
Strauss, S., farmer.
Thirhardt, T., farmer.
Voll, K., farmer.
WALTER FERDINAND, Postmaster and general merchant.
Walter, F., proprietor Bamberg hotel.
Zimmerman, Andrew, brewer.
Zimmerman, Henry, wagon maker.

Banda.—A Village in the Townships of Mulmer and Nottawasaga, County Simcoe. 22 miles from Barrie, and 8 from New Lowell Station, Northern Railway. Population, 50.

Bain, Neil, carpenter.
CLEMENGER, JOHN, Postmaster, wagon maker.
Cloughley, Thomas, blacksmith.
Flack, Robert, farmer.
Graham, Henry, general merchant
Hood, Joseph & Co., general merchant.
Johnson, Thomas.
Lattimer, William, farmer.
Little, William, cabinet maker.
Munro, Hugh, carpenter.
Perry, John, carpenter.
Thomas, John, farmer.
Walker, George, farmer.

Bandon.—A post Village situated on the South branch of the river Maitland, in the Township of Hullet, County Huron. Distant from Goderich, the County Town, 20 miles. Population 50.
ALLEN, JAMES, Postmaster.

Bangor.—A post Village situated in the Township of Pickering, County Ontario.
TURNER, ISAAC, Postmaster.

Bannockburn.—A post Village situated in the Township of Madoc, County Hastings.
CARPENTER, W. H., Postmaster.

Bark Lake.—A Post-office in Jones' Township, County Hastings, on the Madawaska river, 74 miles from Sand Point and 124 miles from Ottawa, on the Ottawa and Opeongo road.

Conway, Michael, farmer.
Donaldson, Archibald, farmer.
Donaldson, James, farmer.
Dunn, William, farmer.
Dupré, Peter, farmer.
Ofrie, Joseph, farmer.
Prishan, Antoine, farmer.
Reed, James, hotel keeper.
Sayya, Jacob, farmer.
Skuce, John, hotel keeper,
SKUCE, RICHARD, sen., Postmaster.

Barnett.—(See Ennotville.) A Post-office in the Township of Nicol, County Wellington.
ELMSLIE, JAMES, Postmaster.

Barriefield.—A small Village in the Township of Pittsburg, County Frontenac, 1½ miles from Kingston. Population about 150.

Allan, Thomas, blacksmith.
Bower, Rev. E. J., (Church of England.)
Esford, Thomas, blacksmith.
Finley, Alexander, grocer.
Hutton, William, inn keeper.
Johnson, Walter, teacher.
McRossie & Co., saw mill proprietors.

Barrie.—The County Seat of Simcoe, and a station of the Northern Railway, pleasantly situated on Kempenfeldt Bay, Lake Simcoe, in the Township of Vespra. It has a fine appearance from the opposite side of the bay, the rising ground bringing every part of the town distinctly into view. Distance from Toronto 64 miles, from Collingwood 31, and from Orillia 27. Steamers to the Muskoka Territory, Orillia, &c. Stages to Penetanguishene. Population 3000.

Albiston, James, agent Northern Railway.
Alexander & Co., druggists.
Anderton Bros., brewers.
ARDAGH & ARDAGH, barristers.
Armstrong, Joseph, grocer.
ARNALL, ALFRED, prop. Queen's Hotel. (See adv)
Ashton, George.
Ball, George, builder.
BANK OF TORONTO, J. M. Smith, agent.
BANK OF COMMERCE, Edmund S. Lally, agent.
BARRIE ADVANCE, D. Crew, publisher.
BARRIE EXAMINER, W. M. Nicholson, editor and proprietor.
Bennett, Humphrey, clothier.
Bingham, A. R., prop. Wellington hotel.
Bingham Bros., butchers.
Bird, Henry, boots and shoes.
Boon, John, inn keeper.
Booth, John, fanning mills.
BOYS, HENRY R. A., County Treasurer.
BOULTON, LOUNT, BOYS & STEWART, barristers, &c.
Brett, Wm., butcher.
Brelley, Samuel, inn keeper.
Bryant, Adam, carpenter.
Burnett, A., stoves and tinware.
Burton & Smith, props. steamer *Ida Burton*.
Butt, Albert, wagon maker.
Byrnes, George, shoemaker.
Campbell, John, brickmaker.
Carpenter, L., lumber merchant.
Carey, Robert, shoemaker.
Caldwell, Wm., blacksmith.
Carson, James, boots and shoes.
Cavanagh, John, farmer.
Chalaupka, Prof., music teacher.
CLARKSON, JOSHUA, proprietor Commercial Hotel (See adv.)
Cooper, George, grocer.
Cotter, J. R., barrister, County Crown Attorney.
Coulter & Pearcey, painters.
Cox, Wm., miller.
Creswicke, Henry, P. L. S.
CREW, D., Editor *Advance*.
Crookshank, J. S., M. D.
CROSBY, WM. H., livery (see adv.)
Cundle, Thos., lumber merchant.
Cunio, Andrew, barber.
Dougal, David, cabinet maker,
Dunn, William, baker,

Durham, John, prop. saw mills.
EDWARDS, JAMES, J. P., Postmaster.
Farragher, D., prop. Farragher's Hotel.
FRASER, HENRY, prop. Exchange Hotel.
Garton, David B., photographer.
Georgen, T. W., druggist.
GOWAN, JAMES R., judge County Court.
Graham, Andrew, tanner.
Graham, Alexander, builder.
GRAHAM, JAMES N., flax and carding mills.
Graham, T., dry goods and groceries.
Grant, J. G., lumber merchant.
Graver, Edward, hardware.
Griffith, Thomas, plasterer.
Grubbe, H. W.
Gunn, Allan, lumber merchant.
Hall, Robert G., agricultural implements.
Hamilton, Alexander, M.D.
Harrison, C., general merchant.
HASTINGS, JOSEPH W., watchmaker (see adv.)
Heinrich, Henry, music teacher.
Henderson, J., general merchant.
Hickling, Charles, farmer.
Hinds, Bernard, general merchant.
Hinds, Edward, general merchant.
Hodson, Robert C., general merchant, bookbinder.
Holt, William, commission agent, broker, &c.
Hubbard, William, innkeeper.
Huggard, John, innkeeper.
Hunter, William, grocer.
Irwin, William, A.M., teacher.
Johns, J. H., proprietor Victoria Hotel.
Johnson, James, grocer.
Johnson, Martin, brickmaker.
Johnson, Thomas, fruits and confectionary.
Johnson, William M., farmer.
KELMAN & CO., druggists.
King & Crabb, general merchants.
King, Nathaniel, prop. Temperance Hotel.
King, Robert, baker.
Leey, James, blacksmith.
Laird & Morrow, grocers, grain dealers, &c.
Laird, John, pork and grain dealer.
LALLY, EDMUND S., agent Bank of Commerce, insurance agent, issuer marriage licenses.
Lane George, merchant tailor, town clerk.
Lane, Jonathan, clerk County Court.
Lee, John, builder.
LLOYD, THOMAS D., clerk Division Court.
Locke, Joseph, general merchant.
Locke, Mrs. J., ladies' school.
Lount, Gabriel T., clerk Registrar.
Lount, Geo. J. P., County Registrar.
Lount, Samuel, Deputy Registrar.
LOUNT, WM., M. P. P.
Lowe, John, farrier.
Lowe, Thomas, butcher.
Lynn Bros., photographers.
McAvoy, P., grocer.
McBride, Chas., shoemaker.
McBride, P., merchant.
McCARTHY & McCARTHY, barristers.
McCausland, J. C., dentist.
McConkey & Co., merchants.
McCormick, Thos., carpenter.
McCormick, Thos., general merchant.
McFetridge. Wm., produce dealer.
McGuirck, John, lime burner.
McHenry, Robt., saddler.
McIntosh, Peter, lumber merchant.
McKinley, Duncan, carpenter.
McLAUGHLIN, M., prop. Simcoe House.
McVity, Wm. B., Clerk of the Peace.
McWatt, John, superintendent Barrie Hotel.

Manahan, Mrs. J. A., grocer.
Mann, W. & Son, books and stationery.
Marks, Mrs. E., proprietor Barrie Hotel.
Marrin, James, general merchant.
Marrin, Thos., shoemaker.
Marston, James, carpenter.
Melady, P., dry goods and groceries.
MEEKING, EDWIN S., auctioneer and general merchant. (See adv.)
MONTREAL TELEGRAPH CO., Jas. Albiston, agent.
Morgan, Rev. Edward, (Church of England.)
Morrow, Alex., insurance agent.
Morrow, David, inspector of inland revenue.
MORROW, JAMES C., attorney.
Morrow, John, merchant.
Morton, E. D., M. D.
Moore, John, shoemaker.
Moore, Martin, saddler.
Neil, Robert, shoemaker.
NICHOLSON, W. M., editor and proprietor Barrie *Examiner*.
Northgraves, Very Rev. Dean (Roman Catholic)
O'Brien, William, barrister
O'Connor, Michael, merchant.
O'Neill, John, carpenter.
OLIVER, LLEWELLYN, M.D., coroner.
Oxenham, R. J., plasterer.
Pae, Peter, general merchant.
Palmer, William, blacksmith.
Pass, Walter, grain merchant.
Payne, John, grocer.
Plaxton, George, stoves and tinware.
Powell & Thompson, groceries and liquors.
Pullen, J., gunsmith.
RAWSON, THOMAS E., stoves and tinware (see adv.)
Riddell, Walter, potash factor.
Robinson, Thomas, miller.
Robinson, W. C., stave factory.
Rogers, Joseph, high bailiff.
Root, William, saddler.
Ross & Gilchrist, general merchants.
Ryan, James, carpenter.
Sanders, L. S., watchmaker.
Saunders, Wm., P. L. S.
Seadon, K., farmer.
SEWRY, HENRY & CO., iron founder (see adv.)
Sheridan, Bernard, merchant.
Sherran, John, saddler.
Sigsworth, Thomas, baker.
Simpson, R., brewer.
Simpson, Thomas, brewer.
SMITH, BENJAMIN W., sheriff.
SMITH, J. M., agent Bank of Montreal.
Soules, David, farmer.
SPENCER, M. H., groceries, wines and liquors (see adv.)
Stevens, Francis, insurance agent.
STEWART, HAMILTON D., barrister.
Strong, W. E., M.D.
Summers, George, carriage maker.
Summers, Joseph, bricklayer.
Summersett, Thomas, blacksmith.
Swan, Mrs. J., grocer.
Sweeney, John, shoemaker.
Thompson, Archibald, lumber merchant.
Thompson, Wm., grocer.
VAN EVERY, DAVID, livery stables (see adv.)
Watson, Mrs., butcher.
WEAYMOUTH, JOHN, livery stables.
Westley, Samuel, constable.
Whitebread, Richard, wheelwright.
Willson, Andrew, lumber merchant.
Willson, John, carpenter.

Bartonville.—A Village in the Township of Barton, County Wentworth, 8 miles from Hamilton and 14 from Grimsby. Population 80.

Burkholder, Jacob, farmer.
Burkholder, William, farmer.
Condy, James, blacksmith.
Crossett, Daniel, farmer.
Crossett, Harvey, farmer.
Crossthwaite, Henry, farmer.
Depew, Abraham.
Depew, Peter, general merchant.
Gage, John, trader and farmer.
Gage, Peter, school teacher.
GAGE, W. J., Postmaster.
Oliver, John, hotel keeper.
Thomas, James, inn keeper.
Waller, George. farmer.
Williams, Rev. D., (Episcopal Methodist.)
Wilson, William, farmer and hotel keeper.

Bath.—An incorporated Village and port of entry on the north shore of the Bay of Quinté, in the Township of Ernestown, County Addington, 12 miles from Napanee and 18 from Kingston. Stages daily to Kingston and Picton. Money Order office. Population 750.

Aishton, Thomas, M.D.
Armstrong, Thomas.
Athos, A. butcher.
Bain, Thomas, sheomaker.
Barrass, Rev. E., (Wesleyan).
Belfour, G., J.P.
BELFOUR, JOHN, Postmaster, telegraph operator.
Belfour, W., accountant.
Belfour & Armstrong, general merchants.
Blair, William, tailor.
Burley, Silas, livery stable proprietor.
Burrowes, Frederick, teacher.
Campbell, D. J., grocer.
Chinnery, A., butcher.
Cunningham, L. L., carpenter,
Davy, P. R.
Davy, W. H., commission merchant.
Davy, W. H., jun., accountant.
Dungan, John, boiler maker.
Ferren, E. G., proprietor City Hotel.
Finkle, R. R., steamboat agent.
Forward, D. T., stock dealer.
Foster, M., tanner.
Gardiner, Joseph, cabinet maker.
Harper, Rev. W. F. S., (Church of England.)
Hawley, Joseph.
Hoselton, H. A., commission and general merchant.
Hough, Mrs., dressmaker.
Houleghan, J., shoemaker.
Howard, T. E.. commission, and gen. mercht.
Huffman, Henry.
Injinean, Lewis, willow ware.
Johnston, J. J., saddler.
Johnston, Robert, soap and candle manufacturer.
Johnston, T. C., saddler.
Johnston, William, wines and liquor.
Kennedy, Roderick, M.D.
Kitson, R. shoemaker.
Laird, Billings, gunsmith.
Laird, J. McC., carpenter.
Lasher, John, general merchant.
Lauder, G. H., telegraph operator.
Lewis, Allen, steamboat agent,
McBride, Daniel, grocer.
McFarlane, D., accountant.
McKenty, E., general merchant.
McQuirk, P. shoemaker.
McTaggart, Miss, dressmaker.
Millar, Samuel, stock dealer.
Milligan, Moses. seedsman.
Mott, Robert, saddler.
Murduff, John, architect.
Noble, J. D., Division Court clerk.
O'Rourke, M., liquor dealer.
Pappa, Peter, tailor.
Parks, Thomas, carpenter.
Peterson, W. F., J.P.
Price, Elias.
Price, R. B., dentist.
Purdy, H. W.
Richards, Miss, dressmaker.
Ridley, Rev. John, (Wesleyan).
Rogers, C. L., accountant.
Rogers, Hudson, dry goods.
Rogers, Samuel, general merchant.
Ross, J. G., general merchant.
Rose, W.
Rouse, D. T., general merchant.
Rouse, John, S., baker.
Shebley, W., saddler.
Sheppard, John, cabinetmaker.
Symonds, Mrs., dressmaker.
Symonds, A., painter.
Thurston, William, woolen factor.
Trimlet, Joseph, tailor.
Tuttle, Miss, teacher.
Urquhart, Donald.
Wemp, Duncan, proprietor Lion Hotel.
Wilcox, R. D., general agent,
Wright, Edward, division court clerk, grocer, &c.

Battersea.—A Village in the Township of Storrington, County Frontenac, situated at the outlet of Loboro' Lake, 16 miles from Kingston. Stage to Kingston. Bi-weekly mails. Population 200.

ANGLIN, W. J., Postmaster, merchant.
Ansly, John, carpenter.
Bates, Timothy, sash and door manufacturer.
Brewer. John, hotel keeper.
Chapman, John, shingle maker.
Chapman, William, carpenter.
Davis, Robert, lumber merchant.
Ginnis, George, hotel keeper.
Hewton & Davis, woolen factory.
Hughes, Edward, blacksmith.
Lattimer, H., stage driver.
McBride, William, weaver.
Smith, John L., lumber merchant.
Spooner, John, storekeeper.
Vanluven, Cornelius, carding mill.
Vanluven, Henry, miller.
Walker, David, wagon maker.
Wright, Z., tanner.

Bayham.—A Post-office in the Township of Bayham, County Elgin, E. R.
LAING, GEORGE, Postmaster.

Bayfield.—A Village in the Township of Stanley, County Huron, situated at the mouth of the Bayfield river, on Lake Huron, 12 miles from Goderich, 10 from Clinton, and 16 from Seaforth. It is a port of entry and vessels touch here on their route from Detroit to Goderich. Stages daily to Seaforth. It is a Money Order Office and Savings Bank.

Adams, John, carpenter.
Ahrens, Fritz, hotel keeper.
Armstrong, William, hotel keeper.
Ballantyne, Donald, laborer.
Baxter, Robert, butcher.
Beaton, Donald, boat builder.
Brikle, M., laborer.
Bettchin, Jacob J., wool and carding manufacturer.
Biggart, John, laborer.
Brunston, A. B., fruit grower.
Burgess, Thomas, cooper.
Cameron, Miss Mary, store keeper.
Cameron, D. & A., saddlers.
Carson, Mrs. William, weaver.
Carson, William, laborer.
Connor, W. W., J.P.,
Crawford, Miss Sarah, teacher.
Crooks, James, carpenter.
Crooks, Richard, carpenter.
Cullens, David, blacksmith.
Daunt, Rev., (Church of England.)
Deising, Peter, tanner.
Dresser, Charles, fisherman.
Duncan, Rev. James, (Free Church).
Duncan, William, teacher.
Dupie, Sylvester, farmer.
Eagleson, Robert, weaver.
Eberhardt, Charles E., baker.
Elliott, Thomas, shoemaker.
Elliott, Edward, hotel keeper.
Egan, F. L., general merchant.
Erwin, James, carpenter.
Eason, John, farrier.
Falkner, Alexander, carpenter.
Ferguson, John, blacksmith.
Foy, William, shoemaker.
Gafe, Mr. tailor.
GAIRDNER, J., Postmaster.
Geirdner, C., general merchant.
Gairdner, M. D.
Ganenhart, John, carpenter.
Gibson, Rev. H., (Presbyterian.)
Gordon, Mrs.
Grainger, James, farmer.
Haacke, Arthur, constable.
Haacke, David, laborer.
Haacke, Henry, trader.
Homan, Valentine, tinsmith.
Irvine, George, blacksmith.
JOSLIN, JOHN, hotel keeper
Jacques, Rev., (Wesleyan.)
King, William, hotel keeper.
Leaker, U. Duncan, teacher.
Lockhart, Richard, weaver.
McAuley, Norman, fisherman.
McAuley, Neil, fisherman.
McDonald, John, fisherman.
McDonald, James, fisherman.
McDonald, James, tailor.
McDougal, Daniel, bailiff.
McDougal, Mrs. D., dressmaker.
McKeown, William, wagon maker.
McLeod, Hugh, fisherman.
McLeod, Daniel, fisherman.
McLeod, James, wool carder.
McPherson, Peter, tailor.
Marks, T., general merchant.
Martin, Abel, laborer.
Miller, E. R., general merchant.
Millar, Henry, cooper.
Mitchell, Thomas, undertaker.
Middleton, Charles, J.P.
Mitchell, Mrs. George, dressmaker.
MORGAN, JOHN, hotel keeper. (See adv.)
Morrison, R., general merchant.
Morrison, William, cabinet maker.
Moore, Rev., (Primative Methodist.)
Murray, Angus, fisherman.
Osmond, Zacariah, carpenter.
Philips, William, cabinetmaker.
Podock, James.
Rankin, W. N., general merchant.
Reid, William, wagon maker.
Ritchie, D. H., clerk Division Court.
Rogers, Solon, carpenter.
Rath, —, brewer.
Rutledge, Andrew, general merchant.
Rylie, H., carpenter.
Sellers, Robert, laborer.
Shaw, Charles, plow manufacturer.
Stanbury, Richard, M.D.
Thompson & Faliere, millers, etc.
Wainright, Henry,
Walmon, A. shoemaker.
Watteford, Richard, miller.
Wellman, David, carpenter.
Whitten, James, wagon maker.
Williamson, James, hotel keeper.
Woods, Frederick, teacher.
Woods, Nivian, M.D.

Beachburg.—A Village in the Township of Westmeath, County Renfrew. Distant from County Town, 15 miles, from Ottawa, 80 miles, from Toronto, 348 miles. Stages to Pembroke and Sand Point. Average price of land, $8. Money order office. Population, 250.

Badgley, Rev. E. J. (Methodist Episcopal)
Beach, Abel, J. P.
Burnett, William, butcher.
Cameron, Rev. Hugh (Presbyterian)
Cannon, William, notary public, &c.
Colquhoun, Miss Mary, dressmaker.
Condie, Alexander, lumber dealer.
Condie, James, sen., miller.
Condie, James, jun.
Condie, Malcolm.
Dowe, Victor, saddler.
Dunn, James.
Eggleston, Newton, carpenter.
Forbes, George, M.D.
Fraser, Donald, general merchant.
Gardiner, Charles, saddler.
Gill, James, carpenter.
Heenan & Legge, general merchants.
Johnston, Andrew, proprietor Johnston's Hotel.
Johnston, James W.
Johnston, John.
Lavender, Robert, wagon maker.
Legerwood, Daniel, teacher.
McLaren, Peter, shoemaker.
McLean, Daniel.
Munro, James, wagon maker.
Murray, T. & W., general merchants.
Simpson, Rev. J. H. (Church of England.)
Sullivan, Thomas, proprietor Pembroke Hotel.
SURTEES, GEORGE, Postmaster and gen. merch't.
Taylor, Thomas, tailor.
Tomblyn, Rev. Wm., (Wesleyan.)
Wiglesworth, John, J. P.

Beachville.—A Village on the Great Western Railway and River Thames, in the Township of W. Oxford, County Oxford, containing 1 flour mill, 1 flax mill, 1 foundry, 2 saw mills, 2 tanneries, 4 churches, 2 common schools, 3 hotels, &c. Distant from County Town, 4 miles, from Toronto, 100 miles. Stages to Embro, Brookadale, and Stratford. Average price of land, $30 to $40. Money Order office. Population, 700.

Barlow, Miss C., dressmaker.
Bennett, Robert, proprietor Royal Exchange Hotel.
Blackwall, D. W., millwright.
Bland, Luke, stock dealer.
Bremner, Alexander, lime manufacturer.
Brink, Charles, farmer.
Brown, Isaac W., M.D.
Brown, John H., proprietor flax mill.
Burton, John, tanner.
Canfield, Steward, farmer.
Carroll, John, farmer.
Case, Harrison, carpenter
Caswell, Albert, farmer
Clemenhegg, Nathan, blacksmith
Collier, James, proprietor Oxford House
Conrad, H. A. (Baptist)
Creighton, Alexander, carpenter
Dark, John, mason
Dean, Solomon, match manufacturer
Dickie, James, wagon maker
Dodge, John, farmer
Dodge, William, farmer
Downing, T., mason
Elsey, J., general merchant.
Evatt, James, grocer.
Fairbairn, James, grocer.
Fassie, William, painter.
Fox, Philip., farmer
Gilbert, E. teacher.
Gould, W. R., cabinet maker.
Gray, Mrs., dressmaker.
Gray, J., lumber dealer.
Green, Hiram, mason.
Greig, Major, George.
Hamilton, Rev. Wm., D.D., (Presbyterian.)
Harp, Henry, carpenter.
Henry, John, tailor.
Henry, Warren, shoemaker.
Hill, William H., grocer.
Hook, William, miller.
Jovering, James, baker.
Karn, Freeman, farmer.
Karn, James, proprietor Railway Hotel.
Lewis, Erwin, farmer.
Lick, John, farmer.
Light, Alexander.
McCombs, Hiram, millwright.
McDonald, John, blacksmith.
McLean, Robert, millwright.
Martin, Calvin, J. P.
Martin, H. F., farmer.
Martin, S. C., farmer.
Martin, William, butcher.
MASON, CHARLES, Postmaster, J. P.
Matheson, J. G., teacher.
Middough, William, blacksmith.
Millar, T. D., commission merchant.
Nellis, E. E. & Co., general merchants.
Nott, James, lime merchant.
Parsons, William, express agent.
Perry, Stephen, shingle manufacturer.
Phelps, Joel, match manufacturer.
Phelps, Uriah, constable.
Phelps. Uriah & Son, blacksmiths.
Rutherford, L., farmer.
Ryan, Mrs., dressmaker.
Secord, Abraham,, match manufacturer.
Slater, John, tailor.
Snider, W. F., carpenter.
Taylor, James & Son, shoemakers.
Walls, Alexander, millwright.
Watson, Rev. W. C., B.A., (Wesleyan.)
Whitelaw, Robert, iron founder, millwright, &c.
Young, Thomas, brick manufacturer.

Beaverton.—A Village on the Eastern shore of Lake Simcoe, at the mouth of the Beaver river, in the Township of Thora, County Ontario, 45 miles from Whitby, 30 from Bell Ewart and 75 from Toronto. It is the terminus of the Port Hope, Lindsay and Beaverton Railway. The steamer *Emily May* plies daily between this point and Bell Ewart station, Northern Railroad. Stages daily to Whitby and Oshawa. Money Order office and Savings' Bank. Population 700.

Adams, John N., shoemaker.
Adams, John, tannery.
Anderson, James, tannery.
Arbuthnot, D. & Co., general merchants.
Bates, James, blacksmith.
Burchard, Anson. blacksmith.
Calder, Alexander, farmer.
Calder, Duncan, farmer.
Cameron, A. general merchant.
Cameron, Alexander, farmer.
CAMERON, DONALD, Postmaster.
Cameron, James, stoves and tinware.
Cameron, Col. Kenneth
Cameron & Bruce (Alex. & G. F.) general merchants
Davidson, C. H., farmer
DAVISON, PETER, M. D. (See adv.)
Ellis Geoffrey, carding mills
Farquharson, D., dry goods.
Glaves, D., hotel keeper
Gordon, N. & W., general merchants
HAMILTON, ALEXANDER, prop. Hamilton house
LOWES, J. S., eclectic physician
McDonald, D. G., general merchant
McKAY, ALEX., M. D., coroner, druggist. (See adv)
McKinnon, A., blacksmith
McLachlan, Rev. John, (Canada Presbyterian)
Miller, J. G., general merchant.
Murray, Peter, blacksmith
Orde, Charles V., barrister
Paterson, Norman F., barrister
PROCTOR, G. R., general merchant
Proctor George, grist and saw mills
Proctor, James R., farmer
Proctor, John A., flour mills
ROBINSON, CHARLES, J. P. clerk 6th Div. Court, com. in B. R., conveyancer, valuator Canada permanent building and saving society
Todd, John & James, carriage makers
Watson, Rev. Mr., (Presbyterian)
Way, J. B., saw mill proprietor
Williamson, David, tailor

Beamsville.—A Village on the Great Western Railway, in the Township of Clinton, County Lincoln. Distant from County Town, 13 miles, from Toronto, 83 miles. Average price of land in vicinity, $45. Money Order office and Savings' Bank. Population 550.

Amiss, Jeremiah, seedsman.
Bosche, A., painter.
Boughner, William, cooper.
Bonghun, Patrick, shoemaker.
Boyer, Matthias, shoemaker.
Burns, James, tailor.
Carter, James F., saddler.
Colladay, Jacob, carpenter
Comfort, W. A., M.D
Conse's,—, proprietor Conse's Hotel.
Cornwall, Miss Minnie, teacher.
Eddy & James, saw mill proprietors
Frigoli, Thos., watchmaker.
Hearle, William, tinsmith.
Henry, James S., general merchant.
Henry, Michael, carpenter.
Henry, Robert, carpenter.
Hewitt, Wm., proprietor saw mill.
Hipple, Jacob, teacher.
Hodge, Archibald, general merchant.
Hunn, Isaac, broom maker.
Ismond, J. J., stock dealer.
Kerr, John C., telegraph operator.
Kerr, William, wagon maker.
Kilbourne, Cyrus, cabinet maker.
Kilborne, R., J. P.
King, William, cooper.
Konkle, Matthias, grain merchant.
Krotz, Abraham, broom maker.
Little, Miss, dressmaker.
Little & Sons, potters.
McBoughner, T., tailor.
McLean, J. G., M. D.
Mackie, Rev. Jas., (Baptist.)
Merrill, R. S., stock dealer.
Morrow, William, shoemaker.
Moyer, Jacob S., broom maker.
Moyer, Jonas, mason.
Moyer, M. W., painter.
Moyer, Samuel S., broom maker.
Murray, Rev., (Presbyterian)
OSBORNE, J. B., Postmaster & general merchant.
Reid, James, insurance agent.
Rodger, J., proprietor Rodger's Hotel.
Rodgers, B., brick maker.
Russ, Cyrus, shingle maker.
Schwabb, William, potter.
Shephard, R., proprietor Station Hotel.
Smith, William, J.P.
Spotton, H. B., teacher.
Sutton, George, butcher.
Tallman, William, mason.
Tinline, William S., carpenter.
Walker, J. S., J.P.
Walker, William, butcher.
Walker, William, wagon maker.
Zimmerman, Jeremiah, proprietor saw mill.

Bear Brook.—A Village in the Township of Cumberland, County Russell. Distant from L'Orignal, the County Town, 52 miles, from Ottawa 18 miles, from Toronto 297 miles. Average price of land, $14 to $25. Population 150.

Brick, J. B., carpenter.
Carter, John, carpenter.
Chauron, Joseph, cooper.
Cobourn, Francis, farmer.
Daust, C., mason.
Dunning & Co., general merchants.
Ferguson, James, M.D.
Fletcher, William H., proprietor Cottage Inn.
Garrett, Rev. T., (Church of England).
Goslin, M., carpenter.
GRIER, BROCK, Postmaster.
Grier, J. & B., general merchants.
Hamilton, Robert, shingle manufacturer.
Haney, William, shingle manufacturer.
Hill, Alfred, teacher
Lone, Nathaniel, farmer
Lowry, Rev. T., (Presbyterian)
McElroy, David, farmer
McNally, Henry, farmer
McNeigh, Peter, J.P.
Middleton, Thomas, farmer
Nelson, Gilbert, farmer
Renney, Rev. J., (Wesleyan)
Shea, Dennis, farmer
Smiley, John, farmer.
Walsh, John, farmer
Wilson, Andrew, farmer
Yates, David, shoemaker.

Belfast.—A Village in the Township of Ashfield, County Huron. Distant from Goderich, the County Town, 18 miles, from Toronto, 154 miles. Stages to Goderich and Lucknow. Average price of land $35 to $40. Population, 50.

Atherington, Miss Eliza Jane, teacher.
Johnston, Samuel, carpenter.
McCrostie, John, farmer.
McHARDY, JOHN, Postmaster.
McHardy, John & Co., general merchants.
Phillips, Samuel, lumber dealer.
Reid, W. H., sen., J.P.
Rinciman, David, lumber dealer.
Sturgeon, Robert, proprietor Belfast hotel.
Woods, William, carpenter.

Belford.—A post Village in the Township of Markham, County York, 23 miles from Toronto, and 3 miles from Markham Village. Population 50.

Boyd, James, J.P.
BURTON, ISRAEL, Postmaster.

Belfountain.—A Village on the River Credit, in the Township of Caledon, County Peel. Distant from Brampton, the County Town 20 miles, from Toronto 40 miles. Stages to Erin and Georgetown. Average price of land $20. Population 100.

Baker, Michael, jr., farmer.
Blair, John, farmer.
Blair, P., farmer.
Brock, Meadows, farmer.
Brock, Robert, cabinet maker.
Bush, T. J., farmer.
Byam, J. F., grocer.
Currie, D., farmer.
Dodd, Thomas, miller.
Frank, Archibald, farmer.
HERRING, NOAH, Postmaster.
Herring, N. I. teacher.
Knox, Rev. Mr., (Methodist Episcopal).
Long, William, carpenter.
McLare, Andrew, farmer.
McLaren, Alexander, farmer.
McTaggart, Peter, wagon maker.
Merry, Thomas P., J.P.
Nugent, Rev. Mr., (New Connexion).
Ramsay, Malcolm, carpenter.
Redick, F. C., proprietor Belfountain House.
Reid, Rev. Hugh, (Baptist).
Sanderson, William, farmer.
Smith, John, farmer.
Steele, James, tanner.
Walker, W. N., farmer.

Belgrave.—A Village on the Maitland river and Buffalo and Lake Huron Railway, in the Township of Morris, County Huron. Distant from Goderich, the County Town, 23 miles, from Toronto 106 miles. Stages to Wingham, Teeswater, Riversdale and Kincardine. Average price of land $20. Population 50.

ARMSTRONG, SIMON, Postmaster & gen. merch't
Bell, C., carpenter.
Brandon, Matthew, farmer.
Corbet, Christopher, J.P.
Coulter, Samuel, shingle maker.
Gleeson, W., general merchant.
McCartney, David, general merchant.
McCrea, John, farmer.
McCrea, William, farmer.
McLean, Rev. Mr., (Presbyterian,)
Morrison, G. W., proprietor of the Half-Way House.
Owens, James, farmer.
Robertson, Donald, cabinet maker.
Smith, Miss Annie, teacher.

Belhaven.—A post Village in the Township of North Gwillimbury, County York, North Riding,
PROSSER, DANIEL, Postmaster.

Belleville.—The County Town of Hastings, situated on the Bay of Quinte, at the mouth of the river Moira, in the Township of Thurlow. It posssses some of the best water privileges in the Province and at different points on the river various extensive manufactories are established. It is a port of entry and does a large business in imports. The chief exports are lumber, flour and produce. Having communication with the principal ports of the Province and the United States, both by water and railway, it is one of the most flourishing towns in the country. The Grand Trunk Railway has a station here, and during the summer, steamers ply daily to and from Kingston and intermediate ports. Distance from Toronto 113 miles, and from Montreal 220 miles. Money Order office and Savings' Bank. Population, 7000.

Ackerill, D., veterinary surgeon.
Adams, George, dealer in stoves, tinware, &c.
Adamson, Mark, grocer.
ÆTNA MARINE INSURANCE CO., (Hartford.) John Thomas, agent.
AGRICULTURAL MUTUAL ASSURANCE ASSOCIATION OF CANADA, John Thomas, agent.
ALBERT COLLEGE, Rev. Bishop Smith, D.D., Rev. Bishop Richardson, D. D., Presidents, Rev. J. Gardiner, Secretary.
Alford, William, shoemaker.
Allcock, Henry, saloon.
Alport, F. F., commission merchant.
ATKINS, H. R., (G. C. Holton & Co)
Bain, Mrs. Jane, milliner
BAKER, JAMES, (John Carscallen & Co)
Baker, Sanford, lumber merchant
Baker, W. J., carriage maker, &c
BANK OF MONTREAL, W. K. Dean, manager
BARRINGER & CO., proprietors Dafoe House
Barrodaile, G. C., prop. Dominion House
Bartley, James, Assistant Postmaster
Bates, Mrs. T., prop. Railway House
Bates, R. J., tailor
Beamish, W. A., landing waiter
Becket, Paul, saddler
Belch, Samuel, grocer and soda water manufacturer
BELL, JOHN, (Ross, Bell & Holden), solicitor Grand Trunk Railway
Bellair, Mrs. Margaret, milliner, &c
BENJAMIN, ELLIS R., collector internal revenue
Bennett & Bain, brewers
Bennett, R. N., butcher
Bennett, Richard B., saloon
Benson, S. M., P. L. S.
Blackley, Mrs. James, grocer, &c
Blacklock, James, town treasurer, agent Phœnix (Hartford) Insurance Co
Blaind, William, painter
Bleasdell, J. H. T., barrister, &c
Bleeker, Wm., proprietor saw mill
Bogart, A. L., J. P.
Bogart, C. V., boot and shoemaker
Bogart, D. D.

Boner, John, grocer
Boswell, Wm., slater
Bonter, John C., hotel keeper
BOWELL, M. M. P. P., Editor and prop. of *Belleville Intelligencer* (daily and weekly) and County of Hasting's Gazetteer and Directory
BOYD, TURNER, barber and hairdresser
Brehmer, Charles, tobacconist.
BRENNAN, D., (W. H. Campbell & Co)
Brennan, Rev. John (Roman Catholic)
Brennan, Rev. Michael (Roman Catholic)
Brenton & Spear, provisions
Briley, Miss Matilda, milliner
Britton, Edward, butcher
Brown, George A. (Brown & St. Charles)
BROWN, G. & P., proprietors Brown's foundry and machine shop (see adv.)
BROWN, JAMES, M.P. (G. & J. Brown)
Brown, James, grocer
Brown, J. W., tailor
Brown & St. Charles, carriage makers
Brown, W., shoemaker
Brydon, William, baker,
Bull, Samuel J., barrister
Bullen, R., boarding house keeper
Bullen, W. H., shoemaker
Bullen, Wesley, groceries, liquors
Burdett, D. E., M.D.
BURDETT, S. B., barrister
Burdon, Alexander, principal grammar school
BURRELL, E., axe factory (see adv.)
Byrne, M., tailor
Campbell, G., discount clk. Merchants' Bk. of Canada
Canniff, Philip, baker
CAMPBELL, W. H. & Co., forwarders, commission merchants.
CANADA PERMANENT BUILDING & SAVINGS SOCIETY, John Thomas, appraiser.
CARSCALLEN, JOHN & Co., builders, &c (see adv.)
Chandler E., chemist and druggist
Chapin, C. G., watchmaker
Charters & Webster, druggists
Cherry, Thomas, cabinet maker
Chesebro, D. D., boots and shoes, groceries, provisions, &c.
Chown, George, stoves, tinware, &c.
Clarke, C. A. (McKinnon & Clarke)
Clarke, Francis, carriage maker
Clark, James A., butcher
Clarke, James, grocer.
Clark, Robert, blacksmith
Clark, William, tailor
Cockburn, general merchant
Coleman, Charles L., barrister, County Attorney, Clerk of the Peace
Coleman, E. H., druggist
Coleman, William H., wine and spirit merchant
Colling, William, carriage and wagon maker
COMMERCIAL UNION FIRE AND LIFE INSURANCE COMPANY, John Thomas, agent
Condon, E., tobacconist
Conger Brothers, (Roger D. and James A.) grocers
Conger, Peter D., dry goods
Conner, William, shoemaker
Cook, John, grocer and provision dealer
Copeland John, saddler
CORBY, H., M.P.P.
CORBY, H. & SON, millers, distillers and produce dealers
Cornell, Henry, painter
Craig, James, builder
Cronk, Jacob, photographer
Croan, M. H., saloon
Crozier, John A. G., clerk Crown timber office
4
Cummins, James, saddler
DAFOE HOUSE, Barringer & Co., proprietors
Dafoe, Zenas, turnkey
Davy, R. B., commission merchant
Deacon, William, (Watson & Deacon)
DEAN & GILBERT, (W. W. & B. S.) barristers
DEAN, W. W., (Dean & Gilbert), Master in Chancery
DeField, Mrs., Ferry house
DEMPSEY, M. O., books, stationery and fancy goods
DENMARK, GEORGE, (Ponton, Falkiner & Denmark
Diamond, A., senr., sash and door factory
DIAMOND, A., (Diamond & Dickson), police magistrate
DIAMOND & DICKSON, (A. Diamond and George D. Dickson), barristers, attorneys, etc.
DICKSON, GEORGE D., (Diamond & Dickson), official assignee
Dickens, William, baker
Docter, William, grocer and hotel keeper
Dorland, P. V., M. D
Dougall, A. R., barrister
DOYLE, JOHN, proprietors International Hotel. (See adv)
Dupont, Edward, agent Home of New Haven, fire Insurance Company.
Dupont, Misses, select school
Egan, W. F., accountant bank Montreal
Ellis, Alfred, butcher
Ellis, William, marine store
Elliott, R., dry goods
Elliott, Thomas, dry goods and groceries
Elvins, Richard, groceries
Empey, Miller M. (Robertson & Empey)
Evans, John D., P. L. S
Evans, Thomas, Civil Engineer
Fahey, Peter, mason
FALKINER, N. B., (Ponton, Falkiner & Denmark)
Fanning, F., hotel
Fanning, Walter, stage proprietor
FINN, JOHN, barrister, &c
FLETCHER, A. & Co., (A. Fletcher and H. Pretty) produce dealers &c. (See adv.)
FLINT, HON. BILLA, Senator
Flint, E. C., manuf. melodeons and cabinet organs
Flint & Robertson, (John J. B. Flint, David B. Robertson) barristers, &c.
FLINT & YEOMANS, lumber merchants
Ford, Frederick, gunsmith
Foran, John, builder
Forrest & Lozo, (Lorenzo Forrest & Alexander Lozo) photographers, &c.
Fox, John, dry goods and clothing.
Foxton, H. P., chief police
FRALECK, BALDWIN, B.A., (Maclellans & Fraleck)
Frederick, John, harness maker
Frith, H., millinery and fancy goods
Frost, Abraham, leather and findings
Frost, Frederick, cabinet maker
Gardner, Thomas, plasterer
Garratt, C. & Co., general merchants
Gibson, George, boots and shoes
Gillen, Michael, hardware
Glass, James, hardware
Graham & Grainger, general merchants
Graham, W. H. & I. B., general merchants
Grainger, Joseph, butcher
Grainger, J. K., butcher
Grant, James, grist mill proprietor
Greatrix, Richard, baker
Grier, Rev. John (Church of England)
Hadden, Richard, saddler

Haines, John J., jun., boots and shoes
Hambly, J. H., chemist and druggist
Hambly, Philip, confectioner and saloon keeper.
Hamilton, L. & Co. (L. Hamilton and J. L. Reed), soda water manufacturers
HAMPTON, HENRY D. (John Carscallen & Co.)
Hannan, Sylvester, shoemaker
Harrison, E., stationery
Harper, Richard, book keeper, Victoria foundry
Harry, Joseph, grocer
HASTINGS CHRONICLE (weekly), Miles & Mason, editors and proprietors.
HASTINGS HOUSE, P. O'Brien, prop. (see adv.)
Hay, Rev. — (New Connexion)
HAYMES, G. H., hatter and furrier (see adv.)
Hayward, Walter J., barrister, &c.
HEIVLY & BROTHER (D. F. & A. G.) photographers
Heller, Andrew, dyer
Henderson, George E., barrister
Henderson, L. H., attorney at law
Henry, Adam (Jones & Henry)
Henry, C., accountant and teller Bank of Montreal
Herald, Alexander, cooper
Higley, P. C., bailiff
Hodge, John, grocer, &c.
Hogg, James, merchant tailor
Hogg, Wm., baker and confectioner
Holbrook, T. A., prop. Anglo American House
HOLDEN, R. & CO., wholesale and retail druggists
HOLDEN, RUFUS, M. D. (R. Holden & Co)
HOLDEN, JAMES C., (R. Holden & Co)
HOLDEN, THOMAS, (Ross, Bell & Holden,) agent Phœnix (England) Fire Insurance Co
HOLTON, G. C. & CO., dry goods and groceries (see adv.)
HOME INSURANCE COMPANY, (New Haven) John Thomas, agent.
Hope, William, M. D.
Howe, Robert, butcher
Hulme, R. Croft, clerk division court
Hume, Mrs. Thos., grocer
IMPERIAL FIRE INSURANCE CO., (London, Eng.,) J. Parker Thomas, agent
Innes, Robert L., civil engineer and architect
INTELLIGENCER, (daily & weekly), M. Bowell, M.P.P., editor
INTERNATIONAL HOTEL, John Doyle (see adv.)
Ireland, J. B., engraver, &c.
IRWIN, C. & CO., sewing machine manufacturers (see adv.)
Jack, Henry, merchant tailor and clothier
James, Mrs. F., photographer
James, George, High Constable County Hastings
James, H., M. D.
JELLETT & BROTHER, (Robert P. & Morgan,) barristers
Jones & Henry, (W. W. Jones and Adam Henry) gen. merchants
Jones, Nathan, dry goods and groceries
Jones, Rev. S., (Church of England)
JONES, WM. (A. S. Page & Co)
KEITH, GEORGE, (Walker & Co.)
KELSO, THOMAS (Pitceathly & Kelso)
Kennedy, James, & Co., dry goods and groceries
KEYES, ANDREW, auctioneer and commission merchant (see adv.)
Kyle, Samuel, proprietor Willard House
Laferte, M., dry goods and groceries
Lanigan, James, butcher
Lanktree, James, shoemaker
Laving, J. P., tailor
LAZIER, JOHN, proprietor Belleville woolen factory
LAZIER & LAZIER, (T. A. & S. S.) barristers, &c.
Legate & Price, grocers
Lester, James, M. D.
LEVER, JOHN P., proprietor cheese box factory. (See adv.)
LEWIS, JOHN, hardware &c.
Linklater, Thomas, stoves and tinware.
LLOYD & STEWART, (Robert R. Lloyd and George M. Stewart) exchange brokers
Lockerty, Thomas, tobacconist
LONDON & LANCASHIRE LIFE INSURANCE COMPANY. John Thomas, agent
McANNANY, F., County Treasurer
McArthur, G. A., proprietor Bull's Head Hotel
McArthur, Neil, grocer
McCaffrey, Raymond, grocer.
McCarthy, Charles, shoemaker and grocer
McComb, James, fancy goods
McCormick, Mrs. A., general merchant
McCormick, Joseph, dry goods and groceries
McCruden, John, Sergeant police
McFee, Allan, watchmaker
McFee, Angus, watchmaker
McGurn, John, butcher
McInnes, John A., clerk crown timber office
McInninch, Henry, blacksmith
McIntosh, Thomas (Read & McIntosh)
McKeown, John, (McKeown & Robertson)
McKeown & Robertson, boot and shoe manufacturers
McKinnon & Clarke, grocers
McKinnon, John, (McKinnon & Clarke)
McLaren, Rev. William, (Free Church Presbyterian)
McMullen, S. S., marble cutter
Mabey, Samuel, grocer
Mackie, James, market clerk
MACLELLAN, A. L. (Maclellan & Fraleck)
MACLELLAN, DUNCAN, (Maclellans & Fraleck)
MACLELLANS & FRALECK, barristers, &c., Belleville and Madoc.
MACOUN, JAMES, (Walker & Co)
Maiden, Joseph, grocer
Marlow, L., hotel keeper
MARTIN, CHARLES, foundry and machine shop. (See adv)
Mason, J. R., (Miles & Mason)
Maxfield, Mrs. Sarah M., M.D
MEACHAM, J. H., Postmaster
Meagher, James, grocer
MERCHANTS' BANK OF CANADA, Andrew Thomson, manager
MEUDELL, JAMES, hatter and furrier. (See adv)
Meudell, William F., collector of customs
Meyers, E. W., jailor
Mikel, W. Y., grocer
MILES & MASON, (E. Miles & J. R. Mason,) editors and proprietors Hastings *Chronicle*
Miller, C. E., clerk sheriff's office
Miller, John, butcher
Mills, Parker, shoemaker
MONTREAL MARINE ASSURANCE CO., John Thomas. agent
Moore, John G., foreman *Intelligencer*
Moore, John S. A., marble works
Morice, J. F. B., manager G. A. Simpson & Co
Morrice, Alexander, shoemaker
Muir, John & Co., clothier
Mullin, C., hotel keeper
NANTES, W. H., Customs broker
Neilson, George, contractor
Neven, P. & M., proprietors Union Hotel
NEW YORK LIFE ASSURANCE CO., J. Parker Thomas, agent
Nichol, Thomas, M.D., homœopathic physician
Northrup, A. G., Clerk County Court, Deputy Clerk Crown and Pleas, Registrar Surrogate

Northgraves, W. J., watchmaker
Nosworthy, James, leather dealer
Nulty, Michael, auctioneer and commission merchant
NULTY, P. M., barrister
O'BRIEN, PATRICK, proprietor Hasting's House. (See adv)
O'CARROLL, MISS M. A., milliner
OSTROM, SYLVESTER, woolen factory
Overell, James C., fancy goods and stationery
PAGE, A. S. & CO., lumber merchants
Papineau, Charles, Terrapin saloon
Patterson, R.
Patterson, R. S.
PEARD, JAMES, dry goods and millinery. (See adv)
Pearson, Henry, hatter
Perkins, E., saloon
Perkins, William, shoemaker
PHILLIPS, N. W., flour and feed
Phippen, F. J., soap and candle factory.
PITCEATHLY & KELSO, (David Pitceathly and Thomas Kelso), wholesale grocers
PONTON, FALKINER & DENMARK, (W. H. Ponton, N. B. Falkiner and George Denmark) barristers
PONTON, W. H., (Ponton, Falkiner & Denmark), County Registrar
PONTON, J. W., deputy registrar
Pope, G. H., (superintendent A. S. Page & Co.)
POTTS, GEORGE J., M.D.
Powell, William, wagon maker
Power, James, M.D.
PRETTY, HENRY, (A. Fletcher & Co.)
PRICE, REES, grocer & provision merchant. (See adv.
Pringle, A. N., sash and door factory
Proctor, A. E.
Rankins, Miles, foreman Victoria foundry
Rankin W. W., engineer fire department
Ranny, George W., sup't Trent public works
Read & McIntosh, (Robert Read & Thomas McIntosh), grain merchants
READ, HON. ROBERT, M.P.P
Redick, James, sash, door and blind factory
Redner, J., grocer and shingle manufacturer
Reed, J. L., (L. Hamilton & Co.) grocer
Reeves, George, builder, etc.
REEVES, WILLIAM, builder, etc. (See adv)
Relyea, G. V. N., dentist,
Ridley, Charles, M.D.
Ritchie, George & Co., dry goods
ROBERTSON & EMPEY, dry goods and groceries
ROBERTSON, JAMES, (Robertson & Empey)
Robertson, William (McKeown & Robertson)
ROBERTSON & STEWART (Alexander Robertson, D. E. Kinnear Stewart), barristers
Roche, George W. W., hatter
Roenigk, Lewis, cabinet maker, &c,
ROSENBERG, H., watchmaker and jeweler (see adv.)
ROSS, BELL & HOLDEN, barristers, solicitors Bank of Montreal, and Merchants' Bank
Rous, F. H., crockery and glassware
Roy, Robert, Maitland, town and police clerk
Rutherford, Thomas, builder
Savage, J. G., cabinet maker
Sawyer, J. H. (M. Sawyer & Co.)
Sawyer, M. & Co. (M. Sawyer and J. Sawyer), chemists and druggists.
Scholes, Wm. H. (Wallbridge & Scholes)
Scott, W. H., accountant Merchants' Bk. of Canada
Sherwood, Hon. George, Judge County Court
Simpson, Geo. & Co., propr's Bay of Quinté elevator.
Simpson, H. (G. A. Simpson & Co.)
Simpson, J. H., barrister.
SMEATON, EDWARD (Walker & Co.)
Smith, A. L., founder.
Smith, C. F., stoves and tinware
Smith, S. B., stoves and tinware
St. Charles, James (Brown & St. Charles)
Stapely, A. J., architect and builder
STAPELY, ROBERT W., sash, door & blind factory
Starling, C. J., contractor
Stevenson, Hugh, carriage maker, &c.
Stewart, Robert, M.D.
SUTHERLAND, J. & W., dry goods (see adv.)
Symons, William, tailor, &c.
Tannahill, R., produce and grain merchant
Taugher, M. & J. (Michael and John)
Taylor, George, Sheriff County Hastings
Taylor, John, watchmaker
Taylor, John, Deputy Sheriff County Hastings.
Templeton, William, general merchant.
Terwilligar, A.M., photographer.
Thomas, Mrs. George, grocer.
THOMAS, JOHN, insurance agent, appraiser Canada Permt. Blg. and Savings Society. (See advt.)
THOMAS, J. PARKER, barrister, attorney, solicitor, &c., Official Assignee County Hastings. (See advt)
THOMPSON, J. W., agent Canadian Express, Montreal Telegraph and Montreal Steamship Co's.
Thompson, M. M., book-keeper A. S. Page & Co.
THOMSON, ANDREW, Manager Merchants' Bank of Canada.
Thomson, Robert, teller Merchants' Bank of Canada.
TICKELL, G. S., cabinet maker, upholsterer, &c.
TRAVELLERS' LIFE AND ACCIDENT INS. Co. (Hartford) J. Parker Thomas, agent.
Truaisch & Zoller, saloon keepers.
Turner, Jeremiah, general blacksmith.
Vair, George, dry goods and groceries.
Van Allen, Thomas, Walker & Co.
Van Norman, Frank, bookseller and stationer.
Vapor, J. C., merchant tailor.
Vermilyea, W. H., carriage builder.
Verner, J. W. Surveyor Customs.
Walker, Rev. A., (Presbyterian.)
Walker, Hugh, grocer.
WALKER, J. M. & CO., (J. M. Walker, Jame, Macoun, Thomas Van Allen, Edward Smeaton, George Keith,) proprietors Belleville foundry.
WALLACE & BRO., (D. J. & J. C.) photographers.
Wallace, Daniel L., grocer, &c.
Wallace, James, prop. Sidney flouring mill
Wallbridge, George, (Walbridge & Scholes).
Wallbridge & Scholes, grocers and wine merchants.
WALLBRIDGE & WALLBBIDGE, (Hon. L. & Adam H.) barristers, &c.
Wallbridge, W. H., prop. Victoria foundry.
Walters, Thomas, tailor,
Walton, George S., sash and door factory.
Ward M,D., dentist
Watson & Deacon, bakers and confectioners
Watson, William (Watson & Deacon)
Watters, Alexander, blacksmith.
WAY, J. F., Crown timber agent.
Weber, Michael, provision dealer and butcher.
Weese, John, hotel keeper
Wensley, William, painter
White, L. J., manager Belleville stone ware works
Wild, Rev. Joseph, (Episcopal Methodist)
Wilkins & Dolan, plasterers
Williams, L. J., brewery
Wills, Thomas, County Clerk
Wilson, Charles, hair dresser
Wilson, John, baker and confectioner
Wilson, Miss M., grocer and fancy goods
Wright, William, saddler
YARWOOD, A. F., cabinet maker
Yeomans, Horace, (Flint & Yeomans)
Zoller, Peter, (Truaisch & Zoller)

Bell Ewart.—A Village and Station of the Northern Railway, on Lake Simcoe, in the Township of Innisfil, County Simcoe, 12 miles from Barrie. The steamer *Emily May* connects here with the Northern Railway. Daily stage, running to Orillia, Beaverton, &c., in connection with the steamer to the Muskoka Territory. One of the largest saw mills, owned by Messrs. Sage & Co., is located here. Money order office. Population, 500.

Aston, Mrs. John, hotel keeper
Barr, Jonathrn, gunsmith
Beeman, E. W.
Bostwick, J. R., builder
Brant, J., merchant
Campbell, Daniel, mariner
Doolittle, Alva
DRAKE, P. E., Postmaster, mercht. and lumber dealer
Dushan, Louis, butcher
Hager, George, merchant
Hugg, E. F., agent Sage & Co
Jebb, W., engineer Sage & Co
Kermott, C. H., teacher
Law, E. M., clerk
Lawrence, W. D., surveyor
Linn, D. W., superintendent Sage & Co
Macbean, Alexander, foundry
Montgomery, J. M., M.D
Ostrander, Charles, farmer
Reddington, Matthew, lumber merchant
Sage, H. W. & Co., lumber merchants
Spooner, W. A., superintendent mill
Willson, Alfred, farmer

Bellrock.—A Village on the Napanee River, in the Township of Portland, County Frontenac, with a large trade in lumber and farm produce. Distant from County Town, 24 miles, from Toronto, 150. Stages to and from Harrowsmith.

Boyce, Caleb, farmer
Brooks, W., farmer
Coffey, Mrs. Mary, proprietor Bellrock Hotel
Craig, Robert, woolen factor
Freeman, Barnabas, general merchant
Grant, Elizabeth, teacher
Grant, George, farmer
Grundill, Edward, carpenter
McCaul, Patrick, general merchant
Milligan, William, blacksmith
Moir, George,
Percy, John, blacksmith
Percy, William
POMEROY, WILLIAM, Postmaster and general merchant
Sanderson, Rev. E., (Methodist Episcopal)
Shory, Silas
Switzer, Orrin, carpenter
Wheeler, J.
Willson, Peter

Belmont.—A Village in the Townships of Westminster and Dorchester, Counties Middlesex and Elgin, 14 miles from County Town, 8 from nearest railway station, 14 from London, and 120 from Toronto Stage to London daily. Improved land $50 and wild $40 per acre. Kettle Creek affords good water power. A grist mill is required. Population, 400.

Black, James, insurance agent
Campbell, James, saddler
Campbell, James B., M.B.
Cline, Daniel D., M.D.
Courson, J., general merchant
Creamer, Robert, hotel keeper
Currie, Rev. Alexander (Presbyterian)
Dawson, A. W., general merchant
Dumaw, Simeon, wagon maker
Dyer, Omi, notary public
Dyer & Adell, general merchants
Eckert, W. D., teacher
Harkness, Adam, farmer
Hawkins, George, merchant tailor
House, Jacob, cabinet maker
Hoover, D. L., butcher
Hungerford, Eli B., cabinet maker
Kindree, J., boots and shoes
Kennedy, Rev. James (Wesleyan)
McIntyre, A., carpenter
McKellar, A., carpenter
McKellar, D., general merchant
Manning, J. G., farmer
Mohr, William, painter
Murray, J. W., carpenter
Nichol, Brothers, flax millers
Nugent, W, T., general merchant
ODELL, W. H., Postmaster
Olmstead, Lewis, hotel keeper
Pearson & Silk, woolen factory
Seeman, Henry, carriage maker
Simpson, James S., tailor
Sleeth, Robert, blacksmith
Smith, Rev. J. P. (Episcopal)
Spencer, Charles B., M.D.
Walker, James, blacksmith
Watcher, George, painter
Yerex, W. N., general merchant
Yex, Isaac, stationery, books, &c.

Belmore.—A Village in the Townships of Culross and Carrick, County Bruce, 16 miles from Walkerton and 40 from Goderich. Population 150.

Calman, F., general merchant
Found & Fitzgerald, saw mill proprietors
Graham, William, carpenter
Hall, Joseph, blacksmith
Huston, Samuel, plasterer
Irwin, F. W., J. P.
Kay, John T., M. D.
Lark, Henry, pump maker
Lloyd, Henry, carpenter
Luxton, John, wagon maker
McNally, Wm., shoemaker
Ontrim, D. J., shoemaker
Proctor, John, carpenter
PERRIFF, PETER, Postmaster, hotel keeper

Bell's Corners.—A Village in the Township of Nepean, County Carleton. Distant from County Town, 10 miles, from Toronto, 300 miles. Stage line from Ottawa to Perth. Money order office. Population, 120.

ARNOLD, GEORGE, Postmaster and general mercht
Bearman, James, J.P
Bearman, John
Brownlee, William, shoemaker
Corbett, William, hotel keeper
Crowe, Robert, shoemaker
Dawson, John, J.P
Dowler, Rev. J. A. (Wesleyan)
Draffin, Richard
Gourlay, Rev. J. L., M.A., (Presbyterian)
Graham, Thomas
Graham, William
Harmer, F. W., Municipal Clerk
Keeman, D., teacher
Lafleur, Andrew, wagon maker
Moodie, Robert, hotel keeper
Patton, Henry, cooper
Pettit, Rev. C. B., M.A., (Church of England)
Pratt, A. D., teacher
Pratt, Isaiah, shoemaker
Robertson, John, farmer
Spittall, Alexander, wagon maker
Spittall, R. P., carpenter
Wright, Albert, tanner

Benmiller.—A Village in the Township of Colborne, County Huron, 6 miles from Goderich. Semi-weekly mails. Population 150.

Adams, Rodney, cradle maker.
Cottle, James, blacksmith.
DeGray, Joseph, cooper
GLEDHILL, J. E. J. & T., woolen mills
Guischbush, Joseph, tanner
Hedeger, Jacob, painter
Heddle, Andrew, carpenter
Kerr, Thomas, shoemaker
Madle, G., tanner
Miller, Jonathan, innkeeper, grocer
Nagle, Joseph, mason
Robertson, William, blacksmith
Rogers, David, miller
Scott, John, weaver
Stewart, John, gardener

Bennie's Corners.—A Village in the Township of Ramsay, County Lanark, distant from County Town 30 miles, from Toronto 265 miles. Average price of land $22 to $40. Population 50.

Anderson, William, farmer
Baird, John, miller.
Cummings, Robert, shoemaker
Cunningham, John, lime manufacturer
Gilmour, John, butcher
Glover, John, cooper
Henderson, Robert, miller
LEISHMAN, A., Postmaster and general merchant
Philip, William, blacksmith
Rothwell, A. T., teacher
Snedden, David, proprietor Rose Bank Hotel
Steele, John, farmer
Toshack, Æneas, farmer
Young, Peter, farmer

Bensfort.—A Village in the Township of Monaghan, County Northumberland, distant from Cobourg the County Town, 25 miles, from Toronto 80 miles. Average price of land $40. Population 100.

Anderson, Hugh, farmer
Castle, Charles, shingle maker
Caswell, Rev. James. (New Connexion)
Creba, William, blacksmith
Dodds, Thomas, farmer
Emberson, William, farmer
Farris, James, shingle maker
Finnie, Andrew, farmer
Huggins, David, shingle maker
McBAIN, JAMES W., Postmaster, bookseller, &c.
Moncrief, George, shoemaker
Morrison, David, farmer
Morrison, William, farmer
Richards, John, tailor
Riddell, Walter, farmer
Rutherford Walter, sash and door manufacturer
Turnbull, James, carpenter
Turnbull, John A., farmer
Wood, Henry, shingle manufacturer
Wood, William, farmer

Bentley.—A Post-office in the Township of Harwich, County Kent, 18 miles from Chatham and 200 from Toronto. Improved land in the vicinity averages $30 per acre.

BENTLEY, S., Postmaster.

Berkeley.—A Post-office in the Township of Holland, County Grey, 20 miles distant from Owen Sound and) 100 miles from Toronto.

FLEMING, JOHN, Postmaster
Jackson, Rev. Thomas, (New Connexion Methodist

Berlin—The County Town of Waterloo and a station of the Grand Trunk Railway, 24 miles from Stratford, 67 miles from Toronto, and 11 miles from Galt. Money Order office and Savings' Bank. Population, 3000.

Aldous, John, manufacturer
ANDREWS, H. M., (Bowlby & Andrews)
Armstrong, John S., detective
Armstrong, Thomas, bailiff
Ballin, August, M.D
Barnhold, Hy, shoemaker
Beeking, William, wagon maker
BERLIN TELEGRAPH, Alexander McPherson publisher
BERLINER JOURNAL, Rittinger & Motz, editors & proprietors
BOEDECKER & STEUBING, wholesale fancy goods, &c
BOND JOHN, general merchant
Borth, Andrew, cabinet maker
BOWLBY & ANDREWS, (W. H. Bowlby, H. M. Andrews) barristers
Bowlby, David S., M.D
BOWLBY, W. H., (Bowlby & Andrews) county attorney
Bowman, Israel D., county clerk, & insurance agent.
BOWMAN, W. H., chemist and druggist
Breithaupt, Lewis, tanner
Brickwer, Henry, cooper
Bramm, John, brick maker
BRAUER, B., prop. Railroad Station Hotel, (see advt)
Brauer, Henry, cooper
BROWN & DEBITT, (Frederick Brown, Joseph Debitt) mattress manufacturers. (See advt)
Brubacher, Henry, farmer
Brubacher, Samuel, farmer
Colquhoun, James, Clerk of County Court.
COMMERCIAL HOTEL, John Roat, prop.
D'Esterre, Duncan, station master G.T.R.
Davidson, George, sheriff.
Dopp, George, hotel keeper.
Eby & Co., pump makers.
Eby, John, farmer.
EBY, JOHN W., chemist and druggist.
Erb, Menno, farmer.
Evans, Rev. —, (Church of England.)
FEICK, JOSEPH K., dry goods and groceries.
FEICK, MISS M. W., milliner.
FENNELL, JOHN, hardware, wholesale and retail.
FOX AUGUST, watchmaker and jeweller, (See adv.)
Funcken, Rev. Dr. Eugene. (Roman Catholic.)
Gaul, Wm. tailor.
Gauntley, Mrs. H., berlin wool and fancy goods.
Gauntley, Henry, saddler
Geddes, Charles R., news depot
Glowalski, Rev. Edward (Roman Catholic)
Gow, Robert, shoemaker
Gwynne, James W., barrister
Haller, John, hatter
Haugh & Roat (John Haugh, Edward Roat) saddlers
Heit, Louis, baggage master G. T. R.
Heller, Casper, proprietor Royal Exchange Hotel
Heller, John & Son, watchmakers, &c.
Hett, Henry, painter
Hett, John B., carpenter
HOFFMAN, ISAAC, dry goods, groceries and hardware, also steam furniture factory
Huber, H. S, general merchant
Hughes, S. L., M. D.
Hunsick, J. C., books and stationery
Hunsicker, John, variety store
Hymmer, Peter, tinsmith
JACKSON, H. F. J., pioneer tobacco factory
JAFFRAY, WILLIAM, Postmaster, Express and Insurance agent, telegraph operator
Kaessman, Rev. C. F. A.
Kaunengiesser, John, Berlin wool and fancy goods
Keyser, William, proprietor Berlin Hotel
Kimmel, Henry, hotel keeper.
King, John, pump maker
Klein, George, butcher
Klippert, John, High Constable
Knell, Henry, watches, &c.
Knowles, William H. G., dry goods
KRAUZ, C. & Son, general merchants, agents for Hamburgh and American Packet Co, (see adv.)
Krauz, Hugo, (C. Krauz & Son)
Kraueger, John, butcher
Lake, Frederick, mason, builder and contractor
Lang, Peter, broom maker.
Levan, Jacob, & Co., blacksmiths
Linprecht, Frederick, American Hotel
McDougall, D., County Registrar
McGuire, John, carriage maker.
McKie, John A., general merchant
McPHERSON, A., editor and proprietor *Berlin Telegraph*
Merchants Bank of Canada, Robert N. Rogers, agent
Meredith, J. S., teller Merchants Bank.
Messner, Martin, baker.
Metzinger, John F., teacher.
Miller, Alex, barrister
Mogk, William, shoemaker
Moore, Hugh E., photographer
Moore, William, insurance agent
Motz, John, (Rittinger & Motz)
Mowat, Alex, Deputy Clerk of the Peace.
Mowat, Alexander H., general agent
Moyer, Abraham, farmer
Mylius, Rudolph, M.D
Nahrgang, Henry & Co., tailors
Neville, C. E., B.A., principal grammar school
NICHOLAUS, ANDREAS, St. Nicolas Hotel
Niehaus, William, boots and shoes
Ott, Cyrus, tobacconist
PETERSON, A. J., Clerk Division Court, Registrar Surrogate, Com. in B.R., Notary Public, agent Standard Life Ass. Co. (See advt)
Potter, James, farmer
Rickert, John, farmer
Ringle & Stroh, tanners
RITTINGER & MOTZ, (Frederick and John) editors and proprietors Berliner *Journal*
ROAT, JOHN, prop. Commercial Hotel
Robinson, John, farmer
ROGERS, ROBERT N., agent Merchants' Bank
ST. NICOLAS HOTEL, Andrew Nicholaus, prop
Schmitt, John, shoemaker
Schmitt, Leopold, blacksmith
Schmitt, Rev. William, (Wesleyan)
Schneiker, Conrad, hotel keeper.
Schofield, M. C., surveyor
Schwenn, H. & J., brick makers
Schwieger, A. W., civil engineer
Scully, Thomas, tanner
Seiler, Louis, miller
Seip, George, brewer
Shantz, David, farmer
Shantz, Jacob, farmer
Shuh, Benjamin, farmer
SIMPSON & ALDOUS, (William and John) cabinet chair and pump factory
Simpson & Son, (Martin & Tendill) shoemakers
Sippel, Henry, weaver
SNYDER, FREDERICK, stoves & tinware, (see advt)

Spetz, Joseph, lager beer brewer
STANDARD LIFE ASSOCIATION COMPANY, A. J. Peterson, agent
STANTON, CHARLES, County Treasurer
Stein & Gottlieb, (William & Frederick) tailors
Strickler, Henry, woolen and flax mills
STUEBING, CONRAD, (Boedecker & Stuebing)
Stuckhart, John, cooper
Tagge, Peter N., general agent
Thomas, John H., boots and shoes
Tuerk, Rev. F. W., (Swedenborgian)
Tyson, Abram, grocer
VanCamp, Lewis, dentist
Voglesang, Emil, vegetable ivory button factory
Wagner, Anslein, potter
Weaver, J. S., prop. Franklin Hotel and Livery
Wells, Walter, insurance agent
Werner, Justus, wagon maker
Wieland, Charles, mason
Winger, John, manufacturer
Woelfle, John J., plough maker
Wright, Charles,
Wright, Francis,
YOUNG & GOOD, (William & Peter H.) groceries wines and liquors
Zeigler, Enoch, carriage maker

Berne.—A Village in the Township of Hay, County Huron, 21 miles from Goderich and 16 from Seaforth station Grand Trunk Railway. Population 50.

Bleam, Christian, farmer
Bleam, David, farmer
Bleam, Jacob, farmer
Douglas, Allan, farmer
Douglas, Peter D. R., farmer
Duncan, Rev. Mr., (Presbyterian)
Erwin, William, wagon maker
Foster, Joseph, farmer
Hep, Andrew, carpenter
Hep, George, sen., cabinet maker
Hunter, John, farmer
Mitchell, Allan, general merchant
MURNER, GOTLEIB, Postmaster
Jaker, Rev. Mr., (Methodist)
Johnstone, Edward, farmer
Roir, Andrew, farmer
Scott, Robert, teacher
Styles, Micheal, farmer
Tapp, Christian, tailor
Witwer, Samuel, tanner, &c.

Bervie.—A Village situated in the Township of Kincardine County Bruce, South Riding.

McINTYRE, NICHOL, Postmaster

Berwick.—A village in the Township of Finch, County Stormont, distant from County Town, 30 miles, from Toronto, 300 miles. Average price of land, $8 to $10. Population, 150.

Bates, Joseph, shoemaker
Blay, Charles, butcher
Campbell, Donald, blacksmith
Campbell, Kenneth, carpenter
Cavanagh, John
Cavanagh, Michael
Clark, Alexander, teacher
COCKBURN, ALEXANDER A., Postmaster, general merchant, &c.
Cockburn, A. J., J. P.
Cockburn, Isaac
Connell, Stewart, general merchant
Cryderman, Jacob
Fleming, Thomas
Fleming, William, general merchant
Gray, Alexander, lime manufacturer
Hamblin, Jesse
Henery, Thomas, carpenter
Jackson, Robert, tanner
James, James, wagon maker
Kelly, Patrick, blacksmith
Kittel, William
Lamont, Rev. Hugh (Presbyterian)
Lewis, William
McGillivray, Duncan, tinsmith
McKinnon, Alexander, carpenter
McLeod, Murdoch, stone mason
McMulligan, Robert
Mellersh, William, proprietor Berwick Hotel
Munroe, John C., M. D.
Murphy, Francis, auctioneer
Patterson, John, shoemaker
Scott, David, shoemaker
Scott, Miss Mary A., dressmaker
Steen, James, shingle merchant
Thistlewart, W. B., lime manufacturer

Bethany.—A Village and Station of the Port Hope, Lindsay and Beaverton Railway, Township Manvers, County Durham, 31 miles from the County Town and 88 from Toronto. A stream passes through the village, affording ample power for machinery. This is a good position for a foundry, agricultural implement works, and a tannery. Improved lands, $35 per acre, wild, $25. Population, 300.

Barr, Andrew, tailor
Bleakly, Francis, general merchant
Brearton, C. H., M. D.
Brown, Andrew, forwarding and commission merchant, railroad agent
Buggins, Rev. George (New Connexion)
Byers, James, farmer
Cain, C. C., flouring mill proprietor
Craig, John, chandler
Craig, William, J. P.
Crosier, James, farmer
Copeland, John, blacksmith
Davis, William, farmer
Ewing, Rev. John (Presbyterian)
Fell, James, farmer
Gardiner, W. F., auctioneer
Graham, Jeffrey, farmer
GRAHAM, WILLIAM MORTON, Postmaster, gen. merchant, and general agent
Graham, W. W., shingle maker

Grandy, R. & J., general merchants
Hunter, William
Kelly, James, forwarding and commission merchant.
Kennedy, Robert, blacksmith
Lamb, John, builder
Lee, Thomas, sash, door and blind factor
McAlister, Michael, J. P.
McCullough, H., wagon maker
McMahon, George, mason
McMullen, David, farmer
Miller, John, builder
Niland, Robert, shoemaker
Preston, R. J., general merchant
Raper, John, wine merchant
Richardson, Alonzo, wagon maker
Richardson, Joseph, sash, door and blind factor
Ryley, Alfred, notary public, general agent
Stafford, Henry, builder
Strike, William, tailor
Sutton, Robert, butcher
Vance, S. C., insurance agent
White, Hamilton
Wilson, William, teacher
Winters, James, shoemaker
Wrightman, S., grocer

Bewdley.—A Village at the head of Rice Lake, in the Township of Hamilton, County Northumberland Distant from County Town 12 miles, from Toronto 75 miles. Average price of land $35 to $40. Population 100.

Barrelthrope, Rev. Mr., (New Connexion)
Benson, James, J.P., insurance agent, &c
Hancock, John, shoemaker
Hancock, Phillip, grocer
Hancock, Thomas, shoemaker
Hannah, Philander, proprietor Farmers' Hotel
Henderson, William, teacher
Ley, George, J.P
Sackville, James, lumber dealer
SIDY, JOHN, Postmaster
Tabscot, Rev. Samuel, (Baptist)
Wright, Robert, proprietor Bewdley Hotel

Billings' Bridge.—A Village on the Rideau River, in the Township of Gloucester, County Carleton. Distant from the County Town 3 miles, from Toronto 236 miles. Average price of land $30. Population 100.

Angus, William, blacksmith.
Campbell, James, farmer
Cuthbert, Mrs., dressmaker
Fairbairn, Peter, farmer
Hepinstall, George, carpenter
Longley, Miss Sarah M., teacher
McKellar, A., farmer
Masson, Hugh, blacksmith
SMITH, WILLIAM, Postmaster and gen. merchant.
Taylor, David, saddler.
Whalen, Matthew, farmer.

Binbrook.—A Village in the Township of Binbrook, County Wentworth, 13 miles from Hamilton. Population 100.

Barlow, Albert, wagon maker
Bigger, R. H., M.D
Brown, John, general blacksmith
Buntin, John, traving agent
Carle, J. S., Franklin House
Chesney, Rev. A., (Baptist)
Gawley, James, wagon maker
HALL, HENRY, Postmaster and gen. merch't
Hoey, James, merchant
McGann, John, blacksmith
McKenzie, Mrs., general merchant
Russell, James, M.D
Sallett, Robert, shoemaker
Stafford, Theodore, harness maker
Wickett, Robert, Union Hotel

Birkham.—A Village in the Township of Moore, County Lambton. Distant from Sarnia, the County Town 12 miles, from Toronto, 180 miles. Average price of wild land improved, $8 to $30. Population, 50.

Brown, J. B., teacher
Farquharson, J., farmer
Galloway, John, J. P.
Gould, P., farmer
McBean, A., carpenter
McBean, J., farmer
McBean, Lewis, carpenter
McDermid, Rev. Peter (Presbyterian)
McDiarmid, J., farmer
McDonald, James M., farmer
McDonald, Wm. P., grocer
McKenzie, J., teacher
McKENZIE, FINLAY, Postmaster
Manning, D., shingle manufacturer
Thomson, W., farmer
Warren, Duncan, farmer
Watson, A., carpenter
Watson, J., teacher
Watson, P., carpenter
Welsh, James, shoemaker

Bishop's Mills.—A Post-office in the Township of Oxford, County Grenville.
BISHOP, ASA W., Postmaster.

Birmingham.—A Village in the Township of Pittsburgh, County Frontenac. Distant from Kingston 12 miles, from Toronto 170 miles. Stages to Kingston and Whitefish. Average price of land $25 to $30 Population 80.

BIRMINGHAM, JAMES, Postmaster
Bower, Rev. E. C. (Church of England)
Chambers, Rev. T. C. (Presbyterian)
Foster, J., miller
Franklin, W. H., farmer
Graham, Miss, teacher
Joyce, J., farmer
Joyce, L., farmer
Joyce, Matthew, J. P.
Kennedy, Rev. David (Methodist)
McNeill, P., farmer
Mundell, J., teacher
Robb, D., teacher
Smyth, W., farmer
Todd. Miss M., teacher
Todd, Samuel, farmer
Todd, T., farmer

Birr.—A Post Village in the Township of London, County Middlesex, situated on the Proof Line Road, 10 miles from London. Population 25.

Dixon, William, hotel keeper
Winters, Daniel, blacksmith
YOUNG, JOSEPH M., Postmaster and gen. mercht.

Black Creek.—A Village at the mouth of Black Creek, and on the Erie and Niagara Railway, in the Township of Willoughby, County Welland. Distant from St. Catherines, the County Town 12 miles, from Toronto 60 miles. Average price of land, $50. Population 100.

ALLEN, ISAAC H., Postmaster and gen. mercht.
Barnhard, Michael B.
Gonder, Michael D., J. P.
Kraft, Francis, carpenter
Leiber, Christopher, painter
McLaughlin, Thomas, customs officer
Parker, John J., carpenter
Smith, Rev. Robert (United Brethren)

Black Heath.—A Post-office in the Township of Seneca, County Haldimand.

POTTS, T. S., Postmaster.

Blair.—A Village on the Grand River, in the township of Waterloo, County Waterloo. Distant from Guelph, the County Town, 6 miles, from Toronto 70 miles. Stage to Preston and New Dundee. Average price of land $45. Population 200.

Adams, J. W., teacher
Bechtel, Isaac, constable
Bechtel, Moses, lumber dealer
Blaschka, Joseph, butcher
Bowman, J. B., lumber dealer
Bowman, Samuel B., farmer
Bowman, Wendell, farmer
Burkholder, Samuel, carpenter
Clements, Oliver, farmer
Cornell, Erastus, farmer
Eshleman, Moses, farmer
Evans, Rev. James, (Christadelphian)
Gress, Peter, weaver
Gress, Philip, carpenter
Kiefhaber, Adam, cooper
Lamb, John, tailor
McNally, Henry, J.P.
McNally, Rev. John, (Mennonite)
McNally & Co., dyers, etc.
Myers, John, wagon maker
Quirmbach, Charles, proprietor Blair Hotel
Reith, Miss Mary A., dressmaker
RENSHAW, JOHN, Postmaster and general merchant
Shirk, Peter, miller
Sipes, John, farmer
Thomson, Hugh, blacksmith
Tilt, William, accountant
WILKES, MATTHEW, Gentleman
Wismer, David, farmer

Blantyre.—A Village in the Township of Euphrasia, County Grey, 22 miles from Owen Sound, 9 from Meaford and 25 from Collingwood. Stages to Meaford. Population 50.

Aiser, Andrew, farmer
Bree, William, farmer
Brown, Rev. A., (Presbyterian)
Clarke, Andrew, farmer
Clarke, Robert, farmer
Davis, Richard, farmer
Douglass, John, farmer
Falls, Alexander, farmer
Harnden, Rev. W. F., (Methodist)
Jenkins, John, blacksmith
McIntosh, William, farmer
Marshall, Samuel, farmer
Mick, John, farmer
Murray, Robert, farmer
Paterson, James, merchant
Paterson, William, shoemaker
Percy, John, farmer
Storey, Walter, farmer
Walter, Philip, farmer
White, Charles, carpenter

Blairton.—A Village and Station of the Cobourg, Peterboro' and Marmora Railroad, in the Township of Belmont, County Peterboro', situate on Marmora Lake, 40 miles from Peterboro', the County Town, and 115 from Toronto. The village is in the immediate vicinity of the richest iron mines in the Dominion, and miners and laborers are in great demand. The land in the vicinity is almost all taken up. Stages to Norwood and Marmora, distance 21 miles. Money order office and savings bank. Population 500.

Armstrong, W. W., baker and hotel keeper
BATES, ROGER, Postmaster and agent C. P. & M. R. R.
Bell, Thomas, carpenter
Brown, J., M. D.
Duff, William, shoemaker
Featherston, Thomas, cabinet maker
Givin, Mrs., grocer
Halstead, Rev. William, (Wesleyan)
Leach, William, butcher
Learmouth, Thomas R., general merchant
McBride, Andrew, grocer
Meikle, James, general merchant
Powell, Edmund, butcher
Powell, Miss Mary, teacher
Rea, Miss Elizabeth, teacher
Scott, D. D., livery stable
Shaw, William, clothier
Sloan, Robert, general merchant
Turner, John, general merchant
Weller, Gilbert, hotel keeper
Whitmarsh, Levi, livery stable
Wilson, D., M.D.
Wynn, William, builder

Blessington.—A Post-office in the Township of Tyendinaga, County Hastings, E. R.
LALLY, JOHN, Postmaster.

Bloomfield.—A Village in the Township of Hallowell, County Prince Edward. Distant from County Town 5 miles, from Toronto 140 miles. Stages to Brighton and Picton. Average price of land $100. Population 600.

Bethune, Rev. Mr., (Methodist)
Boneman, Gideon, wagon maker
Boneman, Stephen, butcher
Bull, Albert, carpenter
Bull, Gilbert, grocer
Clark, J. F., M.D
Clark, W. G., architect and builder
Cooper, John, miller
Cooper, Obediah, J.P
Cooper, Thomas
Dorland, Joshua
Hare, Dexter, saddler
Hare, Peter S., J.P
Keith, E., proprietor Keith's Hotel
Lake, S. K., M.D
Leavett, Rev. U. D., (Universalist)
McFaul, Peter
McGivern, John, cooper
Morgan, Thomas, miller
Noxon, Samuel
Noxon, Thomas H., agent
Noxon, William, iron founder
Reynolds, Mrs., dressmaker
Reynolds, J. S., dentist
Sargent, G. A., auctioneer
Saylor, A. B., general merchant
Stephens, George, carpenter.
STRIKER, JONATHAN, Postmaster.
Sykes, W., tanner
Tomputt, John, butcher
Varney, Levi, crockery, &c
Watson, C. E., shoemaker
Williams, John P., seedsman.
Winters, Mrs., dressmaker
Winters, J. C. tailor,

Bloomingdale.—A Village in the Township of Waterloo, County Waterloo, 5 miles from Berlin, and 8 from Breslau Station. Population 50.

Bowman, John, farmer
Bowman, Menno, farmer
Bowman, Moses, farmer
Brierley, William, shoemaker
Erb, William, farmer
Hauffer, Jacob, farmer
McKay, Donald
MEYER, JOHN G., Postmaster and hotel keeper
Snyder, Benjamin, farmer
Snyder, Benjamin J., farmer.
Snyder, J., farmer
Snyder, M., farmer.

Bloomington.—A Village in the Township of Whitchurch, County York. Distant from Toronto 30 miles. Average price of land $40. Population 50.

Barns, Jacob, farmer
Browning, Henry, shoemaker
Cool, Mrs., dressmaker
Cummings, Mrs., dressmaker
Cummings, John, wagon maker
Fairliss, Thomas, farmer
Fenton, Wake, M.D.
Fockler, John, farmer
Fockler, Johnson, agent sewing machines
Gee, Rev. E. F., (Wesleyan)
Johnson, Robert, blacksmith
Jones, Maxson, blacksmith
Law, Isaac, farmer
Lemons, Jonathan, farmer
McMurray, Alexander, teacher
Patterson, James M., auctioneer
PATTERSON, SAMUEL, Postmaster
Patterson, Thomas H., general merchant
Stapleton, Robert, farmer
Storry, William, farmer
Tatton, Rev. J., (Christian)
Tranmer, Robert, farmer

Bloomsburg.—A Village on Culver's Creek, in the Township of Townsend, County Norfolk. Distant from Simcoe, the County Town, 5 miles, from Toronto 94 miles. Average price of land $40. Population 75.

Bacon, Gad S., blacksmith
Bacon & Griffin, proprietors cheese factory
Culver, Loder, proprietor cheese factory
Culver, Mahlon, tanner
Culver, Ranston, farmer
Gilbert, J., teacher
Griffin, Rev. Stephen, (Baptist)
Heath, Ansley, stock dealer
Hunter, Alexander, farmer
Ireland, Frederick, carpenter
Ireland, George, carpenter
Kellum, Jason, J.P.
KITCHEN, L. W., Postmaster and general merchan
Kitchen, William, farmer
Lee, Thomas, farmer
Robinson, George, butcher
Saltzberry, Henry, carpenter
Skirrow, William P., farmer
Slaght, Rev. Aaron, (Baptist)
Smith, Albert, woolen factor.
Tate, James, painter
Ward, Henry, shoemaker
Widner, Wesley, stock dealer
Young Robert, J.P.

Bluevale.—A village in the Township of Turnberry, County Huron, distant from Goderich, the County Town, 32 miles. Money order office. Population about 200.

Barron, Thomas, general merchant
Brown, George T., hotel keeper
Bruce, Alexander, shoemaker
Duncan, George, blacksmith
Hastie, Rev. James, (Presbyterian.)
Johnston, James, hotel keeper
Leach, W. H. & J., mill owners
MESSER, JOHN, Postmaster and general merchant
Redmond, James, wagon maker
Redmond, Thomas, blacksmith
Sherriff, Charles, miller
Sibbald, Robert T., shoemaker
Smart, Duncan, fulling mills
Tindal, Edward, wagon maker
Wright, Jacob, grocer

Bobcaygeon.—A Village on Bobcaygeon river, between Lakes Pidgeon and Sturgeon, in Township of Verulam, County Victoria, with a good trade in lumber, limestone, hides, grain, &c. The well-known Galway lead mine at Bobcaygeon is now worked night and day. Distant from County town, 22 miles, from Toronto 110 miles. Stages to Lindsay, Peterboro, and Minden, and in summer, boats to Lindsay and Peterboro'. Average price of land $20. Money order office. Population 800.

Aitken, J. & J., grocers
Arnberg, A., boiler maker
Arnberg, A., tinsmith
Bick, George, J. P.
Bottum, E., grocer
Bonnell, —, M. D.
Boyd, Mossom, proprietor saw mill
Bradfield, Charles, insurance agent
Bradfield, C., dry goods merchant
Breden. James, farmer
Breden, John, farmer
Brown, Joseph, general merchant
Clements, Joseph, lock master.
Cheetham, Thomas, carpenter
Chittuk, James, blacksmith
Cumming, Charles, carpenter
Daley, M.
Daley, M., J. P.
Dawkins, H., tailor
Dykes, James, general merchant
Edgar, Mrs. W., dressmaker.
Emsar, N., general merchant
Fair, —, M.D
Fairbairn, Charles, farmer
Garden, Joseph, shoemaker
Gooley, Miss, dressmaker
Graham, Joseph, Crown Lands agent
Graham, S. S., attorney, &c
Green, Edward, butcher
Green, George, gunsmith
Green & Brothers, carpenters
Green & Son, blacksmiths
Harlow, Thomas, saddler
Hoskins, Rev., (Church of England)
Hunter, Robert, constable
Johnston, Christopher, dentist
Johnston,, S. dry goods merchant
Junkin, Irvin, general merchant
Kelley, Edward, farmer
Kennedy, J. & J., carpenters
Kennedy, William, proprietor saw mill
Kelso, Joseph, farmer
Law, D., tailor
Larkin, Miss, dressmaker
Lee, Wesley, farmer
McClaverty, J., tanner
McClelland, S., grocer
McConnell, John, baker
McConnell, Matthew, proprietor Queen's Hotel
McDonald, Duncan, blacksmith
McKinnon, Hugh, carpenter
Macnamara, Mrs., Lizzie, teacher
Montgomery, James, butcher
Moore, E., painter
Nicholas, Ebenezer, wagon maker
Nye, George, cooper
Oakes, Merrit, farmer
Orr, Alexander, general merchant
Patterson, Rev., (Presbyterian)
Rapley, James, butcher
Read, J. L., general merchant
Read, W. B., general merchant
Robinson, Mrs., fancy goods
Russell Cornelius
Sheridan, Rev., (Wesleyan)
Simpson, John, proprietor Forest House
Snowden, William, proprietor Rokeby Hotel
Steel, Thomas, general merchant
Stephens, J., tallow chandler
Linkell & Perrin, druggists booksellers, &c.
Thomson, M. H., teacher
TUPPER, A., LaTouche, Postmaster
Ward, Seth, shingle manufacturer
Wilson, James, shoemaker

Blyth.—A Village in the Townships of Morris and Wawanosh, County Huron, 17 miles from Goderich, and 10 from the nearest station on the Grand Trunk Railway. Stages to Clinton, 10 miles, and Wingham, 10 miles, fare 37 cents. Improved land in vicinity averages $30 per acre. Mechanics and laborers required. The surrounding country is excellently adapted for agriculture. Money order office. Population 350.

Clarke, J., hotel keeper
Clewart, Rev. Mr., (Methodist)
Drummond, William, general merchant
Gurney, George, tailor
Headley, John, hotel keeper
HOLMES, RICHARD W., Postmaster and general merchant.
Holmes, Thomas, J. P., general and insurance agent and auctioneer
Kelly & Heeney, proprietors steam flour mill
Luxford, J., butcher
McKinnon, D. B., general merchant
McLean, Rev. Mr., (Presbyterian)
McQuarrie, James, woolen manufacturer
McTavish, N., wagon maker
Mitchell, R., saddler
Moore, P., general agent
Murphy, Rev. Mr., (Episcopal)
Polson, W., clothier
Poulton, H., tailor
Quinn, George, teacher
Ritchey, Thomas, farmer
Rome, James, stone and lime dealer
Ross, Peter, carpenter
Shane, William, hotel keeper
Sherritt, John, shoemaker
Sloan, William, M. D., druggist
Thompson, J., M. D., druggist
Urquhart, G., carpenter
White, Thomas, tinsmith
Whitehead, L., lumber dealer
Winters, John, cooper

Blytheswood.—A Post office in the Township of Mersea, County Essex.
ROBERTSON CHARLES, Postmaster.

Bogart.—A small Village in the Township of Hungerford, County Hastings, 27 miles from Belleville Iron abounds in the vicinity. Population, 50.

BOGART, A. L., Postmaster
Bogart, C. O., merchant
Cheatham, William, brickmaker
Empry, Christopher, blacksmith
Empry, F. W., farmer
Hart, O., teacher
Hill, Rev. John, (Methodist)
Hill, Joseph, wagon maker
Rutten Abram, farmer

Bolingbroke.—A Post-office in the Township of Sherbrooke, and County Lanark, S. R.
KORRY JOHN, Postmaster.

Bolsover.—A Village on the Talbert River, and on the line of the proposed Toronto and Nipissing Railway, in the Township of Eldon, County Victoria. Distant from Lindsay, the County Town, 28 miles from Toronto, 80 miles. Stage to Woodville. Average price of land $5 to $16. Population, 150.

Burton, Joseph, cooper
Crowther, Peter, tinsmith
Dalgleish, Robert, auctioneer
Dickson, William, farmer
Donely, Cornelius, hotel keeper
Folliott, H. W., wagon maker
Folliott, Thomas, carpenter
Foster, Henry
Gibson, Thomas
Gibson, William, farmer
Kilingworth, Donely & Co., tanners, &c
McBurney, Alexander, carpenter
McRea, Duncan, general merchant
McReady, W.
MARSH, G. F., Postmaster, and general merchant
Marsh, John, butcher
Milligan, Misses, A & B., dressmakers
Milligan, Maxwell, tailor
Mitchell, Donald, carpenter
Moncrieff Hugh, shoemaker
Munroe, Donald, carpenter
Nichols, John, farmer
Jabez, Oliver, M. D
Russell, J. S., general merchant
Scott, Robert, general merchant
Smith & Davis, shingle makers
Thomas, William, saddler
Ward, W. A., distiller
Young, W. Y., hotel keeper

Bomanton.—A small village in the Township of Haldimand, County Northumberland, 13 miles from Cobourg. Daily stage to Cobourg. Tri-weekly mails. Population 30,

Brenton, John, shoemaker
Forbes, Thomas, blacksmith
Iveson, Rev. D., (Wesleyan)
KNIGHT, RICHARD, Postmaster and general merchant
Williams, Rev. W. M., (Presbyterian)

Bolton.—(Albion P. O.)—A Village on the River Humber, and on the line of the proposed Toronto, Grey and Bruce Railway, in the Township of Albion, County Peel. Distant from County Town 16 miles, from Toronto 28 miles. Stages to and from Weston. Average price of land $40 to $50. Population 700.

Alexander, Robert, cabinet maker
Beemish, J., butcher
Bee, Rev. W., (Primitive Methodist)
Bell, J. J., shoemaker
Bolton, L. R., accountant
Bolton, Samuel, carpenter
Booth, R. H., bookseller
Buist, William, woolen factor
Cairns, J., carpenter
Card, John L., farmer
Clark, John, farmer
Coates, George, blacksmith
Cooper, Mrs., dressmaker
Cooper, Thomas, tailor
Cummings, T., tailor
Curlis, T., proprietor Albion Hotel
Curlis, W., proprietor Masonic Hotel
Dalton, W. H., M.D
Dempster, T., butcher
Dick, William & Bros., iron founders
East, Samuel, shoemaker
Eaves, T , fancy goods
EVANS, GEORGE, Postmaster and prop. Exchange Hotel
Frazer, H., proprietor Ontario Hotel
Friar, J., shoemaker
Griffin, William, weaver
Guardhouse, John. general merchant
Hardwick, M., carpenter
Harper, John, saddler
Hickman, E., M.D
Hilliard, John, weaver
Jaffray, Wyatt, general merchant
Johnson, James, J.P
McDonald, Francis, cooper
McDougall, John, farmer
McKee, Alexander, farmer
McKeown, David, blacksmith
McTavish, Miss Margaret, teacher
McTavish, Peter, teacher
Maltby, Joseph, baker
Martin, C. A., tailor
Morgan, E., attorney
Newlove, James
Noble, George, butcher
Norris, William, shoemaker
Norton, David, brick manufacturer
Osler, Rev. H. B., (Episcopal)
Owens, James, pump manufacturer
Parrett, James, potash factor
Sanderson, M., wagon maker
Seymour, William, wagon maker
Sherlock, Rev. B., (Wesleyan)
Shields, John, general merchant
Shore, Henry, farmer
Shore, John, farmer
Smith, G., painter
Sterne, William, T., prop. Railway Hotel
Stewart, Samuel, farmer
Stork, J., druggist
SWINARTON, THOMAS, M.P.P
Switzer, J. C.. carpenter
Taylor, Walter, general merchant
Waflord, S. A., bookseller
Walford, S. A. & Son, tallow chandlers
Warbrick, J., J.P
Warbrick, Joseph, tanner
Wilson, George, tinsmith
Wheeler, Rev. J., (Presbyterian)
Wolf, James, blacksmith

Bongard's Corners.—A Village on the Bay of Quinté, in the Township of Marysburgh, County Prince Edward. Distant from Picton, the County Town, 10 miles, from Toronto 150 miles. Stages to Picton, and steamers to Kingston and Belleville. Average price of land $30 to $50. Population 100.

Anglin, Miss Eliza, general store
Anglin, Robert D., teacher
Bongard, Conrad, J. P.
BONGARD, JOHN, Postmaster
Bongard, J. D., farmer
Campbell, Rev. Thomas, (Wesleyan)
Carney, —, wagon maker
Carson, Thomas G., carpenter
Clark, E , miller
David, Henry, B., farmer
David, Peter, farmer
Harrison, Edward, farmer
Hart, James, wagon maker
Hobson, William, carpenter
Hodgins, Rev. —, (Church of England)
Johnson, John, farmer
Kerr, William, J. P.
Minaker, Nazareth, harness maker
Pearce, John, wagon maker
Solems, Harvey, shoemaker
Solems, Sidney, wagon maker
Tobey, Henry, farmer
Turner, Cornelius, shoemaker
Vanblack, Elias, J. P.
Vangesen, Henry, farmer
Weldon, Rev. Isaac, (Wesleyan)
Young, Rev. —, (Church of England)

Boston.—A Village on Boston Creek, in the Township of Townsend, County Norfolk, 12 miles from Simcoe. Tri-weekly mails. Population 150.

Bailey, Mrs., milliner
Barber, H. J., general merchant
Bowler, James, trader
Butler, Isaac, laborer
Colton, Allen, tinsmith
Duncombe, S. C., M. D.
Generow, L., carpenter
Honney, James, shoemaker
Horis, George, cheese factor
Johnson, Joseph, sen., farmer
Johnson, Joseph, jun., farmer
Lutes, William, wagon maker
Pereton, George, pump maker
Reddick, Rev. Joel (Baptist)
ROUSEN, OLIVER C., Postmaster, merchant
Rusling, David, blacksmith
Southern, William, cabinet maker
Stevens, R., cooper
Tobin, Martin, butcher
Woodley, Israel, farmer

Bondhead.—A Village in the Townships of Tecumseth and West Gwillimbury, County Simcoe, 22 miles from Barrie, 6 from Bradford station, Northern Railway, and 42 from Toronto. Stages dailyto Bradford. Money Order office and Savings' Bank, Population 350.

Brunskill, Thomas, M. D.
Carter, J. & H., general merchants
Davidson, Rev. John, (Episcopal)
Dixon, W. J., saddler
Edmonds, W., painter
FENTON, WALTER R., prop. Fenton House
FRASER, REV. WILLIAM, (Canada Presbyterian)
Jamieson, W. R., boots and shoes
Kline, Anthony, agricultural works
Lewis, G., blacksmith
LOUNT, Hiram, Postmaster and general merchant
McCracken, John, builder
McGeary, James, wagon maker
McMunn, John, tinsmith
Manning, Joseph, merchant
Manning, Samuel, hotel keeper
Nelson, William, founder
Nelson, William C., carriage maker
Orr, Joseph R., M. D.
Pearson, William, blacksmith
Richardson, L. & A., carriage makers
Robertson, George, shoemaker
Scholfield, Thomas C., M. D., Coroner
Shields, Robert, mason
Sprole, J. & R., flour and saw mills
St. Clair, William and James, general merchants
Stevenson, Richard, saddler
Sutton, John, cabinet maker
Vaughan, James, carriage maker.
Watson, George, J. P.
Watson, Moses, blacksmith

Bookton.—A Village in the Township of Windham, County Norfolk. Distant from Simcoe, the County Town 18 miles. Average price of land $25 to $40. Population 200.

Bertram, D. & W., farmers
Book, L., farmer.
Crane, J. & C., farmers
Dalby, George, carpenter
Donald, Rev. William, (Presbyterian)
Dunlop, Alex, carpenter
Elliott, Philander, carpenter
Hall, J., farmer
House, Robert, carpenter
Kelly, D. W., farmer
Kelly, E., farmer
Kelly, R., farmer
Kelly, Samuel, farmer
McCurdy, S., farmer
McINTOSH, PETER N., Postmaster and general merchant
Maddaugh, J., farmer
Maddaugh, Miss N., teacher
Marlatt, A. & W., farmers
Mingle, W., farmer
Moore, Miss S., teacher
Moore, W., farmer
Morrison, Rev. F. W., (Wesleyan)
Osborne, Rev. W. T., (Baptist)
Root, A., shingle manufacturer
Russell, W., farmer
Sweet, Henry, carpenter
Tufford, A. W. J. & R., farmers
Watson, R., farmer
Wheeler, T., farmer

Borelia.—A Village in the Township of Reach, County Ontario, 17 miles from Whitby. Daily stage. Money Order office. Population 350.

Benson, Thomas, shoemaker
Bower, John, farmer
Bowman, James, pump maker
Corson, A. T., farmer
Cottingham, J. D., druggist
Crandell, Caleb, farmer
Crandell, Clark, farmer and drover
Crandell, Stephen E., cabinet maker
Haight, Harrison, gardener
Harrington, Andrew J., hotel keeper
Hilborn, James, millwright
Jamieson, Rev. George (Presbyterian)
JEWETT, JAMES, Postmaster, hotel keeper
Johnston, Henry, blacksmith
Kirkpatrick, Matthew, shoemaker
Lund, Richard, J. P., farmer
Major, Edward, auctioneer
Morrish, George, vineyard proprietor
McConnell, Thomas, farmer
Neale, Frederick, grocer
NOTT, JOHN, cabinet maker
Palmer, George, painter
Post, Israel, grocer
Smith, George, carpenter
Swan, James, blacksmith

Bosworth.—A Post-Village in the Townships of Peel and Maryborough, County Wellington, 26 miles from Guelph, the County Town, the nearest railway station. The Conestogo river, near the Village affords excellent water-power, not yet utilized. There is a Wesleyan Methodist Church in the neighborhood. Stages to Saugeen and Walkerton. Improved land $25 per acre. Population, 100

Armstrong, David, butcher, hotel keeper
DRAPER, CHARLES, Postmaster
Green & Goulding, general merchants
Jackson, Rev. Thomas, (Wesleyan)
Johnston, William, builder
Lowry, J. W., cabinet maker
Lundy, Miss C., teacher
Proctor, Albert, general merchant
Schneider, Martin, hotel keeper
Stubbs, John, sen., builder
Stubbs, John, jun., builder
Taylor, William, saddler

Bornholm.—A Village on the Thames, in the Township of Logan, County Perth. Distant from Stratford, the County Town, 25 miles, from Toronto 113 miles. Stage to Mitchell and Listowell. Average price of land, $16 to $30. Population 150.

Cashon, John, teacher
Cerhon, John, auctioneer
Ferguson, J. W., insurance agent
Gaffoney, T., shingle manufacturer
Gilmartin, J., painter
Haggerty, J.
HAGGERTY, T., Postmaster and hotel keeper
Hornibrook, J.
Hornibrook, T.
Hunt, P., saddler
Jones, K., J. P.
Lyons, J.
McCormack, E., shingle maker
Morrison, Sills & Brown, millers
Rock. G., planing mill
Ruinn, T., telegraph operator
Seger & Zimmerman, wagon makers
Sodwater, John, butcher
Shoults, G.
Snubb, B.
Wade, J.
Ward & Hebden, carpenters

Botany.—A Village in the Township of Howard, County Kent. Distant from Chatham, the County Town 15 miles, from Toronto, 169 miles.

Armstrong, Andrew, farmer
Atkinson, William, farmer
Becket, Rev. J., (Presbyterian)
McBrayne, Archibald, farmer
McBRAYNE. C., Postmaster and general merchant
McKerracher, William, J.P., farmer
Mowbray, William, farmer
Orme, Rev. W., (Wesleyan)
Robertson, J. , farmer

Bothwell.—A Town and station of the Great Western Railway, in the Township of Zone, County Kent Electoral District of Bothwell. The town was incorporated in 1865. Bothwell is the centre of the principal oil region in the Province. Distance from Chatham, 22 miles, and from Toronto, 152. Money Order office and Savings Bank. Population, 1600.

Allen, Henry, cabinet maker
Avery, N. H., tailor
Badder. James, fancy goods
Ball Miss, teacher
Batzner, J., prop. Perkin's House
Bennett, A., carpenter
Benson, Rev, Elder M., (Episcopal Methodist)
Bodman, Richard, grocer
Boon, Thomas, cabinet maker
Bray, W., druggist
Cassmere, Louis, tailor
Clark, C., provisions
Coleman, James, blacksmith
Conover, C. A., insurance agent
Crotty, John, general merchant
Drummond, John, proprietor Masonic Hotel
Duncan, Alexander, proprietor Duncan's Hotel
Finnegan & Dadsell, butchers
Fleming, J., shoemaker
Gay, Walter, cabinet maker
Gordon, J. D., general merchant
Griffith, Thomas, proprietor Royal Hotel
Lughton, William, general merchant, agent American Express Co
Lavin, William, general merchant
Lebu, Mutty, livery stable
Lick, John L., stock dealer
Luke, James, wagon maker
McCattie, John, teacher
McColl, J. T., general merchant
McCraney, D., attorney, &c
McDonald, Angus, carpenter
McDonald, James, carpenter
McLardy, D., shoemaker
McQueen, Mrs., teacher
McQueen, Miss, teacher
Marcus, R., hotel keeper
Miller, George, cooper
Miller, John, R., teacher
Nichol, Robert, attorney
Pope, F. H., M.D
Pratt, A. R., Secretary Land and Patent Office
Railton, George, attorney
Raney, Rev. Father, (Roman Catholic)
Reid, Colin, sash and door manufacturer
Rice, Rev. E. M., (Baptist)
Rowe, W. J., M.D
Roseburgh, William, tinsmith
Scott, John, tailor
Smith, H. F., grocer
Smith, H. F,, book and job printer
Smith, Stokes, builder
Snyder, Philip, blacksmith
Spence, W. C., butcher
Sutherland, E. B., carpenter
Sutherland, Miss Maggie, dressmaker
Tallman & Brant, watchmakers
TAYLOR, JOHN, Postmaster
Thomas, S, J., auctioneer
Trout, James, wagon maker
Tucker, Henry, watchmaker
Vizena, Louis, carpenter
Waite, J. R., telegraph operator
Warden, Rev. Robert H., (Presbyterian)
Webster, John, (Wesleyan)
Wesner & Pope, druggist
Whiting, Ezra, proprietor Martin House
Wood, James E., builder
Wright, Rev. J. T., (Church of England)
Wright, Rev. M. E., (Methodist Episcopal

Bowmanville.—A Town, and Station of the Grand Trunk Railway, situated on the north shore of Lake Ontario, in the township of Darlington, County Durham. It possesses a good harbor, and there is extensive water power in the vicinity. The surrounding country is very fertile. Distant from Cobourg 27 miles, from Whitby 14, and from Toronto 43 miles. Money order office and Savings Bank. Population about 3500.

Allin, John, grocer, etc.
Allison, William, M.D.
Alma Hotel, Thomas Shaw, proprietor
Andrews, Joseph B., groceries and fancy goods
ARMOUR, ROBERT, Registrar West Riding County Durham, issuer of tavern licenses and issuer of marriage licenses
ARMOUR & LOWE, (Robert Armour and William H. Lowe), barristers, etc., solicitors Royal Canadian Bank
Banbury, W. H., boots and shoes
BARKER, CEPHAS, editor and publisher of *The Observer*, (weekly)
Bassett, William, (Basset & Brown)
Bassett, Thomas & Co., (Thomas Bassett and Robert Young), hardware
Bassett & Brown, (Wm. Bassett and John Brown), carpenters and builders
Batting, Thomas, dry goods.
Beith, Alexander, M.D.
BENDER, G. C., manufacturer of cigars, dealer in tobaccos, fancy goods etc.
Berry, —, brick manufacturer
Booth, Charles R. D., Deputy Registrar
Bounsall, Mrs. C., milliner
BOUNSALL, CHRISTOPHER, prop. Bowmanville marble works, and agent Briton Medical Life Association. (See adv.)
BOWMANVILLE MILLS, Capt. Raynes, proprietor, D. Towns, manager
BOWMANVILLE (THE) FURNITURE MANUFACTURING COMPANY, (limited), Thomas Johnston, manager
Bowmanville Union School, (Grammar and Common), Edward T. Crowle, Principal
Bradshaw, Samuel B., hardware merchant, manufacturer and dealer in stoves, etc.
Brent, Miss Jane, milliner
BRIMACOMBE, J. M., surgeon dentist. (See adv)
Brodie, Thomas, senr
BRODIE'S HOTEL, Thomas Brodie, junr., proprietor. (See adv)
Brooke, L. F., dry goods
Brown, John, (Bassett & Brown)
Buckler, Aaron, watchmaker and jeweller
Bunner, Henry, boot and shoemaker
Canada Life Assurance Co., R. & H. O'Hara, agents
Canada Permanent Building and Savings Society; R. & H. O'Hara, agents
Canadian Express Company, W. A. Neads, agent.
Canadian Statesman, (weekly) W. R. Climie, Editor and Proprietor
Cawker, Charles, butcher
Chapman, L. B., wholesale and retail stay manuf.
CHRISTIE, THOMAS, coroner, official assignee, insurance and general agent, auctioneer and appraiser, collector, commissioner in B. R. &c., &c. office McFeeters block, opposite Town Hall.
Clark, Charles, clerk Division Court
Climie, W. R., editor and prop. *Canadian Statesman*
Consaul & Co., (P. W. Consaul and J. Milne) grocers wine and spirit merchants, &c.
Cornish & Son, (William Cornish and Lewis Cornish) watchmakers and jewellers
Cowle, F. Y., dry goods and clothing
Crowle, Edward T., A.M. L.R.C.P., Principal Union School
CUBITT, F. C., mayor
Darch, Richard, blacksmith
Darlington, Josiah, grocer
Darlington, Thomas, grocer and provision merchant
Davidson, — M. D.
Davies, Morgan, wholesale tea and general commission merchant
Depoty, H., carpenter
DICKSON, R. O., Secretary and Treasurer the Bowmanville Furniture Manufacturing Company (Limited)
DIXON, ANTHONY, J. P., Collector of Customs, agent Queen Insurance Company, Royal Insurance Company, and agent Provincial Permanent Building Society of Toronto
Dodd, Thomas, accountant Royal Canadian Bank
Dunstan, Thomas, boots and shoes, and fancy goods
Eastern House, Daniel Jeffery, proprietor
EASTON, ROBERT, wholesale hoop skirt manuf.
Edwards, William, barber
Emery, Gordon, physician and surgeon
FAIRBAIRN, J. B., Postmaster and manager Montreal Telegraph Office
Fairweather, Christina, teacher, Union School
Fanson & Northey, tanners and curriers
FAREWELL, J. E., (Farewell and McGee)
FAREWELL & McGEE, (J. E. Farewell and R. McGee,) barristers, attorneys, solicitors & notaries
Farmers' Exchange and livery stables, Joseph Maynard, proprietor
Farmers' Hotel, Francis Henderson, proprietor
FISHER, D. cashier Ontario Bank
Fletcher, Alexander, baker
Fletcher & Swan, (John Fletcher, jr. and George Swan) general grocers
Foley, Richard D., produce merchant
Forbes, David, merchant tailor
Forman, James G., cooper
FRANK, FREDERICK, (McFeters & Frank)
Galbraith, Elizabeth, teacher Union School
Galbraith, John Keith, barrister, &c
Galbraith, Miss Mary A., fancy store
GIBSON & CO., grocers. (See adv)
Griffiths, John J., saddle and harness maker
Haines, George, carriage maker
Hamley, Richard, brickmaker
Haynes, George, Deputy Reeve
Hartford Fire Ins. Co., R. & H. O'Hara, agents
Heal, Samuel, carpenter
Helson, Thomas H., teacher Union School
Henderson, Francis, prop. Farmers' Hotel and livery stable
Henrey, George, photographer
Higginbotham, John, chemist and druggist
Hill, S. F., general merchant
Hoar, Thomas, blacksmith
Hocridge, John, prop. Neptune Inn, Port Darlington
Holden, J., saw mill proprietor
HOSKIN, F. T., stoves and tinware
James, R. W., dealer in agricultual implements and grain
Jeffery, Daniel, proprietor Eastern House
Jeffrey, Joseph, merchant tailor
Johnston, James (Mortin & Johnston)
JOHNSTON, THOMAS, manager The Bowmanville Furniture Company (Limited)
Jones, T. J., surgeon dentist

Jones, W. J., teller Ontario Bank
Jose, Joseph H., merchant tailor
Kyle, Jane, teacher, Union School
Kyle, William, teller Royal Canadian Bank
Loscombe, Charles R., deputy coroner, for Counties of Durham and Northumberland
Loscombe, Robert R., barrister, &c.
LOWE, WILLIAM H., (Armour & Lowe)
Lynden, Joseph, boarding house
McArthur, F. F., dry goods merchant
McClellan, James, landing waiter Custom House
McClellan, John, Harbor Master Port Darlington
McClellan, William, telegraph operator G. T. R. station
McClung, James (McClung Bros)
McClung, John (McClung Bros)
McClung, Samuel (McClung Bros)
McClung, Thomas (McClung Bros)
McClung, William, carriage maker
McClung, Bros., (James, Thomas, John and Samuel) dry goods and grocery merchants
McCullough, J. & Co., general merchants
McDOUGALL, J., proprietor Fouldin Flouring Mills
McFEETERS, JAMES, (McFeeters & Frank)
McFEETERS & FRANK, (James McFeeters & Frederick Frank) produce and commission merchants
McGEE, R., (Farewell & McGee)
McGill, G., accountant Ontario Bank
McLeod, John, hardware merchant
McMillan, B., telegraph operator
McMillan, D., telegraph operator G.T.R.
McMurtry, John, grocer and provision dealer
McMurtry, William, dry goods
Manning, Robert S., cabinet maker
Manning, Thomas cooper and stave manufacturer
Martin, Richard, confectioner
Mason, Samuel, saddle and harness maker
Mayer, Marcus, cap manufacturer and furrier
Maynard, Joseph, proprietor Farmer's Exchange
Millard, Alice, teacher Union School
MONTREAL TELEGRAPH OFFICE, J. B. Fairbairn manager and Postmaster
Moorcraft, Sarah H., teacher Union School
Morris, James, carriage and wagon maker
Mortin, Philip, (Mortin & Johnston)
Mortin & Johnston, (Philip Mortin & Jas. Johnston), merchant tailors
Murdoch, John, (Murdoch Brothers)
Murdoch, Peter, (Murdoch Brothers)
Murdoch Brothers, (John and Peter), grocers and seedsmen
Neads, Jacob W., iron founder
Neads, W. A., agent Canadian Express Company
O'HARA, HENRY, (R. & H. O'Hara)
O'HARA, ROBERT, (R. & H. O'Hara)
O'HARA, R. & H., (Robert and Henry), booksellers, stationers, photographers, gen'l insurance agents, agents Canada Permanent Building Society, sewing machine agents, and stock and money brokers. (See adv)
ONTARIO BANK, (head office), D. Fisher, cashier
Orr, Robert, teacher Union School
Paton, George, M.D.
Patterson, Bradford, M.D.
Patterson, Thomas, dry goods
Peate, Richard, tailor
Percy, John, blacksmith
Perry, W. G., station master G. T. R.
Pethick, William, tailor
Pierce, William, carpenter
Pirie, William, tailor
Pollock, Jane, teacher Union School
Porter, George, assistant accountant
Port Darlington Custom House, office Bowmanville, Anthony Dixon, Collector of Customs
Porter, Marshall, saddle, harness and trunk maker
PORTER, WILLIAM, iron founder and stove manuf.
POST OFFICE, J. B. Fairbairn, Postmaster
Prout, Mark J., carpenter
Quick, Lewis, (Yellowlees & Quick)
Ratcliffe, A. G., grocer and segar manufacturer
Ratcliffe, F. W., produce dealer and grocer
RAYNES, F., superintendent Capt. Raynes Bowmanville mills
Reed, Richard, manuf. and dealer in boots and shoes
REGISTRY OFFICE FOR WEST RIDING County of Durham, Robert Armour, Registrar
Reid, Henry, M.D.
Robins, Paul, bookseller, &c.
Rose, William A., veterinary surgeon
ROYAL CANADIAN BANK, (Bowmanville branch) Robert Young, manager
Rundell, William, (Williams & Rundell)
Scott, William, boot and shoe maker
Shaw, Thomas, proprietor Alma Hotel
Silver, Edward, pump maker
Simson, T. E., grocer, wine and spirit merchant
Spalding, Charles D., law student
Stott, David, druggist
Stott, Houston, carriage painter
Stoughton, Miss M. G., fancy store
Sumter, J., assistant accountant
Thomas, Thomas, blacksmith
THOMPSON & BURNS, (Willam Thompson and William Burns) produce merchants
Tod, Charles, baker
TOTTERDALE, THOMAS, proprietor Totterdale House, (see adv.)
TOWNS, DAVID, prop. Caledonia oatmeal and grist mills, Clinton street, and manager Bowmanville mills
Travelers Life and Accident Insurance Co., Hartford, R. & H. O'Hara, agents
Treleven, M., manufacturer and dealer in boots and shoes
Trewin, —, boot and shoemaker
Trick, John, butcher
Upper Canada Bible Society, in connection with the British and Foreign Bible Society, R. & H. O'Hara, Depository, King
WEBSTER, GEORGE, manager, T. Bassett & Co.
Westcott, Isaac, carriage and wagon maker
Western Assurance Company of Toronto, R. & H. O'Hara, agents
Williams, Mark, (Williams & Rundell) butcher
Williams & Rundell, (Mark Williams & W. Rundell) butchers
WILSON, CHARLES R., (Wilson & Bro.)
WILSON, Joseph C. (Wilson & Bro.)
WILSON & BROTHER, (Charles R. and Joseph C.) grocers and provision dealers
WINDATT, RICHARD, Town Clerk and Collector.
Wright, Miss Agnes, milliner and dressmaker, King
WRIGHT, WILLIAM, bookkeeper Murdock & Bro.
Wyllie, James, baker and confectioner
Yellowlees, Thomas, (Yellowlees and Quick)
Yellowlees & Quick, (Thomas Yellowlees and Lewis Quick) fancy goods
YOUNG, ROBERT, Manager Bowmanville Branch Royal Canadian Bank, agent Home Ins. Co. of New Haven, Conn., Commercial Union Ass. Co. of London, Eng., European Assurance and Guarantee Co. of London, Eng., office, R. C. Bank
Young & Co., butchers, Market Building
Young, Charles, Britton

Bracebridge.—A Village on the Muskoka River, in the Township of Macaulay, County Victoria Distant from Toronto 140 miles. Stages in winter and boats in summer from Barrie to Washago. Average price of wild land, $2 to $5; improved, $10. Money Order office. Population 150.

BAILEY, ALEXANDER, Postmaster and general merchant
Bailey, A., hotel keeper
Chenier, F., grocer
Frazer, John, teacher
Glass, James, general agent
Gow, George hotel keeper
Herritt, William, farmer
Holditch, S., general merchant
Johnston, John, blacksmith
LOUNT, C. W., J.P.
Lymington, —, cabinetmaker
McDonald, A. H., hotel keeper
McDonald, H. J., grocer
McNichol, Robert, farmer
Scarlet, William, accountant
Sharpe, Walter, farmer
Tait, W., blacksmith
Teviotdale, John, general merchant
Teviotdale, —, cabinetmaker
Gibson, G., accountant
Winfield, John, architect
Way, Rev. —, (Church of England)
Wright, Rev. —, (Presbyterian)

Bradford.—An incorporated Village and Station of the Northern Railway, in the Township of West Gwillimbury, County Simcoe, 22 miles from Barrie and 38 from Toronto. Stages daily to Bond Head. Money Order office and Savings Bank. Population 1000.

Abbott, James G. & J., tanners
Adams, J. M., tin ware
Algeo, Robert, hotel keeper.
Archard, W. Y., druggist
Atkinson, J., sash factory
Armstrong, John, farmer
Barnard, B., dry goods and groceries
Barry, J. W. & Son, tanners
Bingham, Robert, hotel keeper
Bingham, Edward, tanner
Boudy, John, dry goods and groceries
Booth, J. D., teacher
Borrowman, J. & A., marble dealers
BUTTERFIELD, L., foundry and machinist
Brimson, William, pianoforte maker
Campbell, Alexander, groceries and provisions
Clement, Lewis, M. D.
Cockerline, M. B., grist and carding mill
Cook, Gibson, groceries and provisions
Deacon, Joseph, druggist
Dissette, Edward, carriage maker
DOUGLAS, MRS. ANN, Postmistress
Dobson, R., grammar school teacher
Driffield, Thomas & Sons, hardware merchants
Durham, James, saw mills
EDMONSON, WILLIAM, baker and confectioner
Falconbridge, J. R., dry goods and groceries
Fisher, E. J. T., M.D.
Flemming, Miss, school teacher
Goodchild, J. & W., groceries and provisions
Goodfellow, John, farmer
Herrick, Thomas, tailor
Hockridge, John, carriage maker
Husband, George, dentist
Kilkenny, Thomas, cabinet maker
Kilgoe, Robert, hotel keeper
Lamont, Mrs, tinware
Long, William, merchant
McBrien, John, boots and shoes
McKee, Alexander & Son, groceries and liquor store
Manning, H. W., bailiff Division Court
Marrow, Edward, station agent, N. R. Co.
Montgomery, John, boots and shoes
Morris, Job, hotel keeper
MORTON, GEORGE D., M. D., coroner
Morgan, G. W., druggist
Murphy, John, dry goods and groceries
Ormsby, J., boots and shoes
Orr, A. & W., dry goods and groceries
Paul, Rev. R., (Primitive Methodist)
PORTER & BROUGHTON, props. *South Simcoe News*
Rawe, James, photographer
Ruttan, Rev. C., (Church of England)
SCANLON, MARK, barrister, attorney-at-law, &c.
Scott & Graham, saddlers
SMALL, DANIEL, proprietor North American Hotel
Smith, H., fruit and fancy goods
Spence, John, painter
Stephens, John, photographer
Stephenson, John, harness maker
Stibbs, John, baker and confectioner
Stevenson, W. M., dry goods and groceries
Stewart, Robert, grocery and liquor store
Stodders, Andrew, hotel keeper
Strong, William, boots and shoes
Swallow, John, hardware
"SOUTH SIMCOE NEWS," (weekly) Porter and Broughton, editors
Syme, James, M. D.
Trott, W., tailor
Turner & Cockerell, groceries and glassware
Walker, R. & W., cabinet makers
Walker & Overton, tin ware
Wilcock, James, watchmaker
WILSON, J. W. H., attorney-at-law
Wright, C. W., groceries and glassware
York, Eli, blacksmith
Youmans, Rev. J., (Wesleyan)

Braemar.—A Village in the Township of East Zorra, County Oxford. Distant from Woodstock, the County Town, 8 miles, from Toronto 91 miles. Average price of land, $25. Population 75.

ANDREW, ALEXANDER, Postmaster and general merchant
Forbes, Robert, farmer
Harrington, John, J.P.
Leslie, William, farmer
McKay, Alexander, farmer
McKay, George, carpenter
McKay, James B., farmer
McKay, John B., carpenter
McKellar, Hugh, teacher
McKenzie, Rev. —, (Presbyterian)
Munro, William, teacher
Ross, Andrew, farmer
Ross, Thomas, tailor
Sewel, Samuel, farmer
Sutherland, John, farmer
Whaly, Hugh, farmer
Wilkison, John, J.P.

Box Grove.—A Village on Rouge Creek, in the Township of Markham, County York. Distant from County Town 20 miles. Stages daily to Markham Village. Average price of land $50. Population 100.

Break, David, farmer
Break, Joseph, farmer
Glenn, George, shingle manufacturer
Hudley, William, butcher
McCAFFREY, JOHN, Postmaster and general merchant.
Morrison, Rev. W., (Wesleyan)
Raymer, A., farmer
Reesor, Frederick, teacher
Reesor, J. S., farmer
Reesor, Samuel, farmer
Roberts, W. M., farmer
Smith, Edward, tailor
Spry, Joseph, shingle manufacturer
Sutton, Julius, woolen factor
Tomlinson, A. M., farmer
Tomlinson, Cicero, farmer
Tomlinson, Sylvester, farmer

Bowood.—A Post office in the Township of Lobo, County Middlesex.
McLEAN, HUGH, Postmaster.

Boyne.—A Post office in the Township of Trafalgar, County Halton.
EMMETT, S., Postmaster.

Brampton.—The County Town of Peel, a Station of the Grand Trunk Railway, in the Township of Chinguacousy, 20 miles from Toronto. The country in the vicinity is an excellent agricultural one. The County buildings, recently erected, are of freestone and white brick, and are generally admitted to be equal in every respect to any similar structures in the Province. Money Order Office and Savings Bank. Population 1800.

Addy, William, cooper
Agar, T. A., clerk 1st Division Court
Alexander, James, carpenter
Anderson, A., wagon maker
Anthony, John, wagon maker
Anthony, William, blacksmith
Armour & Dawson, builders
Arnold, Rev. Robert, (Church of England)
ATKINS, S. & CO., hardware
AUSTIN, J. A., Deputy Clerk of the Crown, Clerk County Court
Baird, W. M., cabinetmaker
Bates, John, agent sewing machines
BARNHART, S. J., editor and proprietor *Review*.
BECK, SAMUEL, proprietor Revere House
Bell, Henry, grocer
Bell, John, carriage maker
Beynon, J. W., barrister
Boyle, Rev. R., (Primitive Methodist)
BRAMPTON TIMES, George Tye, proprietor
Bright, Lewis, gunsmith
Broddy, Robert, Sheriff
Bullermont, Thomas, grocer
Burnett & Sons, cabinetmakers
Campbell, D. F., County Registrar
CHISHOLM, K., Postmaster
CHISHOLM, K. & CO., (K. Chisholm & M. Elliot), general merchants, flour mill proprietors, produce dealers, etc.
CLARK, JACOB P., (Cummins, Coyne & Clark)
Clark, John, blacksmith
COATES, JOHN, veterinary surgeon and grocer. (See adv)
Cole, J. W., photographer
Carson, J. W., M.D
Coyne, John, boots and shoes
COYNE, JOHN, M.P.P., (Cummins, Coyne & Clark)
Craig, Donald, photographer
Crozier, David, tailor
CUMMINS, COYNE & CLARK, barristers, &c.
CUMMINS, J. P., (Cummins, Coyne & Clark)
Curry, R. C., M.D
Dawson, Charles, fruits, &c
DODDS, J. G., liquor merchant
DUGGAN, WILLIAM, Deputy Clerk of the Peace, Com. in B.R., issuer of marriage licenses
Elliott, John, farmer
ELLIOTT, M. M., (K. Chisholm & Co)
ELLIS, EDWARD, chief constable, auctioneer
Fawcett, Rev. M., (Methodist)
Fenton, David, farmer
Ferguson, William, carpenter
Fewson, John, brewer
Fitzgerald, R. C., agent Royal Canadian Bank
Galbraith, Robert, H., watchmaker
Gilkinson, Joseph, livery stable prop.
Glenn, James, cooper
Golding, James, baker
Gooderham, George, grocer
Graham, George, County Treasurer
Graham, Joseph, general merchant
Graham, Thomas. J.P
GRAHAM, W. K., (Trotter & Graham)
Grant, John, sen., M.D
GREEN, GEORGE, barrister, Clerk of the Peace, County Attorney
Green, James, shoemaker
HAGGERT, BROTHERS, iron founders and merchants. (See adv.)
HAGGERT, JAMES, general merchant
Hamilton, James, carpenter
Harris, Thomas, cooper
Heggie, David, M.D
HANNAH, J. R., prop. British Arms Hotel
Henderson, Robert, general merchant
Hodgson, Joseph, tailor
Holmes, Mrs. M. R, select school
Hossie, W. N., Deputy Sheriff
Hughes, Stewart, bricklayer
HUGHES, WILLIAM, general merchant
Hull, Anthony, carpenter
Hurst, William, grocer
Johnston, William, M.D., coroner
Jones, Robert, prop. Exchange Hotel

Kennedy, James, carpenter
Kennedy, James, cabinet maker
Kleiser, Augustus, watchmaker
LeBert, Joseph, baker
Lewis, John, blacksmith
Lewis, William, stage proprietor
Lillie, William, grocer
Lindsay, William, J.P., County Clerk
Lowes, Robert, farmer
Lundy, William T., general merchant
McBride, Donald, shoemaker
McCauley, Isaac, carpenter
McClellan, George, grocer
McClelland, George, grocer
McDonald, James, hotel keeper
McKechnie, Archibald, tailor
McMann, Robert, carpenter
McMurray, Thomas C., watchmaker
Mahaffy, William, blacksmith
Maloy, P. W., shoemaker
Marshall, William, farmer
Mathers, John, merchant
Menzies, R., proprietor Farmers' Inn
MORPHY & FLEMING, barristers
Murdock, Charles, shoemaker
Nelson, James, saddler
Newcombe, Christopher, farmer
Norton, T. R., blacksmith
Pace, Henry, watchmaker
Patterson, Samuel, farmer
Pattullo, Alexander, M.D.
Paul, Thomas J., attorney-at-law
Peaker, William, stoves and tinware
Pickard, A. John, carpenter
Pimm, Jacob, watchmaker
Playter, W. J., dentist
Porter, John, tailor
Pringle, Rev. James, (Presbyterian)
REVERE HOUSE, S. Buck, proprietor
REVIEW, (the) weekly, S. J. Barnhart, editor
Robertson, John H., saddler
Savage, John, machinist
Scott, A. B., P.L.S
Scott, A. F., County Judge
SCOTT, DAVID L., attorney-at-law
Scully, Henry, carpenter
Seath, John, principal grammar school
Shaw, John, farmer
Shepperd, Thomas, carpenter
Smith, David, farmer
Smith, James, carpenter
Smith & Robertson, bricklayers
SNELL, JOHN, drover. (See adv)
Sparks, Vipond, blacksmith
Spelman, J. A., carpenter
Sproule, J. G. C., butcher
Stewart, John, cooper
Stoneham, Richard, carpenter
Stork, Christopher, druggist
Stuart, Robert, carpenter
Summerville, S., shoemaker
Thistle, J. A
Tilt, James, boots and shoes
TROTTER & GRAHAM, dentists, insurance agents. (See adv)
TROTTER, RICHARD, J.P., (Trotter & Graham)
TYE, GEORGE, proprietor *Brampton Times*
Walsh, E. J., prop. Canada Hotel
Ward, Richard, cooper
White, David, butcher
White, George, shoemaker
Whitehead, Thomas, general merchant
Wigley, A. H., tanner
Williamson, William, cattle dealer
Wilmot & McGurn
Wilson, John, shoemaker
Wilson, S. S., saddler
Wilson, Thomas, marble works
Wood, J. E., barber
Woods, P. L., bookseller
Wright, George, grocer
Wright, Joseph, attorney-at-law

Branchton.—A Village on the Great Western Railway, in the Township of S. Dumfries, County Waterloo. Distant from Berlin, the County Town, 17 miles, from Toronto, 65 miles. Average price of land $50. Population, 250.

Aikins, Thomas, carpenter
Arthur, Hugh, farmer
Beamer, Joseph, planing mill
Brown, C. W., shoemaker
Buchanan, John, farmer
Buchanan, T., farmer
Burnett, Arthur, farmer
Cope, James, carpenter
Crozier, James, butcher
CUMMING & CORNELL, general merchants
CUMMING, D. W., Postmaster
Davis, Henry, engraver
Deacon, J. S., general merchant
Duplan, Charles, station master G. W. R
Farley, George, dyer
Goodall, Robert, farmer
Hunt, James, livery stable proprietor
Jenkins, J., proprietor Jenkins' Hotel
McDeish, George, farmer
McLeish, Robert, teacher
Middleton, George, accountant
Morgan, James, wagon maker
RATHWELL, WILLIAM, teacher
ROSEBURGH, WILLIAM, miller
Sales, Peter, architect
Simpson, George, farmer
Steel, John, dyer
Turnbull, Thomas, wagon maker
White, Hugh, farmer
Wilcox, Richard, butcher
Willard, Charles, painter

Brechin.—A Village in the Township of Mara, County Ontario, 60 miles from Whitby, and 30 from Bell Ewart, a Station on the Northern Railway. Tri-weekly mails. Population 50.

Barker, Joseph, shoemaker
Birney John, hotel keeper
Birney, John, blacksmith
Campbell, Rev. K. A. (Roman Catholic)
FOLEY, J. P., Postmaster and general merchant
McGrath, Michael, weaver
McGrath, Patrick, wagon maker
O'Donnel, Edward, gardener
Parsons, Jacob, farmer
Roach, Thomas, hotel keeper
Thomson, Joseph, general store.

Brantford.—The County Town of Brant, is situated on the Grand River, at the head of navigation and is a station of the Buffalo and Lake Huron Railway. Its name is derived from the celebrated Mohawk Chief, Joseph Brant. The site of the town, 807 acres, was surrendered by the Indians to the Crown, 19th April, 1830, and was surveyed the same year. The Grand River Navigation Canal, commenced in 1840, added materially to the early prosperity of the town, its object was to remove the obstruction caused by the falls on the Grand River; its length is about three miles and it is capable of admitting vessels of three and a-half feet draught to the town. Brantford is situated in the centre of one of the best agricultural sections of the Province, and possesses first-class manufacturing facilities, and having direct railway and water communication with all parts of the Province and the United States, must, at no distant day, become one of the most important towns in the Western Province. Stages to Hamilton and Simcoe. Population 7000. The following are the principal manufacturing establishments:—*Brantford Engine Works*, C. H. Waterous & Co., established 1844, employing 100 hands; steam engines, saw and grist mills, shingle, lath, and stave machines. Steam power 40 horse. *Victoria Foundry*, William Buck, established 1856, employing 80 hands; stoves, ploughs, castings, tin and copper ware, machinery, &c. *Brittania Foundry*, B. & G. Tisdale, established 1851, employs 25 hands; steam power, stoves, &c. *A. Spence*, carriage maker, employs 12 hands. *James Tutt*, planing mill and sash factory, steam power 10 horse employing 35 hands. Money order office and Savings bank.

Adams & Brophy, boots and shoes
Allan, P. C., books and stationery
AMERICAN HOTEL, A. G. Hatch, prop. (see adv.)
Armitage, W., butcher
Ash, W. H. & Co., distillers
Ashworth, G. L., hosiery, &c
Atchison, Mr.
Barden, Rev. P. (Roman Catholic)
Barnfather, David, tailor
Bates, Richard, marble works
Batson, H., hotel keeper
Baxter, J. & W., livery stable keepers (see adv.)
Beglan, Joseph, grocer
Belding, W. W.
Bell, W., tailor
Bellhouse, C. E., grocer
Bellhouse, James, builder
Bellhouse & Large, builders
Bellows, Mr.
BINGHAM HOUSE, Job Bingham, proprietor
BINGHAM, JOB, proprietor Bingham House.
Blackader, F. F., accountant Bank Montreal
Blackwell, Miss, teacher
Botham, Thomas & Co., groceries, &c.
Boulby, J. W., law office
BRADLEY, A., livery stable keeper. (See adv.)
BRANT HOTEL, G. Fleming proprietor. (See adv.)
BRANTFORD COURIER AND GENERAL ADVERTISER, published every Saturday. Subscription $2.00 per year. Henry Lemon, editor and proprietor
BRANTFORD EXPOSITOR, Stewart and Mathison publishers. Weekly terms $2.00 per year.
Brendon, Frederick, chemist and druggist.
Brethour, H. W. & Co., dry goods, millinery, clothing, &c.
Brockington, E., hotel keeper
Bromwich, W., hair dresser
Brooke, Thomas, grocer
BUCK, WILLIAM, stove and agricultural implement manufactory. (See adv.)
Bunnell, A., produce dealer
Calder, William, produce dealer
Callahan, Daniel, boots, shoes, leather and findings
Cameron, Ewen, Montreal Telegraph Office.
Cantillon, W. D., wholesale & retail dealer in liquors
Carnegie, John, accountant B. B. N. A.
Cleghorn, A. & J., hardware merchants
Cleland, William, dry goods
CLEMENT, A. D., Postmaster
Clement, C. H., Assistant Postmaster
Clinch, Ralph, grocery and provisions
Cochrane, Rev. W. (Zion Presbyterian)
Cockshutt, J., dry goods, groceries, hardware, &c,
Coday, Miss, teacher
COLBORNE PLANING MILLS, JAMES TUTT, proprietor
Collis, G. S., blacksmith
Comerford, John, grocer
COMMERCIAL HOTEL, J. C. Palmer, proprietor
CORRIGAN, FRANCIS, Robinson Hall Hotel
Corson, W. C., M.D.
Cowherd, Thomas & Son, copper and tinsmith
Cox, Alfred, watchmaker and jeweller
Cox, F. T., grocer and provision dealer
Creyh, James, watchmaker and jeweller
Crooks, H. P. S., boots and shoes
Crown and Anchor Hotel, Edward Campbell, prop.
Curtis, Daniel, collector of customs
Cusack, Mrs., grocery
Dalrymple, William, cabinet maker
Davis, E., tailor
DELL, WILLIAM, Grand Trunk Hotel
Digby, Dr.
Drake, W. A., baker
Dunn, P., blacksmith
Dutton, William, Ontario Hotel
Edgar, John, china and glassware
Edy, A. & J., photographers
ELLIOTT, JOHN, contractor
Evans, R., agent B. & L. H. R. R.
EXCELL, JAMES P., umbrella maker (see adv.)
Fair, A., groceries and liquors
FARR, JOSEPH, wholesale and retail hardware merchant (see adv.)
Finnessy, M., grocer
Flestner, John, grocer
Fitch, B. F., barrister, &c.
Fleming, George, livery stable keeper
FLEMING, G., Brant Hotel (see adv.)
FORDE, J. & BROTHER, grocers and provision dealers
FORDE, R. J. & CO., grocers and provision dealers
FOSTER, GEORGE, groceries and produce
Gemley, Rev. John (Wesleyan)
Gilbert, Benjamin, barber
Gill & Gardner, saddlers
Gillan, Miss E., school teacher
Glassco, George, hatter and furrier
Glassco, Thomas, tax collector
Gorman, Robert, boots and shoes
GRAND TRUNK HOTEL, William Dell, prop.

Gray, Robert, grocer and butcher
Greirson, G., baker, &c.
Griffiths, Henry, boot maker
Griffith, James, watch maker
Hall, J., agent American Express
Hardy, A. S., barrister
Hardy, G., fruit and fish dealer
Hardy, Thomas J., hatter and furrier
Hart, Dacres W., Collector Inland Revenue
Hartman, C., fruit and confectionery
HATCH, A. G., prop. American Hotel (see adv.)
Hawkins, John J., groceries, provisions, wines and liquors.
Hayd, Benjamin, general store
HAYDEN, J. C., dealers in groceries, wines and liquors, provisions, &c.
Hazall, J., Ontario Hotel
Hazelton, A. W., soap and potash factory
Hebden, J. J., teller Bank British North America
Hext, T. & J., carriage makers and blacksmiths
Hill, A. A., M. D.
Hocking & Bates, Brant Marble Works
Howell, W., groceries, wines and liquors
Hudson, Andrew, books and stationery
Hunter, John, grocer
Hurst, W. B., groceries and liquors
Hutchinson, Alex., Montreal Telegraph Co.
Imlach & Good, vinegar and starch manufacturers
Imlach, W. J., Deputy Reeve
Jackson, L., Assistant Postmaster
Jackson, Robert G., carriage maker
Jackson, Samuel, dry goods and clothing
James, Thomas, Assessor
Jarvis, C., jr., soap, candle and potash manufacturer
Jenkins, John, merchant tailor
Jex, Johnston, blacksmith
Jones, J., locomotive foreman B. & L. H. R. R.
JULL, J. H., Railway Hotel
Kenny, T., Dominion Hotel
Kerr, W. H. C., insurance agent.
Kerr, W. H., Brant Bakery
Kerr's Music Hall
KESTER, E., auctioneer, &c. (see adv.)
KING, GEORGE, King's Hotel
KING'S HOTEL, Railway station Brantford, George King, proprietor
Kirby's Mills, Thomas Robson, proprietor
Kirchnee, J. J., cigar maker
Lacey, Rev. S., (Primitive Methodist)
Lane, C., groceries and provisions
Larmour, R. assistant superintendent B. & L. H. R. R.
LAUTERBACH, G., coffee, dining and oyster saloon
Leeming, H. B., of Leeming & Paterson
Leeming & Paterson, confectioners
LEMON, HENRY, editor Brantford *Courier*
Leonard, Francis H., Reeve
Lewis, J., tailor
LINES, W., grocer, provision dealer
Loney, J., grocery and provisions, wines & liquors
Long, William, shoemaker
Lyons, Woods, carriage maker
McCann, A., tailor
McCollum, William, McCollum's Hotel
McKay, Donald B., saddlery and hardware
McKay, Duncan, Town Treasurer
McLEAN, THOMAS, wholesale and retail dry goods millinery and clothing
McLean, Samuel, fancy goods
McMahon, H., barrister, &c
McMahon, T. B., barrister
McMeans, A., groceries and liquors
McMeans, James, Police Magistrate
McMeans, Thomas, Chief Constable
McGuire, S., fruit and refreshment rooms

Marter Walter, collector Inland Revenue
Martindale & Brother, dealers in plaster
Mason, M. D.
Mason & Hamilton, chemists and druggists
Masterson, William, gunsmith
Matthews, W., J. P., Mayor, Auctioneer and Issuer of Marriage Licenses
MATHISON, ROBERT, editor Brantford *Expositor*
MEACHAM, J. B., dentist. (See adv)
Menzies, George, clerk B. B. N. A.
METROPOLITAN SALOON & OYSTER ROOMS, James Weyms, proprietor
Minore, John, confectionery and fancy store
Moore, M., teacher
Montreal House, Benjamin Hunn, proprietor
MORTON, A. & J. Y., wholesale and retail hardware merchants. (See adv)
Noble, John, painter, &c
Norwood, C., barber
OCCIDENTAL SALOON and Billiard Parlor, Welsh and Walsh, proprietors
Orchard, John, tailor and clothier
Ormerod, John, provision dealer
Ott, John, tanner and dealer in wool
Oxley & Co., grocers and dealers in wines & liquors
PALMER, J. C., proprietor Commercial Hotel
PALMER, STEPHEN, fish dealer and ice merchant (See adv)
Park, S., photographer
Paterson, W., (Leeming & Paterson)
Peel, R., mason
Pendlebury, H., boot and shoe maker
Pierce, W., undertaker
Plewes, D., grain merchant
Plummer, Walter, hotel keeper
Poole, G., tailor
Potts, Thomas, tinsmith
Prince of Wales' Hotel, John Brown, proprietor
Queen's Arms Hotel, Charles Farrell proprietor
Quinlan, Joseph, groceries, wines & liquors
RACEY, H. & Co., auctioneers, &c. (See adv)
RAILWAY HOTEL, near Railway Station, John H. Jull, proprietor
RANSFORD, E. V., Piano-forte agent
READ, JOSEPH, marble works
Reed, Samuel, agent Bank of Montreal
Ritchie & Russell, plumbers and gas fitters
Robertson, Alexander, Manager Bank B. N. A.
Robinson, J., commission merchant and grocer
Robson, M., hotel
Rolph, W. V., paymaster B. & L. H. R.R.
Royal Exchange, John Beer, proprietor
Royal Saloon and Oyster Rooms, J. Humburch, prop
Sanderson, W., seedsman
Savage, A., track inspector, B. & L. H. R.R.
Sayles, John, butcher
Scott, W. P., grocer and butcher
Sears, C. W., Sear's Hotel
Shackell, R., lager beer saloon
Shannon, R., grocer
Shuttleworth, James, butcher
Simms, E., conveyancer, commissioner in B.R., &c.
Simmons, Simon, grocer
Sims Edwin, confectioner
Smith, A. W., exchange broker
SMITH, JAMES, saddle, harness & trunk manufactory. (See adv.)
Smith, John, Sheriff
Smyth, Margaret, groceries
Sowden, John, butcher
SPENCE, A., carriage and wagon maker. (See adv.)
SPENCER, HUGH, groceries, wines and liquors
Spencer, T., West Brantford Brewery
Stapleton, John, boots and shoes

STEWART, C. E., *Brantford Expositor.* (See adv.)
STOCKWELL & BROTHER, dyers & cleaners
STRATFORD, JOHN H. & Co., dealers in oil
STRATFORD, W. H. wholesale grocer and druggist
Strong, T., boots and shoes
Struthers, J., baker, &c.
Stubbs, Thomas, blacksmith
Stubbs, W., blacksmith
Stuttard, James, grocery, &c.
Sunter & Edgar, china and glassware
Sullivan, Dion C., L. L.B., prin. Grammar School
Sutherland, J., books and stationery
Sutton, Dr., dentist
Tairish, John, painter
Tapscott, S. & Co., druggists
TATE, T. H., groceries, provisions, wines and liquors, flour and feed (see adv.)
Taylor, John, dry goods, &c.
Taylor, John, baker
Ternandt, G., provisions,
Terrapin Lunch Room, W. Deaty, proprietor
"THE SHADES," J. P. Excell, proprietor
Tisdale, B. G., founder
Tooze, John, butcher
TOWLER, SAMUEL, boot and shoe maker (see adv.)
Triggerson, J. T., saddler
TUTT, JAMES, door, blind and sash factory
Union Inn, C. Doeringer, proprietor
Usher, Rev. James C. (Church of England)
VanNorman, C. R., barrister, &c.
Vaughan, James, tailor
VICTORIA FOUNDRY, Wm. Buck, proprietor
WALSH, F., Fountain saloon
WALSH, F. & CO., tobacconists, &c.
Wallace, James, leather dealer
Wash, W. E.
WATEROUS, C. H. (C. H. Waterous & Co.)
WATEROUS, C. H. & CO., Brantford Steam Engine Works (see adv.)
Watson, Hargrave, butcher
WATT, GEORGE, wholesale grocer, wine and spirit merchant (see adv.)
Watt, W., planing mill, builder, &c.
WATTS, ALFRED, Reeve
WATTS, A., soap and candle factory (see adv.)
Wear, James, shoemaker
Wehling, Edward, butcher
Weinang, John V., butcher
Welding & Belding, stoneware pottery
Welding, W. E.
Wellington Hotel, H. Woods, proprietor
Welsh, Robert
Weyms, Thomas, Metropolitan Saloon
WHITHAM, H. F., soda water manufactory
Whitham, Matthew, variety store
Whittaker, W., tinsmith
WILKES, GEORGE H., (Waterous & Co.)
Wilkes, G. S.
WILKES, JAMES, J. P., general insurance agent
Wilkie, Mrs., straw milliner
Wilson, A. L., clerk customs
WILSON, C., boot and shoe maker. (See adv)
Wilson, E. C., confectioner.
Wilkinson, John W., watchmaker
WOOD, HON. E. B., M. P., Treasurer Province of Ontario
Wood, Rev. John, (Congregational)
WOODYATT, JAMES, Town Clerk
Worden, Peter, general merchant
Worthington, John, grocery
Wright, J., shoemaker
WYE, JOHN, H. M. D.

Brentwood.—A Village on the Northern Railway, in the Township of Sunnidale, County Simcoe. Distant from Barrie the County Town 18 miles, from Toronto 76 miles. Average price of land $25. Population 150.

Auger, Awie, farmer
Auger, Lewis, jobber
Brown, Thomas
COOK, CHRISTOPHER & Co., lumber dealers
Cullen, Patrick, farmer
Davidson, David, general merchant
Davidson, Joseph, lumber dealer
Desjardins, Paul, farmer
Desourdis, Francis, farmer
DUBOIS, LOUIS EMILE, Postmaster
Forest, Felix, cooper
Harris, E., farmer
Hefferen, John, farmer
Jennings, Abel, butcher
Keenion, Thomas, proprietor Farmers' Inn
Lane, Daniel, farmer
Leggatt, William, farmer
McBride, John, farmer
McGinniss, Miss Catherine, teacher
Middlebrook, Joseph
O'Connell, John, farmer
Orser, John, farmer
O'Shea, Patrick, farmer
Robillard, Joseph, farmer
Ross, George, proprietor Ross Hotel
Scott, William, farmer
Smith, Daniel, butcher
Switzer, Philip, farmer
Warner, John, general merchant
Wiggins, Edward, farmer

Breslau.—A Village situated in the Township of Waterloo, County Waterloo, distant 4 miles from Berlin, the County Town, and 58 miles from Toronto on the Grand Trunk Railway. Population 150.

Bemer, John, cooper
Cottrell, George, Station Master G. T. R.
ERB, EPHRAIM, Postmaster and J. P.
Erb & Bricker, general merchants
Friedland, Christopher, shoemaker
Grey, Miss A., school teacher
Gerster, Charles, hotel keeper and cabinet maker
Hagey, Rev. Joseph, (Mennonite)
Kreuson, Charles, lime burner
Miller, Abram, patent right agent
Shoemaker, John, F., carpenter and builder

Brewster.—A post town in the Township of Stephen, County Huron, South Riding.
McDOUGALL, W., Postmaster.

Brewer's Mills.—A Village on the Rideau Canal, in the Township of Pittsburgh, County Frontenac. Distant from County Town 17 miles, from Toronto 180 miles. Stages to and from Kingston. Population 100.

ANGLIN, ROBERT, sen., Postmaster
Anglin, Robert, jun., general merchant
Beaupree, Joseph
Brown, William, prop. carding mill
Connor, Rev. Father, (Roman Catholic)
Dean, Patrick, lock master
Dillon, Francis, farmer
Dillon, John, farmer
Foster, Thomas, prop. grist mill
Frill, Amos, farmer
Hartnett, Joseph, farmer
Hill, David, farmer
Jordon, Charles, hotel keeper
Keagin, Patrick
Kennedy, Rev. James, (Methodist)
Keys, James, assistant lock master
McLoughlin, William, hotel keeper
McMinn, Samuel, cordwood dealer
McReever & Son, blacksmiths
Maxwell, Richard
Milne, James, contractor
Stetwell, H. B., proprietor saw mill
Willman, Thomas, lumberman

Bright.—A Village situated in the Township of Blandford, County Oxford, and on the Grand Trunk Railroad, 15 miles from Woodstock the County Town. Money order office.

Baird, George, general merchant and stave factor
Berk, Jacob, tailor
Cowan, John, hotel keeper
Cuthbertson, hotel keeper
Gerrie, Rev. John, (Baptist)
Guhl, C., blacksmith
McKee, Robert blacksmith
Rostrock, G., merchant tailor
Rowe, George, boot and shoe maker
Sharp, H. R. & Co., general merchants
SHARP, W. A., (H. R. Sharp & Co.) Postmaster
Simeon, James, harness maker

Bridgeport.—A Village on the Grand River, in the Township and County of Waterloo, two miles from Berlin and 62 from Toronto. The river and Laurel Creek afford first-class water power, which is extensively used. This would be a good opening for a foundry, cotton and woolen mills. Improved land in the vicinity averages $50 per acre. Population, 350.

Abel, Herman, dyer
Abel & Euler, wine dealers
Albert, John, carpenter
Alderson, James, J.P
Beck, Philip, tailor
Bierensteil, Adam, potter
Diefenbacher, Philip, brick maker
EBY, ELIAS, Postmaster
Eby, Elias & Co., lumber merchants, millers, storekeepers, &c.
Fleischhauer, John Otto, general merchant
Froehlich, G., hotel keeper
Heiser, Stephen, carpenter
Hollinger, George, cooper
Hollinger, Philip, cooper
Huff, Adam, tailor
Huff, John, shoemaker
Kreitzweiser, Michael, carpenter
Murray, Adam, woolen factor
Polaender, John, shoemaker
Randolph, Henry, stone and lime dealer
Rosbach, Adam V., saddler
Scheuerman, Frederick, leather dealer
Schiedel, Noah, hotel keeper
Schultz, Karl, shoemaker
Smith, John, hotel keeper
Speissman & Shautz, planing mill props
Thornan, E., carpenter
Velter, Adolph, painter
Wellein, John, carriage maker
Wendling, Jacob, woolen factor

Bridgewater.—A Village on the Grand Trunk Railroad and Scootamotto River, in the Township of Elzivir, County Hastings. Distant from Belleville the County Town 30 miles, from Toronto 140 miles. Stages to Belleville. Average price of land $1.25. Money order office. Population 450.

Barrie, Robert, farmer
Bragg, John and George, tanners
Burns, Francis, farmer
Burns, John, farmer
Chanque, Michael, cooper
Cullen, Rev. Thomas, (Wesleyan)
Empy, Francis, shoemaker
Finch, Henry, carpenter
FLINT, HON. B., mill owner
Frost, Joseph, wagon maker
Garrett, William, iron founder
Gorsline, Norman, carpenter
HARRISON, JAMES. Postmaster
Higinbotham, Andrew, M. D.
Humphries, W., wagon maker
Langley, Michael, farmer
Kerr, George, carpenter
Kerr, William, sen., carpenter
Kerr, William, jr., carpenter
Klinstuber, Ernest, shoemaker
Klinstuber, Julius, shoemaker
McFee, John, tailor
Minie, M., cooper
Rath, William, lime manufacturer
Record, Rice, miller
Rosevair, Joseph, wagon maker
Sager, Alexander, miller
Spencer, William, saddler
Tucker, Francis, lime manufacturer
Turner, Joshua W., tinsmith
Turner, William J., grocer
Tuttle, Leslie, teacher
Wemp, William B., proprietor Bridgewater Hotel
Wolfe, George, woolen factor

Bridgenorth.—A Village on Chemong Lake, in the Township of Smith, County Peterboro'. Distant from County Town 6 miles, from Toronto 100 miles. Stages to and from Peterboro'. Steamers to and from Lindsay. Average price of land $40 to $60. Population 150.

Brumwell, Jacob, carpenter
DEAN, M. S., Postmaster and general merchant
Dunbar, Asa, hotel keeper
Grey, George, cooper
Kelly, S. S., general merchant
McCall, Charles, butcher
McCall. James, carpenter
McCall, William, shoemaker
McDonald, Neil, blacksmith
McFadden, Hugh, boatbuilder
McFadden, John, boatbuilder
Moffatt, William, painter
Moreland, James, cooper
Pearson, Richard, carpenter
Pope, John, proprietor Bridgenorth Hotel
Watson, John N., painter

Brighton.—A Village and station of the Grand Trunk Railroad, and Port of Entry on Presque Isle Bay Lake Ontario, in the Township of Brighton, County Northumberland. Distant from Cobourg the County Town 24 miles, from Toronto 94 miles. Steamboat line to Rochester, U. S. Stages to Picton and Campbellford. Average price of land in the vicinity $80 to $100. Money order office and Savings Bank. Population 1600.

Ames, Robert, cabinet maker
Anderson, Edward, carpenter
Barker & Auston (Robert Barker, John Auston) chemists and druggists
Blizard, John, blacksmith
Bowles, W. C., general merchant
Bowger, Rev. Robert, (Church of England)
Buckley, S., farmer
Bullock, C. E., grocer
Butler, William, carding and saw mills
Carey, W. H., sash and door factor
Chapman, David, tailor
Chapman, J., grocer
Cole, John, vessel owner
Cook, Herman, M. D.
Cook, Josiah, tanner
Cotter, Hiram, carpenter
Coyle, William, blacksmith
Dalton, Thomas, barrister
Davidson, Peter, constable
DEAN, N. B., M.D.
Demill, J. B., hardware
Drewry, George, J.P.
Edwards, E., insurance agent, plaster mills
Ewing, Benjamin, insurance agent
Eyre, John M.P.P., attorney-at-law
FERRES, M., general merchant
Fife. A. E., M.D.
Firman, Charles, carpenter.
Flagler, John, blacksmith
Forbes, Alexander, attorney-at-law
Franklin, Bildad, J.P.
George, Edward, vessel-owner
Good, A., carpenter
Gross, A., photographer
Gross, P., M.D.
Gross, Picton, senr., nurseryman
Gross, S. P., general merchant.
Hardcastle, George, carter
HARPER, CHARLES, Stage House, daily to Campbella and Picton. (See adv.)
Hodges, O. A., bailiff
Hunk, Frances, grocer
Jones. Rev. — (Methodist Episcopal)
KETCHUM, HIRAM E., prop. Ketchum House—livery
Ketchum, John B., billiard rooms
Ketchum, M. P., general merchant, exchange broker
Langman, William, bricklayer
Leslie, D. Y., Collector Customs
Lewis, Henry, carriage maker
Lockwood, M. K., notary public, conveyancer
Lockwood, J. C., stationery and fancy goods
McAlese, John, blacksmith
McCallum, Alexander, commission merchant
McCullough, S., blacksmith.
McKenzie, Daniel, wharfinger
Martin, Alexander, Deputy Sheriff
Morrison, Gilbert H., hotel keeper
Nesbitt, James, dry goods and groceries
Nix, Henry, blacksmith
Norman, Rev. — (Episcopal Methodist)
OCCIDENTAL HOTEL & livery stables, J. H. Sanford
Olsen, S. E., watchmaker
Persons, John F., boat builder
Platt, Willett, lumber merchant
Proctor, Isaac C., dentist
Proctor, I. R., farmer
Proctor, I. S., grocer
PROCTOR, JOHN E., J. P., general merchant, wharfinger, &c.
Purdy, David, general merchant
Purkis, James, station and express agent
Purdy, L. A., general merchant
Quick, John, vessel owner
Quick, William, vessel owner
SANFORD, J. H., prop. Occidental Hotel, livery and sale stables
Sanford, T. D., farmer
Shears, James, hotel keeper
Sherman, J. F., hop grower
Singleton, A. C., farmer
Smith, Rev. A. (Wesleyan)
Smith, Jacob, baker
Smith, James, commission merchant
Solomon, James, painter
Sparrow, Rev. — (Episcopal Methodist)
Spencer, Augustus, carpenter
Squires, H.
Stanley, James, saddler
Thayer & Brother (I. B. & I. B.), hardware, groceries. &c.
Thayer, N., nurseryman
Thompson, A., blacksmith
Van Horn, C.
Van Horn, James, boots and shoes
Wade. William. stage proprietor
WEBB, A. C., P. L. S., & C. E.
Webb, Henry, general merchant
Webb, Thomas, general merchant
Webb, W. W., grocer
Weeks, William, butcher
Wellington, I. M., baker
WYNN, R., manufacturer and dealer in boots and shoes, grocer
Young, J. B., general merchant

Brinkworth.—A Village in the Township of Rawdon, County Hastings. Distant from Belleville, the County Town, 20 miles, from Toronto, 110 miles. Stages to and from Campbellford. Average price of wild land, $10, improved, $20. Population, 50.

Adams, Rev. Q., (Methodist)
Bradley, George, teacher
Edmonds, Rev. E., (Methodist)
Huffman, J., farmer
Merrick, J., farmer
Ranney, C., farmer
Wescott, S., farmer
Wescott, W., farmer
White, P., farmer
WILLIAMS, A., Postmaster, and proprietor Temperance Hotel
Williams, C., farmer
Williams, M. B., farmer
Woodbeck, E., farmer

Brinsley.—A Post-village situated in the Township of McGillivray, County Middlesex, and on the Sauble River, 24 miles from London. Mails semi weekly. Population, 100.

Brewer, A., blacksmith
BROWN, GEORGE, Postmaster and merchant
Dixon, William, farmer
Lewis, C., farmer
Morgan, E., hotel keeper
Pierce, Moses, farmer
Ryan, P., shoemaker
Shouldice, A., carpenter
Slack, George, miller
Small, William, carpenter

Brisbane.—A Village in the Township of Erin, County Wellington. Distance from Guelph, the County Town, 16 miles, from Toronto, 40 miles. Stages to Georgetown and Guelph. Average price of land, $20. Population, 70.

Ashley, Joshua A., veterinary surgeon
Bently, Godfrey, farmer
BOOMER, WILLIAM, Postmaster
Boomer, William & Henry, carpenters
Briggs, Thomas, farmer
Brown, James C., farmer
Burt, John, lumber dealer
Higgins, William, proprietor Sportsman's Hotel
Kenned., Robert, farmer
Kennedy, William, manufacturer wood ware
Lang, George, farmer
Leeson, Manasseh, proprietor British House
Mackelcan, G. J., general merchant
Nurse, Thomas, farmer
Reid, Rev. Hugh, (Baptist)
Ryckman, Elijah, gunsmith
Ryckman & Norton, wagon makers
Smith, Henry, farmer
Taylor, John, insurance agent
Wardell, Jacob, veterinary surgeon
Wheeler, Aaron, farmer

Britannia.—A Post-village in the Township of Toronto, County Peel. Distant from Brampton, the County Town, 6 miles, from Toronto, 26 miles.

Fish, Rev. Charles, (Wesleyan)
McMillan, James, teacher
MUIR, JOSEPH, Postmaster
Robinson, John, farmer

Brock.—A Post-village of the Township of Brock, County Ontario.

JONES, JOHN, Postmaster.

Brockton.—A Post-village situated on Dundas Road, 3 miles from Toronto market, in the Township of York, County York. Population 50.

Abbs, William, farmer
Armstrong, Col. Arthur, J.P.
Boland, Thomas, farmer
Butler, William, mail conductor Grand Trunk R.R.
Cameron, William J., boot and shoemaker
CHURCH, MRS. ANN, Postmistress and proprietor Church's Hotel.
Clary, Walter, toll-gate keeper.
Crealock, John, cattle dealer
Dean, Thomas, drover
Duggan, Daniel, groceries and provisions
Dunn, William, butcher
Hill, Alexander, market gardener and nurseryman
Hilton, Rev. John, (Church of England)
KENNEDY, FRANK, propr Brockton Club House
McGreggor, Archibald, rope walk
Nolan, Michael, grocer and saloon
Oxenham, William, butcher
Russell, William, baker.

Brockville.—A Town and station of the Grand Trunk Railway, situated on the river St. Lawrence, in the Township of Elizabeth, County Leeds. It is the County Town of the United Counties of Leeds and Grenville, and a port of Entry. The steamers plying between Montreal, Kingston, Toronto and Hamilton, stop here daily. It is connected with Smith's Falls, Perth, Almonte, Carleton Place and Sandy Point, by the Brockville and Ottawa Railway. A steam ferry plies every half hour in summer between Brockville and Morrisburg, N. Y. Distant from Almonte, 52 miles; from Carleton Place, 41; Perth, 40; Smith's Falls, 28; Kingston, 48; Montreal, 125; and from Toronto, 208 miles. Money Order office and Savings Bank. Population, 5,000.

Anderson, William, shoemaker
Andrews, J., inn keeper
BANK OF MONTREAL, J. N. Travers, Manager
Barr, Henry, stoves and tin ware
Beecher, W. F. & Co., founders
Bennett, Thomas, produce dealer
Bigg, W. R., teacher
Birney, William, flour and feed
Blyth, B. & R., dry goods
Botsford, W., hardware
Branniff, Thomas, saloon keeper
BRITISH CANADIAN, (weekly), R. W. Kelly editor and proprietor
Broadick, Thomas, baker
BROCKVILLE MONITOR, (weekly), McMullen & Co., proprietors
BROCKVILLE RECORDER, (weekly), D. Wylie, editor and proprietor
Brophy, James, shoemaker
BUELL, J. D., barrister, attorney, etc.
BURNS, A., dentist. (See adv.)
CAMPBELL'S HOTEL, J. L. Campbell, proprietor. (See adv).
CAMPBELL, J. L., proprietor Campbell's Hotel
CHILDS, EDWARD A., (Hall & Childs)
Clayes, E. D., produce and wool dealer
Clinton, James, boots and shoes
Coates, William, watchmaker
Colborne, B., inn keeper
Cole, A., grocer
Cole, A. G., photographer
Cole, J. A., hotel keeper
Cole, W. H., tinsmith
COMSTOCK, W. H., dealer in patent medicines. (See adv.)
Connor, Robert, hotel keeper
Cook, William, baker
Crawford, Hon. George, Senator
Crawford, James, M. P.
CRAWFORD, JOHN, Postmaster
Culbert, John, grocer
Cunningham, Thomas, grocer
Daley, T. D., carriage maker
Dana, A. B.
Dana, George A., leather dealer
Deacon, Joseph, barrister
DeRinzy, E., boots and shoes
Dickinson, Frederick G., Sheriff
Donaldson, A., general merchant
Dowsley, G., shoemaker
Easton, George, Collector Customs
Easton, George, Clerk. Customs
Easton, S. D., baker
Edmondson, Robert, M.D.
Evans, Richard, grocer
Fairbairn, J. K., baker
Fell, Samuel, proprietor Dominion Restaurant
Finley, T., grocer
Fitzsimmons, R. & Son, grocers
Fitzsimmons, William, M.P.P.
FLETCHER, CHRISTOPHER, hardware, groceries and lumber
Fraser, C. F., barrister
French, C. H., painter
Fulford, Hiram, billiard rooms
Fulford, W. M., druggist
Gilmour, F. & Co., grocers
Glazier, S., painter
Gordon, Hugh A., M.D.
Gordon, John, builder
Graham, James, saloon
Grant, R. W., stoves and tin ware
Green, Joseph, M.A., Principal Grammar School
Griffin, G. R., hatter
Groves, William, butcher
HALL, JAMES, (Hall & Childs)
Hall, J. D., M.D.
HALL & CHILDS, (Jas Hall and Edw. A. Childs), Ontario glove works. (See adv)
Harding, T. J. B., druggist
HAWKES, JAMES, druggist. (See adv)
Hayes, D. F., dentist
Henderson, James, butcher
Hope, W. W., boots and shoes
Hover, E. & Co., comb makers
HOUSTON, GEORGE & CO., wines and liquors. (See adv)
Hume, —, station agent B. & O. R.
Hurd, William H., match factory
Hutcheson, George, dry goods.
Jamieson, P. B., tailor
Jessup, James, Clerk of the Peace
Johnson, J., barber
Johnston & Green, produce dealers
Jones, David
Jones, Herbert C., barrister
Jones, Rev. John, (Canada Presbyterian.)
Jones, J. B., Clerk Division Court
JONES, ORMOND, barrister, Registrar
Jones, S. F., commission merchant
Jordan, J. H., news depot
KELLY, R. W., editor and prop. *British Canadian*
Kelly, Thomas, hotel keeper
Kennedy, Edward, boots and shoes
Kincaide, J. E., frame maker
King, Thomas, & Son, grocers
Kinney, R., M.D.
Knowles, H. E., accountant Bank of Montreal
LALONDE, A. D., L. D. S., surgeon dentist (see adv.)
Landon, A. W., general merchant
LANDON, GEORGE L., saloon keeper. (See adv.)
LeRoy, O. R., grocer
Lipsett, Robert, shoemaker
Lothrop, F. L., auctioneer
McCready, A. G., tanner
McCullough, William, manufacturer scythes, &c
McDougall, W. C., tinsmith
McElhinney, John, tinsmith
McGillivray, Rev. Daniel, (Presbyterian)
McGregor, Rev. Alexander, (Congregational)
McGregor, Joseph, tailor
McIntyre, A. C., photographer
McKee, M. saloon
McKenney, James, grocer
McLennan, William, general merchant
McMullen & Co., books and stationery

Malloch, George, County Judge
Manley, William, tailor
Marshall, Norton, general merchant
Marshall, Uriah, hotel keeper
Miller, H., blacksmith
Mitchell, W. H., barber
Moore, Frederick L., County Auditor
Morden, John H., M. D.
Murphy, Michael, butcher
Murray, G. B., fancy goods
Murray, John, agent Montreal Telegraph Company and Canadian Express
O'Brien, Rev. John, (Roman Catholic)
O'Brien, William, job printer
O'Reilly, Mrs. Ann, grocer
Odell, Amos, saddletrees, &c
Odell, D., M. D.
Overell, E., news depot, stationery, &c
Parr, Arthur, saddler
Percival, William, hotel keeper
Pierce, Joseph, tavern keeper
Quigg, James, cabinet maker
Reid, George, hardware
Reilly, Thomas, tailor
Reynolds, Samuel, jr., clerk County Court, deputy Clerk Crown
Rhodes, J. grocer
Richey, Isaac, hotel keeper
Ross, John, general merchant
Schofield, James L., County Treasurer
Schofield, W. A. coroner
Seaman, S. J., cabinet maker
SENKLER, E. J. jr., barrister, County Attorney
Sheffield, J. R., general merchant
Shepherd & Kyle, general merchants
Shepherd, Robert, grist mill proprietor
Sherwood, A.
Sherwood, T., grocer
Sherwood, William, barrister
Shields, E., shoemaker
SMART, JAMES, Novelty Works. (See adv.)
Smart, Thomas, tailor
Smart, Thomas, & bro., machinists
Soper, R. R., hotel keeper
Sparham, E. B., M. D
Sparham, T., M. D
Steacy, T. B., watchmaker
Stagg, John, butcher
Starr, A. H., & G. A., confectioners
Steele & Redmond, attornies
Tane, Rev. F. R., (Church of England)
TRAVERS, J. N., manager Bank of Montreal
Taylor, John, boots and shoes
TURNER, ALLEN & Co., druggists, wholesale and retail. (See adv)
Vanarnum, Thomas, general merchant
Wadsworth, William, grocer
White, Alexander, grocer
White, John, gaoler
Whitney, H., watchmaker
Whittemore, N., saddler
Wilkinson, Thomas, manager gas works
Woods, R. & B., tobacconists
WYLIE, D., editor and proprietor *Recorder*

Brodhagen.—A Village on Brodhagen river, in the Township of Logan, County Perth. Distant from Stratford, the County Town; 30 miles, from Toronto 120 miles. Population 100.

Beneris, L., hotel keeper
Boedecker, Rev. J., (Bible Christian)
BRODHAGEN, CHARLES, Postmaster and prop. flax mill
Brodhagen, Ernest, hotel keeper
Brodhagen, William, general merchant
Byerman, Louis, shingle manufacturer
Grouscopp, A., shoemaker
Grouscopp, H., farmer
Hannel, Christian, cooper.
Hoball, John, saddler
Huffman, Joseph, J. P.
Jacob, Francis, shingle manufacturer
McInnes, Miss, dressmaker
Manly, A., farmer
Murray, Thomas, farmer
Newman, Theodore, wagon maker
Oreimus, F., M. D.
Rapen, John, farmer
Rigby, Christian, carpenter
Reck, George, miller
Schnider, Adam, tailor
Smith, John, farmer
Suer, Christian, carpenter
Warneker, Henry, shoemaker
Wiesenbury, William, farmer
Wright, George, farmer

Bronte.—A Post Village and station on the Great Western Railway, on the shore of Lake Ontario, Township of Trafalgar, County Halton, 14 miles from Hamilton, 25 from Toronto, and 12 from Milton, the County Town. Population about 200.

ADAMS, SAMUEL, blacksmith
Ainsley, Parry, teamster
Anderson, Robert, boot and shoemaker
Bronte House Hotel, Joseph N. Friller, prop.
Butler, Rev. James, (Methodist Episcopal)
Clements, Thomas C., painter
Dorland, John Y., dentist
Griffin, Joseph, merchant
Jones, Charles, machinist
Kemp, Peter, cooper
McCauley, Andrew, shoemaker
McCay, A. G.
McCraney, M. S., general store
McDONALD, MRS. ELIZA, groceries, &c.
McDonell, Alex B., mail carrier
McKay, Thomas
Oakley, Rev. John, (Baptist)
Oakley, Reuben, botanic doctor
Robinson, George, tailor
Shaw, Thomas, station master
Sovereign, Charles, J. P.
THOMPSON, E. C., Postmaster & general merchant
Thompson, Marshall, captain
TRILLER, JOSEPH, captain
Vanleet, Isaac, joiner
Vanleet, John, turner
Warden, Jesse, joiner
Weatherson, John, G. W. R.
Weller, Dr., botanic
Williams, Henry, farmer
WRAY, JOHN, proprietor Bronte Station Hotel
Wright, William, grocery
Wylie, John, captain

Brooklin.—A Village on Campbell's Creek, Township of Whitby, County Ontario, 5½ miles from Whitby, the County Town, and 36 miles from Toronto. Stages daily to and from Whitby, fare 25c. Money Order office and Savings' Bank. Population 750.

Allems, Charles A., miller
ALLIN, THOMAS, (Allin & Thompson)
ALLIN & THOMPSON, (Thomas Allin and William Thompson) props. Ontario tannery. (See adv)
Bailey, Edmund, ginger beer manufacturer
Beaness, George, tailor
BICKELL, JAMES B., Township Reeve and Warden County Ontario
BICKELL, JAMES B., prop. "Mill Hill" Mills (flouring)
Bickle, Henry, prop. Centre (flouring) mills
Bowerman, W. D., woolen factor
Brooklin Literary Hall
Brockenshier, William, photographer
Barnett, Alexander, teacher
Barnett, Leonard, teacher
Campbell, Robert, J.P., mill owner
Campbell, Aaron, J.P., farmer
Campbell, John, retired
Campbell, Calvin, J.P., farmer
Campbell, John P., prop. Brooklin flour mills.
Campbell C. A., dentist and telegraph operator
Card, Chester W., pump maker
Chambers, Rev. A. C., (Wesleyan)
Chamberlin, Daniel F., blacksmith.
COLE, JOHN, prop. Brooklin tannery. (See adv)
Croxall Brothers, (James and John) farmers
Cuttle, James, printer and grocer
Dale, John, harness maker
DARLINGTON, ROBERT, Postmaster & Treasurer County Whitby
Dawes, John, druggist, &c
Dockham, Rev. Henry, (Methodist Episcopal)
Dryden, John, farmer, Deputy Reeve Tp. Whitby
Fisher, Timothy, Township Councillor
Foote, Jonathan, M.D.
Fountain, James, constable
Francis Bros., (Peter and Henry) props. Kent Oatmeal Mills
Fraser, Isaac A., wagon maker
Goldsbro, William T., boot and shoe maker
Grainger, John, horse farrier
Groat, Alfred, butcher
Groat, Miss Phœbe, teacher
Harrison, Richard T., Township Clerk and J.P
Hault, William, foreman Brooklin planing mill
Hayward & Tyler, (Edgar R. B. Hayward and Joseph Tyler) general merchants
Hayward, Edgar, R. B., (Hayward & Tyler)
HEPINSTALL, W., watchmaker
Hepburn & Roberts, (George Hepburn and George Roberts) blacksmiths and wagon makers
Hepburn, George, (Hepburn & Roberts)
Hodgson, Thomas, captain
Holliday, Daniel, sr., insurance agent and farmer
Holliday, Daniel, jr., farmer
Kester & Son, (Isaiah & William) carpenters
KETCHEN, ALEXANDER, blacksmith and wagon maker.
Manning, William, shoemaker
Maybee, James A., harness maker
McBrien, George, painter
McBrien, William, shoemaker
MacDonald, George D., com. merch't and valuator
Murray, Mrs., dressmaker
Nicholls, William, farmer
Phippen, Nicholas, furniture dealer
POWELL, JAMES, prop. Globe Hotel. (See adv)
Roberts, George, (Hepburn & Roberts)
Robson, Thomas, dealer in stoves and tinware
Shaw, John A., school teacher
Smith, Rev. Philander, (Methodist Episcopal)
Smillie, John, tailor
Spears, J. V., Township Councillor
THOMAS, C. C., J. P., ins., land and gen. agent
Thomas, Nelson H., prop. Brooklin planing factory
Thomas, John, photographer
Thomas, Stephen M., general merchant
Thomas, John L. H.,
THOMPSON, WILLIAM H., (Allin & Thompson)
Turner, Alfred, constable
Tyler, Joseph, (Hayward & Tyler)
Vickery, Charles, prop. Brooklin Hotel
Warren, Henry, M.D
Wickett, William, butcher
Willis, John, Township Councillor

Brougham.—A Village in the Township of Pickering, County Ontario. Distant from Whitby the County Town, 12 miles, from Toronto, 27 miles. Average price of land, $50 to $60. Money Order office. Population 400.

Armstrong, Thomas, M. D.
Barclay, E.
Blandon, Willard
Bodell, William, shoemaker
Brignall, William
Brown, Robert, wagon maker
Burton, Thomas, butcher
Churchill, Mrs. Ellen, dressmaker
Daniels, Mrs., dressmaker
Daniels, D., general merchant
Ferrier, D. W., M. D.
Gould, John, butcher
Grove, S. G., saddler
Hand, H. P., general merchant
Harris, John
Herrick, A. C., teacher
Hubbard, Thomas C., J. P.
Hubbard, William
Jackson, Robert
Johnston, J.
Lamoreaux, T., manufacturer wooden ware
Matthews, Charles, auctioneer
Matthews, C. W., proprietor Brougham Hotel
Miller, D.
Miller, Miss Elizabeth, dressmaker
Miller, J.
Patterson, Andrew, tanner
Philips, C.
Philips, John
Sherrard, S. W.
Smith, J. C., general merchant
Stobbs, Rev. T. (Wesleyan)
Stock, G. B., planing mill
Tatton, Rev. Jesse (Christian)
TAUN, RICHARD, Postmaster
Turner, Jacob
Webb, Samuel, wagon maker
Woodruff, Bentley & Co., druggists
Woodruff, Mrs. P., proprietor Central Hotel

Brooksdale.—A Post-office in the Township of West Zorra, County Oxford. Mails bi-weekly. Distance from Embro, 5 miles, and from Woodstock, the County Town, 14 miles. Population 20.

BANNERMAN, SAGE, Postmaster
Davidson, James, general blacksmith
Heal, William, tailor

Brownsville.—A Village in the Township of Dereham, County Oxford, with a large trade in cheese. Distant from Woodstock, the County Town, 22 miles, from Toronto 140 miles. Average price of land, $35 to $45.

Andrews, R.
BARR, CHARLES, Postmaster
Barr, William, general merchant
Brown, E. B., farmer
Brown, J. A., farmer
Clark, Charles
Fewater, Richard, farmer
Fursman & Larkworthy, wagon makers
Glover, Jacob
Hall & Andrews, carpenters
Helmka, Henry, carpenter
Lish, George
McDiarmid, E., tailor
McDiarmid & Clark, general merchants
Nims, Frederick, butcher
Pearson, Simon, shoemaker
Sharp, George, proprietor Royal Hotel
Smith, David, paint r
Winder, Jonat an, farmer
Woolley, Lewis, farmer

Brucefield.—A Village on Peters' Creek, in the Township of Tuckersmith and Stanley, County Huron, Distant from Goderich, the County Town 18 miles, from London 42 miles, from Toronto 145 miles. Stages to Clinton, Seaforth, Bayfield and London. Average price of land $35 to $45. Population 250.

Briggs, Edward, shoemaker
Cameron, D. tailor
Cameron, Henry, teacher
Dallas, James, farmer
Ferguson, James, teacher
Ferguson, Robert, teacher
Frazer, Miss, dressmaker
Hayter, T. N., shoemaker
Kennard, Mrs., dressmaker
Kennard, Thomas J., carpenter
McCartney, James, carpenter
McCowan, Samuel, constable
McDonald, Daniel, carpenter
McDonald, Donald, carpenter
McIntosh, Hugh, carpenter
McIntosh, J., general merchant
McKay, Donald, farmer
McLagan, Alexander, farmer
McLagan, John, farmer
McTavish, Peter, farmer
MARKS, R. W., Postmaster and general merchant
Miller, James, tailor
Munro, Neil, M. D.
Murdoch, James, farmer
Mustard, Hugh, farmer
Mustard, William, farmer
Payne, David, farmer
RATTENBURY, J., proprietor Crown Inn
Ross, Rev. J., (Presbyterian)
Ross, Neil, farmer
Scott, W. & Co., general merchants
Swan, Andrew, farmer
West, Robert, proprietor Exchange Hotel
Westcott, William, farmer
Young, John, farmer
Yuill, W. R., teacher

Brunner.—A Station on the Buffalo and Lake Huron Railway, in the Township of Ellice, County Perth. Distant from Stratford, the County Town 14 miles, from Toronto 100 miles. Average price of land $16.

BRUNNER, JACOB, Postmaster
Brunner & Kuhry, lumber dealers
Gropp, Henry, farmer
Hanna, Robert, farmer
Herr, Louis, proprietor Boundary Hotel
Kerr, Colin, farmer
Kreuter, Frederick, farmer
Nichol, Angus, teacher
Shine, Daniel, auctioneer
Vogt, Henry, farmer

Brunswick.—A Village on the Port Hope, Lindsay and Beaverton Railway, in the Township of Manvers, County Durham. Distant from Port Hope, the County Town 30 miles, from Toronto 70 miles. Average price of land $25. Population 80.

Buggins, Rev. George, (Wesleyan)
Ewing, Rev. —, (Presbyterian)
Graham, Mark, farmer
Ingram, William, farmer
Lee, Joseph, farmer
McCann, Rev. A., (Wesleyan)
McRory, John, farmer
Magill, Joseph, farmer
MIDDLETON, GEORGE, teacher
Morrow, —, proprietor shingle factory
Preston, Isaac, J.P.
Rowan, William, farmer
THOMPSON, FRED., Postmaster and gen. mercht.
Twigg, George, farmer
Vance, John.
Wallace, Rev. —, (Wesleyan)

Bruce Mines.—Noted chiefly for its extensive copper mines, is situated near the head of Lake Hurons in the District of Algoma, opposite the lower end of the Island of St. Joseph, 45 miles from Sault St. Marie the judicial seat and 400 miles from Toronto; the chief mode of travel is per steamer "Algoma," Messrs. Perry & Carruthers, proprietors; the "Waubuno," J. & W. Beatty, proprietors; and the "Chicora," Messrs. Milloy Bros., proprietors, which run regularly during the summer season. Average fare from Toronto to Sault Ste Marie, cabin passage $10, deck $5. Bruce Mines is a port of entry and is rapidly becoming a point of great importance. Messrs. John Taylor & Co. of London, England, have now three mines in active operation. The chief minerals found here being copper ore, gold, magnetic and micaceous iron. The land in the vicinity is at present in a semi-uncultivated state, improved lands being worth from $2 to $6 per acre. Mails during the summer bi-weekly, winter bi-monthly. Population 1400.

Abelson, W., shoemaker
BAXTER, REV. FATHER, (Roman Catholic)
BENNETT, JAMES, J. P.
Biggings, Edward, bailiff, &c
BOWKER, JOHN, insurance agent, Custom House officer
Carpenter, T., cooper
Coatsworth, Joshua, clerk Division Court
Cox, Robert, farmer
CREIGHTON, REV. K., (Wesleyan)
DAVIDSON, JOHN, J. P.
DOBIE, W. C., Postmaster
Fisher, Richard, farmer
Frechette, Stephen, cooper
Flasson, Miss, dressmaker
Goyne, John, carpenter
Hallam, John, carpenter
HAMILTON, H., M. D.
Harris, Thomas, carpenter.
Harris, William, carpenter
Hoig, Miss Mary, teacher
Hoskins, Joseph, carpenter
Jackson, D., butcher
JACKSON, R., proprietor Ashburton Hotel
Jones, Miss Emma, teacher
Jones, H., farmer
Kennedy, Miss, dressmaker
King, Joseph, sen., cooper
King, Joseph, jun., cooper
KOHLER, REV. FATHER (Roman Catholic)
Lobb, S., butcher
McDonald, A., tailor
MARKS, THOMAS, & BROS., general merchants
Murray, Gordon, sen., farmer
NICHOLSON, PETER, general merchant
Paynter, Joseph, cooper
Paynter, Thomas, cooper
PHIPPS, J. C. & CO., general merchants
RICHARDS, JOHN, druggist
Richardson, M., farmer
SHEPHERD, W., express agent
Sullivan, Misses, dressmakers
SUTHERLAND, R. G., teacher
THORLEY, REV. W. (Primitive)
TRELEASE, E. A., proprietor Trelease's Hotel
Tweed, George, painter
Vaughan, W., tailor
Vivian, John, accountant
WARD, THOMAS, watchmaker
Wickett, Misses, dressmaker
Williams, H., shoemaker
Wyllie, James, farmer

Brudenell.—A Village in the Township of Brudenell, County Renfrew. Distant from Pembroke, the County Town 36 miles, from Ottawa 108 miles. Stages to and from Renfrew. Average price of land in village $50. Population 100.

Carty, Francis, farmer
Carty, James, farmer
Carty, John, farmer
Donovan, Thomas, shoemaker
Dorner, James, farmer
Dorner, John, farmer
Fallon, James J., teacher
Foley, Miss, teacher
Grace, James, proprietor Brudenell Inn
Harriett, William, general merchant
Kelly, Patrick, general merchant
Williams, James, teacher
Kinder, Joseph, M.D.
Kilt, John, saddler
McCormack, Rev. J., (Roman Catholic)
McGuire, James, farmer
McNamara, Patrick, shoemaker
Moran, John, general merchant
O'Boyle, John, teacher
O'Brien, Miss, teacher
Payett, D., proprietor British Hotel
Reynolds, Bernard, farmer
Reynolds, James, carpenter
REYNOLDS, JOHN, Postmaster
Reynolds, John, farmer
Ring, Edward, farmer
Scharbonne, John, shoemaker
Watson, John S., miller
Whelan, John, farmer

Bryanston.—A Post Village in the Township of London, County Middlesex, 12 miles from London and 7 from Granton Station. Mails tri-weekly. Population 51.

Chiney, John, blacksmith
Glass, M., hotel keeper
Kennedy, Charles, carpenter
Loveless, W., shoemaker
Sanborn, H., wagon maker
Stanfield, L. & W., general merchants
STANFIELD, JOHN, Postmaster

Buckhorn.—A small Post Village in the Township of Raleigh, County Kent. Distant from Chatham, the County Town, 11 miles. Daily stage to Chatham. Population 50.

Bameron, Malcolm, hotel keeper
Cleveland, James, mason
Creford, Philander, Managing Director Buckhorn Dock Co.
Creford, Samuel, President Buckhorn Dock Co.
LEE, EDWARD L., Postmaster and general merchant
Merrifield, Joseph, hotel keeper
Ranson, Amos, blacksmith
Willey, Richard, blacksmith

Bullock's Corners.—(See Greensville Post Office.)

Burford—(Kelvin P. O.)—A Village on Whiteman's Creek, in the Township of Burford, County Brant. Distant from Brantford, the County Town 9 miles, from Toronto 77 miles. Stages daily to and from Paris. Average price of land $40 to $60. Money Order office. Population 500.

Bingham, Jacob, iron founder
Brown, Rev. Mr. (Congregational)
Byrne, —, farmer
CATTON, JOHN, Postmaster
Chrysler, —, M. D.
Cox, Henry, general merchant
Daniel, Charles, farmer
Day & Sons, general merchants
Dunn, —, cooper
Flewelling, S., carpenter
Flewelling, T. G., carpenter
Fonger, William, flax mill
Foster, Alonzo
Fowler, —, M. D.
Fowler, G. P., butcher
French, G., butcher
Green, Bridget, teacher
Green, Miss Elizabeth, teacher
Grove, —, proprietor Claremont House
Haun, —, farmer
Harbottle, —, M. D.
Hearne, —, cabinet maker
Hipkins, H., M. D.
Horton, J., carpenter
Howard, —, tinsmith
Jones, T., shoemaker
LINTON, JOHN, teacher
Lloyd, Jones T., farmer
Lloyd, J., wagon maker
McCaffray, —, tailor
McGill, Mrs., dressmaker
McGinn, —, shoemaker
McWilliams, farmer
Mills, —, painter
Montgomery, shoemaker
Munger, M.D
Padfield, Rev. Mr., (Episcopal)
Padfield, J. H., dentist
Perley, Colonel
Perley, Charles, miller
Perley, Thomas, brickmaker
Phillip, Rev. Mr., (Methodist)
Ratchie, farmer
SMITH, MATTHIAS, farmer
Stuart, farmer
Sulman, —, baker
Tisdale, Miss, dressmaker
Towler, William, saddler
Whale, J., artist
Whale, Robert, artist
Williams, —, proprietor Albion Hotel
Wilson, M.D
Winskill, —, farmer
Wooden, Mrs. Ira, dressmaker
Yuigh, —, farmer.

Burgessville.—A Village in the Township of North Norwich, County Oxford, 12 miles from Woodstock.

Burgess, E. W., J.P., blacksmith
Burtis, S. S., farmer
CAMPBELL, J., Postmaster
Clark, Rev. Elijah, (Baptist)
Coulson, James, carpenter
Dennis, J. R., farmer
Dennis, W. H., general merchant
Doxsie, A., shoemaker
Easton, William, farmer
Force F., farmer
Garthwaite, William, wheelwright
Griffin, Isaac, butcher
Griswold, H. B., carpenter
Manly, William, wool carder
Nichols, S.; farmer
O'Neil, E., hotel keeper
Pollard, A., woolen factor
Pollard, W., carpenter
Snyder, E. H., farmer
Terwilliger, Rev. S., (Methodist Episcopal)
Thompson, James, tailor
Thrall, J. H., M.D
Watson, J. E., pump maker

Burgoyne.—A Post Village in the Township of Arran, County Bruce.

SHELL, ALFRED, Postmaster.

Burleigh.—A Post Office in the Township of Burleigh, County Peterboro', 30 miles from Peterboro', the County Town.

Clegg, D., J. P.
COLBORNE, JAMES, Postmaster and merchant.
Giles, Henry, miller
Giles, Thomas, miller

Burnstown.—A Village on the Madawaska River, in the Township of McNab, County Renfrew. Distant from Pembroke, the County Town 56 miles. Population 80.

Anderson, John
Braden, Richard, teacher
Davis, William, tailor
Douglas, James, general merchant
Duff, J.
Fisher, John, warden
Leckie, Alex, hotel keeper
Leckie, William, blacksmith
McCallum, John, shoemaker
McGregor, Colin
McGregor, John
McKay, James
McLaughlin, John
McLean, Robert, shoemaker
McNab, John A., Constable
McNaughton, Donald
McNevin, Alex
McRAE, DONALD, Postmaster and gen. merchant
Rochester, George, general merchant
Stewart, John
Stewart, Robert, Constable
Wallace, John
Wilson, William, hotel keeper

Burritt's Rapids.—A Village in the Township of Oxford, County Carleton, situated on the Rideau river and Canal, 30 miles from Brockville, 10 from Kemptville, and 5 from Merrickville. Population 300.

Bishop, Joshua, builder
Brown, Mrs., innkeeper
Burritt, Colonel, Henry
Campbell, R. O., teacher
Collins, Denis, J. P.
Collins, S., inn keeper
Corme, Hugh, shingle maker
Dowel, John, tanner
Falker, George, shoemaker
Guest, John, weaver
Guest, Richard, tanner
Harris, Erastus, merchant.
Healy, John, merchant
Hurd, Stephen, J. P.
Johnston, Noble, hotel keeper
Kerr, Alex., woolen mills
Kidd, W., saw mills
Lane, A. & Son, blacksmiths
McGowan, P. H, bridge tender
Mack, Matthew, saddler
Manes, James, tailor
MEIKLE, JOHN, Postmaster and merchant
Mills, James, shoemaker
Mills, John, tailor
Moffatt, John, weaver
Newans, Thos., lawyer
O'Brian, John, cooper
Patterson, James, blacksmith
Proctor, George, carriage maker
Reid, J. K., J. P.
Shannon, James, carriage maker
Sheppard, George, Lock Master
Thompson, Robert, grist mills
Waldo, R., millwright

Burnbrae.—A Village in the Township of Seymour, County Northumberland. Distant from Cobourg, County Town 40 miles, from Toronto 112 miles. Stages to Stirling, Campbellford and Belleville. Average price of land $16 to $20

Bedford, Gilbert, insurance agent
Brumby, William, grocer
Chaplin, Thomas, teacher
Clark, John, farmer
Clough, James C., farmer
Clough, William, farmer
Craighead, George, farmer
Crossin, James, lime manufacturer.
DONALD, ALEXANDER, Postmaster and general merchant
Hume, Thomas, farmer
Johnstone, John, prop. Stephen House
Lock, Jasper, farmer
Mitchell, George, mason
Morrison, John, farmer
Neill, Rev. Robert, (Presbyterian)
Rannie, George, farmer
Shillinglaw, James, carpenter
Whitton, James, farmer
Wilson, William, carpenter
Young, L. G., teacher.

Burnhamthorpe.—A Post Village in the Township of Toronto, County Peel.

Colson, E., general merchant
SAVAGE, GEORGE, Postmaster

Burnley.—A Post office in the Township of Haldimand, County Northumberland.

GRIMSHAW, R. H., Postmaster, proprietor flour and saw mills.

Burns.—A small Village in the Township of Mornington, County Perth, 22 miles from Stratford and 11 from Listowel. Population 40.

GIBSON, JOHN, Postmaster.

Burtch's Corners.—A Post Village in the Township of Brantford, County Brant. Distant from County Town 6 miles, from Toronto 70 miles. Population 30.

Baker, William, blacksmith
Burtch, Daniel, farmer
Burtch, David, farmer
Dewer, David, farmer
Hoag, William, wagon maker
TAYLOR, GEORGE, Postmaster and genl. merchant

Burton.—A Village in the Township of Manvers, County Durham, 10 miles from Bethany Station. Population, 80.

McGILL, JAMES, Postmaster and merchant
McQuade, Robert, farmer
Neal, James, blacksmith
Taylor, A., farmer
Wallis, Rev. W., (Wesleyan)
Windel, Rev. W. C., (Presbyterian)

Bury's Green.—A Post office in the Township of Somerville, County Victoria, 23 miles from Lindsay and 17 from Fenelon Falls. Weekly mail.

Cavanagh, George, farmer
Fell. Charles, farmer
FELL, JOHN, Postmaster and merchant
Flett, William, farmer
Gransden, A., farmer
Hoskins, George, farmer
Hoskins, Rev. B. S., (Church of England)
Howie, Thomas, farmer
Lamb, Richard, farmer
Lorden, Peter, farmer
Moffatt, Robert, farmer
Smith, Malcolm.

Buttonville.—A Village on the Rouge River, in the Township of Markham, County York. Distant from Toronto, 18 miles. Average price of land $60. Population 100.

Amos, Samuel, tanner
Black, Robert
Black, James, carpenter
Breden, Rev. J., (Wesleyan)
Button, Francis, senr.
Button, Francis, junr., auctioneer
Couch, William, carpenter
Dean, John, hotel keeper
Duncan, Rev. F., (Presbyterian)
Fishburn, Rev. J., (Lutheran)
Garbet, Rev. —, (Wesleyan)
Hart, Henry, shingle maker
Hunter, John
Kelly, John, shingle maker
Nicholl, William, teacher
Sanderson, Edward, auctioneer
Sanderson, John, general merchant
Stiver, Josiah
THOMSON, THOS., Postmaster and gen. merchant
Wilkinson, B., miller
Willmot, Joseph
Young, Alexander.

Buxton.—A Village in the Township of Raleigh, County Kent. Distant from Chatham, the County Town, 10 miles, from Toronto, 191 miles. Average price of land, $10 to $14. Population, 100.

Broadbent, John, farmer
Carter, John, farmer
Carter, William, proprietor Ontario House
Coutts, George, general merchant
Echlin, Daniel C., general merchant
Kersey, John, carpenter
King, Rev. William, (Presbyterian)
KING, WILLIAM, Postmaster
McSwan, William, teacher
Pardo, Andrew, farmer
Riley, Isaac, farmer
Rowe, John, farmer
Sanborn, George, lumber dealer
Scott, Thomas, shoemaker

Byng.—A Village on the Grand River, in the Township of Dunn, County Haldimand, one mile from Dunnville, with which it is conneted by a bridge of 750 feet in length. Population, 150.

Armour, Matthew, mill proprietor
Band, Robert, Alloa mill
Brown, George, J.P., farmer
Cokley, S., hotel keeper
Drake, Thomas, blacksmith
Fite, Henry, carpenter
Hannah, James, shoemaker
Logan, Peter, carpenter
Murdy, Robert, bridge tender
Rogers, William, farmer
Sheehan, W. B., custom officer
THOMPSON, J. M., Postmaster and grocer

Byng Inlet.—A Post-office of the District of Algoma.

LITTLE, CHARLES, Postmaster.

Byron.—A Village in the Township of Westminster, County Middlesex. Distant from London, 5 miles, from Toronto, 140 miles. Average price of land $20 to $30. Population, 150.

Cameron, Miss Flora, teacher
Colville, James, farmer
Duffton, J. & J., woolen factors
Glover, Joseph, proprietor Byron Hotel
Griffith, John & Brothers, woolen factors
Hallywood, A., farmer
Harrington, A., general merchant
Kains, Archibald, farmer
McNamee, L., farmer
Martin, William & Son, shoemakers
Montague, John, farmer
SADLER, ROBERT, Postmaster and gen. merchant
Savage, Rev., (New Connexion)
Shephard, George, farmer
Stephens, John, farmer
Wells, T. B., constable

Cæsarea.—A Village on Lake Scugog, in the Township of Cartwright, County, Durham. Distant from Durham, the County Town, 18 miles, from Toronto 60 miles. Stages to Cartwright, Enniskillen, Hampton and Bowmanville. Average price of land $25 to $30. Population 100.

Crozier, George
DEMARA, EPHRAIM, Postmaster & gen. mercht
Elliott. John, wagon maker
Emerson, Matthew
Graham, George, tailor
Herron, Edward, tinsmith
Irwin, John
Irwin, Robert
Keys, John, hotel keeper
McDonald, Rev. J., (Wesleyan)
Martin, William, lumber dealer
Muirhead, Jacob, shingle manufacturer
Prout William
Thior, Paul, carpenter

Cainsville.—A Village and Station on the Grand Trunk Railway, pleasantly situated on the Grand River, in the Township of East Brantford, County Brant, three miles from Brant, the County Town. It contains Episcopal and Methodist churches, and paper, flouring, and woolen mills. Improved lands in the vicinity average $50 per acre. Stages to Brantford and Hamilton. Population 300.

Brown, Walter, wagon maker
Clark, Mrs. J., grocer
Clotworthy, Rev. W., (Church of England)
Colebeck, John, farmer
Cornish, Rev. G. H., (Wesleyan)
Dresser, J. D., accountant
Duncan, A., general merchant
Elliott, A. & Co., flax mills
Elliott, M., tailor
Filer, R., farmer
Fitch, J. D., proprietor flour mills
GRENNY, M., Postmaster and general merchant
Hare, J. O., shoemaker
Hassard, A., shoemaker
Hamilton, R., nursery and seedsman
Hildred, William, farmer
Hobson, James, butcher
Imlach, Henry, farmer
Langs, J., shingle maker
McConkey, C., carpenter
Orr, John, prop. American Hotel
Peatman, Henry, auctioneer
Ramsay, A., lumber merchant
Reid, James, wagon maker
Rich, J. H., proprietor paper mills
Smithson, R., farmer
Steneboursgh, J., hotel keeper
Thomas, Joseph, J.P
Thomas & Ash, distillers
Westbrook, P., J.P
Whiting, Isaac, general merchant
Wright, S., rope and cordage manufacturer

Caintown. A post Village in the Township of Yonge, County Leeds. Distant from Lyn 7 miles, and from Brockville, the County Town, 14 miles. Population 200.

TENNANT, WILLIAM, jr., Postmaster.

Caistorville.—A Village on Chippewa Creek, in the Township of Caistor, County Lincoln. Distant from St. Catherines, the County Town, 33 miles, from Toronto 60 miles. Average price of land $12 to $20. Money order office. Population 100.

Adams, Robert J., blacksmith
Asher, James, farmer
Cleland, Henry W., carpenter
Cleland, William L., carpenter
Gillespie, Thomas M, teacher
Haney, Robert A., M.D
Hurlburt, Rev. Thomas, (Wesleyan)
Johnston, John, jr., teacher
Kaufman, Jacob, shoemaker
Leigh, Robert, farmer
Lesser, Peter, farmer
Lymburner, J. G. farmer
Mitchell, James, lumber dealer
Park, James, farmer
Park, J., general merchant
SCOTT, M.G., Postmaster and gen. mercht
Spears, Adam, J.P
Stevenson, William J., farmer
Tice, Richard C., blacksmith

Caledon.—(Also called Charleston.)—A Village in the Township of Caledon, County Cardwell, 17 miles from Brampton. Money order office. Population 150.

Arkell, George, tailor
Dawson, Edward, innkeeper
Dodds, W. B., blacksmith
Dyner, John, blacksmith
Hammond, James, prop. saw mill
Harris, Isaac, J.P., general merchant
Harris, John, general merchant
Johnson, James, carriage maker
Johnson, John, shoemaker
McFaul, Rev. A., (Canada Presbyterian)
McLEAN, HUGH, Postmaster, fancy goods. (See adv)
McQuarrie, John, general merchant
Noble, William, teacher
Rayburn, John, carpenter
Rice, George, shoemaker
Shoenlank, Samuel, general merchant
Wanless, John, carpenter

Calabogie.—A Post-office situated in the Township of Bagot, County Renfrew.
DILLON, D., Postmaster.

Calder.—A Post-office in the Township of Delaware, County Middlesex.
CAMPBELL, WILLIAM, Postmaster.

Caldwell.—A post Village situated in the Township of Caledon, County Peel. Distant from Brampton 13 miles, and from Toronto 36 miles. Population about 85,
MURPHY, PATRICK, Postmaster.

Caledon East.—A Village in the Township of Caledon, County Peel. Distant from Brampton the County Town, 17 miles, from Toronto 33 miles. Stages to Mono Mills and Malton. Average price of land $40. Population 100.

Allison, Samuel, M. D.
Amie, Rev. — (Primitive Methodist)
Broddie, Alexander, auctioneer
Bullivant, James, carpenter
Campbell, Peter C., general merchant
Cranston, Alexander, hotel keeper
Dodsworth, William, painter
Fleetham, John, tailor
Greer, Craig, farmer
Hackett, James, shoemaker
Jones, Hiram wagon maker
Judge, Thomas, farmer
McConnell, Rev. — (Presbyterian)
McCue, Thomas, farmer
MUNSIE, JAMES, Postmaster
Nixon, Henry, farmer
Pearen, Henry, insurance agent
Pettigrew, Henry, J. P.
Scott, John, saddler
Stone, William, general merchant
Walker, James, farmer
Watson, James, farmer

Caledonia Springs.—A Village on the Des Atacos, in the Township of Caledonia, County Prescott. Distant from L'Orignal, the County Town, 9 miles, from Montreal, 72 miles, from Ottawa, 68 miles, from Toronto, 330 miles. Stages to and from L'Orignal. Average price of land $25. Population, 100.

Butler, Nicholas, hotel keeper
CAMERON, J. D., Postmaster and general merch't
Gianelli, A. M. F., hotel keeper
McDonald, George M., telegraph operator
McDonald, William J., teacher
Rochon, Joel, hotel keeper

Camborne.—A Post-Village in the Township of Hamilton, County Northumberland. Distant from Cobourg, the County Town, 5 miles. Daily mail. Population, about 250.

Camden East.—(See Clark's Mills)—A Post-office in the Township of Camden, County Addington.
CLARK, BENJAMIN, Postmaster.

Caledonia.—(Seneca post office). An incorporated Village and station of the Grand Trunk Railroad, on the Grand river, in the Township of Seneca, County Haldimand, 12 miles from Cayuga the County Town, 14 from Hamilton and 20 from Port Dover. There is an Indian reserve of several thousand acres in the vicinity. Gypsum is found in the neighborhood in large quantities. Stages to Hamilton. Port Dover and Cayuga. Money Order Office and Savings Bank. Population 1400.

Adams & Co., grocers
Aldridge, James, clerk Division Court, insurance agt.
Aldridge, William, farmer
Alexander, John, carpenter
Alhambra Saloon, William Thomson, jr., prop.
Ashbaugh & Adams, millers
Ball, S., general merchant
Black, Rev. James, (United Presbyterian)
BOOTH, JOHN, Union Hotel, stage proprietor and livery keeper
Britain, Matthew, hotel keeper
Broderick, D. E., merchant tailor
Brown, W. & J., general merchants
Buck, A. C., general merchant, insurance agent and druggist
Builder, John, cabinet factory
CAMPBELL, JOHN, Railway Hotel
Campbell, William, cooper
CHAMBERS, HENRY, hotel heeper
Chrystal, George, teacher
DILLABOUGH, E. H., M. D., Druggist
Donely, M., agent G. T. R.
Donely, M., senr.
Doyle, John, grocer
Elwood, George, shoemaker
Farrell, John, hotel keeper
Fulton, Samuel, carriage maker
Furlong, E., attorney-at-law
Garland, N. & T., general merchants
Grand River Sachem, (Wednesday) Thomas Messenger, editor and proprietor.
Green, E. D., dentist
Harvey, William, accountant
Hayes. James, shoemaker
Heddle, Thomas, blacksmith
Hicks, W. L., & Co., flour millers and merchants
Hill, Rev., B. C., (Church of England)
Holden, W., flour merchant
Howard, John, shoemaker
Howard, Matthew, saddler
Howells, W. E., M. D.
Hull, Henry, saddler
Hull, J. W., saddler
Ince, Henry, J., auctioneer
Jackson, William, assistant Postmaster
Kean, David, baker
Kennedy, Hugh; farmer
Knipe, Oliver, prop. Seneca House
Knipe, Soloman, blacksmith
Lees, Thomas, woolen factory
Leith, William, hotel keeper
McBay, Alexander, shoemaker
McCargow, William, M. D.
McCargow, William, farmer
McDonald, Donald, lime dealer
McDonald, John, shoemaker
McDonald, Malcolm, shoemaker
McKinnon, John M., insurance agent
McKINNON, RONALD, manufacturer, mill owner
McKinnon, J., general merchant
McKinnon, R. A
McLERNON, WILLIAM, general merchant
McNeil, C., produce dealer
McNulty, Rev. J., (Roman Catholic)
McPherson, William, M.D
McQuarin, Donald, miller
Martineau, R., cooper
Mercer, F. C., watchmaker
MESSENGER, THOMAS, editor and proprietor *Grand River Sachem*, coroner and ins. agent
Mitchell Nelson, painter
Mohun, James, merchant tailor
Moore, William, farmer
Morrison, Hector, cooper
Mullen, Robert, carpenter
MUNRO, WILLIAM, prop. Mansion House
Murphy, Peter, hotel keeper
Mutchmor, J. T., lumber merchant
Neilson, James, proprietor International Hotel
Old, James, jun., auctioneer
Palmer, Henry, M.D
Paterson, Samuel, carpenter
Patter, Rev, Robert, (Wesleyan)
Rennelson, W. H., principal grammar school
Rolston, Alexander, farmer
Rosser, John, general merchant
SCOTT, JOHN, Postmaster
Scott, John & Co., foundry
Seldon, Richard, baker
Senn, George, carpenter
Seyright, James, carpenter
Schoots, George, carriage maker
Slater, William, builder and contractor
Smart, W. R., attorney-at-law
SMITH, W. H., stage proprietor and general agent
TAYLOR, ALEXANDER, insurance agent and plaster merchant
THOMSON, WILLIAM, JUN., proprietor Alhambra Saloon
UNION HOTEL, John Booth, proprietor
WALKER, R. E., tinsmith
WATTERS, JAMES, general merchant
WHELAN, ROBERT, grocer
Wickett, Nathan, butcher
Willer, Robert, tinsmith
Wilson, William, sash factory
Young, Christopher, J.P., prop. American Hotel
Young, David, farmer
Young, Frederick, general merchant
Young, Stephen, saloon keeper,
YOUNG & PATTERSON, (J. Young & Samuel Patterson) carriage makers and blacksmiths

---

Camilla.—A Village on the Nottawasaga River, in the Township of Mono, County Simcoe, 6 miles from Orangeville and 28 from Brampton. Stages bi-weekly to Whitfield, Orangeville and Owen Sound. Population 75.

Anderson, Thomas, wagon maker
Christie, Rev. W. M. (Methodist)
CURRIE, HUGH, Postmaster, general store, hotel
Hamilton, Rev. W. (Presbyterian)
Neil, Alexander, carpenter
Orme, John, shoemaker
Turnbull, Alexander, saw mill proprietor

Cambray.—A Village on Goose Creek, in the Township of Fenelon, County Victoria. Distant from Lindsay, the County Town, 8 miles, from Toronto 80. Stages to Fenelon Falls and Carden, fare $1. Money Order Office. Population 100.

Armstrong, George, sawyer
Austin, J., shoemaker
BATEMAN, J. M., Postmaster and merchant
Birkley, M. H., proprietor grist and saw mills
Burley, William, blacksmith and wagon maker
Butler, ——, M.D.
Butler, Richard, saddler
Calder, Andrew, carpenter and joiner
Clendenon, Edwin, farmer
Clendenon, John, farmer
Coals, A., farmer
Curry, Miss, milliner and dressmaker
Dent, George, tanner
Dillingham, Sidney, proprietor saw mill
Dillingham & Smith, proprietors saw mill
Douglass, Thomas. general merchant
Hilborn, J. C. E., proprietors saw mill and tannery.
Holmes, John, wagon maker
Hunter, William, carpenter
Jarvis, Thomas, farmer
McIntyre Duncan, hotel keeper
McKinnon, John, general merchant
McLauchlin, A., miller
McMillan, James, hotel keeper
McQuay, John, teacher
Manney, Walter, carpenter
Moffatt, James, blacksmith
Morgan, John, shoemaker,
Newson, John, farmer
Newson, William, farmer
Phillips, William, shoemaker
Playter Waterman, proprietor saw mill
Pomeroy, Rev. J. C., (Methodist Episcopal)
Powell, Elias, carpenter
Powell, J. Y., dentist and photographer
Russell, George, saddler
Scott, Rev. J. R., (Bible Christian)
Scott, Miss Sophia, teacher
Shawl, John, engineer
Sinclair, John, blacksmith and carriage maker
Sinclair, John, sen., farmer
Smith, Isaac, proprietor shingle factory
Stoddart, William, cabinet maker
Wilkinson, Joseph, prop. saw mill and shingle factory

Campbellford.—A Village on the River Trent, in the Township of Seymour, County Northumberland. Distant from Cobourg, the County Town 40 miles, from Toronto 100 miles. Stages to Brighton daily, and to Stirling tri-weekly. Average price of land $16 to $24. Money Order office and Savings' Bank. Population 700.

Abbott, G. W., general merchant
Anderson, James, carpenter
Archer, Miss, teacher
Arsher, James
Beatty, James, cabinet maker
Beatty, W., teacher
Benor, James, carpenter
Bogart, —, M. D.
Boucher, F.
Buller, C. G.
Cassan, M. S.
Clark, William, contractor
Cook, Robert, J.P
Cockburn, R., miller, general merchant, &c
Cogan, John, boots and shoes
Collins, Daniel, sen., prop. Campbellford Hotel
Collins, Daniel, jr., prop. Phœnix Hotel
Costley, William, wagon maker
Dale, Arthur, accountant
Davidson, J., tailor
Denmark, A
Dickson, John, iron founder
Dinwoodie, James, contractor, miller, &c
Doxsee, C., cabinet maker
Doxsee, W., saddler
Dunlop, John, painter
Elly, R. J., cabinet maker
FERRISS, J. M., Postmaster
Ferriss, J. M. & Co., general merchants
Fraser, Henry, carpenter
Frederick, B., tailor
Free, Robert, carpenter
Gibb, John, general merchant
Grigor, James, butcher
Harry, Richard, boots and shoes
Hawley, M. A., hardware merchant
Hawn, G. S., carpenter
Heathcote, Edward, attorney, &c
Hooper, James, saddler
Irvine, Robert, general merchat
Irwin & Fletcher, general merchants
Johns, Charles, saddler
Johns, Thomas, butcher
Johnston, John, seedsman
Johnston, Robert, wagon maker
Keating, E., tailor
Kennedy, D., insurance agent, &c
Kiernan, Edward, boots and shoes
Lauder, John, saddler
Leffer, Augustus, brick manufacturer
Linton, Robert, wagon maker
Logan, William, cooper
McCarthy, John, boots and shoes
McColl, Mrs. dressmaker
McKay, Mrs., dressmaker
McKelvie, F., carpenter
Martin, G., tailor
Massie, A., carpenter
Maybee, Thomas, butcher
Mitchell, George, lime manufacturer
Morris, J. H., tailor
Mirfield, Samuel, woolen factor
Nadoo, William, carpenter
Nancarrow, Walter, tanner
Norman, Jackson, cooper
Ogilvie, Miss, teacher
Oulton, C., iron founder, &c
Rendle, A. H., druggist
Reynolds, M. A., cooper
Rosinblath, John, manufacturer willow ware
Sevesconte, J. M., J. P.
Shillinglaw, R. carpenter
Skinner, H. E., general merchant
Smith, George, cooper
Smith, Peter, cooper
Stanbury, Aenry, general merchant
Stettman, Robert, general merchant
Temple, Mrs., dressmaker
Temple, Joseph, cooper
Tice, G. F. A., general agent
Tobias, S. boots and shoes
Wallace, — M. D.
Wellman, John, carpenter
Willman, G., proprietor Victoria Hotel
Wilson, W., M. D.
Young, John, boots and shoes

Camlachie.—A small Village and station of the Grand Trunk Railway, two miles from Lake Huron, Township of Plympton, County Lambton. It is 15 miles from Sarnia, the County Town. Average value of improved land, $25 per acre.

Campbell, James, teacher
DOUGLAS, WILLIAM, Postmaster, gen. mercht.
Hastie, William, farmer
McLean, James, teacher
Robinson, James, hotel keeper
Scott, Rev. Robert (Presbyterian)
Smith, J. A., agent G. T. R.
Symington, William, J. P.
Trusler, Alvah, farmer

Cameron.—A small Village in the Township of Fenelon, County Victoria, 9 miles from Lindsay, th County Town. Population 30.

Bice, George, innkeeper
BRYSON, JAMES, Postmaster
Flack, Mrs., grocer
Moffatt, Peter, blacksmith

Campbellville.—A Village at the head of Sixteen-mile Creek, in the Township of Nassagaweya, County Halton. Distant from Milton, the County Town, 7 miles, from Toronto 40 miles. Stages to Wellington Square and Guelph. Average price of land $20. Population 200.

Abrey, G., miller
Bellwood, Christopher, shoemaker
Betts, Rev. J., (Wesleyan)
Buck, William, tailor
Callaghan, Patrick, wagon maker
Cooke, John, proprietor Farmers' Arms
COOPER, JAMES H., Postmaster and gen. mercht.
Davidson & Brothers, woolen manufacturers
Deforest, A., manufacturer willow ware
Doty, Pharis, agent lumber mill
Easterbrook, William, proprietor Campbellville Inn
Hewson, Rev. —, (Church of England)
Hopkins, George, auctioneer
Hubbert, Michael, shoemaker
Kidney, William, general merchant
Little, Rev. J., (Presbyterian)
McGregor, Peter, dentist
McIlverey, George, farmer
McLaren, A. L., teacher
McPhee, Alexander, teacher
Menzies, James, blacksmith
Munn, David, J.P.
Schram, Adam, shingle manufacturer
Scriver, Samuel, carpenter
Skinner, Richard, farmer
Smith, William, carpenter
Smitton, R., butcher
Stribbling, Henry, farmer
Winn, —, M.D.

Campden.—A small Village in the Township of Clinton, County Lincoln, 11 miles from St. Catherines, the County Town, 65 from Toronto and 5 from Beamsville and Jordan Stations, G.W.R. Improved lands in vicinity average $40 per acre, unimproved $30. Population 70.

Albright, Daniel, shoemaker
Barrie, Rev. Francis, (Wesleyan)
Dean, Andrew, flour mill proprietor
Eddy, Edward, shingle manufacturer
Grobb, Joseph, general merchant
Hagerman, Daniel, blacksmith
Hagerman, George, carriage maker
High, William, farmer
Hipple, Jacob, teacher, melodeon agent
Hipple, John, carriage maker
Hipple, William, farmer
Houser, John, farmer
Houser, Michael, farmer
Hummel, H. S., melodeon, etc., agent
Hunsburger, Michael, shingle maker
McFulton, James, farmer
Moyer, David L., cooper
MOYER, HENRY W., Postmaster, and auctioneer
Moyer, Israel, painter
Moyer, Jacob S., broom maker
Moyer, John, farmer
Moyer, Joseph H., farmer
Moyer, S. B., broom maker
Moyer, S. M., farmer
Moyer, Tilman W., carpenter
Moyer, W. W. & Co., tobacconists
Nash, Joseph, sewing machine agent
Nash, S. S., teacher
Oill, James T., farmer
Orth, Daniel, potter
Orth, John, farmer
Rittenhouse, Jacob F., farmer
Smith, John, carpenter
Smith, William, J.P.

Canboro'.—A Post-village, situated in the Township of Canboro,' County of Haldimand. Distant from Cayuga, the County Town, 10 miles. Mails, tri-weekly. Population, 130.

Baldwin, George, shoemaker
Bordsall & Mellick, merchants
Carmody, Daniel, wagon maker
FOLINSHEE, JOHN, Postmaster, J.P
Goss, Jesse F., bailiff
Hazleton, J. G., shoemaker
Mellick. D., blacksmith
Rogers, Matthew, farmer
Smith, Frederick, inn keeper
Smith, Seth, merchant
Sevick, William, butcher

Campbell's Cross.—A Village in the Township of Chinguacousy, County Peel. Distant from Brampton, County Town, 9 miles, from Toronto 36 miles. Stages to Brampton and Orangeville. Average price of land $40.

Bradley John
Campbell, Abraham
Campbell, Francis
Campball, Joseph
Campbell, Seth
Ceasor, John, blacksmith
French, Thomas, stone cutter
Garvey, Peter & Philip, brick manufacturers
Hackett, John, shoemaker
HAGYARD, E. T., Postmaster and general merch't.
Hagyard, Thomas, M.D.
Hagyard, T. C.
Jeffers, Rev. Thomas, (Wesleyan)
Jewitt, George
Johnson, George, butcher
Jordan, Thomas, teacher
Loughed, William, proprietor Dublin Castle
McCollum, R. C., J.P.
McCollum, R. J., general merchant
McDougall, John, carpenter
McKechnie, Archibald
Martin, Joseph, wagon maker
Reynolds, James, shingle manufacturer
Robson, James
Robson, Thomas, stock dealer
Sage, John
Smith, Andrew
Snyder, Abraham, insurance agent

Canfield.—A Village in the Township of Cayuga, County Haldimand, and the proposed crossing point of the Grand Trunk and Southern Railways. Distant from Cayuga, the County Town, 6 miles, from Toronto, 70 miles. Stages to and from Cayuga. Average price of land $15 to $20. Money order office. Population, 150.

Abbott, J. T., teacher
Adron, Mark, mason
Badgely, L. M., lumber dealer
Badgely, Matthew, farmer
Baldwin, James, farmer
Bullock, William, farmer
Canfield, A., shingle manufacturer
Coates, John, blacksmith
Coverdale, William, carpenter
Dryer, Edward, blacksmith
Flanders, G. E., tailor
Flanders, Nelson, farmer
Haney, John, farmer
Haynes, William, farmer
Humphries, Thomas, brick manufacturer
King, Henry, farmer
Leith, Rev. H., (New Connexion)
McDiarmid, Kenneth, shoemaker
McDiarmid & Oxley, grocers
Nelles, Robert L., express agent
Philips, W. A., teacher
Richardson, Rev. W. R., (Wesleyan)
Rose, Mrs., dressmaker
Rose, Henry, match manufacturer
Rose, William, proprietor Railway Hotel
Sabines, M. J., painter
Schram, P., livery stable proprietor
Street, S., farmer
Switzer, Jacob, clerk
Switzer, John, farmer
Switzer, M. D., general merchant
Tenney, Robert, shoemaker
Weaver, Adam, mason
Weaver, Adam, sen., farmer
WILSON, JOHN, Postmaster and general merchant
Wilson, J. C., telegraph operator
Young, Henry, proprietor Royal Hotel

Cannifton.—A Village on the Moira River, Township of Thurlow, County Hastings, three miles from Belleville, the County Town. Stages, to Bridgewater, Stirling and Belleville. Population, 600.

Becket, N. J., miller and grocer
Betts, Rev. L. A. (Episcopal Methodist)
Brooks, E., woollen factory
Brown, George S., farmer
Bullis, W. L., teacher
Canniff, Daniel, farmer
Canniff, John, clerk
CANNIFF, JONAS, jun., Postmaster
Canniff, J. A., blacksmith
Coon, C., carpenter
Dale, Thomas, farmer
Fairman, R. C., Farmer's Inn
Fairfield, J. K., teacher
Farnham, T.
Gillespie & Smith, pumpmakers
Gunsolius, John J., blacksmith
Howell, Rev. J. E. (Wesleyan)
Kane, William, shoemaker
Lake, N., grocer
Larn, T., cooper
Lingham, William, miller
McLigret, R., carpenter
Naylor, Thomas, blacksmith
Naylor, William, shoemaker
Pake, S. S., carpenter
Powers, William, hotel keeper
Stinson, William, saw mill proprietor
Stimers, J. L., hotel keeper
Sills, Jacob, saw mill proprietor
Sutherland, A., saw mill proprietor
Sutherland, William, farmer
Walsh, James, carriage maker
Wilson, A., J. P.

Canning.—A Village on the River Nith, in the Township of Blenheim, County Oxford, 16 miles from Woodstock, the County Town, and 4 from Princeton station, Great Western Railway. The immediate neighborhood contains some good water privileges. Average value of improved land in the vicinity, $40 per acre. Population 150.

ALLCHIN, SAMUEL, Postmaster, proprietor saw and grist mills
Davidson, James, farmer
Johnson, H., farmer
Martin, Charles, butcher
Martin, Donald, farmer
Matthewson, George, mason
Mitchell, Charles, farmer
Oliver, Adam, farmer
Rickert, John, farmer
Roberts, James, leather dealer
Scott, Walter, farmer
Simpson, James, carpenter
Slingsby, William, woolen factor
Smake, Samuel, farmer
Spears, Thomas, farmer
Strong, J., general merchant
Taylor, William H., nurseryman
Turner, Judson, wagon maker
Waldron, John, carpenter
Weatherell, William, hotel keeper
Whitehead, David, farmer
Whitehead, James, farmer
Williams, Joseph, farmer
Wills, Martin, farmer
Wright, Thomas, miller

Cannington.—A flourishing Village in the Township of Brock, County Ontario, on the Beaver River and line of the proposed Toronto and Nipissing Railway, 38 miles from Whitby, the County Town, and 18 from Lindsay. Money Order office. Population 600.

Brandon, Christopher baker
Brown, David S., tanner
Brown, Neil, general merchant
Burnham, Charles, Clerk Division Court
Card, S. W., carding mills
Cavanagh, Allen, carpenter
Clift, Thomas, wagon maker
Corvan, Matthew, J.P.
Davidson, Lachlan
Davidson, P., miller
DeLease, John, brewer
Donald, William, carpenter
Ellis, John W., general merchant
Forman, Thomas C., general merchant
French, Frederick, builder
GIBBS, CHARLES, Postmaster, Commissioner in B. R., agent Western Assurance Co., Toronto.
Gillespie, Donald, M.D.
Harris, Edward, shoemaker
Hay, John, wagon maker
Hefner, Charles, shoemaker
Holmes, John, blacksmith
Hoyle, Henry W., cabinet maker
Hunt, Reuben, wagon maker
Johnston, Robert, shoemaker
Jolliff, John
Jones, Robert, carpenter
Keller, Charles C., solicitor
Lucas, Joseph, grocer
McDougall, John, flour mill proprietor
McKay, Archibald, grocer
McKechnie, Alexander, teacher
McKenzie, Thomas, tailor
Marsh, A. F., general merchant
May, William, tailor
Maybee, Henry, carding mill proprietor
Maybee, Henry W., saddler
Maybee & Graham, stoves and tinware
Munro, Hugh, flour and saw mills
Nimmo, —, proprietor saw mills
Ross, Alexander, builder
Silverthorn, George, carpenter
Silverthorn, John, carpenter
Silverthorn, William, blacksmith
Sharp, John
Smith, George, general merchant
Smith, George, bailiff
Taylor & Lindsay, saddlers
THOMPSON, JOHN H., M.P.P.
Thorne, Thomas, miller
Walsh, Thomas H., tailor
Walton, George
Ward, John, hotel keeper
Willson, J. A., M.D.
Wyatt, Alfred, druggist

Canton.—A Village on Smith's Creek, in the Township of Hope, County Durham. Distant from Port Hope, the County Town, 5 miles, from Toronto 60 miles. Average price of land $50. Population 100

Bragg, M., farmer
Bray, W., farmer
Colman, J., farmer
Campbell, J., farmer
Crawford, S., farmer
Currelly, T., sen., farmer
Currelly, T., jr., farmer
DEACON, W., Postmaster and general merchant
Eascott, R., farmer
Gibbs, R. H., cooper
Graham, Rev. J., (Wesleyan)
Harris, Charles, J.P
Hawkins, M., farmer
Henwood, J., farmer
Johnston, E., farmer
Johnston, J., carpenter
Lowes, J., farmer
McMaster, J., carpenter
Martin, J., farmer
Martin, Thomas, prop. Canton Hotel
Martin, T., cooper
Peters, N., teacher
Pethie, H., farmer
Plain & Powers, lumber dealers
Powers, Mrs. S. S.,
Powers, T. B., M.D
Salter, G. B., miller
Tindall, Mrs, dressmaker

Cape Rich.—A Village in the Township of St. Vincent, County Grey, situated on Nottawasaga Bay, Georgian Bay, 20 miles from Owen Sound, the County Town, and 37 from Collingwood. There are extensive fisheries here. Steamers call daily in connection with the Northern Railway. All kinds of mechanics are required. Average value of improved land $20, unimproved $10 per acre. There is a very superior clay abundant here, suitable for brick or pottery work. Population 180.

Avery, Thomas, cooper
Avery, William, cooper
Boyd, Samuel, farmer
Burns, H., farmer
Carson, J., farmer
Cooper, William, farmer
Dodger, David, farmer
Doran, A., farmer
Downing, William, farmer
Foster F., farmer
Irwin, Robert, farmer
Kennedy, Gilbert, carpenter
McIntosh, Angus, carpenter
McIntosh, G. P., commission merchant
McIntosh, Gilbert, carpenter
McLAREN, DONALD, Postmaster
McLaren, James, shingle maker
Mitch, John, cooper
Nicol, John, painter
Ross, Rev. Robert (Baptist)
Stephen, Adam S., teacher
Terry, J. C., dentist
Tottenham, F. R., farmer
Watson, Col

Carlingford.—A Village in the Township of Fullarton, County Perth, 11 miles from Stratford, the County Town, and 6½ from Sebringville Station. •Bi-weekly mails. Population 100.

Babb, William, blacksmith and wagon maker
DAVIDSON, WILLIAM, Postmaster and general merchant
McInnes, William, innkeeper
Hamilton, Robert, shoemaker
Terry, Frederick, saw mill proprietor

Carleton Place.—A Village on the Mississippi River, in the Township of Beckwith, South Riding County Lanark, a station of the Belleville and Ottawa Railway, 22 miles from Perth, the County Town, 28 from Ottawa and 275 from Toronto. Money Order office and Savings' Bank. Population 800.

Anderson, R., notary public, commissioner in B. R.
Beck, William, carpenter
Bobier, Samuel, painter
Boggart, D. P., M.D.
Bredin, William, grist and oat mills
Brian, Edward, carpenter
Brown, John, general merchant
Burke, John, cooper
Burke, Maurice, cooper
CARLETON PLACE HERALD, (Wednesday), Jas. Poole, proprietor
Carswell, Rev. T., (Canada Presbyterian)
Cavers, John, carpenter
Cragie & Stephinson, shingle makers
Craig, D., butcher
Crampton, Robert, general merchant
Crane, James, farmer
Crane, William, carpenter
Devlin, James, blacksmith
Dunlop, James, carpenter
Findlay, David, founder
Galvin, Patrick, clothing
Gillis & McLaren, lumber merchants
Glover, William, blacksmith
Graham, John, carriage maker
Grant & McLaren, founders
Gray, William B., painter
Greig, J.
Halpeny, R. W., general merchant
Hurd, W. H., M.D.
Kelly, William, hotel keeper
Kilpatrick, James, cooper
King, Colin, farmer
Leden, William, J. P.
Lang, Alexander, blacksmith
Lavelle, N., hotel keeper and auctioneer
Leslie, Jacob, cabinet maker
Lowe, George, agent B. & O. R. R., telegrapher, American express company agent
McArthur, A., J. P.
McDonald, Allen, dyer
McDowell, Rev. H., (Methodist)
McEwan, John, farmer
McEwan, John, grocer
McKay, James, baker
McLaren, P., B.A., principal grammar school
McLaren, Robert, carpenter
McNeeley, Bryce, leather dealer
McPherson, George, bailiff
McVean, J., M. D.
Metcalf, Robert, grocer
Metcalf, R., hotel keeper
Moore, Hugh, merchant tailor
Moore, Richard, shoemaker
Moore, William H. shoemaker
Morris, Rev. E
Muirhead, William, farmer
Munro, James, carpenter
Neelin, William, general merchant
Patterson, William, cabinet maker
Pattie, William, carpenter
Pitland, Joseph, carriage maker
Poole, James, proprietor *Herald*
PRESTON, REV. J. A., (Church of England)
Rorrison, William, carpenter
Ross, Rev. W., (Presbyterian)
Scott, John, carriage maker
Scott, Walter, merchant tailor
Sinclair, Colin, clothing
Stewart, Rev. J., (Baptist)
STRUTHERS, PATRICK, Postmaster
Summer, M. W., general merchant
Taylor, William, china and glassware
Taylor, William, tinsmith
Tucker, Patrick, shoemaker
Tooley, Charles, butcher
Wallace, James, farmer
Wilson, William, M.D.
Waugh, Samuel, saddler

Carlisle.—A Village in the Township of East Flamboro', County Wentworth, on Twelve-mile Creek, 8 miles from Waterdown Station, Great Western Railway, 12 from Hamilton, the County Seat, and 42 from Toronto. Population 150.

Boyer, Anderson, butcher
Burton, John, farmer
Carson, Henry, mason
Cranston, Henry, painter
CROOKER, JOHN C., Postmaster, dry goods and groceries
Davis, William, wagon maker
Dawson, F. K., blacksmith
Duffy, Michael, butcher
Eaton, Daniel, hotel keeper
Edgar, William,
Ellis, John, mason
Ellison, Thomas, J.P., farmer
Hood, Henry, farmer
Hood, John, shoemaker
Mahon, William, blacksmith
Millard, D. B., blacksmith
Mills, W. F., hotel keeper
Newell, William P., farmer
Ross, John, general merchant
Sullivan, James, farmer

Carden.—A Post office in the Township of Carden, County Victoria.
CARLIN, JAMES, Postmaster.

Carlow.—A Post office in the Township of Colborne, County Huron. Distant from Goderich, the County Town, 6 miles. Population about 150.

McDONOUGH, JAMES, Postmaster and innkeeper.
Ross, John, hotel keeper.

Carlsruhe.—A Village in the Township of Carrick, County Bruce, 8 miles from Walkerton the County Town. Tri-weekly mails. Population 200.

Brunner, Wendel, blacksmith
Bruder, George, shoemaker
Goet, Albert, plough maker
Goet, Emil, blacksmith
Gross, William, brickmaker
Grossman, Peter, basket maker
Hauck, Henry, teacher
Hogen, Matthew, carpenter
Hesser, Philip, wagon maker
Hesch, Jacob, mason
Hoffarth, Conrad, farmer
Hoffarth, John, farmer
Klungy, John, cabinet maker
KORMANN, IGNATIUS, Postmaster, gen. mercht.
Kuntze, Jacob, brewer
Leulitts, Xavier, farmer
Lobsinger, A., hotel keeper
Lobsinger, Louis, saw mills
Metzger, Michael, farmer
Newman, John, carriage maker
Rassarts, Rev. F., (Roman Catholic)
Roeser, Philip, tailor
Ropel, Jacob, farmer
Schneider, John, cooper
Schmitzler, Peter, brewer
Schwan, William, mason
Ward, Lawrence, contractor

Carluke.—A small Post Village in the Township of Ancaster, County Wentworth, 11 miles from Hamilton, the County Town, and 50 miles from Toronto. Daily mails. Population about 75.

CALDER, JAMES, J.P. and Postmaster
Calder, John, farmer
Calder, Robert, farmer
Grittman, Jacob, blacksmith
Harvie, William, general merchant
McLaren, James, cooper
McLogan, Peter, J.P.
Moffatt, James, farmer
Moffatt, William, farmer
Morton, James, farmer
Renton, William, farmer
Russell, John, farmer
Stewart, John, steam flour and saw mills
Taylor, James, wagon maker
Thomas, H. A., teacher
Prentice, John, groceries and dry goods
Walker, James, farmer
Walker, John, farmer
Wilson, W., blacksmith

Carnarvon.—A post-office in the Township of Stanhope, County Peterboro'.
BARNUM ANDREW, Postmaster.

Carnegie.—A post-office in the Township of Elderslie, County Bruce.
EWART, SAMUEL, Postmaster.

Carp.—A village in the Township of Huntley, County Carleton, 20 miles from Ottawa, County Town. Stages to Ottawa and Pakenham. Population 125.

Alexander, T. C., carriage-maker
Bell, Rev. R., (Wesleyan)
Brown, Thomas, wheelright
Brown, Thomas, bookkeeper
Butler, J., druggist
Evoy, W., shoemaker
Falls & Stewart, blacksmiths
Featherston, W. J., lumber and general merchant
Godfrey, Rev. J., (Church of England)
Green, Edward, blacksmith
Green, John, hotel keeper
Kidd, Richard, J.P., farmer
Law, William
McBride, H., J.P.
Mealy, George & Brother, general merchants
Newton, E. J., saddler
Roberts, J. E., cabinet maker
Sinclair, Rev. J., (Presbyterian)
Taylor, T., hotel keeper
Wilton, G., pump maker

Carronbrook.—A Village and Station on the Buffalo and Lake Huron Railway, in the Township of Logan, County Perth. Distant from Stratford, the County Town, 17 miles, from Toronto 100 miles. Stages to Cromarty and Brodhagen. Money order office. Population 100.

Baker, Elijah, butcher
Belt, Henry, bookseller
Biles, John, wagon maker
Carpenter, James shoemaker
Carpenter, William, butcher
Carpenter, W., proprietor Donegana Hotel
Carroll Timothy, railway agent
CARRONBROOK TIMES, (Friday), R. L. Smith, editor
Caulfield, Rev. R. H., (Church of England)
Coleman, Robert, accountant
Comber, Edward, marble works
Conlogue, Patrick, carpenter
Conlogue, William, carpenter
Cronin, Daniel, M.D.
Davidson, John, cooper
Dewitt, Thomas, shoemaker
Donkin, R., J.P.
Drummond, Hugh, dealer in stone and lime
Eaton, James, shingle maker
Fegan, Bernard, carpenter
Ferguson, J., insurance agent
Flaherty. J. & Co., general merchants
Flynn, Thomas
Freill, Neil, carpenter
Gallagher, F., prop. Railway Hotel
Harbor, John, brickmaker
Harris & Son, general merchants
Henderson, O. G., & Co., planing mill proprietors
Hoskin, Rev. James (Methodist)
Howard, James, distiller
Howard, William, cabinet maker
Johnston, Frederick, baker
Keating, Stephen, tailor
Kennedy, J., prop. Metropolitan Hotel
Kennedy, Solomon, shoemaker
KIDD, JOSEPH, J.P., Postmaster, general merchant and miller
Kidd, George, telegraph operator
King, Henry, real estate agent
King, Thomas, express agent
King, T. & L., general merchants, agents American Exchange Company
Lambert, Henry, shoemaker
Looby, Edward, wagon maker
McCarron, F. J., auctioneer
McCardy, James, general merchant
McDonald, George A., attorney at law
McLaren, John, accountant
McNevin, Donald, tailor
Malcolm, John, mason
Maldoon, Frank, distiller
Matthews, Thomas, carpenter
Milne, James & Co,. general merchants
Murphy, John, painter
Nevin, Mrs., proprietor Union Hotel
Nevin, P., proprietor Albion Hotel
Oughton, M., cabinet maker
O'Leary, Denis, druggist
Peirce, James, founder and machinist
Platt, W. B., lumber merchant
Pursell, James, saddler
Reading, J. F., general merchant
Reid, Samuel, builder, & sash factory
Robinson & Co., hardware
Rundle, P. L., general merchant
Ryan, Thomas, shoemaker
Smith, Henry, fancy goods
Smith, Isaac, general merchant
SMITH, R. L., editor *Times*
Smith, W. D., tinsmith
Thompson & Co., general merchants
Tole, John
Williams, James, carpenter
Williams, Matthew, carpenter

Carthage.—A Village on Smith's Creek, Township of Mornington, County Perth, 26 miles from Stratford the County Town. Tri-weekly mails. Population 120.

Armstrong, John, blacksmith
Atchison, Stewart, shoemaker
Baillie Hugh, engineer
Balance, Alexander, farmer
BROWN, C., Postmaster, hotel keeper & cooper
Donaghan, Bernard, general merchant
Eslie, Henry, cooper
Gamble, James, miller
Glenn, Charles, farmer
Hamilton, Thomas, farmer
Harvey, Andrew, farmer
Hosier, William, shoemaker
McDonald, Alexander, farmer
Meloin, David, miller
Patterson, Samuel, general merchant
Phillip, George H., carpenter
Phillip, Oran, carpenter
Robertson, Alexander, farmer
Schneider, Charles, general merchant
Sheppard, Rev. W. W., (Methodist)

Carrville.—A Village on the west branch of the Don, in the Township of Vaughan, County York. Distant from Toronto, the County Town, 17 miles. Average price of land, $40 to $50. Population, 50.

Ansley, Thomas, teacher
Atkinson, George
Bone, John
Bone, Thomas
Campbell, John
Combs, John
COOK, THOMAS, Postmaster
Cook, William
Johnston, Rev. William, (Primitive)
Keffer, Joseph
Lund, William, general merchant
Rumble, Joseph, miller
Rupert, Peter, jun
Yateman, Richard

Cartwright.—(See Williamsburgh.)—A Post office in the Township of Cartwright, County Durham.
VANCE, WILLIAM, Postmaster.

Cashel.—A post Village in the Township of Markham, County York. Population about 100.

Crosby, M. B., general merchant
Jennings, Samuel, J.P
Walker, Francis, blacksmith

Cashmere.—A Village on the River Thames, in the Township of Moss, County Middlesex. Distant from London, the County Seat, 40 miles, from Toronto 154 miles. Average price of land $50. Population 200

Bell, Thomas, teacher
Campbell, Alexander, farmer
Campbell, Donald, carpenter
Carson, Samuel, farmer
Downie, Robert, farmer
Farewell, Thomas, prop. Cashmere Hotel
Ferguson, John, miller
Fleming, George, farmer
Fleming, G. B., farmer
Fleming, John, farmer
Fleming, William, farmer
Ford, Thomas, carpenter
Gardiner, James, lumber dealer
Gibb, Singleton
Lewis, Alonzo T., constable
McIntyre, John
McNeil, Hector, wagon maker
MANSFIELD, GEORGE, Postmaster & gen. mercht
Meyer, Abraham
Pucksey, William
Ward, G. G., insurance agent
Wood, James E., cabinet maker

Casselman.—A post Village in the Township of Cambridge, County Russell. Distant from L'Orignal 40 miles, and from Ottawa 26 miles,
CASSELMAN, JOHN SAXON, Postmaster.

Castleford.—A Village on the Ottawa River, in the Township of Horton, County Renfrew.

Fox, John, shoemaker
Hannock, John, hotel keeper
JOHNSTON, ELLIOTT, Postmaster
McDonald, Martin, hotel keeper
McWilliams, James, merchant
Macklem, George, carpenter
Wilson, John, gunsmith
Young, Archibald, merchant

Castleton.—A Village in the Township of Cramahe, County Northumberland, 18 miles from Cobourg, the County Town. Stages to Colborne and Norwood. Money order office. Population, 300.

Andrews, W. H., carpenter
Armstrong, Samuel, blacksmith
Black, E. H., J.P., general merchant
Bowen, W. R., general merchant
Cole, C., general merchant
Cole, R. A., tailor
Coleman, Hiram, shoemaker
Deviney, William, painter
Dorland, A. T., grist and saw miller
Dixon, Samuel, teacher
Eralick, A. C, baker
Gould, C. M., M.D.
Gould, H. P., general merchant.
Griffiths, William, carpenter
Ingersoll, H., blacksmith
Jones, Willis, general agent
Lapp. Chester, flour mill proprietor
McDonald, Samuel, wagon maker
Mitchell, Wesley, butcher
Moore, S., hotel keeper
Nichol, William, blacksmith
Pennock, George W., general merchant
PENNOCK, JOHN C., Postmaster, insurance agent
Pennock, L. J., grocer
Pettibone, Jacob, wagon maker
Pomeroy, Henry, carpenter
Robison, Edward, shoemaker
Scripture, George, grocer
Simmonds, A. W., Temperance Hotel
Stimers, J. W., saddler
Truesdell, Benjamin, carpenter

Castlemoor,—A post Village in the Gore of Toronto, County Peel. 9¾ miles from Brampton, the County Town. Mails bi-weekly. Population 74.

HASSARD, FRANK, Postmaster and hotel keeper.

Cataraqui.—(formerly Waterloo)—A Village in the Township of Kingston, County Frontenac, 3 miles from Kingston, the County Town. Population 200.

Beamish, William, M. D.
Brown, Marshall S., M. D.
Caldwell, Andrew, farmer
Caldwell, William, farmer
Case, Rev. George (Wesleyan)
Clyde, Thomas, farmer
Daly, Mrs. J., hotel keeper
Day, Johnson, J. P., farmer
Ealey, Samuel, tailor
Ferris, J. P., farmer
Hennessey, Mrs., hotel keeper
Marriott, George, farmer
Marriott, Stephen, farmer
Martin, Mrs., hotel keeper
McKIM, PETER, J. P., Clerk Division Court
NORTHMORE, JOSEPH, Postmaster. gen. mercht.
Reilly, Edward, blacksmith
Simpson, John, jun., J. P., farmer
Stewart, John, shoemaker
Walker, George, fanning mill manufacturer

Cavan.—A small Village in the Township of Cavan, County Durham, 30 miles from Cobourg and 3½ from the Port Hope, Lindsay, and Peterboro' Railway. This is a good place for mechanics of all kinds. Improved land averages $40 per acre. Population 150.

Allen, Rev. T. W. (Church of England)
Caswell, Rev. J. (N. C. Methodist)
Coe, John, farmer
Dexter, John, carpenter
Fee, William, farmer
GRAHAM, WILLIAM, Postmaster, general store
Graham, William, farmer
Grandy, Thomas, farmer
Haggarth, Thomas, wagon maker
Hutchison, William, hotel keeper
Lough, William, flour mill proprietor
Manen, George, leather dealer
Newton, James, tailor
Rowan, Thomas R., M. D.
Smith, Richard, druggist
Stapes, Richard, farmer
Swain, John, farmer
Thompson, C.
Thompson, James, cabinet maker
Young, Charles, teacher

Cayuga.—The County Town of Haldimand, situated on the Grand River in the Township of North Cayuga, 25 miles from Hamilton, and 6 from Canfield station on the Buffalo and Lake Huron Railroad. A large quantity of grain and plaster is shipped annually. Money Order office and Savings Bank. Population 700.

Baird, Alexander, tinsmith
Baker, Thomas, builder
Barnes, W. A., barber
Baxter, J., M. D. and J. P.
Baxter, R., M. D.
BURGESS, J. L., saddle and harness maker (see adv)
CAMERON, D., chemist and druggist, agent Montreal Telegraph Company
CAMPBELL, E. C., proprietor Haldimand *Advocate*
Campbell & Smith, hotel keepers
CAMPBELL HOUSE, Joshua Mason prop. (See adv)
"CAYUGA SENTINEL," (Friday) George A. Messenger editor and proprietor
Collins, William, hotel keeper
COLTER, C. W., principal grammar school
DeCew, John, dry goods and clothing
Dochstader, H., hotel keeper
DOMINION HOTEL, A. T. Jones proprietor
Durlong, J., hotel keeper
Farrell, A. P., County Treasurer
Gibbons, Joseph, tailor
Gibney, Miss, teacher
GIBSON, G. A., wine and spirit merchant
Grant, Rev. Mr., (Methodist)
Griffith, R. V., clerk County Court and deputy Clerk Crown
Haldimand Advocate (Friday) E. C. Campbell prop
H—ry, Charles, blacksmith
Hill, Rev., Mr., (Church of England)
Hoshall, John, teacher
Hurssell, Joseph, produce merchant
Hurssell, Joseph
JONES, A. F., hotel keeper
Lawrence, William, gaoler
Leith, Rev. M. (N. C. Methodist
Lightall, P., baker
McClung, D., butcher
McCLUNG, W. R., boot and shoe maker
McDonald, Angus
McGillivray, D., tailor
McMullen, Daniel, hotel keeper
Martin, J. R., County Attorney, Clerk of Peace
MARTIN, RICHARD, Sheriff
MASON, JOSHUA, prop. Campbell House and Stage proprietor (see adv.)
Mason, William, mail conductor
MESSENGER, GEORGE A., Postmaster, editor *Sentinel*, book, job and ornamental printer
Orr, Thomas, painter
Park, Paul, butcher
Robinson, Mrs. J., Commercial Hotel
Rogers, J. H., J. P.
Soyers, Edmund M., general merchant
Stevenson, J. G., County Judge
THOMPSON, DAVID, M. P. P.
Walters, John, general merchant
Younglove, S., watchmaker

Cataract.—A Village on the River Credit, in the Township of Caledon, County Peel, 9 miles from Brampton, the County Town, and 45 from Toronto. Stages to Brampton and Orangeville. Population 100.

Cameron, D., farmer
Cameron, James, farmer
CHURCH, RICHARD, Postmaster & gen. mercht.
Hammond, James
Hunt, William, builder
Keys, Robert, hotel keeper
Little, John, builder
McNichol, H. J., farmer
McSorley, P., farmer
Mallison, Thomas, carpenter
Morrow, Thomas, farmer
Murphy, William, shoemaker
Scott, Isaac, farmer
Smith, J., farmer
Vernon, William, farmer

Cathcart.—A Village in the Township of Burford, County Brant, 14 miles from Brantford, the County Town. Population 150.

MUIR, THOMAS, Postmaster.

Cawdor.—A Post-village in the Township of Kaladar, County Addington.

CAMPBELL, ARCHIBALD, Postmaster.

Cedar Grove.—A Village on the Rouge River, in the Township of Markham, County York. Distant from Toronto the County Town, 20 miles. Average price of land $60. Population 40.

Allison, Andrew, farmer
Burrows, James, farmer
Clark, James, farmer
LAPP, DAVID, Postmaster and general merchant
Lapp, Joseph, farmer
Milroy, John, farmer
Perry, William, farmer
Reesor, Peter, farmer
Reesor, Samuel, farmer
Reesor, Simeon, farmer
Whaley, David, farmer

Cedar Hill.—A small Post Village in the Township of Pakenham, County Lanark. Distant from Perth, the County Town, 30 miles, from Ottawa 150 miles, and from Montreal 150 miles. Population about 80.

CONNERY, JAMES, Postmaster.

Centre Augusta.—A Village in the Township of Augusta, County Grenville, 16 miles from Brockville, the County Town, 12 from Prescott and 6 from Spencerville. Lands in the vicinity average $24 per acre, improved $35. Stages daily to Prescott, fare 25c., to Spencerville 20c. Population 200.

Black, O'Neil, farmer
Brady, James. farmer
Brown, S., wagon maker
COMMONS, AARON B., Postmaster
Commons, Abraham, farmer
Davis, B., shingle maker
Davis, Marcus, shingle maker
Gay, Thomas, hotel keeper
Haud, W., butcher
Kingston, Paul, farmer
Lane, Charles, J.P.
McGrath, Maurice, farmer
McLean, J., wagon maker
McLean, Solomon, C., teacher
McLean, William, farmer
Murphy, Michael, farmer
O'Reilly, Terence, farmer
Roach, Rev. E. P., (Roman Catholic)
Steele, Joseph, farmer
Steele, S., carpenter
Stevenson, F., J.P.
Throop, B., farmer

Centreton.—A Village in the Township of Haldimand, County Northumberland, 16 miles from Cobourg, the County Town, and 100 from Toronto. Average value of land in vicinity, $25 Population 100.

Burns, Patrick, farmer.
Bradley, William, agent
Brewster, John, J.P., farmer
Campbell, Rev. Mr., (Episcopal Methodist)
Coffee, Thomas, farmer
Finn, Rev. William, (Episcopal Methodist)
Holland, William, farmer
McAULEY, THOMAS H., Postmaster, gen. mercht.
McBride, William, farmer
McCann, Abraham, shoemaker
Purdy, Smith, shingle manufacturer
Sargent, Willis, J.P., farmer
Slade, Alfred, farmer
Thomas, James, farmer
Wills, Thomas, farmer
Workman, George, teacher

Cedarville.—A small Post Village in the Township of Proton, County Grey. Distant from Owen Sound the County Town, 46 miles, and from Toronto 60 miles. Population about 30.

ROGERS, THOMAS, Postmaster and gen. merchant. | Rogers, W. & T., merchants and mill owners.

Centreville.—A Village on Whelan's Creek, in the Township of Camden, County Addington. Distant from Napanee, the County Town, 15 miles, from Toronto, 180 miles. Stages to Kingston, Napanee, and Tamworth. Average price of land $30. Population 150.

Ash, John R., M.D.
Carswell, Samuel, wagon maker
Cunningham, —, prop. Cunningham's Hotel
Dowling, Misses E. & H., dressmakers
HAWLEY, JAMES M., Postmaster
Hawley & Bros., general merchants
Hassard Miss C., dressmaker.
Lapum, Jamas N, general merchant
Loughead, James, carpenter
McNamara, John, teacher
O'Connor, William, teacher
Parks, Jerome, saddler
Prout, John, teacher
Reid, R., prop. Reid's Hotel
Reynolds, George, teacher
Robertson, Samuel, cooper
Rupert, Rev. E. S., (Wesleyan)
Switzer, Wilson J., M.D.
Toomey. Rev. John, (Roman Catholic)
Whelan, William, Village Clerk
Whelan, J., prop. Whelan's Hotel
Wills, George, carpenter
Wright, Rev. Peter, (Methodist Episcopal)

Chandos.—A small Post Village of the Township of Chandos, County Peterboro', E. R.
MAXWELL, H., Postmaster.

Charing Cross.—A Village on the line between the Townships of Raleigh and Harwich, County Kent, 7 miles from Chatham, the County Town, and 5 miles from Blenheim. Average value of improved land in the vicinity $35 per acre. Population 100.

Bennett, William, carriage maker
Chapman, Rev. William, Methodist
Drewry, Robert, farmer
Frampton, John, teacher
GAY, J., Postmaster
Knott, John, farmer
McCallum, Rev. Edwin, Methodist
Mancill, William, hotel keeper
Roe, Thomas, hotel keeper
White, Cyrus, butcher
White, Henry, farmer
White, Stephen, farmer

Charleston.—A Village on Charleston Lake, in the Township of Escott, County Leeds, 18 miles from Brockville. Population 100.

Beale, Benjamin, saw mill prop.
Booth, A. C., J. P.
Booth, R. L., inn keeper
Burrows, William, grist mill prop.
GREEN, P. F., Postmaster, general merchant
Hamilton David, J. P.
Hicks, William, wagon maker
Johnston, Henry, J. P.
Melvina, John, inn keeper
Slack & Foster, saw mill props.

Charleville.—A Village on Nation River, in the Township of Augusta, County Grenville. Distant from Prescott, County Town, 12 miles, from Ottawa 45 miles, from Toronto 200 miles. Population 150.

Alden, Miss Jane, teacher
Alder, Miss Levice, dressmaker
Alden, William
Anderson, Jesse
Barton, John
Bass, David
Bass, Henry
Bass, James
Bass, J.
Birks, Edward B.
Birks, Richard
Carson, John
Covill, Stephen
Dakins, Elisha
Kirby, Wilson
Lane, Charles, J. P.
Lane, James
Lane, Joseph
Mosher, James
Perrin, Ebenezer
Place, Wright
Stevenson, Thomas
Tanney, William
Throop, Benjamin
Throop, Justus
Throop, Samuel
Whitney, Calvin
Whitney, Samuel
Wiley, John
Young, Joseph
Young, William

R. Y. ELLIS & BROTHER,

WHOLESALE AND RETAIL DEALERS IN

Shelf and Heavy Hardware,

PAINTS, OILS, GLASS, &c.,

Corner of King and Thames Streets,

INGERSOLL.

S. G. READ'S,

No. 1 Store, Pool's Block, Thames Street, Ingersoll, Ontario.

IS THE RIGHT PLACE TO BUY

STAPLE AND FANCY DRY GOODS.

A GOOD STOCK OF CLOTHING ALWAYS ON HAND.

A beautiful selection of TWEEDS and CLOTHS at extremely low prices. CLOTHING MANUFACTURED TO ORDER, IN THE VERY BEST STYLE, and all Cloths bought at the Store, CUT FREE OF CHARGE.

S. G. READ, Thames St., No. 1 Store.

HEARN'S ROYAL HOTEL,

AND GENERAL STAGE HOUSE.

H. HEARN, - - - - PROPRIETOR.

Free Omnibus to and from Trains. Livery attached.

INGERSOLL, ONT,

Music Hall and Billiard Room attached.

JACOB TURNER & CO.,

DEALERS IN STOVES!

AND MANUFACTURERS OF

Cheese Vats and Dairymen's Implements!

Also, TIN, COPPER and JAPAN WARE; and dealers in LAMPS, COAL OIL, &c.

Thames Street, north of G. W. R. Station, Ingersoll. Ont.

Chatham—The County Town of Kent, is advantageously situated on the River Thames, at the head of navigation, and is one of the most important towns on the Great Western Railway. Large quantities of grain and farm produce of every description, and stave and square timber, are exported from this place. The Churches are numerous, and handsomely constructed. The Merchants' and the Royal Canadian Banks have each established branches here. Chatham is also noted for its mechanical prosperity. There are three large flouring mills, viz: the Kent, City and Union Mills, two carding and woolen mills, the Chatham machine works of Messrs. Hyslop & Ronald, who manufacture reaping and mowing machines extensively, several other foundry and machine shops, tanneries, breweries and numerous saw mills, the manufacture of lumber is carried on here very extensively. The steamer *Dominion* plies regularly during the season of navigation between Chatham, Windsor and Detroit. Chatham is distant from Toronto, per Great Western Railway, 179 miles, from London 64, and from Hamilton 140. Daily stages to Morpeth, Wallaceburg, St. Thomas and Dresden. Port of Entry. Money order office and Savings' Bank. Population about 5,000.

Abbs, Richard, farmer
Adams, John, fanning mill maker
Adam, Robert (Downie & Adam)
ADAMS, WILLIAM, groceries, wines, liquors, &c.
ADDIS, SALEM G., saw miller
Allen, James, currier
Allen, Robert, photographer
Alexander, John, dry goods
American Express Office, Thomas McCrae, agent
Anderson, Levi, cooper
ANDREAE, RUDOLPH, dyer and scourer
Askin, Charles J. S., M.D.
Atkinson, Alexander W., clerk registry office
Baker, W. P , photographer
Ball, William, saw miller
Ball, William, stoves and tinware
Baird, Mrs. Robert, straw and felt worker
BARFOOT, SAMUEL R., Postmaster
Barr, Robert, M.D.
Bartlett, Henry, machinist
Bartlett, Lewis, builder and carpenter
Baxter, A. B., dry goods
Baxter, Henry, mason
Baxter, John, carpenter and builder
Baxter, James H., miller
Baxter, James, carpenter
Baxter & Reed, grocers
Baxter. Thomas H., carpenter
Baxter, William, flour mill proprietor
Beaver, —, M.D.
Beaver Mutual Insurance Company, John J. J. Thompson, agent
Bennett, Thomas, distiller
BERARD, AUGUSTUS, prop. St. Charles Restaurant
Berry, Mrs. J. W., milliner
Berry, William, livery stable
Berube, George, book keeper
Biles, J , auctioneer
Birch, James, teacher
BISSELL, F. R., prop. Rankin House. (See adv.)
BLACKBURN, L. A., groceries and provisions
BLACK, HARRY, exchange broker, cigars & tobacco (See adv)
BOGART, A. D., flour, feed and provisions
Bogart, Alfred carpenter
Bogart, James
BOYD, GRANDISON, hides, wool and provision dealer
Bogart, Nicholas, salesman A. D. Bogart
Brady, John, shoemaker
Brady, John, carpenter and contractor
Brady, Thomas, cattle dealer
Brady, P., mechanic
Bradley, P., butcher
Bray, John L., M. D., coroner
Bridges, John, carpenter
BRIGHT, J. C., M. D., chemist and druggist
Brown, Richard C.
Brown, J. W., exchange broker
Buckle, George, St. George's Saloon
Burns, James, boots and shoes
Bush, Rev. F., (Baptist)
Caledonia Hotel, Alexander McIntosh, proprietor
Cameron, Donald. dry goods
Campbell, Duncan, farmer
Campbell, Kenneth, groceries and provisions
Campbell, P. McVean, barrister
Campbell, William, (McColl & Campbell)
CAMPBELL, K., groceries and provisions
Cartier, Charles
Carr, Hugh, grocer
Carruthers, William, station master G.W.R.
Chapman, John, photographer, chemist and druggist
CHARTERIS, JOHN C., commission & general agent
Chatten, Robert, boots and shoes
"CHATHAM BANNER," J. R. Gemmell, Jr., editor and proprietor. (See adv.)
CHATHAM PLANET, (weekly and tri-weekly) Rufus Stephenson, M. P. P., editor and proprietor (See adv.)
Charity, James H., boot and shoemaker
Charteris, A
Charteris, Charles G , County Treasurer
Chinnick, William, saloon
Chrysler, H., tax collector,
City Flouring Mills, Draper & Castle, proprietors
Cleeve, James, lumber dealer
COATE & LAMONT, wholesale dealers in pot and pearl ashes. (See adv.)
Coate, Philip S., (Coate & Lamont)
Connilleau, Rev. C.S., S. J. Rector, (R. C.)
Conroy, Samuel, tailor
Cooper, Ezekiel C., groceries, &c
Cooper, Robert, bookseller and stationer, and agent Montreal Telegraph Company
Courtilette, John L., gardener
Courtelette, L., confectioner
Cowan, Samuel, harness maker
CUDMORE, RICHARD, auctioneer & commission merchant
Cumming, H. F., dry goods, clothing, boots & shoes
Cunningham, John, blacksmith
Craddock & Somerville, sash, doors, blinds, planing, &c
Crandall, Henry. carpenter
Cresswell, R. H., Teller Merchants' Bank
CROW, JAMES E., Prop. Star Billiard Saloon. (See adv.)
Cross, Thomas, M.D.
Crow, Mrs. Ann, groceries

Crow, Mrs., milliner
Dalgarno James (Dalgarno, Parkinson & Co.)
Dalgarno, Parkinson & Co., founders and machinists
Day, Wesley, hotel keeper
Davis, Isaac, stove founder
Dennis, S. F., painter
Delabays, Rev. Joseph, (Roman Catholic)
Delos, Louis, tailor
Degge, John, grocer
Dixon, James, grocer, &c
Dickson, Thomas, carpenter
Donovan, James, toll keeper, Old bridge
Dolsen, Joseph, waggon maker
DOLSEN, O. J. V., book keeper *Planet* office
Douglas. James, M. D., coroner
Douglass, William, barrister & attorney, Clerk of Peace
DOWNIE & ADAM, hardware, iron & steel. (see adv)
Downie, John, (Downie & Adam)
Downie, James, (Downie & Adam)
DRAPER & CASTLE, proprietors City flouring mills (See adv)
DRAPER & CASTLE, flour and grain merchants (see adv)
Duck, George, book keeper Register office
Duck, J., landing waiter
Duff, Robert, butcher
DUNLOP & BRO., grocers
DUNHAM, J. D., prop. Parsons House. (see adv.)
Dumortier, Rev. François, (Roman Catholic)
Earl, R. J., commercial traveller
Eberts, Charles, sailor
Eberts, Henry, saw miller and ship owner
Eberts, H. J., general merchant
Eberts, J. M., book keeper H. J. Eberts
Eberts, Captain Walter
ELLISON, J. B., local editor Chatham *Planet*
Escott, William H., confectioner
Etna Fire Insurance Company (Dublin) E. W. Scane, agent
Evans, Israel, livery
Everest, Henry M., shoemaker
FABER, M., proprietor Faber's Hotel
Farrell, Richard, leather findings, boots and shoes
Fonteneau, E., blacksmith
FORDHAM, DANIEL, boot and shoe maker
Fordham, Miss Mary, milliner, &c
Forsyth, Daniel, tax collector
Fountain, E., groceries and provisions
FRASER, WILLIAM, watchmaker and jeweller
Frances, William P., butcher
FREEMAN & FREEMAN, barristers, &c
Freeman, George O., (Freeman & Freeman)
FULLARTON, JAMES, prop. Royal Exchange Hotel (see adv)
GARDINER & BROTHER, (W. E. & S. F.) bankers and exchange brokers. (see adv)
Garner, John, proprietor Kent Brewery
Gemmell, James, carriage maker
GEMMELL, J. R., Jr., prop. Chatham *Banner*
Gernay, L., tailor
Gernay, R., merchant tailor
Gillett, Edward, stage proprietor
GLASFORD, ROBERT, prop., Farmers & Mechanics Hotel, North Chatham
Gonne, William, carpenter
GARY, WILLIAM, carriage maker
Green, William, fruits and confectionery
Goodyer, John, chief of police
Gordon, A. G., dry goods
Guttridge, David, tailor
Guttridge, Thomas, blacksmith
HADLEY, SYLVESTER, proprietor planing mill. (See adv)
Hart, James, County Clerk
Harper, James, painter
Harris, James, Agent fruit trees and nurseryman
Hawkins, Nathaniel, grocer
Haylock, Rev. J. (Primitive Methodist)
Higgins, James, boots and shoes
Hill, A. L., landing waiter and florist
Hillman, John, grocer
Hoag, A. N., planing mill
Hoig, William, tailor
Holmes, A. S., J.P., barrister
Holmes, Thomas, flouring mill
Holmes, Tecumseth K., M.D.
HOON, JOHN A., groceries and provisions
Hooper, John, saddler
Howard, William J., boots and shoes
Hughes, E., clerk Merchants' Bank
HYSLOP, JOHN, general dry goods, etc. (See adv)
HYSLOP & RONALD, founders and machinists, agricultural implement manufacturers
IRELAND, THOMAS A., Clerk County Court and Deputy Clerk of the Crown
Ireland, W. S., manager Merchants' Bank
JAQUES, FRANCIS, saddle and harness maker. (See adv)
Jahnke, A., cabinet maker
Jones, Arthur, P.L.S.
Jones, Charles A., clerk Registry Office
Jones, Irvin, barber
Jones, James M., gunsmith
Jones, Francis, barber
KELLY, JOHN B., dry goods, boots and shoes
Kemp, D., accountant Merchants' Bank
Kent, Lubin, groceries wines and liquors
KENT MILLS, Robert Lowe, proprietor
Kitson, Jonathan, grocer
KOGELSCHATZ F. W., cigars and tobacco
Lamont, Archibald
Lamont, Donald
Lamont, H. & M., (Hector & Malcolm) gen. merchts.
LAMONT, JAMES, dealer in grain, wool and provisions, general agent. (See adv)
Lamont, L. C., grain buyer
Lennox, Charles P., dentist
Leonard, Julius, groceries, provisions and liquors
LOWE, ROBERT, prop. Kent flouring mills
McColl, Rev. Angus, (Canada Presbyterian)
McCormick, Mrs. James, milliner
McCrae, Thomas, Police Magistrate
McCrae, William A.
McCrea, Hon. Walter, (McCrea & Robinson)
McCrea & Robinson, barristers
McCROSSAN, THOMAS, dealer in dry goods, groceries, hats, caps, &c
McCully, S. E., M. D., coroner
McDONELL, A., P. L. S. and agent Royal Ins. Co.
McDonell, J. A., C. H. broker
McGregor, A. R., landing waiter & clk Custom House
McIntosh, A. B., wholesale and retail grocer
McIntosh, Alexander, proprietor Caledonia Hotel
McIntosh, John, saddler
McKAY, JOHN, prop. North American Hotel
McKAY, SAMUEL, prop. Star Restaurant. (see adv)
McKELLER, PETER D., County Registrar
McKEOUGH, J. & W. (Jno & William) gen. hardware
McKERRAL, M., saloon
McKerral, John, groceries and provisions
McKerral, P. E., prop, McNaughton's Hotel & grocer
MacNab, Thomas C., clerk Registry Office
McNaughton, Dougald, grocer
McNaughton, D., proprietor Market Hotel
McPherson, A., clerk Rankin House
McQuade, Rev. F. S. J., (Roman Catholic)

Maguire, John, traveller & auctioneer
Malcolmson, Hugh, general merchant
Marling, S. A., M.A., principal grammar school
MARQUAND, J., watchmaker and jeweler (see adv)
Martin, J. W., (Wall & Martin)
MARTIN, THOMAS, bookseller and stationer
Mason, Mrs. Charlotte, toll gate keeper
Medary, Richard, dyer
Merchants' Bank of Canada, W. S. Ireland agent
MERCER JOHN, sheriff
MERRILL, SOLOMON. prop. Union Restaurant
Middlemiss, Robert, foreman cooper
MILES, JAMES W., saloon keeper
Milner, James, grain buyer and constable
MILLER, H. L., constable and detective
Miller, Miles, printer
Miller, R. O. & A. M., dry goods
MONSELL, W. H., agent Royal Canadian Bank
Montreal (Marine) Insurance Co., John J. Thompson, agent
Monck, Richard, land agent
Monk, Henry, gardener
MORRISH, JOHN, post office book store, stationer, &c
Morton, John A., (R. Morton & Co)
Morton, Robert, (R. Morton & Co)
MORTON, R. & CO., general hardware
Mulholland, C., wagon maker
Murphy, —, M.D
Murray, Nathaniel, shoemaker
Nichol, Thomas, gunsmith
Northwood, Henry, lumber merchant
Northwood, John M., grocer
NORTHWOOD, JOSEPH, lumber merchant, dealer in groceries and provisions (see adv.)
Northwood, William
Northwood, William, jun., general merchant
O'HARA, ROBERT, barrister and insurance agent
O'Reilly, Charles P., boot and shoemaker
Oldershaw, James, lime dealer
Orr, George S., pump maker
Oswald, James, carpenter
Oswald, John, painter
Owen, Mrs., milliner
Parkinson, Robert (Dalgarno, Parkinson & Co)
PARSONS HOUSE, J. D. Dunhamprop. (see adv)
PATCHING, WILLIAM J., saloon and restaurant G. W. R. depot
Payne, Robert K
Payne, William, grocer
PEGLEY, CHARLES G., barrister
Pegley, R., M.D., chemist, druggist and coroner
Pennefather, J. G., collector custom house
Phœnix Fire Ins. Co., John J. J. Thompson, agent
Pierce, John S., flour miller
Pierce, Joseph M, wheat buyer
Pile, Charles, boots and shoes
POSTOFFICE, S. BARFOOT, Postmaster
Primoe, Julius, fanning mill maker
Primoe, S., blacksmith
PRIMOE, THEODORE, groceries, provisions, wines and liquors
Quinn, Miss H., milliner
QUIRK, MATTHEW T. (Small & Quirk)
RADLEY, S. D., apothecary
RANKIN HOUSE, F. R. Bissell, proprietor. (See adv)
RANNIE, WILLIAM, dry goods and millinery
Reardon, Mrs. G., boarding house
Reeves, George, blacksmith
Regnier, Rev. F. (Roman Catholic)
REID, JAMES R., merchant tailor. (See adv)
Rice, John, dry goods, boots, shoes, etc.
Richardson, W., (Smith & Richardson)
Riggs, David P., marble works
ROCHE, EDWARD, prop. St. Nicholas Restaurant
Ronald, John, (Hyslop & Ronald)
Rolls, Arthur M., chemist and druggist
ROLLS, JAMES A., barrister
Rolls, J. A., M.D., coroner, chemist and druggist
Rose, George D., general merchant
Ross Miss A., milliner and dressmaker
RUTLEY, THOMAS R. G., prop. Rutley House
Royal Canadian Bank, W. H. Monsell, agent
Sandys, Rev. F. W., D.D., R.D., (Church of England)
Scane, E. W., barrister
Schneider, John, carriage trimmer
Scribner, George W., organs and melodeons
Shackleton, Mrs. M. A., prop. Court House Hotel
Shadd, Isaac D., groceries and provisions
Sherriff Brothers, carriage and wagon makers
Shotwell, G., cabinet maker
Singer, W., grocer
Siverwright, James H., M.D
Slade, John, manuf. and dealer in boots and shoes
Slade, Mrs. J., photographer
SMALL & QUIRK, pumps, flour barrels, staves, straw cutters, &c., (see adv)
Smith, Andrew, blacksmith
Smith, Charles, cooper
Smith, David, grocer
Smith, Frederick F., shoemaker
Smith, Henry
Smith, Isaac, (Smith & Richardson)
SMITH, JOHN & SONS, tanners and curriers, patentees of leather horse nets, saddlers, &c
Smith, John, gardener
Smith, John, farrier
Smith, John, (J. Smith & Sons)
Smith, James M., foreman tanner
Smith, Joseph, blacksmith
Smith, R. O., cabinet maker and undertaker
Smith & Northwood, photographers
Smith & Richardson, (Isaac Smith and W. Richardson) merchant tailors
Snook, Thomas, grocer
SONTAR, JAMES & CO., dealers in agricultural implements, patent rights, seeds, &c
SPARKS, J. W., watchmaker and jeweler
Springer, Oliver, M.D
Stammelen, Mrs. Ignatius, hotel proprietress
Stanton, Thomas, marble cutter
Stark, L. F., founder & machinist (Sontar & Co)
Steinhoff, J. W., captain steamer Dominion
STEPHENSON, RUFUS, M.P.P., editor and proprietor Chatham *Planet*
Stevens, J. J., grocer
Stewart, Mrs. E., groceries
Stringer, George, commission merchant
Stringer, John, proprietor Great Western hotel
STONE, THOMAS, general merchant
Sturman, G. J., proprietor Farmers' Exchange
Sutherland & Richards, bakers and confectioners
Swan, James, weaver
Taylor, Ingram, farmer
Taylor, John, proprietor Farmers' Hotel
Taylor, John W., barber
Taylor, Robert, photographer
Taylor, Captain William J.
TAYLOR, THOMAS H. & CO., woolen manufacturers and dealers in wool (see adv)
Taylor & Williamson, grocers
Tetrault, N. dry goods
Thacker, John, carpenter
Thompson, John D., wagon maker
Thompson, John J. J., general insurance agent

Tilt & Baxter, builders and contractors
Tissiman, John, town clerk and insurance agent
Traxler, Isaiah, grain merchant
Traxler, Salem, grain merchant
Turner & Lambert, sodawater manufacturers
Union Ins. Co., John J. J. Thompson, agent
URQUHART, KENNETH, groceries, glass and crockery (see adv)
Van Allen, Daniel, lumber merchant
Van Allen, John P., foreman *Planet* office
Verrall, Henry, clerk postoffice.
Verrall, George W., job printer
Verrall, S., grocer
Walker & Leith, tanners and curriers
WALLACE, STEPHEN, hotel keeper
Wanless, Thomas K., shoemaker and constable
Wall & Martin, dry goods and clothing
Warren, Duncan,
Warren, James, attorney
WELLS, WILLIAM BENJAMIN, Judge of County Court,
Weaver, Henry, grocer
Wells, William B., law student
Weir, J. C., clerk American Express Company
Westcott, F., teller Royal Canadian Bank
White, William W., dentist
Whitworth, Rev. W. E., (Primitive Methodist)
Williams, George, attorney-at-law & clk Surrogate Ct
Williston, Louis, proprietor Chatham Arms Hotel
Wilson, Archibald, barber
Windsor, E., (Dalgarno, Parkinson & Co)
Windsor, F., (Dalgarno, Parkinson & Co)
WINSLOW, GEORGE S., billiards, (see adv)
Winter, Alfred, blacksmith
Winter, George, hatter and furrier
WOODS & CAMPBELL, (R. S. Woods & P. McVean Campbell,) barristers
Wortley, Robert, groceries and provisions
YOUNG, GEORGE E., groceries, wines and liquors
Young, W. & J., wagon makers
Younger, Mrs. Mary, boarding house

Chatsworth.—A Village in the Townships of Holland and Sullivan, County Grey. Distant from Owen Sound, the County Town 9½ miles, from Toronto 98 miles. Stages to Owen Sound, Durham and Guelph. Average price of land $12 to $16. Money order office. Population 170.

Baskerville, Rev. James, (New Connexion)
Brese, Stephen H., general merchant and proprietor California House
Bristol, Edward, blacksmith
Burgess, John A., M.D.
Cameron, Alexander, general merchant
Cameron, Rev. James, (Presbyterian)
Campbell, —, saddler
Campbell, Alexander, proprietor Carriboo House
Cardwell, David, photographer
CARDWELL, HENRY, Postmaster
Casserly, Michael, farmer
Cummings, James, teacher
Curtis, George, wagon maker
Duffie, Joseph, blacksmith
Foster, Samuel, shoemaker
Foster, Samuel C., farmer
Freeman, Richard, plasterer
Gibson, Thomas, tinsmith
Graham, Samuel, teacher
Graham, Simon, teacher
Hill, Rev. Joseph, (Wesleyan)
Hopkins, John, shoemaker
Hopkins, Joseph, prop. Queen's Arms Hotel
Kingsberry, Stephen, tanner
Leggett, Gore, wagon maker
McGill, Andrew, iron founder
McGregor, Duncan, M.D.
Merriam, Justus, cabinet maker
Merriam, Manchester, carpenter
Morehouse, George, carpenter
Mulholland, Rev. A. H. R., (Church of England)
Redfern, James, cooper
Richardson, Samuel, blacksmith
Shouldice, John, farmer
Thorpe, Charles, farmer
Van Felson, Charles, druggist

Cheapside.—A Village in the Township of Walpole, County Haldimand. Distant from Cayuga, the County Town, 13 miles, from Toronto 75 miles. Stages to Port Dover and Dunnville. Average price of land $20. Population 70.

Blackman, Theodore, teacher
Buckley, James
Buckley, John
Buckley, Robert
Byrers, Rev. —, (Wesleyan)
Day, Samuel, saddler
Dick, John, blacksmith
Hammond, Thomas, teacher
Hobbs, Aaron, miller
Puysley, Rev. W. (Baptist)
PUYSLEY, W., Postmaster and general merchant
Schissler, Martin, shoemaker
Sheek, George, M.D.
Shilderick, James, blacksmith
Silverthorn, George
Sloan, William, auctioneer
Steele, Edward E., wagon maker.

Cheltenham.—A Post Village on the River Credit, in the Township of Chinguacousy, County Peel. Distant from Brampton, the County Town, 12 miles, from Toronto 38 miles. Daily mail. Population about 200. (See Villages too late, at the end of the work.)

CAMPBELL, JOHN, Postmaster.

Cherry Creek.—A Village in the Township of Innisfil, County Simcoe, 14 miles from Barrie, the County Town, 4 miles from Lefroy Station, Northern Railway, and 51 miles from Toronto. Average value of improved lands in the vicinity $25 per acre. A creek in the neighborhood affords good power for machinery. Population 100.

Beatman, Thomas, sen., farmer
Beatman, Thomas, jr., farmer
Clement, Lewis, J.P
Kell, William, farmer
Kirkpatrick, Francis, farmer
Lennox, Lambert, teacher
Lynn, Isaac, farmer
Main, John, carpenter
Main Richard, farmer
Main, W. B., gunsmith
MAIN, WILLIAM, postmaster
Matthews, William, farmer
Sawyer, John, farmer
Tapper, William, farmer
Wilson, Lambert, farmer
Milliken, Robert, shoemaker

Cherry Valley.—A Post-office in the Township of Athol, County Prince Edward.
INSLEY, ISAIAH P., Postmaster.

Chepstow.—A Post Village in the Township of Greenock, County Bruce.
HENESEY, WILLIAM, Postmaster.

Chesley.—A Village in the Township of Elderslie, County Bruce, situated on the north branch of the Saugeen River, 15 miles from Walkerton, the County Town, and 120 from Toronto. Mechanics of all kinds and laborers are required in this section. Improved land in the vicinity averages $20 per acre. Stage to Hanover, 12 miles, fare 75 cents. Population 150.

Adolph, John, wagon maker
Anderson, Duncan, carpenter
Blackwell, T. B., saddler
Cameron, Rev. P., teacher
Campbell, G. dealer in lime and stone
Carter, Henry, tinsmith
Cass, —, carpenter
Clark, A., wagon maker
Cooke, George, M.D
Dobbie, John, farmer
Elliott, J. H., miller
Graham & Co., tailors
Halliday, D. M., general merchant
Irwin, Rev. Mr., (Wesleyan)
Kerr, W., painter
Long, David, carpenter
McDonald, W., shingle maker
McGaw, Joseph, hotel keeper
McLagan, John, farmer
McLagan, P., farmer
McLean, Allen, cooper
McLean, Rev. Mr., (Canada Presbyterian)
McManus, J., farmer
McMANUS, MARK, Postmaster
McManus & McNaughton, general merchants
Quirk, John, shoemaker
Rauhn, Christopher, cabinet maker
Riley, A., wagon maker
Shea, John, shoemaker
Jhoeder, Martin, cooper
Wallace, —, cabinet maker
Winters, Rev. Mr., (Free Church)

Chesterfield.—A Postoffice in the Township of Blenheim, County Oxford, 18 miles from Woodstock, the County Town.
BROWN, WM., Postmaster and Commissioner in B. R.

Churchville.—A Village in the Township of Toronto, County Peel, 5 miles from Brampton the County Town, and 26 from Toronto. The river Credit passes through the Village, affording excellent power for manufacturing purposes. Average price of improved land in vicinity $40 per acre. Stages daily to Malton 9 miles. Population 200.

Anderson, Alexander, shingle maker
Arnett, James, farmer
Atchinson, John, prop. North American Hotel
Fish, Rev. Charles (Wesleyan)
Fogarty, F. A., wagon maker
Frazer, John, carpenter
Hall, Fletcher, farmer
Hall, L. S., farmer
Hall, Salmon, blacksmith
Hardy, William, blacksmith
Harris, Stephen, prop. Revere House
Joice, Maurice, blacksmith
Lake, Rev. Mr., (Episcopal Methodist)
Leslie, John, farmer
Letty, Edward, shoemaker
McClure, James, sen., farmer
McClure, John, jr., farmer
McHugh, John, farmer
Madden, Richard, carpenter
Norton, James, butcher
POINTER, J. E., Postmaster
Pointer, J. E., & R., tanners
Reeve, J. T., farmer
Robinson, Rev. George, (Wesleyan)
Shaw, Rev. Mr., (Episcopal Methodist)
Temple, E., shoemaker
Tisdale, William, farmer
Trew, S. J., teacher
Wilson, John, farmer

Chippawa.—An incorporated Village, on the Erie and Niagara branch of the G. W. R., at the confluence of the Welland and Niagara rivers, in the township of Willoughby, County Welland. Distant from Welland, the County Town, 13 miles, 4 from Niagara Falls, and 82 from Toronto. There is a very extensive distillery here, owned by Messrs. John Thomas & Co., and two tanneries employing a large number of men. Money order office and Savings' Bank. Population 1,200.

Aberdeen, Robert, M.D., druggist
Abraham, W. H., wagon maker
Anderson, James, farmer
Amm, James, tailor
Amm, William, painter
Bartle, John & Co., tanners and curriers
Bond, H., blacksmith
Bosse, Charles
Box, H., grocer
British American Hotel, George Gordon, proprietor.
Caistor, Mrs., grocer
Cameron, Rev. J. Y. (Presbyterian)
Carter, John, blacksmith
Carnochan, A., carpenter
CHIPPAWA DISTILLERY, John Thomas & Co., proprietors
Crane, R. & B., proprietors lumber yard
Cummings, James
Davidson, Thomas, planing mills
Deakers, R., shoemaker
Dobbie, John, farmer
Flemming, William, cabinet maker
FLETT, JOHN, dry goods, groceries, ready-made clothing, boots and shoes (see adv)
Forbes, John, R. N., M.D.
Gerrard, William, teacher
Gilmore, William, blacksmith
Glasher, A., tailor
Glassco, George, farmer
Glosser, William, tailor
GORDON, G., prop. British American hotel (see adv)
Greenwood, William
Hackart, Adam, painter
Herbold, A., dentist
HERBOLD, ADAM, baker, grocer, and flour and feed (see adv.)
Herber. Herman, grocer and cooper
Hill, John, G. W. R.
Higgins, John, grocer
Hume, Mrs., grocer
Hujoe, Thomas, grocer
Ives, Alfred, grocer
Kipp, John, shoemaker
KIRKPATRICK, J. C., J. P.
Kirkpatrick, John C., general merchant
Knarff, John, watchmaker
Lannor, James, cooper
Lauzan, F., cooper
Lennox, E.
Logan, Robert, grocer
Lyons, J., shoemaker
McCredie, Thomas, farmer
MACKLEM, J. F., notary public, banker and money broker
MACKLEM, J. S., Postmaster
MACKLEM, J. S. & L., insurance agents and general merchants (see adv.)
MACKLEM & KIRKPATRICK, tanners
MACKLEM, STREET S., M. D.
MacLeod, Rev. D. J. F. (Church of England)
Marshall, William, farmer
Mater, Rev. M. (Methodist)
Mater, M., gunsmith
Massey, A., wagon maker
Oldfeild, F., butcher
Overholt, Simon, barber
Penrod, Eli, saddler
Peters, E., cabinet maker
PHŒNIX INSURANCE COMPANY, John Thomas & Co., agents
Pierce, Israel, tinsmith
Ross, John, dry goods merchant
Schacht, C., painter
Schurnacher, L., proprietor Railroad House
Shainholdts, E., farmer
Slater, J., farmer
Speck, J., proprietor Exchange
Spitzer, C., grammar school
Swava, G., tailor
THOMAS, JOHN E., insurance agent
THOMAS, JOHN, distiller and rectifier
THOMAS, J. & CO., malsters and grain merchants
Thompson, William, collector inland revenue
Thomas, W. H., (J. Thomas & Co)
Vanwyck, V., cooper
Vinidei, H., shoemaker
Weinbremer, L., gunsmith
Wells, John, farmer
Wells, F., farmer
Welsh, J., Wellington Inn
Wylie, Samuel, butcher
Yarwood, St. George C., Collector of Customs

Church Hill.—A Village in the Township of Innisfil, County Simcoe, 12 miles from Barrie, the County Town, and 2 miles from Lefroy Station, Northern Railway. Population, 120.

Allan, Gavin, J.P., farmer
Boyce, Richard, farmer
Clement, James, general merchant
Coalter, James, carpenter
Cregg, John, hotel keeper
Hempenstall, Robert, blacksmith
Kirkup, James, farmer
McDougall, Daniel, tinsmith
Mathers, John M., wagon maker
Miller, John, blacksmith
Ross, James, M.D
Sheltz, August, potter
SLOAN, HENRY, Postmaster and wagon maker
Sloan, John, farmer
Werner, Lewis, carpenter
Willson, Wellington, farmer
Wray, Samuel, farmer

Clachan.—A small post Village in the Township of Aldborough, County Elgin, distant from St. Thomas, the County Town, 35 miles.

McPHAIL, D., Postmaster

Claremont.—A Village in the Township of Pickering, County Ontario, 16 miles from Whitby, the County Town, and 10 from Frenchman's Creek Station Grand Trunk Railroad. Money Order Office. Population 200.

Appleby, Thomas, butcher
Barry, John, saw mill
Bundy, George, cabinet maker
Bundy, Joshua, tinsmith
Digby, James, saddler
Dowswell, Ambrose, hotel keeper
Dowswell, William, wagon maker
Ecker, Mrs. Isabella, bonnet maker
Eldon, Robert, merchant
Forfar, John, shingle factory
Gerow, George, pump maker
Gerow, John, carpenter
Hopper, George, teacher
Johnston, Thomas, tailor
Lumley, William, painter
McCausland, David, blacksmith
McGregor, J. W., tub and pail factory
McPherson, J., merchant
MACNAB, JOHN M., Postmaster
Macnab, J. & D.. general merchants
Michell, John C., merchant and miller
Michell, William H., conveyancer
Morgan, Alexander, blacksmith
Palmer, John W., shoemaker
Paterson, John, carpenter
Russell, J., oatmill proprietor
Spencer, William, wagon maker
Stafford, Rev. C., (Primitive Methodist)
Stobb, Rev. Thomas, (Wesleyan)
Taylor, Dugald, shoemaker
Watson, William, tailor

Clarence.—A Village in the Township of Clarence, County Russell, distant from Ottawa 27 miles. Averag price of land $7. Money Order office. Population 75.

Boucher, Rev. O. J. (Roman Catholic)
Edwards, W. & G., general merchants
Edwards, W., J. P.
Naubert, F., general merchant
Ramage, J., J. P.
Ross, Rev. J. (Baptist)
Surtees, C., hotel keeper
WILSON, T., Postmaster and general merchant
Woodley, R., hotel keeper

Clarksburg.—A Village on Beaver River, in the Township of Collingwood, County Grey. Distant from Owen Sound, the County Town, 30 miles, from Toronto, 110 miles. Stages to and from Collingwood. Average price of land $20 to $30. Money Order office. Population 300.

Albery, Robert, saddler
Appleby, Rev. Thomas (Church of England)
Barber, Franklin, cabinet maker
Calverly, John, carpenter
Clark, W. A., woolen factor
Cumming, D. N.
Dixon, James, cooper
Donaldson, John, teacher
Elvin, Thomas
Fraser, Hugh, woolen factor
Hazzard, William, proprietor Clarksburg Hotel
Hines, F. W., shoemaker
Hogg, Nicholas, wagon maker
Hunt, R. H., B. M.
HUNTER, WALTER, Postmaster, insurance agent
LeRoy, Frank, proprietor Beaver Valley Hotel
LeRoy, John B., carpenter
Little, William, carpenter
McMaster, James
Marsh, W. J.
Mitchell, Alexander, auctioneer
Rorke, Joseph, attorney-at-law
Sheeres, G. H., carpenter
Sparling, Richard, architect
Sparling, William, carpenter
Tyson, Walter L., miller

Clark's Mills.—(P. O. Camden East)—A Village on the Napanee River, in the Township of Camden, County Addington, 9 miles from Napanee, the County Town. Stages to Kingston, Tamworth, and Napanee. Population 500.

Andrews, Samuel, brewer
Andrews, Thomas, chair maker
Bicknell, Nathan, M. D.
Burgoyne, Joseph, millwright
Bush, William, tanner
Calder, William, tailor
CLARK, BENJAMIN, Postmaster, grocer (see adv.)
Clark, Peter H., manufacturer
Davern, M., miller
Denroche, E. A., teacher
Duncan, Hugh, shoemaker
Duncan, Seth, general merchant
Dunning, A. B., general merchant
Gray, Rev. James (Methodist)
Hamilton, Edward, hotel keeper
Haydon, James, general merchant
Hooper, E. J., M. P. P.
Johnston, Peter, Township Clerk
Kinner, John, blacksmith
Lew, Benjamin, baker
Lewis, Joseph, saddler
Lockwood, Isaac, Clerk Division Court
Lockwood, Jonas, blacksmith
MacDowell, John, Commissioner in B. R.
Nimmo, James, farmer
Reilly, Charles, shoemaker
Robertson, William, painter
Robson, E., butcher
Shaw, Rev. W. (Methodist)
Stanton, Rev. Thomas (Methodist)
Weir, Peter, hotel keeper
Williams, L. D., farmer
Wilson, Charles, carpenter

Clarence Creek.—A Post Village in the Township of Clarence, County Russell.
NEAUBERT, FIRMIN, Postmaster.

Clarke.—(see Newtonville)—A Post Village in the Township of Clarke, County Durham. Money Order office
LOCKHART, JAMES, Postmaster.

Claude.—A Village in the Township of Chinguacousy, County Peel. Distant from Brampton, the Counnty Town, 10 miles, from Toronto, 36. Stages to Brampton and Orangeville. Population 60.

Campbell, James, farmer
Caslor, Hiram, miller
Clunis, Alexander, blacksmith
Croll, Rev. R. (Presbyterian)
Embree, John, shoemaker
Graham, David, woolen factor
Lewis, Joseph, wagon maker
McBride, Daniel, farmer
McCollum, P. J., J.P.
McKechniey, Neil, farmer
Manning, Henry, proprietor Claude hotel
PERDUE, HENRY, Postmaster and general mercht
Robinson, Charles, M.D.
Robinson, George, farmer
Ross, Joseph, tailor
Shipley, John, farmer
Smith, John, farmer
Sutton, William, brick maker
Wiggins, John, farmer

Clavering.—A Post office in the Township of Amabel, County Bruce.
SHACKLETON, JOHN, Postmaster.

Clayten—A Village on the Indian River, in the Township of Ramsay, County Lanark. Distant from Perth, the County Town, 23 miles, from Toronto 260 miles. Average price of land $8. Population 160.

BANNING, OZIAS, Postmaster and general mercht
Bellamy, Edward, farmer
Blair, Edward, carpenter
Blair, Timothy, carding and fulling mill
Bolger, Samuel, farmer
Bussy, John F., shoemaker
Coulter, Thomas, proprietor Coulter's hotel
Cowie, Francis, potash manufacturer
Cram, Henry, wagon maker
Dickson, Mrs. Esther, groceries, &c.
Drummond, D., miller
Drummond, John, farmer
Foster, Edward, farmer
Foster, Edward, shoemeker
Gemmell, John, proprietor Gemmell's hotel
Gibbs, Catherine, dressmaker
Giles, Robert W., blacksmith
Gillon, John, carpenter
Gunn, George, farmer
Hogan, Patrick, tailor
Hopkins, Miss S., teacher
Lelond Xavier, cooper
Letang, Edward, cooper
McClary, James, carpenter
McDonald, Alexander, blacksmith
McDowel, Rev. —, (Wesleyan)
McNeil, George, tanner
McWilliams, Hugh, blacksmith
McWilliams, Joseph, farmer
O'Donnell, Andrew, blacksmith
Saunders, Rev. —, (Church of England)
Shean, John, shoemaker
Watt, Daniel, cabinet maker
Wilson, R. P., miller

Clearville.—A Village in the Township of Orford, County Kent, 30 miles from Chatham, the County Town, 12 miles from Bothwell, and 17 from Thamesville station. Clear Creek, passing through the Village, affords good water power. Average value of land, $30 per acre. Stage to Thamesville, fare, $1 25. Money order office. Population, 105.

Baily, Robert, shingle maker
Berry, Joseph, tailor
Bogart, John, farmer
Burns, C. S., farmer
Bury, E. A., coal dealer
Bury, William, shipper
Campbell, D., farmer
Gesner, D., J.P
Gunder & Gibson, millers
Henry, George, general merchant
Humber, A., cooper
Landon, C., cabinet maker
Laycock, Joseph, hotel keeper
McFarlane, —., blacksmith
McKellar, D., carpenter
Redley, E. A., J.P
Robinson, Robert, farmer
Ruthven, A., carpenter
Smith, H. D., stock dealer
Smith, John C., stage house
Stokes, Robert, farmer
WATSON, H. T., Postmaster and merchant

Clear Creek.—A small village in the Township of Stoughton, County Norfolk, 30 miles from Simcoe, the County Town, 90 miles from Toronto, and 40 from the nearest railway station. There is an abundance of water power in the vicinity. Mechanics of every kind are needed in the neighborhood

BRIDGMAN, J., Postmaster and general merchant
Bridgman, R. E., general agent
Bridgman, T. R. E., auctioneer and insurance agent
Brooks, A., carpenter
Farr. Aaron, cooper
Folger, Rev. S. W., (Baptist)
Jackson, J., J.P
Laycock, Brothers, lumber merchants
Louch, A., blacksmith
Lountbury, S., butcher
McCall, William, teacher
Misener, A., flour mill
Mitchener, A., brickmaker
Pierce, Thomas, carpenter
Pierce, Warren, carpenter
Stephens, W., blacksmith
Treadwell, Rev. W. H., (Baptist)
White, M. W., J.P
Wilson, A., jun., cabinet maker
Wilson, T., wagon maker

Clifton.—A Town and Station on the Great Western and the Erie and Ontario Railways, on the west bank of the Niagara River, about a mile and a-half below the celebrated Falls, in the Township of Stamford, County Welland. Canada is here connected with the State of New York by two suspension bridges, which rank next to the Victoria tubular at Montreal, as the most scientific works of the kind on the continent. The principal is suspended in the air, 250 feet above the river, by four wire cables, each ten inches in diameter, from towers seventy-five feet in height, a distance of 822 feet from tower to tower. the total length of wire in these cables being 4,000 miles. There are two roadways, one above the other, the upper having a railway with three different gauges, and the lower one for waggons, &c. The other, erected in 1868, is situated near the Clifton House, distance between the towers 1200 feet, it is intended for foot passengers and carriages. Clifton is the eastern terminus of the Great Western Railway, and connects with the railways of the State of New York to all parts of the continent. Money order office and savings bank. Population 1,000.

ALBION HOTEL, M. M. Buckley prop. (see adv)
American Express Company, W. A. Gray agent
American Hotel, E. M. Bromley proprietor
ATWOOD, AMASA., prop. Western Hotel, Suspension Bridge (see adv)
Atwood, James, carpenter
Barnett, Sydney, fancy store & photographic views
BARNETT, THOMAS, museum fancy store and water-proof clothing
Barnett, Thomas, jun., artist
Bell, Rev. George, (Presbyterian)
Biggar, Alanson, water works
BIGGAR, A. H., plumber and gas fitter
Booth, James, taxidermist
Bowan. Uriah, butcher, &c
Bower, T., tailor
BROMLEY & SHEARS, (D. H. Bromley & George P. Shears) props. Clifton House
Bromley, E. R., exchange office
BUCKLEY, M. M., prop. Albion Hotel
Buckley, William, grocer, &c
Bush, J. T., prop. Zimmerman grounds
Butters, Thomas, freight agent
Cameron, John E., landing waiter
Central House, B. Hull, prop
Clar,k George W., prop. Elgin House
CLIFTON HOUSE, Bromley & Shears, proprietors (see adv)
Colsan, John, baker
CRICKETERS' HOTEL, J. Jones, prop
Davis, C., clerk Table Rock Hotel
Davis, Edward, clerk, Table Rock Hotel
DAVIS, SAUL, prop. Table Rock Hotel
Drew, John, mason
Farley, Mrs. Mary, temperance saloon
Ganter, Joseph, shoemaker
Gardner, William, chief constable
GRAHAM, F. H., prop. Suspension Bridge Hotel (see adv)
Gilmore, Thomas, carpenter, etc.
Gorman, John, cab proprietor
Hall, Charles, telegraph agent
Hall, Ralph, ticket clerk
Henderson, George, clerk
Henderson, George, jun., gate keeper Susp. Bridge
Hooey, T. G., telegraph operator
Hull, B., prop. Central House
JONES, J., prop. New England Hotel. (See adv.)
Jones, W. Martin, United States Consul
Kelly, Michael, flour and feed store
Law, R., grocer
Leggatt, William, J.P.
Lewis & Biggars, Clifton water works
Lewis, Z. B., coroner
Life Association of Scotland, Jas. Mackenzie, agent
MacKenzie, James, Custom House and forwarding agent
McLeod, Rev. D. J. F., (Church of England)
Mahoney, Timothy, general store
Marston, G. W., butcher
MURRAY & HART
Muchlheim, John, hotel keeper
NIAGARA FALLS MUSEUM, Thos. Barnet, prop.
Neilson, Peter, station agent
NEW ENGLAND HOTEL, J. Jones, proprietor. (See adv)
Newson, Mrs., prop. Great Western House
Oliver, —, M.D.
Preston, F. I., groceries and liquors
Richmond, J., Erie and Niagara Railroad
Robinson, Robert, teacher
Rosli, G., prop. Rosli's Hotel
Rosskelly, William, butcher
Simpson, Wright, station master
Stein, Charles, groceries, provisions, crockery and liquors
Stiff, William, cashier
SUSPENSION BRIDGE HOTEL, Rail-way Station, F. H. Graham, proprietor
TABLE ROCK HOTEL, S. Davis proprietor
Treaton, Henry, Custom House, broker, exchange agt
Walker, Sarah, confectioner, &c
Wallace, Andrew, flour and feed store
Webster, George, superintendant locomotive depart.
WESTERN HOTEL, Suspension Bridge, N. Y., A. Atwood, proprietor
WOODRUFF, W. W., Postmaster, dry goods and groceries.

Clifford.—A Post-Village in the Township of Minto, County Wellington, situated on the Red River, 47 miles from Guelph, the County Town. Average price of improved land in vicinity, $30. Stages to Guelph, Walkerton, and Southampton. Money order office. Population, about 200.

Andrews, Joseph, blacksmith
Appleby, Charles, carpenter
Beck, Frederick, tanner
BROWN, FRANCIS, Postmaster, miller, and hotel keeper
Bullock, Noah, farmer
Caldwell, Robert, J.P
Campbell, Donald, tailor
Cockerell, John, lime dealer
Crandell, Dr
Cusack, John, carpenter
Dolmage, Anson, general merchant
Dolmage, J. H., general merchant
Depew, Rev. Mr., (Methodist)
Fglesham, Hugh, farmer
Fraser, William, farmer
Graff, W. F., shoemaker
Gray, A., miller
Hale, John, farmer
Hallard, James, carpenter
Hay, Rev. Mr., (Presbyterian)
Hillhouse, John, farmer
House. J., carpenter
Hunsberger, Paul, farmer
Knight, James, carpenter
Lugg, Samuel, farmer
McDonald, George, general merchant
McEachren, Bros., general merchants
McIntyre, Alexander, farmer
Morrison, Dr.
Patmore, Henry, blacksmith
Pearson, J., shingle maker
Pearson, John, farmer
Pearson, Samuel, shingle maker
Phink, M., cabinet maker
Renny, William, teacher
Rose, James, shoemaker
Seiple, George, cooper
Sherman, George, tailor
Sparrow, Sylvester, general agent
Stewart, William, hotel keeper
Thompson, Alexander, carpenter
Walton, R., wagon maker
Ward, John, farmer
Weber, Jacob, butcher

Clinton.—A prosperous Village and station of the Buffalo and Lake Huron Railroad, in the Townships of Tuckersmith, Hlulet and Goderich, County Huron. It is the centre of a rich agricultural district, distant from Toronto 120 miles; and from Goderich the County Town 12. Money Order Office and Savings Bank. Population 1500.

Bacon, Henry, shoemaker
Biddlecombe, J., watchmaker
Bowers, G. M., painter
BROWN, GEORGE, proprietor Clinton brewery
Brown, George, J. P
Buchanan, D., carpenter
Buchanan, James, shoemaker
Callender, Robert (Callender & Scott)
Callender & Scott, (Robert Callender, Hugh Scott) dry goods and groceries
Cantlon, H., (of Cantlon & Bro)
Cantlon, William, (Cantlon & Bro)
Cantlon & Bro., carriage and waggon makers
Cassels, Mark, carpenter
Charlesworth, —, manager Blythe flour mills
Chidley, Joseph (M. McTaggart & Co)
CLINTON BREWERY, GEORGE BROOM, prop.
Clinton Mills, James Fair, proprietor
CLINTON NEW ERA, EDWARD HOLMES, editor and proprietor
CLINTON WOOLEN MILLS, T. R. FOSTER, proprietor
CLINTON TANNERY, O. S. DOAN, proprietor
Coates, William, general merchant
Cole, R., M.D.
Commander, Charles (Commander & Elder)
Combe, J, H,, chemist and druggist
Commander & Elder (Charles Commander and John Elder) dry goods
Counter, C., shoemaker
COOPER, THOMAS, proprietor Prince of Wales hotel.
Cruickshank, Charles, boots and shoes
Cunningham, John, grocer
Date, S., clerk
Davis, Silas (Searle & Davis)
Dayment, Charles, builder
DOAN, O. S., prop Clinton Tannery (see adv)
Elder, John, (Commander & Elder)
Fair, James) proprietor Clinton Mills
FAIR, THOMAS, Postmaster
FARMERS' HOTEL, JAMES ROSS, proprietor
FARRAN, W. W., Clerk 10th Division Court and insurance agent (see adv)
Fisher, A. S., general merchant
Fitzsimon, H., sawyer
Forbes, James, general merchant
FOSTER, T. R., proprietor Clinton Woolen Mills
Fullerton, J. W., photographer
Fulton, H. H., teller Royal Canadian Bank
Grant, Peter, blacksmith
Grassick, William (Grassick & Twitchell)
Grassick & Twitchell (William and James) saddlers
Griggs, William, blacksmith
Gunn, Alexander, grocery
HALE, HORATIO, conveyancer, real estate agent, commissioner in B. R.
Harland, Brothers (William S. & John T.) stoves and tinware
Hartt, Charles A., attorney, solicitor, Royal Canadian Bank
Helyar, Charles, blacksmith
Hine, William H., produce dealer
Hodgins, John (Irwin & Hodgins)
HOLMES, EDMUND, editor and proprietor Clinton *New Era*
Hovey, C., assistant manager Clinton Foundry
Hudson, Henry, plasterer
Hunt, George, manager Huron flour and oat mill
Irwin, Richard (Irwin & Hodgins)
Irwin & Hodgins (Richard Irwin, John Hodgins) dry goods and groceries
Jackson, John, shoemaker
Jackson, Thomas, merchant tailor
Johnson, Philip, grocer
Jones, Stephen, butcher

Jones, Thomas, bricklayer and plasterer
King, A. R., painter
Lane, Thomas, proprietor Railway Hotel
Laycock, George, books and stationery
Lee, Roger, saddler
Leslie, John (Rumball & Leslie)
Levin, Thomas, wagon-maker
Loveless, John, tailor
LOUGH, MATTHEW, agent Royal Canadian Bank. agent North British and Mercantile Insurance Co
McCallum, Malcolm, merchant tailor
McDonald, Rev. A. D. (Presbyterian)
McGarva, John, groceries
McMillan, William, assist. man. Clinton Foundry
McMurchie, Alexander (M. McTaggart & Co.)
McMurchie, D., M. D.
McPherson, Alexander, asst. man. Clinton Foundry
McTaggart, M. & Co.(M. McTaggart, Joseph Chidley, (Alexander McMurchie) props. fanning mill factory
McTavish, Donald, iron plough maker
Mack, Mrs. Frances, confectioner
Malcolmson, S., barrister
Matheson, Archibald, blacksmith
Miller, John, saddler
MOONEY, JOHN, cattle merchant
Mountcastle, S. H., farmer
Mullins, E., station master, telegraph operator
Murray, William
Nosworthy, Henry, tailor
Paterson, J. W., grocer
Paterson, R., baker
Patton, David, general merchant
Patterson, Mrs., proprietor Commercial Hotel
PRINCE OF WALES HOTEL, Thomas Cooper, prop
RACEY, JAMES B., groceries, wines and liquors
Racey, R. M., hardware
Railway Hotel, Thomas Lane, proprietor
RANCE, SAMUEL, manager Royal Canadian Hotel
RANSFORD, RICHARD
RATTENBURY, ISAAC, prop. Royal Canadian Hotel
RATTENBURY, ISAAC, farmer
Rattenbury, William, proprietor Clinton Hotel
Ridout, Charles, civil engineer
Ridout, George
Robson, N., groceries, wines and liquors
ROSS, JAMES, prop Farmers' Hotel (see adv)
Ross, Miss, dressmaker
ROYAL CANADIAN BANK, M. Lough, agent, H. Fulton, accountant
Royal Canadian Hotel, Isaac Rattenbury, prop
Rowell, James, blacksmith
RUMBALL & LESLIE, (Frederick Rumball and John Leslie) carriage and wagon makers
Salt, Thomas B., moulder
Salt, Mrs. T. B., grocer
Scott, Hugh, (Callender & Scott)
Searle, W. C. (Searle & Davis)
Searle & Davis. (W. C. Searle and Silas Davis) tinsmiths
Sharp, H. F., photographer
Smith, James, merchant tailor
Stanbury, Thomas, grocer
Steep, John, boots and shoes
Stevens, Henry, carpenter
Stevenson, Thomas, cabinet maker
Strathy, D. B., general merchant
Sturgein, R., pump maker
Spooner, Charles, butcher
Taylor, Alexander, wagon maker
Taylor, William, blacksmith
THWAITES, RICHARD, J. P., issuer of marriage licenses, insurance agent, appraiser Can. Permanent Building and Saving's Society
Twitchell, James, (Grassick & Twitchell)
Walker & Smith, Misses, dressmakers & milliners
WALKER & BROTHER, (H. R. and J. S.) props. stave factory, builders (see adv)
Watts, W. R., Montreal Telegraph Company
WATTS & CO., chemists and druggists
WILKIE, J. Z., M.D., surgeon dentist (see adv)
Williams, John, moulder
WHITEHEAD, JOSEPH, M.P.P., prop. Blythe mills
White, Frederick, attorney and solicitor

Clifton House.—A post office located in the Clifton House, County Welland, for the use of the guests; closed during the winter.

SHEARS, J. Postmaster

Cloyne.—A Village in the Township of Barrie, County Frontenac. Distance from Kingston, County Town 70 miles, from Toronto, 235 miles. Average price land, $1 to $4. Population, 100.

Benny, Charles, carpenter
Benny, Joseph
Benny, Miss Sarah, dressmaker
Bishop, George
Boisley, Francis, proprietor Dominion House
Brintnall, John, proprietor British American Hotel
Campbell, William, lumber dealer
Clark, Bibbin, general merchant
CLARK, ELI, Postmaster
Clrak, Rev. J. F., (Methodist Episcopal)
Clifford, John
Corbett, Rev. J., (Wesleyan)
Cornell, John, carpenter
Cowan, Alexander, marble cutter
Cummings, Charles S., carpenter
Dempsey, W
Dunham, Miss Jane, teacher
Earl, John, teacher
Gaylord, Levi, wagon maker
Hawley, Davis, shingle manufacturer
Herbert, George
Jackson, Calvin, shingle manufacturer
Lewis, Miss Melissa, teacher
Lucas, John, shoemaker
McMillen, Donald, cabinet maker
Meek, Denison, carpenter
Miller, Adolphus, cooper
Miller, Francis, cooper
O Donald, John, prop. Barrie Hotel
Perry, Bowen, lumber dealer
Perry, Edward
Snider, Charles, lumber dealer
Trimpo, William
Winters, John, lime manufacturer
York, Miss M., teacher

Clontarf.—A Village in the Township of Sebastopol, County Renfrew, 35 miles from Pembroke, the County Town, and 120 from Toronto. Improved land in the vicinity averages $6 per acre, wild, 75cts. Money order office. Population, 50.

Benson, Thomas, shingle maker
Hotterman, C. F., general merchant
McCormick, Rev. James, (Roman Catholic)
McDonald, Angus D., carpenter
McDonald, Archibald, wagon maker
McDonald, Daniel, farmer
McDonald, John B., leather dealer
McDONALD, R., Postmaster and hotel keeper
McDonald, Ronald, wagon maker
McDougall, —., shoemaker
Moran, James, farmer
Plant, X., hotel keeper
Potter, John, gunsmith
Ryan, Stephen, J.P
Roebotham, —., shoemaker
Ryan, Patrick, farmer
Sellar, Carroll, farmer
Sinclair, John, carpenter
Varney, John, engraver

Clover Hill.—A Post Village, Township of Tecumseth, County Simcoe, 18 miles from Barrie, the County Town, 11 miles from Gilford Station, N. R. C., and 50 from Toronto. Land in the vicinity averages $35, unimproved, $20 per acre. Money order office. Population, 80.

Campbell, Robert, carpenter
Cobb, Henry, shoemaker
Dinwoody, George, farmer
Dinwoody, William, farmer
Duff, George, farmer
Duff, John, farmer
McLean, Robert, farmer
McLean, William, farmer
RITCHEY, EDWARD J., Postmaster and general merchant
Seabury, Richard, cooper
Stephenson, John, blacksmith

Clyde.—A Village in the Township of Beverly, County Wentworth. Distant from Hamilton the County Town, 23 miles, from Toronto 70 miles. Stages to Galt and Puslinch. Average price of land $35. Population 100.

Bryce, James, farmer
Common, James, farmer
Conkey, Alexander, farmer
Elliott, George, general merchant
Ferguson, Archibald, farmer
Galbraith, John, blacksmith
Hunter, Robert, auctioneer
Law, Thomas, shoemaker
McDonald, Alexander, farmer
McPherson, Daniel, farmer
McPHERSON, WILLIAM, Postmaster and general merchant
McQuillan, W., shingle manufacturer
McWilliams, Robert, teacher,
Mathewson, Andrew, proprietor Clyde Hotel
Mathewson, A., blacksmith
Murray, James C., tailor
Scott, John, farmer
Scott, Joseph, farmer
VanMeter, Ira, constable

Cobourg.—The County Town of the United Counties of Northumberland and Durham, on the line of the Grand Trunk Railway, and the Southern terminus of the Peterboro' and Cobong Railway, 7 miles from Port Hope, 100 from Kingston, 70 from Toronto, 24 from Peterboro', and 60 from Rochester, N.Y. The Town is beautifully situated on Lake Ontario, and the adjoining Country is unsurpassed for fertility. The educational establishments are numerous and are well supported. Money order office and Savings Bank. Population 6,000.

Agnew, James, carter
Alexander, William, saloon keeper
Allan, J., grocer
Allen, Henry, accountant
Andrews, Matthew, grocer
Armour, John D., Q.C., barrister, Co. attorney, &c.
Arnold James, painter
Arrol, James, shoemaker
AUSTON, JAMES, barrister, clk 5th Div. Court
Avaril, Chilli, saddler
Bain, Abraham J., teacher
BAIN, JOHN, painter and paper hanger (see adv)
Baird, John, dyer
Ball, Thomas, boots and shoes
BANK OF MONTREAL, John Porteous, manager
BANK OF TORONTO, J. H. Roper, manager
Barber, James R., railway superintendent
Barr, Alexander, wagon maker
Barr, William M., wagon maker
Barron, Frederick W., teacher
Battell, Thomas, grocer
Battell, William, sen., sash and door factory
Battell, William, jun., builder
Beatty, John, M.D
Beatty, Edmund J., attorney-at-law
Beaufort, Ernest L., G.T.R. saloon keeper
Benedict, Henry W., accountant
Bennett, Glover, tailor
Benson, R. L., Deputy Sheriff Counties Northumberland and Durham
Benson, William, Surveyor of Customs
Bevan, Thomas G., prop. Bevan's Hotel
Bird, Gilbert, painter
Blenkhorn, William, carpenter
Boate, Alexander, music teacher
Boggs, William (Cockburn, Loscombe & Boggs)

Bolster, John, gardener
Bolster, Thomas, saddler
Bolster, William, carpenter
Bond, William, builder
Boswell, Augustus G., barrister
Boswell, Charles M., clerk post-office
Boswell, David, clerk post-office
Boswell, George M., County Judge
BOSWELL, JOHN C., Postmaster
Boswell, John S., insurance agent
Boswell, J. Vance
Boulton, Darcy E., barrister
Boulton, Edward T., barrister
Boulton, Hon. George S., Registrar
Bounsall, John, tailor
Bounsall, Mrs. M. A., straw milliner
Boyd, Robert, shoemaker
Boyd, William, shoemaker
Brass, James, cooper
Bray, Benjamin, carpenter
Bray, Edward, gardener
Brewer, John G., bricklayer
BRODIE, DAVID, Town Clerk and Treasurer
Broughall, Lewis, cooper
Brown, George, tailor
Buchanan, William, proprietor Railroad Hotel
Burke, Michael, proprietor Queen's Arms Hotel
Burn, David, actuary Savings Bank
Burnham, Hon. Asa A., Senator, County Treasurer
Burnham, Asa A., jun.
BURWASH, REV. N., M.A., prof. Victoria College
BUTLER, JOHN, insurance agent and Deputy Clerk of the Peace
BUTLER, WILLIAM (Winans & Butler)
Calcutt, James, brewer
Calcutt, Edward, express messenger
CALCUTT, KINGSLEY, brewer and maltster
Calcutt, William S. K., brewer
Caldwell, William P., tailor
Callender, T. G., dentist
CANADA PERMANENT BUILDING & SAVINGS SOCIETY, G. M. Goodeve, agent
Carlisle, M. L., proprietor restaurant
Carson, Archibald, rope maker
Carson, Thomas, proprietor rope walk
Carswell, William, shoemaker
Chapman, George, machinist
Chatterton, Richard D., Deputy Clerk Crown and Clerk County Court
Clark, George M., Judge Division Court
Clark & Wade (Richard H. and William,) physicians and surgeons
CLENCH, FREEMAN S., cabinet maker
CLENCH, THOMAS B., cabinet maker
Clyme, Thomas, tailor
COBOURG SENTINEL, D. McAllister editor and proprietor
COBOURG STAR, Wm. H. Floyd, pub. & prop.
COBOURG SUN, Thomas McNaughton, editor and proprietor.
COBOURG WORLD, Henry Hough, editor & prop.
COCKBURN, HON. JAMES, Speaker House of Commons
COCKBURN, JAMES, Q.C. (Cockburn, Loscombe & Boggs)
COCKBURN, LOSCOMBE & BOGGS, barristers, &c
Coles, John, wagon maker
COLLINGS, S. & CO., wagon makers
Comrie, James, plasterer
Conlan, Nicholas, blacksmith
Connell, Richard, carpenter
Connell, Mrs. R., dressmaker
Cooney, Edward, Chief Constable
Cooper, George, bailiff
Corrigal, William, Deputy Registrar
Corson, Rev. Robert, (Wesleyan)
Coventry, George, Custom House broker
Covert, Henry
Cox, Aaron, express agent
Craig, Henry, prop. Market Tavern
Crawshaw, John, (Fraser & Co.)
CROSSEN, JAMES, iron founder
Cullingford, John, druggist
Culver, Abraham B., bailiff
Curley, Charles, weaver
Cuthbert, Alexander, groceries and liquors
Daintry, George S.
Daintry, John S., P.L.S.
Daveney, Arthur B., station agent G.T.R.
Dawe, Samson, tailor
Deer, Samuel, painter
Deering, William, boots and shoes
Delaney, Henry, gunsmith, etc.
Densmore, Jonathan, farmer
Dickson, Adam, flour and feed
Dinner, Mrs. C., milliner and dressmaker
Dixon, H., proprietor Dominion Hotel
Doak, Joseph, blacksmith
Dooly & Hewson, dry goods and millinery
Dooly, Mrs. Dora, (Dooly & Hewson)
Downing, William, tinsmith
Doyle, John, tailor
Dumble, John H., barrister
Dumble, Thomas, sen., contractor
Duncan, James, confectioner
Eakins, James
Easton, Henry, Collector Customs
ELLIOTT CHARLES, harbor master, agent Royal Mail Line steamers, Ocean Inman Line, and general ticket agent
Ely, Edward, carpenter
Evans, Henry, carpenter
EWART, SAMUEL L., proprietor Rochester House. (See adv)
Fairbrother, George, blacksmith
Farmer, William, general merchant
Farry, Edward, carpenter
Featherstone, John G., painter
Fee, James, carpenter
FIELD, CORELLI C. (Field & Brother)
Field, John
FIELD, JOHN C., (Field & Bro.)
FIELD & BRO., (John C. and Corelli C.) dry goods and groceries
Field, William, clerk Field & Bro.
FLANIGAN, JAMES, proprietor Commercial House
Fleming, Mrs. Mary, proprietor Cobourg Hotel
Fletcher, John, groceries, boots and shoes
Flood, James, gunsmith
FLOYD, WILLIAM H., publisher and proprietor *Cobourg Star*
Forrest, William, saddler
Fowler, John, shoemaker
Fowler, Robert, tailor
Fox, John, boots and shoes
FRASER, ALEXANDER, M.P.P
FRASER & Co., (Alexander Fraser and John Crawshaw) proprietors Ontario Woolen Mills
Gale, Francis, boots and shoes
Galt, Thomas, barrister
Gilbard, Thomas, merchant tailor
Giddings, James, shoemaker
Giddy, Thomas, farmer
Gilchrist, James A., M.D
Gillard, Herbert, painter
Gillard, James, tailor
Gogett, Caesar, cooper
Goodeve, George M., insurance agent and accountant

Gordon, James, grocer
Gowans, James, cabinet maker
Grant, John & Co., general merchants
Graveley, J. Vance, sen., excise officer
Graveley, J. Vance, jr., barrister
Greenwood, John, saloon keeper
Greenwood, Thomas, proprietor British Hotel
Greenwood, William T., contractor
Grieve, David, tailor
Grieve, George, carpenter
Grieve, James, proprietor Court House Hotel
Guillet, George, general merchant
Gummow, James, wagon maker
Gummow, Robert, grocer
Guy, Michael, cooper
Hales, Richard, blacksmith
Hall, Joseph, grocer
Halliday, Andrew, saddler
Hambly, Edwin, tailor
Hamilton, George, blacksmith
Hargraft & Co. (William Hargraft and John Urquhart) grocers
Harper, Thomas, grocer
Harrison, Simon, bookbinder
Hawthorn, Thomas, boots and shoes
Hawthorne, William, blacksmith
Hayden, John, dealer in pictures, paints, oils, &c.
Hayter, Edmund, J., watchmaker & melodeon agent
Hayter, Mrs. E. J., milliner and dressmaker
Helm, John, iron founder and machinist
Henderson, William, carpenter
Henwood, Roger, boots and shoes
Hewitt, John, gardener
Hewitt, William, painter
Hewson, Andrew (Dooly & Hewson)
Higgins, William, grocer
Highet, Robert, hardware
Hitchens, William, grocer
Hoare, Richard, shoemaker
Hobart, Matthew T., cabinet maker
Holman, Mrs. John, dry goods and clothing
HOLMES, ADAM, forwarder and commission mercht
Home, Thomas, tailor
Hooey, John
Hooey, Stuart, groceries and dry goods
Hopper, William, blacksmith
Hoskins, Henry, bricklayer
Hossack, James, barrister
HOUGH, HENRY, editor and prop. *Cobourg World*
HOUSE, FRANKLIN, bookseller
Howard, Rev. V. B., (Wesleyan)
Howell, Stanley S., grocer
Hull, Edward C., auctioneer
Hunter, William, mason
Hutchison, Samuel, cooper
Irwin, Samuel, cooper
Jakes, William, proprietor North American Hotel
Jackson, John, cabinet maker
James, John
Jeffrey & Co., hardware
Jewell, Thomas, soda water manufacturer
Jex, Frederick, carpenter
Jex, William, barrister
Johns, Jacob, carpenter
Johnston, David, teacher
Jones, George E., broker
Jones, Rev. Richard, (Wesleyan)
Keenan, James, grocer
Kennedy, Abel S., boots and shoes
Keown, John, blacksmith
Kerr, John W., barrister
KERR, WILLIAM, barrister, Mayor
KINGSTON, WILLIAM, M.A., Professor Victoria College
Kershaw, Thomas, grocer
Kobald, Leopold, butcher
Koerber, Louis, music teacher
Laing, Rev. John, (Presbyterian)
LAUDER, JOHN, grocer, produce and com. mercht
Laverty, Robert, carpenter
Lawes, Charles, photographer
Lee, William, carpenter
Lilly, Bernard, prop. Ontario Hotel
Linton, Richard, weaver
Little, R. S., photographer
LOSCOMBE, W. C. (Cockburn, Loscombe & Boggs)
Lossee, Bateman, gardener
Lyons, George, butcher
McALLISTER, DANIEL, editor and prop. *Cobourg Sentinel*
McBride, Dugald, teacher
McCallum, Peter, & Son, general merchants
McCaughey, John, wagon maker
McConnell, James, carpenter
McConnell, William, druggist
McCullough, George, grocer
McDonald, Arthur, notary public
McDonald, James, auctioneer
McFiggin, John, plasterer
McIntosh, James, wagon maker
McKechnie, Henry, prop. Victoria brewery
McKeown, Samuel, brewer
McLeod, John, blacksmith
McNachton, Edmund A., County Clerk, official assignee, &c.
McNAUGHTON, THOMAS, barrister, editor & prop. *Cobourg Sun*
McNeillie, Michael, teacher
McNight, William, carpenter
Maguire, John, carriage maker
Martin, James J., tinsmith
Mason, Henry, insurance agent
Medcalf, William, farmer
Mickleborough, Daniel, hatter
Miller, Jacob, shoemaker
Minaker, & Brother, (David H. and Calvin) dry goods and clothing
Mitchell, John, market clerk
Moore, Charles C., M. D.
Morden, Benjamin, grocer
Morrow, Thomas, saddler
Muldoon, Mrs., groceries
Mulholland, & Brown, (Robert and Peter) hardware and groceries
Munson, Alfred E., contractor
NELLES, REV. S. S., D.D., Pres. Victoria College
Nixon, J. J. & Co., saddlers
Noble, John, boots and shoes
Northrope, Augustus B., manufacturer of musical instruments
O'Flynn, Patrick, teacher
O'Neil, John, general merchant
O'Neill, Timothy, livery stable
Oliver, Frederick S. H., express agent
ORMISTON, DAVID, B.A., head master Grammar School
PAUWELS, EDWARD, proprietor Pauwels' House
Payne, William L., carriage maker
Pearce, James, tailor
Perry, George, landing waiter
Pengelley, John, blacksmith
Phillips, Edward, proprietor Enniskillen Hotel
PHŒNIX FIRE INSURANCE COMPANY, (of London England), Winans and Butler, agents
Plews, Robert, grocer
Polkenhorn, John, grocer
Polkenhorn, Richard, grocer
Pollard, Misses, select school

Pomeroy, William, carpenter
Porteous, John, manager Bank of Montreal
Postlethwaite, Thomas, cabman
POWELL, NEWTON, W., M. D.
Powell, Orrin W., butcher
Pratt, Alexander, confectioner
Pratt, John, baker
Pratt, John, farmer
Pringle, Alexander, watchmaker
Pringle, James, surgeon
Pugh, Frederick, M. D.
Quinn, Patrick, blacksmith
Regan, Patrick, livery stable
Retallack, Samuel, grocer
Retallack, Thomas, bricklayer
REYNAR, REV. ALFRED H., prof. Victoria Coll.
Reynolds, Francis, teacher
Reynolds, John H., flour and feed
Richardson, William, bailiff, Inspector Weights and Measures
Riley, John, shoemaker
Roberts, John D., seedsman
Roberts, Samuel P., proprietor Bank Saloon
Robinson, Henry, veterinary surgeon
Robinson, James, blacksmith
ROCHESTER HOUSE, Samuel L. Ewart, proprietor (see adv.)
Rolls, Charles, sen., M. D.
Rolls, Charles, jun., druggist
Rolls, Jones, druggist
ROPER, J. H., manager Bank of Toronto
Ross, David, merchant tailor
Ross, Walter, merchant tailor
Rowe, Thomas, dentist
ROY, REV. JAMES, B.A., teacher grammar school
ROYAL CANADIAN BANK, Alfred Stow, agent
Rundell, Henry W., shoemaker
Rush, Warren J., grocer
Ruttan, Hon. Henry
Ruttan, Henry Jones
Ruttan, Richard, barrister
Sailsbury, Jonathan, bookseller
Saunders, John, blacksmith
Scoon, Alexander, grocer
Scott, Joseph S., dentist
Service, John, boots and shoes
Sidey, James, accountant
Simmons, George N., saddler
Simpson, Rev. James, (Methodist Episcopal)
Smith, Henry, barrister
Smith, Robert, cabinet maker
Smith, William, livery stable
Smith, William, blacksmith
Stanton, Oliver, farmer
Stanton, William Irvine, barrister
Stennett, Rev. Walter, (Church of England)
Stephens, George, agent pianos and melodeons
Stephens, George J., cabinet maker and upholsterer
Stephenson, Joseph, veterinary surgeon
Stickle, Henry, wagon maker
Stock, Zachariah, gardener
STORR, ALFRED, agent Royal Canadian Bank
Stuart, Charles H., marble cutter
Summons, George, saddler
Sutherland, J. & Co., grocers
Tanner, Henry, farmer
Taylor, Mrs, K., groceries
Thomas, William, butcher
TILDEN, WILLIAM & NEPHEW, manufacturers of varnishes. (See adv)
Timlin, Rev. Michael, (Roman Catholic)
Tourje, Wilbur F., tinsmith
Tourje, William, tinware and stoves
Trebilcock, Paul, sen., shoemaker
Tripp, Henry, carriage maker
Underwood, John, farmer
UNIVERSITY OF VICTORIA COLLEGE, Rev. S. S. Nelles, D.D., President
Urquhart, John, (Hargraft & Co.)
Van Ingen, Abraham J., auctioneer
Van Ingen, William, auctioneer
Waddall, William, barber
Waddell, Archibald, broker
Waddell, R. N., Sheriff
Wade, William, M.D.
Waldie, John, baker and confectioner
Wall, William, tailor
Wallace, Daniel, painter
Wallace, John S., agent
Walsh, Thomas, blacksmith
Ware, John, cooper
Waters, —, M.D.
Weller, William H., barrister, Master in Chancery
Weller, Thomas M. T., telegraph agent
West, William, bricklayer
Western, Thomas, plasterer
White, Christopher, saddler
White, Henry B., accountant
White, J. C., farmer
Whitelaw, John, tinsmith, gas manufacturer
Wicks, George, farmer
Wicks, Thomas, engraver
Williams, Matthew, carpenter
Williams, Matthew B., saddler
Willis, Alfred, boots and shoes
Willis, George, boots and shoes
WILSON, JACOB, general broker
WILSON, JOHN, M.A., Professor Vic. College
Wilson, John, Excise officer
Wilson, John, carriage maker
Wilson, Richard, druggist
Wilson, Robert M., M.D
WINANS, EDWARD S., (Winans & Butler) U. S. Consular agent
WINANS & BUTLER (E. S. Winans and William Butler) commission merchants & insurance agts.
Winch & Brother, butchers
Winn, Charles, grocer
Wood, James, tailor
Woods, Mrs. William, hotel keeper
Woodruff, Thomas, tailor
Wright, John, confectioner
York, James, shoemaker
York, William, barber and dealer in fancy goods

Cobden.—A post Village on Muskrat Lake, in the Township of Ross, County Renfrew. Distant from Pembroke the County Town, 20 miles, from Ottawa 70 miles, from Toronto 190 miles. Population 50.

Aril, Antoine, wagon maker
Boulton, George, steamboat agent
Crawford, John, general merchant
Graffe, John, tailor
Hurst, George W., teacher
McDONALD, JOHN R., Postmaster
McDonald, John R., carpenter
Overman, C. E., J. P.
Rankin, John, general merchant
Rankin, John, proprietor Rankin House

Coboconk.—A small post Village in the Township of Bexley, County Victoria, distant from Lindsay the County Town, 25 miles, and from Toronto 80 miles. Population about 80.

Cronk, J. & J. H., sawmillers
LEROY, JOHN, Postmaster

Codrington.—A Village in the Township of Brighton, County Northumberland. Distant from Cobourg, the County Town, 40 miles, from Toronto 110 miles. Stages to Campbellford, Meyersburg, Hilton and Brighton. Average price of land, $10 to $50. Population 100

Alison, Mrs. Rachel, hotel keeper
Clark, W. R., farmer
Cooney, John, tailor
Creag, Samuel, cooper
Donohoe, Patrick, wagon maker
Dulmage, O., farmer
Heaton, Lyman, wagon maker
Holleran, Thomas, farmer
Hutchinson, Thomas, shoemaker
Kavanagh, A. blacksmith
Kempt, A. F., lumber dealer
Kempt, C. B., J.P.
KILBANK, WILLIAM, Postmaster and gen. mercht
King, George, brick manufacturer
King, Isaac, farmer
Lahay, Miss J., teacher
Morrum, John, farmer
Parsall, William, farmer
Shay, Miss Johanna, teacher
Sullivan, James, blacksmith
Sterling, William, farmer
Young, Miss J., teacher

Colborne.—An incorporated Village in the Township of Cramahe, County Northumberland, Colborne harbor on Lake Ontario is two miles distant, from Cobourg, the County Town, 15 miles. Daily mail. Money Order Office and Savings Bank. Population about 1000.

Bennett, Norman, farmer
Bethune, A. N., M. B.
BYWATER, R. E., druggist and watchmaker
Cameron & Fuller, (C. P. Cameron and J. K. Fuller) general merchants
Campbell, Donald, farmer
Campbell, William, carpenter
Carnell, George, tailor
Casey, H. N., broker and lumber merchant
Chapin, O. A., cabinet maker
Chapman, John, wagon maker
Cockburn, George, farmer
"COLBORNE EXPRESS," (weekly) George Keys editor and proprietor
Crandell, R., farmer
Dailey, Daniel, grocery and book store
Deans & Deans (James and Robert Deans) druggists and general merchants
Dewey, J. B., plaster and flouring mills
Donaghy, Mrs. W. H., milliner
Donaghy, W. H., cabinet maker
Duncan, Rev. Peter, (Presbyterian)
EASTON, W. D., grocer
Errington, William, carriage maker
FORD, CHARLES R., Postmaster, agent Montreal Telegraph Company
Fowler, G. C., pottery
Fowler, Rev. R., (Wesleyan)
Gibson & Campbell, tanners
Gilley, John, flouring mill
Gordon, G. N., stoves, tin and hardware
Gould, E., cooper
Greer, Thomas, farmer
GROVER, JOHN M., Registrar East Northumberland
Hart, Edwin, innkeeper
Hawkins, W. A., shoemaker
HICKS, H., proprietor Hicks Hotel. (See adv)
Higgins, William, wagon maker
Huyck, Selim, general merchant
Jackson, Benjamin, cheese factory
JOHNSTON, WILLIAM, photographer and frame dealer. (See adv)
Keeler, J., M.P.P., forwarder
KEYES, GEORGE, editor and proprietor *Colborne Express*
King, Adam, baker
Lawrence, —, grist mill prop.
Leake, E. W., baker and confectioner
Leith, Robert, hotel keeper
McHUGH, JOHN, proprietor Marion Hotel. (See adv)
McRae, F., general merchant
McDonald, J. L., dentist
Male, Joseph, blacksmith
MARION HOTEL, John McHugh, proprietor. (See adv)
Massie, John, M.D.
Miller, Samuel, butcher
Milligan, A., tailor
Murray, A., grammar school teacher
NICHOL, D., dry goods
Niles, W. H., flouring mill and stave factory
Payne, S. H., attorney at law
Peterson, Fletcher, farmer
Peterson & Huyck, blacksmiths
Peterson, T. H., general merchant
Powers, J. P., M.D.
Robertson, Donald, general merchant
Scott, Reuben, founder
Scougal, James, carriage and harness maker
Scripture, S. R., founder
Shannon, R., merchant tailor
Simpson, Rev. J., (Methodist Episcopal)
Sinclair, John, tailor
Spilsbury, Francis B., farmer
Strong, W. G., farmer
Tuttle, W. W., boots and shoes
Webb, J. G., general merchant
Wells, Alfred, butcher
Wilson, Rev. John, (Church of England)
Vars, A., grocer and provision dealer

Colchester P. O.—(See Oxford Village.)

MECKLE, JOHN, Postmaster.

Coldstream.—A Post Office in the Township of Lobo, County Middlesex, on Bear Creek, 15 miles from London, the County Seat.

Cutler, Amos, farmer
Cutler, E., miller
McCollum, Lafayette, wagon maker
McKinley, Donald, carpenter
MARSH, JACOB, Postmaster and gen. mercht.
Marsh, John, cabinet maker
Rutherford, Alexander, brick maker
Wood, John J., teacher
Zavitz, Daniel, seedsman

Coldwater.—A Village in the Township of Medonte, County Simcoe, on the Coldwater River, about a mile from the Georgian Bay, 30 miles from Barrie, the County Town, and 15 from Orillia. Population, 300.

Caswell, George, hotel keeper, lumber merchant and miller
Christie, Alexander R., lumber merchant
Darling, —, hotel keeper
EPLET, JOHN, Postmaster and general merchant
Hall, William, lumber merchant
Rutledge, William

Colebrook.—A flourishing Village situated on the Napanee River, in the Township of Camden East, and County Addington. Distant from Dingston, 20 miles, and from Napanee, the County Town, 16 miles. Stage to Kingston daily. Population about 250.

Brooks, H. C., merchant
Degraff, Wilson, saddler
Freeman, M., agricultural implements
Lario, J. & P., coopers
Newman, John, general merchant
Shibley, Charlers, saw miller
Smith, James, blacksmith
Walrath, G., lumber merchant
WARNER, CHARLES, J.P., Postmaster and issuer marriage licenses and com. in B.R.
Warner, D. S., general merchant and saw mill prop,
Wartman, Peter, lumber merchant

Coleraine.—A Village in the Gore of Toronto, County Peel. Distant from Brampton, the County Town, 11 miles, from Toronto, 22 miles. Stages to Bolton and Weston. Average price of land $35. Pop. 50.

Birch, F., shoemaker
Calluum, Zachariah, blacksmith
Cole, Thomas
Devins, Isaac, teacher
Gibson, John
Gould, David, proprietor Bee Hive Inn
Gowland, Matthew
GUARDHOUSE, JOHN, Postmaster
Hodgson, Rev. J., (Wesleyan)
Hughes, W. C., general merchant
Kersey, William
Leighton, George
Sandiman, Kirby
Thornburn, A., hotel keeper
Toppin, John
Young, Joseph, weaver

Coleridge.—A Post Village in the Township of Amaranth, County Wellington, distant from Guelph, the County Town, 50 miles, from Toronto, 60 miles. Average price of wild land $10, improved $20. Population 50.

Abernethy, John, farmer
Braiden, James, farmer
Coleman, John, farmer
Fittle, A., farmer
Graham, Thomas, carpenter
Hall, William, J. P.
Hosley, Thomas, farmer
Irwin, Joseph, farmer
Large, J., J. P.
Montgomery, James, farmer
Nixon, M., carpenter
Stones, George hotel keeper
Torrence, Thomas, cabinet maker
TRUEMAN, JOSEPH W., Postmaster

Colinville.—A Village on the River St. Clair, in the Township of Moore, County Lambton. Distant from Sarnia, the County Town, 10 miles, from Toronto 178 miles. Average price of wild land $9, improved $25. Population 60

Alexander, James, farmer
Armstrong, Rev. David, (Church of England)
Butler, James, farmer
BUTLER, JOHN, Postmaster
Dodds, John, wagon maker
Garrett, James, farmer
Henry, John, farmer
Kerr, John, carpenter
Kerr, Peter, carpenter
McDiarmid, Archibald, farmer
Smith, R. S., farmer
Watson, James, teacher
White, James, blacksmith
White, John, farmer

Collingwood.—A Town at the terminus of the Northern Railway, situated on the Georgian Bay, in the Township of Nottawasaga, County Simcoe; 95 miles from Toronto, and 33 from Barrie the County Town Steamers to Meaford, Owen Sound, Penetanguishene, Parry Sound, Byng Inlet, Sault Ste Maria, Fort William, &c. Stages to Durham, Thornbury and Owen Sound. Money Order Office and Savings Bank. Population 2500.

Bain, Peter, M. D.
Barker, J. J., general merchant
Barnhart, Noah, flour mills
Bassett, Thomas, blacksmith
Benway, Anthony A., boat builder
Birnie, John, carpenter
Bourchier, W., lumber merchant
Brown W. A. & Bros., butchers
Burnside, Robert, cooper
CAMERON, CHARLES, proprietor North American Hotel, stage proprietor. (see adv)
Campbell, Colin, general merchant
CARPENTER, E. R., chemist and druggist, (see adv)
Cleland, Hugh M., stoves and tinware
Collins, Allen, proprietor International Hotel
Cooper, M., watchmaker
Crone, William, general merchant
CUNNINGHAM, JAMES, agent N. R. R.
Curtis, Arthur, boots and shoes
Dickinson, C. R., M.A., principal Grammar School
Dougherty, Patrick, brick maker
Dudgeon, Adam, auctioneer
Duffey, Charles, cabinetmaker
Earle, John, carpenter
Edwards James, carpenter
ENTERPRISE (Weekly), John Hogg editor & prop.
Ferguson, Peter
Fleming, John, P. L. S.
Florance, E. C., boots and shoes
Foster, William, general merchant
Gamon, Charles, estate agent
GAMON & DALLAS, barristers, &c.
Geldart, William, carpenter
Gillson, H., prop. saw mills
Gordon, Robert, general merchant
Grant, Duncan, cooper
Grant, John, boots and shoes
GREAVES, JOSEPH, chemist and druggist (see adv.)
HAMILTON, W. B., Postmaster and ins. agent
Hardie, W. H., carpenter
Harrison, Matthew, carpenter
Hartelow, Thomas A., merchant tailor
Henry, James, merchant tailor
Heitman, H., seedsman
Hewitt, John, commission merchant
HEWITT, J. T., books and stationery
Hewser, P., painter
Hill, John, carpenter
Hocking, Henry, carpenter
HOGG, JOHN, Editor
HOTCHKISS & PECKHAM, lumber merchants
JARDINE, JOSEPH, general merchant
Jones, Enos, stone and lime dealer
Jones, Stephen, Victoria Hotel
Keen, William, carpenter
Kelly, D., prop. Commercial Hotel
Kennedy, R., pump maker
Kirk, Robert, planing and saw mills
Knox, Robert, cooper
Leonard, P. C., saddler
LAWRENCE, JOSEPH H., town clerk, estate agent and auctioneer
LeRoy, Eugene. saddler
LETT, REV. STEPHEN, L.L.D., (Church of Eng.)
Liddell, William, baker
Lindsay, James, general merchant
Lockerbie, Andrew, blacksmith
LONG, THOMAS & BRO., general merchants
McIntyre, John, carpenter
McKinnon, Angus, carpenter
McLEAN, GODFREY, watchmaker, (see adv)
McMaster, John, general merchant, agent Vicker's Express
Macdonell, Charles, commission merchant
MELVILLE, FAIR & Co., (Andrew and Thomas W. millers and general merchants
MELVILLE, DAVID, general merchant
Merrill, John, proprietor Huron Hotel
Moberly, Arthur, M. D.
Moberly, George, barrister
MONTGOMERY, DAVID
Mulholland, Edward, merchant tailor
Munson, Jared, carriage maker
Neff, Edmund, general merchant
Nettleton, John, merchant tailor
NORTH AMERICAN HOTEL, Charles Cameron, proprietor
PAGET, WILLIAM P., photographer and merchant
Palin & McMillan, leather merchants
Parlane, William A., accountant
Parrott, Edwin, tinsmith
Patterson, W. G., commission merchant
RAILWAY HOTEL, J. P. Ryley, prop.
ROBERTSON, HENRY, LL.B., barrister
Rochester, Andrew, cooper
Rodger, Rev. R., (Presbyterian)
Rowland, John, prop. Globe Hotel
RYLEY, J. P., prop. Railway Hotel
Seward, J. P., butcher
Smith, George, accountant
Smith & Mulholland, broom makers
STEPHEN, A. R., M.D.
Strong, William A., carpenter
SUTHERLAND, A. M., general merchant
SWAIN, WILLIAM, general merchant
Sykes, Royal, blacksmith
Sykes & Brown, carriage makers
Telfer, Andrew, carpenter
Telfer, Hall, baker
Telfer, James, agent
Telfer & Wiggins, general merchants
Trott, H. J., cabinet maker
Turner, Rev. Charles, (Wesleyan)
Tyson & Post, stave factory
WATSON, GEORGE P., J.P., Mayor
Watts, William, boat builder
Wainsley, W. H., painter
White, Thomas B., carpenter
Wolfe, Thomas P., commission merchant

Colpoy's Bay.—A Post Office of the Township of Albemarle, in the County Bruce, N R
KRIBBS, G., Postmaster.

Coldsprings.—A Village in the Township of Hamilton, County Northumberland, 7 miles from Cobourg, the County Town, and 7 from Harwood. Population 100.

Ainslie, Archibald, farmer
Eagleson, R., carpenter
Gage, G., carpenter
Graham, Robert, J. P.
Iredale, Dr.
McCune, H., butcher
McIntosh, Allen, J. P.
McINTOSH, D., Postmaster, general merchant
Neill, Christopher, J. P.
Nixon, George, farmer.
Philips, J., carpenter
Ramsay, William, hotel keeper
Sidney, D., general merchant

Collin's Bay.— A small Village on the Bay of Quinté, and a station of the Grand Trunk Railway, in the Township of Kingston, County Frontenac, 4 miles from Kingston, the County Town. Improved land in vicinity averages $30, and unimproved $20 per acre. Population 150.

Aiken, Clarke, farmer
Ashley, A., dentist
Carline, Cornelius, farmer
Case, Rev. G. (Wesleyan)
Davy, Peter W., J.P.
Everitt, John, farmer
Grass, John, farmer
Hamilton, David, farmer
Hassard, Rev. R. (Primitive Methodist)
Heck, John, butcher
HERCHMER, LAWRENCE, Postmaster and grocer
Jaquith, Edward, blacksmith
Jaquith, William, carriage maker
Lamb, George, livery stable
McGuin, Antony, farmer
Marsh, George hotel keeper
Purdy. James. carpenter
Rankin. David. farmer
Rankin. Hugh. farmer
Smith. James H.. farmer
Smith. John. farmer

Columbia, (Coventry Post Office).—A Village in a branch of the Humber, in the Township of Albion, County Peel. Distant from Brampton, the County Town, 20 miles, from Toronto 30 miles. Average price of land $40. Population 100.

Arnett, Simeon, shoemaker
Bown, Robert, general merchant
Brown, Robert, tailor
Campbell, Duncan, blacksmith
Elliott & Swinarton, tanners
Elliott, Robert, shoemaker
Kitchen, William, blacksmith
Linn, Andrew, teacher
McAllister, William, general merchant
McGinnis, Joseph, carpenter
McKEE, WILLIAM, Postmaster
Magovern, E., proprietor Columbia Inn
Potter, William, miller
SWINARTON THOMAS, M.P.P.

Columbus.—A thriving Village in the Township of East Whitby, County Ontario, 10 miles from Whitby, the County Town, 40 from Toronto, and 8 from Oshawa station, Grand Trunk Railway. Improved land in the vicinity averages $60 per acre. Money order office. Population 350.

Adams, Joseph, farmer
ASHTON, ROBERT, Postmaster and gen. merchant
Beull, James, mason
Beull, William, notary public, conveyancer, &c.
Bickle, John, flour mills
Bright, John, carriage maker
Bryce, McMurrich & Co., Empire Woolen Mills
Calder, John, shoemaker
Chesterfield, Stephen, shoemaker
Cole, Edward, prop. saw mill
Cruse, John, carriage maker
Doidge, George, farmer
Doolittle, Elisha, farmer
Edmondson, Rev. J. (Canada Presbyterian)
Gaskin, Matthew, blacksmith
Goodman, James, proprietor flour mill
Grass, Lewis C., farmer
Harper, Richard, farmer
Hawkey, L. C., saddler
Hawkins, James and William, shoemakers
Hill, Walter, farmer
Hodgson, Robert, proprietor Crown Inn
Hugre, Stephen, tailor
Hull, Rev. F. C. (Bible Christian)
Joynt, John, potash factor
Kerslake, William, carriage maker
McLaren, Duncan, carpenter
McLean, William, carpenter
Milne, James, proprietor saw mill
Nankeville, Edwin, bricklayer
Passmore, Thomas, shoemaker
Porteous, Alexander, blacksmith
Ratcliff, John, J.P.
Roberts, John, butcher
Rowse, John, general merchant
Scarrah, Charles, cooper
Scarrah, Joseph, cooper
Slater, Rev. J. C., (Wesleyan)
Smith, Allen G., farmer
Smith, William, farmer
Stokes, C. Scott, M.D.
Wherry, John, tailor
Wickett, Samuel R., tanner
Wilcockson, Thomas, farmer

Combermere.—A small Village on the Madawaska River, in the Township of Radcliffe, County Renfrew, 54 miles from Pembroke, the County Town, 54 from Renfrew, and 71 from Sand Point. Bi-weekly mails. Population 54.

Bellisle, Joseph, hotel keeper
Cameron, A. & Co., general merchants
Denison, Henry, farmer
Denison, John, sen., farmer
Denison, John, jun., farmer
Glenn, William, shoemaker
JOHNSON, DANIEL, Postmaster and gen. mercht.
Kelly, Cornelius, blacksmith
Kelly, Thomas, millwright
Seeley, Justus, hotel keeper

Comber.—A Post Village in the Township of East Tilbury, County Essex. Distant from Sandwich, the County Town, 12 miles. Money order office. Population 100.

McALISTER, D., Postmaster.

Conestogo.—A Village in the Township of Woolwich, County Waterloo, situated at the confluence of the Conestogo and Grand Rivers, 8 miles from Berlin, the County Town, 7 from Breslau Station Grand Trunk Railway, and 70 from Toronto. There are first class water privileges in the village and neigborhood. The 7th Division Court of the County is held here. Improved lands in the vicinity average $55 per acre, unimproved $40. Money Order office. Population 300.

Bergman, August, carriage maker
Bowman, John K, lime dealer
Cole, Isaac, carriage maker
Cole, Nelson, carriage maker
Dechir, Philip, carpenter
Eby, William & Cyrus, potters
Fields, James & Son, distillers
Haack, Carl, brick maker
Hahn, George, cooper
HENDRY, CHARLES, Postmaster and general merchant
Hollé, Felix, carpenter
Klemmer, John, shingle maker
Kuntz, Jacob, cooper
Lippert, Jacob, shoemaker
Musselman, David, farmer
Musselman, Peter, farmer
Musselman, Solomon, farmer
Oswald, Philip, hotel keeper
Ritzer, Joseph, tailor
Ruby, E., teacher
Schweizer, Martin, hotel keeper
Shoemaker & Good, carriage makers
Shoemaker, John, shoemaker
Snider, John, farmer
Snyder, J. B. & Co., general merchants
Steuernagel, Christian, hotel keeper
Stroh, Conrad, farmer
Weaver, Daniel, farmer
Weaver, Peter, farmer
Wiegand, William, cabinet maker
Wright, George, farmer

Coningsby.—A Village in the Township of Erin, County Wellington, 16 miles from Guelph the County Town, and 10 from Acton station Grand Trunk Railroad. Stage to Georgetown, 13 miles. Population 100.

Barbour, Robert, J. P.
Baughman, Charles, carpenter
Baughman, Henry, cabinet maker
Bingham, Robert, lime dealer
BURT, J. W., Postmaster, J. P.
Burt, J. & D., shingle makers
Clark, Edward, farmer
Ferguson, Donald, farmer
Harper, John, wagon maker
McGill, John, farmer
McGil, Neil, farmer
McLean, P., teacher
Smith, J., farmer
Smith, Jacob, lime dealer
Smith, M., carpenter
Smith, William, farmer
Thompson, Angus, farmer
Thompson, Dugald, farmer

Conner.—A Village in the Township of Adjala, electoral division of Cardwell. Distant from Barrie the County Town, 35 miles, from Toronto 38 miles. Average price of land $20. Population 75.

Beaton, Kenneth, teacher
Caberon, John, farmer
Collins, Rev. M., (Wesleyan)
Darrach, James, farmer
Elliott, James, farmer
Elliott, Joseph, farmer
Hamilton, Rev., (Presbyterian)
Hunt, Rev. D., (Wesleyan
Jackson, George
Leggett, Joseph farmer
Leggett, William, farmer
McGIBBON, WALTER, Postmaster, and general merchant!
McGilvray & Parsons, millers
McLaughlin, John, miller
Mercer, Robert, farmer
Smith, W. E., teacher

Conroy.—A small Village in the Township of Downie, County Perth, 6½ miles from Stratford, the County Town. Average price of improved land in vicinity $30 per acre. Stages to Stratford, fare 50 cents.

Bradshaw, Thomas, farmer
Blair, William, hotel keeper
Boyes, John, shoemaker
Calahan, John, shoemaker
Cole, H. H., farmer
Coonan, Michael, farmer
Fahey, Timothy, carpenter
Fox, James, farmer
Harrison, John, farmer
Iredale, Joseph, miller
Kane, Timothy, farmer
Knott, Richard, farmer
Moran, Patrick, teacher
O'Grady, John, wagon maker
SMITH, PETER, Postmaster
Thistle, Robert, farmer

Concord.—A small Post Village in the Township of Vaughan, County York. Distant from Toronto 14 miles. Daily Mail.

DUNCAN, JOHN, Postmaster

Consecon.—A Village on Consecon Creek, between the lake of the same name, and Weller's Bay, in the Townships of Ameliasburg and Hillier, County Prince Edward. Distant from Picton, the County Town, 21 miles, from Toronto, 140 miles. Stage to Brighton, Picton and Wellington. Money order office, Population 300.

Arthur, Charles, general merchant
Arthur, Hugh, J.P.
Arthur, James
Bailey, Levi C., painter
Beard, James, sen.
Beech, D.
Beech, P. V.
Boothe, Robert, shoemaker
Byers, John, carpenter
Cadman, J. M., J.P.
Carnike, John, baker
Chase, Jacob, shingle manufacturer
Clark, Henry, cooper
Cotton, W., M.D.
Dipple, —, wagon maker
Firman, Thomas, bailiff
Hays, George, wagon maker
Harrington, J., butcher
Hicks, John, saddler
Hiram, Edward, proprietor Prince Edward hotel
Huyck, Jessie, teacher
Loveless, Hiram, tailor
McDonald, —, M.D
McDonald, David, tailor
McGrath, Mrs., groceries
MARSH, ABRAHAM, Postmaster
Marsh, Edmund, carpenter
Marsh, Edmund, jun., telegraph operator
Marsh, Matthias, wagon maker
Maybee, John, saddler
MEACHAM, W. W., teacher
Miller, Joseph, tinsmith
Miller, Martin, carpenter
Morrison, John & Co., wagon makers
Osborne, F. J., miller
Osborne, John T.
Parliament, Henry
Porter, Robert, proprietor Globe Hotel
Quackinbush, Calvin, tailor
Robinson, Mrs., groceries
Smith, William
Squier & Whittier, general merchants
Squires, H., carpenter
Viant & Mastin, butchers
Weeks, Morris, cooper
Weeks, Solomon, butcher
Weeks, S. S.
Young, M., shingle manufacturer

Constance (see Kinburn).—A Post Office in the Township of Hullet, County Huron, 20 miles from Goderich, the County Town.

THOMPSON, ROBERT, Postmaster.

Conway.—A Post Office in the Township of South Fredericksburgh, County Lennox. 15 miles from Napanee the County Town, and 15 from Earnestown Station Grand Trunk Railroad, on the Bay of Quinte.

Barrass, Rev. Edward, (Wesleyan)
Chamberlain & Sills, patent medicines
Clark, James, farmer
Ham, George, J. P., farmer
Harding, Rev. Robert, (Church of England)
Harwood, George, farmer
Ingersoll, Marshall, farmer
Ingersoll, W. H., farmer
McDowall, Robert, potash manufacturer
Neilson, Alexander, potash manufacturer
Neilson, John, potash manufacturer
Phippin, William, potash manufacturer
Phippin, Richard, potash manufacturer
Sills, Conrad, farmer
SILLS, G. B., Postmaster, &c.
Sloane, William J., farmer
VanDyck, Henry, J. P., farmer
Wright, Solomon, potash manufacturer
Young, Robert, potash manufacturer

Cookstown.—A Village situated at the corners of the Townships of Essa, Innisfil, Tecumseth and West Gwillinbury, County Simcoe, 15 miles from Barrie, the County Town, 13 from Bradford, and 8 from Gilford station, Northern Railway. Stages to Gilford. Money order office. Population 400.

Armstrong, William, blacksmith
Bailey, Thomas, photographer
BOYS, T. T. A., barrister (see adv)
BANTING, COL. ROBERT T., County Clerk
Bradshaw, James, stage proprietor
Buchanan, C. W., M.D.
Campbell, Rev. A. R., (Wesleyan).
CLEMENT, STEPHEN, general merchant
Coleman, E., proprietor hotel
Cook, Christopher
Cook, James, farmer
Cook, Thomas, farmer
Dales, William, blacksmith
Daniels, Elijah, teacher
Dawson, Alexander, farmer
Ferguson, Thomas R., M.P.P.
Ferris, James, farmer
Fidler, Rev. A. J., (Church of England)
Graham, Robert, proprietor hotel
Hamilton, Charles, saddler
HARPER, HENRY, Postmaster, druggist
Hughes, Robert, cooper
Kidd, James, J.P.
Kidd, William F., wagon maker
Leadbetter, William, general merchant
Lenshner, Paul, watchmaker
McCracken, Alexander, wagon maker
McCracken & Heaslip, carpenters
McFarlane, Finlay, J.P.
McKee, Hugh, carpenter
Montgomery, William, shoemaker
NICHOL, H. A., M.D.
Norris, J. W., M.D.
Parkin, William, proprietor hotel
Proctor, John, saddler
Ralston, Peter, shoemaker
Ralston, William, potashery
Ross, John, J.P.
Ross, William, farmer
Ross & Sanders, general merchants
Strong, James G., general merchants
Tate, James, tailor
Watson, John, general merchant
Whitelock, Christopher

Cooksville.—A Village in the township of Toronto, County Peel, 10 miles from Brampton, the County Town, 16 from Toronto and 3 from Port Credit station, Great Western Railway. The Vine Growers Association, established here in 1863, have about 30 acres under culture. Stages daily to Streetsville and Port Credit. Money Order office. Population 400.

Codling, Thomas, butcher
Colwell, Charles, wagon maker
Cook, Jacob
Cook, M. W., manager Cooksville Vine Growers' Association
Coombe, Mark, butcher
Cox, William, baker
DeCourtney, J. M., vine grower
Faulkner, Elias
Galbraith, John, general merchant
Harris, James, ship carpenter
Harris, Timothy, shingle maker
Howard, Rev. T. S., (Wesleyan)
King, Thomas D., J.P., general merchant
Lewis, Thomas, M.D
MORLEY, F. B., Postmaster
Ogden, —, M.D
Parker, Melville, J. P
Peaker, William & Son, tinsmiths
Romain, P. Z., general merchant
Schillar, John, hotel keeper
Soady, James, shoemaker
Weeks, William, shoemaker

Cooper.—A Village on Black and Cooper Creeks, in the Township of Madoc, County Hastings. Distant from Belleville, the County Town, 34 miles, from Toronto 147 miles. Daily Stage to and from Madoc. Average price of land $25. Population 100.

Adams, Robert, cooper
Allen, Charles
Allen, Robert S
ALLEN, THOMAS, Postmaster
Allen, William
Allen, William J
Bacon, Samuel, sen
Bacon, Samuel, jun., lime manufacturer
Bateman, J., constable
Blair, William
Cooper, Miss Sarah Ann, teacher
Deprose, Joseph
Elliott, Thomas, teacher
Fowler, Amos, shoemaker
Kellar, Isaac, carpenter
Ketcheson, J. R., town clerk
Kinnear, Robert, grocer
McDonald, D., constable
Mullett, —, tanner
Remington, John, grocer
Rutledge, Miss Fanny, teacher
Vankleek, B., J.P
Vankleek, Peter
Wood, William, carpenter

Coplestone.—A Village on North Creek, in the Township of Enniskillen, County Lambton. Distant from Sarnia, the County Town, 17 miles. Average price of land $12 to $30. Principal manufacture coal oil.

Elliott, W., carpenter
Graham, John
Johnson, William, teacher
Mitchell, Aquila
Morrison, John
Slack, John
SMITH, RICHARD P., Postmaster
Tracy, John
Wolsey, John, carpenter
Wolsey, Thomas

Copetown.—A Village and Station on the Great Western Railway, on the line between the Townships of Ancaster and Beverly, County Wentworth, 10 miles from Hamilton, the County Town and 50 from Toronto. Average value of improved land in the vicinity $50 per acre. Population 300.

Aikman, Charles, M.D
Armitage, J. W. D.
Bawtinhimer, Adam, wagon maker
Bowman, Joseph, saw mill prop
Burrows, Joseph, grocer
Cope, Jacob, farmer
Cronan, John, hotel keeper
Elliott, H. N., prop. Railroad Inn
Field, Solomon, farmer
Hall, Rev. John, (N. C. Methodist)
Head, Robert, shingle maker
Inksetter, Robert, farmer
Kennedy, Thomas, farmer
Ketchen, H. H., J. P
McAllister, Rev. J., (N. C. Methodist)
Milne, Thomas, J.P., general merchant
Phelp, N. & O. J., saw mill proprietors
Pritchard, John, carpenter
Vandusen, Zena, teacher
Vinton, J., carpenter
Vinton, Newell farmer
Williams, William, shoemaker
Wood, Peter, prop. saw mill

Corinth.—A Post Village in the Township of Bayham, County Elgin, E. R.

BEST, F. A., Postmaster.

Cornabuss.—A Village in the Townships of Glenelg and Artemesia, County Grey, 32 miles from Collingwood, situated on the Saugeen River, which affords good water privileges. Stages to Orangeville, Owen Sound, Collingwood and Durham. Money Order office. Population 200.

Allen, James, hotel keeper
Benson, John, carpenter
Black, John, weaver
Brown, William, general merchant
Burns, James, carpenter
Dundas, William, saddler
Eaton, A. W., blacksmith
Edwards, J. S., Commissioner in B. R.
Gillie, Rev. W. (Wesleyan)
Hackett, Brothers, tinsmiths
McBride, Robert, barber
McFARLAND, W. J., Postmaster, general merchant
Mathews Thomas, saddler
Noble, Alfred, wagon maker
Reynolds, Clark, general merchant
Richardson, Mark, blacksmith
Ritchie, William, wagon maker
Rordan, Thomas, M. D.
Rutledge, Alexander, hotel keeper
Shelder, Hiram, cooper
Stewart, Henry, weaver
Thibodeau, J. B., general merchant
Vardon, Thomas, M. D.
Waldie, James, miller
Wright, George, carpenter

Cornwall.—A Town on the River St. Lawrence, and Grand Trunk Railroad, in the Township of Cornwall, County Stormont. It is the chief Town of the United Counties of Stormont, Dundas and Glengarry. Distance from Montreal 68 miles, from Toronto 265. Money Order Office and Savings Bank. Population 2000.

Adams, P. E., baker and grocer
Allan, William C., M. D.
Atchison, William & Co., proprietors steamer British America
Austin, Rev. Henry. (Church of England)
Bailey, J., general merchant
BANK OF MONTREAL, James Cox, Agent; Evelyn Vardon, accountant
Bartley, Henry, grocery
Bergin, D., M. D.
BERGIN, J., Solicitor, Insurance Agent and Master in Chancery
Bethune, Angus, flour and grist mill
BETHUNE, JAMES, barrister, Clerk Peace and County Attorney
Bethune, W., solicitor
Bradbury, J. L., principal grammar school
Broderick, John, proprietor International Hotel
Bullock, R. K., Collector Customs
Butler, J. R., watchmaker
Cadwell, A. E., iron founder
Callaghan, Owen, blacksmith
Carpenter, David, livery
Carpenter, George, blacksmith
Chisholm, William, attorney-at-law
Cline, Samuel, general merchant
Cline, William, general merchant
CORNWALL WOOLEN MANUFACTURING CO., E. M. Hopkins, President, George Stephen, Vice-President, John Warwick, Manager, James P. Watson, Secretary
COX, JAMES, agent Bank of Montreal
CRAIG, JAMES, M.P.P.
Craig, Robert, tannery
CUSHMAN, J. W., watchmaker and jeweler
Darois, Peter, hairdresser
Davy, John, shoemaker
Dennany, John, innkeeper
Dennison, Joseph, ashery and grocery
Dickinson, J. J., M.D.
Dingwall, James, barrister
Dixon, Rev. James, (Wesleyan)
DUNKIN, THOMAS, proprietor Ottawa Hotel
Duncan, William, livery
Flack & Van Arsdale, (D. A. Flack & Isaac H. Van Arsdale) stone ware manufacturers
Gilley, James & Son, blacksmiths
Gilley, Peter, blacksmith

Gollinger, William, blacksmith
Hepburn, H., proprietor Commercial Hotel
Hessell, William, butcher
Heudebourck, Rev. W. H., (Canada Presbyterian)
HILL, WILLIAM, general merchant
Hodge, Andrew, flour and grist mills
Hollister, W. G., agent Montreal Telegraph Co
Hunter, John, tinsmith
Irons, William, painter
Irving, James, carriage maker
James, C. H., general merchant
Jarvis, George S., judge County Court
Johnston, James C., builder
Joyce, Miss Margaret, confectionery and fancy goods
KEWIN, EDWIN, general merchant (see adv)
Kilgour, J. & Son, (J, Kilgour & James Kilgour) general merchants
Kissock, James, marble works
LEWIS, JOHN W., barber
Littlefield, Mrs. Mary, billiard room
Lonney, John, blacksmith
Lynch, Rev. Michael, (Roman Catholic)
Lynskey, Thomas, agent G. T. R
McArthur, A. A., grocer
McCracken, David, butcher
McDonald, Alexander, cabinet maker
McDonald, R., County Treasurer, Clerk County Court and Deputy Clerk Crown and Pleas
McDonell, Angus, coronor
McDonell, G. & D., general merchants
McDonell, J. A., tailor
McDougall, Alexander, dry goods and crockery
McDougall, John S., boots, shoes, harness and leather dealer
McEniry, Michael, Railway Hotel
McFarlane, Arch & Co., general merchants
McIntosh, J. A., insurance and general agent
McIntyre, D. E., Sheriff
McLEAN, ALEXANDER, editor and proprietor of the *Freeholder*
McLean, Neil, insurance agent
McLennan, Duncan, jailer
McLENNAN, JOHN B., (McDonald & McLennan)
McMahon, Thomas, harness maker
McMillan, D. & Co., general merchants
McPhaul, Angus, general merchant
McPhee, John, hardware and tinware
Macdonald, Æneas, M.D.
MACDONALD, HON. J. SANDFIELD, Q.C., M.P., M.P.P. (McDonald & McLennan)
Macdonald, R., M.D.
MACDONALD & McLENNAN (Hon. J. Sandfield Macdonald, Q.C., and John B. McLennan), barristers
Macdonell, D. A., general merchant
Macdonald, R. G., forwarder and grain merchant G.T.R.
Mack, William, flouring and grist mills
Martin, P. B., paper manufacturer
Mattice, William & Sons (William Mattice, C. J. Mattice and Gregor Mattice) general merchants
Mea, T. M., tailor
Meyers, James, mason
Miller, Donald, brick manufacturer
Morsell, John, prop. foundry
Munro, Duncan
OTTAWA HOTEL, THOMAS DUNKIN, prop
Park, William M., watchmaker
Patton, Very Rev. J., D.D. (Church of England)
Phelan, J. A., collector of canal tolls
Pollock, Samuel, chief constable
Porteous, A. T., photographer
Poole, Charles, clerk Divison Court
Pringle & Hawkes, (George Pringle, M.D., & James Hawkes,) druggists
Pringle, Jacob F., assistant judge County Court
Rattray, Charles, M.D
Robishaw, Oliver, baker
Ross, A. P., carriage maker and blacksmith
Ross, Gordon, mason
Ross, William, barrister
Skeith, J., druggist
Skeith, John, stoves and tinware
Smary, John, steamboat agent
Smith, Daniel M.D
Smith, William, carriage maker
Smythe, Robert, shoemaker
Snetsinger, John, builber
Styles, Homer, blacksmith
Sullivan, Daniel, painter
Talbot, Angus, carpenter
Talbot, John, carpenter
THE FREEHOLDER, (weekly) Alexander McLean, editor and proprietor
Turner, N., hardware
Urquhart, Rev. Hugh, D.D., (Presbyterian)
Van Alstine, John, baker
Wagner, Adam, innkeeper
WAGNER, WILLIAM J., watchmaker and jeweler (see adv)
Warrington, William, proprietor Farmer's Hotel
WARWICK, JOHN, manager Cornwall Manuf. Co.
Wegant, R. G., dentist
Weber, H. W., photographer
Wildon, Thomas, tailor
Wilson, D., baker and grocer
WOOD, GEORGE C., Postmaster and Registrar County Stormont
Worsley, John, shoemaker

Cotswold.—A Village in the Township of Minto, County Wellington, distant from Guelph, the County Town 35 miles, from Toronto 82 miles. Stages to Guelph and Walkerton.

Allen, Rev. H. W. P. (Wesleyan)
Currie, John, teacher
Frazer, Alexander, general merchant
McKENZIE, PETER, Postmaster
McLellan, Rev. George (Presbyterian)
Mackillop, A.
North, S. R., carpenter
Smith, John

Coulson.—A small Village in the Township of Medonte, County Simcoe, 20 miles from Barrie, the County Town, and 86 from Toronto. There is excellent water power in the neighborhood. Average value of improved land $20, wild $5 per acre. Population 40.

COULSON, JAMES, J. P., Postmaster, general merchant, dealer in lumber, stone, lime, &c.
Coulson, William, carpenter
Carmichael, Dugald, farmer
Fagan, John, farmer
Tudhope, John, shingle maker
Walker, Joseph, farmer

Corunna.—A thriving Village on the River St. Clair, in the Township of Moore, County Lambton, 6 miles from Sarnia, the County Town. Large quantities of staves and timber are annually exported, and thousands of cords of word are sold, chiefly to American steamers. Daily mails. Population 200.

Andreaux, Rev. Father, (Roman Catholic)
Baxter, John, tailor
Bennett, John, farmer
Beattie, William, cabinet maker
Britton, Joseph, boot and shoemaker
Brown, William, teacher
Chambers, John, farmer
Chislett, John, boot and shoemaker
Countois, Albert, grocer
Edwards, Davids, sportsman
Ellis, Henry
Ellis, Henry, jun., sailor
Farquharson, Alexander, sailor
Farquharson, John, carpenter
FISHER, DR. ALFRED, Postmaster Sarnia
Gilbert, William, weaver
Hagan, John, shipbuilder
Haney, John, plasterer
Havers, John, butcher and grocer
HUGHES, J. W., general merchant
Jackson, Joseph, tailor
Kingston, Thomas, engineer
Lewis, John, teacher
McGill, John, farmer
McNiel, John, shipbuilder
Marson, John T., gardener
Mitge, Richard C. E., teacher
MILLER, H. J., Postmaster and general merchant
Miller, John P., tin pedler
Minton, Thomas, hotel proprietor
Morris, John, blacksmith
Moylan, John, inn keeper
Porter, James, farmer
Proctor, George, carpenter
Proctor, James, general merchant
Proctor, Merza, millwright
Richards, Peter, carpenter
Scott, William, M. D.
Simpson, Alexander, mechanic
Simpson, James, sailor
Skirving, James, blacksmith
Stanley, Lawrence, wood merchant
Taylor, John, wood merchant
Wallace, James, bricklayer
Wallace, John, blacksmith
Watson, Joseph, farmer

Courtland.—A Village in the Township of Middleton, County Norfolk, 19 miles from Simcoe, and 20 from Ingersoll station Great Western Railway. Stages to Straffordville and Delhi. Average value of improved land in the vicinity $20, unimproved $15 per acre. Population 150.

Campbell, Henry, carriage maker
Connor, Thomas, hotel keeper
Cowan, James, flour and saw mills
Cozens, George, carpenter
Cutting, Stephen, carpenter
Dean, Percy, Township Treasurer
Flaherty, William, tailor
Glover, Pierce, carpenter
Graydon, William, carriage maker
Hall, Daniel, saddler
HARRIS, CHARLES S., Postmaster, clerk 4th Div. Court, Commissioner in B. R., general merchant
Helminck, B., blacksmith
Herron, John, general merchant
Herron, John C. H., shoemaker
Herron, Thomas, farmer
Mills, William, farmer
Ranson, George, farmer
Ranson, Thomas B., farmer
Ranson, William, farmer
Reigh, John, farmer
Standen, James, farmer
Tisdale, Lot, farmer
White, Thomas, general merchant
Wilson, James, hotel keeper

Coventry.—A post office in the County of Cardwell. (See Columbia.)

Craighurst.—A Village in the Township of Medonte, County Simcoe. Distant from Barrie the County Town, 13 miles, from Toronto 75 miles. Stage daily to Barrie and Penetanguishene. Average price of wild land $4, improved $40. Money order office. Population 200.

Archer, Edward, farmer
Bishop, Stephen, farmer
Casey, Michael, general merchant
Clark, John, lumber dealer
CRAIG, JOHN, Postmaster
Craig, Thomas, farmer
Craw, Rev. George, (Presbyterian)
Daly, Mrs., proprietor Farmers' Arms
Firth, George, wagon maker
Frawley, P. J., shoemaker
Green, & Bros., general merchants
Gunn, James, shoemaker
Harris, Rev. R. H., (Church of England)
Hutton, John, tailor
Johnson, Lawrence, farmer
Johnson, William, farmer
Laing, John, blacksmith
McClean, John, blacksmith
McLean, George, farmer
McLean & Johnson, lumber dealers
Matheson, Rev. James, (Wesleyan)
Miller, Alexander, teacher
Mintie, Robert, farmer
Morrison, Mrs. C., proprietor Queen's Arms Hotel
Morrison, William, carpenter
Powell, Richard, general merchant
Rodgers Peter, tinsmith
Rush, Joseph L., carpenter
Sproule, T. S., M. D.
Thornton, John, wagon maker

Craigleith.—A small Village in the Township of Collingwood, County Grey, situated on the Georgian Bay, 6 miles from Collingwood station Northern Railroad, and 38 from Owen Sound the County Town. Average value of wild lands in vicinity $10, and improved $30 per acre. Stages to Owen Sound and Collingwood. Population 50.

FLEMING, A. G., Postmaster
Spong, George, teacher

Cowal.—A post office situated in the Township of Southwald, County Elgin.

McBRIDE, N., Postmaster.

Craig Vale.—A Post Village and Station on the Northern Railway, in the Township of Innisfil, County Simcoe, 7 miles from Barrie, the County Town. Messrs. Thomson, Smith & Son, of Toronto, do an extensive lumber business here. Daily mails. Population about 120.

Bell, Charles, carriage maker
Craigvale Hotel
Griffin, James, blacksmith
McCraw, R. G., tailor
Maneer, Samuel, blacksmith
MUNSIE, ROBERT, J.P., Postmaster, issuer of marriage licenses, auctioneer, general merchant, etc.

Cranbrook.—(Grey P.O.)—A Village in the Township of Grey, County Huron, on the Maitland River, 44 miles from Goderich, the County Town, and 20 from Seaforth Station, Grand Trunk Railway. Good water power. Population 150.

Armstrong, Joseph, carpenter
Barker, John, shoemaker
Dambs, William, hotel keeper, butcher, etc.
Ferguson, Rev. —, (Presbyterian)
Guners, Jacob, carpenter
Gowanlock, Andrew, farmer
Hicks, James, shoemaker
Hogan, Michael, farmer
Hunter, Alexander, carpenter
Huter, F., carpenter
Johnston, John, carpenter
Knight, Joseph, farmer
Leadbeater, Thomas, general merchant
LECKIE, JOHN, Postmaster
McDonald, Daniel, teacher
McLaughlin, John, farmer
McNair, Alexander, teacher
Miller, Henry, A., saw mill proprietor
Mullisan, David & Co., general merchants
Mulholland, Miss, teacher
Schesser, Rev. John, (German Wesleyan)
Seale, George, cooper
Slemons, Samuel, farmer
Tuck, James, hotel keeper
Woodriff, Daniel, farmer

Cranworth.—A Post office in the Township of South Burgess, County Leeds, 35 miles from Brockville, the County Town. Land in the vicinity averages $8 per acre. Phosphate of lime, plumbago, mica, and other minerals abound in the neighborhood.

Baker, George W., shingle maker
Gutridge, Robert, farmer
Hart, Richard, farmer
Jones, Joseph, farmer
Jones, John, farmer
Jones, Peter, farmer
KYLE, THOMAS M., Postmaster and teacher
McKenney, John, farmer
Morrison, James, farmer
Toffey, George, farmer

Crawford.—A Post office in the Township of Bentinck, County Grey, 28 miles from Owen Sound, the County Town. Wild land in the vicinity averages $3 and improved $12 per acre.

Anderson, George, farmer
Coutts, Alexander, farmer
Coutts, John, farmer
Honess, Stephen, farmer
McQuarrie, Lachlan, farmer
McRAE, HECTOR, Postmaster
Shewell, Edward, farmer
White, James, farmer

Creek Bank.—A Village in the Township of Peel, County Wellington. Distant from Guelph, the County Town, 20 miles, from Toronto 65 miles. Stages to and from Guelph. Average price of land $40. Population 50.

Burt, Thomas, carpenter
Crane, Rev. Isaac, (Wesleyan)
Fisher, Alexander, J.P
GRAHAM, JAMES, Postmaster and gen. mercht
Jackson, Rev. Thomas, (Wesleyan)
Miller, Jacob, prop. Creek Bank Hotel

Crediton.—A Village in the Township of Stephen, County Huron. Distant from Goderich, the County Town, 37 miles, from Toronto 169 miles. Average price of land $80. Population 200.

Ales & Lloyd, carpenters
Back, John, general merchant
Bish, George, painter
Bissett, Robert, brick manufacturer
Brown, Charles, general merchant
Campbell, George W., M.D
Eilber, C., general merchant
Eilber, Jacob, carpenter
Foster, Samuel E., teacher
Gaum & Krause, woolen factors
Gaum, V., cabinet maker
Heitzman, C., cooper
Hooper, Rev. William, (Bible Christian)
Klumpp, John, shoemaker
Krause, F. & Bros., architects
Kreider, Mrs., dressmaker
Kreider, John, carpenter
Lloyd, Mrs., dressmaker
Mellon, Henry, tailor
Mitchell, William, brick manufacturer
Murlock, Julius, wagon maker
PARSONS, JOHN, Postmater & general merchant
Press, Simon, prop. Crediton Hotel
Schmidt, Michael, wagon maker
Schnider, William, carpenter
Schœlly, George, saddler
Schwandt, Rev. William, (Dutch Evangelical Ass.)
Schwitzer, Charles, butcher
Schwitzer, Henry, lumber dealer
Schwitzer & Wirt, brick makers
Trevethick, John, wagon maker
Well, Henry, carpenter
White, Robert, cooper
Zwiker, Christian, shoemaker

Credit.—*(See Springfield)*—A Post village in the Township of Toronto, County Peel. Distant from Brampton, the County Town, 13 miles, from Toronto 19 miles. Money Order office.

TAYLOR EMERSON, Postmaster.

Creemore.—A Village on the Mad River, in the Township of Nottawasaga, County Simcoe. Distant from Barrie, the County Town, 26 miles, from Toronto 85 miles. Stages to and from Stayner. Tri-weekly mails. Average price of land $50. Money Order office. Population 200.

Briggs, Rev. S. R., (Episcopal)
Coupland, John
Currie, James, J.P
Currie, Malcolm, teacher
Dack, E. B., M.D
Day, John
Fox, C., cooper
Galloway, T., shoemaker
Gillespie, A., general merchant
Gowan, William, prop. Gowan's Hotel
Hysey, Samuel
Kelly, William, prop. Exchange Hotel
Kitching, T., shoemaker
Langtrey, W., butcher
Lawrence, William, painter
McBeth, John
McManus, G. C., M.D
Madill, R., J.P
Neelands, H
Newton, Edward
Parker, Charles
Patterson, R., saddler
Smith, R., general merchant
Thornbury, F. C. & Co., general merchants
THORNBURY, W. H., Postmaster & gen. mercht
Walker, R., shingle maker
Watts, Rev. J. M., (Methodist Episcopal)

Creighton.—A small Village in the Township of Medonte, County Simcoe, 24 miles from Barrie, the County Town, and 10 from Orillia. Average value of improved land in the vicinity, $12; unimproved, $6 per acre.

Bell, John, J.P.
Brotherson, David, tanner
CAVANAGH, THOMAS, Postmaster and general merchant
Clapham, William, dyer
Cook, John, saw mill prop.
Duddy, Thomas, farmer
Goss, Joseph, farmer
Harris, Rev. Mr., (Church of England)
Livingston, Dugald, farmer
McKay, Dugald, teacher
O'Connor, James, saw mill prop.
O'Connor, John, farmer
Thompson, John, woolen mill

Cressy.—A small Post Village in the Township of Marysburgh, County Prince Edward. Distant from Picton, the County Town, 9 miles. Population about 40.

CARSON, S. W., Postmaster and merchant.

Crieff.—A small Post Village in the Township of Puslinch, County Wellington.

McLEAN, JOHN, Postmaster.

Crinan.—A small Post Village situated on the River Thames, in the Township of Aldboro', County Elgin. Distant from St. Thomas, the County Town 30 miles. Population 30.

McGill, D., blacksmith
McINTYRE, DUNCAN, Postmaster and tailor

Cromarty.—A small Village in the Township of Hibbert, County Perth, 24 miles from Stratford, the County Town, and 100 from Toronto. Average value of land in the vicinity, $35 per acre. Population about 50.

Allen, Benjamin, wagon maker
Bell, John, farmer
Currie, Hugh, farmer
Currie, John, farmer
Ferguson, Alexander, insurance agent
Fotheringham, Rev. John, (Presbyterian)
Hamilton, George, J.P.
Hamilton, Robert, farmer
McKellar, Duncan, farmer
McLaren, Alexander, farmer
McNicol, Walter, shoemaker
McVey, Charles, insurance agent
PARK, ALEXANDER, Postmaster and carpenter
Reading, Joseph, general merchant
Rigg, John, farmer
Walker, Oswald, farmer
Whyte, John, farmer

Crosshill.—A Village in the Township of Wellesley, County Waterloo. Distant from Berlin, the County Town, 16 miles, from Toronto 75 miles. Stages to and from Berlin. Average price of land $40. Population 200.

Barbour, William, farmer
Bird, Benjamin, painter
Boyd, Rev. James, (Presbyterian)
Cleghorn, S. A., proprietor Union Hotel
Couts, William, farmer
Hastings, William, J.P.
Hewatt, William, farmer
Hutchison, Adam, farmer
Kerr ,Andrew, wagon maker
Lee, Joseph, nurseryman
Logan, Rev. —, (Church of England)
McCUTCHEON, JAMES, Postmaster
McCutcheon, R. A., farmer
Mackie, John A., general merchant
Milliken, Rev. Andrew, (Wesleyan)
Oakley, George, proprietor Queen's Arms Hotel
Rannie, S. W., carpenter
Rathwell, W. J., teacher
Sutcliffe, Edward, nurseryman
Tilt, Nathaniel, insurance agent
Wood, Elizabeth, groceries, etc.

Croton.—A small Post Village in the Township of Camden, County Bothwell. Distant from Chatham, the County Town, 20. Daily mails. Population about 80.

Butler, John S., shoemaker
Greenwood, Ira, shoemaker
How, L., blacksmith
JOHNSTON, J. H., J.P., Postmaster, gen. mer and saw mill owner
Woodford, Joseph, cooper

Crowland.—A Post office in the Township of Crowland, County Welland.

BOARDMAN, LUTHER, Postmaster.

Croydon.—A Small Village in the Township of East Camden, County Addington, 15 miles from Napane the County Town. The Salmon river affords excellent manufacturing facilities. Woolen, paper and saw mills are required in the neighborhood. Population 100.

Beeman, Milton J., teacher
Campbell, James, farmer
Close, John, farmer
Cunningham, William, farmer
Doupe, Jacob, farmer
Drader, John, cooper
Estes, George, prop. Croydon House
Feskey, James, teacher
Feskey, Joseph, farmer
Hanna, Robert, farmer
Keller, Peter S., farmer
Lockwood, James, wagon maker
Lockwood, Lorenzo, wagon maker
McCabe, Mrs., California House
Mendell, Carlos, farmer
Miller, William, tailor
Rupert, Rev. Edmund S,, (Wesleyan)
Shannon, Robert, farmer
Smith, M., agent flour mills
Vanest, Elisha, carpenter
WILLIAMS, IRA, Postmaster, gen. mercht, Commissioner in B. R., conveyancer, &c
Williams, John M., prop. flour mills

Crysler.—A Village on the River Nation, in the Township of Finch, County Stormont. Distant from Cornwall the County Town, 40 miles, from Toronto 220 miles. Average price of land $60. Population 200.

Bingham, E. W., general merchant
Brown, E., shoemaker
Craig, A., general merchant
Crysler, J. R., farmer
Fisher, Rev. A., (Church of England)
Farney, Henry, hotel keeper
Graham, Edward, carpenter
Hay, J., farmer
Johnston, A., farmer
JOHNSTONE, E. R., Postmaster, general merchant
Johnstone, John, farmer
Johnstone, William, farmer
Stark, A., teacher
Stevenson, J. L., farmer
Stevenson, William, farmer
Stewart, R., farmer
Waldragg, Z., tailor
Wright, James, wagon maker
Wright, James, carpenter
Wright, James, sash and door manufacturer

Culloden.—A Village in the Township of Dereham, County Oxford, 20 miles from Woodstock, the County Town, and 105 from Toronto. Average price of land in vicinity, $35 per acre. Population 200.

Barnes, Thomas, & Son, coopers
Betts, Rev. J. E. (Wesleyan)
Bradburne, James, gen. mercht and agent patent rights
Broadway, James, painter
Conrad, Joseph, chandler
Darker, James, painter
Davy, John, insurance agent
Dillon, M., auctioneer.
Heaton, A. A., saddler
Hogarth, Isaac, wagon maker
Hopkins, Benjamin, J.P.
Lancaster, D. H., M.D.
Lindsay, W., shoemaker
Livingstone, W., shoemaker
Lune, George, carpenter
McArthur, R., hotel keeper
McDonald, S., M.D.
Magwood, Rev. J. (Wesleyan)
Nichol, E., carpenter
Palmer, S., cabinet maker
Palmer, S. H., painter.
Peck, Levi, carpenter
Pritchard, J. F., teacher
Smart, J. B., tailor
Staples, Francis, lumber merchant
Staples, Robert, wagon maker
Tripp Brothers, flour mill
WILLIAMS, R. T., Postmaster and gen. mercht.

Cumberland.—A Village on the River Ottawa, in the Township of Cumberland, County Russell. Distant from Russell, the County Town, 40 miles, from Ottawa 16¼, from Toronto 300. Stages to Ottawa, L'Orignal and Russell. Average price of wild land $3 to $4. Improved $30. Money order office. Population 200.

Allan, John, shoemaker
Cameron, J. S., Clerk Division Court
Chene, Rev. A. (Roman Catholic)
Culbert, John, jun., insurance agent
Ducssin, Theophile, teacher
DUNNING, G. G., Postmaster (see adv)
Dunning, G. G., & Sons, general merchants
Dunning, Walter, telegraph operator
Dunning, W. H., general merchant
Ferguson, James, M.D.
Fournier, Thomas, carpenter
Grier, J. & B., general merchants
Hubert, William, lime manufacturer
La Rocque, F., cooper
Lough, William, jun., miller
Lowry, Rev. Martin, (Presbyterian)
Lumsden, James, teacher
McCallum, Archibald, bailiff
McKee, Henry, carpenter
McNeil, Miss Isabella, teacher
Major, Edward, cooper
Moreau, Alexander, shingle manufacturer
Poirier, André, lime manufacturer
Seguin, Gabriel, shingle manufacturer
Smith, Rev. James C. (Presbyterian)
Swain, Hugh, carpenter
Toutloffe, Francis, sen., butcher
Wilson, William, general merchant
Windsor, John, hotel keeper

Cumminsville.—A Village on Mill Creek, in the Township of Nelson, County Halton. Distant from Milton, the County Town, 8 miles, from Toronto 40 miles. Stages daily to Hamilton and Milton. Average price of land $40 to $50. Population 100.

Baker, F.
Coffee, Andrew
Cummins, Titus G., J. P.
Earls, A. H.
Fleming, Henry, grocer
Flynn, John
Foley, Thomas
Foster, Henry
Frazer, Alexander, teacher
Harris, John
Houston, George
King, Thomas, shingle manufacturer
Leslie, Thomas, tailor
McGregor, William, M.D.
Nichol, James, general agent
Savage, Hugh
Tait, William, proprietor Victoria Mills
THOMSON ROBERT, Postmaster and genl. mercht.
Thompson, Miss, proprietor "Dusty Miller" hotel
Wall & O'Neil, tinsmiths, &c.

Curran.—A Village in the Township of North Plantagenet, County Prescott. Distant from L'Orignal, the County Town, 21 miles, from Toronto, 250 miles. Stages to and from Pendleton. Average price of land $20. Population, 250.

Allard, Joseph, farmer
Allerie, John, gunsmith
Anderson, James, J.P
Bertrand, Rev. P., (Roman Catholic)
Boucher, Francois, painter
Chatelin, John, farmer
Chatelin, Joseph, farmer
Desjardins, F., wagon maker
Desjardins, M., tanner
Des Lés, Derniers, general merchant
Des Lès, Obliere Regis, butcher
Desmouchette, Emma, dressmaker
Ethier, Calixte, M.D
Gallagher, Patrick, farmer
Goulet, Leon, wagon maker
Lacroix, Leander, wagon maker
Leroux, Joseph, shingle manufacturer
McKinley, John, farmer
McLaren, Alexander, M.D
McLean, A., insurance agent
Matte, Louis, wagon maker
Meilleur, Alexander, baker
Muldoon, M., stock dealer
O'BOYLE, JOHN, Postmaster
O'Boyle, T. O., proprietor Curran Hotel
Portelance, Joseph, farmer
Presley, George, farmer
Rochon, A., farmer
Scott, Rev. Thomas, (Presbyterian)
Thibeau, Alfred, tinsmith

Cumnock.—A Post Office in the Townships of Nichol, County Wellington.
ANDERSON, JOHN, Postmaster.

Dacre.—A Post Village in the Township of Brougham, County Renfrew, 50 miles from Pembroke, the County Town. Mails tri-weekly. Population, 45.

Foy, Michael, farmer
Lane, William, weaver
Lewin, Samuel, carpenter
McCormack, Rev. John, (Roman Catholic)
McWILLIAMS, THOMAS, Postmaster and general merchant
McWilliams, Mark, hotel proprietor and plasterer
Mills, James, hotel proprietor and cabinet maker
Morrow, John, general merchant
Siam, Peter, shoemaker
Stoodley, Robert, sen., stone mason
Stoodley, Robert, jun., stone mason

Dalhousie Mills.—A Post Village in the Township of Lancaster, County Glengarry. Distant from Cornwall, the County Town, 30 miles. The De Lisle River passing through the Village affords good facilities for manufacturing purposes. Mails tri-weekly. Population, 89.

Anderson, Rev. L., (Free Church)
Bathurst, William, general merchant
Belhumere, Joseph, cooper
Cattenach, A., general merchant
CHISHOLM, WILLIAM, Postmaster
Ferguson, Alexander, M.D
McCrimon, Alexander, blacksmith
McQuaig, Alexander, tanner and currier
McDonald, Archibald, farmer
McIntosh, John, carriage maker
McKay, Rev. Alexander, (Presbyterian)
McMaster, Rev. John, (Roman Catholic)
McRae, Alexander, teacher
McRae, Donald F., blacksmith
McVean, John, farmer
Millar, John, mill owner
Munro, George, farmer

Dalkeith.—A Village situated on the River DeGrasse, Township of Lochiel, County Glengarry.

Anderson, Rev. A. R. (Baptist)
Campbell, Donald, farmer
Carry, Thomas, teacher
Deguire, William, butcher
Donovan, James, farmer
Jamieson, John, wagon maker
Jamieson, William, wagon maker
Laselle, Antoine, carpenter
McArthur, C., teacher
McArthur, Hugh, carpenter
McDonell, John, shoemaker
McDougall, Duncan, carpenter
McGillivray, Duncan, farmer
McLennan, Jonathan, farmer
McPhee, Norman, farmer
Robertson & McLennan, general merchants
ROBERTSON, WILLIAM, J. P., Postmaster
Stewart, John, J. P., farmer

Dalston.—A Post Office in the Township of Vespra, County Simcoe, 9 miles from Barrie, the County Town. Improved land in the vicinity averages $25 per acre. Stages to Barrie, Orillia and Penetanguishene.

CLIFFORD, HENRY A., Postmaster
Gow, F., hotel keeper

Darrell.—A Post Office situated in the Township of Chatham, County Kent, 7 miles from Chatham, the County Town.

Campbell, Duncan, J. P.
Fisher, John, J. P.
French, John, carpenter
Green, William, carpenter
HALL, EDWARD, Postmaster
Larwell, Joseph, school teacher

Dartford.—A Village in the Township of Percy, County Northumberland, 27 miles from Cobourg, the County Town. Improved land in the vicinity averages $16 per acre. Stages tri-weekly to Colborne and Norwood. Population 100.

BAILEY, WILLIAM, Postmaster, leather merchant
unningham, Thomas, carpenter
Dorland, D. B., carpenter
Humphries, J. C., farmer
Kelly, William, prop. saw and grist and saw mills
Masters, John, shingle maker
Masters Samuel, shingle maker
Thompson, Sylvester, carpenter
Walker, John, cooper
Zuefelt, John, carriage maker

Danforth.—A Post Office in the Township of Scarboro', County York.

HOGARTH, HENRY, Postmaster.

Davenport.—(Carlton Village.)—A Village and Station on the Northern Railway, in the Township of York, County York, 5 miles from Toronto. Population 100.

Bartlett, Mr., nurseryman
Blake, Chancellor
Brown, Joseph, general merchant
Brown, William, auctionner
Bull, Bartholemew, farmer
Bull, B., jun., J.P
Bull, Thomas, barrister
Bull, William & Sons, wagon makers
Damp, John, contractor
Farr & Taylor, butchers
Grimsby, Henry, cattle dealer
Hayden, John
Hugill, Joseph, teacher
Johnson, Rev. Mr., (Church of England)
Johnstone, James hotel keeper
oliffe, James & Son, carpenters
Kearns, Patrick, constable
Keele, William S., barrister
Lowcock, Johnson, shoemaker
McNabb, John, barrister
McNamara, John, nurseryman
Nightingale, M., hotel keeper
Rapple, Matthew, saddler
ROSS, HON. JOHN
Shedden, John, farmer
Sinclair, C., blacksmith
Toxwell, Albert, farmer
Tuer, Thomas, hotel keeper
Turner, Robert, barrister
Wakefield, William, auctioneer
Watt, John, farmer
Wood, Rev. Dr
Yearly, David, butcher
YEARLY, GEORGE S., Postmater, insurance agent

Dawn Mills.—A Village in the Township of Camden, County Kent, situated on the River Sydenham, 16 miles from Chatham, the County Town. Average price of land $20 per acre. Population 100.

Anderson, Arthur, J.P
Arnold, D. & C., props. saw and grist mills
ARNOLD, T. S., Postmaster
Blackburn, Peter, farmer
Blackburn, Robert, farmer
Boylan, William, farmer
Chambers, William, farmer
Craft, Isaac, farmer
Ecclestone, J. W., hotel keeper
Galbraith, Dr
Gilford, William, farmer
Hicks, Samuel, farmer
Holmes, John, farmer
Hugh, Rev. Thomas, (Church of England)
Kerch, Henry, hotel keeper
Kerr, Rev. Mr., (Methodist)
Prangley, Charles, farmer
Smith, James, J.P
Ward, W. A., general merchant
Webster, Henry, J.P

Daywood...A Post Office in the Township of Sydenham, County Grey, N.R.

CAMERON, A. S., Postmaster.

Dealtown.—A Post Office in the Township of Tilbury East, County Kent. Distant 20 miles from Chatham, the County Town.

RUSSELL, ISAAC, Postmaster.

De Cewsville—A Village in the Township of North Cayuga, County Haldimand, 3 miles from Cayuga, the County Town, and 9 from Canfield Station. Average value of land in the vicinity, improved $30, wild $10 per acre. Population 120.

Barnett, G., farmer
Best, D., farmer
Bingleman, G., proprietor hotel
Campbell, D., farmer
De Cew, John, butcher
De Cew, R. & E., millers
DIER, THOMAS B., Postmaster and genl. merchant
Finley, J., carpenter
Foster, A., farmer
Gardiner, G., insurance agent
Jack, James, sash factory
Kindree, William, J.P.
Kinnear, James, farmer
Kinnear, John, teacher
McClung, D., farmer
McFarlane, John, teacher
McGovern, J., carpenter
Nunn, William, patent rights agent
Petheran, R., shoemaker
Robertson, Robert, painter
Rose, A., hotel keeper
Stannaman, D., carpenter
Strohm, G., farmer
Vanderburgh, A., farmer
Ward, John, farmer
Watson, John, wagon maker
Wharton, G., farmer
Wharton, T., farmer

Deerhurst.—A Village in the Township of West Gwillimbury, County Simcoe. Distant from Barrie the County Town, 16 miles. Mails tri-weekly. Population 500.

Baynes, Richard, farmer
Bell, James, farmer
Bolton, John, hotel keeper
Clement, L., M.D.
Cronan, Michael, farmer
Croxon, Henry, auctioneer
Duck, Robert, farmer
Fennell, Joseph, J.P.
Fisher, E., M.D.
Glassfin, John, hotel keeper
Hambly, Joseph, farmer
Henderson, —, teacher
Huff, Henry, shingle maker
Kelly, James, shingle maker
McBeath, John, J.P.
McConchie, Thomas, nurseryman
McKee, Rev. William (Presbyterian)
Morn, Patrick, carpenter
Morton, D., M.D.
Neilly, John, farmer
Neilly, William, teacher
Paul, Rev. Mr. (Primitive Methodist)
Roberts, Thomas, carpenter
Ruttan, Rev. C. (Church of England)
Tindal, Joseph, farmer
Touse, Bethuel, J.P.
WALKER, SAMUEL, Postmaster and gen. mercht.
Wood, James, farmer
Youmans, Rev. Mr. (Wesleyan Methodist)

Delaware.—A Village in the Township of Delaware, County Middlesex, in the valley of the Thames, 12 miles from London, the County Town, and 3 from Komoka Station G. W. R. Money Order office. Population 300.

Acres, Henry, farmer
Agnew, N., M. D., coroner
Albey, George, builder
Billington, George, M. D.
Bullen, W. F., sen., J. P., Clerk 4th Division Court, Commissioner in B. R., Notary Public
Dain, J., merchant
Davis, Robert, Delaware Mills
Francis, A. McD., druggist
Godfrey, George, auctioneer
Godfrey, Mrs. G., teacher
Grant, Rev. George (Canada Presbyterian)
Grant, William, farmer
Harris, George, farmer
Hill, George, brickmaker
Jennings, John, butcher
Johnstone, Henry
Johnstone, John
Kirk, William, blacksmith
LADD, CALVIN P., Postmaster, druggist
Lawson, David, shoemaker
Livingston, William, J. P., insurance agent, notary
McKay, M., innkeeper
Maleck, John, cabinet maker
Miller, Thomas, carpenter
Newman, Rev. E. E. (Church of England)
Paine, Benjamin, shoemaker
Peocock, Charles, shoemaker
Pennock, George, butcher
Phelps, A., wheelwright
Rawlings, Henry, baker
Robertson, Charles, shoemaker
Rogers, W. S., builder
Sanagan, Louis, cooper
Tupholme, Cordley, hotel keeper
Uptigrove, William, wagon maker
Vail, John, merchant
Vanderveer, David, wagon maker
Whittaker, William, saddler

Delhi.—(see Fredericksburg)—A Post Office in the County Norfolk. Money Order office.
WHITESIDES, JAMES, Postmaster.

THE LEADER.

THE DAILY LEADER

Is published every Morning, at $4.50 a year in advance.

THE WEEKLY LEADER,

PUBLISHED EVERY FRIDAY, AT $2.00 A YEAR IN ADVANCE.

Contains carefully selected News from the Daily Editions, with Agricultural matter and Market Reports.

THE PATRIOT,

Published every Wednesday, at $1.00 a year in advance.

JAMES BEATY, Proprietor, 63 King Street East, Toronto.

JOB PRINTING

EXECUTED IN ALL ITS BRANCHES.

THE CANADIAN FREEMAN

IS PUBLISHED

EVERY THURSDAY MORNING

By JAMES G. MOYLAN, Editor and Proprietor,

At No. 74 CHURCH STREET,

OVER THE TORONTO SAVINGS BANK,

TORONTO.

TERMS.—Two Dollars per annum, if paid within Six Months; or Two Dollars and Fifty Cents at the end of the year.

RATES OF ADVERTISING:

One column per year, with quarterly changes	$120 00
One-half do do do	70 00
One-quarter do do do	40 00
Above ten lines, first insertion, per line	08
Each subsequent insertion, per line	02
Business Cards, six lines and under, per annum	4 00
For six months	3 00

BOOK AND JOB PRINTING

Executed in the highest order of the art, and at reasonable rates.

☞ All letters to be addressed CANADIAN FREEMAN OFFICE, Toronto, Ont., and to ensure attention must be post-paid.

Delta.—A Village in the Township of Bastard, County Leeds; beautifully situated on a small stream between two small lakes, the waters of which empty into the St. Lawrence at Gananoque. 24 miles from Brockville, the County Town, 19 from Irish Creek station Brockville and Ottawa Railway, and 40 from Kingston. Large deposits of iron, plumbago and mica are found in the neighborhood. Stages to Brockville and Westport. Money Order office. Population 300.

Allyn, C., marble works
Barnum, B. C., general merchant
Beckett, R., carriage maker
Bell, J. A., general merchant
Bell, William, J. P.
Bouh, Robert, tailor
Bush, P., boots and shoes
Caris, H., general merchant
Coleman, Anson, leather dealer
Comstock, Levi, hotel keeper
Curtis, G., general merchant
DENAUT, W. H., Postmaster, miller, Clerk Div. Court, Commissioner for taking Affidavits
Hazelton, John, boots and shoes
Hicock, Philo, iron founder
Lang, W., carriage maker
Mott, Henry, hotel keeper
O'Hara, Rev. Mr. (N. C. Methodist)
Quinn, Reuben, carpenter
Ross, Samuel, general merchant
Sinclair, J. M., M. D.
Stevens, V., saddler
Whaley, Isaac, J. P.

Demorestville.—A Village situated on the outlet of Fish Lake, Township of Sophiasburg, County Prince Edward, 9 miles from Picton, the County Town, 49 from Kingston, 9 from Shannonville station, Grand Trunk Railway, 12 from Belleville, and 4 from Northport, on the Bay of Quinte. There are good water privileges in the village and neighborhood, affording a good location for any kind of machinery. Mechanics wanted. Improved land averages $30 per acre. Stages daily to Northport, fare 25c., and in winter daily to Picton, fare 50c., and Belleville 75c. Population 350.

Ackerman, George, architect
Baker, William, baker
Barton, James J., agent Rochester nurseries
Barton Bros., wagon makers
Boulter, James, brickmaker.
Boulter, Wellington, farmer
Butler, Brothers, wagon makers
Clark, H. B., librarian
Cotter, Samuel, farmer
Curlett, J. F., M.D.
Dingman, Rev. J. G. (Wesleyan)
Dunning, Henry, farmer
Fox, Henry P., farmer
Greeley, A., M.P.P.
Gordon, Edward, grocer
Hamilton, J., lime dealer
Hamilton, Israel, auctioneer
Hart, J., general merchant
Hill, Rev. J. (Episcopal Methodist)
Hunt, Samuel, shoemaker
Joyce, Valentine, carpenter
Lazier, George N., farmer
Leatch, Hugh, shoemaker
McDowall, R. J., general merchant, lumber dealer, potash and soap manufacturer
McDowall & Stortts, carding and flour mills
Moore, Thomas, M.D.
Morden, George, proprietor hotel
Nixon, E. R., tailor
Peck, A., hotel keeper
Simonds, Allen, carpenter
SMITH, BENJAMIN, Postmaster
Smith, David, general agent
Sprague, George, farmer
Sprague, James S., teacher
Sprague, N., J.P.
Thompson, Charles, carpenter
Wright, J. G. & Son, saddlers

Denbigh.—A Post Office in the Township of Denbigh, County Addington, 68 miles from Napanee, the County Town.

HUGHES, DAVID, Postmaster.

Denfield.—A Post Village in the Township of London, County Middlesex, 16 miles from London, the County Town, and 120 miles from Toronto. Population 20.

Griffith, Mrs., milliner
Matthews, P., J.P.
Morgan, Miss M., teacher
Moor, James, tailor
Noyes, W., carpenter
Parker, Edward, shoemaker
Robson, William, saloon
Rosser, Miss M., teacher
ROSSER, BENJAMIN W., Postmaster
Rosser, Thomas, shoemaker
Rowland, Rev. D. W. (Baptist)
Shipley, W. J.P.
Telfer, J., teacher
Waugh, Robert, flax and woolen miller

Derryville.—A Post Village in the Township of Brock, County Ontario.

ALLIN, THOMAS, Postmaster.

Deniston.—A Post office in the Township of Hinchinbrook, County Frontenac, 30 miles from Kingston, the County Town. Average price of improved land in the vicinity, $7; wild, $2 per acre. Iron and plumbago are found in the neighborhood. Stage to Harrowsmith, 16 miles, fare 40c.

Buttrell, George, carpenter
FREEMAN, B. C., Postmaster
Giles, John, carpenter
Godfrey, Chester H., J.P.
Goodfellow, David, hotel keeper
Goodfellow, James, hotel keeper
Hamilton, John, J.P.
Matthews, Adam, hotel keeper

Derry West.—A Post office in the Township of Toronto, County Peel.
WILSON, WILLIAM, Postmaster.

Derwent.—A Post office in the Township of Westminster, County Middlesex. Distant 10 miles from London, the County Town, 115 from Toronto.

Allen, John, farmer
Beattie, Edward
Black, A., teacher
Craig, James, J.P.
Crews, Rev. —, (Wesleyan)
Dibbs, John, farmer
Kernohan, William, stock dealer
McKilty, Rev. —, (Methodist Episcopal)
Moore, John, J.P.
Tibits, Alonzo, carriage maker
Walker, David, farmer
WILLSIE & BULLARD, general merchants
WILLSIE, LEWIS, Postmaster and stock dealer

Deux Rivieres.—A post office in the District of Nipissing, on the river Ottawa, 30 miles from des Joachim. There is no conveyance except by canoes and during the winter by sledges. The land in the vicinity is unfit for cultivation.

Bell, David
Bell, Joseph
Johnson, T. H., J. P., District officer
Maguire, Charles
RANSON, ROBERT, Postmaster, and prop. Albion Hotel

Devizes.—A post office in the Township of London, County Middlesex, 6 miles from Granton station, Grand Trunk Railroad.

Baker, Henry, general merchant
Bisbee, Reuben, farmer
COSTELLO, JOHN, Postmaster, general merchant
Gearing & Harding, millers
McMillan, Neal, carpenter
Nelson, William, wagon maker

Devon.—A Village in the Township of Stephen, County Huron, situated on the gravel road from London to Goderich; 33 miles from Goderich the County Town, and 27 from London. Improved land in the vicinity $40 and wild $25 per acre. Population 100.

Bissett, Robert, stock dealer
Coughlin, Timothy, stock dealer
Edwards, Rev. E., (Wesleyan)
GREENWAY, T. W., Postmaster, general merchant
Harris, Henry, farmer
Hockey, Henry, farmer
Holman, Lewis, farmer
Hooper, Rev. William, (Bible Christian)
Huxtable, John, farmer
McPhee, Hugh, flour mills
McWilliams, W. T., farmer
Martin, William, farmer
Prowty, Chester, teacher
Sando, Richard, carpenter
Sando, Thomas, carpenter
Trivitt, Thomas, clerk Division Court
Ward, Thomas, carriage maker
Webber, George, shoemaker

Dexter.—A Village on Lake Erie in the Township of Yarmouth, County Elgin, 10 miles from St. Thomas the County Town, and 150 west of Toronto. Population 250.

Armstrong, William, farmer
Bailey, Edward, farmer
Bell, John, shoemaker
Fisher, Benjamin, farmer
Gilbert, T. W., teacher
McLean, John, cooper
PARKER, NELSON, Postmaster, grocer
Parker, Rodney, shoemaker
Parker, Wellington, farmer
Parker, William, farmer
Pfeffer, John, cooper, hotel keeper
Robins, Caleb, cooper
Vansyckle, John, farmer
Vansyckle, Isaac, farmer

Diamond.—A Post Office in the Township of Fitzroy, County Carleton, 30 miles from Ottawa, the County Town, and 9 miles from Pakenham, the nearest station on the Brockville and Ottawa Railway. There are two churches, Church of England and Wesleyan Methodist in the vicinity, and a Common School.

Baird, George & John
Emery, Rev. C. P. (Episcopal Methodist)
Gourley, William, farmer
Green, Thomas, farmer
McMillan, Alexander & Donald, farmers
WALKER, ROBERT, SEN., farmer
WALKER, ROBERT, JUN., Postmaster, general merchant and manufacturer
Young, Joseph, carpenter

Desmond.—A Post office in the Township of Camden East, County Addington, 14 miles from Napanee, the County Town.

BELL, J. W., Postmaster
Irwin, William, boot and shoemaker

Dickinson's Landing.—*(See Villages too late for regular insertion, at the end of the work.)*

Dingle (see Ainlayville).—A Post Office in the County Huron. Money order office.

GRANT, WILLIAM, Postmaster.

Dixie (formerly Sydenham).—A small Village in the Township of Toronto, County Peel, 12 miles from Brampton, the County Town, 14 from Toronto, and 4 from Port Credit station Great Western Railway. Improved land in the vicinity averages $45 per acre. Stage daily to Toronto, fare 38c. Population 150.

Bennett, John, teacher
Bell, John, wagon maker
Collis, John, innkeeper
Elgie, Mrs. J., storekeeper
Farr, Joseph, farmer
Gillies, Thomas, tailor
Gould, John, farmer
Hawkins, John, J.P., farmer
KENNEDY, WILLIAM, Postmaster, general merchant and innkeeper
Silverthorn, Joseph, farmer
Wilson, John, stock dealer
Wilson, Samuel, shoemaker

Dixon's Corners.—A Village in the Township of Matilda, County Dundas. 36 miles from Cornwall, the County Town. Improved land in the neighborhood averages $30, and unimproved $15 per acre.

Allerous, William, wagon maker
Baker & Co., general merchants
Brinston, Thomas, store and hotel
Coad, William, wagon maker
Crobar, George, shoemaker
Crobar, Matthew, shoemaker
Dixon, E., hotel
Donaldson, George, hotel
Doyle, Cornelius, constable
Empey, Peter, collector
Flatt, Thomas, carpenter
Fulford, W. & H., carpenters
Gilson, John, wagon maker
Harkness, Adam, clerk
Harkness, John, M.D.
Hialmager, Joseph, shoemaker
Lochead, Rev. John (Presbyterian)
McNulty, A., general merchant
Mead, Rev. M. (Roman Catholic)
Morton, Rev. W. (Wesleyan)
Patterson, William, assessor
Rathbun, Hugh, cooper
Salter, William, shoemaker
Shaw, Alonzo, wagon maker
Shaw, Daniel, carpenter
Thompson, David, carpenter
Thompson, E., carpenter
Whenton, Thomas, general merchant
Williams, Rev. W. H., (Wesleyan)
WOOD, WILLIAM, Postmaster

Donegal.—A Post Village in the Township of Elma, County Perth, 26 miles from Stratford, the County Town, and 100 from Toronto. Population 60.

Anderson, William, farmer
Buchanan, William, farmer
Gilchrist, John, farmer
Henry, Hugh & R., farmers
Hemphill, A., farmer
McGill, George, teacher
MASON, MRS. MARY, Postmistress
Stewart, William, farmer

Dobbinton.—A Post Office situated in the Township of Elderslie, County Bruce.

DOBBIN, JAMES, Postmaster.

Don.—A small Village in the Township of York, 8 miles from Toronto, the County Town, near the Don river. Average value of land in the vicinity, $50 per acre.

Bond, Thomas, farmer
Brown, William, potter
Castick, Daniel, shoemaker
Cole, Peter, dyer
Craig, William, carpenter
Craig, John, carpenter
Cudmore, George, potter
Duncan, David, farmer
Duncan, Henry, farmer
Edgar, Rev. James (Methodist)
Elliott, David, general merchant
Elliott, Edward, farmer
Fitzpatrick, Albert, carpenter
Gray, Alexander, farmer
Gray, James, farmer
Gray, John, farmer
Gray, William, miller
HOGG, JOHN, Postmaster and general merchant
Hogg, Robert, farmer
Homely, R., farmer
Laird, Hugh, farmer
Maginn, C. D., general merchant
Meredith, W. H., teacher
Milne, Peter, farmer
Milne, William, general merchant
Milne & Sons, woolen factors
Morrow, Richard, farmer
Muirhead, James, farmer
Sampson, James, farmer
Sampson, John, farmer
Smith, A. M., mill proprietor
Smith, John, farmer
Taylor, Brothers, paper manufacturers
Walker, Rev. J. W. (Primitive Methodist)
Witherspoon, Adam, tailor

Doon.—A Village and Station of the Doon branch of the Grand Trunk Railway, in the Township of Waterloo, County Waterloo, 6 miles from Berlin, the County Town, 33 from Hamilton, and 65 from Toronto. It is situated at the confluence of the Grand and Doon rivers, and possesses excellent manufacturing facilities. Average value of improved lands in the vicinity $40 per acre. Population 200.

Bryer, J. L., shoemaker
Jamison, Andrew, hotel
Lamb, John, tailor
McGarvey, William, hotel
McKenzie, Rev. William (Presbyterian)
Martindale, Martin, shoemaker
Mulloy, N., M.D.
Osborne, William, miller
Padder, Joseph, carpenter
Perine, Brothers, linen factors
SLEE, THOMAS, Postmaster
Vipont & Slee, general merchants
Walker, James A., tailor

Doran.—A Post-office in the Township of Bathurst, County Lanark, 15 miles from Perth, the County Town.

Crosson, J. T., grist mill proprietor
Dickson, William, carpenter
DORAN, WILLIAM, Postmaster, gen. mercht
Murphy, Richard, innkeeper
Spencer, Bernard, shingle maker

Dorchester Station.—A Post-office and Station on the Great Western Railway, in the Township of Dorchester, County Middlesex, 10 miles distant from London, and 107 from Toronto. The Village contains several excellent mill sites. Tri-weekly stage to Aylmer, Lyons and Springfield. Daily Mail. Population 220.

Beal, James, stone mason
Beddlecombe, Charles, shoemaker
Cartwright, William J., J.P., mill owner
Chittick, Francis, boots and shoes
Chittick, George, toll gate keeper
Ferguson, Alexander, grocer
Fordyce, William, wood turner
Foster, George, carpenter
Freeman, Alfred
HARDY, JOSEPH, J.P., Postmaster
Huffman, Christopher, hotel keeper
Hunt, James, blacksmith and wagon maker
Hunt, Peter, farmer
Hunter, Charles, carpenter and builder
Lewis, Oliver, farmer
McCall, Alexander, school teacher
McCann, E., carder and cloth dealer
McCutcheon, James
McLean, Robert, hotel keeper
McRae, A., lumber merchant and saw mill prop.
Merrills, John
Mitchell, Joseph, blacksmith
Painter, John, grocer
Partlow, W., flouring mill
Sweet, Nathan, harness maker
Vanson, Joseph, station master G.W.R
Wade, William, shingle factory and saw mill owner
Ward, Richard, builder
Williams, Reece, section master G.W.R

Dorking.—A Post-office in the Township of Maryboro' County Wellington, N. R.

GATSCHENE, JOHN, Postmaster.

Dornoch.—A Post Village in the Township of North Oxford, County Oxford, 9 miles from Woodstock, the County Town, and 100 from Toronto. Population 50.

Campbell, James, dry goods and groceries
GARDNER, PETER, Postmaster and grocer
Gilchrist, J., cooper
McDonald, John, carpenter
McDonald, Robert, hotel keeper

Douglas.—A Village situated on the River Bonnechere, Township of Bromley, County Renfrew, 27 miles from Pembroke, the County Town, 70 miles from Perth and 75 from Ottawa. The river supplies excellent water power. Average value of improved land $10, wild $4 per acre. Stage to Eganville, 10 miles fare, 50c.; Renfrew Village, 16 miles, fare 75c. Money Order Office. Population 800.

Bell, Rev. C. R., (Church of England)
Bolam, Thomas H., general merchant
CAMERON, DONALD, Postmater, gen. mercht
Culbertson, Thomas, hotel keeper
Gilchrist, Peter, miller
McEachren, S., J.P
McGregor, John, hotel keeper
Philip, John, carpenter
Queceley, John, general merchant
Rose, Rev. E., (Episcopal Methodist)
Thompson, W. S., teacher

Dover South.—A small Post Village in the Township of Dover, County Kent. Distant from Chatham the County Town, 6 miles. Population about 90.

GERVAIS, S., Postmaster.

Downeyville.—A Village in the Township of Emily, County Victoria, 8 miles from Lindsay, the County Town, and about 100 from Toronto. Population 75.

Cameron, James & Co., wagon makers
Coyle, Rev. R., (Roman Catholic)
Crowley, T. & P., shoemakers
Fox, John, farmer
Herlihan, William, gunsmith
Holland, William, farmer
McCARTHY, J. S., Postmaster and grocer
McCarthy, T., hotel keeper
Pigott, Edmond, farmer
Powers, Michael, farmer
Richardson, William, hotel keeper
Scully, Denis, farmer
Scully, Jeremiah, farmer
Scully, John, farmer

Downview.—A Post-office lately established in the County of York, a few miles distant from Toronto.

Drayton.—A Village on the Conestogo River, and on the line of the proposed Wellington, Grey and Bruce Railway, in the Townships of Peel and Maryborough, County Wellington. Distant from Guelph, the County Town, 28 miles, from Toronto, 75 miles. Stages to and from Elora, 15 miles, fare 50cts. Money order office. Population, 500.

Adams, W. E., carpenter
Anderson, Rev. William, (Bible Christian)
Connor, C. M., shoemaker
Crane, Rev. J., (Wesleyan)
Crull, Theodore, cabinet maker
Dales, Edward, farmer
Dales, John, farmer
Dales, Robert P., architect
Deeble, Henry, carpenter
Doan, Jacob, general merchant
Dolton. T., watchmaker
Eby, Lemuel. tailor
Echlin, James, cabinet maker
Emes, S. P., M.D
Fawcett, J. D., carpenter
Fisher, George, shoemaker
Fisher, John, baker
Fox, Martin, proprietor Drayton Hotel
Gardner, A., general merchant
Gordon, J. F., dentist
Haight, John, gereral agent
Halliday, James, teacher
Hambly, W. L., farmer
Harrison, John L., proprietor British Hotel
Hartney, J. H., general merchant
Healey, Almond, farmer
Jackson, Rev. J., (Wesleyan)
Marshall, Stephen, wagon maker
Matthews, Rev., M. H., (Primitive Methodist)
Montgomery, John, farmer
Moodie, Alfred, saddler
Nocker, Louis L., architect
Richards, John, carpenter
Samis, Solomon, farmer
Smith, J., M.D.
Smith, Alfred, auctioneer
Smith, Alfred & Son, coopers
Tate, John, baker
Tuck, E. N., farmer
Whales, John, carpenter
White, John, general merchant
Wittich, John, carpenter
WORTLEY, W. C., Postmaster and gen. merchant

Dresden.—A flourishing Village on the Sydenham River, in the Township of Camden, County Kent, 18 miles from Chatham the County Town, 200 from Toronto, and 16 from Thamesville Station, Great Western Railway. Improved land in the vicinity averages $20 per acre. Stages to Chatham, fare 75c. Money order office. Population 650.

Anderson, Rev. Peter, (Wesleyan)
Arnald, C. F., teacher
Bodkin & Adams, wagonmakers.
Bow, Solomon, carpenter
Bradley, U. H., farmer
Brown, J., proprietor Livingston Hotel
Carroll, James, constable
Carroll, William, carpenter
Clancy, William, carpenter
Clancy, C. M., proprietor City Mills
Clancy, James, grocer
Clarke, Sibree, M. D., druggist
Craig, J. H. & F., lumber merchants
Davis, Rev. S. H., (Baptist)
Davis, T. W., dry goods merchant
Deacon, John, shoemaker
Feladeau, P., proprietor Dresden Hotel
Francis, William, shoemaker
Graham, G. M., carpenter
Graham, G. M., photographer
Green, George, carpenter
Hall, J. H., carpenter
Hazlett, J. B., grocer
Hart, Thomas, wagon maker
Henson, Josiah, farmer
Holland, J. W. bookseller
Huff & Campbell, grocers
Hughson, W. A., M.D.
Hughes, Rev. Thomas, (Church of England)
Huston, Edward, auctioneer
Johnston, J. H., general merchant
Kerr, Rev. (Wesleyan)
Lyman, Rev. B. (Methodist)
McDonald, John A., J.P.
McInnis, T.R., M.D.
McIntosh, Charles, carpenter
McKay, William, wagon maker
McWha, Robert, butcher
Merrils, D. P., cabinet maker
Merritt, A. E., general merchant
Mooney, M., grocer
Moore, Miss teacher
Mount Albert, carpenter
Mountier, William, butcher
Nellis, William, saddler
Osborne, S., cabinet maker
Richey, Sandford, grocer
Roberts, Lewis, wagon maker
Scratch, John T., farmer
Smith, Mrs. Mary, grocer
Stewart, Daniel, farmer
Trevice, Alexander, J.P.
Trevice, Isaac, lime manufacturer
Trevice & Wright, lumber merchants
Van Allen. Henry, farmer
Van Duze, H. H. & T
Verley, George, proprietor brickyard
Watson, A. & Co., general merchants
WATSON, C. P., Postmaster
Watson, David, cabinet maker
Watson, J. A., proprietor Dresden House
Webster, Joseph, shoemaker
Webster & Watson, tanners
Weese, Thomas, farmer
Wells, Miss Amanda, dressmaker
Williston, J. W., general merchant
Windover, W. H., general merchant
Winter, H. E., M.D

Dromore.—A Post Village in the Township of Egremont, County Grey, 41 miles from Owen Sound, the County Town, 56 miles from Guelph Station, Great Western Railway, 40 from Collingwood Station, Northern Railway. Improved land in the vicinity averages $15, wild $7 per acre.

Camp, Joseph, saw mill proprietor
Clark, Duncan, shoemaker
Delong, Ephraim, nursery
Isaac, James, patent rights agent
Isaac, William, patent rights agent
TAYLOR, ALEXANDER, Postmaster and general merchant

Drumbo.—A Village and Station of the Buffalo and Lake Huron branch of the Grand Trunk Railway, in the Township of Blenheim, County Oxford, 17 miles from Woodstock, the County Town, and 9 from Paris. Money order office. Population, 400.

Adams, Dr
Bailey, Rev. H., (Church of England)
Barr, Greville E., cabinet maker
Bastendorff, John P., tailor
Brown, S. D., iron founder and planing mill
Capron, John B., hotel keeper
Chipman, John, tinsmith
Clark, J. W
Colwell, J., cooper
Harrison, George, shoemaker
Irving, P., hotel keeper
Johnston, Andrew, groceries and liquors
Keetch, Rev. J. S., (Primitive Methodist)
Kelley & Harvey, tanners
Laidlaw, John
McCarty, James, carpenter
McKENZIE, JAMES, Postmaster, druggist, agent, American Express Co., telegraph agent
McQuarrie, Rev. H., (Canada Presbyterian)
Markle, Alexander S., carriage maker
Mumа, Henry, estate agent
Muma, Nelson, carpenter
Munn, R. S., general merchant
Pattullo, G. R., teacher
Peck, Almon, carpenter
Pollock, John, baker
Rathbun, Charles
Robertson, D., general merchant
Rogers, James, wagon maker
Rounds, J. B., M.D
Shaw, Daniel, carpenter
Smith, G. W. general merchant
Smith, Rev. Mr., (Baptist)
Stevenson, William, brickmaker
Tibeaudo, J. W., station agent G. T. R
Vanderlip, William, hotel keeper

Drummondville West.—A Village in the Township of Stamford, County Welland, within a short distance of the Erie and Ontario Railroad, and 1 mile from the Falls of Niagara, 14 miles from Welland—the County Town, and 50 miles from Toronto. Manufacturers of all kinds are greatly needed, facilities being first class. Average value of land in the neighborhood $35 per acre. Money order office. Population 1,000

BEATTY, WILLIAM, M. P. P.
Bigger, Charles H., cooper
Biggar, John, tailor
Blanton, Thomas, carpenter
Bowman, James, carpenter
BROKENSHAW, LUKE, Postmaster
Brown, Henry, carpenter
Cameron, Rev. James Y., master grammar school
Carr, John, J.P.
Centre House, Dan. Mahoney, proprietor
Cole, Edwin, boot and shoemaker
Cole, Mrs. Edwin, milliner
Cole, Thomas, boot and shoemaker
Cole, Thomas H., marble cutter
Cook, H. C., dentist
Curry, Matthew N., M.D.
Curry, Amos, painter
Dalton, George, carpenter
Eagles, Rev. Charles, (Church of England)
DUNCAN, G. W. J., general merchant
Earley, General, late C. F. S. A.
ELLIS, THOMAS F., proprietor National Hotel. (See adv)
England, John, watchmaker and photographer
Evans, John, proprietor Exchange Hotel
Fralick. James, proprietor Battle-ground Hotel
Fralick, Robert, shoemaker
Forsyth, E., teacher
Garner, Robert, J.P.,
GARNER & CAMPBELL, tin, copper and sheet iron smiths, dealers in stoves & hollow ware. (See adv.)
Girven, James, baker
Hartman, Jacob, saddle and harness maker
HENDERSHOT, PETER, wholesale and retail dealer in dry goods, groceries, ready-made clothing, boots and shoes, etc.
Henley, Richard, druggist
Hixon, Timothy J., J.P.
Ingles, Rev. C., (Church of England)
International Hotel, Michael Kick, proprietor
Jackson, Moses, woolen goods
Ker, John
Kerr, Peter, general merchant
Kick, Michael, proprietor International Hotel
Laird, Rev. J., (Wesleyan)
Latshaw, E.
Latshaw, James, carpenter
Latshaw, John, carpenter
Lemon, Wilson
Lowell, William
Lundy, L. S., J. P.
McGarry, James, surgeon
McGilley, L., proprietor Railroad House
McGlashan, John T., J. P.
McGuane John, proprietor Farmers' Inn
McHAY, WILLIAM, dry goods merchant
McKenzie, Donald, carpenter
Malone, John, J. P.
Mason, John J., dentist
Mason, John & Jacob, carriage makers
Mewburn, Frank C., surgeon
Morse, Edward, painter
Moss, Austin, cabinet maker and undertaker
NATIONAL HOTEL, T. F. Ellis, prop. (See card)
Norris, M. B., teacher common school
Orchard, J. A., Clerk Division Court and auctioneer
Oswald, James, proprietor Whirlpool Hotel
Pen, John, J. P.
PIPER, ALEXANDER, carriage maker. (See card)
Prowse, William, painter
Robert, Rev. John, (Baptist)
Rowe, Miss Eliza Jane, milliner and dressmaker
RUSSELL, WILLIAM, proprietor Drummondville Brewery. (See adv)
Rysdale, George, proprietor brickyard
Sargent, James, dry goods
Smith, Mary, proprietor Rose Inn
Spence, Henry
STREET, THOMAS C., M. P.
Sutton, Hiram, butcher
Sutton, Philip, butcher
Sutton, Stephen, butcher
Taylor, G. W.
Thompson, Captain, boards National Hotel
Trice, Henry, carpenter
Tucker, Jacob, saddle and harness maker
Vanderburg, John
WEIR, GEORGE, flour and feed store (see adv.)
White, George, brewer
Willox, James, proprietor Niagara Falls Mills
WILLS & KERBY, dealers in groceries, wines and liquors, crockery; hardware, &c. (see adv).
Winn, Joseph
Woodruff, J. C., general merchant
Woodruff & Co., general merchants
Wright, Henry, cabinet maker

Drumquin.—A small Post Village in the Township of Trafalgar, County Halton. Distant from Milton, the County Town, 8 miles. Population 50.

Bell, William, farmer
Brown, Charles, blacksmith
Cottherd, John, farmer
Hood, William, farmer
TOLSON, W. J., Postmaster and hotel keeper

Drury.—A Post Village in the Township of Oro, County Simcoe, 9 miles from Barrie, the County Town, and 72 from Toronto. Average value of land in the vicinity, $25 per acre.

DRURY, RICHARD, Postmaster.

Dryden.—A Post Office in the Township of Wallace, County Perth, N.R.

JOHNSTON, RICHARD, Postmaster.

Duart.—A Post Village in the Township of Oxford, County Kent. 28 miles distant from Chatham, the County Town, and 140 from Toronto. Land in this vicinity averages from $20 to $30 per acre. A flouring mill would pay here, the surrounding county being extremely fertile. Money order office. Population 350.

Ball, John, carriage maker
Ball, Miss, dressmaker
Benson, Rev. Mr. (Wesleyan Methodist)
Blue, John
Bray, Miss, dressmaker
Cunningham, Archibald D.
Cunningham, H. D., J.P.
Cunningham, John, lumber dealer
Curtis, William, policeman and butcher
Fallon, Edward, carpenter
Ford, Thomas A., nurseryman
Genge, R. S., cabinet maker
Gisner, J. S., hotel proprietor
Graham, J. W., M. D.
Graham, N. & Co., fancy goods
Hicks, John F., M. D.
Hill, Horace, cooper
Johnston, George, carpenter
Kennedy, William, carriage maker
Kerr, Peter
Lankin, William, boots and shoes
Leitch, Dugald, tailor
Leitch, James, hotel keeper
Livingston, John, hotel proprietor and cooper
McCallum, Edward, general merchant
McDonald, Alexander, teacher
McDonald, Archibald
McLaren, Daniel, builder
Patterson, Miss, dressmaker
Patterson, Isaac, general merchant
Pollard, Rev. Mr., (Baptist)
Reycroft, Joseph, boots and shoes
Risk, William, teacher
TAIT, DANIEL M., general merchant
TAIT, JAMES, Postmaster
Wright, Maurice, teacher

Dufferin.—A post Village in the Township of Oneida, County Haldimand, 7 miles from Cayuga the County Town, and 60 from Toronto. Land averages from $30 to $35 per acre. Population 100.

Baird, James, farmer
Brooks, F., sewing machine agent
Campbell, William, school teacher
COSSAR, WILLIAM, Postmaster and general agent
Grant, Rev. Alexander, (Presbyterian)
Grant, William, J. P
Hamilton, William, farmer
Herod, William, farmer
Knox, John, farmer
Martin, Hugh, farmer
Murray, Andrew, farmer
Turnbull, David, teacher
Williamson, James, farmer

Dumblane.—A Post office in the Township of Saugeen, County Bruce, North Riding.

FRASER, JOHN, Postmaster.

Dunbar.—A Post office in the Township of Williamsburgh, County Dundas.

ALLISON, A. C., Postmaster.

Dunbarton.—A Village in the Township of Pickering, County Ontario, 9 miles from Whitby, the County Town, 20 from Toronto. Average value of land in vicinity, $50 per acre. There are several excellent water powers in the neighborhood. Money Order office. Population 120.

Allison. William
Annan, Thomas, farmer
Dunbar, William
Falconer, James, saddler
Fawcett, John
Henderson. Thomas, carpenter
Holmes, Jonathan, teacher
Lawson, David, farmer
McConochie, Hugh, farmer
Marquis, John, farmer
Milne, James, tailor
Muir, William, leather dealer
Nisbet, Peter, farmer
Oddie, John, agent G.T.R.
Palmer, Thomas R., general merchant
PARKER, JOHN, J.P., Postmaster, general merchant and insurance agent
Secker, Robert, hotel keeper
Tripp, Reuben, carpenter
Tripp, Thomas, general merchant

Duncrief.—A small Post Village in the Township of Lobo, County Middlesex, in the centre of a good farming district, and on a never-failing stream. Distant 16 miles from London, the County Town, and 12 from Strathroy. Population about 90.

BARNES, JAMES, Postmaster and general merchant.

Dundalk.—A Village in the Township of Melancthon, County Grey, 44 miles from Owen Sound, the County Town, 40 from Collingwood Station Northern Railway, and 48 from Brampton. Stage Monday and Thursday to Orangeville. Population 100.

Airth, William
Bell, Clement, farmer
Bowler, William, tailor
Breen, Lawrence
Corbett, James, hotel keeper
Dane, James, farmer
Hill, Rev. Rowland, (Church of England)
Hughes, William, farmer
Irwin, Christopher, cooper
King, James, farmer
Lowry, Charles, farmer
McAuley, Alexander, farmer
McAuley, Norman, farmer
McDowell, John, J.P., farmer
McKee, Thomas, hotel keeper
McQuarrie, John, general merchant
MULHOLLAND, JAMES, Postmaster and farmer
Noble, Edward, farmer
Oldfield, Michael, druggist
Palmer, Charles, teacher
Redmond, Sylvester, tailor
Russell, Robert, teacher

Dundas.—An incorporated Town, in the Township of West Flamboro', County Wentworth, at the head of the Desjardins Canal, and on the line of the Great Western Railway, 5 miles from Hamilton, the County Town, 79 from London, 44 from Toronto, and 49 from Suspension Bridge. Dundas is noted for its celebrated manufacturing establishments. The water privileges are unlimited. Money Order Office and Savings Bank. Population about 3500.

AITKIN & POST, (William Aitkin and Chas. Post), manufacturers woolen machinery, &c.
Allen & Skinner, (James Allen and John Skinner), watchmakers
American Express Co., Post office building
Babington, J. M., accountant
Baillie, William
Baird, Mary L., grocer
Baird, N. G., barber
Baker, R., axemaker
Barnwell, Job, farmer
Barrie, William, blacksmith
Barton, George M., barrister
Baskerville, Thomas, butcher
Bayley, William, tailor
Beach, George L., dentist
Began Peter, shoemaker
Begue, A. F., J. P., Clerk Second Division Court.
Bennett, Alfred, billiard saloon
Berry, George, blacksmith
Bickell, George, pattern maker
Bickell, George, sen., pattern maker
Bickell, David, carpenter
BILLINGTON, J. P., manager Canada Screw Co.
Bishop, William B., cabinet maker
Bland, Rev. H. F., (Wesleyan Methodist)
Bloomfield, Peter
Booth, H. G.
Boyle, Patrick, general blacksmith
Brady, Peter, stoves and tinware
Brinkworth, William, watchmaker
Brooke, R. S., photographer
Borthwick, Walter, baker
Brown, Michael, shoemaker
Bryce, James, telegraph and express agent
Brydges, William, wagon maker
Burns, James, grocer
Burns, John, boots and shoes
Butler, Rev. John, (Baptist)
BURROWS, G. F., accountant and insurance agent
Burton, Adam, blacksmith
Burton, Peter, peg maker
Cain, Patrick, innkeeper
Calder, Alexander D., druggist
Calder, Duncan
Callaghan, John, grocer
CAMERON, A. D., commission merchant
Campbell, D. M., blacksmith
Campbell, John, carpenter
Cantwell, James, general merchant
Cardwell, William, tailor
CANADA PERMANENT BUILD'G & SAVINGS SOCIETY. George F. Burrows, agent
CASEY & MERCER (William Casey & Jas. Mercer), general merchants
Cass, Patrick, carpenter
Chalmers, Alexander, tanner
Chanells, John, paper makers
Chamberlin, W. H., baker
Chegwin, Mrs. Ann, dry goods, &c,
Cherry, Blaney, paper maker
Clark, Edward, shoemaker
Cody, Richard, cooper
COLEMAN, JAMES, flour mills and stave and barrel factory
Collier, Thomas, lumber dealer
Collins, B., innkeeper
COLLINS & BENNETT (Peter Collins & Henry Bennett), publishers, *Wentworth News.*
Conley, Bernard, shoemaker
Conley, John, boots and shoes
Cook, Rev. Richard (Presbyterian)
Cooper, Jesse, grocer
Crandell, James H., grocer
Crann, Francis, blacksmith
Crow, J. J., book-keeper
Cummings, Edward, shoemaker
Cummings, John, brewer
Davis, J. H. & Son, boots and shoes
Davis, Edward, manager cotton mills
DICKIE, JOHN, grocer
DICKIE, J. C. & CO., grocers
Dingle, Richard, butcher
Dodgson, John, whip maker
Duggan, Michael, tailor
Duncan, Mrs., hotel keeper
Dundon, James, cooper
Egerson, Robert, plasterer
ENRIGHT & BROTHER (John & William Enright), saloon and livery
Evan, John, machinist
Fahey, F., cooper
Fields, Daniel, sen.
Fields, Daniel, plasterer
Fisher, John & Son, paper mills
Forest, John, wire worker
FORSYTH, JOHN, agricultural implement and woolen machinery manufacturer
Forsyth & Co., card clothing manufacturers
Foulds, Mrs. John, fancy goods
Fraley, Mrs. C., grocer
Freed, William S., tinsmith

GARTSHORE & CO. (John and Alexander Gartshore) founders and machinists
Geddes, F., station master Great Western Railway
Geddes, J. C., station master Great Western Railway
Gilleland, Thomas, miller
Gleeson, James, Dundas and Hamilton Express
Goos, Henry, cabinet maker
Gordon, Captain John
GORE DISTRICT MUTUAL INSURANCE COMPANY, George F. Burrows, agent
GRAFTON, J. B. & J. S., dry goods
Graham, Andrew, grocer
Gray, W. R., manufacturer agricultural implements
GREENING, TIMOTHY, Dundas wire works
Griffin, Miss E. C., teacher
Griggs, F., tobacconist
Gwyn, W. B., collector of customs
Hall, William, tanner
HAMILTON, JAMES, M.D.
Hamilton, Robert, painter
Harper, James, painter
Harvey, B., general merchant
Hazlewood, William, blacksmith
Heffernan, John, cooper
Herald, Rev. James (Presbyterian)
Hollingshead, Robert, potter
HOME FIRE AND MARINE INSURANCE COMPANY, New Haven, Connecticut, George F. Burrows, agent
HOME LIFE INSURANCE COMPANY, New York, George F. Burrows, agent
Hopkins, D. W.
Hourigan, Jeremiah, edge tool manufacturer
Howard, Benjamin, painter
Howard, H. H. and R. T., carriage makers
HUNTER, J. H., M.A., head teacher Grammar School
Hurst, Samuel, boarding house
INNES, HUGH, official assignee and agent
Innes, W. P.
Johnson, William, blacksmith
Joyce, William, shoemaker
Kelly & Patterson (John Kelly and Charles Patterson) painters
Kent, Mrs., innkeeper
King, Alonzo, grocer
Knowles, John, carpenter
Knowles, H., shoemaker
Knowles, William, tanner
Laidlaw, William P., tax collector
Lamarche, Joseph, cooper
Latshaw, Isaac, cabinet maker
Laven, Richard, axe maker
LAWRY, CHARLES, leather and findings (see adv.)
Lesslie, John
LITTLER & MAW, machinists
Looney, J. B., teacher
Lyon, Mrs. William, stoves and tinware
McArdell, John, shoemaker
McCarthy, J. C., lumber merchant
McCullough, Alexander, founder
McDONNELL, H., livery stable and hotel keeper
McINTOSH, L., hotel keeper
McKECHNIE & BERTRAM (Robert McKechnie and John Bertram) manufacturers machinists' tools (see adv.)
McKenzie, Thomas H., commission merchant
McMAHON, JAMES, M. D., coroner (see adv.)
McMahon, Philip, cooper
McManus, Mrs., hotel keeper
McMillan, D., photographer
McMillan, D., confectioner
McTaggert, Archibald, tailor
Macdonald, J., founder
Marshall, John, saddler
Martlin, W. B., builder
Martlin, W. J., builder
Marquis, John A., accountant
MEACHAM & BURROWS (J. B. Meacham and C. J. Burrows), druggists and stationers
MERCER & CASEY, builders, &c.
Millman, James, saddler
MOORE, H. & SON (H. & H. H. Moore) gen. merchts.
Morrish, Edwin, fruiterer
Morrison, —, retired
Moss, Charles, saloon keeper
Moss, Joseph, baker
Mountain, Thomas, painter
Nawn, Mrs. Jane, grocer
Newitt, William, butcher
Niblett, W. C., druggist
Nisbet, James, blacksmith
O'Connor, Patrick, blacksmith
O'Leary, Thomas, grocer
O'Neill, Michael, mason
O'Reilly, Rev. John, (Roman Catholic)
Osler, Rev. F. L., rector St. James'
OSLER & BEGUE, (B. B. Osler & T. A. Begue)
Overfield, S
Parker, E. B., pumpmaker
PARMENTER, W. E., morocco leather and glove manufacturer (see adv.)
Passmore, William saddler
Patterson, David, hotel keeper
Pirie, George M., grocer
Quarry, John, saddler
Quinn, Patrick, grocer
Randell, James H., painter
RANKIN, JOHN, dry goods
Ratcliffe, Rev. Frederick, (Baptist)
Reynolds, James, engineer
Ridler, George, assessor
RILEY, P. B., prop. Riley's Hotel.
ROBERTSON & WARDELL, (Thomas Robertson & A. R. Wardell,) barristers
Rolph, George
Russell, Abram, insurance agent
Rutherford, H. C., M.D
Sanders, Richard, hotel keeper
Seace, George F., hotel keeper
SCOTT, JAMES, agricultural implement manufacturer
Smith, John H., hotel keeper
SMITH, J. F., general hardware (see adv.)
Smith, William, cabinet maker
SOMERVILLE, JAMES, publisher *True Banner*
Suter, R. W., secretary and treasurer Canal Company and insurance agent
Thompson, James, accountant
THORNTON, JOHN M., Postmaster
TRUE BANNER newspaper (weekly), James Somerville editor and proprietor
Urquhart, A., blacksmith
Van Noble, David, boiler maker
Wagstaff, John, tinsmith
WALKER, A. H., M.D (see adv)
Watson, David, farmer
Watson, L. B., tailor
Webster, Joseph, flour mill proprietor
Willbey, Thomas, carriage maker
Wilson, John, prop. Wentworth mills
WILSON, RICHARD T., grocer wholesale and retail
Wilson, Wilson, grocer
Wood, John, bailiff First Division Court
WOODHOUSE, EDWARD, town clerk
Woods, Andrew, agent
Wright, John, boiler maker
Wyatt, Robert, engineer
Wynne, Dominick, laborer

Dunnville.—An incorporated Village and station of the Grand Trunk Railway, situated on the Grand River, at its junction with the feeder of the Welland Canal, in the Township of Moulton, County Haldimand, 15 miles from Cayuga, the County Town, 40 from Hamilton, and 40 from Buffalo, N. Y. Money Order office and Savings Bank. Population 1500.

AMSDEN, JABEZ, general merchant, auctioneer and appraiser
Armour, John, Clerk Division Court
ARMOUR, THOMAS, Postmaster
Barker, Edgar, attorney at law
Beemer, Rev. A. (Episcopal Methodist)
Beebe, Nelson, dentist
Bolger, John, saloon keeper
BOYLE, A. & CO., dry goods and groceries
Braund, J., insurance agent
BRAUND, W. & CO., hardware and general dealers
Brown, George, lime dealer
Brown, J. R., grocer
Brownson, A., commission merchant
Bushell, James, hotel keeper
Cairns, Samuel, blacksmith
Callowhill, W., watchmaker
Carlisle, Thomas, general merchant
Chambers, Richard, flour mill prop.
Clemo, James, bailiff
Cormick, Samuel, shoemaker
CRAYSTON, THOMAS, general merchant
Culver, Peter, saloon keeper
Cunningham, Rev. S. (Baptist)
DUNNVILLE LUMINARY (weekly), Thomas Messenger, editor and proprietor
Duval & Irwin, saw mill proprietors
Ebershott, Peter, butcher
Edgar, John, builder
Everingham, James A., miller
Farran, John, barber
Farrell, J. T., M.D
Fleming, Rev. Robert, (Presbyterian)
Flood, Rev. John, (Church of England)
Ford, A. B., tinsmith
Fry, W., M.D
Gash, Matthew, butcher
Gamble, William, restaurant
Gibbs, M., saloon keeper
Hanly, James, photographer
HENDERSHOTT, P. H., dry goods, clothing and groceries, agent Wanzers' sewing machines
Hodder, E., butcher
Hodder, George, butcher
Hood, John, surveyor
Hopkins, N., M.D
Hopkins, N., jun., M.D
House, W., carpenter
Jarden, Z., watchmaker
Johnson, M. B., general merchant
JOHNSON, JOHN T., dry goods and groceries
Kennedy, Rev. George, (Wesleyan)
King, R., grocer
Lawe, Henry, P.L.S., insurance agent
Laidlaw, James, foreman *Luminary*
Leaver, Rev. J. J. A., (N. C. Methodist)
LINDSAY, JAMES, draper
Litster, John, tailor and grocer
LIVINGSTON, ANGUS, blacksmith
McCALLUM, G. A., M.D
McCrae, W. A., Customs Collector
McLaughlin, Alexander, M. D.
McNeil, C., saloon keeper
McNeil, Robert, grocer
McNulty, Rev. J. (Roman Catholic)
Macartney, A. T., dry goods and groceries
May, Richard, baker
Montreal Telegraph Company, J. R. Brown, agent
Morris, James, shoemaker
Murphy, J., landing waiter
Moote, W. M., grocer
NEVENS, JAMES H., prop. Nevens' Hotel (see adv.)
Nevens' Hotel, near Railway Station
NEW DOMINION CABINET WAREROOM, James Schofield & Son
Noble, J., grocer
Old, F. W. M., tinsmith
PENNY, H., boots and shoes
PERRY, CORNELIUS, groceries and liquors (see adv.)
Phipps, Job, shoemaker
PIGEON, MRS. E., prop. Queen's Hotel
Price, D. S., hotel keeper
Price, David, boarding house keeper
QUEEN'S HOTEL, Mrs. E. Pigeon prop.
Ramsay, Francis, deputy sup. Public Works
Randell, N. B., grocer
Reed, J. F., grocer
ROOT, HARMAN, livery stables (see adv.)
SCHOFIELD, JAMES & SON, marble works, steam cabinet factory
Scott, George, woolen factor
Scott, J. S. & Co., cabinet makers
Simms, George, farmer
Smith, George, shoemaker
Smith, John F., druggist, issuer of marriage licenses
Smith, M. A., saw mill proprietor
SMITHERS, RICHARD, boots and shoes
Soper, W., gunsmith
Sowerby, John, carriage maker
STEVENS, CHARLES, saddler, &c
Stevenson, F., attorney-at-law
Thewlis, Allan, grocer
Tipton, Thomas, L. M., collector canal tolls
Upper, M. C., attorney-at-law
Walker, George, painter
WALTHO, SAMUEL, woolen factor
Watson, David, proprietor mills
Weatherby, Miss, milliner
Webber, B. H., flour and feed
Wheeler, Samuel, watchmaker
Whipple, James, carriage maker
WHITE, WILLIAM, merchant tailor
Yocum, James, agricultural implements

Dundela.—A post office in the Township of Matilda, County Dundas.
WHARTON, THOMAS, Postmaster.

Dunkeld.—A Post-office in the Township of Brant, County Bruce, S.R.
BELL, HUGH, Postmaster.

Dundonald.—A Village in the Township of Cramahe, County Northumberland, 25 miles from Cobourg the County Town, and 90 from Toronto. Improved land in vicinity averages $35, unimmproved $12 per acre.

Avery, Anson, farmer
BARKER, JOHN, Postmaster, general merchant
Bedell, D. R., J. P.
Bellamy, Andrew, carpenter
Campbell, D., grist prop. mill
Chesterfield, Henry, shoemaker
Coons, W., saw mill prop.
Dudley, Levi, farmer
Farrow, George, farmer
Harden, William, shingle maker
Hinman, S. J. P.
Ives, William, carpenter
Lane, C. T., wool carder
Murphy, G. T., farmer
Phillip, William, J. P.
Potts, I., saw mill prop.
Purdy, David, farmer
Robson, Rev. Mr., (Wesleyan)
Simpson, Rev. I., (Episcopal Methodist)
Sprung, John, cooper
Stimers, James, lime dealer
Thorne, John T., farmer
Walker, William, farmer
Watson, S. E., telegraph operator

Dungannon.—A Village in the Township of Ashfield, County Huron, 18 miles from Goderich the County Town, and 162 from Toronto, situate on Nine Mile creek, which affords good water power. Improved land in the neighborhood averages $40 per acre. Money order office. Population 250.

Anderson, Thomas, farmer
Barr, Rev. William, (Presbyterian)
Black, Anthony, hotel keeper
CLENDINNING, R., J. P., Postmaster, gen. mercht
Crawford, William, wagon maker
Daunt, Rev. Mr., (Church of England)
Davidson, Robert, farmer
Disher, Thomas, woolen factor
Forbes, Robert, teacher
Garvey, Andrew, cooper
Johnston, Thomas, general merchant
Kerr, & McGrattan, shoemakers
Kitson, George, brick yard
McArthur, William, carpenter
McKay, James, M. D.
McLean, John, farmer
McMath, Hugh, woolen factor
McMath, S., saddler
McPherson, Alexander, tailor
Mallough, William, J. P.
Miller, George, shoemaker
Pentland, Alexander, farmer
Pentland, Thomas, farmer
Roberts, J. W., & Co., general merchants
Saunley, S. B., miller
Sproule, Andrew, cabinet maker
Swift, Dean, hotel keeper
Trealeaven, John, general merchant
Whyford, James, tinsmith
Wiggins, Robert, farmer

Dunvegan.—A Post-office in the Township of Kenyon, County Glengarry.
McLEAN, HECTOR, Postmaster.

Duntroon.—(Formerly Bowmore.)—A Post Village in the Township of Nottawasaga, 5 miles from Stayner the nearest Station on the Northern Railway, and 22 miles to Barrie by road. Daily Mail. Population 90.

Belfry & Co., general merchants
Briggs, George, shoemaker
Clunes, John, blacksmith
Johnson, William, merchant
McCausland, John, carpenter
McDonald, William, machinist
McDonald, William, jun., carpenter
McKeggie, John, J.P
Mackenacher, Alexander, M.D
Neff, Isaiah, inn keeper
RUSSELL, JAMES, Postmaster, gen. mercht
Smith, Donald, tailor

Dunsford.—A small Village in the Township of Verulam, County Victoria, 2 miles south from Sturgeon Lake, 10 miles from Lindsay, the County Town, and 12 from Bobcaygeon. Improved lands in the neighborhood average $25, and wild $12 per acre. Stages to Lindsay and Bobcaygeon. Population 30.

Bell, James, carriage maker
GRAHAM, WILLIAM, Postmaster and storekeeper
McCrea, Donald, teacher
Thurston, Jabez, J.P.

Dunsinane.—A Post Office in the Township of Huron County Bruce, S. R.
McDONALD, JAMES L., Postmaster.

Durham.—A Village on the main branch of the Saugeen River, in the Townships of Bentinck and Glenelg, County Grey. Distant from Owen Sound the County Town, 28 miles, from Toronto 100 miles. Stages to Guelph, fare $3, and Collingwood, fare $2. Average price of farming land $20. Park l $_0$ $75. Money Order Office and Savings Bank. Population 1200.

Anderson, Rev. J., (Wesleyan)
Anderson, W., blacksmith
Bain, James, general merchant
Baldwin, John, carpenter
Barrett & Park, attorneys-at-law
Burnett, A. H., blacksmith
Boulder, Thomas, carpenter
Brown, Alexander, grocer
Brown, James, general merchant
Carson, John, general merchant
Chittick, Christopher, blacksmith
Cochrane, Alexander, J. P.
Cochrane, Asa, proprietor planing mill
Cochrane, A. & A., wagon makers
Cole, Henry, proprietor Exchange Hotel
Colles, W. H. & Co., broom manufacturers
Crawford, J., M. D.
"DURHAM CHRONICLE," White & Johnston, Editors and proprietors
Edwards, —, bookseller
Edwards, J. H., watchmaker
Elvidge, Lockwood, livery stable
Evans, Rev. W., (Church of England)
Findlay & Jones, booksellers
Finlay, R., telegraph operator
French, P., tailor
Gunn, James, M. D.
Harper, C., attorney-at-law
Harris, Thomas, tinsmith
Hunter, Archibald
Hunter, J. H., general merchant
Hyndman, John, general merchant
Isaacs, George, saddler
Jack, John, painter
Jackson, David, J.P.
JACKSON, GEORGE, M.P.
Jackson, William, Crown Land agent
Jamieson, J., carpenter
Jamieson, W., wagon maker
Jones, James, cabinet maker
Jones, Thomas, shoemaker
Kelly, John, lumber dealer
Legate, S. E., painter
Limin, Charles, butcher
McCullough, John, carpenter
McDonald, J. W., carpenter
McFarlane, A., wagon maker
McFarlane, R., wagon maker
McIntyre, D., tailor
McKay, Hugh, auctioneer
McKechnie, A. & G., general merchants
McKelvy, Robert, carpenter
McKENZIE, ARCHIBALD, Postmaster and general merchant
McKenzie, Donald, shoemaker
McKenzie, Roderick, farmer
MacDonnell, D., attorney-at.law
Mahuet, Rev. P., (Roman Catholic)
Meredith, —, grocer
Middough, J. H., proprietor International Hotel
Moodie, John, accountant
Orton, Richard, M. D.
Parke, Rev. W., (Presbyterian)
Parker & Cattle, chemist
Parrot, John, tinsmith
Paterson, Peter, lumber dealer and woolen factor
Perry, J., general merchant
Porter, —, M. D.
Robertson, John, tailor
Rose, Alexander, tailor
Ross, J., shoemaker
Rombough, W. R., teacher
Rowland, John, auctioneer
Russell, George, general merchant
Shewell, John, cabinet maker
Sidsworth, J. baker
Smith, Thomas, tanner
Spence, James, proprietor British Hotel
Stoddart, T., proprietor Durham Hotel
Storey, Henry, wagon maker
Sullivan, J., tinsmith
Surveyor, David, teacher
Sutherland, R., baker
Tucker, G., cooper
Turner, Wilton, teacher
Turner, & Richardson, general merchants
Walker, Rev. J., (New Connexion)
WHITE & JOHNSTON, publishers and proprietors, *Durham Chronicle*
Whitmore, Thomas
Willey, G. G., shoemaker

East Hawkesbury.—A Village in the Township of East Hawkesbury, County Prescott, 14 miles from L'Orignal, the County Town.

Albright, Archibald, farmer
Allison, William, J.P.
Bertrand, Leonard, carpenter
Bertrand, Leonard, jun., carriage maker
Burwash, Caroline, dressmaker
Burwash, Nelson, J.P.
Cameron, John, farmer
Chalmers, Rev. William (Methodist)
Cook, James, painter
Cooke, James, architect
Cunning, William, cooper
Fournier, Peter, cooper
Garrett, Rev. Mr. (Methodist)
Grout, Solomon, farmer
Kirkconnell, John, farmer
Lablond, Pierre, leather dealer
Laflame, Antoine, shingle maker
Le Roy, Frank, carpenter
McADAM, JOHN, Postmaster, boot and shoe maker
McKinnon, —, M.D.
McLennan, Harriet, teacher
McRae, Alexander, teacher
Maneeley, Michael, hotel keeper and genl. merchant.
Ogden, Mrs., milliner
Ralston, Elizabeth, school teacher

Easton's Corners.—*(See Villages too late for regular insertion, at the end of this work.)*

Eagle.—A Post Village in the Township of Aldboro', County Elgin, distant 24 miles from St. Thomas, the County Town. Population 75.

Edwards, Robert, painter
Lindaman, P., dry goods, &c.
McCallum, J., carpenter
MOWBRAY, WILLIAM, Postmaster and carpenter
Mulholland, G. A., cabinet maker and wagon maker
Siegel, Frederick, boots and shoes
Stewart, J. H., carpenter and builder

East Oro.—A small Post Village in the Township of Oro, County Simcoe, 16 miles from Barrie, the County Town. Population 60.

SIMPSON, WILLIAM, Postmaster.

Eastville.—(Holt P.O.)—A Village in the Township of East Gwillimbury, County York, 40 miles from Toronto, the County Town, and 5 from Sharon. Stage to Newmarket. Population 50

Armitage, Joshua, inn keeper
Douglas, Samuel, farmer
Fields, Thomas, farmer
Hopkins, James, farmer
Lepard, John, farmer
Lepard, Leonard, carpenter
Morris, Evan, carpenter
QUIBELL, JOHN, Postmaster and general merchant
Rowen, Richard, farmer
Thompson, Kemp, farmer
Traviss, Charles, farmer

East Williamsburgh.—*(See Villages too late for regular insertion, at the end of the work.)*

Eastwood.—A Post Village in the Township of East Oxford, County Oxford, and a Station on the Great Western Railway, 4 miles distant from Woodstock, the County Town. Population about 100.

Fowler, James, shoemaker
Hyde, William, farmer
Robinson, John, blacksmith
Smith, Hiram, blacksmith
Shaw, John, general merchant
VANSITTART, HENRY, Postmaster

Eden.—A Post Village in the Township of Bayham, County Elgin. Distant from St. Thomas, the County Town, 24 miles. Daily mail.

NETHERCOTT, JOHN, Postmaster.

Eden Mills.—A Village in the Township of Eramosa, County Wellington, 7 miles from Guelph, the County Town, and 4 miles from Rockwood Station, Grand Trunk Railway. A branch of the River Speed passes through the village, and affords good mechanical power

Boyle, Andrew, blacksmith
Campbell, Malcolm, shoemaker
Cook, Frederick, cabinet maker
Cook, Othello, cabinet maker
Gokey, Frank, cooper
Hampson, George, stone and lime dealer
Harris, John, hotel keeper
Harris, Thomas, cooper
Hough, Rev. M., (Wesleyan)
Jackson, Anthony, general merchant
McKay, Samuel, general merchant
Martin, George, wagon maker
MEADOWS, SAMUEL, Postmaster
North, James, carpenter
Richardson, Ralph, wagon maker
Roberts, Daniel, carpenter
Thomas, George, dentist
Wilkinson, Rev. M., (New Con. Methodist)
Wilson, Peter, dyer

Edgecombe.—A Post Office in the Township of Mornington, County Perth, distant 20 miles from Stratford, the County Town. Population 30.

Coulter, Robert, farmer
Dunbar, Mrs., accouchante
Gallop & Brother, carriage makers and blacksmiths
GALLOP, CORNELIUS, Postmaster
Hamilton, William, farmer
Kompff, Louis, carpenter and builder
Kennedy, Thomas, hotel proprietor
McFadden, Uriah, J. P. and farmer
McKenzie, Duncan, stone mason
Montgomery, Joseph, plasterer
Martin, Robert, farmer
White, Robert, stonemason
White, Samuel, teacher

Edmonton.—A Post Village in the Township of Chinguacousy, County Peel, 4½ miles from Brampton, the County Town, and 30 from Toronto. The Brampton and Orangeville stages pass through the Village daily. Population 140.

Cameron, E., general merchant
COLLINGBOURNE, JAMES, Postmaster
Duckworth, James, farmer
Gascoyne & Quinn, carriage makers
Humphries, Edwin, cabinet maker
Huxley, John, boot and shoe maker
Jordan, —, teacher
Knox, William, hotel keeper
Lundy, James, hotel keeper
McCallum, R. C., Township Clerk and Treasurer
McLellan, James, hotel keeper
Newton, George, boot and shoemaker
Quinn, R., J.P
Shields, Thomas, farmer
Snell, B. & E., farmers
Snell, John, farmer
Watson, Benjamin, farmer
Watson, James, farmer
Watson, Robert, farmer

Eddystone.—A Post office in the Township of Haldimand, County Northumberland.

Edwardsburg.—*(See Villages too late for regular insertion, at the end of the work.)*

Effingham.—A Village in the Township of Pelham, County Monck, 7 miles from St. Catherines, the County Town, and 72 from Toronto. Improved land in the vicinity $55 per acre. Population, 50

Atkins, John, farmer
Beckett, Whiston, farmer
Beckett, William, wool factor
Metlar, David, farmer
REDPATH, GEORGE, Postmaster
Sanderson, John, farmer
Ward, Nehemiah, farmer
Wilson, Alexander, farmer

Eganville.—*(See Villages too late for regular insertion, at the end of the work.)*

Egbert.—A Post Office in the Township of Essa, County Simcoe.
STRACHAN, JAMES, Postmaster.

Egerton.—A Post Office in the Township of Luther, County Wellington.
HUNTER, JAMES, J.P., Postmaster and general merchant

Eglington.—A Village on Yonge Street, Township of York, 4 miles from Toronto. Population, 200.

Campbell, James, blacksmith
Coulter, James, shoemaker
Douglass, William, carriage maker
Hargrave, Joseph, shoemaker
Harris, Rev. James
Jackes, W., J.P
Lawrence, Jacob, farmer
Lawrence, John, farmer
McBride, Charles, proprietor Prospect House
Martin, Joseph, farmer
Martin, William, farmer
Maughan,, N., carpenter
Nightingale, Henry, butcher
Snider, Edwin, farmer
Snider, Edward, farmer
Snider, Elia, farmer
Ward, George, farmer

Egremont.—A Post-office in the Township of Normanby, County Grey. Distant from Owen Sound, the County Town, 42 miles, from Toronto 90 miles. Stages daily to and from Guelph. Average price of land $15. Population 60.

Allan, John, farmer
Anderson, William, farmer
Cooper, Mrs. M., hotel keeper
Cringle, James, hotel keeper
Dawson, Robert, farmer
Dickson, John, miller
Lumley, William, farmer
McFarlane, George, farmer
McKellar, Neil, farmer
ROBERTSON, JOHN, J.P
Ryan, W. H., J.P
Sefton, Miss Martha, teacher
SMITH, THOMAS, Postmaster and gen. mercht
West, Rev. Mr., (Methodist)

Egmondville.—A Village adjoining Seaforth Station, Buffalo and Lake Huron Railway, on the Bayfield River, in the Township of Tuckersmith, County Huron, 22 miles from Goderich, the County Town. The The Village was settled in 1845 by Constant Louis Van Egmond. The river affords good water power. Average value of land in vicinity, $40 per acre. Stages to Bayfield, Brucefield and Varna. Money order office. Population, 500.

Allen, Thomas, butcher
Badger, William & Brothers, potash and soap factory
Bohler, V., potter
Bowden, John, brickmaker
Brett, Robert, tanner
Brown, William, miller
Cameron, S., tailor
Carter, James, lumber merchant
COLBERT, HENRY, proprietor Huron Brewery
Duncan, David, carpenter
Ewing, George, butcher
Fulton, Robert, blacksmith
Graham, Rev., (Presbyterian)
Gray, John, plow maker
Heffler, Christopher, wood and willow ware
Hill, Thomas, blacksmith
Holcombe & Hamilton, grocers
JACKSON, GEORGE E., Postmaster
Jackson, G. & H., general merchants
Krusi, C., cooper
McDonald, Solomon, cooper
Merkans, Leopold, tanner
Neff, J., hotel keeper
Robinson, Mrs., hotel keeper
Rudolph, Martin, manufacturer of syrups and cordials
Rudd, William, wagon maker
Shaffler, Paul, carpenter
Smith, Andrew, saddler
Sparrow, Edward, carpenter
Steel, John, shoemaker
Tinkess, Levi, pump maker
Van Egmond, August, fulling mills
VAN EGMOND, C. L., proprietor flour mill
Van Egmond, Leopold, proprietor saw mill
Vercoe, H., M.D
Watson, C. W., sheepskin tanner

Eldorado.—A Village in the Township of Madoc, County Hastings, on the road from Belleville to the Madawaska, and in the heart of the celebrated gold mining region. The Richardson and the Belleville and Richardson mines are now in course of working. The village is 34 miles from Belleville, the County Town, and 153 from Toronto.

Bacon, Charles
Bacon, John
Best, J. R.
Best, J. S
Borland, Samuel, J., dry goods, &c
Chambers, James
Chambers, Joseph
Cooke, Henry
Cooke, John
Craig, W., hotel keeper
DICKSON, ADAM, Postmater
Ellis, William
Gonsolus, Andrew
Gonsolus, Peter
Hassard, Richard
Impey, Servius
Knight, Overton, M.D
Lightburne, Stafford, attorney-at-law
McCarthy, H., hotel keeper
McInroy, John
Moore, Alexander
Moore, James
Moore, John
Moore, John M
O'Brien, John, hotel keeper
Pine, William
Richardson, John
Rupert, Charles
Rupert James
Sandford, Charles
Simmonds, N., hotel keeper
Scott, Robert, grocer, &c
Scott, Thomas, grocer, &c

Elgin.—A Village in the Township of South Crosby, County Leeds, 38 miles from Brockville, the County Town, and 4 from Philipsville. Population 200.

Austin, C. S., general agent
Baker, R. H., shoemaker
Burns, Arthur, farmer
Connors, Thomas, shoemaker
Dargand, Brothers, general merchants
Dargavel, R., bookbinder
Earl, James F., cabinet maker
Halladay, B., carriage maker
Halladay, James, carriage maker
Howard, Rev. N. H. (Episcopal Methodist)
Hunter, Israel, blacksmith
Kelvey, S., saddler
Laishley, Henry, general merchant
Leavitt, A. S., M.D., druggist
Leavitt, T., insurance agent
Leggett, Benjamin, carriage maker
Leggett, Robert, hotel keeper
Merriman, A., brickyard
McGhie, B. T., M.D.
Murphy, James, shoemaker
Mustard, William, carpenter
Newman, A. S., general merchant
Pennock, A. W., cooper
PENNOCK, PHILEMON, Postmaster
Pennock, William, farmer
Rennick, Sterling, builder
Ripley, C. T., J. P.
Savage, Rev. W. (Methodist)
Seel, S., blacksmith
Sexton, T., general merchant
Sly, David, saddler
Warren, J. B., farmer
Withie, A., carpenter

Elfrida.—A Post-office in the Township of Saltfleet, County Wentworth. Tri-weekly mail. Population 50.

Elder.—A Post Village in the Township of Mono, County Simcoe, 35 miles from Barrie, the County Town and 50 from Toronto.

CONN, COURTNEY, Postmaster
Elder, Thomas, J.P
Ewin, John, lime dealer
Lewis, William, J.P., teacher
Mullin, Edward, lime burner

Elginburg.—*(See Villages too late for regular insertion, at the end of this work.)*

Elginfield.—A Post Village in the Township of London, County Middlesex, 14 miles from London, the County Town, and 3 from Lucan, a station on the Grand Trunk Railway. A stage from London to Clinton passes daily. Population 50.

Atkinson, William, blacksmith
Benn, H. & Sons, brickmakers
McCarthy, William, innkeeper
McCormack, Stephen, general merchant
Nangle, Thomas, general merchant
Ryan, W. H., Postmaster, farmer and innkeeper
Scott, W., potash manufacturer
Tracy, Thomas, carpenter

Elizabethville.—A small Village in the Township of Hope, County Durham, 13 miles from Port Hope, the County Town, and 65 from Toronto. Average value of improved land in the vicinity, $45 per acre. Population 75.

McMURTY, JOHN, Postmaster.

Ellengowan.—A post office in the Township of Brant, County Bruce, South Riding.

BROWNLEE, JAMES, Postmaster

Ellesmere.—A post office in the Township of Scarboro, County York.

GLENDINNING, ARCHIBALD, Postmaster.

Elmvale.—A small Village in the Township of Flos, County Simcoe, 22 miles from Barrie, the County Town, and 82 from Toronto. The river Wye, in the neighborhood, affords good water power.

HARVEY, WILLIAM, Postmaster.

Elmira.—A Village in the Township of Woolwich, County Waterloo. Distant 12 miles from Berlin the County Town, and 66 miles from Toronto. The Village is fast growing into importance and numbers at the present time about 450 inhabitants.

Boehler, Jacob, cooper
Canadian Maple Leaf, Thomas Hilliard, proprietor
CHRISTMANA, JOHN, livery proprietor
Detwiler, A. T. & Co., founders and machinists
Dunke, Henry, carriage maker
Ellis, W. D., hotel keeper
ELMIRA JOINT STOCK grist and flouring mill company
Ernst, Rev., Mr., (Luthern)
Girling, John, saddles and harness maker
Graham, Rev. Mr., (Presbyterian)
Hergert, Caspar, tailor
HILLIARD, THOMAS, editor and proprietor *Canadian Maple Leaf*
Johnston, C., teacher
Kempf, Frederick, carpenter
Kuffer, Matthias, hotel proprietor and butcher
Levan, Peter & Co., stoves and tinware
Martin, Hiram, carpenter
Martin, Henry, carpenter
Race, Rev. Mr., (Lutheran)
Rose, Conrad, proprietor Dominion Hotel
Ruppel, John, general merchant
Russell, Charles, carpenter
Savage, John Y., chemist and druggist
Shumacher, John S., painter
Simon, Louis, tailor and saddler
Simpson, James, cabinet maker
Smiley, Rev. Mr. (Wesleyan)
Stork, John, carriage maker
Sutherland, Robert, general merchant
Voght, George, proprietor Union hotel
Wachsmuth, William, boot and shoe maker
Walmsley, David L., M.D.
Warner & Epting, boot and shoe makers
Wenz, Jacob, cooper
Whiting, James A., M.D.
Winger, Isaac, general merchant
WINGER, PETER, Postmaster
Winger & Weaver (Peter Winger and Samuel S. Weaver), general merchants, wool and saw millers
Woodward, George W., teacher
Woodward, Harriet A., teacher

Elm Grove.—A small Village in the Township of Essa, County Simcoe, situated on the Nottawasaga River which supplie some good water privileges. It is distant 19 miles from Barrie the County Town, and 60 from Toronto. Population 20.

Hunt, E., agent R. Love
LOVE, RICHARD, Postmaster, and gen. merchant
Mooney, John, school teacher
McNaughton, Thomas, hotel keeper
Woods, Henry, boot and shoe maker

Elmwood.—A Post Village in the Township of Brant, County Bruce, 12 miles distant from Walkerton, the County Town, and 125 from Toronto. It is situated on a branch of the Saugeen river, which affords excellent water power. The surrounding country is extremely fertile. Stages to Hanover, Scone and Chesley. Population 30.

Bannister, Samuel, shingle maker
Barton, Hugh N., stone cutter
Brown, Rev. (Baptist)
Dalgleish, Robert, potash maker
DIRSTEEN, JOHN, Postmaster and mill owner
Eveligh, Joseph, mill-wright
Gustour & Co., cabinet makers
Huscher & Co., boots and shoes
Huscher, Frederick, accountant
Kempkes, Herman, wagon maker
Kerr, Alexander, teamster
Kerr, John M., painter
Pepper, William, lime burner
Puttock, David, blacksmith
Reinhardt,, John, general store
Reinhardt, Jacob, mason
Robertson, Alexander, blacksmith
Robertson, John, stonecutter
Smith, Thomas, contractor
Smith, William, weaver
Watson, Thomas, carpenter

Elora.—An incorporated Village in the Township of Nichol, County Wellington, beautifully situated near the junction of the Grand and Irvine rivers, 13 miles from Guelph, the County Town, 3 from Fergus, 36 from Listowell, and 52 from Walkerton. Daily stage from Guelph. Money Order Office and Savings' Bank. Population 1,500.

Allan, Charles
ANDREW, JOHN, watchmaker
Arkell, James, miller
BAIN, JOHN, sen., prop. Elora Hotel
BAIN, JOHN, & SON, carding, fulling and woolen mills (see adv).
BAIN, JOHN, Jun. (John Bain & Son)
Bank of Montreal, W. P. Newman, manager
Barron, George, J.P.
Beck, Fred, carpenter
Beck, Thomas, carpenter
BIGGAR, THOMAS, prop. Commercial Hotel (see adv)
Blake, George, mason
BOWES, JOHN, dry goods, groceries, &c.
Brown, George, proprietor marble works
Brown, John, constable
Buckley, John, weaver
BURNS, EDWARD (McMillan & Burns)
Bye, George, grocer
CASSCADEN, JAMES, prop. Farmer's Hotel
Cattanach, Mrs. Mary, dressmaker
Cheeseman, Charles, cabinet maker
Chinnech, Robert, tailor
CLARK, JAMES, miller
COMMERCIAL HOTEL, Thomas Biggar, proprietor
CONNELL, ANDREW, hardware
Connor, Thomas, painter
COOK, ROBERT A., hotel keeper
CULLODEN, W. G., editor and proprietor *North Wellington Times*
Cuthbert, Alexander, blacksmith
Cuthbert & Noble, wagon makers
DALBY, FRANK, proprietor Dalby House (see adv.)
DALBY HOUSE, Frank Dalby, proprietor
Dalby, Robert, tanner
Douglass, Moses
DREW, GEORGE A. (Drew & Jacob)
DREW & JACOB (George A. and John), barristers, attornies, notaries public, &c.
Duff, Rev. John (Presbyterian)
Duncan, John
Duncan, William, mason
Eby, Jonas, carpenter
Eby, William, carpenter
Elliott, William, veterinary surgeon
ELORA HOTEL, John Bain, proprietor
Farrow, Benjamin, pump maker
Farrow, Edward, pump maker
Finlay, David, bailiff
FINLAYSON, JOHN, M. D., Postmaster
Foote, David, farmer
Forbes, George, tailor
Ford, George, carpenter
Fraser, Alexander, miller
FRASER, J. M., miller and distiller
FRASER, J. M. & Co., merchants
Fraser, Peter, miller
Fuller, George, cooper
Garrard & Son, wagon makers
Gay, A. W., agent Elora mills
German, Rev. J., (Wesleyan)
Gerrie, James, shoemaker
Gerrie, Robert, farmer
Gibbson, William
Glick, Lewis, distiller
Godfrey, John, shoemaker
Gordon, A., saddler
Gordon, John W., photographer
Gray, William, mason
Halley, Maurice, grocer
Hamilton, H., blacksmith
Haslem, Charles, carpenter
Hay, George, carpenter
HELE, JOHN W. & Co., chemists and druggists
Henderson, J., merchant
Henderson Bros., merchants
Henneberry, J. & Co., proprietors flax and grist mills
Hicks, John, cooper
Inch, Charles, cooper
JACOB, JOHN, (Drew & Jacob)

Johnston, Joseph, blacksmith
Kelly, Thomas L., brewer
Kenning, J. & R., blacksmiths
Kerr, Robert, tanner
Kerr, William, boots and shoes
Kilpatrick, William, carpenter
Kirk & Clarke, merchants
Kirkendall, Joseph
KNOWLES, WILLIAM, hardware mercht. (see adv)
Land, Henry, shoemaker
La Penotiere, W. H., P. L. S.
Lawrence, Charles, bricklayer
Leach, William, chair maker
Leslie, George, farmer
Lown, Jacob, tailor
McBain, D., mason
McCulloch, James, packer
McDonald, John, carpenter
McGregor, M. O., barrister
McGREGOR, REV. J. G., head master gram'r school
McIlroy, Samuel
McIntosh, James, millwright
McKinlay, George, carpenter
McLean, John, clerk Division Court
McLeod, John, farmer
McMicken, William, carpenter
McMILLAN, A. G., (McMillan & Burns)
McMILLAN & BURNS, (A. G. and Edward) barristers, attorneys, &c.
McNeil, John, cabinet maker
Martin, Thomas, stoves, tinware, &c
Maw & Fenwick, (Robt. B. & Wm.) merchant tailors
Middlemass, Rev. J., (Canada Presbyterian)
MIDDLETON, William G., M. D.
Mitchell, Robert, saddler
MITCHELL & ROBERTSON, general merchants
Modeland, Isaac, iron founder
MUNDELL, JOHN, cabinet maker
NEWMAN, E. H., auctioneer
NOBLE, GEORGE, wagon maker (see adv.)
Paget, A. H., M.D.
Patmore, Levi, carpenter
Pitcher, Richard, painter
Potter, D. M., iron founder
Purviss & McIntyre, teamsters
Roberts, Hugh, farmer
Ross, Arthur, farmer
Ross, James
Ross, John M., miller and distiller
Scott, Charles, carpenter
Scott, Henry, painter
SHAW, J. M., editor and prop. *Lightning Express*
Shepherd, Jacob, carpenter
SHEPPARD, M., watchmaker and jeweller (see adv.)
Sheppard, William, carpenter
Simpson, Peter, carpenter
Sinclair, George, merchant
Smart, Alexander, potash manufacturer
Smith, James, cabinet maker
SMITH, JOHN, editor and proprietor *Elora Observer* (see adv.)
Smith, John A., carpenter
Smith, R. J., stationery and drugs
Somers, J. G., tailor
Spalding, Alexander, carpenter
Stafford, William, bricklayer
STEPHENSON, S. E., watchmaker and jeweler
Tait, J., teacher
Taylor, Benjamin, merchant
Taylor, John, farmer
Thompson, Rev. C. E., (Church of England)
THOMSON, GEORGE, boots and shoes
Topham, Robert, shoemaker
Tribe, Jonathan, farmer
Veitch, James, cooper
Vicars, Francis, teamster
VICKERS, THOMAS, prop. Royal Hotel
Waddell Bros., (Alexander & John) carpenters
Webster, Samuel, tin and coppersmith
Whitlaw, Charles, prop. Elora Mills
Young, James

Embro.—An incoporated Village situated on a branch of the Thames, in the Township of West Zorra, County Oxford, one of the finest agricultural sections of the Province, 10 miles from Woodstock, the County Town, 6 miles from a station of the Great Western Railway. Money Order office. Population 600.

Adams, Henry, M.D., druggist
Adams, James, treasurer municipality
Bartley, Joseph, farmer
Campbell, George, carpenter
Campbell, James, carpenter
Chisholm, Walter, farmer,
Cody, E., grocer
Pent, Lieut.-Col. John D
Duncan, George, M.D
Duncan, John, farmer
Farmsworth & Murney, founders
Forrest, George, general merchant
Fraser, Duncan, grocer
Geddes, William, carriage maker
Grant, William, tailor
Gunn, John, farmer
Henderson, Augus, tinsmith
Herron, Thomas, dry goods
Hicks, Thomas, proprietor flour mills
Hodgkinson, John, farmer
Johnson, Rev., J. B., (Wesleyan)
Laycock, Joseph, proprietor flour mills
McAulay, Hugh, tinsmith
McDonald, A., councillor
McDonald, John, manufacturer woolen goods
McDonald Roderick, carpenter
McDonald & Urquhart, carriage makers
McKay, A. A., councillor
McKay, Daniel, painter
McKay, John, grocer
McKay, Robert, farmer
McKenzie, Rev. Donald, (Free Presbyterian)
McPherson, D. R., insurance agent
Mann, James, general merchant
MATHESON, D., Postmaster, estate agent
Middleton, Donald, farmer
Midgly, William, stock dealer
Midgly, William, saddler
Mitchell, Peter, hotel keeper
Munro, Donald, butcher
Munro, James S., tailor
Patton & McKenzie, general merchants
Ross, Henry, teacher
Ross, David, carpenter
Ross, John M., proprietor flour mills
Sanders, Mrs. hotel keeper
Shary, William, brick yard
Straubel, Charles, saddler
Sutherland, W. E. & H., cabinet makers
Thorne, John H., carpenter
Welch, William, cooper

Elsinore.—A small Post Village in the Township of Arran, County Bruce, 32 miles from Walkerton, the County Town, and 140 miles from Toronto. It is situated on the Stage route from Owen Sound to Southampton. Population 30.

Beatty, James, hotel proprietor
Forsyth, Robert, carpenter
Hamilton, Alexander, carpenter
Luxon, John, general merchant
McLeod, Donald, farmer
MONTGOMERY, ROBERT, Postmaster
Nelson, William, farmer
Pallister, Matthew, carpenter

Embrun.—A Post office in the Township of Russell, County Russell.

LALONDE, JOSEPH, Postmaster.

Emerald.—A Post office in the Township of Amherst Island, County Lenox, 18 miles from Napanee, the County Town.

HITCHEN, JOHN, Postmaster.

Enfield.—A Post Village in the Township of Darlington, County Durham, 12 miles from Port Hope, the County Town, and 40 miles from Toronto. Stage to Oshawa tri-weekly. Population, 80.

Arnott, John, farmer
Bray, John, farmer
Bray, Jonathan, carpenter
Curtiss, Rev. J., (Bible Christian)
Dyer, Daniel, butcher
Dyer, James D., farmer
Hull, Rev. J., (Bible Christian)
HYMERS, JONATHAN, Postmaster and general merchant
Jessup, Elisha, teacher
James, John, farmer
McCullough, George, farmer
McDonald, Mary milliner
Neddery, Robert, J.P., farmer
Ormiston, Robert, farmer
Powell, Benjamin, farmer
Storkes, Charles, farmer
Tapp, William, bootmaker
Thompson, John, shingle maker
Thorne, Thomas, carpenter

Enniskillen.—A Post Village in the Township of Darlington, and West Riding of the County Durham. The surrounding country is extremely fertile. Distant from Cobourg, the County Town 36 miles, and from Toronto, 52 miles. Daily stages to Bowmanville and Cartwright. Mails daily. Population, 300.

Bigham, William, cooper
Burton, William, auctioneer
Couch, J., boot and shoemaker
Flintoff, William, carriage maker
Hannah, Robert, farmer
Hiller, William, M.D
Hugo, Richard, tailor
Hull, Robert, farmer
Hutchinson & Brisbane, general merchants
Kenedy, Robert, boot and shoemaker
McLaughlin, James, M.D
McLaughlin, Robert, carriage maker
McLEOD, D. W., Postmaster, foundry and machine shop, and general merchant
Mallory, Charles, carpenter and builder
Martin, John, flouring miller
Mills, Samuel, harness maker
Morley, Mrs. Ann, hotel proprietor
Osborne, Alexander, teacher
Potter, Philip, farmer
Preston, John, carpenter
Salter, David, farmer
Sandycock, Alexander, butcher
Sharp, James, cabinet maker
Trewin, Samuel, general merchant
Virtue, Archibald, farmer
Virtue, William, hotel proprietor

Ennotville.—(Barnett Post Office.) A Village in the Township of Nichol, County Wellington; distant from Guelph the County Town, 8½ miles, from Toronto 58½ miles. Stages to Fergus and Guelph. Average price of land $40 to $80. Population 50.

Beattie, John, J. P., insurance agent, &c
Beattie, William
Broadfoot, Samuel, J. P.
Campbell, Samuel
Cook, John
Cunningham, John
Cunningham, Robert
Cunningham, William
Davie, John, innkeeper
Davidson, Alexander, grocer
Dow, James
Dow, William, J. P
ELMSLIE, JAMES, Postmaster
Gunn, John
Loghrin, Thomas
McNee, Archibald, carpenter
Scanlon, Eugene, J. P
Scott, James
Sherrat, Archibald, blacksmith
Talbot, Richard, teacher

Ennismore.—A Village in the Township of Ennismore, County Peterborough; 10 miles from Peterborough the County Town, and 80 from Toronto. Average price of land in the vicinity $20 per acre. Mechanics of all kinds are needed. Stages to Peterborough and Bobcaygeon. Population 50

Clarke, Alexander, farmer
Coley, David, farmer
Coyle, Rev. B., (Roman Catholic)
Corkery, Martin, J. P., farmer
Crough, Michael, frrmer
Donoghue, John, hotel keeper
Dow, Humphry, hotel keeper
Lawson, Henry, saw mill
LEHANE, THOMAS, SARSFIELD, Postmaster, general agent
O'Reilly, Michael, farmer
Rivington, George, farmer
Reynolds, William, carpenter
Waters, George, brickmaker

Enterprise.—A Village in the Township of Camden, County Addington, situated on Jackson's Creek, 20 miles from Napanee the County Town. Average value of improved land in the vicinity $30 per acre. Stages to Newburgh and Napanee. Population 150.

Ash, J. R., M. D.
Card, Joseph, carpenter
Clancey, C., farmer
Clark, Mercus, teacher
Cousins, James, farmer
Cox, Eugene, cabinet maker
Dopking, Nateaniel, farmer
Dunn, Michael, farmer
Evans, James, stock dealer
GRAHAM, ROBERT, Postmaster
Graham & Woolfe, general merchants
Grass, Christopher, hotel keeper
Hawley, E. P., general merchant
Hulin, Rev. James, (Episcopal Methodist)
Lockwood, J., wagon maker
O'Dea, P., lumber dealer
Odekirk, Isaac, shingle maker
Parks, Henry, farmer
Pike, James, shoemaker
Reid, Robert, lumber dealer
Retan, John, shingle maker
Rupert, Rev. Mr., (Wesleyan)
Shannon, James, farmer
Snider, Thomas, shingle maker
Switzer, W. J., M. D.
Vannest, John, farmer
Vanolstine, James, wagon maker
Wager, George
Wager, M. O. B., farmer
Wager, Peter, carpenter
Wager, Sanford, carpenter
Wager, William N., carpenter
Walker & Co., wood and willow ware
Wisnom, Samuel, tailor
Wolfe, E. P., farmer

Epping.—A Village in the Township of Euphrasia, County Grey. Distant from Owen Sound the County Town 30 miles, from Toronto 90 miles. Average price of land $20 to $30. Population 50

Ball, Richard
Boyd, James
Brownell, Rev. D., (Wesleyan)
Gilray, Robert, J. P.
Loughead, John
McKnight, James
McKnight, Samuel
McSorley, John
MARSHALL, J. W., Postmaster & general merchant
Masoles, George W., teacher
Neil, John
Neil, Joseph
Piper, S., shoemaker
Robinson, T.
Smith, George

Epsom.—A Village in the Township of Reach, County Ontario, distant from Whitby, the County Town, 15 miles, from Toronto 35 miles. Stages to Whitby and Uxbridge. Daily mail. Population 120.

Bolton, William, hotel keeper
Costello, William, carriage maker
Earchman, Adam, farmer
English, John, farmer
Huckins, J. C., Postmaster and general merchant
McDowall, T. H., shoemaker
Mortson, John, blacksmith
Munro, Timothy, J. P.
Reid, Rev. H. (Wesleyan)
Walker, Archibald, blacksmith
Williams, Rev. — (Wesleyan)
Wilson, T. N., teacher

Erbsville.—A Post Village in the Township of Waterloo, County Waterloo, 8 miles from Berlin, the County Town. Population 110.

Browman, Joseph, tailor
Dipp, Valentine, wood and willow ware
ERB, JOHN L., Postmaster and lumber merchant
Hett, Henry, farmer
Knechtel, Miss V.
Mitchell, William, hotel proprietor
Nixdorf, Ernst, tailor
Sands, Henry, shingle maker
Schnarr, Baltzer, brick maker
Schnarr, Demetrius, cabinet maker
Schnarr, G., farmer

Eramosa.—A small Village in the Township of Eramosa, County Wellington, 5 miles from Guelph, the County Town. Average price of improved land $40 per acre. Stages to Guelph and Erin.

ANDERSON, JOHN, Postmaster
Armstrong, James, hotel keeper
Benn, John, hotel keeper
Bolton, James, farmer
Carter, Henry, farmer
Coghlin, George, carriage maker
Cockburn, James, tailor
Day, David, farmer
Dryden, Robert, hotel keeper
Duffield, John, farmer
Forsyth, William, blacksmith
Johnson, John, farmer
Parkinson, Joseph, farmer
Parkinson, Lazarus, farmer
Scott, George, farmer
Scott, Henry, farmer
Smith, Archibald, J. P.
Thompson, Adam, shoemaker
Tolton, Henry, farmer
Tolton, William, farmer

Erie—A Post Office in the Township of Walpole, County Haldimand, 9 miles from Cayuga, the County Town, and 70 miles from Toronto.

Aikins, William, farmer
Biggar, James, farmer
Caldwell, David, farmer
Caldwell, John, farmer
Finch, Andrew, farmer
Fleming, Henry, farmer
Hastie, John, farmer
McBURNEY, R., Postmaster
McRubie, Rev. John (Presbyterian)
Stuart, George, farmer
Weir, Archibald, farmer

Erin.—A Village situated in the Township of Erin, County Wellington, 20 miles from Guelph, the County Town, 35 miles from Toronto, and 12 miles from Georgetown, the nearest station on the Grand Trunk Railway. Stage to Guelph 20 miles. Fare 75c. Daily mail. Money order office and Savings' Bank. Population 600

Alton, S., hotel proprietor
Ames, Mrs., milliner, &c,
Blashill, William, watches and jewelry
Broddy, James, auctioneer
Campbell, A. & D., clothiers
Campbell, A., farmer
Carbery & Crozier, groceries and crockery
Clark, J., hotel proprietor
Cooper, A., painter
CORNOCK, WILLIAM, Postmaster, J. P., steam flour mill prop.
Crozier, H., hotel keeper
Davis, James, farmer
Ferguson, C., general merchant
Gibbs, George, auctioneer
Harvard & Walker, hardware merchants
Holden, J., druggist
Hood & McKinnon, general merchants
How, William, general store
Hurd, G., farmer
Irwin, Thomas and Samuel, coopers
Kennedy, William, tinsmith
Lennon, J., attorney-at-law
McArthur, A., tailor
McKinnon, Miss, milliner, &c
McLean, Miss, milliner, &c
McLean, John, carpenter and builder
McMillan, A., farmer
McMillan, Charles, farmer
McMillan, D,, carriage maker
McMillan, D. & J., lumber dealers
McMillan, Hugh, farmer
McNaughton, H., M.D
Mann, John, teacher
Matthews, William, harness
Medley, R., boots and shoes
Meloy, Hugh, carriage and wagon maker
Overland, Charles, carpenter and builder
Shingler, J., farmer
Shingler, William, lime manufacturer
Smith, James, harness maker
Thomas, D., dentist
Thompson, A., boot and shoe maker
Thompson, J., farmer
Tyler, William, J.P
Vanderlip, J. H., grocer and provision dealer
Walker, John S., foundry and machine shop
White, E., farmer
Willis, John, butcher
Wood, R., druggist

Escott.—A Post Village in the Township of Escott, County Leeds. Distant from Brockville, the County Town, 30 miles. Population 40.

Abrahams, Thomas, proprietor Escott Hotel
Graham, Daniel, carpenter
McMickle, John, farmer
Mallory, James, saddler
Mallory, Norton, farmer
Nickleson, David, farmer
Oliver, William, shoemaker
Parr, William, farmer
Storey, Thomas, farmer
Sumerby, William, teacher
Todd, Andrew, general merchant

Esquesing.—(See Stewarttown.)—A Post office in the Township of Esquesing, County Halton. Distant from Milton, the County Town, 12 miles, from Toronto 30 miles.

MURRAY, JOHN, Postmaster.

Erinsville.—A Village in the Township of Sheffield, County Addington, on the Salmon River, 18 miles from Napanee, the County Town. The river affords good power, and manufacturers and mechanics are required in the vicinity. Average price of land $20 per acre. Population 150.

Berry, John, cooper
Clark, Andrew, tailor
Cumming, Alexander, farmer
Donovan, Alexander, hotel keeper
Gaffney, Mrs. P., grocer
Hooley, Michael, farmer
Hughes, Lawrence, shoemaker
Killoran, James, farmer
Knight, Cornelius, M.D.
Lockridge, Robert, carpenter
McGarvey, James, shingle maker
McKewan, Michael, storekeeper
McKewan, William, farmer
McMullen, Patrick, J.P., farmer
Milling, S., farmer
Murphy, John, J.P., farmer
Murphy, Michael, shoemaker
Palmatier, John, farmer
Paul, Robert, painter
Phelan, Nicholas, storekeeper
Russel, George, architect
Stanton, Rev. M., (Roman Catholic)
Stewart, Archibald, farmer
WALSH, PATRICK, Postmaster and gen. merchant
York, David, carpenter

Errol—A Post Village in the Township of Plympton, County Lambton, 12 miles from Sarnia, the County Town. Population 50.

Cameron, John, farmer
Campbell, James, teacher
Cronkhite, Wellington, farmer
Emsley, Mrs, grocer
Richardson, John, farmer
WHITING, GEORGE, Posmaster

Etobicoke.—(See Lambton Village.)—A Post office in the Township of York, County York. Money Order office.

HOWLAND, F. A., Postmaster.

Eugenia.—A Village on the Beaver River, in the Township of Artemisia, County Grey, 40 miles from Owen Sound, the County Town. The village site is a lot of 800 acres, belonging to Government, a large portion of which is still unsold, and offered to actual settlers at nominal prices. The facilities for manufacturing are first class, there being 334 feet fall in the distance of one mile of the village plot, one being a beautiful cataract of 70 feet perpendicular height. Manufacturers, mechanics and laborers wanted. Stages to Collingwood Station, Northern Railway. Population 70.

Akitt, Michael, general merchant
Fulford, Rev. E. J., (Methodist Episcopal)
Green, Rev. M., (Wesleyan)
Hambley, W. S., carpenter
Henderson, James, teacher
Knowles, Rev. Mr. (Presbyterian)
Purdy, Alexander, M.D.
PURDY, R. McLEAN, J. P., Postmaster, miller, real estate agent, etc.
Sanders, John, carpenter
Sanders, William, carpenter
Sloan, Jacob, carpenter

Evelyn.—A Post Office in the Township of Nissouri West, County Middlesex, 10 miles from London, the County Town. Improved land in vicinity $36 ; wild $25 per acre.

Belcher, Rev. S. (Church of England)
Carlin, Edward, J. P.
Clipperton, William, farmer
Douglas, James, farmer
Evans, James, M.P.P.
HENSHAW, GEORGE, Postmaster
Henshaw, Samuel, farmer
James, Hugh, farmer
McMaster, Alexander, farmer
Purdy, S., farmer
Scott, Henry, farmer
Seymour, Rev. John (N. C. Methodist)
Taylor, Thomas, farmer
Webster, James, farmer

Eversley.—A Post Village in the Township of King, County York, 24 miles from Toronto, the County Town. Population 26.

Bales, John, shingle maker
Ferguson, John, farmer
Leigh, John, carriage maker
Riddett, Robert, carriage maker
Rogers, Timothy, farmer
Scott, Thomas, farmer
Shanless, Thomas, blacksmith
Tawse, Rev. John, M.A. (Presbyterian)
TINLINE, JAMES, Postmaster and gen. merchant
Trowbridge, Henry, butcher
Wells, James, farmer
Wells, James P., M.D.
Wells, Joseph, farmer
Yule, Andrew, blacksmith

Ethel.—A Post office in the Township of Grey, County Huron, 45 miles from Goderich, the County Town, and 70 from Toronto. The Wroxeter and Seaforth stage passes by the office.

SPENCE, JAMES, Postmaster.

Everton.—A Village in the Township of Eramosa, County Wellington, S. R., distant 11 miles from Guelph, and 40 by rail from Toronto. Land averages in the vicinity $20 per acre. Stage to Guelph. Population 150.

Gibson, —, proprietor Everton Hotel
Gokey, A. H., cooper
McCulloch, Dr.
McKay, —, general merchant
Nairn, A., miller
Richardson, —, carpenter
STEWART, D. F., Postmaster
Stewart, Miss, dressmaker
Warden, —, carpenter
Wheeler, Miss, dressmaker
Wheeler, Miss M., teacher

Exeter.—A flourishing Village in the Township of Stephen, County Huron, on the river Aux Sable. The location of the Village is healthy, and the surrounding country productive. Distant from Goderich, the County Town, 30 miles, and from Toronto 120. Daily stage to London, fare $1, and to Clinton, 19 miles, 75c. Daily mail. Money order office and Savings' Bank. Population 120.

Balkwill, Richard, farmer
Balkwill, William, hotel keeper
Bawden, Joseph, butcher
Bissett, Robert, brick maker
Bissett, W. R., tinsmith
Boulton, H. C., druggist
Brown, John, tailor
Brown, Mrs., milliner
Browning, J. W., M.D.
Brownlee, James, auctioneer
Bryant, Richard, flouring mill prop.
Carling, Isaac, general merchant
Clarke, C. F., barrister and land agent
Clark, Mark, boot and shoe maker
Collins, Rev. James (Bible Christian)
Cowan, Y., M.D.
Crocker, James V., carpenter
Crocker, John V., carpenter
Davis, Richard, carriage maker
Down, James, carriage maker
Drew, Edred, planing mill
Drew, William, hotel proprietor
Dyer, A. G., carpenter
Eacrett, Charles, harness maker
Eacrett, George, harness maker
Eacrett, M., painter
Edwards, Rev. Andrew (Wesleyan)
Elliott, B. V., barrister and insurance agent
Elston, Mr., teacher
Elston, Robert, baker
Fanson, William, harness maker
Floyd, George, farmer
Freeman, A. D., general merchant
Gidley & Bro., planing mill and cabinet makers
Gidley, Thomas, farmer
Gorden, James, hotel keeper
Gould, John, manuf. soap and candles
Green, C., painter
Greenway, Miss Jane, teacher
Greenway, John, butcher
Grigg, William, fancy goods, clothing, &c
Hamilton, C., druggist
Harris, John, carriage maker
Harwood, George, cabinet maker
Harwood, Mrs., milliner
Hooper, Rev. William, (Bible Christian)
Hopkins, Mrs., milliner
Hutton & Hilder, props. flouring mills
Hyndman, John, M.D
Johns, David, tinsmith
Kelly, W., farmer
Keys, Rev. George, (Church of England)
Kilpatrick, George, woolen mills prop
Kingdom, George, farmer
Lewis, A., painter
Logie, James, general merchant
Logie, Rev. John (Presbyterian)
McBride, J., hotel keeper
McDonald, A. D., M.D.
McDonald, Peter, teacher
McDonnell, Miss Susan, teacher
McDonald, William, carpenter
McLeod, Miss, milliner
McNabb, James, cabinet maker
Martern, C. G., general merchant
Milne, James, general merchant
Mitchell, William, brickyard
Osborne, T., teacher
Pickard, James, general merchant and lumber dealer
Pickard, James, farmer
Ramsay, James, carpenter
Rowe, C., tailor
Rumley, Miss, milliner
Sanders, A., grocer
SANDERS, WILLIAM, Postmaster
Sharp, George, boot and shoe maker
Sharp, Miss, milliner
Shoobrook, James, carpenter
Simpson, William, farmer
Smallcombe, W. G., tailor
Snow, John, boot and shoe maker
Southcott, C., grocer
Spackman, John, auctioneer
Switzer, Henry, brickyard
Tait, S., fancy goods
Tait, Sinclair, cooper
Taylor, William, tailor
Towers, James, hotel keeper
Treble, John, boot and shoe maker
Trick, John, carriage maker
Trevitt, Thomas, barrister
Verity, W. H., founder and machinist
Vine, B. D., wines and spirits
Vosper, George, carpenter
Walrond, George, boot and shoe maker
Wannacott, John, dentist
Ward, Thomas, carriage maker
Welsh, William, carpenter and builder
Willis, George, farmer
Winans, H. B., druggist and insurance agent

Fairfield.—(See Troy.)—A post village in the Township of Harwich, County Kent, 18 miles from Chatham the County Town.

Burt, R. P., commission merchant
BURT, S. M., Postmaster
Lambert, S., cooper
Swartout, J., lumber merchant

Fairfield Plain.—A post Village in the Township of Burford, County Brant, South Riding.
HOWELL, ALEXANDER, Postmaster

Fairview.—A post office in the Township of Downie, County Perth, 7 miles from Stratford the County Town, and 107 from Toronto.

Bell, William, farmer
Dunsmore, Joseph, hotel keeper
FORREST, RICHARD, Postmaster
Houck, Richard, farmer
Monteith, Samuel, farmer
Nichol, William, teacher
Robb, Samuel, J.P.
Thamer, Henry, farmer
Young, James, farmer

Falkenburg.—A Post Office in the Township of Monck, County Victoria, N.R.
GEORGE, ROBERT, Postmaster.

Falkirk.—A Village in the Township of East Williams, County Middlesex, 21 miles from London, the County Town. Population, 150.

Baker, Thomas, chandler
Brown, Thomas, shoemaker
Calhoun, G., carpenter
Chatham, Rev. James, (Primitive Methodist)
Davis, Rev. M., (Church of England)
Fletcher, Rev. W., (Presbyterian)
Harket, Joseph, hotel keeper
Hodgson, John, shoemaker
Jones, Thomas, farmer
Kelly, John, saddler
Lambert & Son, woolen mill proprietors
Leach, John, farmer
McCandless, F., M.D
McGuire, E., shoemaker
McFarlane, James, farmer
Merrill, Thomas, shoemaker
O'Leary, R., carpenter
Overholt, Peter, shoemaker
Owens, Rev. Thomas, (Church of England)
Pemperbatton, S., butcher
PRIESTLY, JAMES, Postmaster
Parkes, T., carpenter
Shepley, Lionel, prop. grist mills
Smith, W., M.D.
Stephenson, Thomas, tailor
Stewart, Alexander & Duncan, farmers
Turner, Henry, shoemaker
Westcott, James, flour mill prop.
Wilson, James, carriage maker

Farmersville.—A Village in the Township of Yonge, County Leeds, 15 miles from Brockville, the County Town. Stages to Delta, Philipsville, Forfar and Westport. Money order office. Population, 300.

Addison, R. R., M.D
Alguire, H., farmer
Boddy, Samuel, saddler
Cadwell, N. S., willow ware
Chamberlain, A. A., M.D
Chrysler, F. H., principal grammar school
Cooke, Hiram, dyer
Decker, James, shoemaker
Denovan, John, hotel keeper
Draper, Luke, tailor
Duggan, James, shoemaker
Fisher, Duncan, wagon maker
Gardner, Rev. James, (Methodist Episcopal)
Giles, J. G., M.D
Giles, William, saddler
Gilroy, E., wagon maker
Green, William, farmer
Halladay, S. & E., hotel keeper
Hugill, Rev. Joseph, (Wesleyan)
Jones, John & Son, leather dealers
Judson, Rufus D., grocer
Kincaid, Archibald, tinsmith
Lamb, James P., dentist
Landers, John, cooper
Logan, James, builder
Mansell, David, general merchant and clerk Division Court
Nash, George, farmer
PARISH, ARZA, J.P., Postmaster, general merchant
Parish, William, carpenter
Plumasteel, Henry, druggist
Plumasteel, William, shoemaker
Pronson, Henry, grocer
Redmond, James, teacher
Saunders, William, grist mill prop.
Stafford, George, painter
Stevens, H. J., cabinet maker
Strong, P. W., general merchant
Taplin, Sidney A., general merchant
Wilter, A. D., J.P
Wilter, Edward, butcher
Yates, Stephen, general merchant

Farquhar.—A small Village in the Township of Usborne, County Huron, 35 miles from Goderich, the County Town. Population 30.

EDMOND, WILLIAM, Postmaster, gen. mercht
Davis, James, hotel keeper
Gullett, James, shoemaker

Falkland.—A Post office in the Township of Brantford, County Brant, S. R.
STALLY, M., Postmaster.

Farmington.—A Post-office in the Township of Amaranth, County Wellington, N.R.
MAY, JAMES, Postmaster.

Fenelon Falls.—*(See Villages too late for regular insertion at the end of this Work.)*

Fergus.—An incorporated Village on both banks of the Grand River, in the Township of Nichol, County Wellington. The river affords unlimited water power, and the Village possesses a large number of manufacturing establishments. Distant from Guelph, the County Town, 13 miles, and from Elora 2 miles. Money order office and Savings' Bank. Population 1,500.

Adams, John, shoemaker
ANDERSON, ALEXANDER, distiller
Anderson, Francis, miller
ANDERSON, GEORGE (Dobbin & Anderson)
Anderson, Matthew, blacksmith
Angel, Hercules, tailor
Angel, Samuel, carpenter
ARGO, JAMES, merchant (see adv.)
Armstrong, George, nurseryman
Ashbury, John, mason
Bank of Montreal, George D. Ferguson, agent
Beames, Henry, plasterer
Beames, Elisha, plasterer
Beattie, John, insurance agent
Beattie, William, carpenter
Berry, John, carpenter
Black, Hugh, mason
BLACK, JOSEPH, proprietor Fergus Arms hotel
Black, William, farmer
Boland, James, cooper
CADENHEAD, ALEXANDER, Clerk Division Court and insurance agent
Calder, John, carpenter
Campbell, D. S.
Campbell, Neil, tanner
Cardy, William, tanner
Cattenach, James
Cooper, Rev. H. D., (Episcopal)
CRAIG, JOHN (Craig Bros.)
CRAIG, ROBERT (Craig Bros).
CRAIG, BROS., (John and Robert) editors and proprietors *Fergus News Record.*
CREIGHTON, JOHN A., general merchant
Cross, James F., barrister
Camming, Alexander, millright
Dalziel, Robert, teamster
Dass, James, merchant tailor
Dass, William, tailor
Davie, Andrew, carpenter
Davie, John, prop. boarding house
DOBBIN S. LEONARD (Dobbin & Anderson)
DOBBIN & ANDERSON (S. L. & George), general merchants (see adv).
Dryden, Andrew, teamster
Edwards, William, shoemaker
FERGUS ARMS HOTEL, Joseph Black, proprietor
Fergus Mills, William Robertson, proprietor
FERGUS NEWS RECORD, Craig Bros. editors and proprietors
Ferguson, G. D., agent Bank of Montreal
Fergusson & Watt
FERRIER, A. D., County Clerk
Fleming, Henry, butcher
Forbes, Alexander, boots and shoes
Fordyce, A. D., school superintendent
Forrester, Andrew, mason
Forrester, Charles, watchmaker
Fredrum & Huffman, chemists, &c.
Garvin & Boomer, general merchants
GERRIE, ALEXANDER, saddle and harness maker
GERRIE, JOHN, prop. St. Andrew's Hotel
Gilmour, John, cabinet maker
Gordon, James F., D. D. S.
Gordon, Thomas, A. W., barrister
Gordon, Thomas H., D.D.S.
Gow, Robert, currier
Graham, James, cooper
Grain, William, proprietor saw mills
Grant, J., flour, &c.
GRIEVE, PETER, prop. Ontario House
Grindley, James & Co., iron founders
Grose, John, miller
Hamilton, William, jun., carpenter
Harrison, Benjamin, brickmaker
Hay, William, carpenter
HEFFERNAN, P , prop. Wellington Hotel (see adv
Hoehn, Marcel, barber
Hunt, John, blacksmith
Ironside, John, general merchant
Jamieson, John, bricklayer
Johnston, James, blacksmith
JOHNSTON, J. T. (McKay & Johnston)
JOHNSTON, THOMAS W., tanner
Kay, Charles, prop. saw mills
Kidd, William, teacher
Lingwood, Robert
Lingwood, William H., tanner
Little & Wilson, wagon makers
Logan, William, mason
McCrory, Henry, saddler
McCutcheon, J. K. A., general agent
McDonnell, Rev. George (Presbyterian)
McInnes, George, wagon maker
McInnes, Malcolm, blacksmith
McIntosh, Donald, carpenter
McIntosh, James, carpenter
McIntyre, Archibald, miller
McKAY, THOMAS (McKay & Johnston)

McKAY & JOHNSTON (Thomas and J. T.), merchants
McMillan, James, tailor
McMillan, John A., boots and shoes
McQUEEN, JAMES, Postmaster
McTaggart, D., bailiff
McWilliam, Alexander, baker
McWilliam, John, baker
Mack, Charles, cooper
Marshall, John, general merchant
Mennie, Alexander, currier
Mennie, John, shoemaker
Michie, Henry, merchant
Miller, Moses, baker and grocer
Mills, Matthew, butcher
Milne, James G., attorney
Milne, Thomas, tailor
Minor, Silas, B.A., principal of Grammar School
Moffatt, A., carpenter
Moffatt, J. & A., cabinet makers
MONTREAL TELEGRAPH CO., Watt & Sons, operators
Moore, Garrett, prop. Elgin Hotel
Moore, Richard, shoemaker
Morris, James, mason
Munro, James, saddler
Munro, John, M.D.
Munro, L. C., chemist and druggist
Murdoch, Robert, saddler
Murray, Robert, wagon maker
Murray, William, shoemaker
Noble, Peter, shoemaker
Noble, P. C., photographer
NORTH AMERICAN HOTEL, James Whyte, prop.
ONTARIO HOUSE, Peter Grieve, prop.
Orton, George T., M.D.
Patterson, Archibald, carpenter
PATTISON, WILLIAM, prop. Glenlivat distillery, and dealer in dry goods, groceries, &c.
Phelan, Edmund, painter
Phelan, James, fanning mill manufacturer
Philip, James, conveyancer, commissioner in B. R.
Philip, Robert, druggist
Porter, John, bricklayer
POWNEY, CHARLES, general hardware, oils, &c. (see card)
RAMORE, DOMINICK, merchant
Reid, Robert, miller
Rennie, William, carpenter
Renton, James, blacksmith
Richardson, Alexander, general merchant
Richardson, Thomas, wagon maker
Robertson, Alexander, tailor
Robertson, William, miller
Ross, James, carpenter
Ross, John, weaver
Ross, Thomas, carpenter
ROSS, WILLIAM, village clerk
ST. ANDREW'S HOTEL, John Gerrie, prop.
Sampson, T. J., shoemaker
Scott, Gideon, butcher adv.)
Sherwood, T., merchant
Shields, George, cooper
Shortreed, Robert, farmer
Slater, John, carpenter
Smellie, Rev. George (Presbyterian)
Snaden, James, teamster
Somerville, Samuel, shoemaker
Steel, Robert, flax miller
STEWART, ALEXANDER, boots & shoes (see adv)
Sweeney, William, shoemaker
TAYLOR, ALEXANDER, tailor and clothier
Temple, John, prop. Queen's Arms Hotel
Templeton, John, blacksmith
Thompson, John, carpenter
Thorp, George W., horse dealer
Todd, Arthur, shoemaker
Todd, David, moulder
Todd, Matthew, farrier
Vickers, George, watchmaker
WATSON, THOMAS, steam tannery (see adv)
Watt, James, merchant
Watt, John, merchant
Webster, Henry, sen., tinsmith
Webster, Henry, jun., stoves, tinware, &c.
WELLINGTON HOTEL, P. Heffernan, prop. (See adv.)
WHYTE, JAMES, prop. North American Hotel
Wilkie, Alexander, blacksmith
Wilkie, George, carpenter
Wilson, Hugh, wagon maker
Wilson, James, miller and woolen factor
Wilson, John, blacksmith
WYLLIE, GEORGE G., distiller and rectifier (see adv)
Young, Charles, mason
Young, Thomas A., book-keeper

Ferguson's Falls.—A Post office in the Township of Drummond, County Lanark, 12 miles from Perth, the County Town. Average value of land in the vicinity $24 per acre.

Chisholm, Rev. Dr., (Roman Catholic)
Craig, Robert, leather dealer
HICKS, ROBERT, Postmaster, general merchant
Hollinger, Charles, hotel keeper
O'Connor, Edward, hotel keeper

Fernhill.—A Village in the Township of Lobo; County Middlesex, 20 miles from London, the Count Town. Average value of land in the vicinity $30 per acre.

Armstrong, Richard, farmer
Campbell, John, farmer
Crawford, James, farmer
Duigman, John, farmer
Fenshaw, Rev. Dr., (Methodist Episcopal)
Gray, Archibald, tailor
Lynch, Walter, farmer
McArthur, A., lime dealer
Moore, Neil, teacher
Neff, Isaac H., farmer
OWEN, JENKIN, Postmaster, general merchant
Owen, Rev. T. R., (Baptist)
Preharme, John, farmer
Ross, D. M., J. P.
Rowland, Rev. D. W., (Baptist)
Woodward, Henry, farmer
Woodward, Thomas, sen., J. P
Woodward, Thomas, stone and lime dealer

Feversham.—A Village on the Beaver River, in the Township of Osprey, County Grey, 40 miles from Owen Sound, the County Town, 22 from Collingwood and 120 from Toronto. Average value of improved land in vicinity $20, wild $10 per acre. Stage to Collingwood. Population 80.

Alister, George, farmer
Brown, Robert, farmer
Clark, William, teacher
Colgate, Daniel, farmer
Davidson, George, farmer
Davidson, William, farmer
Edwards, George, cooper
Fisher, A., hotel keeper
Fulford, Rev. E. J., (Church of England)
Hudson, Henry, farmer
Hudson, Joseph, farmer
Knowles, Rev, Robert, (Canada Presbyterian)
LOGIE, JAMES, Postmaster, general merchant
McRobert, Donald, carpenter
Ross, John, carpenter
Speer, John, auctioneer
Thompson, David, farmer
Thompson, George, farmer

Fermoy.—A small post Village in the Township of Bedford, County Addington, distant 50 miles from Kingston.

BOTTING, EDWARD, Postmaster.

Fingall.—*(See Villages too late for regular insertion at the end of this Work.)*

Fish Creek.—(Village Prospect Hill.) A Post Office in the Township of Blanshard, County Perth 18 miles from Stratford, the County Town. Population 150.

Arthur, James, carpenter
Bell, John, farmer
Bell, Thomas W., general merchant
Bisbee, R., brickmaker
Bugg, T., farmer
Byfield, E., blacksmith
Cowper, Rev., — (Church of England)
Crandon, John, butcher
Dennison, James, auctioneer
Draper, John, farmer
Findley, Rev. A., (Canada Presbyterian)
Gilmour, John, carriagemaker
Hagerty, Dennis, hotel keeper
Harding, William H., gunsmith
Hardy, Henry, butcher
Hartshorn, D., blacksmith
Hayes, George, farmer
Hayes, John, farmer
Hollingshead, D., farmer
Hughes, T., farmer
Johnston, P., farmer
Langford, Elijah, dentist
Little, John, J. P.
McCallum, Rev. — (Wesleyan)
McConnell, A., farmer
McDonald, Dr.
McLaughlin, John, J. P
Mossey, Joseph, farmer
Padfield. Alfred, carriage maker
Peacock, W., farmer
Robinson, Andrew, shoemaker
Smith, Rev. — (New Connexion)
Somerville, R., J. P
Stanley, Samuel, carriage maker
Warren, A., carpenter
Willis, Joseph, farmer

Fitzroy Harbour.—A Village beautifully situated between the Ottawa and Carp Rivers, in the Township of Fitzroy, County Carleton; 33 miles from Ottawa the County Town, 10 from Pakenham and 10 from Arnprior Railroad Station. Average price of improved land in the vicinity $25 per acre. Population 200.

Atkinson, Henry, prop. flour mill
Aylwin, D., M. D
Baird, Daniel, general merchant
Barnes, John, shingle maker
Campbell, William, hotel keeper
Cockburn, William, carpenter
Copps, John, farmer
Curry, Rev. Erastus, (Wesleyan)
Daly, James, tailor
Drummond, James, carpenter
Dubord, D., M. D
Emery, Rev. Charles P., (Church of England)
Flint, Robert, carding mill
Hawley, Andrew, hotel keeper
Henderson, Andrew, farmer
Hines, James, farmer
Hyland, Henry, lime and stone dealer
Kirby, John, blacksmith
Learmouth, George, merchant, saw and grist mills
McDonald, John, saw mill proprietor
McFarlane, David, dentist
McFarlane, David, farmer
McLaren, David, general merchant
Nicholson, John, cabinet maker
Robertson, John, general merchant
Sheriff, Allen, farmer
Sheriff, Alexander, general agent
SHERIFF, ROBERT, Postmaster
Smith, James, shoemaker
Somerville, William, general merchant
Tait, Rev. James, (Presbyterian)
Tait, Ralph, teacher
Teevens, John, hotel keeper
Tripp, Henry, farmer
Wark, James, shoemaker
Weir, Thomas, blacksmith

[F]isherville.—A Village in the Township of Rainham, County Haldimand, 7 miles from Cayuga, the County Town. Average value of improved lands in vicinity $35 per acre. Population 60.

[...]ndt, Rev. W., (Lutheran)
[...]LSWORTH, JAMES, Postmaster
[...]st, George, farmer
[...]ble, Henry, farmer
[...]llenbacker, Jacob, farmer
[...]ller, A. B., teacher
Phillips, Peter, famer
Rath, Andrew, farmer
Shurr, Samuel, farmer
Sitter, Peter, farmer
Winger, Jacob, farmer

[F]lesherton.—A Village in the Township of Artemisia, County Grey, at the head waters of Beaver River, 31 miles from Owen Sound, the County Town, 29 from Stayner, and 30 from Collingwood. Stages daily to Collingwood and Deerham and bi-weekly to Orangeville and Chatsworth. Money Order office. Population 160.

[...]sley, Julian, farmer
[Ar]mstrong, J. W., J.P., Clerk Division Court
[...]rtham, Richard, farmer
[Ca]mpbell, Peter, carding mills
[Ch]ristie, W. S., M.D.
[...]rk, William, carpenter
[...]rton, William, shoemaker
[...]awoody, John, farmer
[...]s, Samuel, farmer
[...]ds, John, cooper
[FL]ESHER, W. K., Postmaster, notary public, grist and saw mills
[...]en, Rev. J., (Wesleyan)
[...]ard, John H., wagon maker
Jones, John, general merchant and hotel keeper
Keefer, George, carpenter
Larman, A. L., M.D.
Matthew, H. & Son, shingle makers
Munshaw, Aaron, hotel keeper
Pickle, Wilmot, farmer
Redeoff, Rev. Richard, (New Connection)
Richardson, Matthew, general merchant
Richardson, Mrs., milliner
Stewart, George, farmer
Trimble, Robert, general merchant
William, Rev. David, (Wesleyan)
Wright, William, general merchant

[F]lora.—A Post Village in the Township of Woolwich, County Waterloo, on the Kannakajaique River, 16 miles from Berlin

DEVITT, ISAAC, Postmaster.

[F]lorence.—A Village in the Township of Euphemia, County Lambton, on the River Sydenham, 34 miles from Sarnia, the County Town. Average price of improved lands in the vicinity $25 per acre. Money Order Office. Population 350.

[...]sden & Drake, general merchants
[...]e, Frederick, marble dealer
[Ca]mpbell, Peter, carpenter
[...]y, Hosea, farmer
[...]ter, Miss C., milliner, &c
[Da]vidson, M., prop. steam saw mills
[Da]vidson, Myers, M.D.
[...]ckrell, Joseph, wagon maker
[...]w, James, shoemaker
[...]l, Robert, teacher
[...]sworth & Webster, blacksmiths
[...]sher, John, farmer
[...]den & Merrell, props. steam shingle manufactory
[...]nion, Charles, druggist
[...]rdon, William A., general merchant
[...]y, James, prop. steam flouring mill
[...]ne, Rev. John, (Church of England)
[...]ne, Robert, general agent
[...]son, M., prop. Florence Exchange Hotel
[...]lston, Joseph A., wagon maker
[...]by, George P
[...]by, Squire, prop. brick yard
[...]mont, David, teacher
[...]mont, James C. G., saddler
[...]le, William, shoemaker
Livesly, Robert, general merchant
McCrea & Dunbar, blacksmiths
McGuire, Andrew, tailor
McGregor, John, farmer
Mead, James, prop. Farmer's Exchange Hotel
Mead, Robert, butcher
Morrison, Alexander, manufacturer of woolen goods
Morris, William, M.D
Paul, James, farmer
Pinhale, George, butcher
Proctor, John, farmer
Rheintgen, Gerhard, cabinet maker
Shaw, James, fancy goods, toys, &c
Sheply, Joseph, shoemaker
Smith, Rev. Frederick, (Episcopal Methodist)
Smith, Henry, carpenter
Sturgeon, James, farmer
Tennant, Rev. Elisha, (Wesleyan)
Warden, Rev. Robert, (Canada Presbyterian)
Webster, James T., J.P., carpenter
Webster, William, general agent
Whitehouse, George, druggist
Young, Answorth, general merchant
YOUNG, JOHN A., Postmaster

[Fo]ley.—A Post office of the Township of Whitby, County Ontrrio, S. R.

WILLIAMSON, THOMAS, Postmaster.

Flinton.—A Village in the Townships of Kaladar and Anglesea, Counties Lennox and Addington, situated on Scootomotto Creek, 40 miles from Napanee, the County Town. Average value of improved land in the vicinity $12 per acre. Population 150.

Beckwith, James, broom maker
Brushy, Charles, farmer
Bryden, John, dentist
Corbett, Rev. John, (Wesleyan)
CARSCALLEN, JOHN N., J.P., Postmaster and real estate agent
Davidson, Robert, carpenter
Diailetts, Francis, cabinet maker
Dorland, Levi, cooper
Flint, B., dry goods dealer
Fuller, James, gunsmith
Grant, Charles, soap and candle maker
Layop, Moses, clothing dealer
McDonell, George, butcher
McLucky, William, wagon maker
Matthews, E. J., teacher
Miller, P. W., carpenter
Miller, S. H., carpenter
Ruttan, M. S., M.D.
Smith, B. F., shingle maker
Smith, F. H., shingle maker
Wagar, William, carpenter
Watson, James, farmer
Williams, Albert, butcher
York, M. G., druggist and hotel keeper

Fonthill.—A Village in the Townships of Pelham and Thorold, County Welland, situated on Twelve Mile Creek, in the centre of one of the best agricultural districts in the Province, 5 miles from Welland, the County Town, and 4 from Port Robinson Railway Station. Money order office. Population, 500.

Brown, John, farmer
Buckner, S. W., J.P., farmer
Canby, Thomas, accountant
Church, William G., farmer
Cook, William, saddler
Creighton, Rev. John, (Church of England)
Currie, John M., attorney-at-law
De LaMaittie, Henry, teacher
Dentz, Benedict, carpenter
D'Everardo, Dexter, J.P., attorney-at-law
Emmett, James O., M.D
Frazer, John, M.D
Gadsby, E. W., painter
Giles, Harold, cabinet maker
Giles, Henry, farmer
Gore, John, cabinet maker
Habbershaw, David, shoemaker
Hausler, George W., J.P., farmer
Hobson, Robert, Sheriff Co. Welland
Hunt, Henry, saddler
Keefer, Rev. B. B., (Wesleyan)
Kinsman, A. B., carriage maker
KINSMAN, DAWSON, Postmaster and gen. mercht
Killman, Adam, farmer
Lay, James H., tailor
McCombs, John, carpenter
Moisley, William, shoemaker
Muir, Rev. William, (Baptist)
Oxley, Albert, farmer
Oxley, Henry E., farmer
Oxley, John B., farmer
Page, Joseph C., accountant
Page, William, nursery
Parks, C. C., general merchant
Pearson, William, tailor
Potter, Dexter D. E., accountant
Price, James H., J. P.. farmer
Price, Woodruff, J.P
Randall, Nathan, carpenter
Reilly, James, shoemaker
Rice, Samuel, J.P., farmer
Robertshaw, George, carriage maker
Ross, H. T., architect
Schofield, Adam K., J.P., general agent
Smith, James, hotel keeper
Smith, Thomas, hotel keeper
Starr, Rev. J. H., (Wesleyan)
Steele, James, J.P., farmer
Sterling, Arthur, painter
Swayze, Fletcher, insurance agent
Swayze, M., J.P
Watson, David, carpenter
Weidman, Michael, carpenter
Willson, Daniel, J.P., farmer
Willson, John H., farmer

Forester's Falls.—A Village in the Township of Ross, County Renfrew, on McNaughten's Creek, 2 miles from Pembroke, the County Town. Population 100.

Bennett, John, shoemaker
Boyce, Henry, carding mill
Brown, Delorma, shoemaker
Bulmer, Edward, farmer
Cartman, Robert, farmer
Cameron, Rev. H. (Presbyterian)
Devlin, James, carpenter
Elliott, Thomas, farmer
FORESTER, OLIVER, Postmaster
Forester, Oliver, lumber merchant
Grant, James, sen., insurance agent
Howard, Philander, carpenter
Hunter & Co., general merchants
Huntington, E., farmer
Jack, James, farmer
Jameson, Archibald, blacksmith
Kerr, John, farmer
Knight, William, general merchant
McKay, Owen, teacher
McLelland, John, cooper
McMartin, John, shingle manufacturer
Murdock, James, farmer
Olmstead, Myman, hotel keeper
Smith, Thomas, stone and lime dealer
Thomson, Alexander, jun., M.D.
Wark, James, farmer

Fordyce.—A Post Office in the Township of Wawanosh, in the County of Huron, N.R., 12 miles from Goderich, the County Town. Wild land in the neighborhood averages from $10 to $18 per acre, clear from $20 to $30. Farm laborers much needed here.

Anderson, Alexander, farmer
Armstrong, John, general merchant
Baxter, James, farmer
Beecroft, John, farmer
Brophy, William, farmer
Callin, John C., teacher
Chamney, Richard, farmer
FARQUHARSON, WILLIAM, Postmaster & farmer
Jefferson, John, carriage maker
Jamieson, Thomas, farmer
Mason, John, farmer

Forest.—A Village and Station of the Grand Trunk Railway, in the Township of Plympton, County Lambton, 24 miles from Sarnia, the County Town. Money order office. Population 259.

Brush, Thomas, prop. Farmers' Inn
COLCLOUGH, W. H., station and express agent
CONKLIN, JAMES D., general merchant
CROTTY & HOLCROFT, general merchants
Davidson, James, carriage and wagon maker
Dickey, R. R., merchant
DIER, ROBERT, Postmaster and general merchant
EDGAR, MRS. T., British Queen Hotel
Hewer, Henry, carpenter
Hill & Dier, flouring mill
Hodgins, E., commission merchant
Holdworth, Thomas, farmer
HUTTON, JAMES, M.D., druggist and coroner
JENNINGS, T., clerk British Queen hotel
Johnson, Rev. Richard (Church of England)
Livingston, John, farmer
Livingston, Daniel, carpenter and grocer
Lochead, William, tinsmith
McFadden, L., farmer
McPherson, Allen, farmer
McPherson, Allen and Dugal, flouring mills
McPherson, John, farmer
Mallory, S. C., photographer
Messier, Isaac, planing mills
Morrison, Alexander, telegraph operator G. T. R.
NASH, H. J., M.D
Phelan, John, blacksmith
Revington, David J., saddler
Salmon, Rev. Dr. (Congregational)
Say, Edwin, butcher
Shaw, Mrs., groceries
Smith, C. F., shoemaker
Smith, John, cabinet factory
Stephenson, Hugh, auctioneer
Stephenson, T. J., butcher
Stephenson, Thomas, butcher
Stevenson & Brodie, carriage and wagon makers
TRIPP, JESSE, general merchant
Vivian, Thomas L., shoemaker
Walker, William, cooper
West, Mrs. Anna, milliner, &c.
Wichmann, Charles, tailor
Williams, M., potashery
Wilson, John, blacksmith
Woodroofe, J. A., general merchant
Yoder, William, blacksmith

Forfar.—A Village in the Township of Bastard, County Leeds, 33 miles from Brockville, the County Town and 40 from Kingston. Stages to Westport and Brockville. Population 100.

Davidson, H. S., J.P., farmer
Delong, Jesse, J.P
Deusette, W. P., farmer
Gale, John, farmer
HALES, RICHARD, Postmaster, farmer
Mattice, E., farmer
Poole, J. W., farmer
Robbins, R. D., farmer
Singleton, George, general merchant
Young, W. H. farmer

Formosa.—A Village in the Township of Carrick and Culross, County Bruce, 8 miles from Walkerton, the County Town, and 40 from Seaforth station, Grand Trunk Railway. Stages to Wroxeter, Walkerton and Seaforth. Population 200.

Anstell, A., accountant
Anstell, F. A., bookbinder
Anstell, Joseph, farmer
Anstell & Beninger, general merchants
Beninger, L., hotel keeper
Beninger, M., farmer
Brick, N., farmer
Frank, Silvester, cooper
Gibson, Robert, carpenter
Giesler, A. & F. R., books, &c
Giesler, George, carpenter
Gurk, Frank, cooper
Kirch, John, shoemaker
Klein, Joseph, tinsmith
Klein, John M., farmer
Kratzmeir, Joseph, shoemaker
Kroetsch, J. B., prop. flour mill
Marter, Lewis, hotel keeper
Mesner, A., J.P
Mesner, A. & F. X., general merchants
MESNER, F. X., Postmaster
Mesner, Wendel, farmer
Mosack, John, wagon maker
Mosack, Joseph, hotel keeper
Mosack, Michael, farmer
Nicklous, B., cooper
Prainer, J. B., tailor
Rich, Christopher, farmer
Scharbach, Simon, shoemaker
Schierhart, J. F. carpenter
Schich, Martin, cabinet maker
Seeber, G., attorney at-law
Smitz, Rev. J. J., (Roman Catholic)
Urich, Charles, shoemaker
Wells, Joseph, cabinet maker
Zettel, Andrew, J.P

Forestville.—A Village in the Township of Charlottville, County Norfold, 14 miles from Simcoe, the County Town, and 90 from Toronto. Average value of improved land in vicinity, $40 per acre. Stages daily to Brantford and Paris. Population 150.

Beauford, Edward, cooper
Brown, M., hotel keeper
Donelly, William, M.D.
Dunnett, Rev. —, (Close Communion Baptist)
Dunnett, Miss Martha, teacher
Griffin, G. W., J.P.
Heath, James, brick maker
Horton, John, flouring mill
Knapp, Amos, cooper
Lee, John, hotel keeper
Petty, Curtis, shoemaker
Shaw, Rev. E., (N. C. Methodist)
Simmons, Jonathan, carpenter
Taylor, Jasper, wagon maker
WHITE, CALVIN A., Postmaster, carpenter

Fort Erie.—A Village in the Township of Bertie, County Welland, on Lake Erie, at the head of the Niagara River, nearly opposite Black Rock, N.Y. It is a station of the Grand Trunk Railway and the terminus of the Erie and Niagara Railway. Money Order Office. Population 1000.

Barker, William, U.S. Vice-Consul
Blake, F. N. American Consul
Bristow, Henry, boot and shoe maker
Bristow, Henry, prop. Niagara House
Clarke, William, wagon maker
Cullen, J. T., school teacher
Dargavel, Robert, boot and shoe maker
Dessart, Rev. Father, (Roman Catholic)
Dougal, James, agent G.T.R
Douglas, William, M.B.
Douglas, John, barrister and attorney
Eden, William, assessor and Customs officer
Elliott, John, M.B.
Elsessor, John, marble cutter
Ferris, J. P., dandelion coffee manufacturer
Fitch, Henry, proprietor Royal Exchange Hotel
Gallaher, John, telegraph operator T.T.R station
Graham, Richard, J.P., Collector of Customs, and Commissioner in Chancery
Greeman, Rev. M., (Church of England)
Grogan, William, tinsmith
Hanley, Thomas, saloon keeper G.T.R. station
Harris, Henry, butcher
Hemming, Henry, U. S. consular agent
Johnson, S. W. & Co., dandelion coffee manufacturers
Kohl, John C., butcher
LEWIS, GEORGE, Postmaster and general merchant
Lewis, George, clerk of village
McDougall, John C., machinist
McDougall & Russell, Niagara mowing machine wks.
McKinley, John, baker
McLaren, Duncan, grocer, wine and liquor dealer and provision merchant
McNairn, Bernard, prop. saloon and billiard room
Magwood, John, preventive officer
Magwood, Robert, proprietor Frontier House
Mahony, C. G. T., dining saloon
Murray, William, landing waiter
Nelles, George, telegraph operator G.T.R. station
Noble, O., saloon keeper
Ottley, Thomas M., produce merchant
Perkins, Mrs., saloon keeper G.T.R. station.
Radican, Pat, prop. Canada House
RAINSFORD, WILLIAM, dealer in dry goods, groceries, wines and liquors, boots and shoes, and ready-made clothing
Rose, Francis, refreshment rooms
Russell, William, machinest
Russell, William, lumber dealer
Schryer, Joseph, artist
Smith, Henry
Stewart, Robert, painter
Tracy, J. B., freight clerk G.T.R.
TREBLE, CHARLES, J.P., agent for London and Liverpool and Globe, Provincial, and Victoria Mutual Insurance Company.
TREBLE, CHARLES
Treble, Charles, officer of customs
Treble, William, grocer and liquor dealer
Tolmie, C. E., Erie and Niagara Railway agent
Turner, Benjamin, collector
Tutton, Joseph, blacksmith
Vosburgh, Eli, City Hotel
WARD, JOHN D., grocer and liquor dealer (see adv)
Warren, Robert Grant, landing waiter

Fournier.—A Village in the Township of South Plantagenet, County Prescott, on Plaxton's Creek, 20 miles from L'Orignal, the County Town. Population 150.

Fortier, Alfred, hotel
Gemieux, Bernard, flour mills
Gemieux, Joseph, carpenter
Johnstone, Alexander, saddler
Landriault, Fabien, blacksmith
Levi Harris, general merchant
McLENNAN, A. S., general merchant
Philips, Rev. S. (Roman Catholic)
Ryan, John, J.P.
Scott, John, shingle maker

Foxboro'.—A Post Village in the Township of Thurlow, County Hastings, E.R.
DUFFY, WILLIAM, Postmaster.

Fort William.—A Village situated at the mouth of the Kaministoquoi River, in the District of Algoma, access to which is obtained by steamer, distant from Toronto 900 miles. It is noted for its extensive mineral resources. The principal mines are situated at Thunder Bay about 6 miles distant, in which can be found Silver and Copper in good paying quantities, Lead, Iron and Amethysts are also found in the vicinity. Les Pères Jesuites have a very successful mission here. About two miles above the Fort on the opposite side of the river there is a good Church and 60 or 70 houses, chiefly occupied by half-breeds and Indians, also a good school and resident Priest.

The Hudson's Bay Company have a large farm here and grow oats, barley and all kinds of roots, and there is no doubt wheat can also be raised here; fish are abundant both in the Bay and River.

Dawson, S. J., superintendent Government Works
Dixon, E., agent Thomas Marks
Duroquet, Rev. Father, (Roman Catholic)
Flaherty, J., wine and spirit merchant
Hudson's Bay Company's general store
McAllister, William, explorer
McDonald, Capt. D., supt. Thunder Bay mine
McIntyre, J., J. P., agent Hudson Bay Company
McKellar, Dr., explorer
McKellar, J., explorer
McKellar, P., explorer
McKinney, D. Cape and Shunea mine
McLaren, John, general merchant
McVICAR, MISS C., Post mistress
McVicar, George, explorer
Marks, Thomas, general merchant
Neddo, Rev. Father, (Roman Catholic)
Savigney, H. P., P. L. S
Shune, Rev. Father, (Roman Catholic)

Franklin.—A Post Village in the Township of Manvers, County Durham, 30 miles from Cobourg, the County Town, and 90 from Toronto. Stage to Mount Horeb, distant 6 miles. Population 100.

Armstrong, T. L., teacher
Burgin, Rev. George (New Connexion Methodist)
Fallis, James, farmer
Lytle, James, farmer
Maguire, Miss Margaret, milliner
MAGUIRE, WILLIAM, Postmaster, coroner, J.P., and general merchant
Maguire, William, insurance agent
Middleton, George, teacher
Morrow & Graham, shingle makers
Milligan, Mrs. E., hotel keeper
Noble, Archibald, farmer
Russell & Argue, lumber dealers
Russell, Thomas, J.P.
Stewart, James, farmer
Veals, John, farmer
Windrum, Coll., farmer
Woods, Joseph, farmer
Woods, Thomas, farmer

Franktown.—A Village on Goodwood Creek, in the Township of Beckwith, County Lanark, 15 miles from Perth. Lands in the vicinity average $12 per acre. The Brockville and Ottawa Railway have a station near the Village. Population 200.

Allan, William, engraver
Anderson, Matthew, blacksmith
Budd, Joseph, telegraph operater
Burrows, Dominic, stock dealer
Cameron, Allan, farmer
Campbell, A., farmer
Cavanagh, Robert, general merchant
Clarke, B., druggist
Clarke, Thomas, shoemaker
Clark, Thomas, hotel keepor
Edwards, John, cabinet maker
Ferguson, Duncan, auctioneer
Flegg, Thomas & Bros., coopers
Forde, Miss, milliner
Griffith, Thomas, blacksmith
Hawkins, Henry, butcher
Huhchback, Edward, wood and willow ware manuf.
Jackson, James, soap and candle maker
James, Thomas, saddler
Kidd, George, J. P
Lawford, John, sash, door and blind factory
Leaver, Henry, cabinet maker
Lowe, Phineas, farmer
McDonald, John, farmer
McDonnell, R., stock dealer
McEWEN, EWEN, J. P., Postmaster, commissioner and conveyancer
McEwen, F., insurance agent
McEwen, Hugh, telegraph operator
McEwen, John, farmer
McEwen, Neil, farmer
McEwen, Peter, real estate agent
McGregor, D., sash, door and blind factory
McKenna, Hugh, soap and candle maker
McKenzie, D. & Sons, painters
McKercher, J., J. P.
McLaughlan, Robert & Sons, carpenters
McMahon, J., agent B. & O. R. R.
May, William, farmer
Michael, Murray, shoemaker
Moore, W., leather dealer
Moore, William, hotel keeper
Morris, Joseph, blacksmith
Muirhead, William, farmer
Neilson, J. A., M. D.
Neilson, M., dentist
Nesbitt, Rev. A. C., Church of England
Nesbitt, George, M. D.
Nesbitt, Thomas, general merchant
Nowlan, George, broom maker
Pierce, Thomas, & Sons, rope makers
Roach, Thomas; shoemaker
Roe, Thomas, & Sons, shingle makers
Ross, Rev. Walter (Presbyterian)
Saunders, Thomas, wagon maker
Stewart, Duncan, tailor
Stewart, James, farmer
Stewart, John, J.P.

Frankford.—A Village on the river Trent, in the Township of Sidney, County Hastings, 14 miles from Belleville, the County Town. Stage daily to Trenton Station, Grand Trunk Railway. Average price of improved land $30 per acre.

Bryant, Joseph, butcher
Byam, G. F., carriage maker
Campbell, A., teacher
Campbell, Rev. A. (Methodist Episcopal)
Chapman, John, shoemaker
Clark, George, hotel keeper
Consaul, J., carriage maker
Craske, Walter, grist mill
Dorland, C. H., dentist
Farnsworth, Richard, butcher
Foster, Thomas, baker
Fraser, G. E., general merchant
GILBERT, WILLIAM, Postmaster
Golding, Hiram, hotel and livery
Golding, S., hotel
Goldsmith, G., general merchant
Grass, R., general merchant
Grout, Rev. Mr., (Church of England)
Howard, Thomas J., J. P., general merchant
Huffman, James C., manufacturer of woolen goods
Kinney, William, general merchant
Lafa, A., cooper
Near, J., cooper
Oronhyatekha & Co., druggists, booksellers, &c
Oronhyatekha, Dr. M.B
Outwater, A., tinsmith
Pettet, P. P., carpenter
Phillips, Rev. S. C., (Wesleyan)
Roblin, Edward, farmer
Roblin, M. B., insurance agent
Shorey, J., cooper
Sills Brothers, props. paper mills
Stevens & Sons, tailors
Stillwell, J., general merchant
Sweetman, James, carpenter
Turley, P., farmer
Walter, William, general merchant

Frankville.—A Village in the Township of Kitley, County Leeds, 18 miles from Brockville, the County Town, and 240 from Toronto. Improved land in the vicinity average $60 per acre. Population 300.

Baker, John, Robinson House baker
Bain, A., dentist
Brennan, H. H., general merchant
Burges, Rev. T. (Church of England)
Connor, Miss M., millinery, &c.
Connor & Insper, leather dealers
CONNOR, SAMUEL, Postmaster, grocer and dealer in boots and shoes
Carley, Miss K., millinery, &c.
Downsly, David, carpenter
Dowsly, David H., teacher
Dixon, Adolphus, shoemaker
Dixon, G. A., general merchant
Dixon, Isaac, wood and willow ware
Dixon & Stewart, painters
Dowsly, William, brickmaker
Farren, John, butcher
Ferguson, John, J.P., Crown Inn
Hugill, Rev. J. (Wesleyan Methodist)
Humphries, Henry, blacksmith
Hunt, Absalom, wagon maker
Kilborn, H. A., farmer
Kilborn, James, carpenter
Kilborn, Levi S., blacksmith
Kilborn, Truman, brick maker
Kilborn, Vincent H., blacksmith
Kilborn, Virgil, blacksmith
Kilborn, Warren, M.D.
Lauder, N., M.D.
Logan, James, proprietor Globe Inn
McCrea, Hiram, attorney-at-law
Parker, Robert, carpenter
Rathwell, Robert, saddler
Richards, Christopher, teacher
Soper, John, lime and stone dealer
Southworth, S. J., J.P.
Stewart, B. F., wagon maker
Willmott, Rev. William, (Methodist New Con.)

Fredericksburg.—(Post Office Delhi)—A Village in the Township of Middleton, County Norfolk, and on the Rowan River. It manufactures and has a large trade in sawn lumber, the river supplying good water power. Distant from Simcoe, the County Town, 12 miles, Hamilton 50 miles, London 52 miles and from Toronto 100 miles. Daily stages to Straffordsville and Oakland. Mails daily. Money Orde office. Population 300.

Blake, W. H., M.D., coroner
Burkhart, Magdalene, innkeeper
Church, Joseph, cabinet maker
Conlin, Edward, tanner
Cook, Luke, general merchant
Crozier, James, blacksmith
DeWitt, Jonathan, pump maker and butcher
Durkee, Warren, harness maker
Gilbert, Rev. C. W. M., (Wesleyan)
Hayes, James A., collecting agent
Hazelton, Rev. William P., (Baptist)
Hillaker, H. C., wagon maker
Homey, Israel M., blacksmith
Hubbard, John, tailor
Kemp, James A., hotel keeper
Lambert, Jacob, butcher
Long, Alexander, harness maker
Long, David, carpenter
Owen, Egbert, grocer
Power, Robert, innkeeper and bailiff 4th Div. Court
Redman, Lawrence, shoemaker
Sanderson, John B., wagon maker and blacksmith
Sayles Edwin, hotel keeper
Schmidt, Frederick, shoemaker
Shaw, Rev. C., (N. C. Methodist)
Silbert, Rev. C., (Wesleyan)
Smith, Lewis H., baker
Sovereen, Jacob, grist and saw mill and cloth factory
Ward, William founder
WHITSIDE, JAMES, Postmaster (see adv)
Wilkesson, William, cabinet maker and builder
Wilson, Daniel & Edgar, general merchants
Winslow, Clark, carpenter
Wood, George W., M.D

Freelton.—A Village in the Township of West Flamboro, County Wentworth, 12 miles from Hamilton, the County Town, and 11 from Dundas Station Great Western Railway. Population, 120.

Addison, Christina, milliner and dressmaker
Addison, Mrs. Ellen, hotel keeper
Allen, Michael, shoemaker
Atkinson, E. S., M.D
Brady, James and John, wagon makers
Brown, David, carpenter
Carrill, George, blacksmith
Dands, Peter, carpenter
Flock, C. W., M.D
Freel, Patrick, J.P., hotel keeper
Ferguson, James, carpenter
Hirst, J. and E., general merchants
HIRST, JAMES, Postmaster
McLean, Rev. Alexander, (Presbyterian)
McMonnils, James, tailor
Maynard, Roger, teacher
Morgan, Bros. & Co., steam flouring mills
Pannaker, Lewis, saw miller and lumber dealer
Rowley, James, general merchant
Wood, Rev. George, (Primitive Methodist)
Yokom, David & Co., general merchants

Freeport.—A Village in the Township of Waterloo, County Waterloo, on the Grand River, 4 miles from Berlin, the County Town, and Preston Railway Stations. Population, 60.

Allison, A. B., blacksmith
Axford, Miss Lucy, teacher
Bowman, Rev. J. B
Bowman, J. L., J.P., principal Freeport Academy
Edwards, Rev. Abel, (Wesleyan)
Evans, James, teacher
Gehl, Richard, farmer
Gunbel, Bartel, farmer
Howard, Rev. T., (Wesleyan)
Kropp, Rev. H., (United Brethren)
Lutz, Henry, carpenter
Plowman, Rev. R. G.
Schlichter, Rev. J. B., Secretary Freeport Academy
SCHLICHTER, J. B., Postmaster, stationer and general merchant
Sherk, Rev. A. B., President Freeport Academy
Shupe, E., insurance agent
Shupe, Isaac, patent right agent
Snyder, E. B., farmer
Weaver, Amos, farmer
Weaver. Rev. A. C.
Whitaker & Zyrd, manufacturers of woolen goods

Fregmore.—A Post Office in the Township of Toronto, County Peel, on the River Credit, 15 miles from Brampton the County Town, 6 from Port Credit Station Great Western Railway, and 6 from Streetsville. Average value of improved land in the neighbourhood $45 per acre. The Credit affords excellent water privileges. Population of vicinity 200. 21 miles from Toronto.

ANDERSON, C. E., J. P., notary public, farmer
ANDERSON, C. ELLIOTT
ANDREWS, WILLIAM, farmer
Andrews, Thomas
Axford, Miss Lucy, teacher
AXFORD, WILLIAM, Postmaster and wagon maker
Bell, William, farmer
Brownridge, William, farmer
CAMERON, DONALD, J. P., farmer
CAMERON, WILLIAM, farmer
CLIFTON, JOHN, farmer
Conover, Albert, farmer
Conover, James, farmer
Conover, Samuel, farmer
Curran, Patrick, farmer
Davis, Robert, pensioner
Edwards, Rev. Abel (Wesleyan)
FALCONER, GEORGE, farmer
FRASER, JAMES, farmer
Gill, John, farmer
Howard, Rev. T. (Wesleyan)
Johnson, Charles, farmer
Johnson, Robert, farmer
Marlatt, George, farmer
MARLATT, SAMUEL, farmer
MITCHELL, COL. CHARLES, J.P.
Moss, John, farmer
Munn, George, farmer
Neil, John, farmer
Phœnix, George, farmer
Rowe, James, blacksmith
Shain, Charles, farmer
Shain, William, farmer
Stafford, Ira, farmer
Taylor, H., dentist
Taylor, Henry, hop grower and farmer

Frome.—A Post Office in the Township of Southwold, County Elgin, 7 miles from St. Thomas, the County Town.

Birch, David, teacher
Cdim, Rev. —, (Episcopal Methodist)
Firth, T., farmer
Hindley, Rev. J. (Congregational)
HORTON, ANDREW, Postmaster
Horton, N., carpenter
Horton, P., farmer
Kettlewell, R., nursery
Lawson, G., tailor
McLean, N., tailor
Morse, E. A., tailor
Morse, James, carpenter
Payne, William & Henry, props. steam flouring mills
Randall, F., J.P
Sharon, F., farmer
Sharon, H., farmer
Sharon, T., farmer
Shipley, Rev. J., (Wesleyan)
Sutton, J., farmer
Silcox, W., farmer and carpenter
Silcox, J. B., teacher

Fullarton.—A Village on the River Thames, in the Township of Fullarton, County Perth, 16 miles from Stratford, the County Town, 12 from St. Mary's and 6 from Mitchell. Average value of land in the vicinity $40 per acre. Population 200.

Baird, John, carpenter
Buchan, John, general merchant
Burns, Alexander, M.D
Chisholm, Hugh, insurance agent
Clark, Rev. Mr., (Bible Christian)
Davidson, Alexander, inn keeper
Dyer, Rev. Mr., (Wesleyan)
Ford, Thomas
Green, Rev. Thomas, (Baptist)
Hugill, Charles. J.P
Hugill, William, shoemaker
Jeffrey, John, shoemaker
Kerr, William, tanner
McLellan, Alexander, M.D
Porteous, William, J. P., farmer
Rice, George, general merchant
Rice, Robert
Rigg, Anthony B., carpenter
Vanstone, William, wagon maker
WOODLEY, JAMES, Postmaster

Fulton.—A Post office in the Township of Grimsby, County Lincoln, 30 miles from St. Catherines.

Berry, Rev. Francis, (Wesleyan)
Buckbee, A. P., farmer
Buckbee, J. H., farmer
Culp, William, pottery
Greenman, S. G., farmer
Hughson, W., bricklayer
King, Thomas, grocery
Lee, James, carpenter
Merritt, Alanson, farmer
Miller, P., farmer
Miller, John, shingle maker
Miller, Robert, insurance agent
Nelson, R., farmer
Riddle, —., wagon maker
Service, Rev. R., (Methodist Episcopal)
Snyder, E., farmer
Stephenson, W. C., farmer
White, C., farmer
WHITE, JOHN E., Postmaster

Freeburg.—A Post Office in the Township of Waterloo, County Waterloo.
ROMBACH, FERDINAND, Postmaster.

Galt.—A Town and Station of the Galt and Guelph branch of the Great Western Railroad, on the Grand River, in the Township of North Dumfries, County Waterloo; 11 miles from Berlin the County Town, 30 from Hamilton and 14 from Guelph. The surrounding country is remarkable for its fertility. Galt is the largest Town in the County, and in regard to its manufacturing establishments, one of the principal in the Province. The water power is unlimited. The Town is regularly laid out and the employment o stone in building which abounds in the neighborhood, gives it a remarkably substantial appearance Money Order Office and Savings Bank. Population 4000.

Atcheson, Rev. Robert, (Presbyterian)
Adams, Amos, proprietor Farmers' Inn
Adams Rev. Thomas, (Methodist)
Adams, John, wheat buyer
ADDISON, ALEXANDER, cabinet maker and librarian Mechanics' Institute
Aikens, Thomas, proprietor Union Hotel
Ainslie, James, farmer
Allan, Daniel, builder
Allan, James, carpenter
ALLAN, JOHN, editor and prop. *Dumfries Reformer*
Allan, Robert C., clerk
Allison, John, drover
AMERICAN EXPRESS COMPANY, James G. Fraser, agent
Anderson, James, carter
Anderson Bros., (John & Isaac) dealers in syrups and cigars
Andrich, Martin, butcher
ARNOT, ALEXANDER, D. prop. Galt Brewery
Austin, Adam, millwright
Austin, Samuel. fishmonger
BAILEY, JOHN A., barber and hairdresser
Baker, Thomas, veterinary surgeon
Baker Bros., (W. H. & John) grocers
BALL, A. T. H., barrister, &c
BARBOUR, John, cabinet maker
Barry, Thomas, tailor
Bell, Andrew, teamster
Bell, William, teamster
BENN, WALTER H., prop. Inkerman Inn
Bernhardt, William, prop. Alhambra saloon
Billing, John, tanner
Black, Francis, blacksmith and farrier
BLAIN, JAMES
BLAIN, RICHARD, prop. Dickson Mills
Blain, Thomas, wheat buyer
BOOMER, REV. MICHAEL, (Church of England)
BREIMER, F. H., barber and hair dresser
Brennan, Hugh A., clerk
Brodie, Miss Agnes, confectioner
BROOMFIELD, R., (McDougall & Broomfield)
BROWN, DAVID, book-keeper
Brown, James, photographer
Brown, John, butcher
Brown, R. S. dentist
BROWNLOW, THOMAS, merchant
Brydon & Yeaman, (Walter & William) wagon makers
Buchanan, Alexander
BURNETT, WALTER, tanner and currier
BURNETT, ALEXANDER, market clerk
Caldwell, David, nurseryman
Cant, Adam, pattern maker
CANT, HUGH, saddle and harness maker

Cant, John, trimmer
Carlyle, William, principal Central school
Carrick, Alexander, farmer
Carter & Todd, produce and commission merchants
Cheeseman, John, carpenter
CLARK, JOHN, prop. Young Canadian Saloon
Claden, James, farmer
Connell, David, innkeeper
COOKE, WILLIAM, manager Merchants' Bank
Coulthard, William, carpenter
Cowan, James, farmer
Cowan, Thomas, collector
Crane, Henry, carpenter
CROMBIE, JAMES & CO., woolen factors, millers,
Curliss, James, teamster
Dalgleish, James, builder
Dalgleish, Thomas, builder
Date, H. H., manufacturer of edge tools, axes, &c.
DAVIDSON, JOHN, Postmaster and manager Gore Bank
Davidson, William, saddler
Davis, J. W. & Co., iron founders, tinsmiths, &c.
DEAN, O. S., dealer in fruit, confectionery, &c.
Deans, W. Carter, M. D.
Deary, James, prop. North American hotel
Dennis, Henry, teamster
DICKSON, WILLIAM
Dill, Mrs. Julia, boarding house
Distin, William L.
Dixon, James, carpenter
Dowker, John
DRYDEN, ANDREW, lumber dealer
Dryden, Thomas, carpenter
DUMFRIES FOUNDRY, Goldie, McCulloch & Co., props
DURAND, CHARLES A. (Durand & Philip)
DURAND & PHILIP (Charles A. & George S.) barristers, &c.
DYKES, JOHN G., town Clerk
ELLIOT, WILLIAM, Photographer (see adv)
ELLIOTT, ANDREW.
Elliott, Mrs. C., boarding house
ELSLIE, ALEXANDER G., (J. Fleming & Co.)
Fairgreave, George, carpenter
Ferguson, D. & Co., painters, etc.
Ferguson, John, clerk
Field, Thomas, collector
Fisher, George F., clerk
FISHER, THOMAS S., dry goods, groceries, etc.
FLEMING, JOHN, dry goods, groceries, etc.
FLEMING, JOHN & CO., booksellers & stationers
FOX, CHARLES A., watchmaker and jeweller, (see adv)
Fraser, James G., agent American Express Company and telegraph operator
GALT REPORTER, Jaffray Bros., editors & proprs.
Gash, Mrs. Elizabeth, boarding house
Gay, William, band master and music teacher
Geddes, James D., accountant Gore Bank
Gilholm & Hogg, (Luke and Francis), proprs. steam saw mill
Gillespie, J. B., dry goods
Gillies, Peter, wagon maker
Girdlestone, C. W., book-keeper
GOLDIE, JOHN, (Goldie, McCulloch & Co.)
GOLDIE, McCULLOCH & CO., proprs. Dumfries Foundry
Goodall, George, farmer
Goodall, John, farmer
Gordon, Thomas, shoemaker
Gore District Mutual Fire Insurance Co.. Thomas M. Simons, secretary
GORE BANK, John, Davidson manager
Gorth, Frederick, shoemaker
Gourlay, John, machinist
Graham, David, carpenter
Graham, William, carpenter
Grant, Alexander, mason
Gray, Mrs. Alice, fancy goods
Gray, Robert, carpenter
Grisch, John, shoemaker
Guggisberg, Frederick, dry goods
Habbick, John, dry goods, millinery, &c
Hardy, James, weaver
HARRIS, T. W., Assistant Postmaster
Havill, James, plasterer
Hay, Peter, machinist
Heinhold, William, furrier
Henderson, Archibald, farmer
Henderson, James, carpenter
Henderson, James & Co., booksellers, &c
Henshelwood, Peter, teamster
HETHERINGTON, JAMES, prop. Galt Hotel
Hohl, Jacob, carpenter
Holland, John, painter, &c
Hood, Adam, sen., carpenter
Houseman, John, painter
HOWELL, DANIEL, (Robinson & Howell)
Hume, Gavin, general merchant
HUNTER, JAMES, provision dealer and money broker
HUSBAND, GEORGE E., M. D., homœopathic physician (see adv)
Irving, Matthew, mill stone builder
JAFFRAY BROS., (G. H. & R.) editors and props. *Galt Reporter*
Jaffray, James, book binder
Jamieson, George, farmer
Jardine, John & Walter, blacksmiths
Jeffrey, Peter, weaver
JOB, CHARLES C., M.D., homœopathic physician
JOHNSON, W. H., gunsmith (see adv)
Kay, James, carriage maker
Kay, John, watchmaker and jeweler
Kay, Mrs. William, groceries, &c
Keachie, John B., carpenter
Keefer, Peter, clerk Division Court
KER, ADAM, mayor
Knapp, F. A., accountant
KNOX, THOMAS, baker and confectioner
Laidlaw, Walter, prop. saw mill
LAIDLAW, WILLIAM W., prop. Waterloo sash, door & blind factory (see adv)
Laird, George, carpenter
Lammond, John, machinist
Lavin, Peter, prop. Albion Hotel
Leatherdale, James, carpenter
Lister, Thomas, drover
Lithgow, Alexander, tailor
Little, David, tailor
Little, Thomas, cabinet maker
Little, William, mason
Livett, S. C., grocer
LOWELL, FRANCIS, prop. Queen's Arms Hotel
LUTZ, MORRIS C., J.P
LUTZ & CO., iron founders, agricultural implement makers, &c,
McBROOM, WILLIAM, grocer
McCrea, William J., seedsman and grocer
McCrum, Henry, book-keeper
McCULLOCH, HUGH (Goldie, McCulloch & Co.)
McDonough, L., chief constable
McDougall, Adam, carpenter
McDougall, D., boots and shoes

McDOUGALL, ROBERT (McDougall & Broomfield)
McDOUGALL & BROOMFIELD (Robert & Robert), carpenters and saw mill props
McFarlane, Mrs. J., boarding house
McFeiggan, James, book-keeper
McIlwraith, Andrew, book-keeper
McIntosh, Thomas, gardener
McKeand, Donald, accountant
McKendrick, James, plasterer
McLachlan, William, tailor
McMillan, James, farmer
McMillan, Thomas, seedsman, &c.
McRae, George, gardener
McRae, James, teacher
McTague, James, stoves, tinware, &c.
McWilliams, Charles, tailor
MacGregor, Alexander, insurance and general agent
Maitland, Hugh, music teacher
Malcolm, A., cabinet maker
MECHANICS' INSTITUTE, A. Addison, librarian
Meikle, John, saddler
Mellish, Robert, painter, &c.
MERCHANTS' BANK OF CANADA, W. Cooke, manager
Middlemas, Thomas, station master G.W.R
MILLER, HENRY & CO., druggists
MILLER, JAMES & JOHN, barristers, &c.
MILLER, WILLIAM, County Judge
Miller, William, baker
MILLER, W. NICHOLAS, barrister, &c.
Morris & Jackson, (Thomas & John) boots and shoes
Muir, Rev. J. B., pastor (St. Andrew's Church)
Mundel, J., freight clerk, G. W. R.
Munro, George, carpenter
MURDOCH, HUGH, baker and confectioner
MURDOCH, REV. W. T., pastor (Melville Church)
Murray, Robert, cooper and grocer
Murray & Atcheson, (Hugh & George M.) dry goods
Myles, Thomas, coal yard
Neilson, James, baker
Nelles, R. F., collector of Inland Revenue
Oates, Mrs., confectionery
OLFORD, JOSEPH, boots and shoes
Oliver, Andrew, druggist
Oliver, George, drover
OLIVER, SIMON, manuf. soap, candles, potash, &c
Osborne, William, proprietor Doon Mills
Ovens, Robert, builder
Ovens, William, millwright
PATRICK, ROBERT, woolen factor
PATTERSON, GEORGE H., manager Royal Canadian Bank
Patterson, James, carpenter
PECK, THOMAS, maltster
PHILIP, GEORGE S., (Durand & Philip)
PHILIP, JOHN ROY, M. D.
Pollock, James, P. L. S.
Polson, Angus, dry goods
POLSON, & LAVIN, (Robert & Peter) grocers
QUARRIE, WILLIAM, saddle and harness maker
QUEEN'S ARMS HOTEL, Francis Lowell, prop.
Ramsay, James, drover
RAMSEY, S. F., M.D.
REID, ROBERT, surgeon dentist, (see adv)
Richardson, Samuel, M.D.
Robinson, Edward, shoemaker
ROBINSON, WILLIAM, (Robinson & Howell)
ROBINSON & HOWELL, (William and Daniel), woolen manufacturers
ROBSON, R. & J., builders, sash, door and blind factory, (see adv)
Ross, Malcolm, carpenter
Sampson, Theophilus, J.P.
SCOTT, JOHN, prop. Galt marble works, (See adv)
Scott, John, cattle dealer
SCOTT, T. F., barber and hairdresser
Scott, Walter, carpenter
SCOTT, WILLIAM, (James Scott & Son)
SCOTT, JAMES & SON, carpenters, bobbin manuf. etc. (See adv)
Scringer, James, farmer
Scringer, John, farmer
Scringer & Main, (William and Henry M.) props. livery stable
Scrogie, George, drover
Seagram, Edward, book-keeper
Seagram, Joseph
Seagram, Thomas, M.D.
Sheils, James, drover
SIMONS, T. M., Sec. Gore District Mutual Fire Insurance Co.
Slade, Thomas, carpenter
Smith, Rev. J. K., (Presbyterian)
Smith & Young, (Joel B. and James) props. Victoria Works
Snell, Edmund, butcher
Sparrow, Thomas, issuer of marriage licenses
Sproule, James, shoemaker
Stevens, George, proprietor livery stable
Stewart Charles, weaver
Stewart, Thomas, proprietor Dumfries Mills
Stoddard, Henry, proprietor Western Hotel
Strickland, George T., auctioneer, &c
Strong, R. S., chemist and druggist
Sutherland, Mrs. Elizabeth, confecitoner
Sutherland, John, lumber dealer
Tait, John, blacksmith and agricultural implement maker
TASSIE, WILLIAM, M.A., head master Galt Grammar School
TAYLOR, ROBERT, merchant tailor
Thompson, James J. & Co., woolen factors
Tindel, John C., clerk
Trotter, James, watchmaker and jeweler
Thompson, Peter, blacksmith
Trotter & Scott, (William T. & Robert) stoves, tinware
Turnbull, George, hosier
Uren, Thomas, machinist
Urquhart, Alexander. blacksmith
Veitch, John, plasterer
Wagner, Joseph, tanner
Wallace, Robert, distiller
Warnock, Adam, (James Crombie & Co)
Warnock, James & Co., hardware
WATSON, WILLIAM, tailor
Webber, Charles, broker and insurance agent
Webster, Robert, builder
Wells, James, tool temperer
Whitney, F. L. & Co., ale and porter vaults
WILKINS, N. & E. J., merch't tailors and clothiers
WILKINS, W. H. & S., merch't tailors and clothiers
Wilkinson, Robert, cooper
WILLIAMS, MORGAN, photographer
Woodruff, Mrs. Ann, boarding house
Woods, James, book-keeper
WRIGHT, THOMAS, mathematical master Galt Grammar School
Yorston, Alexander, carpenter
YOUNG, JAMES, M.P.P
Young, William & Co., paper collar manuf
Younie, James, gardener

Gad's Hill.—A Village in the Township of Ellice, County Perth, 6 miles from Stratford, the County Town. Population 100.

Bullard, B , innkeepr
Crinkley, A. & W. B., lumber dealers
CRINKLEY, W. B., Postmaster
Deibrich, George, farmer
Hartling, Charles, farmer
Hattung, Philip, farmer
Kirkpatrick, James, farmer
Kneisel, Henry, farmer
Kollman, Jacob, lumber dealer
Lautenschlager, Adam, cooper
Leisemer, Henry, general merchant
Pfeffer, Conrad, dentist
Ratz, Henry, planing mills
Schmidt, B., farmer
Schmidt, Henry, farmer
Schnarr, N., innkeeper
Whitlenfer, Henry, farmer

Galway.—A Post-office in the Township of Galway, County Peterboro', 42 miles from Peterboro', the County Town. Average value of improved land in the vicinity $3 per acre.

Gneffis, Andrew, inn keeper
McGee, Henry, carpenter
Maxwell, John, inn keeper
Maxwell, Robert, shingle maker
PROBERT, THOMAS, J.P., Postmaster
Stewart, Robert, painter

Gananoque.—An incorporated Village and port of entry, situate on the river St. Lawrence, and distant three miles from a station of the Grand Trunk Railway, in the Township of Leeds, County Leeds. The steamers plying between Montreal, Toronto and Hamilton, call here daily. The proximity of the Village to the magnificent scenery of the Thousand Islands make it a favorite resort for tourists. The water power here is almost unlimited and a large portion has been utilised. Distant from Montreal 155 miles, from Toronto 179 miles and from Kingston 18 miles. Money Order Office and Savings Bank. Population 2,250. The following are the principal manufacturers:—*E. E. Abbott*, machinists' tools, power presses, water wheels, nuts, bolts, &c., and employs a large number of hands; *Cowan & Britton*, nails and hinges; *Isaac Briggs*, steel carriage springs; *D. F. Jones*, spades, shovels, forks, &c.; *George Mitchell*, "Excelsior" mattrass filling, sash and door factory; *Byers & Matthew*, wagon skeins, iron and copper rivets, &c.; *William Bullock*, kettle ears, felloe plates, &c.; *Peter O'Brien*, "Excelsior" mattrass filling; *Robert Brough*, hay rakes, wheel heads, &c.; *Henry Collard*, agricultural implements; *Gordon & Kirkham*, woolen batting; *Skinner & Co.*, scythe snaths, grain cradles, hames, &c.

ABBOTT, E. E., manuf. machinsts' tools, power presses, water wheels, mill gearing, bolts, nuts, &c. (see adv)
Acton, Joseph, ship owner
Acton, Robert, boots and shoes
ALBION HOTEL, Bernard Shiels, prop. (see adv)
ASSELSTINE, G. N., watchmaker, agent Montreal Telegraph Co
Auchinvole, Gilbert, prop. tannery
Bain, Brothers, dentists and photographers
Battams, Samuel, tailor
Beaumont, George, lumber merchant
Bennett, Isaac, tinsmith, stoves, &c
Bockus, C. N., general merchant, agent Mutual Life Insurance Co., of Hartford
BRIGGS, ISAAC, manuf. carriage springs, pumps,
BRITTON, D. F., Postmaster, general merchant, forwarder, &c
BRITTON, FREEMAN, job printer, bookseller, newsdealer, wools, fancy goods, and small wares (see adv).
Brophy, Denis, restaurant
BROUGH, ROBERT, manufacturer patent wheelheads, hay rakes and general wood turning
BROUGH, WILLIAM, general merchant, prop. Gananoque flouring mill
Brown, Andrew F., hotel keeper
Bullock, William, manufacturer of kettle ears, felloe plates, mop sticks, &c.
BYERS & MATTHEW (W. Byers and W. G. Matthew) manufacturers carriage and wagon axles and skeins, iron and copper rivets, &c.
BYERS, R., clerk J. Briggs
Carroll, Rev. John (Episcopal)
CARROLL, W. B., agent Commercial Union Association, England
Calhoun, J. C., prop. Calhoun House
Campbell, Henry, butcher
CHEVERS & McADAM, props. Provincial House
Cheevers, M., tailor
CHEVERS, THOMAS, J.P., treasurer (see adv)
Chevers, Thomas H., carriage maker
Church, Joseph, hotel
COLLARD, HENRY, manufacturer of agricultural implements
Cotton, R. P., woollen factor
COWAN & BRITTON (O. D. Cowan and C. E. Britton) manufacturers nails, hinges, &c.
Crysler, Charles B., general merchant
Damien, Thomas, shoemaker
Edwards, William, cabinet maker
Ellis, Mrs., confectioner
Fairman, Daniel, manufacturer spoons
Fairman, Warren, saw mill proprietor
Gordon, Rev. Henry, (Presbyterian)
GORDON & KIRKHAM (John H. Gordon and Thomas C. Kirkham) manufacturers carded woolen batting for mattrasses and general upholstering
Goulette, A., shoemaker
GOULETTE, O. V., manufacturer hickory chisel handles, buggy spindles and bureau knobs, tobacconist and fancy goods, &c.
Haig, David, hotel
Heaslip, S., manufacturer carpenter's patent braces
Hiscocks, John, general merchant
Hunt, J. D., hotel keeper

Hurst, George, grocer and baker
Huyler, E. B., manufacturer sewing machines
Inwood, John, hotel
JONES D. FORD, manufacturer spades, shovels, &c.
Kirkes, James, shoemaker
Laurie, Robert, blacksmith
Landon, E., saddler
Lindsay, George, wagon maker
McCAMMON, S., chemist and druggist, clerk 3rd Division Court (see adv).
McClary, Charles, saddler
McCleverty, J., tailor
McCrum, Robert, M.D., coroner
McDonald, Rev. Davidson (Wesleyan)
McDonnell, John, builder
McKenzie, William, cabinet maker
Mack, William, hotel keeper
MILLER, H. C., general merchant. (See adv)
MITCHELL, GEORGE, builder, sash and door factory, manufacturer Excelsior mattrass filling. (See adv)
O'BRIEN, PETER, proprietor Exchange Flouring Mill, cooperage, barrel heading and stave factory and general merchant. (See adv)
O'Connor, Rev. Michael, (Roman Catholic)
O'Neil, L., baker.
Ormiston, John, Collector of Customs
Parmenter, James W., J.P., commisioner in B. R. and conveyancer
Parmenter, Joel D., farmer
POTTER, WILLIAM, M.D., coroner
PROVINCIAL HOUSE, Chevers & McAdam, props. (See adv)
Richmond, Thomas, M.D.
Rogers, Samuel, grocer
Rogers, W. N. & Co., general merchants
Sheridan, James, blacksmith
SHIELS, B., proprietor Albion House. (See adv)
SKINNER & CO., (S. & S. C. Skinner), manufacturers saddlery, hardware, agricultural implements etc.
Skinner, A., clerk
Stunden, George, blacksmith
Stunden, J. & C., general merchants
Sytz, Joseph, shoemaker
Taylor, Brother & Co., general merchants
Traveller, Rev. Mr., (Methodist Episcopal)
Treneman, John, station agent
Turner & Taylor, (James and George), gen. merchants
Waddie, J., stage proprietor
Wilkinson, William, barber.
Wing, John, butcher
Wright, Robert, builder

Garafraxa, (Douglas Village).—A Village in the Township of Garafraxa, County Wellington, on the Grand River, 21 miles from Guelph, and 14 from Rockwood Station, Grand Trunk Railway. Money order office. Population 150.

Alpane, John, farmer
Black, R. J., farmer
Brown, George, general merchant
Brown, Rev. Robert, (Congregational)
Clark, Rev. —., (Wesleyan)
Connolly, Thomas, livery stable proprietor
Cassiday, William, steam saw mill proprietor
Cowse, Paul, farmer
Cowse, Peter, innkeeper
Curry, Duncan, general merchant
Gerrie, Peter, farmer
Jupp, O., wagon maker
LIGHTBODY, ANDREW, Postmaster, gen. mercht
Lightbody, John, surgeon
Lindsay, James, farmer
Lovie, James, farmer
Lovie, Michael, farmer
McClanacahm, James, farmer
McGrigor, William, blacksmith
Melican, Rev. William, (Canada Presbyterian)
Mence, George, innkeeper
Michie, William, J.P., grist mill
Rathburn, W. H., dentist
Reid, John, teacher
Rodgers, William, blacksmith
Sargent, Cyrus, farmer
Sargent, Henry, farmer
Sargent, John, farmer
Strachan, Robert, carpenter
Thom, John C., M.D.
Thompson, Theodore, innkeeper
Todd, Alexander, shoemaker
Ward, William, mason

Garden Island.— A Post Office in the Township of Garden Island, County Frontenac.
CUMMING, GEORGE, Postmaster.

Garden River.—An Indian Village, beautifully situated at the confluence of the Garden and Ste. Marie Rivers, in the District of Algoma, 12 miles below the Sault Ste. Marie. The former river runs through the village from north to south, emptying into the latter, which runs from west to east in front of the village, conveying the surplus waters of Lake Superior to Lake Huron. The Ste. Marie separates the State of Michigan from Canada, and is navigable for vessels of every description. Canadian and American steamers are supplied with wood by the Indians, who are christianized and have attained to a high degree of civilization. Population about 400.

AUGOSTO, Chief
CHANCE, REV. J., (Church of England Missionary)
Finley, Alexander, farmer
Holdcroft, Thomas, farmer
PEQUCHININIE, Chief
ROHLER, REV. A., (Roman Catholic Missionary)
Rush, William, farmer
Sanders, John, farmer
WAHBEMAMA, chief

Gemley.—A Post Office in the Township of Clarendon, County Frontenac, 75 miles from Kingston, the County Town. Wild lands in the vicinity average $1, and improved $8 per acre.

Bucher, William, general merchant
Cuheron, C., general merchant
Lockie, C., hotel keeper and cooper
Lockie, William, distiller
Perry, Mrs., innkeeper
Perry, Rev. C. (Wesleyan)
Plotz, William, cabinet maker
Rington, E., M.D.
Shaw, William, general merchant
STALKER, JAMES, Postmaster
Ward, William, shingle maker

Georgetown.—An Incorporated Village and Station of the Grand Trunk Railway in the Township of Esquessing, County Huron, on the River Credit, 12 miles from Milton, 28 from Toronto, and 37 from Hamilton. Population 1500. The extensive premises of Messrs. Barber Brothers occupies an area of an acre, employing 40 hands in the manufacture of every description of book, writing, printing, manilla and wrapping papers.

Allen, William, shoemaker
Anderson, Alexander, grocer
Anderson, Belden, farmer
Anderson, Robert, carpenter
Andrews, John, clothdresser
Armour, Nicholas, watchmaker
Badern, Joseph, shoemaker
Bailey, Isaiah, tailor
Bailey, Thomas, painter
BARBER, JAMES, paper manufacturer
BARBER, JOHN R., reeve
BARBER, JOSEPH, paper manufacturer
BARBER, JOSEPH, Sen., paper manufacturer
BARBER, WILLIAM, & BROTHERS, paper manufacturers (see adv)
BARCLAY, FRANCIS, merchant
Barclay, George A., shoemaker
Baines, Peter N. R., carpenter
Burns, William, constable
Baxendale, Richard, paper manufacturer
Benham, Alfred, livery stable
Bird, John, shoemaker
Blewa, John, shoemaker
Brasbie, Rev. Denis L.
Brinkerhoff, Robert, brewer
BRITTON, N. R., barrister
Brown, George N., blacksmith
Brown, W. R., carriage and wagon maker
Burchell, Robert, grocer
BUTCHART, DAVID, photographer
Calder, Alexander, marble dealer
Calder, Asa, marble dealer
Calder, Charles, marble dealer
CALDER & SON, marble dealers
Campbell, Alexander, printer
Campbell, James A., printer
Carbeneau, Philip, shoemaker
CHASE, JOHN H., innkeeper
Clark, Duncan, livery stable
CLARK, THOMAS, innkeeper
Cook, Thomas, barber
Corry, John, farmer
CRAIG, JOSEPH (J. Craig & Bro.)
CRAIG, J. & BRO., publishers and proprietors *Halton Herald*
Creach, Samuel, tanner
Cross, David, tanner
Crowley, Patrick, wheelwright
Culp, Hiram, blacksmith
Culp & McKenzie, carriage makers
Cummings, —, retired
Cushman, George, painter
De Pottie, James A., merchant
Dade, Rev. Charles
Dalton, Catherine, dressmaker
Dayfoot, G. C.
DAYFOOT, PHILIP W., tanner
Dundas, William, carpenter
Evans, Peter L., merchant
Ewing, Rev. Robert
Forsyth, George, carpenter
Forsyth, John, carpenter
Forsyth, Joseph, carpenter
FREEMAN, WILLIAM, M.D.
Gain, Henry, shoemaker
Gain, William, shoemaker
Galbraith, A., watchmaker
Geddes, Robert, town clerk
Graham, William, butcher
Grandan, H., shoemaker
Grant, Lachlan, grocer
Grieve, Alexander, blacksmith
Hardaker, Jonathan, shoemaker
Hayes, John, fishmonger
Hayes, John, shoemaker
Heartwell, Lewis, farmer
HENDERSON, PHILIP, merchant
Higgins, James, innkeeper
Higgins, John, innkeeper
HILLOCK, JOHN C., tanner
HOOD & McKINNON, general merchants
Johnston, John, carpenter
Joyce, William,
Kennedy, James W., farmer
Kennedy, John, farmer
Kennedy, Rev. Morris
Kennedy, Samuel, sen.
Lee, John, painter
Long, Robert, cooper
McCann, Peter, carpenter
McCulloch, Robert, M.D.
McDermid, John, grocer
McGaw, Robert, carpenter
McKAY, HUGH, grocer and insurance agents
McKay, Walter, carpenter
McKechnie, A., tailor
McKenzie, Daniel, carriage maker
McKENZIE, G. C., iron founder (see adv)
McKinnon, David, merchant
McKinnon, Donald, blacksmith
McLeod, William, merchant
McMaster, William, grocer
Maw, F. & W., founders and machinists
Meadows, John, baker
Miller, Charles, marble cutter
Moore, James, bailiff
Morrison, Rev. S.
NOBLE, WILLIAM, shoemaker (see adv)
Norwich, Henry, painter
O'Leary, Thomas, shoemaker
Orr, Edward A., marble dealer
Page, Solomon, merchant

Parker, John G., merchant
Ranney, Malcolm, M.D.
Reid, Dougald, merchant
Redding, R. A., tailor
Roe, William W., auctioneer
ROSE, LAWRENCE, miller
Rose, Thomas, blacksmith
Rue, John, tailor
RUSHTON, THOMAS, druggist
Rushton & Rose, hop growers
Ryan, Charles, station master
St. John, James, shoemaker
Shea, William M., manufacturer
Sparting, Christopher, butcher
Stall, Henry B., carpenter
Standish, Joseph Y, merchant
STARR, MILTON H., M.D. (see adv)
Stathem, Silas, tinsmith
Tantardini, Abel, blacksmith
Taylor, Isaac, shoemaker
Taylor, John F., saddler
Thayer, Charles, cabinet maker
Thomas, Daniel, carpenter
THOMPSON, BENJAMIN, innkeeper
Travis, David S., turner
Travis, Elijah, retired
Unsworth, Rev. Joseph
Wadsworth, Joseph, carpenter
Walker, Elias, tanner
Wason, Thomas, shoemaker
Webbe, Rev. Henry
Whittaker, Thomas, merchant
Wright, William C., M.D.
Young, James, J.P.
Young, Robert, Division Court Clerk
Young, Thomas, merchant

Georgina.—(See Sutton)—A Post office in the Township of Georgina, County York. Money order office.
BOUCHIER, J. O. B., Postmaster.

Gifford.—A Post office in the Township of South Cayuga, County Haldimand, 6 miles from Cayuaga, the County Town.
FREDENBURGH, C. B., Postmaster.

Gilbert's Mills.—A Post village in the Township of Sophiasburg, County Prince Edward.
GILBERT, JOHN D., Postmaster.

Gilford.—A Post village in the Township of West Gwillimbury, County Simcoe, and a station on the Northern Railway, 16 miles from Barrie, the County Town, and 49 from Toronto. Daily stage to Cookstown. Population 100.

Banker, J. W., carpenter
Brimmer, William, carpenter
Fraser, Alexander, station master
Graham, William, general merchant
Huff, Alvah, carpenter
MACONCHY, THOMAS, Postmaster and proprietor saw mills
Neely, William, farmer and saw miller
NELSON, R., merchant and grain buyer
Rogers, John, innkeeper
Russell, William, farmer
Stevenson, John sawyer
Swallman, Henry, carpenter

Gladstone.—A Village in the Township of North Dorchester, County Middlesex, 14 miles from London, the County Town. Population 80.

Boothy, Jesse, carpenter
Brodie, Alexander A., farmer
Cameron, John, farmer
Demary, Deacon William
Hill, William, farmer
Jackson, William, farmer
Jemarr, James, farmer
McCallum, Hugh, farmer
McDonald, Mrs., dressmaker
McMurray, James
McMURRAY, LEVI, Postmaster and gen. merchant
McMurray, Morris, farmer
Marsh, Deacon William
Marsh, Randall, farmer
Noble, Benjamin, farmer
Perrin, Rev. Andrew, (Baptist)
Scott, Thomas, cooper
Shipp, Thomas, farmer
Swales, William
Tooley, Richard
Ward, Jonathan, general merchant
Ward, Peter, farmer
York, Gustavus, farmer
York, William, jr., farmer
Young, Charles, blacksmith

Glanford.—A Post-office in the Township of Glanford, County Wentworth. (See Village of Mount Hope.)
ATKINSON, JOHN, Postmaster.

Glammis.—A Village in the Township of Bruce, County Bruce, 17 miles from Walkerton, the County Town. Improved lands in the vicinity average $20 per acre. Population 50.

Berton, Richard, farmer
Campbell, Duncan, farmer
CRAWFORD, JAMES, Postmaster
Currie, Rev. Mr., (Presbyterian)
Harrison, Richard, general merchant
Jeffers, Rev. J., (Methodist)
McLennan, Alexander, farmer
McLennan, Donald, farmer
Preston, John, farmer
Ross, Allan, farmer

Glanmire.—A Village in the Township of Tudor, County Hastings, 48 miles from Belleville, the County Town.

TAPP, EDWARD, Postmaster

Glanworth.—A Post Village on the London and Port Stanley Railway, in the Township of Westminster, County Middlesex. Distant 8 miles from London, the County Town. Daily mail. Population 150.

Caulfield, Rev. St. George, M.A. (Church of England)
Ferguson, Colin, farmer
Fisher, Vicars, J.P
Glenn, Michael, farmer
Jackson, W., J.P.
Kerr, Murdoch, farmer
Mechan, Edward, carriage and wagon maker
Murdoch, Alexander, tailor
Quinn, Terence, J.P
Regan, Cornelius, farmer
Regan, Dennis, farmer
Reid, John, blacksmith
Rose, Daniel, farmer
Sweeney, John, shoemaker
Sweeney, Patrick, farmer
TURNBULL, JOHN, Postmaster

Glascott.—A Post Village in the Township of Glenelg, County Grey, S.R.

ENGLISH, JOHN, Postmaster.

Glenallan.—A Village in the Township of Peel, County Wellington, on the Conestogo river, 24 miles from Guelph, the County Town, and 22 from Berlin. Daily stages. Money Order Office. Population 300.

ALLAN, GEORGE, J. P., Postmaster, clerk Division Court and general merchant
Badley, George, general merchant
Barlow, Michael, carpenter
CANADA MAPLE LEAF, (Friday) Thomas Hilliard editor
Cookman, James, grain cradle manuf
Ford, George, wagon maker
Gibson, John C., J.P., gen. mercht., and ins. agent
Greig, Peter, shoemaker
Harvey, Samuel A., M.D.
Hewit, Robert, hotel keeper
HILLIARD, THOMAS, editor and proprietor *Canada Maple Leaf*
Howlet, William, butcher
Janson, Matthias, grain cradle manufacturer
Kinney, Jesse, stone and lime dealer
Love, James, painter
McLachlan, Hugh, tailor
Manderson, John, lumber dealer
Mann, Robert, dry goods
Martin, C. S., saddler
Mellis, George, auctioneer
Minis, Robert, tailor
Moore, W. M., teacher
Peffers, Neil, cabinet maker
Rankin, John, carpenter
Reid, Robert, woolen manufacturer
Ryckman, John, shoemaker
Squires, B., nurseryman
Sutherland, W. S., J.P., grist mill proprietor
Tanner, John, leather dealer
Ward, William, wagon maker
Watson, William, innkeeper

Glenburnie.—A small Village in the Township of Kingston, County Frontenac, 6 miles from Kingston, the County Town.

Blacklock, W., farmer
Case, Rev. George (Wesleyan)
Collins, Charles, wagon maker
Cordukes, Robert T., carpenter
Crozier, Rev. Mr. (Presbyterian)
Doyle, J., J.P.
Draper, R., farmer
Ellice, Arnot, cabinet maker
Fair, J. M., J.P.
Heward, George, farmer
Hickey, J., farmer
Hunter, George, farmer
HUNTER, GEORGE, Sen., Postmaster
Joseland, Rev. Mr. (Wesleyan)
Martin, Rev. Mr. (Methodist Episcopal)
Mucleverty, Thomas, teacher
Pope, Rev. Mr. (Methodist Episcopal)
Rankin, W., farmer
Shannon, R., innkeeper
Spooner, C. N., farmer
Spooner, R., stock dealer
Stinson, J., innkeeper
Sturges, Joel, lime and stone dealer
Waggoner, Col. E., J.P.
Waggoner, Thomas F., butcher.

Glenarm.—A Post Office of the Township of Eldon, County Victoria, distant 18 miles from Lindsay, the County Town. Average price of land, $18 per acre.

COOPER, W., Postmaster.

Glencairn.—A Village in the Township of Tossorontio, County Simcoe, adjacent to the Mad River, 19 miles from Barrie, the County Town, and 85 from Toronto. Land in the neighborhood averages $20 per acre. Population 150.

Bayne, Neil, carpenter
Frame, J. F., accountant
Grainger, W. N., farmer
Grieve, William, hotel keeper
Handy, Benjamin, farmer
Linn, Adam, shingle maker
McBride, James, farmer
McKinley, Charles, shingle maker
Ritchie, David, farmer
STEPHENS, M. W., Postmaster, J.P., gen. merckt.
Stewart, John, farmer

Glencoe.—A Village and Station of the Great Western Railway, in the Townships of Ekfrid and Mosa, County Middlesex, 30 miles from London, the County Town, and 150 from Toronto. Money Order office. Population 500.

Bredin, R., G. W. R.
Cameron, Miss, millinery, &c.
Campbell, J. W., saddler
Coyne, J., dentist
Currie, N., J.P., M.P.P.
Crouse, Oliver, carpenter
Cuthbert, A., shoemaker
Dewar, J., carpenter
Drummond, J., general merchant
Frederick, S., teacher
Freele, George, shoemaker
Gross, H., telegraph operator
Harris, G., tailor
Lawton, Charles & W., coopers
Leitch, M., tailor
McCallum, John, farmer
McCracken, Alexander, general merchant
McDonald, A. P., M.P.P.
McDougall, A. R. & Brother, general merchants
McGee, William, lumber dealer
McIntyre, —, M.D.
McKinnon, H., hotel keeper
McLeod, Rev. J. (Kirk of Scotland)
McNeil, John, tailor
McPlin, Miss, millinery, &c.
McRAE, D., Postmaster, general merchant
McRae, John R., J.P.
Mottashed, J., shoemaker
Munroe, M., stock dealer
Mullett, Lucy, teacher
Riddel, A., painter
Ross, P., hotel keeper
Simpson, William J., J.P.
Slimhoff, F., wagon maker
Sutherland, Rev. N., (Presbyterian)
Thorburn, J., cabinet maker
Walker, John, farmer
Walker, John S., farmer
Walker, Johnston, carpenter
Walker, Samuel J., carpenter
Wandeley, John, brick maker
Wright, Rev. William

Glenlyon.—A small Post Village in the Township of Carrick, County Bruce. Distant from Walkerton, the County Town, 9 miles and from Guelph 50 miles. Population about 80.

Markle, Edward, saw mill proprietor
Pepper, William, agricultural implement manufr.
SHENNAN, J., Postmaster
Shiel, Charles, tailor

Glen Morris.—A thriving Village situated on the Grand River, in the Township of South Dumfries, County Brant, 12 miles from Brantford, the County Town, and 75 miles from Toronto. Daily stage to Galt and Paris. Population 350.

Benham, M. B., carpenter
Corcoran, Patrick, proprietor, flouring mills
Dunbar, Rev. John, (Canada Presbyterian)
Flanagan, John, wagon maker
FLEMING, G., J.P., Postmaster and gen. merchant
Forbes, William, carpenter
Geddes, George N., wagon maker
Germain, A. & S., manufacturers of woolen goods
Griffith, E., proprietor Farmer's Inn
Henderson, Mrs., milliner
Lapraik, Miss, milliner
McIntosh, Hugh, farmer
McKinnon, D., proprietor Waverly Hotel
McMillan, James shoemaker
Murray, John, tailor
Scott, Thomas, carpenter
Sharp, James, J.P
Smith, Frederick, tailor
TOPPING, WILLIAM M., teacher
Trotter, Mrs., milliner
Wallace, Robert, distiller

Glen Tay.—A Post office in the Township of Bathurst, County Lanark, S. R.

MAYBERY, HENRY, Postmaster.

Glennevis.—A Post village in the Township of Lancaster, County Glengarry, 25 miles distant from Cornwall, the County Town. Population 25.

Brown, Michael, teacher
McDonald, D., foundry
McDonald, John, wagon maker
McMillan, D., lumber dealer
McRAE, A. D., Postmaster and general merchant
McRae, D., butcher
McRae, W., general merchant
O'Kavanagh, John, shoemaker
O'Kavanagh, P., saddler
Thompson, D., carpenter
Thompson, D. & L., gunsmith

Glenvale.—A small Post Village in the Township of Kingston, County Frontenac, 9 miles from Kingston, the County Town, and 150 from Toronto. Daily stage to Kingston. Population 100.

Ayoist, Alfred, J.P.
Bumington, George, farmer
CARRUTHERS, JOHN,
Carruthers, Ellen J., teacher
Clark, George, hotel keeper
Curran, Robert, farmer
Davidson, J. O., farmer
Derbishire, Hiram, carpenter
Foster, Thomas, grocer
GIBSON, ROBERT, J.P., Postmaster and farmer
Gordon, Christopher, farmer
Heath, Richard, wagon maker
Jackson, Edward, flouring miller
Langwith, Joseph, Farmer's Inn
Lindsay, Mary, teacher
McCaugherty, Hugh, farmer
Moon, Robert, farmer
Orson, Thomas, farmer
Robinson, Henry, J.P.
Robinson, Lucy, teacher
Shorbine, J., teacher
Thirburn, Joseph and Robert, carpenters
Wartman, B., shingle maker
Wartman, C., dentist
Wartman, Peter, farmer
Weinechie, W., tinsmith

Glen William.—A Village on the River Credit, in the Township of Esquesing, County Halton, 1½ miles distant from Georgetown Station, on the Grand Trunk Railway, 14 miles from Milton, the County Town, and 30 miles from Toronto. Daily mail. Population about 500.

Ackert, George and Nelson, lime and stone dealers
Alexander, Thomas, wagon maker
Bell, Walker, farmer
Cook, Alfred, farmer
Cook, Daniel, farmer
Cook, John, general merchant
Forster, James, farmer
Grant, William, dyer
Herald, John, tailor
Hunt, Bradshaw & Brown, pump and bobbin manufacturers
Kerr, William, tinsmith
Lake, Rev. (Wesleyan)
Leslie, John, farmer
McClure, W., shingle maker
McMaster, William, general merchant
McMurchy, Thomas, cabinet dealer
Malloy, P. W., shoemaker
Murray, John, wagon maker
Roden, William, general merchant
Selway & Tredale, last factory
Shaw, Rev. (Episcopal Methodist)
Smith, J. & W., shingle maker
Standish, J., teacher
Sterrett, Alexander, farmer
Thompson, Joseph, shingle maker
Tweedle, Joseph, lumber dealer
Watkins, William, general merchant
WILLIAMS, CHARLES, Postmaster, J.P., manufacturer of woolen goods and lumber dealer
Williams, Joel, carpenter
Williams, Joseph, flouring mills

Goble's Corners.—A Post Village in the Township of Blenheim, County Oxford, 10 miles distant from Woodstock, the County Town, and 78 miles from Toronto. The Village is within a short distance of the Great Western Railway. It is surrounded by a good farming country and possesses several flouring and saw mills. Population about 500.

Bastedo, Mrs. E. J., teacher Union School
Brown, J. L., painter
Brown, William, butcher
Burns, James, J.P., farmer
Flannigan, William, teacher
Goble, George, blacksmith
Goble, J. G., farmer
GOBLE, W. L., Postmaster, gen mercht
Goble, W. L. & Sons, coopers, turners and painters
Kane, James, farmer
Kipp, James, general merchant
Kipp, Robert, J.P
Laycock & Bros., props. flouring mill
Lewis, Brothers, lumber dealers
Lucas, A., hotel keeper
McIntyre, David, agent G.W.R
Miller, John, farmer
Oliver, Robert, farmer
Palmer, David, carpenter
Patten, Rev. George, (Baptist)
Rains, John, farmer
Robinson, Robert, shoemaker
Rutherford, John, waggon maker
Selby, George, farmer
Shirk, Rev. W. B
Underhay, George, farmer
Walker, William, farmer and real estate agent
Ward, G. N. blacksmith

Glenmeyer.—A Post Office in the Township of Houghton, County Norfolk, 21 miles from Simcoe, the County Town. Average price of improved land $25 per acre.

Gavit, A., farmer
Harvey, Andrew, J.P., farmer
House, J., teacher
McCumber, Daniel, carpenter
Munsell, Nathan, carpenter
HEYER, G. E., Postmaster and farmer
Staght, James, farmer
Smith, J., farmer
Whitney, S., farmer
Willis, Robert, farmer

Goderich.—The County Town of Huron, Township of Goderich, is situated on Lake Huron, at the mouth of the Maitland River. It is a port of entry, has a good harbor, and being the terminus ofthe Buffalo and Lake Huron Railway, affords excellent facilities for the transportation of merchandise, grain, &c. to and from the Western States, by way of Chicago and Milwaukee. In summer it has daily communication by steamer with Detroit, Sarnia, Kincardine, Saugeen, &c. It is surrounded by a fine wheat growing country, which, with its fisheries, and the immense salt beds recently discovered, have added materially to the prosperity of the town. Distant from Stratford, 44 miles; Sarnia, 65; Toronto, 130; Buffalo, N. Y., 160. Money order office and Savings Bank. Population 4,500.

Acheson, William, saddle and harness maker
Acheson, & Smith, (George Acheson, R. B. Smith,) general merchants
Adams, David, merchant tailor
Adamson, Peter, County Clerk
Addison, James, bailiff
Allcock, Thomas, U. S. Consul
Amann, Martin, cabinet maker
Andrews, Thomas, butcher
Archibald, C. E., general merchant
Arthur, William, boarding house
Bain, W. R., barrister
Barrie, George, furniture dealer
Bates, George, cooper
Bell, David, (Shannon & Bell
Bennett & Stett, millers
Benton, J. C., grocers
Bingham, Edwin, fruit and confectionary
Bingham, William, painter
Bissett, George, carpenter
Brooks, James, tailor
Brophy, John, carpenter
Blake, John
Brough, Seckar, Judge County Huron
Buchanan, James, carpenter
Burns, William, cabinet maker
Butler, John, books and stationery
CAMERON, M. C., M.P.P., barrister
Campaigne, Edward, jailor
Campbell, Daniel, photographer
CASSADY, FRANCIS, boots and shoes (see adv)
Cattle, George, chemist and druggist
Clifford, Edwin, baker and confectioner
Collins, A., shoemaker
Cowdry, N. H., teller Royal Canadian Bank
COX., W. T., editor *Signal*
CRABB, CHRISTOPHER, J.P., general merchant
Craig, John, Steamboat Hotel
Cressman, Moses, wagon maker
Crichton, Miss A., dress maker
Dancy, Thomas, prop. salt works
Dark, Mrs. R., prop. Western Hotel
Dark, T. (Dark & Snell).
DARK & SNELL (T. Dark and William Snell) props. Dark's hotel.
Davis, G. N., tinsmith, stove dealer, &c.
Davison, John, barrister
DEAN, JOEL (Dean & Smart)
DEAN & SMART (Joel Dean and W. F. P. Smart) banking and exchange brokers (see adv)
DETLOR, J. C. & CO. (John C. and Thomas Detlor) general merchants
Detlor, J. V. (Rumball & Detlor)
Detlor, S. H. (Rumball & Co.)
DICKSON, ARCHIBALD, Postmaster
Dickson, James, Registrar County Huron
Dixon, Thomas, boots and shoes
Dobson, Isaac & Son, broom factory
Dobson, Stoddard, (I. Dobson & Son)
DONAGHY, WILLIAM, editor and prop. *Goderich Star*. (See adv)
Donogh, Andrew, proprietor North American Hotel
Donogh, John, proprietor Albion Hotel
Doty, D., Collector Customs
DOYLE, B., (Doyle & Squier)
DOYLE & SQUIER, (B. Doyle & W. R. Squier), barristers, etc.
DUNLOP, HUGH, merchant tailor and clothier
Edward, J. H., grocer
Elwood, Rev. E. L., (Church of England)
ELWOOD, GEORGE V., clerk Crown Land agency
ELWOOD, J. Y., barrister, etc., agent Standard Life Insurance Co
Ferguson, Charles, musician
Ferguson, Daniel, grocer
Finlay, James H., accountant Bank of Montreal
Fitz Williams, J., grocer
Fletcher, Charles, town treasurer
FRASER, ANGUS, Deputy Sheriff County Huron
Frazer, Donald, Deputy Registrar
Frederick, Isaac, watch maker and jeweler
Furse, Samuel, boots and shoes
GARDNER, H. & CO., hardware
Gibbons, Robert, M.P.P., Warden County Huron
Gooding, D. S., barrister, attorney, etc.
Gooding, J. K.
Gordon, Daniel, cabinet maker
GORDON, JOHN B., barrister, attorney, solicitor, &c
GRANDY, JOHN, agent sewing machines and musical instruments
Grant, George, groceries, wines and liquors
Graham, George, carpenter
Graham, E., grocer
HALDAN, JOHN, official assignee, general land and insurance agent, notary public, commissioner in B. R., &c.
HALDAN, J. F. C., barrister
Harris, John, general merchant
HAYS, WILLIAM TORRANCE, M.P.P., barrister
Hayes, James, grocer
Hazlehurst, B., auctioneer
Hick, Walter, carpenter
Hilton, George, butcher
Hincks, Ralph, proprietor Royal Canadian Hotel

HORTON, HENRY, grocer
HORTON, HORACE, insurance agent (see adv.)
HOSKER, EDWARD H., proprietor Maitland Hotel (see adv.)
HOWELL, HARVEY, manager Dominion Salt Works
Jessup, George, shoemaker
Johnson, E. L., photographer
Johnston, J. W., photographer
JOHNSTON, HUGH, Clerk County Court, Registrar Surrogate, Deputy Clerk Crown,
JORDAN, FRANCIS, chemist and druggist
Kay, W. & J., general merchants, agents American Express Company
Kerr, William, groceries, wines and liquors
Kirkbride, Alexander, blacksmith
Kydd, Thomas, clerk
LEFROY, ANTHONY, barrister
Lewis, Ira, barrister, crown attorney
Lizars, Daniel, Clerk of the Peace
Logan, Thomas, prop. woolen factory
Logan, William
Longworth, John
McCormack, B., merchant tailor
McDermott, Henry, barrister, master in chancery
McDONALD, JOHN, sheriff
McDougall, P. A., M.D.
McIntosh, Charles, mariner
McIntosh, J. C., general grocer
McKay, Angus, collector and assessor
McKELLAR, JOHN A., principal commercial academy.
McKidd, Rev. A., (Presbyterian)
McKenzie, G., general merchant
McKenzie, John, cabinet maker
McLean, Allen T., merchant tailor
McLean, M.D.
McLeod, John, wagon maker
McMath, William, blacksmith
McMicking, —, M.D.
McPherson, James, blacksmith
McVicar, Adam, mason
Macara, John, barrister
Marlton, Edward, shipbuilder
Marlton, Henry, shipbuilder
Martin, A., (Martin & Whitely)
MARTIN, GEORGE H., bakery (see adv).
MARTIN, ISAAC, prop. Union Hotel
Martin, William, saddler
MARTIN & WHITELY, carriage and wagon makers (see adv)
Middleton, William, carpenter
Miller, James, machinist
Mitchell, John, flour and feed
Moore, Elijah, builder
MOORE, LEWIS C. (Toms & Moore)
Moorhouse, Theodore J., books, stationery, &c
Moss, William, shoemaker
Nicholson, Malcolm, surgeon dentist
O'Dea, P., dry goods and groceries
Ord, L. W
Oster, John, barber
Nolan, Peter, carriage maker
NORTH AMERICAN HOTEL, Andrew Donogh, proprietor (see adv)
Parks, Robert
Parsons, George H., merchant
PENTLAND, SAMUEL, boots and shoes
PHARIS, J. W., Hotel keeper
POLLEY, A. M., livery and sale stables (see adv)
Pollock, Samuel, official assignee
Pollock & Johnston, (S. Pollock and T. Johnston, general merchant
Poole, Rev. Wm. H., (Wesleyan)
Radcliff, Richard, customs officer, agent Scottish Amicable Life Assurance Co
Ralph, John, stoves, tinware, &c
Reid, Harry, prop. Ontario House
Reed, Mrs., grocer
Richardson, W., agent Bank of Montreal
ROBINSON, WILLIAM, groceries and provisions.
Ross, A. M., agent Royal Canadian Bank, County Treasurer
Rumball & Co., (G. Rumball, J. V. Detlor and S. H. Detlor), forwarders, etc.
Runciman, James
Runciman, R., founder
Runciman, R. & Co., founders
SAUNDERS, JAMES, fish curer and dealer (see adv)
Saunders, James, tinsmith, plumber and stove dealer
Savage, W. M., general merchant
Seegmiller, Jacob, farmer
Seymour, W. & Co., (W. & B. Seymour) commission merchants, forwarders, etc.
SHANNON & BELL, (W. D. Shannon and D. Bell) groceries, wines and liquors
Shannon, G. C., M.D.
Shipwood & Strachan, (James Shipwood and D. C. Strachan), groceries, etc.
Sinclair & Walker, barristers, etc.
Sloane, Samuel, produce dealer
SMAILL, JAMES, architect
SMART, W. F. P., (Dean & Smart)
Smith, Abraham, merchant tailor
SNELL, WILLIAM, (Dark & Snell)
Snyder, Rev. P., (Roman Catholic)
Snyder, W., grocer, agent Montreal Telegraph Co.
SQUIER, W. R., B.A. (Doyle & Squier)
Stewart, William, dry goods
STORY, J. & J., hardware, tinsmiths
Stotts, William, saddler, livery stables
Sturdy, T., shoemaker
Sutton, John, dry goods
Swanson, George, carpenter
Thompson, Charles, proprietor Colborne Hotel
Tobin, M. J.,
TOMS & MOORE, (J. F. Toms, Lewis C. Moore) barristers, &c.
Trines, B., chief constable County Huron
TRUEMAN, G. M., auctioneer, land agent. (see adv)
Ure, Rev. R., (Presbyterian)
WADDELL, ANDREW, vessel owner
Watson, James, general merchant
Watson, L. W., dry goods and groceries
Western Hotel, Mrs. R. Dark, proprietor
Wetherall, Thomas, civil engineer
White, William, J.P
Whitely, R. J., (Martin & Whiteley)
WIDDER, CHARLES, Crown Land Agent and collector Inland Revenue
Williams, J. H., hair dresser
Wilson, George, farmer
Wilson, Mrs. E., milliner
Woodcock, E., clerk registry
Worden, William, produce merchant
Wright, J. J., proprietor Huron Hotel

Golden Creek.—A post office in the Township of Bosanquet, County Lambton, 30 miles from Sarnia and 170 from Toronto.

Cornell, S., teacher
Hunt, Rev. George, (Episcopal Methodist)
Kennedy, Allen, Postmaster, J.P., flouring mills

Goldstone.—A post Village in the Township of Peel, County Wellington, distant 24 miles from Guelph the County Town. Daily mail. Population about 50.

Close, Mark, carpenter
Coates, Milner, tavern keeper
Douvard, James, mason
FRANKLAND, THOMAS, Postmaster and general merchant
Greenley, James, carriage and wagon maker

Goodwood.—A post Village in the Township of Uxbridge, County Ontario, 25 miles from Whitby the County Town, and 35 from Toronto. Stage to Stouffville and Bloomington. Population about 100.

Armitage, David, hotel keeper
Barkey, Jacob, blacksmith
CHAPMAN, MICHAEL, Postmaster, gen. mercht.
Degeer, Charles, carpenter
Downwell, George, farmer
Dyke, John, saw mill proprietor
Field, George, farmer and auctioneer
Frazer, George, carpenter
Hamill, James, hotel keeper
Lehman, D. B., saw mill proprietor
McCullough, James, general merchant
Peterson, William, cooper
Sangster, John A., J.P., farmer
Sangster, J. A. & William, wood and willow ware
Shaver, John, shoemaker
Smith, Thomas C., teacher
Stapleton, Henry, steam saw mill proprietor
Stover, Abram, farmer
Wagg, John, farmer
Wagg, Joseph, farmer
Wagg, Thomas, farmer
Watson, W. B., farmer
Weighall, John, farmer

Gore's Landing.—A Post Office and Village in the Township of Hamilton, County Northumberland, N. R.
GABETIS, SARAH, Postmistress.

Gormley.—A Post Village situated in the Township of Markham, County York, 23 miles from Toronto, the County Town. Mails bi-weekly. Population about 80.

Brillinger, Peter, saw mill proprietor
Bruce, Robert, flour mill proprietor
Chebine, Andrew, saw mill proprietor
Collard, George, carpenter
Duncan, Alexander, blacksmith
Farmer, Thomas, planing mill proprietor
Fisher, Charles, shoemaker
Franey, William, hotel keeper
Giles, William, boot and shoemaker
GORMLEY, JAMES, J.P., Postmaster, &c.
Hendry, Thomas, blacksmith
Innes, Leslie, carpenter
Joice, John, blacksmith
Lewis, Thomas, saw miller
Marwood, William, tailor
Oliver, William, carriage and wagon maker
Quantz, George, storekeeper
Watson, John, general merchant

Gorrie.—A Post Office in the Township of Howick, County Huron (see Howick Village).

Gourock.—A Post Office in the Township of Guelph, County Wellington, 3½ miles from Guelph, the County Town, and 5 from Hespeler.

Blachford, Richard, innkeeper
Botterell, Thomas, farmer
Dooley, Martin, farmer
Green, Jonathan, farmer
Hearn, William, drover
Keogh, James, innkeeper
McGarr, Joseph, ropemaker
McGarr, Patrick, farmer
MEWHORT, JAMES, Postmaster, dry goods, groceries, wines, liquors, &c.
O'Farrell, Andrew, farmer
Snelling, George, farmer

Gowanstown.—A Village in the Township of Wallace, County Perth.
GOWAN, MRS. M. A., Postmistress.

Gower Point.—A small Post Village in the Township of Westmeath, County Renfrew, North Riding, distant from Pembroke, the County Town, 25 miles. Population about 100.

Carswell, Thomas M., J. P., Postmaster
Chambers, John, tailor
Mansell, Alfred
Wright, N.
Wright, Samuel, shoemaker

MUGRIDGE & LORIMER,

IMPORTERS OF

GROCERIES, WINES, LIQUORS,

AND MANUFACTURERS OF

CORN BROOMS,

HAMILTON, ONT.

AGENTS FOR DAWS' CELEBRATED ALE AND PORTER.

R, MILNE,

PHOTOGRAPHER!

HAMILTON. ONTARIO.

ALL KINDS OF PHOTOGRAPHS TAKEN IN THE BEST STYLE.

MR. MILNE has now one of the Finest Establishments in the Province; the Reception Rooms and Gallery being on the First Floor. From his long experience (18 years) in Hamilton, his work can always be relied on.

E. KRAFT,

IMPORTER, WHOLESALE AND RETAIL DEALER AND MANUFACTURER OF

SADDLES, HARNESS & HORSE CLOTHING,

TRUNKS, VALISES and BAGS,

OF THE LATEST AND MOST IMPROVED STYLES,

Hose, Military Equipments, &c

York Street, Sign of the Big Collar, near the Market,

HAMILTON, ONTARIO.

Gosfield.—A Village in the Township of Gosfield, County Essex, on Lake Erie, 32 miles from Sandwich, the County Town, and 32 from Windsor. Daily stage.

Atkinson, Rev. Thomas, (Wesleyan)
Alwarth, Edward, M.D
Barnett & Bashlan, shoemakers
Berlin, A. B., dentist
Broadwell, Joel, butcher
Branner. Abraham, broom maker
Cady, James, saddler
Clark, Rev. William, (Wesleyan)
Coats, Thomas, carpenter
Coatsworth, G. W., farmer
COATSWORTH, JOHN, J.P., Postmaster
Coatsworth, Solomon, carpenter
Cooper, Arthur, hide and leather dealer
Cooper, George, tailor
Craney, Thomas, shoemaker
Curtis, Reuben, cooper
Deming, Warren & Wate, general merchants
Drake, William H., M.D
Foster, George, broom maker
Fox, & Co., proprietors livery stable
Fox, Charles, farmer
Fox, J. M., lime and stone dealer
Fox, G. M., farmer
Fox, Hugh, hotel keeper
Fox, John W., hotel keeper
Greener & McVey, tinsmiths
Greenville, William A painter
Harris, H., baker
Harrison, Jason, shoemaker
Hart, Patrick, saddler
Herman, Joseph, cooper
Herrington, Rev. R., (Baptist)
Herrington, R. D., general merchant
Kennedy, Mrs., milliner, &c
Kennedy, William, druggist
King, James, notary public
King, Sidney, M.D
Lawless, Levi, hotel keeper
Longland, William, carpenter
Lypps, —, prop. lumber yard
Lypps, F., prop. flouring mill
McNutt, John, general merchant
Marks & Morse, soap makers
Malott, George, hotel keeper
Mallott & Wigle, props. flouring mill
Pike & Co., props. planing mill
Price, James, carpenter
Pulford, Alfred, wagon maker
Pulford, Edwin, wagon maker
Pulford, Frank, wagon maker
Scratch, A. M., general merchant
Scratch, Joseph, farmer
Stewart, Simon, hotel keeper
Thornton & Wigle, general merchants
Tuffelmire, George, shoemaker
Upcott, —, prop. lumber yard
Whittle, John, farmer
Wigle, Andrew, dentist
Wigle, A. M., farmer
Wigle, A. R., farmer
Wigle, Charles, farmer
Wigle, Daniel, lime and stone dealer
Wigle & Malott, lumber yard
Wigle, M. J., farmer
Wigle, J. S., hotel keeper
Wigle, James, carpenter
Wigle, John W., farmer
Wigle, Solomon, M.P.P., farmer
Wigle, S. S., farmer
Wigle, W., farmer
Williams & Cumiford, shingle makers
Woodbridge, A., general merchant
Woodbridge, Miss E., teacher
Woodiwis, John, cooper
Wye, James, shoemaker
Wye, R. C., wagon maker

Grafton.—A Village and Station of the Grand Trunk Railway, in the Township of Haldimand, County Northumberland, 7 miles from Cobourg, the County Town, and 77 from Toronto. Money Order Office. Population 300.

Aird, James, carpenter
Allen, E., agent G.T.R
Barnum, E., farmer
Beatty, William, farmer
Blacklock, John, tailor
Clitheroe, James, painter
Clitheroe, Miss, millinery, &c
Craig, Garvin, farmer
Doolittle, Samuel, J.P
Downie, H., shingle maker
Drummond, C., farmer
Fisher, J., farmer
Fraser, Charles, tailor
Fraser. William, shoemaker
Gillard, James & Son, general merchants
GILLARD, JOSIAH, Postmaster
Gillespie & Brothers, props, flouring mills
Godard, A. H., accountant
Gould, Abram, teacher
Greenwood, H. & G., manuf. woolen goods
Halliday, James, M.D
Hoyt, Asa, wagon maker
Hildreth, T. F., M.D
Hucheson, William, butcher
Johnston, Brothers, general merchants
Johnston, William, cabinet maker
Lawless, Thomas & Henry, general merchants
McCullough, Andrew, flouring mills
McDonald, W. H., hotel keeper
McFarlane & Co., distillers and rectifiers
Massy, J. G., flouring mills
Mulholland, John, farmer
Monroe, Miss, milliner
Niles, W. H., flouring mills
Patterson, William, hotel keeper
Reid, William, carpenter
Rogers, J. G., J.P
Rogers, R. Z., farmer
Rooney, John, foundry
Ross, Andrew, carpenter
Smith, Rev. John, (Presbyterian)
Spitsle, William, wagon maker
Standley, R. W., farmer
Stewart, John, farmer
Taylor, James, planing mills
Willoughby, William, M.D
Wilson, Rev. J., (Church of England)

Gosport.—A Post Office in the Township of Adolphustown, County Lenox, on Hay Bay, 18 miles from Napanee, the County Town.

Bogart, M. C., J.P.
Collins, Robert, J.P., farmer
GERMAN, GEORGE, J.P., Postmaster
German, G. M., farmer
Kelly, Rev. Thomas (Wesleyan)
Scott, Rev. William (Wesleyan)

Grahamsville.—A Village in the Toronto Gore, County Peel, 7½ miles from Brampton, the County Town, 22 miles from Mono Mills, and 20 from Toronto. Population 60.

Anderson, C., farmer
Armstrong, A., auctioneer
Bell, H., farmer
Bell, Robert, hotel keeper
Brown, John, farmer
Brougham, M. E., accountant
Clifton, Thomas, shoemaker
Dalton, W., farmer
De La Haye, A., M.D.
Dorsey, Thomas, wagon maker
Herbert, Andrew, painter
LAMPHIER, PETER, J.P., Postmaster and general merchant
McCaffrey, Robert, shoemaker
Mitchell, James, blacksmith
Payne, T., farmer
Philips, —, M.D.
Proctor, Henry, teacher
Sims, John, farmer

Grantley.—A Post Office in the Township of Grantley, County Dundas. 18 miles from Morrisburg, the County Town.

Brown, Aaron, mason
Bruce, George, P.L.S.
Carr, Alexander, carpenter
Carr, Alexander J., farmer
Carr, Henry, farmer
Carr, Hugh, carpenter
Carr, Jonathan, blacksmith
Carr, Thomas, lime burner
Casselman, P. A., farmer
Collins, James, farmer
Collins, Thomas, farmer
Gordon, Alexander, farmer
Munro, George, J.P., farmer
MUNRO, J. O., Postmaster and general merchant
Robinson, Z., teacher
Russell, Thomas, bricklayer
Sutherland, James, farmer

Granton.—A Village and Station of the Grand Trunk Railway, in the Township of Biddulph, County Middlesex, 20 miles from London, the County Town. Average value of land in vicinity, $45 per acre.

Armitage, James, lumber yards
Barron, William, telegraph operator
Blackwell, B., commission merchant
Brooks, John, wagon maker
Dearness, John, farmer
Dowryer, Michael, painter
Germyne, Henry, carpenter
Grant, N., commission merchant
Grant, A., farmer
Grant, J., farmer
Grant, James, telegraph operator, agent G. T. R. and Am. Ex. Co.
Grant, William, farmer
Hart, Rev. —, (Episcopal Methodist)
Hewit, Rev. — (Wesleyan)
Hodgins, Samuel, hotel and livery stable keeper
Findlay, Rev. Allen (Presbyterian)
Forman, C., farmer
Forman, G., farmer
Fulton, Thomas, carpenter
JAMIESON, JAMES, Postmaster, shoemaker
Leavitt, William, butcher, flour and provision store
Leavitt, William, farmer
McIntosh, Henry, carpenter
McIntyre, James P., hotel keeper
Mowbray, P., farmer
Murray, Matthew, tailor
Silley, Samuel, teacher
Stanly & Hodgins, general merchants
Stanley, R., commission merchant
Stewart, Alexander, saddler
Webb & Garrett, general merchants
Woodgate, J. R., M.D.

Gravenhurst.—A Village in the Township of Muskoka, District of Muskoka, beautifully situated on Lake Muskoka, and in the vicinity of the picturesque lakes Rosseau and Joseph. It is a favorite resort for pleasure seekers, abounding in game, and the lakes plentifully supplied with fish. The steamers Wenonah and Camilla call here during the summer months. Distant from Barrie 52 miles, and from Toronto 110. Population 100.

Brown, D., hotel keeper
COCKBURN, P., Postmaster
Fuller, S., general merchant
Harvie, J., livery stable keeper
Horton, J. B., hotel keeper
Horton, Miss, teacher
Knott, R., painter
Piercy, J., farmer
Pimbolt, George, agent *Wenonah* steamboat
Scott, John, J.P
Sharpe, J., farmer
Wright, D. farmer

Greenbank.—A Village in the Township of Reach, County Ontario, 20 miles from Whitby, the County Town, and 50 from Toronto. Improved land averages $40 per acre in the vicinity. Population 100.

Anderson, William, architect
ASHLING, JOHN, Postmaster
Bailey, John, wagon maker
Blake, William, teacher
Dusty, Edward, shoemaker
Ferguson, William, butcher
Hall, Henry, wagon maker
Murta, Robert, hotel keeper
Read, Rev. J., (Wesleyan)
Smith, Rev. B. J., (Primitive Methodist)
Vanevery, Rev. Mr. (Church of England)

Greenbush.—A Village in the Township of Elizabethtown, County Leeds, 40 miles from Brockville, the County Town. Population 100

Abbott, J. N., J.P., painter
Blanchard, A. W., farmer
Blanchard, Daniel, farmer
Blanchard, Daniel, wagon maker
Blanchard, Emery, farmer
Blanchard, Thompson, teacher
Codd, Richard, cooper
Connor, Thomas, shoemaker
Cook, Andrew, carpenter
Keoler, J. M., farmer
Kerr, G., farmer
Kerr, Miss, L., teacher
Kerr, R., farmer
Loverin, Norris, farmer
Loverin, Simeon, farmer
Mott, N., tailor
Patterson, John, farmer
Peer, Reuben, livery stable
Powell, Miss E., teacher
Robinson, William, lumber yard
Shetford, Henry, shoemaker
Smith, Thomas, carpenter
Taylor, George, shoemaker
WHITE, E. L., Postmaster, general merchant

Greenock.—A Village in the Township of Greenock, County Bruce, 8 miles from Walkerton the County Town, 130 miles from Toronto, and 20 from Kincardine. Improved land in vicinity $20 per acre. Stages to Walkerton, Seaforth and Kincardine. Population 100.

Black, Thomas, carpenter
Black & Munro, wagon makers
Bradin, A., blacksmith
Colter, James, farmer
Cunningham, Samuel, J.P., farmer
Dermid, Rev. M., (N. C. Methodist)
Forbes, A. G., (Presbyterian)
Grundy, William, blacksmith
Hawthorn, Samuel, hotel keeper
Hornell, William, general merchant
McDonald, John, accountant
McIntyre, William, plasterer
Montgomery, Hugh, farmer
MONTGOMERY, HUGH, Sen., Postmaster, J. P., general merchant
Montgomery, Hugh, jun., steam saw miller
Montgomery, James, farmer
Montgomery, Robert, hotel keeper
Pinkerton, Robert, J.P., farmer
Ritchie, J. B., farmer
Ritchie, P., farmer
Ritchie, William, carpenter
Rolston, Rev. D. D., (N. C. Methodist)
Stewart, Rev., (Baptist)
Trotter, Willirm, shoemaker
Wisser, W., shoemaker

Greenwood.—A Village in the Township of Pickering, County Ontario, 10 miles from Whitby, the County Town, and 20 from Toronto. Population 200.

Adamson, Samuel, brickmaker
Ballard, George, saw mill proprietor
Boddy, John, shoemaker
Byers, Samuel, flouring and grist mill proprietor
Clark, William, farmer
Doyle, Owen, proprietor British Arms Hotel
FULLERTON, ADAM, Postmaster, J.P. and M.D.
Graham, Robert, shoemaker
Green, Fred, J.P., farmer
Green, Samuel J., flouring and grist mill
Hill, Rev. — (Methodist)
Jackson, Edward, farmer
Lennon, Robert, cooper
Larkin, Patrick, farmer
McCann, Vere Ward, farmer
McKay, Alexander, tailor
McKittrick, Andrew, farmer
McKittrick, Eliza, milliner, &c.
McMurray, James, carpenter
McMurray, Thomas, farmer
McRaid, John, farmer
Meen, Frederick, general merchant
Meen, Frederick, telegraph operator
Mitchell, John, flouring and grist mill
Montgomery, J. R., insurance agent
Philip, Sylvanus, teacher
Ready, Patrick, wagon maker
Saddler, James, carpenter
Saddler, William, farmer
Shea, Henry, cooper
Snell, Samuel, carpenter
Somerville, Samuel, farmer
Slatter, Jacob, barrel, stave and hoop manufacturer
Sterling, James, general merchant
Sterling, Judith, hotel keeper
Stobbs, Rev. —, (Church of England)
Tate, Sophia, milliner, etc.
Wilson, George, farmer
Wilson, Richard, farmer

Green Grove.—Post office Thistletown (formerly McKaysville), a settlement in the Township of Vaughan, 15 miles distant from Toronto. Daily mail. Population about 80.

Bauldry, Alfred, carpenter
Fox, William, farmer
Hardy, James, sen., farmer
Hardy, James, jr., farmer
JOHNSTON, RICHARD, Postmaster
Nichol, Robert, farmer
Strong, James, farmer
Smithson, Thomas, farmer

Green Point.—A small Post Village in the Township of Sophiasburg, County Prince Edward.
ROBLIN, PHILIP, Postmaster

Greensville.—A Post Village in the Township of West Flamboro', County Wentworth, 7 miles distant from Hamilton, the County Town, and 1½ miles from Dundas Station, on the Great Western Railway. It has a good flour and grain trade. Mails daily. Population about 500.

Anderson, James, lime and stone dealer
Armstrong, James, hotel keeper
Ashbourne flouring and grist mills, J. Webster, prop
Ballantyne, Thomas, jun., cooper
Barr, Frederick, tailor
Betzner, Samuel, farmer
Brown, M., wagon maker
Clark & Langly, manufacturers of woolen goods
Cochnour, Jacob, saddler
Coulson, George, farmer
Fraser, Hugh, general merchant
Globensky, Lewis, cooper
Graham, James, cooper
Green, Abraham, farmer
Green, John S., farmer
Gurney, Charles, farmer
Higgins, Henry, wagon maker
Hore, F. W., saw mill and lumber dealer
Hume, Miss Mary, teacher
JOYCE, JAMES, Postmaster and general merchant
Lackey, John, weaver
McCarty, Charles, teacher
McCarty, Miss Eliza, teacher
McMasters, Charles, mason
Mann, W. M., lime and stone dealer
Morden, Jonathan, flouring and saw mills
Morden, M., farmer
Markle, E., hotel
Morin, T., blacksmith
Moxly, O., farmer
Peet, Thomas, carpenter
Perry, A., wood turner
Post, George, cooper
Ray, Francis, lime and stone dealer
Sanderson, M. paper mills
Snisdel, Joseph, clerk and auctioneer
Soper, George, carpenter
Steel, John, distiller
Steen, John, wood turner
Surarus, J. D., farmer
Thompson, William, mason
Town, James, distiller
Tunis, John, farmer
Vincent, Henry, engineer
Wales, James, flouring miller
Webster, J., Ashbourne Flouring Mills
Wilson, Joseph, tinsmith
Wishart, K., general merchant

Gresham.—A Post office in the Township of Bruce, County Bruce, 25 miles from Walkerton, the County Town. Average price of wild land in the vicinity, $6; improved, $12 per acre.

Austin, John, carpenter
Bowen, J., shingle maker
BROWN, G. J., Postmaster
McLeod, John, teacher
Matthewson, Rev. William, (Canada Presbyterian)
Mills, Richard, blacksmith
Pace, James, wagon maker

Gretna.—A Village in the Township of North Federicksburgh, County Lenox, 5 miles from Napanee, the County Town. Population 60.

Aylsworth, Rev. J. B., (Episcopal Methodist)
Cole, C. B., J.P.
Hambly, Samuel, farmer
Hough, Charles, butcher
Hough, Jacob, farmer
Hough, John, carpenter
Kelly, Rev. James, (Wesleyan)
Kinerley, Charles, lime and stone dealer
MELLOW, W. J., Postmaster and general merchant
Mellow, W., farmer
Miller, Samuel, farmer
Randall, J., farmer
Scott, Rev., (Wesleyan)
Williams, Edward, tailor
Withers, Daniel, farmer

Grey.—(See Cranbrook)—A Post office in the Township of Grey, County Huron.
LECKIE, JOHN, Postmaster.

Griersville.—A Post Village in the Township of St. Vincent, County Grey, 25 miles distant from Owen Sound, the County Town, and 120 miles from Toronto. Population about 150.

Brinkman, William, shoemaker
Brownell, Rev., (Wesleyan)
Byers, John, farmer
Gauld, Rev., (Presbyterian)
GRIER, ANDREW, Postmaster
McConnell, N., carpenter
McDonald, Miles, farmer
McKinley, Andrew, farmer
McLean, Robert, hide and leather dealer
Marshall, James, wagon maker
Mitchel, Henry, blacksmith
Mitchel, Robert farmer
Noland, Arthur, teacher
Rattray, Alexander, hotel keeper
Spike, Bryan, farmer
Stirling, D. & Co., general merchants
Taylor, William, farmer
Terry, George, blacksmith
Wright, G. W., M.D

Grimsby.—A Village and Station of the Great Western Railway at the junction of Forty-mile Creek with Lake Ontario, in the Township of Grimsby, County Lincoln, 17 miles from St. Catharines, the County Town, 18 from Hamilton and 46 from Toronto. The surrounding country is unsurpassed for fertility in the Province. All kinds of fruit are grown in great abundance. W. W. Kitchen, Esq., is extensively engaged in the manufacture of wine, turning out about 500 barrels of a very superior article per annum; the vineyard occupies 11 acres. Money Order office and Savings Bank. Population 1000.

Allison, R. H., wagon maker
Anderson, Charles, farmer
Anderson, H. H., farmer
Anderson, M. J., Collector Customs
Bouslaugh, W. H., saw mills
Brown, John, T. C., P.L.S.
Campbell, Daniel, master Grammar School
Chambers, J., blacksmith
Clarke, Rev. John S., (Wesleyan)
Cline, David P., baker
Cole, George, wagon maker
Cole, W. A., blacksmith
Fitch, J. D., chemist and druggist
Fitch, W., M.D.
Forbes, W., general merchant and insurance agent
Green, Dr., dentist
GRIMSBY MANSION HOUSE, A. Randall, prop. (See adv)
GRANT, JOHN H. & CO., foundry and agricultural implement manufactory. (See adv)
Gurney & Nelles, grist mills
Kitchen, Jacob, wine maker
Kitchen, W. D., farmer
KITCHEN, W. W., vine grower and wine maker (see adv)
Konkle, William, hotel keeper
Laboreau, Rev. W., (Roman Catholic)
Larin, John D., telegraph operator
Little, B. painter
Locke, Rev. J. H., (Wesleyan)
Looseley, E. D., tailor
McFarlane, A., farmer
McKay, A. J., collector
McNinch, John, shingle maker
Mabey, George, butcher and hotel keeper
Marlatt, P. D. hotel keeper
Mihell, E. M., tinsmith
Miller, W. H., blacksmith
Millward, W. E., M.D
Murray, Rev. J. G., (Presbyterian)
NELLES, H. E., Postmaster
Nelles, J. W. G., farmer
Nelles, P. B., miller
Nelles, S. A. & Co., produce dealers
NELLES, W. H., (John H. Grout & Co)
Nixon, D., farmer
Oman, C. C., wagon maker
Orr, Robert, station master G.W.R
Palmer, D. & Co., canned fruit
PALMER, E. J., general mercht and produce mercht
Petit, J. R., farmer
Petit & Muir, (H. A. & A. P.) props. cheese factory
Racey, C. S., generel agent
RANDALL, A., prop. Grimsby Mansion House Hotel (see adv)
Randolph, Ralph W., butcher, &c
REED, REV. CANON, (Church of England)
Smith & Vandusen, nurserymen
Soper, John
Spillett, W. S.,
Taylor, J. & J., groceries and liquors
Vandyke, John & George, wagon makers & blacksmiths
Westlake, George, saddler
Wilson, W. grist mill
Whittaker, S., shoemaker
Wilson, W., saw mills
Woolverton, C. E., nursery
Woolverton, A., M.D.
Woolverton, J., M.D.

Grovesend.—A post office in the Township of Malahide, County Elgin; distant 20 miles from St. Thomas the County Town.

Borten, George, farmer
Bordick, A. D., farmer
Chappison, Rev. D., (Wesleyan)
Lyon, C. M., farmer
Lyon, W. B., farmer
LYON, W. B., Postmaster
Morkle, R. L., farmer
Parks, A., shoemaker
Smith, Rev. W., (Wesleyan)

Guelph.—The County Town of Wellington, situated on the River Speed, a branch of the Grand River, in the Township of Guelph, was laid out by the late Mr. Galt, the projector of the Canada Company, in the year 1828. The situation was well chosen, being in the midst of a fine undulating country, high, dry and healthy. The town is a station of the Grand Trunk and the northern terminus of the Galt and Guelph branch of the Great Western Railway. It is connected with Fergus, Elora, Southampton, Owen Sound, &c., by stage. In the immediate vicinity are inexhaustible quarries of limestone, of which several of the public buildings are constructed. Commercially, Guelph will compare favorably with any inland town in the Province. The chief manufacturing establishments are: *Wellington Foundry*, Evatt, Inglis & Co., steam and water, 40 hands; *Guelph Steam Foundry*, Mills & Melvin, 30 hands; *Guelph Foundry*, Robertson & Sons, steam, 15 hands; *Guelph Mills* (flour and distillery), David Allan, steam and water, 20 hands; *Stewart's Planing Mills*, steam, 12 hands, capacity 600,000 feet per annum. *Raymond's Sewing Machine Factory*, steam, 40 hands, manufacturing 35,000 machines per annum. *Armstrong, McCrae & Co.*, extensively engaged in the manufacture of lamb's wool, hosiery, woolen goods, &c. Distant from Toronto 47 miles, Hamilton 30, Galt 14, and Owen Sound 85. Money Order office and Savings Bank. Population 6000.

Ainly, Richard, lumber merchant
Albig, John, merchant
Alexander, William, cabinet maker
ALLAN, DAVID, miller, distiller and rectifier (see adv.)
Allan, James D., miller
Allan, John C., machinist
ALLAN, WILLIAM, manager Guelph Mills
Allen, Robert, shoemaker
AMERICAN AND CANADIAN EXPRESS COMPANIES, John Grant, agent
Anderson, James, baker and confectioner
Anderson & Wilkie (George and William) grain and produce dealers
Andrews, Randall, agent and clerk Raymond's factory
Andrich, Adam, pork butcher
Archambault, Rev. S. B. (Roman Catholic)
Arms & Worswick (E. H. and Thomas) sewing machine manufacturers
Armstrong, Andrew, baker and grocer
ARMSTRONG, J. B., proprietor Excelsior Carriage Warerooms
Armstrong, William, blacksmith
ARMSTRONG, McCRAE & CO., woolen factors (see adv.)
Baine, George, fruit dealer
Baker, Alfred A., Clerk Division Court
Balkwill, George, miller
Ball, Rev. W. S. (Free Church)
BANK OF MONTREAL, E. Brough, manager.
Barclay, James, carpenter
Bauer, Joseph A., prop. Farmers' hotel
Beattie, G. (Galbraith & Beattie)
Beattie, Thomas, painter
Bell, Wood & Co. (William Bell, R. Bell, R. B. Wood and Robert McLeod), melodeon manufacturers
BERRY, HENRY, baker and confectioner (see adv)
Bish, P., dry goods
BLACK, GEORGE, prop. Dominion hotel
Blanchford, Thomas, shoemaker
BOND, JOHN M. & CO., hardware
Bookless, John, saloon keeper
BOULT, STEPHEN, planing mill prop.
BREADON, THOMAS, painter
Brennan, L. J., bookbinder
BRIDGEFORD, J. S., carpenter
Brill, James T., produce merchant
BRODIE, P. B., station master G.W.R.
BROUGH, E., manager Bank of Montreal
Brown, Thomas, boots and shoes
Brownlow, William, carpenter
Bruce, George, tailor
Bruce, George A., carriage maker
Bruce, G. & Sons, carpenters
Bucham, A. O., dry goods
BUNYAN, D., saloon keeper
Burgess, William, photographer
BURNS, ROBERT, grocer
Busby, Thomas, painter
Campbell, Christopher, tallow chandler
CAMPBELL, Dr. R., surgeon dentist
CANADIAN BANK OF COMMERCE, G. W. Sandilands, manager
Carl, Moses, butcher
Carrier, Charles H., shoemaker
Carroll, Edward, quarryman
CARROLL, E. & Co., grocers, wine and spirit merchants. (see adv)
Carthew, Edward, Collector of Customs G. W. R
Casey, Michael, proprietor Harp of Erin Hotel
CHADWICK, F. G., (Davidson & Chadwick)
Chance, Robert, merchant
Chipchase, George, saddler
Clark, William, M.D
Cochrane, Robert, cattle dealer
Coffee, Denis, prop. Wellington Hotel & wagon maker
Collins, R. H., veterinary surgeon
Colson, James W., tailor
Congalton, William, mason
Conieham, Joseph, conductor G. W. R
Conway, Patrick, shoemaker
Cook, John, boiler maker
Cooper, Edwin, County Auditor
Cooper, T. W., P. L. S.
Copp, Edwin, machinist
CORMACK, JAMES, merchant tailor and clothier
Couling, L., furniture dealer
COULSON, R. B., proprietor Coulson's Hotel, general stage office, &c
COWAN, W. B., M.D., homœopathic physician and surgeon (see adv)
Crawford, William, carpenter
Creichton, Alexander, cattle dealer
CRIDIFORD, JOHN, boots and shoes
CROFT, N., merchant tailor and clothier (see adv)
Cullen, Paul, cooper
Curtain, Jeremiah, cooper
CUTHBERT, ROBERT, watchmaker and jeweller
Dadson, Samuel, hatter
Darby, Henry, tanner
DAVIDSON, CHARLES (Davidson & Chadwick)
Davidson, John, prop. Guelph marble works
DAVIDSON, J. & T., woolen factors
DAVIDSON & CHADWICK (Charles and F. G.) insurance agents
Dawson, Peter, mason

Day, Daniel, mason
DAY, T. J., bookseller and stationer
DEADY, MARTIN, prop. Deady's hotel
Delabays, Rev. F. (Roman Catholic)
Desroche, William S., photographer
Dickson, David, grain merchant
Dobbie, J., millwright
Dobbie, Thomas, mason
Doran, M. J., grocer
Dudgeon, William, butcher
Duffy, Robert, cooper
DUNN, J. M., head master Grammar School
Eldredge, William H., distiller
Elliott, George, J.P.
ELLIS, THOMAS, prop. American Hotel
EVATT, FRANCIS, (Evatt, Inglis & Co)
EVATT, INGLIS & Co., props. Wellington foundry
EVENING ADVERTISER, J. Wilkinson, editor and proprietor
Ewing, James, teamster
Ewing, John, teamster
FEAST ALFRED, marble works
Fennell, Charles, butcher
Fenwick, Theodore, fruit dealer
Ferguson, Alexander, miller
Ferguson, Alexander, tailor
Ferguson, James, teacher
Frame, John, provision dealer
Fraser, G. B. & Co., dry goods
Fraser & Waterson, cabinet makers
FREEMAN & FREEMAN, (S. B. Freeman, Q.C. and G. O. Freeman) barristers, attorneys, &c
FURNESS, JOHN, conductor G.W.R
Galbraith, Francis, (Macklin, Galbraith & Co)
Galbraith, F. W., (Galbraith & Beattie)
Ganhan, Francis, grain merchant
Garland, Francis, hatter and furrier
GAY, JAMES, naturalist, taxidermist, and locksmith
Galbraith & Beattie, saddle and harness makers
GOLDIE, JAMES, prop. Peoples' Flour Mills
GORE BANK, William Smith, agent
Gouck, Douglas, painter
GOW, JAMES, Collector Inland Revenue
GOW, PETER, M. P. P
GOWDY & STEWART, lumber merchants
GOWDY, THOMAS, (Gowdy & Stewart)
GRAHAM, WM. K., (Trotter & Graham)
GRAND, EDWARD, wine and spirit dealer
Grange, Frank, Deputy Sheriff
Grange, George F., Sheriff County Wellington
GRANT, JOHN, agent Montreal Telegraph and American & Canadian Express Cos.
GREAT WESTERN HOTEL, Robert Oakes, prop.
GUELPH HERALD, George Pirie, editor and prop. (See adv)
GUELPH MERCURY, (McLagan & Innes) (See adv)
GUTHRIE DONALD, barrister attorney, etc.
Hadden, G. & A., (George and Alexander), general merchants.
Hales, John, butcher
Hall, John, contractor
Hall, Col. J. B.
Hall, J. W., barrister
HARRIS, JOHN J., baker and confectioner. (See adv)
Harvey, Edmund, chemist and druggist
Hatch, Henry, money broker, insurance agent, etc.
Hazleton, James, cabinet maker
HEATH, CHARLES, lumber merchant, flour and feed dealer
HEFFERNAN, D., proprietor Victoria Hotel
Heffernan Brothers, (Thomas and Joseph) dry goods
HEROD, GEORGE S., M.D.
HEWAT, WILLIAM, Treasurer Co. Wellington
Hewer, John, tanner and currier, prop. Crown Hotel
Higbee, C. H., exchange broker
HIGINBOTHAM, N., chemist and druggist
HOBSON, JOSEPH, P.L.S. and C.E.
Hogg, Hugh, flour and feed
HOGG, JOHN, dry goods
Hogg, Rev. John, (Presbyterian)
Holden, James, chemist and druggist
HOLLIDAY, THOMAS, brewer and maltster
Hood, George, cattle dealer
Hoover, William, cabman and livery
HORSMAN, JOHN, hardware, oils, &c
Hosken, William, librarian Mechanics' Institute
Hough, James, town clerk and treasurer
Howard, George, stoves, tinware, &c.
Howitt, John, M.D
Hunter, Mrs. John, Berlin wool and fancy goods
INGLIS, JOHN, (Evatt, Inglis & Co)
Ingram, Thomas, auctioneer
INNES, JAMES, (McLagan & Innes)
Jackson, A. M., (Thompson & Jackson)
Jackson, John, exchange broker
Jackson & Hallett, grocers
Jeanneret, Robert J., watchmaker and jeweler
JONES, WILLIAM, proprietor Red Lion Hotel
Kay, John, brass founder
Keables, M. A., foreman Raymond's sewing machine factory
Keating, Thomas, registrar
Kelly, Jonathan, chief constable
Kennedy, A. H. R., flour and feed
King, Walter, market clerk
KINGSMILL, WILLIAM, Postmaster
Kirkland & Millington, wagon makers
Knowles, W. S. G., auctioneer
Kribs, David, pump maker
LEMON, ANDREW, (Lemon & Peterson)
LEMON & PETERSON, (Andrew & Henry W.) barristers, attorneys, &c
LEWIS, JOHN L., general merchant
Lynch, James, Sheriff's bailiff
LYNCH, THOMAS H., proprietor Ontario Hotel
McCrae & Murton, grain buyers
McCulloch, James, Vinegar Works
McCURRY, P., (McCurry & Mitchell)
McCurry, William, surveyor
McCURRY & MITCHELL, (P. & Robert) barristers, attorneys, &c
McDonald, A., Judge County Court
McFarlane, Duncan, commission merchant
McGill, William & Co., general merchants
McGuire, E. W., M. D
McKenzie, James, book keeper
McLAGAN & INNES, editors and proprietors *Guelph Mercury*. (see adv)
McLAGAN, JOHN C., (McLagan & Innes)
McLeod, Robert, cabinet maker
McNeil, John, boots and shoes
MACKENZIE, ALEXANDER, book-keeper Guelph Mills
Macklin, William (Macklin, Galbraith & Co.)
Macklin, Galbraith & Co., co-operative store
Marriott, Henry, saddler
Marriott, William, grain buyer
Marshall, W., photographer
MARTIN, E. R., attorney, insurance agent, &c
Martin, John, teacher
MASSIE, JAMES & Co., wholesale and retail grocers
MELVIN, ROBERT, (Mills & Melvin) Mayor

MEREDITH, C. & T., (Charles & Thomas) grocers
Metcalf, Henry, saddler
MILLER, JOHN, prop. Queen's hotel
Miller, W., wagon maker
MILLS, W. H. (Mills & Melvin)
MILLS & MELVIN,(W. H. & Robert) iron founders
Mimmack, Joseph, barber and hairdresser
Mitchell, John, carpenter and builder
MITCHELL, ROBERT (McCurry & Mitchell)
Mitchell, William, merchant tailor
Molton, D., tanner
MONTREAL TELEGRAPH COMPANY, John Grant, agent
MORRIS, EDMUND, manager Ontario Bank
Murphy, P., prop. Albion hotel
Murton, George, jun., (A. Thompson & Co.)
Naismith, Daniel, ham curer
Naughton & Goughton, grain dealers
Newton, Edwin, official assignee, insurance agent
Newton, Henry, prop. G. T. R. Hotel
Nicholls, William, hotel keeper
O'CONNOR, EDWARD, barrister
O'CONNOR, WILLIAM, billiard rooms
O'Neil, James, prop. Anglo-American Hotel
OAKES, ROBERT, prop. Great Western Hotel and saloon
ONTARIO BANK, E. Morris, manager
Orton & Clark, physicians and surgeons
Oxnard, George A., station agent
Pallister, Thomas, prop. Commercial Hotel
PALMER, REV. ARCHDEACON, St. George's
Palmer & Lillie, barristers, &c.
Parker, Abel, shoemaker
Parker, Robert, wagon maker
Peacock, James, butcher
Perry, D., commission merchant
PETERSON, HENRY W. (Lemon & Peterson)
PETRIE, A. B., chemist and druggist
PIRIE, GEORGE, editor and prop. *Guelph Herald*
Prest & Hepburn, boots and shoes
RAYMOND, CHARLES, sewing machine manuf.
Reynolds, William, Deputy Registrar
Roberts, A., potash manufacturer
ROBERTSON & SONS, props. Guelph foundry
Rodger, George, blacksmith
ROMAIN, C. E., Inspector of Excise for London District
Rose, L., produce and commission merchant
Ross, William, freight agent, G. T. R.
SANDILANDS, G. W., manager Canadian Bank of Commerce
SAUNDERS, T. W., Police Magistrate
SAVAGE, DAVID, watchmaker and jeweller
SAXON, J. F., barrister, insurance agent, &c.
SAYERS, THOMAS, house and sign painter
SHARPE, C. & A., seedsman
Shaw, Samuel (A. Thompson & Co.)
Sherlock, Rev. F. (Roman Catholic)
Shewan, Christopher, merchant
Shields, Malcolm, dyer and scourer
SILVER CREEK BREWERY, George Sleeman & Co., proprietors
Simpson, William, baker
SLEEMAN, GEORGE, & CO., proprietors Silver Creek Brewery
SMITH, GEORGE, Town Collector
Smith, Thomas, photographer
SMITH, WILLIAM, manager Gore Bank
Smith & Metcalf, saddlers
Snelling, William, prop. eating saloon
Snider, W. M., grain buyer
Steele, William, carpenter
Stein, William, cooper
STEVENSON, WILLIAM, prop. Maple Bank Nursery
STEWART. JAMES, (Gowdy & Stewart)
Stewart, John, grain buyer
STEWART, R. & J., props. planing mill (see adv)
STEWART & THOMSON, dry goods and clothing
STIRTON, DAVID, M.P.P
STONE, F. W., stock dealer
Stovel, Edward, pump maker
Sully, John, blacksmith
SUNLEY, WILLIAM, stoves, tinware, &c
SUNLEY, N. & Co., props. Guelph Nursery
SUMER, W. H., prop. Cosmopolitan Shaving Saloon
TAYLOR, WILLIAM G., veterinary surgeon
Thompson, Robert, (Thompson & Jackson)
Thompson & Jackson, (Robert & A. M.) land, loan and general agents
THORNTON, J. B., books and stationery
THORP, JAMES, prop. livery and sale stables
Tovell, N., carpenter and undertaker
TROTTER, R., (Trotter & Graham)
TROTTER & GRAHAM, (R. & W. K.) dentists (see adv)
VICARS, REV. JOHNSTONE, (Church of England)
Von Hoxar, H. G., teacher of languages
WALD, VALENTINE, prop. Bay Horse Hotel
WALKER, CHARLES, teacher
Walker, Hugh. oyster depot
Ward, George, grocer
Watson, John, baker
WEBSTER, JAMES, solicitor
Webster, John, stoves, tinware, &c.
Webster, William, flour and feed
WELLS, ARTHUR, deputy Postmaster
WEST, JOHN, cattle dealer
Wilkinson, George, grocer
WILKINSON, J., editor and proprietor *Evening Advertiser*
Woods, John A., grocer
Workman, William, grocer
Wright, Samuel, baker

Griffith.—A small Post Village in the Township of Griffith, County Renfrew, 60 miles from Pembroke, the County Town. Population about 120.

Adams, James, farmer
Adams, Thomas, farmer
ADAMS, W. H., Postmaster
Adams, W. H., jun., farmer
Joyce, Thomas, farmer
McCook, Edward, farmer
Marsellar, Peter, farmer
Varin, Joseph, farmer

Guysboro.—A Post Office in the Township of Middleton, County Norfolk, 25 miles from Simcoe, the County Town.

Ball, Charles, farmer
Ball, Lewis, butcher
Brim, William, farmer
Dean, R. C., farmer
DOYLE, J. W., Postmaster, general merchant and shingle manufacturer
Doyle, J., hotel keeper
Garnham, Henry, farmer
Garnham, Robert, farmer
Garnam, S. K., steam saw mill
Jefferson, David, farmer
Johnson, W. B., shingle maker and saw mill
Ostrander, John, J.P., grist mill
Richardson, John, farmer
Weaver, Richard, steam saw mill prop.
Weston, John, farmer

Hagersville.—A Post Village in the Townships of Oneida and Walpole, County Haldimand, 9 miles from Cayuga, the County Town, and 23 from Hamilton. Money Order office. Population about 200.

Almas, David, stage proprietor
Baptie, John, tailor
Boyer, Henry, tailor
Giles, John, wagon maker
Glindon, Richard, blacksmith
Graham, Richard, blacksmith
HAGER, RICHARD, Postmaster and farmer
Harrison, William, shoemaker
Hemstreet, Benjamin, innkeeper
Kenner, John, blacksmith
Lewis, John, grocer
Lewis, Lewis, carpenter
Lewis, Thomas, carpenter
McCardy, James, cabinet maker
McDonald, A., innkeeper
Proud, R. H., general merchant
Pyne, Thomas, M.D.
Seymour, Joseph, wagon maker
Turnbull & Amos, merchants
Walters, L. T., tailor

Haldimand (Byng Post Office).—A Village on Sulphur Creek, in the Township of Dunn, County Haldimand, distant from Cayuga, the County Town, 18 miles, from Toronto, 60 miles. Stages to Dunnville and Port Dover. Average price of land $50. Population 200.

Aikins, William J., J.P.
Armour, Matthew, miller
Band, Robert, miller
Blair, Thomas, tailor
Brown, Edward, constable
Brown, George, J.P.
Cokley, Samuel, prop. Byng Hotel
Davis, John, cooper
Drake, John, wagon maker
Drake, Thomas
Fite, Henry, carpenter
Foy, Rev. Thomas, (New Connexion)
Hamilton, T. Q., teacher
Hammond, John, lime manufacturer
Hannah, James, shoemaker
Lyons, Samuel, shoemaker
Murdy, Robert
Ramsay, Francis
Scott, George
Secord, John, constable
Sheehan, Albert, carpenter
Sheehan, T., grocer
THOMSON, J., Postmaster and general merchant
Thomson, William, carpenter

Half Island Cove.—A Post Office in the County of Guysboro'.

DIGDON, JOHN, Postmaster.

Haliburton.—A Village in the Township of Dysart, County Peterboro, beautifully situated on the shore of Lake Kashagawigamog, one of the most picturesque of the numerous small lakes of Central Canada. The Township is one of ten, the property of the Canadian Land Company, Stages bi-weekly to Peterboro 70 miles. Population 60.

Austin, W., carpenter
Cashmer, W. brickmaker
Croston, J., shoemaker
Dover, F., general agent
Dover, J., general merchant
Garrett, A., general merchant
Hohand, James, hotel
Lucas & Co., shingle makers
Lucas, W., grist and saw mill prop.
STEWART, R. C., Postmaster
Wood, W., tinsmith
Young, J., general merchant

Halloway.—A Village in the Township of Thurlow, County Hastings, 10 miles from Belleville, the County Town. Stages daily to Belleville. Population 40.

Barnum, S., proprietor Halloway Hotel and livery stable
Bennet & Co., butchers
Creery, William, blacksmith and wagon maker
Falkner, M., farmer
Fisher, M., farmer
Griffin, M., farmer
Hamilton, M., farmer
Hopkins, J. P., Postmaster and general merchant
Kimmerly, M., farmer
Morden, Miss, teacher
Parks, J., farmer
Welbourne, William, farmer

Hall's Corners, (Binbrook Post Office.)—A Village in the Township of Binbrook, County Wentworth distant from Hamilton, the County Town, 13 miles, from Toronto 53 miles. Average price of land $40. Population 150.

Aikins, William, farmer
Bayley, George, cooper
Bayley, Thomas, cooper
Barlow, Albert, wagon maker
Barlow, Richard, J.P.
Bell, D., teacher
Bell, William, teacher
Bigger, R. H., M.D.
Bunton, John, general agent
Carle, John S., prop. Franklin House
Cooper, James, boiler maker
Edmunds, John, miller
Fletcher, George, insurance agent
Fletcher, Robert, teacher
Flock, John, farmer
Gawley, James, wagon maker
HALL, HENRY, Postmaster and general merchant
Harney, Charles, farmer
Hoey, James, auctioneer
Johnston, G. W., teacher
Lellett, Robert, shoemaker
Marshall, Samuel, farmer
Moore, James, farmer
Russell, James, M. D.
Shaw, Thomas, teacher
Simpson, —, grocer
Stafford, Theodore, saddler
Wickett, Robert, prop. Union Hotel
Woolger, John, farmer
Wright, Charles, farmer
Wright, William, teacher

Hall's Bridge.—A Post Office in the Township of Harvey, County Peterboro', East Riding.
HALL, JOHN, Postmaster.

Hamburg.—A Post Office in the Township of Fredericksburg, County Lennox.
FRASER, A. D., Postmaster.

Hamilton.—One of the chief Cities of the Province of Ontario, and the judicial seat of the County of Wentworth, is beautifully situated on Burlington Bay, the Western terminus of Lake Ontario. It was laid out in 1812 and occupies a plateau of elevated ground winding round the foot of Burlington Heights, which form the back ground of the City; the distance between the Heights and the Bay is about two miles, and on the area thus included stands, in point of population, wealth and importance, the second City in the Western Province. Burlington Bay is a beautiful sheet of water, navigable in all parts to within a few feet of the shore, forming one of the safest and most commodious harbors on the Lakes There are several lines of Steamers in the summer, plying regularly between the City and Montreal, and intermediate ports. The Great Western Railway, from Suspension Bridge to Windsor, has its offices and machine shops here, and the Company has recently erected extensive rolling mills for the purpose of manufacturing its own rails, employing in the aggregate about one thousand workmen. The head office of the Gore Bank is stationed here, and the Bank of British North America, Montreal, Ontario, Royal Canadian, and Canadian Bank of Commerce, have branches here; some of the largest wholesale an manufacturing establishments in the Province are located here. On the rising ground approaching the mountain are a number of elegant residences with grounds beautifully laid out and tastefully ornamented. The City is well supplied with water and gas. The Desjardines Canal connects Hamilton with Dundas, and has a navigation of about 4 miles in length. This is a port of entry. Post office, Money Order and Savings Bank. Distant from Niagara Falls 45 miles, London, 76 Toronto by rail 39, Windsor 183, and from Montreal 378. Population about 26,000.

CITY CORPORATION.

Mayor—James E. O'Reilly.

R. W. Kerr, Chamberlain; George McKay, assistant do.; Thomas Beasley, City Clerk; Alfred H. Hills, assistant do.; Alexander Stuart, tax collector; D. Dawson, assistant do.; John Moore, license inspector; C. Smith, city messenger; William Haskins, city engineer and manager water works; A. Rutherford, assistant do.; R. Ralston, water rate collector; S. McNaier, inspector of weights and measures; J. Cahill' Police Magistrate; R. Davis, Chief of Police; W. T. Sunley, Police Clerk. Thomas Tindill and Peter Balfour, Assessors; R. N. Law and J. J. Mason, Auditors; J. A. P. McKenna, Chief of Fire Brigade; J. Hastie, Street Inspector and Health officer; J. McCracken, high Bailiff; J. Amor, caretaker of Fire apparatus.

CITY COUNCIL.

St. Patrick's Ward: J. E. O'Reilly, Mayor, James Mullin and John Winer. St. George's Ward: John Mitchell, G. Mills and George Murison. St. Andrew's Ward: Robert Chisholm, Hutchinson Clark and D. B. Chisholm. St. Mary's Ward: Kenny Fitzpatrick, William Edgar and George Sharpe. St. Lawrence Ward: Robert Kelly, Robert Nisbet and Patrick Crawford.

COUNTY OFFICERS.

Township of Glanford, Alexander Bethune, Reeve. Township of Beverley, John Clement, Reeve, W. C. Merriam, Deputy Reeve. Township of East Flamboro, Thomas Stock, Reeve, Matthew Burns, Deputy Reeve. Township of West Flamboro, Thomas Miller, Reeve, Matthew Peebles, Deputy Reeve. Township of Binbrook, George Fletcher, Reeve. Township of Barton, R. R. Waddell, Reeve and Warden, Thomas Lawry, Deputy Reeve. Township of Saltfleet, A. D. Lee, Reeve, A. G. Jones, Deputy Reeve. Town of Dundas, Robert McKechney, Reeve; George Bickell, Deputy Reeve. Village of Ancaster, Alonzo Egleston, Reeve, John Heslop, Deputy Reeve. James Kirkpatrick, County Treasurer; D. C. O'Keefe, County Engineer; G. S. Counsell, County Clerk.

EDUCATIONAL.

Upper Canada Institute for the Deaf and Dumb, Dundurn Castle: Board of Commissioners, Rev. Dr. Ormiston, chairman; Rev. E. Ryerson, Judge Logie, the Mayor, E. Stinson, John McKeown, George Ryal, M.D. Secretary of the Board of Medical Superintendents; J. B. McGann, resident Superintendent, James T Watson, J. J. G. Terrill, instructors. *Wesleyan Female College*—Edward Jackson, President; Dr. C. McQuesten, M.D., Vice-president; Joseph Lister, Treasurer; Rev. S. D. Rice, Governor; Miss M. E. Adams, Principal; Rev. W. P. Wright, Augusta M. Adams, Miss A. L. Mason, Miss Maria O. Allen, Miss Ellen Hardie, Teachers; German, Rev. G. Goepp, B.A.; French, Mdlle S. Higgs; Fine Arts, Misses Ellithorpe and Reid. Music, R. S. Ambrose. *Loretto Convent*, Mount St. Mary, Hamilton; under the superintendence of the ladies of Loretto, Rev. Mother J. M. Stanislaus, Superioress. Grammar School, Head Master, J. M. Buchan, M.A.: second Master, E. G. Patterson, M.A.; English Master, Thomas McKee. Central School; Archibald Macallum, M.A., Principal: in connection with this institution are nine Primary or Ward Schools, all under the immediate charge of the Principal. Roman Catholic Schools: Park Street and John Street Schools under the charge of the Sisters of St. Joseph; Peel Street School, Andrew Doyle, Principal.

CHURCHES.

Christ Church, (Church of England,) James Street, Rev. J. G. Geddes, M.A., Rector; Rev. T. S. Cartwright, Curate; services 11 a. m. and 7 p. m. Church of the Ascension, (Church of England,) Hannah Street, Rev. John Hebden, M.A. Rector; services 11 a. m. and 7 p. m, (Church of England,) Emerald Street, Rev. Dr. Neville, Rector; services 11 a. m. and 7 p. m. St. John's, (Church of England,) King, corner Queen street, Rev. J. G. D. McKenzie, M.A. St. Andrew's, (Church of Scotland,) James street, Rev. Robert Burnet, minister, services 11 a.m. and 7 p. m. Knox's Church, (Canada Presbyterian,) corner of James and Henry streets, Rev. A. B. Simpson, minister; services 11 a. m. and 6:30 p.m. Central Presbyterian Church, corner of McNab street and Maiden Lane, Rev. W. Ormiston, D.D., pastor; services 11 a.m. and 6:30 p.m. McNab Street Presbyterian Church, Rev. David Inglis, pastor; services 11 a.m. and 6:30 p.m. Congregational Church, corner of Hughson and Henry streets, Rev. Thos. Pullar, pastor; services 11 a.m. and 6:30 p.m. Baptist Church, Park street, Rev. George Richardson, pastor; services 11 a. m. and 6. 30 p.m. Wesleyan Methodist, King corner Wellington streets. Centenary Church, Main street, between James and McNab, Rev. John Potts, superintendent, and Rev. G. H. Bridgman; services 10 a.m. and 6:30 p.m. New Connexion Methodist, Main street, near Nelson, Rev. Charles McKelvey; services 11 a.m. and 6:30 p.m. Wesleyan German Church, Nelson, corner Rebecca streets, Rev. Charles Allum; services 10 a.m. and 6:30 p.m. Primitive Methodist Church, Gore street, Rev. Walter Reid; services 10½ a.m and 6.30 p.m. Methodist Episcopal Church, John street, Rev. J. Gilray, pastor; services 10.30 a.m. and 6.30 p.m. Evangelical Association; Church on Market street, Rev. Augustus Spies; services 10 a.m. and 7 p.m. Mountain Mission; services at 2 p.m., pastors various. Jewish Synagogue, King street west, Mr. Groos, president, Mr. Roos, vice-president; services, 8 a.m. 4.30 p.m., and 6.30 p.m. Church of St. Mary of the Immaculate Conception; Rt. Rev. John Farrell, bishop.

BANKS.

Bank of British North America: King, between James and Hughson, W. N. Anderson, manager, James S. Lockie, accountant. Bank of Montreal, King street; W. J. Buchanan manager, T. J. Tate accountant, Merchants' Bank of Canada, James, corner of Main street; James Bancroft manager, Charles Crookhall, accountant. Ontario Bank, King street east; Robert Milroy manager, C. C. Holland accountant. Royal Canadian Bank, James street: Henry McKinstry, agent, J. Ellis Lancely, accountant. Canadian Bank of Commerce, King, near John street, Charles R. Murray, manager, W. Roberts, accountant. Gore Bank, King street; Samuel Reid, manager.

INSURANCE COMPANIES.

Canadian Life Assurance Company: capital $1,000,000; President, John Young; vice-president, John Ferrie; manager, A. G. Ramsay. Victoria Mutual Fire Insurance Company of Canada: George H. Mills, president; Levi Lewis, vice-president; W. D. Booker, secretary and treasurer. Canada Farmers' Mutual Fire Insurance Company: Thomas Stock, president; Wm. Macklem, vice-president; P. Street, secretary and treasurer.

CUSTOM HOUSE.

Custom House, situated on the corner of Stewart and McNab streets, William H. Kittson, collector, Wm. Beatty, surveyor, C. R. M. Sewell, chief clerk.

POST OFFICE.

Situated on James street, opposite Merrick street, Edmund Ritchie, Postmaster; E. Ritchie, assistant postmaster; Henry Colbeck, money order clerk.

MISCELLANEOUS.

City Hospital, foot of John street: Charles O'Reilly, M.D., C.M., physician; T. Luckens, superintendent. *House of Refuge*, Cherry street; William Skinner, superintendent. *Hamilton Orphan Asylum*, Park street, under the care of the Sisters of St. Joseph: Sister Mary Phillip, superioress. *Hamilton Board of Trade*, King street east: President, John Stuart; vice-president, Matthew Leggat; secretary, William MacKay. *Hamilton Gaslight Company*: President, John Young; vice-president, Sheriff Thomas; manager, T. McIlwraith. *Hamilton Water Works*: William Haskins, manager; Adam Rutherford, assistant; Robert Ralston, collector. Office, City Hall Building. *Hamilton and Gore Mechanics' Institute*, James street: Thomas McIlwraith, president; Judge Logie, vice-president; Alexander Rutherford, superintendent.

ABBS, REV. GEORGE, editor *Christian Advocate*, Ferguson avenue
Abraham, Charles F., produce and commission merchant, 56 King east
Adam, James, plumber, steam and gas fitter, Hughson, between King and King William
Adams, Miss A. M., teacher Wesleyan Female Coll.
Adams, Miss M. E., principal Wesleyan Female Coll.
Adams, Robert W., barrister, attorney and solicitor, James, opposite Gore
Ætna Insurance Company, Hartford, W. F. Findlay, agent, James, opposite Gore
Ætna Life Insurance Company, Hartford, James Garvin, agent, 50 James n
Aitchison, W. & D., box manufacturers, Bond nr King
Allan, David, flour and feed, 9 & 11 York
Allan, William, contractor, Concession bet James and McNab
Allan & Co., builders, Rebecca, bet John & Catherine
Allen, Benjamin, broker (second-hand) 116 King e
Allum, Rev. Charles (German Wesleyan) 87 Rebecca
AMBRIDGE, T. A., broker, insurance agent, and issuer of marriage licenses, King bet James and McNab
Ambrose, Robert S., professor of music, Wesleyan Female College
Ambrose, William, barrister, attorney and solicitor, 16 King east
AMERICAN EXPRESS COMPANY, J. D. Irwin, agent, James, opposite the Gore
Amery, John F. F., B.A., private school, Temperance Hall, McNab, corner King
Ancaster Knitting Company, office 2 King west
Anderson, James, carpenter, McNab nr Cannon
Anderson, William, pump maker, Grove, bet Liberty and Wellington
Anderson, William J., butcher, City Market
ANDERSON, W. N., manager Bank of B. N. A., s s King
ANGUS, J. & J., hats, caps, furs and straw goods, 56 King w
Appleyard, Thomas, building stone dealer, Tyburn corner Walnut
Armitage, William, second-hand broker, corner King and Caroline
ARMSTRONG, CHARLES, shipping agent, Hughson, between Main and King
Armstrong, Isaac, wholesale china, glass, and earthenware, 20 York, bet McNab and Park
Armstrong, Peter, waggon maker, King east, bet Walnut & Wellington
Armstrong, Walter, house, sign and ornamental painter, cor Main and Cherry
Armstrong, John, hotel keeper, s s Market Square
Arthur, Colin, butcher, City Market
Arthurs, James, hotel keeper, Merrick, s s bet James and McNab
Ash, Isidore, furrier and fur dyer, 33 King west
Ashbaugh, F. A., wholesale and retail grocer, s s Market Square
Askins, A. H., civil engineer G. W. R
Atchison, William, retail grocer, Napier, bet Caroline and Hess
Atchison, W. & D., props. planing mills, Bond, bet King and Main
Atkinson, Mrs., dealer in sewing machines, 71 King west
Atkinson, Joseph, house, sign and ornamental painter, Wellington, near Willson
Atkinson, William, basket maker, 71 King w
Atlantic Mutual Life Ins. Co., J. W. Wilson, agent King, cor John
Attwood, M. W., watches, clocks, jewelry, and musical instruments, Royal Hotel blgs, James
AUSSEM, J. H., wholesale and retail baker and confectioner, Florence Block, King w (see adv)
Austin, Mrs. E., boarding house, Merrick, bet Park and Bay
Axford, George, butcher, n s Pearl, cor King
Aynsley, James J., boots and shoes, King e, bet Nelson and Walnut
Bagwell, John B., corner Park and Market
Baine, John W., hardware, James opposite Market
Baker, James, pork dealer, City Market
Balfour, Peter, carpenter, Market near Bay
Ball, F. A., insurance agent and secretary and treasurer Western Permanent Building Society
Ballantine, R. M., news and periodical depôt, James s of Post Office
Bampfylde, Charles, flour and feed, John bet Augusta and Catherine
BANCROFT, JAMES, manager Merchants' Bank of Canada
BANK OF BRITISH NORTH AMERICA, W. N. Anderson, manager, s s King, bet James and Hughson
Bank of Montreal, s s King bet James and McNab
Banner of Faith, published monthly, printed at *Spectator* office
Barber, E. & Co., tobacco manufacturers, King e bet Cathcart and Wellington
BARBOUR, CHARLES J., shirt manufacturer (see adv)
Barker & Lemessurier, house, sign and ornamental painter, Main bet McNab and James
Barlow, William E., carpenter, 52 John s

BARNARD, P. B. & H., dry goods, millinery, 34 King w
Barnes, George & Co., books, &c., James cor Mkt Sq
Barr, John, barrister, attorney and solicitor, James
Bastedo, Walter, furrier and fur dyer, Wellington cor King
Bastien, H. L., boat builder, Phelan's boat house
Bateman, William, baker and confectioner, King n e Cathcart
Bates, James, M.D.. Gore bet Hughson and John
Bates, William, second hand broker, 118 King e
Batty, Benjamin, watches, clocks and jewelry, 40 King w
BAUER, HENRY, grape wine manufacturer, Main bet James and Hughson (see adv)
Bauer, Leopold, Ontario Brewery, Catharine bet East Bay and Base Line
Beardmore, George L., leather and findings, King bet James and McNab
BEARMAN, F. W., prop American Hotel, King cor Charles (see adv)
Beasley, Richard S., pork dealer, York bet Bay and Caroline
BEASLEY, THOMAS, city clerk, office City Hall
Beatty, O., retail grocer, James cor Wilson
Beatty, Thomas, hotel keeper, s e cor Main and John
Beck, George, prop. Crystal Palace Brewery, King cor Margaret
Beckett, C., prof. of music, n s Henry nr Hughson
Becket, William, fruit and confectionery, 64 James
BECKET, F. G. & CO., founders and machinists, James, nr Simcoe (see adv.)
Beer, Frank, butcher, King, east of Walnut
Beer, John, baker and confectioner, e s James, nr Lind
Bell, John, & Co., Burlington Brewery, Catherine, corner Tyburn
BELLING, B. M., watches, clocks and jewellery, James, nr Main (see adv.)
Belnap, N. M., hotel keeper, John nr King William
Benner, Richard, insurance agent and commission merchant, Wentworth Chambers
BEVIER, DENNIS, livery and sale stable, 77 King west (see adv.)
Berry, John, ice dealer, w s John, nr Hospital
Best, Andrews, & Co., auctioneers and commission merchants, King, corner John
Bible, Robert, coal and wood dealer, Main, corner Charles
BICKLE, T. & SON, wholesale druggists, 6 King e
BIGELOW, ALBERT, wholesale china, glass, and earthenware, Hughson, bet Main and Tyburn
BILLINGS & TURNER, wholesale tobacco manufacturers (see adv.)
Billings & White, physicians and surgeons, James corner Henry
Billington, John, boots and shoes, n s Merrick, bet Park and Bay
BILTON, HENRY W., soda water manufacturer, Market, nr McNab
Bingham, A., stove, tin, copper and sheet iron manufacturer and dealer, McNab, between King and Market
BINNY, ANDREW (Buchanan & Co.) res Victoria Terrace, King
BIRELY, N. F., shipping agent, Brock nr Bay
BIRELY & CO., vinegar manufacturers, James, bet Peel and Augusta (see adv.)
BIRGE, C. A. & M. B., wholesale cigar and tobacco manufacturers, 48 James n
Bishop, J. B., tin, copper, sheet iron, &c., King William, e of Hughson
Blake, William, butcher, City Market
BLACK, DANIEL, proprietor Club House, e s James n of P. O. (see adv.)
Blaicher, Peter C., druggist, John, south of Peel
Blake & McCauley, retail grocers, Peel, cor Cherry
Blanchford, John, undertaker, McNab bet King and Main
Bland, John H., barber and hairdresser, 8 Hughson n corner King
BLANDFORD, HENRY, picture frame manufacturer, 59 James n (see adv)
Bliss, Horace C., patent medicines, Wellington bet Henry and Little Gore
Blum, Christopher, butcher, King cor Park
Blythe, Thomas A., P.L.S., s s Bold bet James and McNab
Boase, Mrs. Jane, retail grocer, Caroline cor Napier
Bogart, D. A., dentist, Hughson cor Rebecca
BOICE, WILLIAM & CO., importers of fancy goods, 3 King e
Bolingbrooke, Charles cabinet maker, 90 King w
Bond, James, butcher, City Market
Bond, Silas, butcher, City Market
BOOKER, W. D., sec. and treas. Victoria Mutual Fire Insurance Company, James
Bowden, Aaron, brick maker, Canada nr Garth
Bowers, J., pork dealer, York bet Park and Bay
Bowman & Howe, sewing machine agents, James opp Mechanics' Hall
Bowron, A. & Son, stove, tin, copper and sheet-iron manufact'rs and dealers, King William nr James
BOYCE, D. R., U. S. consular agent, office at G. W. R. station
Boyd, David, cooper, 10 John n
Boyd, Thomas, grocer, King William cor John
Boyd, Thomas, trunk maker, cor King William and John
BRADSHAW, JAMES, grocer, James opp Market
Brandford, Henry, gilt and stained moulding, 59 James n
Brandum, B. R., barber and hairdresser, 54 John s
Brayley, James, machinist and blacksmith, top of mountain
Brazener, E. L., horse collar maker, 120 King e
Brennen. Michael, sash, door and blind manufactory, rear 10 John n
Bridgewood, George, carriage builder, Tyburn near Hughson
Bridgman, Rev. George H., M.A., (Wesleyan), Maiden Lane
Briers, Thomas, house, sign and ornamental painter, e s Catherine bet Gore and Henry
BRIGGS, G. C. & SONS, wholesale druggists, King Willam, nr James
BRITISH AMERICA ASSURANCE CO., (Fire & Marine,) A. F. Forbes, agent, cor James and King William
British America Insurance Co., fire department, E. Ritchie, agent, Post Office
Britt, Edward, boots and shoes, York, bet Bay and Caroline
BRONSON, S., manager Royal Hotel, James
Brodwell, J. W., accountant, N. Hammond
Brookes, Charles, retail grocer, York bet Caroline and Hess
Browne, E., wharfinger, Royal Mail Line, Brown's Wharf
Brown & Bautz, lithographers, King William corner James
BROWN, GILLESPIE & CO., wholesale grocers, King corner James
BROWN, W. & CO., booksellers and stationers, 46 James n

Bruce, Alexander, barrister, attorney and solicitor, Canada Life Assurance Co's. Buildings
Bruce, John M., barrister, attorney and solicitor, 3 King w
Bruce, Magnus, clothier, 7 James n
BRUCE, WILLIAM, Commercial College, James opposite Gore
BRUCE, JOHN A. & CO., seedsmen and florists, 52 King w
BUCHAN, J. M., M.A., head master Grammar School
BUCHANAN, HON. ISAAC, (Buchanan & Co.), res Auchmar House
BUCHANAN, JOSHUA G., local editor *Spectator*, bds Merrick nr Park
BUCHANAN, PETER T., (Buchanan & Co.), res Auchmar House
BUCHANAN, W. J., manager Bank of Montreal
BUCHANAN & CO., dry goods and groceries, (wholesale) King, cor Catherine
Buckingham, William, butcher, City Market
Bull, Hon. Harcourt B., h Hughson
BUNTIN, GILLIES & CO., wholesale stationers, 23 King e
Burdett, Joseph, brush maker, 35 King w
Burgess, John, professor of music, Hughson, between Tyburn and Peel
Burness, George, & Co., Royal Canadian Livery Stable, 79 James
Burnet, Rev. Robert, pastor St. Andrew's (Church of Scotland)
Burns, Henry, barber and hairdresser, 24 York, nr Park
BURNS, ROBERT, head clerk G.W.R., h Catherine
Burridge, James, pork dealer, McAllister's block, York
BURROW & STEWART, malleable iron founders, Caroline between Miller and York
BURROWS & BROTHER, auction and commission merchants, Merrick, opposite Market
Burton, George W., Q.C. (Burton & Bruce)
BURTON & BRUCE, barristers, attorneys and solicitors, Canadian Life Assurance Co.'s Buildings, James
Butcher, Robert, carpenter, Nelson, between East Market and Rebecca
Caddy, Captain J. H., artist, Main, between Charles and McNab
Caddy, J. St. V., Provincial Land Surveyor, Wentworth Chambers
CAHILL, JAMES, Police Magistrate, James
CALDER, JOHN (McInnes, Calder & Co.)
Campbell, Alexander, retail grocer, York, bet Park and Bay
Campbell, George, wagon maker, King e, between Walnut and Wellington
Campbell, Mrs. Jane, boarding house, King, between Caroline and Bay
Campbell, John, curer of hams and bacon, James, between Main and Tyburn
CAMPBELL, R. & CO., hollow ware enamellers, Mary Street Foundry
Campbell, William, potter, Garth nr Duke
Campbell, W., Clerk of Assize
Canada Christian Advocate, Rev. G. Abbs, editor, John nr King
CANADA FARMER'S MUTUAL INSURANCE CO., Commercial Buildings, James
CANADA LIFE ASSURANCE COMPANY, A. G. Ramsay (F. I. A.) manager, James, nr Main, Isaac Mills, agent
CANADIAN BANK OF COMMERCE, C. R. Murray, Manager, King cor John
Canadian Coal Oil Company, (wholesale) 17 King w
Canning, George, carpenter, 11 Wellington
CAREY, WILLIAM, proprietor Robinson Hall, Market Square
Carlisle, George, carpenter, Caroline bet Napier and York
Carmichael, John W., boots and shoes, King William bet Hughson and John
CARPENTER, E. & Co., importers of fancy goods, 39 King w
Carrigan, Mrs., Hellen, fancy goods, 10 King w
Carruthers, John, flour and feed, 2 King William
Carruthers, Miss, milliner, 67 King w
Case, William J. A., M. D., King cor Walnut
CASSELLS, WALTER G., Gore Bank
Catchpole, George, copper plate printer, 8 Rebecca
Chadwick, John A., dry goods, millinery, &c., John nr King
Chambers, D., plasterer, Bay nr Concession
Chambers, Rev. L. C., (Methodist Episcopal)
CHAMP, WILLIAM S., paymaster G. W. R
Chapman, William M., undertaker, 23 King w
CHARLTON, B. E., vinegar manufacturer, cor King and Wellington
CHARLTON, JAMES, general agent Great Western Railway
Cherrier & Bro., wholesale and retail grocers, s s Market Square
CHILMAN, ISAAC C., wholesale baker and confectioner, King bet Bowery and Caroline
CHISHOLM, D. B., (Chisholm & Lazier) (see adv.)
Chisholm, Robert, contractor, McNab bet Concession and Colborne
CHISHOLM, WILLIAM, lumber dealer, James cor Colborne
CHISHOLM & LAZIER, (D. B. Chisholm & S. F. Lazier, L.L.B.) barristers, attorneys, &c., Lister's buildings, James
CHITTENDEN, C. S., dentist, King e Corby's blk
City of Glasgow Life, R. Benner, agent, Canada Life Assurance buildings
Clark, John & C. O., commission merchants and insurance agents
Clark, Hutchinson, architect and civil engineer, 23 Hughson
Clarke, Thomas, pork dealer, e s James bet Stinson and Barton
Cleary, Mrs. M. A., boarding house, John cor Gore
Clohecy, Thomas, trunk manufacturer, 6 York
Clucas, William, builder, s s Miles bet Caroline and Hess
Cockbin, Thomas H., barber and hairdresser, McNab bet Cannon and Mulberry
Cochrane, Josiah, barber and hairdresser, 41 King w
Cochren, William I. & Co., importers of wines and liquors, McNab nr King
Colbeck, Henry, money order clerk P. O.
Colvin, John, proprietor billiard parlor and sample rooms, 8 King w
Colvin, Patrick, grocer, Hughson cor Wood
COLVIN, PETER, saloon, w s McNab bet King and Market
Commercial Union Assurance Co., T. C. Livingstone agent, Wentworth Chambers
Commercial Union of England, J. J. Mason, C. R. Murray and W. G. Crawford, city agents
Conley, Peter, boots and shoes, 14 King William
CONNECTICUT MUTUAL LIFE INSURANCE CO., Hartford, Conn., N. Hammond, agent, Commercial bdgs, James (see adv)
Connolly, Patrick, plasterer, Little Market nr Lock
Connor, James, dyer and scourer, 77 James

Cook, John B., butcher, City Market
COOK, MRS. WILLIAM, proprietress Cook's Hotel, 64 and 66 King w (see adv)
Cook, William, house, sign and ornamental painter, Vine nr McNab
Cooper, Christopher, grocer, King cor Queen
Cooper, H. G. & Co., carriage builders, Bond bet King and Main
Cooper, R. C. & Co., wholesale and retail grocers, McNab bet King and Market
Co-operative Association, groceries, s s Market square
Copeland, George, rope and twine manufacturer, Wellington bet Henry and Barton
COPP & BROTHER, stove founders and dealers in stoves and tinware, 15 John n
Cosmor, Robt., boots and shoes, York bet Park Bay
Coumbs, George, plasterer, 70 Rebecca
Counsell, Charles M., manager Stinson's Savings' Bank
Counsell, George S., county clerk, h Catherine
Court House, Main, bet Hughson and George
Courtenay, John, dry goods, millinery, &c., Market square
Coutts, Andrew, livery and sale stable, Main nr John
Cox, John, retail grocer, King e
COX, JOHN, photographer, 8 King e (see adv).
Craftsman, The (Masonic), semi-monthly, published by T. and R. White, *Spectator* office
CRAIGIE, JAMES, retail grocer, 72 King e
Craigie, William (Freeman & Craigie)
CRAMPTON, JOHN, general freight agent G.W.R.
Crawford, John, leather and findings, cor East Market and Nelson
Crawford, Patrick, alderman, Elgin
Crawford, W. G., commission merchant, Royal Hotel Buildings, Merrick
Creech, Richard, hotel keeper, Hughson s Main
Creed, James, butcher, King bet Cathcart and Wellington
Cricketers' saloon and restaurant, Thomas Gillesby, prop., Market nr Park
CRICKMORE, CHARLES G., barrister, &c., Commercial buildings, James
Crocket, R. & J., silver platers, n e cor McNab and King
Crockford, John, secondhand broker, John nr Peel
Crooker, T. M., M.D., James bet Main and Tyburn
Crossley, John, dry goods, millinery, &c., James cor King William
Crowther, W. T., professor of music, Market bet Park and Bay
Cuff, Robert C., pork dealer, 60 Market Shed
Cummings, James, Canadian Oil Co., h Main near Wellington
Cunningham, McKichan & Co., paper bag manufacturers, Charles between King and Main
Curry, William, retail grocer, Walnut cor Peel
Curtis, W. R., cigars and tobacco, 66 King w
Cusack, William, boots and shoes, Mulberry between James and McNab
Cuzner, John, hides and wool, 10 York
Dallas, Mrs. J., boarding house, 48 Hughson
Dalley, Edwin, retail grocer, York bet Queen and Ray
Dalley, Edwin, wholesale druggist, s s York bet Queen and Ray
Dallyn, Charles, barber, John near King
Dallyn, J. E., proprietor Great Western Hotel, James corner Murray
Dallyn James, bellows maker Murray bet McNab and James
Dampier, Richard G., Deputy Registrar, Surrogate Court
Darrow, John, livery and sale stable, Rebecca between James and Hughson
Davidson, Alexander, artist, James corner Main
Davidson, John, boarding house, Bay bet Market and York
Davies, John T., pork packer, (Isaac Atkinson, manager), Wentworth nr G. W. R
DAVILLE, T. W., wholesale and retail grocer, 70 King w (see adv)
DAVIS, D., M.D., Merrick bet James and McNab
Davis, William, house, sign and ornamental painter, John bet Lind and Barton
DAVIS, JOHN H. & CO., commission merchants, King e, bet James and Hughson
Davis, Ralph, chief of police
Dayfoot, P. W. & Co., boots and shoes, 52 King e
Day & McComb, marble cutters and dealers, Merrick corner Bay
Debus, George, boots and shoes, James n of Mulberry
Dennison, Jonathan, hotel keeper, Bay cor Cannon
Devlin, James A., M. D., Park bet Merrick and Vine
Dewey, Daniel O., ice dealer, King bet Bowery and Caroline
Dewey, John, saloon and restaurant, Hughson bet King and King William
Dicker, William, boots and shoes, n s King bet Mary and Nelson
Dillon, James, retail grocer, John bet Union and Wilson
Dillon, John, retail grocer, Bay n of Caroline
Dingle James, butcher, John St. Market
Dingle, Joseph A., butcher, City Market
Dodd, William, hotel keeper, McNab bet Park and Merrick
Dodman, James, retail grocer, cor Caroline & Hunter
Dodson, Miss, milliner, 62 King w
Dodson, James, retail grocer, York cor Ray
Dodsworth, John H., cabinet maker, York cor Hess
Doherty, Thomas A., coffee and spice mills, n s Catherine bet Henry and Lind
Donahoe, John, retail grocer, 10 John s
Donahoe, Mrs. J., milliner, 8 John s
Donnelly, G. J., M. D., head of Walnut
Doran, William, retail grocer, King bet Nelson and Cathcart
Doly, John, carriage axle manufacturer, York bet Bay and Caroline
Dow, David, plasterer, Caroline bet Main and Maiden Lane
Dow, Robert, plasterer, Little James w of Queen
Drake, James, butcher, City Market
Drenian, Mrs. Ann, retail grocer, 20 Hughson
Drysdale, Alexander, upholsterer, McNab cor Vine
Dudbridge, Benjamin, retail grocer, Elgin nr Henry
Duff, John, retail grocer, York bet Caroline and Hess
Duffy, Thomas, hotel keeper, McNab cor Merrick
Duggan, T., M.D., president Western Permanent Building Society
Duncan & Galloway, commission merchants, s s Mkt Square
Dunphy, James, hotel keeper, Cannon cor McNab
Dunstan, R. Jewell & Co., manufacturers' agents, Royal Hotel Buildings
Duval, Henry, barrister, King bet John and Hughson
Easson, Allan, broom manuf., King cor Caroline
Easter, Samuel, hotel keeper, 36 James n
Eastwood, J. & Co., booksellers and stationers, 16 King opposite Fountain
ECCLESTONE, W. E., wholesale confectionary manufactory, 10 King e
ECKERSON, LUTHER, photographer, 7 James n (see adv)

Eckhardt, Edward, brewery, Western Limits
Edgar, David, carpenter, York corner Locomotive
EDGAR, WILLIAM, chief clerk, general agency office, G. W. R
Edgar, William, lumber dealer, Caroline cor York
Edgecomb, O. W., house, sign and ornamental painter King cor Catherine
Edinburgh Life, Isaac Mills, agent, Wentworth Chambers
Edwards, Charles P., boots and shoes, 88 King w
Egan & Bartindale, dry goods, millinery, 12 James n
Egan & Jeffery, hats, caps, furs and straw goods, 8 King e
Egener, F. & C., billiard parlor and saloon, King bet Catherine and Walnut
Eichhorn, Max, professor of music, Hess cor King
Elms, E., boots and shoes, Hughson cor Tyburn
Etna Fire Insurance Co. of Dublin, John Clark & Co. agents, John corner King
Evans, Daniel, merchant tailor, 89 James n
Evans, Robt., commission merch,t, Royal Hotel Blk
Evans, Thomas, second hand broker, 91 King e
Evans, William, hotel keeper, York near Bridge
Fairgrieve, John, commission merchant, McNab bet King and Market
Fairweather, John, carpenter, Main bet Bond and Charles
Farley, John, stoves, tin, copper, and sheet iron manufacturer and dealer, McNab bet King and Market Square
Farmer, William, plumber, steam and gas fitter, 98 and 100 James n
Farrell, Right Rev. John (Roman Catholic Bishop,) Bishop's Palace, Sheaffe
Faulkner, Joseph, builder, Broadway cor Pearl
Faustmann, Ernest, vinegar manufacturer, John bet Rebecca and Gore
Fearman, Frederick W., commission merchant, McNab nr Market
Fearnside, Edward C., real estate agent,, e Market bet Stephen and Ashley
Fell, Henry K., watches, clocks and jewelry, s s Mkt Square
FELL, WILLIAM, copper, steel, and wood engraver s s Market Square. (see adv)
FERGUSON, J. W., barrister, (Martin & Ferguson) King, cor James
FERGUSSON, JOHN W., M. D., (Homœopathist) Gore bet James and Hughson
FERGUSSON, JOHN W., M. D., editor *Messenger*
Ferrie. John, vice president Canada Life Assurance Company, James
FIELD & DAVIDSON, saddle, harness and trunk makers, 18 James n
Fielding, Joseph, hats, caps, furs and straw goods, King cor Bond
Fields, John C., leather and findings, 32 King w
FILGIANO, T. LE. P., dentist, n e cor James and King. (see adv)
FINDLAY, WILLIAM F., accountant, insurance agent, official assignee, &c., James, opp the Gore. (see adv)
Finley, C. J., hotel keeper, McNab cor Burlington
Fitch, John, hotel keeper, Burlington Beach
Fitzgerald, William, hotel keeper, King opp Charles
Fitzpatrick & Bro., house, sign and ornamental painters, 33 York
Fleming, John, retail grocer, Catherine cor Barton
Fletcher, George, china, glass and earthen ware, John bet King and King William
Fletcher, George, coal oil and lamps, John bet King and King William
Fletcher, Joseph, boots and shoes, York, bet Bay and Caroline
Flook, William, hotel keeper, s s Stuart opp G.W.R. station
Forbes, Alexander, potash manufacturer, Barton cor King
FORBES, A. F., stock broker and insurance agent, cor James and King William
Forbes, F. J. B., auction and commission merchant, Anglo American Hotel Block
Ford, James, hotel keeper, 45 James north
Forrest, James, hotel keeper, Bay bet Murray and Stuart
FORSTER, A. M., manufacturer boiler compound, Stuart bet Mary and Catherine
Forster, G. J. & Co., wholesale grocers, wine and spirit merchants, cor King and Charles
Fossier, Julius, prof. of music, John bet Catherine and Maria
FOSTER, CHARLES, merchant tailor, King corner McNab
Fowkes, Thomas, dry goods, millinery, &c., 11 King William
Foyster, John, hotel keeper, James cor Burlington
Francis, William H., barber and hair dresser, Hughson nr *Times*'office
Fraser, P. & Co., china, glass and earthenware, James cor King
Fraser, William, grocer, 9 John s
Freeborn, Thomas, house, sign and ornamental painter, cor Willson and Elgin
FREEMAN, S. B., Q.C., (Freeman & Craigie)
Freeman & Brother, grocers, e s James bet Henry and Lind
FREEMAN & CRAIGIE, barristers, &c., Main bet James and Hughson
Freeman & Mahony, boots and shoes, 26 King east
Frier & Dale, wholesale dry goods, King bet McNab and Charles
Furlong, Moses, hotel keeper, foot of James
FURNER, G. H. & Co., millinery, (wholesale) D. McInnis' Block, King
Furnival, Thomas George, merchant tailor, 85 James
Gage, Robert R., barrister, King corner John
Gaines, Joseph H., barber, 24 King w
Galbraith, D. B., commission agent, h s s Main cor Cherry
Galbraith, John, patent medicines, Hughson corner Augusta
Galbraith & Co., hats, caps, furs and straw goods, (wholesale), King bet James and McNab
Gardner, George, butcher, City Market
Gardner, John, fancy goods, King between Bond and Bowery
Garret, James S., produce and commission merchant, Wentworth Chambers
Garrett, John & Co., wholesale boot and shoe manufacturers and dealers, King nr Bank of Montreal
Garvin, James, insurance agent, 50 James n
Gates, F. W. & Co., wholesale dry goods, Commercial Buildings, King w
Geddes, Rev. J. G., M.A., rector (Christ Church), John between Lind and Henry
Geddes, W. A,, barrister, Wentworth Chambers
Getz, George, watches, clocks and jewelry, 22 York
GIBSON, JOHN M., barrister, Wentworth Chambers (see adv)
Gildea, Charles T., grocer, King corner Pearl
Gildon, Henry, grocer East Market corner Nelson
Gillesby, Thomas, proprietor Cricketers' Saloon and training stables
Gillesby, William, flour and feed, w s John s of King

GILLESPIE, GEORGE H., (Brown, Gillespie & Co.)
Gillespie, Hugh, grocer, McNab cor Wilson
Gillies, William, grocer, King corner Pearl
Gilmore, William, boots and shoes, 1 John n
Gilmour, Wm., commission merch't, James, opp. Gore
Gilray, Rev. James, (Methodist Episcopal), John
Glackmeyer, Mrs. E., private school, Park n e cor Sheaffe
Glass, Mrs., boarding house, Bay bet Sheaffe and Colborne
Glassco., W. H. & Son, hats, caps, furs and straw goods, wholesale, corner King and Hughson
Goepp, Rev. Godfrey, B.A. (German Lutheran), Hess nr King
GOERING, JOHN W., saloon & restaurant, 53 John n
Gordon, Robert, carpenter, Wellington bet Peel and O'Reilly
Gordon, William, cooper, n s King William bet Hughson and John
GORE BANK, Samuel Read, manager, King, cor Hughson
Gore District Mutual Life, D. Wright, agent, James n
Gorvin, John, boots and shoes, James opp Gore
Gould, D. A., confectioner, 64 James
Grant, W. W., sail loft, Bay, bet McCauley and Burlington
GRANT & MIDDLEWOOD, props. Spring Brewery, office Bay cor Mulberry
Gray, Robert, merchant tailor, James nr Main
Grayson, George, steel spring maker, Bond bet King and Main
Green, Alfred J., brush maker, 16 and 18 John n
Green, John, fancy goods, King bet Mary and Nelson
Green, John W., watches, clocks, & jewelry, 28 King w
Green, Richard, grocer, Bay cor Little Main
GREEN, W. M., accountant, Hughson nr Main
Greening, Benj., wire mills, Peter cor Hess office York
Greer, Daniel G., real estate agent, King bet James and Hughson
Greer, J. H., Registrar of County Court
Gregory, S. E., commission merchant, 35 King e
Grell, Lorenzo, lager beer saloon, 10 John n
Griffith, Henry, boots and shoes, 82 King e
Griffin, John, fruit and confectionery, John opp wood market
Gross, Rabbi L., Catherine
GROSSMAN, AUGUSTUS, dealer in piano-fortes, 61 James n (see adv)
Grossman, Peter, music and musical instruments, 61 James n
GROVER, LUTHER, wholesale cigars and tobacco, 51 James n (see adv)
Gunner, Wm., leather & findings, ss Market square
GURNEY, E. & C., founders and machinists, e s John n bet King William and Rebecca
GURNEY, WARE & CO., scale makers, 88 James n, office John bet King William and Rebecca
Haigh, Richard, bookbinder, *Spectator* buildings, cor Main and Hughson
HAMILTON CITY & WENTWORTH COUNTY GAZETTEER AND DIRECTORY, (Annual). C. E. Anderson & Co., Publishers. H. McEvoy, Compiler. Directory Branch, *Daily Telegraph* Office, Toronto. (see adv.)
HAMILTON EVENING TIMES, (daily and weekly) C. E. Stewart & Co., proprs., Hughson (see adv)
Hamilton, John M., M. D., R. N., Bay cor McNab
HAMILTON POWDER COMPANY, Benjamin Clark, Secretary, 2 King w
Hamilton, A. & Co., wholesale druggists, King cor James
Hancock, Joseph, flour and feed, cor John and Pearl
HAMMOND, N., commission merchant and insurance agent, Commercial building, James. (see adv)
Hancock, William, builder, York bet Pearl and Lock
Hannan & Bro., stoves, tin, copper and sheet iron manufacturers and dealers, John nr King Wm.
Hardiker, John, commission mercht & broker, James
HARDING, HENRY, plumber, steam and gas fitter, James cor Rebecca
Hardy, Charles, provision dealer, York cor McNab
Harkin, John, hotel keeper, s s Market Square
Harper, Andrew, butcher, City Market
Harris, Henry, butcher, John Street Market
HARRIS, JOHN W., manager *Times* office, Hughson
HARRIS, WILLIAM, baker and confectioner, s s Market Square
Harris, G & Son, bent stuff manufacturers, cor Bay and Stuart
Harrison, Andrew, grocer, cor James and Barton
Harrison, Edward, flour and feed, 12 John s
Harrison, Henry, grocer, John s
Hartford Fire Insurance Company, A. McKeand, agt 9 James n
Hartford Live Stock Insurance Company, McKenzie & McKay, 9 King e
Harvey, John, commission merchant, 11 King e
HARVEY, STUART & CO., wholesale grocers, 21 King e
HASKINS, WILLIAM, city engineer and manager of water works
Hawkins, George D. & Co., hoop skirt manufacturer, 54 King w
Hearn, William, grocer, King cor Lock
Hebden, Rev. John, M. A., rector (Church of the Ascension) Hannah
HEFFERNAN, PATRICK, saloon and restaurant, 90 King e
Henderson, D., proprietor Station Hotel, Stuart opp Depot
Henderson, Robert R., grocer, Bay bet Main and Little Market
HENDRIE, & Co., railway cartage agents, King cor McNab
Henery, John & Co., boots and shoes, 62 King e
Hennessey, Hugh, machinist and blacksmith, Hughson s of King William
Henwood, Edwin, M.D., Main bet James and McNab
Herman, William, steamship agent, 39 King west
HERRON, JOSEPH, merchant tailor, 4 John n
Heys, Mrs. J., milliner, James bet Lind and Barton
Hill, Henry, butcher, cor Rebecca and Mary
Hill, Jasper, butcher, City Market
Hill, Mark, baker and confectioner, McNab bet King and Main
Hill, Thomas, cabinet maker, 32 John s
Hill, Thomas S., sen., watches, clocks and jewelry, John cor Wood Market
Hills, Albert H., architect and civil engineer, Charles bet Maiden Lane and Hunter
Hines, Charles H., butcher, City Market
Hines, H. H., butcher, City Market
Hiscox, James, prop. Victoria House, John cor Catherine
Hitchcock, H. L., hats, caps, furs, and straw goods, Henry bet Hughson and John
Hobson & McPhie, plumbers, steam and gas fitters, James cor Main
HOGAN, J. H., clothier, 68 King cor John (see adv)
Hogan & O'Neill, clothiers, 6 James north
Hogben, Henry, prop. Shades Restaurant, 60 James
Holbrook, Jas., dry goods, millinery, &c., 22 King e
Holcomb, W. H., house, sign and ornamental painter 24 Hughson

Holbrook & Stark, druggists, King cor Hughson
Holden, John R., barrister, &c., James opposite Fountain
Holland, James, gunsmith, John cor King William
Holleran, Patrick, grocer, cor Lind and John
Holton, Warren, prop. Hamilton nursery, King cor Wellington
Home and Colonial, (limited) A. F. Forbes, agent, King William
Home District Mutual Fire Ins. Co., D. Wright, agent, James n
Home Inland Marine Insurance Company, James D. Pringle, agent, Wentworth Chambers
Home Insurance Co., New Haven, Conn., A. McKeand, agent, James
Hooker, Abraham, confectioner, 31 York
Hooker, George, confectioner, York bet Park and Bay
Hooper, Samuel, barber and hair dresser, 84 King e
HOPE, ADAM & CO., hardware, (wholesale) King cor Catherine
Hopkins, Robert, boots and shoes, 8 James n
Horning & Ryckman, wholesale and retail grocers, e s McNab bet Market and King
HOWARD, GEORGE H., general manager's, assistant G. W. R., h Park
HOWARD, JAMES, general purchasing agent G. W. R., h Park
Houlch, William, grocer, Mary cor Rebecca
Howie, A. & Co., gold and silver platers, 3 King w
HOWLES, MATTHEW, stoves, tin, copper and sheet iron manufacturer and dealer, Florence Block, King w
HUGGARD, JOSEPH, proprietor Tecumseh House, James near Merrick (see adv)
Hughes, John, grocer, cor McNab and Burlington
HULL, CHESTER H., editor *Evening Times*, h Tyburn
Hume, James, veterinary surgeon, 1 York
Hurd & Roberts, marble cutters and dealers, York junction of Merrick
Hurrell, Jasper P., professor of music, Main between McNab and James
Hutchinson, James, hats, caps, furs and straw goods 3 James n
Hutton, Charles, proprietor Metropolitan Hotel, cor Stuart and Bay
Hutton & Moon, merchant tailors, Hughson bet King and King William
Hyslop, D. A., dry goods and millinery, 15 James n
Imperial (Fire) Insurance Co., R. Benner, agent, Canada Life Assurance Buildings
Inglis, Rev. David, (Canada Presbyterian) James between Bold and Duke
IRVING, ÆMILIUS, Q.C., barrister, G. W. R. office
IRWIN, J. D., agent American Express Co., James opposite Gore
Izard, William, grocer, West Avenue nr Henry
Jack, William, grocer, Park cor Colborne
Jackson, Thomas, builder, Victoria Avenue cor Main
Jarvis, John, cabinet maker, King bet Nelson and Cathcart
Jarvis, Mrs. John, second-hand broker, King, cor Cathcart
JAMES, GEORGE, dry goods and millinery, 16 James n
JEFFS, FREDERICK, proprietor Dominion Hotel, s s Stuart, opposite G. W. R. station (see adv.)
JENKINS, GEORGE (Johnson & Jenkins)
Jennings, David J., carver, G. W. R.
Jennings, D. J., professor of music, James, between Barton and Lind
Jennings, George J., hotel keeper, McNab, corner Mulberry
Johnson, Mrs. Jacob, milliner, John, bet Peel and Tyburn
Johnson, William, barrister, &c., 3 James n
JOHNSON & JENKINS, cabinet makers, Bay, cor York
JOLLEY, JAMES, saddle, harness and trunk manufacturer, John
JONES, CHARLES T., & CO., stock, bill and exchange broker, Mechanics' Hall
Jones, Rev. Robert (Baptist)
JUDD, W. H. & BROTHER, soap and candle manufacturers, Bay, bet Cannon and York (see adv.)
Kain, Peter, grocer, corner Peel and Catherine
Kavanagh, William, wagon maker, York cor Park
Kelk, Edward, prof. of music, James, s of Stewart
Kelk, William, prof. of music, Mara, cor Walnut
Kelly, Joseph, boots and shoes, 74 James n
Kelly, Patrick, grocer, Willson cor Wellington
Kelly, Robert, Alderman
Kemp, John, hotel keeper, James, opposite Vine
Kempster, Christopher W., sash, door, and blind manufacturer, Main bet Catherine and Walnut
Kendel, Francis, merchant tailor, 104 King w
Kendall, Joseph, prop. Hamilton Brewery, Peel, corner Catherine
Kendall, Thomas, grocer, John, bet Lind and Barton
Kennedy, James, patent medicines, Merrick opp Market
Kent, E. R., hardware, 74 King west
Kent, Joseph, King, cor Lock
KERNER, JOHN, hotel keeper, 72 King w (see adv.)
Kerr, Alexander, grocer, Mary nr Henry
Kerr, Murray A., coal oil and lamps, 53 King w
Kerr, Robert W., City Chamberlain
KERR, BROWN & McKENZIE, dry goods and groceries (wholesale) King e, near James
KERSHAW & EDWARDS' SAFES, Arch. McKeand, agent, 9 James w
KILGOUR, J. & R., dealers in sewing machines, 37 King e (see adv.)
Kilroy, J., second-hand broker, King William, bet James and Hughson
Kilvert, Francis E., barrister, &c., Hughson, bet King and Main
King, Robert, baker and confectioner, John bet Peel and Tyburn
King, William, clothier, 26 John s
King, G. H. and G. A., whip manufacturers, Rebecca bet John and Catherine
Kinrade, H. E., grocer, cor John and Augusta
Knott, John, piano forte manufacturer, Main cor Catherine
Knowles, Henry, wholesale cigars and tobacco, Catherine
Knox, David, commission merchant, Merrick
KRAFT, ERNEST, saddle, harness and trunk maker, 5 and 7 York, bet McNab and Park (see adv)
Laing, James B., M.D., Cannon bet Park and Bay
Lamond, Finlay, grocer, cor Mary and Rebecca
Lancashire Fire and Life, Isaac Mills agent, Wentworth chambers
Land, William, flour and feed, McNab nr King
Langberg, Frederick, cabinet maker, 83 King e
Langberg, John, pork dealer, John, near Peel
Lamphier, William H., grocer, 66 King e
Largay, Michael, secondhand broker
Laurie, Thomas, millwright, Murray bet James and McNab
LAW, R. W., barrister, &c., James cor Merrick
Lawrence, Thomas & Co., druggists, Stinson's Block, King e
Lawry & Stroud, butchers, city market
Laws, John, flour and feed, King e nr Catherine

LAWSON, A. & Co. (A. Lawson and Alexander Mars), book and job printers, 3 King w
LAWSON, BROS., wholesale clothiers, King corner James
Lazier, S. F., M.A., barrister, &c., Lister's Buildings, James
LEE, GEORGE, fish, oysters and game, wholesale, 4 and 6 King w
Lagrice, John, grocer, John bet Peel and Tyburn
Lees, George, flour and feed, 16 John s
LEES, THOMAS, watches, clocks and jewelry, 5 James n
Lees, William, baker and confectioner, Main opp. Court House
Leggo, William, barrister, &c., John cor King
Leitch, John, machinist, John cor Rebecca
Leitch, William, architect and civil engineer, West ave. bet Willson and Rebecca
Lemon, Charles, barrister, &c., King cor John
Levy, H. & A., watches, clocks and jewelry, 7 John s
Levy, Isaac, clothier, 22 King w and Market Square
Lewis, Levi, Vice-President Victoria Mutual Fire Ins. Co., James
Lewis, Thomas, cigars and tobacco, 88 King e
Life Association of Scotland, A. F. Forbes, agent, King William cor James
Lister, Claude, carpenter, 29 Hughson
Little, Alfred, brickmaker, Garth bet Main and King
Little, John, grocer, cor King and Wentworth
Little, Vincent, brickmaker, Main nr w limits
Liverpool and London and Globe Insurance Co., F. A. Bull, agent
Livingston, T. C., civil engineer, 4 Tuckett's block, Bay
Lockman, William, carpenter, Little Market nr Pearl
Logan, George, flour and feed, 76 King w
Logie, Alexander, Judge County Court, h Markland
London Assurance Corporation (establ. 1720), W. F. Findlay agent, James opp Gore
London and Lancashire Insurance Co., W. G. Crawford agent, Royal Hotel bldgs
LONG & BISBY, (W. D. Long and G. A. Bisby), wool dealers, McNab nr Merrick
LORETTO CONVENT, Rev. Mother M. J., Stanislaus, superioress, King w
LORIMER, JAMES, (Mugridge & Lorimer)
LOTTRIDGE, J. W. & CO., wholesale and retail grocers, James cor Market square
Love, David, baker and confectioner, John bet Peel and Augusta
Lucas, A. J., barber and hairdresser, 55 James n
Luckens, T., superintendent City Hospital
Lutz, James M., flour and feed, 11 and 13 York
Lyall John, brass founder, York bet Park and Bay
LYGHT, JOSEPH & CO., booksellers and stationers, 36 King e
Lyle, Mrs. Martha, grocer West ave bet Henry and Willson
Lynch, James, hotel keeper, John corner Tyburn
Lyons, Wm., grocer, Tyburn bet Walnut and Cherry
McAllister, D. C., ship smith, Zealand's wharf
McAllister, John, grocer, cor York and Caroline
McAllister, John, grocer, McNab bet Mulberry and Colborne
McAuliffe, Jeremiah, grocer, Park cor Sheaffe
McAuliffe, Patrick, grocer, cor Hughson and Guise
McCann, John, boots and shoes, 99 James n
McCANN, THOMAS E., confectioner and saloon keeper, 4 and 6 John s
McCarthy, Dennis, grocer, King cor Wentworth
McCarthy, Dennis, hotel keeper, King William bet James and Hughson
McCRACKEN, HENRY, proprietor Anglo American Hotel cor McNab and Market. (see adv)
McCRAE, COLIN, merchant, h Ferguson ave
McCue, James, grocer, Bay cor Little Main
McCulloch, Peter, hotel-keeper, York cor Park
McCurdy, J. & W., carpenters, King William nr John
McCallum, Archibald, M.A., principal of Central School
McDonald, Alexander, contractor, s s York bet Caroline and Hess
McDonald, David, cigars and tobacco, Bay cor York
McDougall, James, coal oil and lamps, King cor McNab
McDonald, John A., grocer, James opp Vine
McDonald, Walter R., barrister, &c., James s opp Gore
McDonough, Luke, saloon, King William bet James and Hughson
McFadden, John, grocer, Hughson cor Wood
McGANN, EDWARD W., res Dundurn Castle
McGANN, J. B., superintendent U. C. Institute for the Deaf and Dumb
McGIVERIN, EDWARD, carriage hardware and trimmings, 56 King e
McGiverin, William & Co., hardware wholesale, 13 & 15 James opp Gore
McGlogan, Cornelius, kotel keeper, King William, bet James and Hughson
McGlogan, Patrick, hotel keeper, Market Square and Hughson s
McGolpin, John, baker and confectioner, 94 King w
McGrath, Edward, wagon maker, cor James and Tyburn
McGuire, Francis, second hand broker, King William nr James
McHenry, Peter S., grocer, Park cor Cannon
McILWRAITH THOMAS, manager Hamilton Gas Light Company
McINNES, ALEXANDER, (Sanford, McInnes & Co)
McINNES, D. & CO., wholesale merchants and manufacturers, King corner John
McINNES, DONALD, (D. McInnes & Co., and McInnes, Calder & Co)
McINNES, HUGH, (McInnes, Calder & Co)
McINNES, CALDER & CO., wholesale dry goods, King cor John
McKaig & Hislop, blacksmiths, n s York bet Park and Bay
McKay, Robert, plasterer, Caroline cor Robinson
McKEAND, ARCHIBALD, banker and exchange broker, 9 James n
McKee, John, hotel keeper, 48 John
McKee, Thomas, English master grammar school
McKelvey, Rev. Charles (N. C. Methodist) Catherine
McKenzie, Rev. J. G. D., M.A., pastor (St. John's Church)
McKENZIE & MACKAY, commission merchants and insurance agents, 9 King e
McKeown, Hugh, saddle, harness and trunk maker, John s of Peel
McKeown, John, barrister, &c., Commercial Buildings, James
McKichan, John R., paper bag manufacturer, McNab nr King
McKillop, David (John Thomas & Co).
McKINSTRY, HENRY, agent Royal Canadian Bank, James
McLean, George, flour and feed, 76 King w
McLellan, Donald, bookseller and stationer, 26 King w
McLean, Hugh, accountant, James opp the Gore
McLeod, A., dyer and scourer, James cor Cannon
McMahon, Hugh, carpenter and builder, 20 Wellington s
McMahon, W. F., watches, clocks and jewelry, 86 King e

McMillan, Archibald, grocer, Bay bet Broadway and Little Main
McMillan, William, director Western Permanent Building Society
McMillan, John, grocer, King nr Wentworth
McNair, Samuel, inspector of weights and measures, City Hall
McNiece, William J., M.D., McNab cor Mulberry
McPherson, Mrs., boarding house, Park bet Cannon and Mulberry
McPherson, John & Co., wholesale boot and shoe manufacturers and dealers, 51 and 53 King e
McTaggart, Miles F., M.D., Park bet Merrick and Vine
MACABE, JAMES, proprietor Volunteer Hotel, King bet Bay and Caroline
Macabe, Thomas & Co., carriage builders, King w
Macdonald, John D., M.D., w s James bet Hunter and Bold
MACKAY, ANEAS D., wharfinger, foot of James
Mackelcan, George L., M.D., Gore bet James and Hughson
Mackelcan, Francis (Mackelcan & Gibson)
Mackelcan, John, M.D., Gore between Hughson and James
MACKELCAN & GIBSON, barristers, &c., Wentworth Chambers, James cor Main
MacKenna, John E., barrister, &c., 22 John s
Mackintosh, David, M.D., John nr Henry
Mackintosh, Hugh, fancy goods, 84 King e
Maclean, Hugh, real estate agent, James opp Gore
Macklem, William, vice-president, Canada Farmer's Mutual Insurance Company, James
Macnabb, Duncan A., commission merchant, Royal Hotel buildings
Magee, William, flour and feed, e s James, between Stinson and Barton
Magen, Christopher, butcher, City Market
Magill, Charles, dry goods, millinery, &c., 76 King e
MAGILL & BROTHER, hardware, 38 King e
Main, Alexander, & Co., rope and twine manufacturers, Mary, corner Oak
Malcolm, John, hotel keeper, McNab, bet Merrick and York
Malcolm, William, plumber, steam and gas fitter, corner Hughson and Augusta
Mallary, William, second-hand broker, John, between Peel and Augusta
Manning, F. E., builder, Tyburn, bet Cherry & Spring
Mansfield, Charles, lager beer saloon, 92 King e
Marrows, Mrs. David F., fancy goods, 39 York
MARS, ALEXANDER (A. Lawson & Co.)
MARSDEN, THOMAS, gilt and stained mouldings, James n (see adv)
Marshall, George, commission merchant, King, bet Catherine and Maria
Marshall, George H., hotel keeper, John, cor Tyburn
Marshall, Joseph, grocer, King, nr Queen
Marshall, Thomas, hotel keeper, cor John and Peel
Martin, Edward, barrister, &c., 2 King w
Martin, Henry, butcher, City Market
MARTIN, HUBERT, lager beer saloon, King, nr Florence Block
Martin, J. B., hotel keeper, s s Market Square
Martin, P., pork dealer, cor John and King William
MARTIN, RICHARD (Martin & Ferguson)
Martin & Bruce, barristers, &c., 2 King w
MARTIN & FERGUSON, barristers, &c., King, cor James
Maslin, Samuel, hotel keeper, James, cor Cannon
Mason, John J., M.D., Augusta, between James and Hughson
Mason, John J., accountant, insurance agent, official assignee, &c., King cor James
Mason, Joseph, bellhanger, 96 King e
MASON, THOMAS, hats, caps, furs and straw goods, 12 James n
MASONIC HALL, n e cor John and Main
Matthews, Joseph B., livery and sale stables s s Mkt nr Park
Matthews & McMenneny, house, sign and ornamental painters, McNab bet King and Market
MATHEWS, R. S., AGENT DOMINION TELEGRAPH CO., 13 King nr Hughson
Meakins, George H., lock manufacturer, Cathcart
Meakins & Sons, cabinet makers, King bet Nelson and Cathcart
MECHANICS' INSTITUTE, James bet Market and Merrick
Meldrum, Henry, druggist, 74 King e
Meldrum, T., hotel keeper, McNab cor Stuart
MENDON, L. C., dealer in sewing machines, 2 Royal Hotel Buildings
MERCHANTS' BANK OF CANADA, James Bancroft, manager, James, cor Main
Messenger, The, (semi-monthly) devoted to the cause of temperance, drawer 69, Hamilton P.O
Meston, Charles, flour and feed, 25 and 27 York
Milhorn, Robert, merchant tailor, James, opp the Gore
Miller, Miss A., milliner, McNab, nr King
Miller, John, butcher, Willson, bet James and McNab
Miller, Mrs. Robert, boarding house, Park, cor Vine
Milne, Robert, photographer, James n
MILLS, GEORGE H., president Victoria Mutual Fire Insurance Company, James
MILLS, ISAAC, insurance agent, James, cor Main
Mills, James, butcher, City Market
Mills, James H., barrister, &c., Charles, cor Main
MILLS, JOSEPH, hats, caps furs, and straw goods, 7 James n
MILLS, HON. SAMUEL, senator, cor Charles and Main
MILLS, WILLIAM H., barrister, &c., s s Main bet Queen and Ray
MILROY, ROBERT, manager Ontario Bank, King
Minnes, Thomas, blacksmith, Main, bet Catherine and Walnut
Minty, Francis C., (Taylor & Minty)
Mitchell, A. A., plasterer, Little Market bet Pearl and Lock
Mitchell, John, alderman, Main nr Charles
Mitchell, Thomas, broom and brush manufacturer, 21 King w
Molzalm, Charles, boots and shoes, 89 King e
Montreal Marine Insurance Co., Maitland Young, jr. agent, 35 King e
MONTREAL TELEGRAPH COMPANY, George Black, manager, James opp the Gore
Moodie, John, variety store, 36 King w
Moore, John, license inspector, City Hall
Moore & Davis, land and general agents, cor James and King William
MOORE, D. & Co., founders and machinists, Catherine cor Lind
Moore, Lyman & Brierly, druggists, 14 King e
Moore, Lyman & Mundy, druggists, James nr King William
Moore & McCauley, ice dealers, cor Main and Catherine
Morden, John, hotel keeper, York bet Pearl and Bay
Morgan, Benjamin, flour and feed, Main bet Cherry and Walnut
Morgan, R. & W., flour, grain and seeds 22 and 24 John s
Morgenroth, Mrs. hotel keeper, York cor Lock
Morris, John G., flour and feed, 25 York
Morris, Lewis, butcher, 32 City Market

Morris, Louis, sash, door and blind manufacturer, King e nr Wellington
Morris, Philip, grocer, cor John and Lind
Morris & Brother, flour and feed, King Williamand Wellington, cor East Market
Morrison, F., hotel keeper, York nr Cemetery
Morrison, Joseph B., stoves, tin, copper and sheet-iron manufacturer and dealer, 7 John n
Morrison Thomas, flour and feed, John cor Wood Market
Morton, David, soap and candle manufacturer, Emerald e of Main
Mossman, Mark, boots and shoes, Hughson cor Gore
Mowat, William, carpenter, Mary bet Rebecca and Henry
MUGRIDGE, C. W., (Mugridge & Lorimer)
MUGRIDGE & LORIMER, (Charles W. Mugridge and James Lorimer) importers of groceries, wines and liquors, McNab nr Merrick (see adv)
Muirhead, Walter, butcher, City Market
Mullin, James, contractor, Main between Cherry and Spring
Mullin, John A., M.D., n s James, bet Cannon and Mulberry
Mundie, William, architect and civil engineer, King near Catherine
Munro, Hugh, grocer, Stuart corner James
Munro, Richard H. R., barrister, &c., Main, between James and Hughson
MUNRO & HENDERSON, clothiers, 28 King e
Munzinger, John M., bookbinder, York, bet McNab and Park
Murdoch, John, grocer, John, corner Union
Murison, George, carpenter, Hughson, nr Catherine
Murphy, Michael, prop Rob Roy Hotel, John cor Peel
Murphy & Murray, wholesale and retail grocers, 78 King e
MURRAY, CHARLES R., manager Canadian Bank of Commerce
MURRAY, A. & CO., dry goods, millinery, &c., 18 King e
MURTON, JOHN W. (W. Reid & Co.) h Catherine
Mutter, Mrs. Philip, second-hand broker, King, cor Cathcart
Myles, Alfred, grain merchant, Bay
Myers, Robert, boots and shoes, James, nr Barton
Myles, Thomas, coal and wood dealer, Myles' wharf, and Main, corner Hughson
Nash, Samuel, beef and pork packer, Market, corner McNab
National Travelers' Insurance Company, New York, W. G. Crawford, agent, Royal Hotel Buildings
Nelligan, Dennis, hotel keeper, John, between Peel and Tyburn
Neville, Rev. Dr., rector St. Thomas Church, Main, between Catherine and Walnut
New, Henry & J., brickmakers, Garth, between Main and King
Niblett, Charles W., barrister, &c., Commercial Buildings, James
Nicholls, Mrs., confectioner, McNab, between King and Market
NICHOLSON, DONALD, (Canadian Oil Co.) h Maria
NOBLE, WILLIAM, Metropolitan Saloon and Restaurant, James, corner Merrick
North British and Mercantile, J. D. Pringle, agent, Wentworth Chambers
NORTH, SAMUEL, stove, tin, copper and sheetiron dealer, McNab nr Merrick (see adv)
Northern Assurance Co., of London and Aberdeen, A. F. Forbes, agent
Northey, George, founder and machinist, Wellington cor East Market
Noyles, J. & Son, butchers, 112 King e
Nowlan, O., hotel keeper and prop. livery stable John cor King William
O'Brien, Henry, gunsmith, John bet Tyburn and Pea,
O'Brien, Luke, hotel keeper, King bet Catherine and Mary
O'Callaghan, F., fruit, wholesale and retail, 14 King w
O'Donohoe, John, auctioneer, Market Square
O'Heir, Peter, saddle, harness and trunk maker, 5 John n
O'Keefe, D. C., P.L.S., C.E., 2 John s
O'Neill, Henry, grocer, York cor Pearl
O'REILLY, CHARLES, M.D., City Hospital
O'REILLY, J. EDWIN, barrister, Mayor, 8 King w
O'REILLY, MILES, barrister, etc., 8 King w
O'REILLY & O'REILLY, barristers, etc., 8 King w
Oliphant, D., publisher *Banner of Faith*
ONTARIO BANK, Robert Milroy, manager, King cor John
ORMISTON, REV. W., D.D., pastor Central Presbyterian Church, h Maiden Lane
Orr, Mrs. A., fancy goods, 14 John n
Orr, Daniel, hotel keeper, John bet Base and Guise
Osborne, James, wholesale and retail grocer, James nr King
Osborne, Mrs. Mary, grocer, Catherine bet Barton and Stinson
OSBORNE, ROBERT, watches, clocks and jewelry, James opp Fountain
Osler & Osler, barristers, etc., King e opp Fountain
OUTERBRIDGE, A. E., patent electric battery for steam boilers, James
Padden, Patrick, grocer, corner Cherry and Maria
Page, James, butcher, York, near Bay
Palm, William, lager beer saloon, Bay, corner King
PAPPS, GEORGE S., LL.B., barrister, &c., King, near James
Parker, Mrs. M. A., boarding house, King William, between James and Hughson
Park, William, grocer, John, near Main
Parks, D., boots and shoes, Lind, between John and Catherine
Passmore, Richard, butcher, City Market
Paterson, Peter, grocer, York, bet Bay and Caroline
Patterson, E. G., teacher Grammar School
Pattison, Zaccheus, wholesale baker and confectioner
Pauling, Richard A., artist, Wentworth Chambers
PEACOCK, JOHN, dry goods, millinery, &c., e s McNab, between King and Market
Pearson, James, fancy goods, 87 James n
Pearson, John & Co., variety store, 58 King w
Peat, Thomas, carpenter, north end Hess
Peden, John, grocer, York, corner Pearl
PEIRCE, C. E. & Co., clothiers, James, near King William (see adv.)
Pentecost & Son, house, sign and ornamental painters, King, near McNab
PERKINS & CLARK, Excelsior Coffee and Spice Mills, Catherine, corner Rebecca
PETERSEN, A., agent A. & S. Nordheimer's pianoforte establishment, James
Pettit, J. H., commission merchant, 2 John s
Penchen, Clark & Co., importers of wines and liquors, John, corner King
Phelan, James P., Royal Hotel Saloon and Billiard Parlor
Phillips, David, carpenter, Ferguson ave. bet East Market and Rebecca
Philips, George R., Variety Store, King nr Mary
PHILP, JAMES, (Philp & Robertson)
PHILP & ROBERTSON, saddle, harness and trunk manufacturers, James nr King William (see adv).
Phœnix Insurance Company of London, England, Brown, Gillespie & Co., agents cor King and James

Phœnix Insurance Company of Brooklin, N. Y., E. Brown, agent Brown's wharf
Phœnix Marine, McKenzie & Mackay, agents, 9 King e
Phœnix Ocean Marine Insurance Co. of Brooklin, N.Y., J. D. Pringle, agent, Wentworth Chambers.
Phœnix Mutual Life Insurance Company, Hartford, Connecticut, W. G. Crawford, agent, Royal Hotel Buildings
Pike, Richard. cigars and tobacco, 12 King w
Pilgrim, Robert A., grocer and soda water manufacturer, King cor Cathcart
POST OFFICE, James opp Merrick
Potts, Rev. John (Wesleyan)
Powell, T. S., lumber dealer, Hughson bet Tyburn and Peel
Powell, William R., grocer, e s Bay bet Sheaffe and Colborne
Price, Charles, prop. Mountain View Hotel
Priddis, John, grocer, McNab cor Vine
PRINGLE, J. D., barrister, insurance agent, &c., Wentworth Chambers (see adv).
PROCTOR, JOHN, wharfinger, Commercial wharf
PRONGUEY, J. P., carriage builder, Park nr Market
Proudfoot, William, barrister, &c., Main bet James and Hughson
Proudfoot & Munro, barristers, &c., Main bet James and Hughson
Provincial Fire Insurance Company, Isaac Mills, agent, Wentworth Chambers
Provincial Fire and Marine, J. D. Pringle, agent, Wentworth Chambers
Pullar, Rev. Thomas (Congregational), Wellington
Queen Fire Insurance Company, McKenzie & Mackay, agents, 9 King e
Quimby, Alfred C., wholesale cigars and tobacco, 43 James n
Quinn, Mrs., hotel keeper, John opp Wood Market
Rae, Richard H., Emigration Agent, G. W. R. wharf
RAMSAY, A. G., F. I. A., manager Canada Life Assurance Company, James nr Main
Ramsay, Robert, butcher. City Market
Rastrick, Frederick J., architect and civil engineer, Maria bet John and Hughson
Rauch, Joseph, leather and findings, 8 John n
RAW, ROBERT, JUN., book and job printer, 8 James
Reeves, Arthur L., baker and confectioner, Walnut nr Pearl
READ, SAMUEL, cashier Gore Bank, King
Reid, Alexander C., M. D., cor Hughson and Rebecca
Reid, C., hotel keeper, John opp Wood Market
Reid, George Lowe, chief engineer G. W. R.
Reid, James, butcher, King cor. Bond
Reid, Rev. Walter, (Primative Methodist) Hughson
Reid, William & Co., coal and wood dealers, Mary bet Henry and Rebecca
Reliance Mutual Life Assurance Company, (London England), John Clark & Co., agents, John cor King
Rice, M. E., marble cutter and dealer, cor Park and Merrick
Rice, Dr. S. D., governor and principal Wesleyan Female College, h Emerald
Richardson, Rev. George, pastor Park street (Baptist Church)
Richardson, Thomas, auction and commission, Merrick nr James
Richardson, William, carpenter, Market bet Park and Bay
Riddel, John, stock, bill and exchange broker, 20 King e
Riddle, John, grocer, cor Rebecca and Mary
Ridley, Henry F., M. D., s e cor Main and Charles
Ridler, William, grocer, Wentworth bet Lock and Pearl
RITCHIE, EDMUND, Postmaster, res Post office, James
RITCHIE, FREDERICK E., assistant Postmaster
Rigsby, John, builder, e Market bet Mary and Nelson
Roach, George, saloon and restaurant, G.W.R. station
Robb, James, barrister, &c., Wentworth Chambers
Robbins, N. B., grate manufacturer, Mary cor Willson
Roberts, Mrs. Ellen, fancy goods, 44 John
Robertson, A. M., ship builder, Zealand's wharf
Robertson, James, dry goods, millinery, &c., 20 King e
ROBERTSON, WILLIAM, (Philp & Robertson)
Robinson, William, boots and shoes, John bet Peel and Tyburn
Rodger, John, blacksmith, 1 York
Rodgers, W. H., butcher, outside City Market
Ronald. William, grocer, 15 York
Ronan, Andrew, grocer, corner Stuart and Hughson
Ronan, Michael, grocer, corner Wellington and Henry
Ronan & Brother, flour and feed, 2 York
Roos, Rabbi L.
Roseburgh, J. W., M.D., James, between Maiden Lane and Hunter
Ross, Andrew, dry goods, millinery, &c., Lister's Block, James
Ross, Miss J., boarding house, Bay, n w cor Cannon
Ross, Samuel F., lumber dealer, Napier, between Hess and Queen
Ross & Smith, hardware, 54 King e
Roy, Robert & Co., wholesale dry goods, James, opp Fountain
ROYAL CANADIAN BANK, H. McKinstry, agent, Canada Life Assurance Company's Buildings
Royal Dominion Commercial College, James, corner King William
Royal Hotel Billiard Rooms, James P. Phelan, proprietor, Merrick, corner James
Royal Insurance Company, George A. Young, agent, Royal Hotel Buildings
Rudel, William Henry, jeweler, manufacturer, King, corner James
Ruse, Mrs. M. A., boots and shoes, 30 King w
Russell, Richard, jeweler, James, opp Fountain
Rutherford, Alexander, superintendent Mechanics' Institute and Reading Room, h Tyburn
RUTHERFORD, G. & CO., bottle manufacturers, Hamilton Glass Works, Hughson corner Warren (see adv)
Ruthven, Peter, bookbinder, 51 Hughson
Rutley, George, hotel keeper, Wellington, nr East Market
Ryall, George, M.D., Main, near Catherine
Ryall, Isaac, M.D., Main, near Catherine
Ryckman, John, flour and feed, King, between Hess and Queen
Rymal, D., hotel keeper, 12 York
Sadleir, Charles A., barrister, &c., Hughson, between King and Main
Sanford, McInnes & Co., wholesale clothiers, 47 & 49 King e
SAWYER, L. D. & CO., manufacturers of agricultural implements, Wellington, north of G. W. R.
Schaupp, John, saloon, Bay, between Concession and Stinson
Schrader, Frederick J., wholesale cigars and tobacco, McNab, between Hunter and Bold
Schumacher, George, butcher, Market, bet McNab and Park
Schwarz, Edward, boots and shoes, 106 King w
Schwarz, Frederick, tobacco manufacturer, Florence Block, King w
Schwarz, Louis, wholesale cigars and tobacco, 81 James n

Scott, Samuel, grocer, West ave. cor East Market
Scottish Provincial Assurance Company, J. D. Pringle, agent, Wentworth Chambers
SCRIVEN, P. L., copper, steel and wood engraver, 28 King w
Seaman, S. L., clothier, 19 York and King w
Secord & Davis, grocers, cor John and Main
Security Insurance of New York (Marine), E. S. Gregory, agent, King e, next door to Bank of Commerce
Sellett, George H., grocer, 21 Rebecca
Semmens & Co., sash, door and blind manufactory, Sophia nr Inchbury
SERVICE & WYLD, importers of cloths, King bet James and McNab
Shannon, Peter, hotel keeper, McNab bet York and Merrick
Sharp, William, grocer, John bet Tyburn and Peel
Sharp & Murison, carpenters and builders
Sharpe & Secord, wholesale and retail grocers, 31 King e
Shill, John, brush maker, Mulberry cor McNab
Shire, Bernhard, carpet shoes, John bet Gore and Henry
Sillett, Mrs., milliner, 23 Rebecca
Simpson, Rev. A. B. (Canada Presbyterian), Henry bet James and Hughson
Simpson, James, importer of wines and liquors, John cor King
Sinclair, Isaac, barber and hairdresser, 66 King w
Skinner, James A., & Co., china, glass, earthenware and fancy goods, wholesale, 27 King e
Skinner, William, superintendent House of Refuge
Small, Thomas, butcher, Main bet Lock and Pearl
Smallwood, Alexander, dealer in wood, hay and straw, King William nr Main
Smallwood, George, prop. Victoria saloon, fruit and oyster depot, 14 John s
Smart, Mrs. George, confectioner, 42 John
Smith, Alexander, grocer, cor John and Peel
Smith, Charles, city messenger
Smith, Donald, clothier, 50 King e
SMITH, GEORGE, stove, tin, copper and sheet-iron manufacturer and dealer, McNab cor Cannon
SMITH, GEORGE, grocer, s s Market Square
Smith, James B., private school,
Smith, Mrs. Jane, tin, copper, sheet iron, &c., 4 York
Smith, John & Co., commission merchants, King cor John
Smith, Robert, tin, copper, sheet iron, &c., King William, bet James and Hughson
Smith, Samuel, hotel-keeper, York cor Bay
Sneath, Mrs. confectioner, 85 James n
Snelgrove, E. L., undertaker, Court House square
Somerville, J. H. & Co., dry goods, millinery, &c., 14 James n
Spectator, The (daily, morning and weekly), T. & R. White, *Spectator* Buildings (see adv)
Spears, Samuel and John, ship smiths, foot of McNab
Speis, Rev. Augustus, Evangelical Association
Spencer, Henry, tin, copper, sheet iron, &c., n s King William bet James and Hughson
Spier, Samuel & John, blacksmiths, McNab nr Burlington Bay
Spink, Mrs. Margaret, boarding house, Market bet Park and McNab
Spittal, William, baker and confectioner, Florence Block, Bay
SPOHN & BELL, barristers, &c., Commercial chambers
Squire, C., flour and feed, 4 Florence Block, King w cial chambers, James
SPOHN, JACOB V. (Spohn & Bell)
Stacy, James B. P., butcher, 71 King e
Stally, Martin, boat builder, foot of James
Stanbury & Co., dry goods, millinery, &c., 30 King e
Stapley, Edward, grocer, cor Wellington and Rebecca
Start, John E., barrister and city recorder, Commer-
Steel, George, boots and shoes, 16 York
Steinger, Joseph, stock, bill and exchange broker, Stewart nr Bay
Stephenson, Charles, contractor, Wellington bet Peel and Tyburn
Sterling, George, inspector of hides, Catharina bet John and Hughson
Stevenson, Charles, builder, 14 Wellington
Stevenson, George, grocer, Peel e of James
Stevenson, James, accountant and general agent, n e cor King and James
Stewart, C. E. & Co., book and job printers, *Times* office, Hughson bet King and King William
Stewart Geo., saddle, harness & trunk maker; 42 John
Stewart, James & Co., founders and machinists, McNab cor Vine
STEWARD, T. B., watches, clocks and jewelry; Goldsmith's Hall, 12 King e
Stinson, Mrs. Elizabeth, Elgin
STINSON, JAMES, proprietor Stinson's Savings Bk, James, cor King William
Stinson, Mrs. Thomas, cor Queen and York
ST. MARY'S ORPHAN ASYLUM, Sister Mary Phillip, superioress, Park
Stock, Thomas, president Canada Farmers' Mutual Insurance Company, James
Stokoe, Charles H., director, Western Permanent Building Society
Storrer, F. M., fancy goods, King cor McNab
Storer, Henry M., chief of police G. W. R., h York
Strange, Henry, M. D., King cor Mary
Summers, William W., builder, Main bet Bond and Bowery
SUTHERLAND, ANGUS, wholesale and retail grocer, 50 King w
SUTHERLAND, JAMES & Co., directory publishers, 3 King w
Sutterby, John, hotel keeper, McNab nr Merrick
SWINYARD, THOMAS, general manager G. W. R., Hunter bet Bond and Charles, res Central House
Taylor, John, contractor, Bowery cor Main
Taylor, John D., billiard parlor, James
Taylor, John E., variety store, 61 King w
Taylor, Joseph, watches, clocks and jewelry, 52 James n
TAYLOR, JOSEPH, secretary to general manager G. W. R
Taylor & Minty, bankers, exchange and insurance brokers, James
Taylor, William, variety store, King bet Bond and Bowery
TECUMSEH HOUSE, J. Huggard, prop. (see adv)
Temple, John & Co., livery and sale stables, Catherine bet King William and Rebecca
THOMAS, C. L., western piano forte factory, 76 and 78 King w. (see adv)
THOMAS, E. CARTWRIGHT, sheriff, Court House
THOMAS, JOHN & CO., founders and machinists, Rebecca, between John and Catherine
Thompson, Mrs., boarding house, Park
Thompson, Greger, boots and shoes, 82 King e
THOMSON, JAMES R. (Thomson & Kilvert)
THOMSON, BIRKETT & BELL, wholesale dry goods, Macnab cor Merrick
THOMSON & KILVERT, barristers, &c., Hughson, between King and Main
Thomson, Thomas & Co., dry goods, millinery, &c., 32 King e

Thomson, John, grocer, corner Bay and Cannon
Thorburn, James, flour and feed, John, between Peel and Tyburn
Thorn, William, china, glass and earthenware, 30 York, between McNab and Park
Thornton & Green, organ builders, 3 Florence Block, Bay
TIFFANY, EDWARD H., barrister, &c., Hughson, between King and Main
Tindill, William, hotel keeper, King, cor Wentworth
Tompkins, George, coal oil and lamps, James, near Murray
Torrence, Thomas, saddle, harness and trunk maker, John, corner Tyburn
Towersey, Mrs. Joseph, milliner, 9 King William
Travelers' Insurance Company, Hartford, A. McKeand, agent, 2 King w
Travers, Denis, grocer, John, between Augusta and Catherine
Tremlett, William, boots and shoes, 20 King w
Truman, William, wholesale and retail grocer, McNab, Market Square
Trumpeler, David, grocer, cor Wellington and Henry
Tuckett & Billings, tobacco manufacturers, 100 & 102 King w
Turnbull & Co., founders and machinists, Mary, cor Little Gore
Turner, Alfred, grocer, corner James and Simcoe
Turner, James & Co., wholesale grocers, Hughson, between King and Main
Urlin, Mrs. A. E., private school, James, between Peel and Augusta
Urry, Henry, barber and hairdresser, Anglo-American Hotel
Vernon, Elias, M.D., w s James bet Hunter and Bold
Victoria House, s s King bet Catherine and Walnut
VICTORIA MUTUAL FIRE INSURANCE COMPANY, W. D. Booker, treasurer and secretary, Wentworth Buildings
WADDELL, R. E., (Waddell & Lemon), s e cor King and John
Waddell, William W., produce and commission merchant, John nr King
WADDELL & LEMON, barristers, &c., cor King and John
Wakefield, John, butcher, City Market
Wakeman, Thomas H., butcher, City Market
Waldhoff, William, dealer in wood, hay and straw, Rebecca cor Hughson
Walker, A. A., M.D., D.D.S., 8 King e
Walker, Charles E., confectioner, 18 John s
Walker, George, grocer, Bay bet Cannon and Mulberry
Walker, James, soap and candle manufactory, Main cor Bowery
Walker, James, wholesale dry goods, 33 King e
Walker, Miles, grocer, corner James and Augusta
Walker, Robert, waggon maker, Walnut bet Main and King
Walker, Robert, grocer, s s York bet Queen and Bay
Walker, William, grocers, Merrick cor Park
Wall & McCarthy, wagon makers, John cor Tyburn
Walsh, Mrs. James, fruit & confectionery, 60 King w
Wanzer, R. M. & Co., sewing machine manufacturers King, cor Catherine
Ward, William, butcher, 33 City Market
Warry, Miss E. R., fancy goods, 26 King w
Waterworth, John, carpenter, Little Market nr Pearl
Watson, Mrs. Ann, boarding house, Park bet Colborne and Concession
Watkins, T. C., dry goods, millinery, &c., 10 James n
Watson, John & Sons, veterinary surgeons, Mary cor King William
Way, James, house, sign and ornamental painter, East Market cor Mary
Webber, E., builder, Maria nr John
Webster, James, builder, Union bet Hughson and John
Western Assurance Company of Toronto, McKenzie & Mackay, agents, 9 King e
WETENHALL, HENRY, barrister, &c., Hughson bet King and Main
Whipple, E. S. (J. Temple & Co.), John nr Rebecca
White, Mrs. A., boarding house, cor Peel and Catherine
White, Thomas W., organ builder, 38 King w
White, T. & R., book and job printers, *Spectator* office, Hughson, cor Main
White, W. C., carpenter, w s McNab bet Cannon and Mulberry
Widger, James, boots and shoes, King cor McNab
Wilkinson, George, barber and hairdresser, 8 York
WILLIAMS, CHARLES F., Shades saloon, Prince's Square, Main (see adv).
Williams, John, grocer, cor Peel and Walnut
Williams, J. M., M.P.P., Canadian Oil Company
Williamson, James, commission merchant, Brock
Wills, J., boots and shoes, 58 King e
WILLSON, F. M., stock, bill and exchange broker, 5 James nr King
Willson, J. W., commission merchant, King cor John
Wilson, Robert, boots and shoes, 40 John s
Winckler, Julius, saloon, 18 York
WINER, J. & CO., wholesale druggists, 25 King e (see adv)
WOOD & LEGGAT, hardware, n s King e of Hughson
Woodley, Samuel, boots and shoes, 22 James n
Woods, W. B., director Western Permanent Building Society
Woolverton, Mrs. E. H., homœopathic pharmacy, 86 King e
WRIGHT, C. H., photographer, 34 King w (see adv.
Wright, David, insurance agent, James opp. Mechanics' Institute
Wright, William, butcher, West ave., bet King and East Market
Yaldon, William, prop. City Arms Hotel, McNab cor Murray
Yale, Mrs. D. C., fancy goods James nr Main
Yates & Garson, carpenters, Duke nr McNab
Young, Charles, grocer, James nr Murray
YOUNG, GEORGE A., insurance and general agent, Royal Hotel Buildings
Young, Jacob, wharfinger, Zealand wharf
Young, Miss J., milliner, 73 King w
Yaung, Maitland, jr., commission merchant, King e
Young, R., prop. Ontario Hotel, Prince's Square
YOUNG, THOMAS, saloon and restaurant, 20 John s (see adv)
YOUNG & BRO., plumbers, steam and gas fitters, John cor King William
YOUNG, H. & R., brass founders, McNab nr Stuart's foundry (see adv)
YOUNG, LAW & CO., props Dundas Cotton Mills Co., McNab, cor Merrick
Youngman, Samuel, flour and feed, Merrick bet Park and Bay
Zingsheim, Jacob, cabinet maker, Florence Block
Zwich, W. H., fruit and confectionery, McNab nr King

HAMILTON CLASSIFIED BUSINESS DIRECTORY.

Marked thus * are Wholesale.

Accountants.

Findlay, William F., James opp Fountain
Green, W. M., Hughson
McLean, Hugh, James opp the Gore
Mason, John J., s s King cor James
Stevenson, James, n e cor King and James

Agencies.

Outerbridge, A. E., patent electric battery for steam boilers, James

Agent, Consular, U. S.

Boyce, D. R., office at G. W. R. Station

Agent, Emigration.

Rae, Richard H., G. W. R. wharf

Agent, Express.

Irwin, John D., James opp Gore

Agents, Insurance.

Ambridge, T. A., King bet James and McNab
Ball, Frederick A., King bet James and McNab
Benner, Richard, Wentworth Chambers
Browne, E., Browne's wharf, foot of McNab
Clark, John & Co., John cor King
Crawford, W. G., Royal Hotel Buildings, Merrick
Findlay, William F., James opp Gore
Forbes, A. F., King William cor James
Garvin, James, 50 James n
Gregory, S. E., 35 King e
Jones, Charles T. & Co., Mechanics' Hall
McKeand, Archibald, 2 King w
McKenzie & Mackay, 9 King e
Mason, John J., King cor James
Mills, Isaac, James cor Main
Pringle, J. D., Wentworth Chambers
Proctor, John, Royal Hotel Block, Merrick
Smith, John & Co., King cor John
Taylor & Minty, James
Wright, David, James opp Mechanics' Institute
Young, George A., Royal Hotel Buildings

Agents, Passage.

Armstrong, Charles, Hughson bet Main and King
Browne, E., Browne's wharf
Herman, William, 39 King w
McKeand, Arch. 9 James n
Proctor, John, Merrick
Willson, Frederick M., 5 James n
Young, George A., Royal Hotel Buildings

Agents, Sewing Machines.

Atkinson, Mrs., 71 King w
Bowman & Howe, James opp Mechanics' Hall
Kilgour, J. & R., King e
Mendon, L. C., Royal Hotel Buildings

Agents, Shipping.

Armstrong, Charles, Hughson bet Main and King
Birely, N. F., Brock nr Bay
Knox, David, Merrick
McKay, Æneas D., foot of James
Proctor, John, Royal Block, Merrick

Agents, Steamship.

Browne, E., Royal Mail Line, Browne's wharf
Herman, William, 39 King w
McKay, Æneas D., McKay's wharf
McKeand, Arch., 9 James n
Proctor, John, Merrick
Willson, Frederick M., 5 James n

Agricultural Implements (Manufacturers and Dealers.)

Copp & Bro., 15 John n
Sawyer, L. D. & Co., Wellington n of G. W. R.
Turnbull & Co., Mary cor Little Gore

Architects and Civil Engineers.

Clark, Hutchison, 23 Hughson
Hills, Albert H., Charles bet Maiden Lane and Hunter
Leitch, William, West ave. bet Wilson and Rebecca
Mundie, William, King near Catherine
Rastrick, Frederick J., Maria bet John and Hughson

Auction and Commission.

Andrews, W. A. & Co., 75 James n
Burrows & Brother, Merrick opp Market
Forbes, F. J. B., Anglo American Block
Richardson, Thomas, Merrick nr James

Baby Carriage Manufacturers.

Semmens, John & Co., Pearl nr King

Bakers and Confectioners.

Aussem, J. H., Florence Block, King
Bateman, William, King nr Cathcart
Beer, John, e s James nr Lind
Chilman, Isaac C., King bet Bowery and Caroline
Ecclestone, W. T., 10 King e
Freeman & Brother, e s James n bet Lind and Henry
Gould, D. A., 64 James
Harris, William, s s Market Square
Hill, Mark, McNab bet King and Main
Hooker A., n s York bet McNab and Park
Hooker, George, s s York bet Park and Bay
King, Robert, John bet Peel and Tyburn
Leegrice, John, John bet Peel and Tyburn
Lees, William, Main opp Court House
Love, David, John bet Peel and Augusta
McGolpin, John, 94 King w
Pattison, Z., Cannon
Reeves, Arthur L., Walnut nr Pearl
Sharp, William, John bet Tyburn and Peel
Spital, William, Florence Block, Bay
Stevenson, George, Peel e of James

Banks.

Bank of British North America, s s King bet James and Hughson
Bank of Montreal, s s King bet James and McNab
Canadian Bank of Commerce, King cor John
Gore Bank, King cor Hughson
Merchants' Bank of Canada, James cor Main
Ontario Bank, King cor John
Royal Canadian Bank, Canada Life Assurance Co.'s Buildings

Bankers and Dealers in Exchange.

Jones, Charles T. & Co., Mechanics' Hall
McKeand, Archibald, 9 James n
Steinger, J., Stuart bet Bay and Caroline
Taylor & Minty, James
Willson, Fred. M., 5 James n

Bank (Savings.)

Stinson's Savings Bank, James cor King William

Barristers, Attorneys and Solicitors.

Adams, Robert W., James s opp Gore
Ambrose, William, 16 King e
Young, George A., Royal Hotel Buildings
Barr, John, James cor King
Barry, John, 8 King w
Burton George William, Q.C., Canada Life Assurance Buildings
Burton & Bruce, Canada Life Assurance Buildings, James
Bruce, Alexander, Canada Life Assurance Buildings
Bruce, John Milne, 3 King w
Cahill, James, office City Hall
Chisholm, D. B., Lister's Buildings, James
Chisholm & Lazier, Lister's Buildings, James
Craigie, William, Main bet James and Hughson
Crickmore, Charles G., Commercial Buildings, James
Duval, Henry, King William bet John and Hughson
Ferguson, J. W., King cor James
Freeman & Craigie, Main bet James and Hughson
Freeman, S. B., Main bet James and Hughson
Gage, Robert, R., King cor John
Geddes, W. A., Wentworth Chambers
Gibson, John M., Wentworth Chambers
Holden, John R., James s opp Fountain
Irving, Æ., Q.C., G.W.R. office
Johnson, William, 3 James n
Kilvert, Francis E., Hughson bet King and Main
Law, R. N., James cor Merrick
Lazier, S. F., M.A., Lister's Buildings, James
Leggo, William, John cor King
Lemon, Charles, King cor John
McDonald, Walter R., James s opp Gore
McKeown, John, Commercial Buildings, James
Mackelcan, Francis, Wentworth Chambers
Mackelcan & Gibson, Wentworth Chambers
MacKenna, John E., 22 John s
Martin, Edward, 2 King w
Martin, Richard, King w cor James
Martin & Bruce, 2 King w
Martin & Ferguson, King cor James
Mills, George H., Wentworth Chambers, James cor Main
Mills, James H., Charles cor Main
Mills, William H., s s Main bet Queen and Bay
Munro, Richard, H. R., Main bet James and Hughson
Niblett, Charles W., Commercial Bdgs., James
O'Reilly, J. Edwin, 8 King w
O'Reilly Miles, 8 King w
O'Reilly & O'Reilly, 8 King w
Osler & Osler, King e opp Fountain
Papps, George S., LL B., King cor James
Pringle, James D., Wentworth Chambers
Proudfoot, Wm., Main bet James and Hughson
Proudfoot & Munro, Main bet James and Hughson
Robb, James, Wentworth Chambers
Sadleir, Charles A., Hughson bet King and Main
Spohn, Jacob V., Commercial Buildings, James
Spohn & Bell, Commercial Chambers
Start, J. E., Commercial Chambers
Thomson, James R., Hughson bet King and Main
Thomson & Kilvert, Hughson bet King and Main
Tiffany, Edward H., Hughson bet King and Main
Waddell, Robert R., s e cor King and John
Waddell & Lemon, cor King and John
Wetenhall, Henry, Hughson bet King and Main

Beef and Pork Packers.

Nash, Samuel, Market cor McNab
Ontario Pork Factory, Township Barton

Bellows Makers.

Dally, James, Murray, bet McNab and James
Dallyn, Joseph & Son, Murray cor James

Bent Stuff, Manufacturers of

Harris, G. & Son, cor Bay and Stuart

Berlin Wool Dealers.

Carpenter, E. & Co., 39 King w
Moodie, John, 36 King w
Pearson, John & Co., 58 King w
Warry, Miss E. R., 16 King w

Billiard Parlors.

Colvin, John, 8 King w
Egener, F. & Co., King bet Catherine and Walnut
Royal Hotel Billiard Rooms, James P. Phelan, Merrick cor James
Taylor, John D., James opp Mechanics Hall
Tecumseh House, J. Huggard, prop.

Boat Builders.

Bastien, H. L., Phelan's boat house
Stalley, Martin, foot of James

Boilermakers.

Beckett, F. G. & Co., Simcoe bet James and McNab
McAllister, David C., Zealand's wharf
Northey, George, Wellington cor East Market
Thomas, John & Co., Rebecca bet John and Catherine

Boiler Compound.

Forster, A. M., Stuart bet Mary and Catherine

Bookbinders and Blank-book Manufacturers.

Barnes, George & Co., James cor Market Square
Brown, W. & Co., 46 James n
Eastwood, J. & Co., King e opp Fountain
Haigh, Richard, *Spectator* Buildings, cor Main and Hughson
Lawson, A. & Co., 3 King w
Munzinger, John M., York bet McNab and Park
Ruthven, Peter, 51 Hughson

Booksellers and Stationers.

Ballintine, R. M., 62 James
Barnes, George & Co., James cor Market Square
Brown, W. & Co., 46 James n
Eastwood, J. & Co., 16 King opp Fountain
Lyght, Joseph & Co., King cor Hughson
McLellan, Donald, 26 King w

Boot and Shoe Manufacturers and Dealers (Wholesale.)

Garrett, John & Co., King nr Bank of Montreal
McPherson, John & Co., 51 and 53 King e

Boot & Shoe Manufacturers and Dealers.

Aynsley, Jas. J., King e bet Nelson and Walnut
Billington, John, n s Merrick bet Park and Bay
Britt, Edward, York cor Bay and Caroline
Carmichael, John H., King William bet Hughson and John
Conley, Peter, 14 King William
Cornor, Robert, York bet Park and Bay
Cusack, William, Mulberry bet James and McNab
Dayfoot, P. W. & Co., 52 King e
Debus, George, James n of Mulberry

Boot & Shoe Manufacturers, &c.—(Continued)

Dicker, William, n s King bet Mary and Nelson
Edwards, Charles P., 88 King w
Elms, E., Hughson cor Tyburn
Fletcher, Joseph, York bet Bay and Caroline
Freeman & Mahony, 26 King e
Gilmore, William, 1 John n
Gorvin, John, Mechanics Hall Building
Griffith, Henry, 82 King e
Henry, John & Co., 62 King e
Hennessy, John, 60 King e
Hopkins, Robert, 8 James n
Kelly, Joseph, 74 James n
McCann, John, 99 James n
Molzhan, Charles, 89 King e
Mossman, Mark, Hughson cor Gore
Myers, Robert, James nr Barton
Parks, D., Lind bet John and Catherine
Robinson, William, John bet Peel and Tyburn
Ruse, Mrs. M. A., 30 King w
Schwarz, Edward, 106 King w
Shire, Bernhard (carpet shoes), John bet Gore and Henry
Steel, George, 16 York
Thompson, Gregor, 82 King e
Tremlett, William, 20 King w
Widger, James, King cor McNab
Wills, J., 58 King e
Wilson, Robert, 40 John s
Woodley, Samuel, 22 James n

Box Manufacturers.

Aitchison, W. & D., Bond nr King

Brass Founders.

Howie, A. & Co., 3 King w
Lyall, John, York bet Park and Bay
Malcolm, William, Hughson cor Augusta
Young, H. & R., McNab nr Stewart's Foundry

Brewers.

Bauer, Leopold, (Ontario Brewery), Catherine bet East Bay and Bay Line
Beck, George, (Crystal Palace Brewery,) King cor Margaret
Eckhardt, Edward, western limits
Grant & Middlewood, (Spring Brewery), Peel cor Mulberry
Kendall, Joseph, (Hamilton Brewery, Peel cor Catherine

Brickmakers.

Bowden, Aaron, Canada nr Garth
Little, Alfred, Garth bet Main and King
Little, Vincent, Main nr Western limits
New, Henry & J., Garth bet Main and King

Bristles, Russian, Importers.

Carpenter, E. & Co., 39 King w

Brokers.

Ambridge, T. A., King bet James and McNab
Crawford, W. G., Royal Hotel Buildings, Merrick
Davis, John H. & Co., King bet James and Hughson
Forbes, A. F., King William cor James

Brokers, (Stock, Bill and Exchange.)

Forbes, A. F., n e cor King William and James
Jones, Charles T. & Co., Mechanics' Hall
McKeand, Archibald, 9 James n
Riddel, John, 20 King e
Steinger, Joseph, Stuart nr Bay
Taylor & Minty, James
Willson, F. M., 5 James nr King

Broom Manufacturers.

Easson, Allan, King cor Caroline
Mitchell, Thomas, 21 King w
Mugridge, & Lorimer, McNab bet Merrick & Vine

Brush Manufacturers.

Burdett, Joseph, 35 King w
Green, Alfred J., 16 and 18 John n
Meakins & Sons, King bet Nelson and Cathcart
Mitchell, Thomas, 21 King w
Still, John, Mulberry cor McNab

Builders and Contractors.

Allan & Co., Rebecca bet John and Catherine
Chisholm, Robert, McNab bet Concession and Colborne
Clucas, William, s s Miles bet Caroline and Hess
Edgar, David, Locomotive cor York
Faulknor, Joseph, Broadway cor Pearl
Hancock, William, York bet Pearl and Lock
Jackson, Thomas, Victoria ave cor Main
Kempster, C. W., Main bet Catherine and Walnut
Lister, Claude, Hughson bet Gore and Henry
Manning, F. E., Tyburn bet Cherry and Spring
Murison, George, Hughson cor Catherine
Richardson, William, cor Market and Caroline
Rigsby, John, east Market bet Mary and Nelson
Sharp & Muirson, Bay bet Merrick and Vine
Stevenson, Charles, 14 Wellington
Summers, William W., Main bet Bond and Bowery
Webber, E., Maria near John
Webster, James, Union bet Hughson and John
White, W. C., McNab bet Cannon and Mulberry
Yates, Robert, Charles bet Maiden Lane and Hunter
Yates & Garson, Duke nr Bond

Building Society (Western Permanent).

T. Duggan, M.D., President; Thomas McIlwraith, Vice-President; F. A. Ball, Secretary and Treasurer. Directors—William McMillan, David Wright, W. B. Woods, E. S. Whipple, Charles H. Stokoe

Cabinet Makers and Upholsterers.

Bolingbroke, Charles, 90 King
Dodsworth, John H., York cor Hess
Hill, Thomas, 32 John s
Jarvis, John, King bet Nelson and Cathcart
Johnson & Jenkins, Bay cor York
Langberg, Frederick, 83 King e
Meakins & Sons, King bet Nelson and Cathcart
Noyes, J. & Son, 112 King e
Reid, James, King cor Bond
Schumacher, George, Market bet McNab and Park
Stacy, James B. P., 71 King e
Wright, William, West ave bet King and East Market

Carriage and Coachbuilders.

Bridgewood, George, Tyburn nr Hughson
Cooper, H. G. & Co., Bond bet King and Main
Macabe, Thomas & Co., King w
Pronguey, J. P., Park cor Market

Carriage Axle Manufacturer.

Doty, John, York bet Bay and Caroline

Carvers and Gilders.

Blandford, Henry, 59 James n
Jennings, David J., G. W. R.
Marsden, Thomas, 50 James n
Thompson, James R., Maiden Lane cor Queen

Chemists and Druggists.

*Bickle, T. & Son, 6 King e
Blaicher, Peter C., John South of Peel
*Briggs, G. C. & Sons, King William nr James
*Dalley, Edwin, s s York bet Queen and Bay
*Hamilton, A. & Co., King cor James
Holbrook & Stark, King cor Hughson
Lawrence, Thomas & Co., Stinson's Block, King e
Meldrum, Henry, 74 King e
Moore, Lyman & Brierly, 14 King e
Moore, Lyman & Mundy, James nr King Wm
*Winer, J. & Co., 25 King e

China, Glass and Earthenware.

Armstrong, Isaac, 20 York bet McNab and Park
Bigelow, Albert, Hughson bet Main and Tyburn
*Daville, T. W., 70 King w
Fletcher, George, John bet King and King Wm
Fraser, P. & Co., James cor King
*Skinner, James A. & Co., 37 King e
Thorn, William, 30 York bet McNab and Park

Cigars and Tobacco.

Birge, C. A. & M. B., 48 James n
Curtis, W. R., 66 King w
Chilman, I. C., King w bet Bowery and Caroline
Grover, Luther, 51 James n
Knowles, Henry, Catharina bet Catherine and John
Lewis, Thomas, 88 King e
McDonald, David, Bay cor York
Pattison, Z., Cannon bet Park and Bay
Pike, Richard, 12 King w
Quimby, Alfred C., 43 James n
Schrader, Frederick J., McNab bet Hunter and Bold
Schwarz, Louis, 81 James n

Civil Engineers.

Askins, A. H., G. W. R.
Haskins, William, city engineer, King cor West Ave.
Hills, Albert H., Charles bet Maiden Lane and Hunter
Livingston, T. C., 4 Tuckett's Block, Bay
O'Keefe, D. C., 2 John s
Rastrick, Fred., J., Maria bet John and Hughson
Reid, George Lowe, (chief engineer, G. W. R.,)

Clothiers.

Bruce, Magnus, 7 James n
Foster, Charles, King cor McNab
Hogan, Jeremiah H., 68 King cor John
Hogan & O'Neill, 6 James n
King, William, 26 John s
Lawson, Bros., 2 and 4 King n e cor James
Levy, Isaac, 22 King w and Market Square
Munro & Henderson, 28 King e
Murray, A. & Co. 18 King e
Peirce, C. E. & Co., James cor King William
Seaman, S. L., 19 York and King w
Smith, Donald, 40 King e
Somerville, James H. & Co., 14 James n

Coal Oil and Lamps.

Farmer, William, 98 and 100 James n
Fletcher, George, John bet King and King Wm
Harding, Henry, James cor Rebecca
Hobson & McPhie, s s Market Square
Kerr, Murray A., 53 King w
McDougall, James, King cor McNab
Spencer, Henry, King William bet Hughson and James
Tomkins, George, James nr Murray
Young & Bro., 24 and 26 John n, cor King Wm

Coal Oil, (wholesale.)

Canadian Coal Oil Co., 17 King w

Coal and Wood Dealers.

Bible, Robert, Main cor Charles
Browne, E., Browne's wharf
Knox, David, Merrick
Mackay, Æneas D., Mackay's wharf
Myles, Thomas, Myles' wharf, and Main cor Hughson
Proctor, John, Zealand's wharf
Reid, William & Co., Mary bet Henry and Rebecca

Coal Grates.

Robbins, N. B., Mary nr Willson

Coffee and Spice Mills.

Doherty, Thomas A., w s Catherine bet Henry and Lind
Excelsior, Coffee and Spice Mills, Perkins & Clark Catherine cor Rebecca

Commercial Schools and Colleges.

Bruce, William, James opp Gore
Royal Dominion Commercial College, James cor King William

Commission Merchants.

Andrews, A. & Co., King cor John
Benner, Richard, Canada Life Assurance Buildings, James
Clark, John & Co., John cor King
Crawford. W. G., Royal Hotel buildings, Merrick
Davis, John H. & Co., King e bet James and Hughson
Duncan & Galloway, s s Market Square
Evans, Robert, Royal Hotel block
Fairgrieve, John, NcNab bet King and Market
Fearman, Frederick W., McNab nr Market
Gilmour, William, James opp Gore
Gregory, S. E. 35 King e
Hammond, N., James
Hardiker, John, w s James nr Mulberry
Harvey, John, 11 King e
Knox, David, Merrick
McKenzie & Mackay, 9 King e
Macnabb, Duncan A., Royal Hotel buildings
Marshall, George, King bet Catherine and Maria
Pettit, J. H., 2 John s
Proctor, John, Merrick w of James
Smith, John & Co., King cor John
Williamson, James, Brock nr Bay
Willson, J. W., King cor John
Young, Maitland, jr., King e

Contractors.

Allan, William, Concession bet James & McNab
Chisholm, Robert, McNab bet Concession and Colborne
Hendrie & Co., King cor McNab
MacDonald, Alexander, s s York bet Caroline and Hess
ullin, James, Main bet Cherry and Spring
Stephenson, Charles, Wellington bet Pearl and Tyburn
Taylor, John, Bowery cor Main

Coopers.

Boyd, David, 10 John n
Faustman, Ernst, John bet Rebecca and Gore
Gordon, William, n s King William bet Hughson and John

Drum Heaters, Patent.

North, Samuel, McNab nr Merrick

Dentists.

Bogart, D. A., Hughson cor Rebecca
Chittenden, C. S., King e Corby's block
Filgiano, Theophilus Le P., n e cor James and King
Walker, A. A., D.D.S., 8 King e

Dry Goods, Millinery, etc.

Barnard, P. B. & H., 34 King w
Chadwick, John A., John nr King
Courtenay, John, Market Square
Crossley, John, James cor King William
Egan & Bartindale, 12 James n
Fowkes, Thomas, 11 King William
Holbrook, James, 22 King e
Hyslop, D. A., 15 James n
James, George, 16 James n
Lawson Brothers, King cor James
McMillan, Archibald, Ray bet Broadway and Little Main
Magill, Charles, 76 King e
Murray, A. & Co., 18 King e
Peacock, John, e s McNab bet King and Market
Robertson, James, 20 King e
Ross, Andrew, Lister's Block, James
Roy, Robert & Co., James opp Fountain
Somerville, J. H. & Co., 14 James n
Stanbury & Co., 30 King e
Thomson, Thomas & Co., 32 King e
Watkins, T. C., 10 James n

Dry Goods, (Wholesale).

Buchanan & Co., King e cor Catherine
Chadwick, John A., John nr King
Frier & Dale, King bet McNab and Charles
Gates, F. W. & Co., Commercial Bdgs. King w
Kerr, Brown & Mackenzie, King e nr James
McInnes, Calder & Co., King cor John
Roy, Robert & Co., James opp Fountain
Thomson, Birkett & Bell, McNab cor Merrick
Walker, James, 33 King e

Dyers and Scourers.

Connor, James, 77 James
McLeod, A., James cor Cannon

Enamellers, Hollow Ware.

Campbell, R. & Co., Mary Street Foundry

Engravers, Copper, Steel and Wood.

Fell, William, s s Market Square
Scriven, P. L., 28 King w

Envelope Manufacturers.

Buntin, Gillies & Co., 23 King e

Express Companies.

American Express Company, J. D. Irwin, agent, James opp Gore

Fancy Goods, Importers of

Boice, William & Co., 3 King e
Carpenter, E. & Co., 39 King w
Furner, G. H. & Co., D. McInnes' Block
Skinner, James A. & Co., 27 King e

Fish, Oysters and Game (wholesale).

Lee, George, 4 and 6 King w

Flax Brokers.

McKenzie & Mackay, 9 King e

Flour and Feed.

Allan, David, 9 and 11 York
Bampfylde, Charles, John bet Augusta & Catharina
Carruthers, John, 2 King William
Doran, William, King bet Nelson and Cathcart
Gillesby, William, w s John south of King
Hancock, Joseph, cor John and Peel
Hardy, Charles, McNab cor York
Harrison, Edward, 12 John s
Hill, Mark, McNab bet King and Main
King, Robert, John bet Tyburn and Peel
Land, William, agent, McNab nr King
Laws, John, King e nr Catherine
Lees, George, 16 John s
Little, John, cor King and Wentworth
Logan, George, agent, 76 King w
Lutz, James M., 11 and 13 York
McLean, George, 76 King w
Magee, William, e s James bet Stinson & Barton
Meston, Charles, 25 and 27 York
Morgan, W. & R., 22 and 24 John s
Morgan, Benjamin, Main bet Cherry and Walnut
Morris, John G., 25 York
Morris & Bro., 5 King William and Wellington cor east Market
Morrison, Thomas, John cor Wood Market
Ronan, & Bro., 2 York
Ryckman, John, King bet Hess and Queen
Sharp, William, John bet Tyburn and Peel
Squire, C., 4 Florence block King w
Thorburn, James, John bet Peel and Tyburn
Youngman, Samuel, Merrick bet Park and Bay

Forwarding, Shipping and Commission Merchants.

Birely, N. F., Brock nr Bay
Browne, Edward, Browne's wharf
Mackay, Æneas D., Mackay's wharf
Williamson, James, Brock nr Bay

Founders and Machinists.

Beckett, F. G. & Co., James nr Simcoe
Burrow & Stewart (malleable iron), Caroline bet Miles and York
Doty, John (carriage axles and boxes), York bet Bay and Caroline
Gurney, E. & C., e s John bet King William and Rebecca
Moore, D. & Co., Catherine cor Lind
Northey, George, Wellington cor east Market
Stewart, James & Co., McNab cor Vine
Thomas, John & Co., Rebecca bet John and Catherine
Turnbull & Co., Mary cor Little Gore
Young, H. & R., McNab nr Stewart's Foundry

Fruits (Wholesale and Retail).

Lee, George, 4 and 6 King w
O'Callaghan, F., 12 King w

Gents' Furnishing Goods.

Egan & Jeffery, 8 King e
Foster, Charles, King cor McNab
Hogan, J. H., King cor John
Hogan & O'Neill, 6 James n
Pierce, C. E. & Co., James cor King William
Storror, F. M., King cor McNab

Glass Manufacturers.

Hamilton Glass Works, Rutherford & Co., Hughson cor Warren

Gold and Silver Platers.

Howie, A. & Co., 3 King w

Grain Merchants.

Abraham, Charles F., 55 King e
Birely, N. F., Brock nr Bay
Davis, John H., 13 King e
Myles, Alfred, Bay
Waddell, William W., 2 John s
Williamson, James, Brock nr Bay
Wilson, J. W., King cor John

Grape Wine Manufacturer.

Bauer, Henry, Main bet James and Hughson

Grate Manufacturers.

Gurney, E. & C., John
Robbins, N. B., Mary cor Willson

Grocers (Wholesale.)

Brown, Gillespie & Co., King cor James
Buchanan & Co., King cor Catherine
Forster, G. J. & Co., King cor Charles
Harvey, Stuart & Co., 21 King e
Kerr, Brown & McKenzie, King e
Perkins & Clark, cor Catherine and Rebecca
Turner, James & Co., Hughson bet King & Main

Grocers, (Wholesale and Retail.)

Ashbaugh, F. A., s s Market Square
Cherrier & Brother. s s Market Square
Cooper, R. C. & Co., McNab, bet King and Market
Daville, T. W., 70 King west
Horning & Ryckman, e s McNab, bet Market and King
Lottridge, J. W. & Co., James cor Mkt Square
Mugridge & Lorimer, McNab, bet Merrick and Vine.
Murphy & Murray, 78 King east
Osborne, James, James, near King
Sharp & Secord, 31 King east
Sutherland, Angus, 50 King west
Truman, William, McNab, Market Square

Grocers, (Retail.)

Barr, John, James bet McAulay and Picton
Boyd, Thomas, King William cor John
Bradshaw, James, James opp Market
Cooper, R. C. & Co., w s McNab bet King and Market
Co-operative Association, s s Market Square
Craigie, James, 72 King e
Dalley, Edwin, York bet Queen and Bay
Donahoe, John, 10 John s
Doran, William, King bet Nelson and Cathcart
Fraser, William, 9 John s
Freeman & Bro., e s James bet Henry and Lind
Lauphier, William H., 66 King e
McAllister, John, cor York and Caroline
McAllister, John, McNab bet Mulberry and Colborne
McAuliffe, Jeremiah, Park cor Sheaffe
Marshall, Joseph. King cor Queen
Monro, Hugh, Stuart cor James
Morris, Philip, cor John and Lind
Morris & Bro., Wellington cor East Market
Morrison, Thomas, John cor Wood Market
Murdoch, John, John cor Union
Park, William, John nr Main
Pilgrim, Robert A., King cor Cathcart
Ronald, William, 15 York
Secord & Davis, cor John and Main
Sellett, George H., 21 Rebecca
Smith, George, s s Market Square
Walker, Robert, s s York bet Queen and Bay
Walker, William, Merrick cor Park
Young, Charles, James n of Murray

Gunsmiths.

Holland, James, John, cor King William
O'Brien, Henry, John, bet Tyburn and Peel
Leitch, John, John, near Rebecca

Hams and Bacon, Curers of

Campbell, John, James, bet Main and Tyburn
Fearman, F. W., McNab, bet King and Market
Hardy, Charles, McNab, cor York
Nash, Samuel, Market, cor McNab

Hardware.

Baine, John W., James, opp Market
Chadwick, John A., John, near King
Hope, Adam & Co., King, cor Catherine
Kent, E. R., 74 King west
McGiverin, Edward, 56 King east
McGiverin, William & Co., 13 and 15 James, opp Gore
Magill & Brother, 38 King east
Ross & Smith, 54 King east
Wood & Leggat, n s King, east of Hughson

Hats, Caps, Furs and Straw Goods.

Angus, J. & J., 56 King west
Egan & Jeffery, 8 King east
Fielding, Joseph, King, cor Bond
Glassco, William H. & Son, 19 King east
Hitchcock, H. L., Henry, bet Hughson and John
Hutchison, James, 3 James north
Mason, Thomas, 12 James north
Mills, Joseph, 7 James north

Hats, Caps, Furs and Straw Goods (Wholesale.)

Galbraith & Co., King, bet James and McNab
Glassco, W. H. & Son, cor King and Hughson

Homœopathic Pharmacy.

Woolverton, Mrs. E. W., 86 King e

Hoop Skirt Manufacturers.

Hawkins, George D. & Co., 54 King w

Hosiery Manufacturers.

Ancaster Knitting Company, off 2 King w

Hotels and Proprietors.

American Hotel, E. W. Bearman, prop., King cor Charles
Anglo-American Hotel, cor McNab and Market, Henry McCracken
Balmoral House, T. Meldrum, prop., McNab cor Stewart
British Exchange, John Morden, York bet Park and Bay
British Hotel, Thomas Beatty, s e cor Main and John
City Arms Hotel, William Yaldon, McNab cor Murray
Cook's Hotel, Mrs. William Cook, prop. 64 and 66 King w
Dominion Hotel, Frederick Jeffs, prop., s s Stuart opp G. W. R. Station
European Hotel, John Kerner, prop., 72 King w
Farmer's Hotel, John Sutterby, prop., McNab nr Merrick
Ford's Hotel, James Ford, 45 James n
Fountain Hotel, Samuel Easter
Great Western Hotel, J. E. Dallyn, James cor Murray
Harkin's Hotel, John Harkin, prop., s s Market Square
James Street Hotel, Samuel Maslin, James cor Cannon
Manchester Hotel, James Forrest, Bay bet Murray and Stuart
Market Hotel, Thomas Duffy, prop., McNab cor Merrick
Metropolitan Hotel, Charles Hutton, cor Stuart and Bay
Mountain View Hotel, Charles Price, prop.
Nelligan, Dennis, John bet Peel and Tyburn
Nelson Hotel, John Armstrong, prop. s s Market Square

Hotels and Proprietors—(*Continued.*)

North American Hotel, O. Nowlan, John cor King William
Ontario Hotel, William Flook, s s Stuart opp G. W. R. Station
Ontario House, James Arthurs, Merrick s s bet James and McNab
Orr, Daniel, Ship Inn, John bet Base and Guise
Palm's Hotel, William, Palm, King cor Bay
Railroad Hotel, Moses Furlong, foot of James
Rob Roy, Michael Murphy, prop. John cor Peel
Royal Hotel, S. Bronson, manager, James cor Merrick
Shakspeare Hotel, J. B. Martin, s s Market Square
Station Hotel, D. Henderson, Stuart opp Depot
Steamboat Hotel, C. J. Finley, McNab cor Burlington
Tecumseh House, J. Huggard, James nr Merrick
Three Horse Shoe, Peter McCullock, York cor Park
Volunteers' Hotel, James Macabe, King bet Bay and Caroline
Wentworth Hotel, Richard Creech, Hughson s of Main
Western Hotel, Samuel Smith, York cor Bay
Wexford House, Luke O'Brien, King bet Catherine and Mary
White Horse Inn, Peter Shannon, McNab bet York and Merrick
Yaldon, William, City Arms Hotel, McNab nr Murray
Young, R., Ontario Hotel, Prince's Square

Ice Dealers.

Berry, John, w s John, nr Hospital
Dewey, Daniel O., King bet Bowery & Caroline
Foyster, J., Burlington nr James
Moore & McCauley, cor Main and Catherine

Inspectors.

Moore, John, (licenses) City Hall
McNair, Samuel, (weights & measures) City Hall
Stirling, George, (hides), Catharina bet John and Hughson

Insurance Companies and Agencies.

Ætna Life Insurance Co., Hartford, James Garvin, agent, 50 James n
Ætna Insurance Co., Hartford, W. F. Findlay, agent, James opp Gore
Atlantic Mutual Insurance Co., J. W. Willson, agent, King cor John
British America Insurance Co., Fire Department, E. Ritchie, agent, Post Office
British America Marine, A. F. Forbes, agent, cor James and King William
Canada Life Assurance Co., A. G. Ramsay, F.I.A., manager, James nr Main, Isaac Mills, agent
Canada Farmers' Mutual Insurance Co., Commercial Chambers, James
City of Glasgow (Life), R. Benner, agent, Canada Life Assurance Buildings
Commercial Union, of England, J. J. Mason, C. R. Murray and W. G. Crawford, city agents
Edinburgh Life, Isaac Mills, agent, Wentworth Chambers
Etna Fire Insurance Co., of Dublin, John Clark & Co., agents, John cor King
Gore District Mutual (Life), D. Wright, agent, James n
Hartford Fire Insurance Co., A. McKeand, agent 9 James n
Hartford Live Stock Insurance Co., McKenzie & Mackay, 9 King e
Home District Mutual Fire Insurance Co., D. Wright, agent, James n
Home and Colonial (limited), A. F. Forbes, agent, King William
Home Inland Marine Insurance Co., James D. Pringle, agent, Wentworth Chambers
Home Insurance Co., New Haven, Conn., A. McKeand, agent, 9 James n
Imperial (Fire), R. Benner, agent, Canada Life Assurance Buildings
Lancashire Fire and Life, Isaac Mills, agent, Wentworth Chambers
Life Association of Scotland, A. F. Forbes, King William cor James
Liverpool and London and Globe Insurance Co., F. A. Ball, agent, T. A. Ambridge, acting agent, King bet James and McNab
London Assurance Corporation (1720), W. F. Findlay, James opp Gore
London and Lancashire Insurance Co., W. G. Crawford, Royal Hotel Buildings
Montreal Marine Insurance Co., Maitland Young, jr., 35 King e
National Travellers' Insurance Co., New York, W. G. Crawford, agent, Royal Hotel Buildings
North British and Mercantile, J. D. Pringle, agent, Wentworth Chambers
Phenix Insurance Co., of Brooklyn, N. Y., E. Browne, agent, Browne's wharf
Phenix Marine, McKenzie & Mackay, agents, 9 King e
Phenix Ocean Marine Insurance Co., of Brooklyn, N. Y., J. D. Pringle, agent, Wentworth Chambers
Phœnix Insurance Company, of London, England, Brown, Gillespie & Co., agents, King cor James
Phœnix Mutual Life Insurance Co., Hartford, Conn., W. G. Crawford, agent, Royal Hotel Buildings
Provincial, (Fire), Isaac Mills, agent for County of Wentworth, Wentworth Chambers
Provincial, (Fire and Marine), J. D. Pringle, agent, Wentworth Chambers
Queen Fire Insurance Co., McKenzie & Mackay, 9 King e
Reliance Mutual Life Assurance Co., London, England, John Clark & Co., agents, John cor King
Royal Insurance Co., George A. Young, agent Royal Hotel Buildings
Scottish Provincial Assurance Co., J. D. Pringle, agent, Wentworth Chambers
Security Insurance Co., of New York, (Marine), S. E. Gregory, agent, King e next door to Bank of Commerce
Taylor & Minty, James
Traveller's' Insurance Co., Hartford, A. McKeand, agent, 2 King w
Victoria Mutual, (Fire), Wentworth Buildings, W. D. Booker, treasurer and secretary
Western Assurance Company, of Toronto, McKenzie and Mackay, agents, 9 King e

Insurance Companies (Home)

Canada Farmers' Mutual Insurance Co., Commercial Buildings, James, R. P. Street, secretary and teasurer
Canada Life Assurance Co., A. G. Ramsay. F. I. A., manager, James nr Main
Victoria Mutual, (Fire), Wentworth Buildings, W. D. Booker, treasurer and secretary

Iron Founders.

Beckett, F. G. & Co., Simcoe bet James and McNab
Burrow & Stewart, (malleable iron), Caroline bet Miles and York
Copp & Bro., Bay cor York
Doty, John, York bet Bay and Caroline
Gurney, E. & C., John bet King William and Rebecca
Moore, D. & Co., Catherine nr Lind
Stewart, James & Co., McNab cor Vine
Turnbull & Co., Mary cor Little Gore
Thomas, John & Co., Rebecca bet John and Catherine

Iron, Steel and Metals.—(*See also Hardware.*)

McGiverin, William & Co., 13 and 15 James opp Gore
Magill, & Bro., 38 King e
Ross & Smith, 54 King e
Wood & Leggat, n s King, e of Hughson

Jewelers, Manufacturing.

Batty, Benjamin, 40 King w
Belling, B. M., w s James bet King and Main
Rudel, William Henry, King cor James
Russell, Richard, James s opp Fountain
Steward, T. B., 12 King e

Leather, Hides, Skins, Findings, &c.

Beardmore, George L., King bet James and McNab
Crawford, John, cor East Market and Nelson
Cuznor, John, York bet Park and McNab
Fields, John C., 32 King w.
Gunner, William, s s Market Square
Rauch, Joseph, 8 John n

Lithographers.

Brown & Bautz, King William cor James
Eastwood, J. & Co., King east opp Fountain
Lyght, Joseph & Co., King cor Hughson

Livery and Sale Stables.

Bevier, Dennis, 77 King w
Burness, Geo. & Co., James bet Merrick and Vine
Coutts, Andrew, Main nr John
Darrow, John, Rebecca bet James and Hughson
Mathews, Joseph B., s s Market nr Park
Nowlan, O., cor John and King William
Temple, John & Co., Catherine bet King William and Rebecca

Lock Manufacturers.

Meakins & Sons, King nr Cathcart
Meakins, George H., Cathcart

Lumber Merchants.

Chisholm, William, James cor Colborne
Edgar, William, Caroline cor York
Powell, T. S., Hughson bet Tyburn and Peel
Ross, Samuel F., Napier bet Hess and Queen

Machinists.

Beckett, F. G. & Co., Simcoe nr James
Doty, John, York bet Bay and Caroline
Howie, A. & Co., 3 King w
Leitch, John, John nr Rebecca
McAllister, D. C., Zealand's wharf
Northey, George, Wellington cor King William
Stewart, James & Co., McNab Street Foundry,
Thomas, John & Co., Hamilton Iron Works, Rebecca bet John and Catherine
Turnbull & Co., Mary Street Foundry

Machinists' Blacksmiths.

Brayley, James, top of Mountain
Hennessy, Hugh, Hughson s of King William

Malleable and Grey Iron Manufacturers.

Burrows & Stewart, e s Caroline bet York and Miles

Manufacturers' Agents.

Dunstan, R. Jewell & Co., (British and Canadian manufacturers), Royal Hotel Buildings

Marble Cutters and Dealers.

Day & McComb, Merrick cor Bay
Hurd & Roberts, York junction of Merrick
Rice, M. E., cor Park and Merrick

Marriage Licenses (Issuer of).

Ambridge, Theodore A., King w bet James and McNab

Melodeon Manufacturers.

Thornton and Green, Florence Block, Bay
White, Thomas W., King w cor McNab

Merchant Tailors.

Bruce, Magnus, 7 James n
Evans, Daniel, 89 James n
Foster, Charles, King cor McNab
Furnival, Thomas G., 58 James
Gray, Robert, James nr Main
Herron, Joseph, 4 John n
Hogan, Jeremiah H. & Co., 68 King e
Huton & Woon, Hughson bet King and King William
Kendel, Francis, 104 King w
King, William, 26 John s
Lawson Brothers, King cor James
Milborn, Robert, James, opp the Gore
Munro & Henderson, 28 King east
Murray A. & Co., 18 King east
Pierce, C. E. & Co., James, nr King William
Smith, Donald, 40 King east

Milliners and Millinery Goods.

Carruthers, Miss, 67 King west
Dodson, Miss, 62 King west
Donahoe, Mrs. J., 8 John south
Heys, Mrs. J., James, bet Lind and Barton
Johnston, Mrs. Jacob, John, bet Peel and Tyburn
Lawson Bros., King cor James
Miller, Miss A., McNab nr King
Mills, Joseph, 7 James n
Murray, A. & Co., 18 King east
Sillett, Mrs., 23 Rebecca
Towersey, Mrs. Joseph, 9 King William
Yale, Mrs. D. C., James nr Main
Young, Miss J., 73 King west

Millinery (Wholesale.)

Furner, G. H. & Co., D. McInnes' Block

Music and Musical Instruments.

Brown, William & Co., 46 James north
Grossman, Peter, 61 James north
White, Thomas W., 38 King west

Newspapers and Periodicals.

Banner of Faith, published monthly, printed at *Spectator* office
Canada Christian Advocate, John street, Rev. G. Abbs, editor
Craftsman (Masonic), semi-monthly, published by T. & R. White, *Spectator* office

Ancaster Woollen Machine Manufactory,

H. & A. EGLESTON,

ARE MANUFACTURING ALL KINDS OF

WOOLLEN MACHINERY,

VIZ.:

Roll Carding Machines, Manufacturing Machines, Power Looms, Giss, Nappers, &c., &c., from entire new patterns, embracing all the modern improvements.

ALSO

AGRICULTURAL IMPLEMENTS,

Such as Cultivators, Ploughs, various kinds of Root Cutters, &c., at low prices.

H. & A. EGLESTON, Proprietors.

EYRE THURESSON,

MANUFACTURER OF SUPERIOR COTTON AND WOOL

All Cards made at this Establishment are of

best Wire, & of English Oak Tanned Leather

MACHINE CARD CLOTHING,

ANCASTER, ONTARIO.

The Proprietor established his Factory in 1863, and has at present at work 38 machines, including Horse Card, Diamond Point, Sheet, Fillet and Doffer Ring Machines. In the manufacture of Card Clothing, E. Thuresson uses only English Oak Tanned Leather in preference to all other kinds; employing twelve hands, and consuming 125 sides of leather weekly.

The following points for square foot, have been generally adopted by manufacturers for all ordinary carding purposes, and unless otherwise ordered, will be filled accordingly:—

No. of Wire.	Points in a square foot.	No. of Wire.	Points in a square foot.
28	34,560	34	62,208
30	41,472	35	69,120
32	48,384	36	76,032
33	55,296		

ANCASTER HOTEL,

JOHN CRAM, Proprietor,

ANCASTER, ONT.

Good accomodation for travellers. Excellent Stabling.

[ANCASTER HOTEL (OR STONE TAVERN,]

CHARLES PHILLIPS, PROP.,

ANCASTER, ONTARIO,

First-class stabling attached.

VICTORIA HOTEL,

ANCASTER, ONTARIO,

RICHARD IRWIN, PROPRIETOR.

Choice Wines and Liquors. Good stabling.

Newspapers and Periodicals—*(Continued)*

Hamilton City and County of Wentworth Directory, (annual) C. E. Anderson & Co., publishers. Directory Branch *Daily Telegraph* office, Toronto

Hamilton Evening Times, (daily, evening and weekly) C. E. Stuart & Co., Hughson

Messenger (semi-monthly), devoted to the temperance cause, drawer 69 Hamilton P.O.

Spectator (daily, morning and weekly), T. & R. White, *Spectator* Buildings

Nurserymen.

Bruce, John A. & Co., 52 King west
Hamilton Nurseries, Warren Holton, prop., King, cor Wellington

Oil Manufacturers and Refiners.

Canadian Oil Company, 17 King west

Organ Builders.

Thornton & Green, 3 Florence Block, Bay
White, Thomas W., 38 King w

Oysters and Game (Wholesale.)

Lee, George, 4 and 6 King w
O'Callaghan, F., 14 King w

Painters, House, Sign and Ornamental.

Armstrong, Walter, cor Main and Cherry
Atkinson, Joseph, Wellington nr Willson
Barker & Lemessurier, Main bet McNab & James
Briers, Thomas, e s Catherine bet Gore & Henry
Cook, William, Vine nr McNab
Davis, William, John bet Lind and Barton
Edgcomb, O. W., King cor Catherine
Fitzpatrick & Bro., 33 York
Freeborn, Thomas, cor Willson and Elgin
Holcomb, W. H., 24 Hughson
Mathews & McMenemy, McNab bet King and Market
Pentecost & Son, King nr McNab
Way, James, East Market cor Mary

Paper Bag Manufacturers.

Buntin, Gillies & Co., 23 King e
Cunningham, McKichan & Co., Charles bet King and Main
McKichan, John R., McNab nr King

Patent Medicines.

Bliss, Horace C., Wellington bet Henry and Little Gore
Briggs & Sons, King William nr James
Dully, Edwin, York bet Queen and Ray
Galbraith, John, Hughson cor Augusta
Kennedy, James, Merrick opp Market

Photographers.

Cox, John, 8 King e
Eckerson, Luther, 7 James n
Milne, Robert, James n
Wright, C. H., 34 King w

Physicians and Surgeons.

Bates, James, Gore bet Hughson and John
Billings & White, James cor Henry
Case, William J. A., King cor Walnut
Crooker, T. M., James bet Main and Tyburn
Davis, D., Merrick James and McNab
Devlin, James A., Park bet Merrick and Vine
Donnelly, G. J., Head of Walnut
Fergusson, John W., (Homœopathic), Gore bet James and Hughson
Hamilton John M, R. N., Bay cor McNab
Henwood, Edwin, Main bet James and McNab

17

Laing, James B., Cannon bet Park and Bay
McNiece, William J., McNab cor Mulberry
McTaggart, Miles F., Park bet Merrick and Vine
Macdonald, John D., w s James bet Hunter and Bold
MacKelcan, George L., Gore bet James and Hughson
MacKelcan, John, Gore bet Hughson and James
Mackintosh, David, John nr Henry
Mason, John J., Augusta bet James and Hughson
Mullin, John A., w s James bet Cannon and Mulberry
O'Reilly, Charles, City Hospital
Reid, Alexander C., cor Hughson and Rebecca
Ridley, Henry T., s e cor Main and Charles
Rosebrugh, J. W., James bet Maiden Lane and Hunter
Ryall, George, Main nr Catherine
Ryall, Isaac, Main nr Catherine
Strange, Henry, King cor Mary
Vernon, Elias, w s James bet Hunter and Bold

Piano-Forte Manufacturers.

Knott, John, Main cor Catherine
Thomas, C. L., Western Piano-forte Factory, 76 and 78 King w

Piano-Fortes, Dealers in

Brown, William & Co., 46 James n
Grossman, Augustus, 61 James n
Petersen, Adolph, Royal Hotel Buildings
Thomas, C. L., 76 and 78 King w
White, Thomas W., 38 King w

Planing Mills.

Aitchison, W. & D., Bond bet King and Main
Brennan, Michael, rear of 10 John n
Kempster, Charles W., Main bet Catherine and Walnut
Semmens & Co., Sophia bet Inchbury and York
Sharp & Murson, Bay bet Merrick and Vine

Plumbers, Steam and Gas Fitters.

Adam, James, Hughson bet King and King William
Farmer, William, 98 and 100 James n
Harding, Henry, James cor Rebecca
Hobson & McPhie, James cor Main
Malcolm, William, cor Hughson and Augusta
Young & Bro., John cor King William

Pork Dealers.

Baker, James, City Market
Beasley, Richard S., York bet Bay and Caroline
Bowers, J., York bet Park and Bay
Burridge, James, McAllister's Block, York
Campbell, John, James, s of Main
Clark, Thomas, e s James bet Stinson and Barton
Cuff, Robert C., 60 Market Shed
Langberg, John, John n of Peel
Martin, P., cor John and King William
Mills, James, City Market

Pork Packers.

Campbell, John, James s of Main
Davies, John T., Isaac Atkinson, manager, Wentworth nr G. W. R
Martin, P., cor John and King William
Nash, Samuel, Market cor McNab

Portrait Painters.

Davidson, Alexander, Wentworth Chambers
Panting, Richard A., Wentworth Chambers

Potter.

Campbell, William, Garth nr Duke

Potash Manufacturers.

Forbes, Alexander, Barton cor Wellington
Judd, W. H. & Bro., w s Bay bet Cannon & Vine

Powder Manufacturers.

Hamilton Powder Company, James cor Main

Printers (Book and Job).

Canada Christian Advocate, John bet King and King William
Lawson, A. & Co., 8 King w
Raw, Robert, jun., 8 James
Stewart, C. E. & Co., *Times* office, Hughson bet King and King William
White, T. & R., *Spectator* office, Hughson cor Main

Printers (Copper-plate.)

Catchpole, George, 8 Rebecca
Fell, William, s s Market Square

Produce and Commission Merchants.

Abraham, Charles F., 55 King east
Davis, John H. & Co., King e, bet James and Hughson
Duncan & Galloway, s s Market Square
Fairgrieve, John, McNab, bet King and Market Square
Garrett, James S., Wentworth Chambers
Lottridge, J. W. & Co., James, cor Mkt Square
Pettit, J. H., 2 Upper John
Smith, John & Co., King, cor John
Waddell, William W., John, nr King
Williamson, James, Brock nr Bay
Willson, J. W., King, cor John

Provincial Land Surveyors

Blythe, Thomas A., s s Bold, bet James and McNab
Caddy, J., St. V. Wentworth Chambers
O'Keefe, D. C., cor King and John

Pump Maker

Anderson, William, Grove, bet Liberty and Wellington

Railway Cartage Agents

Hendrie & Co., King, cor McNab

Rope and Twine Manufacturers.

Copeland, George, Wellington bet Henry and Barton
Main, Alexander, & Co., Mary cor Oak

Saddle, Harness and Trunk Makers.

Field & Davidson, 18 James n
Jolley, James, Prince's Square, John
Kraft, Ernest, 5 and 7 York bet McNab and Park
McKeown, Hugh, John south nr Peel
O'Heir, Peter, 5 John n
Philp & Robertson, James nr King William
Stewart, George, 42 John
Torrence, Thomas, John cor Tyburn

Saddlery Hardware

Field & Davidson, 18 James n
McGiverin, William, & Co., 13 and 15 James opp Gore

Sail Loft.

Grant, W. W., Bay bet McCaulay and Burlington

Saloons and Restaurants.

Black, Daniel, prop. Club House, e s James north of P. O.
Colvin, John, 8 King w
Colvin, Peter, w s McNab bet King and Market
Cricketer's, Thomas Gillesby, propr., Market nr Park
Dewey, John, Hughson bet King & King William
Fleming, John, Catherine cor Barton
Forest, Thomas, Bain prop. James opp Mulberry
Goering, John W., 53 James
Grell, Lorenzo, John nr King William
Heffernan, Patrick, 90 King e
Hogben, Henry, "Shades Restaurant" 60 James
Lee, George, 4 and 6 King w
McCann, Thomas E., 6 John s
McDonough, Luke, King William bet James and Hughson
Malcolm, John, McNab opp Market
Noble, William, "Metropolitan," James cor Merrick
Roach, George, G. W. R. Station
Robinson Hall, Wm. Carey prop. Market Square
Royal Hotel, James P. Phelan, proprietor
Schaupp, John, Bay bet Concession and Stinson
Smallwood, George, 14 John south
Williams, Charles F., "Shades Saloon," Prince's Square, Main
Winckler, Julius, 18 York
Young, Thomas, 20 John s

Sash, Blind and Door Manufacturers.

Brennen, Michael, rear 10 John n
Kempster, Christopher W., Main bet Catherine and Walnut
Semmens & Co., Sophia nr Inchbury
Sharp & Murison, e s Bay bet Merrick and Vine

Scale Makers.

Gurney, Ware & Co., 88 James north, office John bet King William and Rebecca

Seedmen and Florists.

Bruce, John A. & Co., 52 King w
Cooper, R. C. & Co., McNab bet King and Market
Gillesby, William, w s John s of King
Hardy, Charles, McNab cor York
Morgan, R. & W., 22 John south

Sewing Machine Manufacturers.

Wanzer, R. M. & Co., King cor Catherine

Ship Builder.

Robertson, A. M., Zealand's Wharf

Ship Smiths.

McAllister, D. C., Zealand's Wharf
Spears, Samuel & John, foot of McNab

Soap and Candle Manufacturers.

Judd, W. H. & Bro., Bay bet Cannon and York
Morton, David, Emerald s of Main
Walker, James, Main cor Bowery

Soda Water Manufacturers.

Bilton, Henry W., Market nr McNab
Pilgrim, R. A., King e bet Walnut & Wellington

Stationers (Wholesale).

Buntin, Gillies & Co., 23 King e

Steamship Agencies and Agents.

Anchor Line to Glasgow, F. M. Willson, agent, 5 James n
Chaffey, George & Co.'s, line of steamships and barges, John Proctor, agent, Merrick and Commercial Wharf
Canard Line, C. T. Jones & Co., agents, James n
Hamburg American Packet Company, William Herman, agent, 39 King w
Inman Line to Liverpool and Cork, F. M. Willson, agent, 5 James n

Steamship Agencies & Agents—*(Continued)*

Jacques, Tracy & Co.'s line of steamers, John Proctor, agent, Merrick & Commercial Wharf
London and New York Steamship Co., Archibald McKeand, agent, 9 James n
Montreal Freight and Passenger Line, Æ. D. Mackay, agent, Mackay's wharf
Montreal Ocean Steamship Co., George A. Young agent, Royal Buildings, James
National Steamship Co., to and from Queenstown and Liverpool, Archibald McKeand, agent, 9 James n
New York and Antwerp, William Herman, agt., 39 King w
North American Steamship Co., for California, (opposition line), Archibald McKeand, agent, 9 James n
North German Lloyd, William, Herman, agent, 39 King w
Pacific Mail Steamship Co., to San Francisco, California, Australia, New Zealand, China, and South American ports, via Panama, F. M. Willson, agent, 5 James n
Royal Mail Line, between Hamilton and Montreal, Archibald McKeand, agent, 9 James n

Steam Engine Builders.

Beckett, F. G. & Co., Simcoe bet James and McNab
Northey, George, Wellington cor East Market
Thomas, John & Co., Rebecca bet Catherine and John

Steel Spring Makers.

Grayson, George, Bond bet King and Main

Storage, Forwarding and Shipping.

Birely, N. F., 55 King e
Browne, E., Browne's wharf
Mackay, Æ. D., Mackay's wharf
Proctor, John, Commercial wharf
Williamson, J., Brock nr Bay

Stove, Tin, Copper and Sheet Iron Manufacturers and Dealers.

Bingham, A., McNab bet King and Market
Bowron, A. & Son, King William nr James
*Copp Bros., 15 John n
Farley, John, McNab bet King and Market Sq.
*Gurney, E. & C., John bet King William and Rebecca
Hannan & Bro., John nr King William
Howles, Matthew, Florence block, King w
*Moore, D. & Co., King e nr Catherine
Morrison, Joseph B., 7 n John
North, Samuel, McNab nr Merrick
Smith, George; McNab cor Cannon
*Stewart, James & Co., McNab cor Vine

Straw Goods (Wholesale).

Galbraith & Co., King bet James and McNab
Furner, G. H. & Co., D. McInnes' bock

Tailors and Drapers.

Fraugott, Richard, 26 York
Gallagher, Robert, York bet Bay and Caroline
Howard, William H., 10 Rebecca
Karschner, John, 23 York
Milborn, Robert, James opp Gore
Myers, James, 42 John s
O'Neill, Arthur, John bet Peel and Tyburn
Roddick, William, e s James between Stinson and Stuart
Seaman, S. L., 19 York and 20 King w
Vogt, John, John nr Main

Tanners and Curriers.

Brown, James, East Avenue nr King
Humphrey & Newberry, Tyburn

Telegraph Companies.

Dominion Telegraph Co., 13 King nr Hughson
Montreal Telegraph Co., James opp Gore

Tinmen's Tools and Materials.

Moore, D. & Co., King nr Catherine

Tinmen's Tools and Machines (Manuf's of).

Moore, Samuel J., Mary bet Little Willson and Henry

Tin, Copper, Sheet Iron, etc.

Bingham, A., McNab bet King and Market
Bishop, J. B., King William e of Hughson
Farley, John, McNab bet King and Market sq
North, Samuel, McNab nr Merrick
Smith, George, McNab cor Cannon
Smith, Mrs. Jane, 4 York
Smith, Robert, King William bet James and Hughson
Spencer, Henry, n s King William bet James and Hughson

Tip Printing.

Haigh, Richard, *Spectator* Buildings

Tobacco Manufacturers.

Barber, E. & Co., King bet Cathcart and Wellington
Billings & Turner
Schwarz, Frederick, Florence Block, King w
Tuckett & Billings, 100 and 102 King w

Umbrella Makers.

Catchpole, George, Rebecca nr James

Undertakers.

Blachford, John, McNab bet King and Main
Chapman, William M., 23 King w
Snelgrove, E. L., Court House Square

Upholsterers.

Drysdale, Alexander, McNab cor Vine
Hill, Thomas, John opp Prince's Square
Jarvis, John, King bet Nelson and Cathcart
Meakins & Sons, King nr Cathcart
Reid, James, King cor Bond
Snelgrove, E. L., Court House Square
Stacy, James, B. P., 71 King e

Variety Stores.

Mackintosh, Hugh, 84 King e
Moodie, John, 36 King w
Pearson, John & Co., 58 King w
Philips, George R., King nr Mary
Taylor, William, King bet Bond and Bowery
Taylor, John E., 61 King w

Veterinary Surgeons.

Hume, James, 1 York
Watson, John & Sons, Mary cor King William

Vinegar Manufacturers.

Birely & Co., James bet Peel and Augusta
Charlton, B. E., cor King and Wellington
Faustmann, Ernest, John bet Rebecca and Gore

Wagon Makers.

Armstrong, Peter, King e bet Walnut and Wellington
Campbell, George, King e bet Walnut and Wellington
Kavanagh, William, York cor Park
McGrath, Edward, cor James and Tyburn
Walker, Robert, Walnut bet Main and King
Wall & McCarthy, John cor Tyburn

Watches, Clocks and Jewelry.

Attwood, M. W., Royal Hotel Buildings, James
Batty, Benjamin, 40 King w
Belling, B. M., James nr Main
Fell, Henry K., Market Square
Getz, George, 22 York
Green, John W., 28 King w
Hill, Thomas S., sen., John cor Wood Market
Lees, Thomas, 5 James n
Levy, H. & A., 7 John s
McMahon, W. F., 86 King e
Osborne, Robert, James opp Fountain
Steward, T. B., 12 King e
Taylor, Joseph, 52 James n

Wharfingers.

Browne, E., Browne's Wharf, foot of McNab
Mackay, Æneas D., foot of James
Proctor, John, Commercial Wharf
Young, Jacob, Zealand's Wharf

Whip and Whip-lash Manufacturers and Dealers

King, G. H. & H. A., Rebecca bet John & Catherine
Quimby, A. C., 43 James n

Wines and Liquors (Importers of and wholesale dealers in.)

Brown, Gillespie & Co., King cor James
Cochren, William I. & Co., McNab nr King
Forster, G. J. & Co., King cor Charles
Goering, John W., 53 James n
Kerr, Brown & Mackenzie, King e
Peuchen, Clark & Co., John cor King
Simpson, James, McNab w s Market Square
Turner, James & Co., Hughson

Wire Mills.

Greening, Benjamin, Peter cor Hess office York

Wool Merchants and Brokers.

Abraham, Charles F., 55 King e
Cusner, John, 10 York
Davis, John H. & Co., 13 King e
Gillesby, William, w s John s of King
Harvey, John, 11 King e
Long & Bisby, 42 James n
McKenzie & Mackay, 9 King e
Pettit, J. H., 2 Upper John

Hamlet.—A post office in the Township of Burgess, County Lanark, South Riding
BYRNE, JOHN, Postmaster.

Hammond.—A small Village in the Township of Elma, County Perth, 27 miles from Stratford, the County Town, and 27 from Berlin. Average value of improved land in the vicinity $30 per acre. Population 25.

Aitchison, Andrew, saw mills
Burnett, William, farmer
Gray, Daniel, blacksmith
Hammond, James, J.P., farmer
HAMMOND, JAMES, JUN., Postmaster
Hone, William, farmer
Keating, J., farmer
Keating, John, farmer
Keating, W., farmer
Keith, J., farmer
McCauley, John, farmer
Melrose, Thomas, farmer
Robinson, Alexander, farmer

Hampton.—A Village in the Township of Darlington, County Durham, 28 miles from Cobourg, and 40 from Toronto. Stages to Bowmanville and Cæsarea. Money order office. Population 500.

Ashton, Samuel, general merchant
Beer, William, blacksmith
Bell, John, hotel keeper
Bigham, Hugh, M.D.
Bradley, Thomas, stock dealer
Bunt, R., cooper
Cann, Thomas, J.P
Clark, Thomas, blacksmith
Cole, John, tailor
Courtice, Rev. R. T., (Bible Christian)
Cryderman, J.,
ELLIOTT, HENRY, sr., Postmaster, J.P., and prop. flouring mill
Elliott, Henry, jr., gen. merchant and Ins. agent
Ellis, F. L., teacher
Farley, John, sash, door, and blind manufacturer
Fawke, E. S., cabinet maker
Fawke, Thomas, dealer in hides and leather
Gulley, Francis, carpenter
Hill, William, grocer
Hoidge, Rev. J., (Bible Christian)
Hooper, Henry, shoemaker
Jenkins, Mrs., milliner,
Jennings, William, shoemaker
Jennings, William, carpenter
Johns, John, wagon maker
Johns, Samuel, cooper
Joliffe, Rev. Mr., (Wesleyan)
Martin, William, shoemaker
Merrill, C. C., general agent, auctioneer, &c
Merrill, Charles M., general agent
Olford, T., shoemaker
Pethick, Miss E., milliner
Phillips, H. F., hotel keeper, auctioneer and stock dealer
Rogers, W. H., J.P.
Stonehouse, T. G., auctioneer
Territt, Joshua, butcher
Thomas, W. C., saddler
Vanstone, William, wagon maker
Ward, Samuel, grocer
Ward, Thomas, butcher
Washington, Anthony, J.P.
Webster, Louisa, teacher
Williams, D., carpenter
Williams, James, manufacturer of woolen goods
Williams, William, notary public
Wright, Thomas A., carpenter

Hampstead.—A small Village in the Township of North Easthope, County Perth, 10 miles from Stratford, the County Town, and 6 from Shakspeare. Population 45.

Amos, Robert, farmer
Bonner, Henry, blacksmith
Carroll, Henry, farmer
Fraser, D. B. teacher
Gilbert, William, wagon maker
Hofman, Peter, hotel keeper and blacksmith
LIESEMER, HENRY, J.P., Postmaster and general merchant
Lillico, James, farmer
McLaren, Alexander, farmer
Neebe, Henry, farmer
Stewart, James, farmer

Hammettsholm.—A Post Office in the Township of Markham, County York, East Riding.

HAMMETT, JAMES, Postmaster.

Hannon.—A Post Village in the Township of Glanford, County Wentworth, 7 miles distant from Hamilton, the County Town, and 48 miles from Toronto.

COWIE, THOMAS, Postmaster.

Hanover.—A Village in the Townships of Bentinck and Brant, Counties of Grey and Bruce, on the Saugeen River, 40 miles from Owen Sound, 6 from Walkerton, 37 from Southampton and 50 from Collingwood. Stages to all the above places. Average value of land in vicinity $25 per acre. Money order office. Population 500.

Adams, George W., carpenter
Adams, H. P., proprietor flouring mill
Becker, Henry, carpenter
Black, James, cabinet maker
Bottrell, James, butcher
Brawn, G., Evangelical Association
Brehm, S., hotel keeper
Buck, Abraham, farmer
Campbell, Donald, farmer
Campbell, D., manufacturer of woolen goods
Campbell, Duncan, proprietor foundry
Campbell, Peter, druggist
Campbell, William M., tinsmith
Clark, Rev. A. (Baptist)
Clark, James C., wagon maker
Coppinger, Thomas L., general merchant
Davis, I. B., farmer
Deacon, William, hotel keeper
Devlin, William, carpenter
Doberer, Andrew, tailor
Dresch, Valentine, brick maker
Eidt, Lewis, cooper
Ellis, John, farmer
Gilson, John, farmer
Goodeve, E. A., general merchant
GOTTWALS, A. Z., Postmaster and insurance agent
Gottwals & Hood, general merchants
Hahn, John, farmer
Hahn, John, jun., carpenter
Halsted, I. F., M.D.
Hasenjager, C., farmer
Hollinger, George, hide and leather dealer
Hood, John, saddler
Hopkins, R. E., saddler
Huscher, William, shoemaker
Irvine, Rev. W., (Wesleyan)
Johnston, David, farmer
Johnson, John H., carpenter
Kern, C., tailor
Kerr, John, painter
Kisenmeyer, Rev. —, (Baptist)
Knechtel, Daniel, jun., cabinet maker
Kuehner, Conrad, potter
Landerkin, George, M.D.
Lawson, William, grocer
Lockhart & Maywell, brewers
Lynn, Samuel, blacksmith
McDonald, Daniel, teacher
McDonald & Jost, general merchants
McKay, John, carpenter
McKelvie, John, hotel keeper
McNally, Robert, wagon maker
McNally, Samuel, blacksmith
McNicol, John, general merchant
Mackenson, Rev. W. (Lutheran)
Mitchell, P. W., saddler
Newert, Valentine, cooper
Norsworthy, Samuel, shoemaker
Oppertshauser, Conrad, wagon maker
Scarborough, Charles, brickmaker
Schuhmann, Frederick, shoemaker
Schwegler, J. F., general merchant
Small, John, contractor
Softley, Rev. E. (Church of England)
Spry, John, farmer
Sterling, Henry, butcher
Stewart, Charles, shoemaker
Tindal, Rev. W. (Episcopal Methodist)
Tweedie, Sarah, teacher
Wagner, Anthony, blacksmith
Walker, John, cabinet maker
Younge, Simon, tailor

Harcourt.—A Post-office in the Township of Ross, County Renfrew, N.R.

SQUIRES, JOHN W., Postmaster.

Hardinge.—A Post-office in the Township of Barrie, County Addington.

TAPPING, THOMAS, Postmaster.

Harlem.—A small Village in the Township of Bastard, County Leeds, 32 miles from Brockville, the County Town, and 14 from Irish Creek station, Brockville and Ottawa Railway. Population 60.

Austin, Harvey, prop. grist mill
Brown, Roswell, general merchant
Derbyshire, Isaac, general merchat
Gill, Frederick, farmer
Grainsford, William, shoemaker
Green, John, farmer
Janson, W. F., teacher
KINCADE, WILLIAM, Postmaster, shoemaker
Moss, James, shoemaker
Smith, G., lumber dealer
Smith, Israel, cabinet maker
Sweet, Hiram, farmer
Watts, Thomas, farmer
Wetheral, Ruel, blacksmith
Wolfe, Squire, shoemaker

Harley.—(Sometimes called Derby.)—A small Post Village in the Township of Burford, County Brant, S. R., 14 miles from Brantford, the County Town. Daily Mails. Population 50.

Anklin, B., hotel keeper
Bennett, Josiah, carpenter
Denby, John & Joseph, shoemakers
Epps, Daniel, farmer
Epps, Richard, farmer
Groom, William, blacksmith
Hilles, Thomas, carpenter
McLELLAN, J. L., Postmaster and gen. merchant
Parlee, John, farmer
Steedman, Abraham, tailor
Stewart, James, farmer
Whittaker, H. L., wagon maker

Harmony.—A Village in the Township of South Easthope, County Perth, 4 miles from Stratford, the County Town, and 90 from Toronto. Population 50.

Adair, Joseph, farmer
Blair, William, blacksmith
Dunsmore, E., farmer
Dunsmore, James H., farmer
CORBETT, EDMUND, Postmaster, manufacturer of woolen goods

Harold.—A small Village in the Township of Rawdon, County Hastings, 23 miles from Belleville, the County Town.

BUCK, RICHARD, Postmaster
Hesson, John, grocer
Lupton, John, farmer
McKay, Murdoch, teacher
Odbert, William, farmer
Pinder, John, flouring mill
Price, Rev. W. (Wesleyan)
Rankin, David, farmer
Russell, Leonard, pump maker
Sitzer, Edmund, insurance agent and accountant
Wilson, Thomas, farmer

Harper.—A Village in the Township of Bathurst, County Lanark, 7 miles from Perth, the County Town Population 70.

Bailey, Samuel, shoemaker
Baird, Matthew, manufacturer woolen goods
Bolton, William, farmer
Cameron, John, farmer
Campbell, John, farmer
Chant, Rev. E. (Wesleyan)
Churchill, Henry, cooper
Ferguson, Duncan, carpenter
Fisher, John, farmer
Fisher, Malcolm, farmer
Guinness, Christopher, farmer
Harper, Joseph, farmer
Layton, Myles, hotel
Lee, James, lime dealer
McDonald, C., hotel
McNer, Peter, farmer
Marguerat, Louis, sash factory
Menzies, John, farmer
Steele, John, manufacturer woolen goods
WARREN, JOSEPH, Postmaster and gen. merch't
Watts, Edward, shoemaker

Harrietsville.—A Village in the Township of North Dorchester, County Middlesex, 18 miles from London, the County Town, and 7 from Dorchester Station Great Western Railway. Stages to Aylmer and Dorchester. Population 150.

Ballentyne, Hector, blacksmith
Barr, C., general merchant, Com. in B.R.
Barr, William, farmer
Bewe, John, blacksmith
Evans, John, farmer
Facy, Robert, cheese factory
Irwin, William, wagon maker
Jelly, John J., general merchant
Jelly, William, hotel keeper
Kincaid, John, farmer
McMillan, Henry, farmer
McMILLAN, JOHN, J.P., Postmaster
McPherson, Adam, pump maker
Wallace, Isaac, shoemaker

Harrington West.—A Village in the Township of West Zorra, County Oxford, on a branch of the Thames, 21 miles from Woodstock, the County Town, 10 from Stratford, 30 from London and 10 from St. Marys. Population 200.

Anderson, Thomas, farmer
Batrage, William, brick maker
Clufford, John C., farmer
Darling, George, farmer
Harrington & McIntee, hotel keepers
Heron, Robert, general merchant
Horbes, George, lumber dealer and wagon maker
Houpe, George, cabinet maker
Kerr, Angus, general merchant
McCabe, John, coal dealer
McKay, John, farmer
McLeod, H. M., M.D.
Meldrum, Norman, teacher
Meldrum, Rev. William, (Free Presbyterian)
Mills, William, farmer
Morris, Matthew, cabinet maker
Morray, R. A., insurance agent
Pitt, John, J.P., farmer
Rands, A. H., stock dealer
REID, DANIEL, Postmaster, auctioneer and dealer in boots and shoes
Ross, William, farmer
Wadland, William, farmer

Harrisburg.—A Village and Station of the Great Western Railway, on Fairchild's Creek, in the Township of South Dumfries, County Brant, 9 miles from Brantford, the County Town, and 58 from Toronto. Population 150.

Arnold, George, telegraph operator
Basstie, David, teacher
Bowman, Jacob, carpenter
Burt, Robert, J.P., farmer
Coleman, J., hotel keeper
Durham, Joseph, farmer
GALLOWAY, JAMES, Postmaster and gen. mercht.
Griffin, James, shoemaker
Hall, Rev. J. (N. C. Methodist)
Hurley, Mrs. B., groceries
Laurason, Miller B., farmer
Lyall, John, agent American Express
McAllister, Rev. J. (N. C. Methodist)
McLeod, John, carpenter
Shaver, Walter, carpenter
Smith, Simon, farmer
Starr, Frederick, butcher
Starr, George, farmer
Vrooman, A. M., farmer
Vrooman, Daniel, hotel keeper

Harrow.—A Village in the Township of Colchester, County Essex, 30 miles from Sandwich, the County Town, 13 from Amherstburgh and 9 from Kingsville. Average value of improved lands in the vicinity, $16 per acre. Population 50.

Culbert Rev. T., (Wesleyan)
Ferris, William, butcher
FULLMER, E. M., Postmaster and gen. merchant
Hughson, S., miller
Quick, David, butcher
Quick, John B., carpenter
Robertson, R. A., M.D.
Thrasher, John, hotel keeper
Thompson, Lennox, J.P.
Wright, W. G., general merchant
Woughte, T. C., millwright
Yokum, Jesse, cooper

Harrowsmith.—A Village on Spring Creek, in the Township of Portland, County Frontenac, 16 miles from Kingston, the County Town, 32 from Westport and 20 from Parham. Iron, lead and plumbago are found in the vicinity. Population 200.

Babcock, J., proprietor Dominion Hotel
Baker Ira, cabinet maker
Burnett, John, carpenter
Campbell, W., shingle manufacturer
Carscallen & Rogers, saddlers
Charlton, John, farmer
Clark, L., wagon maker
Clark, W. & Co., wagon maker
Cooke, James, teacher
Crozier, Rev. J., (Presbyterian)
Davis, W., painter
Day, A., farmer
Donnelley, John, farmer
Easton, W., cooper
Faris, D., shoemaker
Grant, T., engraver
Herchmer, John, farmer
Hollister, N. P., saddler
Lake, D., farmer
Miller, Rev. W. W., (Wesleyan)
Parkin, R., tailor
Phillips, A., painter
Phillips, R. J., wagon maker
Rogers, F. F., carpenter
Shelby, Charles, farmer
Shelby, E., grocer
Shelby, J., proprietor Albion Hotel
Simpkins, H., carpenter
Smith, J. R., M.D
Spike, A., farmer
Stewart, C., stock dealer
Stewart, G. D., farmer
Stewart, S. general merchant and lumber dealer
STEWART, S. F., Postmaster, notary public, &c
Vandewater, R. W., general merchant
Walsworth, H. J., lime manufacturer

Harriston.—A Village on the Maitland River, and proposed line of the Wellington, Grey and Bruce Railway, in the Township of Minto, County Wellington, 40 miles from Guelph, the County Town, 16 from Listowell, and 26 from Walkerton. Stages to all the above places. Money Order office. Population 275.

Allan, James, proprietor hotel and livery stables
Arnold, William, J. P., and general merchant
Baily, James, saddler
Bateman, Miles, farmer
Brown, James, farmer
Caldwell, Robert, farmer
Connell, James, farmer
Connell, H. & W., shoemakers
Cowan, James, M.D.
Craig, John. tailor
Curry, John, teacher
Denny, T. G., baker
Depew, Rev. F. T., (New Connexion Methodist)
Dow, Alexander, farmer
Dunham, John, teacher
French, William, brick maker
Gowan, Edward and William, architects
Gordon, Hugh, carpenter
Gordon, William, wagon maker
Gray, Benjamin, carpenter
Haig, Robert, accountant
Hall, Miss Catharine, milliner
Hotson, Walter, shoemaker
Johnson, John, lime and stone
Kay, Henry C., accountant
Lee, George, butcher
Livingston, John, insurance agent and auctioneer
Longeast, James, lime and stone
McLennan, Rev. George, (Presbyterian)
Mallaby, J. J., hotel keeper
Markle, A. G., prop. hotel and livery stable
MACREADY, ALEXANDER, Postmaster and gen. merchant
Meiklejohn, Alexander, general merchant
Meiklejohn, Mrs., milliner
Moncrief, Thomas, farmer
Moore, James, farmer
Morrell, Thomas, wagon maker
Morrison, William G., teacher
Nelson, Allan, carpentor
Patmore, Martin, wagon maker
Prentice, James, lime and stone
Preston, James B., lumber dealer
Purdy, Thomas, cooper
Reeve, Matthew, shingle maker
Robinson, Alexander, tinsmith
Robinson, Thomas, steam flouring mills
Smith, George, shingle maker
Steager, John, cooper
Taylor, William, general merchant
Walker, John W., teacher
Webb, John, farmer
Weber, Jacob, butcher
Welte, Silas, cabinet maker
Wright, Malcolm, farmer

Hartford.—A Village in the Township of Townsend, County Norfolk, 18 miles from Simcoe, the County Town. Population 100.

Burke, John, farmer
Burke, John W., shoemaker
Cross, Nelson, carpenter
Merrill, R. J., farmer
Nicholson, John, farmer
Osborne, James, M.D.
Osborne, John, wagon maker
Stafford, Dean, farmer
THOMAS, B. W., Postmaster and general merchant
Vanloon, Adam, farmer
Vanloon, B., carpenter
Vanloon, Benjamin, blacksmith
Vanloon, James, carpenter
Vanloon, John, hotel keeper
Vanloon, William, farmer
Willcox, John, farmer
Willcox & Barnhard, lumber dealers

Hartington.—A Post Office in the Township of Portland, County Frontenac, 19 miles from Kingston, the County Town. Average value of land in vicinity, improved $80, wild $5 per acre.

KENNEDY, WILLIAM, Postmaster.

Hartley.—A Post Office in the Township of Eldon, County Victoria, N. R.

CAMPBELL, ARCHIBALD.

Hartman.—A Post Office in the Township of East Gwillimbury, County York, 40 miles from Toronto, the County Town.

Campbell, Hugh, blacksmith
Graham, Allan, farmer
Luefra, Stephen, blacksmith
Moorhead, James, farmer
Pegg, Isaac, farmer
Robinson, John, farmer
Rolling, John, farmer
Rose, Albert, carpenter
Rose, Isaac, farmer
Scott, Seth, farmer
Shillinglaw, David, farmer
Stiver, John, farmer
TERRY, DAVID, Postmaster and farmer
Thirsk, George, carpenter
Thirsk, William, farmer
Tool, Moses, farmer

Harwich.—A small Village in the Township of Harwich, County Kent, 12 miles from Chatham, the County Town.

Campbell, Robert, tailor
HUTCHINSON, JAMES, Postmaster, merchant
McKay, Mrs., hotel keeper
Rutherford, James, M.D.

Harwood.—A Village and Station of the Cobourg, Peterboro' and Marmora Mining Co. Railway, in the Township of Hamilton, County Northumberland. Average price of land in the vicinity $30 per acre. Population 200.

Brady, E., hotel keeper
DROPE, R., Postmaster and prop. Harwood House
Seed, J. S., railway agent and telegraph operator

Hastings.—A Village on the River Trent, in the Townships of Asphodel and Percy, Counties of Peterboro and Northumberland; 24 miles from Peterboro, 30 from Cobourg and 100 from Toronto. There are several extensive manufacturing establishments here. Money order office and Savings Bank. Stages to Colborne and Peterboro. Population 900.

Askey, D., manufacturer of woolen goods
Baragus, Patrick, baker
Barker, L. D., carpenter
Becket, James, general merchant
Bleasdale, —, M. D
Blacklock, John, manufacturer of knitted goods
Brennan, Dennis, hotel keeper
Brennan, Patrick, hotel keeper and dealer in lime and stone
Brough, A., sash, blind and door manufacturer
Brown, James C., teacher
Clark, Mathew, accountant
Coughlan, T., J. P
Daily, Timothy, tailor
Fife, J. M., grocer
Ford, B., tailor
Fowlds, Bro., steam boat agents and lumber dealers
FOWLDS, HENRY, Postmaster, and proprietor flouring mill
French, —, M. D
Fuller, J., painter
Graham, John, lime and stone
Green, John, carpenter
Griffiths, James, cabinet maker
Griffiths, S. D., wagon maker
Hamilton, James, carpenter
Hardy, A., brickmaker
Harrison, J. C., hotel keeper and butcher
Hawley, A. D. C., druggist
Hill, William, carpenter
Houston & Dunning, shoemakers
Hurley, Timothy, general merchant
Jackson, George, shoemaker
Kemp, J. A., tinsmith
Kennedy, Philip, general merchant
Londerville, Samuel, cooper
Magrath, Miss, milliner, &c.
Morrison, D., accountant
Nelson, D. S., carpenter
Nelson, Mrs. D. S., milliner, &c.
Peters, John, general merchant
Quirk, Rev. John (Roman Catholic)
Sedgewick, Hiram, saddler
Sharpe, John, accountant
Short, Rev. William (Methodist)
Slater, John T., general merchant
Smithett, Rev. W. (Church of England)
Steele, James, carpenter
Steele, Samuel, grocer
Sullivan, D. A., shoemaker
Sullivan, Miss, milliner, &c.
Toms, Isaac, leather dealer
Tracy, John, cooper
Tracy, P. cooper
Whitehead, W. J., proprietor of cotton mills
Wilson, Alexander, tailor
Young, Rev. W. C. (Presbyterian)

Haultain.—A Post Office in the Township of Burleigh, County Peterborough, 25 miles from Peterborough the County Town.

STONE, MILES, Postmaster.

Havelock.—A small Post Village in the Township of Belmont, County Peterborough, distant from Peterborough, the County Town, 27 miles. Population about 50.

PEARCE, PETER, J.P., Postmaster and mill owner.

Hawkstone.—A small Village, beautifully situated on Kempenfeldt Bay, in the Township of Oro, County Simcoe, 16 miles from Barrie, the County Town.

HOUSTON, JAMES, Postmaster
Williamson, James, prop. grist and saw mill

Hawksville.—A Village on the Conestogo River, in the Township of Wellesley, County Waterloo, 12 miles from Berlin, the County Town. Stages tri-weekly to Listowell, and daily to Linwood and St. Jacobs. Money Order Office. Population 400.

Ament, Jacob, farmer
Ament, John, lime manufacturer
Anderson, Duncan, carpenter
Ball, Nicholas, farmer
Biensteikle, Henry, saddler
Borth, Andrew, boots and shoes
Bond, Josiah, wagon maker
Boomer, W. R., J.P., farmer
Brandle, John, boots and shoes
Carter, Henry, druggist
Cornell, Albert, druggist
Cornell, W. F., insurance agent
Diefenbacher, George M., wagon maker
Donald, Fred. K., farmer
EMPEY, M. P., J.P., Postmaster and gen. mercht.
Ford, Michael, carpenter
Fowler, William, farmer
Gager, Henry, hotel keeper
Griger, Henry, baker
Halmel, Gottlieb, lime manufacturer
Haid, A. H., farmer
Hall, James, boots and shoes
Hawk, John, J.P.
Hilborn, J. B., leather dealer
Huffner, Peter, tailor
Hughes, George, farmer
Jamieson, David, general merchant
Kabel, Conrad, hotel keeper
Lickner, William, farmer
Lount, Gabriel, M.D.
Ludwig, Albert, carpenter
Ludwig, Jacob, sen., cooper
Ludwig, Jacob, jun., cooper
McCulloch & Wilson, proprietors woolen and flouring mills
McDonald, Thomas, carpenter
Markham, Thomas, carpenter
Matin, James, boots and shoes
Martinson, Henry, farmer
Martinson, John, farmer
Muir, James J., teacher
Newton, Harry, boots and shoes
Oaks, John W., tinsmith
Ovens, Eliza, milliner, &c.
Pearson, J. W., farmer
Peterson, H. W., farmer
Proudlove, Thomas, farmer
Scott, John, dyer and scourer
Snyder, Sidney, farmer
Stone, A., farmer
Thompson, Richard, farmer
Vardon, W. H., J.P., M.D.
Vatter, Nicholas, farmer
Vatter, Philip, farmer
Voight & Pflaum, brick yard
Watson, David, hotel keeper
Welliver, Chester K., saddler
Wilson, John, farmer
Winn, Joshua, farmer
Woodward, E. G., farmer
Woodward, W. S., farmer

Hay.—A Post Office in the Township of Hay, County Huron. Improved land in the vicinity averages $40 per acre.

Brownlee, James, auctioneer
Campbell, William, farmer
Case, Bon, farmer
Case, Miss Emily, teacher
Case, William, farmer
Hawkins, George, farmer
Hawkins, W., farmer
Henderson, P., farmer
Houlds, Robert, farmer
Jackell, William, farmer
Kouston, John, teacher
Logie, Thomas, farmer
Logie, William, farmer
McLeod, George, farmer
McTaggart, James, farmer
Murray, James, farmer
MURRAY, JAMES, Postmaster
Murray, Robert, farmer
Russell, James, farmer
Tyndle, A. J., farmer
Webster, H., farmer
Wilkie, James, farmer
Willis, John, farmer

Haydon.—A Village on Big Creek, in the Township of Darlington, County Durham, 39 miles from Port Hope, the County Town, 50 from Toronto. Stages daily to Bowmanville. Population 160.

Bickle, John, proprietor flouring mill
Bread William, general merchant
Fleming, John, farmer
Hallier, Mr., flax and flouring mills
Harper, James, hotel keeper
Jolliffe, Rev. —, (Bible Christian)
LUKES, JOHN, Postmaster and general merchant
McLaughlin, James, farmer
Maroney, Patrick, wagon maker and painter
Maloney, John, farmer
Mitchel, John, teacher
Motley, William, lumber dealer
Rice Rev. —, (Bible Christian)
Robinson, John, shingle maker
Rundle, J., farmer
Simpson, Rev. J., (Disciple)
Slimon, William, farmer
Sweet, Frank, lime and stone
Thompson, Rev. William (Disciple)
Tole, Isaiah, farmer
Trewm, William, farmer
Tuer, Joseph, farmer
Tuer, William, farmer

Hawkesbury.—An incorporated Village and Station of the Carleton and Grenville Railroad, on the river Ottawa, in the Township of West Hawkesbury, County Prescott, 5 miles from L'Orignal, 60 from Ottawa, and 88 from Lancaster. Money order office and Savings' Bank. Stages to Lancaster. Population 1200.

Agden, A., carpenter
Armstrong, Rev. J. G. (Church of England)
Bargeron, G., hotel keeper
Benton, James, saddler
Bronette, Felix, wagon maker
Brown, C. W., saddler
Burwash, Miss, teacher
Campbell, James, baker
Chalmers, Rev. Mr. (Methodist)
Clark, John, sash, door and blind manufactory
Clark, Mrs., milliner, &c.
Dewitt, William, manufacturer of woolen goods
Doule, Denis, general merchant
Ewing, William, M.D.
Fraser, Miss, teacher
Fraser, Mrs., milliner, &c.
Freeman, S. L., hotel keeper
Furguson, Rev. Mr. (Presbyterian)
Giles, Henry, saddler
Hamilton, Bros., props. foundry and machine shops and flouring mills
Hamilton, Samuel, butcher
Harbic, Felix, general merchant
Hersey, C. R., leather dealer
HERSEY, Z. S. M., Postmaster
Hersey, Z. S. M. & Son, general merchants and proprietors flouring mill
Higginson & Bros., general merchants
Higginson, J. W., J.P., prop. planing mill and manufacturer of woolen goods
Higginson, Thomas, insurance agent
Hudgeons, George, cabinet maker
Kimball, A.
Laducere, T., butcher
Ledward, Charles, baker
Ledward, Henry, baker
Lefarre, M., carpenter
Lortie, Vincent, general merchant
Lough, H
Lough. William
McKerarche, John, teacher
McMahon, S. J., tinsmith
Munro, James F., teacher
Park, R. S., general merchant
Park, William, tailor
Patter, R. P., farmer
Porter, Misses, milliners, &c
Roberts, E. T., M.D., and insurance agent
Robertson, F., J.P., farmer
Rutherford, R., farmer
Ryan, James, cabinet and wagon maker
Walker, Robert, tailor
Wyman, Thomas, telegraph operator

Haysville.—A Village on Smith's Creek, in the Township of Wilmot, County Waterloo, 14 miles from Berlin, the County Town, 60 from Toronto, and 3 from Hamburg station, Grand Trunk Railway. Population 200.

Allan, Sarah, teacher
Baird, Alexander, tailor
Bergie, David, teacher
Blatchford, John, waggon maker
Brown, James, general merchant
Cleland, A. W., manufacturer of woolen goods
Hays, John, hotel keeper
Mellish, Rev. H. F. (Church of England)
O'Connor, Dr., M.D.
Plum, W. R., hotel keeper
SOMERVILLE, M., Postmaster, general merchant
Thompson, William, shoemaker
Tye, F. E., butcher
Wesley, Joseph, carpenter

Hazledean.—A small Village in the Township of Goulbourne, County Carleton, near the River Carp, 12 miles from Ottawa, the County Town. Population 40.

Abbott, A. J., jeweler and bookbinder
Bradley, George, saddler
Bradley, Joshua, farmer
Bradley, W. B., lumber dealer and manufacturer of woolen goods
Bradly, Robert, shoemaker
Butler, Richard, farmer
Church, C. M., J. P. and M. D
Clark, John, farmer
Colbert, John, farmer
Colbert, William, farmer
Cowan, Andrew, carpenter and wagon maker
Cummings, John, wagon maker and painter
Cuthbert, W. F., J. P
Dowler, Rev. Mr., (Methodist)
Duncan, James, farmer
Egleson, William, teacher
Gilbert, Henry, gunsmith
Godfrey, Rev. J., (Church of England)
Gow, Alexander, tailor
Graham, Innis, saddler
Grant, Robert, J. P., farmer
Hodgins, John, N. P. and farmer
Kemp's Hotel, John Kemp, proprietor
Kemp, John, lime and stone dealer
Lewis, James, butcher
Mulligan, James, farmer
Royal Victoria Hotel, William Watt, proprietor
Shore, Robert, shoemaker
WATT, WILLIAM, Postmaster, general merchant
Young, John, farmer
Young, John, general agent

Headford.—A Village in the Township of Markham, County York, 18 miles from Toronto, the County Town, and 21 from Richmond Hill. Population 70.

Burr, John C., farmer
Clark, John, farmer
Eyre Bros., props. fulling mills and foundry
Henrich, Adam, farmer
MONTGOMERY, JOHN, Postmaster
Monkman, George, farmer
Munro, William, farmer
Phillips, Henry, farmer
Willmott, Peter, J.P., farmer

Head Lake.—A Post-office in the Township of Luxton, County Victoria, 40 miles from Lindsay, the County Town.

Adair, George farmer
Bailey, John, farmer
Burgess, Edward, farmer
Burnett, Augusta, teacher
Casey, James, farmer
Copp, Samuel, carpenter
Donaldson, Benjamin, carpenter
Gillespie, Hugh, carpenter
HALLADAY, WILLIAM, Postmaster
Inglis, Francis, carpenter
McCoughey, James, general merchant
McCrae, Archibald, cooper
Maxwell, William, accountant and general merchant
Nugent, Celia, teacher
Parks, John, farmer
Peel, Richard, tinsmith
Perkins, Ida, teacher
Sinclair, Donald, general merchant
Slocum, Charles, shingle maker
Staples, Robert, carpenter
Trace, James, carpenter

Heathcote.—A Village on Beaver River, in the Township of Collingwood, County Grey, 30 miles from Owen Sound, the County Town, and 17 from Collingwood. Average price of improved land $25 per acre. Stages bi-weekly to Clarksburg. Population 100.

Appleby, Rev. T. M. (Church of England)
Brewster, Edward, boots and shoes
Clinton, William De Witt, M.D.
Davidson, Rev. J. (Presbyterian)
Hilts, Rev. Mr. (Society of Friends)
Hurish, William, general merchant
McCarroll, Thomas & Co., general merchants
Odell, John, carpenter
RORKE, THOMAS, Postmaster and gen. merchant
Rorke, William, notary public and land agent
Strachan, George, school teacher

Hebron.—A Post Office in the Township of Mornington, County Perth, North Riding.

CONNOLLY, BERNARD, Postmaster.

Heckston.—A Village on the north branch of the Nation River, in the Township of South Gower, County Grenville, 30 miles from Brockville. Population 100.

ADAMS, GIDEON, Postmaster and gen. merchant
Adams, H. H., farmer
Adams, John S., farmer
Adams, Joseph, farmer
Adams, William, farmer
Anderson, J. J., farmer
Anderson, Samuel, blacksmith
Beach, William, saw mill proprietor
Biggs, John, cooper
Campbell, Hector, shingle maker
Conn, John, school teacher
Cook, Joseph, J.P.
Cumming, P., farmer
Eager, George, blacksmith
Eagen, James, farmer
Grant, Daniel, flouring mill
Howes, Rev. J., (Methodist)
Hughes, Hugh, general merchant
Moses, William, J.P.
Shaver, Gordon, farmer
Smith, Alexander, boots and shoes
Smith, Elijah, boots and shoes
Smith, James W., shingle maker
Smith, Joseph W., saw miller
Wilson, Mrs. S. A., hotel keeper

Heidelburg—*(See Villages too late for regular insertion at the end of this Work.)*

Henry.—A Post Office in the Township of Longueuil, County Prescott, 4 miles from L'Orignal, the County Town.

Allan, Richard, J.P.
Amlin, Felix, farmer
Bancroft, Abel, farmer
Bancroft, Asa, sen., farmer
Bancroft, Asa, jun., farmer
Barton, Gustavus, farmer
Brown, John, butcher
Chalmers, Thomas, lime dealer and stone mason
Clarke, Justin, farmer
Cross, Harrison, farmer
DICKSON, WILLIAM, J.P., Postmaster
Dunning, Gregory, butcher
Fouriner, Antoine, cooper
Golden, Lizzie, milliner
Leavitt, Mary, teacher
McAdam, Samuel, farmer
McCann, Mary Ann, teacher
McNally, Fanny, teacher
McNally, Henry, farmer
McNally, James, farmer
Pattie, John, farmer
Potts, James, farmer
Ramsay, John, farmer
Ross, Catherine, milliner
Ross, Robert, wheelwright
Steel, Robert, farmer
Walker, Henry, farmer
Walker, William, farmer

Hepworth.—A Post Office in the Township of Keppel, County Grey, N. R.

SPENCER, WILLIAM, Postmaster.

Hespeler.—An Incorporated Village on the River Speed, and Guelph branch of the Great Western Railway. in the Township of Waterloo, County Waterloo. Distant from Berlin, the County Town, 10 miles, from Toronto 70 miles. The Speed affords first class water-power, and the village contains several large manufacturing establishments. The woolen factory of J. Hespeler & Son is one of the lrrgest of the kind in the Province, employing 100 hands; capacity 1000 yards daily. The knitting mills of Randall, Farr & Co. employ 100 hands, and power equivalent to 75 horse. Land in the vicinity averages $60 per acre, Money order office and Savings Bank. Population 1200.

Adams, S., woolen factor
Allendorf, G., woolen factor
Anderson, J., wagon maker
BAKER'S HOTEL, Mrs. Baker, proprietor
Baltzer, J. tailor
Barrett, John, sen., farmer
BARRON, A. F., general merchant
Bergey, E., shoemaker
Bechtel, S., farmer
Bolduc, P., cooper
Brewster, A. J., teacher
CHAPMAN, JOHN, general merchant
Demmick, Mrs., bookseller
Ellis, William, farmer
Fields, H., constable
Fields, Robert, teamster
Germania House, C. Pabst, proprietor
GLICK, MRS., proprietor Union Hotel
Green, B., butcher
Guenther, George, cabinet maker
Haller, M., hotel keeper
Hummitt, T., farmer
Henry, John, baker
HESPELER, GEORGE, J. P
HESPELER, JACOB, J. P
HESPELER, J. & SON, proprietors Hespeler woolen mills, distillers, millers, &c
Heuther, L., wagon maker
HOWAT, A. G., station master G. W. R
Hunter, J. wagon maker
Johnston, J. P., wagon maker
Kannageiser. C., cooper
Karch, C., J.P.
KRIBS, LEWIS, architect, prop. saw mills, etc.
Lacker, C., tailor
Laney, G., lime manufacturer
McCarthy, J., shoemaker
McINTYRE, R., M.D.
MacKenzie, Rev. M. (Presbyterian)
Marr, F., dyer and scourer
Martin, George, saddler
Miller, J., farmer
NAHRGANG, MRS. C., Postmistress
Ohlman, J., hotel keeper
Pabst, C., proprietor Germania House
Pannabaker, A., pound keeper
Phin, J. P., sen., farmer
Phin, J. P., jun., farmer
Picken, P., shoemaker
RANDALL, FARR & CO., manufacturers of woolen goods, hosiery, etc.
Renwick, W., butcher
Rife, H., dentist
Sacks, A. & Co., carpenters
Schofield, J., woolen factor
Seagle, C., farmer
SHAW, ADAM, groceries, &c
Smith, C. E., general merchant
Shetly, G., painter
Stuemphle, John, shoemaker
Traplin, J., cooper
Union Hotel, Mrs. Glick, proprietress
Weir, William, dyer and scourer
Witmer, D. H., farmer
ZRYD, J., stoves, tinware, &c

Hiawatha.—A small Village on the north shore of Rice Lake, in the Township of Otonabee, County Peterboro', 11 miles from Peterboro', the County Town. The Village is on an Indian Reserve. Population, chiefly Indians, 120.

Anderson, John, farmer
Braithwaite, William
Cowie, Daniel, farmer
Crawford, Lewis B., farmer
Hatrick, Richard
McCue, Abram, farmer
Nangon, Richard, farmer
PAUDUSH, CHIEF G. M.
Reynolds, John E., teacher
REYNOLDS, REV. JOSEPH (Wesleyan)
Rice, John, farmer
Soper, Robert, farmer
Taylor, Charles
Thomson, Walter
Throop, John

High Falls.—A Village on the Madawaska River, in the Township of Bagot, County Renfrew, 70 miles from Pembroke, the County Town. Good water power for manufacturing purposes. Wild land in the vicinity averages about 80 cents per acre. Population 50.

Dillon, Denis, hotel keeper
DILLON, T. H., Postmaster
Halliday, John, J.P.
Kennedy, P., dry goods
Lynn, Dr.
McCowan, G., carpenter

Hereward.—A Post Office in the Township of Garafraxa, County Wellington, C. R.

ALLEN, JOHN, Postmaster.

Highfield.—A Post Office in the Township of Etobicoke, County York, 15 miles from Toronto.

Ackrow, John, farmer
Allen, Rev. W. C. (Methodist)
Bailey, Thomas, hotel keeper
Bolton, Thomas, farmer
Boys, Rev. — (Primitive Methodist)
Brooks, Rev. James (Baptist)
Cranswick, Matthew, farmer
Dutchburn, Henry, boots and shoes
Ellis, Miss, school teacher
Gardhouse, James, farmer
Gardhouse, Thomas, carpenter
Nichol, John, butcher
Preston, Mrs. C., milliner, &c.
Russell, Henry, farmer
Smith, Joseph, farmer
Stonehouse, Thomas, tailor
Stubart, Robert, farmer
Taylor, Thomas, farmer
Thomas, Richard, farmer

Highgate.—A Village in the Township of Oxford, Electoral District of Bothwell, 36 miles from Chatham. Population 100.

Athridge, William, farmer
ATKINSON, ANTHONY, Postmaster
Benson, Rev. M. (Wesleyan Methodist)
Gosnell, James, farmer
Gosnell, Lawrence, J.P.
Grout, J. C., carpenter and builder
Haughton, W., painter
Hughson, Rev. W. D. (Episcopal Methodist)
Lee, John, farmer
McDonald, Alexander, blacksmith
McLaren, William, steam saw miller, planing, &c.
Mickle, Thomas, blacksmith
Orme, Rev. J. (Methodist New Connexion)
Phenix, John, farmer
Rutledge, Thomas, farmer
Scott, Frederick, farmer
Stone, John, J.P.
Stone, Robert, farmer
Tape, James, shingle maker
Tape, Thomas, farmer

Highland Creek.—A Village on the creek of the same name, in the Township of Scarboro', County York, 14 miles from Toronto, the County Town, and 2½ from a station of the Grand Trunk Railway. Salt is found in the vicinity. Population 200.

Chamberlain, William, butcher
Cheesewright, Sarah, general merchant
Closson, Stephen, farmer
Collins, John, blacksmith
Craven C., school teacher
Dixon, Robert, farmer
Elliott, John, general merchant
Elliott, Thomas, farmer
Halliwell, William, J.P., flour mill prop.
Heron, William, farmer
Keeler, William, hotel keeper
Lasky, Thomas, cooper
Leslie, Joseph, boots and shoes
McArdle, Joseph, painter
Muir, William, general merchant
Parker, Thomas, butcher
Richardson, James, farmer
Shackleton, Eli, hotel keeper
Shackleton, James, carriage maker
Stephenson, D. G., auctioneer
Stephenson, John, lumber dealer
TREDWAY, WILLIAM, Postmaster and gen. mer.
Walsh, John, boots and shoes
Wilson, John, farmer

Hillier.—A Village in the Township of Hillier, County Prince Edward, 18 miles from Picton, the County Town, and 20 from Brighton Station Grand Trunk Railway. Population 100.

Arthur Mathew, J.P.
Arthur Thomas, wagon maker
Baker, Rev. E. H. M. (Church of England)
Beard, Mrs. S. E., teacher
Byam, John W., teacher
Cameron, Aaron P., farmer
Delong, Isaac, shoemaker
Dorland, Robert J., manufacturer of woolen goods
Dulmage, Edward, wagon maker
FLAGLER, SOLOMON, Postmaster, insurance agent and hotel keeper
Gaddis, Mathew, cooper
Gardner, William, saddler
German, Orrin, teacher
Graydon, Miss Rhoda A., milliner, &c.
Hardy, Thomas, farmer
Tripp, Gilbert, cooper
Hubbs, Abram, proprietor flouring mills
Johnson, Rev. Robert (N. C. Methodist)
Jones, George, farmer
Jones, Robert, farmer
Jones, Samuel, J.P., farmer
Lay, James B., general merchant
Leavens, Paul, farmer
McComb, James, sash, door and blind manufacturer
McComb, William, carpenter
Monaghan, Hugh, cooper
Niles, S. P., farmer
Noxon, Richard, flouring mills
Palmer, Henry, flouring mills
Simpson, Charles O., farmer
Stapleton, Joseph D., farmer
Titus, Joseph, stock dealer and butcher

Hillsboro'.—A Post Village in the Township of Plympton, County Lambton, 20 miles from Sarnia, the County Town, and 5 miles from Forest, the nearest railway station. Mails tri-weekly. Population about 80.

Adams, Robert, cabinet maker
Anderson, Horatio, blacksmith
Galloway, James, carpenter
Gibson, Edward, M.D.
Hart, George, J.P., commissioner in B. R.
HILL, THOMAS L., Postmaster
Hill, Milward, spirit merchant
Hill, Samuel C., farmer
Irvine, James, carpenter
Jones, John, J.P.
Jones, Samuel, shoemaker
Jones, Thomas, merchant
Kendall, Thomas, constable
Reid, Charles, miller
Sanderson, Andrew, wagon maker
Wood, Thomas, innkeeper

Hillsburg.—A Village in the Township of Erin, County Wellington, 22 miles from Guelph, the County Town, and 50 from Toronto. Stage to Georgetown. Money Order Office. Population 300.

Barnham, Dr
Bates, Rev. J. W., (Baptist)
Campbell, John, mason
Edmunds, Joseph, baker
Gaud & Brother, tanners and leather dealers
Green, John, carpenter
Hill, Robert, hotel keeper
How & Bro., gen. merchts and props. flouring mill
How, William, sen., J.P
Kelly, Brown & Co., general merchants
Kilgour & Tell, general merchants
Kirk, John, hotel keeper
Lacy, George, general merchant
Leason, Samuel, hotel keeper
McClellan, C., carpenter
McMillan, Charles. J. P
Pearson, A., cabinet maker
Robertson, Colin, grocer
Rogers, William, mason
Sinclair, Alexander, carpenter
Thurhan, Rev. Donald, (Old Kirk)
Viner, James, gunsmith
Viner, John, furniture dealer
Worts, George; prop. flouring mill
York, Dr.

Hillsdale.—A Village in the Township of Medonte, County Simcoe, 16 miles from Barrie, the County Town. Population 65.

Archer, Edward, farmer
Blackstone, Dr.
Craw, Rev. George, (Presbyterian)
Davis, Miss, teacher
FARAGHER, JOHN, Postmaster and gen. mercht.
Hamilton, John, farmer
Hill, Alexander, hotel keeper
Hill, T., farmer
Hutton, John, tailor
Lillico & Dickey, sash, blind and door factory
Lillico, William, painter
Marlow, James, farmer
Marlow, John, farmer
Morrison, Charles, wagon maker
Plaxton, William, farmer
Preston, James, farmer
Tucker, Z. M., farmer
Walker, James, general merchant
Williams, Lillico & Dickey, carpenters

Hill's Green.—A Post-office in the Township of Hay, County Huron, 3½ miles from Berne.

Hagan, John, farmer
Henderson, Joseph, farmer
Hill, William, farmer
Hudson, Robert, farmer
LOWE, HUGH, Postmaster
McLeod, James, farmer
Roy, E., farmer
Smith, Henry, general merchant
Smith, Neil, general merchant
Troyer, John, general merchant

Hilton.—A Village in the Township of Brighton, County Northumberland, 30 miles from Cobourg, the County Town, and 5 from Brighton Station, Grand Trunk Railway. Population 50.

Bale, William, farmer
BECKER, A. A., J.P., Postmaster and gen. mercht
Becker, C. S., farmer
Chatterson, George, farmer
Clarke, R. G., wine and spirit dealer
Cryderman, W. C., J.P.
Fiddick, Charles, farmer
Johnson, C. W., shoemaker
Johnson, G. L., carpenter
Langdon, W., J.P.
Mowan, R. G., farmer
Mowan, R. J., hotel keeper
Newcomb, J. W., prop. flouring mill
Norris, Rev. J. S. (Episcopal Methodist)
Pansicklin, Thomas, shoemaker
Phelp, John, farmer
Potts, Robert A., farmer
Purdy, Henry, teacher
Richmond, L., farmer
Richmond, Sylvester, carpenter
Short, John E., wagon maker
Simpson, Abijah, wagon maker
Sparrow, Rev. J. P. (Episcopal Methodist)
Thorne, Edmund, farmer
Thorne, G. C., farmer
Webster, J. M., farmer
Webster, Joshua, J.P.

Hoath Head.—A Post Office in the Township of Sydenham, County Grey, North Riding.
HOATH, R., Postmaster.

Hockley.—A Village in the Township of Adjala, County Cardwell, on the Nottawa River, 40 miles from Barrie, and 42 from Toronto. Average value of land $30 per acre. Population 150.

Beatty, David
Beatty, Benjamin
Dunn, Robert, blacksmith
Egner, W. H., dentist
Goodeve, J
Hackell, Thomas, shoemaker
Irwin, John A., farmer
Irwin, Robert, shingle maker
Lindsay, J. B., farmer
Linn, Mrs. A., milliner, &c
MARTIN, THOMAS, Postmaster, general merchant
Palmer, George, tailor
Quigley, John, farmer
Stewart, L., general merchant
Sutherland Mrs. G., milliner, &c
Taylor, George, carpenter
Wilson, James, soap and candle maker

Holbrook.—A Village in the Township of Norwich, County Oxford, 10 miles from Woodstock, the County Town. Population 150.

Brady, Nicholas, hotel keeper
Chambers, Robert, J.P
Chapin, James M., cheese manuf
Dennis, John, farmer
Dickson, Joseph K., farmer
Ditchfield, Samuel J., saddler
Flemming, Archibald, insurance agent
Gagnier, Jerome, blacksmith
Heath, James, waggon maker
Heath, John, wagon maker
Henderson, Joseph, weaver
Madgwick, Elias, carriage trimmer
Montillo Nesbit, insurance agent
Nesbit, J. W., J.P.
Stover, A. C., farmer
WHITFIELD, A. M., Postmaster and manager Denmark Co-operative Association

Holland Landing (St. Albans).—An incorporated Village and Station of the Northern Railway, on the west branch of the Holland River, in the Township of East Gwillimbury, County York, 38 miles from Toronto, the County Town. Money Order office. Population 800.

Ayerst, Francis, baker
Bacon, Henry, mason, builder and lime dealer
Beaton, Donald, farmer
Beach, Robert, shoemaker
Breckon, Joseph, store keeper
Carry, Rev. John (Church of England)
Chapman, Henry, hop grower
CHAPMAN, JOSHUA, brick manufacturer
Conway, D., brewer
Corbiere, Eli, shoemaker
Dennis, William, tanner
Dixon, Alexander, farmer
Dolan, John, miller
Ellerby, David, proprietor woolen mill
Evans, Beverly, carpenter
Evans, J. B., farmer
Fitzgibbon, Michael, weaver
Gilrie, Andrew, carpenter
GLEASON, JOHN, farmer
Gray, James & Richard, well sinkers
Hamilton, Alexander, farmer
Jakeway, Aaron, manufacturer tin, copper and sheet iron ware
Jerome, J.
Johnston, Joseph, trapper
Kelly, Thomas, tailor
KENNEDY, JAMES, clerk municipality
Lane, John, cooper
Lane, Thomas, cooper
Little, John, tailor
Lloyd, Henry, tanner
Lount, Franklin, lumber merchant
Luck, William, wagon maker
McCLURE, JAMES, auctioneer and gen. merchant
McGuigan, John, grocer
McKenzie, John, general land agent
Moore, Robert, farmer
Moore, Thomas, mason
Murphy, Patrick, farrier
O'Keefe, Mary, grocer
Ough, John, mason
Ough, Thomas, farmer
PARNHAM, JAMES, J.P. and farmer
Parsons, William, sexton
Phelps, Alfred, builder
PLAYTER, CAPTAIN, R. B. C., prop. Masonic Arm's Hotel
PORTER, W. H., L.D.S., vice-president Dental Association, Ontario
Pulford, George, miller.
Richardson, William, farmer
Riley, James, farmer
ROSS, D. S., station-and express agent
Salter, John, carpenter
Sexsmith, Samuel, cooper
SHEPPARD, JOHN, builder and prop. Royal Hotel
SLOANE, E. B., Postmaster
SOMERVILLE, C. C., general merchant
Sutherland, Alexander, farmer
Sweesey, George and John, farmers
Sykes, John, lumber merchant
Taylor, Martin, builder
Tate, William, blacksmith
THOMPSON, THOMAS, general merchant, dealer in furs, pelts, &c.
Thorn, B. H., general merchant and flour mill prop.
Thorn, William C., miller
West, John A., trapper
White, George, shoemaker
WILLIAMS, ALEXANDER, supt., tannery, book-keeper
Willson, Colonol R. T.
Winch, Thomas
Wornsop. Thomas, tanner
Wright, Silas, farmer

Holmesville.—A village in the Township of Goderich, County Huron, on the River Maitland, 8 miles from Goderich, the County Town. Populotion 50.

Cantellor, Peter, butcher
Cantleton, William, farmer
Churchill, John, J.P., farmer
Colback, J., farmer
Ford, Henry, J.P., farmer
Ford, Thomas, farmer
Ford, William, farmer
Holmes, John, farmer
Holmes, T., farmer
KELLY, EDWARD, Postmaster
Kelly, Mrs. E., bookseller and stationer
Proctor, William, hotel keeper
Shephard, John, farmer
Shephard, William, farmer
Sherman, G., teacher
Stanley, G., farmer
Young, H., farmer
Young, Joseph, farmer

Holstein.—A Village in the Township of Egremont, County Grey, 35 miles from Owen Sound, the County Town. Population 40.

Cushrie, John, teacher
Kerr, R., wagon maker
McKenzie, W. D., general merchant
Stonehouse, M. L., hotel keeper

Holt (see Eastville).—A Post Office in the Township of East Gwillimbury, County York, 40 miles from Toronto, the County Town.

QUIBELL, JOHN, Postmaster.

Holyrood.—A Post Office in the Township of Kinloss, County Bruce, South Riding.

ELLIOTT, WILLIAM, Postmaster.

Homer.—A Post Office in the Township of Grantham, County Lincoln.

CAVERS, PETER A., Postmaster.

Honeywood.—A Post Office in the Township of Mulmur, County Simcoe, distant 30 miles from Barrie, the County Town.

Lawrence, George & Bro., general merchants
LAWRENCE, R., Postmaster.

Hopefield.—A small Post Village in the Township of Brudenell, County Renfrew, South Riding.

READ, HENRY Y., Postmaster.

Hopetown.—A small Post Village in the Township of Lanark, and County of Lanark, distant from Perth, the County Town, 18 miles, and from Ottawa 60 miles. Population about 50.

Hornby.—A Village in the Township of Esquesing, County Halton, 6 miles from Milton, the County Town, and 28 from Toronto. Stages daily to Georgetown Station, Grand Trunk Railway, 8 miles. Population 80.

Anderson, John, carpenter
Anderson, William, shoemaker
Brain, Bros., brewers
Cook, George, lumber dealer
Cowan, Richard, J.P.
Fox Anthony, M.D.
Galloway, Rev. Mr. (Baptist)
Hall, Robert, J.P.
Justin, John, wagon maker
Lindsay, James B., hetel keeper
Lyon, Thomas G., teacher
McClosky, Henry, potter
McCollan, Thomas, hotel keeper
McCulland, Mrs., milliner, &c.
McMILLAN, JOHN, Postmaster and gen. merchant
Pickard, William, cheese manufacturer
Robertson, Thomas, tailor
Rutledge, Robert, shoemaker
Stewart, Rev. Mr. (Presbyterian)
Story, John, cheese manufacturer
Thurston, Hiram, shingle maker
Tremaine, Rev. Mr. (Church of England)
Wallace, James, shoemaker

Horning's Mills.—A Village at the head of Pine River, in the Township of Melancthon, County Grey. 58 miles from Owen Sound, the County Town, and 25 from Stayner Station, Northern Railroad. Stages to Collingwood and Orangeville. Population 160.

Addison, Rev. Peter (Wesleyan)
AIRTH, WILLIAM, J.P., Postmaster, general merchant and proprietor flouring mill
Allen, Robert, farmer
August, John, carpenter
Barr, John, M.D.
Bates, Henry, J.P., farmer
Bowley, Arnold, shingle maker
Campaigne, James, auctioneer
Emerick, John, butcher
Hill, Rev. Rowland (Church of England)
House, Philip, carpenter
Hudd, Stephen, farmer
Jarvis, David, tailor
Jarvis, Henry, general merchant and tailor
Johnston, Miss E., teacher
McGhee, Robert, farmer
Marshall, George, shoemaker
Marshall, Robert, carpenter
Mason, Mrs. hotel keeper
Morrow, John, saddler
Norton, Thomas, teacher
Page, Elijah, farmer
Page, Reuben, shingle maker
Polley, Hugh, farmer
Polley, Richard, farmer
Rill, Rev. Ephraim (Episcopal Methodist)
Shepherd, George, prop. flouring mill
Silks, William, farmer
Simmenter, John, cooper
Stubbins, William, shoemaker

Houghton.—A Village in the Township of Houghton, County Norfolk, 33 miles from Simcoe, the County Town. Population 350.

Adams, Adam, teacher
Allan, J., farmer
Beckett, Samuel, leather dealer
Bell, Ezra, general merchant
Bradfield, H., farmer
Brady, D. C., farmer
Brawlenhermer, Rev. P., (Wesleyan)
Bridgeman, T. R. E., teacher
Buchner, P., farmer
BUNDY, GEORGE, Postmaster, shoemaker
Callam, P., farmer
Chamberlain, Thomas, J.P., general merchant
Emory, H., farmer
Fick, Miss A., teacher
Finch, T., farmer
Francis, J., farmer
Freeland, William, insurance agent
Gates, Calvin, general merchant
Gates, Clark, painter
Gates, E. D., fancy goods, toys, millinery, &c.
Guest, H., farmer
Hill, Jeremiah, hotel keeper
Hutchinson, J. J., farmer
Jackson, David, hotel keeper
Jackson, James, hotel keeper
Jackson, Willison, leather dealer
Mercer, R., farmer
Merrill, A., farmer
Montgomery, Robert, carpenter
Moore, Hiram, farmer
Nelson, R., farmer
Park, Philip, farmer
Payne, Ephraim, wagon maker
Rice, Ebenezer, shoemaker
Sharp, William, shoemaker
Smith, D., farmer
Smith, Rev. — (Baptist)
Smith, Samuel, farmer
White, Richard, shoemaker
Williams, W. W., farmer

Howick Village (Gorrie Post Office) is situated in the Township of Howick, County Huron, 50 miles distant from Goderich, the County Town, and 180 miles from Toronto. The Maitland River passes through the village, supplying excellent water privileges. A good woolen factory would pay well here. Daily stages from Worcester. Population 350.

Anderson, William farmer
Barber, Miss, milliner, &c.
BESANSON, HENRY, Postmaster.
Bowger, Thomas, lime and stone dealer
Carson, William, general merchant
Condy, John, Queen Arms Hotel
Dickson & Gray, general merchants
Douglas, Robert, Royal Canadian Hotel
Greer, George, farmer
Greer, John, farmer
Greer, Samuel, farmer
Hunt, H. M., general merchant
James, Richard, foundry
Johnston, R. J., hide and leather dealer
Kain, Mrs., milliner, &c.
Lamb, John, butcher
Leech, Edward, insurance agent
Leech, R. & Co., flouring and planing mills and dealers in lumber
McGill, James, butcher
McLaughlin, William, carpenter
McMichael, M. D.
Magwood, Charles, farmer
Miller, Rev. Mr. (Church of England)
Oliphant, William, painter
Perkins, Henry, saddler
Perkins, James, shoemaker
Pickford, C. W., general merchant
Powell, Mrs., teacher
Rea, H. W., general merchant
Roberts, R. G., teacher
Sanderson, Thomas, farmer
Saunders, Rev. Nelson, farmer
Savage, Rev. J. W., (Wesleyan)
Shaw, Sidney, cabinet maker
Smith, Alexander, cooper
Smith, Henry, farmer
Stirling, Archibald, farmer
Stinson, John, wagon maker
Strong, James, farmer
Tindell, Rev. W., (N. C. Methodist)
Wilson, Samuel, tinsmith

Hubbell's Falls.—A Post-office in the Township of Fitzroy, County Carleton, 33 miles from Ottawa, the County Town.

Carss, Robert, J.P
Dickson, Robert, farmer
Forbes, Andrew, farmer
Forbes, John, carpenter
Groves, William, gunsmith
Herrick, M., grocer
Holliday, Francis, general merchant
Hubbell, James, prop. carding mill
Mohr, Charles, hotel keeper
Montfort, R., hotel keeper
Richey, John, farmer
Riddell, Archibald, farmer
RIDDELL, JAMES, Postmaster, farmer
Shields, Alexander, cooper
Somerville, T. G., general merchant
Steen, James, lumber merchant

Hullsville.—A small Post Village in the Township of Walpole, County Haldimand.

Buck, J. W., farmer
Canfield, D. W., merchant
Carroll, Thomas, farmer
Ferguson, Joseph, carpenter
Helm, Walter, farmer
HULL, JOHN, Postmaster
Lounsberg, Oliver, farmer
Murray, David, mechanic
Park, E., farmer
Ryan, William, inn keeper
Trimmer, D., wagon maker

Humber.—A Village on the west branch of the River Humber in the Township of Etobicoke, County York, 17 miles from Toronto, the County Town, 4 from Thistletown, 7 from Weston and 10 from Bolton. Average price of land $40 per acre. Population 150

Allen, Rev. J. W., (Primitive Methodist)
Black, William H., dentist
Boyes, Rev. R., (Primitive Methodist)
Brooks, Rev. Joseph, (Baptist)
Burns, Martin, saddler
Croue, William N., carpenter
De La Haye, A., M.D
De La Haye, J. P., J.P.
Hengill, Daniel, carpenter and auctioneer
Joliff. Rev. William, (Primitive Methodist)
LINTON, JOHN, Postmaster general merchant
McCann, Rev., (Roman Catholic)
McDonald, Angus, butcher
McKay, M.D.
Murphy, Richard, farmer
Nichol, John, butcher
Robinson, John, cabinet maker
Royal, C. P., hotel keeper
Smyth, P., hotel keeper
Thomas, Henry, farmer
Treadgold, George, teacher
Treadgold, Martin, broker and stationery
Treadgold, M., teacher
Watson, William, farmer
Wilks, R., clothing dealer
Wolff, Charles, cabinet maker

Humberstone.—A Village in the Township of Humberstone, County Welland, 4 miles from Welland, the County Town, 1 mile from Lake Erie, and the Welland Canal, and about the same distance from Port Colborne Station, Grand Trunk Railway. Population 400.

Augustine, Elias, wagon maker
Augustine, Simeon, farmer
Baker, John, vinegar manufacturer
Bender. Andrew, cooper
Barth, A., saddler
Boerker, A , gunsmith
Boniberg, William, bricklayer
Breisacher, C., shoemaker
Cutler. Rev. J. B., (Methodist Episcopal)
Ehrhoff, C., shoemaker
Ellsworth, John M., farmer
Farbach, P., blacksmith
Fry, D., blacksmith
Ganger, L., painter
Haney, M. F., J.P., M.D.
Hoffmeyer, Frederick, teacher
Irvine, W. S., tailor
Kinnaird, J. D., harness maker
Klee, J. F., hotel keeper and dealer in boots and shoes
Knisely, O. F., farmer
Kramer, John, blacksmith
Kuss, Rev. A. C. (Evangelical Lutheran)
Law, John, general merchant
Mann & Killmer, butchers
Merer, William, tailor
Mellanby, William
Meddlestadt, A., wagon maker
Miller, Henry
Misener, Isaac, flour and feed
Morgan, George, carpenter
Neff, Abraham, farmer
Neff, Jonathan, proprietor foundry and machine shop
Priestman, Joseph, general agent
Reeb, Michael, grocer
Reid, William, teacher
Rochland, George, ashery
Rother, J. G., blacksmith
Schooley & Augustini, proprietors steam saw mill
Schooley, Benjamin, carpenter
Schooley, Isaac, general merchant
Sherman, F., baker
Snider, H., blacksmith
Snider, Henry. grocer
Staff, A., wagon maker
Stone, Henry, farmer
Stoner, Joseph, farmer
Thompson, Charles, teacher and accountant
THOMPSON, JOHN, Postmaster, J. P., and insurance agent
Tries, Augustus, cooper
Uhrig, Joseph, butcher
Weaver, Samuel, farmer
White, T. hotel keeper
Whiteman, George, farmer
Whiteman, Jacob, hotel keeper
Zerter & Co., cabinet makers

Howe Island.—A Post Office of the Township of Pittsburg, County Frontenac.
URQUHART, R., Postmaster.

Hunsdon.—A post Village in the Township of Albion, County Cardwell.
PREST, WILLIAM, Postmaster

Huntley (Carp Village).—A Post Office in the Township of Huntley, County Carleton, 20 miles from Ottawa, the County Town, and 20 from Packingham. Stage to Packingham. Population of Carp 50.

Alexander, Thomas, wagon maker
Bradley, W. B., proprietor lumber yard
Brown, Thomas, wagon maker
Brown, T., hotel keeper
Featherston, W. J., general merchant
Graham, A., lime dealer
Green, J., hotel keeper
Holmes, J., J.P.
HUESTON, J., Postmaster and general merchant
Johnston, J., lime and stone dealer
Kidd, Richard, J.P.
McBride, Henry, J.P.
Months, Mrs., milliner
Newton, Eli, saddler
Rainberg, O., dealer in hats, caps and furs, and tailor
Taylor, T., hotel keeper
Wilson, Thomas, hide and leather dealer

Huston.—A Village on the River Conestogo, in the Township of Maryboro', County Wellington, 32 miles from Guelph, the County Town. Population 150.

Beldon, S., hotel keeper
Callaway, David, general merchant
Clark, George, brickmaker
Crane, Rev. Isaac (Wesleyan)
Davison, W. J., hotel keeper
Deckherd, George, wagon maker
Ferguson, James, farmer
Graham, George, farmer
Graham, John, farmer
Gray, Matthew, grist mill proprietor
Henry, Charles, flax mill proprietor
Johnston, John C., auctioneer
Johnston, Richard, hotel keeper
Krull, Theodore, cabinet maker
LANDERKIN, JOHN, Postmaster
McBeth, Alexander, J.P.
Nesbitt, Edward, M.D.
Nesbitt, Rev. George, (Church of England)
Robinson, John, general merchant
Walker, Thomas, farmer
Wast, Thomas, shoemaker

Hyde Park Corner.—A Village in the Township of London, County Middlesex, 6 miles from London, the County Town. Population 100.

Barclay, John, farmer
Brown, William, butcher
Edward, George, farmer
Ellis, John, farmer
Elson, Peter, potter
Fisher, James, farmer
Forbes, Duncan, farmer
FRASER, ANGUS, Postmaster and tailor
Hanson, Henry, physician
Hanson, Thomas, physician
Hamble, John, hotel keeper
Lamley, William, general merchant
McDonald, James, farmer
McDougal, John, hotel keeper
McKenzie, D. A., J.P.
McMillan, William, J.P.
Morehouse, James, farmer
Morris, Thomas, butcher
Murch, Henry, blacksmith
Porter, John, farmer
Ramsay, William, farmer
Smith, James, blacksmith

Ida.—A Post-office in the Township of Cavan, County Durham, E.R.
BAPTIE, ALEXANDER, Postmaster

Indiana.—A Village on the Grand River, in the Township of Seneca, County Haldimand, 3 miles from Cayuga, the County Town, and 62 from Toronto. Stages to Caledonia and Cayuga. Money Order Office. Population 200.

Barry, Mrs., inn keeper
Devine, Andrew, shoemaker
Farrell, Patrick, general merchant
Fenlen, Miles, hotel keeper
KINNEAR, A. M., Postmaster
Kirkland, James, distiller
Lester, Thomas, prop. saw mill
McClorey, James, blacksmith
McGovern, Edward, hotel keeper
Madigan, Michael, general merchant
Shipway, Morris, shoemaker
Slaven, Edward, teacher
Thompson, David, M.P.P., prop. flour mills

Ilderton.—A small Post Village in the Township of London, County Middlesex, about 12 miles from London. Mails semi-weekly. Population 30.

Nicol, James, blacksmith
ORD, GEORGE, Postmaster and gen. merchant
Scott, Robert, wagon maker
Severn, Henry, mail carrier

Ingersoll.—A flourishing incorporated Town, in the Township of North Oxford, County Oxford, South Riding, beautifully situated on the River Thames, and a station on the Great Western Railway; distant from Woodstock the County Town, 10 miles, from London 19 miles, and from Toronto 106 miles; a good road passes through the Town to Lake Erie, 33 miles distant. Wheat and other grain and sawn lumber are exported extensively, and during the last three years the manufacture of cheese has engrossed the attention of capitalists; thousands of tons are annually exported, chiefly for the English market. The Town contains 10 Churches, a Grammar, Union and Common schools. The buildings including the Churches are mostly good substantial structures, and many of the private residences display excellent taste and considerable wealth. Stages to Tilsonburg, Vienna and Port Burwell. Money Order Office and Savings Bank. Population 4000.

Ackert, John, pump maker
ADAIR, JOHN, proprietor Adair's Hotel (see adv.)
ADAIR & CAIRNS, (Samuel Adair, Robert Cairns) groceries, provisions, &c
Adkins, James, stove dealer
Agar, Robert, banker and exchange broker
Badden & Delaney, (James Badden, Wm. A. Delaney) carriage and wagon makers
Bailey, George, carriage and wagon maker
BAKER, FREDERICK A., photographer
Barker, Edward, jr., boots and shoes
Barker, Joseph, (Browett & Barker)
Barnes & Bro., (Minor and Nelson) livery and sale stables
Barraclough, Thomas H., boots and shoes
BEAVER MUTUAL INSURANCE COMPANY, (Toronto) Chas. E. Chadwick, director and agent
Bell, William C., (A. Oliver & Co.)
Bennett, Mrs. Mary, fruits and confectionery
Benson, James, barrister
Berry, W., tailor
Bixel, Bro., (Matthew and Leonard) brewers
Blair, William, night station master G. W. R. depot
Bloor, Charles, shoemaker and grocer
Bluer, C., boots and shoes
BOLES, JOHN, merchant tailor
Bowers, Dr.
Bradbury, Fred. B., (Waterhouse, Bradbury & Co).
Brady, James, proprietor Brady's Hotel & auctioneer
Brady, John, proprietor Royal Exchange Hotel
Browett & Barker (Joseph Browett & Joseph Barker) general hardware
BROWN, JAMES, brewer
Brown, James, jun., baker
Brown, Thomas, tanner and currier
Brown & Wells, (P. J. Brown & Thomas Wells), barristers
Buchanan, J. & A., stoves and tinware
Buchanan, John, stoves and tinware
Buckhurst, A. & Co., (A. H. Buckhurst & Peter Sherk), marble cutters
Byre, Thomas
Caldwell, E., musician
Caldwell, O. B., drugs and chemicals
Callaghan, John, general merchant and butcher
Campbell, Homer, general merchant
Campbell, Homer, jun., tin, copper and sheet iron ware
CANADA CHEESE MANUFACTURING CO., president, James Harris; secretary, Daniel Phelan, treasurer; Charles E. Chadwick
Canada Permanent Building and Saving Society, Charles E. Chadwick, appraiser
Canfield, James, attorney-at-law
Carey, Charles C., oyster saloon
Carroll, Daniel W., M.D
Casswell, Edwin, general merchant
CHADWICK, CHARLES E., agent Niagara District Bank and insurance agent
Chapman, John M.
Childs, James, teamster
CHOWN, J. G. & Co., hardware
Christopher, Aaron, (J. Christopher & Bros).
Christopher, J. & Bros., (John, Aaron & George), planing and saw millers
Christopher, John, (J. Christopher & Bros)
Clark, G. A., M.D., (Eclectic)
Clark, Hugh, cabinet maker
Commercial Union Assurance Co., Charles E. Chadwick, agent
Cook, Simeon, lumber merchant
Cragg, Charles, saddle and harness maker
Crotty, H., farmer
CROTTY, WILLIAM, general merchant
Daley House and general Stage Office, A. Daly, prop.
Delaney, William A., (Badden & Delaney)
Doty, Edwin, agt. American & Canadian Express Co.
Douglas, William, proprietor Douglas' Hotel
Dufton, Joseph (Waterhouse, Bradbury & Co.)
Dundas, Alexander, blacksmith and farrier
Dundas, William (Wait & Dundas)
Dunn, J., boot and shoe maker
Dutton, Joseph M., boots and shoes, leather & findings
EASTWOOD, W. & Co., manufacturers of agricultural implements
Edinburgh Life Assurance Co., S. B. Newcombe, agt.
ELLIS, R. Y. & BROTHER (R. Y. & H. Ellis), heavy and shelf hardware (see adv.)
Elliott, John N., groceries and provisions
Elliott, S. A., butcher
Fawkes, Thomas F., watchmaker and jeweller
Ferguson, John J., dry goods and clothing
Ferris, McLean & Co. (George Ferris, John McLean), groceries, provisions, wines and liquors
Fletcher, Thomas, grocer, auctioneer and lumber dealer
Foster, George, blacksmith
GAINES, ROBERT R., barber and hairdresser
Galliford, John, manufacturer and dealer in boots and shoes
Gallagher, William, hotel proprietor
Garvey, John, clerk E. Robinson
Gayfer, John, chemist & druggist, books & stationery

Gerger, J. G., blacksmith
Gibson, Miss, toys and fancy goods
Goble, John, wagon maker
Gordon, Alexander, merchant tailor
Gordon, James, accountant and teller Niagara District Bank
Grant, Benjamin
GRANT, JAMES M., proprietor Great Western Hotel and livery
Grant, Miss Mary, Berlin wool store
Greenaway, Isaac R., boots and shoes
Groppi, Philip, boots and shoes
GURNETT, J. S., editor and proprietor *Ingersoll Chronicle* (see adv.)
Hall, Charles P., watches, clocks and jewellery, fancy goods, musical instruments, &c.
Harris, Alexander, builder
Harris, E. J., surgeon dentist
HARRIS, JAMES, president Canada Cheese manufacturing Company
Hartford Fire Insurance Company, Hartford, Conn., Charles E. Chadwick, agent
Hayes, N., general insurance agent
HEARN, HENRY, prop. Hearn's Royal Hotel (see adv.)
Hearn, William L., fancy goods
Hicks, Miss Margaret, dressmaker
Hoagg, William (J. Turner & Co.)
Home Insurance Company, New Haven, Conn., C. H. Sorley, agent
Hoyt, J. J., M.D.
Hugill, John, photographer
INGERSOLL CHEESE COMPANY, James Harris & Co., proprietors
INGERSOLL CHRONICLE, J. S. Gurnett, editor and proprietor (see adv).
James, Stephen W., blacksmith
Jarvis, Joseph, M.D.
Keating, Robert, hotel proprietor
Kennedy, C., dentist
Kennedy, Peter, prop. Kennedy's Hotel
Kerr, A. R., dry goods, millinery, &c.
Kerr, Daniel, carriage and wagon maker
Kerr, John, wagon maker
Kerr, Hugh, book-keeper, A. Oliver & Co.
Kerscadden, Thomas, prop. Thompson House
King, James, miller and flour barrel maker
Kneeshaw, Robert, agent, chemist and druggist, books and stationery
Lewis, Francis G., photographer
Lewis, John, station master G. W. R. depot
Lister, Archibald, telegraph operator G. W. R. depot
Little, Thomas, boot and shoe maker
McCAUGHEY & WALSH (James McCaughey and Michael Walsh), barristers, &c.
McCausland, Marshal, M.D., (Scott & McCausland)
McDonald, James, hats, caps and furs
McDONALD, JAMES F., barrister, &c
McDONALD, JOHN, J.P
McDonald, Robert, merchant
McINTYRE, JAMES, cabinet maker and furniture dealer, undertaker (see adv)
McKindsey, T. & Co., dry goods, millinery, &c
McLean, Allan, books and stationery, wall paper, picture frames, &c
McLean, John, (Ferris McLean & Co)
McSherry, Andrew & George, plow makers
Macniven, James, dry goods, millinery
Marr, W. & B. & Co., groceries and provisions
Marshall, John J., baker and confectioner
Meally & Carr, Misses, dressmakers
Meridy, George, prop. skating rink
MERCHANTS' BANK, & Savings Bank, Charles H. Sorley, agent
MILLAR, T. D., produce and commission merchant
Miller, Matthew, groceries and provisions
Montreal Telegraph Office
MORREY, JAMES F., cabinet maker and furniture dealer
Morrison, William & Neil, saddle and harness makers
Myers, Stephen, (Waterhouse, Bradbury & Co)
NEWCOMBE, S. B., barrister, &c
NIAGARA DISTRICT BANK, Charles E. Chadwick, agent
Nichols, Mrs. Catharine, groceries, &c
Noe, Louis, fruits and varieties
NOXON BROTHERS, (J. & S.) founders, machinists, and agricultural implement manufacturers
O'Connor, Arthur, grocer
O'Connor, Henry, dry goods
OLIVER, ADAM, (A. Oliver & Co)
OLIVER, A. & CO. (Adam Oliver, William C. Bell and Hugh Sutherland) lumber manufacturers, builders, &c.
O'Neill, Jeremiah, groceries, wines, liquors, &c.
Paine, Mrs. S. E., milliner and dress maker
Paton, Thomas S., dry goods, &c.
Perkins, George E., dry goods
Petrie, Edward A., teller Merchants' Bank
Phelan, Daniel, secretary Canada Cheese manufaturing Co.
Post, Jacob, baker and confectioner
READ, S. G., dry goods and clothing (see adv)
Reid, Alexander, dry goods, millinery and clothing
ROBINSON, Edward, general merchant
Robinson. Ephraim, cabinet maker
Rodenhurst, William, cigar manufacturer
Ross, George, coal and salt dealer
Scott, Henry H., M.D., (Scott & McCausland)
Scott & McCausland, physicians and surgeons
Seely, Miss, dressmaker
Sharp, Thomas A., constable and collector
SHRAPNELL, G. J., grocer, butter, cheese and bacon factor
Slawson & Beel (Charles H. Slawson and William J. Beel), lumber, lath and shingles
Smith, Robert
Softley, Robert, manager Penitentiary boot and shoe store
SORLEY, CHARLES H., agent Merchants' Bank, and insurance agent
Standard Life Insurance Co., (Edinburgh), Charles H. Sorley, agent
Stephenson, Miss A., fruits, confectionary & stationery
STEPHENS & CO., dry goods
Stephens, J., (Stephens & Co.)
Stimson, George G., general merchant, oil refiner
Stuart, Francis, tailor
Stuart John, miller
Stuart, Robert, groceries, flour and feed
Sutherland, Hugh, (A. Oliver & Co.)
Taylor, John, ashery
THIRKELL, JOSEPH, Postmaster
Thompson, L., painter
Tillson, Edwin D., lumber merchant
Tune, James, confectioner
TURNER, GEORGE A., stoves and tinware (see adv)
TURNER, JACOB & CO., stoves and tinware (see adv)
Turner, Jeremiah, machinist
Travellers' Insurance Co., Hartford, Conn., Charles Chadwick, agent
Trick, William, prop. Farmers' Hotel

Vance, Robert, baker and confectioner
Veitch, William, boot maker
Vogt, Henry, watchmaker and jeweller
Wait & Dundas (Nelson Wait and William Dundas), groceries, wines and liquors
Walbank, Samuel S., M.D.
Walker, I. R., M.D.
Walker, John, cooper
Walker, Thomas, prop. Royal Oak Hotel
Walley, George W., crockery and glassware
WALSH, MICHAEL (McCaughey & Walsh)
Waterhouse, Bradbury & Co., woolen mills
Waterworth, William, agent for E. D. Tillson, lumber merchant
WATSON, WILLIAM, dry goods, millinery, &c. (see adv)
Webster, George H., cabinet maker
Welder, David, butcher
Wells, Thomas (Brown & Wells)
White, David, dry goods, millinery and clothing
Williams, Arthur T., M.D.
Williams, Isaac, news agent and fancy goods
Williams, J. Arthur, M.D.
Wilson, Josiah G., carriage maker
Wilson, John W., carriage and wagon manufacturer
Wiseman, George, prop. Carroll Hotel
Wood & Co., prop. Thames Oil Works
WOODCOCK, RALPH A., books, stationery and periodicals, post office, book store, agent for Canada Life and Western Insurance Company
Worth, Humphrey, butcher
Young, Robert H., saddle and harness maker

Ingoldsby.—A Post-office in the Township of Minden, County Peterboro' E.R.
SMITH, RICHARD, Postmaster.

Inistioge.—A Post-office in the Township of Artemesia, County Grey, S.R.
ARMSTRONG, GEORGE, Postmaster.

Inkerman.—A Village in the Township of Mountain, County Dundas, on the north branch of the Pettite Nation River, 50 miles from Morrisburgh, the County Town. Improved land in the vicinity averages $30 per acre. Stages to Iroquois, 16 miles. Population 150.

Baldwin, Albert, wagon maker
Bishop, Thomas, J.P., prop flouring mill
Cook, Ira, cooper
Cook & Sullivan, lumber dealers
Fletcher, W. J., hide and leather dealer and tanner
Harr, C., teacher
Heys, John, shoemaker
Hitchcock, Rev. Z. B., (Episcopal Methodist)
Hows, Rev. John, (Wesleyan)
Kinsey, —, M.D
Lock, John, hotel keeper
Loppel, William, carpenter
Merkley, Almira, milliner, &c
Merkley, & Durant, general merchants
Rennick, John, J.P., general merchant
Sullivan & Co., general merchants
Wharton, William, H., general merchant

Innerkip.—A Village in the Township of East Zorra, County Oxford, on the River Thames, 8 miles from Woodstock, the County Town. Population 200.

Barr, Rev. — (Church of England)
Beggs, Mrs. Sarah, general merchant
Bell, James, carpenter
Callan, John & Thomas, lime and stone
Clement, W. D., M.D.
Corving, William, farmer
Davis, James, farmer
Davidson, William, shoemaker
Edwards, Mrs. Mary, milliner, &c.
Ego, Jacob, shingle maker
Ego & Town, lime and stone
Emerson, Andrew, farmer
Hart, Thomas, farmer
Hislop, Mrs. Ann, milliner, &c.
Hislop, John, hotel keeper
Hotson, Alexander, teacher
Hudson, George, cooper
Isbister, James, carpenter
Keough, Rev. T. T. (Wesleyan)
King, Ellis, painter
Lock, William, wagon maker
McCraig, Rev. T. (Presbyterian)
McKay, Alexander R., carpenter
McKay, James, teacher
McLean, Calvin, farmer
Malcolm, Francis, J.P.
Hogg, T., hotel keeper
Mills, Thomas, farmer
Mitchel, T. T., farmer
Moore, John, flouring mill proprietor
Murray, Robert, M. D
Nichol, James, painter
PERRY, D. K., Postmaster, general merchant
Perry, Julius, cooper
Robson, John, tailor
Ross, John, farmer
Sawnby, John, carpenter
Sclater, James, carpenter
Scollen, John, teacher
Skillings, James, shoemaker
Taylor, John, M. D
Thomson, Andrew, steam flouring mill and lumber dealer
Town, Edward, carpenter
Tree, Stratton, teacher
Tunnell, H. C., teacher
Vincent, Charles, J. P

Innisfil.—A post office in the Township of Innisfil, County Simcoe.
ROSS, BENJAMIN, Postmaster

Innisville.—A post office in the Township of Drummond, County Lanark, South Riding.
CODE, THOMAS, Postmaster.

Inverary.—A Village in the Township of Storrington, County Frontenac; 12 miles from Kingston the County Town. Average price of land in the vicinity, $25 per acre. Stage to Kingston. Population 100.

Bayley, John, butcher
Bond, Allan, farmer
Bond, William, farmer
Campbell, Henry A., farmer
Campbell, James, farmer
Clayton, John, farmer
Clayton, William, teacher
Conklin, Thomas, farmer
Day, Lewis E., hotel keeper
Duff, David, shoemaker
Duff, William, farmer
Edward, John, shoemaker
Hughson, Elizabeth, milliner, &c.
Kniffer, Thomas, wagon maker
Lattimer, William, farmer
Martin, Rev. E. (Methodist Episcopal)
O'Loughlin, Rev. A. (Church of England)
Osborne, Robert, hotel keeper
Purdy, Marshall, saddler
Scott, William, tailor
Spring, John, J.P.
Tupell, Isaac, carpenter
Tupell, William, M.D.
WALKER, D. J., J.P., Postmaster and gen. mer.

Inverhuron.—A Village on the river Sauble, in the Township of Bruce, County Huron, 28 miles from Walkerton, the County Town, and 44 miles from Goderich. Improved land in the neighborhood averages $30, wild $10 per acre. Money order office. Population 120.

Alexander, James, farmer
Chapman, S. P., farmer
Funk, Mrs. S. A., milliner, &c.
Gray, Alexander, lime and stone
Gray, William, flouring and saw mills
Green, B., shoemaker
McDonald, John, leather dealer
McLaw, Angus, farmer
McLellan, Alexander, hotel keeper
McLellan, D., shingle maker
McRae, H., hotel keeper
McRae, John, farmer
McRAE, PETER, J.P., Postmaster and gen. mer.
Matheson, Hugh, cabinet maker
Nettle, William, shoemaker
Oliver, V., cooper
Sample, William, farmer
Scott, David, carpenter
Scott, Michael, carpenter
Scott, J., proprietor saw mill and farmer
Sinclair, Miss Isabella, teacher
Thorrington, John, farmer
Urquhart, John, farmer
Watson, James, cooper
Woolf, Wellington, farmer

Invermay.—A Village on the Sauble River, in the Township of Arran, County Bruce, 24 miles from Walkerton, the County Town, and 125 from Toronto. Stages to Southampton, Owen Sound and Kilsyth. Average value of wild land in the vicinity $12; improved $25 per acre. Money Order office. Population 275.

Andrew, John, J.P.
Bogsley, J., shoemaker
Brown, John, carpenter
Bunton, W. A., farmer
Cooper, Rev. R. S. (Church of England)
Cummer, H. E., flouring mills
Cunningham, John, butcher
Dick, David, J.P.
Dick, Peter, wagon maker
Dunn, J. W., saddler
Dyer, Frank, carpenter
Francis, W. S., M.D.
Freeborn, A., J.P., leather dealer
Gardner, L., farmer
Gardner, S. N., farmer
Graham, James, hotel keeper
Hall, John, shoemaker
Henderson, Isaac, shoemaker
Hoar, W. H., farmer
Irwin, Rev. William (Wesleyan)
James, William, teacher
Keough, Thomas M., farmer
Keys, R., carpenter
Kilborn, James, leather dealer
Kilborn, J. M., insurance agent
Kilborn & Stirk, general merchants
Linton, J. W., farmer
McCartney, Rev. James, (Wesleyan)
Martin, John, farmer
Mitchel, John, cooper
Miller & Brown, cabinet makers
Miller, G. S., carpenter
NEELANDS, A., Postmaster, general merchant and general agent
Neelands, Samuel, auctioneer
Nickelson, Thomas, J.P.
Riddell, William hotel keeper
Sanderson, R., tinsmith
Stirke, George, farmer
Taylor, James, M.D.
Williams, B. H., tinsmith
Willson, Horace, druggist
Weisner, John, leather dealer

Iona.—(*See Villages too late for regular insertion at the end of this Work.*)

Ireland. (McGillivray P. O.)—A Village in the Townships of McGillivray and Biddulph, County Middlesex, 20 miles from London, and 3 from Lucan Station, Grand Trunk Railway. Money order office. Population 250.

Barber, Mrs., milliner
Bice & White, wagon makers
Butler, P., shoemaker
Flanagan, J., grocer and Clerk Division Court
Hicks, John, saddler
Hodgins, James, blacksmith
Howard, William, carpenter
Johnston, Henry, general merchant
Jones, F., cabinet maker
Jordon, J., plasterer
McFadden, Samuel, tailor
Mann, A., wagon maker
Murphy, Matthew, proprietor flour mill
Saunders, Rev. T. E., (Church of England)
SHOFF, D., Postmaster, Commissioner in B. R., notary public
Sutton, D., J.P., farmer
Sutton, James, M.D.

Iroquois.—An incorporated Village and Station of the Grand Trunk Railway, on the St. Lawrence River, 36 miles from Cornwall, the County Town, and 234 from Toronto. Stages to Dixon's Corners, South Mountain and Inkerman. Money Order Office and Savings' Bank. Population 800.

Abbott, Daniel. general merchant
Ault, Guy, farmer
Bailey, Doran & Cameron, general merchants and flouring mill
Baldwin, Joseph, farmer
Beaver, Rev. E. W. (Church of England)
Bell, Robert, clothing dealer
Binions, William, farmer
Blackburn, James, telegraph operator
Boyd, S. J., jewelry, watches, clocks, &c.
Brault, Oliver, sash, door and blind manufacturer
Brouse, C. C., telegraph operator
Brouse, Guy C., farmer
Brouse, G. W., farmer
Brouse, Jacob, farmer
Brouse, John G., hotel keeper
Brouse, N. N.. shoemaker
Brown, James, butcher
Carman, Daniel, shingle maker
Carman, John A. & Co., general merchant
Carman, P., J.P., farmer
Carman, Philip, leather dealer
Carman, Peter, lime and stone
Carman, Rufus, attorney-at-law
Carson, John, cabinet maker
Carstairs, Robert, grocer
Cooms, Mathew, J. P., farmer
Davy, N. M., general merchant
Dillabough, Reuben, hotel keeper
Elliot, Andrew, flax mills
Feader, Lucas, farmer
Graves & Shea, shoemakers
GRIER, JAMES, J.P., Postmaster, grocer
Grier, William, telegraph operator
Haines, Benjamin, wagon maker
Halliwell, Rev. John (Methodist Episcopal)
Heartly, William, carpenter
Lilly, Chancey, carpenter
Lowery, Robert, general merchant
McClain, S. C., teacher
McNulty, John, shoemaker
Mason, Mills & Co., general merchants
Mills, Mason, insurance agent
Milligan, Robert, hotel keeper
Morten, Rev. William, (Wesleyan)
Murray, John, clothing dealer
Patton, A., general merchant
Patton, John, cooper
Patton, William, cooper
Perken, Miss, milliner, &c
Ross, J. H. & Co., general merchants
Ross, John S., J. P
Sandon, Samuel, tinsmith
Scott, John, dyer and scourer
Servis, G. G., general merchant
Shaver, William J., saddler
Stephens, George & Co., flax mills
Stephenson, James, M. D
Thurman, Ezra, butcher
Thurman, N. G., wagon maker
Tooley, Martin, butcher
Tuttle, John N., general merchant
Whitecomb, C. H., grocer
Whitney, William A., teacher
Whyte, Paul, agent G. T. R. and Canada Ex. Co
Wylie, John, general merchant
Wylie, William, baker

Islay.—A small Village in the Township of Fenelon, County Victoria, 16 miles from Lindsay, the County Town. Population 30.

SPENCE, DONALD, Postmaster.

Ivy.—A small village in the Township of Essa, County Simcoe, 10 miles from Barrie, the County Town. Population 80.

Banting, Thomas, farmer
Blackstock, John, teacher
Burton, R. & John, wagon makers
Campbell, Rev. J., (Wesleyan)
DAVIS, GEORGE, Postmaster, J.P.
Drury, Thomas, general merchant
Fletcher, John, carpenter
Gibson, George, tailor
Lennox, James, farmer
Lennox, John, farmer
Ritchie, Charles, general merchant

Islington.—A Village on the River Mimico, in the Township of Etobicoke, County York, 9 miles from Toronto, the County Town, 3 from Mimico Station Great Western Railway and 4 from Carlton Station Grand Trunk Railway. Stages to Toronto and Cookstown. Population 250.

Anderson, Jacob, farmer
Bigham, Samuel, farmer
Cooper, Rev. H. C., (Church of England)
Dempster, Hugh, pot ashery
Dempster, Thomas, butcher
Dunn, John, farmer
Ferrier, John C., baker
Gemmel, Robert L., veterinary surgeon
Hoy, William, shoemaker
Ide, Willis A., blacksmith
Johnston, Benjamin, farmer
Kynoch, John, general merchant
Lord, Henry, butcher
McBride, N., farmer
McBride, Patrick, drover
McFarlane, Alexander, J. P., farmer
McFarlane, Donald, J. P., farmer
McKeown, Mrs., general merchant
Mathers, Adam, farmer
Mathers, James, mason
Mercer, S. A., J. P., farmer
Montgomery, William J., farmer
Moore, George, farmer
Moore, James, farmer
Moore, John, farmer
Musson, Edward, J. P., farmer
MUSSON, THOMAS, Postmaster
Newlove, John, farmer
Pellett, F., farmer
Shaver, Charles, farmer
Shaver, George, farmer
Shaver, Peter, farmer
Siddall, Henry, wagon maker and manufacturer agricultural implements
Smith, Thomas, farmer
Stallard, Edward, butcher
Streight & Ide, builders
Thompson, Alexander, farmer
Thompson, F. A., farmer
Twig, William, shoemaker
Ward, John, farmer
White, Francis, barber
Wilson, Robert, proprietor Islington Hotel
Wilson, William, farmer
Wood, Samuel, farmer

Ivanhoe.—A Post Office in the Township of Huntingdon, County Hastings, 20 miles from Belleville, the County Town, and 80 from Toronto. Stages daily to Madoc and Belleville. Average price of improved land $30 per acre.

Archibald, James, farmer
Bodle, Rev. J., (Bible Christian)
EMO, THOMAS, Postmaster, J.P., gen. merchant
Ford, Rev. J., (Wesleyan)
Frederick, Henry, cooper
Fuller, Benjamin R., general merchant
Fuller, Charles, teacher
Gardner, Samuel, teacher
Garver, Jeremiah, grocer
Geary, Catherine, milliner
eary, John, carpenter and painter
Goldie, Rev., —, (Presbyterian)
Howard, Jones, shingle maker
King, James, shoemaker
Lawson, Rev. Thomas, (Wesleyan)
Lidster, John J., wagon maker
Lummon, Samuel, carpenter
Newton, Richard, farmer
Ranson, Samuel, tailor
Rutledge, James, general merchant
Sargent, William, shingle maker
Shaw, John, shoemaker
Vaughan, William, cabinet maker
Wood, John, J.P., farmer

Janetville.—A small Village in the Township of Manvers, County Durham, 45 miles from Cobourg, the County Town, and 66 from Toronto. Improved land averages $30 per acre. Population 50.

Armstrong, Robert, farmer
Burn, John, prop. saw mill
How, Thomas, farmer
Irwin, William, farmer
Lyon, Thomas, J.P.
McDERMID, JOHN, Postmaster
McDermid, John, prop. saw mill and farmer
McDermid, John and Neal, props. flouring and grist mills
McDermid, N., farmer
McGuire, Adam & Sons, manufs. of woolen goods
McIntyre, N., M.D.
Magill, David, general merchant
Magill, Robert, farmer
Magill, William, farmer
Scott, James, teacher
Stinson, William, farmer
Syer, Thomas, farmer
Taylor, John, farmer
TIMMINS, THOMAS, Deputy Postmaster
Timmins, R. & T., general merchants and proprietors of Temperance House

---

Jasper.—A Village and station of the Brockville and Ottawa Railway, in the Township of Wolford, County Grenville, 21 miles from Brockville, the County Town, 11 miles from Merrickville, 4 from Newbliss and 140 from Toronto. Population 100.

Chalmers, M., teacher
Coleman, Rev. M., (Wesleyan)
Cross, G. W. clothing
Cross, Aaron, farmer
Edmunds, G. & W., clothing
Carr, Michael, J.P., farmer
McAdams, James, agent British and American Exchange Companies
Lummax, William H., shingle maker
Olmstead, Ambrose, farmer
Olmstead, D., farmer
Olmstead, Gideon, farmer
Ralph, Joseph
Ralph, William L., clothing dealer
Robinson, A., tailor and hotel keeper
Ware, Rev. Mr. (Wesleyan)

Jarrett's Corners.—A Post Office in the Township of Oro, County Simcoe, 21 miles from Barrie, the County Town.

JARRETT, CHARLES, Postmaster and gen. mer.
Leatherdale, Luke, wagon maker
McCarroll, James, carpenter
McNab, Findley, cooper
Sheirs, Christopher, carpenter

arvis.—A Village in the Township of Walpole, County Haldimand, 15 miles from Cayuga, the County Town, 30 from Hamilton, and 80 from Toronto. Average price of land in the vicinity $30 per acre. Stages to Hamilton. Money order office. Population 200.

Abraham, William, saddler
Armour & Heartwell, general merchants
Buer, Rev. W. (Wesleyan)
Burbridge, James, cabinet maker
Boyd, David, hotel keeper
Canfield, Rial, J.P., general merchant
Elmer, James, wagon maker
Francis, Rev. J., (Chruch of England)
Heasman, John, J.P
Howell, W. A., M.D
Hull, Mrs., milliner, &c
Hull, Samuel, saddler
Jones, David, cabinet maker
Jones, Mrs., milliner, &c
Kenning, John, teacher
Langreil, John A., M.D
McDowell, Miss, milliner, &c
McRobie, Rev. John, (Presbyterian)
Montgomery, Thomas, hotel keeper
Noble, Nelson, wagon maker
Peterson, Mrs., milliner,
Robinson, William, carpenter
bodgers, Edward, brick maker
Rodgers, John, shoemaker
Rooney, Alexander, hotel keeper
Sill, J. & B., general merchants
Sill, J. R., shoemaker
Whitaker, Robert, shoemaker

Johnson's Mills (Lakeview Village).—A Post Office in the Township of Hay, County Huron, 24 miles from Goderich, the County Town, and 20 from Seaforth Station, Grand Trunk Railway.

Baurbet, Rev. (Roman Catholic)
Begans, Francis, farmer
Berthram, Charles, carpenter
Rossenberg, William, hotel keeper
Broderick, William, farmer
Campbell, John, farmer
Collville, John, teacher
Green, Henry, cabinet maker
Grunner, John, farmer
Hartman, John, farmer
HEYNOCK, HENRY, Postmaster and proprietor saw mill
Heynock, Oswald, blacksmith
House, James, fish dealer
Jacoby, John, stone mason
Krug, Amadeus, carpenter
Launsberry, James, cooper
Maul, Andrew, carpenter
Melick, John, sen., farmer
Meyers, Joseph, farmer
Moss, Peter, farmer
Shade, John, carpenter
Spencer, David, general merchant and wine and spirit dealer
Turnbull, William, nursery and seedman
Van Valdenburg, Henry, cooper
Wilson, Andrew, tinsmith

Jordan.—A Village and Station of the Great Western Railway, on Twenty-mile Creek, in the Township of Louth, County Lincoln, 7 miles from St. Catherines, the County Town, and 68 from Toronto. Population 200.

Bradsford, J., leather dealer
Caskey, Robert H., carpenter
Doughty, Isaac, carpenter and butcher
Eckhardt, George A., saddler
Fegan, R. A., shoemaker
Foley, Thomas, teacher
Goss, S. D., general merchant
Gross, John, pump maker
Haynes, John, farmer
High, A., farmer
High, Rev. D. (Menonite)
High, J., farmer
Honsberger, Samuel, farmer
Johnson, Jacob, farmer
Krapp, John, cabinet maker
Lansey, Michael, blacksmith
Laws, John, general merchant
Matlock, J., leather dealer
Miller, C., tailor
Motter, M., grocer and tailor
Moyer Joseph, painter
Oliphant, Rev. D., (Church of the Disciples)
Petty, John H., wagon maker
Pitcher, C. P., M. D
Simpson, Andrew, shoemaker
Smith, D. G., general merchant
Snure, C., general agent for Bradt's standard bee hive and leather dealer
SNURE, JACOB, Postmaster
Spence, D., hotel keeper
Walrath, Jacob, M. D
White, J., hotel keeper
Wilkinson, Rev. Mr., (New Connexion Methodist)
Wismer, John, farmer
Zimmerman, Mrs., D., milliner, &c
Zimmerman, Peter, farmer
Zimmerman, P., blacksmith

Jerseyville.—A Village in the Township of Ancaster, County Wentworth, 14 miles from Hamilton, the County Town. Population 50.

Bloce, E., cooper
Howell, Levi, general merchant
Howell, M. H. & Co., lumber dealers
Keys, —, M.D.
Lurty, John, wagon maker
McCay, Hugh, teacher.
Miller, George, carpenter
Waugh, John & Co., painters
YOUNG, H. F., Postmaster and general merchant

Johnson.—A Post Office and small settlement in the Township of Sydenham, County Grey, North Riding
JOHNSTONE, WILLIAM, Postmaster.

Jura.—A small Village in the Township of Bosanquet, County Lambton; 26 miles from Sarnia the County Town, 6 from Forest and 7 from Widder Stations Grand Trunk Railroad. Wild lands in the vicinity averages $14; improved $35 per acre

Boyd, Robert, farmer
Brown, Philip, farmer
Campbell, Hugh, farmer
Campbell, Peter, farmer
Calt, Henry, farmer
Hayworth, Rev. A., (Primitive Methodist
Lewis, T. J., teacher
McCardie, Nathaniel, farmer
McCARDIE, JAMES, Postmaster, J. P., and farmer
Middleton, Rev. E., (Primitive Methodist)
Phillips, Thomas, farmer
Thomas, Greenwood, farmer
Thomas, John, farmer

Kaladar.—A Post Office in the Township of Kaladar, County Addington.
DUNHAM, E. F., Postmaster.

Kars.—A Village in the Township of North Gower, County Carleton, on the Rideau River, 21 miles from Ottawa, the County Town, and 280 from Toronto. Population 200.

Boyce, Ira, carpenter
Boyce, John, cooper
Brown, David P., carpenter
Brown, Mrs. D. P., milliner
Bush, J. W., sewing machine agent
Callender, Alexander, wagon maker
Eastman, A. J., prop. steam saw mill, brewery and malt house
Eastman, Almond, carpenter
Eastman, McKenzie, tailor and clothing dealer
Eastman, R. J., J.P. and dentist
Kerr, Alexander, shoemaker
Kerr, John, teacher
Knapp, Joseph, carpenter
Latimer, James, carpenter
Lindsay, James, sen., farmer
Lochead, Rev. William, (Presbyterian)
McCullum, James, farmer
Martin, Cyrus, wagon maker
Martin, Stephen, carpenter
Merritt, Rev. D. P., (Church of England)
Morrell, Oliver, carpenter
O'Callaghen, John, farmer
O'Conner, Daniel, farmer
Rose, John, butcher
Sutherland, John, wagon maker
Taggert, Rev. Charles, (Methodist)
Wallace, Robert, farmer
WOOD, W. D., Postmaster
Wood, W. D. & Co., general merchant

Keene.—A Village in the Township of Otonabee, County Peterboro', on Keene River, 12 miles from Peterboro' the County Town and 9 from Harwood. Stages to Peterboro' and Harwood. Money Order Office and Savings Bank.

Andrews, Rev. F., (Presbyterian)
Armstrong, David, shoemaker
Burnham, Henry H., miller
Campbell, McNeill & Co., general merchants
Campbell, Alexanker, general merchant
Dean, M. P., M.D
EVANS, GEORGE, Postmaster, general merchant
Forsyth, Andrew, carpenter
Gale, John, hotel keeper
Gunn & Poe, steamboat owners
Helson, George, farmer
Lang, George, carpenter
Laing, Alexander, blacksmith
Londerville, Peter, cooper
McCrea, Amos, M.D
McLachlan, John, hotel keeper
Nelson, George, carpenter
Partliff, John, blacksmith
Read, George, M.P.P.
Renwick, Walter, bailiff
Short, Thomas, miller
Sinclair, James, saddler
Wilson, Rev. S., (Wesleyan)

Katesville.—A Village on the River Sydenham, in the Township of Metcalf, County Middlesex, 8 miles from London, the County Town. Tri-weekly mails. Population 100.

Bentley, Robert, J.P., farmer
Branbin, R. W., J.P., farmer
Callum, James, farmer
Clark, William L., wagon maker
Dodd, George
Elliott, James, merchant
Ellis, I., carpenter
Fenerty, Patrick, tailor
Fury, B., innkeeper
Gripton, Henry, farmer
Kent, David, J.P., farmer
Kent, Sidney, lumber merchant
Knight, Barnabas, farmer
McCLATCHEY, WILLIAM, Postmaster, druggist
Mann, John, farmer
Pike, Thomas, lumber merchant
Sessions, A., blacksmith
Webster, Willliam, innkeeper

Kelvin (see Burford).—A Post Office in the Township of Burford, County Brant.
ARMOUR, J., Postmaster.

Kemptville.—An incorporated Village on the south branch of the river Rideau, and a station of the St. Lawrence and Ottawa Railway, in the Township of Oxford, County Grenville. Distant from Brockville, the County Town, 40 miles, from Ottawa 27, and from Prescott 23 miles. Stages to Oxford Mills, Burritt's Rapids and Merrickville. Money Order Office and Savings' Bank. Population 1000.

Adams, Thomas, proprietor Adams' Hotel
Agnew, Henry, wagon maker
Anderson, W. R., merchant tailor
Barnes, William J., wagon maker
Beckett, Thomas, brewer
Bedingfield, R. H., saddle and harness maker
Bissell, W. H., marble cutter
Blackburn, A., general merchant
Bower, (Porter & Bower), general merchant
Boyd, David, boots and shoes
Burness, S., hide and leather dealer
Byce, Mrs., dressmaker
Christie, John, merchant tailor
Clancy, John, telegraph operator
Clothier, A., general merchant
Clothier, A. & Son, iron founders
Cochran, William H., saddle and harness maker
Courtney, Miss, dressmaker
Craig, Thomas, dealer in hides and leather
Curry, J. H., general merchant
Dunn, William, tailor
Ebertson, G. W., dentist
Fannin, L., teacher
Fannin, William, tailor
Fenton, Erastus, brick manufacturer
Ferguson, C. F., M.D.
Gibson, James, butcher
Gilmor, Miss, dressmaker
Grant, Lewis, miller
Hagan, James, tinsmith
Harding, John, miller
Harty, Rev. W. (Roman Catholic)
Hemenway, A., teacher
Hemenway, H., carpenter
Hunter, Anthony, boots and shoes
Hurd, Mrs, dressmaker
Hurd, M., baker
Johnston, Mrs., dressmaker
Johnston, Arthur, boots and shoes
Joly, J. W., teacher
Jones, Edward, carpenter
Keating, G., general merchant
Keenan, M., painter
Kennedy, A. & J., blacksmiths
Kernahan, R., J.P.
Kerr, R., proprietor Farmer's Hotel
Laing, William, agent Canadian Express Co.
Lamping, L., iron founder
Landon, James P., carpenter
Lattimer, E. A., teacher
LESLIE, ROBERT, Postmaster
Longley, M., baker
McGregor, C., baker
McGregor, Rev. M. (Baptist)
McGregor, W., proprietor Kemptville Hotel
McKeon, H., wine and spirit merchant
Magee, John, tailor,
Magee, William J., butcher
Maley, Thomas, boots and shoes
Maley, Bro. & Co., general merchants
Malton, John, butcher
Martin, S.
Mills, Isaac A., general merchant
Morton, Henry, druggist,
O'Connor, John, tailor
O'Connor, M., cooper
Parkinson, Robert, dyer
Perry, Joseph, miller
Prosser, M., cooper
Rath, John, carpenter
Robinson, William, wagon maker
Rowans, Joshua, carpenter
Sanders, John, tinsmith
Sanderson, George, carpenter
Sanderson, William
Scott, W. J., attorney-at-law
Sellick, John, proprietor Sellick House
Sparham, E. B., M. D
Spencer, Rev. J., (Church of England)
Spottswood, William, blacksmith
Stannage, Rev. J., (Church of England)
Steet, John, blacksmith
Story, William, boots and shoes
Sypes, E., watchmaker
Taylor, George, blacksmith
Tewsan, M. M., steamboat agent
Thom, James, wagon maker
Waddle, Rev. R. (Methodist)
Walmsley, William, cooper
Wetherell, R. H., bookseller and stationer
Wolfe, John, cabinet maker

Keenansville.—A Village in the Township of Adjala, County Simcoe, 33 miles from Barrie, the County Town, and 40 from Toronto. Stages to Bradford Station, Northern Railway. Population 120.

Brown, Brothers, props. woolen mills
Burk, A. W., auctioneer and carpenter
Burton, James, farmer
Casserly, M., farmer
Colgan, John, cooper
Creenan, E., bricklayer
Curran, B., shoemaker
Curran, F., tailor
Deblare, Thomas, carpenter
Doyle, M., milliner, &c
Durass, V., farmer
Eagan, Kieran, farmer
Fehely, Elizabeth, milliner, &c
Hart, James C., teacher
Holland, D., farmer
Holland, J., farmer
HUGHES, GEORGE P., Postmaster, J.P., general merchant, and prop. South Simcoe *Observer*
Hughes, P., farmer
Keenan, R., J.P
Keogh, P., farmer
King, P., farmer
Lowe, T., carpenter
Medley, W., farmer
Morrow, F., farmer
O'Connor, Rev. R. A., (Roman Catholic)
Skelly, James, farmer
Skelly, T., auctioneer
Sigsworth, James, J.P
Tomlinson, E., hotel keeper and prop. livery stable
Towns, E., general merchant

Kendal.—A Village in the Township of Clarke, County Durham, 60 miles from Toronto. Population, 150.

ANDERSON, J. R., Postmaster, general agent
Armour, Samuel, teacher
Boyd, James, cooper
Boyd, William, cooper
Carscadden, J., proprietor Queen's Arms Hotel
Carscadden, John, farmer
Chestnut, John, carpenter
Cooper, John, carpenter
Dickey & Comstock, proprietors flouring mills
Dickey, T., shingle maker
Finlay, John, farmer
Halliday, James, farmer
Henderson, Thomas, proprietor Kendall House
Hodge, R., J.P., farmer
Irwin, Henry, farmer
Jackson, W., lumber dealer and carpenter
Jennings, Hugh, farmer
Loper, Frank, shingle maker
Lyness, John, teacher
McLean, James, wagon maker and painter
McLean, James, farmer
Muldrew, W. & Co., general merchant
Olin, Benjamin, shingle maker
Patterson, Thomas, farmer
Patterson, William, farmer
Scott, Hugh, farmer
Scott, William, farmer
Smith & Trew, general merchant
Stanton, Thomas, shoemaker
Thompson, William, farmer
Underwood, Thomas, farmer
Watson, Miss Bella, milliner
Willcock, S. G., shingle maker
Wilson, R. J. J., (New Connexion Methodist)

Kenilworth.—A Village in the Township of Arthur, County Wellington, 32 miles from Guelph, the County Town. Improved land averages $52, wild, $12 per acre. Population 50.

Batho, Joseph, farmer
Batho, James, accountant
Brown, David, farmer
Bunston, Thomas, general merchant
Caughlan, William, general merchant
Christie, Matthew, shingle maker
Coates, Eli, farmer
Dogherty, Thomas, general merchant
Dogherty, Thomas, M.D.
Dunbar, R. H., teacher
Edwards, William, brick maker
Elliott, George, farmer
Elliott, Rev. —., (New Connexion Methodist)
Galloway, William, carpenter
Gordon, Robert, J.P., farmer
Hains, Edward, farmer
Hartly, R. & Son, lumber dealers
Harvey, W., teacher
HAYWARD, ROBERT, Postmaster, general merchant and express agent
Irwin, Charles, general merchant
Kennedy, Patrick, tailor
Langdale, Charles, farmer
McGuire, Robert, shingle maker
McLeod, Alexander, farmer
Neagle, R., saloon keeper
O'Brien, Miss, teacher
Stack, James, carpenter
Stephenson, R., wagon maker
Stephenson, Thomas, J.P.
Thomas, Hiram, hotel keeper
Turner, Walter, carpenter

Kent Bridge.—A Village in the Township of Chatham, County Kent, 10 miles from Chatham, the County Town, and 5½ from Thamesville Station, Great Western Railway. Population 45.

Arnold, Frederick, farmer
Baikie, J. R., hotel keeper
Courtney, Elijah, cabinet maker
Crowe, David, farmer
Eglin, Richard, hotel keeper
Killam, Jacob, merchant
Kohell, Henry, shoemaker
Lachance, John, blacksmith
Lyons, Thomas
SHAW, J. B., Postmaster, merchant
White, John, farmer

Kenmore.—A Village in the Township of Osgoode, County Russell, 25 miles from Ottawa. Stages to Gloucester and Russell. Population 200.

Bowen, George, carpenter
BRANNEN, J. B., Postmaster, general merchant and druggist
Brannen, P. B., accountant
Brannen, T., saddler
Gillespey, Patrick, shoemaker
Jackson, G., engraver
Kearn, James, farmer
Kearn, W. F., farmer
KinCade, Robert, farmer
McArthur, Donald, manuf. farming implements
McDiarmid, John, lumber, dealer and prop. flouring mills
McDougall, John, farmer
McGill, F., shoemaker
McGregor, D., general merchant
McIntyre, James, farmer
Pillar, F., teacher
Rushford, John, shingle maker
Stenhouse, James, farmer
Stewart, Archibald, nurseryman
Tobin, J., prop. Victoria Hotel
Tobin, Joseph A., general merchant
Wishart, D., painter and carpenter
Wishart, John, waggon maker

Kerrwood.—A Village and Station of the Sarnia branch of the Grand Trunk Railway, in the Township of Adelaide, County Middlesex, 26 miles from London, the County Town, and 6 from Napier. Population 150.

Allan, R., shoemaker
Allan, James, grocer
Bully, John, farmer
Edwards, Thomas, butcher
Foster, Charles, J.P., farmer
Foster, George, farmer
Foster, Samuel, proprietor Dominion Hotel
Galbraith, Robert, farmer
Harris, Isaac, lumber dealer and cabinet maker
Irving, J. & J., proprietors steam flouring mill
IRVING, JAMES, Postmaster and general merchant
Morgan, John, J.P., farmer
Richardson, Benjamin. proprietor machine shop
Tyler, John, farmer
Whitney, John, wagon maker
Williams, John, farmer
Williams, Roger, farmer

Kerry.—A Post Office in the Township of Caledonia, County Prescott.
BRODIE, WILLIAM, Postmaster.

Kertch.—A small Village in the Township of Plympton, County Lambton, 18 miles from Sarnia, the County Town, and 163 from Toronto. Population 75.

Anderson, Duncan, farmer
Bryson, James, farmer
Dewar, Alexander, farmer
Dewar, John, farmer
DONNELLY, WILLIAM, Postmaster
Doyle, J., cabinet maker
Hart, J., farmer
Johnstone, Charles, carpenter
Jones, E. A., farmer
Manily, Arthur, farmer
Molton, William, shoemaker
Rogers, Jacob, farmer and hotel keeper
Tendell, James, teacher
Williamson, James, wagon maker

Keswick (Village Medina).—A Post Office in the Township of North Gwillimbury, County York, 60 miles from Toronto, the County Town, and 3 from Belhaven. Stages to Newmarket and Beaverton. Steamers to Bell Ewart. Population 70.

Anderson, James, lumber dealer
Bayley, J., J.P., farmer
Bradford, Robert, proprietor Medina Hotel
Draper, Henry, J.P., farmer
Jewel, Lewis, shingle maker
Jordan, Robert, carpenter
Knight, John, lumber dealer
Major, H. F., proprietor Bell Haven Hotel
Mann, Caleb, farmer
MOORE, HIRAM, proprietor saw mill and Sportsman's Home Hotel
Moore, Peter, carpenter
Moore, William, carpenter
Morton, Friend, farmer
Morton, John, farmer
Morton, S., farmer
Purdy, J. P., farmer
Ritchie, Rev. Mr.
Sprague, Daniel, stock dealer
STENNETT, HENRY, Postmaster
Stennett, R. M., general merchant and builder
Tomlinson, G., farmer
Willoughby, John, stock dealer
Willoughby, J., carpenter
Young, M., shingle maker
Young, William R., carpenter

Kettleby.—A Village in the Township of King, County York, 32 miles from Toronto, the County Town, 7 from Lloydtown, and 7 from Aurora Station, Northern Railway. Improved land averages $45 per acre. Stages to Lloydtown and Aurora. Population 100.

Bogart, Elias, farmer
Bogart, Peter, farmer
Edwards, Peter, farmer
Floyd, Charles, farmer
Floyd, David, teacher
Green, John, dealer in lime and stone
Hay, Rev. William (Methodist)
Hayner, Rev. Mr. (Christian Church)
Heacock, Seth, farmer
Hilborn, Peter, pump manufacturer
Hughes, Aaron, carpenter
Judd, Reuben, sash, door and blind manufacturer
Robertson, Robert, shoemaker
Shrigley, Jesse, farmer
Smith, John W., wagon maker
Smith, Malcolm, teacher
Smith, Oliver J., carpenter
Sparling, Rev. Mr. (Methodist)
Stokes, Joseph, J.P., prop. flouring and grist mills
Stokes, William, farmer
Temow, Simon, farmer
Timdy, S. H., teacher
Van Allen, James, proprietor planing mills
WALTON, JACOB, Postmaster and gen. merchant
Walton, Mrs. Mary, milliner, &c.
Wardell, Paul, hotel keeper
Webb, Albert, farmer
Webb, Mrs. Mary, proprietor planing mills

Keyser.—A Post Office in the Township of Adelaide, County Middlesex, 30 miles from London, the County Town.

Batram, William, farmer
Brock, David, J.P.
COOPER, S., Postmaster
Duggan, Samuel, farmer
Evans, James, farmer
Glover, James, farmer
Harrington, Truman, farmer
Keyser, John, brickmaker
Langan, James, farmer
Murray, Patrick, farmer
Ogden, John, harness maker
Smith, J. S., farmer
Stewart, James, farmer
Whiting, Henry, farmer

Kilbride.—A Village in the Township of Nelson, County Halton, 7 miles from Milton, the County Town, 9 from Wellington Square and 40 from Toronto. Stages to Hamilton and Milton. Population 250.

Baker, Francis, J.P., farmer
Beattie, W., M.D
Calderwood, William, saddler
Caldwell, William, lumber merchant
Duffis, John, plasterer
Haynes, Rev. T., (Wesleyan)
Hunter, Thomas, saddler
Liddell, David, turner
Matthews, John, shoemaker
Mills, F. W., hotel keeper
Montgomery, W. P., prop. woolen factory
Sinclair, R., tailor
Simpson, Rev. W. H., (Presbyterian)
Stewart, Charles, carpenter
Thompson, W. B., tailor
White, John, shoemaker
WHITE, T. L., Postmaster, general merchant
Worthington, A., wagon maker

Killarney.—(Or Shebawanahning.)—Is beautifully situated on the main shore of Lake Huron, 25 miles from Wekwemikong, District Algoma. The Village is hemmed in by mountains on all sides. It has a convenient steamboat landing and a good Catholic church. The population, numbering about 100, chiefly Indians and half-breeds, live chiefly by fishing and hunting. Agriculture is neglected except as regards the usual vegetables for domestic use.

THEBO, SOLOMON, Postmaster.

Killean.—A Village on Mill Creek, in the Township of Puslinch, County Wellington, 9 miles from Guelph the County Town. Population 150.

Blue, William, wagon maker
Bowsey, Alexander, farmer
Campbell, James, carpenter
Copp, William, farmer
Currie, Niell, tailor
Currie, John, cabinet maker
Ellis, Thomas, J.P
FERGUSON, DONALD, Postmaster, gen. mercht
Kenedy, John, carpenter
McIntyre, Alexander, teacher
McIntyre, John, hotel keeper
McIntyre, William, telegraph operator
McKelan, A., farmer
McLellan, Mrs., milliner, &c
McLeod, Rev. Andrew, (Church of Scotland)
McLorty, D., farmer
McLorty, John, shingle maker
McMaster, John, farmer
Thompson, John, farmer

J. W. SMYTH,

Marble Works,

ESTABLISHED 1854.

Dundas Street, opp. Strong's Hotel, London, O.

Head Stones, Monuments, &c. Satisfaction guaranteed or customers need not accept. Free Stone for Building Purposes.

BENJAMIN BRYAN,

Dealer in Stoves, Tinware, Coal Oil, &c.,

House-Furnishing Goods of every description—Cheap for Cash.

MANCHESTER, ONTARIO.

J. J. JOHNSTON & CO.,

Builders and Contractors,

SASH, DOOR & BLIND FACTORY,

Meaford, -- Ontario.

British American House

JOHN W. STUBBS, Proprietor.

MEAFORD, ONTARIO.

This house is situated in the business part of the Village, and near the steamboat landing, and affords excellent accommodation for travelers.

STUBBS' line of Stages twice daily, during winter, to Collingwood and Owen Sound.

Commercial Hotel.

WILLIAM McDONALD, PROPRIETOR.

MEAFORD, ONT.

Good accommodation for travelers. Good stabling. Terms moderate.

A. MILNE & SON,

Dealers in Hardware, Dry Goods, Groceries, Crockery, Ready Made Clothing, Boots, Shoes, &c.,

Meaford, Ontario.

MEAFORD HOTEL.

JOHN PAUL, PROPRIETOR.

Meaford, Ont.

First-class Sample Rooms for Commercial Travelers. Horses for Hire.

H. EASTMAN,

Merrickville, Ont.

Manufacturer of

Flour, Oatmeal, Cornmeal

AND

SHINGLES.

☞ Freighting done from Kingston to Ottawa City.

C. R. SING,

Notary Public, Land Agent

ISSUER OF MARRIAGE LICENSES &c.,

Meaford, Ontario

L. B. WARNICA,

Jeweler & Engraver

Dealer in Watches, Clocks, Jewelery, Fancy Goods Musical Instruments, &c.,

MEAFORD, ONTARIO.

Repairing of all kinds neatly, cheaply and promptly executed.

THOMAS H. STOREY,

Confectioner, and dealer in

Foreign and Domestic Fruits, Taxidermist, &c., Painter, Glazier and Paper Hanger,

All done in first-class style.

Kells Street, Millbrook, Ont.

Kilmanagh.—A Post Village in the Township of Chinguacousy, County Peel. Distant from Brampton, the County Town, 13 miles and from Toronto 34 miles. Population 46.

Benson, Richard, builder
Ceaser, James, cattle dealer
Hackett, James, boots and shoes
Kerr, Robert, tailor
LOWES, ISAAC, Postmaster
Marshall, A., builder sash doors and blinds
Parker, Abraham, shingle and stave maker
Sanderson, Thomas, general merchant
Willey, Robert, blacksmith.

Kilmarnock.—A Village in the Township of Wolford, County Grenville, 34 miles from Brockville, the County Town, on the Rideau Canal. Population 60.

Brannock, Mrs., teacher
Edmonds, Silas, farmer
Ferguson, Joseph, farmer
Fields, Nelson, blacksmith
Graham, Miss, teacher
Haskins, N., farmer
McCarthy, John, farmer
NEWSOME, GEORGE, Postmaster
Tullman, Charles, farmer

Kilmartin.—A Post Village in the Township of Metcalfe, County Middlesex, 35 miles from London, and 4½ from Glenco Station, Great Western Railway.

McCallum, Dougald, carpenter
McKELLAR, DOUGALD, Postmaster and farmer
Purcell, Archibald, blacksmith
Stewart, Rev. Archibald (Presbyterian)
Stewart, Donald, hotel propr. and general merchant

Kilsyth.—A Village in the Township of Derby, County Grey, 7 miles from Owen Sound, the County Town. Population 50.

Anderson, James, carpenter
Armstrong, John, hotel keeper
Beaton, William, general merchant
Black, Hugh, farmer
Bolgour, G. C., tailor
Coulter, Robert, carpenter
Finch, Abraham, tailor
Fleming, William, general merchant
Flenny, John, farmer
Flenny, William, insurance agent
Follies, Edwin, carpenter
Hilts, L., farmer
Lin, Robert, farmer
Moore, Henry, teacher
Morrison, Rev. Duncan (Church of Scotland)
SLOAN, THOMAS, Postmaster, general merchant
Todd, James R., farmer.
Walmsley, William, potter
Wiggins, John, farmer
Young, James, carpenter

Kimberley.—A Post Office in the Township of Euphrasia, County Grey, North Riding.

PURDY, WILLIAM, Postmaster.

Kinburn.—A Post Office in the Township of Fitzroy, County Carleton, 28 miles distant from Ottawa, the County Town. Mails daily.

FRASER, ALLEN, Postmaster.

Kinburn (Constance Post Office.)—A small Village in the Township of Hullett, County Huron, 20 miles from Goderich. Improved lands in the vicinity average $40 per acre. Population 80.

Coates, William, carpenter
Dodds, James, lime burner
Gibson, John & Edward, cabinet makers
Hays, John, wagon maker
Johnson, James, farmer
Lawson, Alexander, weaver
Scott, R., shoemaker
Snell, J., farmer
Stanley, Thomas, shoemaker
Stephenson, Raphael, farmer
THOMPSON, R., Postmaster
Thompson & Stanley, general merchants
Tramer, Thomas, teacher
Tyerman, Aaron, carpenter
Williams, John, wagon maker
Willison, Walter, teacher
Yeo, C., hotel
Young, John, M.D.

Kincardine.—An incorporated Village on the river Penetangore, in the Township of Kincardine, County Bruce, 27 miles from Walkerton, the County Town, 28 from Goderich Station Buffalo and Lake Huron Railroad, 28 from Southampton, and 154 from Toronto. Extensive salt beds are found in the vicinity. Lumber and produce form the chief trade. Money Order Office and Savings' Bank. Population 3,000.

Allen, Robert, butcher
Andrew, Albert, bookseller and stationer
Baird, Robert, J.P., lumber dealer
Barker, C. R., notary public, auctioneer, insurance agent and dealer in wines and liquors
Barker, Joseph, accountant
Barton, John, cabinet maker
Black, Hugh, bookbinder
Bluet, proprietor billiard room
Brick, B., general merchant
Bricker, Moses, hotel keeper
Brown & Bone, manufacturer of woolen goods
Brown, William P., attorney-at-law
Browning, William, wagon maker
Burn, A., brewer
Cameron, Duncan, general merchant
Campbell, Alexander, commission merchant
Campbell, Rev. Archibald
Campbell, John, general agent and accountant
CARTER, BENJAMIN, hotel keeper and proprietor billiard room
Chandle, —, architect
Chesley, A. A., attorney-at-law
Christie, John, dentist
Cook, Joseph, general agent
Cook, —, hotel keeper
Coombe, Benjamin, baker
Coulter, John, teacher
Denning, James, dealer in boots and shoes
Design, George, saddler
Donald, James, dealer in boots and shoes
Driscol, J. W, dealer in hardware, cutlery, &c
Elliott, Robert, baker
Ellums, James, sash, door and blind manufacturer
Ellums, William & Son, carpenters
Evans, A. L., carpenter
Ewan, Charles, sash, door and blind manufacturer
Ferguson, Rev. Mr., (Presbyterian)
Fergusson, Roderick, carpenter
Fisher, Ira & E., props. foundry and machine shop
Fraser, Rev. John, (Canada Presbyterian)
Gordon, William, carpenter
Graham, Angus, dealer in boots and shoes
Graham & Humphries, props. foundry & machine shop
Hamilton, Miss, teacher
Hamlin, L. E., architect
Henderson, Robert, carpenter
Hodginson, Rev. —, (Church of England)
Huntley, H. F., jewelry, watches and clocks
Hurdon & Bros., general merchants
Hurdon, F., M. P.
Hurston, William & John, druggists
Inglis, Rev. Walter, (Canada Presbyterian)
Isard, Albert, butcher
Johnston, Miss, teacher
Johnston, Mrs, milliner
Kay, William, cooper
Keays, James, proprietor brick yard
Keays, Joseph & Son, lime and stone dealers
Keival, Mrs., milliner
Keival, William, painter
Kelly, Rev. —, (Roman Catholic)
Kendrich, Matthew M., insurance agent
Kibbon, William, dealer in boots and shoes
Kitchen, John, cooper
Lang, Joseph, dealer in books, stationery, fancy goods and toys
Lardy, William, tailor
Large, Rev. —, (Episcopal Methodist)
Leadbeater, —, hotel keeper
Legears, James, J.P.
McAuley, John, dealer in boots and shoes
McClure, & Crozier, saddlers
McCosh, John, patent right agent
McInnis, P. D., general merchant
McInnis, P. & N., general merchants
McIntosh, Richard, telegraph operator
McKenzie, Donald, wagon maker
McKenzie, Duncan, cabinet maker
McKerracher & Evans, proprietors planing mills
McKerracher, James, carpenter
McLardy, William, clothing dealer
McLaren, Duncan, hotel keeper
McLean, Alexander, painter
McLean, Archibald, general merchant
McLean, M. & A., proprietors brick yard
McLean, Neil John, carpenter and painter
McLean, Samuel, painter
McLennan, Roderick, carpenter
McLeod, Donald, cooper
McLeod, —, butcher
McPherson, James A., attorney-at-law
McPherson, Malcolm, J.P.
McPherson, M. & John, prop. flouring and grist mill
McPherson, William, hide and leather dealer
Malcolm, Robert, groceries, crockery, glassware, &c.
Mann, A., dry goods
Martyn, De Witt, M.D.
Matheson, A., accountant
Macklem, William, proprietor steam flouring mill
Miller, John, butcher
Morrison, John, teacher Grammar School
Morrison, Robert, tailor
Patterson & Brother, wagon makers
Paterson, Charles, cooper
Peterbaugh, John, patent right agent
Pubelow, George, carpenter
Rastall, William, J.P., notary public and general agt
Reed, David, dealer in boots and shoes
Rice, Rev. L. C., (Wesleyan)
Robertson, Donald, general merchant
Robertson, Peter, general merchant
Robertson, Ross, general agent and com. mercht
Rookledge, Mrs., fancy goods, toys, &c
Rookledge, W. & G., cabinet makers
Ross, E., cabinet maker
Ross, H. M., M. D., druggist
Ross, Jackson, architect
Ruettel, John, tailor
Rutherford, R., general merchant and prop brick yard
Secord, Solomon, M. D
Sellery, John, hide and leather dealer
Scott, William & J., proprietors marble works
Small, James, tailor
Smith, Mrs., hotel keeper
Speers, Robert, butcher
Stewart, —, butcher
Sturgeon, George, J. P., tinsmith
Taylor, John, carpenter
Thomson, Robert, auctioneer
Vanstone, James & Bro., proprietors planing mills
Watson, John, cabinet maker
Williamson, Mrs., milliner
Wilson, Robert, general merchant
Wilkins, William, clothing dealer
Withers, William, J.P.
Young, Robert, lime and stone dealer

Kingston.—The Chief Town of County Frontenac, is situated at the head of the River St. Lawrence, where Lake Ontario, the last link of the chain of the inland seas of Western Canada, together with the Bay of Quinté and the Great Cataraqui Creek, is united with the channel which conveys and empties their waters into the Gulf of St. Lawrence. It is one of the oldest settled localities in Ontario, and occupies the site of the French Fort of Frontenac; was founded in 1784, and incorporated in 1838. Opposite the City are Wolfe Island and Garden Island; and between them and Kingston, a distance of three miles, lies the Bay, a beautiful sheet of water, forming a safe and commodious harbor of every draught. Additional and improved wharves have lately been constructed; which, together with those previously in use, render it in every respect well calculated for an extensive shipping trade. Kingston, at no distant day, promises to be an important manufacturing City. Already the trade of ship building has arrived at great proficiency. Sailing vessels and steamboats of every capacity are here built and fitted out with every requisite, ready for Lake or Ocean navigation. The Marine Railway Company has at different times built and fitted out vessels which have been loaded and sent direct from Kingston to England; and the largest steamboats that now navigate Lake Ontario and the River have been built and furnished with everything necessary at the same establishment. There are two ship building yards in Portsmouth, a flourishing Village within a mile of the limits of the City. The timber necessary for the construction of vessels—oak, pine, cedar, elm, for knees, masts, &c.—is brought from the neighboring Townships; and the iron work, including every description of machinery for steamboats, &c., is furnished by the different foundries in the City. The sail and cordage lofts are kept well supplied; and in short, all the means and appliances for the complete outfit of every sized vessel are always ready at hand. The Grand Trunk Railway passes within two miles of the City; connecting with the City by a branch. As a place of defence, Kingston stands next in strength to Quebec. The batteries of Fort Henry are calculated for the reception of numerous cannon and mortars of the largest calibre. These, together with neighboring martello towers, form a formidable and efficient defence against any aggressive movement which might be directed against the City or neighboring country. The City possesses two Colleges, Queen's and Regiopolis. It has several magnificent public buildings; amongst which may be enumerated the City Buildings, New Court House, &c. There are branch establishments of the Banks of British North America, Montreal Merchants and Royal Canadian. It is in lat. 44° 8' N., lon. 78° 40' W. from Greenwich. Distant from Montreal 198 miles, and from Toronto 165 miles. Population 15,000.

Abraham, James, care taker Mechanics Institute, Princess
Adair, Alexander, grocer, Barrie
Adams, William, boot and shoe maker, Brock
Agnew, James, barrister, Bagot
Allen, William, tinsmith, Wellington
Allen, Miss A. E., hoop skirt manufacturer, Brock
Allen, S., furrier, Wellington
Allen, William, boot and shoemaker, Brock
ALMA MATER SOCIETY, QUEEN'S COLLEGE, Professor McLean, M. D., L.R.C.S.E., President; W. H. Fuller, B.A., Secretary
American Express Company, G. T. Oliver, agent, cor King and Brock
AMERICAN HOTEL, W. Woollard, prop., Princess
Anderson, D., baker and confectioner, Ontario
ANDERSON, GEORGE, (I. Swift & Co.) agent Marine British America Insurance Co., of Toronto, St. Lawrence Wharf
Anderson, Mrs., grocer, Barrie
Andrews, George W., merchant tailor, Wellington
Anglin, Mrs. C., dry goods and millinery, Wellington
Anglin, R. & Co., lumber merchants and saw mill proprietors, cor Wellington and Bay
ANGLO AMERICAN HOTEL, E. Milsep, proprietor cor Ontario and Johnson (see adv)
Atlantic Wharf, foot Princess
Austin, James, innkeeper, cor Queen and Wellington
Bailey, B. & Co., broom makers, Princess
BAILIE, BROS., (Isaac and Henry) book and job printers, Wellington
Bajus, Jacob, brewer, Wellington
Bamford, Alexander, agent G. T. R., Ontario
BANK OF BRITISH NORTH AMERICA, James Riddell, manager, Ontario
BANK OF MONTREAL, R. M. Moore, manager; J. P. C. Phillips, accountant; J. J. Christie, ledger keeper; E. A. Colquhoun, teller; W. D. Antrobus, J. O. Mowat, clerks, cor King and William
BARKER, DR. E. J., City coroner, editor and prop *British Whig*
Barker, Robert W., clerk P. O. Inspector
Barrow, R. W.
BAWDEN, JOSEPH, solicitor, attorney, notary, etc. King. (See adv)
Beaufort, Edward, refreshment saloon railway station
Beaupre, R., proprietor Farmers' Hotel, 4 Brock
BEAVER MUTUAL FIRE AND LIVE STOCK ASSOCIATION, of Toronto, R. I. Jordan, agt., 162 Princess
BECKER, CHRISTIAN, (Rappe, Weber & Co.)
Begg, William & Co., (W. Begg and P. R. Henderson), groceries and liquors, Brock
Bell, Robert, police sergeant
Bennett, James, policeman
Benson, P. M., teacher Provincial Penitentiary
Bertrim, John, shoemaker, Brock
Blondheim, S. H., saloon, Brock
Bousfield, Rev. T., (Church of England), in charge of Diocesan Depository
Bowen, Mrs. G. H., hotel keeper, King
Bower, Rev. E. C., (Church of England), Barriefield
Bowes, Timothy, boots and shoes, Brock
Boyle, Rev. John P., (Roman Catholic)
Braden, John, stock dealer
Brame, Henry, cabinet maker, Princess
Brand, G., cabinet maker, King
Brannigan, Dennis, harness maker, 151 Princess
Breene, Maurice, grocery, Queen

Briggs, Thomas, agent Liverpool and London and Globe Fire and Life, Briton Med. and Gen. Life Ass. of London, Assurance Companies, Ontario
BRITISH AMERICAN HOTEL, Capt. H. E. Swales, proprietor, cor King and Clarence
BRITISH WHIG, (daily and weekly) Dr. Edward J. Barker, editor and proprietor, Bagot
BRITTON & PRICE, (B. M. Britton & C. V. Price), barristers, King
Brock, Rev. Thomas, (Wesleyan), William
Brown, George, hardware, Princess
Browne, James & Co., groceries and liquors, Market Square
Bunt, Richard, blacksmith
Brunett, Archibald, shoemaker, Brock
BURNETT HOUSE, R. R. Stephens, proprietor, Ontario (see adv)
Burns, Robert J., P. O. clerk
Butler, Mrs. Mary, grocer, Princess
Butner, L., Steward Kingston General Hospital
CALVIN & BRECK, (D. D. Calvin and I. A. Breck) ship builders, lumber merchants, forwarders, &c., Garden Island, Ontario
CAMPBELL, MOWAT & McDONNELL, (Hon. Alexander Campbell, Q.C., George L. Mowat and G. M. Macdonnell) barristers, &c.
Campbell, James, grocer, Ontario
Campbell, Matthew, grocer & liquor dealer, Princess
Campbell, Patrick, grocer, King
CANADIAN CHURCHMAN, (Wednesday) J. H. Parnell, publisher, Rev. T. A. Parnell editor, Clarence
CANADIAN ENGINE AND MACHINERY Co., James Tandy, superintendent, Charles Gibson, secretary and treasurer, Ontario.
Canadian Express Company, G. T. Oliver, agent, cor King and Brock
CANADIAN NAVIGATION CO., Hon. John Hamilton, manager, C. F. Gildersleeve, vice-President, St. Lawrence Wharf
Cannon, William, tailor, Princess
CAPE VINCENT FERRY WHARF, foot Brock
CARRUTHERS, JOHN & CO., merchants, props. Kingston Marine Railway, Ontario
CARSON, ROBERT, grocer, flour and feed, 133 Princess
Cartmill, Nathaniel, grocery, Bay
Cartwright, R. J., M.P.
CASWELL, J. D., carriage maker, Princess (see adv)
Chaffey, George & Brother, forwarders, dealers in wood, coal, iron ore, insurance agents, Atlantic wharf
Chanonhouse, Robert, Chief of Police and High Bailiff
Chown, Arthur, general hardware, dealer in stoves, &c., Bagot
CHOWN, EDWIN, (Chown & Cunningham)
Chown, Robert, fruit store, Princess
Chown, S. & Sons, hardware, Princess
CHOWN & CUNNINGHAM, Victoria Stove Works cor King and Queen

Christian Association, Princess
CHRONICLE AND NEWS, (daily and weekly) James Neish, M.D., editor and prop. Princess
Cicolari, Alexander, saloon keeper and confectioner, Market Square
CITY HOTEL, R. A. Irwin, prop., Princess (see adv)
City of Kingston Gas Co., J. A. Henderson, pres., Samuel Muckleston, vice-pres., John Kerr, manager, Queen

Clark, J. C., cor Union and Centre
CLEMENTS, L., L.D.S., Wellington (see adv)
Cline, F. C., Exchange broker, Ontario
Cockburn, John, tin and copper smith, King
Conelly, Michael, professor of English Elements, Regiopolis Roman Catholic College, Brock
Connor, Michael, groceries and liquors, Market Sq.
Conroy, P., grocer, Princess
Conway, Thomas, tailor, King
Cooke, H., tailor, Queen
Corrigan, Patrick, butcher, Wellington
Costello, William, grocer, Wellington
Couper, Mrs. C., grocer, Barrie
Cousineau, Francis (R. Waddell & Co.)
Coverdale, William, architect, King
Craig, A. W., baker and confectioner, Market Square
Craig, Major John, clerk County Council, office Court House
Crawford, Alexander H., agent G.T.R.
Creighton, George W., brewery, King w
CREIGHTON, JOHN, police magistrate, city book store, job printer, King
Cridiford, J., ornamental hair manufacturer and fancy goods, King
Crombie, Alexander, M., Merchants' Bank of Canada Earl
Cronin, M., innkeeper, Ontario
Crown Land and Emigrant Agency, James McPherson, agent, William
Cullen, Garrett, grocer, Bay
Cummings, George A., city registrar
Cunningham, David, mason and builder
Cunningham, David, policeman
CUNNINGHAM, HENRY, J.P., (Chown & Cunningham).
Cunningham, John, mason and builder
Cunningham, John, agent sewing machines, King
Cunningham, William, manufacturer iron-clad piano fortes, Princess cor Ontario
CUSTOM HOUSE, W. B. Simpson, collector, cor King and Clarence
Dacey, M., shoemaker, Ontario
Daly, Patrick, merchant tailor, Princess
David, J. J. E., second-hand broker, Princess
David, W. M., second-hand broker, Princess
Davidson, Andrew, builder, Queen
Davidson & Doran, proprietors Kingston Foundry, Ontario
Davis, James, shoemaker, Barrack
Davis, James, dry goods, Princess
Davis, Rev. Thomas (Roman Catholic)
Davis, Thomas, dry goods, Princess
DAY, W. B., M.D., L.D.S., President Dental Board, Examiner for Ontario, Princess
DEACON, ROBERT, Postmaster
Detlor, G. H., appraiser customs
Devana, John, grocer, Princess
DICKSON, JOHN R., M.D., M.R.C.P., &c., surgeon Provincial Penitentiary, Johnson
Dillon, Joseph, boot and shoe manufacturer, Princess
Dinnis, James, flour and feed, Princess
Dockrill, John, grocer, King
Dolan, Martin, harness maker, Princess
Donnelly, Felix, grocer, Ontario
Doolan, Timothy, Commercial Hotel, Princess
Doran, Mrs. B. & Co., dry goods and millinery Princess
Douglass, Henry, hotel, Princess
Doyle, J., millinery, Princess
DRENNAN, S. T., cabinet maker, Princess
DRIVER, THOMAS, boots and shoes, Princess
Driver, William, tailor, Wellington

DRUMMOND, T., accountant, Rockwood Asylum College
DUFF, JOHN, Clerk Division Court, office Court House
Dufours, Lucas, A. M. A., professor of English literature and history, Regiopolis Roman Catholic College, Brock
Dumble, Henry, confectioner, Brock
Dunbar, John, merchant tailor, Princess
Dunlop, James M., grocer, cor Ontario and Princess
Dunn, John, hotel, cor Barrick and Wellington
Dunn, Thomas, grocer, Bay
Dunoon, John, merchant tailor and clothier, Brock
Dupuis, Nathan F., M.A., prof. Chemistry, Queen's University
Dupuy, H., agent Canada Life Assurance Company, Ontario
Durand, James, Registrar, office Court House
East, John, innkeeper, King w
Elliott, Isaiah, saloon
Elmer, J. D., baker, Princess
Ennis, James, grocery, Wellington
FAHEY, MICHAEL, merchant tailor and clothier, Market Square
Falconer, James, sail maker
Farmer, Peter, hotel-keeper, Brock
Farrelly, Very Rev. James, V.G., Bishop's Palace
Fee, S. H., M.D., Princess
Fenwick, G. W., Chequered Hotel, corner Ontario and Gore
FENWICK, T. M., M.D., corner King and Queen
FENWICK, HENDRY & CO. wholesale grocers, Ontario
Ferguson, Mrs., fancy goods, Wellington
Ferguson, William, sheriff County Frontenac, office Court House
Ferns, Mrs. Christiana, Berlin wool, fancy goods, and millinery, Princess
Fields, Arthur, barber, Ontario
Filtz, George, cabinet maker, Princess
Flanagan, J., deputy warden Provincial Penitentiary
Flanagan, M., City Clerk
Foley, Mrs. Ann, grocery, Wellington
Folger, Brothers, ship owners, exchange brokers, Ontario
Foot, Henry, baker, Princess
Ford, William, jun., Cataraqui Tannery, leather dealer, Market Square
Fowler, A. D., clerk customs
Fowler, Fife, M.D., corner Clergy and Brock
Fraser, David, innkeeper, Market Square
Fraser & George, hardware, Princess
FROILAND, J. D., goldsmith, Princess
Frontenac Lead Mining Company, James Romanes, provisional secretary and treasurer, Brock
Frontenac Loan and Investment Society, Thomas Briggs, Manager; Thos. Kirkpatrick, President; J. A. Henderson, M.D., Vice-President, Ontario
Gage, Matthew, watchmaker, King
Galloway, James, proprietor Belfast House, Ontario
Gardiner, R. & J., dry goods, Princess
Garrigan, James, boot and shoemaker, Princess
Gauthier, Rev. Charles H., Director and Professor Theology Regiopolis R. C. College
Gee, Robert, proprietor Montreal House, Ontario
GERALDI, L., proprietor Geraldi House
GERALDI HOUSE, L. Geraldi, prop., cor Princess and Montreal (see adv)
GIBSON, CHARLES, sec. and treas. Canadian Engine and Machinery Co., Bagot
Gibson, David, grocer, Princess
Gilbert, Mrs. Jane, hotel keeper Barrie
GILDERSLEEVE, C. F., proprietor steamers *Bay of Quinte* and *Norseman*, agent Standard Life Assurance Co., Clarence
GILDERSLEEVE & WALKEM, (J. P. Gildersleeve and Richard T. Walkem), barristers, etc., Clarence (see adv)
GLASSFORD, JAMES A., (Glassford, Jones & Co.) res. Montreal
GLASSFORD, JONES & CO., forwarding and commission merchants, Ontario
Goodearle, H., picture frame maker, Wellington
Gowdey, James, butcher, Princess
Grady, Michael, butcher, Princess
Graves, Reuben, harness maker, Princess
Gray, Rev. P., (Canada Presbyterian)
Green, J., tailor, King
Greenfield, James, dry goods and clothing, Princess
Greenwood, Andrew, provisions, Princess
Griffin, Mrs., hotel keeper, Brock cor Ontario
Grigor, Charles, fancy goods, Princess
Grimason, Mrs. E., hotel keeper and grocer, Princess
Grimm, Henry, butcher
Groh, William, hatter and furrier, Princess
GUNN, ALEXANDER, (J. Carruthers & Co.)
Gurney & Glidden, (A. N. Gurney and J. N. Glidden), forwarders and commission merchants, Atlantic wharf
Hackett, Johnston, shoemaker, Barrie
Halliday, J., hospital overseer Provincial Penitentiary
HALLIGAN, JOHN, groceries and liquors, Anchor Buildings
HAMILTON, HON. JOHN, senator, Maitland
HANCE, MAJOR S. B., United States Consul, cor King and Union
Harper, Samuel, book-keeper J. Carruthers & Co.
Harty, J. & Co., grocers, Ontario
Harty, P. & Co., dry goods, Market Square
Hatch, Charles H., ticket agent, St. Lawrence wharf
Hay, William, merchant tailor, Brock
Hayward & Downing, (William & James), brewers, King w
Heath & Gunn (J. & W. A.), druggists, Princess
Henderson, Henry, photographer, Princess
HENDERSON, JAMES A., D.C.L., barrister, master in chancery, chancellor diocese of Ontario, Princess
HENDERSON, JOHN, bookseller, stationer and news agent, Princess
Henderson, W. P., Registrar Trust and Loan Co., Wellington
Henley, M., berlin wool and fancy goods, Wellington
Hewitt, Robert, grocer, Princess
Higgins, Rev. Bernard (Roman Catholic)
Hillier, S. C., M.D., house surgeon General Hospital res same
Hilton, Thomas, grocer, King w
HOBART, G. S., druggist, Princess
Hogan, James, innkeeper, Ontario
Holder, Benjamin, cabinet maker, Princess
Hope, James, boots and shoes, Princess
Hopeson, William, baker, Princess
Hopkirk, J., clerk customs
Horan, Right Rev. E. J., D.D., Bishop of Kingston
Horsey, Edward, architect
Horsey, R. M., hardware, Princess
Howard, Rev. J. J., Regiopolis College
Howland, Thomas, innkeeper, Brock, cor Division
Hoyle, William, policeman
Hume, Walter, shoemaker, Barrack
HUNTLEY, CHARLES, Cosmopolitan Saloon, Wellington (see adv.)
Hayman, Solomon, hatter and furrier, Princess

Illsey, Charles, policeman
Inglis, Rev. William M., (Presbyterian)
Innis, John C., city engineer
Ireland, O., accountant Trust and Loan Co., Johnson
Ireland Thomas, engraver, Princess
Ireland,, Willam, chamberlain
Irvine, John, treasurer County Frontenac, office Court House
IRVING, W. & SON, (William sen., William jun.), builders and manufacturers of house furnishing goods, cor Clergy and William (see adv)
IRWIN, R. A., City Hotel, Princess (see adv)
Irwin, William, grocery and saloon, Princess
James, Martin, grocery, Queen
JARVIS, COLONEL S. P., assistant adj. general militia, Ontario
Jeffers, L. W., prop. St. Lawrence House, Johnston
Jenkins, Edward, blacksmith, Princess
Jenkins, John, carriagemaker, Princess
Jennings, P. J., general merchant, ship chandlery, cor Ontario and Brock
Johnson, James, Deputy City Registrar
Johnson, J. B., barber, Wellington
Johnson, William, barber, Johnson
Johnston, James, watchmaker, Wellington
Johnston & King, (John H. Johnston, William King), dry goods, Princess
Jones, J. E., cigar dealer, Brock
Jones, John, blacksmith
JONES, J. J., BIRKETT, (Glassford Jones & Co.), residence Montreal
Jordon & Co., general sewing machine, agents, 162 Princess (see adv)
Jordon, Mrs. R. I., dress and mantle maker, 162 Princess (see adv)
Jordon, Miss B., milliner, Barrie
Kain, Francis, boot and shoemaker, Brock
Kane, Dennis, wagon maker, Wellington
KARCH, J. A., (J. A. Karch & Co.), coffee and spice mills, Earle (see adv)
KARCH, J. A. & CO., general merchants, 50 Princess (see adv)
Kavanagh, John, flour and feed, Market Square
Kearns, James, agent Montreal Telegraph Company
Kearns, P., innkeeper, Montreal
Keenan, D. F., foreman *Canadian Churchman*, cor Wellington and Earl
Kelly, John, post office clerk
Kelly, J., barber, Wellington
KEMP, GEORGE, (Kemp & Co).
KEMP & CO., carriage manufacturers, Sydenham (see adv).
Kennedy, R., M.D., Queen's University
Kennedy, Robert, fruit store, Barrie
KERR, JOHN, manager Gas Company, Queen
Kidd, J., landing waiter
Kieltz, Rev. William, Roman Catholic Regiopolis College
King, J. G., chemist and druggist, King
King, Patrick, grocery, Montreal
KINGHORN, G. M., forwarder, shipowner, general merchant, Brock
Kinghorn, John, book-keeper, Cape Vincent wharf
KINGSTON GENERAL HOSPITAL—Directors, Hon. R. S. Cartwright ; T. Kirkpatrick, J. Fraser, H. Sweetnam, H. Yates, M.D., S. C. Hillier, M.D., house surgeon
Kingston Water Works Company, James Wilson, superintendent, Ontario
Kinnear, Mrs. J., clothing, Wellington
Kirk, William, boot and shoe dealer, Princess
KIRKPATRICK, MICHAEL (Kemp & Co.)
KIRKPATRICK, ALEXANDER S., barrister, county attorney
KIRKPATRICK & KIRKPATRICK, (T. Kirkpatrick and G. A. Kirkpatrick), barristers, solicitors in chancery, Ontario
LACEY, W. P. & CO., dry goods, Princess
Laird, John, painter, Princess
Lane, T., policeman
Lanigan, A., caretaker city buildings
Lansing, E. C., barber, cor King and Clarence
Lark, Edward, mason and contractor
Laverty, Edward, clerk express
Lawler & McCaul, butchers, Princess
Laws, William T., messenger P. O.
Legassick, John, shoemaker, Princess
LEHEUP, J. A., watchmaker, Princess
Leonard, Rev. John Francis, Professor of Philosophy Regiopolis R. C. College, Brock
Levey, A. A., clothing, Wellington
Lewis, Rt. Rev. J. Travers, D.D., Bishop of Ontario, King w
Lightfoot, William, book and job printer, Wellington
Lindsay, John, shoemaker, Princess
Lindsay, Patrick, letter carrier
LINTON, J. J., auctioneer and commission mercht., cor King and Clarence (see adv)
Little, Francis, hotel keeper, Barrie
LIVINGSTON, ARCHIBALD, grocer, Princess
Livingston, Charles, merchant tailor
LONERGAN, JAMES, (Rappe, Weber & Co.)
Loynes, Mrs. Rebecca, grocer, Barrie
Lynch, D., prop. Crown and Anchor Inn, Johnston
Lynch, D., landing waiter
Lyster, Very Rev. James, Dean of Ontario and Rector of Kingston
McArdle, James, gunsmith, King
McArdle, Mrs., gentlemen's furnishing goods, Brock
McArthur, James, Auditor County Frontenac
McAuley, Thomas, bookbinder, King
McBride, James, flour dealer, Barrack
McCarthy, C., hotel keeper King w
McCauley, Hugh, police sergeant and detective
McColl, E., landing waiter
McComb, William, fancy goods, Princess
McCORKELL, A., boat builder, Ontario (see adv)
McCormick, A., agt. Kingston brewery and distillery
McCREA, T. W., carriage builder, head of Princess, (see adv)
McCummiskey, Mrs. Alice, inn keeper, Ontario
McCutcheon, J., ashery, Wellington
McDERMOTT, JOHN F., general blacksmith, King
McDermott, Thomas, cabinet maker, Ontario
McDonagh, John, professor versification and syntax, Regiopolis R. C. College
McDonald, Mrs. Anne, grocer, Wellington
McDonald, Peter, groceries and liquors, Market Square
McDONELL, A. B., dry goods, millinery, &c., King
McDowall, J. A., hatter, furrier, Brock
McEwen, D. & Son, boiler makers, Queen
McFarlane, William, foreman *British Whig*
McFaul, A. D., new and second-hand store, Princess
McGarvey, John, shoemaker, Wellington
McGowan, James, hotel, Brock
McGowan, Thomas, hotel, Princess corner Barrie
McGurn, Alexander, P. O. clerk
McIntosh, D., accountant, Provincial Penitentiary
McINTYRE, JOHN, barrister, Princess
McINTYRE, R., grocer, Princess (see adv.)
McKAY, JOHN, jun., hides, leather and findings, Princess (see adv.)
McKeever, Thomas, flour and produce, Market Square
McKillop, A., innkeeper, Johnston

McKELVEY & BIRCH (John McKelvey, Samuel Birch), stoves and tinware (see adv.)
McKinley, John, watchman City Station
McLaughlin, William, policeman
McMahon, G., builder
McMahon, John, carpenter and builder, Sydenham
McMAHON, SAMUEL, cutter, Brock
McMAHON, THOMAS, painter, &c., Barrie corner William (see adv.)
McManus, E., professor French and procurator, Regiopolis R. C. College, Brock
McMillan, John, grocer, Ontario
McMillan & Son (John & Charles), merchant tailors, Princess
McMurtry, William, checker, City R. R. Station, Princess
McNamara, Michael, second-hand dealer, Brock
McNeil, Mrs., groceries, &c., Ontario cor Johnson
McNEIL, NEIL, plumber, brass founder and copper smith, Brock (see adv.)
McNeill, John, grocer, Princess
McNinch, A., hotel, Princess
McPherson, Allen, Sydenham
McPherson, James, Crown Land and Emigrant agent William nr Ontario
McRae, T. W., carriage maker Princess
McRae, W. R. & Co., grocers, Princess
McROSSIE, WILLIAM & CO., lumber merchants, Ontario cor William
McWhirte, D. A., accountant, Queen
MACAROW & SULLIVAN, (Daniel Macarrow, William Sullivan) barristers, &c., Princess
MACDONALD, SIR JOHN A., K. C. B., Minister of Justice, Attorney General
MACDONALD, PATTON & MACHAR, (Sir John A. Macdonald, Q. C., Hon. John Patton, Q. C., Jahn M. Machar) barristers, &c., Clarence
Macdonald, J. G., manager Merchants Bank of Canada, King
McDonell, A. R., assistant clerk Prov. Penitentiary
MacDonell, D. Æ., Warden, Provincial Penitentiary
MacKay, Donald, merchant tailor
MacKenzie, Alexander, kitchen-keeper, Provincial Penitentiary
Mackey, John, shoemaker, King
McLean, Andrew, grocer, Ontario
MACLEAN, DONALD, M. D., Princess
MACNEE & WADDELL, (James Macnee, James Waddell, James Minnes) importers and dealers in dry goods, wholesale and retail, Princess
Macpherson, James, Crown Land Agent
MaGinnis, Owen, innkeeper, Ontario
Main, Adam, cabinet maker, Wellington
Makins, Robert, grocer, Ontario
Makins, Thomas, prop American Hotel, Ontario
Maloney, John, innkeeper and grocer, cor Queen and Wellington
Marks, Capt. John, Brock
MARRISON, WILLIAM J., (Kemp & Co.)
Martin, H., grocer, Princess
Martin, William, wholesale grocer, Princess
Massie, William, planing factory, Barrie
Matthews, John, clerk G. T. R.
MEADOWS, B., soap and candle manufacturer, grocer, &c., Princess
Meagher, Jeremiah, clerk Post Office Inspector
Meagher, T., landing waiter
Megeat, Patrick, police sergeant
Merchants Bank of Canada, J. G. Macdonald, manager; Joseph Rorke, accountant; A. M. Crombie, teller; N. A. Bailey, ledger keeper
MEVES OTTO, jeweler, Princess
Millane, Denis, policeman
Mills, John, grocer, Barrie
MILSEP, E., prop Anglo-American Hotel
Mingaye, W. R., surveyor of customs
Mink, George, saloon, Princess
MINNES, W. P., tax collector
Mitchell, W., mason and contractor
Moffatt, Rev. W. B. (Church of England)
Molland, James, innkeeper, King w
Montgomery, Robert, dyer, Princess
Montreal Telegraph Company, James Kearns, agent, cor Ontario and Johnston
MONTREAL TRANSPORTATION COMPANY, J. M. Kinghorn and George Chaffey, agents, Atlantic wharf
Moore, John, steward, Bagot
Moore, Mrs. M. J., milliner, Barrie
Moore, R. M., manager Bank of Montreal, King cor William
MOORE, THOMAS, merchant tailor and clothier, Brock
Moore & Skinner, (James Moore and John Skinner), dry goods, cor Wellington and Princess
Morgan, William F., grocer, Earl cor Bagot
Morley, James, grocer, Colborne
Morrison, M., flour and feed, Princess
Mostyn, Thomas, inspector weights and measures
MUCKLESTON, SAMUEL, importer of hardware, Princess
MUDIE, JOHN, barrister, Clarence
Mulkins, Rev. H., chaplain Provincial Penitentiary
Mulock, Rev. J. A. (Church of England), Queen
Murray, Rev. Edward H., Roman Catholic Chaplain to the Forces
Murray, James, innkeeper, Brock
Murray, Peter, saw filer, &c., Wellington
Murray, William, auctioneer and commission merchant, Anchor Buildings
Neish, James, M.D., editor and proprietor *Daily News* and *Chronicle and News* (weekly), Princess
NELLIGAN, B., fruits and confectionery, King
NELLIGAN & CO., carriage and wagon makers (see adv).
NELLIGAN M. D., carriage maker
Newlands, George, mason and contractor
Newman, John, saloon, Brock
Newman, Robert, grocer, Princess
NOEL, JOHN V., insurance agent, accountant, etc., Clarence (see adv)
O'BRIEN, M., supt. Anglo American Hotel
O'Connor, Mrs., boots and shoes, Brock
O'Donnell, Mrs. Ellen, grocer, Barrie
O'Donell, John, grocer, Bay
O'Donoghue, Mrs. Margaret, grocer, Princess
O'GORMAN, M., boat builder, Simcoe (See adv)
O'REILLY & DRAPER, (James O'Reilly, Q.C., and Frank C. Draper), barristers, etc., Anchor bldgs.
O'Reilly, Patrick, shoemaker, Colborne
O'Reilly, Peter, sen., Deputy Clerk Crown and Clerk County Court, office Court House
O'Sullivan, D., grocer, William cor Bagot
OBERNDORFF, SIMON, cigar manufacturer and watchmaker, Princess
Ockley, M., fruit dealer, Princess
Ockley, Vincent, grocer, Princess
Offord, George, Penitentiary boot and shoe store, Princess and Brock
Oldreive, S. W., sail maker, Ontario
Oliver, Alfred S., M.D., King
Oliver, J. K., M. D., Ontario
Oliver, G. T., agent Canadian and American Express Cos., cor Brock and King

Orme, Mark Antony, grocer, Princess
Orr, Johnston, grocer, Princess
Overend, Thomas, builder, Princess
Parkhill, James, grocer, Princess
Parker, E. H., chemist and druggist
PARNELL, J. H., publisher *Canadian Churchman*, Clarence
PARNELL, REV. T. A., (Church of England) clerk and sec. Synod of Ontario ;
PATON, JOHN, Commissioner Trust and Loan Co., Emily
Patterson Robert, marine inspector, Princess st wharf
PERCY, W. J., merchant tailor, Brock
Phenix Insurance Co., (marine) Geo. Chaffey & Bro., agents, Atlantic wharf
PHILLIPS, MAJOR W. P., District Quarter Master and Provincial store keeper, Ontario
PHIPPEN, JAMES & SON, (James and Samuel), soap and candle factory, Johnson (see adv)
Pillar, William, baker, Princess
PIPE, WILLIAM, druggist & confectioner, Princess
Pisati, George, sausage maker, cor Brock and Bagot
Porter, John, policeman
Power, John, architect, Queen
PRICE, ISAAC, barrister, 5 Anchor Buildings
Quigley, Joseph, innkeeper, nr G. T. R. Station
Quigley, Owen, porter city station
Quinn, Michael, grocer, Market Square
Ramage, John, watchmaker
Randall, Jared, distiller, King w
RAPPE, CHARLES, (Rappe, Weber & Co.)
RAPPE, WEBER & CO., piano forte manufactory, cor Princess and King (see adv)
Reed, L. G., soda water manufacturer and confectioner, Princess
Rees, F. S., grocer, 157 Princess
Rees, William, innkeeper, Ontario,
Reid, James, cabinet maker, 152 Princess
REGIOPOLIS, COLLEGE, Right Rev. E. J. Horan, president
Reilly, Daniel, barber
Renard, John, grocer, Barrie
Reyner, Joseph, manufacturer church and parlour organs, melodeons, &c., Princess
Richardson, James, grain dealer, Atlantic wharf
RIDDELL, JAMES, manager Bank of British North America
Rigney, W., grocer, Princess
RIGNEY & SLAVIN, (Daniel Rigney, Patrick Slavin), dry goods and clothing, cor Wellington and Brock
Robb, Alexander, prop. St. Lawrence Hotel, Market
Robb, James, hotel keeper, King
Robb, Sergeant Major John, police
ROBERTSON, GEORGE & SON, importers and wholesale grocers, coffee and spice, steam mills, Ontario
Robinson, Thomas, house, sign and ornamental painter, Clarence
Robinson, William, painter, Bagot
Rogers, Mrs. M., prop. Victoria House, Ontario
Rogers, Rev. R. V., (Church of England)
ROSE, EDWIN, boots and shoes, Princess (see adv)
ROSE, R. M., Official Assignee, music teacher, &c., 5 Anchor Buildings (see adv)
Ross, A., dry goods, Princess
Ross, Mrs. E., bakery, Queen
Rourke, J. D., ashery, Wellington
ROYAL CANADIAN BANK, agency, R. G. Fitzgerald, manager
ROYAL COLLEGE OF PHYSICIANS AND SURGEONS, (affiliated to University of Queen's College) James Dickson, M.D., M.R.C.P., Lon., president
Royal Fire and Life Ass. Co., M. W. Strange, agent, Clarence
Royce, John, inn keeper, Ontario
Runians, Norman, grocer, Princess
RUMRILL, GEORGE A., blacksmith, manuf. of patent iron ladders, lightning rods, etc., Wellington, (see adv)
Ryan, Joseph, auditor County Frontenac
Ryckman, Rev. J. B., M.A., (Wesleyan) Johnston
SAVAGE, THOMAS, painter, William, (see adv)
SAVAGE, WILLIAM H. G., painter, Brock (see adv)
Scott, Mrs. Eliza, inn keeper
Shanahan, John, saloon, Ontario
Shanahan, William, saloon, Ontario
Shannon, James, official assignee
Shannon, William, Post-office Clerk
Shaw, Lieut.-Col. David, Brigade Major, Ontario
SHAW, JOHN, notary public, coroner, agent Western, of Toronto, Canada Life and Star Life, of London, Eng., insurance companies, Wellington
Shaw, Samuel, baker, Barrie
Sheldon & Davis, (H. R. Sheldon and R. F. Davis) photographers, King
Sheridan, Bernard, grocer, Wellington
Shirl, John, stoves and tinware, King
SIMPSON, ISAAC, J.P., banker, notary public, agent London, (Eng.,) Assurance Corporation, (Fire and Life) sec. and treas. County Frontenac agricultural society, Clarence (see adv)
Simpson, W. B., collector of customs, Custom House
SKINNER, HENRY, M.D., chemist and druggist, 16 Princess (see adv)
Skinner, James, whitesmith, Princess
Slaven & Mackin, (James and Arthur) merchant tailors, Wellington
Sleith, Samuel, dry goods, Princess
Smeaton, J., tailor, Queen
Smith, Alexander, boot and shoemaker, Brock
Smith, Archibald, harbor master
Smith, James, Victoria Hotel, Brock
Smith, John, hotel keeper, Brock
Smith, Patrick, grocer, Ontario
Smith, W., watchmaker, King
SNOOK, TUNIS L., barrister, Princess cor King
Sommerville, F., grocer, Princess
Spangenberg, George, watchmaker, King
Spencer, Robert, second hand store, Princess
Spohn, John L., photographer, Wellington
Spottiswood, George, billiard room, Wellington
Spratt, Thomas, professor, Belles Lettres Regiopolis Roman Catholic College, Brock
St. George's Hall, Wellington
ST. LAWRENCE WHARF, foot Johnston
Stacey, Edward, books and stationery, King
Stacey, John, policeman
Stafford, Reuben, mes'ger, Merchants Bank of Canada
Stephens, Charles L., Post Office clerk
STEPHENS, R. R., proprietor Burnett House (see adv)
STEPHENS, R., clerk Burnett House
Stevenson, Adolphus, fruiterer, Princess
Stewart, Alexander, grocer, Montreal
Stewart, John, M. D.
Stewart, William, care taker Government Army Stores Department, Princess
STRANGE, MAXWELL, W., M. P. P., (Strange & Rogers) Clarence
STRANGE & ROGERS, (Maxwell W. Strange, R. Vashon Rogers) Clarence
Strange, O. S., M. D., King
Stratford, Henry, grocer & tavern keeper, 136 Princess
Stratton & Co., (I. J. Stratton, Joseph Danson, John Harkes) china, glassware, &c., Princess
SULLIVAN, MICHAEL, M. D., King

BURNETT HOUSE,

ONTARIO STREET, KINGSTON, Ont.,

R. R. STEPHEN'S, PROP.

(LATE OF THE "ISLAND POND HOUSE," ISLAND POND, VER.)

This House has been recently refitted and refurnished, and is now ready for the reception of guests.

CONVENIENT TO ALL THE STEAMBOAT LANDINGS.

Trusty PORTERS IN ATTENDANCE at Cars and Boats.

NEW DOMINION CARRIAGE FACTORY.

J. D. CASWELL,

Manufacturer of all kinds of

Plain & Fancy Carriages, Wagons, Sleighs.

PRINCESS STREET, KINGSTON, ONT.

Orders from any part of the Dominion promptly executed with neatness and dispatch.

N. B.—Constantly in receipt of the latest English and American styles of carriages.

S. PHIPPEN & SON,

CITY SOAP & CANDLE WORKS,

KINGSTON, ONT.,

(ESTABLISHED 1832.)

A LARGE ASSORTMENT OF SOAP AND CANDLES ALWAYS ON HAND.

Orders Promptly Attended to.

S. PHIPPEN. J. F. PHIPPEN.

G. A. RUMRILL,

MANUFACTURER OF PATENT IRON LADDERS

For eve y description of buildings, which in point of safety, neatness and durability cannot be surpassed by any ladders now in use. Also, manufacturer of the most Improved Lightning Rods. All orders by mail or otherwise, promptly attended to.

Wellington Street opposite National Hotel,

KINGSTON, ONT.

General Blacksmithing Done on the Premises

H. SKINNER,

WHOLESALE DRUGGIST

AND DEALER IN

Drugs, Oils, Coal Oil, Lamps, Dyes, Patent Medicines, &c., &c.,

COUNTRY MERCHANTS DEALT WITH ON LIBERAL TERMS.

13 PRINCESS STREET, KINGSTON, Ont.

Sullivan, T., bowling saloon, Wellington
Summerville, Alexander, grocer, 153 Princess
Sutherland, Alexander, boots and shoes, 23 Princess
SWALES, CAPTAIN H. E., prop. British American hotel, corner King and Clarence
Swanston, Adam, baker, Princess
SWEETNAM, MATTHEW, post office inspector
SWIFT, J. & CO., wharfingers, commission merchants, insurance agents, dealers in wood and coal, St. Lawrence Wharf
Swift, Rev. J. R. (Primitive Methodist)
TANDY, RECHAB, marble worker, builder, &c., Barrie (see adv.)
Thibodo, A., Collector Inland Revenue, Ontario
THIBODO, WILLIAM B., barrister, &c., Clarence
Thomson, A., merchant tailor and clothier
Thompson, George, wines and liquors, King
Thompson, Thomas, boot and shoemaker, Brock
THOMPSON, W. J., tailor and broker, Princess
Thornton, Samuel, Albion restaurant, King
Thurston, George, foreman ship builder
Tierney, Owen, grocer, Ontario
Tipson, A. P., tailor, Princess
Tomkins, Robert, grocer, Barrie
TORONTO MUTUAL FIRE INSURANCE CO., R. I. Jordan, agent, 162 Princess
Tossell, Richard, stone mason and contractor
Town, Richard, fruit, oysters and game, Ontario
Tracy, Francis, general blacksmith, King
TRUST AND LOAN CO. OF UPPER CANADA, head office, cor Princess and King, John Paton, commissioner; O. Ireland, accountant; W. P. Henderson, registrar
Tweddell, Mrs. Mary J., furrier, 32 Princess
UNITED STATES CONSULATE, Major S. B. Hance, consul, Ontario
UNIVERSITY OF QUEEN'S COLLEGE, Very Rev. William Snodgrass, D.D., principal
U. S. PLATE GLASS INSURANCE COMPANY (Philadelphia), R. I. Jordan, agent, 182 Princess
Varney, Richard, grocer, Place D'Armes
Voight, H. C., official assignee, Ontario
Waddell, R. & CO., dry goods, corner Princess and Wellington
Wafer, Francis M., M.D., Queen's College
WALKEM, RICHARD T. (Gildersleeve & Walkem), solicitor in chancery
Walker, Robert, harness maker, Princess
Wallis, J. D., photographer, King
Watkins, John
Watson, William, shoemaker, Wellington
WEBER, GEORGE (Rappe, Weber & Co.)
Welch, E. R., marble cutter, Princess
White, Edward, carriage maker, Princess
WESLEYAN LITERARY ASSOCIATION, Rev. E. B. Ryckman, president, W. Tandy, jun., secretary, Queen
White, Robert, druggist, Princess
White, R., dyer, Princess
White, S. P., tobacconist, 30 Princess
Whitehead, J. J., storekeeper, Provincial Penitentiary
Wilkinson, C., harness maker, 18 Princess
WILKINSON, GEORGE M., groceries and liquors, Wellington
Williamson & Welch contractors, Wellington
Wilmot, N., blacksmith, Princess
Wilson, Rev. Andrew (Free Church)
Wilson, George F., grocer, Colborne
Wilson, Rev. H. (Church of England)
Wilson, James, superintendent Kingston Water Works, Barrie
Wilson, John F., butcher, Ontario
Wilson, F., J.P., notary public, general agent, agent British American Assurance Co., Clarence
Wilton, Henry, harness maker, Princess
Windsor, Rev. S. B. (Church of England)
Woods, S., M.A., principal Grammar School
Woolard, Robert, boots and shoes, Brock
WOOLARD, W., prop. American Hotel, Princess
Woolley, James, agent Northern Transportation Co., Inman Line Steamers and Rome and Watertown Railroad, Ontario
Wray & Warde (Alexander Wray and F. J. Warde), auctioneers, general merchants, dealers in ready-made clothing, Brock and Market Square
Wright, Clark, hatter and furrier, Wellington
Yarker, James S., hardware, Princess
YATES, HORATIO, M.D., cor King & William
Yates, Octavius, M.D., William
Young, William, grain dealer, Ontario

KINGSTON CLASSIFIED BUSINESS DIRECTORY.

Agent (Crown Land).
Macpherson, James

Agents (Railway).
Bamford, Alexander, G. T. R.
Wooley, James, Rome, Watertown, &c., Ontario

Agents (Sewing Machines).
Cunningham, John, King
Jordan & Co., Princess

Architects.
Coverdale, William
Powers, John

Auctioneers, &c.
Linton, J. J., corner King and Clarence
Murray, William, Anchor buildings
Wray & Warde, Market Square

Bakers and Confectioners.
Anderson, D., Ontario
Craig, A. W., Market Square
Dumble, Henry, Brock
Elmer, J. D., Princess
Foote, Henry, Princess
Hopeson, William, Princess
Pillar, William, Princess
Ross, E., Queen
Shaw, Samuel, Barrie
Swanston, Adam, Princess

Banker (Private).
Simpson, Isaac, Clarence

Banks.
British North America, James Riddell, manager
Merchants' Bank of Canada, J. G. Macdonald, agent
Bank of Montreal, R. M. Moore, manager
Royal Canadian, R. G. Fitzgerald, manager

Barristers, Attorneys, Solicitors, &c.
Agnew, James, Bagot
Bawden, Joseph, King
Britton & Price, King
Campbell, Mowat & Macdonnell
Gildersleeve & Walkem, Clarence

Barristers, Attorneys, &c.—*(Continued)*

Henderson, James A., Master in Chancery Princess
Kirkpatrick & Kirkpatrick, Ontario
Kirkpatrick, Alexander S., County Attorney
McIntyre, John, Princess
Macarow & Sullivan, Princess
Macdonald, Patton & Machar, Clarence
Mingaye, W. R
Mudie, John, Clarence
O'Reilly & Draper, Anchor Buildings
Price, Isaac H., Anchor Buildings
Snook, Tunis L., Princess corner King
Strange and Rogers, Clarence
Thibodo, William, Clarence

Blacksmiths.

Bunt, Richard, Brock
Jenkins, Edward, Princess
Jones, John
McDermott, John, King
Ramrill, George A., Wellington
Tracy, Francis, King
Wilmot, N., Princess

Boatbuilders.

McCorkell, A., Ontario
O'Gorman, M., Simcoe

Book and Job Printers.

Bailie, Bros., Wellington
Creighton, John, King
Lightfoot, William, Wellington

Books and Stationery.

Creighton, John, King
Henderson, John, Princess
Stacy, Edward, King

Boots and Shoes, Manufacturers & Dealers

Adams, William, Brock
Allen, William, Brock
Bertram, John, Brock
Bowes, Timothy, Brock
Brunett, Archibald, Brock
Dacey, M., Ontario
Davis, James Barrack
Dillon, Joseph, Princess
Driver, Thomas, Princess
Garrigan, James, Princess
Hackett, J., Barrie
Hope, James, Princess
Hume, Walter, Barrack
Kain, Francis, Brock
Kirk, William, Princess
Legassick, John, Princess
Lindsay, John, Princess
McGarvey, John, Wellington
Mackay, John, King
O'Connor, Mrs., Brock
Offord, George, Brock
Rose, Edwin, Princess
Smith, Alexander, Brock
Sutherland, Alexander, Princess
Thompson, Thomas, Brock
Watson, William, Wellington
Woolard, Robert, Brock

Brewers and Malsters.

Bajus, Jacob, Wellington
Creighton, George W., King
Hayward & Downing, King

Brokers (second-hand).

David, J. J. E., Princess
David, W. M., Princess
McFaul, A. D., Princess
McNamara, Michael, Brock
Spencer, Robert, Princess
Thompson, W. J., Princess

Builders and Contractors.

Cunningham, David
Cunningham, John
Davidson, Andrew
Irving, W. & Son
Lark, Edward
McMahon, G
McMahon, John, Sydenham
Mitchell, W
Newlands, George
Overend, Thomas, Princess
Tandy, Rechab, Barrie
Tossell, Richard
Williamson & Welch, Wellington

Cabinet Makers and Upholsterers.

Brame, Henry, Princess
Brand, G., King
Drennan, S. T., Princess
Filty, George, Princess
Holder, Benjamin, Princess
McDermott, Thomas, Ontario
Main, Adam, Wellington
Reid, James, Princess

Carriage and Wagon Makers.

Caswell, J. D., Princess
Jenkins, John, Princess
Kane, Dennis, Wellington
Kemp & Co., Sydenham
McRae, T. W., Princess
Nelligan & Co
White, Edward, Princess

Chemists and Druggist.

Heath & Gunn, Princess
Hobart, G. S., Princess
King, J. G., King
Parker, E. M., Market Square
Pipe, William, Princess
Skinner, Henry, Princess
White, Robert, Princess

China and Glassware.

Stratton & Co., Princess

Cigars and Tobacco.

Jones, J. E. Brock
Oberndorff, Simon, Princess
White, S. P., Princess

Coffee and Spice Mills.

Karch, J. A., Earl
Robertson, George & Son. Ontario

Dentists.

Day, B. W., Princess
Clements, L., Wellington

Dry Goods, Millinery, Clothing, etc.

Anglin, Mrs. C., Wellington
Davis, James, Princess
Davis, Thomas, Princess
Doran, Mrs. B. & Co., Princess
Doyle, J., Princess
Gardiner, R. & J., Princess
Greenfield, James, Princess
Harty, P. & Co., Market Square
Johnston & King, Princess
Lacey, W. P. & Co., Princess
McDonell, H. B., King

Dry Goods, Millinery, &c.—*(Continued)*

MacNee & Waddell, Princess
Moore & Skinner, Princess
Rigney & Slavin, cor Wellington and Brock
Ross, A., Princess
Sleith, Samuel, Princess
Waddell, R. Co., cor Princess and Wellington

Dyers.

Montgomery, Robert, Princess
White, R., Princess

Engraver.

Ireland, Thomas, Princess

Express Companies.

American, G. T. Oliver, agent, cor King and Brock
Canadian, G. T. Oliver, agent, cor King and Brock
Canadian and American, G. T. Oliver, agent, cor Brock and King

Fancy Goods.

Ferguson, Mrs., Wellington
Ferns, Mrs. C., Princess
Grigor, Joseph, Princess
Henley, M., Wellington
McComb, William, Princess

Flour and Feed.

Dinnis, James, Princess
Kavanagh, John, Market Square
McBride, James, Ontario
McKeever, Thomas, Market Square
Morrison, M., Princess

Forwarding and Commission Merchants.

Chaffey, George & Bro., Atlantic wharf
Carruthers, John & Co., Ontario
Glassford, Jones & Co., Ontario
Gurney & Glidden, Atlantic wharf
Kinghorn, G. M., Brock
Swift, J. & Co., St. Lawrence Wharf

Founders and Machinists.

Canadian Engine and Machine Co., Charles Gibson, superintendent, Ontario
Kingston Foundry, Davidson & Doran, proprietors, Ontario
McEwan, D. & Son, Queen
Victoria Stove Works, Chown & Cunningham, cor King and Queen

Fruits, Confectionery, &c.

Chown, Robert, Princess
Kennedy, Robert, Barrie
Nelligan, B., King
Ockley, M., Princess
Stevenson, A., Princess
Town, Richard, Ontario

Grain Dealers.

Richardson, James, Atlantic Wharf
Young, William, Ontario

Grocers.

Adair, Alexander, Barrie
Anderson, Mrs., Barrie
Begg, William & Co., Brock
Breene, Maurice, Queen
Brown, James, Market Square
Butler, Mrs. Mary, Princess
Campbell, James, Ontario
Campbell, Matthew, Princess
Campbell, Patrick, King
Carson, Robert, Princess
Cartmill, Nathaniel, Bay
Connor, Michael, Market Square
Conroy, P., Princess
Costello, William, Wellington
Couper, Mrs. C., Barrie
Cullen, Garrett, Bay
Davana, John, Princess
Dockrill, John, King
Donnelly, Felix, Ontario
Dunlop, James M., cor Princess and Ontario
Ennis, James, Wellington
Fenwick, Hendry & Co., Ontario
Foley, Mrs. Ann, Wellington
Greenwood, Andrew, Princess
Gibson, David, Princess
Halligan, John, anchor buildings
Harty, J. & Co., Ontario
Hewitt, Robert, Princess
Hilton, Thomas, King
James, Martin, Queen
Jennings, P. J., cor Ontario and Brock
Karch, J. A. & Co., Princess
King, Patrick, Montreal
Livingston, Archibald, Princess
McDonald, Peter, Market Square
McIntyre, R., Princess
McMillan, John, Ontario
McNeil, Mrs., Johnson
McNeill, John, Princess
McRae, W. R. & Co., Princess
Maclean, Andrew, Ontario
Makins, Robert, Ontario
Maloney, John, Wellington
Martin, H., Princess
Martin, William, Princess
Mills, John, Barrie
Morgan, William F., cor Earl and Bagot
Newman, Robert, Princess
O'Donnell, Mrs. Ellen, Barrie
O'Sullivan, D., Bagot
Ockley, Vincent, Princess
Orme, Mark Antony, Princess
Orr, Johnston, Princess
Parkhill, James, Princess
Quinn, Michael, Market Square
Rees, F. S., Princess
Renard, John, Barrie
Rigney, W., Princess
Robertson, George & Son, Ontario
Runians, N., Princess
Sheridan, Bernard, Wellington
Smith, Patrick, Ontario
Sommerville, F., Princess
Stewart, Alexander, Montreal
Summerville, Alexander, Princess
Tierney, Owen, Ontario
Tompkins, Robert, Barrie
Varney, Richard, Place d'Armes
Wilkinson, George M., Wellington
Wilson, George F., Colborne

Gunsmiths.

McArdle, James, King
Skinner, James, Princess

Hardware.

Brown, George, Princess
Chown, Arthur, Bagot
Chown, S. & Sons, Princess
Fraser & George, Princess
Horsey, R. M., Princess
Muckleston, Samuel, Princess
Yarker, James S., Princess

Hatters & Furriers.

Allen, S., Wellington
Groh, William, Princess
Hyman, Soloman, Princess
McDowell, J. A., Brock
McKay, John, Princess
Tweddell, Mrs. M., Princess
Wright, Clark, Wellington

Hotels.

American, W. Woolard, prop., Princess
Anglo American, E. Milsep, prop., cor. Ontario and Johnson
Austin, James, cor. Queen and Wellington
Belfast House, Ontario
Bowen, Mrs. G. H., King
British American, Capt. H. E. Swales, cor. King and Clarence
Burnett House, R. R. Stephens, prop., Ontario
City, R. A. Irwin, Princess
Commercial, Princess
Cronin, M., Ontario
Crown and Anchor, Johnson
Douglass, Henry, Princess
Dunn, John, corner Barrack and Wellington
East, John, King
Farmer, Peter, Brock
Farmer's, Brock
Fenwick, G. W., cor. Ontario and Gore
Fraser, David, Market Square
Gilbert, Mrs. Jane, Barrie
Giraldi House, L. Giraldi, prop., cor. Princess and Montreal
Griffin Mrs., cor. Brock and Ontario
Grimason, Mrs. E, Princess
Hogan, James Ontario
Howland Thomas, Brock
Jeffers, L. W., Johnson
Kearns, P., Montreal
Little, Francis, Barrie
McCarthy, C., King
McCummiskey. Mrs. Alice, Ontario
McGowan, James, Brock
McGowan, Thomas, Princess
McKillop, A., Johnson
McNinch, A., Princess
Maginnes, Owen, Ontario
Maloney, John, Wellington
Molland James, King,
Montreal House, Ontario
Murray, James, Brock
Quigley Joseph, near G. T. R. Station
Rees, Wm Ontario
Robb, James, King
Royce, John, Ontario
Scott, Mrs Eliza, Ontario
St. Lawrence, Alexander Robb, Market Square
Smith, James, Brock
Smith, John, Brock
Stratford, Henry, Princess
Victoria House, Ontario

Insurance Companies and Agents.

Ætna of Hartford (fire and marine), James Swift, agent, St. Lawrence Wharf
Ætna Life (Hartford), J. Swift & Co., agents
British American, T. Wilson, agent, Clarence
British American, George Anderson, St. Lawrence Wharf
Beaver Mutual (fire and stock), R. I. Jordan, agt.
Briton Medical Association of London, Thomas Briggs, agent, Ontario
British American (Toronto), Marine, George Anderson, agent
Canada Life, John Shaw, agent, Wellington
Chaffey, George & Brother, Atlantic Wharf
Canada Life, A. Dupuy, agent, Ontario
Home (Hartford) fire and marine, James Swift, agent, St. Lawrence Wharf
Liverpool and London, and Globe, Thomas Briggs, agent, Ontario
London (England) Assurance Corporation (fire and life), Isaac Simpson, agent, Clarence
Noel, John V., Clarence
Phenix (marine), George Chaffey & Brother, St. Lawrence Wharf
Phœnix London (fire), Thomas Kirkpatrick, agent
Reliance Mutual (life), F. Hooper. agent
Royal (fire and life), Liverpool and London, M. W. Strange, agent, Clarence
Star Life, of London, England, John Shaw, agent, Wellington
Standard Life, C. F. Gildersleeve, agent
Toronto Mutual (fire), R. I. Jordan, agent, Princess
U. S. Plate Glass (Philadelphia), R. I. Jordan, agent, Princess
Western of Toronto, J. Shaw, agent, Wellington

Lumber Merchants.

Anglin, R. & Co., corner Wellington and Bay
Calvin & Breck, Garden Island
McRossie, William & Co., corner Ontario and Wellington

Marble Works.

Tandy, R., Barrie
Welch, E. R., Princess

Merchant Tailors and Clothing Dealers.

Andrews, George, Wellington
Cannon, William, Princess
Conway, Thomas, King
Cooke, H., Queen
Daly, Patrick, Princess
Dunbar, John, Princess
Dunoon, John, Brock
Fahey, Michael, Market Square
Green, J., King
Hay, William, Brock
Kinnear, Mrs. J.
Levey, A. A., Wellington
Livingston, Charles
McArdle, Mrs., Brock
McMillan & Son, Princess
McKay, Donald
Moore, Thomas, Brock
Pearcy, William J., Brock
Slaven & Mackin, Wellington
Thomson, A.
Tipson, A. P., Princess
Wray & Warde, Market Square

Navigation Co.

Canadian, Hon. John Hamilton, president, St. Lawrence Wharf

Newspapers.

British Whig, (daily and weekly), Dr. E. J. Barker
Canadian Churchman, (Wednesday), J. H. Parnell, editor. Rev. T. A. Parnell, publisher, Clarence
Chronicle and News, (daily and weekly), James Neish, M.D., editor, Princess

Organ and Melodeon Manufacturer.

Beyner, Joseph, Princess

Painters, House, Sign and Ornamental

Laird, John, Princess
McMahon, Thomas, Barrie
Robinson, Thomas, Clarence
Robinson, William, Bagot
Savage, Thomas, William
Savage, William H. G., Brock

Patent Iron Ladders and Lightning Rods.

Rumrill, George A., Wellington

Photographers.

Henderson, Henry, Princess
Sheldon & Davis, King
Spohn, John, Wellington
Wallis, J. D., King

Physicians and Surgeons.

Day, B. W.
Dickson, John R.
Fee, S. H. Princess
Fenwick, T. M., cor King and Queen
Fowler, Fife, cor Brock and Clergy
Hillier, S. C.
Kennedy, R.
Maclean, Donald, Princess
Neish, James
Oliver, Alfred S., King
Oliver, J. K., Ontario
Stewart, John
Strange, O. S., King
Sullivan, Michael, King
Yates, Horatio, King
Yates, Octavius, William
Wafer, Francis M.

Piano Forte Manufacturers.

Cunningham, William, cor Princess and Ontario
Rappe, Weber & Co., cor King and Princess

Planing Mill.

Massie, William, Barrie

Plumber, Brass and Copper Smith.

McNeil, Neil, Brock

Saddle and Harness Makers.

Branigan, Dennis, Princess
Dolan, Martin, Princess
Graves, Reuben, Princess
Walker, Robert, Princess
Wilkinson, C., Princess
Wilton, Henry, Princess

Saloons and Restaurants.

Blondheim, S. H., Brock
Cicolari, Alexander, Market Square
Cosmopolitan, Charles Huntley, prop., Wellington
Elliot, Isaiah
Irwin, William, Princess
Mink, George, Princess
Newman, John, Brock
Shanahan, William, Ontario
Thornton, Samuel, King

Soap and Candle Makers.

Meadows, B., Princess
Phippen, James & Son, Johnson

Soda Water Manufacturer.

Reed, L. G., Princess

Tanner.

Ford, William, jun., Market Square

Tin and Copper Smiths, Stove Dealers, &c.

Allen, William
Chown, Arthur, Bagot
Cockburn, John, King
McKelvey & Birch
Shiels, John, King

Watchmakers and Jewelers.

Gage, Matthew, King
Johnston, James, Wellington
Leheup, J. A., Princess
Meves, Otto, Princess
Oberndorff, Simon, Princess
Ramage, John, Brock
Smith, W., King
Spangenberg, George, King

King. (Springhill Village).—A Station of the Northern Railway, in the Township of King, County York, 23 miles from Toronto, the County Town, 8½ from Laskey, and 6 from Nobleton. Average value of improved land $40 per acre. Money order office. Population 150.

Atkinson, James, shoemaker
Bales, John, shingle maker
Blisher, William, hotel keeper
Burks, William, wagon maker
Carley, A., teacher
Collie, William, tailor
Crossley, J. P., farmer
Davis, H. & J., general merchants
Garden, G. L., grocer
Garrow, George, farmer
Hagan, John, hotel keeper
Johnston, D., insurance agent
Johnston, James, carpenter
Kirk, W. C., express and railway agent and telegraph operator
Kingstaff, —, M.D.
LLOYD, B., Postmaster and general merchant
Lloyd, James, farmer
Lloyd, William, farmer
McBride, Isaac, farmer
McCallum, Rev. J. H., (Church of England)
Machell, Samuel, J.P.
Pearce, Franklin, carpenter
Pearce, William, carpenter
Pease, Edward, hide and leather dealer
Ross, John, farmer
Rowe, Mrs., general merchant
Trowbridge, Henry, butcher
Wells, Rev. Gabriel, (Disciples Church)
Wells, G., farmer
Wells, J. P., M.P.P., farmer
Winters, Brothers, farmers

Kingsbridge.—A Post Office in the Township of Ashfield, County Huron, N. R.
McCARRON, MRS. MARY, Postmistress.

King Creek.—A small village on King Creek and the River Humber, in the Township of King, County York, 28 miles from Toronto, the County Town. Good water power. Population 50.

Archibald, John, farmer
Campbell, David, farmer
Carmichael, Rev. James, (O. S. Presbyterian)
Hoover, Henry, shingle maker
Love, David, farmer
McMILLAN, A., Postmaster and general merchant
Rutherford, John, shoemaker
Stokes, James C., farmer
Stokes, William, prop. flouring and grist mill
Willis, Frederick, farmer

Kinglake.—A Post Office in the Township of Houghton, County Norfolk, 30 miles from Simcoe, the County Town. Improved land in the vicinity averages $20, and wild $5 per acre.

Bawtinhimer, Rev. Peter, (Wesleyan)
Carruthers, William, carpenter
Cartright, Ezra, farmer
Dawson, John, shingle maker
Featherstone, John, farmer
Harvey, Andrew, J.P.
King, Charles, farmer
McCollum, Henry, wagon maker
MARTIN, E. T., Postmaster, insurance agent, and general merchant
Osborn, A. G., proprietor grist mill
Perrett, James, hotel keeper and grocer
Pratt, E. & C., coopers
Sims, Thomas, farmer
Truman, James, J.P., farmer
Yager, Isaac, shoemaker

Kingsville.—A flourishing Village and Port of Entry on Lake Erie, in the Township of Gosfield, County Essex, 28 miles from Sandwich, the County Town, and 22 from Amherstburg. Average price of land in the vicinity, $15 per acre. Stages to Windsor and Sandwich. Money Order Office and Savings Bank. Population 800. Nearly opposite the village is Point au Pelé Island, which contains about 10,000 acres of land, owned by the descendants of the late William McCormick.

Allsworth, Edward
Atkinson Rev. Thomas, (Wesleyan)
Baurlaugh, D., shoemaker
Bennett, Thomas, carpenter
Berlin, A. R., dentist
Bowers, M., cabinet maker
Bradwell, Joel, butcher
Bruner, Abram, broom maker
Cady, James, saddler
Clark, Rev. George, (Wesleyan)
Cooper, Arthur, dealer in hides and leather
COOPER, GEORGE, Postmaster and tailor
Craney, T., shoemaker
Cunningford & Williams, shingle makers
Davies, Frank, insurance agent
Doherty, Henry, carpenter
Drake, McDonald, cabinet maker
Drake, W. H., M.D.
Edwards, John, wagon maker
Elliott, David, capenter
Foster, George, sash, door and blind manufacturer
FOX, HUGH, hotel keeper and prop. livery stable
Fox, William G., farmer
Gustin, Calvin, brick maker
Greenville, William, painter
Harris, Henry, baker
Hart, Patrick, saddler
Herrington, Rev. R. D., (Baptist)
Herrington, Rev. Richard, (Baptist)
HERRINGTON, R. D., general merchant (see adv)
Hermann, Joseph, cooper
Iler, H. J., general merchant
Kennedy, Alfred
Kennedy, Margaret, milliner
Kennedy, William, druggist and general merchant
KING, COLONEL JAMES, Collector of Customs, Commissioner in B.R., Clerk 3rd Division Court and issuer of marriage licenses
King, James W., general merchant
King, Sidney A., M.D.
Kingsville Woolen Co., manufacturers of woolen goods
Longland, William, sash, door and blind manufactory
Lonsbury, James, shingle maker
McCall, Matthew, painter
McCormick, D., (Point au Pelé Island)
McDonald, David, nursery and seedsman
McVey, Greener, tinsmith
Malott, George, hotel keeper and auctioneer
Malott, Peter G., farmer
Marks, H., soap and candle maker
Moore, Rufus, carpenter
Price, Henry, carpenter
Pike, Price, proprietor planing and flouring mills
Pulford, Edwin, wagon maker
Pulford, Francis, wagon maker
Rich, A. R., teacher
Rose, Jonathan, baker
Scratch, A., general merchant
Scratch, Eli,
Scratch, Henry, brickmaker
Scratch, John, farmer
Scratch, Leonard, farmer
Scratch, Lucinda, milliner,
Sparks, John G., J.P.
Stratton, A., clothier
Stewart, John, broom-maker
Thornton, John, dyer and scourer
THORNTON, R., general merchant
Thotcher, William, shingle maker
Tofflemure, G., shoemaker
Waggott, George, tailor
Wigle, A., dentist
Wigle, Daniel, farmer, lime and stone dealer
Wigle, Malott, flouring mill
Wigle, Solomon, M. P. P., farmer
Wigle, Theodore, J. P
Wilson, Rev. George, (Baptist)
Woodiwis, John, cooper
Wye, James, shoemaker

Kingston Mills.—*See Villages too late for regular insertion, at the end of this work.*

Kinkora.—A Village in the Township of Ellice, County Perth, 12 miles from Stratford the County Town. Improved land in the neighborhood averages $25 per acre. Population 100.

Bernard, T., farmer
Brown, Edward, blacksmith
Casidy, Bartholomew, butcher
Collins, Patrick, J. P.
Harsnip, William, farmer
Healy, James, shoemaker
Hishon, Mortimer, J. P., farmer
Hishon, Patrick, farmer
Marshall, Thomas, teacher
Milloy, Florence, farmer
MORIARTY, JAMES, Postmaster, teacher and dealer in books and stationery
O'Hara, Patrick, shingle maker
O'Neal, Rev. Mr., (Roman Catholic)
Roache, John, J. P.
Stock, John, farmer
Williams, George, carpenter
Writt, Joseph, carpenter
Writt, Matthew, hotel keeper

Kinloss.—A small Village in the Township Kinloss, County Bruce, 16 miles from Walkerton, the County Town, and 12 from Kincardine. Population 78.

Armitage, James, carpenter
Calcleugh, J., hotel keeper
Cole, William, farmer
Dickie, David, nurseryman
Logan, J., woolen factory
McIntyre, William, farmer
Moore, John, farmer
Sharp, H. R. & Co., merchants
Smith, Alexander, farmer
Spenser, John, farmer
Stauffer, G., proprietor saw mills
Taylor Thomas, mason
Vanston, James, proprietor grist mill

Kinlough.—A Post Office in the Township of Kinloss, County Bruce, S. R.

CORRIGAN, SIMON, Postmaster.

Kinmount.—A small Village on Burnt River, in the Township of Summerville, County Victoria, 40 miles from Lindsay, the County Town, 18 from Bobcaygeon. Wild land in the vicinity averages $1.50 per acre. Stages to Lindsay and Bobcaygeon. Population 50.

Brunter, William, hotel keeper
Gilmour, James, cooper
Gilmour, John A., carpenter
Grogan, Thomas, general merchant
Hallowell, William, tailor
HUNTER, JOHN, Postmaster and prop. flour mills
Switzer, Ralph, general merchant

Kinsale.—A Post Office in the Township of Pickering, County Ontario, S. R. Distant from Toronto 30 miles.

FAIRLESS, JOHN, Postmaster and gen. merchant
Hartop, Samuel, saddler and harness maker
Jewell, James, carriage and wagon maker

Kintore.—A Post Office in the Township of Nissouri, County Oxford, 22 miles from Woodstock, the County Town.

Armstrong, William, farmer
Bean, Daniel, farmer
Chesnut Benjamin, farmer
Cook, Francis, farmer
EASSON, WILLIAM, Postmaster and gen. mercht.
Graves, Jonathan, farmer
Patten, James, farmer
Person, T. H., farmer
Simes, Henry, farmer
Sweezey, Benjamin, farmer

Kippen.—A Post Office in the Township of Tuckersmith, County Huron, 22 miles from Goderich, the County Town. Improved land averages $40, and wild $10 per acre.

Bell, Robert J.P., proprietor grist and saw mill
Blair, W., farmer
Cooper, W. W., farmer
Doig, Robert, farmer
Eakin, Rev. Joseph (Established Church of Scotland)
Edgar, William, wagon maker
Edwards, Rev. A. (Wesleyan)
McIlvaine, James, teacher
McLean, James, farmer
McLean, John, farmer
McMordie, R., farmer
MELLIS, ROBERT, Postmaster and gen. merchant
Shaw, James, hotel keeper
Taylor, —, proprietor saw mill

Kintail.—A Post Office in the Township of Ashfield, County Huron, N. R.

GRANT, WILLIAM, Postmaster.

Kirby.—A small Village in the Township of Clarke, County Durham, 40 miles from Cobourg, the County Town, and 54 from Toronto. Population 50.

Baldwin, Miss S., teacher
Carscadden, James, J.P.
Chapman, Joshua, farmer
Gilbank, Richard, general merchant
Gilbank, R., farmer
Hughson, William, farmer
Hugill, Sarah A., milliner, &c.
Jackson, James, general merchant
Lang, R., carpenter and agent for a patent swing pump
POWERS, H. L., Postmaster, J.P.
Powers, H. L., farmer
Powers, Mary E., milliner, &c.
Pride, William, farmer
Ruddock, R., farmer
Storie, George, blacksmith
Thornton, Thomas, shingle maker

Kirkfield.—A Village in the Township of Eldon, County Victoria, 25 miles from Lindsay, the County Town, 16 from Woodville and 80 from Toronto. Improved land in the vicinity averages $20, and wild $6 per acre. Money Order office. Population 100.

Cadotte, A., general merchant
Cameron, Alexander, shingle maker
Cameron, Ewan, farmer
Cockburn, J. D., accountant
Comerford, Philip, shoemaker
Ellis, Edward, gunsmith and blacksmith
Holland, John, proprietor Bee Hive Inn
King, William, lumber dealer
McDougall, Isabella, teacher
McDonald, John, dentist
McGillvray, John, shingle maker
McKenzie, Alexander, carpenter
McKenzie, Duncan, farmer
McLean, Rev. John (Canada Presbyterian)
McRae, Angus, shoemaker, and proprietor Forest Home Hotel
McRae, C., farmer
Mooney, Patrick, butcher
Munro, Alexander, farmer
Munro, Alexander, tailor
Munro, John, farmer
Munro, Thomas, farmer
RUSSELL, J. S., Postmaster, general merchant and lumber dealer
Sherman, Ira, carpenter
Tuttle, Calvin, shingle maker

Kirkhill.—A Post Office in the Township of Lochiel, County Glengarry, 40 miles from Cornwall, the County Town.

Fraser, Duncan, carpenter
Fraser, Simon, hide and leather dealer
La Claire, —, M.D.
McDonald, Allan R., hotel keeper
McDonald, D. A., proprietor planing mills
McDonald, R., general merchant
McGillvray, Mal., J.P., carpenter
McGillvray, R., lime and stone dealer
McINTOSH, DONALD, Deputy Postmaster and general merchant
McIntosh, Finlay, tailor
McIntosh, James, J.P.
McKenzie, Alexander, attorney-at-law
McKenzie, John B., auctioneer
McKinnon, John, carpenter
McLennan, Duncan, carpenter
McLEOD, WILLIAM, Postmaster
McMillan, —, M.D.
Robertson, —, prop. flouring and grist mill
Simpson, —, M.D.
Stewart, John, insurance agent

Kirkton.—*(See Villages too late for regular insertion at the end of this Work.)*

Kirkwall.—A small Village in the Township of Beverly, County Wentworth, 20 miles from Hamilton, the County Town, and 59 from Toronto. Average price of land in the vicinity $30 per acre. Population 50.

Cameron, James, blacksmith
Dalziell, Walter, tailor
Dickson, John, farmer
Dickson, William, farmer
Gilbert, John, farmer
Hunter, Robert, auctioneer
Jameson, George, farmer
Jameson, Thomas, farmer
LUNDY, JOHN B., M.D.
McBain, Francis, farmer
McQueen, Jones, J.P., farmer
McQueen, Jones, teacher
McQueen, Robert, teacher
MACMILLAN, WILLIAM, Postmaster and general merchant
Martin, David, farmer
Martin, Donald, general merchant
Millord, David, teacher
Parker, Robert, farmer
Porteus, Rev. John, (Canada Presbyterian)
Ramour, Charles, lime and stone dealer
Smith, John A., shoemaker
Softley, David, shoemaker
Tait, Walter, wagon maker

ADVERTISEMENTS.

E. KESTER,

Licensed Auctioneer for the Counties of Brant and Norfolk.

Sale Rooms—North Side Market,

BRANTFORD, ONT.

J. B. MEACHAM,

DENTIST.

Corner Colborne and Market Streets. Entrance on Market Street.

BRANTFORD, ONT.

A. MORTON & CO.,

Wholesale and Retail Hardware Merchants,

(Sign of the Cross Cut Saw,)

COLBORNE STREET, BRANTFORD, ONT.

ROBERT ANGLIN,

Dealer in all kinds of Dry Goods, Groceries, Hardware, Boots and Shoes, Ready-Made Clothing, Crockery, &c.

BREWER'S MILLS, ONT.

CHARLES HARPER,

Hotel Keeper, Brighton, Ontario,

Stages daily to Campbellford and Picton.

STEPHEN PALMER,

Grocer, and Dealer in all kinds of fresh and Smoked Fish in Season.

Families and hotels supplied with ice. Orders solicited.

COLBORNE STREET EAST, BRANTFORD.

H. RACEY & CO.,

Auctioneers, Commission Merchants, and General Agents,

(Opposite the Market),

BRANTFORD, ONT.

JAMES SMITH,

SADDLER, HARNESS AND TRUNK MANUFACTURER,

Colborne Street,

BRANTFORD, ONT.

A. SPENCE,

CARRIAGE AND WAGGON MANUFACTURER,

Colborne Street, East of the Market,

BRANTFORD, ONT.

Horse Shoeing and General Repairing done.

STOCKWELL & BROTHER,

Fancy Dyers and Cleaners,

Market Street, next to Fowler's Boot and Shoe Store,

BRANTFORD, ONT.

T. H. TATE,

Dealer in Groceries, Provisions, Wines & Liquors, and Flour and Feed.

Colborne Street East,

BRANTFORD, ONT.

GEORGE WATT,

Wholesale Grocer,

BRANTFORD, ONT.

C. WILSON,

Boot and Shoe Manufacturer,

Colborne Street,

BRANTFORD, ONT.

A. BURNS,

DENTIST, - - Office, Donaldson's Block,

MAIN ST., BROCKVILLE, ONT.

A. SHERWOOD, Assistant.

W. H. COMSTOCK,

Proprietor of Judson's Mountain Herb Pills,

Mores's Indian Root Pills, McKenzie's Dead Shot Worm Candy, and Carleton's Condition Powder,

MAIN ST., BROCKVILLE, ONT.

ALLAN, TURNER & CO.,

CHEMISTS AND DRUGGISTS.

Manufacturers of White and Colored Paints, Importers of Foreign Drugs, Painter's Colors, Oils and Dye Stuffs,

98 & 100 MAIN ST., BROCKVILLE, ONT.

Klineburg.—A Village on the River Humber, in the Township of Vaughan, County York, 22 miles from Toronto, the County Seat. Improved land in the vicinity averages $50 per acre. Money order office. Population 350.

Barbour, James, hide and leather dealer
Bywater, R., druggist
Cameron, William, farmer
Capner, Joseph, farmer
Clarke, A. B., teacher
Cochrane, John, tinsmith
Crosby, M. B., general merchant
Dalzeal, John, farmer
Fast, M., general insurance agent
Etchmar, Charles, cabinet maker
Fraser, Mrs., milliner, &c
Gough, Alexander, cooper
Groskurth, August, cabinet maker
Hayden, James, hotel keeper
Hodgins, Rev. J., (Methodist)
Howland & Brothers, flouring mills
Howland, H. S., lumber dealer
Hughes George, shingle maker
Livingstone, James, general merchant
McCullum, John, J. P., and wagon maker
McCutcheon, David, farmer
McCutcheon, Patrick, farmer
McDonough, John, wagon maker
McIntosh, Alexander, shingle maker
McKay, Robert, hotel keeper
McVicheren, M., butcher
Nixon, Robinson, hotel keeper
Peffrey, John, farmer
Sharp, William, shoemaker
Stevenson, —, M. D.
Train, John, farmer
Walker, John, farmer
WHITE, THOMAS, Postmaster and gen. merchant
Worster, Christian, saddler

Knatchbull.—A Village in the Township of Nassagaweya, County Halton, 15 miles from Milton, the County Town, and 5 from Rockwood Station Grand Trunk Railway. Improved land in the vicinity averages $35 per acre. Population 35.

Anderson, John, farmer
Campbell & Black, (Archibald and Andrew) carriage makers
Coulson, John, farmer
Curren, Edward, farmer
Easton, Thomas, farmer
Hall, Robert, farmer
Kelly, John, farmer
Reed, Henry, blacksmith
Reed, William, farmer
STEPHENSON, WILLIAM, Postmaster
Wilson, George, farmer
Wilson, Thomas, farmer

Komoka.—A Village and Station of the Great Western Railway, at the junction of the Sarnia branch, in the Township of Lobo, County Middlesex, 10 miles from London, the County Seat, and 50 from Sarnia. Money order office. Population 400.

Alway, George, farmer
Barnum, W., J.P. and clerk Am. Ex. office
Betts, Frederick, telegraph operator
Betts, Mrs., hotel keeper
Butler, John, farmer
Catto, George, carpenter
Challoner, G. O., farmer
Falls, Thomas, shoemaker
Fayette, Rev. J. F. A. L. (Presbyterian)
Foster, James, tailor
Graham, Donald, farmer
Hord, Robert, general merchant
Jackson, Rev. Samuel (Baptist)
Lourie, Alexander, wagon maker
McArthur, James, farmer
McDougall, John, farmer
McKenzie, Alexander, general merchant
McKenzie, Alexander, teacher
McLaren, Peter, general merchant
MATEN, O. D., Postmaster and agent American Express Co.
Mathewson, James, carpenter
Milton, James, hotel keeper
Morrison, Neil, auctioneer
Morris, Robert, butcher
Raymond, Isaac, shoemaker
Ritchie, James, shoemaker
Robertson, Robert, railroad agent and telegraph operator
Robinson, W., proprietor Royal Oak Hotel
ROSS, A. M., proprietor oil refinery
Seaton, Donald, farmer
Shedden, Alexander, painter
Smith, Alexander, cooper
Smith, David, farmer
Smith, R. R., M.D.
Stevenson, William, proprietor Britannia Hotel
Taylor, H. & Co., distillers and rectifiers of oil
Thompson, G., farmer
Tiffany, Dean, lime manufacturer
Trard, H. B., farmer
Urquhart, Alexander, painter
Ward, J. C., proprietor Wellington House
Woodhull, C., farmer
Young, James, manufacturer of woolen goods

Laggan.—A small Village in the Township of Kenyon, County Glengarry, 6½ miles from Alexandria, the County Town. Population 50.

CATTANACH, D., Postmaster and land agent
McDonald, Neil, proprietor saw mill
McSweyn, Malcolm, innkeeper
Wilson, Robert, general merchant

Lafontaine.—A Post Office in the Township of Tiny, County Simcoe. Distant 40 miles from Barrie, the County Town.

MOREAU, P. F., Postmaster.

Lake Dore.—A Post office in theTownship of Wilberforce, County Renfrew.

WALLACE, THOMAS, Postmaster.

Lakelet.—A small Village on a branch of the Maitland River, in the Township of Howick, County Huron 55 miles from Goderich, the County Town. Average price of land in the vicinity $25 per acre. Stages to Seaforth and Wroxeter. Population 40.

Driver, Henry, mason
Ferguson, R., farmer
Hazlewood, W. C., shoemaker
Milne, John, wagon maker
Scott, John, builder
Webster, Bros., proprietors saw mill
Young, E. & Bro., general merchants
YOUNG, MYLES, Postmaster and insurance agent

Lakefield.—(North Douro Post Office.) A Village in the Township of Douro, County Peterboro, 9 miles from Peterboro the County Town, and 100 from Toronto. Daily mail. Population 250.

Beatty & Edmison, carriage makers
Baptie, Peter, carpenter
Blakely, William, hotel keeper, dry goods & groceries
CASEMENT, ROBERT, Postmaster, general mercht
Clarm, John, shoemaker
Clementi, Rev. V., (Evangelical Church)
Garbutt, Isaac, farmer
Goheen, Henry, furniture dealer
Gordon, Thomas, boots and shoes
Graham, Robert, dry goods and groceries
Hamilton, William, stage proprietor
Hendon, James, blacksmith
Hull, John, proprietor flouring mill
Keat, E. O., furniture dealer
Knox, John, proprietor flouring mill
Mann, Dr
Mutchall, Mrs., teacher
Pratt, William, hotel keeper
Sainsburg, F., shoemaker
Saunders, J., teacher
Sawers, John, dry goods and groceries
Schofield, Rev. William H., (Methodist)
Sherin, John C., general merchant
Sherin, Samuel, Clerk Division Court
Shields, George, blacksmith
Smith, D., blacksmith
Stock, Rev. Thomas, (Baptist)
Stone, L., tailor
Strickland & Bro., proprietors saw mill
Strickland, R. & P., shingles and lath
Sutton, John, shoemaker
Thom, Rev. James, (Presbyterian)
Thornhill, J., teacher
Urquhart, Kenneth, tailor
Wilson, A., baker
Wilson, E. B., manufacturer of woolen goods

Lakeside.—A Village in the Township of East Nissouri, County Oxford, 20 miles from Woodstock, the County Town, and 100 from Toronto. There are two small lakes in the vicinity affording excellent water power. Improved land in the vicinity averages $45 per acre. Population 100.

ARMSTRONG, ROBERT, Postmaster
Belcher Rev. S. (Church of England)
Bristol, Rev. B. (Episcopal Methodist)
Carroll, Henry, farmer
Garner, Joseph, mill proprietor
Harris, E., farmer
Harris, E. H., farmer
Petton, S., hotel keeper
Seaton, John
Shaw, Angus, farmer
Sparks, Dr.
Sutherland, W., farmer

Lambeth.—A Village in the Township of Westminster, County Middlesex, 6 miles from London, the County Seat. Stages to Delaware and London. Population 250.

Andrews, Mrs. Adolph, grocer
Armstrong, Walter, farmer
Baker, J. L., general merchant
Beattie, Jeremiah, grocer
Best, John, hotel keeper
Best, S. A., M.D.
Burch, Charles, M.D.
Christian, Anthony, millwright
Daniels, J., druggist
Forman, Rev. J., (Wesleyan)
Freakley, William, painter
Geddes, Arthur, tailor
Halls, Thomas, mason
Heard, Robert, wagon maker
Hunt, James, carpenter
KELLEY, GEORGE, Postmaster and gen. merchant
Lackey, Andrew, shoemaker
Lock, Rev. H., (Methodist Episcopal)
McLean, Rev. John, (Church of England)
Mills, J. & R., brick makers
Morden, Charles, carpenter
Northrup, Robert, insurance agent
Reynolds, Sylvester, hotel keeper
Risdon, J., butcher
Sadler, William, farmer
Thomas, Richard, farmer
Webb, William, farmer
Wilson, George, blacksmith

L'Amaroux.—A Post Office in the Township of York, County York. Distant 13 miles from Toronto. Mails tri-weekly.

Bell, William, farmer
Belt, Rev. W. (Church of England)
Edgar, Rev. James, (Primitive Methodist)
Flynn, James, shoemaker
Long, James, farmer
Mason, Francis, farmer
Moore, Thomas, farmer
Murphy, William, carpenter
Nash, Robert, farmer
Richardson, J., blacksmith
Risbrow, William, farmer
Sherwood, John, farmer
Skelton, Richard, shoemaker
Tomlinson, Rev. G., (Wesleyan)
WILLIAMSON, JOSEPH, Postmaster
Wright, Archibald, wagon maker

Lambton.—(Etobicoke P. O.)——A Village in the Townships of York and Etobicoke, County York, on the River Humber, 7½ miles from Toronto, the County Town. Money Order office. Population 500.

Ashenhurst, George, blacksmith
Atkinson & Bro., founders
Beatty, Thomas, M.D.
Burk, William, hotel keeper
Bryans, Mrs., cooper
Colley, John, hotel keeper
Cornell, William, clerk
Creech, M., carpenter
Darche, Mrs. P., cooper
Dawson, William, book-keeper
DeCourcier, Mrs., hotel keeper
Fisher, E. C., miller
Harwood, William, carpenter
Hewett, William, shoemaker
HOWLAND, F. A., Postmaster
HOWLAND, P. & F. A., general merchants, flour mill proprietors, farmers, etc.
Kyffin, Richard, hotel keeper
Montgomery, Alexander, blacksmith
Rogers, J. G., saddler
Ross, John, teacher
Smith, Thomas, cattle dealer
Tier, Thomas, farmer
Ware, Charles, general merchant

Lanark.—An incorporated Village in the Township of Lanark, County Lanark on the River Clyde, a tributary of the Mississippi, 12 miles from Perth, the County Town, and 258 from Toronto. Money order office and Savings Bank. Population 650.

Ballantine, Matthew, farmer
Bain, James, farmer
Baird, James, boots and shoes
Baird, Thomas, boots and shoes
Bowes, James, carpenter, prop livery stable
Bowes, Patrick, proprietor Union Hotel
Brown, Thomas, painter
Caldwell, A. & Sons, prop. steam flouring and saw mills
Caldwell, B., general merchant
Caldwell & Pollock, general merchants
Caldwell & Watchrom, proprietors woolen mills
Closs, John, lime and stone
Craig, Adam, cooper
Craig, Andrew G., butcher
Craig, Robert, farmer
Crawford, William, carpenter
Croskey, James, boots and shoes
Cullen, Mrs. Ellen, teacher
Cunningham, Bolton, carpenter
Currie. James, farmer
Daily, John, painter
Deachman, John, farmer
Deachman, William, farmer
Dobbie, James, founder
Dobbie, Thomas, wine and spirit dealer
Douglas, Adam, saddler
Drysdale, Alexander, carpenter
Drysdale, Andrew, carpenter
Drysdale, James wagon maker
Drysdale, John, wagon maker
Drysdale, Robert, cabinet maker
Ferguson, Robert B., M.D
Field, William C., cabinet maker
Gallinger, Jacob, blacksmith
Glossop, Daniel, boots and shoes
Gordon, John, carpenter
Hamilton, James, boiler maker
Jamieson, John, saddler
Kelly, Alexander, prop. Victoria Inn
Lacouline, Jacob, blacksmith
Lamont, Mrs. J., prop. Crown Inn
Lewis, Rev. Richard, (Congregational)
Lister, Rev. Alexander, (Wesleyan)
McCurdy, Daniel, farmer
McDonnell, Patrick, prop. livery stable
McEum, Mrs. P., dealer in groceries
McEum, Peter, merchant tailor
McGuire, Thomas, boots and shoes
McInnis, Alexander, wagon maker
McIntyre, Mrs. F., milliner, &c
McLaren, David, carpenter
McLaren, John, farmer
McLaren, Peter, farmer
McMarine, Rev. John R., (Church of England)
Mair, Holmes, general merchant
Mair, James, boots and shoes
Mair, John, Jr., turner
Mallotte, A, cooper
Mullen, Patrick, butcher
Munro, Alexander, M. D., druggist
Munro, David, M. D
Reddитt, Thomas H., teacher
Reid, Emery B., tinsmith
Robertson, John, accountant
Robertson, Mrs. J., milliner
ROBERTSON, WILLIAM, Postmaster, J. P., Commissioner in B. R., Clerk Division Court, Coroner, auctioneer, insurance agent, and Issuer of Marriage Licenses
Sharpe, Richard, grocer
Sinclair, Finley, wine and spirit dealer
Smith, John, tanner
Stewart, Robert, farmer
Storie, Margaret, milliner
Turner, Francis, tinsmith
Turner, Mrs. F., dealer in groceries
Walker, Andrew, merchant tailor
Watt, Thomas, carpenter
Wilson, Rev. James, (Church of Scotland)
Wilson, Thomas, boots and shoes
Wright, John, carpenter

Lancaster.—A Village and Station of the Grand Trunk Railroad, on the the River St. Lawrence, in the Township of Lancaster, County Glengary, 14 miles from Alexandria, the County Town. Steamers plying between Montreal and Cornwall, call here bi-weekly. Average value of land in the vicinity $18 per acre. Population 350.

Anderson, Rev. John, (Canada Presbyterian)
Annand, George, mason and brick layer
Bethune, John, shoemaker
Cameron, Alexander
Campbell, Donald, carpenter
Dunlop, John, shoemaker
Falkner, William, farmer
Ferguson, Alexander, farmer
Fraser, J. S., gen. mercht. and prop. Lancaster Hotel
Gillespie, William, blacksmith and steam boat agent
Harper, William, general merchant
Hibbard, Miss, principal Lancaster Ladies' Seminary
Houlle, Joseph, butcher
Johnson, Edward, farmer
Johnson, Margaret, milliner, &c.
McBain, A. L., farmer
McCrimmon, John, shoemaker
McDonnell, John A., wood dealer
McDonald, R. S., farmer
McEdward, J. W., accountant
McEdward, William
McLean, Alexander, wood dealer
McLean, Hugh, wagon maker
McLean, John, blacksmith
McLean, Thomas, farmer
McLennan, Alexander, hide and leather dealer and tanner
McNaughton, John, P.L.S.
McNeil, Samuel, produce dealer
McPHERSON, K., Postmaster
McPherson, Rev. Thomas (Church of Scotland)
Marquette, J., butcher
Meadows, John, carpenter
Nicholson, William, baker
Parker, George H., painter
Ross, Alexander, saddler
Ross, Donald, wood dealer and steamboat agent
Steele, T. O., teacher and insurance agent
Stewart, John, cabinet maker
Sutherland, Daniel, wagon maker

Langford.—A small Village on Sage's Creek, in the Township of Brantford, County Brant, 8¼ miles from Brantford, the County Town, and 17 from Hamilton. Stages to the above places. Population 75.

Brown, Rev. W. G., (Episcopal Methodist)
Cornett, Rev. E., (Wesleyan)
Cornwell, Morgan, farmer
Davis, Aaron, shingle maker
Herman, Jeptha, blacksmith
Langs, E. R., farmer
Langs, Hiram, farmer
Langs, Nelson, farmer
LANGS, W. W., Postmaster, farmer
Mackay, W., carpenter
Milne, A., general merchant
Milne, A., farmer
Myers, Marther, teacher
Ramsay, A., prop. steam saw mill
Sculey, James, farmer
Vanderlip, E. W., J.P., farmer
Whiting, John, prop. steam saw mill
Yorkum, Rev. Mr., (Episcopal Methodist)

Langside.—A Post-office in the Township of Kinloss, County Bruce.
BLACK, DAVID, Postmaster.

Langton.—A Village in the Township of Walsingham, County Norfolk. Distant from Simcoe, the County Town, 18 miles, from Toronto 100 miles. Tri-weekly Mail. Population 60.

BOUGHNER, DAVID W., Postmaster
Gardner, James, prop. saw mill
Gilmour, James, hotel keeper
Gretton, James, shoemaker
Holsted, E., general merchant
McLean, John & Bro., general merchants
Matthews, James, lumber merchant
Shelby, A., teacher
Smith, William, blachsmith
Stanoffe, John, general merchant

Lansdown.—A Post Office in the Township of Lansdown, County Leeds.
BRADLE, JOSH A., Postmaster.

Lansing.—A Village on Yonge Street, in the Township of York, County York, distant from Toronto, the County Seat, 8 miles, and 6 from Thornhill Station, Northern Railroad. Stages daily to Toronto. Population 100.

Bestard, R., saddler
Harris, W. W., general merchant and miller
Harrison, C., farmer
LAMBERT, R. G., Postmaster
Sheppard, John, proprietor Milton House
Sheppard, Joseph E., general merchant
Weatherall, G., hotel keeper
Weed, Albert C., fanning mill manufacturer
Wincup, B., farmer

Largie.—A Post Office in the Township of Dunwich, County Elgin.
LEITCH, ARCHIBALD, Postmaster.

Laskay.—A Village in the Township of King, County York, on the river Humber, 25 miles from Toronto. Population 100.

BALDWIN, G. S., Postmaster and general merchant
Bruce, W., teacher
Burgess, Thomas, cooper
Cleland, A., shoemaker
Crown, William, shoemaker
McNeely, H., hotel keeper
Matheson, Peter, clothing dealer
Mullen, Alexander, shoemaker
Peterman, D., carpenter
Smelser, Henry, auctioneer
Warren, William, cooper
Watson, William, carpenter
Wood, Joseph, J.P.

Larner.—A Post Office in the Township of Hibbert, County Perth.
LARNER, JOHN, Postmaster.

Latona.—A Post Office in the Township of Glenelg, County Grey, distant from Owen Sound, the County Town, 21 miles, and 140 from Toronto. Stages to Guelph and Owen Sound.

APPLEBY, MARK, Postmaster
Cameron, Rev. James (Presbyterian)
Colles, R. W., teacher
McIntosh, Philip, general merchant
Scott, John, innkeeper

Laurel.—A Village in the Township of Amaranth, County Wellington, distant from Guelph, the County Town, 40 miles, from Brampton 31, and from Toronto 54. Semi-weekly mail. Population 60.

Banks, Joseph, farmer
Bennett, George, farmer
Bowen, David, carpenter
Burdge, Rev. J., (Primitive Methodist)
Grey, M. S., farmer
Grey, Richard, blacksmith
Grey, Robert, farmer
Henderson, Rev. Alex., (Church of England)
Hughes, William, carpenter
Jelly, William B., proprietor saw mill
McCauley, Samuel, teacher
Madill, Benjamin, farmer
Marshall, William, farmer
Matthews, Rev. H. S., (Primitive Methodist)
Morrison, John, boots and shoes
Richardson, William, farmer
RIDLEY, FRANCIS, Postmaster and gen. merchant
Simpson, William, weaver
Wainsborough, Robert, township clerk

Lavant.—A Post Office in the Township of Lavant, County Lanark.
BROWNING, ARCHIBALD, Postmaster.

Lavender.—A Post Office in the Township of Mulmur, County Simcoe, 31 miles from Barrie, the County Town.
MASTIN, L. B., Postmaster.

Leamington.—A Village in the Township of Mersea, County Essex, 32 miles from Sandwich, the County Town, 32 from Windsor and 38 from Rondeau. Money order office. Population 350.

Asrew, John, prop. steam flouring mill
Baker, James, carpenter
Barnum, Rev. William L., (Baptist)
Brown, A. M., grocer
Brown, B. V., butcher
Campbell, Joseph, cabinet maker
Clark, Miss Maggie, teacher
COWAN, SAMUEL, saddler
Curtis, Caleb, cooper
Hooker, Rev. L., (Wesleyan)
Hubbel, Rev. John, (Episcopal Methodist)
Kemp, James A., M.D.
KIMBALL, WARREN, J.P., Postmaster, shoemaker
Lane, John, carpenter
Lane, Julia Ann, milliner
Lane, R., carpenter
Lane, Sarah J., milliner
Ley, Joseph, cooper
Lynn, George, shoemaker
McIntyre, Archibald, tailor
Maxon, G. C., M.D., druggist
Morse, George A., general merchant
Palmer, Corydon, general merchant
Pierce, George, painter
Prosser, William, butcher
Pulford, Walter, wagon maker
Robinson, John, auctioneer
Robinson, Joseph, tailor
Russell, Richard, shingle maker
Russell & Wigle, proprietor lumber yard
TRUAX, LEVI, hotel keeper
Wigle & Emery, tinsmiths
Wigle, L. & Son, general merchants
WIGLE, LEONARD, hotel keeper
Wigle, Robert, livery stable
Wilkinson, John R., carpenter
Williams, Richard, shingle maker

Leaskdale.—A Village in the Township of Scott, County Ontario, 30 miles from Whitby, the Count Town, and 50 from Toronto. Population 60.

Blanchard, James, farmer
Collins, George, general merchant
Douglas, Rev. James, (Canada Presbyterian)
Foster, Robert, hotel keeper
Gale, James, shoemaker
Hackings, John, general merchant
Harrison, George, farmer
Lachlan, Andrew, teacher
LASK, GEORGE, Postmaster, J. P
Lask, James, farmer and lumber dealer
Pirt, Martin, farmer
Shannon, James, shoemaker
Stevenson, George, lumber dealer
Tiffin, John, farmer
Williams, Smith, farmer
Wyewan, Richard, carpenter

Leavens.—A post office in the Township of St. Vincent, County Grey, 15 miles from Owen Sound, the County Town.

Arthur James, farmer
Arthur, John, farmer
Blanchard, A., farmer
Brown, Robert, farmer
CUNNINGHAM, STEPHEN, Postmaster
Leavens, W. B., farmer
Lenny, R. B., farmer
McWilliams, James, farmer
Saunders, F. B., farmer
Vanderburgh, S., farmer

Lefroy.—A Village and Station of the Northern Railway, in the Township of Innisfil, County Simcoe, 12 miles from Barrie, the County Town, 1 from Bell Ewart and 52 from Toronto. Money order office. Population 150.

Bannerman, John, farmer
Barry, Sylvester, shoemaker
Burns, Robert, carpenter
Craighead, James carpenter
Craighead, John, lime and stone
Cronan, J., farmer
DAVIDSON, D., Postmaster
Davidson, &. Co., general merchants
Dodson, James J., wagon maker
Finlay, Samuel, cooper
Fraser, David, saddler
Gartley, Alexander, farmer
Goodfellow, William, farmer
Grose, H., J. P., lumber dealer and farmer
Grose, Richard, farmer
Grose, Robert, farmer
Hamner, E. V., proprietor Northern Hotel & livery stable
Houghton, Edward, shingle maker
Irving, J., farmer
Jacques, Thomas W., M. D., druggist
Laidlaw & Fraser, express agents and gen. merchts
Long, John, farmer
McConkey, J., proprietor Lefroy Hotel
McConkey, Thomas, general agent and prop. of livery stable
McKenzie, Alexander, tailor
McKay, G. P., general merchant
Rogerson, F., J.P
Taylor, G. W., telegraph operator and R.R. agent
Terrell, Thomas, tailor
Thompson, William, farmer
Toad, E., J.P
Wallace, R., farmer
Wightman, Rev. Thomas, (Presbytarian)
Wray, S., farmer

Leith.—A Village on Leith Water, in the Township of Sydenham, County Grey. Distant from Owen Sound, the County Town, 7 miles, 40 from Collingwood and 135 from Toronto. Stages to Owen Sound and Collingwood. Population 140.

Ainslie, Adam, farmer and miller
Brown, Miss E. A., teacher
Burr, Peter, blacksmith
Cameron, Arthur, general merchant
Cameron, George, carpenter
Cameron, Peter, carpenter
Dickson, Leslie, weaver
Hunter, Rev. Alexander, B.A., (Presbyterian)
McKeen, William, shoemaker
Ross, Allan, miller
ROSS, JAMES, sen., Postmaster
Ross, James & Sons, general merchants and grain dealers
Scott, David, brickmaker
Turnbull, John, tailor
Wilson, Thomas, hotel keeper

Lemonville.—A small Village in the Township of Whitchurch, County York, 12 miles from Newmarket and 28 from Toronto, the County Town. Population 75.

Dougherty, Samuel, farmer
Hill, James, farmer
HILL, JOHN, Postmaster
Hill, John & Sons, general merchants
Hill, John, jr., hotel keeper
Hunter, Daniel, farmer
Lemon, George, farmer
McRay, George, prop. flouring mill
McQuillan, Edward, farmer
McQuillen, Patrick, farmer
Macklin, P., J.P
Markham, Rev. James, (Primitive Methodist)
Patterson, Henry, wagon maker
Pipher, George, farmer
Steele, Miss Mary, milliner, &c
White, W. J., shoemaker
Windsor, Rev. J. A., (Primitive Methodist)
Wintersteen, Henry, hide and leather dealer and tanner

Leinster.—A Post Office in the Township of Richmond, County Lennox, 11 miles from Napanee, the County Town. Mails tri-weekly. JORDAN, MICHAEL, Postmaster.

Leskard.—A Village on Spring Creek, in the Township of Clarke, County Durham, 30 miles from Cobourg, the County Town, and 60 from Toronto. Population 200.

Betters, John, wagon maker
Bradley, James, J.P.
Carneth, John, J.P., lumber dealer and proprietor flouring mill
Daney, John, J.P., farmer
Daney, John, accountant
Elliott, James, proprietor flouring mill
Griffin, Alfred, J.P., farmer
Jackson, Mark, farmer
McINTYRE, PETER, Postmaster
Martin, Rosel, carpenter
Neely, James, teacher
Potter, Austin, teacher
Powers, Ransom, hotel keeper
Proctor, John, general agent and merchant
Robbins, H. & J., shingle maker
Stalker, John, proprietor planing mill
Thornton, Thomas, shingle maker
Tigh, William, cooper
Tyerman, David, carpenter

Leslieville (Leslie Post Office)—A Village in the Township of York, County York, 2 miles east of Toronto. The *Toronto Nurseries*, occupying 150 acres, are located here, and are, without exception, the most extensive in the Province, embracing every description of fruit and ornamental trees, shrubs, &c. Money Order Office. Population 400.

Ashbridge, Jesse, farmer
Best, James, farmer
Bird, Edward, butcher
Brockwell, Thomas, brickmaker
Cavanagh, Richard, market gardener
Cockburn, Frank, farmer
Cooper, George, market gardener
Crothers, John, constable
Crothers, Samuel, painter
Elwood, John, brick maker
Everiss, Benjamin, blacksmith
Feltstead, George, farmer
Finucan, Thomas, farmer
Fittinger, McCord & Co., proprietors flouring mill
Fox, Thomas, brick maker
Greenwood, Mrs., proprietor of "The Puritan"
Hastings, Thomas, blacksmith
Hill, Samuel, ice merchant
Hollin, T., butcher
Hunter, William, brick maker
Ingleson, John, farmer.
LESLIE, GEORGE, jun., J.P., Postmaster
LESLIE, G. & SONS, proprietor Toronto nurseries
Lewis Francis, general merchant
Lewis, William J., ice merchant
Love, Mrs., gardener
McKee, Martin, general merchant
Manning, James, J.P.
Morin, James, general merchant
Morley, Walker, brick maker
Muir, Alexander, teacher
O'Neil, Miss Agnes, teacher
Reid, Ross, brick maker
Pape, Joseph & Son, market gardeners, fruit & plant dealers
Rahey, William, farmer
Russell, John, brick maker
Sawdon, John, carpenter
Sedgwick, Mrs., market gardener
Smith, George, proprietor Uncle Tom's Cabin
Strader, John, general merchant
Wagstaff, David, brick maker
Wagstaff, William, brick maker
Wallace, James, carpenter
Withrow, Rev. William H., M.A. (Wesleyan)

Lifford.——A Village in the Township of Manvers, County Durham. Distant from Port Hope, the County Town, 32 miles, from Toronto 65 miles, and 6 from Bethany Station Port Hope, Lindsay and Beaverton Railway. Population 50.

Buggin, Rev. George, (New Connexion)
McCann, Rev. Alfred, (Wesleyan)
MIDDLETON, THOMAS A., Postmaster
Wilson, George, teacher

Limehouse—A Village and Station of the Grand Trunk Railway, in the Township of Esquesing, County Halton, 14 miles from Milton, the County Town, 16 from Guelph and 32 from Toronto.

Bescoby, Edward, lime and lumber dealer
Farquhar, James, builder, prop. lime, freestone and flag quarries
Ford, Robert, blacksmith
Fraser, J. B., general merchant
Haslett, Benjamin, hotel keeper
Heather, R., station agent
Lambert, John, plasterer
Lindsay, James, farmer
McDonald, Myles, carpenter
Marshall, William, lime burner
NEWTON, JOHN, Postmaster
Newton, John & Sons, props. woolen and saw mills
Slater, Edward.

Lime Lake.—A small Village in the Township of Hungerford, County Hastings.

Dunn, William, general merchant
Henderson, John, general merchant
JARMINE, JAMES, Postmaster
Maxwell, John, M.D.

Lindsay.—The County Town of Victoria, and terminus of the Port Hope and Lindsay Railway, on Lake Scugog, in the Township of Ops, 28 miles from Peterboro', and 40 from Port Hope. Stages to Beaverton, 28 miles, Fenelon Falls, 20 miles, and Bobcaygeon 22 miles. Money Order office and Savings Bank. Population 3000.

ADAM, THOMAS R., Postmaster
Adam, James, Deputy Postmaster
Allanby, J., dealer
Anderson, John, furniture dealer
Anderson, Mrs., milliner
Armstrong, William T. (Lisle & Armstrong)
Ayres, Parley, axe maker
BAKER, C. L., grocer, miller, and pork packer
BEALL, THOMAS, bookseller, stationer and watchmaker
Begg, —, carpenter
Bell, William, proprietor Bell's Hotel
BENSON, EDWARD, M.D.
BERTRAM, GEORGE (Bertram & Co.)
BERTRAM, JOHN (Bertram & Co.)
BERTRAM & CO. (John and George Bertram), hardware merchants
Bigelow, O. (S. & O. Bigelow)
Bigelow, S. (S. & O. Bigelow)
BIGELOW, S. & O. (Silas and Obadiah), dry goods and groceries
Binnie, Rev. Robert (Canada Free Church)
Bowen, Hollis, lumber, laths and pickets
Boynton, William, proprietor Boynton's Hotel
Boynton's Hotel, William Boynton, proprietor
Britton, Charles, general merchant
Brooks, Abraham, stave factory and cooperage
Brooks, George, cooper
Browne, David, stoves and tinware
Bruce, John, assistant teacher Union School
Cadotte, E., clothing
Cadotte, Mary, groceries and provisions
Cadotte, Louis H., manager Mary Cadotte
Campbell, J. C., assistant teacher Union school
CANADA LIFE ASSURANCE CO., W. Thirkill, agent
Canadian Post (weekly), C. B., Robinson, proprietor
Carew, Patrick, saloon
Cather, L. M., veterinary surgeon
Chambers, R. W. (Coulter & Chambers)
Chapman. Mrs. Eliza, grocery, William
Chisholm, John, grocer
Cluxton, William (Cluxton & Dundas)
Cluxton & Dundas (William Cluxton and J. R. Dundas), dry goods and general merchants
Connolly, James, boots and shoes
COOPER, JOSEPH, editor and proprietor *Victoria Warder*
Corcoran, T. (T. Corcoran & Co).
Corcoran, T. & Co., general merchants
Costello, J. & Co., dry goods
Coulter, William (Coulter & Chambers)
Coulter & Chambers (William Coulter and R. W. Chambers) chemists and druggists
Crawford, Robert, chief trader Hudson's Bay Co.
Crowley, Patrick, shoemaker
Crown Land Office, G. M., Roche, agent
Cullis, John (J. Cullis & Son)
Cullis, Thomas (J. Cullis & Son)
Cullis, J. & Son (John and Thomas) grocers
Cullon. A, general blacksmith
Davis, Parker, shingle and planing mill proprietor
Dean, M., P.L.S. and civil engineer
Dobbie, Rev. R. (St. Andrew's Church of Scotland)
Dobson, John (Dobson & Niblock)
Dobson & Niblock, (John Dobson and Thomas Niblock), grocers
Dobson, Stephen, foundry and machine shop
Doheny, Mrs. Margaret, saloon
Doris, Mrs. Margaret, dressmaker
DORMER, GEORGE, attorney-at-law, solicitor, notary public, etc,
Downey, Mrs. Mary, fancy store
Duncan, James, hotel keeper
Dundas, J. R. (Cluxton & Dundas)
Duncan, David, cooper
Dunsford, Hartley, County Registrar, agent Bank of Montreal
Fee, Thomas, shingle factory, etc.
Ferguson, Mrs., milliner and dressmaker
Fidler, Joshua, M.D., coroner
Finlay, Miss Ellen, assistant teacher Union School
Foley, Charles, operator Montreal Telegraph
Foley, T. & Co., (Thomas and William), hardware merchants and dealers in furs
Foley, William, (T. Foley & Co.)
Fournier, Treffly, prop. Quebec and Montreal Hotel
Francis, Edward, photographer
Funk, Mrs. Maria, hotel keeper
Gardner, Joseph, boots and shoes
Gemsjugger, A., fancy goods and tobocco
Gillies, Allan, (Gillies & Lancashire)
Gillies & Lancashire, (Allan Gillies and Joseph Lancashire) dry goods and groceries
Gimson, J. F., dry goods, millinery, etc.
Gold, Rev. Matthew, (Baptist)
Gourley, Thomas, photographer
Grace, Wm., clerk County Court and Court of Assize
Greener, Rev. James (Wesleyan)
GREGORY, EDMUND, druggist and seedsman
Gregory, George, grocer
Haisley, John, harness maker
Hamilton, P. & J., (Peter and James) plough and carriage factory
HANLON, T., proprietor Railroad Hotel (see adv.)
Hawke, G.-W., dentist
HEAP, JAMES, (MacKay & Heap) agents Liverpool and London and Globe and Lancashire Insurance Companies
Herriman, E. A., physician and surgeon
Hettger, August, peddler
Holmes, B., barber
Holtorf, Henry, cabinet maker
Hopkins, James, saw mill prop.
HUDSPETH, ADAM, barrister
Hudspeth, Robert
Hurd, P. A., attorney-at-law
Jackson, Andrew, jailor
Jeffrey, George, axe manufacturer
JEWETT, CHARLES S., Jr., prop Jewett House (see adv)
JEWETT, HOUSE, (Charles S. Jewett, jr., prop.,) (see adv)
Jewett's Saloon Restaurant, and Billiard Room, B. F. Jewett, proprietor
Jewett, B. F., prop. Jewitt's saloon and restaurant and billiard room
JOHNSTON, JOHN G., foreman *Canadian Post* printing office
Johnston, John, tailor
Keefe, John, shoemaker
Keeve, C. H., watchmaker and jeweler
Kempt, George, M.P., lumber merchant
Kempt, W., M.D
Kennedy, A., prop. Lindsay Carriage Factory
Kent, Thomas, (T. Foley & Co)
Kimball & Makins, (B. R. Kimball and John Makins) iron founders

Kimball, B. R, (Kimball & Makins)
Kleiser, Augustus, watchmaker and jeweler
LACOURSE, A., barrister, Clerk of the Peace, Crown attorney
Lancashire, Joseph, (Gillies & Lancashire)
Lenihan, James, dry goods, &c., and brewer
Lindsay's Hotel, H. F. Lindsay, prop.
Lindsay, H. F., prop. Lindsay's Hotel
Lisle, Joseph, (Lisle & Armstrong)
Lisle & Armstrong, (Joseph Lisle and William T. Armstrong) tanners and curriers
Lovell, James, harness maker
Lynch, F. J., principal Separate School
Lyons, John, boots and shoes
McCarthy, Jeremiah, cabinet maker
McDermott, Mrs. Isabella, grocer
McDonald, Angus, prop. Dominion House
McDougall, Neil, sheriff County of Victoria
McFeely, Edward, stoves and tinware
McKercher, Duncan, deputy sheriff, Court House
McKibbin, James, Clerk of Division Court
McLennan, John (McLennan & Co.)
McLennan, Donald (McLennan & Co.)
McLennan & Co. (John McLennan and Donald McLennan) hardware merchants
McNeil, William, tanner and currier
Macdonald, D., dry goods merchant
MACKAY, O. J., (Mackay & Heap)
MACKAY & HEAP (O. J. Mackay and James Heap) barristers, attorneys-at-law, etc.
Maguire, John, saloon
Maguire, Lawrence, boots and shoes
Mann, James Tudor, ledger keeper, Ontario Bank
Market Hotel, M. Myles, proprietor
Markham, Martin, boots and shoes
Martin, Caleb (Martin & Tweedie), Caleb Martin and Gilbert Tweedie), physicians and surgeons
Matthie, W. & J. (William and John) cabinet makers and wood turners
Maunder, John, butcher
Mitchell, C. J. grocer
Molony, Daniel, grocer
Montreal Telegraph Co.'s office, Charles Foley, operator
Morison, Malcolm, dry goods merchant
Morris, Edward, butcher
Murray, Hugh, tailor
Murray, Donald, turnkey at jail
Miles, Michael, proprietor Market Hotel
Nagle, Miss, assistant teacher separate school
Neads, Charles, teller Ontario Bank
Needler & Sadler, proprietor Lindsay mills
Needler, William, (Needler & Sadler)
NEELANDS, JACOB, dentist (see adv)
Niblock, Thomas, (Dobson & Niblock)
O'Connell, John, saloon keeper
O'Leary, A. P., township clerk of Ops, student at law
Ontario Bank Branch
Orde, C. B., attorney
Parsons, Samuel, blacksmith
Perrin, Samuel, (Thirkell & Perrin)
Pigott, Edward, grocer
Pitts, T. N., merchant tailor
Polson, G., auctioneer
PORTER, R. S., bookseller and stationer
Pyne, Thomas, proprietor Union Hotel
Quebec and Montreal Hotel, Treffly Fournier, prop
Railroad Hotel, T. Hanlon, proprietor
Randall, A., bookseller and stationer
Reazin, H., principal Union School
Roach, G. M., Crown Land agent
Robinson, Margaret, milliner
ROBINSON, C. B., editor and proprietor *Canadian Post*
Robinson, W. J., grocer
Robson, W. M., grocer
Roche, G. M., Crown Land Agent
RODDEN, J. C., proprietor Victoria Steam Brewery
RUSSELL, W. L., broker, commission merchant and auctioneer, agent Canadian Land and Emigration Company
Rutsay, Mrs., milliner and dress maker
St. Clair, Charles H., confectioner
Sadler, Thomas (Needler & Sadler)
Sanderson, James, grocer
Searl, George W., photographer
Skitch, William, wagon maker
Smith, George, carding mill proprietor
Smith, James, Judge County Court
Spier, Robert, general merchant
Spry, Simon, general blacksmith
Stafford, Rev. Michael (Roman Catholic)
Stephenson, George, tinware and stoves
Strudwick, Henry, clerk
Thirkell, John, carriage maker
Thirkell, W. J. (Thirkell & Perrin), agent Canada Life Assurance Co.
THIRKELL & PERRIN (W. J. Thirkell & Samuel Perrin), druggists, &c.
Thomas, D., dry goods
Trude, Samuel, shingle manufacturer
Truscott, Thomas, grocer
Turcot, R., dry goods
Tweedie, Gilbert (Martin & Tweedie)
Umphrey, Horace, grocer
Union Hotel, Thomas Pyne, proprietor
Veitch, E., proprietor Victoria House
Vicars, Rev. John (Church of England)
Victoria House, E. Veitch, proprietor
Victoria Warder (weekly), Joseph Cooper, editor and proprietor
WALLIS, H. A., grocer, wines and liquors
Ward, W. B., baker and confectioner
Watson, James, general merchant
Welch, George, oyster saloon and grocer
Weller, W. H., master in chancery
Whaley, Francis, assistant teacher Union School
Williamson, Joseph, butcher
Williamson, Samuel, butcher
WOOD, S. C., county clerk and treasurer, official assignee
Workman, H., livery stable proprietor
Wright, Miss Annabella, asst. teacher Union School
Wright, Alfred, boots and shoes
Wright, George, painter

Linton.—A small Village in the Township of King, County York, 33 miles from Toronto, the County Town. Population 35.

Acheson, Samuel, farmer
Adams, Rev. James, (Presbyterian)
Fox, William, farmer
Graham, Donald, farmer
Hay, Rev. William, (Methodist)
Hunter, James, J.P
Hunter, Robert, farmer
LYNN, JOSEPH, Postmaster
McDevitt, William, farmer
McLachlin, Hugh, farmer
McMurchy, James, teacher
McShannock, Archibald, farmer
Perry, William, farmer
Somerville, James, farmer
Stinson, William, farmer

Linwood.—A Village in the Township of Wellesley, County Waterloo, 18 miles from Berlin, the County Town, and 85 from Toronto. Population 200.

Bennett, Thomas, cabinet maker
Boomer, A., farmer
Boomer, A., insurance agent
Boomer, J. E., prop. lumber yard
Brash, James, wagon maker
Brown, John, farmer
Bundy, J., farmer
Bundy, John, wagon maker and painter
Crossman, E., painter
FISH, R. Y., Postmaster and gen. merchant
Gregory, John, prop. steam flouring mill
Hastings, William, J.P
Kidd, J. C., hotel keeper
Lovell, Rev. J., (Wesleyan)
McDonald, Dennis
Millikin, Rev. A., (Wesleyan)
Ovens, William, farmer
Patterson, D., teacher
Patterson, Mrs., milliner, &c
Schenowan, Christian, tailor
Schnurr, John, shoemaker
Scott, Robert, farmer
Shields, William, cooper
Smith, William farmer
Strang, Robert, prop. flax mill
Williams, J. R., farmer
Woodman, L., hotel keeper

Lisadel.—A Village on the river Maitland, in the Township of Howick, County Huron, 50 miles from Goderich, the County Town, and 9 from Wroxeter. Population 200.

Bresbin, Leonard, general merchant
Brown, George (Presbyterian)
Corbett, John, farmer
Dantzer, Joseph, shoemaker
Dilworth, Henry, lime and stone
Downey, James, farmer
Evans, John, farmer
Flood, J. Z., boots and shoes
James, William, waggon maker
Johnston, Alexander, farmer
Johnston, William, farmer
Kibbum, Stephen, hotel keeper
Miller, Rev. A. E. (Church of England)
MITCHELL, ARTHUR, Postmaster, commissioner, proprietor flouring mill and lumber dealer
Simson, J. H., teacher
Sotheran, Samuel, saddler
Sweetman, J. J., general merchant
Thomas, Elijah, wagon maker
Tindall, Rev. William, (New Connexion Methodist)
Walker, W. G., insurance agent
Williams & Driver, hide and leather dealers and tanners
Young, James, carpenter

Lisbon.—A Post Office in the Township of North Easthope, County Perth.

Lisburn.—*(See Villages too late for regular insertion at the end of this work.)*

Listowel.—*(See Villages too late for regular insertion at the end of this work.)*

Little Britain.—A Village in the Township of Mariposa, County Victoria, 10 miles from Lindsay, the County Town, 5 from Port Hoover, and 65 from Toronto. Population 200.

Andrews, John J., M.D.
Blewett & Deymen, blacksmiths
BROAD, JOHN, Postmaster and general merchant
Broad, J., tailor
Cullis, John, proprietor flouring mills
Ford, John, tailor
Foster, William, J.P.
Glass & Lobb, bent stuff manufacturer
Glass, John, farmer
Hambly, Mrs., milliner
Hicks, John, shoemaker
Jackson, William, hotel keeper
Loper, William, farmer
McWatters, James, saddler
McWatters, Mrs., milliner
Mark, John, farmer
Mark, Joseph, farmer
Metherell, L. F., general merchant
Mitherell, Seth, farmer
Morgan & Bro., shoemakers
Morgan, T., insurance agent
Murley, & Blewett, general merchants
Murley, John & Son, carpenters
Prior, James, teacher
Richardson, Mr., carpenter
Riley, John, wagon maker
Rogers, O., farmer
Rogers, Samuel, manufacturer woolen goods
Sailes & Smith, cabinet makers
Schell, George, blacksmith
Snooks, R. N., saddler
Whiteside, R. L., J.P., farmer

Little Current, or Waie-bidgi-wang.—A small Indian Village 12 miles across from La Cloche, on the North Shore of the Great Manitoulin. This is the calling place for all vessels going up the north shore of Lake Huron, and here the steamers usually wood.

BURKETT, G. P., Postmaster.

Little Rideau.—A Village in the Township of East Hawkesbury, County Prescott, 11 miles from L'Orignal, the County Town. Population 200.

Bellaregier, Joseph, hotel keeper
Bloomer, Henry, blacksmith
Cumming, William, cooper
Goudie, James, lime and stone
Gourly, John, blacksmith
Johnstone, Alexander, farmer
Johnstone, S., farmer
Johnstone, William, farmer
Kirby, John M., proprietor livery stable
Kirby, William, farmer
Little, John, farmer
Lovell, William, farmer
Ross, Robert, farmer
ROSS, THOMAS, Postmaster, general merchant
Waddell, John, J. P
Watson, James, carpenter
Wyman, Daniel B., farmer
Wyman, H. B., farmer

Lloydtown.—A Village in the Township of King, County York, 36 miles from Toronto, the County Town, and 12 from King Station Northern Railroad. Money order office. Population 300.

Agnew, W. H., dentist
Anderson, John, blacksmith
Armstrong, Arthur, jr., Clerk Division Court, insurance and commission agent
Ash, John, proprietor Mansion House
Brown, John, blacksmith
Brown, Thomas, (Seymour, S. & Co.)
Carson, Joseph, teacher
Cassidy, John, cooper
Cassidy, Thomas, cooper
Cooper, James, farmer
Davis & Irwin, general merchants
Devling, William, cabinet maker
Dodds, William, wagon maker
Doyle, James, farmer
Doyle, John, shoemaker
Duggan, James, proprietor Lloydtown Inn
Eastwood, Alfred, druggist
EASTWOOD, ANTHONY, J. P., Postmaster and general merchant
Edwards, George, tanner
Fanning, Bernard, hide and leather dealer
Farrier, —, (Seymour, Stogdill & Co.)
Hambler, William, shoemaker
Hay, Rev. William, (Wesleyan)
Henderson, James
Kane, Roger, tinsmith
Lawrence, James, farmer
Lloyd, William, farmer
Lodge, Robert, wagon maker
McDougal, James, farmer
McKenzie, Roderick, butcher
Maher, P., cabinet maker
Maloney, Mrs., milliner, etc.
Maloney, Patrick, shoemaker
Osler, Rev. H. B., (Church of England)
Pinkerton, John, farmer
Ramsey, Robert, wagon maker
Schofield, William, M.D.
Seymour, Stogdill & Co., proprietors woolen mills
Shanks, Peter, carpenter
Shaw, William, carpenter
Smith, John
Sparling, Rev. J., (Wesleyan)
Stogdill, Solomon
Tawse, Henry, proprietor brick yard
Thompson, William, farmer
Tyson, Henry, proprietor flouring mill
Tyson, Thomas W., proprietor flouring mill
Walsh, Robert, P.L.S., conveyancer, etc.
Williamson, Thomas, carpenter
Wright, John, carpenter

Lobo.—A Village in the Township of Lobo, County Middlesex, on the Ox Bow River, 11 miles from London, the County Town, and 5 from Komoka Station, Great Western Railway. Population 150.

Brown, J., farmer
Campbell, J., carpenter
Card, Rev. J., (Wesleyan)
Challoner, T., manuf. sash, doors, and blinds
Coakley, William, shoemaker
Cohoe, A., farmer
Cohoe, B., teacher
Edward, Henry, insurance agent
Edwards, N., real estate agent
Edwards, John N., J.P., farmer
EDWARDS, T. S., Postmaster
Fares, Henry, nurseryman
Fares, N., farmer
Ferguson, A., farmer
Ferguson, R., farmer
Gadsley, C., farmer
Goodhue, G. G., farmer
Graham, Duncan, farmer
Graham, P., teacher
Gray, John carpenter
Irvine, Joshua, architect
Irvine, Joshua, farmer
Johnston, D., farmer
Jackson, Rev. E., (Baptist)
Kelworth, W. M., prop. flouring and grist mill
Livingston, A., tailor
McArthur, A. A., farmer
McArthur, D. & A., proprietors brickyard
McDougall, William, butcher
McIntyre, J. B., wagon maker
McKeith, John, carpenter
McKeith, J. D., proprietor steam saw mill
McKellar, D., lumber dealer
McLeay, J. D., M.D.
McMillan, Rev. D. (Presbyterian)
McMurphy, D., dealer in lime and stone
McNeil, Rev. —, (Methodist)
McPhedrain, J., teacher
Monger, W. F., proprietor American House
Morrison, Neil, auctioneer
Murch, G., blacksmith
Night, B., farmer
Seaton, D., J.P., farmer
Scott, J. W., cheese manufacturer
Simpson, J., dealer in lime and stone
Smith, Alexander, shingle maker
Smith, D., manufacturer of sash, door and blinds
Ward, Hiram, patent right agent
Young, N., manufacturer of woolen goods

Loch Garry.—A Village in the Township of Kenyon, County Glengarry, on Loch Garry, 8 miles from Alexandria, the County Town. Population 100.

FRASER, JAMES, J.P., Postmaster
Grant, Donald, shoemaker
McDonald, John, innkeeper
McDonnell, Alexander, shoemaker
McPherson, Donald, teacher
O'Connor, Rev. J. S. (Roman Catholic)

Lochiel.—A Village in the Township of Lochiel, County Glengarry. Population 300.

Cameron, John, hotel keeper
Chisholm, Angus, proprietor livery stable and grocer
Chisholm, Valentine, tailor
Clark, James, attorney-at-law
Dewer, Robert, dentist and dealer in hardware, cutlery, &c.
Fraser, Donald, sash, door and blind manufacturer
Fraser, Findlay, dry goods dealer
Fraser, Simon, hide and leather dealer and tanner
Fraser, William, carpenter
Jameson, William, wagon maker
Kennedy, A. E., teacher
McBain, Archibald, proprietor flax mill
McCameron, Rev. — (Free Presbyterian)
McCraig, Angus, J.P.
McDonell, Rev. A. (Roman Catholic), J.P.
McDonell, A. R., hotel keeper
McDonell, D., shingle maker
McDonell, Hugh, dyer and scourer
McDonell, Margery, milliner
McGillivray, Malcolm, J.P.
McIntosh, James, J.P.
McKay, Rev. — (Presbyterian)
McKenzie, John, auctioneer
McLeander, Donald, shoemaker
McMillan, D., butcher
McMillan, John, cooper and gunsmith
McNab, Archibald, J.P.
McNeil, Findlay, saddler
McPhee, Alexander, telegraph operator and lumber dealer
Miller & Campbell, tinsmiths
Quigley, Owen, J.P., dealer in groceries, crockery, queen's ware, &c.
Rankin, A., painter
Robertson, William, prop. flouring mill
SIMPSON, JAMES, Postmaster, gen. merch
Simpson, James, jun., M.D
Stewart, John, insurance agent
Urquhart, Allan, teacher

Lockton.—A small Village on the River Humber, in the Township of Albion, County Peel, 20 miles from Brampton, the County Town, and 30 from Toronto. Population 30.

Bambrick, R., hotel keeper
Clary, Rev. R., (Church of England)
Judge, J., general merchant
Kenny, J., farmer
Lock, A., farmer
Lock, W., farmer
Lucy, R., farmer
Squires, W., farmer
Taylor, W., farmer
TUTHILL, J. V., Postmaster, gen. mercht
Wallis, J., farmer

Logierait.—A Post-office in the Township of Moore, County Lambton, 6 miles from Sarnia, the County Town. Improved land averages, $30 and wild $14 per acre.

Bell, C., farmer
Burr, R. N., farmer
Carr, T., farmer
Carruthers, F., carpenter
Cole, William, farmer
Collum, D., farmer
Cruise, J., farmer
Davidson, John, carpenter
Decoursey, P., farmer
Fleck, R., J.P
Gibb, A., farmer
Guanan, Thodore, carpenter
Hossie, A., farmer
HOSSIE, D., Postmaster and nurseryman
Hossie, Robert, J.P., carpenter
Jackson, J., J.P.
McGregor, A., farmer
Millikin, M., farmer
Scott, P., farmer
Simpson, William, farmer
Stewart, William, farmer
Thornton, J., J.P.

Londesboro'.—A Village in the Township of Hullett, County Huron, on the Maitland River, 18 miles from Goderich, the County Town. Population 150.

Asknish, Robert, proprietor brick yard
Brandson & Whenhan, wagon makers
Campbell, James, general merchant
Campbell, James, farmer
Dickson, John, proprietor flouring mill
Graham, William, farmer
Haggard, T., farmer
Hawk, Rev., William, (Wesleyan)
Hill, Thomas, shoemaker
Kellain, Rev. Henry, (Wesleyan)
Knott, Henry, wagon maker
Manning, James, wagon maker
Morrow, Charles, J.P.
NEELAND, JOHN, Postmaster and gen. merchant
Smyth, Charles, shoemaker
Sterling, George, farmer
Walker, David, farmer
Walker, Mrs. Ann, hotel keeper
Walker, John, butcher
Watson, William, lime and stone
Woodman, Arthur, tailor
Witts, Charles, cabinet maker

London.—The chief seat of the County of Middlesex, beautifully situated on the River Thames, was first settled in 1825, and was incorporated as a City in 1855. A desire has evidently been manifested to imitate the metropolis of the British Empire, as the names of the streets and bridges strongly indicate. The public buildings generally as well as many of the private residences are noble specimens of architecture, and are chiefly built of brick or stone; the streets are wide, laid out at right angles, and lighted with gas. The surrounding country is noted for the culture of grain and all other farm produce. London vies favourably with other Cities of Ontario in manufacturing enterprise: there are several extensive foundries and machine shops, four large flouring mills, the celebrated breweries of Messrs. W. & J. Carling and Labatt & Co., several tanneries and oil refineries, and as regards the manufacture of carriages London stands unrivalled. There is a Board of Trade and all the Banks of the Province have branches or agencies here. Three daily papers, besides several weeklies are published here. The *Free Press*, *Prototype* and *Times* being the most influential. The Churches are numerous, all the principal denominations being represented. St. Paul's Cathedral is a handsome Gothic structure built of stone. The other church edifices are also handsomely and substantially built, forming ornaments to the City. The Huron College incorporated May, 1863, provides instruction for candidates for Holy Orders in the United Church of England and Ireland, and also receives students desirous of obtaining instruction in the higher branches of education. The Hellmuth College incorporated 1865 is situated on a beautiful site, the grounds of which comprise ten acres. It was founded by the Very Rev. I. Hellmuth, D.D., Dean of Huron, who is also actively engaged in establishing a similar institution for females, the site of which is already secured. There are also two Roman Catholic Institutions, viz.: the Academy of the Sacred Heart, and the Sacred Heart Convent. The Crystal Palace is a handsome and commodious building, and its grounds spacious and attractive, besides the Provincial Exhibitions being occasionally held here, a local Fair has lately been established with great success, including the County of Middlesex and City of London Associations which is intended to be held annually. London enjoys excellent railroad communications. The Great Western Railway passes through the City, connecting with all points east and west, also with a branch to Sarnia. The Grand Trunk has a branch railroad to St. Mary's, there is also a railway direct to Port Stanley. Distance from Hamilton 76 miles, from Toronto, 115 miles, from Montreal, 447 miles, from Sarnia, 56 miles, and St. Thomas, 15. Population about 18,000.

CITY CORPORATION.

City Hall, Richmond Street, regular Meetings every alternate Monday, J. Christy, Mayor. 1st Ward, Edward Glackmayer, B. Wheeler, Andrew, McCormick; 2nd Ward: S. McBride, J. B. Smyth, John Campbell; 3rd Ward: David Hughes, William Farris, W. Nichol; 4th Ward: Alexander Murray, Hewett Fysh, W. S. Smith; 5th Ward: S. H. Graydon, R. Smith, M. Anderson; 6th Ward: John Christy, T. Peel, George Macbeth; 7th Ward: Thomas Partridge, jun., Thomas Partridge, sen., James Egan. *Police Court:* Police Magistrate, Lawrence Lawrason, Clerk, A. S. Abbott, High Bailiff and Chief of Police, Richard Wigmore. *Fire Brigade*: Chief engineer, Samuel Stewart, Phœnix Company, (Hand Engine), Captain John Ponsons, Forest, City Company, (Steamer), Captain Hewitt Fysh, Hook and Ladder Company, Captain E. S. Bilton.

COUNTY AND JUDICIAL OFFICERS.

County Officers.—County Town, London; Thomas Rutledge, of Medcalfe, Warden; Adam Murray, Treasurer; James Keefer, County Clerk; William Elliot, Solicitor; Charles W. Connor, County Engineer; David Wyllie, and James Johnston, County Auditors; James Ferguson, County Registrar; Dr. Hobbs, Surgeon of Gaol. *Judicial Officers.*—Honourable James E. Small, County Judge; James Shanley, Master-in-Chancery; J. E. Parker, Deputy County Judge; Charles Hutchinson, County Attorney; Wililam Glass, Sheriff; John Guernsey, Deputy Sheriff; John McBeth, Clerk of Crown, Clerk of County Court, and Registrar of Surrogate; Joseph Lamb, Governor of Gaol; John B. Askin, Clerk of the Peace. *County of Middlesex Registry Office.*—James Ferguson, Registrar; office hours, from 10 A.M. to 3 P.M.

EDUCATIONAL.

Academy of the Sacred Heart, conducted by the sisters of the Sacred Heart, Mother Superior Bastide. *Sacred Heart Convent* in connection with the above. *Hellmuth College.*—Visitor the Right Rev. the Lord Bishop of Huron; President of the Corporation, The Very Rev. I. Hellmuth, D.D., Dean of Huron; Head Master, the Rev. Arthur Sweatman, M.A. *Huron College.*—President of the incorporation, the Right Rev. the Lord Bishop of Huron. Officers of the College: Principal and Divinity, Professor Rev. T. Brock, M.A.; Professor of Classics and Mathematics, Rev. W. H. Halpin, M.A.; Bursar, V.

Cronyn, Esq., B.C.L. ; Librarian, John R. Wilson. *Central School.*—Located between King and York, J. B. Boyle, principal ; Primary School, No. 1, Horton St., No. 2, Talbot St., No. 3, Waterloo St., No. 5, Colborne St., No. 6, Bond St., No. 7, Waterloo St., St. Peter's School, Roman Catholic, Richmond St.

CHURCHES.

Church of England, (St. Paul's Cathedral, Richmond Street, Right Rev. Benjamin Cronyn, D.D., Bishop; Very Rev. Isaac Hellmuth, Dean; Rev. J. M. Innes and R. H. Starr, Curates: hours of service 11 a. m. and 6.30 p. m. ; Military service 9 a. m. Christ Church, (Church of England,) Wellington corner Hill, Rev. John Smyth, Incumbent, Rev. Benjamin Bayly, assistant: services 11 a. m. and 6.30 p. m. St. John's Chapel, Huron College, Rev. Prof. Halpin. St. James' (Church of Scotland,) head of Richmond Street, Rev. F. Nicol: services 11 a. m. and 6.30 p. m. Canada Presbyterian, (St. Andrew's Church,) North Street, Rev. John Scott: services 11 a.m. and 6.30 p.m. Canada Presbyterian Church, Clarence Street, Rev. James J. Proudfoot: services 11 a.m. and 6.30 p.m. Roman Catholic Church, (St. Peter's) Richmond, corner Duke Street, clergymen, Right Rev. John Walsh, D.D., Bishop, Very Rev. J. M. Bruyere, V. G. Rev. W. Flannery, Rev. F. O. J. Ouellet, Rev. P. O'Shea: first mass 7 a.m., second mass and sermon for military 8½ a.m., third mass and sermon 10½ a.m., vespers and sermon 6½ p.m. Congregational Church, King Street, Rev. James A. R. Dickson: 11 a.m. and 6:30 p.m. Methodist Episcopal Church, North Street, Rev. P. Smith: services 10.30 a.m. and 6.30 p.m. North Street Wesleyan Methodist, North, corner Clarence Street: services 10.30 a.m. and 6.30 p.m. Adelaide Street Wesleyan Methodist Church: services 10:30 a.m., and 6.30 p.m. Pall Mall Wesleyan Methodist Church: services 10:30 a.m. and 6:30 p.m. New Connexion Methodist Church, Clarence Street: services 10.30 a.m. and 6 p.m. Primitive Methodist Church, King Street: services 10:30 a.m. and 6 p.m. Bible Christian Church, Horton Street, Rev. E. Roberts: services 10.30 a.m., and 6 p.m. Regular Baptist Church, corner Talbot and York Streets, Rev. James Cooper: services 11 a.m. and 6.30 p.m. Free Baptist Church, Clarence Street: services 10.30 a.m. and 6 p.m. Baptist Church, (colored) Horton Street: services 11 a.m. and 6 p.m. Methodist Episcopal Church (colored) Thames Street: services 10 a.m. and 6 p.m.

BANKS.

Bank of Montreal (branch) and Savings Bank, Richmond Street, F. W. Thomas, manager; S. J. Stammers, accountant; Savings Bank, J. T. Boyd, clerk. Bank of British North America, Richmond Street, Hugh Simpson, manager; J. P. Lawless, accountant. Merchants' Bank, Richmond Street, William F. Harper, manager; William Kingsley, accountant. Canadian Bank of Commerce, Richmond Street, H. S. Strathy manager; Henry S. Scadding, accountant.

CUSTOM HOUSE.

Office—Albion Buildings, Richmond Street, south of the Post-office. J. B. Strathy, Collector; Duff Cameron, Surveyor; Richard Abbott, Appraiser; Edward S. Collett, Chief Clerk; Richard Irvine and John Dorothy, Landing Waiters; Henry Boyd, Messenger.

POST OFFICE DEPARTMENT.

London Division.—G. E. Griffin, inspector; George Cox, H. J. Johnson, Andrew Thomson, and Frank Cronyn, clerks.

London Post Office.—Lawrence Lawless, Postmaster; R. J. C. Dawson, Deputy Postmaster; Joseph Gordon, Flemming French, J. D. Sharman, H. D. Dalton, John Hunter, John McLaughlin and R. F. Matthews, clerks; J. Nicholls, letter carrier; Martin O'Meara, porter; office hours, 8 a.m. to 7 p.m.

BOARD OF TRADE.

Annual meeting for the election of officers held on the last Friday in April. General business meeting held every three months.

NEWSPAPERS.

Free Press.—Published daily and tri-weekly, J. & S. Blackburn, editors and proprietors, Richmond street, opposite North street. *Prototype.*—Published daily and weekly, by John Siddons; H. Hunter, editor; office, Dundas, corner of Talbot street. *Advertiser.*—Published every evening. John Cameron, editor and proprietor; Henry Gorman, local editor; office, Dundas, between Ridout and Talbot streets. *Evangelical Witness.*—(The organ of the Wesleyan Methodist New Connexion Body). Rev. J. H. Robinson, editor; published weekly, at the office of the *Advertiser.* *Farmer's Advocate.*—A monthly issue, devoted to the agricultural interests of the country; W. Weld, editor and proprietor; office, Talbot street. *The Educator.*—A monthly periodical, devoted to the interests of practical education, is published on the 15th or the 16th of each month, by Jones & Co., office, Richmond street, opposite City Hall.

HORTICULTURAL AND AGRICULTURAL SOCIETY.

Horticultural and Agricultural Society of the Electoral Division of the City of London.—James Johnson president; James N. Cousins, vice-president; William McBride, secretary, John Stewart, treasurer.

LITERARY SOCIETIES, ETC.

Church of England Young Men's Association, organized March 1st, 1868. President, the Very Rev. I. Hellmuth, D.D., Dean of Huron; vice-presidents, Rev. J. Smyth and Rev. H. Starr; corresponding secretary, J. Dyas; recording secretary, J. Pope; treasurer, G. F. Jewell; librarian, William McMullen; room, Church Society's building, Richmond street. Mechanics' Institute, building on Talbot street, opposite William street. London Literary Society, meet every Wednesday evening, Victoria Buildings, Richmond Street. London Dramatic Club, meet at Clarence House, Clarence street.

SAVINGS AND LOAN SOCIETY.

The Huron and Erie Savings and Loan Society.—Directors: W. Hman, president; Charles Stead, vice-president; William Boyer, managing director; solicitor, V. Cronyn, LL.B.; secretary and treasurer, Charles Murray; accountant, Thomas Boyer.

GAS COMPANY.

London City Gas Company—Office and works, Horton street, corner of Ridout street—Charles Hunt, president; Daniel Macfie, vice-president; Thomas Drought, secretary; Peter Rimmer, manager of works.

LOCAL INSURANCE COMPANIES.

The Agricultural Mutual Association of Canada—Head office, Ridout street, London—Officers: Crowell Willson, president; William R. Vining, vice-president; William Niles, general agent and inspector; F. E. Cornish, solicitor; A. G. Smyth (Auditor City of London), James Hamilton, auditors; Alexander Macdonald, D. C. Macdonald, joint secretaries. *The Ontario Mutual Fire Insurance Company*—Office: Richmond street, opposite City Hall.—Officers: Alderman S. McBride, president; Capt. T. Wilson, vice-president; James Johnson, Esq., secretary and treasurer; A. J. B., Macdonald, Esq., solicitor; Thomas Greene, Esq., general agent and inspector.

Abbott, Alexander R. (Abbott & Maylard) h Talbot
Abbott, Alexander S., city clerk, City Hall
Abbott, Christopher C. (Abbott & Hutchinson)
Abbott, H. G. (Abbott Bros)., h Dundas
Abbott, Richard, appraiser
Abbott, Samuel W., (Abbott Bros.) h North
ABBOTT, BROS., carriage makers, Dundas nr Wellington
Abbott & Hutchinson (C. C. Abbott and Charles Hutchinson) barristers, Dundas
ABBOTT & MAYLARD, groceries and provisions, Market Square
Abraham, William, carriage maker, Bathurst
ACADEMY OF THE SACRED HEART, East Dundas
Adair, John, insurance agent
ADAMS, EDWARD (E. Adams & Co.) h Duke
Adams, Joseph, artist and dentist, Richmond opp North
ADAMS, EDWARD & CO., wholesale grocers, Dundas bet Talbot and Ridout
ÆTNA FIRE INSURANCE COMPANY, of Dublin, F. S. Clarke, agent, Richmond
Ætna Insurance Company (Hartford, Conn.), R. Waddell, agent, Talbot
AGNEW, J. Washington, M.D., Dundas cor Waterloo
AGRICULTURAL EMPORIUM, William Weld, proprietor, Talbot
AGRICULTURAL MUTUAL ASSURANCE ASSOCIATION OF CANADA, Crowell Willson, president, W. R. Vining, vice-president, Alexander and D. C. Macdonald, joint secretary, Ridout
ALANSON, JOHN, grain and commission, York nr Richmond
Alda, John H., grocer, Wellington nr Hill
Allaster, John, brewer, Dundas
ALLEY, HENRY B. B., dry goods, &c., Dundas
AMERICAN EXPRESS COMPANY, James T. Boniface, agent, Richmond
AMERICAN HOUSE, Samuel Grigg, proprietor, Richmond cor York (see adv.)
Amiraux, T., physician, Mill nr George
Anderson, Alexander, M.D., Ridout
ANDERSON, EDWARD (M. & E. Anderson), h Hitchcock
Anderson, James and George, carpenters, Cartwright
ANDERSON, MURRAY (M. & E. Anderson), h Dundas
ANDERSON, M. & E., proprietors Globe Foundry, stove founders, &c. (see adv.)
Anderson, Thomas, painter, South
Andrus, Brothers, melodeon makers, King bet Clarence and Wellington
Ansell, Thomas, fancy goods, Dundas nr Richmond
Anundson, Christian, cabinet maker, Dundas
Arkell, Robert, M.D., h Ridout
Arkell, Robert (Lucas & Arkell), h Ridout
Arscott, Richard, tanner, corner George and Ann
Ashton, A. E., insurance agent, Ridout
Ashton, Charles J., boot and shoe maker, Dundas
Ashston, Miss M., berlin wool, &c., Dundas
Ashworth, John, photographer, Richmond
Askin, John B., clerk of peace, h Westminster
Aston, Thomas, engraver and working jeweler, Dundas
Atkinson, J., pump maker, Richmond cor Hitchcock
Atkinson, Joseph (J. Atkinson & Co.) h e Dundas
ATKINSON, J. & CO., wholesale small wares, dry goods, &c., Dundas, bet Talbot & Market Lane (see adv.)
ATLANTIC PETROLEUM WORKS, Waterman & Brothers, proprietors, Hamilton Road (see adv.)
Bailey, William J., Empire Hop Yard, h Waterloo
Baillie, Hugh, carpenter, Grey
Baker, Isaac W. C., silver plater, stoves and tinware Dundas

Baker, Daniel, prop Brock Hotel, Talbot cor York
Baker, John, bailiff, King
BAKER, JOHN E., fruits and confectionery, Richmond nr P. O.
BALKWILL, WILLIAM, prop. Balkwill's Hotel, Talbot corner King
Ball, John, tailor, Dundas
Ball, William H., county constable, Dundas e of Adelaide
Barnfather, W. C., foreman G. W. R., h Horton
BANK OF BRITISH NORTH AMERICA, Hugh Simpson, manager, Richmond
BANK OF MONTREAL, F. W. Thomas, manager, Richmond corner Fullarton
Barham, Thomas, baker, Ridout
BARKER, SAMUEL (Becher, Barker & Street), h Waterloo
Barker, William, assistant clerk C. H.
BARNARD, PETER C., auction and commission Richmond
BARNWELL, G. T., station master G.W.R., office Depot
Baskerville, William, sergeant police, Mill
BAWDEN, WILLIAM, auctioneer and general agent Talbot, nr Dundas (see adv)
Baxter, H. A., lumber merchant, cor Kent and Mkt Lane
Bayles, Thomas, hairdresser, Richmond
Bayley, Richard, barrister, Ridout
Bayley, Adam & Co., oil refiners
Bayly, Rev. B., A.B., head master Grammar School
BEATTIE, THOMAS, (T. Beattie & Co)
BEATTIE, T. & Co., importers of dry goods, millinery, &c., Dundas
Beatty, John, cooper, King, nr Talbot
BECHER, HENRY, (Becher, Barker & Street) h Thornwood
BECHER, H. C. R., Q.C. (Becher, Barker & Street), h Thornwood
BECHER, BARKER & STREET, (H. C. R. Becher, Q.C., Samuel Barker, W. P. R. Street & Henry Becher) barristers, &c., North
BEDDOME, T. B., broker, insurance and general agent, Albion Buildings, Richmond
BEDDOME & DEMPSTER, agents. Travelers' Ins. Co., Albion Buildings, Richmond
BEECHER, GEORGE, silver plater, Dundas, bet Clarence & Wellington
Begg, William, boots and shoes, Dundas nr Market Lane
Begley, John, confectioner Dundas
Bell, Archibald, barrister, Ridout, cor north
Bell, Rev. James, (N.C. Methodist) h e Horton
Bell, John H., prof. book-keeping London Commercial College
Bell, William, (Davis & Bell) h Horton
Belton, James H., (Willis, Belton & Co.) h King
BELTZ, EDMUND, hatter and furrier, 85 Dundas
BELTZ, HENRY, sr., carpenter, Horton
BELTZ, HENRY, jr., hatter and furrier, 85 Dundas
Bennett, Charles, undertaker, King bet Richmond and Clarence
Benson, William D., h Burwell
Bentley, Henry, grocery, King bet Richmond & Talbot
Bergin, Patrick, Simcoe
Besott, Frederick, Talbot
Bickell, John, fruiterer, Richmond
Bilton, E. S. & Co., (E. S. and Joseph), soda water manufacturers Dundas nr Wellington
Birkett, Mrs. Mary Ann, boarding house e Horton
BIRRELL, JOHN, (John Birrell & Co.), h Westminster
BIRRELL, GEORGE S, (John Birrell & Co.)
BIRRELL, W. H., (John Birrell & Co., h Westminster
BIRRELL, JOHN & CO., (John, George and W. H.) wholesale dry goods, North
Bishop, Rev. J. H., (Wesleyan)
BLACKBURN, JOSIAH, (J. & S. Blackburn), h Ridout, cor Market
BLACKBURN, STEPHEN, J. & S. Blackburn), h Dundas, bet Waterloo and Colborne
BLACKBURN, J. & S., (Josiah, and Stephen), editors and proprietors *Free Press*, Richmond opp North
Blair, John, city collector, office City Hall
Blakeney, Thomas, book-keeper Merchants' Bank
Block, Louis, butcher, Wellington, cor Grey
Blount, Rev. G. R., (Methodist Episcopal) Bathurst cor Thames
Bodie, Mrs. Margaret, milliner, Clarence cor Simcoe
Bolton, James, carpenter and builder, Talbot, near Hitchcock
BONIFACE, JAMES T., agent American and Canadian Express Cos., Albion bldgs., Richmond
BOSTWICK, EDWARD, saloon and billiards, Richmond opp City Hall
Bowman, Daniel M., commercial traveler, h Adelaide
BOWMAN, WILLIAM, supt. L. & P. S. R. R., h Colborne nr Bond (see adv)
BOWMAN, WILLIAM, Jun., cigars and tobacco, Richmond cor Dundas
Boyd, Archibald, tailor, King nr Richmond
BOYD, JAMES T., clerk Savings Bank, (Montreal), h Cartwright
Boyd, John, policeman, h Grey nr Clarence
Boyd, J. T., cashier Bank of Montreal, Savings Bank, Richmond
Boyd, Robert, merchant tailor, Dundas
Boyd, William, tailor
BOYER, THOMAS, accountant Huron and Erie Savings and Loan Society, h Mill
BOYER, WILLIAM, manager and director Huron and Erie Savings and Loan Society, h Mill
BOYLE, JAMES B., Principal Central School, h Dundas nr Burwell
Bragg, Charles, cooper, Richmond
Bragg, Frederick, cooper, Richmond
Bremner, Alexander J., foreman "Free Press"
Brecklan, Charles, butcher, King cor. Ridout
Briant, Henry (E. Adams & Co.) h Talbot
Brierly, Thomas, oil refiner, Adelaide, nr limits
British America, Assurance Company (Toronto) George B. Scott, Agent, Talbot
Briton Medical and General Life Assurance, A. G. Smyth, Agent, Albion buildings
BROCK, T., M. A., principal Huron College
Brophy, John, grocer, Colborne
Brough, Richard R., solicitor, Dundas
Brouse, C. J., Dundas
Brown, Charles, saloon, City Hall buildings
BROWN, JOHN, city chamberlain, City Hall, h Talbot
Brown, Vesey, M. D., Kent, near Mark Lane
Browne, Richard, Ridout, North
Brummitt R., buggy spring maker, Ridout
Brunton, William Y., Mica miner, St. James
Bruyere, Very Rev., J. M. (V. G.) Bishop's Palace, Duke
Buckle, William D., local editor London "Prototype"
Bunning, John W., fruits and confectionery, Richmond
Burke, Edmond, photographer, Richmond
Burns, George, dry goods, Dundas

Burridge, John, boots and shoes, King cor. Talbot
Burrows, George, band-box maker, Adelaide, near Hamilton road
Burrows, R. W., barrel factory, e Simcoe
Burton, James, grocer, Adelaide
Butler, Henry, h Wellington
Butler, H., money-lender, Richmond cor. King
Butler, H., h Wellington, near Horton
Butler, Gen. Thomas J., (C. S. A.) h Piccadilly
BYRNE, MILES, groceries and liquors, Richmond
Caldwell, Thomas, cabinet maker, King, bet Richmond and Talbot
Campbell, Alexander, manuf. sash, doors, blinds, &c. Bathurst
CAMPBELL, ANGUS M., (J. A. Johnson & Co.) Music Hall, Richmond
Campbell, Clarence T., M.D., office, Richmond
Campbell, Francis, prop. Royal Hotel, Richmond
Campbell, John, watchmaker and jeweler, Dundas nr Talbot
Campbell, John, carriage factory, King nr Talbot
Campbell R., butcher, 16 Market House
Cameron, Duff, surveyor C.H., h James
CAMERON, JOHN, prop. *Evening Advertiser*, Dundas w
Cameron, William, sen., book-keeper *Advertiser*
CANADIAN BANK OF COMMERCE, H. S. Strathy manager, Albion Buildings, Richmond
CANADIAN BUILDER AND MECHANICS' MAGAZINE, Richmond (see adv.)
CANADIAN EXPRESS COMPANY, James T. Boniface, agent, Richmond
CANADA LIFE ASSURANCE CO., F. S. Clarke, Richmond, n of Dundas
Cannell, Miss Jane, milliner, Horton
Carey, George, (McKenzie & Carey)
Carey, William, (E. A. Taylor & Co)
CARLING, HON. JOHN; (W. & J. Carling)
CARLING, W., (W. & J. Carling)
CARLING, W. & J., props. City Brewery, Waterloo
Carpenter, Mrs. Jane, boarding house, Hamilton Road
Carter, Robert, prop. Farmers' Home, Dundas
Cattermole, James, M.D., King nr Waterloo
Chalcraft, Frank, butcher, Hamilton Road
Chalmers, William, saloon keeper, Richmond
Chaplow, James, prop. Court House Hotel
Chapman, Albert T., (Smith, Chapman & Co.) h Hitchcock
CHAPMAN, CHARLES, book binder, stationer, &c. Dundas, nr Talbot (see adv)
Chisholm, Andrew (A. Chisholm & Co) h Kent
Chisholm, Hiram, commercial traveler, Dundas, nr William
CHISHOLM, A. & Co., (A. Chisholm and Alexander J. G. Henderson), dry goods, chothing, etc., Dundas
Church, Frank, prop. Brighton Arms, Wellington
Churcher, Thomas, provision merchant and official assignee, Market Square
City Hospital, Chas. Moore, M.D., physician, Thames
Clare, John, K., accountant *Free Press* office
Clark, Alexander, shoemaker, Hamilton Road
Clark, A. & R., barbers, Richmond
Clark, William, agent Bible and Tract Society
CLARKE, FRANCIS S., banker, exchange broker, and insurance agent Richmond (see adv)
Clegg, John, grocer, cor Clarence and Simcoe
Clegg, Robert E.: fruit and confectionery, Richmond bet King and York
Cleghorn, Andrew, (Ed. Adams & Co.) Dundas cor Colborne
Cobbleditch, William, butcher, Burwell
Code, W. H., lumber merchant, cor Clarence and York
Cole, Edwin, chair maker, Talbot nr York
Collett, David, barrister, h Pall Mall
Collett, Edward S., chief clerk Custom House
Collison, Mrs. M. A., milliner, Dundas nr Clarence
Commercial Union Insurance Co., A. H. Beddome, agent, Albion bdgs
Comstock, Henry, grocer, Talbot
Connor, C. H., B.A., master Hellmuth College
Connor, John, boot and shoe maker, Market Square
Conway, Thomas, boarding house, Bathurst nr Wellington
Cook, J., photographer, Richmond
Cook, Philip, boots and shoes, Dundas w of Clarence
Coombs, William, prop. Bell Inn, Talbot nr York
Cooper Edmund H., blacksmith, King cor Talbot
COOPER, FRANK, photographer, Richmond opp City Hall (see adv)
Cooper, Rev. James, (Baptist), Talbot cor Horton
COOPER, JOHN, photographer, Dundas, bet Richmond and Clarence
Cooper, William D., (Mahan, Hillson & Cooper) h William
Co. Operative Association of London, Dundas w, of Market Lane
Coote, William, prop. livery stable, Dundas nr Clarence
CORNISH, FRANCIS E., (Cornish & Macdonald) h Talbot
CORNISH & MACDONALD, (F. E. Cornish & Alex. J. B. Macdonald) barristers, Dundas nr Talbot
Corrigan, Christopher S., barrister, Dundas, bet Ridout and Talbot
Cottrell, George, assistant collector inland revenue, h King, cor William
COUSINS, JAMES M., pump, fanning mill and straw cutter manufacturer, Bathurst nr Talbot
Cousins, Job B., pump maker, Wellington
Cousins, John, fanning mill maker
Cowan & Wright, (James Cowan & James Wright) general hardware, Dundas
Cox, Joseph, carpenter, Dundas, nr Wellington
Craig, James & Co., manufs. of botanic medicines, Dundas, nr Talbot
Crawford, Lambert F., homoeopathic physician, Richmond, opp P.O
Cregg, John L., hotel keeper, Burlington
CRESSALL, JOSEPH, manager Penitentiary boot and shoe store, Dundas (see adv)
Crittle, William, grocer, Dundas, cor Burwell
Crocker, James, broker, Ridout
Crofts, Benjamin, (Green, Crofts & Co) h Simcoe
CRONYN, RIGHT REV. BENJAMIN, D.D., Lord Bishop of Huron, res See House Westminster
CRONYN, BENJAMIN, (Cronyn & Cronyn) h Adelaide, cor North
CRONYN, VERSCHOYLE, (Cronyn & Cronyn) h Dundas
CRONYN & CRONYN, barristers, Dundas bet Talbot and Ridout
Crook, John, blacksmith, King nr Talbot
CROOKS, HIRAM, manuf. of Wahoo Bitters, Rich mond, bet York and King
Currie, Donald, agent Hendrie & Co., cartage agent G.W.R. freight office
Currie, William L., bookseller, Richmond
Curtis, Henry, C., grocer, Dundas nr Wellington
CUSTOM HOUSE, Albion Buildings, Richmond J B. Strathy; collector
Dalton, Charles (Dalton Brothers)

Dalton, Joseph, butcher, 4 Market House
Dalton, Joseph D., (Dalton Brothers)
Dalton, Joshua D. (Dalton Brothers)
Dalton Brothers, manufacturers of soap and candles, cor York and Thames
Darch, Mrs. J., saddles and harness, Talbot opposite Market
Darch, Robert, saddle and harness maker, King bet Richmond and Talbot
Dark, William P., plasterer, h York
DART, ROGER, prop., Dominion Carriage Works, Dundas, bet Wellington and Waterloo (see adv)
Darvill & Robb, founders and machinists, King bet Ridout and Talbot
Davidson, R. S. T. & Co., dry goods and clothing, Dundas cor Richmond
Davies, Mrs. David, boarding house, Wellington
Davis, Henry, watchmaker and Jeweller, Dundas e of Richmond
Davis, Dr. Elisha, Dundas near Ridout.
Davis & Bell, (John Davis and William Bell) barbers, Dundas
Dawson, Benjamin, h North
DAWSON, RICHARD, J. C., assistant Postmaster, h Dundas
Dawson & Brother (M. D. & W. Dawson) book & job printers, Richmond
Deadman, James, painter, Talbot
Dean, William, grocer, Mark Lane
DELL, FREDERICK J., groceries and liquors, Richmond cor King (see adv.)
DEMPSTER, WILLIAM, insurance agent, Albion buildings, Richmond
Denison, George H., agent for Voltaic soles and bands
Denton, John M., merchant tailor, Albion buildings, Richmond
DERBY, JAMES C., manager Tecumseh House, Richmond cor York
Devlin, Robert, with E. Beltz, Dundas
Dewey, William, goldsmith, Dundas near Talbot
Dewyer, William, marble cutter, h Colborne
Diprose, Henry, grocer, Wellington cor South
Dodd, John C., & Son, carpenters and builders, e North near Clarence
Dodson, William, (Dodson & Perkin) Dundas cor Wellington
Dodson, & Perkin, butchers, 17 and 18 Market bdgs
Dorothy, John, landing waiter G. T. R
Douthwaite, Charles, soap and candles, Adelaide opp Duke
Doyle, John, saddle and harness maker, King bet Richmond and Talbot
DRANGER, JOHN, new and second hand clothing plated ware, &c., Dundas bet Clarence and Wellington (see adv)
Drought, Thomas, secretary Gas Company, Talbot bet York and King
Drury, Thomas, h Hill bet Waterloo and Colborne
Duffield Brothers, oil refiners, Hamilton Road
Dulmage, John, proprietor Ontario Hotel, King bet Richmond and Talbot
Dundas, James F., proprietor Central Inn, Dundas nr Wellington
Dunn, James, saddler, Market Square
Dunnett, Charles, proprietor Baths foot of Dundas
Durand, William, boots and shoes, Dundas
DUTTON, SAMUEL, saloon and restaurant, Dundas bet Talbot and Ridout
DYAS & WILKENS, (T. W. Dyas, P.L.S., and H. A. Wilkens) architects and patent agents, Richmond (see adv)
Dyer, Wm., groceries & provisions, Hamilton Road
DYSON, WILLIAM, stoves and tinware, manufacturer of cheese vats, milk cans, &c., Dundas nr Richmond (see adv)
Eastman, Rev. C. S., (Episcopal Methodist) h Waterloo nr King
Eckley, Henry K., commission merchant, Richmond
Edinburgh Life Assurance Company, L. Lawrason, agent, Albion building, Richmond
Edwards, John, stoves and tinware, Richmond opp Roman Catholic Church
Edwards, William, grocer, cor Wellington and Simcoe
Efner, Abraham, bending factory, York e of Adelaide
Egan, James, photographer, Dundas
Eldridge, John, baker, Clarence nr King
Elliott, James, teacher, London Commercial College
ELLIOTT, JOHN, proprietor Phœnix Foundry Bathurst cor Wellington
Elliott, Joseph H., wool and commission, n w cor Market Square
Elliott, William, stone and brick builder and roofer, Wellington nr Dundas
ELLIOTT, BROS., (John B. and Charles H.), groceries and liquors, 90 Dundas
Elliot & Fraser, (William Elliot and James H. Fraser) barristers, cor Richmond and Dundas
Ellwood, Garner, J.P., King, e of Adelaide
Elson, John, sen., butcher, Market
Elson, John, jun., butcher, Market
Emery, Arthur S., auctioneer and land agent, Dundas bet Ridout and Talbot
ERITH, WILLIAM T., manufacturer of patent malt and herbalist, Bond cor Colborne
European Life and Guarantee Assurance Society, E. Baynes Reed, agent, Albion bdgs, Richmond
EVANS, MAJOR R. J., sec. and treas. Hellmuth College, h Grosvenor
Fairbairn, Walter, tailor, Richmond
Farmers' Advocate, William Weld, editor and propr., Talbot s of Dundas
Farrar, David, M.D., Dundas
Farrell, Mrs. L., (wid John), grocer, Richmond
Farris, Samuel
Farris, William, sewing machine agent, Dundas w of Richmond
Ferguson, James, Registrar County Middlesex, Court House Square
Ferguson, John, undertaker, etc., Richmond
Ferguson & Co., (W. H. and M. H. Ferguson), groceries and liquors, Dundas e of Richmond
Fergusson & Co., (Jas. Fergusson and E. W. Hyman) pork packers, King nr Ridout
Finlayson, Alexander, dry goods, etc., Dundas bet Richmond and Talbot
Fish, Robert, grocer, Dundas
Fitzgerald, Fred. A., (Fitzgerald & Scandrett), King bet Wellington and Waterloo
Fitzgerald, William, civil engineer, George
Fitzgerald & Scandrett, (F. A. Fitzgerald and John Scandrett), groceries, wines and liquors, Dundas e of Richmond
Flannery, Rev. W., St. Peter's church, res Bishop's Palace, Richmond
Fleming, John, axe and edge tool maker, Ridout bet King and York
FLOCK, JAMES H., barrister, attorney and notary public, Albion bdgs, Richmond (see adv)
Flock, John R., M.D., e Dundas bet Clarence and Wellington
Flock, William, Dundas nr Clarence
Flood, James, barrister, bds cor Dundas and Adelaide
Flory, Samuel, lime and brick dealer, Dundas
Forknell, Edward G., fish dealer, Market

Foster, George, carpenter
Fraser, James H. (Elliot & Fraser)
Fraser, Thomas, city collector, City Hall
Frazer, Thomas, flour and feed, Richmond
Fuller, Hugh P., butcher, Market Square
Furness, George, produce and commission, Dundas
FURNESS, WILLIAM C., manager Montreal Telegraph Company. Albion Buildings, Richmond
Fysh, Henry, flour and feed. and proprietor Middlesex mills, Proof Line Road
Fysh, Hewitt, confectioner, wholesale and retail, Dundas nr Clarence
Gardiner, Thomas, proprietor Dominion House, Mark Lane
GAULD, ALEXANDER, merchant tailor, Dundas
Geary, John (Geary & Moncrieff)
Geary & Moncrieff (John Geary and George Moncrieff) barristers, Dundas nr Ridout
Geen, Thomas, butcher, Market House
Gibbins, Mrs. S. A., books and stationery, Dundas between Richmond and Clarence
GILL, WILLIAM, C. L., registry office, City Hall
Glass, David, barrister, etc., Dundas w of Talbot
Glass, Graham, saloon, Market Lane s of Dundas
Glass, Samuel, h e North
Glass, Samuel, jun., deputy sheriff, King bet Ridout and Thames
Gleeson, James, grocer, Richmond cor Bathurst
GLEN, JAMES, merchant tailor, Dundas e of Ridout
Going, Henry, M.D., Dundas bet Wellington and Waterloo
Goldner, Joseph, clothier, Richmond and Dundas
Goodacre, George, saloon, Market Square
Goodhue, Charles, barrister, King opp Market
Goodhue, Hon. George
Gordon, William, Talbot bet Kent and Market
GORMAN, HENRY, local editor *Advertiser*
Gough, William, second-hand store, Talbot
Gould, Martin, tailor and grocer, Wellington
Gould, Richard, grocer, Hamilton road
GOWAN, T., & Co., groceries, wines and liquors, Dundas, near Market Lane
GRAND TRUNK R. R. City Ticket Office, Richmond, n of King
Grannan, William, second hand store, King nr Ridout
Graves, Otto B., carver and gilder, Richmond
Gray, Anthony, barber, Richmond
Gray, George B., plow manufacturer, Fullarton
Graydon, Simson, H., barrister, Dundas, e of Ridout
Green, H. C., lumber merchant, cor Clarence and Bathurst
Green, John (Green, Crofts & Co.) h North
Green, Peter, grain buyer
Green, Thomas, manufacturer sash, door and blind, Bathurst near Clarence
Green, Crofts & Co. (John Green, Benjamin Crofts & A. B. Powell) dry goods, h Dundas
Grey, George (Muirhead & Grey) miller
GRIFFIN, GILBERT E., Post Office Inspector's Office, London Post Office
GRIFFIN, JAMES, seedsman, florist and nurseryman, store City Hall, Richmond
Griffith, Richard, painter and dealer in paints, oils, glass, &c., Dundas
GRIFFITHS, JOHN H., photographer and dealer in photographic stock, Dundas, cor Market Lane, (see adv)
GRIGG, SAMUEL, prop. American House, cor Richmond and York (see adv)
Griswold, Dr. Edgar B., conductor, G. W. R., h North
Groves, Frederick, saloon, Richmond
Groves, Henry, high constable and bailiff h York
Groves, Richard, inn-keeper, near cemetery
Grube, F. W., B. A., Master Hellmuth College
Gunn, George M., agent Scottish Provincial Life Assurance Company office, Talbot n of Dundas
Gurd, John, & Son (John & William) sewing machine repairers, gunsmiths and rifle makers, Dundas
Hagarty, Daniel, M. J., M.D., Richmond cor King
Hamilton, John, proprietor Kent Brewery, Ann
Harens, John, photographer, Richmond cor King
Harper, A., M.D., Hitchcock nr Mark Lane
HARPER, W. F., manager Merchants' Bank
Harris, Edward, (Harris & Magee)
Harris, George B., (Harris & Magee)
Harris, John, fruits and confectionery, Richmond n of York
HARRIS & MAGEE, barristers, etc., Dundas
Hart, Miss Kate, milliner, etc., Dundas nr Richmond
Hartford Fire Insurance Co., W. Dempster, agent, Albion bdgs, Richmond
Harvey, Thomas, carpenter, Talbot nr North
Haskett, James, painter, King cor Wellington
Hassell, James, individual ledger keeper, Bank B. N. A., Richmond
Hasty & Perley, coopers and stave manufacturer, York adj Leonard's Foundry
Hawkins, George, commission merchant, King bet Richmond and Talbot
HAWTHORN, WILLIAM, prop. Strong's Hotel, Dundas (see adv)
Hay, Miss, milliner, etc., Dundas
Hayden, Thomas T., hotel keeper
Haystead, David, prop. Haystead's Hotel and Brewery, King cor Ridout
HEATHFIELD, M. W., importer and wholesale dealer in drugs and chemicals, Dundas nr Richmond (see adv.
HELLMUTH COLLEGE, St. James bet Wellington and Waterloo
HELLMUTH, VERY REV. I., D.D., President Hellmuth College
Hemphill, Zachariah, agent A. & S. Nordheimer's piano fortes
Hendershot, Abraham, boarding house, Clarence bet Bathurst and Horton
Henderson, Alexander J. G., (A. Chisholm & Co.), h Talbot
Henry, Bernard, books, stationery and exchange broker, Richmond s of Dundas
Hibbert, John, grocer, Horton, cor Clarence
Hill, William, inn keeper, Adelaide
Hilliard, William M., (Hilliard & Saunby), h Clarence
Hilliard & Saunby, (William M. Hilliard and J. D. Saunby), props. Mill Branch Mills, office Richmond
Hine, Abel, taxidermist, Clarence
HISCOX, GEORGE T., livery stable, Dundas
Hiscox, Thomas, North nr Clarence
Hobbs, John, L.R.C.S.I., h Hitchcock
Hockin, Samuel, cooper, Wellington
Hodgens, Thomas D., carriage and wagon maker, Richmond
Hodgins & Brown (Elijah Hodgins and James H. Brown), livery, Clarence
Hogg, Edward, butcher, Market
Hogg, Isaac, watchmaker, Mark Lane
HOLMES, CALVIN D., barrister, Dundas nr Talbot
Home Insurance Company, (New Haven, Conn.), Beddome & Dempster, agents, Albion Buildings, Richmond
Hope, Adam & Co., iron and hardware merchants, North nr Talbot

Hooper, John, foreman *Advertiser*
Horton, William, city recorder, h Westminster
Horton & Wilson (William Horton and David Wilson), barristers, Talbot
Howe, Michael, boarding, York
Humphrey, Charles C., clerk Strong's Hotel
Hunt, Charles, produce, commission and groceries, and proprietor city mills, Richmond
Hunter, Hamilton, excise officer, Albion Buildings
HUNTER JOHN, coal oil and lamps, Richmond (see adv)
Hunter, Rev. W. J. (Wesleyan Methodist), h Fullarton
Huntley, A. T., agent Thompson & Duff
Hurlbit, Mrs. Matilda, boarding house, King nr Talbot
HURON AND ERIE SAVINGS AND LOAN SOCIETY, E. W. Hyman, president, Charles Stead, vice-president, Charles Murray, secretary and treasurer, Dundas nr Talbot
HUTCHINSON, CHARLES, county crown attorney, (Abbott & Hutchinson), res Westminster
HYMAN, ELLIS W., leather merchant and tanner, City Hall Buildings, Richmond
Imperial Fire Insurance Company, George B. Scott, agent, Talbot
Irvine, Richard, landing waiter G. W. R., freight depot
Irving, Thomas T., barrister, Dundas
Ison, Mrs. Dr., boarding house, Wellington
Jacobs, Joseph E., Petersville
James, Robert, grocer, Wellington
Jarman, Benjamin, undertaker and grocer, Richmond cor Kent
Jeffers, Arthur, West End Saloon, Dundas
JEFFERY, JOSEPH, banker and exchange dealer, land and general broker, Palmer's Blk, Richmond
Jerome, Charles C., proprietor National Bitters
Joanes, William, carpenter and builder, e North nr Colborne
JOHNSON, JAMES, (Rowland & Johnson) secretary and treasurer Ontario Mutual Fire Insurance Co., Richmond opp City Hall (see adv)
Johnson, John, freight agent G. W. R., h Colborne
JOHNSON, J. A. & Co., universal shuttle sewing machines, 4 Music Hall, Richmond
Johnston, Alexander, leather and findings, Richmond opp Post Office
Johnston, Rev. W. R., Grammar School teacher
JONES, JOHN, baker, Wellington cor South (see adv)
JONES, J. W., principal, London Commercial College, Wellington
Joyce, Mrs. G., boarding house, Dundas nr Ridout
Judd, Hubert H., (Roe & Judd)
Kains, William K., produce merchant, York
Kay, Alexander R., secretary London Pressed Brick Company, Richmond cor King
Kearns, W., photographer, Talbot
KEEFER, JAMES, County Clerk, office Court House
Keenleyside, A., (Spencer & Keenleyside)
Kennedy, Rev. Andrew, agent for Presbyterian Board of Publication, Richmond
KENNEDY, D. M., (Ross & Kennedy)
KERSHAW & EDWARDS, safes, A. G. Smyth, agt Albion buildings, Richmond
King, Mrs. Eliza, boarding house, Talbot nr York
Kingsley, Wm., accountant, Grosvenor cor Burlington
KIRKPATRICK, ROBERT, boots and shoes, Dundas nr Richmond (see adv)
Kohl, Richard L., cigars and tobacco, Dundas nr Richmond
Korn, Henry, cigar manufacturer, Market
Labatt, Mrs. (widow, J. K.), h Grey
LABATT, GEORGE, brewer, h Grey
LABATT, JOHN (Labatt & Co.), Simcoe
Labatt, Miss Louisa, boarding house, Ridout
LABATT & CO., proprietors London Brewery, foot of Talbot (see adv)
LAING, LOCKHART & CO., (John B. Laing, James Lockhart, J. B. Sutherland), importers of dry goods)
Lake, Rev. John N., York bet Ridout and Talbot
Lancaster, Joseph J., M.D., (Homœpathist), Richmond nr City Hall
Land, George P., (O'Brien & Land)
Large, A. T. & Co., soda water manufacturers and pork butchers Dundas cor of Wellington
Landor, Henry, M.D., h John
LAW, JOHN, brass founder, Richmond bet King and York (see adv)
Lawless, John P., accountant Bank B. N. A.
LAWLESS, LAWRENCE, Postmaster, h Kent bet Market Lane and Talbot
LAWRASON, LAWRENCE, police magistrate, official assignee, Albion Buildings, Richmond
LAWRASON, WILLIAM L., attorney and solicitor, Albion Buildings, Richmond
Leathorn, Robert, butcher, 1 Market
Leeds, James, grocer, e Hill
Leeder, Asaph, M.D., Bathurst
Lenfesty, Henry, broker and commission merchant, Talbot
Lentall, Thomas, carpenter, Richmond
Lentall, Mrs. T., grocer, Richmond
Lendall, Thomas, carpenter, Richmond
Leonard, Hon. Elijah, founder, York
Leonard, James E., (L. C. Leonard & Co.), h Hitchcock
LEONARD, LEWIS C., (L. C. Leonard & Co.), h Hitchcock
LEONARD, L. C. & Co. (Lewis C. & James C. Leonard) oil refiners, coal oil and lamps, Richmond opposite North
Leslie, R. A., teller, Bank British North America
Lester, Daniel, grocer, York cor Burwell
Lewis, Robert, painter and glass stainer
Ley, John D., barber, Richmond
LILLEY, CHARLES, groceries and provisions, cor Burwell and Dundas
Linfoot, George, butcher, 15 Covent Market
Lively, John, prop. Waterman's Arms, Clark's Bridge
Liverpool and London and Globe Insurance Company, A. G. Smyth, agent, Albion Buildings, Richmond
Lloyd, Thomas L., prop. Sun Inn, Dundas
Lockhart, James, (Laing, Lockhart & Co) h King
Logan, Alexander, barber, King
London, Ass. Corporation, Waddell & Gunn, agents, Talbot nr Dundas
LONDON CITY AND COUNTY OF MIDDLESEX DIRECTORY, C. E. Anderson & Co., publishers, H. McEvoy, compiler, Directory Branch, *Daily Telegraph* office, Toronto (see adv)
LONDON CITY GAS WORKS, Thomas Drought, secretary, Horton cor Ridout
LONDON FREE PRESS AND WESTERN ADVERTISER, J. & S. Blackburn, editors and proprietors, Richmond opp North (see adv)
LONDON PRESSED BRICK MANUFACTURING CO., works, Westminster, office Richmond
LONG, HENRY D., (Edward Adams & Co.) h Colborne

Long, Mrs. Mary, grocer, Dundas cor Ridout
Loughrey, Archibald, harness and saddle maker, Richmond
Loughrey, William, grocer, Petersville
Lounsbury, Rev. E., (Methodist Episcopal) h North nr Waterloo
Loveless, Robert, grocer, Sarnia
LOYD, THOMAS, livery stable, prop. American House, Richmond cor York (see adv)
Lucas & Arkell, maltsters, Ridout
Lucas, William J., carpenter, Maitland nr e North
Luxton, Richard, butcher, 10 Market
McArthur, Daniel, second hand broker, Talbot opp Market
McArthur & Christie, grocers, Higgins' Block, Dundas
McBride, Alexander, (S. & A. McBride,) h Fullarton
McBride, Samuel, (S. & A. McBride,) h Ridout
McBRIDE, S. & A., stoves, tinware, oils and lamps, Richmond opp City Hall
McBride, William, City Assessor, Office City Hall h Fullarton
McCann, Peter, saloon, Richmond
McCann, Philip, hats, caps and furs, Dundas near Market Lane
McCLEARY, JOHN, (J. & O. McCleary), h Westminster
McCLEARY, J. & O., stove founders and tinsmiths, Wellington bet King and York
McCLEARY, OLIVER, (J. & O. McCleary) h Dundas
McCleary, William, surveyor, bds O. McCleary
McCONACHIE, DAVID, dry goods, Dundas nr Talbot (see adv)
McCormick, Andrew, grocer, Richmond cor York
McCormick, Thomas, manuf'g confectioner, Clarence
McCormick, William, grocer, Richmond nr Bathurst
McCROSSON & CO, hatters and furriers, Albion Block, Richmond (see adv)
McCue, John G., prop. McCue's Hotel, Kent corner Mark Lane
McDermott, Patrick, contractor, h Mill
McDonald, Alexander, Deputy Registrar County Middlesex, h Ridout
McDONALD, A. J., boots and shoes, Dundas
McDonald, H. F., travelling inspector Huron and Erie S. and L. Society
McDonald, John, proprietor Market Saloon and fish dealer, Market Square
McDonald, Richard, proprietor Petersville Hotel
McDonell, Allan J., boots and shoes, Dundas nr Richmond
McDONOUGH, JOHN K., (McDonough & Shoebotham), h Richmond
McDonough, Thomas J., wholesale grocer, Dundas w of Richmond
McDonough, William, wholesale grocer, Richmond n of Dundas
McDONOUGH & SHOEBOTHAM, (John K. McDonough and William B. Shoebotham) dry goods and groceries, Dundas nr Market Lane (see adv)
McDowell, Mrs. Eliza, boarding house, Talbot
McDowell, James, hotel keeper, Richmond
McGLOGHLON, WILLIAM D., watches, clocks and jewelry, 77 Dundas (see adv)
McGregor, Daniel, provision dealer, Market Square
McHugh, Peter, variety store, Market Square
McIntosh, Alexander, (A. & J. G. McIntosh & Co.), h e Dundas
McIntosh, John G. (A. & J. G. McIntosh & Co.) h King
McIntosh, Mrs. Julia, groceries, &c., Great Market, near Colborne
McIntosh, W. J., circulation agent "Advertiser"
McIntosh, A. & J. G. & Co., importers of dry goods, &c., 57 and 59 Dundas
McIntyre, Archibald, silver plater, King near Ridout
McKellar & Stewart, carriage and waggon manufacturers, Richmond, opposite English Cathedral
McKenzie, Andrew, M. D., h York
McKenzie, Donald, butcher, Market Square
McKenzie, & Cary, grocers, Dundas
McMartin, Peter, hotel-keeper, King near Richmond
McMechan, John, boots and shoes, Dundas near Clarence
McMillan, Duncan, commission merchant, Talbot
McMillan, William, oil refiner, Dundas between Burwell and Maitland
McNab, Robert, M.D., Lichfield
McPhail, Archibald, lumber merchant, York near Clarence
McPherson, Archibald, dry goods, Dundas e of Talbot
McPherson, George, boots and shoes, Dundas opposite Market Lane
McPherson, Robert (Stewart, Bruce & Co.) h Market near Talbot
McPHERSON, J., & CO., (John McPherson, E. W. Hyman and Daniel Sterling) wholesale manufacturers of boots and shoes, Dundas
McVeigh, Edward, second-hand store, King
McVeigh, Francis, second-hand store, King
McAdams, Alexander, lumber merchant, Bond
Macbeth, George, h Bond opposite Cartwright
MACBETH, JOHN, clerk of County Court Department, Clerk of Crown and Common Pleas, and Registrar of Surrogate Court, office Court House
MACBETH & WALKER, (George Macbeth, John Walker) agents Canada Chemical Manufacturing Co., and Ontario Chemical Works, Richmond
MACDONALD, ALEXANDER, Secretary Agricultural Mutual Assurance Association of Canada, Ridout
MACDONALD, ALEXANDER J. B. (Cornish & Macdonald) h Talbot
MACDONALD, D. C., Secretary Agricultural Mutual Assurance Association of Canada, Ridout
Macfie, Daniel, importer of dry goods, Dundas cor Talbot
MACHATTIE, DR. A. (Machattie & Co.) h King
MACHATTIE, HENRY, Ontario Starch Works (see adv)
MACHATTIE & CO., Ontario Chemical Works, s of Hamilton Road
Mackenzie, Philip, barrister, e of Ridout
Mackey, Thomas H., grocer, Mark Lane
Macmillan, Duncan, barrister, Dundas e of Ridout
MAGEE, JAMES (Harris & Magee), h e Dundas
Mahan, Hillson & Cooper, proprietors Gore Oil Refinery, Trafalgar
MANLEY, ROBERT, dry goods, Dundas w of Market Lane
Mann, James A., photographer, Dundas e of Market Lane
Mann, S. D., professor of penmanship London Commercial College, King nr Clarence
Marrs, David, boots and shoes, Richmond, bet Dundas and King
Marsh, Rev. J. W. (Church of England) Waterloo
Mason, John, proprietor Western Hotel, Richmond opp English Cathedral
Mathewson, Henry, advertising agent *Free Press*, h e North
Matthews, John, proprietor Britannia House, Wellington cor York
Maylard, Philip F. (Abbott & Maylard, h e North

MEARNS, WILLIAM, furniture dealer and upholsterer, Richmond bet King and York (see adv)
MERCHANTS' BANK, W. F. Harper, manager, Richmond cor William
Meredith, Edmund, barrister, bds Burlington cor Thames
Meredith, John C., No. 1 Division Court Clerk, Dundas nr Ridout
Meredith, William R. (Scatcherd & Meredith), h Talbot
Merritt, John C., book-keeper J. McPherson & Co., h Richmond
Metharell, John, grocer, Dundas bet Clarence and Wellington
Metzger, John G., tailor
Millar, John (T. & J. Millar), h Dundas
Millar, Thomas (T. & J. Millar), h Hitchcock
MILLAR, T. & J. (Thomas & John), stoves and tinware, Dundas bet Richmond and Clarence
Miller, Edward, fancy goods, Dundas nr Richmond
Mills, Francis, grocer, Dundas e of Clarence
Mills, John, books and stationery, exchange office, Richmond bet Dundas and King
Milroy, William, manufacturer childrens carriages, Richmond n
Minhinnick, J. R. & Co., Crown Oil works
Mitchell, B. A., chemist and druggist, Dundas e of Talbot
Mitcheltree, Joseph, butcher, 9 Market
Moncrieff, George, (Geary & Moncrief) h Burwell
MONTREAL ASSURANCE COMPANY, (Marine branch) R. Waddell, agent, Talbot
MONTREAL TELEGRAPH COMPANY, C. Furness manager, Albion buildings, Richmond
Moore, Charles, M. D., Wellington, bet Dundas and King
Moorehead, Alexander, blacksmith, King bet Talbot and Ridout
MOOREHEAD, GEORGE, cabinet maker and furniture dealer, King bet Richmond and Clarence (see adv)
Moran, Jeremiah H., (Thompson & Moran) h Clarence
Morden, Ralph, J. P., homœopathic physician, e North cor Clarence
Morgan, Morgan L., glass stainer, h King
Morkin, Edward, hotel keeper, Wellington cor Duke
Morkin, John, blacksmith, Richmond
Morkin, Thomas, grocer, Mark Lane
Morphy, Andrew, watches and jewelry, Dundas
Morris, Robert, hotel keeper, Westminster
Morrison, Peter, merchant tailor, Dundas w of Clarence
Morrison, Thomas, wagon maker, e North
Mortimer, William, second hand broker, Market Sq
MOSSOP, JONATHAN, (J. & T. Mossop) City Hotel
MOSSOP, THOMAS, (J. & T. Mossop) City Hotel
MOSSOP, J. & T., (Jonathan and Thomas) proprietors City Hotel, Dundas cor Talbot
Moule, John, grocer, Dundas nr Richmond
Mountjoy, Richard, fruits and confectionery, Richmond opp City Hall
Moyle, Thomas, Warden County Middlesex, office County buildings
Muirhead & Grey, prop. oatmeal mill, Colborne bet Horton and Simcoe
Mullins, John, grocer, King, nr Clarence
Mummery, Stephen, naturalist, Talbot cor Market
Mundy, John, photographer, Richmond
Murphy, Edward, boots and shoes, Richmond n Dundas
MURRAY, ADAM, county treasurer, opp Court House
Murray, Alexander, carpenter, Wellington cor e North
MURRAY, CHARLES, secretary and treasurer Huron and Erie Savings and Loan Society, Dundas nr Talbot
MURRAY, HUGH S., watches, clocks, and jewelry, Palmer's Block, Richmond (see adv)
Murray, Robert S., upholsterer, dry goods importer, &c., Dundas cor Talbot
Mustill, John, farrier and blacksmith, Ridout bet King and York
Nagle, Thomas, grocer, York bet Ridout and Thames
Neilson, Hugh, manager telegraph office
Nelles, Henry H., D.D.S., Dundas bet Richmond and Talbot
Nelles, John A., M.D., e Dundas
Nesbit, Bros., coopers, Horton bet William and Adelaide
Nicholls, John, P.O. Depot, h Blackfriars
Nickels, George, livery and sale stables, Richmond
Niles, William, general agent Agricultural Mutual Assurance Ass. of Canada, h Ridout
NITSCHKE, JOHN, piano forte manuf., Dundas
Noble, William, grocer, Hamilton Road
Noone, Mrs. C., grocer, Market Lane
Norris, George, tailor, Clarence nr Dundas
North British & Mercantile Fire and Life Ins. Co., H. S. Strathy, agent, Bank of Commerce
O'Brien, Thomas, (O'Brien & Land) Richmond
O'Brien & Land, (Thomas O'Brien & George P. Land) barristers, Richmond opp City Hall
O'Callaghan, Thomas E., groceries and fruit, Dundas
O'Connor, James, saloon keeper, Richmond
O'Donohue, John, saloon keeper, York
O'Donohue, John, auction and commission merchant, Dundas nr Richmond
O'Higgins, Joseph P., (F. Smith & Co.), h Dundas
O'Shea, Rev. J., St. Peter's Church
Offord, George & Co., Penitentiary boot and shoe store, Dundas
Oliver, James, boots and shoes, Dundas
ONTARIO CHEMICAL WORKS, Machattie & Co., proprietors, s of Hamilton Road
ONTARIO MUTUAL FIRE INSURANCE CO., S. McBride, President; Capt. T. Wilson, Vice President; James Johnson, Secretary and Treasurer; office Richmond opp City Hall (see adv)
ONTARIO STARCH WORKS CO., Adelaide, (see adv)
Ormsby, Nicholas, saloon, City Hall
Ouellett, Rev. F. O. J., St. Peter's Church, h Bishop's Palace
Oxley, Michael, grocer, King nr Clarence
Pacey, John P. (Plummer & Pacey), h Hitchcock
Pannell, John, proprietor City Arms Hotel, King opp Market
PARKE, E. JONES, barrister, Dundas e of Ridout
Parker, David H., merchant tailor and sewing machine agent, 2 Music Hall
PARTRIDGE, THOMAS, solicitor, notary public, etc., Dundas cor Market Lane
Partridge, Thomas, St. James nr William
Paul, Samuel, lumber merchant, York
Pavey, Edwin, (Pavey & Sons)
Pavey, Eli, (Pavey & Sons)
Pavey, Emanuel, (Pavey & Sons)
Pavey & Sons, carriage makers, King nr Talbot
Peacock, James, Berlin wool, Richmond s of North
Peel, John R., marble cutter, Richmond opp Duke
PEEL, THOMAS, merchant tailor, Dundas (see adv.)
Pendergast, John, (Bolton & Pendergast), h Hill
Percival, James, flour and feed, North nr Clarence
Percival, William, grocer, Dundas nr Clarence

Perrin, Daniel S., wholesale confectioner and biscuit baker, Richmond nr York
Perrin, Darius, surgeon dentist, Dundas e of Clarence
Peters, George M., baker, Richmond s of Kent
Peters, Samuel, F.L.S., Albion bdgs, Richmond
Peters, S. & Co., oil refiners, Adelaide
Phair Henry, saloon, Market Square
PHILLIPS, THOMAS, M. D., Fullarton bet Mark Lane and Talbot
Philipps, William H., general engraver, Dundas e of Clarence
PHŒNIX FOUNDRY, John Elliott proprietor, Wellington cor Bathurst
Phœnix Insurance Company of England, J. C. Meredith, agent, Dundas
Pigott, Thomas, butcher, Market Lane
PLUMMER, EPHRAIM, (E. Plummer & Co.,) h Hitchcock
PLUMMER, JOHN, (Plummer & Pacey) h Hitchcock
PLUMMER, E. & Co., chemists and druggists, Dundas e of Richmond
PLUMMER & PACEY, carriage, wagon, hub and spoke manufacturers (see adv)
Pope, John, master Hellmuth College, h Wellington
Powell, Ambrose B., (Green, Crofts & Co.) h Clarence
Powell, George S., (G. Powell & Son) h Wellington
Powell, George jr., (G. Powell & Son) h Wellington
Powell, Thomas, proprietor Hiscox's Hotel, Dundas
Powell, G. & Son, marble dealers, Richmond cor King
Priddis, Charles, dry goods, Dundas nr Richmond
Priestley, John H., chemist, h e North
Pritchard, R. & G., commission merchants, King bet Richmond and Talbot
Proudfoot, Alexander, grocer, Petersville
PROVINCIAL INSURANCE COMPANY, R. Waddell, agent, Talbot
Puddicombe, Abraham, King nr Wellington
PUDDICOMBE, ROBERT W., chemist and druggist, Albion buildings, Richmond (see adv)
Quick, Robert, butcher, Market House
Railway Passenger's Insurance Company, Hartford, Conn., Beddome & Dempster, agents, Albion buildings
Redman & Riley, Misses, dressmakers, Dundas
REED, EDMUND BAYNES, barrister and insurance agent, Albion buildings, Richmond
Reed, Thomas, Coffee House, Market Square
Regan, Daniel, boots and shoes, Dundas w of Richmond
Reid, John, proprietor Reid's Hotel, Ridout
Reid, Robert, books and stationery, Dundas nr Talbot
Reid, William, stationer, h Burlington
Reid, W. J. & Co., china, glass and queensware, Richmond
Rendall, John, manager Thompson & Duff, Dundas
Revere House, Edwin Woodbury, proprietor, Richmond cor King
Reynolds, George J., grocer, Richmond nr King
Reynolds, Nelson, pump-maker, Wellington cor Simcoe
Reynolds, Richard, grain and wool, Petersville
RICH, ROBERT, general produce merchant, Maitland, between Dundas and King (see adv.)
Rimmer, Peter, manager London Gas Works, h Horton
ROACH, GEORGE, proprietor refreshment rooms G. W. R. depot
Robb, John G. (Darvell & Robb), h King
Robertson, J. S., oil refiner, Bathurst
Robinson, Egerton R., manager Robt. Walker & Sons, Dundas
Robinson, Henry E. (W. H. Robinson & Co.)
Robinson, George, dry goods and clothing, Dundas nr Richmond
Robinson, Henry S., agent Gore Mutual Insurance Company, res Westminster
Robinson, William H. & Co., chemists and druggists, Richmond opp City Hall
Rock, Warren, barrister, Dundas e of Ridout
Roe, George, proprietor Waterloo Hotel, Richmond nr King
Roe & Judd, carriage and wagon makers, Wellington, bet King and York
Rogers, Edward, plumber and gasfitter, Dundas w of Talbot
ROOKS, WILLIAM H., proprietor Terrapin restaurant, Dundas bet Richmond and Clarence
ROSS, A. M. (Ross & Kennedy)
Ross, George W., general agent *Advertiser*
Ross, John, saddle and harness maker, Dundas, Smith's Block, Dundas
ROSS & KENNEDY (A. M. Ross and D. M. Kennedy), proprietors Dominion Oil Refinery
Rourk, John, saloon, Richmond
ROWLAND, ALFRED, china, crockery, lamps and oils, Richmond n of Dundas (see adv.)
ROWLAND, EDWARD, Montreal boot and shoe store, agent Singer sewing machines, Dundas e of Richmond (see adv)
ROWLAND, FREDERICK, wholesale and retail grocer, Richmond cor Dundas ; grain merchant, York ; and pork packer, King cor William (see adv)
ROWLAND & JOHNSON, (Fred Rowland & James Johnson), oil warehousemen, William corner Bathurst off Richmond opp City Hall
ROWLEY, W., proprietor Senate Saloon and Billiards, Richmond
Royal Insurance Co., F. B. Beddome, agent Albion, bds Richmond
RUDD, CHARLES, veternary surgeon, Hitchcock (see adv)
Ryan, James, hotel keeper, Clarence cor King
SABINE J. B., dentist, Dundas e of Talbot
Salter, John, chemist and druggist, Dundas e of Richmond
Santo, John, butcher, Market
Saunby, Joseph D., (Hilliard & Saunby)
Saunders, James, h King nr Wellington
SAUNDERS, WILLIAM, chemist and druggist, Dundas bet Richmond and Clarence
Savage, Rev. D., (New Connexion Methodist), h Ridout
Scandrett, John, market clerk, (Fitzgerald & Scandrett), h King nr Wellington
Scanlan, John, soap factory, Hill
Scatcherd, Thomas, (Scatcherd & Meredith)
Scatcherd & Meredith, (Thomas Scatcherd & W. R. Meredith) barristers, Dundas e of Ridout
Scott, George B., insurance agent and notary public, Talbot n of Dundas
Scott, Rev. John, (Free Presbyterian), h e North nr Waterloo
Scottish Provincial (Life) Assurance Co., George M. Gunn, agent, Talbot n of Dundas
Scragg, John G., prop. Corn Exchange Hotel
Seddon, Mrs. George, carver and gilder, Dundas nr Talbot
Service, Alexander, gaocer, Wellington bet Simcoe and Grey
Shain, Hiram, grocer, Hamilton Road
SHANLY, JAMES, master in chancery and barrister, Ridout
Shanly, Colonel James, Dundas cor Maitland

Sharpe & Stenabaugh, grocers, Dundas e of Talbot
Shattuck, John, M.D., Richmond
Shaw, Archibald, dry goods, h Richmond
Shaw, Benjamin, commission merchant, King bet Talbot and Richmond
Shaw, George, grocer, Dundas nr Richmond
Shaw, C. D. & Co., hardware, iron and steel, Dundas bet Richmond and Talbot
Shedden, John & Co., John Grey, agent, cartage agts Richmond cor York
Shoebothem, Thomas, St. James cor Colborne
Shoebothem, William, (McDonough & Shoebothem) h east Dundas
Shopland & Beutly, hub factory, e North nr Wellington
SIDDON, JOHN, prop. *Prototype*, office Dundas nr Talbot (see adv)
Sime, William, boots and shoes, Dundas nr Richmond
Simmons, R. P., prop. Northern Hotel, e North
Simpson, J. F., flour and feed, Richmond
SIMSON, WALTER, (W. & R. Simson & Co.) h Westminster
SIMSON, WILLIAM, (W. & R. Simson & Co.) h Hitchcock
SIMSON, W. & R. & Co., groceries, wines and liquors, Dundas bet Talbot and Richmond
Sippi, Charles A., M.D., Alma nr St. James
Sippi, C. A., L.A.H.D., master Hellmuth College
Slater, Edward K., painter and paper hanger, h Fullarton
Slater, James, produce dealer, King nr Richmond
Slater, Samuel, boots & shoes, Dundas nr Wellington
Small, Hon. James C., judge, h Hitchcock nr Talbot
SMALLMAN, THOMAS H., station agent L. & P. S.R.R
Smart, John, grocer, Maitland n of Dundas
Smith, Alexander, grocer, Westminster
Smith, Charles, cooper, York cor Waterloo
Smith, Charles P., (Smith, Chapman & Co.) h Talbot
Smith, Edward, butcher, 7 Market House
Smith, Mrs. E., milliner and dressmaker, Dundas cor Wellington
Smith, George W., John cor George
Smith, Henry A., commission merchant, Talbot nr Horton
Smith, James, cooper, William nr Richmond
SMITH, JAMES, prop. Albion Restaurant and billiard saloon, Richmond adj P.O. (see adv)
SMITH, WILLIAM SIMPSON, importer and wholesale grocer, Dundas bet Market Lane and Talbot and Market sq.
Smith Chapman & Co., general hardware, Dundas, nr Richmond
STRONG, H. B., h William
Smith, F. & Co., importers of groceries, wines and liquors, Dundas
Smith & Gordon, carriage makers, King bet Talbot and Ridout
Smith & Jamieson, proprietors London and Clinton stage, Hayden's Hotel
SMYTH, ALFRED G., insurance and shipping agent, Albion Buildings, Richmond
SMYTH, REV. JAMES, incumbent Christ Church, h Maitland
SMYTH, JOHN B., groceries, wines and liquors, Talbot s of Dundas (see adv.)
SMYTH, JOHN W., marble dealer, Dundas bet Richmond and Clarence (see adv)
Smyth, Thomas & Co., grocers, Richmond
Southcott, James, grocer, Talbot bet Dundas and Market
Spence, N. C., exchange broker, Richmond
Spencer & Keenleyside, oil refiners, Hamilton Road
Springer, Benjamin, P.L.S.. h Ridout nr Fullarton
SPRY, ABRAHAM W., merchant tailor, Dundas nr Clarence (see adv.)
Stammers, S., accountant, Bank of Montreal
Stedwell, J. D., oil refiner, Hamilton Road
Steinhoff, Samuel H., grocer, Mark Lane
Stephens, Richard, proprietor Westminster Bridge tannery
Stevenson, Hugh, Market nr Mark Lane
Stevenson, James, M.D., Market nr Mark Lane
Stewart, Alexander (Stewart, Bruce & Co.)
Stewart, James, carpenter, Burlington
Stewart, John (McKellar & Stewart and Stewart, Bruce & Co.)
Stewart, Bruce & Co., founders and manufacturers of agricultural implements, Fullarton
Stone, Ashbel C., M.D., dentist, Dundas nr Clarence
STRATHDEE, JOHN, agent Adam Hope & Co., cor North and Talbot
Strathy, Henry S., manager Bank of Commerce
STRATHY, JAMES B., collector of customs, res The Pines, Dundas
STREET, WILLIAM P. R., (Becher, Barker & Street), h Piccadilly
Strong, Henry, drugs and patent medicines, Picton nr Duke
STRONG'S HOTEL, William Hawthorne, proprietor Dundas nr Richmond (see adv)
Stuart, John, clerk wood market
Sulphur Springs Baths, C. Dunnett, proprietor, foot of Dundas
SUTHERLAND, GEORGE D., dry goods and clothing, Dundas cor Richmond
Sutherland, James B., (Laing, Lockhart & Co.)
Sweatman, Rev. Arthur, M.A., head master Hellmuth College
SYMMONDS, JOHN, grocer, Dundas bet Clarence and Wellington
SYMMONDS, JOHN, sole agent for the Dominion for Littlewood's Washing Crystal, Smith's block Dundas
Symmons, William H., second hand furniture, Talbot
Tanton Bros., (John and Thomas) commission merchants, &c., Talbot opp Market
Tapp, Thomas, grocer, Pall Mall
Taylor, Benjamin, grocer, Simcoe cor Colborne
TAYLOR, CHAS., pork packer, Ridout bet Bathurst and York
TAYLOR, HENRY, exchange broker, Richmond opp City Hall
Taylor, John, pump maker, cor Sarnia and Mill
Taylor, Lieut. Col. John B., District Staff Officer of Militia, Albion buildings
TAYLOR, E. A. & Co., booksellers, and stationers bookbinders, &c., Richmond cor North
Teale Charles, marble cutter
Teale, Christopher, sen., Maitland nr Gt Market
Teale, Christopher, Jr., artist, Maitland nr Bond
TEALE, EMANUEL, (Teale & Wilkens) h Maitland nr Bond
TEALE & WILKENS, (E. Teale & H. A Wilkens) marble dealers, Dundas opp Strong's Hotel (see bottom lines)
Tecumseh House, B. F. Moore, proprietor, James C. Derby, manager, Richmond cor York
Thomas, Edward, proprietor Great Western Hotel, Richmond nr G. W. R.
THOMAS, F. W., manager Bank of Montreal, Richmond
Thomas & Co., undertakers, Talbot

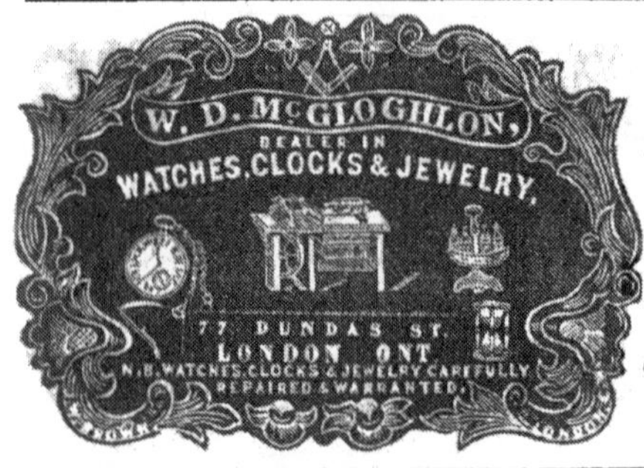

THE BEST AND CHEAPEST HOUSE IN THE WEST,

WATCHES, CLOCKS, JEWELLERY, &C.,

MASONIC APRONS, JEWELS AND EMBLEMS,

ON HAND AND MADE TO ORDER.

77 Dundas Street, London, Ontario.

WILLIAM BAWDEN,

AUCTIONEER,

LAND, HOUSE, AND GENERAL AGENT,

TALBOT STREET,

LONDON, ONTARIO.

N.B.—Registry kept for parties having Houses to let. Inventories taken, and valuations of all kinds made.

FRANK COOPER,

PHOTOGRAPHIC ARTIST,

Richmond Street, 2 doors North of Revere House,

London, Ontario.

Pictures taken in all the latest styles of the Art. Satisfaction given, or no charge.

Particular attention given to the position of the sitter.

T. BEATTIE & CO.,

Direct Importers of British and French

DRY GOODS,

MILLINERY, MANTLES, SILKS, SHAWLS, REAL LACES, KID GLOVES, &c.

Dundas Street, Opposite Market Lane,

London, Ontario.

Liberal terms to Wholesale Millinery Customers.

F. J. DELL,

General Dealer in

GROCERIES,

Wines and Liquors,

Butler's New Brick Block, Corner Richmond and King Streets,

LONDON, ONTARIO.

NEW GROCERY WAREHOUSE,

(WHOLESALE AND RETAIL,)

ALEX. TYTLER,

Family Grocer, Tea, Coffee, Wine, Spirit, and Provision Merchant, and Dealer in Crockery, Importer and Bottler of

GUINNESS'S DUBLIN PORTER,

DUNDAS ST. WEST, 2 DOORS EAST R. S. MURRAY,

LONDON, ONTARIO.

Thompson, A. K., livery stable, William
Thompson, Thomas, (T. & J. Thompson) h Westminster
Thompson, William J., (Thompson & Moran), Dundas bet Clarence and Wellington
THOMPSON & DUFF, publishers' agents, Dundas bet Clarence and Wellington
Thompson & Moran, carriage and wagon makers, Dundas bet Clarence and Wellington
Thompson, T. & J., gen. hardware, Dundas cor Talbot
Thornton, Wm., proprietor Locomotive Inn, Clarence
Tomlinson, Thomas, saw filer, Market Square
Traher, John, artist, Dundas
Traher, William, merchant tailor, Dundas bet Richmond and Clarence
Travelers' Insurance Company, of Hartford, Conn., Beddome and Dempster, agents, Albion bdgs
Trebilcock, George, merchant tailor, Dundas nr Richmond
Trebilcock, Mrs. Harriet, groceries, etc., Dundas
Trebilcock, William, grocer, Dundas
Trimble, George, prop. Queen's Arms Hotel, Horton cor Waterloo
Trotman, Samuel, grocer, Colborne nr Bond
Turville, William S., proprietor Hartley Mills, Burlington, n of limits, store King nr Market
TYTLER, ALEXANDER, groceries, provisions, wines and liquors, Dundas e of Talbot (see adv)
Underhill, Joseph, proprietor Young Briton Hotel, Wellington
Vanvalkenburgh, Thaddeus, detective, h Dundas
VINING, W. R., Vice President Agricultural Mutual Assurance Association of Canada
WADDELL, ROBERT, general insurance agent, accountant, conveyancer, commercial agent and money broker, Talbot bet Dundas and North
Waddell & Gunn, insurance agents
Wakeling, William, oil and commission, Market Lane
Walker, A., M.D., Maitland bet Hill and South
Walker, James A., produce merchant, Talbot
Walker, John (Machattee & Co.), h King
WALKER, ROBERT, & SONS, dry goods, Dundas
Walker & Anderson, carpenters, King nr Clarence
Wallace, Arthur, city assessor, City Hall, h Waterloo
Wallace, Peter, match manufacturer, e of Limits
Walmsley, John, conductor G. W. R., h York
WALSH, RIGHT REV. JOHN, D.D., bishop Diocese of Sandwich, res Palace, Richmond
Ward, James, tailor, Richmond
Ware, David T., watches, clocks and jewelery, and agent Wheeler & Wilson's sewing machines, Dundas, w of Clarence
Waterman, Herman (H. Waterman & Bro.)
WATERMAN, H. & BRO., Atlantic Petroleum Works, office Music Hall, Richmond (see adv)
Watson, George, architect, King nr Richmond
Weatherhead, William, grocer, Westminster
Webb, Thomas, manufacturer boots and shoes, Dundas bet Richmond and Clarence
Webb, William, prop. Wellington House, Wellington cor Bathurst
Webster, George, wood yard, Wellington nr North
Webster, Isaac, flour and feed, Market Lane
WELD, WILLIAM, editor and prop. *Farmers' Advocate*, and prop. Agricultural Emporium, Talbot s of Dundas (see adv)
Wescott, Thomas R., barrister, Ridout nr North
Western Assurance Co., of Toronto, F. B. Beddome, agent, Albion Buildings
WESTLAKE, FRANCIS, biscuit baker and confectioner, Dundas bet Market Lane and Talbot and Hitchcock and Talbot
Westlake, William, hoop skirt manufacturer and tailor, Dundas bet Richmond and Talbot
Westlake, Mrs. W., millinery and dry goods, Dundas bet Richmond and Talbot
Westland, G. P., M.D., (homœopathist), Dundas bet Richmond and Clarence
WESTMAN, ALFRED, umbrella repairer, saw manufacturer and filer, &c., Dundas nr Talbot
Weston, Amos, second hand furniture, Talbot
Whale, Mrs. Ellen, hotel keeper, Hamilton Road
Whan, James, jeweler, London
WHAN, THOMAS (Whan & McLean), h Waterloo
WHAN & McLEAN (Thomas Whan and John McLean), importers of dry goods, etc., Dundas w of Richmond
Whately & Meredith, attorneys-at-law, Albion Buildings, Richmond
Wheeler, Alfred, (Duke) saloon, Market Square
Wheeler B., boots and shoes, Dundas e
Wheeler, Henry, baker, Ridout bet King and York
Wheeler, Bros., boots and shoes, Dundas between Richmond and Clarence
Whetter, Richard, butcher, 8 Market House
Whiskard, Thomas O., new and second-hand clothing, Dundas e
White, John, proprietor Olympic saloon, Richmond
Whiting, Mrs. E., dry goods and millinery, Dundas cor Clarence
Wigmore, Richard, Chief of Police, City Hall
WILKENS, H. A. (Teale & Wilkens), h Dundas
Wilkinson, Edward, blacksmith, Richmond bet King and York
Wilkinson, Nicholson, sheepskin tanner, Horton
Willcox, Amos, sen., cabinet maker, King bet Talbot and Ridout
Williams, John, chemist & druggist, Dundas opp Market Lane
Willis, Robert, boarding-house, Richmond nr Horton
Willis & Belton, lumber merchants, York bet Clarence and Wellington
Willis, Belton & Co., manufacturers of lath and shingles, Acton, Ontario; office, York
Willson, Crowell, president Agricultural Mutual Assurance Association of Canada, Ridout
Wilson, Mrs., groceries, Simcoe cor Burwell
Wilson, David (Horton & Wilson) bds Clarence
Wilson, Henry (Wilson & Code), h Wellington
Wilson, John, proprietor White Ox Inn, Hamilton Road
Wilson, William, proprietor livery stable, Dundas
Wilson & Code, lumber merchants, Clarence cor York
Wilson & Davis, soap and potash manufacturers, Bathurst cor Thames
Winnett, John, lumber merchant, York bet Richard and Clarence
WINNETT, THOMAS, city weighmaster and license inspector, Market Square
Wood, C., inn keeper, Waterloo nr Oxford
Woodbury, Miss A., hoop skirts, King under Revere House
Woodbury, Edwin, prop. Revere House, Richmond cor King
Wood's International Hotel, J. G. Wood, prop., also grocer, Dundas cor Clarence
Worthington & Martin, barbers, Tecumseh House
Wright, James (Cowan & Wright)
Wright, John, butcher, Market
Wright, Mrs. M., boarding house, Fullarton
Wright & Durand, builders and contractors, North cor Wellington
WYCKOFF, PETER, watches, clocks and jewelery, Dundas, w of Richmond
Yealland, Edmund, tailor, Dundas bet Clarence and Wellington
Yirrell, Thomas, boots and shoes, Richmond nr King
Young, Joseph, boots & shoes, Dundas nr Wellington

LONDON CLASSIFIED BUSINESS DIRECTORY.

Marked thus * are Wholesale.

Agents, Cartage.

Hendrie & Co., G. W. R. freight office
Shedden, John & Co., cor Richmond and York

Agents, Express.

Boniface, James T., (Canadian and American), Albion buildings, Richmond

Agents, Insurance.

Ashton, A. E., Ridout bet Dundas and North
Beddome, F. B., Albion buildings, Richmond
Caldwell, D. M., 41 Dundas
Clarke, Francis S., e s Richmond n of Dundas
Dempster, William, Albion buildings, Richmond
Gunn, George M., Talbot bet Dundas and North
Lawrason, L., (Edinburgh Life), Albion bldgs, Richmond
Macdonald, Alexander, Agricultural Mutual Assurance Association of Canada, Ridout
Macdonald, D. C., Ridout
Meredith, John C., Dundas nr Ridout
Reed, E. Baynes, Albion buildings, Richmond
Smyth, Alfred G., Albion buildings, Richmond
Waddell, Robert, Talbot, bet Dundas and North

Agents, Sewing Machines.

Campbell, A. M., Music Hall
Lake, John N., s s Dundas n of Richmond
Moore, Walter B., Palmer's Block, Richmond
Parker, David H., Music Hall Blgs Richmond
Rowland, Edward, n s Dundas, e of Richmond
Ware, D. T., Dundas, bet Richmond and Talbot

Agents (Shipping.)

Smyth, Alfred G., Albion bgs, Richmond

Agricultural Implements.

Gray, George B., Fullarton
Kinney, Brainard & Co., 3rd con., tp. London
Leonard, Elijah, York bet Waterloo and Colborne

Architects, Civil Engineers and Surveyors

Peters, Samuel, Albion blgs, Richmond
Watson George, s s King, bet Richmond and Talbot

Auctioneers, &c.

Barnard, Peter C., e s Richmond, opp City Hall
Bawden, William, Talbot, s of Dundas
Emery, Arthur S., n s Dundas, bet Talbot and Ridout
O'Donohue, John, n s Dundas, bet Richmond and Clarence

Axe Manufacturer.

Fleming, John, Ridout, bet King and York

Bakers and Confectioners.

Barham, Thomas, Ridout, bet King and York
Dean, William, Mark Lane, bet Lichfield and Market
Eldridge, John, Clarence, bet King and Dundas
Eitzgibbon, James, n e cor Ridout and York
Jones, John, Wellington, cor South
Peters, George M., w s Richmond, s of Kent
Ranahan, John, s s Dundas, w of Wellington
Soule, Robert, n s Dundas, w of Wellington
Wheeler, Henry, Ridout bet King and York

Banks (Savings.)

Bank of Montreal, J. T. Boyd, clerk, cor Richmond and Fullarton
Merchants' Bank, Richmond cor William

Banks.

Bank of British North America, H. Simpson, manager, Richmond, cor e North
Bank of Montreal, F. W. Thomas, manager, Richmond cor Fullarton
Canadian Bank of Commerce, H. S. Strathy, manager, Richmond
Merchants' Bank, William F. Harper, manager, Richmond cor William

Barristers, Attorneys, Solicitors, &c.

Abbot & Hutchinson, s s Dundas, e of Ridout
Bell, Archibald. Ridout cor North
Becher, Barker & Street, East North
Brough, Richard R., n s Dundas, bet Ridout and Talbot
Brown, John J., Richmond cor King
Corrigan, C. S., Dundas, bet Talbot and Ridout
Cornish & Macdonald, n s Dundas, bet Talbot and Ridout
Cronyn & Cronyn, n s Dundas, bet Talbot and Ridout
Elliot & Fraser, n e cor Richmond and Dundas
Flock, James H., Albion blgs, Richmond
Geary & Moncrieff, n s Dundas, e of Ridout
Glass, David, s s Dundas, bet Talbot and Ridout
Graydon, Simpson H., n s Dundas, e of Ridout
Harris & Magee, s s Dundas, bet Talbot and Ridout
Holmes, Calvin D. n s Dundas, bet Talbot and Ridout
Horton & Wilson, e s Talbot, nr Dundas
Irving, Thomas T., s s Dundas, bet Talbot and Ridout
Lawrason, William L., Carling's Block, Richmond
Mackenzie, Philip, Robinson Hall, Dundas
MacMillan, Duncan, s s Dundas e of Ridout
O'Brien & Land, Richmond opp City Hall
Parke, E. Jones, s s Dundas, e of Ridout
Partridge, Thomas, Dundas, cor Market Lane
Reed, E. Baynes, Albion buildings, Richmond
Rock, Warren, n s Dundas, e of Ridout
Scatcherd & Meredith, Dundas, e of Ridout
Shanley, James, Ridout
Whately & Meredith, Albion buildings, Richmond

Baths.

Sulphur Springs Baths, foot of Dundas

Bending Factories.

Efner, Abraham, York e of Adelaide
Plummer & Pacey, Ridout near Fullarton

Berlin Wools.

Ashton, Miss M., s s Dundas, e of Clarence
Gibbons, Mrs. S. A., Dundas, near Clarence
Miller, Edward, n s Dundas, e of Richmond
Peacock, James, w s Richmond, s of North

Billiard Saloons.

Bostwick, Edward, Richmond opp City Hall
Rowley, William, Richmond n of King
Smith, James, Albion, Richmond, adjoining P.O.
Strong's Hotel, Dundas
Tecumseh House, Richmond, cor York
Woodbury, E., Revere House.

Bitters, Syrups and Cordials.

Crooks, Hiram, e s Richmond, bet York and King

Blacksmiths.

Cooper, Edmund H., n s King, between Talbot and Ridout
Crook, John, King bet Talbot and Richmond
Davies, David, Wellington, bet King and York
Moorehead, Alexander, n s King between Talbot and Ridout
Morkin, John, Richmond opposite R. C. Church
Morrison, Thomas, s s e North, bet Clarence and Wellington
Mustell, John, w s Richmond, bet King and York
Wilkinson, Edward, w s Richmond, bet King and York

Boarding Houses.

Davies, Mrs. David, w s Wellington, bet King and York
Flock, William, Dundas, between Clarence and Wellington
George, Mrs. Fanny, n w cor Wellington and Bathurst
Hendershot, Abraham, w s Clarence bet Bathurst and Horton
Hurlbit, Mrs. Matilda, n s King, bet Talbot and Ridout
McDowell, Mrs. Eliza, cor King and Ridout
Ison, Mrs., Wellington, bet Dundas and e North
Joyce, Mrs. E., n s Dundas, bet Ridout and Talbot
King Mrs. Eliza C., Talbot bet York and Bathurst
Paul, A. B., Clarence bet King and Dundas
Proudfoot, Mrs. Sarah, Ridout, bet North and Fullarton

Bookbinders.

Chapman, Charles, s s Dundas, bet Talbot and Ridout
Reid, Robert, n s Dundas, bet Richmond and Talbot
Taylor, E. A. & Co. Richmond cor North

Booksellers and Stationers.

Carrie, William L., Richmond
Henry, Bernard, e s Richmond, s of Dundas
Mills, John, e s Richmond, bet King and Dundas
Reid, Robert, n s Dundas, bet Richmond and Talbot
Taylor, E. A. & Co., Richmond, cor North

Boots and Shoes, Manufacturers & Dealers Wholesale.

McPherson, J. & Co., Dundas e of Richmond

Boots and Shoes, Manufacturers & Dealers Retail.

Ashton, Charles J., n s Dundas, bet Clarence Wellington
Begg, William, s s Dundas, bet Market Lane and Talbot
Cook, Philip, n s Dundas, w of Clarence
Cressall, Joseph, Penitentiary boot and shoe store, Dundas
Durand, William, s s Dundas
Kirkpatrick, Robert, n s Dundas w of Clarence
McDonell, Allen J., n s Dundas, bet Richmond and Clarence
McMechan, John, n s Dundas, bet Richmond and Clarence
McPherson, George, n s Dundas, opp Market Lane
Oliver, James, s s Dundas, w of Market Lane
Regan, Daniel, s s Dundas, e of Richmond
Rowland, Edward, n s Dundas e of Richmond
Sime, William, s s Dundas bet Richmond and Clarence
Taylor, William, e s Talbot s of Dundas
Webb, Thomas, s s Dundas bet Richmond and Clarence
Wheeler, Bros., Dundas nr Richmond
Yirrell, Thomas, w s Richmond bet King & York
Young, Joseph, Dundas nr Clarence

Brewers and Maltsters.

Allaster, John G., Dundas e of Adelaide
City Brewery, W. & J. Carling, Waterloo cor Pall Mall
Hamilton, John, Ann bet Sarnia and Talbot
Haystead, David, prop Victoria Brewery, s w cor King and Talbot
Labatt & Co., props London Brewery, foot of Talbot
Lucas & Arkell, Ridout cor York

Brickmakers.

London Pressed Brick Manufacturing Company, Westminster

Broker, Land and General.

Jeffery, Joseph, w s Richmond, Palmer's Block

Brokers, Stock, Bill and Exchange.

Beddome, F. B., Albion Buildings, Richmond
Bunning, John W., w s Richmond s of Dundas
Clarke, Francis S., e s Richmond n of Dundas
Henry, Bernard, e s Richmond s of Dundas
Jeffery, Joseph, w s Richmond, Palmer's Block
Lawrason, L., Albion Buildings, Richmond
Mills, John, e s Richmond bet King and Dundas
Spence, N. C., Richmond
Taylor, Henry, Richmond opp City Hall

Builders and Contractors.

Anderson, James and George, Cartwright bet Bond and Duke
Bolton and Pendergast, s s King bet Ridout and Talbot
Campbell, Alexander, Bathurst bet Talbot and Richmond
Castle, James, King bet Talbot and Ridout
Cox, Joseph, Dundas w of Wellington
Dodd, Joseph C. & Son, n s e North bet Clarence and Wellington
Ellwood, Garner, King e of Adelaide
Foster, George, n e cor Bathurst and Thames
Hoskins, Richard, h n s e Horton bet William and Maitland
Joanes, William, s s North bet Colborne and Waterloo
Lentall, Thomas, Richmond opp R. C. Church
Lucas, William J., Maitland bet e North and Duke
McMillan, Archibald, Maitland s of Great Market
Murray, Alexander, cor Wellington and e North
Palmer, Edward, h w s Burwell bet e Horton and E. Simcoe
Stewart, James, Burlington s of Cheapside
Taylor, George, e s Talbot bet Bathurst and Horton
Walker, William C., n e cor Clarence and King
Walker & Anderson, n s King bet Richmond and Clarence
Wright, John, h n s King bet Waterloo and Colborne
Wright & Durand, cor e North and Wellington

Cabinet Makers and Upholsterers.

Anundson, Christian, n s Dundas bet Talbot and Ridout
Caldwell, Thos., King bet Richmond and Talbot
Coombs, Henry, n s King bet Richmond and Talbot

Cabinet Makers, &c.—(*Continued*)

Ferguson, John, w s Richmond bet Dundas and King
Mearns, William, Temperance Hall, Richmond
Morehead, George, King nr Clarence
Wilcox, Amos, s s King bet Talbot and Ridout

Carriage and Wagon Makers.

Abbott Brothers, n s Dundas bet Wellington and Waterloo
Campbell, John, s s King bet Talbot and Ridout
Dart, Roger, s s Dundas bet Wellington and Waterloo
Hodgens, Thos. D., cor Market and Mark Lane
McKellar & Stewart, opp English Cathedral
Morrison, Thomas, s s East North, bet Clarence and Wellington
Pavey & Sons, King bet Talbot and Ridout
Plummer & Pacey, Ridout nr Fullerton
Roe & Judd, w s Wellington bet King and York
Thompson & Moran, s s Dundas bet Clarence and Wellington

Carriage Spring Manufacturer.

Brummett, R., Ridout cor Bathurst

Carvers and Gilders.

Graves, Otto B., w s Richmond nr City Hall
Seddon, Mrs., n s Dundas bet Ridout and Talbot

Chemists and Druggists.

Crittle, William, Dundas, s w cor Burwell
Heathfield, M. W., Dundas opp Strong's Hotel
Mitchell, B. A., n s Dundas e of Talbot
Puddicombe, Robert W., Albion bdgs, Richmond
Plummer, E. & Co., n s Dundas e of Richmond
Robinson, William H., Richmond opp City Hall
Salter, John, s s Dundas e of Richmond
Saunders, William, n s Dundas bet Richmond and Clarence
Strong, Henry, Picton nr Duke
Williams, John, n s Dundas opp Market Lane

Chemical Works.

Canada Chemical Works, office Richmond nr King
Machattie & Co., office Richmond nr King

China, Glass and Earthenware.

Reid, W. J. & Co., Richmond adj City Hall
Rowland, Alfred, e s Richmond n of Dundas

Cigars and Tobacco.

Bowman William, jun., s e cor Dundas and Richmond
Kohl, Richard L., s s Dundas bet Richmond and Market Lane

Clothing, New and Second-hand.

Dranger, John, Dundas nr Wellington
Whiskard, Thomas G., Dundas.

Collector of Inland Revenue.

McClery, Peter, Albion Buildings, Richmond

Commercial College.

London Commercial College, w s Wellington bet Bathurst and York

Commission Merchants.

Clark, Henry & Co., Victoria Blgs., Richmond
Eckley, Henry K., Ann
Elliott, Joseph H., n w cor Market Square
Hawkins, George, King bet Richmond and Talbot
Lenfestey, Henry, Talbot opp Market
McMillan, Duncan
Pritchard, R. & G., s s King bet Richmond and Talbot
Shaw, Benjamin, King, bet Talbot and Richmond
Smallwood, James
Tanton Bros., Talbot opp Market

Confectioners, Wholesale.

Fysh, Hewitt, n s Dundas bet Richmond and Clarence
McCormick, Thomas, e s Clarence s of Duke
Perrin, Daniel S., e s Richmond bet York and King
Westlake, Francis, s s Dundas bet Market Lane and Talbot

Dentists.

Adams, J., Richmond opp North
Nelles, Henry H., D.D.S., n s Dundas bet Richmond and Talbot
Perrin, Darius, Dundas e of Clarence
Sabine, J. B., n s Dundas
Stone, Ashbel C., M.D., Dundas nr Clarence

Dry Goods, Wholesale.

Birrell, John & Co., North nr Talbot
Laing, Lockhart & Co., North cor Talbot

Dry Goods, Retail.

Alley, Henry B. B., n s Dundas bet Richmond and Talbot
Beattie, T. & Co., Dundas opp Market Lane
Burns, George, n s Dundas w of Richmond
Chisholm, A. & Co., Dundas opp Market Lane
Davidson, R. S. T. & Co., n w cor Richmond and Dundas
Finlayson, Alexander, n s Dundas e of Talbot
Green, J. & Co., n s Dundas opp Market Lane
Higginson, William, s w cor Richmond & Dundas
Mactie, Daniel, Dundas cor Talbot
Manley, Robert, Dundas w of Market Lane
Murray, Robert S., Dundas cor Talbot
McDonough & Shoebothem, s s Dundas bet Market Lane and Talbot
McIntosh, A. & J. G. & Co., 57 and 59 Dundas
McPherson, Archibald, n s Dundas e of Talbot
Priddis, Charles, s s Dundas w of Richmond
Reid, W. J. & Co., adj City Hall, Richmond
Robinson, George, e s Dundas bet Richmond and Market Lane
Smith Mrs. E., s s Dundas cor Wellington
Sutherland, George D., s s Dundas bet Talbot and Market Lane
Walker, Robert & Sons, s s Dundas bet Richmond and Market Lane
Westlake, Mrs. William, n s Dundas bet Richand Talbot
Whan & McLean, n s Dundas w of Richmond

Engraver—Copper, Steel and Wood.

Aston, Thomas, n s Dundas bet Wellington and Waterloo

Express Companies.

Canadian & American Express Co., James T. Boniface, agent, Albion buildings, Richmond

Fancy Goods.

Atkinson, J. & Co., Dundas nr Talbot
Jackson, John H., Dundas e of Talbot
McHugh, Peter, n s Market Square
Miller, Edward, n s Dundas e of Richmond
Peacock, James, w s Richmond s of North
Reid, W. J. & Co., adjoining City Hall, Richmond

Fanning Mills, Manufacturers of.

Stewart, Bruce & Co., Hitchcock, bet Mark Lane and Talbot

Flour and Feed.

Butler, Henry, Richmond n of King
Frazer, Thomas, w s Richmond bet Bathurst and Horton
Fysh, Henry, n s Market Square
Percival, James, North bet Clarence and Wellington
McCormick, Andrew, Richmond cor York
Sharp, James, Sarnia bet Mount Pleasant and Ann
Southcott, James, Talbot bet Dundas and Mkt
Webster, Isaac, Market Lane

Foundries and Machine Shops.

Those marked thus * are Brass.

Anderson, M. & E., proprietors Globe Foundry, e Dundas
Bruce, D. & Co., Fullarton bet Talbot & Ridout
Darvill & Robb, King bet Ridout and Talbot
Elliott, John, proprietor Phœnix Foundry, s e cor Bathurst and Wellington
*Hobbs, W. C., Clarence, opp N. C. Methodist Church
*Law, John, w s Richmond, bet King and York
Leonard, Hon. Elijah, York bet Waterloo and Colborne
McCleary, J. & O., York bet Wellington and Clarence
*Rogers, Edward, Dundas w of Talbot

Fruits, Oysters, Game and Confectionery.

Baker, John E., Palmer's Block, Richmond
Bickle, John, Richmond n of York
Bunning, John W., w s Richmond s of Dundas
Clegg, Robert E., e s Richmond bet King and York
Harris, John, e s Richmond n of York
Mountjoy, Richard, Richmond opp City Hall
O'Callaghan, Thomas E., Dundas cor Mkt Lane
Spence, N. C., Richmond opp City Hall

Gold and Silver Platers.

Baker, Isaac W. C., n s Dundas w of Clarence
McIntyre, Archibald, King bet Ridout and Talbot
Beecher, George, n s Dundas bet Clarence and Wellington

Grain Merchants.

Alanson, John, York bet Richmond and Talbot

Grocers, Wholesale.

Adams, Edward & Co., s s Dundas bet Talbot and Ridout
McDonough, Thomas J., Dundas w of Richmond
Rowland, Frederick, n e cor Richmond & Dundas
Simson, W. R. & Co., s s Dundas bet Richmond and Talbot
Smith, F. & Co., n s Dundas bet Richmond and Talbot
Smith, W. Simpson, Dundas and Market Square
Tytler, Alexander, s s Dundas e of Talbot

Grocers, Retail.

Agnew, Washington, s w cor Dundas & Waterloo
Bentley, Henry, King bet Richmond and Talbot
Byrne, Miles, Richmond opp City Hall
Castle, James, King bet Talbot and Ridout
Clegg, John, s w cor Clarence and Simcoe
Cleghorn, Andrew, Ridout bet Kent and Market
Comstock, Harvey, e s Talbot s of Dundas
Curtis, Henry C., s s Dundas w of Wellington
Dean, William, Mark Lane bet Lichfield and Market
Edwards, William, s w cor Wellington & Simcoe
Elliott, Bros., s s Dundas bet Richmond and Market Lane
Fitzgerald & Scandrett, s s Dundas e of Richmond
Gleeson, James, cor Richmond and Bathurst
Hibbert, John, s w cor Horton and Clarence
Howard, Thomas, s w corner Wellington & Grey
Jarman, Mrs. Richmond opp R. C. Church
Lake, Alfred, Westminster
Lentall, Mrs. T., Richmond opp R. C. Church
Lester, Daniel, n e cor York and Burwell
Lilley, Charles, s e cor Burwell and Dundas
London Co-operative Association, 41 Dundas
Loughrey, William, Petersville
McCormick, Andrew, Richmond cor York
McCormick, William, Richmond bet G. W. R. and Bathurst
McDonough & Shoebothem, s s Dundas bet Market Lane and Talbot
McDonogh, William, e s Richmond bet Dundas and North
McKenzie, Roderick, Richmond opp City Hall
Metharell, John, n s Dundas bet Clarence and Wellington
Moule, John, n s Dundas bet Richmond and Talbot
Mullin, John, n s King bet Clarence and Wellington
Mullin & Smyth, Richmond opp City Hall
Noble, William, Hamilton Road bet Maitland and William
Nagle, Thomas, York bet Ridout and Thames
O'Callaghan, Thomas E., Dundas cor Market Lane
Oxley, Michael, s s King bet Clarence and Wellington
Percival, William, n s Dundas bet Clarence and Wellington
Proudfoot, Alexander, Petersville
Reynolds, George J., e s Richmond bet King and York
Service, Alexander, w s Wellington bet Simcoe and Grey
Sharpe & Stenabaugh, s s Dundas e of Talbot
Shaw, George, s s Dundas bet Richmond and Clarence
Smith, Alexander, Westminster
Smyth, John B., e s Talbot s of Dundas
Southcott, James, Talbot bet Dundas & Market
Symmonds, John, n s Dundas bet Clarence and Wellington
Taylor, Benjamin, n w cor E. Simcoe and Colborne
Trebilcock, Mrs. H., n s Dundas bet Clarence and Richmond
Trebilcock, William, s s Dundas w of Clarence
Weatherhead, William, Westminster
Westby, William, n w cor Dundas and Ridout
Wood, John, Dundas nr Clarence

Gunsmiths.

Gurd, John & Son, s s Dundas, opp Strong's Hotel

Hardware.

Cowan & Wright, Dundas opp Market Lane
Hope, Adam & Co., North bet Talbot & Ridout
Shaw, C. D., & Co., Dundas bet Richmond and Talbot
Smith, Chapman & Co., s s Dundas bet Richmond and Market Lane
Thompson, T. & J., Dundas n w cor Talbot

Halls.

City Hall, Richmond
Music Hall, Richmond bet York and King

Hatters & Furriers.

Beltz, Edmund, 85 Dundas
McCann, Philip, s s Dundas bet Richmond and Market Lane
McCrossin & Co., Albion Block, Richmond

Hoop Skirt Manufacturers and Dealers.

Claypole, Mrs. Mary Ann, Mark Lane bet Lichfield and Market
Green, J. & Co., n s Dundas opp Market Lane
Westlake, William, n s Dundas bet Richmond and Talbot
Woodbury, Miss Abigail, under Revere House

Hop Yards.

Bailey, William, w s Waterloo bet e King and Dundas

Hotels.

American House, Samuel Grigg prop., s e cor Richmond and York
Baker, Daniel, prop. Brock Hotel, n w cor Talbot and York
Baldeg, John, prop. Westminster Hotel, s s King nr Ridout
Balkwill, William, prop. Balkwill's Hotel, n w Talbot and King
Boyce, John, prop. Westminster Abbey Inn, Clark's Bridge, Westminster
Bradt, P. H., prop. Anglo American Hotel, n w cor York and Wellington
Campbell, Francis, prop Royal Hotel, w s Richmond bet G. W. R. and Bathurst
City Hotel, J. & T. Mossop, props. Dundas cor Talbot
City Arms Hotel, J. Pannell, prop., King opp Market
Dulmage, John, prop. Ontario Hotel, King, bet
Dundas, James, prop. Central Inn, n s Dundas bet Wellington and Waterloo
Essery, William A., prop. Montreal House, York
Hayden, Thomas, prop. Hayden's Hotel, cor King and Talbot
Haystead, David, prop. Haystead's Hotel, s w cor King and Ridout
Hiscox Hotel, Thomas Powell, prop., Dundas, bet Richmond and Clarence
International Hotel, (Wood's), J. Woods, prop., Dundas cor Wellington
McDonald, Richard, prop. Petersville Hotel, Petersville
Matthews, John, prop. Britannia House, s w cor Wellington and York
Revere House, E. Woodbury, prop., Richmond cor King
Simmons, R. P., prop. Northern Hotel, North e of Richmond
Strong's Hotel, William Hawthorne, prop., n s Dundas bet Richmond and Clarence
Tecumseh House, B. F. Moore, prop., James C. Derby, manager, Richmond cor York
Thomas, Edward, prop. Great Western Hotel, e s Richmond bet G. W. R. and Bathurst
Western Hotel, J. Mason, prop. Richmond
White Ox Inn, John Wilson prop., Hamilton Road e of limits

Hubs and Spokes, Manufacturers of

Plummer & Pacey, Ridout nr Fullarton
Shopland & Bentley, s s North bet Wellington and Clarence

Insurance Companies and Agents.

Ætna Fire Ins. Co., of Dublin, E. Baynes Reed, agent, Albion blgs Richmond
Ætna Fire Ins. Co., Hartford, Conn., R. Waddell, agent, Talbot
Agricultural Mutual Assurance Association of Canada, Ridout n of Dundas
Briton Medical and General Life Assurance, A. G. Smyth, agent, Albion bdgs, Richmond
Canada Life Assurance Co., F. S. Clarke, agent, Richmond n of Dundas
Commercial Union Insur'ce Co., A. H Beddome, agent, Albion bdgs, Richmond
Edinburgh Life Association, L. Lawrason, agent, Albion bdgs, Richmond
European Life and Guarantee Assurance Co., E. Baynes Reed, agent, Albion bdgs, Richmond
Hartford Live Stock Insurance Co., D. C. Macdonald, agent, Ridout
Hartford Fire Insurance Co., Hartford, Conn., W. Dempster, agent, Albion bdgs, Richmond
Home Insurance Co. of New Haven, A. G. Smyth agent, Albion bdgs, Richmond
Liverpool and London and Globe, A. G. Smyth, agent, Albion bdgs, Richmond
London Assurance Corporation, (London, Eng.) Waddell & Gunn, agents, Talbot bet Dundas and North
Montreal Assurance Co., (marine), R. Waddell, agent, Talbot
Ontario Mutual Fire Ins. Co., James Johnson, Sec. and Treas., Richmond opp City Hall
Phœnix Insurance Co., of England, John C. Meredith, agent, Dundas
Railway Passengers' Insurance Co., Hartford, Conn., Beddome & Dempster, agents, Albion bdgs, Richmond
Royal Insurance Co., F. B. Beddome, agent, Albion bdgs, Richmond
Scottish Provincial Life Assurance Co., George M. Gunn, agent, Talbot bet Richmond and North
Travelers' Insurance Co., of Hartford, Conn., F. B. Beddome, agent, Albion bdgs, Richmond
Western Assurance Co. of Toronto, F. B. Beddome, agent, Albion bds, Richmond

Lamps and Oil.

Baker, I. W. C., n s Dundas w of Clarence
Dyson, William, Dundas opp Strong's Hotel
Edwards, John, Richmond opp R. C. Church
Hunter, John, Richmond
Leonard, L. C. & Co., e s Richmond, adjoining *Free Press* office
McBride, S. & A., e s Richmond bet Dundas and King
Peters, S. & Co., Adelaide cor York
Rowland, Alfred, e s Richmond bet Dundas and North
Stewart, Samuel, e s Richmond n of Dundas

Leather and Findings.

Dunnett, Charles, Sulphur Spring Baths
Hyman, E. W., City Hall bdg
Johnston, Alexander, e s Richmond opp P. O.

Livery Stable Keepers.

Coote, William, Dundas opp Strong's Hotel
Wilson, W., s s Dundas bet Richmond and Clarence
Hiscox, George T., n s Dundas bet Richmond and Clarence
Hodgens & Brown, Clarence

Livery Stable Keepers—*(Continued)*

Loyd, Thomas, American House, s e cor Richmond and York
Nickel, George, e s Richmond bet King and York
Thompson, Andrew K., William bet Richmond and Talbot
Woods, John, Clarence s of Dundas

Lumber Merchants.

Baxter, H. A., cor Kent and Mark Lane
McPhail, Archibald, s s York bet Clarence and Wellington
Paul, Samuel, York bet Richmond and Talbot
Willis Belton & Co., s s York bet Clarence and Wellington
Wilson & Code, n w cor Clarence and York
Winnett, John, York bet Richmond and Clarence

Marble Cutters and Dealers.

Peel, John R., Richmond nr Simcoe
Powell, G. & Son, Richmond cor King
Smyth, John W., s s Dundas bet Richmond and Clarence
Teale & Wilkens, s s Dundas opp Strong's Hotel

Melodeon Manufacturers.

Andrus, Bros., s s King bet Clarence and Wellington

Merchant Tailors.

Boyd, Robert, n s Dundas bet Richmond and Clarence
Denton, John M., Albion Buildings, Richmond
Gauld, Alexander, Dundas bet Talbot and Market
Glen, James, s s Dundas e of Ridout
Morrison, Peter, Dundas
Parker, David H., 3 Music Hall, Richmond
Peel, Thomas, n s Dundas bet Richmond and Clarence
Spry, Abraham W., n s Dundas bet Richmond and Clarence
Traher, William J., Dundas w of Clarence
Trebilcock, George, n s Dundas bet Richmond and Clarence

Mica Miner.

Brunton, William Y., h St. James cor Alma

Mills, Flour, Grist and Oatmeal.

Hilliard & Saunby, North Branch Mills, office Richmond
Hunt, Charles, City Mills, foot of Talbot
Muirhead & Grey, e s Colborne, bet e Horton and e Simcoe
Turville, William S., propr Hartley Mills, Burlington n of limits; office King

Newspapers and Periodicals, Publishers.

Educator, J. W. Jones & Co., editors and proprietors, Richmond opp City Hall
Farmers' Advocate, W. Weld, editor and prop., Talbot
Free Press, J. & S. Blackburn, editors and props, Richmond opp North
London City and County Middlesex Directory, C. E. Anderson & Co., publishers, H. McEvoy, compiler. Directory Branch, *Daily Telegraph Office*, Toronto, Ontario
London Prototype, office, Dundas nr Talbot, John Siddons, proprietor
London Evening Advertiser, office, Dundas bet Talbot and Ridout, John Cameron, prop.

Nurserymen, Seedsmen and Florists.

Leslie, Alexander, Petersville
Griffin, James, Richmond

Official Assignees.

Churcher, Thomas, Market Square
Lawrason, L., Albion Buildings, Richmond

Oil Warehousemen.

Rowland & Johnson, William, cor Bathurst, office Richmond opp City Hall

Oil Refineries.

Forest City Oil Refinery Co., Duffield Bros., Hamilton Road
Leonard, L. C. & Co., Crescent Oil Refinery, Hamilton Road
Mahan, Hillson & Cooper, Gore Oil Refinery
Peters, S. & Co., Adelaide cor York
Ross & Kennedy, Hamilton Road
Spencer & Keenleyside, Hamilton Road
Stedwell, J. D., Hamilton Road
Thompson, I. V., Adelaide nr s e limits
Waterman, H. & Bro., Atlantic Petroleum Works, office Music Hall Richmond

Painters, House, Sign and Ornamental

Deadman, James, Talbot opp Market Square
Griffith, Richard, n s Dundas, bet Richmond and Clarence
Haskett, James, s e cor Wellington and King
Johnston, Joseph, Great Market near Colborne
Lewis, Robert, e s Richmond opp P. O.
Slater, Edward K., n s Dundas, w of Wellington

Photographers.

Ashworth, John, Albion buildings, Richmond
Cooper, Frank, Richmond n of King
Cooper, John, n s Dundas, bet Richmond and Clarence.
Egan, James, n s Dundas, opp Market Lane
Griffiths, John H., Dundas, cor Market
Mann, James A., s s Dundas e of Market Lane

Photographic Materials.

Egan, James, n s Dundas, opp Market Lane
Griffiths, John H., Dundas, cor Market Lane

Piano Fortes, Manufacturers & Dealers in.

Andrus Bros., s s Dundas, opp Market Lane
Nitschke, John, n s Dundas, bet Richmond and Clarence

Physicians and Surgeons.

Anderson, Alexander, Ridout bet North and Fullarton
Brown, V., Kent nr Talbot
Campbell, C. T., Homœopathic, Richmond opp North
Cattermole, James, h n s King, bet Waterloo and Colborne
Davis, Elisha, n s Dundas, bet Talbot and Ridout
Farrar, David, Dundas w of Richmond, h s w cor King and Waterloo
Flock, John R., s s Dundas, bet Clarence and Wellington
Harper, A., Hitchcock, bet Mark Lane and Talbot
Hobbs, John
Lancaster, Joseph J., Homœopathic, w s Richmond, near City Hall
Leeder, Asaph, h n s Bathurst, bet William and Maitland
Moore, Charles, w s Wellington, bet Dundas and King
Morden, Ralph, J. P., homœopathic, e North cor Clarence
Payne, Samuel, boards Balkwill's Hotel
Phillips, Thomas, Fullarton, bet Mark Lane and Talbot

Physicians and Surgeons—*(Continued)*

Sippi, Charles A., e s Alma, nr St. James
Westland, G. P., M. D., homœopathic, Dundas, bet Richmond and Clarence
Woodruff, William, e s Clarence, bet Dundas and King

Plumbers and Gas Fitters.

Law, John, Richmond, bet King and York
Rogers, Edward, n s Dundas, w of Talbot

Pork Packers.

Ferguson, James & Co., props. Ontario Pork Packing House, n s King, bet Talbot and Ridout
Rowland, Frederick, Bathurst, cor William
Shaw, Benjamin, h n s King, bet Maitland and William
Taylor, Charles, Ridout

Printers, Book and Job.

Blackburn, J. & S. *Free Press*, Richmond opp North
Cameron, John, *Advertiser*, Dundas, w of Talbot
Dawson Bros., Richmond, opp City Hall
Siddons, John, *Prototype*, North, w of Talbot

Produce and Commission Merchants.

Elliott, Joseph H., n w cor Market Square
Hilliard & Saunby, Talbot, bet Dundas and King
Kains, William K., York bet Clarence and Wellington
Slater, James, King, bet Richmond and Talbot
Tanton Bros, Talbot, opp Market
Walker, James A., Talbot bet Dundas and North

Pump Makers.

Atkinson, J., Richmond cor Hitchcock
Cousins, James N., Bathurst nr Talbot
Quick, James, Adelaide nr eastern limits
Reynolds, Nelson, Wellington nr Grey
Taylor, John, s w cor Sarnia and Mill

Roofers' Materials, Slate, Metal and Felt.

Elliott, Wm., Wellington bet Dundas and North
Smyth, John W., Dundas bet Richmond and Clarence

Saddle and Harness Makers.

Darch, Mrs. J., Talbot opp Market
Darch, Robert, n s King bet Richmond & Talbot
Doyle, John, n s King bet Richmond and Talbot
Dunn, James, n s Market Square
Loughrey, Archibald, Richmond bet Dundas and North
Ross, John, n s Dundas Smith's Block

Saloons and Restaurants.

Bostwick, Edward, Richmond opp City Hall
Brown, Charles, City Hall, Richmond
Dutton, Saml., s s Dundas bet Talbot and Ridout
Glass, Graham, Market Lane
McDonald, John, s s Market Square
O'Connor, James, Richmond cor King
Ormsby, Nicholas City Hall
Roach, George, G. W. R. Depot
Rooks, William H., s s Dundas bet Richmond and Clarence
Rowley, William, e s Richmond n of King
Smith, James, "Albion," adjoining Post Office, Richmond

Sash, Door and Blind Manufacturers.

Campbell, Alexander, Bathurst, bet Talbot and Richmond
Green, Thomas, n s Bathurst bet Clarence and Wellington

Savings and Loan Society.

Huron and Erie Savings and Loan Society, n s Dundas bet Ridout and Talbot

Shingle and Lath Manufacturers.

Willis, Belton & Co., s s York bet Clarence and Wellington

Small Wares, Wholesale.

Atkinson, J. & Co., Dundas nr Talbot

Soap and Candle Manufacturers.

Dalton Bros., n w cor Thames and York
Douthwaite, Charles, Adelaide opp Duke
Wilson & Davis, s w cor Bathurst and Thames

Soda Water Manufacturers.

Bilton, E. S. & Co., Dundas nr Wellington
Large, A. T. & Co., s s Dundas w of Wellington

Stage Proprietors.

Smith & Jamieson, proprietors London and Clinton stage, Hayden's Hotel

Starch Factory.

Ontario Starch Works Co., Adelaide s e of limits

Stoves and Tinware.

Anderson, M. & E., n s Dundas bet Ridout and Talbot
Baker, I. W. C., n s Dundas w of Clarence
Dyson, William, Dundas opp Strong's Hotel
Edwards, John, Richmond opp R. C. Church
Hunter, John, Richmond cor King
McBride, S. & E., e s Richmond bet Dundas and King
McCleary, J. & O., w s Wellington bet King and York
Millar, T. & J., n s Dundas bet Richmond and Clarence
Stewart, Samuel, e s Richmond n of Dundas

Tailors and Drapers.

Ball, John, s s Dundas e of Clarence
Davey, George, s s King bet Ridout and Talbot
Gould, Martin, w s Wellington bet Bathurst and Horton
Norris, George, w s Clarence bet King and Dundas
Yealland, Edmund, s s Dundas bet Clarence and Wellington

Tanners and Curriers.

Hyman, Ellis W., City Hall Building
Stephens, Richard, prop Westminster Bridge Tannery, Westminster
Wilkinson, Nicholas, Horton, cor Thames

Telegraph Company.

Montreal Telegraph Co., office Albion Buildings Richmond

Watchmakers and Jewelers.

Casson, John E., s s Dundas e of Clarence
Davis, Henry, s s Dundas e of Richmond
Hogg, Isaac, Market Lane
Jackson, John H., n s Dundas e of Talbot
McGloghlon, William D., 77 Dundas
Morphy, Andrew, s s Dundas w of Richmond
Murray, Hugh S., w s Richmond, s of North
Ware, D. T., n s Dundas nr Wellington
Wyckoff, Peter, s s Dundas w of Richmond

Wine and Spirit Merchants.

Bergin, Patrick, n s E. Simcoe bet Maitland and Burwell
Byrne, Miles, Richmond opp City Mills

J. ATKINSON & CO.,

Importers and Wholesale Dealers in

EUROPEAN AND AMERICAN SMALL WARES,

DRY GOODS, FANCY GOODS,

CUTLERY, STATIONERY, &c.,

AN EXTENSIVE ASSORTMENT ALWAYS ON HAND.

The NEW SERIES of CANADIAN SCHOOL BOOKS at SPECIAL RATES.

DUNDAS STREET, LONDON.

All Work WARRANTED.

GUARANTEED. SATISFACTION

WILLIAM DYSON,

MANUFACTURER OF

CHEESE VATS,

Dairy Utensils

Also Tin and Copper Smith, and dealer in every description of Stoves.

DUNDAS STREET, Opposite Strong's Hotel, - LONDON, ONT.

AMERICAN HOUSE.

SAMUEL GRIGG, Proprietor.

RICHMOND STREET, cor. YORK, convenient to the G. W. R. Station

London, Ontario.

Excellent Accommodation for the travelling public. In connection with this House is a First Class LIVERY AND SALE STABLE, with Horses and Vehicles to hire at all hours.

Wine and Spirit Merchants—*(Continued)*

Elliott, Bros. Dundas bet Richmond and Market Lane
Fitzgerald & Scandrett, Dundas, e of Richmond
Hibbert, John, s w cor Horton and Clarence
Lester, Daniel, n e cor York and Burwell
McDonough, Thos. J., n s Dundas nr Richmond
McDonough, William, e s Richmond bet Dundas and North
McKenzie, Roderick, Richmond opp City Hall
Mackay, Thomas H., n w cor Mark Lane and Market
Morkin, Thomas, cor Mark Lane and Lichfield
Mullin & Smyth, Richmond opp City Hall
Moone, Mrs. Catherine, Mark Lane
O'Callaghan, Thomas E., Dundas cor Market Lane
Proudfoot, Alexander, Petersville
Rowland, Frederick, n e cor Richmond & Dundas
Service, Alexander, Wellington bet Simcoe and Grey
Sharpe & Stenabaugh, s s Dundas e of Talbot
Simson, W. & R. & Co., s s Dundas bet Richmond and Talbot
Smith, F. & Co., n s Dundas bet Talbot and Richmond
Smith, William Simpson, s s Dundas bet Market Lane and Talbot
Smyth, John B., e s Talbot s of Dundas
Taylor, B., n w cor Simcoe and Colborne
Tytler, Alexander, s s Dundas e of Talbot
Weatherhead, William, Westminster

Wood Merchants.

Flowers, John, n w cor Wellington and South
Odle, Edwin, South bet Clarence and Wellington
Webster, George, n s Wellington bet Duke and North
Westby, Thomas, Petersville

Long Island Locks.—A Village on the Rideau River in the Township of Gloucester, County Carleton, 15 miles from Ottawa, the County Town. Land in the vicinity averages $20 per acre. Population 175.

Armstrong, Thomas, farmer
Brown, John, shoemaker
Butler, Michael, hotel keeper
Byers, Thomas, farmer
Clark, Nicholas, farmer
Clossin, W. T., wagon maker
Clothier, A., carpenter
Collins, Alexander, farmer
Findley, Alexander, farmer
Findley, William, farmer
Gamble, John, farmer
GAMBLE, MOSES, Postmaster, tailor
Gamble, Robert, farmer
Hall, David, merchant

Longwood.—(Melbourne Village.)—A Station on the Great Western Railway, in the Township of Ekfrid and Caradoc, County Middlesex, 21 miles from London. Population 125.

Beaumont, Robert, blacksmith
Bedford, James, painter
Brodie, James tailor
Brodie, J. W., teacher
Clark, Adam, farmer
Clarke, Alexander, farmer
Cornell, Christopher, farmer
Gentleman, David, tailor
Gibbs, John, cooper
Goodwin, William, saddler
Gordon & Begg, general merchants
GORDON, THOMAS, Postmaster, J.P
Gorman, Thomas, carpenter
Haigh, Thomas, teacher
Hearns, Thomas, carpenter
Kennedy, Rev. (Wesleyan)
Lacey, Joseph, shoemaker
McKenzie, John, hotel keeper and gen. mercht
McNulty, Peter, farmer
Miller, Jonathan, farmer
Robinson, J., farmer
Scott, John, wagon maker
Simmons, George, blacksmith
Sinclair, D. A., M.D.
Stewart, Rev. John (Canada Presbyterian)
Sutherland, John, shoemaker
Urquhart, William, tailor
Walker, Rev. R., (New Connexion Methodist)
Walker, William, cooper
Wellman, William, carpenter
Wilkinson, William, sen., J.P., farmer
Young, Benjamin, hotel keeper

Lonsdale.—A Village in the Township of Tyendinaga, County Hastings, on the Salmon River, 18 miles from Belleville, the County Town, and 131 from Toronto. Improved land in the vicinity averages $30 per acre. Population 100.

Aylesworth, Bowen, carpenter
Brown, D., farmer
Bruin, John, wagon maker
Casey, Patrick, wagon maker
Dawson, William, blacksmith
Doxsee, William, general merchant
Empey, Misses, milliners, etc.
Grant, William, cooper
Haight, Benjamin, blacksmith
Kimmerly, Peter, cooper
Lawrenson, John, general merchant
Lazier, James A., J.P., proprietor flouring mill
McFarren, Neal, farmer
McGinnis, James, carpenter
McGivin, Edward, teacher
Mabee, James, farmer
Nash, Patrick, hotel keeper
Randall, William T., tailor
Robinson, Rev. — (Wesleyan)
Ross, J. & J., manufacturers of woolen goods
Steward, Morgan, dyer and scourer
Sweeny, Miles, lime and stone
Sweeny, Miles, & Son, shoemakers
Turnbull, Rev. J. (Presbyterian)
Waldman, R., bookseller and stationer
West, William, blacksmith
West, John, farmer
Whitman, James, farmer
Whiteman, John, shoemaker
WILDMAN, RICHARD, Postmaster and gen. mercht,

Longwood Station.—A Village and Station on the Great Western Railway, in the Township of Caradoc, County Middlesex, 20 miles from London, the County Town, and 133 from Toronto. Daily mail. Population 100.

Alcock, R., general merchant
Campbell, —, teacher
Griffith, L. L., lumber merchant
Middlemas, G., cooper
Pratt, John, shoemaker
Vigor, R., hotel keeper
WHITE, J. A., Postmaster and general merchant
White, O., station master

Loretto.—A Village in the Township of Adjala, County Simcoe, 33 miles from Barrie, the County Town, 18 from Bradford Station, Northern Railway, and 42 from Toronto. Population 75.

Casserly, M. J., teacher
Casserly, William, proprietor Ontario House
Derham, P., J.P., general merchant
Doyle, B., proprietor Loretto Hotel
Doyle, P., farmer
Duggan, H., farmer
Gamble, J., J.P., farmer
Holland, John, farmer
Kelly, J., farmer
KELLY, P. D., J.P., Postmaster, insurance agent, and general merchant
McCabe, P., carpenter
McKenna, Charles, M.D.
Malone, J., farmer
Morrow, F., farmer
Nevins, J., farmer
Patton, James, farmer

L'Orignal.—The County Town of Prescott and Russell, in the Township of Longueil, on the Ottawa River, 59 miles from Ottawa, 66 from Montreal, 36 from Lancaster Station Grand Trunk Railroad, and 9 from Caledonia Springs. Money order office and Savings Bank. Population 850.

Aird, John, farmer
Bone, F., butcher
Brunet, Rev. A., (Roman Catholic)
Butterfield, John, attorney-at-law and insurance agt
Byers, R. D., farmer
Cameron, James, farmer
Campbell, D. P., M. D
Campbell, Robert, architect
Cass, Alfred, J. P., farmer
Castelloe, M. J., telegraph operator
Chalmers, Rev. D., (Wesleyan)
Clare, F., farmer
Clare, F. saddler
Daniell, James, County Judge
Dartnell, E. T., barrister, Co. Attorney, Clerk Peace
Fabien, J. butcher
Ferguson, Rev. G. D., (Old Kirk Presbyterian)
Grant, Allan J., barrister
Grant, A. J., farmer
Hall, Robert, tanner
Hamilton, William, architect
Hannam, Miss, milliner
Hayes, James, painter
JOHNSON, CHAUNCEY, Postmaster, J. P., and general merchant
Johnson, L. H., grocer and baker
Johnson, S. M., general merchant
Labelle, Wilfred, prop. Ottawa Hotel
Little, W., editor and publisher of *The Advertiser*
Lowiolette, Edward, prop. Ontario House and livery stable
McNab, F. F., principal grammar school
Marston, Jeremiah, painter
Marston, J. C., farmer
Marston, J. W., J.P., County Treasurer, Registrar Surrogate, &c., insurance agent
Maxwell, Miss E., teacher
Meyette, Felix, prop. L'Orignal House
Millar, John, general merchant
Murray, James, farmer, lime and stone dealer
O'Brian, D. J., general merchant
O'Brian, John, lumber dealer and prop. flouring and grist mill
O'Brian, Peter, barrister, County Clerk
Sonlier, Michael, carpenter
Steel, T. O., insurance agent
The Advertiser, published every Wednesday by W. Little, editor and proprietor
Treadwell, C. P., Sheriff
Unsworth, Parker, butcher
Walsh, James, tailor
Wright, William, shoemaker

Lorraine.—A Village in the Township of Mono, County Simcoe, 34 miles from Barrie, the County Town, and 50 from Toronto. Population 150.

Alexander, James, farmer
Anderson, James, farmer
Campbell, William, farmer
Colburg, Rev. —, (Wesleyan)
Hunt, Rev. D., (Wesleyan)
Mumford, Charles, farmer
MILLS, JOHN, Postmaster, cabinet maker and farmer
Quinn, James, farmer
Summerville, John, farmer
Stewart, Robert, farmer

Lowbanks.—A Post Office in the Township of Moulton, County Monck.

Ayers, William, farmer
Burket, A., farmer
Burrick, B., farmer
Furry, L., farmer
Logan, Thomas, J.P.
Michener, Isaac, carpenter
OVERHOLT, HENRY, Postmaster
Pew, R., farmer
Wallace, Alexander, farmer
Williams, J., farmer

Lowville.—A Village on Twelve-mile Creek, in the Township of Nelson, County Halton, Distant from Milton, the County Town, 6 miles, and from Toronto 46. Stages to Hamilton and Milton. Pop. 275.

Black, Miss, teacher
Blackstock, Rev. W. S. (Wesleyan)
Clement, Rev. Benjamin (Wesleyan)
Culloden, A. B., general merchant
Emerson & MacNair, blacksmiths
Gilmore & Burkholder, iron founders
Glass, —, saddler
Greer, James wagon maker
Lee, George, tanner
McKAY, OSCAR, Postmaster and general merchant
McLaren, J., general merchant
MacDaid, Henry, hotel keeper
Oliver, J. B., general merchant
Pembroke, John, shoemaker
Plewis & Warcup, millers
Rumpell, W. E., cabinet maker

Lucan.—A Village and Station of the Grand Trunk Railway, in the Township of Biddulph, County Middlesex, 16 miles from London, the County Town, 15 from St. Marys, and 55 from Sarnia. It is surrounded by an excellent agricultural district, and is rapidly increasing in importance. The principal business is the exportation of grain, produce and timber. Money Order office and Savings Bank. Population 900.

Armitage, James, teacher
Armitage, James, general merchant
ARMITAGE & O'NEIL, general merchants
Atkinson, Edward, wagon maker
Atkinson, Thomas, farmer
Bean, Hugh, prop. brickyard
Bowey, William, architect
Bryanton, Robert, cooper
Butler, P., farmer
Cavanagh & Armitage, grain merchants
Cobleigh, H. W., commission merchant
Collins, Henry, tinsmith
Cranican, M., grocer and liquor dealer
Curry, Robert W., principal Lucan Academy
Dagg, James, butcher
Davis, Samuel, nurseryman
Dight, Thomas, commission merchant
Drought, John, cabinet maker
Ellwood, William, tailor
Fairburn, Henry, baker
Farrell, John, druggist
Farrell, Patrick, bookseller and stationer
Fox, Robert, general merchant and agent
Frank, William, general merchant
Galloway & Mason, founders and machinists
Gemmell, F., general merchant
Gibson, S., carpenter
Gibson, Thomas, cooper
Gibson, T., carpenter
Girard, Rev. Joseph (Roman Catholic)
Goodacre, A., cabinet maker
Gordon, Mrs., prop. Royal Hotel
Heays, Mrs., teacher
Henry, David, saddler
Hersey, S. C., commission merchant
Hodgins, George, proprietor Dublin Hotel
Hodgins, George, farmer
Hodgins & Neville, blacksmiths
Hodgins, Thomas, grocer
Hoskins, R., carpenter
Hossack, Thomas, M. D
Hunter, Richard, stock dealer
Hutchins, W. H., wagon maker
Jackson & Rodgers, machinists and founders
Jamieson, William, architect
Johnston, William, barber
Lucan Gazette, published by E. Penton & Co
Lund, Rev. William, (Wesleyan)
Lynch, Joseph, auctioneer
McCosh, D. J., general merchant
McDonald, D. & Co., general merchant
McIlhargey, P., J. P., grocer
McLaughlin, William, proprietor Australian Hotel
McLean, Robert, proprietor Central Hotel
McRoberts & Armitage, commission merchants
McRobert & Bro., commission merchants
McRobert, Charles, stock dealer
McRoberts, David, grocer
Mills, Charles, cooper
Moore, William, druggist
Munro, F., grocer, wine and spirit dealer
Neil, R. B., blacksmith
NELIN, JOHN, proprietor Dominion Hotel
NICOL, ALEXANDER, (Nicol & Gemmel)
NICOL & GEMMEL, general merchants
O'DONOHUE, JOHN, prop. Queen's Hotel
O'Loane, James, attorney-at-law and N. P.
O'Neil, R. A., J.P., commission merchant
Oliver, Isaac, shoemaker
Pashley, C. F., bookseller and stationer
Pashly, C. F., painter
Penton, E., attorney-at-law and N.P.
Penton, E. & Co., publishers of Lucan *Gazette*
Porte, George, farmer
PORTE, WILLIAM, Postmaster, general agent and issuer of marriage licenses
Pratt, W. H., butcher
Pringle, G. D., dealer in jewellery, watches, clocks, &c.
Quarry, H. B., general merchant
Quarry, William B., M.D.
Quigley, Denis, shoemaker
Reid, Miss B., milliner, &c.
Reid, William, boots and shoes
Reynolds, John, station and express agent
Roache & Hodgins, lumb'r dealers & props. plan'g mills
Roche, W. E., general merchant and planing mill
Robin & Alway, soap and candle makers
Robinson, James, blacksmith
Robins, Orlando, lumber dealer
Sanders, C.W., general merchant and insurance agent
Sanders, Rev. Thomas E. (Church of England)
Seale, Mrs. E., milliner
Shaffer, A., painter
Shea, D., tailor
Smyth, M., carpenter
Sparling, J., butcher
Sproat, Thomas, nurseryman
Stanley, B., J.P. (Stanley, Dight & Co.)
Stanley, Dight & Co., general merchants, props. steam flouring mill
Stanley, William, J.P., (Stanley, Dight & Co)
Stewart, Thomas A., carpenter
Taylor, William, merchant tailor
Tennent, William, carpenter
Thomas, Thomas, carpenter
Thompson, Richard, carpenter
Trevithick, S., blacksmith
Tyler, Miss, milliner, &c
Walden, Francis, J.P., M.D
Walker, W. E., hotel keeper
Young, James, shoemaker
Young, Miss K., teacher

Loughboro.—A Post-office in the Township of Loughboro', County Frontenac.

Amey, Nicholas, J.P., farmer
Ash, David, M.D
Blake, John, farmer
Chown, Lewis, general merchant
Cook, Rev. William, (Primitive Methodist)
Copping, Thomas, tailor
Dawson, John, tailor
Dunlop, Neil, M.D
Fillion, E. N., painter
Grant, James, J.P
Ginley, Walter, general merchant
Grinnell, A., hotel keeper
Henstridge, J. W., teacher
Ivey, John, tailor
Joiner, Charles, J.P., farmer
Lahey, James, J.P., general merchant
Loughlin, Rev. Anthony, (Church of England)
Madden, Daniel H., wagon maker
MADDEN, HUGH, Postmaster, general merchant
Ockley, George, hotel keeper
Williams, Cornelius, wagon maker
Wood, James, prop. flouring mills
Wood, William, farmer
Young, Rev. S., (Methodist Episcopal)

Louisville.—A Village and Station on the Great Western Railway, on the River Thames, in the Township of Chatham, County Kent, 6 miles from Chatham, the County Town, and 160 from Toronto. Stages to Chatham, Kent Bridge, Dawn Mills and Dresden. Population 85.

Allan, F., carpenter
Arnold, Lewis, proprietor Royal Oak Hotel
Bedford, Eben, farmer
Dickson, T. K., grocer
Everitt, Samuel, farmer
Everitt, William, brick maker
Everitt, William A., J.P., farmer
Fleming, Andrew, farmer
Fleming & Lamb, steam flouring mill
Grover, T. B., farmer
Hardy, John A., farmer
Huston, William, M.D.
Knapp, S. M., J.P., farmer
Langford, Rev. Alexander, (Wesleyan)
McDiarmid, Rev. William, (Baptist)
Merritt, George B., telegraph operator
Merritt, William, farmer
Mitchell, Rev. George, (Wesleyan)
Shaw, Sylvanus, prop Louisville Exchange Hotel
Simson, F., shoemaker
STRUTHERS, ROBERT C., Postmaster and general merchant
Traxler, T. B., carpenter
Williston, Silas, farmer
Wright, Maurice, teacher

Lucknow.—A thriving Village in the Township of Kinloss, County Bruce, on Nine Mile River, 27 miles from Walkerton, the County Town, and 22 from Goderich. Stages to Kincardine, Walkerton, Goderich, and Bluevale. Money Order Office and Savings Bank. Population 750.

Armstrong, Leonard, insurance agent
Armstrong, Walter, general merchant
Berry, G. B., druggist and dealer in fancy goods, toys, &c
Bingham & Little, general merchants
Brown, Rev. N. (Wesleyan)
Burgess, George, carpenter
Burgess, Mark, tailor
Burgess, Sarah, teacher
Cameron, Duncan, tailor
Cameron & Miller, wagon makers
Campbell, James, hotel keeper
CAMPBELL, MALCOLM, Postmaster, J.P., and general merchant
Colerick, Samuel, painter
Cunningham, R. S., prop. Lucknow Hotel
Dochstader, Rev. J. W., (N. C. Methodist)
Dunoon, Donald, wagon maker
Fletcher, Thomas, jewelery, watches and clocks
Garner, J. H., M.D.
Geddas, William, cooper
Grundy, John, wagon maker
Greenash, J., shoemaker
Graham, Robert, shoemaker
Hale, Miss, milliner
Hays, William, shoemaker
Hood, Robert, lime and stone
Johnson, William, carpenter
Kelty, Miss, milliner
Kerr, George, clothing dealer
Lees & Douglass, manufacturers of woolen goods
McCradey, Robert, carpenter
McGregor, Norman, M.D.
McGregor, John, carpenter
McHaffie, William, general merchant
McKenzie, John, prop. Western Exchange Hotel
McKinnon, Alexander, tailor
McLean, Charles, wagon maker
McMillan, D., tailor
McNab, Rev. J., (Presbyterian)
Meredith, Mankin, lime and stone
Millan, D. M., druggist
Miller, James, carpenter
Miller, Ralph, hotel keeper
Mooney, Charles, tinsmith
Murray, Alexander, general merchant
Orr, William, butcher
Patterson, D., photographer
Proctor, Robert, saddler
Reed, John, saddler
Reed, John M., cabinet maker
Robertson, Thomas, hide and leather dealer & tanner
Secord, Charles, general merchant
Shepherd & Gledhall, cabinet makers
Somerville, James, J. P., general agent
Tennant, John S., M. D.
Treleavan, W., lumber dealer and proprietor flouring mills
Walker, William, baker
Warren, James, teacher
White, P. G., proprietor livery stable
Williamson, James, cabinet maker

Lumley.—A Village in the Township of Usborne, County Huron, on the River Sauble, 30 miles from Goderich, the County Town, 10 from Carronbrook and 12 from Seaforth Station Grand Trunk Railroad, Stages to Exeter. Population 160.

Allison, John, nurseryman
Barker, George, blacksmith
Bishop, Archibald, J. P
Bolton, Samuel, dentist
Dinnin, Mary Ann, milliner
DINNIN, WILLIAM, Postmaster, and general merchant
Dinnin, William & Sons, carpenters
Fanson, Richard, farmer and stock dealer
Fife, John & Son, woolen goods manufacturer
Glenn, John, farmer
Gray, Rev. Henry, (Presbyterian)
Love, Samuel, farmer
Marquiss, Richard, lime and stone
Pollard, Thomas, farmer
Smith, George, cooper
Steacy, George. farmer
Stewart, James, tailor
Strang, David, farmer
Strang Thomas, shoemaker.

Lunenburg.—A village and station of the G. T. R., in the Township of Osnabruck, County Stormont 14 miles from Cornwall, the county town, 19 from Crysler. and 260 from Toronto, Population 450.

Adams, Joseph J. P., farmer
Akins, Edward, boots and shoes
Alguire, Mrs. A. F., general merchant
Andrew, Rev. William, Methodist
Blake, Robert, carpenter
Bradshaw, William, architect
Cairns, William, cabinet maker
Canthart, Jonah, waggon maker
Delaney, Henry, boiler maker
Delaney, J. A., cheese manufacturer
Eaman, J. R., butcher
Gardiner, Edward, waggon maker
Garrett, Rev. Richard, Church of England
Grant, James, farmer
Hamilton, Martha, teacher
Hagerty, Edgar, hide and leather dealer and tanner
Hawn, John, boots and shoes
Hawn, Sidney, proprietor commercial exchange
Hough, Simeon, farmer
Hutchins, Hiram, boots and shoes
KIRKPATRICK, FRANCIS, Postmaster, saddler
McPherson, James, architect
McPherson, James, jun., attorney-at law
Mattice, William, carpenter
Monk, John, architect
Pyper, William, teacher
Rombough, J. J., farmer
Shaver, Jacob H., general merchant
Shaver, John, farmer
Shaver, W. S., farmer
Wood, J. K., farmer
Wood, J. R., founder and machinist
Wood, William H., farmer
Wood, William S., farmer

Lurgan.—A Post Office in the Township of Huron, County Bruce, 38 miles from Walkerton, the County County Town.

Blair, George, farmer
Campbell, James, farmer
Hicks, John, miller
McCRINDLE, JAMES, Postmaster
Welsh, Thomas, farmer

Luther.—A Post Office in the Township of Luther, County Wellington, 28 miles from Guelph, the County Town. Improved land in the vicinity $18, wild $6 per acre

McPherson, William, general merchant
STUCKEY, S., Postmaster

Luton.—A Post Office in the Township of Malahide, County Elgin, 15 miles from St. Thomas, the County Town.

Causland, John M., J.P.
Clendining, J. L., waggon maker
Court, Edward, farmer
Dinnis, William B., carpenter
Doolittle, Ira, farmer and dealer in lime and stone
Fairchild, Rev. John F. (M. Episcopal)
Garrett, James, farmer
Harvey, Joseph, J.P.
Harvey, William, J.P., farmer
Haun, Charles H., distiller and rectifier
Haun, John C., cabinet maker
Haun, Mrs. J., tailoress
Hill, A., proprietor flouring and grist mill
McCausland, John, farmer
McCausland, John, insurance agent
McCausland, Wesley, farmer
Murdie, William, auctioneer
Richardson, Thomas, farmer
Staley, Peter, shingle maker
Tyrrell, L., cooper
TYRELL, L. S., Postmaster and general merchant
Vanpatter, John, farmer

Lyndhurst.—A Village in the Township of Lansdowne, County Leeds, on the Gananoque River, 28 miles from Brockville, the County Town, and 187 from Toronto. Population 150.

Godkin, James, shoemaker
Hesselgrave, Rev. Henry (Episcopal Methodist)
Howard, Alpheus, M.D.
Lee, Christopher L., cooper
Roddick & Green (John & Henry), general merchants, flour and saw mill proprietors
RODDICK, JOHN, Postmaster
Sheffield, William, farmer
Stafford, John C., carpenter
Struthers, Calvin, J.P.
Wetherell, William, carriage maker
Wight, George P., hotel keeper

Lyn.—A Village and Station of the Grand Trunk Railway, on Coleman's Creek, in the Township of Elizabethtown, County Leeds, 6 miles from Brockville, the County Town, and 204 from Toronto. Money Order Office and Savings Bank. Population 750.

Armstrong, J. F., turner
Armstrong, John, blacksmith
Bagg, Edwin, cabinet maker
Baxter, Nathan, auctioneer
BELL, J. SEYMOUR, Postmaster
Brown, C. B., farmer
Brown, Ira, farmer
Bryson, Robert, tailor and clothing dealer
Buell, George S., J.P., grocer
Bullis, Jeremiah, J.P., butcher and prop. livery stable
Bullock & Coleman, proprietor planing mill
Bullock, Frederic G., accountant
Clow, Archibald, carpenter
Clow, David, farmer
Clow, Duncan, farmer
Coleman, Charles M., accountant
Coleman, Norman, J.P., saddler
Coleman, R., nurseryman
Coleman, Walter E., nurseryman
Coleman, W. F., M.D
Coleman, William, farmer
Collier, William, hide and leather dealer and tanner
Cook, Erastus, manufacturer of woolen goods
Coward, L. W., tinsmith
Cumming, James, hide and leather dealer and tanner and prop. flouring mill
Curtis, E., hotel keeper
Densdale, Mrs., milliner, &c
Edgers, Wesley, cabinet maker
English, Rev. William, (Wesleyan)
Gardiner, Charles, farmer
Gilhooley, John, boots and shoes
Gillertain, James, prop. Lyn House
Glashan, J. C., teacher
Gray, William, carpenter
Holliday, John, general merchant
Harvey, Edwin, wine and spirit merchant
Harvey, William, prop. Dominion House
Haskin, Sidney, painter
Horton & Taylor, shingle makers
Jones, Rev. R. L., (Church of England)
Lane, Rev. B., (Episcopal Methodist)
Leslie, J. & Co., general merchants
McCrady, Alexander, farmer
McCrady, David, farmer
McCrady, John, carpenter
McLean, George, telegraph operator
McNish, George, founder and machinist
Mitchell, George, boots and shoes
Murphy, Jeremiah, R.R. and express agent
Nash, Edwin, carpenter
Orton, Celsus, saddler,
Palmer, John, carpenter
Pergan, Paul, cooper
Pergan, Peter, boots and shoes
Scott, Stephen, carpenter
Thompson, William, wagon maker
Trickey, A. T., druggist and dealer in books and stationery
Widdis, Robert, wagon maker
Wilson, Charles R., hide and leather dealer & tanner
Wilson, Darwin, farmer

Lynedoch.—A Village on Big Creek, in the Township of Charlotteville, County Norfolk, 12 miles from Simcoe, the County Town, and 55 from Hamilton. In the vicinity there are strong sulphur springs, equal to any on the continent, which have proved very effectual in the cure of chronic diseases, especially those resulting from impurity of the blood. The flow of water is about six gallons a minute. The chief business of the place is the manufacture of lumber. Stages to Brantford, Simcoe and Paris. Money Order Office. Population 150.

Bottomley, John, hotel keeper
Brown, Joshua, farmer
Burwash, Rev. N. S. (Wesleyan)
Charlton, George G. & Co., general merchants
Charlton, John, farmer
Cowan, William, farmer
Crysler, E. M., farmer
Cunliff, P., miller
Disho, Ira, cooper
GRAY, GEORGE, Postmaster
Hagerman, N. C., M.D.
Hagerman, S. F., farmer
Ingram, Edwin, blacksmith
Louks, W. H., farmer
McKown, J.P., farmer
McMaster, P., farmer
Marsland, John, farmer
Patient, Benjamin, shoemaker
Reid, Archibald, carpenter
Roche, William, teacher
Schull, C., wagon maker
Wilson, Abner, proprietor flouring mill
Wilson, James H., blacksmith
Wood, George, farmer

Lynnville.—A small village, in the Township of Windham, County Norfolk, 6¼ miles from Simcoe the county town, and 80 from Toronto. Population 70.

Axford, George, farmer
Axford, Wellington, dry goods dealer
Axford, Wellington, painter, wagon maker
Bangner, Nelson, capenter
CROOKER, WILLIAM L., Postmaster and prop. Farmer's Inn
File, George, farmer
Fonger, Joel, farmer'
Gibson & Brothers, farmers
Gibson, William and D., props. steam saw mill
Hall, C., farmer
Hilliker, John, farmer
Larmer, J. W., general merchant
Miller, David, carpenter
Rand, John, farmer
Wardell, Peter, shoemaker
White, William, farmer and prop. steam shingle manufacturer
Willson, Asa, blacksmith

Lynden.—A Village and Station of the Great Western Railroad, in the Township of Beverly, Count Wentworth, 15 miles from Hamilton, the County Town, 10 from Brantford, 12 from Paris and 15 from Galt. There is a large business done here in the lumber trade. Money order office. Population 400.

Barrett, William, wagon maker and painter
Berrington, John, agent American Express Co.
Berry, Robert, butcher
Bigger, George F., M. D
Bishop, N. H., proprietor brick yard
Blasdell, B., lumber dealer
Blasdell, Daniel, farmer
Blasdell, George, farmer
Blasdell, Jacob, farmer
Blows, Lewis, carpenter
Bradwin, J. & E., potters
Clement, William, manufacturer of woolen goods
Cornell, Miss E. A., milliner
Cornell, Jeremiah, general merchant
Cornell, Jesse, farmer
Daseff, Josephus, carpenter
Dayman, Peter, proprietor brick yard
Dyment, Nathaniel, lumber dealer and farmer
Dyment, Peter, grocer
Glass, Alexander, baker
Hanes, Alexander, J.P., farmer
Hendershott, A., patent right agent
Horning, William, boots and shoes
Howard, Henry, farmer
Howard, Charles, dentist
Howell, J., dentist
Lemon, Thomas, butcher
Lemon, William, jewelery, watches, clocks, etc.
McDonald. Mrs. Christina, prop. Western Hotel
McLean, John, teacher
McRae, Charles Andrew, M.D
McRAE, WILLIAM commercial traveler
May, William, grocer
Misener, J., proprietor New Dominion Hotel
Montgomery, William, tailor
Nisbet, Adam, farmer and lumber dealer
Orr, James E., dealer in clothing, boots and shoes
Orr, Wesley F., general merchant and insurance agt
Patterson, Robert L., boots and shoes
Shaver, James W., telegraph operator
Shaver, Robert, general agent
Skea, James, carpenter
Smith, P. P., grocer
Stewart, J. W., carpenter
VANSICKEL, B., J.P., Postmaster, gen. merchant, farmer and lumber dealer
Vansickel, William, carpenter
Walburg, John, patent right agent and carpenter
Wood, Robert, saddler
Woolams, Daniel, proprietor flouring mill

Lyons.—A Village in the Township of North Dorchester, County Elgin, 17 miles from St. Thomas, the County Town, and 110 from Toronto. Population 60.

Appleford, George, farmer
Caghill, Robert, shoemaker
Cline, Benjamin, farmer
Cloppeson, Rev. C., (Wesleyan)
Cronk, J., shoemaker
Doan, Albert, teacher
Emery, Charles, farmer
Fullerton, Richard, farmer
Gunn, Daniel, farmer
Martin, E., farmer
Putnam, Henry, farmer
PUTNAM, PETER J., Postmaster and prop. Lyons Exchange
Smith, Rev. G., (Wesleyan)
Wilkinson, Thomas, wagon maker
Winder & Lee, general merchants
Winder, Thomas, carpenter

McDonald's Corners.—A Post Office in the Township of Dalhousie, County Lanark.

CHALMERS, WILLIAM, Postmaster.

McGillivray.—(See Ireland).—A Post Office in the Township of McGillivray, County Middlesex. Money Order office.

SHOFF, D., Postmaster.

McIntyre.—A Post Office in the Township of Osprey, County Grey.

POTTS, EDWARD, Postmaster.

Maberly.—A Village on Fall River, in the Township of South Sherbrooke, County Lanark, 16 miles from Perth, the County Town. Population 100.

Dixon, John, auctioneer
Goldemo & Goldberg, general merchants
McConnell, Robert, carpenter
McGREGOR, JOHN, J.P., Postmaster and propr. shingle factory
McMorin, Rev. W., (Church of England)
McNichol, Hugh, wagon maker
Morrison, George, hotel keeper
Morrison, Henry, shoemaker
Morrow, James, farmer
Morrow, John, hotel keeper and prop. flouring mill
Park, H., cooper
Shannon, Rev. V., (Wesleyan)
Smith, Rev. W., (Methodist Episcopal)
Spencer, —, M.D.
Welsh, Thomas, wagon maker
Williams, Miss, teacher

Macton.—A Village in the Township of Peel, County Wellington, 25 miles from Guelph, the County Town 18 from Berlin and 80 from Toronto. Stages to Berlin and Listowell. Population 128.

Auman, Nicholas, shoemaker
Connolly, John, farmer
Connolly, N., farmer
Cowan, R. F., teacher
Francis L., prop. Farmers' Inn
McCORMICK, J. M., Postmaster, hotel keeper
McCormick, James, farmer
McCormick, Patrick, farmer
McGeehan, Ellen, teacher
Nolen, James, farmer
O'Brien, John, bricklayer
O'Connor, David, farmer
O'Toole, Peter, blacksmith
Scott, James, farmer
Sweeney, C., farmer

McNab-Glengary.—A Post Office in the Township of Lochiel, County Glengary.
FRASER, SIMON, Postmaster.

Macville.—A Post-office in the Township of Albion, County Cardwell.
WILSON, SETH, Postmaster.

Madoc.—A Village on Deer Creek, in the Township of Madoc, County Hastings, 27 miles from Belleville, the County Town, 7 from El Dorado and 150 from Toronto. The Village is situated in the midst of the best mineral region, as yet discovered in Ontario, gold, iron and lead have been found. Stages to Belleville, Thanet and El Dorado. Money Order Office and Savings Bank. Population 750.

Adams, Harvey, carpenter
Allan, Miss, milliner, &c
Atkins, W. H., dealer in clothing and boots & shoes
Aylswith, C. F., P.L.S
Baalam, Miss, milliner
Bateman, Joseph, proprietor brick yard
Begg, Peter, teacher
Bentliff, Edward, accountant
Black, John, boots and shoes
Bristol, Wellington & Co., blacksmiths
Brooks, George, grocer
Caverly, Joseph, blacksmith
Coe & McPherson, real estate agents
Cross, Thomas, general merchant
Dale, James, tinsmith
Dale, John, J. P., dealer in hardware, cutlery, &c
Deans, Gray & McGregor, general merchants
Declare, M., butcher
Dingman, Henry, farmer
Driscoll, S., tailor
Dunn, John H., J. P., farmer
Eastwood, Miss, milliner
Elms, W. H., M. D
Fitzgerald, James, attorney-at-law
Fitzgerald, Joseph, sash, door and blind manufacturer
Ford, Rev. W. J., ((Wesleyan)
Forneri & Kennedy, P. L. Surveyors
Foster, Alexander, boots and shoes
Franklin, Edward, lumber dealer
Fraser, Sylvester, carpenter
Gillen, Miss, milliner
Gray, Walter, carpenter
Gream, Charles, real estate agent and attorney-at-law
Griffin, Spencer, carpenter
Gustin, S., prop. livery stable and pump maker
Harper, John, grocer and baker
Heyworth, James, painter
Heyworth, John, cabinet maker
Hodgins, William, prop. North American Hotel
Huffman & Son, prop. Huffman House
Kirk, Charles, prop. flouring mill
Lawler, Rev., Roman Catholic
Lawson, Rev. T., Wesleyan
Lewis, D. P., carpenter
Loomis, J. S., M. D.
McBeath, Miss, milliner, &c.
McQuillin, Robert, M. D.
Mancey, E., tailor
MADOC MERCURY, published every Saturday by Albert Smallfield
Marrin, Owen, boots and shoes
Maybee, Alonzo, painter and engraver
Maybee, cabinet maker and prop. planing mill
Mitchell, T. A., grocer
Mockridge, Rev. Charles H., (Church of England)
Moon, A., prop., Hastings House
Mullet, Sylvanus, hide and leather dealer and tanner
O'Bryan, James, cooper
O'FLYNN, E. D., Postmaster, J.P., insurance agent and general merchant
O'Hara, James, J. P., farmer
Orr, William, blacksmith.
Patterson, R., & Co., props. flouring mill
Pemeroy, Rev. D. (Episcopal Methodist)
Rawe, G. D., dealer in jewelery, watches, clocks, &c.
Reed, Stephen, blacksmith
Ross, A. B. & Bros., general merchants
Seymour, F. E., farmer
Seymour, Horace, farmer
Sinclair, Misses, milliners
Sinclair, Peter, saddler
Sills, Bryant, painter and general agent
SMALLFIELD, ALBERT, editor and publisher *Madoc Mercury*
Smith, Jacob, draftsman and engraver
Soames, Mrs., milliner
Sparrow, Rev. P. L. (Episcopal Methodist)
Suttan, H. H., M.D.
Tabor, Samuel, cooper
Tassie, John, farmer
Tuller, W., farmer
Tumilty, W. H., J.P.
Van Kleeck, B. H., farmer
Vanorman, Allan & Co., shingle makers
Ward, William, boots and shoes
White, George, carpenter
White, John, founder and machinist, and proprietor planing mill
Wilson, C. G., druggist and dealer in books and stationery
Wilson, C. G., telegraph operator
Wishart, Rev. David (Presbyterian)
Wise, Louis, boots and shoes
Wood, A. F., J.P., and insurance agent
Wood, A. F. & Co., general merchants
Wright, Andrew, baker and grocer

Madrid.—A post office in the Township of Sebastopol, County Renfrew.

Connolly, James, farmer
Connolly, Patrick, farmer
Foran, Edward, farmer
Gallaghar, John, J. P
Gallagher, William, farmer
McCAWLEY, PATRICK, Postmaster, gen. mercht
McCormac, Rev. James (Roman Catholic)
O'Connor, Martin, farmer

Maidstone.—A Post Office County Essex (see Sandwich East).

Maitland.—A Village on the River St. Lawrence and Station of the Grand Trunk Railroad, in the Township of Augusta, County Grenville, 4½ miles from Brockville, the County Town. Population 200.

Adams, H., farmer
Baker, J., shoemaker
Bamfield, J., tailor
Byers, William, farmer
Cunningham, J., farmer
Dumbrill, J., general merchant
Eldridge, C., hotel keeper
Ferrier, J., grocer
Fletcher, Hoag & Co., distillers
Foster, Captain
Huntington, Rev. —, (Wesleyan)
Jones, D., farmer
Lewis, Rev. R., (Church of England)
LONGLEY, G. C., Postmaster
McClone, H., grocer
McDougall, A., farmer
McHenry, G., general merchant
McManus, F., cooper
Pearson, A., farmer
Ryrie, J., farmer
Sales, John, hotel keeper
Smith, William, butcher
Suddley, F., shoemaker
Wells, J. B., general merchant
Wood, J. L., carpenter

Mallorytown.—A Village and Station of the Grand Trunk Railroad, in the Township of Yonge, County Leeds, 12 miles from Brockville, the County Town, 9 from Rockport, 5 from Escott and 190 from Toronto. Stages to Escott and Rockport.

Andress, E., wagon maker
Andress, James, proprietor brick yard
Avery, R., general merchant
Bruce, W., telegraph operator, railroad and express agent
Filer, A. D., teacher
Hadigan, M., stock dealer
Haight, E. B., M. D
Holmes, Thomas, wagon maker
Huntly, John, wagon maker
Keys, A., shoemaker
LEE, F. F., Postmaster
Mallory, H. W., stock dealer
Mallory, G. L., general merchant
Mallory, Ira, J. P
Mallory, Mrs. G. L., milliner
Monfort, J., tinsmith
Monfort, P., farmer
Mune, A. A., general merchant
Munro, William, cooper
Pennet, George, farmer
Proctor, J. W., carpenter
Purvis, E., J. P
Swatfyer, G., general merchant
Thomas, E. S., farmer
Wickwire, G., painter

Malone.—A Village on the River Moira, in the Township of Marmora, County Hastings. Distant from Belleville, the County Town, 35 miles. Stages to Madoc and Belleville. Weekly mail. Population 60.

Bowerman, Henry, prop. grist mill
Caldwell, W. M., engineer
Christie, W. J., farmer
De Cew, James
Dollan, Thomas, miner
Doxey, Rev. —, (Wesleyan)
Elan, Joseph, miner
Heigle, L.
McDermott, John, miner and assayer
McFaul, A., miner
McGregor, George, tavern keeper
Minchin, W. H., teacher
Murphy, Ira, carpenter
Nightingale, Thomas, book keeper
Nixon, T., miner
POWELL, D. N., Postmaster
Powell, M. H., miner
Richardson, George, general merchant
Severn & Caldwell & Co.. prop. quartz crushing mill
Watson, John

Malvern.—A small Village in the Township of Scarboro', County York, 14½ miles from Toronto, the County Town, and 5 from Scarboro' Station, Grand Trunk Railway.

Burton, William, cooper
McDermid, Peter & David, physicians
Milne, David A.. proprietor saw mill
Milne, William, lumber merchant
SMITH, THOMPSON, Postmaster, merchant and proprietor Temperance Hotel
Wyper, Joseph, saddler

Malton.—A Village and Station of the Great Western Railroad, in the Township of Toronto, County Peel, 6 miles from Brampton, the County Town, and 15 from Toronto. Stages to Tullamore, Sandhill, Mono Mills, &c. Population 200.

Aikins, John, J. P., farmer
Allen, Daniel, farmer
ALLEN, JOSEPH B., Postmaster
Allen. T. B. & Co., general merchants
Armstrong, Adam, auctioneer
Aull, Rev. John, (Presbyterian)
Blain George, farmer
Boyce, Rev. James S., (Primitive Methodist)
Brocklebank, Townley, farmer
Brown, Richard, painter
Bunker, Thomas, teacher
Cook, Thomas, carpenter
Dawson, George, J. P
Ellabey, John, saddler
Foster, Joseph, wagon maker
Foster, William, farmer
Graham, John, butcher
Halliday, Richard, hotel keeper
Heydon, James, saloon keeper
Ibson, Richard, farmer
Jennings, Franklin, American Express and G. T. R. agent
McDonald, Alexander, farmer
McDonald, William, farmer
Moore, Samuel, farmer
Mulholland, Thomas, farmer
Robinson, John, shoemaker
Tomlinson, David, farmer
Wisly, James, carpenter

Manchester (Auburn P. O.)—A Village on the Maitland River, in the Townships of Wawanosh and Hullet, County Huron. Distance from Goderich, the County Town, 11 miles, from Toronto, 143 miles. Average price of land $25 to $30, Population 100.

Anderson, Thomas, proprietor Railroad Hotel
Ballantine & Borland, wagon makers
Boyce, Richard W., farmer
Caldwell, Samuel, general merchant
Davidson, James, farmer
Dey, A., blacksmith
Downs, Robert, blacksmith
Downs, William, farmer
Elkins, Æneas, farmer
Elkins, J. & G., millers
Farrow, Henry
Hoar, Thomas, farmer
Jones, Isaac, farmer
McDonald, John, farmer
Marshall, Samuel, farmer
Merriot, Thomas, farmer
Scott, James, J.P.
SUTHERLAND, JAMES, Postmaster and general merchant
Tunney, Thomas, farmer
Whiting, Rev. —., (Wesleyan)
Wilson, W. J., shoemaker
Young, Rev. Stephen, (Presbyterian)

Manchester.—A Village in the Township of Reach, County Ontario, 16 miles from Whitby, the County Town, and 45 from Toronto. Stages to Whitby, Uxbridge, Oshawa, and Beaverton. Money Order Office, Population 175.

Boyard, A., butcher
BROWN & CHRISTIAN, general merchants
BROWN, JOHN H., (Brown & Christian)
BRYAN, BENJAMIN, agent, dealer in stoves, tinware, and coal oil (see adv)
Byam, William H., carriage maker
Campbell, James, (R. & J. Campbell)
Campbell. Robert, (R. & J. Campbell)
Campbell, R & J., general merchants
Christie, Donald E., farmer
Christie, John, township clerk and conveyancer
CHRISTIAN, SAMUEL H. (Brown & Christian)
Currie, George, township treasurer
Daniels, John, boots and shoes
Davis, William, blacksmith
Dawson, Cornelius (Dawson & Co.)
Dawson & Co. (Cornelius Dawson and William Yates), chemists and druggists
Dobson, Joshua, farmer
Ensign, Ranson, farmer
Ewers, A. W., farmer
Ewers, George, carpenter
Fidgett, Hiram, farmer
Fitkin, Fuller, harness maker
GORDON, ADAM, Postmaster and general merchant
Golding, John, bricklayer
Graham, Alexander, farmer
Graham, Frederick, farmer
Graham, George, carpenter
Harper, Henry, farmer
Hiscock, Charles, baker and confectioner
Jeffery, Richard, carriage maker
Jennings, Denis, teacher
Kimberly, John, painter
Kimberly, Misses, milliners, &c.
Lamb, Henry, farmer
Lamb, Hiram, farmer
Leach, Lewis, boots and shoes
Leonard, James, photographer
Lisle, Henry, farmer
Lock, Henry, farmer
Mozier, John, farmer
Parkin, James, carriage and wagon maker
Parks, W. H., cabinet maker
Paul, Andrew, prop. grist mill
PLANK, BARTHOLOMEW, prop. Revere House
Powson, William, attorney, &c
Shaw, Joel, farmer
Smith, Rev. Mr., (Primitive Methodist)
Steel, William, wagon maker
Spins, James, tailor
Straiton, Thomas B., manager for R. & J. Campbell
St. John, George, farmer
Squire, James, tailor
Thompson, Henry, prop. Union Hotel
Torrance, Alexander, tailor
Torrance, Andrew, manager for Joshua Wright
Ures, Abraham, farmer
Vernon, Nathaniel, farmer
Wright, Joshua, boots and shoes
Yates, William, (Dawson & Co.)

Mandamin.—A Village and Station on the Great Western Railway, in the Township of Plympton, County Lambton, 10 miles from Sarnia, the County Town. Population 100.

Bird, John, farmer
Chalmers, James, farmer
Donald, T., farmer
Duncan, John, farmer
Dunlop, James, general merchant
McLerie, William, farmer
Paul, John, farmer
Quinn, James, farmer

Malakoff.—A post office in the Township of Marlborough, County Carlton; distant 26 miles from Ottawa.
PIERCE, W. J., Postmaster

Manilla.—A Village in the Townships of Mariposa and Brock, Counties of Ontario and Victoria, 32 miles from Whitby and 14 from Lindsay. Stages to Oshawa, Beaverton, Lindsay and Woodville. Money Order Office. Population 500.

Allen, G. farmer
Bowes, E., general merchant
Brown, M. E., teacher
Calhoun, J. hotel keeper
Campbell, Rev. H. (Canada Presbyterian)
Caster, G., general merchant
Chesterfield W., shoemaker
Clarke, A., clothier
Clarke, J., J.P., blacksmith
Conway, S., hotel keeper
Coone & Bros., wagon makers
Douglas, A., insurance agent
Douglas, G., general merchant
DOUGLAS, MARY, Postmaistress
Douglas, Misses M. & E., milliners, etc.
Duncon, D. cooper,
Edwards, G. P., general merchant
Edwards, R., general merchant
Ghent, W., carpenter
Glover, Rev., T. W., (Bible Christian)
Graham, W. S., cabinet maker
Harper, R., B.A., teacher
Holliday, J., butcher.
Horne, G., farmer
Keeler, C., farmer
McBain, James, auctioneer
McDonald, H., J.P., blacksmith
McEachern, L., carpenter
McFadyen, Rev. A. (Baptist)
McFadyen, Mrs. T., milliner
McGregor, Rev. D. (Congregational)
McLean, D. C., wagon maker
McLean, M., tanner
McQuarrie, H., teacher
May, T., saddler
Maybee, R., saddler
Michael J., farmer
Oakley, F., M.D.
Pearce, G., shoemaker
Skinner, Joseph T., tinsmith
Smith, J., proprietor steam flouring mill
Stabback, J., farmer

Manitowaning.—A small settlement beautifully situated at the head of Heyward Sound, on Manitoulin Island, District of Algoma, 150 miles from Sault Ste. Marie, 30 from Little Current, and about 140 from Toronto. It contains only the residence of the officers of the Indian Department, and a few Indian houses. Government lands on the island are offered at 20 cents per acre. Mails weekly in summer, and fortnightly in winter. Steamers to Collingwood and Sault Ste. Marie.

Ironside, A. McG., Clerk Div. Court and interpreter
Plummer, William, local superintendent Indian Affairs, land agent and fishery overseer
Simpson, Thomas, M.D.
SIMPSON, T., Postmaster

Mannheim.—A Village in the Township of Wilmot, County Waterloo, 6 miles from Berlin, the County Town, 4 from Petersburg Station, 14 from Galt, and 81 from Toronto. Population 100.

Backert, Martin, farmer
Bergey, Jacob, farmer
Bleam, Jonathan, farmer
Boehmer, Valentine, cooper
Bowman, Joseph L., farmer
Bowman, Moses L., farmer
Eckhardt, John, tailor
Ernst, John, farmer
Ferrier, John L., teacher
Fallman, John, farmer
Geiger, Daniel, farmer
Gerbig, John, hotel keeper
Gofton, Robert, farmer
Huether, Nicholas, shoemaker
Hoffman, Joseph, general merchant
Kausman, Rev. C. F. A. (Evangelical Lutheran)
KNECHTEL, DANIEL L., Postmaster
Knechtel, Jonas, cabinet maker
Kropp, Isaac, farmer
Miller, Michael, farmer
Peppler, George, blacksmith
Pimper, William, weaver
Riekert, John, farmer
Ringler, Benjamin, farmer
Schiedel, Joshua, farmer
Schweitzer, Jacob, farmer
Sehl, Peter, mason
Shantz, A. D., proprietor flax mill
Shantz, John D., proprietor flax mill
Shantz, Samuel L., proprietor saw mill
Ware, John, blacksmith

Manotick.—A Village on the Rideau River, in the Township of North Gower, County Carleton, 15 miles from Ottawa, the County Town. Population 200.

Atkinson, Francis, shoemaker
Beanbry, Dennis, blacksmith
Cameron, M., farmer
Condie, William, farmer
Cowan, John, general merchant
Cowan, Samuel, M.D
Davidson, Alexander, hotel keeper
Dickinson, M. K., general merchant, lumber dealer, and prop. flouring and planing mills
Fortune, William, tailor and clothing dealer
Jennings, John J., druggist
Latimer, James, carpenter
McCorkall, Thomas, wagon maker
Mansfield, Thomas, farmer
Mansfield, William, farmer
Mooney, James, cooper
O'Grady, Michael, hotel keeper
PARKER, G. L., Postmaster
Peyment, Louis, blacksmith
Pollock, Miss, milliner, &c
Rickey, George, teacher
Shearer, John, painter
Williams, George, general merchant
Willson, William, farmer

Mansfield.—A small Village in the County of Middlesex.

Baily, Thomas, blacksmith
Loughead, James S., proprietor hotel
Mansfield, J. & G., general merchants
Prigley, George, proprietor hotel

Mansfield.—A Post Village in the Township of Mulmur, County Simcoe. Distance from Barrie, the County Town, 27 miles. Population about 40.

Anderson, David, shoemaker
Campbell, Robert, blacksmith
Gallagher, Paul, general merchant
GILBERT, WILLIAM, Postmaster, general merchant
Morrow, John W., shomaker
Wilson, W. H., prop. woolen factory

Maple.—A Village in the Township of Vaughan, County York, 18½ miles from Toronto. Money Order Office. Population 150.

Aiken, Rev. William, (Church of England)
Barlow, R., general merchant
Buttery, Thomas, blacksmith
Cousins, John, shingle maker
Develin, William, J.P.
High, William, shoemaker
Humphreys, J. D., telegraph operator R. R. and express agent
Hunter, William, tailor
Irvine, Andrew, shoemaker
Lochhart, John, wagon maker
Logan, George, hotel keeper
Lowry, Joseph, teacher
McArtney, Valentine, tailor
McDonald, John, carpenter
McDonald, L. A., carpenter
McQuarrie, H., J.P.
Matherson, Misses, milliners
Moore, Patrick, manufacturer of woolen goods
NOBLE, JOSEPH, Postmaster and general merchant
O'Neil, Hugh, manufacturer of woolen goods
Raith, Thomas S., blacksmith
Richardson, Leeds, saddler
Rupert, J. P., J.P., general merchant
Rupert, O., M.D.
Rumble, R., hotel keeper and proprietor livery stable
Vailes, Richard, painter
Waterhouse, John, general merchant
Willson, Albert, teacher
Woods, James, blacksmith
Wood, William, blacksmith

Maple Hill.—A Post Office in the Township of Brant, County Bruce, 3 miles from Walkerton, the County Town.

CLEMENT, ROBERT B., Postmaster and gen. mer.
Hall, William, saw mill proprietor
Lalonde, T., carpenter
Scarborough, Charles, brickmaker
Simpson, George, carpenter
Wright, Samuel, hotel keeper

Mapleton.—A small Village in the Township of Yarmouth, County Elgin, 10 miles from St. Thomas, the County Town. Average value of land $45. Population 30.

APPLEFORD, WILLIAM, Postmaster and prop. cheese factory
Bray, T. B., farmer
Caughill, Peter, J.P.
Charlton, William, farmer
Culver, Edwin, farmer
Deo, Dennis, carpenter
Dexter, D., farmer
Fawcett, J. G., general merchant
Gilbert, G. H., teacher
Hughes, Thomas, butcher
Leam, Charles, farmer
Luton, Robert, teacher
Lymon, Philip, farmer
McClelland, John, farmer
McGregor, D., farmer
Mackay, E., teacher
Thompson, Daniel, shoemaker
White, Frederick, J.P., carpenter
Wismer, John, J.P., farmer

Marchmont.—A Village on North River, in the Township of North Orillia, County Simcoe, 27 miles from Barrie, the County Town, 6 from Orillia, and about 87 from Toronto. Stage to Orillia and Coldwater. Population 70.

Bailey, William, farmer
Black, Alexander, carpenter
Campbell, W. P., shingle maker
Clarke, A., farmer
Clarke, Ellen, milliner, etc.
Coleman, John, farmer
De Gear, William, farmer
Drinkwater, Thomas, J.P.
Fox, William, wagon maker
Gillott, William, farmer
Golden, Thomas, farmer
Hall & Brothers, lumber dealers
Hamilton, F. J., farmer
Hopkins, Thomas, farmer
Izzard, James, farmer
Joyce, Patrick, farmer
Kean, John, J.P., proprietor grist mill
Nelson, John, farmer
Nixon, C., general merchant
Noyes, —, wagon maker
Orser, J., hotel keeper
Overend, William, butcher
POWLEY, CHARLES, Postmaster
Powley, Jacob, lumber dealer
Price, Thomas, proprietor Farmer's Inn
Price, William, lime and stone
Randall, John, carpenter
Rix, George, farmer
Rix, John, farmer
Smith, George, farmer
Smith, Henry, farmer
Stewart, Rev. A., (Episcopal)
Teskey, John, farmer
Teskey, William, teacher
Ward, John, farmer
Wright, George, farmer

Marden.—A Post-office in the Township of Guelph, County Wellington.

BLYTH, C. McD., Postmaster.

Markham.—A Village on the River Rouge, in the Township of Markham, County York, 20 miles from Toronto, and 10 from Scarboro' Station, Grand Trunk Railway. The 2nd Division Court is held here. Stage to Toronto. Money Order Office and Savings Bank. Population 1000.

Anthony, John, carpenter
Armstrong, Miss, dressmaker
Armstrong, Robert, tinsmith
Armstrong, William, farmer
Ash, S. C., tailor
Bambridge, G. T., blacksmith
Burk, Ebenezer, general merchant
Barker, A., J.P. and notary public
BARKER, JAMES J., J.P., Postmaster, clerk division court
Barker, James J., general merchant
Barnes & Flumerfelt, general merchants
Beecher, John, painter
Browning, William, watchmaker
Byron, Mrs. Joseph, tailoress
Caldwell, G. C., veterinary surgeon
Calvert, W., butcher
Campbell, Rev. J;, (Presbyterian)
Carson, H. R., accountant
Cash, D., J.P.
Commiskey, Dr.
Coupe, Samuel, butcher
Crosby, C., farmer
Crosby, L., seedsman
Cumming, Peter, saddler
Dack, John, shoemaker
Digby, George, saddler
Doherty, Dr.
Doherty, Miss Emily, teacher
Fawcett, Rev. M. (Wesleyan)
Fogg, John, baker
Forster, John, cabinet maker
Freel, Dr.
Hall, H., proprietor Franklin House
Hall, Rev. J. (Wesleyan)
Holden, S., J.P.
Holden, S., druggist
Hutton, H. H., teacher
Jerman, Henry, blacksmith
Lane, Henry, general merchant
Lumley, George, painter
McCallum, Rev. J. (Congregational)
McCausland, Dr.
McGill, Hugh, wagon maker
McMahon, R., cooper
Mairs, A., attorney-at-law
Mardon, William, shoemaker
Marshall, John, proprietor livery stable
MARKHAM ECONOMIST, Hon. D. Reesor, prop., (Thursday)
Maxwell, James, carpenter
Miller, George, farmer
Miller, T. H. & Co., general merchants
Milne, T. A., proprietor flouring mill
Morgan, T. & G., blacksmiths, etc.
Musselman, D. & S., dentists
Nichols, John, butcher
Pollard, John, saddler
Pringle, R. & G., wagon makers
Rainer, A. B., shingle manufacturer
REESOR, HON. D., J. P., proprietor *Markham Economist*
Reesor, David, jun., fruit tree agent
Reesor, John, farmer
Roebotham, J. S., proprietor Wellington Hotel
Robinson, James, tanner
Robson, W. B., proprietor livery stable
Scott, Adam, teacher.
Smith, Mrs. A., teacher
Smith, F. J. D., attorney-at-law
Smith, John D., painter
Smith, Matthew, cabinet maker
Snowball, John, brick maker
Speight & Sons, sash and door manufacturers
Tocque, Rev. P., (Church of England)
Todd, Thomas, founder and machinist
Wales, H. R., wagon maker
Willis, A., real estate agent
Wilson, Henry, general merchant
Wilson, Mrs. Henry, dressmaker
Wilson, Robert, general merchant
Wilson, W., carpenter
Wooten, D., proprietor Anglo American hotel
Workman, William, tailor

Maple Valley.—A Post Office in the County of Grey.
DICK, JAMES, Postmaster.

Marathon.—A Post Office in the Township of Huntly, County Carleton
WOODS, SAMUEL, Postmaster.

March.—A Post Office in the Township of March, County Carleton, 15 miles from Ottawa.

Armstrong, John, general merchant
Bury, W. H., brewer
Holmes, John, hotel keeper
Kirwin, William, general merchant
McMurty, David, general merchant
Richardson, Frederick, J.P.
Sharp, Alexander, hotel keeper
Smith, Thomas, hotel keeper

Marlbank.—*(See Villages too late for regular insertion at the end of this work.)*

Marmion.—A post office in the Township of Sullivan, County Grey, 20 miles from Owen Sound, the County Town.

Berry, John, farmer
Casson, Robert, farmer
Cochran, Robert, teacher
Crittenden, E., shingle maker
Foster, John, farmer
Foster, Thomas, farmer
Harrison, John, farmer
Hemstock, George, farmer
Hislop, John, farmer
Hill, Rev. Joseph, (Wesleyan)
McBain, David, farmer
Melburn, John, farmer
Osborne, William, farmer
Wait, Rev, G. (United Brethren)
WARD, JAMES, Postmaster, farmer
Wild, William, farmer
Wright, Joseph, farmer

Marmora.—A Post Village on the Township of Marmora, County Hastings.

Hawley, J., general merchant
JOHNSON, BENJAMIN, Postmaster
Loucks & Hough, general merchants

Marston.—A flourishing Village on Venison Creek, in the Township of Walsingham, County Norfolk, 20 miles from Simcoe, the County Town, and 14 from Port Rowan. Population 25.

Beemer, James, farmer
Beemer, Oran, farmer
Brown, Ruth, milliner, etc.
Franklin, Welland, stock dealer
GARDNER, JOHN, Postmaster, P. L. S., lumber dealer and proprietor saw mill
Gardner, Matthew, M.D., dentist
Houk, Harvay, butcher
Louis, John, farmer
Mills, William, farmer
Roher, Jacob, farmer
Seymour, John, farmer
Tick, Jacob, cabinet maker
Williams, Henry, farmer
Williams, W. P., farmer
Winch, John, general merchant
Winch, Richard, baker
Winters, Harry, farmer
Winters, Miss L. J., teacher

Martintown—A Village on the River Raisin, in the Township of Charlottenburgh, County Glengarry, 12 miles from Cornwall, the County Town. Money Order office. Population 450.

BLACKWOOD, ROBERT, Postmaster and general merchant
Brown, John, blacksmith
Brown, Peter, innkeeper
Burnett, Rev. Mr. (Presbyterian)
Conroy, Peter W., general merchant
Cresswell, Daniel, general merchant
Foulds, John, general merchant
Grant, A. G.
Kennedy, Alexander, teacher
McCallum, Duncan, general merchant
McDonald, Charles
McDonald, Duncan, blacksmith
McDonald, Samuel, wagon maker
McLeod, Angus, wagon maker
McPhardon, Charles, general merchant
McPherson, John, M.D.
McRae, John, shoemaker
McVean, Angus, saddler
Martin, Duncan M., general merchant
Patterson, Rev. Mr. (Free Church)
Rayside, James
Robertson, John, shoemaker
Smith, William, blacksmith
Urquhart, John, general merchant
Wilson, Alexander, general merchant

Marnoch.—A Village in the Township of Wawanosh, County Huron.

PORTERFIELD, PETER, Postmaster and general merchant.

Marshville.—A Post Office in the Township of Wainfleet, County Monck.

LEE, EDWARD, Postmaster.

Marysville.—A Post Office in the Township of Tyendinaga, County Hastings.

Allison, B. J., corn merchant and general agent
Allison, W. H., telegraph operator
Anderson, Alexander, proprietor sash, door and blind manufactory
Anderson, George, general merchant
Buckley, William, blacksmith
Dessey, Thomas, farmer
Hayes, Miss B., milliner, &c
Kelly, John, farmer
KEMP, JOHN, Postmaster, telegraph operator, G.T.R. and Can. Ex. Co.'s agent and prop. livery stable
Kilmurray, Peter, farmer
Lamphier, John, farmer
Lyman, C. P., general merchant
McAllister, John, shoemaker
McGuinness, John, carpenter
Mackey, Rev. Mr. (Roman Catholic)
Mullens, James, carpenter
Nealon, Joseph, prop. sash, door and blind factory
Nealon, Michael, farmer
Roberts, A. L., J.P., farmer
Roberts, A. W., farmer
Sweeney, Charles, farmer
Sweeney, Michael, farmer
Welsh, Edward, blacksmith and wagon maker
Woodcock, Sandford, carpenter

Massie.—A Post-office in the Township of Holland, County Grey.

MASSIE, A., Postmaster.

Matawatchan.—A Post-office inthe Township of Matawatchan, County Renfrew, 70 miles from Pembroke, the County Town.

Barry, Walter, farmer
Fraser, Thomas, farmer
Hunter, David, farmer
Hunter, H., farmer
McDonald, Archibald, farmer
McGregor, James, farmer
McGREGOR, JOHN, Postmaster
McKellar, George, farmer
Thomson, William, farmer
Willson, John, farmer

Maxwell.—A Village in the Township of Osprey, County Grey, on the Beaver River, 40 miles from Owen Sound, the County Town, 22 from Collingwood and 120 from Toronto. Stages to Collingwood and Durham. Money Order Office. Population 100.

Blazes, —, hotel keeper
Bowes, G. L., general merchant
Bradbury, Duke, boots and shoes
Bunker, Francis, boots and shoes
Clarke, Thomas, tailor
Crossley, James L., farmer
Deer, A., blacksmith
Davis, Miss, milliner
Flesher, Thomas, teacher
Fields, Henry, hide and leather dealer and tanner
Fisher, Alexander, butcher
Gamey, Miss M., milliner
Gamey, Thomas, J.P.
Gilbert, Rev. C. D. (Primitive Methodist)
Gordon, James, accountant
Guy, William, blacksmith
Hannah, Alexander, agent Vicker's Express Co., and prop. North American Hotel and livery stable
Heron, D., farmer
Heron, D., gunsmith
Heron, R., sash, door and blind manufactory
Heron, R., farmer
Heron, Thomas, carpenter
Heron, William, manufacturer of woolen goods
Hill, Rev. Rowland (Church of England)
Irwin, J. G., painter and wagon maker
Izzard, —, farmer
Johnston, Rev. D. A. (Wesleyan)
Johnston, William, boots and shoes
Kerr, B. S., M.D., dentist
Kerton, J., farmer
Keston, W. F., carpenter
Knowles, Rev. R. (Canada Presbyterian)
Long, H., farmer and dealer in lime and stone
Long, Wesley, sash, door and blind manufacturer
McRoberts, A., proprietor flouring mill
Mathew, Robinson, boots and shoes
MAXWELL, JOSEPH, Postmaster and attorney-at-law
Maxwell, J., farmer
Rudley, George, butcher
Raymond, —, fruit tree agent
Reid, Rev. J. J., (Primitive Methodist)
Saigeon, Joseph, farmer and wood dealer
Selkirk, Alexander, accountant and bookbinder
Spear, John, auctioneer
Sproule, T. S., M.D., dentist and druggist
Sutherland, J. N., general merchant
Thompson, George, saddler

Mattawa.—A small Village and depot of the Hudson's Bay Company, in the District of Nipissing, at the junction of the Ottawa and Mattawa Rivers, 154 miles from Sand Point.

BANGS, JOHN, Postmaster, general merchant, clerk 2nd division court and hotel keeper
Belanger, Alexis, carpenter
Burritt, Elihu A., carpenter
Carney, Augustus, bailiff
Simmons, Noah, general merchant, hotel keeper

Mayfield.—A small Village in the Townships of Chinguacousy, County Peel, 7 miles from Brampton, the County Town, and 27 from Toronto.

Archdekin, F., hotel keeper
Archdekin, P., farmer
Duncan, G., farmer
Gray, W., farmer
Hearn, William, farmer
Hiscocks, Robert, general merchant
Ludlow, J., farmer
Spiers, Adam, farmer
SPIERS, WILLIAM, Postmaster

Maynard.—A Post Office in the Township of Augusta, County Grenville. Tri-weekly mails.

BIRKS, CHARLES, Postmaster.

Maynooth.—A Post Office in the Township of Hastings, County Hastings.

DOYLE, MICHAEL, Postmaster.

Meadowvale.—A Village in the Township of Toronto, County Peel, on the River Credit, 23 miles from Toronto, 5 from Brampton, the County Town, and 5½ from Malton Station Grand Trunk Railroad. Stages to Malton. Money order office. Population 250.

Birdsell, Col., J. P
Brown, Samuel, farmer
Carthew, William, carpenter
Chapman, William, tailor
Cheyne, C.
Davidson, Walter, shoemaker
Elliott, W., J. P
Elliott, W. E., farmer
GOODERHAM, C. H., Postmaster
Gooderham & Worts, proprietors flouring mill and general merchants
Griffith, H., saddler
Hardy, John D., wagon maker
Hopper, James, carpenter
Hull, A. M., accountant
Johnson, James, cooper
Johnson, Thomas, cooper
Laidlaw, Matthew, general merchant
Leslie, William, teacher
Ramsay, George, wagon maker
Simpson, John, proprietor planing mills
Spelum, John, cooper
Strong, Moses, proprietor Commercial Hotel
Turisson, W. H., cooper
Wilson, John, farmer

Medina.—A post office in the Township of East Nissouri, County Oxford, 25 miles from Woodstock, the County Town.

BECK, J. H., Postmaster, general merchant
McKay, Alexander, farmer

Medonte.—*(See Villages too late for regular insertion at the end of this work.)*

Melancthon.—A post office in the Township of Melancthon, County Grey.

BROWN, JAMES, Postmaster.

Melrose.—A Village in the Township of Tyendenaga, County Hastings, 13½ miles from Belleville, the County Town. Population 100.

Anderson, Donald, farmer
Anderson, Rev. — (Methodist Episcopal)
DUNCAN, GEORGE, Postmaster, general merchant
Eaton, Jacob, J. P
Forrester, James, farmer
Haight, Robert, farmer
Hollingsworth, Edward, shoemaker
McFarlane, John, farmer
McLachlan, W. G., teacher
McLaren, Alexander, J. P., farmer
Morden, Israel, farmer
Morden, Philip, carpenter
Osborn, Robert, farmer
Turnbull, Rev. John, (Presbyterian)
Ward, William, hotel keeper

GEORGE MOORHEAD,

Manufacturer and dealer in all kinds of

PARLOR, DRAWING AND BED-ROOM

FURNITURE.

New Sale and Show Rooms, Richmond St., opposite City Hall. Factory, King St. between Richmond and Clarence,

LONDON, ONT.

T. NEELANDS,

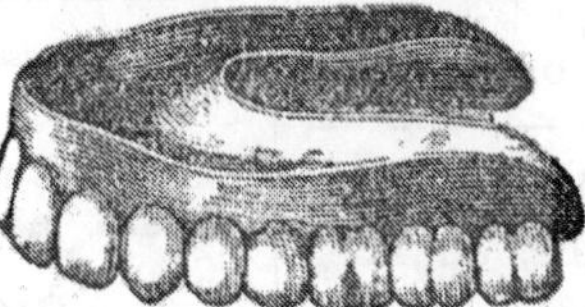

Surgeon Dentist,

Walton Street, Port Hope.

T. J. WINSHIP,

Wholesale and Retail Tobacconist,

Dealer in all kinds of Cigars, Tobacco, Snuff, Meerschaum and Briar Pipes, &c.,

George Street, Peterboro', Ontario.

GEORGE TAYLOR,

Manufacturer of Pumps, and general Wood Turner,

Corner of Simcoe and Aylmer Sts.,

PETERBORO', ONT.

Royal Canadian Hotel,

Simcoe Street, Peterboro', Ontario.

WILLIAM McDONALD, - - PROPRIETOR.

First-class Stabling in connection, and every accommodation for the travelling public.

Peterboro' Livery Stable,

ROBERT WHITE, PROPRIETOR.

Good Horses and comfortable conveyances, with or without driver, furnished at reasonable prices for cash. Stable in rear of Casse's Hotel, Peterboro', O.

W. H. PAULL,

Dealer in general Groceries, Crockery, China and Glassware, &c.,

Dixon's Block, George Street,

PETERBORO', ONT.

THOMAS MENZIES,

Bookseller and Stationer,

Peterboro', Ontario,

Sterling and American Exchange Bought and Sold. Drafts on New York at low rates.

EDWARDS MERRILL,

Barrister and Attorney-at-Law, Solicitor in Chancery and Insolvency, &c.,

Picton, Ontario.

Prompt attention given to collections.

J. R. ORMOND & CO.,

Importer of Watches, Clocks, Jewellery, Fancy Goods, &c.,

Peterboro', Ont.

OAKVILLE HOUSE,

OAKVILLE, ONT.,

John Williams, - - Proprietor.

Good accommodation and excellent Stabling.

THOMAS REYNOLDS & SON,

Dealers in Groceries, Wines, Liquors, &c.,

Colborne Street,

OAKVILLE, ONT.

JOHN WALSH.

COLBORNE STREET, OAKVILLE, ONT.,

WAGON MAKER,

All kinds of Wagons and Carriages made to order. Job Work done on shortest notice.

MAITLAND McCAULEY,

Solicitor, Attorney & Notary Public,

ORANGEVILLE, ONT.

PAISLEY HOUSE,

JOHN PAISLEY, - - PROPRIETOR.

ORANGEVILLE, ONT.

Newly furnished and refitted. Every accommodation for Guests. First class sample rooms.

T. S. MOFFATT, P. M.,

GENERAL MERCHANT,

Dealer in Raw Furs, &c., Issuer of Marriage Licenses, &c., Sign of the Elephant, corner of Front and Mississaga Streets.

ORILLIA, ONT.

THOMAS DALLAS,

Clerk 7th Division Court, Commissioner in B.R., Agent Western Insurance Co., and Freehold Permanent Building & Savings Society of Toronto.

ORILLIA, ONT.

R. JAMES RIGGS,

Merchant Tailor,

DEALER IN

Gentlemen's Outfitting & Underclothing

Simcoe Street, near King,

OSHAWA, ONT.

THOMAS DALLAS,

Clerk 7th Division Court,

General Insurance Agent, Commissioner in B.R.

Mississaga Street, ORILLIA, ONT.

JAMES B. KEDDIE,

Harness, Saddlery and Carriage Trimming Establishment,

OSHAWA, ONT.

A good assortment of everything in the trade constantly on hand, or made to order, Collars made easy, safe and durable. Trimming done in the best of styles. Repairing done with neatness end despatch. All work warranted.

P. TAYLOR,

WATCHMAKER AND JEWELLER,

Simcoe Street,

OSHAWA, ONT.

Horizontal, Duplex, Lever, Lapine and all kinds of Watches and Clocks repaired.

J. P. JOHNSTON,

WATCHMAKER AND JEWELER,

Dealer in English and French Watches, Clocks, Jewelry, and Fancy Goods,

KING STREET WEST, - - OSHAWA, ONT.

Watches and Jewerly repaired and warranted.

WILLIAM BEEN,

Flour, Feed & Commission Merchant,

King Street West,

OSHAWA, ONT.

RAILROAD HOUSE,

Near G. T. R. Station, SOUTH OSHAWA, ONT.

MICHAEL BROOKS, Proprietor.

Meaford.—A thriving Village, at the mouth of the Bighead River, on the South East shore of the Georgian Bay, in the Township of St. Vincent, County Grey; 19 miles from Owen Sound, the County Town, 22 from Collingwood, and 120 from Toronto. The Village is the Depot of an excellent agricultural district, and possesses all the elements of prosperity. Trade local. Stages daily during winter to Collingwood and Owen Sound, Messrs. Stubbs and Bookless, proprietors. Money order office. Population 1200.

ALBERLY, JOHN, Township Clerk, land agent, notary public, &c
Anderson, James, tanner
Andrus, Nicholas
Arthur, John, farmer
BARBER & HARRIS, (Charles Barber & Thomas Harris), props. Georgian Iron Works (see adv)
Bird, Henry, cabinet ware
Bishop & Hopkins, (E. W. & John) saddlers
Blanshard, Ira, teamster
BLANCHARD, J., baker, groceries and liquors
Bowser, —., brickyard
Bower, Mrs. Elizabeth, grocer
Bright, T. G., dry goods and groceries
BRITISH AMERICAN HOTEL, John Stubbs, prop (see adv)
Brown, Thomas, butcher
Brownell, Rev. Daniel, (Wesleyan)
Burns, Charles, shoemaker
Burritt, A., blacksmith
CAIN, J. C., book and job printer (see adv)
Cain, W. F. & Co., saddlers
CARRE, THOMAS, chemist and druggist
CASWELL, G. A. & BRO., boots and shoes
CASWELL, JOHN A., (G. A. Caswell & Bro.)
Chapman & McDonald, (Benjamin F. & Hector), saddlers
Chisholm, H. & Co., general merchants
Christie, Peter, farmer
Clark, Ebenezer, farmer
Clark, Frederick, J.P., farmer
Clelland, James, stoves, tin and hardware
COMMERCIAL HOTEL, William McDonald, prop. (see adv)
Corby, James, J.P., farmer
Cox & Grant, (James & James), blacksmiths
DAVIS, J. H., photographer
Davis & Ellis, photographers
DICKSON, ROBERT, prop. Meaford flouring mills
DONOVAN, THOMAS, provincial land surveyor and civil engineer
DUNLOP, THOMAS (Noxon & Dunlop)
Eagles, Samuel, J.P., farmer
Ellis, Frank, blacksmith
Flower, Samuel, baker
Foster, R. H., chemist, druggist and seedsman
Fuller, Peter, insurance agent
Fulton, R. & H., general merchants
Gauld, Rev. Mr. (Presbyterian)
GEDDES & WILSON (James & John S.) barristers
Gifford, A., insurance and general agent
Hamilton, Rev. Thomas (New Connexion)
Hawkins, William, brickyard
Helstrop, Robert, wagon maker
Hill, John, proprietor British Hotel
Howe, Thomas & Sons, farmers
Hurd, Kilburn, general merchant
Jewell, W. C., dentist
Jones, John, barber
JOHNSON, ALEXANDER, general merchant
JOHNSTON, J. J. & CO. (J. J. Johnston, W. Whetham and David McCann) proprietors sash, door and blind factory, builders and contractors (see adv)
La Rush, Charles, hotel keeper
LAYTON, D. L., Postmaster and general merchant
Leavens, Reuben (W. F. Cain & Co.)
Lindsay, John, dry goods and groceries
Livingstone, W. F., hotel keeper
Lochead, Robert, prop. shingle factory
Lowe, James, brick yard
Lynn, R. F., P.L.S.
McCANN, DAVID, (J. J. Johnston & Co.)
McCausland, Alexander, farmer
McDonald, Miles, farmer
McDONALD, WILLIAM, prop. Commercial Hotel
McDonald & McGee, (William and John D.) carriage makers
McIntosh, Robert, M.D.
McKnight, Robert, drugs, groceries, etc., Commisr. in B. R.
McKinney, Bradshaw, tanner
McKinney, James, shoemaker
McLean, C. R., M.D.
MEAFORD HOTEL, John Paul, proprietor
MEAFORD MONITOR, (weekly), H. Watt, prop.
MILNE & SONS, (Alexander, James and Robert), dry goods, groceries and hardware (see adv)
Minturn, John, painter
NOXON, DORLAND, (Noxon & Dunlop)
NOXON & DUNLOP. (Dorland and Thomas) dry goods and groceries
Patton, John, cabinet maker
PAUL, JOHN, proprietor Meaford Hotel
Pillgrem, William, general merchant
PLUNKETT, THOMAS, bookseller and stationer, official assignee, agent Montreal Telegraph Co., Clerk Division Court and Township Treasurer
POLLARD, W. D., attorney, solicitor etc.
PURDY, JESSE T., J.P., proprietor flour, woolen, and saw mills
Purdy, Marshall B., proprietor saw mill
Purdy, William H., farmer
Read, Nicholas, farmer
Robinson, George, shoemaker
ROBINSON & LAYTON, (M. and J. W.), wharfingers, forwarders, shipping and express agents, dealers in lumber, coal, etc.
Saunders, Samuel, farmer
Sheppard, C. & Co., dry goods and clothing
Shepphird, Jethro, tailor
Sinclair & Adamson, founders
SING, C. R., notary public and land agent (see adv)
Smith, John N., carpenter
Speer, Samuel D., J.P., farmer
Stephens, William, stoves and tinware
STEWART, J. & W., general merchants and produce dealers
Stovel, J., tailor
STUBBS, JOHN, prop. British American Hotel (see adv)
Symes, Thomas F., M.D.
Tait, Adam, blacksmith
Taylor, Rev. Charles, (Methodist Episcopal)
Thompson, Alexander, lumber merchant
Tottenham, F. R., J.P., farmer
Trout, Rev. M., (Disciples)
TYSON, JOHN, prop. steam saw mill
Vanderburgh, Stephen, farmer
Ward, John, farmer
WARNICA, L. B., watchmaker, jeweler and engraver (see adv)

Watson, Rev. Thomas, (Church of England)
Watson, Colonel William, J.P
Watt, Andrew, bailiff
Watt, Charles, manufacturer fanning mills
WATT, H., editor and proprietor *Monitor*
Watt, James, carpenter
WETHAM, W., (J. J. Johnston & Co.)
Whitlaw, William, farmer
Wilcox & Anderson, (T. C. & J. P.), tanners, boots and shoes
Williams, James, proprietor Meaford woolen mills
Wood, W. S., carriage and wagon maker

Melville.—A Village in the Township of Hillier, County Prince Edward, on Consecon Lake, 14 miles from Picton, the County Town. Population 100.

Burdett, E. J., farmer
Carly, W. E., grocer
Cooper, R. B., J. P., proprietor flouring mill
Danare, A. B., insurance agent
Henderson, William, farmer
How, Daniel, farmer
JOHNSON, CALEB, Postmaster and farmer
Johnston, Rev. Robert (New Connexion Methodist)
Lewis, John, carpenter
Miller, W. R., teacher
Morton, George, farmer
Post, C. B., farmer
Post, J. R., teacher
Stratton, Rev. F. B. (Methodist Episcopal)
White, E. B., shoemaker

Menie.—A Post Office in the Township of Seymour, County Northumberland, 50 miles from Cobourg, the County Town.

Atkinson, Edward, general merchant
Barnett, James, cooper
Bell, John, teacher
Brunton, Alexander, tailor
MATHER, JAMES, Postmaster and gen. merchant

Merivale.—A Post Office in the Township of Nepean, County Carleton, 6 miles from Ottawa.

Bayne, Robert, farmer
Clarke, John, farmer
Clarke, Thomas, farmer
Collins, Samuel, J.P.
Gourley, Rev. J. S. (Presbyterian)
Greer, Joseph, tailor
HOPPER, EDWARD B., Postmaster and farmer
Hopper, George B., watchmaker, jeweler, &c.
Hopper, William, farmer
Johnson, Walter, J.P.
Kennedy, Donald, brick maker
Lemoine, Charles, wagon maker
Lemoine, Edward, wagon maker
Lemoine, William, wagon maker
McFarlan, John, proprietor Merivale Hotel
McKibben, Robert, teacher
McKibben, William, teacher
Morris, Rev. J. A., (Church of England)
Nelson, John, farmer
Quinlon, Joseph, farmer
Scott, Archibald, farmer
Scott, William, farmer
Waddell, John, wagon maker

Merlin.—*(See Villages too late for regular insertion at the end of this work.)*

Merritton (Thorold Station).—A Village and Station of the Great Western Railroad, in the Township of Grantham, County Lincoln, on the Welland Canal; 3 miles from St. Catherines, the County Town. Population about 1000. The Lybster Cotton Mills established here employ 200 hands, combined steam and water power; capacity 10,000 yards of cotton cloth, and 1000 lbs. cotton warp, together employing 200 looms daily. The Beaver Cotton Mills, employ 80 hands and 50 horse power. The St. Catherines Paper Mill employs 60 hands, turning out 2½ tons of paper daily.

Ball, Bernard, general merchant and insurance agent
Ball, Peter, J. P
Betts, G., bookseller
Bowie, Rev. Mr. (Bethel Church)
Brown, Alexander, farmer
Campbell, John, shoemaker
Connors, Andrew, J. P., farmer
Corbin, D. W., brick manufacturer
Crow, —, farmer
Delaney, Andrew, blacksmith
Fields, Rev. George(Wesleyan)
Gordon & McKay, proprietors Lybster Mills
Haylitt, J., butcher
Lenbrock, H., proprietor Welland Valley Hotel
Leo, —, general merchant
Parnell, William, proprietor planing mills
Reid, —, G. W. R
Riordan, J., proprietor paper mill
Roberts, Rev. T. A., (Church of England)
Schooley, —, general merchant
STEPHENS, S. M., Postmaster and gen. merchant
Stokes, G. H., farmer
Wait, W. W., proprietor Beaver Mills
Wallace, G. H., teacher
Wilson, George, farmer
Winslow, John, general merchant

Merrickville.—An incorporated Village on the Rideau River, in the Townships of Wolford and Montague, County Grenville, 28 miles from Brockville, the County Town, 15 from Kemptville and 9 from Irish Creek Station Brockville and Ottawa Railway. Stages to Irish Creek and Kemptville. Money Order office and Savings Bank. Population 750.

Armstrong, James, proprietor City Hotel
Ballantyne, J. F., manufr. of staves and headings
Barton, Joseph, saddler
Bissell, Alpheus, farmer
Boyd, Joseph, grocer
Brennan, Edward, carpenter
Brownlee, James, cabinet maker
Bunhill, John, J.P., P.L.S., farmer
Bunhill, Michael, butcher
Church, M K., M.D.
Culbert, Thomas, general merchant
Cummins, Albert, cooper
Cummins, Elijah, cooper
Dangerfield & McCrea, manufacturers of scythe-snaths hames, &c.
Derrick, Aaron, farmer
Deritt, Edward, butcher
Dowdall, P., auctioneer
Driscoll, William, carpenter
Duke, Francis, butcher
Duke, John, boots and shoes
Engley, Mrs., groceries
Engley, William, cooper
Eagleton, James, proprietor Exchange Hotel
Eastman, Robert G., wagon maker
Easton, Hiram, J.P., proprietor oat mill
Erritt, Edward, lumber dealer
Forrest, Rev. Charles (Church of England)
French, T. J., attorney-at-law and insurance agent
Gilroy, E. J., millinery, &c.
Gwynne, David, teacher
Haddon, Rev. Thomas (Wesleyan)
Hall & Wright, publishers *Merrickville Chronicle*
Halnan, Jason, boots and shoes
Hamilton, Rosanna, milliner, &c.
Harrison, Robert, saddler
Heaney, Charles, hide and leather dealer and tanner
Holden, Charles
Holden, Horatio, proprietor garden vineyard, &c.
Jacques, H. W., druggist
JAKES, SAMUEL, Postmaster and gen. merchant
Johnston, John, lockmaster
Kelly, E. J., M.D.
Kirkland, William J., boots and shoes
Langford, Samuel, carpenter
Linginfelter, —., painter
McCrea, Alexander, farmer
McCrea, Edward, farmer
McDonald. —., dealer in wine and spirits
McGee & Pearson, founders and machinists and props. planing mill
McGee, Simon, boots and shoes
McIntyre, Bridget, prop. Rideau Hotel
McKibbon, Robert, boots and shoes
Mahoney, Mrs., milliner
Meikle, J. & T., general merchants
Merrickville Chronicle, (Wednesday), Hall & Wright, publishers
Merrick, Aaron, J.P., general merchant
Merrick, Henry, manufacturer of woolen goods
Merrick, Plumer, farmer
Merrick, Stephen, prop. North Merrickville Hotel
Merrick & Ward, proprietor flouring mill
Mills, John, cabinet maker
Miskelly, William, dealer in stoves and tinware
Montgomery, George A.
Nickleson, William, carpenter
Oliver, Mrs., groceries
Parker, Asa, nurseryman
Read, N. C., insurance agent
Reel, Daniel, tailor
Roach, John, lime and stone
Robson, Rev. Ebenezer (Wesleyan)
Sebra, Alexander, carpenter
Somerville, Richard, baker
Smith, H. D., M.P.P., proprietor cheese factory
Weir, William, M. D
Whitmarsh, E. H., J. P., insurance agent
Whitney, —, proprietor hop yard
Winn, William, lime and stone

Mersea.—A Post office in the Township of Mersea, County Essex, 14 miles from Sandwich, the County Town, and 14 from Stoney Point

Miller, John, merchant
ROBERTSON, CHARLES, Postmaster, gen. mercht.
Yelland, John, blacksmith

Metcalfe, (Osgoode Post Office).—A Post Office in the Township of Osgoode, County Carlton, 9 miles from Osgoode Station on the Ottawa and Prescott Railway, and 20 miles from Ottawa City. Daily mail. Money order office. Population 300.

Allan, Joseph, M. D
Allan, William & Hugh, general merchants
BAKER, ADAM J., J. P., Postmaster, com. in B.R.
Cameron, Peter, blacksmith
Campbell, W. F., general merchant
Carson, John, photographer
Cousins, Dr.
Imily, Andrew, boots and shoes
Ireson, Timothy, saddler
McDougall, Peter, M. D
McEwan, Robert, boots and shoes
McPherson, Charles, blacksmith
Morgan, Ira, J. P., clerk 6th Division Court, commissioner in B. R
Morgan, W. W., proprietor hotel
Stringer, William, tanner
Sweeney, John & Michael, boots and shoes
Wallace, William, general merchant
Watson, S., boots and shoes
York, John, grocer
York, William, grocer and hotel keeper

Meyersburg.—A Post Office in the Township of Seymour, County Northumberland.
OLIVER, THOMAS, Postmaster.

Michipicoten River.—A small Village in the District of Algoma, and a trading depot of the Hudson's Bay Company, on the Michipicoten River, Lake Superior, 120 miles from Sault Ste. Marie and 530 from Toronto.

BELL, P. W., Postmaster, Agent Hudson's Bay Company.

Middleville—A Village in the Township of Lanark, County Lanark, 20 miles from Perth, the County Town. Population 135.

Affleck, George, shoemaker
Affleck, James, J.P., farmer
Affleck, Robert, farmer
Aitkinson, George, proprietor Farmers' Inn
Anderson, Edward, shingle maker
Blackburn, John, cabinet maker
Blackburn, John, dentist
Borrowman, James, blacksmith
Borrowman, William, farmer
Brimer, William, shingle maker
Campbell, James, farmer
CROFT, WILLIAM, Postmaster and gen. merchant
Deachman, Thomas, constable
Douglas, Rev. James (Congregational)
Guthrie, Edward, wagon maker
Guthrie, William, shoemaker
McEwen, John, teacher
McLachlan, Peter, council messenger
McLean, A. C., teacher
McLean, Rev. D. J. (Presbyterian)
Mathers, John, farmer
Middleton, William, carpenter
Millotte, Alphonse, cooper
Muir, James, auctioneer
Rankin, James, J.P., farmer
Rankin, John, farmer
Robertson, Thomas, cabinet maker
Rodgers, James, farmer
Scott, William, carpenter
Somerville, John, farmer
Somerville, Robert, farmer
Stewart, James, general merchant
Watt, Robert, poulterer
Williams, Moses, wagon maker

Midhurst.—A Village on Oliver's Creek, in the Township of Vespra, County Simcoe, 5 miles from Barrie, the County Town, and 65 from Toronto. Population 100.

Appleby, Guy, carpenter
Bond, William, farmer
Culham, John, farmer
Cummings, Amos, farmer
Cummings, James, carpenter
Garvin, David, lumber dealer
Gill, John, farmer
Gordon, William, farmer
Leadlar, Robert, lumber dealer
Locke, Silas E., farmer
McGowen, John, farmer
McGowen, Robert, carpenter
Partridge, John, shingle maker
Russell, Andrew, lumber dealer
Robinson, Thomas, J.P., lumber dealer and proprietor flouring mill
SNEATH, GEORGE, J.P., Postmaster and insurance agent
Truman, William, teacher
Woodsworth, Rev. W. (Wesleyan)

Mildmay.—A Post Office in the Township of Carrick, County Bruce.

DOLMAGE, J. H., Postmaster.

Milford.—A Village on Black Creek, in the Township of Marysburgh, County Prince Edward, 7 miles from Picton, the County Town. Steamer to Belleville, 37 miles. Stage to Picton. Money order office. Population 300.

Bond & Minaker, shoemakers
Bongard, G. F., general merchant
Bradon, M.D.
Burley, Emerson, saddler
Campbell, Rev. Thomas (Wesleyan)
Clapp, Robert, J.P.
Clapp, Robert, shoemaker
Cook, James, J.P.
Crabb, S. V., cabinet maker
Craig, A., grocer
Craig, James, shoemaker
Curry, Matthew, hotel keeper
Dodge, Nelson, J. P
Empey, Harvey, hotel keeper
Fegan, J. W., carpenter
Goldsmith, David, grocer
Hicks, Lewis, J. P., wagon maker
Hudson, A., cooper
Hudgin, Rev. W. G., (Episcopal Methodist)
Lake, John C., general merchant
McKibbin & Knox, general merchants
Minaker, William, teacher
Palen, Duncan, carpenter
Rose, David, shoemaker
Smith, James, grocer
Tighe, Rev. S., (Church of England)
Wildon, Rev. Isaac, (Wesleyan)
Wilmer, W. H., cooper
Young, Rev. —, (Episcopal Methodist)

Mill Bridge.—A Post Office in the Township of Tudor, County Hastings.

NORMAN, R. M., Postmaster.

Millbank.—A Village in the Township of Mornington, County Perth, 17 miles from Stratford, the County Town, and 21 from Berlin. Stages to Stratford and Berlin. Money order office. Population 500.

Alexander, William, teacher
Alexander, William, farmer
Atchison, Stewart, boots and shoes
Bloomingthal, Francis, proprietor Rob Roy Hotel
Caulfield, T. F., proprietor Commercial Hotel
Crawford, John, boots and shoes
Crowley, Rev. M., (Presbyterian)
Davidson, John, tailor
Drake, James, carpenter
Fraser, Gordon, saddler
Freeborn, George, boots and shoes
Freeborn, John, J.P., general merchant
Freeborn, Robert, farmer
Gibson, James, carpenter
Gordon, William, general merchant
Johnson, James, M.D.
Logan, Rev. W., (Church of England)
Loder, Peter, proprietor steam flouring mill
Lovel, Rev. Isaac, (Wesleyan)
McKee, John, farmer
McKee, Robert, farmer
Milliken, Rev. A. (Wesleyan)
Mitchell, James C., general merchant
Nichol, David, carpenter
Poole, Thomas, carpenter
Reid, James, farmer
RUTHERFORD, WILLIAM, Postmaster and general merchant
Rutherford, William, farmer
Smith, Hugh J., carpenter
Stewart, James L., architect
Stewart, William, architect
Urquhart, Thomas, proprietor Millbank Hotel
Wood & Kells, general merchants

Mill Brook—A Village and Station of the Port Hope, Lindsay and Beaverton Railway, on Deyell's Creek, in the Township of Cavan, County Durham, 25 miles from Cobourg, the County Town, 17 from Port Hope, 17 from Peterboro' and 83 from Toronto. Money Order office and Savings Bank. Population 1200.

Allen, Rev. Thomas, B.A., (Church of England)
Armstrong, Robert, J.P., farmer
ARMSTRONG, ARCHIBALD, dry goods
Armstrong, R. J., prop. saw mill and lumber mercht
Atkins, Henry, livery stable
Bateson, William, carpenter
Brakey, James, shoemaker
BURROWS, PHILIP P., M.D., coronet
Burton, James, proprietor Clifton House
Campbell, George, collector
Christie, Miss, teacher
Clark, John, shingle maker
Collins, T. B., general merchant
Coombe & Richard, merchant tailors
Cossford, Rev. Thomas, (Wesleyan)
Crocker, Mrs., hotel keeper
CRUMMER, THOMAS, proprietor Farmers' Hotel (see adv)
Davey, Richard, tanner and currier
Dawson, William, farmer
Dean, Armstrong, boot and shoe maker
Doak, J., blacksmith
Douglas, Rev. James, (Presbyterian)
EYRES, THOMAS, general merchant and insurance agent
FAIR, GEORGE, iron founder
Fallis, Richard, auctioneer
FARMERS' HOTEL, Thomas Crummer, proprietor, (see adv)
Ferguson, Alexander, carriage maker
Gillott, John, cabinet maker
Gillott, Thomas, cabinet maker
Gorden, William, proprietor Montreal House
Gott & Deyell, grocers
Greer, T. H., shoemaker
Guy, Richard, watch maker and jeweler
HAYTER, ALFRED E., editor and proprietor *Millbrook Messenger*
Hetherington, George, J. P., farmer
HOWDEN, RICHARD, Postmaster
HOWELL, RICHARD, grocery and tinware
HOWELL, S. J. & BROTHERS, general merchants
Judd, H. W., woolen factory and carding mill
Kellett, Robert, saddler
Kerr, James, treasurer
Matthews, Ezra, butcher
Medd, Thomas, farmer
MIGHT, JAMES, physician, surgeon and coroner
Might, William, saddler
MILLBROOK MESSENGER, Alfred E. Hayter, editor and proprietor
Mitchell, Benjamin, jr., manufacturer wood sawing machines
Montreal House, William Gordon, proprietor
Muirs, James, general blacksmith
Needler, George, miller
Russell, E. W., photographic artist
Scott, Charles, butcher
Smith, William, blacksmith
Southeran, J. W., township clerk and insurance agt.
Sowden, William H., J.P.
Staples, William, bailiff 4th Division Court
Story, John, blacksmith
STORY, THOMAS H., nurseryman, confectioner dealer in fruits, taxidermist, etc. (see adv)
Taylor, William, station master P. H., L. & B. R.
Taylor, William, jun., telegraph operator
TURNER, HENRY, M.D.
Turner, William, Clerk 4th Division Court
Vance, William, teacher
Walsh, Samuel, wagon maker
Walsh, Silas H., dentist
Watson, H. S., painter
Wood & Kells (Archibald Wood and T. G. Kells), general merchants

---

Mill Grove.—A Village in the Township of West Flamboro, County Wentworth, 6 miles from Hamilton, and 40 from Toronto. Improved land $30. Population 150.

Berney, W. H., general merchant
Black, Joseph, hotel keeper and general merchant
Black, William, butcher
Brown, William, teacher
Cumming, Charles, carpenter
Foster, William, carpenter
Orr, William, carpenter
Pete, Thomas, hotel keeper
Richardson, Rev. J., (New Connexion Methodist)
Smith, Rev. —, (Episcopal Methodist)
THOMPSON, ORON, Postmaster
Thompson, William, shoemaker
Worthington, J., wagon maker
Willowby, Rev. William, (Wesleyan)

Mille Roches.—A Village on the Long Sault, or Cornwall Canal, and Station of the Grand Trunk Railway, in the Township of Cornwall, County Stormont, 6 miles from Cornwall, the County Town, and 261 from Toronto. Money Order office. Population 450.

Andrews, Rev. W, (Wesleyan)
Annable, Hiram, farmer
Armstrong, James, farmer
Bisbee, S. W., cabinet maker
Brill, Rev. John, (Church of England)
Brooks, W. D., cabinet maker
Cutler, Guy, wagon maker
Derousie, Louis, general merchant
Frank, Martin, cooper
Gravity, John, farmer
Harrison, Henry, general merchant
Kegar, W., general merchant
McConnell, Hugh, tailor
McDonald, D. D., carpenter
McNairn, Elisha, farmer
McRea. Duncan, general merchant
Marsh, John, farmer
MOSS, S. H., Postmaster
Mendoch, Alexander, shoemaker
Phillips, H. G., proprietor Travelers Home Hotel
Prosser, W. O., teacher
Robertson, Theodore & James, proprietors flouring and saw mills
Roys, Evan, farmer
Roys, William, farmer
Roys, William A., farmer
Snetsinger, J. G., general merchant
Tait, David, J. P., farmer
Tait, Mary M., general merchant
Tilton, Joseph, sen. farmer
Tilton, Joseph, carpenter
Wood, William D., proprietor saw and flouring mills
Wood, W. D. & J., manufacturers of woolen goods

Mill Haven.—A Village on the Bay of Quinte, and Mill Creek, in the Township of Earnest Town, County Lenox, 14 miles from Napanee, the County Town, and 15 from Kingston. The creek affords excellent water power. The Village is within 1½ miles of a Station of the Grand Trunk Railway. Population 175.

Amey, B., farmer
Amey, Levi, wagon maker
Amey, J., farmer
Armstrong, William, farmer
Clement, William, farmer
Forward, D. C., farmer
FORWARD, G. B., J.P., Postmaster
Garbutt, Thomas, carpenter
Henderson, Messrs. & Co., prop. grist and saw mills
Miller, Sebastian, J.P.
Milligan, S., farmer
Parrott, W., farmer
Patterson, Allice, general merchant
Phillips, Albert, shoemaker
Ritchey, James, carpenter
Vanclerk, William, shoemaker
Vent, James, farmer
Wemps, B., hotel keeper

Milliken.—A Post Office in the Township of Markham, County York, 16 miles from Toronto.

Bain, Rev. James, (Church of Scotland)
Chapman, N., farmer
Gennie, S., farmer
Gibson, F., carpenter
Goodenough, S., farmer
GORVETT, WILLIAM, Postmaster, gen. merchant
Hood, William, farmer
L'Amoreaux, C. L., farmer
McPherson, A., farmer
Macklin, James, farmer
Miller, S., farmer
Milliken, N., hotel keeper
Mitchell, William J., J.P.
Woodhall, William, cabinet maker

Millington.—A Post Village in the Twnship of Mara, County Ontario.

Mill Point.—A Village in the Township of Tyendinaga, County Hastings, on the Bay of Quinté, 20 miles from Belleville, the County Town, 7 from Napanee and 129 from Toronto. Population 500.

Aylesworth, Peter, steamboat agent
Beeman, T., insurance agent
BOWEN, JAMES, Postmaster
Bower, James, farmer
Brisbane, William, wagon maker
Clark, William F., shoemaker
Cook, Joseph, butcher
Carscallen, Thomas, painter
Devanport, Miss Lucy, teacher
Donaghue, Florence, general merchant
Dryden, Charles, butcher
Felson, Frank, saddler
Gratien, J., carpenter
Jacques, C., shoemaker
Jager, Jacob, general merchant
Monck, James saddler
Morrison, David, telegraph operator
Nichols, J., farmer
Oliver, Andrew, carpenter
Oliver, C., hotel keeper
Rathbun, H. B., prop. steam saw mill
Rathbun, H. B. & Son, general merchants
Richardson, James, tailor
Roberts, L. W., farmer
Scott, Rev. John, (Presbyterian)
Stafford, Phillip, carpenter
Stevens, John, wagon maker
Stuart, Mrs. Mary Ann, general merchant
Tracy, Edward, butcher
Vanalstine, Anna Louisa, tailoress
Weldon, George R., hotel keeper
Wells, Edward H., saddler
Williams, M. H., accountant
Wilson, Lewis, farmer

Milnesville.—A Post Office in the Township of Markham, County York.

Barkey, Joseph, farmer
Byers, David, farmer
Byers, John, farmer
Calvert, George, blacksmith
Clacy, William, farmer
Gregory, John, farmer
Hoover, Christopher, farmer
Hoover, John, farmer
Kock, John, farmer
Milne, Peter, farmer
PEARCE, THOMAS, Postmaster and shoemaker
Rayner, A. B., farmer
Rayner, David S., farmer
Read, William S., farmer
Wideman, Samuel, farmer

Milton.—The County Town of Halton, in the Township of Trafalgar, 38 miles from Toronto, 11 from Bronte Station G.W.R., 12 from Georgetown Station G.T.R., and 25 from Hamilton. Money Order Office and Savings' Bank. Population 1000.

Abrey, B. G., P.L.S.
Anderson, William, shoemaker
Andrews, George, butcher
Armstrong, William, carpenter
Bastedo, Jacob, farmer
Bastedo, J., hatter
Bell, Hugh
Bews & Halcro (William & Peter), merchant tailors
Blackstock, Rev. William S. (Wesleyan)
Boak, William
Bones, E., cabinet maker
Booth, Edmund, baker
Brothers & Hatton (Joseph & J. S.), founders
Burger, William, bailiff and butcher
Burns, Nelson, principal Grammar School
Burrows, George, photographer
Callaghan, Owen
Carter, J. S., M.D.
Center, Socrates, pot-ash factor
Christie, D. D., general merchant
Clarkson, George, hotel keeper
Currie, Angus, shoemaker
Dewar, John, barrister
Dewer, John, jr., barrister, Clerk Peace and County Attorney
Downie, David
Eager, W. L. P., County Treasurer, Clerk County Court, Deputy Clerk Crown, Registrar, Surrogate, insurance agent
Edmunds, E. B., confectioner
Farley, Samuel, carpenter
Freeman, Clarkson, M. D.
Gillespie, Rev. John (Presbyterian)
Halcro, P., merchant tailor
Harrison, Johnston, farmer
Henderson, Thomas D., carpenter
Holgate, John, Clerk Division Court, agent Canada Life Assurance Company
Hollinrake, James, general merchant and agent Scottish Provincial Assurance Company
Horner, John, hotel keeper
Iamond, William
Jones, Benjamin, cabinet maker
Jones, John F., agent
Jones, Richard, saddler
Kay, Rev. John (New Connexion)
Laidlaw, William, barrister
Little, David, tailor
Little, William, saddler
Lyon, Robert A., merchant
LYON, WILLIAM D., Postmaster and gen. mercht
McCallum, Finlay, County Treasurer
McCann, Logan, proprietor woolen mills
McDermott, Patrick, tinsmith
McGuffin, James, merchant
McKay, Peter M., grocer
McKindsey, G. C., sheriff
Marshall, John, proprietor livery stable
Martin John, farmer
MATHESON, ROBERT, editor *Champion*
Matheson, Thomas G., barrister
Matheson & Dixon, barristers
Miller, Thomas, Judge County Court
Niehaus, F. W., barrister
Panton, William, County Clerk
Plewis & Warcup, millers
Racey, Thomas, County Registrar
Robertson, David, M.D.
Roper, John P., grocer
Sanderson, Francis, butcher
Scott, William, farmer
Smiley, William, lumber merchant
SMITH, G., mayor, general merchant, agent Standard Life Insurance Co.
Stearn, William J., tanner
Street, William H., M.D.
Taylor, Samuel F., tanner
Thompson, Charles H., hotel keeper
Tremayne, Rev. F., (Church of England)
Van Allen, Eli, builder
Van Allen, Joshua, tailor
Waldie, James, blacksmith
Wallace, John, hotel keeper
White, John, M.P.P.
White, Thomas, M.D.
Willcox, William P., watchmaker
Willmott, James B., druggist, dentist, telegraph and insurance agent
Wilmott, Robert, farmer
Yeoman, William, agent
Zimmerman, J., carpenter

Mimico.—A small Village and Station of the Great Western Railway, 7 miles from Toronto. Population 25.

Bellman, Anthony, farmer
Cooper, Rev. H. C. (Church of England)
Edwards, Rev. A. (Wesleyan)
Hendry, Andrew, teacher
Hendry, George, farmer
KYNOCK, JOHN, Postmaster, agent G.W.R.
McDowell, William, proprietor Royal Hotel
Martin, William, farmer
Randle, John, farmer
Scott, George, grocer and carpenter
Stock, Edward, farmer
Wood, James, farmer

Minden.—A Post Village in the Township of Snowden, County Peterboro. Money Order Office.

Andrews, G. & H., general merchants
Bell, Andrew, proprietor hotel and dealer in boots and shoes
Dumble, William, general merchant
Eastman, Lewis, proprietor hotel
Langton, J., general merchant
Leary, Thomas, proprietor hotel
Mason, Francis, general merchant
Pearce, W. H., proprietor flouring mill, tanner, &c.
PECK, S. S., Postmaster
Soyer, Benjamin, proprietor hotel

Mitchell.—An incorporated Village and Station of the Buffalo and Lake Huron Railway, on the River Thames, in the Townships of Logan and Fullarton, County Perth, 12 miles from Stratford, the County Town, 22 from Goderich, 103 west of Toronto and 128 from Buffalo, N.Y. The 2nd Division Court is held here. Stage to Listowel, 22 miles. Money Order Office. Population 1,590.

Abbott, J., J.P
Abbott, William, saddler
Aikens, J., tanner
Allcock, I., prop. Melborne House
Anderson, G. S., broker
Archer, Mrs. E., baker
Ault, M. M., general merchant
Awty, F
Babb, T., J.P., general merchant
Barge, James, prop. British Hotel
Bailey, William, grocer
Barrett, George, grocer
Bennett, L., grocer
Bennett, Thomas, saddler
Birt, W. H., tinsmith
Botterell, P
Boyd, James, cabinet maker
Brickers, H., prop. mill
Brisbin, Nelson, bookseller
Bullard, C., livery stable
Burns, John, bailiff
Campbell, H., cabinet maker
Caulfield, Rev. H. (Church of England)
Cheesman, T., architect
Christie, R., accountant
Clark, Rev. A. (Bible Christian)
CLARK, P. H., grocer
Clegg, Mrs., dressmaker
Clegg, William, insurance agent
Colwell, William, bookseller
COMMERCIAL HOTEL. John Hicks, proprietor
Coon, D., M. D.
Coppin, J. S., constable
Cunningham, James, shoemaker
Davidson, John, druggist
Davison, S. W., M. D.
DENT, ABRAM, attorney, &c.
Dowling, Thomas, carpenter
Dudney, P., proprietor International Hotel
Dunsmore, J. M., teacher
Dyre, Rev. W. (Wesleyan)
Edwards, S., proprietor planing mill
Egglaton, J., baker
Elder, Miss C., teacher
Ellison, J. B., carpenter
Engles, A., druggist
Etty, W., brick manufacturer
Fishleigh, F., tailor
Fitz, John, cabinet maker
Flagg, J. H., J.P. and general merchant
Green, E. B., accountant
Green, Rev. T., (Bible Christian)
GRIFFITH, S. F., attorney
Haley, Rev. E. A., (Wesleyan)
HICKS, JOHN, prop. Commercial Hotel (see adv)
HICKS, JOHN, Postmaster
Hocking, William, butcher
Hollands, F., proprietor mill
Honey, S., wagon maker
Hornibroook, E., M.D.
Hurd, J., general merchant
Hooking, John, butcher
Hoflich, W., butcher
Holmes, J. F., carpenter
HOOD, J., general merchant
Hoskin, James
Huston & Paterson, general merchants
Jackson, James
James, E., grocer
Keeler, R., general merchant
Ketterson, J.
Keisag, E., shoemaker
Larkworthy, W., butcher
Lemon, J., tailor
Livingtone, William. hotel keeper
Lockhart R. G., watchmaker
Lynde, C., general merchant
McDonel, T., crockery
McGeorge, Miss M., teacher
McIntyre, D., shoemaker
McPhail, Daniel, auctioneer
McQuade, John, shoemaker
Matheson, J., J.P.
Mitchell, Rev. J. W. (Presbyterian)
Mitchell Advocate, (Friday), Davis & Bro., props
Morter, James, grocer
Mulheron, A. & J., cabinet makers
Murphy, J., stock dealer
O'Connor, J. M., general merchant
Potts, William, painter
Reid, William, butcher
Rich, Thomas
Roffe, J. H., baker
Russell, W., tailor
Sarvis, B. B., general merchant
Sedgwick, William, painter
Shanly, P., proprietor Farmers' Hotel
SILLS, G. F. & J., lumber dealers
SILLS, J., J.P.
Small, Miss, dressmaker
Smith, James, cooper
Smalls, W., proprietor mill
Smith, John, carpenter
STEPHENS, A., druggist
Stewart, D. H., general merchant
Stewart, R., cooper
STILES, BEGG & CO., wagon makers
TAIT, J. B., proprietor carding mill
Thompson, W., proprietor oatmeal mill
Thompson & Williams, founders
Walkinshaw, J., tailor
Whitehead, Charles, watchmaker
Wills, H. L., tailor
Wills, W. H., painter
Williams, J. R., saddler
Williams & Thompson, founders
Winstanley, E., lumber dealer
Woods, E. J., agent American Express Co
Yeo, J., wagon maker

Minesing.—A Village in the Township of Vespra, County Simcoe, 10 miles from Barrie, the County Town. Population 250.

Johnston, John, plasterer
Johnston, William, farmer
Johnston, Thomas, farmer
Kent, John, farmer
Lawson, George, farmer
Lawson, L., farmer
Livingston, Donald, shoemaker
McLean, Miss, teacher
Morren, John, teacher
Orchard, James, farmer
Parkhouse, H., farmer
RONALD, A., farmer
Standen, John, blacksmith
Woodsworth, Rev. James (Wesleyan)

Mimosa.—A Post Office in the Township of Erin, County Wellington.

REED, HENRY, Postmaster.

Moffatt.—A small Village, in the Township of Nassagaweya, County Halton, 13 miles from Milton, the County Town, and 19 from Guelph. Population 60.

Allison, Jacob, farmer
Allison, John, farmer
Anderson, John, weaver
Cottrell, John, farmer
Cusick, William, farmer
Donovan, John, farmer
Dunn, Robert, farmer
Elliott, George, farmer
Gordon, James, farmer
Gould, Peter, farmer
Hunter, James, carpenter
Kean, B. H., farmer
Laing, Adam, farmer
LITTLE, PETER, Postmaster, gen. merchant
McLaren, Peter, farmer
Moffat, James, blacksmith
Moffat James, farmer
Sheridan, Robert, farmer
Simpson, Thomas, farmer
Wallace, Hiram, shoemaker
Weir, James, farmer

Mohawk.—(Mount Pleasant.)—A Village on Spring Creek, in the Township of Brantford, County Brant, 5 miles from Brantford, the County Town, 20 from Simcoe, and 75 from Toronto. Stage to Simcoe and Brantford. Money Order Office. Population 500.

Andrews, Rev. Alfred, (Wesleyan)
Briggs, Albert T., teacher
Bingham, George, shoemaker
Briggs, Alexander, hotel keeper
Bryce, George, blacksmith
Clotworthy, Rev. William, (Church of England)
Cook, A. H., M.D
Ellis, John R., J.P., cabinet maker
Fear, Samuel W., wagon maker
Gamon, George, cooper
Haight, Elijah, clothing dealer
JONES, WILLIAM L., Postmaster, dry goods, &c
McGeary, John, dry goods, &c
Peatzie, Rev. William, (Can. Presbyterian)
Phelps, Hiram, farrier
Racey, Thomas, nurseryman, &c.
Rouse, Julius, grocer
Saylis, Solomon, hotel keeper
Stow, John, wagon maker
Stow, M., wagon maker
Tennent, Richard, shoemaker
Townsend, A., waggon maker
Wray, William, butcher

Moira.—A Village in the Township of Huntington, County Hastings, 16 miles from Belleville, the County Town, and 120 from Toronto. Stages to Plainfield and Belleville. Population 100.

Clark, Timothy, J.P., farmer
Dean, W. H., inn keeper
Foster, James
Foster, John C.
Griffin, Samuel, merchant
Hoskins, Ira, blacksmith
Howard, William, merchant
Irwin, Alexander, wheelwright
Ketcheson, James, farmer
Ketcheson, Philip, farmer
McTaggart, Allen, fanning mill manufactory
OSTROM, HENRY, J.P., Postmaster, farmer
Ryan, J. J., Clerk 7th District Court
Vandewater, James

Molesworth.—A small Village in the Township of Wallace, County Perth, 40 miles from Stratford, the County Town, and 28 from Seaforth and Mitchell Stations Grand Trunk Railroad. Population 75.

Bell, Rev. J. W. (Presbyterian)
France, Thomas, hotel keeper
Gardner, John J., blacksmith
LIVINGSTONE, N. M., Postmaster and gen. mercht
Loughead, Samuel, shoemaker
Mitchell, John, saw mill proprietor
Smith, Rev. W. W. (Congregational)

Monckland,—A Post Office in the Township of Roxborough, County Stormont, on a branch of the Aux Raisin River, 13 miles from Cornwall, the County Town

Logan, John, M.D.
Maloney, Martin, shoemaker
McDonald, Archibald, farmer
McDonald, Neil, farmer
McDonell, Alexander J., farmer
McDonell, Alexander R., farmer
McDonell, Allen, farmer
McDonell, Allen J., farmer
McDonell, Donald J., farmer
McDonell, Dougal, farmer
McDonell, George, wagon maker
McDonnell, John, farmer
WEEGAR, ZACHARIAS, Postmaster and gen. mer.

Monck,—A Post Office in the Township of Luther, County Wellington, 36 miles from Guelph, the County Town.

BRAIN, GEORGE, Postmaster

Moneymore.—A Post Office in the Township of Hungerford, County Hastings.

HARIGAN, JOHN, Postmaster.

Mongolia.—A small Village in the Township of Markham, County York, 26 miles from Toronto. Population 25.

Bell, Robert, hotel and storekeeper
CURTIS, ROBERT, Postmaster and gen. merchant
O'Dwyer, James, hotel keeper

Monkton.—A Post Office in the Township of Elma, County Perth, 22 miles from Stratford, the County Town.

Armstrong, Adam, wagon maker
Bennett, Joseph, hotel keeper
Burns, Charles, carpenter
Collinson, John, proprietor West Monkton Hotel
Empberry, B., cooper
Erskine, Andrew, general merchant
Foster, W. & J., builders
Fox, John, hide and leather dealer and tanner
Fox, Thomas, proprietor planing mills
GREENSIDES, EDWARD, Postmaster & gen. mer.
Love, George, proprietorhotel
McDonough & Co., general merchants
Morrison, Robert, general merchant
Priest, Mrs., prop. Sportsman Inn
Renwick, Rev. Robert (Presbyterian)
Schriener, Paul, shoemaker
Smith, W., teacher
Stewart, W. A., butcher
Weir, Walter, general merchant
Wells, H. & Co., grocers
Winstanley, Edward, lumber dealer

Mono Centre.—A small village in the township of Mono, County Simcoe, 45 miles from Barrie, the County Town, 32 from Brampton and 50 from Toronto. Stage to Camilla and Orangeville. Pop. 50.

Barclay, John, farmer
Glover, Hugh, farmer
Glover, William, farmer
Laidlaw, Alexander, farmer
Paterson, Aaron, farmer
Still, David, farmer
Turnbull, Thomas, farmer
WILSON, JOHN, Postmaster, general merchant
Wilson Thomas, farmer

Mono Mills.—A village on the river Humber, in the township of Caledon, County Peel, 23 miles from Brampton, the County town, and 24 from Malton Station, G. T. R. Stage to Malton. Money Order Office. Population 175.

ALEXANDER, JOSEPH, Postmaster, general merchant.
Allen, James & John, general merchants
Campbell, William, & Sons, proprietors Mono Mills Tannery
Clark, James, waggon-maker
Clayborne, John, shoemaker
Cleary, Rev. Richard, (Church of England)
Cobean, Andrew, harness maker
Dwyer, Michael, hotel keeper
Farley, William, shoemaker
Henderson, William, blacksmith
Hunt, Rev. David (Wesleyan)
Jeffers, James, builder
Kidd, John, hotel keeper
Lennox, William, hotel
McConnell, Rev. Mr. (Free Church)
McLaughlin, Michael, prop. grist and fulling mills
McLaughlin, Patrick, general merchant
McLaughlin, Philip general merchant
Patterson, John, builder
Peacock, Mrs., milliner
Squires, William, hotel keeper
Stevenson, William & John, wagon makers
Stewart, Alexander, M., druggist
Vance, Matthew, teacher

Montague.—(See Roseville).—A Post Office in the Township of Montague, County Lanark.
CLARK, PETER, Postmaster.

Montreal, Q.—(See Appendix)—NOTE.—The Publishers of the Ontario Gazetteer have concluded to give a Business Classification of the City of Montreal for the convenience of merchants generally.
C. E. A. & Co.

Montrose.—A Post Office in the Township of Stamford, County Welland.
THOMPSON, ARCHIBALD, Postmaster

Moore.—A Village on the River St. Clair, in the Township of Moore, County Lambton, 11 miles from Sarnia, the County Town. Steamers to Detroit and Port Huron. The 7th Division Court is held here. Money-order office. Population 450.

Abernethy, William, farmer
Armstrong, Rev. David, (Church of England)
Baby, Raymond, farmer
Barr, Mitchell, shoemaker
Boulton, John, farmer
Boulton, Thomas, farmer
Bowen, Nelson, carriage maker
Brightwell, Richard, butcher
Courtney, John, general merchant
Cranston, Samuel, carpenter
Crapper, Thomas, painter
Cronkhite, Jordan, carpenter
Dale, Henry, baker
Egan, M. C., teacher
Fisk, James & Son, shingle makers
Gallino, Alexander, proprietor Farmer's Hotel
Gamble, A. W., M. D
Gratten, Robert, shoemaker
Hadden, John, farmer
Hicks, Rev. William, (Wesleyan)
Hurst, William, farmer
McRae & Cunningham, woolen factors, saw mill proprietors
MORRISON, JOHN, Postmaster
Nisbet, John, grocer
Oliver, Edward, M.D.
Reilley, Charles, proprietor Mooretown Hotel
Richmond, Robert, carriage maker
Scarlett, Richard, china and glassware
Smith, James, butcher
Solis & Bro., general merchants
Sutherland, John, sash and door factory

Moose Creek.—A small Village on the River St. Lawrence, in the Township of Roxborough, County Stormont, 25 miles from Cornwall, the County Town. Population 50.

Aubee, Alexander, cooper
Beauchamp & Co., cabinet makers and furniture dealers
Begg, James, J.P., auctioneer
Belshy, Elias, general merchant
Buchanan, Archibald, farmer
Davis, Rev. —, (Roman Catholic)
Dewar, K., farmer
Grant, D., farmer
Grant, Jennette, milliner
Grant, John, carpenter
McIntosh, James, attorney-at-law
McKILLICAN, WILLIAM, Postmaster
McKillican, William, farmer
McLean, John, farmer
McLeod, James, farmer
McMillan, D., proprietor flouring mill
McRae, Daniel, manufacturer of lime and farmer
McRae, John, tailor
Sinclair, Rev. — (Free Presbyterian)
Stewart, John, farmer
Stewart, P., farmer
Urquhart, William, general merchant
Van Steenburgh, Levi, general merchant
Vineberg, Alexander, general merchant
Vineberg & McMillan, lumber dealers

Moray.—A Post Office in the Township of McGillivray, County Middlesex.
HAGERMAN, H., Postmaster.

Morganston.—A Post Office in the Township of Cramahe, County Northumberland, 23 miles from Cobourg, the County Town.

Finn, George, carpenter
Church, Oliver, carpenter
Gould, James, cooper
NEWMAN, WILLIAM T., Postmaster and grocer
Pollock, William, J.P.
Turney, John, cooper

Morningdale Mills.—A Village in the Township of Mornington, County Perth, 18 miles from Stratford, the County Town, 21 from Berlin, and 85 from Toronto. Stages to Berlin and Stratford. Population 100.

Alexander, William, teacher
Armstrong, John, farmer
Barr, David, farmer
Bearinger, C., carpenter
Bearinger, Noah, carpenter
Campbell, John, cooper
Carson, James, farmer
Cooney, Mrs. M., milliner, etc.
Glenn, Edward, farmer
Good, John, cooper
Gordon, John, hotel keeper and shoemaker
Gray, George, farmer
Kerr, William, farmer
Leggitt, John, farmer
McMullin, William, farmer
Mack, John, auctioneer
Milliken, Rev. — (Wesleyan)
NICKLIN, JOHN, Postmaster, J. P., proprietor steam flouring mill and general merchant
Stewart, William, farmer
Wright, James, proprietor steam shingle manufactory

Morewood.—A Post Office in the Township of Winchester, County Dundas.

M'KAY, A., Postmaster.

Morley.—A Post Office in the Township of St. Vincent, County Grey, 15 miles from Owen Sound, the County Town.

Almond, James & Edward, wine and spirit dealers
Bingham, J. W., teacher
Johnson, George, farmer
Johnson, William, farmer
Kirvan, William L., farmer
Leflar, Nelson, farmer
LEMON, JAMES, Postmaster
Taylor, Rev. —, (Episcopal Methodist)
Tizzell, John, farmer
Veil, Thomas, shingle maker
Wade, Charles, hotel keeper

Morpeth.—A Village in the Township of Howard, County Kent, 22 miles from Chatham, the County Town. Stages to Thamesville, Chatham and St. Thomas. Money Order Office and Savings' Bank. Population 600.

Addeman, George, butcher
Addeman, John, carpenter
Bennett, John, proprietor southern railway hotel
Benson, Rev. M., (Wesleyan)
Boyd, John. tailor
Bury, Edward, farmer
Call, Frederick, farmer
Call, Samuel, farmer
Call, William, farmer
Campbell, Duncan, farmer
Campbell, Neil, proprietor steam flouring mill
Cornwall, Hiram, farmer
Cottier, John, tailor
Cullis, William, potter
Davidson, John, boots and shoes
Davis, James J., cabinet maker
Davis, Rev. —, (Episcopal Methodist)
Duck, John, J.P., insurance agent
Edmonds, Mrs., milliner, etc.
Harrison, Thomas, patent right agent
HEYWARD, ANDREW, Postmaster and druggist
Hill, Austin, farmer and coal dealer
Hill, David, lime and stone dealer
Hill, Erastus, farmer
Johnston, William J., fancy goods, toys, etc.
Kitchen, John, general agent
Kitchen, Samuel, general merchant
Knight, John, carpenter
Lampman. John, farmer
Lloyd, John, founder and machinist
Liebner, Augustus, cabinet maker
McCollum, F. A., general merchant
McDonald, Edwin, boots and shoes
McNeil, Malcolm, M.D
Mason, John, farmer
Metcalf, James, farmer
Nation, Edward, farmer
Nation, James C., general merchant
Palmer, John, farmer
Pierce, George, farmer
Precour, Louis, baker
Reynolds, James R., tailor
Richardson, Charles, farmer
Ross, William, jeweler, engraver, &c
Sexton, Daniel W., prop. Sheldon House
Shaw, Charles, wagon maker and wine and spirit dealer
Shields, Edward, cooper
Simons, Walter B., prop. steam flouring mill
Smith, Cyrus, farmer
Smith, David, prop. Dominion House
Smith, Israel, farmer
Smith, James M., M.D
Stewart, James, farmer
Taylor, Thomas, butcher
Taylor, William J., boots and shoes
Teer, Thomas, tinsmith
Teetzel, John, patent right agent
Teetzel, William, proprietor Commercial Hotel
Thatcher, Stephen, farmer
Traxler, Michael, saddler
Walters, Robert, farmer
Wilson, Matthew, farmer
Wilson, William, general merchant
Wilson, Rev. Robert J., (Church of England)
Wood, George C., saddler
Wood, William K., boots and shoes

Morrisburg.—An incorporated Village, Port of Entry and Station on the Grand Trunk Railway, on the River St. Lawrence, in the Township of Williamsburgh, County Dundas, 30 miles from Cornwall, the County Town. Stages to West Winchester and Dunbar. Money Order Office and Savings Bank. Population 1,800.

Balen, N., farmer
Barry, John, general merchant
Bedsted, T. W. H., farmer and dealer in lime and stone
Bockus, Abraham, cabinet maker and dealer in furniture
Bradfield & Bros., general merchants
Bradfield, F., J.P
Brodie, William, general merchant
Brouse, G. W., druggist
Burns, S., carpenter
Burns, Stephen, dealer in boots and shoes and hides and leather
Capell, John, general merchant
Carman, N., wagon maker
Carroll, Paul, general merchant
Casselman, B., general merchant
Casselman, Richard, prop. flouring mills
Casselman, W., J.P., farmer
Chalmers, James, dealer in jewelry, watches & clocks
Chamberlain, T. F., M.D., dentist and druggist
Clement, A., general merchant
Casselman, Warner, wagon maker
Cutler, S., prop. American House
Cutler, S., farmer
Dain, A., founder
Davidson, Rev. John, (Presbyterian)
Dick, John, tailor
Dillon, George, general merchant
Dillon, John, boots and shoes
Dundas Courier, (Friday), Hugh C. Kennedy, editor
Durdis, Thomas, J.P., stock dealer
Empy, A., prop. Dundas Exchange Hotel
Farlinger, A., farmer
Fetterley, P., general merchant
Fetterley, John, accountant
Flynn, William, prop. marble works
Foley, Jeremiah, boots and shoes
Ford, William, butcher
Garvey, S., general merchant
Gillard, F., carpenter
Gillard, William, carpenter
Gillispie, Thomas, architect
Gilson, William, J.P., prop. steam flouring mill
Glasford, James, general merchant
Gormley, John, tanner
Gormley, P., accountant
Henderson, John, coal dealer
Hesson, John, saddler
Hickey, George L., general merchant
Hickey, R. J., M.D.
Hilliard, D., tailor and dealer in clothing
Howson, Bros., tinsmiths
HOLDEN, JAMES, Postmaster and gen. merchant
Holt, G. A., tinsmith
Hopper, Jacob, farmer
Hunson, R., painter
Kellogg, E. A., carpenter and lumber dealer
KENNEDY, HUGH C., editor *Dundas Courier*
Kingston, William, proprietor International Hotel
Kinney, James P., general merchant
Livingston, Rufus, general merchant
Loucks, Rev. E., (Church of England)
Lyle, R., painter
Lyons, P., butcher
McDonell, A. G., notary public and real estate agent
McDonell, Thomas, general merchant
McGill, Rev. William, (Wesleyan)
McKenzie William, proprietor planing mill
McLaren, John, telegraph operator, express and railway agent
McMartin, Alexander, proprietor billiard room
Martin, R., tanner
Matthews, S. K., baker
Merkley, H. G., lumber dealer
Merkley, James, farmer
Meikle & Bro., general merchants
Millar, James W., commission merchant and steamboat agent
Millar, J. F., founder
Moffat, G, proprietor marble works
Nash, Edward A., M.D.
Nash, Henry, cabinet maker and dealer in furniture
Nash, Joseph, proprietor flouring mill
Nash, R. G., machinist
Nash, W. A., grocer
Perkins, J., general merchant
Perrin, William J., carpenter
Piper, John, wagon maker
Pitts, H., dealer in hardware, cutlery, &c
Pitts, William, general merchant
Pitts, William, carpenter
Plantz, William A., general merchant
Purkis, Mrs., select school
Robertson, A., architect
Rose, J. W., J. P., farmer and nurseryman
Rubidge, Thomas S., architect
Saxe, M., general merchant
Scott, W. E., teacher Grammar School
Sherman, A. B., M. D
Shinnick & Co., general merchants
Smith, Gilbert, tailor and clothing dealer
Southers, J., attorney-at-law
Stevens, Henry G., general merchant
Stevens, H. G., farmer
Styles, William, teacher
Swayne, E., saddler
Tyrrell, F., attorney-at-law
Ulman, G., proprietor Union Hotel
Vanallan & Son, boots and shoes
Wallace, James, carpenter
Warner, J. C., butcher
Weaver, J., proprietor Empey House
Wegant, Herman, dentist
Wegar, A., saddler
Wegar, B., general merchant
Wegar, Michael, butcher
Wilkins & Co., general merchants
Wilson, John, boots and shoes

Morrisbank.—(*See Villages too late for regular insertion at the end of this work.*)

Morriston.—A Village in the Township of Puslinch, County Wellington, 9 miles from Guelph, the County Town, and 22 from Hamilton. Money Order Office, Stages to Guelph and Hamilton. Population 400.

Atkin, Thomas, (Baptist)
Bach, Valentine, painter
Brown, B., shoemaker
Calfus, Charles, farmer
Campbell, Hugh, wagon maker
Clark, John, farmer
Clark, Peter, proprietor planing mills
Eckhart, John, shingle maker
Feeler, Henry, shingle maker
Fisher, G. cabinet maker
Gayer, J., shoemaker
Grier, Thomas M., general merchant
Hardy, Miss Kate, milliner, etc.
Harrison, Rev. —. (Church of England)
Howe, John, carpenter
Jacob Benjamin, farmer
Jacob, William, farmer
Keating, Thomas A., M. D.
McDonald, Rev. Kenneth, (Canada Presbyterian)
McFarlane, David, teacher
McKenzie, Alexander, tailor
McKenzie, Angus, tailor
Martin, Charles & Frederick, butchers
Merlihan, Thomas, hotel keeper
Mitchell, James B., hotel keeper
MORISON, R. B., Postmaster
Morison, R. B. & Co., general merchants
Rathermill, C., carpenter
Roberts, John, farmer
Scott, John T., saddler
Stein, John, cooper
Stratton, William, carpenter
Thompson, James, farmer
Tyrrell, Edward, hotel keeper
Winer, John, farmer

Mortlake.—A Post Office in the Township of Scarboro, County York, 8 miles from Toronto.

Alderson, James, farmer
Ashbridge Isaac, farmer
Auburn, Henry, hide and leather dealer
Brewer, Joseph, butcher
Dixon, William, farmer
Lapsley, —, M.D.
McClure, Joseph, farmer
McClure, V., farmer
Morgan, D., carpenter
Neal, William, farmer
Norris, W. H., J.P.
Pherrill, A., farmer
Pherrill, David, farmer
Stibbort, Thomas, shoemaker
Swallow, John, saddler
Thompson, James W., proprietor Halfway House
Thompson, James W., farmer
THOMPSON, MRS. MARY A., Postmistress
Tully, Mrs., general merchant
Tully, P., cooper

Morton.—A Village in the Township of South Crosby, County Leeds, 15 miles from Gananoque Station Grand Trunk Railway. Stages to Kingston and Delta. Tri-weekly mail. Population 150.

Davies, R. D., butter merchant
Denny, Antoine, cooper
Foley, William, saddler
Judd, Amos G., commissioner
Kelly, William, carriage manufacturer
LEAKE, JAMES R., Postmaster and gen. merchant
Lowe, Rev. Mr. (Church of England)
Manuel, D. H., blacksmith
Mand, James A., cheese-box manufacturer & sawyer
Morton, George, general merchant, proprietor cheese manufactory and saw and grist mill
Niblock, Arabella, teacher
Redmond, James, shoemaker
Somerville, John, miller
Wood, William, hotel keeper and prop. livery stable

Morven.—A Post Office in the Township of Ernestown, County Addington.

Davy, John M., farmer
Gordanier, William, farmer
Gordanier, James, farmer
Gordanier, William R., farmer
HENWOOD, DANIEL, Postmaster and blacksmith
Irish, Seth, farmer
Irish, Tillotson, farmer
Kaylor, Frederick, farmer
Neilson, P. F., farmer

Moscow.—A village in the township of Camden, County Addington, 18 miles from Napanee, the County Town. Population 60.

Abrams, William, teacher
Amey, Edward, farmer
Amey, Jacob, farmer
Amey, L., farmer
Burns, James, J.P., farmer
Garrison, George, farmer
Jackson, James, blacksmith
Kain, Hugh, hotel keeper
Lake, George, J. P.
Lemon, Joseph, shoemaker
McConnell, George, shoemaker
Millsap, Hicks, farmer
Palmer, Walter, waggon maker
Peters, William W., blacksmith
Van Luven, Peter, farmer
VANLUVEN, ZARA, Postmaster and general merchant

Mossley.—A village in the Township of North Dorchester, County Middlesex, 15 miles from London and 5 from Dorchester Station, Great Western Railway. Population 100.

Amoss, James, teacher
AMOSS, JOHN, Postmaster, general merchant
Barr, Samuel, farmer
Coates, William, farmer
Cooper, Joseph, carpenter
Crews, Rev. T., (Methodist)
Graham, William, farmer
Greer, William, farmer
Hardy, John, tailor and clothing dealer
Lane, James, farmer
McMillen, Thomas, lime and stone
Meakes, John, blacksmith
Meakes, Jonathan, farmer
Mossop, John, farmer
Mossop, John, carpenter
Plaxton, George, butcher
Plaxton, George, farmer
Plaxton, John, farmer
Plaxton, William, farmer
Rawson, S. F., painter
Ross, Rev. J. S., (Methodist)
Scott, William, auctioneer
Spencer, James, farmer
Spring, Daniel, farmer
Topkins, Peter, farmer
Venning, Thomas, carpenter
Ward, S., farmer

Motherwell.—A post office in the Township of Fullarton, County Perth, 14 miles from Stratford, the County Town. Improved land in the vicinity averages $35.

Anderson, James, farmer
Baird, Charles, farmer
BROWN, JAMES, Postmaster, J. P., farmer
McIntyre, John, J. P., farmer
Nairn, James, farmer
Rogers, George, farmer
Rogers, Robert, farmer
Thompson, Samuel, farmer
Watson, William, farmer

Mountain Grove.—A post office in the Township of Olden, County Frontenac, 51 miles from Kingston.

Cronka, —, hotel keeper
GODFREY, E. L., Postmaster
Horn, T. hotel keeper
Peters, Rev. Mr., (Wesleyan)

Mountain View.—A post office in the Township of Ameliasburgh, County Prince Edward.

WAY, W. H., Postmaster.

Mount Albert.—A Village in the Township of East Gwillimbury, County York, 45 miles from Toronto.

Bell, Joseph, butcher
Crawford, William, teacher
Digby, Henry, painter
Eckardt, George & Bro., hide and leather dealers and tanners
Eckardt, T. H. & N. P., general merchants
Ford, J. W. & C. L., manuf, woolen goods
Forest, R. W., M.D
Forrest, William, teacher
Hamill, John, prop. Valey Mills Hotel
Hamilton, Rev. C., (Wesleyan)
Harris, Frederick, cooper
Hortop, Samuel B., saddler
Huff, Peter, cooper
Hunter, George W., prop. planing mill
Hunter, Hamilton D., general agent
Hunter, John, boots and shoes
HUNTER ROBERT, Postmaster, J.P
Jennings, —, boots and shoes
Johnston, —, carpenter
Leek, John, general merchant
Leek, Mrs., milliner, &c
McCallum, F. C., M.D
McKeown, John C., prop. Royal Oak Hotel
Marwood, William, tailor
Miller, Anthony, hide and leather dealer and tanner
Mirk, George, carpenter
Porter, Matthew, tailor
Rose, Albert, carpenter
Shields, James, general merchant
Shuttleworth, John, carpenter
Stephenson, William, wagon maker
Stokes, George, J.P.
Summerfelt & Brown, prop. flouring and grist mill
Summerfelt, William H., prop. flouring and grist mill
Willson, Mrs., general merchant

Mount Albion.—A small Village in the Township of Saltfleet, County Wentworth, 6 miles from Hamilton, Population 60.

Bruce, William P., farmer
Cheyne, Rev. George, (Canada Presbyterian)
COOK, JAMES R., Postmaster
Davis, Jonathan, J.P., farmer
Draper, Rev. —, (Methodist Episcopal)
Fletcher, John, lime and stone
Fletcher, Orlando, teacher
Govan, J. & J., general merchants
Grassie, C., wagon maker
Johnston, —., proprietor Victoria House
Kenny, Henry, shoemaker
Laing, William, tailor
Neil, Levi, auctioneer
Stewart, Thomas, lime and stone
Stirling, Daniel, carpenter
Stirling, William, carpenter
Turner, Dougald, wagon maker, prop. Albion Hotel
Turner, John, farmer
Vanduzen, Robert, farmer
Willson, David, carpenter

Mount Brydges.—A Village and Station of the Great Western Railway, in the Township of Caradoc. County Middlesex, 16 miles from London, the County Town. Stages to Muncey and Delaware. Money Order office. Population 600.

Agnew, N., M.D.
Anderson, Miss Jane, milliner
Arnold, John, lumber dealer
Attwood, P. H., auctioneer
Badge, John
Banghart, Andrew, proprietor Farmers' Hotel
Bateman, Edward C., farmer
Billington, George
Bolton, Alfred, carpenter
Brady, Rhoda, saddler
Branston Brothers, agents American Express Co.
Branston, H. E., telegraph operator
BRANSTON, J., Postmaster
Burwell, J. B., farmer
Cade, Robert, proprietor Grove Hotel
Clark, J., proprietor flouring and grist mill
Clark, Samuel, prop. steam flouring and grist mill
Darrack, John, teacher
Darrack, Miss Jennett, milliner
Fisher, William, farmer
Forbes, Thomas, general merchant
Francis, William, farmer
Gamble, James, wagon maker
Grans, Rev. George (Presbyterian)
Hadden, Joseph, section foreman
Handy, Edward, J.P., real estate and insurance agent
Hockin, Joseph, cooper and proprietor stave factory
Hutton, G. Y., insurance agent
Jackson, Rev. Samuel, (Baptist)
Jarvis Frank, proprietor livery stable
Jordan, Daniel, butcher
Kennedy, Rev. James, (Methodist)
Krooman David, North American Hotel
Krooman, John, stock dealer
Laing, Joseph, baggage master
Lee Elijah, carpenter
Lee Jeremiah, carpenter
Lockwood, George, farmer
Lodge Thomas, cooper
London, Franklin, carpenter
London, Jeremiah, proprietor steam saw mill
Lundie, William, general merchant
McCracken, Samuel, farmer
McKay, Thomas, tailor
Miller, Robert, butcher
Miller, C. J., accountant
Mills, Mathew, general merchant
Mines, James, carpenter
Moore, George, farmer
Nash, E.
Northcott, Thomas, J. P.
Paine, John, shoemaker
Price, William, accountant
Pullen, Richard, farmer
Randall, Rev. Lewis, (Methodist Epispocal)
Riley William, farmer
Robinson, James, cooper
Robertson, William E., general merchant
Rockey, E., proprietor flouring and grist mill
Rowles, Charles, general merchant
Rowles, Mrs. William, milliner, &c.
Rowles, William, butcher
Seabrook, Sidney, stock dealer
Sutherland, Alexander, farmer
Thompson, Frank, farmer
Tuck, Edward, general merchant
Turk, Josiah, manufacturer of woolen goods
Webb, Richard, agent, G. W. R. R.
Williams, Richard, farmer

Mount Charles,—A small Village on the Etobicoke Creek, in the Township of Toronto, County Peel, 6½ miles from Brampton, the County Town, and 20 from Toronto. Stages to Malton and Churchville. Population 50.

Boyle, Rev. R. (Primitive Methodist)
Campbell, A. F., teacher
Condale, William, shoemaker
Dale, John, farmer
Foster, Joseph, wagon maker
Fish, Rev. C. (Wesleyan)
Hornly, William, farmer
Irvine, Charles, farmer
Johnston, James, J.P.
KING, CHARLES, Postmaster and gen. merchant
King, Charles, sen., farmer
McBride, T. Z., farmer
McLeod, Robert, carpenter
Nixon, William, J.P.
Savage James, wagon maker

Mount Elgin.—A Village in the Township of Dereham, County Oxford, 17 miles from Woodstock, the County Town, 26½ miles from Port Burwell, and 8 from Ingersoll Station G.W.R. Money Order Office. Population 125.

Bain, Richard, farmer
Benson, Rev. William (Methodist Episcopal)
Bodwell, A. E., J.P., farmer
Bodwell, E. V., J.P., M.P.P.
Bodwell, J. V., farmer
Bucknell, D, A., teacher
Caverhill, William, farmer
Cody, C. G., J.P., farmer
Collins, Josiah & Son, general merchant
Collins, Josiah, farmer
Dodge, Charles, shoemaker
Duncan, Rev. Abraham (Baptist)
Elliott, David, farmer
Elliott, Rev. Isaac (Baptist)
Hadcock, Isaac, farmer
Hadcock, William, farmer
Harris, William, farmer
McCawley, Bartley, shoemaker
Miles, Robert, wagon maker
Morrison, Douglas, farmer
Murray, Donald, proprietor Mount Elgin Hotel
Oxford, S. R., farmer
SMART, JAMES, Postmaster
Terryberry, J. G., M.D.
Tripp, Adams, farmer
Waggoner, Isaac, farmer
Whitelock, James, butcher

Mount Forest—An incorporated Village in the Townships of Egremont, Normanby and Arthur, County Wellington, on the River Saugeen, 41 miles from Guelph, the County Town, 67 from Hamilton, 83 from Walkerton, 16 from Durham and 27 from Fergus. It is one of the most enterprising villages in the West and though commenced as recently as 1854, now has a population of 1,700. Stages daily to Guelph and Owen Sound. Money Order Office and Savings Bank.

Ainley, T., tanner
Anderson, A., prop. Anderson House
Begg, George & M., cabinet makers, props. planing mill
Bently, W., patent right agent
Bishop, William, butcher
Bissell, Amos, stoves and tinware
Bond, Rev. J., (Wesleyan)
Campbell, J. M., bookseller and stationer
Chambers, James, lime dealer
Clewe, John D., barrister
Colcleugh, James, druggist
Colcleugh, William, telegraph operator
Conklin, Jonathan, auctioneer
Costello, Thomas, grocer
Coyne, Isaac, prop. North American Hotel
Crawford, J. M., tinsmith
Crichton, George, hide and leather dealer
Crossin, butcher
Dale, R. J., watchmaker
Demage, J., dentist
Dickson, Peter, baker
Doyle, James, cooper
Doyle, Richard, wagon maker
Dunbar, James, prop. livery stable
Dunbar, S., M.D.
Eeroyd, Alfred E., M.D.
Elliott, Rev. J., (Wesleyan)
Evans, William, proprietor Palmerston House
Forster, Rev. R. W., (Church of England)
Garland, J., teacher
Giles, Charles, painter
Godfrey, Alexander, tavern inspector
Gowanlock, R. R., painter
Graffe, Thomas, G., real estate agent
Gregory, A. T., proprietor nursery
Gribben, John, tailor
Gruer, William, carpenter
Hampton, Josiah, grocer
Hartley, Richard, proprietor Vulcan foundry
Hewitt, William, proprietor Hewitt's Hotel
Honey & Poole, wagon makers
Humphreys, A., carpenter
Ireland, Isaac, patent right agent
Kennedy, J., barrister
Kilgour, Robert, proprietor Mount Forest Foundry
Lee, William C., farmer
Lilley, William, tailor
Little, Robert, butcher
McAdams & McLaren, publishers Mount Forest Examiner
McFadyen, John, barrister
McGill, Thomas, carpenter
McLaren, Daniel, grocer
McLaren, John, dealer in hardware, cutlery, etc.
McMillan, C. P., barrister
McMillan, Rev. John, (Free Presbyterian)
McMullen, James, J.P., general merchant
Mahent, Rev. S. P., (Roman Catholic)
Marshall, Anthony, saddler
Martin, John, prop. flouring and grist mill
Millar, A. H., M.D.
Miller, Thomas R., barrister
Mount Forest Examiner, (Thursday), McAdams & McLaren, proprietors
Murray, Rev. J. A., (Presbyterian)
Naismith, John, general merchant
Patterson, J. W., fancy goods and toys
Riddle, W. H., insurance agent
Roberts, William, hotel keeper
Robinson, John, general merchant
Robinson, William, butcher
Rogers, John, saddler
Sadler, I. G., watchmaker and engraver
Scott & Morrison, general merchants
Scott & Reid, general merchants
Sheppard, John, collector and auctioneer
Sherwood, E., grocer
Simmons, Smith, cooper
SMITH, THOMAS G., Postmaster, insurance agent and accountant
Smith, Mrs. T. G., milliner
Smith, W. & R., general merchants
Smith, William, carpenter
Spence, D., general merchant
Stovel, H. H., M.P., insurance agent and general merchant
Swan, Thomas, wagon maker
Tlett, John, carpenter
Wait, Rev. E. G. (Methodist Episcopal)
Watt, Thomas, wagon maker
Wilkes, J. C., notary public and insurance agent
Williams, J. A., accountant
Wilson, H., insurance agent
Winfield, W. W., general merchant
Wylie, William
Yarlet, Henry, carpenter
Yeoman, D., lumber dealer and prop flouring mill
Yeoman, Horace P., M.D.
Yeoman, L. H., druggist

Mount Hurst,—A small Village in the Township of Albion, County Peel, 18 miles from Brampton, the County Town.

Avery, Rev. —, (Primitive Methodist)
Bee, Rev. —, (Primitive Methodist)
Bentley, William, shoemaker
Bradley, Arthur, shingle maker
Byrne, Thomas, farmer
Clarke, Thomas, butcher
Colly, John, J.P.
Dwyre, Charles, hotel keeper
Downey, Henry, farmer
Duke, William, farmer
Hanna, John, farmer
Millington, William, farmer
McCabe, Alexander, J.P.
Maxwell, James, teacher
Monkman, Andrew, farmer
Monkman, James, farmer
Noble, Andrew, architect
Phillips, Rev. W. (Wesleyan)
Sherlock, Rev. B. (Wesleyan)
Suggett, Jones & Roadhouse, wagon makers
WALLACE, JOHN, Postmaster, J. P., gen. mercht
Wallace, William, farmer
Wilson, Henry, farmer

Mount Healy.—A Village on the Grand River, in the Township of Oneida, County Haldimand, 4 miles from Cayuga, the County Town,. Stage to Caledonia and Cayuga. Gypsum abounds in the neighborhood. Population 150.

Dochstader, W., hotel keeper
Donaldson, J. & W., props. grist, saw & plaster mills
Elliott, S. & M., miners
Kirkland, James, distiller
Russell, William, general merchant
THOMPSON, A. W., Postmaster, County Warden

Mount Hope—(P. O. Glanford.)—A Village in the Township of Glanford, County Wentworth, 8 miles from Hamilton, on the Hamilton and Caledonia Plank and Gravel Road. Mails daily. Population about 150.

Armstrong William, blacksmith
ATKINSON, JOHN, Postmaster and grocer
Bethune, Alexander, M.D.
Brierly, George butcher
Brierly, William, butcher
Carroll, Nichol, hotel keeper
Case, J. S. & D. G., general merchants
CRAIG, WILLIAM, proprietor Mount Hope Stage Hotel (see adv)
Davidson, Alexander
Dunn, John, farmer
Every, John, hotel keeper
Frazer, Jacob, farmer
Gillen, David, blacksmith
Gordon, John, weaver
Hibbard, B., carpenter
Hibbard, Richard, carpenter
Hibbard, William, carpenter
McClement, John, shoemaker
Martin, Adam, farmer
Mulholland, William, farmer
Neale, John, wagon and carriage maker and general blacksmith
Potts, Charles D., merchant
Shafer, Jacob, butcher
Smith, William L., M.D.
Snider, Joseph, farmer
Taylor, William & Son, weavers
Wilcox, Samuel, carriage and wagon makers
Young, William, farmer

Mount Horeb.—A Village in the Township of Ops, County Victoria, near Pigeon Creek, 9 miles from Lindsay, the County Town, and 72 from Toronto. Population 50.

Beamish, John, farmer
Burns, Rev. N. (Wesleyan)
Green, John, farmer
Gundy, Rev. S. (N. C. Methodist)
Lees, Thomas, blacksmith
Lindsay, James, hotel keeper, bricklayer and plasterer
REYNOLDS, WILLIAM, Postmaster
Skuce, James, farmer
Skuce, William, farmer
Southam, James, tailor
Southam, Richard, farmer
Wilson, George, farmer
Wilson, Thomas B., teacher

Mount Pleasant.—A Village in the Township of Cavan, County Durham, 30 miles from Cobourg, the County Town, and 90 from Toronto. Population 200.

Best, Mrs. A., milliner
Best, Hamilton, farmer
Best, Jacob, general merchant
BEST, SAMUEL G., Postmaster
Best, Thomas, jr., prop. saw mill
Bland, Joseph, farmer
Cossford, Rev. Thomas, (Wesleyan)
Courtney, Edward, hide and leather dealer & tanner
Ewing, Rev. J., (Canada Presbyterian)
Garnett, John, farmer
Goodwin, John, manuf. of woolen goods
Jameson, George, J.P., farmer
McCormick, Samuel, prop. Mount Pleasant Hotel
McFaul, Daniel, butcher
McLean, James, J.P., ins. agent and gen. mercht
McLean, James, tailor
McLean, John, shoemaker
McPherson, John, farmer
Miller, William, tailor
Mills, Robert, farmer
Sanderson, Joseph. teacher
Shields, John, farmer
Shields, Joseph, prop. saw mill
Thuxton, Robert, farmer
Webster, Abraham, farmer
Wilson, J. W., carpenter

Mount St. Louis.—A Village on Sturgeon River, in the Township of Medonte, County Simcoe, 20 miles from Barrie, the County Town. Stages to Barrie and Penetanguishene. Tri-weekly mail.

Blue, Duncan, oil refiner
Coulson, James, farmer
Dunn, James, farmer
Ennis, Frank
Fitzgerald, James, farmer
Fitzgerald, John, farmer
Fitzgibbon, John, blacksmith
Flanegan, Patrick, blacksmith
Frawley, Patrick, farmer
Gore, Frederick
HUSSEY, JOHN PATRICK, Postmaster, gen. mer.
Hussey, Michael, farmer
Kinghorn, John, carpenter
McDonald, William, weaver
Miller, Robert, weaver
Ross, George
Shanahan, John, blacksmith
Sullivan, Daniel, farmer

Mountsberg.—A small Village in the Township of East Flamboro', County Wentworth, 17 miles from Hamilton. Population 50.

Campbell, James, J.P.
Dawson, S., farmer
Fearnley, Charles, farmer
Forsyth, Rev. W., (Baptist)
Green, G. W., shingle maker
Hallum, John, farmer
Hart, J. N., farmer
Hewings, John, farmer
Hopkinson, George, auctioneer
McCormick, James, manuf. of sash, doors and blinds
McIntosh, Donald, tailor
McLaren, John, wagon maker
McLean, James, teacher
McNiven, Colin, farmer
PAINE, J. W., Postmaster, general merchant
Pitts, J., carpenter
Smith, F. M., (Episcopal Methodist)
Smith, James, farmer
Trask & Paine, butchers

Mount St. Patrick.—A Post Office in the Township of Brougham, County Renfrew.
BRADY, BRIDGET, Postmistress.

Mount Salem (Late Salem).—A Post Office in the Township of Malahide, County Elgin.
WHITE, W. W., Postmaster.

Mount Vernon.—A Village on Whiteman's Creek, in the Township of Brantford, County Brant, 7 miles from Brantford, the County Town, 7 from Paris, and 82 from Toronto. Stage to Paris. Money order office. Population 200.

Allen, Mrs., dealer in fancy goods, toys, &c
Andrews, Rev. A., (Wesleyan)
Armour, Robert, shoemaker
Ainsleybrooke, George, hotel keeper
Bingham, J., founder and machinist
Bone, Edward, shoemaker
Collins, John, tailor
Downing, J., cabinet maker
Fowler, C., butcher
Hittle, William, hotel keeper
Irwin, Matthew, wagon maker
Johnston, Henry, hotel keeper
Jones, Levy C., carpenter
McIntosh, James, tailor
McWilliam & McAllister, general merchants
Manas, David, wagon maker
Miles, William, farmer
Munson, L., manufacturer woolen goods
Nelles, W. G., farmer
Parsons, Robert, teacher
Penn, William & Co., boots and shoes
Perrin, Andrew, farmer
Perrin, David, farmer
PERRIN, THOMAS, Postmaster, manufacturer of woolen goods, and prop. flouring and grist mill
Perrin, William & Co., general merchants
Thompson & Kellogg, dry goods dealers
Townsend, Henry, farmer
Waters, George, farmer
Weetman, Joseph, cooper

Mount Webster.—A Post Office in the Township of Landsdown, County Leeds.
WEBSTER, ROBERT, Postmaster.

Mulgrave.—A Post Office in the Township of Bertie, County Welland, 14 miles from Welland, the County Town, and 70 from Toronto.

Barnhart, Adam, farmer
Johnston, Joseph, farmer
Kennedy, James, farmer
Learn, Benjamin, farmer
LEARN, PETER, Postmaster, cheese factor and farmer
Lavitz, John, farmer

Mulmur.—A small Village in the Township of Mulmur, County Simcoe, 35 milles from Barrie, the County Town, and 52 from Toronto. Population 40.

Bader, Mrs. Mary, hotel keeper
Ewins, John, farmer
Jennings, Thomas, shoemaker
Little, Edward, farmer
Little, James, farmer
Little, Robert, farmer
LITTLE, WILLIAM, Postmaster, farmer
McCleary, Rev. John, (Church of England)
Murphy, John, farmer
Neely, John, shoemaker
Parson, William, cabinet maker
Robinson, Samuel, auctioneer
Wilkinson, Arthur, teacher
Wilson, W. H., clothing dealer

Munster.—A Post Office in the Township of Goulbourn, County Carleton.

Brownlee, J. S., butcher
Brown, Rev. W. D., (Wesleyan)
Butler, F., farmer
Butler, W., farmer
Conly, Thomas, teacher
Douris, James, hotel keeper
Edwards, John, general merchant
Higgins, W., farmer
Hill, R., farmer
Jordan, Benjamin, butcher
Seabrook, R., shingle maker
McRory, D., carpenter
McFarlane, W., farmer
Rutledge, J., farmer
Sample, William, shoemaker
Scott, John, J. P
Shillington, J., stone dealer
Shillington, Thomas, farmer
TUBMAN, THOMAS, Postmaster, lime and stone
Williams, W., farmer

Muncey.—*(See Villages too late for regular insertion at the end of this work).*

Murray.—(Village, Carrying Place).—A post office in the Township of Murray, County Northumberland, 34 miles from Cobourg, the County Town, 25 from Picton, and 6 from Trenton Station Grand Trunk Railroad. The Village is beautifully situated at the head of the Bay of Quinté, the site occupying the isthmus, 1¼ miles wide, connecting the County Prince Edward with the mainland. Across the isthmus, the projected Murray Canal, connecting Lake Ontario and the Bay of Quinté will run when completed. Stages to Brighton and Kingston. Population 300.

Alley & Bonter, butchers
Barter, R. C., shoemaker
Biggar, J. L.
Bouter, Shuter S., painter
Buchanan, Thomas, farmer
Buchanan, William, farmer
Cobb, Rev. Thomas, (Wesleyan)
Corrigan, R. J. M., farmer
Davern, J. D., grocer and hotel keeper
Davis, Charles, carpenter
Dench, J., farmer
DICKSON, RICHARD O., Postmaster
Fitzgerald, John, farmer
Germain, Miss M., teacher
Griggs, Reuben, blacksmith
Hall, Francis, farmer
Hay, Richard, farmer
Hunt, Henry B., farmer
Lawson, Job, farmer
Murray, J., teacher
Phipps, Thomas, carpenter
Plees, Rev. H. E., B. A. (Church of England)
Rowe, Benjamin, farmer
Rowe, John, farmer
Rowe, Joseph, carpenter
Rowe, Peter, farmer
Shears, George, proprietor Shear's Hotel
Sheriff, C. N., marble dealer
Smith & Empey, farmers
Stewart, Mrs., grocer
Wragg, Thomas B.
Young, Reuben, tanner

Murvale.—A Village in the Township of Portland, County Frontenac, 12 miles from Kingston. Population 200.

Davis, Isaac, farmer
DAVY, M., Postmaster
Ferguson, D., farmer
Griffith, R., farmer
Guess, F., farmer
Hicks, B., farmer
Irwin, W., farmer
Lake, N., farmer
Murton, James, farmer
Murton, John, farmer
McArthur, C., farmer
Peters, S., farmer
Stafford, Z., farmer
Taggert, H., farmer
Vanluven, F., farmer

Muskoka Falls.—A Village on the east branch of the Muskoka River, in the Township of Draper, County Victoria, distant from Lindsay, the County Town, 54 miles, and 125 from Toronto. Stages to Barrie and Bracebridge. Population 20.

Cameron, William, hotel keeper
Chettle, William, blacksmith
McMurray, Thomas
NAPIER, GEORGE, Postmaster
Thompson, John, farmer
Trethewey, James, miller
Trethewey, Samuel, sawyer
Wright, Rev. Walter (Presbyterian)

Myrtle.—A Post Village in the Township of Whitby, County Ontario. It is situated on the gravel road leading to the Town of Whitby, and is distant therefrom 9 miles. Population 75.

Holburt, Reuben, grocer
Kehoe, John, blacksmith
PIKE, FRANCIS L., Postmaster
Scirrah, Frederick W., blacksmith

Musselburg.—A small Village on the North River, in the Township of Mornington, County Perth, 14 miles from Stratford, the County Town. Population 50.

Boshart, Joseph, teacher (German)
Burghman, William, shoemaker
Croly, Rev. J. E. (Canada Presbyterian)
Foss, Theodore, tailor
Hehn, George, blacksmith
Logan, Rev. W. (Church of England)
Milligan, Rev. M. (Wesleyan)
Seignor, George E., shoemaker
SHEARER, GEORGE, Postmaster and gen. mer.
Shine, Daniel, auctioneer
Shuchart, M., tinsmith
Thamer, Henry, wagon maker
Watt, Robert, teacher

Nairn.—A Post Village situated on the River Aux Sables, in the Township of East Williams, County Middlesex, 3 miles from Ailsa Craig, and 22 from London. It is surrounded by an excellent farming country. Money order office. Mails weekly. Population 200.

BELL, ARCHIBALD, Postmaster and carpenter
Brady, James, cooper
Carmichael, Allen, proprietor City Hotel
Davidson, Roderick, agricultural implement manufacturer and blacksmith
Dimond, John, J.P., general merchant and flouring mill proprietor
Foster, V., millwright
Frazer, Donald
Frazer, Angus, shoemaker
Frazer, David, brickmaker
Frazer, Hugh, blacksmith
Gilchrist, Hugh, general merchant
Gilchrist, John, proprietor Nairn Hotel
Halbert, Miss, milliner
Livingston, John, wagon maker
McKeith, Peter, shoemaker
McKenzie, Donald, shoemaker
McKenzie, Colin, wagon maker
Munro, D., carpenter
Parson, John, miller and millwright
Sands, Richmond, M.D.
Wylie, David, Township Clerk

Nanticoke.—A Village on Nanticoke Creek, in the Township of Walpole, County Haldimand, 18 miles from Cayuga, the County Town, 8 from Port Dover and 26 from Dunnville. Stages to Port Dover, Caledonia and Dunnville. Population 230.

Acker, James, proprietor New Dominion Hotel
Adams, Rev. E. (Episcopal Methodist)
Banfield, James, wagon maker
Banfield, John, boots and shoes
BOURNE, C. E., Postmaster, gen. merchant, com. in B.R. and general agent
Bradley, Henry, boots and shoes
Cooper, T. G., farmer
Clark, Harry, proprietor Victoria House
Cummer, A. G., farmer
Crabtree, George, teacher
Evans, Charles, carpenter
Francis, Rev. John (Church of England)
Hall, G. B., proprietor flouring mill
Harris, Thomas, wagon maker
Harris, William, boots and shoes
Howcutt, John, proprietor flouring mill
Husband, J. W., teacher
Jackson, Henry, carpenter
Jackson, John, farmer
Livingston, Hugh, wagon maker
Low, Col.
Low, N. E., P.L.S.
McLean, John, carpenter
Meneke, J. W., J.P., farmer
Monck, John W., J.P.
Newby, Thomas, carpenter
Ross, James, carpenter
Saunders, Samuel, J.P., farmer
Sloan, William, auctioneer
Thurston, William, butcher
Turner, A., general merchant
Wakeling, Thomas, saddler
Walker, James, M.D.
Ward, V. C., carpenter
Willmott, Rev. J. C., (Wesleyan)
Wood, David, farmer

Napanee.—The County Town of the United Counties of Lennox and Addington, on the Napanee River, is a Port of Entry, and Station of the Grand Trunk Railway. The river, flowing through the Town, empties into the Bay of Quinté, affording first-rate water power, and is navigable to the town for vessels of six feet draught. The vicinity was first settled in 1782, and the town plot was laid out in 1832. The chief trade is in flour, grain, lumber and woolen goods. Money Order office and Savings Bank. Population 2000

Aylesworth, J., grocer and leather dealer
Ashton, Clark, jailor
Anderson, Joshua, grocer
Bartles, W., butcher
Beeman, Truman, com. in B. R., notary public
Benn, Duncan, blacksmith
Blewett, James, grocer
Blewett, John, grocer
Blewett, William & Bro., prop. livery stables
Bogart, Rev. J. J., (Church of England)
Bowen, Edward, grocer
Bower, J., druggist
Bowie, William, hotel keeper
BOYLE & WRIGHT, (H. Boyle and R. G. Wright) stoves, hardware, tinware, water lime &c. (see adv)
Briggs, B., shoemaker
BRISTOL, A. S., M.D
Brown, Rev. J., (Roman Catholic)

Burgess, James, baker
Burrowes, J. J., judge county court
Byrnes, L., saloon keeper
CAMPBELL, F. W., barrister, &c
CAMPBELL HOUSE, Archibald McNeil, proprietor (see adv)
CARMAN, T. S., editor and prop. *Weekly Express*
CARNALL, MATTHEW, watchmaker (see adv)
Cassidy, John, grocer
Chamberlain, Thomas, M.D
CHAMBERLAIN, W. R., barrister
Chatterson, Robert, butcher
CLEMENTS, S. T., L.D.S., dentist
Clow, P., prop. saw mill
Coates, J. & Co., saddlers
Conger & Bro., masons and bricklayers
Culhane, James, grocer
Davis, A. C., general merchant, clothing
DAVY, B. C., (Davy & McKenzie)
DAVY & McKENZIE, (B. C. Davy, Fred'k McKenzie) barristers, &c
Davy, John
Davy, Mrs., hotel
DETLOR, WILLIAM V., County Clerk, Notary Public, Agent Provincial, Western and Ætna (of Hartford) Insurance Companies, grain dealer
Detlor & Scott, druggists
Dickens, Edwin, baker
Douglass, H., general merchant
Downey, R., dry goods
Duncan & Day, tanners
Dunning, George, provisions
Ellsworth, Rev., (Episcopal Methodist)
Foster, Rinaldo, dry goods and groceries
Fralick, D. W. & J. F., blacksmiths
Fralick, E. M., grocer
GIBBARD, J. & SON, cabinet makers, planing mill and sash, door and blind factory
Grange, James, M.D.
Grange Brothers, druggists
Green, J. C., cabinet factory and planing mill
Haig, Robert, grocer
Hamilton, Gerrard, carriage maker
Hamilton, H., carriage maker
Heslam, William, hotel
Haycock, L. C., grocer
Henwood, Daniel, blacksmith
HENRY & BROTHER, editors and proprietors *Napanee Standard*
HERRING, JOHN, founder and machinist
Hooper, Edward, County Treasurer
Hooper, E. & Son, general merchants
HUFFMAN, J. C., J.P., druggist and chemist
Hughes, provincial land surveyor
James, Charles, clerk First Division Court, agent Standard Life Assurance Company, Secretary Lennox Agricultural Society.
JUDD, W. S., watchmaker and jeweler, (see adv)
Killoran, Thomas, hotel keeper
Lawson, Alexander, carpenter
McBain, Charles, cabinet maker
McDonald, Robert, saloon
McGUIN, JOHN B., Clerk County Court and Deputy Clerk Crown, Agent (of Hartford) Insurance Company
McMULLIN, WILLIAM, general merchant
McNamara, M. J., attorney-at-law
McNEILL, ARCHIBALD, prop. Campbell House
McNeil, A., grocer
Madden, S. S., tannery
Martin, James, groceries and liquors
MERCHANTS' BANK OF CANADA, Alexander Smith, agent
Miller, D. H., flour mill
Miller, William, dry goods and groceries
Minor, H. S.
Moyle, Mrs., grocer
Neville, A. & Co., manfr patent burners, lamps, etc.
Murphy, C. G. & Co., merchant tailors
NAPANEE STANDARD, Henry & Bro., editors and proprietors
O'Connell, T. F., station agent G.T.R. and express agent
O'Dwyer, John, founder and machinist
O'Reilly & McNamara (James O'Reilly, Q.C. and M. J. McNamara) barristers, &c
Paisley, Charles, hotel keeper
Parkes, J. C., grocer
Parrish, William, stoves and tinware
PERRY, JAMES S., prop. carding and fulling mills, dealer in land plaster
Phelan, J., saloon keeper
Powell' J. W., photographer
Preston, D. H., barrister
Pruyn, M. W., deputy sheriff
Pruyn, Oliver T., sheriff
Quackinbush, George H., general merchant
Ralson, Hugh, U. S. Consular agent
Rennie, R. & Co., general merchants
Richardson & Judd, photographers
ROBERTSON, T. J., attorney-at-law
Robinson, William S., official assignee, accountant
Roblin, Marshall P, county registrar
Rogers, M. T., general merchant
Roney, James, wagon maker
Ross, John, prop. flour mill
ROSS, WILLIAM, proprietor Glencoe flouring mill
RUTTAN, ALLEN, M.D.
Schriver, Mrs., grocer
Scott, Rev. John, (Presbyterian)
Scott, Thomas, attorney-at-law
Scott, Rev. —, (Wesleyan)
Searle, E. & Co., hardware.
Saxsmith, G. S., tailor
Shannon, Neil, baker
Smith & Andersen, grocers
SOBY, JOHN, proprietor Soby House
SOBY HOUSE, John Soby, proprietor (see adv)
STEVENSON, HON. JOHN, M.P.P., Speaker Legislative Assembly, Ont.
STEVENSON, WILLIAM & GEORGE, merchants
Templeton, Mrs. grocer
Templeton, William, foreman *Weekly Express*
Thynne, Thomas W., auctioneer
Tremble, Thomas, butcher
Truesdale, J. D., M.D.
Vivian, Samuel, stationer, printer and bookbinder
Waddell, D. T., saddler
Warner & Brother, grocers
Webster & Boyes, (John Webster and Robert Boyes), carriage makers
WEEKLY EXPRESS, (Thursday), T. S. Carman, editor and proprietor
Wegands, C., cabinet maker
Wilkinson, William H., (Wilkinson & Reeve) Clerk Peace and County Crown Attorney
WILKINSON & REEVE, (William H. Wilkinson, William A. Reeve) barristers, &c
WILLIAMS, W. S., (Williams & Morden) official assignee
WILLIAMS & MORDEN, (W. S. Williams, A. L. Morden) barristers
Wilson, George, general merchant
Wilson, Mrs. H., grocer
Wilson, J. & W., shoemakers
Wilson, S. B., boots and shoes
WRIGHT, H. M. & Co., manufacturers and dealers in water lime, proprietors saw mill

Napanee Mills.—A Village on the Napanee River, in the Township of East Camden, County Addington, 5 miles from Napanee, the County Town, and 17 from Tamworth. Stages to Napanee, Newburgh, Centreville, and Tamworth. Population 100.

Bruton, James, painter
Burgoine, William, architect
Carr, John, wagon maker
Cook & Cochran, proprietors saw mill
Cook, Joseph, M. D
Fox, M., butcher
Granger, A. C., farmer
Hulin, M. H., general agent
Jackson, J., farmer
Jackson, W., farmer
Johnston, W., attorney-at-law
Lloyd, B. C., farmer
McAvoy, P., farmer
Madden, Robert, J. P., farmer
Madden, H., farmer
Miller, James, prop. livery stable
Miller, Peter, farmer
Mott, O. W., accountant
Norman, William, farmer
O'Neal, John P., shoemaker
Pybus, William, soap and candle factory
Spencer, Homer, teacher
Wales, Robert, gunsmith
Woodward, H., dentist
WRIGHT, H. M., Postmaster
Wright, H. M. & Co., lime and stone
Wright, Ruben, farmer

Napier.—A Post Village in the Township of Metcalf, County Middlesex. Distant from London 35 miles, and Strathroy, 12 miles. The River Sydenham passes through the Village affording excellent water privileges. Mails daily. Money Order Office. Population about 175.

Arthurs, Alexander, issuer of marriage licenses, Commissioner in B. R., insurance agent
ARTHURS, JOHN, J.P., Postmaster
Brock, Robert, blacksmith
Brown, William, boot and shoemaker
Brown, Thomas, cradle maker
Burwell, John, pump maker
Case, Ira, blacksmith
Cook, George, cabinet maker
Freely, Thomas, boot and shoemaker
Field, Joseph, innkeeper
Galdrick, Edward, J.P., merchant
Hutton, John, merchant
Jackson, Thomas, cigar maker
Knapston, Charles, boots and shoes
Laird, Rev. James, (Wesleyan Methodist)
Mackey, Thomas, contractor and builder
Munroe, John, blacksmith
Nixon, Alexander, M.D.
Roch, Reuben, innkeeper
Shaver, Stephen, merchant
Sinclair, Lauchlin, M.D.
Smith, William, wagon maker
Sutherland, James G., mill proprietor
Temple, Samuel, brickmaker

Nassagaweya.—A Village in the Township of Nassagweya, County Halton, 12 miles from Milton, the County Town, 13 from Guelph, and 45 from Toronto.

Abrey, George, prop. flouring mills
Cargill, Henry, lumber dealer
Carner, Henry F., farmer
Coon, Charles, boots and shoes
Cusick, Christopher, general merchant
Daley, James, general merchant
EASTERBROOK, ELIAS, Postmaster
Easterbrook, George, J.P. and farmer
Easterbrook, John, general merchant
Fletcher, Jeremiah, farmer
Hutcheon, Robert, farmer
Irving, Robert, butcher
Laren, Alexander, teacher
Lister, Samuel R., J.P. and general agent
Little, James, farmer
Little, Rev. James (Free Presbyterian)
Little, Peter, general merchant
Lyons, Michael, proprietor Halton Hotel
McGlashen, Archibald, farmer
McNair, Donald, auctioneer
McPhederan, Duncan
McPhederan, Jeremiah, farmer
Meade, Robert, general merchant
Pearse James, farmer
Player, William, tailor
Stingel, Henry, cabinet maker
Stranger, George, farmer
Spiers, William H., prop. North American Hotel
Thomas, George, dentist
Wallace, Hiram, boots and shoes
Wilkinson, Rev. Henry (New Connexion Methodist)
Winn, Theophilus, M.D.

Navan.—A Post Office in the township of Cumberland, County Russell.

O'MEARA M., Postmaster.

Nelson.—A Village in the Township of Nelson, County Halton, 13 miles from Milton, the County Town, 5 from Wellington Square, and 12 from Hamilton. Population 120.

Atkinson, Stephen, farmer
Bastedo, David, farmer
Burger, James E., hotel keeper
Campbell, N. J. & Bros., dairy farmers
Cartwright, Frederick, blacksmith
Early, John, farmer
Ellis, Daniel, shoemaker
Furness, William, shoemaker
Glass & Watts, saddlers
Gordon, John, farmer

Haddon & Fraser, saw mill props
Haddon, H. & Son, dairy farmers
Ireland J., farmer
McCauley, Hugh, farmer
McCulloch, Peter, farmer
McCready, Henry, hotel keeper
McLean, David, J.P
Miller. Thomas, township clerk
Mitchell, Richard, farmer
Richardson, William, M.D
Smith, M., wagon maker
Springer, Adam, farmer
Springer, David R., farmer
SPRINGER, DAVID W., Postmaster, gen. mercht
Stinson, Abraham, farmer

Netherby.—A Village in the Township of Humberstone, County Welland, 6 miles from Welland, the County Town, and 60 from Toronto. Population 150.

Baners, Michael, carpenter
Beam, Samuel, broom manuf
Bembeck, P. Z., shoemaker
Box, Edward, carpenter
Burns, Martin, constable
Burns, S. E., teacher
Current, Nelson, J.P
Drummond, John, farmer
Fares, J., J.P
Findlay, James, farmer
Green, Rueben, J.P
HOUSE, JOSEPH, Postmaster, general merchant
House, Lewis, accountant
House, Mary E, milliner
Hurt, Alexander, shingle maker
Learn, Jacob, farmer
McKenney, B., wagon maker
Neff, Alpine, wagon maker
Pauley, John, shoemaker
Schiel, Jacob, carpenter
Smith, Frederick, prop. Humberstone House
Sturges, Benjamin, constable
Young, Adam, cooper
Zantz, J., J.P.

Neustadt.—A Village on the south branch of the Saugeen River, in the Township of Normanby, County Grey, 45 miles from Owen Sound, the County Town. The village was settled about 12 years ago by D. Winkler, and the population, chiefly German, numbers about 500. Money Order Office.

Dellinger, Nicholas, hotel keeper
Denner, Adam, blacksmith
Dopher, John, farmer
Dunneman, Henry, cabinet maker
Ecksteen, Daniel, farmer
Enler, Adam, hotel keeper
Fellman, Rev. Mr. (Baptist)
Fisher, Andrew, cabinet maker
Forster, Martin, brick manufacturer
Francis, Rev. Mr. (Roman Catholic)
Franz, John, sash and door manufactory
Stendry, William, flax mill
Kelberg, Carl, shoemaker
Heintzman, George, painter
Heuther, Henry, brewer
Kalbfleisch, George, general merchant
Klein, John, teacher
Knapp, Daniel, farmer
Lensing, Nicholas, wagon maker
Loas, John, sash and door manufacturer
Loas, Louis, wagon maker
McEdwards, Alexander S., general merchant
Marklinger, Gottlieb, saddler
Meister, George, cooper
Merkle, Jacob, blacksmith
Neocker, George, hotel keeper
Nestor, Frank, blacksmith
Pfaff, Adam, shoemaker
Puschinskey, W. F., general merchant
Puschinskey, F. W., tinsmith
Rekoph, George, blacksmith
Seaman, John, farmer
Scherfle, Andrew, sash and door manufacturer
Shearsmith, Carl, cooper
Shurman, George, tailor
WACHTER AM SAUGEEN, Lang & Heise, props
Wahn & Heise, iron founders
Weler J. N., farmer
Weinert, John, shoemaker
Whidmeyer, Englebit, farmer
Weigand, A. A., tailor
WINKLER, DAVID, J.P., Postmaster
Winkler, J. C., shoemaker
Wolf, Adam, wagon maker
Wunderlich, Rev. — (Lutheran)
Zettlar, Andrew, hotel keeper

Nevis.—A Post Office in the Township of Oro, County Simcoe, 18 miles from Barrie, the County Town.

Cotton, Samuel, farmer
Crawford, George
Crawford, William, farmer
Fletcher, Alexander, farmer
GREENSHIELDS, JAMES, Postmaster
Jarmy, Samuel, farmer
Jarmy & Clarke, proprietor saw mills
Lawrence, Dr.
McKay, Findlay, farmer
Morningstar, George, inn keeper
Rouse William, farmer
Scott, Michael, J.P.
Shane, Peter, farmer

Newark.—A Post Village in the Township of North Norwich, County Oxford.

HENDERSON, HENRY, Postmaster, and general merchant
Henderson, Joseph, merchant
Hill, William, blacksmith
Hilliker, Enoch, farmer
Holmes, Benjamin, J.P.
Pritchard, Thomas, farmer
Saxton, James, wagon maker
Smith, Seneca, boot and shoe maker

New Aberdeen.—A Village in the Township of Waterloo, County Waterloo, 5¼ miles from Berlin, the County Town. Population 54.

Davidson, George, lumber dealer
Gerrie, John, teacher
Grant, Robert, farmer
Hamacher, Peter, shoemaker
Israel, George, farmer
KEY, WILLIAM, Postmaster
Key, William, wagon maker
Leadt, John, shingle maker
McDougal, D., dyer and scourer
Marshall, William, carpenter
Scott, Thomas, farmer
Thomson, James, farmer
Thomson, Johnson, boots and shoes
Thompson, Joseph, farmer
Wildfong, Joseph, farmer
Wylde, Henry, grocer

Newbliss.—A Village on Irish Creek, in the Township of Kitley, County Leeds, 24 miles from Brockville the County Town, and 4 from the nearest Railway Station. Average price of land in the vicinity $30 per acre. Population 300.

Balf, Patrick, farmer
Bruce, Robert, woolen manufacturer
Cade, Joseph, accountant
Campbell, William, accountant
Carnochan, John, farmer
Church, William, M.D.
Daly, Richard, cabinet maker
Daly, Mrs., tailoress
Davison, John, sen.
Driver, William, J.P., farmer
Edgar, John, J.P. and general merchant
Edgar, J., jun., insurance agent
Edgar, Mrs., tailoress
Foster, Richard, tinsmith
Gunnis, Thomas, wagon maker
Johnston, Joseph, watch maker
Jones, William, proprietor, Newbliss hotel
Jones & Davison, general merchants
Kerr, Abraham, farmer
Kinch, Edward, shoemaker
King, W. J., proprietor lumber yard
Latrace, Isaac, baker
Latrace, Mrs. Isaac, dressmaker
Latrace, James, brewer
Latrace, Septimus, tanner
Lerikey, John J., cooper
Lockwood, E., fancy goods
Luckey, William, watchmaker
Mackay, Charlotte, teacher
Mackay, John, sen., engraver
Mackay, John, teacher
Mackie, David, farmer
Moore, James, tallow chandler
Moore, Mrs., tailoress
MORAN, WILLIAM, Postmaster
Parker, Andrew, dyer
Quinn, John, painter
Quinn, T., saddler
Ross, Andrew, farmer
Ross, C. carpenter
Ryan, William, gunsmith
Ryan, Mrs., dressmaker
Shanks, James, farmer
Smith, Charles, carpenter
Stewart, Ansley, architect
Stewart, George, hardware
Tate, Alexander, farmer
White, Rev. William, (Presbyterian)
Wright, John, butcher

Newbridge.—A Post Office in the Township of Howick, County Huron.
CARSON, JAMES, Postmaster.

Newburgh.—An incorporated Village on the Napanee River, in the Township of Gamden East, County Addington, 6 miles from Napanee, the County Town, and 180 from Toronto. Stages daily to Napanee, Kingston and Tamworth. Money Order Office and Savings' Bank. Population 1000.

Aylesworth, J. B., Councillor
Beaudet, D. A., carriage maker
Black, John & Son, tanners
Campbell, John, M.A., principal grammar school
Caton, Allen, druggist
Caton, Miles, general merchant
Dunlop, Miss, teacher
Eakins, George, cabinet maker
Empey, Nathan, general merchant
Finkle, Henry, carriage maker
Fullerton, Joseph, cabinet maker
Gray, Rev. James, (Wesleyan)
Ham, John D., J.P., general merchant
Hanlin, Rev. James, (Wesleyan)
Hooper, Douglas, J.P., general merchant
Hope, A. F., hotel keeper
HOPE, R. F., J.P., Postmaster
Hope, W. A. & Co., general merchants
Huyck, Miss, teacher
Jones, Edward, prop. planing mill
McCannon, James, druggist
McGee, John, principal Model School
Madden, George, farmer
Madden, Sylvester, carder
Miller, C. H., Councillor
Paul, James, grocer and provision dealer
Pepin, Daniel, tailor
Porter, W. H., grocer and provision dealer
Powell, Ruell, tinsmith
Powers, James, hotel keeper
Russell, Andrew, tailor
Scott, Thomas, carriage maker
Shorts, Nelson
Stickney, D. B., Councillor
Wells, John, saddler

Newboro'.—A Village in the Townships of North and South Crosby, on the Rideau Canal, County Leeds, 40 miles from Brockville, the County Town, and 20 from Perth Station, Brockville and Ottawa Railroad. Stage to Brockville. Money order office. The 8th Division Court is held here. Population 350.

Adams, Edward G., blacksmith
Bain, A., dentist
Bell, Abraham, farmer
Bell, A. W., N. P., general agent & general merchant
Bell, Robert, boots and shoes
Bilton, James, J. P.
Bilton, William, farmer
Blake, Richard, general merchant
Bolton, Henry, boots and shoes
Brown, Arthur, teacher
Butler, Joseph H., tinsmith
Cannon, George, general merchant
Cannon, Thomas, clothing dealer and tailor
Davison, R. S., general merchant
Denby, Badley, painter
Denby, William, grocer
Donahoe, John, farmer
Douglas, Samuel, boots and shoes
Draffin, John, general merchant
Dunham, Charles I.
Dunham, George, M.D.
Elliott, James, carpenter
Elliott, Miss, miliner, &c.
Fessant, Rev. E. (Wesleyan)
Forster, Alfred, lock master
Foster, Thomas, carpenter
Heron, John, blacksmith
Hopkins, Robert, general merchant
Kennedy, Owen, prop. Newboro Hotel and cabinet maker
Kilborn, Miss Hettie, telegraph operator
Kilborn, Horace, druggist and Division Court Clerk
Kilborn, Col. John, farmer
Knapp, Harvey, farmer
Leech, Richard, farmer
Legget, Henry, saddler
Legget, James, hide and leather dealer and tanner
Lewis & Co., general merchants
McDonald, David, J.P.
McGregor, John, auctioneer
McKian, Patrick, grocer and cabinet maker
McManus, William B., tailor
Moran, Daniel, carpenter
O'Connor, William, stock dealer
O'Hara, Rev. James (New Connexion Methodist)
Paul, William, cooper
Pielow, William, saddler
Poole, John N., farmer
Preston, J. W., grocer
Preston, Robert H., M.D.
Shaver, J. H., wagon maker
Staunton, George, carpenter
Staunton, Thomas, carpenter
Stephenson, Rev. F. L. (Church of England)
Telt, Benjamin, M.P.P.
WEBSTER, THOMAS, Postmaster and gen. mercht
Webster, W. J., general merchant
Whitmarsh, John G., butcher
Wing, George, accountant
Wright, Edward, carpenter
Wight, J. R., proprietor Dominion House
Wright, Sampson, watchmaker, jeweler, &c.

Newboyne.—A Post Office in the Township of Bastard, County Leeds, 29 miles from Brockville, the County Town. Improved land in the vicinity averages $20 per acre.

Cawley, John, J.P., farmer
Davis, John, tailor
Gardiner, Robert, farmer
Joynt, John B., farmer
Layng, John, J.P., farmer
Lyons, John, farmer
Lyons, Joseph, teacher
Lyons, Michael, grocer
LYTLE, JAMES, Postmaster
Moss, George, tailor
Robinson, Thomas, farmer
Rogers, George, farmer
Rogers, John, farmer
Rogers, Thomas, farmer

Newbury.—A Post Village and Station on the Great Western Railway in the Township of Mosa, County of Middlesex, 36 miles distant from London, and 152 from Toronto; it is the centre of a fine agricultural country, and large quantities of grain, lumber, and square timber are shipped from this point. Daily mails. Money Order Office and Savings Bank. Population 800.

Adair, Robert, boots and shoes
Anderson, John D., accountant
Archer, Henry R.
Archer, John, general merchant
Archer, John J., general merchant
Armstrong, Alexander, M.D.
Babcock, David, prop. Union Hotel
Ball, S. J., station master
Banning, George E., flouring and saw miller
Bigger, Dr., M.D.
Bracken, John, carpenter
Bradshaw, William, blacksmith
Brown, Mrs., milliner and dressmaker
Brown, W. W., cabinet maker
Campbell, Colin, hotel keeper
Clayson, William, gun and pistol maker
Clements, John R., general merchant
Clements, William, veneer manufacturer
Cusack, H., hoop merchant
Davis, John P., carriage and wagon maker
Davis, Miss M., teacher
Davis & Fleming, wool carders and cloth dressers
Deming, Prosper, collector
Fleming, Samuel, (Davis & Fleming)
Gay, John, blacksmith
Green, Farmer, boots and shoes
Guppy, William J., flour, feed and groceries
Guy, Benjamin, flour and feed
Hall, Thomas & Henry, cabinet makers
Heywood, William, prop. Heywood's Hotel
Irwin, William, stave buyer
Kelly, Joseph B., general merchant
Lawrence, Rev. Benjamin, (Methodist Episcopal)
Lawrence, Jamin, general merchant
Leech, J. M., teacher
Lince, Rev. M. J., (Baptist)

Little, James, shoemaker
McMurray, Samuel, soap and candles
McNorton, Titus, agricultural implements
McRae, Alexander, general merchant
Macdonald, Robert, tailor
Maggs, Thomas, confectioner
Merritt, William H., saddler
Miller, Jacob, watchmaker
Modeland, Thomas, wagon maker
Morris, E. & Co., soap and candles
Mounteer, John, butcher
Mounteer, William, confectioner
Mylne, John, druggist
Nelles, R. A., stoves and tinware
Nelles, R. A. & Co., general merchant
Ollis, William, baker and confectioner
O'Mara, John, P. L. S.
Palmer, Mrs. M., milliner
Palmer, Wm. L., farrier
Patterson, James, grocer
Purdy, David A., lumber and veneer
Randall, Thomas, boots and shoes
Randall, Thomas, general merchant
Rickerby, John, merchant tailor
ROBINSON, THOMAS, Postmaster, general merchant, commissioner in B. R., express agent, etc.
ROBINSON & CO., props. saw mill
Roome, W. F., M.D.
Ruth, Salem, tinsmith
Schwader, John, butcher
Smith, George J., conveyancer and com. in B. R.
Stafford, Rev. E. A., (Wesleyan)
Storey, Thomas, proprietor Albion Hotel
Toles, Jerome, carpenter
Tucker, Henry, watchmaker and jeweler
Urquhart, Donald R., general merchant
Ward James C., inn keeper
Ward, Joseph M., proprietor Clarendon House

Newcastle.—An incorporated Village, Port of Entry, and Station of the G. T. R. on Lake Ontario, in the Township of Clarke, County Durham, 23 miles from Cobourg, the County Town, 17 from Port Hope, 5 from Bowmanville, and 48 from Toronto. Money Order Office and Savings' Bank. Population 1,300.

Adams, Joshua
Allen, Charles, cabinet maker
Allin, Daniel, cabinet maker
Allin, D., cabinet ware, stationery and fancy goods
Anderson, C.
Arnold, J., butcher
Arnot, Duncan
Barrie, Thomas
Bayly, George J., dry goods and general merchant
Barfett, John Rice, saddle and harness maker, dealer in general hardware
Batten, Charles, blacksmith and wagon maker
Bayley, G. J., general merchant
Beeman, Edwin, nurseryman
Bellwood, John
Bones, S. & Brother, brick manufacturers
Bowen, Bradford
Bowis, James, carpenter
BRADLEY, W. R., express agent
Bradley & Douglas (Wilson Bradley and Thomas Douglas), livery stable
Bradley, Wilson, (Bradley & Douglas)
Brent, Rev. Henry, (Church of England)
British and Foreign Bible Society (Newcastle Branch) John Templeton, Depository
Brown, George, tailor
Brown, William, boots and shoes
Carr, Henry, boots and shoes
Casselman, Miss, teacher Union School
Casselman, Jacob, dry goods and groceries
Chambers, Richard, boot and shoemaker
Chandler, Stephen B., dentist
Clark, Robert, (Poole & Clark)
Cleghorn, Rev. Thomas (Wesleyan)
Commercial Hotel, R. Grose, proprieter
Dickson, James
Dodd, John, M.D.
Douglas, Robert, proprietor livery stable
Douglas, Thomas, (Bradley & Douglas), express agent
Downing's Hotel, Thomas Downing, proprietor
Downing, Thomas, proprietor Downing's Hotel
Durham Woolen Manufacturing Company, Charles Wood, manager
Eilbeck, Robert, telegraph operator
Eilbeck, J.
Ellsworth, Alfred, photographer
Fairbairn, Robert, J.P., general merchant
Farncombe, Frederick, Collector of Customs
Foster, Horace, chemist and druggist, and agent Edinburgh Life Association of Scotland, and Sec. Durham Woolen Manufacturing Co.
FOTHERGILL, ROBERT, chemist and druggist,
Galbraith, David, M.D.
Gibson, Capt. Frank, vessel owner
Gibson, Thomas
Gillespie, John, butcher
Glendenning, John, proprietor Wellington Hotel
Gorman, E., hardware merchant
Grant, William, boot and shoe maker
Gray, George, grocer
Grose, Richard, proprietor Commercial Hotel
Henry, M., watch maker and jeweler
Hill, Richard
HODGES, HIRAM, J.P., Postmaster, agent Montreal Telegraph Co
Hunter, A. H., grocer
Ivory, P
Ivory, William, farmer and prop. carding mill
Jacobs, George A., produce dealer
Jackson, James, grocer
Lidsay, William, brickmaker
Little, Robert, merchant tailor
Lockhart, A. & Son, prop. flour mills
Lovekin, James, J.P., produce dealer
LYMAN, JOHN, (Northrop & Lyman)
McClung Bros, dry goods, groceries, boots and shoes
McCullough, Rev. William, (Wesleyan)
McDONALD, JOHN, (McDonald & Metcalfe)
McDonald, William, baker
McDONALD & METCALFE, (John McDonald and George Metcalfe) marble manuf. (see adv)
McGill, Robert, butcher
McNaughton, Andrew, prop. Newcastle flouring mills
Martin, T. J., prop. Wellington House
MASSEY, H. A., prop. Newcastle agricultural and machine works, and coroner for the United Counties of Northumberland and Durham
METCALFE, GEORGE, (McDonald and Metcalfe)
Middleton, Henry
Miller, Thomas, general merchant
Monagan, Mrs. C., milliner and dressmaker
Monro, Henry
Montreal Telegraph Company, Hiram Hodges, agent
Moore, Samuel, blacksmith

NEWCASTLE AGRICULTURAL & MACHINE WORKS, H. A. Massey, proprietor
NEWCASTLE POST OFFICE, King street, Hiram Hodges, Postmaster
Nicholson, Francis, wharfinger
NORTHROP, HENRY S., (Northrop & Lyman)
NORTHROP & LYMAN, (Henry S. Northrop, and John Lyman) wholesale manufacturers and dealers in patent medicines
O'Meara, Charles, telegraph operator, G.T.R. station
Olford, Joseph, boots and shoes
Parsons, J. H., teacher, Union School
Philp, James, station master, G. T. R.
Pond, Edmund, barber and painter
Poole, John (Poole & Clark)
Poole & Clark, (John Poole & Robert Clark)
Riddle, Rev. J., (Presbyterian)
Robson, J. J., J.P.
Rose, William N., physician surgeon and coroner
Rowe, Thomas, wagon maker
Simmons, E., carpenter
Stillwell, Frederick, blacksmith
Strowger, Louis, proprietor Globe Hotel
Tamblyn, Thomas, J.P., hide and leather dealer
Tamblyn, W. W., M.A., principal, Union School
TEMPLETON, GEORGE, (G. Templeton & Co.)
TEMPLETON, JOHN, (G. Templeton & Co.)
TEMPLETON, G., & Co. (George Templeton & John Templeton) general store
Toll, J., boots and shoes
Treleaven, John, planing mill proprietor
Tremaine, E. G., telegraph operator G. T. R.
Trickey, J. M., gunsmith
Wallbridge, Asa F.
Walls, Wm.
Wagstaff, William, miller
Walbridge, John E., farmer
Warner, W. H., Town Clerk
Warren, Richard, painter
Warren, Wm., painter
Wellington House. F. J. Martin, proprietor
Wilkinson, R. T., barrister
Willmot, A.
Wilmot, Samuel, Clerk of Division Court, issuer of marriage licenses and insurance agent
Wood, Charles, manager Durham Woolen Manuf. Co.

New Dundee.—A Village on Alder Creek, in the Township of Wilmot, County of Waterloo, 12 miles from Berlin, the County Town, and 6 from Petersburg station, Grand Trunk Railway. Population 125.

Arnold, J., cooper
Bader, J., tailor
Bead, Lyman, J.P.
Becker, Jacob, saw mill
Bettscher, Gott, agent for fruit trees
Bettscher, Jacob, J.P.
Bettscher, Jacob F., watchmaker
Boehmer, Valentine & Son
Brickner & Son, F. and G., millers
Butcher, Frederick, butcher
Cassel, Jesse B., farmer
Cressman, J., farmer
Cressman, Samuel, farmer
Dirstein, Elias, carpenter
Fisher, Henry, shingle manufacturer
Gix, H., tailor
Glanser, Benedick, shoemaker
Hunsberger, Samuel H., carpenter
Kriesel, Frederick, tinsmith
Lantenschlage, P. S., general merchant
Lenghas, L. O., M.D.
McDonald, D., farmer
McTavish, Douglas, teacher
MOYER, A. Postmaster
Millar, John, farmer
Moyer, Bros., general merchants
Poth, Andrew, cabinet maker
Reichard, Jacob, saw mill
Rosenberger, C. D., farmer
Sauer, John, proprietor Anglo-American Hotel
Schlichter, Rev. Samuel
Schlumnie, August, wagon maker
Smith, S., cooper
Studer, Peter, proprietor Dundee Hotel
Tilt, John, farmer
Trusseler, Bros., saw mill proprietor
Watson, Tilt & Adsett, woolen manufacturers
Weber, John M., wagon maker

New Edinburgh.—A Village in the Township of Gloucester, County Russell, on the Rideau River, 1 mile from Ottawa, and 60 from L'Orignal. The Village, for electoral purposes, is in the County Russell, but judicially in County Carleton. Money order office. Population 400.

Aird, Matthew, proprietor New Edinburgh Hotel
Allen, James, general merchant
Ballantyre, G., cooper
Bell, William R., M.D.
BLACKBURN, JAMES, Postmaster and general merchant
Blackburn, Robert, general merchant
Bray, John, blacksmith
Burritt, Henry O., farmer
Butler, T. O., mail conductor
Clark, Robert, plasterer
COOKE, ALANSON C., Deputy Postmaster
Currier, Benjamin, manager saw mills
CURRIER, J. M., M.P., lumber merchant
Currier, T. W., sash factory
Dawson, F. W., carpenter
Dickinson, M. K., commission merchant
Duff, Robert, carpenter
Farmer, Thomas, master tug *Bytown*
Ferguson, John, fire warden
French, George, miller
Higginson, Rev. George N., (Church of England)
Holmes, William, carpenter
Keefer, T. C., president street railway
McClymont, William & Co., proprietors flouring and grist mill
McDonald, Peter, farmer.
McEwan, George & Son, tinsmits, dealers in stoves
McIlroy, John, carpenter
McKay, Joseph & Bro., manufact'rs of woolen goods
McLeod, Dugald, miller
Newell, Hugh W., carpenter
Patterson, John, tailor
Phillips, Rev. T. D. (Church of England)
Proctor, J. W. & Co., general merchants
Redmond, Patrick, pound keeper
Sherwood, Joseph
Sinclair, James, agent J. McKay & Bros.
Smith, Richard, farmer
Surtees, Robert, architect
Tubman, Thomas, teacher
Urie, William, general merchant

New Durham.—A Village on Big Creek, in the Township of Burford, County Brant, 18 miles from Brantford, the County Town, and 18 from Paris. Population 140.

Adams, Oliver, tanner
Allen, C. E., carpenter
Bertram, E. J., teacher
Brown, Rev. J., (Congregational)
Cochran, Charles, teacher
Douglas, David, saddler
Douglas, John, baker
Haight, Hiram, farmer
Hartley, J., general merchant
Hartley, William, wagon maker
Henry, J. B., farmer
Kelly, Philip, farmer
Lawrason, P. M., insurance agent
Marsh, Joseph, farmer
Mason, William B., farmer
Moore, E. F., shoemaker
Morrison, Rev. —, (Methodist)
Robbins, J., farmer
Secord, A., carpenter
Secord, J. C., J. P
Schoorley, A., general merchant
Sims, Solomon, farmer
Siple, E., proprietor New Durham Exchange

New Hamburgh.—An Incorporated Village on the River Nith, and Station on the Grand Trunk Railway, in the Township of Wilmot, County Waterloo, distant from Berlin, the County Town, 18 miles, from Toronto 75. Money Order Office and Savings' Bank. Population 1,400.

ALLCHIN, JOHN, Clerk Division Court
Allen, S., teacher
Boechler, C., proprietor Union Hotel
Boehler, Xavier, potter
Bogue, H. M.D.
Boullie, W. H., M.D.
Broeckner, Peter, bookbinder
Brown, H. R. D., com. merchant
CAMERON, CHARLES, general merchant
COMMERCIAL HOTEL, Jacob Seyler, proprietor
De Guehery, Rudolph, teacher
Dietz, J. H., cabinet maker
Ernst, Charles, general merchant
ERNST, C., Postmaster
Fennel & Co., hardware
Flock, Henry, watch maker
Funken, Rev — (Roman Catholic)
Gartung, Ernst, prop. Clarendon Hotel
GOODMAN, KENNETH, attorney-at-law
Graf, Frederick, watchmaker
GUGGISBERG, W. & CO., general merchants
Harlen, Rev. E. (Wesleyan)
Heimbecher, Peter, blacksmith
Hoeffler, F, C., general merchant
Hopf, William, soap manufacturer
Hunter, William, general merchant
Klein, Lewis, general merchant
McCALLUM & CAMERON, druggists
Merner, F., wagon maker
Merner, Samuel, iron founder
Morley, John, bailiff
Morrison, D., miller
Niebel, Jacob, boots and shoes
Nopper, John, iron founder
Otto, Henry, blacksmith
Parker & Wilson, millers
Rally, Rev. W. B., M.A. (Church of England)
RAW, STEPHEN, prop. North American Hotel
RAW, STEPHEN & SONS, brewers
Read, G. A., woolen factor
Robertson, Rev. — (Presbyterian)
Ruchty, George, boots and shoes
Schmidt, J. A., teacher
SEYLER, JACOB, proprietor Commercial Hotel
Spring, Rev. C. F. (Lutheran)
Steinberg, George, boots and shoes
Stiefelmeyer, Ulrich, M.D.
Tappe & Peine, boots and shoes
Wagner, Frederick, boots and shoes
Wagner, Jacob, prop. City Hotel
Wagner, John, wagon maker
Wredow, William, tobacconist
Young, W. & C., tanners

New Lancaster.—(See Riviére Raisin P.O.)

New Lowell.—A Village and station on the Northern Railway, on Coates' Creek, in the Township of Sunnidale, County Simcoe, 17 miles from Barrie, the County Town and 79 from Toronto. Population 200

Bell, Angus, teacher
Coyle, Thomas, farmer
Gill, Patrick, carpenter
Guilfoy, Michael, fa.mer
Harkin, Martin, farmer
Harkin, N., farmer
Hill, R. J. A., telegraph operator and railroad agent
Jacques & Hay, proprietors saw mill, turning factory
Jennings, Able, butcher
Kee, Matthew, farmer
Langtry, James, carpenter
McIlroy, Daniel, farmer
Macham, Thomas, J.P., farmer
Martin, John, hotel keeper
Mason, Joseph, shingle maker
Mother, James, general merchant
O'Brien, James, shoemaker
Paton, Andrew, general merchant
PATON, PETER, Postmaster
Prentice, A., lumber dealer
Scott, Isaac, shingle maker
Stephens, M. W., lumber dealer

Newington.—A village in the Township of Osnabruck, County Stormont, 10 miles from Dickinson's Landing. Population 60.

BAKER, JACOB, Postmaster, general merchant and prop. Wellington Hotel
Foster, Leshy, farmer
Hawn, Joseph, shoemaker
Hill, James, carpenter
Jardine, Ferguson, farmer
Jardine, J., farmer
McDonald, R., stock dealer
McIntyre, Miss Mary, milliner
McLaughlin, Daniel, farmer
Morton, Miss Mary Ann, milliner
Parker, John, painter
Ross, W., wagon maker
Ruth, Charles, M.D
Snetsinger, Frederick, farmer
Snetsinger, George, farmer
Snetsinger, John, farmer
Snetsinger, M., carpenter

Newmarket.—An incorporated Village and Station of the Northern Railway, in the Township of Whitchurch, County York, on the east branch of the Holland River, 34 miles from Toronto. It is one of the most flourishing villages on the Northern line, the amount of business being equal to that of any other on the route. Money Order Office and Savings' Bank. Stages to Pine Orchard, Stouffville, Sharon, Keswick, Sutton, and in winter to Beaverton. Population 2500.

Anderson, W. W., principal Grammar School
Airth, Graham, dealer in fish, oysters, &c.
Alexander, Robert, teacher
Allen & Hendry (James & Thomas) iron founders
Arnott & Fox, coopers
Atkinson, Thomas, insurance and general agent, auctioneers, &c.
Argue, Rev. T., (Methodist Episcopal)
Bach, George H., carpenter
Bentley, John, M.D., J.P., druggist and grocer
BINNS, GEORGE M., Editor *Courier*, book and job printer, book-binder and dealer in books, stationery, &c.
Bishop, Thomas, mason
Bishop, William, mason
Bond, Mrs. J., millinery and mantles
Botsford, Joseph, cabinet maker
Botsford, Nelson, carpenter
Botsford, Timothy, saddler
BOULTBEE, ALFRED, barrister, attorney, etc
Bowden, W. H., baker and confectioner
Brelsford, Charles, proprietor North American hotel
Brimson, John, carriage maker
Brown, Rev. John, (Presbyterian)
Budge, Alexander, blacksmith
Burk & Harrison (D. and Henry) general merchants
Burn, Alfred, general merchant
Cain, Patrick, tinsmith
Caldwell, James B., painter
CAMPBELL & LOUNT (E. C. Campbell and G. W. Lount) barristers
Campion, J. L., attorney
CAWTHRA, JOSEPH, agent Royal Canadian Bank
Chambers, Rev. A. B., (Wesleyan)
Chantler, Joseph, builder
Clubine, John, farmer
Cook, John, Clerk Division Court, Notary Public, Commissioner in B. R.
DAVISON, JOHN, proprietor Davison House
Denne, Vincent, butcher
Dennis, John, pump maker
Dieterle, Wm., watches, clocks, jewelery & fancy goods
Dudley, Walter, station agent N. R. R
Dudley, Walter, jr., attorney
ELVIDGE, Charles, (Sykes & Elvidge)
Forsyth, Mrs. M., proprietor Railroad Hotel
FYFE, ARCHIBALD, assistant Postmaster
Gamble, N. A., farmer
Gorham, Charles, woolen factor
GORHAM, NELSON, prop. woolen and carding mills
Hackett, James, M. D., druggist
HANMER, CLARK, proprietor Eagle Hotel
Harris & Culverwell, grocers
Harrison & Sykes, (Henry and Samuel) props saw mill
Hartry & Co., tanners and curriers
Henderson, Andrew, books, stationery and fancy goods, insurance agent
Haynor, Rev. C., (Christian)
Hodge, J. & J., stoves and tinware
Hoggard, George, proprietor Royal Hotel
Hughes, J. W. & Co., general merchants
Hunter, James J., M. D
Hutchcroft, George B., carriage maker
IRWIN, EDWIN, P., farmer
IRWIN, JARED, farmer
JACKSON, ERASTUS, editor and proprietor *Newmarket Era*, dealer in blank books and stationery, issuer marriage licenses, coroner York and Peel
Jackson, John, groceries and provisions
Jackson, John F., foreman *Era*
JAMES, JAMES, chemist & druggist, (Dr. Hackett)
Johnson, Jacob N., carpenter
Johnson, Nelson, carpenter
JONES, WILLIAM, L., photographer (see adv)
Joy, Robert B., hairdresser
Kean, Rev. P. J. (Roman Catholic)
Kirk, Thomas, blacksmith
Lewis, John E., farmer
LOUNT, G. W. (Campbell & Lount)
LUKES, WM., proprietor steam flouring mills
McCracken, Alexander J., livery, stage proprietor and carriage maker
McLaughlin, Richard, tinsmith
McMaster & Lockard (William McMaster, jr. and C. H. Lockard), general merchants
Marsden, J. W., miller, produce & commission mercht.
Martin, Philip, tinsmith
MECHANICS' INSTITUE. E. Jackson, president.
MILLARD, JOSEPH & SON, cabinet makers
Mitchell, David, carpenter
Mosier, Thomas, proprietor Newmarket Hotel
Murray, Robert, wagon maker
Nash, John, chemist and druggist
NEWMARKET ERA (weekly). E. Jackson, editor and proprietor. (See adv.)
Nixon, James, groceries and provisions
Orr, Wm. & A. B., general merchants
PEARSON, JAMES J., registrar North Riding, County York, and insurance agent
PEARSON, N., surgeon and dentist. (See adv)
Pearson, P. P., J.P.
Peck, P. B., surgeon and dentist
Pockham & Hoeg, lumber merchants
Peterson, Thomas, merchant

Philips, John H., piano-forte and melodeon manuf.
Poole, Miss, Elizabeth, milliner, &c.
RAMSAY, REV. CANON (Church of England)
Raper, Thomas, tailor
Reeder, M. M., butcher
REID, A. N. & CO., marble dealers (see adv)
REID, DAVID W. (A. N. Reid & Co.)
Richardson, Henry, carpenter
Richardson, Major W. N.
ROADHOUSE, SAMUEL, cabinet maker and undertaker (see adv)
ROE, WILLIAM, Postmaster, general merchant and com. in B. R.
ROGERS, D. L., M.D.
Saxton, John, jeweler
Scott, Dr., eclectic physician
Sharpe, Ingham, groceries and liquors
SIMPSON, C. H., druggist and general merchant
Simpson, Henry, brewer
Simpson, R., general merchant
Simpson, Theodore, baker
Smith, Mrs., milliner, etc.
Smith, Robert H., J.P.
Southard, William V., agent
Spencer, Eli, merchant tailor
Spencer, Israel C., barrister
Srigley, Robert, farmer
Stead, J. G., merchant
Stickwood, Isaac, brick maker
Summers, Horatio G., general merchant
Sutherland, Alexander, tailor
Sutherland, Donald, J.P., grain merchant
SYKES & ELVIDGE, (Samuel Sykes and Charles Elvidge), founders and machinists
Thompson, Henry, saddler
Wallace, W. B., tanner and currier
Wallis, Robert, inspector
Wallis, William, saddler
Warner, Thomas, cabinet maker
Webster & Bond, (S. & W.) sewing machine agents
Wetherall, J. S., blacksmith and carriage maker
Williams, George, farmer
Willson, James H., tailor
Willson, John, shoemaker
Withy, William, blacksmith
Wood, George, painter
Wood, Joseph, painter

Newport.—A Small Village in the Township of Brantford, County Brant, on the Grand River, 3 miles from Brantford, the County Town, and 70 from Toronto. Population 60.

Chapin, Lyman, J.P.
Gantlet, James, shoemaker
Gill, Joseph, shoemaker
Hearns, John, wagon maker
Holding, T., general merchant
MILLOY, COLIN, Postmaster, hotel keeper
Robarts, David, cabinet maker
Sager, John, hotel keeper
Watt, Thomas, cooper
Woodley, George, general merchant

New Ross.—A Post Office in the Township of Matilda, County Dundas, 58 miles from Cornwall, the County Town. Improved Land in the vicinity averages $15 per acre.

Anderson, Richard, cabinet maker
Burk, Walter, farmer
CURRIE, THOMAS, Postmaster
Gordon, John, farmer
Gordon, Richard, farmer
Gormley, Patrick, farmer
Lennox, Thomas, farmer
McGregor, Christopher, farmer
McShane, James, farmer
Wright, Robert, farmer

Nerwy.—A small Village in the Township of Elma, County Perth, 28 miles from Stratford, the County Town, and 7 miles from Listowell. Population 50.

Coulter, C., farmer
FALCONER, D., Postmaster and general merchant
Foster, J. R., hotel keeper
Fullarton, S., teacher
Harvey, M., farmer
Morrison, John, blacksmith
Simpson, J., farmer

New Sarum.—A Village in the Township of Yarmouth, County Elgin, 6 miles from St. Thomas, the County Town, Stages to St. Thomas and Aylmer. Population 200.

Cloes, O'N., farmer
Coll, M. D., builder
Elliott, T., farmer
Frances, T., farmer
Gilbert, T., farmer
Graghbury, Leenbury, butcher
House, C., farmer
Leitch, Thomas, teacher
Norton, John, architect
O'Neal, C., J.P
Oakes, Garrett, J.P., farmer
Oakes, Robert, brewer
Stephenson, J. H., J.P
Stokes, John, farmer
Smith, J., prop. New Sarum Hotel
Whitsell, Nelson, broom manuf
Wilcox, George, farmer
Wilcox, J., prop. Farmers' Inn
WILTON, SAMUEL, Postmaster, gen. mercht

Newton Brook.—A Village in the Township of York, County York, 9 miles from Toronto. Stage to Toronto. Population 500

Agar, Mrs. Margaret, store keepe
Anderson, Alexander, wagon maker
Cameron, W. W., shoemaker
Clement, Rev. R. E., (Wesleyan)
Cooper, James, miller
CUMMER, W. W., Postmaster, gen. merchant
Drury, Michael, cooper
Finby, James, prop. Finch's Hotel
Finch, John, farmer
Flynn, Miss C., dressmaker
Flynn, D., shoemaker
Francis, John, farmer
Graham, William, shingle manufacturer
Humberstone, Thomas, potter
Husband, George, dentist
James, John, farmer
James, Joseph, farmer
James, William, J.P., farmer
Jovin, Rev. James (Wesleyan)
Lankey, John, carpenter
Lauder, John, farmer
McBride, David, farmer
McCague, Miss, dressmaker
McDonell, Joseph, wagon maker
Mulholland, David, farmer
Munroe, George, shoemaker
Parsons, Charles, miller
Powell, Charles, agent
Robinson, William, farmer
Routliffe, George, farmer
Smith, Joseph, painter
Steele, Thomas, proprietor Green Bush Hotel
Street, William, farmer
Taber, R. D. M., teacher
Watson, W., watchmaker
Woods, John, mason

Newtown Robinson.—A Village in the Township of Tecumseth, County Simcoe, 19 miles from Barrie, the County Town, and 47 from Toronto. Stage to Bondhead. Population 120.

Cobourn, James, carpenter
Faulkner, William, tailor
Hipwell, H. J., teacher
HIPWELL, J. R., Postmaster and general merchant
Hudson, John, hotel keeper
Law, James, J.P.
McCarthy, J. S., J.P.
McLean, Richard, carpenter
Merrick, John, carpenter
Proctor, Thomas
Towns, W. C., woolen factory

Niagara. A flourishing incorporated Town in the Township of Niagara, County Lincoln, and beautifully situated at the mouth of Niagara River on Lake Ontario. It is one of the oldest Towns in Ontario, it lies on a plain and is noted for its healthy position, making it a favourable resort in the summer for invalids. Distant from Toronto by water 36 miles, Hamilton by rail 50 miles, St. Catherines the County Town 12 miles, and from Niagara Falls 16 miles. Daily mails. Money order office and post office savings bank. Population about 2000.

Alma, John L., liquor merchant
Best, Robert, butcher
Bishop, John, butcher
Carnathan, Robert, proprietor hotel
Carnochan, James, carpenter
Chisholm, Mary, proprietor American Hotel
Clement, George A., hardware, &c
Crysler, H. P., general merchant
Donnelly, William G., proprietor livery stable
Follett, Stephen A., groceries
Fraser, Mrs. John, proprietor hotel
Hewitt & Dorley, boots and shoes
Kirby, William, printer
Longhurst, George, butcher
Mackin, Edward, blacksmith
Moffatt, Mary, proprietor hotel
Monroe, John R., grocer
Morson, Fred, physician
McClelland, William, general merchant
McConnell, John, tailor
McCulloch, John, wholesale and retail groceries and liquors
O'Neil, Richard, baker
Paffard, Henry, druggist
Betley, Joseph W., dry goods and trimmings
Platt & Son, carriage makers
Rousseau, John, hotel keeper and livery stable
Rowland, Thomas M., dry goods
Senior, William, variety store
Stocking, J., groceries and liquors
Walsh, James, boots and shoes
WARREN, ROBERT, Postmaster
Whitelaw, Francis M., books and stationery
Wright, James, photographer

Nicolston.—(Commonly called Underhill).—A small Village in the Township of Essa, County Simcoe, on the Nottawasaga River, 20 miles from Barrie, the County Town, and 53 from Toronto. Population 75.

Blakeley, Thomas, farmer
Boaks, Benjamin, farmer
Cunningham, William, farmer
Garbutt, John, painter
Graham, John, blacksmith
Hayden, T.
Heaslip, Rev. John K., (Presbyterian)
Irwin, James, hotel keeper
Lattimer, Robert, farmer
McKee, Robert, farmer
NICOL, JOHN, Postmaster, and gen. mercht, miller
Rodgers, Samuel, farmer
Upton, George, woolen factor
Upton, John, dyer

Newtonville (Clark P. O.)—A Village in the Township of Clark, County Durham. Distance from Port Hope, the County Town, 12 miles, from Toronto, 53. Money Order Office. Population 200.

Cleghorn, Rev. Thomas, (Wesleyan)
Convey, Ephraim, blacksmith
Dicky, T., farmer
Downing, Jonathan, wagon maker
Gindall, William, farmer
Hancock, George, saddler
Jacobs' Joseph, J.P., issuer of marriage licenses and Commissioner in Q. B.
Johnson, Andrew, cooper
Jones, W., farmer
Jones, Samuel
Lockhart, Hugh
LOCKHART, JAMES, Postmaster and gen. mercht
Love, William, teacher
Low, D. B, merchant tailor
McAldin, Isaac, wagon maker
McBrien, W. W., M.D.
McClang, Rev. James, (Wesleyan)
McMurty, James, farmer
Moorehead, William, shoemaker
Morgan, Robert, mason
Muldrew, W. & Co., (William Muldrew & John Muldrew), general merchants and merchant tailors
Muldrew, William, merchant tailor
Quackinboss, James, blacksmith
Ramsay, Samuel, proprietor Traveler's Rest
Robinson, Mark, prop. Queen's Arms Hotel
Smith, Noble C., general merchant
Spooner, George, M. D
Sterling, John, shoemaker
Sylvester, Charles, tailor
Thompson, James, hotel proprietor
Walters, Mrs., dressmaker

Nile.—A small Village in the Township of Colborne, County Huron, 8½ miles from Goderich, the County Town. Population 30.

Allen, F., innkeeper
Bell & Gilmour, lumber merchants
Burritt, G., farmer
Cartlon, J., farmer
Clark, William, farmer
Girvin, C., J.P.
Jackman, William, farmer
Matthews, William, farmer
Pentland, R., farmer
Sheppard, G., farmer
Stewart, C., farmer
Stratton, J., carpenter

Nilestown.—A Post Village, situated on the line between the townships of Dorchester North and Westminster, County Middlesex, distant 7½ miles from London, and 4½ from Dorchester Station, the nearest Railroad point. The River Thames passes through the Village supplying excellent water power. Stages from London to Belmont. Daily mail. Population about 150.

Burdick, Albert, farmer
Burdick, Smith, farmer
Burdick, Willard, wine grower
Burns, George, teacher
Cameron, Henry
Cannon, Elijah
Craig, William, wagon maker
Crouse, Nelson, millwright
Edwards, Thomas, miller
Gilmore, Andrew, dairyman
Coulding, Thomas, inn keeper
Henry, John, general merchant
Lane, John, proprietor Nilestown Hotel
Le Lievre, Henry, 7th Division County Clerk
McNab, David, carpenter
Moore, Samuel, M.D.
MORWOOD, JOHN, Postmaster and gen. merchant
Niles, Henry, J.P., farmer
Niles, William, J.P., farmer
Niles, Willott, agricultural implement agent
Odell, Frederick, blacksmith
Pearson, Thomas, prop. flouring and woollen mills
Perrin, Rev. Christopher (Baptist)
Pigott, Henry, farmer
Pigott, William, farmer
Pixley, Robert, farmer and hop grower
Reynolds, Henry, miller
Richmond, Richard, shoemaker
Rolph, William, wagon maker
Rowatt, Joseph, farmer
Sage, Nelson, farmer and cheese maker
Snell, William, cooper
Waterland, Edward, blacksmith

Nobleton.—A Village in the Township of King, County York, 28 miles from Toronto. Population 100.

Adams, Rev. James, (Canada Presbyterian)
Bushby, James, prop. British Empire Hotel
Childs, William, wagon maker
Crosby, William, carpenter
Godfrey, E. Y., saddler
Graham, Charles, blacksmith
Hambly, Charles, general merchant
Hambly, George, glove maker
Hawman, Jacob, butcher
Hollingshead, Robert, carpenter
McMurchy, Mary, milliner
McNaughton, Alexander, general merchant
Mahaffy, John, M.D.
Milligan, James, farmer
MUNSIE, WILLIAM, Postmaster, J.P., and general merchant
Osler, Rev. H. B., (Church of England)
Payne, Thomas, painter
Perry, R. S., teacher,
Phillips, John, farmer
Ritt, John, blacksmith
Snider, Isaac, J. P.
Stannett, T. C., proprietor Nobleton House
White, Robert, carpenter

Nissouri.—A Post Office in the Township of Nissouri, County Oxford, on a branch of the Thames, 16 miles from Woodstock, the County Town.

Fletcher, John M., shoemaker
HOWES, JOSEPH, Postmarter
McBrayne, Archibald, general merchant
McKenzie, John, blacksmith
McQuorqudale, Alexander, J.P.
Morrison, James, teacher

Nithburg.—A river on the river Nith, in the Township of North Easthope, County Perth, 14 miles from Stratford, the County Town. Population 175.

BROWN, JAMES, J.P., Postmaster and gen. mer.
Brown, James, carpenter
Brown, James L., assistant postmaster
Brown, John C., accountant
Chatterton, Henry, wagon maker
Detze, Adam, proprietor Nithburg Hotel
Drummond, Rev. A. A. (Presbyterian)
Farrell, William, butcher
Fink, Henry, lime and stone
Forrest, Robert, farmer
Frazer, Duncan, teacher
Gabel, John, lumber dealer
Hart, John, farmer
Kumpf, William, cooper
McDonald, James, farmer
McDougall, Thomas, dealer in boots and shoes
McDougal, William, general merchant
Milne, John
Milne, James, farmer
Milne, John, cheese manufacturer
Milne, Rev. William (Baptist)
Muter, P. J., M.D.
Robertson, D., farmer
Robertson, Robert, farmer
Rush, Elias, carpenter
Stalley, Daniel, shingle maker
Stocks, George, shoemaker
Swan, Robert, tanner
Younker, Frederick, farmer

Norham.—A Village on Salt Creek, in the Township of Percy, County Northumberland. Distant from Cobourg, the County Town, 30 miles, 16 from Colborne, and 100 from Toronto. Stages daily to Colborne. Population 300.

Alexander, Rev. Thomas, (Presbyterian)
Bailey, James, wagon maker
Bailey, William, blacksmith
Boyes, G. B., farmer
Curtis, John, farmer
Dalton, John, blacksmith
Demorest, Rev. Thomas, (Wesleyan)
DEMOREST, DR. B.G.G., Postmaster
Dingman, A., blacksmith
Douglass, Alexander, general merchant
Gerow, Timothy, hotel keeper
Graham, John, teacher
Gunner, John, farmer
Harcomb, N., farmer
Harris, David, grocer
Harris, Jacob, blacksmith
Hess, Jacob, wagon maker
Raymond, Mrs. J. A., dressmaker
Sills, Rev. W. A., (Methodist Episcopal)
Smith, H. S., shoemaker
Snelgrove, John, teacher
Tierney, Mathew. shoemaker

Norland.—A Village on Gull River, in the Township of Laytop, County Victoria, 30 miles from Lindsay, the County Town. Stages to Lindsay and Trenton Falls. Population 70.

Adair, John, wagon maker
Bowins, H. & C., shingle makers
Briggs, George, farmer
Halliday, T. I., general merchant
McLAUCHLIN, A. A., Postmaster, prop. grist and saw mill
Sawyer, Hiram, innkeeper

Normandale.—A small Village in the Township of Charlottville, County Norfolk, 10 miles from Simcoe, the County Town. Average price of improved land in the vicinity $30 per acre. Population 75.

Guyler, William, J.P.
Mesmore, Rev. Mr., (Methodist)
Post, John D., general merchant
SHEPPARD, JOHN W., Postmaster, innkeeper
Shaw, John, miller
Wilcox. H. P., carpenter

Normanton—(See Port Elgin.)—A post office in the Township of Saugeen, County Bruce.

ROY, ARCHIBALD, Postmaster.

North Adjala.—A Post Office in the Township of Adjala, County Cardwell.

DONEHY, WILLIAM, Postmaster.

North Augusta.—A Post Village situated on the south branch of the Rideau River, in the Township of Augusta, County Grenville. Distant from Prescott, the County Town, 17 miles, and from Toronto 250 miles. Daily mail. Money Order office. Population 350.

Baldwin, Samuel, carpenter
Bellamy, H. H., hotel keeper
Bellamy, J. B., proprietor flouring mill
Bellamy, L. H., proprietor saw mill
BELLAMY, SAMUEL J., Postmaster
Blake, Henry, boots and shoes
Botham, John, tailor
Caper, Peter, tailor
Chapman, John, general merchant
Colborne, Benjamin, proprietor planing mill
Crozier, George, cooper
Davis, Ralph, general merchant
Dunn, A. G. M.D., druggist
Gillett, Jesse, grain cradles, etc.
Hill, M. W., general merchant
Humphries, James, carriage maker
Humphries, William, hotel keeper
Joyce, Thomas, boots and shoes
Love, Alpheus, blacksmith
Lyman, Mrs., milliner
McCully, Andrew, cabinet maker
Mott, Samuel, harness maker
Morton, S. W., general merchant
Pardee, A. B., tanner, boots and shoes
Whitworth, John, blacksmith

North Bruce.—A post office in the Township of Bruce, County Bruce, 35 miles from Walkerton, the County Town.

McCarrol, D., hotel keeper
McTAVISH. DONALD, Postmaster
Siebert, Joseph, cooper

North Douro,—(See Lakefield.)

Northfield.—A Small Village in the Township of Cornwall, County Stormont, 14 miles from Cornwall, the County Town. Population 35.

Alguire, M., shoemaker
Baker, J. & Co., general merchants
Bartle, William, M.D.
Hough, John, J.P.
Latrace, N., farmer
Laughlin, D. M., farmer
Myers, A., carpenter
Runion, B. G., farmer
Rupert, A., farmer

North Glanford.—A Post Office in the Township of Glanford, County Wentworth, 5½ miles from Hamilton.

Bates, John, farmer
Bates, Joseph, farmer
Binkley. A., J.P.
Bradt, D., farmer
Brigham, W., farmer
Chase, Henry, farmer
Choate, T., farmer
DICKINSON, EDWARD, Postmaster, gen. merch.
Dickinson, E. & Son, carpenter
Ellis, H., farmer
Finch, E., farmer
French, A., farmer
French, T., farmer
Hess, T., farmer
Kelly, A., farmer
Kelly, R., farmer
Kern, David, farmer
King, Stephen, Insurance agent
McFeggan, B., farmer
McKee, H. farmer
Mann, Samuel, carpenter
Maricle, J., farmer
Robins, L., shingle maker
Shafer, P. C. teacher
Smith, E., farmer
Smith, L. C., farmer
Smith, O., farmer
Smith, Robert, farmer
Springer, Richard, J.P.
Terryberry, J., proprietor Farmer's Hotel
Woodman, J., proprietor Homestead House
Wright, E., farmer

North Keppel.—A small village in the Township of Keppel, County Grey, 20 miles from Owen Sound, the County Town. Population 60.

Denoon, James, miller and merchant
Dewar, David, Postmaster
Finley, James A., shoemaker
Horn & Lymber, lumber merchants
Patterson, Garrett, cooper
Stevens, John A. shoemaker
Totten, William, general merchants

North Montague.—A Post-office in the Township of Montague, County Lanark.

STEWART, W. H., Postmaster.

North Gower.—A Village on Stephen's Creek, in the Township of North Gower, County Carleton, 23 miles from Ottawa and 7 from Osgoode station, Ottawa and Prescott Railway. The 5th Division Court is held here. Money Order Office. Stage to Osgoode. Population 600.

Anderson, William, carpenter
BEAMAN JAMES, Postmaster
Beaman & Wallace, general merchants
Beaman, William & Son, wagon makers
Bruce, Thomas, carpenter
Cayes, Lewis, cabinet maker
Conley, Thomas, tailor
Cowan, William, J.P
Craig & Cryderman, tanners and manuf. boots and shoes, harness, &c
Craig, James, farmer
Craig, Robert, J.P., farmer
Craig, R., saddler
Crawford, Francis, cooper
Cullander, Alexander, blacksmith
Dixon, Robert, farmer
Edward, James, general merchant
Elliott, William, hotel keeper
Forde, R. F., teacher
Glasier, W. S., general merchant
Griffitn, Mrs. E., grocer
Hicks, John, general merchant
Johnson, James, prop. Union Hotel
Kennedy, James, brick maker
Lochead, Rev. William. (Presbyterian)
McGowen, Albert, saddler
McCartney, George, general merchant
Merritt, Rev. D. P., (Church of England)
Mills, Thomas, cooper
Montgomery, Robert, farmer
Morphey, Joshua, shoemaker
Neelin, W. general merchant
Phelan, John, farmer
Roche, W. P., M.D.
Scott, Hiram, general merchant
Teggart, Rev. C., (Wesleyan)
Trimble, James, farmer
Trimble, William, farmer
Wallace, John, blacksmith
Wright, John, shoemaker and tanner
Wright, Thomas, carpenter

North Lancaster.—A village on the River Beaudet, in the Township of Lancaster, County Glengarry. Distant from Alexandria, the County Town, 24 miles; 10 from Lancaster Station, and 300 from Toronto. Stage to McDonald's Corners. Population 200.

Campbell, Angus
Daoust, Emilien, hotel keeper and blacksmith
Grant, Peter, township clerk
Kennedy, W. F., hotel keeper
Leclair, Alexander, general merchant
LECLAIR, CHARLES, Postmaster, J.P., gen. merch.
McCuaig, Kenneth, hewer
McDonald, Alexander, farrier
McDonald, Angus, hewer
McDonald, John, cabinet maker
McDonald, Ronald, shoemaker
McLennan, Donald, watchmaker
McLeod, Duncan, councillor
McLeod, Samuel, bailiff
McRae, Alexander E,, deputy reeve
McRae, Donald, J.P., farmer
McRae, Miss, teacher
Masterson, Rev. J., (Roman Catholic)
Morrison, Donald, blacksmith
Neveux, Noel, pearl and potash factor
Richardson, Robert, hotel keeper
Robinson, George J., book-keeper
Rozon Xavier, carpenter
Thomson, Donald & John, millwrights
Villeneuve, Louis, cooper
Watier, E., carpenter

North Mountain.—A Post-office in the Township of Mountain, County Dundas
CLELLAND, JAMES, Postmaster.

North Pelham.—A Post-office in the Township of Pelham, County Mock.
McQUEEN, Mrs. M. A., Postmistress.

North Port.—A Village on the Bay of Quinte, in the Township of Sophiasburg, County Prince Edward, 13 miles from Picton, the County Town, 12 from Belleville, and 5 from Shannonville Station, Grand Trunk Railway. Steamers to Belleville and Kingston. Money Order Office. Population 200.

Ashley, Egbert, teacher
Baker, David, carpenter
Baker, John, carpenter
Brooks, S. R., tinsmith
Cronk, John M., shoemaker
Crysdale, J. J., tailor
Forbes, Mrs. N., tinware, &c.
Leslie, Alexander, proprietor Ontario Hotel
Morden, R. & W. H., general merchants
Robinson, John
Robinson, John, jr., carpenter
Ruttan, D. W., J.P.
Solmes, Samuel, J.P.
SOLMES, SAMUEL, Jr., Postmaster and gen. mer.
Spencer, Richard, wagon maker

North Ridge.—A Post Office in the Township of Gosfield, County Essex.
CUMMIFORD, JAMES, Postmaster.

North Seneca.—A Post Office in the Township of Seneca, County Haldimand.
TUCKER, JOHN, Postmaster.

North Williamsburg.—A Village in the Township of Williamsburgh, County Dundas, 70 miles from Cornwall, the County Town. Stages to Dunbar and Winchester. Population 100.

Bell, Thomas, general merchant
Blacklock, Dr.
Casselman, William J., J.P.
Chamberlin, Dr.
Davidson, Rev. John (Presbyterian)
Eastwood, Henry, wagon maker
Empey, Abner, shoemaker
Ford, Christopher, hotel keeper
Ford, W. H., hotel keeper
GORDON, WILLIAM, J.P., Postmaster
Hollister, Chesley, auctioneer
McHaffie, William, tailor
Magee, Samuel, wagon maker
Merkley, George, farmer
Smith, George, leather dealer
Stewart, George, shoemaker
Sutherland, George, cooper
Whittaker, Simeon, shoemaker
Winegard, Isaac, proprietor planing mills

Norwich.—A Village on Otter Creek, in the Township of North Norwich, County Oxford, 17 miles from Woodstock, the County Town. There are several cheese factories in the neighborhood and 13 in the Township. Stage to Woodstock. Money Order Office and Savings Bank. The 4th Division Court is held here. Population 850.

Adams, H. J., saddler
Addison, William, cabinet maker
Aikman, R. S. & Son, bakers
Anderson, Edward, boots and shoes
Ballard, Austin, farmer
Barr, Edward, saddler
Barr & Collins, props. steam flouring mill and shingle factory
Barr, James, J.P., N.P., and clerk Division Court
Barr, James, farmer
Barr & Watson, founders and machinists
Beard, G. S., M.D
Bleakley, George, prop. Bleakley House
Boomer, George C., insurance agent
Bradley, Robert, painter
Brown, Andrew, cooper
Brown, Robert, cooper
Bungay, S. F., tinsmith
Caker, W. F., proprietor Farmers' Hotel
Carroll, James, M.D.
Carter, Samuel, proprietor livery stable
Chambers, Solomon, carpenter
Charlton, Matthew, boots and shoes
Clark, F. J., accountant and librarian
Clark, Mrs. F. J., fancy goods, toys, etc.
Close, William, brick and tile maker
Cook, E., M.D.
Cotton, Henry, grocer
Dawson, Robert, farmer
Dean, A. W., teacher
Dean, M., shingle maker
Donald, Daniel, carpenter
Donald, Rev. W., (Presbyterian)
Douglass, John, tanner
Duncan, Gilbert, cheese manufacturer
Duncan, John, accountant
Dykeman, A., carpenter
Farrington, Harvey, cheese manufacturer
Frey, John, painter
George, William H., tailor
Green & McCausland, general merchants
Haight, Thomas, wagon maker
Hand, William, & Co., boots and shoes
Jackson, L. J., general merchant
Lackrider, Charles, manager co-operative association
McAuley, John D., wagon maker
McKee, Hugh, nursery
McKee, John, farmer
Miller & Co., general merchants
Miller, William, butcher
Montrose, Joshua, wagon maker
MOORE, GILBERT, Postmaster
Morrison, Rev. W. F., (Wesleyan)
Padfield, C. W., M. D
Palmer, J. B., farmer
Peath, Rev. Edwin, (Church of England)
Pitcher, Seneca, general merchant
Powers, William, painter
Roddy, David, tailor
Rogers, D., butcher
Scarff, William S., wagon maker
Scott, Robert, auctioneer
Shields, Mrs., dyer and scourer
Smith, Samuel, cheese manufacturer
Stevenson, David, carpenter
Stevenson, H., carpenter
Stevenson, James, carpenter
Stover, A. J., farmer
Stroud, William, farmer
Sutton, Granville C., watchmaker, jeweler, &c
Sutton, John, farmer
Swartwout, Lorenzo, carpenter
Templeton, N. J., proprietor Stroud's Hotel
Tidy, Claudius, general agent
Tidey, George, shingle maker
Tidey, John A., druggist
Topham, Brothers, founders and machinists
Vail, Walter S., painter
Vanvalkenburgh, Hiram, J.P.
Vanvalkenburg, Truman, carpenter
Vedin, Andrew, engraver and goldsmith
Walker, George, cabinet maker
Walker & Wood, boots and shoes
Wickham, Mrs., milliner, &c.
Will, Joseph S., boots and shoes
Woodrow, Simcoe J., nursery
Yates, John F., tailor

Norval.—A Village and Station of the Grand Trunk Railway, on the river Credit, in the Township of Esquesing, County Halton, 12 miles from Milton, the County Town, and 26 from Toronto. Money Order Office. Population 250.

Alexander, Rev. J. (Presbyterian)
Brady, P., agent G.T.R.
CLAY, WILLIAM, Postmaster
Forster, John, J.P.
Fry, William, butcher
Gallop, Eli, saddler
Hewson, Thomas, saddler
Holmes, John, hotel keeper
McConnell, George, potter
McPherson, Alexander, cooper
Maccarthur, Rev. J. G., (Church of England)
Matthews, George, hotel keeper
Mitchell, Thomas, cooper
Noble, Robert, prop. grist mill
Smith, Thomas, teacher
Snow, Thomas, tailor
Switzer, James R., saddler
Vokes, James T., saddler
Webster, Samuel, M.D

Norway.—A Village on the Kingston Road, in the Township of York, County York, 4 miles from Toronto Population 100.

Brown, J. broom maker
Chester, Matthew, wagon maker
Colander, H., farmer
Goodchild, Charles, butcher
Knight, George, butcher
O'Sullivan, D., farmer
Renton, Thomas, blacksmith
ROYNE, JOHN, Postmaster and proprietor Stage House
Smith, J., farmer
Smith, Thomas, prop. Norway Hotel
Stevens, Thomas, blacksmith

Norwood.—A Village on the River Ouse, in the Township of Asphodel, County Peterboro, 20 miles from Peterboro, the County Town, and 30 from Colborne. Stages to Peterboro and Colborne. Wild lands in vicinity, $4; improved, $12 per acre. Money Order Office and Savings Bank. Population 700.

Bell, T. J., teacher
Brown, John P., carpenter
Buchan, John, general merchant
Buck, James A., general merchant
BUTTERFIELD, J. A., Postmaster, &c.
Calder, John, tanner
Crowther, James, cooper
Dewart, Thomas, carpenter
Douty, Henry, tinsmith
Douty, John, shoemaker
Eaton, Wm., tailor
Elliott, Abraham, general merchant
Ewins, Michael, carpenter
Frazer, Thomas, tinsmith
GROOVE, P. M., M.P.P.
Harper, J. & J., carpenters
Hartley, E. R., prop. Globe Hotel
Henderson, George, wagon maker
Hill, R., proprietor British Hotel
Johnson, J. A., proprietor International Hotel
McLauchlin, James, cooper
McLauchlin, Robert & Co., props. Morrison House
Moore, Charles, physician
Moore, O. W., cabinet maker
Moffatt, Briston, shoemaker
Mullins, Michael, proprietor Norwood House
Nicoll, Matthew, wagon maker
Nicoll, William, general blacksmith
Bruce, Joseph B., general merchant
Peters, Charles, tinsmith
Philp, Rev. S. C., (Wesleyan)
Pierson, Mrs., dressmaker
Raddon, James, baker
Reynolds, P. W., general merchant
Roxbrough, William E., general merchant
Scott, Mrs. Margret, dressmaker
Scott, Matthew, tanner
Scott, S., M.D.
Starke, Dr.
Stephenson, William H., general merchant
Smith, C., tailor
Smith, Thomas, general merchant
Thom, J. H., teacher
Tudhope, R., teacher
Udy, W., shoemaker
Wilson, Robert A., saddler
Wood, John, carpenter
Young, Rev. W. C., (Presbyterian)

Nottawa.—A Village on Pretty River, in the Township of Nottawasaga, County Simcoe, 30 miles from Barrie, the County Town, and 3 from Collingwood Station Northern Railroad. Population 160.

Bourchier, William, proprietor Batteaux mills
Bruce, Jamieson, cabinet maker
Buck, George, cooper
Crone, Wesley, brick maker
Crone, William, brick maker
Holden Benjamin, carpenter
Holden, S. O., carpenter
Jardine, Andrew, J.P., Clerk Fourth Division Court
Kerr, William, saddler
Kirkland, Dr.
McAlister, Dougald, carpenter
McAlister, L., M.D.
McIntyre & Currie, general merchants
MELVILLE, A., Postmaster
Melville, Fair & Co., proprietors steam flour mills
Nash, Richard, hotel keeper
Ovas & Oliver, general merchants
Rowbotham, Edward, butcher
Scott & Frame, general merchants
Walker, Peter, shingle maker
Wells, David, hotel keeper
Wiggins, C. & H., general merchants
Wiggins, Henry, hotel keeper

Notfield.—A Post Village situated at the head of River de Lille, in the Township of Kenyon, County Glengary, distant from Alexandria, the County Town, 14 miles. Population about 150.

Begg, Alexander, general merchant
Campbell, Samuel, M.D.
Craig, Robert, Tanner
Currier, Paul, tanner
Draper, S. T., general merchant
Kelly & Freedman, general merchants
KENNEDY, PETER, Postmaster, blacksmith
McConnell, Neil, carpenter
McDonald, Donald, general merchant
McEwan, Duncan, blacksmith
McIntyre, John, carpenter
McMullen, Duncan, carriage maker
McNaughton & McLaren, proprietors planing mill
Sernie, Louis, boots and shoes
Teniac Louis, boots and shoes

Oak Ridges.—*(See Villages too late for regular insertion at the end of this work.)*

Oakville.—A Town, Port of Entry, and Station of the Great Western Railroad, situated at the confluence of Sixteen Mile Creek with Lake Ontario, in the Township of Trafalgar, County Halton, 16 miles from Milton, the County Town, 21 from Georgetown, 18 from Hamilton, and 18 from Toronto. Money order office and Savings Bank. Population 2000.

Arnott, David, dry goods and clothing
Baker, George J., livery stable proprietor, express agt
BALMER, J. S., assistant post office
BALMER, ROBERT, Postmaster, Town Clerk, Clerk 2nd Division Court, agent Montreal Telegraph Company, insurance agent, Commissioner, Notary Public, &c
BARCLAY, JOHN, (Barclay & Lawrie)
BARCLAY & LAWRIE, (John Barclay and William A. Lawrie) dry goods and general merchants
Boon, Isaac, proprietor Railroad Inn
Boon, Joseph, proprietor Royal Exchange Hotel
Brown, F. J., (F. J. Brown & Co.)
Brown, F. J. & Co., (Francis J. Brown, Ezra Whiting) brewers
Brown, Rev. T. C., (Episcopal Methodist)
BUTLER, MRS. ANN, baker and confectioner, boarding house, oysters, &c
CANADIAN HOTEL, James Teeter, proprietor
CHISHOLM, DUNCAN, ship builder and owner
CHISHOLM, COL. GEORGE K., flour & grist mills
Chisholm, R. K., Collector of Customs
Connor, John, general grocer, wines and liquors
COSLEY, JOHN, barber and hair dresser, proprietor indian root shrub, toys, gunsmith, &c
DOTY, JOHN, foundry and machine shop (see adv)
DOTY, PHARIS, manager Thompson & Smith's steam saw mill
Ferrah, Robert, baker and confectioner
Fitzgerald, Miss Norah, dressmaker and milliner
Fletcher, Rev. John, M.A., rector English Church
Frampton & Son (John Frampton, sen., John Frampton, jr.) house, sign and ornamental painters
GORING, ARTHUR, proprietor Victoria House
Graham, John, baggage-man G.W.R.
GULLEDGE, HENRY, saddle and harness maker
HAGAMAN, JEREMIAH, carriage maker
Hagaman, W. E., general merchant
Harcus, Mrs. Mary, teacher
Hillmer, E., butcher
Howes & Pollard (Joseph & Erastus D.) grocers, &c.
Howes, Joseph (Howes & Pollard)
Hubner, John, boot and shoemaker
Johnson, David (McDougald & Johnson)
LAIDLAW, WALTER, station master G.W.R.
Lawrie, William A. (Barclay & Lawrie)
Lusk, Charles H., physician and surgeon, &c.
Lyon, Peter, captain
McCay & Bro. (W. F. & G. C.) job printers
McDougald, Peter A. (McDougald & Johnson)
McDougald & Johnson (P. H. McDougald & David Johnson), general merchants
McGill, William (M. Robinson & Co.)
McNab, Samuel, general blacksmith
Mason, John, butcher
Matthews, Aaron, watchmaker and jeweler
Meikle, Rev. William (Canada Presbyterian Church)
Milbourne, Joseph, Customs officer
MILBOURNE, WILLIAM, manufacturer of patent and enamelled leathers, &c. (see adv.)
Mills, Miss Mary, teacher
Morgan, James C., M.A., head teacher Grammar School
Moore, John, & Co., stoves and tin ware
Mason, John, butcher
Narraway, J. W., teacher
OAKVILLE HOUSE, John Williams, proprietor
Orr, William A., & Co. (W. A. Orr & C. H. Moore)
Patterson, David, carpenter and joiner
Patterson, Thomas, millinery store
Puddefoot, Charles, tinsmith
REYNOLDS, THOMAS, & SON (Thomas Reynolds, jr., Thomas Reynolds, sr.), dealers in groceries, wines, liquors and produce (see adv.)
RIACH, JAMES, saddle and harness maker
Robertson, William, hardware merchant
Robinson, M. & Co. (Michael Robinson, Wm. McGill) boots and shoes
Romain, William F., general merchant
Ryan, Rev. J. (Roman Catholic)
Sumner, George J., chief constable
Sutherland, T. J., physician and surgeon
TEETER, JAMES, proprietor Canadian Hotel
Thomas, Thomas D., spinning wheel manufacturer
URQUHART, JOHN, chemist and druggist
WALSH, JOHN, carriage maker and general jobber, &c. (See adv.)
Walsh, William, grocer and boot and shoe maker
WASS, WILLIAM, auctioner, land and estate agent, broker and notary, insurance agent, &c.
Williams, Justus S. W., M.D., coroner for the County of Halton
Williams, Justus W., treasurer
WILLIAMS, JOHN, prop. Oakville House. (See adv.)
Williams, Mrs. Eliza, dry goods and clothing
Willoughby, Rev. William (Wesleyan)
Wilson, Eleanor, dressmaker
Wilson, James, tailor
WOOD, RICHARD SHAW, chemist and druggist, prop. planing mills, &c. (See adv.)
Wright, D. D., physician, surgeon, &c., coroner County of Halton
Young, W. H., grocer, bookseller, &c.
Ziller, George, cabinet maker

Oakland.—A village in the Township of Oakland, County Brant, 9 miles from Brantford, the County Town, and 14 from Simcoe. Money Order Office. Population 250.

Abbott, W. J., general merchant
Abbott, W., shoemaker
Beebe, J., hotel keeper
Beebe, S. farmer
Chapin, Charles, farmer
Cowles, Richard, tailor
Knox, Robert, painter
McMichael, J., teacher
Malcolm, E., farmer
Malcolm, S. D.
Nobbs, Robert, wagon maker
Prosser, John, general merchant
Saigner, R., hotel keeper
TOYNE, JOHN, Postmaster and general merchant
Vanderlip, Robert, farmer
Vivian, John, farmer
Vivian, William, carpenter
Vivian, Stephen, carpenter
Westbrook, M., farmer
Wood, Rev. John, (Methodist Episcopal)

Oak Hill.—A Post Office in the Township of Laxton, County Victoria. 31 miles from Lindsay, the County Town.

Acheson, Robert, farmer
Gorbett, S. J., farmer
CORBETT, WILLIAM, Postmaster
Corbett, W. H., farmer
Davey, William, farmer
Lapp, Samuel, merchant
Pile, G., farmer
Pile, H., farmer
Reed, James, farmer
Staples, George, farmer
Staples, Joseph, farmer
Staples, Robert, farmer

Oakwood.—A Village in the Township of Mariposa, County Victoria, 8 miles from Lindsay, the County Town, 9 from Port Hoover, and 75 from Toronto. Stages to Lindsay, Manilla, Little Britain and Port Hoover. Population 400.

Anderson, Peter, clothing dealer
Ashbury, Robert, wagon maker
Banks, William, hotel keeper
Barnard, John, farmer
Bateman, David, farmer
Bateman, George, J.P. and general merchant
BOWS, E. A., Postmaster and general merchant
Cameron, A., general merchant
Cummings, John F., clothing dealer
Degrassi, A. J. M., M.D.
Demery, Richard, farmer
Denison, D. B., hotel keeper
Devitt, Abraham, teacher
Dillman, John, farmer
Eck, John, saddler
Gilbert, C., carpenter
Irwin, Samuel, J.P., patent right agent
Jewell, G., shoemaker
Kells, John, wagon maker
King, David, farmer
Meirs, Joseph, shoemaker
Metherel, Samuel, farmer
McLauchlan, David S., cabinet maker
McLauchlan, W. H., insurance agent
Pascoe, Lewis, hide and leather dealer and tanner
Pillen, Charles, carpenter
Pomroy, Rev. J. C., (Church of England)
Pyper, G. A., J.P., proprietor steam flouring mill
Rear, William, M.D., druggist
Shannon, Thomas, carpenter and painter
Silverwood, W. A., farmer
Taylor, William, accountant and auctioneer
Thorndyke, James, farmer
Weir, James, farmer
Williams, Rev. T., (Wesleyan)
Willmot, Jackson, painter
Woodcock, Rev. E., (Methodist Episcopal)

Oban.—A Post Office in the Township of Sarnia, County Lambton.

CARRICK, WILLIAM, Postmaster.

Odessa.—A flourishing Village in the Township of Ernestown, County Addington, 12 miles from Napanee, the County Town, 12 from Kingston, and 4¼ from Ernestown Station Grand Trunk Railway. Money Order Office and Savings Bank. Population 1200.

Allen, Lewis, grocer
Babcock, L. D., blacksmith
Babcock, Wesley, shoemaker
Black, Samuel, music dealer and piano agent
Booth, B. A., prop. woolen factory
Booth, D. B., M. D., dealer in drugs and hardware
Booth, P. D. & K. J., props. grist and saw mills
Casson, Rev. W., (Wesleyan)
Close, James A., teacher
Darley, T. G., cabinet maker
Davy, D., cooper
Davy, W., carpenter
Derbyshire, Byron, general agent
Dupuis, T. R., M.D
Ellison, J., carpenter
Emmery, Andrew, hotel keeper
Fries, Frederick, shoemaker
Gordon, B., blacksmith
Lee, Edward, contractor
Lee, Joseph, blacksmith
McDonald, A. S., wholesale liquor dealer
McDonough, Henry, blacksmith

McEwen, James, wholesale liquor dealer
McKechnie, James, tailor
McLauglin, B., carpenter
Moore, W. R., marble factory
Ross, T. R., M.D
Snider, Calvin, watch repairer and jeweler
Snider, W. F., dentist and photographer
Stanton, Rev. (Church of England)
Storms, A., sash and door manufactory
Strong, K. S., saddler
Timmerman, W. D., telegraph operator
TIMMERMAN, P. S., Postmaster, gen mercht
Timmerman, A. E., leader brass band
Toplift, James, shoemaker
Walker, C. A., provision store
Walker, S. T., general merchant
Walker, Mrs. J. S., hotel keeper
Watts, J. E., hotel keeper
Watts & Jones, carriage makers
Wycott, F. R., hotel keeper

Offa.—A Post Office in the Township of Stephen, County Huron, 40 miles from Goderich, the County Town Improved land averages $25, wild $10 per acre.

Crowley, James, wagon maker
Franklin, D., farmer
Gerard, Rev. Joseph, (Roman Catholic)
Hall, Thomas, farmer
Hawes, W. H. & J., general merchants
Johnson, Thomas, farmer
Nevill, Michael, blacksmith
O'Connell, P., farmer
Oliver, W., farmer
QUARRY, JOHN G., Postmaster
Regan, C., farmer

Oil Springs.—An incorporated Village on Black Creek, in the Township of Enniskillen, County Lambton, 20 miles from Sarnia, the County Town, 7 from Petrolia Station, Great Western Railway, and 180 west from Toronto. This Village, as its name indicates, owes its rise to the inexhaustible deposits of petroleum found in the neighborhood. The surrounding country is one of the best agricultural sections of the Province. Silver is found in the vicinity. Money Order Office and Savings Bank. Stages to Sarnia and Petrolia. Population 750.

Adamson, E., druggist and fancy goods
Adamson, George, insurance agent
Aikens, James, farmer
Anderson, Peter, carpenter
Barry, H. H., general merchant
Beaurs, Peter, general merchant and cooper
Bishop, H., dry goods and boots and shoes
Blain, Thomas, farmer
Boulton, W., farmer
Braund, John Q., carpenter
Bright, James, general merchant
Brookman, Rev. —, (Church of England)
Brown, Henry, accountant
Cameron, Hugh, proprietor Brantford Hotel
Clark, Adam, telegraph operator
Collyes, N., cooper
Currie, John, grocer
Danks, Isaiah, village clerk
Elliott, Andrew, proprietor steam saw mills
Gilbert, E. E., founder and machinist
Gill, Sampson, painter
Gorsline, R. P., proprietor Sherman House
Hammond, William, agent Hartford Oil Refinery Co.
Hayden, James, proprietor Anglo-American
Hazel, William, shoemaker
HERRING, R., book and job printer
Japes, Rev. H., (Roman Catholic)
KEATING, JAMES, Postmaster, general merchant, real estate agent
Kirby, E. D., J.P.
Knox, T. D.
Lockhart, J., agent Canada Rock Oil Company
McBride, R., lumber merchant
McCann, J., cooper
McDermott, Rev. M., (Presbyterian)
McFarlane, J., cooper
McKellar, Hugh, teacher
Macklem, S. Street, M.D.
Marsland, John, boiler maker
Martin, J., cooper
Martin, Samuel, boots and shoes
Miller, Alexander, assessor
Miller, Walter, farmer
Moore, James, carpenter
O'GRADY, S. G., agent Wyoming Oil Refining Co., cooper
Osborne, G., agent Black Creek Oil Refining Co.
Owens, E., grocer
PARKER & TOWNSEND, general agents & shippers
Parry, H. H., baker
Palmer, George, cooper
Peet, Hiram, grocer
Powers, P., farmer
Radcliffe, Mary, milliner
Rait, A., proprietor Oxford Hotel
Richardson, R. A., tailor
Richardson, William, real estate agent
Robertson, Christopher, farmer
Robinson, Henry, painter
Salmon, Thomas, saddler
Sefton, J. W., agent Black Creek Oil Refining Co.
Seib, Charles, cooper
Sheppard, John
Simms, Luke, woolen, soap and candle manufacturer
Smith, C., proprietor Alexander hotel
Stevenson, Leonard, farmer
Sutherland, George, tailor
Thompson, E., farmer
Thompson, Joseph, cooper
Vaughan, L. B., banker and real estate agent
Waddell, J., tailor
Walker, H. B., agent Aneline Co
Wheeler, Henry, nurseryman
Yates, George, collector

Old Montrose.—A Post-office in the Township of Romney, County Kent, 38 miles from Chatham, the County Town.

MILLS, HORATIO, J. P., Postmaster.

Olinda.—A Post-office in the Township of Gosfield, County Essex, 2d miles from Sandwich, the County Town.

Bruner, Abram, broom maker
Bruner, John, carpenter
Bruner, Reuben, broom maker
Brund, Thomas, farmer
Coats, Thomas
Crone, Joseph H., J.P
Fox, John C., J.P., general merchant
Fox, John E., farmer
Fox, John, J., farmer
Fox, Michael G., farmer
Jeffrey, Matthew, farmer
Johnson, John E., teacher
Ryal, Charles, farmer
Squire, Thomas, farmer
Stewart, John, broom maker
Wigle, John W., farmer

Omemee.—A Village and Station on the Port Hope, Lindsay and Beaverton Railroad, on Pigeon Lake, in the Township of Emily, County Victoria, 12 miles from Lindsay, the County Town and 93 from Toronto. Money Order Office and Savings Bank. Population 500.

Adams, F., wine and spirit dealer
Balfour, G. & Son, carpenters
Beatty, William, J. P., dealer in hardware, cutlery
Bently, William, general merchant
Best, William, J. P., farmer
Blackwell, Catherine, hotel keeper
Black, W. A., M. D
Blood, William, baker
Burns, Rev. William, (Wesleyan)
Burton, William, railroad agent and telegraph opr.
Bradburn, Mary Ann, hotel keeper
Campbell, Joseph, tinsmith
Clarke, William, hotel keeper and prop. livery stable
Comstock, John, wagon maker
Cottingham, William, J. P., proprietor flouring mill and lumber dealer
Cottingham, William S., general merchant
Curry, William, general merchant
Davidson, Col. E., farmer
Delamer, J. H., editor *Omemee Standard*
Dies, Chester, hide and leather dealer and tanner
Disbrow, Rev. Noah, (Church of England)
Dodd & Read, general merchants
Doran, William, blacksmith and gunsmith
Eley, Thomas, engraver
Elliott, William, saddler
English, John, wagon maker
English, Samuel, cradle maker, and carpenter
English, W. H., dealer in groceries, toys, &c
Evans, William, farmer
Ford, Robert, constable
Foster, Edward, constable and butcher
Goodliffe, Charles, carpenter
Goodwin, John, proprietor nursery
GRUNDY, ROBERT, Postmaster
Grundy, Rev. T. S., (N. C. Methodist)
Hanna, Edward, farmer
Hanna, John, cooper
Hawkins, George, proprietor livery stable
Hawkins, Thomas, brick maker
Henderson, James, lime and stone
Hodge, Robert, blacksmith
Kennedy, Thomas, blacksmith
Kent, Joseph, proprietor livery stable
Kincaid, John, architect
Knowlson, C., J.P., general agent and issuer of marriage licenses
Kule, Joseph, boots and shoes
Laidlaw, C., lime and stone
Laidlaw, James, farmer
Lamb, George, hide and leather dealer and tanner
Lusher, N. W. & Co., general merchants
McBrian, John, shoe maker
McCrea, John, cabinet maker
McGue, Samuel, farmer
McNeely, Isaac, J.P., general merchant
Marr, W. N , soap and candle manufacturer
Matchell, Thomas, J.P., druggist
Matchell, William C., notary public
Miller, William, tailor
Mitchell, Thomas A., bailiff and constable
Moore, Henry, farmer
Morrison, George, general merchant
Muir, William N., general merchant
Neil, William, jr., blacksmith
Norris, George A., M.D., druggist
Nory, James, manufacturer of woolen goods
Odell, H. H., watchmaker, jeweler, &c.
Omemee Standard (Friday) J. H. Delamar, prop.
Pope, Martha, general merchant
Quade, Archibald, farmer
Redmond, Alexander, tailor
Redmond, Alexander, blacksmith
Ryan, Barbara Victoria, milliner
Shaw, John, teacher
Sheridan, John, boots and shoes
Sherwood, William, boots and shoes
Simpson, C. A, (Episcopal Methodist)
Stephenson, Thomas, J.P. and general merchant
Switzer, John, farmer
Thornton, David, general merchant
Wallace, James, founder and machinist
Wallace, Mrs., milliner
Williamson, Eli, saddler
Williamson, John, tailor
Wood, Sarah, general merchant

Ompah.—A small Village on Trout Lake, in the Township of Palmerston, County Frontenac, 84 miles from Kingston. Population 40.

Campbell, C., milliner
Cunningham, Charles, general agent
Deshaw, T., cooper
Dunham, H., proprieter Ompah House
Elliott, Archibald. carpenter
L., M.D.
Knight, Rev, D. (Methodist Episcopal)
Lane, Rev. W. M. (Presbyterian)
Penny, Rev. Charles E. (Wesleyan)
Stane, John, teacher
Watt, James, lime and stone

Omagh.—A Post Village in the Township of Trafalgar, County Halton. Distant from Milton, the County Town, 5 miles, from Hamilton 25 miles. Population 75.

LITTLE, THOMAS, Postmaster.

Oneida.—A Village in the Township of Oneida, County Haldimand, 11 miles from Cayuga, the County Town, and 66 from Toronto. Stages to Hamilton and Port Dover. Population 250.

Ball, H., cabinet maker
Bridgit, James, J.P.
Bridgit, Joseph, innkeeper
Buchanan, William, carriage maker
Ince, H. J., auctioneer
MUTCHMORE, T. J., J.P., Postmaster and general merchant
Stewart, Hugh, J.P., lumber merchant
Taggart, Jacob, cooper
West, James, grocer

Orangeville.—An incorporated Village in the Township of Garafraxa, County Wellington, 36 miles from Guelph, the County Town, 60 from Barrie, 40 from Toronto, and 22 from Brampton. It is the centre of an excellent agricultural country, and is rapidly increasing in wealth and population. Orangeville is one of the chief stations of the projected Toronto, Grey and Bruce Railway. Daily stages to Brampton. Money Order Office and Savings' Bank. Population 1300.

Acheson, William J., insurance agent, dealer in fancy goods, stationery, &c.
Anderson, Frank, shoemaker
Anderson, James, shoemaker
Anderson, John, merchant
Armstrong, W., M.D.
Bailey, William, blacksmith
Bell, George
Bennett, Edward, carpenter
BRADSHAW, J. H., editor and prop. *Advertiser*
Brown, Lewis, tailor
Bunt, Charles, teacher
Burris, William, carpenter
Byers, James, wagon maker
Campbell, W. & Son, tanners and boots and shoes
Carbert, Joseph, M.D.
Chisholm, K. & Co., general merchants
Collins, Bernard, potter
Corbett, James, weaver
Crawford & Fitzgerald, cabinet makers
Cullen, C., watchmaker
Daniels, William, fanning mill manufacturer
Dawson, Thomas, farmer
Dnner, Sepho, farmer
Driver, Thomas, cooper
DUNBAR, F. G., architect
Earls, Myron, innkeeper
Fead, James, barrister and real estate agent
Ferguson, James, painter
Fisken, John K., carpenter
Flesher, John, general merchant
FOLEY, JOHN, editor and proprietor *Sun*
Foster, Joseph, mason
Fountain, Benjamin, tailor
Frank, Dr., dentist
Gilchrist & Kent, (John & W. R.)
Henderson, Rev. Alexander, (Church of England)
Henry, James, M.D., coroner
Haley, Hugh, carpenter
Hamilton, Samuel, farmer
Harrop, Robert, photographer
Hewat, W. S., M.D.
Hewitt, Joseph, carpenter
House, J. B., photagrapher
Hughes, William, weaver
Irvine, Robert, painter
Irwin, Francis, general merchant
JACKSON, THOMAS, saddle and harness maker
Jenkins, Jacob, mason
Jones, Andrew, blacksmith
Jones, John, blacksmith
Jull, Orange, miller
Jull, Thomas, flour and saw mill proprietor
Keetch, J. W., watch maker
Kelly, James, proprietor Commercial Hotel
Ketchum, Jesse, real estate agent
Keys, James, carpenter
Knight, Thomas, farmer
Lawrence, Orange, proprietor saw mill
Lennox, Andrew, proprietor Marksman's House
LESLIE, GUY, J. P., Commissioner in B. R.
Lester, James, stoves and tinware
Lindsey, Johnston, general merchant
Lloyd, William R., fancy goods
Longeway Brothers (John & Henry) gen. merch'ts
McADAM, THOMAS, & CO., groceries and liquors
McAuley, Francis, agent agricultural implements
McCARTHY, MAITLAND, Solicitor, Notary Public Insurance Agent (see adv.)
McKay, Rev., William E., (Presbyterian)
McKINNON, STEWART & Co., general merchants
McKittrick Bros., founders and mahinists
McLean, Emery, general merchant
McNab, Peter, carpenter
May, James, saddler
May, John, J.P., com. in B.R., appraiser Canada Permanent Building and Savings Society
Meek, William, cooper
Menary, David, blacksmith and wagon maker
Menary, William, plasterer
Milloy, Daniel, dry goods and groceries
Mortimer, Richard, mason
Nicholson, Isaac, carriage maker
PAISLEY HOUSE, John Paisley, prop. (see adv)
Parsons, John, merchant, prop. saw mill
Parsons, William, stoves and tinware
PATULLO, JOSEPH, barrister, solicitor, conveyancer, &c
Pollard, John B., baker
Poyntz, Thomas G., druggist
Raines, William R., land, insurance and gen. agent
Riddell, James K., painter
Riddell, Robert, mason
Sanders, David, plasterer
Shaw, Joseph, teacher
Shields, John, estate agent
Stevenson, John, prop. fulling mill
Stevenson, Thomas, druggist
Tilt, John, shoemaker
Vanwyck, Samuel, hotel keeper
Whitter, John, prop. Wellington Hotel
Waldick, William, architect
Watson, Robert, carpenter
Wilcox, George, butcher
Wilkins, Matthew, butcher
Wheelock, Charles J., P.L.S.
York, T. G., M.D.

Orillia.—An Incorporated Village, beautifully situated on Lake Couchiching, in the Township of Orillia, County Simcoe, 27 miles from Barrie, the County Town, and 90 from Toronto. The surrounding country is justly celebrated for its romantic scenery and its excellent hunting and fishing grounds, which make it a favorite resort for summer tourists. During the season of navigation, steamers ply daily between this point and Barrie and Bell Ewart, connecting with the Northern Railway, and with the far-famed Muskoka Lake and Falls. A branch of the Provincial Lunatic Asylum is established here. Trade chiefly local. Money Order Office and Savings' Bank. Population 1,200.

ARDAGH, J., M.D., M.R.C.S.E., Medical Superintendent, Lunatic Asylum
Badger, George, Steward Lunatic Asylum
Bailey, J. & Brothers, props. Orillia Planing Mills.
Bailey, R., general merchant
Barter, J.
Beacock, D. V., L.D.S.
Bingham, W., stoves and tinware
Blain, John, flour mill
BOLSTER, GEORGE IEVERS
Booth, George J., builder and cabinet maker
Burton, J., tailor
Campbell, Rev. K. A., (Roman Catholic)
Cockburn, John P., Agent Life Assurance of Scotland, general merchant
Cook, Henry, barber
Cooke, Walter, stoves and tinware
Corbett, G. H., M.D., coroner
DALLAS, THOMAS, Clerk Division Court, com. in B. R., Insurance Agent, (see adv.)
Drinkwater, J.
Dunn, Thomas
Dunn, William, sash and blind factory
Elliott, C. S., M.D., coroner
ELLIOTT, THOMAS, general merchant
Evans, Frank, barrister
Fletcher, Miss M., fancy and dress goods
Fowlie, Albert, P.L.S., and land and general agent
Franklin, John
Fraser, F. S., clerk Provincial Lunatic Asylum
French, R., gunsmith
Goffatt, Mrs., millinery and mantles
Goffatt, Thomas, general agent
Grant, F. J. R., estate agent, conveyancer, &c
Gray, Rev. John (Presbyterian)
Gribbin, F., Royal Hotel
Hammond, J., boot and shoe maker
Harvie, John, stage and livery stable proprietor
Harvie & Millard, stage proprietors
Hind, J. J., general merchant
Humme, Julius, photographer
Husband, Richard, saddler
Jackson, W. W., brewer
JOHNSON HOUSE, J. A. Johnson, proprietor
JOHNSON, J. A., proprietor Johnson House
Jones, Robert, cabinet maker
Kean, Frank, general merchant
KING, ATHENIAS, J.P., general merchant
Landy, John J., barrister
Larard, F., watchmaker
McBrayne, Angus, tailor
McCauley, William, blacksmith
McKinlay, D., wagon maker
McMillan, A., cooper
McMULLEN, JOHN C., notary public, accountant and general agent
Morgaret, A., painter
Mark, Rev. Dr. (Wesleyan)
Miller, Melville, (Thomson & Miller)
Moffatt, A., farmer
MOFFATT, THOMAS S., Postmaster, gen. mercht., issuer of marriage licenses (see adv.)
Moffatt, William, proprietor Green bush Hotel
Monck, Col. S. C
Moore, Christopher, auctioneer
Morrow, A., insurance agent
Mulcahy & Co., general merchants
MURRAY, P., editor and prop. *Expositor* (see adv)
Noble, P. C., watchmaker, agent Montreal Tel. Co.
O'Brien, Lucius R., (O'Brien & Co.) Com. in B. R
O'BRIEN & CO., general merchants
ORILLIA EXPOSITOR, (Friday) P. Murray, editor (see adv.)
Ormesby, Edward, merchant
Parkhill, Robert, merchant tailor
Powley, S. P
Quinn, James, estate agent
Ramsay, Robert, M.D.
Reed, George, wagon maker
Robinson, Samuel S., attorney-at-law
Ross, B. W., prop. Orillia house and Peoples' bakery
Ross, Robert, wagon maker
Rutherford, —, butcher
Sanderson, Dr., coroner
Sanson, D. L., general merchant
SLAVEN, J. W., M. D., chemist
Stewart, Rev. Alexander, (Episcopal)
Stewart, Charles, shoemaker
Tate, Jamrs, shingle makers
Taylor, G. W
Thomson, John, (Thomson & Miller)
Thomson, & Miller, saw mill proprietors
Thomson & Wilson, general merchants
Tindale, Robert
Tite, George, painter
Tudhope & Co., (William sen. and William jr.) hardware
Turner Thomas, boots and shoes
Vick, George, baker and grocer
Wainman, E., farmer
Wainwright, Samuel, tanner
Wallace, Joseph, merchant tailor
Wheeler, B., carpenter
Wilson, L., general merchant
World, John, general merchant

Ongley.—A Post Office in the Township of Brighton, County Northumberland
MAYBEE, PETER H., Postmaster.

Orchard.—A Post Office in the Township of Normanby, County Grey.
CALDWELL, THOMAS, Postmaster.

Onondaga.—A Village and Station of the Buffalo and Lake Huron Railway, beautifully situated in the centre of a rich agricultural district, in the Township of Onondaga, County Brant, 9 miles from Brantford, the County Town. Population 350.

BECKWELL, W. S., Postmaster, insurance agent
Burrell, W. M., farmer
Edwards, D. G. C., farmer
Ford, John, general merchant
Ford, Joseph, general merchant and hotel keeper
Hamilton, Robert, farmer
Henderson & Bradshaw, carriage makers
Herdsman, Richard, J.P.
Hartley, John, farmer
Ireland, George, hotel keeper
Lincoln, George, farmer
McLeod, William, farmer
Merrell, John, farmer
Nevin, Samuel, J.P.
Oliver, Thomas, farmer
Powers, John, carpenter
Scholfield, John, baker
Scholfield, Walter, carpenter
Southwell, William, general merchant
Squires & Harold, general merchants and proprietors flour mills
Tingue, Dr.
Truckle, William, carpenter
Vansickle, George, farmer
Whiting, Matthew & Co., general merchants
Wilson, William, hotel keeper
Wood, William, farmer

Orleans.—A Post Office in the Township of Gloucester North, County Russell.

MCHARRY, H., Postmaster.

Oro.—(See Richardson's corners.) A Post Office in the Township of Oro, County Simcoe.

MORNINGSTAR, LEVI, Postmaster.

Orono.—A Village on Orono Creek, in the Township of Clarke, County Durham. Distant from Cobourg, the County Town, 27 miles, 4½ from Newcastle, and 50 from Toronto. Stages to and from Newcastle Money order office. Population 1000.

Allen & Clark, blacksmiths
Allen, William, architect and wagon maker
Andrus, Edson, pump maker
Andrus, F., painter
Anderson, J., jewelry, watches, clocks, &c.
Beattie, John, cooper
Beattie & Lockhart, stave and barrel head manufrs.
Beer, George, blacksmith
Beer, J., architect
Beer, Miss A., milliner
Billings, D. M., manufr. of springs, wheels, &c.
Billings, W. W., music teacher
Bingham & Cassadon, general merchants
Bingham, J., M.D.
Caswell W., saddler
Chester & Brothers, groceries and liquors
Clarke, L., proprietor saw mill
Cronkhite, J., proprietor of woolen mills.
Curtis, George, hotel keeper
Curtis, Rev. James (Methodist Episcopal)
Cutler, J., proprietor job printing office
Dancaster, Thomas, general merchant
Davids, Isaac, butcher
Donnelly, N., groceries and liquors
Eddy, Hiram, blacksmith
Eddy, James, bricklayer
Fitzpatrick, James, cooper
Gardiner, J. A., general merchant
Gamsby, (A. A. & Bro.) general merchants
Gamsby, L. A., druggist
Gamsby, W. L., photographer
Hale, W. F., merchant tailor
Hallett, James, hotel keeper
Henry, W., general merchant
Herninan, N., M.D.
Herninan, W. L., M.D.
Hill, G., dealer in boots and shoes
Hutton, William, manufacturer of plows, &c.
Kerr, William, hotel keeper
Kirkland & Hockeridge, carriage builders
Knox, A., tailor
Lawrence, Rev. George (Presbyterian)
Leigh, James, founder and machinist
Ley, D., grocer
Linton & Awde, blacksmiths
Long, G. M. & Bro., general merchant
Lyman, George, shoemaker
McClung, Rev. Mr. (Wesleyan)
McCullough, D., shoemaker
McPherson, Miss E., milliner
Manes, G., tailor
Martin, J. & Co., architects
Mason, John, house and carriage painter
Mason, John, grocer and baker
Mason, L. C., saddler
Miller, John, grocer
Moment, R., general merchant
Moulton, Proctor, teacher
Powers, H. H., general merchant
Pringle A. & Brother, stone masons
Robinson & Cornell, Misses, straw workers
Reed, J., general weaver
Renwick, H., M.D.
Rice, Rev. J. J. (Bible Christian)
Sills, Miss F., dress maker
Smith, Miss E., straw worker
Stalker, Miss, teacher
Thomas, J., bricklayer
Thompson, William, tanner and currier
Tonie, Lewis, hardware, stoves, etc.
Townshend & Galbraith, manufacturers and dealers in furniture
Trull, W. W., insurance agent
TUCKER, J. S., Postmaster, prop. flouring & flax mills
Venner, Thomas, general merchant
Walden, F., general weaver
Walter William, wagon maker
Watson, J., hotel keeper
Wilkinson, Miss, teacher
Winters, Robert, merchant tailor

Ormond.—A small Village in the Township of Winchester, County Dundas, 48 miles from Cornwall, the County Town. Average value of land $16 per acre.

Dewar, James, farmer
McArthur, John, farmer
McConnell, Samuel, J.P.
McDonald, Duncan, farmer
McGregor, Donald, farmer
McPhail, R., shoemaker
MORGAN, IRA, Postmaster
Pike, William C., constable
Rodney, John, farmer

Orwell.—A Village in the Township of Yarmouth, County Elgin, 9 miles from St. Thomas, the County Town. Stages to Aylmer and St. Thomas. Money order office. Population 300.

Bingham, D. G., farmer
Bingham, W. F., hotel keeper
Davis, David F., J. P., farmer
Ferguson, Benjamin, carriage maker
Hendershot, Lorenzo, proprietor flour mills
Knight, Benjamin, hotel keeper
Lewis, W., shoemaker
McConnell, Robert, tailor
Morton, Alfred, saddler
Newcomb, Webster, general merchant
Secord, Albert, saddler
Secord, Thomas, butcher
Sinclair, Alexander, shoemaker
Stevens, James C., farmer
SUTHERLAND, DAVID, Postmaster and general merchant
Tupte, James J., farmer
Turnbull & Wickett, proprietors planing mill
White, Robert, brick and tile manufacturer
White, Thomas, proprietor livery stable

Osceola.—A Village on Snake River, in the Township of Bromley, County Renfrew, 18 miles from Pembroke, the County Town, and 30 from Sand Point Railway Station. Population 100.

Aurie, Antoine, carpenter
Foley, James, carpenter
Graff, John, tailor
Graham, William, carpenter
Hawkins, Joshua, cooper
Lashney, George, cooper
McDonald, Donald, hotel keeper
McLAREN, ALEXANDER, Postmaster
McLaren, John, insurance agent
McLaren Brothers, merchants and millers

Osgoode.—A Post Office of Carleton County. (See Metcalfe).

Oshawa.—An incorporated Village, Port of Entry and Station of the Grand Trunk Railway, in the Township of East Whitby, County Ontario, 4 miles from Whitby, the County Town; 2½ from Sydenham Harbor, Lake Ontario; 15 from Manchester, 45 from Beaverton and 33 from Toronto. Money Order Office and Savings Bank. Stages to Beaverton and Lindsay. Population 3000.

Andrews, George, carpenter
Annand, George, station master G.T.R.
Atkinson, E., chemist and druggist
Baker, E., tailor
Bainbridge, Wm., general blacksmith & carriage shop
Baker, Elijah, merchant tailor
Bedford, H. R., student with Farewell & McGee
BEEN, WILLIAM, flour, feed & commission (see adv)
Bond & May, contractors
Boyd, John, saddle and harness maker
Brodie, Thomas, jun., teller Ontario Bank
Brooks, J. F., stock dealer
BROOKS, MICHAEL, Railroad House (see adv)
BURK, D. F., general merchant
Butler, James P., dry goods, clothing, boots and shoes
CANADIAN SON OF TEMPERANCE, (Monthly), Luke & Larke, publishers
Carmichael, James, dry goods and groceries
Carswell, Henry, baker and confectioner
Clark, Joseph, coroner, physician and surgeon.
Coburn, William, physician and surgeon
Collins, John, barber
Co-operative Association Store, M. A. McLean, manager
Cowan, W. F., general merchant
Craig, Joseph, carriage maker
Dean, William, foreman Edward Miall & Co.
Devlin, J. B., surgeon dentist
Dewer, Mrs. Isabella, boarding house
Dickie, William, dry goods, clothing, millinery, boots and shoes
Dillon, J., nurseryman
Dingle, Thomas, carpenter
Dockhan, Rev. H., (Methodist Episcopal)
Eastwood, C. S., physician and surgeon
English, L., barrister
Fairbanks, S. B., barrister and reeve
FAREWELL, J. C., (Farewell & McGee)
FAREWELL & McGEE, (J. E. Farewell, LL.B. & R. McGee, M.A.,) barristers
Farmer's Hotel, James Quigly, proprietor
Felt, A. O., billiard room
Finnemore, Henry, miller, Gibbs & Bro
Finney, James W., peddlar and boarding house
Fletcher, Michael, machinist, dealer in tobacco and cigars, and manuf. of ginger beer
Fowke, J. W., general store
Francis, James, nurseryman
French, Isaac, nurseryman
Garth, George W., butcher
Gibbs, Lieut.-Col. W. H., (Gibbs & Bro)
GIBBS, T. N., M.P.P., (Gibbs & Bro)
Gibbs & Bro., (T. N. Gibbs, M.P.P., and W. H. Gibbs) millers and produce dealers
Gibbs, Lobb & Co., (T. N. Gibbs, W. H. Gibbs, and James Lobb) general merchants
Gibson, James A., P.L.S., dealer in fancy goods, books, stationery, &c
GLEN, F. W., executor estate Joseph Hall, manuf. all kinds machinery and agricultural implements
Gotkin, Mrs., dealer in berlin wools and fancy work
Gott, Robert, boot and shoe manuf

Gullock, John, mason
Gunn, D., telegraph operator Montreal Tel. Co
Gurley, George, merchant tailor
Hawkins, Joseph, blacksmith
Hawthorn, Thomas G., boots and shoes
Henry, James O., photographer, boot and shoe dealer
Hinckson, D., farmer
HINDES, A., prop. Lockhart House, (see adv)
Hoitt, James E., photographer
Honey, Charles H., carriage and sleigh maker
JOHNSTON, JOHN P., watchmaker and jeweler (see adv)
Jordon, William, painter
JOSEPH HALL MACHINE WORKS, manufacturers of agricultural implements and general machinery F. W. Glen, executor
Keddie, James B., saddle and harness maker and carriage trimmer
Kerr, George, accountant, Ontario Bank
King, William, tanner and currier
Kirbey, John (Kirbey Bros.)
Kirbey, Thomas (Kirbey Bros.)
Kirbey, Bros. (John & Thomas), painters
Knox, A., stock dealer
Lang, William, salesman William Dickie
Larard, James, watchmaker
LARARD, REGINALD, watchmaker and proprietor spring mattrass factory (see adv)
LARKE, J. S. (Luke & Larke)
Laughlin & Robson, tanners
Law, Mrs. Susanna, grocer
Liddicott, Samuel, shoemaker
LOCKHART HOUSE, A. Hindes, prop'r (see adv.)
LUKE, SAMUEL (Luke & Larke)
Luke & Bro. (Jesse T. Luke & Joseph Luke) cabinet and chair manufacturers
LUKE & LARKE (Samuel Luke and J. S. Larke), editors and publishers *Oshawa Vindicater* and *Canadian Son of Temperance*
McCabe, William, teacher
McCarthy, Miss Mary, millinery and dressmaking
McCheaney, William H., baker and confectioner
McGee, R. (Farewell & McGee)
McGill, John, auctioneer
McGill, William M., M.P.P, physician and surgeon
McLean, M. A. general merchant
Male, C. S., machinist and grocer
Merritt's Hotel, Daniel Harrison, prop.
MIALL, EDWARD & CO,, cabinet makers (see adv)
MICHAEL, W. D., dry goods, tailoring, millinery, groceries, boots and shoes
MICHAEL & MORGAN, (William D. and E. B.) general merchants
Murray, J. N., book-keeper
Nelson, Rev. J. F., (Christian)
O'Regan, John, cooper
Ontario Bank, George E. Shaw, manager
Oshawa Cabinet Factory, W. H. Gibbs, president
OSHAWA VINDICATOR, (weekly) Luke & Larke, publishers
Pascoe, Rev. W. S., (Bible Christian)
Pedlar, H., stoves and tinware, lamps, coal oil, &c
Pellow, W. H., (Pellow & Walton) agent Edinburgh Life Assurance Association
Pellow & Walton, (W. H. Pellow & Adam M. Walton) general hardware merchants and manufs. and dealers in cheese vats, dairy utensils, tinware and stoves
PRINGLE, JAMES, prop. Commercial Hotel
Prudhomme, Louis, shoemaker
Quigley, James, hotel keeper
Rae, Francis, physician and surgeon
Railroad House, Michael Brooks, prop
Ratcliffe & Co., grocers and provision dealers
RIGGS, JAMES, merchant tailor and dealer in gents outfittings, underclothing, &c. (see adv)
Riordan, D., brickmaker
Robinson, Mark, chemist and druggist
Robson & Lauchland, (James Robson and William Lauchland) tanners and curriers
Sanders, Rev. Joseph L. (Wesleyan)
Shaw, G. E., manager Ontario Bank
Shea, Rev. J. J., (Roman Catholic)
Sheppard, Elder, (Disciples)
Slade, D. D., farmer
Small, A. G., proprietor flour mill
Smith, Andrew (R. & A. Smith)
Smith, C. W., architect
SMITH, DAVID, Postmaster
Smith, Robert (R. & A. Smith)
Smith, R. & A. (Robt. & Andrew) dry goods & groceries
Spurrill, John, hotel keeper
Steele, R. C. & Co., (R. C. Steele, Peter & John Murdock), grocers and seedsmen
Stephenson, George, butcher
Stephenson, William, builder
Stewart, Miss, milliner and millinery goods
Sweet, Samuel, blacksmith
Sykes, John, steam planing mill
Taylor, John, grocer, wine and spirit merchant
TAYLOR, H. B., accountant, E. Miall & Co.
TAYLOR, PHILIP, watchmaker and jeweller, (see card)
Thomas, William H., livery stable
Thornton, John, shoemaker
Thornton, Rev. H., D.D. (Presbyterian)
Trennum, Mrs. Almira, millinery
Trunnan, James, butcher
Taigg, — nurseryman
Vars, & Devlin (C. N. Vars & J. B. Devlin) surgeons and dentists
Wall, Patrick, cooper
Walton, Alfred M. (Pellow & Walton) insurance agent, Hartford Fire, Royal, London, and Liverpool and Globe, Provincial, Canada Life
Warren, William, tanner and currier
Western, Matthew, cooper
Whisler, Thomas, grocer and fancy goods
Whiting & Cowan, (A. S. Whiting & John Cowan), scythe works
Wigg, Walter, furniture dealer
Wilcox, Edward A., blacksmith
Wilkinson, Henry, boot and shoemaker
Willox, James, bookseller and stationer
Wilson, John, brickmaker
Wood, James, (Wood & Brother)
Wood, Samuel, (Wood & Brother)
Wood & Brother, (Samuel & James), general merchants
Warrell, Rev. J. B. (Church of England)

Ospringe.—A Post Office in the Township of Erin, County Wellington.
SYMON, WILLIAM, Postmaster.

Ossian.—A Post Office in the Township of Enniskillen, County Lambton.
McPHERSON, GEORGE S., Postmaster.

Ottawa—The Capital of the Dominion of Canada, is situated on the Ottawa River, 87 miles from its confluence with the St. Lawrence, and where the Gatineau and Rideau Rivers and the Rideau Canal meet. The city, formerly called Bytown, obtained its name from its founder, Colonel By, an officer of the Royal Engineers, commissioned by the Imperial Government, in 1827, to superintend the construction of the Rideau Canal. In 1854 Bytown was created a city, and its present more appropriate name conferred. The canal divides the city into Upper and Lower Town, and enters the Ottawa throug height magnificent stone locks. A massive cut-stone bridge, erected by the Royal Sappers and Miners, crosses the canal. The city is well laid out, the streets are generally wide, regular and uniform, and for the most part intersect each other at right angles. The principal quarters are supplied with gas, and active measures are now being taken for the construction of ample water works. The celebrated Chaudiere Falls, at the western extremity of the city, present a scene of grandeur unsurpassed on the continent, except by the Niagara Falls, which in many respects they rival. A suspension bridge, erected by the Provincial Government, at an original cost of $66,448, spans this foaming chasm, and unites the Provinces of Quebec and Ontario. At the north-east end of the city are two other Falls, over which the waters of the Rideau River are precipitated into the Ottawa, and although inferior to the Chaudiere, they are not wanting in interest. Altogether the scenery around the city is of unequalled beauty—wild, romantic and picturesque. —presenting a variety rarely to be met with. The commerce of Ottawa is constituted almost wholly of lumber, which passes through the city from the vast forests in the rear. More of this staple is manufactured in the district of which Ottawa is the emporium, than in any other part of Canada, and the supply furnished here is the main dependence of the spring and fall fleets which arrive in this country for return cargoes to Europe. Of sawn lumber, the mills at the Chaudiere and Rideau Falls send out every year about one hundred millions of feet, board measure. The mills in the vicinity send out about seventy million feet of deals, and several smaller mills through the country about twenty millions more, for all of which Ottawa is the commercial centre. In addition, vast quantities of square timber are also annually exported. The future of Ottawa is not difficult to foresee. Situated in the centre of a fertile and rapidly developing country; holding, as it were, the key of the lumber trade; possessing unlimited water power, which men of enterprise and capital are yearly turning to account, as also every facility of communication with the principal cities of the Dominion and with the United States, it is destined to become a place of immense manufacturing operations. The natural capabilities of defence are great and important. The Parliament Buildings, recently erected, are magnificent specimens of architecture, there is no modern Gothic purer of its kind, nor less sullied with fictitious ornamentation. They consist of three buildings, forming three sides of a quadrangle, but they are not joined, the vacant spaces at the corners being of considerable extent. The fourth side opens upon one of the principal streets of the city. The total frontage of the quadrangle, including the side buildings, is 1200 feet. The centre buildings, having a frontage of 475 feet, are occupied as the Houses of Parliament, and the side buildings as Goverment offices. The buildings stand upon a rock rising almost perpendicularly 170 feet, looking immediately down upon the river, though they are approached from the city without any ascent. The St. Lawrence and Ottawa Railway was opened in 1854, and adds materially to the prosperity of the city. There is a daily line of steamers between Ottawa, Montreal and Kingston, and trains twice a day to Prescott, connecting with the Grand Trunk and Ogdensburgh Railways. Ottawa is distant from Montreal 126 miles, from Quebec 296, from Kingston 95 and from Toronto 233 miles. Population 22,000.

CITY CORPORATION.

Mayor.—Henry J. Friel. *Aldermen.*—James Cunningham, Abraham Pratt, John Rochester, C. W. Bangs, Frs. Abbott, C. T. Bate, William Mosgrove, J. G. Robinson, J. P. Featherstone, Isidore Traversey, John Heney, E. J. Martineau, J. B. Guerrard, Charles Goulden.

Corporation Officers.—W. P. Lett, City Clerk; William Routh, Assistant Clerk; R. Ross, High Bailiff; W. H. Thompson, Chamberlain; G. H. Preston, Collector; Michael Nile, Messenger.

Police Commissioners.—The Mayor, the Recorder, and the Police Magistrate.

Recorder's Court.—J. B. Lewis, Recorder; W. P. Lett, Clerk; R. Ross, High Bailiff; E. Armstrong, Crier. Days of sitting—First Mondays in March, June, and September, and the third Monday in December.

City Registry Office.—Alexander Burritt, Registrar; Thos. Sproule, Deputy Registrar; Copying Clerks, W. H. Egleston, John Bishop. Office—Elgin Street.

COUNTY OF CARLETON.

J. Holmes, Warden, Huntly; Z. Wilson, Ottawa, Treasurer; Edward Beaman, Ottawa, Clerk; J. B. Lewis, Solicitor, Ottawa. Dr. J. Sweetland, Surgeon to the Jail. A. W. Powell, Governor of the Jail; William Corbett, Inspector of Weights and Measures. Christo her Armstrong, County Judge, Ottawa; R. Lyon,

Deputy County Judge, Ottawa; R. Lees, County Attorney, Ottawa; W. F. Powell, Sheriff, Ottawa; J. Bailiff, Deputy Sheriff, Ottawa; J. Frazer, Deputy Clerk of the Crown, Clerk of County Court and Registrar of Surrogate, Ottawa; John Wilson, Master and Deputy Registrar in Chancery, Ottawa.

County of Carleton Registry Office.—Edward Sherwood, Registrar, Ottawa; W, Schofield, Deputy Registrar, Office hours, from 10 a.m., till 3 p.m.

PUBLIC BODIES.

St. Lawrence & Ottawa Railway.—Thos. Reynolds, Managing Director, Montreal; T. J. Leslie, Secretary and Treasurer, Ottawa; Superintendent, T. S. Detlor, Prescott; C. Dame, Master Machinist, Prescott; William Ronaldson, Road Master, Prescott; Office in Ottawa—Desbarats' Block, Sparks Street.

Ottawa Gas Company.—President—E. McGillivray; Managing Director, F. Clemow; Directors.—Honorable James Skead, Edward Griffin, T. Patterson, H. J. Friel; C. Fellowes, Secretary; J. Perry, Manager of Works; Office—Sparks street.

Custom House.—Duncan Graham, Collector; Archibald Douglas, Surveyor; J. S. Lee, Clerk; Alexander Heney, 1st Landing Waiter; John Lytle, 2nd do.; Benjamin Gordon, Clerk; W. A. McAggy, Appraiser; John Burns, Messenger; Office—Elgin Street.

Rideau Canal Office.—James D. Slater, Superintendent; Martin Carmen, Francis Carmen, Clerks; F. Abbott, Foreman of Works; Paul Cooper, Messenger.

Office of the Superintendent of the Ottawa River Works.—Horace Merrill, Superintendent; David Scott, Clerk.

Association of Lumber Manufacturers.—Allan Gilmour, President; Richard McConnell, Vice-President; David Moore, Joseph Aumond, Levi Young, Hon. James Skead and Robert Conroy, Directors: Robert Skead Treasurer; G. H. Perry, Secretary; Hon. James Skead, David Moore and the Secretary, Audit Committee,

Montreal Telegraph Company.—N. W. Bethune, Manager. Office—Metcalfe Street, between Wellington and Sparks.

Canada Central Railway Company.—John G. Richardson, President; Henry Abbott, Vice-President and Managing Director; Directors, R. W. Scott, M.P.P., J. W. B. Rivers, W. F. Powell, George Lowe, jun., W. R. Worsley, Secretary and Treasurer.

Mutual Building Society of Ottawa.—H. McCormick, President; P. A. Egleson, sen., Vice-President, William Hunton, A. Pratt, John Stewart, William Schofield, Thomas Hanly, Directors; Robert Lees; Solicitor; Bank of British North America, Bankers; James Egleson, Secretary and Treasurer. Loan Meetings, first Thursday of every month. Directors Meetings, second Thursday of every month.

Ottawa Board of Trade.—Hon. James Skead, President; Edward McGillivray, Vice-President; G. H. Perry, Secretary, *pro tem;* H. V. Noel, Treasurer; Council of the Board. S. Howell, C. T. Bate, Alexander Workman, Thomas Patterson, S. Christie, E. P. Remon, H. J. Fried, John Rochester, jun., G. H. Perry, C. R. Cunningham, R. H. McGreevy; Board of Arbitrators, Allan Gilmour, Joseph Aumond, Levi Young, J. M. Currier, M.P., H. F. Bronson, P. A. Egleson, J. F. Caldwell, G. E. Desbarats, James Cunningham, James Hope, W. Pennock.

Ottawa and Gloucester Road Co:—President, Edward McGillivray; Secretary and Treasurer, W. H. Falls.

Canada Bank Note Company.—W. C. Smilie, President; Alfred Jones, Vice President; Henry Earle, Secretary and Treasurer; G. B. Boreland, Manager; Office, corner Wellington and Hugh streets.

Ottawa Street Railway.—President, Thomas C. Keefer; Directors, J. M. Currier, M.P., Robert Blackburn, Thomas Reynolds, W. G. Perley, Horace Merrill, Henry O. Burritt; Secretary, Robert Surtees; Messrs. Lyon & Remon, Solicitors.

Bytown and Nepean Road Company.—President, George Arnold; Secretary and Treasurer, Charles Pinney.

Crown Timber Office.—A. J. Russell, Agent and Inspector of Crown Timber Agencies, Canada; C. S. McNutt, Assistant; L. A. Russell, Draughtsman; James Ritchie and Edward Smith, jun., Clerks. Office, corner of Queen and Hugh streets.

CHURCHES.

Christ Church, (Church of England), Sparks Street, Rev. J. S. Lauder, M.A., Rector; Parsonage adjoining Church. Chapel of Ease, (Church of England), Sussex Street, Rev. J. S. Lauder, M.A., Rector. St. Albans, (Church of England), corner of Daly and King Streets, Rev. Dr. Jones, Rector. New Edinburgh Parish, (Church of England), Rev. J. N. Higginson, M.A. Church of St. James, Hull, (Church of England), Rev. J. Johnson. St. Andrew's Church, (Church of Scotland), Rev. D. M. Gordon. Knox's Church, Free, Daly Street, Rev. Thomas Wardrope. (Church of Scotland), Bank Street, Rev.

William Moore. Congregational Church, corner of Elgin and Albert Streets, Rev. Edward Ebbs. Wesleyan Methodist Church, corner of Metcalfe and Queen Streets, Rev. Mr. Harper. Methodist Episcopal Church, corner of York and Dalhousia Streets, Rev. Mr. Stone. Baptist Church, Queen Street, between Elgin and Metcalfe, Rev. D. McPhail. Methodist Episcopal Church, LeBreton's Flats, Rev. T. W. Pickett. St. Andrew's Church, (Roman Catholic), Rev. J. Collins, P.P. Cathedral of Notre Dame, the Bishop and Parochial Clergy; Mr. Gustave Smith, organist. St. Joseph's Church, (Roman Catholic), Rev. J. F. Guillard, P.P. University of Ottawa, Patron, the Bishop of Ottawa; Principal, the Rev. Pere Tabaret, O.M.I. Church of Notre Dame de Bonsecours, (Roman Catholic), Hull, Resident Priest, Rev. H. Reboul. Chaplain to General Hospital, Rev. F. H Grennier. Hudson Bay Mission, Resident Priests, Rev. Peres J. M. Piau, L. Lebret, C. Guegnuen; residence, St. Claude, on the Temiskaming river, P. Q. Shanty Mission, two of the Rev. Peres Oblats visit the shantymen for a few weeks every year.

RELIGIOUS AND CHARITABLE SOCIETIES.

Ottawa Auxiliary Bible Society.—Patron, His Excellency, the Governor General; George Hay, President; William Clegg, William Hamilton, Hon. S. L. Tilley, James Johnson, W. A. McAgy, Vice-Presidents; Rev. Thomas Wardrope, Corresponding Secretary; Rev. D. M. Gordon, B.D., Recording Secretary; George May, Treasurer; J. Durie, Depositary.

Magdalen Asylum.—Sisters of the Good Shepherd, Ottawa street, between Gloucester and Chapel streets.

St. Patrick's Orphans' Home.—Church street, between Dalhousie and Sussex streets.

Protestant Orphans' Home.—Albert street, near Elgin street.

Ottawa Convent.—Corner of Sussex and Nunnery streets.

General Hospital.—Under the superintendance of the Sisters of Charity; Dr. Hill, Consulting Physician; Dr. Beaubien, Surgeon.

County of Carleton, General Protestant Hospital, Ottawa.—President, Judge Armstrong; Vice-President; George Hay; Treasurer, Alexander Workman; Secretary, Roderick Ross; Stewart, George Sadler; Matron, Miss Sadler; Consulting Physicians, Drs. Hill and Van Cortlandt; Attending Physicians, Dr. Grant, M.P., Drs. McGillivray, Henry, Leggo and Codd; Elected Directors, Judge Armstrong, George May, Alexander Workman, Thomas Patterson, James Dyke, John Roberts, Edward Gillivray, W. H. Walker, James Peacock, George May, John Durie, H. V. Noel; Directors for life, Roderick Ross, James McCracken, Richard Bishop, A. M. Dole, James Rosamond. The Board meets first Tuesday in each month, at the Hospital, at 4 p. m. The Directors visit the Hospital two together, daily, each two taking a week in succession. There is a Finance and Supply Committee, annually appointed—these are the only two standing Committees.

BANKS.

Ontario Bank: Ottawa Branch—William Wade, Manager; A. C. Mowbray, Accountant; S. A. McMurtry, Teller; G. Mann, Actuary in Savings' Department; John S. Lytle, Ledger Keeper. Office—Corner of Sparks and Metcalfe streets. Bank of British North America: Ottawa Branch—Office, 140 Wellington street; A. C. Kelty, Manager; P. Robertson, Accountant; John Black, Teller. Bank of Montreal: Ottawa Branch—Office, 202 Wellington street; A. Drummond, Manager; F. A. Stewart, Accountant; G. R. Bartlett, Teller; F. W. Cotton, H. A. Matheson, H. Drummond, G. H. Griffin, G. W. Dodwell, J. Graham, Clerks. Quebec Bank: Ottawa Branch—H. V. Noel, Manager; Octavius Newcombe, Accountant; C. V. Noel, Teller; Thomas Mackinnon, Deposit Ledger Keeper; A. Green, Discount Clerk. Royal Canadian Bank: Ottawa Branch—Office, Desbarat's Block, 77 Sparks street; Acting Manager, Charles Grassett; Clerk, J. Kavanagh.

NATIONAL SOCIETIES, ETC.

St. George's Society.—Incorporated by Act of the Provincial Parliament, 24th Victoria, chap. 144. Dr. Sweetland, President; E. C. Barber, 1st Vice-President; James Slocombe, 2nd Vice-President; Thomas Painter, Secretary. Committee of Management.—Henry Gough, James Salmon, George Bott, T. Hallandal, J. Skinner, John Bray and George Bartlett; Chaplain—Rev. C. C. Codd; Physician—Dr. Van Courtlandt; Solicitor—E. P. Remon; Auditors—James F. Brown and Thomas Birkett; Stewards—W. B. Howes, T. Satchetl, R. W. Stevens, and S. Rogers.

St. Andrew's Society.—James Fraser, President; J. Thorburn, 1st Vice-President; A. C. Wilson, 2nd Vice-President; A. Mann, Treasurer; J. P. Robertson, Secretary; Rev. W. Gordon, Chaplain; Drs. MacDonald and Grant, Physicians; R. Lees, Solicitor.

Ottawa Natural History Society.—J. Langton, M.A., President; Edmund Meredith, 1st Vice-President; J. A. Grant, M.D., F.G.S., M P., 2nd Vice-President; Edward Van Courtlandt, M.R.C.S., Curator; James Ogilvy, Treasurer; William White, Recording Secretary; Arthur Harvey, F.S.S., Corresponding Secretary; Members of Council, John Thorburn, M.A., Lieut.-Col. Thomas Wiley, C.S.R.

Irish Protestant Benevolent Society.—W. F. Powell, President; P. A. Egleson, sen., 1st, Vice.-President; A. Pratt, 2nd Vice-President; H. McCormick, Treasurer; Thomas Sproule, Recording Secretary; Thomas Thompson, Assistant Recording Secretary; Samuel Rothwell, Corresponding Secretary; Rev. J. S. Lauder, Chaplain; Messrs. Magee and Woodburn, Auditors.

French Canadian Institute.—J. W. Peachley, President; Dr. P. St. Jean, 1st Vice-President; Pierre Roque, 2nd Vice-President; H. Lapierre, Corresponding Secretary; M. Tetu, Recording Secretary; E. Tetu, Treasurer; L. A. Grison, Librarian. Committee of Management—Messrs. Leprohon, Martineau, N. Tetu, L. Cadieux, I. Champagne, A. Roque. Library Committee—L. A. Grison, W. Fanning, J. V. Michaud, L. Berthelot, P. Marier.

Independent Order of Good Templars.—Ottawa Lodge No. 403. Robert Crain, W. C. T.; Julia Murphy, W. V. T.; George B. Shaw, W. S.; G. Maclean Rose, W. T.; George Crain, W. F. S.; Ira W. Starr, W. M; Kate Minore, W. I. G.; Alexander McDonald, W. O. G.; William Minore, W. C.; Eliza Lockwood, W. A. S.; Marion Young, W. D. M.; Almira Lockwood, W. F. H. S.; Maggie McLaren, W. L. H. S., Edward Storr, P. W. C. T.

Bytown Division Sons of Temperance, No 224.—Edward Batterill, W.P., ; Dr. John Leggo, Treasurer; Dr. C. Leggo, Financial Scribe; G. Topley, Recording Scribe; F. Hunter, Assistant Recording Scribe; Edward Storr, Chaplain; John Young, P.W.P.; George B. Shaw, Conductor; Alfred Leggo, I.S.; Mr. Floyd, O. S.

St. Patrick's Literary Association.—Thomas Tuerin, President; William Kehoe, 1st Vice-President; Patrick Baskerville, 2nd Vice-President; Peter Aiken Egleson, Treasurer; W. H. Waller, Corresponding Secretary; John Kelly, Recording Secretary; William D. O'Brien, Assistant Recording Secretary; Mr. McStravick, Librarian. Trustees.—P. E. Ryan, William Kehoe, J. Casey, P. Quinn, J. L. P. O'Hanley, J. Lyons, W. White, T. Coffee, M. Starrs, M. O. Keefe, F. McCaffrey and P. Smith. Committee of Management.—William Kehoe, P. Quinn, M. Starrs, W. White, and J. L. P. O'Hanly.

Mechanics' Institute.—W. White, President; A. S. Woodburn, 1st Vice-President; E. P. Remon, 2nd Vice-President; James Cunningham, Treasurer; D. Matheson, Corresponding Secretary; G. Kennedy, Recording Secretary; J. Thorburn, Honorary Librarian; J. W. Finlay, Curator; Managing Committee. —R. Hunter, Chairman; D. Matheson, W. White, James Porter, J. G. Whyte, G. Kennedy; J. B. Stacy, Custodian and Librarian.

Ottawa Grammar School.—John Thorburn, M. A., Principal; John McMillan, B. A., 1st Assistant Master; Hamilton Allan, 2nd Assistant Master; M. Berthelot, French Master.

EDUCATIONAL.

Ottawa College.—Very Rev. J. H. Tabaret, President; Rev. F. Lepers, Professor of Moral Theology; Rev. A. Lemoine, Professor of Dogmatic Theology; Rev. N. Martens, Bursar; Rev. J. B. Laroie, Prefect of Studies; Rev. P. Froe, Professor of Mental Philosophy; Rev. L. Chaborel, Prefect of Discipline; Rev. J. Barrett and A. Lecompte, Professors of Greek and Latin; Rev. A. Riordan and P. Gladu, Professors of Belles Letters; Rev. J. McKernan and Rev. P. Brennan, Professors of English Language; Rev. J. B. Duhairne and L. Marion, Professors of Frrnch Language; Mr. A. Smith, Professor of Piano; Mr. M. De Barillon, Professor of Drawing.

MILITIA.

District Staff, District No. 4.—Commandant.—Lieut.-Col. Atcherly, D.A.A.G.; Lieut.-Col. Jackson, Brigade Major; Lieut.-Col. McDougall, District Paymaster; Capt. Stoddart, District Quartermaster.

OTTAWA FIRE BRIGADE.

John Langford, Superintendent; Paul Favreau, Assistant Superintendent. *Rideau Fire Company.*—L. A. Grison, Captain, Pierre Jobin, Lieut. Alexis Folsy, Secretary and Treasurer. *Queen Engine Company.*—James Egleson, Captain; James Fogarty, 1st Lieutenant; Eustache Dearneault, 2nd Lieutenant; Napoleon Berichon, Secretary and Treasurer. *Ottawa Engine Company.*—J. Walsh, Captain; P. S. Slattery, 1st Lieutenant; William McCaffrey, 2nd Lieutenant; R. Reardon, Secretary; John Kehoe, Treasurer. *Chaudiere Engine Company.*—Francis Link, Captain; Philemon Wright, Lieutenant; Henry Livings,

Secretary; E. C, McGillivray, Treasurer; James Hendrick, Engineer. *Lower Town Hook and Ladder Company.*—Eamas Roy, Captain ; J. B. Doucette, Lieutenant; Xavier Groulx, Secretary and Treasurer. *Central Hook and Ladder Company.*—William Langstaff, Captain; 1st Lieutenant, J. Harvey ; 2nd Lieut., F. Prodrick ; J. L. G. Robertson, Secretary ; John Nicholson, Treasurer ; J. Marshall, Engineer.

AGRICULTURAL.

City of Ottawa Agricultural Society.—(Established 1865.)—J. B. Lewis, President; John Ashworth, Vice-President; J. M. Currier, M. P., 2nd Vice-President; Directors—James Skead, R. W. Scott, M. P. P., Alonzo Wright, M. P., John Rochester, jr., A. McKellar, Ira Morgan, Robert Kenny,; A. S. Woodburn, Secretary and Treasurer.

County of Carleton Agricultural Society.—D. Kennedy, President ; T. M. Robertson, Vice-President ; James Davidson, 2nd Vice-President; Directors.—John Dawson, Thomas Clark, E. Watson, W. Graham, R. Bayne, John Nelson, Hugh Gourlay ; A. S. Woodburn, Secretary and Treasurer.

ABBOTT, FRANCIS, foreman Rideau Canal Works, Wellington
Abbott, Henry, managing director Canada Central Railway Co.
Abbott, John B., blacksmith, George
Acres, George, policeman
Ahern, J. & W., blacksmith, Duke
Allan, William, china and glassware, 51 Rideau
Angus, William, boots and shoes, 226 Wellington
Angus & Huckell (Andrew Angus and Thos. Huckell) boots and shoes, 15 Sussex
Angus & Son (Robert, sen. & Robert, jun.) cabinet makers, 22 Rideau
Ansell & Michaels (Assher & Henry), tobacconists, cor Spark & Elgin
Ardill, John, plasterer, King
Armstrong, E., crier Recorder's Court
Armstrong, Christopher, Judge Co. Carleton, Court House
ARMSTRONG, GEORGE, proprietor Union House, cor Queen and Elgin
Armstrong, Thomas, blacksmith, Besserer
ARNOLDI KING, wine merchant and architect, Metcalfe (see adv)
Ashfield, John, grocer, Duke
Atcherly, Lieut.-Col. D. A., A.G. Militia Dept
ATKINSON, H. & CO., lumber merchts, 130 Sussex
Atkinson, Neil, policeman
AUDY, A. O. & CO., wholesale tea and coffee merchants, Elgin
Aumond, Joseph, lumber merchant, Rideau
Aumond, William, clerk Militia Department, Rideau
Austin, George F., P.L.S., Victoria Terrace
Austin, William, P.L.S.
Bailiff, James, deputy sheriff, Court House
Baldwin, A. H. & Co., lumber merchants, Chaudiere Island
BANGS, C. W. & CO., hatters & furriers, 34 Sussex
BANK OF BRITISH NORTH AMERICA, A. C. Kelty, manager ; P. Robertson, accountant ; J. Black, teller, Wellington
BANK OF MONTREAL, Andrew Drummond, manager ; J. A. Steward, accountant ; G. R. Bartlett, teller ; H. A. Matheson, F. M. Cotton, H. M. Drummond, G. H. Griffin, J. A. Graham, G. W. Dodwell, clerks, Wellington
Bannon, John, policeman
Barnes & Feck (William and George), plumbers and gasfitters, William
Barrett, James, tailor, Hull
Barrett, Michael, hotel keeper, 44 York
Barry, Robert, plasterer, 248 Rideau
Bartlett, George, confectioner, 37 Sussex
Baskerville, George, grocer, Duke
Baskerville, Patrick, grocer, cor Church and Cumberland
BATE, C. T. & Co., (C. T. & H. M. Bate) wholesale grocers, Canal Basin
Bate & Co., grocers, 52 Sparks
Beament, Thomas & Co., (Thomas and George) gent's furnishings, 25 Sparks
BEARMAN, EDWARD, County Attorney, Court House
Beatty Thomas, grocer, cor Parry and Nelson
Beaubien, Cleophas, M. D., York
Beaucaire, Benjamin, inn-keeper, Murray
Beaudouin, Dr., Hull
BEAVER HOTEL, F. X. Lapierre, 75 Sussex
Beckett, Dr. J. A., dentist, 10 Sparks
BELL, W. R., A. M. Ph. D., M. D., C. M., D. S., D. O., New Edinburg
BELL & WOODBURN, (T. G. & Alexander G.) book and job printers, Elgin
Bellemare, T., boots and shoes, 67 Sussex
Bermingham, James, auctioneer, 72 Sussex
Bertrand, N., Chaudiere Hotel, Head
BESSERER & COWAN, (L. W. Besserer, Andrew Cowan) general hardware, 18 Rideau (see adv)
Bethune, N. W., agent Montreal Telegraph Company, Augusta
Billings, Bradish, architect, Elgin
BINKS, JAMES, tobacconist, 62 Rideau
Bison, Moise, proprietor carding mill, Hull
Blasdell, N. S. & Co., founders, Middle
Blyth, G. R., dry goods, 234 Wellington
BLYTH & KERR, (George J. & William) plumbers, gas and steam fitters, tin and coppersmiths, bell hangers, &c. ; dealers in house furnishing hardware, 25 Rideau
Boland, William, butcher. Byward Market
Booth, John R., lumber merchant, Chaudiere Island
Booth, Robert R., gen. mercht., Bridge cor Montreal
BORBRIDGE, S. & H., saddle, harness and trunk manufacturers, 39 Rideau (see adv.)
Bott, George, fruit and provision, cor Rideau and Dalhousie
Boulton, J. F., barrister, cor. Sparks and Metcalfe
Bourget, James, billiard parlor, Russell House
Bourque, Edward, tinsmith, 58 Rideau
Boyden, Joseph, Variety Hall, 34 Sussex
BOYLE, MICHAEL, butcher, By Ward Market (see adv)
Bradbury, William, butcher, By Ward Market
Brading, H. F. & Co., brewers, George
Bradley, R. A., solicitor in chancery, Elgin
Brennan, Patrick, blacksmith, Clarence
BRITISH AMERICAN BANK NOTE COMPANY, (Montreal and Ottawa).—W. C. Smillie, president ; Alfred Jones, vice-president ; Henry Earle, secretary and treasurer ; G. B. Burland, manager, cor Wellington and Kent
Bronsons & Weston, saw mill props., Middle

Brown, Alfred, general merchant, 69 Sparks
Brown, Archibald, saloon keeper, cor Wellington and George
Brown, H. M., teacher, cor Sparks and Metcalfe
Brown, John, police sergeant
Brown, James, druggist, 67 Sparks
Brown, John, architect, Hull
Brown, John, soap and candle factor, York
Brown, Thomas, Crown Hotel, 56 Rideau
Brule, Thomas, blacksmith, York
Brown, W. W., barber, 39 Sparks
BROWNE, D. T. & CO. (D. J. Browne and Henry C. Symmes), grocers and wine merchants, 16 Rideau (see adv)
Buchanan, James, grocer, 222 Wellington
Buck, George A., livery, Rideau cor Ottawa
BUCK & SANGER (George A. and William H.), proprietors Revere House
Buckley, William, confectionery, Wellington
Bufton, J., butcher, Wellington Market
Bureau, Joseph, foreman *Canada Gazette*
BURGESS, WILLIAM, clerk *Times* Printing Company, Daly
Burke, George R., Clerk 1st Division Court, Court House
BURKETT, THOMAS, hardware, paints, oils, &c., 24 Rideau
Burns, John, messenger Customs
BURRITT, ALEXANDER, City Registrar, Elgin
BURSTALL, EDWARD, lumber mercht, 134 Sussex
Cahill, John, prop. Terrapin Saloon, cor Sparks and Elgin
CALDWELL, J. F. & Co., clothing and dry goods, 72 Sussex
CAMERON, A. F., book keeper Hamilton Brothers, Cathcart
CAMERON, HON. MALCOLM, Queen's printer, agent Provincial Insurance Company of Canada, Desbarats' buildings
Cameron, William, saloon, Murray
CAMPBELL A. & Co., (A Campbell & Joseph Sleeman) wholesale and retail grocers, 53 Sussex
Campbell, Thomas, turner, Metcalfe
CANADA GAZETTE, (weekly) printed by authority, Desbarats' buildings
CANADIAN EXPRESS COMPANY, C. C. Ray, agent, Elgin
Crandell & Co., lumber merchants and saw mill props. Hull
Cardinal, Felix, hotel keeper, York
Carlton, Christopher, hotel keeper, Canal Basin
Carmen, G. Arthur, col'r Tolls, Rideau Canal, Locks
Carmen, Martin, clerk, Rideau Canal Works
Carson & Wilson, shoemakers, Duke
CASSELS, R. S., president and manager Union Forwarding and Railway Company, Wellington
Cassidy, P. H., inn-keeper, York cor Dalhousie
Cauthrey, Benns., butcher, Byward Market
Cavillier, X., carriage maker, Hull
CHALMERS & Co., coal oil, lamps, berlin wool and fancy goods, 62 Sparks
Chambers, Thomas J., general merchant, Clarence
CHAMPAGNE, ANTOINE, Hotel Cartier, Murray, (see adv)
Champagne, Seraphin, carriage maker, 96 Clarence
CHAMPNESS, WELDON, British Lion Hotel, 61 Sparks, (see adv)
Chapais, Hon. J. C., Minister of Agriculture
Chepmell, Henry, secretary Union Forwarding and Railroad Company
Chesley, George, M. D., 25 Rideau
Chevrier, Alexander, inn-keepér, St. Patrick
Chevier, L., hotel keeper, St. Patrick
Chevier, N., clothier, 50 Sussex
Chisholm, Duncan, grocer, 118 Sussex
Christie, S., com. mercht and general agent, Russell House Block
Ciappy, John, grocer, Duke
CITY HALL, Michael Nile in charge, Elgin
CITY REGISTRAR'S OFFICE, Alexander Burritt, registrar, Elgin
Clark, W. C., music teacher, O'Connor
Clarke, George, hotel keeper, 5 York
CLEMOW, FRANCIS, official assignee, general agt, 19 Sparks
Coates, Mrs. W., watches, jewelry, &c., Sussex
Cockburn, John, boatbuilder, Chaudiere Island
Cochrane, John C. T., insurance agent, Elgin
Codd, Alfred, M.D., Rideau
CODD, D. & CO., solicitors for patents of invention and parliamentary agents, Elgin (see adv)
Coffey, Thomas, pork and grain, Clarence
Coleman, A. O. F., veterinary surgeon, York
Collins, Rev. J., P.P., (Roman Catholic)
COLLINS, PETER, grocer, Sussex
Connelly, James, butcher, By Ward Market
Cordelet, W. G., tinsmith, Sussex
COTTON, JAMES, managing director *Times* printing and publishing company
COUNTY CARLETON PROTESTANT GENERAL HOSPITAL, Rideau
Cowan, Thomas, butcher, Hull
COWARD, D. W. & CO., com. merchants, ins. agts and exchange brokers, 17 Sparks (see adv)
Cox, George, engraver, Elgin cor Sparks
Craig & McKenzie, (John C. and Robert) tailors, 73 Sparks
Crane, G. W., books and stationery, Wellington
Cross, John, prop. planing mill, Duke
Cruice, R. W., commission merchant, Sparks
Culbard, William G., tanner, manuf. lambskin mats, Sandy Hill
Cummings, Robt., carriage maker, Cummings' Island
Cunningham, James, book-keeper, Gilmour & Co
CUNNINGHAM & LINDSAY, (Chartres R. and James), importers of British and foreign dry goods, 14 Rideau
CURTIS, JOHN, hair dresser and manufacturer of hair work, 57 Rideau (see adv)
CURRIER, J. M., M.P., lumber merchant, New Edinburgh
Cussans, Henry, confectioner, 60 Rideau
CUSTOM HOUSE, Elgin
Cuzner, Luke, boots and shoes, 29 Rideau
Dalglish, George, grocer, Wellington
Dalglish & Russell, (James & Thomas), grocers, 213 Wellington
D'Amour, Elice, blacksmith, Clarence
Damontier, H., blacksmith, Hull
Darpentier, B., prop. Hull Hotel, Hull
David & Co., grocers, Duke
Davidson & Daniel, (F. R. & R. F.) druggists, 41 Rideau
Davis, Frederick, police sergeant
Day, Samuel, colporteur, Gloucester
Delude Charles, baker, Hull
Demaris, Leonard, grocer, Murray
DESBARATS' BUILDINGS, corner Sparks and O'Connor
DESBARATS, GEORGE B., *Canada Gazette*, wholesale and retail stationer, bookbinder, printer and publisher, Desbarats' Buildings
DICKINSON, M. K., flour merchant, and sawed lumber and shingle manufacturer, Sussex

DOLE, A. M., agent firm Hamilton Bros., Sussex
DOLEN, MICHAEL, general merchant, 38 York
Donaldson, R., produce, Hull
Dorion, C. P., stoves and tinware, 58 Sparks
Dorion, J. Edmond, M.D., Clarence
Dorion, —., photographer, Duke
Douglas, Archibald, Surveyor Customs, h River View Nepean
Dow, Donald, builder and contractor, Besserer
Dow, James, grocery, 244 Wellington
DRIVER, THOMAS, boots and shoes
DRUMMOND, ANDREW, manager Bank Montreal
DRUMMOND, GEORGE P., insurance agent, exchange broker, 19 Sparks
DUFF, ALEXANDER, (O'Meara & Co.)
Dufour, Peter, carriage maker, 114 Rideau
Duhamel, J., butcher, Hull
Duhamel, Louis, carriage maker, Murray
DUKE HOUSE, John B. Le Duc, prop., Duke
Dunn, Edward, plasterer, McTaggert
Dunn, Robert, plasterer, Cathcart
Dunn, Thomas, plasterer, Gloucester
DUNNING, A. J., barrister, Court House Avenue
DURIE, JOHN & SON, books and stationery, agents Phœnix Life Assurance Co., Sparks
Durocher, Celestin, policeman
Durocher, Oliver, boots and shoes, 77 Sussex
DUVERNAY, BROS., (L. N. & L. D.) publishers *Le Canada*, booksellers and stationers, 26 York
Dyke, John, saloon keeper, York
EARLE, HENRY, secretary and treasurer B.A. Bank Note Co., Bay
Eastman, R., photographer, York
EASTON, HIRAM, prop. flour, oat and shingle mills, Canal Basin (see adv)
EASTON, M. G., (W. H. Easton & Co)
EASTON, W. H. & CO. forwarding and com. merchants, Canal Basin (see adv)
Eaton, R., paints, oils, &c., Elgin
Ebbs, Rev. Edward (Congregational)
EDDY, E. B., manuf. sawn lumber, matches, pails, tubs, &c., Hull
Edwards, Solomon, grocer, Wellington
Egleson, Mrs., ladies clothing, Rideau
Egleson, P. A. & Son, (P. A. and James) grocers, 80 Sussex
Egleson, W. H., clerk City Registrar
ELLIOTT, ROBERT, hotel keeper, York
ELLIOTT & HAMILTON, (George E. and William) dry goods, Rideau
ELSON, WILLIAM, book-keeper *Canada Gazette*, O'Connor
Enwright, Mrs. Ann, stoves and tinware, Wellington
Esmond, Bros., (J. P. and J. R.) stoves and tinware, 43 Sparks
Etna, of Dublin, Fire and Life Ins. Co., N. McKinnon, agent, 41½ Sparks
Evans, Jeremiah, carriage maker, Sparks cor Bank
Evans, Samuel, pork packer, Rideau
Falls, W. H., student-at-law
Farley, James F., book-keeper, Robert Skead, Sparks
FEATHERSTON, JOHN P., chemist of the Pharmaceutical Society, London, Eng., 57 Sussex
Feeby, George, shoemaker, Hull
Fellowes, G. B. L., Q.C., barrister
Fest, Mrs., confectioner, Rideau
FINGLAND & DRAPER, (William and Benjamin J.), dry goods and lumber merchants, 9 and 11 Sussex
Fink, John P., plasterer, Parks
Fisher, Benjamin, agent E. Burstall, 134 Sussex
Fitzpatrick, Hugh, proprietor Exchange Hotel, Hull
Fleck, Alexander, founder and machinist, Wellington
Foisey, A., shoemaker, Sussex
Foote, James, grocer, Rideau.
Forrest, A. G., P.L.S., O'Connor
Fraser, Andrew, blacksmith, York
Fraser, James, Clerk County Court, Deputy Clerk Crown and Pleas, Registrar, Surrogate, Clerk of Assize, County Carleton, Pres. St. Andrew's Society
Fraser, H. D., locksmith, York
Fraser, James, 52 Sussex
Frederick, Theodore, brass finisher and plumber, William
FRIEL, HENRY J., mayor, agent Royal Insurance Co., London, Eng., Sussex
Fripp, Sidney B., architect, Wellington
Gaffney, Bernard, tailor, Sussex
GALLAGHER, THOMAS, contractor and builder Metcalfe
GARLAND, MUTCHMOR & CO. (J. M. & Alexander) dry goods, 20 Sparks
GARVEY, JAMES, M.D, 94 Rideau
Gelhausen & Dupuy, (Peter & Peter) 31 Rideau
Gendreau, A. E., hair dresser, 206 Wellington
GENERAL HOSPITAL, (under the direction of the Grey Nuns), Sister Laube, directress, Boulton
Germain, E., tanner, Clarence
GERMAIN, N., tin and coppersmith, gas-fitter, dealer in stoves and hardware, 25 Sussex
Gibb, Alexander, barrister, Rideau
Gilligan, B., grocer, Murray
Gillihan, W. S., bank note engraver
GILMOUR, ALLAN, lumber merchant, president Association Lumber Manufacturers
GILMOUR & CO., lumber merchants props. saw mills, etc., Wellington cor Kent
GILPIN, ROBERT, prop. Old Red Lion Hotel, Little Sussex cor St. Paul's (see adv)
GOODE, DANIEL, prop. Goode's Hotel, St. Paul
Gordon, Benjamin, chief clerk customs
Gordon, Rev. D. M., (Church of Scotland) pastor St. Andrews
Gorman, Philip, inn keeper, 58 Clarence
Gough, Henry, brick maker, Biddy
GOUIN, JAMES A., prop. Russell House, cor Sparks and Elgin
Goulden's Hotel, cor Sussex and Bolton
Gouldthrite, Samuel, saloon keeper, Elgin
GOWAN, H. & J., carvers and gilders, manuf. looking glass and picture frames, dealers in musical instruments, &c., 54 Sparks (see adv)
GOWAN'S ASSEMBLY ROOMS, H. & J. Gowan props., 54 Sparks
Graham, Alexander, collector inland revenue, Elgin
Graham, Andrew, prop. St. Lawrence Hotel, cor Rideau and Nicholas
Graham, Archibald & Co., dry goods, 48 Sparks
Graham, C. E., M.D, Hull
Graham, Duncan, customs collector, Elgin
Graham, John, prop. Albion Hotel, Nicholas
Graham, R., hotel keeper, 108 Sussex
GRAHAM, WILLIAM, prop. City Hotel, Clarence
Graham, William, manuf. square timber, Gloucester Township
GRANT, DONALD M., agent Imperial Fire Ins. Co. of London, England, Elgin, h 188 Rideau n (see adv)
Grant, Edward, watchmaker, 321 Wellington
GRANT, JAMES A., M.D., M.P., &c., Rideau
Grant, Mrs. Jane, hotel keeper, George
Grant & Henderson, (Lewis and John S.) dry goods, 20 Rideau

Grassett, C. B., accountant in charge Royal Canadian Bank, Hugh
Gravelle, H., axe factory, Hull
Graves, Thomas, grocer, Wellington
Groulx, Toussaint, boots and shoes, 67 Sussex
Green, John, grocer, Rideau
Grennier, Rev. F. H., chaplain General Hospital
Grennier, J. B., hotel-keeper, Hull
Griffin, Mrs. Ann, grocery, St: Andrew
GRISON, LOUIS A., insurance agent and collector, Sussex and York (see adv)
GRIST, HENRY, solicitor for patents of invention and draughtsman, cor Elgin & Sparks (see adv)
Grubert, Bros. (Arthur & Lawrence), manufacturers boots and shoes, Elgin
Guerard, J. Bte., general merchant, cor Church and Dalhousie
Guerin, Thomas, engineer, Sparks
GUIGUES, MOST REV. JOSEPH E., R. C. Bishop, diocese of Ottawa
Guillard, Rev. J. F., P.P., (Roman Catholic), St. Joseph's
Guindon, —, butcher, By Ward Market
Gundry, Charles, baker, Hull
Hall, Edward, confectioner, Wellington
Hallendal, Francis, innkeeper, Wellington
HAMILTON, HON. JOHN, (Hamilton Bros.), res Montreal
HAMILTON, ROBERT (Hamilton Bros.) res Quebec
HAMILTON, BROS. (Robert & John), saw mill proprietors and lumber merchants, Sussex
Handy, Peter, moccasin maker, 108½ Sussex
Haram, Robert, cabinet maker, Rideau
Harper, Rev. E. B., M.A. (Wesleyan)
Harris, James, veterinary surgeon, 72 Clarence
HARRIS & CAMPBELL (R. P. Harris and Thomas Campbell), cabinet makers and upholsterers, Sussex (see adv)
Hartford Fire Insurance Company, W. Wade, agent
Hauser, A., news depot, 56 Sparks
HAY, GEORGE, importer of general hardware, agent Kershaw & Edwards' safes, 21 Sparks
Haycock, R. H., barrister, Elgin
Hayes, T. B., translator House of Commons, Daly
HEARN, WILLIAM, market drug store, 22 York (see card)
Heney, John, wood merchant, Canal Basin
Heney, & Co., harness makers 24 York
Henry, Alexander, landing waiter
Henry, John B., exciseman, Elgin,
Henry, William J., M. D., Kent
Herbert, Patrick, Rideau Hotel, 46 Rideau
Herrick, Brush & Co., (G. H. and Charles E.) commission merchants, brokers, insurance agents, &c., Rideau
Hick, Robert, jr., attorney-at-law, Elgin
HICK, H. & Co., Occidental bankrupt stock emporium, cor Rideau and Sussex (see card)
HIGGINSON, JAMES, dry goods and clothing, 47 Sussex
Higginson, Rev. J. N., M.A., (Church of England) New Edinburgh
Hill, Hamett, M. D., M.R.C.S, Eng., Victoria Terrace
Hilliard, John, butcher, By Ward Market
Holbrook, George, merchant tailor, Elgin
Holland, William, policeman
HOPE, JAMES & CO., bookbinders, booksellers and stationers (see adv)
HOTEL, CARTIER, A Champagne, Murray (see adv)
Howe, George, house painter, Augusta
Howe, George & Son, boots and shoes, 10 Rideau
Howe, William, painter, George
HOWELL, SAMUEL & CO., (S. Howell, John C. Brennan) grocers, cor Sussex and Rideau
Hoy, Charles, baker, Wellington cor Bay
Huckell, Benjamin, flour and feed, cor Sussex & York
Hughes, W. S., saddler, 6 York
Humphries, George, carriage maker, 45 Daly
HUNTON, THOMAS & WILLIAM, dry goods, cor Sparks and Metcalfe
Hurley, J., green grocer, 42 York
Hurtibise, R., painter, Cumberland
HUTCHISON, DR. GEORGE., dentist, 41½ Sparks (see adv)
Iliffe, Thomas, baker, Dalhousie
IMPERIAL FIRE INSURANCE COMPANY OF LONDON, ENG.; Donald M, Grant, agent, Elgin (see card.)
INSTITUT CANADIEN FRANCAIS D'OTTAWA, Sussex
Irvine, George, innkeeper, Wellington
ISAAC, THOMAS, furnishing ironmonger, Sparks, (see card)
Jackson, Lieut.-Col., Brigade Major, Militia Department
JAMIESON, R. E. & J. C., grocers & bakers, Victoria Terrace
Johnson, F. W., flour and produce, Hull
Johnson, Rev. J. (Church of England), Hull
Johnson & Shaw, general merchants, Hull
Johnston, Rev. J. (Church of England), Hull
Johnston & Law (Joseph and John), shingle factory, Queen
Jolicœur, Octave, shoemaker, 67 Rideau
Jones, Alfred, vice-president B. A. Bank Note Co., Princes' Terrace
Jones, Rev. T. B., L.L.D. (Church of England), rector St. Albans
JONES & HOLLAND (S. J. & George C.), news agents and booksellers, Post Office block
Jordan, John, policeman
Joyce, Edward F., picture and fancy goods, 105 Rideau
Kavanagh, M., Queen's Restaurant, Wellington cor Metcalfe
Kavanagh, Timothy, flour dealer, 54 Rideau
Kaye, Thomas, watchmaker, 246 Wellington
KEARNS & RYAN (Peter Kearns and J. H. Ryan), dry goods, &c., cor Sussex and York
Keefer, Augustus, barrister, Queen
Kehoe, John, blacksmith, Nicholas
Kehoe, William, blacksmith, George
KELTY, A. C., manager Bank of British North America, Wellington
Kenly, Robert, cooper, Queen
Kenly, Robert, jun., watchmaker and jeweler, 33 Sparks
Kennedy, John, butcher, Byward market
Kennedy, Patrick, butcher, Rideau
KERR, DAWSON, prop. *Volunteer Review*
Kilby, Francis T. prop. Ontario Saloon, 12 York
Kilduff, P., blacksmith, 34 York
Killeen, John A., tobacconist, Rideau
Kipp, Wilfred, stoves and tinware, Duke
KIRBY, THOMAS H., (C. W. Bangs & Co)
Labelle, Henry, hotel keeper, 41 York
Laberge, O., hotel keeper, Murray
Lacey, Thomas, butcher, By Ward Market
Lachance, Samuel, butcher, By Ward Market
Lamb, W. A., boots and shoes. 28 Sussex
Langford, John, builder
Langlois, Edward, inn keeper, St. Patrick
Langrell, Thomas, chief of police
Lapierre, E. A., groceries and liquors, Rideau
Lapierre, F. X., prop. Beaver Hotel, 75 Sussex
LAPIERRE, HORACE, barrister, &c., cor Sussex and York
Lapierre, R., merchant tailor, 106 Sussex

Lapointe, Moses, fish dealer, Market Square
Laporte, Victor, prop. Farmers' Inn, grocer Rideau
La Rèvière, B. B., prop. Canada Hotel, Sussex
Latchford, James, grocer, Victoria Terrace
Latimer, William, boots and shoes, Wellington
Latremouille, Octave, clothier, 152 Sussex
Lauder, Rev. J. S., M.A., (Church of England), rector Christ's Church, Sparks
Laurie, S., boots and shoes, 39 Sussex
Lawrence, R., jr., boots and shoes, 4 York
LEAVENS, D. R., coal oil, lamps, watches, jewelry, &c.
LE CANADA, (tri-weekly) Duvernay Bros., publishers, 26 York
LE DUC, JOHN B., prop. Duke House, Duke
L'Hôpital Generale, under the supervision of the Sisters of Charity, Nunnery
Lee, J. S., customs clerk
Lee & Dawson (Thomas and William) saddlers 55 Rideau
LEES & GEMMELL, (Robert Lees, John J. Gemmell) barristers, etc., Court House
Leblanc, Joseph, hotel keeper, 120 Sussex
Leblanc, Pierre, innkeeper, St. Patrick
Leclaire, Theophile, butcher, cor Dalhousie and St. Andrew
Leggo, Christopher, M. D., Rideau
Leggo & Mondelet (John Leggo, Charles Mondelet) dentists, Sparks
Lessard, David, grocer, Bolton
Lesslie, John, watchmaker, 25 Sparks
LESLIE, THOMAS G., secretary and treasurer St. Lawrence and Ottawa Railroad Company, Sparks
LETT, W. P., City clerk
Levielle, Arsene, butcher, Byward Market
Lewis & Pinhey, (John B. Lewis, Charles H. Pinhey) barristers, Elgin
Lindsay, W. B., Clerk House of Commons, opp St. Patrick's Hall
LINK, NICHOLAS, book keeper, Hamilton Bros., Cathcart
Litle, John, landing waiter
Lockwood, A., photographer, Sparks
Logan, George, M. D., O'Connor
Long, James & Co., painters, Duke
Loucks, H. L., produce, Hull
Loyer, Paul, builder, Bolton
LYON, ROBERT, M. P. P
LYON & REMON, (Robert Lyon, M. P. P., Edward P. Remon, barristers, solicitors Ontario Bank, and Canada Permanent Building and Savings Society, Elgin
Lyons, John, grocer, 28 York
McAmmond, John, innkeeper Wellington
McCAFFREY, WILLIAM, hotel keeper, York
McCarron, James, builder, Bolton
McCarthy, James, general merchant, Wellington
McCarthy, John, tailor, Queen
McClelland, Samuel, innkeeper, York
McComb, Mrs. E. A., fancy goods, Sussex
McCormick, Andrew, grocer, 63 Sparks
McCormick, Henry, flour mill, Hull
McCormick, H., miller and grain dealer, 65 Sparks
McCormick, Mrs. William, millinery, 83 Rideau
McCracken, James, agent H. Atkinson & Co., Metcalf Square
McCULLOUGH, HENRY, superintendent British Lion Hotel
McCullough, James, tannery, Park
McCullough, R., grocer, Bank
McDonald, Bros., auctioneers, Sussex
McDONALD & CO., proprietors St. Lawrence Dye Works
McDougal, Lieut.-Col. P. L., District Paymaster Militia Department, Augusta
McDOUGAL & CO. (Francis & A. R. McDougal) hardware merchants, 33 Sussex
McDOUGALL, HON. WILLIAM, C.B., Minister of Public Works, Daly
McEdward, G., book-keeper H. Atkikson & Co., 19 George
McFarlane, John, grocer, Rideau
McFarlane, William, marble works, Rideau
McGee, Mrs. F., innkeeper St. Patrick
McGILLIVRAY, DONALD, M.D., 128 Wellington
McGILLIVRAY, EDWARD, general merchant, 269 Wellington
McGilton, Thomas, boots and shoes, Mosgrove
McGREEVY, ROBERT H., builder and contractor, Rideau
McIsaac, John, Grand River Hotel, cor Sussex and Clarence
McKay, Thomas, Ottawa grist mills and flour and feed merchant, 132 Sussex
McKAY, WILLIAM, house and decorative painter, importer paper hangings, 43 Rideau (see adv)
McKechnie, Mrs., grocer, Rideau
McKenna, Mrs., saloon, 66 Sparks
McKever, Patrick, butcher, By Ward Market
McKINNON, NEIL, commission and exchange broker and insurance agent, 41½ Sparks
McLARDY, H. J., editor *Citizen*
McLaughlin, R., wood turner, Sussex
McLEAN, HECTOR, auctioneer and land agent, 13 Sparks
McMaster, D., saddler, York
McNaughton, Capt. Malcolm, agent Sincennes & McNaughton, (Montreal) Canal basin
McNutt, C. S., assistant Crown Timber agent, Queen
McPhail, Rev. D., (Baptist)
McVittie, William, policeman
McWade, Daniel, shoemaker, Duke
MacAgy, W. A., Appraiser Customs, preventive officer and warehouseman
MacCarthy, H. F., druggist, 236 Wellington
MACDONALD & CO., St. Lawrence Dye Works, Elgin
Macdonell, Æneas, M.D., Rideau
Mackay, Thomas, merchant miller, Chaudiere Island
Mackenzie, Andrew, M.D.
MACPHERSON, KENNEDY & CHRISTIE (James Macpherson, George Kennedy & A. J. Christie), barristers, Elgin
Manuel, John, clerk Gilmour & Co.
Mars, Edward A., arcihtect, Rideau
MARSTON, G. J., Postmaster, Hull
Martel, John Byward Market
Martin, Dr. C. A., surgeon dentist, 53 Sussex
Martin, James & Co., grocers, Sussex
MARTIN, DR. OLIVER, surgeon dentist, 48 Sparks (see adv)
Martin, Thomas, flour dealer, 69 Rideau
MARTINEAU, EUGENE, dry goods and clothing, cor Sussex and Clarence
Martineau, Mrs. Margaret, innkeeper, Murray
Mason, John, builder and contractor, Sandy Hill
Mason, R. & G., saw mills, cor Montreal and Bridge
Mason, William, boat builder, Chaudiere Island
MASSEY, W. M., chemist and druggist, 28 Sparks (see adv)
Masson, A., flour and feed, Wellington
Matheson, W. M., barrister, Elgin
MATHEWS, THOMAS, prop. Mathews' Hotel, York
Matthewman & Co., painters, Elgin
May, George, leather and findings, 31 Sussex
Meadows, H. & Co., stoves, &c., 35 Sussex
MECHANICS' INSTITUTE AND ATHENÆUM; Edward Stacey, librarian, Sparks
Merrill, Thomas, superintendent Ottawa River Works

Metcalfe, Joseph, dry goods, 59 Sparks
Miller, David, hoop skirt and corset manufacturer, 43 Sparks
Miles, Edmund, lessee theatre, music dealer, &c., Wellington
Mills, J. C., fruit dealer, 60 Sparks
Mills, Willaim, account ordnance, George
Minore, William, city express, Queen cor O'Connor
MITCHELL, CHAS. W., foreman *Times*, Bank
Moisan, J. B., tanner, Church
Montgomery, J., innkeeper, Wellington
MONTGOMERY, R. S., saddle and harness maker, 59 Rideau
MONTREAL AND OTTAWA FORWARDING CO.; D. Murphy, agent, Canal Basin
MONTREAL TELEGRAPH CO.; N. W. Bethune, agent, Metcalfe
Mooney, Joseph, insurance and general commission agent, Sparks
MOORE, DAVID, lumber merchant, 12 York
Moore, Rev. William (Free Church)
MORRISON, W., prop. Ottawa City Flour mills, Duke
Mortimer, A. bookbinder and paper ruler, Metcalfe
MORTIMER, GEORGE, chemist and druggist, 41 Sussex
MOSGROVE & TAILLON (William Mosgrove and George Taillon), barristers, 41 Rideau
Mowat, A. & Son, merchant tailors, 30 Sussex
Mullin, Bernard, dry goods and clothing
MURPHY, D., agent Montreal and Ottawa Forwarding Co
Murphy, George, boots and shoes, 20 York
MURPHY, JOSEPH J., attorney-at-law, solicitor, &c., 18 Rideau
Murray, Mrs., billiard saloon, Metcalfe
MUSGROVE, JOHN M., prop. Ottawa business college, Sparks
Mutual Building Society of Ottawa, H. McCormick, pres., James Egleson, sec. and treas
Naubert, A., general dealer, Sussex
Nellis, Thomas F., barrister, solicitor Quebec Bank, Metcalfe
Nelson, Thomas, boots and shoes, 333 Wellington
Newbanks, William, hotel keeper, York
Noel, H. V., manager Quebec Bank
North British and Mercantile Ins. Co., George P. Drummond, agent, 19 Sparks
Notman, William, photographer, cor Wellington and Metcalfe
Nye, L. N., tobacconist, fruits, &c., 43 Sussex
O'CONNOR, DANIEL, barrister, Rideau
O'Connor, John R., contractor, Duke
O'Connor, William, prop Ottawa Hotel, Clarence
O'CONNOR & WALLER, (R. E. O'Connor and W. H. Waller) ins. agents, brokers, and commission merchants, 27 Sussex (see adv)
O'GARA, MARTIN, barrister, police magistrate, Rideau
O'Gara, Michael, grocer, cor Dalhousie and St. Patrick
O'HANLY, J. L. P., P.L.S., C. E. Railway, practice office, Elgin cor Sparks
O'Hara & Whelan, (John and Peter) grocers, Duke
O'Keefe, Dennis, policeman
O'Meara, P., saloon keeper, Rideau
O'MEARA & CO., dry goods and clothing, 50 Sparks
O'Neil, E. J., detective
O'Neill, John, grocer, St. Andrew
O'Reilly, J., grocer, Church
Offord, Jonathan, boots and shoes, 68 Sparks
OLD RED LION HOTEL, R. Gilpin, proprietor, Little Sussex (see adv)
Oliver & Annable, cabinet makers, Chaudiere Island
ONTARIO BANK, William McWade, manager, S. A. McMurty, teller, J. J. Little, ledger keeper, cor Sparks and Metcalfe
ORME, J. L. & SON, (J. L. & George L. Orme), piano forte, music and fancy goods, next to J. Durie & Son, 8 Sparks
OTTAWA BOARD OF TRADE, Hon. James Skead, president
OTTAWA BUSINESS COLLEGE, John Musgrove, principal, Sparks
OTTAWA CANCER INFIRMARY, O. C. Wood, M.D., Maria (see adv)
OTTAWA CITIZEN, (daily and weekly), I. B. Taylor, proprietor, Rideau
OTTAWA GAS CO., Edward McGillivray, president, C. L. Fellowes, secretary, office 19 Sparks
Ottawa Permanent Building Society, James Fraser, president, Wm. Hay, secretary, Sparks
OTTAWA TIMES, (daily and weekly), Alexander Robertson, editor, 36 Sparks
Owens, Arthur, butcher, 72 Rideau
Painter, Thomas, stone cutter, Albert
Palmer, Henry A., toys and fancy goods, Rideau
Papillon, S., grocer, cor Church and Dalhousie
Paquette, Henry, boots and shoes, 48 Rideau
Pardey, Mrs. William, boarding house, Wellington
PATTERSON, THOMAS, groceries and liquors, 26 Rideau (see adv)
Peacock, James, hatter and furrier, 28 Rideau
Peltier, Herrick, tinware, 70 Clarence
Pennock, J. T. & William, solicitors for patent and copyrights, insurance agents and exchange brokers, 19½ Sparks
Perkins, Edward L., foundry, Sparks
Perkins, H. B., grocer, Wellington
PERLEY & PATTEE, (William G. Perley, Gordon B. Pattee), lumber merchants, Head
Perry, G. H., city engineer, secretary Association Lumber Manufacturers
Philion, Alexis, carding mill, Montreal, L. B. F.
Pichet, T., innkeeper, St. Patrick
Pickett, Rev., T. W., (Methodist Episcopal) Le Breton's Flats
Pidgeon, Thomas C., contractor, Cathcart
Pinard, Alophe, policeman
Pinard, J. A. & Co., merchant tailors, dry goods, &c., 17 Sussex
Pinard, H. Adolphe, general merchant, Bolton cor Dalhousie
Pipus, George, plasterer, Chapel
Porter, Henry, blacksmith, Hull
Porter, John, P. L. S., 36 Metcalfe
POULIN, PIERRE, groceries and provisions, Market House, Clarence
POULIN, PIERRE & CO., wine merchants, Clarence
Powell, Alexander W., gaoler
POWELL, WILLIAM F., Sheriff County Carleton, Court House
Pratt, A., dry goods, 60 Sparks
PRESTON, GEORGE H., City collector, dealer in boots and shoes, 12 Rideau
Prodrick, William, confectioner, 38 Sussex
Proulx, Edward, axe factor, Duke
Pudvin, Francis, butcher, Byward Market
QUEBEC BANK, H. V. Noel, manager; Octavius Newcombe, assistant; C. V. Noel, teller; Thos. MacKinnon, ledger keeper; A. Green, clerk, Wellington
Quignan, Mrs., boarding house, cor Bank and Sparks
Quinn, Hugh, grocer, Ottawa
Raitt, J., tailor, Wellington
Rajotte, T., merchant tailor, 34 Sparks
Rathier, Abraham, hotel keeper and grocer, cor Bolton and Cumberland

RAY, C. C., agent Canada Express Company, Elgin
Reardon, W. & R., broom and brush manufacturers, York
Rebeul, Rev., (Roman Catholic), Hull
Registry office, County Carleton, Edward Sherwood, Registrar, cor Nicholas and Daly
Reliance Mutual Insurance Company, N. McKinnon, agent, 41½ Sparks
REVERE HOUSE, Buck & Sanger, proprietors, cor Rideau and Ottawa
Rice, Daniel, barber, 81 Sussex
Richardson, John G., President Canada Railway Co.
Richardson, Robert, butcher, Wellington Market
RIDEAU CANAL OFFICE, J. D. Slater, superintendent, 126 Wellington
Rideau Club, 200 Wellington
RIGGS, ALEXANDER, editor and proprietor *The United Service Gazette*, Besserer
Riopell, Andrew, hotel keeper, 120 Sussex
Robert, Stanislaus, butcher, 87 Rideau
Roberts, C. E., P.L.S., C. E., Hull
Roberts, Rev. E. J. (Apostolic) Hull
Roberts, John, druggist, Rideau
ROBERTSON, ALEX., editor, *Times*, Besserer
Robertson, A., tobacconist, Elgin
ROBERTSON N., merchant tailor, opposite Russell House (see adv)
Robillard, A., M.D., York
Robinson & Co. (James G. Robinson and John Hill) grocers, Sussex
Rochester, John, tannery and shingle factory, Richmond Road
Rochester, J. & J., brewers, Richmond Road
Rochon, Flavien, carver, St. Patrick
RODNEY, B. B., merchant tailor
Rogers, Samuel, cabinet maker and upholsterer, 70 Rideau
Rogers, Samuel, cabinet maker, Wellington
Roos, John, tobacconist, 26½ Sparks
Ross, Hugh, grocer, Wellington
Ross, Roderick, high bailiff
Ross, Thomas, issuer marriage licenses
ROSS & PARSONS, (Alex. Ross and Albert Parsons) attorneys, solicitors, etc., Elgin
Routh, Edward, Assistant City Clerk
Rowet, John, contractor, Duke
Rowe, Amos, auctioneer and commission merchant, 42 Rideau
Roy, Augustin, hotel keeper, 12 St. Patrick
Roy, Leon, saloon, 79 Sussex
ROYAL CANADIAN BANK; C. B. Grasett, accountant; W. Kavanagh, clerk, 11 Sparks
Russell, A. J., agent and inspector of Crown Timber Agencies, Canada, office, Hugh cor Queen
Russell, George H., upholsterer, William
Russell, Lindsay, P.L.S.
Russell, William, gunsmith, 59 York
RUSSELL HOUSE; James A. Gouin, proprietor Sparks cor Elgin
RYAN, CARROLL, editor *Volunteer Review*
Salmon, James, hotel, York
SATCHELL, BROTHERS (Charles and Francis), butchers, Byward Market
Scott, Mrs. A., fruits and confectionary, 15 Sparks
SCOTT, R. W., M.P.P.
SCOTT & ROSS (R. W. Scott, M.P.P. and W. A. Ross), barristers, Elgin (see card)
SEALE, GEORGE; Ottawa Cabinet Warehouse, Rideau
Schofield, William, Deputy Registrar, Co. Carleton
Sharon, V., hairdresser, 126 Sussex
Shearer, John, builder and contractor, Wilbrod
Sheldon, George A., hatter and furrier, 26 Sparks
Sherwood, Edward, Registrar, cor Nicholas and Daly
Shouldis, George, baker, 186 York
Simon & Campbell, general merchants, Hull
Sinclair, C. J., books and stationery, 240 Wellington
Sinclair, Donald, P.L.S., Bank
Sinclair, Duncan, P.L.S.
SKEAD, HON. JAMES, lumber merchant, Duke and Chaudiere Island
SKEAD, ROBERT, lumber merchant, Sparks
Skinner, Joseph, druggist, 242 Wellington
SLATER, JAMES D., P.L.S., superintendent Rideau canal, Wellington
Slattery, Miles, grocer, 68 Clarence
Slattery, William, butcher, By Ward Market
SLEEMAN, JOSEPH (A Campbell & Co.)
Slocombe & Stevens, tavern, Rideau
SMILLIE, WILLIAM C., President B. A. Bank Note Co., Victoria
Smith, Gustave, music teacher, cor Rideau and King
Smith, J. C., carriage maker, Bank
SMITH, JAMES, butcher, By Ward Market
Smith, James W., butcher, By Ward Market
Smith, W. A. D., woodturner, Cumberland
SMITH, W. G., book-keeper Queen's Printing-Office, Victoria Terrace
Smith, Thomas, merchant tailor
Soucy, Clement, second-hand broker, 15 Clarence
SPARKS, NICHOLAS, barrister, attorney, solicitor, &c., Elgin (see adv).
Sparks, Robert, P.L.S., Elgin
Spencer, E., photographer, 24 Sparks
Sproule, Thomas, deputy registrar, Elgin
St. Andrew's Society, James Fraser, president, J. P. Robertson, secretary
St. Jacques, Frank H., book-keeper Union House
St. Jacques, M. H., hotel, 128 Sussex
St. Jean, P., M.D., St. Patrick
St. Jean Baptiste Society, George E. Desbarats, president
St. Joseph's Academy, Sister Olier, directoress, Daly
St. Joseph's Orphan Home, Sister Thibodeau, directoress, cor Sussex and Cathcart
ST. LAWRENCE DYE WORKS, Macdonald & Co., Elgin
ST. LAWRENCE AND OTTAWA RAILWAY COMPANY, Thomas Reynolds, managing director, office, Sparks
St. Louis Hotel, Church
St. Mary's Academy—under the supervision of the Grey Sisters; Sister Mary of the Immaculate Conception, Superioress, Wellington
St. Pierre, Adolphe, innkeeper, Murray
Stacpoole, John Massy, farmer
Stapledon, John & Philip, builders, Gloucester
Star Life Assurance Society of London, England, George P. Drummond, agent, 19 Sparks
Starmer, Thomas, boots and shoes, Rideau
Starrs, Michael, proprietor Ottawa House, Clarence
STEPHENS, A. J. & Co., boots and shoes, 51 Sparks
Stephen, R. W., sewing machine agent, 37 Sparks
Stiff, Brothers, (Thomas P. and Phil S.) photographers, 56 Sparks
Stockdale, John, livery, Queen,
Stoddart, Capt., District Quarter-master, Militia Department
Stone, Rev. S. G., (Methodist Episcopal)
Storey, George, general merchant, Clarence
STOREY, THOMAS, merchant tailor, 59 Sussex
Sullivan, John, grocer, St. Patrick
SUTHERLAND, GEORGE S., watchmaker, leader Sutherland's Brass and String Band, 63 Rideau
Sutherland, William, merchant tailor, 61 Rideau
Sutton, James T., commission agent, Sussex
Swalwell, Anthony, cabinet maker, 35 Sparks
Sweetland, John, M. D., Mosgrove

Sweetman, John, dyer, Sparks
Tackaberry, I. B., auctioneer, commission merchant, real estate agent, &c., 36 Rideau
Taylor, Alexander, hotel keeper, 84 Clarence
TAYLOR, I. B., proprietor *Citizen* and stationer
Taylor, James M., station agent, St. L. and O. R
Taylor, William, carding mill, Montreal L. B. F
Terrance, John, butcher, Byward Market
Tetreau, N., Notary, Hull
Thayer, J. & Co., groceries and provisions, Duke
Thistle, W. R., P. L. S., C. E., cor Sparks & Metcalfe
Thompson, James, dry goods and clothing, 55 Sussex
Thompson, John, groceries and provisions, 27 Rideau
Thompson, T. W., solicitor, Elgin
Thompson, W. H., City Chamberlain, City Hall
TIMES PRINTING AND PUBLISHING CO., James Cotton, managing director, 38 Sparks
Todd, Samuel, policeman
Topley, W. J., agent W. Notman
Toronto House, Mrs. Trotter, proprietress, 71 Sparks
Townsend, Charles, blacksmith, Pooley's Bridge
Tracy, James, watchmaker, 19 Rideau
Tracy, William, watchmaker, 14 York
Traunweiser, F., jeweler, Sparks
Traversy, Isidore, general merchant, 94 Sussex
Trayler, Alfred, builder, Rideau
Trudell, J. B., baker, Hull
Turgeon, N., photographer
Turner, Frederick E., photographer, 83 Rideau
UNION FORWARDING & RAILWAY CO., R. S. Cassels, pres. and manager, H. Chepmell, sec., Wellington
UNION HOUSE, George Armstrong, prop., cor Queen and Elgin
UNITED SERVICE GAZETTE, Alexander Riggs, editor and proprietor, 36 Sparks
UNIVERSITY OF OTTAWA, Rev. Pierre Tabaret O. M. I., principal
Valvade, F. X., M.D., St. Patrick opp Bishop's
Valiquette, Joseph, boots and shoes 88 Sussex
VALIQUETTE & POITRAS, (Joseph Valiquette and Peter Poitras) tin and coppersmiths, stove dealers &c., 48 Rideau
Van Courtlandt, Edward, M.R.C.S., Eng., consulting Physician, Protestant Hospital
Vermette, Jean Baptiste, grocer, Murray
Victoria Terrace, Richmond Road
Volunteer Review, (Monday) D. Kerr, prop., Carroll Ryan, editor, Rideau
WADE, WILLIAM, manager, Ontario Bank
WALKER & PENNOCK (W. H. Walker and P. Pennock) barristers, etc., Rideau (see adv)
WALL, WILLIAM, groceries and liquors, cor Nicholas and Rideau
Wallingford, George, butcher, By Ward Market
Ward, J. W., barrister, Elgin
Wardrope, Rev. Thomas (Free Church) Pastor Knox's Church
Warnock, James, flour and feed dealer, 82 Sussex
Warren, Mrs., fruits, oysters, etc., 107 Rideau
Warwicker, Thomas, saddler, 319 Wellington
Washburn, Sexton, axe factory, Chaudiere Island
Webster, John, buildier, Ottawa
Western Assurance Co. of Canada, George P. Drummond, agent, 19 Sparks
Whalley & Sharp, contractors and masons
Whelan, Denis, grocer, 44 Rideau
White, George, blacksmith, Queen
White, John, carver, Hull
White M., shoemaker, 41 Sparks
Whiteside, H. & Co., manfrs. childrens' carriages, 64 Rideau
Whitty, James, hotel keeper, 12 Murray
White, James J., books and stationery, 34 Rideau
Wigmore, J., confectioner, Wellington
Wills, William J., immigation agent, Metcalfe
Wilson, A., Chief Clerk, St. L. & O. R., Sparks
Wilson, John, Master and Deputy Registrar, Court House
Wilson, L., Treasurer County Council, Court House
Wily, Lieut. Col. Thomas, commaudant, Daly
Wolff, James F. W., M.D., Albert
WOOD, O. C., M.D., cancer infirmary, 41½ Sparks (see adv.)
Wood & Rossiter (Wm. C. Wood and W. M. Rossiter) groceries and liquors, 38 Rideau
Woodland, Richard, tannery, St. Paul
Woodland, Stewart, butcher, Wellington
Woodland, Thomas, butcher, Wellington
Woods, Mrs., meat market, Wellington
WORKMAN, ALEXANDER, & CO., general hardware, manfrs. agents, 30 Rideau and Wellington (see adv.)
Wright, Alonzo, M.P., Hull
Wright, C. B. water lime works, Hull
Wright, Philemon, saddler, Hull
Wright, P. W., shingle factory, Hull
Wright & Lynott, butchers, Hull
Wright, T. C., prop. Wright House, Hull
Wright, William McKay, barrister, Hull
Wright & Batson, steam saw mill, Hull
Yielding, John, butcher, 65 Rideau
Young, James, foreman bindery *Canada Gazette*
YOUNG, RIGHT HONORABLE SIR JOHN, BART, P.C., K.C.B., G.C., M.G., Governor General Dominion of Canada, residence Rideau Hall
Young, John, grocer, cor St. Andrew & Cumberland
Young, Levi, proprietor saw mills, Middle
Young, Bronson & Co., flour mills, Le Breton Flats
Young & Radford, (William & J. J.), watchmakers, 30 Sparks

OTTAWA CLASSIFIED BUSINESS DIRECTORY.

Marked thus * are Wholesale.

Agent (Emigration).
Wills, William J., Metcalfe

Agents (General).
Christie, Samuel, Russell House block
Clemow, Francis, 19 Sparks
Dole, A. M., Sussex
Fisher, Benjamin, 134 Sussex
Mooney, Joseph, Sparks
Sutton, James T., Sussex

Agents (Patent Rights & Parliamentary).
Codd & Co., Elgin.
Grist, Henry, Elgin cor Sparks
Pennock, J. T. & William, 19½ Sparks

Architects.
Arnoldi, King, Metcalfe
Billings, Bradish, Elgin
Brown, John, Hull
Fripp, Sidney B., Wellington
Mara, Edward A., Rideau

Auctioneers.
Birmingham, James, 72 Sussex
McDonald & Brother, Sussex
McLean, Hector, 18 Sparks
Rowe, Amos, 42 Rideau
Tackaberry, I. B., 36 Rideau

Axe Makers.

Gravelle, H., Hull
Proulx, Edward, Duke
Washburn, Sexton, Chaudiere Island

Bakers.

Delure, Charles, Hull
Gundry, Charles, Hull
Hoy, Charles, Wellington
Iliffe, Thomas, Dalhousie
Jamieson, R. E. & J. C., Victoria Square
Shouldis, George, 186 York
Trudell, J. B., Hull
Warnock, James, 82 Sussex

Banks.

British North America, A. C. Kelty, manager, Wellington
Montreal, Andrew Drummond, manager, Wellington
Ontario, William Wade, manager, Sparks cor Metcalfe
Quebec, H. V. Noel, manager
Royal Canadian, 77 Sparks

Bank Note Engravers.

British American Co., W. C. Smillie, President, Wellington

Barristers, Attorneys, Solicitors, &c.

Bearman, Edward, County Attorney
Boulton, J. F., Sparks
Bradley, R. A., Elgin
Dunning, A. J., Court House
Fellowes, G. B. L., Q.C., Metcalfe square
Gibb, Alexander, Rideau
Haycock, R. H., Elgin
Hicks, Robert, jun., Elgin
Keefer, Augustus, Queen
Lapierre, Horace, Sussex cor York
Lees & Gemmill, Court House
Lewis & Pinhey, Elgin
Lyon & Remon, Elgin
Macpherson, Kennedy & Christie, Elgin
Matheson, W. M., Elgin
Mosgrove & Taillon, 41 Rideau
Murphy, Joseph, 18 Rideau
Nellis, Thomas E., Metcalfe
O'Connor, Daniel, Rideau
O'Gara, Martin, Rideau
Ross & Parsons, Elgin
Scott & Ross, Elgin
Sparks, Nicholas, Elgin
Thompson, T. W., Elgin
Walker & Pennock, Rideau
Ward, J. W., 15 Elgin
Wilson, John, Court House
Wright, W. McKay, Hull

Boatbuilders.

Cockburn, John, Chaudiere Island
Mason, William, Chaudiere Island

Book and Job Printers.

Bell & Woodburn, Elgin
Hunter, Rose & Co., Sparks

Bookbinders and Blank Book Manufacturers.

Desbarats, George E.
Hope, James & Co., Sparks cor Elgin
Hunter, Rose & Co., Sparks
Mortimer, A., 38 Metcalfe

Booksellers and Stationers.

Crane, G. W., Wellington
Desbarats, George, Desbarats' buildings
Durie, John & Son, Sparks
Duvernay, Brothers, 26 York
Hauser, A., 56 Sparks
Jones & Holland, Post Office block
Sinclair, C. J., 240 Wellington
Whyte, James J., 34 Rideau

Boots and Shoes, Manufacturers & Dealers

Angus, William, 236 Wellington
Angus & Huckell, 15 Sussex
Bellemare, T., 67 Sussex
Carson & Wilson, Duke
Cuzner, Luke, 29 Rideau
Durocher, Oliver, 77 Sussex
Feeley, George, Hull
Foisey, A., Sussex
Grennier, J. B., Hull
Groulx, Toussaint, 67 Sussex
Grubert, Brothers, Elgin
Howe, George & Son, 10 Rideau
Howe, & Son, Rideau
Jolicoeur, Octave, 67 Rideau
Lamb, W. A., 28 Sussex
Latimer, William, Wellington
Laurie, S., 39 Sussex
Lawrence, R., jr., 4 York
McGilton, Thomas, Mosgrove
McWade, Daniel, Duke
Murphy, George, 20 York
Nelson, Thomas, 333 Wellington
Offord, Jonathan, 68 Sparks
Paquette, Henry, 48 Rideau
Preston, George H., 12 Rideau
Starmer, Thomas, Rideau
Stephens, A. J. & Co., 51 Sparks
Valiquette, Joseph, 88 Sussex
White, M., 41 Sparks

Brewers and Maltsters.

Brading, H. & Co., George
Rochester, J. & J., Richmond Road

Builders and Contractors.

Dow, Donald, Besserer
Gallagher, Thomas, Metcalfe
Langford, John
Loyer, Paul, Bolton
McCarron, James, Bolton
McGreevy, Robert H., Rideau
Mason, John, Sandy Hill
O'Connor, John, Duke
Pigeon, Thomas, Cathcart
Rowat, John, Duke
Shearer, John, Wilbrod
Stapledon, John and Phillip, Gloucester
Trayler, Alfred, Rideau
Webster, John, Ottawa
Whalley & Sharp

Cabinet Makers, Upholsterers, &c.

Angus & Son, 22 Rideau
Haram, Robert, Rideau
Harris & Campbell, Sussex
Oliver & Annable, Chaudiere Island
Rogers, Samuel, Wellington
Russell, George H., William
Ottawa Cabinet Warehouse, George Seale, Rideau
Swalwell, Anthony, 35 Sparks

Carding and Fulling Mills.

Bison, Moise, Hull
Philion, Alexis, Montreal
Taylor, William, Montreal

Carriage Makers.

Cavillier, X., Hull
Champagne, Seraphin, 96 Clarence
Cummings, Robert, Cumming's Island
Dufour, Peter, 144 Rideau
Duhamel, Louis, Murray
Evans, Jeremiah, cor Sparks and Bank
Humphries, George, 45 Daly
Smith, J. C., Bank
Whitesides, H. & Co., 64 Rideau

Chemists and Druggists.

Browne, James, 67 Sparks
Davidson & Daniel, 41 Rideau
Featherston, J. P., 57 Sussex
Hearn, William, 22 York
MacCarthy, H. F., 236 Wellington
Massey, W. M., 28 Sparks
Mortimer, George, 41 Sussex
Roberts, John, Rideau
Skinner, Joseph, 242 Wellington

Coal Oil, Lamps, &c.

Chalmers & Co., 62 Sparks
Leavens, D. R., 73 Rideau

Commission Merchants.

Boyden, Joseph, 34 Rideau
Christie, S., Russell House Block
Coward, D. W. & Co., 17 Sparks
Cruice, R. W., Sparks
Easton, W. H. & Co., Canal Basin
Herrick, Brush & Co., Rideau
McDonald, Bros., Sussex
Mooney, Joseph, Russell House Block
O'Connor & Waller, 27 Sussex

Commission, Forwarding and Shipping Merchants.

Dickinson, M. K., Sussex
Easton, W. H. & Co., Canal Basin
McNaughton, Captain Malcolm (Sincennes & McNaughton), Canal Basin
Murphy, D., Montreal and Ottawa Forwarding Line, Canal Basin
Sutton, James T., agent Ottawa River Navigation Co., Queen's wharf
Union Forwarding and Railway Company, R. S. Cassels, president, 183 Wellington

Confectioners, Wholesale.—*(See also Bakers.)*

Bartlett, George, 37 Sussex
Buckley, William, Wellington
Cussans, Henry, 60 Rideau
Fest, Mrs., Rideau
Hall, Edward, Wellington
Prodrick, William, 36 Sussex
Wigmore, J., Wellington

Dentists.

Beckett, Dr. J. A., 10 Sparks
Hutchison, Dr. George, 41½ Sparks
Leggo & Mondelet, Sparks
Martin, Dr. C. A., 53 Sussex
Martin, Dr. Oliver, 48 Sparks

Dry Goods, Clothing, Millinery, &c.

Blyth, G. R., 234 Wellington
Caldwell, J. F. & Co., 72 Sussex
Cunningham & Lindsay, 14 Rideau
Egleson, Mrs., Rideau
Elliott & Hamilton, Rideau
Fingland & Draper, 9 & 11 Sussex
Frazer, James, 52 Sussex
Garland, Mutchmor & Co., 20 Sparks
Graham, Archibald & Co., 48 Sparks
Grant & Henderson, 20 Rideau
Higginson, James, 47 Sussex
Hunter, Thomas, & Son, Sparks cor Metcalfe
Kearns & Ryan, Sussex cor York
McCormick, Mrs. William, 83 Rideau
Magee & Russell, 29 Sparks
Martineau, Eugene, Sussex cor Clarence
Metcalfe, Joseph, 59 Sparks
Mullin, Bernard, Duke
O'Meara & Co., 50 Sparks
Pinard, J. A. & Co., 17 Sussex
Pratt, A., 60 Sparks
Thompson, James, 55 Sussex

Dye Works.

McDonald & Co., Elgin
Sweetman, John, Sparks

Engraver.

Cox, George, Elgin cor Sparks

Exchange and Money Brokers.

Coward, D. W. & Co., 17 Sparks
Drummond, George P., 19 Sparks
Herrick, Brush & Co., 3 Rideau
McKinnon, Neil, 4½ Sparks
O'Connor & Waller, 27 Sussex
Pennock, J. T. & William, 19½ Sussex

Express Companies.

Canadian Express Co.; C. C. Ray, agent, 10 Elgin
Minore, Wm., City Express, Queen cor O'Connor
Whiteside, H. & Co., City Express

Fancy Goods.

Boyden, Joseph, 34 Sussex
Chalmers & Co., 62 Sparks
Joyce, Edward F., 125 Rideau
Leslie, John, 25 Sparks
McComb, Mrs. E. A., Sussex
Orme, J. L. & Son, 8 Sparks
Palmer, Henry A., Rideau

Flour and Grain Dealers.

Coffey, Thomas, Clarence
Dickinson, M. K., Sussex
Donaldson, R., Hull
Easton, Hiram, Canal Basin
Huckell, Benjamin, Sussex cor York
Jamieson, R. E. & J. C., Victoria Terrace
Johnson, F. W., Hull
Kavanagh, Timothy, 54 Rideau
Loucks, H. L., Hull
McCormick, Henry, Hull
McKay, Thomas, 132 Sussex
Martin, Thomas, 69 Rideau
Masson, A., Wellington
Ottawa City Mills, W. Morrison, prop., Duke
Warnock, James, 82 Sussex
Young, Bronson & Co., Le Breton Flats

Founders and Machinists.

Blasdell, N. S. & Co., Middle
Fleck, Alexander, Wellington
Perkins, Edward L., Sparks

Fruit Dealers.

Mills, J. C., 60 Sparks
Nye, L. L., Sussex
Scott, Mrs. A., 15 Sparks
Warren, Mrs., 107 Rideau

General Merchants—(Those who keep a stock of Groceries, Dry Goods, etc.)

Booth, Robert R., Bridge
Brown, Alfred, 69 Sparks
Chambers, Thomas, Clarence
Dolen, Michael, 38 York
Guerard, J. Bte., Dalhousie, cor Church
Johnson & Shaw, Hull
McCarthy, James, Wellington
McGillivray, Edward, 269 Wellington
Naubert, Amie, Sussex
Pinard, H. Adolphe, Bolton
Simon & Campbell, Hull
Storey, George, Clarence
Traversy, Isidore, 94 Sussex

Grocers, Wholesale.

Bate, C. T. & Co., Canal basin

Grocers, Wholesale and Retail.

Ashfield, John, Duke
Baskerville, George, Duke
Baskerville, Peter, Church
Bate, & Co., 52 Sparks
Beatty, Thomas, Parry
Browne, D. T. & Co., 16 Rideau
Buchanan, James, 222 Wellington
Campbell, A. & Co., 53 Sussex
Ciappy, John, Duke
Collins, Peter, Sussex
Dalglish, George, Wellington
Dalglish & Russell, 213 Wellington
David & Co., Duke
Demaris, Leonard, Murray
Edwards, Solomon, Wellington
Egleson, P. A. & Co., 80 Sussex
Foote, James, Rideau
Gilligan, B., Murray
Graves, Thomas, Wellington
Green, John, Rideau
Howell, Samuel & Co., Sussex cor Rideau
Jamieson, R. E. & J. C., Victoria Terrace
Lapierre, E. A., Rideau
Laporte, Victor, Rideau
Latchford, James, Victoria Terrace
Lyons, John, 28 York
McCormick, Andrew, 23 Sparks
McCullough, R., Bank
McFarlane, John, Rideau
McKechnie, Mrs. Rideau
Martin, James & Co., Sussex
O'Gara, Michael, Dalhousie
O'Hara & Whelan, Duke
O'Neill, John, St. Andrew
O'Reilly, J., Church
Papillon, S., Church
Patterson, Thomas, 26 Rideau
Perkins, H. B., Wellington
Poulin, Pierre, Clarence
Quinn, Hugh, Ottawa
Robinson & Co., Sussex
Ross, Hugh, Wellington
Slattery, Miles, 68 Clarence
Sullivan, John, St. Patrick
Thayer, J. & Co., Duke
Thompson, John, 27 Rideau
Wall, William, Rideau cor Nicholas
Whelan, Denis, 44 Rideau
Wood & Rossiter, 38 Rideau
Young, John, St. Andrew

Hardware, Dealers in

Besserer & Cowan, 18 Rideau
Blyth & Kerr, 25 Rideau
Burkett, Thomas, 24 Rideau
Germain, N., 25 Sussex
Hay, George, 21 Sparks
Isaac, Thomas, Sparks
McDougal & Co., 33 Sussex
Workman, Alex. & Co., Rideau and Wellington

Hatters & Furriers.

Bangs, C. W. & Co., 34 Sussex
Peacock, James, 23 Rideau
Sheldon, George A., 26 Sparks

Hides, Leather, and Findings.

Cuzner, Luke, 29 Rideau
Howe, George & Son, 10 Rideau
May, George, 31 Sussex
Offord, Jonathan, 68 Sparks
Preston, George H., 12 Rideau

Hotels, Taverns and Proprietors.

Albion Hotel, John Graham, prop., Nicholas cor Daly
Barrett, Michael, 44 York
Beaucaire, Benjamin, Murray
Beaver Hotel, F. X., Lapierre, prop., 75 Sussex
British Lion, Weldon Champness, prop., 61 Sparks
Britannia Inn, Francis Hallendel, proprietor, 251 Wellington
Canada Hotel, B. B. La Riviere, Sussex
Cardinal, Felix, York
Carlton, Christopher, Canal Basin
Cassidy, P., York cor Dalhouse
Champagne, Antoine, Murray
Chaudiere Hotel, N. Bertrand, prop., Head
Chevrier, Alexander, St. Patrick
City Hotel, William Graham, Clarence
Commercial Hotel, Robert Elliott, prop., York
Crown, Thomas Brown, 56 Rideau
Darpentier, B., Hull
Duke House; J. D. Le Dac, proprietor, Duke
Exchange; Hugh Fitzpatrick, Hull
Farmer's Inn; Victor Laporte, Rideau
Gilpin, Robert, Little Sussex
Goode's Hotel; Daniel Goode, prop., St. Paul
Gorman, Philip, 58 Clarence
Goulden's Hotel; Sussex
Graham, R., 108 Sussex
Grand River; John McIsaac, Sussex cor Clarence
Grant, Mrs. Jane, George
Hotel Cartier; A. Champague, prop., Murray
International Hotel; Geo. Clark, prop., 5 York
Irvine, George, Wellington
Labelle, Henry, 41 York
Laberge, O., Murray
Lablanc, Joseph, 120 Sussex
Lablanc, Pierre, St. Patrick
Langlois, Edward, St. Patrick
McAmmond, John, Wellington
McCaffrey, William, York
McClelland, Samuel, York
McGee, Mrs. F., St. Patrick
Martineau, Mrs. Margaret, Murray
Mathews, Thomas, York
Montgomery, J., Wellington
Newbanks, William, York
Old Red Lion; R. Gilpin, prop., Little Sussex
Ottawa; William O'Connor, prop., Clarence
Ottawa House, Michael Starrs, Clarence
Pichet, T., t. Patrick
Revere House, Buck & Sanger proprietors
Rideau, Patrick Herbert proprietor, 46 Rideau
Riopell, Andrew, 126 Sussex
Roy, Augustin, 12 St. Patrick
Salmon, James, York

Hotels, Taverns & Proprietors—*(Continued)*

Slocombe & Stevens, Rideau
St. Jacques, M. H., 128 Sussex
St. Lawrence, Andrew Graham prop., Rideau cor Nicholas
St. Louis Louis, Church
St. Pierre, Adolphe, Murray
Taylor, Alexander, 84 Clarence
Union House, Geo. Armstrong, Queen cor Elgin
Whitty, James, 12 Murray
Wright, T. C., Hull

Insurance Companies and Agents.

Cochrane, John, Elgin
Coward, D. W. & Co., 17 Sparks
Drummond, George P., 19 Sparks
Etna of Dublin, (fire and life) N. McKinnon, agent, 41½ Sparks
Grison, Louis A., Sussex cor York
Hartford Fire, W. Wade agent
Herrick, Brush & Co., Rideau
Imperial Fire of London, Donald M. Grant agent Elgin
McKinnon, Neil, 41½ Sparks
Mooney, Joseph, Sparks
North British and Mercantile, George P. Drummond agent, 19 Sparks
O'Connor & Waller, 27 Sussex
Phœnix Life Assurance Company, John Durie & Son, agents, Sparks
Provincial of Canada, Hon. Malcolm Cameron
Reliance Mutual, N. McKinnon, agent, 41½ Sparks
Royal of London, England, Henry J. Friel, agent, Sussex
Star Life of London, England, George P. Drummond, agent, 19 Sparks
Western of Canada, G. P. Drummond, agent, 19 Sparks

Livery and Sale Stables.

Buck, George A., Rideau
Stockdale, John, Queen

Lumber Merchants.

Atkinson, H. & Co., 130 Sussex
Aumond, Joseph, Rideau
Baldwin, A. H. & Co., Chaudiere Island
Booth, John R., Chaudiere Island
Bronsons & Weston, Middle
Burstall, Edward, 134 Sussex
Candell & Co., Hull
Currier, J. M., New Edinburgh
Dickinson, M. K., Sussex
Easton, Hiram, Canal Basin
Eddy, A. B., Hull
Gilmour & Co., Wellington
Graham, William, Gloucester Township
Hamilton, Bros., Sussex
Mason, R. & G., Montreal cor Bridge
Moore, David, 12 York
Perley & Pattee, Head
Skead, Hon. James, Chaudiere Island
Skead, Robert, Sparks
Wright & Batson, Hull
Young, Levi, Middle

Merchant Tailors and Clothiers.

Barrett, James, Hull
Beament, Thomas & Co., 25 Sparks
Caldwell, J. F. & Co., 72 Sussex
Chevrier, N., 50 Sussex
Craig & McKenzie, Sparks
Gaffney, Bernard, Sussex
Hick & Co., Rideau cor Sussex
Holbrook, George, Elgin
Lapierre, R., 106 Sussex
Latremouille, Octave, 102 Sussex
Mowat, A. & Son, 30 Sussex
Pinard, J. A. & Son, 17 Sussex
Rajotte, T., 34 Sparks
Robertson & Lawrence, opp Russell House
Smith & Rodney, Elgin
Story, Thomas, 59 Sussex
Sutherland, William

Music and Musical Instruments.

Gowan, H. & J., 24 Sparks
Miles, Edmund, Wellington
Orme, J. L. & Son, 8 Sparks

Newspapers.

Canada Gazette, (official), weekly
Le Canada, (tri-weekly), Duvernay Bros., props., 26 York
Ottawa Citizen, (daily and weekly), I. B. Taylor, proprietor, Rideau
Ottawa Times, (daily and weekly), Alexander Robertson, editor, 36 Sparks
Times Printing Co., James Cotton, managing director, 38 Sparks
United Service Gazette, (weekly), Alex. Riggs, editor, 36 Sparks
Volunteer Review, (weekly), Dawson Kerr, prop.

News and Periodical Depots.

Durie, John & Son, 10 Sparks
Hauser, Augustin, 60 Sparks
Jones & Holland, Post Office block

Painters, Plain and Ornamental.

Eaton, R. & Co., 7 Rideau
Howe, George, Augusta
Howe, William, George
Lang, James & Co., Duke
McKay, William, 43 Rideau
Matthewman & Co., Elgin

Photographers.

Dorion, —, Duke
Eastman, R., York
Lockwood, A., Sparks
Notman, William, Wellington
Spencer, E., 24 Sparks
Stiff, Brothers, 56 Sparks
Turgeon, Narcisse, Rideau
Turner, Frederick E., 83 Rideau

Physicians and Surgeons.

Beaubien, Cleophas, York
Beaudouin, —, Hull
Bell, W. R., New Edinburgh
Chesley, George, 25 Rideau
Codd, Alfred, Rideau
Dorion, J. Edmond, Clarence
Garvey, James, 94 Rideau
Graham, C. E., Hull
Grant, James A., Rideau
Henry, William J., Kent
Hill, Hamett, Victoria Terrace
Leggo, Christopher, Rideau
Logan, George, O'Connor
McGillivray, Donald, 128 Wellington
Macdonell, Æneas, Rideau
Mackenzie, Andrew
Robillard, A., York
St. Jean, Pierre, St. Patrick
Sweetland, John, Mosgrove
Valade, F. X., St. Patrick
Van Courtlandt, Edward
Wolff, James F. W., Albert
Wood, O. C., 41½ Sparks

Piano Fortes, Manufacturers & Dealers in

Miles, E., Wellington
Orme, J. L. & Son., 8 Sparks

Plumbers, Gas and Steam Fitters.

Barnes & Feck, William
Blyth & Kerr, 25 Rideau
Frederick, Theodore, William
Germain, N., 25 Sussex

Provincial Land Surveyors.

Austin, George F., Victoria Terrace
Austin, William
Forrest, A. O.
O'Hanly, J. L. P., Elgin
Porter, John, 36 Metcalfe
Roberts, C. E., Hull
Russell, Lindsay
Sinclair, Donald, Bank
Slater, James D., Wellington
Sparks, Robert, Elgin
Thistle, W. R., Sparks cor Metcalfe

Saddle and Harness Makers.

Borbridge, S. & H., 39 Rideau
Henry & Co., saddlers, 24 York
Hughes, W. S., 6 York
Lee & Dawson, 55 Rideau
McMaster, D., York
Montgomery, R. S., 59 Rideau
Warwicker, Thomas, 319 Wellington
Wright, Philemon, Hull

Saloons and Restaurants.

Brown, Archibald, William
Cahill, John, Sparks cor Elgin
Cameron, William, Murray
Dyke, John, York
Goldthrite, Samuel, Elgin
Kavanagh, M., Wellington cor Metcalfe
McKenna, Mrs., 66 Sparks
Murray, Mrs., Metcalfe
O'Meara, P., Rideau
Ontario, F. T. Kilby, prop., 12 York
Roy, Leon, 79 Sussex

Soap and Candle Factory

Brown, John, York

Stove Dealers, Tin, Copper and Sheet Iron Smiths.

Blyth & Kerr, 25 Rideau
Bourque, Edward, 58 Rideau
Cordelet, W. G.
Dorion, C. P., 58 Sparks
Enright, Mrs., Wellington
Esmonde, Brothers, 43 Sparks
Germain, N., 25 Sussex
Kipp, Wilfred, Duke
Meadows, H. & Co., 35 Sussex
Peltier, Herrick, 70 Clarence
Valiquette & Poitras, 48 Rideau

Tanners and Curriers.

Culbard, William G., Sandy Hill
Germain, E., Clarence
McCullough, James, Park
Moisan, J. B., Church
Rochester, John, jun., Richmond Road

Tea and Coffee Merchants (Wholesale.)

Andy, A. O. & Co., Elgin

Tobacconists.

Ansell & Michaels, Sparks cor Elgin
Binks, James, 62 Rideau
Gelhausen & Dupuy, 21 Rideau
Killeen, John A., Rideau
Nye, L. H., 43 Sussex
Robertson, A., Elgin
Ross, John, 26½ Sparks

Veterinary Surgeons.

Coleman, A. G. F., York
Harris, James, 72 Clarence

Watchmakers and Jewelers.

Coates, Mrs. W., Sussex
Kaye, Thomas, 246 Wellington
Kenly, Robert, jun., 33 Sparks
Leavens, D. R., 73 Sussex
Leslie, John, 25 Sparks
Poulin, Pierce, Clarence
Sutherland, George S., 63 Rideau
Tracy, James, 19 Rideau
Traunweiser, F., Sparks
Young, Radford, 30 Sparks.

Otterville.—*(See Villages too late for regular insertion at the end of this work.)*

Oustic.—A Post Office in the Township of Eramosa, County Wellington.

WHITEHEAD, THOMAS, Postmaster.

Oungah.—A Post Office in the Township of Chatham, County Kent. Distant from Chatham, the County Town, 7 miles, from London 60, and from Toronto 175.

KINNEY, THOMAS, Postmaster.

Outram.—A Post Office in the Township of Brant, County Bruce.

Ferguson, James, J.P. | SMITH, DAVID, Postmaster.

Overton.—A Post Office in the Township of Camden, County Addington.

FOX, S. D., Postmaster.

BRITISH LION HOTEL,

Nos. 61 and 63 Sparks St., Ottawa, Ont.

WELDEN CHAMPNESS, - - - - - - - PROPRIETOR.

EVERY ACCOMMODATION! EVERY COMFORT OF A HOME!

MODERATE CHARGES.

From the fact of this House being so Centrally Situated,

BEING IN THE IMMEDIATE VICINITY OF THE POST OFFICE, TELEGRAPH, EXPRESS AND PARLIAMENT BUILDINGS, RENDERS IT THE BEST HOUSE FOR TRAVELLERS.

Remember the BRITISH LION when you come to the Capital of our New Dominion.

LOUIS A. GRISON,

AGENT FOR THE

FRENCH JOURNAL "LE CANADA,"

FOR THE

Scottish Provincial Assurance Company,

FOR THE

rench Canadian Institute, etc., etc.

OFFICES—York and Sussex Sts,

OTTAWA, ONT.

H. & J. GOWAN,

Carvers & Gilders, Looking Glass

AND

ICTURE FRAME MANUFACTURERS.

DEALERS IN

MUSICAL INSTRUMENTS, &c., &c.,

nd lessees of Gowan's Assembly Rooms, 54 Sparks Street, OTTAWA, ONT.

H. & J. GOWAN are prepared to furnish Brass nd String Bands at the shortest notice.

DR. O. C. WOOD,

Physician, Surgeon & Accoucheur

OTTAWA, ONTARIO.

AY OFFICE.—Opposite the Times Office, Sparks Street, Centre Town.

IGHT OFFICE.—At his Residence, Maria Street, Centre Town.

CANCERS CURED without the use of the knife, y a new but certain, speedy and almost painless rocess. References given to parties successfully reated, if required.

D. CODD & CO.,

Patent and Parliamentary Agents

AND SOLICITORS,

OTTAWA, ONT.

Models, Specifications, Drawings,

And all other Business in connection with obtaining Letters Patent of Invention, attended to on the shortest notice. Personal attendance in Ottawa not required.

REFERENCES.—Chief Justice Fisher, St. John's, N. B.; James A. Grant, M.D., M.P., &c., Ottawa; J. A. Snow, P.L.S., Hull; Hon. Jas. Skead, Ottawa.

D. T. BROWNE & CO.,

(Late Browne & Hardy)

GENERAL GROCERS,

Wine and Spirit Merchants,

DEALERS IN

PORK, FLOUR, TEA, ETC., ETC.,

NO. 16 RIDEAU STREET.

OTTAWA, ONT.

D. T. BROWNE. H. C. SYMMES.

ROBERTSON & LAWRENCE,

MERCHANT TAILORS

OPPOSITE

RUSSELL HOUSE,

OTTAWA, ONTARIO.

Owen Sound.—The County Town of Grey, and a Port of Entry, situated at the mouth of the Sydenham River, on the South side of the Georgian Bay, Lake Huron, in the Township of Sydenham. It was first settled in the year 1840, and has rapidly increased in wealth and population. The exports are principally grain and timber. The water power in the vicinity affords excellent facilities for manufacturing purposes and several establishments are in operation adding greatly to the prosperity of the Town. Steam communication daily with Collingwood and Meaford by steamer *Frances Smith*, and in winter by daily stage; by steamer *Algoma* weekly with Bruce Mines and Sault Ste Marie, and tri-weekly with Colpoy's Bay, by steamer *Champion*. Daily stage to Guelph, Southampton, &c., Distant from Collingwood by land 41 miles, by water 60; from Meaford 28; Colpoy's Bay 40; Guelph 84; Sault Ste Marie 250, and Bruce Mines 220. Money Order Office and Savings Bank. Population 3000.

Adams, W. F., photographer
Adams, J. F., photographer
Allen, Benjamin, dry goods and clothing
Anderson, William, baker and confectioner
Armstrong, William, Clerk of the Peace
Allen, R. H., (Allen & Co.,) patentee forest cultivator agent Canada Farmer's Insurance Company
Barnhart, C. E., M. D.
Barnhart, J., M. D
Benner, Henry, foreman *Advertiser*
Bishop, E. W
Bishop, William, saddler
Boak, Charles, (Boak & Woods)
Boak & Woods, general merchants
Bond, J. & W., dry goods and groceries
BOOKLESS, W. A., proprietor Bookless' Hotel
Boyd, J. W., photographer
Boyd & Tobey (Thomas M. Boyd, James Tobey) grocers
Brown, Ezra, J. P.
Brown, John & Co., general merchants
Brown, James, blacksmith
Buchan, J.
Burlingham, L., dentist
BUTCHART, ANDREW, stoves & tinware (see adv)
BUTCHART, GEORGE M., stoves, tin and hardware (see adv)
Cain, W. C., photographer
CATON, JAMES & CO., dry goods and groceries crockery, glassware, &c
Cavers, Thomas, blacksmith
Chambers, —, master brig *Hero*
Chatwin & Comely (Thomas G. Chatwin and David Comely) cabinet makers
Chisholm, John, commission merchant
Chisholm, T. A., wharfinger
Christie, David, founder and machinist
COATES & DUNN (John Coates, William Dunn) saddlers (see adv.)
COBEAN SAMUEL, hotel keeper
CORBET, GEORGE, jun., (Henning & Corbet)
CORBET & SONS, (George, John and James) Grey Foundry
COULSON, J. P., proprietor British hotel
COWPER, GEORGE C., (Ormiston & Co.)
Crawford, Robert, grocer
CREASOR D. A., barrister and attorney at law, solicitor in chancery, etc.
CREASOR, JOHN, barrister, etc., County attorney
CREIGHTON, DAVID, (Rutherford & Creighton)
Creighton, George, P., general merchant
Creighton, James, shoemaker
Creighton, John, shoemaker
Crichton, Alexander, general merchant
Crosby, Henry, elder (B. Wesleyan)
Crosby, J., saw framer
Dass, R., merchant tailor
Davis, Andrew, carpenter
Davis, Mrs. Jane, milliner
DAVIS, W. H., (Davis & Hodgins) proprietor Commercial Hotel
DAVIS & HODGINS (W. H. Davis, John Hodgins) proprietors Propeller "Champion"
Dawson, John, Union hotel
DeCourcey, Reuben, M.D.
Denoon, D., Royal saloon
Douglas, James, Deputy Registrar
Douglas, James, merchant tailor
Doyle, R. J., Insurance agent
Dowsley, T. B., carriage and wagon maker
Dunn, William, master tug Okrone
Evans, E. W., dry goods and groceries
Forhan, Michael, watchmaker
Fox, Charles, plasterer
Francis, John G., forwarding and commission merchant
Frizzell, James, boot and shoes
Frost, J. W., dry goods and groceries
Frost, John & Son, general merchants and tanners
Gale, G. J., County Clerk and auctioneer
GILSON, MICHAEL, saddler
Gimby, Charles, shoemaker
GORDON, THOMAS, town clerk, Commissioner in B. R. and coroner
Gould, William, moulder
Granottier, Rev. F. X., (Roman Catholic)
Harper, Rev. C. M., (British Episcopal Methodist)
Harris, Scarff & Co., (A. B. Harris, F. Scarff), dry goods
HARRISON, BROS., (Wm. & John), lumber and flour merchants
Hawkins, Rev. J., (New Connexion)
HEALEY, M. J.
Henderson, H. G., dry goods and groceries
HEMING & CORBET, (H. P. Hening, George Corbet, jun.), hardware, wholesale and retail
Hopkins, B., butcher
Horne, James, Buck's Head Hotel
Hunt, Rev. S. T. A., (Wesleyan)
Inglis, Peter, mill proprietor, Clerk Surrogate
Johnson, James, groceries and liquors
JOHNSON, WILLIAM, barrister and attorney-at-law
Jones, Benjamin, clerk
Kennedy, James, wagon maker
KENNEDY, WILLIAM & SON, iron founders, millwrights and machinists, sash, door and blind factory
Kough, William, hardware, wholesale and retail
LANE, S. G., County Warden
LANE & STEPHENS, (S. G. Lane, John Stephens), barristers
Lawson, E., grocer
Leask, John, blacksmith
LE PAN, FREDERICK, County Treasurer
Lethbridge, Charles, proprietor Victoria Hotel
Lister, Rev. C., (Disciples)
Little, J. H. & Co., editors and proprietors *Advertiser*
Lunn, Thomas, County Registrar
McClean Bros., (S. and W. A.) groceries and liquors
McFadden, —, barrister
McInnis, John, millwright & machinist, Arnott P. O.

McMeekin, W., hotel keeper, township Derby
McPherson, Henry, Judge County Grey
Malone, Henry, brewer
Malone, Mrs., milliner
Markle, John, saloon
Maughan, Joseph, Sheriff County Grey
MEIR, JOHN, groceries and provisions
MERCHANTS' BANK OF CANADA, John Pottenger, agent
Miller, George S., (Miller & Moe)
Miller, George, wagon maker
Miller, James C., clerk
MILLER, JOHN, groceries, liquors and hardware
Miller, John, jailer
Miller, T. B., clerk
MILLER & MOE, (Geo. S. Miller and Husted Moe), forwarding and commission merchants
Mitchell, James, bookbinder
MITCHELL, R. E., groceries and provisions
MOE, HUSTED, (Miller & Moe)
Moore, C. H., Deputy Sheriff
Morrison, Rev. Duncan, (Presbyterian)
Mouck, Ernest, captain *Champion*
Mulholland, Rev. A. H. R. (Church of England)
Munro, David, blacksmith
Neving, D. & T., butchers
Notter, R., groceries, wines and liquors
Ollernshaw, Thomas, grocer
ORMISTON & CO., dry goods and groceries
OWEN SOUND ADVERTISER, J. H. Little & Co., publishers and proprietors
OWEN SOUND TIMES, Rutherford & Creighton, publisers and proprietor (see adv)
Park, James, grocer
Parke, Simon, groceries and liquors
PARKER, J. W. (Parker & Cattle)
PARKER & CATTLE, chemists, druggists, and wine merchants
Patterson, J. W., shoemaker
Paynter, Charles & Sons, coopers and stave factors
Pearson, John, warehouseman
Pengelly, William, tailor
Platt, Samuel, student-at-law
Pottenger, John, agent Merchants' Bank of Canada
Pratt, C. J. & W., grocers
Preston, James, B.A., principal Grammar School
Price, George, dry goods and groceries
Rae, Robert S., tailor
Rankin, C., P.L.S.
Rankin, George, blacksmith
Riddell, John, brewery
Robertson, Francis, brewer and maltster
Robertson, James J., barrister, &c.
ROBERTSON, W. T., clerk steamer *Frances Smith*
Robinson, Rev. R. (Congregational)
ROSSITER, R. W., sash, door and blind factory
RUTHERFORD & CREIGHTON (John Rutherford and David Creighton) editors and proprietors *Owen Sound Weekly Times* (see adv)
Sadlier, Robert, architect
Scagel, George, livery stables
Scagel, S. C., general merchant
Scott, Thomas, M.P.P.
Scurry, H. J., barber
Seldon, William, propriètor Owen Sound Hotel
Shaw, Mrs. Jane, confectionery
SLOAN, JOHN, organ and melodeon factory (see adv)
Smith, J. A., shoemaker
Smith, Lewis, general merchant
SMITH, W. H., master steamer *Frances Smith*
Snider, George, M.P.P.
Spencer, David, cabinet maker
Spencer, George, lumber merchant, com. mer., conveyancer, com. in B. R.
Spencer, Walter, music teacher
Spragg, John C., County Auditor
Spry, William, P.L.S. and civil engineer
Stephens, A. M. & Co., hardware, wholsale and retail
STEPHENS, HENRY, stoves and tin ware (see adv)
STEPHENS, J. C., clerk
Stephens, R. E., agent
STEPHENS, W. A., Collector of Customs, Agent Provincial, British America, Fire Mutual and Queen's Ins. Co's.
Stephenson, Rev. Thomas (Presbyterian)
Strang, H. I., B.A., principal, grammar school
Sumner, W. C. & Co., general merchants
Sutherland, James, grain dealer
Symes, W. B., master steamer *Wabuno*
Taylor, Henry, tailor
Telfer, Gideon, blacksmith
Thompson, James, barber
TODD, EDWARD, books and stationery, agent Montreal Telegraph and Vicker's Express Cos.
Trout, William, machinist
Tucker, John, shoemaker and grocer
Tucker, William, baker and confectioner
Trotter, Thomas, dentist
Van Dusen, Frederick, foreman, *Comet*
Van Dusen, Owen, prop. and publisher *Comet*
VICK, J. K., watchmaker, jeweler, engraver, &c.
Vickers & Johnson (Thos. Vickers and Daniel Johnson) general merchants
Warner, Moseley, agent
Williams & Manders, (Thos. Williams and William Manders) marble works
Wilkinson, William, Anglo-American Saloon
Wightman, Robert, chemist and druggist
Wilkes, Charles R., Clerk First Division Court
Williams, George, dry goods and groceries
Wilson, James, hotel keeper
Woodside, Thomas, boarding house
Wright, D. W., painter

Oxenden.—A Small Village on Gleason River in the Township of Keppel, County Grey, 21 miles from Owen Sound, the County Town. Steamers to Collingwood and Owen Sound. Population 50.

Allison, Amos, teacher
Atkey, George, farmer
Atkey, James, farmer
Brooks, William, carpenter
Craig, James, farmer
Dinsmore & Hodgins, gen. merchants
Flaherty, William, farmer
Guilford, J. C., prop. sash aud door factory
McDougal, Peter, carpenter
Mallard, D. J., prop. British Hotel
North, Alfred R., farmer
Ogilvie, Dr
Patterson, Thomas, prop. grist and saw mills
Scott, John W., farmer
Sims, W. W., farmer
Soper, Almon, farmer
STANLEY, JOHN M., Postmaster
Stanley & Gilford, general merchants
Williams, Dr
Winter, James, carpenter
Wyburn, William, farmer

Oxford.—(Colchester P.O.)—A Post Village in the Township of Colchester, County Essex, 26 miles from Sandwich, the County Town, 26 from Windsor and 250 miles from Toronto. The Village contains a Baptist and Episcopal Methodist Church. Daily Mail. Population about 200.

Adams, Matthew, boots and shoes
Aikman, David, farmer
Aikman, Oliver, farmer
Baldwin, Rev. J. (Baptist)
Baldwin, W., farmer
Bell, James, clerk 4th Division Court
Buchanan, John G., J.P.
Duff, W., farmer
Ferris, Miss Georgiana, school teacher
FERRIS, PHILIP, wharfinger, &c.
Goodyear, Thomas, carpenter
HACKETT, ALEXANDER, steamboat agent
HACKETT & CO., general merchants
Hawkins, Thomas, J.P. & M.D.
Hall, John, gunsmith, turner, &c.
Henrich, George, boots and shoes
Howie, James, farmer
Huffman, R., farmer
Lockhart, J. H., farmer
Lodge, John, blacksmith
Loveless, J., boots and shoes
McAnnany, Robert, machinist and engineer
MICKLE, JOHN, Postmaster
MORSE, A. D., general merchant
Reneau, Charles, blacksmith
Reynolds, Rev. William (Wesleyan Methodist)
Robertson, R. A., M.D.
Russell, Hugh, hotel and flour mill proprietor
Seneca, Edward. hotel proprietor
Woodbridge, W. W., farmer
Wright, John, austioneer
Wright, S. L., general merchant
Wright, William, saddler

Oxford Centre.—A Post Office in the Township of East Oxford, County Oxford.

GARBUTT, WILLIAM, J.P., Postmaster
Hazlow, James, blacksmith
Scheoley, Nelson, innkeeper

Oxford Mills.—A Village on the south branch of the Rideau River, in the Township of Oxford, County Grenville, 22 miles from Brockville, the County Town, and 4 from Kemptville Station, St. Lawrence and Ottawa Railway. Population 120.

Anderson, Henry, farmer
Anderson, Thomas, shoemaker
Boyd, A., cooper
Buck, Samuel, blacksmith
Christie, John, farmer
Davis, G. H., innkeeper
Edwards, Joseph, wagon maker
Fletcher, James, shoemaker
Foley, John, tailor
GAIR, MURDOCH, Postmaster
Gilmer, John, farmer
Goodspeed, Rev. J. B., (New Connexion)
Grant, Allan, farmer
Hanlon, Michael, farmer
Harris, Thomas, farmer
Hurd, Alonzo, blacksmith
Jones, Charles, tailor
Jones, C. & Co., general merchants
Lindsay, John, blacksmith
Spry, Samuel, painter
Stannage, Rev. John, (Church of England)
Stephens, W., carpenter
Tripp, James, cooper
Vance, George, wine merchant
Watterson, John, teacher
Waugh, Richard, proprietor flouring mills
Waugh, W. W., J.P., lumber dealer

Oxford Station.—A Post Village on the line of the St. Lawrence and Ottawa Railway, in the Township of Oxford, County Grenvile. Land in the vicinity averages $15 per acre.

Black, William J., farmer
Clair, R. R., agent P. & O. R. R.
Cummerford, B., tailor
Fraser, Allen, wagon maker
Gerdner, John, farmer
Gardner, Robert, carpenter
HOLMES, ANDREW, J.P., Postmaster and hotel keeper
Irwin, Henry, carpenter
Johnston, David. farmer
Johnston, Isaac, farmer
Johnston, James, shoemaker
Johnston, John, J.P.
Johnston, Simon, farmer
Kelly, Michael, tailor
McGarvin, Owen, farmer
McGindley, Andrew, farmer
Maneeley, Hugh, carpenter
Sanderson, John, farmer
Sanderson, William, shingle maker

Oznabruck Centre.—A small Village in the Township of Oznabruck, County Stormont, 17 miles from Cornwall, the County Town. Population 80.

Barker, Gordon, general merchant
Barker, William, general merchant
Brills, Rev. M. (Wesleyan)
Clarke, James, farmer
Cryderman, John, farmer
Hutchins, William. painter
Hutchins, W. A., auctioneer
Myers, Tobias, hotel keeper
Plimadore, Joseph, carpenter
POAPS, JACOB J., Postmaster
Poaps, W. E., nurseryman
Sledge, Thomas, butcher
Warner, Adam, farmer
Warner, Frederick, farmer
Warner, Peter, farmer

Paisley.—A Post Village on the Saugeen and Elora Road at the junction of the Saugeen and Teeswater Rivers, in the Township of Elderslie, County Bruce, 16 miles from Walkerton, the County Town, and 128 from Toronto. The surrounding country is extremely fertile and the water privileges fine. Stages to Walkerton and Southampton, fare 75 cts. Mails daily. Money Order Office and Post Office Savings Bank. Population 1200.

Allan, D., proprietor, Victoria Hall
Bain, Hugh, shoemaker
Bain, J., surgeon
Barbour, James, wagon maker
Bates, J., proprietor, Anglo-American Hotel
Bone, James, tanner
Bradley, J., foundry
Bremner, Rev. George (Canada Prebyterian)
Briggs, George, saddler .
Brockie, J. & A., general merchants
Bruce, William C., general merchant
Buchanan, John, blacksmith
Cordner, Rev. R. (Church of England)
Deans, John, wagon maker
Dick, Robert, general merchant
Farr, T. R., grocer
Fisher, Duncan, proprietor, grist and saw mill
Floor & McLaren, general merchants
Gibson, David, blacksmith
Gilhuly, Joseph, wagon maker
GOLDIE, RICHARD, proprietor Paisley *Advocate*
Hanna, Rev. Thomas (Wesleyan)
Hay, R. M., general merchant
Hornell, William, baker
Irving & Hogg, general merchants
Jeffries, Rev. T. M., (N. C. Methodist)
Johnson, John, hotel prop-
Key, William, grocer
McArthur, John, blacksmith
McCalder, J., hotel keeper
McDonald, Joseph, blacksmith
McGavin. James, saddler
McGregor, D., blacksmith
McKechnie, John, shoemaker
McKechnie, N., general merchant
McLaren, P., M.D.
McLean, Rev. M. W., (Canada Presbyterian)
McLeod, Hugh, prop. grist mill
McMillan, J., prop. saw mill
McNamara, M., watchmaker, jeweler, &c
McNamara, Robert, tailor
McNeil, Rev. Donald (Baptist)
Maher, William, cabinet maker
Mallock, G. W., prop. saw mill
Martin, John, axe manuf
Mitchell, R., prop. Dominion Hotel
Mitchell, Robert, hotel keeper
Murdoch & Orchard, prop. woolen factory
Mudie, Thomas, tinsmith
ORCHARD, THOMAS, Postmaster, gen. merchant
Pasmore, W. J., surgeon
Porteous, Robert, general merchant
Ralston, C., general merchant
Rattray, John, baker
Reid, Peter, tailor
Saunders, James, teacher
Sargeson, W., proprietor British Hotel
Scott, William, proprietor hotel
Scott, William, shoemaker
Shannon, Samuel, grocer
Sherwood, George, general merchant
Smith, G. & W., general merchants
Steel, James, blacksmith
Steel, Samuel, wagon maker
Urquhart, G. C., druggist
Valentine, J., proprietor grist and saw mill
Wallace, Robert, proprietor saw mill
Wilson, H. A., druggist
Young, H. C., proprietor Union Hotel

Pakenham.—A village a station of the Brockville and Ottawa Railway, on the Mississippi River, in the Township of Pakenham, County Lanark, 40 miles from Perth, the County town, and 36 from Ottawa. Money Order Office and Savings Bank, Population 800.

Ayre, John, farmer
Blackwood, D., M.D.
Bolton, George, tinsmith
Bradly, Thomas, blacksmith
Brown, Robert, J.P.
Brown & Scott, general merchants
Burns, Dr., coroner
Chatterton, S. D., proprietor Ontario House
Clark, Robert, shoemaker
Cowan, James, tinsmith
Cowan, William, shoemaker
Cameron, Miss, dressmaker
Canton, J. H., general merchant
Carswell, A., farmer
Cockle, J., farmer
Cross, C., general merchant
Dack, George, blacksmith
Dack, William, shoemaker
Davie, R. H., tailor
Dickson, William, hotel keeper
Doherty, C. O., agent B. & L. H. R. R.
Donoher, B., cabinet maker
Drysdall, Alexander, blacksmith
Dunnet, James, general merchant
Edwards, Robert, cabinet maker
Elliott, John, constable
Ellis, James, J.P.
Ellis, R., farmer
FOWLER, ALEXANDER, Postmaster and druggist
Francis, Jonathan, farmer
Gemmill, John A., attorney
Gibson, E. B.,, M.D.
Gordon, Alexander, general merchant
Graham, Robert, wagon maker
Hartney, James, general merchant
Harvey, Matthew, shoemaker
Hillard & Dickson, millers
Hillard, Daniel, farmer
Kelly, Simon, carpenter
Kirtland, D., M.D.
Lavin, Rev. —, (Roman Catholic)
Lindsay, John, farmer
Low, John, bailiff
Lynch, Michael, cooper
McArthur, Arthur, farmer
McEwan, Robert, saddler
McKibbin, J., farmer
McKim, Uriah, farmer
McManigal, John, proprietor Pakenham House
McNicol, Duncan, carpenter

McVicar, John, farmer
McVicar, William, farmer
Mann, Rev. A., M.A., (Presbyterian)
Masson, Rev. James, (Wesleyan)
Mayne, R. H., baker
Nairn, Thomas, farmer
Ogilvey, David, farmer
O'Neil, John, wagon maker
Parker, George, cooper
Quigley, James, carpenter
Quigley, Miss, teacher
Richey, James, farmer
Riddell, John, carpenter
Riddell, R., farmer
Robertson, Miss, dressmaker
Ryan, D., farmer
Ryan, Francis, farmer
Scott, James, tanner
Scott, Y., J.P.
Sherlock, James, butcher
Sliter, Alonzo, teacher
Smith, Daniel, general merchant
Smith, James, M.A., teacher
Smith, John, wagon maker
Stobs, R., general merchant
Tait, William, tailor
Templeman, William, tailor
Woods, James, farmer
Woods, William, farmer
Woods, Robert, farmer

Palermo.—A Post Village in the Township of Trafalgar, County Halton, 8 miles from Milton, the County Town, and 30 miles from Toronto. Land in the vicinity averages $40 per acre. Money Order Office Population 300.

Buck, Anson, M.R.C.S., London
Campbell, Bernard, butcher
Dolmage, Robert, general merchant
Hager, A., hotel keeper
Harris, Henry, tailor
Lawrence, Jacob & Son, iron founders
Lawrence, Jacob, J.P.
SWITZER, H. M., J.P. and Postmaster and gen. mer.
Teetzel, William, general merchant
Vanallen. John, hotel keeper

Paris.—An incorporated Town, beautifully situated on the Grand River, in the Township of Dumfries, County Brant. It is a Port of Entry and an important Railway Station, being at the intersection of the Great Western Railway by the Buffalo and Lake Huron Railway. The water privileges in the neighborhood are unlimited, affording ample power for several extensive mills, woolen factories, &c. Paris derives its name from the large quantities of Plaster of Paris, or Gypsum, found in the vicinity and several mills are constantly employed grinding it for farming purposes. Money Order Office and Savings Bank. Population about 3,200.

Adams, Peter, wagon maker and blacksmith
ADAMS, W. E. (Penman & Adams)
Acres, J. W., B.A., L.R.C.P., principal Union school
Anderson, John, commission merchant
Angus, George, builder and contractor
Allworth, Rev. Mr., (Congregational)
Baker, John, boot and shoe maker
Baird, A. H
Batty, William, tin and iron plate worker
Barclay, R., watchmaker
Barclay, Robert, manager sewing machine factory
Beamer, J. E., hair cutter
Beare, M., fruit and fancy store
Bell, George, baker
Betts, Joseph Y., general merchant
Borland, Miss & Co., fancy store
Boswell, Thomas N.
BRADFORD'S HOTEL, O. D. Bradford, proprietor (see adv)
Bradford, O. D., hotel and stage office
BRITISH AMERICAN HOTEL, Paris Station, Jas. A. Young, proprietor (see adv)
British American Sewing Machine Factory, Robert Barclay, manager
Brown, Dickson & Co., tobacco manufacturers
Brown, W., butcher
BROWN, W. & CO., livery stable keepers (see adv)
Buckley, John, tinware and stove dealer
BULLOCK, JOSEPH, wholesale and retail dealer in groceries, wines and spirits (see adv)
Burdsnall, George, general merchant
Campbell, A., boot and shoemaker
CAMERON, MONTOMERY & CO., dry goods and millinery
Canadian Hotel, T. Mayberry, proprietor
Capron, C., farmer
CAPRON, WALTER, produce merchant
Capron, W. H.
CARR, M, X., J.P., Postmaster, Paris station
Chambers, John, baker
CHAMBERS, RICHARD, New Dominion Saloon (see adv)
Clarkson, Charles, teacher
Clarke, Thomas, tinsmith
COLEMAN, THOMAS W., prop. plaster mills (see adv.)
Davey, Mrs., milliner and dressmaker
Dickson, D. R., general insurance agent
Dickson, James, M.D., physician and surgeon
Dow, John, ticket clerk Paris Station
Dowling, Rev. T. (Roman Catholic)
DUMFRIES' HOUSE, Thomas P. Gray, proprietor
Eddington, James G., accountant Royal Canadina Bank
Evans, Robert, freight clerk
Fagan, J. S., cabinet maker, etc.
Farmers' Hotel, James Batty, proprietor
Farmers' Exchange Hotel, R. Storr, proprietor
Fawkes, G. H., watchmaker and jeweller
FINLAYSON, HUGH, SEN., M.P.P.
FINLAYSON, HUGH & CO., tanners, etc.
Finlayson, Hugh' saddle, harness and trunk maker
Finlayson, John, clothier and fancy goods
Flanagan, Charles, saddler and harness maker
Fleming, Pierce, wagon maker
FLOREY, G. T., miller, etc.
Flueling, Mrs. N., proprietor Queen's Arms Hotel
Gleason, Lyman, hotel keeper

Gill, Alexander, monager Coleman's plaster mill
Gouinlock, Walter, groceries, wines and liquors
Gray, T. P., auctioneer, etc
Granton, John, groceries, wines and liquors
GRAHAM, T. & J. H., dry goods, clothing, liquors, stationery, &c.
Green, Michael, proprietor Paris Hotel
Griffiths, George, proprietor Robinson Hotel
Hall, Thomas, dry goods
Hamilton, N.
HART, HENRY, attorney, solicitor and notary pub.
Havill, Henry, carpenter
Havill, James, carpenter
Havill, William, carpenter
Haycock, F. H., Collector of Customs
Haycock, T. H., farmer
Henderson, Alexander, grist mill
Henderson. Rev. Thomas (Baptist)
Hoffman, George & Co., general store
Huson, Albert, bailiff, Division Court
James, Rev. J. (Presbyterian)
Jamieson, A., stone cutter
JONES, S. J., Judge Division Court
Lawrence, John, physician
Liverpool, London and Globe Insurance Company; W. Stanton, agent
Loughead, J., hotel keeper
McCOSH, JOHN, attorney, solicitor in Chancery and conveyancer
McCosh, Thomas, grocer and general dealer
McGlory, Roger, wagon maker
MARTIN, W. S., agent G.T.R.
Martin, W., farmer
Manse, Lewis, groceries and provisions
Maxwell, David, machinist,
MAXWELL & WHITELAW, machinists and manufacturers of agricultural implements (see adv)
Mechanics' Institute; C. Hubbard, librarian.
Mills, Rev. W. (Wesleyan)
Miller, Francis, carpenter
Miller, Gideon, carpenter
Miller, James, carpenter
Millburn & Co., money brokers & dealers in exchange
Mitchell, George, clothier
Mitchell, J. C.
MONTGOMERY & CO., dry goods
Murphy, W., farmer
Murray, Thomas, cattle dealer
Nash, A., boots and shoes, hats and furs
NEW DOMINION SALOON; Richard Chambers, proprietor
NEW PARIS MILLS; C. Whitelaw, proprietor
Newton, W., livery stable keeper
O'Brien, Timothy, butcher
O'Neil, D., farmer
O'Neil, Thomas, com. merchant
Oakley, G. W., ticket clerk, G. W. R., Paris Station
ONTARIO HOUSE, Paris Station, Walter Capron, proprietor
Penford, Edward, boot and shoemaker
PENMAN & ADAMS, knitting factory
Parker & Cattle, druggists, teas and tobacco, J. S. Parker, manager
PARIS STAR, W. Powell, editor and proprietor
Patton, Andrew, farmer
Patton, David, iron monger
Patton, D., farmer
Patton, Edward, cabinet makers
Patton, J., farmer
PATTERSON, WILLIAM, dentist, (see adv)
PENMAN, JOHN
PENMAN & ADAMS, proprietors, knitting factory
Penton, Henry, Clerk Division Court
Penton, Henry, groceries, crockery and liquors
Penton, J., farmer
Philip, F., license inspector
Powell, W. G., issuer of marriage licenses, *Star* office
POWELL, W. G., auctioneer, *Star* Office
Qua, S.
Railton, G. W., Agent G. W. R., Paris Station
Railroad Saloon, Paris Station, Wap, John, prop.
Rendall, James, chief constable
Robertson, Rev. W. (Presbyterian)
Roberts, J., collector
ROYAL CANADIAN BANK, Norman, Totten, agt.
Ryle, James, commission merchant
Ryall, Thomas, J.P., general merchant
Scott, G. S., druggist and importer crockery & gls'ware
Schaffer, James
Settle, J. J., farmer
Shannon, J., artiste
SINCLAIR, R., prop. Gore Hotel (see adv)
Smith, N
Sovereign, L., farmer
Stapleton, W., boots and shoes
STANTON, GEORGE, Postmaster
Stanton, George, agent Montreal Telegraph Co
Stewart, J
Storr, R., prop. Farmers' Exchange Hotel
Taylor, W. H., groceries, crockery, wines and liquors
Telfer, George, landing waiter Paris Station
Thompson, butcher and drover
TOTTEN, HENRY, barrister and solicitor
TOTTEN, NORMAN, agent Royal Canadian Bank
Townley, Rev. Dr., (Episcopal)
Turnbull & Thompson, builders and machinists
Union Hotel, J. Loughead, proprietor
Walton, W., gunsmith
Wass, John
Watt, John, M.D., physician and surgeon
Watts, C., groceries, wines and liquors
West, A., variety store
Whitelaw, Andrew, machinist
WHITELAW, CHARLES, Mayor
White, W., freight clerk, G.W.R. station
Winter, W. & J., dealers in fruit and oysters
Winter, W., express agent
Wood & Fudger, dry goods, clothing and groceries
WYNN, H. C., agent G.W.R
Wynn, H. C., farmer
YOUNG, JAMES, prop. British American Hotel (see adv)

Panmure.—A small settlement in the Township of Fitzroy, County Carleton, 25 miles from Ottawa.

Boyle, William, farmer
Checkly, Charles, farmer
Dean, Miss Jane, teacher
Devine, P., farmer
Emerry, Rev. M. P.
Graisgen, W. farmer
Green, John, farmer
Holmes, Alexander, farmer
Hudson, John, farmer
Hudson, Matthew, farmer
Lumney, Edward, farmer
Magrath, Michael, farmer
Moorehouse, John, farmer
Nagle, M.D., farmer
RING, JAMES, Postmaster
Ring, John, cooper
Ring, Robert, farmer
Storey, David, farmer
Storey, William, farmer
Whalen, Peter, farmer

Paris Station.—A Village at the junction of the Great Western and Buffalo and Lake Huron Railways, on Smith's Creek, in the Township of South Dumfries, County Brant, 1 mile from Paris.

Capron, Hiram
Capron, Horace, farmer
CAPRON, WALTER, proprietor Ontario House
CARR, M. X., Postmaster
Cole, Solomon
Conium, George, switchman G. W. R.
Gleason, Lyman, hotel keeper
Haycock, Frederick, Collector of Customs
Hoffman, George, general merchant
Kyle, James, wool dealer
Manse, Lewis, grocer
Martin, William, station agent G.T.R.
MURPHY, WILLIAM
Nixon, W. S., general merchant
O'Connor, P., grain dealer
O'Neil, Thomas, wool and grain dealer
Richards, saloon keeper
Ryall, Thomas, insurance agent and grain dealer
Sutton, R. T., patent right agent
White, John, foreman freight department G. W. R.
White, J., freight clerk G. W. R.
Wynne, J., agent G. W. R.

Parham.—*(See Villages too late for regular insertion at the end of this work.)*

Park Hill.—A thriving village in the Township of West Williams, County Middlesex, on the Grand Trunk Railway, 49 miles from London, by rail, via St. Mary's, and about 30 miles in a direct line. It is becoming the centre of a large and increasing business, a large trade being done in the exportation of wheat, lumber, staves, etc. Improved land, averages $25 per acre. Money order office. Population about 400.

Arrand, Charles, carpenter
Bell, James, tailor
Bullen, F., fancy goods
Burns, Robert, auctioneer
Burns, Thomas, J.P.
Butler, James, saddler
Cameron, John, farmer
Campbell, A., carpenter
Campbell, D. M., shoemaker
Carter, Gilbert, produce merchant
Caw, William, M.D.
Clement, J., carpenter
Colvin, Charles, J.P. and farmer
Connell, D. C., watchmaker
Cornish, W. R., notary public
Cramer, C., carpenter
Cruikshanks, P., druggist
Cunningham, Mrs., dressmaker
Deo, Benjamin, cabinet maker
Dickinson, J., woolen manufacturer
Douglas, Dougald, blacksmith
Eckardt, E., wagon maker
Elliott, G., attorney
Elliott, William, brick maker
English, John, tinsmith
Fairburn, T., baker
Galbraith, Rev. — (Wesleyan)
Gibbs, John, general merchant
Gleason, James, carpenter
Harrison, John, produce merchant
Hastings, William, hotel keeper
Hawkey, John, wagon maker
Hayes, George, cooper
Howley, John, watchmaker
Kelly, F., watchmaker
Keyser, F. J., butcher
Long, Miss, dressmaker
McBain, Rev. R. F., (Presbyterian)
McClure, Daniel, tailor
McClure, Donald, J. P.
McDonald, A. A., general merchant
McInnis, Dougald, blacksmith
McIntyre, John, tailor
McKellar, A. & M. D., coal dealers
McKellar, M. & A. D., hardware
McKee, Rev., (Baptist)
McKinnon, John, grocer
McKinnon, Donald, grocer
McLeod, Donald, general merchant
McLeod, Simon, hotel keeper
McPhail, A., shoemaker
MacAlpine, R. S., M. D
Manies, E., painter
Mathews, Abram, blacksmith
Maybury, T. A., general merchant
Meggo, C., butcher
Merredith, Edmund, attorney
Mott, John, butcher
Mott, Smith, hotel keeper
Munro, Brothers, general merchants
NOBLE, JOHN, Postmaster
Oaks, J., painter
Paxman, Adam, auctioneer
Perry, G., farmer
Phippen, Edward, cooper
Phippen, Robert, cabinet maker
Porte, Robert, general merchant
Raymon, A., blacksmith
Reeves, G. B., agent G.T.R.
Robertson, George, painter
Rogers, Rev. R. B. (Methodist)
Ross, James, shoemaker
Ross, Miss, teacher
Scoon, John, druggist
Scott, John, wagon maker
Shaw, P., teacher
Shoults, William, produce dealer
Siddell, Joseph, J.P., produce dealer
Smith, Alexander, carpenter
Smith, Nelson, shoemaker
Soda, J., shoemaker
Streeter, Henry, tanner
Taylor, James, hardware
Taylor, Porte & Co., planing mills
Thompson, A., lumber merchant
Wade, Charles A., seeds, &c.
Welsh, Donald, hotel keeper
Wilson, F. J., attorney

Park Head.—A Postvillage in the township of Amabel, County Bruce, 30 miles from Walkerton, the County Town, and 134 from Toronto.

Anderson, Duncan, farmer
Blakeley, Edward, farmer
Brown, Rev. George M., (Wesleyan)
Carry, Miss A. M., teacher
Clifford, James, farmer
Connelly, Thomas, farmer
Cribbis, James, farmer
Cribbis, John, farmer
Kennedy, Alexander, farmer
Kirkland, Hugh, farmer
Lewis, Henry, farmer
McIvor, William, farmer
SIMPSON, WILLIAM, Postmaster
Smart, L., farmer
Smith, David, farmer
Spencer, Edwin, farmer
Street, John, farmer
Street, W. A., farmer
Willie, John, farmer

Parker.—A Post Office in the Township of Peel, County Wellington, 23 miles from Guelph, the County Town.

Blackwell, W. J., J.P.
LAIRD, G. M., Postmaster
Lundy, Miss E. M. B., teacher
McKim, R., J.P., M.P.P.

Parma.—A Post Office in the Township of South Fredericksburg, County Lenox.

GRIFFITH, DAVID, Postmaster.

Parry Sound.—A Village in the Township of McDougall, District of Algoma, on the River Seguin, 70 miles from Collingwood and 165 from Toronto. Steam to Collingwood, fare $2, and Stage to Orillia, fare $3. Government lands are free to the amount of 100 acres, over that number 50c. per acre. The Village is close to lake navigation and the water power is almost unlimited. Copper and iron is supposed to exist in the neighborhood, at present the chief trade consists of lumbering. Money Order Office. Population 200.

Armstrong, J. H., farmer
Armstrong, Samuel, farmer
Beatty, J. & W. & Co., general merchants
BEATTY, WILLIAM, J.P. and M.P.P
Blair, Miss E., teacher
Bowers, William, farmer
Burrett, Alfred, farmer
Burrett, Henry, prop. Seguin Hotel
Caton, T. R., carpenter
Cole, Joseph, shoemaker
Cook, William, farmer
Dawson, J. B. P., M.D.
Field, John, carpenter
Hunt, Joseph, farmer
McAllister, Robert, farmer
McClelland, John, druggist
Misho, John, cooper
Moore, John, wagon maker
Rogerson, Joseph S., cooper
Slade, George, farmer
Stephens, A. G., M.D
WAKEFIELD, N. P., Postmaster, &c
Wilcox, William, farmer
Wilson, James tailor

Patterson.—A Post Village in the Township of Vaughan, County York, 17½ miles from Toronto, and 2 miles east of Richmond Hill Station, Northern Railway. The whole village, comprising 100 acres, is owned by Messrs. Patterson & Bro., agricultural implement manufacturers. The residents are chiefly employed in the same establishment. Daily mail. Money order office. Population 175.

Bassingtwait, William, farmer
Drury, James, farmer
Graham, William, farmer
Metcalf, Robert, farmer
PATTERSON & BRO. (Peter and Alfred S. Patterson) manufacturers of agricultural implements
PATTERSON, P., Postmaster
Rumble, William, farmer
Vilie, J., farmer

Peepabun.—A Post Office in the Township of Luther, County Wellington, 28 miles from Guelph, the County Town. Average price of improved land $15 per acre.

DICKSON, ROBERT, Postmaster.

Pefferlaw.—A Village in the Township of Georgina, County York, 30 miles from Newmarket, and 60 from Toronto. Stage to Newmarket tri-weekly. Average price of improved land $30 per acre. Population 130.

Armstrong, Thomas, carpenter
Bathgate, Andrew, farmer
Bathgate, James, farmer
Boyd, John, farmer
Burnie, John, farmer
Donnell, James, farmer
Greer, Michael, miller
Griffith, Christopher, farmer
Hart, George, farmer
JOHNSTON, GEORGE, J.P., Postmaster and general merchant
Johnson, William, dyer
Johnston, Robert, general merchant
Laviolette, Charles, farmer
Laviolette, Peter, farmer
Lloyd, John, farmer
Lloyd, Thomas, farmer
Reekie, James, carpenter
Scott, Miss Annie, teacher
Switzer, Tobias, shoemaker
Way, R. B., farmer
Way, William, farmer
Way, Thomas, farmer
Winfield, James, proprietor Pefferlun Exchange

Pembroke.—The County Town of Renfrew, situated at the confluence of the Ottawa and Muskrat Rivers, 90 miles from Ottawa and 32 from Portage du Fort. This is the chief depot of the extensive lumbering operations of the upper Ottawa. The scenery in the neighborhood is unequalled for diversified and romantic beauty. Steamers tri-weekly from Ottawa, and from Pembroke to Des Joachim. Money Order Office and Savings Bank. Population 2000.

Angus, Robert, painter
Ansell, Michael, tobacconist
Bell, Joseph, lumber merchant
Bell, William, P.L.S.
Boucher, Rev. Olivier (Roman Catholic)
Bourke, Edward, gaoler
Chamberlain Bros., general merchants
Chapman, W. D., tinsmith
Clarke, Edward, saddler
Clarke, Thomas, dry goods
Clendinnen, J. D., M.D.
Coleman, James, butcher
Conner, J. W., principal Grammar School
Cooke, James, carpenter
Copeland, James, proprietor Ottawa House
Cormack, John S., druggist
Crombie, E., agent Quebec Bank, insurance agent
Cunningham and Flanuery, general merchants
Cushing, E. T., hotel keeper and grocer
Deacon, John, Judge County Court
Deacon, Thomas, attorney-at-law
Delahay, Robert, general merchant
Dennison, R. A., baker
Dewar, John, boots and shoes
Dickson, James, cooper
Dickson, W. W., M.D.
Dougherty, J. E., grocer
Duck, William, barrister and Clerk of Peace
Duggan, Captain, steamer "Pembroke"
Evans, Andrew, clerk Division Court and ins. agent
EVANS, S. F. A., P.L.S. and ins. agent (see card)
Forbes, Andrew, dry goods
Ford, George, agent Montreal Telegraph Company
Foster & Walker, tinsmiths
Frazier, Hugh, carriage maker
Garth, Guido, painter
Gebel, S., gunsmith
Gibbons, William, butcher
Godkin, Samuel, cooper
Gorman, Michael, forwarder and com. merchant
Gorman, Michael, tinsmith
Grieves, James, carpenter
Hawkins & Leach, hotel proprietors
Heenan, James, general merchant
Henderson, Rev. William (Church of England)
Herrick, Brush & Co., forwarders
Hickey, John, County Clerk
Howarth, Thomas, watchmaker
Hughes, M., cabinet maker
Hunt John, watchmaker
Hunter, W. A., general merchant
Irving, A., Registrar
Irwin, James, M.D.
Leeney, E., saddler
Leitch, David, shoemaker
Loucks, H. H., attorney-at-law
McDougal, Mrs., boarding school
McConnell, Benjamin, lumber merchant
McDermid, J., cabinet maker
McEwen, Rev. John, (Presbyterian)
McDowell, Rev. D. C., (Wesleyan)
McGregor, Daniel, brickmaker
McIntosh, Isaac, fancy goods
McIvor, Dr.
McKenzie, E., M.D.
McLaren, Thomas, tailor
McLeod, J., blacksmith
Millar, Alexander, general merchant
Mitchell, S. & E., booksellers
MOFFAT. ALEXANDER, Postmaster, flour mill proprietor
Montreal Telegraph Co., George Ford, agent
Morgan, Robert, cabinet maker
Morris, James, sheriff
Murray, T. & W., general merchants
Nasmith, L., carpenter
O'Driscoll, M., attorney-at-law
O'Kelly, Christopher, lumber merchant
O'Meara, M. & Co., general merchants
Patterson, W. H., grocer
PEMBROKE OBSERVER, (Friday), Beeman Bros., publishers
Potter, J. W., marble works
Quebec Bank, E. Crombie, Agent
RENFREW UNION (Friday)
Sayers, George, baker
Scott, Francis, attorney-at-law
Shields, Charles, shoemaker
Sparling, William, carpenter
Stewart, J., tinsmith
Supple, John, sen., M.P.P.
Supple, John, lumber dealer
Thompson, Archibald, Clerk, County Court, Deputy Clerk Crown, Registrar, Surrogate
Trieve & Rodden, flour mill proprietors
Walford, W. M., engraver
Whelan, Charles B., watchmaker
White, —, attorney-at-law
White, P., sen., J.P.
White, Richard, grocer, insurance agent
Winters, Capt. Fletcher, steamer *Allumette*
Wright, John E., auctioneer

Pendleton.—A village on the South Nation River, in the Township of South Plantagenet, County Prescott, 28 miles from L'Orignal, the County Town, and 320 from Toronto. The vicinity is rich in minerals, particularly lead, plumbago and asbestos. Saline and sulphur springs are also numerous. Population 400.

Anderson, Alexander, hardware merchant
Anderson, James, J.P.
Barton, Oliver, farmer
Belanger, A., baker
Byrnes, Thomas, farmer
Cheesman, William, shoemaker
Collins, Miss M., dressmaker
Cummings, J., M.D.
DELES, DERNIER, J. M. C., Postmaster, general merchant
Dillon, William, proprietor Exchange Hotel
Falkner, James, carpenter
Farrell, Charles, cooper
Fletcher, Kenneth, farmer
Franklin, Alexander, brewer
Franklin, Mrs., dyer
Gordon, Campbell, watchmaker
Hill, Miss E., teacher
Hinckey, Miss M. A., dressmaker
McCormack, James, carpenter
McEwan, Rev. P., universalist
McLean, Hugh, farmer
McLennan, A. S., M.D.,
McLennan, Mrs. A. S., dressmaker
McPhee, Alexander, saddler
McQueen, John, farmer
McFall, James, farmer
Minton, Mick, butcher
Moffatt, J. & H., general merchants
Monette, Joseph, general agent
Nichol, John, M.D
Ollard, John, carpenter
Pendleton Academy
Robillard, J. B., prop. Pendleton Hotel
Ryan, Dennis, farmer
Scott, Rev. Thomas, (Presbyterian)
Shane, John, farmer
Shane, Maurice, farmer
Smith, Miss E., teacher
Story, William, tanner
Wells, H. H., accountant

Pelham Union.—A Post Office in the Township of Pelham, County Monck.
BUCKBEE, J. C., Postmaster.

Penetanguishene.—*(See Villages too late for regular insertion at the end of this work.)*

Penville.—A Post-office in the Township of Tecumseth, County Simcoe, 26 miles from Barrie, the County Town, and 42 from Toronto. Average price of land in the vicinity $75 per acre. Population 120.

Ausman, Abram, general merchant
Ausman, Conrad, dentist
Ausman, John, farmer
Bramin, Charles, farmer
Carson, John H., teacher
Coon, M., farmer
Dewart, S. H., teacher
Dunham, W. C., dentist
Flatt, James, shingle maker
Havelock, T. C., wagon maker
Hill, E., farmer
Hill, Rev. Mr., (N. C. Methodist)
McDermitt, John, carpenter
McMinn, Samuel, farmer
McMinn, Samuel, carpenter
Mills, John, J.P.
Morton, Thomas, saddler
Penfield, H., proprietor Black Horse Inn
Penfield, L., farmer
Richardson, R., farmer
Rogers, J. B., J.P.
Smith, T. W., proprietor Mansion House
Strangways, F., J. P.
Stone, Isaac, farmer
Sydie, Alexander, blacksmith
TURNER, EDWARD T., Postmaster and gen. mer.
Winans, H., farmer

Perrytown.—A Village in the Township of Hope, County Durham, 16 miles from Cobourg, the County Town, and 70 miles from Toronto. The village contains good water privileges. Improved land in the vicinity averages $50 per acre. Daily mails. Population about 120.

Adams, Mrs., prop. hotel
Caldwell, John D., wagon maker
Caldwell, Samuel, farmer
Cantling, Miss, teacher
Choate, Aaron, J.P., farmer
CORBETT, R. ASTLEY, M.D., Postmaster
Corbett, Samuel, J.P.
Corbett, S. C., M.D.
Dyer, James, manufacturer woolen goods
Everett, Robert D., farmer
Gale, Rev. —, (Bible Christian)
Graham, Rev. William, (Wesleyan)
Gray, James, farmer
Gray, W., farmer
Hamill, William, J.P.
Irvin, John, shoemaker
Lewis, Richard P., butcher
Lochead, Rev. William, (Canada Presbyterian)
Lucas, John W., wagon maker
McElroy, John, proprietor flouring mill
Purcell, William, shoemaker
Scott, J. soap and candle maker
Sleep, Samuel, blacksmith
Thompson, William, cooper
Veal, John, grocer
Wilson, Robert, tailor

Perth—The County Town of Lanark, is pleasantly situated on the River Tay, in the Township of Drummond, distant from Brockville 40 miles, Smith's Falls 12 miles, and from Ottawa 50 miles. Mails daily. Money Order Office and Savings Bank. Population 2500.

ALLAN, HENRY, manufacturer of boots and shoes (see adv)
Allan, James, baker
Allan, James, general merchant
ASPDEN, THOMAS, Managing Director Ontario Concentrated Tannin Co.
Bain, Rev. William, (Presbyterian)
Balderson, M., hotel keeper
BANK OF MONTREAL, William Munro, agent, Benjamin Tassie, teller
Bell, James, registrar S. R. Lanark
Bell, Thomas & John, blacksmiths
Berford & Elliott, attorneys-at-law
Berford, W. R. F., Clerk Peace and County Surveyor
Berford, William, County Auditor
Bothwell, Joshua, cooper
BRITISH STANDARD (weekly); Burton Campbell, editor
BROOKE, THOMAS, Town and Township Clerk
Buell, W. O., barrister
Butler, George, tinsmith
Butler, William, tinsmith
Byron, Owen, saloon
CAIRNS, THOMAS, Postmaster
Caldwell, Rev. William (Baptist)
CAMPBELL, BURTON, editor *British Standard*
Campbell, James, mangle, pump and washing machine manufacturer
Campbell, Archibald, official assignee
CANADA BOLT COMPANY; W. J. Morris, manager (see card)
Chisholm, Rev. James, D.D. (Roman Catholic)
Consitt, G. A., attorney-at-law
COOMBS, JOHN S., chemist and druggist
Corry, George, axe maker
Cromwell, J. M. C., P.L.S.
Davies, J. & Co., marble works
Davis, Francis, grocer
Devlin, William F., blacksmith
Dodds, M. R., grocer
DORAN, JOHN, agent Liverpool, London and Globe, Provincial, Home & Canada Life Ins. Co.
Dougherty, Edward, saddler
Douglas, J. W., barrister
Dunnet, George, general merchant
Enwright, T., tailor
Fairbairn, J. & Co., saloon and grocers
Farrell, William, saddler
Ferland, A. L., general merchant
Ferland, Leverin & Co., general merchants
Ferrier, John, harness maker
Fiddler, Miss Margaret, milliner
Field, W. W., painter
Fraser, Donald, County Attorney
Fraser, William, County, Treasurer
FREEMAN, R. D., manager Royal Canadian Bank
Gamsby, G A., general merchant
Gordon, Mrs. R., innkeeper
Graham, Richard, grocer
GRANT, W., M.D., C.M. (see adv)
Gray, James, manager Merchants' Bank
Griffin, Patrick, merchant tailor
HART, JOHN, books and stationery (see adv)
Hart, Rev. Thomas, principal Grammar School
Henderson, J. T., grocer
Henrichon, Felix, blacksmith
Hicks, James, general merchant
Hicks, Thomas, wagon maker
HICKS, WILLIAM, prop. Hicks' Hotel (see adv)
Holliday, David, shoemaker and tanner
Holmes, M., tailor
Howden, Robert, M.D.
James, E., blacksmith
Jamieson, A., shoemaker
JAMIESON, THOMAS, saddler (see adv)
KELLOCK, J. D., M.D., & Co., chemists and druggists (see adv)
Kellock, Robert, gaoler
Kennedy, Edward, general merchant and hotel keeper
Kennedy, J. T., dentist
Kerr, George, general dealer
KILPATRICK, PETER, tanner and currier
Kippen, Alexander, sash factory
LANE, FREEMAN, druggist & stationer (see adv)
Laurie, James, baker
Lee, U. C., station master
Lillie, Robert, moulder
Love, E., hair dresser
McArthur, Andrew, tinsmith
McCullough, John, carriage maker
McDermott, Peter, hotel keeper
McDonogh, Miss Mary
McIntosh, Duncan, hotel keeper
McLaren, John A., distiller
MALLOCH, EDWARD G., barrister
Malloch, John G., County Judge
Martindale, William, hardware
Mattheson, R. J., general merchant
Meighen, A. & Brothers, general merchants
Meighen, Charles, grocer
Menzies, John, Registrar N. R.
MERCHANTS BANK OF CANADA, James Gray, Agent
Moffatt, Robert, Clerk 1st Division Court
Morris & Radenhurst (Alex. Morris, M.P., and Wm. H. Radenhurst) barristers, etc.
Morris, John, P.L.S.
MORRIS, W. J., manager Canada Bolt Co. (see adv.)
Morrison, Ezekiel, photographer
Morrison, Mrs. Rebecca, milliner
Morrison, William, auctioneer
MUNRO, WILLIAM, Agent, Bank Montreal
Murray, Rev. Charles (Roman Catholic)
Neilson, C., watchmaker
Nichol, John, M.D.
NORTHGRAVES, G. & SON. watchmakers (see adv)
NORTHGRAVES, WM. (G. Northgraves & Son)
O'Brien, William, boots and shoes
O'Neill, Patrick (J. Fairbairn & Co.)
PERTH COURIER, (weekly), G. L. Walker & Bro., publishers
PERTH EXPOSITOR, (weekly), Thomas Scott, editor and proprietor
Philp, Henry, cabinet maker
RICE, CHARLES, Deputy Clerk Crown, Reg. Surr. Court
RIDDELL, JOHN, cabinet maker (see adv)
ROYAL CANADIAN BANK, R. D. Freeman, manager, R. E. Johnston, teller
Rudd, John, tailor
Rutherford & Miller, blacksmiths
Ryan & Devlin (Patrick Ryan and George Devlin), general merchants
SCOTT, THOMAS, editor and proprietor *Expositor*
Scott, John, millwright
Selley, A. E., telegraph and express agent, broker

Shaw & Hall, barristers
Shaw & Matheson (C. A. Matheson and Henry D. Shaw), general merchants
Shaw, Richard, founder
Sibbitt, Robert, general merchant
Spalding, James, brewer
Spillman & Dennison, painters
Stanley, Dick & Co. (John & Matthew Stanley and James Dick), carriage makers
Stevenson, Rev. R. L. (Episcopal)
Sutherland, Mrs. James, grocery
Templeton, G. & J., tanners
Thompson, James, sheriff
Thompson, R., general merchant
Thompson, William J., photographer
Thornton, John, cooper
Thornton, William, M.D., teacher common school
Urquhart, D. W., general merchant
Wade, Mrs. R., milliner
WALKER, G. L. & BRO., editors Perth *Courier*
Walsh, William, general merchant
Watson, W., shoemaker
Wilson, James, M. D
Wright, H. B., hatter
Yates, Abel, hotel keeper
WEATHERHEAD, T. & CO., general merchants

Perch Station.—*(See Villages too late for regular insertion at the end of this work.)*

Petawawa.—A Village in the Township of Petawawa, County Renfrew, 10 miles from Pembroke, the County Town. It is situated on the Petawawa River, a tributary of the Ottawa, 50 miles distant from Arnprior, the fare from which place by boat is $2. Population 48.

Bellefulle, G., general merchant
Bellefulle, T., hotel keeper
Blais, Joseph, hotel keeper
Bowan, John, lumber dealer
Brannan, Charles, farmer
Brannan, Samuel, farmer
DEVINE, SOLOMON, Postmaster and prop. hotel
Egan, Edward, farmer
Evans, Robert, farmer
Lance, Michael, shingle maker
McClelland, David, farmer
McGregor, James, farmer
McIntyre, William, farmer
Youler, John, farmer

Peterboro'.—The County Town of Peterboro' on the Peterboro' branch of the Port Hope, Peterboro' and Lindsay Railroad, is situated on the Otonabee River, in the Township of Monaghan. It is a place of considerable importance, and is rapidly improving in wealth and population. Large quantities of manufactured lumber are annually exported. Peterboro' was first settled in the year 1825, and incorporated in 1850. Stages to Norwood, Lakefield, Keene, &c. Money Order Office and Savings Bank. Population 5,000.

Alexander, Charles Albert, groceries and provisions
Allen, Edmund R., marble cutter
Ames, James H., boots and shoes
Anthony, John, boots and shoes
Armour, S., clerk Ontario Bank
Arnot William, chief constable
Arnot, William, jun., confectioner
Bakewell, E., cutter J. W. Dunnet
BANK OF MONTREAL, R. Richardson, agent
BANK OF TORONTO (Branch), Alexander Smith, manager
BARLEE, GEORGE, Deputy Registrar
BARNSTON, P. S., accountant and teller Bank of Montreal
Barrie, William J., photographer
Beattie, Miss, teacher
Beatty, T., groceries and provisions
Beck, Rev. John W. R., (Church of England)
Bell, George, clerk
Bell, William, chemist and druggist
Bertram, John, hardware merchant
Best, James, dry goods and groceries
Black Horse Hotel, Malcolm McKellar, proprietor
BLOMFIELD, CHARLES J., secretary Canada Land and Emigration Co.
Bloomfield, John, veterinary surgeon
Borrowman, Miss, teacher Union School
Boucher, Robert, medical student
Bradburn, Thomas, dry goods and groceries merchant
Brodie, Robert, proprietor Auburn woollen mill
Brook, Daniel, proprietor Peterborough woollen mill
Brown, John, furniture manufacturer
Brown, Robert, barber
Burnham, George, jun., physician and surgeon
Burnham, George, sen., physician and surgeon, and coroner
Burnham, John, barrister
Byrne James, proprietor Ontario House
Caisse's Hotel, Jewett & Turver, proprietors
CAMERON, CHARLES, (McKellar & Cameron)
Cameron, John, grocer
CAMPBELL, JAMES, grocer
Campbell, A. H. & Co., (A. H. Campbell, J. C. Hughson, I. S. Huntson) proprietors Nassau saw mills
Canadian Express Co., George A. Cox, agent
Cantlon, Rev. David (Bible Christian)
CARNEGIE, JOHN, jun., M.P.P.
Carnochan, Miss Janet, teacher Union School
CARVER, S. J., Postmaster
Chambers, Miss, teacher Union School
Chambers, Thomas (Thomas Chambers & Son)
Chambers, William (Thos. Chambers & Son
Chambers, Thomas & Son (Thos. and Wm. Chambers) grocery and bakery
Clark, Jemima, milliner
Clark, Matilda, milliner
Clark, William, watchmaker
Clarke, John, watchmaker
Clementi, Theodore, surveyor
Clifford, John, grocer and provision merchant
Cluxton, William, dry goods and groceries
COLLINS, JOSHUA D., Deputy Registrar
Collins, Thomas, grocer
COMMERCIAL HOUSE, George Cronn, proprietor
Comstock, Aaron, furniture dealer
Connal, Peter, grocer

Conners, Professor, barber
Cook, John, proprietor, Dickson's saw mill
Coulter, William, druggist
Course & Morgan (Wm. Course and Alfred Morgan) confectioners and saloon
COX, GEORGE A., Agent, Montreal Telegraph Co's. and insurance agent
Cox, Henry, painter
Croft, William, proprietor Croft's Hotel
CRONN, GEORGE, proprietor Commercial Hotel and Billiard Room
Curtin, John, saloon
Dawson, Alexander (Munro & Dawson)
Delaney, John, blacksmith
Dennis, Henry, agent John Dennis
Dennis, John, patent pump manufacturer
Dennistoun, Robert, county judge
DENNISTOUN, JAMES (Dennistoun, Fairbairn & Cassels)
Devlin, A. P., solicitor
Dixon, J. B., M.A., principal Union School
Doharty, John, wagon maker and blacksmith
Douglas, John, carriage and wagon maker
DONNELLY, THOMAS, wholesale and retail dealer in sadlery, hardware and trunks, saddles, harness, &c. (see adv)
DONELLY, THOMAS, agent for Wheeler and Wilson and Singer's sewing machine (see adv)
Dumble, D. W., barrister
DUNNET, JAMES W., dry goods and clothing
Dunsford, George, lawyer
Eastland, William, dry goods merchant, and dealer in produce and raw furs
EASTWOOD, D. S., manager Ontario Bank
EDMISON, GEORGE, attorney-at-law
Edwards, James, town clerk and treasurer
English, John, blacksmith
English, James, blacksmith
English, William, boatbuilder
Errett, R. W., insurance agent
Erskine, John, dry goods
Evans, Henry T., marble manufacturer
FAIRBAIRN, T. M. (Dennistoun, Fairbairn & Cassels)
Fairweather, William & Co., dry goods
Faucher, D., proprietor St. Lawrence Hotel
Fitzgerald, Gideon, carpenter
Fitzgerald, Tobias, carriage manufacturer
Fitzgerald & Bolger, surveyors
Flavelle, Mrs., teacher, Union School
Fletcher, John, boots and shoes
Flynn, James, carriage and wagon maker
Fortye, Thomas, custom house officer
GALVIN, PATRICK, carriage and wagon maker
Giles, Philip, provision dealer and gardener
GILMOUR, J. W., chemist and druggist
Glover, Lewis, grocer
Goodwin, Wright M., confectioner and telegraph opr.
Graham, Mrs., milliner and dressmaker
Green, Benjamin, soap, candle and potash manufr.
Green, W. J., grocer and confectioner
GREEN & ROACH, dry goods
Grubb, R. W., teller, Bank of Toronto
Haffey, Patrick, merchant tailor and clothier
Hall, Albert, confectioner
HALL, JAMES, Sheriff County of Peterborough
HALL, JAMES A., deputy sheriff
Hall, John J., Division Court Clerk
HALL, WILLIAM, (Nicholls & Hall)
HALL, WILLIAM, general merchant
Hamilton, James, manuf. agricultural implements
Hamilton, Robert, hardware merchant
HAMILTON, WILLIAM, iron founder (see adv)
Hardie, Robert, B. A., teacher Union School
Harvey, Alexander, physician, surgeon and coroner
HATTON, D. G., (Weller & Hatton)
Holtain, Col
Helm, William, prop. Helm's foundry and machine shop
Henthorn, David, prop. livery stable
Henthorn, James T., J.P
Henthorn, William H., saloon keeper
Heubach, Frederick, cabinet maker and upholsterer
Hill, E. C., lessee Music Hall
Hodgen, William H., (Minaker & Hodgen)
Howie, J. R., homœopathic physician and surgeon
Howie, Ryerson, M.D., homœopathic
Hughson, Joseph, prop. livery stable
JAMES, JOHN & SON, (John James and William E. James) cabinet makers and upholsterers
Jardine, James, ledger keeper, Toronto Bank
Jayes, Samuel, groceries, liquors, &c
Jeffers, James, saloon keeper
Johnston, George, (W. & G., Johnston)
Johnston, Rev. J. H., M.A., (Wesleyan Methodist)
Johnston, William, (W. & George Johnston)
Johnston, George & Son, (Robert & Willism), dry goods
Johnston, W. & G., (William & George), tailors
Kelly, Very Rev. Oliver, (Roman Catholic)
Kempt, A. W., chemist and druggist
Kennedy, James C., painter
Kennedy, John, J.P.
Kennedy, Joseph H., painter
Kennedy, William N., law student
Kidd, —., bookseller and stationer
Kincaid, Robert, coroner, physician and surgeon
Kingan, Robert, hardware merchant
Langford, George, umbrella and parasol repairer
Lannin, Thomas, manufacturer of tin, sheet iron and copperware, and dealer in stoves
Larmour, Robert, shoemaker
Lawder, Edward, (C. Lawder & Co.)
Lawder, E. & Co., (Edward Lawder & John Ryan), dry goods and clothing
Leake, John, boot and shoemaker
Lech, William, furrier
Lemay, David, confectioner
Lemay, Francis, dry goods and clothing
Leonard, Thomas, shoemaker
Lilley, Miss, milliner
Lilley, William
Lundy, R. B., tanner and currier
Lundy, William, general merchant
McClelland, John, watchmaker and jeweler
McCullough, John R., M.D.
McDonald, Angus, groceries, wines and liquors
McDONALD, WILLIAM, proprietor Royal Canadian Hotel (see adv)
McFaul, John, teacher, Union School
McGregor, Lewis, stage and livery stable proprietor
McKELLAR, DONALD (McKellar and Cameron)
McKellar, Malcolm, proprietor, Black Horse Hotel
McKELLAR & CAMERON (Donald McKellar and Charles Cameron) groceries, hardware and commission merchants
McMillen, William, barber
McNab, R. A., produce merchant
McNab, John, M.D.
McWilliams, James, carriage and wagon maker
McWilliams, James, jailor
McWilliams, John B., bailiff
Macdonnell, Rev. D. J., (Church of England)
Macdougall, A. H., teller, Royal Canadian Bank
Maloney & Brothers (Daniel and William) grocers and wine merchants

Mahoney, Thomas, grocer
Martin, Miss Mary Ann, dressmaker
Martin, William (Robertson and Martin)
MARVER, EDWARD
MENZIES, THOMAS, bookseller & stationer (see adv)
Mercer, William & Brothers (Wm., Frank and John) mer. tailors and dealers in gents' furnishing goods
Meyetta, L., barber
Minaker, William H. (Minaker & Hodgen)
Minaker & Hodgen (Wm H. Minaker and Wm. H. Hodgen), builders and manufacturers Kinney's Patent Harrows
MITCHELL, GEORGE, prop. St. George Saloon
Mitchell, William H., harness maker
Moffat, James, wagon and carriage maker
Moffat, John, blacksmith
Moloney, Michael, dry goods and groceries
MONTREAL HOUSE, dry goods and clothing; J. W. Dunnet, proprietor
MONTREAL TELEGRAPH COMPANY; George A. Cox, operator
Moore, W. H., solicitor
Morris, E., manufacturer Botanic medicines
Morrow, R. A.
Mungovan, Patrick, news agent
Munro, George (Munro & Dawson)
Munro & Dawson (George Munro and Alexander Dawson), proprietors Ontario Grist Mill
New Dominion House; John Reid, proprietor
NICHOLLS, ROBERT (Nicholls & Hall)
NORTH BRITISH AND MERCANTILE FIRE AND LIFE INSURANCE COMPANY; R. Richardson, agent
Norton, Henry, turnkey
O'Beirne, Ivan, secretary of Town Trust Commissioners
O'Brien, David, blacksmith
O'Donnell, J., L.D.S., surgeon dentist
O'Neill, Miss Mary A., dressmaker
Ogilvy, W., manager Royal Canadian Bank
ONTARIO BANK; D. S. Eastwood, manager
Orde, G. F., general agent
ORMOND, CHARLES (Ormond & Walsh)
Ormond, J. R. & Co., watchmakers and jewelers (see adv)
ORMOND & WALSH (Charles Ormond and William Walsh), chemists and druggists
Owen, Henry, washing machine manufacturer
Parnell, Richard, miller
Paterson, W. & Son, tanners
Patterson, George, grocer and provision merchant
Patterson, Robert, boots and shoes
Pearse, E., county clerk
Pengelly, James, saddler
Pentland, David, dentist
PERRY, CHARLES, M.P.
PETERBOROUGH EXAMINER, (weekly), James Stratton, editor and proprietor
Peterborough Music Hall, E. C. Hill, lessee
PETERBOROUGH REVIEW, (weekly), Robert Romaine, proprietor
Peters, Charles, law student
Phelan, E., proprietor Phelan's Hotel
POOLE, EDWIN, manufacturer and dealer in cabinet ware, upholstering and undertaking
POOLE, EDWIN, Lieut.-Col. 57th battalion Volunteer Militia
Reid, John, proprietor New Dominion House
RICHARDSON, R., agent Bank of Montreal, and agent North British and Mercantile Fire and Life Insurance Co.
Robertson, William (Robertson & Martin)
Robinson, Edward, grocer and provision merchant
Robinson, J. & Co., dry goods and groceries
Robertson & Martin (William Robertson and William Martin), planing mill and sash and blind manufacturers
Rogers, Rev. J. M. (Free Church)
ROMAINE, ROBERT, proprietor *Peterboro' Review*
Rose, Mrs. Mary, milliner and dressmaker
Ross, George, proprietor Ross's Hotel
Rowe, Robert, contractor
ROYAL CANADIAN BANK, W. Ogilvy, manager
ROYAL CANADIAN HOTEL, William McDonald, proprietor (see adv)
ROYAL INSURANCE CO., (Fire and Life), Alex. Smith, agent
RUBIDGE, CHARLES, Registrar
Rush, T., veterinary surgeon
Rutherford, Miss, teacher
Ryan, Patrick, tanner and currier
Ryan, John, (E. Lawder & Co.)
ST. GEORGE'S SALOON, George Mitchell, prop.
St. Lawrence, Hotel, D. Fancher, proprietor
ST. LAWRENCE HOTEL, E. Shaver, proprietor
Sanderson, Miss, milliner
SCOTT, WILLIAM A., lumber merchant
SCOTT, WILLIAM H, Mayor, attorney
Sexsmith, Alice, dressmaker
Sexsmith, Mary A., private school
SHAVER, E., proprietor St. Lawrence Hotel
Sheridan, W., County Treasurer
SMITH, ALEXANDER, manager Toronto Bank and insurance agent
Smith, Henry H., law student
SMITH, SIDNEY, Q.C., barrister and Inspector of Registry offices
Stalker, Joseph
STANDARD LIFE ASSURANCE COMPANY, Alexander Smith, agent
Stinson, R. & Son, manufacturers and dealers in boots and shoes
Stephens, James, printer
Stephens, James A., book and job printer and bookbinder
Stethern, George, & Co., hardware merchant
Stevenson, James, stoves and tinware
Stewart, G. A., P. L. S., county surveyor
Stinson, groceries and provisions
Stock, Rev. Thomas (Baptist)
STRATTON, J., publisher "Peterborough Examiner"
Strickland, H. (Strickland & Brothers) lumber merchts
Sullivan, John, proprietor Farmer's Home
Tamblyn, John, teller Ontario Bank
Tanner, George, cabinet maker
Taylor, Frederick, teacher Union school
TAYLOR, GEORGE, pump maker and wood turner (see adv)
Taylor, Robert, tailor
TAYLOR, JOHN, boots and shoes
Thompson, Robert, photographer
THOMPSON, W. G. (W. G. Thompson & Co.)
THOMPSON, W. G. & CO., (William G. Thompson, Robert Nicholls and William Hall) dry goods
Tierney, William, proprietor Tierney's Hotel
Uin, Hamilton, proprietor Stewart House
Waddell, William, saddler
WALSH, WILLIAM, (Ormond & Walsh)
WALTON, ROBERT, hardware, stoves, tin house furnishing, saddlery, lamps and oil
WELLER, C. A., (Weller & Halton)
WELLER & HALTON, (C. A. Weller and D. G. Halton) barristers
Wells, John, boot and shoe maker
WESCOTT, ROBERT, potter
WHITE, ROBERT, prop. livery stable (see adv)
White, Samuel, boots and shoes, sewing machine agt
White, Thomas, collector of Inland Revenue

Whyte & Hamilton, (John White and William Hamilton) iron founders
Wilson, Miss R., milliner
Winright, Mrs., milliner
WINSHIP, T. J., tobacconist (see adv)
Wrighton, W. H., grocer and provision merchant
Yelland, William, blacksmith

Petersburg.—A Village and Station of the Grand Trunk Railway, in the Township of Wilmot, County Waterloo, 6 miles from Berlin, the County Town, and 80 from Toronto. Daily Mail. Population 300.

Bauer, Conrad, prop. livery stable
Doell, Peter, blacksmith
Ernst, Henry, general merchant
Ernst, Hiram, telegraph operator
ERNST, L., Postmaster and hotel keeper
Gottschalk, Elias, wagon maker
Kranter, Jacob, teacher
Martin, Jacob, painter
Platt, J. C., telegraph operator
Platt, William, agent G.T.R. and Can. Ex. Co
Poll, C., shoemaker
Schaefer, Jacob, tailor
Toeger, Christopher, tanner
Voll & Bro., weavers and dyers

Peterson.—A Post Office in the Township of Stanhope, County Peterboro'.

Peterson's Ferry.—A Post Office in the Township of Sophiasburg, County Prince Edward.
PETERSON, PAUL C., Postmaster.

Petrolea.—An incorporated Village and Station of the Great Western Railway, on Bear Creek, in the Township of Enniskillen, County Lambton, 20 miles from Sarnia, the County Town, and 170 from Toronto. It is situated in the celebrated Western Oil Region, and a large number of wells are sunk in the Village. Money Order Office and Savings Bank. Population 1,000.

BARCLAY, P., Postmaster and banker
Barker, Rev. D., (Episcopal Methodist)
Bishop, H., dry goods merchant
Blackmar, —., agent Hillsdale Oil Co.
Bolt, John, conveyancer
BOULTON, JOHN, proprietor Internationl Hotel
Boyce, William, prop. Great Western Hotel
Brown & Kennedy, boots and shoes
Brown, William, hotel keeper
Canneff, H., watchmaker and jeweler
Chamberlain & Simley, proprietors oil wells
Chisholm, —., agent Toronto Rock Oil Co.
Cooley & Simmons, dealers in lubricating oil
Dale, John B., druggist
Dale, R., telegraph operator
Davis, S. E., boots and shoes
Drader, E., grocer
Draper & McKenzie, founders and machinists
Duggan, Michael, farmer
Dunlop & Polley, proprietors oil wells
Ellwood & Parsons, proprietors oil wells
Fairbanks & Bennett, hardware and groceries
FLETCHER & BOSWELL, props. American Hotel
Fraser, Miss, milliner, etc.
Graham, Thomas, proprietor, oil works
Hamilton, John, tailor
Hartry, Alfred, wagon maker
Herring, R. O., printer
Houston, Robert, farmer
Hunt, H. H., tinsmith
Hutchinson, Rev. John (Wesleyan)
Hyde, John C., proprietor, oil works
Keith, Jonathan, baker
Kimball, —, agent, Hartford Oil Co.
King, Thomas, boots and shoes
Lancaster, J. A., teacher
Lancy, —, proprietor, oil wells
Lawson, James, proprietor, oil wells
Lindsay, W., grocer
McCallum, James, soap and candle manfr.
McCormack, Charles, cabinet maker
McDonald, John, boiler maker
McGarvey, H. H., general merchant
McGill, James, carpenter
McKenzie, John, general merchant
McMillan, John, agent, Standard Oil Refinery
McQueen, E., general merchant
Manning, R., butcher
Marshall & Goodrich, proprietors oil wells
Montgomery, James, farmer
Morrison, John, farmer
Murphy, George E., J.P.
Naylon, J., proprietor Murray's Hotel
Nelson, J. H., boots and shoes
Noble, John D., proprietor oil wells
Oliver, W. H., M.D.
Oliver, Walter, lumber dealer
PARKER, MELVILLE, notary public
PARKER & TOWNSEND, general merchants, agents and dealers in lubricating oils
Penson, Thomas, lumber dealer
Reynolds, William, Variety Store
Rispin, John, agent G.W.R.
Schmidt, Franklin, cooper
Simpson & Lumbard, proprietor United States hotel
Slack, R., grocer
Sovereign, Cyrus, general merchant
Spencer & Smith, oil refiners
Sproul, Jacob, butcher
Stewart, John, farmer
Stokes, S., tank digger
Stover, A. R., dealer in lubricating oil
Taylor, Peter, proprietor oil wells
Tracy, John, land agent
Van Tayl & Hayes, prop. Michigan Exchange Hotel
Waddell, James, tailor
Walters & Palmeter, books and stationery
Webster, Daniel, grocer
Woodley, John, prop. steam flouring mill

Petworth.—A Village on the Napanee River, in the Township of Portland, County Frontenac, 17 miles from Kingston, and 18 from Napanee. Stage to Kingston. Population 200.

Aaron, Rev. Mr. (Wesleyan)
Back, John, miller
Beattie, William, teacher
Brown, Sylvester, grocer
CARSCALLAN, E. L., Postmaster
Dunbar, James, farmer
Ferrell, Hiram, farmer
Foster, James, cooper
Foster, James, painter
Garrison, George, lime manufacturer
Garrison, John, grocer
Hulon, Rev. W. (Episcopal Methodist)
Knight, Alfred, assistant postmaster
Lott, George, J.P. and general merchant
Lott, L., farmer
McDonough, James, farmer
Miller, Rev. Mr. (Wesleyan)
O'Loughlin, Rev. A. (Church of England)
Peters, Absalom, blacksmith
Roberts, William, cabinet maker
Rush, M., farmer
Smith, Ira, blacksmith
Snider, Solomon, shingle manufacturer
Sweet, Judson, shoemaker
Upham, John, dyer
Vanest, James, sen., M.D.
Wager, George, cabinet maker
White, Rev. Mr. (Episcopal Methodist)
Youman, Samuel, farmer

Philipsburg.—A small Village in the Township of Wilmot, County Waterloo, 12 miles from Berlin, the County Town.

Armbrecht, Henry, wagon maker
Bechtel, N., farmer
Berg, H., farmer
Boettinger, J., tailor
Bunsho, Jacob, carpenter
Doering, Adam, farmer
Doering, Andrew, farmer
Doering, E., J.P.
Doering, C. & Son, tanners and general merchants
DOERING, G. C., Postmaster
Eidt Conrad, farmer
Eidt, J. C., farmer
Eidt, J. S., farmer
Forler, Philip, carpenter
Germann, J., general merchant
Graff, G. M., farmer
Grimms, J. E., proprietor Phillipsburg, Inn
Hoffman, Henry, wagon maker
Jundt, George, shoemaker
Lantz, George, farmer
Lohr, Daniel, shoemaker
Moran, John, teacher
Schmidt, Rev. G. (Lutheran)
Schmidt, H. R., farmer
Wettlanfer, C., farmer

Philipsville.—A Village in the Township of Bastard, County Leeds, 30 miles from Brockville, the County Town, and 15 from Westport. Stages to Brockville and Westport. Population 150.

Alguire, W. W., accountant
BROWN, GEORGE, Postmaster and general mercht
Curtis, Franklin, shoemaker
Downey, Patrick, wagon maker
Earl, Edward, saddler
Farnham, Mrs. E., milliner
Graham, Rev. —, (Roman Catholic)
Halladay, Alvin, lime and stone
Hart, John, hotel keeper
Haskin, C., carpenter
Haskin, Samuel W., proprietor flouring mill
Howard, Rev. William, (Episcopal Methodist)
Janson, Rev. William T. (Baptist)
Johnston, C., cabinet maker
Livingston, Miss Mary, milliner
Ludbrook, William H., cooper
McDonald, Joseph, shoemaker
McEachron, James E., tanner
Murphy, Warren, teacher
Nolan, Michael, lime and stone
Philips, D., J.P.
Porter, James, wagon maker
Warren, Joshua, general merchant
Whitmore, George, shoemaker
Willows, Thomas, J.P.

Pickering.—A Post Village in the Township of Pickering, County Ontario, 6 miles distant from Whitby, the County Town, and 23 from Toronto. Average price of land $60 per acre. Daily mails. Money order office. Population 300.

Bunting, B., J.P., general merchant
Conway, Rev. Mr., (Roman Catholic)
Cuthbert, William, boots and shoes
Ferguson, William, carpenter
Gibbons, Mrs., milliner, &c
Gordon, John & Sons, coopers
Grant, Lewis M., wagon maker
Haight, John, dyer and scourer
Hartrick, John, carpenter
Head, Mrs. John, prop. flouring mill
Henderson, Joseph, carpenter
Hodgson, James, saddler
Jennings, Thomas, blacksmith
Johnson, George, tailor
Kennedy, Rev. A., (Canada Presbyterian)
Leonard, Richard, hotel keeper
Lepper, John, general merchant
Linton, Joseph, boots and shoes
Lipsey, John, brewer
Lossee, Mrs. M., milliner
McGann, Bartlett, boots and shoes
Margach, Alexander, blacksmith
Mason, Andrew, hotel keeper
Matthews, Francis, millinery goods, &c

Mockridge, Rev. Mr., (Church of England)
Peart, Thomas, butcher
Peters, Albert, teacher
Pollard, James, boots and shoes
Pope, Frederick, telegraph operator
Rex, George, painter
Ross, Rev. William (Church of Scotland)
Rua, Michael, blacksmith
Smith, Moses, proprietor flouring mill
Stobbs, Rev. -- (Wesleyan)
Sullivan, Patrick, wagon maker
Thorpe, James L., general merchant
Tucker, David, M.D.
Westlake, Nicholas, butchar
WHITING, ELIZABETH, Postmistress
Whitmore, John, general merchant
Williams, Rev. — (Bible Christian)
Wright, Edward, general merchant

Picton.—The County Town of Prince Edward, on the Bay of Quinté, in the Township of Hallowell, 20 miles from Belleville, 30 from Trenton and 45 from Kingston. Stations G.T.R. Steamers to Belleville and Kingston daily, to Oswego tri-weekly, and to Montreal weekly. Stages daily to Brighton and Belleville. Money Order Office and Savings Bank. Population, 3000.

Ackerman, G., professor German and Drawing, Ontario College
Allen, John H., commission merchant
Allison, Rev. Cyrus (Wesleyan)
ALLISON & GIBSON (W. H. R. Allison and Stephen Gibson), barristers, &c. (see card)
Allison & McDonald, druggists
Babitt, Richard, mariner
BANK OF MONTREAL; F. A. Despard, agent; Fred. White, teller; W. Ross, jun., ledger keeper
BARKER, DAVID, Postmaster
BARRER & SHANNON (D. Barker and Thomas Shannon), Prince Edward foundry
Beaton, William A., grocer
Beringer, J. F., watchmaker
Blanchard, Mrs. J., Globe Hotel
Bog, T., produce and commission merchant
Bond, Rev. W., Ontario College
Booth, William, Deputy Registrar
BOWERMAN, ELIAS, L.D.S.
BOYLE, ROBERT, county clerk, editor and proprietor *Picton Times*
Bristol, Almond, merchant
Brooks, G., shoemaker
Campbell, Thomas, tailor
Carrington, John, tannery
Carter, J. N., hardware
Carter, William, grocer
Carter & Clute, general merchants
Case, F. H., merchant
Chadd, George, baker
Chapman, C. A., chemist and druggist
Chapman, R. J., county treasurer
Clapp, John, grocer
Clapp, Robert, U. S. Consular agent
Clute, John S., collector customs
Colden, Thomas, grocer
Cook, Willett A., painter
Conger, J. W., printer
CONGER, S. M., editor and prop. *Picton Gazette*
Crozier, St. G., professor of music Ontario College
Curran, William, grocer
Davis, John, saddler
DESPARD, F. A, agent Bank of Montreal
Dingman, Dugald, photographer
Donnelly, Thomas, general merchant
Dougall, William
Downes, Captain, Bursar, Ontario College
Downs, John, blacksmith
Downes, J. P., Clerk, Division Gourt
Dunlop, James, & Co., clothiers
Elliott, John, shoemaker
Eyre, R. H., fancy goods
Fairfield, D. L., County Judge
Faughan, Sergeant, drill instructor and house steward, Ontario College
FITZGERALD, R. J., barrister
Fralick, Brothers carriage makers
Gaw, Hugh, treasurer
Gearing, Colin, general merchant
GIBSON, STEPHEN, (Allison and Gibson)
Gilbert, R. S. & J. N., cabinet makers
Gillespie, B., grocer
Gillespie & Browne, tanners
Glenn, James, shoemaker
Goodmurphy, Lawrence, dry goods and clothing
Greeley, A., M.P.
HAIGHT, CANNIFF, chemist and druggist
Hart & Son, carriage makers
Henderson, John, grocer
Ingersoll, F., M.D.
Ingram, C. W., silver plater
Irving, Andrew, builder and contractor
Jamieson, T., grocer
Kemp, W. G., dry goods and groceries
Kelly, George, mason and contractor
Lalor, Rev. M. (Roman Catholic)
Lennox, —, principal Grammar School
Lent, J. E., marble works
Long, Claude, 2nd master Ontario College
LOW, PHILIP, barrister, County Attorney, Clerk Peace, Clerk County Court
McCuaig, Paul F., forwarder, etc.
McDonald, Charles A., grocer
McDonald, Henry, jailer
McDonald, C. J., grocer
McFaul, T., grain merchant
McGillivray, Charles, grocer
McGowan, William, boots and shoes
McKee, James, builder
McKenzie, Walter, merchant
McMechan, Rev. John, (Presbyterian)
Macaulay, Rev. William (Church of England)
MERRILL, EDWARD S., barrister
MERRILL, SAMUEL, barrister
Moore, Thomas, M.D.
Morden, J. B., M.D.
Morden, J., bailiff
Mottashed, J., hotel keeper
Mulholland, James, dry goods and groceries
Mullett, John, tanner
Nash, J. Platt, M.D.
NEW NATION, (weely), Platt & Way, editors and proprietors
Norman, R. A., boots and shoes
Noxon, Richard, (Dunlop & Co)
O'Reilly, James, grocer
O'Shea, D., shoemaker
ONTARIO COLLEGE, president, the Lord Bishop of Ontario
Owens, William, lumber merchant
Patterson, William, baker

Peck, James, dry goods and groceries
Phillips, Thomas, tinsmith
Phillips, Vincent, mariner
PICTON GAZETTE, (weekly) S. M. Conger, editor
PLATT & WAY, (G. D. Platt and B. Way, editors props. *New Nation*
PORTE, J. A., master steamer *J. Greenway*
Porte, W. J., watchmaker
Porter, James, leather dealer
Powers & Hughes, builders
RANKIN, A., M.D
RANKIN, C. E., P.L.S., civil engineer
Rawson, Luther, shoemaker
Redmond, Joseph, grocer
Redmond, William, ship builder
Reid, Thomas, grocer
Reynolds, J. G., grocer
Reynolds, William, prop. brick yard
Reynolds, W. P., dry goods and groceries
Roblin, F. P., hardware
Roblin, John P., county registrar
Ross, Walter, M.P.
Ross, Walter & Co., merchants
Ross, W., jun., discount clerk Bank of Montreal
Sawyer, Rufus, cabinet maker
Seeds, William, blacksmith
Shaw, Mrs., matron Ontario College
Sills, Elisha, dry goods
Simonds, W. B., veterinary surgeon
Smith, E. B., master steamer *St. Helen*
Southard, Abram, cabinet maker
Southard, Archibald, farmer, president Prince Edward Agricultural Society
Stanton & Ruttan, steam grist and saw mills
Stickney, S. C., watchmaker
Striker, G.
Sullivan, Denis, grocer
Synott, William, dry goods and groceries
Taylor, Francis, butcher
Thomas, John, carriage maker
Thorne, George P.
Thorpe, Henry J., sheriff
TIMES, THE (weekly) Robert Boyle, editor and prop
Tracey, W., M.R.C.P., Eng., (Ontario College)
Treusdale & Branscombe, photographers
Turney, John, grocer
TWIGG, JOHN, Deputy Clerk Crown and Pleas, Clerk County Court, Registrar Surrogate, secretary Prince Edwaad Mutual Insurance Co.
Vanblaricum, Robert, saddler
Vanblaricom, Thomas N., blacksmith
Vandusen, C., grocer
Van Patten, Peter, hotel
Wait, Charles, stoves and tinware
Ward, Patrick, mariner
Washburn, Paul
Welch, Robert, jun., mason and contractor
WHITE, FREDERICK, teller Bank of Montreal
Wilson, C. S., J.P.
WOOD, HENRY T., L.D.S., registrar R. C. D. S. Ontario
Woods, Francis, hatter
Wycott, Nelson, hardware
Willoughby, Rev. N. R. (Wesleyan)
Yarwood & Co., clothing, &c.

Pine Grove.—A Village on the river Humber, in the Township of Vaughan, County York, 18 miles from Toronto, 7 from Thornhill Station Northern Railway, and 9 from Weston Station Grand Trunk Railway. Population 200.

Balmer, George, accountant
Bearman, George, mechanic
Blain, Seward, blacksmith
GOODERHAM, A. L., Postmaster
Gooderham & Worts, general merchants and millers
Graham, James, farmer
Graham, Thomas, M.P.P., farmer
Hay, Rev. R. (Congregational)
Hinchy, James, millwright
McClure, Hamilton, saddler
Mayward, John, proprietor Pine Grove Hotel
Smith, Thomas, farmer
Stegman, John
Stegman, Thomas, manager Gooderham & Worts
Sterling, William, proprietor Commercial Hotel
Stuart, William, miller
Tollon, James, farmer
Watt, Charles, shoemaker
Witherspoon, David, farmer
Wilson, Albert, teacher
Willy, Thomas, farmer

Pine Orchard.—A Post Office in the Township of York, County York

Lundy, Samuel, carpenter
May, Nelson, carpenter
Randall, C., Postmaster
Widdifield, William, blacksmith

Pinkerton.—A Post Village in the Township of Greenock, County Bruce, 11 miles from Walkerton, the County Town, and 140 from Toronto. Average price of improved land $25 per acre. Population 80.

Banting, W., farmer
Bentley, J., farmer
Bowes, W., farmer
Douglass, J. G., M.D
Fleming, James, shoemaker
Garland, R., farmer
Geary, Thomas, cabinet maker
Jeffers, Rev
KING, SAMUEL A., Postmaster
McCormick, W. C., hotel keeper and gen mercht
McKechnie, O'Neil, teacher
McKenzie, Roderick, shoemaker
Pinkerton, David, farmer
Pinkerton, Joseph, prop. flouring mill
Pinkerton, M., farmer
Pinkerton, Thomas, lumber dealer
Smith, Joseph, carpenter
Willson, James, carpenter
Willson, Wellington, carpenter

Pine River.—A Post Village in the Township of Huron, County Bruce. Distant 34 miles from Walkerton, the County Town, and 159 from Toronto. Improved land averages from $10 to $25 per acre. Population 50.

Armstrong, J., farmer
Ballantyne, J., farmer
Beatty, J., farmer
Bell, W., farmer
Carleton, D., farmer
Harding, Robert, farmer
Huggans, Rev. W. (Primitive Methodist)
Hurron, F., farmer
Hyslop, William, carpenter
Ingles, Rev. W., (United Presbyterian)
Irwin, W. H., farmer
McCOSH, A. G., Postmaster
McCosh, W., farmer
McDonald, A., farmer
McDermid, D., farmer
McKay, William, prop. Huron Inn
Montgomery, G., farmer
Montgomery, W., farmer
Moore, J., farmer
Patterson, T., farmer
Smith, John, J.P
Taylor, Samuel, teacher
Telford, J., farmer
Telford, T., farmer
Thompson, J., farmer
Watson, J., farmer

Pittsferry.—A Post Office in the Township of Pittsburgh, County Frontenac.
ROOT, DANIEL, Postmaster.

Plainfield.—A Village on the Moira River, in the Township of Thurlow, County Hastings, 10 miles from Belleville, the County Town, and 20 from Bridgewater. Stage to Bridgewater. Population 200.

Barnes, James, lumber dealer and prop. flouring mill
Bradsham, William, farmer
Caverly, P. K., wagon maker
Chamberlain, Mrs., groceries
Clapp, S., lumber dealer
Fox, W., farmer
Gardiner, G., proprietor, planing mill
Garrison, W. H., J.P., carpenter
Gould, Andrew, shoemaker
GOULD, E. N., Postmaster
Hall, A., farmer
Hall, T., farmer
Hall, Mrs., groceries
Hicks, Joshua, farmer
Hinds, A. C., carpenter
Latta, G. & G., lumber dealers
McCradie, Edward, teacher
McDannitt, William, farmer
Parks, A., farmer
Ross, G., hotel keeper

Plattsville.—A Village on Smith's Creek, in the Township of Blenheim, County of Oxford, 16 miles from Woodstock, the County Town, and 80 from Toronto.

Ames, Rev. W. (Wesleyan)
Baker, Mrs., milliner, &c.
Baker, Nelson, brick maker
Brundle, Joshua, tinsmith
Brymner, James, cooper
Burton, —, tailor
Caspary, Henry, cooper
Chambers, Walter, carpenter
Chilby, Martin, cooper
Climons & Veech, druggists and general merchants
Coxson, George, farmer
Cramp, William, butcher
Dalton, —, tailor
Dodge, Mrs., proprietor Plattsville House
Flinn, Conrad, saddler
Ford, Michael, shoemaker
Freed, N. & Co., proprietors flouring mill, and sash, door and blind manufactory
Gatzke, Andrew, livery stable
Gatzke, Anderson, shoemaker
Gofton, R., farmer
Greenfield, —, carpenter
Gullingbaugh, Frederick, painter
Harvey, John, farmer
Hayward, James, painter
Hoffman, Henry, cooper
Holshour, John, cooper
Kilborn, J., J.P., N.P.
Lake, Thomas, grocer
Lipp, Henry, cooper
McDonald, J. J., teacher
McGinnis, Daniel, carpenter
Masters, George, carpenter
Mellish, Rev. W. (Church of England)
Morrison, John, M.D.
Motherall, James, shoemaker
Nicholl, Thomas, farmer
Parks, R., tanner
Patton, Robert, farmer
Philips, —, M.D.
Platt, Edward, lumber dealer
PLATT, SAMUEL, Postmaster, proprietor saw mill
Poor, Joseph, carpenter
Reynolds, A., grocer
Richardson, Rev. E. (Wesleyan)
Robinson, John & Co., general merchants
Seaman, Thomas, wagon maker
Sellers, Miss, milliner, &c.
Shantz, David P., farmer
Smart, John, general merchant
Smart, John, farmer
Snider, Amos, farmer
Speir, Mrs., milliner
Stouffer, A. R., proprietor flouring mill
Taylor, Thomas, wagon maker
Thomas, Rev. C. A. (Lutheran)
Treffey, R., farmer
Vanevery, W., accountant
Walden, R. S., general agent
Warnock & Co., manufacturer of woolen goods
Wilrich, W., prop. Commercial Hotel
Workman, Thomas, farmer

Playfair.—A small Village on the Mississippi River, in the Township of Bathurst, County Lanark, 12 miles from Perth, the County Town. Improved land averages $45, and wild $12 per acre. Population 50.

Anderson, Robert, shingle maker
Boulton, Samuel, farmer
Buffam, George, carpenter
Buffam, William, carpenter
Elliott, Robert, shoemaker
Gibson, Andrew, teacher
Jackson, Marshal, farmer
Jackson, William, cooper
Laden, John, farmer
Lees, William, J.P., shingle maker
Lester, Rev. Alexander, (Methodist)
McDonald, John, farmer
MILLS, G. C., Postmaster, grocer, and cabinet maker
Playfair, Elijah, farmer
Shanks, Alexander, farmer
Sheridan, Richard, farmer
Smith, William, hotel keeper
Welsh, Edward, shingle maker

Plantaganet.—*(See Villages too late for regular insertion at the end of this work).*

Pleasant Hill—*(See Villages too late for regular insertion at the end of this work.)*

Plum Hollow.—A Post Office in the Township of Bastard, County Leeds.

ALGUIRE, MRS. LYDIA, Postmistress.

Port Abino.—(Ridgeway Village)—A Station on the Buffalo and Lake Huron Railroad in the Township of Bertie, County Welland, 18 miles from Welland, the County Town, 8 from Fort Erie, and 10 from Port Colborne. The Station is called Bertie. Land in the vicinity averages $40 per acre. Population 450.

Aberry, C., boots and shoes
Auger, Alexander, blacksmith
Balfour & Bibly, general merchants
Brewster, N., M.D.
Brown, T. W., tailor
Clark, John, proprietor, brick yard
Cutler, E., prop. flouring mill, sash, door and blind manfr. and general merchant
Cutler, N., wagon maker
Dickout, H. C., J.P.
Disher, B. M., general merchant
DISHER, R., Postmaster
Fortier, Sarah, milliner, etc.
Gervin, C. A., tinsmith
Graff, E. H., boots and shoes
Gray, John, wagon maker
Hershey, Andrew & Co., founders and machinists
Hershey, Benjamin, carpenter
Hershey & Co., proprietor, planing mill
Hibbard, H. M., patent right agent
Huffman, Alfred, proprietor, livery stable
Huffman, G., Ridgeway Hotel
Jackson, John, butcher
Johston, Joseph, stock dealer
Matthews, C., boots and shoes
Mattison, A., general merchant
Mutchner, —, M.D.
Moore, E. F., wagon maker
Nagle, S., cabinet maker
Our, D., tailor
Seymour, Vanbleck & Co., International Lime Co.
Sloan, W. M., J.P.
Snyder, B. P.. blacksmith
Spading, M., butcher
Tait, A., shingle maker
Teal & Co., wine and spirit dealers
Teel, Zachariah, grocer
Teull, J., gunsmith
Wilkins, C., tanner
Willson, A., proprietor City Hotel
Willson, R. B., saddler

Point Alexander.—A Post Office in the Township of Rolph, County Renfrew.

LANE, JOHN, Postmaster.

Point Edward.—A Village and Station of the Grand Trunk Railway, at the confluence of Lake Huron and the River St. Clair, in the Township of Sarnia, County Lambton, 2 miles from Sarnia, the County Town.

Beyer, A., shoemaker
Clement, P., hotel keeper
Crouch, I., shoemaker
Empey, D., carpenter
Ernst, W. F., general merchant
ERNST, LOUIS, Postmaster and grocer
Fitzgibbon, D., hotel keeper
Holden, James, hotel keeper
Johnston, John, carpenter
Livingston, D., grocer
Mathewson, G. N., Custom House officer
Salter, Rev. T. R. (Church of England)
Spetz, Jacob, hotel keeper and painter
Thompson, Rev. John (Presbyterian)
Turnbull, D., boiler maker
Wiley, T., hotel keeper

Point Petre.—A Post Office in the Township of Athol, County Prince Edward, on the shore of Lake Ontario, 13 miles from Picton, the County Town. Point Petre lighthouse is situated here, and there is an extensive fishery in the vicinity.

Campbell, Rev. —, (Wesleyan)
Collier, Edward, cooper
Collier, James, waggon maker
Edmonds, John, carpenter
Garrison, G. A., carpenter
Garrison, Samuel, carpenter
Garrison, William, farmer
Kinney, John, teacher
Kinney, William, J.P.
McCormick, George, farmer
McGivern, Francis, cooper
McKibbon, Thomas, farmer
Martin, Alexander, carpenter
Martin, Charlotte, teacher
Martin, Stephen, farmer
Palen, W. A., J.P., farmer
Reid, Thomas, cooper
Reusan, Henry, cooper
SCOTT, JAMES, Postmaster, lime and stone dealer and farmer
Starks, L., lime and stone
Tuttle, Henry, carpenter
Weldon, Rev. Isaac (Wesleyan)

Pomona.—A Post Office in the Township of Glenelg, County Grey.

ROSS, JAMES, Postmaster.

Point Traverse.—A Post Village in the Township of Marysburgh, County Prince Edward, 17 miles from Picton, the County Town, and 150 from Toronto. Stage to Milford. Average price of land $25 per acre. Population 50.

CASE, HARMON, Postmaster, shingle maker
Moran, E., teacher

Poland.—A Post Office, in the Township of Dalhousie, County Lanark.

Bingley, Charles, carpenter
Gavin, Robert, farmer
Lennon, Michael W., teacher
McINTOSH, DUNCAN, Postmaster, prop. Barmoral Inn
McIntosh, John, farmer
Ogilie, Robert, farmer
Paul, John, farmer
Paul, Moses, farmer
Regan, John, farmer
Stewart, James, farmer
White, Gilbert, grocer

Ponsonby.—A small Village in the Township of Pilkington, County Wellington, 9 miles from Guelph, the County Town, 7 from Fergus and 4 from Elora. Improved land in the vicinity averages $35 per acre. Population 50.

HALLEY, JAMES, L., Postmaster, general mer.
Hirst, G., hotel keeper
McKenzie, George, J.P.
McPherson, J., teacher
Maitland, J. & W., wagon maker
Michie, William, J.P.
Neagle, James, farmer]
O'Connor, C., farmer
Telfer, W. B., farmer
Wallace, Donald, assessor

Port Bruce.—A small Village in the Township of Malahide, County Elgin, 18 miles from St. Thomas, the County Town. Good manufacturing facilities are afforded by Catfish Creek. Average value of improved land $40, and wild $30 per acre.

Camp, John, farmer
Chappison, Rev. J. (Wesleyan)
Clemens, Elijah, farmer
Copeland, George, farmer
Copeland, Joseph, farmer
Copeland, Mark, farmer
Davis, S. H., commission merchant
Eakins, John A., general merchant
Egbert, William J., farmer
Elliott, William, teacher
Gooden, Charles, farmer
Gooden, S. S., farmer
Harding, Rev. F., (Church of England)
Hewett, Edward, New Dominion hotel
Hicks, Robert, prop. sash, blind and door manufac.
Homer, Abram, carpenter
Homer, Andrew, commission merchant
Jones, Peter, farmer
Laidlaw, Thomas, farmer
Loucks, Wellington, carpenter
Meston, William, J.P.
Moore, L., farmer
Murdie, William, patent right agent
Murdie, W., farmer
Nairn, T. M., general merchant
Nickerson, Alfred, farmer
Norman, Joseph, shoemaker
Percy, William, farmer
Roberts, Robert, farmer
Shaver, John, cooper
Smith, B. F., grocer
Smith, Charles A., proprietor Commercial Hotel
Teeple, William, farmer
THOMPSON, THOMAS, Postmaster, patent right agent and commission merchant
Trim, Samuel, butcher
Young, S., lime and stone dealer

Poole.—A Post Village, in the Township of Mornington, County Perth. Distant 13 miles from Stratford, the County Town, and 200 from Toronto. Stage to Stratford; fare 50 cents. Average price of land $30 per acre. Mails tri-weekly. Population 200.

Bashart, Charles, shoemaker
Burnett, Andrew, farmer
Chalmers, John, J.P.
Dehr, George, wagon maker
Douglass, Robert, farmer
Dunlop, William, carpenter
Farrell, James, farmer
Foss, Theodore, tailor
Holmes, Christian, wagon maker
Manser, George, butcher
MATHEWS, DANIEL, Postmaster, proprietor Poole Hotel and general merchant
Miliken, Rev. —, (Wesleyan)
Misner, Henry, farmer
Montgomery, James, J.P.
Northrop, Rev. Charles (Baptist)
Poppe, Ernst, cabinet maker
Roup, Joseph R., farmer
Roup, Joseph U., farmer
Segnor, Frederick, cooper
Shrine, Daniel, auctioneer
Talbert, William, shoemaker
Walker, Robert, farmer
Watt, Robert, teacher

Port Albert.—A Village on Nine Mile River, in the Township of Ashfield, County Huron, 10 miles from Goderich, the County Town, and 22 from Kincardine. Stages to the above places. Population 150.

Bennett, Arthur, farmer
Bennett, John, farmer
Caldwell, George, farmer
Coltart, John, teacher
Crawford, James, proprietor saw mill
Draper, George, farmer
Graham, James, farmer
Hawkins, A. C., real estate agent
HAWKINS, THOMAS, Postmaster and gen. mer.
Hayden, W. J., farmer
Kennedy, William, farmer
McMillan, John, farmer
McRea, Duncan, proprietor Port Albert Hotel
Martin, Stephen, shingle maker
Pierce, Edward, proprietor Grove Inn
Quaid, Andrew, weaver
Simpson, Thomas, farmer
Small, John, shingle maker
Young, Richard, shoemaker

Port Burwell.—A Village and Port of entry at the mouth of Big Otter Creek and Lake Erie, in the Township of Bayham, County Elgin, 30 miles from St. Thomas, the County Town, 30 from Ingersoll, 40 from Simcoe, and 150 from Toronto. Daily stage to Ingersoll. Money Order Office and Savings' Bank. Population 1000.

Allan, John, boots and shoes
Andrews, John, cabinet maker
Ault, John, farmer
Bawtinheimer, Rev. Peter (Wesleyan)
Bradfield, Bros., grocers
Burwell, L., farmer
Cameron, Thomas, carpenter
Carew, Robert, boots and shoes
Cosseboom, W. H., carpenter
Davis, George, proprietor planing mill
Deacon, William, general merchant
Dunham, A., telegraph operator
Dunham, E. A., insurance agent
Eager, Edward, proprietor brick yard
Ferguson, Alexander, general merchant
Fitch, Rev. H. P. (Baptist)
Franklin, Benjamin, M.D.
Freeman, Daniel, barrister, notary public and insurance agent
French, Robert, proprietor Erie Hotel
Halstead, William, tinsmith
Hamilton, W. H., lumber dealer
Hankinson, C. H., boots and shoes
Hankinson, Samuel, carpenter
Hare, George, teacher
Hobson, John, cabinet maker
Hotchkiss, Benjamin, carpenter
Hotchkiss, Thomas, carpenter
Keefer, T. D., M.D.
Lake, Mrs., milliner
Lewis, William, watchmaker, jeweler, etc.
Leybourne, Samuel, butcher
Long, A., constable
McBride, Alexander, com. merchant and gen. agent
McCollum, W. A., druggist
McCoombs, William, lime and stone
McDermid, Lemuel, carpenter
McDonald, Alexander
McMatle, John, painter
Mallafont, Richard, baker
Mason, Mrs., milliner
Mason, William, broom manufacturer
Merrill, A., proprietor livery stable
Millard, David, proprietor American Hotel
Moore, William A., teacher
Newcomb, Isaac, carpenter,
PILCHER, THOMAS, Postmaster
Pierce, Lewis, grocer
Pontine, George, carpenter
Reace, David, farmer
Rediker, Elias, cooper
Ross, Charles, tailor
Schulte, Rev. —, (Church of England)
Snelgrove, Jacob, wagon maker
Sullivan, Miss N., milliner
Sutherland, Alexander, J.P.
Stephens, Charles, baker
Stephenson, Jonathan, carpenter
Taylor, Job, wagon maker
Tomlinson, R., soap and candle maker
Tripp, T. W., M.D.
Wells, J., dentist
Wildern, A., wagon maker
Wildern, Job, fancy goods and toys
Wrong, J. W., general agent and commission merchant
Yonell, W. & Co., props. flouring mill and general merchants

Port Colborne.—A Village situated at the head of the Welland Canal, and Junction of the Buffalo and Lake Erie with the Welland Railway, in the Township of Humberstone, County Welland. It has an extensive grain trade, and an elevator is here erected capable of transferring 7,000 bushels of grain per hour from vessels to cars. Distant from Welland 8 miles, from Hamilton 60 miles, and from Buffalo, N. Y., 20 miles. Money Order Office and Savings Bank. Population 1,600

Ault, George, ship carpenter
Barth, A., harness maker
Blanchard, Rev. Samuel (Methodist)
Boardman, Luther, carpenter and builder
Bonleau, James, telegraph operator
Boyle, John, saloon
Boywey, A., innkeeper
Carter, C. H., tug proprietor
Carter & Haun, grocers
CARTER, L. G., J.P., Postmaster and general merchant, agent American Express Co
Chase, George, ship carpenter
Cook, Hugh, saloon
Cook, John, saloon
Cook, Samuel, grocer
Cook, William T., groceries and provisions
Cooper, Rev. W. E. (Church of England)
Conn, Miss, milliner and dressmaker
Derkinn, Miss, teacher
Dessart, Rev. —, (Roman Catholic)
Deterling, John, brickmaker
Fares, D. W., M.D. and druggist
Faulkenhagen, Charles, brickmaker
FURRY, ELISHA, J.P., grocer, flour and feed store (see adv)
Ganger, Lewis, painter
Gibbons, D. & Co., grocers
GIBBONS, PETER, J.P., general merchant (see adv)
Gordon, John, steamboat agent and wood merchant
Gordon, Robert, M.D., druggist
Green, Miss E. L., milliner
Greenwood, Thomas, butcher
Hannaford, George, evening shade saloon
Hardison, James, hotel keeper
Henning, John, steamboat agent
HIGGINS, SAMUEL, harbour master
Holmwood, John, artist
Hopkins, S. J., dentist
Hopkins, William, general merchant
Howey, Joseph, baker
Hughes, David, agent Welland Railway
Jones, William H., stoves and tinware
Jordan, John, telegraph operator
Kappel, F., watchmaker and jeweler
KARR, JOHN C., general merchant (see adv)
Kennard & Misner, harness makers
Kirby, Jane, saloon
Langdon, John, teacher
Lawson, A. & W., boots and shoes
Lawson, Alexander, notary public and agent for the London and Lancashire Life Insurance Co.
Lawson, William, boots and shoes
LEACH, R. H., proprietor, Leach's Hotel (see adv)
LEACH'S HOTEL, R. H. Leach, prop. (see adv)
LEARN, JOHN, grocer, flour and feed (see adv)
Lewis, Mrs., milliner and dressmaker
LEWIS, WILLIAM, barber
McCain, D. W., carpenter and builder
McCarthey, Michael J., ship smith, etc.
McFall, D., boots and shoes
McRae, John, general merchant
Mann, William, butcher
Matthews, John, farmer
Muir, Rev. William (Baptist)
Neff, Henry, carpenter
Neff, J. B., M. D
Neff, Jonathan, foundry and machine shop
NORTH, JACOB, brewer and maltster, lake shore road (see adv)
O'Connor, John, carpenter
O'Neil, John, saloon
O'Neil, John, butcher
O'Neill, Thomas, boots and shoes
Port Colborne Petroleum Company
Price, Miss, teacher
Priestman, Joseph, jr., general and patent right agent
Ramey, James, hotel keeper and livery proprietor
RICHARDSON, MATTHEW, machinist, proprietor planing and saw mills (see adv)
Reeb, John, lime manufacturer
Ruth, William A., collector of customs
Schofield, James S., clerk and landing waiter
Schofield, Thomas, baker and grocer
Schofield, Thomas, J.P
Schooley, Benjamin, carpenter
Shickaluna, S., ship carpenter
SMADES, SAMUEL S., notary public, J. P., com. Queen's Bench, issuer of marriage licenses, bookseller, and insurance agent
Smith, A. C., stock dealer
Smith, E., auctioneer
Smith, F. R., teacher
Sperry & Co., coal dealers and com. merchants
Sperry, J. H
Thom, James, agent G.T.R
Troup, Peter, prop. steam flour mill
Twohy, James, prop. Welland House
Voisard, Rev. J. A., (Roman Catholic)
Willson, Gordon, clerk and landing waiter
Wintermute, George, lumber merchant
Woods, Frederick, blacksmith

Port Credit.—A Village and Station of the Great Western Railway, on the River Credit and Lake Ontario, in the Township of Toronto, County Peel, 14 miles from Brampton, the County Town, 13 from Toronto and 27 from Hamilton. Large quantities of grain are annually shipped from this point. The port is one of the best on the lake. Stages to Cooksville and Streetsville. Population 350.

BETHUNE, REV. C. J. (Church of England) res Springfield
Blakely, Alexander, ship carpenter
COTTON, ROBERT, J.P.. notary public and farmer res Indian Village
Grafton, C., hotel keeper
HAMILTON, JAMES, Postmaster and gen. mercht.
Johnston, George, blacksmith
Lynd, R., hotel keeper and general merchant
McAuliff, Patrick, carpenter
McCully, Patrick, shoemaker
McEwan, Robert, teacher
McFarlane, A., station agent G.W.R.
O'Leary, Timothy, tailor
Shaw, James R., general merchant
STEVENS, STYLE, hotel keeper
Thompson, John, wharfinger

Port Dalhousie.—An incorporated Village and Port of Entry on Lake Ontario, in the Township of Grantham, County Lincoln, 3 miles from St. Catharines, the County Town, 30 by water from Toronto and 30 from Hamilton. It is the terminus of the Welland Canal and Welland Railway. The chief trade is in lumber, flour and grain. Money Order Office and Savings Bank. Population 1,200.

Andrews, S., dry dock
Apply, H., reeve
Barnes, John, butcher
Bethel, N., farmer
Black, John, cooper
Buckbee, Palmer, farmer
Burson, Rev. G., (Presbyterian)
Clifford, John, carpenter
Cole, Samuel, proprietor Astor House
Consadine, Dr.
Dacey, John, saddler
Denton, John, clothier and tailor
Dixon, Rev. C. (Church of England)
Groom, Miss, teacher
Harris, Richard, wagon maker
Howse, H., tinsmith
Johnson, Joseph, shoemaker
Laurie, John, J.P., insurance agent
McGrath, B., proprietor Murray House
McMahon, Owen, proprietor livery stable
MARTINDALE, C. H., Postmaster and gen. merch[t]
May, George, farmer
May, Joseph, farmer
Morrison, Marshall, proprietor livery stable
Morrison, Mrs., milliner, etc.
Muir, Alexander, dry dock
Pawling, Nathan, J.P., general merchant
Pawling, Nathan H., farmer
Read, George W., telegraph operator
Read, W. H., farmer
Runchey, William, proprietor Pickwick House
Smith, John, butcher
Todd, E. H., hotel keeper
Walkerly, Joseph, proprietor None-Such Hotel
Walt, David, carpenter
Wood, John, carpenter
Wood, Richard, baker
Woodall, Jonathan, shoemaker
Young, H. Y., painter

Port Elgin (Normanton P.O.)—A Village on Lake Huron, in the Township of Saugeen, County Bruce, 30 miles from Walkerton, the County Town, 30 miles from Owen Sound, 25 from Kincardine, and 5 from Southampton. Stages to the above places. Steamers to Goderich and Southampton. Money Order Office. Population 650.

Allen, William, prop. Elgin House
Anthers, Rev. Jacob (Evangelical Association)
Atkinson, George C., saddler
Becker, Henry, tailor
Begg, Miss, teacher
Betznor, Jacob, prop. flouring mill and lumber dealer
Bricker, Dillmore O., commission merchant
Cameron, William, general merchant
Campbell, John, tailor
Campbell, William J., tanner
Craig, George, general merchant
Crick, William, boots and shoes
Currie, Donald, farmer
Currie, Duncan, carpenter
Currie, John C., general agent
David, John D., farmer
Dent, George, general merchant
Detwiler, John R., proprietor Steamboat House
Detwiler, Noah, carpenter
Douglass, Robert, M.D.
Douglass, Robert, sen., farmer
Eby, Enoch, farmer
Eby, Martin F., telegraph operator
Eby, Martin F., druggist
Eby, Rev. Solomon (Menonite)
Ewald, Daniel, teacher
Falconer, Angus, lime and stone
Frazer, Rev. Alexander (Presbyterian)
George, James, boots and shoes
Gould, Rev. — (Wesleyan)
Gowanlock, William, sen., farmer
Guyer, George, cabinet maker
Hall, William H., butcher
Hoover, Martin, commission merchant
Hunter, Matthew, auctioneer
Johnston, Albert, cooper
Kennedy, John C., wagon maker
Kinsey, D. S., carpenter
Larrock, D. & C., general merchants
Larrock, James, cabinet maker
Laurison, Rev. W. W. (United Brethren)
Sehnent, Rev. J. J. (New Jerusalem)
McCarroll, Daniel, butcher
McClure & Stewart, manufacturers of woolen goods
McGillivray, Peter, farmer
McIntosh & Detwiler, wagon makers
McKnight, Charles, boots and shoes
McLachlan, Robert, founder and machinist
McLean, Mrs., milliner
McPhail, Neil, farmer
Muir, James, carpenter
Noble, William, tailor
Philips, Elias, baker
Prendis, Pascal, carpenter
Rae, Neil A., attorney-at-law and insurance agent
ROY, ARCHIBALD, J.P., Postmaster, general and steamboat agent
Ruby & Hilker, general merchants
Schmidt, B., proprietor brick yard
Sebastian, William A., fancy goods, toys, etc.
Sehnen, J. J., insurance agent
Shiels, Andrew, cabinet maker
Siefort, Clement, cooper
Smith, Jesse, proprietor North American Hotel
Stafford, Mrs. A. P., milliner
Stafford, Frederick, grocer
Stafford, John, farmer
Stafford, Robert, proprietor Dominion House
Stevens, H., tanner
Stewart, John R., druggist
Stirton, John, farmer
Weaver, Rev. —, (N. C. Methodist)

Port Dover.—A Village and Port of Entry on Lake Erie, in the Township of Woodhouse, County Norfolk, 8 miles from Simcoe, the County Town, 25 from Dunnville, 38 from Hamilton and 24 from Caledonia. Stages to the above places. Money Order Office and Savings Bank. Population 1000.

ABEL, DAVID, Postmaster and grocer
Allison, John, painter
Arnot, A., cabinet maker
Ansley, C., tinsmith
Bagley, William, telegraph operator
Bannister, William, carpenter
Barrett, T. B., Deputy Collector Customs
Battersby, Arthur, farmer
Beaupre, John, farmer
Becker, J., proprietor Commercial Hotel
Bowlby, Lewis, commission merchant
Brougham, Miller, cabinet maker
Brown, Edward, baker
Caley, Mrs. milliner, etc.
Caley, William, boots and shoes
Carleton, J., teacher
Carleton, William, teacher
Carpenter, G. M., farmer
Christie, Mrs., milliner
Craig, W., proprietor North American Hotel
Cragie, Rev. William, (Presbyterian), superintendent public schools
Crawford, —, principal Grammar School
Crossland & Lyons, proprietor Norfolk Woolen Mills
Delow, E., broom manufacturer
Ellis, F. W., auctioneer
Fairchild, —, prop. Farmer's Hotel and brick yard
Fleming, Mrs., milliner
Follensby, L. B., proprietor livery stable
Frayne, Richard, saddler
Gamble, Samuel, N.P. and general agent
Gillies, T. S., wagon maker
Gunnel, Rev. —, (New Advent)
Guy, T. F., proprietor grist mill
Hall, Edward, commission merchant and lumber dealer
Harris, J. C., boots and shoes
Hart, E. G., publisher *New Dominion*
Harvey, Jaffrey, farmer
Hussey, Henry, carpenter
Hellyer, R., steamboat agent
Higman, W. H., collector of customs
Hillyer, R., commission merchant
Hoffman, Louis, cabinet maker
Hume, John, carpenter
Jenkins, William, carpenter
Innes, Andrew, carpenter
Ladd, Michael, wagon maker
Laird, Rev. William, (Wesleyan)
Lange, N. L., proprietor livery stable
Law, Robert, carpenter
Law, William, carpenter
Lawson, Adam, carpenter
Lawson, Peter, American Consul
Lawson, Peter, proprietor steam tannery
Leaney, William, grocer
Long, M., butcher
McCoy, P., J.P.
McKitterick, Robert, carpenter
Mann, James, farmer
Marr, Francis, farmer
Marr, R., lime dealer
Milton, Samuel, painter
Morgan, Henry, J.P.
Mulford, C., tailor
Mulkins & Ritchie, commission merchants
Naughton, Thomas, boots and shoes
NEW DOMINION, (Friday), E. G. Hart, proprietor
Passmore, George, boots and shoes
Petrie, J., tailor
Powell, B., general merchant
Riddell, James, J.P., auctioneer
Riddell, R., general merchant
Roberts, Henry, farmer
Ross, J., proprietor Railroad House
Salt, John, carpenter
Scofield, N. B., general merchant
Sidway, J., broom manufacturer
Skey, F., druggist
Slocumb, Henry, carpenter
Smith, Robert, proprietor livery stable
Sovereign, H. H., farmer
Stewart, J. W., M.D.
Stephens, Richard, architect
Stevenson, John, clothier and tailor
Stringer, Henry, carpenter
Thompson, Andrew, farmer
Thurlow, —, butcher
Tibbetts, Rev. William (Church of England)
Varey, Brian, carpenter
Vatcher, S., baker
Waddell, R., broom manufacturer
Walker, N. C., M.D.
Walsh, C., landing waiter
Wilson, George, general merchant
Watts, W., butcher
Williams, H., butcher
Winton, C., proprietor Norfolk House

Port Elmsley.—A Village and Station of the Brockville and Ottawa Railway, on the River Tay, in the Township of North Elmsley, County Lanark, 6 miles from Perth, the County Town. Population 200.

Allan, John, manufacturer of woolen goods
Devlin & Co., tanners
ELLIOTT, JOHN, Postmaster and farmer
Heatherington, William, shoemaker
Hunter, W., farmer
Irving, William, carpenter
Lowe, David, carpenter
McCormick, Mrs. J., proprietor hotel
McIlhenney, James, proprietor flouring mill
McKenzie & Campbell, lumber dealers
O'Hara, H., farmer
O'Hara, W. G., farmer
Sherwood, H. N., lumber dealer
Weatherhead, W., farmer
Werkes, A. F., grocer and hotel keeper
White, Rev. George B. (Church of England)

Porter's Hill.—*(See Villages too late for regular insertion at the end of this work.)*

Port Franks.—A small Village at the mouth of the Aux Sables, Township Bosanquet, County Lambton, distant from Widder 6 miles. Population about 200.

Bell & McKellar (John Bell and P. McKellar), lumber merchants
Moore, Charles, hotel keeper
Smith & Utter (S. Smith and John Utter), saw mill proprietors
Taylor, Joseph, hotel keeper

Port Granby.—A Village on Lake Ontario, in the Township of Clarke, County Durham, 1 mile from Newtonville Station, Grand Trunk Railroad, and 16 from Cobourg, the County Town. Population 200.

Barrie, John, farmer
Bellamy, George, farmer
Brown, James, farmer
Boon, Abraham, farmer
Caughton, Cornelius, farmer
Caughton, Dennis, farmer
Cotton, John, farmer
Elliott, George, farmer
Evans, James, farmer
Goodenough, Richard, farmer
Gray, Charles, farmer
Henderson, Willram, farmer
Jacobs, George, farmer
Johnston, J., farmer
Johnston, R., J. P., farmer
Keable, Edward, station agent
Kimball, Austin, farmer
Lancaster, Jonathan, farmer
Lockhart, Andrew, farmer
McCullough, James
McFarlane & Gordanier, props. steam flouring mill
MARCH, DAVID, Postmaster, proprietor hotel and commission merchant
Meadows, Francis, farmer
Milligan, James, farmer
Price, Rev. (Baptist)
Quantrill, David, farmer
Robinson, William, farmer
Tapp, Rev. —, (Baptist)
Thomas, Andrew, farmer
Thompson, J. M., teacher
Thompson, Moses, farmer
Wade, John, farmer
Wallace, Thomas, farmer
Welch, Thomas, farmer
Williams, John, farmer

Port Hoover.—A Post Office in the Township of Mariposa, County Victoria.
ROGERS, ELIAS, Postmaster.

Port Hope.—An incorporated Town in the township of Hope, County Durham, beautifully situated in a small valley on Smith Creek, the mouth of which forms an excellent harbor on Lake Ontario. It is a Station of the Grand Trunk Railway, and the terminus of the Port Hope, Lindsay and Beaverton Railway. There is a fine agricultural section in the vicinity and an extensive trade in lumber and farm produce is centered here. Distant from Cobourg, 7 miles; from Peterboro, 29; from Lindsay, 42; from Toronto, 63; and from Kingston, 98 miles. Port of Entry. Money Order Office and Savings Bank. Population 5000.

Abercrombie, William, dry goods and clothing
Abbott, Miss Margaret, milliner and dressmaker
Allen, A., teller, Ontario Bank
Anderson, James, baker, etc.
Anderson, W., dry goods
Austin, James, butcher
Badgley, Rev. C. H. (Church of England)
BAIRD, JAMES, bookseller and stationer, Fire, Life, and Marine General Insurance Agent
Baker, Erastus A., groceries and provisions
Bank of Montreal, W. P. Crombie, agent
BARNETT, E. W. & CO. (E. W. Barnett and Wm. Craig) glue manufacturers (see adv)
Barrett, William, prop. Barrett's mills and woolen factory
Beamish's Mills, Joseph G. King, proprietor
Beamish, Francis, prop. Beamish's Plaster Mill
Beatty, James, carpenter
Beggs, Miss A. E., millinery
Bennett, William, dry goods
Benson, Frederick A., law student
BENSON, THOMAS M., barrister (see adv)
Bethune, Rev. F. A. (Church of England)
BIRSS, J. H., produce merchant
Black, Charles, teacher, Union School
Blackham's Hotel, WilliamMartin, proprietor
BLETCHER, WILLIAM, produce merchant
Bletchford & Boney (George B. and Richard W.), general blacksmiths and wagon makers
Brent, Charles, chemist and druggist
BRITISH CANADIAN (weekly); J. B. Trayes, editor and proprietor
Brown, J. A., surgeon, dentist and dealer in pianofortes and melodeons
Brownscombe, James, shoemaker
BUCKETT, FREDERICK JOHN, manager Hasting's House
Budge, Edward, merchant, tailor
CAISSE'S HOTEL, L. Caisse, proprietor
Calcutt, James, jun., proprietor Calcutt's Brewery
Campbell, Archibald, agent B.R.R.
Cameron, Charles, M.D.
CANADA BUTTON COMPANY; E. G. Chaut, manager
Canadian and American Express Company; Stanley Paterson, agent
Carson, John, grocer
Carveth, J. S., butcher
Carveth, William, butcher
Chalk, Robert, carriage and wagon maker
Charlesworth & Gamett (H. G. C. and G. R. G.), grocers and provision merchants
CHISHOLM, D., barrister
Clemes, Charles, grocer and provision merchant
Clemesha, John W., physician and surgeon
Coad, George, shoemaker
Cochrane, Andrew, harbor master
Cochrane, Rev. William, (Presbyterian)
Cochrane, James, hotel keeper and produce buyer
Cole, Miss Harriet, milliner

Commercial Hotel, J. S. German, proprietor
Commercial Union Fire and Life Insurance Co., D. Smart, agent
Coots, W. J., boot and shoemaker
COSBY, A. M., manager Bank of Toronto
CRAIG, WILLIAM & SONS (W. Craig, T. Craig, W. Craig, jun.) wood dealers and leather manufacturers
Craick, James, dry goods
Crawley, Elias, saloon keeper
Crombie, William Picton, agent Bank of Montreal
Davis, Miss, milliner
Dempsey, Rev. J. (Baptist)
Dewar, John F., physician and surgeon
Dickson, R, saddle and harness maker
Doebler, Charles, hatter and furrier
Dowling,, Miss, childrens' clothing
Duck, Michael, grocer
Earle, Thomas, saddler
East Durham Registry Office, George C. Ward, Registrar
Elliott, Mrs. J., hoop skirt manufactory
Ellis, Thomas F., telegraph operator G. T. R.
Evans, William, blacksmith
Evatt, W. W., law student
Evatt, William Henry, M.D., physician and surgeon
Farmers' Inn, Richard Foster, proprietor
Farquharson, Murray, marble manufacturer
Ferguson, Mrs. Wallace, fancy stamping and embroidery
Fisk, G. L., train dispatcher P. H. L. & B. Railway
Fitzsimmons, Hugh, hairdresser
Fogarty, Miss Susan, dressmaker and milliner
Forbes, Henry, customs' surveyor
Foster, Francis, variety store mill
Foster, Richard, proprietor Farmer's Inn
FOWLER, W. J., produce and commission merchant, broker, &c. (see adv)
Furby, George M., bailiff 2nd Division Court and insurance agent
Furby, William H., cabinet maker
Geale, John, fancy dry goods
George, J. G., builder and undertaker
German & Doyle, proprietors Royal Hotel
Gibson, William, groceries, wines and liquors
Gilchrist, Charles, head-constable
Gillett, Hiram, dry goods and millinery
Givins, Henry C., accountant R. C. B.
Goheen, Thomas H., livery stables
Gray, E., general ticket and freight agent P. H. L. & B. Railway
Gray, Joseph, secretary and treasurer P. H. L. & B. Railway
Gray, N., conductor P. H. L. & B. Railway
Green, C., weaver
Grierson, Mrs., teacher Union School
Griffin, Martin, proprietor Griffin's Saloon
Griggs, H. P., eclectic physician
Hagerman, C. A., groceries and provisions
Hales, H. B., saddle and harness maker
Hall, J. G., law student
Hamly, Bros., (J. R. Hamly and Thomas Hamly) boots and shoes
Hanna, Jane, grocer
Hartford Fire Insurance Company, David Smart, agt
Haw, Lawrence, proprietor Ontario House
Hawthorne, Edward, blacksmith
Hayden, Thomas, founder
Healy, J. M., accountant Ontario Bank
HELM, J., JR., foundry and machine shop (see adv)
Henderson George, livery stable proprietor and steam boat agent
Herchmer, G. S., teller Bank of Toronto
Hetherington, John, saloon
HEWSON, CHARLES, grocer and provision mercht (see adv)
Hewson, John, grocer and baker
Higgins, R. W., teacher Union School
Hiland, William, grocer and confectioner
Hill, R., tailor
Hill, Robert, tailor
Hockin, N., dry goods, boots and shoes
Hoffman, Jacob, dealer in fancy goods and manufacturer of cigars
Howell, R. S., forwarding, shipping and insurance agent
Howell, R. S., grocer and provision merchant
Hume, Robert, grain buyer
Hunter, Charles, cooper
IRWIN, J. M., lumber merchant
James, Thomas F., produce and commission merchant and insurance agent
Jarvis, C. R., hardware
Jenkins, A., weaver
JOHNSTON, J. S. (W. S. & J. S. Johnston)
JOHNSTON, W. S. (W. S. & J. S. Johnston)
JOHNSTON, W. S. & J. S., editors and proprietors *Port Hope Guide*
Jones, Thomas P., U. S consular agent
Kane, Rev. Michael (Roman Catholic)
Kellaway, Philip, carpenter and builder
KING, JOSEPH G., proprietor Beamish's Mill
Kirchhoffer, John N., law student
KIRCHHOFFER, NESBITT, barrister (see adv)
Knight, Charles, grocer and baker
Lambert, Charles, proprietor Black Horse Inn
Lauder, George P., landing waiter
Lee, John, proprietor Lee's Hotel
Lees, John, boot and shoe maker
Lelean, W. & S., (William and Samuel), dry goods and millinery
Leonard, Thomas, blacksmith
Lewis, F. G. & Co. (F. G. and M. A. Lewis), photographers
Libby, John, horse shoer, &c.
Libby, R. S., watchmaker and jeweler
Little, Thomas, boots and shoes
Lodge, J. N. G., insurance agent
LYDON, JOHN, dealer in groceries, wines, dry goods, provisions, &c. (see adv.)
McCabe, Peter, proprietor Ontario flouring mill
McCarthy, Mrs. Margaret, grocery
McCormick, E. E., telegraph operator, G.T.R.
McCreary, Robert, proprietor Commercial Hotel
McCreery, Thomas, billiard saloon
McFarlane & Gardanier (McFarlane and H. H. Gardanier), millers
McGuire, A. S., teacher
McHenry, James S., confectioner
McKay & Hewson (Robert McKay and John Hewson), boot and shoe makers
McLennan, Donald, hardware
McLennan, Donald J., grocer and provision merchants
McMaster, James, second hand broker
McMurtry, John F. & Brother (John F. and J. A.), lumber merchants
McNeil, Miss M., milliner and dressmaker
Macdougall, A. H., manager Royal Canadian Bank
MACKIE, WILLIAM, proprietor Mackie's Hotel
MACKIE'S HOTEL; William Mackie, proprietor
Maguire, Albert B., house and sign painter
Maitland, Hugh, wagon maker
Marshall, David, saloon
Marshall, John, boot and shoe manufacturer
Martin, Thomas, carpenter
Martin, William, proprietor, Blackham's Hotel
Mathews & O'Brien (Benj. R., and James) carriage makers

Mayhew, Anthony, planing mill, sash, blind and door manufactory
Menhenitt, Thomas, grocer, baker, etc.
Meredith, H. V., accountant, Bank of Montreal
Merchants Union Express Co., Stanley, Patterson, agent
Mitchell, F. R., grocer
Mitchell, George and John, druggists
Molson, W. M., proprietor flouring mill
Monahan, William, boot and shoemaker
Montreal Ocean Steamship Co., Stanley, Patterson, agent
Montreal Telegraph Co., Stanley, Patterson, agent
Morris, John, butcher
Morse, F. W. & Co., chemists and druggists
Mulligan, John
Mulligan, Robert, groceries, wines and liquors
Murphy, F., auctioneer and Inland Revenue Inspector
NEELANDS, F., dentist (see adv)
O'Brien, James (Mathews & O'Brien)
O'Donnell, P. J., bookseller and stationer, dealer in fancy goods, &c.
O'Keane, Rev. M., (Roman Catholic)
O'Meara, Rev. Dr. (Church of England)
O'Neill, J. & R. (James and Richard), dry goods and groceries
Ontario Bank, John Smart, manager
Orr, Robert, manager Molson's mills
Pack, John, proprietor Simpson's Hotel
Parsons, William, blacksmith
Paterson, Stanley, banker, exchange broker, agent Canadian and American Express Companies
PEPLOW, EDWARD, JUN., (E. Peplow & Son)
PEPLOW, EDWARD, SEN., (E. Peplow & Son)
PEPLOW, E. & SON (Edward, sen. and Edward, jr.) proprietors Viaduct Mills
Perks, George, M.D.
Perry, Horace, watchmaker and jeweller
Philp, William, music teacher
Phœnix Hotel, Edward Theobald, proprietor
Pillsworth, Daniel, boot and shoemaker
Pitts, T. N., merchant tailor and dealer in gentleman's furnishing goods
PORT HOPE GUIDE, (weekly), W. S. & J. S. Johnston, editors and proprietors (see adv)
Port Hope Post Office, Robert Wallace Smart, Postmaster
Porter, Archibald, agricultural implements
Price, Rev. A. (Bible Christian)
Pringle, A. W., watchmaker and jeweler
Provincial Insurance Co., Cornelius Quinland, agent
Purslaw, Adam, principal Union School
Quay, William, groceries, stoves and tinware
Quinlan, Cornelius, manufacturer and wholesale and retail dealer in stoves, tin and copperware
RANDALL, P. R., bookseller, stationer and music dealer
Raymond, M., boot and shoemaker
Read, W., (Simpson & Read)
Reynolds, John, hotel keeper
Reynolds, W., conductor P. H. L. & B Railway
RIORDAN, JOHN, proprietor Ontario Brewery
Robertson, James, tanner and currier, and dealer in shoe findings
Robertson, Miss Kate, teacher
Rose, Harvey Milton, boots and shoes
ROSS, LEWIS, dry goods and groceries
Rowland, William, painter
Royal Canadian Bank, Archibald Campbell, agent
RUSSELL, H. C., importer and dealer in pianos, melodeons and organs
Ruskell, Henry, butcher
RUSSELL, H. C. & BRO. (H. C. Russell & G. R. Russell), upholsterers and cabinet makers
Russell, James L., dry goods and groceries
Sager, John, proprietor Queen's Hotel
SANDS, ARCHIBALD, secretary and treasurer Port Hope Gas Co., and insurance agent
Saunders, H. V., town clerk, insurance agent
Sculthorp, Samuel, solicitor
Shenick, Miss A., teacher
Shepherd, William, clerk 3rd Division Court
Shepherd, James, Moleson's mills
Simson, John, station master G. T. R
Simpson, William (Simpson & Read)
Simpson & Read, (W. Simpson and W. Read) grocers
Simpson's Hotel, John Pack proprietor
Skitch, William, merchant tailor
Smart, David, barrister
SMART, GEORGE, commission agent in grain and dealer in lumber
Smart, J. B., market clerk
SMART, ROBERT W., Postmaster
Smith, Robert, photographer
Standard Life Assurance Company, J. Baird, agent
Steven, John, confectioner
Stevenson, John, tinware, stoves, &c
Stevenson, William, merchant tailor
SUMMERVILLE, THOMAS, distiller
Tapscott, Rev. S., (Baptist)
Taylor, Erastus, agent Worthen and Baker
Taylor, H. G., master mechanic P. H., L. & B. R
TEMPEST, W. S., grocer, wine and spirit merchant
Theobald, Edward, proprietor Phœnix Hotel
Tinker, Stephen, engine driver P. H. & P. R
Toronto Bank, A. M. Cosby, manager
Trayes, J. B., editor and proprietor *British Canadian*
TRINITY COLLEGE SCHOOL, Rev. C. H. Badgley head master
Tripp, David, shoemaker
UNITED STATES CONSULAR AGENCY, Thomas P. Jones, agent
Van Norman, Miss, teacher
Vindin, Edmund S., lumber and commission mercht
Wallace, R., produce agent
Walker, John, cabinet maker and upholsterer
WARD, GEORGE C., Registrar East Durham and issuer of marriage and tavern licenses
Ward, Thomas W., Deputy Registrar
Warmington, Charles (Charles Warmington & Bro.)
Warmington, John (Charles Warmington & Bro.)
Warmington, Charles & Bro., (Charles and John), manufacturers of mineral water, Mount Royal bitters and ginger wine
WATERS, REV. D., M.A., LL.B. (Canada Presbyterian)
Watson, Thomas, teacher
Whitehead, F. L., accountant
Whitehead, M. F., Collector Customs
WILLIAMS, A. T., general superint. P.H.L. & B.R.
WILLIAMS, ARTHUR T. H., M.P.P.
Williams, James, barber and hairdresser, dealer in pipes, tobacco and fancy goods
Wilson, William, leather dealer
Winters, Nicholas, proprietor Victoria Inn
Wittman, John, sausage maker
Woods, G. A. (G. A. Woods & Co.)
Woods, William G. (G. A. Woods & Co.)
Woods, G. A. & Co., (G. A. and Wm. G.), planing sash, doors, blinds and fanning mills
WOON, JOHN C., book-keeper
Worthen & Baker, (Sanborn Worthen and R. H. Baker), loom manufacturers
Wright, John, attorney, etc.

Portland.—A Village on the Rideau Canal, in the Township of Bastard, County Leeds, 30 miles from Brockville, the County Town, 25 miles from Smith's Falls; 16 from Irish Creek, and 8 from Newboro Stages to Brockville and Westport. Population 200.

Brown, Robert, wagon maker
Chipman, S. E., cooper
Donovan, James, inn keeper
Dorway, John, shoemaker
Grant, John, blacksmith
Heath, E., cooper
Johnson, Richard, general merchants
Kinney, Patrick, cooper
Morris, Samuel, blacksmith
Rape, Michael, inn keeper
SCOVILL, S. S., Postmaster, J.P., general merchant
Sherwood, W. H.
Stratton, J. W., grocer
Trotter, Richard, wagon maker
Whiting, Arza, tanner

Port Maitland.—A Post Office in the Township of Sherbrooke, County Monck.

Doughn, W., hotel keeper
MOSS, JAMES, Postmaster

Port Perry.—A large and flourishing Village situated at the head of Lake Scugog, and terminus of the Port Whitby and Scugog Gravel Road, in the Township of Reach, County Ontario. It is the centre of a good agricultural country and possesses excellent water power. It contains several extensive flour, grist and saw mills, a woolen mill and foundry. Distant from Whitby, the County Town, 18 miles, and from Toronto, 48. Stage to Whitby, fare 75 cents. Steamers to Lindsay during navigation. Daily Mail. Money Order Office. Population 1000.

Addison, William, blacksmith
Allison, J. W., general merchant
BIGELOW, BROTHERS (Joseph and Palmer Bigelow), general merchants
BIGELOW, JOSEPH (Bigelow, Brothers), manager Royal Canadian Bank
BIGELOW, JOSEPH (Bigelow, Brothers), proprietor saw mills, shingle and heading factory
BIGELOW, PALMER (Bigelow, Brothers)
Bullen, Thomas, tailor
Burnham, Harris, Clerk 3d Division Court
Charles Henry, general merchant and issuer of marriage licenses
Christian, Miss H. J., school teacher
COCHRANE & COCHRANE (Samuel H. & William M.). barristers, &c.
COCHRANE, WILLIAM M. (Cochrane & Cochrane)
COCHRANE, SAMUEL H. (Cochrane & Cochrane)
Coady John, harness maker
Cook, John, butcher
Davis, Isaac J., telegraph operator
DAVIS, JOHN W., cabinet maker, &c.
EBBELS, HUBERT L. (Spencer & Ebbels)
Ebbels, W. D., school teacher
Flett & Hutchison (John Flett and William Hutchison), general blacksmiths
Flett, John (Flett & Hutchison)
Forneri, Rev. R. S. (Episcopal)
Foy, Henry, boot and shoe manufacturer
GEROW, CORNEILUS B. (Hoitt & Gerow)
Gibson, Adam M., foreman Port Perry Agricultural Works
Gibson, George, P.L.S. and C.E.
Good, James, brick maker and bricklayer
GORDEN, HENRY, Postmaster
Henley, George, baker, &c.
HOITT & GEROW (John Hoitt and C. B. Gerow), provisions, groceries, wines and liquors (see adv)
HOITT, JOHN (Hoitt & Gerow)
Hutchison. William (Flett & Hutchison)
Ireland, Daniel, hotel keeper
Jamieson, Rev. George (United Presbyterian)
JONES, GEORGE W. (Paxton & Jones)
Jones & Jones (George W., M.D. and Richard, M.D.), physicians, druggists, &c.
Jones, George W., M.D. (Jones & Jones)
Jones, Richard, M.D. (Jones & Jones)
King, Rev. Joseph (Baptist)
Lazier, J. B., cradle and barley fork maker
Marsh, Charles (Marsh & Trounce)
Marsh & Trounce (Thomas Marsh and W. J. Trounce) general merchants, lessees Union flouring mills and shingle manufacturers
MAW, HARRISON (H. Maw & Son)
MAW, H. & SON (Harrison and John H.) contractors and builders (see adv)
Maw, Robert H., carpenter and builder
MAW, JOHN H. (H. Maw & Son)
McKenzie, Charles, livery stables
McKenzie, Henry, photographic artist
Moore, Anson, painter, &c.
Mundy, Edward, editor and proprietor *Standard*
Parrish, W. T., dealer in hardware, tinware & stoves
PAXTON, THOMAS, M.P.P. (Paxton, Tate & Co.)
PAXTON & JONES (Thomas C. Paxton & George W. Jones), general merchants (see adv)
PAXTON, THOMAS C. (Paxton & Jones)
PAXTON, THOMAS (Paxton, Tate & Co.) proprietor Port Perry saw mills
PAXTON, TATE & CO. (Thomas Paxton, William Tate and Charles Paxton), Port Perry agricultural works
PAXTON, CHARLES (Paxton, Tate & Co.)
Perkins, David, tailor
PORT PERRY STANDARD (weekly), E. Mundy, editor
Robinson, George, sash, door and blind manufacturer
Sanderson, Rev. G. (Methodist Episcopal)
SEXTON, ALLEN N., manager W. S. Sexton
SEXTON, WILLIAM S., lumber merchant
Shaw, Mrs. J. J., proprietress Royal Canadian Hotel
Shipman, W. H., fishery overseer
SINCLAIR, NEIL, proprietor Railroad Hotel
SPENCER, T. H. (Spencer & Ebbels)
SPENCER & EBBELS (T. H. Spencer & H. L. Ebbels), barristers, &c. (see adv)
Stout, Samuel, hairdresser
TATE, WILLIAM (Paxton, Tate & Co.)
Trounce, William J. (Marsh & Trounce)
WHITE, GEORGE URIAH, carriage maker, &c.
Wilson, Corneilus, painter
YOUNG, C. T., proprietor Port Perry woolen factory
Youmans, J. R., grammar school teacher

Port Nelson.—A Post Office in the Township of Nelson, County Halton, on the shore of Lake Ontario 32 miles from Toronto, and 8 from Milton, the County Town, a considerable trade is carried on especially in lumber and grain. Daily Mail. Population 150.

Cline, Jacob, agent
COTTER, HUGH, J.P., Postmaster, produce and lumber merchant
Douglass, William, general merchant
Green, Rev. T., LL.B. (Church of England)
Green, John, sen., forwarder
Irving, William, captain
Johnston, William, sen., captain
Kurtz, John P., carpenter
Land, Hiram, pump maker
Lane, Jeremiah, carpenter
Le Clair, Alexander, ship builder
Mosher, B. F., painter
Royal, Mrs., inn keeper
Well, Caleb, carpenter

Port Robinson.—A Village and Station of the Welland Railway, on the Welland River, in the Township of Thorold, County Welland, 4 miles from Welland, the County Town, and 56 from Toronto. Money Order Office and Savings' Bank. Population 500.

Abbey, Alexander, carpenter
Bell, W. H., proprietor Bell's Hotel
Bennett, C. B., accountant
Blake, J. A., commission merchant
Boos, George L., tailor
Bradfield, Jonathan, farmer
Clark, Oliver, broom manufacturer
Coleman, D., prop. Mansion House and grocer
Cook, Warren, painter
Coulter, Andrew, farmer
Coulter, Robert, grocer
Dean, Cyrus, architect
Elliott, Andrew, butcher
Elliott, George, teacher
Elliott, Robert, general merchant
Farr, Walter, carpenter
Feeney, Edward, tailor
Griffith, Thomas, butcher
Grisdale, G., carpenter
Hill, William, J. P., general agent
Hill, John, farmer
Hixon, William, farmer
Holditch, Henry, farmer
Jordan, Mrs. E., proprietor British Hotel
Jordan, George A., station agent and telegraph oper.
Jordan, William, painter
Kimball, J. J., proprietor livery stable
King, R. S., M. D.
Linger, Freeman, boots and shoes
Linger Isaac, carpenter
McCOPPEN, JAMES, Postmaster, J. P., gen. mercht
McCoppen, Mrs. James, milliner
McCullough, W. A., deputy Postmaster
McGill, Rev., (Presbyterian)
McKee, Vilroy, wagon maker
McFarland, Duncan, farmer
McFarland, J. C., M. D.
Morrin, P. H., accountant
Roberts, Rev. T. B., (Church of England)
Saunders, John, grocer
Stark, Joseph, carpenter
Star, Rev. J. (Wesleyan)
Stark, Robert, cabinet maker
Stuart, Mrs., milliner
Wamsley, John, farmer
Watson, John, farmer
Willson, Mrs. E. A., select school
Wood, Mrs., milliner

Port Rowan.—A post office in the Township of Walsingham, County Norfolk. Money Order Office and Savings Bank.

McCLENNAN, ANDREW, Postmaster.

Port Royal.—A small village on Lake Erie, in the Township of Walsingham, County Norfolk, 22 miles from Simcoe, the County Town, and 90 from Toronto. Population 100.

ABBOTT, R., Postmaster, general merchant
Anderson, H., farmer
Anderson, J., farmer
Bingham, Charles, J.P.. Real Estate and Insurance Agent
Bingham G., farmer
Bingham, W., farmer
Bowers, C., farmer
Bowers, H., farmer
Burch, Titus, shoemaker
Dewitt, J., farmer
Ellis, A., proprietor Port Royal Hotel
Fick, Gilbert, broom manufacturer
Fick, P. F., farmer
Folger, Rev. S. W. (Baptist)
Hanson, William, proprietor Western Hotel
Overlaugh, W., tanner
Spencer, Miss S., milliner, etc.
Spencer, L., farmer
Woodward, James, teacher

Port Ryerse.—A Village on Young's Creek, in the Township of Woodhouse, County Norfolk, 6¼ miles from Simcoe, the County Town, and 80 from Toronto. Population 200.

Burgess, John, teacher
Cutting, James, hotel keeper and coal dealer
Franklin, B. B., telegraph operator
Green, Mary, proprietor Port Ryerse House
Heart, Norman, butcher
Holmwood, Walter, commission merchant and steamboat agent
Leaney, Henry & Co., grocers
Marlatt, Abram, potter
Peggs, Robert, teacher
Ryerse, Edward P., J.P., collector Inland Revenue
Ryerse, Rev. George J. (Baptist)
RYERSE, W. H., Postmaster, general merchant and insurance agent
Stickney, Amos, farmer
Stickney, James, proprietor livery stable.

Portsmouth.—An incorporated Village situated on Portsmouth Bay, in the Township of Kingston, County Frontenac, 2 miles distant from Kingston. The new Provincial Asylum is located here. The bay forms a deep and well sheltered harbor, and good facilities are offered for the building and launching of vessels of the largest size. Daily mail. Population 1200.

Agnew, John, M.D.
Allen, Rev. J. G. (Church of England)
Baiden, Eli, market gardener
Baker, William, foreman C. & G.'s tannery
Bannister, E., keeper Penitentiary
Bastrick, Thomas, guard Penitentiary
BEAUPRE, EDWARD, grocer, innkeeper and collector
Cameron & Murdie, builders and props. sash, door and blind factory
Campbell, Ellen, grocer
Carruthers & Gunn (J. C. & A. G.), tanners
Carter, Thomas, guard Penitentiary
Cox, Mrs., private school
Craig, John, accountant and clerk of the corporation
Crawford, William, guard Penitentiary
Culcheth, John, baker
Dobbs, Rev. F. W. (Church of England)
Drennan, S. T., cabinet maker
Dunlop, Robert, guard Penitentiary
Elliott, Elizabeth, hotel keeper
Evans, William C., prop. Lock Manufactory
Finn, Michael, plasterer
Fisher, James & Son, brewers
Fitzsimmons, James, guard Penitentiary
Flanigan, John, deputy warden Prov. Penitentiary
Funnell, Jesse, tailor
Grant, William E., boots and shoes
Horsey, Edward, architect
Howard, Richard, ship carpenter
Howard, Thomas, ship carpenter
Johnson, Absalom H., M.D.
Litchfield, J.P., M.D., medical superintendent Rockwood Lunatic Asylum
Lowe, Samuel, boots and shoes
McCammon, Thomas, baker
McCarthy, James, grocer
McCarthy, Thomas, keeper Penitentiary
McConnell, William, grocer
McDonald, Archibald, deputy clerk Penitentiary
McDonell, D. A. C., warden Penitentiary
McDonell, John, M. D.
McIntosh, Donald, clerk Penitentiary
McKay, Miss, milliner
McLeod, Alexander, guard Penitentiary
McLEOD, GEORGE, Postmaster, J. P., gen. mercht
Marks, John, general merchant
Mitchell, Peter, prop. Portsmouth marine R. R
Mooney, John, foreman G. Offord & Co.
Mowat, Rev. John, (Presbyterian)
Mudie, John, attorney-at-law
Newton, John, M. D
Nicholson, John, ship carpenter
Nicholson, Thomas, ship carpenter
Offord, George & Co., boots and shoes
Pugh, John, boots and shoes
Quinn, Patrick, hotel keeper
Ramsden, George, wagon maker
Schroeder, James, butcher
Sexton, George, butcher
Short, James, grocer
Steward, Robert, blacksmith
Sullivan, William, keeper Penitentiary
Van Strabenzie, Major Bowen, late 100th Regiment
Walsh, Patrick, keeper Penitentiary
Wilkinson, William, grocer
Wishart, John, ship carpenter

Port Stanley.—A village and station of the London and Port Stanley R.R., in the Townships of Yarmouth and Southwold, County Elgin, situate on Lake Erie, distant from St. Thomas, the County Town, 10 miles; Toronto, 157; London, 26; and Hamilton, 110. Communication by steamer with American Ports on the Lake. Average value of improved lands in the neighborhood, $40. There are Episcopal, Wesleyan Methodist, and Congregational churches in the village. Population 400.

Arkell, Henry, general merchant
Berry, M., saddler
Berry, Mrs., hotel keeper
Bostwick, J. R., J.P.
Brown, Charles A., butcher and grocer
Cameron, Ewan, J.P.
Chandler, Thomas, commission merchant, forwarder, insurance agent
Edgcombe, James, painter
Edgcombe, Thomas, wagon maker
Ellison, John, builder
Finlay, John, general merchant
Gunn, Angus, station master, insurance and marine agent
Harding, Thomas, proprietor flour mills
Hemphill, John, collector customs
Jackson, John, butcher and grocer
Kerr, Samuel, butcher and grocer
Latimer, Rev. James, (Wesleyan)
Leitch, John, shoemaker
Leitch, L., teacher
Long, Conrad, cooper
Lloyd, George, hotel proprietor
Lloyd, George, shoemaker
McCallum, John, tailor
McCorkell, Robert, livery proprietor
McCorquodale, Duncan, cooper
Martin, R., hotel proprietor
Mason & Earnshaw, woollen manufacturers
Miller, Dr., physician
Nixon & Ferguson, nurserymen
Payne, Alfred, sash, door and blind factory
Payne, James, hotel proprietor
Payne, Manuel, telegraph and general agent
Price, Samuel, jun., general mercht., insurance agent
Sexsmith, Rev. George, (Wesleyan)
Shepard, S., forwarding and commission merchant
Sutherland, Dr.
Sweeney, John, grocer
TENNENT, JOHN, Postmaster
Thomson, Robert, forwarding and commission mercht
Wade, M. A., druggist
Webb, Robert, baker and grocer
Wilson, John, stone and lime dealer
Yavitz, Jesse, proprietor flour mills

Port Union.—A village in the Township of Pickering, County Ontario, 12 miles from Whitby the County Town and 17 from Toronto. Population 100.

Annes, A., farmer
Annes, L., farmer
Brennan, W., telegraph operator
Chester, Isaac, farmer
Cowan, William, farmer
Dickson, R., farmer
Dudley, T. G., farmer
Gibson, Robert, carpenter
Hemming, William, teacher
Laskey, Thomas, hotel keeper and cooper
McDonald, Alexander, farmer
Mitchell, J.
Moon, Joseph, hotel keeper
Neilson, R., farmer
Pullen, Mrs. N., groceries
PULLEN, N. L., Postmaster
Stratton, Alexander, agent G.T.R.

Port Talbot.—*(See Villages too late for regular insertion, at the end of this work.)*

Pot Leg.—A small Village in the County of Essex, 2 miles distant from Colchester. Population 50.

Bert, Josiah, blacksmith
Brown, James, farmer
Drummond, J., teacher
Ferris, John, farmer
FERRIS, MATTHEW, general merchant
Longburg, C., saddler
Quick, Amos, blacksmith
Quick, William J., farmer
THRASHER, WILLIAM, general merchant

Powell.—A Post Office in the Township of Huntley, County Carleton.
EGAN, DENNIS, Postmaster.

Prescott.—A Town and Port of Entry on the River St. Lawrence, situated near the Junction of the Grand Trunk and St. Lawrence and Ottawa Railroads, in the Township of Augusta, County Grenville, opposite the City of Ogdensburgh, N.Y. The steamers plying between Montreal and Hamilton stop here daily, and ferries pass every hour between Prescott and Ogdensburgh. Distant from Brockville, the County Town, 12 miles, Ottawa 45, Montreal 113 and from Toronto 220. Money Order Office and Savings Bank. Population 3,000

Anderson, D., oysters, fruit, &c
Armstrong, William, landing waiter
Babcock & Co., props. Prescott Tannery
Bacon, Ebenezer, prop. tannery
BAINES, J., Medical Hall, chemist and druggist
Baudry, S., shoemaker
Benson, W., produce
Bertrand, S., axe maker
Birks, George, chemist and druggist
Blakely, Robert, harness maker
Blakey & Skinner, groceries and liquors
Bolton, George, contractor
Boswell, Rev. E. J., D.D., (Church of England)
Boyd, Rev. Robert, (Presbyterian)
BOYLE, J. P., groceries and provisions
BRADY CONCERT HALL, I. D. Purkis, prop. (see adv)
Brady, John, grocer
BROCK, REV. JAMES, (Wesleyan)
Brouse, H. A., express agent, confectioner
BROUSE, W. H., M.D., Postmaster
Buckly, John, general merchant, and forwarder
Burke, S. E. & Co., dry goods
Burton, Rev. Mr., (Presbyterian)
BYRNES, PETER, editor Prescott *Telegraph*, bookseller and stationer
Cairns, James, builder and lumber merchant
Camp, William, accountant
Carlin, William, shoemaker
Chartier, A., grocer
Clarke, Macniel, M.P.P., barrister
Coates, T., tinsmith
Conlon, P., carpenter
Coons, S. M., furniture dealer
Coughlan, Patrick, saddler
Dame, C., supt. locomotive works St. L. & O. R.R.
Daniels, David, groceries and liquors
DANIEL'S HOTEL; L. H. Daniels, prop.
DANIELS, L. H., prop. Daniels' Hotel (see adv.)
Davis, Albert, tailor
Davis, A., grocer
DETLOR, T. S., supt. St. Lawrence & Ottawa R.R.
Dillon, John, butcher and drover
Dixon, T., sash, door and blind factory
DOWSLEY, JOHN, agent Royal Insurance Co.
Dowsley, M., agent Liverpool and London and Globe; Western of Canada and Commercial Union Insurance Companies
Dubois, Narcisse, cooper
Duffy, John, shoemaker
DUNN, JAMES, Union Hotel
DUNN, WILLIAM, farmer
Easton, John, M.D.
Egert, A. S. (J. P. Wiser & Co.)
Ellis, William, contractor
Elwood, James G., landing waiter
Ewart, Frank, saddler
Fell, William, barber
Ferguson, A. W., photographer
Ferguson, John, groceries and hardware
Ford, Francis, grocer
Ford, John, grocer
Ford, William, butcher
Ford, Brothers, exchange brokers, R. R. and steamboat agents
Fortier, F., wheelwright
FRANCIS, JOHN, proprietor Ottawa Hotel, Junction (see adv)

Fraser, Allan, M.D.
French, Benjamin, farmer
Gallagher, P., tailor
Geare, Frederick, dry goods
Geralds, A. S., preventive officer
Geralds, William, landing waiter
GIBSON, L., Manager, Merchants Bank of Canada, agent Life Association of Scotland
Graham, Walter, barber
Grant, T. E., barber
Gray, Charles, billiard and bowling saloon
Gray, Matthew, dry goods
Gray, John, attorney-at-law
Green, B. F., foreman Prescott distillery
Hackett, T. H., grocer
Harding, George, druggist
HARRISON, THOMAS, clerk 2nd Division Court, agent Canada Life Assurance Company
Hayden, P., grocer
HAYNEN, JOSEPH, merchant tailor, and clothier (see adv)
Headlam, W. C., saloon
Henderson, R. S., barrister
Henning, W., tailor
HIGBEE & McCOY, dealers in tin, copper, and sheet iron ware (see adv.)
HILLYARD, JOSEPH, manufacturer and dealer in boots and shoes, leather and findings
Hodgetts Alfred, brewer, (R. P. LaBatt)
Hoey, Thomas, grocer
Hollingsworth, Samuel, livery stable
Hooker, Alfred, real estate agent
Horan, Daniel, shoemaker
Hughes, John, butcher
Hulbert, Samuel, proprietor Prescott foundry
Hutchins, H., fancy goods
IRWIN, JAMES
Jenkisson, J., shoemaker
Jessup, H. D., M. D., Collector Customs
JOHNSON, J. S., proprietor Johnson House
JOHNSTON, G. E., general merchant (see adv)
Jones, J. S., dentist
Jones, William E., watchmaker
Jones, William J., M.D.
JONES & DOWSLEY (Edwin Jones and M. Dowsley) proprietors Grenville Foundry
Kavanagh, Thomas, dry goods
KEELER & PEAKE (Marcus R. Keeler and Levi Peake) dry goods
KEILTY, BROS., groceries and liquors
Kelly, Daniel, butcher
Kilbourn, A. L., proprietor Kilbourn House
Labar, S. D., tobacconist
LA BATT, R. P., brewer, maltster and hop dealer (see adv)
Lancier, G., blacksmith
Leslie, Edward, station agent G.T.R.
McCarthy, John, & Co., distillers
McDermott, D., grocer
McFarland, J., stock dealer
McGrory, Edward, sen., baker
McGrory, Edward, jun., grocer
McGregor, Robert, saddler
McKeon, Edward, produce dealer
McLaughlin, John, confectioner
McLEAN, JOHN NEIL, barrister
McParlan, John, cattle dealer
MACGREGOR, JOHN, agent Montreal Telegraph and Travelers' Insurance (Hartford) Companies (see adv)
MAYBERRY, JOHN, groceries, liquors, hardware
MELVILLE, T. R., chemist and druggist
MERCHANTS' BANK OF CANADA, L. Gibson, manager, and J. F. Harper, teller
MERRILL, S. B., collector inland revenue, Prescott Division
Miller, J. S., proprietor Dog and Duck Inn
Mooney, Hugh, potter
Mooney, John, potter
Moran, Peter, grocer
Mowat, William, proprietor North American Hotel
MURPHY, JOHN, boots, shoes and leather
Northup, N., auctioneer and commission merchant
O'Brien, Patrick, groceries and liquors
O'Leary, John, livery stable proprietor
O'Riley, Miles, grocer
Ormiston, Alexander Custom House broker
Ormiston, J. B., freight agent St. L. & O. R.
Peck C. H., farmer
Plumb, C., soap and candle maker
PLUMB, ISAAC, Captain ferry *Prescott*
Pond, Charles C., clerk Johnson House
Post, M. J., dealer in hides, skins and furs
PURKIS, I. D., forwarder and commission merchant, dealer in flour and grain, proprietor ferry *Prescott*
Reynolds, James, barrister
Roache, Rev. E. P. (Roman Catholic)
Roblin, D., book-keeper Customs
Ryder, William, constable
Satchell, John, butcher and drover
Savage, John, grocer
Scott, John, grocer
Scott, W. J., Registrar County Grenville
Shaver, Charles, dry goods
Smalls, James, grocer
Smith, James, painter
Stentiford, Charles, stationer, etc.
Stitt, John, bailiff
STRIKER, A. N., Inspector Inland Revenue, Kingston District
TELEGRAPH (weekly), P. Byrnes, editor
Tinkus, Jehiel, chief constable
Torr, Thomas, baker
Twomley, George, surveyor Customs
Tyrie, J., baker
UNION HOTEL, James Dunn, proprietor
UNITED STATES CONSULATE, James Weldon, consul
Walter, W. L., tin and hardware
Walton, J., cabinet maker
Ward, Nestfield, builder and contractor
WELDON, JAMES, U. S. Consul
WHITE, B., town clerk, agent Scottish Provincial (Life), Provincial of Canada (Fire), and Home (New Haven) Insurance Companies (see adv)
Whitney, Albert, accountant Prescott Distilleries
Wilkinson, D. C., proprietor Junction Hotel
Willard, Charles, farmer
Willard, N., dry goods, and hardware
Wells, Alexander, proprietor St. Lawrence Hotel and ticket and exchange broker
Wise, F. A., engineer St. L. & O. R. R.
Wiser, J. P. & Co., distillers
Wright, N. J., grocer
Yule, A. R., station agent G. T. R. and St. L. & O. R. R., and Montreal Telegraph Co., Prescott, Junction

Preston.—An Incorporated Village and Station on the Great Western Railroad, situated at the confluence of the Speed and Grand Rivers, in the Township of Waterloo, County Waterloo, 8 miles from Berlin, the County Town; 28 from Hamilton, and 75 from Toronto. It was settled in the year 1833, by German Emigrants. The water power is ample and several Mineral Springs possessing remarkable medicinal qualities are found in the Village and vicinity. Money Order Office and Savings Bank. Population 1400.

Abbey, Moses A., hop grower
Anderson, William, wagon maker
Andrich, Andrew, butcher
Bauman, Abram, tanner
Bauman, Peter, sash, door and blind manufacturer
Bernhardt, Henry, brewer
Blackwood, Robert, teacher
Boos, Jacob, cooper
Brauns, Henry, carpenter
Clare & Beck, founders and machinists
Clare, John, J.P.
Clochmore, W.
Cowan, James
Deis, John, butcher
Doemer, August, general merchant
Erb, A. A. & Brothers, general merchants, props. flouring mill and lumber dealers
Ewald, Martin, carpenter
Folsom, Hugh, R., M.D.
Fricker, Samuel, boots and shoes
Goldsmith, Miss, milliner, etc.
Guggisberg, Frederick, cabinet maker
Heise, Henry, cabinet maker
Henning, Michael, boots and shoes
Herman, John, butcher
Hunt, Elliott & Co., rope and cordage manufacturers
Husband, William A., insurance agent
Jell, Robert; agent G.W.R.
Jones, Miss, milliner
Kannel, Peter V., tailor
Kelsey, Richard, tanner
Klotz, James, insurance agent
KLOTZ, OTTO, J.P., notary public and proprietor Klotz' Hotel
Koetsch, E. A., M.D.
Kremer, Charles, cabinet maker
Kress, C., proprietor Great Western Hotel
Lamb, John, stock dealer
Langrill, Peter, stock dealer
Maas, Claus, organ builder
Mahler, Geoege, lime and stone
Martin, Jacob, cooper
Miller, Charles, boots and shoes
NISPEL, CONRAD, Postmaster, druggist and general merchant
Roos, Charles, boots and shoes
Roos, George, proprietor Roos' Hotel
Roos, G. M., proprietor Preston Hotel
Roos, Jacob, brewer
Roos, John, general merchant
Schlueter, William, agent American Express Co.
Schlueter, William C., general merchant
Schlueter, W. C., telegraph operator
Schultz, Charles, wagon maker
Stahlschmidt, William, teacher
Stehle, George, painter
Stumpfle, Michael, potter
Volkmann, John, carpenter
Vonelrau, Conrad, cooper
Whan, Valentine, founder and machinist
Wares, George, auctioneer
Weirster, Rev. E., (Evangelical Lutheran)
Williamson, J. D., general merchant
Winters, A., lime and stone
Wright, Alexander, manufacturer of woolen goods

Prince Albert.—A large and important Village in the Township of Reach, County Ontario, 18 miles from Whitby, the County Town, and 46 from Toronto. It is the centre of a fine agricultural country and commands an excellent trade in merchandise. Stage to Whitby, fare 75c. Daily Mail. Money Order Office. Population about 700.

Adams, John, (J. & D. Adams)
Adams, J. & D., money brokers, &c
Adams, D. (J. & D. Adams)
Archer, John, cooper
BAIRD & PARSONS (James Baird and Henry Parsons) publishers Ontario *Observer*
Baird, James, (Baird & Parsons)
Baldwin, William H., M.D. (Brathwaite & Baldwin)
Barber, Samuel P., farmer
Billings, John, solicitor, &c
Bongard, Abram, butcher
Bongard, Jacob, butcher
Boynton, Robert, farmer
Braithwaite & Baldwin, (Francis H. Braithwaite, and William H. Baldwin), physicians
Brathwaite, Francis H., M.D., (Brathwaite & Baldwin.)
Bruce, George, photographer
Bullon, Jonathan, tailor
Cantlon, Rev. David, (Bible Christian)
Carswell, John
Cash, Elijah, pump and fanning mill maker
Courtice, Thomas, harness maker, telegraph operator
COX, JAMES, dealer in boots and shoes, &c
CURRIE, GEORGE, (Currie & Ross)
CURRIE & ROSS, (Geogge Currie and A. Ross), general merchants
Daliey, D. V., dentist
Dawson, Cornelius (Dawson & Co.)
Dawson & Co. (Cornelius Dawson and William Yates) chemists and druggists
Daynes, George (Daynes & Snell)
Daynes & Snell, boot and shoe makers
Decker, Mrs. William, watches and jewelery
Eddy, Rice H., farmer
EMANEY, JAMES, carriage maker (see adv)
Forman, Charles, tailor
FORMAN, THOMAS C., general merchant
Graham, Alexander, farmer
Graham, Frederick, farmer
Graham, Henry, shoemaker
Haskin, Richard, shoemaker
Heal, John, tailor
Heard, John, blacksmith
Hickey, Martin, tanner
Hiscocks, Charles, baker and confectioner
Holman, James, farmer
Houck, Lewis S., farmer
Hurd, Abner
Hurd, Abner, jun., law clerk

Jamieson, Rev. George (United Presbyterian)
Jeffrey, John, farmer
Jones, George W., M.D.
Jury, John, builder, etc.
Langdon, Rev. John
Langdon, Richard V., teacher
McCaw, Albert E., tinsmith
McCAW, HUGH H., Postmaster
McCaw, James, shoemaker
McConnell, James, merchant tailor
McDonald, John, millwright
McGill, Donald, tailor
McKinley, Robert, wagon maker
MARSH, WILLIAM H., ornamental painter, etc. (See adv)
MOGGRIDGE, JOHN, prop. Anglo American Hotel
Nutting, Miss Victoria, teacher
ONTARIO OBSERVER, (weekly), Baird & Parsons, publishers
Palmer, Miss Emma, teacher
Park, William H., dealer in furniture, &c.
Parrish, William, farmer
Parsons, Henry (Baird & Parsons)
Pound, Walter, farmer
Reid, Rev. Henry (Wesleyan)
Robson, Matthew G., insurance agent, money broker
Rolph, John, harness maker
ROSS, AARON (Currie & Ross)
Rose, J. W., retired
Rose, Miss Nettie, music teacher
Sanders, James, wagonmaker & blacksmith
SCOTT, WILLIAM, proprietor Victoria Hotel
Sinclair, Archibald, grocer
Smith, Andrew, carpenter
Snell, Robert (Daynes & Snell)
Stevenson, Neil, wagon maker
Taylor, John F., farmer
Tomlinson, Thomas, currier
TOMLINSON, WILLIAM A., chemist and druggist (see adv)
Ware, John E., M.D.
Wightman, William M. & Co., general merchants
Wightman, William M. (Wm. M. Wightman & Co.)
Wilcox, William M., bailiff 3rd Division Court
Williams, Rev. J. (Wesleyan)
Wright, Joshua, shoemaker and tanner
Yarnold, Benjamin
Yarnold, William E., P.L.S.
Yates, William (Dawson & Co.)
Youmans, John E., principal Grammar School

Primrose.—A Post-office in the Township of Mono, County Simcoe.

Priceville.—A Village on the Saugeen River, in the Township of Artemesia, County Grey, 38 miles from Owen Sound, the County Town. Stage to Collingwood. Money order office. Population 400.

Bishop, James, tanner
Burns, Dr.
Cameron, Rev. Charles, (Presbyterian)
Cameron, John, general merchant
Conkey, Matthew, boots and shoes
DIXON, JOSEPH, Postmaster, general merchant
Evans, Robert, wagon maker
Fenis, Robert, auctioneer
Fergusson, William, J. P
Ghent, D. A., general merchant
Ghent, Dr.
Gray, J. D., tailor
Lee, W. B., lime and stone dealer
Little, Williams, carpenter
McConnell, N, J. P
McDonald, D., proprietor flouring mill
McFadyen, Duncan, boots and shoes
McIntyre, Rev. Robert, (Baptist)
McKay, John, proprietor steam flouring mill and lumber dealer
McLane, Donald, carpenter
McMillan, C. B., hotel keeper
McNeal, John, carpenter
Robinson, Thomas, hotel keeper
Simpson, John, cabinet maker
Tryon, S., butcher
Wait, Francis, gunsmith
Watson, Mrs. milliner
Watson, William, wagon maker
Wright, Ferguson, teacher
Yeoman, G. M., general merchant

Princeton.—A Village and Station of the Great Western Railway, in the Township of Blenheim, County Oxford, 12 miles from Woodstock, the County Town, and 80 from Toronto. Money order office. Population 500.

Bartlett, Rev. H. (Church of England)
Benham, George, M.D.
Brogan, William, wagon maker
Burk, P., tailor
Campbell, Rev. A. (Wesleyan)
Cheeswright, F., tailor
Clark, Daniel, M.D.,
Clubb, C. N., painter
Cowan, Thomas & Co., gen. merts. and lumber dealers
Cowherd, Thomas, tinsmith
Dake, J., hotel keeper
David, William, blacksmith
Forsyth, H. C., shoemaker
Galbraith, Francis, general merchant
Gissing, A. W., druggist
Henderson, James S., carpenter
Hull, E. D., shoemaker
Johnson, Benjamin, hotel keeper
Kelly, William & Sons, tobacconists
Lawrence, H., saddler
LINDSAY, J. L., Postmaster
Logan & Milburne, butchers and proprietors livery
Loney, Joseph, hotel keeper
McLean, Rev. J. (Episcopal Methodist)
Mann & Travers, general merchants
Matthews, C. M., groceries and provisions
Mosier, J. G., pump maker
Pattullo, G. R., teacher
Robertson, George, sheep skin tanner
Ryerson, J., teacher
Scott, T. O., grocer
Strode, John, hotel keeper
Wallace & Houghton, tanners
Whitehead, William, carpenter
Winters, Henry, wagon maker and blacksmith

Progreston.—A Village in the Township of Flamboro East, County Wentworth, 6 miles from Waterdown station on the Great Western Railway, and 12 from Hamilton. The twelve mile creek here furnishes an abundant supply of water power. Population 150.

Ashbury, William, blacksmith
Beatty, Henry, sawyer
Burton, William C., proprietor peg factory
Campbell, Rev. Daniel
Campbell, John, sawyer
Campbell, William, proprietor flouring and saw mills
Crooker, Wesley, farmer
Edgar, John, sawyer
Fleming, Adam, miller
Griffin, Barney, teamster
Launy, Charles, proprietor peg factory
McIntosh, Robert, peg maker
McIntosh, John, proprietor flouring mill
Missouri, Thomas, builder
Tansley, Joseph, farmer
Thompson, William, farmer
Zimmerman, Isaac, teamster

Prospect.—*(See Villages too late for regular insertion at the end of this work.)*

Purdy.—A post office in the Township of Bangor, County Hastings.
LAKE, W., Postmaster.

Purpleville.—A post office in the Township of Vaughan, County York.

Puslinch.—A Village in the Township of Puslinch, County Wellington, 11 miles from Guelph, and 20 from Hamilton. Stages to the above named places. Population 100

Bannatyne, Alexander, blacksmith
Dixon, John, farmer
Ferguson, Lewis, general merchant
Forbes, Robert, shingle and barrel heading manuf
Gates, James, farmer
Leslie, George, lime and stone dealer
LESLIE, WILLIAM, Postmaster, J. P., general agt and general merchant
McDonald, John A., manager of general store
McPherson, D., farmer
Martin, William, farmer
Marshall, John, farmer
Mickle, Charles, farmer
Miller, Charles, proprietor saw mill
Micklen, Richard, propsietor saw mill
Paxton, John, tailor
Pirie, William, proprietor British Hotel
Stratton, William, carpenter
Suartz, Edward, shoemaker
Watson, Robert, farmer

Putnamville.—A Village on Reynold's Creek, in the Township of Dorchester, County Middlesex, 16 miles from London, and 5 from Ingersoll Station, Great Western Railway. Population 200.

Beckett, James, butcher
Choate, John, J.P.
Clifford, Thomas, carpenter
Collins, David, boiler maker
CRAIK, ROBERT, Postmaster and general merchant
Deacon, F. M., teacher
Dundas, John, brick maker
Hadwin, Rev. T. (Wesleyan)
Hannon, G. E., wagon maker
Longfield, Joseph, carpenter
McKee, Thomas, prop. shingle factory
Menhennick, Thomas, manager shingle factory
Osborne, D. L., carpenter
Orr, J. L., prop. New Dominion hotel
Putnam, Thomas, J.P.
Rath, John, carpenter
Rath, Matthew, carpenter
Richardson, Thomas, proprietor Farmers' Home
Rumball, Josiah, prop. flouring mill and lumber merchant
Wade, Rev. W. (Bible Christian)
Waite, Joel, shoemaker
Wolfe, Miss M. A., milliner

Queensborough.—*(See Villages too late for regular insertion, at the end of this work.)*

Queenston.—*(See Villages too late for regular insertion, at the end of this work.)*

Queensville.—A Village in the Township of East Gwillimbury, County York, 37 miles from Toronto, and 7 from Newmarket Station, N.R.R. Stage to Newmarket. Population 300.

AYLWARD, JAMES, J.P. and general merchant
AYLWARD, JAMES H., Postmaster and farmer
Cowieson, John, farmer
Cunningham, Andrew, blacksmith
Cuthbertson, Samuel, general merchant
Degeer, Peter, farmer
Deverell, William, general merchant
Doan, E. H., farmer

Evans, David, farmer
Evans, William, farmer
Eves, N., farmer
Fogg, Wright, shoemaker
Fuller, John, hotel keeper
Garrick, James, general merchant
Hamilton, Rev. C. (Wesleyan)
Hendry, William J., teacher
Kavanagh, James, butcher
Miller, A. J., blacksmith
Peregrine, David, farmer
Ritchie, David, hotel keeper
Sanderson, R., farmer
Silver, James, painter
Stiles, H. D., J.P. and general merchant
Terry, Stephen, blacksmith
Turner, William, shoemaker
Wallace, John, shoemaker
Wright, George, carriage maker

Raglan.—A Post Village in the Township of East Whitby, County Ontario, distant from Whitby, the County Town, 14 miles, and from Toronto 40 miles. Stage to Oshawa Population 150.

Burns, James, farmer
Cooper, Thomas, general merchant
Couch, J., boots and shoes
Dowling, J., blacksmith
FOSTER, L., Postmaster and general merchant
Greenwell, John, blacksmith
Hastop, John, blacksmith
Hodgson, Thomas, general merchant
Hodgson, T., farmer
McBrine, James, teacher
Pomroy, Rev. —, (Methodist Episcopal)
Sanderson, Rev. Mr. (Methodist Episcopal)
Smith, A., farmer
Smith, Moses, miller
Taylor, T., proprietor hotel
Walker, R., farmer

Railton.—A Village near Loughboro' Lake, in the Township of Loughboro', County Frontenac, 12 miles from Kingston. Population 100.

Carey, James, farmer
Conway, Patrick, wine and spirit dealer
Donahue, Rev. M. (Roman Catholic)
Harrison, D. N., wine and spirit dealer
Harrison, David N., farmer
Keely, James D., farmer
Keely, Martin, proprietor Keely's Inn
Lyons, James, farmer
McCaulay, Francis, farmer
McConnell, James, farmer
O'Brien, James. farmer
O'Brien, Lawrence, carpenter
WALSH, JOHN, Postmaster, teacher
Walsh, Patrick, carpenter
Walsh, William, farmer

Rainham.—A Post Office in the Township of Rainham, County Haldimand.

Bessey, William, general merchant
File, Jacob, auctioneer
Fitzgerald, Gerald, farmer
Fitzgerald, William, carpenter
Fox, Rev. (N. C. Methodist)
Hagney, Cornelius, cooper
Havill, Richard A., painter
Havill, Richard, wagon maker
HANSBERGER, ISAAC, Postmaster, gen. merchant
Phillips, D. B., teacher
Raible, Martin, cabinet maker
Schneider, Frederick, shoemaker
Siebert, Frederick, tailor
Smith & Wardell, general merchants
Stevenpiper, Philip, carpenter
Wardell, Peter, brick yard

Rainham Centre.—A small Village in the Township of Rainham, County Haldimand, 8 miles from Cayuga, the County Town. Stages to Dunnville and Port Dover. Population 100.

Booker, Thomas, wagon maker
Clouse, Ira, proprietor Lake Erie House
Culver, Austin, general merchant
Culver, Guy, farmer
Culver, N., farmer
Culver, Peter, farmer
Elfner, George, blacksmith
Emerick, Rev. J. M. (Baptist)
Evans, Joseph, farmer
Foreman, Christopher, blacksmith
Forster, Jesse, farmer
Franklin, Jacob, farmer
Hansberger, D. O., farmer
Hartwick, Valentine, confectioner
Hoist, Jacob, blacksmith
Kennedy, David, tanner
Law, John, J.P.
Neil, John, cabinet maker
Ross, Alexander, farmer
Stewart, James, farmer
Stewart, Joel, farmer
THOMSON, WILLIAM J., Postmaster and general merchant.

Rama.—A Post Office in the Township of Rama, County Ontario.

McPHERSON, JAMES, Postmaster.

Ranelagh.—A Post Village in the Township of Windham, County Norfolk, 17 miles from Simcoe, the County Town, and 84 from Toronto. Population 59.

Buckburrough, John, farmer
Cornell, William, farmer
Hoggard, John, farmer
LAKE, BENJAMIN, Postmaster
Shaver, James, farmer
Tull, James, farmer
Winshell, John, farmer

Ratho—A Post Village in the Township of Blandford, County Oxford, 14 miles from Woodstock, the County Town, and 80 miles from Toronto. It is a Station on the Buffalo and Lake Huron Railroad. Population 100

Adam, Johnston, wagon maker
Allshire, Thomas, carpenter
Baird, Hugh, butcher
Bean, Daniel, farmer
Brast, David, farmer
Brast, Joseph, farmer
Currie, John, blacksmith
Davidson, William, farmer
Endress, Peter, cabinet maker
Hamilton, James, carpenter
Henderson, John, teacher
Hepworth, Joseph, boots and shoes
Hebertson, Andrew, farmer
Hughes, William, hotel keeper
Kerr, James, general merchant
Lensler, Christian, farmer
McCuaig, Rev. Finlay (Canada Presbyterian)
Oliver, John, J.P.
Peat, Thomas, farmer
Pettigrew, Robert, teacher
Prentice, William, blacksmith
Russell, J. R., teacher
Sellars, Thomas, farmer
Smith, William, carpenter
Steedsman, George, carpenter and lumber dealer
Tye, Frank, butcher
WILLIAMS, JOSEPH, Postmaster, gen. merchant

Ravenna.—A Post Office in the Township of Collingwood, County Grey, 35 miles from Owen Sound, the County Town, and 117 from Toronto. Land in the vicinity averages $30 per acre. Population 60.

Alcock, Robert, wagon maker
Armitage, G., blacksmith
Eachrin, P. W., teacher
Hutchinson, G., weaver
Lyne, Edward, general merchant
McKain, Archibald, carpenter
Reid, William, J.P.
Weir, Mrs. P., general merchant
Weir, William, hotel keeper

Ravenswood.—A Post Village in the Township of Bosanquet, County Lambton, 25 miles from Sarnia, the County Town, 145 from Toronto, and 5 from Widder Station Grand Trunk Railway. The average price of land is $25 per acre. Population 65.

Abbott, Joseph, shoemaker
Armstrong, William, teacher
Bogart, John P., farmer
Charlton, Rev. William (Wesleyan)
Clemms, Henry, farmer
Feathers, Rev. T. (Wesleyan)
Goodfellow, Rev. P. (Presbyterian)
Holbrook, Edwin, proprietor steam saw mill
Hollingshead, William, farmer
JARVIS, P., Postmaster, general merchant
Kawling, Allan, stock dealer
Lapham, Alfred, farmer
McIntosh, John, tailor
McIntyre, Dougal, farmer
McMullin, Daniel, wagon maker
Millburn, William, carpenter
Shervington, Peter, farmer
Staley, George, shingle maker
Virgo, William, carpenter
Williamson, Daniel, wagon maker
Woodson, Smith, farmer

Reading.—A Post Village in the Township of Garafraxa, County Wellington, 27 miles from Guelph, the County Town, and 50 from Toronto. Stage to Georgetown, fare $1. Improved land in the vicinity averages $30 per acre. Mails daily. Population 120.

Cook, Benjamin, teacher
Cunningham, Robert, insurance agent
DONALDSON, ROBERT, Postmaster, and prop. Reading Hotel
Edwards, Rev. W. W., (Wesleyan)
Gillies, Archibald, tailor
Johnston, James, James, farmer
King, Henry, general merchant
King, Richard, farmer
Lawson, George, farmer
Lawson, Robert, boots and shoes
Leeson, Isaac, general merchant
McCormack, William, general merchant
Nodwell, John, farmer
Nodwell, Samuel, farmer
Petrie, Alexander, teacher
Simpson, John, farmer
Vicars, Rev. Johnston, (Church of England)
Watson, Thomas, farmer
Westover, William, boots and shoes

Renfrew.—An incorporated Village on the Bonnechére River, in the Township of Horton, County Renfrew, 37 miles from Pembroke, the County Town, and 60 from Ottawa. It is the centre of a fine agricultural district. Money order office and Savings' Bank. Stages to Farrell's Landing, Douglas and Eganville. Population 900.

Addison, Matthew, jewelry, watches, clocks, &c.
Airth, David, councillor
Airth, H., sen., farmer
Airth, William, general merchant
Archer, Richard, jun., farmer
Archer, R. C., baker
Barr, Robert, blacksmith
Bassan, Charles, proprietor brick yard
Bellamy, J. H. & Co., dealers in stoves and tinware
Bellerby, H., J.P., town clerk
Bellerby, Henry, farmer
Bellerby, Mrs., private seminary
Biggan, George, general merchant
Bremner, John, farmer
Brisban, O., carpenter
Bromley, James, sen., attorney.at-law
Bromley, James, painter
Bronscan, John, saddler
Buffum, Henry, hotel keeper
Burns, John, treasurer
Campbell, M., soap and candle maker
Carney, James, boots and shoes
Carswell, Robert, carpenter
Chesser, Charles, patent right agent
Cheshire, D., soap and candle maker
Churchill, I., cooper
Combs, Samson, lime and stone
Costello, J. W. & Co., general merchants
Desroche, A., boots and shoes
Devine, Felix, general merchant
Docherty, James, brewer
Dougall, Peter, blacksmith
Dunlop, Gabriel, shingle maker
Duple, Francis, carpenter
Duple, Miss, milliner
Drysdale, Robert, cabinet maker
Eady, George, jun., general merchant
Edwards, William, coal dealer
Farquharson, Mrs., proprietor lumber yard
Feachney, William N., collector and auctioneer
Ferguson, Alexander, carpenter
Fitzmaurice, Michael, wagon and plow manufacturer
Fitzmaurice, Michael, veterinary surgeon
Francis, Samuel, axe manufacturer
Freer, Benjamin, teacher grammar school
Freer, Rev., principal grammar school
Freer, Thomas, M.D.
French, Francis, tailor
Frood, William, carpenter
Gibbons, James, farmer
Gibbons, William, farmer
Gillies, Patrick, boots and shoes
Gordon, R., blacksmith
Gorman, Simon O., cooper
Goulett, H., cooper
Gravall, H., proprietor hotel
Groves, Henry L., grocer
Groves, Henry, farmer
Gruble, Rev. (Church of England)
Halpenny, William, J.P., Reeve and general mercht.
Harris, William, Crown Land agent
Hillman, Miss, miliner, &c.
Huston, Moses, saddler
Hynes, Thomas, cabinet maker
Jamieson, Alexander, clothing dealer and tailor
Jamieson, John, weaver
Jamieson, William, farmer
Johnston, James, shingle maker
Jourda, K., carpenter
Kelly, Patrick, proprietor livery stables
Knight, Joseph, farmer
Leach, Robert, farmer
Logan, William, proprietor woolen mills
Lynn, Dr.
McAndrew, John, general merchant
McDonald, John D., attorney-at-law
McDougall, John, boots and shoes
McDougall, J. L., prop. flouring mill & gen. mercht.
McDougall, Miss, milliner, &c.
McGee, James, boots and shoes
McInnes, John, tanner
McInnis, Mrs., telegraph operator
McIntyre, Gregor, farmer
McIntyre, Patrick, druggist
McIntyre, Robert & Co., general merchants
McIntyre & Stewart, general merchants
McKAY, WILLIAM, Postmaster and gen. merchant
McLellan, Adam, architect
McMillan, Hugh, proprietor flouring mill
McNab, John, M.D.
McRae, John, proprietor flouring mill
McTavish, Adam, blacksmith
Matherson, Mrs., milliner
Mills, John, butcher
Mills, William, carpenter
Moore, Dr.
Morris, Thomas, proprietor sash, blind and door factory
Muir, T. B., tailor
Munro, Alexander, architect
Murphy, Joshua, saddler
New, Thomas, farmer
New, William, farmer
O'Hara, John, blacksmith
Park, John, teacher
Reeves, William, lime and stone
Reynolds, J., painter
Robertson, James, boots and shoes
Ross, Mrs., milliner, etc.
Rougier, Rev. P. (Roman Catholic)
Ryan, P., proprietor British Hotel
Scott, John, butcher
Seymour, Joseph, boots and shoes
Smith, John, tanner and proprietor flouring mill and Exchange Hotel
Stewart, Donald, butcher
Stewart & Dixon, general merchants
Stewart & Johnston, general merchants
Stewart & Knight, axe manufacturers
Thibadeau, Mrs., grocer
Thomson, Rev. George, (Presbyterian)
Traynor, Mrs, milliner
Walker, Rev. T. H., (Wesleyan)
Walford, S. & J. H., drugs and fancy goods
Wallace John, architect
Ward, James, tanner
Watt, James, cabinet maker
White, Rev. G. H., (Episcopal Methodist)
Wright, Mrs. O., proprietor Renfrew House

Renton.—A post office in the Township of Townsend, County Norfolk, 5 miles from Simcoe the County Town, and 6 miles from Port Dover.

Raymond.—A Post-office in the Township of Watt, Muskoka District, 14 miles from Bracebridge and about 150 from Toronto. Parties visiting this portion of the country in summer take steamer from Barrie to Washago, fare $1.25, thence to Gravenhurst by stage, fare 75c., thence to Bracebridge by steamer, fare 50c., and stage to Raymond; in winter per stage the whole way from Barrie, fare $3., there is also a stage from Bracebridge to Parry Sound, distance 52 miles, fare $3. Government land in the vicinity is chiefly free granted, the remainder 50c. per acre. There are numerous water privileges here, and though the resources of the country at present are undeveloped, this district promises to become of considerable importance at no distant day. The vicinity is a favorite resort for summer tourists, affording excellent hunting and fishing.

Alexander, Samuel, farmer
Atkinson, Robert, farmer
Bogart, Jacob H., farmer
Galloway, Matthew, farmer
Gaffney, James, carpenter
Giles, Robert, farmer
Giles, Thomas H., carpenter
Gott, James, farmer
Hamilton, Edward, farmer
Hammill, John, farmer
Lance, Robert, shoemaker
Smith, William, farmer
SUFFERN, ANTHONY, Postmaster
Wilson, George, carpenter

Ravenshoe.—A Post Office in the Township of East Gwillimbury, County York.
OLIVER, J. B., Postmaster.

Rednersville.—A Post Village in the Township of Ameliasburg, County Prince Edward, 21 miles from Picton, the County Town, and 120 from Toronto. Population 160.

Austin, Mrs. James, prop. Rednersville Hotel
Crowter, James, tinsmith
Dalmay, H., teacher
Kitcheson, E. C., accountant
Redner, James, general merchant
Roblin, P., J.P
Snider, Isaac, tailor
Thompson, Rev. James, (Wesleyan)

Reekie.—A small Village on the Penetangore River, in the Township of Kincardine, County Bruce, 27 miles from Walkerton, the County Town. Population 75.

Avery, Samuel, wagon maker
Bennett, Caleb, gen. mercht and prop. steam flouring mill
Bennett, Joshua, baker
Edmonds, James, carpenter
Emmons, J., tailor
Fraser, Rev. John (Presbyterian)
Griffith, Henry, farmer
Griffith, William, farmer
Hall, R. D., teacher
Hume, John, shingle maker
Large, Rev. R. (Methodist Episcopal)
McKay, Mrs., manufacturer of woolen goods
Reekie, William, J.P., farmer
Robinson, W. R., manufacturer of woolen goods
Scott, John, manufacturer of woolen goods
Shin, John, farmer
Shin, Joseph, farmer
Shin, Mrs., clothing dealer
Stuart, Thomas, farmer
Took, Robert, sen., shoemaker
Took, William, carpenter
Trans, Charles, carpenter
Watson, Peter, cabinet maker
Wayburn, P., carpenter
Wilson, Leonard, farmer

Richmond.—A Village situated on the Goodwood River, in the Township of Goulborn, County Carleton. The village was founded in 1819 by the Duke of Richmond, who died in a barn three miles below the village from the effects of the bite of a pet fox. Distant 20 miles from Ottawa. Per stage fare $1. Improved land averages $50 per acre. Daily mail. Money order office. Population 300.

Armstrong, J., farmer
Bains, C. T., attorney-at-law
Baxter, M., saddler
Beatty, D., M.D.
Bennet, H., farmer
Bennett, J., farmer
Bennett, T., farmer
Brogan, John, carpenter
Brogan, Mrs., milliner
Brown, Thomas, wagon maker
Brown, W., painter
Brown, Rev. W. D. (Methodist)
Burrows, John, auctioneer
Butler, John, principal grammar school
BUTLER, W. H., Postmaster, tanner, leather dealer and general merchant
Byers, W., farmer
Davidson, J., farmer
Davis, T., farmer
Elliot & Little, proprietors flouring mills and lumber dealers
Good, W., farmer
Hill, J., farmer
Hinton, J., J.P.
Lewis, Thomas, general merchant
Lowry, Peter, teacher
Lyon, P. E., auctioneer
McDonald, K., farmer

McDougall, P., wagon maker
McElroy, H,, J.P. and general merchant
McElroy, P., notary public
McLean, James, cabinet maker
McRea, A., farmer
McRea, D., farmer
McRea, Samuel, tailor
Maxwell, J., farmer
Miller, Thomas, shoemaker
Milligan, James, general merchant
Mills, J., farmer
Mullin, Rev. E. (Presbyterinn)
O'Connell, Rev. P. (Baptist)
Pettet, Rev. C. B. (Church of England)
Rieley, Edward, proprietor hotel
Scott & Brother, carpenters
Scott, John, farmer
Shillington, W., butcher and baker
Stewart, John, proprietor hotel
Wilson, W., general merchant
Wright, A., carpenter

Richmond (Bayham Post Office).—A Village in the Township of Bayham, County Elgin, situated on Otter Creek, 20 miles from St. Thomas and 20 from Ingersoll, by stage. Population 200.

Anderson, P., farmer
Cook, S., hotel
Doan, George A., farmer
Hamilton, John, shoemaker
High, Andrew, farmer
LANG, GEORGE W., Postmaster and merchant
Leach, Job, flour mills
Mann, P. M., M.D.
Moore, Andrew, farmer
Morse, William D., carriage maker
Pauling, James, wagon maker
Pound, William, farmer
Procunier, G. M., J.P.
Scriver, James, carpenter
Simmonds, Richard, flour mills
Summers, Alexander, farmer
Wallace, John, wagon maker
Woods, James H., cabinet maker
Woods, Henry, general merchant

Richmond Hill.—A flourishing Village in the Township of Markham and Vaughan, (Yonge St. dividing the Townships) County York, distant 16 miles from Toronto, and 3 from Richmond Hill Station. Northern Railway fare to Toronto by rail 25 cents, by stage 50 cents. Improved lands average from $60 to $75 per acre—the surrounding country is extremely fertile. There are two creeks near the Village affording excellent water privileges. Daily mail. Money Order Office and Savings Bank. Population 900.

ATKINSON, W., general merchant
Appleby, George H., proprietor flouring mills
BARNARD, GEORGE A., general merchant
Bernard, Hiram G., farmer
Bernard, J. G., general merchant
Boyle, David, proprietor saw mill
Bredin, Rev. John (Wesleyan)
Bridgford, Lieutenant Colonel
Campbell, Mrs., ladies' school
Christian, James, hotel keeper
Christian, Mrs., hotel keeper
COGHLAN, THOMAS, grocer and furniture dealer
Cook, Thomas, proprietor Richmond Hill Hotel
Cooper, William, painter
COULTER, JOHN, merchant tailor and clothier
Cox, William, butcher
Crookshank, Lieut. Colonel
CROSBY, ISAAC, general merchant
CROSBY, PARKER, J.P.
Davidson, Benjamin, millwright
Dick, Rev. James (Presbyterian)
Dolmage, Gideon, hotel keeper
Dolmage, Tobias, boots and shoes
Duncumb, John, M.D.
Freek, James, proprietor brick yard
Gray, R. A., teacher
Hall, Mrs., fancy goods and toys
HALL, R. H., druggist
Hamilton, John, cooper
Harrington, John, farmer
Harrison, William, saddler
Henderson, A., watchmaker, jeweler, &c
Hopkins, David, grocer
Hopper, Robert, butcher
Hostetter, John, M.D
Humphreys, J. D. station agent
Hutchins, John C., wagon maker
Lafferty, A. M., M.A., principal grammar school
Langstaff, James, M.D
Law, A., J.P., insurance agent
LAWRENCE, JAMES, clerk 3rd division court and clerk and treas. township Vaughan
Lymburner, Robert, prop. livery stable
Lynett, Nicholas, farmer
McBeath, Andrew, wagon maker
McNair, Matthew, architect
Marsh, Robert, J.P., farmer
Morgan, Thomas, grocer
Morris, Rev. T. J., (Roman Catholic)
Munshaw, William, blacksmith
Myers, Mrs., milliner
Myers, W. H., saddler
Newton, Henry, general merchant
Newton, James, sen., architect
Newton, James, jun., leather dealer and tanner
Nichol, George B., barrister
Pogue, William, cooper
Raymond, Robert, hotel keeper
Russell, William, farmer
Scott, Alexander, editor and prop. York *Herald* and dealer in books, stationery, &c
Seedman, Thomas, wagon maker
Shanklin, Rev. R. (Church of England)
Siver, Robert, boots and shoes
Soules, George, baker
Storey, John W., carpenter
TEEFY, M., J.P., Postmaster, commissioner in B. R., conveyancer, and general merchant
Trench, William blacksmith
Vandeburg, Richmond, farmer
Vetie, John, hotel keeper
Warren, W. S., J.P.
Williamson, Miss, milliner
Williamson, Robert, boots and shoes
Wright, Amos, J.P., M.P.
Wright, William, farmer
YORK HERALD, (Friday), Alexander Scott, editor and proprietor

Riceville.—A small Village in the Township of South Plantaganet, County Prescott, 24 miles from L'Orignal. Population 50.

Coote, George, farmer
Corgar, S., shoemaker
Draper, S. T., prop. flouring mill and general mercht
Dyson, Joseph, farmer
Franklin, Benjamin, proprietor brick yard and farmer
Franklin, Henry, farmer
Frith, C., farmer
McDougall, Miss, C., teacher
McLAURIN, P., Postmaster
McLean, H. J., general merchant
Metcalfe, C., farmer
Metcalfe, H., farmer
Rawe, William, sen., farmer
Rawe, William, jr., farmer
Rome, Thomas, farmer
Scott, George, farmer
Shorts, Rev. A. (Episcopal Methodist)
Wells, R., cabinet maker

Richview.—A Village in the Gore ofthe Township of Toronto, County Peel. Distant from Toronto 15. miles, and from Brampton, the County Town, 11 miles. Land in the vicinity averages $40 per acre. Daily mails. Population 75.

Aikins, Hon. J. C., J.P.
Aikins, J. C., farmer
Arth, A., farmer
Bamane, J., farmer
Bamane, P., farmer
Bateman, J., shoemaker
Burgess, J., farmer
BURGESS, R. M., Postmaster
Cook, W., farmer
Coulter, J., farmer
Crowley, M., farmer
Cullham, J., farmer
Ellerby, J., tailor
Garbutt, D. H., farmer
Garbutt, G., farmer
Gowland, G., proprietor Richview Hotel
Graham, J., J.P., farmer
Graham, T., farmer
Hagan, Miss E., teacher
Jackson, H., farmer
Marron, M., shoemaker
Mellow, S., farmer
Peacock, J., wagon maker
Ramage, T., carpenter
Trueman, D., carpenter
Trueman, J., wagon maker

Richwood.—A thriving Village and Station on the Buffalo and Lake Huron Railway, in the Township of Blenheim, County Oxford. The River Nith runs near the Village, affording excellent water power Distant from Woodstock, the County Town, 19 miles, and from Paris 8. Daily Mail. Population 300

Ainslie, M. F., teacher
German, Rev. J., (Wesleyan)
Key, William, insurance agent
LAYCOCK, J. H., Postmaster
McCaw, Gabriel, blacksmith
Mills, Rev. J., (Wesleyan)
Rupert, C., farmer
Scott, Robert, general merchant
Taylor, William, shoemaker
Thompson, John, blacksmith
Wright, David, general merchant

Ridgeville.—A post office in the Township of Pelham, County Monck, 6 miles from Welland, the County Town, and 70 from Toronto. Average price of land $50 per acre. Population 60.

Beckett, Samuel, farmer
Brown, L. F., proprietor planing mill
Brown, Peter, blacksmith
Collins, Andrew J., carpenter
Cushing, Pierce, wagon maker
Fry, William, teacher
Haist, Michael, farmer
Hill, S. W., tanner
Holdrich, Robert, general merchant
Moore, Whitson, farmer
Rinker, Rolson, general merchant
STEELE, JONAS, J.P., Postmaster
Swayze, Samuel, farmer
Taylor, Alexander L., farmer
Thompson, John, carpenter
Townsend, George, grocer
Vanevery, William A., farmer
Ward, Clark, blacksmith
Ward, Josiah, farmer
Willson, Z., tanner

Ringwood.—A Post Office in the Township of Whitchurch, County York, 26 miles from Toronto. Stages to Markham and Toronto. Population 100.

Brown, O. J., teacher
Button, N., J.P., proprietor Ontario House
Gould, James, teacher
Gould, R., teacher
Grove, Jacob, carpenter
Homer, Emanuel, carpenter
Lehman, Christian, butcher
Lehman, Ludwig, general merchant
Lehman, S. W., proprietor planing mills
McPherson, Hugh, carpenter
SILVESTER, G. H., Postmaster, general merchant3
Skene, William, prop. Ringwood House
Widerman, P., J.P., and prop. marble yard
Yakely, J., shoemaker

Ridgetown.—A village in the Township of Howard, County Kent, 21 miles, from Chatham, the County Town. Stages to Thamesville and Morpeth. Land in the vicinity averages $20 per acre. Mails daily. Money order office. Population 500.

Atkins, James, farmer
Beaton, Hugh carpenter
Bedford, David, general merchant
Benton, N. S., proprietor Western Hotel
Benson, Rev. Manley, (Wesleyan)
Bevans, John, blacksmith
Brach, A., general merchant
Britton, Ephraim, saddler
Cavan, Rev. William, (Presbyterian Free Church)
Colby, Philander, proprietor brick yard
Coleman, Walter, cabinet maker
Dodge, H., proprietor hotel
HANCOCK, L. S., Postmaster, dealer in books, stationery, stoves and tinware
Hawkins & Graham, carpenter
Heyward, A., general merchant
Jackson, Alexander S., tanner
Jackson, George, proprietor livery
Jackson, Joseph, butcher
Lake, C., M.D.
Lozier, George, proprietor saw mill
McEwen, James, boots and shoes
McLachlan, J. B., general merchant
Mitton, James, blacksmith
Mitton, John, farmer
Mitton, William, farmer
Moody, John, manufacturer of woolen goods, prop. steam flouring mill
Moore, T., proprietor hotel
Morgan, Mrs., milliner
Morgan, W. H. B., clothing dealer
Orendorf, P. J., carpenter
Page, John & Son, soap and candle makers
Page, Miss, milliner
Phelps, Richard, J. P
Rich, E. K., general merchant
Rockey, George, wagon maker
Schlenker, Thomas, saddler
Sinclair, Rev. D., (Disciples Church)
Smith, Jacob, M. D., druggist
Smith, John, carpenter
Stewart, Elihu, teacher
Sutherland, George, wagon maker
Tylhurst, Edward, farmer
Waterworth, David, farmer
Wetson, George, general merchant
Watson, —, farmer
Wilber, Clark, boots and shoes
Weston, John, carpenter
Young, James, blacksmith
Young, John, blacksmith

Ripley.—A Post-office in the Township of Kinloss, County Bruce.

Riversdale.—A Post Village in the Township of Greenock, County Bruce, 12 miles from Walkerton, the County Town. Stages to Walkerton, Kincardine, Goderich and Wingham. Improved land averages from $20 to $25 per acre. Daily Mail. Money Order Office. Population 80

Braden, O., farmer
Charhand, R., hotel keeper
Cosgrove, John, insurance agent
Crysler, James H., constable
Forbes, Rev. A. G., (Presbyterian)
Griffith, W. J., prop. Riversdale Hotel
Hornell, David, general merchant
Kelly, Rev. Hugh J., (Roman Catholic)
McDonald, Peter, shingle maker
McKenzie, Charles, teacher
McLennan, Miss E., teacher R. C. school
Mason, Anthony, prop. steam saw mill
Miller, James, farmer
O'CONNOR, H. B., Postmaster, clerk division court auctioneer and general agent
Pringle, William, farmer
Robins, Ezra, carpenter
Ross, Paul, farmer
Snodgrass, W. O., farmer
Watson, W. J., farmer

Riviere Raisin.—(Village New Lancaster.)—Is situated in the Township of Lancaster, County Glengary, 16 miles from Cornwall, the County Town and 279 from Toronto. The Grand Trunk Railway runs through the Village. Stage to Martintown, 12 miles, fare 75c. Daily Mail. Population 350.

Anderson, John, watchmaker, jeweler, &c
Bertrand, Oliver, shoemaker
Cameron, Alexander, farmer
Chapman, R., proprietor Clair Hall Hotel
Falconer, A., M.D.
Fraser, Duncan, tailor and clothier
Kavanagh, P., saddler
Kensella, Peter, saddler
Key, William, butcher
Leclair, A. D., general merchant
Loucks, Thaddeus, telegraph operator
McBain, A. L., farmer
McCrimmon, Donald, shoemaker
McDonald, A. S., proprietor Commercial Hotel
McDonald, D. A., general merchant
McDonald & Devine, wagon makers
McDonald, R. S., farmer
McDougal, R. J., general merchant
McGillis, Neil, stoves and hardware
McGregor, Alexander, cabinet maker
McGregor, Daniel, blacksmith
McGregor, Miss, milliner
McInnes & Le Roy, blacksmiths
McLeod, Peter, watchmaker, jeweler, etc.
McMillan & McDonald, grocers
McMillen, Hugh C., carpenter
McMillen, Hugh D., carpenter
McNaughton, Donald, general merchant
McPherson, A., insurance agent
McPherson, Daniel, farmer
McPHERSON, JAMES, Postmaster, grocer and insurance agent
McPherson, D. F. & W., general merchant
McPherson, John, farmer

McRae, E., proprietor New Lancaster Hotel
Maxwell, Archibald, shoemaker
Morrison, Donald, carpenter
Murdoch, R., farmer
O'Neill, Patrick, tailor
Odett, B., painter
Richardson, H., agent British Am. Ex. Co. & G. T. R.
Roderick, Cameron. farmer
Roell, Francis, carpenter
Ross, Thomas, M.D., druggist
Stewart, Miss, milliner
Tobin, A., proprietor Grand Trunk House
Urquhart, James, grocer
Wilson, J., baker

Roblin.—A Village on Salmon River, in the Township of Richmond, County Lennox, 10 miles from Napanee, the County Town. Population 150.

Anderson, Thomas, foreman for H. B. Rathburn & Son
Beeman & Paul, lumber dealers
CARD, EBENEZER, Postmaster, general merchant
Chambers, T., miller
Dafoe, Peter, general merchant
Hart, Miles, shoemaker
Hughes, John, carpenter
Jackson, Walter, carpenter
Lee, Rev. —, (Primitive Methodist)
McBride, George D., teacher
McConnell, James, farmar
McConnell, John, farmer
McCutcheon, Alexander, farmer
Orr, Charles R., constable
O'Brien, James, proprietor hotel
Paul & Beeman, lumber dealers
Paul, W., butcher
Rathburn & Son, H. B., lumber dealers
Shorts, Robert, cooper
Shorts, Rev. S. D. (Episcopal Methodist)
Spencer, E. A., proprietor saw mills
Spencer, E. H., J.P.
Spencer, Henry, general merchant
Spencer, N. and E. H.. proprietor flouring mills
Spencer, N. E., farmer
Vader, William, proprietor saw mill
Wheeler, Seth, proprietor hotel
Windover, N., farmer
Woods, S. L., turner and cheese box manufacturer

Rob Roy.—A Post Office in the Township of Osprey, County Grey.

McGOWAN, DAVID, Postmaster.

Rochester.—A Post Village in the Township of Rochester, County Essex, and a Station on Grand Trunk Railroad, 20 miles from Sandwich, the County Town, and 215 from Toronto. Daily mail. Population 400.

Chevalier, Antoine, sen., grocer
Chevalier, Antoine, jun., saddler
Chevalier, N., councilman
Chevalier, Samuel, blacksmith
Clontier, R., grocer
Clontier, William, blacksmith
Crae, John, general merchant
Cullen, Henry, proprietor hotel
DUMONCHELLE, P., Postmaster and gen. mer.
Haines, Nicholas, watchmaker
Hamell, Xavier. councilman
Harrison, Rev. W. (Presbyterian)
Hart, Raphael, blacksmith
Johan, Rev. C. L. M. (Roman Catholic)
Johnson, J. W., general merchant
Marentelle, P., shoemaker
Menan, L. & M., blacksmiths
Meward, S., shoemaker
Mousseau, F. X., teacher
Ouellette, J., blacksmith
Ray, Joseph A., reeve
Simons, Christian, councilman
Stone, John, proprietor Rochester Hotel
Taylor, John, grocer and proprietor Western Hotel
Welsh, Edward, station master
Wilcox, Samuel, councilman

Rockton.—A Village in the Township of Beverly, County Wentworth, 15 miles from Hamilton. Pop. 100.

Ames, Charles, shoemaker
Atkins, William, blacksmith
Bannor, Patrick, farmer
Barnaby, G. H., butcher
Bell, Alexander, teacher
Brown, John, wagon maker
CARNELL, BENONI, Postmaster and gen. mercht.
Carruthers, John, farmer
Crawder, Rev. F. J., (United Brethren)
Dickson, Peter, farmer
Draper, Rev. J., (Methodist Episcopal)
Fetheringham, Mrs. S. J., milliner
Fry, Christopher, wagon maker
Grummit, James, proprietor Rockton House
Harrison, Rev., (Church of England)
Headworthy, Lewis, wagon maker
Henderson, William, J. P., farmer
Hunter, R., auctioneer
Jackson, Thomas, farmer
Kernaghan, Andrew, farmer
Lundy, J. B., M. D.
McDonald, W., J. P., insurance agent
McCusker, Thomas, proprietor Farmers Inn
McManaly, John, farmer
McQueen, James, teacher
Mattren, Andrew, blacksmith
Riddel, Walter, lime and stone
Robinson, John, blacksmith
Robinson, William, blacksmith
Smith, J. T., farmer
Stockwell, George, cooper
Stockwall, Washington, carpenter
Stockwell, Westley, carpenter
Swinton, Thomas, farmer
Teepel, John, J. P

Rockford.—A Post Office in the Township of Townsend, County Norfolk, 11 miles from Simcoe, the County Town.

Bowlby, William, & Bros., props. flouring mill
Cook, Martin, prop. sash, door and blind manuf.
Downey, James, carpenter
GREATHEAD, JOSEPH, Postmaster and gen. mer.
Henderson, John, blacksmith
Higgins, Henry, shingle maker
Lee, William, weaver
Lemon, James, blacksmith
Nurser, B., weaver
Parsons, D. W., teacher
Powell, William, proprietor brick yard
Ross, B., shoemaker
Smith, James, carpenter
Somers, R. J., general merchant
Thompson, John F., proprietor flouring mill
Watson, Rev. C. (Wesleyan)
Wood, Rev. E. (Church of England)

Rockingham.—A Village in the Township of Brudenell, County Renfrew, 50 miles from Pembroke, the County Town. Population 100.

Acton, Arthur, farmer
Acton, Richard, farmer
Bond, John, weaver
Burton, James, proprietor Rockingham Hotel
Crosier, A. P., hotel keeper
Decharm, L., blacksmith
Huckway, R. K., carpenter
James, Richard, farmer
James, Richard, teacher
James, William, carpenter
Kinder, Joseph, farmer
Kitt, John, saddler
Larwell, A., farmer
Murphy, John, farmer
Murphy, William, farmer
Watson & Co., proprietors carding mill
WATSON, JOHN, Postmaster, proprietor flouring and saw mills and general merchant

---

Rockport.—A Village on the River St. Lawrence, in the Township of Escott, County Leeds, 20 miles from Brockville, the County Town, and 9 from Mallorytown Station Grand Trunk Railway. Improved land averages $25 per acre. Population 200

Burtch, Alfred, farmer
Carnegie, A. B., proprietor Rockport Hotel
Cornwall, Charles, J.P., commission merchant
Cornwall, C. & Co., general merchants
CORNWALL, WILLIAM, M.D., Postmaster
Dollinger, Lewis, general merchant
Higgins, Charles, farmer
Leaman, John, farmer
Lear, Thomas, farmer
Natty, Edward, customs officer
Scott, James, farmer
Skinner, W. M., farmer
White, George, ferryman

Rockside.—A Post Office in the Township of Caledon, County Cardwell.
KIRKWOOD, D., Postmaster.

Rockwood.—A Village and Station of the Grand Trunk Railroad, on a branch of the River Speed, in the Township of Eramosa, County Wellington, 8 miles from Guelph, the County Town, and 41 from Toronto. Marble is found in the neighborhood and there is excellent water power in and adjacent to the Village. Money order office. Population 600.

Barry, James, cooper
Benner, R. M., shoemaker
Carson, William, carpenter
CLARK, DAVID, J. P., proprietor flouring mill
Cunningham, John, tailor
Daly, Mrs., milliner
DUFFIELD, S., hotel keeper
Duncan, John, telegraph operator, G. T. R. and American express agent
Ellis, John, butcher
Farish, William, proprietor flouring mill
Gibson, J. M., teacher
Gregory, Thomas, teacher
Harris & Co., manufacturers of woolen goods
Hough, Rev. J., (Wesleyan)
JONES, C. A., M.D. and druggist
Joseland, Henry, lime and stone
Knowles, James W., saddler
Landrum, Richard, shoemaker
McCAIG & McMILLAN, prins. Rockwool Academy
McCarthy, William, general merchant
McLeod, John, general merchant
McMacken, Thomas, cooper
McMorry, Charles, butcher
Morris, Samuel, wagon maker
NAIRN, ALEXANDER, proprietor Kelvin mills
Nealan, Thomas, wagon maker
Nelson, John, tailor
PASSMORE, ROBERT, Postmaster
Passmore Brothers, general merchants
Perkins, William, M.D.
Reeve, Rev., (Presbyterian)
Robinson, George, blacksmith
ROCKWOOD ACADEMY, McCaig & McMillan, principals
Rowland, Binna, shoemaker
Russell, James, farmer
Stout, Eli, tinsmith
Stovel, William, hotel keeper
Strange, Henry, J.P.
Turner, John, blacksmith
Vicars, Rev. J. (Church of England)
Warner, Andrew, grocer
Warden & Ostrander, blacksmiths
Williams John, shoemaker
Wright, J. & W., baker

Rodgerville.—A Post Office in the Township of Usborne, County Huron. Money Order Office.
BONTHRON, JAMES, Postmaster.

Rodney.—A Post Office in the Township of Aldboro', County Elgin.
HUMPHREY, A., Postmaster.

Roebuck.—A Post Office in the Township of Augusta, County Grenville.

Barton, George, farmer
Bovaird, James, farmer
BOUVAIRD, JAMES, jun., Postmaster, grocer
Bovaird, Richard, farmer
Bovaird, William, farmer
Brown, Sylvester, grocer
Heck, Jacob, proprietor saw mill
Jackson, William, farmer
Johnson, Robert, farmer
Kelso, Hugh, farmer

Rokeby.—A small Village in the Township of South Sherbrooke, County Lanark, 18 miles from Perth, the County Town.

ADAMS, A., Postmaster
Boles, William, general merchant
McKay, John, blacksmith

Rolph.—An almost extinct Village in the Township of Middleton, County Norfolk, 21 miles from Woodstock. (Post Office discontinued.)

Romney.—A Post Office in the Township of Romney, County Kent.

Backus, Elijah, proprietor steam flour mill
Coatsworth, Alfred, farmer
COATSWORTH, CALEB, Postmaster
Coatsworth, John, farmer
Coatsworth, Joseph, farmer
Cooper, Samuel, brick maker
Dawson, James, farmer
Dawson, Joseph, farmer
Dawson, Randolph, J.P.
Edwards, Meredith, innkeeper
Hetherington, Joseph, farmer
Jackson, Moses, grape grower
Mills Horatio, J.P.
Renwick, Thomas, farmer
Robinson, John, farmer
Robinson, William, farmer
Shanks, James, farmer
Shaw, William, brickmaker
Smith, John, farmer
Switzer, John W., teacher

Ronaldsay.—A Post-office in the Township of Proton, County Grey.

Anderson, John, collector
Armstrong, William, constable, pound keeper, and tavern inspector
Black, Robert, farmer
Brown, William, farmer
Campbell, Andrew, farmer
Campbell, Francis, farmer
Campbell, George, farmer
Campbell, James, farmer
Campbell, John, farmer
Campbell, Thomas, farmer
Dingwall, Andrew, farmer
Dyce, James, dealer in lime and stone
Fullerton, Archibald, butcher
Fullerton, Neil, butcher
Giles, Alexander, assessor
King, James, councillor
McARDLE, JOSEPH, Postmaster, township clerk, general agent and com. merchant
McAuley, Donald, teacher
McDonald, Donald, farmer
McDonald, William, reeve
Morrison, Rev. John (Presbyterian)
Peer, John, carpenter
Scarlett, Robert, carpenter
Smith, George G., carpenter
Vert, J. R., general merchant

Rondeau Harbour.—A Village in the Township of Harwich, County Kent, distant from Chatham, the County Town, 17 miles, and 190 from Toronto. Stages daily to and from Chatham. Average value of land in vicinity $50. Population 360.

Bay, Jonathan, proprietor Rondeau Hotel
Bell, David, farmer
Gerow, Allen, blacksmith
Gerow, Charles, farmer
Lloyst, William, farmer
McIntyre, Daniel, teacher
Maxwell, James, carpenter
Muckle, D., farmer
Stapley, David, farmer
STODDARD, E. L., Postmaster, general merchant and lumber dealer
Story, Thomas, farmer

Rondeau.—A Village in the Township of Howard, County Kent, 12 miles from Chatham, the County Town, 10 from Morpeth, and 5 from Rondeau Harbor, Lake Erie. Stages to Chatham. Money Order Office. Population 750.

Ayres, Charles, carpenter
Baird, William, shoemaker
Benedict, Archibald, shoemaker
Bernett & Kenney, carpenters
Bisnett & Kenney, prop. flouring and planing mills
Brunell, S., lumber dealer
Cameron & Montford, stock dealers
Chapman, Rev. Mr. (Wesleyan)
Cox, James, wagon maker
Doolittle, M. T., jewelry, watches, clocks, &c.
Duke, Stephen, painter
Earl, E., carpenter
Fennecy, James, cooper
Finley, R. S., teacher
Flater & Fennecy, shingle makers
Flater, G. & N., wagon makers
Hall, C., farmer
Hicks, Thomas, farmer
Hill, Rev. J. (Episcopal)
Hungerford & Anderson, wagon makers
Hughner, R., prop. flouring mill
Jackman, Aaron, saddler
Jackson, Thomas R., farmer
Jackson, T. C., proprietor livery stable
Kinnard, F. C., carpenter
Lee, E. L., general merchant
Lee & Sewell, butchers
McGeorge, W. G., P.L.S.
McGregor, John, farmer
McGregor, William, farmer
McInnis, L. R., M.D.
McKelvey, George, tailor
McMichael, John, J.P., farmer
Malcom, S., P.L.S.
Maxwell, James, carpenter
Maxwell, William, carpenter
MORRIS, J. K., Postmaster, lumber dealer, general agent and general merchant
Osborne, E. W., cabinet maker
Pinckney, T. Y., general merchant
Putnam, A. E., grocer
Rock, C., carpenter
Sheldon, J., hotel keeper
Shipley, J. W., carpenter
Stevens, N. H., general merchant
Van Velson, D. J., M.D.
Waddle, Rev. R. (Presbyterian)
Watson & Brown, tinsmiths
Wharm, F., tailor

Rosa.—A post office in the Township of Murray, County Northumberland, 40 miles from Cobourg, the County Town.

Arnott, William, blacksmith
Chisholm, A. T., proprietor Murray Hotel
FIELDHOUSE, HENRY, Postmaster, Township clk
Fieldhouse, M. H., teacher
Gartshore, John L., J. P., prop. flouring and saw mills
Kenny, Miss, teacher
McColl, John, reeve
Meyers, Thomas, blacksmith
Roberts, Edward, auctioneer
Weaver, M. B., clerk Division Court and bailiff

Rosebank.—A small Village in the Township of Brantford, County Brant, 4½ miles from Brantford, the County Town. Population 50.

ALMAS, ALMON, Postmaster
Campbell, George, farmer
Charlton, Seth, farmer
German, George, manufacturer of woolen goods
Harris, Rev. J., (Wesleyan)
Jones, Rev. E. (Wesleyan)
McDonald, Miss J., teacher
McLaughlin, George M., farmer
McLean, John, teacher
Shipman, Mrs. J., hotel keeper
Sturgis, Miss C., milliner

Rosedale.—A Post office in the Township of Fenelon, County Victoria, 19 miles from Lindsay, the County Town.

McNEIL, MOSES, Postmaster.

Rosedene.—A Post Office in the Township ot Gainsboro, County Monck, 12 miles from St. Catherines the County Town.

McKAY, CORNELIUS, Postmaster.

Roseneath.—A Village in the Township of Alnwick, County Northumberland, 20 miles from Cobourg, the County Town. Improved land in the vicinity averages $20 per acre. Population 75.

Black, David, carpenter
Burkett, George, wagon maker
Dair, John, shoemaker
HARSTONE, JOHN, Postmaster, gen merchant
Kennedy, Alexander, J.P
Lepper, James, hotel keeper
Liscombe, George, carpenter
McCreevy, James, shoemaker
Noden, William, M.D
Stevenson, Frederick, tailor

Rosement.—A Village in the Township of Mulmur, County Simcoe, 30 miles from Barrie, the County Town, and 18 from Angus Station R.R. Population 100.

Aberdeen, James, blacksmith
Amess, Joseph, shoemaker
Armstrong, Dr.
Bowes, Edward P., general merchant
Brown, John, blacksmith
Brown, Mrs. J., general merchant and proprietor Rosemont Hotel
Corbet, Richard, general merchant
Cumberland, James, saddler
CUMMING, GEORGE, Postmaster and gen. mercht
Duncan & McLaren, carpenters
Gowan, Thomas, & Co., general merchants
Gowan, Thomas, carpenter
Hellock, John, tailor
Henderson, Thomas, general merchant and proprieto "Globe" Hotel
Holmes, Robert, teacher
McCleary, John Rev. (Church of England)
McLennan, Rev. A. (Presbyterian)
Morrison, Hugh, farmer
Morrison, John, farmer
Ogden, Dr.
Robinson, Samuel, auctioneer
Solomon, William, farmer
Tate, Joshua, farmer
Thomas, Dr
Wright, William, wagon maker

Rosetta.—A Village in the Township of Lanark, County Lanark, 20 miles from Perth, the County Town Population 50.

Campbell, David, farmer
McFARLANE, ROBERT, Postmaster

Roseville.—A Post Village in the Township of North Dumfries, County Waterloo, 7 miles from Berlin, the County Town and 50 from Toronto. Population 200.

Barton, James, lumber dealer
Betchel, Jacob, shingle maker
Bricker, Benjamin, farmer
Bricker, Jacob, farmer
Bricker, John, farmer
Clemons, Jacob, prop. Globe Inn
Detweiler, Jacob, farmer
GINGERICH, MOSES, Postmaster, gen. merchant
Hallman, Benjamin, farmer
Hallman, Jacob, carpenter
Joice, Josiah, prop. Roseville Hotel
Kaiser, Frederick, wagon maker
Kaiser, John, cooper
Leicht, William, wagon maker
Linger, William, shoemaker
Lucht, William, farmer
Richardson, Robert, teacher
Scharer, William, cooper
Smith, Rev. Mr. (United Brethren)
Snider, Samuel, farmer
Ward, George, auctioneer

Rossville—A Village in the Township of Montague, County Lanark, 18 miles from Perth, the County Town, and 5 from Smith's Falls Station Brockville and Ottawa Railway.

Barton, William, general merchant
Canunduff, Robert, farmer
Chalmers, Edward, farmer
CLARK, PETER, J.P., Postmaster
Conners, Thomas, tailor
Davis, Elias, farmer
Davis, John, farmer
Ferguson, John, insurance agent
Gill, William, teacher
Livingston, Robert, farmer
Loucks, John, farmer
Lumsden, Thomas, cooper
McEachran, John, tanner and shoemaker
Scott, James, saddler
Scott, John, shoemaker
Shields, John, J.P., farmer
Sweeney, Oliver, general merchant
Vandusen, N. P., farmer
Wylie, William, carpenter

Roslin.—A small Village in the Township of Huntington, County Hastings, 14 miles from Belleville, the County Town. Stages to Bridgewater and Belleville. Average value of land $30 per acre. Population 75.

Anderson, A., farmer
Bond, Rev. William, (Church of England)
Campbell, John, farmer
Campbell, William, J.P., farmer
Carnahan, B., shoemaker
Chisholm, William F., proprietor flouring mill
Duncan, George, farmer
Duncan, Robert, farmer
Embury, Allen, carpenter
Emyey, William, saddler
GILROY, WILLIAM, Postmaster, general merchant
Hudson, Charles, farmer
Hewitt, John, farmer
Hudson, William, wagon maker
McCready, Thomas, farmer
McNellis, L., cabinet maker
Martin, William, proprietor hotel
Masson, A., farmer
Nixon, William, painter
Thompson, Rev. J. R., (Church of Scotland)
Vair, George, general merchant
White, John, founder
Wilson, B. S., M.D.
Wilson, J. M., teacher

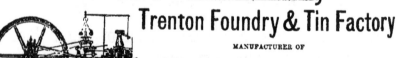

Ross.—A post office in the Township of Ross, County Renfrew, 28 miles from Pembroke, the County Town

Bailly, Robert, councilor
Cameron, Rev. W., (Church of Scotland)
Grant, James, insurance agent
Hill, John, councillor
Huntington, E., hotel keeper
McLeese, William, mill-wright
Marshall, John, councillor
Rankin, John, reeve
Thompson, Alexander, M.D.
Wallace, William, councillor
Work, J., hotel keeper

Rosseau.—A Post Office in the Township of Humphrey, County Simcoe, 90 miles from Barrie, the County Town.

Bailey, Benjamin, farmer
Cameron, A., farmer
Irwin, Richard, farmer
MILNE, GEORGE, Postmaster

Rothsay.—*(See Villages too late for regular insertion at the end of this work.)*

Rouge Hill.—A Post Office in the Township of Pickering, County Ontario.
GRAHAM, HUGH, Postmaster.

Round Plains.—A Post Office in the Township of Townsend, County Norfolk, 7 miles from Simcoe the County Town.

Berry, Rev. F. (Freewill Baptist)
Brooks, H., farmer
Burr, W. H., general merchant
Coy, C., proprietor Round Plains Hotel
Earle, Wellington, teacher
Langs, Henry, farmer
Lefler, Daniel, farmer
Lewis, Levi, shingle maker
Messerer, Job, farmer
Munroe, J., farmer
Osbourne, Rev. W. (Baptist)
Scovill, W., farmer
Serles, Moses, farmer
WEVER, JOHN, Postmaster and proprietor Farmers' Inn
Wood, Rev. J. (Episcopal Methodist)

Ruthven.—A Village in the Township of Gosfield, County Essex, 28 miles from Sandwich, the County Town, and 30 from Windsor. Money Order Office. Stage to Windsor. Population 250.

Atkinson, Rev. T., (Wesleyan)
Dawson, Thomas, J.P.
Deming, H. V., general merchant
Dever, E., butcher
Drake, W. H., M.D.
Harrington, Jason, shoemaker
Harrington, J., farmer
Hawke, John, hotel keeper
Heatherington, John, carpenter
LOVELESS, LEVI, proprietor Ruthven Hotel
Lypps, F., lumber dealer
Lypps, F. A., proprietor flouring mill
McLeod, W. S., cabinet maker
McNult, John, general merchant
Malott, George, auctioneer
Pulford, A., wagon maker
Pulford, C., painter
RUTHVEN, HUGH, Postmaster
Sanburn, Charles, painter
Stewart, Charles, broom manufacturer
Stewart, Thomas, carpenter
Wate, M. grocer
Wigle, C. R., wagon maker
Williams, John, carpenter
Williams, Thomas, brick maker

Rugby.—A Village in the Township of Oro, County Simcoe, 21 miles from Barrie, the County Town. Population 75.

BALL, JAMES, Postmaster and general merchant
Bone, David, farmer
Brown, George, farmer
Cameron, Daniel, carpenter
Gray, Rev. J. (Presbyterian)
Horn, William, farmer
Jackson, Peter, shoemaker
Johnson, William, farmer
Litster, George, farmer
McIntosh, David, teacher
McIntosh, William, blacksmith
Mark, Rev. Robert (Methodist)
May, William, farmer
Portas, T. H., proprietor flouring mill
Robertson, Andrew, farmer
Robertson, George, farmer
Robertson, John, carpenter
Sanderson, Rev. J. G. (Congregational)
Tudhope, George, J.P.

Russell.—A Village on Caistor River, in the Township of Russell, County Russell, 60 miles from L'Orignal, the County Town. Improved land $18, wild $6 per acre. Population 200.

Boulton, G. S., teacher
Boulton, P., J.P., farmer
Campbell, P., general merchant
Cheny, John, farmer
Craig, W. & A., general merchant
Dickinson, George, M.D.
Duncan, John, sash, blind and door manufactory
Duncan, William, teacher
Eadie, William, farmer
Fetterby, Sidney, baker
Fitzpatrick, H., tailor
Garrott, Rev. D. (Church of England)
Green, T., proprietor British Hotel
Hamilton, William, J. P., farmer
Harrison, David, farmer
Helner, N., general merchant
HELNER, RICHARD, Postmaster, farmer
Helner, William B., lumber dealer
Henderson, W., farmer
Keays, James, J.P., Clerk Division Court
Kelly, James, proprietor Albert House
La C lle, Felix, shoemaker
Low John W., proprietor flouring mill
McDonald, John, proprietor Russell House
McQuarie, Mrs., milliner
Mattin, Charles, carpenter
Moore, Thomas A., butcher
Pattyson, Rev. W. M. (Wesleyan)
Perry, A., cooper
Pelton, C., baker
Pelton, Hiram, shoemaker
Powell, William, farmer
Ravin, William, carpenter
Ronan, H. B., town clerk and tanner
Ross, Miles, teacher
Rowat, Rev. A. (Presbyterian)
Simpson, Robert, proprietor woolen factory
Sutherland, Alexander, wagon maker
Sutherland, George, wagon maker
York, S., wine and spirit dealer
Young, Robert, farmer

Rutherford.—A Post Office in the Township of Dawn, County Bothwell.

Bloom, J., farmer
Bloom, Robert, farmer
Cook, J., farmer
Cary, H., farmer
Duff, Robert, teacher
Graham, W. J., farmer
Huff, S., farmer
McDONALD, ALEXANDER, Postmaster
Mawlan, Henry, J.P.
Proctor, John, farmer
Rheinleyen, John, teacher
Walker, William, farmer

Ryckman's Corners.—A small Village in the Township of Barton, County Wentworth, 4 miles from Hamilton. Population 75.

Binckley, Alexander, farmer
Carr, John, proprietor Royal Oak Hotel
Cowie, Thomas, general merchant
Dawson, George, wagon maker
Gage, John, farmer
Gage, William, farmer
Kerns, Josiah, farmer
Kerns, Samuel, farmer
McKee, Henry, proprietor Barton House Hotel
Marshall William, farmer
Moore, Miss, teacher
Ryckman, Hamilton, farmer
Rymal, Ira, farmer
Rymal, Joseph, farmer
Shafer, Philip, farmer
Skinner, George, blacksmith
Smith, Jacob, farmer
Tilman, John, farmer
Tilman, Peter, farmer
WELLS, WILLIAM, Postmaster, builder and wagon maker
White, William, farmer
Young, Calvin, farmer

Rylstone.—A Post Office in the Township of Seymour, County Northumberland, 52 miles from Cobourg the County Town.

ALLAN, DAVID, Postmaster, proprietor grist and saw mill
Haughton, Robert, farmer
Hay, James, farmer
Lisle, John, farmer
Loucks, Peter, farmer
Meiklejohn, William, farmer
Richards, Miss, teacher

St. Anns.—A Village on the River Jordan, in the Township of Gainsborough, County Lincoln, 16 miles from St. Catherines, the County Town, and 11 from Grimsby. Stages to Grimsby and Welland Port. Population 100.

Heaslip, James D., tanner
Kerr & Notman, lumber dealers
Lister, Edward, general merchant
Malcolm, Rev. James (Presbyterian)
Secord, George, M.P.P.
Snyder, J. H., carpenter
Snyder, O., milliner
Upper, Jacob, J.P. and general merchant

St. Agatha.—A Village in the Township of Wilmot, County Waterloo. Distant from Berlin, the County Town, 8 miles, from Toronto 70, and 1½ from Petersburg Station, Grand Trunk Railway. Population 250.

Brueckner, Oscar, teacher
Bruxer, Dominic, mason
Bury, John, painter
Dietrich, Gregor, farmer
Dietrich, Theobald, farmer
Doll, Berhard, farmer
Dorschel, Joseph, carpenter and builder
Dorschel, Lucas, cabinet maker
Döersam, Adam, blacksmith and innkeeper
Funcken, Rev. Eugene (Roman Catholic)
Hirteis, Joseph, mason
Horn, Henry, shoemaker
Jantzi, Michael, farmer
KAISER, ANTONI, J.P., Postmaster and commissioner in B.R.
Kaiser, John A., innkeeper
Kaiser & Herres, general merchants
Kohlbrenner, Henry, weaver
Kress, Adam, carpenter
Kuenemann, Joseph, farmer
Lenhart, Adam, blacksmith
Lichti, Christel E., farmer
Lichti, Nicholaus, farmer
Litwiller, Peter, farmer
Meyer, John August, teacher
Pioth, Michael, weaver
Roth, Chrystel L., farmer
Schrank, Charles, saddler
Seip, Adam, farmer
Seip, Justin, farmer
Studer, Amandus, shoemaker
Strub, Joseph, farmer
Tschirhart, Peter H., innkeeper
Uberschlag, Joseph, farmer
Weinstein, Raphael, weaver
Zimmer, Henry, wagon maker

St. Andrews.—A Post Village in the Township of Cornwall, County Stormont. Mails tri-weekly. Population 20.

MASTERMAN, L., Postmaster.

St. Catherines.—The County Town of Welland, in the Township of Grantham, on the Welland Canal, and a station of the Great Western Railway. It is beautifully situated on a tract of table land above the valley through which the canal is cut, and in the midst of a district which, for its fertility and cultivation, has been called the garden of Canada. The town is celebrated for its mineral springs and its hotels. It is well built, and has numerous manufacturing establishments, in excellent trade. Ship-building is carried on extensively. Distance from Niagara 11 miles, from Hamilton 22, from Buffalo, N.Y., 36. Population 8500.

ABELL, CHANDLER, machinist (see adv.)
ABBOTT, JOHN W. & CO., manufacturers sewing machines (see adv.)
Adams, C. S., J.P.
ADAMS, THOMAS, paymaster Welland Canal
Ahren, W., C.E.
Arnold, C. M., Niagara District Bank
Allen & Bro., photographer
Allen, Thomas E., M.D.
Allan, William B., architect
American Express Co., M. E. Kellogg, agent
American Hotel, James Grubb, proprietor
Anderson, John, hairdresser
Arcade Saloon, J. Melvin, proprietor
Ashford, James, St. James saloon
Avary, George, ship carpenter
BACK, JOHN, confectioner
BALL, G., Postmaster and County Treasurer
BANK OF MONTREAL, A. B. Buchanan, manager
Bannister, Charles, teacher
Bauvan, Hugh, cooper
Barr, Mrs. James, millinery, &c.
Barr, James, money broker
Barr, William, cabinet maker
Barber, James, cabinet maker
Barker, James, grocer
BARON, WILLIAM, marble merchant and stone cutter
Barries, Thomas, mason
BARWICK, H. C., manager Bank of Commerce
Bate, Thomas B., brewer
Beadle, D., nursery
Beatie, Thomas, boot and shoemaker
Beaver Mills, Thomas R. Merritt, proprietor
Beckett, William, woolen factory
Bedell, C., soda water manufactory
Beeton, William R., druggist
Begy, Frank P., painter, etc.
Begy, G. A., sash, door and blind factory
Begy, W., cooper
Benson, C. J., barrister
Benson, James B., (J. R. Benson & Co.)
Benson, James R., M.P.
Benson, James R. & Co., ironmongers
Berhalter, Joseph, lager beer saloon
Berryman, Edgar, P.L.S.
Berston, W. J. (Harris and Berston) dealer in tobacco and cigars
Betts, George, leather and findings
Bishopirc, James, soap and candle maker
Bixby, D. W., bookseller, etc.
BOLES, WILLIAM, merchant tailor
Boyle, Arthur, druggist
Boyle's Hotel, James Boyle, proprietor
BRADT, SIMON, Idaho Saloon
Braund, Henry, machinist
Brooks G., cabinet maker
Brown & Hamilton (Calvin and Charles K.) barristers
Brown, Mrs. J., dressmaker
Brown's Hotel, Thomas Brown, proprietor
Brownlee, Henry, grocer
BROWNLEE, THOMAS R., groceries, provisions, crockery and glassware (see adv)
Byrne & Willey, patent medicine manufacturers
Byson, Ross, manager, estate F. Coy.
BUCHANAN, A. B., agent Bank of Montreal
Buchanan, Irwin, sash, blinds, etc.
Bullock, Charles, shoemaker

Bunting, T., leather, hides, etc.
Bumgras & O'Donnell, painters
Burgoyne, Henry, builder
BURNS, CHARLES, saloon
Burns, Thomas, Mayor and Police Magistrate
Burrow, Chatfield & Co., copper smiths
Benson, Rev. George, (Canada Presbyterian)
Butler, W., vinegar maker
Camidge, John, teacher
CANADIAN BANK OF COMMERCE, H. Barwick, manager
Cahill, M., cabinet maker
Cairns, James
CAIRNS, HOUSE, W. May, proprietor
Camp, L. C., insurance agent
Campbell, Roderick, hotel keeper
Carlisle, Henry, dry goods and clothing
Carnall, Rebecca, berlin wool and children's dresses
Carnathan, R., proprietor Shickluna House
Carroll, Rev. John (Wesleyan)
Casselman, R. D., proprietor flouring mill
Casey, Thomas B., barber
Caulton, Dr. F. G. (Homœopathic)
Cavers, Charles, sewing machine agent
Cawker, J., tailor
Chapman, T., tailor
Chisholm, W. A.
Clark, James, surveyor customs
Clark, John S., landing waiter
Clark, Richard A,, issuer of marriage licenses
Clark, Thomas, M.D.
Clench, F. A. B., Clerk County Court
Clifford, F. J., grocery, wines and liquors
Clifford, Francis James, groceries, wines and liquors
Clipper Shades Saloon, W. F. Robertson, proprietor
Cloney, Thomas, grocer
CODLING, WILLIAM M., tailor and clothier
Coffin, T. C., clerk Quebec Bank
COLLIER, H. H., lumber merchant, general dealer in groceries and crockery, and provisions
Collins, Matthew A., manager for W. Beckett
Collver, A. P., oil merchant and collector market fees
Congle, P., tailor and clothier
Connor, Francis, boot and shoe maker
Conway, Frank, grocer
COOK. J. R., groceries, provisions and crockeryware
Cooke, William, mail contractor
Coombs, Thomas, saloon
Copeland, John, collector
COPELAND, W. L., Postmaster
COPELAND, W. L. & CO., booksellers & stationers
Cornish, Joseph, butcher
Coy, Francis (estate of), hardware
Crawford, James, watch maker
Cuff, J. E.,
Culloden, L. P., agt. Connecticut Mutual Life In. Co
Culver, J. D., broker
Currie, J. G., barrister
Cuthbert, John, bookbinder
Dabt, William, wagon maker
DAILY EVENING JOURNAL, W. Grant & Co., proprietors
DAILY TIMES, John Fitzgerald publisher and prop
Dale, John, shoemaker
Dawson, S. S., assessor
Davis & Co., omnibus proprietors G. W. R
DAVIS, WILLIAM, provisions and crockery
Decatur, William, proprietor saloon and livery stables
DILLON, JAMES, boot and shoe manufacturer
Disher, George, photographer
Disher & Haight, manufacturers of woolen goods
Dimmons, William, shoemaker
DOLSON, S. G., builder and contractor
Dougan, James, carpenter and builder
Dougan, William, M.D., C.M.
Douglas, James, watchmaker and jeweler
Douglas & MacMullin, watchmakers and jewelers
Dudley, Thomas, assistant Montreal Telegraph Co.
Duggan, James, builder
Duhee, James, butcher
Dunn, A., shipper
DURHAM, JOHN, dry goods merchant
Eccles, W. M., barrister
Ecclestone, Francis E., confectioner
ELLIS, ALFRED, grocer and liquor dealer
Ellis, Charles R., landing waiter
ELLIS HOUSE, A. Ellis, proprietor (see adv)
Emricks, R., oyster and ale depot
Estate of late Francis Coy, hardware merchant
EUROPEAN DINING ROOMS, Thomas McCoomb, proprietor (see adv.)
Fairfield, Benjamin C., (Copeland & Co.)
Farmer, G. A., accountant and teller Bank of Montreal
Finn, P., crier of court
Fish, L. W., boot and shoemaker
FITZGERALD, D. & J., variety store
Fitzgerald, Daniel, variety store
Fitzgerald, James
FITZGERALD, JOHN, publisher and proprietor *Weekly Times*
Fitzgerald, Maurice, proprietor livery stable
Fitzgerald, R., groceries, provisions, &c.
Flack, James, carpenter
Flemming, John, cooper
FLINT, J., saw manufacturer (see adv)
Flummerfelt, Joseph, Farmers' Inn
Fowler, J. B., jeweler
Fraser, Alexander, G.W.R. telegraph office
Fuller, W., accountant Bank of Commerce
Gadsby, Benjamin C., painter
Gadsby, E., bricklayer
Gadsby, W., shoemaker
Gammon, Charles, butcher
Garken, Henry, billiard room
GIBSON, C. M., cashier and accountant Welland Railway and Steamboat Co.
GILES, HENRY MARTIN, secretary and treasurer Niagara District Mutual Fire Insurance Co.
GOLDSMITH, S., importer of seeds, foreign and domestic (see adv)
Goodman, E., M.D.
Goodman, J. A., agent Royal Canadian Bank
GORDON, CHARLES E., restaurant and saloon
Graham & Smith, butchers
GRAVES, O. C., manager Stephenson House
Gray, J. P., Glasgow warehouse
Graydon, Thomas H., inspector Niagara District Mutual Fire Insurance Co.
Greenwood, W., carriage maker
Greenwood, W. W., druggist
Grobb, James, proprietor American Hotel
GROBB, JOSEPH, auctioneer and appraiser
GROSS'S DINING SALOON (see adv)
GROSS, MRS., tavern keeper, &c.
Groves, George, accountant and estate and insurance agent
Gwinner, John, tailor
Haines, A., shoe store
Hanagan, Mrs. T., groceries and liquors
Hanagan, Timothy, painter
HANNIFAN & LAUGHLIN, proprietors Terrapin restaurant (see adv)
Harold, James, prop. Union Hotel
HARDY, ELIZA M., hat and fur store

Hartford Fire Insurance Company, Peter McCallum, agent
Hartford Live Stock Insurance Company, Peter McCallum, agent
Harris & Berston, tobacco and cigar dealers
Harris, James, butcher
HARVEY, U. A.
HAYNES, D. CURTIS, banker and broker
HAVENS, MAHLON, livery stable keeper (see adv)
Healey, Timothy, manuf. boots and shoes
HELLEMS, C. W., sen., lumber merchant
Helliwell, A. teller Bank of Commerce
Helliwell, F. L., clerk Quebec Bank
Helliwell, Thomas L., insurance agent
Hembold, George P., treasurer
Hodgins, Joseph, flour and grain
Holland, Rev. H. (Church of England)
Holder, John, nurseryman
Holmes & Greenwood, carriage makers
Holmes, Josiah, carriage maker
Hostetter, Thomas, prop. flour mill
HOUGHTON, E., prop. Pickwick House (see adv.)
Howse, J. H., tinsmith, &c
Howse, J. R., tinsmith
HUFF, DR. WILLIAM W, prop. livery stable (see adv)
Hunniford, John, dealer in groceries and provisions
Hynes, Charles, prop. Commercial Hotel
Hutchinson, Alexander, flour and feed
International Hotel, S. Clark, proprietor
Isaacs, W., bricklayer
Ivey, William, merchant tailor, &c
Jackson, James W., watch and clock maker
James, W., tailor
Jabut, V., shoemaker
Jeffrey, A., hardware merchant
Johnston, A. (Laurie & Johnston)
Jones, A. C., pork dealer
Jones, John B., agent
Jones, Moses, lager beer saloon
Jones, P., blacksmth
Jones, S., wagon maker
JUKES, AUGUSTUS, M.B.
Junkin, John
Junkin, John & Co., importers of crockery & grocers
KANE & BROTHER, grocers, liquor merchants and general dealers (see adv.)
Karshner, John, tailor
Keeley, Thomas, painter
Kellog, Moses E., agent American Express Company
Kelly, T., painter
Kerris, Charles, lock-keeper
Kilroy, William, blacksmith
KIRBY, JAMES, cabinet maker (see adv.)
Knapp, R., carpenter
Konkle, Adam, fishmonger
Lamb, James, Collector of Customs
Larkin, Peter & Co., dealers in groceries, &c.
Larue, P. & Co., general merchants
LAUGHLIN, MARTIN, Terrapin Saloon
Lauder, J. M., County Judge
Lawrence, C., fancy dry goods
Lawrie, James (Lawrie & Johnston)
Lawrie, J. (R. & J. Lawrie)
Lawrie, R. (R. & J. Lawrie)
Lawrie & Johnston, grocery and liquor dealers
Lawrie, R. & J., flour and grain merchants, farm and garden seeds
Leavenworth, E. S., printer
Leavenworth, H. F., oil merchant
Lee, James, general merchant
Lee, James, fruits
Leggett, Thomas M., landing waiter
Lepper, Arthur, (John Lepper & Co.)
Lepper, John, (John Lepper & Co.)
Lepper, John & Co., merchant tailors
Lilcoln Mills, Thomas R. Merritt, proprietor
Lindsay, Nathaniel A., boots and shoes
McCALLUM, PETER, insurance agent (see adv)
McCame, Henry, bridge tender
McCann, P., messenger Quebec Bank
McCarthy & Brownlee (Thomas and W. H.) groceries and provisions
McCarthy, Peter, barrister
McCarty, E., blacksmith
McCarty, Mrs., dressmaker
McCarty, T., blacksmith
McClelland, Robert, teacher
McClive, W. H., barrister, etc.
McCOOMB, THOMAS, restaurant (see adv)
McCORMICK, MATTHEW, builder (see adv)
McCourt, James, sail maker
McEmery, D. B., shoemaker
McElroy, N. L., blacksmith
McFarland, Thomas, shoemaker
McGhie, William, insurance agent
McGHIE & FINN, auctioneers and general commission agents, money brokers and land agents fo the Western States and Canada
McGRATH, J. G., general manager Welland Railway and Steamboat Co.
McGuire, D., groceries, wines and liquors
McINTYRE & SONS, cabinet makers (see adv)
McKINLEY, R. & CO., Novelty Works, steam bending and spoke factory
McLaughlin, James, shoemaker
McLean, John, grocer
McMullin, R. H., jeweler
McNamara, John M., groceries
McNamara, Mrs., millinery
McPhail, John, station master G. W. R
Macdonald, F. W., Master in Chancery
Macdonald, Ronald, Clerk of Peace
Mack, F. L., M.D
Mack, T., M. D
Madden & Ball, barbers
Mahon, T. D., grocer
Mahoney, Thomas, tailor and clothier
Maloney, Patrick, grocery
MANSION, HOUSE, B. O'Loughlin, prop. (see adv)
MAY, ANDREW, dentist (see adv)
May, Charles, book keeper Cairns House
MAY, W., Cairns House (see adv)
Meadows, James, carpenter
Meadows, Maria, eating house
Mechanics Institute, D. W. Bixby, secretary
Merritt, Nehemiah, director Gas Company
MERRITT, THOMAS R., M.P
Mills, A., machinist
MILLS, A. M., pump maker (see adv)
Mills, James, chemist and druggist
Miller, James A., agent North British Insurance Co.
Miller & Miller, barristers
Mittleberger, W. A., clerk of Div. Court
Monro, Fisher, bakery and grocery
MONRO, JOHN, importer of wines and liquors and general groceries (see adv)
Montgomery, A., chief Constable
Montreal Telegraph Company, W. Smith, agent
Morey, Nathan, foreman at S. G. Dolson's
Muir, W., cabinet maker
Nasmith, T. H., accountant Royal Canadian Bank
Niagara District Bank, C. H. Arnold, manager
NIAGARA DISTRICT Mutual Fire Insurance Co., T. Mack, President
Nelson, C. G. & Co., soda water manufacturer
Norris & Neelon, flour merchants
Norton, Rev. R. (Presbyterian)

NOVELTY WORKS, R. McKinley & Co., props.
O'Donnell, T., painter
O'LOUGHLIN, B., prop. Mansion House (see adv)
O'Neil, Thomas, police constable
O'Reily, H., grocer
OILL, G. N., iron founder and steam engine manufr.
Oill, Jerome, foreman at G. N. Oills
Oille, Lucius, M.D.
Ontario Saloon, W. Decatur, proprietor
Orr, James, sign painter
Orr, Thomas. saddle, harness and trunk maker
Oswald, Thomas, police constable
Owens, P. B. & Co., dry goods merchants
PAGE, G. H., proprietor Dew Drop Inn
PAGE'S DEW DROP INN, Page, G. H. prop. (see adv)
Patterson, R., groceries and liquors
Payne, J., boots and shoes
Peterson, Richard, butcher
Phelps, N. & O. J., lumber merchants
PICKWICK HOUSE, E. Houghton, prop. (see adv.)
Powell, John, Registrar
Powell, W., Deputy Registrar
Provincial Insurance Company, Peter McCallum, agt.
Purvis, A., mantle, straw and fancy goods
QUEBEC BANK, D. Reerekie, agent
Rason, John, St. Charles Hotel
REEKIE, R. J., M.D., Managing Director Welland Railway and Steamboat Cos.
REEREKIE, D., agent, Quebec Bank
Reid, John, tailor and clothier
Riley, George, grocer, wines and liquors, crockery and glassware
Riley, John, saloon keeper
Riley, Patrick
RIORDAN, JOHN, paper manufacturer
Robinson, J., attorney and notary
Robinson, Storrs, auctioneer
Rollinson, John, town clerk
Rogers, Elkanah, wood merchant
Ross, G., blacksmith
ROSS, JOHN, importer and general dealer in dry goods and millinery
Rykert, G. Z., P.L.S.
Rykert, J. C., warden, M.P.P
St. Catharines Brewery, Taylor & Bate, proprietors
ST. CATHARINES CONSTITUTIONAL, James Seymour, publisher and proprietor
ST. CATHARINES HOUSE, Thomas Westall prop
St. Catharines Rock Oil, Refinery, Leavenworth and Collver, proprietors
St. Catharines and Welland Gas Light Co., president H. R. Goodman, M.D
St. Catharines Woolen Factory, W. Beckett, prop
St. John, A. S., conveyancer
St. John, S. L., money broker
Scholfield, Thomas C., M.D
Scott, Benjamin, clerk American Express Co
Scully, John K., printer
Secord, Charles B., registrar Surrogate
Secord, James B., general agent
SEWING MACHINE FACTORY, John W. Abbott & Co., proprietors, (see adv)
SEYMOUR, JAMES, publisher and prop. weekly *Constitutional*.
Shaw, Thomas, merchant
SHEA & CAIN, bakers and confectioners
Shickluna, Lewis, ship builder
Simpson, C. P., barrister
Sinclair, A., tailor
Smiley, S., dentist
SMITH, GEORGE, carriage works (see adv)
Smith, John, butcher
Smith, Simon C., upholsterer and cabinet maker
Soper, L. N., dealer in sewing machines, melodeons, etc.
Standbrook, G. H., butcher
Starr, Cyrus, miller
Starr, J. E., groceries and provisions
STEPHENSON HOUSE, Beverly Tucker, proprietor (see adv.)
Stevenson, C. N., manufacturer of agricultural implements
Stinson, Francis, wine and spirit merchant
Stinson, —, proprietor livery stables
Struthers, Robert, dry goods merchant
Sullivan, Thomas, M.D.
Tait, J. L., draper
Taylor, James, brewer
Taylor, Peter, tinsmith, etc.
Taylor & Bate, brewers
Terington, John, miller
The Lancashire Insurance Co., Peter McCallum, agt.
The Dominion Saloon, James McMullen, proprietor
Thomas, J., proprietor Hartford House
Thompson, J. S., dry goods
Thompson, W., accountant
Thomson, W., collector Inland Revenue
TIMES, (Thursday), John Fitzgerald, editor and proprietor
Town Hall Exchange Saloon, W. Haynes, proprietor
Tracy, Michael, proprietor Great Western Hotel
Travelers' Insurance Co., Peter McCallum, agent
Tucker, Beverly, proprietor Stephenson House
Vanderlip's Hotel
Vine, F., butcher
Wald, John, pork merchant
Walker, Rev. Charles, (Baptist)
Wallace & Brothers, butchers
Welch, R., tailor
Welland House, Charles Norton, proprietor
Welland View House, McGlenn, F. proprietor
WESTALL, THOMAS, St. Catherines House
Western Insurance Company of Toronto, Peter McCallum, agent
Whitmore, John A., dealer in dry goods
Whittaker, John, baggageman
Wilson, G., builder
WILSON, HARPER, grocer
WILSON, HENRY, grocer
WILSON, HENRY & BROTHER, grocers
WILSON & ROBERTSON, (George B. Wilson, William J., Robertson) flour and feed store
Wing, R. D., freight clerk
Wingrove, James, pork dealer
Wingrove, & Jones, pork merchants
Woodruff, Joseph A., Sheriff, County Lincoln
Woodruff, S. D., superintendent Welland Canal
Woodruff, R. & Co., staple and fancy dry goods
Woods, George, saddler
Woods, G. & J., saddlers, harness and trunk makers
Woods, James, saddler
Yale & Co., ironmongers and founders
Yorkshire House, Harrison, Henry, proprietor
YOUNG, ROBERT, saloon keeper

St. Clements.—A Post Village in the Township of Wellesley, County Waterloo, 10 miles from Berlin, the County Town, land in the vicinity averages $40 per acre. Daily Mail. Population 200.

Adam, Joseph, potter
Bowman, Matthew, wagon maker
Brenner, George, blacksmith
Brenner, John, farmer
Bush, Nicholas, farmer
Daub, C., blacksmith

Daub, Joseph, proprietor Anglo-American Hotel
Doerr, George, J.P., farmer
Essig, G., tailor
Fisher, Philip, farmer
Freyburger, Joseph, proprietor British Arms Hotel
Glowalski, Rev. E. (Roman Catholic)
Greyerbiehl, Joseph, prop. Great Western Hotel
Heckler, John, shoemaker
Hele, Simon, shoemaker
Kuntz, John, farmer
McNab, M., general merchant
Meyer, Jacob, farmer
Miller, J., farmer
Mindell, Christopher, tailor
Murmann, E. & Co., general merchants
Oelschlanger, William, J.P.
Offholder, J., teacher
Rau, John, shoemaker
Rosenblatt & Son, John, cabinet maker
Simmer, John, farmer
Skalitzky, Francis, tailor
Starr, John, wagon maker
Starr, Samuel, carpenter
STROH, JOHN, Postmaster, J.P., proprietor British Crown Hotel
Wiederkehr, Henry, tinsmith
Zarnke, Frederick, carpenter

St. Eugene.—A post Village in the Township of East Hawkesbury, County Prescott, 18 miles from L'Orignal the County Town, and 270 from Toronto. Land in the vicinity averages $18 per acre. Population 275.

Allison, W., J. P
Baizenne, J. B., painter
Baizeune, Miss S., milliner
Bouthier, Adolphe, general merchant
Burwash, Nelson, farmer
Cameron, C., J. P
Clermont, A., farmer
Daoust, J. B., carpenter
Dencault, Jean Baptiste, cooper
Desormeau, Francois, wagon maker
Duhamel, Rev. J. J., (Roman Catholic)
Finn, D. E., dressmaker
Gamble, J., J. P
Kelly, Bernard
Labrosse, E., baker
Labrosse, Mrs. A., teacher
LABROSSE, SIMON, Postmaster, general merchant
Labrosse, Paul, auctioneer
Labrosse, Pierre, farmer
LaDoucear, J. B., butcher
LaFlamure, S., carpenter
LaLande, A., farmer
LaToulippe, C. N., carpenter
Lavallie, Xavier, tanner
Laverne, Felix, saddler
Leblanc, Michael, tanner
Leroux, Mrs. A., manufacturer of woolen goods
McBean, Archibald, J.P., commissioner, clerk of Division Court, general merchant and proprietor grist mill
McDonald, H. R., J.P.
McEntee, B., farmer
McKinnon, H., M.D
McKinnon, J. S., shoemaker
Mark, W. J., hotel keeper
Milinder, Mrs. E., tailoress
Mongemais, N., M.D
Proulx, X., shoemaker
Quesnel, Hilaire, hotel keeper
Raizenne, F. B., wagon maker
Routhis, A., wine and spirit dealer
St. Denis, A., dressmaker
St. Denis, E.. farmer
Steele, David, town treasurer and general merchant
Turcotte, M., J.P.
Villeneuve, P., cabinet maker
Villeneuve, Theodore, farmer

St. George.—A Village on Big Creek, in the Township of South Dumfries, County Brant, 9 miles from Brantford, the County Town, 8 from Paris, 10 from Galt, and 3 from Harrisburgh Station, Great Western Railway. Money Order Office. Population 500.

Austin, W., prop. flouring mill
Batty, C., general merchant
Bell, Benjamin, J.P., prop. planing mill and foundry
Bell, George, farmer
Bryden, R. C., accountant
Buckberry, Samuel, wagon maker
Cameron, Allen, founder and machinist
Clinton, John, carpenter
Culham, J., prop. Great Western Hotel
Dougherty, Rev. J. G., (Baptist)
German, George, manuf. of woolen goods
Glass, William, farmer
Haas, F., boots and shoes
Harris, Rev. James (Wesleyan)
Howell, Thomas W., farmer
Hume, Rev. Robert (Presbyterian)
Hunter, David, teacher
Huson, Albert, auctioneer and insurance agent
Kay, John, butcher
Keefer, J. N., general merchant
Kitchen, E. E., M.D.
Lawrason, P. D., farmer
Lorimer, Samuel, prop. sash, blind & door factory
McPherson & Dewar, general merchants
McRoberts, Alexander, general merchant
Mainwaring, H., farmer
Mainwaring, N. E., M.D., proprietor flouring mill
Mullin, W. A., farmer
Notman, John, cabinet maker
O'Hara, J. M., proprietor St. George's Hotel
O'Reilly, Michael, tailor
Reid, David, cabinet maker
Richardson, John, farmer
Rymal, D. M., farmer
Smith, John, farmer
Smith, Rachel, teacher
Snowball, Robert, farmer
Snowball, William, wagon maker and prop. flouring and flax mills
STANTON, S., Postmaster
Stinson, E., M.D.
Stinson, James, M.D.
Thomas, D., proprietor Union Hotel
Thompson, John, butcher
Thomson, J. C., painter
Wilson, James, saddler

St. David's.—A Village in the Township of Niagara, County Lincoln, 8 miles from St. Catherines, the County Town, 43 to Toronto by water and 82 by rail. The Erie and Niagara Railway passes within 1½ miles of the Village. Land in the vicinity averages $35 per acre. Daily mail. Population 309.

Ball, Robert N., farmer
Barbeau, Anthony, proprietor flouring mill
Barbeau, Louis, proprietor flouring mill
Brown, S. J. J., Reeve
Dunn, Luther, sen., carpenter
Bunn, Luther, jun., wagon maker
Fairlie, Andrew, farmer
Fairlie, James, tailor
FISHER, C., Postmaster and grocer
Fitch, E., proprietor St. David's Hotel
Fisher, Thomas W., shoemaker
Harvey, U. V. & C., manufrs. of machine leather belting
McIntosh, William, blacksmith
Middaugh, John, sen., farmer
Misener, Rev. D. W. (Episcopal Methodist)
Mowers, George, carpenter
Pew, Robert, teacher
Prest, George D., farmer
Read, S. J., saddler
Servos, Alexander
Shorburn, David, Township Clerk and Treasurer
Willox, Edward, proprietor flouring mill
Woodruff, George
Woodruff, Henry, general merchant
Woodruff, W. H., farmer
Woodruff, Richard, sen.

St. Helens.—A Post Village in the Township of Wawanosh, County Huron, 20 miles from Goderich, the County Town, and 150 from Toronto. Average price of improved land $30 per acre. Population 100.

Allen, William, farmer
Blue, Malcom, carpenter
Clark, R. C., blacksmith
Cummings, James, farmer
Devereux, Patrick, shingle maker
Gordon, John, farmer
GORDON, WILLIAM, Postmaster, general merchant
Humphrey, William, farmer
Irwin, John, carpenter
Leaver, Hiram, hotel keeper
Lusk, Rev. Robert (Canada Presbyterian)
McDonald, Angus, farmer
McDonald, Hugh, farmer
McHardy, N. & Co., general merchants
Mathers, Henry, J.P.
Patterson, James, teacher
Ramage, James, carpenter
Rutherford, John, blacksmith
Somerville, Thomas, proprietor flouring mill
Spurrie, James, shoemaker
Stark, William, farmer
Todd, T. & D., proprietors steam saw mill
Webster, James, carpenter
Wilson, Robert, farmer

St. Ives.—A Post Office in the Township of West Nissouri, County Middlesex.

HOWARD, THOMAS, Postmaster.

St. Jacobs.—A Village on the Conestogo River, in the Township of Woolwich, County Waterloo, 8 miles from Berlin, the County Town. Stages to Berlin and Elmira. Money order office. Population 500.

Abitz, William, butcher
Auman, Nicholas, blacksmith
Berges, Anthony, boots and shoes
Betzner, David, farmer
Bowman, J. E., J.P., M.P., commissioner in B. R.
Bowman, S. P., teacher
Bowman & Zinkan, hide and leather dealers & tanners
Brubacher, David, wagon maker
Burkholder, Benjamin, teacher
Cress, Ephraim, farmer
Cress, Peter, manufacturer of spinning wheels
Eby, C. & D. E., proprietors planing mill
Eby, David E., carpenter
Eby, Peter
Gabel, John, tailor
Gleiser, Peter, general merchant
Hahn, John G., tailor
Hanck, Frederick, farmer
Hanch, Rev. Theobald (Evangelical Association)
Heller, George, saddler
Herris, Valentine, proprietor Albion Hotel
Kinzinger, Joseph, boots and shoes
Levan, D. S. & Co., tinsmiths
Martin, P. G., farmer
Menger, George, blacksmith
Moyer, Rev. S. N. (Evangelical Association)
Ortwein, John, lime and stone
Puttock, Jesse, boots and shoes
Reitzel, Anthony, farmer
Rendlinger, Daniel, cooper
Robinson, William O., M.D.
Schaefer, Adam B., carpenter
Schlitt, Henry, tailor
Seibert, Adam, carpenter
Snyder, B. D., proprietor flouring mill
Snyder Brothers, manufacturers of woolen goods
Sticker, M., farmer
Voelker, Andrew, boots and shoes
Wanner, Louis, cooper
Weber, Jacob, farmer
Witz, John George, wagon maker
Weaver, Levi, proprietor Farmers' Inn
WIDEMAN, JOHN L., Postmaster, Clerk Division Court and general merchant

---

St. Johns.—A Village in the County of Middlesex.—(See Arva Post Office.)

St. Johns—(St. Johns West P. O.)—A Village in the Township of Thorold, County Welland, 7 miles from Welland, the County Town, and 77 by rail from Toronto. Daily mail. Population 250.

Angleman, Thomas, boots and shoes
Beckett, Miss Ellen, milliner
Brooks & Haney, flour mill proprietors
Brooks, James, mill owner
Brown, George, farmer
Brown, N., farmer
Carl, Nelson, miller
Carl, William, carriage and wagon maker
Collis, Henry, manufacturer of woolen goods
Carrick, Richard, tailor
Fell, Charles
Foss, W. D., teacher
Gainer, John, farmer
Gilmore, W. H., blacksmith
Ginter, John, farmer
Ginter, Peter, farmer
Haney, James, mill owner
Haney, Smith, mill owner
HANEY, STEPHEN, J.P., Postmaster, agent Clinton Mutual Insurance Co.
Haney & Vanderburgh, proprietors flour mill
Harper, John, tailor
Johnson, John, farmer
Keefer, Rev. B. (Wesleyan)
Kellens, David
Laws, Henry, farmer
Miller, Conrad, farmer
MOORE, DAVID, assistant Postmaster, and general merchant
Morehouse, Samuel, carriage and wagon maker
Phillips, Rev. J. R. (Methodist Episcopal)
Riley, Philip, tailor
Schram, Miss Margaret, milliner
Seabourn, Matthew, J.P.
Seabourn, Thomas, farmer
Smith, Joseph, proprietor St. Johns Hotel
Starr, Rev. J. Herbert (Wesleyan Methodist)
Summers, F. G., farmer
Summers, Hayatt, J.P.
Swayze, John
Swayze, Johnson, saw mill owner
Vanderburgh, Leonard, mill owner
Wilkison, John, clothier
Williams, John, mason

St. Marys.—A Town on the River Thames and station of the Grand Trunk or Buffalo and Lake Huron Railway, in the Township of Blanshard, County Perth, 12 miles from Stratford, the County Town, 21 from London, 70 from Sarnia, and 99 from Toronto. Large quantities of grain are annually shipped from this point. There are extensive quarries of limestone in the immediate vicinity. Stages to Mitchell 22 miles and Exeter, 24 miles. Money Order Office and Savings Bank. Population 4,007.

Abbott, S. A., M.D
Adams, Mrs. J., prop. Empire Hotel
Alexander, Thomas
Andrews, William & Co., watchmakers
Atkins, William, dry goods and clothing
Bailey, Thomas, cabinet maker
BAYLY, WILLIAM A., R.R. station agent
BANK OF MONTREAL, Robert Hillyard, agent
Barnes, A. J., boots and shoes
Barron, J. L., cooper
Bartlett, John, baker
BEATTY, ALEXANDER, general merchant
BELCH, ALEXANDER J., editor and prop. St. Marys *Argus* and the North Middlesex *Review*
Berry, J. B., barber, auctioneer
Bickell, Mrs. T., fancy goods, toys, &c
Bickell, Thomas, soap factory
BIRTCH, ELI, wood merchant and contractor
Box, Richard, J.P
Brown, William, cabinet maker, insurance agent
Carlisle, Robert, cooper
Carr & Heney, carriage makers
Cartell, R. T., cooper
Case, David, saddler
Case, Mrs., millinery
CLENCH, L. M., barrister, attorney-at-law, ins. agt
Coleman, J., clerk, Third Division Court
Coleman, William, butcher
Cook, John, boarding house
Cooper, E., proprietor Royal hotel
Constable, William, proprietor Ontario hotel
CRAIG & HAMILTON, (James Craig; James Hamilton) builders and contractors, proprietors planing mill and sash, door and blind factory (see adv.)
Crawford, William, grocer
Crittenden, L., town clerk
Curran, Rev. J. P. (Church of England)
Currie, William, grain dealer
Day, Lewis, boots and shoes
Demmick, Rev. M., (Episcopal Methodist)
Dudley, John, farmer
Dudley, O., farmer
Duffy, Michael, farmer
Dunbar, James, tailor
Eaton, James, general merchant
Eaton, Robert, cabinet maker
Eaton, Robert, grocer
Egan, M., constable
Falconer, Alexander, carpenter
Falconer, William, mason
FORD, A. E., M.D.
Ford, Robert, farmer
Ford, William H., notary public, real estate agent and conveyancer
Forrester, Andrew
Garner, J. S. cooper
Garner, William, proprietor saw mills
German, A. M., proprietor New Dominion hotel
Gibb, William, veterinary surgeon
Gilpin, R. W., boots and shoes
Gilpin, T. R., tinsmith
Goodbow, P., saddler
Gordon, William, general merchant
Graham, William, tailor
Grant, Alexander, mason
Grant, John, mason
Grice, James, carpenter
Guest, J. W., proprietor St. Marys brewery
Guest, Robert, grocer
Guest, T. B., farmer
Guest, William, farmer
Gunn, Donald, manufacturer woolen goods
HAGGART, W. & T., founders and machinists
Hall, J. J., M.D.

Hammitt, George A., tinsmith
Hanley, John A., mail carrier
HARDING, J. E. & BRO., barristers
Harrison, A., saddler
HARRISON, D. H., M.D., C.M., coroner
Harrison, John & Son, manufacturers woolen goods
Harrison, Milner
Harstone, Robert, hardware, issuer marriage licenses
Hayns, Richard, grocer
Helps, John, farmer
HILL, ARUNDEL, Postmaster
HILLYARD, ROBERT, agent Bank of Montreal
Hodgetts, James, accountant Bank of Montreal
HUDSON, J. B., proprietor Grand Trunk Hotel
Hutton, Theodore, general merchant
Hutton, William L., commission and forwarding merchant, tanner and insurance agent
HUTTON, WILLIAM VEAL, proprietor flour mills
Ingersoll, Charles
Ingersoll, James
Ingram, Joseph, grocer
Iredale, Thomas, grain merchant
Irvine, William H., carpenter
Jackson, Andrew, farmer
Jardine, James, blacksmith
JARVIS, J., grain merchant
Johnson, Thomas, grocer
JONES & McDOUGALL (C. S. Jones & Alfred McDougall), barristers
Jones, Thomas J., books and stationer
Junor, K., teacher
Kennedy, James, proprietor Union Hotel
Kerr, R. S., carpenter
Knowlton, William, painter
Kunz, David, cabinet maker
Lambie, W. H., insurance agent
Laughton, Malcolm, tailor
Lagear, Jacob, farmer
Lennox, George, farmer
Lockhart, R. G., watchmaker
Long, Edward, general merchant and insurance agent
McCALLUM, CUTHBERT, druggist
McCallum, Rev. J. W. (Wesleyan)
McConnell, David T., hardware
McCormick, James, carriage maker
McCracken, Michael, potash factory
McDonald, John, grocer
McDonald, Rev. P. (Baptist)
McDougall, Daniel
McDougall, Horace, telegraph operator
McEVOY, HENRY, teacher
McIntosh, William, dry goods
McIntyre, George, boots and shoes
McIntyre, James, tailor
McIntyre, L. A., agent Canadian Express Co.
McIntyre, Thomas, official assignee and general agent
McKillop, R., painter
McLaren, Joseph, baker
McLarty, Daniel, carriage maker and proprietor livery stables
McLean, G. S., druggist
McLean, John, bookbinder
McLean, William, telegraph operator
McNally, G., dry goods
Malcolm, William, farmer
Manly, Thomas & John, painters
Mara, T. A., grocer
Marshall, Charles, farmer
Miller, Duncan, carriage maker and proprietor livery stables
Mitchell, James, carpenter
Moore, James D., provisions
MOORE, JOHN & SON, proprietors steam flouring mill, founders and machinists (see adv)
Morphy, John, boots and shoes
Morshead, William, farmer
Niven & Hart, P. L. Surveyors, insurance and estate agents
Noel, Peter, painter
Oddy, Jacob, proprietor British Hotel
Oliver, James, baker
Paddell, Mrs., fruit dealer
Pierson, W., proprietor St. Mary's Hotel
Poole, J. W., teacher
ROBERTSON, ALEXANDER, prop. flax mill
Robertson, D., proprietor National Hotel
Rodgers. Nicholas, farmer
ROSE, D. D., glue merchant
RUPERT, D. S., surgeon and dentist
Sanderson, John, lumber merchant
Sharp, H. F., books and stationery
Simpson, George, proprietor flour mill
Sinclair, John, M.D.
Size, George, boots and shoes
Smith, Abiel, grain merchant
SMITH, G. B., general merchant
SMITH, J. FOX, barrister
Smith, Martin, tanner
Smith, Thomas, farmer
Smyth, Rev. E. (N. C. Methodist)
Smyth, Rev. William (N. C. Methodist)
Somerville, William, grain merchant
Sparling, James W., farmer
St. John, Adam, farmer
ST. MARYS' ARGUS, (Thursday) A. J. Belch, editor and proprietor
ST. MARYS' STANDARD (Saturday) Joseph Bowes editor and proprietor
Stafford, Joseph, saddler
Stevens, Allan, farmer
Stevens, Nathan, farmer
Stoddart, Archibald, druggist
Tate, Joseph, auctioneer
Taylor, D. S., glove factor
Treanor, M., grocer
VON GUNTEN, CHARLES, watchmaker and engraver
Von Gunten, L., watchmaker
Vanzant, J. H., pump maker
Walsh, John, groceries, wines and liquors
Watt, James, auctioneer
Weir, John, cheese factor
Whelihan, P., merchant
Whillans, J., grain dealer
Whillans & Smibert, groceries and provisions
Whitston, James, marble works
Willis, John, lumber dealer
Wilson, Daniel, M.D
Wilson, George, prop. billiard rooms
Willson, Levi, baker
Woolway, Thomas, grain merchant
Wright, Peter, principal grammar school

St. Raphael.—A Post Office in the Township of Charlottenburgh, County Glengarry, 9 miles from Alexandria, the County Town, and 7 from Lancaster Station, Grand Trunk Railway. Daily mail.

Bane, Alexander, farmer
Bane, James, farmer
Chisholm, Miss Annie, teacher
McDONALD, MISS ALLEN, Postmistress
McDonald, John A., farmer
McDonald, John R., farmer
McPherson, Roderick, farmer
McRae, Angus, farmer
McRae, Duncan, farmer

St. Thomas.—The judicial seat of the County of Elgin, in the Township of Yarmouth, is pleasantly situated on Kettle Creek, and is a station of the London and Port Stanley Railroad, 15 miles from London, and 120 from Toronto. It contains four churches, viz., Episcopal, Roman Catholic, Presbyterian and Wesleyan Methodist. A central and grammar school. Two ably conducted newspapers are supported here, and the Merchants' Bank has a branch in the town. It is the centre and market for a rich agricultural district, the price of land averaging $40 per acre. Daily stages to Aylmer, Fingal, Chatham and Sparta. Population 2000.

Abbott, S. J.
Allen, Bros., photographers
Allworth, A. J., station master L. & P. S. R.R.
Anderson, Mrs. Elizabeth, grocer
Arkell, Thomas, mayor, general merchant
Askew, Charles, auctioneer
Baikie, J. D., P.L.S.
Barr, Walter, merchant tailor
Barrett, William, wagon maker
Bennett, George, blacksmith
Bishop, Luke, nurseryman
BLEAKLEY, J. Y., flour and feed dealer, and depot of Elgin mills
Blue, Archibald, assistant editor *Canadian Home Journal*
Boggs, G. W.
Borbridge, Henry, saddle and harness maker
Brown, D., drover
BROWN, HENRY, stoves, tinware, hardware, house-furnishings, &c.
Bromell, William, wines and liquors
Burns, A., dentist
Cameron, Ewen, principal Central School
CAMPBELL, W. F., groceries and provisions
Carrie & Pollock (James Carrie & H. B. Pollock), general merchants
Caulfield, Rev. St. George, LL.D. (Church of Eng.)
Chambers, John, baggage master L. & P. S. R.R.
CLARIS, GEORGE T., County Treasurer
Clark, Willoughby, prop. Clark's Hotel & billiards
Cole, John, proprietor Cole's Hotel
Cole, Thomas, billiard saloon
Coles, S., blacksmith
Colinson, William, sheep skin tannery
Comford, Hiram, woolen carding and foundry
Corbett, Stephen, boots and shoes
Coyne, William, dry goods, clothing, millinery, &c.
Crocker, John & Son, tanners and curriers
Cruise, James E., merchant tailor and dealer in Singer Sewing Machines
Cusick, Robert, butcher
Cuthbertson, Rev. George (Presbyterian)
Davis, William, hair dressing saloon
Davy, R. B., boot and shoe maker
Day, Samuel, wagon maker
Dodd, James
Drake, Daniel, proprietor livery stable
ELGIN MILLS; E. M. Yarwood, proprietor
Ellis, Henry F., attorney
Ellison, Freeman, lumber dealer
ERMATINGER, EDWARD, Postmaster
ERMATINGER, F. E. & CO., commission and forwarding merchants
Farley, James, Clerk of the Peace and Clerk 3d Division Court
Farley, John, barrister
Ferguson, Leonard, painter
Gardner, David, baker
Gilbert, M. A. & Co., com. and forwarding merchants
Going, F. B., M. D.
Goodwin, Mis., dressmaker
Gundy, Rev. J. J., (Baptist)
Gusten, E. W., M. D
Hagar, Rev. J., (Wesleyan Methodist)
Hall, Miss Elizabeth, teacher
Hay, Thomas, baker
Hanvey, D., issuer of marriage licenses, revenue inspector, &c
Harte, Charles W., berlin wool and variety store
Henderson, Alexander, saloon and groceries
Henderson, William, teller Merchant's Bank
Hillis, J., wagon maker
HILLIS & METCALFE, (William Hillis, Thomas Metcalfe), planing, sash, doors and blinds
HOME JOURNAL, A McLaughlin, editor and prop.
HORSMAN, RICHARD, importer of bar iron, hardware, paints, oils, glass, lamps, and house furnishings
Horton, Edward, barrister
Hughes, D. J., County Judge
Hutchinson, James, clerk Hutchinson House
Hutchinson, Richard
Hutchinson William, proprietor Hutchinson House
Ivor, Samuel
Jackson, William, cabinet maker
Kains, George, maltster
Kains, John A., barrister
Kains, Joseph O., groceries and provisions
Kains, Thomas, ashery
King, John, jailor
Laing & Blake, (W. Laing and John Blake) general merchants
Laing, Joseph, auctioneer
LINDOP BRO., (Thomas Henry and Charles) general merchants, dry goods, groceries, boots and shoes
Lindop, W. E., photographer
Lipsey, William, J. P.
Lord & Baillie, carriage makers
Love, A., cooper
Love, Mrs., milliner
Love, Neil, market clerk
Love, W., cabinet maker
Luton, L., M.D
McAdam, James, groceries, provisions, liquors
McClure, Rev. John, head master grammar school
McColl, A., tailor
McCully, Robert, saddle and harness maker
McCrone & Smellie, (Edward McCrone and John R. Smellie) general merchants
McCrone, Mrs., milliner
McDonald, John, agent Merchants' Bank and agent Life Ass. of Scotland
McIntosh, D., drover
McIntyre, A., insurance agent
McKay, John, county registrar
McKay, William, county clerk
McKenzie & Still, (D. K. McKenzie and J. H. Still) dry goods, clothing, millinery, &c
McKenzie, M.
McLachlan, Archibald, editor and proprietor *Canadian Home Journal*, bookseller and stationer
McLEAN, JOHN, barrister and town treasurer
McRoberts, Joseph, tailor
Macdougall & Hallowell, (Calvin Macdougall and J. S. Hallowell) barristers
Mann, Jehiel, barrister

Marlatt, N., groceries and provisions
Martin, J. P., insurance agent
Meek, Bros., (William and Thomas) saddlers and harness makers
Merchants' Branch Bank and Savings Bank, J. McDonald, agent
Metcalfe, George, cooper
Midgley, John, merchant and clothier
Mitchell, Thomas, prop. Caledonia Hotel
Moore, M. T., tanner and currier
Moore, N. W., dealer in leather, shoe findings, saddle, harness, trunks, &c
Morgan, George W., boots, shoes and trunks
MORRILL, CHARLES A., U.S. Consular agent
Munro, Colin, sheriff
Meal, Mrs. C., milliner
Nelson, Robert, watches, clocks and jewelry
O'Boyle, Andrew, boots and shoes
Paddon, Samuel, butcher
Parish, D., general insurance agent
Perine & Young, flax mills
Pettifer, Peter
Pierce, Leslie, brickmaker
Pincombe, John, butcher
Pollock, H. B. (Carrie & Pollock)
Potticary, Charles, jr., soap and candles
Powell, Miss E. J., teacher
Price, Samuel, official assignee
Pringle & Son (George and Robert), watchmakers and jewelers
Rhycard, George C., groceries, provisions, liquors, &c
Richard, Charles G., chemist and druggist, bookseller and stationer
Rieser, William, brewer
Robinson, Jabel, lumber merchant and dealer in stoves and tinware
Roe, Charles, produce dealer
Roe, Peter, J.P., general merchant
Rowe, John, bootmaker
Sanagan, W., cooper
Scarff, George, deputy sheriff
Scott, George, farmer
Sinclair, A., drover
Sinclair, D., blacksmith
Southwick, George, M.D.
ST. THOMAS DISPATCH, P. Burke, editor & prop.
Stacey & Reeks (Joseph Stacey and William Reeks), Elgin Iron Works
Stacey, Thomas, carriage maker, blacksmith, lumber dealer, &c.
Stanton, James, barrister and county crown attorney
Stewart, Archibald, groceries and provisions
Thompson, Surranus, cabinet maker
Thompson, David, proprietor Thompson House
Thompson, Leonard
Thornton, H., livery stable
Turner, George S., boots and shoes
Turville, Richard, flour and grist miller
Union School, John McClure, principal
Vail, Mrs., proprietor Royal Exchange Hotel
Van Buskirk, Henry
Van Buskirk, William, M.D.
Walker, Miss Eliza, teacher
Waller, Miss E., teacher
Walthern, J., painter
Warner, Rev. W. (Wesleyan Methodist)
Warren, Thomas D., Deputy Clerk of Crown and County Court
Wegg, David, teacher
Whipple, M. P., L.D.S., surgeon and dentist
White, John, merchant tailor
WHITE, WILLIAM J., attorney (see adv)
WIENER, CHARLES, proprietor St. Thomas brewery
Williams, Thomas, J.P.
Wilkinson, John, fruit and confectionery
WILSON, J. H., M.D.
Wimbush, John R., baker
Wimbush, William, baker
Wegg, George, jun., carriage and wagon maker
Worthington, Charlotte, dyer
Yarwood, E. M., proprietor Elgin Mills
Youmans & Rowley (William Youmans & George Rowley), books, stationery, exchange and telegraph office
Zuker, Rev. Charles (Roman Catholic)

Sable.—A Post Office in the Township of West Williams, County Middlesex, 30 miles from London, the County Town, and on the Aux Sable River, 5 miles from Park Hill Station Grand Trunk Railway. The locality is rapidly becoming settled, land averages from $30 to $40 per acre.

Allison, Hugh, farmer
Gray, John, farmer
Lake, Stephen, J.P., farmer
Love, John, farmer
McCallum, Peter, shoemaker
McCubbin, John, farmer
McDONALD, ALLAN, Postmaster, farmer
McIntyre, S. C., J.P., general merchant
McIntyre, R., farmer
McKenzie, Donald, farmer
McLellan, John, Port Dalgetty Inn
McMillan, Angus, farmer
McPherson, Rev. S. (Presbyterian)
Morrison, R., proprietor Highlanders' Inn

Saintfield.—A Post Village in the Township of Reach, County Ontario, 25 miles from Whitby, the County Town, and about 50 miles from Toronto. Daily Stage to Whitby, fare $1. Average price of land $45 per acre. Daily Mail. Population 90.

Beecroft, Alvery, carpenter
Blyth, John, proprietor saw mill
Bunker, Amos, carpenter
Campbell, Donald, hotel keeper
Craig, John, weaver
Cronsberry, Elijah, farmer
Eck, Charles, saddler
Graham, James, farmer
Houldershaw, Richard, farmer
Horne, Alexander, weaver
Hunter, Christopher, farmer
Kenally, John, farmer
McKay, Donald, general merchant
Moffatt, William, farmer
Patterson, George, farmer
Phillips, William, farmer
SANDERS, WILLIAM, Postmaster
Stone, Amos, butcher
Thomas, Archibald, teacher
Vanzant, William, shingle maker
Watson, Alexander, blacksmith

Salem (now called Mount Salem).—A Village in the Township of Malahide, County Elgin, 18 miles from St. Thomas, the County Town. Improved land averages $35 per acre. Population 100.

Baldwin, Joseph, farmer
Benner, John, farmer
Boughisan, Jacob, farmer
Brown, J. T., farmer
Brown, W. H., proprietor Salem Hotel
Buch, James, farmer
Chalk, James, farmer
Chalk, Phinnie, carpenter
Denniss, William, carpenter
Dolon,, Albert, broom manufacturer
Ellsworth, John, farmer
Esseltine. Jacob, farmer
Fairchild, Rev. J, (Union Church)
Gerhard, Ghristian, tailor
Grass, James, farmer
Grass, J. C., proprietor hotel
Harvey, Joseph, J.P.
Harvey, William, J.P.
Hill, Ambrose, proprietor flouring mill
Hunt, Thomas, farmer
Kelly, John, farmer
McInnis, Thomas
McLim, —, shoemaker
Mathewson, M., constable
Rockey, Emanuel, wagon maker
Sanders, Thomas, proprietor flouring mill
Smades, Benjamin, shingle maker
Smades, Joel, shoemaker
Smith, W. H., cabinet maker
Spencer, Andrew, farmer
Sweed, Henry, farmer
Warburton, W., teacher
Ward, W., butcher
WHITE, W. W., Postmaster, general merchant
White, W. W., farmer

Salem (formerly Wynford Post Office).—A Village beautifully situated on the Irvine River, in the Township of Nichol, County Wellington, distant from Guelph, the County Town, 13 miles, from Elora 1 mile, and 63 from Toronto. Stages to Guelph, Walkerton and Hollen. Average price of improved lands in the vicinity $50. Village plots $100. Population 800.

Allan, William, general merchant
Beck, Adam, cooper
Bell, Robert, boots and shoes
Benerlein, Charles, proprietor sash and door factory
Bennie, James, carpenter
Bitzer, Mrs., proprietor Ontario House
Bradley, E., general merchant
Brown, George, proprietor marble works
Callaghan, John, lime burner
CHEESMAN, J. M., proprietor stave factory
Clark, William
Crowley, Jerome H., carpenter
Danforth & Lee, last manufacturers
Daul, Joseph, tailor
Davidson, James, bookbinder
Dixon, C. F., baker
Doerbecker, Conrad, J.P., brick manufacturer
EBY, JACOB B., proprietor Salem mills
Eddleston, George, tinsmith
Ernest, Gilbert, cooper
Findlay, James, J.P.
Findlay, Robert, carpenter
Fisher, Christian, cabinet maker
Flad, George, brewer and prop. Rising Sun Hotel
Fraser, Miss, milliner and dressmaker
Fraser, John, general merchant
Frazer, Hugh, boots and shoes
French, Josias
Gibbs, Robert, teacher
Griffith, J. W., M.D.
HILBORN, DAVID, prop Salem Hotel (see adv)
IRVINE FOUNDRY, Isaac Modeland, proprietor
IRVINE MILLS, J. & E. Wissler, props. (see adv.)
Johnston & Simpson, wagon makers
Keelmy, Charles, carpenter
Keil, John W., proprietor Union Hotel and cooper
Keith, John
Kilpatrick, Robert, wagon maker
Knox, Robert
Lawrence, Charles, cooper
Lawrence, John H., tailor
Lee, James, painter
Lindlay, David, auctioneer
McQueen, James
Massie, David M., baker
Middleton, Gavin, proprietor sash and door factory
Middleton, James
MODELAND, ISAAC, proprietor Irvine Foundry
Moir, James
Moore, S. & P., proprietors flax mills
Mulligan, Henry, butcher
Munro, John, wagon maker
Mutch, James & Son, boots and shoes
Nichol, William, carpenter
Quinlan, Daniel, proprietor Farmers' Inn
Renter, Jacob, proprietor Salem Brewery
Roberts, W., baker
Rodenbiller, Phillip, carpenter
SALEM HOTEL, David Hilborn, prop. (see adv)
SALEM MILLS, Jacob B. Eby, proprietor
Schuler (Charles & Christian), whip manufacturers
Simpson, Robert, carpenter
Sims, Bros., woolen factors
Sutherland, George, mason
Taylor, Barbara, teacher
Trenholm, Samuel, carpenter
Watt, Alexander, stock dealer
Webster, John, carpenter
Whiteley, William, J.P., saddler
Whiteley, W., & Son, rope manufacturer
WISSLER, J. R., J.P., Postmaster
WISSLER, J. & E., general merchants, tanners and proprietors Irvine mills (see adv)

Sandhurst.—A Post Office in the Township of South Fredericksburg, County Lennox.
ALLAN DAVID, Postmaster.

Salford.—A Village in the Township of Dereham, County Oxford, 14 miles from Woodstock, the County Town. Stages to Ingersoll and Port Burwell. Population 120.

BOON, WILLIAM, Postmaster
Dickhout, Richard, grocer
Donoker, George, general merchant
Fills, John, carpenter
Hill, Calvin, G., farmer
Kennedy, James, carpenter
Kennedy, William, carpenter
Lighthart, Edward, butcher
McLean, Rev. Hugh, (Methodist)
Mayberry, John, wagon maker
Miller, John A., carpenter
Rainney, Hiram & Homer, cheese makers
Swadling, Robert, carpenter

Salmonville.—A Village on the River Credit, in the Township of Chinguacousy, County Peel, 12 miles from Brampton, the County Town, and 5 from Georgetown Station Grand Trunk Railway. Good water power. Population 100.

Campbell, George, farmer
Henderson, Robert, farmer
Lyons, Thomas, farmer
Rutledge, John, farmer
Smith, Archibald, farmer
Smith, Daniel, farmer
Stringer James, farmer
Townsend, Edward, farmer

Sandfield.—A Post Office on La Graise River, in the Township of Lochiel, County Glengarry, 40 miles from Cornwall, the County Town.

Baker, Donald, farmer
McDanale, H. R., general merchant
McGillis, Duncan & John, shingle makers
McIntyre, Miss Maggie, teacher
McKenzie, Major, farmer
McLeod, Alexander, farmer
McRae, Alexander, farmer
McRAE, ANGUS, Postmaster and general merchant
McRae, Donald, farmer
McRae, Malcolm, farmer
McRae, Jonathan, farmer

Sandford.—A Post Office in the Township of Scott, County Ontario, 35 miles from Whitby, the County Town.

Burnham, T., farmer
Faron, John, shoemaker
Flumerfelt, S., proprietor saw mill
Harwood, R., blacksmith
Hurd, W., farmer
Irvine, J., proprietor Sandford House
Irvine, T., farmer
McCallum, J. S., teacher
McKee, Rev. R., (Primitive Methodist)
Moore, A. W., farmer
Moore, John, farmer
Porteous, W., farmer
Smith, George, farmer
Smith, Rev. James, (Primitive Methodist)
Stark, J., blacksmith
Stark, John, wagon maker
Stewart, Mrs. M., milliner
Tame & Taberbram, shingle makers
TAYLOR, EDWARD, Postmaster, general mercht
Week, James, township clerk, farmer

Sand Hill.—A Post-office in the Township of Chinguacousy, County Peel, 14 miles from Brampton, the County Town, and 29 from Toronto. A Stage from Malton to Mono Mills passes through the Village. Daily Mail. Population 150.

Bowles, Thomas, reeve, farmer
Boyd, Edward, merchant tailor
Elliott, James, carpenter
Elliott, Joseph, boots and shoes
Elliott, T. & W., general merchants
Hanna, William, J.P., commissioner, farmer
Harrington, Thomas, saddler
Hennesy, Samuel, M.D
Hennesy, Thomas, M.D
Hewitt, John, J.P., farmer
Hodgson, Robert, blacksmith
McKee, Alexander, J.P., farmer
Mitchell, William, blacksmith
ORR, JOHN, Postmaster
Parker, George, proprietor Commercial Hotel
Philips, Rev. R., (Wesleyan)
Porter, James, bricklayer
Rutherford, William, councillor
Sanderson, J., teacher
Sherlock, Rev. —, (Wesleyan)
Thompson, John, carriage maker
Wells, W. W., general merchant

Sand Point.—*(See Villages too late for regular insertion at the end of this work.)*

Sandwich.—The County Town of Essex, is beautifully situated on the Detroit River, in the midst of a fine and well settled agricultural country, about 2 miles below Windsor and 9 below Lake St. Clair. This is one of the oldest towns in the West. The trade of the surrounding country consists principally of agricultural products, all kinds of grain and fruit growing in Canada, maize, grapes, and tobacco. There is a celebrated spring of great medicinal excellence here, possessing curative powers equal to any on the Continent. It is upwards of 500 feet deep, and flows 25 feet above its surface, suitable baths, &c., are established, and all convenience for patients being of a high order, it will doubtless prove advantageous to the Town and vicinity. Distance from Toronto 222 miles; from Hamilton, 188; from Woodstock, 140; from Chatham, 50; and from Detroit, 3. Stages to Amherstburg, Kingsville, &c. Steamers to Detroit and all other points. Money Order Office and Savings Bank. Population 1200.

Allison, Mrs. Ann, grocery
Askin, James W., Deputy Registrar
Askin, John, County Registrar
Askin, Mrs. Joseph
Atkin, George, County Warden
Baby, Charles, barrister, Clerk Peace
Baby, William
Bain, William, founder and machinist
Bartley, O., P.L.S., and C. E.
Benito, Cleophus, blacksmith
Bochmann, Theodore, painter
Boismier, Joseph, blacksmith
Brown, George, farmer
Bruyére, Very Rev. J. M., Vicar-General
Chalmers, James
CHEWETT, C. W
Clark, J., proprietor steam flour mill
CLARK, W. & J. B., shoemakers
Cowan, M., Customs
Cowan, W., Custom House broker
Cutter, James, saloon keeper
DALEITEN, J., baker
Devlin, Thomas, shoemaker
Dobson, Cyrus, farmer
Donaldson, John, hotel keeper
Doonan, Thomas, shoemaker
Dugray, Louis, carpenter
Dugray, Severe, carpenter
Duprat, Rev. C., (Roman Catholic)
Dupres, Louis, farmer
ELLIS, A. C., saddler and harness maker
ELLIS, J., harness maker
Elliott, Rev. F. G., ((Church of England)
Fellers, George
Fluett, J. L., atterney, &c
Gauthier, J. B., general merchant
Girardot, T., teacher
Gluns, R., tanner
Golibois, L., wagon maker
Gray, Moses, farmer
Green, Edward
GUILLOTT, H. C., general merchant
GUILLOTT, JAMES P., druggist and gen. merchant (see adv)
Haggert, Charles H., general merchant
Hann, G., farmer
Hartley, William, miller
Hawkins, Henry, farmer
Henderson, Mrr. W., grocery
Holden, W., general merchant
Jessop, George, hotel keeper
Labelle, Charles, cooper
Lamb, C. W., tinsmith, &c.
Lasaline, S., cabinet maker
Lauvan, G., shoemaker
Laughton, J. B., proprietor Essex House
LEECH, GEORGE O'CALLAGHAN, governor jai
Leduc, Napoleon, wagonmaker
LEGGATT, W. G., County Judge
McDonald, S. S., County Attorney
McEWAN, JOHN, sheriff County Essex
McKee, Thomas, Clerk Division Court
McKillop, Malcolm, principal grammar school
McMULLEN, D. A., barrister, Dep. Clerk Crown, &c
Mansur, J. W.
Marcon, E., insurance agent
Marcon, F. E., barrister, &c.
Morcotte, Henry, wagon maker
Marentette, P., J.P., &c.
Marseille, Rev. J. (Roman Catholic)
MASON, GEORGE W., grocer, &c.
Mason, Thomas, general merchant
Mears, William, proprietor Albion Hotel
Mercer, Mrs. Joseph
Miller, J., general merchant
Monferton, Craig, carpenter
Moore, Michael, tailor
MORIN, P. H., H. M. Customs
Ouellette, A. B., blacksmith
Ouellette, Joseph, carpenter
Ouellette, Theodore, Inland Revenue Inspector
Overton, Thomas, tailor
Parent, Mrs. Fabin
Parent, George, farmer
Platt, C., saloon
ST. LOUIS, CALIXTE, Postmaster, general merchant
Salter, A. P., P.L.S. & C.E.
SANDWICH EXCHANGE, Jacob Stuttz, prop.
Lemande, D., shingle manufacturer
Shields, John, farmer
Smith, David, mason
STEWART, D., proprietor Western Hotel
STUTTZ, JACOB, prop. Sandwich Enchange
Sutherland, Mrs., storekeeper
Teakle, Henry, carpenter
Vandum & Ellis, brewers
Vernor, Arthur
Waldrum, J., cabinet maker
Wilkinson, Alexander, P.L.S.
Winters, J., butcher
Woodbridge, Thomas
WRIGHT, THOMAS H., County Treasurer

Sarawak.—A Post Office in the Township of Sarawak, County Grey, 12 miles from Owen Sound, the County Town.

Lundy, Joseph, farmer
McKENZIE, JOHN, Postmaster, steamboat agent, accountant and general agent
McKenzie, John, farmer
McNaught, William, J.P., farmer
Roy, William, farmer
Scagel, John, farmer
Smith, E. L., teacher
Sutton, William, farmer
Webb, George, cooper
Wilson, John, farmer

Sarepta.—A Village in the Township of Hay, County Huron, 30 miles distant from Goderich, the County Town, and 180 from Toronto. Improved land in the vicinity averages $30 per acre. Population 28.

Breckerick, J., teacher
Brown, J., farmer
Cheetham, Rev. J., (Primitive Methodist)
Edworthy, G., farmer
Ewing, John, general merchant
Fenwick, J., farmer
Fried, Absalom, proprietor flouring mill
Gill, J., farmer
Heist, C., cabinet maker and carpenter
Hull, E., farmer
Martin, P., farmer
Raider, Philip, farmer
REYNOLDS, WILLIAM, Postmaster, prop. Farmers' Inn
Rollings, J., teacher
Trimner, A., farmer

Sarnia.—The County Town of Lambton, in the Township of Sarnia, at the head of the River St. Clair, near its junction with Lake Huron. It is immediately opposite the City of Port Huron, State of Michigan, with which it has constant communication by a steam ferry, at all seasons of the year, the navigation at this point never being obstructed by ice. The town was laid out in 1833, and is situated on a healthy site at an elevation of eighteen feet above the river. Possessing excellent facilities for transportation, and one of the best harbors on the Lakes, its commercial and manufacturing advantages cannot be overrated. The buildings are numerous, and several of them of a superior kind. The streets are well paved and regular, crossing at right angles. Sarnia is the terminus of the Grand Trunk and the Sarnia branch of the Great Western Railway, both Companies having extensive depots here. Distant from Detroit 60 miles, and from Goderich 60. Money Order Office and Savings Bank. Population 3000.

Abrams, Richard, potashery
ADAMS, DANIEL, steam flouring mill
ADAMS, J. F., proprietor carding and fulling mill)
ADAMS & SEAGER (Joshua Adams; Charles Seager barristers (see adv)
Alexander, Andrew, proprietor Alexander House
Allair, A., grocer
Allen, Samuel, governor jail
Baker, F. W., proprietor St. Clair Hotel
Ball, Alfred, butcher
Balster, J. C., watchmaker
Barrie, James, general merchant
BARRON, JOHN, photographer (see adv)
BELCHAMBER, JAMES, prop. Belchamber House
Benning, H., tailor
Blaikie, Francis, founder
BRYCE & CO. (W. & David Bryce) Exchange Brokers (see adv)
BUCKE, JULIUS P., barrister, county attorney (see adv.)
Buck, Richard M., M.D., C. M.
CAMERON, JOHN, land agent, conveyancer
CARMAN, GEORGE A., insurance and general agent, exchange broker, etc., (see adv)
Carter, G. W., saloon
Caupp, J., drover and butcher
Chalmers, R. S., hardware
Chapman's, restaurant and billiard rooms
Chester, John, grain and flour merchant, agent (Atkinson, Gaddis & Hodgins)
Clark, A. C., general merchant
Clark, Daniel, grocer
CLARK, William B., importer and general merchant (see adv.)
Climie, Andrew, grocer
Copland, James, baker
Corbould, William, accountant Bank of Montreal
Crawford, John, dry goods
Cross, Henry, book-keeper
CURTIS, CLARK, turner, pump maker, etc
DAVIS & WATT, (James Davis and Frederick Watt) barristers, etc
Delmage, Arthur, constable
Donnelly, William, agent, (D. C., Thompson, Q)
Douglas, P. B., student-at-law
DUGGAN, E. W., U.S., consul
Elliott, F., dry goods
Farr, C. A., proprietor livery
Farr, William, wagon maker
Faulkner, James, cooper
Ferguson, D., photographer
FISHER, A., J.P., Postmaster, com. in B.R., issuer marriage licenses
Fisher, Charles, clerk P.O
FLEMING, M., agent American Express Co. and Canadian Express Co., agent Montreal Telegraph Co., and exchange broker (see adv)
Flintoff, James, sheriff County Lambton
Foulds, James, baker and grocer
Francis, John J., P.L.S
GEMMELL, J. R., J.P., dep. clerk crown and pleas, clk Co. court and editor and prop. *Observer*
Gleeson, J., groceries and liquors
Glynn, Richard, rifle maker
GOWANS, JAMES, (Pardee & Gowans)
Gray, David, shoemaker
Gustin, H., stage proprietor
Hall, H., cabinet maker
Hall, Brothers (Richard and Morrison), tanners
HARKNESS, ROBERT, prop. propeller "Sea Gull"
HARKNESS, WILLIAM G., billiard saloon and livery (see card)
Hickinbotham, G., general agent
Hickinbotham, Mrs., music teacher
Highwarden, S., pawnbroker
Hitchcock, S., crier Court
Holden, John, plasterer and lime burner
Hudson, W. H.. student-at-law
Ireland. William, builder and contractor
JOHNSTON, THOMAS W., M.D., Registrar County Lambton
Jones, E. R., P.L.S.
KEAYS & CO, (W. J. Keays and R. Harkness), forwarders, commission merchants, steamboat agents, &c. (see adv.)
Kelly, James, grocer
Kelly, W, H., groceries and liquors
Klumpp, F., drover and butcher
Lambert, James, tailor
Leys, Alexander, dry goods, &c.

McCARTHY & MASON,
(Late C. McCarthy),
FURNISHING UNDERTAKERS,
Warerooms and Residence 155 Queen West,
opposite College Avenue, Toronto.
Funerals Attended.

BOATS TO LET.
Boats Built, Repaired & Painted
Oars, Row-Locks, &c., for sale.
FRANK A. NOVERRE, *Proprietor.*
Foot of Simcoe Street, West of Union Station,
Toronto, Ont.

T. H. O'NEIL,
William III. Hotel,
56 and 58 Adelaide St. East,
TORONTO,
Opposite the Court House.
Boarders taken by the Day or Week.

S. H. OLIVER,
GENERAL COMMISSION MERCHANT,
Dealer in Flour and Feed, Split Peas, Pot Barley, Buckwheat Flour, Oat and Corn Meal, and Produce of all kinds.
Cash Advanced on Produce consigned for Sale.
289 Queen St. West, Toronto, Ont.

Dolphin Saloon and Billiard Parlor,
JOS. PALMER (LATE OF BARRIE), PROP.,
131 King St. East, Toronto, Ont.
The best Brands of Wines, Liquors and Cigars, Oysters, Game, &c., &c., &c.

R. T. POCKNELL,
Manufacturer of French and English Confectionery,
33 KING WEST,
TORONTO, ONTARIO.

MAPLE LEAF SALOON.
No. 6 Adelaide St. West, near Yonge, Toronto, Ont.,
ALEXANDER PURSE, PROPRIETOR,
Best Brands of Wines, Liquors and Cigars, two First-Class Bagatele Tables.

ROBERT CARMICHAEL,
GENERAL COOPER,
No. 9 Adelaide Street East,
TORONTO, ONTARIO.

JOHN PEARCY,
(Late of the Firm of G. Pearcy & Son,)
House, Sign and Ornamental Painter, Paper Hanger, General House Decorator, &c.,
No. 8 Hayter Street, Toronto, Ontario.

THOMAS REED,
DEALER IN GROCERIES, PROVISIONS, &C., &C.,
Sign of the Yorkvile "Tea Pot,"
630 Yonge Street, Toronto, Ontario.

HUGH P. SAVIGNY.
Provincial Land Surveyor and Mining Engineer,
32 Exchange Buildings, Toronto Ontario.

PETER A. SCOTT,
BUILDER AND CONTRACTOR,
Lumber Merchant, Dealer in Drain Tiles, &c.,
618 Yonge St., Toronto, Ontario.

PROF. G. W. SMITHS,
Fashionable Hair Dresser and Shaving Saloon, Warm and Cold Baths, all the year round,
No. 134 King West, Toronto.

Queen Street Coal and Wood Yard,
HUGH SPENCE, PROPRIETOR,
Coal and Wood always on Hand at lowest Prices,
199 Queen Street West, Toronto, Ont.

CHARLES SPROAT,
PROPRIETOR SPADINA BREWERY,
145 Vanauley Street, Toronto, Ontario.

TIDEY'S HOTEL,
W. J. TIDEY, PROPRIETOR,
365 Yonge Street, Toronto, Ont.
The choicest Wines, Liquors and Cigars, always on hand.

Leys, George, merchant tailor
LIPSCOMB, FRANCIS, station agent G.W.R.
LISTER, JAMES F., barrister, &c. (see adv.)
Lowrie, Joseph, blacksmith and wagon maker
Lucas, Henry, grocer
Luscomb, William, butcher
McElheron, W. J., proprietor Western Hotel
McCarty, Daniel, grocer
McClellan W., saloon
McDONALD, DUNCAN, prop. McDonald's Hotel
McGlashan, Peter, collector inland revenue
McKENZIE, DANIEL, groceries
McLagan, Alexander, builder
McLagan, C. A., grocer
McLean, G. S., druggist
McMASTER, D., fancy goods, jewelry, musical instruments, stationery, etc.
McMULLEN, ROBERT C., com. in B. R., notary public, coroner, general law and land agt (see adv)
McVicar, S. A., deputy Sheriff
MacKenzie, Alexander, M. P.
MacKenzie, James, oil refiner
MacKenzie, John & Charles, hardware, oil refiners
MACKENZIE, ROBERT, (R. & H. MacKenzie) Indian agent
MACKENZIE, R. & H., builders, saw mill props., cabinet makers
MacKenzie & Gurd (J. A. MacKenzie, R. S. Gurd), barristers, etc.
Mahoney, John, stoves and tinware
Masuret, M., groceries and liquors
Minten, Thomas, hotel keeper
Neal, H., watchmaker
Nicholson, Miss M., fancy, goods, mantles, etc.
Oliver, Robert, builder
PARDEE, T. B., M.P.P., (Pardee & Gowans)
PARDEE & GOWANS, (T. B. Pardee, M.P.P., Jas. Gowans), barristers
PETERSON, N. C., proprietor Sarnia foundry
Porter, James
Pottinger, Samuel, grocer
Pretty, W. J., shoemaker
Poussette, A. C., M. D
Poussett, E. P., clerk peace, master in chancery
Poussett, E. W., druggist
POUSSETT, HENRY M., groceries and liquors
Rigney, W., tailor
Robinson, Charles, Judge County Lambton
Rogers, James, marble works
RUSSELL, GEORGE, proprietor Sarnia brewery
Sanders & Bassett (C. & E.), cabinet makers
SARNIA OBSERVER (Friday), A. Gemmill, prop.
Saulter, Rev. George A. (Church of England)
Scully, J., Collector Customs
Sheehan, James, dry goods
SHOEBOTHAM, HENRY, M.D.
Skilbeck, R., secretary Lambton Permanent Building and Investment Society
Smith, Hugh, County Clerk, valuator Huron and Erie Savings and Loan Society
Smith, James H., Deputy Registrar
Smith, Thomas L., proprietor National Hotel
Sproule, Walter, blacksmith
STEVENSON, GEORGE, official assignee, land agent, broker and conveyancer
Stewart, William, dry goods
SULLIVAN, M., barrister (see adv)
Symington, T. & J. S., dry goods
Taylor, Charles, painter
Terry, Charles, blacksmith
Thatcher, Jared S., auctioneer and com. merchant
Thomas, G. J., clerk P.O.
VIDAL, E. A., Clerk County Treasurer, insurance and general agent
VIDAL, HON. ALEXANDER, agent Bank of Montreal, County Treasurer, agent Liverpool and London and Globe Insurance Co.
VIDAL, WILLIAM P., barrister (see adv)
Wanless, Henry, grocer
Wanless, R. & Co., grocers
Ward, William, livery
WATSON, E. P., auctioneer and bookseller (see adv)
Wenino, Paul, grocer
WHYTE, EDWARD A., bookkeeper and agent Sarnia Brewery
WOOD, J. H., editor and proprietor *British Canadian*
Young, Archibald, general merchant
Young, Archibald, jun., insurance agent

Saugeen.—(Southampton Village)—Is situated on Lake Huron at the mouth of the Saugeen River, in the Township of Saugeen, County Bruce; it is a Port of Entry from which large quantities of wheat, pork and lumber are shipped annually. The Village is 24 miles west of Owen Sound and 60 north of Goderich with both of which places it is connected by good gravel roads; Walkerton, the County Town, is distant 32 miles. The mode of travel during summer is by steam to Goderich and Collingwood, and by Stage in winter. Money Order Office and Savings Bank. Population 600.

Adair, Thomas, commission merchant
Angus, A. & P., proprietors planing mill
Belcher, Walter, telegraph operator
Bowes, Joseph, baker
Burwash, James A., com. merchant
Busby, William, auctioneer
Byers, John, saddler
Canaden, Thomas, iron founder
Cartwood, John, fishery overseer, Div. Court Clerk, insurance and general agent
Causley, J., shingle manufactory
Conway, James T., J.P.
Davis, Thomas, cabinet maker
Denny, John, proprietor flour mill
Douglass, & Co., general merchants
Drake, R. A., wagon maker
Fleming, James, carpenter
Fraser, Archibald, lime and stone dealer
Gibbons, Richard, proprietor brickyard
Gilbert, Joseph, proprietor Royal Hotel
Granville, Augustus, cooper
Granville, Gabriel, cooper
Harrison, Joseph, tailor
Head, Thomas, lumber dealer
Hilbert, Mary A., proprietor Masonic Hotel
Hogg, James, tailor
Jackson, H., butcher
Jock, James, boots and shoes
Kennedy, Edward, wagon maker
Koiley, James, proprietor British Hotel
Lawrie, Andrew, carpenter
LEE, THOMAS, Postmaster, commission merchant and steamboat agent
Le Veaux, G. Victor, teacher
Lindsay, Andrew, general merchant
McDonald, J. A., tailor

McGregor, Peter, boots and shoes
McIntyre, George, tanner
McLean, John, painter
McLeod, Mrs., milliner and dressmaker
McNabb, Alexander, crown land agent
Morrison, Thomas, carpenter
Noesly, Anthony, cooper
Porteous & Co., general merchants
Proudfoot, F., barrister
Scott, W. S., M.D.
Sinclair, Alexander, general merchant
Slee, C. A., attorney-at-law
Stafford, Adam, proprietor, Revere House
Stewart, John R., chemist and druggist
Treckelton, J. D., M.D.
Tuck, Frederick, tinsmith
Wallace, William, agent Vicker's Express
Wallace & Stirton, general merchants
Wetherall, Samuel, baker
Wilson, Byron, insurance agent

Sault Ste Marie.—The County Town of the District of Algoma, is situated on the north shore of St. Mary's River, at the foot of the rapids which obstruct navigation from Lake Huron to Lake Superior, which are, however, overcome by a canal constructed on the United States side of the river. The town settled by the French in 1668, is a port of entry, and now numbers, 400 inhabitants, consisting principally of French Canadians and half-breeds. The mode of travel during the summer months is by steamer from Collingwood, distance about 370 miles. fare $8.50. The minerals of this section of the province consist of iron, lead, copper, silver, gold, nickel and cobalt ; the chief products, wheat and all kinds of grain, lumber, furs, etc., fish and game are abundant. Government lands are worth 20 cents per acre, and improved about $10. There is a Roman Catholic chapel, and priest in attendance, with a large congregation. Protestant services are held in the Court House and school house, the latter place was built by private subscription and has a large attendance of pupils. The value of exports from this port for the year ending June 30th, 1868, amounted to $303,429.

Bampton, C. J., builder and hotel proprietor
BORRON, EDWARD, mining engineer
BROWN, PETER, landing waiter
CAMERON, ALEXANDER, hotel keeper
CARNEY, JOHN, general merchant
CARNEY, RICHARD, sheriff
Carney, William, jailor
COUSINS, JOHN, clerk Division Court
COUSINS, JOHN, landing waiter
DAVIDSON & TOWERS, general merchants
ELLIOTT, E., merchant tailor
Fear, Rev. Samuel (Wesleyan Methodist)
Grose, —, cooper
HAMILTON, JOHN M., crown attorney, barrister and insurance agent
HYNES, ANDREW, bailiff
Lapier, William, cooper
Lloyd, J., carpenter
McCulloch, Thomas, farmer
McKay, J., butcher
McNab, Donald, farmer
Mayville, Joseph, farmer
MORRISON, JOHN, prop. Anglo American Hotel
PILGRIM, HENRY, clerk district court and registrar surrogate court
PIM, DAVID, Postmaster and collector inland rev
PRINCE, HON. JOHN, Q.C., J.P., district judge
SAVAGE, JOHN M., J.P, registrar
STEAM FLOURING AND GRIST MILL
Stratton, William, farmer
TOWERS, T. A. P., agent Vickers' Express
TREW, C. N., M.D.
TROTT, JOSHUA, general merchant
TURNER, WILLIAM, teacher
WILSON, JOSEPH, J.P., collector H. M. Customs and Crown Land agent

---

Scarboro'.—A Post Village in the Township of Scarboro', County York, situated on the Markham Road, and adjacent to the Grand Trunk Railway. Distant from Toronto 10 miles. Stage from Rouge Hill to Toronto, fare 50c. Daily Mail. Money Order Office. Population 150.

Annes, Jeremiah, farmer
Beard, Jonathan, hotel keeper
Belt, Rev. William, (Church of England)
Bowen, C. C., farmer
Chamberlain, William, butcher
Chester, George, general merchant
Clossan, L. D., M.D
Hall, William, farmer
Harris, Rev. A. G., (Wesleyan Methodist)
Humphrey, James, farmer
Luke, Wallace, carpenter
Maberly, Charles, boots and shoes
MACLEAN, DONALD, Postmaster, general merchant
Montgomery, James, teacher
Purdy, Mrs., milliner [illegible]
Read, T. M., agent British American Express Co.
Ross, Alexander, carriage and wagon maker
Swallow, John, harness maker

Scone.—A Post Office in the Township of Brant, County Bruce.

BEARMAN, THOMAS, Postmaster.

Scotch Block.—A Village in the Township of Esquesing, County Halton, 6 miles from Halton, the County Town. Improved land averages $40 per acre. Daily mails. Population 20.

Gordon, George, teacher
HUME, THOMAS, Postmaster, prop. flouring mill
McCall, George, teacher
Steel, Robert, proprietor flouring mill
Stewart, John, J.P.
Stewart, Jones, proprietor steam flouring mill

Schomberg.—A post Village in the Township of King, County York, 40 miles distant from Toronto. Stage from Aurora Station Northern Railway, 14 miles, fare 50 cents. Improved land in the vicinity, averages $60 per acre. Daily mail. Money order office. Population about 350.

Armitage, Eli, general merchant
Armitage, Stephen W., baker
Baxter, Charles, proprietor Ontario Hotel
Bond, John, R., druggist
Botham, M., tailor and clothier
Brown, G., proprietor flouring mill
Brown, John R., farmer
Burns & Hayman, farmers
Campbell, John H., general merchant
Cochron, William, painter
Collins, John A., cabinet maker
Cranney, Thomas, founder and machinist
Crawford, Andrew, tailor and clothier
Davis, Samuel, farmer
Dennis, D., proprietor Victoria Hotel
Dennis, Samuel P., manufacturer of woolen goods
Fair, Robert, tailor
Finch, Charles, planing mills
Foucar, J. P., tinsmith and dealer in stoves
Grant, Alexander, wagon maker
Hawkins, James, books and stationery, bookbinder and proprietor printing office
Hay, Rev. William (Wesleyan)
Hill, Rev. R. W. (New Connexion)
Hollinshead, William, farmer
Housegan, Daniel, boots and shoes
Hughes, Clarkson, farmer
Hughes, George, J.P.
Hughes, George L., saddler
Hughes, John S., cabinet maker
Hughes, John W., general merchant
Hulce, H., prop. St. George's Hotel and livery stable
Kilpatrick, Robert, watchmaker, jeweler, &c.
Leonard, Sidney, general merchant
Leonard, Stephen, farmer
LOCKHARD, W. S., Postmaster and gen. merchant
Longbottom, T. B., proprietor brick yard
McMinn, John, tinsmith and dealer in stoves
Meganty, F., tailor
Moore, William, J.P. and general merchant
Pearson, George, farmer
Pearson & Robinson, dentists
Phillips, Isaac S., farmer
Phillips, Joel, J.P.
Pinkerton, Matthew, farmer
Playter, Edward, M.D.
Robertson, Thomas, wagon maker
Ross, James, general merchant
Schomberg Standard, (Friday), James Hawkins, prop.
Shannahan, James, boots and shoes
Shelson, Robert, cooper
Skinner, George, butcher and soap and candle manufacturer
Spring, William, wagon maker
Sproul, William J., farmer
Tegart, Anderson, saddler
Vaux, Henry, M.D.
Vincent, D. H., teacher
Walton, William M., insurance agent

Scugog.—A Village in the Township of Scugog, County Ontario, 26 miles distant from Whitby, the County Town, and 65 from Toronto. Stages to Whitby and Oshawa, fare 75c. Daily mail. Population 100.

Betts, Miss, teacher
Bond, Jones, butcher
Cantling, Rev. —, (Bible Christian)
Cleghorn, A., teacher
Dunn, William, saddler
Earl, Rev. W. C. (Christian)
FINLEY, ISAAC, Postmaster, general merchant and prop. sash, door and blind factory & livery stable
Finley, Thomas, carpenter
Foster, E., farmer
Foy, John, township clerk
Fralick, Solomon, farmer
Hall, Rufus, farmer
Harper, Charles, farmer
Hope, Thomas, farmer
Hull, Henry, shingle maker
Jackson, David, farmer
McKinley, Moses, carpenter
McPaul, John, carpenter
Nesbit, Charles, farmer
Pringle, E., teacher
Read, Rev. Mr. (Wesleyan)
Sanderson, R. (Methodist Episcopal)
Sexton, William L., J.P., reeve
Taylor, William, farmer
Taylor, William, jun.
Thorn, Joseph, lime and stone
Wakeford, Samuel, cooper
Wallace, William, carpenter
Watson, Thomas, farmer
Williams, Peter, farmer
Winn, Samuel, cooper

Seaforth.—An incorporated Village, and Station of the Buffalo and Lake Huron Railroad, in the Townships of Tuckersmith and McKillop, County Huron, 22 miles from Goderich, the County Town, 16 from Bayfield, and 27 from Wroxeter. A large trade in lumber and grain is done here, and the village is rapidly increasing in importance. Stages to Bayfield and Wroxeter Money Order Office and Savings' Bank. Population 1800.

Beattie, John
BENSON, JAMES H., barrister (see adv)
Bell, Thomas, cabinet maker
Broadfoot, John (Broadfoot & Gray)
BROADFOOT & GRAY (John and Adam) props. planing mill (see adv)
Bonthron, James & Son, dry goods and groceries
Brine, J. P., auctioneer
Broughton, Edward P., station master, telegraph opr.
BULL, T. P., watchmaker
Ault, William, grocer
Campbell, John, saddler
CAMPBELL & SMITH (Wm. and H. H.) merchant tailors
CARDNO, ALEXANDER, baker and prov. dealer
Carmichael, Robert, hotel and livery
Carnochan, Robert, farmer
Cash, Edward, merchant
Chesney, W., farmer
CHUBB, THOMAS, books, stationery and fancy gds.

Cleghorn, James, tailor
Cleghorn, James, tailor
Clough, Richard, farmer
Colbert, H., brewer
Coleman, T. T., M.D.
Collier, R. H., general merchant
Collins, John, miller
Collins, R. W., proprietor billiard room
Corby, G. R., general merchant
COUNTER, M. R., watchmaker and jeweler (see adv)
Coventry, Thomas, shoemaker
Creswell, Edwin, farmer
CULL, C. H., book and job printer, express and telegraph agent
Curry, Andrew, butcher
Currie & Pringle(Thomas and James), commission merchants and grain dealers
Davis, Griffith, dry goods
Dewar, Archibald, teacher
Dickson, James, farmer
DICKSON, SAMUEL, Postmaster
Dodds, James, lime manufacturer
Downey, Thomas, livery stables
Duncan, Julius, grain dealer
Duncan, J. & Co., boots and shoes
Dunnett, C., tanner
Elder, J., cooper
Elliott, James, grocer
Ewing, George, butcher
Fee, J. D., hardware
Ferguson, Thomas, carpenter
Ferris, W. K., carpenter
Fisher, Robert, carpenter
Foster, Thomas, hotel
Gills, O. L., life assurance agent
Gowenlock, Robert, farmer
Gowenlock, W. C., M.D.
Grant, Hugh, architect
Grassie, William, blacksmith and wagon maker
Gray, Adam (Broadfoot & Gray)
Grieve, Thomas, lime manufacturer
Guthrie, Miss Jane, teacher
Guthrie, R., clothes dealer
Harris, G. W., dentist
Hayhurst, Rev. William, (Wesleyan Methodist)
Haynes, R. T., grocer
Hays, Robert, J. P.
Hazelwood, Edward, grain dealer
Herrfeldt, William, commission merchant
HICKSON, E. & Co., (E. and John Hickson) druggists and general merchants
Hill, Alexander, carpenter
Hill, William, general merchant
Holmsted, F., attorney-at-law
Houghton, —, proprietor Lloyd's Hotel
Jacobs, Sidney N., tinsmith
Jarvis, G. T., land and general agent
Jarvis, T. J., grocer
Johnston, Rev. C. C., (Church of England)
JOHNSTON, THOMAS, grain merchant
Johnstone & Bros., hardware
Kellogg, W. M., grocer
Kennedy, S. L., photographer
Kidd & McMulkin, general merchants
Killoran & Ryan, (John Killoran, Thomas Ryan) groceries, wines and liquors
Lamb, A., grocer
Lancaster, William, hotel keeper
Logan, John, dry goods and groceries
Losby, E., carpenter
LUMSDEN, R. & Co., booksellers and stationers
McAdam, Gordon, assistant Postmaster
McBride, James, proprietor Seaforth House (see adv)
McCallum, John (Zapfe & McCallum)
McCaughey, S. G., barrister
McCLEARY, W. J., attorney-at-law
McConnell, William, farmer
McDonald, Rev. Alexander D. (Baptist)
McDougall, Archibald, general merchant
McDougall, A. G., insurance agent
McGregor, J. M. & J., grocers
McIntosh & Morrison (James & M. C.), carriage makers
McNaught & Teeple (D. and J. S.) carriage makers
McPhillips, George & William, P.L.S.
Metherell, A., veterinary surgeon
Metherell, Charles, M.D.
MEYER, FRANZ A., saddler
Moodie, Robert B., freight clerk G.T.R. and insurance agent
Morrison & Conor, bakers
Murray, John, blacksmith
PALTRIDGE, F., photographer
PENTON, CHARLES, editor *Seaforth Expositor*
PORTER, JOHN S., hide and wool dealer (see adv)
POTTS, JOHN, hotel keeper
Powell, Simon, clerk
Ramsey, Peter, lumber dealer
Reid, William O., hardware
RIDLEY, J. D. McGILL, agent Royal Canadian Bank
Robert, Hugh, sash and door manufacturer
Robertson, Matthew, cabinet maker
Robertson, W. S., groceries, wines and liquors
Rogers, R. P., dry goods and groceries
ROSS, H. H., clerk
ROYAL CANADIAN BANK, J. D. McGill Ridley, agent, Charles Hunter, teller
SCOBIE, BROTHERS (John and William) millers
Scott, Alexander, carpenter
SCOTT, ROBERT, grain dealer
SEAFORTH EXPOSITOR, Penton & Colborne, editors and proprietors
SEAFORTH HOUSE, James McBride, prop. (see adv)
Seatter, John, druggist and ins. agt., exch. broker
SEEGMILLER, FREDERICK, oat and barley mill
Shannon & Sparling (Thos. & G. W.) cabinet factory
Sharp, R. L., proprietor Sharp's Hotel
SHEARSON, W. A. & CO., millers
SILLS, D. L., produce merchant and insurance agt.
Simons, R. H., painter
Smith, John, wagon maker
Smith, U. R., M.D.
Spragge, H., shoemaker
Sproat, George, farmer
Stark, Samuel, leather dealer
St. John, James, brick manufacturer
STEPHENS, THOMAS, grain merchant, (see adv)
Stewart, Alexander, blacksmith and wagon maker
STRONG, ALONZO, livery and sale stables
Tait, R. P., harness maker
Tennison, David, carpenter
Tracy, Robert, M.D.
Trott, S., cooper
Vanston, James, lumber dealer
Veal, Frederick, grocer
Walsh, James, hotel keeper
Watkinson, A., painter
Watson, C. W., leather dealer
Watson, W. N., insurance agent
Welsh, James, carpenter
Whiting, E., tinsmith
Williamson, G., blacksmith and wagon maker
Williamson, Rev. S. (Methodist Episcopal)
Wilson, Alexander, lime manufacturer
Wilson, D. D., produce dealer
Zapfe & McCallum, (A. and John), foundry

Sebringville.—A Village in the Townships of Ellice and Downie, County Perth, 4½ miles distant from Stratford, the County Town, and 93 from Toronto. The Buffalo and Lake Huron Railway passes within a quarter of a mile of the village. The water privileges are excellent, and several factories are in course of erection. Daily mails. Population 350.

Alles, Rev. P. (Evangelical)
Armstrong, J., farmer
Barthel, J. T., merchant tailor
BENNETT, J., Postmaster and general merchant
Boas, M. & Co., nurserymen
Boeker, L., farmer
Bowes & Sanderson, patent pump manufacturers
Durst, J., carpenter
Eby, A., M.B.
Elder, Miss Jane, teacher
Goettler, A., J.P., proprietor steam flour mill
Goetz, Andrew, attorney-at-law
Goetz, J., nurseryman
Gourlay, A., sen., farmer
Heist, C., cabinet maker and prop. planing mill
Hengerer, Rev. J. A. (Evangelical Lutheran)
Hill, Brothers, proprietor steam flour mill and carriage maker
Hoffman, J. R., general merchant
Inman, J., cabinet maker
King, J. G., agent B. & L.H.R.
Klien, J., farmer
Koch, G., saddler
Koch, J., blacksmith
Laugenbash, Frank, harness maker
Lebing, D., lumber dealer
Lensemmier, J., carriage and wagon maker
Menning, F. L., vinegar works
Mortz, J., boots and shoes
Moritz, J. T., tanner
Pearson, J., farmer
Pigeon, P., hotel proprietor
Rowley, P., farmer
Rohfrietch, P., carpenter
Rohfrietch, Theobold, carpenter
Rohfrietch, T., prop. hotel, builder and contractor
Scarth, Brothers, general merchants
Scarth, H., farmer
Scarth, J., grocer
Scheke, A., merchant tailor
Sebring, John, farmer
Smith, Ernst, leather dealer
Studer, H., brewer
Woods, George, butcher
Yauch, C., general merchant, jeweler & hotel keeper

Scotland.—*(See Villages too late for regular insertion, at the end of this work.)*

Seeley's Bay.—A Village in the Townships of Leeds and Lansdown, Counties of Leeds and Grenville, 36 miles from Brockville, the County Town, and 200 from Toronto. Stage to Kingston, fare 75 cents. Improved land averages $50 per acre. Population 250.

Anglin, Jane, milliner
Beebe, Guy, blacksmith
Campbell, Hugh, farmer
Chapman, John, J.P., farmer
Church, Albert, blacksmith
COLEMAN, WILLIAM, Postmaster
Colinson, David, farmer
Ferguson, William, teacher
Gilbert, Albert, farmer
Gilbert, Edward, carpenter and grocer
Gilbert, John, carpenter
Gilbert, William, carriage, wagon maker and carpenter
Gray, Dr., physician and surgeon
Harkins, Samuel, shingle maker
Hussey, Robert, carpenter
King, John, carpenter
Molton, James, J.P.
Neddo, E., butcher
Palmer, William, cooper
Richardson, William, boots and shoes
Russell, T. H., livery
Saridge, Rev. William (Wesleyan)
Wellwood, William, painter
Wright, John, hotel keeper

Selkirk.—A Village in the Township of Walpole, County Haldimand, 12 miles from Cayuga, the County Town, and 70 from Toronto. Stage to Dunnville, fare 75c. Average price of improved land $25 per acre. Money Order office. Population 50.

Baxter, Lewis, steam flour mill proprietor
Boecker, N., tailor
Boyer, Joseph, boots and shoes
Brett, Charles, blacksmith
Clark, George, watches and jewelry
Conschofter, August, cabinet maker
Crawford, Joseph, blacksmith
Dell, Levi, painter
Fry, J., M.D.
Gadsby, Amos, carriage and wagon maker
Graham, Mrs., proprietor Travelers' Home
Harrison, T. T. S., M.D.
Holmes, William, farmer
Hoover, Jesse, V., J.P.
Horst, S., lime dealer and stone mason
Kent, Henry, general merchant
Kent, James, jun., general merchant
Kinsely, H., proprietor Union Hotel
Miller, Samuel, carpenter
Moody, Rev. M. H. (Primitive Methodist)
Richmond, Rev. Hugh (Baptist)
Shavalear, John, harness maker
Spears, Samuel J., auctioneer
Steinhoff, B. F., dentist
Stratton, George, livery stable proprietor and butcher
Troller, Henry, tailor
WILKIE, JAMES, Postmaster
Wilson, John, stoves and tinware
Winyard, R. J., general merchant
Wood, William S., teacher
Yager, L., carpenter
Yocum, W. H., blacksmith

Selby.—A Village in the Township of Richmond, County Lenox, 4 miles from Napanee, the County Town. Population 125.

Baker, R., farmer
Bride, Rev. William (Wesleyan)
Chisholm, Rev. F. (Church of England)
McKim, John, farmer
Rose, James, farmer
Rose, William, farmer
Russell, A., teacher
WARTMAN, DAVID, Postmaster

Selton.—A Post Village in the Township of Howard, County Kent, 169 miles from Toronto. Stages from Morpeth to Thamesville pass through the Village. Average price of land $25 per acre. Population 50.

Colby, Philander, gunsmith
Dick, Alexander, farmer
Ferguson & Campbell, lumber dealers
Gillis, Duncan, hotel keeper
Jenks, Edward, farmer
Kennedy, George, farmer
Latimer, U., insurance agent
Latimer, U. H., farmer
Latimer, William, J.P.
Lawton, S., broom manufacturer
McKay, Alexander, farmer
Mills, Nathaniel, teacher
Ogletree, Rev. H. (Methodist Episcopal)
Orme, Rev. J. (N. C. Methodist)
Reed, William, farmer
Robinson, Arthur, farmer
ROBINSON, JAMES, Postmaster, gen. merchant
Smith, David, shingle maker

Selwyn.—A Post Village in the Township of Smith, County Peterboro', 12 miles from Peterboro', the County Town, and 120 from Toronto. Average price of land $40 per acre. Population 50.

Baker, Samuel, farmer
Bell, James, general merchant
Bell, William, farmer
Bluet, Josias, farmer
Davis, John, cooper
Gibbons, James, blacksmith
Isbister, John, blacksmith
Jones, Rev. C. E. (Methodist)
McDougall, Thomas, teacher
McGrath, Patrick, carpenter
McIlmoyle, Nathan, farmer
McIlmoyle, William, carpenter
McKee, Andrew, farmer
McKee, William, farmer
Manning, Samuel, farmer
Middleton, John J., teacher
Moore, John, J.P.
Morrison, Peter, carpenter
Northy, James, farmer
Northy, John, farmer
NORTHEY, RICHARD, Postmaster, gen. merchant and hotel keeper
Northy, William, farmer
Roberts, Rev. E. (Baptist)
Sanderson, Edward, farmer
Sanderson, Francis, farmer
Thom, Rev. J. (Roman Catholic)

Seneca (see Caledonia).—A Post Village in the Township of Seneca, County Haldimand. Money Order Office and Savings Bank.

Severn Bridge.—A Village on the River Severn, in the Township of Morrison, County Simcoe, about 42 miles from Barrie, the County Town, 12 from Washago, the head of navigation, 22 from Bracebridge, and 11 from Muskoka Falls. The Village is situated on the Severn River and Muskoka Colonization Road. Steamers from Gravenhurst, 11 miles to Bracebridge. The government lands north of this point are very fertile, and are offered at one dollar per acre. Mill sites are numerous and timber abundant. Population 10C.

Bayley, James I., farmer
Blackaby, Richard, farmer
Davis, Moses, carpenter
Fellows, Isaac, carpenter
JACKSON, JAMES H., Postmaster & gen. mercht.
McKenzie, Charles, proprietor hotel
Morden, James, cabinet maker
Wasdel, Joseph, farmer

Shamrock.—A Post-office in the Township of Admaston, County Renfrew.

GOWAN, P., Postmaster.

Shanick.—A Post-office in the Township of Marmora, County Hastings.

BAILEY, JAMES, Postmaster.

Shakspeare.—A Village and Station of the Grand Trunk Railway, in the Township of North Easthope, County Perth, 8 miles from Stratford, the County Town; 50 from Hamilton and 82 from Toronto. Money Order Office. Stages to Hamburgh and Nithburg. Population 600.

Battram, B. S., plow maker
BROWN. GEORGE, Postmaster, Clerk Div. Court, com. in B.R. and conveyancer
Brown, M., grocer
Campbell, J. S., mason
Cairncross. James, cabinet factory
Cairncross & Offord, general merchants
Clapperton, William, blacksmith
Collin, J. A., shoemaker
Donald, James hotel keeper
Donaldson, F. W., carpenter
Drummond, Rev. A. G., (Canada Presbyterian)
Eiler, John, tinsmith
Flynn, Richard, hotel keeper
Gelt, F., shoemaker
Grosch, C. H., general merchant
Holwell, Thomas, tailor
Kleinkecht, A., prop. steam tannery
Lehman, Charles, pump maker
Leslie, Alexander, teacher
Lyall, John, butcher
Milne, Rev. Walter, (Baptist)
Minchin, George, carriage maker and blacksmith
Mippan, Alexander, drover
Muter, P. J., M.D
O'Rorke, John, drover
Ralley, Rev. W. B., (Church of England)
Rattelbron, C., shoemaker
Scott, Alexander, general merchant
Trow, James, J.P., M.P.P., com. in B.R., conveyancer

Shanly.—A Post-office in the Township of Edwardsburgh, County Grenville.

CLARK, WILLIAM, Postmaster.

Shannonville.—A Village in the Township of Tyendinaga, County Hastings, 9 miles from Belleville, the County Town, and 120 from Toronto. It is a station on the Grand Trunk Railway. Money Order Office. Population 750.

Anderson, Rev. A. H., (Episcopal Methodist)
Appleby, N. S., prop. flouring mill
Beckwith, Henry H., wagon maker
Beckwith, M., proprietor shingle mill
Blighe, W. H., teacher
Boulton, Alexander, carpenter
Bowen, William, carpenter
Clark, Chester E., boots and shoes
Clanson, David, cooper
Channonhouse, Thomas, M.D.
Craig, James D., boots and shoes
Crampton, Thomas, tailor and grocer
Creeper, Thomas, boots and shoes
Demill, Daniel N., tinsmith
Dornan, James, cooper
Doreen, John, proprietor Dundas Hotel
Doxsee, George A., wagon maker
Earle, George R., farmer
Earle, Thomas, proprietor flouring mill
Earle, William A., blacksmith
Easton, Joseph, blacksmith
Embury, Andrew, carpenter
Garrison, Richard, carpenter
Geddes, James, farmer
Gonsolus, S., proprietor Commercial Hotel
HOLDEN, HIRAM, J.P., Postmaster & gen. mercht
Jeffers, W. C., M.D.
Jenkins, William, tanner and dealer in boots and shoes
Kennedy, William, cooper
Lazier Brothers, proprietors flouring mill
Lazier, Richard L., farmer
Leroy, Charles, blacksmith
Lewen, Rev. William (Church of England)
Little, Joseph, butcher
Lyons, Richard, carpenter
McCance, James, general merchant
Meyers, Herman, butcher
Hunnelly, Mary, grocer
Pearsall, Amos, farmer
Pearsall, James, grocer and painter
Pegan, Robert, founder
Pegan, Robert F., J.P., cabinet maker and proprietor planing mill
Randall, A. B., wagon maker
Redner, Horace, M.D., druggist
Reed, Joseph, butcher
Roberts, John H., general merchant
Robinson, Charles, general merchant
Robinson, Rev. Robert (Wesleyan)
Roblin, Nathan, wagon maker
Roblin, William, blacksmith
Shaw, S. R., proprietor Albion Hotel
Smith, B. C., grocer
Smith, David, J.P., farmer
Smith, Samuel, agent G. T. R.
Sweetnam, William, saddler
Vallean, Peter, baker
Wallbridge, Francis, lumber dealer
Williams, Peter, saddler
Wright, George C., teacher
Young, John, carpenter
Young, Lewis, proprietor Farmer's Hotel

Shanty Bay.—A Post Office in the Township of Oro, County Simcoe.

HEARD, WILLIAM, Postmaster.

Sharon.—A Village in the Township of East Gwillimbury, County York, 35 miles from Toronto, and 4 from Newmarket Station, Northern Railway. Improved land averages $50 per acre. Money Order Office. Population 400.

Beller, Ira, painter
Brammar, Edward, blacksmith
Brammar, Joseph, proprietor saw mill
Cavanagh, James, carpenter
Collins, J. J., teacher
Doan, E., farmer
Doan, George, farmer
Doan, Judah, farmer
EDMAND, J. W., general merchant
Edmand, W. R., farmer
Gollinger, R., carriage and wagon maker
Graham, Charles, L.D.S.
Haines, C., farmer
Hamilton, Rev. C. (Wesleyan Methodist)
Helmer, Mrs., milliner
Hogaboom, J. C., farmer
Kays, John, hotel keeper
Kester, George, boots and shoes
Lundy, Judah, farmer
Lundy, Reuben, proprietor flouring mill
McClure, Rev. W. (N. C. Methodist)
Malloy, W., auctioneer
Morris, J., tinsmith
Morris, R., harness maker
Noble, H., M.D.
Proctor, Samuel, carpenter
Robinson, C., general merchant
Rowen, William, carriage maker
Selby, William, farmer
Smith, G. P., general merchant
STOKES, JOHN T., Postmaster, architect, builder
Terry, J., J.P.
Watson, H., prop. Mansion House
Willows, J., farmer
Willson, H., farmer
Willson & Graham, general merchants
Willson, John D., farmer

Sharpton.—A Village in the Township of Kingston, County Frontenac, 11 miles from Kingston and 144 from Toronto. Population 50.

Babcock, D., farmer
Bell, John, sen., J.P., farmer
Bell, John, jr., farmer
Bell, William, farmer
Gordon, James, farmer
Harker, Thomas, farmer
Harker, William, farmer
McKECHNIE, ROBERT, Postmaster, farmer
McRae, D., farmer
Raymond, Caleb, J.P., farmer
Sharp, T., farmer
Vrobman, John, farmer
Wagner, Miss T., teacher
Wilson, William, farmer

Sheridan.—A Village in the Township of Trafalgar, County Halton, 15 miles from Milton, the County Town, and 20 from Toronto. Land in the vicinity averages $40 per acre. Daily mail. Population 150.

Bethune, Rev. C. J. (Church of England)
Brown, Rev. T. C. (Methodist Episcopal)
Brownridge, —, farmer
Edwards, Rev. Abel (Wesleyan)
Flynn, John, butcher
Flynn, John F., grocer
Harris, Arthur, farmer
Harris, Captain John, farmer
Hepburne, Miss, teacher
HILL, ERASTUS D., Postmaster and gen. mercht.
House, Miss, teacher
Howard, Rev. Thomas (Wesleyan)
Lawrence, Ferris, insurance agent
Lee, John, farmer
Long, George, boots and shoes
Long, John, carpenter and wagon maker
Oughtred, Stephen, blacksmith
Pollard, Joshua, J.P., insurance agent
Shane, Samuel, farmer
Shook, Conrad, farmer
Shunk, George, farmer
Skinner, John, farmer
Wilson, Richard, farmer

Shelburne.—A village in the township of Melancthon, County Grey, 55 miles from Owen Sound, the County Town, and 61 from Toronto, a stage runs to Brampton Station Grand Trunk Railway, 37 miles, fare $1·50 ; to Orangeville, 16 miles, $1·00 ; to Flesherton, 22 miles, $1; and to Horning's Mills, 7 miles, 37 cents. Average price of land $18. Money order office. Daily Mail. Population 70.

Carr, Robert, farmer
Caslor, Robert W., blacksmith
Chartres, George, farmer
Coleman, John, farmer
Cummings, John, shingle maker
Gabriel, Matthew, farmer
Gillespy, John, farmer
Hains, William, farmer
Hall, William, sen., J.P., farmer
Hall, William, jun., farmer
Jelly, Andrew, farmer
Jelly, Simon, stock dealer
JELLY, WILLIAM, Postmaster, proprietor British Canadian Hotel
Latta, Archibald, farmer
Latta, Mrs., manufacturer of woolen goods
McFadden, Angus, shoemaker
McKaig, George, blacksmith
McKaig, Mrs., milliner
Madill, William, farmer
Merkly, George, carpenter
Mooney, Robert, teacher
Pashak, Joseph, farmer
Parkinson, Adam, general merchant
Petigrew, John, farmer
Silks, Henry, farmer
Silks, Jacob, farmer
Timberry, George, farmer
Trible, John, farmer
Westercot, George, proprietor brick yard

Sheffield.—A Village in the Township of Beverly, County Wentworth, 19 miles from Hamilton, the County Town, 6 from Galt and 55 from Toronto. Average price of land $40 per acre. Population 140

Abbs, Frederick, tailor
Armstrong, Benjamin, farmer
Armstrong, Joseph, teacher
Benner, Hunson, carpenter
BOND, EDWIN, Postmaster, general merchant
Chapman, George, boot and shoe and hide and leather dealer
Crawford, John S., general agent
Crowder, Rev. J. (United Brethren)
Dania, David, & Son, blacksmiths
Drury, James, proprietor Sheffield House
Faulkner, A. W., grocer
Gomock, Alexander, patent right agent
Harrison, Rev. H., (Church of England)
Hemis, Rev. James, (Wesleyan)
Lloyd, Griffith, farmer and stock dealer
Lloyd, John, grocer
LUNDY, F. B., M.D.
Main, D. W., farmer
Middlemess, Robert, proprietor planing mill
Mudge, B. H.. insurance agent
Munson, Lent, farmer
Rentoul, David, sen. farmer
Rentoul, David, wagon maker
Richards, Joseph, farmer
Ricker, Christopher, farmer
Shannon, Jacob, butcher
Willard, John, painter
Will, E., farmer

Sheldon.—A Village in the Township of Adjala, County Simcoe, 43 miles from Barrie, the County Town, and 50 from Toronto. Population 50.

Beaty Thomas, saw mill proprietor
Bullock, George, farmer
Ewen, Samuel, farmer
Henderson, James, blacksmith
Hetherington, James, blacksmith
Hetherington, William, farmer
McCabe. J., farmer
Maguire, William, farmer
Newall, John, proprietor saw mill
Parker, George, saw mill owner and farmer
Webb, J., farmer
WEBSTER, M., Postmaster and general merchant
Young, Mrs., proprietress hotel

Sherkston.—*(See Villages too late for regular insertion at the end of this work).*

Shetland.—A Post Office in the Township of Euphemia, County Lambton.
DREW, JOHN, Postmaster.

Shipley.—A Post Office in the Township of Wallace, County Perth.

Allison, John, farmer
Booth, Robert, teacher
BRISTOW, EDWARD, Postmaster
Dupernelle, Rev. F. (Lutheran)
Gardiner, John, farmer
Hensworth, Albert, farmer, sash and blind factor
Hensworth, C. M., township clerk and land agent
Hensworth, Elias, farmer
Hensworth, M. T., farmer
Hensworth, William, farmer
Miller, Rev. A. E. (Church of England)
Piggot, James, farmer
Sharick, Rev. David (Menonite)
Shepherd, Rev. William W. (Wesleyan)
Strong, Richard, farmer
Wilson, Robert, farmer

Shrigley.—A Village in the Township of Melancthon, County Grey.
AUGUST, WILLIAM, Postmaster.

Sillsville.—A Post Office in the Township of S. Fredericksburg, County Lennox, 10 miles from Napanee, the County Town, and 169 from Toronto,

Clute, David A., farmer
Donney, Thomas, farmer
Pringle, Andrew, farmer
SILLS, DONOVAN, Postmaster
Sills, G. B., farmer

Silver Creek.—A Post Village in the Township of Esquesing, County Halton.
DEAN, JOHN, Postmaster.

Silvershoe.—*(See Villages too late for regular insertion, at the end of this work.)*

Silver Hill.—A Post Office in the Township of Charlotteville, County Norfolk, 11 miles from Simcoe, the County Town, and 100 from Toronto.

COLE, MRS. ELIZABETH, Postmistress
Holiday, David, blacksmith
Smith, William, teacher

Simcoe.—The County Town of Norfolk is pleasantly situated on the River Lynn, in the Township of Woodhouse. It is distant 25 miles from Brantford, by Stage, fare $1.25; from Paris Station, Great Western Railway, 28 miles, fare $1.25; from Hamilton, 40 miles, fare $3.00; to Port Rowan, fare $1.25. The surrounding country is in a high state of cultivation and furnishes large quantities of wheat and other grains. Improved lands are worth from $40 to $125 per acre. The River furnishes excellent water privileges and capitalists would find this a good spot for manufacturing. The Gore and Montreal Banks have each established agencies here. Money Order Office and Savings bank. Population 2100.

Adams, George, cooper
Alexander, John, saloon
Algeo, David, leather dealer
American Express Co., A. J. Donly, agent
Anderson James, boots and shoes
Andrews, Miss, milliner
Ansley, J. H., barrister, &c.
Ausborne, Mrs. M. A., fancy goods
Austin, Jonathan, druggist
Austin & Scott, carriage and wagon makers
BANK OF MONTREAL, Buchanan, —, manager
Battersby, George, proprietor Suffolk House
Beemer, W. H., carriage and wagon maker
Bowlby, Hiram, farmer
BRITISH CANADIAN (Wednesday) William Kelly, editor and proprietor
Brooks & Son, flax millers
Brown, Mark, cooper
Brown, M. C., J.P., harness maker and saddler
Brown & Son, woolen manufacturers
Buchanan, —, manager, Bank of Montreal
Brethour, H. W., dry goods
Burton, Mrs. T, baker
CAMPBELL, DUNCAN, agent Gore Bank
Carnochan, Misses, milliners
Carpenter, John B., farmer
Carr, Mrs., teacher
Carter, Henry, boots and shoes
Cattle, John, leather dealer
Chadwick & Ansley, stoves and tinware
Chadwick, James T., prop. livery stable
Church, Mrs., milliner
Clark, John, M.D
Clouse, Israel, saloon keeper
Coates, Joseph, carriage and wagon maker
Collins, John, cabinet maker
Cook, Asa, stoves and tinware
Courtland, H. N., asst. principal Union School
Covernton, Charles, M.D
Craigie, Rev. W., B.A., (Free Church)
Culver, George, farmer
Culver, John M., farmer
Culver, Joseph, farmer
Curtis, John, insurance agent
Curtis, John, grocer
Darling, George L., watchmaker and jeweler
Dean, James, prop. Shepherd's Hotel
Deedes, Edmund, sheriff
Donly, A. J., books, drugs, etc., official assignee
Douglass, Miss, ladies' academy
Dredge, George, proprietor Mansion House
Durward, Alexander, dry goods
Dyer, Miss, milliner
Ermatinger, James, county clerk
Falls & Tocher, general merchants
Finley, William
FOLEY, HON. M. H., barrister
FULLER, C. J. (Walker & Fuller), barrister, attorney-at-law, notary public, &c. (see adv.)
Galbraith, Robert, boots and shoes
Gallagher, P., boots and shoes
Gardner, Samuel, marble dealer
Gibbons, William, soap and candle manufacturer
GORE BANK, Duncan Campbell, agent
Grasette, Rev. E., M.A., rector (Church of England)
Groff, Henry, county treasurer, insurance agent
Hambridge, George, butcher
Hardy, H. A., county attorney and barrister
Hardy, Henry, barrister
Harmon, Misener & Kendall, architects
Harris, William, boots and shoes
Harrison, Miss, telegraph operator
Hart, A., livery proprietor
Hawley, Alexander, leather dealer
Hayes, James, M. D.
Heath, A., farmer
Heath & Widner, drovers
Hebblewhite, Thomas, hardware
Hodgson, R., tailor
Holmes, Hugh, general merchant
Hooker, William, prop. flouring mill
Hurd & Adams, carriage and wagon makers
Hunt, L. H., J.P., general agent
Hutton, R., painter
Ilton, William, butcher
JACKSON BROS., builders, sash and blind manufs. prop. planing mills, etc
Jackson, E., town treasurer
Jackson, James, painter
Jackson, R. P., barrister, &c
KELLY, WILLIAM, editor and prop *British Canadian*
Kendall, Misses, milliners and dressmakers
Kent, Edwin, brewer
Kirk, David, general merchant
Lamson, N., insurance and general agent
Landon, Z., farmer
Lansdell, Frederick F., grocer
Lear, Henry, watches and jewelry
Lee, W. E., barrister
Lewis James, barber
Livingstone, Rev. Martin, M.A., (Kirk)
Livingstone, R. T., township councilor, barrister, &c
Livingstone, William, town clerk
Long, Miss, milliner
Luscombe, Samuel, butcher
Lyons, Brothers, general merchants
Lyons, James A., general merchant
McCallum, John, tailor
McCool, John, carpenter and builder
McGill, Mrs., school teacher
McIntosh, B., teacher grammar school
McKay, — maltster
Mair, James, patent plow manufacturers

Marlatt, John
Marf, Oliver T., farmer
Mathar, E., & Son., tailors
Matthews, Daniel, county warden, farmer
Merrill, Amos A., general mercht. and lumber dealer
Millar, William, baker
Minett, Amos A., general merchant
Misener & Kendall (Harmon, Misener & Kendall), builders and contractors, planing mills, etc.
Moore, Robert, stoves and tinware
Mulholland, Miss, private school
MULKINS, HENRY, Postmaster
Murphy, John, & Son, auctioneers, insurance and general agents
Nevills, William, proprietor Nevills' Hotel
Nickerson, W. F., butcher
NORFOLK REFORMER (Thursday) Reuben Thoroughgood, editor and proprietor
Norris, John, baker
O'Shea, Rev. Father, (Roman Catholic)
Park, John J., woolen manufacturer
Parker, J., pound-keeper
Perry, J. E., groceries, wines, liquors, etc.
Pettit, Isaac, farmer
Pettit, William, brick maker
Pierce, John, carpenter and builder
Polly, A. Y., township councillor
POLLEY & MADDEN, founders and machinists
Pursell, Asa A., proprietor livery stable
Puzey, Thomas, farmer
Rapelje, C. P., Clerk County Court and Deputy Clerk Crown
RITCHIE, FORD & CO., general merchants, flouring millers and distillers
Roberts, William, groceries, wines and liquors
Robinson, J., butcher
Salmon, James, M.D.
Schiler, Charles, butcher
Scott, John, Township Councillor
Scott, Rev. Mr. (Baptist)
Sharpe, William, insurance agent
Smith, George, barber
Sovereign, Lemon B., fancy goods
Sovereign, Lemon G., general merchant and lumber dealer
Stanton, F. G.
Stanton, George, M.D.
Steele, Matthey, harness maker and saddler
Steinhoff, F., harness maker and saddler
Steinhoff, Finley, farmer
Steinhoff & McDowell, planing mills
Sullivan, John, boots and shoes
Sutton, Paul, tailor
Thompson, John & Walter, architects, sash and blind manufacturers and builders
Thompson, Steinhoff & McDowell, carpenters
THOROUGHGOOD, REUBEN, editor *Norfolk Reformer*
Tisdale, David, barrister
Tisdale, James M., auctioneer, insurance and general agent
Todd, James, cattle dealer
Townly, Thomas, tailor
Tune, Robert, baker
Wadsworth, W., M.A., principal union school
Wakefield, Rev. Mr. (Wesleyan Methodist)
Walker, D. M., barrister
WALKER & FULLER (D. M. Walker, C. J. Fuller), barristers (see adv.)
Walker, John J., gunsmith
Walsh, F. L., county registrar
Walsh, T. W., insurance agent
Waters, Mrs. (widow J.) baker
Watts, The Misses, milliners and dressmakers
Weatherly, Miss, dressmaker
Weatherly, J., tailor
Wells, Lyman, dentist
Wells, Miss, teacher
Wesley, Daniel, farmer
Weston, William, leather dealer
Wilkinson, Rev. Mr. (Episcopal Methodist)
Williamson, John, saloon and billiards
Wilson, Augustus
Wilson, James F. & Co., booksellers and druggists
WILSON, JOHN, M. D., Reeve of Simcoe Township
Wilson, William
Wood, Edward, farmer
Wood, T. D., gaoler
York, W., M. D.

Singhampton.—A Village in the Township of Nottawasaga, County Simcoe, 50 miles from Barrie, the County Town, and 108 from Toronto. Stages to Collingwood and Durham. Money order office Population 130.

Algco, James, shoemaker
Armstrong, Mrs., milliner
Bell, Angus, accountant, general agent
Chesnut, Alexander, wagon maker
Darrock, Sarah, teacher
Grant, David, J.P., carpenter
HAMILTON, JAMES, Postmaster, gen. merchant
Londrie, Eli, grocer
McIntyre, Alexander, general merchant
Middleton, W. J., proprietor Exchange Hotel
Pearson, William, proprietor flouring mill
Richmond, Mrs., milliner
Sing, J. K., lime and stone
Thornby, Thomas, M.D.

Skipness.—A Post Office in the Township of Amabel, County Bruce.
REID, DONALD, Postmaster.

Skye.—A small Post Village in the township of Kenyon, County Glengary. Stage to Lancaster Station, Grand Trunk Railway, 28 miles, fare $2. Average price of land, $8.50.

Campbell, John, farmer
Chisholm, John, farmer
Douglass, Robert, architect
Douglass, William J., painter
Macdonald, John and Charles, coopers
MACKENZIE, JAMES R., Postmaster, N. P., attorney-at-law and general agent
McCuaig, John, farmer
McDonald, Duncan, architect
McKenzie, Alexander, farmer
McLeod, Duncan, farmer
McLeod, Miss Mary, teacher
McMaster, John, architect

Sleswick.—A small Post Village in the Township of Caledon, County Peel, 20 miles from Brampton, the County Town, and 35 from Toronto. Stage from Malton to Mono Mills, via this Village, 22 miles, fare $1. Population 25.

Bible, John, J.P., farmer
Brown, John, J.P., farmer
Drummond, Peter, farmer
Evans, John, J.P., farmer
Evans, Richard J., hotel keeper and gen. merchant
Evans, Robert, farmer
Evans, Robert, teacher
Lindsay, James, farmer
Little, Thomas, farmer
Moffatt, John, farmer
Moffatt, William, farmer
Morgan, William, farmer

Sligo.—A Post Village in the Township of Caledon, County Peel, 13 miles from Brampton, the County Town, and 38 from Toronto. Stage to Brampton, fare 50c. Mails Daily. Population 50.

BELL, THOMAS, Postmaster, farmer
Bell, William, farmer
Nunn, Samuel, farmer
Smith, Miss, teacher
Stokes, William, miller and farmer

Smithfield.—A Village in the Township of Brighton, County Northumberland, 23 miles from Cobourg, the County Town and 105 from Toronto. The Grand Trunk Railway passes within 4 miles of the Village. Stage from Brighton to Picton, via Smithfield, 36 miles. Population 400.

Barber, James, general merchant
Bate, William, butcher
Clarke, James, blacksmith
Coulter, H., farmer
Dean, Homer, carpenter
Drury, William, prop. Renfrew flouring mill
Farley, William, farmer
Groff, Arnold, lime manuf
Ireland, James, farmer
Johnson, Henry, general merchant
Joy, Theodore, wagon maker and blacksmith
Lochlan, James, J.P., blacksmith
Marsh, A. H., teacher
Marsh, E., farmer
Marsh, S. E., lumber dealer
Miller, Archibald, cooper
Miller, Frank, proprietor brick yard
Moffatt, Thomas, shoemaker
Murray & Brighton, cheese manufacturers
Palmer, Wilson, proprietor Smithfield flouring mill
Phillips, A. M., teacher
Purdy, R., lumber dealer and farmer
Smith, Abijah, sen., grocer
SMITH, DRUMMOND, Postmaster
Smith, D., farmer
Smith, Mary, teacher
Smith, Robert, farmer
Vantassel, Henry, farmer
Washborne, Joseph, tailor
Watt, James, butcher
Watt, Reuben, farmer
Weller, Asa, shoemaker
White. John, farmer
White, Thomas, farmer
Young, Jacob, painter

Smith's Falls.—An incorporated Village situated on the Rideau Canal, in the Township of Elmsley, County Lanark, and a station of the Brockville and Ottawa Railroad; distant from Perth the County Town 12 miles, and from Toronto 250, from Ottawa and Kingston each 60 miles by canal. The Village contains several large manufacturing establishments, the water privileges being almost unlimited, and there are still great inducements for capitalists to invest. The celebrated agricultural works and stove foundry of Messrs. Frost & Wood are located here doing an extensive business, and employing a large number of hands. Money order office and Savings Bank. Population 1400.

Acton, Robert, general merchant
ANDERSON, W. J., M. D.
Armstrong, Walter, farmer
Arnold, H., farmer
Atcheson, James, M. D.
Bain, Rev. James (New Connexion)
Baird, Henry, carpenter
Ballantyne, F., farmer
Ballantyne, J., farmer
Barnes, Rev. S. M., (New Connexion)
Bartlett, Russell, cabinet maker
Bourke, Julia, teacher
Bourke, Thomas, brewer
Boyd, Abram, grocer
Boyd, A., sash factory
Boyd, Mrs., milliner and fancy goods
Bradley, John F., photographer
Brennan, John, boots and shoes
Brown, Archibald, farmer
Brown, Mrs., milliner
Burritt, W. H., M.D.
Butler, Ira B., watchmaker
Campbell, Daniel, farmer
Carley, William, butcher
Carnduff, Robert, farmer
Carroll, Michael, hotel keeper
Casey, B., cooper
Caswell, James W., carriage maker
Chalmers & Barnes, blacksmith
Chalmers, Henry, blacksmith
Chambers, J. McGill, notary public
Chambers, J. A., M.D.
Chambers, James A., grocer
Chambers, J. McGill, notary public
Chevrefils, Victor, general merchant
Coleman, Rev. F. (Wesleyan)
Copeland, R. W., grocer
Cornell, George A., grocer

Church. Jeremiah, farmer
Clark, Alexander, general merchant
Clark, Hugh, farmer
Clark, Peter, farmer
Clune, Rev. Michael, (Roman Catholic)
Code, Stephen, carriage maker
Code, William, blacksmith
Coleman, Rev. Francis, (Wesleyan)
Collins, Rufus S., axe maker
Coombs, Joseph, druggist
Corbett, James, mail contractor
Cornell, George A., general merchant
Cossitt & Brother, (G. M. and Newton), founders and machinists
Craine, John, painter
Davis, Elias, farmer
Davis, John, farmer
Davis, Levi, blacksmith
Dodds, John, carpenter
Donohoe, Jeremiah, general merchant
Donovan, Rev. Joshua (Baptist)
Edgar, William, trader
Edmonds, Elisha, farmer
Edmonds, Thomas, farmer
Ferguson & Gilroy (Duncan A. & William) general merchants
Foster, George, tailor
Foster, James, farmer
FROST & WOOD (Francis T. Wood, Charles B. Frost and Alexander Wood), founders and machinists, general merchants and proprietors Pike's Falls saw mills (see adv)
Garrett, John, cooper
Garrett, Samuel, cooper
Garvin, Martin, carriage maker
Gilroy, Edward, butcher
Gilroy, William, general merchant
Goodfellow, Archibald, carpenter
Gould, James H. and Jason, millers
Graham, Robert, farmer
Graham, William, farmer
Guthrie, C., grocer
Guthrie, James C., shoemaker
Harper R., conveyancer and general agent
Harris, James, saddler
Hazeltine, Andrew, trader
Healy, Peter, general merchant
Healy, Phillip, painter
Hourigan, James, farmer
HOURIGAN, JOHN, proprietor Hourigan House
HOURIGAN HOUSE, John Hourigan, proprietor
Hyslop, John, boots and shoes
Jacob, Thomas, tannery
Jarvis, William H., cabinet maker and insurance agt
Johnson, William, farmer
KEITH, WILLIAM M. editor *Smith's Falls Review*, books and stationery
Kelly, Thomas, boots and shoes
KETCHUM, STEPHEN, tanner and currier (see adv)
Kirkwood, John, boots and shoes
Landon, Henry, insurance agent
Lewis, Robert, blacksmith
Loucks, David, farmer
Loucks, John, farmer
McDonald, George, blacksmith
McDonald, William, farmer
McEnroe, James, saloon
McGillivray, John, general merchant
McGillivray, William, farmer
McGregor, Duncan, farmer
McGregor, John, farmer
McKenzie, Hugh, carpenter
McNulty, Hugh, carpenter
Maitland, Peter, farmer
Midgley, J., tinsmith
Midgley, W. H., tinsmith
Moag, Mary, teacher
Moag, Stewart, teacher
Morgan & Washburn, general merchants
Morton, Thomas, druggist
Mylne, Rev. S. (Presbyterian)
Niblock, James, boots and shoes
O'Neill, Bartholemew, blacksmith
Percy, Thomas, merchant tailor
Pratt, John. baker
Publow, John, carpenter
Raines, T. W., dentist
Rath, James, general merchant
Raymond, T., dyer
Read, E. B., tinsmith
Robinson, James, tailor
Ross, Hugh
Rutherford, George, farmer
SHAW, JAMES, Postmaster, general merchant and insurance agent
Shepherd, William, cabinetmaker
Shields, Charles, general merchant
Shields, James, general merchant
Shields, John, farmer
Shields, Peter
Shields, Russell, farmer
Sinnott, J., tailor
Sinnott, William, tailor
SMITH'S FALLS FOUNDRY AND AGRICULTURAL WORKS, Frost & Wood, proprietors (see adv)
Smith, David, shingle maker
Smith, John, carpenter
Splane, John, carriage maker
Sparham, William H., station master, agent Canadian Express Co.
St. Denis, Joseph, butcher
Story, Gilbert, farmer
Taylor, George, saddler
Templeton, Allen, proprietor tannery
Tenny, Daniel, farmer
Trott, James, carriage maker
Tweedy, Thomas, innkeeper
Tyker, William, teacher
Vandusen, Benjamin, carpenter
Walker & Co., woolen factors
Wall, Michael, butcher
WARD, ABEL R., J.P., proprietor grist, carding and saw mills
WARD, GEORGE A., farmer
Ward, James, grocer
Ward, J. A., stave and shingle maker
Ward, Truman R., proprietor flour mill
WARD, WILLIAM M. & BRO. (William M. and John B.) proprietors flour, saw and carding mills (see adv)
Watkins, Henry, barber
Webster, Asa, farmer
White, Rev. G. W. (Church of England)
White, John, boots and shoes
Whitson, Andrew, shingle manufacturer
WILLIAMSON, WILLIAM, stave factory (see adv.)
Williscraft, John, watchmaker

Southampton Village.—(See Saugeen Post Office.)

Smithville.—A Post Village in the Township of Grimsby, County Lincoln, 19 miles from St. Catherines, the County Town, and from Grimsby Station on Great Western Railway, 8 miles per stage. Average price of land in vicinity, improved $35, unimproved $30 per acre. Daily mail. Money order office. Population 500.

Adskins, Edward, butcher
Alcock, Robert, boots and shoes
Alway, J. W., M.D.
Bates, J. S., hotel proprietor
Berry, Rev. F. (Wesleyan)
Brant, George, general merchant, furniture dealer and insurance agent
Breheny, Edward, boots and shoes
Buckbee, W. P., hotel proprietor
Cooper, William, hotel proprietor and butcher
Copeland, George, carriage and wagon maker
Cruickshank, William, teacher
Curran, Mrs. M., grocer
Draper, Rev. E. (Episcopal Methodist)
Edmonds, John, proprietor flouring mill
Graves, J. J., general merchant
Griffin, J. W., grocer
Griffin, R. C., J.P.
Hare, W. V., grocer
Knott, Rev. William (Universalist)
Laboureau, Rev. T. (Roman Catholic)
Lacey, A. H., dentist
Lally, Martin, general merchant
Lounsbury, Robert, cooper
McAlister, Catherine, teacher
McAlister, Grace, teacher
McLean, Sarah, boot and shoe dealer
McPherson, G. D., M.D.
Middleton, James T., general merchant
Morgan, Richard, carpenter
Morse, M. J., J.P.
Murgatroyd, R. & M., general merchants
Murray, Charles, cooper
Newton, F. E., boots and shoes
Rool, Andrew, cabinet maker
Russ, William, founder and machinist
Tanner, John, harness maker
Teeter, Solomon, carpenter
Telfer, W. W., carpenter
THOMPSON, ROBERT, J.P., Postmaster and insurance agent
Walker, Thomas, cooper
Wardell, J. S., carriage maker
Williams, Nathan, butcher

Sombra.—A Village in the Township of Sombra, County Lambton, 20 miles distant from Sarnia, the County Town. Land averages from $30 to $50 per acre. Daily mail. Money order office. Population 200.

Bourton, Rev. Thomas, (Episcopal Methodist)
Brock, William, carpenter
Burnham, M. L., cabinet maker
CATTANACH, PETER, Postmaster, farmer
Cornwall, H., shoemaker
Dawson, James, J. P., farmer
Dawson, J. & D., general merchants
Gemmill, Duncan, general merchant
Hicks, Rev. William, (Wesleyan)
Hughes, Henry, carpenter
Kerby, Aaron S., cabinet maker
Kerby, N., auctioneer
Miller, James, carpenter
Newcomb, James, shingle maker
Roberts, Joshua, shingle maker
Sawesberry, James, butcher
Smith, Andrew, general merchant
Watson, Arthur W., J. P., farmer
Whitley, Samuel, grocer and proprietor hotel

Sonya.—A post office in the Township of Brock, County Ontario, 26 miles from Whitby the County Town, and about 55 from Toronto. Stage to Oshawa 26 miles, fare $1.50. Land averages $40 per acre. Population 40.

Currie, Rev. Archibald, (Canada Presbyterian)
HARPER, LEWIS, Postmaster, general merchant
McLean, Hugh, carpenter
McLean, Miss, milliner
McCluston, N., M.D.

South Cayuga.—Commonly called Fry's Corners, is situated in the Township of South Cayuga, County Haldimand, 12 miles from Cayuga, the County Town, and about 80 from Toronto. Stages to Dunville, 6 miles, fare 25 cents; and to Selkirk, 11 miles, fare 50 cents. Daily Mail. Population 40.

Albright, Samel, farmer
Beck, Frederick L., farmer
Culp, Rev. Jacob (Menonite)
Cook, Robert, farmer
Cook, William, J.P., farmer
Fry, Elias, carriage and wagon maker
FRY, ISAAC, Postmaster, J.P., general merchant
Fry, Miss Matilda, teacher
High, Rev. Abraham (Menonite)
Honsberger, Henry, farmer
Honsberger, Valentine, J.P.
Nash, Abraham, J.P., farmer
Overholt, Isaac, farmer
Widrich, John, boots and shoes

South Douro.—A Post Office in the Township of Douro, County Peterboro', 9 miles from Peterboro', the County Town. Population about 20.

HANNAHAN, THOMAS, Postmaster.

South Elmsley.—A Post Village in the Township of South Elmsley, County Leeds, 28 miles from Brockville, the County Town, and about 200 from Toronto; it is within 6¼ miles of a Station on the Brockville and Ottawa Railway. Daily Mail. Population 100.

Campbell, Miss A. B., teacher
Carroll, Matthew, lime and stone dealer
Code, Joseph, carriage and wagon maker
Coleman, Rev. —, (Wesleyan)
Covell, A. W., shingle maker
Duffield, John, farmer
Duffield, Thomas, boots and shoes
GAROM, WILLIAM, Postmaster, general merchant
Green, Miss A., milliner
Lemott, James, tailor
Loles, Mrs. William, grocer
McKinney, William, farmer
Marshall, John, farmer
Miller, Rev. William, (Presbyterian)
Newman, W. K., boots and shoes
O'Reilly, Thomas, hotel proprietor and auctioneer
Patterson, James, farmer
Rutherford, George, farmer
Salmons, Thomas, farmer
Shields, James, dry goods
Simpson, Peter, flour mill proprietor
Tetlock, Henry, hotel proprietor
Vickery, L., farmer
Weeks, E. F., J.P., fire insurance agent
White, Rev. G. W., (Church of England)
Willis, Joseph, dry goods, books, etc.

South Dummer.—*(See Villages too late for regular insertion, at the end of this work.)*

South Finch.—A post village in the township of Finch, County Stormont, 27 miles distant from Cornwall, the County Town and 14 from Dickinson's Landing, Station Grand Trunk Railway, fare per stage 75 cents. Daily Mail. Population 50.

Cameron, Rev. Donald (Presbyterian)
Campbell, Duncan, tailor
Duffy, Edward, gunsmith
Empey, Philip, farmer
Irvin, David, farmer
Lamont, Rev. Hugh (Presbyterian)
Link, John, hotel keeper
McKay, James, farmer
McLeod, Angus, farmer
McLeod, Miss Mary, teacher
McMILLAN, DUNCAN G., Postmaster, gen. mer
McMillan, John R., J.P
Munro, George, J.P
Munro, John C., M.D
Park, Hugh, farmer
Pitts, Robert, general merchant

South Gloucester.—A Post-office in the Township of Osgoode, County Russell.

STANLEY, THOMAS, Postmaster.

South Gower.—A Post-office in the Township of South Gower, County Grenville.

WALLACE, JAMES, Postmaster.

South Lake.—A Post-office in the Township of Leeds, County Leeds, 40 miles from Brockville, the County Town, and 180 from Toronto.

Anderson, Robert, councillor
Birmingham, James
BIRMINGHAM, WILLIAM, Postmaster
Birmingham, William, jr., teacher
Carroll, Rev. John, (Church of England)
Darragh, Miss Laura, teacher
Johnson, David, teacher
Trenamon, John, telegraph operator

South March.—A Post Village in the Township of March, County Carleton, 2 miles distant from the Ottawa River, and 15 from Ottawa City, per stage, fare $1. Improved lands average $20 per acre. Population 500.

Armstrong, James, farmer
Armstrong, John, general merchant
Berrey, W. H., brewer
Cutlon, James, shoemaker
Easking, W., farmer
Gamsford, Hugh, farmer
Gow, Alexander, tailor
Graham, E., saddler
Holmes, J., J.P., hotel keeper
Huckel, B., hotel keeper
Kirvin, William, general merchant
McAdams, John, teacher
McMurtry, David, general merchant
May, Rev. John (Church of England)
Moley Rev. — (Roman Catholic)
Monk, G. W., farmer
Monk, G. W., insurance agent
Morgan, H., farmer
Richardson, J. W., J.P.
Riddell, O., farmer
SCISSON, SAMUEL, Postmaster
Smith, J., hotel keeper
Sprool, Thomas, wagon maker
Younghusband, John, farmer
Younghusband, Nicholas, shoemaker
Younghusband, Nicholas, tanner

South Middleton.—A Post Office in the Township of Middleton, County Norfolk. Improved land averages $14 per acre.

Armstrong, Cornelius, J.P.
Beecraft, David, blacksmith
Boyle, William, blacksmith
Bristow, John carpenter
Burwash, Rev. N. S. (Wesleyan)
Butler, P., proprietor steam shingle mill
Canneillor, T., farmer
Cronkright, Peter, lime and stone
Fisher, James, farmer
Gilbert, C. W. M., supt. Wesleyan church
Holtby, Mathias, supt. Wesleyan church
Johnson, W. B., proprietor steam shingle mill
McKim, Philip, farmer
McKIM, ROBERT, Postmaster and farmer
McKinly, John, clothier
Millar, Rev. — (Episcopal Methodist)
Murphy, Alexander, farmer
Potter, E. H., proprietor steam saw mill
Storey, Rev. H. (Methodist Episcopal)
Wallace, James, farmer
Wilson, John, farmer
Wilson, Samuel, farmer

South Monaghan.—A small Post Village in the Township of South Monaghan, County Northumberland, 20 miles from Cobourg, the County Town, and 80 from Toronto. Improved land averages $40 per acre. Daily mail. Population 100.

Brown, W., farmer
Clark, John, hotel keeper
Clark, Joseph, farmer
Clegg, Mrs. M., milliner
Crossley, Joseph & Holden, general merchants
Deyell, T., farmer
Douglass, Rev. James (Canada Presbyterian)
Fair, William, farmer
Hall, John, farmer
Lancashire, R. S., carpenter
Lang, Alexander, brickmaker
Lightfoot, John, farmer
O'Brian, Thomas, farmer
Tate, J., farmer
Tate, T. C., farmer
WADDELL, ROBERT, J.P., Postmaster, gen. mer.

South Mountain.—A Village on Petite Nation River, in the Township of Mountain, County Dundas, 8 miles from Oxford Station Ottawa and St. Lawrence Railroad, and 17 from Matilda Station Grand Trunk Railway. Population 300.

Adams, E. B., general merchant
Beggs, Robert, carpenter
Blow, Robert, carriage maker
Blow, Samuel, blacksmith
Bowen, E. A., general merchant and steam saw mill owner
Bullis, C. S., M.D.
Caldwell, Henry, teacher, Town Clerk & commissioner
Carmichael, Samuel, blacksmith
Christie, W. B., general merchant
Cleland, David, carriage maker
Cleland, John, innkeeper
Crawford, John, carpenter
Curtis, Lewis, painter
Fell, James, machinist
Ferrall, D. & E., tinsmiths
Gilroy, William, wagon maker
Graham, David, proprietor saw and shingle mill
Harty, Rev. William (Roman Catholic)
Henderson, Chancey, innkeeper
Howe, Rev. H. (Wesleyan)
Hyndman, Joseph, J.P., grist and saw mill owner
Hyndman, Joseph J., miller
Larue, Anthony, jun., boot and shoe maker
Larue, Anthony J., sen., cooper
Lemon, Miss, milliner
McKenzie, Rev. F. (Church of England)
Moore, Henry, tanner and currier
MORROW, JOHN, Postmaster and gen. merchant
Ranson, Robert, tailor
Ridley, William J., Clerk Division Court
Smith & VanCamp, fullers and carders
Story, John, mason
Walker, James, boots and shoes
West, James, P.L.S.

South Zorra.—A Post Office in the Township of East Zorra, County Oxford, 5 miles distant from Woodstock, the County Town. Land in the vicinity averages from $40 to $50 per acre. Population 20.

Armstrong, Arthur, farmer
CROSS, THOMAS, Postmaster and teacher
Farquhar, Rev. F. D. (Church of England)
Harrington, John, farmer
Wilkinson, John, farmer

Speedie.—A post Village in the Township of Sydenham, County Grey, 6 miles from Owen Sound the County Town, and about 120 from Toronto. Average price of improved land $30 per acre. Daily mail. Population 60.

Armstrong, Charles, farmer
Armstrong, David, farmer
Beatie, Andrew, farmer
Biggar, Andrew, farmer
Clark, Robert, wagon maker
Davidson, James, wagon maker
Dewar, Rev. Robert, (Presbyterian)
Harkness, Gideon, farmer
Lemon, Charles, hotel keeper
Mooney, Patrick, shoemaker
Nesbit, George, farmer
Sloane, A. C., M.D.
SPEEDIE, WILLIAM, Postmaster
Telford, James, wagon maker
Telford, William, teacher
Vanwick, Robert, hotel keeper

Sparta.—A Post Village in the Township of Yarmouth, County Elgin, 10 miles from St. Thomas, the County Town, and about 120 from Toronto. A stage leaves daily for White's Station, London and Port Stanley Railway, fare 25 cents; also daily stage to St. Thomas. Daily mail and Money Order Office. Population about 500.

Armstrong, James, J.P.
Arthurs, Thomas, grocer
Bates, John, wagon maker and blacksmith
Bell & Carr, shoemakers
Bobier, John, stock dealer
Boddington, —, M.D.
Burt, D., proprietor brick yard
Carr, J., shoemaker
Climpson, James, tailor
Coakley, Henry, dentist
Durdle, James, hotel keeper
EAKINS, J. A., Postmaster, notary public, general agent, general merchant, lumber and grain dealer and pork packer
Eakins & Murray, founders
Edge & Coakley, druggists
Fraser, Alexander, conveyancer and accountant
Hall, George, painter
Henderson, F. A., carpenter
Jay, Alfred, wagon maker and blacksmith
Jay, A. H., glove maker
Lincoln, James, carpenter
McDowell, John, hotel keeper
Martyn, J. P., insurance agent
Meyer, Joseph, carpenter
Mills, Minard, auctioneer
Mordinger, L., cabinet maker
More, Silas, proprietor stage and mail carrier
Morgan, Edward, broom manufacturer
Moyer, Mrs., milliner
Murray, & Co., blacksmiths
Murdie, William, auctioneer
Oill, E. W., cabinet maker
Oill, John, J. P., blacksmith
Oill, John & Son, wagon makers
Ross, Meredith, saddler
Sanderson, —, M. D.
Smith, H. B., general merchant
Smith, Isaac, broom manufacturer
Smith, N. B., lumber dealer
Smith, William, blacksmith
Straffon, R. J., cabinet maker
Trim, Samuel, butcher
Town, John, proprietor oil well
Welding H. B., proprietor flouring mill
Wood, A. J., manager co-operative association

Speedside.—A Post Office in the Township of Eramosa, County Wellington, 10 miles from Guelph, the County Town, and 48 from Toronto.

Armstrong, William, farmer
Barrie, Rev. William, (Canada Presbyterian)
Brown, John, general merchant
LOUGHRIN, JAMES, J.P., Postmaster
Loughrin, Thomas, farmer
Wood, Joseph, teacher

Spencerville.—A Village in the Township of Edwardsburgh, County Grenville, 22 miles from Brockville, the County Town. Land averages $10 per acre. Population 100.

Armstrong, Mrs., milliner
Bennett, John, J.P., general merchant
Bennett, Miss M., milliner
Carmichael, Andrew, carriage and wagon maker
Depencier, S. T., teacher
Fairbairn, Andrew, farmer
Fairbairn, Gideon, farmer
Fairbairn, James, carriage and wagon maker
Fairbairn, Robert, proprietor flouring mill
Graham, Rev. — (Methodist Episcopal)
Helmes, Rev. John (Wesleyan)
Hunter, Thomas, proprietor Spencerville Hotel
IMRIE, MRS. W. B., Postmistress and gen. store
Keeler, James, farmer
Laidlaw, Andrew, farmer
Lawdon, John, carpenter
McShane, Henry, boots and shoes
Miller, James, farmer
Millar, John, farmer
Mollan, Rev. James B., (Presbyterian)
Robertson, George F., carriage and wagon maker
Robertson, James, painter
Robertson, Thomas, J.P., grocer
Snyder & Millar, general merchants
Spencer, David, farmer
Stitt, Miss Mary, milliner
Stitt, William, J.P., prop. Victoria Hotel
Tripp, Archibald, cooper
Wallace, J. McL., M.D

Spring Arbour.—A Village in the Township of Walsingham, County Norfolk, 22 miles from Simcoe, the County Town, and 105 from Toronto. Daily Mails. Population 90.

Auger, Frederick, cabinet maker
Argyle, George, innkeeper
Bennett, A. M., farmer
Bennett, Henry, farmer
Cox, George, sash maker
Hazen, Elijah, blacksmith
Hazen, G. N., farmer
Hazen, Jacob W. ,farmer
HAZEN, JOHN W., Postmaster
Hazen, Matthias, farmer
McKay, James, farmer
Smith, William, general merchant
Smith, J., prop. flour mill
Terrett, —, lumber merchant

Springbank.—A Post-office in the Township of East Williams, County Middlesex.
WELLS, W., Postmaster.

Springfield.—A Village in the Townships of South Dorchester and Malahide, County Elgin, 18 miles distant from St. Thomas, the County Town, and 114 to Toronto. Stage to Dorchester station, Great Western Railway, 16 miles, fare 75c., to Aylmer, 6 miles, fare 25c. Daily Mail. Population 400.

Anderson, David, hide and leather dealer, butcher
Anderson & Foy, boot and shoe manufs. and dealers
Allen, J. & W., stoves and tinware
Baker, Isaac. carpenter
Blett, John, boots and shoes
Clumas, Archibald, farmer
Clumas, John, J.P.
Cook, John, J.P.
Dennis, James, cooper
Dexter, George, farmer
Fanning, Edward, cabinet maker
Fleckenstein, George, carriage and wagon maker
Fuller, Sarah, milliner
GRAVES, W. H., Postmaster and gen. merchant
Gunn, John, farmer
Herrick, S., proprietor hotel
Hindley, Miss Phœbe, teacher
Johnson, Reuben, J.P.
Leeson, John, teacher
Lyon, J. C., teacher
McEown, J. G., general merchant
McEown, Lyman, general and lumber merchant
McIntosh, James, general merchant
McIntosh, Robert, carpenter
McIntosh, William, farmer
McKenny, R. C., stock dealer and farmer
Mills, Cornelius, teacher
Mills, J. B., M.D.
Nigh, George, farmer
Pritchard, William, farmer
Scott, Robert, farmer
Smart, James B., tailor
Weaver & Kenzie, props. steam flouring and saw mills
Yocum, Rev. J. W. (Episcopal Methodist)
Yoder, Joshua. carpenter
Yoder, Moses, farmer

Springfield (Credit Post Office).—A Village on the River Credit, in the Township of Toronto, County Peel, distant from Brampton, the County Town, 13 miles, from Toronto 19 miles. Stages to Port Credit and Streetsville. Average price of land $30 to $40. Population 150.

Adamson, Alfred, farmer
Bethune, Rev. C. J. S. (Episcopal)
Blair, Benjamin, painter
Brain, Miss Anna, teacher
CAMERON, DONALD, J.P.
Clarkson, Warren, farmer
Cox, Robert, farmer
Crozier, George, farmer
DIXIE, B. W. B., M.D.
Evans, Robert, farmer
Faulkner, George, farmer
Featherston, Joseph, butcher
Galbraith, William, shoemaker
Hall, William, farmer
Hammond, Oliver, J.P.
Hammond, Thomas, farmer
HARRIS, CAPT. J. B., J.P., res Benares
Hayes, John, farmer
Hickey, Lawrence, butcher
Hickey, William & Bro., masons
Higgins, Albert, blacksmith
Hunt, Charles, painter
Johnson, William, carpenter
King, Edward, farmer
Lewis, Thomas, general merchant
McCarty, Richard, shoemaker
McGill, Thomas, farmer
McGRATH, WILLIAM, res Erindale
Mayhew, John, cabinet maker
Mercer, Miss Annie, teacher
Messenger, Thomas, J.P.
MITCHELL, COL. CHARLES, J.P., res Hawthorn Park
Murphy, Michael, general merchant
Newman, Thomas, farmer
Shook, Henry, cooper
TAYLOR, EMERSON, Postmaster and proprietor Exchange Hotel
TAYLOR & McGILL, lumber dealers
Wilson, John, blacksmith
Woodruff, John, carpenter

Springford.—A village in the township of South Norwich, County Oxford, 16 miles distant from Woodstock the County Town, and 50 from Toronto, Stage to Woodstock, fare $1. Daily mail. Money order office. Population 200.

Benson, Rev. W., (Methodist Episcopal)
Bryan, A., carpenter
Crossett, John, boot and shoemaker
Gillard, William, commission merchant
Haley, E. C., cabinet maker
HAMILTON, A. H., Postmaster and gen. merchant
Haycock, Rev. C. W. (Baptist)
Hoskiss, Mrs., milliner
Jenvey, Charles, brickmaker
Kennedy, Nathan, carpenter
Latimer, W. R., teacher
McFarlane, Alexander, blacksmith
McFarlane, Miss, milliner
McFarlane, Peter, blacksmith
Morris, Robert, saddler
Mudge, Philip, carpenter
Nelson, Charles, hotel proprietor
Oatman, W. W., boot and shoe maker
Rice, James, hotel proprietor
Wilcox, A. L., general store
Wilcox & Collins, proprietors cheese factory
Woodward, Lucas, blacksmith
Woodward, Washington, carriage maker

Springhill.—(See King Post Office).

Springtown.—(Bagot Post Office.)—A Village on the Brockville and Ottawa Railroad, and Madawaska River, in the Township of Bagot, County Renfrew. Distant from Pembroke the County Town, 54 miles, from Ottawa 58 miles. Average price of land $5 to $10. Population 50.

Anderson, John, carpenter
Costello, Catherine, teacher
HOLLIDAY, JOHN, Postmaster
Kennedy, Patrick, general merchant
McCrea, E., proprietor Madawaska Hotel
Wigney, Joseph, cooper

Springville.—A Village situated on the gravel road between Peterborough and Port Hope, in the Township of North Monaghan, County Peterborough, 7 miles from Peterborough the County Town, and 83 from Toronto. The Millbrook branch of the Port Hope and Peterborough Railway passes within 1 mile of the Village. Average price of land $40 per acre. Daily mail. Population 200.

Bennett, John, dentist
Bedgrove, William, blacksmith
Blain, Rev. William, (Presbyterian)
Clarke, William, farmer
Corneil, J. C., teacher
Dundas, James, farmer
Dundas, Capt. John, farmer
Fowler, William, farmer
Gent, Edward, tailor
Gibson, Robert, carpenter
GOODFELLOW, ARCHIBALD, Postmaster, and general merchant
Jameson, John, weaver
Leitch, John, weaver
McCall, Robert hotel keeper
McCamus, William, M. D.
McBain, William, farmer
McDonald, John, blacksmith
McIndoe, Robert, farmer
Mahony, William, blacksmith
Scott, Sorel, hotel keeper
Walsh, John, J.P., farmer
Wilson, David, farmer
Young, George, farmer

Staffa.—A Village in the Township of Hibbert, County Perth, 20 miles from St. Mary's, the County Town, and 100 from Toronto. Land in vicinity averages $25 per acre; the Village is within 5 miles of a Station on the Buffalo and Lake Huron. Population 100,

Chade, Abraham, general merchant
Chubb, William, blacksmith
Drake, John, farmer
Dyer, Rev. J. E. (Wesleyan)
Hamilton, James, shoemaker
Hammond, Thomas, dealer in lime and stone and cooper
Hatham, R., farmer
Henderson, Mrs., milliner
Hodges, James, teacher
Luffin, Charles, farmer
McCurdy, John, general merchant
McTavish, Dr.
Morris, James, farmer
Pillow, J., hotel keeper
Pillow, James, farmer
RUNDLE, R. F., Postmaster and general merchant
Sadler, John, carpenter
Warden, William farmer
Webb, R. & Son, proprietors steam flouring mill
Woods, D., farmer

Stamford.—A Village beautifully situated in the Township of Stamford, County Welland, 2 miles from Niagara River, and 4 from the Falls. Population 500.

Badger, J., blacksmith
Berryman, Thomas, lime and stone and wine and spirit dealer
Bowen, C., baker
Calvert, James, farmer
Church, M., farmer
Collard, John, teacher
Collins, George, blacksmith
CORRELL, P. A., Postmaster and gen. mercht.
Corry, Dr.
Dee, John, real estate agent
Dougan, Robert, boots and shoes
Duff, Miss, teacher
Ellis, George, proprietor flouring mill
Gilchrist, A., tailor
Gillehurst, Miss A., milliner
Gorman, Miss C., private school
Hyatt, George, farmer
Ingles, Rev. J. (Episcopal)
Johnston, William, boots and shoes
Jones, Edward, farmer
Hular, H., farmer
Laird, Rev. J. G. (Wesleyan)
McDonald, S., boots and shoes
McGill, Rev. J. (Presbyterian)
Mahoney, D., proprietor hotel
Martin, George, stock dealer and butcher
Mewburn, H. C.
Mitchel, J., farmer
Morrison, Alexander, farmer
Oswold, James, hotel keeper
Parker, James, farmer
Parker, William, farmer
Pew, L., general merchant
Pew, Thomas, farmer
Redhead, William & Co., wagon makers
Shrimpton, George, carpenter
Shugg, John, general merchant
Smith, Thomas, carpenter
Stewart, George, general agent
Swain, William, saddler
Taylor, G., J.P.
Thompson, John, farmer
Thompson, S. M., tailor
Trimpton, George, farmer
White, George, brewer
Wilson, John, wagon maker

Stanley's Mills.—A Village on the Humber River, in the Township of Chinguacousy, County Peel, 8 miles from Brampton, the County Town, and 4½ from Malton, Station Grand Trunk Railway. Stages to Mono Mills and Malton. Population 200.

Anderson, William, farmer
Allison, John, shoemaker
Balfour, James, farmer
Balfour, Miss, milliner
Brodie, James, teacher
Burbridge, John, wagon maker
BURRELL, CHRISTOPHER, J.P., Postmaster
Dale, George, carpenter and proprietor Union Hotel
Dale, John, butcher
Elder, David, proprietor flouring mill
Ewart, James T., general merchant
Fleming, M., farmer
Harrison, Emanuel, farmer
Holtby, Thomas, J.P.
Holtby, Mathias, wagon maker
Hostrawser, William, carpenter
James, William, farmer
Johnston, James, farmer
McDonald, Benjamin, farmer
McFadden, Rev. W. (Wesleyan)
Moore, William, farmer
Morrison, J. W., dentist
Pearen, John, farmer
Pearen, M., farmer
Sanderson, John, farmer
Saul, John, farmer
Somerville, James, farmer
Stubbings, John, blacksmith
Sutherland, Rev. D. G. (Wesleyan)
Taylor, John, general agent
Tigg, Joseph, tanner
Tippling, James, blacksmith
Trudgeon, William, shoemaker
Vernon, James, farmer
Walker, James, farmer
Watkins, William, proprietor flouring mill
Woodhall, William, farmer

Stafford.—*(See Villages too late for regular insertion at the end of this work.)*

Stanton.—A Village in the Township of Mulmur, County Simcoe, 40 miles from Barrie, the County Town. Land in the vicinity averages $25 per acre. Population 100.

BEATTY, W. H., Postmaster, general merchant
Bradshaw, William C., teacher
Campaign, George, farmer
Cotton, William, J.P.
Creary, Edward, farmer
Freeland, John, farmer
Graham, C., township reeve
Hall, William, carpenter
Hand, Thomas, farmer
Hand, William, farmer
Kirkpatrick, James, township assessor
Love, John A., general merchant
McClinton, John, farmer
McCutcheon, D., farmer
McKee, Samuel, farmer
McMulkin, E., flouring mill proprietor
Noble, John, farmer
Pearson, William, cabinet maker
Renwick, John, carpenter
Roadhouse, Rev. J. (Primitive Methodist)
Robinson, H., dentist
Rutledge, George, J.P.
Sims, James, carpenter
Snidles, John, carpenter
Summersett, Robert, carriage and wagon maker
Walker, John, farmer
Walker, Thomas, farmer
Walker, William, farmer

Stayner.—A village and station of the Northern Railway, Township Nottawasaga, County Simcoe, 24 miles from Barrie and 86 from Toronto. The village is rapidly increasing in importance and possesses excellent facilities for manufacturing. The surrounding country is unsurpassed for agricultural purposes. Improved lands $40 per acre, wild lands, $25. Population 600.

ALGEO, JOHN, hotel keeper
Beaton, A. H., M.D.
Beaton, D. J., brickyard
Beaton, D. J., teacher
Bennet, J. W., saddler
Boomer, Isaac, carpenter
Briggs, Rev. S. (Church of England)
Buffy, William, carpenter
CLUSKEY, JAMES, tinsmith (see adv.)
Cole, R. J., telegraph agent
Coleman, Mrs., hotel keeper
Collins, George, hotel keeper
Colwell, Jabez, tailor
Crawford, John, carpenter
Darrah, John, wagon maker
Devitt, John, cabinet maker
DOMINION, WEEKLY (Thursday); A. Wallace & Co
Doner, John, steam flour mill
Earl, T., general merchant
Geyer, Alfred, painter
Greenfield, Rev. James (Presbyterian)
Hannah, R. B., tanner
Heisie, Michael, butcher
Henderson, Hugh, shoemaker
Henry, William, saddler
Hill, Andrew, tailor
Horray, John, carpenter
Ingersoll, A. M., tanner
LAIDLAW, J. D., general merchant (see adv.
Lawrence, William, painter
Lewis, Thomas, grocer
LONG & BROTHER, general merchants
LOSSIE, LAWRENCE, tinsmith (see adv.)
McArthur, Peter, constable
McDonald, L. A. & Co., general merchant
McEachern, Roderick, tailor
McKeggie, J. H., agent Vicker's Express
McKEGGIE, JOHN, Postmaster

McLeod, Martin, carpenter
McSherry, Patrick, proprietor billiard room
Mathers, John, cabinet maker
Mathers, John, wagon maker
Murray, John, lumber merchant
Parkinson, R. J., general merchant
Parsons, Thomas, general merchant
Phillips, Gideon, cabinet maker
Reid, William, grocer
Roadley, Thomas, saddler
Smith, John, shoemaker
Smith, William, grocer
Struthers, Alexander, proprietor steam flour mill
Thompson, A., hotel keeper
Tucker, Rev. Samuel, (Wesleyan)
Wallace, Alexander, grocer
WALLCE, A. & CO., editors *Dominion Weekly*
Williamson, William, druggist
Wilson, Archibald, baker

Steele.—A Post Office in the Township of Oro, County Simcoe Improved land in the vicinity averages $10 per acre.

ROBINSON, C., Postmaster.

Stella.—A Village on the Bay of Quinté in the Township of Amherst Island, County Addington. Steamers call here daily in passing between Kingston and Belleville. Distant from Kingston 16 miles, and from Toronto, 175. Mails semi-weekly. Population 120.

Fowler, Daniel, artist
Fowler, Adjutant Reginald
Fowler, Lieut. Col. William
Hamilton, Robert
Hitchens, John, hotel keeper
McGuinnes, John, general merchant
McIntosh, Rev. James, (Canada Presbyterian)
Patterson, Capt. Robert
PERCIVAL, WILLIAM, J. P., Postmaster, township reeve
Walters, John, councillor
Wright, George, general merchant

Stevensville.—A Village on Black Creek, in the Township of Bertie, County Welland, 12 miles from Welland the County Town. Population 100.

Barnhart, Peter, farmer
Baker, Benjamin, farmer
Baker, Jeremiah, farmer
Baker, Levi, farmer
Baker, Michael, farmer
Beane, S. W., farmer
Cline, Jacob
Cropley, William, tanner and currier
Eberly, George, farmer
Fripp, James, wagon maker
Gaforth, Alexander, attorney-at-law
Gilmour, John, shoemaker
Gaforth, Franklin, M. D.
Haun, M. J. & J. H., proprietors flouring mill
Hendershot, John
Hendershot, Peter, soap and candle manufacturer
House, R. B., painter
HOUSE, W. F., Postmaster
Huffman, J. F., proprietor hotel
Huffman, Peter, wagon maker
Johnston, John
Johnston, Samuel, stock dealer
Krafft, F. W., carpenter
Law, John, grocer
McKenzie, Jane, teacher
Rodgers, John, cooper
Shisler, Peter, J.P.
Shisler, J. W. general merchant
Smith, Rufus (U. B. Church)
Tytherleigh, Charles, shoemaker
Wade, Frank, butcher
Wade, Robert, painter
Wade, William, tailor

Stewartown (Esquesing Post Office.)—A Village on the River Credit, in the Township of Esquesing, County Halton, distant from Milton, the County Town, 12 miles, from Toronto 30 miles. Daily stages to Milton and Georgetown. Average price of land $40 to $50. Population 300.

Austin, William, shoemaker
Barnes, William, carpenter
Bessy, J. R., J.P.
Bessy, J. S.
Campbell, Robert
Cross, David, tanner
Dundas, F., proprietor British Union Hotel
Fee, John, cabinet maker
Graham, Richard
Henry, John, grocer
Hood & McKinnon, millers
Hull, James, wagon maker
Huston, F.
Jeffers, Rev. T. (Wesleyan)
Johnston, John, lumber dealer
McArthur, Rev. J. G. (Episcopal)
McGinnis, David, teacher
Mitchell, Peter, cooper
MURRAY, JOHN, Postmaster
Nixon, Edward, saddler
Reed, Alexander, shoemaker
Rowe, P. M.
Sparrow, Thomas, saddler
Thompson, George, J.P.
Tost, Henry, carpenter
Whaley, George, proprietor Stewartown Hotel
Wilson, James, carpenter
Young, William, shoemaker

Stirling.—An Incorporated Village on Salmon Creek, in the Township of Rawdon, County Hastings, 15 miles from Belleville, the County Town, 12 from Trenton Station, Grand Trunk Railway. Stages to Belleville, Marmora and Campbellford. Money Order Office and Savings Bank. Population 1000.

Ackers, John, cooper
Adams, Rev. J. Q. (Episcopal Methodist)
Allen, E. D., councilor
Allen, G. D., manufacturer fanning mills
Austee, A., farmer
Barlow, Jesse, farmer
Berry, W. H., barber
Blakeley, James, hop grower
Boldrick & Fiddler, general merchant
Boldrick, James, telegraph operators
BOULTBEE, Dr. J.P., M.P.
Bradley, —, M.D.
Bradley, T. H., proprietor livery stable
Brydon, A., baker
Buchan, Rev. A. (Presbyterian)
Burrow, Stephen, mason
Butler, Charles, bailiff
Caldwell, J. T., carpenter
Carr, Rev. J. (Wesleyan)
Cash, Robert, farmer
Chard, Peter
Chard, Thomas, farmer
Chard, William, farmer
Chard, Wellington Smith & Geary, manfrs. of window shades
Church, A., proprietor Exchange Hotel
Cosly, Miss M., teacher
Couley, George, farmer
Craig, C., general merchant
Craigie, Charles, foundry
Crooks, S., watchmaker
Declair, John, mason
Demill, S., boot and shoe maker
Demorest, Dr.
Dempsey, Michael, farmer
Downs, Thomas, proprietor Mansion House
Eaton, Isaac, hop grower
Fanning, John, farmer
Feeney, Joseph, wagon maker
Finch, R., boots and shoes
Gallagher, J., M.D.
Geary, J., carpenter
Gerow, Mrs., baker and confectioner
Gilbert, Mrs., dressmaker
Glass, A., boots and shoes
Green & Brown, general merchants
Green, Darius, farmer
Green, Ebenezer, farmer
Green, Jedediah, hop grower
Green, John, farmer
Grout, Rev. W. G., (Church of England)
Hannah, J. W., shoemaker
Heagle & MacCauley, wagon makers
Horton, Samuel, farmer
Houghton, Miss, dressmaker
Houghton, H. B., B.A., teacher
Hough, John V., blacksmith
JUDD, W., Postmaster, clerk of court & gen. mercht
Kyle, James, farmer
Kyle, William, farmer
Lake, Nicholas, farmer
Lake, Richard, farmer
Langman, Richard, manufacturer spring wheels
Loucks, Jacob, butcher and grocer
Lavine, Francis, stone cutter
McDougall, D., miller
McDougall, T., councillor
McKeown, James, tailor
McRony, Charles, hotel keeper
Martin, David, tinsmith
Martin & Son, harness makers
Martin, William, cabinet maker
Milne, James, general merchant
Mitchell, W. A., prop. billiard saloon
Montgomery, James, farmer
Montgomery, Thomas, farmer
Mott, James, blacksmith
Naylor, James, blacksmith
Parker, F. B., township clerk
Parker, Mrs. W. R., prop. Stirling House
Parker, Dr
Potts, E. F., grocer and liquor dealer
Potts, James, farmer
Rosebush, Edward, farmer
Roy, R. M., photographer
Scott, Thomas, farmer
Sine, G. W., teacher
Smith & Bro., general merchants
Smith, H., carpenter
Stedman, B., general merchant
Stickle, C. F., general merchant
Stickle, Mrs., dressmaker
Thurber, H. B., grocer
Tucker, Luther, farmer
Turner, Mrs., dressmaker
Vantassel, J. R., issuer of marriage licenses
Wescott, S. N., farmer
Weaver, Peter, farmer
Wilson, George, farmer
Wheeler, T., wagon maker
White, David, carpenter
White, George, carpenter
Wilson, Dr.
Wolever, Isaac, general merchant
Wright, Anson, farmer
Wright, Uriah, farmer
Young, Rev. W., (Baptist)

Stirton.—A Post Office in the Township of Peel, County Wellington.

LUXSON, JOHN, Postmaster.

Stisted (late Rowan Mills).—A Post Office in the Township of Walsingham, County Norfolk.

FRY, JAMES, Postmaster.

Stittsville.—A small Village in the Township of Goulburn, County Carleton, 15 miles from Ottawa. Population 80.

Alexander, A., farmer
Alexander, James, tanner
Alexander, T., shingle manufacturer
Alexander, William, lime manufacturer
Allen, P., shingle manufacturer
ARGUE, JOHN S., Postmaster and general merchant
Argue, William, farmer
Bobier, Gregory, proprietor Stittsville House
Bradley, John, farmer
Borroughs, G. A., painter
Brown, Rev. W. D. (Wesleyan)
Cherry, Robert, farmer
Church, C., M.D.
Cuthbert, William F., J.P., farmer
Dennison, William, farmer
Eastman, W. & W., blacksmith
Harten, A., farmer
Harten, James, cooper
Hodgins, John, notary, etc.
Lewis, J., stock dealer
McEnally, G., farmer
Nolan, James, auctioneer
Pettit, Rev. C. B. (Episcopal)
Poole, J. F., farmer
Pool, John F., shoemaker
Ramburg, O., tailor
Sawyer, Mrs. A. E., dressmaker
Sinclair, Rev. —, (Presbyterian)
Stenzel, William, shoemaker
Warren, Thomas, wagon maker
West, R. L., teacher
Winchester, Edward, shoemaker

Stockdale.—A Post Village in the Township of Murray, County Northumberland, 40 miles from Cobourg the County Town, and 100 from Toronto. Average price of land $40 per acre. Population 140.

Anderson, Joshua, farmer
Bates, C., farmer
Benedict, David, farmer
Campbell, Rev. —, (Episcopal)
Creller, David, farmer
Loveless, J. W., farmer
Moran, M. B., teacher
OSTERHOUT, J. D., Postmaster
Philp, Rev. —, (Wesleyan)
Rourke, Robert, farmer

Stoco.—A Post Village in the Township of Hungerford, County Hastings, 25 miles from Belleville, the County Town, and 275 from Toronto. Population 200.

Bennett, B., shoemaker
Brown, George, hotel keeper
Brown, Margaret, woolen manufacturer
Corrigan, J., wagon maker
Hines, Henry, carpenter
Huffman, P., farmer
Humphry, Dr.
Irwin, William, wood and willow ware
Lawlor, Rev. E. B. (Roman Catholic)
Murphy, Ann, dressmaker
MURPHY, FRANCIS, Postmaster, general merchant
Mulrooney, Thomas, farmer
Murphy, Patrick, general merchant
Palmer, Benjamin, hotel keeper

Stony Creek.—A Village beautifully situated in the Township of Saltfleet, County Wentworth, 6 miles from Hamilton, and 2 from Lake Ontario. Money Order Office. Population 220.

ALEXANDER, REV. JAMES L. (Church of England)
Bradley, John J., Clerk Division Court and general merchant
Bridgman, Irwin, M.D., coroner
Brown, Thomas, dentist
Campbell, D. W., M.D.
Carpenter, George, farmer and proprietor saw mill
Carpenter, Gershom, farmer
Coombs, Horace, carpenter
Coombs, John, carpenter
Corman, James, farmer
Crawford, Patrick, farmer
Davis, George, farmer
Davis, Thomas, farmer
Davis, William, farmer
Gibson, Rev. James D., (Church of England)
Glover, George, farmer
Green, William, farmer and carding
Green, Samuel, farmer
Hopkins, J. Wesley, J.P.,
Hopkins, Silas, farmer
Hull, Henry, proprietor Exchange hotel
JONES, A. G., P.M., and general merchant
Lee, Abram, farmer
Lee, David, blacksmith
Lee, Hamilton, blacksmith
Lee, James, sen., & Sons, blacksmiths
Lee, James, jun., blacksmith
Lee, Jeremiah, farmer
Lee, Samuel, farmer
Logan, Samuel M., farmer
Lottridge, William, farmer
Loudon, Daniel, farmer
Lutz, Henry, farmer
McMillan, E. M., proprietor Acacia House
Marlatt, Albert, proprietor Canada House
Morgan, William, farmer
Nash, Samuel, farmer
Nash, William, farmer
Olmstead, M., farmer
Penfold, Joseph, farmer
Place, Ebenezer, farmer
Spera, Henry, J. P
Spera, William, farmer
Springstead, Oliver, carpenter
Utter, Henry, farmer
Utter, Palmer, farmer
Vanwagner, Peter, J. P
Vanwagner, T., farmer and proprietor saw mill
Wallace, Joseph, blacksmith
Williamson, John, J. P

Stony Point.—A Village and Station of the Great Western Railway, on Lake St. Clair, in the Township of Tilbury West, County Essex, 28 miles from Sandwich the County Town, Population 100.

Andrieux, Rev. P., (Roman Catholic)
Aubry, Stephen, J. P., commissioner in B. R., issuer of marriage licenses, conveyancer, real estate agt., and lumber dealer
Belleau, Michael, teacher
Chevalier, H., general merchant
Chevalier, Joseph, farmer
DESJARDIN, HENRY, Postmaster, general mercht
Desjardin, Israel, farmer
Drain, Daniel, boots and shoes
Kenville, A., carpenter
McGuire, Samuel, carpenter
Mailloux, Antoine, farmer
Mailloux, Francis, general merchant
Mailloux, Xavier, general merchant
Parent, D., farmer
Rondot, E., farmer
Seguin, Joseph, carpenter
Trudell, Peter, farmer

Stouffville.—A Village on the Town Line, in the Townships of Markham and Whitchurch, County York, 28 miles from Toronto, 20 from Newmarket and 20 from Whitby. Stages daily to the above places. Money Order Office and Savings Bank. Population 500.

Barnes, Richard, carpenter
Besan, George, cooper
Brooks, Heal, carpenter
Brownlee, Thomas, cooper
Bruels, John A., wagon maker
Burgess, John, cooper
Burkholder, Samuel, cabinet maker
Campbell, Rev. John, (Presbyterian)
Chinn, F., prop. North American Hotel
Daly, James, shoemaker
Davis, Philip, cabinet maker
Day, Rev. B. W., (Congregational)
Flint, Rev. George, (Primitive Methodist)
Flint, George, sen., J.P., prop. planing mill
Flint, George & Son, cabinet makers
Freel, S. L., M.D.
Gee, Rev. D. E. F., (Wesleyan)
Gould, John, carpenter
Grant, James, watchmaker, jeweler, &c
Hand, John, baker
Johnstone, James, farmer
Knill, R., prop. Havelock Hotel
Leaney, Edward, general merchant
Leamon, John, cooper
Lloyd, A. C., M.D
Lloyd, R. C., M.D.
Loaze, R. N., butcher
McCallum, George, tailor
McKinnell, David, farmer
McKINNELL, GEORGE, Postmaster & gen. mercht
McMurdy, Donald, tanner
Mann, John R., teacher
Nichols, James, farmer
O'Brien, James, cabinet maker
Patterson, James M., auctioneer
Patterson, T., carpenter
Roddick, William, wagon maker
Sanders, Edward B., general merchant
Sanders, William, tailor
Sangster, John A., wood and willow ware
Shaw, Thomas, druggist
Stevens, Chauncey, tailor
Stock, Mrs. Joel, dry goods and millinery
Tinkler, Thomas, butcher
Urquhart, Hector, wagon maker
Urquhart, John, wagon maker
Van Zant, G. R., tinsmith and dealer in stoves
Wheeler, Edward, J.P., general merchant and proprietor steam flouring and saw mills
Wideman, Joseph, potter
Williams, Edward, carpenter
Williams, R., dry goods
Williams, Mrs. R., milliner
Yake, A., proprietor Union Hotel
Yake, Calvin, proprietor Stouffville Hotel
Yake, John, general merchant

Straffordville.—A Village on the Little Otter River, in the Township of Bayham, County Elgin, 22 miles from St. Thomas, the County Town, 5 from Vienna, 34 from London, and 8 from Port Burwell. Money-Order office. Population 400.

Arn, Charles, lime and stone
Brawn, Rev. E. F. (New Connexion)
Brown, John, M. D.
Brown, Rev. Joseph (Methodist Episcopal)
Campbell, J. O., teacher
Dennis, Thomas, farmer
Drake, Daniel, blacksmith
Emry, W. Y.
Garnham, Edward, stock dealer and farmer
Garnham, Robert, J.P., farmer
Garrett, William, blacksmith
Gray, Edwin, lumber dealer
GRIFFIN, WILLIAM, Postmaster, saddler, tanner and leather dealer, grocer, etc.
Hatch, L. J., general merchant
Henry, George, M.D.
Henry, John, tinsmith
Hoag, W. C., general merchant
Hodgins, Eli, farmer
Howey, Robert, farmer
Hubbard, M., prop. Eastern Hotel and livery stable
Huntsberger, Enos, farmer
Johnson, Peter, gunsmith
Johnson, Peter M., blacksmith
Jones, Jacob S., notary public
Jones, J. H. & Co., proprietors oil well
Ketchabau, John, tanner and leather dealer
Kingsworth, John, boots and shoes
Land, S. W., boots and shoes
Lane, William, clerk
Leach, M., proprietor Straffordville Hotel
Louis, King, blacksmith
McBurley, William, cooper
McBurley, William, blacksmith
McCollum, Henry, wagon maker and painter
McNaughton, R. J., J.P., insurance agent
McNorton, R. J., gen. agt, tailor, prop. flouring mill
Mann, —, Deputy Reeve

Mitchell, Thomas, shingle maker
Olwood, George, cooper
Philips, G. K., real estate agent
Price, Charles, constable, proprietor planing mill and wagon maker
Rammage, William, sash, blind and door manfr.
Ribble, David, constable, saddler
Ribble, Edwin, saddler
Robinson, Henry, general agent
Roe, Daniel, councillor
Saunders, M. N., general merchant
Shingler, Wallace, farmer
Silverthorn, D. F., constable, boots and shoes
Silverthorn, James, butcher
Sloan, James, auctioneer
Smoak, Robert, prop. Ontario House and livery stable and nursery
Stansell, Riley, cabinet maker
Stratton, Henry, Deputy Reeve
Turnbull, —, councillor
Wade, Mathew, wagon maker
Ward, W. D., patent right agent
Whaley, E. C., tailor
Yager, Adam, blacksmith

Strangford—A Post Office in the Township of York, County York.
BLAIR, ISAAC, Postmaster.

Stratford.—The County Town of Perth, is situated on the river Avon, at the corners of the Townships of Downie, Ellice and North and South East Hope. The Grand Trunk and the Buffalo and Lake Huron Railways cross each other here. thus giving the town railway facilities equal to those of any place in the Province. It is a port of entry, and being surrounded by a fine agricultural region, has an excellent trade. It is a well-built and rising town. Distant from Toronto 88 miles, from Sarnia 80, London by rail 39, and from Goderich 115 miles. Money order office and Savings' Bank. Population 4000.

ABBOTT, J. B., proprietor *Orange Gazette*
Abraham & Hepburn, cabinet makers
Adams, John, tailor
Albion Hotel, D. M. White, proprietor
Alcock, Mrs., hotel keeper
Anderson, John, grain dealer
ARGO, A. L., proprietor Stratford flouring mills
Bailey, D. T., assessor
Baird, George, proprietor packing house
Baker, Abraham
Ballantyne, Thomas, proprietor cheese factory
Bank of Montreal, James Hogg, agent
Barker, George, blacksmith
Barker, Henry, shoemaker
Beatty, Samuel, boots and shoes
Bell, Rev. J. P. (Primitive)
BENNOCH, JAMES, produce dealer
Berry, Joseph, shoemaker
Birch, J. & P., tinsmiths
Boag, John, proprietor Wilmot flouring mill
Brandenberger, William, butcher
Brazier, George, grocer
Brown, John, deputy registrar
Brown, Magnus, carpenter
Browning, Charles, builder and hotel keeper
Buchannan, C., teller R. C. Bank
BUCKINGHAM, WILLIAM, editor *Beacon*
Burritt, D. B., clerk division court and ins. agent
Byers, George W., tinsmith
Byrne, Miss S. M., milliner
CALE, THOMAS, photographer (see adv)
Campbell, David, cabinet maker
Campbell, John, carpenter
Campbell, Robert, mason
Campbell, Stewart, county clerk
Carrall & McCulloch, barristers
Cartwright, C., dentist
Cassels, David, merchant tailor
Cavanagh, John, baker
Caven, Alexander, insurance agent
Chowen, Richard, prop. Market Hotel
Clark, John J., dry goods and groceries
Clark, Thomas, auditor
Clements, James, grocer
Codd, John, ale and porter, wholesale
Constable, A. M. H., job printer
Cooper, John, councillor
Corcoran, James, grocer
Corey, T. F. & Co., manufs. patent medicines
CORRIE, JOHN, prop. Queen's Arms Hotel
Counter, John, proprietor Commercial Hotel
Craib, John, councillor
Crerar, James, J.P.
Crinnan, Rev. P. V. G. (Roman Catholic)
Croker, N. G., proprietor Rose's Hotel
Daly, J. C. W.
Daly, Thomas Mayne, mayor
Daly, T. M., wholesale grocer
Davis, David, grocer
Dean, Charles, agent Spring Brewery, Hamilton
Dearlove, John
Dempsey, Hugh, proprietor cheese factory
Dennis, Mrs., boarding house
Donaldson, Ralph, tailor
Down, William, provision and fruit dealer
Dunn, Peter, wagon maker
Duperow, Charles, blacksmith
Durrant, Rev. John (Congregational)
Dutton, John, chemist and druggist
Easson, William, proprietor saw and planing mill
Edwards, John, proprietor Stratford Hotel
ELDER, G. & J., steam cooperage (see adv.)
Ellison, G. & J., props. refreshment rooms, R.R.
Faulkner, William & Co., boots and shoes
Fisher, Joseph, proprietor Junction Coffee House
Forbes, J. & R., proprietors livery stables
FORMAN, GEORGE, Clerk Registry
Fortune, W. W., produce and commission merchant
Fraser, John, tailor
Fraser, John M., millinery and fancy goods]
Fuller, S. S., deputy reeve
Fuller, T. R., hardware
Gandy, John, marble cutter
George, Rev. James, D.D., (St. Andrews)
Gibson, Henry, confectioner
GIBSON, JOHN, baker
Gladders, Robert, prop. Stanfield House
Glendenning & Chrispin, painters
Gordon, James, dry goods
Gourlay, Alexander, farmer

Graber, F. X., fancy goods
Hamilton, John, collector of customs and inland rev
Hamilton, William, grocery and saloon
Hammer, Jacques, blacksmith
Hammond, H., grocer
HANOVAN, M. J., M.B., (see adv)
HANVEY & SMITH, (William H. and George) physicians and surgeons
Harrison, W. D., chief constable, auctioneer, &c
Hay, G., undertaker
HAYES, M., county attorney and Clerk of the Peace
HAYES & O'LOANE, barristers
HAYWARD, LYSTER
Hegi, Charles, jeweler
Hepburn, Alexander, architect
HEPBURN, WILLIAM, upholsterer
Hesson, S. R., general merchant
Hildebrand, George, contractor
HILTON, G. A., tanner (see adv)
Hitchcock, Henry, proprietor Daly House
Hoffman & Son, dry goods and groceries
HOGG, JAMES, agent Bank of Montreal
Holliday, Thomas, proprietor Corn Exchange Hotel
Holmes, John, contractor
Home Insurance Company, L. Haynan, agent
HOPWOOD, THOMAS, boots and shoes
Horne & Clark, dry goods
Hossie, John, deputy sheriff
Humphrey, John, blacksmith
HUNTINGTON, J. E., L.D.S., surgeon dentist
Hyde, J., M.D., coroner
IDINGTON, JOHN, L.L.B., (Macfarlane & Idington)
INNES, JOHN, proprietor oat and barley mills
Irwin, J. T., carpenter
Jackson, George A., barber
Kyle, James, grain merchant
Larkworthy, George, butcher
Lawrence, George W., solicitor
Lawson, Thomas, boots and shoes
Lean, R., manufacturer agricultural implements
Lee, Charles, merchant tailor
Lizars, Daniel H., County Judge
LOCKHART, MARION, fancy goods
Lynn & Goodwin, wagon makers
McCallum, William, books and stationery
McCarthy, Thomas, farmer
McCauley, James, proprietor Victoria Hotel
McCauley, John, butcher
McCauley, William R.
McColl, Rev. E. C. W. (Congregational)
McCracken, F., chandler
McCulloch, J. A., councillor
McDonald, D. B., carpenter
McGregor, Alexander, grocer
McGregor, C. J., principal grammar school
McKay, Angus, merchant
McLaurin, Rev. John (Baptist)
McMair, A. & Co., dry goods
McNaughton, William, miller
McPherson, J. C., farmer
McPherson, Rev. Thomas C. (Presbyterian)
Macdonald, James, dry goods
MACFADDEN, JAMES, clerk County Court
MACFARLANE, ROBERT, M. P. P., (Macfarlane & Idington)
MACFARLANE & IDINGTON, (Robert and John) barristers, solicitors, &c.
MacGregor, R. A., teller Bank of Montreal
MADDOCKS & ELLISON, com. merchts (see adv)
Marshall, Andrew, grain merchant
Marshall, John, merchant
Marshall, Walter, produce merchant
Marshall, William R., general merchant
Marshall, & Fuller, proprietors flax mill
Megan, J. & P., grocers
MERCHANTS' BANK, Charles H. Ransom, agent
Miller, A., principal common school
Miller, Thomas, accountant, official assignee, &c
Miller, Bros., wagon makers
Milne, John, grocer
Moderwell, Robert, sheriff
MONTEITH, ANDREW, M.P.P., County Treasurer
Morrison & Co., dry goods and groceries
Morrow, Henry, general merchant
Mowat, William, secretary County Perth Mutual Fire Insurance Company
Myers, Robert, tanner
O'Higgins, John, wholesale and retail grocer
O'LOANE, LAWRENCE T., Postmaster
O'Neil, Rev. J., (Roman Catholic)
OWEN, JOHN, photographer (see adv)
Paeckert, Edward, gunsmith
Parker, John, tinsmith
Patterson, Rev. E., (Church of England)
Patterson, Mrs., general merchant
Pethick, William, hotel keeper
Perick, Daniel, pump maker
Porter, W. T., teller Merchants' Bank
Powell, James, clerk customs
Price, Rev. William (Wesleyan)
Provincial Insurance Co., G. W. Lawrence, agent
QUEEN'S ARMS HOTEL, John Corrie, proprietor (see adv.)
Rankin, James, J.P.
RANSOM, CHARLES H., agent Merchants' Bank
REDFORD, JAMES, M.P.P.
REDFORD & McDONALD, brokers, conveyancers, commission merchants, insurance agents, &c.
Reid, John, councillor
Rice, George, butcher
Rice, George, saddler
Rieby, Augustus F., watchmaker
Riggs, Isaac, councillor
Robarts, Samuel, boarding-house
Robb, John M., editor and proprietor *Herald*
Roberts, William H., watchmaker
Roffey, William, proprietor Union Hotel
Ross, J., produce merchant
Royal Canadian Bank, J. Young, agent
RUTHERFORD, JAMES S., produce and commission merchant
Salkeld, Joseph, farmer
Sayers, John, grocer
Scholz, John F., whipmaker
Scott, David, produce merchant
Scott, John A., commission merchant
Scown, Daniel, tavern-keeper
SCRIMGEOUR, BROS., proprietors planing mill
Service, R. S., brigade major
Sewell, Henry, town clerk
Sewell & Hooper, flour and feed
Sharman, John, crown land agent
SHARMAN, JOSEPH, prop. Stratford Agricultural Works
SHAVER, P. R., M.D., coroner
Smiley, William, commission merchant
SMITH, ALEXANDER, tanner (see adv)
Smith, J. G., dry goods
Smith, R. & J. G., barristers
Smithwick, Peter J., grain merchant
Stephenson, George, agent G.T.R.
Stewart, James, boarding house
Stewart & Stewart & Sewell, barristers
STONEY, JOHN L., grocer
STONEY, THOMAS, reeve, saddler
Stoney, Thomas, saddler
TAYLOR, C. B. & CO., dry goods

Taylor, George, shoemaker
Taylor, James
TEUSCHER, JACOB, editor *Colonist*
THOMPSON, RICHARD, grain and seeds
Transon, Thomas, prof. of music
TRIPP, M. E., M.D., (see adv)
Trow, James, M.P.P
Turner, Joseph G., billiard rooms
Uberlacker, H., butcher
Vanstone, John, jr., wagon maker
Vanton, William, saddler
Wade, W. G., accountant, R. C. Bank
Wanzell, William F., auctioneer
Watson, Mrs., private school
Watson, Joseph, general merchant
Watson, Peter
Waugh, George J., druggist
Wenningers, J., druggist
White, D. M., proprietor Albion Hotel
Whitehead, E. S., watchmaker
Williamson, Alexander, merchant tailor
Willis, J. L., baker
Wilmot Mill, John Boag, proprietor
Wilson, John, hotel keeper
Wilson, Thomas, grocer
WINKLER, FREDERICK W., painter
Winter, Thomas, insurance and express agent
WOODS & FISHER, barristers
WORKMAN, W. & F., hardware merchants
Worth, J., butcher
Yeandle, Thomas, blacksmith
Young, James, agent Royal Canadian Bank

Strathallan.—A Village on a branch of the River Thames, in the Township of East Zorra, County Oxford' 7 miles from Woodstock, the County Town, and 7 from Tavistock. Population 150.

Badgero, Justin, teacher
Bartholemew, D., carpenter
Caldwell, William, blacksmith
Cook, A. B., farmer
Cook, C. H., M.D.
Dunn, Thomas, farmer
Fox, Thomas
Hamilton, Hugh, accountant
Hooper, C. H., shoemaker
Kennedy, Andrew, farmer
Lappin, James, hotel keeper and grocer
McKay, Donald, blacksmith
Murray, James, carpenter
Murray, John, carpenter
Plasket, Timothy
Shadwick, Adam, farmer
Tuddington, Josiah, farmer
Tuddington, Josiah
VAN DEEOR, J. C., Postmaster, stoves and tinware, hardware, grocer, etc.

Strathroy.—A large and enterprising Town, situated on the River Sydenham, on the borders of the Townships of Adelaide and Caradoc, and the principal station on the Sarnia branch of the Great Western Railway in the County of Middlesex. Distant from London 22 miles, and from Sarnia 40 miles. Strathroy is rapidly improving both in size and importance, and contains several extensive establishments for the manufacture of agricultural implements, woolen goods, leather, sash, doors and blinds, etc. The lumber business is also carried on here to a great extent, and square timber exported in large and increasing quantities. Money Order office and Savings Bank. Population about 2500.

Aikins, John, wagon maker
Aldwell, Edward D., stoves and commission agent
American Express Co., John Lenfesty, agent
Andrews, James, butcher
Armstrong, W. A., revenue inspector
Atwood, P. H., auctioneer
Auld, Adam, woolen factor
Bailey, Thomas, blacksmith
BANK OF COMMERCE; J. S. Small, agent
Banghart, Michael, proprietor Union House
Baskerville, Thomas, boots, shoes and leather
Baskerville, Thomas H., boarding house
Beattie, Alexander F., auctioneer and ins. agent
BELL, ARCHIBALD, barrister, &c. (see adv.)
Bettridge, William, M.B.
Black & Mitchell, lumber merchants
Bolem, Isaac, barber
Bond, John, baker and confectioner
Bradley, W. J., photographer
Brown, Cornelius, groceries, &c.
Brown, James, butcher
Brown, Joseph, butcher
Bullard, Luther, livery
Cameron, Rev. A. A. (Baptist)
Cameron & Ritchie, boots and shoes
Campbell, Mrs., boarding house
Canada Permanent Building and Savings Society; J. B. Winlow, appraiser
Carre, Thomas, druggist
Clarke, W. J., barber
Cooper, Cornelius, blacksmith
Cooper, Henry, carpenter
Colter, Charles, dentist
Cooper, J. C. (A. Robb & Co.)
Cowan, Richard, M.D.
Crawford, Samuel, manufacturer of agricultural implements
Crispin, Thomas, stoves and tinware
Crone & Wilson, lumber, lime and coal
Decow, Daniel, tanner and currier
Decow, John L., stoves and tinware
Degroot, James, well-digger
Dell, Solomon, spinning wheel manufacturer
DEWAN, J. D., wholesale grocer
Donley & Cuddy, groceries and liquors
Dubois, Joseph & Son, coopers
Dumbrill, Richard, hardware
Dunn, James D., grocer
Dupil, Xavier, painter
Drynan & Ross, dry goods
Edwards, E. G., M.D.
Edwards, Henry F., saddler
ELLIOTT & CRAWFORD, agricultural implement manufacturers and founders
Elliott, J. B., grocer
English, James, station master
Ewer, William H., bookseller, &c
Ferguson, John N., watchmaker

FAWCETT, THOMAS & CO., builders, lumber merchants and manufacturers of sashes, doors, blinds, shingles, &c. (see adv)
Fitzpatrick & Gatford, hotel proprietors
Forbes, Thomas, dry goods
Frank, Francis, saw miller
FRANK, JOHN, land owner
Frank, Solomon, rake, snaith, and cradle manuf
Fraser, Alexander, carpenter
Furry, Barber, constable and auctioneer
Gatford, Richard, hotel keeper
Geary, T. J., chemist and druggist
Geddes, Mrs. Martha, boarding house
German, G. G., boots and shoes
Gilzean & Bro., dry goods and groceries
Goodwin, Abram, groceries, wines and liquors
Gough, James, express agent
Gowrie, John H., blacksmith
Green, S. S., manager Peddie & Co
Griffiths, Rev. A. E., (Episcopal Methodist)
Hardy, Thomas E., gunsmith
Harrison, F. L., undertaker and cabinet maker
Hayden, Albert, leather and findings
Henderson & Co., dry goods, groceries, &c
Henderson, Gregg, M. D
HILL, ROBERT, upholsterer, cabinet maker and undertaker
Hilton, Friend, boots and shoes
HILTON & EAKINS, cabinet makers, & upholsterers
Hull, William W., cabinet maker
Humphrey, Arthur W., photographer
Humpidge, Frederick, chair factory
Humpidge, Walter, billiards
Irvine & Saul, butchers
JACKSON, L. F., proprietor Commercial Hotel
Jeffrey, David, cattle dealer
JOHNSTON, ALEXANDER, banker and exchange broker
Johnston, Charles L., builder
Johnston, William M., land agent and notary public
Keefer, James, J.P., County Clerk
Kelly, William H., watches, clocks and jewelry
Kenny, Theodore M., grocer
KNAPP, CHARLES, proprietor Western Hotel (see adv)
Koyl, G. B., accountant
Laird, W. P., solicitor
Lauler, J. D., wagon maker
Learoyd, Rev. John (Wesleyan Methodist)
Legallee, Thomas (Lenfestey & Legallee), tanner
Lemon, William, grocer
LENFESTY, JOHN, grain and general merchant
LENFESTEY, JOHN, JUN., insurance and American Express Co. agent
LENFESTY & LEGALLEE, tanners and curriers (see adv)
Long, William, proprietor Exchange Hotel
LONGHEAD, JAMES S., proprietor of Market
Lyddy, G. P., P.L.S.
McCOLL, HUGH, publisher *Strathroy Age*
McCully, Wright, carpenter
McGhee, William, grocer
McIntosh, James, merchant tailor
McIntyre, Dugald
McIntyre, John C., carpenter
McKELLAR, D. S., M.D.
McKillop, Donald, grocer
McKINDSEY, JOHN, barrister
McLAREN, H. & A., dentists and manufacturers of patent artificial limbs (see adv)
McLeod, William, builder
McMARSHALL, THOMAS, merchant tailor
MACINTOSH, CHARLES H., Postmaster and editor and prop. Strathroy *Despatch* (Thursdays) (see adv)
Mann, Eli D., livery
Mann, G. A., stoves, plows, lamps and oils
Mann, Henry, founder and agricultural implement maker
Mann, John
Mann, Moses, shoemaker
Manner, R. C., conveyancer
Mansfield, J. G., dry goods
Manson, James
Meek, William H., builder
Meekinson, Andrew, fruiterer
Mitchell, W. L., agent Scottish Provincial Ins. Co.
Moore, Rev. B. C., M.E.
MOORE, ISAAC, prop. Albion House, Front cor Thomas (see adv)
Mothersill, Joseph, M.D.
MURRAY, W. H., dry goods
Music Hall; Dr. D. S. McKellar, proprietor
Nicholson, Robert, lumber merchant
Noble, James, dry goods and groceries
O'Callaghan, John, grocer
O'Donovan, Rev. D. (Roman Catholic)
O'Keefe, Patrick, grocer
Orchard, George, chemist
Page, Mrs., milliner
Patterson, Rev. R. S. (Church of England)
Pearce & Polley, dry goods
Peddie & Co., general merchants
Phillips, William, carpenter
Pike, Charles, tailor
Pincombe, Richard, prop. Strathroy flouring mills
Piper, H. P., watches and jewelery
Prangley, George, hotel proprietor
PROVINCIAL INS. CO., J. Lenfesty, jun., agent
Purcell, Bros. (W. & W. J.) dry goods and clothing
Randall, John, carpenter
Ratley, William, grain merchant
Ray & Irwin, photographers
Richards, Robert, auctioneer
Richardson, Robert, chairmaker
RICHARDSON, THOMAS (W. G. Van Staden & Co)
Ritchie, Robert (Cameron & Ritchie)
ROBBS, ALEXANDER (A. Robbs & Co.)
ROBBS, A. & CO., props. Strathroy woolen mills
Robertson, Donald, contractor
Sadleir, Thomas, saddler
Sample, David F., cooper
Saul, Richard, butcher
SCATCHERD, ROBERT C. (Scatcherd & Bro.)
SCATCHERD & BRO., barristers, &c.
Schultheis, Francis, marble worker
Scoon, John A., J.P., conveyancer and commissioner in B. R.
Scott, C. G., dry goods
Scott, T. B., grocer
Sewell, Mrs. M., boarding house
Sharpe, Thomas H., provisions
Small, Joseph C., clerk 6th division court, conveyancer and com. in B.R
SMALL, JOSEPH S., agent Bank of Commerce
Smith, L. H., grain merchant
Smith & McPherson, staves, pumps, etc
Snell, Thomas, brewer
Sommerville, J. A., M.D
Spurr, William, grocer and shoemaker
Stephenson, Bros., saddlers
Stewart, William, dry goods, &c
Stonehouse, Edward, solicitor and agent Commercial Union, European Life and Guarantee Ins. Cos

STRATHROY AGE, Hugh McColl, publisher
STRATHROY DISPATCH, Charles H. Mackintosh editor and proprietor
Stuart, W. H., baker and confectioner
Thompson, Edward, iron and hardware
Thompson, G. W., books and stationery
Turner, Cornelius, builder
VANSTADEN, W. G. & CO., hub, spoke and bending factory (see adv)
Van Wyck, John, livery prop.
WILSON, JOSEPH, (Wilson & Cruikshank) warehouseman, and dealer in coal, lime, &c
WILSON & CRUIKSHANK, manufs. sash, doors, blinds and bending materials, planing and saw mill props., etc
WINLOW, JACOB B., fire and life insurance agent, issuer of marriage licenses and appraiser Canada Per. B. and S. Society
Woodward, James, butcher
Wright, James, boots and shoes
Wynn, Ambrose, prop. Hazelton House
Young, R. W., teacher grammar school

Strathburn.—A Village situated on the River Thames, in the Township of Moss, County Middlesex, 30 miles from London, the County Town, and 2½ miles from Glencoe Station, Great Western Railway. Mails tri-weekly. Population 100.

Beckton, Thomas, farmer
Clark, George, trader
Coulthard, George & John, mill owners
Coyne, John, dentist
Ferguson, Robert, blacksmith
Graves, Peter, farmer
Hickey, Robert, farmer
Kelley, Abner, cradle maker
McKenzie, Norman, cooper
McRae, James R., carpenter
McRAE, HUGH, Postmaster, gen. mer. & hotel prop
Murchison, John, merchant tailor
Scarlett, W. H., cabinet maker
Steinhoff, Jacob, shoemaker
Stewart, Duncan, brick maker
Sutherland, Rev. William R. (Presbyterian)
Webster, David, dry goods
Webster, William, farmer

Strathnairn.—A Post Office in the Township of St. Vincent, County Grey.
HARTMAN, JOHN W., Postmaster.

Streetsville.—An incorporated Village on the River Credit, in the Township of Toronto, County Peel, 10 miles from Brampton, the County Town, and 24 from Toronto. The river affords first-class water power. Money Order Office and Savings Bank. Population 1,000.

Allen, George, tailor and clothier
Atkinson, William, boots and shoes
Bays, John, cooper
Ballinger, John, farmer
Bamford & Sons, sash, blind and door manufacturers
Barber, William, J.P.
Barnhart, John, M. D., reeve
Battice, John, blacksmith
Beaty, Robert K., J.P., wine and spirit dealer
Beaty, Thomas K., proprietor flouring mill
Blackwell, John A., saddler
Blyth & Son, wood and willow ware
Brown, John, proprietor Streetsville hotel
Butcher, John, baker
Crumbie, John, J.P., M.D.
Cunningham & Bro., tinsmiths and dealers in stoves
Douglas, Charles M.D.
Douglas, Donald, farmer
Douglass, George, farmer
Dundee, Thomas, painter
Elliott, Robert, carpenter
Embleton & Brother, telegraph operators and general merchants
Fish, Rev. Charles, (Methodist)
Franklin, Bennett, farmer
Glendenning, John, farmer
Gooderham & Worts, proprietors flouring mill and general merchants
Graydon, William, sen., farmer
Graydon, William, boots and shoes
Grimshaw & Lewis, wagon makers and proprietors Telegraph Hotel
Harris, William, proprietor Globe Hotel
Halloran, P. O., tailor
Howard, George, wagon maker and blacksmith
Hoy, A., boots and shoes
Irwin, Robert, potter
Kerr & Bro., cabinet makers
Lewis, R. H., wagon maker and prop. livery stable
McAuley, George, teacher
McDonell, Miss, milliner
McKay, Rev. W., (Presbyterian)
Middleton, Rev. J., (Church of England)
Montgomery, James, proprietor brick yard
Patterson, James, farmer
Penny, William J., town clerk and treasurer
Ramsey, Robert, farmer
Robinson, & Co., founders and machinists
Rutledge & Graydon, books and stationery, fancy goods toys, &c
Rutledge, Henry, farmer
RUTLEDGE, JAMES E., Postmaster, J.P., gen. agt,
Simpson, A., J. P.
Sparling, James, butcher
Sterling, John E., auctioneer and stock dealer
Taylor, Miss, milliner
Wadsworth, D., teacher
Woods, J., M. D., druggist
Worthington, James, carpenter

Stromness.—A Village on the feeder of the Welland Canal, in the Township of Sherbrooke, County Haldimand, 19 miles from Cayuga, the County Town, and 2 from Feederbridge Station Buffalo and Lake Huron Railway. Population 100.

Benner, Robert, blacksmith
Benson, Albert, blacksmith
Cunningham, Rev. S. (Baptist)
Dodge, Henry W., blacksmith
Galbraith, A., farmer
Galbraith, Archibald, jun., prop. Stromness Hotel
Galbraith, Daniel J., teacher
Kavanagh, Felix, saddler
Leaver, Rev. J. J. A. (N. C. Methodist)
Logan, Thomas, J.P.
McCallum, L., M.P., lumber dealer and tug boat owner
McDonald, A., J.P., Reeve, farmer
Moss, M., proprietor Farmers' Hotel
Niece, Abner, farmer
Niece, Charles, farmer
Niece, William, farmer
NIMMO, ROBERT, Postmaster

Stretton.—A post office in the Township of Reach, County Ontario

---

Sullivan.—A small Village in the Township of Holland, County Grey, 14 miles from Owen Sound, the County Town. Population 60.

Bell, Joshua, blacksmith
Buchanan, William, sen., farmer
BUCHANAN, WILLIAM, Postmaster
Buchanan, John, tailor
Bumsted, Samuel, farmer
Carson, J., teacher
Davidson, William, weaver
Donald, John, farmer
Elliott, A. S., prop. flouring mill and carding mills
Frost, William, general merchant
Gillies, Robert, general merchant
Gorsline, William, teacher
Hilliard, Rev. William (Baptist)
Hopkins, Nicholas, shoemaker
McLauchlan, James, farmer
McClure, David, carpenter
Markle, Walter, hotel proprietor
Pears, George, proprietor saw mill
Sproule, Joseph, proprietor Ontario Hotel
Totten, John, proprietor saw mill
Wilson, Mrs., farmer

Summerstown.—A Village on the River St. Lawrence, in the Township of Charlottenburgh, County Glengarry, 10 miles from Cornwall, the County Town, and 7 from Lancaster Station, Grand Trunk Railway. Average value of land $28 per acre. Population 100.

Baker, A. J., general merchant
Blondin, Isaac, shoemaker
Cameron, A. J., J.P.
McDermid, William, teacher
SUMMERS, ANDREW, Postmaster
Summers, Mrs. D., innkeeper

Summerville.—A Village on the Etobicoke River, in the Township of Toronto, County Peel, 14 miles from Brampton, the County Town, and 7 from Port Credit Station, Great Western Railway. Population 100.

Aikens, Dr.
BEMROSE, WILLIAM, Postmaster, general mercht
Bennett, John H., teacher
Clarkson, William, farmer
Edwards, Rev. A. (Wesleyan)
Howard, Rev. A. (Wesleyan)
Johnson, John, farmer
Johnson, Thomas, farmer
Kennedy, William, farmer
Kern, D., hotel keeper
More, Robert, farmer
Pallett, Robert, farmer
Shaver, W. L., farmer
Wilcox, Allan, farmer

Sunbury.— A Post Office in the Township of Storrington, County Frontenac, 12 miles from Kingston,

Chambers, Rev. Thomas L. (Presbyterian)
Craig, Robert. shoemaker
Crowe, Francis, carpenter
Edward, Robert, teacher
Fisher, James, carpenter
Gay, Robert, wagon maker
Hodgson, John, shingle maker
Jackson, John, shingle maker
Leach, Rev. S. K. (Wesleyan)
McBRIDE, JOHN, Postmaster and gen. merchant
McNeely, John, J.P. and farmer
McWalters, Samuel, farmer
Moreland, James, farmer
Murdock, Edward, farmer
Smith, Charles, farmer
Smith, James, farmer
Waldron, John, farmer

Sunnidale.—A small Village and Station of the Northern Railway, in the Township of Sunnidale, County Simcoe, 25 miles from Barrie, the County Town, and 85 from Toronto.

Armstrong, John, lumber dealer and farmer
Bell, Alexander, farmer
Fleming, T., blacksmith
Fyfe, James, farmer
Gilchrist, Alexander, farmer
GILLESPIE, ALEXANDER, Postmaster
Gillespie, Samuel, lumber dealer and farmer
Glenn, J., hotel keeper
McNeill, Archibald, lumber dealer

Sutherland's Corners.—A Post Office in the Township of Euphemia, County Lambton.

Anderson, Donald, farmer
Armstrong, Adam, shingle manufacturer
Armstrong, William, J.P. and teacher
Dillon, Thomas, hotel keeper
Dobbyn, John, farmer
Gage, James A., shoemaker
McAuslin, Andrew, farmer
McDonald, James, farmer
McKeown, Henry, cooper
McKeown, James, shoemaker
Moorehouse, T. P., farmer
Moorehouse, William, farmer
Smith, Dougall, auctioneer
Stafford, Rev. Mr. (Methodist)
WALKER, JAMES, Postmaster
Warden, Rev. R. (Presbyterian)

Sweaburg.—*(See Villages too late for regular insertion at the end of this work.)*

Switzerville.—A Village in the Township of Ernestown, County Addington, 6 miles from Napanee, the County Town. Population 200.

Bush, C., farmer
Empey, Thomas, farmer
Fralick, Mr., teacher
Gray, Rev. Mr. (Wesleyan)
Kenny, John, farmer
MILLER, CALVIN W., J.P., Postmaster, issuer of marriage licenses and commissioner in B. R.
Miller, C. W., farmer
Miller, M. N., farmer
Neville, M., farmer
Shaw, Rev. Mr. (Wesleyan)
Switzer, C., farmer
Switzer, John G., farmer
Thompson, Joseph, farmer
Williams, B., J.P.
Williams, David, farmer
Williams, R., farmer

Sylvan.—A Village on Silver Creek, in the Township of West Williams, County Middlesex, 34 miles from London, and 5 from Widder Station Grand Trunk Railway. Population 100.

Burns, John, cabinet maker
Corby, James, boots and shoes
DAWSON, JOHN, Postmaster
Elliott, Andrew, lumber dealer
Hall, John, farmer
Howland, T. F., farmer
James, Henry, farmer
McKee, Rev. — (Baptist)
Mackie, Mathias, farmer
Mason, Jabez, carpenter
Odell, Charles, general merchant
Oliver, Andrew, wagon maker
Proctor, E. M., lumber dealer and shingle manufactr
Randall, Samuel, proprietor brick yard
Rogers, Rev. — (Methodist Episcopal)
Whitelaw, Alexander, farmer
Wilson & Blanchard, hotel keeper

Talbotville Royal.—A Village in the Township of Southwold, County Elgin, 3 miles from St. Thomas, the County Town. Population 100.

Boughner, John, hotel keeper
Bowlby, Alexander, farmer
Bowlby, Samuel, farmer
Godfrey, Edward, cabinet maker
Jackman, Joseph, farmer
Milly, R. C., farmer
Payne, William, proprietor flouring mill
Roberts, Walter, carpenter
Smith, John, J.P., farmer
Smith, William, blacksmith
White, Rev. James (New Connexion)

Tamworth.—A Village on the Salmon River, in the Township of Sheffield, County Addington, 20 miles from Napanee, the County Town, and 35 from Kingston. Average price of land in the vicinity $15 per acre. Money Order Office. Population 300.

Abraham, E., gunsmith
Adair, John, farmer
Aylsworth & Huffman, druggists, etc.
AYLSWORTH, JAMES, Postmaster
Belch, James, general merchant
Bird, Rev. W. (Episcopal)
Bolger, George, shoemaker
Byrens, James, farmer
Cameron, D., Clerk Division Court
Carscallen, James A., auctioneer

Copeland, James, dyer
Douglas, A. C., general merchant
Douglas, H. J., proprietor Addington House
Drader, John, cooper
Embury, V. D., baker
Floyd, John, tailor
Fowler, P. J., J.P.
Gilmore, D., farmer
Grange, R., proprietor planing mill and lumber mill
Hannah, George, farmer
Harvey, Patrick, tailor
Jones, Henry A., attorney, etc.
Jones, Richard, woolen manufacturer
Joyner, H., iron founder
Knight, James, M.D.
Layes, S., Canada Co
Lloyd, Peter, carpenter
McKim, Elias, wagon maker
McKim, E., hotel keeper
McMullen, —, com. general merchant
Martin, Mrs. S. M., dressmaker
Martin, S. M., wagon maker
Miller, George E., carpenter
Neely, R. N., J.P.
Perry, E., crown land agent
Peterson, Rev. A. S. (Wesleyan)
Phillips, D., tinsmith
Ring, David, cabinet maker
Rose, W. A., general merchant
Sherman, John, general merchant
Shields, C., painter
Shields, James, wagon maker
Smith, L. H., proprietor lumber yard
Smith, R., M.D., teacher
Smith & Smith, general merchants
Tuple, Peter, carpenter
Wheeler, Alonzo, shoemaker
Wheeler, L. A., proprietor Tamworth hotel
Wheeler, W. R., cabinet maker
Wordsworth, M. J., proprietor livery stable
Young, Norman, carpenter

Tapleytown.—A small village in the Township of Saltfleet, County Wentworth, 11 miles from Hamilton. Population 60.

Benson, Rev. Charles E., (Methodist Episcopal)
Calvery, Joseph, butcher
Clark, John, farmer
Clark, John B., general merchant
Combs, William, carpenter
Dewitt, George, farmer
Dougherty, Henry, farmer
Gollan, Alexander, J.P.
Harris, Samuel, teacher
Jameson, John, shoemaker
Norton, John, farmer
Paterson William, farmer
Penfold, John, farmer
PTOLEMY, JOHN, Postmaster, and general mercht.
Service, Rev. Richard, (Episcopal Methodist)
Soules, John, farmer
Springstead, John, farmer

Tara.—A Village on Sauble River, in the Township of Arran, County Bruce, 35 miles from Walkerton the County Town. Average value of land $15 per acre. Stages to Owen Sound 15 miles, and Southampton 15 miles. Population 300.

Allen, James W., carpenter
Brinkman, William, farmer
Brown & Thomas, wagon makers
Cairns, Thomas, farmer
Chesterfield, Peter, cabinet maker
Clerihue, James, general merchant
Douglass, John, farmer
Douglass, Robert, farmer
Drinkwater, George, lumber dealer, proprietor steam saw mill and planing mill
Feathers, A., hotel keeper
Gerolamy, W. A., manufacturer of fanning mills
Grier, John, shoemaker
Grier, Michael, shoemaker
Hamilton, John, farmer
Hanley, John, weaver
Heglers, Sebastian, leather dealer and tanner
Hill, John, carpenter
Hiscocks, Rev. J. (Episcopal Methodist)
Kennedy, James, mason and brick layer
Kennedy, John, farmer
Lennox, H., weaver
Lumsden, John M., farmer
McClosky, James, potter
McCrea, Archibald, farmer
McDonald, prop. flouring mill
McFarlain, William, weaver
Moore, — prop. ashery
Nelson, John, hotel keeper
Newton, Thomas, carpenter
Richards, John, mason and bricklayer
Richards, Thomas, mason and bricklayer
Richie, David F., teacher
Robbins, Daniel, butcher
Shaw, Isaac, wagon maker
Smith, Thomas, farmer
Spier, John, painter and carpenter
Taylor, James, M.D
Thomas, William, wagon maker
Thompson, Thomas, manuf. of woolen goods
Toby & Gerolamy, general merchants
TOBY, JOHN, Postmaster
Tolmie, Rev. A., (Canada Presbyterian)
Urquhart, Misses, milliners
Vandusen, W., general merchant

Tarbert.—A Post-office in the Township of Luther, County Wellington, 34 miles from Guelph, the County Town.

Bellamy, Elizabeth, teacher
Dammand, C., shingle maker
Luxton, William, farmer
McDougall, Hugh, J.P., farmer
McDougall, John, farmer
McKenzie, E., farmer
McLellan, Angus, farmer
McLellan, Donald, farmer
McMURCHY, MALCOLM, Postmaster
Martin, Archibald, farmer
Osborne, William, cooper
Simpson, Robert, farmer

Tatlock.—A Post Office in the Township of Darling, County Lanark, 28 miles from Perth, the County Town.

Barr, Peter, farmer
Beaton, John, teacher
Caldwell, John, farmer
GUTHRIE, MRS. MARGARET, Postmistress
Guthrie, Peter, farmer
Longstaff, John, farmer
Murray, Patrick, shoemaker
Oliver, John, farmer
Pretty, Daniel, farmer
Rentoul, John, J.P.
Rentoul, William, farmer
Robertson, John, farmer

Tavistock.—A Village and Station of the Buffalo and Lake Huron Railway, in the Township of South Easthope, County Perth, 8 miles from Stratford, the County Town. Average value of land in the vicinity $45 per acre. Population 300.

Asmus, August, tailor
Caspar, Henry, cooper and shingle maker
Freinder, Jacob, tanner
Frohr, sash, door and blind manufacturer
Gerhard, John, farmer
Hausuld, Valentine, general merchant
Irwin, John, farmer
Kerby, A. N., agent B. & L.H.R. and telegraph operator
Klein, John, general merchant
McCracken, James, commission merchant
McKellar, John, farmer
Malcolm, George, proprietor flouring mill
MATHESON, G. D., Postmaster and agent American Express Co.
Matherson, G., proprietor hotel
Mohr & Gerhard, general merchants
Moslock, William, J.P.
Murray, Alexander, carpenter
Nash, Abraham, teacher
Pamper, William, saddler
Reid, Robert, commission merchant
Roedding, Henry, shoemaker
Rubbing, Henry, wagon maker
Rutherford, Johnston, grocer and com. merchant
Schnurr, W., blacksmith
Scott, Duncan, farmer
Sharp, John, brick maker
Shantz, Benjamin, proprietor flax mill
Smees, A., hats, caps and furs
Smith, John, blacksmith
Spark, V., wagon maker
Stenupf, Rev. John (Baptist)
Weitzel, Adam, farmer
Wetlaeyfer, George, cooper
Wetlaeyfer, John, shoemaker
Woon, John, farmer
Zoelner, Charles, proprietor hotel

Taylorholme.—A Post Office in the Township of Gloucester, County Russell.

TAYLOR, CHARLES, Postmaster.

Tecumseth (Clarksville Village).—A Post Office on a branch of the Nottawa River, in the Township of Tecumseth, County Simcoe, 25 miles from Barrie, the County Town, and 12 from Bradford Station, Northern Railway. Stages to Bondhead and Keenansville. Population 226.

Aylesworth, Rev. I. B. (Wesleyan)
Barton, W. J., general merchant
Byer, lumber dealer
Clark, Henry, cooper
Conklin, A. J., carpenter
Davidson, Rev. John (Church of England)
Dunham, William, carpenter
Dunn, Francis, carpenter
Evans, Selby, farmer
Falls, Nicholas, painter
Ferguson, Robert, carpenter
Forsyth, T., pumpmaker
Frazer, Ebenezer, teacher
French & Matchell, shingle makers
Fry, Henry, painter
Hammell, Francis and Robert, blacksmiths
Hammill, William, farmer
Hill, Robert, farmer
Irwin, John, millwright
Irwin & Reed, wagon makers
JONES, D. A., Postmaster and general merchant
Jones, J., lumber dealer
Jones, William, farmer
Lambert, Charles, tailor
Latimer, Francis, carpenter
Lowery, James, blacksmith
McCarty, Perry, J.P.
Major, William H., hotel keeper
Matchett, James, carpenter
Moodie, Rev. James (Canada Presbyterian)
Morrow, Thomas. hotel keeper
Owen, Isaac & Jacob, coopers
Ramer, J., lumber dealer
Robinson, R. H., teacher
Silvester, H., general merchant and insurance agent
Smart, William, farmer
Smith, James, farmer
Sproule, Robert, lumber dealer
Steel & Cotton, shingle makers
Stevens, F. S., Clerk of Court
Strong, William, wagon maker
Whiteside, W. N., M.D.

Teeterville.—*(See Villages too late for regular insertion at the end of this work.)*

Teeswater.—A small Village on the River Tees, in the Township of Culross, County Bruce, 16 miles from Walkerton, the County Town, and 21 from Clinton Station, Grand Trunk Railway. Stages to Wingham and Riversdale. Average price of land $20 per acre.

Ballagh, Alexander, farmer
Ballagh, Fleming, farmer
Brown, P. B., J.P., prop. flouring mill and lumber dealer
Carson, Rev. R. (Wesleyan)
Clarke, William, hotel keeper
Colvin, George, shoemaker
Cragg, Rev. Edward (Wesleyan)
Delayer, Joseph, saddler
Fairbairn, D., founder and machinist
FAIRBAIRN, THOMAS, J.P., editor and publisher *News Boy* and general agent
Flemming, Neil, M.D.
Fraser, J., founder and machinist
Fulford, Jessie, farmer
Gibson, Alexander, farmer
Gilles, John, M.D.
Gordon, William, general merchant
HADWEN, MATHEW, Postmaster, gen.merchant
Kirkland, Samuel, carpenter
Logan, John, farmer and general agent
McCremmon, Angus R., teacher and insurance agent
McDonald, D. A., shoemaker
McKay, Rev. Adam (Free Presbyterian)
McKague, Thomas, tinsmith and dealer in stoves, etc.
McKibbon, George, general merchant
McLean, Allan, general merchant
McLean, J. K., general merchant
McQue, John, prop. Teeswater Hotel
McVicar, John, tailor
Mack, John, shoemaker
NEWS BOY, (alternate Friday) Thomas Fairbairn, proprietor
Oliver, John, grocer
Sclanders, James, sash, door and blind manuf.
Sclanders, Mrs., milliner
Sharp, James, farmer
Shelton, Francis, cabinet maker
Spence & Douglas, shoemakers
Stevens, Thomas, saddler
Weir, Thomas, wagon maker
Wilson, D. R., prop. Wilson House
Young, E. T., carpenter

Telfer.—A Post-office in the Township of London, County Middlesex.

Nichols, Joshua, shoemaker
TELFER, ADAM, Postmaster, gen merchant

Tempo.—A Post-office in the Township of Westminster, County Middlesex

Bennet, Benjamin, farmer
Bennet, James, farmer
Bundle, Thomas, farmer
Dangerfield, Jabez, farmer
Davis, A. C., auctioneer
Davis, Amos, hotel keeper
Davis, Benjamin, farmer
Davis, James, farmer
Down, William, farmer
Ling, Joseph, farmer
Little, William, carpenter
McBride, Malcolm, shoemaker
Nevilles, Isaac, carpenter
Orr, James, farmer
Orr, Thomas, farmer
Pennock, Willliam, J. P., farmer
REMEY, ABRAHAM, Postmaster and carpenter
Remey, Silas, farmer
Riley, Miss Ann, teacher
Sutton, William, farmer
Vail, George, farmer
Weldon, Thomas, farmer
Wilson, Jeremiah, J. P., farmer

Tennyson.—A post office in the Township of Drummond, County Lanark.

Buchanan, Duncan, farmer
Devlin, Charles, farmer
Devlin, Thomas, blacksmith
McGREGOR, DONALD, Postmaster and carpenter
McKinnon, John, farmer
McNaughton, John, farmer
McPherson, John, farmer

Teston.—A Village in the Township of Vaughan, County York, 21 miles from Toronto. Population 100.

Andrews, Benjamin, farmer
Armstrong, Thomas, farmer
Bates, Thomas, boot and shoe maker
Breden, Rev. John, (Wesleyan)
Develin, William, J. P
Kenney, James, shingle maker
Kenney, Joel, carpenter
Lund, Joseph, wagon maker
McEchren, Hugh, hotel keeper
Malloy, James, farmer
Marwood, William, farmer
Murray, Isaac, farmer
Richards, John, farmer
Ross, David, blacksmith
Walkington, John, farmer
WILSON, GEORGE, Postmaster, general merchant

Teviotdale.—A small Village in the Township of Minto, County Wellington, 32 miles from Guelph, the County Town.

Laird, J., innkeeper
MILLER, M. S., Postmaster and general merchant
Watt, A., shingle maker
Wood, John, teacher

Texas Landing.—A steamboat landing on the Detroit River, in the Township of Anderdon, County Essex, 2 miles from Amherstburg. Large quantities of wood and stone are shipped from this place.

DeCourtney, J. M., vine grower
Morgan, J., farmer
NORVAL, DALLAS, wood and fish merchant (see adv)
WHITE, T. B. & CO., general merchants, wood and stone dealers (see adv)

Thamesford.—*(See Villages too late for regular insertion at the end of this work.)*

Thamesville.—*(See Villages too late for regular insertion at the end of this work.)*

Thanet.—A Post Office in the Township of Wallaston, County Hastings, 56 miles from Belleville.

Burgher, James, farmer
Fitzgibbon, James, farmer
Hepburn, James, farmer
McKILLICAN, B., J.P., Postmaster, hotel keeper
Menzie, A., hotel keeper
Murphy, Charles, farmer
Murphy, John, farmer
Nugent, Patrick, farmer
Sweet, B., shingle maker
Thwaites, W., hotel keeper

Thistleton.—A Post Office in the Township of Etobicoke, County York.

JOHNSTON, RICHARD, Postmaster.

Thomasburg.—A Village in the Township of Hungerford, County Hastings, 17 miles from Belleville, the County Town. Population 150.

Ashton, H. G., general merchant
Ashton, J. B., farmer
Barber, J., farmer
Brason, Joseph A., tanner
Butler, John, farmer
Clark, J., farmer
Clure, Thomas, J.P.
Clure, Thomas H., carpenter
Coulter, Andrew, J.P.
Davis, George W., harness maker
Eaton, Alexander, shoemaker
Embury, John, farmer
Graham, George, farmer
Graham, J. & T., blacksmiths
Graham, Thomas, farmer
Harrison, John, farmer
Henry, Benjamin, general merchant
Holbert, N., blacksmith
Lowry, John J., farmer
McGuire, James, hotel-keeper
McMillan, John, shoemaker
Mains, John, wagon maker
Morton, Alexander, farmer
Morton, John B., teacher
Morton, Thomas, farmer
ROBERTSON, JOHN, Postmaster and tailor
Ryan, Rev. David (Wesleyan)
Ryan, Rev. William (Wesleyan)
Sherry, James, shoemaker
Sherry, William, shoemaker
Stocks, George, farmer

Thompsonville.—A Post Office in the Township of Tecumseth, County Simcoe.

SCHMIETENDORF, J. T., Postmaster.

Thornbury.—A thriving Village on the Beaver River, in the Township of Collingwood, County Grey, 27 miles from Owen Sound, the County Town, and 14 from Collingwood Station, Northern Railway. The river affords first-class water power. Daily mail to Collingwood. Population 350.

Andrews & Cummer, flour mill proprietors and lumber merchants
Appleby, Rev. J. H. (Church of England)
Armstrong, George, general merchant
Beaker, Rev. J. (Wesleyan Methodist)
Brownridge, G., carpenter
Bull, H., carpenter
Bush, David, cabinet maker
Campbell, James, brickmaker
Campbell, John, tailor
Carless, Charles, carpenter
Davidson, J., carriage and wagon maker
Dennismore, Abram, cooper
Fletcher, D., farmer
Fraser, Hugh, woolen manufacturer
Gauld, Rev. J. (Presbyterian)
Hill, John, farmer
Hill, Joseph, stone mason
Hilts, Rev. J. H. (Primitive Methodist)
Hovey, John, cooper
Hunt, J., farmer
Hunt & McCausland, carriage and wagon makers

Kew, William
Land, John, butcher
Leemiug, William, farmer
Lewis, J., tailor
McCormick, John, carpenter
McCort, J., hotel proprietor
McFarlane, Peter, teacher
McKenny, J., nurseryman
McKENNY, THOMAS, Postmaster, druggist and telegraph operator
Murdy, J., agent Vicker's Express and prop. hotel
Osborne, George, farmer
Polley, George, dyer
Riddle, James, mason
Rorke, J.
Rutherford, James, boot and shoe maker
Shaver, Walter, farmer
Shaver, William, farmer
Shaver, W. W., shingle maker
Shearer, Robert, carpenter
Stephenson, J., hotel keeper and insurance agent
Stephenson, James, attorney-at-law
Wales, Samuel, painter
Walter, William
Webb, Samson, tailor
Wheeler, John, cooper
White, William
Wright, James
Youmans, David, farmer
Youmans, Miss H., milliner
Youmans, J. H. & Co., general merchants
Young, John, stoves and tinware

Thorndale.—A small Village in the Township of West Nissouri, County Middlesex, 11 miles from London. Population 75.

Brien, John, farmer
Condon, D., wagon maker
Cunningham, James, farmer
Ferguson, Robert, general agent
Fitzsimmons, Thomas, farmer
Forester, Dr.
Fox, James, farmer
Harrison, J., bookseller
HARRISON, THOMAS, Postmaster, gen. merchant
Harrison, William, carpenter
Henry, William, hotel keeper
Huston, William, farmer
Jackson, William, tailor
Jackson, J., painter
Logan, George, farmer
Logan, William, farmer
McCarthy, D., grocer
McCrae, J., lumber dealer
McGurdie, Thomas, shoemaker
McGuirk, John, farmer
McRae, John, station agent G.T.R
Moore, William, J.P
Owen, Charles, carpenter
Rathbon, J., general agent
Steel, Thomas, shoemaker
Syms, J. & Co., woolen factors
Switzer, B., J.P
Vining, W. R., J.P
Wilson, R., lime and stone

Thornhill.—A Village on Yonge Street, in the Townships of Vaughan and Markham, County York, 12 miles from Toronto, and 3 from Thornhill Station Northern Railway. Stages daily to Toronto. Money Order Office and Savings Bank. Population 750.

ARNOLD, ROBERT J., J.P.
BRUNSKILL, JOHN, proprietor Pomona flour and saw mills
Campbell, A., tinsmith
Carman, Alfred, carriage maker
Carr, Thomas, general merchant and druggist
Chapman, Isaac, J.P., farmer
Cockerline, Thomas, tailor
Cogswell, Mason E., carriage maker
Cook, John W., cabinet maker
Coyle, Thomas, blacksmith
Dick, Rev. Robert, (Presbyterian)
Ellston, John, crockery and glassware
Farr, James, farmer
Gallanough, Archibald, general merchant
Garbutt, Rev. T. (Wesleyan)
Garton, John, insurance agent
Heron, Henry, hotel keeper
Holdsworth, John, shoemaker
Kirby, William, farmer
Kirkpatrick, William, saddler
LANE, JOHN, J.P., farmer
Lane, William, farmer
Langstaff, John, proprietor planing mills
LEMON, HENRY, proprietor Thornhill Hotel
Ludford, Caleb, saddler
Lumley, John, painter
McDOUGALL, DAVID, proprietor Thornhill flour and saw mills
Morgan, John, farmer
Morris, Rev. T. J., (Roman Catholic)
Mundey, Joseph, farmer
Parsons, John, proprietor
Pearson, John, farmer
PURKISS, JOSIAH, P.M., general merchant, insurance agent, &c
Shanklin, Rev. R., (Church of England)
Shuter, James, general merchant
Suddaby, W., tailor
Webster, Charles, butcher
West, Robert A., general merchant
Williams, Michael, butcher

Thornton.—A Village in the Township of Innisfil, County Simcoe, 9 miles from Barrie, the County Town Population 100.

Armstrong, William, J.P
BANTING, THOMAS M., Postmaster, gen mercht
Doan, Lambert, farmer
Fyfe, Joseph, J.P
Henry, Thomas, farmer
Hill, Arthur, farmer
Lennox, Ignatius, farmer
Lennox, Thomas, farmer
Walker, Aaron, farmer

Thorold.—An incorporated village on the Welland Canal, and a station of the Great Western and Welland Railways, in the Township of Thorold, County Welland, 12 miles from the County Town, 3 from St. Catharines and 75 by rail and 45 by water from Toronto. The village possesses first-class water power and an excellent opening is offered for all kinds of manufactures. The chief at present are three cotton mills; a paper mill; 3 flour mills; a plaster and cement mill; a tannery, a foundry, etc Population 2000

Arnold, James, groceries and liquors
Baker, Henry, potter
Ball, Bernard, grocer
Ball, J. H., teacher grammar school
Band & McArthur, flouring mill
Barter, George, attorney-at-law
Batten, John, butcher
BAXTER, GEORGE, barrister and attorney-at-law, solicitor, &c
Beatty, Henry, farmer
Beatty, John
Beatty, William, M.P
Beatty & Son, hide and leather dealers
Bell, Thomas, cooper
Birbeck, Richard, stoves and tinware
Booth, Thomas A., carpenter
Boyle, John, manager P. Bowen's
Bridden & Booth, potters
Brown, John, contractor and prop. of cement mills
Brown, John, collector
Browne, J. E., druggist & agent Montreal Telegraph Company.
Buchanan, Samuel, agent Welland Railroad
Burley, George, carpenter
Campbell, James & C., manufacturer of cotton yarns
Campbell, William, carpenter
Carroll, William, accountant
Carter, John
CITY HOTEL LIVERY STABLES, Fitch & Rogers proprietors (see adv)
CITY HOTEL, A. Lock, proprietor
Cloy, John, general merchant
Cloy, John, baker
Cockburn, Mrs., millinery
Comerford, John, carpenter
Comerford, Richard, carpenter
Cowan, William, miller
Crawford, Charles tailor
Curry & Hawse, soap and candle makers
DOBBIE, A., manufacturer of steam engines, mill gearing and iron turbine water wheels
DOUGAN, ROBERT, grocery, hardware, crockery
Elwiss, William, cabinet maker
Fields, William, Thorold House
Fish, W. F., accountant
FITCH & ROGERS, livery stable keepers (see adv)
Flannery, Matthew, painter
Friday, Theodore, saddler
Garden, Arthur, general merchant
GRAHAM, JOHN & CO., publishers *True Patriot*
Gray, George, carpenter
Grenville, John, wagon maker
Gribben, Rev. J. J. (Roman Catholic)
Happell, George, boots and shoes
Hendershot, C. E., general merchant
Hendershott, M., groceries, boots and shoes
Hendershott, W., saw mill proprietor
Henderson, Alexander, teacher
Hennessy, Michael, carpenter
Howell, William, wagon maker
James, H., agent American Express Co.
James, William, farmer
Jenkinson, Thomas, Royal Exchange Hotel
Johnston, R. J., M.D.
Jones, Clement A., nursery
Keefer, Rev. B. B. (Wesleyan)
Keefer, H. F., general merchant
KEEFER, JACOB, Postmaster
Keefer, John, farmer
Kisby, Henry, dyer
Lampman, Frederick, attorney-at-law
Lawson, James, miller
Lawson, William, tailor
Lawson & Cowan, flour merchants
Lear, Daniel, grocer
Leeson, Richard, general merchant
Lemon, Adam, carpenter
Lemon, B. H., M.D.
Leonard, T. S. & Co., clothiers
Lepper & Co., John, dry goods
LOCK, A., proprietor City Hotel (see adv)
McBride, James, cooper
McCarthy, Mrs., proprietor Mansion House
McDonagh, John, proprietor saw mill
McFARLAND, GEORGE, groceries, liquors, hardware, boots and shoes, etc. (see adv)
McGovern, John, saloon and grocery
McINDOE, ARCHIBALD, block maker
McIntosh, Alexander, saddler
McIntyre, James, tailor
McKague, Neil, butcher
McPherson & Weir, proprietors flouring mill
Mackay, Thomas, butcher
Millar, James, tailor
Millar, James. horse dealer
Moore, Jones, wholesale grocer
Moran, Michael, teacher
Morley, Isabella, boots and shoes
Morley, John, plow manufacturer
Munro, James, dry goods and clothing
Norris & Neelon, flour merchants
Ogg, James D., baker
Ontario Cotton Warp Mills, James Campbell & Co., proprietor
Owens, P. B., dry goods
Palmer, L. L., M.D.
Parnall, William, planing mill
Parnall, William, sash, door and blinds
PATTERSON & FOTHRINGHAM, manufacturers of all kinds of bent stuff for carriage making, also dealers in hubs, spokes, &c.
Pew, Robert, teacher
Pike, William, cooper
Radley, Stephen, Bailiff Division Court
Radley, Stephen, prop. Mail Bus, G.W.R.
Reid, W., agent G. W. R.
Roberts, Rev. T. T. (Church of England)
Rogers, Matthew, teacher
Rolls, Henry, M.D.
Sands, P., barber
Sanders, Joseph, boot and shoe maker
SAUNDERS, W. Sr (Saunders & Phelps)
SAUNDERS & PHELPS, hub, spokes, fellowes, bent work and carriage fifth wheel manufactory
Schooley, Gilbert, groceries
Schaaf, John, jeweler
Schwaller, A., groceries, liquors and hardware mercht
SCOTT, T. D., confectioner (see adv)
Sharp, David, clothing dealer
Shordes, E. S., dentist
Stanley, Alexander, insurance agent
Stanley, Alfred, painter
Starr, Rev. J. H. (Wesleyan)
Stewart, James, general merchant
Stevenson, John, carpenter
Stevenson, William J., general merchant

TAGGART, JAMES L., boot and shoe maker
TAGGART'S SALOON; James L. Taggart
Theal, L., blacksmith
Thompson, W. H., Welland Hotel
THOROLD TRUE PATRIOT, (weekly) John Graham & Co., proprietors
WAIT, W. W.
Weeks, James, saddler
Wells, Russell, carpenter
Whitelock, John, carpenter
Williams, James, carpenter
WINSLOW, WILLIAM, British Hotel (see adv)

Thorold Station.—(See Merritton).—A Village in the Township of Grantham, County Lincoln.
STEPHENS, S. M., Postmaster.

Thurlow.—A Village in the Township of Thurlow, County Hastings, 13 miles from Belleville, the County Town. Ten Mile creek in the immediate vicinity affords good water power. Average value of land $20. Population 200.

Betts, Rev. L. A., (Episcopal Methodist)
Cadman, A., butcher
Caldwell, John F., insurance agent
Casey, James, farmer
Casey, John, farmer
Casey, Miss Martha, telegraph operator
CASEY, WILLIAM T., Postmaster, wagon maker
Casey, Willot, farmer
Chapman, William, farmer
Davis, Daniel, shingle maker
Denyes, Peter, farmer
Embury, Allen, carpenter
Giffard, Abraham, broom manufacturer
Goman, Richard J., teacher
Ham, D., farmer
Hazlitt, Joseph, farmer
Howell, Rev. Jacob E., (Wesleyan)
Huntly, Charles, teacher
McAmmond, Rev. T., (Episcopal Methodist)
McGunnion, Peter, leather dealer and shoemaker
McMichael, R. C., cabinet maker
McReady, Mary, teacher
Miller, Morgan, carpenter
Palmer, John D., insurance agent
Palmer, P. R., insurance agent
Palmer, P. R., farmer
Parks, John, carpenter
Phillips, George, J.P.
Phillips, James, farmer
Phillips, Marcus, farmer
Phillips, Robert, farmer
Phillips, William, farmer
Phillips, William H., saddler
Sills, Robert, farmer
Sills, William, J.P., farmer
Thrasher, Gilbert, farmer
Van Allen, Mrs. Susan, M.D.
Wells, William C., Patent Right agent and saddler
Willson, B. S., M.D.

Tilbury East.—A Post Office in the Township of Tilbury East, County Kent.

Ainslie, James, insurance agent
Daly, Bernard, teacher
Fletcher, John, real estate agent
Jackson, Benjamin T., M.D.
Kerr, John, J.P.
Laing, Alexander, carpenter
Letorneau, Solomon, shingle maker
Martin, Matthew, J.P.
Mazary, Carlo, painter
Reid, Robert, carpenter
Sales, George, carpenter
SMITH, JAMES, Postmaster, general merchant and lumber dealer
Smith, Robert & Bros., proprietors steam flouring mill
Stevenson, Andrew, cooper
Stewart, James, general merchant
Vaughan, William, cooper
Waddell, Robert H., J.P.
Wands, Alexander, wagon maker

Tilsonburg.—(Dereham P. O.)—A Village on Otter Creek, in the Township of Dereham, County Oxford 25 miles from Woodstock, the County Town, and 15 from Ingersoll Station, Great Western Railway, Lumber is the principal business, excellent water power in the vicinity. Improved land in the neighborhood averages $35; wild, $10 per acre. Stages to Ingersoll, Vienna and Port Burwell. The Tilsonburg *Observer* is published every Thursday. Money Order Office and Savings Bank. Population 1000.

Armstrong & Wardle, general merchants
Ault, J. Mc., M.D.
Bain, Th mas B., general merchant
Beaupre, T., shoemaker
Best, George, farmer
Betts, Rev. J. E. (Wesleyan)
Bjorck, N. F., leather dealer
Bouser, George, livery
Brook, B., woolen factory
Brown, T. L., dentist
Barnes, F., butcher
Burke, R. H. & Co., founders and machinists
Carpenter, S. B. W., carpenter
Cowan, Alexander, farmer
Crosset, Peter, farmer
Darrow, J. & W., founders
Dewar, John, tailor
Dillon, M., auctioneer
Dobie, T. W., M.P.
Dyke, T. J., telegraph operator
Ferguson, C. W., general merchant, insurance agent
Forshee, J. N., hotel keeper
Garnett, John, insurance agent
Goodwin, C., farmer
Goodwin, John, farmer
Graham, P., North American Hotel
Hardey, Thomas, J.P.
Harrick, Ira, farmer
Harvey, W., carpenter
Hawkins, C., J.P.
Hawkins, F. R., carpenter
Hayes, J., farmer

Hayes, W., farmer
Hill, Charles, carpenter
Hogan, H., farmer
Jeffery, John, farmer
Jones, Rev. Henry (Church of England)
Kellet, W., farmer
Kelso, D., cabinet maker
Kern, S., farmer
LAW, W. S., editor *Tilsonburg Observer*
Leduc, T., teacher
Lindop, J. C., general merchant
Livingstone, S., farmer
Luke, J., brewer
McDonald, William, tailor
McDonald & Norris, barristers
McLean, L., com. merchant, insurance agent
McMullen, B., carpenter
Malcolm, F., farmer
Maybee, O. P., farmer
Marett, F.
Moran & Hillman, bakers
Musselman, A., hotel keeper
North, William, saddler
Paine, T. L., grocer
Pease, C. J., painter
Pettit, D., brickmaker
Pryor, W. A., shoemaker
Richardson, Rev. W. (Presbyterian)
Robinson, George, grocer
Ruggles, Levi, sash factory
Sanders, J. M., farmer
Sharp, F., butcher
Shattuck, H., farmer
Sinclair, L. C., M.D.
Smith, J. & L., millers
Smith, M. S., general merchant
Taylor, George, shoemaker
Thompson, John, saddler
Tillson, E. D., general merchant, flour and planing mills
TILSONBURG OBSERVER (Thursday), W. S. Law, editor
Tweedale, J. M., M.D., druggist
VAN NORMAN, BENJAMIN, Postmaster
Vansittart, J. G., barrister
Waller, H., shoemaker
Waller. R., tinsmith
Watts, W. Z., cabinet maker
Weeks, Joseph, farmer
White, Absolom, shingle maker
Wilcox, J. D., farmer
Williams, R., farmer
Willson, A., butcher
Younie, George, carpenter

Tiverton.—A Village in the Township of Kincardine, County Bruce, 27 miles from Walkerton, the County Town. Stages to Kincardine 9 miles, Southampton 20, Pinkerton 15, and Inverhuron 3 miles. Population 150.

Ballantyne, Robert, boots and shoes
Curie, Rev. H. (Presbyterian)
Dodds, Thomas, woolen mill proprietor
Fraser, Rev. William (Baptist)
Gifford, C., proprietor steam flouring mill
Kennedy, N., general merchant
McAuley, John, stoves and tinware
McBain, A., general merchant
McDonald, John, leather dealer
McDougall, A., carpenter
McEwen, Daniel, teacher
McFayden, A., proprietor hotel and livery
McINNES, N., Postmaster
McInnes, P. & A., general merchants
McIntyre, A., carriage and wagon maker
McIntyre, J. C., carpenter
McKinnon, J., J.P.
McLellan, D., J.P.
Paterson, D., grocer
Paterson, J. Rae, M.D.
Rice, Rev. Luther O. (Wesleyan)
Robertson, J., tailor
Stroner, J., tailor
Turner, Mrs., proprietor Tiverton House
Wickham, J., shingle maker
Wickham, C., J.P.
Wright, John, boots and shoes

Toledo.—A Village on Irish Creek, in the Township of Kitley, County Leeds, 20 miles from Brockville, the County Town; 8 from Jasper Station, Brockville and Ottawa Railway. The Creek affords excellen water power. Land averages $40 per acre. Population 200.

Baker, L., proprietor hotel
Bellamy, Chancey, lumber dealer
Bellamy, Chancey and James, props. flouring mill
Cornell, S. S., M.D.
Dayton, John H., dyer and scourer
Denaut, Stephen, cooper
Derbyshire, Matthew, teacher
Drewery, Thomas, tailor
Hillis, James, cooper
Hillis, Thomas, cooper
Hillis, William, prop. sash and door factory
Judson, Silas, cabinet maker
Judson, Wesley, saddler
Kincade, James, saddler
King, James, cooper
Knapp, S., famer
Koye, James, butcher
Lewis, Rev. J. (Wesleyan)
Lockwood, Norton, carpenrer
Lockwood, Walter, carpenter
Loucks, R., farmer
Lyman, Z., J.P.
McCrum, James, cooper
McCrum, William, shoemaker
McLEAN, MRS. C. A., Postmistress
Marshall, Josiah, farmer
Marshall, M., farmer
Raney, Rev. William (Wesleyan)
Reed, A., farmer
Read, David R., general merchant
Read, William, carpenter
Robinson, Horatio, leather dealer and tanner
Robinson, Stephen, shingle maker
Robinson S., proprietor Stage House
Robinson, William, carpenter
Sailman, Frank, butcher
Stewart, George J.P.
Stratton, James, general merchant and wagon maker
Stratton, William, wagon maker
Stratton, Y., farmer
Webster, Beecher & Code, general merchants
White, Rev. William (Presbyterian)
Williams, D., farmer
Williams, H., farmer
Willson, David, shoemaker
Willson, M. J., saddler

Topping.—A Post Village in the Township of North Easthope, County Perth, 10 miles from Stratford, the County Town. Mails tri-weekly. Population 60.

CROZIER, S., Postmaster
Crozier, T., constable
Mohr, Charles, innkeeper

Toronto.—The chief city of the Province of Ontario, is situated in latitude 43° 39' 24" north, and longitude 79° 21' 30" west, on the north-west shore of Lake Ontario, and facing the Bay, a beautiful and spacious sheet of water, oval in form, and accessible to craft of all kinds. It was founded by Lieutenant-Governor Simcoe, who, having formed extensive plans for the improvement of the colony, resolved upon the foundation of a Provincial capital, and caused the first survey of the site to be made in 1793, by Bouchette, of the Royal Engineers. The place was called York until 1834, when it was incorporated, and the name changed to Toronto. In 1813 York was captured by the Americans, under General Pike, who was killed at the storming of the fort, but was held only for a few days, while in the meantime the Government House, public buildings, and all stores that could not be carried away, were burned. The site of the city is nearly level, sloping gently from the water's edge. The form is that of a parallelogram, the streets intersecting at right angles; the two chief thoroughfares, containing the principal mercantile establishments, are named King and Yonge: the former runs parallel with the Bay, and the latter intersects it, extending northwards for upwards of thirty miles, forming a sort of irregular village, and passing through a rich and prosperous country. The public buildings are numerous, and many of them very handsome. The principal are University College, a spacious Gothic structure, standing amidst the retired retreats of the Queen's Park, with beautiful avenues leading from Yonge and Queen Streets, Trinity, Upper Canada and St. Michael's Colleges, the Provincial Normal School Buildings, the Magnetical Observatory, situated in the Queen's Park, established by the British Government at the request of the Royal Society of England in 1840, the General Hospital, St. James' and St. Michael's Cathedrals, and the numerous churches, Osgoode Hall, the seat of the Superior Courts of Law and Equity for Ontario; the Crystal Palace, built for the use of the Provincial Exhibition, the Provincial Lunatic Asylum on Queen Street and its branch in Queen's Park, the St. Lawrence Hall, Mechanics' Institute, Masonic Hall, Merchants' Exchange, Western, British American, Royal, and Edinburgh Insurance Buildings, the *Telegraph* and *Globe* printing offices, and the several banking establishments. The Queen's and University Parks, the Horticultural Gardens and Normal School Grounds are tastefully laid out and open to all for pleasure and recreation. Toronto is the seat of the Provincial Government, and the several public departments are located here.. The industrial establishments are extensive, thriving and rapidly extending their capacity and improving their productions. The city is well supplied with water, and is lighted by gas. The spacious land-locked harbor affords every facility for any possible extension of trade and the connection with all parts of the Dominion and the United States, by means of the Grand Trunk, Great Western and Northern Railways, and by navigation in summer, combined with the steady energy and enterprise of her citizens, and her centralized position, make the future of Toronto progressive and prosperous. Estimated city assessment, $25,000,000. Distant from Montreal 333 miles, Kingston 165 miles, Hamilton 45 miles, London 114 miles, Collingwood 93 miles, New York 500 miles, Boston 593 miles. Population 60,000.

CITY GOVERNMENT.

ELECTED JANUARY 1869.

Council meets in the City Hall every Monday evening.

Mayor—Samuel B. Harman.

St. Andrew's Ward.—Aldermen—Harman, Boulton and Bell.

St. David's Ward.—Aldermen—Hynes, Adamson and Lepper.

St. George's Ward.—Aldermen—Smith, Vickers and Clements.

St. James' Ward.—Aldermen—Sheard, Boustead and Henderson.

St. John's Ward.—Alderman—Boxall, Riddell and J. E. Smith.

St. Lawrence Ward—Alderman—Strachan, Medcalf and Manning.

St. Patrick's Ward.—Alderman—Baxter, Dickey and Harrison.

OFFICERS OF THE CORPORATION.

City Clerk.—John Carr.

Assistant Clerk.—Stephen Radcliff.

Assistant Clerks.—F. B. Orris, Robert Roddy and Martin Merry.

Chamberlain.—A. T. McCord.

Assistant Chamberlain.—M. B. Hicks.

Assistant Clerks.—John W. Hetherington and Wm. Jardine.

License Inspector.—Ogle R. Gowan.

Assistant License Inspector—Robert Beard.

City Engineer—Joseph H. Bennett.

Assistant in Engineer's Office.—George H. Booth.

Clerk Engineer's Office.—Robt. Wilson.

Chief Engineer of Fire Brigade.—James Ashfield.

Health Officer.—John Reed.

Weigh Master.—Charles Fisher.

Police Magistrate.—Alexander McNabb.

Police Clerk.—J. T. Nudel.

Chief of Police.—W. S. Prince.

Auditors.—George A. Barber and William R. Orr.

Collectors.—St. David's Ward—Charles McCaffrey. St. Lawrence Ward—George Hulme. St. Andrew's Ward—William J. Turner. St. James' Ward—A. Jardine. St. George's Ward—John Nixon. St. John's Ward—Andrew Fleming. St. Pattrick's Ward—John Henry.

City Coroners.—Dr. Hallowell, Dr. Lawlor, Dr. Riddell, and Dr. Buchanan.

Clerk of the Peace for the County of the City of Toronto, and a Commissioner for *dedimus Potestatem* for the administration of Oaths of Office, Stephen Radcliffe.

Sheriff.—F. W. Jarvis.

Crier.—James Severs.

Lessees of Markets.—St. Lawrence and Wood Markets, Thomas Beatty; Hay, Fish and Cattle Markets, Robert Guy.

The Police Court, old Mechanics' Institute, Court Street. Alexander Macnabb, Police Magistrate.

The Police Office, old Mechanics' Institute, Court street.

The Eastern Station House is under the City Hall. *The Western Station House* is on Queen street, between Peter and Brock streets. *The Yonge Street Station House* is opposite Edward street.

STANDING COMMITTEES *and Boards of the Council of the Corporation of the City of Toronto*, 1868.—*Finance and Assessment.*—Alderman Boxall, chairman; Messrs. Boulton, Boustead, Dickey, Manning, Vickers.

Board of Works.—Alderman Sheard, chairman: Messrs. Baxter, Bell, Hynes, Riddell, Strachan, T. Smith.

Jail Inspectors.—Alderman Strachan, chairman; Messrs. Bell, Boxall, Harrison, Lepper, Sheard, T. Smith.

Fire, Water and Gas.—Alderman Dickey, chairman; Messrs. Adamson, Bell, Boustead, Clements, Manning, J. E. Smith.

Wharves and Harbors.—Alderman Bell, chairman; Messrs. Boxall, Clements, Dickey, Henderson, Lepper, Strachan.

Licenses.—Alderman Vickers, chairman; Messrs. Boulton, Harrison, Henderson, Lepper, Medcalf, Riddel.

Walks and Gardens.—Alderman Baxter, chairman; Messrs. Boulton, Hynes, Sheard, J. E. Smith, Strachan, Vickers.

Public Buildings.—Alderman Adamson, chairman; Messrs. Boulton, Boxall, Harrison, Henderson, Manning, T. Smith.

Public Markets.—Alderman T. Smith, chairman; Messrs. Boulton, Baxter, Dickey, Henderson, Lepper, Medcalf.

Board of Health.—Alderman Boustead, chairman; Messrs. Baxter, Bell, Hynes, Riddell, T. Smith, Strachan.

Printing.—Alderman Clements, chairman; Messrs. Boulton, Boustead, Harrison, Lepper, Manning, Riddell.

SCHOOL TRUSTEES.

CHAIRMAN: JOHN BAXTER.

St. Lawrence Ward.—Thomas Winfield, Dr. J. Ross.

St. David's Ward.—Emerson Coatsworth, Dr. H. H. Wright.

St. James Ward.—James Bain, Walter S. Lee.

St. Andrews' Ward.—Henry Godson, W. B. McMurrich.

St. John's Ward.—Arbuckle Jardine, Thomas Spence.

St. George's Ward.—Hon. John McMurrich, Dr Joseph Adams.

St. Patrick's Ward.—Alderman John Baxter, Dr. W. W. Ogden.

Secretary of the Board, George A. Barber. Local Superintendent, Rev. James Porter.

SCHOOLS AND NAMES OF TEACHERS.—*St. Lawrence.*—Palace St. School.—Head Master, M. Gill; Head Mistress, Miss J. Armstrong; Assistant Teacher, Miss H. Wilkinson.

St. David—George Street School.—Head Master, J. F. Jeffers; Head Mistress, Miss M. J. Keown; Assistant Teachers, Miss M. Hamilton, Miss A. L. Armstrong; Junior Assistants, Miss C. Scarlett, Miss A. Henning.

St. David.—The Park School.—Head Master, William Anderson; Head Mistress, Miss M. Robertson; Assistant Teacher, Miss Boddy: Junior Assistants, Miss M. A. Anker, Miss M. Buik.

St. James.—Victoria Street School.—Head Master, William Spotton; Head Mistress, Miss G. Round; Assistant Teachers, Miss M. A. Kennedy, Miss E. Kennedy; Junior Assistants, Miss M. Robinson, Miss A. O'Flagherty.

St. John.—Louisa Street School.—Head Master, Henry Browne; Head Mistress, J. S. Morrison, Assistant, Teachers, Miss L. Pyper, Miss P. McGee; Junior Assistants, Miss A. Hall, Miss C. Spotton.

St. John.—Elizabeth Street School.—Head Master, Robert McCausland; Head Mistress, Miss M. Greenlees; Assistant Teacher, Miss Sarah McBride, Miss S. M. Hamilton.

St. George.—John Street School.—Head Master, S. McAllister, Head Mistress, Miss M. Ferguson; Assistant Teacher, Miss Agness Kelloch; Junior Asistants, Mrs. J. Hamilton, Miss M. Elliott.

St. Patrick.—Phœbe Street School.—Head Master, Samuel Coyne; Head Mistress, Miss C. M. Churchill; Assistant Teachers, Miss A. Rogers, Miss O. Dunn; Junior Assistants, Miss E. Frazer, Miss Eliza Thompson, Miss Fanny Lawrence.

St. Patrick.—Givins Street School.—Head Master, James Anderson; Head Mistress, Miss R. Thompson.

TORONTO POST OFFICE.

Postmaster.—Joseph Lesslie.

Assistant Postmaster.—G. H. Backas.

Clerks.—John H. Davis, John Carruthers, Alfred Cooper, Alfred Barley, Aylmer Langley, Benjamin Langley, Alfred Corke, Joseph Saulter, John Forsyth, Archibald Harstone, Henry Falkiner, Donald P. Ross, William Wright, Henry Boulter, Charles R. Butler, William Loudon, Augustus Webber, B. M. Armstrong, C. J. W. Winstanley, John Monaghan, George A. Ross, Jas. A. Brodie, E. D. James.

Letter Carriers.—John McCloskey, John Ross, Peter Ross, Robert Stephens, James Alston, John Bazley, J. Clode, A. Brown, John Hudson.

Box Collectors.—Thos. Crotty, J. Hodgkinson.

Housekeeper and Messenger.—Joseph Roden.

Assistant Messenger.—Geo. Wm. Groth.

INSPECTOR'S OFFICE, TORONTO DIVISION.

P. O. Inspector.—John Dewe.

Chief Clerk.—Wm. Cuppage.

Clerks.—Daniel Spry, John McLochlin, G. J. Mason, H. W. Jackson.

Messenger.—John Buchan.

CUSTOM HOUSE.

Collector.—Jas. E. Smith.
Surveyor.—Thomas C. Scott.
Chief Clerk.—John Douglas.
Clerks.—G. Henderson, C. K. Mackay, A. Munro, J. Woodhouse, D. Delamere, Russell Inglis, John Beaty.
Appraiser.—Alexander Macpherson.
Chief Landing Waiter.—J. P. Dunn.
Landing Waiters.—T. McCarthy, H. Sinclair, J. Christie, J. W. Hogan, W. Howe, Bouchette Anderson; J. Milbourne, Landing Waiter at outport Credit; George Watson, Landing waiter at outport Collingwood.
Lockers.—J. Stitt, R. G. A. Paton, Alex. Duff.
Messenger and Housekeeper.—Wm. Mackay.

BOARD OF TRADE EXCHANGE.

Wellington Street.

OFFICERS FOR 1869.

President.—James G. Worts.
Vice-President.—William Elliott.
Treasurer.—John Turner.
Secretary.—Chas. Robertson.
Members of Council.—A. R. McMaster, Thos. C. Chisholm, John Gordon, A. M. Smith, Robert Wilkes, Chas. Robertson, Henry S. Howland, John Laidlaw, J. C. Fitch, Hon. John McMurrich, Noah Barnhart, W. J. McDonell.
Board of Arbitration.—F. W. Coate, W. D. Matthews, J. D. Merrick, James Adamson, H. S. Howland, James Young, C. W. Bunting, J. C. Campbell, Charles Parsons, J. C. Fitch, J. C. Griffith, W. J. Shaw.
Harbor Commissioners.—Messrs. J. G. Worts and Thomas D. Harris.
Hospital Trustee.—Henry S. Howland.

INLAND REVENUE OR EXCISE OFFICE.

EXCHANGE BUILDINGS.—OFFICERS.

Assistant Commissioner.—Alfred Brunel, Brock Street.
District Inspector.—Henry Godson, 200 Richmond Street West.
Collectors.—George P. Dickson, 12 Gerrard Street; James Shaw, Wellington Street.
Deputy Collectors.—John Morrow, Spadina Avenue; R. A. Hartley.
Excise Officers.—W. M. Gorrie, Exchange Buildings; F. H. Mickleburgh, Temperance Street; Maxwell McCord; Richard Woodsworth, Church Street; Angus D. McDonell, Dundas Street; Sam'l Grey, Church Street; R. R. Dixon, Queen Street; John McDonnell Campbell, Bay Street; C. T. Dixon, 12 Gerrard Street; P. M. Robins, Yonge Street.

HARBOR COMMISSIONERS.

Office, Front Street, nearly opposite the Custom House, J. G. Worts, Esq., Chairman.
Commissioners appointed by the Board of Trade.—T. D. Harris, J. G. Worts.
Commissioners appointed by the City Council.—Ald. Smith and Manning.
Commissioner appointed by the Government.—Wm. Cawthra.
Harbor Master.—Hugh Richardson.
Deputy Harbor Master.—James Smith, junr.
Light-house Keeper, and Deputy Harbor Master, Queen's Wharf.—Robert Kerr.

TORONTO FIRE DEPARTMENT.

Chief Engineer.—James Ashfield; residence, No. 8 Temperance Street; Office, south-west wing City Hall Buildings.
Assistant Engineer.—Richard Ardagh.
22 branchmen, 11 hook and ladder men, 1 bugler, 2 engineers of steam fire engines, 2 firemen of steam fire engines, 2 drivers of horses for steam fire engines, 3 drivers of hose carts, 1 driver of hook and ladder truck, 1 caretaker, in all 47 men, with three steam fire engines, hose carts, hose, hook and ladder apparatus, and 7 horses.
Two Stations.—No. 1 Station, at Bay Street Fire Hall, corner of Temperance Street; No. 2 Station, at Court Street Fire Hall.

METROPOLITAN WATER COMPANY.

Offices, 21 and 22 Exchange Buildings; J. Evans, Clerk of the Company; L. G. Bolster, Superintendent; W. H. Stotesbury, Collector.

CONSUMERS' GAS COMPANY.

Office, Toronto street, east side. E. H. Rutherford, President; James Austin, Vice-President; Hon. Wm. McMaster, George Duggan, L. W. Smith, W. Cawthra, I. C. Gilmor, J. T. Smith, J. H. Mead, James Henderson, John Eastwood, A. Lepper, Directors; Henry Thompson, Manager; W. H. Pearson. Book-keeper; F. D. Whittemore, Assistant Book, keeper; John Henderson, Foreman.

HURON AND ONTARIO SHIP CANAL CO.

Provisional Directors: F. C. Capreol, W. J. Macdonell (manager Toronto Savings Bank), Hon. Donald McDonald, Thomas R. Ferguson, M.P.P., Thomas Grahame, M.P.P., Adam Crooks, Q.C., Henry Fowler, John Hawkshaw and A. M. Kendall, of London, England, Consulting Engineers; Wm. Sykes, Resident Engineer; A. Luders Light, C. E., Woodstock; Hon. William Cayley, Honorary Secretary; Messrs. Crickmore, Boyd & Stayner, Solicitors.

CANADA MERCANTILE PROTECTIVE ASSOCIATION.

Office, 20 Toronto street, Toronto. President, A. K. Boomer; Board of Directors: Messrs. Joseph Hurd (Hurd & Leigh), Thomas Webb, W. P. Marston, John Kay, A. K. Boomer, Wm. Hewitt, J. Storell, Wm. Strachan, Wm. Awde; Solicitors: O'Connor, Warmoll & Givens; Managers, Messrs. Cupples & Hunter.

BANKS.

Bank of British North America, corner of Yonge and Wellington streets. S. Taylor, Manager; Lewis Moffatt, Frederick Perkins, Local Directors; Larratt W. Smith, Solicitor; Thomas S. Hill, Accountant; J. A. Codd, First Teller; J. G. Orchard, Second Teller; E. W. Syer, Discount Clerk; E. Wickens, Ledger Keeper; A. A. Nicholson, O. Weir, Clerks; Robert Parks, Messenger.

Bank of Montreal, corner of Yonge and Front streets. Head Office, Montreal. T. B. Anderson, President; E. H. King, General Manager. Capital-$6,000,000. Toronto Branch—George W. Yarker, Manager; S. J. Stammers, Accountant; G. H. Wilson, First Teller; M. Heaton, Second Teller; D. Glass, Third Teller; J. C. Vankoughnet, Assistant Accountant; W. G. Telfer, Ledger Keeper (Credit); R. B. Crombie, Deposit Ledger Keeper; W. G. Telfer, Teller's Assistant; George Drummond and A. Jarvis, Clerks; P. McBrien, Messenger.

Bank of Toronto.—Directors: William Gooderham, James G. Worts, Hon. A. A. Burnham, William Cantley, William Fraser, William Cawthra, and A. T. Fulton; William Gooderham, President; James G. Worts, Vice-President; George Hague, Cashier; Hugh Leach, Assistant Cashier; W. R. Wadsworth, Accountant; William Simpson, Inspector; J. T. M. Burnside, First Teller; W. M. Harman, Second Teller; G. W. Hodgetts, Third Teller; D. Campbell, Discount Clerk; John Adams, Assistant Discount Clerk; C. W. Arnold, Ledger Keeper; Joseph Henderson, Collection Clerk; C. J. Page, J. A. Johnston, E. C. B. Fetherstonhaugh, Clerks. Bank, corner of Wellington and Church streets.

Bank of Upper Canada.—Trustees' Office, Ontario Hall, Church street.

Canadian Bank of Commerce—Opened May 1st, 1867. Hon. William McMaster, President; Henry S. Howland, Vice-President; R. J. Dallas, Cashier; John C. Kemp, Inspector; Wm. Smith, Accountant; W. G. Boswell, Assistant Accountant; Robert C. Jennings, First Teller; Robert C. Miller, Second Teller; W. J. Robertson, Transfer Clerk; J. H. Plummer, Discount Clerk; L. Bolster, Ledger Keeper; L. Buchan, T. M. Watson, B. Jennings and R. O. Greet, Clerks; J. Blackwell, Messenger.

City Bank, Montreal.—South-west corner of Bay and Wellington streets. John Moat, Manager; G. W. Manning, Teller; W. C. Kennedy, Discount Clerk; Clifton Shears, Ledger Keeper; J. Ardill, Messenger.

Merchants' Bank, 13 Wellington street west. James G. Harper, Manager; F. Cresswell, Accountant; W. Scadding, Teller; H. R. Morton, Corresponding Clerk; John Morphy, Discount Clerk; D. Miller, Branch Accountant; J. Henderson, Messenger.

Ontario Bank, corner of Wellington and Scott Streets. A. Fisher, Manager; Hon. W. P. Howland, C.B., Local Director; Patton, Osler & Moss, Solicitors; G. H. McVity, Accountant; George Hamilton, Ledger Keeper; J. F. Feilde, Paying Teller; W. B. Wallace, Receiving Teller; W. H. Holland, Discount Clerk; G. Lovekin, Junior Clerk; F. Guest, Messenger.

Quebec Bank, Bank of Toronto Building. Head Office Quebec. Capital, $1,478,725. S. Stevenson, Cashier; R. H. Bethune, Manager; J. Price, Accountant; J. H. Kane, Teller; J. H. Miller, Ledger Keeper; William Nicholls, Clerk.

Royal Canadian Bank.—Discount days, each day. James Metcalfe, President; Hon. D. McDonald, Vice-President. Directors: Wm. Barber, James Crombie, R. A. Harrison, Alexander Manning, A. M. Smith; T. Woodside, Cashier; John Michie, Assistant do.; Alexander Campbell, Accountant; Arch. Campbell, Inspector; George Burn, J. M. G. Ridley; F. A. Ridley, Tellers; F. A. Knapp, General Ledger; John Graham, Stock do.; W. M. Peterkin, Discount do.; W. C. Pridham, Deposit do.; F. A. Reesor, Collection Clerk; James Scott, Secretary.

SAVINGS BANKS.

Government Post Office Savings Bank.—Office at Toronto Post Office.

Toronto Savings Bank.—Office, 72 Church Street. William J. MacDonnell, Manager; James Mason, Assistant. Interest at rate of 5 per cent.

Merchants' Savings Bank, Wellington street, in connection with the Merchants' Bank of Canada. Capital, $6,000,000. J. G. Harper, Manager. C. Scadding, Actuary.

Interest at the rate of four per cent. per annum will be allowed on all deposits of four dollars and upwards.

Interest will commence from the day of deposit and allowed to the date of withdrawal. Deposits may be withdrawn at any time at the pleasure of the depositor.

Depositors of one hundred dollars and upwards may obtain a higher rate of interest by a special arrangement, the particulars of which will be made known on application.

BUILDING, SAVING AND INVESTMENT SOCIETIES.

Frehold Permanent Building and Savings Society.—Incorporated May, 1859, pursuant to the Act of the Provincial Legislature, 9th Victoria, chapter 90, and amendments. Office, corner of Church and Court streets. Capital, $500,000, in shares of $100 each. Hon. William McMaster, *President;* James Michie, *Vice-President;* Charles Robertson, *Secretary;* John Leys, *Solicitor;* W. D. Taylor, *Cashier;* R. R. Cathron, *Bookkeeper. Directors*—Hon. Wm. McMaster, Hon. Henry S. Howland, James Michie, W. J. Macdonell, Alexander Murray, James Austin, A. T. Fulton. *Bankers*—Bank of Commerce.

Canada Permanent Building and Savings Society—Incorporated by authority of Parliament. Capital, $1,100,000. Invested on Real Estate, $1,400,000. Annual Income, $400,000. Office, Masonic Hall, Toronto Street, Toronto. *Board of Directors*—Joseph D. Ridout, *President;* Peter Paterson, *Vice-President;* James G. Worts, Edward Hooper, Samuel Nordheimer, Joseph Robinson, A. M. Smith, E. H. Rutherford; Jonas Ap Jones, *Solicitor;* J. Herbert Mason, *Secretary and Treasurer. Bankers*—Bank of Toronto; Bank of Montreal.

Commercial Building and Savings Society.—The Hon. John McMurrich, *President;* John Burns, *Vice-President;* John Rains, *Secretary and Treasurer.* Office, corner of Yonge and Adelaide streets.

The Provincial Permanent Building and Savings' Society.—*Directors*—A. Thornton Todd, *President;* C. S. Gzowski, *Vice-President;* C. J. Campbell, F. W. Cumberland, Manager Northern Railway, W. Ince, Messrs. F. & G. Perkins & Co., Herbert Mortimer. *Solicitors*—Messrs. Patton, Osler & Moss. *Bankers*—Bank of British North America. *City and County Valuator*—C. Unwin, P.L.S. *Auditors*—W. B. Phipps and S. Spreull. *Secretary and Treasurer*—E. Bradburne. Head Office, Toronto street, Toronto (first door south of the Post Office.

Union Permanent Building and Savings' Society.—Incorporated under the Act of the Parliament of Canada. Office, 82 King street east. Directors—F. Richardson, President; A. Lepper, Vice-President; A. Henderson, T. Henning, I. C. Gilmor, J. C. Fitch, Geo. Goulding; Wm. Mortimer Clark, Solicitor; Wm. Pyper, Secretary and Treasurer.

Western Canada Permanent Building and Savings' Society.—Directors—Hon. George W. Allan, President; John Worthington, Vice-President; Wm. Gooderham, James E. Smith, Francis Shanly, Sam'l Platt, Hon. D. L. Macpherson. Solicitors—Messrs. Robinson, Robinson & O'Brien. Bankers—Bank of Toronto; Royal Canadian Bank. Walter S. Lee, Secretary and Treasurer. Offices, No. 70 Church street, Toronto.

Metropolitan Permanent Building Society.—Incorporated pursuant to Acts of Provincial Parliament. Hon. William Cayley, President; Frank Shanly, of Toronto, Vice-President; Mathew Crooks Cameron, Solicitor; James Fraser, Secretary and Treasurer. Office, 4 King street west (next door to Fulton, Michie & Co.) Shares, $50 each, payable either in advance or by monthly instalments of $4 per share, and a deposit of $2 per share at time of entering. New members may come in at any time. No entrance money or management fee.

LOAN, LAND AND CREDIT COMPANIES.

Canada Landed Credit Company.—Incorporated by Act of Parliament, 1858. Capital, $1,000,000. Subscribed capital, $500,000. President, Lewis Moffatt, Esq. Vice-President, John Macdonald. Directors: The Hon. G. W. Allan, William Alexander, The Hon. Asa A. Burnham; C. S. Gzowski, Judge Gowan, Hon. W. P. Howland, C.B., Lewis Moffatt, Hon. William McMaster; J. B. Osborne, Samuel Spreull, Larratt W. Smith, D.C.L. Bankers: Messrs. Smith, Payne & Smith, London; Bank of Commerce, Toronto. Solicitor, Stephen Maule Jarvis. Auditors, Wm. Wilkinson, Charles Robertson. Secretary, John Symons. Head Office, 22 King street, Toronto. London Agency, Messrs. Brunton & Son, 32 Cornhill, London, E.C.

Colonial Securities Company of London, England—£500,000 sterling. Invests money upon security of improved farm lands or good city property for five years, at moderate rates of interest; charges not to exceed 20 dollars on new loans and 12 dollars on renewed loans. Deposits on account of principal taken at a fixed rate of interest. For further information apply to R. J. U. Chipman, Secretary, Toronto, or to any of the Company's valuers in Ontario. *Office*—Edinburgh Life Assurance Building, Wellington Street, Toronto.

COUNCIL OF THE AGRICULTURAL AND ARTS ASSOCIATION OF ONTARIO.

ELECTED MEMBERS.

No. 1 District---George McDonald, Cornwall.
2 " Hon. J. Skead, Ottawa.
3 " Andrew Wilson, Maitland.
4 " Edwin Mallory, Napanee.
5 " John Walton, Peterboro'.
6 " George Grahame, Brampton.
7 " James Cowan, Waterloo.
8 " J. C. Rykert, M.P.P., St. Catherines
9 " Hon. David Christie, Paris.
10 " Robert Gibbons, Goderich.
11 " Lionel Shipley, Falkirk.
12 " Stephen White, Charing Cross.

Ex-Officio Members.—Hon. John Carling, Commissioner of Agriculture; George Buckland, Professor of Agriculture, Toronto University; Dr. Beatty, President of Mechanics' Institute Association, Cobourg: W. A. Mills, President of Fruit Growers' Association, Hamilton: Rev. Dr. Ryerson, Chief Superintendent of Education for Ontario.

Officers.—President, E. Mallory, Napanee; Vice-President, Lionel E. Shipley, Falkirk; Treasurer, George Graham, Brampton; Secretary, Hugh C. Thomson, Toronto; Professor Croft, University College, Consulting Chemist; Andrew Smith, L.E.V.C., Veterinary Surgeon and Referee; James Fleming, Toronto; Bankers, Bank of British North America; W. A. Cooley, General Superintendent of the Exhibition; James Fleming, Superintendent of Grain, Roots, and the Horticultural Department; J. E. Pell, Superintendent of Arts and Manufactures Department.

Toronto Horticultural Society.—President, Hon. G. W. Allan; Vice-President, James Fleming; 2d Vice-President, P. Armstrong; Corresponding Secretary, W. S. Lee; Recording Secretary, J. A. Simmers; Treasurer, James E. Ellis.

City of Toronto Electoral Division Society.—President, George Leslie, jr.; 1st Vice-President, Mayor A. Shaw; 2d Vice-President, Captain J. B. Boustead; Secretary and Treasurer, W. Edwards; Directors, P. Armstrong, Colonel R. L. Denison, John Gray, senr., Alderman Strachan, James Fleming, H. C. Thomson, James Forsyth, George Fair, John Forsyth.

This Society holds a Summer Exhibition of Horticultural Products, and a Fall Exhibition of Agricultural and Mechanical Products.

Membership, $1.00 per annum, admitting Member and Lady to all the Society's Exhibitions.

Canada West Poultry Association.---Officers for 1869: President, James Graham; Vice-President, Colonel R. L. Denison; Honorary Secretary, Thomas McLean; Treasurer, A. M. Howard; Auditors, M. B. Hicks and James Beswick; Committee, Lieut. Col. Hassard, Rice Lewis, A. McL. Howard, P. Armstrong, R. A. Wood, John McDonald, County Treasurer, J. E. Withers, B. Bull, T. McLean, J. Beswick, T. Shivers Birchall, James Graham.

Meetings of the Association are held on the first Thursday in each month at the Agricultural Hall, corner of Yonge and Queen streets.

BENEVOLENT AND CHARITABLE INSTITUTIONS.

Provincial Lunatic Asylum—Is 2¼ miles from the City Hall, on Queen street. Property vested in the Crown. The institution is now under the management and support of the Local Government of Ontario, who frame by-laws for its government, and appoint an Inspector to thoroughly examine the Asylum and report to His Excellency the Lieutenant-Governor. The admission of patients is regulated by Cap. 122, Con. Stat. U. C., which requires that the patient be examined by three licensed medical practitioners, verified by Reeve or Mayor, collectively, who certify to the insanity.

Officers of the Institution.—Medical Superintendent, Joseph Workman, M.D.; Assistant Physician, B. Workman, M.D.; Clinical Assistant, J. Workman, junr.; Bursar, J. McKirdy; Steward, James Henry; Matron, Mary Ann Parkes.

Note.—A Branch of this Asylum has been established in the old University Buildings, under the same management. Robert Blair, Steward; Eliza Blair, Matron.

Toronto General Hospital.---Trustees: Hon. Justice Wilson, Chairman; E. H. Rutherford; J. Merrick (appointed by Government); John McDonald (appointed by the Board of Trade); Alderman Boxall (appointed by the City Council.)

The Orphan's Home and Female Aid Society---Established in 1853. Situated on Sullivan street. Is under the patronage of the Church of England, and at present has 26 girls and 36 boys in attendance. Officers of the Society---Patroness, Her Excellency, Lady Young; Visitor, Lord Bishop of Toronto; First Directress, Mrs. Murray; Second Directress, Mrs. Vankoughnet; Treasurer, Mrs. Kingston; Secretary, Mrs. Hoskins; Chaplain, Archdeacon Fuller; Medical Officer, Dr. Ogden. Committee of Council---Rev. S. Lett, Ven. Archdeacon Fuller, D.D., Messrs. J.

Crickmore, M. R. Vankoughnet, R. A. Harrison, Andrew Fleming, and such of the Churchwardens of Churches within the City of Toronto, as are members of the Corporation, Matron, E. M. Large.

House of Providence.---Power street. Under the direction of the Sisters of St. Joseph.

Superior, Mother de Chantel.

Number of Sisters, 16; orphans, 240; infirm, blind, lame and incurables, 110; deaf and dumb in the school of the institute, 9.

Toronto House of Industry.---Established in 1837, corner of Elizabeth and Elm streets.

Officers for 1869.---Rev. Dean H. J. Grasett, Chairman; Edward Hobson, Deputy Chairman; Henry Rowsell, Treasurer; Rev. A. J. Broughall, Secretary.

Ward Visitors. --For St. Lawrence Ward, Mr. W. J. McDonell, 50 Front street; for St. David's Ward, Hon. G. W. Allan, Moss Park; for St. James' Ward, Mr. John Shea, 109 Seaton street; for St. George's Ward, Rev. Alex. Williams, 22 Mercer street; for St. Andrew's Ward, Mr. J. Tyner; for St. John's Ward, Mr. E. Hobson, 5 Agnes street; for St. Patrick's Ward, Rev. A. J. Broughall, St. Stephen's Parsonage; Mr. C. Duckett, General Superintendent.

The Weekly Committees meet on Tuesdays and Fridays, at 9 o'clock, a. m.

The Board or Managers meet on the third Thursday of each month, at half-past 3 o'clock, p. m.

Boys' Home.---Located east side of George near Gerrard street. For the training and maintenance of destitute boys not convicted of crime.

Board of Mangement.---Lady Patronesses, Mrs. Stisted, and Mrs. Draper; Directress, Mrs. McCutcheon, Mrs. Watson, Mrs. Dunlop, Mrs. Hodgins, Mrs. Gzowski, Mrs. John Ridout, Mrs. Cosens, Mrs. Davidson; Treasurer, Mrs. Mulholland; Secretary, Mrs. A. H. Coulson; Managers, Mrs. E. Baldwin, Mrs. Beardmore, Mrs. Brunskill, Mrs. Beard, Mrs. Crombie, Mrs. Cosens, Mrs. A. H. Coulson, Mrs. Dunlop, Mrs. Davidson, Mrs. Freeland, Mrs. Grasett, Mrs. C. Gamble, Mrs. Gzowski, Mrs. R. Gilmour, Miss Gordon, Mrs. Hodgins, Mrs. Hagarty, Mrs. James Leslie, Mrs. McCutcheon, Mrs. Mulholland, Mrs. V. B. McMurrich, Miss Mitchell, Miss Michie, Mrs. Ryerson, Mrs. Rutherford, Mrs. John Ridout, Mrs. James Strachan, Mrs. A. M. Smith, Mrs. D. Wilson, Mrs. Watson, Miss E. Wilson; Honorary Managers, Mrs. G. W. Allan, Mrs. John Baldwin, Mrs. Cawthra, Mrs. I. C. Gilmor, Mrs. Henning, Mrs. Lewis Moffat; Solicitor, C. Robinson; Medical Officer, James Thorburn, M.D.; Bankers, Bank of Toronto; Matron, Mrs. Munro.

Girls' Home and Public Nursery.---Located on Sherbourne street. Board of Managers for 1869.---Honorary Member, Mrs. Wm. Elliott; 1st Directress, Mrs. McCaul; 2nd do., Mrs. A. R. McMaster; 3rd do., Mrs. R. Gilmour; Secretary, Miss Elliott; Treasurer, Mrs. Kerr; Treasurer of Building Fund, Mrs. Cassidy.

Lying-in Hospital.---Located at the corner of Richmond and Shepherd streets. 1st Directress, Mrs. Grasett; 2nd do., Mrs. Hodder; Treasurer, Mrs. Cumberland; Secretary, Mrs. J. Ridout; Matron, Mrs. Black.

Toronto Magdalene Asylum.---Yonge Street, Yorkville, north of Toll Gate. Office Bearers.---Honorary Visiting Managers, Mrs. J. Baldwin, Mrs. McCutcheon, Mrs. Blake, Mrs. Topp; Directresses, Mrs. Dunlop, Mrs. McMurrich, Mrs. Alcorn, Mrs. Freeland; Treasurer, Mrs. James Leslie; Secretary, Mrs. Thomas Ewart; Visiting Physician, Dr. Robinson.

NATIONAL SOCIETIES.

St. George's Society.---Office Bearers, 1869.---President, James Young; Vice-Presidents, 1st, S. G. Wood; 2nd, F. Osler; 3rd, S. Hammond. Chaplains, Rev. Provost Whittaker, M.A., Rev. W. S. Darling, Rev. S. J. Boddy. Physicians, Dr. Berryman, Dr. Rowell and Dr. Tempest. Treasurer, E. Bradburne. Secretary, H. Mortimer. Committee: Messrs. G. Frankland, J. H. Mason, W. Rowland, James Russell, John West, John Whitley, John W. Young. Stewards: Messrs. A. R. Boswell, G. Chanter, F. B. Cumberland, Joseph Hurd, T. C. Patteson, R. P. Stephens. Auditors: Messrs. H. Pellatt and William Hope. Standard Bearers: Messrs. John Symonds and H. Jackman.

St. Andrew's Society.—List of officers of the St. Andrew's Society, of the City of Toronto, in the County of York, and Province of Ontario: President, the Hon. David L. Macpherson, Senator; 1st Vice-President, Mr. Robert Hay; 2nd Vice-President, Mr. W. Mortimer Clark; Managers, Messrs. C. Carnegie, J. Patterson; Chaplains, Rev. John Barclay, D.D., Rev. John Jennings, D.D., Rev. A. Topp; Physicians, James Thorburn, M.D., J. L. Lizars, M.D.; Treasurer, Isaac C. Gilmor; Secretary, James F. Smith, Jr.; Committee of Accounts, W. B. McMurrich, John Paterson, A. McPherson; Standard Bearers, T. M. Pringle, George McMurrich, J. D. Edgar, R. Maitland. The Society holds quarterly meetings every year, viz.: On the second Thursday in February, May, August and November, the last of which is called "The Meeting preparatory to the Anniversary Assembly." Thirteen members constitute a quorum. Officers to be chosen annually from among the resident members at the Preparatory Meeting, and to be installed on the Festival of St. Andrew next ensuing.

St. Patrick's Society.—Office-bearers for 1869-70. President, Frank Smith; 1st Vice-President, John A. Donaldson; 2nd Vice-President, Major McMaster; Treasurer, Robt. Wilkes; Corresponding Secretary, Thos. Maclear; Recording Secretary, Wm. Halley; Assistant Secretary, Jno. Donaldson. Committee of Management, Thos. Wilson, J. D. Merrick, James Kerr, Robert Sullivan, A. McMaster, William McMaster, John Canavan, John O'Donohoe, John Carr, J. B. Cook, Lieut.-Col. Gilmor, Alderman Dickey, Robert Wilkes, L. G. Bolster, George Harding, Thomas McCrosson; Stewards, Lieut.-Col. Gilmor, Robert Sullivan, J. D. Merrick, Major McMaster, Alderman Dickey, R. A. Harrison, J. B. Cook, and several others. Meetings: Committee Meetings held every Monday Evening, at 4 p.m., at the Office of the Society, for the transaction of the special business of the Society. Applications for aid received only at these meetings. Monthly meetings: First Friday in every month. Quarterly Meetings: First Friday in every third month, including every Third Monthly Meeting, both held for general business of the Society. Annual Meeting: 17th March. Election of officers, First Monday in March in every year.

Young Irishmen's Catholic Benevolent Association.—Established 1869.—President, John Davey; Vice-President, J. Mallon; Secretary, Thos. McDonell; Financial Secretary, Edward Donelon; Treasurer, Daniel Hartnett.

Hibernian Benevolent Society.—Established 1858. —President, Patrick Boyle; Treasurer, Daniel Moriarty. Meetings, monthly, at Hibernian Hall, St. Lawrence Hall Buildings.

Sons of St. Patrick.—Established 1869.—President, William Mitchell; Secretary, Thomas Clarke. Meet in their Rooms, Bathurst street, weekly.

SCIENTIFIC AND RELIGIOUS INSTITUTIONS.

Toronto Mechanics' Institute.—Officers for 1869: President, Hon. G. W. Allan; 1st Vice-President, W. P. Marston; 2nd Vice-President, D. Spry; Treasurer, W. Edwards; Directors, C. W. Bunting, W. P. Marston, H. E. Clarke, William Halley, John Withrow, W. H. Sheppard, R. W. Elliott, F. W. Cumberland, Thomas Davison, Thomas McCrosson, H. Langley, N. L. Piper, Chas. Carnegie. Richard Lewis, Secretary; Wm. Ellingsworth, Keeper.

Young Men's Christian Association.—Rooms, 34 King street east. Free Reading Room, open daily from 8 a.m. to 10 p.m.

Meetings.—Weekly Meeting, for devotional exercises, reading essays, and discussion thereon, every Tuesday evening, at eight o'clock. Prayer Meeting every Saturday evening, from 8 to 9 o'clock. Cottage Prayer Meetings are held every week in Berkeley street Fire Hall; on Britain street, Sayer street, &c. Prayer Meeting every Sabbath afternoon, at 3 o'clock. Bethel Service held every Sabbath afternoon (during season of navigation) on board steamer "City of Toronto," Yonge street wharf. Young men are cordially invited to visit the Rooms, and attend the weekly meetings and Bible Class. Persons desirous of joining the Association, can obtain forms of application for membership, in accordance with Article 1 of By-laws, at the Rooms, or from the Recording Secretary.

Officers for 1869-70—President, Daniel Wilson, LL.D.; Vice-Presidents, Robert Baldwin, James Carlyle, M.D., B. Homer Dixon, K.N.L., George Hague, John Macdonald, Robert Walker; Corresponding Secretary, J. C. Hamilton, M.A.; Recording Secretary, Walter B. Copp; Treasurer, John K. Macdonald; Librarian, F. W. Kingstone; Directors, Wm. Anderson, W. J. Murphy, Wm. Grainger, Jno. Laird, Geo. Chaffey, Jr., Richard Faircloth, W. J. Robertson, E. J. Joselin, John Beattie, City Missionary; Wm. Robinson, Assistant Librarian, 34 King street east.

Upper Canada Bible Society.—Office-bearers for 1869: President, the Honorable George W. Allan; Vice-Presidents, Right Rev. Dr. Cronyn, Bishop of Huron; Very Rev. Dean Grassett, Revs. J. Richardson, D.D., James Harris, A Lillie, D.D., E. Wood, D.D., J. Jennings, D.D., R. Burns, D.D., M. Willis, D.D., LL.D., A. Sanson, A Green, D.D., E. Ryerson, D.D., LL.D., J. H. Robinson, T. S. Ellerby, R. A. Fyfe, D.D., Lachlan Taylor, D.D., Wellington Jeffers, D.D., William McClure, E. Baldwin, M.A., W. Reid, M.A.; W. A. Baldwin, Hon. Wm. McMaster, Hon. W. H. Blake, Hon. Oliver Mowat, George Buckland, John Macdonald, Daniel Wilson, LL.D., A. T. McCord; Treasurer, the Honorable William McMaster; Secretaries, the Rev. Wm. Reid, M. A., J. George Hodgins, LL.B., George Hague; Travelling Agents, S. B. Johnson, Esq., Rev. W. Brookman, Rev. T. Goldsmith; Depository, Mr. James Carless; Directors—all Ministers of the Gospel who are members of the Society, Messrs. John Tyner, Wm. Osborne, A. Christie, James Foster, H. Mortimer, Alex. Rattray, G. L. Beardmore, M. Pearson, Samuel Rogers, H. Graham, F. W. Kingstone, Robert Wilkes, B. Homer Dixon, Dr. C. B. Hall, R. Baldwin, J. J. Woodhouse, J. McBean; Kingston Auxiliary, Very Rev. William Snodgrass, D.D., Rev. K. M. Fenwick, M. Sweetnam, Esq.

Upper Canada Religious Tract and Book Society.—Office-bearers for 1869: President, Rev. Jas. Richardson, D.D.; Vice-Presidents, Right Rev. Dr. Cronyn, Bishop of Huron, Very Rev. H. J. Grasett, B.D., Dean of Toronto, Rev. James Harris, Rev. A. Lillie, D.D., Rev. R. Burns, D.D., Rev. J. Jennings, D.D., Rev. E. Wood, D.D., Rev. R. A. Fyfe, D.D., Rev. W. Reid, A.M., J. C. W. Daly, Esq., Honorable J. McMurrich, Hon. Wm. McMaster, A. T. McCord, Esq., Wm. Osborne, Esq., John Tyner, Esq., J. F. Marling, Esq.; Treasurer, Hon. John McMurrich; Secretaries, Rev. T. F. Caldicott, D.D., John K. McDonald, Esq.,; Agent, Rev. Peter Kerr; Depository, Mr. James Carless; Directors, all Ministers of the Gospel who are Members of the Society, Messrs. C. Walker, A. Christie, J. Brown, S. Rogers, W. T. Mason, J. J. Woodhouse, R. Baldwin, Dr. Tempest, Jas. Foster, H. Graham, D. Buchan, G. L. Beardmore.

MISCELLANEOUS ASSOCIATIONS.

Toronto Typographical Union, No. 91.—Originally established February 9, 1844.—Officers for 1869: President, Wm. DeVere Hunt; Vice-President, John Farrell; Corresponding Secretary, J. S. Williams; Financial Secretary, W. Douglass; Recording Secretary, C. A. Harcourt; Managing Committee, C. Blackhall, R. J. Milligan, Thos. Todd.

Licensed Victuallers' Association of Ontario.—President, William Balkwill, London; First Vice-President, J. W. Goering, Hamilton; Second Vice-President, John Paul, Meaford; Grand Treasurer, John MacDonald, London; Grand Secretary, James Smith, London.

Licensed Victuallers' Association of Western Ontario.—Toronto Division.—Officers for 1869: Chairman, Capt. W. Cox; Vice-Chairman, John Cornnell; Treasurer, M. Macfarlane; Secretary, Thos. Brown; Warden, Eli Hussey; Committee, Messrs. John Mercer, S. Higgins, A. Purse, J. W. Brown, Jacob Schaefer, J. Gilbert and Thos. Moor. Directors, Jas. Croker, John Bolam, J. Ick Evans, Geo. Jones, Samuel Higgins, John Mercer, John Cornnell, Thos. Brown, Robt. Taylor and M. Macfarlane; Stewards, Messrs. L. W. Bergfeld, Geo. Giddings and John Smith; Auditor, Richard Walsh; Master of Ceremonies, George Hall; Marshall, John H. Meyer.

CHURCHES.

ENGLISH CHURCHES.

Cathedral of St. James, King street east.—Very Rev. H. J. Grassett, B.D., Dean of Toronto, Rector; Assistant Ministers. Rev. Canon, Baldwin, M.A., Rev. J. L. Trew. Services at 11 a.m. and 7 p.m.

Church of the Holy Trinity, Trinity Square.—Rev. H. Scadding, D. D., Incumbent; Rev. W. S. Darling, Rev. H. W. Davies, B.D. Services on Sundays, early celebration of Holy Communion, 8 a.m. in Summer, 8:30 in Winter; regular services, 11 a.m. and 7 p.m. Daily morning prayer, 8 a.m.

St. George's Church, John street.—Ven. Archdeacon Fuller, D.D., Rev. T. S. Ellerby. Services at 11 a.m. and 7 p.m.

St. Peter's Church, Carlton street.—Rev. S. J. Boddy, M.A. Services at 11 a.m. and 7 p.m.

Trinity Church, King street east.—Rev. Alexander Sanson. Services at 11 a.m. and 7 p.m.

St. John's Church, Victoria Square.—Rev. Alex. Williams, B.A. Services at 11 a.m. and 7 p.m.

St. Stephen's Church, College street.—Rev. A. J. Broughall, M. A. Services at 11 a.m. and 7 p.m.

Trinity College Chapel.—Rev. Provost Whitaker, M.A., Rev. John Ambery, M.A., Rev. Wm. Jones, M.A.

St. Anne's Church, Dundas street, near Brockton. —Rev. John Hilton.

St. Paul's and Old St. Peter's Church.—Rev. Saltern Givins, Rev. J. Langtry, M.A.

CATHOLIC APOSTOLIC.

South side of Richmond street, near Yonge.—Rev. George Ryerson, Pastor. Services, Sundays, 10 a.m. and 5 p.m.; daily, 5 p.m.

ROMAN CATHOLIC CHURCHES.

St. Michael's Cathedral, Bond Street.—Right Rev. J. J. Lynch, D.D., Bishop: Very Rev. J. F. Jamot, V.G., Rector; Rev. M. J. White, Rev. J. R. Lee, Assistants.

St. Paul's, Power Street, Very Rev. F. P. Rooney, V.G., P.P.; Rev. P. Conway, Assistant.

St. Mary's, Bathurst street, Rev. J. B. Proulx, P.P., Chaplain to H. M. Forces; Rev. J. O'Donohoe, Assistant.

St. Patrick's, Dummer street, Rev. J. M. Laurent, P.P.

St. Basil's, Clover Hill, Church of the Basilian Fathers, Rev. C. Vincent, Superior; F. M. Ferguson.

PRESBYTERIAN CHURCHES.

Bay street Church, corner of Bay and Richmond streets. Rev. John Jennings, D.D. Services at 11 a.m. and 7 p.m.

Knox's Church, Queen street, near Yonge.—Rev. Alexander Topp, A.M. Services at 11 a.m. and 7 p.m.

Cooke's Church, Queen street, between Church and Nelson.—Rev. Wm. Gregg, A.M. Services at 11 a.m. and 7 p.m.

Gould street Church, corner of Gould and Victoria streets.—Rev. Robert Wallace. Services at 11 a.m. and 7 p.m.

West End Church, Queen street, corner of Denison Avenue.—Rev. Robert Wallace. Services at 11 a.m. and 7 p.m.

St. Andrew's Church, corner of Church and Adelaide streets.—Rev. John Barclay, D.D. Services at 11 a.m. and 7 p.m.

Reform Presbyterian Church, James street, corner of Louisa.—No regular pastor.

Charles Street Church.—Rev. John Campbell, A.M., Pastor.

METHODIST CHURCHES.

EAST CIRCUIT.—*Adelaide street Wesleyan Methodist Church*, corner of Adelaide and Toronto streets.—Services at 10:30 a.m. and 6.30 p.m.

Yorkville Wesleyan Methodist Church, Bloor street, Yorkville.—Services at 10:30 a.m. and 6:30 p.m.

Berkeley street Wesleyan Methodist Church, corner of Queen and Berkeley streets.—Services at 10.30 a.m. and 6:30 p.m.

WEST CIRCUIT.—*Richmond street Wesleyan Methodist Church.*—Services at 10:30 a.m. and 6:30 p.m.

Queen street Wesleyan Methodist Church.—Services at 10:30 a.m. and 6.30 p.m.

Elm Street Wesleyan Methodist Church.—Services at 10:30 a.m. and 6.30 a.m.

Cooper's Wesleyan Methodist Church.—Services at 10:30 a.m. and 6:30 p.m.

Seaton street Wesleyan Methodist Church.—Services at 10:30 a.m. and 6:30 p.m.

Queen street west Wesleyan Methodist Church.—Services at 10:30 a.m. and 6.30 p.m.

New Connexion Methodist Church.—Services at 10:30 a.m. and 6:30 p.m

Primitive Methodist Church, Alice street near Yonge.—Services at 10:30 a.m. and 6:30 p.m.

Primitive Methodist Church, Yonge street, Yorkville.—Services at 10:30 a.m. and 6:30 p.m.

Methodist Episcopal Church, William street, Yorkville.—Services at 10:30 a.m. and 6:30 p.m.

Parliament street Church, Primitive Methodist.—Services at 10:30 a.m. and 6:30 p.m.

British Methodist Episcopal Church (African), 84 Sayer Street.—Services at 10:30 a.m. and 6:30 p.m.

EPISCOPAL METHODIST.

Sayer Street Church.—Rev. Mr. Bannon. Service at 11 a.m., 3 p.m., and 7 p.m.

Richmond Street Church.—Rev. Mr. Carto. Service at 11 a.m. and 7 p.m.

BAPTIST CHURCHES.

Alexander street Church.—Rev. G. A. McNutt, Pastor. Public worship, 11 a.m. and 6.30 p.m. Sabbath School, 2:30 p.m. Weekly prayer meeting, Thursday, at 7:30 p.m., in basement.

Bond street Church.—T. F. Caldicott, D.D., Pastor. Prayer meeting in basement from 10 a.m. to 11 a.m. Public worship at 11 a.m. and 6.30 p.m. Sabbath School at 2:30 p.m. Weekly prayer meeting, Thursday, at 7:30 p.m., in basement.

Queen street Church.—Rev. J. H. Magee. Public worship at 11 a.m. and 3 p.m. Sunday School, 2 p.m. Prayer meeting on Wednesday evening, at 8 p.m.

CONGREGATIONAL CHURCHES.

Zion Church, Adelaide street, corner of Bay.—Rev. J. G. Manley, Pastor. Public worship at 11. a.m. and 6.30 p.m.

Bond street Church, corner of Crookshank.—Rev. F. H. Marling, Pastor. Public worship at 11 a.m. and 6.30 p.m.

Wood street Church, corner of Church.—Rev. R. T. Thomas, Pastor. Public worship at 11 a.m. and 6.30 p.m.

DISCIPLES.

The congregation of Disciples meet every Lord's Day, at the brick Meeting House, on the corner of Victoria and Shuter streets, at 11 a.m. and 6 p.m. Seats free.

JEWISH SYNAGOGUE.

155 Yonge street.—M. Gorfenkel, Reader. Public worship on Saturdays at 9 a.m., and holidays.

EVANGELICAL UNION.

Situated on Albert street, near Yonge.—Rev. Henry Melville, Pastor. Hours of service 11 a.m. and 6.30 p.m.

BRETHREN.

Meeting Room situated on Alexander street, between Yonge and Church, north side.

NEW JERUSALEM.

Albert street.—Mr. John Parker. Service at 11 a.m. and 6.30. p.m.

GERMAN LUTHERAN.

Bond street.—Rev. C. F. W. Rechenberg. Service at 11 a.m. and 7 p.m.

UNITARIAN CHURCH.

Jarvis street, above Cruickshank.—Rev. J. R. Lavelle. Service at 11 a.m. and 7 p.m. Sunday School in connection, at 2:30 p.m.

TORONTO JAIL MISSION, for holding Bible classes among the prisoners, meet at the Jail every Sunday morning, at 9 a.m. Superintendent, J. George Hodgins, LL.B.; Treasurer, Sheriff Jarvis; Teachers and Messengers: George Hague, Esq. (Bank of Toronto), Mrs. J. H. Howe, Mrs. Buell, Mrs. Price, Mr. Lugsdin, Mr. McNaught, Mr. Venn, and others.

CHURCH SOCIETY.—DIOCESE OF TORONTO.

Patrons.---His Excellency the Governor General; the Venerable Society for Promoting Christian Knowledge; the Venerable Society for the Propagation of the Gospel in foreign parts.

President.---The Right Reverend the Lord Bishop of the Diocese.

Vice-Presidents.---The Very Reverend Dean of Toronto; the Venerable Archdeacon of Toronto; the Venerable Archdeacon of Niagara; the Rural Deans; Rev. Dr. Beaven; Rev. Provost Whitaker, M.A.; the Hon. Chief Justice Draper; the Hon. Chancellor Vankoughnet; the Hon. Vice-Chancellor Spragge; the Hon. G. S. Boulton; the Hon. J. H. Cameron; the Hon. G. W. Allan; Henry Rattan; J. W. Gamble; J. R. Williams; E. G. O'Brien; L. Moffatt; Colonel Kingsmill.

Standing Committee and Mission Board.---His Lordship, the President; the Archdeacon of Toronto; the Archdeacon of Niagara; the Rural Deans; one Clerical Delegate for each District Branch; one Lay Delegate for each District Branch; Rev. Dr. Beaven; the Reverend the Provost; Rev. J. Davidson, M.A.; Rev. J. D. Cayley, M.A.; Rev. J. H. McCollum, M.A.; W. Gamble; R. B. Denison; Charles Magrath; John Carter; H. Mortimer.

Land and Investment Committee.---The Very Rev. the Dean of Toronto; the Venerable Archdeacon Fuller; Rev. Canon Read; R. B. Denison; H. A. Joseph; W. Gooderham; P. Paterson; W. Gamble.

Clergy Trust Commutation Committee.---The Archdeacon of Toronto; the Archdeacon of Niagara; Rev. Dr. McMurray; Rev. F. L. Osler, M.A.; Rev. J. G. Geddes, M.A.; Rev. Canon Brent, M.A.; Rev. H. Holland, B.A.; Rev. Canon Baldwin, M.A.; I. W. Gamble; C. J. Campbell; T. C. Street; F. Farncomb, William Ince, William Gooderham, H. R. O'Reilly.

Book and Tract Committee.---Rev. Dr. Beaven; Provost Whitaker; Rev. Canon Read; Rev. Canon Baldwin; Rev. Dr. O'Meara; Rev. William Belt, M.A.; Rev. Alexander Williams, M.A.

Episcopal Endowment Committee.---Venerable Archdeacon Palmer; Venerable Archdeacon Fuller; Rev. Canon Read; Peter Paterson; Lewis Moffatt; Charles Magrath.

Rectory Lands Committee.---The Dean of Toronto; Rev. Canon Read, D.D.; Rev. F. L. Osler, M.A.; Charles Magrath; Robert Denison; Herbert Mortimer.

Secretary.---W. P. Atkinson.

Treasurers.---Venerable Dean Grassett; C. J. Campbell; L. Moffatt.

Auditors.---W. Gamble and J. W. Browne.

Note.---By an Act of the last Session of the Legislature of Ontario, the Synod of the Diocese of Toronto has been incorporated, and the Church Society of said Diocese united with the Synod, under the name of the "Incorporated Synod of the Diocese of Toronto."

ROMAN CATHOLIC INSTITUTIONS.

St. Michael's College---Clover Hill: Superior, Rev. C. Vincent; Professor of Moral Theology, Rev. C. Vincent; Professor of Dogmatic Theology, Philosophy and Greek, Rev. R. Frachon; Professor of Natural Philosophy and Chemistry, Rev. D. O'Connor; Professor of Rhetoric, Rev. M. J. Ferguson; Professor of 1st Latin Class, Mr. O'Gorman; 2d Latin Class, Rev. M. Mulcahy; 3d Latin Class, Mr. L. Brennan; Professor of 1st Commercial Class, Mr. J. McCoy; 2d Commercial Class, Mr. W. Brennan; 3d Commercial Class, Mr. E. Murray; Professor of Mathematics, Mr. Kennedy; Professor of French, Rev. R. Challandard; Professor of Music, Rev. R. Challandard and Mr. E. Murray; Painting and Drawing, Mr. Kennedy; Master of Discipline, Mr. John Morrow; Number of Students, 100.

Christian Brothers.---Rev. Brother Arnold, Director; 14 in number conduct five schools, viz.: Academy, Nelson street, 162 pupils; St. Mary's, Bathurst street, 125; St. Paul's, Power street, 95; St. Michael's, Richmond street, 126; St. Patrick's, Dummer street, 93; all free except the Academy.

Convent and Academy of the Nuns of Loretto.---Boarding School at Abbey of the Holy Family, Wellington place, near Brock street; Rev. Mother Teresa Dease, Superioress; Religious, 18, Boarders, 50. Day school at the Convent, Bond street; Mother Ignatia, superioress; Religious, 22; Day Pupils 178. Free school conducted by the Nuns of Loretto; on Bond Street; average attendance 180. *Sisters of St. Joseph*, Albany street Clover Hill, Mother Antoinette, Superioress; Religious 32; House of the Novitiate, 19, boarders, 45, day pupils, 27. Select school, St. Mary's, 30 pupils. The Sisterhood likewise conduct the following schools: *St. Basil's*, attached to Convent; *St. Alphonsus*, Stanley street; *St. Paul's*, Powerstreet; *St. Patrick's*, Dummer street; *St. Mary's*, Bathurst street; average attendance, 900. *House of Providence*—Rev. Mother DeChantal, Superioress; Religious, 16; Orphans 250; Old and Infirm, 100. *Deaf and Dumb Institution.*---Sisters St. Joseph, pupils 10.

St. Joseph's Society.---Established 1869, object, mutual improvement of its members, meet every Tuesday at the Academy of the Christian Brothers, Nelson street, President James J. Costello; Vice-President, Thos. Lalor; Secretary D. J. O'Connell; Treasurer, J. J. Terry; Chaplain, Rev. W. J. White.

St. Nicholas Home, Stanley street, Object, a home for destitute industrious children, under the care of the Bishop.

UNIVERSITIES COLLEGES, ACADEMIES AND SCHOOLS

UNIVERSITY OF TORONTO.---*Chancellor*---Hon. Jos. C. Morrison.

Vice-Chancellor---Adam Crooks, Esq., LL.D.

Bursar.---David Buchan.

McCROSSON & CO.,

111 KING STREET EAST,

Opposite St. James' Cathedral, **TORONTO.**

Branch, Albion Buildings, London, Ont.

DIRECT IMPORTERS

FROM

ENGLAND, FRANCE AND UNITED STATES.

The Largest, Choicest and most fashionable stock in Toronto.

RAW FURS BOUGHT FOR CASH AT HIGHEST MARKET PRICES.

Members of the Senate.---John Langton, M.A.; Rev. J. McCaul, LL.D.; Hon. James Patton, LL.D., Q.C.; Hon. David Christie, Senator; Sir Wm. E. Logan, D.C.L., F.R.S.; James J. Hayes, M.D.; Rev. A. Lillie, D.D.; Rev. E. Ryerson, D.D.; The Principal of Queen's College; Rev. S. S. Nelles, M.D.; Very Rev. A. McDonell; G. R. Cockburn, M.A.; William T. Aikins, M.D.; H. H. Croft, D.C.L., F.C.S.; J. B. Cherriman, M. A.; Daniel Wilson, LL.D.; Rev. John Jennings, D.D.; Hon. O. Mowat; G. Herrick, M.D.; Ira Lewis, M.A.; Larratt W. Smith, D.C.L.; S. S. Macdonell, LL.D.; Rev. H. B. Jessop, M.A.; J. Helliwell, M.A.; W. G. Draper, M.A.; T. A. McLean, M.A.; John Boyd, M.A., B.C.L.; D. McMichael, LL.D.; J. E. Thomson, B.A.; E. C. Jones, B.A.; J. D. Armour, B.A.; J. J. Kingsmill, B.A.; Hon. W. Cayley, Rev. W. McClure; Rev. Dr. Fyfe; J. H. Morris, M.A.; E. Blake, M.A.; Rev. Dr. Barclay; Rev. W. F. Checkley; Right Rev. J. Walsh; Rev. A. Carman, B.A.; T. H. Bull, M.A.: Rev. John Davison; Very Rev. Dean I. Hellmuth, D.D.

Officers of the Senate.---John E. Thompson, M.A., Librarian; T. Moss, M.A., Registrar.

Scholarships offered at Examinations of the University.---Faculty of Law, 4: 1 for Matriculants, 1 for Students one year's standing, 1 for Students two year's standing, 1 for Students 3 year's standing. Faculty of Medicine, 4: 1 for Matriculants, 1 for Students two year's standing, 1 for Students three years' standing. Faculty of Arts, 24; at the Junior Matriculation Examination, 1 in Classics, 1 in Mathematics, 2 for general proficiency in all the subjects appointed for Junior Matriculants; at the Senior Matriculant Examination, 1 in Classics, 1 in Mathematics, 2 for general proficiency in all the subjects appointed for Senior Matriculants; at the Examination for the first year, 1 in Classics, 1 in Mathematics, 2 for general proficiency; at the Examination of the second year, 1 in Classics, 1 in Mathematics, 1 in Natural Science, 1 in Modern Languages, with History, 1 in Logic, Metaphysics and Ethics, 1 in general proficiency; at the examination of the third year, 1 in Classics, 1 in Mathematics, 1 in Natural Sciences, 1 in Modern Languages, with History, 1 in Metaphysics and Ethics, with Civil Polity, Natural Theology and History, 1 for general proficiency. Value of each Scholarship, $120, and tenable for 1 year only.

UNIVERSITY COLLEGE, TORONTO.---*President*---Rev. John McCaul, LL.D.

Professors, &c.---Rev. John McCaul, LL.D., Professor of Classical Literature, Logic and Rhetoric; Rev. James Beaven, D. D., Professor of Metaphysics and Ethics; H. H. Croft, D.C.L., Professor of Chemistry and Experimental Philosophy; George Buckland, Esq., Professor of Theory and Practice of Agriculture; J. B. Cherriman, M. A., Professor of Natural Philosophy; Daniel Wilson, LL.D., Professor of History and English Literature; Rev. William Hincks, F.L.S., Professor of Natural History; E. J. Chapman, Ph. D., Professor of Mineralogy and Geology; G. T. Kingston, M. A., Professor of Meteorology, and Director of the Magnetical Observatory; Dr. Oldright, Acting Lecturer on Italian and Spanish; J. M. Hirschfelder, Lecturer on Oriental Literature; W. H. Vandersmissen, M. A., Acting Lecturer on German; Emile Pernet, Acting Lecturer on French; James Loudon, M.A., Mathematical Tutor and Dean; G. S. Goodwillie, M.A., Classical Tutor; David Buchan, Acting Registrar; Henry Rowsell, printer, bookseller and stationer.

TRINITY COLLEGE.---*Corporation of Trinity College:* The Right Rev. the Lord Bishop of Huron, The Right Rev. the Lord Bishop of Ontario; The Right Rev. the Lord Bishop of Toronto.

Trustees.---The Very Rev. the Dean of Toronto; the Hon. G. W. Allan; Lewis Moffatt.

Council.---Honorary members; John Arnold, Ex-officio Members: The Hon. John Hilliard Cameron, Chancellor of the University; the Rev. the Provost of Trinity College; the Rev. John Ambery, M.A., Professor of Classics; the Rev. William Jones, M.A., Professor of Mathematics.

Members from the Diocese of Toronto.---Professor Bovell, M.D.; the Very Rev. the Dean of Toronto; the Hon. G. W. Allan; Lewis Moffatt, Esq., the Hon. Mr. Vice-Chancellor Spragge; James M. Strachan; the Hon. Mr. Justice Hagarty, D.C.L.; Samuel Bickerton Harman, B.C.L.; *the Ven. the Archdeacon of Niagara; the Rev. W. McMurray, D.D., D.C.L.; the Rev. S. Givens; the Rev. J. G. Geddes, M.A.; James Henderson; C. J. Campbell; Christopher Robinson, M.A.; the Ven. the Archdeacon of Toronto.

Members from the Diocese of Ontario.—The Venerable H. Patton, D.C.L. Archdeacon of Ontario; James A. Henderson, D.C.L; the Rev. Wm. Bleasdell, M.A.; the Rev. Edward Jukes Boswell, D.C.L.; the Very Rev. James Lyster, LL.D., Dean of Ontario. Nominated by the Bishop of Toronto; the other members from the Diocese of Toronto being elected by the Corporation.

Secretary, Charles Magrath, D.C.L.; Provost, Rev. George Whittaker, M.A.; Professor of Divinity; The Provost; Professor of Classics; Rev. John Amberry, M.A.; Professor of Physiology and Chemistry; James Boyell, M.D.; Classical Lecturer, Rev. A. J. Broughall, M.A.; Professor of Music, G. W. Strathy, Mus. Doc.; Lecturer in French, Mons. Emile Pernet; Lecturer on Drawing and the Fine Arts, Mr. George Gilbert.

UPPER CANADA COLLEGE.—Founded 1829.—*Visitor.*—His Excellency the Governor General.

Principal—George R. R. Cockburn, M.A.

Masters---William Wedd, M.A., first Classical Master; James Brown, M.A., Mathematical Master; C. W. Connon, LL.D., English Classical Master; John Martland, B.A., second Classical Master and resident Master in College boarding-house; Michael Barrett, M.A., M.D., first English Master and Lecturer on Chemistry and Physiology; C. J. Thompson, second English Master; Rev. E. Schluter, M.A., French and German Master; J. A. Paterson, M.A., Assistant Mathematical Master; R. Baigent, Drawing Master; Major Goodwin, Gymnastics, Fencing and Drill; Bursar, D. Buchan, Esq.; Janitor and Messenger, James Marshall.

Fees.---The fee for all the regular subjects taught is, per term; one pupil, $10; two brothers, $9; three brothers, $8 each; the fee for Ornamental Drawing, $2 per term extra.

College Boarding House.---Fee (inclusive of Tuition,) $45 per term.

N. B.—All fees, whether for board or tuition, are payable strictly in advance to the Bursar of the Institution. Boys entering during any term are charged after a certain period only for the unexpired portion of that term at the above rates.

Terms.—The autumn term begins September 1st. The winter term begins November 10th. The spring term begins February 5th. The summer term begins April 21st.

Knox College.—Principal and Professor of Systematic Divinity, Rev. M. Willis, D.D., LL.D.; Emeritus Professor of Church History, Rev. E. Burns, D.D.; Apologetics and Exegetical Theology, Rev. W. Caven; Lecturer on Evidences, Rev. R. Ure; Lecturer on Homiletics, Rev. J. J. A. Proudfoot; Chairman of College Board, Rev. D. Inglis, Hamilton; Secretary, Rev. W. Reid, A.M. Session opens on the first Wednesday of October and closes on the first Wednesday of April.

Provincial Normal and Model Schools, for the Instruction and Training of Teachers.—*Normal School:* J. H. Sangster, M.A., M.D.; Head Master; Rev. H. W. Davies, D.D., Second Master; J. G. Hodgins, L.L.B., Lecturer on the School Law of Upper Canada; Samuel Clare, Teacher of Book-keeping and Writing. William Armstrong, C.E., Drawing Master; H. F. Sefton, Teacher of Vocal Music; Major H. Goodwin, Teacher of Gymnastics and Calisthenics. *Model Schools*, in which *the Normal School Students practice the art of Teaching:* J. Carlyle, M.D., Master of the Boys' School; James Hughes, First Assistant; Charles Archibald, Second Assistant; Mrs. Martha Cullen, Mistress of Girls' School; Clara Clark, First Assistant; Caroline E. McCausland, Second Assistant, and the Teachers of Writing, Bookkeeping, Drawing, Music, Gymnastics and Calisthenics in the Normal School.

The Sessions of the Normal School commence on the 8th of January and the 8th of August, and close on the 15th of June and 15th of December in each year.

Council of Public Instruction for Upper Canada.—Rev. Egerton Ryerson, D.D., LL.D., Chief Superintendent of Education; Right Rev. John J. Lynch, D.D., R. C. Bishop of Toronto; Very Rev. Dean Grasset, B.D.; Hon. Mr. Justice Morrison; Rev. J. Jennings, D.D.: Rev. J. Barclay, D.D.; Hon. Wm. McMaster and Rev. W. Ormiston, D.D., members for the purposes of the Grammar School Act; Rev. John McCaul, LL.D., President of University College, and the Presidents of the Colleges affiliated with the Toronto University. A. Marling, LL.B., Recording Clerk.

Department of Public Instruction, Ontario.—For the general administration of the Grammar and Common School Laws.

Education Office.—Rev. Egerton Ryerson, D.D., LL.D., Chief Superintendent of Education; John George Hodgins, L.L.B., F.R.G.S., Deputy Superintendent of Education and Editor of the *Journal of Education* for Ontario; Alexander Marling, L.L.B., Chief Clerk and Accountant, having also charge of Grammar School Meteorological Returns; A. J. Williamson, Clerk of Correspondence; F. J. Taylor, Clerk of Statistics; J. T. R. Stinson, Assistant Clerk of Correspondence; Office Messenger, James Moore.

Depository Branch.—S. P. May, M.D., Clerk of Libraries; Edward B. Cope, Depository Salesman; Edward J. Russell, Assistant Clerk of Libraries; Henry Wilkinson, Assistant Depository Salesman; Edward J. Russell, Assistant Clerk of Libraries; G. Barber, Depository Packer and Messenger.

Offices in the Victoria Square, Toronto.

Number of public libraries, 1868, 1,035; number of volumes, 221,037.

Educational Museum.—Connected with the Educational Department is a Museum, containing specimens of school apparatus and furniture, a valuable collection of Italian, Dutch and Flemish oil paintings and statuary casts and busts. The Museum is freely open to the public.

Grammar Schools.—Each of these schools (which form the intermediate link between the Common Schools and the Universities) is managed by a Board of Trustees, appointed jointly by the County and Town Councils. In cities, the Trustees are all appointed by the City Council, except where there is only one school in the county. The Head Master must be a graduate of a British or Colonial University, unless certified and appointed by the 18th September, 1865. Besides fees, local rates or contributions to the extent of half the Government grant must be raised for the master's salary. The grant is payable to those schools only which attain a certain standard, and is based on the average attendance of pupils in the prescribed studies. An extra grant is provided for masters taking certain meteorological observations, and giving military instruction. Pupils attending these schools are prepared for matriculation in the Univesities.

Canadian Institute.—President, Professor H. Croft, D.C.L.; First Vice-President, J. N. Agnew, M.D.; Second Vice-President, J. Thorburn, M.D.; Third Vice-President, Professor E. J. Chapman, Ph.D.; Treasurer, Samuel Spreull; Recording Secretary, W. Mortimer Clark; Corresponding Secretary, L. Heyden.; Curator, A. E. Williamson; Librarian, Rev. H. Scadding, D. D.; Council, Professor G. T. Kingston, M.A.; Professor Daniel Wilson, LL.D.; Professor J. B. Cherriman, M.A.; W. H. Cumming, M.D.; C. B. Hall, M.D.; Andrew Russell; Rev. Prof. W. Hincks, F.L.S., and ex-Editor *Journal*; Assistant Secretary, James Johnson; Editing Committee: General Editor, Rev. William Hincks, F.L.S., E. J. Chapman, LL.D., Ph. D., Professor of Geology and Mineralogy, University College; Rev. Wm. Hincks, F.L.S., Professor of Natural History, University College, Toronto; Dan'l Wilson, LL.D., Professor of History and English Literature, University College, Toronto; G. T. Kingston, M.A., Director of Magnetic Observatory, Toronto; Henry Croft, D.C.L., Professor of Chemistry and Experimental Philosophy, University College, Toronto; J. B. Cherriman, M.A., Professor of Natural Philosophy, University College, Toronto; Jno. Barrett, M.D.

Medical Section.—Organized April, 1863. The leading English and American medical and scientific journals taken for the use of members. The session commences on the second week in October, and meetings are held every alternate week for six months. Officers for 1868-69: Chairman, James Thorburn, M.D.; Secretary, Wm. Tempest, M.D.; Committee of Management, Drs. Agnew, Rosebrugh and Cummings.

Private College, No. 133 Victoria street, Toronto.—Principal, J. P. Cleveland, M.D.

Trinity College Association of Alumni.—Officers for 1869: President, James Henderson, Jr., B.C.L.; Vice-President, Rev. H. W. Davies, B.D.; Secretary, A. Lindsay, B.A.; Treasurer, Beverley Jones, B.A.; Members of General Committee, Messrs. S. J. Vankoughnet, B.C.L.; W. P. Atkinson, B.A.; R. W. Hindes, B.A.; Rev. J. Langtry, B.A.; C. H. Badgley, B.A.; C. Thomson, M.A.

Ontario Literary Society.—President, Kenneth MacKenzie, Q.C.; First Vice-President, John E. Rose, M.A.; Second Vice-President, J. H. Macdonald; Treasurer, James J. Foy; Secretary, A. McPherson King; Corresponding Secretary, C. J. Christie; Assistant Secretary, W. M. Elliott, M.A.; Librarian, Jno. Nicholson; Executive Committee, B. Jones, B.A.; A. W. Francis, M. Hutchinson, Samuel Platt, Junr.

MEDICAL SCHOOLS AND INSTITUTIONS.

VICTORIA UNIVERSITY.—Medical Department, at Yorkville, Toronto. The Medical Department of Victoria College is also in affiliation with Toronto University The certificate of qualification of this School confers the right of registration under the Medical Act for Upper Canada. Each of the Medical Lecturers is connected with one or more of the hospitals, dispensaries, and charities of the city. The Lectures commence on the first day of October, and continue six months. Graduation, Spring and Fall, when the Examinations will be both written and oral. Dean, Hon. John Rolph, 20 Gerrard street west, to whom apply for any further information.

THE TORONTO SCHOOL OF MEDICINE—In affiliation with the University of Toronto, incorporated by Act of Parliament, 1851. Lectures delivered in Medical School Building, University Park, from 1st October to 31st March. President, Wm. T. Aikins, M.D.; Secretary, H. H. Wright, M.D.; Lecturers, Joseph Workman, M.D., Superintendent Provincial Lunatic Asylum, Emeritus Lecturer on Psychological Medicine; M. Barrett, M.A., M.D., Emeritus Lecturer on Institutes of Medicine; E. M. Hodder, M.D., F.R.C.S., England, Obstetrics and Diseases of Women and Children; Wm. T. Aikins, M.D., principles and practice of Surgery, and Clinical Surgery; H. H. Wright, M.D., L.C.P.S., Ont., principles and practice of Medicine and Clinical Medicine; James H. Richardson, M.D., M.R.C.S., Eng., General and Descriptive Anatomy; Uzziel Ogden, M.D., Materia Medica and Therapeutics; J. Thorburn, M.D., Edin., and Toronto University, Medical Jurisprudence; James Bovell, M. D., L.R.C.P., Eng., Institutes of Medicine; James Rowell, M.D., Surgical Anatomy, and demonstrator of Anatomy; Prof. A. H. Croft, D.C.L., F.L.S., Chemistry and Experimental Philosophy; and Prof. William Hincks, F.L.S., Botany, &c., both at University College. The degrees of the University are recognized in Great Britain.

HOMŒOPATHIC MEDICAL BOARD OF CANADA.—Established 22 Vic., ch. 47. President, Duncan Campbell, M.D., Edin., Member General Council University of Edinburgh, L.R.C.S.E., 103 Bay street, Toronto; Secretary and Treasurer, William Springer, M.D., Ingersoll, Ont. G. C. Field, M.D., Woodstock, Ont.; J. P. R. Morden, London, Ont.; Joseph Adams, M.D., Toronto, Ont. The Board meets in Toronto, on the first Tuesdays in January and July of each year, for the examination of candidates for Diplomas and Provincial License, who must have lodged their certificates of study with the Secretary at least one month before the meeting of the Board. The election of Members of the Board takes place, in accordance with the Act, at the January meeting in each year. All letters on matters connected with the Board to be addressed to the Secretary, Dr. J. Springer, Ingersoll, Ont.

ECLECTIC MEDICAL BOARD.—Established 24 Vic., ch. 110. G. A. Carson, M.D., Whitby; J. J. Hall; M.D., St. Mary's; N. Hopkins, M.D., Dunville; Wm. H. Hurd, M.D., Carleton Place; R. H. Clark, M.D., Cobourg; W. B. Weir. M.D., St. Mary's; and S. S. Cornell, M.D., Toledo. Board meets in Toronto, semi-annually, on the second Tuesday in October and the third Tuesday in June. All letters on matters connected with the Board to be addressed to the Secretary, N. Hopkins, M.D., Dunville.

VETERINARY SCHOOL—In connection with the Board of Agriculture, Toronto, Ontario. Professors: Andrew Smith, V. S., Edinburgh, Anatomy and Diseases of Farm Animals; J. Thorburn, M.D., Veterinary Materia Medica; James Bovell, M.D., Animal Physiology; George Buckland, Professor of Agriculture, University College, the History, Breeding and Management of the Domesticated Animals.

THE TORONTO EYE AND EAR DISPENSARY.—This is a public charity supported by private subscription, under the management of a Board of Directors, as follows: A. T. McCord, President; A. Dredge, Vice-President; W. T. Mason, Secretary and Treasurer; R. Wilkes, W. J. Macdonell, James Bain, E. J. Palmer, Robert Walker, John Macdonald, J. W. Mason, A. R. McMaster, William Elliott, Dr. Rosebrugh, Surgeon; Drs. Reeve and Cummings Assistant Surgeons. The Dispensary is open every day (Sundays excepted) at 9 o'clock a.m. and 6:30 p.m.

TORONTO BOARD OF HEALTH.

Principal Office, City Hall; Branch Office, York street, corner of Richmond. Alderman J. Boustead, Chairman; Dr. James Rowell, 306 Yonge street; Dr. William Tempest, Yonge street; John Reed, Inspector; F. B. Orris, Secretary.

CLUBS.

TORONTO DRAMATIC CLUB.—Stage Manager, P. Roberts; Secretary, R. B. Butland. Meet, on call, in Temperance Hall.

TORONTO CLUB.—Incorporated by Act of Parliament, for social purposes, 27 Vict., cap. 92.) C. S. Gzowski, President; Committee, T. P. McKenzie, Hon. J. H. Cameron, C. S. Gzowski, Hon. H. H. Killaly, N. Kingsmill, Lewis Moffatt, J. H. Morris, G. P. Ridout; A. Thornton Todd, Secretary and Treasurer.

TORONTO CRICKET CLUB.—Officers for 1869: President, J. O. Heward; 1st Vice President, J. Martland; 2nd Vice-President, Robert Spratt; Secretary, Robert Bethune; Treasurer, R. C. Henderson; Committee, Messrs. Baines, G. Harman, Yarker, Blake and Chandler. Ground on Avenue Road, Caer Howell. Practice every day during Summer season.

TORONTO CURLING CLUB.—President, John Shedden; 1st Vice-President, Thomas McGaw; 2nd Vice-President, D. S. Keith; Secretary and Treasurer, R. H. Ramsay; Chaplains, Rev. Drs. Barclay and Jennings; Committee of Management, Messrs. Forbes, Macpherson, Gardiner and Keith; Skips, Duncan Forbes, Alex Macpherson, John O. Heward, and Capt. Chas. Perry. The President is, *ex-officio*, Skip. Represented members, D. Mair and George Denholm, Montreal

ROYAL CANADIAN YACHT CLUB.—Esplanade, between Yonge and Scott. Officers for the year 1869: Commodore, E. M. Hodder; Vice-Commodore, G. H. Wyatt, Captain, B. R. Clarkson; Secretary, Arthur R. Boswell; Treasurer, Wm. Hope.

CLASPER ROWING CLUB OF TORONTO.— , President; John Maughan, 1st Vice-President; Geo. Holman, 2nd Vice-President; W. A. Wilson, Secretary; C. E. Anderson, Junr., Treasurer.

TORONTO ROWING CLUB.---Organized August 23, 1865. List of Officers for 1869: President, Angus Morrison, M.P.P.; Vice-Presidents, P. T. Shivers Birchall and Geo. H. Wyatt; Secretary and Treasurer, W. M. Davidson.

ONTARIO LACROSSE CLUB.---List of Officers for 1869: President, Capt. W. Arthurs; Vice-President, W. McNaught; Field Captains, Joseph Lugsden, Thomas Brown; Secretary, J. S. Ewart; Committee, J. Hornibrook, C. S. Murray and J. F. Hornibrook.

TORONTO LACROSSE CLUB.---W. D. Otter, President; R. M. Sutherland, Vice-President; George Massey, Secretary-Treasurer; P. Campbell, J. Erskine, T. Mitchell, Committee.

WEST END LACROSSE CLUB OF TORONTO.---Romain Buildings. A. D. Holman, President; C. W. Winstanley, Vice-President; C. E. Anderson, Jr., Secretary and Treasurer; W. A. Wilson, 1st Captain; A. S. Fortier, 2nd Captain; R. Tinning, B. Anderson, R. J. Tinning, Committee.

RAILWAYS.

GREAT WESTERN RAILWAY OF CANADA.—Thos. Swinyard, General Manager; G. H. Howard, Assistant Manager; Joseph Price, Treasurer; W. Wallace, Traffic Superintendent; John Crampton, Freight Superintendent; W. M. Pennington, Assistant Freight Superintendent; W. A. Robinson, Locomotive and Car Superintendent; Jas. Howard, Purchasing Agent; Nicholas Weatherston, Station Master; John Bryson, Assistant Station Master; J. S. Champ, Cashier Freight Department.

NORTHERN RAILWAY OF CANADA.---Head Office, Brock street, corner of Front street. Fred. W. Cumberland, Manager Director. Passenger and freight depots and locomotive department, Esplanade, foot of Brock street; passenger station, rear of City Hall. John Harvie, Train and Traffic Master; J. J. Ross, Through Freight Agent; J. F. McDonald, Local Freight Agent; A. Rolph, General Ticket Clerk; George Parker, Baggage Master.

GRAND TRUNK RAILWAY.---Head Office, Montreal. C. J. Brydges, Managing Director: Joseph Hickson, Secretary and Treasurer. Branch offices, Western Division, 62 Bay street Toronto; W. S. Spicer, Local Superintendent, Montreal to Detroit, Buffalo to Goderich; P. S. Stevenson, General Western Freight Agent, Toronto. Passenger station, Union station, foot of York street, Toronto; H. Bourlier, Station agent. Freight station, Esplanade, between Simcoe and John sts.; J. H. McNairn, Freight agent.

STAGE ROUTES.

Stage for Thornhill, leaves Bay Horse Hotel, Yonge street, 3:20 p.m., every day, Sundays excepted. Fare 30 cents.

Stage for Richmond Hill, leaves Bay Horse Hotel, Yonge street, at 3:30 p.m., every day, Sundays excepted. Fare 50 cents.

Stage for Cooksville, leaves Bay Horse Hotel, Yonge street, at 3:30 p.m., daily, Sundays excepted.

Stage for Rouge Hill, leaves Monkhouse's Hotel, at 3:30 p.m., daily.

Stage for Stouffville, leaves Albion Hotel, at 3 p.m., daily.

HOME INSURANCE COMPANIES.

PROVINCIAL INSURANCE COMPANY OF CANADA—Established 1849. Head Office, corner Toronto and Court streets, Toronto. Hon. J. H. Cameron, M.P., President; Lewis Moffatt, Vice-President; Hon. Malcolm Cameron; C. J. Campbell; George Duggan; A. T. Fulton; H. S. Howland; A. B. McMaster; W. J. MacDonell; Angus Morrison; John Worthington; Directors. James Sydney Crocker, Manager and Secretary; C. R. Dickson, Assistant Secretary. Fire Insurances effected on every description of property. Marine Insurances---inland and to the lower ports, New Brunswick, Nova Scotia, and the West Indies, and by steam vessels to Europe. Rates as moderate as those of any other respectable Insurance Company. Losses promptly settled. Inspectors: Fire---John Turnbull; Marine---A. M. Macgregor.

WESTERN ASSURANCE COMPANY.---Incorporated 1851. Fire, Inland and Ocean Marine Insurance. Head Office, corner of Church and Colborne streets, Toronto. Hon. John McMurrich, President; Charles Magrath, Vice-President; Directors: A. M. Smith, John Fisken, James Michie, A. Manning, R. J. Dallas, Robert Beatty, N. Barnhart; Bernard Haldan, Secretary; John Maughan, jr.; Assistant Secretary; Inspectors: Fire---William Blight; Marine---Captain J. T. Douglas; James Pringle, General Agent.

BRITISH AMERICA ASSURANCE COMPANY, Fire and Marine, oldest chartered Upper Canadian Company; head office: corner of Church and Court Streets, Toronto.—Board of Directors: Hon. G. W. Allan, Richard S. Cassels, E. H. Rutherford, G. J. Boyd, A. Joseph, Thomas C. Street, Hon. William Cayley, Peter Paterson, G. Percival Ridout; Governor, G. Percival Ridout; Deputy Governor, Peter Paterson. Trustees, E. H. Rutherford, Hon. William Cayley: G. J. Boyd; Marine Inspector, Captain Courneen; T. W. Birchall, Managing Director.

TORONTO MUTUAL FIRE INSURANCE COMPANY, No. 20 Toronto street, Toronto.—President, C. E. Chadwick, Vice-President, David Thurston; Directors: A. Barker, C. E. Chadwick, R. L. Denison, Joseph Gregory, John Paterson, Dr. A. A. Riddel, Henry Rowsell, D. Thurston, Managing Director; Secretary, H. Hancock; Fire Inspector, W. Henderson; Inspector of Risks, S. S. Frost; City Agent, C. Unwin, Adelaide street, opposite Court House.

BEAVER MUTUAL FIRE INSURANCE COMPANY, 20 Toronto street, Toronto. — President: Charles E. Chadwick; Vice-President, David Thurston; Managing Director: S. Thompson; Board of Directors: C. E. Chadwick, Ingersoll; D. Thurston, Toronto; A. Barker, Markham; Hon. Oliver Blake, Townsend; Hon. J. H. Cameron, Toronto; Jos. W. Collins, Newmarket; Richard L. Denison, Lippincott; H. Rowsell, Toronto; John Snell, Edmonton; George Snider, Owen Sound; S. Thompson, Toronto. Honorary Directors: W. H. Berry, March; T. Bowles, Reeve, Chinguacousy; Hon. Geo. Bryson, M.L.C., Pontiac; James Dryden, Whitby; William Edwards, Clarence; T. Higginson, West Hawkesbury; H. S. Howland, York; Thos. McConkey, M.P., Barrie; J. McDermot, Reeve of Wallace; Hon. J. Simpson, Senator, Bowmanville; Alfred O. Stephens, Tecumseh; Treasurer, T. J. Thompson; Secretary, W. T. O'Reilly; Fire Inspector, W. Henderson; Bankers, Ontario Bank.

HOME DISTRICT MUTUAL FIRE INSURANCE CO.—John Rains, Secretary, Yonge street, corner of Adelaide.

Aaron, Morris, jeweler, 368½ Yonge
Ablett, William, grocer, 266 King e
Abraham, Joseph, prop. N. E. Omnibus h 12 Elm
Adair, Mrs. A., boarding, 45 Richmond e
ADAM, STEVENSON & Co., booksellers and publishers, 61 King e
Adams, D. S. & B., gent's furnishing goods, 156 Yonge and 51 King w
Adams, James, sail mkr, Tinning's Wharf, Esplanade
Adams, Mrs. Jane, Grape saloon, 38 Adelaide e
Adams, Joseph, M.D., Homœopathist, 54 Bay
Adams, Robert, boarding house, 242 King e
ADAMS, WILLIAM, wholesale grocer, E. Market square
ADAMS, W. C., dentist, 95 King e
Adams, W. M., tinsmith, 424½ Queen w
Adamson, James, wharfinger, St. Lawrence wharf, Esplanade
Adamson, William, City Agent of Globe Printing Co.
Adamson, William, wharfinger, St. Lawrence wharf, Esplanade
Adelaide Street Wesleyan Methodist Church, Adelaide cor Toronto
ÆTNA INSURANCE CO., of Hartford, Conn., W. Rowland, agent, Front cor,. Church
ÆTNA LIFE INSURANCE CO., John Garvin, general agent, Whittemore's Buildings, Toronto
ÆTNA LIVE STOCK INSURANCE CO., Scott & Walmsley, agents, Ontario Hall, Church
AGNEW, JOHN N., M.D., Richmond w, cor Bay
Agricultural Hall, Yonge, cor Queen
Aikenhead James, wood mercht., St. Lawrence wharf
Aikens, J. R., provisions, 621 Yonge
Aikens, James, wood merchant, St. Lawrence wharf
Aikin & Kirkpatrick, produce and general commission merchants, 2 Ontario Chambers, cor Front and Church
Aikins, William, M.D., 70 Queen w
Aitkins, William, baker, 72½ Queen w
ALDWELL & CO., props. William street brewery, 122 William (see adv)
Alexander, Mrs. Jeannette, grocer, 370 Queen w
Alexander, J. A., second hand store, 30 Queen w
Alexander, William (Blaikie & Alexander)
Allan, John, & Co , cloths, 81 Colborne
ALLCOCK, S., C. LAIGHT & CO., manufacturers and dealers in fishing tackle, needles, &c., 39 Colborne (see adv.)
Allen, George L., governor County Jail
Allen, James, M.D., 206 Queen e
Allen, John, eating house, 22 w Market
Allen, Robert M., barrister, Court
Allen, F. H., produce merchant, 4 Bank of Toronto Buildings
Alley, Henry, clerk Provincial Secretary's office, Parliament Buildings
Alley, Jeremiah, clerk Crown Lands Department, Parliament Buildings
Alley, Jerome, clerk Crown Lands Department, Parliament Buildings
Allington, Robert, M.D., Yonge nr Bloor, Yorkville
Allison, Absalom G., train despatcher, G. T. R.
Amberry, Rev. John, classical master, Trinity College
AMERICAN HOTEL, David Walker, proprietor, Yonge cor Front
AMERICAN MERCHANTS' UNION EXPRESS COMPANY, J. D. Irwin, agent, 57 Yonge
American Steam Guage Company, George Harding, agent, 77 King w
ANDERSON, C. E., broker and commission merchant, *Daily Telegraph* Buildings, Bay
Anderson, James, principal, Givins' Street School
ANDERSON, C. E., jr. (C. E. Anderson & Co.) *Daily Telegraph* Buildings, Bay
ANDERSON, C. E. & CO. (C. E. Anderson, jr., J. Ross Robertson, and J. B. Cook), Directory and Gazetteer Publishers, Directory Branch *Daily Telegraph*, Bay cor King
Anderson, John H., barber, 130 King w
Anderson, Joseph, grain buyer, 28 Richmond e
Anderson, J. B. Bouchette, customs' officer, G.T.R., Club Chambers, York
Anderson, Robert W., photographer, 45 King e
Anderson, William, head teacher, Park School
Andrews, R. J., M.D., 169 Queen w
Andrews & Son, (Andrew & Andrew O.) auctioneers and commission merchants 109 Yonge
Antoinette, Rev. Mother, superieress convent of St. Joseph, St. Alban's
Appleton, Mrs. Edward, grocery, 560 Queen w
Archbold, David, sergeant police, 33 Queen e
Archbold, L., T.P.F., h 11 Duke
Archibald, Charles, second asst. Boys' Model School
Ardagh, William, saloon, basement Police Court
Arkel, George, wood contractor, G T.R., 461 King w
Armitage, George, marble and stone-cutter, 8 Gould
Armitage, William, second-hand store, 194 Queen w
Armstrong, George, grocer, 48 Richmond w
Armstrong, James D., grocer, 148 King e
Armstrong, J. R. (J. R. Armstrong & Co.), h 78 Peter
Armstrong, J. R., & Co., City Foundry, stoves, tin and hollowware, 161 Yonge
Armstrong, Thomas, inspector cab licenses, City Hall Buildings
Armstrong, William, artist and civil engineer, 42 King e
ARNOLD, REV. BROTHER, director Christian Brothers Academy and Schools, Nelson
Arnold Richard, passenger agent G. T. R., Scott cor Front
Arnoldi, F., entering clerk Registrar's Office, Court of Chancery, Osgoode Hall
Arnott, David, wholesale dry goods, 39 Yonge
Arthurs, Thomas, carpenter, 23 Douro
Arthurs, William & Co., dry goods, 25 King e
Ash, William, grocery, 220 Queen w
Ashall, Mrs. M. A., books and stationery, 284 Yonge
Ashby, Mrs. Annie, boarding-house, 135 Adelaide w
Ashfield, James, chief engineer, Toronto Fire Dept., City Hall Buildings
Atchison, Mrs. Elizabeth, confectioner, 630 Yonge
Atkinson, John, builder, 37 Edward
Atkinson, S., lumber merchant, 69 Wood
ATKINSON & BOSWELL, barristers, 74 King e
ATTORNEY GENERAL'S OFFICE, Hon. John Sandfield Macdonald, Q.C., Attorney-General, King nr Simcoe
August, Alfred, carpenter and builder, Sheppard nr Adelaide
Ault, William, solicitor in Chancery, Yonge cor King
Austin, James, collector, &c., No. 1 Bank of Toronto Buildings.
Authors, James, coal oil and lamps, 270 Yonge
Awde, W., butcher, 458 and 460 Queen w
Aykroyd, Henry, boat builder, Yonge street wharf
BACH, E., saddler, 10 King w
BACKAS, C. A., stationer and news dealer, Whittemore's block, Toronto
Backas, George H., assist't Postmaster, 26 Alexander
Baigent, R., drawing master U. C. College
BAILEY, HENRY, sole agent C.W. Williams & Co., wax thread sewing machines and Lamb's knitting machines, 28 King w
Bailey, John, butcher, 286 Queen w

Bailey, J. T., hair dresser, 22½ King w
Bailey, Thomas, fruit dealer, 296 Queen w
Bailey, T. J., civil engineer
Bailie, John. hardware, 266 Yonge
Bain, James, bookseller and stationer, 46 King e
BAIN, JAMES & CO., boots and shoes, 125 King e
Bain, John, (Paterson, Harrison & Bain)
Bain, John, baker, 311 Queen w
Baines, Christopher C., accountant, 6 Wellington e
Baines, Hugh, manager Toronto steel, iron and railway works, h 2 Strachan ave
Baird, Alexander, hotel keeper, 141 Portland
Baker, Guy S., lumber merchant, 240 Richmond w
Baldwin, Rev. E., (Church of England), 51 Duke
Baldwin, W. Wilcox, law stamp distributor, Osgoode Hall
Ball, John, grocer, 216 Queen w
BANK OF BRITISH NORTH AMERICA, S. Taylor, manager, Yonge cor Wellington
BANK OF TORONTO, George Hague, cashier, Wellington cor Church
BANK OF UPPER CANADA, Trustees' office Ontario Hall, Church nr Court
Banks, C. C., local supt. locomotive dept. G.T.R., h 425 King w
Banks, William H., assistant librarian Mechanics' Institute
BANSLEY, CHARLES, hair dresser, toys and fancy goods, 71 King w
Baptist Book Room, H. Lloyd, steward, 11 King w
Barber, Charles, potash manufacturer, Little Don
Barber, George, librarian Normal School
Barber, G. A., secretary Board of School Trustees and City Auditor. 59 Colborne
Barchard, William, box manufacturer, 121 Duke
Barclay, Rev. John, D.D. (Established Church of Scotland), 92 Adelaide w
BARKER, F. T., printer, advertising agent and publisher Exhibition Advertiser, 70 King e
Barker, George & Co., fancy and straw goods, 40 Yonge and 14 Front e
Barnard, John, confectioner, 71 Nelson
Barnhardt, Noah L., miller and produce dealer, Manning's Block, Front
Barr, Matthew, insurance agent, Ontario lane
Barr, W. J., shoemaker, 313 King e
Barrett, Mrs. James, dressmaker. 390 Yonge
BARRETT MICHAEL, M.A., M.D., First English Master and Lecturer on Chemistry and Physiology, Upper Canada College
Barrett & Evans, barristers, Exchange Alley, cor Colborne
Barrick, E. J., M.D., 276 Yonge
Barron, John, boots and shoes, 38 West Market Square and 149 King e
Barron, William. boot and shoemaker, 215 King e
Barry, Thomas B., barrister, 5 York Chambers, Court
Barry, W, M., oil merchant, 295 Yonge
Bartlett, W. R., Superintendent and Commissioner Indian Affairs, Jordan cor King
Barton, Charles L., conductor G.T.R., 275 Yonge
Barton, G., carpenter and builder, 10 Louisa
BARTON, GEO. H., stage manager, Royal Lyceum
Barton, John, broom manufacturer, 9 and 11 Dundas
Barwick, F. D., barrister, Romain buildings, King w
BASSETT & KEEBLE (Thomas Bassett and Harry Keeble), proprietors Platt's Hotel, 50 and 52 Nelson
Basso, Antonio, brush maker, 584 Yonge
Bate, the Misses M. & M., ladies hair dressers and manufacturers, 31 King w
Baxter, Alderman John, St. Patrick's Ward, h 30 St. Andrews
BAY HORSE HOTEL; Thomas Best, proprietor, 137 and 139 Yonge
Bayley, William, broker, 7 Toronto
Baylis, James & Co., carpets and oil cloths, wholesale, 16 Colborne; retail, 81 King e
BAY STREET FIRE HALL, e s Bay cor Temperance
Beale, Francis, hotel keeper, 331 King e
Beard, E. & Co., stoves and tinware, 31 East Market Square
Beard, E. & Co.. coal and wood dealers and founders, Beard's Wharf, Esplanade
Beardmore, G. L. & Co., wholesale leather and findings, 6 Wellington w
Beatty, Adam, grocer, Queen cor Parliament
Beatty, Adam, grocer, 69 Berkerley
Beatty, Charles, baker, Berkeley bet Queen and Sydenham
Beatty, Charles, boots and shoes, 162 Yonge
Beatty, Luke, prop. Beatty's Hotel, 108 Adelaide e
Beatty, Robert, shoemaker, 133 Sumach
Beatty, Thomas, lessee of Market, 40 Nelson
Beatty & Chadwick, barristers, 58 King e
Beatty & Forsyth (Thomas Beatty & William Forsyth), props. Commercial Hotel, 54 & 56 Nelson
Beatty & Townly, house, sign & carriage painters, 48 Queen w
BEATY, JAMES, M.P., prop. *Leader* and *Patriot*, King e (see adv.)
Beaty, Robert & Co., exchange brokers, 53 King e
Beauchamp, Richard, furniture dealer, 91 Queen w
Beaumont, W. R., M.D., 134 Wellington w
BEAVER DRUG MILLS & LABORATORY, Lyman, Elliott & Co., proprietors, Palace
BEAVER MUTUAL INSURANCE ASSOCIATION, W. T. O'Reilly, secretary, 20 Toronto
Beaver Soda Water Works, Riddell & Burns, props. 406 Yonge
Beck, Samuel, contractor for wells and drains, 79 Boulton
Beckett, Edward, prop. Globe Foundry, 42 Queen w
Beckford, E. O., contractor, h 242 Victoria
Bee, David, grocer, 309 Church
Beekman, Robert, accountant, 5 King w
BELFORD, ALEXANDER, clerk *Daily Telegraph*
Belford, Chas., editor *Leader*, h 4 Carty's Blk., George
Bell, Anthony, butcher and provision dealer, 358½ Yonge
Bell, George, house furnishing, 323 Queen w
BELL, THOMAS, wood and coal dealer, 199 Queen w and 150 Simcoe (see adv)
Bell, William, builder, 371 Yonge
BELL & CO., book and job printers and publishers, 70 King e (see adv)
Bell, Crowther & Tilt, barristers, cor Church and King
Belton, John, leather and findings, 308 Yonge
Bender, Charles (Heintzman & Co.), King w
Bennett, James, tavern-keeper, 18 Terauley
Bennett, Joseph H., city engineer, 43 Agnes
Bennett, Robert, barrister, Gwynne, Yorkville
Bergen, James, butcher, 387 King e
Bergfield, Lewis A., 212 Queen w
Berrie & Brisbane, bakers, 383 Queen w
Berry, Alfred, carriage, house and ornamental painter, 15 Agnes
BERRYMAN, CHARLES V., M.D., Jarvis, Yorkville
Berthon, G. T., portrait painter, 43 King w
Bertram, Thomas, grocer, 179 Centre
Bescoby, Edward, lime and stone dealer, Esplanade cor Market w

BEST, THOMAS, prop Bay Horse Hotel, 137 and 139 Yonge
Beswick, James, groceries and liquors, 26 w Market Square
BETHELL, FRANCIS, watchmaker and jeweller, 234 Yonge
BETHUNE, RIGHT REV. A. N., D.D., D.C.L., Episcopal Bishop of Toronto, 80 Beverley
Bethune, R. H., manager Quebec Bank, h Beverley cor Baldwin
Betz, John, prop Betz' Hotel, Esplanade cor Simcoe
Bevan, John W., cooper and wine manufacturer, 622 Yonge
Bickerstaff, Joseph, grocer, 375 Yonge
Bickerstaff & Bro., grocers, 243 and 245 Queen w
Bickford, E. O., railroad contractor, Whittemore's Building, Toronto
BIGELOW, N. GORDON, M.A., LL.B., barrister, Whittemore's Buildings, Toronto
Bills, T. H., butcher, 60 Queen w
Bilton, John, painter and glazier, 82 Agnes
Bilton, William, importer foreign and domestic fruits, confectionery, &c., 121 King e and 188 Yonge
Binsted, John, furniture, 321 Yonge
Birch, Charles, prop Sportsman's Saloon, 85 Yonge
BIRCHALL, T. W., managing director B. A. Insurance Co., Church cor Court
BIRD, CHARLES G., professor violin, 65½ North Park nr Parliament
Bird, E. B., butcher, 323 Yonge
Bird, Henry, butcher, 378 Queen w
Bird, Peter, fruit dealer, 279 Queen w
Bird, Peter, provision dealer, 34 St. Lawrence Market
Bird, W. J., butcher, 235 Yonge
Birney, J. & J. L., milk depot, 70½ Queen w
Birnie, Mrs. Grace, boarding school, 100 Bond
Birtch, Robert S., barrister, Court cor Toronto
Bishop, James, 249 King e
Blachford, Anthony, boots and shoes, 107 King e
BLACK, NORRIS, artificial limbs, and sewing machines, 18 King e (see adv.)
Blackbird, George, hotel keeper, 234 Front w
BLACKBURN, JOHN, City Steam Press, 96 Yonge
Blackburn, Robert, professor of music, 101 Terauley
Blackhall, Charles, proof reader *Globe*
Blackhall, J., bookbinder, 74 King e
BLAIKIE & ALEXANDER, (John L. Blaikie; William Alexander) accountants, brokers and estate agents, Jordan
BLAIN, FERGUSON & PARKINSON (David Blain, Thomas Ferguson & Robert W. Parkinson), barristers, 74 Yonge
Blair, Hugh, keeper branch Lunatic Asylum
Blair, John, prop. Blair's Hotel, 73 and 75 Nelson
BLAKE, EDWARD, M.A., Q.C., M.P., and M.P.P., resides Township York
Blake, J. N., barrister 64 Church
Blake, R., grain merchant, 520 Queen w
BLAKE, KERR & WELLS, (E. Blake, Samuel H. Blake, James K. Kerr, R. M. Wells) barristers, Masonic Hall
Blakey, John, prop. Liverpool hotel, 56 Wellington e
Blakely, John, provisions 155 Berkeley
Bland & Leask, dry goods and clothing 176 Yonge
Blevins & Duggan (John Blevins; George F. Duggan) barristers, City Building
Blight, William, inspector Provincial Insurance Co., h 52 North
Blong, George, grocer, 222 Queen e
BLONG, H. & E., butchers 3 and 5 St. Lawrence market
Blume, Michael, druggist, 117 Queen w
Blumenthal, Ady, general dealer, King e
Boatman, Charles, blacksmith, 485 Queen w
Boddy, Rev. S. J. (Church of England) 112 Winchester
BOECKH, CHARLES, brush manufacturer, 98 Berkeley (see adv)
Bolam Hotel, Bernard Sullivan, manager, cor Church and Adelaide e
Bolam, John, Butchers Arms' Hotel, cor East Market Square and Palace
Bolster, Launcelot G., supt Metropolitan Water Co., 20, 21 and 22 Toronto Exchange
Bolton, J. P., grocer, 18 Palace
Bond, John, cabinetware, 209 King e
Bond, John, blacksmith, 52 Queen w
Bond, John, prop Ontario Livery Stables, Sheppard
Bond St. Congregational Church, Bond cor Cruickshank
Bond Street Regular Baptist Church, Rev. T. F. Caldicott, pastor
Bonnell, W., agent Smith & Cochrane, boots and shoes, Montreal, 37 Yonge
Bonnick, Joseph, butcher, 377 Yonge
Bonter, Isaac, baker, 597 Yonge
BOOMER, A. K., commission merchant, and agent Fairbank's Scales and Kershaw & Edwards's Safes 93 King w
Booth, John, confectioner, 131 York
BOOTH & SON (H. G. and George) coppersmiths, 26 Richmond w
Bostwick, Amos (Henderson & Bostwick), h 642 Yonge
Bostwick, George, J.P., Yonge, Yorkville
Boswell, George, steward General Hospital
Boulton, Hon. H. P., prop Royal Dominion Mills, Bay cor Esplanade, h 61 Wellington w
Boulton, James, barrister, 170 King w
Boulton, W. H., John
BOURLIER, H., station master G. T. R., agent Montreal Ocean Steamship Company
Boustead, J. B., provisions and commission merchant (wholesale), 82 Front e
Bovell, James, M.D., Denison Avenue
Bowden, John W., grocer, 127 York
Bowdway, Gilbert, blacksmith, 218 Dundas
BOXALL, JOHN, stoves, tinware, &c., 50 Queen w (see adv)
Boyd, A., blacksmith, 621 Queen w
Boyd, John, wood dealer, Albert
Boyd, Robert, grocer and contractor, 231 King e
Boyd, William, barrister, h 84 Wellington w
BOYD, JOHN & CO. (John Boyd, Alexander M. Munro and C. W. Bunting), wholesale grocers. 61 and 63 Front e
Boyd & Stayner, barristers, 70 King e
BOYLE, PATRICK, editor and proprietor *Irish Canadian*, book and job printer, Exchange Alley
BOYS' HOME, Mrs. Munroe, matron, George
Brabington, R., groceries and provisions, Gerrard
BRADBURNE, E., agent Canada Life Assurance Co., Whittemore's Building, Toronto
Bradbury, James R., mining agent, 6 Wellington e
Bradford, J. W., flour and feed, 211 King e
BRADFORD, ROBERT, flour and commission merchant and City Express, 75 Yonge & 211 King e
Bradley, John, furniture dealer, 313 George
BRADSTREET, J. M. & SON, improved mercantile agency, 32 Wellington e
BRAY, JOSIAS, n w cor King and Church
Breen, James, butcher, 448 Queen w
Breen, P. and D., butchers, 21 St. Lawrence Market

Brennan, Lawrence, professor St. Michael's College, St. Josephs
Brent, Mrs. E., proprietor Turkish Baths, Bloor
Brent, J. W., sec'y General Hospital, 86 King e
Brew, Thomas, tailor, 269½ Queen w
Bridge, J. G., grocer, 38 Denison ave
Bridgeland, J. W., supt. Colonization Roads, Parliament Buildings
Bridgman, J. W.. portrait painter, 39 King w
Bridgewater, Thomas, clothing store, 325 Yonge
Briggs, Dr. J., surgeon and chiropodist, 6 King w
Briggs, Robert, gunsmith, 203 King e
BRIGGS, SAMUEL R.. lumber dealer, shipper and commission merchant, 37 Toronto Exchange
BRIGGS, THOMAS, wholesale and retail dealer in lumber, laths, shingles, flooring, &c., 17 to 24 Edward (see adv)
Bright, William, butcher, 63 Seaton
Briggs, W. H., grocer, 303 Yonge
BRIMER, JOHN, merchant tailor, 171 Yonge
Brimstin, Hugh, cutler and bell hanger, 288 Yonge
Briscoe, William, blacksmith and wagon maker, 129 Queen w
BRITISH AMERICAN ASSURANCE COMPANY; governor, George Percival Ridout, deputy-governor, Peter Paterson; managing director, Thomas W. Birchall; 54 Church cor Court (see adv. inside front cover)
BRITISH AMERICAN & BRYANT, STRATTON & ODELL COMMERCIAL COLLEGE, Odell & Trout, proprietors, 57 Yonge & Toronto cor King
Briton Medical and General Life Association, James Fraser. agent, 5 King w
Britton, James, butcher, 13 and 15 St. Lawrence Market
Broadwell, J. W., insurance agent, Canada Life, office Toronto
Brock, Henry, hotel keeper, 556 Queen w
Brock, Llewellyn, M.D., editor and proprietor *Dominion Medical Journal*, office 9 Trinity square
BROMFIELD, E. T. & Co., publishers *Canadian Journal of Commerce*, 48 King e
BRONSDON & PATON, (J. L. Bronsdon and J. W. Paton) paints, oils, German and English plate, etc., 84 Yonge (see adv)
Brooks, James, second-hand dealer, 222 Queen w
Brooks, Joseph, grocer, 90 Church
Brooks, Mrs. S., boarding house, 36 Richmond w
Broom, James, dry goods, 246 Yonge
Broom, R., lock smith and bell hanger, 26 and 28 Colborne
Broughall, Rev. A. J., (Church of England), St. Stephen's Parsonage
BROWN, CHARLES, (C. P. Reid & Co.) h 190 Church
BROWN, GEORGE, saloon and billiard parlor, Queen's Hotel
BROWN, HON. GEORGE. managing director *Globe* Printing Co., h 270 Wellington w
Brown, Henry, butcher, Yonge, Yorkville
Brown, James, M.A., mathematical master U. C. College
BROWN, JAMES, JUN., produce merchant, 24 Toronto Exchange
Brown, John, librarian Law Society, Osgoode Hall
Brown, John, builder, 72 Victoria
Brown, John, temperance saloon, 370½ Queen w
Brown, John, M.D., 321 Queen w
BROWN, J. GORDON, editor-in-chief *Globe*, 26 and 28 King e
Brown, J. W., proprietor British Hotel, cor King and Simcoe
Brown, J. R., boots and shoes, 42 King w
Brown, Robert, hotel keeper, 326 Queen w
Brown, Thomas, proprietor Metropolitan Hotel, King cor Bay
Brown, William, builder, 38 Agnes
BROWN, WILLIAM, carriage hardware, 72 King e
Brown, William, dry goods, 416 Queen w
BROWN BROTHERS, bookbinders, stationers and blank book manufacturers, 66 and 68 King e (see adv)
Browne, J. O., P.L.S., Whittamore's bdgs, Toronto
BROWN, PHILIP & CO., bankers and exchange brokers, 67 Yonge
Brownlee & Conn (Harvy Brownlee & Joshua Conn), clothing and furnishing goods, 151 King e
Bruce, James, dry goods, 315 Yonge
BRUNEL, LIEUT. COL. ALFRED, 10th Royals, Assistant Commissioner Inland Revenue, Toronto Exchange, h Bathurst nr Front
Brumell, H. P., druggist, 13 King e
Brunskill & Kirby, commission merchants, 78 Front
BRYCE, McMURRICH & CO., wholesale importers of dry goods, 34 Yonge
BRYSON, JOHN, assistant station master and telegraph operator G. W. R., Yonge St. Station
BUCHAN, DAVID, bursar University and Colleges, Simcoe cor Adelaide
Buchanan, C. W., M.D., coroner, 57 Adelaide w
Buckland, Professor George, secretary Bureau Agriculture, 335 Jarvis
Buckley, John, cab owner, York cor Wellington
Buckley, Joseph, blacksmith, 45 James
Buell, Andrew Norton, Master in Chancery, Osgoode Hall
BUGG, CHARLES, fruits and confectionery, books and stationery, 296 Yonge (see adv)
Bulman, William, grocer, 51 Elizabeth
Bulmer & Douglas, brick, tile and pipe manufacturers, Yorkville
Bunce, Prof. H. T., M.D., 23 Frederick
Buntin Brother & Co., wholesale stationers and paper manufacturers, 63 and 65 Yonge
BURKE, WILLIAM, lumber merchant and builder, sash, door and blind factory, Sheppard cor Richmond (see adv)
Burness & Sons, bakers, Queen cor Jarvis
Burns, Charles, prop York Street Inn, 115 York
Burns, James, wholesale and retail grocer and commission merchant, 5 and 6 City Hall Buildings
Burns, James, grocer, 202 Palace
Burns, John, grocer, 28 Queen w
Burns, Patrick, prop Lord Nelson Hotel and coal and wood merchant, 226 Queen cor John
Burns, Rev. Robert, D.D., professor of Church History, Knox's College
Burns, G. & Co., grocers, 4 Palace
Bury, William, confectionery, 418 Queen w
Butchart, D. C., photographer, 145 King e
BUTLAND, RICHARD B. importer of music and musical instruments, 37 King w
Butler, Alfred, news dealer, 85 Queen w
Butler, Patrick, shoemaker, 272 Queen w
BUTLER, WILKIN B., Division Court, house, land and mercantile agent, 2 Leader buildings
Butt, Ephraim, carriage maker, 15 Agnes
Butt, James, blacksmith, 100 Victoria
Byers, W. A., grocer and tavern keeper, 94½ Church
Byrnes, T., Messenger Legislative Assembly, Parliament buildings
Cadow, William, merchant, h 325 Jarvis
Cain, James, watchman, Parliament buildings
Calder, Duncan, blacksmith, 22 Beverley

Caldicott, Rev. T. F., D.D., (Baptist) h Bond cor Gould
Callaghan, Hugh, shoemaker, 318½ Queen w
Callard, Mrs. John, dealer in fancy goods 166 Queen w
Callard, Josiah, cutler, 316 Queen w
Callaway, Mrs. M., milliner and dressmaker, 339 Yonge
Cameron, Alan, clerk of process, Osgoode Hall
Cameron, Donald M., local reporter *Globe*
CAMERON, HARMAN & MURRAY, (Hon. J. H. Cameron, Q.C., M.P., S. B. Harman & W. H. Murray) barristers, &c., Romain bldgs., King w
CAMERON, HON. J. HILLYARD, Q.C., M.P., (Cameron, Harman & Murray) h Meadows, 342 Queen w
CAMERON & HOLMSTED, (Alexander Cameron & George S. Holmsted) King, cor Church
CAMERON & McMICHAEL, (Hon. M. C. Cameron, Q.C., M.P.P., Daniel McMichael, D.C.L., & C. McMichael) barristers, &c. 44 Church
CAMERON, McMICHAEL, FITZGERALD & HOSKINS (M. C. Cameron, Q.C., Daniel McMichael, D.C.L., Edward Fitzgerald, M.A., LL.B., and Alfred Hoskins) barristers and solicitors in Chancery, 44 Church
CAMERON, HON. M. C., Q.C., M.P., (Cameron & McMichael) and (Cameron, McMichael, Fitzgerald & Hoskins) Provincial Secretary and Registrar, h 64 Duke
Cameron & Smart, barristers, Whittemore's building, Toronto
Camidge, John, Mus. Doc., Cantuar (Eng.) h Parliament
Campbell, Alexander, blacksmith, 338 King e
CAMPBELL & CASSELS, (Charles J. Campbell & Walter G. Cassels) bankers and brokers, 60 King e
Campbell, Duncan, M.D., president Homœopathic Medical Board, h 108 Bay
CAMPBELL, G. L., gold and silver plater, 20 Toronto
Campbell, James & Son, wholesale publishers, and booksellers, 9 Toronto
Campbell, John, brickyard, Yonge, between Beverley and Cottingham Road, Yorkville
Campbell, John, boots and shoes, 26 Wellington e
Campbell, M., china, glass and earthenware 254 Yonge
Campbell, William, grocer, 14 Palace
Campbell, W. A., clerk of assize, County York, res e s Avenue Road, nr Bloor, Yorkville
CAMPTON, B. H., butcher and pork packer, 167 King w
Campton, James, butcher, 133 York
CANADA COMPANY, Hon. W. B. Robinson and Hon. G. W. Allan, commissioners, 202 King e
CANADA FARMER (monthly), Globe Printing Co., publishers and proprietors, 26 and 28 King e
CANADA INLAND STEAM NAVIGATION COMPANY'S OFFICE, N. Milloy, agent, 8 Front e
CANADA LANDED CREDIT COMPANY, Lewis Moffatt, President; H. S. Howland, Vice-President; John Symons, secretary, 22 King e
CANADA LIFE ASSURANCE COMPANY, E. Bradburne, agent, Whittemore's block, Toronto
CANADA PERMANENT BUILDING & SAVINGS SOCIETY, Joseph D. Ridout, President; Peter Paterson, Vice-President; J. Herbert Mason, Secretary and Treasurer, Masonic Hall (see inside front cover)
CANADA PRESBYTERIAN CHURCH, Bay cor Richmond
CANADA SUNDAY SCHOOL ADVOCATE, semi-monthly
CANADIAN ALMANAC, W. C. Chewett & Co., 17 & 19 King e
CANADIAN BANK OF COMMERCE, Hon. William McMaster, President; Henry S. Howland, Vice-President; R. J. Dallas, Cashier, Yonge cor Colborne
CANADIAN BAPTIST (weekly), H. Lloyd, editor and proprietor, 11 King w
CANADIAN EXPRESS COMPANY, J. D. Irwin, agent, 57 Yonge
CANADIAN FREEMAN, J. G. Moylan, editor and proprietor, 74 Church
CANADIAN INDEPENDENT MAGAZINE (mo.), Rev. F. H. Marling, editor
CANADIAN INSTITUTE, Prof. H. Croft, D.C.L., F.C.S., President, 44 Richmond e
CANADIAN JOURNAL, alternate months, conducted by the editing committee of the Canadian Institute; A. Lovell & Co., printers
CANADIAN JOURNAL OF COMMERCE, E. T. Bromfield & Co., Publishers, 43 King e
CANADIAN MERCANTILE TEST (fortnightly), John Kerr, editor and proprietor, British America Assurance Company's Bdgs, Court cor Church
CANADIAN MONETARY TIMES and Insurance Chronicle, Robertson & Cook, Publishers for the Company, Bay nr King
CANADIAN PHARMACEUTICAL JOURNAL, J. M. Trout, publisher, *Daily Telegraph* office, Bay, E. B. Shuttleworth, editor
Canavan, John, attorney-at-law, 58 King e
Canniff, —, M.D., 111 Church
Capon, William B., dealer in decalcomanie materials and picture frames, 93 Yonge
CAPREOL, FREDERICK C., President Huron and Ontario Ship Canal Co., 16 & 18 Wellington e
Carlaw, John A., cashier G. T. R. office, Union Station, h 207 Jarvis
Carless, James, depository U. C. Bible and Tract Society, 102 Yonge
CARLISLE, GEORGE W., prop Terrapin Restaurant, 87 and 89 King e
Carlyle, James, M.D., principal Boys' Model School
Carmichael, Capt., steamer *Champion*, h 44 Wood
Carmichael, Robert, cooper and dealer in woodenware, 9 Adelaide e
Carnegie, Charles, watchmaker and jeweller, 14 King e
Carr, John, city clerk, h 23 Denison Avenue
Carrol, Robert, builder and contractor, h e s Sheppard
Carroll, Charles I., barrister, North cor Bloor
Carroll, John, supt *Leader* office, h 172 Berkeley
Carroll, John, prop Rochester House, 20 Front w
CARRUTHERS, E. M., & CO., (E. M. Carruthers, George Ewart and Charles Perry), props steamer *Algoma*, 55 Front e
CARRUTHERS, E. M. (E. M. Carruthers & Co.), wharfinger, Queen's Wharf
Carruthers, John, contractor, h 14 Don
Carson, James, prop Turf Club Hotel, 40 King w
Carson, Wallice, prop Rising Sun Hotel, 626 Yonge
Carter, Mrs. Amelia, milliner, dressmaker and ladies' hair dresser, 292½ Yonge
Carter, George, barber, 25 King e and Queen's Hotel
Carter, John, professor of music, h 137 Simcoe
Carter, M. & A., milliners and mantle makers, 362 Yonge
Carto, Benjamin, fancy goods, 260 King e
Carto, Mrs. B., manufac'r hair jewellery, 260 King e
CARTY, J., & CO., manufacturers soap and candles, cor Queen and George
Cary, G. W., barber, 10 Front e
Cassels, Robert, Jr., barrister, 56 Church, h 517 Jarvis

CASSELS, WALTER G. (Campbell & Cassels), 60 King e
Cassidy, J. J., M.B., physician to House of Providence, 118 Church
Caswell, Wm., boarding-house, 153 Adelaide w
Cathcart, James, innkeeper, 356 Queen w
CATHRON, ROBERT R., accountant Freehold Permanent Building and Savings Society, h 169 Mutual
Cattanach, Alexander J. (Crooks, Kingsmill & Cattanach), 17 Wellington w
CATTO, JOHN, & CO., dry goods, 59 King e
CAULKINS & SANDERSON (J. B. Caulkins and P. K. Sanderson), broom and brush manufacturers, 434 Yonge
CAULKINS, J. R. (Caulkins & Sanderson), h 432 Yonge
CAVEN, REV. W., professor Exigetical Theology, Knox's College, h Victoria
Cawthra, William, h 91 Bay cor King
CAXTON PRESS; Thomas Hill & Son, proprietors, King cor Nelson
Cayley, John, res Castle Frank, rear of Cemetery
Cayley, Hon. William, Clerk Surrogate Court, h n s D'Arcy w Beverly
Carberry, Kennedy, grocer, 228 Sayer
CHAFFEY & BROTHER, coal and wood merchants, 49 Front e
Challandard, Rev. Pierre, professor St. Michael's College, St, Joseph
Chaloner, Mrs. Henry, dry goods, 372 Queen w
Chambers, Daniel, hotel, 202 Queen w
CHAMP, J. S. & CO., roofing material, cor Front and Church
Chandler & Platts, dry goods and clothing, 165 King east
CHAPMAN, EDWARD J., Ph. D., professor of minerology and geology, University College
Chard, Charles, fruits and confectionery, 318 Yonge
CHARLESWORTH, JOHN, & CO., wholesale importers of dry goods and millinery, 44 Yonge & 3 Wellington w
CHERRIMAN, J. B., M.A., professor Natural History, University College, h 49 Bloor
Cherry, Raspin R., proprietor Cumberland House, Yonge w, Yorkville
Chesnut, T. G., boarding and day school, Murray
CHEWETT, W. C. & CO., booksellers, stationers, book and job printers, lithographers, publishers *Canadian Almanac*, 17 and 19 King e
Childs & Hamilton (W. S. Childs, C. Brown and W. B. Hamilton), boots and shoes wholesale, 7 Wellington e
CHIPMAN, R. J. U., secretary and manager Colonial Securities Company, Edinburgh Assurance Company's Buildings, Wellington w
Chisholm, Thos. C., commission merchant, 88 Front e
Christian Brothers' Academy; Rev. Brother Arnold, principal, 98 to 102 Nelson e
Christian Brothers' School; Rev. Brother Arnold, principal, Bathurst bet Adelaide and Queen
CHRISTIAN GUARDIAN; Rev. W. Jeffers, D.D., editor, 80 King e
Christian, Thomas, mathematical and telegraph instrument maker, 27 Exchange, h 115 Victoria
Christie, Alex. R., lumber merchant, h 287 King w
CHRISTIE, A., accountant, commission and patent agent, 34 King e (see adv)
CHRISTIE, BROWNE & CO., wholesale biscuit manufacturers, 626 Yonge
Christie, The Misses, boarding and day school, Cruickshank
CHURCH CHRONICLE (THE), monthly, printed for the Church Society by Henry Rowsell, 76 King e
CHURCH OF THE HOLY TRINITY, Trinity Square, w of Yonge
Church Society's Office, Diocese of Toronto, W. P. Atkinson, secretary, 76 King e
Church Street Wharf, Scott & Gorrie, props., Esplanade, foot of Church
CITY BANK MONTREAL, John Moat, manager, s w cor Bay and Wellington
CITY BATHS AND GYMNASIUM, Donald Grant, superintendent, Adelaide w nr Yonge
City Larder and Lunch Rooms, William Yielding, proprietor, Post Office Lane
City of Glasgow Assurance Co., J. E. Smith & Co., agents, 34 Church cor Colborne
City Police Court, Court
City Registrar's Office, Charles Lindsay, City Registrar, Royal Ins. Co's. Blgs., Yonge cor Wellington
City Telegraph, P. McEachran, prop., 34 King e
Clare, Isaac, farrier, 309 Queen w
CLARK, ALLISTER M., barrister, 3 Wellington Chambers, Jordan
Clark, Bros., carriage makers, 151, 153 and 155 York
Clark, H. D., grocer, 95 Church
CLARK, J. & A. (James & Angus), produce and commission merchants, 53 Wellington e
Clark, John, saloon keeper, 171½ Yonge
Clark, Joseph, marine store, 14 Adelaide w
Clark & McConnell, fruit, oysters, &c., 294 Yonge
Clark, P. M., merchant tailor, King w
CLARK, S. C. DUNCAN- & CO., agents for Mott's Lubricating Oils, and general agents Lancashire Insurance Co., 96 King cor Church
Clark, Thomas, confectioner, 383 Yonge
Clark, William Mortimer, barrister, 48 King e
CLARK, WHITE & CO., lumber merchants, 14 and 15 Ontario Chambers, cor Front and Church
CLARKE, H. E., trunks and valises, 103 King w
Clarke, F., boots, shoes, trunks, &c., 86 Yonge
Clarke, J. P., Mus. Bac., h Bloor nr Yonge, Yorkville
Clarke, Miss M. A., boarding house, 100 Church
Clarke, William, shoemaker, 131 Queen w
Clarke, Rev. W. F., editor *Ontario Farmer*, address *Ontario Farmer* office
CLARKSON, THOMAS & CO. (Thomas Clarkson & B. R. Clarkson), produce and commission merchants, 83 Front
CLARKSON, THOMAS, (Thomas Clarkson & Co.) official assignee
Cleary, Michael, 2 Renfrew cor Queen
Cleary, Walter M., 202 Queen w
Clegg, Thomas, fruit store, 227 King e
Clements, John, builder, prop Atlas Wood Works, door, sash, blind, planing and saw mill, Front opp Queen's Hotel
Cleveland, J. P., M.D., private college, 133 Victoria
Cleveland, John, shoemaker, 143 Adelaide w
CLINDINNING, JOHN A., boatbuilder, s s Esplanade cor Scott (see adv)
Clinkunbroomer, Charles, watchmaker, 156 Queen w
Close, P. G., wholesale and retail grocer, 10 Palace
Clunie, Wiliam, M.D., 208 Church
Coate, F. W. & Co., auctioneers and commission merchants, 51, King e.
Clyne, Wm., groceries and provisions, 112 Caroline
Coates, C. W., clerk Wesleyan book room, 78 King e
Coates, Robert, proprietor City Arms Hotel, 36 west Market Square
Coatsworth, Emerson, carpenter and lumber dealer, 359 King e

Coates, Thomas, prop Western Hotel, 648 Queen w
COBB, WILLIAM W., agent Colonial Securities Company, bds Rossin House
Cobley, Henry & Co., cask manufacturers, (wholesale) 55 Front e
COCKBURN, GEORGE R. R., M.A., Principal U. C. College, King cor Simcoe
Cocker, William, M.D., 36 Bond
Cochran, Alexander, Lord Nelson Hotel, 8 Palace
Coddington, Luther C., proprietor Richmond House, 29 Victoria
COFFEE, L. & CO., (Laurence Coffee & T. Flynn), produce and commission merchants, 2 Manning's block, Front e (see adv)
Coghill, Robert, carriage manufacturer, 163 King w
Coldwell, William, assistant editor and Parliamentary reporter *Globe*
Cole, Rev. Henry J., chaplain to H. M. forces, h 7 Douro
Coleman, Arthur, builder, h 179 Dalhousie
Coleman & Co., hatters and furriers, 55 King e
Coleman, George, confectioner, 99 King w
Coleman, J. & Sons, melodeon manufacturers, 56 King w
Coles, George, baker, flour and feed, 627 George
Collar, Miss Eliza, ladies' school, 147 Church
Collard, Joseph, butcher, 299 Yonge
Collett, M., & Son, bacon curers, 468 Yonge
Collins, John, steam gauge and brass works, 112 Bay
Collyer, John, prop Clifton House, 80 Colborne
COLONIAL SECURITIES' COMPANY, R. J. U. Chipman, secretary, Edinburgh Assurance Co.'s Buildings, 17 Wellington w
Colwell, Henry, lumber merchant, 414 Front w
Colwell, W. W., wholesale lumber merchant, Front w bet Brock and Portland, res Sunnyside
COMMERCIAL BUILDING AND INVESTMENT SOCIETY, Hon. John McMurrich, Pres.; John Burns, Vice-Pres.; John Rains, sec. and treas.; 120 Yonge
COMMERCIAL HOTEL, Beatty & Forsyth, props., 54 & 56 Nelson
COMMERCIAL UNION ASSURANCE CO'Y, of London, England, Wm. Westmacott, agent, 72 King e
Commissariat Staff Corps, office 53 York
Congdon, R. D., h 5 Alice
Conlin, Henry, grain merchant, h 96 Duke
Conlin, Henry, jun., produce dealer, 74 Palace
Connell, William E., watchmaker and jeweller, 150 Yonge
Connon, C. W., LL.D., English Classical Master, U. C. College
Connor, Miss Joanna, boarding-house, 97 Ann
CONSUMERS' GAS COMPANY'S WORKS, Henry Thompson, manager, e s Parliament bet Little Front and Palace; office, 20 Toronto
Constantinides, P., M.D., 369 Yonge
Convent of St. Joseph, St. Albans, Rev. Mother Antionetta, superioress
Conway, Rev. P., assistant St. Paul's, Power
Coo, William, wire-worker, 208 Queen w
Cook Bros. (Hiram H., John and George), lumber merchants, 56 Bay
COOK, JAMES B. (Robertson & Cook), *Daily Telegraph*
Cooke's Church (Presbyterian), co Mutual & Queen e
Cooke, John, leather dresser and fancy colored sheep-skin mat manufacturer, h 33 Oak
Coombe, John, Medical Hall, 104 Yonge
Cooper, Charles W., barrister, reporter Chancery Chambers and legal repor'r *Globe*, h 32 Alexander
Cooper, James (Sessions, Turner & Co.), h 265 Queen e
Cooper, Mrs. Mary A., boarding-house, 53 Queen e
Cooper, Wm. A., photographer, 45 King e
Cooper, William J., house, land, estate, patent and parliamentary agent, Romain Buildings, King w
COPLAND, WILLIAM, prop East Toronto Brewery, h 314 King e
Copley, J., barber and hairdresser, 238 Yonge
Copping, G. H., packing-box maker, 10 Queen w
Corbett, William, wood merchant, 196 Elizabeth
Corcoran, John, boots and shoes, 222 King e
Corin, Charles, sign writer, 16 Queen w
Corin, J. L., sign painter, &c., 34½ Queen w
CORNNELL, JOHN (Wallis & Cornnell), proprietor Cornnell's Hotel, West Market Square
Cornish, J. H., boots and shoes, 240 Yonge
Cornish, T. W., boots and shoes, 637 Yonge
Cornor, Edward, scale manufacturer and tobacconist, 254 Yonge
COSGRAVE & CO., props West Toronto Brewery, 619 Queen w
Cosgrove, Owen, grocer, 180 Queen w
Cottrell, William, tinsmith, 60 King w
Couch, Richard, builder, &c., 132 and 134 Adelaide w
Couthard, John, wines and spirits, 30 Francis
Courneen, R., marine inspector B. A. Assurance Co., h 233 Richmond w
Courtenay, John, dry goods and millinery, 118 Yonge
Court Street Fire Hall, Court
Couture, Mrs. A. & Co., oyster and fruit dealers, 82 Queen w
Cowan, D., & Co. (David Cowan and William Sidery), wholesale provision and commission merchants, 29 Church
Cowan, Robert, shoemaker, 277 Queen w
Cowdry, Thomas, M.D., 354 Queen w
Cowper, George B., Crown Lands Department
COX, G. & J. W., &. CO., importers of dry goods and manufacturers of millinery, mantles and clothing, 115, 117, 119 and 121 King e
Cox, James, confectioner, 165 Yonge
Cox, Captain William, prop Black Horse Hotel, 24 and 26 Palace
Coxall, McRae & Co., grocers, 101 King e
COXON, GEORGE, soda water, 361 Yonge (see adv)
Coxon, Samuel, sausage maker and grocer 220 King e
Coyne, Thomas, 121 Queen w
Craig, James, F. confectioner, 91 Church
Crane, Samuel, coal and wood, 103 Queen w
Crane, William, Holman Opera Troupe, 1 Ritchie's Terrace
Crapper, James, plumber and gas fitter, 88 Adelaide e
CRAPPER, JAMES, plumber and gas fitter, 88 Adelaide e (see adv.)
Crawford, Archibald, baker, 381 Queen w
CRAWFORD, ARTHUR, toys and fancy goods, 164 Yonge (see adv)
CRAWFORD & CROMBIE, (John Crawford Q.C., and Ernestus Crombie, M.A.,) barristers 9 and 10 Masonic Hall
CRAWFORD, D. & Co., spice mills, soap, candle, and oil manufacturers, Palace cor Princess
Crawford, George G., M.D. 109 Elm
CRAWFORD, JOHN, Q.C., M.P., (Crawford & Crombie) h cor Wellington and Simcoe
Crawford, John, butcher, 418 Queen w
Crawford, Richard, butcher, 164 Agnes
Crawford, Samuel, butcher, 100 Caroline
Crawford & Smith, dry goods, 91 King e
Crawford's Wharf, Esplanade foot of Berkeley
Creys, Isaiah, wagon maker, 8 and 10 Edward
Crickmore, John, barrister, 70 King e

Crocker, James, prop. Albion Hotel, 55 East Market
CROCKER, JAMES SYDNEY, secretary and manager Provincial Insurance Company of Canada, Toronto, cor. Court, h Brock, cor. Wellington Place
Crocker, Sydney, jr., clerk, Provincial Insurance Co., of Canada
CROFT, HENRY, M.A., D.C.L., F.C.S., professor of Chemistry, University College
Croft, William, & Co., needles, fishing tackle, &c., 37 Colborne
CROMBIE, ERNESTUS, (Crawford & Crombie)
Crombie, M., barrister, h 181 John
CROOKS, ADAM, Q.C., (Crooks, Kingsmill & Cattanach, h 41 Grange Road)
CROOKS, KINGSMILL & CATTANACH (Adam Crooks, Q.C., Nichol Kingsmill, M.A. and Alexander J. Cattanach, M.A.), barristers, &c., Edinburgh Assurance Co's. Blgs., 17 Wellington w
Crowe, William, Maple Leaf Saloon, 246 Queen w
Crown Inn Hotel. Edward Jackson, Davenport Road, Yorkville
Crown Timber Agency Office, 53 Duke
CRUMPTON, HENRY, wholesale and retail confectioner, 171 King e (see adv)
Cuff, W. H., provision dealer, 48, 50 and 52 St. Lawrence Market
CUMING & WELLS, plumbers and gasfitters, 175 King w (see adv.)
CUMBERLAND, FREDERICK W., managing director Northern Railway Company, h Pendarvis, College
Cumberland House, R. B. Cherry, Yonge bet Scollard and Beverly
Cummer, F. D., produce and commission merchant, 8 and 9 Ontario Chambers
Cumming, William H., M.D., 82 Adelaide w
Cummins, Sergeant Major Patrick, T. P. F., No. 1 Station, h 122 Jarvis
Cunningham, D., local reporter *Globe*
Cuppage, William, chief clerk P. O. Inspector's Office, h 131 Bay
CUPPLES & HUNTER (Joseph Cupples & Lewis Hunter), Mercantile Protective Association, 20 Toronto
CURRIE, NEIL, boiler maker, Esplanade, near Church (see adv.)
Currie, Charles, 34 Agnes
CUSTOM HOUSE WHARF, W. Higinbotham & Co., proprietors, foot of Yonge
Cuthbert, Richard, bookbinder, 42 Carlton
Cuthbert, Simon, bootmaker, 367 Yonge
Cuttell, Thomas & Son, book and job printers, s s Change Alley, cor Colborne
D'Allien, A. J., proof reader *Globe*
Dack, Edward, boots and shoes, 73 King w
Daley, Charles & Co., leather dealers, 56 Yonge
Dallas, Angus, wholesale dealer in wooden ware and fancy goods, 74 York
Dalton, R. G. Clerk Crown and Pleas, Queen's Bench, Osgoode Hall
DALTON, WILLIAM, fruit, confectionery, ice cream &c.. 364 Yonge
Daly, Mrs. Ann, boarding house, 109 Simcoe
Daly, Edward, contractor, 79 Peter
Damele, John, looking glass manufacturer, h 218 Sayer
Damer & Co., wholesale boots and shoes, 97 Yonge
Damer, J. & W., boots and shoes, 144 Yonge
Damoreau, C. F., engraver on wood, 87 Bay cor King
Dane, John, grocer, Osgoode cor Sayer
DARLING, REV. W. S., rector Church of Holy Trinity, res Parsonage, Trinity Square
Darlington, W. D., felt roofing manufacturer, Clare and 35 Queen e
DAVIDGE, WILLIAM, JUNR., comedian, Holman Opera Troupe
DAVIDS, JOSEPH, chemist and druggist, 169 King e (see adv)
DAVIDSON, DAVID, com. merchant, 80 Front e
DAVIDSON, McVITTIE & CO. (William Davidson, Thomas McVittie and J. M. Davidson), importers of coach and saddlery hardware, 11 King e (see adv)
Davies, C., watchmaker, jeweler and dealer in fancy goods, 284 Yonge
Davies, Brothers, wholesale grocers and seed merchants, 6 Palace
Davies, F. N., butcher, 237 Yonge
DAVIES, REV. H. W. W., B.D., second master Normal School and Curate Church of Holy Trinity, 5 Breadalbane.
DAVIES. THOMAS & SON, maltsters and brewers, Don Brewery, River
Davies, William & Co., pork packers, 37, 39 & 41 Palace
Davis, A., provision dealer and pork butcher, 316 Queen w
Davis, Daniel, tailor, 34 King w
Davis, Isaac, designer and stamper, 288 Yonge
Davis, James, city assessor St. Lawrence Ward, 17 Sherbourne
Davis, J., inspector of distilleries, 36 Exchange Bldg
Davis, J. F., fruit store, 32 Queen w
Davis, Robert & Co., grocers and liquor dealers, 55 King w
Dawbarn, Charles & Co., seedsmen and florists, 124 King w
Dawson, S. J., C. E. & P. L. S., 38 Exchange Bldgs
DAY, JAMES E., proprietor Day's Commercial and Telegraph Institute, 82 King e
DAY'S COMMERCIAL COLLEGE; James E. Day, proprietor, 82 King e (see adv.)
Deacon, A. T., Clerk Indian Office, Jordan
Dean, George, grocer, 174 Parliament
Dee & Herbert, paint shop, 353 Queen
DEGRASSI, ALFIO, general broker, shipping and insurance agent, 52 King e
DeGrassi, George, M.D., 292 King e
Delanay, Thomas, groceries, 385 King e
De LaHunt, Thomas, barber, &c., 70 Colborne
De La Porte, A. V., broker and commission merchant, 57 Front e
Delude, Remi, machinist, 257 Queen
Deneler, Gottlieb, prop. German Hotel, 24 York
Denison, George T., barrister, 11 Wellington Chambers
DENISON, COL. GEORGE T., commandant volunteer garrison, 5th Military District, Ontario, Wellington Chambers, "Rusholme," Dundas
Denison, Robert B., Brigade Major, "Bellevue," head of Denison Avenue
Denison, W. L., grocer and feed store, Dundas
Denison, Richard L., "Lippincott," Brockton
Denyer, William, butcher, 289 Yonge
Dever, William, butcher, 36 King w
Devine, Thomas, surveyor-in-chief, Crown Lands Department, Parliament Buildings
Dewdney, R., blacksmith, 99 and 103 Parliament
DEWE, JOHN, Post Office Inspector, Toronto Division, office Post Office
Dexter, Thomas, butcher, h 155 Jarvis
Diamond, J. S., M.D., 38 Spadina Avenue

DICK, CAPT. THOMAS, prop Queen's Hotel
Dickey, Neill & Co. (J. I. Dickey, John Neill and Nat. Dickey), props Soho Foundry, 18 and 28 Beverley
Dickson, Charles R., accountant Provincial Ins. Co. of Canada, cor Court
Dickson, George P., collector Inland Revenue, Toronto Exchange
Dickson, James H., auction and commission, 121 Yonge
DILLON, JOHN, jun. (Reford & Dillon), res Montreal
DILWORTH, JAMES, clerk *Daily Telegraph*
Dingwall, James, barrister, Ontario Hall, Court
Dineen, Jeremiah, hatter and furrier, 92 Yonge
DINEEN, W. & D., hatters and furriers, 80 Yonge
DINNIS, RICHARD, builder and lumber merchant, 48 Bay
Disciples' Church, Shuter cor Victoria
Dixon Bros., carriage builders, 70 and 72 King w
DIXON, B. HOMER, Consul for Netherlands, "Homewood," Wellesley
DIXON, F. E., 72 King e
DIXON, JOHN L., 72 King e
Dixon, William, produce, flour and feed, 249 King e
Doane, Henry, livery, rear of 40 King w
Dobbie & Carrie, (James A. Dobbie and Robert Carrie) wholesale dry goods, 45 Yonge and 3 Wellington e
DOBSON, JAMES, J.P., Postmaster, com. Court of Queen's Bench, Yorkville
Dodgson, Shields & Co., (John Dodgson and James Shields) wholesale and retail grocers, &c., 138 Yonge cor Temperance
Doel, John, 38 Adelaide
DOLPHIN SALOON, Joseph Palmer, prop., 131 King e (see adv.)
Dominion Medical Journal, (monthly) Dr. L. Brock editor, office No. 9 Trinity Square
DOMINION TELEGRAPH CO., Hon. Wm. Cayley, president; H. Reeve, secretary, Wellington e;
Dominion Telegraph Institute, 84 King e and cor York and King
Donaldson, J. A., emigration agent, 53 York
Donaldson, James, barrister, bds 98 Queen
DON BREWERY, Thomas Davies & Son, props., e s River nr Queen, (see adv)
Doughan, Samuel, butcher, 307 Church
Donnelly, John, fancy goods, 12 St. Lawrence Arcade
Donohoe, Francis P., shoemaker, 33 Queen w
Donohoe, William, blacksmith, 14 Edward
Donovan, Joseph A., barrister, Ontario Hall, Court
DON STATION, G. T. R., Thomas Meagher, station agent, Little Front cor East
Dorcey, Mrs. Matthew, grocer, 73 Stanley
Dorsey, John, grocery, 142 York
Dosser, W. R., grease manuf., 300 King
Douglas, Captain J. T., marine inspector W. A. Co. 25 Winchester
DOUGLAS, JOHN, chief clerk Custom House, Walton bet Terauley and Elizabeth
DOUGLAS, JOHN & Co., auctioneers and commission merchants, 92 Yonge (see adv)
Douglas, L., boarding house, 16 Front e
Douglas, Sarah M., boarding house, 51 Richmond e
Doughty, Mrs. Jane, groceries, 554 Yonge
DOW, W. H. & CO., dry goods, 1 King w
Downey, Mrs. Mary, boarding house, 116 King w
Downey, Mrs. Mary, hotel keeper, cor Victoria and Stanley
Downing, Thomas, boots and shoes, 256 Yonge
Dowson, Edward, cor Queen and Victoria

Doyle, James H., barrister, 20 Toronto
Doyle, Laurence, Ontario Hotel, 52 Adelaide e
Doyle, Patrick, books and fancy goods, 6, 8 and 10 St. Lawrence Arcade
Doyle, Thomas, hotel keeper, 78 Colborne
Draper, Hon. William Henry, C.B., Chief Justice of Ontario, h Hazeldean e s Gwynne, Yorkville
Dratt, B. F., proprietor employment and real estate agent, Nelson cor King
Draycott, C., proprietor Star Hotel, Front w
DREDGE, A. & CO., wholesale stationers and bookbinders, 53 Yonge (see adv)
Drew, Mrs. Amelia, fancy goods and servants' registry, 362½ Yonge
Drouillard, Felix, tobacconist, 13 King w
Drummond, John, h Victoria
Duckett, Charles, superintendent House of industry, Elm cor Elizabeth
DUDLEY & BURNS, (James and John), proprietors New Commercial Printing House, Victoria Hall, Melinda
Duckworth, Mrs. John, milliner, 324 Queen w
Duffey, Charles. butcher, 4 St. Lawrence Market
Duffey, James, Church cor Carlton
Duffin & Ferguson, (Robert Duffin and Henry Ferguson), sail makers, foot of Yonge
DUFFIN, W. W., general commission agent, 65 Colborne (see adv)
Duggan, George, City Recorder, h 272 Wellington w
Duggan, Joseph, hotel keeper, 248 King e
Duggan & Meyers, barristers, Court cor Toronto
Dugdale, William, grocer, 44 Nelson
DUN, WIMAN & CO., mercantile agency, John Moss, manager, 4, 5 and 6 Toronto Exchange
Dunbar, Richard, grocer, 32 West Market Square
DUNCAN, P. & CO., groceries and liquors, 349 Queen w (see adv)
Dundas, Alexander, grocery, 92 Church
Dunlop, Rev. John J. (Presbyterian), 100 Church
Dunlop, William, lamps, oil, &c., 631 Yonge
Dunn, Daniel, blacksmith, 5 Church
Dunn, David, grocery, 562 Queen w
Dunn, G. W., hoop skirt manufacturer, dry goods, 206 and 208 Yonge
Dunn, J. R., butcher, 377 Queen w
Dunn, Justus, oysters, fruit, game and confectionery, 130 King w
Dunn & Scott (Wm. Dunn and Jno. Scott), butchers, St. Patrick's Market, Queen w
Dunning, C. H., butcher, 10 St. Lawrence Market
DUNSPAUGH & WATSON (Wm. H Dunspaugh & James Watson), wholesale druggists, 3 Front e
Durand, Charles, barrister, 1 Adelaide e
DWIGHT, H. P., supt. Montreal Telegraph Co., Exchange Buildings, h 231 Jarvis
East, H. W., umbrella and parasol manufacturer, 298 Yonge
Eastwood, John, & Son, dry goods and clothing, 122 King e
Eaton, T. & Co., wholesale dry goods, 14 Front w
Edinburgh Life Assurance Co., David Higgins, secretary, 17 Wellington w
Edmunds, Elisha, barber & hairdresser, 292½ Yonge
EDWARDS, H., hat block manufacturer and carver, 202 Terauley (see adv)
Edwards, J., books and stationery, 136 Yonge
Edwards, Thomas, butcher, 406 King e
Elliot, George L., Dentist, 31 King e.
ELLIOT, J. W., dentist, 43 King w (see adv)
Elliott, J., saddler, 56 Nelson
ELLIOTT, W., painter, frescoer, church and house decorator, Cruickshank cor Victoria

ELLIS, GEORGE, upholsterer and mattress maker, 179 Yonge (see adv)
Ellis, James, Royal Oak Saloon, 268 Yonge
ELLIS, JAMES E., watchmaker and jeweller, 48 King e
Ellis, John E., editor *Canada Farmer*, *Globe* office, King e
ELLIS, MRS., ladies' hair manufacturer, 179 Yonge
Ellison, W. J., groceries, wines and liquors, 388 Queen w
Emerson, James, second-hand store, 216 King e
Emery, Robert, M.D., druggist, 62 Queen w
English & Foster (C. E. English, M.A. and Wm. A. Foster, L.L.B.), barristers, Ontario Hall, Church
Equi, Louis, groceries, wines and liquors, 263 Yonge
Erwood, Simon, second-hand furniture, 61 Queen w
European Assurance Society. London, England; W. T. Mason, agent, 5 Ontario Hall
European Express Company; J. D. Irwin, agent, 57 George
EVANS, EDWYN (Evans, Sherwood & Co.), bds Queens' Hotel
Evans. George, tinsmith, 419 Queen w
EVANS, J. ICK, commission agent, 11 Douro
Evans, John, clerk Metropolitan Water Company, 20, 21 and 22 Toronto Exchange
EVANS, SHERWOOD & CO. (Edwyn Evans, L. P. Sherwood), commission merchants, insurance and general agents, 15 Wellington e
Evans, Simon, prov. dealer, 29 & 30 St. Lawrence mkt
EVENING TRIBUNE; Moyer & Co., publishers, 30 King e
EVES, JAMES, soda water manufacturer and dealer in old coins, Indian and other curiosities, 107 Yonge (see bottom lines)
Ewing, Benjamin, tailor, 182 Terauley
Ewing, Robert D., photographer, 150 King
Fahey, James, local reporter *Globe*
Fair, J. John, 187 Yonge, h 131 Bay
Faircloth, George S. & Son, sign and house painters and glaziers, 12 Adelaide e
Fairfield, Alfred E., groceries & provisions, 322 Yonge
Fairfield, Henry B., Fountain restaurant and billiard saloon, 69 King e
Fanson & Northy (E. Fanson and H. Northy), wholesale and retail seed merchants, 4 City Hall bldgs
Faragher. Thomas, watchmaker, 178 King e
Farley, Arthur, variety hall, 291 Qeen w
Farley, James, builder, Jarvis cor Shuter
Farley, William, grocer, 481 Yonge
Farquharson, James, tailor, 179 Queen w
Farquharson, Peter, grocer, 194 Adelaide w
Farrant, John, stationer, 283 Yonge
Farrell, S. W., commission merchant, 78 Front e
FAULKNER & CO., boots and shoes, 3 King w
Fawkes, S., undertaker, 337 Yonge
Fayrann, Frederick, assistant librarian Mechanics' Institute
Fee, John, groceries and liquors, 437 King e
Fee, Joseph, groceries and produce, 451 King e
Fee, Lucas, provision dealer, 30 and 32 St. Lawrence Market
Feintuch, Marcus, watches, clocks and jewelry, 129 King e
Fenner & Co., photographers, 146 Yonge
Fenson, John, engineer and machinist, 35 Adelaide w
Ferguson, Rev. Michael, prof. St. Michael's College
Ferguson, Robert, tailor, 18 Adelaide w
Ferguson, Robert, dry goods, 371 Queen w
Ferry, Thomas, groceries and provisions, 114 Duchess
Field, Richard, grocer, 116 York
Finch, W. S., merchant tailor and clothier, 6 King e
FINCH, F., law stationer and law lithographer, 44 Church opp. St. James' Cathedral
Finn, William, groceries and provisions, 470 Queen w
Firstbrook & Reed, props. planing mill, 265 King e
FISHER, ALEXANDER, manager Ontario Bank, 24 Wellington e cor Scott
Fisher, Charles, market inspector, 27 Terauley
Fisken, John & Co. (John Fisken & Thomas Gordon) rock oil and commission merchants, 15 Wellington e
Fitch, J. C., wholesale grocer, Wykeham Lodge, Yonge
FITTINGER, H. McCORD & CO., manufacturers of vinegars, whiskey, beer, &c., Leslieville
Fitzgerald, John, grocer, 87 Pine
Fitzgerald, John, blacksmith, 48 Queen w
Fitzhenry & O'Donohoe (W. T. Fitzhenry & Martin O'Donohoe), distillers, 61 Little Front
Fitzsimmons, George J., variety store, 135 York
Fitzsimmons, C. J., manufacturing jeweler, 81 King e
Flanagan, Mrs. Susan, grocer, 172 Queen w
Flavell, John, groceries and liquors, 99 Elizabeth
Fleming, Andrew, collector, 129 University
Fleming, James, seed store and Yonge street nursery 348 and 350 Yonge
Fleming, J. & Co. (James Fleming, Geo. W. Buckland) seedsmen and florists, 180 Yonge
FLEMING & WARD (John Fleming, David Ward) pawnbrokers, 58 Adelaide
Fletcher, Hugh R., mining geologist and assayer, office 109 Mutual
Flood, Edward and Co. wines and liquors, 45 Colborne
Foad, William, tavern keeper, 591 Yonge
Forbes & King, bankers and exchange brokers, 30 King e
Forbes, William, dairyman, 454 Yonge
Ford, Wm., M.D. accountant and cashier, Crown Lands department, Parliament bdgs
Forneri, Dr. James, 126 William
Forrest, John, 15 Masonic hall
Forrest, Lorenzo, photographer, Church, cor. King
FORSTER, JAMES, general commission agent, 13 Wellington east
Forsyth, George, builder, 103 Adelaide e
FORTIER, CAPT. CHARLES G. general agent, Phenix Ocean and Inland Marine Insurance Co. 6 and 7 Ontario Chambers, cor. Church and Front (see adv.)
Foster, C. C., Inspector of Agencies, Edinburgh Assurance Co., 17 Wellington w.
Foster, Hetherington, agent, 37 Louisa
Foster, James, mathematical and telegraph instrument maker, 27 Toronto Exchange
Foster, John, grocer, 167 Queen st. w
Foster & Son, hardware merchants, 145 King e
Foulds and Hodgson, importers of small wares and fancy goods, 10 Wellington w
Fowler, Robert, contractor and builder, 398 Yonge
Fowler, Mrs. Robert, milliner and dressmaker, 39 Yonge
Fowles, R., grocer, 411 Queen st. w
Fox, Edward, surveyor and draughtsman, Crown Land Department, Parliament bdgs
FOX, GEORGE, slater, builder and contractor, prop. Don Vale Hotel, Gravesend
Foy, Patrick, merchant, 186 Jarvis
Foy, William, saloon keeper, 167 York
Frachon, Rev., Regis. Prof. St. Michael's College, St. Joseph's
Francis William, W., flour and feed, 7 Queen w

Francis, Thomas, new and second-hand manufacturer plated ware, 197 Yonge
Frankland, G., butcher, 24 St. Lawrence Market
Franklin, Walter W., local editor *Journal of Commerce*
Fraser, James, agent Liverpool and London ins. co., 5 King w
Fraser, Robert, barrister, 44 Church
FREEHOLD PERMANENT BUILDING AND SAVINGS SOCIETY, Charles Robertson, sec. and treas., Ontario Hall, Church
Freeland, W., barrister, *Leader* Buildings
FRENCH CONSULAR AGENCY, W. J. MacDonell agent, 72 Church
Frisby & Bartlett, tailors and men's mercers, 198 Yonge
Frith, William, furniture dealer, 170 Queen w
Fry, John, cabinet maker, 33½ Queen w
Fuller, Charles, lithographer, W. C. Chewett & Co
Fuller, Mrs. Julia M., boarding and day school, 72 Gloucester
FULLER, The Venerable Archdeacon, T. B., D.D. D.C.L., rector St. George's, res. John
Fullerton & Co., publisher's agency, 30 King e
FULTON. MICHIE & CO., (A. T. Fulton and James Michie) grocers, wine and spirit merchants, 7 King w
Funston, William, prop. Grand Trunk Inn, 144 Little Front
Gaby, Joseph, prop. Railroad Hotel, Yonge, Yorkville
Gaffney, John, hotel keeper, 26 Church
Gagnier, Theodore C., tobacconist, 67 King e
Galagher, John, butcher, 185 Parliament
Galbraith, William, gen. com. mercht, 6 Manning's Block, Front e
Gale, James W. gents' furnishing, 58 King w and Yonge cor Adelaide
GALT & HENDERSON, (Thomas Galt, Q.C., and James Henderson, jun.) barristers, &c., Royal Ins. Co.'s Blgs, Yonge cor Wellington
GAMBLE & BOULTON, barristers, Court cor Church
GAMBLE, CLARKE, (Gamble & Boulton) h Holland House, 61 Wellington w
Gamble, Thomas, homœopathist, 42 Ann
Gamble, William, general broker, 24 Toronto Exchange
Gauge, Samuel, grocer, Davenport Road
Gannon, M. E., prop. Ontario House, 44 Palace
Garbutt, Joseph, news depot, 296½ Queen w
GARDNER & RAMSAY, produce, provision and commission merchants, 4 Manning's Block, Front e
Garton, John, pork and fish smoker, 326 Yonge
GARVIN, JOHN, general agent Ætna Life Insurance Company, Whittemore's building, Toronto
Gates, G. W. & Co., sewing machines, 14 King e
Gearing, Joseph, builder and lumber dealer, 421 Yonge
Gee, Mrs. Ann, confectionery, 448 King e
GEMMELL, ALEXANDER, boots and shoes, 97 King w (see adv.)
General Wolfe Hotel, John Irwin, cor Church and Colborne
GEORGE, DAVID J., dry goods, etc., 277 Yonge cor Cruickshank
Gerry, James, groceries and provisions, Yonge
Gibbs, Malcolm, dry goods, 210 Yonge
Gibson, Alexander, grocer, 227 Parliament
Gibson, D., plumber and gasfitter, 28 Adelaide e
Gibson, John, 31 Elizabeth
GIBSON, JOSEPH, marble works, cor Winchester and Parliament
Gibson & Son, harness makers, 207 Yonge
Giddings, George, Dew Drop Inn, 223 Yonge cor Shuter
Gilbert, A., butcher, 22 St. Lawrence Market
Gilbertson, George, photographer, Adelaide head of Toronto
Gill, John, hotel keeper, cor Front and Simcoe
GILLESPIE, J. & CO., hats, caps, furs and straw goods, wholesale, 64 Yonge
Gillet & Allen (Fred. Gillet and J. Allen) bakers and confectioners, 147 Yonge
GILLMOR, LT.-COL. CHARLES T., Queen's Own Rifles, Clerk Legislative Assembly, Parliament buildings
GILMOR, ISAAC C., real estate and insurance agent, 59 Colborne (see adv.)
Gilverson, M.R., provision dealer, 22 St. Lawr'e Mkt
Glackmeyer, F. J., Sergeant-at-arms Legislative Assembly, Parliament bldgs
Glenn, Mrs. Jane, boarding house, 10 Bond
GLOBE HOTEL, Joseph Ross prop., 163 Yonge
GLOBE NEWSPAPER, morning, evening and weekly published by Globe Printing Co., 26 and 28 King e
GLOBE PRINTING COMPANY, 26 and 28 King e
Gloster, Thomas, boot and shoe maker, 13 and 15 Melinda
Godfree, G. R. carpenter and builder, 65 & 67 Queen w
Godfrey, Michael, grocer, 163 York
Godson, George, sen., flour and feed, 152 Queen w
Godson, Henry, District Inspector of Excise, Toronto Exchange
Goodwin, Mrs. Mary, dry goods, Yonge, Yorkville
Golding, J., Balaklava Hotel, 564 Queen w, cor Strachan.
Goldsmith, Alfred W., wood turner, 552 Yonge
Goldsmith, Edward, vestry clerk, S. James', h 8 Ontario e
GOOCH, R. N., broker, general insurance agent and notary public, 32 Wellington e
Good, James, prop. Good's Foundry, 4, 6 and 10 Queen e
GOODERHAM, GEORGE, (Gooderham & Worts
GOODERHAM, ROBERT T., manger Gooderham & Worts, bds s s Little Front, bet Parliament & Trinity
GOODERHAM'S WHARF, Esplanade, foot of Trinity
GOODERHAM, Wm., sen., (Gooderham & Worts) h 4 Little Front.
GOODERHAM, Wm., jun., manager Gooderham & Worts, h 4 Little Front
GOODERHAM & WORTS, (Wm. Gooderham, sen. George Gooderham, and James G. Worts), Toronto Distillery, Esplanade, cor Trinity, and 10 and 12 Toronto Exchange.
Goodwin, Major, gymnastic, fencing and drill instructor, U. C. College
Goodworth, L. B. & Co., paper, twine, &c., 41 Colborne
Gordon, McKay & Co., (John Gordon, Donald McKay & Hugh McDonald), wholesale dry goods, 11 & 13 Wellington e
Gorrie, Wm. M., clerk Inland Revenue, 26 Toronto Exchange
Goslen, John, asst Editor *Globe*
Gospel Tract Depository, Mr. F. W. Grant, manager, 390 Yonge
Goulding, George, millinery, 175 and 177 Yonge
Gourlay, David, grocer and confectioner, 262 Yonge
GOURLEY, W. H., carriage painter, 299 Queen w
GOVERNMENT EMIGRATION OFFICE, J. A. Donaldson, agent, 53 York

Gowan, H. P., hotel, 81 Colborne
Graham, James, 314 Jarvis
Graham, S. & Co., carpet warehouse, 3 King e
Graham, W. & J., props. Montreal House, 148 King w.
GRAND, JOSEPH, Royal Horse Bazaar, Riding Academy, Livery Stable, and Velocipede School, 98 Wellington w
GRAND TRUNK RAILWAY OFFICE, H. Bourlier, agent, Esplanade, foot of Yonge
Grant, Alexander, Registrar Court of Chancery, Osgoode Hall
GRANT, DONALD, superintendent City Baths, Adelaide w, nr Yonge
Grant, J. M., Clerk, Crown Lands' Department, Parliament buildings
Grant, William, barrister, h Napier
Grantham, E., oil lamps and glassware 170
GRASSETT, VERY REV. DEAN, Rector St. James' cathedral, h 97 Adelaide w
Gray, George H., proprietor Victoria Hotel, 460 and 462 Yonge
GRAY, ROBERT H., hoop-skirt manufacturers and fancy goods 43 Yonge (see adv)
Gray, Thomas, clerk, Registrar's Office, Court of Chancery, Osgoode Hall
Grayson, Isaac, groceries and dry goods, 267 Queen w
GREAT WESTERN RAILWAY PASSENGER & FREIGHT STATION, Offices foot of Yonge
Greene, Columbus H., barrister, 40 Adelaide e
Greer, John, coal and wood merchant cor Nelson and Adelaide e
Gregg, George R., assistant editor *Leader*, Leader buildings
Gregg, Rev. William, (Presbyterian) h 116 Mutual
GREGORY, JOSEPH, agent Star Life Assurance Co., 78 King e (see adv)
Greig & Carlyle, steam cabinet and packing box factory, 61 Ontario e
Griffith, John C., & Co., importers of groceries, wines and liquors, 219 and 221 Yonge
GRIFFITH, ROBERT, (W. & R. Griffith) Ontario block
Griffith, T. B., commission merchant, 82 Front e
Griffith, Thomas, & Co., wholesale grocers, 37 and 3 Front e
Griffith, Thomas, (Thomas Griffith & Co.)
Griffith, W. & R., wholesale grocers, Front cor Church
Griffith, W., (W. & R. Griffith & Co.)
Grossmith, Charles W., perfumer, 34 King e
Grundler, G., butcher, 98 Church
Guinane, William, boots and shoes, 105 Yonge
GUNDRY & LANGLEY (Thomas and Henry) architects and civil engineers, Jordan nr King (see ad)
Gunn, Murdoch, crockery, 207 King e
Gunther, F. & E., wholesale jewellers, 9 King e
Gurney, E. C., stove founders, 91 Yonge
Gustin, Andrew J., superintendent rolling mills, h 120 George
GWYNNE, ARMOUR & HOSKIN, (John W. Gwynne, Robert Armor, John Hoskin) barristers and solicitors, Jordan nr King
GWYNNE, HUGH, secretary and treasurer, Law Society, Osgoode Hall
GZOWSKI & CO. (C. S. Gzowski, D. L. Macpherson), railroad contractors and proprietors Rolling Mills, Romain buildings, 87 King w
Hackman, Diedrich, cigar manufacturer, 122 York
Hackett, John, grocery and school, 87 Queen w
HAGARTY, HON. J. H., D.C.L., Judge Court Queen's Bench, h 61 William
HAGUE, GEORGE, cashier Bank of Toronto, h Queens' Park
Halbhaus, Theodore, farrier, 89½ Yonge
Haldan, Bernard, secretary and treasurer Western Assurance Company, h 7 Breadalbane
Hale, George W., dentist, 9 Temperance
Hall, Cyrenius B., M.D., Sheppard cor Adelaide
Hall, John, M. D., homœopathist 33 Richmond e
Hall, Joseph, N. & Co., hardware, wholesale, 58 Yonge
Hall, Mark, builder, 78 Seaton
Hall, Thomas, second hand broker, 256 King e
Hall, William, dry goods and millinery, 4 Rossin House block
HALLAM, JOHN, dealer in leather and hides, Esplanade, nr City Hall
Hallamore, John, druggist, 374 Queen w
HALLATT, G., saw maker and repairer, 12 Victoria
HALLEY, WILLIAM, dealer in printers' materials, 83, 85 and 87 Bay
Halliday, Mrs. Marion, dry goods, 430 Queen w
Hallowell, William, M. D., 14 Gloucester Row, Ontario, nr Duke
Halse, Mrs. Isabella, ladies' and children's clothing, 125 Yonge.
Ham, Joseph M., tailor, 300 Queen w
HAMBLY, WILLIAM, night foreman, news dept., *Daily Telegraph*
HAMILTON, ALEXANDER, painter, paper hanger, and dealer in paints, oils, paper hangings, &c., 183 King e (see adv)
Hamilton, Arthur, boots and shoes, 475 Yonge
Hamilton, Sidney S., wharfinger, Esplanade, bet Scott and Church
HAMILTON THOMAS, secretary N.R.C.
Hamilton, William, blacksmith, 14 Queen w
HAMILTON, WILLIAM & SON, St. Lawrence Foundry, 138 to 152 Palace
HAMLIN, EDWARD H., fruits and confectionery, 107 King w
HAMLIN, & Co., fruits and confectionery, 119 Yonge
Hammond, Alfred, baker, 314 Yonge
Hammond, Samuel, baker and confectioner, 69 King west
HAMPTON, WM. B., M.D., resident medical supt. Toronto General Hospital
HANCOCK, H., secretary Toronto Mutual Fire Ins. Co., 20 Toronto
Hancock, John W., barrister, 22 Toronto
Hand, Wm., saddler, Yonge, Yorkville
HANLON, MRS. E.
Hanratty, J. J., & Co., dry goods and clothing, 137 and 139 King e
Harbour Commissioners' Office, Hugh Richardson, harbour master, 4 Front w
Harcourt, George, merchant tailor, 65 King e
Harding, George, plumber and gasfitter, 77 King w
Hardy, Mrs., milliner and dressmaker, 201 Yonge
Hare, John, weaver, r 580 Yonge
Harley, Mrs. J., boarding-house, 12 Temperance
Harley, T. H., barber, 77 Yonge
Harman & Hagarty (George Harman and John H. Hagarty), barristers, 56 Church
Harnett, Maurice, shoemaker, 89 Church
Harper, Daniel, general store, 149 York
HARPER, JAMES G., manager Merchants' Bank of Canada, h 15 Wellington w
Harper & Son, architects, Romain Bdgs, King e
Harris, E., china, glass and queensware, 49 King st e
Harris, J., produce broker and commission merchant, 85 Front e

SEASON 1869-70.

LESSEE AND MANAGER - GEORGE HOLMAN.

Also of the Holman English Opera Troupe.

CROWDED NIGHTLY

By the Elite.

NEW FEATURES. NEW FACES.

OPERA, DRAMA, BURLESQUE,

BALLET, FARCE AND PANTOMIME.

Performance every Evening.

FOR PARTICULARS SEE DAILY PAPERS AND PROGRAMMES.

GOD SAVE THE QUEEN.

HARRISON, ROBERT A., Q.C., M.P., Spadina Avenue
Harris, Rusk, barrister, 64 Church
Harris, Samuel, boots and shoes, 160 King e
Harris, T. D., insurance agent, Clare
Harris, W. H., dyer and scourer, 152 King w
HARRISON, GLOVER, china and glassware, 71 & 73 King e
Harrison, Martin, fancy goods, 304½ Queen w
Hart, Joseph, gen. agent and accountant, 28 Duchess
Hartley, Philip, steward Trinity College
HARTNEY, H. J., Queen's Printer, Parliament Blgs, bds Rossin House
Harvard, Albert, druggist, 290 Queen w
HARVEY, ST. GEORGE, gen. broker, 36 Colborne
Hassard, Richard, painter & glazier, 146 Richmond w
Hasson, Mrs. Eliza, grocer, 90 Bay
Hasson, John, blacksmith and grocer, 17 Adelaide w
Hastings, Edward A., professor of music, 218 George
Hastings, James, sergeant-major T. P. F., No. 3 police station, Queen w
Hawke, George M., office 65 Colborne
Haworth, T. & Co., wholesale hardware merchant, 52 Yonge
Hartill, Alexander, manufacturers' agent, 8 and 9 Ontario Chambers, Front cor Church
Hartill, A. Junn & Co., commission merchants, 8 and 9 Ontario Chambers, Front cor Church
Hay, Robert (Jacques & Hay), h 28 Wellington e
Hay, R. J., photographer, 27 King e
Hayden, Charles, superintendent Toronto Necropolis Winchester
Hayes, William, shoemaker, 304 Queen w
Hays, Dennis, 246 Palace
Hays, Owen, oyster saloon, basement 53 Wellington e
Heal, George, dealer in horns, tails and glue pieces, &c., 34 George
Heap, R. & Co., ale and porter bottlers, *Leader* lane
Heaslip, Thomas, tavern keeper, Esplanade n Scott
Heath, Charles W., barrister, Beverley cor D'Arcy
Hector, John, Q.C., barrister, 11 King w
Hector, Thomas, chief clerk in charge land claims and sales in old Townships, Crown Land Department, Parliament Buildings
HEINTZMAN & Co., pianoforte manufacturers, King adj Rossin House
Helliwell, John, M.A., barrister, notary public, solicitor for Bank of Toronto, Bank Toronto Bldgs
HENDERSON, ANDREW, auctioneer, appraiser and commission agent, 65 Yonge
Henderson, Alexander, 36 Gerrard e
Henderson & Bostwick (John Henderson and Amos Bostwick), wholesale manufacturers of hats, caps, mantles, straw goods, general millinery and fancy goods, 18 and 20 Wellington w
Henderson, Elmer (McLennan & Henderson)
Henderson, G., wholesale and retail grocer, 328 Queen w
Henderson, George, grocer, 59 Sayer
Henderson, James, junr. (Galt & Henderson)
Henderson, John, foreman Consumers Gas Co
Henderson, Mrs. John, boarding house, 237½ Church
Hendrie, John & Co., cartage agents G.W.R., 41 Scott
Hennessy, John, shoemaker, 558 Queen w
HENNING, THOMAS, treas, Globe Printing Co., 26 King e
Hennings, George, taxing officer Court of Chancery
Henrich, Tobias, groceries and provisions, 462 King e
Henry, John, city collector, St. Patrick's Ward
Herbert, Peter, grocer, King w cor Portland
Herdman, Joseph, grocer, 376 Queen w
HERSON, J., butcher, 18 St. Lawrence Market
Hessin, William, wholesale confectioner, 7 Front e
Heward, Francis H., manager Royal Ins. Co., Yonge cor Wellington
Heward, John O., office, 18 Toronto Exchange, h Bloor, Yorkville
Heward, W. B., clerk of Practice Court and Chambers, Osgoode Hall
Hewitt, W., hardware merchant, 111 Yonge
Heyden & Defoe, (L. Hayden and D. M. Defoe) barristers, 74 Church
Hickey, Mrs. Hannah, grocery, 552 Queen w
Hickling, Charles, gen. provision store, 219 Palace
Hickman, William, jr., fruit store, 92 Queen w
Higgins, David, sec. Edinburgh Life Assurance Co., Wellington w
Higgins, Mrs. fancy goods, 254½ Yonge
Higgins, Samuel, prop. Grand Trunk House, York nr Union Station
Hill, George, saloon keeper, 169 York
Hill, Samuel, ice merchant, Esplanade bet George and E Market
Hill, Thomas S., accountant Bank of British North America
HILL, THOMAS & SON, props. Caxton Press printing establishment and manufs. parchment labels, tags, &c., Nelson cor King (see adv)
Hilton, Rev. John, pastor St. Ann's Church, Dundas
HIME HUMPHREY L., estate and insurance agent, stock broker, 6 Wellington e, h Robert w s opp Russell
Hinchcliffe, Benjamin, hotel keeper, Yonge cor Richmond
Hincks, William, F.L.S., Professor Natural History, University College
Hirst, John, Yorkshire Stingo Hotel, 14 Francis
Hoag, Isaac M., (Peckham & Hoag), and (Hotchkiss, Peckham & Co.) res Newmarket, Ont
Hobbs, James, blacksmith, 25 and 27 Adelaide w
Hodder, Edward M., M.D., 159 Queen w
Hodgetts, George, chemist and druggist, 279 George
Hodgins, George, watch maker and jeweller, 169 King e
Hodgins, John George, LL.B., Deputy Superintendent of Education for Ontario, Pembroke nr Wilton Crescent
Hodgins, Miss M., milliner and dressmaker, 1 Rossin House block
HODGINS, THOMAS, barrister, Masonic Hall
Hodgins, Thomas, shoemaker, 303 Queen w
Hodgins, William, grocer, 310 Queen w
Hodgson, Joseph, stoves and tinware, 185 Yonge
HOLCOMB, SAMUEL F., forwarding and commission merchant, 2 Exchange bdgs, h 115 Wellington w
Holiwell, Mrs. M. J. H., ladies' boarding school, cor John and Wellington
Holland, George B., inspector and superintendent London and Lancashire Assurance Company, h 149 Sherborne
Hollin, David, barber, East Market Square
Hollingshead, Silas, M.D., (eclectic), 274 Yonge
Hollins, David, grocer, 96 Queen w
HOLMAN, ALFRED D., Holman Opera Troupe, 1 Richie Terrace
HOLMAN, ALFRED, treas Holman Opera Troupe, 1 Richie Terrace
HOLMAN, GEORGE, lessee Royal Lyceum, King w, h 1 Richie Terrace (see adv)
HOLMES, JOHN, boots and shoes, 180½ Yonge (see adv)
Holmes, Norman L., druggist, etc., 216 Queen e
HOLMSTED, GEORGE S. (Cameron & Holmsted)

Home and Colonial Fire and Life Insurance Company, T. D. Harris, agent, e s Clare
Home District Mutual Fire Insurance Co., 120 Yonge
Home and Foreign Record of the Canadian Presbyterian Church, published monthly, by A. Lovell & Co., for the Canadian Presbyterian Church
HOME INSURANCE CO., of New Haven, Conn., W. Rowland, agent, 55 Wellington and 58 Front, cor Church
HOOPER, E. & CO., druggists, 43 King w
Hope, A. & C. J. & Co., wholesale hardware merchants, 53 Front e
Hope, Rev. H. P., (Church of England), h 248 Wellington w
Hopkirk, Thomas, milling, &c., 176 King e
Hornby, R., M.D., 174 York
HORNIBROOK & LEPAN, general grocers and spirit merchants, 167 Yonge
Horton —., local reporter *Globe*
Horton, Mrs., principal Bishop Strachan School
Hoskins, R. A. & Co., wholesale dry goods, 5 Wellington e
HOTCHKISS, PECKHAM & CO. (Lewis Hotchkiss, J. S. Peckham & Isaac M. Hoag), manufacturers and dealers in lumber, 11 Toronto Exchange
HOTCHKISS, LEWIS (Hotchkiss, Peckham & Co.), res. Birmingham, Conn., U.S.
Houel, A. T., foreman job department *Globe*
HOUSTON & TAYLOR (Thomas Houston & Robert F. Taylor), merchant tailors, 121 King w
How, John Y., grocer, 435 Yonge
HOWARD, ALLAN McLEAN, Clerk Division Court, office, Court House
Howard, James, hotel keeper, 222 and 226 Front
Howard, J., George and Dragon Hotel, 28 John
Howard, Mrs. M., milliner, 334 Yonge
HOWARD, SMITH & CO., brokers, 4 Ontario Chambers, cor Front and Church
Howard, Walter P. (Macdonald, Stephens & Howard), Wellington Chambers
HOWARTH, J., chemist and druggist, 243 Yonge
HOWE, MRS. H. J., young ladies' select school, 161 Jarvis
HOWLAND, HENRY S. (Howland, Bros.), 27 Church
HOWLAND, HIS EXCELLENCY HON. WILLIAM P., C.B., LIEUT. GOVERNOR OF ONTARIO, res. Government House
HOWLAND & BROS., millers, Kleinburg, 25 and 27 Church
HOWLAND & FITCH, wholesale grocers and commission merchants 25 and 27 Church
Howson, Joseph, M.D., druggist, 86 Queen w
Hozock, Luke, grocer, 446 Queen w
Hubasheck, A. & Co., vinegar manufacturers, 92 and 98 Adelaide w
Hubbard & Harney, 195 Yonge
Hubbard, A. M., carpenter, 236 Queen w
HUBERTUS, W. L. & CO., distillers, Esplanade, Church (see adv.)
Hubbard, Charles H., gold leaf manufacturer, 26 Adelaide w
Hughes, Brothers, wholesale dry goods, 62 Yonge
Hughes & Co., importers of dry goods, 128, 130 and 132, King e
Hughes, Mrs. Sarah, boarding house, 390 Church
Huggins, John, groceries, 417 Queen w
Hulme, Mrs., furniture dealer, 194 King e
Hulme, George, 134 Palace
Humphry, Simon, carpenter and builder, 13 James
Humphries, Mrs. Victoria, boarding and day school, 18 Magill
HUNT, MRS. DEV., Ladies' School, 171 Richmond west
Hunter, H., grocer, 296 Yonge
Hunter, Robert, second hand clothing, 38 Queen w
Hunter, Robert, shoemaker, 42 Nelson
HUNTER, ROSE & CO., parliamentary book and job printers, bookbinders, &c., 86 King w
Hunter, Samuel, tavern keeper, 293 Queen w
Hurbert, Albert, confectioner, 121 York
HURD, E. E. W., barrister, York Chambers, Court
HURD, LEIGH & CO., importers china, glass and earthenware, and china enamellers, 72 Yonge
Hurd & Goodall, (L. H. Hurd, and W. H. Goodall), patent agents, 74 Church
HURON AND ONTARIO SHIP CANAL COMP'Y. Frederick C. Capreol, President, 16 and 18 Wellington e
Hurrell, C. T., agent Goderich Salt Company, 82 Front e
Hurst, James, plumber and gas fitter, 104 Adelaide e
Hurst, John, hotel keeper, 14 Francis
HUSSEY, ELI, proprietor University Inn, 400 Yonge
Hutchinson, Matthew, carriage builder, James
Hutty & Gray, butchers, 8 St. Lawrence Market
Hyland & Boylan, milliners furnishing store, 95 Yonge
Hynes, Michael, grocer, 218 Queen e
Ibbotson, George, saw maker and repairer, 12 Francis
Ince, Thomas H., barrister, &c., 6 Wellington e, h Cecil w nr Spadina Avenue
Inglis, Rev. W.. assistant editor, *Globe*
Inland Revenue Office, 13, 14, 16 and 17, Toronto Exchange
IMPERIAL INSURANCE COMPANY of England, J. E. Smith & Co., agents, cor Church and Colborne
Iredale, Mrs. Mary, tin shop, 47 Queen st. w
Iredale, William, lastmaker, 239 Yonge
IRISH CANADIAN (weekly), Patrick Boyle, editor and prop. 37 Colborne
Ires, Mrs. Hester, fancy goods, 40 Queen w
IRISH, MARK H., Manager Queen's Hotel, Toronto, and Queen's Royal Hotel, Niagara
IRVING, A. S. books and stationery, 35 King w
Irving, Wm., architect, 120 Yonge
Irwin, B., portrait painter
IRWIN, J. D., Agent American Merchants' Union Express Co., 55 & 57 George
Irwin, John, peop General Wolfe Hotel, 34 Church
Irwin, Miss S. boarding house, 86 Adelaide w
Irwin, William, general broker, *Leader* Buildings
Irwin, William, tavern keeper, 79 Church
IRWIN, WILLIAM H. directory publisher, *Daily Telegraph* Buildings
Island, Mrs. proprietor Sligo Inn, 235 King e
Jackman and McGann (Frank Jackman and John McGann) ship brokers, &c., Esplanade, near Church
Jackson & Henry, 478 Jarvis
JACKSON, J. H., watches, clocks, jewelery, fancy goods, Masonic regalia, &c. 83 King e (see adv.)
Jackson, John, tinsmith, 248 Queen w
Jackson, M. B., Clerk of Crown, Osgoode Hall
Jackson, Thomas, bill poster, 31½ Queen w
Jacobi, Philip, leather and findings, 103 Yonge
Jacques, Alexander, foreman pressman, *Globe* office
JACQUES & HAY, furniture warerooms, 19 & 21 King w
Jaffray, Robert, wholesale and retail grocer, 244 Yonge
JAMES, ROBERT, jun. agent for patent portable self-acting fire extinguisher, 6 Wellington e, h Isabella cor Church

James, Silas, Superintendent York Roads, Church between Isabella and Charles
Jamot, Very Rev. J. F., V. G. St. Michael's Cathedral
JANES, S., P. L. S.
JANES, BRAYLEY & NEWCOMBE, dry goods, 51 King e
Jaques, George E. & Co., forwarders, 50 Front e
Jardine, Alex. groceries and prov. 28 West Market
Jardine, A., grocer, 88 Queen w
Jarman, William, ticket agent G. T. R., Union Station
JARVIS, E. J., land agent, broker, etc., Whittemore's bldg., Toronto
JARVIS, FREDERICK W., sheriff, office Court House
JARVIS, S. M., barrister, 22 King e
Jefferss, J., hair-dresser, 256 Yonge
Jeffers, Rev. Wellington, D.D., editor *Christian Guardian*
JEFFERY, W. H., manager, Reford & Dillon, 12 and 14 Wellington e
Jennings & Brandon (James Jennings and John Brandon) dry goods, wholesale, 38 Yonge
Jennings, George J., patentee, 187 Yonge
Jennings, James, dry goods, 178 Yonge
Jennings, Rev. John (Canada Presbyterian) 153 Jarvis
Jewell & Timms (Fred. Jewell and John Timms) props. Shades, 24 Melinda
Johns, Robert, stationer, 301 Yonge
Johnson, Mrs. Sophia, hotel keeper, 228 Front
Johnson, Neil, produce and comn. merchant, 3 Manning's block, Front e
Johnston, D. B., saloon keeper, 347 Queen w
Johnston, E. & R., flour and feed mers. 11 Palace
Johnston, James, eating saloon, St. Lawrence Market
Johnston, James A., assistant sec. Canadian Institute, h 44 Richmond e
Johnston, W. S., assistant editor *Globe*
Jolly, Edward, groceries, etc., 224½ Queen w
JONES, BROTHERS (Jonas Ap., Clarkson and Beverley Jones) barristers, Masonic Hall
Jones, Charles B., M.D., 37 Richmond e
Jones, George, hotel keeper, 152 Queen w
Jones, Henry J., clerk, Crown Lands Department
Jones, William, butcher, 142 and 144 King e
Jones, Mrs. William G., fancy goods, Yonge
Jordan, Robert & Co., grocers, 10 and 11 Rossin House Block, King w
Jory, Samuel, photographer, 75 King e
Jose, Richard, confectioner, 285 Queen w
Joseph, Frank, barrister, Jordan
JOSEPH, HENRY, exchange and money broker and official assignee, 82 King e
JOSEPH, J. G. & CO., watchmakers and jewellers, 5 King e and 46 Yonge
JOURNAL OF EDUCATION, monthly, Rev. Dr. Ryerson, assisted by J. G. Hodgins, M.A., editors, A. Lovell & Co., printers, 67 Yonge
Juby, Mrs., dry goods, 516 Queen w
Judah, A. H., grocery, 163½ York
Kader, Anthony, grocer, 82½ Queen w
Kain, S. S., grocery, 298 Queen w
Kane, Francis, grocer, &c., cor Sumach and Queen e
Kassel, M., dry goods and clothing, 307 Queen w
Kauffman, William A., architect, Masonic Hall
Kavanagh, John, pawnbroker, 45 Queen w
Kavanagh, Mrs. Hannah, milliner, &c., 106 Church
KAY, JOHN, dry goods, millinery, carpets, 1 King e
Kay, John, agent British America and Scottish Assurance Companies, Church cor Court
Kearney, James, supt. St. James' Cemetery, Lodge St. James' Cemetery
Keenan, Patrick, hotel keeper, 74 Colborne
KEITH, D. S., plumber and gasfitter, 109 King w
KEIGHLEY, WILLIAM H., manager Reford & Dillon, h 49 Cruickshank
Keith, George, groceries, &c., 23 East Market Square
Kelly, John, grocer, 102 Strachan
Kelz, John, merchant tailor, 352 Yonge
Kennedy, grocer and wood yard, 307 Queen w
Kennedy, David, lumber yard, 423 Queen w
Kennedy, Francis, "Never too late to mend," general repairer, 58 King w
Kennedy, John E., M.D., 295 Queen w
Kennedy, Thomas, grocer, 205 Queen w
Kennedy, Thomas, coml. traveller. 109 Parliament
Kenny, Mrs. Ann, 18 Duchess
Kenny, Mrs. Michael, rags, old iron, &c., 12 William
Kent, John, carpenter, 286½ Yonge
KERBY, HENRY J., saloon, cigars and tobacco, 81 King w
KERR, JOHN, publisher Mercantile Test and official assignee, Court cor Church
Kerr, John, baker, 288 Queen w
Kerry. Crathern & Co., wholesale druggists, 41 Yonge
KERSHAW & EDWARDS' safes, A. K. Boomer, agent, 93 King w
KERSTEMAN, WILLIAM, mining agent, 60 and 62 Church
Kilfeder, Robert, wagon and carriage maker, 149 Queen w
Kincade, Robert, boots and shoes, 356 Yonge
KING, G. W. & CO., white wire clothes lines, 90 King e
King, James, grocer, &c., 88 Caroline
King, John L., M.D., M. R. C. S. Eng., King cor Nelson
King, Rev. John, pastor Gould street Presbyterian Church, 326 Jarvis
King, Mrs. J. G., private school, 101 Dalhousie
King, William, butcher, 36 St. Lawrence market
King, Wm. & Alex., second-hand brokers, 26 Queen w
Kingsberry, James, groceries and liquors, 494 King e
Kingsley, William, 323 and 325 Queen e
KINGSMILL, GEO. R., sub-editor daily *Telegraph*
KINGSMILL, NICOL (Crooks, Kingsmill & Cattenach), 17 Wellington w
KINGSTONE, F. W., barrister, 62 Church
Kingstone, G. T., director observatory, Queen's Park
Kinsman, D., watchmaker, 365 Yonge
Kinsman, William, grocer, Terauley cor Walton
Kinzinger, Jacob, English bun house, 100 York
KLEISER, S. P., watches, clocks and jewelery, 130 Yonge
Klopp, William, tobacconist, 27 King w
Kneally, Andrew, grocer, 48 Bathurst
Knox, John, shoemaker, 468 Queen w
Knox's Church, Queen bet Yonge and Bay
Kœrber, Louis, boot and shoemaker, 120 York
KRAUSS, FRANK, assistant editor *Globe*
Kupitz, Edward, butcher, 27 Queen w
L'Estage, William J., commission merchant and broker, York Chambers, Court
La Penotiere, Frederick, solicitor, Court cor Toronto
Laidlaw, Douglas, wheat merchant, 80 Front e
Laidlaw, George, commission merchant, 51 Wellington e and 54 Front e
Lailey, Thomas & Co., wholesale clothing, hats, caps, &c., 11 Wellington w
LAIRD, R. W., carver and gilder, 79 King w
Lake View House, John McCaffrey, prop., Parliament cor Winchester
Lalor, L. J., blacksmith, &c., 22 King w
LAMB, PETER R. & CO., manufs. blacking, glue, &c., Amelia nr Necropolis (see adv.)

Lamb, John, boots and shoes, 183 Yonge
Lancashire Fire and Life Ins. Co., S. C. Duncan-Clark & Co., n w cor King and Church
Langston, Thomas, shoemaker, 224 King e
Langtry, Rev. J., M.A., Church bet Alexander and Maitland
Lash, John F., (J. G. Joseph & Co)
Latch, William, lumber merchant, 22 King w
Lauder, Abraham W., (Ross, Lauder & Mulock)
Laurent, Rev. J. M., pastor St. Patrick's R. C. Church, h 148 Dummer
Lavelle, Rev. John R., (Unitarian) h 53 Alexander
Lavin, Thomas, grocer, 89 Nelson
Law, James, prop. Niagara House, 24 Front e, cor Scott
Lawlor, Michael, M.D., 187 Richmond w
Lawrence, J. W., 360 Yonge
Lawrence & Mitchell, (Richard and Alexander) builders, house movers, &c., Queen w nr Spadina Av
Lawson, Edward & Sons, confectioners, 93 King e
Lawson & Hargrave, grocers, 170 King e
Lawson, Meredith & Co., wholesale and retail grocers, 242 Yonge
LAYTON, H. U., proprietor Caer Howell Hotel, College Avenue
LEADER BUILDINGS, cor King e and Leader lane
LEADER, morning, evening and weekly, James Beaty, proprietor and publisher, 63 King e
LEADER AND PATRIOT, James Beaty, proprietor, 63 King e
Leadlay, E., wool, hides, &c., 87 Front e
Leadlay, Henry, dealer in hides, sheep skins and wool, Dundas
LEASK, JAMES, Toronto Bottling Company, 55½ Yonge
Leath, John, lamps and oils, 24 Queen w
Leckie, John, importer of gilling threads, seine and sturgeon twines, 6 Front w
LEDYARD, HENRY, barrister, secretary Wellington Gold Mining Company, h 44 Gerrard e
LEDYARD, THOMAS D., barrister, 74 Yonge
Lee, Rev. J. R., assistant St. Michael's Cathedral
Lee, J. R., chemist and druggist, 337 King e
LEE, WALTER S., secretary Western Canada Permanent Building & Savings Society, 70 Church
Lee, William A., grocer, 512 Queen w
Leigh, Edmund G., (Hurd Leigh & Co.)
Leith, Alexander, (Leith & Kennedy)
Leith & Kennedy, (Alexander Leith, Thomas S. Kennedy) barristers, 41 Melinda
Lendreville, Joseph, cooper, 438 Queen w
Lendrevine, G., grocer, 257 Queen w
Lengston, Thomas, shoemaker, 229 King e
Lenhardt, George, spring mattrass manufacturer, 101 Adelaide w
Lennox, William, dry goods, 382 Yonge
Lenny, Mrs., boarding house, Bishop's buildings, cor Simcoe and Adelaide
LePan, Henry, (Hornibrook & LePan)
Leslie, Alexander, boots and shoes, 81½ King e
LESLIE, GEORGE H., chemist and druggist, Bloor cor Yonge, Yorkville (see adv)
Leslie, J., boots and shoes, 113 King w
Leslie, James E., Hayter
Leslie, John, commercial traveller, 479 Yonge
Leslie, Miss Christiana, milliner, 180 Queen w
LESSLIE, JOSEPH, Postmaster, Toronto
Levack Brothers, butchers, 351 Queen w
LEVEY, CHARLES & CO., machinery, brokers, engineers, etc., 73 Adelaide w
Levi, Harris, tailor, 114 York
Lewis, George, grocery, 175½ York
Lewis, Henry, ice merchant, 353 King e
Lewis, Henry, locksmith and bell hanger, 453 Yonge
Lewis, Isaac T. manager, Kerry, Crathern & Co.
Lewis, J. D. & Co. (John D. Lewis and Robert P. Thomas) tobacco mnfrs., 64 Nelson e
Lewis, Joseph, barber, 384 Queen w
LEWIS, RICE & SON, hardware, 52 and 54 King e
Lewis, Richard, secretary and librarian Mechanics' Institute, Church
Leys, John (Rice Lewis & Son)
LEYS, McMURRICH & ROBERTSON, barristers, cor King and Church
License Inspector's Office, East Market
LIFE ASSOCIATION OF SCOTLAND, R. N. Gooch, agent, 32 Wellington e
Likens, James, prop. Clyde Hotel, 158 King e
Lillie Frederick W., grocer, 74 Queen w
Lindsay, Charles, City Registrar, h 171 Church
Lindsay, G. E., clerk, Crown Lands Department, Parliament bldgs
Lindsay, Henry, grocer, 56 King w
LINTON, J. D., woodenware, toys, fancy goods, etc., 23 King w
Liston, William, grocer, 317 King e
Little, Andrew, carter and provision dealer, cor Portland and Little Richmond
LIVERPOOL AND LONDON AND GLOBE INSURANCE CO., and Briton Medical and General Life Association, James Fraser, agent, 5 King w
Livingston, Johnston & Co., wholesale clothing merchants, 51 Yonge
LLOYD, BENJAMIN, hotel keeper, 2 Bathurst
LOANE, SAMUEL, hotel keeper, 162 King w
Loane, William, boots and shoes. 171 King w
Locke, F., groceries and provisions, 165 King w
Logan, J., wholesale fruits, flowers, etc., 38 King w
London Central Agency of England, Scott & Walmsley, agents, Church
Loretto Abbey, Front w
Loretto Convent, Bond
Lersch, David, second-hand clothing, 12 Queen w
Louder, Hannah, confectionery, 191 King e
Lovatt, Joseph, tailor, 142 King e
Love, N. C., chemist and druggist, 129 George
LOVELL, A. & CO., book and job printers and binders, 67 Yonge
Loveys, Samuel, boat builer, Esplanade foot of Church
Lownsbrough, William, shoemaker and dealer, 93 Queen w
LUCAS, GEORGE D., sign and fresco painter, 43 Queen w (see adv)
Lugsden, J. & J., hatters and furriers, 101 Yonge
Lumbers, John, flour and feed depot, 111 and 113 Adelaide e
Lumbers, J. & T., grocers, 146 King e
LUMSDEN, JOHN H., foreman job department *Daily Telegraph*
Lund, Richard, M.D., chemist and druggist, 337 King e
Lying-in Hospital, Sheppard, cor Richmond, Mrs. Black, matron
LYMAN, ELLIOT & CO., (Benj. Lyman, William Elliot and W. Elliot), chemists and druggists; retail department, 155 King e; office and sample room, 157 King e; warehouse, 81 and 83 Front; mills, Palace
LYNCH, RIGHT REV. JOHN JOSEPH, Roman Catholic Bishop of Toronto, St. Michael's Palace, Church

LYMAN & MACNAB, (Wm. Lyman and John Macnab), wholesale hardware merchants, 5 Front e
LYNES, WILLIAM, clerk Common Pleas, office Osgoode Hall
LYON, JAMES F. & CO., wholesale druggists and perfume manufacturers, 57 Richmond e
McBean, James, builder, cor Buchanan and Terauley
McBean, John, lumber merchant, 11 and 13 Adelaide w
McBride, Francis, butcher, Queen w nr Bishop
McBride, James, barrister, etc., 40 Adelaide e
McBride, John, barrister, 38 Adelaide e
McBride, Samuel, coal and wood merchant, office Adamson's wharf
McCabe, Peter, second-hand store, 41 Queen w
McCabe, Terence, tavern keeper, 225 King e
McCaffrey, Charles, tax collector and high bailiff, 147 Berkeley
McCaffrey, John, prop Lake View House, Parliament cor Winchester
McCann, Thomas, grocer, 258 Lumley
McCARTER, JOHN, butcher, 7 and 9 St. Lawrence Market
McCarthy, Mrs. M. A., artist, 376 Yonge
McCARTHY & MASON, undertakers, 155 Queen w (see card)
McCaul, Rev. John, D.D., President University College
McCAUSLAND, JOSEPH, glass stainer and painter, 8 King w
McCaw, Hugh, merchant tailor, 89 Queen w
McCleary, Robert, grocer, Elizabeth nr Gerrard
McCLEARY, W., local reporter *Daily Telegraph*
McClennan, Mrs. C., dressmaker, 376 Adelaide w
McClelland, John, grocer, Sydenham, cor Berkeley
McClelland & Co., stencil cutters, 48 King e
McConkey, George, photographer, 147 King e
McConvill, Bernard, Crystal Hotel, cor Francis and Adelaide e
McCORD, A. T., City Chamberlain, office City Hall
McCord, Maxwell, excise officer, Inland Revenue Office, Exchange Buildings
McCormack, T. G., groceries and provisions, 342 Yonge
McCormack, Thomas G., grocer and boarding-house, 129 Church
McCormick, Richard, boot and shoemaker, 175 York
McCrea, James, confectioner, 5 St. Lawrence Arcade
McCROSSON & CO., hatters and furriers, 111 King e and London, Ontario (See adv)
McCutcheon, Peter McGill, barrister, &c. 40 Adelaide e
McDONALD & CHADWICK (D. Mitchell McDonald and Austin C. Chadwick), barristers, Whittemore's Block, Toronto
McDonald, Hugh, merchant, 90 Wellington w
McDonald, Peter, grocer, 103 Church
McDougall, Colin, lumber inspector W. Latches' lumber yard, cor Queen and James
McDunnough & James, wholesale and retail importers of carpets, 31 King e
McEACHREN, NEIL, merchant and military tailor, 191 Yonge
McEachren, P., supt. Dominion Telegraph Co., 34 King e, and cor York and King
McEntee, John, boots and shoes, 133 Yonge
McEVOY, HENRY, publisher and compiler of directories and gazetteers, *Daily Telegraph* blgs., Bay
McEvoy, Henry, tavern keeper, 104 Church
McFarlane, John, ticket clerk G. W. R., Yonge St. Station
McFarlane, L. M., M.D., 278 Yonge
McFarren, Andrew, grocer, 195 King e
McGAW, THOMAS, bookkeeper Queen's Hotel
McGinn, James, proprietor Golden City Billiard Parlour, 41 King w
McGowan, Samuel, 59 Agnes
McGrath, Charles, barrister, 65 Colborne
McGREGOR, PATRICK, barrister, 26 Adelaide e
McGrotty, James, butcher, 233 King e
McGuire, Francis, refreshment saloon G.W.R. Depot
McIlmurray, James, M.D., 19 Richmond w
McIlroy, Mrs. H., confectioner, 154 King w
McIntosh, Charles, 28 Walton
McINTOSH, WILLIAM, flour and feed, 209 Yonge
McKay, John M., wholesale grocer and hop merchant, 7 Manning's Block, Front e
McKay, Thomas, foreman press department, W. C. Chewett & Co.
McKAY, S., importer and wholesale dealer in groceries, wines, liquors, &c., general commission merchant, 13 Wellington e (see adv).
McKee, Alexander, fruit and provisions, 161 Yonge
McKenzie, William, grocer, 112 York
McKindless, James, 31 Queen w
McLauchlin, John, innkeeper, cor George and Duchess
McLean, A. G. & T. A., barristers, 12 Melinda
McLean, James, shoemaker, 320½ Yonge
McLEAN, W., financial manager *Daily Telegraph*
McLean, William, auditor and accountant, 13 Masonic Hall
McLean, William G., butcher, 1 St. Lawrence Mkt.
McLear & Co., booksellers and stationers, 11 King w
McManus, James, cooper, 25 Queen w
McMASTER, A. R. & BROTHER, wholesale dry goods, 32 Yonge
McMaster, Hon. William, M. L. C. h College, Yorkville
McMichael, Daniel, Q. C. D. C. L. (Cameron & McMichael) and (Cameron, McMichael, Fitzgerald and Hoskins) h 252 Wellington w
McMichael, Robert, grocer, 168 Queen w
McMullen, Archibald, grocer, 343 Queen w
McMurray & Rae (J. Sauren McMurray and George Martin Rae) barristers, &c., York Chambers, Court
McNab, D. 24 and 26 Front e
McNab, Murray & Jackes (John McNab, George Murray, Joseph Jackes) barristers &c. Court House
McPHAIL, ROBERT, publisher of school books and dealer in stationary and fancy goods, Change Alley, near King
McPherson, Hon. D. L. (C. S. Gzowski & Co.) 87 King w
McQueen, Thomas, brass finisher, 270 Queen w
McSherry, James, Proprietor Sailors' Home Hotel, e s George near Esplanade
MacCrea, John O., broker and commission merchant, and commissioner for taking affidavits for superior courts, Lower Canada, 16 Ontario Chambers, cor Church and Front
MacCuaig, R. C. W. Manager Bradstreet's Mercantile Agency, Bank Toronto Buildings
MacDavitt, Frank, Manager Virtue and Yorston
MacDonald, A. W., produce and commission merchant, 59 Front e
MacDonald, C. fireman, Parliament Buildings
MacDonald, Major George, Staff Officer of Pensioners' h 26 Seaton
MACDONALD, JOHN K., Treasurer County York, Office Court House
MACDONALD, JOHN & CO., wholesale importers of dry goods, 21 and 23 Wellington e
MacDonell, Alexander, barrister, 56 Church

MacDonald, Stephens & Howard (John MacDonald, R. P. Stephens & W. P. Howard) barristers &c. 9 & 10 Wellington Chambers, Jordan
MacDonell, John P. Clerk Master's Office, Osgoode Hall
MacDonell, W. J. Manager Toronto Saving's Bank and French Consular Agent, 72 Church
MacDougall & Skae, Civil Engineers and Architects, Provincial Insurance Buildings, Toronto
MACFARLANE, MALCOLM, groceries and liquors, 95 Nelson
MacGregor, Alexander M., Marine Inspector Provincial Insurance, Co. of Canada, Toronto, cor Court
Mack, Mrs. Thomas, oysters, fruit & cigars, 26 Francis
Mackay, Charles B., clerk Custom House foot of Yonge
MACKENZIE, KENNETH, Q.C. (Mackenzie & Scott)
MACKENZIE & SCOTT, barristers, Provincial Insurance Buildings, Toronto cor Court
Mackenzie, Misses Helen & Elizabeth, ladies' boarding school, 72 Bond
MACLENNAN & HENDERSON (James Maclennan and Elma Henderson), barristers, Ontario Hall, Court
Macnabb, Alexander, Police Magistrate (Macnabb & Morgan)
Macnabb & Morgan (Alexander Macnabb and T. Kearton Morgan), barristers, &c., Court
Macnutt, Rev. G. A., pastor of Alexander street Baptist Church, h 2 Carlton
McPherson, Alexander, appraiser customs, excise warehouse
MADDISON, G. L., Scottish Provincial Life Assurance Company, 84 Bay
Magdalen Asylum, Yorkville
Maguire, John, grocery & provision store, 56 Gerrard w
Maguire, John, baggage master G. W. R., Yonge street station
Maher, Thomas, station master G.T.R.
Mainprice, Charles, butcher, 444 Queen w
Maitland, Robt., general broker, 35 Toronto Exchange
MAKINSON, GEORGE, Makinson's Hotel, 340 Yonge cor Elm
MALCOM, R., saddles, harness, valises and trunks, 181 King e and 8 Rossin House block (see adv.)
MALLON, JOHN & CO., butchers, 12, 14 and 16 St. Lawrence market
Malloy, William, barrister, 78 King e
Malone, Martin, British mail agent to New York, h 504 Yonge
Maloney, John M., merchant tailor, 81 Bay
Maltman, John, band-box mkr, 38 High cor Vananley
Manly, Rev. John G. (Congregational), 227 Church
Manley, Mrs. John, honiton lace manufr., 380 Yonge
Manley, John, tailor, 380 Yonge
Manning, Alexander, contractor, 89 Wellington w
Manning, J., insurance agent, 40 Adelaide e
Mara, Thomas, house and land agent, 158 John
Mara, William, groceries, wines, &c., 288 Queen w
March, Charles, house, sign and ornamental painter, grainer and paper hanger, 76 Adelaide e
MARGACH, J. L., wholesale and retail drugs and chemicals, 44 King e
Marks, Joseph, locomotive inspector, 145 Brock
Marks, Robert, grocer, 108 Agnes
Marks, Wm., leather belting manuf., 34 Temperance
Marling, Alexander, L.L.B., chief clerk education office, 16 Sultan
Marling, Rev. Francis Henry (Congregational), h 279 Church
Marling, J. W., general agent Canada Life Assurance Company, h 254 Wellington w
Marriott, J. G., meat store, 111 Queen e
Marsh, John, grocer, 50 Parliament
Marshall, John S., baker, 99 Church
Marshall, Hendrick, accountant, h 151 Jarvis
MARSTON, W. P., importer and manufacturer of guns, rifles, pistols, &c., 132 Yonge (see adv)
Martin & Ecklin, dry goods, 147 King e
Martin, George, boot and shoemaker, 96 York
Martin, Henry, teacher of music and drawing, Mechanics' Institute
MARTIN, JAMES & SON (James, sr. and James, jr.), proprietors Ontario foundry and machine shop, 209 Queen e and 3 Ontario lane
Martin, Joseph, merchant tailor, 636 and 638 Yonge
Martin, Thomas M., portrait painter, 22 King e
Martland, John, B.A., second classical master and resident master in college boarding house, U. C. College
MASON, ALFRED J., cashier Canada Permanent Building and Savings Society, Masonic Hall
Mason, John, boots and shoes, 215 King e
MASON, J. HERBERT, secretary and treasurer Canada Permanent Building and Savings Society, Masonic Hall (see adv. inside front cover)
MASON, WILLIAM T., accountant and official assignee and agent European Assurance Society, London, England, 5 Ontario Hall
MASONIC HALL, Toronto opp Court
Masters, Theodore, confectioner, 261 King e
Matthew, John, groceries, provisions, &c., Dundas
Matthews, James, prop. Robinson House, 109 and 111 Bay
Matthews, William, dealer in piano-fortes, 378 Yonge
Matthews, William, toys and fancy goods, 384 Yonge
Matthews, H., bookseller, 241 Yonge
MATTHEWS, H. J., picture framer, gilder, &c., 189 Yonge
Matthews, William, soap and candle manufacturer, Berkeley, bet Esplanade and Palace
MATTHEWS, W. D., & Co., (W. D. Matthews and R. C. Hamilton) produce and commission merchants, 16 Front e
Matheson, A., chemist and druggist, 140 King w
MATHESON, HUGH, merchant tailor and clothier 16 King e (see adv)
Maunders & Brother, (William & T. Maunders) painters and glaziers, 93 Church
May, Samuel P., M.D., Education Office
May, Thomas, prop. hotel and pawn broker, 119 Queen w
May, Thomas, & Co., (Thomas May & James Paterson) fancy dry goods and millinery, 68 Yonge
Mead, John, hardware, 156 King e
MEADOWS, SAMUEL, gas fitter, diamond setter, &c., 21 and 23 Queen w
Meagher, William, oil lamps, &c., 32 King w
Meakin, William, dry goods, 181 Yonge
MECHANICS' INSTITUTE AND LIBRARY, cor Adelaide and Church
MEDCALF, E. & A., (Edward & Alfred) proprietors Don Foundry, 489 King e
Medcalf, F. H, alderman, 448 King e
Meehan, John, butcher, 26 St. Lawrence market
Meehan, Neil, saloon keeper, 137 Queen w
Meek, Thomas, prop. Meek's hotel, East Market square
Melady, P. & N., dry goods, 141 King e
Melander, John, watches and jewelry 344 Yonge
Mellich, James, grocer, 201 Elizabeth
MENDON, L. C., agent for Ontario, for Howes' Sewing Machines, 3 Rossin House (see adv)
MERCANTILE PROTECTIVE ASSOCIATION, Cupples & Hunter, 20 Toronto
Mercer, James, prop. eating house, 24 Church

MERCANTILE TEST, (semi-monthly) John Kerr, publisher, British America Assurance Buildings, Court cor Church, printed by W. C. Chewett & Co., King e
MERCER, ANDREW, issuer of marriage licenses, h Wellington cor Bay
MERCER, JOHN, prop. Yonge Street Inn, 253 Yonge
MERCHANTS' BANK OF CANADA, James G. Harper, manager, 13 Wellington w
MERCHANTS' DISPATCH FAST FREIGHT LINE J. D. Irwin, agent, 57 Yonge
MERCHANTS' SAVINGS BANK, Charles Scadding actuary, 13 Wellington w
MERRICK, J. D. & Co., wholesale millinery and fancy goods, 42 Yonge
MERRICK BROTHERS, dry goods, 47 & 49 King e
Merrifield, Robert, boots and shoes, 190 Yonge
METROPOLITAN WATER COMPANY, Launcelot G. Bolster, supt., 20 21 & 22 Toronto Exchange
Metropolitan Hotel, Thomas Brown, proprietor, cor King and Bay
METROPOLITAN PERMANENT BUILDING SOCIETY, James Fraser, sec. and treas., 5 King west
Meyer, John H., hotel keeper, York cor Front
Michael, George, optician, 51½ King e
MICHIE, GEORGE & CO., (Alex. F. Fulton and James Michie) wholesale grocers, cor Front and Yonge
Middleton, Francis, baker and confectioner, 158 King w
Military Hospitals, 36 Front w and 490 Queen w
Millar, J. W., watchmaker and jeweler, 135 King e
MILLER, ADAM, bookseller and stationer, 62 King e
MILLER, A., new and second hand clothing, plated ware, &c., 226, 228 and 230 King e
MILLER, HUGH & CO., chemists and druggists 167 King e
Miller, James, bookseller and fancy goods, 272 Yonge
Miller, R. B., attorney-at-law, 86 King e
Miller, Young & Co., cabinet makers and undertakers, 280 Yonge
MILLICHAMP, WALLACE, gold and silver plater, 80 Queen w
Milligan, A. & Co., wholesale and retail grocers and commission merchants, 1, 2 and 3 City Hall Buildings
Milligan, Frederick, 108 Adelaide w
Milligan's Hotel, A. Milligan, prop., 10 w Mkt Sq
MILLOY, NICOL, agent Canadian Inland Navigation Company, Front e
MILLOY & CO. (Donald Milloy, and Thomas Burke,) shipping agents, Yonge st wharf
Mills, John, grocer, 24 Francis
Mintz, A. J., second hand broker, 32½ Queen w
Mintz, Isaac, pawn-broker, 105 Queen w
Mishaw, Thomas B., groceries, wines and liquors, 329 Yonge, cor Gould
Mitchell, Mrs. B., grocer, 173 King w
Mitchell, George, merchant tailor, 219 Yonge
Mitchell, Mrs. Rebecca, boarding, 168 King w
MITCHELL, WM., dry goods, mantles, millinery, &c., 103 King e
MOAT, JOHN, manager City Bank of Montreal, s w cor Bay & Wellington
MOFFAT, MURRAY & BEATTIE, wholesale dry goods, 36 Yonge
Moloney, Mrs. E., fancy goods, 218 King e
Moloney, Jeremiah, Lovejoy hotel, 108 York
MONETARY TIMES & INSURANCE CHRONICLE, J. M. Trout, publisher, 60 and 62 Church
Monkhouse, Mrs. Alice, prop. Eastern Hotel, 172 King e
Monteverd, Michael, wire worker, 381 Yonge
Montgomery, John, blacksmith, Yonge, bet Bloor and Jarvis
Montgomery, Richard, blacksmith, Queen w, opposite Asylum
MONTREAL, BANK OF, G. W. Yarker, manager, Yonge cor Front
Montreal House, W. & J. Graham props., 148 King w
MONTREAL MARINE ASSURANCE COMPANY, R. N. Gooch, agent, 32 Wellington e
MONTREAL TELEGRAPH CO., H. P. Dwight, supt., 3, 15 and 30, Toronto Exchange
MONTREAL TYPE FOUNDRY, Charles T. Palsgrave, prop., W. D. Stethem, manager, 33 Colborne
Mooney, Owen, grocer, 40 Victoria
Moore, Alexander, shoemaker, 477 Yonge
Moore, Berry, (Charles Moore & Co.), h 60 Bond
MOORE, CHARLES & CO., (Charles Moore & Berry Moore), wholesale importers of groceries, wines & liquors, 5, 7, & 9 Wellington w
Moore, David, furniture, 307 Yonge
Moore, G. F. & Co., pickle and sauce factory, 187 Yonge
Moore, Henry, butcher, 28 St. Lawrence Arcade
Moore, John W., mattrass maker, 79 Queen w
Moore, Mrs., dry goods, &c., 408 Queen w
Moore, Richard, blacksmith, Palace
Moore, Thomas, tavern keeper, 55 and 57 Elizabeth
Moore, William, grocer, 283 Queen w
MORAN, JAMES, tallyman, N. R. C
Morey, Robert, grocer and broom maker, 64 Agnes
Morell, A. & Co., auctioneers and jobbers, 148 King e cor Nelson
Morell, M. S., dry goods, 254 Queen w
MORISON, FARQUHAR, mercht tailor, 12½ King w
Morison, John, grocer and liquor merchant, 5 Manning's block, Front e
Morison, John, grocer, 38 and 40 Wellington e
MORISON & CO., ale & porter bottlers, Masonic Hall
MORPHY, E. M., watches, clocks and jewelry, 141 Yonge
MORPHY, G. & H. B., barristers, 57 Yonge
MORPHY, SULLIVAN & FENTON, (George and Henry B. Morphy, Robert Sullivan and Henry Fenton) barristers, &c., Express buildings, Yonge
Morris, Thomas, confectioner, 345 Yonge
Morris & Smith, barristers, &c., Wellington Chambers Jordan
MORRISON, ANGUS, M. P., (Morrison & Sampson) h Windsor Place, Windsor
MORRISON, ANGUS G., junior clerk Legislative Assembly, Parliament buildings
MORRISON, DANIEL, editor daily *Telegraph*
MORRISON, JAMES, plumber, steam and gas fitter, cor Bay and Temperance
Morrison, John, soap manufacturer, Palace nr East
Morrison, John, grocer, 234 Queen w
MORRISON, HON. JOSEPH C., Judge Queen's Bench, h Woodlawn, Yonge, Yorkville
MORRISON & SAMPSON, barristers and attorneys-at-law, solicitors, &c., 61 Colborne (see adv)
MORRISON, TAYLOR & CO., wholesale provision and com. merchants, 5 Manning's block, Front e
MORRISON, W. C., gold and silversmith and jeweler 12 King w
MORSE, H. J. & CO., bankers and exchange dealers, 50 King e

MORTON, BENJAMIN, secretary and treasurer, trustees B. U. C., Ontario Hall
MORTIMER, HERBERT, stock broker and notary public, secretary and treasurer Madoc Gold Mining Company, and secretary St. George's Society, Victoria Hall, Melinda
Mortimer, Philip, cabinet maker, 262 Queen w
Moses, Andrew, grocer, 562 Yonge
Moses, W. W., basket maker, 291 Yonge
Moss, John, manager, Dun, Wiman & Co., h 98 Terauley
Moss, Thomas, M.A., (Patton, Osler & Moss), Registrar University College, Toronto, h 21 Bloor e
Mosiman, J. F., tinsmith, Colborne
Mossman, James, grocer, 205 Church
Mottram, J. H. H., general agent *Globe* Printing Co.
Mowat, Hon. Oliver, Vice-Chancellor, h head of College, Yorkville
Moxon & Reeves (Henry Moxon and Alfred Reeves), butchers, 20 St. Lawrence Market
Moyer & Co. (P. E. W. Moyer and R. L. Patterson), publishers *Evening Tribune*, 30 King e
MOYLAN, JAMES G., editor and prop *Canadian Freeman*, 74 Church, h 145 Church
Mullaney, James B., clerk *Leader*
Mullen A., boots and shoes, 347½ Yonge
Mulvey, John, grocer, 479 Queen w
Mulvey & Fleming, marble dealers, 8 Cruickshank
Murdock, Alexander, band master 164 King w
Murphy, Jeremiah, pawnbroker, 45 Queen w
Murphy, John, prop Cooper's Arms Hotel, 20 and 22 Wellington e
Murphy, John, 349 Yonge
Murphy, John, janitor Normal School
Murphy, Mrs., hotel keeper, Esplanade cor Church
MURPHY, N. E., barrister, &c.
Murphy, Thomas, boots and shoes, 442 Queen w.
Murphy, Thomas, boots and shoes, 122 Yonge
Murphy, William, cooper, 351 Yonge
Murray, Edmund, prof. St. Michael's College, St. Joseph
Murray, James, tinsmith, 224 Yonge
MURRAY, W. A. & CO., dry goods, 21 & 23 King e
Murray, William, confectioner, 225 Yonge
Mutton, Samuel, coal and wood, Queen e cor Sherbourne
MYERS, WILLIAM, dentist, 45 King e
Myles, James, coal and wood, Esplanade cor Church and Toronto cor Adelaide
Myles, William, coal and wood, s s Front w bet Yonge and Bay
Manton, Edward, broker and com'n merchant, e s Change Alley s of Colborne
Nash, Edward A., clerk, Canada Company, h 53 Duke
NASH, JOHN R., crown timber agent, 53 Duke
NASMITH, JOHN, bread and biscuit baker, 66 Nelson
Nasmith, M., baker and confectioner, 372 Yonge
Nelson, Henry, hair-dresser, 82½ King w
Nelson, J. B., engraver, 22 King e
Nelson, Wood & Co. (branch) wholesale importers of woodenware, fancy goods, etc., 74 York
NERLICH, H. & CO., wholesale fancy goods, 2 Adelaide w and 5 Rossin House
Newbigging, William, boarding house, 32 Front e
Newcombe, James, M.D., 105 Church
NEW YORK CASUALTY INSURANCE CO., Pellatt & Osler, agents, 86 King e
Niagara House, James Law, prop., 24 Front e cor Scott
Nichol, J. J., coal and wood merchant, cor Front e and Scott
Nichols, Simon, saddler and saloon keeper, 107 Queen w
Nichols, Robert, saddler and collar maker, 32 Church
Nicol, William B., barrister, *Leader* Building
Nightingale, Thomas, brick and tile manfr., Yorkville
Nixon, Thomas, dealer in hides and wool, 79 Colborne
Noble, Andrew, cutter, J. Renilson, bds 9 Louisa
Noble, G. & Co., dry goods, 214 Yonge
Noble, Thomas H., railway contractor, 384 King e
NORDHEIMER, A. & S., piano fortes and music, 15 King e
NORTH BRITISH AND MERCANTILE INSURANCE CO., Life department, H. L. Hime, agent, 6 Wellington e
NORTH BRITISH AND MERCANTILE INSURANCE CO., Fire department, R. N. Gooch, agent, 32 Wellington e
NORTH-WESTERN EXPRESS, J. J. Vickers, proprietor, 55 Yonge
NORTHERN FIRE AND LIFE ASSURANCE CO., William Rowland, agent, 57 Wellington
NORTHERN RAILWAY OFFICES, cor Brock and Front w
NORTHERN RAILWAY PASSENGER STATION, Esplanade bet East and West Market
NORTHERN RAILWAY WHARF AND ELEVATOR, F. P. G. Taylor & Co., wharfingers, Esplanade opp Portland
NOTMAN & FRASER, photographers, 120 King e
Notman, John, assistant clerk Legislative Assembly
Noverre, Augustin, prof. of dancing, h 250 Wellington w
NOVERRE, F. A., boat builder, Esplanade foot of Simcoe (see adv)
Noverre, John H., (Noverre & Smith), h 250 Wellington w
Noverre, Misses, ladies' school, 250 Wellington w
Noverre & Smith, photographers, 31 King e
Nudel, John T., clerk Police Court, h 34 Wood
Nurse, Richard, proprietor Cottage Inn and grocer, 314 Church, cor Ann
O'Brien, E. R., fire inspector B. A. Insurance Co.,
O'Brien, Henry, barrister and reporter com. law, 68 Church
O'Brien, Mrs., proprietor Railway Hotel, York cor Esplanade
O'Brien, James, cooper, 263 King e
O'Brien, Michael, cooper, 19 and 21 Palace
O'Brien, Mrs. Margaret, grocer, 94 Church
O'Connell, Mrs. Mary, proprietor O'Conriel's Inn, 56 Adelaide w
O'Connor, Charles, cabinet maker, 226 Yonge
O'Connor, John, grocer, 10 Queen w
O'Connor, John, brickmaker, 12 South Park
O'Connor, Rev. Dennis, prof St. Michael's College, St. Joseph
O'Connor, T. J., chemist and druggist, 251 King e
O'CONNOR, THOMAS, groceries and provisions, 197 and 199 King e (see adv)
O'Connor, Warmoll & Givins, barristers, Ontario Hall, Church
O'Connor, William, photographer, *Leader* Blgs
O'Dea, Miss Ann, confectionery, 7 and 9 St. Lawrence Arcade
O'Dea, Miss Margaret, fruit and confectionery and registry office for servants, 78 Church
O'DONHOE & DEVLIN, (J. O'Donohoe and A. P. Devlin) barristers, 62 Adelaide e
O'Donohoe, Rev. J., assistant St. Mary's, Bathurst
O'Donnell M., dry goods, 182 Yonge
O'Gorman, Michael, Prof. St. Michael's College, St. Joseph
O'Grady, J. A., prop. Shakespeare Hotel, King cor York

O'Hagan, James, grocer, 326 Queen cor Pine
O'Halloran, Michael, baker, 130 Jarvis
O'Keefe & Co., props. Victoria Brewery, cor Gould and Victoria
O'Leary, Thomas, grocer, 119 and 121 Nelson
O'Leary, Timothy, grocer, 181 Queen w
O'Leary, Timothy, tinsmith, cor King and Caroline
O'Malley, John, dry goods, 76 Queen w
O'Neill, Edward, hatter, 84 Church
O'Neill, Terence, inspector of prisons, h 40 Duke
O'NEIL, T. H., proprietor William III Hotel, 56 Adelaide e (see adv)
O'REILLY, WILLIAM T., secretary Beaver Mutual Insurance Co., 20 Toronto
OATES, R. H., mill stone manuf. and Bolting Cloth depot, corner Church and Esplanade
Odd Fellows' Hall, Toronto opp Court
Odell & Trout, props. British American Commercial College, Whittemore's Blgs, Toronto
Office of Trustees Bank of Upper Canada, Benjamin Morton, sec. and treas., Ontario Hall, Church
Ogden, Uzziel, M.D., 57 Adelaide w
Ogden, William W., M.D., 242 Queen w
Oldright, William, M.D., prof. Spanish and Italian University College, h 65 Nelson
Oliphant, D. S., M. D. (homœopathist) 175 Church
Oliver, John D., broker, h 32 Wellington w
OLIVER, J. S. Ontario Seminary, 328 Yonge
OLIVER, S. A., produce and commission merchant, 289 Queen w (see adv.)
ONTARIO BANK, A. Fisher, manager, 24 Wellington e cor Scott
ONTARIO GAZETTEER AND DIRECTORY, C. E. Anderson & Co. publishers. H. McEvoy, compiler, *Daily Telegraph* Office (see adv)
Ontario Law List and Canadian Conveyancer (The) 88 King e
Ontario Livery and Sale Stables, John Bond, prop. Sheppard
Orr, William R., mercantile academy and city auditor, h 12 Mutual
Osborne, William, notary public and land agent, h 159 Jarvis
Osborne, William, prop. Union Station Hotel, York near Front
OSLER, EDMUND B., (Pellatt & Osler)
Osler, Featherston, (Patton, Osler & Moss) h 23 Avenue
Oulcott, John, crockery and glass ware, 291 Yonge
Ovens, Mrs. Eliza, boarding house, 88 Richmond e
Ovens, John, fancy goods, 126 Yonge
Oxenham, William, butcher, 100 Queen w
Page & Parnell, dry goods, 194 & 196 Yonge
PALMER, E. J. photographer, and dealer in materials, 115 King e
Palmer, John, painter, 121 Adelaide w
Palmer, John, boarding house, 26 Temperance
PALMER, JOSEPH, prop. Dolphin restaurant and billiard parlor, 131 King e (see adv.)
Palmer, Miss Lucy, boarding house, 206 Church
Palmer, Thomas, prop. Woodbine Saloon, 88 Yonge
Palgrave, C. T., printers' warehouse, 33 Colborne
PAPE, J., fruit dealer, 38 & 40 St. Lawrence market and 49 King w
Parker, George, baggage master, N.R.C. h 151 Brock
Parker, Joseph L. hotel keeper, 215 Yonge
PARKER, JOHN O., brass founder and finisher, 148 York (see adv.)
PARKER, SIR HENRY, BART., h 23 William
Parkes, William R., grocer, 246 King e
Parkinson, Mrs. Emily, prop Island Hotel, the Island
Parkinson, Reuben, wagon maker, h 128 Duke
Parliament Buildings, Wellington nr John

Parry Brothers, butchers, 331 Yonge
PARSON BROTHERS (William and Henry) wholesale dealers and manufacturers of oils, paints, colors, lamps and glassware, 51 Front e
Parsons, Samuel N., night station master and telegraph operator G. W. R., Yonge street Station
Passmore, F. F., P.L.S., 23 Duke
Passmore, J., crockery and glassware, 297 Yonge
Passmore, Samuel W., naturalist, 232 Yonge
PATERSON, HARRISON & BAIN, solicitors in Chancery, Ontario Hall, Court
PATERSON, HARRISON & PATERSON, (James Paterson, R. A. Harrison, Q.C., John Paterson), barristers, Ontario Hall, Court
Paterson, J. A., B.A., assistant mathematical master U. C. College
Paterson, James, grocer, 128 and 130 York
Paterson, P., & Son, hardware, iron and steel, 24 King e
PATERSON, W., & CO., bankers and brokers, insurance, passage and general agents, n w cor King and Church (see adv)
Patterson, Alexander, groceries & liquors, 287 Yonge
Patterson & Beaty, barristers, 3½ King w
PATTERSON, BEATY & HAMILTON (C. S. Patterson, James Beaty, jun., and J. C. Hamilton), barristers, solicitors in Chancery, 5 King w
Patterson, J. & J., boots and shoes, 148 King e
Patterson, John, grocery, 166 York
PATTERSON, JOHN H., solicitor York Chambers Court
Patterson, Thomas C., Asst. Prov. Secretary and Deputy Registrar, 17 Avenue
PATRIOT, WATCHMAN, AND NEWS OF THE WEEK (THE), Jas. Beaty, prop, 63 King e
Patton & Co., importers glassware and crockery, 64 King e
PATTON, HON. JAMES, Q.C. (Patton, Osler & Moss), (and Macdonald, Patton & Machar), Kingston, res Kingston, Ontario
PATTON, OSLER & MOSS (Hon. James Patton, Q.C., Featherston Osler and Thomas Moss, M.A.), barristers, solicitors, &c., 7, 8 and 9 Toronto Exchange
Peacock, Charles, tavern keeper, 633 Yonge
Peacock, James, City Express, 55½ Yonge
Pearcy, Gilbert, painter, 11 and 13 Richmond e
PEARCY, JOHN, painter, Hayter, nr Yonge (see adv)
PEARS, GEORGE, Ontario Coffee and Spice Mills, Alexander, cor Yonge
Pearson, M. & E., dry goods, 158 Yonge
Pearson, Wm. T., seedsman, 22 Sydenham
Peay, Walter, wire worker, 61 Lumley.
Peck, A. C., gardener, s s Wellington w bet Windsor and Peter
PECKHAM & HOAG, (J. S. Peckham & Isaac M. Hoag) lumber merchants, 11 Toronto Exchange
PECKHAM, J. S., (Peckham & Hoag) and (Hotchkiss, Peckham & Co.), h 67 Shuter
Pedlow, Mrs. I. E., confectionery 96 Yonge
Pedlow, Thomas, carpenter, 51 McMahon
Peiler, Carl, music teacher, Yorkville
Peland, James, cigars, 116½ King w
Pell, James, frame maker, 106 York.
PELLATT & OSLER, (Henry Pellatt, Edmund B. Osler), stock brokers insurance agents, accountants, &c., 86 King e
Penfold, Mrs. Phœbe, confectioner, 122½ York
Penrose, James, photographer, 58 King e
PEOPLES & CO., wine and spirit merchants, 311 Yonge

Perkins, Charles, locksmith and bell-hanger, 14 Adelaide e
Perkins, Frederick, director Bank B. N. A., h College cor Beverley
Perkins, F. & G. & Co., wholesale grocers, 41 & 43 Front e
Pernet, Emile, prof. of French, 139 Beverley
PERRY, CHARLES, & CO., commission merchts & managers of steamer "Algoma," 55 Front e
Perry, Mrs. Mary, boarding house, 44 Alice
Peters & Donald, grocers, 134 King e
Peter, Robert, grocer, 434 Queen w
Peterkin, J. F., wood carver, 22 Queen w
Pettigrew, Samuel & Co., carpenters and joiners, 113 Richmond w
Philbrick, C. J., M.D., F.R.C.S.E., h Bloor e, Yorkville.
PHILLIPS, JOSEPH, Joseph W., builder, sash, door, and blind factory, Hayter, nr Terauley.
Phillips, M., M.D., 70
Phillips, Mrs., boarding house 78 Agnes
PHILLIPS, R. picture frame and washable gilt moulding manufacturer, 53 King w (see adv.)
Phillips, Thomas, housekeeper and chief messenger Legislature Assembly, Parliament Buildings
Phipps, George, cabinet maker and broker 84 King w
Phipps, John, provision dealer, 35 St. Lawrene Mkt.
PHIPPS, W. B., banker and exchange broker, 5 Toronto
Phœnix Fire Insurance Co. of London, Moffatt, Murray & Beattie, agents, 36 Yonge
PHŒNIX INSURANCE CO. OF BROOKLYN, N. Y., Charles G. Fortier, agent, 6 and 7 Ontario Chambers
Phœnix Mutual Life, Hartford (Conn.), A. DeGrassi, agent, 53 King e
PIDDINGTON, A., dealer in second-hand books, stationery, and fancy goods, 248 and 250 Yonge
Piddington, George, manufacturing jeweler, 1 *Globe* lane
Pierce, Felix, pork and provisions, 233 Yonge
PIM, HENRY, general smith, 453 Yonge
Pim, John, wagon maker, h 453 Yonge
PIPER, H. & CO., wholesale house furnishing goods, 81 Yonge
PIPER, HIRAM, house furnishing and hardware, 83 Yonge (see adv)
Piper, N. L. & Son, house furnishing goods, 169 Yonge
Playter, John, grocer, 27 Palace
Plenderleith, J., carpenter and builder, Sayer nr Edward
Plunkett, John, tinware, 2 St. Lawrence Arcade
POCKNELL, R. T., confectioner, 83 King w (see adv)
Police Station, No. 1, Sergeant Major Cummins, City Hall Buildings
Police Station, No. 2, Sergeant Major J. McPherson, 309 Yonge
Police Station, No. 3, Sergeant Major Hastings, 249 Queen w
Pollard, Mrs. Mary, Berlin wool and fancy goods, 4 King e
Pollock, D. J., M.D., 144 Bay
Pollock, James, cashier *Globe* Printing Co.
Porter, Rev. James, local superintendent City Public Schools, office Western Insurance Blgs., Colborne, h 13 Wood
POST OFFICE, Joseph Lesslie, Postmaster, Toronto bet King and Adelaide
Potter, Charles, optician, 20 King e
Powell, John S., employment agent, 139 York
Power, Joseph, hotel and grocer, 454 and 456 Queen w
PRICE, GEORGE W., mail clerk daily *Telegraph*
Price, George, grocer, 244 Queen w
Price, James, boarding house, 388 Yonge
PRIESTMAN, JOHN, superintemdent J. M. Bradstreet & Sons improved mercantile agency, Wellington e
Primitive Methodist book rooms, Rev. W. Rowe, steward, 89 Yonge
PRINCE, CAPT. WILLIAM S., chief Constable, office, Police Court
Pringle, T. M. & Co., dry goods, 153 King e
Protestant Orphans' Home, Sullivan bet Beverley and Commons
Proulx, Rev. J. B., parish priest and chaplain to H. M. forces, h 102 Bathurst
PROVINCIAL FIRE AND MARINE INSURANCE COMPANY, Scott & Walmsley, agents, Ontario Hall
PROVINCIAL INSURANCE BUILDINGS, Toronto cor Court
PROVINCIAL INSURANCE COMPANY OF CANADA, Hon. J. Hillyard Cameron, President; James Sydney Crocker, Secretary and manager; Toronto cor Court (see page 3)
PROVINCIAL LUNATIC ASYLUM, Queen, western limits
PROVINCIAL NORMAL AND MODEL SCHOOLS, Gould, bet Victoria and Church
PROVINCIAL PERMANENT BUILDING SOCIETY, E. Bradburne, agent, Whittemore's block
Postlethwaite, Colin W., storekeeper, N. R. C
Pullen, Joseph, brush maker and fancy goods, 260 Yonge
PUNSHON, REV. W. MORLEY, h 64 Bond
Purdy, Mrs. Margaret, innkeeper, 266 Queen w
Purdy, Mrs. William, milliner, 330½ Queen w
PURSE, ALEXANDER, Maple Leaf Saloon, 6 Adelaide w (see adv)
Purvis, Robert W., station master, City Hall Station N. R. C
Pyper, William, secretary and treasurer, Union Building and Savings Society, 82 King e
QUEBEC BANK, R. H. Bethune, manager, Bank of Toronto Buildings
QUEEN FIRE AND LIFE INSURANCE COMP'Y, W. Rowland, agent, 55½ Wellington and 58 Front cor Church
QUEEN'S HOTEL, Thomas Dick, proprietor; Mark H. Irish, manager, Front bet Bay and York
QUEEN'S OWN HOTEL, Robert Taylor, prop., 101 King w
Queen's Wharf, Esplanade foot of Bathurst
Queen's Wharf Hotel, Edward Williams, prop. Front cor Bathurst
Quigley & Miles (T. Quigley and C. F. Miles) comn merchants, 12 and 16 Ontario Chambers cor Front and Church
Quinn, John, grocer and butcher, 144½ York
Quinn, John, prov. dealer, 25 St. Lawrence Market
Radford, Miss Elizabeth, dressmaker, 42 Wellington w
RAFFAN, JOSEPH, chemist and druggist, 134 Queen w
Rahelley, Gerald, boots and shoes, 145 Yonge
Railway Passenger Accident Assurance Co., William Rowland, agent, 57 Wellington e
RAINS, JOHN, manager, Home District Mutual Insurance Co., and Commercial Building and Investment Society, 120 Yonge
Ramsay & Farquhar (David and Wm.) stone cutters and builders, foot of Church
Ramsay, James, tavern keeper and grocer, 118 and 120 Sayer

Ramsay, John J., merchant tailor, 370 Yonge
RAMSAY, WILLIAM & CO., wholesale grocers, wine and spirit merchants, 84 and 86 Front e
Randall, John W., St. Lawrence Hotel, 29 East Market Square
Rankin, Mrs. E., boarding house, 156 Adelaide w
Rattray, F. A., groceries and liquors, 220 Yonge
Ray, J. E., M.D., 22 Richmond e
Read & Boyd (D. B. and John Alex.) barristers, 77 King e
Reading, John, hoop skirts and fancy goods, 204 Yonge
Real Estate Journal, J. M. Trout, publisher, 60 and 62 Church
Rechenberg, Rev. C. F. W., in rear Ev. Lutheran Church, 104 Bond
REED, THOMAS, groceries and provisions, 630 Yonge (see adv.)
Rees' Wharf, Esplanade foot of York
Rees, William, M.D., Simcoe bet Front and Esplanade
Reeve, Alfred, wholesale clothing dealer, h 45 Cruickshank
Reeve, Miss Ann, boarding and day school, 45 Cruickshank
Reeve, Richard A., M.D. (Rosebrugh & Reeve), h 24 Shuter cor Victoria
Reeves, William, M.D., Front foot of Simcoe
REFORD & DILLON (Robert and John, jun.) importers and wholesale grocers, 12 and 14 Wellington e
REFORD, ROBERT, (Reford and Dillon) res Montreal
Registry Office, County York, John Ridout, Registrar, Toronto
REID, CALVIN P., (C. P. Reid & Co.)
REID, C. P. & Co., (C. P. Reid & Charles Brown) importers and wholesale dealers in wines, liquors and cigars, 30 Wellington e
Reid, J. B., barrister, 62 Church
REID, JOHN, fruits and confectionery, oysters, 111 King w
Reid, M. & E., milliners and dressmakers, 202 Yonge
Reilly, E., hotel, Douro cor Tecumseh
Reiley, Thomas, hoop-skirt manufacturer, 35 Colborne
Reliance Mutual Life Assurance Co., William Henderson, agent, King cor Yonge
Renilson, John, merchant tailor, 236 Yonge
Rennardson, George, gun and rifle maker, 182 King e
Rennardson, Robert, boat builder, Esplanade
Rennie, Mrs. Anna M., fancy dry goods, 351 Yonge
Reynolds, Richard, boots and shoes, 152 Yonge
Reynolds, W., 332 Yonge
Rice, William H., wire works, 35 Grosvenor
Richards, Henry, grocer, Yonge cor McGill
Richards, Hon. W. B. Chief Justice, Common Pleas, 409 Yonge
RICHARDS, HON. STEPHEN, Q.C., (Richards & Smith) Commissioner of Crown Lands, Ont., 74 Yonge
RICHARDS & SMITH, barristers 74 Yonge
Richardson & Brother, (C. & J.) butchers 200 Queen e
Richardson, David G., grocer, 31 Terauley
Richardson, Hugh, harbor master, 4 Front w
Richardson, James H., M.D., M.R.C.S., Eng., 116 Bay
Richardson, Rev. James, Bishop, Methodist Episcopal church, 34 St. Joseph
Riddel, A. A., M.D., coroner, Emigration agent New Zealand, 217 Queen e
Riddell & Burns (Francis Riddell & Alexander Burns) Beaver Soda Water Works Buchanan cor Yonge
Riddell, Frank, baker, 60 Edward
Riddel, C. J., & Co., chemists and druggists, cor Queen e and Ontario
Riddell, J., merchant tailor, 15 King w
Riddell, Joseph, grocer and liquor store, 60 Edward
Ridout, Aikenhead & Crombie, general hardware, 2 King e
Ridout, George P., governor British American Assurance Company, h 86 Wellington w
Ridout, John, Registrar County York, h 111 Wellington w
Ridout, Joseph D. (Ridout, Aikenhead & Crombie), h 86 Wellington w
Ridout, Samuel G., supervisor of assessments, 202 Seaton
Riley & May, proprs. Revere House, and managers of billiard tables, King w cor York
Ringham, G., stoves and tinware, 324 Yonge
Rising Sun Hotel, W. Carson, 632 Yonge
Risley, Samuel, government inspector steamboat boilers, 54 York
RITCHIE, John, plumber and gas fitter, 192 King e
Ritchey, Louis, blacksmith and wagon maker, 355 Queen w
Rivers, William, veterinary surgeon, 76 South Park
Roach, John, Roach's hotel, 20 Palace
ROAF & DOWNEY (John Roaf, Q.C., and John Downey), barristers, Mechanics' Institute, Church
Robb, James, groceries and provisions, 177 Centre
Roberts, C. S., foreman news depot *Globe*
Roberts, George, cabinet maker, 168 Yonge
Roberts, W. R. jeweler, 59 King w
Robertson, Alex., bootmaker, 9 Rossin House block
Robertson, Bros., grocers & confectioners, 258 Yonge
ROBERTSON, CHARLES, secretary and treasurer Freehold Permanent Building Society and secretary to Board of Trade, Ontario Hall, Church
ROBERTSON & COOK, publishers and proprietors *Daily Telegraph*, Bay cor King (see adv.)
ROBERTSON, DAVID D., engraver, Yorkville
Robertson, Jardine & Co. (Gideon Robertson and Alexander Jardine), importers and jobbers of teas, commission merchants, &c., 1 Manning's block, Front e
ROBERTSON, J. ROSS (Robertson & Cook)
ROBERTSON, JOHN, SON & CO., wholesale dry goods, 70 Yonge
ROBERTSON, STEPHEN & CO., importers of dry goods, 32 Wellington e (see adv)
Robertson, W., tinware, &c., 285 Yonge
Robinson, Alfred, barber, King e
Robinson & Brown, butchers, 2 St. Lawrence Arcade
Robinson, Charles, crockery, &c. 346 Yonge
Robinson, Charles, jr. jeweller and paper box manufacturer, 346 Yonge
Robinson, Christopher, Q. C. barrister, 68 Church
Robinson, Hon. J. B. barrister, 68 Church
Robinson, J. D. dry goods, 213 King e
Robinson, Mrs. juvenile clothing, 336 Yonge
Robinson & Pearson, boots and shoes, wholesale, 54 Yonge
Robinson, T. C. jeweller and paper box manufacturer, 96 Yonge
Robinson, T. dry goods and clothing, 127 Yonge
Robinson, Thomas, barber, 14 Queen w
Robinson, Thomas S., M. D. 21 Gould
ROBINSON, W. S., chemist and druggist, ws Yonge, Yorkville
Rochester House, John Carroll, prop. 20 Front w
Rock, Michael, grocer, 359 Queen w
Rockwell, Mrs. R. A., portrait painter, 39 King w
RODGERS, S. & G., cutlery, saw makers, machinists, 166 King e

Rodden, W. H., manufacturers' agents, King e
Rogers, C. K., hatter and furrier, 133 King e
Rogers, James H., hatter and furrier, 109 King e
Rogers, William D., painter, 103 Bay
Rollo, James, agent, Travellers' of Hartford Insurance Co. 62 Gerrard e
Rolph, Adam, ticket agent, N. R. C.
ROLPH, HON. JOHN, L. L. D. M. D. M. R. C. S., Dean Medical Faculty, Victoria College, 20 Gerrard w
Rolph, J. T. engraver and lithographer, 11 King w
Rolph, J. Widmer, M. D. 20 Gerrard
Romain Buildings, 81 & 93 King w
Roman Catholic Cathedral, (St. Michael's) cor Church and Shuter
Rooke, Thomas, cabinet maker, 361 Queen w
Roome, Thomas F. organ builder h 634 Yonge
Rooney, James, flour and feed, 81 Church
Rooney, N. & F. wholesale dry goods, 60 Yonge
Rooney, Very Rev. F. P., P. P. St. Paul's, Power
RORDANS & CO., law stationers and booksellers, 88 King e (see adv)
Rosbach, George A., butcher, 78 Queen w
Rose, H. J., pharmaceutist, Yonge cor Richmond
Rose, Mrs. J., boarding and day school, 3 Gerrard w
Rose, John E., barrister, 78 King e
Rose, Rev. Samuel, steward and manager Wesleyan book room, 80 King e
Rosebrugh, Abner M., M.D., (Rosebrugh & Reeve), h 117 Church
Rosebrugh & Reeve, (A. M. Rosebrugh, M.D., and R. A. Reeve, M.D.), 55 Queen e, cor Church
Ross, Alexander M., M.D., C.M., 159 Church
Ross, David, grocer, 55 Queen w
Ross, David, confectioner, 191 Queen w
Ross, George, fruiterer, 227 Yonge
Ross, James, M.A., assistant editor *Globe*
Ross, James, M.D., 74 Caroline
Ross, Hon, John, Q.C. (Ross, Lauder & Mulock)
ROSS, JOSEPH, proprietor Globe Hotel, 163 Yonge
ROSS, LAUDER & MULOCK, barristers, Masonic Hall
ROSSIN HOUSE HOTEL, G. P. Shears, lessee and manager, cor King and York
Rough, James, flour and grain inspector, 50 Front e
Rowe, Rev. William, secretary Primitive Methodist Missionary Society, 89 Yonge
Rowell, George, 306 Yonge
Rowell, James, M.D., 306 Yonge
Rowland, John, dry goods, 173 Yonge
ROWLAND, WILLIAM, fire, marine, accidental and life insurance agent, 55 Wellington and 58 Front cor Church
ROWSELL, HENRY, bookseller and stationer, 76 King e
ROYAL CANADIAN BANK, James Metcalfe, M.P., President, Hon, Donald McDonald, Vice-Pres., T. Woodside, Cashier e s Toronto
Royal Engineers' department, Purveyor's department and Garrison Surgery, Wellington w, cor Dorset
Royal Insurance Co. of England, Francis Heward, manager, Yonge cor Wellington
Royle, James, dyer, 104 York
ROYAL LYCEUM, George Holman, lessee and manager, King w (see adv)
Ruddell, Joseph, fruit dealer, 366 Queen w
Rudolph, A., goldsmith, 64 Adelaide e
Ruse, Charles, grocer, 379 Queen w
Rush, F., grocer, 415 Queen w
Russell, Andrew, assis't Commissioner Crown Lands, Parliament Buildings
Russell, A. W., wholesale watches & jewelry, 55 Yonge
Russell, J. P., M. D., 148 Bay
Russell, John, confectionery and glassware, St. Lawrence Arcade
Russill, John, market gardener, Yonge
RUTHERFORD, ANDREW, stoves, tin and hardware, house furnishing goods, &c., 126 King e (see adv)
Rutherford, E. H., President Consumers Gas Company Provincial Insurance Companys bldgs, Toronto
Ryan, Jeremiah, grocer, 17 Melinda
Ryan, John, grocer, 98 Parliament
Ryan, John, grocer, 174 and 176 Parliament
Ryan, Martin, grocery, 162 Queen w
Ryan, Michael, grocer, 125 Queen w
RYAN & OLIVER, retail hardware, 114 Yonge
Ryder, Thomas, carriage maker, 186 Queen w
Ryerson, Rev. Egerton, D. D., chief superintendent of Education, Ontario, h 151 Victoria
Sadd, James, cigars and tobacco, 65 King w
SAIT, EDWARD, anatomical shirt and collar maker, 7 Rossin Block, King w
Sale, Julian, commission agent, h 63 Elizabeth
SAMUEL, M. & L., (Mark and Lewis) commission and general merchants, 49 Wellington e, 52 Front e and 28 South Castle street, Liverpool, England
Sanderson, G., grocer, 158½ Teraulcy
Sanderson, George, melodeon maker, h 9 Renfrew
Sanderson, George, grocer, 556 Yonge
SANDERSON, P. K., (Caulkins & Sanderson), h 432 Yonge
SANGSTER, JOHN H., M.A., M. D., head master Provincial Normal and Model Schools, h w s College, Yorkville
Sanson, Rev. A., incumbent Trinity Church, h Erin cor King
Saunders, B., merchant tailor, 89 King w
Saunders, S., tailor, 320 Yonge
Saulter, R. & W. (Richard & William) coal and wood merchants, s.s. Esplanade, foot of Church
Saulter, Thomas, prop. ferry steamer, "Bouquet"
SAVIGNEY, HUGH P., C. E. surveyor and mining engineer, 32 Exchange buildings (see adv.)
SAVINGS BANK (MERCHANTS') Charles Scadding, actuary, 13 Wellington w
SAWDON, GEORGE, house furnishing lamps, oils, &c. 385 Yonge
Sawdon, George, jr. tinsmith, 385 Yonge
Scadding, Charles, actuary, Merchants' Savings Bank, h 162 Jarvis
Scadding, C. A., engraver and manufacturer printers' materials, 6 Richmond e
SCADDING, REV. HENRY, D. D., incumbent Church of Holy Trinity, h 10 Trinity
Scales, Joab, & Co., wholesale manufacturers of tobacco, 45 Palace
Scarlett, E. C., lumber dealer, 497 Queen w
Schadel, Charles, cigar manufacturer, 98 York
Schluter, Rev. E. M. A. French and German master, U. C. College
Schomberg, Henry A. cabinet maker, 187 Yonge
Schultz, A. & Co. grocers, 405 Queen w
Schuster, Leopold, cigars and tobacco, 339 and 341, Queen w
SCOLEY, EDWARD K. grocer 37 and 39 St. Lawrence Market
Score, R. & Son (Richard & Richard J.) merchant tailors and clothers, 95 King e
SCOTT & GORRIE, wharfingers, Church st. Wharf
SCOTT, JAMES, book-keeper, C. E. Anderson & Co. bds 121 Simcoe
SCOTT, PETER A., builder and lumber merchant, 618 and 620 Yonge (see adv)

Scott, James, dry goods, 99 King e
SCOTT, T. C., Surveyor of Customs, h e s Pembroke near Gerrard
SCOTT & STOLLERY (Alexander Scott and W. A. Stollery) builders, contractors, wharfingers, &c. Esplanade, cor Bay (see adv)
SCOTT & WALMSLEY, general insurance agents, Travellers' Life and Accidental Insurance Co. &c. agents for M. C. Hickie, wine merchant, London, England, Ontario Hall, Church
Scottish Provincial Life Assurance Company, G. L. Maddison, agent, 84 Bay
Scoville, J. & N. C. (John and Nathaniel Church Scoville) car wheel works, Esplanade, opposite Queen's Hotel
Seaborn, Thomas, hotel keeper, 116 King w
Seath, John, plumber and gas fitter, 202 Church
Seels, John, saloon keeper, 67 King
SEGSWORTH, J., watchmaker and jeweler, 113 Yonge
Sellers, Charles, groceries and provisions, 73 Gerrard
Selway, Matthew, last maker, 24 Adelaide w
SESSIONS, JARED D., (Sessions, Turner & Co) res Maiden, Mass
SESSIONS, TURNER & CO., (Jared D. Sessions, John Turner and James Cooper) wholesale boot and shoe manufs., 8 Wellington w
Severn, Henry, prop. Yorkville Brewery
Shades Restaurant, Jewell & Timms, props., 24 Melinda and 33 King w
Shannessy, John, prop. Royal Restaurant, 9 King w
Shannon, John, Buchanan
SHAPTER & OWEN (J. T. Shapter & John T. Owen) chemists and druggists, 78 Yonge
SHARP, WILLIAM & SON, undertakers, 115 Queen w and 477 Yonge (see adv)
Sharpley, Benjamin, baby carriage manuf., 616 Yonge
Shaver & Bell, dry goods and clothing, 159 King e
SHAW, ALEXANDER, lending library, books and stationery, 29 King w
Shaw, James, assistant collector inland revenue, Toronto Exchange
Shaw, John L., prop. European Hotel, 110 York cor Boulton
Shaw, John P., dry goods, &c., 99 Yonge
Shaw, John & Co., wholesale dry goods, 10 Wellington east
Shaw & Campbell, (W. J. Shaw & E. J. Campbell) grocers, 135 Yonge
Shaw & Roberts, architects, 64 King e
SHEARS, GEORGE P., lessee and manager Rossin House, cor King and York
SHEDDEN, JOHN & CO., cartage agents G.T.R., 42 Front e
Sheppard, Matthew, prop. York Hotel, 648 Yonge
SHEPPARD, ROBERT, prop. marble works, 171 Queen w (see adv)
SHEPPARD, WILLIAM H., prop. marble works, 173 Queen w (see adv)
Sheppard & Daguere, (Robert & J. F.) photographers 117 King e
SHERWOOD, L. P., (Evans, Sherwood & Co.) h 140 Adelaide w
Shewan, M., books and stationery, 1 St. Lawrence Arcade
SHEIL, C. J. MAHER, agent C. E. Anderson & Co., bds 24 Louisa
SHIELDS, GEORGE W., day foreman news department *Daily Telegraph*
Shipway, Charles, lamps and oils, 290 Yonge
Short, Mrs., King cor Bathurst
Shortiss, Edward, solicitor, 84 Exchange bdgs
SHORTISS, THOMAS, 32 Toronto Exchange
Sibbet, Mrs. Mrs. Mary, grocer, 200 Queen w
Sievert, Louis, cigar manufacturer, 62½ Queen w
Silvas, M., harness maker 253 King e
Simmers, J. A., seedsman and florist, 20 West Market Square
SIMPSON, JOSEPH, knitting and yarn factory, 35 Front e
Simpson, Thomas, propr. Old Countrymen's Home, 124 York
Simmington, —, block maker, 12 Church
Sinclair, John, toys, china, glassware, 254 George
Sinclair, J. & F. G., wholesale and retail grocers, 12 Palace
Skaith, Mrs. Phœbe, groceries and provisions, Yonge cor Wood
Skerry, W. J., grocer, provisions, flour and feed, 634 Yonge
Skinner, Colin, grocer and provision dealer, 271 Yonge
Skinner, Henry, Deputy Sheriff, h Jarvis bet Wellesley and Isabella
Skinner, The Misses, private school, 20 Gerrard w
Skinner, R., grocer, 149 George
Slatter, James, baker 359 Yonge
Sloan, James A., grocer, 195 and 197 Queen w
Small, John T., M.D., M.R.C.S.E., h 144 Simcoe
Smallpeice, Henry E., saddler, 58 Nelson
SMALLPEICE, HENRY, clerk *Daily Telegraph*
Smart, John, hair dresser and wig maker, 46 King w
Smedley & Sutherland, (Joseph Smedley and John Sutherland), packing box manufacturers, Richmond e
Smellie, Mrs. Euphemia, milliner and straw bonnet maker, 376 Yonge
SMITH, ALEXANDER, brush manufacturer, Dundas (see adv.)
Smith, Andrew, veterinary surgeon, 37 Temperance nr Bay
Smith, Andrew, saddler, 550 Queen w
Smith, A. M., Director Royal Canadian Bank
Smith, D. W., Toronto Dye Works, 75 King w
Smith, Edwin, hotel keeper, 156 King w
Smith, Elias, boarding house, 138 York
Smith, Fair & Co. (John Smith, Thomas W. Fair and Andrew Melville), wholesale grocers, 65 Front cor Church
SMITH, FRANK & CO., importers of teas, groceries, wines and liquors, Front cor Scott
Smith, George H., barber, 134 King w
Smith, Henry, painter, 229 Yonge
Smith, H. T., plumbing and brass finishing, 95 Queen w
SMITH, JAS. E., Collector of Customs, h Wellesley
SMITH, J. E. & CO., wholesale grocers, wines and liquors, 31 Church
Smith, James Lamond, Land Superintendent Bank Upper Canada
Smith, James, refreshment saloon, Union station
Smith, James, jun., deputy harbor master 4 Front w
Smith, James, architect, 11 King w
Smith, John, boots and shoes, 123 Yonge
Smith, John, proprietor Victoria saloon, 44 King w
SMITH, JOHN B., lumber merchant, planing mills, &c., Front w nr Bay
Smith, John E., M.D., 184 King e
SMITH, LARRATT W., D.C.L. (Smith & Wood), h Summerhill House
Smith, Mrs., boarding house, King n w cor York
Smith, Richard, innkeeper, 440 Queen w
Smith, Thomas, house, sign and ornamental painter, 22 and 24 Wellington w

SMITH, THOMPSON & SON (Thompson, Smith and Egbert A. Smith), lumber merchants, Esplanade bet Bay and York
Smith, W., M.D., M.R.C.S., Eng., 292 Yonge
Smith, William, prop Fermanagh Inn, 11 Victoria
Smith & Wills, wholesale and retail confectioners, 244 Yonge
SMITH & WOOD (Larratt W. Smith, D.C.L. and Samuel G. Wood, L. L. B.), barristers, &c., solicitors for the Bank of British North America, 4 Wellington e
Smith, Prof. William H., lightning rod manufacturer, Rochester House
Smith, W. W., oyster and fruit store, 94 Queen w
Snarr, John, coal and wood dealer, 9 Front
Snarr, Thomas, 168 George
Snelling, Richard, L. L. B., barrister, Leader bldgs, King e
Snider, M. Edward, surgeon dentist, 81 King e
Soleder, John, undertaker, 240 King e
Solomon, Ward, auction & com. mercht., 146 King e
Somers, John, grocer, 184 Terauley
Sommerville, William, tavern keeper, 426 Front
SORLEY, J. B., leather com. merchant, 25 Front e
Southard, C., receiving clerk, American Ex. Co.
Soyer, A., confectioner, 131 Yonge
Spadina Brewery, Charles Sproatt, proprietor, 145 Vanauley
Sparling, Christopher, contractor, 67 Victoria
Sparrow & Whatmough, house furnishers, 87 Yonge
SPACKMAN, J. R., acting manager Royal Lyceum, h 136 Adelaide w
SPENCE, HUGH, wood and coal, 199 Queen w (see adv)
Spence, James, City Assessor St. John's Ward, 65 Elizabeth
Spence, James, British Lion Hotel, 56 Queen w
Spence, Mrs. John L., juvenile clothing and fancy goods, 437 Yonge
Spencer & Bull, (T. H. Spencer and T. H. Bull) barristers, Masonic Hall
SPIRIT OF THE AGE, J. Blackburn, printer, 96 Yonge
Spooner, James, tobacconist, 41 King e
Spragge, Hon. J. G., Vice-Chancellor, 299 King e
Spratt, Robert, flour dealer and comn. merchant, 31½ Church
SPREULL, SAMUEL, accountant, Jordan cor King
SPROATT, CHARLES, prop. Spadina Brewery, 145 Vanauley (see adv)
Spry, Daniel, clerk, Inspector's Office, Post Office
St. Andrew's Church (Presbyterian) fronting on Church, cor Adelaide e
St. Ann's Church of England, Dundas
St. Basil's R. C. Church, St. Joseph
St. George's Church (Episcopal) John bet Queen and Grange Road, Rev. Archdeacon Fuller, minister
St. George's Society Office, H. Mortimer, secretary, 1 Victoria Hall, Melinda
St. Germain, Alfred H., Canadian Advertising Agency 34 King e
St. James' Cathedral, King cor Church
St. James' Cemetery, John Kearney, supt., Parliament
St. James' Parochial School, Church cor Adelaide
St. John the Evangelist (Church of England) Victoria Square
St. John, Mollyneux, assistant editor *Globe*
St. Joseph's Convent, St. Albans nr Breadalbane
St. Lawrence Hall, King e bet Church and Nelson
St. Lawrence Wharf, James Adamson, prop., foot of West Market Square
St. Michael's Cathedral, Shuter cor Bond
St. Michael's College, St. Joseph, Clover Hill
St. Mary's (R. C.) Church, Bathurst nr Adelaide
St. Mary's Industrial School, McDonald Square
St. Patrick's Market, Queen w
Stalker, John, retail dry goods, 192 Yonge
STANDARD LIFE ASSURANCE CO., AND COLONIAL LIFE ASSURANCE CO., Pellatt & Osler, agents, 86 King e
STANLEY, ROBERT, boots and shoes, 392 Yonge (see adv)
Stanley, William, furniture broker, 150 York
Stanway, George & Co., brokers, 3 Ontario Chambers cor Front and Church
Star Life Assurance Co., Joseph Gregory, agent, 78 King e
Stanton, William H., barrister, Court cor Toronto
STAUNTON, M. & SON, manufs. paper hangings, &c., manufactory Front w, store Yonge cor King
Staunton, S., importer of berlin wool and fancy goods, 2 King w cor Yonge
STAYNER, F., crown lands timber office, 11 Wood
STAYNER, F. W., land agent, 31 Exchange Blgs
Steel, John, groceries and provisions, 366 Yonge
Steele, William H., attorney, clerk Cameron and McMichael
Steiner, N. L., prop. Marble Works, 275 Yonge
Stephens, Robert, grocer, 33 Elizabeth
Stephenson, Edward, builder, 448 Parliament
STEPHENSON, JAMES, agent Robertson, Stevens & Co., Montreal, h Grosvenor
Stephenson, James, asst. supt. G.T.R., 215 Parliament
Stephenson, Rev. William, pastor Adelaide Street W. M. Church, h 239 Jarvis
Sterling, John, hide and leather inspector, 210 Church
STERN, SAMUEL, importer and wholesale dealer in fancy goods, 14 Wellington w cor Jordan (see adv.)
Stevens, James, prof. of music, 95 Ann
Stevenson, Holmes, contractor, 181 Seaton
Stevenson, John, commission merchant, 46 North Park
Stevenson, John, tailor, 251 King e
Stewart, Alexander, grocer, 380 Queen w
Stewart, Frederick J., tea and commission broker, 33 Church
Stewart, George H., grocer, 174 Yonge
Stewart, Miss Ida A., boarding house, 43 Richmond e
Stewart, Mrs. Olive, ladies' boarding school, Duke cor George
STEWART, P. H., printer and publisher, Shuter cor Yonge
Stibbs, James, notary public and money broker, 20 Adelade w
STIBBS, WILLIAM, architect and civil engineer, 20 Adelaide w
STISTED, MAJOR GENERAL, HENRY WILLIAM, C.B., Com. H. M. Forces, Ontario, 168 King w
Stock, James, wholesale and retail grocer, 16 Palace
Stokes, George, tailor and clothes cleaner, 22 Adelaide e
Stoner, Henry, Avenue House, 146 Queen w
STOODLEY, S., manager Allcock, Laight & Co.
Storm, Thomas, builder and contractor, 141 Queen e
Storm, W. G., architect, Romain blds, King w
Stotesbury, W. H., collector, Metropolitan Water Co., 20, 21 and 22 Toronto Exchange
Stovel, Joseph, merchant tailor, 63 King w
Stow, Frederick P., stock broker, 22 Toronto
Stow, Mrs. F., private school, Jarvis

Stowe, Mrs. Emily, M.D., 39 Richmond e
Strachan, William, groceries and liquors, 168 King e
Strachan, William & Co., groceries, wines, and spirits, 150 King e
Strathy, G. W., Mus. Doc., 44 Bond
Strathy, John, barrister, Adelaide cor Simcoe
Stratton, William, brass finisher and locksmith, 199 Yonge
Strong, Edgar & Graham (S. H. Strong, Q. C., J. D. Edgar and R. Graham) barristers, Wellington Chambers
Stubbs, Miss Anna B., ladies' school, 45 Grange Road
Stupart, Capt. R. D., secretary, Association Canadian Underwriters, 5 Ontario Chambers
Sturzaker, James, saddler, 102 York
Stuart, A. H., solicitor, 39 King w
SUNDAY SCHOOL DIAL, THE, an illustrated religious paper for children, monthly; address A. Christie, P.O. box 696, Toronto
SUNDAY SCHOOL ADVOCATE (Wesleyan), 80 King e
Summerville, Mrs. Margaret, boarding house, 8 Bond
Sutherland, Donald, housekeeper Osgoode Hall
Sutherland, George, butcher, 239 Church
Sutherland, John, packing box manufacturer 59 Richmond e
Sutherland, W. W., merchant tailor, 100 Yonge
Sutherland & Marshall, (Alexander Sutherland and Samuel Marshall), soap and candles, 11 Denison avenue
Swann, John H., baby linen and ladies' outfitting, 57 King w
Swan Brothers, grocers, 162 and 164 King e
Swinbourn George Henry, mathematical instrument maker, 24 Adelaide e
Switzer, Benjamin, broker, 42 Bond
Switzer, Charles A., forwarding clerk American Express Co.
Sydere, A. H., routine clerk, Parliament bdgs
SYLVESTER, BROTHER & HICKMAN, vessel owners, agents and general brokers, 1 Ontario Chambers, cor Front and Church
Taggart, Charler, baker and confectioner, 316 Yonge
Tallen, James, assistant station master G.T.R., Don station
Taylor, Capt. Archibald A., coal and wood merchant, Palace
TAYLOR, F. P. G. & CO., lumber and commission merchants, inspectors and general forwarders, office, Northern Railway wharf
Taylor, George, stoves and tinware, 225½ Yonge
Taylor, Hugh R., tavern keeper, 98 Caroline
Taylor, F. J., clerk of statistics Education Office
TAYLOR, JOHN & BROS., paper manufacturers and dealers, cor Colborne and W. Market Square (see adv)
TAYLOR, J. & J., patent fire and burglar proof safe manufacturers, 198 and 200 Palace (see adv opp title page)
Taylor, L. J., confectioner, 363 Yonge
Taylor, Rev. Lachlin, D.D., (Wesleyan Methodist), bds 56 Gerrard
Taylor, Robert, proprietor Queen's Own Hotel, 101 King w
TAYLOR, SAMUEL, manager Bank of British North America, 2 Wellington e, cor Yonge
Taylor & Shipley, wholesale collar and gig saddle manufacturers, 250 King e
Taylor, T. W., Judges Secretary Court of Chancery, Osgoode Hall
Taylor, W. D., cashier Freehold Permanent Building Society, cor Church and Court
Taylor, Watson, merchant tailor, 82 Yonge
Taylor, William, fish, oysters and fruit, 94 Yonge
Taylor, W. S., commercial editor *Globe*
TAYLOR & WILSON (Joseph and Samuel) wholesale and retail manufacturers of cigars 124 Yonge (see adv)
Tarleton, William, boots and shoes, 232 Queen w
TELEGRAPH, MORNING, EVENING AND WEEKLY, Robertson & Cook, props., Bay, cor King
Tempest, William, M.D., 330 Yonge and City Medical Health Officer, office, City Hall bldgs
Temple, Dr., 33 Temperance
Tenison & Hunter, dry goods and clothing, 105 King e
TERRAPIN SALOON, G. W. Carlisle, proprietor, 87 and 89 King e
TERRY'S EXPRESS AND CITY PARCELS DELIVERY, West End Depot, Adelaide cor Yonge, East End Depot, King cor Caroline (see bottom lines)
TERRY, JOHN, flour, feed and produce and comn, prop. Terry's Express and City Parcels Delivery, Adelaide cor Young and King cor Caroline (see bottom lines)
The Scottish Provincial Assurance Co., G. L. Maddison, agent, 6 Wellington e
Thom, Charles, prop. Target Hotel, Yonge, Yorkville
Thomas, John, pianoforte maker, Elizabeth cor Gerrard
THOMAS, M. A., prop. English Chop House, 30 King w
Thomas, R. P., barber, 27 East Market Square
Thompson & Allen (Hugh Thompson and Thomas Allen) props. East End Brewery, 5 River
Thompson, A. J., 431 Yonge
Thompson, Charles, grocer, 75 and 77 King e
Thompson, Christopher J., second English master U. C. College
Thompson, D., chemist and druggist, 386 Yonge
Thompson, Edward, grocer, 97 Church
Thompson, F. J., treasurer Beaver Mutual Insurance Co., 20 Toronto
Thompson, Henry, manager, Consumers Gas Co., h 159 Palace
Thompson, James, 406 Queen w
Thompson, James E., plumber and gas fitter, h 24 Gerrard
Thompson, Joseph, hotel and bagatelle table mnfr., 406 Queen w
THOMPSON, T. P., local reporter *Daily Telegraph*, and secretary Hastings Gold Mining Company, bds 240 King e
Thompson, Robert, provision and commission merchant, 33 Church
Thompson, Thomas, saddles, harness and trunks, 185 King e
Thompson, Thomas, treasurer Beaver Mutual Insurance Company, h Yorkville
Thompson, Thomas & Son, importers of dry goods, clothing, boots and shoes, 136 and 138 King e
Thompson, William, wagon maker, 464 Queen w
Thompson, William, melodeon maker, h 2 Osgoode
THOMSON & BURNS (William Thomson and John Burns), wholesale hardware, crockery and fancy goods, Front w opp Custom House
Thomson, James, painter and glazier, 358 Yonge
Thomson, John E., barrister, &c., York Chambers, Court
Thorburn, James, M.D., lecturer on medical jurisprudence, Toronto School of Medicine, h 119 Church
THORNE, PARSONS & VENNOR, wholesale leather merchants, 79 Front e

Thorne, Horace, barrister, Court
Thorn, W., produce and commission merchant, 1 Manning's block, Front e
Thornhill, E., tavern keeper, Nelson cor Richmond
Thrall, Walter, boarding house, 126 King w
Threlkeld, Joseph, whip and trunk manufacturer, 390½ Yonge
Thurman, Mrs. H., pie & crumpet maker, 625 Yonge
THURSTON, D., U. S. Consul, Masonic Hall
TIDEY, WILLIAM J., hotel keeper, 305 Yonge (see adv)
Tietzner, Henry W., dry goods, 412 Queen w
TILBURY, GEORGE F. & CO., agents for Ives & Allen, Montreal; D. A. Ansell, Montreal; the Provincial hardware manufacturing company, sample rooms 11 and 12 Ontario Chambers, Front cor Church (see adv)
Timpson, T. B., mathematical instrument maker, 63 Queen w
Tinning, R. & Brothers (R. Thomas and John), wharfingers and wood dealers, Tinning's wharf, Esplanade ft of York
Tinning's wharf, s s Esplanade w ft of York
Tinsley, John M., grocer, 77 Agnes
Todd, Andrew, h 88 Wellington w
Todd, R. M., second hand store, 192 Queen w
Todd, William, grocer & provision dealer, 105 Nelson
Tollis, Henry, landscape gardener and florist, 65 Gerrard w
Topp, Rev. Alexander, pastor Knox's Church, h 38 William
Toronto Board of Health Office, City Hall, branch York cor Richmond
Toronto Car Wheel Works, J. & N. C. Scoville, props Esplanade, opp Queen's Hotel
TORONTO CENTRAL SASH, DOOR & BLIND AND MOULDING FACTORY, J. P. Wagner prop., 71 and 73 Adelaide w (see adv)
TORONTO CITY DIRECTORY, (annual) C. E. Anderson & Co., publishers, H. McEvoy, compiler, Bay cor King (see adv)
TORONTO CITY EXPRESS, Robert Bradford, prop., 75 Yonge
Toronto City Steam Mills and Distillery, Gooderham & Worts, props, Palace
Toronto Club, John Brown, steward, 77 York
Toronto Corn Exchange, Thomas Clarkson, pres., 19 and Rotunda Toronto Exchange
Toronto Cricket Club, Grounds Queen's Park, College Avenue
Toronto Dispensary, 162 York
Toronto General Hospital, William B. Hampton, M.D., resident medical superintendent, h cor Don and Sumach
Toronto Grammar School, Rev. Arthur Wickson, L.L.D., rector, Dalhousie nr Gould
Toronto Grey and Bruce Railway Company, provisional directors: John Gordon, pres., James E. Smith, vice-pres., W. S. Taylor, secretary, 46 Front e
Toronto Homœopathic Pharmacy, 171 Yonge
Toronto Horticultural Gardens, Thomas Tillman, gardener, s s Carlton bet Jarvis and Sherbourne
TORONTO LEADER, James Beaty, M. P., prop. 63 King e
Toronto Lying-in-Hospital, Mrs. Black, matron, Richmond cor Sheppard
Toronto Magdalene Asylum, Yonge, Yorkville
TORONTO MAGICAL DEPOT, James Eves, prop., 107 Yonge (see bottom lines)
TORONTO MUTUAL FIRE INSURANCE CO., H. Hancock, secretary, 20 Toronto
Toronto Mining Exchange, Josias Bray, pres., S. C. Duncan, clerk, sec. and treas., York Chambers, Court
Toronto and Nipissing Railway Company, provisional directors: John Crawford, pres., W. F. McMaster, vice-pres., Charles Robertson, secretary, 46 Front e
TORONTO POST OFFICE, Joseph Lesslie, Postmaster, Toronto opp Court
Toronto Rolling Mills, C. S. Gzowski and Hon. D. L. McPherson, props., Little Front bet East and Cherry
Toronto Savings Bank, W. J. MacDonell, manager, 72 Church
Toronto School of Medicine, in affiliation with University, Queen's Park
Toronto Steel, Iron and Railway Works, foot of Strachan Avenue
Toronto Street Railway, offices Yorkville and Ontario Hall, Church
Toronto Temperance Reformation Society, Temperance Hall, Temperance
TORONTO TYPOGRAPHICAL UNION, No. 91, Rooms Temperance Hall, Temperance
Toronto Water Works, Exchange Buildings, engine house Esplanade foot of Peter
Totilman, F., jr., prof. of music, h n s Sydenham, Yorkville
Touzeau, William, engraver, 1 *Globe* lane
Toye, Benjamin B., chief operator Montreal Telegraph Company, h 169 Mutual
Toye, Charles, tailor, 64 Queen w
Toy, Samuel, butcher, 17 and 19 St. Lawrence Mkt
Tracie, Uri J. & Co., groceries and provisions, 157 Yonge
TRAVELERS' (ACCIDENT) INSURANCE CO'Y, Hartford, Conn., W. Rowland, agent, 55 Wellington, and 58 Front cor Church
Travelers Life and Accident Insurance Company, Scott & Walmsley, agents, Ontario Hall, Church
TREES, SAMUEL & CO., importers saddlery hardware, 69 Colborne (see adv)
Trenor, Peter, lumber dealer, cor Nelson and Duke
TRINITY CHURCH, King, bet Erin and Trinity
TROTTER, ROBERT G., L.D.S., dentist, 53 King e (see adv.)
TROUT, J. M., business manager, "The Canadian Monetary Times and Insurance Chronicle," 60 and 62 Church, h 176 Victoria
Trump, Daniel, grocery, 145 York
TUCKER, DANIEL, stationery, postage and bill stamps, &c., 65 Colborne Street, up stairs
Tucker, Edward, confectioner, 28½ Yonge
Tully, Kivas, architect and superintendent of Public Works, Parliament Buildings
Tulley, Robert, butcher, h 20 Elizabeth
Turner, Alexander, photographer, Adelaide e
TURNER, JOHN, photographer, 74 Yonge (see adv.)
Turner, John, machinist, 447 and 449 Yonge
TURNER, JOHN (Sessions, Turner & Co.) h 23 Grenville
Turner, W., butcher, 28 St. Lawrence Market
Tushingham, Richard, builder, 108 Bay
Union Permanent Building and Savings Society, William Pyper, secretary, 84 King e
Union Railway Station, Esplanade, foot of York
Union Station Hotel, William Osborne, prop., York
University and College Bursar's Office, David Buchan bursar, Simcoe cor Adelaide
UNIVERSITY INN, E. Hussey, prop., 400 Yonge
UNITED STATES CONSULATE, D. Thurston, Consul, Masonic Hall, Toronto

Unwin, Charles, sen., land and insurance agent, Adelaide e opp Court
Unwin, C., insurance agent, 42 Adelaide e
Upper Canada Bible and Tract Society Depository J. Carless, agent, 102 Yonge
Upper Canada Common Pleas Report, printed and published by Henry Rowsell, 76 King e
Upper Canada Law Directory, published every alternate year, by J. Rordans, law stationer, Church, W. C. Chewett & Co., printers
Upper Canada Law Journal, monthly, R. A. Harrison, B.C.L., and W. A. Ardagh, editors and and proprietors; W. C. Chewett & Co., printers and publishers, 17 and 19 King e
Upper Canada Local Courts Gazette, R. A. Harrison, B.C.L., and W. A. Ardagh, editors and proprietors; W. C. Chewett & Co.. printers
Ure, Rev. R., lecturer on Homoletics, &c., Knox's College
Urry, Henry, tailor, 123 York
Valentine, John, M.D., 39 King w
Vance, James J., clerk of committee Leg. Assembly Parliament Buildings
Vandersmissen, W. H. German lecturer University, bds 165 Bay
VANKOUGHNET & LASH, (M. R. Vankoughnet Z. A. Lash) barristers, 74 Yonge
Vankoughnet, Hon. Philip, M. M. S., chancellor Ontario, h 283 King w
Vankoughnet, S. J., barrister, 64 Church
Vannevar, J. jun., bookseller and stationer, 338 Yonge
Varcoe, R., prop. Varcoe's Hotel, 153 Yonge
Vaughan, Patrick, grocer, 452 Queen w
Verner, F. A., artist, 64 King e
Vernon, Norton, manufacturing jeweler, 159 Yonge
Verrall, Walter, carriage builder, h 139 University
Vickers, J. J., prop. North Western Express, 55 Yonge
Victor, Thomas, Sumach cor King
Victoria Brewery, O'Keefe & Co., props. Gould cor Victoria
Victoria Hotel, G. H. Gray, prop., 460 & 462 Yonge
Villiers & McCord, (John Villiers and A. T. McCord, jun.) manufacturers and dealers in hoop skirts and fancy goods, 37 Yonge
Villiers, Thomas, carpenter and joiner, Prov. Ins. Chambers, Court cor Toronto
Vincent, Very Rev. C., Superior St. Michael's College, Clover Hill
Virtue & Yorston, publishers and importers, 55 Yonge
Volunteers' Drill Shed and Military School, s s Wellington w of Simcoe
Vyse, James, pattern maker, 39 Queen w
WADSWORTH & UNWIN, P.L.S., C.E., land and general agents, 42 Adelaide e
Wadsworth, Vernon R., P.L.S. and C.E., h 254 Wellington w
WAGNER, JACOB P., proprietor Toronto Central sash, blind and door manufactory, 71 and 73 Adelaide w (see adv)
Wainwright, James, shoemaker, 310 King e
Wakefield, W., civil engineer, 39 King w
Walker, C. & W., dry goods and clothing, 7 King e
WALKER, DAVID, proprietor American Hotel, Yonge cor Front
Walker, George, tobacco worker, 171 York
Walker, John, agent Ætna Life Insurance Company, Whittemore's bldgs
Walker, Robert & Sons, (Robert, Joseph and Robert I.), dry goods and clothing; wholesale, Nos. 18 and 20 Colborne; retail, 33 to 37 King e
Wallace, Hugh, clerk *Globe* Printing Co., King e
Wallis, A. W., druggist, 287 Queen w
Wallis & Cornnell, props. Queen Street Brewery, 619 Queen w
Wallis, John, M.P.P., Queen w
Walls, Thomas & Co., (Thomas Walls and Thomas Walsh), importers of woolens and dry goods, 28 Wellington e
Walsh & Co., (James Walsh and Christopher Willerton), soda water manufacturers, Clare
Walsh, J., pork dealer, 78 Front e
Walsh, John, captain and owner *Princess of Wales*
WALSH & LOVEYS, (James Walsh and George Loveys), lumber merchants, 88 and 90 King w
Walsh, Patrick, grocer, n s Queen nr Lumley
WALSH, RICHARD, Metropolitan Hotel
WALTON, BENJAMIN, builder and dealer in roofing, slates, slabs, &c., 221 Jarvis (see adv)
Walton, George A., agent Wheeler & Wilson's Sewing Machines, 105 King w
Walton, Henry, cutter, C. & W. Walker, 7 King e
Walters, L., new and second hand store, 180 King e
Walton, Matthew, insurance agent, h 24 Walton
WALZ, JOHN & CO., lager beer brewery, 74 Duchess
Wanless, John, watchmaker, 172½ Yonge
Ward, David, second hand broker, 281 Yonge
Ward, Edward, grocer, 24 Victoria
WARD, G., manufacturing jeweler, 60 Adelaide e (see adv)
Ward, James, butcher, 252 Yonge
Ward, Mrs. D., millinery and dress maker, 231 Yonge
Wardell, Jacob, variety and second hand broker, 213 King e
WARDELL, O., auctioneer, Jarvis
WARE, G. B., law stationer and lithographer, Masonic Hall, Toronto (see adv)
Warren, Nathaniel, grocer and provisions, 312 Yonge
Warrington, Misses Mary and Emma, ladies' boarding school, 6 Bond
Warwick, Mrs. Anna, boarding house, 11 Teranley
Warwick, Frederick, teacher, clerk St. James' Cathedral, h 59 Seaton
Warwood, James, manufacturer of bricks and sewer pipes, h Yonge r Cottingham, Yorkville
Washington, J., barber, 163½ York
Wathey, H. C., legal editor *Globe*
Watkins, John H., groceries and liquors, 300 Yonge
Watkins, Mrs. Henrietta, groceries, 267 Church
Watkins, L. A., grocer, 443 Yonge
Watson, Henry, prop. St. George's Saloon, 6 Richmond w
Watson, James, coffee and spice manufacturer, 85 Ann
Watson, Richard, tinware, 232 King e
Watt, Thomas A., upholsterer, 50 Edward
Waudby, Henry, marble cutter, Yonge w Isabella
Way, James, dry goods and groceries, 271 Queen w
Webb, Thomas, baker and confectioner, 302 Yonge
Webster, Mrs. Edward, dressmaker, 151 Yonge
Wedd, William, M.A., first classical master, U. C. College
Weekly Visitor (The) printed and published by G. H. Stewart, Louisa cor Yonge.
Weir, Alexander, boots and shoes, 603 Yonge
Weir, Thomas, commissary general, h 25 Windsor
Wellington Chambers, w s Jordan nr King
Wellington Gold Mining Co., of Madoc (limited) H. S. Ledyard, manager, sec. and treas., 74 Yonge
Welsh, Patrick, grocer, 466 Queen w
Wenman, Charles, butcher, 11 St. Lawrence Market
Wesleyan Book Rooms, Rev. S. Rose, steward, 78 King e

Wesleyan Mission Office, Rev. Enoch Wood, D.D., gen. supt., Rev. Lachlin Taylor, D.D., sec. and treas. Temperance r Richmond St. Church
Wesbroom, Mrs. W., dry goods, 220 Queen e
WEST END LA CROSSE CLUB rooms, Romain bldgs, King w
West, John, butcher, St. Patrick's Market, Queen w
West Toronto Brewery, Cosgrave & Co., props., cor Queen and Niagara
West, W. & Co., boots and shoes, 200 Yonge
West, William, furniture broker, 21 Adelaide e
Western Assurance Co., Hon. John McMurrich, pres.; Chas. Magrath, vice-pres.; B. Haldan, sec., J. Maughan, jun., assist. sec., 28 Church
Western Canada Permanent Building and Savings Society, W. S. Lee, sec. and treas., 70 Church
Western Marine Insurance Co., William Rowland, agent, 57 Wellington e
WESTMACOTT, W. M., agent Commercial Union Insurance Co., 72 King e
Westman, Joseph, bellows maker, 35 Queen w
Westman, Samuel, saw sharpener and umbrella repairer, 177 King e
WESTON, W. H., dealer in fruits, confectionery flowers, &c., 445 Yonge
Wetkowske, Louis, tailor, 66 Adelaide, e
WHARIN, W. & CO., watchmakers and jewelers, 11 King e
Wheeler, Thomas, wood engraver, 48 King e
WHITE, W. A., dealer in sewing machines, 90 King e
White, Rev. W. J., assistant St. Michael's Cathedral
Whitehead, Charles J., 113 Wellington w
Whitehouse, C. J., manuf. of tinware, 193 King e
Whitehouse, Nathaniel, pocket book manufacturer, 6 Richmond e
Whitley & Esten, (John Whitley and J. H. Esten), barristers, 64 Church
Whitney, George, land agent, 392 Church
Whitney, J. W. G., estate agent, Court cor Church
WHITTAKER, REV. GEORGE, M.A., professor of Divinity, Provost Trinity College, Trinity College, Queen
Whittemore's Buildings, Toronto cor King
Wickson, Rev. Arthur, L.L.D., Rector Toronto Grammar School, h 74 Church
WICKSON, JOHN, butcher, 6 St. Lawrence Market
Wickson, Samuel, solicitor, 74 Church
Widdowson, A., painter and glazier, 1 Shuter
Widgery, William M., oysters and fruit store, 72 Queen w
Wiesner & Co., wholesale hats, caps & furs, 35 Yonge
Wightman, George, produce and commission mercht, 36 Colborne
Wilby, Edward, children's carriage maker, 108 and 110 Richmond w
Wiley & Rowley, painters, 24 James
WILKES, R., wholesale jeweler, 48 and 50 Yonge
Wilkins, George, grocer, 335 King e
Wilkins, John, grocer, cor Palace and Trinity
Wilkinson, James, oysters and fruits, 222 Yonge
WILLCOCK, STEPHEN, watches and watch materials, 4 King e
Wilcocks, S., merchant tailor, cor Victoria & Adelaide
Williams, Rev. Alexander, (Church of England) 22 Mercer
Williams, C. M., undertaker, 193 Yonge
Williams, Edward, prop. Queen's Wharf Hotel, cor Front w and Bathurst
Williams, George, hotel keeper, 8 West Mkt Square
Williams, G. W., upholsterer, 601 Yonge
Williams, Isaac, boarding house, 98 Queen w
Williams, J. J., undertaker, 302 Queen w
Williams, Philip, grain merchant, 64 Duke
Williams, R. S., melodeon and organ dealer and dealer in musical instruments, 143 Yonge
Williams, Thomas R., hotel keeper, 176 Queen w
Williams, William, berlin wools and fancy goods, 184 Yonge
Williams, William, fancy goods, 127 King e
Williamson, A. J., M.D., clerk of correspondence, Education office, 15 Gould
Williamson, G. T., accountant Western Canada Permanent Building and Savings Society, 70 Church
Williamson, J., M.D., 15 Gould
WILLIS, REV. DR. MICHAEL, King w bet John and Peter
Willmott, Charles W., undertaker, 268 and 270 Adelaide w
Willmott, Edward, butcher, Yonge n s bet Bloor and Sydenham
WILLMOTT, GEORGE, groceries, provisions, wines and liquors, 374 Yonge (see adv)
Wills, G. S. & A., biscuit manufacturers, Adelaide w cor Bay
Wilson, Hon. Adam, judge Court Common Pleas, h Spadina Avenue
Wilson, Alfred, P.L.S., s s Church nr Isabella
Wilson, Andrew, grocery, 66 Agnes
WILSON, CHRISTOPHER, scale manufacturer, Toronto nr Adelaide (see adv)
WILSON, DANIEL, L.L.D., prof. of history, &c., University College, 107 Bloor
Wilson, David, boots and shoes, 27 King e
WILSON, GEORGE, prop. New Dominion Hotel, 66 and 68 Colborne (see adv)
WILSON, HON. JOHN, judge Court Common Pleas 29 Gould
Wilson, John & Co., pork and provisions, 77 Colborne
Wilson, John A., barber, 224 Queen w
Wilson, Mrs. Isabella, grocer, 130 Simcoe
Wilson, S. J., grocer, 516 Queen w
Wilson, Thomas, (Frank Smith & Co) cor Front e and Scott
WILSON, WILLIAM, vinegar manufacturer and manufr of cigar boxes, 115 and 117 Bay (see adv)
Windeat, William, photographer, 39 King w
Wingfield & Thomas, upholsterers cabinet makers and spring manfrs., 151 Yonge
Winstanley, O. S., M.D., 331 Yonge
Winter, Charles, soap factory, Palace
Withers, J. E., agent Lake Superior Silver Mines, 28 and 29 Exchange bldgs
Withrow & Hillock, builders and lumber merchants, 59 and 61 Adelaide w
WOOD, FREDERICK JAMES, hotel keeper, 461 and 463 Yonge
Wood, H. J., tinsmith, 113 Queen w
WOOD, HON. E. B., M.P.P., Provincial Treasurer, Ontario, Parliament bldgs
Wood, J. O., chemist and druggist, 61 King w
Woods, John, grocer Dundas cor Dover Court Road
Wood, R. A., chemist and druggist, 230 Yonge
Wood, Rev. Enoch, D.D., (Wesleyan Methodist) Davenport Road
WOOD, SAMUEL G., LL.B. (Smith and Wood) h 300 Jarvis
Wood, T. R., agent Ætna Fire Insurance Co. of Hartford, 58 Front e
Woodcock, Mrs. A., dry goods and millinery, 134 Yonge
Woodcock, James, hotel keeper, 2 Palace
Woodhouse, Henry, blacksmith, 10 Church

WOODLAND, G. & SON, boots and shoes, 303 Queen w
WOODSIDE, THOMAS, cashier, Royal Canadian Bank, Toronto
Woolgar, George E., second-hand broker, 96 Agnes
WORKMAN, BENJAMIN, M.D., Assistant Medical Superintendent, Provincial Lunatic Asylum
WORKMAN, JOSEPH, M.D., Medical Superintendent, Provincial Lunatic Asylum
Workman, Joseph, jun., clinical assistant, Lunatic Asylum
Worthington, John, contractor, Queen's Park
Worthy, Francis T., civil engineer, 19 Cruickshank
WORTS, JAMES G. (Gooderham & Worts) vice-pres. Bank of Toronto, h cor Front and Trinity
Wright, George H., hair dresser, 54 Adelaide e
Wright, George, M. D., cor Queen and James
Wright, H. C. & Co., paper bag manufacturers and printers, 22 Francis
Wright, Henry H., M. D., 187 Queen e
Wright, John, gas fitter, 387 and 389 Yonge
Wright, James, grocer, King cor Caroline
Wright, John T., barber, cor Church and Colborne
Wright, Mrs. J., dry goods, boots & shoes, 373 Yonge
Wright, Mrs. William, dry goods, 424 Queen w
Wright, William, tavern keeper, cor King e and Parliament
Wright, William, proprietor Welcome Home Inn, 327 and 329 King e
WRIGLEY, JOHN & WILLIAM, manufacturers of cotton and wool batting, woolen carpets, cotton and wool wadding, felt cloths, and dealers in general manufacturers stock, 68 and 70 Nelson
Wyatt, G. H., ship broker and freight agt 48 Front e
YARKER, GEORGE W., manager Bank of Montreal, cor Yonge and Front
YIELDING, WILLIAM, proprietor City Larder and lunch room, Post Office Lane
Yonge Street Whrf, Milloy & Co., (Donald Milloy & Thomas Burke)
Yorkville Brewery, Henry Severn, proprietor, Yonge, Yorkville
Yorkville Inn, Mrs. Elizabeth Kerr, Yonge, Yorkville
YOUNG, JAMES, produce and commission mercht, 42 Wellington e
Young Men's Christian Association rooms, F. W. Kingstone, librarian, 34 King e
YOUNG, ROBERT, manuf boots & shoes, 110 Yonge

TORONTO CLASSIFIED BUSINESS DIRECTORY.

Marked thus * are Wholesale.

Accountants.

Blaikie & Alexander, Jordan cor King
Christie, Alexander, 34 King e
Ebbels, John L., Yonge cor Adelaide
Fraser, James, 5 King w
Kerr, John, 3 British America Assurance Blgs., Court
Mason, William T., 5 Ontario Hall, Court
Pellatt & Osler, 86 King e
Spreull, Samuel, Jordan cor King

Agents.

Canada Machinery—
Levey, Charles, 73 Adelaide w

Canada Starch Company—
Crawford, D. & Co., Palace cor Princess

Cartage—
Hendrie, J. & Co., 19 Wellington e
Shedden, John & Co., 42 Front e

Collecting—
Butler, Wilkin B., *Leader* Buildings
Cupples & Hunter, 20 Toronto

Commission—
Christie, Alexander, 34 King e
Hope, W., 2 Victoria Hall
L'Estrange, W. J., 16 York Chambeas, Court

Emigration—
Donaldson, John A., York

Express—
Irwin, J. D., 57 Yonge

Fire Extinguisher—
James, Robert, jun., 6 Wellington e

House, Land and Estate—
Blaikie & Alexander, Jordan cor King
Butler, Wilken B., 2 *Leader* Buildings
Christie, Alexander, 34 King e
Cooper, William J., Romain Buildings
DeGrassi, A., 58 King e

Agents—*(Continued)*
Hime, Humphrey L., 6 Wellington e
Hope, William, 2 Victoria Hall
Jarvis, E. J., Whittemore's Block
Maitland, Robert, Toronto Exchange
Powell, John S., 139 York
Shortiss, Thomas, Toronto Exchange
Wadsworth & Unwin, 42 Adelaide e
Whitney, J. W. G., 2 British America Assurance Buildings

Insurance—
Bradburne, E., Toronto
Bradwell, J. W., Toronto
Clark, S. C. Duncan & Co., n w cor King and Church
Davidson, A., 49 Front e
DeGrassi, A., 33 King e
Fortier, Charles G., Ontario Chambers, Front corner Church
Fraser, James, 5 King w
Garvin, J., Whittemore Buildings, Toronto
Gilmor, Isaac C., 59 Colborne
Gooch, R. N., 32 Wellington e
Gregory, Joseph, 78 King e
Hime, H. L., 6 Wellington e
Jarvis, A., Whittemore's Building, Toronto
Maddison, G. L., 84 Bay
Mason, William T., 5 Ontario Hall, Court
Rollo, James, 62 Gerrard e
Rowland, William, cor Front and Church
Scott & Walmsley, Ontario Hall, Church
Smith, J. E. & Co., 81 Church
Unwin C., 42 Adelaide e
Westmacott, William M., 72 King e

Knitting Mashines—
Bailey, H., 28 King w

Lubricating Oils—
Clark, S. C. D., & Co., King cor Church

Agents—(*Continued*)

Mercantile—

Bradstreet, J. M., & Son, Bank of Toronto bdgs. Wellington e
Dunn, Wiman & Co., Exchange building, Wellington

Patent—

Christie, Alexander, 34 King e
Hancock, J. W. 20 Toronto

Piano Fortes—

Heintzman & Co., King w, adjoining Rossin House
Nordheimer, A. & S., 15 King e

Safes—

Boomer, A. K. (Kershaw & Edwards) 93 King w
Lewis, Rice & Son (J. & J. Taylor) King cor Toronto

Scales—

Boomer, A. K., 93 King w

Publishers—

Virtue, Yorston & Co., 57 Yonge

Sewing Machines—

Bailey, H., 28 King w
Black, Norris, (Singer) 18 King e
Boomer, A. K., 93 King w
Gates, G. W. & Co., manufacturers, office 14 King e
Mendon, L. C., (Howe & Wanzer), 3 Rossin House Block
Walton, G. A., 105 King w
White, W. A., 90 King e

Steamships—

Bourlier, Henry, Union Station
Clark, S. C. D. & Co., cor King & Church
Milloy, Nicol, 8 Front e
Scott & Walmsley, Ontario Hall, Church
Sylvester, Bro. & Hickman. 1 Ontario Chambers

Agricultural Implements,

(*See also Hardware Merchants.*)

Dawbarn, Charles & Co., 124 King e

Ale and Porter Vaults and Bottlers.

Morison, Malcolm, 12 Toronto
Heap, R. & Co., Leader alley
Toronto Bottling Co., James Leask, prop. 65½ Yonge

Architects, Civil Engineers & Surveyors.

(*See also Provincial Land Surveyors.*)

Armstrong, William, 42 King, e
Browne, John O., Whittemore's Buildings, Toronto
Gundry & Langley, Jordan, cor King
Harper & Son, Romain Buildings, King w
Irving, William, 120 Yonge
Kauffman, W., 14 Masonic Hall
Savigny, Hugh P., 32 Exchange Buildings
Shanly, Francis, 54 York
Shaw & Roberts, 64 King e
Smith, James, 11 King w
Stibbs, William John, 20 Adelaide w
Storm, William G., Romain Buildings, King w
Wadsworth & Unwin, 42 Adelaide e

Artificial Limbs.

Black, Norris, 18 King e

Artists.

Armstrong, William, 42 King e
Berthon, George T., 43 King w
Bridgman, J. W., 39 King w
Damoreau, Charles F., Bay cor King
Forbes, John, Romain Buildings, King w
Gilbert, George A., 48 Gerrard e
Halford, Josiah, 14 Alexander
Irwin, B., King w
Kane, Paul, 40 Wellesley
Martin, Thomas M
Verner, F. A.

Auction and Commission.

Andrews & Son, 109 Yonge
Coate, F. W. & Co., 57 King e
Dickson, J. H., Yonge
Douglas J. & Co., 92 Yonge
Henderson, Andrew, 65 Yonge
Morell, A. & Co., 148 King e
Solomon, Mark, 142 King e

Bakers.

Aitken, William, 72 Queen, w
Bain, John, 311 Queen w
Beatty, Charles, Berkeley
Bee, David, corner Church and Magill
Berrie & Brisbane, 333 Queen w
Booth, John, 131 York
Burness, Henry, Queen cor Nelson
Carrick, Mrs. M. A., 49 Richmond w
Christie, William, 526 Yonge
Coleman, George, 99 King w
Coles, William, Yonge
Compton, Arthur, 171 King e
Gibb, Lawrence, 74 Adelaide w
Gillett & Allen, 147 York
Hammond, Samuel, 69 King w
Herbert, John, 148 Queen w
Hope, Edward, Yonge, Yorkville
Kinzinger, Jacob, 100 York
Marshall, J. S., 99 Church
Middleton, Francis, 158 King w
Murray, W. H., 225 Yonge
McDonald, Donald, 265 Queen w
Nasmith, John, 66 Nelson
Nasmith, Mungo, 372 Yonge
O'Halloran, John, 381 Queen w
O'Halloran, M., 130 Jarvis
Rattray, Alexander, 148 Yonge
Reed, Alexander, 5 McMahon
Reeves, Richard, 60 Centre
Reynolds, Frank, 1 Gould
Riddell, Francis, 60 Elizabeth
Slater, James, 359 Yonge
Sutherland & Marshall, 15 Denison av

Banks.

Bank of British North America, Yonge cor Wellington
Bank of Montreal, cor Yonge and Front
Bank of Toronto, Wellington cor Church
Bank of Upper Canada, trustees' office, Ontario Hall, Church
Canadian Bank of Commerce, Yonge cor Colborne
City Bank, Montreal, cor Bay and Wellington
Merchants' Bank, 13 Wellington w
Ontario Bank, Wellington cor Scott
Quebec Bank, Wellington nr Church
Royal Canadian Bank, Toronto opp Post Office

Banks, Savings.

Merchants Savings Bank, 18 Wellington w
Toronto Savings Bank, 72 Church

Bankers.—*(See also Brokers, Stock, Money and Exchange.)*

Beaty, Robert, 53 King e
Browne, P. & Co., 67 Yonge
Campbell & Cassels, 60 King e
Forbes & King, 30 King e
Joseph, Henry, 82 King e
Morse, H. J. & Co., 50 King e
Paterson, William & Co., King nr Church
Phipps, W. B., 5 Toronto

Barbers and Hairdressers.

Bailey, J. A., 28½ King w
Bansley, Charles, 71 King w
Cain & Carter, 172 Yonge
Carter, George, Queen's Hotel
Cary, G. W., 10 Front, e, and 154 Yonge
Casey, Thomas P., Rossin House
Copley, James, 238 Yonge
De La Hunt, Thomas, 70 Colborne
Edmunds, Elisha, 292½ Yonge
Harley, T. H., 77 Yonge
Hollin, David, 39 East Market Square
Nelson, Henry, 32½ King w
Robinson, Alfred, King e
Robinson, Thomas, 147 Yonge
Scott, William, 47 George
Smart, J., King w
Smith, W. G., 134½ King w
Thomas, Robert, East Market Square
Washington, James, 173½ York
Wilson, John, 222½ Queen w
Wright, George H., 54 Adelaide e
Wright, John, cor Church and Colborne

Barristers, Attorneys and Solicitors.

Allen, Robert Mahon, York Chambers, Court
Anderson, J. T., Osgoode Hall
Armour & Hoskin, Jordan, cor King
Atkinson & Boswell, 62 King e
Ault, William, Yonge cor King
Barrett & Evans, Colborne, cor Exchange Alley
Barry, Thomas, York Chambers, Court
Barwick, Frederick D., Romain Buildings, King west
Beatty & Chadwick, 58 King e
Bell, Crowther & Tilt, s e cor Church and King
Bigelow, N. Gordon, cor King and Toronto
Birtch, R. S., Court
Boulton, James, 44 Church
Boyd & Stayner, 70 King e
Blain, Ferguson & Parkinson, s w cor King and Yonge
Blake, Kerr & Wells, 4 & 5 Masonic Hall
Bull & Williams, 1 and 2 Masonic Hall
Blevins & Duggan, 39 Church
Cameron, Harman & Murray, Romain Buildings, King w
Cameron & Holmested, cor King and Church
Cameron & McMichael, 44 Church
Cameron, McMichael, Fitzgerald & Hoskin, 44 Church
Cameron & Smart, Whittemore's buildings, Toronto.
Canavan, John, 58 King e
Capreol, J. L., 3 York Chambers, Court
Clark, Alister M., 4 Wellington Chambers, Jordan
Clark, William M., 48 King e
Crawford & Crombie, Masonic Hall
Crickmore, John, 70 King e
Crooks, Kingsmill & Cattenach, 19 Wellington w

Barristers, Attorneys, &c.—*(Continued)*

D'Allain, A. J., cor King and Toronto
Denison, George T., jun., 8 Wellington Chambers
Dingwall, J., M.A., Ontario Hall
Doyle, J. H., 20 Toronto
Duggan & Meyers, Provincial Insurance Buildings, cor Court and Toronto
Durand, Charles, 1 Adelaide e
English & Foster, Ontario Hall, Church
Fraser, Robert, 44 Church
Freeland, William, *Leader* Buildings, King e
Galt & Henderson. Royal Insurance Buildings, Yonge cor Wellington
Gamble & Boulton, Court, cor Church
Greene, C. H., 40 Adelaide, e
Harman & Hagarty, Church
Hancock, John W., 22 Toronto
Harris, Rusk, 64 Church
Heath, C. W., D'Arcy
Hector, John, 11 King w
Helliwell, John, cor Church & Wellington
Heyden & De Foe, 74 Church
Hodgins, Thomas, 6 Masonic Hall, Court
Hurd, E. E. W., York Chambers
Ince, T. Henry, 6 Wellington e
Jarvis, Stephen M., 22 King e
Jones, Bros., 7 & 8 Masonic Hall
Kingstone, F. W., 62 Church
La Penotiere, Frederick J., Court, cor Toronto
Ledyard, Thomas D., 74 Yonge
Leith & Kennedy, 41 Melinda
Leys, McMurrich & Robertson, s e cor King and Church.
Macdonald, Stephens & Howard, 9 and 10 Wellington Chambers, Jordan
Macdonnell, Alexander, 56 Church
Mackenzie & Scott, 19 Toronto
Maclennan & Henderson, 8 and 9 Ontario Hall
Macnabb & Morgan, Court
Magrath, Charles, 65 Colborne
Miller, Robert, 86 King e
Morphy, Sullivan & Fenton, Express Buildings, 55 Yonge
Morris & Smith, 1 Wellington Chambers, Jordan
Morrison & Sampson, Western Ins. Co.'s bdgs
McBride, John, 40 Adelaide e
McCaul, G. Lefroy, 85 King e
McCutcheon, P. McGill, 40 Adelaide e
McDonald & Chadwick, Whittemore's Buildings, Toronto
McGregor, Patrick, 26 Adelaide e
McLean, A. G. & T. A., 12 Melinda
McMurray & Rae, York Chambers, Court
McNab, Murray & Jackes, Court House
Murphy, N., Adelaide e
Nicol, William B., 60 Adelaide w
O'Brien, Henry, 68 Church
O'Connor, Warmoll & Givins, 44 Church
O'Donohoe & Devlin, 62 Adelaide e
Paterson, Harrison & Bain, Ontario Hall, Court
Paterson, Harrison & Paterson, Ontario Hall, Court
Patterson, John H., York Chambers, Court
Patterson, Beaty & Hamilton, 8½ King w
Patton, Osler & Moss, 7 and 8 Exchange Bdgs., Wellington e
Reid, John B., 62 Church
Read & Boyd, 77 King e
Richards & Smith, cor King and Yonge
Roaf & Downey, Mechanics' Institute, Church
Robinson, Christopher, 68 Church

Barristers, Attorneys, &c.—(*Continued*)

Robinson, Hon. J. B., 68 Church
Rose, John E., 78 King e
Ross, Lauder & Mulock, Masonic Hall
Shortiss, Edward, Exchange bdgs
Smith & Wood, 4 Wellington e
Snelling, Richard, *Leader* bdg, King e
Spencer & McDonald, 1 and 2 Masonic Hall
Stanton, William H., Provincial Insurance bdgs, Court
Strathy, John, 119 Simcoe
Strong, Edgar & Grahame, 7 and 8 Wellington Chambers, Jordan
Taylor, T. W., Osgoode Hall
Thorne, Horace, Court
Vankougnet & Lash, Yonge cor King
Vankoughnet, S. J., 64 Church
Wickson Samuel, 74 Church
Whitley & Esten, 64 Church

Basket Maker.

Moses, Walter W., 291 Yonge

Baths.

Brent, Mrs. G. W., (Turkish), Bloor, Yorkville
City Baths, 10 and 12 Adelaide w
Rossin House, King, cor York

Bellows Maker.

Westman, Samuel, 35½ Queen w

Berlin Wools.

Ashall, Mrs. E., 284 Yonge
Ovens, John, 126 Yonge
Pollard, Mrs. S., 4 King e
Williams, William, 127 King e

Billiard Rooms.

Brown, George, Queen's Hotel
Fairfield, H. B., (Fountain), 69 King e
McGinn, James, Golden City Billiard Parlor, 41 King w
Palmer, Joseph, 131 King e
Riley & May, Revere House, cor King and York
Rossin House, cor King and York
Thomas, M. A., English Chop House, 30 King w

Billiard Table Manufacturers.

Riley & May, York nr King

Bill Posters.

Jackman, Henry, 68 Agnes
Jackson, Thomas, 31½ Queen w

Biscuit Bakers. (*See also Bakers & Confectioners.*)

Christie, Brown & Co., Yonge
Dodgson, Shields & Co., Yonge cor Temperance
Lawson, Edward, 93 King e
Nasmith, John, Nelson
Wills, G. S. & A., 121 Bay

Blacking Manufacturers.

Lamb, Peter R. & Co., rear Necropolis

Blacksmiths.

Ablitt, George, 326 Richmond w
Ash, Mrs. Rebecca, 164 Queen w
Berry, James, 111 Richmond w
Boatman, Charles, 485 Queen w
Briscoe, William, 127 and 129 Queen w
Dewdney, R., 99 and 103 Parliament
Donough, William, 14 Edward
Dunn, Daniel, 5 Church
Fitzgerald, John, 52 Queen w
Gellatly, David, 564 King w
Hobbs, James, 25 Adelaide w
Hodgson, Robert, lane off Scott
Holman, Joseph, 358 Queen w
Moore, Richard, Palace nr George
Oulstar, Peter, 7 Richmond w
Pim, Henry, 453 Yonge
Thomas, Victor, cor King and Sumach
Walker, Thomas, 79 George
Woodhouse, Henry, 10 Church
Woods, Wm., cor. Queen and Dundas
Wootton, Joel, 52 Queen w
Wright, Charles, 82 Richmond w

Blank Book Manufacturers.—(*See also Book-binders.*)

Brown Bros., 66 & 68 King e
Chewett, W. C., & Co., 17 & 19 King e
Dredge, A., & Co., 53 Yonge
Lovell, A., & Co., 67 Yonge
McPhail, Robert, Exchange Alley

Boarding Houses.

Adams, Robert, 242 King e
Alderdice, Mrs. M., 138 John
Ashley, Mrs. Ann, 135 Adelaide w
Barker, Mrs. R., 14 Temperance
Barlow, Miss Sarah, 126 Brock
Boyd, A., Queen w, nr Niagara
Briggs, Henry, 105 Sayer
Burns, Patrick, 28 Francis
Butters, Mrs. Sarah, 226 Church
Carfrae, Margaret J., 34 Scott
Carter, John, 88 Bay
Casper, Samuel, 23 Adelaide w
Clarke, Mrs. Anne, 4 Spadina Avenue
Clarke, Miss M. A., 100 Church
Cooper, Thomas, 51 Queen
Cosens, Mrs. Mary, 68 Shuter
Cunningham, Mrs. M., 14 Shuter
Dosser, W. R., 47 Richmond e
Douglass, Miss Ellen, 111 Bond
Douglass, Mrs. S. M., 51 Richmond e
Duncan, Mrs. Charlotte, 227 Palace
Dunlop, Mrs. Elizabeth, 73 Bay
Elliott, Humphrey, 16 Richmond e
Feehan, Mrs. C., 17 Richmond e
Glann, Mrs. J., 10 Bond
Graham, Mrs. E. rear 30 King w
Graham, Patrick, 44 Scott
Gravison, Mrs. M., 499 Yonge
Grey, Mrs. Jane, 51 Queen e
Haslip, Thomas, East Esplanade
Hewton, Mrs. M., 168 Richmond w
Holmes, Miss Catherine, 150 Queen w
Hudson, James, 75 Peter
Huggins, Mrs. John, 432 Queen w
Humphries, Mrs. V., 18 Magill
Hurley, Mrs. Janet, 12 Temperance
Irwin, Miss Susan, 86 Adelaide w
Joice, Thomas, 70 Bond
Kerby, Mrs., 49 Richmond e
Layton, Mrs. Emma, 14 Emma
Lennox, Mrs. E., 166 Mutual
Lenny, Mrs. G., 121 Simcoe
Lovelock, Wm., 73 Peter
Lowe, Mrs. J. F., 92 Bay
Major, Mrs. C. B., 164 York
Mason, James, 28 Victoria
Miller, Mrs. Rebecca, 204 Victoria
Mitchell, Rebecca, 168 King w
Morley, Mrs. Ann, 84 Richmond w
Mullen, Mrs. 6 Shuter
Murray, Mrs. J., 7 Albert

Boarding Houses—(*Continued*)

Murray, Mrs. M., 300 Jarvis
McClune, Miss M.' 131 Victoria
McCoy, Mrs. Hester, 158 Berkeley
McPherson, Miss Jessie, 151 Church
Newbigging, Wm., 32 Front e
Newlove, Mrs. Charlotte, 73 George
Noden, Miss M., 188 Church
Ovens, Mrs. Eliza, 88 Richmond e
Palmer, John, 26 Temperance
Palmer, Miss Lucy, 206 Church
Penfold, Mrs. P., 122 York
Pettet, Mrs. Annie, 40 Nelson
Phair, Mrs. Margaret, 112 Victoria
Phillips, Mrs., 78 Agnes
Ramsay, Mrs. 61 Ann
Rankin, Mrs. Eliza, 156 Adelaide w
Scath, John, 202 Church
Shannon, James, 105 Adelaide e
Shaw, Miss Charlotte, 49 Queen e
Smith, Elias, 138 York
Smith, Mrs. Jane, 60 Bay
Smith, Mrs. Mary, 134 King w
Stewart, Miss Ida A., 43 Richmond e
Stewart, Miss Lucy, 60 Albert
Summerville, Mrs. Margaret, 8 Bond
Taylor, Mrs. E., 121 Church
Taylor. Mrs. Jane, 39 Alice
Thomas Mrs. W., 173 Church
Thompson, Mrs. Mary, 12 Front e
Timmons, Miss Mary, 144 York
Turriff, Mrs. L., 21 Adelaide w
Wadsworth, Mrs. 79 Victoria
Walker, Mrs. M., 31 Temperance
Walker, Mrs., 47 Queen e
Walsh, Mrs., 56 Richmond e
Woods, Ann, 86 Berkeley
Wylie, Mrs., 129 Church
Yates, Mrs., 68 Albert

Boat Builders.

Akroyd, Henry, Yonge-street wharf
Clendinning, John A., Esplanade, foot of Scott
Loveys, Samuel, Esplanade, foot of Church
Noverre, Frank A., Esplanade, nr Simcoe
Rennardson, Robert, Esplanade, foot of George

Boiler Makers.

Currie, Neil, Esplanade foot of Church
Dickey, Neil & Co., 22 Beverley

Bolting Cloths.

Oates, R. H., cor Esplanade and Church

Bone Manufacturers (ground).

Lamb, Peter R. & Co., rear Necropolis

Bookbinders.

Blackhall, J., 74 King e
Brown Bros., 66 and 68 King e
Chewett, W. C. & Co., 17 and 19 King e
Christian Guardian Office, 80 King e
Dredge, A. & Co., 53 Yonge
Lovell, A. & Co., 67 Yonge
McPhail, Robert, & Co., Exchange Alley

Bookbinders' Materials.

Brown Bros., 66 and 68 King e

Booksellers and Stationers.

*Adam, Stevenson & Co., 61 King e
Backas, C. A., 3 Toronto
Bain, James, 46 King e
Baptist, Book Room, 11 King w
*Campbell, James & Son, 9 Toronto
Carless, J., Bible and Tract Depository, 102 Yonge
Carswell, Robert, 6 King w
*Chewett, W. C. & Co., 17 and 19 King e
Church Society, Diocese of Toronto, Book Room, 76 King e
Donelly, John, St. Lawrence Arcade
Doyle, Patrick, 6, 8 and 10 St. Lawrence Arcade
Edwards, John, 136 Yonge
Irving, A. S., 35 King w
Johns, Robert, 301 Yonge
Maclear. Thomas, Victoria Hall
Matthews, Henry, sen., 241 Yonge
*Miller, Adam, 62 King e
Miller, James, 272 Yonge
Piddington, Alfred, 248 and 250 Yonge
Primitive Methodist Book Room, 89 Yonge
Rowsell, Henry, 74 and 76 King e
Shaw, Alexander, 29 King w
Shewan, M., 1 and 3 St. Lawrence Aarcade
Thompson, R. S., 49½ King w
Wesleyan Book Room, 80 King e

Boot and Shoe Manufacturers and Dealers' Wholesale.

Cobley, H. & Co. (cack), 55 Front e
Childs & Hamilton, 7 Wellington e
Damer & Co., 97 Yonge
Paterson, J. & J., 148 King e
Robinson & Pearson, 54 Yonge
Sessions, Turner & Co., 8 Wellington w
Thompson & Son. 136 and 138 King e

Boot and Shoe Manufacturers and Dealers, Retail.

Bachly, Christian, cor Dalhousie and Queen
Bain, James & Co., 125 King e*
Bain, Patrick, 180½ Queen w
Barron, John, 149 King e
Barron, John, 40 West Market Square
Barron, William, 205 King e
Beatty, Charles, 164 Yonge
Beatty, Joseph, 251 Yonge
Blachford, A., 107 King e
Brooke, C. R. & Co., 115 Yonge
Brownscombe, Henry, 123 King e
Butler, Patrick, 272 Queen w
Callaghan, Hugh, 318½ Queen w
Campbell, John, 26 Wellington e
Clarke, Frederick, 86 Yonge
Corcoran, John, 222 King e
Cornish, Theophilus W., 637 Yonge
Cornish, Joshua H., 240 Yonge
Cowan, Robert, 277 Queen
Curry, Michael, 258 King e
Cuthbert, S., 367 Yonge
Dack, E., 73 King w
Damer & Co., 97 Yonge
Donohoe, Francis, 33 Queen w
Downing, Thomas, 246 Yonge
Durham, Michael, 38 Victoria
Faulkner, William & Co., 3 King w
Gemmell, Alexander. 97 King w
Gilles, Thomas, 51 Edward
Gilmor, William, 100 Lumley
Gloster, Thomas, 17 Melinda
Guinane, William, 105 Yonge
Hamilton, George, 33 Denison Avenue
Harnett, Maurice, 89 Church
Harris, Samuel, 160 King e
Hayes, William, 304 Queen w

Boot & Shoe Manufac'rs—*(Continued)*

Hick, Henry, 9 Sayer
Hodgins, Thomas, 306 Queen w
Holmes, John, Agricultural Buildings, Yonge cor Queen
Hunter, Robert, 42 Nelson
Jack, James, 8 Jordan
Kincade, Robert, 356 Yonge
Knox, John, 468 Queen w
Koerber, Louis, 120 York
Lamb, John, 183 Yonge
Langston, Thomas, 224 King e
Langton, Thomas, 174 King e
Leslie, Alexander, 81½ King e
Leslie, James, 113 King w
Loane, William, 171 King e
Lownsborough, William, 193 Queen w
Martin, George, 96 York
Mason, John, 215 King e
Merrifield, Robert, 190 Yonge
Mullen, Andrew, 347 Yonge
Murphy, Philip, 23 Richmond e
Murphy, Thomas, 122 Yonge
Murphy, Thomas, 442 Queen w
McCormick, Richard, 175 York
McEntee, John, 133 Yonge
Nacy, Thomas, 62 Bathurst
Parr, Edwin, 21 Adelaide w
Paterson, J. & J., 148 King e
Rahelly, Gerald, 145 Yonge
Reynolds, Richard, 152 Yonge
Robertson, A., Rossin House block, King
Rollins, J. H., 119 Yonge
Savage, James, 8 Jordan
Smith, John, 123 Yonge
Smith, John, 142 Little Front
Sparrow, George, 198 Yonge
Spurgeon, John, 296 King e
Stanley, Robert, 386 Yonge
Taylor, Robert, 300 King e
Wainwright, James, 310 King e
Way, James, 271 Queen w
Weir, Alexander, 603 Yonge
Weir, James, Yonge, Yorkville
Wilson, David, 25 King w
Woodland, G. & Son, 303 Queen w
Young, Robert, 110 Yonge

Bowling Alleys.

Bennett, James, 18 Terauley
Layton, H. U., Caer Howell Hotel
Montreal House, 146 King w

Box Manufacturers.

Firstbrook & Read, 265 King e

Brewers and Maltsters.

Aldwell & Co., 126 William
Copland, W. (East Toronto), Parliament cor King
Cosgrave & Co. (West Toronto), Queen w, nr Niagara
Davies, T. & Son (Don Brewery), River
Thompson & Allen (East End Brewery), 192 Beech cor River
O'Keefe & Co. (Victoria), Gould cor Victoria
Severn, H. (Yorkville Brewery), Yorkville
Sproatt, C. (Spadina), 145 Vanauley
Wallis & Cornnell (West Toronto), 619 Queen w
Walz, J. & Co., Duchess cor Caroline

Brokers (General).

Anderson, C. E., *Daily Telegraph* building
Armitage, William, 194 Queen e
Blumenthal, John, 210 King e
Clark, Capt. J., Exchange Buildings
Harvey, S. G., 36 Colborne
Hope, William, Victoria Hall
Howard, Smith & Co., Ontario Chambers, Front cor Church
King, Robert, 379 Yonge
Lynn, Henry S., 80 Church
Macrae, J. C., 16 and 17 Ontario Chambers
Shortiss, Thomas, Toronto Exchange, Wellington e

Brokers (Insurance).

Jarvis, A. M., Whittemore's Buildings, Toronto
Sylvester, Brothers, & Hickman, Ontario Chambers, cor Front and Church

Brokers, Shipping.

Wyatt, George H., 48 Front e

Brokers, Stock, Bill, Money and Exchange

(See also Bankers and Brokers.)

Beaty, Robert, 53 King e
Browne, Phillip & Co., 67 Yonge
Campbell & Cassels, 60 King e
Forbes & King, 30 King e
Joseph, Henry, 82 King e
Morse, H. J. & Co., 50 King e
Mortimer, Herbert D., 1 Victoria Hall, Melinda
Patterson, William, & Co., King e nr Church
Pellatt & Osler, 86 King e
Phipps, William B., 5 Toronto
Rowland, William, cor Front and Church
Stibbs, James, 20 Adelaide w
Stow, Frederick P., Jarvis

Broom Manufacturers.

Barton, John, 11 Dundas
Caulkins & Sanderson, 434 Yonge
Morey, J. W., 83 Queen w

Brush Manufacturers.

Boeckh, Charles, 98 Berkeley
Murphy, Joseph, 140 Centre
Pullen, Joseph, 260 Yonge
Smith, Alexander, 54 Dundas
Wilson, James, 12 Louisa

Builders and Contractors.—*(See also Carpenters and Builders.)*

Adams, John, 91 Elm
Ardagh, Arthur, 230 Queen e
Armitage, John, 423 King e
Armstrong, Robert, 55 Richmond w
Atkinson, John, 27 Edward
Booth, James, 8 Don
Booth, S., 10 Adelaide e
Brown, George, 196 John
Burke, William, 19 Sheppard, cor Richmond
Campbell & Barton, 199 Yonge
Carroll, Robert, Sheppard, nr Richmond
Cavie, William, 40 Magill
Clements, John, Front opp Queen's Hotel
Clements, T. & C., 37 and 39 Nelson w
Coleman, Arthur, 179 Dalhousie
Dinnis, Richard, 48 Bay
Dodds, Robert, 8 Osgoode
Downey, Thomas, 66 Terauley
Emery, George, Alexander
Farley, James, 163 Jarvis
Fowler, Robert, 390 Yonge
Gearing, Joseph, 425 Yonge
Greenlees, John, 108 Terauley
Hall, William, 76 Seaton

Builders & Contractors—*(Continued)*

Harper, John, 161 Simcoe
Joselin, Henry, Alexander
Kerr, John, rear 88 Spadina Avenue
Lamb, William, 183 King w
Leslie, Robert, 35 Terauley
Moulds, William, Mercer, nr John
McBean, James, 33 Walton
McDonald, D. & T., 80 Albert
Parker, Samuel. cor Carlton and Seaton
Petch, Robert, 3 Victoria
Phillips, J. W., cor Terauley and Hayter
Plenderleith, James, Sayer nr Edward
Plenderleith, John, 38 Trinity Square
Rawlin, William, 87 Centre
Robins, William, 126 Richmond w
Scott, Peter A., 618 Yonge
Scott & Stollery, Esplanade cor Bay
Shaw. George, 20 Nassau
Snarr, Thomas, 168 George
Stevenson, Edward, 448 Parliament
Storm, Thomas, 141 Queen e
Synge, Edward, 131 Richmond w
Wagner, Jacob P., 71 and 73 Adelaide w
White, George H., Avenue Road, Yorkville
Wilson, John, 116 McMahon
Worth, Benjamin, 148 Richmond w

Builders' Materials.

Dinnis, Richard, 48 Bay
Gearing, Joseph, 425 Yonge
Scott & Stollery, Esplanade, foot of Bay

Building, Savings, and Investment Societies.

Canada Permanent Building and Savings Society Masonic Hall
Commercial Building and Investment Society, 120 Yonge
Freehold Permanent Building and Savings Society Church cor Court
Metropolitan Permanent Building Society, 5 King w
Provincial Permanent Building and Savings Society, Toronto, adjoining P. O.
Union Permanent Building and Savings Society, 80 King e
Western Canada Permanent Building and Savings Society, 70 Church

Butchers.

Ablett, Fred. & Wm., St. Lawrence Market
Awde, William, 458 Queen w
Bell, Anthony, 356 Yonge
Bells, Thomas H., 60 Queen w
Bergin, James, 387 King e
Bird, H. & E., 323 Yonge
Bird, William J., 235 Yonge
Blong, Henry, 5 St. Lawrence Market
Bonnick, Joseph, 377 Yonge
Boyce, Joseph, 111 Queen w
Breen, P. & D., 21 St. Lawrence Market
Bright, William J., 63 Seaton
Britton, J., 13 and 15 St. Lawrence Market
Campton, Thomas, 133 York
Compton, B. H., 167 King w
Coxon, George, 361 Yonge
Crawford, Samuel, 100 Caroline
Davies, F. N., 237 Yonge
Denyer, William, 289 Yonge
Dever, William, 36 King w
Doughan, S. N., 307 Church
Duffy, Charles, 4 St. Lawrence Market
Dunn, James R., 377 Queen w
Dunning, Caleb H., 10 St. Lawrence Market
Edwards, Thomas, 409 King e
Emery, Joseph, 51 Garrison
Flanigan, Cornelius, 172 Queen w
Frankland, G. F. 20 St. Lawrence Market
Gallagher, John, 185 Parliament
Garton, John, 326 Yonge
Gilbert, Albert, Hayden
Grainger, George, 629 Yonge
Grundler, Gottleib, 98 Church
Harbell, H. W., 120 Church
Herson, J., 18 St. Lawrence Market
Hutty & Gray, 8 St. Lawrence Market
Jones, William, 142 King w
King, William, 36 St. Lawrence Market
Kupitz, Edward, 27 Queen w
Mainprice, Charles, 444 Queen w
Mallon & Co., 12, 14 and 16 St. Lawrence Mkt
Maplebeck, John, 244 King e
Marriott, J. G., 115 Queen w
Meehan, John, 26 St. Lawrence Maket
Moore, Henry, 28 St. Lawrence Market
Moxon & Reeves, 20 St. Lawrence Market
Mumford, James, 261 Yonge
McBride & Emery, 544 Queen w
McCarter, John, 7 and 9 St. Lawrence Market
McLean, William G., 1 St. Lawrence Market
Oxenham, William, 100 Queen w
Palk, Edward, cor Queen w and Brock
Parry Brothers, 231 Yonge
Quinn, John, 25 St. Lawrence Market
Richardson & Brothers, 200 Queen e
Robinson & Brown, 2 St. Lawrence Market
Roberts, George, 168 Yonge
Rosback, George, 78 Queen w
Sieber, Andrew, 226 Adelaide w
Smith, Henry, Avenue Road, Yorkville
Smith, James, 1 St. Lawrence Market
Stellwagen, Mrs. Josephine, 98 Agnes
Thompson, A. J., 431 Yonge
Toy, Samuel, 17 and 19 St. Lawrence Market
Tucker, William, 378 Queen w
Ward, James, 252 Yonge
Watts, George, Parliament cor Beach
Wenman, Charles, 11 St. Lawrence Market
West, John, St. Patrick's Market
Wickson, John, 6 St. Lawrence Market

Cabinet Makers and Upholsterers.—*(See also Upholsterers, also Furniture Dealers.)*

Dewar, Michael, r 47 Queen w
Gibson, H., 15 James
Hulme, Mrs. G. L., 194 King e
Jacques & Hay, King cor Jordan
McRobie, Alexander, 252 Yonge
Schomberg, Henry A., 187 Yonge
Williams, George W., 601 Yonge
Wingfield, J. M., 151 Yonge

Cabs and Childrens' Carriages.

Phipps, George, 84 King w
Sharpley, Benjamin, 612 Yonge
Wilby & Cartwright, 110 Richmond w

Cack Manufacturer.

Cobley, Henry, 35 Front e

Carpets & Floor Oilcloths.—*(See also Dry Goods.)*

Hughes & Co., 128 and 130 King e
Graham, Henry & Co., 3 King e
McDunnough & James, 84 King e
Wrigley, J. & W., 68 and 70 Nelson

Carpenters and Builders.—*(See also Builders and Contractors.)*

August, Alfred, 38 King w
Booth, Samuel, 10 Adelaide
Ellis, William, 14 Sheppard
Finch, John, 59 University
Ford & Forbes, 37 Richmond w
Humphrey, Simon, 13 James
Johnson, T. R., West Market
Kitson, John, sen., 21 Maria
Lees, R. B., 3 Adelaide e
Morrow, John, 21 Elizabeth
Moulds, William, 11 Nelson
McCarthy, Callaghan, 155 Queen w
Oliver, John, Richmond w
Pettigrew, S. & Co 113 Richmond w
Pettit, George, 92 Bay
Reid, George, rear 55 McMahon
Richey, Louis, 355 Queen w
Rooke, Thomas 361 Queen w
Wilkinson, Christopher, 32 Power
Withrow & Hillock, 59 and 61 Adelaide w

Carriage & Coach Builders.—*(See also Blacksmiths and Waggon Makers.)*

Briscoe, William, 127 and 129 Queen w
Butt, Ephraim, 15 Agnes
Clark Brothers, 151 York
Coghill, Robert, 163 King w
Dixon Bros., 70 & 72 King w
Walker, John, Yonge, Yorkville

Carriage Hardware.

Brown, William, 72 King e
Davidson, McVittie & Co., 152 King e
Trees, Samuel, & Co., 69 Colborne

Carriage Trimmings, Wholesale.

Brown, William, 72 King e

Carvers and Gilders.—*(See also Picture Frame Makers.)*

Laird, Robert W., 79 King w
Matthews, Henry J., 189 Yonge
Pell, James C., 106 York
Phillips, R., 53 King w

Car Wheel Manufacturers.

Scoville, J. & N. C., Esplanade

Chemists and Druggists.

Blume, Michael, 117 Queen w
Brumell, Henry P., 13 King e
Coombe, John, 104 Yonge
Davids, Joseph, 169 King e
*Dunspaugh & Watson, 3 Front e
Emery, Robert, 62 Queen w
Hallamore, John, 374 Queen w
Harvard, A., 290 Queen w
Hodgetts, George, 279 Yonge
Holmes, Ninian L., 216 Queen e
*Hooper, E., & Co., 43 King w
Howarth, John, 243 Yonge
Howson, Joseph, 86 Queen w
*Kerry, Crathern & Co., 41 Yonge
Leslie, George H. & Co., Yonge, Yorkville
Love, Neil C., 129 Yonge
Lund, Dr. Richard, 337 King e
*Lyman, Elliott & Co., St. Lawrence Hall, King e
Lyon, J. F. & Co., 57 Richmond e
Matheson, Angus, 138 and 140 King w
*Miller, Hugh & Co., 167 King e
O'Connor, Thaddeus J., 251 King e
Raffan, Joseph, 184 Queen w
Riddel, C., J. & Co., 217 Queen e
Robinson, William S., Yonge, Yorkville
Rose, Henry J., 155 Yonge
Shapter & Owen, 78 Yonge
Smith, William, M.D., 292 Yonge
Wood, John G., 61 King w
Wood, Robert A., 230 Yonge

China, Glass and Earthenware.

Campbell, M., 252 Yonge
Crawford, Arthur, 164 Yonge
Farley, Arthur, 291 Queen w
Gunn, Murdoch, 207 King e
*Harris, Edwin, 40 King e
*Harrison, Glover, 71 and 73 King e
*Hurd, Leigh & Co., 72 Yonge
Passmore, James, 297 Yonge
*Patton & Co., 64 King e
Piddington, Alfred, 248 and 250 Yonge
Robinson, Charles, 346 Yonge
Sinclair, John, 245 Yonge
*Thompson & Burns, Front w

Chiropodist.

Briggs, D. J., 6 King w

Cigar Box Manufacturer.

Wilson, William. 115 and 117 Bay

Cigars and Tobacco.

Carlisle, George W., Terrapin Restaurant
Collis, George A., & Co., Yorkville
*Drouillard, Felix, 13 King, w
Gagnier, Theodore C., 67 King e
Hackmann, D., 120½ York
*Klopp, William, 27 King w
Nerlich, H. & Co., 6 Rossin House Block
Sadd, J., 65 King w
Schadel, Charles, 98 York
Schuster, L., 339 and 341 Queen w
Sievert, Louis, 62½ Queen w
Spooner, James, 41 King e
*Taylor & Wilson, 114 Yonge

Cloaks, Shawls and Mantles.

Cox, G. & J. W. & Co., 115 and 121 King e
Dickson, Crawford & Smith, 91 King e
*Henderson & Bostwick, 11 Wellington w
*Hughes Brothers, 62 Yonge
Kay, John, 1 King e
*Macdonald, John, & Co., Wellington e
Murray, W. A. & Co., 21 King e

Clothes Renovators.

Alexander, Junius, 84 Queen w
Judah, Philip, 163½ York
Newton, George, 29 James
Robson, Hugh, 298 King e
Stokes, George, 22 Adelaide e
Swain, John, 20 Victoria
Wilson, Mrs. Sarah, 116 Church

Clothiers.—*(See also Merchant Tailors.)*

Brimer, John, 171 Yonge
Brownlee & Conn, 151 King e
Eastwood, J. & Son, 122 King e
Finch, William S., 6 King e
Hughes & Co., 128, 130 and 132 King e
Melady, P. & N., 141 King e
Murray, W. A. & Co., 21 King e
Pringle, T. M. & Co., 153 King e
Robinson, Thomas, 127 Yonge
Shaver & Bell, 2 St. Lawrence Hall
Walker, Robert & Sons, 35 and 37 King e

Clothing Wholesale.

Henderson & Bostwick, 11 Wellington w
Hughes Brothers, 62 Yonge
Lailey, Thomas & Co., 11 Wellington w
Livingston, Johnson & Co., 51 Yonge
Thompson & Son, 136 & 138 King, and 2, 4, 6 & 8 Francis
Walker, Robert & Sons, 35 and 37 King e

Coal and Wood, Dealers in.

Aikens, James, St. Lawrence Wharf, foot West Market Square
Beard, E, & Co., foot of Church
Bell, Thomas, 199 Queen West
Burns, Patrick, Queen's Wharf
Chaffey, E. & Co., 49 Front e
McBride, Samuel, Edward, n Elizabeth
Myles, James, Esplanade, near Church, and Toronto, cor Adelaide
Myles, William, Front, bet Yonge and Bay
Nicol, Joshua J., Front e, cor Scott
Snarr, John, Front e, near Yonge
Smith, C. J., Victoria
Tinning, R. & Brothers, Tinning's Wharf, Esplanade, foot of York
Wyatt, George H., Ontario Wharf, Esplanade

Coffee and Spice Mills.

Crawford, D. & Co., Princess, nr Palace
Pears, George, Yonge, cor Alexander

Comb Manufacturer.

Bothwell, Robert C., 112 Yonge

Commercial Colleges.

British American Commercial College, Odell & Trout, Whittemore's Buildings, Toronto, and 55 Yonge
Day, James E., 82 King e

Commission Merchants.—*(See also Forwarding, Shipping and Commission.)*

Boomer, A. K., 93 King w
Boustead, J. B., 82 Front e
Brown, James, jun., 24 Exchange Rotunda
Brunskill & Kirby, 78 Front e
Chisholm, T. C., 88 Front e
Clarkson, Thomas & Co., 83 Front e
Coffee, L., & Co., 2 Manning's block, Front
Cummer, F. D., 8 and 9 Ontario Chambers, Front e
Davidson, David, 80 Front e
Dobson, W. E., Yorkville
Douglas, J. & Co., 92 Yonge
Evans, Sherwood & Co., 15 Wellington e
Evans, J. Ick, 9 Douro
Farrell, Samuel W., 78 Front e
Fisken, John & Co., 58 Yonge
Galbraith, William, 6 Manning's Block, Front
Gooderham & Worts, 10 and 12 Exchange Blgs, Wellington e
Harris, J., 85 Front e
Holcomb, S. F., Toronto Exchange, Wellington e
Howard, Smith & Co., 4 Ontario Chambers, Front cor Church
Howland & Fitch, 10 and 12 Exchange Blgs
Hurrell C. T., 82 Front east
Laidlaw, Douglas, 80 Front e
Lillie, F. W., 74 Queen w
Macrae, J. O., 16 and 17 Ontario Chambers
Matthews, W. D. & Co., 16 Front e
Nixon, Thomas, 79 Colborne
Perry, Charles & Co., 56 Front e
Quigley & Miles, Ontario Chambers
Reford & Dillon, 12 Wellington e
Scott & Gorrie, Church-street Wharf
Sorley, James B., 25 Front e
Spratt, Robert, 31½ Church
Young, James, 42 Wellington

Confectioners.—*(See also Bakers & Confectioners.)*

Chard, Charles, 318 Yonge
Cox, James, 165 Yonge
Craig, James F., 91 Church
*Dodgson, Shields & Co., Yonge cor Temperance
Hamlin, E. H., 107 King w
Haycock, William, Yonge, Yorkville
*Hessin, William, 7 Front
Ives, Esther, 40 Queen w
Jose, Richard, 285 Queen w
*Lawson, Edward & Sons, 93 King e
Murray, William, 225 Yonge
*Pocknell, Richard T., 33 King w
Reid, John, 111 King w
Robertson Bros., 258 Yonge
*Smith & Wills, 264 Yonge
Soyer, Alfred, 131 Yonge
Tucker, Edward, 281½ Yonge
Webb, Thomas, 302 Yonge

Consuls.

Dixon, B. Homer, Consul General of the Netherlands and Consular Agent, Carleton
Macdonell, W. J., French Consular Agent, 24 Church
Thurston, D., United States Consul, Masonic Hall

Contractors.—*(See also Carpenters and Builders.)*

Boyd, Robert, 231 King e
Carruthers, John, 14 Don
Daly, Edward, 79 Peter
Dinnis, Richard, 48 Bay
Ginty, John, 148 Adelaide w
Manning Alexander, 89 Wellington w
Scott & Stollery, Esplanade, cor Bay
Worthington, John, 8 Queen's Park

Conveyancers.—*(See Barristers, Attorneys, &c.)*

Coopers.

Bevan, J. W., 622 Yonge
Carmichael, Robert, 9 Adelaide e
Dathie, Robert, Riordan's Row, Palace
Delaney, Thomas, 361 King e
Hardy, Edward, 7 South Park
Lendreville, Joseph, 438 Queen w
McManus, James, 25 Queen w
O'Brien, Michael, 19 Palace
Reynolds, James, rear 38 Terauley
Thompson, Samuel, Duchess nr George
Williams, John, Yonge, Yorkville

Coroners.

Buchanan, C. W., M.D., 51 Adelaide w
Hallowell, Wm., M.D., Gloucester Row, Ontario
Hodder, E., M.D., 159 Queen w
Lawlor, Michael, M.D., 187 Richmond w
Riddel, A. A., M.D., 217 Queen

Cotton Manufacturers.

Gordon, Mackay & Co., 9 and 11 Wellington e

Cotton Wool and Batting.

Wrigley, J. & W., 68 and 70 Nelson

Cutlers.

Brimstin, Hugh, 288 Yonge
Callard, Josiah, 316 Queen w
Rodgers, S. & G., 166 King e

Dentists.

Adams, W. C., 95 King e
Elliot, George L., 31 King e
Elliot, John W., 43 and 45 King w, h same. References: The Rt. Rev. The Lord Bishop of Toronto; The Rt. Rev. The Lord Bishop of Huron; The Rt. Rev. The Lord Bishop of Ontario
Hale, George W., 9 Temperance
Hopkins, S. J., 137 King e
Myers, William, 45 King e
Snider, Martin, 81 King e
Trotter, R. G., 53 and 55 King e

Designers and Stampers.

Davis, Isaac, 228 Yonge
Pollard, Mrs. Mary, 4 King e

Distillers.

Fitzhenry & O'Donohoe, 61 Little Front
Gooderham & Worts, Trinity cor Esplanade
Hubertus, W. L. & Co., 14, 16 and 18 Church

Drain Pipe, Tile and Brick Manufacturers.

Douglas & Bulmer, Yonge, Yorkville
Nightingale, Thomas, Yonge, Yorkville

Dressmakers.—(*See also Milliners and Millinery Goods*).

Batten, Mrs. Maria, 127 Adelaide w
Chapman, Mrs., 105 Berkeley
Cluskey, Miss Minnie, 23 Centre
Cook, Miss, 307 King e
Cornell, Mrs. T., 154 Centre
Cumming, Miss Mary, 178 King w
Delancey, Mrs. L., r 40 Denison
Donagh, Mrs. E., 9 Emma
Dunn, Mrs. Judith, 63 Emma
Dunn, Miss M. A., 60 Victoria
Egan, Miss M., 46 Albert
Fraser, Miss M., 160 Victoria
Green, Miss C., r 70 Duchess
Guinane, Mrs. Willam, 105 Yonge
Harnett, Miss M., 68 Queen e
Hart, Miss Charlotte, 213 Elizabeth
Heyden, Mrs. M., Elizabeth, n College ave
Hore, Mrs. E., 22 Albert
Ivery, Mrs. M. A., 34 Louisa
Johnson, Miss, 225 Church
Jones, Mrs. T., 97 Parliament
Macarthy, Mary A., 376 Yonge
Mills, Miss Margaret, 68 Terauley
Mortimer, Josephine, 57 University
Munn, Mrs. Elizabeth, 368 Yonge
Munn, Mrs. H., High
McMahon, Eliza, 137 Agnes
Oliver, Miss S. I., 12 Victoria
Parkin, Anne, 25 Renfrew
Pettigrew, Mrs. Louisa, 129 Elm
Radford, Miss Carrie, 42 Wellington w
Radford, Miss Margaret, 42 Wellington w
Robinson, Ann, 336 Yonge
Smith, Mrs., 229 Yonge
Tait, Miss, 70 McGill
Thompson, Jane, 17 Pine
Weaver, Mrs. R., 46 Agnes
Webster, Mrs. E., 151 Yonge
Welch, Mrs. Mary Ann, 17 Shuter
Whitlow, Miss Fanny, 135 Vanauley
Young, Miss Mary, 47 North

Dry Goods, Wholesale.

Arnott, David, 39 Yonge
Bryce, McMurrich & &o. 34 Yonge
Charlesworth, John & Co., 44 Yonge
Dobbie & Carrie, 3 Wellington e and 45 Yonge
Eaton, T & Co., 14 Front w
Gordon, Mackay & Co., 9 and 11 Wellington e
Hoskins, R. A. & Co., 5 Wellington e
Hughes Brothers, 62 Yonge
Jennings & Brandon, 38 Yonge
Macdonald, John & Co., 21 and 23 Wellington e
Moffatt, Murray & Beattie, 36 Yonge
McMaster, A. R. & Brother, 32 Yonge
Robertson, John, Son & Co., 70 Yonge
Rooney, N. & F., 60 Yonge
Shaw, John & Co., 10 Wellington e
Thompson & Son, 136 and 138 King e, and 2, 4, 6 and 8 Francis
Walker, Robert & Sons, 18 Colborne

Dry Goods, Retail.

Aikenhead, Helen, 20 Queen w
Aird, M. J., 66 and 68 Queen w
Arthurs, William & Co., 25 King e
Brown, Francis, 81 Sayer
Brown, William, 416 Queen w
Bruce, James, 315 Yonge
Callard, Harriet, 316 Queen
Catto, John & Co., 59 King e
Chandler & Platts, 165 King e
Cox, G. & J. W. & Co., 115 to 121 King e
Dickson, Crawford & Smith, 91 King e
Dow, William H. & Co., 1 King cor Yonge
Drummond, James, Queen w nr Portland
Dunn, John W., 206 and 208 Yonge
Eastwood, John & Son, 122 King e
Gale, James W., 116 Yonge and 55 King w, cor Bay
George, D. J., 277 Yonge
Gibbs, M., 210 Yonge
Goodwin, Mrs. Mary, Yorkville
Graham, Bernard, St. Lawrence Hall, 161 King e
Grayson, Isaac, 267 Queen w
Halliday, Mrs. M., 430 Queen w
Hanratty, J. J. & Co., 137 and 139 King e
Hewett, William, Yorkville
Hughes & Co., 128 and 130 King e
Janes, Brayley & Newcombe, 57 King e
Jeffrey, William H., 27 Gould
Jennings, James, 187 Yonge
Kay, John, 1 King e cor Yonge
Meakin, William, 181 Yonge
Melady, P. & N., 141 King e
Merrick & Brother, 47 and 49 King e
Mitchell, William, 103 King e
Morell, M. S., 254 Queen w
Murray, W. A. & Co., 21 and 23 King e
McCaffrey, Miss Sarah, 292½ Queen w
Martin & Echlin, 147 King e
Noble, George & Co., 214 Yonge
O'Donnell, M., 182 Yonge
O'Malley, John, 76 Queen w
Page & Pannell, 194 and 196 Yonge
Passmore, Mrs., 232 Yonge
Pearson, M. & E., Yonge cor Richmond
Pringle, T. M. & Co., 158 King e
Robinson, J. D. R., 200 Yonge
Robinson, Thomas, 127 Yonge
Rowland, John, 173 Yonge

Dry Goods, Retail—(*Continued*)

Scott, James, 97 King e
Shaver & Bell, 2 St. Lawrence Hall
Simmons, Miss Clara, Yonge, Yorkville
Stalker, John, 192 Yonge
Tenison, & Hunter, King, e cor Church
Thompson & Son, 136 and 138 King e
Walker, Robert & Sons, 35 and 37 King e
Way, James, 271 Queen w
Wesbroom, Mrs. William, 220 Queen e
Widdy, John, 271 Yonge
Wright, Mrs. Janet, 273 Yonge
Wylie, Robert J., 118 Yonge

Dyers.

Harris, William H., 152 King w
Royle, James, 104 York
Smith, David W., 75 King w

Edge Tool Manufacturers.

Rodgers, S. & G., 166 King e

Elevators.

Northern Railway Co., foot of Bathurst
Shedden, John & Co., Grand Trunk
Taylor, Archibald, foot of George

Enamellers, China and Glass.

Hurd, Leigh & Co., 72 Yonge

Engine Builders (*See also Foundries and Machine Shops*).

Beckett, Edward (Globe Foundry), 44 Queen w
Dickey, Neill & Co. (Soho Foundry), 22 to 30 Beverley
Good, James, 6, 8 and 10 Queen e
Hamilton, William & Son (St. Lawrence Foundry, Palace
Martin, James & Son, Ontario Lane, off 209 Queen e

Engineers, Civil (*See Architects, Civil Engineers and Surveyors*).

Engravers, Copper, Steel and Wood.

Damoreau, C. F. Bay, cor. King
Nelson, J. B., 22 King e
Rolph, Joseph T., 11 King w
Wheeler, Thomas, 48 King e

Envelope Manufacturers.

Buntin, Bros. & Co., 63 and 65 Yonge
Dredge, A. & Co., 53 Yonge

Exchange, Dealers in (*See Brokers, Stock, Bill and Exchange.*)

Express Companies.

American Merchants Union, J. D. Irwin, 55 and 57 Yonge
Bradford, Robert (City), 75 Yonge, and 211 King e
European Express Company, J. D. Irwin, 55 and 57 Yonge
Peacock, James (City), 54 Caroline
Merchants' Despatch, J. D. Irwin, 55 and 57 Yonge
Terry, John (City Parcel), Adelaide cor Yonge, and King cor Caroline
Vickers, John J., N. W. Express, 55 Yonge

Fancy Goods (*See also Berlin Wools*).

Ashall, R. M., 286 Yonge
Barnett, Edward, 358 Yonge
Ellis, Mrs. Margaret, 84 Queen w
Bothwell, Robert C., 112 Yonge
Butler, Alfred, 85 Queen w
Callard, John, 166 Queen w
Carto, Benjamin, 260 King e
Champion, Jones, 330 Queen w
*Cox & Co., 28 Wellington e
Crawford, Arthus, 164 Yonge
Croft, William, 37 Colborne
Davis, Mrs. M. A., 375 Queen w
Harris, William, 310 Yonge
Harsant, M., 304½ Queen w
*Henderson & Bostwick, 18 and 20 Wellington w
Jorrey, Samuel, 234 King e
*Joseph, J. G. & Co., 46 Yonge, and 5 King e
*May, Thomas & Co., 68 Yonge
Miller, James, 272 Yonge
McPhee, Mrs. E., 408 Queen w
Pendergast, Mrs. T., 297½ Yonge
Piddington, Alfred, 248 Yonge
Rennie, Mrs. A. M., 354 Yonge
Sheppard, Charles, 255 Yonge
Solomon, S. M., 264 King e
Spence, Mrs. J. L.. 437 Yonge
*Stern, S., Victoria Hall, Melinda
Thomson, R. S., 49½ King w
Thompson, William, 382 Yonge
Williams, William, 127 King e

Fire Hose and Leather Belting Manufac'trs

Marks, William, 34 Temperance

Fishing Tackle.

Leckie, John, 35 Colborne
Robinson, Joseph & Co., Sheffield House, 15 King w
Wilkes, Robert, 50 Yonge

Flour and Feed.—(*See also Provision Dealers.*)

Bickerstaff, Joseph, 375 Yonge
Bickerstaff & Bro., 243 and 245 Queen w
Bradford, Robert, 75 Yonge and 274 King e
Byers, Allan, 94 Church
Dixon, William, 249 King east
Equi, Louis, 263 Yonge
Fowles, Robert, 411 Queen w
Godson, George, 182, Queen w
McIntosh, W. D., 209 Yonge
Rock, M., 359 Queen w
Rooney, James, 81 Church
Spratt, Robert, 31½ Church
Terry, John, Adelaide cor Yonge, and King cor Caroline
Watkins & Lumbers, 111 and 113 Adelaide e

Flouring Mills.

Boulton, H. J., New Don Mills, Front nr Bay
Gooderham & Worts, 10 and 12 Exchange buildings, Wellington e
Howland & Fitch, 10 and 12 Exchange buildings, Wellington e

Foundries and Machine Shops. — *Thos marked thus (*) are brass.*

Armstrong, J. R. & Co. (City Foundry), 161 Yonge
Beckett, Edward (Globe Foundry), 42 Queen w
*Collins, John, 112 Bay
*Crapper, J., 88 Adelaide e
Dickey, Neill & Co. (Soho Foundry), 22 Beverley
Fensom, John, 33 and 35 Adelaide w
Good, James, Yonge cor Queen
Gurney, E. & Co. (Phœnix), 91 Yonge
Hamilton, William & Son (St. Lawrence Foundry), 136 Palace

Foundries and Machine Shops—(*Continued*).

Medcalf, E. & A. (Don Foundry), 489 King e
*Morrison, James, Bay cor Temperance
*Parker, J. O., 148 York
*Ritchie, John, 192 King e
*Smith, H. T., 95 Queen w

Fish, Oysters, Game and Confectionery.—*See also Confectioners.*)

Bilton, Wm., 121 and 123 King e, & 188 Yonge
Brydon, George, 207 King e
Bugg, Charles, 296 Yonge
Clegg, T., 227 King e
Denneler, G., 24 York
Dunn, Justus, 166 Yonge
Dunn, T. J. & Co., King w cor York
Hamlin, Edward H., 107 King west
Hamlin & Co., 119 Yonge
Lindsay, Henry, 54 King w nr Bay
Moffat, Mary, 426 Queen e
O'Dea, Miss Ann, 7 and 9 St. Lawrence Arcade
Reid, John, 111 King, w
Ruddell, Joseph, 366 Queen w
Russell, John F., 11 St. Lawrence Arcade
Ryan, Hope, 4 and 5 St. Lawrence Arcade
Smith, W. W., 94 Queen w
Taylor, William, 94 Yonge
Widgery, William M., 72 Queen w
Wilkinson, James, 220 Yonge

Furnaces (Hot Air).

Boxall, John, 50 Queen w

Furniture (Manufacturers and Dealers).—(*See also Cabinet makers and Upholsterers*).

Bond, John, 201 and 209 King e
Francis, Thomas, 197 Yonge
Frith, William, 170 Queen w
Hulme, Mrs. G. L., 194 King e
Jacques & Hay, King, cor Jordan
Phipps, George, 84 King w
Roberts, George, 168 Yonge
Schomberg, Henry A., 187 Yonge
Williams, J. J., 302 Queen w

Gas Companies.

Consumers' Gas Company, 19 Toronto

Gents' Furnishing Goods.—(*See also Clothiers and Merchant Tailors.*)

Gale, J. W., King cor Bay

Gilders.—(*See Carvers and Gilders, also Picture Frame Makers.*)

Glass Stainer.

McCausland, Joseph, 8 King w

Glue Manufacturers.

Lamb, Peter R. & Co., r Necropolis
Tiffin, Arthur, 458 King e

Gold and Silver Leaf, and Dental Foil Manufacturer.

Hubbard, Charles H., 28 Adelaide w

Gold and Silver Platers.

Campbell, G. L., 20 Toronto
Millichamp, Wallace, 80 Queen w
Ward, George, 60 Adelaide e

Gold and Silversmiths.—(*See also Watchmakers and Jewelers.*)

Ellis, James E. & Co., 43 King e
Joseph, J. G. & Co., 5 King e
Morrison, W. C., 12 King w
Robinson, Joseph, & Co., 15 King w
Rudolph, A., 72 Adelaide e
Wharin, William, & Co., 11 King e

Grindstones, &c.

Scott & Stollery, Esplanade cor Bay

Grocers, Retail.

Ablitt, William, King cor Ontario
Adams, William, 29 East Market
Alexander, Mrs. Janet, 370 Queen w
Armstrong, George, 48 Richmond w
Armstrong, J. D., 148 King e
Ash, William, 220 Queen w
Aspden, Henry, 120 Victoria
Bartram, Thomas, 179 Centre
Bartrem, David, 38 Centre
Bartrem, Thomas, 18 Christopher
Beatty, Adam, 126 Queen e
Beatty, Adam, 24 Bishop
Beatty, Charles, 222 Queen e
Becket, C. C., Yonge, Yorkville
Bee, David, Church cor Magill
Best, John, 213 Sayer
Beswick, James, 26 West Market Square
Bickerstaff, Joseph, 375 Yonge
Bickerstaff & Brother, 243 and 245 Queen w
Bird, Peter, 279 Queen w
Blong, Mrs., widow, George, Queen cor McMahon
Blumenthal, Ady, 210 King e
Bolton, John P., 18 Palace
Bond, Mrs. Lydia, 114 Elm
Bowden, John, 129 York
Boyd, Robert, 231 King e
Boyd, Mrs. Sarah, 285 Church
Brassington, Richard, Seaton cor Gerrard
Breadon, Thomas, 89 Terauley
Bridge, James T., 38 Denison Avenue
Briggs, William H., 303 Yonge
Brook, Joseph, 90 Church
Brophy, Mrs. Rose, Pine e
Brown, George, 346 King e
Brown, John, 27 Stanley
Bullman, William, 51 Elizabeth
Burgess, Ralph K., Beech
Burns, James, Palace, nr Trinity
Burns, John, 28 Queen
Burns, John, cor Queen w and James
Byers, Allen, 87 Church
Byers, William A., 97 Church
Cameron, James, 136 Brock
Campbell, Wm., 14 Palace
Carberry, Kennedy, 228 Sayer
Carrick, Mrs. M. A., 49 Richmond w
Cathcart, James, 356 Queen w
Clarke, Henry D., 95 Church
Clarke, Joseph C., 136 King w
Clarkin, Bernard, 23 Queen e
Clegg, Joseph, 52 Terauley
Clegg, Thomas, 227 King e
Close, P. G., 10 Palace
Clyne, William, 112 Caroline
Cooper, John, 420 Front
Cooper, William, 249 Queen e
Coxon, Samuel, 220 King e
Cosgrove, Owen, 178 Queen w

Grocers, Retail—(*Continued*)

Crawford, Thomas, 58 Elizabeth
Crawley, Abraham, 60 Dummer
Crooks, James, 12 St. Andrew
Curran, James, 136 Spadina Avenue
Curran, Patrick, 23 Shuter
Curran, Robert, 161 Parliament
Daley, Alexander, 188 Centre
Davies Brothers, 6 Palace
Davis, George W., 17 Scott
Davis, R. & Co., cor King and Bay
Dawson, John, 77 Centre
Dean, John, 6 Osgoode
Dee, Thomas, 42 West Ontario
Delaney, Thomas, 385 King e
Dender, George, 24 York
Denison, G. W., 193 Dundas
Devlin, Hugh, John, cor Adelaide
Dodgson, Shields & Co., 137 Yonge, cor Temperance
Dorsey, John, 132 York
Doughty, Mrs. Jane, 554 Yonge
Douglas, John, 77 Hayter
Duffy, Robert, 148 Beech
Dugdale, William, 44 Nelson e
Duggan, John, 243 Church
Dunbar, Richard, 32 West Market Square
Dundas, Alexander, 92 Church
Emery, Thomas, 462 King e
Equi, Louis, 263 Yonge
Evans, Simon, 215 Queen e
Fairfield, Alfred, 322 Yonge
Farley, Arthur, 291 Queen w
Farley, William, cor Yonge and Maitland
Farquharson, P., 194 Adelaide w
Faulkner, M. B., 342 Yonge
Fee, John, 437 King e
Fee, Joseph, 451 King e
Ferry, Thomas, 114 Duchess
Fife, Hugh, cor Maria and Elizabeth
Flannagan, Mrs. Mary, 491 Richmond
Flavell, John, 99 Elizabeth
Foster, David, 385 Adelaide w
Foster, John, Queen w, cor Simcoe
Fowler, Robert, 411 Queen w
Foy, William, cor Richmond w and York
Fulton, Michie & Co., 7 King w
Gavin, Richard, 204 Queen e
Garry, James, Yonge, Yorkville
Gates, W. E., 262 King e
Gibbings, Thomas, 147 Victoria
Gibson, Alexander, 227 Parliament
Gibson, Joseph, Yonge, Yorkville
Gilmor, William, 100 Lumley
Godfrey, M., 114 Richmond w
Goodman, Mrs., Strachan Avenue
Gorman, Mrs. Ann, 34 Power
Gourlay, David, 269 Yonge
Graham, Isaac, 80 Sayer
Grainger, Mrs. M., 587½ Queen e
Grayson, Isaac, 267 Queen w
Greensides, William, Yonge, Yorkville
Griffith, J. C. & Co., 219 and 221 Yonge
Hackett, John, 87 Queen w
Hague, William, 202 Queen e
Happer & Hutchinson, 149 York
Hasson, John, 17 Adelaide w
Helbert, James, cor Herbert and Bishop
Henderson, George, 328 Queen w
Harbell, Hugh W., 112 Church
Harper, Daniel, 149 York
Herbert, Peter, King w, cor Portland
Hesson, Eliza, 90 Bay
Hewet, Richard, 156 Centre
Hickey, Mrs. H., 552 Queen w
Hickling, Charles, 219 Palace
Hickman, William, junr., 92 Queen w
Hilts, Samuel, 114 Sayer
Hockady, William, 29 Strachan
Hodgins, William, 310 Queen w
Hodkinson, John, 435 Yonge
Hollings, David, 96 Cueen w
Hornibrook & LePan, 167 Yonge
Hozack, Luke, 446 Queen w
Hunter, Hugh, 296 Yonge
Hunter, Mrs. P., 49 Elizabeth
Hynes, Michael, 218 Queen
Irwin, Richard, 58 McMahon
Island, John, 235 King e
Ives, Mrs. Hester, 40 Queen
Jackson, Thomas, 132 Agnes
Jaffray, Robert, 244 Yonge
James, Robert, 177 Centre
Jardine, Alexander, 28 West Market
Jardine, A., 88 Queen w
Jenkins, Frederick, 82 Queen w
Johnston, Alexander J., 135 Sayer
Jordan, R., & Co., King w cor York
Judah, Adolphus A., 163 York
Kain, Mrs. B., Adelaide cor Portland
Kain, Francis, Sumach cor Queen
Keith, George, 23 East Market
Kennedy, Thomas, 205 Queen w
Kennelly, Andrew, 48 Bathurst
Kerr, James, 90 Albert
Kerr, John, 229 Church
King, James, cor Caroline and Duchess
Kingsbury, James, King cor Don
Kingsley, William, cor Queen and Pine
Kinsman, William, 178 Terauley
Lambrick, William, 37 Bishop
Larkin, Thomas, 55 Sayer
Lavin, Thomas, 89 Nelson e
Law, John, 300 Yonge
Lawrence, J. W., 360 Yonge
Lawson, Edward & Sons, 93 King e
Lawson & Hargrave, 170 King e
Lawson, Meredith & Co., 242 Yonge
Le-, William H., 512 Queen w
Lennox, Edward, cor Magill and Church
Lewis, George, 175½ York
Lillie, F. W., 74 Queen w
Lindsay, Henry, 54 King w
Liston, James, 19 Adelaide e
Liston, William, 303 King e
Little, Andrew, Portland cor Richmond w
Little, Robert, 94 Richmond e
Lock, John, Davenport Road, Yorkville
Locke, Francis, 165 King w
Low, John, 300 Yonge
Love, William, 414 Queen
Lumbers, J. & T., 146 King e
Lumsden, James, cor King and Pine
Lusty, Mrs. S., 229 Palace
Lynch, Denis, cor Pine and James e
Macdonald, Peter, 103 Church
Macfarlane, Malcolm, 95 Nelson
Madigan, Patrick, 87 Nelson
Maguire, John, 78 Gerrard
Maher, Patrick, 16 East
Mallick, James, 201 Elizabeth
Mara, Thomas A., 288 Queen w
Marks, Robert, 108 Agnes

Grocers, Retail—*(Continued)*

Marsh, John, 316 King e
Marx, Francis, 125 Queen w
Matthew, J., 56 Dundas
Maxwell, Mrs. E., 383 Parliament
Metcalf, Mrs. E., 29 Camden
Michie, William, cor Albert and Sayer
Miller, John, 280 Yonge
Milligan, A. & Co., 1, 2 and 3 City Hall bldgs
Mills, John, 24 Francis
Mills, John, 228 Pine
Mills, Robert, 315 Church
Milne, William, Spadina Avenue
Mishaw, Thomas B., 388 Queen w
Mitchell, Mrs. A., 410 Queen w
Mitchell, Mrs. B., 173 King w
Mitchell, James, 121 Beech cor Pine
Mitchell, Richard, 84 Edward
Mooney, Owen, 40 Victoria
Moore, William, 283 and 283½ Queen w
Morphy, John, 31 Terauley
Morrison, John, 234 Queen w
Moses, Andrew, 562 Yonge
Mossman, James, 205 Church
Muckle, Mrs. Margaret, 83 Elizabeth
Mulholland, Mrs. Elizabeth, 34 Queen w
Mulvy, John, 479 and 481 Queen w
Murphy, Andrew, cor King and Power
Murphy, Mrs. C., 22 Shuter
McCann, Thomas, 258 Lumley
McCleary, Robert, 191 Elizabeth
McClelland, John, 160 Berkeley
McCormick, Thomas G., 342 Yonge
McDonagh, Mrs. Mary, 74 Elizabeth
McDonald, Peter, 103 Church
McFarren, Andrew, 195 King e
McGowan, Samuel, 59 Agnes
McKenzie, William, 112 York
McMullen, Archibald, 343 Queen w
McNamara, Mrs. A., 380 and 382 Adelaide w
Neil, Joseph, 33 Sayer
Nolan, M., 17 Queen w
North, William, 67 Victoria
Nurse, Richard, 314 Church
O'Brien, Mrs. M., cor Church and Stanley
O'Connor, John, 10 Queen w
O'Connor, Thomas, 197 and 199 King e
O'Dea, Miss M., 78 Church
O'Hagan, James, 326 Queen e
O'Leary, Thomas, cor Nelson and Queen e
O'Leary, Timothy, 181 Queen w
Orton, Robert, 507 Centre
Palmer, Hamilton, 77 Sayer
Parkes, John, 155 Berkeley
Parkes, W. R., 246 King e
Paterson, James, 128 York
Patterson, Alexander, 287 Yonge
Patterson, James, 104 and 106 Adelaide w
Patterson, Thomas, 224 Queen e
Penfold, Mrs. P., 122 York
Peters, Robert, 484 Queen w
Peters & Donald, 140 King e
Playter, J. W. & R., 27 Palace
Powell, John, 348 King e
Power, Joseph, 424 Queen w
Price, George, 244 Queen w
Quinn, John, 150 and 152 York
Ramsay, James, 120 Sayer
Ramsay, William., 126 Berkeley
Rattray, Frederick A., 220 Yonge
Reid, Thomas, 639 Yonge
Reesby, Henry, Yonge, Yorkville
Richards, Henry, Yonge cor Magill
Richards, William M., 329 Yonge
Richardson, David G., 31 Terauley
Richardson, W. P., 246 King e
Riddell, Francis, 60 Elizabeth
Riddell, Joseph, 60 and 62 Edward
Robb, James, 177 Centre
Robertson, William, 205 Bishop
Robertson Brothers, 258 Yonge
Roblin, M. G., 223 Yonge
Rock, Michael, 359 Queen w
Rodgers, Mrs. Ellen, 96 Parliament
Rogers, John, 108 Centre
Rosenbury, C. E., 53 Queen w
Ross, David, 55 Queen w
Rowland, Thomas, 66 and 68 Centre
Ruse, Charles, 379 Queen w
Rush, Francis, 415 Queen w
Ryan, Mrs. B., 71 Stanley
Ryan, John, 176 Parliament
Ryan, John, 98 Parliament
Sanderson, George, 158 Terauley
Sanderson, John, 206 Sayer
Scholes, Richard, 161 Lumley
Shultz & Co., cor Queen w and Portland
Scoley, Edward K., 37 and 39 St. Lawrence Market
Scott, George, Town Hall Block, Yorkville
Sibbet, Mrs. Mary, 200 Queen
Simpson, George, 62 Cherry
Simpson, Thomas, 126 York
Sinclair, H. F. G., 12 Palace
Skaith, Mrs. Phœbe, Yonge cor Wood
Skinner, Rufus, 149 Yonge
Sloan, James A., 195 and 197 Queen w
Smith, Henry, 346 Adelaide w
Smith, William, 1 and 13 Victoria
Somers, John, 184 Terauley
Spence, John, 195 and 197 Queen w
Spence, William, 186 Centre
Stacy, Benjamin, 42 Camden
Staurdy, Frederick, 42 Elizabeth
Steel, John, 58 Agnes
Stennett, Thomas, Yonge, Yorkville
Stephens, Robert, 83 Albert
Stephens, James, 67 Elizabeth
Stewart, Alexander, 380 Queen w
Stewart, George H., 174 Yonge
Stock, James, 16 Palace
Strachan, William, 163 King and 41 East Market Square
Swan Brothers, 162 and 164 King e
Sweetman, Henry, 93 Elm
Swift, Dominick, 489 Queen w
Switzer, Tobias, 39 Terauley
Taylor, Miss H. L., Ann cor Church
Thompson, Charles, 77 King e
Thompson, Edward, 97 Church
Thompson, Hugh, 47 Duchess
Thompson, William R., 153 Berkeley
Tinsley, John M., 77 Agnes
Todd, William, 105 Nelson
Torphy, Daniel, 145 Elizabeth w
Tracie, U. J. & Co., 161 Yonge
Trehor, Mrs. Mary, 38 Bathurst
Trump, Daniel, 145 York
Vaughan, Patrick, 452 Queen w
Walsh, James, 76 Stanley
Walsh, Martin, 690 Queen w
Walsh, Patrick, 376 Queen w
Ward, Edward, 24 Victoria

ANDREW RUTHERFORD,

DEALER IN

STOVES, GRATES,

TIN, JAPANNED, PLANISHED AND WOODEN

GOODS,

Coal & Rock Oils, Lamps, &c.,

AND

HOUSE FURNISHING HARDWARE.

No. 126 KING STREET EAST,

TORONTO, ONT.

ROBERTSON, STEPHEN & CO.,

Dry Goods Importers,

Nos. 19, 21, 23 and 25 Lemoine Street, And Nos. 2, 4 and 6 St. Helen Street, } **Montreal.**

JAMES STEPHENSON, - - AGENT,

Office, 32 *Wellington Street East*,

TORONTO, ONT.

THE

Canadian Conveyancer,

And Handy-Book of New Real Property Law of Ontario ;

Being a selection of concise Precedents in Conveyancing, carefully revised, and adapted to the new Law, forming a Manual of Conveyancing under the new Law, for the use of Students and Country Practitioners, &c.; with introduction and notes.

Price, $2; full bound.—Sent, carriage free, to any part Canada, on receipt of price.

RORDANS & CO., Law Booksellers,

88 *King Street, Toronto.*

SCOTT & STOLLERY,

(LATE JAMES WORTHINGTON,)

Contractors, Builders and Wharfingers.

CUT STONE, OHIO AND GEORGTOWN BLOCK STONE, FLAGS AND HEARTH-STONES TO ORDER

GRINDSTONES,

From 14 lbs., to 4,000 lbs., for Wet or Dry Grinding, and of carefully selected qualities.

SCOTCH AND CANADIAN

Sewer Pipe, Drain Tiles, Fire Brick, Fire Clay, &c.

Esplanade and Bay Street, **Toronto, Ontario.**

Grocers Retail—(*Continued*)

Ward, James, 384 Adelaide
Warren, Nathaniel, 247 Yonge
Watkins, Lloyd N., 443 Yonge
Watkins, Mrs. William, 267 Church)
Way, James, 271 Queen w
White, Mrs. Honora, 27½ Queen w
Wilkins, George, 335 King e
Wilmot, Edward, 268 Queen w
Wilmott, George, 374 Yonge
Wilson, Andrew, 66 Agnes
Wilson, Robert, 189 Parliament
Wilson, Standish G., 515 Queen w
Wright, George, 41 Edward
Wright, James, King e
Wright, William, 327 King
Young, William, 66 Hayter

Grocers (Wholesale.)

Adams, William, 29 East Market Square
Boyd, John & Co., 61 and 63 Front e
Campbell, William, 14 Palace
Close, P. G., 10 Palace
Cowan, D. & Co., 29 Church
Griffith, Thomas & Co., 37 and 39 Front e
Griffith, W. & R., Front cor Church
Howland & Fitch, 25 Church
Michie, George & Co., Front cor Yonge
Moore, C. & Co., 5, 7 and 9 Wellington w
McKay, John M., 7 Manning's Block, Front e
McKay, Samuel, 18 Wellington e
Perkins, F. & G. & Co., 41 and 43 Front e
Ramsay, William & Co., 84 and 86 Front e
Reford & Dillon, 12 and 14 Wellington e
Shaw & Campbell, 135 Yonge
Smith, Frank & Co., Front cor Scott
Smith, Fair & Co., Front cor Church
Smith, J. E. & Co., 31 Church

Gunsmiths.

Marston, William P., 132 Yonge
Rennardson, George, 182 King e

Hair Dressers, Ladies.

Bates, the Misses, 31 King w

Hair Worker.

Ellis, Mrs., 179 Yonge

Harbor Master.

Richardson, Hugh, 4 Front w

Hardware.

Baillie, John, 266 Yonge
Collett, Martin, 468 Yonge
Foster, James & Son, 145 King e
Hall, Joseph N. & Co., 53 Yonge
Haworth, Thomas & Co., 52 Yonge
Hewitt, William, 111 Yonge
Hodgson, Joseph, 135 Yonge
Hope, Adam & Co., Front
Lewis, Rice & Son, King e, cor Toronto
Lyman & McNab, 5 Front e
Meade, John, 156 King e
Morphy, John, 31 East Market Square
Paterson, P. & Son, 24 King e
Piper, Hiram, estate of late, 83 Yonge
Piper, H. & Co., 51 Yonge
Piper, Noah, 169 Yonge
Ridout, Aikenhead & Crombie, 2 King e
Rutherford, Andrew, 126 King e
Ryan & Oliver, 114 Yonge
Sparrow & Whatmough, 87 Yonge
Tilbury, George F. & Co., agents for Ives & Allen, Montreal, and D. A. Ansell, 11 & 12 Ontario Chambers

Hatters and Furriers.

Coleman & Co., 53 King e
Dineen, W. & D., 80 Yonge
Dineen, J., 92 Yonge
Gillespie, J. & Co. (wholesale), 64 Yonge
Halbhaus, Theodore, 89½ Yonge
Lugsdin, J. & J., 101 Yonge
McCrossen & Co., 111 King e
O'Neill, Edward, 84 Church
Rogers, Charles K., 133 King e
Rogers, James H., 109 King e
Wiesner & Co., 35 King e

Hides and Skins. (*See also Leather & Findings.*)

Barry, J. W. & Son, 79 Colborne
Hallam, John, 84 Bond
Leadlay, Edward, 642, Queen w

Hoop Skirt Manufacturers.

Dunn, John W., 206 Yonge
Galloway, David, 212 Yonge
Gray, Robert H., 43 Yonge
Reading, John, 204 Yonge

Hotels and Taverns.

Albion, James Crocker, prop., 33 and 35 East Market Square
Allen, Thomas, 52 Bathurst
American, David Walker, prop., Yonge cor Front
Argyle, Hotel, James Law, Front e
Baird, Alexander, 141 Portland
Platt's Hotel, Bassett & Keeble, props., 50 and 52 Nelson
Bay Horse, Thomas Best, prop., 137 and 139 Yonge
Beale, Francis, 331 King e
Beatty's Hotel, Luke Beatty, prop., 108 Adelaide e
Beatty & Forsyth, 54 and 56 Nelson
Beily, E., Douro cor Tecumseth
Bennett, James, 18 Teranley
Bergfield, Louis W., 212 Queen w
Betz, John, Esplanade cor Simcoe
Bishop, James, 294 King e
Blackbird, George, 234 Front
Black Bull, Mrs. Purdy, 265 Queen w
Black Horse Inn, William Cox, proprietor, 24 and 26 Palace cor George
Blair's John Blair, proprietor, 73 Nelson e
Blakeley, John, 56 Wellington e
Britannia House, T. R. Williams, prop., 176 Queen w
Brock, Henry, 556 Queen w
Brown, George, 76 Front
Brown, J. N., British Hotel, King w cor Simcoe
Brown, Robert, 926 Queen w
Brown, Thomas, Metropolitan, King w cor Bay
Burns, Charles, 306 King e
Burns, Charles, 115 York
Burns, Patrick, 226 Queen w
Butchers' Arms, John Bolam, prop., East Market cor Palace
Caer Howell Hotel, H. U. Layton, prop., College Avenue
Carson, James, Turf Club, 40 King w
Carson, Wallace, 632 Yonge
Cathcart, James, 356 Queen w
City Arms, Robert Coates, prop., 36 West Market Square

Hotels and Taverns—(*Continued*)

Cherry, R. R., Cumberland House, Yonge, Yorkville
Coates, Thomas, 548 Queen w
Collyer, John, Clifton House, 80 Colborne
Cornnell's, John Cornnell, proprietor, West Market Square, near Front
Coyne, Thomas, Queen w, nr York
Doyle, L., 52 Adelaide e
"¡Dew Drop Inn," G. Giddings, prop., Yonge cor Shuter
Doyle's, Thomas Doyle, proprietor, 78 Colborne
Draycott, Charles, Front w, nr Peter
Duffy's, James Duffy, proprietor, cor Church and Carleton
Duggan, Joseph, 248 King e
Foad, William, 591 Yonge
Fox, George, Don Vale
Foy, William, 167 York
Funston, William, 141 Little Front
Gaffney's, John Gaffney, proprietor, 26 Church
Gannon, M. E., 44 Palace
Gannon, P., 177½ Queen w
Gibson, John, 31 Elizabeth
Gill's Hotel, John Gill, proprietor, cor Simcoe
Globe Hotel, Joseph Ross, proprietor, 163 Yonge
Golding, Joseph, 568 Queen w
Goldring's, Charles Goldring, proprietor, George cor Esplanade
Gowan, H., 81 Colborne
Graham, W. & J., 148 King w
Grand Trunk Inn, 144 and 146 Little Front
Gray, G. H., 460 and 462 Yonge
Green Bush Hotel, J. L. Parker, proprietor, 215 and 217 Yonge
Heaslip, Thomas, Esplanade, nr Scott
Higgins, Samuel, York, nr Union Depot
Hill, George, cor York and Richmond w
Hinchcliffe, Benjamin, 160 Yonge
Howard, James, 222 Front
Howard, J., 28 John
Hulme, George, 134 Palace
Hussey, Eli, cor Yonge and Hayter
Irwin, John, 46 Church
Irwin's, William Irwin, proprietor, 79 Church
Jackson, Edward, Crown Inn, Davenport Road, Yorkville
Johnson, Alexander, Maple Leaf, 246 Queen w
Johnson, Mrs., Old Half Way House, 228 Front w
Kennedy, Frank, Brockton
Kenny, Mrs. A., 18 Duchess
King's Hotel, John H. Meyer, Front cor York
Lake View House, John McCaffrey, proprietor, Parliament cor Winchester
Lawrence, Richard, 347 and 349 Queen w
Leeds Arms, Edward Dowson, prop., Victoria
Likens, John, Clyde Hotel, 158 King e
Lloyd, Benjamin, 2 Bathurst cor Front
Loane, Samuel R., 162 King w
Lord Nelson Inn, A. Cochrane, prop., 8 Palace
Macfarlane, Malcolm, 95 Nelson
Makinson's, George Makinson, prop., 340 Yonge
Matthews, J., Robinson House, Temperance, 109 Bay
May, Thomas, York cor Queen
Meehan, Neil, 137 Queen, w
Meek, Thomas, 37 East Market
Mercer, John, prop. Yonge Street Inn, 258 Yonge
Milligan, Archibald, 12 West Market Square
Milligan, Frederick, 108 Adelaide w
Milne, William, 154 Spadina ave
Maloney, Jeremiah, 108 York
Monkhouse, Mrs. Alice, 172 King cor George
Murphy, John, 22 Wellington e
Murphy, Mrs., corner of Esplanade and Church
McCabe, Thomas, 225 King e
McCaffrey, J., Winchester cor Parliament
McEvoy, H., 63 Richmond cor Church
McLaughlin, J., George cor Duchess
McSherry, James, George nr Esplanade
O'Brien, Mrs., York cor Esplanade
O'Connell, Mrs. Mary, 56 Adelaide w
O'Dea, James, 333 King, e
Ontario, Lawrence Doyle, proprietor, Adelaide e
Ontario House, M. E. Gannon, prop., 44 Palace
Patterson, Thomas, 224 Queen e
Peacock, Charles, 633 Yonge
Porter, John, head of Bathurst
Powers, William, Bathurst, corner Queen
Purdy, Mrs. Margaret, 266 Queen w
Queen's, Thomas Dick, prop., Front bet Bay and York
Queen's Own, Robert Taylor, prop., 101 King w
Railroad Hotel, J. Gaby, proprietor, Yorkville
Randall, J. W., St. Lawrence Hotel, 29 East Market Square
Red Lion Inn, William Kirk, prop, Yorkville
Revere House, Riley & May, propra., cor King and York
Richmond House, Luther C. Coddington, prop., 29 Victoria
Roach's, John Roach, proprietor, 22 Palace
Rochester House, J. Carroll, prop, 20 Front w
Rodgers, Mrs. E., 96 Parliament
Rossin House, George P. Shears, lessee and manager, cor York and King
Shaw, J., European Hotel, 110 York
Shakspeare Hotel, John O'Grady, proprietor, cor King and York
Sheppard, Matthew, 648 Yonge
Short, Mrs. Mary, 521 King w
Simpson, Thomas, 124 York
Smith, Edwin, 156 King w
Smith, Richard, 440 Queen w
Sommerville, William, 426½ Front w
Spence, James, 52 Queen w
Squirrel, George, Front nr Peter
Star Hotel, C. Draycott, 264 Front w
Sullivan, B., Church cor Adelaide
Taylor, Hugh, 98 Caroline
Thompson, James, 406 Queen w
Thornhill, Edward, 104½ Nelson cor Richmond
Tidey, William J., 305 Yonge
Toronto House, Samuel Hunter, proprietor, cor Queen and Peter
Union Station Hotel, William Osborne, propr., York nr Front
Warde, James, 384 Adelaide w
William III, T. H. O'Neil, proprietor, 56 and 58 Adelaide e
Williams, Edward, cor Front and Bathurst
Williams, George, 8 West Market Square
Williams, Thomas R., 176 Queen w
Wilson, David, cor George and King
Wilson's, George Wilson, proprietor, 66 and 68 Colborne
Wright, William, 327 King e
Yorkshire Stingo, John Hurst, prop, 14 Francis
Yorkville Inn, Mrs. E. Kerr, Yonge, Yorkville

Ice Dealers.

Hill, Samuel & Co., Palace nr George
Lewis, Henry, 353 King e

House Furnishing Goods.—*(See also Hardware and Stove Dealers.)*

Bell, George, 231 Queen w
Grantham, Ellwood, 170 Yonge
Hewitt, William, 111 Yonge
Lewis, Rice & Son, 52 and 54 King e
Linton, John D., 23 King w
Paterson, P. & Sons, 24 King e
Piper, Hiram, estate of late, 83 Yonge
Piper, H. & Co., 81 Yonge
Piper, Noah L. & Son, 169 Yonge
Rutherford, Andrew, 126 King e
Sparrow & Whatmough, 87 Yonge

Insurance Companies.

Ætna, of Hartford (fire and marine) William Rowland, agent, Front cor Church
Ætna Life Insurance Co., of Hartford, Conn., John Garvin, Whittemore's bldgs, Toronto
Ætna Live Stock Insurance Co., Scott & Walmsley agents, Church
Beaver Mutual Fire Insurance Association, W. T. O'Reilly, sec. Toronto
British America Assurance Co., Thomas W. Birchall, managing director, Court cor Church
Britain Medical and General Life Association, J. Fraser, 5 King w
Canadian Lake Underwriters' Association, Ontario Chambers, Front e
Canada Life Association Co., E. Bradburne, agent, Toronto
Colonial Life Association Co., Pellatt & Osler, agents, 86 King e
Commercial Union Assurance Co, (London, Eng.) William M. Westmacott, 72 King e
Edinburgh Life Assurance Co., David Higgins, sec., 19 Wellington w
European Assurance Guarantee Society (London), W. T. Mason, Ontario Hall, Court
Hartford, of Hartford, Conn. (fire) William Rowland, agent, Front cor Church
Home District Mutual Fire Insurance Co., John Rains, sec., Yonge cor Adelaide
Home and Colonial (fire and life) Insurance Co., T. D. Harris, Clare
Home, of New Haven (fire and marine) William Rowland, agent, Front cor Church
Imperial Insurance Co., of London, Eng., 31 Church, James E. Smith & Co., agents
Lancashire Fire and Life Insurance Co., S. C. D. Clark & Co., general agents for Ontario, 94 King cor Church
Life Association Society of England, J. Gregory, agent, 48 King e
Life Association of Scotland, R. N. Gooch, agt, 32 Wellington e
Liverpool and London and Globe Fire and Life Insurance Company, J. Fraser, 5 King w
London Fire and Life, Isaac C. Gilmor, agent, Colborne
Montreal Fire and Marine Insurance Company, R. N. Gooch, agent, 32 Wellington e
National Union Life Insurance Company, London, England, Scott & Walmsley, Ontario Hall, Church
New York Life Insurance Company, Evans, Sherwood & Co., agents, 15 Wellington e
New York Casualty Insurance Company, Pellatt & Osler, agents, 86 King e
North British and Mercantile Insurance Company, R. N. Gooch, agent, 32 Wellington e
Phœnix Fire Assurance Company, of London, England, Moffatt, Murray & Beattie, 36 Yonge
Phœnix Ocean and Inland Insurance Company, C. G. Fortier, agent, Ontario Chambers
Provincial Fire and Marine Insurance Company, Scott & Walmsley, agents, Church
Provincial Insurance Company, J. S. Crocker, manager, Toronto cor Court
Queen Insurance Company, Liverpool (Fire and Life) W. Rowland, agent, Front e
Railway Passengers' Insurance Company, Hartford, W. Rowland, agt, cor Front and Church
Royal Insurance Company, of England, F. H. Heward, manager, Yonge cor Wellington
Scottish Provincial Assurance Company, G. L. Maddison, agent, 44 Bay
Standard Life Assurance Company, Edinburgh, Pellatt & Osler, agents, 86 King e
Star Life Assurance Society of England, J. Gregory, 48 King e
Toronto Mutual Fire Insurance Company, H. Hancock, Secretary, 20 Toronto
Travellers' Insurance Company (Life and Accident), W. Rowland, agent, Front e
Western Assurance Company, B. Haldan, Secretary, 28 Church
Western Insurance Company, Buffalo, (Fire and Marine), W. Rowland, Front cor Church

Iron Founders.—*(See Foundries and Machine shops*

Iron and Steel, Dealers in.

Hall & Co., Joseph N., 58 Yonge
Hope, Adam & Co., 53 Front e
Lewis, Rice & Son, King cor Toronto
Paterson, P. & Son, 25 King e
Ryan & Oliver, 114 Yonge

Ivory Black and Animal Charcoal Manufacturers.

Lamb, Peter R. & Co., rear Necropolis

Jewellers.—*(See Watchmakers and Jewellers.)*

Jewellers, Manufacturers.

Campbell, G. L., 20 Toronto
Fitzsimons, C. J., 81 King e
Morrison, W. C., 12 King w
Robinson, Charles, 96 Yonge
Vernon, Norton, 159 Yonge
Ward, George, 60 Adelaide e

Juvenile Clothing, Dealers in.

Halse, Mrs. Isabella, 125 Yonge
Robinson, Mrs. Ann, 336 Yonge
Swann, John H , 57 King w

Knitting and Yarn Manufacturers.

Simpson, Joseph, 25 Front e

Lamps and Oils.

Authors, James, 270 Yonge
Boxall, John, 50 Queen w
Cottrell, William, 62 King w
Grantham, Ellwood, 170 Yonge
Jackson, John, 48 Queen w
Meagher, William, 32 King w
Millichamp, Wallace, 80 Queen w
Parson Brothers, 51 Front e
Piper, H. & Co., 81 Yonge
Piper, Hiram, estate of, 83 Yonge
Piper, Noah L. & Son, 169 Yonge
Shipway, Charles, 290 Yonge
Wood, H. J., 113 Queen w

Last Manufacturer.

Selway, Matthew, 24½ Adelaide w

Law Stationers.

Finch, Frederick, 44 Church
Rordans, Joshua, 88 King e
Ware, George B., 16 Toronto

Leather Belting and Fire Hose Manufact'r.

Marks, William, 34 Temperance

Leather and Findings, Wholesale.

Beardmore & Co., 6 Wellington w
Belton, John, 146 Yonge
Childs and Hamilton, 7 Wellington e
Daley, Charles & Co., 56 Yonge
Jacobi, Philip, 103 Yonge
Parsons, Charles, 79 Front e
Sorley, James B., Front e, nr Scott
Thorne, Parsons & Vennor, 79 Front e

Lime, Dealers in.

Bescoby, Edward, West Market, cor Esplanade

Lithographers.

Chewett, W. C. & Co., 17 and 19 King e
Rolph, J. T., 11 King w

Livery Stables.

Bond, John, Sheppard nr Richmond
Doane, Henry, 40 King w
Grand, Joseph, 98 Wellington w

Loan Societies.

Canada Landed Credit Co., 22 King e
Canadian Land & Emigration Co., Bank of Toronto Building
Colonial Securities Co., (London, Eng.) 17 Wellington w

Locksmiths and Bellhangers.

Brimstin, Hugh, 288 Yonge
Broom, James, 26 and 28 Colborne
Lalor, L. J., 22 King w
Lewis, Henry, 3 Walton
Perkins, Charles, 14 Adelaide e
Smith, Frank, 69 Queen w

Lumber Merchants.

Atkinson, S. 69 Wood
Boyd, John, cor Albert and Elizabeth
Briggs, S. R., Toronto Exchange
Briggs, Thomas, 24 Edward
Burke, William, cor Richmond and Sheppard
Christie, Alexander R., 287 King w
Clarke, White & Co., 14 & 15 Ontario Chambers
Colwell, Henry, 414 Front
Colwell, W. W., N. R. Co. wharf, and Front nr Portland
Couch, Richard, 132 Adelaide w
Dinnis, Richard, 48 Bay
Fowler, Robert, 394 Yonge
Gilbert, E. B., 248 Adelaide w
Hotchkiss, Peckham & Co., 11 Exchange Bldgs
Kerr, William, 287 King w
Latch, William, Hayden
McBean, John, 11 Adelaide w
McPhee, Duncan, 408 Queen w
O'Connor, J., 12 South Park
Peckham & Hoag, 11 Exchange Buildings
Scarlett, E., 497 Queen w
Scott, Peter A., 618 and 620 Yonge
Smith, Thompson & Son, Esplanade, bet York and Bay
Smith, John B., Front nr Bay
Taylor, F. P. G & Co., N. R. Co., West Esplanade
Tenor, Peter, cor Nelson and Duke
Walsh & Loveys, 188 and 190 King w

Machinery Brokers.

Levey, Charles & Co., 73 Adelaide w

Map Publishers.

Bell & Co., 70 King e
Chewett, W. C. & Co., 17 and 19 King e

Marble Cutters.

Armitage, George, 8 Gould
Gibson, Joseph, Winchester cor Parliament
Mulvey & Fleming, 8 Cruickshank
Sheppard, Robert, 181 Queen w
Sheppard, W. H., 113 Queen w
Steiner, Newman L., 275 Yonge
Waudby, Henry, Yonge nr Isabella

Marriage Licenses, Issuer of.

Cayley, Hon. W., Court House
Mercer, Andrew, cor Wellington and Bay

Mathematical Instruments, Manufacturers of.

Foster, James, room 27 Exchange Buildings
Potter, Charles, 20 King e
Swinburne, Henry, 24 Adelaide e

Mattrass Manufacturers.

Ellis, George, 179 Yonge
Moore, J. W. 79 Queen w
Wagner, J. P., Adelaide w

Melodeon Manufacturers.—*(See also Music and Musical Instrument Dealers.)*

Coleman & Son, 56 King w
Williams, R. S., 143 Yonge

Mercantile Agencies.

Bradstreet, J. M. & Son, Bank of Toronto Blgs.
Dun, Wiman & Co., 4, 5 & 6 Exchange Blgs

Merchant Tailors—*(See also Clothiers and Tailors.*

Brimer, John, 171 Yonge
Clarke, P. M., 95 King w
Farquharson, James, 179 Queen w
Finch, William S., 6 King e
Frisby & Bartlett, 193 Yonge
Ham, J. M., 300 Queen w
Harcourt, George, 75 King e
Houston & Taylor, 2 Rossin House Block
Kelz, John, 352 Yonge
Loughlin, M. O., 297 Queen w
Maloney, John M., 81 Bay
Matheson, Hugh, 16 King e
Morison, Farquhar, 12 King w
McEachren, N., 191 Yonge
Renilson, John, 236 Yonge
Riddell, John, 17 King w
Saunders, Bernard, Romain Blgs, King w
Score, R. & Son, 95 King e
Stovel, Joseph, 63 King w
Sutherland, William W., 100 Yonge
Taylor, Watson, 82 Yonge
Toye, Charles, 64 Queen w
Walker, C. & W., 7 King e
Wetkowski, Louis, 66 Adelaide e

Metal Merchants and Dealers in Tinners' Stock.

Samuel, M. & L., 52 Front e

Millinery and Millinery Goods.—(*See also Dressmakers and Dry Goods.*)

Anderson, Miss Elizabeth, 6 Temperance
Anketell, Elizabeth, 206 Queen w
Ashall, R. M., 286 Yonge
Barker, George, 10 Wellington w
Brown, Mary, 33 Louisa
Callaway, Mrs. M., 339 Yonge
Carter, M. & A., 362 Yonge
Chaloner, Mrs. H., 374 Queen w
Conway, Miss, 225 Church
Fawcett, Mrs. C., 61 Agnes
Fowler, Mrs. Mary, 390 Yonge
Gegan, Miss Anne, 69 Ann
Goulding, George, 175 and 177 Yonge
Hodgins, Miss, 1 Rossin House block
Hopkirk, Thomas, 176 King e
Howard, Mrs. M., 334 Yonge
Hyland, Mrs. 93 Yonge
Kavanagh, Mrs. Hanna, 106 Richmond e
May, Thomas & Co., 63 Yonge
Mitchell, William, 184 King e
McEvoy, Lavinia L., 41 Terauley
Patton, Miss Elizabeth, 58 Shuter
Purdy, William, 303½ Queen w
Reed, the Misses, 202 Yonge
Robinson, Thomas, 127 Yonge
Strider, Mrs. Sarah, 256 Yonge
Tapscott, Mrs. S., 450 King e
Ward, Mrs. D., 281 Yonge
Woodcock, Andrew, 184 Yonge
Wylie, Mrs. Catharine, 384 Yonge

Millstone Manufacturer.

Oates, R. H., Esplanade cor Church

Morocco Manufacturer.

Barry, J. W. & Son, 79 Colborne

Museum.

Passmore, S. W., 232 Yonge (admission 10c)

Musical Instrument Repairer.

Matthews, William, 378 Yonge

Music and Musical Insturment Dealers.
(*See also Piano-forte Manufacturers and Dealers.*)

Butland, R. B., 37 King w
Coleman, J. & Sons, 56 King w
Heintzman & Co., King w., adg Rossin House
Mathews, William, 378 Yonge
Nordheimer, A. & S., 15 King e
Williams, R. S., 143 Yonge

Mustard Manufacturer.

Crawford, D. & Co., Palace cor Princess

Naturalist.

Passmore, S. W., 232 Yonge

Needles, Fish Hooks, &c.

Allcock, Laight & Co., 39 Colborne
Croft, William & Co., 37 Colborne

News and Periodical Depots.

Backas, C. A., 10 Toronto
Chewett, W. C. & Co., 17 and 19 King e
Chisholm, Colin R., Union Station
Irving, A. S., 35 King w
Thompson, R. S., 49½ King w

Newspapers and Peirodicals, Publishers, &c.

Canada Farmer, monthly, printed and published by the *Globe* Printing Company, 26 and 28 King e
Canada Sunday School Advocate, semi-monthly, printed and published for the proprietor at the *Guardian* office
Canadian Almanac, The, printed and published by W. C. Chewett & Co., 17 and 19 King e
Canadian Baptist, weekly, H. Lloyd, editor and publisher, 11 King w
Canadian, Entomologist, monthly, editor, C. J. S. Bethune; printed by W. C. Chewett & Co., 17 and 19 King e
Canadian Freeman, weekly, J. G. Moylan, editor and proprietor, 74 Church
Canadian Independent Magazine, monthly, Rev. John Wood, editor, printed for proprietors by W. C. Chewett & Co., 17 and 19 King e
Canadian Journal, The, alternate months, conducted by the editing committee of the Canadian Institute. Printed by W. C. Chewett & Co., 17 and 19 King e
Canadian Journal of Commerce, E. T. Bromfield & Co., publishers, 48 King e
Canada Law Journal, The—Monthly, R. A. Harrison, B.C.L., W. D. Ardagh and Henry O'Brien, editors and proprietors, W. C. Chewett & Co., printers, 17 and 19 King e
Canadian Monetary Times and Insurance Chronicle, printed at *Daily Telegraph* office, cor King and Bay
Christian Guardian, published every Wednesday morning, at the Wesleyan book and printing establishment, 80 and 82 King e
Christian Journal (Primitive Methodist), Rev. Thomas Compton, editor, 89 Yonge
Church Chronicle, The, monthly, printed for the Church Society, by H. Rowsell, 79 King e
Daily Telegraph—morning, evening and weekly, Robertson & Cook, proprietors, Bay nr King
Globe, The—morning, evening and weekly, *The Globe* Printing Co., publishers, 26 & 28 King e
Home and Foreign Record of the Canada Presbyterian Church—printed monthly by A. Lovell & Co. for Canada Presbyterian Church
Irish Canadian (weekly)—printed and published by Patrick Boyle, 45 Colborne
Journal of Education (monthly)—Rev. Dr. Ryerson, assisted by J. G. Hodgins, LL.B., F.R. G.S., editor, Educational Department, Ontario, proprietor and publishers; printed by A. Lovell & Co., 67 Yonge
Leader, The—morning, evening, and weekly, James Beaty, proprietor and publisher. John Carroll, printer, 63 King e
Local Courts and Municipal Gazette, The—R. A. Harrison, B. C. L.; W. D. Ardagh and Henry O'Brien, editors and proprietors. W. C. Chewett & Co., printers, 17 and 19 King e
Mercantile Test, The—(semi-monthly), J. Kerr, publisher, British America Assurance Buildings, Court cor Church. Printed by W. C. Chewett & Co., 17 and 19 King e
Ontario Gazette—Hunter, Rose & Co., printers, King w
Ontario Gazetteer and Directory—C. E. Anderson & Co., publishers; Henry McEvoy, editor and compiler, *Daily Telegraph* office Directory Branch, Bay cor King
Ontario Farmer—W. F. Clarke, editor and prop., Hunter, Rose & Co., publishers, 86 King w
Ontario Law List and Canadian Conveyancer, The—88 King e
Patriot, Watchman and News of the Week, The—James Beaty, proprietor, 63 King e

Newspapers, Periodicals, &c—(*Continued*)

Sunday School Advocate, Wesleyan — (semi-monthly), Rev. S. Rose, editor, 80 King e
Sunday School Dial, The—Address, A. Christie, Post Office, box 696, Toronto.
Toronto City Directory, Annual, C. E. Anderson & Co., publishers, H. McEvoy, editor and compiler, *Daily Telegraph* office, Directory Branch, Bay, cor King
Upper Canada Common Pleas Reports—printed and published by H. Rowsell, 76 King e
Upper Canada Law Directory—Published every second year by J. Rordans, W. C. Chewett & Co., printers. 17 and 19 King e.
Upper Canada Law and Equity Reports—Printed by Henry Rowsell, 76 King e
Weekly Visitor—Printed and published by P. H. Stewart, cor Louisa and Yonge

Numismatists.

Eves, James, 107 Yonge
Terry, John, Adelaide, cor Yonge

Nurserymen, Seedsmen and Florists.

Davies Brothers, 6 Palace
Dawbarn, Charles & Co., 124 King e
Fleming, James, 250 Yonge
Fleming, J. & Co., 180 Yonge, cor Queen
Gray, John, Dundas
Simmers, Joseph A., 20 West Market Square
Tollis, Henry, 65 Gerrard
Toronto Nurseries, George Leslie & Son, props, Leslieville

Oculists and Aurists.

Rosebrugh & Reeves, 55 Queen e

Official Assignees.

Clarkson, Thomas, 85 Front
Kerr, John, cor Court and Church
Mason, William T., Ontario Hall, Church
Pellatt & Osler, 86 King e

Oil Manufacturers.

Fisken, John & Co., 58 Yonge.
Parson Brothers, 51 Front e

Oil Stills, &c.

Currie, Neil, Esplanade, nr Church

Oil Refiners, Coal.

Parson Brothers, 51 Front e

Opticians.

Michael, George, 51½ King e
Potter, Charles, 20 King e

Organ Builders.

Coleman & Sons, 56 King w
Lye, Edward, 90 Sayer
Roome, T. F., cor Grosvenor and Yonge

Packing Box Manufacturers.

Barchard, William, Duke
Eales, Walter, 172 York
Edington, William, 81 Queen w
Ryall, James, 80 George
Smedley & Sutherland, 100 Church

Painters (House, Sign and Ornamental.)

Beatty, Samuel, 299 Queen w
Beatty & Townley, 48 Queen w
Booth, G. & W., 47 King w and 32 Adelaide e
Corin, Charles, 16 Queen w
Dee & Herbert, 353 Queen e
Elliott, William, Cruickshank cor Victoria
Faircloth & Son, 12 Adelaide e
Hazard, H., 146 Richmond
Kidd, John, 190 Queen e
Lucas, George D., 43 Queen w
March, Charles, 86 Adelaide e
McCausland, Joseph, 8 King w
Palmer, John, 121 Adelaide w
Pearcy, John, Hayter nr Yonge
Pearcy, G., 4 Richmond e
Rogers, William D., 103 Bay
Smith, Thomas, 22 Wellington w
Thompson, James, 354 Yonge
Widdowson, Andrew, 2 Shuter

Paper Hangings.

Edwards, John, 137 Yonge
Hamilton, Alexander, 183 King e
McPhail, Robert, Exchange Alley
Staunton, M., Front, nr Custom House
Thompson, James, 354 Yonge

Paper Warehouses.

Buntin, Bro. & Co., 61 and 63 Yonge
Taylor, John & Bros, 30 West Market Square

Pawnbrokers.

Fleming & Ward, 58 Adelaide e
Kavanagh, John, 45 Queen w
May, Thomas, cor Queen and York
Mintz, A. J., 105 Queen w

Perfumery, Manufactuers of

Grossmith, C. W., 34 King e
Lyon, James F., & Co., 57 Richmond e

Photographers.

Anderson, Robert W., 45 King e
Bugg, Charles, 137 King e
Butchart, David C., 145 King e
Carswell, R., 6 King w
Cooper, W. A., 45 King e
Ewing, R. D., 150 King w
Fenner & Co., 146 Yonge
Forrest, L., 105 King e
Gilbertson, George, Adelaide opp Toronto
Hay, E. R., 27 King e
Hollingworth, John, 284 Yonge
McConkey, George, 147 King e
Noverre & Smith, 31 King e
O'Connor, William, *Leader* Blgs, 63 King e
Palmer, Eli J., 118 King e
Penrose, James, 53 King e
Sheppard & Daguere, 122 King e
Turner, Alexander, Adelaide
Turner, John, corner King and Yonge
Windeat, William, 39 King w

Physicians and Surgeons.

Those marked thus (*) are Homœopathists.

*Adams, Joseph, 54 Bay
Agnew, John M., 46 Richmond w
Aikins, W. T., 70 Queen w
Allen, James, 206 Queen e
Andrews, R. J., 169 Queen w
Barrett, Michael, west U. C. College
Barrick, E. J., 276 Yonge
Beaumont, William R., 134 Wellington w
Berryman, C. V., Jarvis, Yorkville
Bovell, James, Denison Avenue
Brown, John, 321 Queen w
Buchanan, Charles W., 51 Adelaide w
Buchanan, O. R., 51 Adelaide w
*Campbell, Duncan, 108 Bay

Physicians, and Surgeons—(*Continued*)

Cassidy, J. J., 118 Church
Clunie, William, 208 Church
Constantinides, Peter, 369 Yonge
Cumming, William H., 82 Adelaide w
DeGrassi, George P., 292 King e
Emery, Robert, 62 Queen w
*Gamble, T. C., 42 Ann
Hall, Cyrenius B., 42 Adelaide w
*Hall, John, 33 Richmond e
Hallowell, William, Gloucester Row, Ontario
Hodder, Edward, 159 Queen w
Hollingshead, Silas (eclectic) 274 Yonge
Hornby, Robert, 174 York
Howson, Joseph, 86 Queen w
*Jones, Charles B., 37 Richmond e
King, John, King corner Nelson
Lawlor, Michael, 187 Richmond w
Lund, Richard, 337 King e
McIlmurray, James, 19 Richmond w
Newcombe, James, cor Church and Richmond
Newcombe, William, cor Church and Richmond
Ogden, Uzziel, 57 Adelaide w
Ogden, Winslow, 242 Queen w
Oldright, William, 65 Nelson
*Oliphant, David S., 175 Church
Phillips, M., 70 Bay
Ray, John E., 22 Richmond e
Rees, W., Simcoe nr Front
Richardson, James H., 116 Bay
Riddel, A. A., 217 Queen e
Robinson, Thomas S., 21 Gould
Rolph, Hon. John, 20 Gerrard w
Rolph, John W., 20 Gerrard w
Rosebrugh & Reeves, 55 Queen e
Ross, Alexander M., 159 Church
Ross, James, 74 Caroline
Rowell, James, 396 Yonge
Russell, J. P., 148 Bay
Small, John T., 144 Simcoe
Smith, John E., 184 King w
Stowe, Mrs. E. H., 39 Richmond e
Tempest, William, 330 Yonge
Temple, Dr., 23 Temperance
Thompson, Dr., 386 Yonge
Thorburn, James, 119 Church
Winstanley, O. S., 331 Yonge
Workman, Benjamin, P.L.A.
Workman, Joseph, P.L.A.
Wright, G. W., 1 James
Wright, H. H., Queen e nr Caroline

Piano Forte Manufacturers.

(*See also Music and Musical Instrument Dealers.*)

Heintzman & Co., 105 King w
Nordheimer, A. & S., 15 King e
Stevenson & Co., J. H., Rossin House block, King w
Thomas John, 167 Elizabeth
Williams, R. S., 143 Yonge

Picture Frame Makers.—(*See also Carvers and Gilders.*)

Laird, Robert W., 79 King w
Matthews, Henry J., 189 Yonge
Pell, John C., 53 York
Phillips, R. D., King w

Planing Mills.

Burke, William, Richmond cor Sheppard
Clements, John, Front opp Queen's hotel
Coatsworth, Emerson, 359 King e
McBean, James, Walton
Phillips, J. W., Terauley cor Hayter
Smith, J. B., Front bet Yonge and Bay
Wagner, J. P., 71 and 73 Adelaide w

Plaster of Paris Workers.

Casci, V., 3 Stanley
Talrene, Sebastian, 71 Sayer

Plumbers and Gasfitters.

Collins, John, 112 Bay
Crapper, James, 88 Adelaide e
Cuming & Wells, 175 King w
Harding, George, 77 King w
Hurst, James, 104 Adelaide e
Jackson, John, 248 Queen w
Keith, David S., 109 King w
Meadows, Samuel, 23 Queen w
Morrison, James, cor Bay and Temperance
Ritchie, John, 192 King e
Smith, H. T., 95 Queen w
Wright, John, 387 and 389 Yonge

Porcelain Gilders and Enamellers.

Hurd, Leigh & Co., 72 Yonge

Pork Packers.

Davies, William & Co., Palace, cor Frederick
Sorley, James B., Front e, nr Scott
Wilson, John & Co., 77 Colborne

Potash Manufacturers.

Barber, Charles, 58 South Park
Stone, William, cor South Park and Cherry

Printers, Book and Job.

Barker, Francis T., 70 King e
Beaty, James, *Leader*, 63 King e
Bell & Co., 70 King e
Blackburn, John, 96 Yonge
Boyle, Patrick, Exchange alley
Chewett, W. C. & Co., 17 and 19 King e
Christian Guardian office, 80 King e
Cuttell, Thomas & Son, Exchange alley
Dudley & Burns, Victoria Hall, King w
Globe Printing Company, 26 and 28 King e
Hill, Thomas & Son, (Caxton Press,) King, cor Nelson
Hunter, Rose & Co., 86 King e
Lovell, A. & Co., 67 Yonge
Moyer & Co., 32 King e
Robertson & Cook, *Telegraph*, Bay nr King
Rowsell, Henry, 74 and 76 King e

Printer's Materials.

Scadding, C. E., 6 Richmond e

Printers' Warehouse.

Halley, William, 85 and 87 Bay
Palsgrave, Charles T., 33 Colborne

Produce—(*See also Commission Merchants.*)

Aikin & Kirkpatrick, 2 Ontario Chambers
Allen, F. H., 4 Bank of Toronto Blgs
Barnhart, Noah, 124 Wellington w
Boomer, A. K., 93 King w
Bradford, Robert, 75 Yonge
Chisholm, T. C., 88 Front e
Clark, J. & A., Front e
Coffee, L. & Co. 2 Manning's Block, Front e
Conlin, Henry, junr., 74 Palace
Cummer, F. D., 8 and 9 Ontario Chambers, Front, e
De Laporte, A. V., 57 Front e
Gardner & Ramsay, 4 Manning's Block, Front e

Produce—(*Continued*)
Laidlaw, George, 54 Front e
Meredith, Thomas, 80 Front e
Morrison, Taylor & Co., 1 Manning's Block, Front e
Oliver, S. A., 289 Queen w
Terry, John, cor King and Caroline and Adelaide, cor Yonge
Thompson, Robert- 38 Church
Thorne, William, 1 Manning's Block, Front e
Wightman, George, 36 Colborne
Young, James, Wellington e

Provincial Land Surveyors. (*See also Architects, Civil Engineers and Surveyors.*)
Brown, John O., Whittemore Buildings, Toronto
James, Silas, Church nr Isabella
Passmore, F. F., 23 Duke
Savigny, Hugh P., Exchange Buildings
Unwin & Wadsworth, 42 Adelade e
Wilson, Alfred, Church nr Isabella

Provision Dealers.
Aikens, John R., 621 Yonge
Alexander, Mrs. Janet, 370 Queen w
Bickerstaff & Bro., 243 and 245 Queen w
Boustead, J. B., 82 Front e
Cuff, Henry W., 48, 50 & 52 St. Lawrence Mkt
Davis, A., 314 Queen w
Dexter, Thomas, 155 Jarvis
Evans, S., 29 and 31 St. Lawrence Market
Finn, William, 470 Queen w
Flannagan, Mrs. M., 491 Richmond w
Garton, John, 326 Yonge
Gilverston, Matthew R., 27 St. Lawrence Mkt
Herson, James, 18 St. Lawrence Market
Johnson, N., 3 Manning's Block, Front e
Lawrence, J. W., 360 Yonge
Little, A., cor Portland and Richmond
Morrison, John, 234 Queen West
McFarren, Andrew, 195 King e
Park, James, 47 St. Lawrence Market and 49 King w
Peirce, Felix, 233 Yonge
Phipps, John, 35 St. Lawrence Market
Quinn, John, 144½ York
Ryan, Martin, 162 Queen w
Savery, William, 114 Church
Sloan, James A., 195 and 197 Queen w
Swan, Brothers, 162 King e
Turner, William, 23 St. Lawrence Market

Registry Office for Servants.
Drew, Mrs. Amelia, 370 Yonge
Stubbs, Mrs. Agnes, 17 Adelaide e

Rolling Mills.
Gzowski, C. S. & Co., office, Romain Buildings, King w

Roofer's Composition (Slate and Metal)
Champ, J. S. & Co., cor Front and Church
Darlington, W. D., 35 Queen e
Forbes, Duncan, 21 James
Walton, Benjamin, Jarvis

Saddle and Harness Makers.
Bach, Edward, 10 King w
Davison, Frederick, Yorkville
Elliott, John, 56 Nelson
Gibson & Son, 207 Yonge
Malcom, R., 181 King e and 8 Rossin Block
Nicholls, Robert, 82 Church
Nicolls, Simon, 167 Queen w
Smallpeice, Henry, 58 Nelson
Smith, Andrew, 550 Queen w
Sturzaker, James, 102 York
Thompson, Thomas, 185 King e

Saddlery and Carriage Hardware.
Davidson, McVittie & Co., 152 King e
Brown, William, 72 King e
Trees, Samuel & Co., 69 Colborne

Safes (Fire and Burglar Proof).
Boomer, A. K. (Kershaw & Edwards) 93 King w
Lewis, Rice & Son, King cor Toronto
Taylor, J. & J. (manufacturers), Palace cor Erin

Safe, Lock, & Vault Door Manufacturers.
Lalor, L. J., 22 King w
Taylor, J. & J., Palace cor Erin

Sail Makers.
Adams, James, Tinning's wharf

Saloons and Restaurants.
Ardagh, William, under Police Court
Carlisle, George W. (Terrapin), 69 King e
City Larder, William Yielding, prop., Post Office
Clark, John (Elysium), Yonge cor Queen
Fairfield, H. B. (Fountain), 69 King e
Jewell & Timms (Shades) King w in r of Melinda
Kerby, Henry J., 81 King w
Loane, Samuel R., 162 King w
Maguire, Francis, G. W. R. Depot
Palmer, Joseph, pro. (Dolphin), 131 King e
Palmer, Thomas (Woodbine), 88 Yonge
Purse, Alexander, 4, 6 and 8 Adelaide w
Seels, John, 67 King w
Shannessy, John (Royal), 9 King w
Smith, Edwin, 156 King w
Smith, James, Union Depot
Thomas, M. A. (English Chop House), 30 King w
Varcoe, Richard, 153 Yonge

Sash, Door and Blind Manufacturers.
Burke, William, cor Richmond and Sheppard
Clements, John, Front opp Queen's Hotel
Coatsworth, Emerson, 359 King e
McBean, James, Walton, and Terauley cor Buchanan
Phillips, J. W., Terauley, cor Hayter
Smith, John B., Front near Bay
Wagner, Jacob P., 71 Adelaide w

Saw Makers, &c.
Rodgers, S. & G., 166 King e
Smallwood, T. W. F., 19 Richmond e
Westman, Samuel, 177 King e

Scales (Counter and Platform).—(*See also Hardware Merchants.*)
Boomer, A. K., 93 King w
Cornor, Edward, 254 Yonge
Wilson, Christopher, Toronto nr Adelaide

Schools (Boarding and Day).
Armstrong, Miss, Hayter nr Terauley
Birnie, Mrs. Grace, 100 Bond
Chesnut, T. G., Murray
Christie, The Misses, Cruickshank
Cleveland, J. P., M.D., 133 Victoria
Collar, Miss, 147 Church
Fuller, Mrs. Julia M., 72 Gloucester
Holliwell, Mrs. M. J. H., cor John & Wellington
Howe, Mrs. H. J., 161 Jarvis
Humphries, Mrs. Victoria, 18 Magill

Schools—(*Continued*)

Hunt, Mrs. DeV., 171 Richmond west
King, J. G., 101 Dalhousie
Lee, Patrick, 29 Frederick
Mackenzie, The Misses, 72 Bond
Noverre, the Misses, 250 Wellington w
Oliver, John, 328 Yonge
Orr, W. R., 12 Mutual
Reeve, Miss Ann, 45 Cruickshank
Rose, Mrs. J., 3 Gerrard w
Skinner, The Misses, 20 Gerrard w
Stewart, Mrs. O., cor Duke and George
Stowe, Mrs. F., Jarvis
Stubbs, Miss A., 45 Grange Road
Warrington, The Misses, 6 Bond

Sewing Machine Manufacturers.
(*See also Agents Sewing Machines.*)

Black, Norris, 18 King e
Gates, G. W. & Co., (Victoria) 14 King e and 119 Bay

Shipping, Forwarding and Commission.
(*See also Commission Merchants and Produce Merchts*)

Briggs, S. R., Toronto Exchange
Carruthers, E. M. & Co., 56 Front e
Holcomb, S. T., 2 Exchange Blgs.
Jaques, G. E. & Co., 50 Front e
Matthews, W. D. & Co., 16 Front e
Taylor, Archibald, foot of George
Young, James, 42 Wellington e

Soap and Candle Manufacturers.

Carty, J. & Co., cor Queen and George
Crawford, D. & Co., Princess nr Palace
Matthews, William, Esplanade foot of Berkeley
Morrison, John, Palace nr East
Sutherland & Marshall, 11 Denison Avenue

Soda Water Machine Manufacturer.

Smith, H. T., 95 Queen w

Soda Water Manufacturers.

Campton, Thomas, 96 Adelaide w
Coxon, George, 361 Yonge
Eves, J., cor Yonge and Adelaide e
Riddell & Burns, 406 Yonge
Smith, H. T., 95 Queen w

Stamped Copper Bottom Manufacturer.

Armstrong, J. R. & Co., 161 Yonge
Good, James, 6, 8 and 10 Queen e
Gurney, E. & C., 91 Yonge
Whitehouse, Charles J., 193 King e
Wood, H. J., 113 Queen w

Stationers.—(*See also Booksellers and Stationers*

Brown Brothers, 66 & 68 King e
Buntin Brother & Co., 63 & 65 Yonge
Campbell, James & Son, 9 Toronto
Chewett, W. C. & Co., 17 & 19 King e
Dredge, A. & Co., 53 Yonge
Edwards, John, 136 Yonge
Finch, Frederick, (law), 44 Church
McPhail, Robert, Exchange Alley
Miller, Adam, 62 King e
Rordans, J. (law,) 88 King e
Shewan, Magnus, 1 1 St. Lawrence Arcade
Ware, G. B., (law), 16 Toronto

Stone Yard.

Dinnis, Richard, 48 Bay
Farquhar & Ramsay, foot of Church
Scott & Stollery, foot of Bay

Stencil Cutter.

McClelland & Co., 48 King e

Stoves, Copper, Sheet Iron Manufacturers of.

Adams, W. M., 426 Queen w
Armstrong, J. R., & Co., 161 Yonge
Beard, E. & Co., 31 E Market Square
Boxall, John, 50 Queen w
Cottrell, William, 60 King w
Dunlop, William, 631 Yonge
Evans, George, 415 Queen w
Fluker, John, 92 Terauley
Gurney, E. & C., 91 Yonge
Hodgson, Joseph, 185 Yonge
Iredale, William, 239 Yonge
Jackson, John, 248 Queen w
Meagher, William, 32 King w
Mosiman, J. F., 67 Colborne
Murray, James, 224 Yonge
*Piper, Hiram, (Estate of late), 83 Yonge
*Piper, H. & Co., 81 Yonge
*Piper, Noah L. & Son, 168 Yonge
Ringham, George, 324 Yonge
Robertson, William T., 285 Yonge
*Rutherford, Andrew, 126 King e
Sawdon, George, 385 Yonge

Stove Founders. (*See also Stove, Tin, Copper, and sheet Iron manufacturers and dealers in.*)

Armstrong, J. R. & Co., 161 Yonge
Good, James, 6, 8 and 10 Queen e
Gurney, E. & C., 91 Yonge

Tailors' Trimmings, Wholesale.

Allan, John & Co., 31 Colborne

Taxidermist.

Passmore, S. W., 232 Yonge

Teachers (Music).

Bird, Charles G., 65 North Park
Blackburn, Robert, 101 Terauley
Camidge, John, Mus. Doc., 311 Parliament
Carter, John, 137 Simcoe
Clark, J. P., Mus. Bac., Bloor, Yorkville
Dixon, Miss J. F., 31 Richmond e
Haberstock, Nimrod, (piano forte), 71 Queen e
Hastings, Edward A., 218 George
Humphreys, J. D., 6 Seaton
Kerrison, J. D., 97 Bloor e
Labitzky, William, Sydenham, Yorkville
Martin, Henry, 9 Cruiksnank
Peiler, Carl, Yorkville
Sefton, H. F., 230 Church
Strathy, George W., Mus. Doc., 44 Bond
Toulmin, Frederick, Sydenham, Yorkville

Telegraph Companies.

Dominion Telegraph Company, J. Kirby, manager, 4 Wellington e
Montreal Telegraph Company, Harvey P. Dwight, manager, Exchange Buildings, Wellington e

Theatre.

Royal Lyceum, George Holman, lessee and manager, rear of 101 King w

Tinners' Stock, Wholesale.

Samuel, M. & L., 49 Wellington e

Tobacco Manufacturers.

Collis, G. A. & Co., Yorkville
Lewis, J. D. & Co., 64 Nelson e
Scales, Job & Co., 45 Palace.

Tobacco Machinery, Manufacturers of.
Hamilton, William & Son, St. Lawrence Foundry, Palace

Toys and Fancy Goods.
Bansley, Charles, 71 King w
Crawford, Arthur, (Bazaar) 164 Yonge
Linton, John D., 23 King w
Nelson, Wood & Co., 74 York
Piddington, Alfred, 248 Yonge
Sinclair, John, 245 Yonge

Trunk Makers.
Clarke, F., 86 Yonge
Clarke, H. E., 103 King w
Malcom, R., 181 King e, and Rossin House Block

Umbrella Maker.
East, Henry, 298 Yonge

Undertakers.
Fawkes, S., 337 Yonge
McCarthy & Mason, 155 Queen w
Solleder, John, 240 King e
Williams, C. M., 193 Yonge
Williams, J. J., 302 Queen w
Wilmott, Charles W., 268 & 270 Adelaide w

Upholsterers.—*(See also Cabinet Makers.)*
Ellis, George, 179 Yonge
Williams, George W., 601 Yonge
Wingfield & Thomas, 151 Yonge

Veterinary Surgeons.
Allen, John, Shuter nr Yonge
Smith, Andrew, 40 Temperance

Vinegar Manufacturers.
Fittinger, H., McCord & Co., Lesslieville
Parks, W. & Co., 92 to 98 Adelaide e
Wilson, William, 115 and 117 Bay

Wagon Makers.—*(See also Blacksmith, Carriage and Wagon Makers.)*
Butt, Ephraim, r 15 Agnes
Creys, Isaac, 10 Edward
Eagle, William, 144 Duke
Hamilton, Robert, 31 Adelaide
Kearney, Patrick, Lane off Scott
Kempter, Francis, 457 Yonge
Kennedy, David, 419 Queen w
McGlone, John, 25 Princess
McQuinn, S. F., 357 Queen w
Ryder, Thomas, 186 Queen w
Thompson, William, 485 Queen w

Watchmakers and Jewellers.
Abbott, Morris, 268½ Yonge
Bethell, Francis, 234 Yonge
Carnegie, Charles, 14 King w
Clinkunbroomer, Charles, 156 Queen w
Cornell, William E., 150 Yonge
Ellis, James E., 43 King e
Faragher, Thomas, 178 King e
Feintuch M., 129 King e
Hodgins, George, 169 King e
Jackson, J. H., 88 King e
Joseph, J. G. & Co., 5 King e and 46 Yonge
Kent & Bro., 116 Yonge
Kleiser, S. P., 130 Yonge
Melander, John, 344 Yonge
Millar, Mrs. Jane W., 135 King e
Morphy, Edward M., 141 Yonge
Roberts, W. R., 59 King w
Robinson, Joseph & Co., 15 King w
Russell, A. W., 57 Yonge
Segsworth, John, 113 Young
Wanless, John, 172 Yonge
Wharin, William & Co., 11 King e
Wilkes, Robert, 48 and 50 Yonge

Watchmakers' Tools.
Gunther, F. & E., 9 King e
Kleiser, S. P., 130 Yonge
Wilkes, Robert, 48 and 50 Yonge
Willcock, Stephen, 4 King e

Wharves and Wharfingers.
Adamson, James, St. Lawrence wharf
Adamson, William, Adamson's wharf
Beard, E. & Co., foot of Church
Brown, John & Co., Yonge cor Esplanade
Carruthers, E. M., Queen's wharf and 56 Front e
Dalby, George E., 122 Brock
Hamilton, Sydney S., Hamilton' wharf
Helliwell's wharf, Esplanade, bet West Market Square and Church
Higginbotham, N. & Co., Custom House wharf
Milloy & Co., Yonge street wharf
Northern Railway wharf, John Albiston, Esplanade w
Queen's wharf, ft of Bathurst
Scott & Gorrie, ft of Church
Shaw, Thomas, Leak's wharf, nr Market
Taylor, Archibald, ft George
Tinning, R. & Brothers, Tinning's wharf, Esplanade cor York
Wyatt's wharf, George H. Wyatt, nr Jacques & Hay's factory

Whip Manufacturers.
Threlkeld, Joseph, 390 Yonge

Wig Makers.
Bansley, Charles, 71 King w
Copley, James, 258 Yonge
Smart, John, 46 King w

Wine and Spirit Dealers.
Armstrong, J. D., 148 King e
Boyd, John & Co., 63 Front e
Coulthard, John. 30 Francis
Fulton, Michie & Co., 7 King w
Griffith, J. C. & Co., 219 Yonge
Griffith, Thomas & Co., 39 Front e
Griffith, W. & R., Front cor Church
Hooper, E. & Co., 43 King w
Hornibrook & LePan, 167 Yonge
Howland & Fitch, 25 Church
Hubertus, W. L. & Co., 14 Church
Jaffray, Robert, 244 Yonge
Law, John, 300 Yonge
Michie, George & Co., Front cor Yonge
Moore, C. & Co., 5, 7 and 9 Wellington w
Patterson, Alexander, 287 Yonge
Peoples & Co., 311 Yonge
Perkins, F. & G. & Co., 41 Front
Reford & Dillon, 12 and 14 Wellington e
Reid, C. P., & Co., 30 Wellington e
Scoley, Edward K., 37 and 39 St. Lawrence Mkt
Sinclair, J. & F. G., 12 Palace
Smith, Frank & Co., Front e, cor Scott
Smith, James E., & Co., 31 Church
Stock, James, 16 Palace
Strachan, William, & Co., King e cor Nelson
Thompson, Charles, 77 King e
Watson, John, Exchange Alley

Wire Workers.
Coo, W. H., 203 Queen w
Monteverd, Michael, 381 Yonge
Rice, W. H., 35 Grosvenor

Wood Merchants.
(*See, also, Coal and Wood, Dealers in*)
Aikenhead, James, St. Lawrence Wharf
Anderson, Joseph, 53 Agnes
Bell, Thomas, 199 Queen w and 150 Simcoe
Corbett, William, 196 Elizabeth
Crane, Samuel, 103 Queen w
Holt, William, Edward nr Elizabeth
Hunter, Samuel, 299 Queen w
Kennedy, Thomas, 207 Queen w
Mutton, S., cor Queen and Sherbourne
McBride, Samuel, 135 Elizabeth
Saulter, R. & W., Church nr Esplanade

Wood and Willow Ware.
Linton, John D., 23 King w
Moses, Walter W., 291 Yonge
Nelson, Wood & Co., 74 York
Murphy, William, 351 Yonge

Wool, Hide and Skin Dealers.
Barry, James W., & Son, 79 Colborne
Blake, John, Givens
Leadlay, Edward, 642 Queen w
Nixon, Thomas, 79 Colborne
Wilson & Co., 77 Colborne

Wool Pullers.
Leadlay, John A., Don Bridge

Tormore.—A small Village in the Township of Albion, County Peel, 14 miles from Toronto, and 13 from Weston. Population 60.

Blake, Thomas, farmer
Doyle, Thomas, hotel keeper
GRAHAM, WILLIAM, Postmaster, general mercht.
Hart, Robert, J.P., farmer
Mitchell, James, farmer
Porr, William, farmer
Shuttleworth, Thomas, blacksmith
Thomas, William, farmer
Watson, John, farmer

Totnes.—A Village in the Township of Ellice, County Perth, 8 miles from Stratford, the County Town. Mails semi-weekly. Population, 100.

DENNSTEDT, GEORGE H., Postmaster, general merchant.

Tottenham.—A small Village in the Township of Tecumseth, County Simcoe, 36 miles from Barrie, the County Town, and 10 from Bondhead.

Anston, William, wagon maker
Brown, —, tailor
Carmichel, Daniel, teacher
Casey, Owen, farmer
Conley, B., tailor
Coop, John T., butcher
Eagan, Nicholas, prop. flouring mills
Falls, Nicholas, painter
Farrell, Andrew, soap and candle maker
Greenaway, John, wagon maker
Greenaway, Noble E., cabinet maker
Greenaway, Thomas, farmer
Hill, Rev. R. N. (N. C. Methodist)
Hipwell, A., general merchant
Lavery, Joseph, boots and shoes
Martin, Robert, hotel keeper
Nolan, George A., J.P., prop. flouring mills
Power, John, tanner and hide and leather dealer
Sample, Hugh, farmer
Sandford, W. H., general merchant
Shields, Francis, farmer
Stephens, Alexander, farmer
Stephenson, Thomas, carpenter
Stone, Henry, general agent
Sydie, John, saddler
Sydie, Mrs., milliner
Tegart, George, farmer
Tegart, James, farmer
Tegart, James M., J.P.
Trevor, George, boots and shoes
Walker, John D., general merchant
Willson, Alexander, sash, blind and door manuf
WILSON, JOHN, Postmaster, general merchant.

Townsend Centre.—A post office in the Township of Townsend, County Norfolk.

Barber, William, farmer
Hellzer, W. S., stock dealer
Hennington, R., shingle maker
Lamb, John, proprietor hotel
Lewis, J. S., farmer
Park, Charles, farmer
Petit, Jonathan, brick maker
Rice, Philip, farmer
SLAGHT, H., Postmaster
Slaght, Israel, general merchant
Slaght, Job, carpenter
Slaght, John, carpenter
Smith, James H., farmer
Smith, J. D., teacher
Smith, Philip, farmer
Smith, William H., carpenter

Trafalgar.—A Village in the Township of Trafalgar, County Halton, 12 miles from Milton the County Town, 4 from Oakville and 16 from Georgetown Station Grand Trunk Railroad. Population 80

APPELBE, JAMES, J. P., Postmaster
Appelbe, John R., insurance agent
Bayne, William, butcher
Elliott, George, J. P
Keating, William, farmer
Kilgour, William, flour and grist mill
Kindree, Amos, hotel keeper, farmer
McDuffee, Daniel, farmer
McWilliams, William, hotel keeper, farmer
Pettit, William, farmer

Treadwell.—A small Village in the Township of North Plantagenet, County Prescott, 17 miles distant from L'Orignal, the County Town.

HUGHES, H., Postmaster.

Trenton.—An incorporated village, port of entry and station of the G.T.R., in the Townships of Murray and Sidney, Counties Northumberland and Hastings. The village is pleasantly situated on both sides of the river Trent, at the head of the Bay of Quinté. Large quantities of lumber and grain are shipped from this point. Steamers to Oswego, Montreal and intermediate ports. Distant from Belleville 12 miles, Toronto, 101 and from Kingston 59. Money Order Office, and Savings Bank. Population 1800.

Allan, Daniel, baker
Alley, William, watchmaker
Austin & Hilton, general merchants
Austin, W. H., (Austin & Hilton) forwarding, commission and produce merchant, agent Royal Provincial Insurance Company
Barker, W. T., druggist and apothecary
Bleasdell, Rev. William, M.A. (Episcopal)
Brettargh, Rev. Henry, (Roman Catholic)
Brown & Brock, photographers
Carpenter & Dunham, saloon keepers
Chisholm, James, grocer
Christie, James, agent Montreal Telegraph Company and exchange broker
Clarke, William, store keeper
Cooley, Samuel, J.P
Cobb, Rev. Thomas, (Wesleyan)
COURIER, (Thursday) George Young, editor & prop
Cumming, James, J.P., lumber merchant
Day, W. H., M.D., coroner
Deans, George, M;D., druggist
Delaney, H. W., notary public, conveyancer, &c
DENCH, JOHN, general merchant (see adv)
Dickens & Nelson, groceries, glassware, crockery, &c
Dunlop, A. W., clerk
Flindell, J. F., brewer
Forest, J. T., prop. Forest House
FRANCIS, C., barrister, &c., agent Liverpool and London and Globe Ins. Co., and Standard Life Association Co
Francis, Robert, P.L.S
GALNA, WILLIAM, book-keeper and ins. agent
Garrett & Brock, grocers
Gooding, Samuel, blacksmith
Gordon, George H., miller, dry goods and clothing
Graham, W. H. & I. B., gen merchants
Hill, Calvin, saddler
Hutchinson, John, clerk
Hutchinson, Joseph, baker
Hyde, W. J., shoemaker
Ireland, William M., groceries and provisions
Irish, J. R., dentist
Jeffs & Hume, general merchants
Knox, Uriah, blacksmith
Lawrence, Joseph, mason
Losie, grocer
Lougheed, Robert, grocer
Lyons, William, hotel keeper
McColl, John, station, telegraph and express agent
McCready, Bernard, tailor
McGowan, Francis, shoemaker
McGUIRE, F. J., J.P., general merchant
McKewen, H., hotel
MACAULEY, ALEXANDER, Collector Customs, Commissioner in B.R., issuer marriage licenses
Macauley, Denis
Manning, Peter, shoemaker
Marsh, Charles, saddler
Marsh, James, grocer
Meath, John, builder
Meyers, Adam H., barrister
Miller, Alexander, foreman Trenton Steam Mills
Miller, Joseph, grocer
Miller, Nathaniel, pump maker
Miller, R. P., grocer
Miron, Joseph, lime dealer
Morrison, W., wagon maker
Murphy, Daniel R., barrister
Parent, A. hotel
Papineau, Francis, Commercial hotel
Potter, James, grain merchant
Prieur, L., grocer
Purdy Bros., dealers boots & shoes, props plaster mills
Purdy, R., hardware
Quinlon, James, cabinet maker
Reeves & McCue, saddlers
Roblin, David, village treasurer
Rozitkie, John, butcher
SHEA, WM. P., Trenton Foundry, stamped tin and copper ware (see adv)
Simmons, Jeremiah, Clerk Division Court, Clerk Municipality.
Simpson, James, builder
Smith, G. A., dry goods and groceries
Snelson, William, foreman Trenton Foundry
Snider, C. A., tailor
Snider, H. & Co., hotel keepers
Spencer, A., grocer
Sweet, C., blacksmith
Thompson, J. W., general merchant
Walsh, Patrick, constable
Wert, J. R., saddler
White, James, shoemaker
Williams, R. W., M.B.
Yorston, John, foreman *Courier*
YOUNG, GEORGE, editor and proprietor *Trenton Courier*
YOUNG, JAMES, notary public, com. in B.R., grocer and leather dealer

Trecastle.—A small village in the Township of Wallace, County Perth, 35 miles from Stratford, the County Town, Population 50.

Bishop, James, farmer
Bishop, William, farmer
Brown, Thomas, farmer
Callaway, Thomas, farmer
Cole, William, farmer
COWAN, WILLIAM C., Postmaster
Craig, Joseph H., farmer
Donelly, Matthew, farmer
Gray, William H., farmer
Johnson, John, farmer
Kell, Freeborn, farmer
Knowles, Thomas, shingle maker
McCaughrin, Daniel, lumber dealer
McCombs, John, farmer
Morgan, George, blacksmith
Scholte, farmer
Shields, L. J., general merchant

Trowbridge.—A Village in the Township of Elma, County Perth, 34 miles from Stratford, the County Town, and 22 from Mitchell. Population 200.

Bradley, William, general merchant
Carruth, Joseph, farmer
Clothier, William, carpenter
Cosens, C., lime and stone dealer and farmer
Cosens, Charles, cabinet maker and carpenter
Cosenss George, carpenter
Code, George, saw mill proprietor
Code, George, jun., lime and stone dealer
CODE, GEORGE, SEN., Postmaster
Delyea, Isaac, carpenter
Farrow, Frederick, hotel keeper
Friar, John, general merchant
Gray, Andrew, watch maker
Halfpenny, R., farmer
Large, Jacob, butcher
Large, John, cabinet maker and carpenter
Mann, Thomas, general merchant
Moore, Robert, farmer
Oliver, R. & N., tanners and leather merchants
Smith, Robert, blacksmith
Thompson, Matthew, wagon maker
Tucker, Rev. William (Wesleyan Methodist)
Zulrigg, Gilbert, wagon maker
Zulrigg, John, blacksmith

Troy (Fairfield P. O.)

Burt, R. P., commission merchant
BURT, S. M., Postmaster
Lambert, S., cooper
Swartout, J., lumber merchant

Tuam.—A Village on a branch of the Nottawasaga River, in the Township of Tecumseth, County Simcoe, 36 miles from Barrie, the County Town, 6 from Schomberg, and 50 from Toronto. Population, 100.

Abernethy, Joseph, farmer
Abernethy, Thomas, farmer
Allen, John, soap and candle maker
Allen, Richard, general merchant
Anderson, Robert, patent right agent
Bamby, Richard, carpenter
Brawley, F., founder and machinist
Brawley, Francis, jun., cooper
Brawley, Mrs. M., baker
Brawley. T., wagon maker
Brown, Samuel, distiller
Collard, Clark, M.D.
Collard, John, proprietor planing mill
Cowan, Hamilton, distiller
Dale, William, wagon maker
DeLane, James, farmer
DERHAM, P., Postmaster, J.P., lumber dealer and general merchant
Doyle, Thomas, teacher
Egan, Nicholas & James, props flouring mill
Ellison, W., carpenter
Haffey, Miss, milliner
Hannah George, farmer
Hodgins, J., farmer
Hollingshead, George, J. P.
Hollingshead, Joseph, farmer
Karns, John, farmer
King, D. G., general agent
King, James, sen., attorney-at-law
King, James, weigh master and license inspector
King, John, cabinet maker and prop. livery stables
Lavrey, Joseph, shoemaker
Legewood, Thomas, carpenter
Logan, Robert, proprietor Green Lion Hotel
Lowrey, R., banker
McGarr, Joseph, dentist
McMahon, Hugh, farmer
Martin, Robert, billiard room
Millegan, James, farmer
Millegan, Thomas, general merchant
Millegan. William, painter
Mills, Jesse, tanner, hide and leather dealer
Montgomery, James, attorney-at.law
Palmer, J., painter
Papen, L. A., proprietor Commercial Hotel
Pearson, J., accountant
Percy, Gilbert, cabinet maker
Platt, James, farmer
Rogers, Joseph, farmer
Rogers, Levi, farmer
Rogers, Thomas and James, commission merchants
Scanlon, James,
Shields, F., stock broker
Slattery, Daniel, proprietor oil well
Snowdon, F., principal Willowdale Academy
Urquhart, John, saddler
Walker, J. D., auctioneer
Walls, W., farmer
Wells, W., proprietor brick yard
Wilson, E., wagon maker
Wilson, James, proprietor planing mill
Wilson John & Co., sash, blind and door mnfrs

Trudell.—A Post Office in the Township of Tilbury West, County Essex.

Allen William, carriage maker
Cornwall, John, farmer
Dodd, James F., farmer
Goodrow, M., blacksmith
Manning, John, farmer
Marchand, Jean Bte., innkeeper
Peel Bros., gen merchts, props grist and saw mills
RICHARDSON, H., Postmaster, general merchant
Wilson, Robert, carpenter

Tullamore.—A Village in the Township of Chinguacousey, County Peel, 10 miles from Brampton, the County Town, and 8 from Malton, Stages to Mono Mills and Malton. Money Order Office. Population 100.

Bailey, Mrs., tailor
Brown, Henry, brick yard
Buchanan, H., boots and shoes
Buchanan, Miss, milliner
Bullyman, Thomas, butcher
Burrell, Thomas, carpenter
Chaffee, J. M., general merchant
Chaffee, J. M., farmer
Chamberlain, F., tailor
Corket, George, farmer
Dynes, R., cabinet maker
Ellis, John, carpenter
Endacott, H., saddler
Evans, J., tailor
Grant, Rev. William (Church of England)
Grey, Samuel, gunsmith
Hamilton, George, J.P., proprietor livery stable and nurseryman
Hewson, James, farmer
Hewson, N., farmer
Hogg, George, shoemaker
Jordan, William, wagon maker
Leighton, J., farmer
Lindsay, James, general merchant
Lindsay, William, farmer
LOWTHER, JOHN, Postmaster, general merchant
Mulligan, James, J.P
Mulligan, Joseph, J.P., prop. Commercial Hotel
Mullin, J. F., M.D
Neely, William, J.P., farmer
Rain, R., farmer
Robinson, James, farmer
Sargent, William, farmer
Shields, John, farmer
Thompson, J., farmer
Thompson, T., farmer
Vogan, Joseph, blacksmith
Wilson, J., farmer
Woods, John, prop. Exchange Hotel

Tuscarora.—(Village Middleport).—A Station of the Grand Trunk Railway, on the Grand River, in the Township of Onondaga, County Brant, 11 miles from Brantford, the County Town, 6 from Caledonia and 25 from Port Dover. Population 200.

Allen, William, farmer
Armour, Thomas, J. P
Boyce, John, shingle maker
Brezett, Joseph, carpenter
Deagle, David, general merchant
Dennis, David, carpenter
Douglas, Alexander, farmer
Douglas, William, farmer
Duane, Rev. D. W., (Church of England)
Grant, James, farmer
Hager, Charles, farmer
Hager, James, farmer
Harris, Richard, farmer
McArthur, James, lumber dealer
McLaren, Robert, baker
Matheson, Robert, cabinet maker
MAYNARD, HENRY, Postmaster, general mercht
Mirricle, Robert, farmer
Osborn, John, farmer
Patten, Frederick, M.D
Patterson, James, carpenter
Patterson, John, hotel keeper
Reeker, Frederick, farmer
Sheppard, James, hotel keeper

Tweed.—A Village on the Moira River, in the Township of Hungerford, County Hastings, 25 miles from Belleville, the County Town. The Village is situated in the midst of one of the richest mineral regions in the Dominion. Gold, silver, copper, antimony, &c., being abundant. Several large crushing and smelting mills have been erected and the Village presents every probability of future prosperity. Population 500.

Breen, James, blacksmith
Burr, J. F., farmer
Carleton, John F., saddler
Conners, William, hotel keeper
Cross, Robert, carpenter
Downing, John, hotel keeper
Elliott, Joseph, J.P., farmer
Green, J., blacksmith
Greer, William, carpenter
Hacket, John, shoemaker
Howell, George, M.D.
Jamieson, James, lumber dealer
McCammon, John, carpenter
McCann, Thomas, general merchant
McCormick, R., tailor
McGowan, A., wagon maker
MARSHALL, RICHARD, Postmaster and grocer
Munroe, G. A., hotel keeper
Murphy, Francis, general merchant
Pomeroy, T. E., M.D.
Porter, John, farmer
Potts, William, farmer
Reid, James, general merchant
Rosvere, John, shoemaker
Ryan, Rev. David (Wesleyan)
Spafford, Abijah, baker
Waller, James, blacksmith
Walsh, P., tailor
White, Samuel, tinsmith
White, William, tinsmith
Williams, William, grocer
Wray, William, tailor
Wright, William, general merchant

Tweedside.—A Village in the Township of Saltfleet, County Wentworth.

Allison, Z. B., telegraph operator
Althouse, E., manuf. woolen goods
Althouse, George W., saddler
Althouse, John M., tailor
Althouse, J., farmer
Althouse, S., farmer
Beadle, J., farmer
Beadle, S., farmer
Bridgman, Dr
Carpenter, Andrew, farmer
Carpenter, H. W., farmer
Carpenter, J., grocer
Carpenter, J. & G., prop. saw mill
Clarke, J., grocer
Combs, W., cooper
Cook, James, prop. flouring mill
Cowell, John W., shingle maker
Harris, J. H., cooper
Hart, George, shingle maker
JOHNSON, GILBERT, Postmaster
Johnston, G., farmer
Johnston, J. W., farmer
Lacy, R., farmer
Lawrence, Thomas, hotel keeper
Lowden, N. T., teacher
McKay, Dr
Marlatt, Charles, farmer
Milne, J., prop. livery stable
More, Charles, cabinet maker
Muir, George, dentist
Muir, George W., painter
Muir, M., manuf. woolen goods
Neil, Levi, auctioneer
Owens, R. L., lime and stone dealer
Pettit, J., farmer
Potruff, D., watchmaker
Smith, John, farmer
Smith, Joshua, farmer
Stewart, A., farmer
Stewart, Thomas, farmer
Swazie, J., dry goods
Tolmey, J., grocer
Travis, J. H., painter
Tweedle, F., farmer
Tweedle, J., farmer
Tweedle, R., farmer
Tweedle, W., farmer

Tyrconnell.—A Village in the Township of Dunwich, County Elgin, 18 miles from St. Thomas, the County Town. Improved land in the vicinity averages $30 per acre. Population 200.

Allen, George, farmer
Allen, George, blacksmith
Allen, George, carpenter
Backus, Andrew, farmer
Backus, Stephen, farmer
Barber, James, tanner
Basket, William, butcher
Bate, James, farmer
Bate & Osborne, general merchants
Blackwood, James, farmer
Burnside, William, manufacturer woolen goods
Cameron, Peter, blacksmith
Campbell, Dougald, farmer
Campbell, Dougald, carpenter
Comfort, A., proprietor woolen factory
Conn, M., J. P.
CONN, M., JUN,, Postmaster
Crane, Peter, farmer
Drennan, Rev. A., (Wesleyan)
Duncan, George, teacher
Frome, William, hotrl keeper
Harding, William, hotel keeper
Hawkins, Elias, boots and shoes
Humphrey, Moses, carriage maker
Hunt, George, estate agent
James, Richard, cooper
Kennedy, Rev. J., (Church of England)
Mitchell, Joseph, proprietor fulling and saw mills
Morden, William, lime and stone dealer
Morish, Richard, veterinary surgeon
O'Brien, John, carpenter
Osborne, Walter, teacher
Page, James, blacksmith
Page, Jonas, soap and candle factory
Page & Son, potash factors
Pearse, John, proprietor cheese factory
Quimby, J. L., shingle factory
Ramon, Isaac, carriage maker
Scott, Joseph, grain merchant, leather dealer
Sheridan, Michael, tailor
Winters, Charles, carpenter

Tyrrell.—A Post Office, in the Township of Townsend, County Norfolk.
HEATH, SAMUEL, Postmaster.

Udora.—A Village on Black River, in the Township of Scott, County Ontario 32 miles from Whitby, the County Town, and 54 from Toronto. Population 200.

Brethour, Arnold, proprietor saw mill
Brethour, James, farmer
Brethour, James E., farmer
Brown, William, proprietor saw mill and grocer
Clissold, Samuel, cooper
Cosgrove, M., blacksmith
Fawns, George, farmer
Fairfield, Archibald, hotel keeper
Harrison, Henry, farmer
Harrison, Reuben, teacher
McDowell, Samuel, blacksmith
Phillips, William and Robert, pump makers
Scott, Samuel, farmer
Shire, Jacob, farmer
Shire, William, weaver
Shoddon, William, farmer
Tucker, Michael, proprietor saw mill
Umphrey, Samuel, prop. saw mill and gen. mercht.
Urquhart, Alexander, carpenter
Woodcock, Jacob, shingle maker

Umfraville.—A Post Office in the Township of Dungannon, County Hastings.

Carr, Robert, farmer
Cleak, J. P., general merchant and mill owner
Doyle, Morgan, farmer
Finnegan, Michael, farmer
Hana, William, farmer
Harding, Philip, carpenter
KAVANAGH, D., J.P., Postmaster, gen. merchant
Kelly, Neil, farmer
Long, Eason, carpenter
McCabe, Thomas, farmer
McCormick, Rev. Mr. (Roman Catholic)
Mulcahey, Mrs. farmer
O'Neill, John, farmer
Robinson, Miss Maria, teacher
Robinson, William, farmer and mill owner
Sutton, Rev. Mr. (Church of England)
Sweet, B., shingle maker
Tait, J. R., general merchant
Tait, Miss Sarah, teacher

Uffington.—A Post Office in the Township of Draper, County Ontario.

THOMPSON, ANDREW, Postmaster.

Ulster.—A Post Office in the Township of Wawanosh, County Huron.

McKAY, GEORGE, Postmaster.

Underhill.—A Small Village in the Township of Essa, County Simcoe, 21 miles from Barrie, the County Town.

Burns, James, butcher
Garbut, John, painter
Irwin, James, innkeeper
NICOLS, JOHN, Postmaster
Upton, Joseph, general merchant

Underwood.—A Village in the Township of Bruce, County Bruce, 25 miles from Walkerton, the County Town, Stages to Goderich, 48 miles, Southampton, 15, and Paisley, 13. Population 150.

Cameron, Donald, hotel keeper
COULTHARD, J. H., Postmaster, gen. merchant
McDonald & Co., general merchants
McLean, Charles, auctioneer
Macfarlane, Walter, general merchant
Matheson, John, blacksmith
Munn, M., M.D

Unionville.—A Village on the River Rouge, in the Township of Markham, County York, 19 miles from Toronto. Population 400.

Braithwaite, Mark M., general merchant
Carter, John, auctioneer and butcher
Chant, Christopher, cabinet maker
Crosby, H. P., M.P.P., prop flouring mill
Davison, James M., farmer
EAKIN, GEORGE, P. M., general merchant
Eakin, William, carriage maker
Eckardt, Frederick, farmer
Eckardt, James, farmer
Eckardt, William, farmer
Eckardt, Salem, auctioneer
Eckardt, Thomas P., M. D.
Eckardt, William, J. P., farmer
Fairless, James, general merchant
Fawcett, Rev. M., (Wesleyan)
Fishburn, Rev. J., (Lutheran)
Hill, Rev. George J. G.,, (Church of England)
Hunter, George, blacksmith
Johnson, David, shoemaker
Joyce, John, farmer
Justice, Charles, M. D.
McCallum, Rev. D. (Congregational)
Nicolson, Andrew, cooper
Richardson, Thos, farmer
Robinson, George, carpenter
Size, A., hotel keeper
Size, James, carpenter
Size, John, shoemaker
Size, William, hotel-keeper
Stephenson, John, blacksmith
White, John, general merchant
Woodall, William, cabinet maker

Upnor.—A Post Office in the Township of Carden, County Victoria.

TRESIDDER, THOMAS, Postmaster.

CURRIE BOILER WORKS

AND

STEAM BOILERS,

OF EVERY DESCRIPTION MADE AND REPAIRED.

On ESPLANADE near CHURCH STREET, TORONTO

NEIL CURRIE, Prop.

A. DREDGE & CO.,

WHOLESALE STATIONERS,

BOOKBINDERS,

AND

ENVELOPE MANUFACTURERS,

53 Yonge Street, Toronto, Ontario.

Sole Agents in Canada for SLATER & PALMER'S CELEBRATED PRINTING INKS.

GALLERY OF ART.

R. W. LAIRD,

Mirror and Picture Frame Manufacturer!

79 KING STREET, TORONTO, ONT.

Trade supplied with Picture Frame Mouldings of all descriptions. Send for Samples and prices.

Union.—A Village and Station on the London & Port Stanley Railway, on Beaver Creek, in the Township of Yarmouth, County Elgin, 5 miles from St. Thomas, the County Town. Money Order Office. Population 150.

Atherton, C., general agent
Bailey, Richard, prop. flouring mill
Davidson, James, blacksmith
Fera, W. A., carpenter
Gavitz, Jesse, prop. flouring mill
Graham, Robert, farmer
Green, Thomas, J.P
Green, T. & B., manuf. woolen goods
Hannan, Isaac, saddler
Haight & Wilson, props. of flour mill and manuf. woolen goods
Hathaway, S. B., farmer
Hepburn, Michael, farmer
Long, Elias, farmer
Mandeville, W. H., J.P., carriage maker
Montgomery, R., hotel keeper
Partridge, John, hotel keeper
Sexsmith, Rev. George (Wesleyan)
Steele, Jonathan, farmer
Steel & McKenzie, general merchants
Welding, E. H., farmer
Wintermute, Benjamin, farmer
Young, Matthew, carpenter

Utica.—A Village in the Township of Reach, County Ontario, 14 miles from Whitby, the County Town, and 44 from Toronto. Stages to Uxbridge and Whitby. Population, 150.

Allen, William, blacksmith
Blackburn, Samuel, mason
Broderick, George, farmer
Christie, Duncan, farmer
Christie, Donald, farmer
Currie, George, prop saw mill
Dafoe, Jacob, hotel and storekeeper
Dake, Hiram, hotel keeper
Fagan, Henry, tailor
Kendle, E., farmer
Leach, Temple, shoemaker
McKay, Rev. R. D. (Presbyterian)
McKercher, Farquhar, farmer
Sanders, William, wagon maker
Smith, Malcolm, farmer
Sutliffe, John, general merchant

Utterson.—A Post Office in the Township of Stephenson, District of Muskoka, 140 miles from Toronto. The land in the vicinity is granted free to actual settlers

Galloway, David, shoemaker
George, Thomas, Grocer
HANES, ERASTUS, Postmaster
Hanes, James, farmer
Hanes, Jeremiah, farmer
Hogaboom, David, cooper
Kennedy, S. S., shoemaker
McAlpine, — proprietor grist mill
Snell, John, butcher
Tully, Philip, cooper
Winfield, John M., stone dealer
Rook, John, farmer

Uttoxeter.—A Post Village in the Township of Plymouth, County Lambton.

SHEPHERD, SIMPSON, Postmaster

Uxbridge.—A Village on a branch of Black River, in the Township of Uxbridge, County Ontario, 20 miles from Whitby, the County Town. The village is on the line of the proposed Toronto and Nipissing Railway, also on the line of the Whitby & Port Perry, by a proposed branch. Money Order Office and Savings Bank. Stage daily to Whitby. Population 1500.

Anderson, James, cooper
Annand, W. J., proprietor Uxbridge House
ARMSTRONG HOUSE, E. Armstrong, proprietor. (see adv).
Bagshaw, A., farmer
Baker Jacob, cabinet maker
Bascom, J., Sen.
Bascom, J. M. D.
Beebe, S., blacksmith
Bell, Richard
Bishop, W. H., patent right agent
Bolster, J. & Co., general merchant
Bolster, T., sen.
Bolton, William, blacksmith
Blaire, Rev. L., Roman Catholic, res Vromanton
Brown, J., carpenter
Brown, Johnston, planing mill, sash, door and blind factory
Brown, J. W. C., attorney-at-law, accountant, insurance agent, notary public
Burchall, Thomas, cooper
Bustin, William, carpenter
Button, A. T., planing mill
Button, A. T. & Co., general merchant
Card, D. M., auctioneer and livery stables
Chapman, Ira,
Cleland, Rev. W., (United Presbyterian)
Colcock, T. F., baker
Combe, William, tailor
Cowan, Andrew, general merchant
Crosby, Harman, general merchant
Crosby, J. G., general merchant
Crosby, M. B., butcher
Dickey, Joseph, accountant, insurance agent, etc
Douglass, Rev. J., (Canada Presbyterian)
Dowling, Daniel, cooper

Etwell, Edward, wagon maker
Fawcett, J. C., general merchant
Feasby, J. B., J.P.
Ferguson, W., farmer
Finch, Joseph, innkeeper
Forneri, Rev. R. S., (Church of England)
Gould, J. E.
Gould, Joseph, J.P., flour and grist mill, manufacturer woollen goods
Hamilton, William, general merchant
Hardy, Alexander, carpenter
Harman, J., teacher
Harrison, James, harness maker
Henderson, Andrew, innkeeper
Hilborn, J. P., farmer
Hilliary, J. J., M. D
Jones, Henry, painter
Jones, John, carpenter
Kimmerly, J. A., painter
Kydd, W., farmer
Low & Bertram, boots and shoes
McCann, J. F., harness maker
McCallum, C., carpenter
McCarthy, D., painter
McCulloch, John, shoemaker
McGrath, M., tailor
McGrath, Thomas, brick yard
McGuire, J. & W., cabinet makers
McRucher, John, carpenter
Miller, Henry, Commercial Hotel
Miller, Rev. George, (Methodist Episcopal)
Nation, J., M. D
Nott, Rev. J., (Baptist)
O'Neill, M., blacksmith
Parrish, Samuel, tanner
Peare, C. H., watchmaker
Pearson, Rev. M., (Wesleyan Methodist)
Reeves, Joseph, shoemaker
Rhodes, Joseph, wagon maker
Smith, Andrew, general merchant
Somerville, Adam, carpenter
Stanton, Thomas, brewer
Stone, M., tailor
St. John, T., Anglo Saxon Hotel
Stewart, John, butcher
Spears, Robert, J. P
Thom, Andrew, lime and stone dealer
Thompson, Alexander, carpenter
Thomson, John, teacher
Thompson, Henry, tinsmith
Thompson, John, B.A., teacher grammar school
Thompson, William, boots and shoes
Tuck, William, wagon maker
Umphrey, Robert, grocer
Vicars, M. & Bros., props. foundry and machine shop
WHELER, GEORGE, J.P., Postmaster prop. flour and grist mill
Waid, C. D., watchmaker and dentist
Walker, C. H., painter
Walks, David, wagon maker
Wheler and Tomlinson, job printers
White, William, shingle maker
Weeks, A. D., druggist
Welsh, William, tailor
Willson, W., carpenter

Vandecar.—A small village in the township of East Oxford, County Oxford, 9 miles from Woodstock, the County Town, and 4 from Eastwood station. Population 50.

ARNELL, THOMAS H., P. M., carpenter
Ayling, James, farmer
Bertram, Daniel, farmer
Bertram, William, farmer
Canfield, Joel, farmer
Cate, George, plasterer
Daly, Foed, farmer
Davis, W. J., painter
Fowler, James, shoemaker
Neal, Thomas, farmor
Redpath, Septimus, general merchrnt
Seburg, Stephen, farmer
Smith, George, blacksmith
Thompson, George, farmer
Vandecar, Robert, farmer

Valentia.—A Post office in the Township of Mariposa, County Victoria.

SHARP, H. W., Postmaster.

Valetta.—A Post office in the Township of Tilbury East, County Kent, 16 miles from Chatham, the County Town. Daily Stages to Chatham and Windsor. Daily Mail.

RICHARDSON, JOHN, Postmaster, gen. mercht
Wands, Alexander, blacksmith and wagon maker

Vallentyne.—A Village in the Township of Brock, County Ontario, 36 miles from Whitby, the County Town, and 55 from Toronto. Population 50.

Brethour, Arnold, farmer
Brethour, Henry, farmer
BRETHOUR, SAMUEL, Postmaster, gen. merchant
Conbey, Daniel, wagon maker
Edwards, Thomas, general merchant
Glendinning, Henry, farmer
Miller, John, farmer
Reid, Thomas, hotel keeper
Ryan, J. T., farmer
St. John, Amos
St. John, Julius
Switzer, C. & L., shoemakers
Thompson, George, blacksmith
Thompson, John, sash factory
Thompson, John, prop planing mil
Thompsan, Joseph, farmer
Thompson, William, farmer

Vankleek Hill.—A thriving Village in the Township of Hawkesbury West, County Prescott, 8 miles from L'Orignal, the County town, and 30 from Lancaster. Stages to the above places. Money Order Office and Savings Bank. Population 700.

Armstrong, Rev. J. G., (Church of England)
Barton, Thomas O., general merchant
Boyd, James, J. P., general merchant
Cameron, Hugh. general merchant
Cameron & Cummings, prop. flour mills and general merchants
Campbell, A. B., carpenter and cabinet maker
Chalmers, Rev., (Methodist)
DeLorme, Peter, carpenter and cabinet maker
Gregg, Thomas, hotel keeper
Harkin, William, M.D.
Hays, William, painter
Hepburn, Thomas, saddler
Hersey & Johnson, leather dealers
Higginson, Thomas, farmer
Jamieson, D. J., general merchant
Johnson, Hiram, hotel keeper
Jolly, Emanuel & Son, tailors
Kerr, —, proprietor flour mill
Lumsden, Rev. W. (Congregational)
McCuaig, Malcolm, general merchant
McDonell, Angus, wagon maker
McDONELL, DUNCAN, Postmaster and druggist
McDonell, James A., proprietor American hotel
McDonell, Roderick, hotel keeper
McIntosh, Angus, tailor
McIntosh, James, M.D.
McIntosh, James, boots and shoes
McIntosh, John, boots and shoes
McLaren, James R., boots and shoes
McLaren, John R., general merchants
McLaren, Brothers, general merchants
McRae, William, saddler
McVicar, Alexander, wagon maker
Merondo, Peter, carpenter
Pelon, P., boots and shoes
Potter, John, farmer
Potter, John C., grocer
Robertson, John, general merchant
Ross, Thomas C., tailor
Sample, John, auctioneer
Saucier, P. T., watch maker
St. Denis, butcher
Stewart, Hugh, baker
Stewart, Neil, farmer
Thistlethwaite, Robert
Vankleek, John, farmer
Villeneuve, Michael, carpenter
Waite, William, butcher.
Wells, James P., general merchant, manufacturer of pot and pearlash

---

Varna.—A Village near the Bayfield River, in the Township of Stanley, County Huron, 18 miles from Goderich, the County Town, and 10 from Seaforth Station Grand Trunk Railway. Stage to Bayfield and Seaforth. Population 100.

Armstrong, William, cooper
Cook, Thomas, shoemaker
Crawford, John, shoemaker
Deihl, George, cabinet maker
Logan, David, cooper
Purdy, William, carriage maker
SECORD, J. B., Postmaster and general merchant
Stinson, William, proprietor flour mill
Turner, John, hotel keeper
Turner, William, proprietor flour mill
Willson, A., general merchant

Veighton.—A small Village in the Township of Cumberland, County Russell, 60 miles from L'Orignal, the County Town. Population 80.

Armstrong, Robert, farmer
Baggs, John, tailor
Buckingham, John, farmer
Buckingham, Richard, farmer
Eady, William, farmer
Hamilton, Robert, shingle maker
Henderson, Walter, farmer
James, G., farmer
Lane, James, farmer
McVEIGH, JOHN, Postmaster and hotel keeper
McVeigh, Thomas, pump maker
Marshall, G., farmer
Shaw, George, farmer
Shaw, Robert, farmer
Shaw, William, farmer
Wilson, Richard, farmer
Wilson, Thomas, farmer
York, George, drover

Vellore.—A Small Village in the Township of Vaughan, County York, 20 miles from Toronto. Pop. 50.

Cameron, Archibald, farmer
Constable, William, farmer
Frank, Peter, farmer
Hughes, George, shingle maker
Lamere, Jacob, farmer
McDonald, Archibald, farmer
McDonald, Daniel, carpenter
McDONALD, JOHN, Postmaster, gen. merchant
McDonald Samuel, wagon maker
McKinnon, Alexander, carpenter
McLean, Charles, farmer
McNeil, Arthur, farmer
Snider, John, farmer

Vennachar.—A Post Office in the Township of Abinger, County Addington.
McKENYON, CHARLES, Postmaster.

Ventnor.—A Village on the Petite Nation River, in the Township of Edwardsburgh, County Grenville, 14 miles from Prescott.

Adams, Alexander, carpenter
Adams, Alfred, farmer
Adams, Edward, farmer
Adams, Edwin, blacksmith
Adams, Josiah, lumber merchant and saw mill prop
Adams, Josiah, shingle maker
Adams, Levi, flouring and grist mill
Condell, William T., cabinet maker, agent artificial limbs
Cook, Abel, carpenter
Cook, John, farmer
Davidson, Abraham, farmer
Davidson, James, farmer
Dinwoodi, Wm. C., lumber mer. and saw mill prop
GAMBLE JOHN, Postmaster
Gamble William J., carpenter
Gillespie, James, general merchant
Gillespie, James, farmer
Gillespie, Miss Catharine, teacher
Imrie, John, farmer
Leddie, James & Son, shoemakers
Lockerbie, Matthew, blacksmith
McDougall, Alexander, painter
Macaulay, John, carpenter
Macaulay, John, general merchant
Still, James, wagon maker

Verdun.—A Post Office in the Township of Huron, County Bruce

COLLING, J., Postmaster.

Vernon.—A Post Office in the Township of Osgoode, County Russell.

McDONALD, DUNCAN, Postmaster

Vernonville.—A Post Office in the Township of Haldimand, County Northumberland.

TERRY, HENRY, Postmaster.

Verona.—A small Village in the Township of Portland, County Frontenac; 21 miles from Kingston. Average price of land in the vicinity $20; unimproved, $10 per acre.

Abrams, Howard, teacher
Abrams, J., carpenter
Abrams, William, inn keeper
Card, A., cooper
Carruthers, Miss Ellen, teacher
Folger, Rev. Mr., Primitive Methodist
Grant, Alexander, cooper
Lyons, Francis, painter
Moore, John, cabinet maker
O'Laughlin, Rev. Mr., Church of England
Peters, Eli J., wagon maker
Sanderson, Rev. Mr., Episcopal Methodist
Stanford, A. E., general merchant
WATSON, J., J. P., Postmaster
Watts, William. butcher
Wright, Charles, butcher

Vesta.—A Post Office in the Township of Brant, County Bruce.

Blakeway, Thomas, carpenter
Stevens, W. A., general merchant
CAMERON, ROBERT, Postmaster

Victoria Corners.—A small Village in the Township of Reach, County Ontario, 26 miles from Whitby, the County Town, and 48 from Toronto. Population 30.

Acton, A., farmer
MADILL, HENRY, Postmaster
Mooney, R., farmer
St. John, G., farmer

Victoria Square.—A Village in the Township of Markham, County York, 21 miles from Toronto and 9 from Richmond Hill station Northern Railroad. Population 100.

Allison, Thomas, general merchant
Carpenter, W. H., shoemaker
Cook, John, wagon maker
Fusby, Thomas, lumber merchant
Fusby, William
Hall, Joseph, wagon maker
HEISE, D., Postmaster and general merchant
Heise, Christopher, lumber merchant
Hunt, Thomas
McKenzie, John, blacksmith
Martin, George
Michael, Wallis, hotel keeper

Vienna.—An incorporated Village on Big Otter Creek, in the Township of Bayham, County Elgin, 28 miles from St. Thomas, the County Town, and 28 from Ingersoll. Money Order Office and Savings Bank. Stage to Ingersoll. Population 800.

Abbott, David, sash factory
Appleton, L., carpenter
Appleton, Thomas J., butcher
Baldwin, Levi, farmer
Ball, Jesse P., P.L.S.
Bartlett, Porter, farmer
Bawtinheimer, Rev. P. M. (Wesleyan)
Boyd, W. T. & J., grocers
Brasher, George, farmer
BRASHER, SAMUEL, Postmaster, mercht tailor
Brasher, William, merchant tailor
Broom, William, cabinet maker
Brown, Rev. Joseph (Episcopal Methodist)
Brown, T. T., gen. merchant
Burgess, John, boots and shoes
Carter & McDermand, shingle makers
Chute, Charles, carpenter
Chute, Charles, farmer
Chute, George, baker
Cookson, C. G., general merchant
Crawford, John, barrister
Crawford, John, insurance agent
Creech, Thomas, wagon maker
Douglass, John, founder and machinist
Draeseke, Charles, general merchant
Edison, C. O
Edison, F. W., stoves and tinware
Edison, M. B., prop. livery stable
Edmonds, John, brick maker
Griffin, David, farmer
Griffin, Jacob, farmer
Griffin, Saunders, farmer
Gundry, L. J., druggist and insurance agent
Hawkinson, Haynes, leather dealer
Hawksworth, John, farmer
Hawksworth, Peter, farmer
Hallowood, Charles, farmer
Hallowood, Thomas, farmer
Jenkins, Thomas, lumber dealer
Jenkins, Thomas, saddler
Jewell. Francis, general merchant
Johnson, H. B., lumber dealer
Lambert, James, prop. Francisco House
Light, Lazarus, brick maker
McAllister, H. B., grocer
McCally, R. L., teacher
McConnell, Beni, farmer
McConnell, John, farmer
McCurdy, Leonidas, farmer
McCurdy, Richard, farmer
McDermand, James, carpenter
McKee, J. T., grocer
Marr, Daniel, farmer
Marr, James, farmer
Martin, D. F., carpenter]
Matheson, A., proprietor Exchange
Miller, O. T., principal grammar school
Milne, William, baker
Montreal Telegraph Co., E. J. Brasher, agent
Morrison, James, cooper
Nelles, John
Nelles, Nelson, lumber dealer
Nelles, R. H., leather dealer
Newcomb, Simon, J.P.
Pillman, M. K., merchant tailor
Potter, E. H., lumber dealer
Price, Moses
Putnam & Brasher, lumber dealers
Reynolds, William H. dentist
Roebuck, Henry, farmer
Ross, William, boots and shoes
Schulte, Rev. John, D.D. (Church of England)
Seels, H. & Co., founders and machinists
Stoner, B., carpenter
Stratton, David, farmer
Stratton, Henry, farmer
Suffel & Finch, proprietors flouring mills and genera merchants
Teal, John, farmer
Thornton, George, boots and shoes
Thornwaite, Charles, saddler
Turk, Henry
Tweedie, J. B., M. D
Vail, Charles L., M. D
Van Velson, John, farmer
Van Velson, Raymond, farmer
Volkert, Rev. Mr., (Roman Catholic)
Watts, J. C., brick maker
Watts, William, brick maker
Wallington, E., carpenter
Weinhold, A. G., painter
Wildern, Daniel, boots and shoes
Wright, Francis F., fancy goods
Wright, James F., auctioneer

Vigo.—A post office in the Township of Flos, County Simcoe.
GALLAGHER, JOHN, Postmaster.

Villanova.—A small Village in the Township of Townsend, County Norfolk, 12 miles from Simcoe, the County Town.

Barber, Ira, farmer
Charters, I., butcher
Cortis, T. L., J. P
Dean, P. D., farmer
Hazleton, D., cheese factor
Irwin, David, farmer
Johnson, T. B., M. D
Johnson, William, farmer
McLAREN, J., Postmaster
Smith, William, painter
Upper, J. S., general merchant
Wilkin, Thomas, blacksmith
Woodhouse, W., farmer

Violet.—A Village on Big Creek, in the Township of Ernestown, County Addington, 9 miles from Napanee, the County Town. Stage to Kingston, 17 miles.

Aylsworth, John, J. P.
Bennet, Stephen, painter
Perry, A. B., J. P.
PERRY, D. W., Postmaster
Perry, W. H., J. P.
Rocknell & Perry, builders

Vine.—A small Village in the Township of Innisfil, County Simcoe, 7 miles from Barrie, the County Town.

Armstrong, William, teacher
Brooks, George, farmer
Brooks, William, farmer
Doan, Albert, farmer
Evans, Samuel, farmer
Fletcher, John, farmer
Gibson, William, innkeeper
McClure, John, farmer
Simpson, George, farmer
Simpson, John, farmer
SIMPSON, RICHARD, Postmaster, gen mercht
Snowdown, Robert, tailor
Thomson, William, farmer
Walker, William, farmer

Virgil.—A Village in the Township of Niagara, County Lincoln, 8 miles from St. Catharines, the County Town, and 9 from Clifton Station. Population 100.

Ball, John W., farmer
Ball, R. N., farmer
Ball, J. N., farmer
Bristol, J. M., general merchant
Cairns, George, farmer
Clement, T.M., farmer
Cushman, Isaac, blacksmith
Goodall, David, farmer
Lambert, W. W., hotel keeper
Miller, G. J., farmer
Niven, Robert, farmer
Servos, Alexander, farmer
Servos, Peter, farmer
Stevens, John, farmer
Walker, Francis, wagon maker
Young, John, farmer

Vittoria.—A Village on Young's Creek, in the Township of Charlotteville, County Norfolk, 7 miles from Simcoe, the County Town, and 33 from Port Burwell. Stages to Brantford, Paris and Port Burwell. Money Order Office. Population, 600.

Anderson, H., J.P.
Anderson, T. C., grocer
Battersby, A., M.D.
Boulten, H., butcher
Coleman, A., distiller
Dawson, W., saddler
Duncan, C., carpenter
Duncan, John, hotel keeper
Dunkin, Joseph, hotel keeper
Ewing, W., tailor
Guntin, J., carpenter
Hackett, J. & E., carriage makers
Hewitt, George, saddler
Hewitt, W., druggist
Kelly, H. S., general merchant
Laing, A., insurance agent
Lamport, T., J.P.
McCALL, GEORGE D., Postmaster
McCall, John, farmer
McCall, Joseph, farmer
McCall, S., M.P.P.
McKenna, H. J., tailor
McMahon, J., tailor
Maybee, O., farmer
Miller, W. H., M.D.
Montrose, L. H., stoves and tinware
Nicholson, Jabez, prop flouring mill
Partridge, T., brick maker
Pegg, A., teacher
Potts, E. L., J.P.
Potts, J. E., leather dealer
Reed, A., cabinet maker
Swayze, A., painter
Tisdale, E., farmer
Williams, J., boots and shoes
Young, C. P., telegraph operator
Young, P. E., J.P.
Young, R. E., general merchant

Vivian.—A Post Office in the Township of Whitchurch, County York.

McCORMICK, ROBERT, Postmaster.

Vroomanton.—A Village in the Township of Brock, County Ontario, 38 miles from Whitby, the County Town. Population 150.

Calhoun, William, general merchant
Coleman, Rev. W. (Wesleyan)
Conboy, J., watch maker
Francis, T., blacksmith
Gillespie, M., J.P., farmer
Hunter, J., general merchant
Keenan, M., farmer
Miller, J. farmer
Moore, J., shoemaker
Pangman, S., wagon maker
Sheir, G. farmer
Sheir, L. R., farmer
Speiran, C., miller
Speiran, J., farmer
Speiran, J., shoemaker
Switzer, E., farmer
St. John, J., proprietor saw mill
Taylor, J., farmer
TESKEY, JOHN, Postmaster
Umphrey, J., farmer
Varcoe, J., inn keeper
Vrooman, J., sen., farmer
Vrooman, J., farmer
White, B., farmer

Wabashene.—A Sub-post Office in the Township of Tay, County Simcoe.
HALL, WILLIAM, Postmaster.

Wales.—A Post Office in the Township of Osnabruck, County Stormont.
BAKER, WILLIAM, Postmaster.

Walkerton.—The County Town of Bruce, beautifully situated on the banks of the Saugeen River, in the centre of one of the richest agricultural sections of the Province. The facilities for manufacturing are first-class, the river affording unlimited water-power. Distant from Guelph, 63 miles; Goderich, 47 Seaforth 48, and Southampton 33. Stages to the above named places. Money Order office and Savings Bank. Population 1000.

Anderson, Jonah, carpenter
Barnett, William, carpenter
Benson, James, auctioneer
Bill, Thomas
Blair, James, proprietor flouring mill, founder and machinist
BROWN, WILLIAM, editor *Bruce Herald*
Bruce, John, grain merchant
BRUCE HERALD, (Friday), William Brown, editor
Carter, William, brick maker
Cassady, J. F., M. D.,
Chambers, John, teacher
Clarke, Mrs., fancy goods
Coldwell Morgan, barrister
Collins, William, J. P., clerk first division court
Cochrane, Andrew, boots and shoes
Cooper James G., insurance agent
Cowie, H., grain merchant
Davidson, Hugh, druggist
Davis, J. F., groceries and liquors
Deans, Henry C., druggist
Flett, James, boots and shoes
Foscombe & Hammond, groceries and liquors
Fraser, William, barrister
Gammond, Richard, painter
Geary, Richard, cabinet maker
Georgen, M., baker
Gould. George, county clerk
Griffiths, James, hotel keeper
Gunn, William, deputy clerk Crown and Pleas
Hammond, Frederick, insuaance agent
Hargreaves, Mrs., fancy goods
Hartley, H., hotel keeper
Heffernan, Patrick, merchant tailor
Hibbert, J. G., merchant tailor
Hill, Joshua, stoves and tinware
Johnson, Henry, boots and shoes
Kelly, Rev. H. J., (Roman Catholic)
Kilmer, E., telegraph operator
Kilmer & Hunter, general merchants
Kingsmill, J. J., County Judge
Kirkpatrick, Henry, barrister
Lockhart, William, carriage maker
McCarthy, J. L. D., M. D
McDiarmid, Rev. N. A., (N. C. Methodist)
McLay, John, County Registrar
McLean, Andrew, saddler
McVicar, William, hotel keeper
MACLEAN, MALCOLM, Postmaster
MERCHANTS' BANK OF CANADA, Alexander Sproat, agent
Moffat, Rev. R. C., (Canada Presbyterian)
Moore & Wilson, general merchants
Morrison, James, proprietor Union Hotel and livery
O'Connor, Hamilton P., barrister
Scott, William, builder and lumber dealer
Seed, E., watchmaker and engraver
Shannon, William, saddler
Shaw, Alexander, barrister
Sinclair, L., M. D
Softley, Rev. E., (Church of England)
SPROAT, ALEXANDER, County Treasurer, agent Merchants' Bank of Canada
Stovell, C. W., insurance agent
Richardson, Timothy, stoves and tinware
Richardson, William, butcher
Ross, Donald W., barrister, County Crown Attorney
Ruby, William H., County auditor
Sutherland, Robert, barrister
Sutton, William, sheriff
Thompson, Andrew, leather dealer
Ussher, Henry, M.D.
Walker, Joseph
Wallace, Simon, carpenter
Waterson, James, hotel keeper and livery
Willoughby, Walter, J.P.
Wilson, William, painter
Wisser, L., merchant tailor

Wallace.—A post village in the Township of Wallace, County Perth.

Wallaceburg.—A Village on the River Sydenham, in the Townships of Chatham and North Gore, County Kent. 17 miles from Chatham, the County Town. Money Order Office and Savings Bank. Population 600.

Adams, William, blacksmith
Ayers, William, merchant tailor
Beattie, Joseph H., general merchant and ins. agent
Becker, William, blacksmith
Campbell, Jane, milliner
Campbell, Peter, teacher
Carolan, J. D., tailor
Clancey, Michael, general merchant, lumber dealer and steam grist mill owner
Davis & Little, grocers
Deslaurier, John B., wagon maker
Dolsen, Isaac, carpenter
Dunlop, Catharine, milliner
Farrell, J. & Co., steam shovel handle company

Fisher, John, carpenter
Fisher, Thomas, painter
Forham, Peter, grocer
Forham, Thomas, harness maker
Fraser, Charles, J.P., insurance agent
Gordon, Aaron, brick and lime manufacturer
Havsen, John, hotel keeper
Hay, Alexander, general merchant
JOHNSON, LIONEL H., Postmaster, bookseller and general merchant
Johnson, Daniel, general merchant
Jones, Richard, tailor
Judson, James, carpenter
Judson, Lister, painter
Judson, Samuel, carpenter
Lalonde, S., groer
Lanlonde, Joseph, cabinet maker
Langstaff Miles, general merchent
Lillie, John, J.P., druggist
Little, Albert, grocer
Little, James, butcher
Little, John & Son, general merchants
Lloyd, Lionel, carpenter
McDermand, Charles, carpenter
McDonald, Julia, milliner
McDonnell, William, hotel keeper
McDougall, Alexander, attorney
McIntyre, Henry, carpenter
McLean, Hector, jun., J.P.
McLean & Co., dry goods
McLeod, Angus, hotel keeper prop. livery stable
Martin, Henry, J.P., nurseryman
Martin, Thodore, hide & leather dealer, boots & shoes
Mitchell, George, M.D.
Newman, J. B., M.D.
Niven, Thomas, grocer
Patterson & Lee, foundry
Patterson, William, steam flour mill
Feck, Richard, hotel
Rambo, Peter, carpenter
Ray, George, wagon maker
Smith, Calvin, sash, door and blind manufactory, and carpenter
Smith, John L., baker
Travers, Edwin, blacksmith
Vincent, Joseph, hotel
Wagstaff, Charles, boot and shoe maker
Warner, D. A., hotel
West, Thomas, hotel
Yule, R. H., teacher

Wallacetown.—A Village in the Township of Dunwich, County Elgin, 18 miles from St. Thomas, the County Town. Stages to St. Thomas and Chatham.

Barclay, A. E. S. K., general merchant
Black, James, farmer
Blackwood, Robert, general merchant
Bradt, Robert, wagon maker
Brayen, William & Bro., carpenters
Cameron, Donald, shoemaker
Clay, D., proprietor Ontario Hotel
Crews & McLean, sash, door and blind manufacturers
Crews, O., lumber merchant
Cusack, Thomas & Bro., grocers
Forbes, Duncan, cooper
Graham, John, teacher
Gunn, Alexander, attorney-at-law
Henry, C. G., proprietor Anglo American Hotel
Herron, George, proprietor livery stable and cabinet maker
Hinds, T. & J., plough manufacturers
Lilley, J., tailor
Luten, T., prop. Britannia Hotel
Lyng, Dr., M.D.
McBeath, B. C., dentist
McBeath, Captain
McCall, Samuel, farmer
McCallum, D. J., farmer
McCallum, Miss, milliner
McDairmid, Rev. Neil, (Presbyterian)
McFarlane, Archibald, carpenter
McGill, David, tinsmith
McIntyre, Captain
McIntyre, John C., cooper
McIntyre, Mrs., milliner
McIntyre, S. W., accountant and auctioneer
McKellar & Co., carpenters
McKellar, J. P., teacher
McKillop, D., farmer
McKILLOP, JOHN, Postmaster, general merchant
McLane, David & Bro., builders and wagon makers
McPhail, A. saddler
McPherson, Hector, farmer
McTavish, Angus, shoemaker
McTavish, D., shoemaker
Medwin, John, cabinet maker
Penwarden, J., M.D., druggist
Pierce, John, farmer
Pierce, William, farmer
Rapelge, John, saddler
Robertson, Matthew & Co., general merchants
Ruthven, D. G., M.D., druggist
Urquhart, A. C., tailor

Wallbridge.—A Village in the Township of Sidney, County Hastings, 9 miles from Belleville the County Town. Population 75.

Bleecher, John, bailiff
Bleeker, Mrs. S., hotel keeper
Chisholm, John A., J. P
Clark, James, boots and shoes
Dafoe, William J., patent rights agent
Foster, Theodore, carpenter
Kellogg, Charles P., teacher
Ketchison, Allan F., dentist
Ketchison, David R., bailiff, boots and shoes
Ketchison, Alfred B., carpenter
Ketchison, P. C., Clerk Division Court
Kehoe, Martin, farmer
Lowry, William, butcher
Miller, Stephen, blacksmith
Moon, John, wagon maker and painter
PRIOR, FRANCIS B., Postmaster, grocer, &c
Sidney Town Hall Cheese Factory, S. T. Wilmot, President
Thompson, Rev. James, (Episcopal Methodist)
Ward, Rev. E. A., (Wesleyan Methodist)

Wallenstein.—A small Village in the Township of Wellesley, County Waterloo, 15 miles from Berlin, the County Town, and 18 from Listowell. Population 40.

Bulmer, R.
Fowler, Rev. John
Goodwin, Rev. John, (Wesleyan Methodist)
Lomas, Rev. William, (Primitive Methodist)
Martinson, John
Martinson, William
Mathews, William
OSWOLD, J. B., Postmaster, hotel keeper
Powell, R., J.P.
Shafer, Adam, wagon maker
Tremain, M.

Walmer.—A Post Office in the Township of East Zorra, County Oxford.
PARKER, ROBERT, Postmaster.

Walsh.—A Post Office in the Township of Charlotteville, County of Norfolk.
McCALL, D. W., Postmaster.

Walter's Falls.—A small Village in the Township of Holland, County Grey.
WALTER, MRS. E. H., Postmistress.

Walton.—*(See Villages too late for regular insertion at the end of this work).*

Wardsville.—An incorporated Village on the River Thames, in the Township of Mosa, County Middlesex, 36 miles from London, and three from Newbury Station, Great Western Railway. Money Order Office and Savings Bank. Population 800.

Aitchison, Alexander, flour, feed, and groceries
Aitchison, E., steam flour mills
Barclay, M. F., druggist
Boyd, Joseph, carpenter
Calderwood, R., general merchant
Corneill, Adam, wagon maker
Course, George, physician
Coventry, John physician
Coyne, T., dentist
Dixon, H. C., harness maker
Dufton, E. T., general merchant, woolen factor
Dykes, J., farmer
DYKES, J. M., publisher *Wardsville Investigator*
English, Thomas, wagon maker
Flemming, John, blacksmith
Freckleton, Charles, jeweler
Freckleton, David, baker
George, Adam, boots and shoes
Gibb, David, farmer
Gibson, William D., architect
Gordon, W. A., teacher
Grover, Johnson M., insurance agent
Hall, Thomas, carpenter
HAMMOND, W. D., Postmaster, general merchant and notary public
Harper, William, prop steam flour mill
Henderson, H., blacksmith
Herald, Thomas, boots and shoes
Holmes, James, wagon maker
Howes, W. K., grocer and flour dealer
Humphrey, Francis, blacksmith
Jackson, James, cooper
Kent, T., general merchant
Ladell, H., hotel keeper
Lilly, E., & Co., wagon makers
Loxley, Charles, baker
McIntyre, Alexander, tailor
McKelvey, R., tailor
McKinnon, John, hotel keeper
McKinnon, Rev. N. (Presbyterian)
McLean, James, carpenter
Meston, A., farmer
Munroe, J. H., M.P.P.
Munroe, M. & G., general merchants
Mulligan, T., farmer
Neil, Richard, auctioneer
Nelson, John, carpenter
Nelson & Willing, wholesale flour dealers
O'Malley, Captain Charles, farmer
Palmer, John, Fire Inspector
Pool, John, cabinet maker
Pool, John, farmer
Porter, John, carpenter
Risley, F. B., builder
Shaw, James, cabinet maker
Sheppard, William, harness maker
Sinclair, W., teacher
Smith, Donald, blacksmith
Smith, James, painter
Sole, Rev. John (Baptist)
Stevely, William, tinsmith
Street, John, brickmaker
Tifton, E. D., J.P.
Ward, John, farmer
Ward, John, cabinet maker
Ward, Sheldon, hotel keeper
Wardsville Cheese Factory, John Watterworth, president; W. D. Hammond, secretary
Webster, Rev. J. (Wesleyan Methodist)
Weir, John, butcher
Wilson, Andrew, Clerk 5th Division Court, Com. in B. R. and general agent
Wilson, A., blacksmith
Wright, Rev. J. (Church of England)
Yorke, W. D., stock dealer
Young, J. A., boots and shoes

Walsingham.—A Village on the shore of Lake Erie, in the Township of Walsingham, County Norfolk, 18 miles from Simcoe, the County Town, and 36 from Paris. Stages to Port Burwell and Brantford. Pop. 200.

Anger, Rev. J. (Primitve Methodist)
Backhouse, J. A., J.P.
Brandon, Abraham, blacksmith
Chesterman, J., shoemaker
Collins, William, teacher
Dace, C. J., general merchant
Hazen, James, blacksmith
Huchison, J. B., general merchant
Johnson, J., J.P.
KITCHEN, HENRY L., Postmaster
Kitchen, W. H., hotel keeper
McBurney, William, lumber dealer
McCall, D. A.
McCall, T. C. A., general merchant
McCall, J. G., carpenter
DcDonald, Alexander, blacksmith
McDonald, John, carpenter
McDonald, Warren, carpenter
McLean, J., M.D.
Mason, John, wagon maker
Megamore, Rev. J. (Wesleyan Methodist)
Reeves, H., painter
Reeves, Joseph, tailor
Reeves, T., painter
Wood, Rev. William (Church of England)
Woodward, H. H., hotel keeper

Wanstead.—A Village and Station of the Great Western Railway, in the Township of Plympton, County Lambton, 18 miles from Sarnia, the County Town, and 5 from Uttoxeter. Population 100.

Butler, William, carpenter
Carson, W., hotel keeper
DEWAR, JOHN, Postmaster, express agent and general merchant
McBride, D., teacher
McDonald, Joseph, teacher
McIntyre, Joseph, teacher
Masson, James blacksmith
Johnston, J., hotel keeper
Little, John, cooper
Robertson, D. S., J.P.
Scott, Rev. R. (Canada Presbyterian)
Smith, George, boots and shoes
Smith, J., J.P.
Wallace, John, boots and shoes
Williamson, Joseph, wagon maker
Wynne, H. N., hotel keeper

Wareham.—A post office in the Township of Osprey, County Grey.

BATTRICK, EDWIN, Postmaster.

Warkworth.—A Village on Mill Creek, in the Township of Percy, County Northumberland, 28 miles from Cobourg, the County Town, and 16 from Colborne and Brighton Stations Grand Trunk Railroad. Stage to Colborne. Money order office. Population 400.

Alexander, Rev. Thomas, (Presbyterian)
Aylsworth, George S., sash, door and blind manufr
Banta, A. J., flour mill
Bettes, J. K., tinsmith
Black, A.
Boyce, George B.
Boyce, William H.
Brookmeyer, T., carpenter
Butler, Charles, painter
Burton, R., boots and shoes
Coleman, C. A., teacher
Closson, John, wagon maker
Covert, David, cooper
Covert, Hiram, tailor
Covert, William, cooper
Craig, W., hotel keeper
Cummings, John, J. P
Curtis, John
Dawson, John, flour mill proprietor
Dolman, John, harness maker
Douglass Donald
Farmer, James H., general merchant
Farmer, William, general merchant
Fenes, Mrs., milliner
Ford, George, baker
Ford, John, cabinet maker
Gorman, J. H., general merchant
Grattan, George, hotel keeper
Haight, W. G., baker
Hamilton, James, general merchant
Hill, M., grocer
Hudson, Charles, boots and shoes
Humphries, H. H., sen
HUMPHRIES, ISRAEL, Postmaster, gen. mercht.
Humphries, William
Hurlbert, R. P., insuranse and general agent
Insley, A. W., wagon maker
Jones, Chailes, patent right agent
Kennedy, W., J.P.
Kennedy, W., general merchant
Lord, John, foundry
McCammon, H., druggist
McCrae, James N., physician
McCoy, H. boots and shoes
McDonald, H., hotel
McPherson, Josiah, wagon maker
Mather, Thomas, tailor
Might, J. M., general agent
Might, Rev. Samnel (Wesleyan)
Maybee, Alfred, auctioneer and general merchant
Osborne, Sheldon, cabinet maker
Pickworth, Daniel, carpenter
Pomeroy, Charles, carpenter
Pomeroy, Robert, carpenter
Snodgrass, John
Staples, J. H., flour mill
Sunborne, A. M., dyer
Thompson, Peter
Wicks, J. N., tinsmith
Wiggins, W. T., grocer

Warsaw.—A Village on Indian River, in the Township of Dummer, County Peterboro', 14 miles from Peterboro', the County Town. Stages to Peterboro'. Money Order Office. Population 150.

Campbell, Thomas, wagon maker
Cannon, George, teacher
Choate, J. S., issuer of marriage licenses, and com. in Q.B., &c
CHOATE, THOMAS, Postmaster, gen mercht
Choate, Thomas George, J.P., prop. flour mill
Closson, J., M.D
Dawkins, James, cooper
Edwards, Frederick, farmer
Hamlin, Samuel, blacksmith
Hawthorn, Thomas, farmer
Kennedy, Patrick, blacksmith
Kidd, Archie R., farmer
Kidd, Daniel, blacksmith
Lukey, Sampson, J.P
Lumsden, Frank, farmer
McIlorna, Edward, farmer
McKee, James, general merchant
Payne, Sidney, farmer
Payne, Stephen, shingle maker
Reid, James, tailor
Reid, Washington, general merchant
Smith, Robert, farmer
Snelgrove, William, hotel keeper
Wason, John, general merchant

Warminster.—A Post-office in the Township of Medonte, County Simcoe.
DEACON, WILLIAM GEORGE, Postmaster.

Warner.—A Post-office in the Township of Caistor, County Monck.
SMITH, T. W., Postmaster.

Warrington.—A Post Village in the Township of Nottawasaga, County Simcoe.
RANDOLPH, JOHN, Postmaster.

Warwick.—A small Village on Bear Creek, in the Township of Warwick, County Lambton, 25 miles from Sarnia, the County Town, and 7 from Forest station, Grand Trunk Railway. Stage to Watford station, Great Western Railway 8 miles. Money order office.

Brennan, Rev., (Roman Catholic)
Brent, William, hotel
Broley, Rev. James, (Wesleyan Methodist)
Burns, J. M., general merchant
Campbell, Robert
Douglas, Daniel, wagon maker
Eccles, J. D., J.P.
Elliot, James T., J.P.
Evans, Richard, auctioneer
Gibson, Rev. J. C., (Church of England)
Gordon, William, tailor
Hawkins, James
Hay, Thomas, blacksmith
Hunter, John, wagon maker
Kenward, Thomas, carpenter
Kingston, C. J.
Larrat, James
McKenzie, William, carpenter
Manders, William, boots and shoes
Menery, James, general merchant
MORRIS, JOHN H., Postmaster, general merchant
Restrick, Frank
King, Louis, boots and shoes
Rogers, D., steam grist mill
Rogers, Mrs. D., hotel
Rogers, John, hotel keeper
Rogers, William H., butcher
Rose, John, blacksmith
Scott, Alexander, bleacher
Shannon, Robert, carpenter
Smith, James, butcher
Tanner, James
Tanner, John
Westley, John, wagon maker
Wier, Richard, M.D.
Westley, J., tailor
Wilson, John, harness maker

Washington.—A Village on the River Nith, in the Township of Blenheim, County Oxford, 20 miles from Woodstock, the County Town; 5 from Drumbo Station, Buffalo and Lake Huron Railroad; 9 from Baden Grand Trunk Railway; and 10 from Princeton, Great Western Railway. Population, 150.

Ames, Rev. Williamm (Wesleyan Methodist)
Basteed, Francis, boot and shoe maker
Bourchier, Robert J.
Brundee, John, farmer
Bourchier, Edward, constable
Buchanan, William, farmer
Carson, John, physician
Chamberlain, E. G., boots and shoes
Cochrane, John, teacher
Cornell, Harvey, farmer
Day, John, farmer
DUNN, WILLIAM, Postmaster, general merchant
Gammon, William, wagon maker
Graham, John, carpenter
Harmer, Henry, farmer
Richardson, Rev. E., Wesleyan Methodist
Smith, Richard, H., hotel
Thompson, John, brick maker
Thompson, J. Q., boot and shoe manfr
Wakefield, Daniel, farmer

Waterdown.—A Village and Station of the Great Western Railway, in the Township of East Flambore, County Wentworth, 6 miles from Hamilton; Stages to Carlisle, 6 miles; Cummingsville, 9; and Milton, 16. Money Order Office. Population 1000.

Anderson, Samuel, hotel keeper and livery
Armstrong, John, carpenter
Baker, Abraham, hotel keeper and livery
Baker, Henry, butcher
Baker, James, billiard room and hotel
Baker, Read, rake and cradle factory
Baker, Solomon, baker
Baker, William, agent G. W. R.
Barnes, James, boot and shoe maker
Broadbent, H., boiler maker
Broadbent, Herman, manfr of woolen goods
Brown, Alexander, steamboat agent
Brown, Edward, wagon maker
Brown, John, teacher
Brown, William, nurseryman
Burns, Edward proprietor planing mill
Burns, Mathew, lumber yard
Calbeck Brothers, wagon makers
Caso, S. O., general merchant
Casey, Stephen, hotel keeper
Collier, John, butcher
Creer, John, lumber dealer
Crooker, W. H., grocer and comn merchant
Cummer, L. A., prop. flour mill
Davies, David, cooper
Davis, Andrew
Dernam, Patrick, boot and shoe maker
Eager, J. C., general merchant
Eaton, S. S., tinsmith
Edwards, H., carpenter
Edwards, Henry, hotel keepor
Edmison, Rev. H., (Presbyterian)
English, John, carpenter
Forbes, James
Forfar, Thomas, carpenter
Fraser, Peter, jewelry, watches, &c
Gamble, William, boot and shoe maker
Garvin, John B., boot and shoe maker
Garvin, Thomas, boot and shoe maker
Glasgow, John, J.P
Grant, Rev. R. N., (Can. Presbyterian)
Grieve, Walter, carpenter
Hall, Thomas, M.A., teacher
Heissie, William, grocer
Houston, Rev. S., (Church of England)
Howland, W. P., prop. steam flour mill
Hugh & Broadbent, founders and machinists
Hugh, William, wagon maker
Lee, William H., cabinet maker
McDonald, J., painter
McMonies, James, sen., J.P
McMonies, James, M.P.P
McMonies, James, jr., general agent, auctioneer, and clerk 3rd, division court
Maher, Thomas, cooper
Matrun, Charles, prop. steam flour mill
Nichol, William, carpenter
O'Neil, John, lime manufacturer
O'Reilly, H. R., attorney-at-law
Philip, William, physician
Richardson, Rev. George, (N. C. Methodist)
Rymal, George
Schaler, Ferdinand, carpenter
Shouldice, James, baker
Skinner, Ormond, M.D., druggist
Smith, Joseph, general merchant
Stewart, James, tailor
Stock, Thomas, J. P.
Stonehouse, John, butcher
Stuart, William, J.P.
Thompson, Hugh, harness maker
THOMPSON, JAMES B., Postmaster, general merchant, express agent
Truesdale, H., Carpenter
Walker, Dr. A., dentist
Willoughby, Rev. William, (Wesleyan)
Wilson, Rev., (Wesleyan)
Young, James, wagon maker

Washago.—A Post Village in the Township of Orillia, County Simcoe.

HAMILTON, ALEXANDER, Postmaster

Waterloo.—An incorporated village in the Township of Waterloo, County Waterloo, 2 miles from Berlin, the County Town; 10 from Preston; 20 from Millbank, and 20 from Glenallen. Surrounding country is remarkable for its fertility, and the village is rapidly increasing in wealth and population. Trade chiefly local. Stages to all the above named places. Money Order Office and Savings Bank. Population 2000.

Beisang, Blasius, hotel keeper
Boner, Charles, carpenter
Bowman, B., watches, clocks and jewelry
Bowman, Brothers, general merchant
BRICKER, B. H., proprietors woollen mills
Bricker, Jacob, foundry
Bridgman, J., M.D., coroner
Busch, George, lime manufacturer
Cain, J
CANADISCHE BAURNFREUND (Thursday) J. Kalbfleisch, editor and proprietor
CONRAD, JACOB, stoves and tinware
CRAWFORD, D. J. H., manager Ontario Bank
Dahm, Jacob, carpenter
Devitt, Benjamin, general merchant
Devitt, D., general merchant
Devitt, John, hotel
Doerbecker, George, hotel
Eby, D. B., farmer
Edler, George, butcher
Fairbairn, J. P., baker
Fairman, F., hardware
Fischer, William, J.P., general merchant
Forbes, J., livery stable
GERMAN CANADIAN, William Raich, editor and publisher
German, Julius, harness maker
Gingrich, D. W., architect

Good, Joel, farmer
Good, J., physician
Green, Mrs., milliner
Hamilton, John, merchant tailor
Hasenpflug, John, blacksmith
Hewett, Robert, prop Commercial hotel
Hoffman, George, blacksmith
Hoffman, J., J. P.
Hoffman, John
Hoelsche, Rev. J. (Lutheran)
Huether, F., brewer
Hughes, Jeremiah, inspector and general agent Waterloo Co. Mutual Fire Insurance Co.
Jacobi, John, pottery
Jamieson, R., baker
KALBFLEISCH, JOACHIM, editor and prop *Canadische Baurnfreund*
Kenniff, C., bookseller
Killer, N., carpenter
King, John S., teacher
Klippert, John, auctioneer
KUMPF, C., Postmaster, fancy goods
KUNTZ, DAVID, prop Spring brewery
Lenz, C., carpenter
McDougall, John, J.P., hardware
MacGACHEN, F. STEWART, agent Canada Life and Western Fire Insurance Co's
MacGACHEN & COLQUHOUN (F. Stewart & Frederick) barristers, solicitors, &c. (see card)
Manerer, Rev. M., (German Methodist)
Moerscheimer, Jacob, boots and shoes
Morningstar & Merner, foundry and machine shop
Morris, W. L., accountant Ontario Bank
MOYER C. E. & CO., editors and proprietors *Waterloo Chronicle*
Moyer, Isaac, painter
MOYER, P. E. W.
Murray & Bockus, woolen manufacturers
Newton, Francis B., hop grower
Noecker, Charles, hotel keeper
ONTARIO BANK, D. J. H. Crawford, manager
Peppler, L., blacksmith
Quickfall, R., farmer
RAICH, WILLIAM, editor and publisher *German Canadian*
Randall, G., gen. mercht, distiller & prop flouring mill
Roos, Jacob, boots and shoes
Rupple, Henry, brickmaker
Schade, Martin, hats and caps
Schæfer, H. N., carpenter
Scheren, Michael, foreman *Chronicle*
Scheneman, F. L., hide and leather dealer
Schlote, Frederick, butcher
Schmidt, L., cooper
Schnarr, H., hotel keeper
Schneider, Charles, harness maker
Shuch, John & Co., general merchants
Snider, Elias, steam flour mill
Snider, Samuel S., farmer
Snyder, Daniel
Springer, Moses, J.P., notary public
SPRINGER, MENNO, agent Montreal Telegraph Co.
SPRINGER & SNYDER (Menno & Simon), druggists
Strauhe, V., gunsmith
Stuart, William, blacksmith
Stuebing, William, cooper
Swarts, Amos, painter
TAYLOR, C. M., secretary Waterloo Co., and Mutual Fire Insurance Co.
Thomas, H., boots and shoes
Tisdale, C. G., general agent
Wagner, Jacob, wagon maker
Walden, J. W., M.D.
Walter, Jacob, boots and shoes
Wanless, John, auctioneer
WATERLOO CHRONICLE, (Thursday), C. E. Moyer & Co., editors and proprietors
WATERLOO MUTUAL INSURANCE CO., C. M. Taylor, sec
Weber, Joseph B., teacher
Wegenast, M., prop. planing mill
Wells, Walter, dentist
Welsh, J., nurseryman
Wilson, James
Yeagley, H., M.D
Zoellner, H. A., druggist

Waterloo.—Frontenac Co.—(*See Cataraqui*,)

Watford.—A Village and Station of the Great Western Railway, in the Township of Warwick, County Lambton, 27 miles from Sarnia, the County Town. Principal trade, grain, lumber and staves. Money Order Office. Population 300.

Baker, Herman, stave and timber merchant
Finlayson, R., prop. Watford Hotel
MARSHALL, JOHN, merchant tailor
Mavity, John, general merchant
MERRY, JAMES, Postmaster, general merchant
RAILROAD HOTEL, R. Wiltshire, prop
SHIRLEY, JOSEPH W., M.D., (see adv)
WILTSHIRE, ROBERT, prop. Railroad Hotel

Watson's Corners.—A Village in the Township of Dalhousie, County Lanark, 18 miles from Perth, the County Town. Population 60.

Barrie, James, shoemaker
Blair, George, nurseryman
Craig, John, farmer
Cumming, Peter, farmer
Cumming, Robert, farmer
Forde, William, carriage maker
Gardner, William, auctioneer
Garrow, Charles, cooper
Gilloss, John, flour mill
Hood, John, farmer
Horn, James, farmer
HORN, WILLIAM, Postmaster, general merchant
Jackson, Thomas, cooper
Kelso, John, teacher
McArthur, Charles, cooper
McLean, Rev. D. J., (Church of England)
Munroe, John, general merchant
Nichol, James, hotel keeper
Park, Alexander, farmer
Park, Andrew, farmer
Park, William, carpenter
Penman, Archibald, cabinet maker
Proven, Alexander, farmer
Purdon, Alexander, carriage and wagon maker
Reid James, farmer
Scott, John, hotel keeper
Steed, George, flour mill
Storie, John, tailor

Waterford.—A Village in the Township of Townsend, County Norfolk, 8 miles from Simcoe, the County Town, and 16 from Brantford. Nanticoke creek in the vicinity affords good water power. Stages to Brantford and Simcoe. Money Order Office and Savings Bank. Population 800.

Barber, S. L., cabinet maker
Becker, B.
Becker, L., general merchant
Beemer, H., general merchant
Beemer, Lewis, hotel keeper
Beemer, W. & H., coopers
Blakesbee & Yeatman, carriage makers
Boughner, N.
Boughner, N., J. P.
Boughner, S. N., accountant
Boughner, W. H., stoves and tinware
Bowlby, A., M.D.
Buckberrough, D., insurance agent
Campbell, R., butcher
Chambers, U. J., dentist, watches and jewelery
Chart, H., cooper
Christie, E. G., painter
Church, J. J., harness maker
Clark, N., general merchant
Clark, T., J.P.
Culver, J. C., M.D.
Culver, Lyman, carpenter
Dean, R., blacksmith
Dean, D. K., carpenter
Duncombe, Alexander, prop. flouring mill and lumber dealer
Duncombe, D., M.D.
Emmett, C., boots and shoes
Farnsworth, A., blacksmith
Fergusson, Rev. George, B.A. (Wesleyan Methodist)
Foster, D. R.
Grace, E., blacksmith
Green, J. L. & J. W., founders and machinists, lumber dealers, &c.
Hague, Thomas, shoemaker
Hall, F. A., teacher
Harris, Rev. J. (Church of England)
Heath, Ansley, stock dealer
Horning, L., shoemaker
Johnson, H., hotel keeper
Kimball, J., blacksmith
Leach, David, painter
Leach, P., painter
Lewin, G. W., tailor
Little, A. M., general merchant
Lundy, S. & E. H., harness makers
Lundy, S., insurance agent
McMichael, Aaron, dentist
McMichael, William, farmer
Matthews, Edward, dentist
Merrill, C., general merchant
Merritt, J., M.D
O'Hearn, James, carpenter
O'Hearn, M., blacksmith
Olmstead, J. D., general merchant
Park, C., brick maker
Parney, D., shingle maker
Parney, John, J.P
Pickhaver, George, shoemaker
Purcell, L. P., cabinet maker
Redker, J. P., tailor
Rock, Thomas, prop. flouring mill
Schram, William, harness maker
Shaver, John, general agent
Shrigley, W. O. R., tannery proprietor
Skelly, William, farmer
Slaght, Rev. A., (Baptist)
Slaght, A., nurseryman
Smith, William, carriage maker
Squire, J. W., general merchant
Squire & Boughner, nurserymen
Tobin, M., butcher
Tune, R., baker
Walker, Rev. A. B., (New Connexion Methodist)
Williams, Rev. W., (New Connexion Methodist)
WILSON, DAVID, Postmaster, groceries, stationery and news depot
Yerks, M. painter

Waverly.—A post office in the Township of Flos, County Simcoe, 22 miles from Barrie, the County Town.

Bannister, David, farmer
Bannister, John, hotel keeper
Brisbain, H., pottery, crockery, china and glassware
Chapman, Thomas, farmer
Clark, George, J.P.
Clark, Miss M. A., teacher
Cummings, James, cooper
French, Gabriel
French, Thomas
Gorman, Edward, tailor
Jardine, David, carpenter
KETTLE, ALEXANDER, Postmaster
McCallum, John, grocer
McDonald, John, cooper
McDonald, Owen, shingle maker
Moodie, William
Pew, Thomas
Sibbald, George, carpenter
Train, David
Watt, James
Williamson, Walter T., teacher

Welcome.—A Village in the Township of Hope, County Durham, 10 miles from Cobourg, the County Town, and 3 from Port Hope. Population 100.

Brownscombe, John, pottery
Brown, Thomas, farmer
Day, John T., farmer
Friend, James, blacksmith
Giddey, William, butcher
Giles, John, farmer
Grimason, John, wagon maker
Henwood, Charles, farmer
Martin, John, farmer
Milligan, David, farmer
Oak, Paul, blacksmith
TOM, CHARLES, Postmaster, boot and shoemaker
Vanstone, John, farmer
Westleek, John, wagon maker

Welland.—The County Town of Welland, on the Welland River, Canal and Railway, in the Townships of Crowland and Thorold, situated in the centre of an excellent agricultural section. The water-privilege is almost unlimited, and the town is rapidly increasing in wealth, extent and manufacturing importance. Direct railway communication with Buffalo, St. Catharines, Toronto and Hamilton, and by water, via the Welland River and Canal, to all Lake Ports. Money order Office and Savings Bank. Pop. 1200.

Adrian, John, saddler
Asher, Alexander
Bald, Crptain
Beatty, Matthew, boiler maker and founder
Betts, Moses, planing mill, lumber dealer
Box, Thomas, carpenter
Bridges, James & Co., general merchants
Bridges & McIlvine, grocers
Briggs, Rev. J. (Wesleyan)
Brittin, Smith O., painter
Brookfield, Jacob, J.P., general merchant
Brown, P., carriage and wagon maker
Buchner, Henry, carpenter
Burgar, G. R. E.
BURGAR, THOMAS, J.P., Postmaster and insurance agent
Burgar, W. E., M.D., druggist
Canada Patent Broom Company
Carl, A., harness maker
Carnochan, James, crockery, glassware and groceries
Chipman, J. S., carpenter
Clark, George, butcher
Clayton & Hopkins, hardware and tinsmith
Cooley, Daniel, painter
Cooper, David, proprietor grist mill
Cooper, Mrs. Robert, milliner
Crosby, A. H., J. P.
Craig, Thomas, notary public
Creighton, Rev. J., Episcopal
Crosby, A. H., lumber yard
Cumines, Thomas, chemist and druggist
Dennis, J., tailor
D'Everardo, D., county clerk
DEWHURST, E. R., proprietor Welland Telegraph
Doan, William, Railroad Hotel
Ellenwood, W. C., woolen manufacturer
Ellsworth, George, carpenter
Farr, C. H., boots and shoes
Foster, James, cooper
Garden, W. N., J. P., City Hotel
Girvin, S. R., hardware and tinsmith
Griffith, James, grain merchant
Guest, W. F., butcher
Haney, H., painter
Hann, A. L., foundry
Hellems, E. R., accountant
Hendershot & Bo., general merchants
Hill, A. S., notary public and insurance agent
Hobson, G. L., Deputy Sheriff
Hobson, Robert, Sheriff
Hooker, T. N., brick maker
Hoover, E.
Jeffrey, W. D., wagon maker
Jennings, C. J., carpenter
Kennedy, T., billiard room
Lamartin, J., teacher
Lamont, Robert, J. P.
Lamont, S., boots and shoes
Lampman, George, jewelery
Lansch, C., prop Farmer's hotel
Lamon & Buchner, harness, hide & leather dealers
Lewis, William, basket maker
Lock, H. D., clothing, hats and caps
Logan, J., carpenter
McAlpine, A. J.
McCann, D., boots and shoes
McEwan, David, baker
McGlashan, James, County treasurer
McKey, J., tailor
Mewhinney, J., Ontario hotel
Morwood, R., general merchant
Muir, Rev. William, (Baptist)
Page, Alexander
Page, William, nurseryman
Parsons, Rev. R., (Episcopal Methodist)
Pattison, S. N., billiard room and auctioneer
Phillips, Arthur
Pilbeam, W. H., hardware and tinsmith
Raymond & Eccles, notaries
Raymond, L. D., Q. C., attorney, Clerk Peace
Rink, F. M., tailor
Rose, H. A., dry goods and clothing
Rose, James O., flour and feed
Ross, Henry T., architect
Rounds, O.H., prop planing mill
Russell, Hugh, boots and shoes
Sauter, F. X., cabinet maker
Schneider, J. W. H., patent right & insurance agent
Schooley, J. W., physician
Shrigley, Enoch, druggist
SIDEY, J. J., proprietor Welland *Tribune;* books, stationery and fancy goods
Smith, E., carpenter, auctioneer
Spencer, Alfred, coal dealer
Stephenson, Robert, accountant
Strawn, J. D., boots and shoes
Thompson, Archibald, J. P., grist mill
Tuckey, James, jeweler and engraver
Tufts, D., bridge tender
Tuft, James
Tupper, C., tailor
Tupper, Mrs. C. F., milliner
Vanderlip, J., Commercial Hotel
Vandeburgh, John, agent, W.R.R., and telegraph op.
Vanwyck, A. K., shingle maker and planing mill
Watson, J., lock tender
WELLAND TELEGRAPH, E. R. Dewhurst, prop
WELLAND TRIBUNE, J. J. Sidey, proprietor
Wheatley, Miss, teacher
White & Co., carriage and wagon makers
Wilkinson, H., Welland Hotel
Willett, Alfred, clerk 1st Division Court
Wilson, R
Willson, J. P., deputy Clerk Crown.
Winters, James, carpenter
Wright, J., livery stable
Wright. T., butcher
Yokom, A., carpenter
Yokom, Jesse
Young, Joseph, wooden ware
Zeiter & Co., cabinet makers

Wellman's Corners.—A Post Office in the Township of Rawdon, County of Hastings.

EMPEY, GEORGE, Postmaster.

Welland Port.—A Village on the Welland River, in the Township of Gainsboro', County Lincoln, 18 miles from St. Catharines, the County Town, 10 from Dunnville Station, 12 from Beamsville Station and 50 from Toronto. Stages to Grimsby, 17 miles, Port Robinson, 14 and Canfield, 14. Money Order Office. Population 300.

Bangham, Joseph, carpenter
Beatty, Thomas, M.D
Becker, John L., general agent
Bridgman, Gilbert, teacher
Cavers, Walter, drover
Clarke, Rev. A., (United Brethern)
Collver, John W., M.D
Cushman, Jacob, hotel keeper
Devitt, Joseph, lumber yard
Dochstader, Darius, lumberman
Dunn, David, general merchant
Flumerfelt, Z., hotel keeper
Gillam, Daniel, blacksmith
Haggarty, David, butcher
Heaslip, John L., J.P
Heaslip, Joseph, brick maker
Heaslip, Joseph, jun., painter
Henderson, John
Henry, Calvin
Holmes, D. C., general merchant
HOLMES, SAMUEL, Postmaster
Holmes, Samuel H,, wine and spirit merchant
Horton, F. L., cooper
Imwel, Frederick, tailor
Johnson, John W., boots and shoes
McQuin, John, tailor
Kay, Thomas H., wagon maker
Malcolm, Rev. J., (Presbyterian)
Misener, Jacob, surveyor
Moore, John, carpenter
Parke,, Calvin C., general merchant
Rice, James, lumberman
Robertson, Gavan, accountant
Rose, Thomas, butcher
Stewart, George, blacksmith
Sutherland, B., hotel
Swartz, Peter, boots and shoes
Vaughan, Edmund, shingle maker
Wiggins, Samuel G., J. P.

Wellington Square.—A Village and Station of the Great Western Railway, in tho Township of Nelson, County Halton, pleasanrly situated at the head of Lake Ontario, 15 miles from Milton, the County Town 7 from Hamilton, and 33 from Toronto. It has a good harbor, and large quantities of grain and lumber are annually shipped. Money Order office and Savings Bank. Population 800.

Aikman, R. P., M.D.
Allen, J. & G. (John and George) tinsmiths
Allen, James, wagon maker and general merchant
Baker, William, photographer
Bales, Richard, innkeeper
Bastedo, James, dentist
Bastedo, John T., assistant Postmaster
BASTEDO, WALTER S., Postmaster
Bastedo & Allen, (G. C. Bastedo, L. B. Allen,) dry goods and general merchants
Bates, R.W., prop Bates inn
Baxter, Thomas
Bell, Thomas, boot and shoe maker
Bent, James C., carpenter and joiner
BIBLE, GEORGE, Station Master G. W. R.
Bray, F., farmer
Bulleu, Charles F., M. D.
Bunton, William, grain merchant
BURLINGTON HOTEL, Elias DeGarmo, prop
Campbell, John H., lumber dealer
Cartier, Samuel, M.D.
Cole, Richard, baker and confectioner
Cotter, James W., butcher
Davison, John, general agent
DeGarmo, Elias, prop Burlington hotel
Durkee, M. & Co., nurserymen
Eager, Benjamin, prop saw mill
Ferguson, Rev. T. A., (Wesleyan Methodist)
Fisher, Jacob H.
Flock, William, prop Flock's hotel, G.W.R. station
Freeman, Joseph
Freeman, Joshua
Galloway, Jonathan, general merchant
Gibson, J., farmer
Ganton, S. Y., teacher
GRAHAM, THOMAS, agent Montreal Telegraph co, dealer in fancy goods, insurance agent
Green, Rev. T., (Church of England)
Hales, Joseph H., general merchant
Hall, Miss Margaret, dressmaker
Hall, William, Captain
Halson, Robert, druggist
Haygarth, Thomas, general blacksmith
Henderson, Captain Daniel
Henderson, Joseph, prop. Lake View Hotel
Hendrie, William
Horning, Joseph, farmer
Jeffery, Rev. T. W. (Wesleyan)
Kearns, William, general merchant
Kerr. W. J. Simcoe, barrister, &c.
Kines, Rev. James (Wesleyan)
Kirtz, Michael, carpenter
Kirtz, Peter, carpenter
Lemon, Herbert, Collector of Customs
McCarter, George, wagon maker and gen. blacksmith
Minhinnick, John W., butcher
Moore, Patrick, boot and shoemaker
Murray, John, baggageman, G. W. R.
Ogg, Nelson, cooper
Railton, Edward, carpenter
Rushbrook, George, tailor
Ryan, Rev. Mr. (Roman Catholic)
St. Clair, Alexander, painter
Smith & Brothers, (Wm. and John) gen. merchants
Springe, O. T.
Sullivan, Denis, carpenter
Torrance, D., prop. steam flouring mills
Tuller, John
Waldie, John & Co., general merchants
Waldie, John (John Waldie & Co.)
Weber, Lawrence, farmer
Wills, George, farmer
Wills, Smith, farmer
White & Caldwell, lumber dealers
Wilson, Rev. J. (Episcopal Methodist)
Young, John H., cabinet maker

Wellington.—A Village in the Township of Hillier, County Prince Edward.

CAMPBELL, DONALD, Postmaster
Chadd, George, baker and grocer
Clinton & Stinson, founder
Dunning & Clinton, carriage maker
Flayler, S. W., general merchant
Flayler & Boyce, general merchants
Harris, William, carriage maker
Hicks, Danial, carriage maker
Hollingsworth, S. W., stoves and tinware
Patterson, William, proprietor hotel
Reid, Mrs., proprietor hotel
Ross, Walter, & Co., general merchants
Terry & Co., foundry proprietors
Todman & Clemenson, general merchants

Wellesley.—A Village in the Township of Wellesley, County Waterloo, 17 miles from Berlin, the County Town. Stage to Baden Station, Grand Trunk Railway, 9 miles. Population, 400. Money order office.

Achteberg, Charles, tailor
Anetz, Jantz, brick maker
Berdux, Peter, butcher
Bull, William, tailor
Bushman, A.
Dersau, Peter, cooper
Dersau, William, hotel keeper
Doering, D. & L., flour mill
Doering, Lorentz, bookseller
Doersam, Peter, brewer
Doersam, Valentine, wood and willow ware
Ernst, Christain E., carpenter
Fliehand, John, wagon maker
Fortar, Jacob K., carpenter
Haferweld, Henry, cabinet maker and builder
Koch, Rev, Levi W., Lutheran
Livingston, J. & J. flax mill props.
McKee, S.
Meyer, Alexander, tinsmith
Morton William, physician
Otman, Charles, planing mill
Otman, Mary, soap and candle maker
Pickel, Ernst, rope and cordage manufacturer
Pickel, Miss, milliner
Rainer & Hickey, dyers and scourers
Rose, Frederick, saddler
Schneider, John, boots and shoes
Scott & Kneble, general merchants
Stabby, John, painter
Smith, Lewis, hotel keeper
Tribe, A., jeweler
Wagner, B., shoemaker
Wagner, Barthold, messenger
Wagner, William, butcher
Wagner, William, tailor
Westux, Peter, hotel keeper
Wellinger, M., saddler
ZOEGER, JOHN, Postmaster and general merchant

Wendover.—A Post Office in the Township of Planteagenet, County Prescott.

LAMB, WILLIAM, Postmaster.

West Arran.—A Post Office in the Township of Saugeen, County Bruce.

Campbell, P., J.P.
McINNIS, RICHARD, Postmaster and hotel keeper

West Brook.—A Post Village, in the Township of Kingston, County Frontenac, 7 miles distant from Kingston, and 180 from from Toronto. Daily mail. Population 200.

Bridge, Andrew, cooper
Clarke, Benjamin, grocer and shoemaker
Hall, Mrs. Jane, groceries
Leonard, Hiram, blacksmith
Leonard, Nathanial, wagon maker
McDonald, William, blacksmith
Powley, Henry R., grocer and shoemaker
Sproule, James, hotel proprietor and farmer

West Essa.—A Post Office in the Township of Essa, County Simcoe.

Aitcheson, John, carpenter
DRURY, T., Postmaster
Drury, J., general merchant
Fletcher, Samuel, blacksmith
Gordon, T. A., J.P.
Henderson, D., general merchant
McLeod, Alexander, tailor

Westfield.—A Post Office in the Township of Wawanosh, County Huron.

Brooks, Robert
Carr, William
Densmore, John
Hanaford, George
Harcourt, John
Harrison, John
HELPS, HEZEKIAH, Postmaster
Hoover, Adam
McLaughlin, Thomas
Moss, John
Ramsay, George
Redman, Charles
Redman, John
Taylor, Thomas
Tindel, George, farmer
Tindel, William, farmer
Woods, James

West Flamboro.—A Post Village in the Township of Flamboro' West, County Wentworth, 3 miles from Dundas Station, 8 from Hamilton and 47 from Toronto. Daily Mails. Money Order Office. Population about 500.

Bansley, Mrs. William, paper manuf
Barton, Samuel, blacksmith
Berry, George, blacksmith
Betzner, David, farmer
Bingham, Niel, farmer
Bowman, John, carpenter
Bowman, Stephen, carpenter
Bussy, Samuel, wagon maker
Christie, Rev. Thomas, (United Presbyterian)
Clark, James, weaver
Clark, William, weaver
Colcleugh, William, farmer
Coleman, James, farmer
Coleman, Robert, blacksmith
Cornwall, Vincent, M.D., physician and surgeon
Crooks, Thomas & Son, saw millers and farmers
Durrant, Charles, general dealer in dry goods, groceries, &c
Echlin, Daniel, blacksmith
Edworthy, William, farmer
Ewart, William, carpenter
Fleming, Patrick, farmer
Gillies, William
Gilmore, William, contractor
Graham, William, cooper
Hanes, Abraham, farmer
Hanes, George, farmer
Hodge, Owen, carpenter
Irving, John B., carpenter
Jackson, George, farmer
Jackson, John, butcher
Jones, Alfred, wagon maker
JONES, JOHN, carriage and wagon maker, general blacksmith, &c
Lawrence,, Frederick
Lepointe, Nelson, farmer
Lochrey, Alexander, farmer
Lucas, Thomas, stone cutter
McCormick, Levi W., wagon maker
McNeil, John, farmer
Martin, Mrs., dressmaker and milliner
Martin, Thomas, boot and shoemaker
Miller, W. F., (Thomas & W. F. Miller)
Miller, Thomas & W. F., paper manufs
Miller, Thomas, M.D
Miller & Dickson, physicians and surgeons
Morden, William, sawyer
Morris, Mrs.
Neff, John, sen., farmer
Neff, John, jun., carpenter
Newcombe, Jethro, stone cutter
Newcombe, John, stone cutter
Newcombe, Joseph, stone cutter
Newcombe, Robert, stone cutter
O'Brien, Mrs. boarding house
O'Reilly, J. R., M.D., physician and surgeon
Oram, Hugh, foreman paper mill
Ollimette, Benjamin, blacksmith
PERCY, JOHN, Postmaster merchant tailor
Ross, William, farmer
Smith, J. B., prop. West Flamboro' Hotel
Smith, Alexander, insurance agent
Smith, J. S., merchant
Sullivan, Cornelius, tailor
Sweet, Georg , blacksmith
Turley, Joseph, carpenter
Van Every, Hugh, general dealer in dry goods, groceries, hardware, crockery &c
West Flamboro' House, Jacob B. Smith prop
Wishart, Alexander, contractor
Wishart, Kenneth, farmer and township treasurer

West Huntingdon.—A Post Office in the Township of Huntingdon, County Hastings

Archibald, James
Ashley, John
Ashley, Ruth, teacher
Ashley Simeon
Chisholm, M., hotel
Erno, Thomas, dry goods
Erwin, Alexander, wagon maker
Forgy, Peter
Gay, Robert, general merchant
Gardner, ., hotel
Gardner, Samuel, teacher
Hoggistie, James
Kitchen, Owen, J. P.
Luke, John
LUKE, PHILIP, Postmaster
Luke, P., hotel keeper
McInroy, John, carpenter
McTaggart, Archibald, carpenter
McTaggert, Allen, cooper
Osborn, James, carpenter
Ransom, Samuel
Reid, Nestor
Rutledge, James, dry goods
Ryan, J. G., J. P
Sills, John

West Huntley.—A post office in the Township of Huntley, County Carlton, 26 miles from Ottawa.

Carroll, Patrick
Conboy, Thomas, teacher
Corcrea, Patrick, teacher
Egan, P
Evoy, James, cooper
Fetherston, William J., general merchant
Finners, Patrick, blacksmith
Hewston, John, general merchant
HORAN, EDWARD, Postmaster
Kennedy, John, jr.
Kennedy, Lawrence
Kennedy, Patrick
Kidd, Richard, notary public
Marion. John, J. P.
Mordy, John William
Mordy, Thomas
Murphy, Ellen, teacher
O'Brien, Jeremiah
O'Malley, Rev. Mr. (Roman Catholic)
Oakley, Elizabeth, teacher

West Lake.—A Post Office in the Township of Hallowell, County Prince Edward.

LAMBERT, HENRY, Postmaster.

West McGillivray.—A Post Village in the Township of McGillivray, County Middlesex. Distant from London 20 miles. Population 250.

Baynton, William, shoemaker
Bice, Gilbert, proprietor grist mill
Brewer, Abraham, general merchant and blacksmith
Brown, George, general merchant
Bryant, John, shoemaker
Eckhart, John, shoemaker
Frank, John, general merchant
FRASER, WILLIAM, Postmaster and gen. merchant
Grundy, John, blacksmith
Harcourt, George, shoemaker
Hastings, J., proprietor saw mill
Judge & Robinson, blacksmiths
Lavett, Henry, blacksmith
Macy, John, hotel keeper
Mack, John, hotel keeper and pump maker
Mellon, William, blacksmith
Patterson, John, wagon maker
Pearson, Thomas, shoemaker
Reyan, Patrick, shoemaker
Slack, George, proprietor grist mill
Smith, Alexander, general merchant
Thompson, Andrew, proprietor saw mill
Tweedle, Thomas, blacksmith

West Montrose.—A Village on the Grand River, in the Township of Woolwich, County Waterloo, 12 miles from Berlin, the County Town. Population 100.

Anderson, A. L., teacher
Bear, Samuel, lumber yard and planing mill
Benner, J. & Son, woolen manufactures
Bowman, Noah
Gordon, William, stock dealer
Halm, George, gunsmith
Holm, George, carpenter
KILBURNE, J. B., Postmaster and general mercht.
Kumpf, Frederick, cooper
McKay, Hiram, cooper
Pickert, Philip, cooper
Ryder, N., hotel keeper
Seaton, John, J.P.
Shirk, Abraham (United Brethren)
Veitch, William, J.P.
Woodward, J. M.

Weston.—A Village and Station of the Grand Trunk Railway on the River Humber, in the Township of York, County York, 9 miles from Toronto. Stages to Pine Grove, Albion, Klineburg and Woodbridge. Money Order Office and Savings Bank. Population 1000.

Bank, Dr., teacher
Banks, H., druggist
Barry, John, boots and shoes
Beamish, William, boots and shoes
Brown, John, carpenter
Brown Brothers, pottery
Bull, E., M.D.
Card, W., cooper
Checkley, Rev. W. F., teacher
Conron, James, butcher
Coulter, James, prop. foundry and planing mill
Crane, George, teacher
Crookshank, James, carpenter
Cullerton, Patrick, tailor
Eagle, John, hotel keeper and livery
Ellerly, William, J.P.
English, Rev. N. (Wesleyan)
Flemming, Robert, tailor
Flynn, Robert, boots and shoes
Gracey, James, brewer
Hickey, Z., agent G. T. R.
Huffman, James, saddler
Hodgson, James, teacher
Irwin, William, blacksmith
Jevins, James, painter
JOHNSON, ROBERT, Postmaster, gen. merchant
Johnson, Rev. W. A. (Church of England)
Kennedy, George, livery
Kemp, John, hotel keeper
Kempsall, Michael, blacksmith
Kempsall, Seth, blacksmith
Little, John, hotel keeper
Long, George, telegraph operator
Little, John, livery
Langstaff, Miss, milliner
Maguire David, boots and shoes
Mason, William, general merchant
Macdougal, Robert, grist mill
Musson, E. J., general merchant
Mallaby, Peter, blacksmith
Maulson, John, accountent
Nasen, William, jeweler
Parker, John, carpenter
Peers, Hugh, butcher
Peers, Thomas, constable
Plowman & Hall, foundry
Rowantree, David, butcher
Shuttleworth, James, wagon maker
Smith, Edward, tailor
Smith, Joseph P., butcher
Smith, W. H., general merchant
Stone, David, carpenter
Taylor, Robert, baker
Tyrrell, William, J.P., builder
Wadsworth, C. & W., general merchants, proprietors flour mills
Wadworth, W., J.P.
Watson, Miss, milliner
Wood, George, tinsmith

West Osgoode.—A Village and Station of the St. Lawrence and Ottawa Railway, in the Township or Osgoode, County Carleton, 21 miles from Ottawa. Population 100.

BOWER, J. C., Postmaster and general merchant
Caughley, Thomas, J.P.
Clerand, Hugh, general merchant
Hollen, Arthur, J.P.
Huffey, Thomas, cooper
Mores, Charles, J.P.
O'Connor, Daniel, teacher
Wilson, Elizabeth, teacher

Westover.—A small Village in the Township of Beverly, County Wentworth, 15 miles from Hamilton.

Bell, Alexander, teacher
Bennett, W. H., wagon maker
Burrell, George, general merchant
Chamberland, — physician
Cochrane, William, saw and shingle mills
Henry, William, saw, last and shingle mill
Kemp, Joseph, hotel prop.
Lindsay, John, grist mill
McINTOSH, BENJAMIN, Postmaster
Miles, James, general merchant
Purdy, Thomas, blacksmith
Smith, Rev. H., (Methodist Episcopal)
Wood, Peter

Westport.—(*See Villages too late for regular insertion, at the end of this work.*)

West's Corners.—A Village on Smith's Creek, in the Township of Mornington, County Perth, 17 miles from Stratford, the County Town. Population 300.

Adair, Samuel, carpenter and builder
Brownlee, James, general merchant
Coulter, John, farmer
Deppisch, George, general merchant
Dillabough, James, M. D.,
Dorland, S. G., carpenter and builder
Edwards, George, J. P.,
Edwards, Richard, teacher
Grosh, George, boots and shoes
Hunter, Nelson, farmer
Kertcher, Valentine, lumber yard
Kirchland, Alexander, boots and shoes
Lippert, J., boots and shoes
Miller, Henry, wagon maker
Milliken, Rev. A. (Wesleyan Methodist)
Moss, Robert, hotel keeper
Musgrave, Rev. Peter (Canada Presbyterian)
PIERSON, JOHN, Postmaster and gen. merchant
Pugh, David, farmer
Roe, James, farmer
Roe, Samuel, hotel keeper
Ross, David, teacher
Strong, James, hide and leather dealer
Torrance, William. teacher
Tovil, Rev. Isaac (Wesleyan Methodist)
Whaley, James, sen., farmer
Whaley, Samuel, J.P.
Whaley, Samuel, Division Court Clerk
Wilson, William, hotel keeper

West Winchester.—A Village in the Township of Winchester, County Dundas, 35 miles from Cornwall, the County Town. Population 250.

Amable, Allen, general merchant
Amable, George, farmer
Armstrong, Rev. J. (Wesleyan Methodist)
Baker, Benjamin, stone dealer
Beach, Asa, general merchant
Beach, M. F., proprietor flour and planing mill
BONE, WILLIAM, Postmaster and gen. merchant
Brown, John, shoe maker
Brown, Robert, farmer
Christie, John, sen., carpenter
Dixon, Thomas, hotel keeper
Forth, John, butcher
Forth, Nelson, farmer
Fox, C. J., farmer
Fulford, Alonzo, carpenter
Henderson, Caleb, shoemaker
Hickey, —, M. D.
Hogaboom, Gilbert, cooper
Hughes, James, farmer
Johnston, Rev. W., (Episcopal Methodist)
Laflamme, J. D., general merchant
Laing, George, farmer
Liffiton, J. G., tailor
McDermid, Rev. D., (Baptist)
McPherson, Joseph, tanner
McQuade, Henry, shoemaker
Mallory, Joseph B., tinsmith
Mercill, Henry, wagon maker
Mills, Ezra H., cooper
Mills, John, painter
Mulloy, George, J. P.
Orton & Hunter, wagon makers
Rae, David, J. P.
Robertson, Joseph, tailor
Scott, James, hotel keeper
Scott, William, tailor
Suddaby, Thomas, cabinet maker

Westwood.—A Village in the Township of Asphodel, County Peterboro'. Stages to Keene and Norwood. Tri-weekly mails. Population 75.

Andrews, Rev. Mr., (Presbyterian)
Breckenridge, John, farmer and saw mill proprietor
Brown, Thomas, wagon maker
Cameron, Thomas, miller
Christie, Thomas, tailor
Farrier, Rev. Mr.
Griffin, Samuel, general merchant
Humphreys, Job, farmer
McCamus, J., teacher
Macdonald, Thomas, farmer
O'Grady, Jeremiah, shoemaker
Powell, John, farmer
Powell, Mrs. saw and grist mill prop.
Reid, Thomas, shoemaker
Sargent, Edward, blacksmith
Sharp, William, blacksmith
Short, Rev. Mr. (Methodist)
Weald, Michael, hotel keeper

Wexford.—A small Village in the Township of Scarboro', County York, 9 miles from Toronto. Pop. 50.

Armstrong, Edward, farmer
Barker, Mark, farmer
Beath, James T., grocer
Belt, Rev. W., (Church of England)
Cutting, Charles C., boots and shoes
Edgar, Rev. J. (Methodist)
Frame, George, farmer
Gooderham, George, farmer
Hall, John, farmer
Harris, Rev. —, (Episcopal Methodist)
McBEATH, JAMES T., Postmaster
Maginn, Charles D., J.P.
Martin, Samuel, farmer
Percy, Mathew, farmer
Sanderson, Charles, wagon maker
Sisley, Mrs., grocer
Sylvester, Richard, farmer
Tingle, John, general merchant

Westmeath.—A Post Office in the Township of Westmeath, County Renfrew.
FRASER, ALEXANDER, Postmaster.

Whalen.—A small Village in the Township of Biddulph, County Middlesex, 19 miles from London.

McDonald, A., grocer
Magee, J. J., cradle maker
MILSON, JOHN H., Postmaster and wagon maker
Morley, J., carpenter
Stanly, W. D., teacher
Stevenson, J., carpenter

Wheatley.—A Village in the Township of Mersea, County Essex, 38 miles, from Sandwich the County Town. Stages to Windsor, Chatham and Amherstburg. Population 150.

Bachelder, Thomas, boots and shoes
Backus, E., steam flour mill
Barnum, Elder (Baptist)
BUCHANAN, W. J.P., Postmaster
Calhoun, John, cabinet maker
Collisson, S.
Craig, William, wagon maker
Dales, William, carpenter
Darbyshire, G., farmer
Darbyshire, Willam, farmer
Emerson, J., farmer
Fisher, George, tailor
Foster, Ralph, teacher
Fox, Charles H., general agent
Fox, R. R., farmer
Fox, Thomas M., J.P.
Fox & Co., proprietors saw mill
Harris, J., farmer
Harrison, Thomas, farmer
Hickson, J., farmer
Hooker, Rev. L. (Wesleyan)
Iverson, J., farmer
Julian, Jacob, hotel keeper
Lamarsh, J., farmer
Lane, H.
Malott, Henry, grocer
Marcott & Hutt, carpenters
Middleton, George, general merchant
Overholt, George, M.D.
Piggott, J., farmer
Pisor, Robinson, foundry proprietor
Plant, John, butcher
Robinson, George, grocer
Robinson, Joseph, baker
Setterington, William, farmer
Setterington, H., farmer
Sharp, George E., hotel keeper
Thompson, J. A.
Thompson, John R., hotel keeper
Watson, W., farmer
Wigfield, William, farmer
Wigle, Alexander, farmer

Whitby.—The County Town of Ontario, on Lake Ontario, and a station on the Grand Trunk Railway, is one of the most thriving Towns in the Province. The harbor is one of the best on the lake, and large quantities of grain and produce are shipped from this point. The manufacturing establishments are numerous and extensive. Whitby is the southern terminus of the proposed Whitby and Port Perry Railway, united by a branch with Uxbridge and Beaverton, on Lake Simcoe, which, when completed, will add materially to the prosperity of the Town. Distant from Toronto, 29 miles; Port Perry, 18; and from Beaverton, 45. Daily Stages to Prince Albert, Port Perry, Uxbridge and Beaverton. Port of Entry. Money Order Office and Savings Bank. Population, 3500

ALBION HOTEL, James C. McPherson, proprietor
Alexander, Alexander, Ontario Hotel
Allin, Lewis, books, stationery, wall papers and music
All Saint's Church, (Church of England), Rev. J. D. Cayley, Minister
Annes, George E., proprietor Whitby Brewery
Arnall, John, confectioner
Ayres, George, blacksmith
Bandel, Joseph A., boots and shoes
Beattie, Francis, butcher
Billings, W. H., barrister
Black, James
Blow, John, bookkeeper James Rowe & Co., agent British America Assurance Co.
Blow, William, grain and produce dealer
Borland, James, variety store
British America Assurance Co., Fire and Marine, of Toronto, Levi Fairbanks, jun., agent
BRITISH AND FOREIGN BIBLE SOCIETY, Jas. H. Gerrie, Depository
Brown, Loren, grocer

BROWN, N. W. (Brown & Patterson)
BROWN & PATTERSON, (Nicholas W. Brown, Robert & Rueben Patterson), proprietors Whitby Agricultural Works, (see adv.)
Bryan Jacob
Bryan, John, stoves and tinware
Bryan, William, manufacturer tin, copper and sheet iron ware, stoves, etc
BURNHAM, ZACHEUS, Judge County Court Ontario County
Burns, William, boots, shoes and groceries
Byrne, James, chemist and druggist
Byrne, Rev. James T. (Congregational)
CALDWELL, E. M., proprietor Commercial Hotel, (see adv)
Cameron, Alexander, chief constable
Cameron, George, shoemaker
CAMPBELL, JAMES A., proprietor Dr. Carson's Victoria Wine Bitters
Campbell, R. & J., dry goods and groceries
Canadian Express Office, George Yule, Agent
Card, William H., dentist
CARSON, G. A., M. D.
Cayley, Rev. J. D., (Church of England)
Champion, H. T.
Clarke, James A., photographer
CLAYTON, JAMES, wagon maker (see adv)
Clegg, T. W., harbor master
Cochrane, M. H., dry goods and groceries
COCHRANE, SAMUEL H., barrister and Co. Att'y
Collins, Matthew, boots and shoes
COMMERCIAL HOTEL, E. M., Caldwell, proprietor (see adv.)
Commercial Union Assurance Company of London, England, Fire and Life, Levi Fairbanks, jr., agt
Conway, G. O. S., builder and contractor
Cormack, George, carpenter and builder
Coulthard, Walter, sheriff's bailiff
County Court Office and Surrogate, J. V. Ham, depty clerk of the Crown
Crosby, Henry H., grocer
Cullen, William, baker and confectioner
Danford, Thomas, High Constable Ontario County
DARTNELL, GEORGE H., barrister, Master and deputy Registrar in Chancery
Dawes, Clement
Deverell, Thomas, contractor
Dow, Thomas, accountant Ontario Bank
Draper, Chester, grain dealer
Draper, James, deputy Registrar
Draper, C. & Co., commission and grain merchants, proprietors Ontario Steam Elevator
Dundas, John, tea pedlar
Eastwood, W., M.D.
Edinburgh Life Assurance Company of Scotland; Levi Fairbanks, jun., agent
Etna Fire and Marine Insurance Company of Dublin; T. H. McMillan & Co., agents
FAIRBANKS, LEVI, JUN., insurance agent and auctioneer
Fairbanks, Levi, sen.
Farquaharson, John
Farmers' Inn, Samuel G. Wilkinson, proprietor
Farmers' Victoria Mutual Insurance Company of Hamilton, Yeoman Gibson, agent
Ferguson, John, tailor
Fox, Castle, boot and shoe maker
Francis, Richard, groceries, wines and liquors
Freeman, T. P., carriage painter
Fullerton, Robert, telegraph operator (see adv)
GIBSON, YEOMAN, importer of dry goods, groceries and hardware, produce and grain dealer, commission merchant and insurance agent
GERRIE, JAMES H., mayor, chemist and druggist
Gordon, James K., barrister
Gortzig, Charles, melodeon manufacturer
Grammar School, Thomas Kirkland, head master
Green, Simon P., sewing machine agent
GREENWOOD, J. HAMER, solicitor, dealer in lands, mortgages, money stocks and exchange
Griffith, Charles, gun, locksmith, &c.
Groat, Ira, grocer
GROSE, STEPHEN, planing mill, sash, blind and door manufactory (see adv)
Gross, George C., hardware merchant
Gunn, R. J., M.D.
Ham, John V., Deputy Clerk of the Crown
HAM, GEORGE H., editor and prop. *Whitby Gazette*
Hamilton & Co., dry goods and groceries
Hamlin, Miss B., dressmaker
Hancock, Dr.
Hannam, W. H., painter and glazier
HARPER, MAJOR, manfr. wood working machinery (see adv.)
Hartford Live Stock Insurance Co., Levi Fairbanks, jun., agent
Hatch & Brother (Richard and Samuel) hardware, stoves and tinware
Hewis, George, butcher
HIGGINS, WILLIAM, H., editor and prop. *Whitby Chronicle*
Hill, Samuel, saw mill and flax mill proprietor
Hillary, Michael, M.D.
HOLDEN, JAMES, official assignee, notary public, land and general agent, Deputy Reeve (money to loan) (see adv)
Hopkins, C. A., station master G. T. R.
Howell, John, grocer
HUSTON, THOMAS, town clerk and treasurer
Irvine, Miss E., dressmaker
Jameson, R. H., grocer and spirit merchant
Johnston, Charles, blacksmith
Johnston, James, watches and jewelry
JONES, C. A., barrister, agent Life Association of Scotland
Jones, Rev. C. G., (Church of England)
Keith, John, farrier, wood and coal merchant
KELLER FRANCIS, Postmaster
KING, CHARLES (Rainer & Co.)
King, Rev. M.. (Baptist)
KING, BROTHERS, (Joseph and Charles), tanners and curriers, dealers in shoe findings (see adv)
Knowling, Mrs. Eliza, agent for Madam Briggs' diagrams
Lamon, James, attorney-at-law, land agent, etc.
Law, W. H., M.D.
Law, W. A., accountant James Holden
LAWDER, ROBERT H., commission merchant
Lawler, Thomas, grocer and liquor dealer
Lawlor, Andrew, baker and confectioner
LIFE ASSOCIATION OF SCOTLAND, C. A. Jones, agent
Liverpool and London and Globe Fire and Life Ins Co., Levi Fairbanks, jun., agent
Losie, Miss S. G., millinery, etc.
Lowes & Powell, (John M. Lowes and J. B. Powell), dry goods, groceries, millinery, etc.
Lyne, John, boots and shoes
McDougall, John G., confectioner
McLennan, Rev. K. (Presbyterian)
McMillan, T. H. & Co., dry goods, groceries and liquors, insurance agents
McPHERSON, JAMES C., proprietor Albion Hotel
McPherson, Mrs., millinery and dressmaking
Macdonell, Duncan C., clerk 1st Division Court
Macdonell, H. J., barrister, Clerk of the Peace and Clerk of the County Council County Ontario

Mathison, David, tailor
Montreal Telegraph office, George Yule, jun., agent
Moore, W. A., teller Ontario Bank
Mosure, Miss E., dressmaker
Munro, R. L., auctioneer
Murphy, James J., teacher
Myers, Thomas, auctioneer and commission merchant
Newbury, John, shoemaker
O'DONOVAN, MICHAEL, manufacturer of carriages wagons, sleighs and velocipedes (see adv)
O'NEILL, WILLIAM, proprietor Grand Trunk Hotel G. T. R. Station
ONTARIO BANK, branch, R. F. Lockhart, manager
Ontario Farmers Mutual Insurance Company (Fire) Levi Fairbanks, jr., secretary
Palmer, Samuel, painter
Paxton, William, jr., County Treasurer
PERRY, J. H., Registrar Ontario County
Perry, R. E., produce merchant
Phenix Insurance Company of Brooklyn, N. Y., marine, Levi Fairbanks, jr., agent
Philp, James, saddle, harness and trunk manuf
Pœnix Fire Insurance Company, of London, England, Yeoman Gibson, agent
Pirie, Alexander, blacksmith
Pringle, Alexander, merchant tailor
Proudfoot, John, general blacksmith
RAINER, JOSEPH F., (Rainer & Co.)
RAINER & CO., (Joseph F. Rainer and Charles King) piano forte manufacturers (see adv)
Ray, Nathaniel, livery stable proprietor
Reliance Mutual Association of London, England, T. H. McMillan & Co., agents
REYNOLDS, NELSON G., Sheriff County Ontario, res Trafalgar Castle
Rice, A. K., cabinet maker
Rice, John, blacksmith
RICHARDSON, ARTHUR, agent Royal Canadian Bank
Richardson, Joshua
ROBINSON, JOHN, hairdresser
ROBSON, GEORGE, proprietor Robson House (see adv.)
Roche, Mrs. Sarah, milliner
Ross, Lauder, Mulock & Smith (Hon. John Ross, Q. C., A. W. Lauder, M.P.P., W. Mulock and G. Y. Smith), barristers
Rowland, B., proprietor National Hotel
ROYAL CANADIAN BANK, Arthur Richardson, agent
ROYAL HOTEL, Thomas Walker, prop. (see adv)
Saunders, John, boot and shoe manufacturer
St. John's Church (Church of England), Rev. C. G. Jones, minister
Schoales, Mrs., milliner and dressmaker
Scott, Charles, butcher
Scott, Jerome, butcher
Shaw, John, manufacturer washing machines
Shea, Rev. John J. (Roman Catholic) res. Oshawa
Skinner, John, general merchant
Slater, Rev. — (Wesleyan)
Smith, Bernerd, Victoria Hotel
Smith, George Y. (Ross, Lauder, Mulock & Smith)
Snow, Richard, proprietoe Huron House
STANTON, JOHN, foreman *Whitby Chronicle*
Stearns & Spurrill, manufacturers wine bitters
Thompson, H., pumpmaker
Thompson, William, saddle and harness maker
Thwaite, Metcalfe, tea merchant
TILL & SAMO (John Till and James H. Samo), cabinet makers, &c. (see card)
Till, William, furniture dealer
Tilley, James, junior master Grammar School
TOMLINSON, R. H., Dep. Sheriff, Ontario County
Twohey & Perry (Jerome Twohey and Peter Perry), proprietors daily stages to Uxbridge
Tye, John, tanner and currier
WALKER, THOMAS, prop. Royal Hotel (see adv)
Walkey, Samuel, carriage maker
Walters, Henry, flour, feed and commission merchant
Watkis, John L., dentist
Watson, John, shipping broker and forwarder
Wilson, R. H., photographer
Whalen, James, shoemaker
Whitby, Billiard Parlour, B. Fowle, manager
Whitby Brewery, George Ezra Annes, proprietor
WHITBY CHRONICLE, W. H. Higgins, editor and prop., published every Thursday, subscription $1 50 per annum
WHITBY GAZETTE (weekly), George H. Ham, editor and proprietor
WHITBY POST OFFICE, Francis Kellar, Postmaster
Wilkinson, John, watches and jewelery
Wilkinson, Samuel G., proprietor Farmers' Inn
Wilson, Alexander C., house, sign and ornamental painter and paper hanger
Wilson, R. J., barrister
Wolfender, Jonathan, marble cutter
YARNOLD, R. J., boots and shoes (see adv)
Yule, George, agent Montreal Telegraph Co., agent Canadian Express, and supt. Whitby and Port Perry Telegraph Co.
Yule, George, exchange broker
Yule, William, telegraph operator

Whitehurst.—A post office in the Township of Elizabethtown, County Leeds, 13 miles from Brockville, the County Town.

Bell, James, shoemaker
BELL, JOHN, Postmaster
Bell, Walter, farmer

White Rose.—A village in the Township of Whitchurch, County York, 25 miles from Toronto and 4 from Aurora, station, Northern Railroad. Population 75.

Ashton, Seth, lumber dealer and insurance agent
Hutchison, Henry, teacher
Lloyd, Charles, farmer
Lloyd, George wagon maker
LLOYD, JARED, J.P., Postmaster
Mercer, William, boots and shoes
Richardson, Thomas, tailor
Robinson, William, carpenter
Smith, R., farmer
Steele, Mark, farmer
Steele, P. J., carpenter
Wallace, Stephen, farmer
Young, Joseph

White Lake.—A village in the Township of McNab, County Renfrew, 50 miles from Pembroke, the County Town, and 14 from Arnprior station, St. Lawrence and Ottawa Railroad Large quantities of lumber are exported from this point. Population 150.

Alliston, John, hotel
Bennett, Robert, lime and stone dealer
Best, Mrs., milliner
Bole, George, blacksmith
Box, G. John, general merchant
Browne, John
Cuthbert, James E., general merchant
Lee, John, hotel keeper
Lindsay, William, shingle maker
Lindsay, William, lumber yard
Ludgate, Mrs., milliner
McLauchlan, Duncan
McManus, Dennis, general merchant
McNab, Dugald C., teacher
McRae, John, wagon maker
Monahan, Timothy, blacksmith
Neil, Nicholas, cooper
PARIS, JOHN, Postmaster, lumber dealer
Robertson, Alexander, carpenter
Robertson, Duncan
Shane, Michael, lime manufacturer and stone dealer
Stirling, Alexander, grocer
Stewart, Alexander
Stewart, Donald, lumber dealer

Whitevale.—A Village in the Township of Pickering, County Ontario, 14 miles from Whitby, the County Town, to which place it is connected by daily stage. Daily mail. Population about 300.

Alaway, A., cooper
Allen, John, boot and shoemaker
Bessie, John, sawyer
Bessie, George, sawyer
Burton, Thomas, hotel keeper
Burton, Israel, butcher and mover
Burton, George, farmer
Burton, William, carpenter
Booth, William, wagon maker
Booth, Henry, cabinet maker
Bradshaw, Edward, farmer
Defoe, David, teamster
Ellis, J., superintendent of woolen factory
Ferrier, Amos, teacher
Gilchrist, George, planer
Hilts. F., farmer
Hilts, R., farmer
Hoover, P. R. & Co., cheese factory
Hoover, P. R. (P. R. Hoover & Co.
Major Hotel, Thomas Burton, proprietor
Major, H., farmer
Miller, Mrs. Ann
Moodey, D., boot and shoemaker
Moore, Rev. J. B. (Baptist)
McPHEE, D., Postmaster and merchant
Patten, Joseph, carpenter
Percy, S. T., bookkeeper
Roach, F., blacksmith
Robinson, John, cooper
Rose, J. & Son, merchants and tailors
Spink, W. & J., millers
Squires, Alexander, miller
Strachan, George, farmer
Taylor, James, general merchant
Taylor, D., weaver
Turner, William, sen., farmer
Turner, William, jun., farmer
Vardon, J., carpenter
Vardon, R., planer
Verro, A., farmer
Waters, Thomas, cloth fuller
White, Trumen P., mill and factory owner
Wigmore, S. B., tinsmith
Wilson, M., sen., farmer
Wilson, Joseph, steam carriage factory
Wilson, M., jun., carriage maker
Wonch, J. W., teacher

Whitfield.—A village in the Township of Mulmur, County Simcoe, 35 miles from Barrie, the County Town, 18 from Angus Station Northern Railway, and 17 from Orangeville. Stages bi-weekly to Orangeville. Population 100.

Archer, William, carpenter
Davison, John, farmer
Dean, John, farmer
Ferris, Matthew, J.P., farmer
Graham, Colwell, J.P.
HENRY, P. D., Postmaster
Leighton, P. S., tailor
Levens, Joseph, general merchant
McCutcheon, David, farmer
Middleton, George, carpenter
Noble, William, general merchant and hotel keeper
Oliver, Joseph, farmer
Pollagher & Laing, general merchants
Wilson, George, farmer

Whittington.—A Village in the Township of Amaranth, County Wellington, 40 miles from Guelph, the County Town. Stages to Owen Sound and Orangeville. Population, 100.

Allingham, James, farmer
French, Thomas, farmer
BOWSFIELD, ROBERT, J. P., proprietor Whittington Hotel
Galbraith, John, dentist
Graham, Thomas, carpentar
Jefferson, George, farmer
Johnson, David, farmer
Leader, Joshua, farmer
Macmunn, Charles, blacksmith
Murray, Henry, farmer
Routledge, John, gunsmith
Whitten, Robert, farmer
Whitten, Thomas, farmer

Wiarton.—A thriving Village in the Townships of Amable and Keppel, Counties Grey and Bruce, 60 miles from Walkerton. The Village is beautifully situated at the head of Colpoy's Bay, one of the best natural harbors on the Upper Lakes, in the midst of a beautiful section justly celebrated for its romantic scenery, healthy climate, pure air and pure water. Steamer Champion to Owen Sound. Population, 100.

Dennis, J., wagon maker
Dinsmore, Thomas, hotel keeper
Gilpin, T., lumber dealer
Greenlees, Robert, general merchant
Hodgins, J. W., general merchant
Hurst, F., agent
Kribbs, Henry, shoemaker
Jones, E. C., steamboat agent, forwarding and com. merchant
MILLER, B. B., Postmaster, estate agent
Patterson, Thomas, carpenter
Whitworth, W. B., saddler
Williams, Dr,, proprietor saw mills
Wilmot, Isaiah, carpenter

Wick.—A small Village in the Township of Brock County Ontario, 25 miles from Whitby the County Town.

Brabazon, George, farmer
Carmichael, Peter, proprietor Wick hotel
Hadden, George, farmer
Huntington, James, butcher
Leask, Alexander farmer
Leask, David, farmer
McArthur, Rev. A., (Presbyterian)
Parrish, Lewis, proprietor grist mill
Patterson, J. shoemaker
SHIRE, CALEB, Postmaster, general merchant
Stone, John, farmer
Tipp, William E., painter

Wicklow.—A post office in the Township of Haldimand, County Northumberland, 10 miles from Cobourg, the County Town.

Armstrong John & Son, shoemakers
Bennett, W. C., wagon maker
Davy, John, carpenter
Doolittle, Ephraim, farmer
Doolittle, Samuel, farmer
EWING, C. E., Postmaster
Hale & Wilson, wagon makers
Hall, Alexander, farmer
McCullen, A., grist mill
Massie, John, G., proprietor grist mill
Scripture, S. L. J., founder and machinist
Williams, Isham, grocer

Widder Station (Thedford Village).—A Village on the line of the Grand Trunk Railway, in the Township of Bosanquet, County Lambton, about 3 miles from the River Aux Sables. Distant from Sarnia, the County Town, 32 miles and from Arkona, 7½ miles. Lime, salt and oil are found in the neighborhood. Stage to Arkona. Money Order Office. Population 350.

Adams, A.
ATKINSON & GATTIS, commission and forwarding merchants (see adv)
Bishop, William, farmer
Beattie, Alexander, general merchant
Burns, J. P., insurance agent
BURNS, J. P. & CO., general merchants
Burrow, M., telegraph operator
Cameron, John, woolen manufacturer
CORNELL, JONAS, general merchant
Curtis, George, auctioneer
Dalziel, Andrew, blacksmith
Dalziel, John, shingle maker
Davidson, A.
Davidson, William, farmer
Diller, Anson, carpenter
Dobie, John
DOBBIE, M. A.
DUNN, GEORGE, hotel keeper
Foster & Sills, butchers
Freeman, Rev. B. (Baptist)
Goodfellow, Rev. P. (Presbyterian)
Haney, R., sash and stave factory
Hilburn, Wilson, farmer
Hirkmott, J. V., commission and forwarding mercht
HOLWELL, G. W., hotel keeper
Hunt, Rev. G. (Methodist Episcopal)
Jackson, Frederick, wagon maker
Johnstone, Rev. (Church of England)
Johnston, Edward, blacksmith
Jones & Kennedy, props. steam flouring & grist mill
Kennedy, Caleb, general merchant
Kennedy, Jacob, prop. grist mill
King, S., shingle maker
Kirkpatrick, T., gen. mercht and real estate agent
Kirkpatrick & King, lumber dealers
KIRKPATRICK, THOMAS, J.P., Postmaster and general merchant
Lang, John, accountant
Lee, James, watchmaker
LENNOX & McGREGOR, general merchants
Long, John, accountant
Lyman, Morris, carpenter
McCormick, R., farmer
McIntosh, R., tailor
McKinnon, L., teacher
McLean, J. M., M.D
McNab, J., cabinet maker
Main, David, lime and stone dealer
Markness, Thomas, boots and shoes
Morgan, G. G., tailor
Morgan, W. H., station master, express and ins. agt
Parkinson, M., farmer
Parks, Thomas, boots and shoes
Pikman, George, farmer
Plumb, Paul, carpenter
Powell, J., farmer
Pringle, William E., tailor
RAE, R., J.P., general merchant
Reagan, James B., tinsmith
Ryckman, G., farmer
Southworth, Levi, lime and stone dealer
Southworth, N. E., seedsman
Symanson, A., boots and shoes
Tidball, Richard, boots and shoes
Titus, Christopher, carpenter
Washburn, L., cabinet maker
Watcher, Richard, blacksmith
Watts, John, farmer
WATTSON, MARTIN, cabinet maker & lumber dealer
Willet, Arthur, carpenter
Wilson, Richard, general merchant

Widder.—A Village in the Township of Bosanquet, County Lambton, 32 miles from Sarnia, the County Town, and 1½ from Widder Station. Stages to and from Arkona. Population 200.

Bethune, Donald, grocer
Chase, Asa, hotel keeper
Chester, John, farmer
Crawford, Thomas, farmer
Dalziel, Andrew, blacksmith
Dalziel, John, manager saw mill
Decker Isaac, proprietor saw mill
Donald Archibald, lumber merchant
DUFFUS, ADAM, Postmaster, merchant
Elliott, John, lumber merchant
English, Alexander, farmer
Goodfellow, Rev. Peter (Presbyterian)
Johnson, Hiram, wagon maker
Kier, William, shoemaker
Lackey, John, farmer
Long, John, bookkeeper
Munger, Elijah, tanner
Munnes, W. A., M.D.
McKellar, Donald, farmer
McKELLAR, P., J.P., comn. in B. R.
McMillan, Thomas, saddler and tanner
McNab, James, miller
Owens, John, prop. saw mill
Tidball, Robert, shoemaker

Wilfrid.—A Village in the Township of Brock, County Ontario, 36 miles from Whitby, the County Town. Population 60.

Burgess, F., painter
CHAMBERS, JOHN Postmaster and gen. mercht
Hamil, A., mason
Hart, G., farmer
Hart, R., farmer
Hodgins, T., carpenter
Hunter, J. W., weaver
Lloyd, J., farmer
Lloyd, T., farmer
McCallum, J., surveyor
Nealon, J., farmer
Nugent, T., farmer
Reekie, J., merchant
St. John, P., farmer
Till, William, wagon maker
Vallentyne, John, blacksmith
Way, N. B., farmer
Way, W. lumber dealer

Wilkesport.—A small Village in the Township of Sombra, County Lambton, 20 miles from Sarnia, the County Town.

Brown, Charles, farmer
Brown, Henry, farmer
Butterworth, William, painter
Campbell, J., carpenter
Cullen, Peter, farmer
Eyre, Thomas, carriage maker
Eyre, William, carriage maker
Farr, Joseph, carpenter
KIMBALL, WILLIAM, J.P. and general merchant
McNaughton, John, shoemaker
McQuarrie, Dr.
Parker, Andrew, confectioner
Peattee, Robert M., tailor
Selmon, Samuel, farmer
Selmon, Thomas, saddler
Stone, G. T., tinsmith
Stone, J. W., tinsmith
Sturdevant, Herman, M.D.
Sturdevant, Ira, farmer

Willetsholme.—A Post Office in the Township of Pittsburg, County Frontenac.

ABRAM, JOSIAS, Postmaster.

Williams (Nairn).—A small Village on the River Aux Sable, in the Township of East Williams, County Middlesex, 22 miles from London. Population 130.

BELL, ARCHIBALD, Postmaster, carpenter
Bradley, James, cooper
Carmichael, Allan, hotel keeper
Davidson, Roderick, blacksmith
Drummond, William & Co., general merchants
Fraser, Hugh, blachsmith
Gilchrist, Hugh, general merchant
Gilchrist, John, hotel keeper
McKeith, Peter, shoemaker
McKenzie, Donald, shoemaker
Livingstone, John, wagon maker
Parsons, John, proprietor grist mill
Sands, Richmond, M. D.

Williamsburg.—(Cartwright Post Office)—A small Village in the Township of Cartwright, County Durham, 40 miles from Cobourg, the County Town, and 16 from Bowmanville. Improved lands in vicinity average $40 per acre. Stages daily to Bowmanville, fare 75 cents, Population 100.

Ford, John, general merchant
Kerrigan, Robert, tailor
Lummis, John, flour mill
McPHAIL, HUGH, general merchant
Martin, William, J. P.
Mason, Thomas, hotel keeper
Montgomery, John, M. D.
Moore, Joseph, tailor
Morrison, James, millwright and gunsmith
Spinks, Robert, J. P.
Tooley, John, hotel keeper
VANCE, W., Postmaster
Walker, William tanner

Williamstown.—A Village on the River Aux Raisin, in the Township of Chartottenburg, County Glengarry, 12 miles from Martintown. Population 500.

Barrett, William & Co., carriage and wagon makers
Barston, Lewis, carpenter
Bertrand, Oliver, boot maker
Braseland, David, tailor
Burton, James, wagon maker
Campbell, Daniel, brick maker
Campbell, William, lime and stone dealer
Carron, Thomas, butcher
Cattanach, Lauchlin, wagon maker
Curry, James, baker
Earl, James, shingle maker
Elder, George, gunsmith
Ferguson, George, boot maker
Ferguson, Peter R.
Fraser, A.
Gordon, Francis, cooper
Grant, John A., patent right agent
Gedbois, P. V. D., cabinet maker and gen. merchant
Irons, William, painter
Jamieson, Alexander, teacher
Ladoo, Charles, wagon maker
McBain, James, farmer
McCarthy, Rev. I. J. ((Roman Catholic)
McCrimmon, Duncan, lime and stone dealer
McDonald, Angus, J.P., hotel keeper
McDonald, Donald, boot maker
McDonald, John A. & Co., general merchants
McDonald, Thomas, hotel keeper
McDonald, William, auctioneer
McGregor, John A.
McLaren, John, brick maker
McLENNAN, DUNCAN, Postmaster and grocer
McLennan, Murdoch, farmer
McPherson, James, tailor
McPherson, John, general merchant
McRae, John, carpenter and builder
Maxwell, David, teacher
Murchison, Duncan
Patterson, Rev. Nathaniel (Free Church)
Pigeon, William, boot and shoe maker
Rousson, Adolphus, carpenter
Roussen, Joseph, carpenter
Rousson, Timothy, carpenter
Shaver, Robert, M.D.
Slack, James, tailor
Sullivan, Andrew, tinsmith
Summers, J. A., general merchant
Sylvester & McGillis, steam flour and grist mill
Ward, Alexander, tinsmith
Watson, Rev. Peter (Presbyterian)

Williamsville.—A Village belonging to the Corporation of the City of Kingston, situated one mile from the market. Population 250.

Andrew, Thomas, grocer
Carnovsky, Robert, baker
Hafner, George, butcher
Hance, J. T., innkeeper
O'Laughlin, Miss, school teacher
Purdy, Mrs. Susan, innkeeper
Spotton, Richard, hotel keeper
Ward, Charles, Temperance House

Williscroft.—A Post Office in the Township of Elderslie, County Bruce.

Halliday, James, farmer
McLeed, William, builder
Robb, Alexander, farmer
Shipman, J. B., prop. saw mill
WILLISCROFT, GEORGE, Postmaster, farmer

Wilton.—A village on Big Creek, in the Township of Ernestown, County Lennox, 12 miles from Napanee, the County Town, stage to Kingston and Odessa. Population 200.

Amey, Peter, farmer
Beattie, Dawson, cabinet maker
Brown, Sayer, J.P.,
Cook, Rev., (Primitive Methodist)
Davey, John, saddler
Davey, Stanton, farmer
Histed, William, cooper
Homer, James, teacher
Hurley, Edward, blacksmith
Kellar, Andrew, saddler
Lapan, N., J.P.
Lee, Nicholas, shingle maker
McClement, David, tailor
Miller, James, farmer
Mills, Thomas & Son, potash manufacturers
Owens, Williams, wagon maker
Parrott, Miss Amanda, teacher
Peters, James, blacksmith
Pultz, Henry, farmer
Scott, Charles, blacksmith
Shibley, Jacob, J.P.
Simmons, Austin & Bro, props. flour and grist mill
Simmons, H., prop. Dominion Hotel
Snider, Jeremiah, J.P
Squires, Rev. G. H., (Wesleyan)
Storm, George, farmer
Storm, James, farmer
Thompson, James, carpenter
Thompson, William, sen., sash, door and blind manf
Walker, William, farmer
Ward, Christopher, farmer
Ward, Joseph, J.P., farmer
WARNER, SIDNEY, J.P., Postmaster, gen. merch́t
Wilton, Rev. Richard, (Wesleyan Methodist)

Willowgrove.—A post office in the township of Oneida, County Haldimand.

KEATING, THOMAS, Postmaster.

Willowdale.—A small Village in the Township of York, 9 miles from Toronto. Population 50.

Archer, Rev. E. G. (Episcopal Methodist)
Brest, John
CUMMER, JACOB, Postmaster
Cummer, Joshua
Fenby, James, hotel keeper
Gibson, P. S., carpenter
Holmes, William
Hutten, Rev. J. B., (Episcopal Methodist)
Johnson, Abraham, J.P.
McMurchy, Alexander
Piper, Joseph, shingle maker
Read, H. H., teacher
Sheppard, Joseph, farmer
Wallis, William
Willson, A. L., attorney-at-law

Wilmur.—A Post Office in the Township of Loughboro, County Addington.
HENRY DAVID, grocer.

Wimbledon.—A Post-office in the Township of Sandwich East, County Essex.

Burke, Edward, farmer
Burwell, James, farmer
Chall, Frank, farmer
Chall, William, farmer
Chapman, W., hotel keeper
Dawind, John, J.P
Duneshell, J., brick maker
Jessop, John, farmer
Moore, John, distiller and rectifier
Moore, John, clothing dealer
Ouellette, Joseph, farmer
Penman, James, butcher
Penman, William, butcher
Rounding, C., farmer
Rounding, —, bootmaker
Taylor, Edwin, farmer
Turk, John, farmer
Vollars, Thomas, proprietor steam flour mill

Winchelsea—(Elimville.)—A small Village in the Township of Usborne, County Huron, 30 miles from Goderich, the County Town. Population 50.

Allen, Alfred, carpenter
Andrew, George, wagon maker
Brimacombe, John, boots and shoes
Carpenter, Richard, blacksmith
Cathcart, Henry, blacksmith
Chittick, John, blacksmith
Cook, Thomas, wagon maker
Delbridge, John, farmer
Elliott, Mrs. F., hotel keeper
Evans, Richard, cooper
Godbolt, George, farmer.
Hall, Charles, carpenter
Hall, John, carpenter
Hall, Samuel, carpenter
Hall, Samuel P., teacher
McKee, R. F., farmer
Miller, Joseph, farmer
Miner, William jun., carpenter
Nagle, Thomas, farmer
Penwarder, David, jun., soap and candle maker
Robinson, William and Robert, carpenters
SMITH, ALEXANDER, Postmaster, general merch.
Taylor, Henry, general merchant
Turnbull, Andrew, farmer
Walker, David, J. P.
Watson, George E., carpenter

Winchester.—A Village on the Nation River, in the Township of Winchester, County Dundas, 36 miles from Cornwall, the County Town; and 18 from Williamsburg Station, Grand Trunk Railway. Pop. 500.

Armstrong, Rev. A., Wesleyan Methodist
Ault & Edgerton, carders
Beach, Asa, general merchant
Buish Robert, furniture store
CASSELMAN, CHARLES T., Postmaster and general merchant
Casselman, Solomon, blacksmith
Dwyer, Frank, tailor
Fisher, Joseph, wagon maker
Flynn, John, boots and shoes
Gibbons, Jeremiah J., general merchant
Gillespie & Ray, general merchants
Ginley, James, inn keeper
Graham, James, harness maker
Grant, Donald, physician
Hay, James, teacher
Hillar, William, grist and saw mill
Hugh, Patrick, general merchant
Johnson, Joseph, physician
Johnson, Rev. W. E., Episcopal Wesleyan
McMahon, James, boots and shoes
Moad, Henry W., general merchant
Smith, James, boots and shoes

Winchester Springs.—A Post-office in the Township of Williamsburg, County Dundas.
GREER, JAMES, Postmaster.

Windermere.—A Post-office in the Township of Watt, County Victoria.
McALPINE, JOHN, Postmaster.

Windham Centre.—A Village in the Township of Windham, County Norfolk, 10 miles from Simcoe, the County Town. Population 150.

Baker, B. F., farmer
Baker, Hewit, farmer
Green, Robert, farmer
MARTEE, G. F., Postmaster, general merchant and prop. saw mill
Newall, Hugh, wagon maker
Robertson, Charles, farmer
Shaw, Rev. C., (New Connexion Methodist)
Silverthorne, Lewis, general merchant
Silverthorne, William, carpenter
Smith, P. C., teacher

Windsor.—The largest and most important Town in the County of Essex, is pleasantly situated on the Detroit River, in the Township of Sandwich, opposite Detroit, 46 miles from Chatham, and 110 from London. The Town is built on a high bank from 30 to 40 feet above the river, rendering the situation healthy and desirable as a place of residence. The town was laid out in 1834, and in 1846 contained a population of 300, which increased in 1861 to 2,500, at present it may be estimated at about 5,000. Windsor enjoys excellent facilities for manufacture and commerce, being the western terminus of the Great Western Railway, and also having the benefit of summer navigation to all points. Money Order Office and Savings Bank.

Alard, William, tailor
ANDREWS, ALFRED A., M.D
Angan, George, prop. Shakespere Hotel
Apple, Frederick, carpenter and builder
ARMOUR, JOHN, notary, (see adv)
Askew, Henry
Bailey, Henry, grocer
Bailey, Richard, boots and shoes
Barnet, Ferdinand, blacksmith
Barrett, Edward, prop. Hirons House
BARTLETT, ALEXANDER, town clerk
Bartlett, James, carpenter
Bartlett, William, baker
BATTY, JOHN, cabinet maker (see adv)
Bayfield, J. F., baggage master G.W.R
Baylis, Benjamin, confectioner
Bell, Henry, trader and ice dealer
Bills, John, carpenter
Binner, Etienne, wagon maker
Blackadder, John, merchant
Blay, David, engineer
Bloomfield & Co., auctioneers
Boismer, Lawrence, carpenter
Brennan, James, tailor
Brown, William, carpenter
Butler, D., grocer
Cameron & Thorburn, merchants
CAMERON & CLEARY, barristers, &c
Caron, Francis, police magistrate
CASGRAIN, CHARLES E., M.D
Chater, Thomas, inn keeper
Chater, William, blacksmith
Cherry, Augustus, trader
CLARKE, CHARLES, boots and shoes (see adv)
Clark, John, revenue officer
Clark, Samuel, shoemaker
Clark, John, tailor
Coleman, B., cooper
Collins, Edward, carpenter
Comstock, Levi, coppersmith
Conway, Patrick, merchant
Cooley, A. J., blacksmith
Cooley & Clarke, wagon makers
Corkrell, J. B
Corney, John M., tailor
Cotter, William
Cowley, Thomas, engineer
Cross, F. J., soap and candle manuf
Crow, George, boarding house
Cuthbertson, James
Davenport, Horace
Davies, Evan, tailor
Delisle, Antoine, carpenter
Dennison, John, revenue officer
Dodson, John, track inspector
Donnelly, E. B., M.D
Dougall & Bros., merchants
Douglass, C. D
Dowler, Oliver, mason
Elliott, J. F., collector of customs
Elliott, J. L. G., clerk 7th division court
Farrell, William, shoemaker
Faulkner, Samuel, carpenter
Fergus, Robert, merchant
Finlay, Mrs., saloon keeper
Fletcher, D., tailor
Forbes, James, Capt. steamer *Argo*
FOSTER, F. L., P.L.S., ins. agent, &c., (see adv)
FRASER, JAMES, watchmaker and jeweler (see adv)
Freeman, Coleman, cooper
Frester, H., groceries and provisions
Gauthier & St. Louis, merchants
Gilkes, George P
Girdlestone, G. W., express agent G.W.R
Glover, H. B., mason
Goete, George, carpenter
Gorst, Thomas, photographer
Gossman, George, tailor
Goyean, David, farmer
Grant, George, bookseller and stationer
Graham, Levi, grocer
GRASSE, S. D., M.D
GRASSETT, C. D., agents Merchants' Bank
Graveline, Joseph, carpenter
Green, Robert, engineer
Griffis, Benjamin, carpenter
Hagerty, William, watchmaker and jeweler
HALL, W. G., collector inland revenue
Hathaward, Simon, carpenter
Hayden, Allan, cooper
Head, Thomas, tailor
Helm, John, mason
HIRONS, W. B., liquors, wholesale, (see adv)
Histem, George, blacksmith
Holmes, James S
Holton, W., broker
Horne, C. R., barrister
Huffer, A. J., carpenter
Hughes, Peter, carpenter
Hurst, Rev. John, (Church of England)
Hutton, Albert, tinsmith
Hutton, John
Hyner, Henry, tailor
Irwin, David, ship-builder
Jask, John, tailor
Jeffers, John, blacksmith

Jenking, George, Capt. steamer *Essex*
Johnson, T. N., saloon keeper
Johnston, David, blacksmith
Jones, John, tailor
Jones, George, butcher
Judd, Francis A., painter
Kellett, R., track supt. G.W.R
Kelly, John
Kennedy, H., brewer, wine and spirit merchant
Kennedy & Jones, brewers
Lambert, R., M.D
Lambie, James, merchant
LAND, M. E., photographer (see adv)
Langsberg, A., vinegar manufacturer
Lark, Christopher, engineer
LAURIE, P. G., publisher and prop. *Record and Journal*
Lonsberry, J., blacksmith
Lucier, Charles, carriage maker
McAllister, John, lumber merchant
McCrae, John, insurance agent
McDermott, Thomas, grocer
McDonough, William, grocer
McGREGOR & BRO., bankers, &c., (see adv)
McGREGOR, W. & D., props. livery stable (see adv)
McKay, Donald, machinist
McLellan, William, shoemaker
McMaster, John, merchant tailor
McMicken, A
McMicken G., stipendiary magistrate
McNish. John, carpenter
Macdonell, S. S., barrister, &c
MACDONALD & BUCHAN. tobacco manufacturers (see adv)
Mahan, S. W. & Co., grocers
Marantette, Cesaire
Marantette, Joseph, revenue officer
Mason, William, tinsmith
Meloche & Reeves, (T. X. & S. T.) saddle and harness manufacturers
Miller, T. M
Mills, James
Moore, G. H., mason
Morland, John, mason
Morton, Thomas, teacher
Morton, William, revenue officer
Moting, James, grocer
Mudd, John, tailor
Mulreany, John, conductor Great Western Railway
Murray, George, druggist
Napier, A., butcher
Neiswinker, William, carpenter
Nestler, Paul, locksmith
NEVEUX, LOUIS, hardware, (see adv)
Noll, Adam, shoemaker
Nutson, Samuel, hotel keeper
O'CONNOR & WHITE, barristers, etc
O'Doherty, Daniel, teacher
Offet, Henry, grocer
Ouillette, Charles
Ovington, George, blacksmith
Page, Simon, barber
Paget, Patrick, carpenter
PARENT, A., grocer, and fish dealer, (see adv)
Parent, Neil, carpenter
Park, Joseph, engineer
Pepin, Basil, carpenter
Perkins, Thomas, revenue officer
Polkenham, William, carpenter
Pomfret, John, carpenter
Prest, T., bookseller, manager Montreal Telegraph Co.
Prince, Albert, barrister
Prince, L. D., shoemaker
PULFORD, H. T. L., lumber merchant, (see adv)
RAE, ROBERT, distiller and rectifier
Ramon, P., teacher
Reaume, Hypolite, mason
RECORD AND JOURNAL, P. G., Laurie, prop.
Reed, John, carpenter
Reed, W. A., coppersmith
RICE, F. T., cabinet maker
Rice, Thomas, cabinet maker
Richards, Mark, sen., baker and confectioner
RICHARDS, MARK, Jun., confectioner (see adv)
Rocheford, Michael, saloon keeper
Rolff, H. H., general dealer
Rolff, William, hardware merchant
Roeders, Justus, grocer
Ronalds, Wiley, cooper
Rorison, B. D., mail agent
Sachelon, Andrew, harness maker
Scott, Robert, butcher
Scott, W. G.
Sheeley, Alanson C.
Shipley, George, merchant tailor
Shorland, Walter, marble works
Skitman, Isaac, dray manufacturer
Smith, John F., dentist
Snider, Peter, carpenter
Spry, H., painter
Sterns, C. W., proprietor livery stable
Stewart, Rev. W. W.
St Louis, Damas, merchant
Storey, William, carpenter
STRONG & NOBLE, bankers
Sutton, C. C., druggist
TAYLOR, ROBERT, grocer
Taylor, William
Thompson, James, gardener
Thorburn, John, merchant
Thorp, John, conductor G. W. R
TREBLE, J. M., merchant (see adv)
TROTTER, F. L., P. L. S.
Trump, Louis, carpenter
Tuft, F., dealer in new and second hand goods
Turk, John, hotel keeper
Turk, John, groceries, liquors, &c.
UNSWORTH, RICHARD, prop. National Hotel
Urquhart, J., cashier G.W.R. freight depot
Vrowman, Henry, carpenter
WAGNER, A. H., Postmaster
Wagner, Rev. James T. (Roman Catholic)
WALKER, HIRAM, prop. flour mill and distillery
Watson, John, revenue officer
Weaver, John, carpenter
Webster, John, boarding house
White, Isaac, baggage master G.W.R.
Whitson, William, mason
Wickert, Frederick, cabinet maker
Williamson William, butcher
Wills, Edward, saddler
Willson, Harris, auctioneer
Windsor Castle, T. Ruinsberry
Winter, Joseph, butcher
Winter, J. & Brothers, butchers
Woodbridge, Thomas, saddler
Wright, R. W., carpenter
Wright, Matthias, cooper
Wylie, John, carpenter
Young, Charles, tinsmith
Young, E. W., ticket clerk G.W.R.
Young, David S., oil refinery

Winfield.—A small Post Village in the Township of Peel, County Wellington, distant from Guelph, 25 miles. Population about 75. YOUNG, JAMES, Postmaster.

Wingham.—A Village on the River Maitland, in the Township of Turnberry, County Huron, 28 miles from Goderich, the County town, and 23 from Clinton station, Grand Trunk Railway. Stages to Clinton, Lucknow and Teeswater. Money Order Office. Population 600.

Abraham, Thomas, boots and shoes
Anderson, J., hotel keeper
Ausley, J., foundry
Bailey, Duncan, cabinet maker
Bamers, J., harness maker
Beare, John, painter
Beare, L. P., J. P.
Berkley, W., tailor
Campbell, Malcolm, general mrechant
Carman, John, cooper
Carr, James, boots and shoes
Carrie, Robert, J.P., farmer
Carruthers, Thomas, blacksmith
Cleworth, Rev. W., (Wesleyan)
Copeland, Joseph, hotel keeper
Fisher, Archibald, lumber merchant
Fisher, John, fancy goods, books and stationery
FISHER, PETER, Postmaster, manufacturer of tweeds and flannels, flouring mill prop
Flack, Joseph, tanner
Foster, E. & C., wagon makers
Graham, James, blacksmith,
Green, George, general merchant
Griffin, C., hotel keeper
Hastie, Rev. James, (Presbyterian)
Heppleweighte, John, cabinet maker
Holland, J., hotel keeper
Jackman, J. G., druggist
Jackson, T. J., general merchant, druggist
Johnston, J. & T., blacksmiths
Kent, Styles & Son, general merchants
Kerr, T., tailor
Kirkley, William, general merchant
Langdale, William, watchmaker
Lloyd, J., cabinet maker and brick yard
McGregor, Duncan, tailor
McKinnon & Bros., general merchants, flour and oatmeal mills, and lumber merchants
Maney, Barnabas, tinsmith
Mundle, John, teacher
Murphy, Rev. William (Church of England)
Nichols, Joseph, carpenter
Risdon, Joseph, boots and shoes
Ronderaus, J., boots and shoes
Scott, C. T., general agent, notary public
Sinclair, Rev. Thomas, (Baptist)
Sloan, Robert, M.D.,
Small, Robert, blacksmith
Srigley, N. M.D.
Tamblyn, J., M.D.
Trott, John, tinsmith
Varney, Oglevie, carpenter
Warren, George, general merchant
Welsh, Thomas, blacksmith

Winona.—A post village and station on the Great Western Railway, in the Township of Saltfleet, County Wentworth, distant 12 miles from Hamilton. Mails daily. Population 50.

Carpenter, George D., farmer
CARPENTER, JOSEPH, Postmaster, general merchant, American Express Agent and saw mill proprietor
Harrington, William, locksmith
Morrison, Samuel W., proprietor Ontario House
Smith, Benjamin, J.P.
Smith, E. B., cheese manufacturer
Thompson, George, station master
Williams John, farmer
Wilson, John, farmer

Winterbourne.—A village on the Grand River, in the Township of Woolwich, County Waterloo, 9 miles from Berlin, the County Town. Population 200.

Aris, James, carpenter
Bemis, B. B., hotel
Chalmers, David, J.P.
Chambers, T. W., proprietor flour mill
Dow, J., J.P.
Fromm, J., general merchant
Goukel, C., auctioneer
K.LBURNE, P. S., Postmaster, boots and shoes
Marr, John, carriage maker
Smith, Joseph, carpenter
Stork, George, grocer

Winthrop.—A Village in the Township of McKillop, County Huron.

MURCHIE, ALEXANDER, Postmaster.

Woburn.—A Village in the Township of Scarboro', County York, 12 miles from Toronto. Stages to Toronto, Markham and Stouffville.

Bain, Rev. James (Presbyterian)
Bowden, Joseph, wagon maker
Brooks, Miss Sarah J., dressmaker
Campbell, Henry, teacher
Carnaghan, James, farmer
Chapman, Charles, crockery, china and glassware
Closson, L. D., M.D.
Green, James, farmer
Holloway, John, boots and shoes
Johnston, David, farmer
Johnston, William, hotel keeper
Lapsley, William, M.D.
Lauder, John, tailor
McIlmurray, Captain William
McIlmurray, Henry, seedsman
Mabley, Charles, boots and shoes
Morgan, James
Purves, James, farmer
Scott, Francis, farmer
Secor, Alexander M., J.P.
Secor, George, farmer.
TELFER, ALEX. H., Postmaster and gen. merchant
Wheeler, John P., J.P.
Wood, T., tailor

Wisbeach.—A Post Office in the Township of Warwick, County Lambton.
BOWES, JOANNA, Postmistress.

Wolfe Island.—A Village and Island in the Township of the same name, opposite Kingston, distance 3 miles. Population 300.

Baker, Catherine, general merchant
Baker, Daniel, farmer
Baker, Edward, general merchant
Baker, John, farmer
Bingham, James, M.D.
Briceland, Thomas, farmer
Cattenach, Donald, wagon maker
Coxall, Mrs. general merchant
Coxall, William, general merchant
Coyle, James, farmer
Craine, John, painter
Cuff, James, farmer
Dawson, John, jun., hotel keeper
Dawson, Patrick, farmer
Dawson, Thomas, J.P.
Davis, Albert, hotel keeper
Davis, Joseph L., carpenter
Doyle, John, carpenter
Eaves, John, painter
Eccles, James, J. P
Going, A. H., steam grist mill
Graham, Rev. J. M. (Roman Catholic)
Hawkins, John James, general merchant
Hitchcock, Hiram O., hotel keeper
Holliday, John, J. P
Horne, James, J. P
Horne, John, J. P
Howard, Rev. E. S. (Episcopal Methodist)
Irwin, C., M. D
Irvine, John
King, Patrick, carpenter
Kirkpatrick, Rev. F. M. (Church of England)
Kyle, Joseph, stock dealer
Lawlor, Thomas, teacher
McDonald, James, farmer
McDonell, Duncan R
McKay, James, J.P., farmer
MALONE, GEORGE, J. P., Postmaster
O'Brien, John, teacher
O'Shea, Jeremiah, teacher
Owens, Charles, carpentet
Porteous, Rev. George, Presbyterian
Sandison, H. L., tailor
Spoor, M., J. P
Sweetman, Michael, carpenter
Troy, John, hotel keeper
Watts, Samuel, farmer

Wolverton.—A Post Village situated on Smith's Creek, in the Township of Blenheim, County Oxford. Mails daily. Population about 250.

Bawtinlumer, Absolom, wagon and carriage manuf.
Bawtinlnmer, B. W., general blacksmith
Brown, John H., proprietor flax mill
Cochran, William H., saddle and harness maker
Currey, D. W. & S., proprietors saw mill
Currey, G. N., proprietor grist mill
Dawson, George, builder
Dawson, George, jun., farmer
Dawson, Robert, carpenter
Dawson, Silas, teamster
Dawson, Thomas, farmer
Dawson, William, farmer
Frostick, Henry, farmer
Frostick, Johathan, boot and shoemaker
Hunt, J. H., butcher
LAVERY, JAMES, Postmaster, and gen. merchant
Lovett, John, proprietor lath mill
Meggs, John, Megg's Hotel, and prop. water power saw mill
Warner, Francis, prop. steam stave and shingle fac.
Wolverton, Alonzo, general merchant

Woodbridge.—A Village on the River Humber, in the Township of Vaughan, County York, 17 miles from Toronto, and 8¼ from Weston. Money Order Office. Population 708.

ABELL, JOHN, foundry and agricultural works
Bell, John, hotel keeper
Brown, John, mill owner and lumber merchant
Brown, Neil & Co., foundry and machine shop
Bunt, F. J.
Bunt, Francis, farmer
Bunt, John, sash, door and blind manufacturer
Burkholder, Christopher, farmer
Cartwright, Rev. C. E., (Church of England)
Crawford, John, tailor
Devlin, John, M. D.
Elliott, J., farmer
Elliott, John, blacksmith
English, Rev. Noble F., (Wesleyan Methodist)
Frank, Miss, dressmaker
Gamble, John W., J. P.
Hay, Rev., Robert, (Congregational)
Herbert, A., painter
Holdermess, J., hotel keeper
HOWELL, JOHN F., Postmaster
Husband, George, dentist
Jeffrey, John, farmer
Jeffrey, William, farmer
McCallum, Duncan, clerk Division Court
Mackintosh, Roe J., woolen manufacturer
Martin, Miss, dressmaker
Mason, William, brick yard
Matthews, Robert, carpenter
Orr, Miss, dressmaker
Playter, Thomas, farmer
Roam, Joseph, boots and shoes
Roe, J. & Brother, general merchants
Rose, James, boots and shoes
Roundtree, J., butcher
Saunders, J., general merchant
Shaw, Charles, tinsmith
Smith Samuel, mill owner and lumber merchant
Summers, William, machinist
Wallace, Clark, teacher
Wallace, George, cooper
Wallace, George, farmer
Wallace J. & Brothers, general merchants
Wallace, W., hotel keeper
Wesley, William, tinsmith
Williams, John
Wright, Norman, boots and shoes

Woodburn.—A Village in the Township of Binbrook, County Wentworth, 15 miles from Hamilton, and 60 from Toronto. Land in the vicinity averages $30 per acre. Population 80.

Atter, Samuel, teacher
Benner, Amelia, milliner
Benner, William, wagon maker
Bill, William, teacher
Cooper, James, boiler maker
Edmonds, John, proprietor steam flouring mills
Gibson, Rev. J. D. (Church of England)
Henry, Horace, farmer
Jarvis, Archibald, farmer
Kerr, Jacob, farmer
King, George W., farmer
McGillicuddy, Jordan, general merchant
McKay, Walter, M. D.
Magill, Henry, farmer
Miller, John, shingle maker
Milsop, Robert, tailor
Ptolmey, James, farmer
PTOLEMY, WILLIAM, Postmaster, boots & shoes
Shaw, Robert, farmer
Shaw, Thomas, teacher
Sidney, John, J. P., farmer

Woodford.—A Post Office in the Township of Sydenham, County Grey, 10 miles from Owen Sound, the County Town, and 110 from Toronto. Stage to Owen Sound, fare 50c., to Meaford, fare 50c. Population 20.

Caven, James, farmer
Curry, John prop North American Hotel
Knight, Harris, farmer
McDonald, D., teacher
McLaren, Archibald, farmer
Rogers, J. M., farmer
THOMSON, JOHN, Postmaster

Woodham.—A Village in the Township of Blanshard, County Perth, 22 miles from Stratford, the County Town. Money Order Office. Population 120.

Ash, Michael, wagon maker and blacksmith
Beatton, Daniel, farmer
Beaty, Joseph, farmer
Cammel, John, insurance agent
Daymon, Miss Barbara, teacher
Dodds, William, farmer
Elwin, William, steam flouring and grist mill
Ford, Samuel, constable
Hanes, Stephen
Hicks, John, hotel keeper and carpenter
Kirk, David, farmer
Leaker, James, farmer
Mills, William, carpenter
Morley, Joseph, carpenter
Rodly, Samuel, proprietor grist mill
Sawyer, Aaron
SHIER, JONATHAN, Postmaster and gen. mercht.
Smith, Rev. Mr. (N. C. Methodist)
Stephens, Joseph, carpenter
St. John, William, farmer
Walker, David, J.P.
Wetterington, Robert, farmer
Wickson, Hugh, carpenter

Woodlands.—A Post Office in the Township of Osnabruck, County Stormont.
STEWART, R. H., Postmaster.

Woodstock.—The County Town of Oxford, is situated in the Township of Blandford, and on the line of the Great Western Railway. Distant from Hamilton 48 miles, from Paris 19, from London 29, and from Toronto 88. The Canadian Literary Institute is located here and under the control of the Regular Baptist denomination, average attendance of students 100. The Royal Canadian and Gore Bank have each a branch here. It is a port of entry. Money Order Office and Savings Bank. Population 5,000.

Alexander, Hon. George
AMERICAN MERCHANTS' UNION EXPRESS CO., J. McKay, agent
Anderson, John, tailor
Atlantic Mutual Life Ins. Co., Albany, N.Y., John H. Bryant agent
Ayres, William, blacksmith
BAIN, JOHN, cabinet maker, furniture dealer and undertaker (see adv)
Bain & McKenzie, carpenters
BALL, F. R., J.P., (Ball & Matheson) County Attorney, Clerk of Peace
Ball & Matheson, (F. R. Ball and J. Matheson) barristers, &c
Barnard, Mrs. Harriett, prop. Fireman's Inn
Bates, Rev. John, (Baptist)
Beard, Charles L., insurance and patent agent and secretary Oxford Per. Blg and Savings Society
Beard, Dr , physician and surgeon
Beard, John, general insurance agent
BEARD & NELLIS, (Henry B. Beard & Joseph H. Nellis) barristers, &c
Bee Hive Steam Factory, wooden ware, wash boards, clothes pins, croquet sets, &c
Bettridge, Rev. William, (Church of England)
Bickerton, William, saddle and harness makers
Bickle, John, butcher
Bickle, Joseph, butcher
Bickle, Robert, butcher
Bird, Robert, groceries, wines and liquors
Bishop, William, prop. Bishop's Hotel
Blomeley, Mrs. Elizabeth, toys and varieties

BOWDITCH, GEORGE, hardware, tin, iron and copper
BRAIDWOOD, JOHN, dealer in staple and fancy dry goods, &c
BRYANT, JOHN H., surgeon dentist, Bryant's Block and agent Atlantic Mutual Insurance Company
Broman, S. J., grocer
Brooks, William, butcher
Brotchie, John, tailor
BROWN, B. P., M. D
Brown, John H., proprietor flax mill
Burgess, Samuel, auctioneer
BURNS, J. M., agent Royal Canadian Bank, and general insurance agent
Burtch, Henry T., farmer
Caister House, C. Caister, proprietor
Cameron, John, jailor
CANADIAN LITERARY INSTITUTE, (Reg. Baptists), R. A. Fyfe, principal
Carryer, Charles G., saddles, harness and trunks
Chalmers, John, (Scott & Chalmers)
Chambers, Mrs. Mary, milliner and dressmaker
Church of England Depository for Christian Knowledge Society and Religious Tract Society, Edward Lakeman, depositary
CLARK & DAVIDSON, (Thomas Clark and John Davidson), flour millers
Clark, Thomas J., proprietor Orman flour mills, also oil refiner and steam barrel factor
Clarkson, John, station master and freight agent Great Western Railway
Close, Joseph, proprietor brick yard
Clyde & Crawford, (David Clyde and James Crawford) carriage and wagon makers
Coad, James, manager Scott & Co., apothecaries hall
COADVILLE & CO., gunsmiths
Coghill, Donald, boots and shoes
Coghill, John, insurance agent
Collens, Stephen, proprietor Woodstock Brewery
Cottle, Thomas J., flax miller and oil cake manf.
Couzens, Miss E., teacher
Cox, James, dry goods, clothing, etc
Crane, John, surgical instrument manufacturer
Crane, John E., gunsmith
Crawford, John M
CROOKS & WHITE, (C. J. Crooks & David White) general hardware merchants
Cummings, R. H.
Davis, A. R., painter, etc.
Dawes, A., baker and confectioner
DEASE & CHAMBERS, general merchants
De BLAQUIERE, CHARLES, Postmaster
DENT, ROBERT R., proprietor Montgomery House
DINGWALL, R. A., watches, clocks and jewelry
Donaldson, William, butcher and general dealer
Dorman, D. H., manufacturer of woolen goods
Doston, Thomas, barber and hairdresser
Douglas, John, saddler
Douglas, Robert, saddle and harness maker
Eddie, Joseph, weaver
Ede, Joseph, grocer
Eden, Thomas, boots and shoes
Edwards, William, painter
Fauquier & Co., insurance and commission merchants
Fauquier, Philip, teller Gore Bank
Ferguson, Edward, barber
Field, C., M.D.
Finkle, Henry J., solicitor
Fletcher, Ashton, barrister, etc.
Fletcher, Richard, baker
Forrest, John, oatmeal miller
Forrest, John & Co., grocer
Francis, George, baggage master G.W.R.
Frazer, George J., teacher
Frazel, Samuel
Fuller, T.
Fury, M., grocer
FYFE, R. A., Principal Canadian Literary Institute
Gammond, Henry, saloon and oysters
Gardner & Rose, (William Gardner and Hugh Rose) carriage and wagon makers, general blacksmiths and mill pick makers
Glendinning, John, butcher
GORDON, ADAM, wholesale and retail groceries, wines and liquors, also agent Daw's ale and porter
Gordon, John, accountant
GORE BANK, William Smith, manager
Gough, Mrs. Marian, millinery and fancy goods
Grafenhorst, L., boot and shoemaker
Grant, Thomas, boots and shoes
Gray, George A., barrister
Greig & Bird (John Greig and Robert Bird) barristers
Green William, teamster
GREY, WILLIAM, issuer of marriage licenses, land agent, etc.
Gunn, James, groceries, wines and liquors
Guppy, E. T., boot and shoemaker
Gurnett, George C., bootmaker
Guthrie, Miss G., teacher
Hack, Henry
Hack, Mrs. (wid. David) Prince of Wales Restaurant
Hall, Henry, boots and shoes
Hall, John, telegraph operator
Hargrave, William, Deputy Postmaster
Harknett, Albert, prop. International Hotel
Harrison, John, market clerk
HARWOOD, GEORGE, baker and confectioner, oysters, fruits, etc.
Hay, James, cabinet maker
Hay, John, boots and shoes
Hayward, Arthur, prop. Victoria House
Heatley, James, grocer
Heath, J., wagon maker
Henry, Thomas, carpenter
Hill, J. M., insurance agent
Holling, J. W., cigars and tobacco
Home Fire Insurance Co., New Haven (Conn.) J. M. Burns, agent
Hopkins, Thomas, proprietor Elgin House
Howland, Francis L., M.D.
House, William, gun and locksmith
Huggard, John, provision merchant
Humphrey, Mrs., milliner
INGERSOLL, JAMES, County Registrar
Izard, Henry, teacher
Jackson, E. T., saddles, harness and collars
Jackson, John, farmer
Jeffrey & Brother (Francis & John), general hardware importers
Johnston, Robert, baker
Joy, Sylvanus, M.D.
Kelley, Cornelius, telegraph operator G.W.R. station
Kintrea, James, County Treasurer
Kirton, George, photographer
Kogelschutz, E. A., cigars and tobacco
Kollmyer, S., cabinet maker
Lakeman, Edward, depositary (Church of England)
Life Association of Scotland, J. M. Brown, agent
LODGE, JOHN O., wholesale and retail dealer in boots, shoes, trunks, &c.
London Assurance Corporation, London, England, J. M. Burns, agent
Love, John, cabinet maker
Love, Thomas, cabinet maker
McAllan, William, boots and shoes
McCallum, Malcolm, merchant tailor
McCAUSLAND, W. J., booksellers and stationers, also dealer in melodeons and sewing machines

McCLENEGHAN, ALEXANDER, editor and proprietor *Times*
McCloud, William C., dry goods, hardware and groceries
McDermid, Rev. D. (Presbyterian)
McDonald, John
McIntyre, John, groceries, crockery, wines & liquors
McKay, Alexander M., groceries, wines and liquors
McKay, George, tailor
McKay, Hugh, M.D.
McKay, John, boot and shoe maker
McKAY, JOHN, agent American & Merchants' Union Express Company, also oysters wholesale and retail, and in kegs, broker and exchange office
McKay, William, saddle and harness maker
McKay, J. & Co., groceries, wines and liquors
McKENZIE D., groceries, wines and liquors, wholesale and retail
McKenzie, Hugh, groceries, wines and liquors
McKINNON, MALCOLM, dry goods and millinery
McLeod, W. C., general merchant
McMullen, Rev. William T. (Presbyterian)
McWHINNIE, JOHN, J.P., Col. Inland Revenue
McWHINNIE, ROBERT, editor and proprietor *Woodstock Sentinel*
McWhirter, J. & Co., commission merchant and insurance agent
Mackay, A., blacksmith
Madary, Richard, dyer and scourer
Martin & Co., groceries and crockery
MARTIN, JOHN, baker and confectioner, soda water and ice creams
McKay, R., merchant tailor
Martin, Mrs., teacher of music
Mason, Richard, butcher
Matheson, Gilbert, prop. North American Hotel
Matheson, John, marble cutter
Matthew, Henry, prop. Jolly Farmers' Inn
MAYCOCK, JOSEPH, painter, paper hanger, dealer in fancy goods and wall paper
Midgley, John, boots and shoes
Miller & Finkle (D. G. Miller & Alexander Finkle), barristers
Miller, James & Robert, grain merchants
MILLER, JOHN H., organ and melodeon manuf. (see adv.)
Montgomery, George, boots and shoes
Montgomery, George, machinist
Montgomery, Mrs. George, milliner
Montgomery House, R. R. Dent, proprietor
MONTREAL TELEGRAPH CO., William Nicholson agent
Morris, Richard, tailor
Nasmyth, George, merchant tailor
Nasmyth, William, groceries and provisions
Nellis, Joseph H. (Beard & Nellis)
Newton, Andrew, merchant tailor
New York Store, D. McKenzie, groceries, wines and liquors
NICHOLSON, JAMES, photographer
Nicholson, William, telegraph operator
Nott, James, lime and stone
O'NEIL, JAMES, proprietor, Market Hotel
O'Rourke, James, sheepskin buyer
Oliver & Schell, general merchants
Oliver, Thomas, M.P., wool merchant
Oswald, George, boiler maker
Oswald & Paterson, (George and John Oswald & John Paterson) stove founders
OXFORD PERMANENT BUILDING & SAVINGS SOCIETY, William Grey, President; Charles L. Beard, Secretary
Palmer, Joseph, proprietor American Hotel
Parker, Henry, grain buyer
Parker & Hayes, (Henry Parker & Henry Hayes) flour millers
PARKER & HOOD, importers and dealers in dry goods, clothing, &c.
Parker, John, lumber yard
Parr, George, groceries, provisions, crockery, &c.
Pascoe, George, butcher and general dealer, Market House
Pascoe, John, butcher
Pattison, Rev. R., (Primitive Methodist)
Paterson, John, (Oswalds & Paterson)
Paulin, J. & Co., (J. and W. Paulin & Hiram Prior) proprietors Vulcan Foundry, stoves and agricultural implement manufacturers
Peacock, Daniel, carpenter
Peddie, J. W. & Co., general merchants
Peers, Joseph, farmer
Peirson, Robert, groceries, provisions, etc.
Pettit, William, confectioner
Pierson, William, baker
Pocock, Stephen, blind factory
Pope, Charles, farmer
POST OFFICE, CHARLES DE BLAQUIERE, Postmaster, William Hargrave, Deputy Postmaster
Pott, William, watchmaker, jeweler, & groceries and provisions
Powell, George, blacksmith
Preston, Rev. James, (Wesleyan Methodist)
Price, Mrs Elizabeth, furrier and glove maker
Prior, Hiram (J. Paulin & Co.)
Puckridge, J. & R. W., groceries and provisions, crockery, etc.
Quinn, Daniel, tailor
Rae, Miss, milliner
REID, WM. A., groceries, wines & liquors, (see adv.)
Revell, Robert, (Stark & Revell)
Ravell & Teeple, (Richard M. Ravell and Alanson Teeple,) dentists
Richards, D., groceries and provisions
Richardson, Hugh, barrister
Richmond, D. C., hats, caps, furs, boots and shoes
Rippon, Joseph, dry goods
Robinson, John, flour and feed
Robinson, Joseph, groceries and provisions
Rose, Angus, groceries
Ross, D. & J., (David & James) groceries, provisions, wines and liquors
Ross, Andrew, sheriff
Ross, Hugh, carriage maker
ROSS, HUGH & CO., cabinet makers and manufacturers of all kinds of wooden ware
Ross, Robert, wine and spirit dealer
ROYAL CANADIAN BANK, J. M. Burns, agent
Scarf, William, wagon maker
SCHELL & CLARKE, (Robert S. Schell and Walden Clarke) dry goods, millinery, &c.
Schofield, F. B., planing, sash, doors and blinds
Scott, S. A. & Co., apothecaries hall
SCOTT & SWAN, (Wm. Scott & L. H. Swan,) physicians and surgeons (see adv.)
Scott & White, (Thomas Scott & James White) chemists and druggists
SHAW, A. G., hoop skirt manufacturer
Shelder, Smith, prop Railroad saloon
Short & Chalmers, grain buyers
Silcox, John, soap and candle maker
Smith, George, Prov. Railway hotel
Smith, John, butcher
SMITH, WILLIAM, manager Gore Bank
Snelgrove, William, nurseryman
Snowden, Robert, bookbinder
Stark & Revell, (Robert Stark & Robert Revell,) chemists and druggists
Stearns & Bro., (John E. & F. A.) livery stable props

Stranchon, George, teacher
Sutherland, Alexander, livery stable proprietoor
Sutherland, John S., boots and shoes
Sutherland, Miss Catherine, dress maker and ready-made under clothing
Taylor, William H., seedsman
Teeple, W. B., groceries, provisions, liquors, etc
Thacker, Robert, proprietor Thacker's Hotel
THE TIMES, Alex. McCleneghan, editor and prop.
Thompson, S., inn keeper
Totten, W., barrister
Townsend, Richard, groceries and provisions
Turquand, John, M.D.
Union Mutual Life Insurance Company, Maine, W. J. McCausland, agent
Walker, G. & Co., boots and shoes
Walley, G. W., china, glass and queen's ware
Warwick, William, bookseller, stationer, bookbinder
Weeks & Denyer, blacksmiths, & veterinary surgeons
WEEKS, GEORGE, groceries and provisions, china, glass and queen's ware
Weeks, John, cabinet maker
Whally, W. S., boots and shoes
White, A., proprietor planing mill
WHITE, D., importer, silk mercer, house furnishings
White, David, clerk county council
White, David, Sen., architect
White, John & Co., dry goods, millinery, clothing, etc
White & Robinson, veterinary surgeons
White, William B., veterinary surgeon
WILLIS, ALFRED E., professor of penmanship, (Willis & Bryant), Bryant's block
WILLIS & BRYANT, (A. E. Willis, and J. H. Bryant), photographers
WILSON, WILLIAM, tanner and currier, general dealer in leather, hides, skins, findings, etc
Wilson, William, boots and shoes
Woodroofe, Robert, watchmaker and jeweler
WOODSTOCK HOTEL, D. Matthews, proprietor
Woodstock Mechanics Subscription Library, Thomas Henry, secretary and treasurer, Miss Blomeley, librarian
WOODSTOCK SENTINEL, R. McWhinnie, prop
Wright, Samuel, chemist and druggist

Woodslee.—A Village on Bell River, in the Township of Maidstone, County Essex, 20 miles from Sandwich, the County Town. Population 60.

Bailey, David, carpenter
Chambers, John, farmer
Coller, Michael
Conway, J. & H., lumber merchants
Conway, Miss Ellen, teacher
Donovan, M. & P., farmers
Hogan, J. A., general merchant, hotel keeper and livery stable proprietor
Lambert, John, farmer
Lespiuinee, George, butcher
LINDSAY, W. S., Postmaster and accountant
Little, Robert, general merchant
McAuliffe, Michael, teacher
McCluskey, John, wagon maker
McMahon, John, farmer
Roe, William, auctioneer
Taylor, A., farmer
Wilcox, Samuel, farmer

Woodville.—A Village in the Township of Mariposa, County Victoria, 17 miles from Lindsay, the County Town. Money Order office. Population 250.

Adam, Robert, farmer
Armstrong, J., lumber merchant
Bradway, William, cooper
Brynd, Thomas, wagon maker
Cameron, Donald
Cameron, James, brick yard
Cameron, William, J.P.
Campbell, Archibald, blacksmith and wagon maker
Campbell, G., blacksmith
Clark, J. F., J.P.
Clark, P. H., M.D.
Crouter, Peter, tinsmith
Forman, T. C., general merchant
GILCHRIST, JOHN C., Postmaster, gen. merchant
Grant, Andrew, farmer
Grant, Donald, farmer
Hungerford, R., bailiff and auctioneer
Irish, E. R., J.P., farmer
Jamieson, J., general merchant
Johnson, B., farmer
Lumsden, H. D., P.L.S., real estate agent
McAllister, —, M.D.
McCutcheon, W. A., teacher
McDonald, John, insurance agent
McDougall, Alexander, boots and shoes
McDougall, Rev. N. (Presbyterian)
McDuffie, J., farmer
McKenzie, Sidney, J.P.
McLeod, Angus, druggist
McSweyn, Peter, tailor
McTavish, Rev. J. (Canada Presbyterian)
Maybee, George A., prop. Northern Hotel
Millar, G. W., Clerk Division Court, general agent
Morison, John, farmer
Morison, Malcolm, general merchant
Morison, Thomas, lime and stone dealer
Parker & Campbell, livery stables
Parker, M. S., proprietor Eldon House
Smith, Donald, farmer
Stuart, James, harness maker
Sutherland, William, blacksmith
Whyte, James

Wooler.—A Village in the Township of Murray, County Northumberland, 36 miles from Cobourg, the County Town. Population 120.

Alley, T., general merchant
Alley, William, carpenter
Anderson, William, blacksmith
Burns, Peter, boots and shoes
Cobb, Rev. T. (Wesleyan Methodist)
Ellis, James, blacksmith
Fieldhouse, M. H., teacher
Gould, L. F., wagon maker
Hollinger, John, tanner
McColl, John A., carpenter
Norris, Rev. (Episcopal Methodist)
Rockwell, A., M.D.
Sanderson, Joseph, dentist
Scott, Ruben, merchant
Sharp, J. H., tanner
Smith, R., carpenter
Smith, Thomas, hotel keeper
Sparrow, Rev. M., (Methodist Episcopal)
WESSLES, ALBERT, Postmaster

Wroxeter.—A thriving Village on the River Maitland, in the Township of Howick, County Huron, 46 miles from Goderich, the County Town, 25 from Seaforth Station, Grand Trunk Railway, and 22 from Walkerton. The River affords excellent water power and there are several flourishing manufacturing establishments in and adjacent to the Village. Stages to Seaforth, Walkerton and Lisadel. Money Order Office and Savings Bank. Population 400.

Allen, Nathaniel, cabinet maker
Allen & Hodgson, sash, blind and door manufs
Applebee, Charles, carpenter
Barker, William, leather dealer, boots and shoes
Beauchamp, P. J., druggist, books and stationery
Brown, Rev. George, (Presbyterian)
Brown, James, carpenter
CARROLL, CYRUS, Postmaster, druggist, notary public, real estate, and insurance agent
Chambers, George, hotel keeper
Chambers, William
Dalton, Thomas, jewelry
Day, Mrs., hotel keeper
Dickson, Robert, tailor
Doubledee, James, grocer
Edwards, William H., carpenter
Ferguson, John, general merchant
Forsyth, Robert, dealer in woolen goods
Gibson, George, carpenter
Gibson, Thomas & Robert, props. grist mill and lumber merchants
Gibson & Miller, props. flax mills
Gofton, John, prop. livery stable
Gordon. Miss, milliner
Graham, Robert A., teacher
Griffith, Hamilron, farmer
Hardy, William, farmer
Hasson, William, confectioner
Hay, William D., carpenter
Henderson, David W., wagon maker
Henning, John, carpenter
Hinde, William, butcher
Hodgson, Allen, planing mills
Hodgson, Ralph, cabinet maker
Hood & Conboy, general merchants
Hossack, Samuel, lime and stone dealer
Ingles, G. & J., general merchants
Johnson, William, hotel
Kennedy, J. E., baker
Knutson, John, tailor
Lawrie, William, accountant
Leeper, R. D., general merchant
McDonald, Thomas, butcher
McLaughlin, John, hotel
McNally, William, boot and shoe maker
Martin, G. G., attorney
Miller, John, wood and willow ware
Miller, Robert, carpenter
Milne, Alexander, carpenter
Moffatt, John, commission and forwarding merchant
Morphy, James, stock dealer
Morrow, Adam, farmer
Mosgrove, Thomas, farmer
Outram, David J., boot maker
Parkhurst, James H.
Reuder, Frederick, general merchant
Phippen, Alonzo, cooper
Phippen, George, cooper
Playford, Thomas, auctioneer
Rea, David, farmer
Reuder, William, J.P.
Robinson, A. H. & R., booksellers and stationers
Roy, William A. Y., tailor
Saunders, Thomas B., saddler
Sanderson, Henry, farmer
Sanderson, John, general merchant
Small, Samuel B., M.B.
Smith, Charles A., cooper
Snyder, Rev. Solomon (Congregational)
Terry, William H., tinsmith
Thompson, Joseph, saddler
Vogt, John B., gunsmith
Wark, John, carpenter
Willitts, Charles, wood and willow ware
Worthington, Addison, M.D.
Yeomans, J. Y., painter
Young, James, grocer
Young, William, hotel keeper
Zimmerman, John, hotel keeper

Wyandott.—A small Village in the Township of Maryborough, County Wellington, 38 miles from Guelph.

AYERST, WILLIAM, Postmaster
Bowman, Daniel G., farmer
Hay, Robert, farmer
Johnson, John D., farmer
Langford, Charles, teacher
Leslie, William, farmer
Marks, Thomas, farmer
Phillips, Owen, farmer
Porteous, David, farmer
Turner, Elisha, farmer

Wyebridge.—A Village on the river Wye, in the Township of Tiny, County Simcoe, 27 miles from Barrie the County Town. Stage to Barrie and Penetanguishene. Population, 140.

Blackmore, Ferguson, carpenter
Blay, Angus, potash manufacturer
Casselman, Hiram, farmer and lumber merchant
Casselman, Zacheriah, hotel keeper
Fitzprtrick. Hugh, shoemaker
Flood, Rev. Mr., (Church of England)
Frith, John, wagon maker
Ganton, S., blacksmith
Gognen, — cooper and pearl ashery
Grant. Angus
Hemonerey, John, carpenter
McGregor, D., general merchant
McRae, Nelson, general merchant
Moses, Max, general merchant
PLEWES, JAMES, J. P., Postmaster, mill owner and lumber merchant
Plewes, James S., miller
Rodgers, Lochart, millwright
Sodin, William, shoemaker
Stewart, James, teacher
Tripp, H., blacksmith and hotel keeper
Varty, William, pearl ashery

Wyoming.—A Village in the Township of Plympton, County Lambton, 15 miles from Sarnia, the County Town. It is one of the principal points of the Western Oil Regions. Money Order Office and Savings Bank. Population, 400.

Anderson, D. D., general merchant
ANDERSON' JOHN, Postmaster
Axford, J., shoemaker
Bell, Andrew, blacksmith
Bentley, J. S., shoemaker
Borrowman, D., wagon maker
Brookman, Rev. W., (Church of England)
Casey, S., groceries and liquors
COURSE, J. H., grocer and provision dealer
Dale, J. B., druggist
Dick, Samuel, tailor
DURAND, R. M., hotel keeper
Finlayson, John, shoemaker
Frasier, William, iron works
Gordon, William, shoemaker
Hagar & Cronin, oil refiners
Jolley, Rev. Mr., (Primitive Methodist)
Jones, Rev. T. S., (Wesleyan)
Laing, Alexander, general merchant
McColl, P., oil refiner
McGarvey, E., general merchant
Miller, D., tailor
Mott, G. B., M.D.
Richardson, Rev. G. T., (Wesleyan)
SAUNDERS, ISAIAH, hotel keeper
Taylor, G., oil refiner
Ward, F., oil refiner
Westland, A., general merchant

Yarker.—A Village on the Napanee river, in the Township of Camden, County Addington, 13 miles from Napanee, the County town, and 18 from Kingston. Population 200.

Ansley, H. H., farmer
Babcock, Peter, farmer
Benjamin, E. W., foundry
Booth, A. P., woolen manufacturer
Brown, Miss M. J., milliner
Cambridge, Hugh, tailor
Carroll, John, farmer
Connelly, Joseph, foundry
Estace, J. B., hotel keeper
Gill, Norris, blacksmith
Graham, Robert, shoemaker
Guss, S. S
Irish, A. D., teacher
Irish, Peter, farmer
McVean, A., flouring and grist mill prop
Martin, James, farmer
O'Lauglin, Michael, auctioneer
Scott, A. C., grocer
SHIBLEY, JOHN A., J.P., Postmaster, gen mercht
Shibley, John A., lumber merchant
Waitman, Peter, foreman planing mills
Woodhouse, Edward, wagon maker
Vanluven, A., saddler
Vanvalkenburg, John, carpenter
Veneat, Hiram, carpenter
Veneat, Peter, carpenter

Yarmouth Centre.—A Village in the Township of Yarmouth, County Elgin, 5 miles from St. Thomas, the County Town. Population 150.

Evely, W., veterinary surgeon
Hawley, T., farmer
Heyden, William, farmer
Hughes, M., farmer
Landers, William, carpenter
Leonard, L. S., J.P
McCordie, Isaac, carpenter
McCordie, R., farmer
McCordie, W., farmer
Mann, William, lumber dealer
Marlatt, Jehiel, farmer
Newcombe, A. C., dentist
Newcombe, A., farmer
Newcombe, George, leather dealer
Newcombe, D. W., farmer
NEWCOMBE, WILLIAM, Postmaster, gen. mer.
Parlee, G. A., hotel keeper
Philips, E. C., shoemaker

York Mills.—A Village in the Township of York, County York, 6 miles from Toronto. The west branch of the river Humber passes through the Village, affording excellent manufacturing facilities. Stages to Richmond Hill, Thornhill and Toronto. Population 100.

Armour, James, farmer
Armour, John, farmer
Armour, Walter, farmer
Beckett, A. R., farmer
Breen, Thomas, farmer
Cooper, John, wagon maker
Coppin, N. W., proprietor flour mills
Craig, John, cooper
Craig, William, cooper
Curry, Robert, carpenter
Curry, W., blacksmith
Eden, Charles, blacksmith
Godwin, William, farmer
Hodge, Rev. T. P. (Church of England)
HOGG, JOHN, J.P., Postmaster, general merchant
Hogg, J. & W., proprietors flour and planing mills
Lackie, David, farmer
Leach, Mrs. T., general merchant
Little, J. T., farmer
Monteith, Rev. R. (Canada Presbyterian)
Peebles, Captain A. J. L.
Pennock, Joseph, carpenter
Rightly, Joseph, farmer
Shuttleworth, George, farmer
Stewart, Michael, proprietor York Mills Hotel
Turner, Solomon, farmer
Van Ostram, John C., farmer

York.—A Village on the Grand River, in the Township of Seneca, County Haldimand, 6 miles from Cayuga, the County Town, and 5 from Caledonia Station, Buffalo and Lake Huron Railroad. The River affords excellent water power. Gypsum is found in great abundance in the vicinity. Money Order Office. Population 300.

Brooks, Charles
Campbell, Joseph, tailor
Clark, William, wagon maker
Cormick, J., general merchant
Cuttliff, W., hotel keeper
Davis, A. A., general and insurance agent
Davis, R. H., M.D.
Davis, R. M., J.P.
Duffin, S., farmer
Farmer, John, wagon maker
FINDLEY, HENRY H., saddle and harness maker
Harcourt, M., J.P.
Headley, John, gunsmith
HUDSON, CHARLES L., Postmaster and gen. mer.
Hursell, William, accountant
Kennedy, D., hotel keeper
Kennedy, D., tailor
Kyffin, James, general merchant
Lamond, Alexander, farmer
Lamond, James, carpenter
Lutes, R., blacksmith
Lutes, Walter, M.D.
Lynch, Joseph, wagon maker
McDonald, John, comn mer. flouring and grist mill
Martin, F. O., farmer
Martin, R., sheriff County Haldimand
MARTINDALE, BROTHERS (Thomas and Ralph), manufacturers and dealers in plaster of Paris, coal, &c.
Mellon, Thomas & Son, blacksmiths
Nelles, James, J.P.
Nelles, J. A., general merchant, druggist, &c.
Nelles, J., farmer
Shand, J., farmer
Slacker, Henry, carpenter
Stevins, W., carpenter
Strachan, Thomas, general merchant
Sweet, F., lumber merchant
Trotter, James, hotel keeper
Tuck, John, painter
Wedge, J., shingle maker
Wicketts George, carpenter
Wickett, N. H., butcher
Wiers, Richard, farmer
Williamson, A., shoemaker
Wilson, William, cabinet factory
Young John, carpenter
YOUNG, WILLIAM, proprietor Mansion House

York River.—A small Village on York River, in the Township of Faraday, County Hastings, 80 miles from Belleville, the County Town. Population 50.

Browers, Isaac, carpenter
CLARK, J., Postmaster, general merchant, lumber dealer and proprietor brick yard
Gabel, Godfield, farmer
Gabel, Henry, farmer
George, J. C.
Harding, Philip, carpenter
Moore, Josias, farmer
Powers, John, farmer
Seddons, James, carpenter
Serums, John, farmer
Shears, Isaac, cooper
Spurr, Benjamin, farmer
Sweet, H. & W., shingle makers

Yorkville.—An incorporated Village adjoining the northern limits of the City of Toronto 2½ miles from the City Hall. The Village is connected with the City by a Street Railway. Money Order Office Population about 1000.

Adlington, Robert, M.D., Yonge
Ains, L. (Plant & Warwood), Yonge
Alcorn, Samuel, Bloor
Alston, James, postman, Scollard
Anderson, Mark, laborer, Davenport Road
Andrews, Matthew, merchant tailor, Town Hall Blk. Yonge
Andrews, Thomas, Avenue Road
Archer, William, bookkeeper, Scollard
ARCHIBALD, CHARLES, teacher Boys' Model School, York
Armstrong, E., gate No. 1, Yorkville and Vaughan Plank Road
BACKUS, C. A., William
Back, John, gardener, Sydenham
Bailey, Matthew, prop. Tea Gardens, Bloor w
Bailey, Thomas, commercial traveller, Jarvis
Baldwin, W. Wilcocks, Osgoode Hall, William
Barden, Michael, shoemaker, Yonge
Barrett, R. B. (Barrett & Evans), barrister, Bloor e cor Gwynne
Beaty, John, dry goods merchant, William
Becket, Craven Clark, provision, wine and spirit merchant, Yonge
Berryman, C. V., M.D., Jarvis
Bezley, George P., butcher, William
Blackburn, John, Rosedale
Blackwood, T. F., Jarvis
Blake, Samuel H., barrister, Bloor e nr Sherbourne
Blakely, Miss, matron Magdalen Asylum, Yonge
Bonnick, Joseph, butcher, Yonge
Booth, William, builder, Davenport road
Bocock, Alfred, butcher, Avenue road
Bowling, George, carter, Sydenham
Boyne, Charles, brickmaker, Yonge
Boynes, Charles, brickmaker, (Douglas & Bulmer)
Branton, Thomas, laborer, Davenport Road
Brent, Mrs. Eliza, widow J. W., Turkish baths, Bloor, w
Brown, Henry, butcher, Yonge
Brown, Miss H. C., young ladies' seminary, Jarvis
Brown, Philip, cattle dealer, Yonge
Brown, William, shoemaker, Bellair
BUCHAN, DAVID, Bursar of University, Bloor e, head of Jarvis
Bundy, Patrick, carpenter, Sydenham
Castle, Richard, cattle dealer Sydenham
Cherry, Raspin R., Cumberland House, Yonge
Clark, A. M., barrister, Avenue
Clark, George W., Scollard
Clark, James, carpenter, Sydenham
Clark, James Paton, Mus. Bac., Bloor e

Clark, Thomas, joiner, Davenport Road
Clayton, George Henry, painter, William
Clink, Thomas, carpenter, Yonge
Collett, John, wheelwright (John Walker) Yonge
Convey, Patrick, butcher, Davenport Road
Crawford, Allen, teacher, James
CROFT, HENRY, Professor of Chemistry, University of Toronto, James
Crown, David, shoemaker, Jarvis
Crown, Edward, toll keeper, gate No. 1, Yonge
Crumpton, Arthur, Avenue Road
Daniels, Francis, constable Jarvis
Daniels, John C., county detective, Bloor
Daniels, William, gardener, Avenue Road
Davis, Edward, carpenter, Sydenham
Davis, J. Boyd, barrister, Rosedale
Davison, Frederick, saddler, Yonge
Dawson, Richard, bricklayer, Scollard
Dennis, William, cattle dealer, Sydenham
DOBSON, JAMES, Postmaster, Town Hall Block, Yonge
Dobson, William, corn factor, Scollard
Douglas, John, tailor Sydenham
Douglas & Bulmer, (Roger Douglas & Isaac Bulmer) brick and tile manufacturer, Yonge
Drake, William, carpenter, Sydenham
DRAPER, HON. W. H., chief justice, Gwynne
Dunning, Caleb, butcher, Yonge
Edmonds, John, boot & shoe maker, Yonge
Ellis, John, dairyman, James
Ewart, George, Bloor e
Farrel, John, clerk Street Railway, Yonge
Farrel, William, carpenter, Sydenham
Fihl, John, basket maker, Yonge
Forbes, Hugh, gardener, Cottingham
Fraser, John, teacher, Scollard
Gaby, Joseph, prop Railroad Inn, Yonge
Garsford, Allan, teacher, Yorkville school
Gee, George, cattle dealer, Sydenhrm
Gerry, James, grocer, Yonge
Gibson, Joseph, grocer and provision dealer
Glanville, ohn, butcher, Sydenham
Godfrey, Louis, commercial traveller, Sydenham
Godwin, Mary, dry goods, Yonge
Grainger, Edward, butcher, Town Hall Block, Yonge
Grainger, Frank, carpenter, Yonge
Grainger, William, butcher, William
Greensides, William, brick manufacturer, Yonge
Grey, John, gardener, Sydenham
Grundy, Mrs., young ladies' seminary, Jarvis
Gundry, Thomas, (Gundry & Langley) architect and civil engineer, William
Hancock, John Webster, barrister, patent agent, &c. Yonge
Hand, William, saddler, Town Hall Block, Yonge
Handy, William, boot and shoe maker, Yonge
Harrington, John, brick manufacturer, Davenport road
Harvey, Robert, gardener, Yonge
Hastings, Richard, merchant, Davenport place
Haycock, William, confectioner, Yonge
Heward, W. B., Bloor w
Hector, John, Q.C., Rosedale
Henderson, William, Bloor e
Hewitt, William, dry goods, Yonge
Hill, Thomas S., accountant, Bloor e
HINCKS, WILLIAM, Professor Natural History, University College, Avenue Road
Holmes, Richard, teacher, Cottingham
Hope, Edward, baker, Yonge
HUBERTUS, W. L. (W. L. Hubertus & Co.) Bloor e
Hutchinson, John, blacksmith, Sydenham
Jackson, Edward, Crown Inn, Davenport Road
Jarvis, Edgar, land agent, Rosedale
Jarvis, Samuel, barrister, Yonge
Johnson, Neil, provision dealer, Davenport Road
Jones, James, superintendant Street Railway, Scollard
Keefler, Matthias, book-keeper, Davenport Road
Kerr, Elizabeth, Yorkville Inn, Yonge
Kirk William, Red Lion Inn, Yonge
Kirkpatrick, Andrew, saddler, Yonge
Labitzky, William, music teacher, Sydenham
Lane, William, gardener, Avenue Road
Lawrence, Stephen, gardener, Roxburgh
LESLIE, GEORGE H., & CO., chemists and druggists, Yonge, (see adv)
Luness, William, butcher, Yonge
Madden, Patrick, blacksmith, Sydenham
Magdalen Asylum, Yonge, w. s
MEDICAL COLLEGE, in connection with Victoria University, Hon. Dr. Rolph, Dean
Montgomery, John, blacksmith, Sydenham
Moore, John, gardener, Davenport Road
MORRISON, HON. JOSEPH C., Judge Court of Queen's Bench, Woodlawn, Yonge
Murray, Alexander, (Moffatt, Murray & Beattie) Bloor, east
McCausland, Mrs. Anne Jane, principal girls department, Yorkville School
McCausland, Robert, teacher, William
McPHERSON, HON. D. L., Yonge
Nichols, Joseph, carpenter, New Kent Road
Nichols, James, sen., carpenter, Bellair
Nightingale, Thomas, brick and tile manuf. Yonge
O'Brien, Henry Martin, attorney, Avenue Road
Palmer, Henry H., professor of dancing, Avenue Road
Parsons, Henry, plasterer, Scollard
Peak, Louis C., book-keeper, William
Pickering, James, carpenter, Jarvis
Pickering, Richard, painter, Sydenham
Pierce, Leonard, brick and tile manufacturer, Davenport Place
Piggott, James, gardener, Davenport Road
Plant & Marwood, (James Plant and Stephen James Warwood), pipe manufacturers, Yonge
Playfair, John, S., merchant, Bloor e
Purse, William, gardener, Sydenham
Reasby, Henry, grocer, Yonge
Richards, Hon. Stephen H., barrister, Commissioner Crown Lands, Bloor
Robinson, George, butcher, Cottingham
ROBINSON, W. S., dispensing chemist, nr Town Hall Block, Yonge
SANGSTER, JOHN H., M.A., M.D., Avenue Road
Scott, George, grocer and provision dealer, Town Hall Block, Yonge
SEVERN, HENRY, Yorkville Brewery, Yonge
Simmons, Mrs. Clara, dry goods, Yonge
Skerry, John, gardener, Sydenham
Smart, William Lynn (Cameron & Smart) William
Smiley, Andrew, brick manufacturer, Yonge
Smith, Henry, butcher, Avenue Road
Smith, Robert James, William
Sorley, James Bruce, leather merchant, Yonge
St. Paul's Church, (Church of England) Bloor w
Stather, John, shoemaker, Davenport Road
Stennett, Thomas, grocer, Yonge
Stevenson, Archibald, gardener, Avenue Road
Steward, Thomas, butcher, Sydenham
Sutherland, Rev. A. (Wesleyan), William
Thom, Charles, Target Inn, Town Hall Block, Yonge
Thompson. David, corporation inspector, William
Thompson, Edward, carpenter, Sydenham
Toronto Street Railway, depot, Town Hall block, Yonge
Toulmin, Frederick, music teacher, Sydenham
Townsley, Wm., brick machine maker, Avenue Road
Vare, George, gardener, Roxburgh
Walker, John, wheelwright, Yonge

Walker, Robert, blacksmith, Yonge
Walker, Walter, carpenter and joiner, Yonge
Wallis, James, blacksmith, Yonge
Watson, James, wholesale and retail druggist, Bloor e
Watson, William, jeweler, Yonge
Weir, James, boot and shoe store, Yonge
Wesleyan Methodist Church, Bloor e
West, Thomas, plasterer, Sydenham
Weston, John, upholsterer, Sydenham
White, George H., builder, Avenue Road
Wickson, Samuel, attorney, Yonge
Wilcock, Thomas, market gardener, Davenport Road
Willard, Henry, gardener, Sydenham
Williams, John, cooper, Yonge
Woods, Thos., car inspector, Street railway, Sydenham
Woodhouse, William, gardener, Sydenham
Woolley, Martha, confectioner, Yonge
Wright, James, gardener, Avenue Road

Young's Point.—A small Village in the Township of Smith, County Peterboro, 14 miles from Peterboro, the County Town. Population 40.

Aryatt, Joseph, farmer
Aryatt, J., jun., farmer
Barry, T., teacher
Davis, E., farmer
Davis, John, cooper
Davis, W., farmer
Graham, John, saw mill
Kearney, James, jun., general merchant
Kearney, James, farmer
KEARNEY, PATRICK, Postmaster
Miller, Andrew, butcher
Millage, C., farmer
Pasley, A., farmer
White, Samuel, carpenter
White, T., farmer
Young, Matthew, hotel keeper
Young, Samuel, farmer
Young, T., farmer
Young, William, farmer

Zephyr.—A Post Office in the Township of Scott, County Ontario.

Cunningham, Michael, farmer
Dunckly, Rev. G. (Bible Christian)
Foot, William, farmer
Graham, Newton, farmer
Habson, George, farmer
Hamilton, Rev. (Wesleyan)
Hunter, George W., carpenter
Leatch, George, farmer
March, Alfred, teacher
March, Oliver, farmer
Pearce, Rev. — (Wesleyan)
Pickering, John, farmer
Pickering, Thomas, farmer
Roach, Martin, farmer
Schell, Isaac, farmer
Weller, L., farmer
Wesley, Timothy, farmer
WILSON, JOHN, Postmaster and general merchant

Zetland.—A small Village on the River Maitland, in the Township of Turnberry, County Huron.

BRACE, LEWIS T., Postmaster, and lumber dealer.

Zimmerman.—A Village on Twelve-mile Creek, in the Township of Nelson, County Halton, 8 miles from Milton, the County Town, and 8 from Wellington Square Station Great Western Railway. Population 60

Bower, Charles & William, merchant tailors
Bridgman, John, farmer
Crawford, G. C., manufacturer of woolen goods
Doury, David, carpenter
Edmondson, Rev. Henry (Presbyterian)
Foster, George, farmer
Gowland, George, farmer
Haynes, Rev. Frederick (New Connexion)
Joyce, Samuel, teacher
Lamb, Nathaniel, lime and stone
McLeod, Daniel, J.P.
MILLER, ROBERT, Postmaster
Sharp, George, butcher
Spence, William, farmer
Watson, Thomas, farmer
Zimmerman, Daniel, general merchant
Zimmerman, H. P., J.P., prop. flouring and saw mill
Zimmerman, J., farmer
Zimmerman, James, farmer
Zimmerman, Johnson, dentist
Zimmerman, Philip, carpenter

Zurich.—A Village in the Township of Hay, County Huron, 24 miles from Goderich, the County Town. Money Order Office. Population 200.

Axt, Frederick, blacksmith
Bauer, Charles, wagon maker
Bonnet & Masser, proprietor flouring mill
Broderick, John, teacher
BROWN, ROBERT, Postmaster and gen. merchant
Creiman, Charles, tinsmith
Deichert, John, blacksmith
Deichert, Nicholas, saddler
Direstein, Henry V., teacher
Foster, Nicholas, brick yard
Frang, John, proprietor Victoria Hotel
Freeman, A. D., general merchant
Greb, Henry, carpenter
Hess, Christian, potter
Hess, Frederich, wagon maker
Hyrook, Christian, wagon maker
Kegs & Elliot, general merchants
Sippel, Henry, cooper
Steinbach, Henry, prop. Zurich Hotel
Tee, Walter, J.P.
Wagner, Conrad F., wagon maker
Walper, Abel, tanner
Wibmer, Amos, blacksmith
Wilson, William G., insurance agent and teacher
Witmer, Absolom, carpenter
Witmer, Amos, blacksmith
Zeller, Michael, J.P.
Zimmerman, Henry, tailor

Villages Received too late for Insertion in their proper places.

NOTE.—Villages marked thus * will be found in the body of the Work, but more recent and extended information has since been received.

***Allandale Mills.**—A Village in the Township of Otonabee, County Peterboro', 10 miles from Peterboro', the County Town, and 6 from Keene Station, Cobourg, Peterboro' and Marmora Railway. Population 200

Calder, William, tanner
Chisholm, Alexander, saddler
Connel, Alexander, blacksmith
Shearer & Sons, carpenters
SHORT, RICHARD, Postmaster, saw mill prop
Short, T., founder and miller

***Alma.**—A Village in the Township of Peel, County Wellington, 18 miles from Guelph, the County Town. Stage to Walkerton. Population 175.

Anderson, R., grocer
Anderson, R., blacksmith
Callum, C., carpenter
Cousins, H., carpenter
Downing & Allen, wagon makers
Fairweather, Thomas, farmer
GRAHAME, THOMAS, Postmaster
Isaac, James, blacksmith
Johnston, James, inn keeper
Ledingham & Milne, props. planing mill
McCua, Alexander, J.P., farmer
McElroy, W. J., general merchant
McGowan, D., farmer
Miller, H., carpenter
Rumble, H., carpenter
Smart, P., carpenter
Speirs, Alexander, insurance agent
Steele, J. C., inn keeper
Thacker, James, brickmaker
Toney, David, shoemaker
Toney, Thomas, shoemaker
Wallace, James, M.D
Wilton, James, farmer

***Batchewana.**—A small Village in the Township of Fisher, District of Algoma, 45 miles from Sault St. Marie.

IRONSIDE, GEORGE A., agent Hudson's Bay Co
McKAY, R. T. general merchant

***Bervie.**—A Village in the Township of Kincardine, County Bruce, 20 miles from Walkerton, the County Town. Stages to Goderich and Walkerton. Population 150.

Bottoms, Rev. William, (Wesleyan)
Boyd, A. K., hotel keeper
Bradley, Thomas, dentist, druggist, &c
Carter, George, carpenter
Cave, Edward, tailor
Gammon, Richard, lumber merchant
Hodgins, Joseph, carpenter
Hodgkin, Rev. Dr. (Church of England)
Huggins, Rev. William (Primitive Methodist)
Long, Samuel, butcher
McIntyre, Nichol, J.P.
McPherson, John, carpenter
MADDEN, J., Postmaster
Madden & Sithes, general merchants
Needham, James & Brother, carriage and wagon mkrs
Peterbough, Alexander, shingle maker
Proudfoot & Sons, dyers and scourers
Ralson, James, boots and shoes
Rice, Rev. O. L. (Wesleyan)
Siddon, John, boots and shoes
Stout, William, teacher
Walsh, Stephen, general merchant

Caintown.—A Village in the Township of Yonge, County Leeds, 13 miles from Brockville, the County Town. Tri-weekly Mails. Population 250.

Andress, Edward, wagon maker
Andress, Sylvester, wagon maker
Buell, William S., carpenter and blacksmith
Connolly, M. J., teacher
Davidson, Margaret, general merchant
Dawson, Rev. A. (Methodist Episcopal)
English, Rev. William (Wesleyan)
Ferguson, James, weaver
Huntly, John, wagon maker
McCollum, William, weaver
Miller, Samuel, farmer
Phillips, R. R., wood contractor
Purvis, Henry, carpenter
Thomson, Alexander, wood contractor
Tennant, David D., farmer
Tennant, David T., farmer
Tennant, James, blacksmith
Tennant, Thomas, farmer
Tennant, William, farmer
Thompson, Benjamin, Collector of Township Taxes
Wilson, E. D., shoemaker

heltenham.—A Village in the Township of Chinguacousy, County Peel, 12 miles from Brampton, the County Town. Population 100.

ıker, W. H., cooper
AMPBELL, JOHN, Postmaster
ıeyne, George, blacksmith
›rrigill, P. H., general merchant
aines, Charles
aines, E., prop. saw mill and cabinet maker
aines, Frederick, miller
enry, Hugh, farmer
enry, William, prop. Cheltenham Inn
ing, Charles H., general merchant
Little, Joseph, farmer
Lyons, John, farmer
Lyons, Thomas, farmer
McConnell, Archibald, tanner and shoemaker
McKechner, John, farmer
Mercer, T. L., saddle and harness maker
TRACY, J. S., Postmaster and prop. Ontario House
Wilkinson, Matthew, cabinet maker
Young, Andrew, wagon maker

oldwater.—A Village on the Coldwater River, in the Township of Medonte, County Simcoe, 30 miles from Barrie, the County Town. Stage to Orillia. Population 150.

arber, John, farmer
orland, William, hotel keeper
ush, George, naturalist
ıswell, George, mill owner
ıswell, George, jun., hotel keeper
unlop, John, mill owner and farmer
stell, John, general merchant
Harris, Rev. R. H. (Church of England)
Kent, W. H., farmer
McCall, J., teacher
Marks, Rev. (Methodist)
Nettleton, William, general merchant
Rutledge, William H., reeve and farmer
Wilson, William, farmer

ickinson's Landing.—A Village and Station of the Grand Trunk Railway, on the river St. Lawrence in the Township of Osnabruck, County Stormont, 10 miles from Cornwall; and 77 from Montreal. Money Order Office. Population, 250.

ndrews, Rev. — (Methodist)
ullock, R. R., collector of customs and mill owner
ush, E., teacher
lark, P., teacher
olqohoun, William, general merchant
awson, John and Franklin, tanners
awson, A., saddler
aman, N., farmer
isher, John S., blacksmith
orbas, Peter, general merchant
Ianes, William H., hotel keeper
Iutchins, James, tinsmith
ohnston, Thomas E., butcher
Latrace, William, blacksmith
Lover, M., cooper
Lynch, Rev., Roman Catholic
McMullen, John, tailor
McNairn, J. N., saddler
McQuillan, William, shoemaker
Miller, William E., cabinet maker
Ransom, David, baker
Waldroff, Jacob, farmer
WAGNER CHARLES, Postmaster and general merchant
Wagner, William H., M. D
Warren, Samuel, ship chandler

orking.—A Village on Smith's Creek, in the Township of Wellesley, County Waterloo, 22 miles from Berlin, the County Town; and 12 from Listowell. Stages to the above places. Population, 100.

uke, William, carpenter
dmeston, George, shoemaker
ATSCHINE, JOHN, P. M., proprietor Royal Hotel
lass, Michael, livery
Kennedy, David, farmer
Kennedy, Samuel, farmer
ewis, J., dentist
ove, James, painter
McDonald, Arthur, farmer
Miller, John, farmer
Miller, William, farmer
Roos, John, cooper
Ryan, Nicholas, butcher
Semple, J., general merchant
Snyder, George, lumber dealer
Watson, James, farmer
Watson, John, farmer
Watson, Robert, farmer
Wells, George, wagon maker

East Williamsburgh—A Village on the River St. Lawrence, in the Township of Williamsburgh, County Dundas, 2 miles from Aultsville Station Grand Trunk Railway, and 6 from Morrisburg.

Castleman, William, M.D.
Cook & Son, masons
Cunningham, Robert, blacksmith
Empey, Charles, blacksmith
Hayes, Godfrey, blacksmith
Hickey, R. J., M.D.
PILLAR, LINDSAY, Postmaster, general merchant and saw mill proprietor
Snyder, Elias, carpenter and pump maker
Snyder, John, general merchant
Tracey, George, carpenter
Wells, George, general merchant

Easton's Corners.—A Village in the Township of Wolford, County Grenville, 24 miles from Brockville, the County Town, Money Order office. Population 100.

Brundige, A., hotel keeper
Cameron, A., general merchant
COOLIDGE, ISAAC, Postmaster and cheese manufacturer
Devitt, Thomas, tanner
Edwards, F., photographer
Edwards, J., boots and shoes
Ferguson, Henry, wine merchant
Fortune, Mrs., groceries
Foster, A., boots and shoes
Holliday, James, tailor
Hunt, Edward, carriage maker
Ireland, A. A., blacksmith
Ireland, Isaac, blacksmith
Narings, W., harness maker
Narings, John, hotel keeper
Pearson, Simon, ashery
Putnam, B. S., tanner
Shaw & Sloan, general merchants
Sutton, Miss C., milliner
Watts, John, blacksmith
Wickwire, P., brick maker

Eastwood.—A Village and Station of the Great Western Railway, 4 miles from Woodstock. Pop. 150.

Boulson, Charles, farmer
Burrows, R. W. & A., proprietors grist and saw mills
Desbanes, Rev. T. C. (Church of England)
Draper, B., farmer
Fredinburgh, A., farmer
Hayward, John, inn keeper
Huggart, R. & D., farmers
Hyde, William, carpenter and wheelright
Kipp, R., farmer
Layenby, Thomas, farmer
Leak, J. & R., farmers
Overholt, M. & Sons, farmers and mill owners
Perry, Thomas, farmer
Potter, A., farmer
Robinson, John, blacksmith
Robinson, Richard, farmer
SHAW, JOHN, Posmaster, grocer and shoemaker
Slattery, John, farmer
Smith, Hiram, blacksmith
Ulman, John, carpenter

Edwardsburgh.—A Village and Station of the Grand Trunk Railway, on the River St. Lawrence, in the Township of Edwardsburgh, County Grenville, 21 miles from Brockville, the County Town, and 69 from Kingston. Population 300

AIKEN, WILLIAM S., Postmaster, grocer
Osgoode, H. A., hotel keeper
Benson, W. T., prop. starch factory
Burns, L., general merchant
Glassford, Charles, general merchant
Harbottle, Thomas, blacksmith
McLatchie, James, blacksmith
McPherson, Kenneth, general merchant
Meade, William, cabinet maker
Pearsall, Mrs., milliner
Riddell, William, grocer
Thompson, William, boots and shoes

Eganville.—A Village on the Bonnecheure River, in the Township of Grattan, County Renfrew, 23 miles from Pembroke, and 85 from Ottawa. Money Order Office. Population 800.

Austin, W. W., general merchant
Bonfield, James, general merchant and prop mills
Bonfield & Turner, lumber dealers
Brennan, Patrick, blacksmith
Campbell, Mrs. L., hotel keeper
Channonhouse, John, M.D
Childerhouse, John, prop. carding mill
Dougherty, D., tailor
Gallagher, Hugh, wagon maker
George, Henry, general merchant
Gorman, William, blacksmith
Hetherington, John, groceries, boots and shoes
Judge, John, M.D
Lacy, Daniel, general merchant
Lynn, James, M.D
McDermott, Samuel, tinsmith
McDonald, John J., hotel keeper
McDonald, Robert, hotel keeper
McGregor, Duncan, prop. carding mill
McHugh, Patrick, blacksmith
McNamara, John, boots and shoes
Merrick, C. H., hotel keeper
Mullin, Stephen, saddler
Paul, James, boots and shoes
QUEALY, JOHN, Postmaster, general merchant
Reeves, James, general merchant
Searson, Mrs., groceries and saloon
Smith, John, tanner
Smith, William, saloon keeper
Whalley, Isaac, saddler

Elginburg.—A Village in the Township of Kingston, County Frontenac, 8 miles from Kingston.

BATES, PETER, Postmaster, shoemaker
Jackson, William, carriage and wagon maker
Pope, John, blacksmith

Farran's Point.—A Village situated at the lower entrance of Farran's Point Canal, on the River St. Lawrence, in the Township of Osnabruck, County Stormont. It has good mill privileges. Distant from Cornwall, the County Town, 16 miles, and from Dickinson's Landing 5 miles. Population 150.

Baker, George M., grocer and saddler
Dafoe, Isaiah, carriage maker
Deneney, Edward, hotel keeper
Elliott, David, boots and shoes
Farran, Charles C., prop. saw and grist mill
FARRAN, JOHN, Postmaster and prop. carding mill
Ferris, George, general merchant
Gibson, William, general merchant
Gorrell, George T., general merchant
Gougeon, Joseph, boots and shoes
Kerr, Joseph & Bro., general merchants
McTiernan, J., tanner and dealer in boots and shoes
Robinson, Martin, general merchant
Selkirk, George, cabinet maker

Fenelon Falls.—A Village on Cameron Lake, and Fenelon River, in the Township of Fenelon, County Victoria, 16 miles from Lindsay, the County Town. Money Order Office. Population 500.

Arthurs, Joseph M., hotel keeper
Barker, Rev. T., (Methodist)
Bell, Thomas, blacksmith
Bell, W., hotel keeper
Berks, Rev. Mr., (Bible Christian)
Brandon, A., hotel keeper
Brown, F., farmer
Brownlee & Mowrey, lumber merchants
Campbell & McCallum, boots and shoes
Carville, D., butcher
Cassiday Bros., builders
Davis, H., wagon maker
Deward, W., general merchant
Downey, L., hotel keeper
Ellerby, William, farmer
Everest, W. E., druggist
Eyres, H., farmer
Farmer, W., shoemaker
Fawcett, M., prop. lath factory
Fielding, William, township clerk
Fisk, Julius, farmer
Fitzgerald, James, M.D
Fitzgerald, J. C., clerk division court
Graham, Henry, general merchant
Green & Ellis, lumber merchants
Hand, E. D., grocer
Hodgins, Jonathan, J.P
Hoskins, Rev. B., (Church of England)
Jackson, R., tailor
Jameson, G. S., general merchant
JAMESON, R. B., Postmaster
Jordan, W., farmer
Keith, George, blacksmith
Kennedy, J. W., painter
Lochead, Rev. W., (Presbyterian)
McDermott, B., tailor
McGrane, John, baker and grocer
Naylor, J., J.P., farmer
Palmer, Elias, blacksmith
Reed & Moore, general merchants
Ross, James, grocer
Scully, B., general merchant
Secord, W. E., conveyancer
Smith, J. D., lumber merchant
Smith, R. C. & Co., lumber merchants
Townsend, J., tinsmith
Twomey, J., blacksmith
Ullyott, Dalton, lumber merchant
Webster, Robert, farmer

Fingal.—A Post Village, situated in the Township of Southwold, County Elgin, distant from St. Thomas, the County Town, 7 miles; from London 55 miles, and from Toronto 140 miles. Daily mail. Money Order Office and Savings Bank. Population 600.

Atkins, Henry, harness maker
Bake, James, butcher
Bissel, Stewart, shoemaker
Burtch, James, grocer
Burwell, Adam, harness maker and tanner
Burwell, Samuel E., grocer
Campbell, Malcolm, harness maker
Cochrane, Roderick, general merchant
Collins, Rev, John, (Episcopal Methodiss)
Doyle, William A., stove pedler
Drak, William, wagon maker
Edmonds, Charles, general merchant
Finlay, James P., general merchant
Fowler, L., J. P.
Fulton, A. & J., druggists
Hammill, James, marble cutter
Hooper, Francis, wagon maker
Hyndman, Peter, tailor
Laurence, Thomas, shoemaker
Lewis, Chancy, wagon maker
Linte, Charler, tailor
Longden, Margaret, prop hotel
McAuley, Rev. Ewing, (Canadian Presbyterian)
McColl, Archibald, blacksmith
McDonald, John P., accountant
McGeachy, William, M. D.
McKay, J. W., grocer
McKenzie, George, general merchant
McLachlin, Duncan, wagon maker
McLardy, Archibald, shoemaker
McLaughlin, James, M.D.
McLaughlin, M., M.D.
McPherson, Glasgow & Co., founders
Marshall, William O., cooper
Metcalf, George, cabinet maker and undertaker
Neal, William, merchant tailor
Penwarden, George, proprietor hotel
Risdon & Brotherhood, tinsmiths
Shepley, Rev. Joseph, (Wesleyan)
Smith, Joseph, proprietor hotel
Sutherland, Rev. George, Free Church of Scotland
Timewell, Henry, blacksmith
Tonkin, James & Joseph, millers
TUBBY, SAMUEL, Postmaster, municipal clerk, conveyancer, etc.
Warren, Edward, shoemaker
Wood, A., J.P.
Wood, W., blacksmith
Young, Alexander, shoemaker

Heidelburg.—A village in the Township of Wellesley, County Waterloo, 11 miles from Berlin, the County Town. Population 400.

Allis, Valentine, saddler
Becker, John, blacksmith
Doersam, George shoemaker
Hahn, John, wagon maker
Kabel, Conrad K., jun., brewer
KRESSLER, JOHN, Postmaster and proprietor hotel
Miller, Henry A., general merchant
Muir, J., general merchant
Schafer, Conrad, tailor
Steiss, A., proprietor hotel
Volmer, Peter, blacksmith
Weiss, George, wagon maker
Weiss, Christopher, blacksmith

Iona.—A village on Talbot creek, in the Township of Southwold, County Elgin, 12 miles from St. Thomas, the County Town, and 135 from Toronto. Money Order Office. Stages to St. Thomas and Morpeth. Population 500.

Allen, G., photographer
Beedle, Robert, blacksmith
Black, Duncan, grocer
Brown, Archibald, farmer
Brown, George, cabinet maker
Cascaden, John, M.D.
Chisholm, William, Com. in B.R.
Clark, John, cancer specialist
Clark, Rev. J., (Baptist)
Cole, Henry, grocer
Decow, Daniel, stove and tinware
Decow, Duncan, issuer marriage licenses
Decow, John, prop. livery stable
Edgcombe & Boston, wagon makers and blacksmiths
Harris, Charles, cabinet maker
Kerr, Colin, farmer
Lamb, George
Liddell & Chisholm, general merchants
Lodge, William, farmer
Lowther, James, wagon maker and blacksmith
Lowther, W. D., carpenter
Lumley, E., prop. American Hotel
Lumley, G. O., carpenter
Lumley, Bros., carpenters
Lumley, Thomas, cooper
McColl, Nicol, M.P.P.
McCallum, D., merchant tailor
McIntyre, Samuel, butcher
McKay, Neil, blacksmith
McLandy, N., shoemaker
McSherry & McLean, agricultural implements
Manson, John, M.D.
Mills, John, proprietor Commercial Hotel
Parker & Son, blacksmiths
Philpott, James, Clerk Division Court
PHILPOTT, J. A., Postmaster and conveyancer
Philpott, James, farmer
Roach, E., shomaker
Silcor, George, farmer
Silcor, John, farmer
Simmons, Asa, grocer
Sinclair, Peter, tailor
Smith, Squire, saddler
Stafford, Abel, farmer
Stafford, Richard, teacher
Tait, F. A., general merchant
Taylor, Rev. J. B., (Baptist)
Taylor, William

Kinburn.—A small Village in the Township of Fitzroy, County Carleton, 28 miles from Ottawa.

Douglas, Robert, blacksmith and hotel keeper
FRASER, ALLAN, Postmaster
Scott, Robert, shoemaker
Stepf, John, blacksmith
Thompson & Stanley, general merchants
Williams, John, wagon maker

Kingston Mills.—A Village near the first locks of the Rideau Canal, in the Township of Kingston, County Frontenac, 6 miles from Kingston. Population 200.

BROWNLEY, ROBERT, Postmaster, grocer
Cunningham, Davy, boots and shoes
Cunningham, James, boots and shoes
Cunningham, Peter, grocer
Dean, Mrs., hotel keeper
Latchford, William, blacksmith
Milloy, James, saddler
Smith, Edward, proprietor mills

Kirkton.—A Village on the boundary line between the Counties of Huron and Perth, in the Townships of Usborne and Blanchard, 48 miles from Goderich and 22 from Stratford. Population 100.

Callendar, John, blacksmith
Dewar, James, shoemaker
Gould, John, proprietor hotel
Kirk James, blacksmith
PARK, ROBERT, Postmaster, general merchant
Roadhouse, J., wagon maker
Stubbs, Joseph, M. D., druggist

Lake Dore.—A Post Office in the Township of Wilberforce, County Renfrew.

Davis, Edward, farmer
Denison, John, farmer
Jackson, John, farmer
King, Robert, farmer
Salter, Peter, blacksmith
Shaw, John, miller
WALLACE, THOMAS, Postmaster, innkeeper and farmer

Largie.—A Post Office in the Township of Dunwich, County Elgin.

Crawford, Archibald, farmer
Galbraith, Donald, farmer
Goldie, John, shoemaker
LEITCH, ARCHIBALD, Postmaster, carpenter
Leitch, Angus, farmer
Leitch, Donald, farmer
McCallum, Peter, farmer
McDonald, Angus, farmer
McDonald, Donald, farmer
McIntyre, Duncan, farmer
McLean, John, farmer
McPhail, Donald, farmer
Milligan, Edward, innkeeper

Lisburn.—A Post Office in the Township of Huron, County Perth, distant from Kincardine the County Town, 9 miles, from Hamilton 90, from London 90 and from Toronto 100.

RUTTLE, GIDEON, Postmaster.

Listowell.—An Incorporated Village on the Maitland River, in the Townships of Elma and Wallace, County Perth, 33 miles from Stratford, the County Town; and 22 from Mitchell. Money Order Office, and Savings Bank. Population, 1200.

Alexander, John, general merchant
Bell, Rev. J. W. (Presbyterian)
Bennauair, Henry, harness maker
Bogues, William, potash maker
Brownlow, Thomas, general merchant
Chapman, Newman, boots and shoes
Climie & Billinger, grist and saw mill proprietors
Dawson & Little, wagon makers and blacksmiths
Dempsey, George, groceries and liquors
Danyer, Alexander, grocer and baker
Draper, John, general merchant
Flaherty, John, proprietor hotel
Gibson, W., proprietor hotel
Hacking Brothers, druggists
Hacking, Joseph, editor and pub. *Listowell Banner*
Hacking & Tilt, proprietors *Banner*
HACKING, W. H., Postmaster
Halstead, James A., general merchant
Harvey, Paul, tailor
Hay, D. D., division court clerk
Henderson, John, proprietor saloon
Helper, J., cooper
Herman & Bolton, proprietors woolen factory
Hesseo, W. & G., cabinet makers
Hent. Luke, druggist
Langdale, William, watchmaker
Lee, James, saddler
LISTOWELL BANNER, Joseph Hacking, editor and publisher
Little, E. G., general merchant
Livingston, John, general merchant
McIlraith, Stewart, tanner, boots and shoes
McKay, Alexander, tailor
McKinney, W., boots and shoes
McLeod & Herman, woolen factory
Markle, William, proprietor hotel
Miller, Rev. A. E. (Church of England)
Moore, John, proprietor hotel
Mortimore, G. R., stoves and tinware
Murray, Archibald, shoemaker
Neville, John, merchant tailor
Nichol, John, M. D.
Palmer, Rev. H. B. (Episcopal Methodist)
Philip, John, M. D.
Ryder, John, shoemaker
Robinson, Albert, books and notions
Robinson & Jackson, cabinet makers
Rothwell, B., teacher
Sill, Abraham, M. D.
Schlim, Henry, harness maker
Scott, J. W., general merchant
Shepherd, Rev. W. W. (Wesleyan)
Smith, Samuel, cabinet maker
Snider, F., tinsmith
Thompson, John. general merchant
Towner & Campbell, tanners
Turnbull & Lockie, founders
Vele & Godsave, tanners
Waugh, W. T., general store
White, A. P., proprietor match factory
Winter, James, wagon maker and blacksmith
Zimmerman, John, proprietor hotel

Mansfield.—A Village in the Township of Mulmur, County Simcoe, 32 miles from Barrie, the County town, and 17 from Angus station, Northern Railway. Population 60.

Black, William, farmer
Campbell, Robert, blacksmith
GILBERT, WILLIAM, Postmaster, hotel keeper and general store
Grier, Charlton, farmer
Holdship, Thomas, teacher
Legate, Benjamin, farmer
McCracken, Blair, wagon maker
McCracken, Robert, farmer
McMahon, John, J.P., farmer
McMulkin, Edward, miller, Bayne mills
Morrow, John W., shoemaker
Silks, Joseph, farmer
White, James, farmer

Marlbank.—A Village and Station of the Grand Trunk Railway, on the river Moira, in the Township of Hungerford, County Hastings. Population 100.

ALLAN, WILLIAM G., Postmaster, general merchant.

Medonte.—A small Village in the Township of Medonte, County Simcoe, 25 miles from Barrie, the County Town.

MOON, EDMUND, Postmaster.

Medina (Keswick P. O.)—Situated in the Township of North Gwillimbury, County York. (See Keswick, page 239.)

Anderson, James, proprietor saw mill
Mellen, Peter, blacksmith
Quance, F., general merchant
Smith, Thomas W., hotel keeper
Stennett, R. M., general merchant
Trelan, John, blacksmith
Trelan, Samuel, blacksmith
Yoe, William, boots and shoes

Merlin.—A Post Office in the Township of Raleigh, County Kent.

BENEDICT, E. S., Postmaster.

Morrisbank.—A Post Office in the Township of Grey, County Huron.

Hislop, Alexander, farmer
Miller, John R., farmer
Miller, Richard, farmer
Moffat, Robert, farmer
ORR, JAMES, Postmaster
Simson, Andrew, farmer
Simson, James, farmer
Wright, William, farmer

Muncey.—A small Post Village and Indian Reserve, six miles in extent, inhabited by three tribes of Indians, viz.: the Oneidas, Ojibeways and Munceys. It is situated in the Township of Carradoc, County Middlesex. Distance from London 20 miles.

WHITING, R. E., Postmaster.

***Newburgh.**—An incorporated Village on the Napanee River, in the Township of Camden East, County Addington, 6½ miles from Napanee, the County Town, and 24 from Kingston. Money Order Office and Savings Bank. Population 1,500.

Allen, John, farmer
Ash, David, painter
Ash, Elias, painter
Aylesworth, J., farmer
Aylesworth, John B., farmer
Baker, Richard, butcher
Baregar, George, carpenter
Baughan, John, carriage builder
Bell, David, farmer
Bell, Edward, farmer
Bell, James, farmer
Bell, William, farmer
Benson, Matthew R., laborer
Black, George, tanner
Black, John, tannery
Briser, Walter, boot and shoe manufactory
Brown, John, retired
Burdette, D. A., carriage maker
Carscallen, Archibald, farmer
Carscallen, Luke, farmer
Casey, Hiram, laborer
Caten, Allen, reeve, druggist
Caton, Miles, Village Treasurer, general merchant
Clark, Elias, carpenter
Creigeton, John, general blacksmith and carriage builder
Cummings, George, tanner
Darouche, P., tailor
Davy, James, shoemaker
Davy, John W., leader brass band
Dawe, James, confectioner and baker
Derouch, Pascal, tailor
Detlor, Benjamin, provisions
Detlor, Jacob V., shoemaker
Detlor, William V. P., boot and shoe maker
Dickinson, John A., pump maker
Douglass & Hooper, general merchants
Dowling, John, groceries and crockery
Dowling, Richard & John, potash manufacturer
Dunn, Henry, blacksmith
Eakins, George, cabinet maker
Eakins, William H., cabinet maker
Empey, Nathan, grocer
Evans, Robert, farmer
Farley, John, blacksmith
Files, Benjamin
Files, Chester, farmer
Finkle, Henry, carriage maker
Fullarton, Joseph, senr., cabinet maker
Fullarton, Joseph, junr., cabinet maker
Fullarton, W. B., sec. and treas., brass band
Ham, Robert, stone cutter
Hanes, S., axe maker
Hill, Stephen, laborer
Hillard, Mrs. E. S., milliner and dress maker
Hooper, Douglas, general merchant, and prop flouring mill and woolen manufactory
Hope, R. T., prop Camden house
HOPE, W. A., Postmaster, (W. A. Hope & Co.)
HOPE, W. A. & Co., general merchants, (see card)
Howell, William, carpenter
Huycke, Edward, carpenter
Jackson, John, farmer
Jennings, Isaac, blacksmith

Jones, Edward, contractor and builder
Jones, R., assessor
Lanfear, E. O., pump and harness maker
Lasher, S. N., carpenter
Lockwood, Robert, blacksmith
Loucks, N., painter
McCammon, James, M.D., druggist
McConnel, E., tailor
McConnell, Samuel, carpenter
McGee, John, teacher
McGuire, Peter, laborer
McKeown, Patrick, laborer
Madden, George, proprietor flouring mill
Madden, Mrs. George, bakery
Madden, Sylvester, woolen manufacturer
Miller, Cephas H., J.P., farmer
Miller, Joseph, cooper
Milligan, William, laborer
Moore, Charles, carriage maker
Moss, Robert, tailor
Mulholland, John, laborer
Murdoff, Nicholas, carpenter
Nugent, William, sen., farmer
Nugent, William, jun., farmer
Osborne, R., village clerk
Papa, Daniel, tailor
Paul, James, groceries and provisions
Porter, W. H., grocer
Powers, James. proprietor Empire House
Reuben, Jones, farmer
Richardson, Michael, sawyer
Rook, Richard, watchmaker and jeweler
Russell, Andrew, tailor
Russell, William, painter
Ryan, Matthew, drum major
Scott & Jennings, blacksmith
Scott, Thomas, carriage maker and blacksmith
Shetler, Conrad, farmer
Shetler, Frederick, farmer
Shetler, Matthew, farmer
Shorey, John, carpenter
Shorts, Nelson, butcher
Snider, John O., dealer in stoves and tinware
Spencer, Homer, bailiff fifth Division Court
Stanton, Rev. Thomas
Stickney, David B., manufacturer of agricultural implements, stoves, &c.
Sutton, James, butcher
Taylor, Joseph, proprietor axe manufactory
Tinkle, Henry, carriage maker
Wease, Peter
Wells, John C., saddler and harness maker

North Augusta.—A Village on the Rideau River, in the Township of Augusta, County Grenville, 15 miles from Brockville, the County Town, 4½ from Bellamy's Station, Brockville and Ottawa Railroad, and 224 from Toronto. Money Order Office. Population 500.

Aspinall, James, proprietor North Augusta Hotel
Baldwin, Samuel, cabinet maker
Bellamy, J. B., J. P., proprietor woolen mill and shingle manufactory
Bellamy, L. H., proprietor saw mill
BELLAMY, SAMUEL J., Postmaster
Birks, Rev. U., (New Connexion)
Botham, John, tailor and farmer
Capes, Peter, tailor
Carpenter, D. H., carpenter and joiner
Chapman, John, general merchant and assist. P. M.
Checkley, T. F., issuer of marriage licenses & farmer
Cochran, John, proprietor Victoria House
Colborn, Benjamin, proprietor grist mill, and manuf. of butter firkins
Cooke, Rev. A. W., (Church of England)
Daniels, Henry, farmer
Dixon, James, carpenter
Dowling, William, J.P., Commissioner
Dunn, A. T., M.D
Foxton, John, carpenter
Gillett, Jesse, manufacturer of grain cradles
Harrison, Thomas, bailiff
Hill, T. W., general merchant
Huntington, Rev. S., (Wesleyan)
Johnson, Charles E., blacksmith
Joyce, Thomas, shoemaker
Langstaff, James, shoemaker
Lyman, Mrs., milliner, &c
Lyman, Warren, clerk of Division Court
McCully, Andrew, cabinet maker
McCully, John, carpenter
McIntosh, Matthew, farmer
Melville, John H., teacher
Metcalf, William, carpenter
Miller, Thomas, farmer
Mott, Mrs., milliner and dressmaker
Mott, Samuel, harness maker
Murray, Hugh, plasterer
Murray, William, plasterer
Norton, S. W., general merchant
Pardee, A. B., J.P., farmer and shoemaker
Pardee, F. J., farmer and shoemaker
Parish, Samuel, carpenter
Ralph, David, general merchant
Timblick, Alexander, carpenter
Willson, Rev. F. (Episcopal Methodist)
Wright, Isaiah, township clerk and treasurer

Otterville.—A Post Village in the Township of South Norwich, County Oxford, 20 miles distant from Woodstock, the County Town. It has a large trade in sawn lumber and farm produce. Mails daily. Money Order Office. Population 500.

Bedford, S. & J., hotel keepers
Buck, Robert, cabinet maker
Bullock, James E., agent saw and grist mills and woolen factory
Coller, A. J., M.D.
Comfort, Stephen, hotel keeper
Conklin, W. P., druggist
Cornell, J. H. & S. P., general merchants
Cornell, William, commission merchant
Creighton, William, shoemaker
Durkee, Asa, tanner, harness, boots, &c.
Erb, Abraham, proprietor woolen factory
Fish, John, pump maker
Furlong, John, cooper and shingle maker
Lewis, W., watchmaker
McFarlane, John, blacksmith and wagon maker
Madison, Matthew, proprietor grist mill
Mesecar, A. J., M.D.
Parker, Mary, groceries and liquors
Parker, Peter, hotel keeper
Parsons, William, carriage maker and blacksmith
Southwick, George, general merchant
Swift, Hiram, proprietor saw mill
South Norwich Co-operative Association, John Vanbuskirk, president
Tisdale, A. N., M.D.
Vanbusbirk, John, stoves and tinware

Oak Ridges.—A Post Village of the Township of Whitchurch, County York. Distance from Toronto 21 miles. Population 100.

Curtis, J., hotel keeper
Davy, George, hotel keeper
GREGORY, D., Postmaster
Gregory, Thomas, saw miller
McKenzie, Philip, builder
Mortson, T. & J., proprietor saw mill
O'Connor, William, shoemaker
Routledge, Peter, blacksmith

Parham.—A Village in the Township of Hinchinbrooke, County Addington, 38 miles from Kingston. Weekly mails. Population 80.

Bertram, Alexander, farmer
Bertram, William, farmer
Clow, Oliver, farmer
Cox, George and James, farmers
Grant, Mrs., storekeeper
GRIFFITH, JOHN A., Postmaster, gen. mercht
Hampton, John, farmer
Hampton, Thomas, farmer
Howe, Andrew, farmer
Lee, John, farmer
Ryan, Michael, farmer
Swerkirk, Henry, inn keeper
Vanalstine, John C., inn keeper
Wager, Redford, farmer

Penetanguishene.—A Village on the Bay of the same name, Lake Huron, in the Townships of Tiny and Tay, County Simcoe, 32 miles from Barrie, the County Town, and 97 from Toronto. This Village has long been a place of note, a military fort having been established here during the war of 1812, and kept up until a few years ago, when the garrison was withdrawn. The population consists in a great measure of French Canadians and half-breeds. There are also a considerable number of pensioners, who have neat habitations and small farms in the vicinity. The Provincial Reformatory is located about three miles from the Village. The Bay forms a good harbor and is a beautiful sheet of water, which, with its richly wooded shores forms a magnificent picture. A large trade in furs is carried on here. Stages tri-weekly to Barrie. Money Order Office and Savings Bank. Population 350.

Burke, Sergeant-Major David, drill instructor and guard Reformatory
Cadeau, Andrew, farmer
Carlisle, J., prop. New Dominion Hotel
Columbus, E., blacksmith
Columbus, L., blacksmith
Copeland, George, prop. flouring and saw mills
Corbeau, Francis, wagon maker
Darling, James, general agent
Delorme, C., wagon maker
Dunlop, A., general merchant
Dusome, Mrs., Northern Hotel
Featherstonhaugh, William, clerk and deputy Warden Reformatory
Gilmor, W. R., M. D., surgeon Reformatory
Gleeson, John, stone mason and keeper Reformatory
Hallen, Rev. George, (Church of England)
Jackson, William, ship builder
Jeffery, E. & H. E., general merchants
Jeffery, Henry, clerk Division Court
KELLY, WILLIAM MOORE, Warden Reformatory
Kennedy, Rev. J. P., (Roman Catholic) Chaplain to Reformatory
LaFreier, Antoine, wheelwright
Lannigan, Thomas, assessor and collector
Larush, P., photographer
Leduc, Thomas, farmer
Landrom, M., tanner
Lenioc, Xavier, blacksmith
Lynch, Michael, cooper and keeper Reformatory
McDonald, D. H., lumberer
McDonald, Edward, farmer
McLaughlin, Samuel, steward Reformatory
MITCHELL, D. J., Postmaster and lumber mercht. Agent Hudson Bay Fur Company
Moreau, Toussaint, baker
Mundy, Michael, farmer
Parker, Robert J., keeper Reformatory
Plo‹fe, Eusebe, saddler
Quinn, P., Globe Hotel
REFORMATORY, 3 miles from Village, William Moore Kelly, Warden
Reid. William, ship builder
Rolston Bros, (William & Peter) pot and pearl ash factory
Simpson, William, J. P., Collector Customs, Commissioner in B. R., &c.
Sneath, William C., cutter
Tannant, David, carpenter and keeper Reformatory
Thessier, Gilbert, Canada hotel
Thoscotte, Thos., tinsmith
Triffeau, S., carpenter
THOMPSON, A. A., general merchant
Thompson, H. H., general merchant
Weir, John, tailor
Wicher, Rev. J., (Wesleyan Methodist)
Wilkie, John, blacksmith
Wright, James, butcher

Perch Station.—A Post Office, in the Township of Sarnia, County Lambton.

IRWIN, JOHN, Postmaster.

Peterson's Ferry.—A small Village on the Bay of Quinte, in the Township of Sophiasburg, County Prince Edward, 14 miles from Picton, the County town, 2 from Mill Point, and 9 from Napanee. Population 25.

Black, C., farmer
Brickman, William H., farmer
Burlett, John & Son, carpenters
Carmen, Henry, farmer
Carmen, Thomas, farmer
Cole, Heman, farmer
Cronk, A. W., farmer
Cronk, David J., shoemaker
Cronk, James B., dyer and scourer
Dewitt, B. L., farmer
Dewitt, William L., farmer
Houtland, David, shingle maker
Mason, John, cooper
Noxon, G., farmer
PETERSON, PAUL C., Postmaster
Row, Benjamin, farmer
Solmes, D. B., J. P., insurance agent
Williams, George & Sons, broom manufacturers
Wilson, Isaac, farmer

Plantagenet.—A Post Village situated on the South Nation River, 5 miles from its junction with the Ottawa, in the Township of North Plantagenet, County Prescott. Distant from L'Orignal, the County Town, 18 miles; from Ottawa, 41 miles; and from Toronto, about 255. Money Order Office. Population, 200.

CHAMBERLAIN, W. A., Postmaster and general merchant
Duport, B., blacksmith
Eastman, Robert, tanner
Gauthier, L., shoemaker
Hagar, Albert, general merchant, lumber dealer, &c.
Larocque, Charles, groceries and liquors
Larocque, Joseph, proprietor hotel
Leduc, Pierre, tavern keeper
Lorocque, E., blacksmith
Mackay, Joseph, hotel keeper
O'Keefe, John, harness maker
Prentiss, G. W., M. D.
Yeon & Brother, hotel keepers

Pleasant Hill.—A Village in the Township of Walsingham, County Norfolk, 21 miles from Simcoe, the County Town, and 34 from Ingersoll. Population, 300.

Auger, Rev. N. T., (Primitive Methodist)
Auscomb, Rev. T., (Episcopal Methodist)
Brown, S. D., grocer
Botham, H., saddler
Christmas, George, carriage maker
Clark, H. B., farmer
Deacon, Rev. D., (Church of England)
Dibbell, James, proprietor woolen mill
Perris, George, farmer
Kincaid, R., hotel keeper
Layman, Thomas, farmer
MORGAN, W., Postmaster and general merchant
Russell, John, shoemaker
Smith, H., general merchant
Wilson, W., tanner
Wingrove, George, farmer

Porter's Hill.—A Post Office in the Township of Goderich, County Huron.
HENRY, JAMES, Postmaster and general merchant.

Port Talbot.—A Post Village in the Township of Dunwich, County Elgin.
MACBETH, GEORGE, Postmaster.

Prospect.—A Post Village in the Township of Beckwith, County Lanark.

BURROWS, WILLIAM, Postmaster, hotel keeper
Craig, Thomas, tanner
Craig, George, general merchant
James Brothers, proprietors saw mill
McGregor, Duncan, proprietor saw mill
Moffatt, Thomas, shoemaker
Riley, William, blacksmith
Tomlinson, J., shoemaker

Queenston.—A Village situated on the west bank of the Niagara River, in the Township of Niagara County Lincoln. It is connected with Lewiston, N. Y., by means of a suspension bridge across the river. The scenery in the vicinity is very beautiful. On the heights above the village is the Monument erected to General Brock. Distant from Niagara Falls, 7 miles; from Toronto by water, 48, and from Hamilton, 50 miles. Daily mail. Population about 450.

Boland, John, general merchant
Hunter, John, wagon maker
Kirkland, George, wheelwright
Palmer, William, hotel keeper
Pendergast & Brother, blacksmiths
Sullivan, John, groceries and liquors
Thorburn, Richard, M.D.
Wadsworth, Daniel, hotel keeper
Wadsworth, John, hotel keeper
Wray, Joseph, butcher
WYNN, JAMES, Postmaster and general merchant.

Queensborough.—A Post Village situated on Black Creek, in the Township of Elzevir, County Hastings. Distant from Belleville, the County Town, 36 miles. Population 100.

Jeffs, John, general merchant
Lingham, Thomas, general merchant, lumber, etc.
THOMPSON, DANIEL, Postmaster, proprietor grist and saw mills

Rothsay.—A Village in the Township of Maryboro', County Wellington, distant 29 miles from Guelph, the County Town, the River Conestogo passes through the Village affording excellent mill privileges. Daily Mail. Population 200.

Allen, George, boots and shoes
Barber, Charles, boots and shoes
Cartier, David W., general merchant
Fotheringham, John, wagon maker
Glintz, Frederick, prop. hotel
Gubb, William, miller
Hans, Henry, photographer
Hans Brothers, general merchants
Hastings, David, blacksmith
Haston, Luther, general merchant
Johnson, William, prop. hotel
Kilpatrick, Joseph, blacksmith
Knowles, J. S., general merchant
Lowes, W. H., general merchant
Lowry, Parker, prop. hotel
McKenzie, K., wagon maker
Moore, J. F., tailor
Ogden, John, carpenter
STULL, J. F. A., Postmaster, gen. merchant
Stull & Oliver, general merchants
Watchron, Robert, carpenter

Sandhurst.—A Village on the Bay of Quinte, in the Township of South Fredericksburgh, County Lennox, 12 miles from Napanee, the County Town. Stages to Kingston, 24 miles; and Wellington, 22 miles.

ALLEN, DAVID M., Postmaster
Asselstine, Nicholas, farmer
Chamberlain & Sills, manfrs. Shoshonees Remedy
Downey, Thomas, farmer
Fraser, Andrew, farmer
Ham, Ira, farmer
Harding, Rev. R. (Church of England)
Hickey, John, grocer
Hill, William, farmer
Lasher, B., farmer
Lloyd, R. N., carpenter
McDowell, Robert, shingle maker
Mallory, John, farmer
Murdock, John and Nicholas, carpenters
Neilson, Allen, farmer
Neilson, John, farmer
Phippen, William, potash factory
Rickely, William, cooper
Sills, D., farmer
Smith, Hiram, carpenter
Smith, William, carpenter
Wright, Solomon, farmer

Sand Point.—A Village and Station of the Brockville and Ottawa Railroad, on the River Ottawa, in the Township of McNab, County Renfrew, 45 miles from Pembroke, the County Town, 45 from Ottawa, and 54 from Perth. This was the earliest settled plot in the County, ana is the seat of an extensive lumber trade. Stages to Pembroke and Renfrew. Population 150.

Brown, James, station agent
Durenyi, E., general merchant
FOURDRINER, MRS., Postmistress
Lewis, L. C., hotel keeper
McDonell, Alexander, lumber merchant
McDonell, Duncan, general merchant
Murphy, W. H. & Co., comn and gen. agents
Usborne, John, forwarding and comn merchant
Ward & Scott, props. saw mills
Young, James, hotel keeper

Scotland.—A Village in the Township of Oakland, County Brant, 11 miles from Brantford, the County Town, and 14 from Paris Station. Stages to Simcoe, and Paris. Money Order Office. Population 500.

Bowman, George A., blacksmith
Corbin, C. F., painter
Eddy, C.
Flanigan, John, carpenter
Foster, Alonzo, clerk Division Court and issuer of marriage licenses
Gillespie, Robert, tanner
Grevoir, Jacob, cooper
Hamilton, Alexander, teacher
Hay, Rev. William (Congregational)
Hixon, Henry F., carpenter
Hooker, Albert, carriage maker
Lawrence, Thomas, blacksmith
Loughurst, John, boots and shoes
LYMAN, HENRY, Postmaster, general merchant
McLean, John, M. D.
Malcolm, Augustus, farmer
Malcolm, Eddy, cooper
Malcolm, Edgar & Co., druggists
Malcolm, Eliakim, J. P., farmer
Malcolm, George, general merchant
Malcolm, George, carpenter
Malcolm, Hugh, boots and shoes
Malcolm, J. R., proprietor flouring mill
Malcolm, Marcus, manufacturer woolen goods
Malcolm, William C.
Martin, William, carpenter
Merritt, Isaac B.
Pettet, John G., bailiff
Phillips, George, carriage maker

Pilkey, P. J., hotel and livery
Pollard, A. T., tailor
Powers, John, cabinet maker
Prouse, Thomas O., general merchant
Pretty, Henry, carpenter
Reynolds, William J., carriage maker
Scott, R. & R., saddlers
Sullivan, Robert, blacksmith
Taylor, John, carriage maker
Tegart, E. W., M.D.
Thatcher, J., hotel keeper
Tucker, Richard, tinsmith
Vining, Rev. J. E. (Baptist)
Wheeland, Thomas, farmer
Whiting, Charles, cabinet maker

Sherkston.—A Post Office in the Township of Humberstone, County Welland.
STRINGER, A. O., Postmaster.

Silver Creek.—A Post Office in the Township of Esquesing, County Halton.
DEAN, JOHN, Postmaster
Preston, Mrs., hotel keeper

Silver Shoe.—A Post Village in the township of Sunnidale, County Simcoe, 17 miles distant from Barrie, the County town. Daily mail. Population 100.

Fisk, S., saw miller
Fleming, Andrew, blacksmith
Glen, James, hotel prop.
MATHER, JAMES A., Postmaster, gen mercht, Commissioner in B. R., issuer marriage licenses
Prentice, Alexander, saw mill prop.
Switzer, Robert, hotel prop.

South Dummer.—A Post Office in the Township of Dummer, Counto Peterboro'.
SPEER, W. M., Postmaster.

Stafford.—A Post Office in the Township of Stafford, County Renfrew.

Brown, William, farmer
CHILDERHOSE, ROBERT, Postmaster, farmer
Clark, Andrew, farmer
Hamilton, James, farmer
Mick, Daniel, farmer
Sparling, George, farmer
Teebo, B., farmer
Young, Richard, farmer

Sunnidale.—A Post village in the Township of Sunnidale, County Simcoe, and is a station on the Northern Railway, 25 miles from Barrie the county town and 89 from Toronto. Daily mail. Population 100.

Armstrong, John, farmer
Bell, Alexander, farmer
Blair, Malcolm, teacher
Coleman, John, farmer
Dean, Ephraim, J.P
Ferguson, John, teacher
Tyfe, James, farmer
Gilchrist, Alexander, farmer
GILLESPIE, ALEXANDER, J. P., Postmaster and farmer
Gowan, R., county judge, M.P.P
Greenfield, Rev. J., (United Presbyterian)
Howe, William, farmer
McDonald, Rev. A., (Church of Scotland)
McNeill, Archibald, farmer
Machan, Thomas, J.P
Mather, John, general merchant
Patton, Andrew, general merchant
Shaw, James, farmer
Tucker, Rev. Mr., (Methodist)

Sutton, (Georgina, P.O.)—A village in the Township of Georgina, County York, near Lake Simcoe, 55 miles from Toronto. Daily stage to Newmarket. Money Order Office. Population 850.

Armstrong, Robert, boots and shoes
BOURCHIER, J. O., Postmaster, proprietor grist and saw mills
Brooks, William, boots and shoes
Cole, Warren, tinsmith
Ego, Angus, J.P.
England, George, prop. woollen mills
Fair, Robert, tailor
Fry, George, general merchant
Fry, William
Grant, Alexander, wagon maker
Hill, Moses, tannery and boots and shoes
Kemp, George, butcher
McCardill, James
McCleary, William, wagon maker
McDonald, John, wharfinger
Major, Sidney, proprietor hotel
Moran, James, boots and shoes
Mossington, Miss S., milliner
Nichol, Robert, tailor
Noble, Charles T., M.D.
Orr, W. & A. B., general merchants
Ramsey, Charles & William, builders
RIDDELL, C., J.P.
Ronan, Thomas, boots and shoes
Sheppard, Joseph, hotel keeper
Stevenson, J. R., general merchant
Till, Robert, wagon maker
Trelvar, Henry, J.P., blacksmith

Sweaburg.—A Post village in the Township of West Oxford, County Oxford, 5½ miles from Woodstock, the County Town, and 8 from Ingersoll. Population about 200.

Bastedo, J. R., saw mill and shingle maker
Budd, Joseph, proprietor saw mill
Carr, John, proprietor saw mill
Cody, J. A. general merchant
Collins, John, hotel keeper
FLOOD, HARVEY, Postmaster, general merchant
Thompson, P., proprietor hotel

Teeterville.—A Post village, situated on Big Creek, in the Township of Windham, County Norfolk, 13 miles distant from Simcoe, the County Town, and 7 from Scotland. Population about 150.

Armstrong Edward, shoemaker
Cole, Henry, blacksmith
EDGEWORTH, THOMAS, Postmaster
Edgeworth & Robertson, dry goods
Gray, John, blacksmith
Ireland, R., hotel keeper
McKnight, James, mill owner
Mitchell, Thomas, boot maker
Pugsley, Josiah, cabinet maker
Robertson & Teeter, shingle factory
Robinson, James, general merchant
Robinson, William, general merchant
Snow, Nicholas, wagon maker
Sparrow, J. W., M.D.
Teeter, G. & W. H., proprietors saw and grist mill
Teeter, W. H. & Solomon, props. saw and grist mill
Watts, Henry, blacksmith

Thamesford.—A Village on the River Thames, in the Township of East Nissouri, County Oxford, 12 miles from Woodstock, the County Town, 13 from London, and 5 from Ingersoll. Money Order Office. Population 200.

Baker, James, cooper
Brock, John, grocer
Brown, William, general merchant
Dawes, Thomas, M. D.
Garner, Peter, potash factory
Houghton, Elihu, harness maker
Hull, Hazard, machinist
Hull & Kennedy, blacksmiths and wagon makers
Johns, John, proprietor grist and saw mills
Lee, John, proprietor hotel
McCARTY, N. C., Postmaster, general merchant
McCarty, A. J., painter
McKay, John, tailor
McLellan & Johnson, blacksmiths and wagon makers
McLeod, Joel, proprietor hotel
McMurray, James, sewing machines
Martin, John, general merchant
Shafer, O. F., nursery
Sugden & Son, proprietor woolen mill
Sutherland, Donald, conveyancer

Thamesville.—A Village and station on the Great Western Railway, in the Township of Camden, County Kent, 15 miles from Chatham, the County Town, 50 from London and 12 from Morpeth. About 3 miles from this village is the Indian settlement of Moravian Town, the site of the "Battle of the Thames," in which fell the celebrated Indian warrior, Tecumseth, in the forty-fourth year of his age. Thamesville is a Money Order Office. Mails daily. Population 700.

Adair, Robert, boots and shoes
Barling, James, dealer in wood and coal
Beck, F. T., general merchant
Bedford, John, general merchant
Boosey, J. E., stationer
Decow, Ezekiel, general merchant
DUNCAN, JAMES, Postmaster, gen. merchant
Ferguson & Sons, props. saw mill
Fox, Christopher, saloon keeper
Gillis, L., veterinary surgeon
Hoag, Joseph, wagon maker
Hynes, James, tailor
Kelly, George, wagon maker and blacksmith
Kendrick Absalom, tanner
Kendrick, Solomon, harness maker
Lake, Charles, M.D
Lawrence, Frederick, prop. flouring & carding mills
Lancaster, Richard, hotel keeper
McAnally, Arthur, hotel keeper
McFarlane, Daniel, general merchant
McKinley, William, barrister
Maloche, J. B., blacksmith
Mayhew, F. T., general merchant
Mayhew, William & Co., hardware
Metzner, William, shoemaker
Mimmach, William, wagon maker
Mountford, J. G., hotel keeper
Murray, J., flour and feed
Orr, George M., photographer, stationer, &c
Paupst, Benjamin, merchant tailor
Pulaski, Joseph, cabinet maker
Robinson, Benjamin, prop. grist mill
Sersion, J., harness maker
Shaw, A. J. C., general merchant
Shirren, Andrew, blacksmith
Simpkins, J., blacksmith
Spackman, G. F., hardware, stoves, &c
Swisher, Richard, M.D
Tye, G. A., M.D
Watts, William, hotel keeper
Wilson, J. W., general merchant

Thistletown.—A Post-office in the Township of Vaughan, County York, W.R. (See Village of Green Grove.)

Troy.—A Post Office in the Township of Beverley, County Wentworth, situated on Fairchild's Creek and on the Dumfries and Beverley plank road, 18 miles from Hamilton and 12 from Paris. Population 200.

Bennet, Jesse, shingle maker
Blasdell, John, farmer
Cassady, Isaac, butcher
Clark, George, general merchant
Cornell, Thomas, farmer
Cumming, Mrs. John (widow)
Cumming, John, farmer
Elliott, William, wagon maker
Farmers' Inn, John Patton, proprietor
Gamble, John, farmer
Houghkenberg, F., shoemaker
Johnson, John, farmer
Jones, Andrew, farmer
Jones, William, farmer
Laidlaw, Adam, farmer
Lawrison, James, jun., farmer
Lawrison, James, sen., farmer
Lawrason, Sydney, farmer
McCormick, Michael
Mather, David, blacksmith
Misener, Adam, proprietor saw mill
Misener, Michael, farmer
Misener, Clark & John, farmers
Mulholland, George, farmer
Mulholland, Hugh, farmer
Mullett, John, laborer
NEFF, JOHN, (Neff & Sager), Postmaster
Neff & Sager, general merchants
Nesbet, Barney, farmer
O'Reilly, D., blacksmith
Pirton, John, proprietor Farmers Inn
Rector, William, farmer
Robb, William, farmer
Roelofson, J. & E. B., cabinet makers, etc.
Roelofson, William, farmer
Segar, Dennis
Segar, Malachi, jun.
Segar, Malachi, sen.
Segar, Nathaniel (Neff & Segar)
Sherwas, John, lime burner
Suple, William, farmer
Warner, Thomas, proprietor saw mill
Wilson, James, mill proprietor
Wilson, William, tailor
Wood, George, farmer
Wood, Lewis, farmer
Wood, Samuel, farmer

Tyrone.—A small Village in the Township of Darlington, County Durham. Distant from Cobourg, the County Town, 36 miles, and from Toronto 45 miles. Population 300.

WELCH, JOHN T., Postmaster.

Underhill.—A Village in the County of Simcoe, now commonly called Nicholston, (see page 336)

***West Port.**—A village situated on the Rideau Canal, in the Township of North Crosby, County Leeds. Steamboats pass West Port on the lake, in plying between Kingston and Ottawa. Distant from Brockville, the County Town, 45 miles; from Kingston, 40; and from Ottawa, 60 miles. Daily mail. Pop. 600

Alguire, W. W., general merchant
Arnold, H. T., general merchant
Brash, Robert, carpenter
Cameron, F. A., hotel keeper
Clark, Joel, jr., proprietor woolen mill
Dier, William, blacksmith
Douglass, George, boots and shoes
Fife, William, carriage maker
Foley, Deeland, general merchant
Fredenburgh, W. H., mill proprietor
Hartwell, S. A., general merchant
Jackelo, J., hotel keeper
Kearns, Samuel, carpenter
Kelly, Henry, tailor
Kelly, Mrs. Ann, groceries
Kelly, Peter, carriage maker
Kerr, George, cooper
Leslie, John, hotel keeper
McAllister, Alexander, boots and shoes
McCaw, Thomas, foundry
McGuire, John, boots and shoes
Middleton, E., millwright
Mulvadill, James, groceries and liquors
Murphy, George, blacksmith
Murphy, Patrick, boots and shoes
O'Neil, John, blacksmith
Ripley, Samuel, blacksmith
Scott, M. W., tanner
WHELAN, WALTER, general merchant
WHELAN, JAMES, postmaster

MONTREAL,

PROVINCE OF QUEBEC.

Montreal.—The chief City of British North America, situated on a large and beautiful island of the same name, about 30 miles in length by 10 miles in extreme breadth, formed by the confluence of the Ottawa and St. Lawrence Rivers, and on the north bank of the latter. It is at the head of ocean navigation, and the foot of lake and river navigation, about 90 miles above tide water and 300 miles from salt water, possessing all the advantages of a sea coast City and inland navigation combined. It is accessible by vessels of over 1,800 tons burthen, and has direct communication with London, Liverpool, Glasgow, and all foreign ports. It is the chief manufacturing City of the Province, and many of its establishments will compare favorably with those of any other country. Montreal, as seen from any approach, with Mont Royal in the background, together with the beautiful villas, glittering roofs and domes, tall spires and lofty towers, present, to the beholder, a vast, picturesque, and grand panorama. The principal streets are Great St. James, Notre Dame, St. Paul, Commissioners and McGill. Among such a large number of elegant public buildings we may mention the Bonsecours Market, built at a cost of $287,300, one of the finest buildings on the continent, the Court House, costing $296,569, the French Cathedral, the Bank of Montreal, Bank of British North America, the Custom House, McGill College, Jesuit College, Post Office, St. George's and many other churches, all ornaments to the City. The City is well lighted with gas, and the water works are almost unequalled. The water is drawn from St. Lawrence about a mile and a half above the Lachine Rapids, and through an open canal led into a basin, from which it is forced to the reservoir upon the brow of the mountain, several hundred feet above the level of the City. The harbor and basin are good and safe, and capable of enlargement to almost any extent to accommodate the future wants of the City. The wharves, between one and two miles in length, are surmounted with a massive stone wall, upon the heights of which are a promenade and wide street, affording an excellent view of the river and shipping. There are numerous inclined planes from the wharves to the street above, by which carriages ascend and descend, and the whole for appearance, cleanliness and commodiousness, is unexcelled by any port on the continent. From Point St. Charles, at the head of the harbor, to St. Lambert, on the opposite side of the river, a distance of about two miles, has been built the Victoria Bridge, unsurpassed by any other structure of the kind in the world. It has two long abutments and twenty-four piers of solid stone masonry. The bridge is built of iron, on the tubular principle, and makes a complete line of railway from Sarnia, on the St. Clair River, in the extreme western section of the province, to Portland, Maine, giving Montreal an unbroken railway communication of over 1,100 miles in length, with numerous tributaries and connections. The trains of the Grand Trunk Railway leave Montreal daily for all points, both ways, on the line in Canada and the United States. A line of splendid steamers ply weekly between Montreal and Liverpool, carrying the mails, in summer; and between Liverpool and Portland semi-monthly in winter. In the season of navigation steamers ply daily from Montreal to all the principal towns and cities in the province situated on the lakes and rivers. Montreal is distant from Liverpool, 2,750 miles; Quebec, 180 miles; Kingston, 173 miles; from Toronto, 333 miles; Ottawa, 120 miles; Portland, 292 miles; New York, 400 miles; and from Boston, 334 miles. Population about 130,000.

ABBOTT, HON. JOHN J. C., Q.C., M.P., advocate, 47 St. John

ACADEMIE COMMERCIALE CATHOLIQUE DE MONTREAL, U. F., Archambault, principal, 31 and 33 Cotte

Ackermann & Minough, plumbers, steam and gasfitters, tinworkers, 105 Vitre

Adams, A., hardware merchant, 139 St. Lawrence

Adams, Francis, engraver and copperplate printer, 99 St. Peter

Adams, J. A., manfrs agent, 30 St. Francois Xavier

Adams, James D., gro. and liquors, 257 St. Lawrence

Adams, R., comn merchant, 70 St. Janvier

ADCOCK & ENGLISH, wholesale importers of electro silver plated ware, spoons, forks, etc. 301 Commissioners (see adv.)

ADJUTANT GENERAL'S OFFICE, Colonel Thackwell, 31 Notre Dame

AGNEW, S. A., jewelry and fancy goods, 294, 296 and 374 Notre Dame

Aitken, John & Co., manfrs and imprs of gentlemen's hosiery and ladies' underclothing, 377 Notre Dame

Akin & Kirkpatrick, flour, provn and comn mers., 20 Foundling

Akin, Thomas, grocer, 2 Grand Trunk

ALBION HOTEL, Decker & Co., props. McGill

Alexander, Rev. John, pastor First Baptist Church, 24 St. Monique
Allan, Hugh & Andrew, general shipping agents, and agents, Montreal Ocean Steamship Co., cor Common and Youville
Allan, James, coal and wood mer., 636 Craig
Allan, John, merchant, 425½ Notre Dame
Allan, Thomas, merchant, 133 Richmond
Allard, Charles, carriage maker, 19 Mount Royal
ALLOWAY, ARTHUR WILLIAM, veterinary surgeon, Royal horse bazaar and Riding school, 30 Cotté.
Ambler, Samuel, commission merchant, 67 St. Elizabeth
AMERICAN HOUSE, C. S. Browne, proprietor, cor St. Henry and St. Joseph (see adv)
AMES, MILLARD & CO., wholesale boot and shoe manufacturers, 23 St. Peter
AMOS, A. & E., importers of French calfskins, patent leather, calf, kid and morocco, 25 St. Peter
ANCE, L,ABBE FRANCOIS, 165 Craig
Anderson, James D., merchant tailor, 124 Great St. James
Anderson, John & Co., shipping, importing, forwarding and commission merchants, 86 and 88 McGill
Anderson, Robert, merchant, 67 St. Francis Xavier
Anderson, T. B., President Bank of Montreal, and chairman of London and Liverpool and Globe Ins. Co., corner Gt St James and Place d'Armes
Andrews, H. O., advocate, 330 Bleury
Andrews, John, Professor High School of McGill College, 19 Courville
Angers, Edmond, boot and shoe manufacturer, wholesale and retail, 339 Notre Dame, cor St. Francois Xavier
Angus, Logan & Co., wholesale paper and stationery importers, printing and wrapping paper manufacturers, 378 St. Paul
Angus, Richard B., manager Bank of Montreal, 1 Great St. James
Ansell, D. A., importer of foreign goods, 8 Union buildings, 43 St. Francois Xavier
Antoine, Rev. E., church of the Oblats Fathers, 95 Visitation
Aoustin, Rev. M., Seminary of St. Sulpice, 320 Notre Dame
Archambault, Amable, notary, 10 Little St. James
Archambault, Dr. D. D., 435 St. Joseph
ARCHAMBAULT, P. A. O., advocate, 43 St. Vincent
Archambault, Rev. J., St. James R. C. church, 473 St. Catherine
Archambault, U. E., principal of Montreal Catholic commercial academy, 31 and 33 Cotte
Archer, David, silver and brass plater, and manufacturer of saddlery & carriage hardware, 304 Craig
Archer, F. B., commissary general, 891 Sherbrooke
Archer, Labelle & Co., flour and grain merchants, 10 Port
Archibald & Richardson, grocers, wine and spirit merchants, 392 and 394 Notre Dame, cor St. Alexis
Armstrong, R. J., grocer and wine merchant, 191 McGill
Arnton, John J., auctioneer and real estate agent, 364 Notre Dame
Arrand, Rev., M., procureur Seminary of St. Sulpice, 320 Notre Dame
Art Association of Montreal, Lord Bishop of Montreal president; T. D. King, curator Mechanics Hall, 108 Great St. James
Ascher & Co., wholesale dealers in watches, jewelry, plated ware and fancy goods, 393 St. Paul
Association of Underwriters, 22 St. John, cor. Hospital
Atwater, E. & Co., oil, lead and colour merchants, 17, 19 and 21 St. Nicholas
Aubin, Fred., groceries, liquors, wines, 32 Dupre Lane
Aubry, Charles B., baker, 457 St. Mary
AUERBACH, Z. & CO., watchmakers and jewelers, 422 Notre Dame
Auger, A. J., commission merchant, and dealer in lumber, laths, shingles, etc., Vitre and St. Elizabeth
Auger, J. B. & Co., forwarders and ship builders, office, 85 and 89 Common, ship yard, cor. Etienne and Canal
Auger, Jean Bte., manager Montreal and Ottawa Forwarding Co., 1181 Dorchester
Ault, Charles, M. E., 768 St. Catherine
Austin & Co., wholesale grocers, 26 & 28 St. Maurice, cor. St. Henry
Austin, James, boot and shoe maker, 145 Richmond
Ayer & Beatie, produce merchants, 36 St. Sacrament
AYLWIN, HON. THOMAS C., judge, 34 Notre Dame
Azile St. Antoine, superior and director, Eusèbe de Poorter, 255 to 261 Dorchester
Baccerini, G. & Co., manufacturers of statuary, 14 Gosford
BACON, LIEUT. COLONEL T., brigade major militia, 63 St. Gabriel
BADEAUX, P. B., customhouse agent, office No. 14, 301 Commissioners
Badger, F. H., chief telegraph operator, City Hall, 186 St. Paul
BADGLEY, HON. WILLIAM, judge, 64 McGill college av
Bailey, Henry, local superintendent G. T. R., 951 Dorchester
Baillargeon, Joseph, groceries, liquors and provisions, 458 and 460 St. Mary
Baillie, James & Co., importers of dry goods, wholesale, 480 St. Paul and 401 Commissioners
Baird & Crawford, grocers and wine merchants, wholesale and retail, 123 Great St. James
Baird, James, hardware, 153 Wellington
BAKER, POPHAM & CO., wholesale clothiers, 512 St. Paul
Bakewell, Rev. Frederick, St. Patrick's house 92 St. Alexander
BALCH, REV. CANON, D.D Christ., Church cathedral, 581 Sherbrooke
Baldwin, C. H. & Co., commission merchants, importers and wholesale dealers in wines, groceries and cigars 8 St. Helen
Baldwin, Rev. Maurice S., M.A., incumbent St. Luke's church, 161 Jacques Cartier
Bolfour, Robert, groceries, wines and liquors, 121 St. Urbain, cor Dorchester
Balmain, Rev. John, minister Cross Church, Marlborough, Hochelaga
Baltzly, B. F., photographer, 372 Notre Dame
Bancroft, E. I. & Co., livery and boarding stables, 591 Lagauchetière
Bancroft, Rev. Charles, D.D., incumbent of Trinity Church, and honorary canon of Christ Church cathedral, 26 Berri off Viger sq
Bancroft & Sharpe, city express, and wholesale fruit depot, 93 Gt St James
Bangs, Isaiah L. & Co., felt and composition roofing, 9 Place d'Armes hill
BANK OF BRITISH NORTH AMERICA, Thomas Paton, general manager; A. C. Hooper, manager, 34 and 36 Gt St James

BANK OF MONTREAL, SAVINGS BANK DEPARTMENT, Henry Vennor, manager, Place d'Armes
BANK OF MONTREAL, T. B. Anderson, president; E. H. King, general manager; Richard B. Angus, manager, Place d'Armes
BANK OF TORONTO, J. Murray Smith, accountant, 109 Great St. James
BANQUE DU PEUPLE, B. H. Lemoine, cashier, 9 Gt St James
BANQUE JACQUES CARTIER, H. Cotté, cashier, 49 Gt St James
Barbarin, Rev. A., Seminary of St Sulpice, 320 Notre Dame
Barbeau Edmond J., actuary, City and District Savings bank, 8 Gt St James
Barbeau, F. X., dry goods, 77 St. Joseph
Barcello, H. M., M. D., 402 St. Catherine
Barclay, Capt. John, superintendent Montreal Ocean Steamship Company, 55 Victoria
BARDEY, REV. J., Seminary of St. Sulpice, 320 Notre Dame
Barnard, John G., civil engineer, superintendent Grand Trunk Railway, 917 St. Catherine
Barnard & Pagnuelo, advocates, 487 Craig
Barnjum, Frederick S., professor of physical culture, 259 Aqueduct
Barrett, Rev. B., curate, St. Henri, Tannery, west
Barrett, Richard, commission merchant, 9 William
Barrington, George, manufacturer of trunks, valises, and bellows, 429 Notre Dame
Bartley, W. P. & Co., St. Lawrence engine works, 17 Mill
Bastian, Thomas, boots and shoes, 52 Gt. St. James
Bateman & Cowper, machinists, 53 Dalhousie
Bathgate & Brother, tobacco merchants 9 St. John
Battersby, D , real estate agent and general collector, 67 Great St. James
Baudry, J. U., clerk of appeals, 296 Dorchester
Bayard, Noel, contractor, 202 St. Andre
Bayley, Thomas Way, barrister, 118 St. Bonaventure
Baylis, Henry, Montreal Varnish Company, 18 Latour
Baylis, James, carpet and oil cloth warehouse, 140 Great St. James
Baynes, W. C., M. A., secretary and bursar McGill university,, office, Burnside Hall, Dorchester
Bazin, Dr. James A., surgeon dentist, 36 Beaver Hall Terrace
Beardsall, William Francis, glue, size and neats foot oil manfr. Dominion glue works, 255 Fullum
BEATTY, JOHN, foreman *Daily Witness* 12 Montcalm
Beau, C. & J. B. Hupe, New York Sample Rooms, 573 and 575 Craig
BEAUBIEN, LOUIS, M.P.P., Cote St. Catharine
Beaubien, Pierre, M.D., 606 Craig cor St. Francois Xavier
Beaubien, Rev. C., vicar, St. Vincent de Paul, 85 Fullum
Beauchamp, Alderic, watchmaker and jeweler, 128 St. Lawrence
Beauchamp, Francois X., manufacturing jeweler, 134 St. Francois Xavier
Beauchamps, L. E., & Co., dry goods, 89 Notre Dame
BEAUCHEMIN, C. O. & VALOIS, booksellers, bookbinders and printers, 237 and 239 St. Paul
Beaudoin & Senecal, grocers, 47 St. Mary
Beaudry & Dufresne, watchmakers, jewelers and importers of fancy goods, 180 Notre Dame
Beaudry, G. N. L., advocate, 1 Drummond
Beaudry, J. A. U., surveyor and architect, patent solicitor, 296 Dorchester
Beaudry, J. & Cie, general dry goods, 268 Notre Dame
Beaudry, J. Napoleon, sec-treas. Richelieu Co., 164 Visitation
BEAUDRY, JEAN L., president La Banque Jacques Cartier, 1 Drummond
Beaudry, Louis, managing director, New City Gas Co., office, 223 Notre Dame
Beaudry, Narcisse, watches, clocks and jewelry, 43 St. Lambert Hill
Beaudry, Pierre, prothonotary's office, 71 St. Hubert
Beaudry, Rev. C., St. V., parish priest, Cote, St. Louis
Beaufield & Brodie, notaries, 60 Little St. James
Beaufort, E., wine merchant, 261 St. Antoine
Beaumont & Buchignani, Delmonico lunch room, 79-81 St. Francis Xavier
Becker, Albert, wool card manfr. 14 William
BECKET, JOHN C., printer and pub. 76 Gt. J. James
Bedard, Louis, notary, 10 Little St. James
Bedard, Rev. Pierre J. Bte., vicar, Notre Dame de Grace
Beers, James Crawford, city assessor, 284 St. George
Belair, L. R. dit Plessis, dry goods importer, 283 and 285 St. Lawrence
Belanger & Desnoyers, advocates, 11 Little St. James
Belanger, J. A., C.P.S.G., Cote St. Louis
Belanger, Joseph, soap manfr, Cote St. Louis
Belanger, Rev. Alfred, P.S.V., director of Deaf and Dumb Institution, Cote St. Loius
Belanger, Stanislas, grain merchant, 234 St. Lawrence
Belisle & Haly, dry goods, 61 Notre Dame
Beliveau, Aime, Richelieu Hotel, 47 St. Vincent
Beliveau, Hilaire, gen hardware mer. 193 & 195 St. Paul
Beliveau, Joseph, prop. Jacques Cartier Hotel, 29 Jacques Cartier sq
Beliveau, Louis J. & Co., wholesale and retail hardware mers, 297 and 299 St. Paul
Bell & Higgins, wine merchants, 48 St. Joseph
Bell, J. & T., boot and shoe manfrs, wholesale, Cathedral Block, 273 Notre Dame
Bell, James, assistant superintendent G. T. R., 110 Congregation
Bell, John, M.A., M.D., resident surgeon Montreal general hospital, 422 Dorchester
Belle, Charles E., notary, Crown timber agent, 42 Little St James
Belle, Dr. G. E. A., dentist, 471 Craig
Belle, J. A. Achille, advocate, 7 St Lambert
Belle, Joseph, notary, 471 Craig
Bellemare, Raphael, advocate, collector of inland revenue, 26 Little St James
Bellhouse, David, ironmasters agent, 17 St Sacrament
Bellhouse, J. G., com. merchant, 17 St Sacrament
BELLINGHAM, SYDNEY, M.P.P., Côte St Catherine
BELVIDGE MINING AND SMELTING CO., George B. Cramp, secretary, 59 Gt St James
Benjamin, William & Co., importers of dry goods, wholesale, 493 St Paul
Bennett, J. D., manufacturer of plate chests, cabinets, dressing cases, &c., 26 St Lambert
BENNING & BARSALOU, auctioneers and commission merchants, 48 and 50 St Peter
Benny, MacPherson & Co., wholesale hardware merchants, 392 St Paul
Benson, John W., dry goods, small wares, clocks and chair cane, 398 and 400 St Paul, cor Custom house sq
BENSON, WILLIAM T., of Edwardsburg Starch Co., 37 St Peter
BENTLEY, DAVID, printer, 175 St George
Bernard & Davis, surgeon dentists, 564 Craig
Barry, William, machinist and engineer, printing press and sewing machine manufacturer, 567 Lagauchetiere cor Anderson

Berthelet, Dr. Benjamin, physician and surgeon, 64 St. Denis cor Dorchester
Berthelot, Hon. J. A., judge, 290 Lagauchetiere
Berthiaume & Fils, dry goods, 16 Jacques Cartier sq
Berthiaume, Wilderick & Co., dry goods, 115 Notre Dame
Bertin, Rev. L., Seminary of St. Sulpice, 320 Notre Dame
Bertram, Alexander, chief engineer fire department, City Hall
Bertrand & David, merchant tailors, 98 Notre Dame
Bertrand, Magloire, general dry goods, 139 Notre Dame
Bessey, William E., M.D., C.M., 24 St. Radegonde
Bethune, Strachan, Q.C., advocate, 54 Little St. James
BETHUNE, VERY REV. JOHN, D.D., Dean of Montreal and Rector of Christ Church Cathedral, 44 McGill College ave
Bettes, H., M.D., 232 St. Antoine
BIBAUD, J. G., M.D., prof. anatomy, University of Victoria College, Montreal branch, 12 Cotte
Bibaud, J. J. E., advocate, 386 Jacques Cartier
Bibaud, Maximilian, LL.D., 33 St. Lambert
BILLAUDELE, REV. PIERRE, vicar general, Seminary of St. Sulpice, 320 Notre Dame
Billings, E., F.G.S., paleontologist Geological survey
Billion, Rev. L., Seminary of St. Sulpice, 320 Notre Dame
Binmore, Charles, merchant, 55 City Councillors
Biron, Samuel, grocer, wine and spirit merchant, 57 St. Joseph
Biscornais, Julien, proprietor Quebec Hotel, 171 St. Paul
BISHOP, GEORGE & CO., engravers, lithographers and printsellers, 53 Great St. James (see adv)
Bissett, Alexander, superintendent Lachine Canal, 5 Hanover
Black, James F. D., city treasurer, 184 Mountain
Black, Lewis S. & Thom, wholesale merchants and importers of dry goods, McGill
Black & Locke, leather and commission merchants, 494 St. Paul
Black, Rev. David (Canada Presbyterian Church) Cote St. Antoine
Black, Rev. William M. (Church of Scotland), 98 Mansfield
Blacklock, John, groceries, liquors and provisions, 181 St. Lawrence
Bleakley, John, advocate, 34 Little St. James
BLOMELY, EDWIN, proprietor coal oil stores, 405 and 407 Wellington
BOARD OF AGRICULTURE, George Leclere, M.D., secretary, cor Craig and Chenneville
BOARD OF ARTS AND MANUFACTURES, H. Bulmer, president; A. A. Stevenson, secretary; office Mechanics' hall, 108 Great St. James
BOARD OF NOTARIES, 18 Little St. James
BOARD OF STOCK BROKERS, E. Ford, secretary, Merchants Exchange, 11 St. Sacrament
BOARD OF TRADE, W. J. Patterson, secretary, 1 St. John
Boisseau, Alfred, photographer and portrait painter, 84 Great St. James
BOIVIN, GUILLAUME, manufacturer of boots and shoes, wholesale, 317 and 319 St. Paul
Bolton, George F., M R.C.V.S., veterinary surgeon, 32 Bleury
Bonald, Dr. G. S. de, member of La Société Impériale des Arts, Sciences et Belles Lettres de France; Hydropathic or water cure establishment, 255 Dorchester
Bonar, Rev. James B., minister American Presbyterian church, 916 Dorchester
Bonaventure Street Railway Station, for Grand Trunk and Lachine Railways, off Chaboillez square, bet St. Joseph and St. Bonaventure
BOND, FRANK, stock and share broker, 7 St. Sacrament
BOND, REV. CANON WILLIAM B., A.M., incumbent of St. George's church, and rural dean of Hochelaga, 16 Phillips square
Bondy, D. D., advocate, 585 Craig
Bonin, Edmond, National hotel, 348 Commissioners
Bonnell, Walter, leather and general commission merchant, 3 St. Helen
Bonner, Isaac, agent, Montreal and Ottawa forwarding Co., 107 Duke
BONNEVILLE & GARIEPY, commission merchants, 65 Common
Bonnissant, Rev. Mathurin, Seminary of St. Sulpice, 320 Notre Dame
BONSECOURS DEAF AND DUMB FEMALE INSTITUTION, sister Mary, directress, head of St. Denis
Booker, A., auctioneer and commission merchant, 361 Notre Dame
Borland, Rev. John, 268 Lagauchetiére
Borthwick, Rev. J. Douglass, incumbent St. Mary's Church, Hochelaga
Boswell, H. J., agent Manhattan Life Insurance Co., 66 St. François Xavier
Bothwell, John A., advocate, 119 St. François Xavier
Boucher, George, leather merchant and dealer in shoe findings, 407 St. Paul
Boudreau, A. A., banker and broker, exchange and specie dealer, 62 St. François Xavier
BOUDRIAS, DOMINIQUE, professor and president Union St. Pierre, 389 St. Catharine
Boulton & Goodall, paper collar manufactory, 14 William
Bourbonniere, Narcisse G., notary, 18 St. Therese
Bourbonniere, Toussaint B., notary public, 616 St. Mary
Borgeau, Victor, architect, 106 German
Bourgeois, David & Co., importers of French wines, Paris fancy goods, boots and shoes, 233 Notre Dame
Bourgeois, Louis Phillippe, groceries, wines and liquors, 58 Lagauchetiere
BOURGET, MONSEIGNEUR IGNAC, R. C. Bishop of Montreal, Bishop's Palace, between Cemetery and St. Margaret
Bourgouin, N. H., advocate, 29 St. Vincent
Bourgouin, Octave, contractor, 147 St. Elizabeth
Bourrett, H. A., money order and savings bank department, Post Office, 594 St. Urban
Bouthillier, C. F., advocate, 34 Little St. James
Bouthillier, Jude, advocate, 43 Inspector
BOUTHILLIER, TANCREDE, sheriff, Court House, 177 Notre Dame
Bowie, George, sen., contractor, 44 Bleury
Bowie, W. B. & Co., importers of British and foreign dry goods, 395 Notre Dame
Bowman, Smith & Co., commission merchants, 35 St. Nicholas
Boyce, Michael, notary, 591 St. Joseph
Boyd, Egan & Co., custom house forwarding and gen. commission merchants, 7 Common
Boyd, Robert W., bookseller and stationer, commission agent and general collector, 13½ Place d'Armes
Boyd, Thomas W., gun maker and fishing tackle warehouse, 241 Notre Dame

BOYER, HUDON & CO., wholesale produce, provision and grocery merchants, Customs House Square
Boyer, Louis, M.D., 54 St. Dennis
Boyer, Louis, merchant, 54 St. Denis
BRADSTREET, J. M. & SON, improved mercantile agency, John Glass, manager, Molson's Bank Building, cor Gt St. James and St. Peter
BRAHADI, ABRAHAM, furrier, manufacturer and importer of hats, caps, &c., 247 and 249 Notre Dame cor St. Lambert
Brault, Charles, notary, 99 St. Louis
Brault, L. Napoleon, notary, bds 519 Craig
BRAZEAU, FRANCOIS XAVIER, dry goods, 252 and 254 St. Paul
BREHAUT, WILLIAM H., police magistrate, Clairevue, Cote St. Antoine
Brennan, Francis & Co., importers of woolens, 82 St Peter
BRIGADE OFFICE OF VOLUNTEER MILITIA, lieut. colonel Thomas Bacon, brigade major, 68 St Gabriel
Briggs, Rev. William, Wesleyan minister, 5 St Edward
BRITISH AND AMERICAN EXPRESS CO., Gilman Cheney, superintendent, D. T. Irish, agent, 7 and 9 Place d'Armes
BRITISH COLONIAL STEAMSHIP COMPANY, (limited); Gillespie, Moffatt & Co., agents, 310 St Paul
BROSSARD, MOISE, flour and general merchant, 127 St Paul
Brosseau, Alfred T., M.D., 14 Chaboillez sq
Brosseau, Antoine O., notary, 80 St George
Brouillette, Rev. M. C., vicar, Cote St. Louis
Brousseau, Antoine O., notary, 22 St. Lambert
Brousseau, Jean Bte., advocate, 20 St. Gabriel, h 201 Mignonne
Brown, A., commission merchant and dealer in iron, 58 McGill
Brown, Alfred, commission merchant and railway supplies, 20 St. Sacrament
BROWN & CHILDS, boot and shoe store, St. Peter cor Lemoine, and 106 to 112 Queen cor Ottawa
Brown, John O., auctioneer, broker and commission merchant, 210 Notre Dame
Brown, P. E., M.D., C.M., 81 St. Alexander
Brown, Rev. James, St. Patrick's house, 92 St. Alexander
BROWN, T. S., official assignee, 1 Union buildings, 43 St. Francois Xavier
Brown, William, secretary and superintendent Protestant House of Industry and Refuge, 547 Dorchester
BROWNE, C. S., American house, 20, 22 and 24 St. Joseph, and 47 and 49 St. Henry (see adv.)
Browne, P. D., banker and exchange broker, 18 Great St. James
BROWNING, SAMUEL, proprietor Ottawa Hotel, 148 St. James
Bruce, James & Co., importers of dry goods, small wares and fancy goods, 390 St. Paul
BRUNEAU, HON. JEAN C., judge, St. Laurent
Bruneau, Rev. B. O., Bishop's palace, Cemetery
Brunet, Alexis, advocate, 38 Little St. James
Brush, A. N., United States inspector of customs, 23 College
Brush, George, Eagle Foundry and Engine works, 32 to 40 King, nr Canal basin
Bryant, Stratton & Tasker's Business College and Telegraph Institute, 5 Place d'Armes
BRYMER, ROBERT, confectioner, 230 Notre Dame
BRYDGES, CHARLES J., managing director Grand Trunk Railway, Chandos house, 571 Sherbrooke
BRYMNER, DOUGLAS, editor *Evening Telegraph*, 98 St. Hypolite
Bryson, Alexander, sen., customs appraiser, 15 Common
Bryson, Campbell, dealer in leather, shoe findings and cod oil, 9 Lemoine
Bryson, J. B. & A., general brokers and commission merchants, 33 St. Nicholas
Bryson, T. Macfarlane, merchant, 14 Belmont
BUCHANAN, I. & CO., general merchants, Royal Insurance Blgs., 3 Common
Buchanan, James, Glasgow ham warehouse, 30 Victoria Square
Buchanan, John, architect, 148 St. Elizabeth
Buchanan, William O., commission merchant and manufacturer of foundry facings, 13 St. Helen
Buck, Robertson & Co., produce merchants, 96 McGill cor William
Buck, Walter, general agent of New York Life Insurance Co., h 214 St. George
Buckingham, Thomas, carriage maker, 9 St. Antoine
Buies, A., advocate, 111 Notre Dame
BUILDING ASSOCIATION, MONTREAL, H. A. Nelson, president; W. A. Merry, secretary; office 65 Great St. James
BUILDING SOCIETY, MONTREAL CANADIAN, C. Melancon, president; L. A. Jette, secretary; office 42 St. Vincent
BUILDING SOCIETY, MONTREAL CITY AND DISTRICT, Thomas Mussen, president; W. F. Gairdner, secretary; office 39 Little St. James
BUILDING SOCIETY, MONTREAL MUTUAL, William Turner, president; James Ross, jun., secretary; office 6 Bleury
BUILDING SOCIETY, MONTREAL PERMANENT, Henry Thomas, president; M. H. Gault, secretary; office 77 Great St. James
BUILDING SOCIETY, PERMANENT, OF THE DISTRICT OF MONTREAL, D. E. Papineau, president; F. A. Fauteux, secretary; office 12 Place d'Armes
BUILDING SOCIETY, PROVINCIAL PERMANENT, Hugh Allan, president; G. B. Muir, secretary; office 10 Place d'Armes
Bulmer & Sheppard, steam brick makers, head of Dufresne, office, 244 Parthenais
BUNTIN, ALEXANDER, & Co., wholesale stationers, paper and envelope manufacturers, 338 St. Paul, and 273 Commissioners
BURDEN, GEORGE, editor *Daily News*, 53 City Councillors
BUREAU DE LA FABRIQUE DE MONTREAL, E. A. Dubois, secretary, 38 St. Sulpice
Bureau & Normandeau, notaries and commissioners for Lower Canada, and conveyancers and commissioners for Upper Canada, 96 St. Francois Xavier
BURKE, WALTER, manager New York Life Insurance Company, 51 Great St. James, (see adv. opp. inside back cover)
Burke, John, groceries, wines and spirits, 34 and 36 St. Henry, cor. St. Maurice
Burland, Benjamin, surveyor and landing waiter at Rouse's Point, h 174 Mountain
Burland, Lafricain & Co., engravers, lithographers and printers, 115 St. Francois Xavier, opposite Post Office
Burland, Rev. John, 268 Lagauchetiere
Burns, James, & Co., commission merchants, 17 St. Sacrament

Burnett & Thomson, brokers, 64 St. Francois Xavier
Burrell & Houghan, City Express, office, 24 Foundling, and 157 Great St. James
Burrows & Co., wine merchants, 20 Hospital
BUSINESS COLLEGE, Bryant, Stratton & Tasker, 5 Place d'Armes, cor. Notre Dame
BUSS, J. B., oyster and fruit dealer, 17 Place d'Armes, (see bottom lines)
CABINET DE LECTURE PAROISSAIL, D. F. Palin, director; Jean Thibeaudeau, guardian, 327 Notre Dame
Caldwell, Thomas, manager Merchants' Savings Bank, 642 St. Lawrence
Cameron, A. H., forwarder, 244 Guy
Cameron, H., manufacturer of canvas, cotton and paper bags, 32 Great St. James
Cameron & Ross, produce and commission merchants, 435 Commissioners
CAMIRANT, RAPHAEL, leather, oil and hides, 271 and 273 St. Paul
Campbell, David, agent Canadian Land and Mineral Co., Cote St. Antoine
Campbell, Francis W., M.D., 617 Craig
Campbell, George W., M.D., Dean of Faculty of Medicine, McGill University
Campbell, John, advocate, 42 Bleury
Campbell, John, merchant tailor, 442 Gt. St. James
Campbell, John McDermott, manager rolling mills, 472 William
Campbell, Kenneth & Co., Medical Hall, 23 Great St. James
Campbell, L. J. & Co., manufac'rs of leather belting and fire engine hose, belt leather, lace leather, etc., 17 Lemoine
CAMPBELL, R. & CO., carpet, oil cloth and curtain warehouse, 208 and 210 McGill
Campbell, Rev. Robert, A.M., minister of St. Gabriel church (Church of Scotland), 299 Dorchester
CAMPBELL, ROLLO, printer, 42 Bleury
Campbell, W. A. & Co., coffee roasting and spice mills, 526 Lagauchetiere
Campbell, Wm., insurance inspector, 148 St. Denis
Campion, Rev. Auguste, priest of the parish of St. Brigide 30 Seaton
Canada Fur Dressing Co., 39 St. Jean Baptiste
Canada Glass Company (limited), C. W. Walkem, secretary, 10 St. Nicholas
CANADA HORSE NAIL CO., 29 ill
Canada Hotel, Victor Marcotte, proprietor, 17 St. Gabriel
CANADA LAW JOURNAL, James Kirby, advocate, editor; John Lovell, printer and publisher, 23 St. Nicholas; editorial office, No. 4 Merchants' Exchange, 11 St. Sacrament
Canada Marine Works, A. Cantin, proprietor, 722 St. Joseph
Canada Plumbago Company, G. B. Cramp, secretary, 59 Great St. James
Canadian Engine and Machinery Company, R. Wright, secretarp and treasurer, 67 City Councillors
CANADA EXPRESS CO., G. Cheney, superintendent, D. T. Irish, agent, 7 and 9 Place d'Armes
CANADIAN INSTITUTE, Hon. L. A. Dessaulles, president, 111 Notre Dame
CANADA LAND AND MINERAL COMPANY, D. Campbell, agent, 3 Corn Exchange, 1 St. John
CANADIAN MESSENGER, John Dougal & Son, proprietors, 126 Great St. James
CANADIA NAVIGATION CO., A. Milloy, manager, 73 Great St. James
CANADIAN RUBBER CO., Francis Scholes, manager, office 272 St. Mary

Cantin, Augustin, shipyard, 690 St. Joseph
Cardinal, Calixte, leather merchant, 3 St. Amable Lane
Cardinal, Joseph, leather merchant, 3 St. Amable Lane
Carlisle, J., furniture warerooms, 402 and 404 Notre Dame
CARLISLE, J., prop. Terrapin Restaurant, Crystal Block, 289 Notre Dame
Carmichael, Rev. James, assistant minister St. George's Church, 15 St. Edward
Carroll, M. J., groceries, wines and liquors, 60 Bleury
Carroll, Patrick, London House 414 Commissioners 7
Carson, Andrew, merchant tailor, 58 Great St. James
Carter, C. B., advocate, 8 St. Sacrament
CARTER, EDWARD, Q.C., M.P.P., 31 Cadieux
Carter, George, notarial clerk Mount Royal Cemetery Road
Carter & Hatton, advocates, 353 Notre Dame
Cartier, Pominville & Betournay, advocates 43 St. Vincent
CARTIER, SIR GEORGE E., Bart., 32 Notre Dame
CASSIDY, JOHN L. & CO., importers of china, glass and earthenware, 342 and 343 St. Paul, and 275 Commissioners
Cassils & Cameron, Montreal hoop skirt factory, 9 and 11 Recollet
Caven, James, agent Ottawa and Rideau Forwarding Co., 60 Common
Caverhill, J. & T., merchants, 48 Great St. James
CAYA, JEAN BAPTISTE, wholesale boot and shoe manufacturer, 450 St. Mary
Chaffee, A. B., gen. ins. agent, 85 St. Francois Xavier
CHAMARD, JOHN, comn mer and warehouseman, 13 Common
Chance Brothers & Co., glass manfrs. and lighthouse engineers, B. & S. Thompson, agents, 12 Lemoine
Chanteloup, Ernest, manfr. of bronze goods, brass ornaments, brass founder and finisher, 587 to 593 Craig
Chapeleau, Zephirin, bookseller and stationer, 174 Notre Dame
Chapleau, Rainville & Prevost, advocates, 10 Little St. James
Chaplin, Edward, broker and comn mer., 15 Corn Exchange, 1 St. John
Chapman, Fraser & Tylee, wholesale grocers, 15 Hospital
Chapman, Henry, consul for Italy and the Argentine Republic and vice-consul for Norway and Sweden, 22 St. John
Chapman, Henry & Co., wine, tea and gen. mers. agents, for Lloyds and Glasgow Association of Underwriters, 22 St. John cor Hospital
Chaput, L., Fils & Cie., wholesale grocers, wine and spirit mers., 429 Commissioners
Charbonneau, Liboire L., leather merchant and dealer in shoe findings, 444 St. Paul
Charbonneau, Louis & Co., city jobbing steam mills, 12 St. Charles Borromee
Charbonneau, Louis Henri, groceries, wines and liquors, 32 Jurors
Charest, Samuel, dry goods, 3 St. Lawrence
Charlebois, A. & A. B., general grocery brokers, 16 St. Sacrament
Charlebois, A. & H., groceries, wines and liquors, 110 McGill
Charlebois, Alphonse, hardware merchant, St. Henri, Tannery west
Charlebois, Dr. B. H., 145 Bleury
Charlebois, J. C., broker, 145 Bleury
Charles, Walter, oils, paints, glass, &c., 49 and 51 St. Lawrence

Charpentier, Magloire Eugene, advocate, 10 Little St. James
Cheney, Fiske & Co.'s United States and Canada Express, D. T. Irish, agent, 4 Place d'Armes
CHENEY, GILMAN, superintendent Canadian Express Co., 7 Place d'Armes
Cherrier, Come Seraphin, Q.C., 15 St. Vincent
Childs, Charles, manuf. of lasts, boot-trees, crimps, etc., 112 Queen
Childs, George & Co., wholesale grocers, 20 and 22 St. Francois Xavier
Chipman, J. R., insurance agent, 262 St. Charles Borromee
Chisholm, Colin R. & Co., news agents, Bonaventure depot, St. Bonaventure
Christian, Thomas R., inspector of branches and agencies, Bank of Montreal
Christie, William, prop. soap and candle factory, 36 Jacques Cartier, office 516 Craig
CHURCH OBSERVER, (weekly) published in the interests of the Church of England, lay editor, J. Wright; printed for the proprietors by Penny, Wilson & Co., 51 Gt St. James
CHURCH SOCIETY, Diocese of Montreal, Rev. Canon Balch, D.D., secretary, 77 Gt St. James
CITIZENS' INSURANCE AND INVESTMENT CO, G. B., Muir, manager, 10 Place d'Armes
CITY AND DISTRICT SAVINGS BANK, E. J. Barbeau, actuary, 9 Gt St. James
CITY BANK, William Workman, mayor, president, Ferdinand Macculloch, cashier, Place d'Armes
Clark, Alexander C., broker, 632 Lagauchetiere
Clark, F. A., exch. broker, 125 St. Francois Xavier
CLARK, JAMES P. & CO., importers and wholesale dealers in dry goods, 162 McGill
Clark, O. L. & R. S., bell manufacturers, Cote St. Paul
Clark, T. M. & Co., commission merchants, 5 St. Sacrament
Clarke & Clayton, importers of wines, spirits, etc., 46 St. Peter
Clarke & Dalbec, advocates, 192 Notre Dame
Clarke, Henry J., Q. C., 60 Dubord
Clarke, John G., importer, 32 St. Francois Xavier
Clarke, W. R., dry goods, bonnets, hats, etc., 196 McGill
Clarkson, Rev. J. B., 694 Sherbrooke
Claxton, T. James & Co., wholesale dry goods merchants, Caverhill's Buildings, 59 St. Peter
Clendenning, William, founder and stove manufacturer, 118 and 120 St. James, and 165 William
CLERK, GEORGE EDWARD, editor and proprietor *True Witness*, 126 St. Antoine
Clouston, James S., Hudson Bay Co., 48 Cathcart
Clothier Seraphin, groceries, wines and liquors, 29 and 31 St. Joseph
Cochrane, A. McK., agent St. Lawrence Glass Company, and Anglo-American Peat Company, 388 St. Paul
COCKBURN, BROWN & NAPIER, Canada brass works, brass founders, finishers, gas fitters, plumbers, etc., cor. Craig and St. Antoine
Coderre, J. Emery, M.D., 392 Lagauchetiere
Coghlan & Co., groceries, wines and spirits, wholesale 516 Craig
Cohen, Arthur M., broker, Merchants' Exchange, 11 St. Sacrament
COLE & BRO., stoves and hardware, St. Patrick's hall buildings, 15 Victoria square
COLE, GEORGE F., consulting engineer, machinery, engineering supplies and hardware commission agent, Union buildings, 43 St. Francois Xavier
COLE, FREDERICK, secretary Commercial Union Assurance Co., 387 St. Paul
Colin, Rev. L., Seminary of St. Sulpice, 320 Notre Dame
Collard, Louis Henri, advocate, 30 St. Vincent
COLONIAL CHURCH AND SCHOOL SOCIETY'S MODEL SCHOOL, Rev. Canon W. Bond, superintendent and secretary, 44 St. Bonaventure
Colson, Lamb & Co., tea dealers and commission merchants, 25 St. John cor Hospital
COMMERCIAL UNION ASSURANCE CO., Morland, Watson & Co., general agents, Frederick Cole, secretary, 387 St. Paul
Comte, Benjamin, president Mutual Fire Insurance Co., 100 St. George
Comte, Joseph, commission merchant, 102 St. George
CONNECTICUT MUTUAL LIFE INSURANCE CO., R. Wood, agent, 83 St. Francois Xavier
CONSULATE GENERAL OF THE UNITED STATES OF AMERICA, 23 Great St. James
Continential Life Insurance Company, R. R. Andrew, general agent, 13 Place d'Armes
Copeland, C., sen., shipping agent and agent Whitehall Transportation Co., 5 Common
Copeland & Phymister, general brokers and coal merchants, office 21 St. Sacrament, coal yard, 66 Grey Nun
Corbeil, L. L., advocate, 41 St. Vincent
Corbeille & Beaudry, advocates, 52 St. Gabriel
Corcoran, John, wine merchant, 166 Amherst
Corcoran, William, produce merchant, 23 St. Hubert
Cordner, Rev. John, minister of the Unitarian church Piedmont cottage, ab Durocher
CORISTINE, JAMES & CO., hats, furs and buck mitt manufacturers, 473 and 475 St. Paul
CORN EXCHANGE, William Patterson, secretary, St. John cor St. Sacrament
Cornell, C. A., U. S. inspector of Customs, 28 College
CORNISH, REV. GEORGE, M.A., professor of classics and history in McGill University
CORONER'S OFFICE, Joseph Jones, coroner for the district of Montreal, 44 St. James
CORPORATION OF MONTREAL, Charles Glackmeyer, clerk, City Hall, 187 St. Paul
Costello, Patrick, groceries and liquors, 182 Vitre cor Chenneville
Costen, Thomas & Co., gunsmiths, bellhangers, and fishing tackle warehouse, 27 Great St. James and cor Place d'Armes hill Fortification Lane
Cote St. Paul Shovel Factory and Scythe Works, Frothingham & Workman, props., Cote St. Paul
Coulson, Duncan, manager Bank of Toronto 8
COURSOL, C. J., Judge of sessions, office Court House
Coursolle, Casimir, architect, 218 Panet
COURT & MACINTOSH, accountants, North British and Mercantile Insurance Co.'s buildings, 11 Hospital
Coutu, Gilbert, notary, 16 St. Elizabeth
COWAN & DESAUTELS, manufacturers and importers of hats, caps and furs, 416 Notre Dame cor St. Peter
COWAN, ROBERT C., advocate, 9 St. Lambert
Cox & Collins, scale manufacturers, 9 Chenneville
Cox, James, shirt and collar manufactory, 19 Kent
Cox, James P., broker, 26 St. Sacrament
Coyle, P. J., advocate, 50 Little St. James
CRAIG, ALEXANDER, painter, glazier and paperhanger, 179 Fortification Lane
CRAIG, DAVID J., warehouseman, produce and general comn mer., 26 Foundling

CRAIG, JAMES PETER, pianoforte manfr., 122 and 124 St. Lawrence
Craig, John, comn merchant 23 German
Craik, Robert, M.D., 19 Place d'Armes Hill
Cramp, G. B., advocate, 59 Great St. James
Crane & Baird, com mers. 8 Corn Exchange, 1 St. John
CRATHERN & CAVERHILL, wholesale hardware, agents for Victoria Rope Walk and Vielle Montagne Zinc Co., Caverhill's bldgs, 61 St. Peter
CRAVEN & FARRAR, importers and dealers in all kinds of foreign and domestic fruit, cigars, confectionery, shell fish, etc., 235 McGill
Crawford & Co., mers, 354 St. Paul & 286 Commissioners
Crawford, James & Co., wholesale tea, wine and spirit merchants, 19 St. Sacrament
Crevier, Antoine, groceries, wines and liquors, 266 Jacques Cartier
Crevier & Poitras, tinsmiths and general stove warehouse, 427 Notre Dame
Cross & Lunn, advocates, Merchants Exchange Court, 10 Hospital
Cummings, Joseph, scythe manfr. Cote St. Paul
CUNDILL, FRANCIS & CO., wholesale druggists, 32 Lemoine
Cunningham, W., tobacconist, 124 Notre Dame
CUNNINGHAM, W. & SON general and commission merchants, 4 Union Buildings, 43 St. Francois Xavier
Cunningham, William H., sculptor and dealer in foreign and American marbles, 91 Bleury
Curran & Grenier, advocates, 44 Little St. James
Curran, Rev. W. B., M.A., incumbent of St. Stephen's Church, 22 St. Monique
CURRIE, W. & F. P. & CO., wholesale hardware, 100 Grey Nun
Curry, Benjamin S., managing director Petroleum Gas Co., 156 Great St. James
Curry, W. A., estate agent, 84 Great St. James
Cushing & Trenholm, advocates, 38 St. John
CUSTOM HOUSE, A. M. Delisle, collector, John Lewis, surveyor, Custom House Sq., St. Paul
CUSTOMS EXAMINING WAREHOUSE, 14 Common
CUTHBERT, R. & SON, Dominion Brass Works, 101 and 103 Queen, (see adv)
CUVILLIER & CO., general merchants, 17 St. Sacrament
CYPIHOT & BROTHER, hatters and furriers, 376 Notre Dame
Dagen, Gaspard, notary, 589 St. Catherine
Dagenais, Adolphus, M.D., physician and surgeon, 233 Lagauchtiere
Dagenais, J. C., merchant tailor, 12 St. Lambert
DAILY NEWS, MONTREAL WEEKLY TRANSCRIPT—John Lovell, printer and publisher, 23 and 25 St. Nicholas
Dakers, James, secretary Montreal Telegraph Company, Hochelaga
DALEY, JOSEPH HENRY, Government emigration agent, 303 Commissioners
Dalton, W. & Co., booksellers, stationers and news dealers, 64 Great St. James
Daly, A. D. & Co., crockery, china, and glassware, cutlery, fancy goods, toys, lamps, wholesale and retail, 11 Bleury
Damour, Alfred, notary, 394 St. Mary
Damour, Louis A., notary, 398 St. Mary
Dangerfield. William, boots and shoes, Cathedral Block, 275 Notre Dame
Daniel, Rev. Charles E., assistant minister St. John the Evangelist Chapel, 307 St. Urbain
Daniel, Rev. F., Seminary of St. Sulpice, 320 Notre Dame
DANIS, GEORGE, editor *Le Nouveau Monde*, 286 Dorchester
DANSEREAU ARTHUR, B. C. L., advocate, editor *La Minerve*, 101 St. Louis
Daoust, Oliver, brewer, 51 Amherst
Darey, Professor P. J., McGill University, h 108 University
Darling & Brady, soap and candle manufacturers, 96 St. Charles Borromee
DARLING, WILLIAM & CO., iron merchants, English and German writing and printing papers, stationery, and fancy goods, 30 St. Sulpice
DARRAGH, JAMES, groceries, wines and liquors, 55 Alymer, cor. Berthelet
Dart, Rev. William, B.A., city missionary in connection with St. George's Episcopal Church, 740 St. Catherine
Date, John, plumber, gas fitter, brass founder, and coppersmith, 657 Craig
David, A. H., M. D., 42 Beaver Hall Terrace
David, A. M., importer and general hardware and customs agent, 409 St. Paul
David, E. D., registrar and treasurer Trinity House, Harbor Commissioners Building, 14 Custom House square
David, Edouard, artificial flower and feather manufacturer, 94 Notre Dame
DAVID, FERDINAND, alderman, 195 St. Dennis
David, Fleury, groceries, 81 Montcalm
David, Guillame, general agent, 31 St. Vincent
David, M. F., advocate, 31 St. Vincent
DAVID, TUCKER, coal and general commission merchant, 78 McGill
DAVID & VALOIS, advocates, 20 St. Gabriel
DAVIDSON, ALEXANDER, marine inspector, 63 McGill college ave
DAVIDSON, CHARLES P., advocate, 60 Little St. James
DAVIDSON & KERR, wholesale manufacturers of japanned, planished and stamped tinware, 22 and 30 Hospital
DAVIDSON, LEO. H., barrister, Great St. James (see adv)
Davie, J. G., dry goods, 111 St. Mary
Davis, B. T., commission merchant, 104 Mansfield
Davis, Dr. H. C., dentist, 564 Craig
Davis, Henry, dry goods, 226 Bleury
DAVIS, JAMES, manufacturer and importer of needles, fish hooks and fishing tackle, 13 St. Alexander
DAVIS, NELSON, customs and forwarding agent and commission merchant, 9 Common cor Port
Davison, James, manager Phœnix Fire Assurance agency, 310 St. Paul
DAWES, J. P. & T. A., ale and porter brewers, office 119 Great St. James
Dawes, Robert, commission merchant, 111 Mignonne
Dawson, Benjamin, 41 McGill College ave
DAWSON, BROTHERS, publishers, booksellers, stationers, printsellers, bookbinders, news agents, &c., 55 Great St. James and 516 Craig
Dawson, J. W., LL.D., F.R.S, F.G.S., principal McGill University
Dawson, W. V., agent for Cowan & Co., paper makers, 18 St. John
Day & Day, advocates, 192 Notre Dame
Day, J. J., Q.C., of Day & Day, Casa del Monte, 149 Cote des Neiges road
Day, James, florist, nursery, Cote St. Louis, Mile end

Day, James G., advocate, 40 Durocher
Deaf and Dumb Female Institution, Sister Mary, directress, head of St. Denis
Deaf and Dumb Institution for Males, by the Clercs Paroisseaux de St. Viateur, Cote St. Louis
Dean, Stephen, superintendent of telegraph, Point St. Charles
DeBeaufort, Jean, grain merchant, 73 Visitation
DeBeaumont, Alfred, advocate, 98 Cadieux
DeBellefeuille & Turgeon, advocates, 36 St. Vincent
Decarie, Augustin, & Brothers, Victoria Wire Works, 576 Craig
Decary, A. C., notary, 103 St. Joseph
Decary, Jean, contractor, 267 St. Bonaventure
DECKER & CO., props. Albion hotel, 527 to 533 St. Paul
cutter manuf., r 536 St. Mary
DEGUISE, MICHEL T., contractor, 17 Balmoral
DEGUISE, OLIVIER, flour and grain merchant, 205 Commissioners
DELISLE, A. M., collector of customs, 444 Sherbrooke
Delisle Brothers McGill, hardware merchants, 483 and 485 St. Paul
Delorimier & Duclos, chemists and druggists, 191 and 193 St. Joseph
Delorimer, L. G. V., M.D., 59 Inspector
Delorimier, T. & C. C., advocates, 6 Little St. James
Delorme, Pierre, leather and commission merchant, shoe findings, &c., 418 St. Paul
Delorme, Simeon, leather merchant, 274 St. Paul
Delvecchio & Laviolette, wholesale wine merchants, 394 St. Paul
Demers, Augustin, lumber merchant, 51 Lacroix
DeMontigny, B. Testard, advocate, 35 St. Vincent
DeMontigny, Pierre, grocer, 562 St. Joseph
DENHOLM, GEORGE, produce and commission merchant, 53 St. Francois Xavier
Depatie, Jean Baptiste & Co., lumber merchants, 531 Craig
Deputy Adjutant General's Office, Colonel Thackwell' deputy; Colonel Havelock, assistant deputy, 31 Notre Dame
Deputy Quartermaster General's Office, Col. Lyson's, deputy, 31 Notre Dame
DESEVE, ALEXANDRE, sen., advocate, St. Henri Tannery west
Desjardins & Desjardins, advocates, 10 Little St. James
Desjardins, Dr. J. A., 22 St. Lawrence
Desjardins, Dr. L. A. E., 33 St. Antoine
Desjardins, Magloire, advocate, 50 St. Gabriel
Desmarteau & Bond, importers of fancy and staple dry goods, 456 Notre Dame
Desmarteau, Charles, groceries, flour and liquors, wholesale and retail, 37 and 41 St. Mary
Desmarteau, N & W. & Jodoin, importers of dry goods and groceries, wholesale, 286 and 288 St. Paul, and 231 and 233 Commissioners
DeSola, Rev. A., LL.D., (Jewish Synagogue) 533 Lagauchetiere
Desrosiers, Dr. L. J. P., 391 St Joseph
Dossaulles & Ermatinger, clerk of Crown and Peace, Court House, 177 Notre Dame
DEVANEY & CO., auctioneers and commission merchants, 139 Great St. James
Devins & Bolton, chemists and druggists, 193 and 198 Notre Dame
DEVLIN, BERNARD, advocate, 25 St James (see card)
Devlin, Owen J., notary, 40 St James
Dewar, G. R., manufacturer of shirts and collars, 381 Notre Dame cor St John
Deziel & Vezina, merchant tailors, 131 St. Joseph
Dick, Samuel, lapidary or cutter of precious stones, 576 Craig
Dickson, George R. & Co., com. merchts, 17 Lemoine
Dickson, William, lumber merchant, 125 Richmond
Dinning, John G., secretary Merchants exchange, 179 Bleury
DION'S BILLIARD HALL, 111 Great St James (see adv)
DION, JOSEPH & BROS., (Joseph and Cyrille) 214 Bleury
District Inspector of Musketry Office, capt. J. Grant, 31 Notre Dame
Dobell, Henry, merchant, 33 St. Sacrament
DOHERTY & DOHERTY, advocates, 38 Little St. James, (see adv)
Dolan, Francis, dry goods, 460 Notre Dame
Dominique, Andre, lumber yard, 208 Wellington
Donnelly, James, wholesale dry goods, Dominion Buildings, 130 McGill
Donnelly, P. & F., lumber merchants, 284 Craig cor Wolfe
Donohue, Timothy, grocer, wine and spirit merchant, 161 St. Paul, cor St. Claude
DONOVAN & MORAN, leather manufacturers, 142 Amherst
DONOVAN, PETER, lumber merchant, 39 Inspector
DORAN, JAMES, cashier G.T.R., 134 Amherst
DORAN, S. J., freight agent G.T.R., office St. Bonaventure station
Dorav, Amable, groceries, wines and liquors, 109 St. Paul
Dorion, Beaudry & Co., brewers, 16 Jacques Cartier
Dorion, Dorion & Geoffrion, advocates, 43 St. Vincent
Dorion, Edward, St. Andrew's Hotel, 48 and 49 Common
Dorion, G. T. & Co., watchmakers and jewellers, 86 St. Lawrence
DORION, HON. A. A., M.P., of Dorion, Dorion & Geoffrion, 121 Champ de Mars
Dorman, S. W., advocate, 32 St. James
Dorney, John Frederick, superintendent City Passenger Railway, Hochelaga
D'Orsonnens & Gauthier, physicians and surgeons, 130 and 132 St. Lawrence
Dorval, Medéric, commission merchant, 410 Dorchester
Dorwin, Canfield & Co., bankers 37 St. Francois Xavier
Dorwin, J. H., barometer maker, 59 St. Francois Xavier
Dostaler, Hyacinthe Marc, principal St. Mary academy
Dougall, John & Co., leather, produce and commission merchants, 472 St. Paul
DOUGALL, JOHN & SON, proprietors Montreal Daily Witness, 126 St. James
DOUGLAS, BRO. & CO., lumber merchants, saw and planing mill owners, 342 William
DOUGLASS, JAMES & CO., wholesale grocers, 508 St. Paul
Douglas, Rev. George, (Wesleyan) 79 Bleury
Douglas, William, boots and shoes, 212 McGill and 182 Wellington
DOUGLAS, WILLIAM, jun., general agent for the Dominion of Canada for the National Life Insurance Co., of U. S. A., 32 Great St. James (see adv. opposite inside back cover)
DOUGLAS, JOHN & CO., importers of china, glass and earthenware, 13 and 15 St. Helen
Doutney, W. L., grocer, &c., 28 St. Gabriel

Doutre & Doutre, advocates 20 St. Gabriel
Drapeau, Rev. J. Bte., Long Point
Drummond, George A., sugar refiner
DRUMMOND, HON, L. T., judge, 1126 Dorchester
Dubeau, Charles, tobacconist, 217 St. Lawrence
Dubord, Alexis & Co., manufs. tobacco and cigars, 227 and 229 St. Paul
Dubreuil, Joseph, painter, 226 Montcalm
Dubuc, Charles, M.D., 541 St. Joseph
Dow, William & Co., brewers and distillers, 198 St. Joseph
Dowd, Rev. Patrick, parish priest St. Patrick's Church, St. Patrick's house, 92 St. Alexander
Doyle, James & Co., wholesale grocers, 24 and 26 St. Peter
Drake, J. M., M.D., physician and surgeon, 19 Beaver Hall Terrace
Drescher, H., agent and importer of hardware, 22 and 24 Lemoine
Driscoll, Henry, advocate, Q.C., 20 Barclay
Duclos, H., proprietor Montreal House, 6 and 8 Custom House sq
Duclos, Hiram, jr., Bellevue Hotel, Côte St. Luc road, Côte des Neiges
Dufresne, Gray & Co., importers of fancy and staple dry goods, wholesale and retail, 454 Notre Dame
Dufresne, Joseph, manufacturer of packing boxes, printers' furniture, etc., 12 St. Charles Borromèe
Dufresne, Joseph, notary, 179 Lagauchetière
Dufresne, Léon G., groceries, wines, liquors, etc., 530 St. Catherine
Dufresne & McGarity, grocers, wine and spirit merchants, 221 Notre Dame
Dufresne, Ovide, flour and provision merchant, 209 Commissioners
Dufresne, Thomas, grocer, 39 Sanguinet
Dufresne & Viau, provision merchants, 205 and 207 Commissioners
Dugas, C. Aimé, advocate, 353 Notre Dame
Dugdale, Joseph J., M.D., physician and surgeon, 564 Craig
Duggan, John H., advocate, 40 St. James
Duhamel, Amable, groceries, wines and liquors, 183 Commissioners
Duhamel, Joseph, advocate, 28 St. Vincent
Duhamel, Joseph Napoleon, groceries, wines, liquors and provisions, 144 Lagauchetière cor Visitation
Dulude, A. & Co., dry goods, 53 St. Mary
Dumaine, C. Adolphe, livery stables and express, 1 Campeau
Dumas & Phelan, law stamp commissioners, Court House, 177 Notre Dame
Dumouchel, Louis N., notary, 86 St. Lawrence, St. J. Bte. village
Dumoulin, Rev. J. Philip, assistant minister Trinity Church, 105 St. Hubert
DUN, WIMAN & CO., mercantile agency, James Hedley, manager, Union Buildings, 37 and 39 St. Francois Xavier
Duncan & Forster, wholesale grocers, 12 and 14 St. John and 9 St. Alexis
Dunlop & Browne, advocates, 30 St. James
Dunlop, John, advocate, 67 St. Francois Xavier
DUNN, R. FISH & CO., wholesale jobbers in dry goods, commission merchants and manufacturers agents, 479 St. Paul
Dupras, Calixte, groceries, wines and liquors, 34 St. Mary
Dupuis & Labelle, dry goods, 66 and 68 Notre Dame
Dupuis, Pierre, tobacconist, 208 St. Lawrence
DURACK, PATRICK J., groceries, wines, liquors and provisions, 139 Vitre
Durand, Joseph, notary, 135 St. George
Durand, N., advocate, 18 St. Therese
Durnford, Philip, collector of inland revenue, 1241 Dorchester
Duverger, L. N., dry goods, 65 Notre Dame
DUVERNAY, FRERES, printers and publishers of *La Minerve*, and general job printers, 16 St. Vincent
DYDE, COLONEL JOHN, commandant active volunteer force
Dyde & Major, pot and pearl ash insps. 14 to 22 College
Dyer, William Andrew, chemist, 462 St. Catherine
Eager, W. L., inspector of beef and pork for the City and district of Montreal, 46 Wellington
Eagle Foundry, George Brush, prop. 34 King
EARLE, LIEUT. COLONEL W., military secretary, 22 McTavish
Eastey, David, tobacconist, 15 Place d'Armes
Easton, William, notary, Union bldgs, 45 St. Francois Xavier
EATON, RICHARD, superintendent locomotive department G. T. R.
Eaves, William, watch manfr. and importer of watches, watch materials, etc., 359 Notre Dame
Eckroyd, Thomas, tanner and morocco leather dresser, 154 William
Edson, Hiram, prop. of Eagle Hotel, 23 and 31 College
EDWARDS, CHARLES D., manufacturer of fire and burglar proof safes; factory, cor Inspector and College; office, 17 Victoria square, under St Patrick's Hall (see adv.)
Edwards, Dr. Nelson, 304 Notre Dame
Edwards, John Baker, Ph. D., consulting chemist, 73 St. Alexander
Edwards, Thomas, broker, 83 Fullum
EDWARDSBURG STARCH CO., John Thompson, secretary and treasurer, 37 St. Peter
Egan, Christopher, corn merchant, 47 Richmond sq
Egginton, Enoch, supt. St. Lawrence Glass Works
Ekers, Thomas A., brewer, 409 St. Lawrence
Ellegood, Rev. Jacob, M.A., incumbent St. James the Apostle Church, Episcopal, 1230 St. Catherine
Elliott, John, grocer, wine and spirit merchant, 194 to 198 St. Paul, and 155 and 157 Commissioners
Elliott, Sawtell & Co., hardware, 509 St. Paul
Emery, J. W., & Co., tinsmiths, 629 St. Joseph
EMIGRATION OFFICE, GOVERNMENT, Joseph H. Daley, agent, 303 Commissioners
Empey, G. D., Merchant's Hotel, 51 College
Empey, Johnstone & Co., wholesale importers of staple dry goods, 16 St. Helen
Empson, John, civil engineer, 22 St. Monique
ENGLISH WORKINGMEN'S ASSOCIATION, S. C. Bagg, president; rooms Central Fire station, 607 Craig
Esdaile, J. & R., general brokers, 45 St. Francois Xavier
Esinhart, John, architect, 36 St. Lambert
Espitalier, G., importer of wines, 16 St. John
Esplin, Charles, steam saw and planing mills, and packing case factory, 111 Duke
Etna Fire and Marine Insurance Company of Dublin, T. W. Griffith, manager, cor St. Francois Xavier and St. Sacrament
EUROPEAN ASSURANCE SOCIETY, Life and Guarantee, Edward Rawlings, manager, 71 Great St. James
Evens, Alfred, of Middlemiss & Evans, 811 St. Catherine
EVANS, BROTHERS, firewood, coal and coke, 735 Craig
EVANS, EDWIN, general merchant and manufacturers agent, 23 Hospital

EVANS & EVANS, wholesale hardware merchants, 7 Custom House square
Evans, George & Co., real estate agents, 13 Place d'Armes
Evans, James S. & Co., manufacturers and wholesale dealers in ready made clothing, 146 McGill
EVANS, JOHN HENRY, wholesale and retail hardware, 463 to 469 St. Paul, and 14, 18 and 20 St. Nicholas
Evans, Mercer & Co., wholesale druggists and manufacturing chemists, 265 Notre Dame
Evans, S., boot and shoe warehouse, 160 McGill
Evans, Samuel W., boots and shoes, 19 Bleury
Evans & Son, hardware manufacturers agents, 10 St. Nicholas cor St. Paul
EVANS, WILLIAM, agricultural implement and seed warehouse, over St. Ann's market (see adv)
EVENING TELEGRAPH AND COMMERCIAL ADVERTISER, daily, T. K. Ramsay, Q.C., managing editor, 67 Great St. James
Ewart, Shearer & Co., clothiers, 422 St. Paul
EWING, S. H. & A. S., Montreal coffee and spice steam mills, 102 King (see adv)
Ewing, William, inspector of agencies of North British and Mercantile Insurance Company, 211 Bleury
EXAMINING CUSTOMS WAREHOUSE, 15 Common
EXCISE INSPECTORS AND COLLECTORS OF INLAND REVENUE, 1st Division, R. Bellemare; 2d division, P. Durnford, 26 Little St. James
Express House, Daniel McClanagan, proprietor, 188 St. Bonaventure
Fabre & Gravel, French books, stationery and paper hanging, 46 St. Vincent
Fabre, Gustave R., inspector of hardware, saddlery, carriage furniture, &c., 287 and 289 St. Paul
FABRE, VERY REV. CANON E. C., Bishop's palace, Cemetery
Fahrland, Theophile, architect, engraver and jewellery manufacturer, 552 Craig
Fairbairn, J. & Son, brokers, 6 Corn Exchange, 42 St. Sacrament
FAIRBANKS, RUFUS, broker, 24 St. Sacrament (see adv)
Fairie, James, wholesale depot, coal oils, lamps, shades, lanterns, &c., 100 St Francois Xavier
Farrell, William, wine and spirit merchant, and dealer in cigars, 420 St. Paul
Faucher, Fils & Cie, general hardware and smiths coal, 796 Craig cor Little St. Antoine
Faure, Ferdinand, notary, office Seminary
Fauteux, Pierre Aime, advocate, 88 St. Lawrence, St. J. Bte. village
FENWICK, GEORGE E., M.D., editor *Canada Medical Journal*, 24 Beaver Hall terrace
Feron, Martin, groceries wines and liquors, wholesale and retail, 88 and 90 Bleury
Ferrier & Co., wholesale hardware merchants 24 and 26 St. Francois Xavier
FERRIER, HON. JAMES, senator, M.L.C., and chairman G.T.R., 100 St. Alexander
FESSENDEN, THOMAS, Government steamboat inspector, Canal Office, Windmill Point, opposite Prince
Filer & Co., leather merchants, 510 St. Paul
Filer, Samuel, commission merchant, 29 Kent
Filiatrault, Cyriac, importer of tobacco and cigars, 11 Jacques Cartier square
FINDLAY & McWILLIAM, wholesale confectioners, 516 St. Paul
Fisher, Mark & Sons, manufacturers and importers of woolens, cloths, &c., 461 St. Paul, cor. St. Nicholas
FITTS, C. & Co., biscuit and cracker bakers, 120 and 122 Inspector, cor. St. Antoine, (see adv)
Fleck, Alexander, Vulcan Iron Works, 26 William
Fletcher, Donald, & Co., fancy goods, paper hangings, etc., 221 McGill
Fletcher, E. R. A., principal Dominion Commercial Academy, 63 St. Alexander
Footner, M. A & Co., berlin wool and fancy goods, 336 Notre Dame
Forbes, A. H., heavy hardware, drain pipes, fire bricks and cement, 86 Grey Nun
Ford, E., stock, share, mining and general broker, 18 St. John
Forester, Moir & Co., wholesale grocers, 21 St. Helen and 18 Recollet
Forsyth, Robert, civil and mining engineer, and importer and manufacturer of all kinds of marble and granite, 552 William, and 139 Bleury
FOSTER, T. E., general agent Travellers Insurance Company, 25 St. Francois Xavier
Foulds & Hodgson, importers of dry goods, small wares, and fancy articles, wholesale, 364, 366 and 368 St. Paul
Foulds & McCubbin, wholesale clothiers, 370 St. Paul
Fowler & Roy, architects, 96 St. Francois Xavier
Franchere, Quinn & Co., grain merchants, 279 Commissioners
Francis, W. & B., importers of hardware, cutlery, etc. 490 St. Paul and 407 Commissioners
Franck, J. C. & Co., wholesale grocers, wines and spirits, 25 Hospital
Francheur & Giroux, dry goods, 7 and 9 St. Lawrence
FRANKLIN, F., stock department Bank of Montreal 445 Sherbrooke
Franklin Hotel, F. X. Pardis, proprietor, 31 and 33 Chaboillez Square
Franklin, W, T. & Co., importers and manufacturers of hats, caps and furs, 400 Notre Dame
Fraser, Brothers, grocers, wine and spirit dealers, 182 and 184 Bleury
Fraser, Daniel, lamps, coal oil & crockery, 184 Bleury
Fraser, Edward C., wholesale wine and spirit mercht, 53 St. Bonaventure
FRASER, Francis, hardware wholesale agent for Birmingham and Sheffield manufacturers, jewelry, glassware, fancy goods, 28 St. Sulpice
Fraser, Hugh & Co., importers, 45 St. Sacrament
Fraser, John, importer of dry goods, wholesale, 53 and 55 St. Sulpice
Fraser, Rev. Joshua, chaplain military forces, and minister St. Matthew's church, 9 Balmoral
Fraser, Thomas, commission and produce merchant, 352 Commissioners cor Callières
Fraser, William, M.D., physician and surgeon, 690 Dorchester
Fréchette, Edmond P., notary, 44 St. Vincent
Freeman, Allen, oyster house and saloon, 99 St. James
Freer, Captain Noah, 990 St Catherine
FREER, EDWARD STAYNER, Postmaster
FREER, WILLIAM M. & CO., agents Pacific Mail Steamship Co. of New York, and Star Life Assurance Co. of London ; and general commission merchants, Exchange Court, 10 Hospital
French Canadian Institute, 18 Notre Dame
FRENCH CANADIAN MISSIONARY RECORD, J. C. Becket, publisher, 84 St. James.
Frothingham & Workman, wholesale hardware merchants, 395, 397 and 399 St. Paul
Fuhrer, F. A., commission merchant, 6 St. Elizabeth

Fuller, Alphonse, lamp store, 20 Chaboillez sq
Fuller, Thomas & Co., flour and commission merchts, 482 St. Paul and 403 Commissioners
FULLER, W. H., superintendent India and China Tea Company, Hospital
Fuller, William, M.D., physician and surgeon, 515 Wellington
Fulton, John & Co., commission agents, North British Chambers, Hospital
Furniss, Albert, Côte des Neiges road n tollgate
Fyfe, James, patent scale manuf., r 84 Wellington
Gadoua, Julien, hotel, 105 and 107 St. Paul
Gagnon, G. A., importer of shirts, collars, ties, gloves, and general outfitting, 300 Notre Dame
Gaherty, Mrs., ship chandler and marine store, 311 Commissioners
Gairdner, R. H., commission merchant and broker, 19 St. Sacrament
Galarneau, M. C., leather and shoe findings, 295 St. Paul
Galarneau, P. M. & Co., importers of dry goods, wholesale, 350 St. Paul
Galbraith, John, merchant tailor, 110 Great St. James
Gale, Rev. Thomas, 237 Seigneurs
Galibert, Calixte & Son, tanners, 109 St. Cartherine cor Colborne avenue
Garand, M., notary, 43 St. Vincent
Garult, Maxime, advocate, 6 St. James
Gardner, Dr. William, 474 St. Joseph
Gardner, John, chemist and druggist, 375 Notre Dame
Gardner, Robert, manufacturer of machinery, Novelty Works, 40 to 54 Nazareth
Gareau, Damase & Co., groceries and liquors, St. Louis, cor Bonsecours
Gareau, P. & Co., flour, grain and provision merchts 357 Commissioners
Gariepy, Doctor R., 96 Champ de Mars
Garrison Brigade Office, captain R. C. Healey, brigade major, 27 Gosford
GARTH, CHARLES & CO., plumbers, gas and steam fitters, Dominion metal works, 536 Craig (see adv)
Gaucher & Tellemosse, groceries, wines and liquors, 121 St. Paul
GAULT BROTHERS & CO., importers of fancy and Staple dry goods, 64 and 66 St. Peter cor. Recollet
GAULT, M. H., manager Royal Canadian Bank, 77 Great St. James
Gauthier, George N., agent and collector, 20 St. Gabriel
Gauthier, Mayrand & Co., wholesale grocers and provision merchants, 289 Commissioners
Gauthier, Moise, merchant tailor, 192 Notre Dame
Gauthier, Theophile, advocate, r. 35 St. Mary
GAZETTE, the Montreal Printing and Publishing Company, props., John Lowe, managing director, 67 Great St. James
Gear, Henry J., comn mer. importer and dealer in teas, Havana and German cigars, 32 St. Nicholas
Geddes, C. & C. G., stockbrokers, 32 St. Francois Xavier
Geddes, Henry H., estate agent, 32 Great St. James
Gelinas, Severe, impr of gen. dry goods, 280 St. Paul
GENAND, J. A., editor *L'Ordre*, 30 St. Gabriel
GERAGHTY, & CO., private detective office, Place d'Armes
GIANELLI, ANGELO M. F., prop. Cosmopolitan Hotel, 15 Place d'Armes, and lessee Caledonia Springs Hotel
Giband, Rev. A., Seminary, St. Sulpice, 320 Notre Dame
Gibb & Co., merchant tailors, 50 Great St. James
Gibb, Hunter & Doucet, notaries public and comn for U. C. and Superior courts, 1 and 2 India Chambers, Hospital
GIBERTON, A., importer and comn mer., 7 Custom House sq (see adv.)
Gibson, Rev. J., Munro, pastor Erskine Church, 112 Stanley
Gilbert, E. E., Canada engine works, 735 St. Joseph
Gill & Geen, packing box manufacturers, 27 and 28 St. Bonaventure
Gill, W. P. & Co., auction and commission house, 219 St. Lawrence
GILLESPIE, MOFFATT & CO., general merchants, and agents for Phœnix Insurance Company and British Colonial Steamship Company (limited), 310 to 316 St. Paul, & 251 & 253 Commissioners
GILLIES, JOHN, printer and publisher, of *True Witness*, 696 Craig
Gilman, Frank E., advocate, 60 Little St. James
Gilmour & Co., general merchants, 22 Recollet
Gilmour, James, Caledonia House, 419 Commissioners
Gilmour, James Y. & Co., importers of dry goods and small wares, 375 St Paul
Giraldi, Serafino, sen., wines, liquors, &c., 252 Notre Dame
Girard, Auguste, grain merchant, 17 St. Sacrament
Girard, H., dry goods, 212 and 214 Notre Dame
Girard & Nantais, fancy and staple dry goods and hoisery, 4 Stephens Block, 237 Notre Dame
Girdwood, G. P., M.D., M.R.C.S.L., 630 Lagauchetière
Girouard & Robidoux, advocates, 16 Little St. James
Glackmeyer, Charles, city clerk, 142 St. Denis
Glasgow, W. H., beltmaker, 467 William
GLASS, JOHN, manager J. M. Bradstreet & Son's improved mercantile agency, cor Great St. James and St. Peter
GLASSFORD, JONES & CO., forwarders and commission merchants, 86 Common
Glenora Flour Mills, A. W. Ogilvie & Co., Seigneurs n William
Globensky, L. A. & Co., importers, 396 St. Paul
Goderre, J. Emery, M.D., 392 Lagauchetière
Godfrey, Robert T., M.D., cor St. Catherine and McGill col ave
Goedike, Dennis Benjamin, advocate, Bourget, Coteau St. Augustin
Goheir, Remi, dry goods, 335 Mignonne
Goode, John B., importer of small wares, buttons, cutlery, fancy goods, &c., 57 St. Sulpice
Goodhugh, W. S. & Co., importers of leathers, 34 St. Peter
GORDON, ALEXANDER & CO., patent scale manufacturers, 73 College (see adv)
Gordon, James & Co., brokers and commission merchants, 49 St. Francois Xavier
Gordon, Mrs. Alexander, ladies boarding and day school, 328 Bleury
Gordon, Thomas & Co., general merchants, 4 Corn Exchange building, 43 St. Sacrament
Goudie, John, fancy goods, jewellery and plated ware, 117 St. Lawrence
Gough, Alfred, collector of Lachine Canal tolls, Lachine Canal office
Gould & Hill, sheet music and piano fortes, 116 Great St. James
Goulden, James, chemist and druggist, 177 and 179 St. Lawrence
GOULD, IRA & SONS, city flour mills, south side Canal wharf, office 14 William

Gould, Rev. E., minister New Jerusalem Church, 23 Hanover
Gourre, J. B., manufacturer and importor, and repairer of feathers, 210 St. Lawrence
GOVERNMENT EMIGRATION OFFICE, Joseph H. Daley, agent, 301 Commissioners
Graber, Jacob, jeweler and watchmaker, 825 St. Catherine
Grace, Patrick, grocer, 591 St. Mary
GRAFTON, F. E., publisher, bookseller and stationer 78 and 80 Great St. James
Graham, George, grocer, wholesale and retail, 16 St. Radegonde
Graham, J. Andrew, stationer and dealer in engravings, music, etc., Cathedral Block. 279 Notre Dame
Graham, Robert, wood and coal merchant, 305 Craig and 32 Durham
Graham, Robert & Co., stationers and blank book manufacturers, 47 St. Francois Xavier
Graham, Thomas, china, glass and earthenware, 110 and 112 St. Lawrence
Granby Red Slate Company, Henry Bulmer, president; E. L. Snow, secretary and treasurer, 67 Great St. James
GRANDE SEMINARIE DES ECCLESIASTIQUES, Rev. J. Bte, Larue, director, Sherbrooke n. Guy
GRAND TRUNK RAILWAY COMPANY OFFICES, Point St. Charles; ticket offices at Bonaventure station, and 39 Great St. James
GRAND TRUNK RAILWAY FREIGHT OFFICES, Charboillez square and Albert
Granjon, Rev. Moise Benoit, Seminary of St. Sulpice, 320 Notre Dame
Grant, Hall & Co., Royal flour mills, 111 Mill, and office, 96 Grey Nun
Grant, Henry, watchmaker, jeweler and optician, 303 Notre Bame
GRANT, WILLIAM & CO., gentlemen's haberdashery, 151 Great St. James, (see adv)
Gravel, Freres, dry goods and groceries, 2 St. Lawrence
Gravel, Martin, carriage maker, 75 St. Antoine
Gray, Henry R., dispensing and family chemist, 144 St. Lawrence
Great Manitoulin Oil Co., W. M. Freer, secretary and treasurer, Exchange Court, 10 Hospital
Green, Rev. James, missionary Montreal Bible Society 380 St Antoine
Greenburg, S. R., & Co., dry goods,, 125 St. Lawrence
Greene. Eugene, Cumberland House, 185 St. Bonaventure, cor. Cemetery
Greene, Francis, plumber, steam and gas fitter, 54 St. John
GREENE & SONS, wholesale fur and hat manufacturers and importers, 517 to 521 St. Paul
GREENSHIELDS, SAMUEL, SON & CO., importers of dry goods, wholesale. 46 to 50 St. Sacrament (see adv)
Grenier, George, M.D., 22 St. Denis
Grenier, Jacques & Co., importers of fancy and staple dry goods, wholesale, 300 St. Paul cor St. Jean Baptiste
Griffin, John C., notary and commissioner for taking affidavits, North British Chambers, 11 Hospital
Griffith, T. W., insurance agent, cor St. François Xavier and St. Sacrament
GROSS, FERDINAND, surgical apparatus and truss maker, 36 Victoria sq (see adv)
Grothé, J. M., jeweller, watchmaker and silversmith, 35 St. Lambert
Groves, G. & J., importers of china, glass and earthenware, wholesale and retail, 424 St. Paul and 43 Capitol
Guibord, Louis J., advocate, 6 Little St. James, bds 5 Common
Guilbault's Botanical and Zoological Garden, J. E. Guilbault, manager, entrance St. Lawrence or Upper St. Urbain
Guilmette, Joseph O., dry goods and ready made clothing, 71 Notre Dame
Gundlack, Alexander F., accountant, 82 St. Dominique
GUNDY, REV. SAMUEL B. S., 20 Dupre lane
GUNN, JOHN, commission merchant, 20 Cotte
Gunn, John, produce and general commission merchant, 12 William
Gutman, Moses, & Co., hoop skirt manufacturers, 26 and 28 Lemoine
Guy, Michael P., notary, 113 Mountain
Haeusgen & Gnaedinger, furriers and wholesale manufacturers of hats and caps, 56 St Peter
Hagan, William, hardware merchant, 168 and 170 St. Lawrence
Hagar, Charles, & Co., manufacturers of leather belting and fire engine hose, 107 and 109 Queen
Hagar, Edward, & Co., importers of china, glass and earthenware, 14 and 16 St. Peter cor St. Paul
Hagar, George & Co., general hardware merchants, 520 and 522 St. Paul
HAIGHT, F. S., M.A., Montreal academy, 14 St. Bonaventure
Haines, Brother & Co., general commission merchants, and agents for manufacturers, 90 St. Francois Xavier
Haldimand & Co., general hardware merchants, wholesale and retail, 253 and 255 St. Paul cor St. Vincent
Hall, Joseph N., & Co., wholesale hardware merchants, 10 St. Peter cor St. Paul
Hall, Kay & Co., general metal and tin merchants, Young's buildings, 90 McGill
Hamelin, Flavien, M.D., physician and surgeon, 529 St. Catherine
Hamilton, Rev. William, D.D., principal, institute for young ladies, 5 Oxford terrace, 53 McGill college avenue
Hampson, Robert, commission merchant, and agent for Phœnix (Marine) Insurance Co., New York, 18 Corn Exchange Blgs., St. John
Handly, Edward, dry goods, 203 and 205 St. Paul, and 7 Jacques Cartier Square
Handyside & Co., customs and forwarding agents, 58 St. Francois Xavier
Hanley, Thomas, Kingston Hotel, 74 Common cor Prince
Hanlon, Thomas F., civil engineer, 31 Notre Dame
Hannaford, Edward P., engineer, west, G. T. R., 36 City Councillors
HARBOR COMMISSIONERS OFFICE, H. H. Whitney, secretary, 14 Custom House Square
HARBOR MASTER'S OFFICE, captain A. M. Rudolf, harbor master, Harbor Commissioners Building, 14 Custom House Square
Harper, D. A., importer of electro plate, clocks, watches, fancy good and jewelery, 267 Norte Dame
Harrison, Thomas, dry goods, hosiery, &c., 104 Bleury
Hart, Alexander & Co., wholesale tobacco warehouse, 323 to 827 St. Paul
Hart, Nicholas, commission merchant, 518 St. Mary
Hart, Theodore, insurance agent, 33 St. Nicholas
Hartman, Charles J., commission merchant and general agent, 3 Union Building, 41 and 43 St. Francois Xavier

Hart, James A., chemist and druggist, 396 Norte Dame
Harvey, Horatio Nelson, lumber dealer 6 Union av
Harvey, James, warehouseman and commission merchant, 32 Colborne
Hastie, William, assistant collector of inland revenue, 58 Courville
Hawkins, Thomas, hide and leather inspector, tanner, 196 Ann
Hayes, Andrew, manufacturers agent for cutlery, china, glass and earthenware, 356 St. Paul
HEARN, MRS. C., optician and mathematical instrument maker, 242 Notre Dame (see adv)
HEAVYSEGE, CHARLES, Montreal Witness, 11 Alymer
Hebert & Lamy, groceries, wines and spirits, 623 St. Mary
Helliwell, Charles L., commission agent, 44 Berri
Helliwell & Macphie, commission merchants and importers, 504 St. Paul
Henderson, James H., forwarding and commission merchants, 99 Common cor Dalhousie
Henderson, John & Co., hatters and furriers, Crystal block, 283 Notre Dame
Henderson & Lovelace, coal and commission merchants, and importers of fire bricks and English pipe clay, 30 St. Lambert hill
Henderson, William, lumber merchant, Charlotte cor St. Constant
Hendry, Robert & Co., gold and silversmiths, watchmakers and jewelers, 53 Great St. James
Henry, Philip, dealer in tobacco, &c., 308 Notre Dame cor St. Sulpice
Henry, Simpson & Co., wholesale patent medicines and perfumery, 513 and 515 St. Paul
Henshaw, F. W., ashes broker and general commission merchant, 10 St. Sacrament
HERALD MONTREAL, Edward G. Penny, editor; E. G. Penny & Andrew Wilson, proprietors, publishers and printers, 51 Great St. James
Héroux, Edmond, M.D., 613 St. Catherine
Hervey, James, commission merchant, Mill
Hétu, Léonard Ovide, notary, 16 Little St. James, h 517 St. Catherine
Heubach, George, general shipping agent for Quebec and Gulf Port S. S. Co., 31 St. François Xavier
HEWARD, S. B., commission merchant, 24 St. Sacrament
HIAM, W. H., wholesale importer of fishing tackle and fancy goods, 8 Lemoine
Hibbard & Co., manufacturers and importers of rubber goods, 10 Lemoine
Hibbard, W. R. & Co., trunks, valises, and bag manufacturers, 354 and 356 Notre Dame
HICKS, VERY REV. E. H., Bishop's palace, Cemetery
HICKS, WILLIAM HENRY, professor McGill Normal school, 42 St Bonaventure
HICKSON, JOSEPH, secretary and treasurer Grand Trunk Railway, Point St. Charles
Hieronymus Frere, Friars College, 141 St. Denis
Higgins, Joseph J., axe manufacturer, Côte St. Paul
Hill, C., bookseller, stationer and circulating library 666 Dorchester, cor Brunswick
Hill, C. F. & Co., agents for Eaton's Automatic ventilating stove, 58 St. François Xavier
Hilton, W. & Co., cabinet makers and upholsterers, 61 Great St. James
Himsworth, C. G., advocate, 182 St. Denis
Hingston, W. H., M.D., L.R.C.S., 645 Lagauchetiere
Hirshfeld, H., importer French and English corsets and hoops, 215 Notre Dame
Hobbs, William, agent for British manufacturers, and Lancashire Fire and Life Insurance Company, Muir's Buildings, Place d'Armes
HOBSON, THOMAS, & CO. produce commission merchants, 486 and 488 St. Paul, and 405 Commissioners
Hodson, William H., architect, 59 St. Bonaventure
HOGAN, HENRY, proprietor St. Lawrence Hall, 29 and 31 Great St. James
Hogan, Rev. James, St. Ann's Church, 113 McCord
Holland, Andrew T. & Co., exchange brokers, 29 St. Francois Xavier
Holland, George A., importer of paper hangings, beads and fancy goods, 421 Notre Dame
Holland, M. & Son, wool hat factory, cor St. Francois Xavier and St. Paul
Holland, Richard, importer of paper hangings and fancy goods, 266 Notre Dame
Holtby, William, tobacco, cigars, etc., 6 St. Radegonde
Holton, Edward, advocate, 88 Great St. James
HOLTON, HON. LUTHER H., M.P., h 1043 Sherbrooke
Honey, John, prothonotary, 4 Phillips Square
Hood, Andrew W., soap and candle manufacturer, 57 Amherst
Hood, Mrs. D., saw and planing mill, 276 Craig
Hood, Thomas D., pianoforte warerooms, 79 Great St. James
Hope, John, commission and general merchant, 16 Corn Exchange Building, St. John
Hopkins, Edward Martin, agent Hon. Hudson's Bay Company, bds. 200 Bleury
Hopkins & Wily, architects and valuators, 59 Great St. James
Horan, John, notary, 562 Dorchester
Horne, George, wholesale and retail stationer, account book manufacturer, and picture frame maker, 71 and 73 St. Francois Xavier
HORSEY, E. H., M.D., 44 Beaver Hall terrace
HOSPICE OF ST. VINCENT DE PAUL, Brothers of Charity, brother Eusebe, principal, Mignonne
HOSPICE ST. ANTOINE, Miss Catharine Samson, superioress, 32 Labelle
HOSPICE ST. BATHILDE, Miss Sophia Bissonnette, superioress, 76 Vitre
HOSPICE, ST. JOSEPH, brother Eusebe, superior and director, 255 Dorchester
HOSPICE ST. JOSEPH, Sisters of Providence, for aged priests, 143 Mignonne
HOSPICE ST. JOSEPH, sister Frigon, superioress, Cemetery
HOTEL DIEU DES RELIGIEUSES HOSPITALIERES DE ST. JOSEPH, Mont St. Famille, Hotel Dieust and Upper St. Urbain
Hotel Du Canada, Victor Marcotte, proprietor, 20 and 22 and 24 St. Therese
Hotel Richelieu, A. Beliveau, proprietor, 45 St. Vincent
Houle, Alphonse, advocate, 20 St. Gabriel
Houle & Gauthier, groceries, wines and liquors, 115 Inspector
HOUSE OF INDUSTRY AND REFUGE, PROTESTANT, William Brown, secretary and superintendent, 547 Dorchester
Howard & Furner, wine and spirit merchants, bottlers and packers of Dow & Cos'. ales and porter, 95 St. Peter
Howard, R. P., M.D., L.R.C.P.E., professor of medicine, McGill University, 9 Beaver Hall hill
Howard, Smith & Co., brokers, produce and general commission merchants, 42 St. Francois Xavier

Howard, Thomas, importer, 4 Union Buildings, 43 St. Francois Xavier
Howe, H. Aspinwall, M.A., rector High School, 265 Sherbrooke
Hoyle, William & Co., importers of glass and earthenware, 11 St. Helen
Hus & Richardson, importers of leather, commission merchants, and sole agents for Alexander's kid gloves, 52 St. Peter
Hubbard & Hall, opticians, 113 St. George
Hubert, Papineau & Honey, prothonotaries, 177 Notre Dame
Hubert, R. A. R., prothonotary, 441 Sherbrooke
Hudon & Beliveau, importers of groceries, wines and spirits, 42 Jacques Cartier Square
Hudon, E. Fils & Cie, dry goods, groceries, importers of choice wines and cigars, 260 to 264 St. Paul, and 209½ Commissioners
Hudon, Joseph & Co., wholesale grocers, 246 St. Paul and 199 and 200 Commissioners
Hudon, Victor, importer of groceries, wines, liquors, &c., 306 and 308 St. Paul, and 249 Commissioners
HUDSON BAY COMPANY, E. M. Hopkins, agent, 17 Common
Hughes, Louis, monument builder, 465 St. Lawrence
HUGHES, N. H., deputy chief of police, 347 Dorchester
Hunsicker, J. E., commission mercht, 22 Foundling
Hunt & Brock, wine and commission merchants, 31 St. John
HUNT, T. STERRY, M.A., F.R.S., LL.D., chemist and mineralogist to the Geological Survey, h Crescent
HUNTINGDON, HON. L. S., M.P.P., president Huntingdon Mining Co., 48 Great St. James
HUNTINGDON MINING CO., Hon. L. S. Huntingdon, M.P.P., president; D. Ross Wood, secretary and treasurer, 48 Great St. James
HURON COPPER BAY COMPANY, John G. Burrows, secretary, 2 North British chambers, 11 Hospital
Hurteau, Isidore, N. P., Longueil
Hurtubise & Hamilton, dry goods, wholesale and retail, 8 St. Joseph
Huston, F. & Co., clothiers and outfitters, 68 and 70 St. Lawrence
HUTCHINS, B. & CO., importers of teas and general groceries, 188 and 190 McGill
Hutton, James & Co., agents for Birmingham and Sheffield hardware, 17 St Helen
Ibbotson, Henry J., advocate and clerk of Recorder's Court, 20 Hanover
IMPERIAL FIRE INSURANCE COMPANY OF LONDON, Rintoul Brothers, agents, 24 St. Sacrament (see adv. inside back cover)
India Chambers, 13 Hospital
INDIA AND CHINA TEA COMPANY, 23 Hospital
IRELAND, H. W. & CO., hardware merchants, nail and metal broker, agent for Welland Railway and Steamboat Company, 411 St. Paul and 94 Common
Irish, Charles T., exchange broker, 11 Place d'Armes
Irish, D. T., agent for Cheney, Fiske & Co., National Express Co., and British and American Express Co., 7 and 9 Place d'Armes
Iron, Nail and Spike Works, Thomas Peck & Co., 63 Mill, office 391 St. Paul
Irvine, Rev. Robert, D.D., minister of Knox church, 773 St. Catherine
IRWIN, JAMES, of Irwins' Foundry, 114 Ann
IRWIN'S FOUNDRY, 114 Ann
Isaacson, John H., notary Public, commissioner for receiving affidavits to be used in Ontario, Massachussetts and Kentucky, U. S., 40 St. François Xavier
Isaacson, R. W., Isaacson's Hotel, 67 St. Gabriel
IVES & ALLEN, hardware manufacturers, etc, 113 to 123 Queen
Jackson, Rev. Samuel, ministar of St. Paul's Union Church, Cote St. Paul
Jacobs, H. & Co., importers of cigars and meerschaum pipes, 299 Notre Dame, and 177 McGill
Jacques, Alphonse, advocate, 43 St. Vincent
JACQUES CARTIER BANK, Henri Cotte, cashier, 49 Great St. James
JACQUES CARTIER NORMAL SCHOOL, Abbe H. Verreau, principal, Abbe Routier, assistant principal, 128 Notre Dame
Jacques & Lamontagne, leather and shoe findings, 296 and 298 St. Paul
James, George & Co., wholesale boot and shoe manufacturers, 8 Dollard cor Notre Dame
Jamieson, R. C., & Co., varnish manufacturers, 48 St. Sacrament
Janes, Oliver & Co., commission merchants and flour dealers, 12 Foundling
Janes, W. D. B., coal merchant, 19 McGill and 147 Great St. James
Jacques, G. E., forwarder and commission merchant, 103 to 108 Common
Jeffery, Brothers & Co., general merchants, 44 St. Sacrament
JELLYMAN, RICHARD, paper box manufacturer, 58 Craig (see adv)
Jenking, Thomas, brush manufacturer, 343 Notre Dame
Jenkins, Rev. John, D.D., minister St. Paul's church, Church of Scotland, 749 Dorchester
Jenning's, Emery, inner sole manufacturer, 17 Dorchester cor Colborne av
Jette & Archambault, advocates, 44 St. Vincent
Jobin, A. Damase, notary, 5 St. Therese
Jobin & Mathieu, notaries, 5 St. Therese
Johnson, Alexander, LL.D., professor of natural philosophy in McGill University, 70 McGill College avenue
Johnson, Thomas R., accountant and estate agent, 44 Little St. James, h 258 Bleury
Johnson, W. B., grocer, 46 Beaver hall terrace cor Dorchester
Johnson, William, manufacturer of agricultural implements, 16 and 22 Nazareth
Johnston, James, & Co., importers and wholesale dealers in dry goods, 56 St. Peter cor Recollet
Jones, C. G., real estate agent, 88 Great St. James
Jones, Hon. Robert, 6 Portland Place, 242 St. Antoine
Jones, John M., & Co., leather commission merchts, 20 St. Peter
Jones, Joseph, coroner, and agent for Briton and Britannia Life Assurance Co., 44 Little St. James
Joseph, Jesse, Belgian Consul. 873 Sherbrooke
Joseph, Joseph Olivier, B.C.L., advocate, 38 Little St. James
Judah, Henry, advocate, 51 Little St. James
JUVENILE PRESBYTERIAN, monthly, John Lovell, printer, 23 St. Nicholas
Kahler, Rev. Henry C., 127 St. Dominique
Kalb, Jacob, wholesale dry goods, 414 St. Paul, cor Custom house sq
Kapp, Otto & Co., dealers in cork, 229 Notre Dame
Kavanagh, Michael, soap and candle manufacturer, 39 Chabqoillez sq

Kearney, P. J., auctioneer and broker, 69 St. Peter
Kellert & Friedman, pawnbrokers and Dominion loan office, 184 Notre Dame
Kelley & Dorion. advocate, 16 Little St. James
Kemp & Brown, wholesale and retail grocers, importers, coffees, wines, liquors, &c., 147 McGill
Kemp, G. & Co., shirt and collar establishment, 306 Notre Dame
Kennedy, James, merchant tailor and clothier, 58 and 60 St. Lawrence
Kennedy, McCullagh, groceries and provisions, 108 Wellington
Keroack, Alphonse, leather merchant, 443 St. Paul
Kerr, William H., advocate, 8 St. Sacrament
Kerry Brothers, & Crathern, wholesale druggists, 351 St. Paul
Kidner, J. F., impr. of Paris millinery and mantles, flowers and ribbons, 435 Notre Dame
Kilby, Ralph H., manufacturers' agent, h 45 Drummond
Kimbton, Henry, commission merchant, 332 Lagauchetiere
KING, EDWIN F., post office inspector, 4 McGill College Avenue
KING, EDWIN HENRY, general manager Bank of Montreal, 202 University
KING, THOMAS D., proprietor of *The Spectator*, 144 Peel
Kingan & Kinloch, wholesale grocers, 54 St. Sacrament, cor. St. Peter
Kingan & Scott, money brokers, 66 St. Francois Xavier
Kingston, Frederick, wine and spirit merchant, 28 Hospital
Kingstone & Hatton, barristers-at-law for Upper Canada, office, 353 Notre Dame
Kinmond, W. L. & Co., engineers and railway supply agents, 7 Custom House Square
Kinsella, Nicholas, groceries, wines and liquors, 17 Juros, cor Anderson
Kirby, Charles Henry, sub editor *Montreal Herald*, 211 St. Antoine
Kirby, James, advocate, and editor of the Lower Canada Law Journal, 4 Merchant's exchange, 11 St. Sacrament
KIRUP, JOSEPH, brush manufacturer, 329 St. Paul
Kirkwood, Livingstone & Co., general brokers and commission merchants, 449 Commissioners
Kirkwood, W. W. & Co., foreign produce agents, and commission merchants, 17 and 19 Lemoine
Kollmeyer, Alexander Henry, M. D., 25 Jurors
Labodie, Henri Adolphe, M. D., 6 Little St. James
Labadie, J. A. & J. E. O., notaries, 6 Little St. James
LA BANQUE JACQUES CARTIER, Honore Cotte, cashier, 49 Great St. James
Labelle, Jacques, hotel, 179 St. Dominique
Labelle, Pierre, hotel, 200 St. Lawrence
Labelle, Regis, lumber merchant, 470 St. Joseph
Labelle, Severe, merchant, 409 Lagauchetiere
Laberge & Bertrand, builders and contractors, 64 St. Louis
Laberge, Louis, dry goods, 163 St. Paul
Labine, Jules, dry goods, 166 Notre Dame
Labonte, David, axe maker, St. Marguerite, Tannery west
Labonte, David, tailor and outfitter, 256 St. Joseph
Labranche, Joseph, brushmaker, 195 Jacques Cartier
Labrecque & Maturin, merchant tailors and clothiers, 15 St. Lawrence
Lacan, Rev. J., St. James' R. C. Church, 473 St. Catherine
Lacombre & Clarke's French and English Academies 82 St. Denis
Lacoste, Joseph C., advocate, 29 St. Vincent
Lacroix & Berger, carpenters, 105 St. Louis
LA FABRIQUE DE MONTREAL, E. A. Dubois, agent, 38 St. Sulpice
Laflamme, Alfred, trunkmaker, 129 St. Joseph
Laflamme, Edmond, lamps and paints
Laflamme, R. & G., advocates, 64 Little St. James
Lafleur, Jean Baptiste, advocate, 76 St. Lawrence, St. J. Bte. village
Lafleur, Rev. Theodore, 390 Dorchester
Lafon, Vincent, detective, r 18 St. Constant
Lafond, J. E., exchange broker, 329 Notre Dame
Laframboise, Hon. Maurice, advocate, 32 Little St. James, h 85 Union ave
Lafreynaye & Armstrong, advocates, 10 St. Lambert
Lafrieniere & St. Onge, flour and grain merchants, 291 and 293 Commissioners
Laggatt, Henry, jeweller and goldsmith, 122 Notre Dame, cor Claude
Laidlaw, Middleton & Co., commission merchants, 4 St. Nicholas
Laing & Couper, provision and commission merchants, 338 Commissioners
Lalonde & Valade, Railway hotel, 45 Chaboillez sq
Lamarche, L. E., groceries, wines & liquors, 499 Craig
Lamarche, Rev. G., Bishops palace, Cemetery
Lamarre & Labelle, dry goods, 85 Notre Dame
Lambe, W. B., advocate, 59 Great St. James
LAMERE, J. B., agent Richelieu Navigation Co., 201 Commissioners
LA MINERVE, daily, tri-weekly and weekly, Duvernay Freres, publishers and printers, 16 St. Vincent
Lamontague, C. H., notary, 50 St. Gabriel
Lamothe, Pierre, notary, 34 Little St. James
Lamoureux, Pierre, foreman job department at John Lovell's printing establishment
Lamplough & Campbell, opp Fortification Lane cor St. Lambert Hill
LANCASHIRE FIRE AND LIFE INSURANCE CO., William Hobbs, gen agent, 5 Place d'Armes
Lanctot, H., notary, 231 Notre Dame
Lanctot, Hypolite, notary, 97 St. Constant
Lanctot, Mederic, advocate and editor of *L'Independence Canadienne*, 119 Champ de Mars
Lane, John, deputy commissary gen. 745 Sherbrooke
Lane, William, Liverpool House, 571 Craig
Langford, John, of Langford's advertising and publishing agency, 13 Place d'Armes
Langford's Advertising and Publishing Agency, Place d'Armes Chambers, 13 Place d'Armes
Langlands, James, coffee and spice mills, 36 and 42 St. Gabriel
Langlois, Pierre, grocer, 321 St. Joseph
Langlois, Rev. J. Bte., parish priest of St. Vincent de Paul, 85 Fullum
Lapierre, Rev. P. L., P.P., St. Henri, Tannery west
Lappare, Henri, notary, 25 St. Vincent
Laramee, Alfred, M.D., 541 Lagauchetiere
Lareau & Brother, hotel keepers, 206 St. Lawrence
LA REVUE CANADIENNE, monthly, E. Senecal, printer and publisher, 10 St. Vincent
Lario & Brother, Canada nail works, south side canal
Lariviere & Bourdeau, hardware, paints, &c., 233 and 235 St. Paul
Lariviere, N. & A. C., Canada coach and sleigh factory, 74 St. Antoine
Larkin, Patrick, groceries, wines and liquors, 185 Ottawa
LARMINIE, G. H., editor of *Trade Review* and *Intercolonial Journal of Commerce*, 58 St. François Xavier

Larochelle, D., boots and shoes, 156 Notre Dame
Larocque, Alfred, director City and District Savings Bank, 293 Dorchester
Larocque, Alphonse B., M.D., 585 St. Catherine
Larose, Auguste, contractor, 154 German
Larue, N. & Co., architects and measurers, 181 Great St. James
Laslett, William, importer and commission merchant, 4 Royal Insurance buildings, 1 Common
Lassonde & Favreau, hotel, groceries and liquors, 43 St. Mary
Latham, Richard S., chemist and druggist, 667 Craig
Latour, L. A. Huguet, notary, 40 St. Denis
Laurent, Laforce & Co., pianos, harmoniums and music, 225 Notre Dame
Laurent, M., architect, 36 St. Lambert
LAURIE, A. & CO., wholesale dry goods merchants, 374 St. Paul cor St. Sulpice
Lavender, Henry, merchant tailor, 295 Notre Dame
Laverty, Joseph, groceries, wines and liquors, 110 Bleury cor Bernard
Lavigne, Moise, groceries, wines and liquors, 228 St. Constant cor Mignonne
Law Stamp Office, Norbert, Dumas & Phelan, commissioners; David Tait, manager, Court House, 177 Notre Dame
Law, Young & Co. merchants, 56 and 58 Wellington
LAWLOR, J. D., manufacturer and dealer in sewing machines and all kinds of boot and shoe machinery, findings, wholesale and retail; 365 Notre Dame (see adv.)
Lawton, H. J., importer of coal oil, general lamp goods, English cut glass, &c., 42 St. Sulpice
Leach, R. A., advocate, 16 University
LEACH, VEN. ARCHIDEACON, W. T., D.C.L., LL.D., Christ Church Cathedral, h 16 University
Lebeau, Louis, blacking manufacturer, 545 St. Catharine
Leblanc & Cassidy, advocates, 486 Craig
Leblanc, Dr. Benjamin H., 135 Centre
Leblanc, Joseph, flour merchant, 179 Commissioners
LEBLANC, VERY REV. CANON G., Bishop's palace, Cemetery
Lecavalier & Godin, dry goods, 293 St. Lawrence
L'ECHO DE LA FRANCE, receuil de la literature, sciences, philosophic, beaux arts, historie, religion, politic, &c,, d'Europe; Louis Ricard, directeur, 422 Craig
L'ECHO DU CABINET DE LECTURE PAROISSIAL DE MONTREAL, monthly; C. Thibault, manager, 27 St. Vincent
Leclair, Rev. W., St. Ann's church, 113 McCord
Leclair, F. & J. & Co., wholesale importers of dry goods and groceries, 290 St. Paul, and 235 Commissioners
Leclerc, John A,, leather merchant and dealer in shoe findings, and shoe peg manufacturer, 530 St. Paul
Leclere, Georges, M. D., secretary Board of Agriculture for L. C., 615 Craig
Leduc, Joel, grain merchant, 299 Commissioners
Lee, Charles, produce broker, 30 Foundling
Lee, Thomas. chief accountant Bank of Montreal, 57 Courville
Leeming & Cowie, commission merchants, 40 St. Nicholas
Leeming, John & Co., auctioneers and agents for sale of real estate, 364 Notre Dame
Lefebvre, Francois, wholesale and retail confectioner and tobacconist, 512 and 514 St. Mary
Lefebvre, Jean Bte., & Cie., groceries, wines and liquors, 242 Craig
Lefebvre & Maillet, advocates, 35 St. Vincent
Lefebvre, O., grocer, wine and spirit dealer, 111 Amherst
Leggatt & Reay, grocers, wine, spirit and provision merchants, 431 Notre Dame cor Dollard
Legge, Charles, & Co., civil engineers and solicitors for patents, 48 Great St. James
Lemaire, Touissant, grocer, 413 Jacques Cartier
Leman, C. J., M.D., physician & surgeon, 519 Craig
Lemire, Eustache, M.D., 487 Craig
LEMOINE, P. G. & SON, book and job printers, 34 St. Gabriel
Lenoir, Charles, boot and shoe manufacturer, 406 Notre Dame cor St. Peter
LENOIR, REV. H., St. James R. C. church, 473 St. Catherine
LE NOUVEAU MONDE, daily, tri-weekly and weekly; J. Royal, editor; Andre Senecal, manager, 23 St. Vincent
Leonard & McKinnon, merchant tailors and clothiers, 154 McGill
Lepage, Germain, hardware, stoves, etc., 210 St. Paul
LE PAYS, tri-weekly and weekly; Papineau & Dorion, publishers and printers; Alphonse Lusignan, editor; Andre Senecal, manager, 9 St. Therese
Leprohon, E. Alcibiade, architect, 101 St. Christophe
Leprohon, J. L., M.D., 51 St. Rodegonde cor Lagaucheterie
Lesag, Louis, superintendent Water Works, 24 Wolfe
Leslie, A. C., hardware broker and agent, 30 St. Francois Xavier
LESLIE, HON. JAMES, senator, 36 Parthenais
Letourneux & Cie., importers of hardware and cutlery, wholesale and retail, 259 to 265 St. Paul
L'EVECHE DE MONTREAL, Very Rev. J. O. Paré, secretary, Cemetery off St. Antoine
Levesque, Antoine, customs appraiser, 15 Common
Levesque, Joseph, groceries, wines, liquors and provisions, 43 Bonaventure
Levin, Bernard, hatter and furrier, wholesale and retail, 297 Notre Dame
Levy, Rev. B., St. Constance street synagogue
Lewis, John, Surveyor of customs, 381 Nun
Lewis, Kay & Co., importers of dry goods, and fancy staple goods, wholesale, cor. St. Helen and Recollet
Lewis, W. F. & Co., wine merchants, 84 St. Peter
Lewthwait, Alexander, wheelwright Petit Cote
L'Heureux. Hilaire, agent, 65 Campeau
L'Hussier, Pierre, hatter and furrier, wholesale and retail, 221 St. Lawrence
LIFE ASSOCIATION OF SCOTLAND, P. Wardlaw, secretary, Royal Insurance Buildings, 1 Common. (see adv. inside back cover)
Limoges & Co., general dry goods, 125 and 127 St. Josheph
Linton & Cooper, manufacturers and wholesale dealers in boots and shoes, 524 and 526 St. Paul
Lippe, Camille, groceries, wines and liquors, 218 Montcalm, cor. Mignonne
Little, Thomas, general grocer, 603 and 605 St. Mary
Little, William A., engraver and lithographer, 35 St. John, cor. Notre Dame
Loeser, L. & Co., hat and cap manufacturers, wholesale and retail, 468 Notre Dame
Logan, Angus & Co., paper makers, stationers, and envelope and paper bag manufacturers, 378 St. Paul
LOGAN, SIR WILLIAM E., F. R. S., and G. S., director of the Geological Survey of Canada, 76 St. Gabriel

Lomer, Gerhard & Co., general fur merchants, exporters, importers and manufacturers of buckskin mitts and gloves (New York. 56 Cedar st), 475 St. Paul
Lonergan, Rev. J.. Hochelaga
LOOSEMOORE, REV. CANON PHILIP, senior canon Christ Church cathedral, 103 University
Lorange, Joseph, groceries and provisions, 124 Montcalm cor Sydenham
Lorange, Olivier, groceries, wines and liquors, 115 Dorchester cor Syndenham
Loranger & Loranger, advocates, 29 St. Vincent
Lord, James & Co., commission merchants and general shipping agents, 18 Common
L'ORDRE, tri-weekly and weekly; Plinguet & Laplante, proprietors and printers, 30 St. Gabriel
LOVELL, JOHN, printer and publisher of the *Daily News; Montreal Weekly Transcript;* Montreal Directory; general Book and Job Printer and Blank Book Manufacturer, 23 and 25 St. Nicholas, between St. Sacrament and St. Paul
Low, John W., New York Temperance hotel
LOWE, JOHN, managing director Montreal Printing and Publishing Company, 67 Great St. James
LOWER CANADA AGRICULTURALIST, monthly; Jos. Perrault, editor and proprietor; John Lovell, printer, 22 St. Nicholas
LOWER CANADA JURIST (monthly); John Lovell, proprietor, publisher and printer, 23 and 25 St. Nicholas
LOWER CANADA LAW JOURNAL, quarterly; James Kirby, advocate, editor and conductor; John Lovell, printer & publisher, 23 St. Nicholas
LUSIGNAN, ALPHONSE, editor of *Le Pays*, 9 St. Therese
Lussier, Paul, advocate Hochelaga
Luttrell, Richard, station agent, G.T.R.
Lyman, S., Jones & Co., wholesale drug and commission merchants, and agents for Union Mutual Life Assurance Co., of Boston, 44 St. John
Lymans, Clare & Co., wholesale chemists and druggists, 384 and 386 St. Paul
Macbean, David, B.A., M.D., Sylvan place, 140 St. Monique
Macbean, William, land agent G.T.R., Sylvan place, 140 St. Monique
MacCallum, Duncan C., M.D., physician and surgeon, 520 Craig
McCulloch, F., cashier City Bank, Place d'Armes, cor Great St. James
MACDONALD, de B., & Co., importers and manufacturers of straw goods and steel spring hoop skirts, 19 St. Helen
McDonald, J. M., St. Lawrence dye works, 31 Bleury
McDonald, Rev. Alexander, secretary French Canadian Missionary Society, 82 St. Christophe
McDonnell, Peter L., advocate, and assistant city clerk, City Hall, 186 St. Paul
McDonnell, Richard, advocate, 17 Place d'Armes, hill
McDonnell, Robert L., M.D., physician and surgeon, 889 St. Catherine
McDOUGALL & DAVIDSON, stock and bill brokers and agents for North British and Mercantile Insurance Co., 11 Hospital
McDougall, Hartland S., stock and share broker, St. Sacrament cor St. Nicholas
McEwen, Peter, general manager, Union Bank, 51 McGill college ave
McFarlane, James B., plumber gas fitter, and manufacturer of every description of copper work, 6 Bleury
McFarlan, Walter, & Baird, wholesale clothing, and dry goods, Dominion buildings, 126 McGill
Mackay & Austin, advocates, 34 Little St. James
Mackay, David, customs appraiser, 15 Common
Mackay, John & Co., commission merchants, 33 St. Nicholas
MACKAY, JOSEPH & BRO., wholesale dry goods, 170 McGill
Mackenzie, J. G. & Co., general merchants, 381 and 383 St. Paul
Mackenzie, Richard, manufacturers agent for railway supplies, 356 St. Paul,
Maclean, David E. & Co., produce commission merchants, shippers, and ship agents, 4 St. Nicholas
MacLean, Donald, pianofortes, 7 St. Charles Borromee
MACPHERSON, JOHN, deputy assistant Adj. Gen. of Militia, Brigade Office, 63 St. Gabriel
MacQuisten, P., city surveyor, 164 St. Hubert
MacRae, George, advocate and commissioner for taking affidavits for Ontario, 42 Little St. James
MacTavish Brothers, wholesale dealers in petroleum, kerosene and machinery oils, lamps, &c., 140 St. Lawrence
MacVicar, Rev. D. H., minister of Cotte Street Canada Presbyterian Church, 674 Lagauchetiere
McAdam, Charles, commission merchant, Scotland
McARTHUR, JOHN, & SON, oils, colors, manufacturers and dealers in lubricating oils, paints and window glass, 18 Lemoine
McAVAY, E. F., & CO., manufacturers of New Dominion Cement, 153 St. James (see adv)
McCallum, Duncan, M.D., physician and surgeon, 784 Craig
McCallum, J., & Sons, piano-forte warerooms, 66 Bleury
McClure & Cassils, importers of fancy and staple dry goods, glovers, hosiers, and shirt and collar makers, 393 Notre Dame
McCONKEY, SAMUEL, St. Lawrence cigar store and sample rooms, 30 and 32 Great St. James
McCord, David R., advocate, 486 Craig
McCoy & Vilbon, advocates, 6 Little St. James
McCready, James & Co., leather commission merchts, 503 St. Paul
McCuaig, John F., shipping and insurance agent, 31 St. François Xavier, and 81 Common, canal wharf
McCulloch, Brothers, commission merchants, 10 and 12 Corn exchange
McCulloch, Jack & Co., importers of dry goods, wholesale, 426 and 428 St. Paul
McDonald, Alexander & Sons, contractors and builders, 71 Bluery
McDonald, Dugald, commercial academy, 104 St. Bonaventure
McDonald, John, groceries, wines and liquors, 167 St. Lawrence cor Dorchester
McDonald, R., advocate, 17 Place d'Armes hill
McDONALD, W. C., tobacco merchant and manuf., 340 Notre Dame (see adv)
McDougall, Jas., canal flour mill, 447 Commissioners
McDougall, John & Co., manufacturers of car wheels, works, St. Gabriel locks, office, 22 St. Sacrament
McEachran, D., M.R.C.V.S., veterinary surgeon, 679 Craig
McEvenue, B., deputy postmaster
McFee, Duncan, general commission merchant, 10 William
McGarvey, Owen, chair and furniture warehouse, 11 St. Joseph
McGauvran, J. W. & Co., saw and planing mills, St. Gabriel Locks

McGibbon, Alexander, grocer, wine and spirit merchant, 69 Great St. James, and 44 St. Gabriel
McGibbon, William, grocer, wine and spirit merchant, 218 and 220 Notre Dame
McGILL MODEL SCHOOL, James McGregor, boys' department; Miss Mary Coady, girls department, 30 to 38 Belmont
McGILL NORMAL SCHOOL, professors Hicks and Robins, 30 Belmont
McGILL UNIVERSITY, College buildings, 803 Sherbrooke; Medical faculty, 25 Cotté; High school, cor Dorchester and University; secretary's office, 677 Dorchester
McGregor, Gregor, auctioneer and commission merchant, 90 St. Francois Xavier
McGuire & Co., Metropolitan hotel, 47 St. Jean Baptiste
McIlree, J. D., M. D., inspector of hospitals, and principal medical officer, 31 Notre Dame
McIntosh & Daly, merchant tailors and gent's furnishing goods, 5 St. Patrick's hall, 25 Victoria sq
McIntosh, Edward, notary, 114 St. Joseph
McIntyre, Denoon & French, wholesale dry goods, 399 Commissioners
McIver & Co., hatters and furriers, wholesale and retail, 191 Notre Dame
McKay, Henry & Co., commission merchants, shipping and insurance brokers, 11 St. Sacrament
McKenna, Thomas, plumber, gas and steam fitter, 58 and 60 St. Henry
McKenzie, M., marine and ship chandler, 4 and 6 Grey Nun
McKenzie, William, exchange broker, 98 St. Francois Xavier
McKercher, J. B. & Co., boots and shoes, 228 Notre Dame
McLACHLAN, BROS. CO., importers of staple and fancy goods, small wares, 468 St. Paul
McLAREN, JOHN C., saddlery emporium, and belt and hose manufacturer, 149 Great St. James, h 17 Belmont
McLaren, W. & Co., wholesale boot and shoe manufacturers, 18 St. Maurice
McLaren, William D., groceries, wines and liquors, 247 St. Lawrence cor St. Catherine
McLaughlin, J., chief water police, 12 Grey Nnn
McLea, John & Robert, shipping agents, 8 Common
McLean, D., agent leather, hides and wool, 82 and 84 McGill
McLeod, Rev. J. A., incumbent of St. Thomas Church, 17 Berri
McMahon, Arthur, advocate, 17 Little St. James
McMartin, John, agent for steamer *L. Renaud*, 2 Grey Nun
McMaster, W. J. & Co., importers of staple and fancy dry goods, 16 Lemoine
McMILLAN & CARSON, wholesale clothiers, 150 McGill
McNamara, Daniel, grocer, wine and spirit dealer, 367 St. Joseph
McNamee, Francis B., contractor, 275 St. Antoine
McRae, F. A., wholesale and retail confectioner, 531 St. Mary
McRitchie, Rev. George, pastor Wesleyan Church, 28 St. Monique
McShane, R., wholesale grocer, 109 and 111 McGill
Maguire & Smith, shipchandlers and grocers, 285 Commissioners
Malo, Francis Xavier, merchant tailor, 235 Notre Dame
Mandeville, Elie, book and job printer, 99 Campeau
Mandeville, Francois, notary, 427 St. Mary
MANN, DAVID DANIEL, clothier, 161 McGill (see adv.)
Mann & Son, merchant tailors, 403 and 405 Notre Dame cor St. Peter
Mansfield, Martin, Mansfield House, 215 St. Bonaventure
Manson, William, importer of British and foreign stationery, 58 St. Francois Xavier
Manton, Joseph, gunmaker, 689 Craig
Marchand, L. W., Deputy Clerk, Court of Appeals, Court House, 177 Notre Dame
Marchand, Louis & Son, banking and exchange office, cor St. Francois Xavier and great St. James
Marchand, Mederic, advocate, 4 St. Elizabeth
Marcotte, Victor, prop. Hotel du Canada, 20, 22 and St. Therese cor St. Gabriel
Marcou, Henderson & Co., hats and caps, 186 Notre Dame
Marechal, Rev. Joseph Nap., parish priest, Notre Dame de Grace
Marenda, Francois, Franklin House, 23 to 31 Cemetery
Markgraf, Charles F., M.A., professor McGill University, 335 Dorchester
Marler, G. L., accountant, Seminary St. Sulpice, 320 Notre Dame
MARRIAGE, WALTER, importer of English groceries, 30 Lemoine (see adv.)
MARTEL, JOSEPH, groceries, wines and liquors, 564 and 581 St. Mary
Martin, George, photographic goods, 42 St. John
Martin, John, fur broker, and general commission merchant, 459 St. Paul
Martin & Monat, wholesale dry goods, 220 St. Paul
Martiheau, Rev. F., Seminary of St Sulpice, 320 Notre Dame
Mason, John, shoemaker, 256 St. Patrick
Mason, S. W., account book manufacturer, paper ruler and book binder, 59 St. Francois Xavier
Masson, D., & Co., wholesale grocers and commission merchants, 31 St. Peter
MATHEWSON, J. A., importer and wholesale grocer, 202 McGill
MATHEWSON, JOHN, & SON, soap, candle and oil manufacturers, 10 to 29 Inspector cor College
Mathieson, Rev. Alexander, D.D., minister of St. Andrews' Church, Church of Scotland, 30½ City Councillors
Mathieu, Rev. J. M., Bishop's Palace, Cemetery
Matthews, Richard, perfumer and fancy soap manufacturer, 35 Murray
Matthews, Robert L., deputy assistant Commissary General, 193 Bleury
Matthews, Stephen, merchant tailor, 82 Great St. James
Mauffette, Joseph, principal St. Joseph Academy, 507 to 513 St. Joseph
Mavor, James A., & Co., Montreal Marble Works, cor St. Catherine and St. Alexander
Maxwell, E. J., & Co., lumber merchants, 545 and 715 Craig
May, Joseph, importer of dry goods, wholesale, 449 St. Paul
May, S. H., & Co., importers of paints, oils, glass, brushes, varnish, &c., 474 St. Paul and 395 Commissioners
MAY, THOMAS & CO., importers of straw goods and fancy dry goods, Caverhill's Buildings, 68 St. Peter
Maybank, George, St. Vincent hotel, 48 St. Vincent
MAYOR'S OFFICE, William Workman, mayor, City Hall, 186 St. Paul

Maysenhoelder & Berger, working jewellers and chainmakers, 27 St. Lambert
MECHANICS' BANK, Walter Shanly, president; Alexander Molson, vice-president and managing director, 86 Great St. James
MEDICAL FACULTY McGILL COLLEGE, 25 Cotte
MEDICAL HALL, Kenneth Campbell & Co., proprietors, 23 Great St. James, branch establishment, 8 Phillips Square
Meek, James, prop St. Lambert House, 8 St. Lambert
Meeker, C. J., banking exchange office, 51 St. Francois Xavier
Meikle, John Robert, hotel keeper, 12 Vitre
Meilleur & Co., manufacturers and dealers in stoves, iron, bedsteads, tin and sheet iron ware, 526 Craig
MERCANTILE AGENCY, Dun, Wiman & Co., proprietors; James Hedley, manager, 37 and 39 St. Francois Xavier
Mercantile and Exchange Bank of Liverpool (limited), Prentice, Macdougall & Co., agents, 60 St. Francois Xavier
MERCHANTS' BANK OF CANADA, Jackson Rae, cashier, Place d'Armes cor Notre Dame
Merchants' Exchange, John C. Dinning, secretary, 11 St. Sacrament
Merchants' Hotel, G. D. Empsey, prop., 51 College
Merrill, Dr. J. A., medical electrician, 149 Great St. James
Merrill, H. & H., dry goods, 288 Notre Dame
Merry, W. A., secretary Building Society, 233 St. Antoine
Metivier, J. Baptiste, contractor, 258 St. George
Meunier, David, proprietor Glasgow hotel, 74 and 76 St. Lawrence
Meyer, J. & Co., wholesale importers of dry goods, 525 St. Paul
Meyn & Wulff, manufacturers agents, 351 Commissioners
Michaels & Lyon, auctioneers and importers of carpets, woolens and general merchants, 301 Notre Dame
MILITIA BRIGADE OFFICE, lieut.-col. T. Bacon, brigade major, 63 St. Gabriel
Millar, G. M., commission merchant, 464 St. Paul
Millar, George A., commission merchant, 401½ Craig
Millard, H. R., importer of watch materials, tools, glasses, &c., 48 Great St. James
Millard R. & Co., railroad chairs and spike factory, 147 Prince
MILLAR, ADAM, junr, bookseller, stationer, and dealer in fancy goods, 29 Bleury
MILLER, ALEXANDER, secretary Canadian Navigation Co., 73 St. James
Miller, Charles D. & Co., confectioners, 344 Notre Dame
MILLER, ROBERT, wholesale stationer, school book publisher, book binder and blank book manufacturer, and agent for Lovell's series of school books, 387 Notre Dame
Miller, Thomas, leather merchant, 263 St. George
MILLOY, ALEXANDER, agent Royal Mail Through Line steamers, Montreal to Hamilton, 73 Great St. James
Mills, E. Lyman, broker and merchant, 33 St. Francois Xavier
Minchin, William & Co., importers of china, glass and earthenware, 417 St. Paul
Mireault, Gilbert, advocate, 6 Little St. James
Mitchell, A. & Co., brokers and commission merchants, 327 Commissioners
Mitchell, James, West India and general commission merchant, 7 St. Helen
Mitchell, Lewis, organ builder, 104 St. Antoine, cor Cemetery
Mitchell, Robert, commission merchant and broker, 33 St. Sacrament cor St. John
Mitchell, Robert & Co., Montreal brass foundry, 114 St. Peter cor Craig
Mocock, William, axe and edge tool manufacturer, St. Gabriel locks
MODEL SCHOOL OF COLONIAL CHURCH AND SCHOOL SOCIETY, Rev. canon Bond, 44 St. Bonaventure
MOLSON, ALEXANDER, managing director Mechanics Bank, and agent for International Life Assurance society, 557 Sherbrooke
MOLSON, J. H. R. & BROTHERS, brewers, distillers, vinegar manufacturers and sugar refiners, 222 St. Mary, city office 117 St. François Xavier
MOLSON, WILLIAM, president of Molsons Bank, 342 St. Mary
MOLSON'S BANK, William Molson, president, William Sache, cashier, 100 Great St. James cor St. Peter
MOLSON'S BANK, SAVINGS DEPARTMENT, James Elliott, manager, 100 Great St. James
Monagan, W. F., M.D., M.C.P.S., 77 Upper St. Dominique, St. J. Bte. village
MONDELET, HON. CHARLES, judge Superior Court, 268 St. Antoine
Mondelet, W. H., M.D., 268 St. Antoine
Mondion, Louis Joseph, dry good, 451 and 453 St. Joseph
Monette, Maxime, dry goods, 201 St Paul
MONGEAU, J. N., advocate, 223 Notre Dame
Mongeon, Charles, wharfinger, Lachine canal office
MONK, HON. SAMUEL CORNWALLIS, Judge of Superior Court, 28 Victoria
Monk & Normandeau, advocates, 43St. Vincent
Monk & Rixford, advocates, 34 Little St. James
Montmarquet, A. Edouard, dry goods, 398 St. Catherine
MONTREAL & CHAMPLAIN RAILROAD CO., Grand Trunk Railway office, Point St. Charles
MONTREAL & OTTAWA FORWARDING CO., Isaac Bonner, agent, 69 Common
MONTREAL AND QUEBEC STEAMBOAT OFFICE, Richelieu Co., 201 Commissioners
MONTREAL ASSURANCE CO., fire and marine, W. Murray, manager, 25 Great St. James
MONTREAL AUXILIARY BIBLE SOCIETY, T. Muir, depositary, 713 Craig
MONTREAL AXE AND EDGE TOOL FACTORY, William Mocock, proprietor, cor Seigneurs and Canal
MONTREAL AXE WORKS, Morland, Watson & Co., proprietors; factory on Lachine canal; office 387 St. Paul
MONTREAL BUILDING ASSOCIATION, H. A. Nelson, president, office 65 Great St. James
MONTREAL CANADIAN BUILDING SOCIETY, C. Malancon, president; L. A. Jette, secretary; office 42 St. Vincent
MONTREAL CITY AND DISTRICT BUILDING SOCIETY, T. Mussen, president; office 60 Little St. James
MONTREAL COLLEGE, Rev. Charles Lenoir, director, Sherbrooke, n Guy
MONTREAL COLLEGIATE SCHOOL, Charles Nichols, L. R. C. P., head master; W. Nichols, C.M., vice-principal, 21 Victoria
MONTREAL CORN EXCHANGE, W. J. Patterson, secretary, cor St. John and St. Sacrament
MONTREAL GAZETTE, Montreal Printing and Publishing Company, printers and publishers, John Lowe, managing director, 67 Gt. St. James

MONTREAL GENERAL HOSPITAL, Dr. George Ross. house surgeon; Edward Russell, steward, 422 Dorchester cor St. Dominique
MONTREAL HERALD, Edward G. Penny, editor; E. G. Penny and Andrew Wilson, proprietors, publishers and printers, 51 Great St. James
MONTREAL HORSE NAIL WORKS, Morland, Watson & Co., proprietors, office 387 St. Paul
Montreal House, Hiram Duclos, proprietor, 6 and 8 Custom House sq
MONTREAL, LACHINE AND GRAND TRUNK RAILWAY DEPOT, St. Bonaventure
MONTREAL LEAD WORKS, Montreal Rolling Mills Co., proprietors; Morland, Watson & Co., managing directors; factory on Lochine canal; office 387 St. Paul
MONTREAL NAIL WORKS, Montreal Rolling Mills Co., proprietors; Morland, Watson & Co., managing directors; factory on Lachine canal; office 387 St. Paul
MONTREAL OBSERVATORY, C. Smallwood, M. D., LL.D., D.C.L., 803 Sherbrooke
Montreal Ocean Steamship Co., H. & A. Allan, agts, cor Youville & Common,
Montreal Permanent Building Society, Henry Thomas, president; M. H. Gault, secretary; office 77 Gt. St. James
MONTREAL PRINTING AND PUBLISHING CO., John Lowe, managing director, 67 Great St. James
MONTREAL ROLLING MILLS, Montreal Rolling mills Co., proprietors; Morland, Watson & Co., managing directors; factory on Lachine canal; office 387 St. Paul
MONTREAL SAW WORKS, Morland, Watson & Co , proprietors, office 377 St. Paul
MONTREAL TACK WORKS, Morland, Watson & Co., proprietors, 387 St. Paul
MONTREAL TELEGRAPH CO., connecting with the principal cities and towns in Canada and the United States; Hugh Allan, president; James Dakers, secretary; 12 and 14 St. Sacrament
MONTREAL TYPE AND STEREOTYPE FOUNDRY, C. T. Palsgrave, proprietor, 1 St. Helen
MONTREAL WEEKLY TRANSCRIPT, issued every Thursday afternoon; John Lovell, printer and publisher, 23 and 25 St. Nicholas, bet St. Sacrament and St. Paul
MONTREAL WITNESS, John Dougall, editor; John Dougall & Son, proprietors, publishers and printers, 126 Great St. James
Mooney, J. H., commission merchant and dealer in wool, hides, etc., 85 Grey Nun
Moore, Dominique, hotel, 33 and 35 Cemetery
Moore, G. & J., hats, caps and furs, Cathedral block, 269 Notre Dame
Moore, Semple & Hatchette, wholesale grocers, 2 Dominion buildings, 128 McGill
Moore, Terence, groceries, wines and liquors, 194 St. Bonaventure
Moreau, Ouimet & Lacoste, advocates, 30 St. Gabriel
Moreau, Very Rev. Canon H., Bishop's Palace, Cemetery
Morgan, Henry & Co., dry goods, wholesale and retail, Colonial House, 163 Great St. James cor Victoria Square
Morgan, James Vaughan, importer and general merchant, 23 Hospital
Morin & Co., general brokers and commission merchants, 24 St. Sacrament
MORISON, JAMES & CO., importers of dry goods, 274 and 276 Notre Dame
Moreau, Rev. E., chaplain Bishop's Palace, Cemetery
MORLAND, WATSON & CO., merchants in iron and hardware, proprietors Montreal Saw Works, managing directors Montreal Rolling Mills Co.; general agents Commercial Union Assurance Co. and National Provincial Marine Insurance Co., 387 St. Paul
Morris, David & Co., produce and leather, St. Patrick's Hall, 17 Victoria Square
Morton, Osborne, livery stables, 38 St. Bonaventure
Moseley & Ricker, manufacturers of boot, shoe and carriage leather, 510 St. Paul
MOSS. J. L. & CO., pawnbrokers and city loan office, 84 Notre Dame
Moss, S. H. & J., importers and clothiers, 5 Recollet
Mosseau & David, advocates, 36 St. Vincent
Mousseau des Islet, Rev. Gilbert, 120 German
MUIR, EWAN & CO., wholesale clothirs, 185 McGill
Muir, George B., sec-treasurer Provincial Permanent Building Society, and manager Citizens Insurance Company, 75 University
MUIR, W. & R., importers of dry goods, 166 McGill
MULHOLLAND & BAKER, wholesale hardware merchants, 419 and 421 St. Paul, yard entrance, 27 St. Francois Xavier, (see adv)
Mullarky & McCready, wholesale boot and shoe manufacturers, 8 St. Helen
MULLER, FREDERICK, M. D., homœopathic phpsician, 83 Union Avenue
Mullin, J. E., & Co., wholesale grocers, 30 St. Peter
MUNDERLOH, STEENCKEN & CO., shipping and commission merchants, 301 Commissioners (see adv)
Munro, Alexander, stockbroker, 55 St. Francois Xavier, h Mountain
Munro, Daniel, plumber and gasfitter, 17 St. Bonaventure
Munro, Edwin, M.D., 448 Dorchester
Murphy, A. A., importer of Irish linen, staple and fancy dry goods, 418 and 420 Notre Dame
Murphy, J. J. A., merchant tailor, 9 Bleury
MURPHY, JOHN & CO., hosiery, gloves, ribbon, small wares, gentlemen's haberdashery etc., 405 Notre Dame and 79, 81 and 83 St. Peter
Murphy, Matthew, rope manufacturer, 123 Ontario
Murray & Co., booksellers and stationers, Stationers' Hall, 379 Notre Dame cor St. John
Murray, Daniel D., Hotel du Peuple, 163 Commissioners
Murray, Robert B., wholesale dealer in petroleum, benzine, and lubricating oils, 36 Lemoine
Murray, William, manager Montreal Insurance Co., Cote St. Antoine
Mussen, Thomas, importer of staple and fancy dry goods, 257 and 259 Notre Dame cor St. Lambert
Nagle, S. B., advocate, 50 Little St. James
NATIONAL EXPRESS COMPANY, D. T. Irish, agent, 7 and 9 Place d'Armes
NATIONAL LIFE INSURANCE CO. of the U. S. A., William Douglas, jun., general agent for the Dominion, office Great St. James (see adv. inside back cover)
NATIONAL PROVINCIAL MARINE INSURANCE CO., Morland, Watson & Co., gen. agents, 387 St. Paul
NATURAL HISTORY SOCIETY MUSEUM, J. F. Whiteaves, curator, Wm. Hunter, taxidermist, University cor Cathcart
Neher, Martin, map, print and picture colorer, at John Lovell's 23 and 25 St. Nicholas
Nelson, Alfred, M.D., 12 Little St. James
Nelson & Ballard, architects, 121 Great St. James
NELSON, WOOD & CO., fancy goods, woodenware, clocks, etc., 29 St. Peter

NEW CORN EXCHANGE BUILDING, 43 St. Sacrament cor St. John
NEW DOMINION MONTHLY, annual subscription $1; John Dougall & Son, props., printers, and publishers, 126 Great St. James
NEW ENGLAND MUTUAL LIFE INSURANCE CO., William Douglass, jun., general agent, 32 Great St. James
NEW YORK LIFE INSURANCE CO., Walter Burke, general agent for Dominion, 51 Great St. James (see adv. opp inside back cover)
Nichols, Charles, L.R.C.P., principal of Montreal Collegiate school, 21 Victoria
Nichols, Robinson & Co., banking exchange office, 213 St. Francois Xavier
Nicol, John, brush manfr., 122 Magill
Nield, Edward & Co., imprs. of gentlemen's haberdashery and comn mers. 479 St. Paul
Nimmo, Rev. James (Church of Scotland) 169 St. Elizabeth
Nivin & Co., general comn mers., 484 St. Paul
Nolan, W. P., & Co., commission and provision merchants, 26 St. Sacrament
NORMAL SCHOOL, Professors Hicks and Robins, 30 Belmont
Norman, Rev. R. W. (Church of England), 686 Dorchester
Normandin, Alexis, & Frere, groceries and liquors, 286 to 290 St. Lawrence
Norris, Wm., general broker and commission agent, Exchange Court, 10 Hospital
North British and Mercantile Insurance Co., MacDougall & Davidson, agents, H. J. Johnston, secretary, 72 St. Francois Xavier cor Hospital
Northrup & Russell, commission merchants, Royal Insurance Building, 3 Common
Notman, Wm., photographer & publisher, 17 Bleury
O'BRIEN, JAMES, & CO., wholesale clothiers, 207 McGill cor Recollet
O'BRIEN, JAMES J., furniture dealer, 553 and 555 St. Mary
O'Brien, Rev. Michael, St. Patrick's house, 92 St. Alexander
O'BRIEN, W., agent G.T.R., 39 Great St. James
O'Donnell, John, M.D., physician and surgeon, 49 St. Alexander
O'Farrell, Rev. Michael, St. Patrick's house, 92 St. Alexander
O'HEIR, JAMES, wholesale clothier and outfitting warehouse, 152 Magill
O'Leary, Patrick, M. D.
O'LOGHLAN, MARTIN, grocceries, wines, liquors, &c., 120 Prince cor Ottawa
Oblats, Rev. Peres, St. Peter's church, 95 Visitation
Oertel, Albert C., commission and shipping mercht, Royal Insurance buildings, 2 Common
Ogilvie, A. W. & Co., flour mills, St. Gabriel locks
Ogilvy & Co., importers of dry goods, 495 St. Paul
Ogilvy, James A., dry goods, wholesale and retail, 91 and 93 Mountain
ONTARIO BANK, Henry Starnes, manager, 6 Place d'Armes
Ostell, John, architect and lumber dealer, St. Gabriel locks, office and yard, 761 Craig
OTTAWA AND PRESCOTT RAILWAY CO., Thomas Reynolds, managing director, 60 Little St. James
OTTAWA AND RIDEAU FORWARDING CO., James Caven, manager, 60 Common
OTTAWA HOTEL, Samuel Browning, prop, 150 Great St. James, and 445 Notre Dame
OTTAWA RIVER NAVIGATION CO., R. W. Shepherd, president Mercantile Library building, 14 St. Bonaventure (see adv)
OVERING, THOMAS, Canada Wire Works and Wire Cloth Manufactory, 757 Craig (see adv)
PACIFIC MAIL STEAMSHIP COMPANY OF NEW YORK, William M. Freer, agent, 10 Hospital
PACIFC MUTUAL INSURANCE COMPANY OF NEW YORK, M. H. Gault, agent, 77 Great St. James
PACY, T. B., housefurnishing and builders, hardware, mechanics' tools, 25 St. Lawrence
PAGELS, FREDERICK, tobacconist and dealer in meerschaum and fancy pipes, 113 Great St. James (see adv.)
Paige, E. & B. P., threshing and mowing machines, 84 Wellington
Palatin, Rev. M., Seminary of St. Sulpice, 320 Notre Dame
PALSGRAVE, CHARLES THEODORE, proprietor Montreal Type Foundry, 1 St. Helen cor Lemoine
Papineau, Anthony, grain merchant, 4 St. Henry cor College
PAPINEAU, HON. LOUIS JOSEPH, 92 Champ de Mars
Papineau, L. J. A., prothonotary, Belle Riviere, 52 St. Mary
Papineau, Papineau & Durand, notaries, 32 Little St. James
Poquette, Moise, wines, liquors and spirits, 19 Bonsecours
Paquin, Isidore, ready made clothing and dry goods, 27 St. Lawrence
Paradis, Francois X., Franklin hotel, 31 and 33 Chaboillez square
Pare, Very Rev. J. O., secretary to the Right Rev. the Lord Bishop of Montreal, Bishop's palace, Cemetery
PAREEC, A. DAVIDSON, secretary Scottish Provincial Assurance Company, Toupin's building, 12 Place d'Armes
Parkin, James, importer of British and foreign lace and embroidery, 250 Notre Dame
Parks, J. G., photographer, 84 Great St. James
Parkyn, James, miller and dealer in flour, 669 Craig
Parkyn, William, hydraulic locks, Cote St. Paul
Parslow, John, bookbinder, stationer, paper ruler and account book manufacturer, 442 St. Paul
Parsons, Henry, merchant tailor, 145 Great St. James
PARYS, GEORGE, general agent, 58 St. Francois Xavier
Patenaude, Clement, Empire hotel, 20 Bonsecours
Paterson, J. & Co., blacking and oil manufacturers, 29 Commissioners
Paton, Rev. Andrew, assistant minister St. Andrew's Church (Church of England)
PATON, THOMAS, general manager Bank of British North America
Patterson, William J., secretary Corn Exchange, St. John cor St. Sacrament
PATON, JOHN & CO., china, glass and earthenware, 135 Great St. James
Patton, R., plumber, gasfitter, brass founder and electroplater, bronzing, etc., 742 Craig
Patton, Thomas, & Bro., merchant tailors and wholesale clothiers, 203 McGill
Pauze & Beique, advocates, 38 St. Vincent
Payette, Antoine E., notary, 161 Lagauchetiere
Payne, Edward, commission merchant, 202 St. Denis
Peck, Thomas & Co., manufacturers of iron, nails, ship and railroad spikes, office, 391 St. Paul
Pedlar, S. & Co., managers British American agency, Ætna Life Insurance Co., 20 Great St. James
Pell, A. J., carver and gilder, looking glass and picture frame maker, 345 Notre Dame
Pelletier, Louis & Cie., dry goods, 101 Notre Dame

Pall, J. E., collector and general agent, 91 St. Antoine
Pellisher, Rev. M., 172 Richmond
Pelthier, Hector, M. D., Edin., 632 Craig
PENNY, WILSON & Co., printers, proprietors and publishers of the *Montreal Herald*, and book and job printers, 51 Great St. James
Penton, Frederick W. L., chief of city police, 76 St. Denis
Peres, Oblats, Rev. M. Antoine, superior St. Peter's Church, Visitation, cor. Dorchester
Perkins, J. A., sen., lumber merchant, 27 McGill College Avenue
Perkins & Ramsay, advocates, 60 Little St. James
Permanent Building Society of the District of Montreal, office, 12 Place d'Armes
Perrault, Eloi, leather merchant, and dealer in shoe-findings, 305 and 307 St. Paul
Perrault, Honore, groceries, wines and liquors, 326 Jacques Cartier
PERRAULT, JOSEPH FRANCOIS, proprietor of *Lower Canada Agriculturist* and *Revue Agricole*, 44 St. Denis
Perrault, Leon, groceries, wines, liquors, &c., 496 St. Catherine
Perrault, Louis & Co., book and job printers and publishers, 36 St. Vincent
Perrault & Merrill, dry goods, 131 Notre Dame
Perrin, Charles F., dry goods, wholesale and retail, 123 Notre Dame
Perrin & Frere, hardware and paints, wholesale and retail, 525 St. Mary
Perry, Alfred, inspector Royal Insurance Co., 1 Common
Perry & Co., news depot, stationery, &c., 509 Craig
PERRY DAVIS & SON, Pain Killer depot, 380 St. Paul
PERRY, EDWARD & CO., trunk and valise manufacturers, 371 Notre Dame
Perry, George A., boots and shoes, wholesale and retail, 293 Notre Dame
Petroleum Gas Co., Benjamin S. Curry, managing director, 156 Great St. James
Phillips, Edwin, watchmaker, 237 McGill
PHILLIPS, JAMES Z., dry goods, 129 St. Lawrence
Phillips, Walter, commission merchant and agent for Inman Line of Steamers, St. John cor Hospital
Phœnix Fire Assurance Company of London, Gillespie, Moffatt & Co., agents, James Davison, Manager, 310 St. Paul
Phœnix Marine Insurance Company, Robert Hampson, agent, 18 Corn Exchange Blg, St. John
Picard, F., agent Vermont Central R.R., St. James
Picard, Rev. M., Seminary of St. Sulpice, 320 Notre Dame
Picault & Son, chemists and druggists, and dealers in patent medicines, 74 to 78 Notre Dame cor Bonsecours
Piche Eugene Urgele, advocate, 41 St. Vincent
Pickup, Edmund, news agent and postage stamp depot, 123 and 125 St. Francois Xavier
Pickup, R., news depot, St. Lawrence hall, 31 Great St. James
Pillow, Hersey & Co., manufacturers of cut nails, sheet iron, tacks, &c., 5 Custom house square
Pinet, Dr. Alexander R., 80 Visitation
Pingel, Johan, C., watchmaker and jeweller, 741 Craig
Plamondon, Very Rev. Canon L. T., Bishops Palace Cemetery
PLATE GLASS INSURANCE CO., William Douglas, jun., 32 St. James (see adv)
Plessis Dit Belair L. R., dry goods, 233 and 235 St. Lawrence
Plante & Bourgoin, Stoneyard, 151 St. Elizabeth
Plimsoll, Warnock & Co., straw and fancy dry goods, 18 St. Helen
PLINGUET & LAPLANTE, printers and publishers of L'Ordre, 30 St. Gabriel
PLUNKETT, E. W., engineer, surveyor and patent solicitor 88 St. James
POCOCK, GEORGE, ladies and children's hat and shape manufacturer, 782 Craig
Poitras, J. O., merchant tailor, 60 Notre Dame
POLLOCK & CALVERT, picture frame makers, 13 Bleury
Popham, James & Co., boot and shoe manufacturers, 487 and 489 St. Paul
Popham, John, advocate, 67 St. Francois Xavier
PORT WARDEN'S OFFICE, captain Alexander Schaler, Royal Insurance buildings, 2 Common
Porteus & Co., brokers, agents for manufacturers, 2½ St. Sacrament
Porter & Delesderniers, tanners and leather dealers, 504 St. Paul
POST OFFICE, E. S. Freer, Postmaster, cor St. James and St. Francois Xavier
Potter, H., photographer, 64 St. James
Powell, George, dry goods merchant, 33 St. Joseph
Pratt, John & Co., wholesale leather merchants, 453 St. Paul
Pratt, Noel, cabinet maker and upholsterer, 37 and 39 St. Lawrence
Prefontaine, Perrault & Co., dry goods, 97 Notre Dame
Prentice & McDougall, stock brokers, and agents for Alliance Assurance Co. of London, 60 St. Francois Xavier
PRESBYTERIAN, THE, monthly; Lay Association, prop; John Lovell, printer, 23 St. Nicholas
Prevost, Alphonse, notary, 43 St. Vincent
Prevost, Amable & Cie., wholesale dry goods, 266 and 268 St. Paul, and wholesale groceries, 217 Commissioners
Prevost, Hector, advocate, 43 St. Vincent
Prince, Henry, impr. of music and musical instruments, 305 Notre Dame
Pringle, Thomas, millwright and machinist, 527 St. Joseph
PRIVATE POOR HOUSE, Rev. James Hogan, director, sister Michaud, directress, 35 Prince
PROTHONOTARY'S OFFICE, Hubert, Papineau, & Honey, prothonotaries; George Pyke, deputy prothonotary, S. C., Court House, 177 Notre Dame
PROENCHER, J. A., editor of *La Minerve*, 41 St. Louis
PROVENCHER, JOSEPH N., agent and collector, 180 Vitre cor Chenneville
PROVINCIAL INSURANCE CO. OF CANADA, John F. McCuaig, agent, office 31 St. Francois Xavier
PROVINCIAL PERMANENT BUILDING SOCIETY, Hugh Allan, president; W. Workman, mayor, vice-president; G. B. Muir, secretary, office, 10 Place d'Armes
PROWSE, BROS., dealers in house furnishing hardware, stoves, &c., 128 St. James
PRUD'HOMME, HON. EUSTACHE, senator, Coteau St. Pierre
Prud'homme, Prospere, groceries, wines and liquors, 444 St. Joseph
Pullan, W. G. & Co., pin manufacturers, Seigneurs
Putney, Charles M., wholesale and retail confectioner, 40 Victoria square
Pyke, George, deputy prothonotary, 362 St. Urbain
QUEBEC BANK, William Rhind, manager, 14 Place d'Armes

Queen Insurance Company of Liverpool and London, A. McK. Forbes, resident secretary and general agent, Merchants Exchange, 13 St. Sacrament
Quevillon, Charles, dry goods, 512 Craig cor St Lambert
QUINN, F. A., advocate, 38 Little St. James (see adv)
Quintal, Ferdinand, groceries, wines and liquors, 329 St. Catherine
RADWAY, JOHN, M.D. & CO., patent medicine manufacturers, 14, 16 and 18 St. Francois Xavier cor St. Paue
RAE, JACKSON, cashier Merchants' Bank, cor Notre Dame and Place d'Armes, 154 St. Charles
RAFTER, JOHN A., general dry goods, clothing and haberdashery store, 31 St. Lawrence
RAFTER & KENNEDY, wholesale clothiers and importers of woollens, 30 Lemoine
RAMSAY, A. & SON, manufacturing agents 41 Recollet
RAMSAY, THOMAS K., Q.C., advocate and managing editor of *Evening Telegraph*, 85 University
RAMSAY, W. M., manager Standard Life Assurance Company, 47 Great St. James
BANKIN, JOHN, merchant, 14 St. Helen
Raphael, Thomas W., commission merchant, 19 St. Nicholas
Raphael, William, artist, 67 Great St. James
RATTRAY, J. & CO., manufacturers of tobaccos, cigars snuffs, &c., 206 Notre Dame (see adv)
RAWLINGS, EDWARD, secretary European Assurance Society, 71 Great St. James
Raymond, Oliver, M. D., 566 St. Mary
RAYMORE, & Co., J. F., watches, clocks, jewelry and fancy goods, 270 Notre Dame
Redburn, William, dry goods, 127 Wellington
REDDY, JOHN, M. D., physician and surgeon, 877 St Catherine
REDPATH, P., Canada Sugar Refinery, St. Gabriel locks, office, 11 Hospital
Reed, George, carriage maker, 219 Craig
REED, GEORGE W., slate and metal roofer and wholesale dealer in refrigerators, and tinware, 758 Craig
REED, THOMAS D., chemist and druggist, 40 St. Antoine
REED, WILLIAM, custom house agent, 309 Commissioners
REEKIE, ROBERT JAMES, civil engineer and general contractor, 131 Great St. James
REES, D. & CO., inspectors of beef, pork and butter, and commission merchants, 46, 48 and 60 Grey Nun
REEVES, JOHN J. merchant tailor, 227 Notre Dame
REFORD & DILLON, commission merchants, 23 St. Sacrament
Regnaud, F. J. V., provincial surveyor, 17 St. Dominique
REID, J., millinery and straw goods, 245 Notre Dame
REID, W. & CO., general merchants and dealers in paper, stationery, etc., 84 McGill
REID, WILLIAM, house carpenter and builder, 762 Craig
REINHARDT, G. & SONS, lager beer, ale and porter brewers, 333 German
RENAUD, HON. LOUIS, 686 Laganchetiere
Renaud, Ignace, dry goods, 162 and 164 Notre Dame
RENAUD, LOUIS, Jun., commission merchant, 38 Foundling
Reuter, Lionais & Co., importers of wine and commission merchants, 14 and 16 Hospital
REVUE AGRICOLE, monthly; J. Perrault, editor and proprietor; John Lovell, printer, 23 St. Nicholas

Reynolds & Cleary, grain and flour merchants, 786 Craig
REYNOLDS, THOMAS, managing director, St Lawrence and Ottawa R. R., 60 Little St. James
Reynolds, William, wholesale and retail grocer and provision dealer, 169 McGill
Rheaume, Napoleon, carver, gilder and picture frame maker, 75 St. Lawrence
RHIND, WILLIAM, manager Quebec Bank, 11 Place d'Armes
Rhynas, John, commission and shipping merchant, 9 and 11 St. Helen
Ricard, Arthur G., M.D., 603 St. Mary
Ricard, Louis, advocate, 423 Craig
RICE, BROTHERS, manufacturers of all styles of ladies and gents paper collars, cuffs, fronts, &c., 582 Craig (see adv)
Rice, T. G., wire worker, 522 Craig
Richards, Joseph, merchant tailor, 82 St. Peter
Richardson, Isaac A. & Co., plumbers, gas and steam fitters, &c., 41 St. Lambert hill
RICHARDSON, JAMES, Geological survey, 75 Cathcart
Richelieu Hotel, A. Beliveau, prop., 45 St. Vincent
RICHELIEU NAVIGATION COMPANY, J. B. Lamere, agent: J. N. Beaudry, secretary, 203 Commissioners
Riddell, Thomas & Co., booksellers, stationers and newspaper depot, 54 and 56 Great St. James
Rielle, Joseph, architect, 89 St. Francois Xavier
Rienrard, Felix, notary, 385 St. Catharine
Riley, M. K. & Co., inner soles and counters, 10 Dorchester
Riley, William, comn mer. 55 McGill College av
RIMMER, ALFRED J. P., wine merchant, Danish consul general, 16 St. Sacrament
Rimmer, Gunn & Co., comn mers. 40 St. Peter
Ringland & Co., manfrs. of shirts, collars and ties 398 Notre Dame
RINTOUL BROTHERS, comn mers. agents for Imperial Fire Insurance Co., 24 St. Sacrament, (see adv. inside back cover)
Ritchie, Hew F. K., stationery department, G. T. R.
Ritchie, Thomas W., Q C., 24 McTavish
RITCHOT & TRUDELLE, grocers and grain mers., Hochelaga
RIVARD, S., advocate, 41 St. Vincent
Rivert, Joseph S., notary, 16 Little St. James
Riviere, Joseph Isaie, hotel, 184 Notre Dame
Rixford, E. H., advocate, 34 Little St. James
Robb, Charles, mining engineer, surveyor and patent agent, 96 St. Francois Xavier
ROBB, JOHN, Montreal steam bakery, 55 Dufresne
Robert, Alexis, contractor, 229 Lagauchetiere
Robert, Jean Baptiste, grain dealer, 135 St. Paul
Roberts George, builder and contractor, 499 Laganchetiere
Roberts & Reinhold, lithographers and engravers, 13 Place d'Armes
ROBERTSON, A. & W., advocates, 50 Little St James
Robertson & Beattie, wholesale grocers and comn. mers., 124 McGill
ROBERTSON, DAVID, wholsale grocer, 36 St. Peter
ROBERTSON, JAMES, general metal merchant, Canada Lead Works, 126 to 132 Queen
ROBERTSON, STEPHEN & CO., dry goods importers, St. Helen, cor. Lemoine
ROBERTSON, THOMAS & CO., metal and tube merchants, 26 St. Sulpice, and 379 St. Paul
ROBERTSON, W., insurance agent, 59 St. Francois Xavier
ROBSON, GEORGE, secretary New City Gas Company, 223 Notre Dame

RODGERS, DAVID, M. A., High School
Rodier, Chas. S., manufacturer of threshing machines 62 St. Martin
Rodier, Hon, Charles S., advocate, 228 St. Antoine
Rodier, P. A., lumber merchant, 512 St. Joseph
Roe, T. P., general merchant, Royal Insurance Bds., 1 Common
Rogers & King, iron founders, 645 Craig n Bleury
Rolland, Gabriel L., boot & shoe manufacturer wholesale, 377 St. Paul
Rolland, J. B. & Fils, booksellers, printers and bookbinders, 12 and 14 St. Vincent
Rollin, Dr. Alexis, 591 St. Joseph
Rooney, Patrick, importer of staple and fancy dry goods, 457 St. Paul
ROSE, DANIEL, book and job printer, 7 Dollard
ROSE, HON. JOHN, minister of finance, 107 Simpson
ROSE, RITCHIE & ROSE, advocates, Standard Assurance Blgs., 47 Great St. James
Ross, George, A.M., M.D., house surgeon Montreal General Hospital
Ross, P. S. & Brother, shipchandlers, paints, oils, 10 Grey Nun
Ross, T. & F. & Co., wholesale grocers and commission merchants, 361 Commissioners
Ross, William, notary, commissioner for taking affidavits in the province of Quebec to be used in the province of Ontario, 18 St. Sacrament
Rottot, Jean Philippe, M.D., physician and surgeon, 66 St. Denis
Rosseau, Rev. Rene, Seminary of St. Sulpice, 320 Notre Dame
Rousselot, Rev. M., parish priest, Seminary of St. Sulpice, 320 Notre Dame
Routh, Havilland & Co., commission and general merchants, Royal Insurance buildings, 1 Custom House square
Roy, Adolphe & Co., importers of dry goods, wholesale, 278 St. Paul and 225 and 227 Commissioners
Roy, Euclide, advocate, 1 St. Therese
Roy, F. X., Portland Hotel, 189 Commissioners
Roy, James & Co., wholesale dry goods merchants, 505 St. Paul
Roy & Joseph, advocates, 10 St. Lambert
Roy, Rouer, Q C., city attorney, 479 St. Joseph
ROYAL CANADIAN BANK, M. H. Gault, manager, 77 Great St. James
ROYAL MAIL THROUGH LINE OF STEAMERS, Montreal to Hamilton, Alexander Milloy, agent, 73 Great St. James
RUDOLF, CAPTAIN ALFRED M., harbour master, Harbour Commissioners office, 14 Custom House sq
RUSSELL, EDWARD, steward Montreal General Hospital, 89 St. Dominique
Rutherford & Brother, ready made clothing, 199 McGill
Rutherford, W., lumber merchant, 897 Dorchester
RUTLAND & BURLINGTON, Rensselaer, Saratoga, and Lake Champlain steamers, Cardinal & Bockus, agents, 39 and 41 Great St. James
Ryan, Cornelius, stoves, tin and copper ware, refrigerators, &c., 38 Victoria sq
RYAN, HON. THOMAS, senator, 206 Peel
RYAN, M. P., M.P., produce and provisions, commission merchant, 120 and 122 King
Ryan, Matthew, advocate, 64 Little St. James
Ryland, George H., county registrar, Court House, 177 Notre Dame
SACHE, WILLIAM, cashier Molson's Bank, Sherbrooke cor Drummond
SADLIER, D. &. J., & CO., publishers, booksellers and stationers, 336 and 338 Notre Dame cor St. Francois Xavier

Samuels, William, hatter & furrier, 367 Notre Dame
SANBORN, MYRON H, deputy sheriff, 270 St. Charles Borromee
Sancer & Frere, wholesale and retail hardware merchants, 283 and 285 St. Paul
Sanders, Henry, optician, 141 Great St. James
Sargent, G. A., commission merchant, 25 Great St. James
Saunders, H. & A., jewellers, 295 Notre Dame
SAUVAGEAU & TAYLOR, general commission merchants and produce brokers, 18 St. Sacrament
SAVAGE, ALFRED & SON, oil works, 314 William, office 48 St. Sacrament
Savage, Lyman & Co., watchmakers and jewellers, Cathedral Block, 271 Notre Dame
SAVINGS BANK DEPARTMENT, MOLSON'S BANK, James Elliott, manager, 100 St. James
SAVINGS BANK DEPARTMENT OF THE BANK OF MONTREAL, Henry Vennor, 3 St. James
SAVINGS BANK DEPARTMENT OF THE MERCHANTS BANK, under the management of T. Caldwell, cor Notre Dame and Place d'Armes
Schiller, Charles E., dep clerk crown, 404 Dorchester
Schilling, Dr. Gustavus, 15 Latour
Schmidt, Samuel B., M.D., 539 Craig
SCHOLES, CHARLES, manager, Canadian Rubber Co., 157 University
School and Home of Industry, 476 Lagauchetiere
SCHOOL OF MEDICINE AND SURGERY, E. H. Trudel, M.D., president; H. Peltier, M.D., secretary, 473 Lagauchetiere
Schwob Brothers, importers of watches, Crystal Block, 293 Notre Dame
SCLATER, CAPTAIN ALEXANDER, port warden, 2 Common
SCOTT, GEORGE S., tea broker and commission merchant, 12 Hospital
Scott, S. B., & Co,, agent for Wheeler & Wilson's and Howe's sewing machines, and knitting machines, 345 Notre Dame
Scott, THOMAS S., architect, 44 Little St. James
Scott, W. E., M. D., Professor of Anatomy, McGill University, 34 Beaver Hall Terrace
Sculthorp & Pennington, agents for Bevington & Morris, London, England, 131 Great St. James
Seath, Robert, wholesale clothier and importer, 10 St. Joseph
Seebold, George, pianoforte manufacturer's agent, 45 St. Louis
Seers, Arthur A., notary, 38 Little St. James
Selley, J. B., M.D., 165 Bleury
SEMINARY OF ST. SULPICE, Rev. M. Baile, superior, 320 Notre Dame, n Place d'Armes
Seneeal, Arthur, importer of coal oil, lamps, chandeliers, &c, 303 St. Paul and 172 Lagauchetiere
Seneeal, Cadieux & Cie, grocers wine and spirit merchants, 19 Jacques Cartier sq
Seneeal, Charles, leather merchant, 235 Craig
SENECAL, EUSEBE, book and job printer, and publisher of La Revue Canadienne, 10 St. Vincent
Seneeal & Ryan, advocates, 15 St. Vincent
Sentenne, Rev. A., St. James R. C. Church, 473 St. Catharine
Sewell, Colin, M. D., 22 St. Radegonde
Sewell, H. G., broker and commission merchant, 19 St. Sacrament
SEXTON, JOHN P., recorder for City of Montreal, 144 St. Denis
Seybold, Henry, importer of hardware, 227 and 229 St. Lawrence
Seymour, C. E., commission merchant and dealer in leather, hides and oil, 507 St. Paul
Seymour, Grant, clerk militia department, 19 St. Edward

Seymour, M. H., general commission merchant, and dealer in leather, hides, wool, &c., 403 St. Paul
SHACKELL, HENRY, auditor G.T.R., 95 Union av
SHANLY, WALTER, M. P. P., civil engineer, 31 Great St. James
Shannon, Alexander & Co., wholesale grocers, 102 and 104 McGill
Shannon, Daniel, commission merchant and dealer in produce and provisions, 11 William
Shannon, Neil, wholesale and retail grocer, 455 Commissioners
Sharpley, Rice, jewelery, watches and fancy goods, Crystal Block, 281 Notre Dame
Shaw, David, general shipping agent and commission merchant, 2 Common
Shaw, F. & Brothers, tanners, and dealers in hides, leather and oil, 14 Lemoine
Shaw, George, commission merchant and ship broker, Corn Exchange, 48 St. Sacrament
Shaw, Henry J., auctioneer and commission mercht, 97 Great St. James
Shaw, Rev. W. J., (Wesleyan) 967 St. Catherine
Shearer, James & Co., steam saw and planing mills, cor Seigneurs and Richardson, and 722 Craig
SHEDDEN, JOHN, general railway contractor and forwarder; Thomas Symington, agent Grand Trunk Railway; office for collection and delivery of freight, 40 and 42 Foundling
SHEPHERD, ROBERT W., president Ottawa River Navigation Co., 39 Beaver Hall Terrace
SHEWAN, A. N., M. A., principal of west end academy, 87 McGill college av
Shinnock, John, commission merchant and dealer in oils, coals, &c., 17½ Lemoine
SHIPWAY, J. G. & SON, auctioneers, brokers, and commission merchants, 18 St, Sacrament
SHOREY, H. & CO., wholesale clothing and tweeds, 535 St. Paul
SIDEY, J. G., commission merchant, 33 St. Nicholas
Simard, Joseph, notary, 262 Lagauchetiere
Simms, Robert & Co., general merchants, Royal Insurance Buildings, 1 Common
Simpson & Bethune, general insurance agents, 104 St. Francois Xavier
SIMPSON, WHITEHEAD & CO,, saddlery and carriage hardware, 452 St. Paul
SINCENNES & McNAUGHTON, forwarders and line of tug steamers, 203 Commissioners
Sinclair, Jack & Co., wholesale grocers and commission merchants, 413 St. Paul
Sippell, G. J., civil engineer, 26 Drummond
Slack & Gravel, commission merchants and importers of leather and shoefindings, 409 St. Paul
SMALWOOD, CHARLES, M. D., L. L. D., D. C. L., director of the Meteorological and Magnetic Observatory, 32 Beaver Hall Terrace
Smallwood, John R., M. D., physician and surgeon, 32 Beaver Hall Terrace
Smardon, John, soap and candle manufacturer, 140 St. Urbain
SMITH, COCHRANE & CO., wholesale boot and shoe manufacturers, 45 St. Peter and 51 St. Sacrament
SMITH, COL. W. OSBORNE, Assistant Adjutant General of Militia, 63 St. Gabriel
Smith, C. F. C., resident secretary Liverpool and London and Globe Fire and Life Insurance Co., Insurance Buildings, 16 Place D'Armes
Smith, George, forwarder, Royal Insurance Blgs, 1 Common
Smith, H. B., & Co., china, glass and earthenware, 446 and 448 St. Paul and 369 Commissioners
Smith, James, notary, conveyancer and real estate agent, Mechanics' Bank Chambers, 88 Great St. James
SMITH & PHILLIPS, notaries public, etc., Mechanics' Bank Chambers, Great St. James (see adv)
Smith, W. A., & Co., manufacturers of shirts and collars, and gentlemen's furnishing goods, 496 and 498 St. Paul cor St. Peter
Smith, W. H. & Co., agents for manufacturers of china, glass and earthenware, hardware and electro-plate, encaustic flooring tiles, and general merchants, 18 and 20 Hospital
Smith, W. Howe, general merchant, 6 St. Sacrament
Smith, William, & Brother, sugar refiners, office, 17 William
Smith, William Primrose, M.D., 624 Lagauchetiere
Smyth, George, commission merchant, 75 St. Paul
Snow, E. L., Canadian superphosphate, 93 Jurors
Snowdon, C. C., & Co., hardware merchants, 454 and 456 St. Paul cor St Nicholas
Snowdon & Gairdner, advocates, 60 Little St. James
SOCIETE DE CONSTRUCTION CANADIENNE DE MONTREAL, M. M. C. Melancon, president, 42 St. Vincent
Sowdon, Francis M., local agent Life Association of Scotland, Courville and at St. Lambert
Spearpoint, W. E., merchant tailor and clothier, 32 Victoria Square
Spenard, Charles C., notary, 6 Little St. James
SPICER, WILLIAM J., superintendent G. T. R., 929 St. Catharine
SPENCER, RICHMOND, chemist, importer and dealer in drugs, McGill cor Notre Dame
Springle, J. H., architect, 279 Drummond
ST. ANDREW'S HOME, William Burnet, chairman, 484 Dorchester
St. Antoine Academy, under the direction of the Sisters of the Congregation of Notre Dame, 111 St. Antoine
St. Charles, F. X., flour merchant, 453 Commissioners
ST. DENIS ACADEMY, under the direction of the Congregational Nuns, sister St. Gabriel, superioress, 35 St. Denis
ST. GEORGE'S HOME, 201 Fortification lane
ST. JEAN, L. G., dry goods, 44 Sanguinet
St. Julien, J. T., advocate, 38 Little St. James
ST. LAWRENCE ENGINE WORKS, W. P. Bartley & Co., 17 Mill
ST. LAWRENCE GLASS CO., A. McK. Cochrane, secretary, 388 St. Paul
ST. LAWRENCE HALL, H. Hogan, prop. 31, 33 and 35 Great St. James
ST. VINCENT DE PAUL ASYLUM, Sisters of Providence, sister Charles, superioress, 44 Visitation
STAFF OFFICER OF PENSIONERS, Captain Sweeney, Cote des Neiges road
STARK, CRANSON A., produce, general commission merchant, and ship agent, 10 St. Nicholas
STARK, EDWARD, insurance agent, 6 McGill av
STARKE, JAMES & CO., book and job printers, 54 St. Francois Xavier cor St. Sacrament
Starke, R. J., commission merchant, 5 St. Sacrament
Starke, Smith & Co., tobacco factory, 88 & 92 King
STARNES, HENRY, manager Ontario Bank, 6 Place d'Armes
Steele, T. L., sewing machines, thread, &c., 387 Notre Dame
STEPHEN, GEORGE & CO., Canadian woolens, Albert Buildings, 10 Bonaventure
Stephens, George W., advocate, Exchange Court 10 Hospital
Stephens, Romeo H., agent London Assurance Corporation, and grain inspector, 56 St. Francois Xavier
STETHAM, WILLIAM, Montreal Type Foundry, 57 Aylmer

STEVENSON, A. A., printer and publisher, 70 St. Francois Xavier
Stevenson & Co., importers of dry goods, 12 St. Helen
Stevenson, James Black, commission merchant, 5 St Sacrament
STEWART, A. B., official assignee and accountant, Merchants' Exchange, 11 St. Sacrament
STEWART, ALEXANDER, groceries, wines and liquors, 24 and 26 Chaboillez Square
STEWART, WILLIAM, manufacturers' agent, and dealer in twines, thread, &c., 420 St. Paul
STIMSON & RICHARDSON, leather and commission merchants, 52 St. Peter, (see adv)
Stirling, McCall & Co., importers of British and foreign dry goods, 373 St. Paul
Stodard, D. R., stock broker and real estate agent, 48 Great St. James
Stone, Rev. Alfred, Proprietary College School, The Manse, 35 City Councillors
STONEHAM, T. F., manuf. of transparent window shades, cloth and wire screens, &c., 295 Notre Dame (see adv)
Stratton, F. C., general freight agent, G.T.R., 67 City Councillors
Street, John, watch case maker and manufacturing jeweler, 241 Notre Dame
Stroud, W. D., broker, 35 St. Nicholas
Stuart, Ernest H., notary 66 Little St. James
Stuart, Henry, Q.C., 8 St. Therese
Stuart, James, glue factory, 416 Panet
Stuart, William, plumber, gasfitter, and brassfinisher 704 and 706 Craig
Stuart, William W., produce merchant, St. Nicholas
Surveyor, Louis J. A., house furnishing and shelf hardware, stoves, platedware, tinware manufacturer, etc., 524 Craig
SUTHERLAND, A. C. & CO., wholesale dry goods, 10 St. Helen
SUTHERLAND, FORCE & CO., wholesale dry goods, 480 St. Paul
Sutherland, William, M. D., physician and surgeon, 667 Dorchester, cor. Union Avenue
Swain, Henry, manufacturer of tobacco and cigars, and importer of tobacconists' goods, 309 St. Paul
Tabb, Horatio N. & Co., gold and silver platers, and manufacturers of all kinds of presses, 683 Craig
Tabb, W. R., hardware merchant, 462 Notre Dame
Taft, A. B. & Co., architects, 49 Bleury
Tallet, Rev. M., 30 Seaton
Tambareau, Rev. M., Seminary of St. Sulpice, 320 Notre Dame
TASKER, JAMES, principal, Bryant, Stratton & Tasker's business college, 5 Place d'Armes
Tate & Co., graving docks and shipyard, south side canal, Point St. Charles
Taylor Brothers, brokers and comn mers., Merchants Exchange, 11 St. Sacrament
Taylor, Edward R. & Co., managers, Berkshire Life Insurance Co., 20 Great St. James
Taylor, Edward T., broker, Merchants' Exchange, 11 St. Sacrament
Taylor, Hugh, advocate, 11 Panet
Taylor, John, general storekeeper G. T. R., Clarke ave, Cote St. Antoine
Taylor, Rev. William, D.D., 1054 St. Catherine
Taylor, Robert, brewer, 340 St. Lawrence
Tees, John, groceries and provisions, 359 and 363 St. Joseph
Tempest, John W., Bank of Montreal, 58 University
Terroux, Charles A., deputy prothonotary, 306 Craig
Tessier, Louis, dry goods, 127 Notre Dame
Tessier, S. A., dry goods, 231 St. Lawrence
TETU, J. L., deputy chief of police, 159 Jacques Cartier
TETU, WILLIAM, sub-editor of *The Gazette*, 67 Great St. James
THEATRE ROYAL, J. W. Buckland, lessee and manager, 19 Cotte
Therien, Thomas, commission merchant, 6 Cemetery
Thibault & Auge, advocates, 27 St. Vincent
Thibeault, Dr. A., 15 Visitation
Thibeault, Francis, tanner, Bourget, Coteau St. Augustin
Thomas, Thibaudeau & Co., dry goods, wholesale, 324 to 326 St. Paul, and 265 Commissioners
Thomas, Z. & Brother, contractors, 182 St Constant
Thompson, B. & S. H., agents for Birmingham and Sheffield hardware, 12 Lemoine
Thompson & Conway, merchant tailors, 52 St. Lawrence
THOMPSON & DUFF, publishers, general agents for Blackie & Son, publishers, Glasgow; London Printing and Publishing Co.; and Johnson, Fry & Co., New York; 655 Craig n Bleury
Thompson, E., boots and shoes, wholesale and retail, 248 Notre Dame
Thompson, John, grocer, wine and spirit merchant, 204 and 206 St. Paul
Thompson, John, wholesale grocer, 33 German
Thompson, Murray & Co., general merchants, 42 St. Sacrament
THOMSON, JOHN, secretary & treasurer, Edwardsburgh Starch Co., 37 St. Peter
Thurber & Co., commission merchants, 13 Common
Thurston, I. D., & Co., manufacturers of machine sewed boots and shoes, 19 Lemoine cor McGill
Tiffin, Brothers, general merchants, importers of teas, sugars, wines, &c., 318, 320 and 322 St. Paul, and 259 and 261 Commissioners
Tiffin, Thomas & Co., groceries, provisions, wines, spirits, &c., 214 St. Paul, and 169 and 171 Commissioners
Timmermann, T., commercial agent, North Chambers, Hospital
Tinson, Jean Baptiste, architect and measurer, 423 Lagauchetiere
Torrance, James & Co., general merchants, 27 St. Sacrament
Torrance & Morris, advocates, Merchant's Exchange, Exchange Court and 11 St. Sacrament
Touchet, Louis D., dry goods, 83 and 85 St. Lawrence
Toupin, Rev. Joseph, St. Patrick's House, 92 St. Alexander
Tourville, Louis, grain and spirit merchant, 297 Commissioners
Tracy, T. B., M.D, 158 McGill
TRADE REVIEW AND INTERCOLONIAL JOURNAL OF COMMERCE, weekly, D. Larminie, editor, office 58 St. Francois Xavier
TRANCHEMONTAGNE, J. G., forwarding, commission and general agent, 295 Commissioners
Tregent, P., importer of British and foreign goods, 30 Hospital
Trenholme, E. H., M.D., C.M., 32 St. Radegonde
Trester, M., importer of woolen and fancy goods, wines, &c., 466 St. Paul
TRINITY HOUSE, E. D. David, registrar and treasurer, Harbor Commissioners Building, 14 Custom House sq
Trudel & Carmel, wholesale and retail grocers, wine and spirit merchants, 111 St. Lawrence
Trudel, Eugene Herbule, M. D., 77 Ducord
Trudel, F. X. A., advocate, 223 Notre Dame
Trudel & Vincent, staple and fancy dry goods, wholesale and retail, 96 Notre Dame
TRUST AND LOAN COMPANY OF UPPER CANADA, William Chapman, commissioner; S. W. Woodward, assistant commissioner, 107 Great St. James

TRUE WITNESS, weekly ; George E. Clerk, editor and prop, John Gilles, printer, 696 Craig
TRUTEAU, VERY REV. CANON A. F., vicar general, Bishop's palace, Cemetery
Tucker, Richard, soap and candle manufacturer, 371 Visitation
Tucker, S. & Son, lumber merchants, represented by William Dickson, St. Gabriel locks
Tuckwell, James, wholesale fruit dealer, 119 McGill
Tuggey, Charles H., house and land agent, 61 Great St. James
Turcot, Dr. J. M., 325 Dorchester
Turgeon & Frere, wholesale and retail clothiers, 213 McGill
Turgeon & Grattan, flour merchants, 187 St. Paul
Turgeon, Louis G., M.D., physician and surgeon, 141 St. Lawrence
Turgeon, Nestor, groceries, wines and liquors, 51 Common
Turgeon & Sareault, dry goods, 399 St. Joseph
Turner, William J. N., Montreal commercial school, 975 St. Catharine
Tyre, James, commission merchant and agent for water-proof cloth cover manufacturers, 10 St. Nicholas
UNION BANK, Peter MacEwen, manager, Merchants' Exchange, 11 St. Sacrament
UNITED STATES CONSULATE, Thomas F. Wilson, consul, 25 Great St. James
UNIVERSITY McGILL COLLEGE, Medical Faculty, 25 Cotte ; Faculty of Arts and High School, cor Dorchester and University, University Blgs, 803 Sherbrooke
Urquhart, Alexander, & Co., general merchants, 44 St. Peter
Utley, Maurice H., M.D., 6 Beaver Hall Square
Vallee, Jean Baptiste, advocate, 30 St. Vincent
Vallee, Joseph D., notary, 93 St. Charles Borromee
VALLEYFIELD PAPER MILLS, Alexander Buntin & Co., proprietors, Valleyfield, head of Beauharnois canal, warehouse 338 St. Paul and 273 Commissioners
Varey, George, exchange broker, 90 Great St. James
Vass, Alexander H., produce broker and commission agent, 4 St. Sacrament
Vautier, Philip, shipwright and caulker, lumber, masts, spars, &c., 28 Grey Nun
Vennor, Henry, manager Savings Bank department, Bank of Montreal, Place d'Armes.
VERMONT CENTRAL RAILROAD AND LAKE CHAMPLAIN TICKET OFFICE, F. Picard, ticket agent; George Phippen, freight agent, Gt. St. James
VERREAU, M. L'ABBE H., principal Jacques Cartier Normal school, Old Government
VICTORIA WORKS, iron, nail and spike manufactory, Pillow, Hersey & Co., Mill
VILLA MARIA, educational establishment for young ladies, conducted by the Sisters of the Congregation of Notre Dame, Cote St. Antoine
Villeneuve, Joseph Octave, dealer in groceries, wines, spirits, provisions, and proprietor of Mile End omnibuses, 134 St. Lawrence, cor. Mile End
Villeneuve & Lacaille, grocers, wine and spirit merchants, 200 St. Paul and 161 Commissioners
Villeneuve, Nazaire, groceries and liquors, wholesale and retail, 67 St. Mary
Villeneuve, Professor Alphonse, principal, Maitrise St. Pierre, 8 Rose
Villeneuve, Rev. M., Seminary of St. Sulpice, 320 Notre Dame
Vining, L. R., & Co., wholesale boot and shoe manufacturers, 38 Lemoine cor McGill
Virtue, James & Co., ale, porter, and cider vaults, 39 St. Vincent
Wachtel, E., dry goods, 178 St. George
Waddell & Pearce, general hardware agents, iron, steel, metals and railroad supplies, 27 St. John
Wadsworth, Wm., trader, 119 Amherst
Wagner, William, architect and surveyor, 116 St. Denis
Wainwright, William, private secretary to C. J. Brydges, 972 St. Catherine
Wait George, commission merchant, 2 Young's buildings, McGill cor William
Walkem, C. W., secretary Canada Glass Co., limited, 39 Craig cor Shaw
Walkem, J. B., potash broker, 5 St. Sacrament, 266 Lagauchetiere
Walker, Alexander, importer of dry goods, McGill
Walker, Henry W., chief bookkeeper G. T. R., 945 Dorchester
Walker, James & Co., importers of hardware and house furnishings, 106 Gt St James, cor Peter
Walker, John H., wood engraver, 1 Place d'Armes
Walker, Joseph, hardware commission merchant, 21 St. John
Walker, William, millwright, 325 St. Antoine
Walker, William S., importer of clocks, watches and jewellery, 321 Notre Dame and 41 and 43 St. Lawrence
Waller, Samuel, M. D., 618 St. Mary
Wallis, S. H., G.T.R., 67 City Councillors
Walsh, A. & M., groceries, wines and liquors, 3 St. Antoine
Wand, Peter Charles, builder and contractor, 293 St. Charles Borromee
Wanless, Ewen, room papers and fancy goods, 238 St. Lawrence
Wanless, John, M.D., L.F.P.S., Glasgow, homœopathic physician and surgeon, 646 Lagauchetiere
Ward, Edward C., U. S. claim agent and general agent Atlantic Mutual Life Insurance Company, 25 Great St. James
WARDLAW, P., secretary Life Association of Scotland, Royal Insurance bdgs, 1 Common
WARNER, G. W. & SON, bankers and exchange brokers, 57 St. Francois Xavier
Warner, James, manufacturer of rubber goods, 98 Cadieux
Warren, Horace B., scale manufacturer, 34 St. Patrick cor St. Columba
WARREN, OLIVER, teacher Colonial Church and School Society's Model School, 261 St. Martin
Warren, Samuel R. & Co., organbuilders, 32 and 34 St. Joseph
WATERMAN, H. & BROTHER, Atlantic Petroleum Works, London, Ont., Robert B. Murray, agent, office 36 Lemoine
WATKINS, JOHN, foreman at John Lovell's, 117 Wolfe
Watson, J. R. & Co., exchange and stock brokers, 69 St. Francois Xavier
Watson, John, commission merchant, hardware, 6 Union bdgs, 43 St. Francois Xavier
WATSON, JOHN & CO., china glass and earthenware, wholesale, 5 and 7 Lemoine
WATSON, ROBERT, accountant, assignee and commissioner for taking affidavits for Ontario, Merchants' Exchange, 11 St. Sacrament
WATT, DAVID A. P., produce commission merchant, 6 Corn Exchange, 43 St. Sacrament
Weaver, George W., cloth factory, St. Gabriel Locks
Webb, Dr. Charles W., dentist, 142 St. Lawrence
Weekes, George, notary, 16 Little St. James
Weir, Robert & Co., importers, wholesale stationers and account book manufacturers, 160 and 162 Great St. James
Weir, William, exchange broker, 121 St. Francois Xavier

Welch & Bullock, advocates, 60 Little St. James
West Brothers, tobacco factors and commission merchants, 144 McGill
Whalley & Woods, importers of dry goods, 240 McGill
Wheeler, Thomas B., M.D., 963 St. Catherine
White, John T., publisher, 38 St. George
White & McKay, boiler makers, 12 Colborne
White, Samuel, commission merchant, 51 St. Antoine
Whitehead & Ross, commission merchants, 15 and 17 Lemoine
WHITNEY, H. H., secretary Harbor Commissioners, 943 St. Catharine
Whitney, N. S., wholesale dry goods and leather, 14 St. Helen
Whyte, John, accountant and official assignee, 11 St. Sacrament
Wicksteed, Richard J., advocate, 42 Little St. James
Wilkes, Rev. Henry, D.D., minister of Zion Congregational Church, 249 Mountain
WILKES, ROBERT, importer of watches, clocks, jewelry and fancy goods, 455 St. Paul
Williams' Brewery, Miles Williams, jun., proprietor, 97 College
Williams, C. W. & Co., sewing machines, 347 Notre Dame
Williams, John, Manager Victoria Iron Works, 53 Ottawa
Williams, Thomas, oil manufacturer, 91 Wellington
WILLIAMSON, JAMES, & CO., importers of fancy and staple dry goods, wholesale and retail, 448 Notre Dame
Willis, Charles, rope manufacturer, 423 Commissioners
Willison, Henry, London tea warehouse, 4 Phillips sq
Wills & Mooney, Canada Horse Nail Co, 112 Duke
WILSON, ANDREW, of Penny, Wilson & Co., St. Monique
WILSON & BOURQUE, brush makers 291 St. Paul
Wilson, C. T. & Co., boot and shoe manufacturers, 387 Notre Dame
Wilson & Co., wholesale and retail boot and shoe manufacturers 342 Notre Dame
WILSON, HON. CHARLES, senator, 1180 Dorchester
Wilson, Isaac P., lumber merchant, 49 McGill college avenue
WILSON, JOHN, book and job printer, 42 St. John
WILSON, PATTERSON & CO.. general commission merchants, 875 Commissioners
WILSON & RUMSEY, bankers, and exchange brokers, 104 St. Francois Xavier, (see adv)
Wilson, Thomas, general agent, 58 St. Francois Xavier
Wilson, Thomas & Co., hardware, wholesale and retail 218 St. Paul and 177 Commissioners, cor. Jacques Cartier Square
Windeyer, Richard C., architect, 48 Great St. James
WINDHAM, LIEUT. GENERAL SIR C. ASH, K.C.B., 31 Notre Dame
Winks, George & Co., dry goods, wholesale and retail Albert Buildings, cor. McGill and Victoria
Winn & Holland, general commission merchants, 34 Foundling
WINNING, HILL & WARE, wholesale wine and spirit merchants, 389 and 391 St. Paul (see adv. back cover)
WITHERS, J. P., commission merchant, 28 Hospital
Wolf, Rev. Philip, 239 Bleury
Wood, D. Ross, secretary and treasurer Huntingdon Mining Co., 148 Great St. James
Wood, Peter W., manufacturer of cottons, flannels, yarn, seamless bags, &c., 572 William
Wood, Rev. Edmund, M.A., Incumbent of the (free seat) chapel of St. John the Evangelist, 278 St. Urbain
Wood, Robert, insurance agt, 83 St. Francois Xavier
Woodward, Samuel W., assistant commissioner Trust and Loan Co. of Ontario, 107 Great St. James
WORKMAN, THOMAS, M.P.P., 899 Sherbrooke
WORKMAN, WILLIAM, Mayor of Montreal, and president City Bank, 935 Sherbrooke
Worthington, Richard, bookseller and stationer, 101 Great St James cor St. Peter
Wright & Brogan, notaries, 58 St. Francois Xavier
Wright, Edward & Co., importers of china, glass and earthenware, 492 St. Paul & 409 Commissioners
Wright, Rev. William, M.D., 489 Craig cor St. Dominique
Wright, Robert, secretary-treasurer Canadian Engine and Machinery Co., 67 City Councillors
Wurtele, Jonathan S. C., advocate, 47 St. John
Yates, Benjamin F., merchant, 104 St. Urbain
Young, David, Paymaster G.T.R., 30 Balmoral
YOUNG, HON. JOHN, flour insp'r, 224 Wellington
YOUNG, JAMES A., hoop skirt manufacturer, 505½ St. Paul
Young, John M., merchant, 6 William
ZACHARIAS, M., & CO., manufac'rs of tobaccos, cigars, snuffs, &c., 213, 219 and 234 Notre Dame

HUDSON'S BAY TERRITORY.

This vast Country stretching across the Northern portion of British America, includes nominally, 1st "Rupert's Land," embracing (as granted by the charter of Charles 2nd, in 1670) all the country watered by the Rivers falling into Hudson's Bay. 2nd. The Indian Territories leased in 1821, and including indefinite areas drained by the Mackenzie, Coppermine, Athabaska, Saskatchewan and Red Rivers; extending from the sources of these Rivers to the Arctic Ocean; and from the Rocky Mountains to the Pacific Ocean. 3rd. The whole of British Columbia and Vancouver's Island.

Hudson's Bay is said to have been reached by Sebastian Cabot in 1517. In 1523-4 Verazzani sailed up the coast as far as Davis' Straits, which were reached by Davis in 1585. Various other English navigators sailed northward in search of a north-west passage, but it was not until 1610 that Henry Hudson reached the Straits and Bay now bearing his name. Button, Bylot, Baffin, Fox and James visited the Bay between 1612 and 1631, and traced out and examined the shores and gave their names to portions of the vast inland sea. Connection with Canada was maintained by Canoe, along the Saguenay River and thence overland to the Bay by the Quebec Fur Company, established by Cardinal Richelieu in 1627. Tadousac at the mouth of the River, was their chief trading post in Canada.

The treaty of St. Germains, in 1632, confirmed the whole of the Hudson's Bay Territory to France and De Groselier and Radisson, two French Canadians visited it, but not being successful in their efforts to induce their own Governments to promote the trade in it, they went to England. Prince Rupert entered warmly into their scheme and despatched them on a trading voyage, and their report being favourable, Charles 2nd (though by the treaty of St. Germain's he had relinquished his claim to the territory) granted a Charter to Prince Rupert and others, for traffic in furs and peltry, in the extensive regions then called Rupert's Land. This was the origin of the famous Hudson's Bay Company's charter in 1670, which was in 1690 confirmed by Act of the British Parliament for seven years, but has never since been renewed.

The first consequences of this charter were conflicts between the English and French in the territory. The Chevalier de Troyes was despatched with troops from Quebec, and in 1686 succeeded in capturing the principal forts of the Company. At the treaty of Ryswick, in 1697, and even so late as 1713, the Company had only Fort Albany left. In 1713, by the treaty of Utrecht, the whole of the Hudson's Bay Territory was ceded to Britain and in 1763 the whole of British North America. The Company has since remained in possession, but without any definite title.

The area of the Hudson's Bay Territory may be estimated at about 2,000,000 square miles; its greatest extent from east to west, 3,200 miles; and from north to south, 1,400 miles. The surface of this vast Territory is greatly diversified by ranges of hills, lakes, rivers, prairies, and marshy tracts. The Rocky Mountains on the west, extend from the Arctic Ocean to the United States, but the general slope of the country is in a northerly direction towards the Arctic Ocean and Hudson's Bay.

The most remarkable feature of the Territory is the almost unbroken chain of lakes extending from the head of Lake Superior to the Arctic Ocean. The principal are the Lake of the Woods, Winnepeg, Winnipegosis, Manitoba, Wolleston, Deer, Athabaska, Great Slave and Great Bear Lakes.

The Hudsen's Bay Company have upwards of 100 Forts scattered over the country for the purpose of collecting furs, which form their chief trade, the principal are *Fort Garry*, situated a few hundred yards west of the confluence of the Assiniboine and Red Rivers, and *Stone Fort*, in the colony of Red River. The Company employs about 3,000 persons. The population of this vast country is not more than 200,000, composed to a great extent of Indians and half-breeds. The Indians are the Crees, round the Hudson's Bay, and the Salteaux, further in the interior, both inoffensive tribes, subsisting by hunting, fishing and trapping; and further west, in the boundless prairies, are the more warlike, Sioux, Blackfeet, Flatheads, Crows, and other tribes, living on the products of the chase.

North West Company of Canada.—In 1766, various trades, competitors of the Company engaged in the fur trade. They followed the old French route, and had their head quarters at Montreal. These traders united their several interests, and in 1784, formed the "North Western Company of Canada." This new Company directed its trade chiefly to the North-West—*via.* Lake Superior, towards the Pacific Ocean and Columbia River. They even sent trading ships round Cape Horn. In 1793 Sir Alexander Mackenzie, a partner in the Company, made his famous North-West journey from Canada, across the Rocky Mountains to the Pacific Ocean, (the first ever made north of Mexico), and discovered Fraser River. He afterwards discovered and explored the magnificent river bearing his name. The northern or main branch of the Columbia River was discovered in 1811, by Mr. Thompson, the astronomer, who descended its stream to the Pacific Ocean.

In 1811, Thomas Douglas, Earl of Selkirk, purchased a tract of country from the Hudson's Bay Company, lying between the United States boundary and lakes Winnipeg and Winnipegoos, since called the Red River Settlement. In 1821 he brought settlers from Scotland for the Colony, and, subsequently, numbers of Swiss and French Canadians were introduced. Some time after he appointed Captain Miles McDonell, who was Governor of the Company's District of Assiniboine, sperintendent, who issued a proclamation forbidding the appropriation of provisions except to the use of the Colonists. This assumption of exclusive jurisdiction by the Hudson's Bay Company, excited the bitterest feelings on the part of the rival North-Western Company, and gave rise to a fierce contest between them during the progress of which the Colonists were twice expelled and many lives lost, including that of Governor Semple. Sir George Drummond sent part of a regiment from Quebec to preserve order and to restrain the violence of both companies. The feud ceased by the amalgamation of the companies. On the death of Lord Selkirk, the company resumed the purchase on condition of paying a certain quit rent. The majority of the original settlers left the country, and the Company did not encourage further immigration. Hence, with the exception of an occasional visitor from Minnesota and some slight additions from the interior of the Hudson's Bay Territory, as retired chief factors, traders and clerks, the little colony was left to its own resources and in the course of half a century from its foundation it numbered exactly 10,000 souls.

Red River Settlement.—RESOURCES, CLIMATE, &c.—Our object in the present article is not to discuss the vexed question of the Hudson Bay Company's rights, as events now pending point to the almost certainty of the incorporation of this magnificent territory with the Dominion of Canada, but to furnish general information as to the resources of Rupert's Land, and in so doing it will be shown that though in regard of soil, climate, and general resources, a vast section of it is well adapted for settlement; very little encouragement has been given to immigration. As fine an agricultural country as any we can boast of in Canada, containing somewhere about Forty Millions acres of available land. lies here, almost unappropriated, though two centuries have elapsed since first the Hudson's Bay Company adventured into the region

Rupert's Land, as above stated, includes the whole country from the Rocky Mountains to the shores of Hudson's Bay, and is held to embrace the lands on all waters flowing into Hudson's Bay. The extent of this territory is estimated at 1,077,000 square miles. The population is claimed to be about 43,000 Indians and from 15,000 to 20,000 whites and mixed races. At the outset we must state that in any statistics we furnish of the great north-west in this article, we do not include that part of British North America west of the Rocky Mountains, but confine ourselves to a review of the capabilities and prospects of the country east of the mountains, which is yet comparatively in a state of nature, and of this section, the southern or cultivable part alone need claim our attention. In the icy and inhospitable region north of the 60th parallel the hunter and trapper will never be intruded on by the agriculturist, but, leaving that section out of account, we have, according to Lorin Blodgett, a wedge-shaped tract, commencing two degrees south of the boundary line, inclining north-westward in conformity with the bend of the Rocky Mountains, and terminating not far from the 60th parallel in a narrow line. This is a productive and cultivable region, within easy reach of immigration, the surface of which is said to cover fully 500,000 square miles. Professor Hind, speaking of this great prairie plateau, or "fertile belt" of Rupert's Land, says: that it stretches from the Lake of the Woods to the Mountains, a distance af 800 miles, and that its breadth throughout is from 80 to 100 miles. This extraordinary belt of rich soil and pasturage he estimates at 40,000,000 acres. Dr. Huton says that the winter in this region is not more severe than that experienced in Canada, and in the western districts, which are removed from the influence of the great lakes, the Spring commences a month earlier than on the shore of Lake Superior. which is five degrees further south.

The importance of this great region may be gathered from the further fact that not only is it abundant in agricultural and mineral resources, but it is admitted to be almost the sole remaining theatre of colonization on the continent. Explorations of the regions between the Mississippi and the Rocky Mountains, by the United States Government, have disclosed the facts that the limits of nearly all the available areas for settlement, westward, have been reached. The country west of the 98th parallel, embracing nearly one-half of the entire surface of the United States, is a waste which can never be utilized for agricultural purposes. Professor Henry, of the Smithsonian Institute, calls this section "a wilderness unfitted for the use of the husbandman, although in some of the mountain valleys, as at Salt Lake, by means of irrigation, a precarious supply of food may be obtained. On the northern edge of this great wilderness extends the fertile belt of the Saskatchewan Valley, which contains 64,000 square miles of country, in one continuous strip, available for the purposes of the agriculturist." And, says Professor Hind, "by contrast, with an immense sub-arctic sea to the north, and a desert area to the south, this favored 'Edge of the Woods' country acquires political and commercial importance."

Being a prairie region, this fertile belt offers every facility for the making of roads and railroads, and in addition, has a magnificent water communication, which, with some few improvements, would allow a continuous navigation from Breckenridge, on the Red River, 224 miles north of St. Paul, to the shadows of the Rocky Mountains. The country between Breckenridge and St. Paul is level prairie, now traversed by four-horse coaches, daily, being the means of communication, at present, between Minnesota and the Red River and Saskatchewan region.

There is another channel of communication with this country, used only once a year, we refer to that *via* the ice bound region of Hudson's Bay. By this route one or two vessels belonging to the Company, bring out annually, a large portion of the outfits destined for the support of their trading posts in the interior. A few passengers arrive and depart by this route.

Yet another outlet of this territory, and the one in which Canada is most interested, is that by Lake Superior. This track lies across a series of granitic ridges, in some places as high as 1,400 feet above the level of the lake, which form the height of land between the waters of Superior and Lake Winnipeg and Hudson's Bay. Except on the borders of Lake Superior, however, these ridges do not attain the elevation we have mentioned and there are several fine alluvial valleys scattered through the region, where, in the event of roads being opened up, thriving settlements would before long be located. Concerning this route, its feasibility and cost, a good deal of conflicting opinion has been advanced, some would have it that the difficulties are well nigh insuperable and that the cost would be prodigious, but there are a large number of dissentients from this view, and among them we would refer to Mr. Dawson and Mr, Sandford Fleming, the present engineer of the Intercolonial Railway. The latter shows that by taking Mr. Dawson's recommendations as to the construction of a road between Lake Superior and Fort Garry, with some modification, a road could be made through British territory which would be far shorter than any of the routes by way of the States. The shortest and speediest route to Red River through American territory is by way of Grand Haven, Milwaukee, La Crosse and St. Paul, making a total 1696 miles from Toronto. By the route from Toronto to Nipigon harbor, Lake Superior, and thence by the proposed road and steamboat communication to Fort Garry, the distance would be lessened to 1,050 miles. Showing a saving in distance by the British route over every other of 646 miles. This, of course, would lead to a corresponding diminution in the cost of freight and passenger traffic. Mr. Dawson estimates that by taking advantage of the water communication, by way of Dog Lake, Savanne River, the Lake of a Thousand Islands, the River Seine, Rainy Lake and River, and the Lake of the Woods, or a total of 499 miles, of which 308 are navigable by steamers, a good road might be constructed at a cost of from £50,000 to £80,000. It would cost even less than this sum, for the Red River colonists themselves offered to build the section of the road adjoining Red River, 92 miles in length, and at all events, that section is now being constructed for the Dominion Government, while there has also been a beginning made at the other terminal section on Lake Superior, for which an appropriation of $55,000 was lately made by Government. By the construction of this road it is claimed that the cost of conveying goods to Fort Garry would be reduced to less than $40 per ton from Lake Superior, against $100 from York Factory, and $90 from St. Paul, Minnesota.

There are, also, other projects connected with the Canadian section of this proposed line of communication, which we need not here comment on. Among these are the Ottawa and French River Canal ; a railroad from Ottawa to Fort Garry, passing north of Lake Superior ; and a railroad in a direct line from Quebec to Nipigon River, along the watershed between the St. Lawrence and Hudson's Bay. The latter line, it is averred, would shorten the distance across the Continent 120 miles.

The advocates of railroad communication between Canada and Red River are numerous, one view being that it would avoid all the disadvantages and expense attendant on the frequent transhipments incident to the proposed system of land and water communication. Another advantage of railway travel would be found in enabling Canada to compete favorably with Minnesota in the struggle for the rich trade of the north-west. The construction of such a road would seem to be comparatively easy of accomplishment, for, if narrow guage lines can be built for $15,000, or broad gauge for $25,000 per mile, railroad building through any section would not prove such a formidable task ; and it would be still less so, if, as is stated, the means to build such roads can be obtained merely by the aid of land grants. A railroad through the Lake Superior section westward, and across the Continent, has long been spoken of, and urged on the Imperial authorities. If, as has been frequently set forth, British Columbia is, for the purposes of overland communication, the key to the Pacific, and if, as we believe to be the case, it is absolutely necessary to the continuance of British power and rule on this Continent, that British Columbia and Rupert's Land should be united in the Confederation of British Provinces, then there can be no doubt that the Pacific Railway across the British territory will be built, and the sooner the better, for we have our competitors on the other side of the line pushing forward their Pacific Railway at the astonishing rate of three and four miles a day.

Rupert's Land, as we have stated, is rich in mineral as well as agricultural wealth. Within these sub-arctic plains, says Wheelock, between latitudes 47° to 60° north is reproduced the climate of Western Europe, in the corresponding belt of the temperate zone. Nine tenths of Russia, the main seat of population and resources, lies north of St. Paul, Minnesota ; and the great prairie region of the North-West may in the future, witness similar prosperity. Its agricultural resources have been tested all through the fertile belt, with but one result of which we have heard, unvarying success ; and enough has been revealed of its mineral treasures, with the slightest exploration, to show them to be abundant. Gold, silver, iron, lead, coal, gypsum, petroleum and salt, are found in the Saskatchewan valley. A vast coal bed, according to Sir John Richardson, skirts the base of the Rocky Mountains to a great extent, and is believed to be continued far into the Arctic Sea. The existence of this great coal field, it will be seen, must be of the utmost importance in the future development of a region devoid of timber, for the most part, except along the water courses.

Throughout Rupert's Land there are several small settlements of the white and mixed races. Around the Presbyterian, Roman Catholic, Methodist and Church of England Mission-posts on the Saskatchewan, and here and there in the interior, many families have settled down, built themselves snug homesteads, cultivated farms, and erected churches, chapels and school houses. There are also a few feeble attempts at settlement around most of the Hudson's Bay Company's posts. But, looking at the vast unoccupied domain in which these little beginnings of civilization are originating, they appear the merest specks—the scarcely recognizable vanguard of that vast army of emigration which will one day overrun these magnificent plains, and cause a solitary place to blossom as the rose. The largest settlement in the Territory is that called Red River, on the river of that name. Red River empties into Lake Winnipeg, and is situated in lat. 50° N., and long 97° W. It runs north and south, taking its rise in the affluents of Elbow Lake, Minnesota, on the height of land close to the sources of the Mississippi, and has a course of over 500 miles in length. Fort Garry, as the Red River Colony is sometimes termed, is the Hudson Bay Company's Post, at the confluence of the Red and Assiniboine rivers in the settlement.

The late Alexander Ross, in his work on the Red River Settlement, speaks of it in the most favorable terms. The country, he says, is healthy, the soil rich, and the crops luxuriant; and he cites frequent instances in which from 40 to sixty bushels of wheat to the acre were obtained. The climate of Red River, and even the whole Saskatchewan Valley, is claimed by Blodgett to be nearly as mild in its annual average as that of St. Paul, Minnesota, which would give it a winter mean of 15 degrees, and an annual mean of 44 degrees. This would represent the climate of Wisconsin, Northern Iowa, Michigan, Ontario, and Southern New England. In summer it is warmer than Northern Illinois, Western Wisconsin, Northern New York, or Ontario. The winter, though very cold, is like the corresponding season in Quebec, a very enjoyable and healthy one. With a bright sunshine, and clear dry atmosphere, the season is one of much enjoyment out of doors, and not half-a-dozen times in a winter, perhaps, is travel interrupted by intensely cold or stormy weather. Spring opens at the same time as at St. Paul, and Minnesota, it need hardly be observed, is now one of the largest grain producing States in America.

The Company's nominal selling price for land in the Red River District is 7s. 6d. per acre; but, having no force to enable them to deal with defaulters, the Company never made much out of the land business. If a settler paid up on a notification from the authorities, well and good; if he proved fractious and refused to pay, well and good also. He lived unmolested. Land changing hands between private parties, would in most instances, command a far higher price than that named above. But, for the most part, if a man desires to change his location he goes on to wild land and occupies it as by unquestioned right. As to the agricultural capacity of the District generally, not only is it capable of raising splendid wheat; but also all the great northern staples—corn, oats, barley, potatoes, sheep and cattle; and it has been observed that "cultivated plants yield the greatest product near the northernmost limits of their possible growth." And, for this reason, says Blodgett (and no better authority can be quoted) "it is proved that the Basin of the Winnepeg is the seat of the greatest average wheat product on this continent, and probably in the world." Throughout the Red River Settlement the yield of grain and root crops is prolific, and those taking to the cultivation of the soil have had, as a rule, abundant returns. Not only has this been the case, but for the last ten years at least, farmers have been able to dispose of all they have raised at high prices; wheat for instance, ruling at from 4s. to 10s. sterling per bushel, and other crops in proportion. From a residence of some years in that quarter, the writer of this article can safely say that notwithstanding the good rates obtaining for grain, during no one year of the past eight or ten, has the supply kept pace with the demand; and this has been owing, not to a failure of crops (except in the case of the grasshopper visitation last year), but to a failure to put in enough seed to suffice for the wants of the community, and allow of a limited supply for the interior of the Territory. The settlers in Red River, it must be explained, are not all farmers. Out of 12,000 or 14,000 inhabitants fully one-half follow the chase, and depend on it almost solely for their sustenance the year round. They are nominally farmers also; but a glance at the weed-grown, ill-cultivated patches of soil adjoining their homesteads, will show what an utter farce their farming is. It could not be expected to be otherwise; for hunting and farming are such dissimilar pursuits that the man engaging in both will almost infallibly neglect one. But, until the past four or five years, the hunter could very well afford to neglect his farm. He sallied out to the plains twice or thrice a year with his family and fellow hunters and their families, until their number swelled to the dimensions of a small army. And they hunted and feasted the summer through. Thousands of buffaloes were slain in these expeditions; and the man himself was to blame who did not return home with from two to half a dozen cart loads of buffalo meat. He had thus abundance to keep his family all the year round, for the surplus could be readily bartered for flour, tea, cloth, and all the necessaries of life. But not in the great majority of cases, perhaps, did the supplies last out their term. The hunter's return home was signalized by such prolonged feasting, and his ideas of domestic economy were so extravagant, that two or three months before spring time came starvation stared them in the face and only by short allowances and unlimited credits could Jean Baptiste make both ends meet till the season for hunting came round again. From this class there is a large annual demand for farm produce.

Having glanced thus briefly at the climate, resources and prospects of the Red River Settlement and Rupert's Land generally, we will close our sketch with a few remarks concerning the Government and religious and educational advantages enjoyed by the inhabitants of Red River. Those living in the interior are pretty well provided for by the missions, so far as the means of education and religion are concerned. As to governmental machinery it is not generally needed in the interior of that vast almost untenanted domain. Where it is called for some primitive substitute is found, it is generally satisfactory, and on the whole, justice is done between man and man. In the Red River district affairs are managed by a Governor and Council, the latter being appointed by the Hudson Bay Company in London, from among the settlers, and numbering usually a dozen or more. The Roman Catholic and Episcopal Bishops as well as the Recorder, have seats at this Council Board. The laws are few and simple, and are seldom amended or repealed, and this little Parliament of Assiniboia, as it is sometimes called, is one of the most easy-going, good natured bodies to be found to-day on the face of the Globe. The only imposition in the shape of a tax, is a four per cent. duty levied indiscriminately on all the imports. Occasionally they have discriminated against spirituous liquors and imposed on them a heavy duty. But, as in more civilised communities this only led to smuggling on an extended scale. The funds realised from these sources by the Council are mainly squandered in patching up roads and bridges, and the work performed in this way is of such an excellent character that it has to be done over again every year or so.

The only religious bodies in the settlement are the Roman Catholic, Episcopal, Presbyterian and Methodist, the latter body making its first appearance there last year, and having very few adherents yet. The Roman Catholics number about half the population, and have a fine cathedral, college, nunnery, and several chapels and schools scattered along the Red and Assinobine Rivers. The present Bishop, Taché, once swayed the entire country between the mountains and Lake Superior, but two other Dioceses were carved out of his a few years ago. The Episcopal and Presbyterian Churches may be said to divide the remainder of the Red River population between them. The former denomination boasts an excellent cathedral, college, and a large number of churches and schools—more than ample for the wants of the present number of inhabitants. The Diocese of the Bishop, Machray, extends over all Rupert's Land. The Presbyterian settlers have, also, several churches and schools, and are, generally, the most well-to-do section of the community.

Justice is administered by a Recorder, who holds Quarterly Courts at Fort Garry, and these deal with all cases not coming under the cognizance of the Petty Courts. These last are held monthly, and presided over by the Magistrates of the District. The decisions in these Courts, being, as a rule, given with less regard to strict law than common sense, would occasionally astonish an outsider, but are, on the whole, as satisfactory to those most concerned, as legal decisions usually are.

The Northwest.—By the Rev. Æn. M'D. Dawson, Ottawa.—The "North West Territory," is that portion of British North America which is situated between Lake Superior to the east, the Pacific Ocean and the Russian Dominions (now a portion of the United States) to the west. The 49th parallel of north latitude, and the chain of waters from Rainy Lake to the confluence of Pigeon River with Lake Superior, form the boundary between this territory and the United States on the south. To the north, with the exception of some portions of Alaska (lately Russian America), it has no other limits than those of the globe itself—the ice, the snow, the perpetually frozen seas and lands of the polar regions.

The Principal Rivers.—North Western America is watered by numerous rivers, the greater of which only need here be named. The Columbia, rising in the Rocky Mountains, traverses the Blue Mountains, and the Cascade Mountain chains. It, then, after many windings sometimes in a southerly, sometimes in a westerly direction, loses itself in the Pacific Ocean at Astoria, three degrees south of the boundary line. The treaty which deprived Great Britain of the better part of the Columbia, left to her the right of navigating this noble river in common with the citizens of the United States. The Fraser River also has its source in the Rocky Mountains. After a circuitous course through the Blue Mountains, the Cascade Mountains, and the intervening plains and valleys, it joins the sea at the strait or sound which separates Vancouver Island from the Continent of America. This river is celebrated for its sands of gold. Even as to California and Australia, thousands of adventurers have already been attracted to its banks; and their enterprise has been crowned with success unsurpassed as yet in the annals of gold digging.

Of Pelly River there need be little mention, as it half belongs to a foreign power. It is quite possible, however, that arrangements might be made with that power (the United States) for navigating this great river to its junction with the sea.

The Mackenzie River is wholly within British territory. It is one of the greatest rivers in the world its course being two thousand five hundred miles from its source in the Rocky Mountains to its debouch in the Arctic Ocean. It is navigable for about twelve hundred miles, thus affording easy access in the summer months from the Arctic Sea, and from the Northern Pacific by Behrings Straits, to the interior of the North-West Territory. It flows through a fertile and finely-wooded country, skirted by metalliferous hills. According to the best computation, it drains an area of 443,000 geographical square miles.

The Elk and Peace Rivers, although great and beautiful streams, are only tributaries of the MacKenzie.

The Coppermine and the Great Fish River also discharge their waters into the Arctic Ocean. The former abounds in copper ore and galena. On the banks of the latter, it is credibly said that there is excellent grazing. Next comes the Churchill River which flows from the interior of the country, across the Granite Belt, to Hudson's Bay.

The Saskatchewan with its two branches arising in the Rocky Mountains, drains an area of 363,000 square miles. The Red River and the Assiniboine flowing from the heights near the sources of the Missouri and the Mississippi add immensely to the waters of Lake Winnipeg and thence find their way by the Nelson River to Hudson's Bay.

General Description.—There is admirable unity in the geological appearances of this vast territory. By nature it has been made one land, however much it may be divided by the policy of man. The great chain of the Rocky Mountains extends from its southern to its northern boundary, rising at its highest elevation, to the height of sixteen thousand feet above the level of the ocean. Parallel with these, to the west, rise the Blue and Cascade Mountains, as if intended for a vanguard towards the waves of the Pacific. From the base of the Rocky Mountains, eastward, the country is a gently sloping plain for 800 or 900 miles, to the commencement of the great Crystalline Belt, which taking a north-westerly direction about the head of Lake Superior, continues in this course and almost parellel with the Rocky Mountains as far as fifteen hundred miles, and with only a slight elevation above the neighboring plain until reaching the Coppermine River near the Arctic Ocean, it forms hills eight hundred feet in height. Its average breadth is two hundred miles. On the side that looks towards Hudson's Bay, its outline is pretty much the same as that of the shores of this sea, thus verifying what geologists say as to the waters of this region having been confined within their actual limits by the upheaving of these primary formations. Between this belt or plateau and the Bay, there is a narrow strip of limestone. From this bed of limestone to the sea, the land is low, flat, swampy, and, in part alluvial.

Lakes.—On the western edge of the great Chrystaline Plateau are situated the principal Lakes of the North-western Continent—Winnipeg two hundred and thirty miles in length and forty miles broad; Arthabasca, Great Slave Lake, and the largest of them all, Great Bear Lake, which is intersected toward its North-western extremity, by the Arctic Circle.

To the west of this great chain of water the country is all habitable, and in a northerly direction, as far as the sixty-fifth degree of north latitude. If, indeed, the MacKenzie River should ever be what nature has adapted it for being, the principal channel through which a great portion of the trade of the western world must flow, there may one day be a dense population even so far north as the junction of its waters with the Arctic Ocean.

Country West of the Crystalline Belt, Assiniboia, etc.—The portion of the country that may be first considered is the extensive region bordering on Lakes Winnipeg, Manitoba and Winnipigoos. Its principal rivers are the Assiniboine, which is all within British territory, and the Red River, which only becomes British at Pembina, a small town on the frontier of the United States. The authorities that can be most relied on, speak highly of the climate, the soil, and the beauty of the region. It has been officially reported by the Canadian Exploring Expedition of 1857, that "the summer temperature is nearly four degrees warmer than at Toronto, as ascertained by comparison of corresponding observations." Summer begins earlier and with more regularity than in Canada. We are not surprised, therefore, to learn that "the melon grows with the utmost luxuriance, without any artificial aid, and ripens perfectly before the end of August." (Expedition '57.) Wheat crops have often been known to give a return of fifty bushels to the acre, and farms have been proved to be capable of yielding for eighteen successive years without any diminution of their produce. All kinds of garden vegetables, as well as oats, barley, Indian corn, hops, flax, hemp, potatoes and other root crops are easily raised. "The potatoes, cauliflowers and onions I have not seen surpassed," says Professor Hind, "at any of our Provincial fairs."

The character of the soil cannot be exceeded. It is a rich, black mould, from ten to twenty inches deep, reposing on a lightish-colored alluvial clay, about four feet deep, which again rests upon lacustrine or drift clay, to the level of the water in all the rivers and creeks inspected by the Expedition of 1857 and 1858.

It is far from being true, as has been stated, that there is only some arable or cultivable land along the course of the great rivers. "I frequently examined the soil," writes Professor Hind in his official report, "some miles distant from the rivers along my line of route, and I invariably found the prairie country to exhibit an uniform fertility." This rich and beautiful region which has been described by some travellers, as an unbroken level, watered by numerous tributary streams, and abounding in elm, oak, ash, maple and all the varities of trees known in Canada, is no less than one million five hundred acres in extent. Recent observations also prove that this "paradise of fertility," as it has been called by one of the settlers, is not more than six hundred feet above the level of the ocean.

Passing to the west of the valleys of the Assiniboine and Red rivers, we find a country no less fertile, and even more beautiful, as it possesses the pleasing variety of hill and dale. It is watered by an infinite number of lesser streams, the principal of which are the Swan river, and the higher tributaries of the Assinniboine. This interesting region was likewise visited by the exploring expedition sent by the Government of Canada in 1867-8. In Mr. S. J. Dawson's official report of this expedition, published by order of the Canadian House of Assembly, this extensive portion of the North-West territory is described as being eminently adapted for the purposes of agriculture and colonization. Possessing a milder climate than the more elevated lands to the south of the United States boundary line, all the varieties of cereal crops can be produced without difficulty or risk of failure. According to this gentleman's description, the whole country has more the appearance of a fine park, beautifully varied with lawns, woods, gardens, shrubberies, lakes and streams, than an unreclaimed tract of unbroken wilderness. If the late Governor of the Hudson's Bay Company, Sir George Simpson, had passed through this country, it would undoubtedly have inspired one of his eloquent and glowing pictures of wood-land, lake, and river scenery. If it has not hitherto been colonized to any extent, the blame for such neglect of the interests of humanity must be charged to the Hudson's Bay Company, whose policy, however worthy and meritorious each leading member is known to be, is necessarily hostile to every enterprise that is not calculated to preserve and increase the profitable breed of martens, beavers, muskrats, foxes, wildcats and other vermin, together with the aboriginal races in their rude state, who are the best hunters of such animals and the most expert purveyors of skins and furs for the great fur-dealing company.

The Saskatchewan Country.—This extensive territory stretches from the borders of the granite plateau already alluded to, and from which it is separated by a chain of waters consisting of Cedar Lake, a portion of the River Saskatchewan, Fine Island Lake and Beaver Lake, for a distance of 800 or 900 miles westwards to the Rocky Mountains. It is divided into numerous plains and valleys by the river Saskatchewan, its two great branches, and its numerous tributaries, which rising, for the most part, in the vast mountain range, rush down the innumerable vales and glens on its eastern slope, giving life, beauty and fertility to a region which would otherwise be a rugged and forbidding wilderness.

The travellers who have visited this region bear ample witness to the fertility of the soil. The scenery they describe as "magnificent," and the banks of the river on either side, as luxuriant beyond description. "Vast forests," says Lieutenant Saxon, "cover the hill-tops and fill the valleys. The climate is mild, and cattle keep fat in winter as well as in summer on the nutritious grasses."

Sir George Simpson, who had been for thirty years Governor of the Hudson's Bay Company, in his very beautiful and interesting book (Voyage Round the World), informs us that "the rankness of the vegetation between the forks of the Saskatchewan, savoured rather of the torrid zone, with its perennial spring, than of the northern wilds." He speaks of himself and his fellow-travellers as "brushing the luxuriant grass with our knees, and the hard ground of the surface was beautifully diversified with a variety of flowers, such as the rose, the hyacinth and the tiger lily."

"Towards the foot of the Rocky Mountains," says the same impartial writer, "lies a country capable of being rendered the happy home of millions of inhabitants, when facilities of communication shall be offered which can lead to it."

Dr. King, in his evidence before the select Committee of the House of Commons (1857), gives a very interesting account of a colony which was endeavoring to establish itself near Cumberland House, between Fine Island Lake and the River Saskatchewan. This colony occupied, and had in a high state of cultivation, some fifteen hundred acres, on which they raised excellent wheat. When asked by Mr. Christy whether the cultivation was successful, Dr. King replied, "quite successful; the wheat was looking very luxuriant." Were there any other kinds of crops? "There were potatoes and barley, also pigs cows and horses." In this small settlement, each man had his own particular allotment, and everything, according to the evidence of Dr. King, was in the most flourishing condition. The learned witness, however, further states—"When I was going away they said: 'Cannot you help us? You are a Government officer; the Company have ordered us to quit, and we shall be ruined.'" Of course agriculture and colonization were not the objects of the Company; and, *la raison du plus fort est toujours la meilleure.* What became of this interesting little colony deponent said not. The day may not, perhaps, be far distant when colonization will be undertaken on a greater scale, and under more fostering auspices.'

But it has been stated that owing to periodical inundations which, every spring, lay the whole country under water, for nearly 200 miles from the junction of the Saskatchewan with the lakes, cultivation, the raising of crops,—settlement—are impossible. This objection, if, indeed, it be a serious one, applies only to a very limited section of the country. And, could no means be discovered by which these inundations might be prevented or at least regulated and rendered advantageous? There are falls of great magnitude near the point where the Saskatchewan joins Lake Winnipeg; and although the people at Red River do not think that by removing a certain mill pond in their country, an immense swamp which it dams up would be drained, it is nevertheless beyond question, that if the wants of man required it, the annual floods of the Saskatchewan might be made to find their way into Lake Winnipeg without first inundating the country. But, in a region where it rains so little, the precipitation being in the course of the year only fifteen inches, it might tend more to the raising of abundant crops, to regulate and even extend the rush of the spring tide waters. To what does Egypt owe the fertility of its plains, if not to the Nile's inundations? The whole valley through which the great river flows was wont to be overflowed, and often to excess; yet who ever heard of a famine on the banks of the Nile, or that Egypt was incapable of being, when occasion required, the granary of the world? In order that no inconvenience might arise from excessive inundations, great and stupendous works were erected by the generosity of the kings of Egypt and the ingenuity of her people. Thus were the superfluous waters disposed of and regulated, so as to increase to an amazing extent the fertility of the land. Who knows but, when people if not princes have been multiplied on the earth, similar works may be undertaken in the hitherto neglected regions of the North-West?—and who dare say that the vast countries there, which have known no sound as yet save the lowing of wild cattle and the war-whoop of the fierce red-man, shall not rejoice one day in all the blessings of civilization, and become vocal with the glad accents of millions upon millions of happy beings.

Soil and Climate of the Regions Watered by the MacKenzie River and its Tributaries, the Elk and Peace Rivers.—The valleys of the Elk and Peace rivers, tributaries of the MacKenzie, although much further north than the countries on the Saskatchewan, being situated between the 55th and 58th degrees of north latitude, enjoy a climate and soil adapted to the growth of all the cereals, and all kinds of garden vegetables. Wheat, even, can be raised easily in these valleys, for it grows at Fort Liard, in 60 degrees north latitude, on Mountain River, another tributary of the MacKenzie. Although we have no positive evidence before us which decidedly proves that wheat crops may be relied on at Peace River, there is surely ground for believing that, where the spring is so early, grain, which even cold Siberia refuses not to the labor of man, might be successfully cultivated. Sir Alexander MacKenzie, in his journal of date 10th May, 1793, says that "already the buffaloes were seen with their young ones frisking about them." At this time also, (10th May), "the whole country," he writes, "displayed an exuberant verdure. The trees that bear a blossom were advancing fast to that delightful appearance; and the velvet rind of the branches, reflecting the oblique rays of a rising or a setting sun, added a splendid gaiety to the trees, which no expressions of mine are qualified to describe."

Between the two rivers—the Elk and the Peace—55·56 N. latitude, "the ground rises at intervals to a considerable height, and stretches inward to a great distance. At every interval or pause in the rise, there is a very gently ascending space or lawn, which is alternate with abrupt precipices to the summit of the whole, or at least as far as the eye could distinguish. This magnificent theatre of nature has all the decorations which the trees and animals of the country can afford it. Groves of poplars, in every shape, vary the scene, and their intervals are enlivened with vast herds of Elks and Buffaloes—the former choosing the steep uplands, and the latter preferring the plains."—*Sir Alex. McKenzie's Journal*, 1793.

Extreme Limits of Cultivation.—At Fort Norman, within a few miles of the 65th parallel of north latitude, barley and potatoes have been raised, although, probably, wheat could not be cultivated. It is well known, however, that in Europe it grows to perfection as far north as latitude 59.

But, neither wheat crops nor cereals of any kind are destined to form the resources and wealth of this portion of the country. The navigation of the McKenzie will be its treasure. And surely if the enterprising citizens of the United States find it profitable to convey from the seas which receive the waters of this great river, shiploads of whale oil and other merchandise, it will be still more so for the future inhabitants of the flowery regions of the Saskatchewan, the Assnibone and the Red River to derive like supplies from the Arctic Ocean by means of the McKenzie, which is navigable during the summer months for more than twelve hundred miles; thus affording access to the very heart of the land, whence, in all directions, there are lakes and rivers capale of bearing on their waters the most richly laden merchant ships. Seven millions of dollars yearly, the sum accruing to the United States from the whale fisheries alone, are surely but an inconsiderate fraction of the priceless treasures that might be fished up from the inexhaustable depths of the great Arctic Sea. And this will be, one day, the rich possession of the numerous people who will find their homes on the eastern slopes of the Rocky Mountains, and in the fertile valleys and the prairies which end only where the settled country of Canada begins.

The Way to the North-West.—Hitherto, it has been too generally believed that access to the beautiful countries of the North. West is extremely difficult, if not impossible. This idea may have arisen from the circumstance that the Hudson's Bay Company have been in the habit of travelling thither by long and circuitous, difficult and even dangerous routes. It seems extraordinary that they should have preferred to convey their stores and merchandise round by the stormy waters of the north, with their only port at York Factory on Hudson's Bay, which is almost always frozen, when a more direct way was at their command, by the Canadian lakes and the chain of waters which extend from Lake Superior to the vicinity of their settlement on Red River. This may have led to the belief that there existed no better route. Recent explorations have shewn, however, that the journey from Canada to the North-West is shorter than has been supposed, and comparatively easy; that indeed, where there are *portages* or carrying places, a great highway might be established, only a little longer than the most direct or *air* line from Fort William at the head of Lake Superior to Fort Garry, on the Red River—(Air line, with a little road making, 377 miles—route by land and water, 454 miles).

Nor does this route pass through a barren and inhospitable wilderness, the height of land separating Lake Superior from the countries to the westward once passed, the rivers and lakes are bordered by prairies and luxuriant woods. Nor are these regions without inhabitants. In addition to the Indian tribes who are by no means hostile, there are numerous settlers of European origin, and several missions have been in existence for many years. The colonists of Red River, who are most anxious to hold relations with Canada, would prefer this route to the more circuitous, difficult and dangerous one by Pembina and through the State of Minnesota. They gave proof of this preference by undertaking themselves to make a road ninety miles in length, from that settlement to the Lake of the Woods which constitutes so large a portion of navigable waters, extending to within thirty miles of Lake Superior. The Government of the Dominion of Canada, in consideration of the loss of the crops at Red River this year, 1868, have relieved the settlers from this responsibility and are now actually directing the construction of a road from Fort Garry, in connection with the navigable waters.

This route will in a short time hence, be available for travel and traffic, part of the land road from Thunder Bay, (L. Superior), towards the lake region, which lies between Lake Superior and the Red River country, being already constructed, and an appropriation having been made by the Canadian Government for the construction of 90 miles of wagon road from the last of the chain of lakes (the Lake of the Woods,) to Fort Garry, the chief place in the Red River Settlement.

It is not unreasonable to suppose that, by opening communications with the North West territories, an important amount of trading will be at once established between those regions and Canada. At present the settlers at Red River are dependent for their supplies on the State of Minnesota. Goods can only be conveyed from St. Paul, the chief city of that State, with considerable difficulty and at great expense. The North-western people would find a cheaper and equally well supplied market in Canada; and as has just been shewn, the cost of carriage would be materially less. The able men who direct the energies of the Hudson's Bay Company, would be among the first, undoubtedly, to see the advantages of the new route, and to avail themselves of them. Canada cannot fail to recognize her interest in such great public, even national, improvements. Trade, to the value of many millions yearly, would be directed to her borders, wealth would flow to her from the gold mines of the Fraser, the coal fields of Vancouver, the inexhaustible fisheries of British Columbia, and the fertile plains of the Saskatchewan, the Red River and the Assiniboine—waters which, communicating by means of *portages*, lead all the way to the immediate neighborhood of Lake Superior.

And what if the highway to the distant east—to China and Japan; to the lovely islands of the Pacific; to Borneo; to New Zealand; to golden Australia and our vast Indian Empire—should pass through the beautiful and productive valleys of the North-West?

A railway from Halifax or Quebec to the western coast of the American Continent has been spoken of; and, indeed, such a way could be more easily made along the plains of the Saskatchewan and the northern passes, than through the more mountainous country some degrees farther south. Nor would the Rocky Mountains be an unsurmountable barrier. They could be pierced without any serious engineering difficulties at the sources of the MacKenzie and Fraser Rivers, or at the point where they were traversed by Sir George Simpson, with a long train of horses, wagons and baggage, at the head waters of the Saskatchewan and the Columbia. In the meantime, other kinds of roads and modes of conveyance may be adopted with almost equally great advantage. The more direct way to Red River, by the chain of lakes and rivers which already almost connect the Canadian lakes with the settlement at Fort Garry, once established, as it must be in a year or two, the great highway as far as the Rocky Mountains, and within 200 miles of Fraser River, is complete, the rivers and lakes extending westwards from Red River, being navigable even for vessels of large tonnage, eight hundred miles of the way. At present there is no other route to the rich and populous lands of the Eastern Hemisphere than by the stormy seas of Asia and Africa, across the Isthmus of Panama, round Cape Horn, or through the dangerous straits of Magellan, or by what is called "the overland route," through foreign countries. Whether the nations of Europe will continue to prefer these ways, which, however, long and difficult and dangerous, have the sanction of antiquity, it is obvious that Canada, as she increases in wealth and population, will find the new way, although all but untrodden as yet, more convenient, perhaps even essential, for the wants of her extended trade.

British Columbia.—This territory, which includes Vancouver's Island, formerly belonged to the Hudson's Bay Company, but in 1858 was given up to Great Britain, and formed into a colony. It is bounded north, by the Simpson River, and a branch of the Peace River; west, by the Gulf of Georgia, which separates it from Vancouver's Island; on the south by the State of Oregon, (latitude 49° N); and east, by the Rocky Mountains. The superficial area is about 280,000 square miles; the greatest extent from north to south 500 miles, and from east to west 400 miles. The colony is divided into eight districts, forming five electoral divisions, viz: New Westminster, Hope, Yale and Litton, Cariboo East, Cariboo West, Douglass and Lillooet. The surface of British Columbia is, in general, mountainous and intersected by numerous lakes and rivers. The climate is temperate, and warmer than in the same latitude on the Eastern coast of the continent, and the soil, especially in the interior, is fertile, and well adapted for agriculture and pasturage. It is well wooded, and possesses immense beds of coal and other minerals.

The colony derives its chief importance from the rich gold discoveries which have been made, especially along the source of Frazer's River. The influx of miners and gold-seekers since its discovery, in 1858, has been very great; before that time it was a perfect wilderness, inhabited almost entirely by Indians. The revenue at present (1869) is about $800,000, and the expenditure somewhat in excess *per annum*; the public debt principally incurred in making roads, which are owned by government, is something under $1,500,000. The imports are about $5,500,000, and the exports, including $3,000,000 to $4,000,000 of gold, about the same.

Vancouver's Island is separated from the main coast by Queen Charlotte Sound and the Gulf of Georgia, and from the United States by San Juan de Fuca Straits. The climate is warm and healthy and the soil productive, but as yet not much cultivated, the chief trade consisting of lumber, furs and fish. It owns its chief importance to its extensive coal beds.

No census has been taken of the colony, but the population of the two parts together, may be estimated at about 30,000 whites and Chinese, and 36,000 Indians.

The distance from Halifax, Nova Scotia, to Victoria, Vancouver's Island, is about 4,800 miles by the valleys and mountain passes.

MISCELLANEOUS INFORMATION.

THE QUEEN AND ROYAL FAMILY.

THE QUEEN.—VICTORIA, of the United Kingdom of Great Britain and Ireland, &c., Queen, Defender of the Faith. Her Majesty was born at Kensington Palace, May, 24, 1819; succeeded to the throne June 20, 1837, on the death of her uncle King William IV; was crowned June 28, 1838; and married, February 10, 1840, to His Royal Highness, Prince Albert. Her Majesty is the only child of his late Royal Highness Edward Duke of Kent, son of King George III. The children of Her Majesty are:—

Her Royal Highness Victoria-Adelaide-Mary-Louisa, PRINCESS ROYAL OF ENGLAND AND PRUSSIA, born November 21, 1840, and married to His Royal Highness Frederick William of Prussia, January 25, 1858, and has issue three sons and a daughter.

His Royal Highness Albert-Edward, PRINCE OF WALES, born November 9, 1841; married, March 10, 1863, Alexandra of Denmark (Princess of Wales), born December 1, 1844, and has issue two sons and a daughter; Prince Albert Victor, born January 8, 1864; Prince George Frederick Ernest Albert, born June 3, 1865, and Princess Louise-Victoria-Alexandra Dagmar, born February 20, 1867.

Her Royal Highness Alice-Maud-Mary, born April 25, 1843; married to H. R. H. Prince Frederick Louis of Hesse, July 1, 1862, and has issue three daughters.

His Royal Highness Alfred-Ernest-Albert, Duke of Edinburgh, born August 6, 1844.

Her Royal Highness Helena-Augusta-Victoria, born May 25, 1846; married July 5, 1866, Prince Frederick Christian of Schleswig-Holstein, and has issue one son.

Her Royal Highness Louisa-Caroline-Alberta, born March 18, 1848.

His Royal Highness Arthur-William-Patrick-Albert, born May 1, 1850.

His Royal Highness Leopold-George-Duncan-Albert, born April 7, 1853.

Her Royal Highness Beatrice-Mary-Victoria-Feodore, born April 14, 1857.

George-Frederick-William-Charles, K. G., K. P., G. C. B., G. C. H., G. C. M. G., P. C., D. C. L., DUKE OF CAMBRIDGE, cousin to Her Majesty, born March 29, 1819.

Augusta-Wilhelmina-Louisa, DUCHESS OF CAMBRIDGE, niece of the Landgrave of Hesse and aunt to Her Majesty, born July 25, 1797; married, in 1819, the late Duke of Cambridge.

George-Frederick-Alexander-Charles-Ernest-Augustus, K.G., G.C.H., DUKE OF CUMBERLAND, (ex-King of Hanover), cousin to Her Majesty, born May 27, 1819; married Princess Frederica of Mecklenburg-Strelitz, and has issue a son and two daughters.

Augusta-Caroline-Charlotte-Elizabeth-Mary-Sophia-Louisa, daughter of the late Duke of Cambridge and cousin to Her Majesty, born July 19, 1822; married June 23, 1843, to Frederick Grand Duke of Mecklenburg-Strelitz, and has a son.

Mary-Adelaide-Wilhelmina-Elizabeth, daughter of the late Duke of Cambridge and cousin to Her Majesty, born November 27, 1833; married June 12, 1866, Francis Paul, Prince of Teck, and has issue one daughter.

Leopold II., KING OF THE BELGIANS, maternal cousin of the Queen, born April 9, 1835.

HER MAJESTY'S HOUSEHOLD.

LORD STEWARD'S DEPARTMENT.

Lord Steward..........Rt. Hon. Earl of Tankerville.
Treasurer..........Rt. Hon. Col. Percy Egerton Herbert, C.B.
Comptroller..........Rt. Hon. Viscount Royston.
Master of the Household..........Major Sir John C. Cowell, K.C.B.
Secretary of the Board of Green Cloth..........E. M. Browell, Esq.

LORD CHAMBERLAIN'S DEPARTMENT.

Lord Chamberlain..........Rt. Hon. Earl of Bradford.
Vice-Chamberlain..........Rt. Hon. Lord Claude Hamilton.
Comptroller..........Hon. Spencer Ponsonby.
Chief Clerk..........T. C. March, Esq.
Private Secretary to the Queen..........Lieut.-Gen. Hon. Charles Gray.
Keeper of the Privy Purse..........Major-Gen. Sir Thomas M. Biddulph, K.C.B.
Secretaries..........H. T. Harrison, Esq., and D. C. Bell, Esq.
Paymaster of the Household..........W. Hampshire, Esq.
Captain of the Yeomen of the Guard..........Earl of Cadogan.
Captain of the Gentlemen-at-Arms..........Marquis of Exeter.
Master of the Ceremonies..........Major-Gen. Hon. Sir E. Cust, K.C.H.
Lord High Almoner..........Bishop of Oxford.
Dean of Chapel Royal..........Bishop of London.
Sub-Dean..........Rev. F. Garden, M.A.
Clerk of the Closet..........Bishop of Worcester.
Resident Chaplain..........Very Rev. Dean of Windsor.
Mistress of the Robes..........Duchess of Wellington.
Groom..........Major-Gen. F. H. Seymour.

MASTER OF THE HORSE DEPARTMENT.

Master of the Horse..........Duke of Beaufort, P.C., K.G.
Clerk Marshall..........Lord Alfred Paget.
Crown Equery and Secretary..........Col. G. A. Maude, C.B.
Master of the Buckhounds..........Lord Colville.

PRINCE OF WALES' HOUSEHOLD.

Groom of the Stole..........
Keeper of the Privy Seal..........H. W. Fisher, Esq.
Comptroller and Treasurer..........Gen. Sir Wm. Knollys, K.C.B.
Private Secretary..........H. W. Fisher, Esq.
Attorney General..........Sir W. Alexander. Bart.
Receiver General..........Major General Sir T. W. Biddulph, K.C.B.

DOMINION OF CANADA.

GOVERNOR GENERAL.

The Right Honorable Sir JOHN YOUNG, Bart., of Baillieborough Castle, County of Cavan, Ireland, P.C., K.C.B., G.C.M.G.; formerly M.P., for Cavan, successively Joint Secretary of the Treasury from 1841 to 1844; Chief Secretary for Ireland from 1852 to 1855; from 1855 to 1859, Lord High Commissioner of the Ionian Islands, and since Governor of New South Wales, appointed in 1860; born August, 1807. Residence—Rideau Hall, Ottawa.

In the absence of the Governor General, the Government is administered by Lieut.-General Sir Charles Ashe Windham, K.C.B.

THE QUEEN'S PRIVY COUNCIL FOR CANADA.

The Hon. Sir John Alexander Macdonald, K.C.B., Minister of Justice and Attorney-General.
The Hon. Sir George Etienne Cartier, Bart., Minister of Militia and Defence.
The Hon. Samuel Leonard Tilley, C.B., Minister of Customs.
The Hon. John Rose, Minister of Finance.
The Hon. William McDougall, C.B., Minister of Public Works.
The Hon. Minister of Inland Revenue. } Vacant.
The Hon. Secretary of State for the Provinces. } Vacant.
The Hon. Joseph Howe, President of the Privy Council.
The Hon. Peter Mitchell, Minister of Marine and Fisheries.
The Hon. Alexander Campbell, Postmaster-General.
The Hon. Jean Charles Chapais, Minister of Agriculture.
The Hon. Hector Louis Langevin, Secretary of State of Canada.
The Hon. Edward Kenny, Receiver General.

OFFICERS.—Wm. H. Lee, Clerk of the Privy Council; Wm. A. Himsworth, Assistant do.

CLERKS.—F. Vallerand, J. O. Côté, F. H. Himsworth, H. Alexander, Wm. H. Lee. Doorkeeper, M. Naughton; Messengers, Wm. E. Morgan, Jos. Cairns, Patrick Batterton.

GOVERNOR'S SECRETARY'S OFFICE (Eastern Block).—Denis Godley, Secretary; H. Cotton, Chief Clerk; J. Kidd, 2nd Clerk; J. Burrows, 3rd Clerk; P. St. Hill, Office Keeper; G. Boxall, Messenger; G. Smith, Extra Messenger.

COMMISSIONERS PER DEDIMUS POTESTATEM.—Wm. H. Lee and Wm. A. Himsworth.

THE SENATE.

Speaker—The Honorable Joseph Cauchon.

PROVINCE OF ONTARIO.

Senators.	*P. O. Address.*
John Hamilton	Kingston.
Roderick Matheson	Perth.
John Ross	Toronto.
Samuel Mills	Hamilton.
Benjamin Seymour	Port Hope.
Walter H. Dickson	Niagara.
James Shaw	Smith's Falls.
James R. Benson	St. Catharines.
Hon. Alexander Campbell	Kingston.
David Christie	Paris.
James Cox Aikins	Richview.
David Reesor	Markham.
Elijah Leonard	London.
William MacMaster	Toronto.
Asa A. Burnham	Cobourg.
John Simpson	Bowmanville.
James Skead	Ottawa.
David L. Macpherson	Toronto.
George Crawford	Brockville.
Donald Macdonald	Toronto.
Oliver Blake	Waterford.
Billa Flint	Belleville.
Walter McCrea	Chatham.
George William Allan	Toronto.

PROVINCE OF QUEBEC.

Senators.	*P. O. Address.*
James Leslie	Montreal.
Asa Belknap Foster	Waterloo.
Hon. J. C. Chapais	Ottawa.
Louis A. Olivier	Berthier.
Jacques O. Bureau	St. Remi.
Charles Malhiot	Pointe Du Lac.
Louis Renaud	Montreal.
L. Letellier de St. Just	Riviere Ouelle.
Ulric Joseph Tessier	Quebec.
John Hamilton	Hawkesbury.
Charles Cormier	Plessisville.
Ant. J. Duchesnay	St. Catharines.
David Edward Price	Chicoutimi.
E. H. J. Duchesnay	St. Marie Beauce.
Leandre Dumouchel	St. Therese B'lle.
Louis Lacoste	Boucherville.
Joseph F. Armand	Riviere Prairies.
Charles Wilson	Montreal.
William H. Chaffers	St. Cesaire.
Jean B. Guevremont	Sorel.
James Ferrier	Montreal.
Sir Narcisse F. Belleau	Quebec.
Thomas Ryan	Montreal.
John S. Sanborn	Sherbrooke.

PROVINCE OF NOVA SCOTIA.

Senators.	*P. O. Address.*
Hon. Edward Kenny.............	Halifax.
Jonathan McCully................	Halifax.
Thomas D. Archibald	Sydney, C. B.
Robert B. Dickey..................	Amherst.
John H. Anderson................	Halifax.
John Holmes.......................	Pictou.
John W. Ritchie...........	Halifax.
John Locke...	Shelburne.
Caleb R. Bill.........................	King's County.
John Bourinot	Sydney.
William Miller..	Halifax.

PROVINCE OF NEW BRUNSWICK.

Senators.	*P. O. Address.*
Amos E. Botsford	Westcock, West'l'nd
James Dever.........................	St. John, N. B.
John Robertson.....................	" "
Robert L. Hazen	" "
William H. Odell	Fredricton.
David Wark	Richibucto.
William H. Steeves.........	St. John, N. B.
John Glazier	Sunbury, N. B.
John Ferguson	Bathurst.
Robert D. Wilmot	Belmont, Sunbury.
Abner R. McClellan	Hopewell, Albert Co
Hon. Peter Mitchell	Miramichi.

PERMANENT OFFICERS OF THE SENATE OF CANADA.

John F. Taylor, sen., Clerk of the House, Master in Chancery, also Cashier and Accountant; Robert LeMoine, Deputy Clerk and Clerk Assistant, Master in Chancery, and Chief French Translator; Fennings Taylor, Deputy Clerk and Clerk Assistant, Master in Chancery, and Acting Chief Office Clerk; James Adamson, 1st English Clerk; Peter Miller, 2nd English Clerk; Neil McLean, English Clerk; A. A. Boucher, 1st French Translator and Clerk; Alfred Garneau, 2nd French Translator and Clerk; Victor E. Tessier, Clerk of French Journals; Rene Kimber, Gentleman Usher of the Black Rod and Sergeant-at-Arms; Samuel Skinner, Housekeeper; J. B. Myraud, Postmaster; L. G. Casult, Library Messenger; Peter Rattep, Speaker's Messenger; Peter Dunne, Assistant Housekeeper, News Room, &c.; James Wingfield, Assistant Doorkeeper, Wardrobe, &c.; Frederick Gilbert and Napoleon Boulet, Watchmen and Messengers; Thomas Wheeler, Louis Robitaille, John Dunne, A. Boucher, A. Douhaire, Sessional Messengers; Edward Botterall, Doorkeeper; J. C. Young, J. Wingfield, P. Boulet, J. N. Rattey, Pages.

ADDRESS.—To the Honorable the Senate of the Dominion of Canada, in Parliament assembled.

The Petition of———

[*Place and Date.*] Humbly sheweth, That, &c.

MEMBERS OF THE HOUSE OF COMMONS.

(From Ontario.)

SPEAKER—The Hon. James Cockburn.

Constituencies.	Members.	P. O. Address.
Addington.........	E. Lapum.........	Napanee
Algoma	W. McK Simpson	Bruce Mines
Bothwell...	David Mills.......	Bothwell
Brant, N. R.	J. Y. Bown, M. D	Brantford
" S. R... ...	E. B. Wood.......	"
Brockville, Town.	James Crawford..	Brockville
Bruce, N. R	Alex. Sproat......	Southampton
" S. R.......	Francis Hurdon..	Kincardine
Cardwell	T. R. Ferguson ..	Cookstown
Carleton.	John Holmes.. ...	Bell's Corners
Cornwall, Town...	J. S. Macdonald.	Cornwall
Dundas.....	J. S. Ross.........	Iroquois
Durham, E. R....	F. H. Burton	Port Hope.
" W. R....	Edward Blake....	Toronto
Elgin, E. R.......	S. W. Dobbie. .	Staffordville
" W. R.......	J. H. Munroe....	Wardsville
Essex	John O'Connor...	Windsor
Frontenac	J. Kirkpatrick...	Kingston
Glengary	D. A. Macdonald	Alexandria
Grenville, S. R...	Walter Shanly...	Montreal
Grey, N. R.........	George Snider....	Owen Sound
" S. R.........	George Jackson..	Bentinck
Haldimand.........	D. Thompson	Indiana
Halton	John White	Milton
Hamilton, City...	Charles Magill ...	Hamilton
Hastings, N. R ...	Mack. Bowell	Belleville
" E. R....	Robert Read	"
" W. R...	James Brown....	"
Huron, N. R	Jos. Whitehead ...	Clinton
" S. R........	Wm. C. Cameron	Goderich
Kent	Ruf. Stephenson.	Chatham
Kingston, City ...	Hon Sir J A Macdonald, K C B.	Ottawa
Lambton...	Alex. Mackenzie.	Sarnia
Lanark, N. R.......	Hn W McDougall	Ottawa
" S. R... ..	Alex. Morris.....	Perth
Leeds and Grenville, N. R......	Francis Jones....	Kemptville
Leeds, S. R.........	John Crawford...	Toronto
Lennox	E. J. Cartwright	Kingston
Lincoln..............	M. Merritt........	St. Catherines
London, City......	John Carling.....	London
Middlesex, N. R..	Thos Scatcherd...	"
Middlesex, E. R...	Crowell Wilson..	London
" W. R...	A. P. Macdonald	Glencoe
Monck...............	L. McCallum . ..	Stromness
Niagara, Town ...	Angus Morrison.	Toronto
Norfolk, N. R.....	A. Walsh	Simcoe
" S. R ...	P. Lawson........	Port Dover
Northumberland, E. R.	Joseph Keeler....	Colborne
" W. R.	Hon. J Cockburn	Cobourg
Ontario, N. R....	J. H. Thompson.	Carmington
" S. R.. ..	Thos. N. Gibb...	Oshawa
Ottawa, City......	Jas. M. Currier..	Ottawa
Oxford, N. R.....	Thomas Oliver...	Woodstock
" S. R......	E. V. Bodwell...	Ingersoll
Peel	J. H. Cameron...	Toronto
Perth, N. R	J. Redford.........	Stratford
" S. R......	R. McFarlane....	"
Peterboro', E. R..	P. M. Grover.....	Norwood
" W. R.	Charles Perry ...	Peterboro'
Prescott	J. Hager...........	Plantagenet
Prince Edward ...	Walter Ross......	Picton
Renfrew, N. R ...	John Rankin.....	Cobden
" S. R....	D. McLachlin....	Arnprior

MEMBERS OF THE HOUSE OF COMMONS (ONTARIO)—*Continued.*

Constituencies.	Members.	P. O. Address.	Constituencies.	Members.	P. O. Address.
Russell	J. A. Grant, MD	Ottawa	Welland	T. C. Street	Chippewa
Simcoe, N. R.	T. D. McConkey	Barrie	Wellington, N.R.	G. W. A. Drew	Elora
" S. R.	W. C. Little	Dover Hill	" S. R.	D. Stirton	Guelph
Stormont	Samuel Ault	Aultsville	" C. R.	——	"
Toronto, E.	James Beaty	Toronto	Wentworth, N. R.	J. McMonies	Waterdown
" W.	R. A Harrison	"	" S. R.	Joseph Rymal	Barton
Victoria, N. R.	John Morison	Woodville	York, E. R.	James Metcalfe	Toronto
" S. R.	G. Kempt	Lindsay	" N. R	James P. Wells	King
Waterloo, N. R.	I. E. Bowman	St. Jacob's	" W. R	Amos Wright	Toronto
" S. R.	James Young	Galt			
(From Quebec.)					
Argenteuil	J. J. C. Abbott	Montreal	Montmagny	J. O. Beanbien	Montmagny
Bagot	J. S. Gedron	St. Rosalie	Montmorency	J. Langlois	Quebec
Beauce	E. C. Pozer	Quebec	Montreal Centre	Thos. Workman	Montreal
Beauharnois	M. Cayley	Beauharnois	" East	Sir G. E. Cartier	"
Bellechasse	N. Casault	Quebec	" West	M. P. Ryan	"
Berthier	A. H. Paquet	St. Cuthbert	Napierville	Sixte Coupal	Lacolle
Bonaventure	T. Robitaille	New Carlisle	Nicolet	Joseph Gaudet	Gentilly
Brome	C. Dunkin	Knowlton	Ottawa County	Alonzo Wright	Ironside, Hull
Chambly	M. Benoit	St. Huburt	Pontiac	Edwin Heath	Portage du Fort
Champlain	J. J. Ross	Ste Anne de la Perade	Portneuf	J. T. Brousseau	Quebec
			Quebec Centre	G. H. Simard	"
Charlevoix	S. X. Cimon	Malbaie	" East	P. G. Huot	"
Chateauguay	L. H. Holton	Montreal	" West	Thos. McGreevy	"
Chicoutimi and Saguenay	P. A. Tromblay	Chicoutimi	" County	P J O Cheauveau	"
Compton	J. H. Pope	Cookshire	Richmond and Wolfe	W. H. Webb	Melbourne
Dorchester	Hon. H L Langevin	Quebec	Richelieu	T. McCarthy	Sorel
Drummond and Arthabaska	M. Senecal	Pierreville	Rimouski	George Sylvain	Bic
			Rouville	M. Cheval	St. Hilaire
Gaspe	P. Fortin	Quebec	St. Hyacinthe	A F. Kierskowski	St. Charles
Hochelaga	A. A. Dorion	Montreal	St. Johns	F. Bourassa	Lacadie
Huntingdon	Hon. John Rose	"	St. Maurice		
Iberville	M. Bechard	Iberville	Shefford	L. S. Huntingdon	Waterloo
Jacques Cartier	G. Gaucher	St. Genevieve			
Joliette	F. B. Godin	Joliette	Sherebrooke	A. T. Galt	Sherbrooke
Laprairie	A. Pinsonnealt	Laprairie	Soulanges	L. Masson	Coteau Landing
L'Assomption	L. Archambault	L'Assomption	Stanstead	Charles Colby	Stanstead
Laval	T. H. Bellerose	St. V de Paul	Temiscouata	Charles Bertrand	Isle Verte
Levis	J. G. Blanchet	Levis	Terrebonne	L. R. Masson	Terrebonne
L'Islet	P. Pouliot	L'Islet	Three Rivers		
Lotbiniere	H. G. Joly	Quebec	Two Mountains	J. B. Daoust	St. Eustache
Maskinonge	G. Caron	St. Leon	Vaudreuil	D. McMillan	Rigaud
Megantic	George Irwin	Quebec	Vercheres	F. Geoffrion	Vercheres
Missisquoi	B. Chamberlain	Durham	Yamaska	Moise Fortier	St. David
Montcalm	Jos. Dufresne	St. Julienne			
(From New Brunswick.)					
Albert	John Wallace	Hillsboro'	Restigouche		
Carleton	C. Connell	Woodstock	St. John County	J. H. Gray	St. John
Charlotte	J. Boulton	St. Stephen	" City	S. L. Tilley	Fredricton
Gloucester	T. Anglin	St. John	Sunbury	Charles Burpee	Sheffield
Kent	Auguste Renaud	Buctouche	Victoria	John Costigan	Grand Falls
Kings	George Ryan	Kings	Westmoreland	A. J. Smith	Dorchester
Northumberland			York		
Queens	J. Ferris	Queens			
(From Nova Scotia.)					
Annapolis	W. H. Ray	Annapolis	Hants	Joseph Howe	Halifax
Antigonish	H. McDonald	Antigonish	Inverness	H. Cameron	Port Hood
Cape Breton	J. McKeagney	Sydney	Kings	W. H. Chipman	Cornwallis
Colchester	A. W. McLelan	Londonderry	Lunenburg	E. M. McDonald	Halifax
Cumberland	Hon. C. Tupper, C. B.	Halifax	Pictou	J. W. Carmichael	New Glasgow
			Queens	Jas. Forbes	Liverpool
Digby	A. W. Savary	Clare	Richmond	W. J. Croke	Halifax
Guysboro'	S. Campbell	Guysboro'	Shelburne	Thomas Coffin	Shelburne
Halifax	A. G. Jones	Halifax	Victoria	William Ross	St. Annes
"	P. Power	"	Yarmouth	Thomas Killam	Yarmouth

41

OFFICERS OF THE HOUSE OF COMMONS.

Chief Department—W. B. Lindsay, Clerk of the House; Alfred Patrick, Clerk Assistant, and Chief Clerk of Controverted Elections; D. W. Macdonell, Sergeant-at-Arms. *Law Department*—G. W. Wicksteed, Law Clerk; F. Badgley, Assistant Law Clerk and Chief English Translator; E. P. Dorion, Assistant Law Clerk and Chief French Translator. *Accountants' Department*—Thomas Vaux, Accountant; Josh. Stansfeld, Assistant Accountant and bookkeeper. *Department of Routine and Records*—F. McGillivray, Clerk of Routine and Records. *General Department*—H. Hartney, Chief Office Clerk and Clerk of the Joint Committee of both House of Printing; H. B. Stuart, English Writing Clerk; E. Denechaud, French Writing Clerk; J. H. T. Blais, H. R. Smith, H. Lindsay, J. S. Sloane, C. Panet, William Bowles, Fitzgerald Cochrane, J. E. B. McCready, Junior Clerks. *Committee Department*—J. P. Leprohon, Assistant Clerk of Controverted Elections. *Private Bill Department*—Alfred Todd, Chief Clerk of Committees, and Clerk of Private Bills; T. Patrick, Second Clerk of Committees, and Clerk of Railway Committees; F. X. Blanchet, Third Clerk of Committees. *Votes and Proceedings*—H. Poetter, Clerk of Votes and Proceedings. *French Translators' Department*—W. Fanning, Translator of Votes and Proceedings and Journals; F. G. Coursolles, J. F. Gingras, E. Blain, H. A. McCoy, Assistant French Translators. *English Translators' Department*—William Wilson, F. Hayes, Wm. Wilson, jun., Assistant English Translators; G. H. Macaulay, Assistant English Translator and Secretary to Mr. Speaker. *Journal Department*—W. B. Ross, English Journal Clerk; P. Rivet, French Journal Clerk; A. G. D. Taylor, Assistant English Journal Clerk. *Library Department*—Alpheus Todd, Librarian; A. G. Lajoie, Assistant Librarian; A. Laperriere, Library Clerk. *Post Office Department*—F. N. Belcourt, Postmaster; E. Pelletier, Post Office Messenger. *Department of Sergeant-at-Arms*—A. L. Cardinal, Chief Messenger; M. McCarthy, Assistant Chief Messenger; O. Vincent, Library Messenger; J. O'Connor, Doorkeeper; Joseph Lemonde, Speaker's Messenger; Wm. Graham, Messenger; James Hoy, Library Messenger; Edward Stacey, Messenger, Edward Storr, Assistant Doorkeeper; Etienne Roy, Joseph Turgeon, Joseph Brown, O. Roberge, M. Laflamme, J. Nadeau, E. Botterill, Andrew Elliott, E. Asselin, Messengers; James Fitzsimmons, George Smith, Night Watchmen.

ADDRESS—To the Honorable the House of Commons of the Dominion of Canada, in Parliament assembled.
The Petition of ———
[*Place and Date.*] Humbly sheweth, That, etc.

DEPARTMENT OF JUSTICE.

Hon. Sir J. A. Macdonald, K.C.B., Minister of Justice and Attorney General; Hewitt Bernard, Deputy Minister of Justice; John Stewart, Charles Drinkwater, A. Atcheson, John A. Macdonell, Clerks; Patrick Lynch, F. Curran, Messengers.

FINANCE DEPARTMENT.

Hon. J. Rose, Minister of Finance; W. Dickson, Dep. Inspector General; N. Godard, Chief Clerk and Provincial Book-keeper; J. Drysdale, Book-keeper; M. A. Higgins, Warrant Clerk; Archibald Cary, Book-keeper; F. G. Scott; C. J. Anderson, J. A. Torrance, R. W. Baxter, P. Ryan, W. A. Blackmore, H. A. Jones, G. Ammond, and R. Kilaly, Clerks; D. Ryan, Housekeeper and Messenger; P. Pender, Messenger.

Auditor's Branch—John Langton, Auditor of Public Accounts; John Simpson, Assistant Auditor; Thomas Ross, Clerk of Contingencies; Thomas Cruse, T. D. Timms, Book-keepers; A. Harvey, Statistical Clerk; J. Patterson, E. C. Barber, G. M. Jarvis, J. R. Hall, W. H. Cotton, J. B. Simpson, Clerks; J. Pender, Messenger

DEPARTMENT OF MILITIA AND DEFENCE.

Hon. Sir G. E. Cartier, Bart., Minister of Militia and Defence; Major George Futvoye, Deputy Minister; Col. P. L. Macdougall, Adj. General of Militia; Lieut. Colonel Walker Powell, Deputy Adj. General. *Office of Minister of Militia and Defence*—P. Chapleau and Henry D. J. Lane, Clerks; John W. Gow, Messenger. *Account Branch*—Robert Berry, Chief Clerk and Accountant; C. H. O'Meara, E. Gelinas, D. McClennan, W. H. Aumond, Clerks; Napoleon Cassault, Messenger. *Adjutant-General's Office*—Capt. Stuart, Secretary; W. R. Wright, Grant Seymour, F. X. Lambert, G. E. M. Sherwood, C. Junot, T. C. Larose, Sir J. D. Hay, Clerks; L. Morel and M. Ryan, Messengers. *Store Branch*—Lieut. Colonel Thomas Wily, Superintendent of Stores; G. Grant, W. M. Steers, Joseph Yeomans, Clerks.

DEPARTMENT OF PUBLIC WORKS (WESTERN BLOCK.)

Hon. W. McDougall, C.B. Minister; T. Trudeau, Deputy; F. Braun, Secretary. *Engineering Branch*—J. Page, Chief Engineer; F. P. Fubidge, Assistant Engineer; G. F. Baillairge, Thomas Munro, J. H. Rowan, T. Guerin, E. H. Parent, Engineers; C. McCarthy, J. Le B. Ross, C. E. Michaud, Draughtsmen; S. McLaughlin, Photographer. *Financial Branch*—John Baine, Book-keeper and Accountant; F. Hamel, Assistant Book-keeper and Accountant; J. W. Harper, Clerk and Paymaster. *Corresponding Branch*—T. B. French, Corresponding Clerk; J. F. N. Bonneville, J. R. Arnoldi, F. H. Ennis, George Verret, Charles Pope, O. Dionne, Clerks; H. A. Fissiault, Law Clerk; Patrick Ownes, Chief Messenger; Michael Walsh, Assistant do.; H. Potvin, J. Deslauriers, Messengers.

OFFICE OF SECRETARY OF STATE FOR PROVINCES.

—— Secretary of State; Edmund A. Meredith, L.L.D., Under Secretary of State; G. Powell, Chief Clerk; H. E. Steel, 1st Class Clerk; C. J. Birch, 1st Class Clerk; Nazare Tetu, Clerk; James Dorr, Messenger.

MARINE AND FISHERIES DEPARTMENT.

Hon. P. Mitchell, Minister of Marine and Fisheries; William Smith, Deputy Minister; W. F. Whitcher, Chief of Fisheries Branch; John Hardie, 1st Clerk Marine Branch; John Tilton, Accountant Marine and Fisheries Department; S. P. Bauset, Clerk Fisheries Branch; W. H. Venning, Inspector of Fisheries New Brunswick and Nova Scotia; J. S. Thompson, W. H. Alexander, James Daley and J. R. Tucker, Clerks; George Fisher and Thomas Wheeler, Messengers.

CUSTOMS DEPARTMENT (EASTERN BLOCK.)

Hon. S. L. Tilley, C.B., Minister of Customs; R. S. M. Bouchette, Commissioner; J. W. Peachy, Corresponding Clerk; J. R. Audy, Clerk of Seizures and Forms; T. P. Robarts, Statistical Clerk; H. H. Duffil, Statistical and Canal Office Clerk; G. M. Mailleue, P. E. Sheppard, H. C. Hay, W. A. Bell, J. A. Audy and J. H. Wolff, Check Clerks; H. Kavanagh, Inspector of Ports; R. Bell, Inspector of Canals; J. Walls, Messenger.

COLLECTORS OF CUSTOMS.

Those marked thus are Warehousing Ports.*

*Amherst,** .... J. J. Fox.
*Amherstburg,** .... E. Anderson.
*Belleville,** .... W. F. Meudell.
*Brantford,** .... D. Curtis, Jr.
Brighton, ... D. Y. Leslie.
*Brockville,** .... George Easton.
Burwell, ... E. A. Dunham.
*Bytown,** .... D. Graham.
*Chatham,** .... J. G. Pennefather.
*Chippawa,** .... C. St. G. Yarwood.
Clarenceville, ... Charles Stewart.
Clifton, ... W. Leggett.
*Coaticook,** .... J. Thompson.
*Cobourg,** .... H. Easton.
*Colborne,** .... W. A. Booth.
*Cornwall,** .... R. K. Bullock.
Cramahe, ... J. M. Merriman.
*Dalhousie,** .... J. Lamb.
*Darlington,** .... A. Dixon.
*Dover,** .... W. H. Higman.
*Dundas,** .... W. B. Gwyn.
*Dundee,** .... E. D. Phillips.
Dunville, ... W. A. Macrae.
Elgin, ... R. P. McMillan.
*Fort Erie,** .... R. Graham.
Frelighsburgh, ... H. J. Parker.
Gananoque, ... J. Ormiston.
*Gaspe,** .... J. C. Belleau.
*Goderich,** .... D. Doty.
*Guelph,** .... E. Carthew.
*Hamilton,** .... W. H. Kittson.
Hemmingford, ... M. Sweet.
*Hope,** .... M. Whitehead.
*Kingston,** .... W. B. Simpson.
Kingsville, ... J. King.
Lacolle, ... A. Holden.
*London,** .... J. B. Strathy.
*Montreal,** .... A. Delisle.
Morrisburg, ... Hiram Carman.
Napanee, ... John Benson.
*New Carlisle,** .... John Fraser.
Newcastle, ... H. Farncomb.
*Niagara,** .... J. W. Taylor.
*Oakville,** .... R. K. Chisholm
*Oshawa,** .... C. Walsh.
Owen Sound, ... W. Stephens.
*Paris,** .... F. H. Haycock
Penetanguishene, ... E. Jaffrey.
Philipsburg, ... J. Henderson.
*Picton,** .... J. Robin.
Potton, ... George Gunn.
*Prescott,** .... H. D. Jessup.
*Quebec,** .... J. W. Dunscomb.
*Queenston,** .... P. B. Clement.
*Rimouski,** .... P. L. Gauvreau.
Rowan, ... P. Bennett.
Russeltown, ... R. Rogers.
*Sarnia,** .... J. Scully.
Saugeen, ... W. Keith.
*Sault Ste. Marie,** .... J. Wilson.
*Stanley,** .... J. Hemphill, act'g.
Stanstead, ... C. Bullock.
*St. John's,** .... W. McCrea.
Stratford, ... John Hamilton.
Sutton, ... B. Seaton.
*Toronto,** .... Jas. E. Smith.
*Trenton,** .... A. Macaulay.
Wallaceburgh, ... C. Fraser.
*Whitby,** .... W. Warren.
*Windsor,** ....
*Woodstock,** .... W. H. Van Ingen.

INLAND REVENUE DEPARTMENT.

—— Minister of Inland Revenue; Thomas Worthington, Commissioner of Inland Revenue; Alfred Brunel, Assistant Commissioner and Inspector of Inland Revenue; Dr. L. O'Brien, J. F. Brown, and Alexander Begg, Check Clerks; Richardson Borrodaile, Corresponding Clerk; W. Himsworth, jun., Clerk 4th Class; John Fowler, Messenger.

DEPARTMENT OF AGRICULTURE.

Hon. J. C. Chapais, Minister of Agriculture; J. C. Taché, Deputy Minister, A. J. Cambie, Patent Clerk; S. Drapeau and W. H. Johnson, Statistical Clerks; S. S. Finden, General Correspondence; C. C. Neville, Statistical Returns; Sirinus Ferland, Trade Mark, Copyright and Archivist; N. Boissonnault, Curator of Patent Models; H. Casgrain, Assistant Patent Clerk; J. O'Brien, Blue Book and Translator; E. Tetu, D. Boutier, J. E. D'Auteuil, D. Lanigan, J. B. Jackson, and J. F. Dionne, Clerks; J. E. Lemieux, Office Keeper, W. J. Lynch, Junior Clerk; A. Frichette, Model Repairer, J. Boily, B. Moreau, J. B. Lacroix, Messengers.

INDIAN OFFICE.

Hon. H. Langevin, Superintendent-General of Indian Affairs; William Spragge, Deputy Superintendent; C. T. Walcot, Accountant; L. Vankoughnet, Chief Clerk; J. P. M. Lecourt, Draftsman; S. G. Murray, Clerk; W. R. Bartlett, Visiting Superintendent and Commissioner, Toronto; J. T. Gilkison, do., Brantford; R. Mackenzie, Sarnia; W. Plummer, do., Manitoulin Island; S. Colquhoun, Agent, St. Regis; E. N. DeLorimier, do., Laprairie; D. T. Simpson, Surgeon, Manitoulin Island; McGregor Ironsides, Clerk and Interpreter, Manitoulin Island; H. Andrews, Clerk, Brantford; A. Deacon, clerk, Toronto; J. Jennesseaux, Schoolmaster, Manitoulin Island; Rev. A. Jamieson, Missionary, Walpole Island; Rev. G. A. Anderson, do., Tyendinaga; Rev. H. Chase, do. Carradoc; Rev. Fathers, Boucherds, do., Lorette; Rev. F. H. Marcoux, do., St. Regis; Rev. Joseph Moreault, do., St. Francis; Drs. Dee and McCargo, Medical Superintendents, Grand River Indians.

ORDNANCE LANDS BRANCH, OTTAWA.

W. F. Coffin, Ordnance Land Agent and Chief Clerk; F. P. Austin, Clerk; W. Mills, Bookkeeper, J. Forsyth, Land Bailiff; H. Goodwin, Caretaker, Toronto.

RECEIVER GENERAL'S OFFICE.

Hon. Edward Kenney, Receiver General; Thomas D. Harington, Deputy do.; G. C. Reiffenstein, Chief and Debenture Clerk; T. C. Bramley, Book-keeper; J. B. Stanton, Correspondence and Receipts Clerk; F. Lewis, Warrant and Bank Accounts and Seignorial Tenure Accountant; J. F. Pellant, Assistant do.; L. F. Dufresne, Clerk in charge of Municipal Loan Fund of Provinces of Ontario and Quebec and Dominion Stock Account; C. W. Shay, General Clerk; F. Hunter, Assistant Book Keeper; J. B. H. Neeve, Stamp Acts Clerks; F. L. Casault, Office Keeper and Messenger; F. McCaffrey, Messenger.

PROVINCE OF ONTARIO.

LIEUTENANT-GOVERNOR.

His Excellency William P. Howland, C. B., Toronto.

EXECUTIVE COUNCIL.

Hon. John S. Macdonald, Attorney-General.
Hon. Matthew Crooks Cameron, Sec. and Registrar.
Hon. John Carling, Minister of Agriculture.
Hon. Stephen Richards, Commissioner of Crown Lands.
Hon. E. B. Wood, Treasurer.
(J. Shuter Smith, Clerk).

OFFICERS OF THE LEGISLATIVE ASSEMBLY:

Clerk of the House—Charles T. Gilmor.
Assistant Clerk—John Notman.
Clerk of Committees—J. J. Vance.
Queen's Printer, Chief Office Clerk, and Clerk of Printing Committee—H. J. Hartney.
Routine Clerk—A. H. Sydere.
Junior Clerk—Angus G. Morrison.
Sergeant-at-Arms—F. J. Glackmeyer.
House-keeper and Chief Messenger—Thomas Phillips.
Messenger—T. Byrnes.
Fireman—C. Macdonald.
Watchman—James Cain.

LEGISLATIVE ASSEMBLY.

Constituencies.	Members.	P. O. Address.	Constituencies.	Members.	P. O. Address.
Addington	E. J. Hooper	Napanee	Middlesex, N.R.	J. S. Smith	McGillivray
Algoma	F W Cumberland	Toronto	" W.R.	Mr. Currie	Glencoe
Bothwell	A. McKellar	Chatham	Monck	George Secord	Gainsboro'
Brant, N.R.	H. Finlayson	Paris	Niagara, town	S. Richards	Toronto
" S.R.	E. B. Wood	Brantford	Norfolk, N.R	James Wilson	Waterford
Brockville, town	W. Fitzsimmons	Brockville	" S.R.	S. McCall	Vittoria
Bruce, N.R.	Donald Sinclair	Saugeen	Northumberland,	John Eyre	Brighton
" S.R.	Edward Blake	Toronto	" W.R	Alexander Fraser	Cobourg
Cardwell	T. Swinarton	Bolton's Mills	Ontario, N.R	Thomas Paxton	Port Perry
Carleton	R. Lyon	Ottawa	" S.R.	Dr. McGill	Oshawa
Cornwall, town	Jno S Macdonald	Cornwall	Ottawa, City	R. W. Scott	Ottawa
Dundas	Simon Cook	Morrisburgh	Oxford, N.R.	George Perry	Drumbo
Durham, E.R.	A. T. H. Williams	Port Hope	" S.R.	A. Oliver	Ingersoll
" W.R.	Mr. McLeod	Bowmanville	Peel	John Coyne	Brampton
Elgin, E.R.	D. Luton	New Sarum	Perth, N.R.	James Trow	Stratford
" W.R.	Nicol McColl	Iona	" S.R.	A. Monteith	Shakespeare
Essex	S. Wigle	Amherstburg	Peterboro', E.R.	G. Read	Keene
Frontenac	D. D. Calvin	Kingston	" W.R.	G. Carnegie	Peterboro'
Glengary	James Craig	Cornwall	Prescott	J. Boyd	Vankleek Hill
Grenville, S. R.	M. Clarke	Prescott	Prince Edward	A. Greeley	Picton
Grey, N.R.	T. Scott	Owen Sound	Renfrew, N.R	J. Supple	Pembroke
" S.R.	A. W. Lauder	Toronto	" S.R.	J. L. Macdougall	Renfrew
Haldimand	J. Baxter	Cayuga	Russell	W. Craig	L'Orignal
Halton	W. Barber	Georgetown	Simcoe, N.R.	W. Lount	Barrie
Hamilton, City	J. M. Williams	Hamilton	" S.R.	T. R. Ferguson	Cookstown
Hastings, N.R.	G. H. Boulter	Stirling	Stormont	Wm. Colquhon	Dickinson's L'g
" E.R.	Henry Corby	Belleville	Toronto, East	M. C. Cameron	Toronto
" W.R.	Ketchan Graham	"	" West	J. Wallace	"
Huron, N.R.	Isaac Carling		Victoria, N.R.	A. P. Cockburn	Orillia
" S.R.	W. T. Hays	Goderich	" S.R.	J. Matchett	Omemee
Kent	John Smith	Chatham	Waterloo, N.R.	Moses Springer	Waterloo
Kingston, City	M. W. Strange	Kingston	" S.R.	I. Clemens	Galt
Lambton	J. B. Pardee	Sarnia	Welland	W. Beatty	Thorold
Lanark, N.R.	D. Galbraith	Almonte	Wellington, N.R.	R. McKim	Township of Peel
" S.R.	— Code	Perth	" S.R.	Peter Gow	Guelph
Leeds & Grenville	H. D. Smith	Merrickville	" C.R.	A. D. Ferrier	Fergus
Leeds, S.R.	Benjamin Tett	Newboro	Wentworth, N.R.	R. Christie	Flamboro West
Lennox	J. Stevenson	Napanee	" S.R.	W. Sexton	Ancaster
Lincoln	J. C. Rykert	St. Catharines	York, E.R.	H. P. Crosby	Markham
London, City	John Carling	London	" N.R.	J. McMurrich	Toronto
Middlesex, E.R.	James Evans	"	" W.R.	T. Graham	Woodbridge

ATTORNEY GENERAL'S OFFICE.

Hon. John S. Macdonald, Attorney General; J. Shuter Smith, 1st Clerk; H. Kinloch, 2nd Clerk; Angus McDonnell, Messenger; M. Smith, Housekeeper.

PROVINCIAL SECRETARY'S OFFICE.

Hon. M. C. Cameron, Provincial Secretary; Thomas C. Patteson, Assistant Secretary; Isaac R. Eckart, Chief Clerk.

PROVINCIAL REGISTRAR'S OFFICE.

Hon. M. C. Cameron, Provincial Registrar; T. C. Patterson, Deputy Registrar; Daniel Stevenson, Chief Clerk.

TREASURER'S DEPARTMENT.

Hon. E. B. Wood, Treasurer; Worsley Ebbs, Accountant; George Mathews, Auditor; James Kerr and C. H. Sproule, Clerks; J. Little, Messenger.

DEPARTMENT OF AGRICULTURE AND PUBLIC WORKS.

Commissioner, Hon. John Carling; Secretary Bureau of Agriculture, George Buckland, Professor of Agriculture, Toronto University; Architect and Superintendent of Public Works, Kivas Tully; Accountant and Librarian, Wm. Edwards; Superintendent Colonization Roads, J. W. Bridgland; Messenger, John Balkwell

DEPARTMENT OF CROWN LANDS, ONTARIO.

Commissioner, Hon. S. Richards; Assistant Commissioner, Andrew Russell; Accountant and Cashier, William Ford; Surveyors and Draughtsmen, Thomas Devine, J. W. Bridgland, Edward Fox; Draughtsman, Alex. L. Russell. 1st Class Clerks: Thomas Hector, Henry J. Jones, J. C. Tarbutt, Jeremiah Alley, John Morphy, John Tolmie, Thomas Hammond, F. A. Hall, A. Kirkwood, A. J. Taylor, John C. Miller. 2nd Class Clerks: G. E. Lindsay, F. Norton, J. M. Grant, W. W. Langlois, W. Ebbs, John Innes. 3rd Class Clerks: D. G. B. Ross, R. H. Browne, R. H. Temple, W. H. Cowper. 4th Class Clerk, C W. Hurd. Office-keeper, John Bradshaw; Messenger, A. McDonald.

Crown Timber Agents.—Upper Ottawa—A. J. Russell, Ottawa; C. S. McNutt, Assistant; J. Ritchie, Clerk; L. A. Russell, Draughtsman; E. T. Smith, Clerk; Robert Mills, Messenger. Lower Ottawa—C. E. Belle, Montreal; J. C. Coursolles, Clerk. Ontario—J. F. Way, Belleville; J. A. Macinnes, J. B. Drury, Clerks. Huron, Superior and Peninsula of Ontario—Joseph R. Nash, Toronto; F. W. Stayner, Assistant; J. F. Elliot, Sub-Agent, Windsor.

Crown Land Agents.

Admaston	William Harris.	*Lindsay*	G. M. Roche.
Berlin	H. S. Huber.	*Parry Sound*	N. P. Wakefield.
Bobcaygeon	J. Graham.	*Pembroke*	J. P. Moffatt.
Bracebridge	C. W. Lount.	*Saugeen*	Alex. McNabb.
Cardiff	Wheeler Armstrong.	*Sault Ste. Marie*	J. Wilson.
Durham	William Jackson.	*Sebastopol*	C. F. Holtermann.
Elora	James Ross.	*Stratford*	John Sharman.
Goderich	Charles Widder	*Tamworth*	Ebenezer Perry.
Kingston	James Macpherson.		

BOARD OF EXAMINERS OF P. L. SURVEYORS.

Hon. the Commissioner of Crown Lands, *ex officio;* A. Russell, Assistant Commissioner of Crown Lands; Joseph Bouchette, Deputy Surveyor General; Prof. Chapman, Toronto; J. Stoughton Dennis, Yorkville; T. Devine, Toronto; F. F. Passmore, Toronto; T. F. Gibbs, Adolphustown. Secretary, C. Unwin, Toronto.

DEPARTMENT OF PUBLIC INSTRUCTION, ONTARIO.

For the administration of the Grammar and Common School Law. *Education Office.*—Rev. Egerton Ryerson, D.D., LL.D., Chief Superintendent of Education; John Geo. Hodgins, LL.B., F.R.G.S., Deputy Superintendent of Education and Editor of the *Journal of Education* for Ontario; Alex. Marling, LL.B., Senior Clerk and Accountant, having also charge of Grammar School Meteorological Returns; A. J. Williamson, Clerk of Correspondence; F. J. Taylor, Clerk of Statistics; J. T. R. Stinson, Assistant Clerk of Statistics; W. H. Atkinson, Assistant Clerk of Correspondence; Office Messenger, James Moore. *Depository Branch.*—S. P. May, M.D., Clerk of Libraries; Edward B. Cope, Assistant Clerk of Libraries; Henry Wilkinson, Depository Salesman; R. J. Bryce, Assistant in Depository; S. Barber, Depository Packer and Messenger. Offices in the Victoria Square, Toronto.

PROVINCE OF QUEBEC.

LIEUTENANT-GOVERNOR.

His Excellency Sir Narcisse Fortunat Belleau, Knight, Quebec.

EXECUTIVE COUNCIL.

Pierre Joseph Oliver Chauveau, Secretary and Registrar, and Minister of Public Instruction
Gideon Ouimet, Attorney General
Joseph Octave Beaubien, Commissioner of Crown Lands
Christopher Dunkin, Treasurer.
Louis Archambault, Commissioner of Agriculture and Public Works
C. B. DeBoucherville, President Legislative Council.
George Irvine, Solicitor General.

OFFICERS.

F. Fortier, Clerk of the Executive Council; G. W. Colfer, First Clerk; G. G. Grenier, Second Clerk; Oliver Vallee, Messenger.

LEGISLATIVE COUNCIL.

Divisions.	Councillors.	P. O. Address.	Divisions.	Councillors.	P. O. Address.
Alma	J. L. Beaudry	Montreal.	Mille Isles	F. H. Lemair	
Bedford	Thomas Wood		Montarville	J. B. DeBoucherville	Quebec.
De la Durantaye	J. O. Beaubien	Quebec.	Repentigny	L. Archambault.	"
De la Valliere	J. B. G. Proulx	Nicolet.	Rigaud	J. Prudhomme	Tanneries, Mon.
De Lanaudiere	P. E. Dostaler	Berthier-en-halt	Rougemont	John Frazer	
De Lorimier	C. S. Rodier	Montreal.	Saurel	D. M. Armstrong	Sorel.
De Salaberry	Henry Starnes	"	Stadacona	T. McGreevy	Quebec.
Grandville	Elozee Dionne		Shawinegan		St. Anne de la Perade.
Gulf	J. Leboutillier	Gaspe.	The Laurentides	J. J. Ross	
Inkerman	George Bryson		Victoria	J. E. Gingras	Quebec.
Kennebec	I. Thibaudeau	Quebec.	Wellington	James Ferrier	Montreal.
La Salle	Louis Panet	"		Edward Hall	Sherbrooke.
Lauzon	A. C. DeLery				

OFFICERS OF THE LEGISLATIVE COUNCIL.

G. B. de Boucherville, Clerk, Master in Chancery and Accountant; Pierre Legare, Assistant Clerk, Master in Chancery, French Translator and Assistant Accountant; Thomas W. Lloyd, Second Assistant Clerk, Clerk of the English Journals, and English Translator; Isaie Jodoin, Advocate, Clerk of the Offices and Committees, and Translator; B. Globenski, Advocate, Clerk of French Journals, Clerk of Permanent Orders and Private Bills, and Translator; N. Faucher, jun., Clerk of Special Committees and Petitions, Translator; S. S. Hatt, Gentleman Usher of the Black Rod; T. E. Roy, Sergeant-at-Arms; A. Labelle, Copyist; F. X. Brault, First Messenger; Francis Blais, Richard Clancey, and T. Dion, Messengers.

LEGISLATIVE ASSEMBLY.

Constituencies.	Members.	P. O. Address.	Constituencies.	Members.	P. O. Address.
Argenteuil	S. Bellingham	Montreal	Montgomery	L. Blais	St. Thomas
Bagot	M. Gendron	St. Liboire	Montmorency	J. Cauchon	Quebec
Beauce	C. H. Poser	Quebec	Montreal Centre	Ed. Carter, Q.C.	Montreal
Beauharnois	E. Langevin	St. Thimothee	" East	Sir G E Cartier	"
Bellechasse	Dr. Pelletier	St. Charles	" West	A. W. Ogilvie	"
Berthier	Dr. Moll	Berthier	Napierville	P. Benoit	
Bonaventure	J. Hamilton	New Carlisle	Nicolet	J. Gaudet	Gentilly
Brome	C. Dunkin	Knowlton and Quebec	Ottawa County	Dr. Church	Aylmer
Chambly	— Jodoin	Boucherville	Pontiac	J. Poupore	Chichester
Champlain	Hon J C Chapais	St. Anne de la Perade	Portneuf	Dr. Larue	Cap Sante
Charlevoix	C. Clement	Eboulements	Quebec Centre	G. H. Simard	Quebec
Chateauguay	Dr. Laberge	St. Martine	" East	J. P. Rheaume	"
Chicoutimi and Saguenay	P. Tremblay	Chicoutimi	" West	John Hearn	"
Compton	James Ross	Lingwick	Quebec County	P J O Chauveau	"
Dorchester	Hn H L Langevin	Quebec & Ottawa	Richmond and Wolfe	— Picard	Wotton
Drum. and Artha.	E. J. Hemming	Drummondville	Richelieu	J. Beaudreau	Sorel
Gaspe	P. Fortin	Laprairie	Rimouski	J. Garon	Rimouski
Hochalaga	L. Beaubien	Montreal	Rouville	M. Robert	
Huntingdon	J. Servier	Hemmingford	St. Hyacinthe	M. Bachard	
Iberville	Dr. Molleur	Iberville	St. Johns	F. Marchand	St. Johns
Jacques Cartier	LeCavalier	St. Laurent	St. Maurice	L. Desaulniers	Three Rivers
Joliette	Dr. Lavallee		Shefford	— Bessette	Waterloo
Laprairie	— Therien		Sherbrooke	— Robertson	Sherbrooke
L'Assomption	Maj. Matheu	Lachenaie	Soulanges	D. A. Coutlee	Cedars
Laval	J. Bellerose	St Vinc'nt de Paul	Stanstead		
Levis	Dr. Blanchet	Levis	Temiscouata	E. Mallioux	St. Arsene
L'Islet	P. Verrault	St. Jean	Terrebonne	J. A. Chapleau	Montreal
Lotbiniere	H. J. Joly	Lotbiniere	Three Rivers	C B deNiverville	Three Rivers
Maskinonge	C. Caron	St. Leon	Two Mountains	G Ouimet	Montreal & Q'bec
Megantic	G. Irvine	Quebec	Vaudreuil	A. C. D. L. Harwood	Vaudreuil
Missisquoi	J. S. Brigham	Philipsburg	Vercheres	Dr. Craig	
Montcalm	F. Dugas		Yamaska	M. Senecal	Pierreville

REGISTRATION SERVICE.

Quebec—F. W. Blaiklock, G. A. Bouchette. *Montreal*—J. P. Varin, P. L. Morin, L. W. Sicotte, J. B. Bruneau, E. Lionnais. Extra Clerk,—T. Cherrier.

CROWN TIMBER AGENTS.

St. Maurice—Alphonse Dubord, Three Rivers; Wm. Lamb, Clerk. St. Francis—G. J. Nagle, St. Hyacinthe. Saugenay—George Duberger, Chicoutimi. Chaudiere and Madawaska—C. Dawson, Frazerville, Lower St. Lawrence—C. T. Dube, Trois Pistoles. Baie des Chaleurs—Jos. N. Verge, Carleton, Q. *Collector at Quebec*—McLean Stewart; W. O'Kine, Assistant; John McKay, Clerk. *Supervisor of Cullers*—Wm. Quinn, Quebec; M. Harbeson, Deputy Supervisor; Alexander Fraser, Book-keeper; T. J. Walsh, Cashier; Daniel Carey, Clerk; J. Y. Cooke, James Prendergast, Pierre Miller, Francis Quinn, Wolfred Launiere, Lorenzo Hearne, Edward Duggan, Jos. E. Belland, Eugene Blondeau, Neil Stewart, Z. Levasseur, Specification Clerks. Patrick Jordan, Office Keeper. Charles E. Belle, Deputy Supervisor for Montreal and Sorel, Montreal.

CROWN LAND AGENTS.

Allumette Island	T. Smith.	*Rimouski*	J. B. LePage.
Arthabaskaville	A. Gagnor.	*Robinson*	W. Farwell.
Aylwin	M. McBean.	*St. Anne des Monts*	C. F. Roy.
Bergeronne	R. Boulianne.	*St. Ambrose*	
Calumet	F. X. Bastien.	*St. A. de la Perade*	C. Marcotte.
Carleton	J. N. Verge.	*St. A. de la Pocati*	F. Deguise.
Chelsea	Robert Farley.	*St. Charles*	S. V. Larue.
Chicoutimi	T. Z. Cloutier.	*St. Claire*	F. Roleau.
Clarendon	E. Heath.	*St. Gervais*	F. Lamontagne.
Frampton	Andrew Ross.	*St. G. de Brandon*	J. Laporte.
Frelighsburgh	O. B. Kemp.	*St. Gregoire*	
Gaspe Basin	John Eden.	*St. J. Port Jolie*	C. F. Fournier.
Grenville	D. McMillan.	*St. Gerome*	A. B. Lavellee
Isle Verte	L. N. Gauvreau	*St. Raymond*	Ig. P. Dery.
Lambton	L. Labrecque.	*St. Thomas*	Fras. Tetu.
Leeds	John Hume,	*Three Rivers*	A. Dubord.
New Carlisle	J. A. Label.	*Thurso*	G. W. Cameron.
Quebec	McLean Stewart	*Wendover*	
Rawdon	Alex. Daly.	*Wolton*	J. T. LeBel.

BOARD FOR EXAMINATION OF P. L. SURVEYORS.

Hon. the Commissioner of Crown Lands, *ex officio*; Joseph Bouchette, Dep. Surveyor General; Adolphus Larue, Quebec; C. F. Fournier, St. Jean, Port Jolie; F. W. Blaiklock, C. P. F. Baillarge, E. T. Fletcher, and P. Gauvreau, Quebec, Provincial Land Surveyors; Secretary, William Blaiklock, Quebec; Examiner in Geology and Mineralogy, Sir W. E. Logan, &c.

OFFICERS OF THE HOUSE OF ASSEMBLY.

George M. Muir, Clerk of the House; Etienne Simard, Assistant Clerk; Thomas McCord, Law Clerk; C. A. Pariseau, Clerk; J. B. Frechette, Accountant; Laureant Simoneau, Assistant Accountant; Charles F. Langlois, Chief Clerk, Distributor of Stationery and Superintendent of Supernumeraries; C. J. Ardouin, Alexander Boulanger, Cyrille Pettigrew, Charles Pageau, Th. Prendergast, Copying Clerks; Charles P. Lindsay, Committee Clerk and Clerk of Elections; Edouard Lemoine, Clerk of Private Bills Committee; Edu. Belleau, 1st Assistant Clerk; Joseph Whydden, 2nd Assistant Clerk; Edouard Moreau, Chief French Translator; Benoni Marguette, 1st Assistant Translator; Buteau Turcotte, 2nd Assistant Translator; Wm. Cook, Chief English Translator; J. B. Duggan, Assistant Translator; Edouard Demers, Speaker's Secretary, Assistant Clerk of Committee, and Permanent Copying Clerk; Paul E. Smith, Clerk of the English Journals; O. C. Delacherrotiere, Clerk of the French Journals; Louis Fortier, 1st French Assistant Clerk; Wm. T. McGrath, 1st English Assistant Clerk; Thomas Molony, 2nd English Assistant Clerk; Leon P. Lemay, Librarian; Pierre Chenest, Postmaster; C. Dion, Assistant Postmaster and Permanent Messenger; Charles Garneau, Sergeant at Arms; Oliver Robetaille, Chief Messenger; Alfred Pellitier, Speaker's Messenger; Martial Roy, Edward Littlejohn, Joseph Trudelle and Simeon Gagne, Messengers.

SECRETARY'S OFFICE.

Hon. P. J. O. Chauveau, Provincial Secretary; P. J. Jolicœur, Assistant Secretary; A. N. Montpetit, First Clerk; Oliver Campeau, Accountant; David S. Leach, Second Clerk; J. B. Lenoir, Third Clerk; Joseph O. Laurin, Copying Clerk; Pierre Prevost, Messenger.

PROVINCIAL REGISTRAR'S DEPARTMENT.

Hon. P. J. O. Chaveau, Provincial Registrar; J. B. Meilleur, Deputy Registrar; A. Belanger, First Clerk; Roderick McKenzie, P. M. Bardy, Second Clerks; Etienne Poitras, Messenger.

DEPARTMENT OF PUBLIC INSTRUCTION.

Hon. P. J. O. Chauveau, Minister of Public Instruction; Dr. Louis Giard, Secretary; H. H. Miles, Assistant Secretary; Pierre Chauveau, Clerk of French Correspondence, Assistant Editor of the *Journal de l'Instruction Publique*, and Librarian; Patrick Delaney, Clerk of English Correspondence and Assistant Editor of the *Journal of Education;* Alf. Thomas, Clerk of Accounts and Statistics ; Leopold Devisme, Assistant Clerk of French Correspondence ; J. B. Marcou, Assistant Clerk of Accounts and Statistics; Jacques Lappare, Copying Clerk and Storekeeper; Paul Blouin, Messenger.

TREASURER'S OFFICE.

Hon. Christopher Dunkin, Treasurer; Joseph Elliott, Assistant Treasurer; Gaspard Drolet, Auditor; Henry Hemming and F. D. Tims, Bookkeepers; Arthur Giard, Stanley H. Holt, Joshua E. E. Marmette, and W. A. Davies, Clerks; Henry Hughes, Office Keeper and Messenger; G. Trudelle, Second Messenger.

AGRICULTURE AND PUBLIC WORKS.

Hon. Louis Archambault, Commissioner; Simeon Lesage, Assistant Commissioner ; Pierre Gauvreau, Architect and Superintendent, of Public Works; Boucher de la Bruère, Inspector of Angencis, and Superintendent of Colonization; Edward Lionnais, Corresponding Secretary and Accountant ; J. B. Derome, First Clerk and Accountant; J. B. Derome, First Clerk and Draughtsman ; Charles Lesperance, Clerk ; Thomas J. Nesbitt, Assistant, Secretary; Joseph O. Fontaine, Corresponding Clerk; J. B. Pelletièr, Messenger.

ATTORNEY GENERAL.

Hon. Gedeon Ouimet, Attorney General; Joseph A. Defoy, Assistant of the Law Officers of the Crown; Antoine T. Marsan, Clerk; Pierre E. Watier, Messenger.

DEPARTMENT OF CROWN LANDS.

Commissioner, Hon. J. O. Beaubien; Assistant Commissioner, G. A. Bourgeois; Deputy Surveyor General, Joseph Bouchette; Surveys Branch—E. T. Fletcher, G. G. Dunlevie, J. F. Bouchette, E. E. Tache, William Baron Von Koerber, F. Chassé, T. Morkill; Accountants Branch—J. V. Gale, H. B. Dufort, G. G. Gale ; Land Sales, Western Section—W. F. Collins, T. D. Dugal, W. F. Collins, L. Berthelot ; Registrar—J. J. Prendergast ; Woods and Forests—L. A. Robitaille, A. Pare, Jules Tache ; Land Sales, Eastern Section—L. D. Lemoine, L. L. Rivard, D. C. Mackedie, G. A. Varin, J. Brassard ; House Keeper—P. Potvin; Messengers—P. Cahill, C. Dumontier.

PROVINCE OF NEW BRUNSWICK.

SEAT OF GOVERNMENT—FREDERICTON.

EXECUTIVE COUNCIL.

LIEUTENANT-GOVERNOR—His Excellency Lemuel Allan Wilmot. G. M. Campbell, Private Secretary.

Hon. John McAdam, Chief Commis. Board of Works
Hon. A. R. Wetmore, Attorney General.
Hon. J. A. Beckwith, Provincial Secretary.
Hon. R. Sutton, Surveyor General.
Hon. B. Beveridge, Member of Council.
Hon. A. C. Desbrisay, Member of Council.
Hon. W. P. Flewelling, Member of Council.
F. A. H. Stratton, Clerk.

LEGISLATIVE COUNCIL.

Hon. J. S. SAUNDERS, President.

Counties.	Name.	P. O. Address.	Counties.	Name.	P. O. Address.
Albert	Hon. J. Lewis	Hillsboro'	Restigouche	Hon. W. Hamilton	Dalhousie
Carleton	" C. Perley	Woodstock	St. John	" A. McL. Seely	St. John
Charlotte	" J. J. Robinson	Campo Bello	St. John		
Gloucester	" R. Young	Caraquette	Sunbury	" C. Harrison	Sheffield
King's	" J. H. Ryan	Mill Stream	Westmorland	" D. Hannington	Shediac
Northumberland	" J. Davidson	Oak Point	York	" J. S. Saunders	Fredericton
Northumberland	" W. Muirhead	Chatham	York	" G. Minchin	Fredericton

OFFICERS OF THE LEGISLATIVE COUNCIL.

George Botsford, Clerk ; E. W. Miller, Assistant Clerk ; B. R. Jouett, Usher of Black Rod ; Rev. John M. Brooks, D.D., Chaplain.

HOUSE OF ASSEMBLY.

Hon. Bliss Botsford, Speaker.

Constituencies.	Name.	P. O. Address	Constituencies.	Name.	P. O. Address
Albert (County)..	C. A. Peck	Hopewell	Queen's County..	W. S. Butler	Grand Lake
" " ..	A. A. Bliss	Hillsborough	Restigouche (Co.)	Hon. A. C. DesBrisay	Dalhousie
Carleton (County)	William Lindsay.......	Woodstock	" "	W. Montgomery	Dalhousie
" "	J. R. Hartley	Woodstock	St. John (County)	Hon. C. N. Skinner..	St. John
Charlotte (Co) ...	Hon. J. McAdam	St. Stephen's	" "	J. Quinton	St. John
" "	F. Hibbard	St. George's	" "	J. Coram	St. John
" "	Henry Fry	St. Andrew's	" "	G. King..................	St. John
" "	B. R. Stevenson	St. Stephen's	St. John (City) ..	Hon. A. R. Wetmore.	St. John
Gloucester (Co)...	John Mehan...........	Bathurst	" "	W. H. A. Keans	St. John
" "	W. Taylor..............	Bathurst	Sunbury(County)	W. E. Perley	Blissville
Kent (County) ..	W. S. Caie	Kouchibou-guac	" "	J. Glasier	Lincoln
			Victoria (County)	Hon. B. Beveridge ...	Andover
" "	O. McInerny	Richibucto	" "	L. Theriault...........	Andover
King's (County).	Hon. W. P. Flewelling	Clifton	Westmorl'd (Co.)	B. Botsford	Moncton
" "	J. Flewelling..........	Kingston	" "	A. Landry	Dorchester
" "	G. McLeod	Studholm	" "	A. McQueen............	Westmorland
Northumb'd (Co)	George Kerr	Chatham	" "	J. L. Moore	Dorchester
" "	Hon. R. Sutton	Newcastle	York (County)...	H. Dow.....	Fredericton
" "	W. M. Kelly	Chatham	" "	Hon. J. A. Beckwith.	Fredericton
" "	J. C. Gough	Chatham	" "	A. Thompson	Low. Douglas
Queen's (County)	R. T. Babbitt	Upper Gage-town	" "	J. Pickard	Fredericton

OFFICERS OF THE HOUSE OF ASSEMBLY.

C. P. Wetmore, Clerk; G. J. Bliss, Clerk Assistant; A. T. Coburn, Sergeant-at-Arms; Rev. C. G. Coster, A.M., Chaplain.

GOVERNMENT OFFICERS.

Hon. D. Wark, Receiver General; J. S. Beek, Auditor General; J. Bennett, Chief Superintendent of Schools; George Thompson, Assistant Superintendent of Schools; Robert Gowan, Chief Clerk in Crown Land Office; T. O'Connor, Draughtsman; Asa Coy, Chief Clerk in Board of Works; J. W. Smith, Chief Clerk in Provincial Secretary's Office; G. E. Fenety, Queen's Printer, W. Carman, Clerk of Supreme Court at Law and in Equity.

PROVINCE OF NOVA SCOTIA.

Seat of Government—Frederickton.

Lieutenant Governor—(and Deputy Governor for signing Marriage Licenses)—His Excellency Major General Charles Hastings Doyle. Harry Moody, Private Secretary; Lieut. Col. W. H. Clerke, Nova Scotia Militia, Aide-de-Camp; Major M. B. Daly, (1st Brig. Mil. Artillery), Prov. Aide-de-Camp.

EXECUTIVE COUNCIL.

Hon. William Annand, Treasurer and President.
Hon. Martin J. Wilkins, Attorney General.
Hon. William B. Vail, Provincial Secretary.
Hon. Robt. Robertson, Commissioner of Public Works and Mines.
Hon. R. A. McHeffey, Member of Council.
Hon. Edward P. Flynn, " "
Hon. Jared C. Troop, " "
Hon. John Ferguson, " "
Hon. James Cochran, " "

Retired Members of Council, retaining their rank and precedence, by special permission of Her Majesty.—Hon. Enos Colling, Hon. James W. Johnston, Hon. Joseph Howe, Hon. Charles Tupper, C.B., Hon. Wm. A. Henry, Hon. James McDonald, Hon. Samuel L. Shannon, Hon. Alexander McFarlane, Hon. Adams G. Archibald.

LEGISLATIVE COUNCIL.

Hon. Alexander Keith, President.

	Name.	*P. O. Address.*
Hon.	Robert M. Cutler...........	Guysborough.
"	Staley Brown	Yarmouth.
"	Mather B. Almon..........	Halifax.
"	Alexander Keith	Halifax.
"	Henry G. Pineo.............	Wallace.
"	James McNab...............	Halifax.
"	R. A. McHeffey.............	Windsor.
"	John Creighton..	Lunenburgh.
"	William C. Whitman......	Annapolis.
"	Freeman Tupper............	Liverpool.
"	Samuel Chipman...........	Cornwallis.
Hon.	John McKinnon............	Antigonish.
"	Peter Smyth.................	Port Hood.
"	Samuel Creelman...........	Colchester.
"	William O. Heffernan......	Guysborough.
"	D. McN. Parker............	Halifax.
"	James Fraser................	Pictou.
"	William Annand............	Halifax.
"	William J. Stairs...........	Halifax.
"	Henry Murtell..............	Arichat.
"	Gilbert McManna..........	Shelburne.

OFFICERS.—John C. Haliburton, Clerk; Robert L. Weatherby, Law Clerk and Clerk of Parliament; Rev. George W. Hill, A.M., Chaplain; John J. Sawyer, Gentleman Usher of the Black Rod.

HOUSE OF ASSEMBLY.

Hon. JOHN J. MARSHALL, Speaker.

Constituencies.	Name.	P. O. Address.	Constituencies.	Name.	P. O. Address.
Annapolis	Jared C. Troop	Bridgetown	Inverness	Hiram Blanchard	Halifax
"	David C. Landers	Wilmot	"	Alex. Campbell	Broad Cove, Int
Antigonish	Daniel McDonald	Antigonish	King's	E. L. Brown, M.D.	Wolfville
"	Joseph McDonald	Truro	"	David M. Dickie	Canning
Colchester	Robert Chambers	Londonderry	Lunenburgh	James Eisenhauer	Lunenburgh
"	Thomas F. Morrison	Wallace River	"	Mather B. Desbrisay	Bridgewater
Cumberland	Amos Purdy	Wallace	Pictou	Robert S. Copeland	Merigomish
"	Henry G. Pineo, jr.	Sydney, C. B.	"	Martin I. Wilkins	Pictou
Cape Breton	Alonzo J. White	Sydney	"	Geo. Murray, M.D.	Merigomish
"	John Ferguson	Halifax	Queen's	William H. Smith	Liverpool
Digby	William B. Vail	Clare	"	Samuel Freeman	Liverpool
"	Urbine Doucette	Manchester	Richmond	Edward P. Flynn	Arichat
Guysborough	John J. Marshall	Sherbrooke, StM	"	Josiah Hooper	Fourché
"	John A. Kirk	Beaver Harbor.	Shelburne	Robert Robertson	Halifax
Halifax	Henry Balcan	Halifax	"	Thomas Johnson	Locke's Island
"	James Cochran	Halifax	Victoria	William Kidston	Baddeck
"	Jeremiah Northup	Maitland	"	John Ross	Baddeck
Hants	William Lawrence	Falmouth	Yarmouth	Wm. H. Townsend	Yarmouth
"	Elkanah Young	Antigonish	"	John K. Ryerson	Yarmouth

OFFICERS OF THE HOUSE OF ASSEMBLY.—Clerk, Henry C. D. Twining; Assistant Clerk, Lawrence G. Power; Chaplain, Rev. Canon Cochran; Sergeant-at-Arms, A. M. Gidney; Assistant Sergeant-at-Arms, James L. Griffin.

PRINCE EDWARD ISLAND.

LIEUTENANT-GOVERNOR.

His Excellency GEORGE DUNDAS.

GEORGE D. ATKINSON, Private Secretary.

EXECUTIVE COUNCIL.

Hon. Geo. Coles, President.
" J. Heasley.
Hon. W. W. Lord.
" R. P. Haythorne.
Hon. H. J. Callbeck.
" G. Howlan.
Hon. A. Laird, Jr.

Clerks: Hon. George Coles and Charles DesBrisay. Assistant Clerk: W. DesBrisay.

LEGISLATIVE COUNCIL.

PRESIDENT—Hon. Donald Montgomery.

District.	Name.
Queen's County:	
Charlottetown & Royalty	Hon. Edward Palmer
1st District	Hon. D. Montgomery
Do	Hon. J. Balderston
2nd District	Hon. Geo. Beer.
"	Hon. P. Haythorne.
King's County:	
1st District	Hon. P. Walker
Do	Hon. James Dingwell

District.	Name.
King's County (continued):	
2nd District	Hon. A. McDonald
Do	Hon. D. Gordon
Prince County:	
1st District	Hon. W. W. Lord
Do	Hon. James Yeo
2nd District	Hon. A. Anderson
Do	Hon. Jas. Muirhead

Clerk: John Ball. Black Rod and Sergeant-at-Arms: H. Palmer. Chaplain: Rev. L. C. Jenkins, D.C.L.

(Address the whole, Charlottetown, P.E.I.)

HOUSE OF ASSEMBLY.

SPEAKER—Hon. Joseph Wightman.

Queen's County:
Charlottetown...Hon. F. Brecken, J. T. Jenkins.
1st District ..... " P. Sinclair, D Cameron.
2nd " ...... " H. J. Callbeck, W. S. McNeill.
3rd " ...... " George Coles, F. Kelly.
4th " ...... " James Duncan, B. Davies.
King's County:
George Town, Hons. T. H. Haviland, R. McAulay.
1st District, " Jos. Hensley, E. Kickham.
2nd District, Hon. Ed. Reilly, A. McCormack.
3rd " " L. C. Owen, Jos. Wightman.
4th " " S. Prowse, K. Henderson.
Prince County:
1st District, Hon. G. Howlan, H. Bell.
2nd " " J. Yeo, David Ramsay.
3rd " " Geo. Sinclair, Jos. Arsenault.
4th " " C. Howat, A. Laird.
5th " " C. McLennan, D. Green.

Chief Clerk: John McNeill. Assistant Clerk: K. Morrison. Sergeant-at-Arms: N. Conroy. Chaplain: Rev. Thomas Duncan.

NEWFOUNDLAND.

(Newfoundland is a sufficient Post Office Address for all the following).

LIEUTENANT-GOVERNOR.

His Excellency ANTHONY MUSGRAVE, Esquire.

EXECUTIVE COUNCIL.

Hon. Laurence O'Brien, President.
" Frederick T. B. Carter, Premier.
" Nicholas Stabb.
" John Bemister.
Hon. Ambrose Shea.
" John Kent.
" John Hayward.

LEGISLATIVE COUNCIL.

Honorable Laurence O'Brien.
" Edward Morris.
" Nicholas Stabb.
" Robert Kent.
Honorable James S. Clift
" Richard O'Dwyer.
" Edward White.
" Peter G. Tessier.
Honorable James Cormack.
" James O. Fraser.
" John Winter.
" Edward D. Shea.

Hon. George H. Emerson, Clerk.

LEGISLATIVE ASSEMBLY.

St. John's East, J. Kavanagh, J. Kent, R. J. Parsons.
" West, T. Talbot, H. Renouf, P. Brennan.
Harbor Grace, Mr. Goddin, W. S. Green.
Carbonear, J. Rorke.
Harbor Maine, G. J. Hogsett, C. Furey.
Port de Grave, Robert John Pinsent, Jr.
Bay de Verds, Hon. J. Bemister.
Trinity, S. Rendell, F. J. Wyatt, R. Alsop.
Bonavista, J. H. Warren, J. T. Oakley, J. T. Burton.
Twillingate & Fogo, T. Knight, W. V. Whiteway.
Ferryland, T. Glenn, M. Kearney.
Placentia and St. Mary's, Hon. Ambrose Shea, P. M. Barron, Thomas O'Reilly.
Burin, E. Evans, Hon. Frederick B. T. Carter.
Fortune Bay, Thomas R. Bennet.
Burgeo and Lapoile, Daniel W. Prouse.

John Stewart, Clerk.

GOVERNMENT HOUSE, OTTAWA.

TUESDAY, 28th day of July, 1868.

PRESENT:

HIS EXCELLENCY THE GOVERNOR GENERAL IN COUNCIL.

ON the recommendation of the Honorable the Minister of Customs, and in pursuance of the provisions of the 11th Section of Act 31 Vic. Cap. 6, intituled: "An Act respecting the Customs," His Excellency in Council has been pleased to order, and it is hereby ordered, that the following Regulations respecting the Coasting trade of the Dominion, be and the same are hereby adopted and established.

Certified, WM. H. LEE,
Clerk of the Privy Council.

COASTING REGULATIONS.

1. Vessels and Boats employed solely in the transport of Goods or Passengers from one Port or place to another Port or place within the limits of the Dominion of Canada, shall be deemed to be engaged in the Coasting Trade, and shall be subject to the Regulations governing the same.

2. None but British registered Vessels and Boats, wholly owned by British subjects, can lawfully be engaged in the Coasting Trade of the Dominion of Canada, and the names of such Vessels or Boats and the names of their Ports of Registry, shall be distinctly painted on the Stern of said Vessels or Boats.

3. Such Vessels and Boats, may, without being subject to entry, or clearance as required by law, for Vessels trading between Ports in the Dominion of Canada, as well as with Foreign Ports, carry goods the produce of Canada, or goods duty free, or goods duty paid or passengers from any Ports or places in the Provinces of Ontario and Quebec, to any other Ports or places in the said Provinces, or from any Ports or places in the Province of New Brunswick, to any other Ports or places in the said Province, or from any Ports or places in the Province of Nova Scotia, to any other Ports or places in the said Province, provided always that the owners or masters of such Vessels or Boats, shall take out a license for the season for that purpose from a Collector of Customs in Canada, and that the owners or masters in taking out the said License shall enter into Bonds of $500 conditioned that such Vessels or Boats shall not be employed in the Foreign Trade, and provided also that the Master of every such Vessel or Boat shall keep or cause to be kept, a Cargo Book in the form prescribed by the Customs Department, to be registered by the Collector of Customs who granted the License, in which Book shall be entered at the Port of Lading, an account of all goods taken on board of such Vessel or Boat, stating the description of the packages, the quantities, the descriptions and value of the goods therein, as also of the goods stowed loose, and the names of the respective Shippers and Consignees, as far as any of such particulars shall be known to him: and at the Port of discharge shall be entered in the said Cargo Book, the respective days upon which any such goods shall be delivered out of such Vessel and also the respective times of departure from the Port of Lading and of arrival at the Port of unlading.

4. The Master of any such Vessel or Boat shall produce his License and Cargo Book to any Officer of Customs, whenever the same shall be demanded, and answer all questions put to him, and such Officer of Customs shall be at liberty to note any remark on the Cargo Book which he may deem proper, and if the Cargo Book shall not be kept in the manner hereby required, and the particulars of all Cargo laden and unladen, duly noted therein, the Goods and Vessel shall be forfeited, and the Master shall incur the penalty of $100.

5. Before any Coasting Vessel or Boat shall depart from any Port of Lading in any one of the Provinces of the Dominion of Canada for any other Port in the said Dominion, not in the said Province of departure, an account or Report with a duplicate thereof, in the form or to the effect following, and signed by the Master, shall be delivered to the Collector, who shall retain the duplicate and return the original account or report dated and signed by him: and such account or Report shall be the clearance of the Vessel or Boat for the voyage and the transire or pass for the goods expressed therein, except for goods under Bond or goods liable to Excise or Internal Revenue duty, which shall require the entries and warrants for landing to be signed by the proper Officers as required by Law, and if any such account or Report be false, the Master who signed it shall forfeit the sum of $100.

REPORT and Transire Coastwise for a Registered Vessel or Boat proceeding from one Province to another in the Dominion of Canada.

Port of
Name of Vessel.
Master's Name. Register Tons.
Port of Registry. Whither bound.

Foreign Goods.	
Warehoused Goods removed under Bond.	
Goods liable to duty of Excise.	
Do. removed under Bond.	
Sundry other Goods, Produce of Canada, &c.	

(Signed)
Master,

Cleared the day of 186 .
(Signed)
Collector of Customs for the Port of

COASTING REGULATIONS—*Continued.*

6. Within twenty-four hours after the arrival of any Coasting Vessel or Boat at the Port of discharge, ɪich requires a *transire* as above described, and before any goods shall be unladen, the transire with the ɪme of the place or wharf where the lading is to be discharged, noted thereon, shall be delivered to the ɪllector, who shall note thereon the date of the delivery: and if any of the Goods on board such Coasting ɪssel or Boat shall be subject to any customs duty the same shall not be unladen until due entry has been ɪde at the Custom House and a warrant granted for the landing thereof; and if any of the Goods on Board ch Vessel or Boat be subject to any duty of Excise or Internal Revenue the same shall not be unladen, thout the authority or permission of the proper Officer of Excise; but no entry shall be required at the ɪstom House for any Goods brought Coastwise the produce of Canada or Goods on which the duties whether Customs or Excise have already been paid or which are duty free.

7. Vessels and Boats employed in the Coasting Trade and that shall not have taken out a License for rrying Goods, and obtained a Cargo Book as above provided, shall report inwards and outwards at the arest Port to their place of arrival or destination and require clearances whenever they depart from any ɪrt or place within the Dominion of Canada, and in default of their so reporting the Vessel or Cargo, the aster shall in such cases be subject to the penalty of $100 for departing and arriving without due entry wards or outwards, as the case may be: Provided that when a vessel shall sail from any place where there no Custom House, or officer of Customs, it shall be sufficient for the carrying out of this regulation that the rner or Master of such Vessel do, as soon afterwards as possible, forward to the nearest Custom House a milar report in duplicate, or lodge the same at the first Port at which he shall touch where there is a ɪstom House Officer.

8. Goods under removal Bond from one Canadian Port to another Canadian Port, may be carried in any ritish registered Vessel or Boat, trading Coastwise with a proper License and Cargo Book upon such Goods ɪing properly entered in the Cargo Book and in the account or Transire, in duplicate, the Collector at the ɪrt from which such Goods are removed, being required to forward by Mail, to the Collector of the Port for hich the Goods are destined, all the particulars and description of the Goods so forwarded, and the Packages ɪall be properly marked in Red, as now provided, but no Goods under Bond shall be carried in any Coasting essel or Boat until the Master has delivered an account in duplicate or transire to the Collector of Customs the Port of Lading.

9. No Coasting Vessel or Boat to touch at any Foreign Port unless forced by unavoidable circumstances, ɪd the Master of any Coasting Vessel or Boat which has touched at any Foreign Port, shall declare the same writing under his own hand, to the Collector or other proper Officer of Customs at the Port or Place in ɪnada where his Vessel or Boat afterwards first arrives, under a penalty of $100.

10. If any goods are unshipped from any Vessel or Boat arriving Coastwise, or unshipped or water borne be shipped to be carried Coastwise on Sundays or Holidays, or unless in the presence, or with the authority the proper Officer of Customs, or unless at such times and places as shall be appointed and approved by m for that purpose; the same shall be forfeited and the Master of the Vessel or Boat shall forfeit the sum $100.

11. Officers of Customs may board any Coasting Vessel or Boat in any Port or Place, and at any period the voyage search her, and examine all Goods on board, and demand all the documents which ought to be ɪ board; and the Collector may require such documents to be brought to him for inspection.

12. No Fishing Boat or Boat used in Ferrying under 15 tons burthen, shall, except by Special License permission, carry any Goods from a Foreign Country, which are liable to duty, under pain of seizure, ɪless the same (in the case of Ferry Boats) be for the sole use of some passenger then on board.

13. No Goods can be carried in any Coasting Vessel or Boat, except such as are laden to be so carried at me Port or place in Canada, and no Goods shall be taken into or put out of any Coasting Vessel or Boat hile on her voyage by River, Lake or Sea.

14. The Transire Coastwise required by these Regulations, may in the case of any Steam Vessel carrying Purser, be signed by such Purser with the like effect in all respects, and subject to the like penalty on the ɪurser, and the like forfeiture of the Goods, in case of any untrue statement in the Transire, as if the Transire as signed by the Master; and the word *Master* for the purposes of these Regulations shall be construed as ɪcluding the Purser of any Steam Vessel; but nothing herein contained shall preclude the Collector or proper fficer of Customs from calling upon the Master of any Steam Vessel to answer all such questions concerning ɪe Vessel, passengers, cargo, and crew, as might be lawfully demanded of him if the report had been made y him, or to exempt the Master from the penalties imposed by these Regulations for failure to answer any ɪch question, or for answering untruly, or to prevent the Master from making such report, if he shall see t so to do.

15. The Coasting Regulations of the late Province of Canada dated the 12th April, 1861, and all egulations heretofore existing in the Province of New Brunswick or Nova Scotia in reference to Coasting in ny of the said Provinces are hereby repealed.

(Signed)

S. L. TILLEY,

Minister of Customs.

Regulations Governing Traveller's Carriages, &c., Crossing the Frontier.

To ensure uniformity at the frontier ports, in dealing with "carriages of travellers and carriages laden with merchandise," and to afford the utmost facility to parties visiting the Dominion for transient purposes, consistent with the protection of the Revenue, the MINISTER OF CUSTOMS has approved of the following "Regulations and Restrictions."

1st.—Regular Stages and Hacks, when the owners or the drivers are known to the officers, may be allowed to cross the frontier and return within two days, without being required to make an entry at the Custom House, subject only to the ordinary examination, search and inspection.

2nd.—Travellers intending to remain within the Dominion for a longer period than two days, are required in all cases to report and enter their horses, carriages and travelling equipage; and in cases where they do not intend to leave at the same port at which they enter, or are uncertain on that point, they must deposit with the Collector the full amount of duty on such horses, carriages and other dutiable articles, to be returned only on their furnishing satisfactory evidence that the same articles have been returned unchanged to the United States. Travellers intending to leave at the Port of Entry, may be allowed to enter as above, and in lieu of cash to give a Bond, with an approved resident surety, covering the amouut of duty, and with the additional condition that such Bond shall be enforced if the time specified therein be exceeded.

3rd.—The time to be allowed travellers in either case shall not exceed one calendar month; and if that term be exceeded, the entries shall be considered *bonâ fide* entries for duty, and be included in the accounts of the Port.

4th.—All moneys received by Collectors on deposit, under the above Regulations, shall be, if possible, deposited *ad interim* in a Bank, in the Collector's name; and if there is no Bank available, then in some other place of security under the Collector's control; and a separate account of the receipt and disposal of such deposits shall be sent quarterly to this Department.

5th.—The entry in each case should contain such a description of the horses, carriages, &c., as would enable the Collector or other Officer to identify them on their leaving the Dominion; and a copy shall be furnished the owner or other person making such entry, which shall be his permit for travelling in the Country.

R. S. M. BOUCHETTE,

Commissioner of Customs.

CUSTOMS DEPARTMENT,

OTTAWA, *March 8th*, 1869.

JUDICIARY OF ONTARIO.

THE LAW SOCIETY OF UPPER CANADA.

Visitors.—Hon. W. H. Draper, C.B., president Court of Error and Appeal; Hon. P. M. M. S. VanKoughnet, D. C. L., Chancellor of Ontario; Hon. W. B. Richards, Chief Justice of Queen's Bench; Hon. John Godfrey Spragge, Vice-Chancellor; Hon. J. H. Hagarty, D.C.L., Chief Justice Court of Common Pleas; Hon. J. C. Morrison, Judge Court of Queen's Bench; Hon. Adam Wilson, Judge Court of Queen's Bench; Hon. John Wilson, Judge Court of Common Pleas; Hon. Oliver Mowat, Vice-Chancellor; Hon. John W. Gwynne, Judge Court of Common Pleas.

Treasurer—Hon. John Hillyard Cameron, D.C.L., Q.C.

Benchers.—Hon. Henry J. Boulton, Q.C.; George Ridout; Hon. John Rolph; Hon. George S. Boulton; Hon. James E. Small, Q.C.; David Jones; George Rolph; Robert Berrie; George S. Jarvis; Donald Bethune; Thomas Kirkpatrick, Q.C.; Clarke Gamble; Marcus Fayette Whitehead; George Malloch; George Boswell, Q.C.; Miles O'Reilly, Q.C.; Hon. John H. Cameron, D.C.L., Q.C.; Hon. George Sherwood, Q.C.; James Smith, Q.C.; Hon. Sir John A. Macdonald, K.C.B., Q.C.; Hon. John Ross, Q.C.; Hon. John S. McDonald, Q.C.; Charles Baby; George Duggan; John Crawford; George B. L. Fellowes, Q. C.; Secker Brough, Q.C.; Nesbitt Kirchhoffer; Samuel Black Freeman, Q.C.; Roland McDonald, Q. C.; John Bell, Q.C.; John S. Smith; H. C. R. Becher, Q.C.; Lewis Wallbridge, Q. C.; Richard Miller George W. Burton, Q.C.; Hon. Alexander Campbell, Q.C.; Stephen Richards, jun., Q.C.; Thomas Galt, Q.C; David B. Read, Q.C.; John Hector, Q.C.; Jacob F. Pringle; Hon. John Prince, Q.C.; John Duggan, Q.C.; James A. Henderson; Matthew R. VanKoughnet; Hon. James Patton, L.L.D., Q.C.; Daniel MacMartin; Philip Low; Richard F. Steele; John Miller; Sir James L. Robinson, Bart.; Samuel H. Strong, Q.C.; A. J. Macdonnell; J. B. Lewis; J. J. Burrowes ; D. McMichael, L.L.D ; W. Proudfoot; K. Mackenzie, Q.C.; R. Dennistoun; Angus Morrison; Christopher S. Patterson; John Roaf, Q.C.

Secretary, Librarian and Examiner.—Hugh N. Gwynne, B.A., Trinity College, Dublin.

Examiners and Lecturers.—John T. Anderson, Esq., Common Law; Alexander Leith, Esq., Real Property; Thomas Moss, M.A., Equity.

COURTS.

COURT OF ERROR AND APPEAL.—Constituted for the hearing of appeals, in civil cases from the Court of Queen's Bench, Chancery and Common Pleas, and appeals in criminal cases from the Courts of Queen's Bench and Common Pleas. From the judgment of this Court an appeal lies to Her Majesty in Privy Council, in cases over £1,000, or where annual rent, fee, or future rights to any amount, are affected. *Judges*—Hon. William H. Draper, C.B., Chief Justice of Ontario; Hon. P. M. M. S. VanKoughnet, D.C.L., Chancellor of Ontario; Hon. William Buell Richards, Chief Justice ot the Common Pleas; Hon. John Godfrey Spragge, Vice Chancellor; Hon. John Hawkins Hagarty, D L., Judge Court of Queen's Bench; Hon. Joseph Curran Morrison, Judge Court of Queen's Bench; Hon. Adam Wilson, Judge of the Court of Common Pleas; Hon. John Wilson, Judge of the Court of Common Pleas; Hon. Oliver Mowat, Vice Chancellor. *Clerk and Reporter*—Alexander Grant.

COURT OF IMPEACHMENT.

For the trial of Judges of the County Courts or Recorders in Ontario, under Con. Stat. U. C. cap. 14, and 29 and 30 Vic., cap. 3S. *Judges*—Hon. W. H. Draper, C.B., Chief Justice of Ontario; Hon. Philip M. M. S. VanKoughnet, D.C L., Chancellor of Ontario; Hon. William B. Richards, Chief Justice of the Court of Common Pleas; with provision for other Judges acting in the event of their absence or illness. *Clerk*—W. B. Heward.

COURT OF QUEEN'S BENCH.

The jurisdiction of this Court extends to all manner of actions, causes and suits, criminal and civil, real, personal and mixed, within Ontario, and it may proceed in such, by such process and course as are provided by law, and shall tend with justice and dispatch to determine the same; and may hear and determine all issues of law, and also with the inquest of twelve good and lawful men (except in cases otherwise provided for), try all issues of fact, and give judgment, and award execution thereon, and also in matters which relate to the Queen's Revenue (including the condemnation of contraband or smuggled goods), as may be done by Her Majesty's Superior Courts of Law in England. *Chief Justice*—Hon. W. B. Richards. *Puisne Judges*—Hon. Joseph Curran Morrison and Hon. Adam Wilson. *Clerk of the Crown and Pleas*—R. G. Dalton, Q.C. *Reporter*—Christopher Robinson, Q.C. *Senior Clerk*—John Small. *Junior Clerk*—W. B. Lynes. *Crier and Usher*—Andrew Fleming.

COURT OF COMMON PLEAS.

This Court has the same powers and jurisdiction, as a Court of Record, as the Court of Queen's Bench. Writs of summons and capias issue alternately from either Court. *Chief Justice*—Hon. J. H. Hagarty. *Puisne Judges*—Hon. John Wilson and Hon. John W. Gwynne. *Clerk of the Crown and Pleas*—M. B. Jackson. *Reporter*—S. J. VanKoughnet, M.A. *Senior Clerk*—S. B. Clark. *Junior Clerk*—B. T. Jackson. *Crier and Usher*—Patrick O'Connell.

COURT OF CHANCERY.

This Court has the like jurisdiction as the Court of Chancery in England. in cases of fraud, accident, trusts, executors, administrators, co-partnerships, account mortgages, awards, dower. infants, idiots, lunatic and their estates, waste, specific performance, discovery, and to prevent multiplicity of suits, staying proceeds ings at law prosecuted against equity and good conscience, and may decree the issue, repeal or avoidance of letters patent, and generally the like powers which the Court of Chancery in England possesses to administer justice in all cases in which there is no adequate remedy at law. *Chancellor*—Hon. P. M. M. S. VanKoughnet D.C.L. *Vice Chancellors*—Hon. John G. Spragge and Hon. Oliver Mowat. *Judge's Secretary*—T. W. Taylor. *Special Examiners*—John Hector, Q.C., and James H. Esten. *Registrar and Reporter*—Alexander Grant. *Registrar's Clerk*—Willoughby Cummings. *Clerks*—Arthur Holmstead and Thomas Gray. *Entering Clerks.* F. Arnoldi and Alexander F. McLean. *Usher and House Keeper.*—Donald Sutherland. *Messenger*—Henry Humphreys.

MASTERS OFFICE IN CHANCERY.

Master in Ordinary—Andrew Norton Buell. *Taxing Officer*—George Hemmings. *Master's Clerk*—Walter M. Ross. *Clerk*—J. P. Macdonell. *Local Masters and Deputy Registrars*—*Barrie*—Wm. E. O'Brien. *Belleville*—Wm. W. Dean. *Brantford*—John Cameron. *Brockville*—Jacob Dockstader Buell. *Chatham*—George Williams. *Cobourg*—Wm. H. Weller. *Cornwall*—John McDonell. *Goderich*—H. McDermott. *Guelph*—James W. Hall. *Hamilton*—Wm. Leggo. *Kingston*—James A. Henderson, D.C.L. *Lindsay*—William H. Weller. *London*—James Shanley. *Ottawa*—John Wilson. *Owen Sound*—David A. Creasor. *Perth*—W. O. Buell. *Peterboro*—W. H. Weller. *Simcoe*—David Tisdale. *Sandwich*—Samuel S. Macdonell. *Sarnia*—P. T. Poussett. *St. Catharines*—F. W. McDonald. *St. Thomas*—James Stanton. *Stratford*—G. W. Lawrence. *Sault Ste. Marie, Algoma*—Hon. John Prince, Q. C. *Whitby*—George H. Dartnell. *Woodstock*—H. B. Beard.

ACCOUNTANT'S OFFICE IN CHANCERY.

Accountant General.—Robert J. Turner. *Clerks*—W. C. Crofton and Frank Walker

PRACTICE COURT AND CHAMBERS.

One of the Common Law Judges holds a Court during each Term, called the "Practice Court," for hearing matters relating to the adding or justifying bail, discharging insolvent debtors, administering oaths, hearing and determining matters on motion, and making rules and orders in causes and business depending in either of said Law Courts. Chambers are held each day, and by a recent order, daily in Chancery, by T. W. Taylor, Esq., the Judges' Secretary, in Common Law, and by one of the Judges of the said courts, for such business relating to suits therein as may be transacted by a single Judge out of court. *Clerk, Common Law*—William B. Heward. *Reporter Common Law Chambers*—Henry O'Brien. *Reporter Chancery Chambers*—C. W. Cooper.

HEIR AND DEVISEE COURT.

Commissioners—The Judges of the Superior Courts, and such other persons as may be appointed by commission under the Great Seal. Their duties are to determine claims to lands in Ontario, for which no patent has issued from the Crown in favor of the proper claimants, whether as heirs, devisees, or assignees. Sittings at Toronto, first Monday in January and July in each year. *Clerk of Commissioners*—W. B. Heward.

COUNTY COURTS.

Presided over by a resident Judge in each County. Their jurisdiction extends to all personal actions where the debt or damages claimed do not exceed £50; and to all suits relating to debt, covenant or contract, where the amount is ascertained by the acts of the parties, or signature of the defendant to £100; and to all bail bonds and recognizances of bail given in the County Court, to any amount; but not to cases involving the title to lands, validity of wills, or actions for libel, slander, crim. con., or seduction. An appeal lies to either of the Superior Courts of Law. These Courts also possess equity powers, to the amount of £50, subject to an appeal to Chancery.

SURROGATE COURTS.

The jurisdiction of these Courts relates to all testamentary matters and causes, and to the granting or revoking of probate of wills, and letters of administration of the effects of deceased persons having estate or effects in Ontario, and all mattess arising out of or connected with the grant or revocation of probate or administration subject to an appeal to the Court of Chancery. The County Judges are also Judges of the Surrogate Courts. *Surrogate Clerk*—Sir J. L. Robinson, Bart.

COURTS OF QUARTER SESSIONS.

Chairman, the County Judge in each County, who, with one or more Justices of the Peace, holds a Court of Quarter Sessions in his County four times a year for trials by Jury in cases of felony and misdemeanor, but treason and capital felonies are exempted from their Jurisdiction.

INSOLVENT DEBTORS' COURTS.

By the "Insolvent Acts of 1864 and 1865," 26 and 28 Victoria, cap. 57, and 29 Vic., cap. 18, provision is made "for the settlement of the estates of insolvent debtors, for giving effect to arrangements between them and their creditors, and for the punishment of fraud. In the Province of Quebec this enactment applies to traders only; in Ontario to all persons, whether traders or non-traders. In these Courts the County Court Judge in each County presides—the only appointments made in pursuance of this statute being those of "official assignees," who are to be nominated by the "Board of Trade at any place, or the council thereof, within the county or district adjacent thereto in which there is no Board of Trade." This important statute is proving a great boon to the community in enabling parties, who from unavoidable circumstances find themselves paralysed by hopeless liability, to obtain relief, and recommence business.

DIVISION COURTS.

For the summary disposal of cases by a Judge; but a jury of five persons may be demanded in certain cases. Their jurisdiction extends to actions of debt or contract amounting to £25; injuries or torts to personal

chattels amounting to £10; and personal actions to that amount, if not excepted from their jurisdiction; but not to actions for gambling debts, liquors drunk in a tavern, or notes of hand given therefor, ejectment, title to land, &c., or any toll, custom, or franchise, will or settlement, malicious prosecution libel, slander, crim. con., seduction or breach of promise, or actions against a J.P., or anything done by him in the execution of his office, if he objects to it. Each judicial district is divided into court divisions, and courts are held once in two months in each division, or oftener, at the discretion of the Judge. The Divisions are established by the Courts of Quarter Sessions.

CROWN LAW OFFICER.

Attorney-General—Hon. John S. Macdonald, Q.C.

OFFICERS OF THE COURTS.

Clerks of Assize—The Deputy-Clerks of the Crown are *ex-officio* Clerks of Assize and Marshals in their respective counties.

Deputy Clerks of the Crown—The Clerks of the County Courts will be *ex-officio* Deputy Clerks of the Crown and Pleas of their several counties as the present incumbents vacate by death or otherwise.

Deputy Registrars and Masters in Chancery—These officers are appointed by the Court, for each County, as occasion requires.

Clerk of the Process—For selling and issuing Writs of Summons and other Writs in the Queen's Bench and Common Pleas (alternately)—Allan Cameron. *Assistant Clerk*—A. H. B. Wadsworth. The Clerks of the Crown and Pleas at Toronto and the Deputy Clerks of the Crown in the several counties are supplied with Writs from Toronto, and re-issue the same in their respective counties.

TERMS OF THE COURTS.

Appeal Terms commence on the fourth Thursday next after Hilary, Easter and Michaelmas Terms.

Law Terms—Hilary begins first Monday in February, and ends Saturday of the following week; Easter begins third Monday in May, and ends Saturday of the second week thereafter; Michaelmas begins third Monday in November, and ends Saturday of the second week thereafter. By the Act 24 and 30 Vict., cap. 40, Trinity Term, hitherto commencing on the Monday after 21st August, is abolished; but the same statute gives power to the Court of Queen's Bench and Common Pleas, at their discretion, to hold sittings in *banc* in time of vacation (except long vacation), by virtue of a rule or order of the court, respectively, to be made in or out of the term for the hearing of such special cases or rules for new trials, as shall be named in a list to be attached to any such rule or order; and for giving of judgments in cases previously argued; and for disposing of such other business of the Court, as in its discretion it shall see fit. Notice of such rules to be given in form and manner prescribed by the act, six clear days before the day appointed. Long vacation extends from 1st July to 21st August.

Court of Chancery—This Court sits every week, except during the Christmas vacation from the 24th December to the 6th January, and the long vacation from the 1st July to 21st August, on Mondays for hearings, on Tuesdays for motions, and on Wednesdays for motions for decrees, and on the other days upon any adjourned motions, &c., from the regular days.

County Court Terms commence on the first Monday in January, April, July and October, and end the following Saturday.

CIRCUITS OF THE COURTS.

Law Circuits.—Courts of Assize and Nisi Prius, and of Oyer and Terminer and General Gaol Delivery, shall be held twice a year in each County or union of Counties, in the vacation between Hilary and Easter Terms, and between that period of the vacation after the 21st August and Michaelmas Term, except in the County of the City of Toronto and the County of York, in each of which counties there shall be a third such Court in every year, in the vacation between Michaelmas and Hilary Terms. There are six Circuits, as follows, viz.:—The *Eastern*: Pembroke, Perth, Brockville, Ottawa, Kingston, Cornwall, L'Orignal. *Midland*: Napanee, Belleville, Cobourg, Whitby, Peterboro', Lindsay, Picton. *Niagara*: Milton, Barrie, Hamilton, Welland, St. Catharines, Owen Sound. *Oxford*: Guelph, Woodstock, Berlin, Stratford, Brantford, Cayuga, Simcoe. *Western*: Walkerton, Goderich, Sarnia, London, St. Thomas, Chatham, Sandwich. *Home*: Counties of York and Peel. The Courts in each Circuit shall be presided over by one of the Chief Justices or Judges of the Superior Courts, or in their absence, by some one Judge of a County Court, or some one of Her Majesty's Counsel learned in the law, requested by any one of the Chief Justices or Judges of the Superior Courts to act in that behalf.

Chancery Sittings.—For the Examination of Witnesses and Hearing Causes, are held in the Spring and Fall of each year, as follows:—Toronto, Goderich, Stratford, Sarnia, Sandwich, Chatham, London, Woodstock, Simcoe, Guelph, Brantford, St. Catharines, Hamilton, Whitby, Cobourg, Barrie, Owen Sound, Kingston, Brockville, Cornwall, Ottawa, Belleville, Peterboro', Lindsay. The Courts in each Circuit are presided over by the Chancellor or one of the Vice-Chancellors, or by any one of Her Majesty's Counsel learned in the law, requested by the Chancellor or one of the Vice-Chancellors to act in that behalf.

County Court and Quarter Sessions Sittings.—For the trial of issues of fact, and the assessment of damages, on the second Tuesday in March, June, September and December in each year. The City Sittings take place on the First Tuesday of the same months.

Commissioners in Ontario, for taking Affidavits to be used in Courts of Quebec.—Robert A. Harrison, Barrister, Toronto; Richard Snelling, Barrister, Toronto; Larrat W. Smith, D.C.L., Barrister, Toronto; James Morris, Barrister, Toronto; James A. Henderson, D.C.L., Kington; Hon. George Crawford, Senator, Brockville; James Jessup, Brockville; J. D. Buell, Brockville; W. M. Matheson; George Futvoye, Q.C., Ottawa.

Commissioners in Quebec, for taking Affidavits to be used in Courts of Ontario.—Theodore Doucet, Notary Public, Montreal; J. Court, Montreal; John J. C. Abbott, Advocate, Montreal; George Macrae, Advocate, Montreal; John H. Isaacson, Notary Public, Montreal; William B. Lambe, Advocate, Montreal; Frederick W. Torrance, Advocate, Montreal; P. B. Casgrin, Advocate, Quebec: Frederick C. Vannovous, Advocate, Quebec; Charles G. Holt, Q.C., Quebec; J. B. R. Dufresne, Quebec; Noel Hill Bowen, Notary Public, Quebec; George Futvoye, Q.C., Ottawa; Hewit Bernard, Advocate, Ottawa; E. L. Montizambert, Advocate, Ottawa.

Commissioners in England, for taking Affidavits to be used in Canadian Courts.—Chas. Bischoff (Bischoff, Coxe & Bompas, Solicitors), 19 Coleman street, London, England; John Morris (Ashurst, Morris & Co., Solicitors), 6 Old Jewry, London, England.

Legal Holidays.—Sundays, New Year's Day, Epiphany, Annunciation, Good Friday, Ascension, Corpus Christi, St. Peter, St. Paul, All Saints, Christmas Day, and any day appointed by Proclamation for a general fast or thanksgiving.

DIVISION COURT CLERKS.

ALGOMA DISTRICT.

I.	John Cousins	Sault Ste. Marie
II.	J. Coatsworth	Bruce Mines
III.	A. M. Ironsides	Manitowaning
IV.	——— ———	Fort William

BRANT.

I.	J. Robinson	Brantford
II.	Henry Penton	Paris
III.	Samuel Stanton	St. George
IV.	Wm. H. Serpell	Burford
V.	Alonzo Foster	Scotland
VI.	Matthew Whiting	Onondaga

BRUCE.

I.	Wm. Collins	Walkerton
II.	H. B. O'Connor	Riversdale
III.	Joseph Barker	Kincardine
IV.	John Valentine	Paisley
V.	John Eastwood	Southampton
VI.	Peter Sinclair	Underwood
VII.	W. S. Francis	Invermay

CARLETON.

I.	George R. Burke	Ottawa
II.	Rowland B. Eagar	Richmond
III.	John Fenton	South Huntley
IV.	Wm. D. Pigot	Fitzroy Harbor
V.	Wm. Cowan	N. Gower
VI.	Ira Morgan	Metcalfe, Osgoode
VII.	Frederick W. Harmer	Nepean

ELGIN.

I.	Simon Newcombe	Vienna
II.	——— ———	Aylmer
III.	James Farley	St. Thomas
IV.	James Philpott	Iona
V.	F. McDiarmid	Airey, Aldboro'

ESSEX.

I.	Thomas McKee	Sandwich
II.	Alanson Bottsford	Amherstburg
III.	James King	Kingsville
IV.	G. Buchanan	Colchester
V.	Jonathan Wigfield	Mersea
VI.	Francis Graham	Rochester
VII.	James L. G. Elliott	Windsor

FRONTENAC.

I.	John Duff	Kingston
II.	P. McKim	Cataraqui
III.	Edward Upham	Sydenham
IV.	Samuel Stewart	Harrowsmith
V.	D. J. Walker	Inverary

GREY.

I.	Chas. R. Wilkes	Owen Sound
II.	Wm. Jackson	Durham
III.	Thos. Plunkett	Meaford
IV.	Thomas J. Rourke	Collingwood
V.	John W. Armstrong	Proton
VI.	Henry Cardwell	Chatsworth

HASTINGS.

I.	Robert C. Hulme	Belleville
II.	P. C. Ketcheson	Sidney
III.	Hiram Holden	Shannonville
IV.	Robert McCammon	Tweed
V.	William Judd	Stirling
VI.	George D. Rawe	Hastings
VII.	J. J. Ryan	East Moira
VIII.	John Tulloh	Canniftom
IX.	Jeremiah Simmons	Trenton
X.	Benjamin Beddome	Marmora
XI.	James Mairs	Bridgewater

HALDIMAND.

I.	James Aldridge	Caledonia
II.	G. S. Cotter, jun.	Cayuga
III.	John Armour	Dunnville
IV.	I. Honsberger	Rainham
V.	Seth K. Smith	Canborough
VI.	Chas. E. Bourne	Nanticoke

HALTON.

I.	John Holgate	Milton
II.	Robert Balmer	Oakville
III.	Robert Young	Georgetown
IV.	James Matthews	Acton
V.	S. R. Lister	Nassagaweya
VI.	Robert Miller	Nelson

HURON.

I.	P. A. McDougall	Goderich
II.	Ludwig Mayor	Seaforth
III.	Thomas Trivitt	Exeter
IV.	John Cooke	Dungannon
V.	David H. Ritchie	Bayfield
VI.	W. W. Farran	Clinton
VII.	Benjamin Fralick	Ainleyville and Wroxeter alternately

KENT.

I.	Jas. Sheriff	Chatham
II.	J. Duck	Morpeth
III.	D. Wallace	Dawn Mills
IV.	G. Young	Harwich
V.	John Lillie, jun.	Wallaceburgh
VI.	J. Taylor	Bothwell

LAMBTON.

I.	P. T. Poussett	Sarnia
II.	J. F. Elliott	Warwick
III.	William Webster	Florence
IV.	P. Cattanach	Sombra
V.	Thomas R. Scott	Hillsboro'
VI.	T. Kirkpatrick	Widder Station
VII.	Robert Dale	Moore town
VIII.	Robert Fuller	Petrolia
IX.	John W. Branan	Alvinston

DIVISION COURT CLERKS—(*Continued.*)

LANARK.

I. Robert Moffatt................Perth
II. Wm. Robertson..............Lanark
III. James C. Poole..............Carleton Place
IV. R. Harper.................. ....Smith's Fall
V. R. H. Davie....................Pakenham
VI. John Patterson... ....Ramsay

LEEDS AND GRENVILLE

I. John B. Jones ....Brockville
II. Thos. Harrison ....Prescott
III. S. McCammon......... ....Gananoque
IV. Robert Leslie.................Kemptville
V. Michael Kelly.................Merrickville
VI. W. H. Denaut.................Delta
VII. Hiram McCrea... ....Frankville
VIII. Horace Kilborn . ...Newboro'
IX. David Mansell... ....Farmersville
X. Thos. Robertson..............Spencerville
XI. Warren Lyman........ ......N. Augusta
XII. Alfred A. Munro ....Mallorytown

LENNOX AND ADDINGTON.

I. Charles James .. ..Napanee
II. John D. Noble................Bath
III. Edwin Mallory...... ....Parma
IV. Isaac J. Lockwood............Newburg
V. Wm. Whelan.................Centreville
VI. Henry Pultz... ....Wilton
VII. Charles Skene.................Emerald
VIII. Donald Cameron..............Tamworth

LINCOLN.

I. ....:...............................Niagara
II. W. A. Mittleberger.........St. Catharines
III. Clark Snure....................Jordan
IV. John C. Kerr...................Beamsville
V. Robert Thompson...... .....Smithville
VI. Thomas Pearson..............Abington, Caistor
VII. George Secord.................St. Anns, Gainsb'ro

MIDDLESEX.

I. John C. Meredith...........London
II. Gustavus G. Hamilton......Nairn
III. John Flanagan ....Lucan
IV. W. F. Bullen.................Delaware
V. Andrew Wilson..............Wardsville
VI. Joseph Small.................Strathroy
VII. H. Le Lievre...................Draney's Corners
VIII. W. B. Bernard........... ..St. John's

NORFOLK.

I. Edmund Jackson ... .Simcoe
II. Edward Matthews...... .....Waterford
III. D. W. Freeman..... ....Simcoe
IV. C. S. Harris.....................Courtland
V. W. Hewett......................Vittoria
VI. S. P. Mabee.....................Port Rowan
VII. T. Chamberlin ....Houghton Centre
VIII. Samuel Gamble ....Port Dover

NORTHUMBERLAND AND DURHAM.

I. Charles Clark, sen........... Bowmanville
II. Samuel Wilmot .. ..Newcastle
III. William Shepherd............Port Hope
IV. William Turner...............Millbrook
V. James Auston..................Cobourg
VI. James G. Rogers............. Grafton
VII. William Johnstone............Colborne
VIII. George S. Burrell............Brighton
IX. John Douglas.................Warkworth
X. Manson B. Weaver............Murray
XI. Daniel Kennedy.. ....Campbellford
XII. Sidney Scobbel...............Cartwright

ONTARIO.

I. D. C. Macdonell..............Whitby
II. Joseph Wilson..................Pickering
III. Harris Burnham................Port Perry
IV. Joseph Dickey.............. ...Uxbridge
V. Robert E. Lund.............Canington
VI. C. Robinson.....................Beaverton
VII. Henry E. O'Dell............Atherley

OXFORD.

I. ....Woodstock
II. William H. Landon.........Princeton
III. Donald Matheson... ....Embro
IV. James Barr.... ....Norwichville
V. David Canfield ....Ingersoll
VI. Charles Hawkins ....Tilsonburg

PEEL.

I. T. A. Agar..................... Brampton
II. A. Simpson.......................Streetsville
III. John Harris.......................Charleston
IV. L. R. Bolton......... ....Bolton Village
V. M. E. Brougham........ ......Grahamsville

PERTH.

I. David B. Burritt ....Stratford
II. Thomas Mathieson...........Mitchell
III. J. Coleman ....St. Mary's
IV. George Brown...................Shakespeare
V. Samuel Whaley...............West's Corners
VI. D. D. Hay .... Listowel

PETERBOROUGH.

I. John J. Hall.... ....Peterboro'
II. John A. Butterfield..........Norwood
III. Thomas Campbell.............Keene
IV. S. S. Peck ....Minden
V. Samuel Sherin..................Lakefield

PRESCOTT AND RUSSELL.

I. John Millar .. . .L'Orignal
II. William McRae..............Vankleekhill
III. A. MacBean ....East Hawkesbury
IV. James Von Bridger ....Plantagenet
V. Farquhar McRae..............Cumberland
VI. James Keays ....Russell
VII. Thomas White................Hawkesbury
VIII. Henry Bradley..................Caledonia

PRINCE EDWARD.

I. John P. Downes ....Picton
II. James Cook............. .. ..Milford
III. Samuel Solmes.................Northport
IV. Edward Roblin.................Roblin's Mills
V. William Young.................Wellington
VI. Harvey Spafford...............Cherry Valley
VII. Joshua M. Cadman...........Consecon
VIII. Richard Hill.....................Bongard's Corners

RENFREW.

I. Andrew Irving ....Pembroke
II. William Cannon..............Beachburgh
III. William Halfpenny...........Renfrew
IV. G. E. Neilson........ ....Arnprior
V. John Halliday .. .. Bagot
VI. S. G. Lynn.......................Eganville
VII. John Rankin ....Cob len
VIII. Joseph Kinder ....Brudenell Corners

SIMCOE.

I. Thomas Lloyd ....Barrie
II. Thomas McConchy ....Bradford
III. F. S. Stephens...............Tecumseth
IV. A. Jardine ....Nottawasaga Mills
V. John Craig ....Craighurst
VI. Thomas Dallas..................Orillia
VII. William Little ....Mulmur
VIII. George McManus ... .Mono Mills
IX. H. E. Jeffery ... .Penetanguishene

DIVISION COURT CLERKS—(*Continued.*)

STORMONT, DUNDAS AND GLENGARY.

I.	Archibald Fraser	Williamstown
II.	C. D. Chisholm	Alexandria
III.	Charles Poole	Cornwall
IV.	J. Bockus	Dickinson's Landg
V.	John W. Loucks	Morrisburg
VI.	John S. Ross	Iroquois
VII.	William J. Ridley	Mountain
VIII.	John A. Cockburn	Berwick
XI.	Peter Stuart	Lancaster
X.	William Rae	Winchester
XI.	D. McIntosh	Roxborough
XII.	John A. Macdougall	Kenyon

VICTORIA.

I.	George W. Miller	Woodville
II.	John C. Fitzgerald	Fenelon Falls
III.	W. B. Reid	Bobcaygeon
IV.	T. Matchett	Omemee
V.	James McKibbon	Lindsay
VI.	William Taylor	Oakwood

WATERLOO.

I.	A. J. Peterson	Berlin
II.	Otto Klotz	Preston
III.	Peter Keefer	Galt
IV.	John Wyllie	Ayr
V.	John Allchin	New Hamburg
VI.	M. P. Empey	Hawkesville
VII.	John L. Wideman	St. Jacobs

WELLAND.

I.	Alfred Willett	Welland
II.	S. S. Hagar	Wainfleet, Welland
III.	Thomas Newbigging	Fort Erie
IV.	J. A. Orchard	Drummondville
V.	George Keefer	Thorold

WELLINGTON.

I.	A. A. Baker	Guelph
II.	William Leslie	Puslinch
III.	William McCarthy	Rockwood
IV.	Alexander Cadenhead	Fergus
V.	William Tyler	Erin
VI.	John McLean	Elora
VII.	George Allan	Allansville
VIII.	C. O'Callaghan	Arthur
IX.	Guy Leslie	Orangeville
X.	Henry C. Kaya	Harriston
XI.	James C. Wilkes	Mount Forest
XII.	Edgar N. Tuck	Drayton

WENTWORTH.

I.	William Griffin	Hamilton
II.	Alexis F. Begue	Dundas
III.	J. McMonies, jun	Watertown
IV.	W. McDonald	Rockton
V.	John J. Bradley	Stoney Creek
VI.	L. A. Gurnett	Ancaster
VII.	John Atkinson	Glanford
VIII.	Henry Hall	Hall's Corners

YORK.

I.	Allan Howard	Toronto
II.	J. J. M. Barker	Markham
III.	J. M. Lawrence	Richmond Hill
IV.	John Cook	Newmarket
V.	William Fry	Sutton
VI.	Arthur Armstrong	Lloydtown
VII.	D. McCallum	Burwick
VIII.	John Paul	Weston
IX.	W. H. Norris	Scarboro'

REGISTRARS OF THE PROVINCE OF ONTARIO.

COUNTIES, ETC.	REGISTRARS.	COUNTIES, ETC.	REGISTRARS.
Algoma District	John Savage, Sault Ste. Marie.	London, City	W. C. L. Gill, London
Brant	T. H. Shenston, Brantford.	Middlesex	James Ferguson, London
Bruce	John McLay, Walkerton.	Norfolk	F. L. Walsh, Simcoe
Carleton	E. Sherwood, Ottawa.	Northum, E. R	J. M. Grover, Colborne
Dundas	J. P. Crysler, Morrisburg.	" W. R	William Eyre, Cobourg
Durham, E. R	Geo. M. Ward, Port Hope.	Ontario	William Paxton, jun., Whitby
" W. R	Robt. Armour, Bowmanville.	Ottawa, City	Alexander Burritt, Ottawa
Elgin	John McKay, St. Thomas.	Oxford	James Ingersoll, Woodstock
Essex	J. A. Askin, Sandwich.	Peel	D. F. Campbell, Brampton
Frontenac	James Durand, Kingston.	Perth	William Smith, Stratford
Glengarry	Alex. McKenzie, Alexandria.	Peterborough	Charles Rubidge, Peterboro'
Grenville	W. J. Scott, Prescott.	Prescott	John Higginson, L'Orignal
Grey	Thomas. Lunn, Owen Sound.	Prince Edward	J. B. Roblin, Picton
Haldimand	A. P. Farrell, Cayuga.	Renfrew	Andrew Irving, Pembroke
Halton	Thomas Racey. Milton.	Russell	James Keays, Russell
Hastings	W. H. Ponton, Bellevelle.	Simcoe	George Lount, Barrie
Huron	James Dickson, Goderich	Stormont	George C. Wood, Cornwall
Kingston, City	Geo. A. Cumming, Kingston	Toronto (City	Charles Lindsey, Toronto
Kent	P. D. McKellar, Chatham	Victoria	H. Dunsford, Lindsay
Lambton	T. W. Johnston, Sarnia	Waterloo	D. McDougall, Berlin
Lanark, N. R	John Menzies, Perth	Welland	D. D'Everardo, Fonthill
" S. R.	James Bell, Perth	Wellington	James Webster, Guelph
Leeds	Ormond Jones, Brockville	Wentworth	John H. Greer, Hamilton
Lennox & Addington	M. P. Roblin, Napanee	York, S. R	John Ridout, Toronto
Lincoln	John Powell, St. Catharines	York, N. R	James J. [illegible], Newmarket

COUNTY AND JUDICIAL OFFICERS—ONTARIO.

COUNTIES AND	CO. TOWNS.	TREASURERS.	COUNTY CLERKS.	CO. ATTORNEYS.	CO. JUDGES, &C.	SHERIFFS.	CL'KS OF PEACE.	CL'KS. CO. CT. & DEP. CLK. OF CR.	RGS. SURROGATE
Algoma Dist.	Sault S Marie	Richard Carney.		J. M. Hamilton	Hon. J. Prince.	R. Carney	J. M. Hamilton	Henry Pilgrim.	Henry Pilgrim.
Brant	Brantford	C. R. Biggar	John Cameron	G. R. VanNorman	S. J. Jones	John Smith	John Cameron	W. B. Rubidge	W. B. Rubidge.
Bruce	Walkerton	Alex. Sproat	George Gould	Donald W. Ross	J. J. Kingsmill.	Wm. Sutton	D. W. Ross	William Gunn	William Gunn.
Carleton	Ottawa	Z. Wilson	E. Bearman	R. Lees	C. Armstrong	W. F. Powell	R. Lees	James Fraser	James Fraser.
Elgin	St. Thomas	Geo. T. Claris	William McKay	James Stanton	D. J. Hughes	Colin Munroe	James Farley	T. D. Warren	T. D. Warren.
Essex	Sandwich	Thos H Wright	Thomas McKee	S. S. Macdonell	G. W. Leggatt.	John McEwen	Charles Baby	D. A. McMullin	D. A. McMullin
Frontenac	Kingston	John Irvine	John Craig	A. F. Kirkpatrick	W. G. Draper	Wm. Ferguson	A. Kirkpatrick.	P. O'Reilly	P. O'Reilly.
Grey	Owen Sound	Fred. LePan	Geo. J. Gale	John Creasor, jr.	H. Macpherson.	J. Maughan	W. Armstrong	P. Inglis	P. Inglis.
Haldimand	Cayuga	A. P. Farrell	F. Stevenson	J. R. Martin	J G. Stevenson	R. Martin	J. R. Martin	R. V. Griffith	R. V. Griffith.
Halton	Milton	F. McCallum	W. Panton	John Dewar, jr	Thomas Miller.	G. C. McKindsey.	John Dewer, jr.	W. L. P. Eager	W. L. P. Eager.
Hastings	Belleville	F. McAnnany	Thomas Wills	C. L. Coleman	Geo. Sherwood	Geo. Taylor	C. L. Coleman.	A. G. Northrup	A. G. Northrup
Huron	Goderich	A. M. Ross	P. Adamson	Ira Lewis	Secker Brough	John McDonald	D. Lizars	Hugh Johnston	Hugh Johnston
Kent	Chatham	C. G. Charteris	James Hart	W. Douglas	W. B. Wells	John Mercer	W. Douglas	T. A. Ireland	Geo Williams.
Lambton	Sarnia	Hon Alex. Vidal	Hugh Smith	J. P. Bucke	C. Robinson	James Flintoft	P. T. Poussett.	J. R. Gemmill	J. R. Gemmill.
Lanark	Perth	Wm. Fraser	W. R. F. Berford	D. Fraser	J. G. Malloch	James Thompson.	W R. F. Berford	Charles Rice	Charles Rice.
Leeds and Grenville	Brockville	J. L. Schofield	James Jessup	E. J. Senkler, jr.	Geo. Malloch	F. G. Dickinson	James Jessup	S. Reynolds, jr.	James Jessup.
Lennox and Addington.	Napanee	E. Hooper	W. V. Detlor	W. H. Wilkinson	J. J. Burrowes.	O. T. Pruyn	W H. Wilkinson	J. B. McGuin	J. B. McGuin.
Lincoln	St. Catherines	G. P. M. Ball	F. A. B. Clench	R. Macdonald	J. M. Lawder	J. A. Woodruff	R. Macdonald	F. A. B. Clench	Chas. B. Secord
Middlesex	London	Adam Murray	James Keefer	C. Hutchinson	J. E. Small	W. Glass	J. B. Askin	John McBeth	John McBeth.
Norfolk	Simcoe	Henry Groff	J. Ermatinger	H. A. Hardy	W. M. Wilson	E. Deedes	H. A. Hardy	C. P. Rapelje	C. P. Rapelje.
Northum & Durham	Cobourg	A. A. Burnham	E. Macnachtan	J. D. Armour	J. M. Boswell	R. N. Waddell	J. D. Armour	R D Chatterton	M F Whitehead
Ontario	Whitby	Wm. Paxton, jr	H. J. Macdonell	S. H. Cochrane	Z. Burnham	N. G. Reynolds	H. J. Macdonell	J. V. Ham	J. V. Ham.
Oxford	Woodstock	James Kintrea	David White	F. R. Ball	D. S. McQueen.	Andrew Ross	F. R. Ball	James Kintrea	James Kintrea.
Peel	Brampton	Geo. Graham	W. Lindsey	George Green	A. F. Scott	Robert Broddy	George Green	J. A. Austin	J. A. Austin.
Perth	Stratford	A. Monteith	S. Campbell	M. Hayes	D. H. Lizars	R. Moderwell		Jas. McFadden.	Jas. McFadden.
Peterboro'	Peterboro'	W. Sheridan	E. Pearse	C. A. Weller	R. Dennistoun	James Hall	C. A. Weller	Thomas Fortye.	Thomas Fortye.
Prescott & Russell	L'Orignal	J. W. Marston	Peter O'Brian	E. T. Dartnell	James Daniell	C. P. Treadwell	E. T. Dartnell	J. W. Marston.	J. W. Marston.
Pr. Edward	Picton	R. J. Chapman	Robert Boyle	P. Low	D. L. Fairfield	H. J. Thorp	P. Low	John Twigg	John Twigg.
Renfrew	Pembroke	Andrew Irving	John Hickey	W. Duck	John Deacon	James Morris	Wm. Luck	A. Thompson	A. Thompson.
Simcoe	Barrie	H. R. A. Boys	R. T. Banting	J. R. Cotter	J. R. Gowan	B. W. Smith	W. B. McVity.	Jonathan Lane.	J. Lane.
Stormont, Dundas and Glengarry	Cornwall	R. McDonald	G. S. Jarvis, jr.	James Bethune	Geo. S. Jarvis.	D. E. McIntyre	James Bethune.	R. McDonald	R. McDonald.
Victoria	Lindsay	S. C. Wood	S. C. Wood	A. LaCourse	James Smith	N. McDougall	A. LaCourse	W. Grace	W. Grace.
Waterloo	Berlin	Charles Stanton	I. D. Bowman	W. H. Bowlby	Wm. Miller	Geo. Davidson	W. H. Bowlby.	J. Colquhoun	A. J. Peterson.
Welland	Welland	Jas. McGlashan	D. D'Everardo	L. D. Raymond	H. W. Price	Robert Hobson	L. D. Raymond	I. P. Willson	D. D'Everardo.
Wellington	Guelph	Wm. Hewat	A. D. Ferrier	H. W. Petersen	A. McDonald	Geo. J. Grange	T. Saunders	James Hough	Thos Keating.
Wentworth	Hamilton	Jas Kirkpatrick	G. S. Counsell	S. B. Freeman	A. Logie	E. C. Thomas	S. B. Freeman	S. H. Ghent	George Rolph.
York	Toronto	John Macdonald	John Elliott	John McNab		F. W. Jarvis	John McNab	W. McKenzie	Hon. W. Cayley

POST OFFICE DEPARTMENT—DOMINION OF CANADA.

GENERAL POST OFFICE.

Postmaster General, Hon. Alexander Campbell; Deputy Postmaster General, Wm. H. Griffin; Accountant, H. A. Wicksteed; Secretary, Wm. White; Superintendent Money Order Branch, P. Le Sueur; Superindent Savings Bank Branch, J. C. Stewart; Cashier, John Ashworth. Clerks of First Class, E. C. Hayden, R. Oliver, H. S. Weatherly, J. T. McCuaig, J. Audette, C. W. Jenkins, W. H. Smithson, Wm. D. LeSueur. Clerks of Second Class, J. Brophy, J. Boyd, E. H. Benjamin, B. King, G. H. Hargrave, H. J. Garrett, W. S. Thomas, D. Matheson.

Ocean Mail Service—Book-keeper, Robert Sinclair.

Law and Bill Stamp Branch—Book-keeper, C. Roger.

Inspection Branch—Arthur Woodgate, Nova Scotia Division, Halifax; John McMillan, New Brunswick Division, Fredericton; W. G. Sheppard. Quebec Division, Quebec; E. F. King, Montreal Division, Montreal; M. Sweetnam, Kingston Division, Kingston; John Dewe, Toronto Division, Toronto; G. E. Griffin, London Division, London.

LETTER RATES.

Letters posted in Canada addressed to any place within the Dominion pass, if pre-paid, for 3 cents per ½oz., but if posted unpaid such letters are charged 5 cents per ½oz.

On letters to Prince Edward's Island, the rate is 3 cents per ½oz., if prepaid, 5 cents if unpaid.

The rate on Letters to the United Kingdom is, by Canadian Packet, sailing from Quebec, Portland, or Halifax,

Not exceeding ½oz .... 12½ cents.
Exceeding " and not exceeding 1 oz... 25 "
and so on, increasing one rate of postage for each additional half ounce.

And by Cunard Packet, 15 cents per ½oz, &c.

Letters for the United Kingdom must be prepaid, or they will be charged a fine of 6d. sterling on delivery.

Letters for British Colonies and Possessions beyond Sea, and Foreign Countries, via England, must be prepaid.

The rate on Letters for the United States is 6 cents per ½ oz.

The rate on Letters to Cuba is 10 cents per ½oz.

United States Letters 6 cents, if prepaid, 10 cents if unpaid.

The rate of postage on letters to British Columbia and Vancouver's Island is 10 cents per ½oz., which must be prepaid. An additional charge is made on these letters on delivery, for sea postage on the Pacific side. Newspapers 2 cents each, Books 4 cents per 4 oz.

Red River Letters 6 cents per ½oz; newspapers 2 cents each, or commuted rate if from Red River to regular subscribers in Canada.

MAILS FOR CANADA FROM ENGLAND.

Two Ocean Steamers carrying mails for Canada leave Liverpool in each week, viz.: a Canadian Packet on every Thursday, *via* Derry on Friday, sailing to Quebec in summer and Portland in winter, by which the postage rate is 6d. stg. per ½ oz.; and a Cunard Packet every Saturday, *via* Cork on Sunday, bringing Mails for Canada to New York, by which the postage rate to Canada is 7d. stg. per ½ oz.

A Canadian Packet leaves Liverpool every alternate Saturday for Halifax, calling at Queenstown *en route*. Postage 6d. stg. per ½ oz., same as by Canadian Packet to Quebec or Portland.

The British Post Office forwards letters to Canada by the first packet sailing after the letter is posted, unless the letters bear a special direction—"By Canadian Packet" or "By British Packet"—and in that case they are kept over for the Packet designated. "By Canadian Mail" is not a distinctive superscription; for any Mail for Canada is a "Canadian Mail," by whatever Packet forwarded.

WEST INDIES VIA NEW YORK.

West Indies (British) letters 10 cents per ½ oz.; newspapers 2 cents each. (Foreign) letters, 22 cents per ½ oz.; newspapers 3 cents each. Books (British only) 2 cents per 4 oz.

Letters, &c., prepaid for transmission, *via* New York, are forwarded direct on New York with every mail made up for that Post Office; whence West Indian mails are despatched as follows:

For Havana and the West Indies, *via* Havana, every Thursday afternoon.

For St. Thomas, the West Indies, and Brazil, on the 23rd of every month.

Letters for the West Indies, British and Foreign, are also sent *via* Halifax and Bermuda; postage 12 cents per ½ oz.; newspapers 2 cents each.

REGISTRATION OF LETTERS.

Persons posting letters containing value, should be careful to require them to be registered, and to obtain from the Postmaster a certificate of receipt for Registration.

The charge for Registration, in addition to the Postage, is as follows, viz.:

On Letters to any other place in Canada, or British North America .... 2 cents.
On Letters for the United States................ 5 "
On Letters for the United Kingdom .... 8 "
On Letters for British Colonies or Possessions, sent *via* England.........................25 "
On Letters to France and other Foreign Countries, *via* France, an amount equal to the postage rate.
On parcels, patterns or samples, in Canada, 5 cents.
On book packets and newspapers to United Kingdom, 8 cents.

Both the postage charge and registration fee must in all cases be prepaid.

Registration is not an absolute guarantee against the miscarriage or loss of a Letter; but a Registered Letter can be traced when an Unregistered Letter cannot, and the posting and delivery or non-delivery can be proven. A Registered Letter is thus secured against many of the casualties which, from incorrect address, forgetfulness of the receiver, or other error, may affect an Unregistered Letter.

BOOK POST WITH GREAT BRITAIN, BY CANADIAN PACKET FROM QUEBEC OR HALIFAX.

A Packet weighing not more than 4 oz...... 7 cents
Above 4 oz. but not exceeding 8 oz.......... 12½ "
" 8 oz. " " 12 oz.......... 19 "
" 12 oz. " " 1 lb.......... 25 "
and so on, adding 7 cents for every additional 4 oz.

BY CUNARD PACKET FROM NEW YORK.

A Packet weighing not more than 4 oz...... 9 cents
Above 4 oz. but not exceeding 8 oz.......... 17 "
" 8 oz. " " 12 oz.......... 25 "
" 12 oz. " " 1 lb.......... 33 "
and so on, adding 9 cents for every additional 4 oz.

BOOK POST RATES BETWEEN CANADA, FRANCE, ITALY, GERMAN STATES AND NETHERLANDS.

COUNTRY.	Not exced'g 2 oz.	2 oz. to 4 oz.	4 oz. to 8 oz.	8 oz. to 1 lb.	1 lb. to 1½ lb.	1½ lb. to 2 lb.
	cts.	cts.	cts.	cts.	cts.	cts.
France............	5	10	20	40	60	80
Italy..............	6	18	25	38	50	63
German States.....	6	18	25	50	75	100
Netherlands.......	5	10	17	34	50	67

These rates must invariably be *prepaid* on transmission from Canada. Photographs, *provided they they are not upon glass or in cases containing glass*, may he forwarded to Great Britain, etc., at the *Book rate of postage*. Book Packets addressed to the United Kingdom may be registered on payment of the ordinary registration fee, viz., 8 cents in addition to the postage.

All book packets must be open at *both ends* or *both sides* to allow the inspection of the contents.

MISCELLANEOUS CHARGES.

The charge on Parcels by the Parcel Post, which is limited to places within the Dominion, is 12½ cents per 8 oz. (with 5 cents additional if registered).

One cent per oz., payable in advance by Postage Stamp, is the rate on Printed Circulars (Printed Circulars, if sent in envelopes, whether *sealed* or *unsealed* are liable to letter postage), Prices Current, Hand Bills, and other printed Matter of a like character, and on books, bound or unbound, when posted at a Canadian Post Office, and addressed to any place in the Dominion of Canada, British North America generally, or the United States.

The postage upon Prices Current addressed to the United Kingdom is *two cents each*, which must be prepaid by postage stamps, or they will be sent to the Dead Letter Office, to be returned to the senders.

NEWSPAPERS AND PERIODICALS.

Newspapers published in Canada may be sent by Post from the office of publication, addressed to any place in Canada, at the following rates, *if paid quarterly in advance* by either the publisher at the post office where the papers are posted, or by the subscriber at the delivering post office :

For a paper published 6 times a week, 30 cts. per qr.
" " 3 " 15 " "
" " 2 " 10 " "
" " 1 " 5 " "

When the above rates are not paid in advance by either publisher or subscriber, such Papers are charged one cent each on delivery.

TRANSIENT NEWSPAPERS.

Transient Newspapers—that is to say, Canadian Newspapers posted otherwise than from the office of publication, and American or British papers posted or re-posted in Canada, must be prepaid 2 cents each, by postage stamp, or they cannot be forwarded—except only *British Newspapers* distributed to regular subscribers by Canadian booksellers or News Agents—such papers pass free as they would do if received in the Canadian Packet Mails.

NEWSPAPERS BY MAIL FROM ENGLAND OR UNITED STATES.

Newspapers received from England by the Canadian Packet Mails are delivered free

Newspapers from England by the Cunard Packet Mails are charged 2 cents each for delivery. (This is the American transit charge).

United States Newspapers brought by Mail into Canada, to regular subscribers, are charged one cent each on delivery, transient papers 2 cents each.

PERIODICAL PUBLICATIONS.

The rate on all Periodicals other than Newspapers, passing by mail in Canada, save such as may be addressed to or received from the United Kingdom, is one cent per 4 oz. weight of package containing periodical matter, whether the package contain one or more numbers.

Any fraction of 4 oz. to be charged as a full rate.

After the 31st December, 1868, no periodicals whatever, except exchanges, (*i. e.* periodicals passing between publishers in Canada, and between publishers in Canada and publishers in the United States, Prince Edward Island, or Newfoundand) will be entitled to exemption from postage.

Transient Periodical matter posted in Canada must in all cases be prepaid by postage stamp.

The above rate will be payable on delivery on all periodical matter received from the United States, except that Canadian editors may receive exchange periodicals from the United States free of Canadian postage.

Periodicals, printed and published in Canada, may be posted addressed to any place in the United Kingdom by Canadian packet, on prepayment by postage stamp of two cents each number.

No package of periodicals can be sent through the post, if it exceed 4 lb. in weight.

POSTAGE RATES ON MISCELLANEOUS MATTER.

Patterns or samples of merchandise and goods for sale, not exceeding 24 oz. in weight, may be posted in Canada to be forwarded to any place within the Dominion, on prepayment by postage stamp of a rate of 1 cent per ounce, under the following regulations :

Patterns or samples must be sent in covers open at the ends, so as to be easy of examination. Samples however of seeds, drugs, and so forth, which cannot be sent in open covers, may be enclosed in bags of linen or other material, fastened in such a manner that they may be readily opened ; or in bags entirely closed, provided that they be transparent, so that the officers of the Post Office may be able to satisfy themselves as to the nature of the contents.

The packet may bear on the *outside* the address of the sender, in addition to the address of the person for whom it may be intended ; also a trade mark and numbers, and the price of the article enclosed ; *inside*, there must be no enclosures but the samples or patterns themselves ; the particulars however of the trade marks, numbers and price, may be marked on the articles themselves, instead of on the outside of the packet, at the option of the sender.

Any sample or pattern packet containing a letter, or otherwise violating the conditions of the preceding rules, will be rated and treated as a letter.

The rate of one cent per ounce is to be prepaid by postage stamp, and if such rate be not fully pre-paid by the stamps affixed, the packet is to be rated with the deficient postage and a fine of five cents in addition.

Packets of samples and patterns may be registered on pre-payment by postage stamp of a registration fee of five cents in addition to the postage rate, and provided such packets be duly handed in to the post office for registration.

No packet of samples or patterns must exceed 24 ounces.

These regulations apply only to the transmission of Packets or samples and patterns within the Dominion of Canada, and will not in any manner interfere with the regulations governing the exchange of samples and patterns with the United Kingdom, or with the foreign countries to which the same advantage extends namely, France, Belgium, Italy, German States, Netherlands, Portugal, Switzerland, and Denmark.

No provision as yet exists for the exchange of such matter with the other British Colonies, with the U.S. or with other foreign countries than those above named.

Book and newspaper manuscript, and printers' proof-sheets (whether corrected or not), maps, prints, drawings, engravings, photographs when not on glass or in cases containing glass, and sheet music (whether printed or written), may pass in covers open at the ends or sides, and provided that no letter, or other communication intended to serve the purpose of a letter, be enclosed therein, on pre-payment, when posted in Canada, by postage stamp of the ordinary printed matter rate of one cent per ounce; or upon payment of that rate on delivery of such matter when received in the mails from the United States.

POSTAGE OF BOOKS, PATTERNS AND SAMPLES.

Patterns of merchandise, and samples, may be forwarded between the United Kingdom, France, Italy, German States, Netherlands, Portugal, Switzerland, and Denmark, by the Canadian Packet Mails, at book post rates, and subject to the following conditions:

There must be no writing or printing other than the address of the person for whom the packet is intended, the manufacturer's or trade mark and number and price of the article.

Any infringment of the above regulations will render the packet liable to be treated and charged as a letter.

Samples of seeds, drugs, and similar articles intended for delivery within the United Kingdom, are now allowed to be sent in bags entirely closed, provided such bags be transparent, so that the officers of the Post-office may be able to satisfy themselves of the contents.

The rule which prohibited the transmission through the Post, as patterns of articles of cutlery, &c., has been recinded: and scissors, knives, razors, forks, steel pens, nails, keys, watch machinery, metal-tubing, pieces of metal or ore, and such like articles, are now allowed to be forwarded by the Post as samples, provided they be packed and guarded in so secure a manner as to afford complete protection to the contents of the mail bags, and to the persons of the officers of the Post-office. Such articles, however, must be so packed that they may be easily examined; and it is made a rule that any packet containing such articles, which may be found to be insufficiently guarded, shall not be forwarded through the Post.

None of the articles named in the next preceding paragraph may be sent as patterns or samples to any place abroad, except Germany, Belgium, and the British Colonies, and not to these places when addressed *via* France.

PATTERNS, LIMIT OF SIZE AND WEIGHT.

The limits of weight and size are as follows:

If for Canada, 24 oz.; the United Kingdom, 24 oz; France, 36 oz.; Germany, 8 oz.; the Kingdom of Italy 36 oz.; Belgium, 8 oz.; the Netherlands, 16 oz.; Portugal, 16 oz.; the Azores, 16 oz.; Madeira, 16 oz; Denmark, 48 oz.; Switzerland, 48 oz.

If for Canada or the United Kingdom, 24 inches in length and 12 inches in breadth or depth. If for France, Portugal, the Azores, or Madeira, 18 inches in length and 12 inches in breadth or depth. If for Germany, the Kingdom of Italy, Belgium, the Netherlands, Denmark, or Switzerland, 24 inches in length and 12 inches in breadth or depth.

Any infringement of the conditions laid down as above will render the package liable to be treated and charged as a letter.

Bags entirely closed, even though they may be transparent, must not be used for the transmission of seeds to foreign parts.

No prints or printed matter will be allowed to pass by book post between the United Kingdon and Canada unless printed on paper, parchment or vellum.

MONEY ORDERS IN ONTARIO AND QUEBEC.

All the Money Order Post Offices in Ontario, Quebec and New Brunswick are authorized to draw Money Orders on each other for any sum up to $100, and for as many orders of $100 each as the Applicant may require, upon the following terms, viz.:—in Ontario and Quebec,

On Orders up to		$10	5 cents.
Over $10 and up to		$20	10 "
" 20	"	40	20 "
" 40	"	60	30 "
" 60	"	80	40 "
" 80	"	100	50 "

In New Brunswick, the rate of commission is 5c. for each $10 or fraction thereof.

MONEY ORDERS ON THE UNITED KINGDOM.

The Money Order Offices throughout the Dominion also draw upon all the Money Order Offices in England, Ireland and Scotland, and the Channel Islands, for any sum up to £10 sterling, and grant as many Orders for £10 sterling each as may be needed to make up the amount to be remitted. The terms are as under:—

On Orders up to £2		$0 25
"	over £2 and up to £5	0 50
"	over £5 " £7	0 75
"	over £7 " £10	1 00

MONEY ORDERS ON THE LOWER PROVINCES.

The Money Order Offices in Ontario, Quebec and New Brunswick, draw also upon the Money Order Offices in Nova Scotia, Prince Edward Island and Newfoundland. The Orders, like those of the United Kingdom, are made payable in sterling money, and for sums up to £10 sterling. The terms are:—

For Orders up to £5	25 cents.
" over £5 and up to £10	50 "

The Money Order Post Offices are furnished with Lists of all the Money Order Offices in the United Kingdom, Ontario, Quebec, New Brunswick, Nova Scotia, Prince Edward Island and Newfoundland; and the Postmasters are instructed to afford every information in their power, in respect of the places upon which they draw, together with any other information relating to such issues as the intending Remitters may desire.

POST OFFICE SAVINGS BANKS.

The Post Office Savings Banks, established by statute in the last session of Parliament, commenced operations in Ontario and Quebec on the 1st April, 1868.

The direct security of the Dominion is given by the statute for all deposits made.

At each Savings Bank Post Office the regulations may be read by the public, giving full information with respect to the mode of depositing and withdrawing money, and these regulations are printed on the cover of the pass book supplied to each depositor.

Any person may have a deposit account, and deposits are received daily during the ordinary hours of Post Office business, of any number of dollars, from $1 up to $300, the total amount which can be received from a depositor in any one year, except in cases to be specially authorized by the Postmaster General.

The Postmasters of Savings Banks will act as agents for the receipts of the money deposited for transmission to the Postmaster General, and for the payment by the Postmaster General of money withdrawn by depositors.

Each depositor is supplied with a pass book, and the sums paid in, or withdrawn, are entered therein by the Postmaster receiving or paying the same. In addition, a direct receipt for each amount paid in, is sent to the depositor from the Postmaster General, and the Postmaster General will issue a cheque, payable at any Post Office Savings Bank desired, for any sum withdrawn.

Every depositor's account is thus kept with the Postmaster General, and a depositor may pay into his or her account with the Post Office Savings Bank, at any of the Savings Bank Post Offices which at the time may best suit his convenience, and may exercise the same choice in drawing out money, subject only to the obligation of producing the pass book, in proof of identity—whenever paying or drawing out money.

Interest at the rate of 4 per cent. per annum is allowed on deposits lying in the ordinary deposit accounts, but when a depositor has $100 deposited, he or she may request the Postmaster General to transfer this sum to a special account, and will then receive a certificate of such special $100 deposit, bearing interest at 5 per cent per annum.

Postmasters are forbidden by law to disclose the name of any depositor, or the amount of any sum deposited or withdrawn.

No charge will be made to depositors on paying in, or drawing out money, nor for postage on communications with the Postmaster General in relation thereto.

The Postmaster General will be always ready to receive and attend to all applications, complaints, or other communications addressed to him by depositors or others, relative to the Post Office Savings Bank matters.

Additional Post Offices will from time to time be authorized to act as Savings Bank agencies.

POSTAGE STAMPS.

Postage Stamps are provided for sale of the respective values of 2 cents for Newspapers; 2 cents for Prices Current and periodicals for the United Kingdom; 3 cents for ordinary Dominion Letters; 6 cents for United States rate; 12½ cents for Canadian Packet, and 15 cents for Cunard Packet.

PENAL CLAUSES.

To steal, embezzle, secrete or destroy any post letter, shall be felony; punishable in the discretion of the court by imprisonment in the Penitentiary, for not less than three nor more than five years; unless such post letter contains any chattel, money or valuable security, in which case the offence shall be punishable by imprisonment in the Penitentiary for life, or for a period not less than five years.

To steal a post letter bag, or a post letter from a post letter bag, or a post letter from any post office, or from any officer or person employed in the Canada post office, or from a mail—or to stop a mail with intent to rob or search the same—shall be felony; punishable by imprisonment in the Penitentiary for life, or for a period not less than five years.

To open unlawfully any post letter bag—or unlawfully to take any letter out of such bag—shall be felony; punishable by imprisonment in said Penitentiary for five years.

To steal, embezzle or secrete any parcel sent by parcel post, or any article contained in any such parcel, shall be felony; punishable by imprisonment in the Penitentiary for a period of not less than three years.

To receive any post letter, or post letter bag, or any chattel, money or valuable security, parcel or other thing, the stealing, taking, secreting or embezzling whereof is hereby made felony, knowing the same to have been feloniously stolen, taken, secreted or embezzled, shall be felony; punishable by imprisonment in the Penitentiary for any term not less than five years—and the offender may be indicted and convicted either as an accessory after the fact or for a substantive felony, and in the latter case whether the principal felon hath or hath not been previously convicted, or is or is not amenable to justice. And however such receiver be convicted, the offender shall be punishable as aforesaid.

To forge, counterfeit or imitate any postage stamp issued or used under the authority of this act, or by or under the authority of the government or proper authority of the United Kingdom, or of any British North American Province, or of any Foreign Country,—or knowingly to use any such forged, counterfeited or imitated stamp,—or to engrave, cut, sink or make any plate, die, or other thing whereby to forge, counterfeit or imitate such stamp or any part or portion thereof,—or to have possession of any such plate, die or other thing as aforesaid, except by the permission in writing of the Postmaster General, or of some officer or person who, under regulations made in that behalf, may lawfully grant such permission,—or to forge, counterfeit or unlawfully imitate, use or affix, to or upon any letter or packet, any stamp, signature, initials or other mark or sign purporting that such letter or packet ought to pass free of postage, or at a lower rate of postage, or that the postage thereon, or any part thereof, hath been prepaid or ought to be paid by or charged to any person, department or party whomsoever, shall be felony; punishable by imprisonment in the Penitentiary for life, or for a period not less than five years, and to such felony all the provisions of any Act respecting Forgery shall apply as if such offence were made felony under that act, in so far as the provisions thereof are not inconsistent with this act, and the accessories to any such offence shall be punishable accordingly.

To forge, counterfeit or imitate any post office money order, or advice of such money order, or post office savings bank depositor's book, or authority of the Postmaster General for repayment of a post office savings bank deposit, or any part thereof—or any signature or writing in or upon any post office money order, money order advice, post office savings bank depositor's book, or authority of Postmaster General for re-payment of a post office savings bank deposit, or any part thereof, with intent to defraud, shall be a felony; punishable by imprisonment in the penitentiary for any term not less than two years and not exceeding seven years, and the accessories to any such offence shall be punishable accordingly.

To enclose in or with any letter, packet or other mailable matter sent by post, or to put into any post office any explosive, dangerous or destructive substance or liquid, or any matter or thing likely to injure any letter or other mailable matter, or the person of any officer or servant of the post office, shall be a misdemeanour, unless such offence is or shall be by law constituted a crime of greater magnitude.

To enclose a letter or letters, or any writing intended to serve the purpose of a letter, in a parcel posted for the parcel post, or in a packet of samples or patterns posted to pass at the rate of postage applicable to samples and patterns, or to inclose a letter or any writing to serve the purpose of a letter, or to enclose any thing in a newspaper posted to pass as a newspaper, at the rate of postage applicable to newspapers (except in the case of the accounts and receipts of newspaper publishers, which are permitted to pass folded within the newspapers sent by them to their subscribers), or to enclose a letter in any mail matter sent by post not being a letter, shall in each case be an offence punishable by a penalty of not less than ten and not exceeding forty dollars in each case.

To remove, with fraudulent intent, from any letter, newspaper, or other mailable matter, sent by post, any postage stamp which shall have been affixed thereon, or wilfully, with intent aforesaid, remove from any postage stamp which shall have been previously used, any mark which shall have been made thereon at any post office, shall be a misdemeanor.

It shall not be lawful for any person other than a postmaster to exercise the business of selling postage stamps or stamped envelopes to the public, unless duly licensed so to do by the Postmaster General, and under such conditions as he may prescribe; and any person who shall violate this provision by selling postage stamps or stamped envelopes to the public without a license from the Postmaster General, shall, on conviction before a Justice of the Peace, incur a penalty of not exceeding forty dollars for each offence.

If any person wilfully or maliciously injures or destroys any street letter-box, pillar-box, or other receptacle established by authority of the Postmaster General for the deposit of letters or other mailable matter, such person shall, on conviction, be deemed guilty of a misdemeanor, punishable by fine or imprisonment, or both, in the discretion of the court before which the offender is convicted; and every person who aids, abets, counsels or procures the commission of this offence, shall be guilty of a misdemeanor, and be indictable and punishable as a principal offender.

If any person uses, or attempts to use, in prepayment of postage on any letter or mailable matter posted in this Dominion, any postage stamp which has been before used for a like purpose, such person shall be subject to a penalty of not less than ten and not exceeding forty dollars for every such offence, and the letter or other mailable matter on which such stamp has been so improperly used may be detained, or, in the discretion of the Postmaster General, forwarded to its destination, charged with double postage.

SUGGESTIONS TO THE PUBLIC.

Facility will be given to the Post Office in the discharge of its daily duties, and greater security afforded to the Public, by careful attention to the following recommendations:

Post all letters and newspapers, &c., as early as practicable, especially when sent in large numbers.

When a number of newspapers are addressed to the same office, put them up in one parcel.

When a number of circulars are posted, tie them up in a bundle, with the addresses all in one direction.

Address letters, papers, &c., in a legible and complete manner, always giving the name of the Post Office; and if there be more than one Post Office of that name, the name of the county in which situated. In case of letters going abroad, the name of the country as well as of the town and city should be given in full. Letters for example, if intended for London, England, if simply addressed "London," would be forwarded to London, Ontario, and thus be delayed.

Should it be desired to send a letter or newspaper by any particular line of Packets, or by any particular route, the special address should be clearly written *above* the ordinary direction as "By Canadian Packet."

See that every letter, newspaper, or other packet sent by post, is securely folded and sealed. Every such packet has to be several times handled; and even when in the mail bag, is exposed to pressure and friction. Unless, therefore, the article be light and pliant, it should be enclosed in strong paper, linen, parchment or some other material which will not readily tear or break.

Fasten the covers of newspapers firmly, so as to prevent them from slipping out.

When dropping a letter or newspaper into a letter box, always see that the packet falls into the box, and does not stick in its passage.

Never seal letters for the East and West Indies and other hot climates with wax. Such a practice is attended with much inconvenience, and frequently with serious injury, in consequence of the melting of the wax and the adhesion of the letters to each other. In all such cases use either wafers or gum and advise your correspondents in the country referred to, to do the same.

Never send money or other articles of value through the Post Office, except either by means of money-order or in a registered letter. Carefully secure every letter or packet containing money or value, first with gum and afterwards with good sealing-wax, on which make the clear impression of a seal.

On posting a registered letter or packet always obtain a receipt for the same at the office where posted.

When letters or papers are delayed or missing, at once communicate the fact to the Postmaster General or to the Inspector of the division in which is situated the Post Office at which the delayed or missing letters were posted. In case of a missing letter enclosing value, state the exact contents, the exact address, and the office at which posted, and the day and hour on which posted; the name of the person by whom posted, and the name of the person by whom received at the office. In the case of a delayed letter or paper send the cover or wrapper in an entire state in order that the place of delay may be ascertained by an examination of the post marks. State also the office at which posted, and the day and hour on which posted.

Trouble and loss occasionally arise out of the carelessness or dishonesty of parties employed in the Post Office service; yet instances are not wanting in which it has been shown, to the satisfaction even of the complainants, that the fault at first attributed to the Post Office, in truth rested in other quarters. Thefts by private hands, although very difficult of proof, have not unfrequently been brought to light; and it is greatly to be desired that those who suffer loss, should, in the first instance, and while the circumstances are fresh, endeavour to ascertain with the utmost precision all particulars respecting the despatch or receipt of the lost letters or papers, and lose no time in communicating this information to the Inspector. Indeed, generally speaking, it is only by careful inquiry into minute details that the offender can be detected, whether he be a servant of the Department or not.

The Post Office is a Department which admits of constant improvement and expansion. The public, by sending to the Postmaster General, clear and correct information respecting faulty arrangements, may materially benefit the service. It must be remembered, however, that changes in machinery so extensive and intricate as that of the Post Office, must be made cautiously and with much previous consideration.

Time is generally required to carry out any material change in postal arrangements; for even when decided upon, old contracts, requiring notice of termination, may have to be got rid of, and tenders for new contracts invited by public advertisement, before the decision can take effect.

V.  R.

POST OFFICE SAVINGS BANKS—CANADA.

1.—The following Post Office Savings Banks are open daily for the receipt and repayment of deposits, during the ordinary ours of Post Office business.

2.—The direct security of the Dominion is given by the Statute for all deposits made.

3.—Any person may have a deposit account, and may deposit yearly any number of dollars, from $1 up to $300, or more rith the permission of the Postmaster General.

4.—Deposits may be made by married women, and deposits so made, or made by women who shall afterwards marry, will e repaid to any such woman.

5.—As respects children under ten years of age, money may be deposited :

Firstly—By a parent or friend as Trustee for the child, in which case the deposits can be withdrawn by the Trustee until he child shall attain the age of ten years, after which time repayment will be made only on the joint receipts of both Trustee nd child.

Secondly—In the child's own name—and, if so deposited, repayment will not be made until the child shall attain the age of en years.

6.—A depositor in any one of the Savings Bank Post Offices may continue his deposits at any other of such offices without otice or change of Pass-Book, and can withdraw his money at that Savings Bank Office, which is most convenient to him. For instance, if he makes his first deposit at the Savings Bank at Cobourg, he may make further deposits at, or withdraw his noney through, the Post Office Bank at Collingwood or Quebec, Sarnia, Brockville, or any place which may be convenient to im, whether he continue to reside at Cobourg or remove to some other place.

7.—Each depositor is supplied with a Pass Book, which is to be produced to the Postmaster every time the depositor pays n or withdraws money, and the sums paid in or withdrawn are entered therein by the Postmaster receiving or paying the same.

8.—Every depositor's account is kept in the Postmaster General's Office in Ottawa, and, in addition to the Postmaster's eceipt in the Pass Book, a *direct acknowledgment from the Postmaster General for each sum paid in* is sent to the depositor. f this acknowledgment does not reach the depositor within ten days from the date of his deposit, he should apply immeiately to the Postmaster General, by letter, being careful to give his address, and if necessary renew his application until he eceives a satisfactory reply.

9.—When a depositor wishes to withdraw money, he can do so by applying to the Postmaster General, who will send him y return mail a cheque for the amount, payable at whatever Savings Bank Post Office the depositor may have named in his pplication.

10.—Interest at the rate of 4 per cent. per annum is allowed on deposits in the ordinary Pass Book deposit account, and the nterest is added to the principal on the 30th June in each year.

SPECIAL DEPOSIT ACCOUNT.

11.—Any depositor who has $100 at his credit in his Pass Book, or ordinary account, may request the Postmaster General o transfer that sum to a special account, and will then receive from the Postmaster General a certificate of special deposit for ach $100 so transferred. These certificates bear 5 per cent. interest, and are redeemable on such previous notice as may be hereon expressed. When repayment is required, the $100 will be repaid to the depositor at any Savings Bank Post Office which e may name. The interest on certificates of special deposit is placed to the depositor's credit in his ordinary Pass Book ccount, and becomes principal in that account, on the 30th June in each year.

12.—Postmasters are forbidden by law to disclose the name of any depositor, or the amount of any sum deposited or vithdrawn.

13.—No charge is made to depositors on paying in or drawing out money, nor for Pass Books, nor for postage on communiations with the Postmaster General in relation to their deposits.

14.—The Postmaster General is a ways ready to receive and attend to all applications, complaints, or other communications ddressed to him by depositors or others, relative to Post Office Savings Bank business.

15.—A full statement of the Regulations of the Post Office Savings Bank may be seen at any of the Post Offices named in he following List:

Post Office.	County and Province.	Post Office.	County and Province.
.cton Vale	Bagot, Q	Brampton	Peel, O
.lbion	Peel, O	Brantford	Brant, O
.lexandria	Glengary, O	Brighton	Northumberland, O
.lmonte	Lanark, O	Brockville	Leeds, O
.mherstburg	Essex, O	Brooklin	Ontario, O
.rkona	Lambton, O	Buckingham	Ottawa, Q
.rnprior	Renfrew, O	Campbellford	Northumberland, O
.rthur	Wellington, O	Cannington	Ontario, O
.urora	York, O	Carleton Place	Lanark, O
.ylmer, East	Ottawa, Q	Cayuga	Haldimand, O
.ylmer, West	Elgin, O	Chambly Canton	Chambly, Q
.yr	Waterloo, O	Chatham, West	Kent, O
.arrie	Simcoe, O	Chelsea	Ottawa, Q
.ayfield	Huron, O	Chippawa	Welland, O
.eamsville	Lincoln, O	Clarksburg	Grey, O
.eauharnois	Beauharnois, Q	Clifton	Welland, O
.eaverton	Ontario, O	Clinton	Huron, O
.elleville	Hastings, O	Coaticook	Stanstead, Q
.erlin	Waterloo, O	Cobourg	Northumberland, O
.erthier	Berthier, Q	Colborne	Northumberland, O
.lairton	Peterboro, O	Coldwater	Simcoe, O
.ond Head	Simcoe, O	Collingwood	Simcoe, O
.othwell	Kent, O	Compton	Compton, Q
.owmanville	Durham, O	Cookstown	Simcoe, O
.radford	Simcoe, O	Cornwall	Stormont, O

POST OFFICE SAVINGS BANKS—CANADA—(*Continued.*)

Post Office.	County and Province.	Post Office.	County and Province.
Creemore	Simcoe, O	Ottawa	Carleton, O
Danville	Richmond, Q	Owen Sound	Grey, O
Dundas	Wentworth, O	Paisley	Bruce, O
Dunnville	Haldimand, O	Pakenham	Lanark, O
Durham	Grey, O	Paris	Brant, O
Elora	Wellington, O	Pembroke	Renfrew, O
Erin	Wellington, O	Penetanguishene	Simcoe, O
Exeter	Huron, O	Perth	Lanark, O
Fergus	Wellington, O	Peterboro	Peterboro', O
Fingal	Elgin, O	Petrolea	Lambton, O
Frelighsburg	Missisquoi, Q	Picton	Prince Edward, O
Galt	Waterloo, O	Point St. Charles	Jacques Cartier, Q
Gananoque	Leeds, O	Portage du Fort	Pontiac, Q
Georgetown	Halton, O	Port Burwell	Elgin, O
Goderich	Huron, O	Port Colborne	Welland, O
Granby	Shefford, Q	Port Dalhousie	Lincoln, O
Grimsby	Lincoln, O	Port Dover	Norfolk, O
Guelph	Wellington, O	Port Hope	Durham, O
Hamilton	Wentworth, O	Port Robinson	Welland, O
Hastings	Peterboro', O	Port Rowan	Norfolk, O
Hawkesbury	Prescott, O	Port Stanley	Elgin, O
Hespeler	Waterloo, O	Prescott	Grenville, O
Hull	Ottawa, Q	Preston	Waterloo, O
Huntingdon	Huntingdon, Q	Prince Albert	Ontario, O
Ingersoll	Oxford, O	Quebec	Quebec, Q
Inverness	Megantic, Q	Renfrew	Renfrew, O
Iroquois	Dundas, O	Richmond East	Richmond, Q
Joliette	Joliette, Q	Richmond Hill	York, O
Keene	Peterboro', O	Rimouski	Rimouski, Q
Kemptville	Grenville, O	Riviere du Loup (en bas)	Temiscouata, Q
Kincardine	Bruce, O	Rosemont	Simcoe, O
Kingston	Frontenac, O	St. Andrew's East	Argenteuil, Q
Kingsville	Essex, O	St. Catharines West	Lincoln, O
Knowlton	Brome, Q	St. Hyacinthe	St Hyacinthe, Q
Lachine	Jacques Cartier, Q	St. John's East	St. John's, Q
Lachute	Argenteuil, Q	St Marys Blanchard	Perth, O
Lanark	Lanark, O	St. Paul's Bay	Charlevoix, Q
Laprairie	Laprairie, Q	St. Roch de Quebec	Quebec, Q
L'Assomption	L'Assomption, Q	St. Thomas West	Elgin, O
Leeds	Megantic, Q	Sandwich	Essex, O
Lennoxville	Sherbrooke, Q	Sarnia	Lambton, O
Levis	Levis, Q	Saugeen	Bruce, O
Lindsay	Victoria, O	Seaforth	Huron, O
Listowel	Perth, O	Seneca	Haldimand, O
London	Middlesex, O	Sherbrooke	Sherbrooke, Q
L'Orignal	Prescott, O	Simcoe	Norfolk, O
Lucan	Huron, O	Smith's Falls	Lanark, O
Lucknow	Bruce, O	Sorel	Richelieu, Q
Lyn	Leeds, O	South Quebec	Levis, Q
Madoc	Hastings, O	Stanstead	Stanstead, Q
Manchester	Ontario, O	Stayner	Simcoe, O
Markham	York, O	Stirling	Hastings, O
Meaford	Grey, O	Stouffville	York, O
Melbourne	Richmond, Q	Stratford	Perth, O
Merrickville	Grenville, O	Strathroy	Middlesex, O
Millbrook	Durham, O	Streetsville	Peel, O
Milton, West	Halton, O	Thornhill	York, O
Montmagny	Montmagny, Q	Thorold	Welland, O
Montreal	Hochelaga, Q	Three Rivers	St. Maurice, Q
Morpeth	Kent, O	Thurso	Ottawa, Q
Morrisburg	Dundas, O	Tilsonburg	Oxford, O
Mount Brydges	Middlesex, O	Toronto	York, O
Mount Forest	Grey, O	Trenton	Hastings, O
Murray Bay	Charlevoix, Q	Uxbridge	Ontario, O
Napanee	Lennox, O	Vankleek Hill	Prescott, O
Newburgh	Addington, O	Vienna	Elgin, O
Newbury	Middlesex, O	Walkerton	Bruce, O
Newcastle	Durham, O	Wallaceburg	Kent, O
New Edinburgh	Carleton, O	Wellesley	Waterloo, O
New Hamburg	Waterloo, O	Wardsville	Middlesex, O
Newmarket	York, O	Waterdown	Wentworth, O
Niagara	Lincoln, O	Waterford	Norfolk, O
Norwich	Oxford, O	Waterloo East	Shefford, Q
Norwood	Peterboro', O	Waterloo West	Waterloo, O
Oakville	Halton, O	Welland	Welland, O
Odessa	Addington, O	Wellington Square	Halton, O
Oil Springs	Lambton, O	Weston	York, O
Omemee	Victoria, O	Whitby	Ontario, O
Onslow	Pontiac, Q	Windsor	Essex, O
Orangeville	Wellington, O	Woodstock	Oxford, O
Orillia	Simcoe, O	Wroxeter	Huron, O
Oshawa	Ontario, O	Wyoming	Lambton, O

POST OFFICE DEPARTMENT,
Ottawa.

A. CAMPBELL,
Postmaster-General.

LIST OF POST OFFICES IN ONTARIO.

The Offices printed in Italics are authorized to Grant and Pay Money Orders.
*The Offices marked * are Savings Bank Offices.*

NAME OF POST OFFICE.	ELECTORAL COUNTY OR DIVISION.	NAME OF POSTMASTER.
Aberarder	Lambton	D. McBean
Aberfoyle	Wellington, S. R.	S. Falconbridge
Abingdon	Monck	Thomas Pearson
Acton	Halton	J. Matthews
Addison	Brockville	Coleman Lewis
Adelaide	Middlesex, N.R.	John S. Hoare
Admaston	Renfrew, S. R.	Arch. Patterson
Adolphustown	Lenox	J. J. Watson
Agincourt	York, E.R	John Milne
Ailsa Craig	Middlesex, N.R.	Shackleton Hey
Alberton	Wentworth, S.R.	S. W. Smith
Albion	Cardwell	George Evans
Albury	Prince Edward	James H. Peck
Aldboro'	Elgin, W.R.	Luther Carpenter
Aldershot	Wentworth, N.R	Alexander Brown
Alderville	Northumberland, W.R.	James Curtis
Alexandria	Glengary	A. S. Macdonald
Alfred	Prescott	John Hill
Algonquin	Grenville, S.R.	Silas Wright
Allanburg	Welland	John Rannie
Allandale Mills	Peterborough, E.R.	Richard Short, sen.
Allan Park	Grey, S.R.	Thomas Boddy
Allendale	Simcoe, S.R.	Andrew Miscampbell
Allenford	Bruce, N.R.	William Sharp
Allisonville	Prince Edward	R. C. Hicks
Alliston	Simcoe, S.R.	George Fletcher
Alloa	Peel	Thomas Clarridge
Alma	Wellington, N.R.	Thomas Graham
Almira	York, E.R.	John Bowman
Almonte	Lanark, N.R.	James H. Wylie, jun.
Alport	Victoria, N.R.	A. F. C. Alport
Alton	Cardwell	Mrs. Agnes Meek
Altona	Ontario, S.R.	Joseph Monkhouse
Alvanley	Grey, N.R.	James Webster
Alvinston	Lambton	J. W. Brannan
Amberley	Huron, N.R.	Alexander Fraser
Ameliasburgh	Prince Edward	Owen Roblin
Amherstburg	Essex	James Kevill
Amiens	Middlesex, N.R	Charles McArthur, sen.
Ancaster	Wentworth, S.R.	Anna M. McKay
Anderson	Perth, S.R.	Humphrey White
Angus	Simcoe, S.R.	John Mather
Antrim	Carleton	T. Cavanagh
Appin	Middlesex, W. R.	Angus Campbell
Appleby	Halton	James W. Cotter
Appleton	Lanark, N. R.	Albert Teskey
Apsley	Peterboro', E. R.	E. S. Hall
Apto	Simcoe, N. R.	C. McLauchlin
Arden	Addington	D. Osborne
Ardoch	Addington	F. W. Bucher
Ardtrea	Simcoe, N. R.	William Blair
Argyle	Victoria, N. R.	John McKay
Arkell	Wellington, S. R.	William Watson
Arkona	Lambton	Sarah E. Schooley
Arkwright	Bruce, N. R.	G. D. Kilbourn
Arlington	Cardwell	Thomas Kidd
Arnott	Grey, N. R.	William G. Murray
Arnprior	Renfrew, S. R.	Andrew Russell
Aroe	Victoria, N. R.	Charles McInnes
Arthur	Wellington, N. R	Mrs. Janet Small
Arva	Middlesex, E. R.	W. B. Bernard

LIST OF POST OFFICES IN ONTARIO—(*Continued.*)

NAME OF POST OFFICE.	ELECTORAL COUNTY OR DIVISION.	NAME OF POSTMASTER.
Ashburn	Ontario, S. R.	Edward Oliver
Ashburnham	Peterboro', E. R.	Robert D. Rogers
Ashgrove	Halton	Mrs. Sarah Hunter
Ashton	Carleton	John Sumner
Ashworth	Ontario, N. R.	John Mustard
Athens	Ontario, S. R.	John M. Bell
Atherly	Ontario, N. R.	R. Bingham
Atherton	Norfolk, N. R.	W. C. McMullin
Athlone	Cardwell	John Kidd
Athol	Glengary	M. A. Fisher
Attercliffe	Monck	James Tisdale
Auburn	Huron, N. R.	James Sutherland
Aughrim	Lambton	J. McKeune
Aultsville	Stormont	I. R. Ault
**Aurora*	York, N. R.	Charles Doane
Avening	Simcoe, N. R.	W. H. Thornbury
Avon	Middlesex, E. R.	G. C. Smith
Avonbank	Perth, S. R.	David Muir
Avonmore	Stormont	E. N. Shaver
Avonton	Perth, S. R.	A. Shields
**Aylmer (West)*	Elgin, E. R.	Philip Hodgkinson
**Ayr*	Waterloo, S. R.	Robert Wylie
Ayton	Grey, S. R.	John McPhilips
Baby's Point	Lambton	James Menton, sen
Baden	Waterloo, S. R.	Jacob Beck
Bagot	Renfrew, S. R.	John Halliday, sen
Baillieboro'	Durham, E. R.	James Fitzgerald
Bakersville	Wentworth, N. R.	John Baker
Balderson	Lanark, S. R.	Saunders Watson
Baldwin	Addington	Gordon P. York
Ballantrae	York, N. R	Isaac Lepard
Ballinafad	Wellington, C. R.	John S. Applebe
Ballycroy	Cardwell	J. McClelland
Ballyduff	Durham, E. R.	W. A. Maxwell
Ballymote	Middlesex, E. R.	J. W. O'Brien
Balmer's Island	Renfrew, S. R.	Allan Stewart
Balmoral	Haldimand	George B. Lundy
Balsam	Ontario, S. R.	Robert Dodds
Baltimore	Northumberland, W. R.	John Gilbard
Bamberg	Waterloo, N. R.	F. Walter
Banda	Simcoe, S. R.	John Cleminger
Bandon	Huron, N. R.	James Allen
Bangor	Ontario, S. R.	Isaac Turner
Bannockburn	Hastings, N. R.	W. H. Carpenter
Bark Lake	Hastings, N. R.	Richard Skuce, sen.
Barnett	Wellington, C. R.	James Elmslie
**Barrie*	Simcoe, N. R.	James Edwards
Bartonville	Wentworth, S. R.	W. J. Gage
Bath	Lennox	John Balfour
Battersea	Frontenac	W. J. Anglin
**Bayfield*	Huron, S. R.	James Gairdner
Bayham	Elgin, E. R.	George Laing
Beachburg	Renfrew, N. R.	George Surtees
Beachville	Oxford, S. R.	Charles Mason
**Beamsville*	Lincoln	J. B. Osborne
Bear Brook	Russell	Brock Grier
**Beaverton*	Ontario, N. R.	Donald Cameron
Belfast	Huron, N. R.	John McHardy
Belford	York, E. R.	Israel Burton
Belfountain	Cardwell	Noah Herring
Belgrave	Huron, N. R.	Simon Armstrong
Belhaven	York, N. R.	Daniel Prosser
**Belleville*	Hastings, E. R.	J. H. Meacham
Bell Ewart	Simcoe, S. R.	P. Ed. Drake
Bellrock	Addington	William Pomroy
Bell's Corners	Carlet n	George Arnold
Belmont	Middlesex, E. R.	W. H. Odell
Belmore	Huron, N. R.	Peter Terriff

LIST OF POST OFFICES IN ONTARIO—(*Continued.*)

NAME OF POST OFFICE.	ELECTORAL COUNTY OR DIVISION.	NAME OF POSTMASTER.
Benmiller	Huron, N. R	Edwin Gledhill
Bennie's Corners	Lanark, N. R	Alexander Leishman
Bensfort	Northumberland, W. R	James W. McBain
Bentley	Kent	Samuel Bentley
Berkeley	Grey, N. R	John Fleming
**Berlin*	Waterloo, N. R	William Jaffray
Berne	Huron, S. R	G. Murner
Bervie	Bruce, S. R	Nichol McIntyre
Berwick	Stormont	J. A. Cockburn
Bethany	Durham, E. R	W. M. Graham
Bewdley	Northumberland, W. R	John Sidey
Billings' Bridge	Russell	David Taylor
Binbrook	Wentworth, S. R	Henry Hall
Birkhall	Lambton	F. McKenzie
Birmingham	Frontenac	Mrs. E. Birmingham
Birr	Middlesex, E. R	Joseph M. Young
Bishop's Mills	Grenville, N. R	Asa W. Bishop
Black Creek	Welland	Isaac H. Allen
Black Heath	Haldimand	T. S. Potts
Blair	Waterloo, S. R	J. Renshaw
**Blairton*	Peterboro', E. R	Roger Bates
Blantyre	Grey, N. R	James Paterson
Blessington	Hastings, E. R	John Lally
Bloomfield	Prince Edward	Jonathan Striker
Bloomingdale	Waterloo, N. R	J. G. Moyer
Bloomington	York, N. R	S. Patterson
Bloomsburg	Norfolk, N. R	L. W. Kitchen
Bluevale	Huron, N. R	John Messer
Blyth	Huron, N. R	R. W. Holmes
Blytheswood	Essex	Charles Robertson
Bobcaygeon	Victoria, S. R	A. La. T. Tupper
Bogart	Hastings, E. R	A. L. Bogart
Bolingbroke	Lanark, S. R	John Korry
Bolsover	Victoria, N. R	G. F. Marsh
Bomanton	Northumberland, W. R	Richard Knight
**Bondhead*	Simcoe, S. R	Hiram Lount
Bongard's Corners	Prince Edward	John Bougard
Bookton	Norfolk, N. R	P. N. McIntosh
Borelia	Ontario, N. R	James Jewett
Bornholm	Perth, N. R	Timothy Hegerty
Boston	Norfolk, N. R	Oliver C. Rouse
Bosworth	Wellington, N. R	Charles Draper
Botany	Bothwell	C McBrayne
**Bothwell*	Bothwell	John Taylor
**Bowmanville*	Durham, W. R	J. B. Fairbain
Bowood	Middlesex, N. R	Hugh McLean
Box Grove	York, E. R	John McCaffrey
Boyne	Halton	Stephen Emmett
Bracebridge	Victoria, N. R	A. Bailey
**Bradford*	Simcoe, S. R	Mrs. Ann Douglas
Braemar	Oxford, N. R	Alexander Anderson
**Brampton*	Peel	K. Chisholm
Branchton	Waterloo, S. R	D. W. Cumming
**Brantford*	Brant, S. R	A. D. Clement
Brechin	Ontario, N. R	Jemes P. Foley
Brentwood	Simcoe, N. R	L. E. Debois
Breslaw	Waterloo, N. R	Ephraim Erb
Brewer's Mills	Frontenac	Robert Anglin
Brewster	Huron, S. R	W. McDougall
Bridgenorth	Peterborough, W. R	Marcus S. Dean
Bridgeport	Waterloo, N. R	Elias Eby
Bridgewater	Hastings, N. R	James Harrison
Bright	Oxford, N. R	W. A. Sharp
**Brighton*	Northumberland, E. R	Joseph Lockwood
Brinkworth	Hastings, N. R	Allen Williams
Brinsley	Middlesex, N. R	George Brown
Brisbane	Wellington, C. R	William Boemer
Britannia	Peel	

LIST OF POST OFFICES IN ONTARIO—(*Continued.*)

NAME OF POST OFFICE.	ELECTORAL COUNTY OR DIVISION.	NAME OF POSTMASTER.
Brock	Ontario, N. R	John Jones
Brocton	York, W. R	Mrs. Ann Church
**Brockville*	Brockville	John Crawford
Brodhagen	Perth, N. R.	Charles Brodhagen
Bronte	Halton	E. C. Thompson
**Brooklin*	Ontario, S. R.	Robert Darlington
Brooksdale	Oxford, N. R.	Sage Bannerman
Brougham	Ontario, S. R.	Richard Taun
Brownsville	Oxford, S. R	William Barr
Brucefield	Huron, S. R	Robert Marks
Bruce Mines	District of Algoma	W. C. Dobie
Brudenell	Renfrew, S. R.	John Reynolds
Brunner	Perth, N. R.	Jacob Brunner
Brunswick	Durham, N. R.	S. R. Beamish
Bryanston	Middlesex, E. R	John Stanfield
Buckhorn	Kent	Edward L. Lee
Burford	Brant, S. R	John Catton
Burgessville	Oxford, S. R	Josiah Campbell
Burgoyne	Bruce, N. R	Alfred Shell
Burleigh	Peterborough, E. R	James Golborne
Burn-brae	Northumberland, E. R.	Alexander Donald
Burnhamthorpe	Peel	George Savage
Burnley	Northumberland, W. R	R. H. Grimshawe
Burns	Perth, N. R	John Gibson
Burnstown	Renfrew, S. R	Donald McRae
Burritt's Rapids	Grenville, N. R.	John Meikle, jun
Burtch	Brant, S. R	George Taylor
Burton	Durham, E. R	James McGill
Bury's Green	Victoria, N. R	John Fell
Buttonville	York, E. R.	T. Thomson
Buxton	Kent	Rev. W. King
Byng	Haldimand	James M. Thomson
Byng Inlet	District of Algoma	Charles Little
Byron	Middlesex, E. R	Robert Sadler
Cæsarea	Durham, W. R	Ephraim Demara
Cainsville	Brant, N. R	Margaret Greeny
Caintown	Leeds, S. R	W. Tennant, jun
Caistorville	Monck	M. G. Scott
Calabogie	Renfrew, S. R.	D. Dillon
Calder	Middlesex, W. R	William Campbell
Caldwell	Cardwell	Patrick Murphy
Caledon	Cardwell	George Bell
Caledon East	Cardwell	James Munsie
Caledonia Springs	Prescott	John D. Cameron
Camborne	Northumberland, W. R	
Cambray	Victoria, N. R	George Henderson
Camden East	Addington	Benjamin Clark
Cameron	Victoria, N. R	James Bryson
Camilla	Cardwell	Hugh Currie
Camlachie	Lambton	William Douglas
**Campbellford*	Northumberland, E. R.	James M. Ferriss
Cambell's Cross	Peel	E. T. Hagyard
Campbellville	Halton	ames H. Cooper
Campden	Lincoln	H. W. Moyer
Canboro'	Monck	John Folmsbee
Canfield	Haldimand	John Wilson
Canniffton	Hastings, E. R	Jonas Canniff, jun
Canning	Oxford, N. R.	Samuel Allchin
Cannington	Ontario, N. R	Charles Gibbs
Canton	Durham, E R	William Deacon
Cape Rich	Grey, N R	Donald McLaren
Carden	Victoria, N R	ames Carlin
**Carleton Place*	Lanark, S R	Patrick Struthers
Carlingford	Perth, S R	William Davidson, jun
Carlisle	Wentworth, N R	John C. Crooker
Carlow	Huron, N R	James McDonagh
Carlsruhe	Bruce, S R	I. Kormann
Carluke	Wentworth, S R	James Calder

LIST OF POST OFFICES IN ONTARIO—(_Continued._)

NAME OF POST OFFICE.	ELECTORAL COUNTY OR DIVISION.	NAME OF POSTMASTER.
Carnarvon	Peterboro', E R	Andrew Barnum
Carnegie	Bruce, N R	Samuel Ewart
Carp	Carleton	W. J. Fetherstonhaugh
Carronbrook	Perth, N R	Joseph Kidd
Carrville	York, W R	Thomas Cook
Carthage	Perth, N R	Charles Brown
Cartwright	Durham, W R	William Vance
Cashel	York, E R	M. B. Crosby
Cashmere	Middlesex, W R	George Mansfield
Casselman	Russell	John S. Casselman
Castleford	Renfrew, S R	Elliott Johnston
Castlemore	Peel	Francis Hassard
Castleton	Northumberland, W R	John C. Pennock
Cataract	Cardwell	Richard Church
Cataraqui	Frontenac	Joseph Northmore
Cathcart	Brant, S R	Thomas Muir
Cavan	Durham, E R	William Graham
Cawdor	Addington	Archibald Campbell
*_Cayuga_	Haldimand	G. A. Messenger
Cedar Grove	York, E R	David Lapp
Cedar Hill	Lanark, N R	James Connery
Cedarville	Grey, S R	Thomas Rogers
Centre Augusta	Grenville, S R	A. B. Commins
Centreton	Northumberland, W R	T. H. McAuley
Centreville	Addington	
Chandos	Peterboro', E R	H. Maxwell
Charing Cross	Kent	
Charleston	Leeds, S R	P. F. Green
Charleville	Grenville, S R	Samuel Throop
*_Chatham_	Kent	S. Barfoot
Chatsworth	Grey, N R	Henry Cardwell
Cheapside	Haldimand	William Pugsley
Cheltenham	Peel	John Campbell
Chepstow	Bruce, S R	William Henesey
Cherry Creek	Simcoe, S R	William Main
Cherry Valley	Prince Edward	Isaiah T. Insley
Chesley	Bruce, N R	Mark McManus
Chesterfield	Oxford, N R	William Brown
*_Chippawa_	Welland	J. S. Macklem
Churchill	Simcoe, S R	H. Sloane
Churchville	Peel	James E. Pointer
Clachan	Elgin, W R	D. McPhail
Claremont	Ontario, S R	J. McM. McNab
Clarence	Russell	Thomas Wilson
Clarence Creek	Russell	Firmin Neaubert
Clarke	Durham, W R	James Lockhart
*_Clarksburg_	Grey, N R	Walter Hunter
Claude	Peel	Henry Perdue
Clavering	Bruce, N R	John Shackleton
Clayton	Lanark, N R	O. Banning, jun
Clear Creek	Norfolk, S R	Jonathan Bridgeman
Clearville	Bothwell	Henry Watson
Clifford	Wellington, N R	Francis Brown
*_Clifton_	Welland	W. W. Woodruff
Clifton House (sub) closed during winter.	Welland	J. Shears
*_Clinton_	Huron, S R	Thomas Fair
Clontarf	Renfrew, S R	J. R. McDonald
Clover Hill	Simcoe, S R	Eli Clarke
Cloyne	Addington	W. McPherson
Clyde	Wentworth, N R	John R. McDonald
Cobden	Renfrew, N R	John Leroy
Coboconk	Victoria, N R	J. C. Boswell
Cobourg	Northumberland, W R	William Kilbank
Codrington	Northumberland, E R	J. R. Ford
*_Colborne_	Northumberland, E R	John Mickle
Colchester	Essex	D. McIntosh
Coldsprings	Northumberland, W R	

LIST OF POST OFFICES IN ONTARIO—(*Continued.*)

NAME OF POST OFFICE.	ELECTORAL COUNTY OR DIVISION.	NAME OF POSTMASTER.
Coldstream	Middlesex, N R	Jacob Marsh
*Coldwater	Simcoe, N R	John Eplett
Colebrook	Addington	Charles Warner
Coleraine	Peel	John Gardhouse
Coleridge	Wellington, N. R	Joseph W. Trueman
Colinville	Lambton	John Butler
**Collingwood*	Simcoe, N R	W. B. Hamilton
Collin's Bay	Frontenac	Lawrence Herchmer
Colpoy's Bay	Bruce, N R	L. Kribs
Columbus	Ontario, S R	Robert Ashton
Comber	Essex	D. McAlister
Combermere	Renfrew, S R	Daniel Johnson
Concord	York, W R	John Duncan
Conestogo	Waterloo, N R	Charles Hendry
Coningsby	Wellington, C R	John W. Burt
Connor	Cardwell	W. McGibbon
Conroy	Perth, S R	Peter Smith
Consecon	Prince Edward	A. Marsh
Constance	Huron, N R	R. Thompson
Conway	Lennox	G. B. Sills
**Cookstown*	Simcoe, S R	Henry Harper
Cooksville	Peel	
Cooper	Hastings, N R	Thomas Allan
Copetown	Wentworth, N R	Thomas Milne
Copleston	Lambton	R. P. Smith
Corinth	Elgin, E R	F. A. Best
Cornabuss	Grey, S R	W. J. McFarland
**Cornwall*	Cornwall	G. C. Wood
Corunna	Lambton	H. J. Miller
Cotswold	Wellington, N R	Peter McKenzie
Coulson	Simcoe, N R	James Coulson
Courtland	Norfolk, N R	C. S. Harris
Coventry	Cardwell	William McKee
Cowal	Elgin, W R	N. McBride
Craighurst	Simcoe, N R	John Craig
Craigleith	Grey, N R	A. G. Fleming
Craigvale	Simcoe, S R	Robert Munsie
Cranworth	Leeds, S R	Thomas M. Kyle
Crawford	Grey, S R	Hector McRae
Credit	Peel	Emerson Taylor
Crediton	Huron, S R	John Parsons
Creek Bank	Wellington, N R	James Graham
**Creemore*	Simcoe, N R	W. H. Thornbury
Creighton	Simcoe, N R	Thomas Cavanagh
Cressy	Prince Edward	S. W. Carson
Crieff	Wellington, S R	John McLean
Crinan	Elgin, W R	D. McIntyre
Cromarty	Perth, S R	Alexander Park
Crosshill	Waterloo, N R	James McCutcheon
Croton	Bothwell	J. H. Johnston
Crowland	Welland	Luther Boardman
Croydon	Addington	Ira Williams
Crysler	Stormont	E. K. Johnstone
Culloden	Oxford, S R	R. T. Williams
Cumberland	Russell	G. G. Dunning
Cumminsville	Halton	Robert Thomas
Cumnock	Wellington, C R	John Anderson
Curran	Prescott	John Boyle
Dacre	Renfrew, S R	John Morrow
Dalhousie Mills	Glengary	William Chisholm
Dalkeith	Glengary	William Robertson
Dalston	Simcoe, N R	H. A. Clifford
Danforth	York, W R	Henry Hogarth
Darrell	Kent	Edward Hall
Dartford	Northumberland, E R	William Bailey *
Davenport	York, E R	George S. Yearley
Dawn Mills	Bothwell	T. S. Arnold

LIST OF POST OFFICES IN ONTARIO—(*Continued.*)

NAME OF POST OFFICE.	ELECTORAL COUNTY OR DIVISION.	NAME OF POSTMASTER.
Daywood	Grey, N R	A. S. Cameron
Dealton	Kent	Isaac Lambert
De Cewsville	Haldimand	T. B. Dier
Deerhurst	Simcoe, S R	Samuel Walker
Delaware	Middlesex, W R	C. J. Ladd
Delhi	Norfolk, N R	James Whitesides
Delta	Leeds, S R	W. H. Denaut
Demorestville	Prince Edward	B. Smith
Denbigh	Addington	David Hughes
Denfield	Middlesex, E R	Benjamin W. Rosser
Deniston	Addington	B. C. Freeman
Derryville	Ontario, N R	Thomas Allin
Derry West	Peel	William Wilson
Derwent	Middlesex, E R	L. G. Willsie
Desmond	Addington	J. W. Bell
Deux Rivieres	District of Nipissing	Robert Ranson
Devizes	Middlesex, E R	John Costello
Devon	Huron, S R	Thomas Greenway
Dexter	Elgin, E R	Nelson Parker
Diamond	Carleton	R. Walker, jun.
Dickinson's Landing	Stormont	Charles Wagner
Dingle	Huron, N R	William Grant
Dixie	Peel	W. Kennedy
Dixon's Corners	Dundas	William Wood
Dobbinton	Bruce, N R	James Dobbin
Donegal	Perth, N R	Mary Mason
Doon	Waterloo, S R	Thomas Slee
Doran	Lanark, S R	William Doran
Dorchester Station	Middlesex, E R	J. N. Hardy
Dorking	Wellington, N R	John Gatschene
Dornoch	Oxford, S R	Peter Gardner
Douglas	Renfrew, N R	Donald Cameron
Dover South	Kent	S. Gervais
Downeyville	Victoria, S R	J. S. McCarthy
Drayton	Wellington, N R	W. C. Wortley
Dresden	Bothwelll	C. P. Watson
Dromore	Grey, S R	Alexander Taylor
Drumbo	Oxford, N R	James McKenzie
Drummondville West	Welland	Luke Brokenshaw
Drumquin	Halton	William John White
Drury	Simcoe, N R	R. Drury
Dryden	Perth, N R	Richard Johnston
Duart	Bothwell	James Tait
Dumblane	Bruce, N R	John Fraser
Dunbar	Dundas	A. C. Allison
Dunbarton	Ontario, S R	John Parker
Duncrief	Middlesex, N R	James Barnes
Dundalk	Grey, S R	James Mulholland
Dundas	Wentworth, N R	J. M. Thornton
Dundela	Dundas	Thomas Wharton
Dundonald	Northumberland, E R	John Barker
Dungannon	Huron, N R	R. Clendinning
Dunkeld	Bruce, S R	Hugh Bell
Dunville	Monck	Thomas Armour
Dunsford	Victoria, S R	William Graham
Dunsinane	Bruce, S R	James L. McDonald
Duntroon	Simcoe, N R	James Russell
Dunvegan	Glengary	Hector McLean
Durham	Grey, S R	A. B. McNab
Eagle	Elgin, W R	W. Mowbray
East Hawkesbury	Prescott	John McAdam
Easton's Corners	Grenville, N R	Isaac Coolidge
East Oro	Simcoe, N R	William Simpson
East Williamsburgh	Dundas	Lindsay Pillar
Eastwood	Oxford, S R	John Shaw
Eddystone	Northumberland, W R	
Eden	Elgin, E R	John Nethercott

LIST OF POST OFFICES IN ONTARIO—(*Continued.*)

NAME OF POST OFFICE.	ELECTORAL COUNTY OR DIVISION.	NAME OF POSTMASTER.
Eden Mills	Wellington, C R	Samuel Meadows
Edgecombe	Perth, N R	Cornelius Gallop
Edmonton	Peel	James Collinghourne
Edwardsburgh	Grenville, S R	William S. Akin
Effingham	Monck	George Redpath
Eganville	Renfrew, S R	John Quealy
Egbert	Simcoe, S R	James Strachan
Egerton	Wellington, N R	James Hunter
Eglington	York, E R	Joseph Hargrave
Egmondville	Huron, S R	George E. Jackson
Elder	Cardwell	C. Conn
Eldorado	Hastings, N R	Adam Dickson
Elfrida	Wentworth, S R	Richard Smy
Elgin	Leeds, S R	Philemon Pennock
Elginburg	Frontenac	Peter Bates
Elginfield	Middlesex, E R	W. H. Ryan
Elizabethville	Durham, E R	J. McMurtry
Ellengowan	Bruce, S R	James Brownlee
Ellesmere	York, E R	Archibald Glendinning
Elm Grove	Simcoe, S R	Richard Love
Elmira	Waterloo, N R	Peter Winger
Elmvale	Simcoe, N R	William Harvey
Elmwood	Bruce, S R	J. Dirstein
**Elora*	Wellington, C R	John Finlayson
Elsinore	Bruce, N R	Robert Montgomery
Embro	Oxford, N R	D. Matheson
Embrun	Russell	Joseph Lalonde
Emerald	Lenox	John Hitchin
Enfield	Durham, W R	Jonathan Hymers
Enniskillen	Durham, W R	D. W. McLeod
Ennismore	Peterboro', W R	Thomas S. LeHane
Enterprise	Addington	Robert Graham
Epping	Grey, N R	J. W. Marshall
Epsom	Ontario, N R	Joseph C. Huckins
Eramosa	Wellington, C R	John Anderson
Erbsville	Waterloo, N R	John L. Erb
Erie	Haldimand	R. McBurney
**Erin*	Wellington, C R	William Cornock
Erinsville	Addington	Patrick Walsh
Erroll	Lambton	George Whiting
Escott	Leeds, S R	Andrew Todd
Esquesing	Halton	John Murray
Ethel	Huron, N R	James Spence
Etobicoke	York, W R	F. A. Howland
Eugenia	Grey, S R	R. McLean Purdy
Evelyn	Middlesex, E R	George Henshaw
Eversley	York, N R	James Tinline
Everton	Wellington, C R	D. F. Stewart
**Exeter*	Huron, S R	William Sanders
Fairfield	Kent	Sarah A. Burt
Fairfield Plain	Brant, S R	Alexander Howell
Fairview	Perth, S R	Richard Forrest
Falkenburg	Victoria, N R	Robert George
Falkirk	Middlesex, N R	James Priestly
Falkland	Brant, S R	M. Stally
Farmersville	Leeds, S R	Arza Parish
Farmington	Wellington, N R	James May
Farquhar	Huron, S R	William Edmond
Farran's Point	Stormont	John R. Farran
Felton	Russell	Alexander McGregor, jun.
Fenaghvale	Prescott	James Proudfoot, jun.
Fenella	Northumberland, W R	George Harper
Fenelon Falls	Victoria, N R	R. B. Jameson
Fenwick	Monck	James W. Tayler
**Fergus*	Wellington, C R	James McQueen
Ferguson's Falls	Lanark, S R	Robert Hicks
Fermoy	Addington	Edward Botting

LIST OF POST OFFICES IN ONTARIO—(*Continued.*)

NAME OF POST OFFICE.	ELECTORAL COUNTY OR DIVISION.	NAME OF POSTMASTER.
Fernhill	Middlesex, N R	Jenkin Owen
Feversham	Grey, S R	Mary Sproul
**Fingal*	Elgin, W R	Samuel Tubby
Fish Creek	Perth, S R	
Fisherville	Haldimand	James Elsworth
Fitzroy Harbour	Carleton	Robert Shirreff
Flesherton	Grey, S R	A. McSorley
Flinton	Addington	J. A. Cascallen
Flora	Waterloo, N R	Isaac Devitt
Florence	Bothwell	John A. Young
Foley	Ontario, S R	Thomas Williamson
Fonthill	Monck	Danson Kinsman
Fordyce	Huron, N R	Wm. Farquharson
Forest	Lambton	R. Dier
Forester's Falls	Renfrew, N R	Oliver Forester
Forestville	Norfolk, S R	C. A. White
Forfar	Leeds, S R	Richard Hales
Formosa	Bruce, S R	F. X. Mesner
Fort Erie	Welland	George Lewis
Fort William	Algoma	Miss C. McVicar
Fournier	Prescott	A. S. McLennan
Foxboro'	Hastings, E R	Wm. Duffy
Frankford	Hastings, W R	William Gilbert
Franklin	Durham, E R	William Maguire
Franktown	Lanark, S R	E. McEwen
Frankville	Leeds, N R	Samuel Connor
Freelton	Wentworth, N R	James Hirst
Freeport	Waterloo, S R	J. B. Schlichter
Frieburg	Waterloo, N R	Ferdinand Rombach
Frogmore	Peel	William Axford
Frome	Elgin, W R	Joseph Silcox
Fullarton	Perth, S R	James Woodley
Fulton	Lincoln	J. E. White
Gad's Hill	Perth, N R	Wm. B. Crinkley
**Galt*	Waterloo, S R	John Davidson
Galway	Peterboro', E R	Thomas Probert
**Gananoque*	Leeds, S R	D. F. Britton
Garafraxa	Wellington, C R	Andrew Lightbody
Garden Island	Frontenac	George Cumming
Garden River	District of Algoma	Rev. Jas. Chance
Gemley	Addington	James Stalker
**Georgetown*	Halton	Francis Barclay
Georgina	York, N R	J. O. B. Bourchier
Gifford	Haldimand	C. B. Fredenburgh
Gilbert's Mills	Prince Edward	John D. Gilbert
Gilford	Simcoe, S R	Thos. Maconchy
Gladstone	Middlesex, E R	L. McMurray
Glammis	Bruce, N R	J. Crawford
Glanford	Wentworth, S R	John Atkinson
Glanmire	Hastings, N R	Edward Tapp
Glanworth	Middlesex, E R	John Turnbull
Glascott	Grey, S R	John English
Glenallen	Wellington, N R	George Allen
Glenarm	Victoria, N R	W. Cooper
Glenburnie	Frontenac	George Hunter
Glencairn	Simcoe, S R	M. N. Stephens
Glencoe	Middlesex, W R	Donald McRae
Glenlyon	Bruce, S R	J. Shennan
Glenmeyer	Norfolk, S R	Geo. E. Meyer
Glenmorris	Brant, N R	Gavin Fleming
Glennevis	Glengarry	Alex. E. McRae
Glen Tay	Lanark, S R	Henry Mayberry
Glenvale	Frontenac	Robert Gibson
Glen William	Halton	Charles Williams
Goble's Corners'	Oxford, N R	Wm. L. Goble
**Goderich*	Huron, S R	A. Dickson
Golden Creek	Lambton	Allen Kennedy

LIST OF POST OFFICES IN ONTARIO—(*Continued.*)

NAME OF POST OFFICE.	ELECTORAL COUNTY OR DIVISION.	NAME OF POSTMASTER.
Goldstone	Wellington	Thomas Frankland
Goodwood	Ontario, N R	Michael Chapman
Gore's Landing	Northumberland, W R	Sarah Gabetis
Gormley	York, E R	James Gormley
Gorrie	Huron, N R	Henry Besanson
Gosfield	Essex	Joseph Coatsworth
Gosport	Lenox	George German
Gourock	Wellington, S R	James Mewhort
Gowanstown	Perth, N R	Mrs. M. A. Gowan
Gowerpoint	Renfrew, N R	Thomas M. Carswell
Grafton	Northumberland, W R	J. Gillard
Grahamsville	Peel	Peter Lanphier
Grantley	Dundas	John C. Munro
Granton	Middlesex, N R	James Jamieson
Gravenhurst	Victoria, N R	Peter Cockburn
Greenbank	Ontario, N R	John Asling
Greenbush	Brockville	Eli L. White
Greenock	Bruce, S R	Hugh Montgomery
Green Point	Prince Edward	Philip Roblin
Greensville	Wentworth, N R	James Joyce
Greenwood	Ontario, S R	A. Fullarton
Gresham	Bruce, N R	E. J. Brown
Gretna	Lenox	W. J. Mellow
Grey	Huron, N R	John Leckie
Griersville	Grey, N R	Andrew Grier
Griffith	Renfrew, S R	W. H. Adams, sen
**Grimsby*	Lincoln	H. E. Nelles
Grovesend	Elgin, E R	W. B. Lyon
**Guelph*	Wellington, S R	William Kingsmill
Guysboro'	Norfolk, N R	J. W. Doyle
Hagersville	Haldimand	Charles Hager
Haliburton	Peterboro' E R	C. R. Stewart
Halloway	Hastings, E R	Mary Ann Peck
Hall's Bridge	Peterboro' E R	John Hall
Hamburg	Lennox	A. D. Fraser
**Hamilton*	Hamilton	Edmund Ritchie
Hamlet	Lanark, S R	John Byrne
Hammettsholm	York, E R	James Hammett
Hammond	Perth, N R	James Hammond, jun.
Hampstead	Perth, N R	Henry Liesemer
Hampton	Durham, W R	H. Elliott
Hannon	Wentworth, S R	Thomas Cowie
Hanover	Grey, S R	A. Z. Gottwalls
Harcourt	Renfrew, N R	John W. Squires
Hardinge	Addington	Thomas Tapping
Harlem	Leeds, S R	William Kincaid
Harley	Brant, S R	J. L. McClellan
Harmony	Perth, S R	Edmond Corbett
Harold	Hastings, N R	Richard Buck
Harper	Lanark, S R	Joseph Warren
Harrietsville	Middlesex, E R	John McMillan
Harrington West	Oxford, N R	Donald Reid
Harrisburg	Brant, N R	James Galloway
Harriston	Wellington, N R	A. Macready
Harrow	Essex	Mrs. Ann Munger
Harrowsmith	Addington	Samuel F. Stewart
Hartford	Norfolk, N R	B. W. Thomas
Hartington	Addington	William Kennedy
Hartley	Victoria, N R	Archibald Campbell
Hartman	York, N R	D. Terry
Harwich	Kent	James Hutchison
Harwood	Northumberland, W R	Robert Drope
**Hastings*	Peterboro', E R	Henry Fowlds
Haultain	Peterboro', E R	Giles Stone
Havelock	Peterboro', E R	Peter Pearce
**Hawkesbury*	Prescott	Z. M. S. Hersey
Hawkstone	Simcoe, N R	James Houston

LIST OF POST OFFICES IN ONTARIO—(*Continued.*)

NAME OF POST OFFICE.	ELECTORAL COUNTY OR DIVISION.	NAME OF POSTMASTER.
Hawksville	Waterloo, N R.	M. P. Empey
Hay	Huron, S R.	James Murray
Haydon	Durham, W R.	John Lukes
Haysville	Waterloo, S R.	Margaret Somerville
Hazledean	Carleton.	William Watt
Headford	York, E R	John Montgomery
Head Lake	Victoria, N R.	William Halladay
Heathcote	Grey, N R.	Thomas J. Rorke
Hebron	Perth, N R.	Bernard Connolly
Heckston	Grenville, N R.	G. Adams
Heidelburg	Waterloo, N R.	John Krassler
Henry	Prescott	William Dickson
Hepworth	Grey, N R.	William Spencer
Hereward	Wellington, C R.	John Allen
**Hespeler*	Waterloo, N R.	Conrad Nahrgang
Hiawatha	Peterboro', E R.	Joseph Reynolds
High Falls	Renfrew, S R.	T. H. Dillon
Highfield	York, W R.	H. Dutchburn
Highgate	Bothwell	A. Atkinson
Highland Creek	York, E R.	William Treadway
Hillier	Prince Edward	Solomon Flagler
Hillsboro'	Lambton	Thomas L. Hill
Hillsburgh	Wellington, C R.	William How, sen.
Hillsdale	Simcoe, N R.	John Faraghar
Hill's Green	Huron, S R.	Hugh Love, sen.
Hilton	Northumberland, E R.	A. A. Becker
Hoath Head	Grey, N R.	R. Hoath
Hockley	Cardwell	Thomas Martin
Holbrook	Oxford, S R.	A. M. Whitfield
Holcomb	Peterboro', E R	Jonathan A. Wilde
Holland Landing	York, N R.	Miss E. B. Sloane
Hollen	Wellington, N R.	S. Robertson
Holmesville	Huron, N R.	Edward Kelly
Holstein	Grey, S R.	N. D. McKenzie
Holt	York, N R.	John Quibell
Holyrood	Bruce, S R	William Elliott
Homer	Lincoln	Peter A. Cavers
Honeywood	Simcoe, S R.	George Lawrence
Hopefield	Renfrew, S R.	H. Y. Read
Hopetown	Lanark, N R.	
Hornby	Halton	John McMillen
Horning's Mills	Grey, S R.	William Airth
Houghton	Norfolk, S R.	George Bundy
Howe Island	Frontenac	R. Urquhart
Hubbell's Falls	Carlton	James Riddell
Hullsville	Haldimand	John Hull
Humber	York, W R.	Thomas Bell
Humberstone	Welland	John Thompson
Hunsdon	Cardwell	William Prest
Huntley	Carleton	John Hueston
Huston	Wellington, N R.	John Landerkin
Hyde Park Corner	Middlesex, E R	Angus Fraser
Ida	Durham, E R.	Alexander Baptie
Ilderton	Middlesex, E R	George Ord
Indiana	Haldimand	James Hill
**Ingersoll*	Oxford, S R.	Joseph Thirkell
Ingoldsby	Peterboro', E R	Richard Smith
Inistioge	Grey, S R.	George Armstrong
Inkerman	Dundas	John Renwick
Innerkip	Oxford, N R	James H. Hill
Innisfil	Simcoe, S R.	Benjamin Ross
Innisville	Lanark, S R.	Thomas Code
Inverary	Frontenac	D. J. Walker
Inverhuron	Bruce, N R.	Peter McRae
Invermay	Bruce, N R.	Abraham Neelands
Iona	Elgin, W R.	J. A. Philpott
**Iroquois*	Dundas	James Grier

LIST OF POST OFFICES IN ONTARIO—(*Continued.*)

NAME OF POST OFFICE.	ELECTORAL COUNTY OR DIVISION.	NAME OF POSTMASTER.
Isley	Victoria, N R	Donald Spence
Islington	York, W R	Thomas Musson
Ivanhoe	Hastings, N R	Thomas Emo
Ivey	Simcoe, S R	George Davis
Janetville	Durham, E R	J. McDermid
Jarratt's Corners	Simcoe, N R	Charles Jarratt
Jarvis	Haldimand	James Sill
Jasper	Grenville, N R	George Cross
Jerseyville	Wentworth, S R	H. F. Young
Johnson	Grey, N R	William Johnstone
Johnson's Mills	Huron, S R	Henry Heyrock
Jordan	Lincoln	Jacob Snure
Jura	Lambton	James McCordie
Kaladar	Addington	E. F. Dunham
Kars	Carleton	W. J. Wood
Katesville	Middlesex, W R	William McClatchey
Keenansville	Cardwell	G. P. Hughes
**Keene*	Peterboro', E R	George Evans
Kelvin	Brant, S R	John Armour, jun
**Kemptville*	Grenville, N R	Robert Leslie
Kendal	Durham, W R	W. Trull
Kenilworth	Wellington, N R	Robert Hayward
Kenmore	Russell	John B. Brannen
Kent Bridge	Kent	John B. Shaw
Kerrwood	Middlesex, N R	James Irving
Kerry	Prescott	William Brodie
Kertch	Lambton	William Donolly
Keswick	York, N R	Henry Stennett
Kettleby	York, N R	Jacob Walton
Keyser	Middlesex, N R	Samuel Cooper
Kilbride	Halton	Thomas L. White
Killarney	District of Algoma	Solomon Thebo
Killean	Wellington, S R	D. Fergusson
Kilmanagh	Peel	Isaac Lowes
Kilmarnock	Grenville, N R	George Newsome
Kilmartin	Middlesex, W R	D. McKellar
Kilsyth	Grey, N R	Thomas Sloan
Kimberly	Grey, N R	William Purdy
Kinburn	Carleton	Allan Fraser
**Kincardine*	Bruce, S R	M. McKendrick
King	York, N R	Benjamin Lloyd
King Creek	York, N R	A. McMillan
Kinglake	Norfolk, S R	E. T. Martin
Kingsbridge	Huron, N R	Mrs. Mary McCarron
**Kingston*	Kingston	Robert Deacon
Kingston Mills	Frontenac	Robert Brownley
**Kingsville*	Essex	George Cooper
Kinkora	Perth, N R	James Moriarty
Kinloss	Bruce, S R	
Kinlough	Bruce, S R	Simon Corrigan
Kinmount	Victorio, N R	John Hunter
Kinsale	Ontario, S R	John Fairless
Kintail	Huron, N R	William Grant
Kintore	Oxford, N R	William Easson
Kippen	Huron, S R	Robert Mellis
Kirby	Durham, W R	H. L. Powers
Kirkfield	Victoria, N R	James S. Russell
Kirkhill	Glengarry	William McLeod
Kirkton	Huron, S R	Robert Park
Kirkwall	Wentworth, N R	W. McMillan
Klineburgh	York, W R	Thomas White
Knatchbull	Halton	William Stephenson
Komoka	Middlesex, N R	O. D. Maybee
Lafontaine	Simcoe N R	P. F. Moreau
Laggan	Glengary	Donald Cattanach
Lake Doré	Renfrew, N R	Thos. Wallace
Lakelet	Huron, N R	Myles Young

LIST OF POST OFFICES IN ONTARIO—(*Continued.*)

NAME OF POST OFFICE.	ELECTORAL COUNTY OR DIVISION.	NAME OF POSTMASTER.
Lakeside	Oxford, N R	Robt. Armstrong
L'Amaroux	York, W R	James Taylor
Lambeth	Middlesex, E R	George Kelley
**Lanark*	Lanark, N R	Wm. Robertson
Lancaster	Glengary	K. McPherson
Langford	Brant, S R	W. W. Langs
Langside	Bruce, S R	David Black
Langton	Norfolk, S R	D. W. Boughner
Lansdown	Leeds, S R	Jos. A. Bradle
Lansing	York, E R	R. G. Lambert
Largie	Elgin, W R	Archd. Leitch
Larner	Perth, S R	John Larner
Laskay	York, N R	George S. Baldwin
Latona	Grey, S R	Mark Appleby
Laurel	Wellington, N R	F. Ridley
Lavant	Lanark, N R	Archd. Browning
Lavender	Simcoe, S R	I. B. Mastin
Leamington	Essex	Warren Kimball
Leaskdale	Ontario, N R	George Leask
Leavens	Grey, N R	S. Cunningham
Lefroy	Simcoe, S R	David Davidson
Leinster	Lennox	M. Jordan
Leith	Grey, N R	James Ross, sen.
Lemonville	York, N R	John Hill
Leskard	Durham, W R	P. McIntyre
Leslie	York, E R	George Leslie, jr.
Lifford	Durham, E R	Calvin Hall
Limehouse	Halton	John Newton
Lime Lake	Hastings, E R	James Jarmin
**Lindsay*	Victoria, S R	Thomas Adam
Linton	York, N R	Joseph Lynn
Linwood	Waterloo, N R	Robert Y. Fish
Lisadel	Huron, N R	Arthur Mitchell
Lisbon	Perth, N R	James Zincann
Lisburn	Bruce, S R	G. Ruttle
**Listowell*	Perth, N R	W. H. Hacking
Little Britain	Victoria, S R	John Broad
Little Current	District of Algoma	G. B. Burkitt
Little Rideau	Prescott	Thomas Ross
Lloydtown	York, N R	Anthony Eastwood
Lobo	Middlesex, N R	Thomas S. Edwards
Loch Garry	Glengary	James Fraser
Locheil	Glengary	R. Dewar
Lockton	Cardwell	Adam Parkinson
Logierait	Lambton	D. Hossie
Londesborough	Huron, N R	John Neelands
**London*	London	Lawrence Lawless
Long Island Locks	Carleton	Moses Gamble
Longwood	Middlesex, W R	Thomas Gordon
Longwood Station	Middlesex, W R	L. L. Griffith
Lonsdale	Hastings, E R	Richard Wildman
Loretto	Cardwell	P. D. Kelly
**L'Orignal*	Prescott	C. Johnston
Lorraine	Cardwell	John Mills
Loughboro'	Addington	Hugh Madden
Louisville	Kent	R. C. Struthers
Lovat	Bruce, S R	Thomas Allen
Lowbanks	Monck	Henry Overholt
Lowville	Halton	Andrew Pickett
**Lucan*	Middlesex, N R	William Porte
**Lucknow*	Bruce, S R	M. Campbell
Lumley	Huron, S R	William Dinnin
Lunenburg	Stormont	F. Kirkpatrick
Lurgan	Bruce, S R	James McCrindle
Luther	Wellington, N R	Samuel Stuckey
Luton	Elgin, E R	L. R. Tyrell
**Lyn*	Brockville	John S. Bell

LIST OF POST OFFICES IN ONTARIO—(*Continued.*)

NAME OF POST OFFICE.	ELECTORAL COUNTY OR DIVISION.	NAME OF POSTMASTER.
Lynden	Wentworth, N R	William McRae
Lyndhurst	Leeds, S R	John Roddick
Lynedoch	Norfolk, S R	George Gray
Lynnville	Norfolk, N R	W. L. Crooker
Lyons	Elgin, E R	P. J. Putman
McDonald's Corners	Lanark, N R	William Chalmers
McGillivray	Middlesex, N R	D. Shoff
McIntyre	Grey, S R	Edward Potts
McNab—Glengary	Glengary	Simon Fraser
Maberly	Lanark, S R	John McGregor
Macton	Wellington, N R	J. M. McCormick
Macville	Cardwell	Seth Wilson
**Madoc*	Hastings, N R	E. D. O'Flynn
Madrid	Renfrew, S R	P. McCawley
Maidstone	Essex	Thomas Moran
Maitland	Grenville, S R	George C. Longley
Mal akoff	Carleton	W. J. Pierce
Mall orytown	Leeds, S R	Frederick F. Lee
Malone	Hastings, N R	D. N. Powell
Malton	Peel	J. B. Allen
Malvern	York, E R	Smith Thomson
**Manchester*	Ontario, N R	Adam Gordon
Mandamin	Lambton	
Manilla	Victoria, S R	Mary Douglas
Manitowaning	District of Algoma	Thomas Simpson, M. D.
Mannheim	Waterloo, S R	Daniel L. Knetchel
Manotick	Carleton	G. L. Parker
Mansfield	Simcoe, S R	William Gilbert
Maple	York, W R	Joseph Noble
Maple Hill	Bruce, S R	R. B. Clement
Mapleton	Elgin, E R	William Appleford
Marathon	Carleton	Samuel Woods
March	Carleton	Thomas Read
Marchmont	Simcoe, N R	Charles Powley
Marden	Wellington, S R	C. McD. Blyth
**Markham*	York, E R	James J. Barker
Marlbank	Hastings, E R	W. G. Allan
Marmion	Grey, N R	James Ward
Marmora	Hastings, N R	Benjamin Johnson
Marnoch	Huron, N R	P. Porterfield
Marshville	Monck	Edward Lee
Marston	Norfolk, S R	John Gardner
Martintown	Glengary	Robert Blackwood
Marysville	Hastings, E R	John Kemp
Massie	Grey, N R	A. Massie
Mattawa	District of Nipissing	John Bangs
Maxwell	Grey, S R	Joseph Maxwell
Mayfield	Peel	William Spiers
Maynard	Grenville, S R	Charles Birks
Maynooth	Hastings, N R	Michael Doyle
Meadowvale	Peel	C. H. Gooderham
**Meaford*	Grey, N R	D. L. Layton
Medina	Oxford, N R	J. H. Beek
Medonte	Simcoe, N R	Edmund Moon
Melancthon	Grey, S R	James Brown
Melrose	Hastings, E R	George Duncan
Melville	Prince Edward	Caleb Johnson
Menie	Northumberland, E R	James Mather
Merivale	Carleton	E. B. Hopper
Merlin	Kent	E. S. Benedict
**Merrickville*	Grenville, N R	Samuel Jakes
Mersea	Essex	Jonathan Wigfield
Meyersburg	Northumberland, E R	Thomas Oliver
Michipicoten River	District of Algoma	P. W. Bell
Middleville	Lanark, N R	William Croft
Midhurst	Simcoe, N R	George Sneath
Mildmay	Bruce, S R	J. H. Dolmage

LIST OF POST OFFICES IN ONTARIO—(*Continued.*)

NAME OF POST OFFICE.	ELECTORAL COUNTY OR DIVISION.	NAME OF POSTMASTER.
Milford	Prince Edward	James Cook
Millbank	Perth, N R	W. Rutherford
Mill Bridge	Hastings, N R	R. M. Norman
**Millbrook*	Durham, E R	Richard Howden
Mills Roches	Cornwall	S. H. Moss
Mill Grove	Wentworth, N R	Oron Thompson
Mill Haven	Lenox	George B. Forward
Milliken	York, E R	W. Gorvett
Millington	Ontario, N R	John Warrington
Mill Point	Hastings, E R	James Bowen
Milnesville	York, E R	Thomas Pearce
**Milton West*	Halton	William D. Lyon
Mimico	York, W R	J. Kynock
Mimosa	Wellington, C R	Henry Reed
Minden	Peterboro', E R	S. S. Peck
Minesing	Simcoe, N R	Andrew Ronald
Mitchell	Perth, N R	John Hicks
Moffatt	Halton	Peter Little
Mohawk	Brant, S R	William L. Jones
Moira	Hastings, N R	Henry Ostrom
Molesworth	Perth, N R	N. M. Livingstone
Monck	Wellington, N R	George Brain
Monckland	Stormont	Zachariah Weegar
Moneymore	Hastings, E R	John Harigan
Mongolia	York, E R	Robert Curtis
Monkton	Perth, N R	Edward Greensides
Mono Centre	Cardwell	John Wilson
Mono Mills	Cardwell	Joseph Alexander
Montague	Lanark, S R	Peter Clark
Montrose	Welland	Archibald Thompson
Moore	Lambton	John Morrison
Moose Creek	Stormont	William McKillican
Moray	Middlesex, N R	H. Hagerman
Morewood	Dundas	A. McKay
Morganston	Northumberland, E R	William J. Newman
Morley	Grey, N R	James Lemon
Morningdale Mills	Perth, N R	J. Nicklin
**Morpeth*	Bothwell	Andrew Heyward
Morrisbank	Huron, N R	James Orr
**Morrisburg*	Dundas	James Holden
Morriston	Wellington, S R	R. B. Morrison
Mortlake	York, E R	A. Thompson
Morton	Leeds, S R	James R. Leake
Morven	Lenox	Daniel Henwood
Moscow	Addington	Zara Vanluven
Mossley	Middlesex, E R	John Amoss
Motherwell	Perth, S R	James Brown, sen.
Mountain Grove	Addington	E. L. Godfrey
Mountain View	Prince Edward	W. H. Way
Mount Albert	York, N R	R. Hunter
Mount Albion	Wentworth, S R	James R. Cook
**Mount Brydges*	Middlesex, W R	John Branston
Mount Charles	Peel	Charles King
Mount Elgin	Oxford, S R	James B. Smart
**Mount Forest*	Grey, S R	T. G. Smith
Mount Healy	Haldimand	A. W. Thompson
Mount Horeb	Victoria, S R	William Reynolds
Mount Hurst	Cardwell	John Wallace
Mount Pleasant	Durham, E R	S. J. Best
Mount St. Louis	Simcoe, N R	J. B. Hussey
Mount St. Patrick	Renfrew, S R	Bridget Brady
Mount Salem (late Salem)	Elgin, E R	W. W. White
Mountsberg	Wentworth, N R	James N. Paine
Mount Vernon	Brant, S R	Thomas Perrin
Mount Webster	Leeds, S R	Robert Webster
Mulgrave	Welland	P. Learn, sen.
Mulmur	Simcoe, S R	William Little

LIST OF POST OFFICES IN ONTARIO—(*Continued.*)

NAME OF POST OFFICE.	ELECTORAL COUNTY OR DIVISION.	NAME OF POSTMASTER.
Muncey	Middlesex, W R	R. E. Whiting
Munster	Carleton	Thomas Tubman
Murray	Northumberland, E R	Richard O. Dixon
Murvale	Addington	Michael Davy
Muskoka Falls	Victoria, N R	Mrs. Susan J. Foxley
Musselberg	Perth, N R	George Shearer
Myrtle	Ontario, S R	Francis L. Pike
Nairn	Middlesex, N R	Archibald Bell
Nanticoke	Haldimand	C. E. Bourne
**Napanee*	Lenox	Gilbert Bogart
Napanee Mills	Addington	H. M. Wright
Napier	Middlesex W R	John Arthurs
Nassagiweya	Halton	Thomas Easterbrook
Navan	Russell	M. O'Meara
Nelson	Halton	D. W. Springer
Netherby	Welland	Joseph House
Neustadt	Grey, S R	D. Winkler
Nevis	Simcoe, N R	James Greenshields
New Aberdeen	Waterloo, S R	William Key
Newark	Oxford, S R	Henry Henderson
Newbliss	Leeds, N R	William Moran
Newboro'	Leeds, S R	Thomas Webster
Newboyne	Leeds, S R	James Lytle
Newbridge	Huron, N R	James Carson
**Newburg*	Addington	Robert Hope
**Newbury*	Middlesex, W R	Thomas Robinson
**Newcastle*	Durham, W R	Hiram Hodges
New Dundee	Waterloo, S R	A. Moyer
New Durham	Brant, S R	E. F. Schooley
**New Edinburgh*	Russell	James Blackburn
**New Hamburg*	Waterloo, S R	Christian Ernst
Newington	Stormont	Jacob Baker
New Lowell	Simcoe, N R	P. Paton
**New Market*	York, N R	William Roe
Newport	Brant, S R	Colin Milloy
New Ross	Dundas	Thomas Currie
Newry	Perth, N R	Daniel Falconer
New Sarum	Elgin, E R	Samuel Wilton
Newton Brook	York, W R	W. W. Cummer
Newton Robinson	Simcoe, W R	J. R. Hipwell
**Niagara*	Niagara	Robert Warren
Nicolston	Simcoe, S R	John Nicol
Nile	Huron, N R	Henry J. Kerr
Nilestown	Middlesex, E R	John Morwood
Nissouri	Oxford, N R	Joseph Howes
Nithburg	Perth, N R	James Brown
Nobleton	York, N R	William Munsie
Norham	Northumberland, E R	Dr. B. G. G. Demorest
Norland	Victoria, N R	A. A. McLaughlin
Normandale	Norfolk, S R	John W. Shepherd
Normanton	Bruce, N R	Archibald Roy
North Adjala	Cardwell	William Donehy
North Augusta	Grenville, S R	Samuel J. Bellamy
North Bruce	Bruce, N R	D. McTavish
North Douro	Peterboro', E R	Robert Casement
Northfield	Stormont	
North Glanford	Wentworth, S R	Edward Dickenson
North Gower	Carlton	James Beaman
North Keppel	Grey, N R	David Dewar
North Lancaster	Glengary	Charles Leclair
North Montague	Lanark, S R	W. H. Stewart
North Mountain	Dundas	James Cleland
North Pelham	Monck	Mrs. M. A. McQueen
North Port	Prince Edward	Samuel Solmes, jun
North Ridge	Essex	James Cummiford
North Senaca	Haldimand	John Tucker
North Williamsburg	Dundas	William Gordon

LIST OF POST OFFICES IN ONTARIO—(*Continued.*)

NAME OF POST OFFICE.	ELECTORAL COUNTY OR DIVISION.	NAME OF POSTMASTER.
Norval	Halton	William Clay
Norway	York, E R.	
**Norwich*	Oxford, S R	Gilbert Moore
**Norwood*	Peterborough, E R	J. A. Butterfield
Notfield	Glengary	Peter Kennedy
Nottawa	Simcoe, N R	Andrew Melville
Oak Hill	Victoria, N R	William Corbett
Oakland	Brant, S R	John Toyne
Oak Ridges	York, N R	D. Gregory
**Oakville*	Halton	R. Balmer
Oakwood	Victoria, S R	E. A. Bowes
Oban	Lambton	William Carrick
**Odessa*	Lenox	P. S. Timmerman
Offa	Huron, S R	John G. Quary
**Oil Springs*	Lambton	James Keating
Old Montrose	Kent	H. Mills
Olinda	Essex	John C. Fox
Omagh	Halton	Thomas Little
**Omemee*	Victoria, S R	Robert Grandy
Ompah	Addington	Henry Dunham
Oneida	Haldimand	J. T. Mutchmore
Ongly	Northumberland, E R	Peter H. Maybee
Onondaga	Brant, S R	William S. Buckwell
**Orangeville*	Wellington, C R	Guy Leslie
Orchard	Grey, S R	Thomas Caldwell
**Orillia*	Simcoe, N R	Thomas Moffat
Orleans	Russell	H. McHarry
Ormond	Dundas	Ira Morgan
Oro	Simcoe, N R	Levi Morningstar
Orono	Durham, W R	Joseph L. Tucker
Orwell	Elgin, E R	D. Sutherland
Osceola	Renfrew, N R	Alexander McLaren
Osgoode	Russell	Adam J. Baker
**Oshawa*	Ontario, S R	David Smith
Osprey	Simcoe, N R	James Dick
Ospringe	Wellington, C R	William Symon
Ossian	Lambton	Geo. S. McPherson
**Ottawa*	Ottawa	G. P. Baker
Otterville	Oxford, S R	Gervaise Goodwin
Oungah	Kent	Thos. Kinney
Oustic	Wellington, C R	Thos. Whitehead
Outram	Bruce, S R	David Smith
Overton	Addington	
**Owen Sound*	Grey, N R	George Brown
Oxenden	Grey, N R	G. M. Stanley
Oxford Centre	Oxford, S R	Wm. Garbutt
Oxford Mills	Grenville, N R	Murdoch Gair
Oxford Station	Grenville, N R	Andrew Holmes
Oznabruck Centre	Stormont	Jacob J. Poaps
**Paisley*	Bruce, N R	Thomas Orchard
**Pakenham*	Lanark, N R	Alex. Fowler
Palermo	Halton	H. M. Switzer
Panmure	Carleton	James Ring
Parham	Addington	John Griffith
**Paris*	Brant, N R	George Stanton
Paris Station	Brant, N R	M. X. Carr
Parker	Wellington, N R	George M. Laird
Park Head	Bruce, N R	William Simpson
Park Hill	Middlesex, N R	John Noble
Parma	Lennox	David Griffith
Parry Sound	District of Algoma	N. P. Wakefield
Patterson	York, W R	Peter Patterson
Peepabun	Wellington, N R	Robert Dickson
Pefferlaw	York, N R	George Johnson
Pelham Union	Monck	J. C. Buckbee
**Pembroke*	Renfrew, N R	Alex. Moffatt
Pendleton	Prescott	J. M. C. Delesderniers

LIST OF POST OFFICES IN ONTARIO—(*Continued.*)

NAME OF POST OFFICE.	ELECTORAL COUNTY OR DIVISION.	NAME OF POSTMASTER.
**Penetanguishene*	Simcoe, N R	D. J. Mitchell
Penville	Simcoe, S R	Edward T. Turner
Perch Station	Durham, E R	John Irwin
Perrytown	Lanark, S R	R. A. Corbett
**Perth*	Lanark, S R	Thomas Cairns
Petawawa	Renfrew, N R	Solomon Devine
**Peterboro'*	Peterboro', W R	S. J. Carver
Petersburg	Waterloo, S R	John Ernst
Peterson	Victoria, N R	
Peterson's Ferry	Prince Edward	Paul C. Peterson
**Petrolea*	Lambton	Patrick Barclay
Petworth	Addington	E. L. Carscallen
Philipsburg West	Waterloo, S R	G. C. Doering
Phillipsville	Leeds, S R	George Brown
Pickering	Ontario, S R	Mrs. Elizabeth Whitney
**Picton*	Prince Edward	David Barker
Pine Grove	York, W R	A. L. Gooderham
Pine Orchard	York, N R	C. Randall
Pine River	Bruce, S R	Alexander G. McCosh
Pinkerton	Bruce, S R	Samuel King
Pittsferry	Frontenac	Daniel Root
Plainfield	Hastings, E R	Edward N. Gould
Plantagenet	Prescott	Henry Smith
Plattsville	Oxford, N R	Samuel Platt
Playfair	Lanark, S R	G. C. Mills
Pleasant Hill	Norfolk, S R	J. D. Morgan
Plum Hollow	Leeds, S R	Mrs. Lydia Alguire
Point Abino	Welland	Ralph Disher
Point Alexander	Renfrew, N R	John Lane
Point Edward	Lambton	Louis Ernst
Point Petre	Prince Edward	James Scott
Point Traverse	Prince Edward	Harmon Case
Poland	Lanark, N R	
Pomona	Grey, S R	James Ross
Ponsonby	Wellington, C R	James L. Halley
Poole	Perth, N R	D. Matthews
Port Albert	Huron, N R	
Port Bruce	Elgin, E R	Thomas Thompson
**Port Burwell*	Elgin, E R	Thomas Pilcher
**Port Colborne*	Welland	L. G. Carter
Port Credit	Peel	Robert Cotton
**Port Dalhousie*	Lincoln	John H. Martindale
**Port Dover*	Norfolk, S R	David Abel
Port Elmsley	Lanark, S R	John Elliott
Porter's Hill	Huron, S R	Robert Porter
Port Granby	Durham, W R	David March
Port Hoover	Victoria, S R	Elias Rogers
**Port Hope*	Durham, E R	Robert W. Smart
Portland	Leeds, S R	S. S. Scovil
Port Maitland	Monck	James Moss
Port Nelson	Halton	Hugh Cotter
Port Perry	Ontario, N R	H. Gordon
**Port Robinson*	Welland	James McCoppen
**Port Rowan*	Norfolk, S R	Andrew McLennan
Port Royal	Norfolk, S R	Robert Abbott
Port Ryerse	Norfolk, S R	William H. Ryerse
Port Severn (sub)	Simcoe, N R	Alexander R. Christie
Portsmouth	Frontenac	George McLeod
**Port Stanley*	Elgin, E R	John Tennant
Port Talbot	Elgin, W R	George Macbeth
Port Union	Ontario, S R	Henry L. Pullen
Powell	Carleton	Denis Egan
**Prescott*	Grenville, S R	W. H. Brouse
**Preston*	Waterloo, S R	Conrad Nispel
Priceville	Grey, S R	Joseph Dixon
Primrose	Simcoe, S R	
**Prince Albert*	Ontario, N R	H. H. McCaw

LIST OF POST OFFICES IN ONTARIO—(*Continued.*)

NAME OF POST OFFICE.	ELECTORAL COUNTY OR DIVISION.	NAME OF POSTMASTER.
Princeton	Oxford, N R	J. G. Lindsay
Prospect	Lanark, S R	William Burrows
Purdy	Hastings, N R	W. Lake
Purpleville	York, W R	James Livingston
Puslinch	Wellington, S R	William Leslie
Putnam (late Dorchester)	Middlesex, E R	Robert Craik
Queensborough	Hastings, N R	Daniel Thompson
Queenston	Niagara	James Wynn
Queensville	York, N R	James H. Aylward
Raglan	Ontario, S R	L. Foster
Railton	Addington	John Walsh
Rainham	Haldimand	Isaac Honsberger
Rainham Centre	Haldimand	
Rama	Ontario	James McPherson
Ranelagh	Norfolk, N R	Benjamin Lake
Ratho	Oxford, N R	Joseph Williams
Ravenna	Grey, N R	William Reid
Ravenshoe	York, N R	J. B. Oliver
Ravenswood	Lambton	Paul Jarvis
Raymond	Victoria, N R	Anthony Sufferin
Reading	Wellington, C R	Robert Donaldson
Rednersville	Prince Edward	Simon Meacham
Reekie	Bruce, S R	
**Renfrew*	Renfrew, S R	William Mackay
Renton	Norfolk, N R	
Riceville	Prescott	P. McLaurin
Richmond West	Carleton	W. H. Butler
**Richmond Hill*	York, W R	Matthew Teefy
Richview	Peel	Robert M. Burgess
Richwood	Oxford, N R	J. H. Laycock
Ridgetown	Bothwell	L. S. Hancock
Ridgeville	Monck	Jonas Steele
Ringwood	York, N R	G. H. Silvester
Ripley	Bruce, S R	
Riversdale	Bruce, S R	H. B. O'Connor
Roblin	Lenox	E. Card
Rob-Roy	Grey, S R	David McGowan
Rochester	Essex	P. Dumouchelle
Rockford	Norfolk, N R	Joseph Greathead
Rockingham	Renfrew, S R	J. S. J. Watson
Rockport	Leeds, S R	William Cornwall
Rockside	Cardwell	D. Kirkwood
Rockton	Wentworth, N R	B. Cornell
Rockwood	Wellington, C R	Robert Pasmore
Rodgerville	Huron, S R	James Bonthron
Rodney	Elgin, W R	A. Mumphrey
Roebuck	Grenville, S R	James Bouvaird, jun
Rokeby	Lanark, S R	A. Adams
Rolph	Norfolk, N R	James Cowan
Romney	Kent	C. Coatsworth
Ronaldsay	Grey, S R	Joseph McArdle
Rondeau	Kent	J. K. Morris
Rondeau Harbour	Kent	E. L. Stoddard
Rosa	Northumberland, E R	H. Fieldhouse
Rosebank	Brant, N R	Almon Almas
Rosedale	Victoria, N R	Moses McNeil
Rosedene	Monck	Cornelius McKay
**Rosemont*	Simcoe, S R	George Cumming
Roseneath	Northumberland, W R	John Harstone
Rosetta	Lanark, N R	Robert McFarlane
Roseville	Waterloo, S R	Moses Gingrich
Roslin	Hastings, E R	William Gilroy
Ross	Renfrew, N R	'ames McLaren
Rosseau	Simcoe, N R	George Milne
Rothsay	Wellington, N R	J. F. A. Stull
Rouge Hill	Ontario, S R	Hugh Graham
Round Plains	Norfolk, N R	John Weaver

LIST OF POST OFFICES IN ONTARIO—(*Continued.*)

NAME OF POST OFFICE.	ELECTORAL COUNTY OR DIVISION.	NAME OF POSTMASTER.
Rugby	Simcoe, N R.	James Bell
Russell	Russell	
Rutherford	Bothwell	James McCagey
Ruthven	Essex	Hugh Ruthven
Ryckman's Corners	Wentworth	William Wells
Rylston	Northumberland, E R.	D. Allan
St. Agatha	Waterloo, S R.	Anthony Kaiser
St. Andrews, West	Cornwall	Lackey Masterson
St. Ann's, Lincoln	Monk	Jacob Upper
**St. Catharines*	Lincoln	W. L. Copeland
St. Clements	Waterloo, N R	John Stroh
St. Davids	Niagara	C. Fisher
St. Eugène	Prescott	Simon Labrose
St. George, Brant	Brant, N R	Samuel Stanton
St. Helens	Huron, N R.	William Gordon
St. Ives	Middlesex, E R.	Thomas Howard
St. Jacobs	Waterloo, N R.	John L. Wideman
St. John's	Welland	Stephen Haney
**St. Mary's, Blanchard*	Perth, S R.	Arundel Hill
St. Raphael, West	Glengary	A. McDonell
**St. Thomas, West*	Elgin, E R.	E. Ermatinger
Sable	Middlesex, N R.	A. McDonald
Saintfield	Ontario, N R.	William Sanders
Salem	Wellington, C R	John R. Wisler
Salford	Oxford, S R	William Boon
Salmonville	Peel	
Sandfield	Glengary	Angus McRae
Sandford	Ontario, N R.	Edward Taylor
Sandhill	Cardwell	Robert Dwyer, jun
Sandhurst	Lenox	David Allan
Sand Point	Renfrew, S R	H. J. Fourdrinier
**Sandwich*	Essex	O. St. Louis
Sarawak	Grey, N R	
Sarepta	Huron, S R.	William Reynolds
**Sarnia*	Lambton	Alfred Fisher
**Saugeen*	Bruce, N R.	Thomas Lee
Sault Ste. Marie	District of Algoma	David Pim
Scarboro'	York, E R	Donald McLean
Schomberg	York, N R.	William S. Lockard
Scone	Bruce, S R.	Thomas Bearman
Scotch Block	Halton	Thomas Hume
Scotland	Brant, S R.	H. Lyman
Scugog	Ontario, N R.	Isaac Finley
**Seaforth*	Huron, S R.	Samuel Dickson
Sebringville	Perth, N R.	Isaac Bennett
Seeley's Bay	Leeds, S R	William Coleman
Selby	Lenox	David Wartman
Selkirk	Haldimand	James Wilkie
Selton	Bothwell	James Robinson
Selwyn	Peterboro', W R	Richard Northy
**Seneca*	Haldimand	John Scott
Severn Bridge	Victoria, N R	James H. Jackson
Shakespeare	Perth, S R.	George Brown
Shamrock	Renfrew, S R.	P. Gorman
Shanick	Hastings, N R	James Bailey
Shanly	Grenville, S R	William Clark
Shannonville	Hastings, E R	Hiram Holden
Shanty Bay	Simcoe N R	William Heard
Sharon	York, N R.	John T. Stokes
Sharpton	Frontenac	R. McKechnie
Sheffield	Wentworth, N R	Edwin Bond
Shelburne	Grey, S R	William Jelly
Sheldon	Cardwell	M. Webster
Sheridan	Halton	E. D. Hill
Sherkston	Welland	A. O. Stringer
Shetland	Bothwell	John Drew
Shipley	Perth, N R.	E. Bristow

LIST OF POST OFFICES IN ONTARIO—(*Continued.*)

NAME OF POST OFFICE.	ELECTORAL COUNTY OR DIVISION.	NAME OF POSTMASTER.
Shrigley	Grey, S R	William August
Sillsville	Lenox	Donovan Sills
Silver Creek	Halton	John Dean
Silver Hill	Norfolk, S R	Elizabeth Cole
Silvershoe	Simcoe, N R	James A. Mather
**Simcoe*	Norfolk, N R	Henry Mulkins
Singhampton	Simcoe, N R	James Hamilton
Skipness	Bruce, N R	Donald Reid
Skye	Glengary	J. R. McKenzie
Sleswick	Cardwell	Richard J. Evans
Sligo	Cardwell	Thomas Bell
Smithfield	Northumberland, E R	S. D. Smith
**Smith's Falls*	Lanark, S R	James Shaw, jun
Smithville	Lincoln	Robert Thompson
Sombra	Bothwell	P. Cattanach
Sonya	Ontario, N R	Lewis Harper
South Cayuga	Haldimand	Isaac Fry
South Douro	Peterboro', E R	Thomas Hanrahan
South Dummer	Peterboro', E R	Hugh Drain
South Elmsley	Leeds, N R	William Garvin
South Finch	Stormont	Duncan G. McMillan
South Gloucester	Russel	Thomas Stanley
South Gower	Grenville	James Wallace
South Lake	Leeds, S R	W. Bermingham
South March	Carleton	Samuel Scisson
South Middleton	Norfolk, N R	Robert McKim
South Monaghan	Northumberland, W R	Robert Waddell
South Mountain	Dundas	John Morrow
South Zorra	Oxford, N R	Thomas Cross
Sparta	Elgin, E R	John A. Eakins
Speedie	Grey, N R	William Speedie
Speedside	Wellington, C R	James Loughrin
Spencerville	Grenville, S R	Mrs. Mary Imrie
Spring Arbour	Norfolk, S R	J. W. Hazen
Springbank	Middlesex, N R	W. Wells
Springfield	Elgin, E R	W. H. Graves
Springford	Oxford, S R	John Wood
Springville	Peterboro', W R	A. Goodfellow
Staffa	Perth, S R	R. F. Rundle
Stafford	Renfrew, N R	Robert Childerhose
Stamford	Welland	Mrs. Phœbe A. Correll
Stanley's Mills	Peel	C. Burrell
Stanton	Simcoe, S R	William H. Beatty
**Stayner*	Simcoe, N R	John, McKeggie
Steele	Simcoe, N R	Coll Robinson
Stella	Lenox	William Perceval
Stevensville	Welland	William T. House
**Stirling*	Hastings, N R	William Judd
Stirton	Wellington, N R	John Luxson
Stisted	Norfolk, S R	James Fry
Stittsville	Carleton	J. S. Argue
Stockdale	Northumberland, E R	I. D. Osterhout
Stoco	Hastings, E R	Francis Murphy
Stony Creek	Wentworth, S R	Alva G. Jones
Stony Point	Essex	H. Desjardins
**Stouffville*	York, N R	Edward Wheeler
Strabane	Wentworth, N R	Matthew Peebles
Straffordville	Elgin, E R	O. Whitecomb
Strangford	York, E R	Isaac Blain
**Stratford*	Perth, S R	L. T. O'Loane
Strathallan	Oxford, N R	J. C. Van Decar
Strathburn	Middlesex, W R	Hugh McRae
Strathnairn	Grey, N R	John W. Hartman
**Strathroy*	Middlesex, N R	Charles McIntosh
**Streetsville*	Peel	James E. Rutledge
Stretton	Ontario, N R	
Stromness	Monck	Robert Nimmo

LIST OF POST OFFICES IN ONTARIO—(*Continued.*)

NAME OF POST OFFICE.	ELECTORAL COUNTY OR DIVISION.	NAME OF POSTMASTER.
Sullivan	Grey, N R.	William Buchanan
Summerstown	Glengary	Andrew Summers
Summerville	Peel	William Bemrose
Sunbury	Frontenac	John McBride
Sunnidale	Simcoe, N R.	Alexander Gillespie
Sutherland's Corners	Bothwell	James Walker
Sweaburg	Oxford, S R.	H. Flood
Switzerville	Lenox	Calvin W. Miller
Sylvan	Middlesex	John Dawson
Talbotville Royal	Elgin, W R	John Stacey
Tamworth	Addington	James Aylsworth
Tapleytown	Wentworth, S R.	John Ptolemy
Tara	Bruce, N R	John Tobey
Tatlock	Lanark, S R	Mrs. Guthrie
Tavistock	Perth, S R.	George Matheson
Taylorholme	Russell	Charles Taylor
Tecumseth	Simcoe, S R	D. A. Jones
Teeswater	Bruce, S R	M. Hadwen
Teeterville	Norfolk, N R	Thomas Edgeworth
Telfer	Middlesex, E R	Adam Telfer
Tempo	Middlesex, E R	A. Remey
Tennyson	Lanark, S R	D. McGregor
Teston	York, W R	George Wilson
Teviotdale	Wellington, N R.	M. G. Miller
Thamesford	Oxford, N R.	N. C. McCarty
Thamesville	Bothwell	James Duncan
Thanet	Hastings, N R	B. McKillican, sen.
Thistleton	York, W R	Richard Johnston
Thomasburg, E R.	Hastings	John Robertson
Thompsonville	Simcoe, S R.	J. T. Schmietendorf
Thornbury	Grey, N R.	Thomas McKenny
Thorndale	Middlesex, E R	Thomas Harrison
**Thornhill*	York, W R	Josiah Purkiss
Thornton	Simcoe, S R	T. M. Banting
**Thorold*	Welland	Jacob Keefer
Thorold Station	Lincoln	S. M. Stephens
Thurlow	Hastings, E R.	William T. Casey
Tilbury East	Kent	James Smith
**Tilsonburg*	Oxford, S R.	Benjamin Van Norman
Tiverton	Bruce, N R	N. McInnes
Toledo	Leeds, N R	Mrs. C. A. McLean
Topping	Perth, N R	S. Crozier
Torbolton	Carleton	Samuel D. Haight
Tormore	Cardwell	Wm. Graham
**Toronto*	Toronto	Joseph Lesslie
Totnes	Perth, N R	John Raw
Tottenham	Simcoe, S R	John Wilson
Townsend Centre	Norfolk N R	Hiram Slaght
Trafalgar	Halton	James Appelbe
Treadwell	Prescott	Humphrey Hughes
Trecastle	Perth, N R	W. C. Cowan
**Trenton*	Hastings, W R	James Cumming
Trowbridge	Perth, N R	G. Code
Troy	Wentworth, N R	John R. Neff
Trudell	Essex	Henry Richardson
Tuam	Simcoe, S R	P. H. Derham
Tullamore	Peel	John Lowther
Tuscarora	Brant, N R	Henry Maynard
Tweed	Hastings, E R	Richard Marshall
Tweedside	Wentworth, S R	Gilbert Johnson
Tyrconnell	Elgin, W R	Meredith Conn
Tyrone	Durham, W R	John T. Welch
Tyrrell	Norfolk, N R	Samuel Heath
Udora	Ontario, N R	S. Umphrey
Uffington	Victoria, N R	A. Thompson
Ulster	Huron, N R	George McKay
Umfraville	Hastings, NR	D. Kavanagh

LIST OF POST OFFICES IN ONTARIO—(*Continued.*)

NAME OF POST OFFICE.	ELECTORAL COUNTY OR DIVISION.	NAME OF POSTMASTER.
Underwood	Bruce, N R	J. H. Coulthard
Union	Elgin, E R	E. J. Steele
Unionville	York, E R	George Eakin
Upnor	Victoria, N R	Thomas Tresidder
Utica	Ontario, N R	Jacob Dafoe
Utterson	Victoria, N R	Erastus Haines
Uttoxeter	Lambton	S. Shepherd
* *Uxbridge*	Ontario, N R	George Wheler
Valentia	Victoria, S R	Hugh W. Sharp
Valetta	Kent	J. Richardson
Vallentyne	Ontario, N R	Samuel Brethour
Vandecar	Oxford, S R	
* *Vankleek Hill*	Prescott	Duncan McDonell
Varna	Huron, S R	Josiah B. Secord
Veighton	Russell	
Vellore	York, W R	John MacDonald
Venice	Missisquoi	Thomas Hunter
Vennachar	Addington	Charles McKenyon
Ventnor	Grenville, S R	John Gamble
Verdon	Bruce, S R	J. Colling
Vernon	Russell	Duncan McDonald
Vernonville	Northumberland, W R	Henry Terry
Verona	Addington	Joseph Watson
Vesta	Bruce, S R	Robert Cannon
Victoria Corners	Ontario, N R	Henry Madill, jun
Victoria Square	York, E R	
* *Vienna*	Elgin, E R	Samuel Brasher
Vigo	Simcoe, N R	John Gallagher
Vine	Simcoe, S R	Richard Simpson
Violet	Lenox	D. W. Perry
Virgil	Niagara	James M. Bristol
Vittoria	Norfolk, S R	George D. McCall
Vivian	York, N R	Robt. McCormick
Vroomanton	Ontario, N R	John Teskey
Wabashene (sub)	Simcoe, N R	Wm. Hall
Wales	Stormont	William Baker
* *Walkerton*	Bruce, S R	Malcolm McLean
Wallace	Perth, N R	D. M. Williams
* *Wallaceburg*	Kent	Lionel H. Johnson
Wallacetown	Elgin, W R	John McKillop
Wallbridge	Hastings, W R	F. B. Prior
Wallenstein	Waterloo, N R	Jacob B. Oswald
Walmer	Oxford, N R	Robert Parker
Walsh	Norfolk, S R	D. W. McCall
Walsingham	Norfolk, S R	Henry L. Kitchen
Walter's Falls	Grey, N R	Mrs. E. H. Walter
Walton	Huron, N R	George Bigger
Wanstead	Lambton	John Dewar
* *Wardsville*	Middlesex, W R	W. D. Hammond
Wareham	Grey, S R	Edwin Battrick
Warkworth	Northumberland, E R	Israel Humphries
Warminster	Simcoe, N R	William George Deacom
Warner	Monck	T. W. Smith
Warrington	Simcoe, N R	George Randolph
Warsaw	Peterboro', E R	Thomas Choat
Warwick	Lambton	James Menerey
Washago	Simcoe, N R	Alexander Hamilton
Washington	Oxford, N R	William Dunn
* *Waterdown*	Wentworth, N R	James B. Thompson
* *Waterford*	Norfolk, N R	
* *Waterloo*	Waterloo, N R	C. Kumpf
Watford	Lambton	James Merry
Watson's Corners	Lanark, N R	William Horn
Waverley	Simcoe, N R	A. Kettle
Welcome	Durham, E R	John C. Tom
* *Welland*	Welland	Thomas Burgar
Welland Port	Monck	Samuel Holmes

LIST OF POST OFFICES IN ONTARIO—(*Continued.*)

NAME OF POST OFFICE.	ELECTORAL COUNTY OR DIVISION.	NAME OF POSTMASTER.
* *Wellesley*	Waterloo, N R	John Zoeger
Wellington	Prince Edward	Donald Campbell
* *Wellington Square*	Halton	Walter S Bastedo
Wellman's Corners	Hastings, N R	George Empey
Wendover	Prescott	William Lamb
West Arran	Bruce, N R	
West Brook	Frontenac	Andrew Bridge
West Essa	Simcoe, S R	Thomas Drury
Westfield	Huron, N R	H. Help
West Flamboro'	Wentworth, N R	John Percy
West Huntingdon	Hastings, N R	Philip Luke
West Huntley	Carleton	Edward Horan
West Lake	Prince Edward	Henry Lambert
West McGillivray	Middlesex, N R	Wm. Fraser
Westmeath	Renfrew, N R	Alexander Fraser
West Montrose	Waterloo, N R	J. B. Kilborne
* *Weston*	York, W R	Robert Johnston
West Osgoode	Russell	John C. Bower
Westover	Wentworth, W R	B. McIntosh
Westport	Leeds, S R	James Whelen
West's Corners	Perth, N R	John Pierson
West Winchester	Dundas	William Bow
Westwood	Peterboro', E R	Samuel Griffin
Wexford	York, E R	J. T. McBeath
Whalen	Middlesex, N R	J. H. Milson
Wheatly	Essex	W. Buchanan
* *Whitby*	Ontario, S R	Francis Keller
Whitehurst	Brockville	John Bell
White Lake	Renfrew, S R	John Paris
White Rose	York, N R	Jared Lloyd
Whitevale	Ontario, S R	Donald McPhee
Whitfield	Simcoe, S R	P. D. Henry
Whittington	Wellington, N R	R. Bowsfield
Wick	Ontario, N R	Caleb Shier
Wicklow	Northumberland, W R	C. E. Ewing
Widder	Lambton	Adam Duffus
Widder Station	Lambton	Thomas Kirkpatrick
Wilfrid	Ontario, N R	John Chambers
Wilkesport	Bothwell	William Kimball
Willetsholme	Frontenac	Josias Abrams
Williams	Middlesex, N R	Neil McTaggart
Williamstown	Glengary	Duncan McLennan
Williscroft	Bruce, N R	George Williscroft
Willowdale	York, W R	Jacob Cumner
Willowgrove	Haldimand	Thomas Keating
Wilmur	Addington	
Wilton	Lenox	Sydney Warner
Wimbledon	Essex	
Winchelsea	Huron, S R	A. Smith
Winchester	Dundas	C. T. Casselman
Winchester Springs	Dundas	James Greer
Windermere	Victoria, N R	John McAlpine
Windham Centre	Norfolk	George F. Martee
* *Windsor*	Essex	Alex. H. Wagner
Winfield	Wellington, N R	James Young
Wingham	Huron, N R	Peter Fisher
Winona	Wentworth, S R	Joseph Carpenter
Winterbourne	Waterloo, N R	
Winthrop	Huron, N R	Alexander Murchie
Wisbeach	Lambton	Joanna Bowes
Woburn	York, E R	A. H. Telfer
Wolfe Island	Frontenac	George Malone
Wolverton	Oxford, N R	James Lavery
Woodbridge	York, W R	John F. Howell
Woodburn	Wentworth, S R	William Ptolemy
Woodford	Grey, N R	John Thomson
Woodham	Perth, S R	Jonathan Shier

LIST OF POST OFFICES IN ONTARIO—(*Continued.*)

NAME OF POST OFFICE.	ELECTORAL COUNTY OR DIVISION.	NAME OF POSTMASTER.
Woodlands	Stormont	R. H. Stewart
Woodslee	Essex	W. S. Lindsay
* *Woodstock*	Oxford, N R	Charles DeBlaquiere
Woodville	Victoria, N R	John C. Gilchrist
Wooler	Northumberland, E R	Albert Wessels
* *Wroxeter*	Huron, N R	Cyrus Carroll
Wyandott	Wellington, N R	W. Ayerst
Wyebridge	Simcoe, N R	James Plewes
* *Wyoming*	Lambton	John Anderson
Yarker	Addington	J. A. Shibley
Yarmouth Centre	Elgin, E R	William Mann
York	Haldimand	Charles L. Hudson
York Mills	York, E R	John Hogg
York River	Hastings, N R	James Cleak
Yorkville	York, E R	James Dobson
Young's Point	Peterboro', W R	
Zephyr	Ontario, N R	John Nelson
Zetland	Huron, N R	L. J. Brace
Zimmerman	Halton	Robert Miller
Zurich	Huron, S R	Robert Brown

LIST OF TELEGRAPH STATIONS.

Abercorn ... Q
Acton ... O
Acton ... Q
Adams ... N Y
Adams Centre ... N Y
Ailsa Craig ... O
Ainleyville ... O
Alanburg ... O
Albany ... N Y
Alexandria Bay ... N Y
Almonte ... O
Altona ... N Y
Amherstburg ... O
Ancaster ... O
Angus ... O
Antwerp ... N Y
Arnprior ... O
Arthabaska ... Q
Arthur ... O
Aston ... Q
Aultsville ... O
Aurora ... O
Ausable Forks ... N Y
Aylmer ... O
Aylmer ... Q
Ayr ... O
Baden ... O
Bangor ... N Y
Barrie ... O
Bath ... O
Bathurst ... N B
Batiscan ... Q
Beachburg ... O
Beamsville ... O
Beauharnois ... Q
Becancour ... Q
Belleville ... O
Belleville ... N Y
Bell Ewart ... O
Belœil ... Q
Berlin ... O
Berlin Falls ... N H
Berthier ... Q
Bertie ... O
Bethel ... Me
Bic ... Q
Black Brook ... N Y
Black River ... Q
Bobcaygeon ... O
Bord à Plouffe ... Q
Boston ... Mass
Bothwell ... O
Boucherville Mont ... Q
Boundary Line ...
Bowmanville ... O
Bradford ... O
Bramley ... O
Brampton ... O
Brantford ... O
Brasher Falls ... N Y
Breslau ... O
Bridgewater ... O
Bright ... O
Brighton ... O
Britannia Mills ... Q
Brockville ... O
Brompton Falls ... Q
Brooklin ... O
Brooklyn ... N Y
Brownville ... N Y
Brushes Mills ... N Y
Bryant's Pond ... Me
Buctouche ... N B
Buffalo ... N Y
Burke ... N Y
Burlington ... Vt
Cacouna ... Q
Caledonia ... O
Caledonia Springs ... O
Camlachie ... O
Campbellford ... O
Campbellton ... N B
Canfield ... O
Canton ... N Y
Cape Vincent ... N Y
Carleton Place ... O
Carron Brook ... O
Carthage ... N Y
Castleton ... O
Cayuga ... O
Centreville ... N Y
Chambly ... Q
Champlain ... N Y
Chateauguay ... N Y
Chateauguay Basin ... Q
Chatham ... N B
Chatham ... O
Cheever ... N Y
Chicago ... Ill
Chippawa ... O
Cincinnati ... Ohio
Clarence ... O
Clarksburg ... O
Clayton ... N Y
Cleveland ... Ohio
Clifton ... N Y
Clifton ... O
Clifton House ... O
Clinton ... O
Clinton Mills ... N Y
Coaticooke ... Q
Cobourg ... O
Colborne ... O
Collingwood ... O
Compton ... Q
Consecon ... O
Copetown ... O
Coteau ... Q
Cornwall ... O
Cowansville ... Q
Craigies Mills ... Me
Craig's Road ... Q
Crown Point ... N Y
Cumberland ... O
Dalhousie ... N. B
Dannemora ... N. Y
Danville ... Q
Danville Junction ... Me
Davenport ... O
Deer River ... N. Y
Dekalb Junction ... N. Y
Delaware ... O
Des Rivieres ... Q
Detroit ... Mich
Derby Line ... Vt
Dexter ... N. Y
Dickinson's Landing ... O
Don ... O
Doucet's Landing ... Q
Dresden ... O
Drumbo ... O
Duffin's Creek ... O
Dundas ... O
Dundee ... Q
Dunham ... Q
Dunville ... O
Durham ... O
Durham (G. T. R) ... Q
Ecclesville ... O
Edwardsburgh ... O
Ellenburg ... N. Y
Elizabethtown ... N. Y

Elora ... O
Ernestown ... O
Essex ... N. Y
Etchemin ... Q
Evan's Mills ... N. Y
Exeter ... O
Falmouth ... Me
Farnham ... Q
Father Point ... Q
Fergus ... O
Eorrest ... N. Y
Forest (G.T.R) ... O
Fort Covington ... N.Y
Fort Erie ... O
Fredericton ... N. B
Frelighsburg ... Q
Frenchman's Bay ... O
Galt ... O
Gananoque ... O
Garden Island ... O
Georgetown ... O
Georgeville ... Q
Gilead ... N. H
Gilford ... O
Glencoe ... O
Glen House ... N. H
Goderich ... O
Gorham ... N.H
Gould's Landing ... O
Gouveneur ... N.Y
Grafton ... O
Granby ... Q
Granton ... O
Greenwood ... O
Grenville ... Q
Grimsby ... O
Guelph ... O
Hadlow Cove ... Q
Halifax ... N.S
Hamburg ... O
Hamilton ... O
Hanover ... O
Harrisburg ... O
Hastings ... O
Hawkesbury ... O
Hemmingford ... Q
Henderson ... N.Y
Hespeler ... O
Heuvelton ... N.Y
Holland Landing ... O
Hudson ... Q
Hull ... Q
Huntington ... Q
Industry or Joliette ... Q
Ingersol ... O
Irish Creek ... O
Island Pond ... Vt
Isle Verte ... Q
Kemptville ... O
Keeseville ... N. Y
Kincardine ... O
King ... O
Kingston ... N. B
Kingston ... O
Knapps ... N. Y
Knowlton ... Q
Komoka ... O
L'Acadie ... Q
Lachine ... Q
Lachine Junction ... Q
Lacolle ... Q
Lancaster ... O
Lansdowne ... O
L'Assomption ... Q
Lawrence ... N.Y
Lefroy ... O
Lennoxville ... Q
L'Epiphanie ... Q
Levis ... Q
Lindsay ... O
Lisbon ... N. Y
L'Islet ... Q
Listowel ... O
Little Metis ... Q
London ... O
L'Orignal ... O
Longwood ... O
Lowville ... N. Y
Lucan ... O
Lyn ... O
Lynden ... O
Madoc ... O
Madrid ... N. Y
Magog ... Q
Maitland ... O
Mallorytown ... O
Malone ... N Y
Malton ... O
Manchester ... O
Mansonville ... Q
Mansville ... N Y
Manvers ... O
Markham ... O
Martinsburg ... N Y
Maskinonge ... Q
Massena Springs ... N Y
Matilda ... O
Meaford ... O
Mechanic Falls ... Me
Merrickville ... O
Metapedia ... Q
Methot's Mills ... Q
Metis, (Grand) ... Q
Mexico ... N Y
Millbrook ... O
Mill Cove ... Q
Mill Point ... O
Milton ... O
Milwaukee ... Wis
Mitchell ... O
Moira ... N Y
Moore's Junction ... N Y
Morrisburg ... O
Mount Brydges ... O
Mount Forrest ... O
Montreal ... Q
Napanee ... O
Newboro ... O
Newbury ... O
Newcastle ... O
Newcastle ... N B
New Gloucester ... Me
New Liverpool ... Q
New Lowell ... O
Newmarket ... O
Newtonville ... O
New York ... N Y
Niagara ... O
Niagara Falls ... N Y
Nicolet ... Q
Norfolk ... N Y
North Lawrence ... N Y
North Stratford ... N H
North Troy ... Vt
Northumberland ... N H
Norton ... Vt
Norwood ... O
Oakville ... O
Odessa ... O
Ogdensburg ... N Y
Oil Springs ... O
Omemee ... O
Orillia ... O
Ormstown ... Q
Oshawa ... O
Oswego ... N Y
Ottawa ... O
Owen Sound ... O
Paisley ... O
Pakenham ... O
Park Hill ... O
Paris Depot ... O
Paris town ... O
Pembroke ... O
Perth ... O
Peterboro' ... O
Petersburgh ... O
Petrolia ... O
Philadelphia ... N Y
Philadelphia ... Pa
Picton ... O
Pierrepoint Manor ... N Y
Pierreville ... Q
Plantagenet ... O
Plattsburg ... N Y
Plattsville ... O
Point Claire ... Q
Point Fortune ... Q
Point Levi ... Q
Point St. Charles ... Q
Portage du Fort ... Q
Port Burwell ... O
Port Colborne ... O
Port Dalhousie ... O
Port Dover ... O
Port Elgin ... O
Port Henry ... N Y
Port Hope ... O
Port Huron ... Mich
Portland ... Me
Portneuf ... Q
Port Perry ... O
Port Robinson ... O
Port Rowan ... O
Port Ryerse ... O
Port Stanley ... O
Port Union ... O
Potsdam ... N Y
Potsdam Junction ... NY
Prescott ... O
Prescott Junction ... O
Preston ... O
Prince Albert ... O
Princeton ... O
Pulaski ... N Y
Quebec ... Q
Queenston ... O
Raymondville ... N Y
Renfrew ... O
Repentigny ... Q
Richford ... Vt
Richibucto ... N B
Richland ... N Y
Richmond ... O
Richmond ... Q
Richmond Hill ... O
Richville ... N Y
Ridgway ... O
Rimouski ... Q
Riv. du Loup, en bas ... Q
Riv. du Loup, en haut ... Q
Rochester ... N Y
Rockwood ... O
Rouse's Point ... N Y
Sackets Harbor ... N Y
Sackville ... N B
Sand Point ... O
Sandwich ... O
Sandy Creek ... N Y
Sarnia ... O
Saratoga Springs ... N Y
Scarboro ... O
Seaforth ... O
Shakspeare ... O
Shannonville ... O
Shediac ... N B
Sherbrooke ... Q
Shingle Creek ... N Y
Simcoe ... O
Smith's Falls ... O
Somerset ... Q
Sorel ... Q
Southampton ... O
South Bolton ... Q
South Hinchinbrook ... Q
South Paris ... Me
St. Albans ... Vt
St. Alexander ... Q
Stanbridge ... Q
Stanfold ... Q
Stanstead ... Q
St. Armand ... Q
Stayner ... O
St. Anne, Bt. de l'Isle ... Q
St. Anne de la Pérade ... Q
St. Anne de la Pocat ... Q
St. Catharines ... O
St. Charles ... Q
St. Charles, en bas ... Q
St. François ... Q
St. Hilaire ... Q
St. Hyacinthe ... Q
Stirling ... O
St. Jean Port Joli ... Q
St. John ... N B
St. Johns ... Q
St. Johns ... Nfld
St. Lambert ... Q
St. Marys ... O
St. Ours ... Q
Stottsville ... Q
St. Paschal ... Q
Stratford ... O
Strathroy ... O
Streetsville ... O
St. Thomas ... O
St. Thomas ... Q
Summit ... N Y
Sutton Flats ... Q
Sweetsburg ... Q
Tavistock ... O
Terrebonne ... Q
Thamesville ... O
Theresa ... N Y
Thorndale ... O
Thornbury ... O
Thornhill ... O
Thorold ... O
Three Rivers ... Q
Ticonderaga ... N Y
Tilsonburg ... O
Tiverton ... O

Toronto ....O
Trenton ....O
Trois Pistoles..............Q
Troy...................N Y
Turin ....N Y
Tyendinaga ....O
Underwood ....O
Upton.......................Q
Uxbridge ....O
Valleyfield..................Q
Vandreuil ....Q
Vienna ....O
Vittoria ....O
Wallaceburg ....O
Walkerton.....................O
Wardsville.....................O
Warkworth ....O
Warwick ....Q
Washington............D C
Waterdown ....O
Waterford ....O
Waterloo ....O
Waterloo ....Q
Watertown ....N Y
Waterville ....Q
Watford ....O
Welland..........................O
Wellington ....O
Wellington Square ......O
West Milan...........N H
West Paris...............Me
West Port.............N Y
Weston ....O
Whitby ....O
Whitehall.............N Y
Whitevale ....O
Widder ....O
Williamsburg ....O
Windsor.......................O
Windsor.......................Q
Wingham ....O
Wolf Island ....O
Woodstock....................O
Wroxeter ....O
Wyoming ....O
Yamachiche ....Q
Yarmouth ....Me

CANADIAN NEWSPAPERS.

PROVINCE OF ONTARIO.

PLACE.	NAME OF PAPER.	ISSUED.	PUBLISHER OR PROPRIETOR.
Aurora	Banner	Weekly	E. F. Stephenson
Ayr	Herald	"	James G. Watson
Barrie	Advance	"	D. Crew
"	Examiner	"	William M. Nicholson
Belleville	Intelligencer	Daily & W.	M. Bowell, M.P.
"	Hastings Chronicle	Weekly	Miles & Mason
Bentinck	Standard	"	
Berlin	Telegragh	"	Alexander McPherson
Bowmanville	Statesman	"	W. R. Climie
"	Observer	"	Cephas Barker
Bradford	News	"	Porter & Broughton
Brampton	Review	"	S. J. Barnhart
"	Peel Banner	"	Alexander Dick
"	Times	"	George Tye
Brantford	Courier	"	Henry Lemon
"	Expositor	"	Stewart & Mathison
Brockville	Recorder	"	D. Wylie
"	Monitor	"	McMullen & Co.
"	British Canadian	"	R. W. Kelly
Caledonia	Grand River Sachem	"	Thomas Messenger
Carleton Place	Herald	"	James Poole
Carronbrock	Times	"	R. L. Smith
Cayuga	Sentinel	"	George A. Messenger
"	Advocate	"	E. C. Campbell
Chatham	Planet	"	Rufus Stephenson, M.P.P.
"	Banner	"	J. R. Gemmell, jun.
Clinton	New Era	"	Edward Holmes
Cobourg	Sun	"	Thomas McNaughton
"	Sentinel	"	D. McAllister
"	Star	"	William H. Floyd
"	World	"	Henry Hough
Colborne	Express	"	George Keyes
Collingwood	Enterprise	"	John Hogg
Cornwall	Freeholder	"	Alexander McLean
Dundas	True Banner	"	James Somerville
"	Wentworth News	"	Collins & Bennett
Dunnville	Luminary	"	Thomas Messenger
Durham	Chronicle	"	White & Johnston
Elora	Observer	"	John Smith
"	Lightning Express	"	J. M. Shaw
"	Times	"	W. G. Culloden
"	News Record	"	Craig Brothers
Galt	Reformer	"	John Allen
"	Reporter	"	Jaffray Brothers
Georgetown	Herald	"	J. Craig & Brother
Glenallen	Maple Leaf	"	Thomas Hilliard

PROVINCE OF ONTARIO—(*Continued.*)

PLACE.	NAME OF PAPER.	ISSUED.	PUBLISHER OR PROPRIETOR.
Goderich	Huron Signal	Weekly	W. T. Cox
"	Star	"	William Donaghy
Guelph	Advertiser	Daily & W.	J. Wilkinson
"	Evening Mercury	"	McLagan & Innes
"	Herald	Weekly	George Pirie
Hamilton	Spectator	Daily & W.	T. & R. White
"	Evening Times	"	C. E. Stewart & Co
"	Christian Advocate	Weekly	Rev. G. Abbs
"	Craftsman	Monthly	T. & R. White
Ingersol	Chronicle	Weekly	J. S. Gurnett
"	News	"	Aldrich & Lewis
Kincardine	Bruce Review	"	J. Lang
"	Bruce Reporter	"	A. Andrews
Kingston	British Whig	Daily & W.	Dr. E. J. Barker
"	Canadian Churchman	Weekly	J. H. Parnell
"	Chronicle and News	"	James Neish, M.D
Lindsay	Canadian Post	"	C. Blackett Robinson
"	Victoria Warder	"	Joseph Cooper
Listowel	Banner	"	Joseph Hacking
London	Free Press	D., t-w.&w	J. & S. Blackburn
"	Advertiser	Daily & W.	John Cameron
"	Prototype	"	John Siddon
"	Canadian Builder	Monthly	Dyas & Wilkens
"	Farmers' Advocate	"	William Weld
Madoc	Mercury	Weekly	Albert Smallfield
Markham	Economist	"	Hon. D. Reesor
Meaford	Monitor	"	H. Watt
Merrickville	Chronicle	"	Hall & Wright
Milton	Champion	"	Robert Matheson
Millbrook	Messenger	"	Alfred E. Hayter
Mitchell	Advocate	"	Davis & Bro.
Morrisburg	Courier	"	Hugh Kennedy
Mount Forest	Examiner	"	McAdams & McLaren
Napanee	Standard	"	Henry & Brother
"	Express	"	T. S. Carman
Newmarket	Era	"	Erastus Jackson
"	Courier	"	George M. Binns
Orangeville	Sun	"	John Foley
"	Advertiser	"	J. H. Bradshaw
Orillia	Expositor	"	P. Murray
Oshawa	Vindicator	"	Luke & Larke
"	Son of Temperance	Monthly	Luke & Larke
Owen Sound	Advertiser	Weekly	J. H. Little & Co
"	Comet	"	Owen Van Dusen
"	Times	"	Rutherford & Creighton
Ottawa	Citizen	Daily & W.	J. B. Taylor
"	Times	Weekly	Times Printing and Publishing Co.
"	News	Daily	A. Wilson & Son
"	United Service Gazette	Weekly	Alexander Riggs
"	Le Canada	Tri-weekly	Duvernay Brothers
"	Canada Gazette (official)	Weekly	George B. Desbarats
Paris	Star	"	W. G. Powell
Paisley	Advocate	"	Richard Goldie
Pembroke	Observer	"	Beeman, Brothers
Perth	Expositor	"	Thomas Scott
"	Courier	"	G. L. Walker & Brother
"	Standard	"	Burton Campbell (editor)
Peterboro'	Review	"	Robert Romaine
"	Examiner	"	James Stratton
Picton	Gazette	"	S. M. Conger
"	Times	"	Robert Boyle
"	New Nation	"	Platt & Way
Port Dover	New Dominion	"	E. G. Hart
Port Hope	British Canadian	"	J. B. Trayes
"	Guide	"	W. S. & J. S. Johnston
Port Perry	Standard	"	E. Mundy
Prescott	Telegraph	"	Peter Byrne

PROVINCE OF ONTARIO—*Continued.*)

PLACE.	NAME OF PAPER.	ISSUED.	PUBLISHER OR PROPRIETOR.
Prince Albert...	Observer	Weekly ...	Baird & Parsons
Princeton	Review	"	
Richmond Hill.	Herald	"	Alexander Scott
Sarnia	Observer	"	J. R. Gemmell
"	British Canadian	"	J. H. Wood
Seaforth	Expositor	"	Charles Penton
Simcoe	British Canadian	"	William Kelly
"	Reformer	"	Reuben Thoroughgood
St. Catherines..	Journal	Daily & W.	W. Grant & Co.
"	Times	"	John Fitzgerald
"	Constitutional	Weekly ...	James Seymour
St. Mary's	Perth Standard	"	Joseph Bowes
"	Argus	"	Alexander J. Belch
St. Thomas	Dispatch	"	P. Burke
"	Home Journal	"	Archibald McLachlan
Stratford	Beacon	Weekly ...	William Buckingham
"	Herald	"	John M. Robb
"	Colonist	"	Jacob Teuscher
Strathroy	Dispatch	"	Charles H. Macintosh
"	Age	"	Hugh McColl
Tilsonburg	Observer	"	W. S. Law
Thorold	True Patriot	"	John Graham & Co
Toronto	Canada Farmer	Monthly ..	Globe Printing Company
"	Canadian Baptist	Weekly ...	H. Lloyd
"	Canadian Entomologist	Monthly ...	C. J. S. Bethune
"	Canadian Freeman	Weekly ...	J. G. Moylan
"	Canadian Independent Magazine	Monthly ...	Rev. John Wood
"	Canadian Journal, The	Alt. Mon.	Canadian Institute
"	Canadian Journal of Commerce	Weekly. ..	E. T. Bromfield & Co
"	Canadian Pharmaceutical Journal	Monthly ...	Pharmaceutical Society
"	Canada Law Journal, The	Monthly ...	R. A. Harrison, B.C.L., W. D. Ardagh and Henry O'Brien
"	Canadian Monetary Times and Insurance Chronicle		J. M. Trout
"	Christain Guardian	Weekly ...	Rev. W. Jeffers, D.D.
"	Christain Journal (Primitive Methodist.		Rev. Thomas Compton
"	Church Herald	Weekly ...	Church Printing and Publishing Co
"	Daily Telegraph	M. E. & W.	Robertson & Cook
"	Dominion Medical Journal	Monthly ...	Llewellyn Brock, M.D.
"	Evening Tribune	Daily ...	Moyer & Co
"	Globe, The	M. E. & W.	Globe Printing Company
"	Home and Foreign Record of the Canada Presbyterian Church	Monthly ...	Canada Presbyterian Church
"	Irish Canadian	Weekly ...	Patrick Boyle
"	Journal of Education	Monthly ...	Educational Department
"	Leader, The	M. E. & W.	James Beaty
"	Local Courts and Municipal Gazette, The		R. A. Harrison, B. C. L., W. D. Ardagh. and Henry O'Brien
"	Mercantile Test, The	S-Monthly.	J. Kerr
"	Ontario Gazette		Hunter, Rose & Co
"	Ontario Farmer		Rev. W. F. Clarke
"	Patriot, Watchman, and News of the Week, The		James Beaty
"	Sunday School Advocate (Wesleyan)	S-Monthly.	Rev. S. Rose
"	Sunday School Dial, The	Monthly ...	A. Christie
"	Weekly Visitor	Weekly ...	P. H. Stewart
Trenton	Courier	"	George Young
Waterloo	Chronicle	"	C. E. Moyer & Co.
"	German Canadian	"	William Raich
Walkerton	Herald	"	William Brown
Welland	Telegraph	"	E. R. Dewhurst
"	Tribune	"	J. J. Sidey
Whitby	Chronicle	"	William H. Higgins
"	Gazette	"	George H. Ham
Windsor	Essex Journal	"	P. G. Laurie
Woodstock	Sentinel	"	Robert McWhinnie
"	Times	"	Alexander McCleneghan

PROVINCE OF QUEBEC.

PLACE.	NAME OF PAPER.	ISSUED.	PUBLISHER OR PROPRIETOR.
Arthabaskaville	L'Union	Weekly ...	
Beauharnois ...	Le Courier	" ...	J. M. Camyre
" ...	Journal	" ...	
East Chester ...	Journal de T. R	" ...	
Granby	Gazette	" ...	S. C. Smith
Huntingdon ...	Journal	" ...	James Main
" ...	C. Gleaner	" ...	Robert Lellar
Montreal	Herald	D. S-w. & W	Edward G. Penny
"	Gazette	D. T-w. & W	Montreal Printing & Publishing Co.
"	Witness	D. S-w. & W	John Dougall & Son
"	News	Daily	John Lovell
"	Transcript	Weekly ...	John Lovell
"	Telegraph	Daily	Evening Telegraph Co.
"	La Minerve	Semi-we'ly.	Duvernay Frères
"	Christian Observer	Weekly ...	J. Wright
"	Star	Daily	Marshall & Co.
"	Canada Scotsman	Weekly ...	John Dougall & Son
"	True Witness	" ...	G. E. Clark
"	Le Pays	Tri-weekly.	Papineau & Dorion
"	L'Ordre	W. & Tri-w.	Plinquet & Laplante
"	Trade Review	" ...	D. Laminie
"	Le Noveau Monde		Andre Senecal
Richmond	Guardian	Weekly ...	W. E. Jones
Sherbrooke	Gazette	" ...	J. S. Walton
St G de Rimouski	La Voix du Golfe	Semi-week.	
St. Hyacinthe ..	Gazette	" ...	A. L. C. Papineau
" ..	Courier	Weekly ...	C. Lusseu
" ..	Journal	" ...	L. R. Robinson
Stanstead	Journal	" ...	H. Rose
Sweetsburg	District of Bedford Times	" ...	
Three Rivers ...	Enquirer	" ...	
" ...	Journal	" ...	
Quebec	Chronicle	Daily	J. J. Foote
"	Mercury	" ...	G. T. Cary
"	Gazette	" ...	Middleton & Dawson
"	Le Journal de Quebec	Tri-w. & W	Augustine Côté
"	News	Weekly ...	J. Donahue
"	Le Canadien	Tri-weekly.	Hon. F. Evanturel
"	Le Courier du Canada	" ...	L. Brousseau

PROVINCE OF NEW BRUNSWICK.

PLACE.	NAME OF PAPER.	ISSUED.	PUBLISHER OR PROPRIETOR.
St. Johns	Globe	Daily	John V. Ellis
"	News	Tri-w. & W	Wellis & Davies
"	Morning Journal	Tri-weekly.	William Elder
"	Morning Post	Daily	
"	Le Franco Canadien	Weekly ...	
"	Colonial Presbyterian	" ...	William Elder

PROVINCE OF NOVA SCOTIA.

PLACE.	NAME OF PAPER.	ISSUED.	PUBLISHER OR PROPRIETOR.
Halifax	Acadian Recorder	Tri-weekly.	Blackader Bros.
"	British Colonist	" ...	Alpin Grant
"	Evening Express	" ...	Compton & Co.
"	Reporter	" ...	J. C. Croskill
"	Citizen	" ...	E. M. McDonald
"	Morning Chronicle	Daily	Charles Annand
"	Nova Scotian	Weekly ...	Charles Annand
"	Royal Gazette	" ...	E. M. McDonald
"	Unionist and Halifax Journal	Tri-weekly.	William A. Penney
"	Weekly Citizen	Weekly ...	E. M. McDonald

BANKS IN CANADA—AGENCIES, &c.

PLACE.	BANK.	MANAGER OR AGENT.	PLACE.	BANK.	AGENT OR MANAGER.
Barrie	Toronto	J. M. Smith, manager	Montreal	Ontario	H. Starnes, manager
“	Ca. Commerce	E. S. Lally, agent	“	Toronto	D. Coulson, manager
Belleville	Merchants'	A. Thomson, manager	“	Royal Canad.	M. H. Gault, managr
“	Montreal	W. K. Dean, manager	“	Union	P. MacEwen, manager
Berlin	Merchants'	R. N. Roberts, agent	Napanee	Merchants'	A. Smith, agent
Bowmanville	Ontario	D. Fisher, cashier	N. Glasgow, N.S.	Nova Scotia	J. W. Carmichael, agt
“	Royal Canad.	R. Young, agent	Newmarket	Royal Canad.	Jos. Cawthra, agent
Brampton	Royal Canad.	R. C. Fitzgerald, agt	Oshawa	Ontario	G. E. Shaw, manager
Brantford	B N America	Alex. Robertson, mgr	Ottawa	B. N. America	A. C. Kelty, manager
“	Montreal	S. Read, manager	“	Montreal	A. Drummond, mgr
Brockville	Montreal	J. N. Traverse, mangr	“	Ontario	Mr. Milroy, manager
Carleton, Gaspé	La Nationale	John Meagher, agent	“	Quebec	H. V. Noel, manager
Chatham	Merchants'	W. S. Ireland, mangr	Owen Sound	Merchants'	J. Pottenger, agent
“	Royal Canad.	W. H. Monsell, agent	Paris	Royal Canad.	Norman Totten, agent
Clinton	Royal Canad.	M. Lough, agent	Perth	Merchants'	James Gray, agent
Cobourg	Montreal	Jno. Porteous, mangr	“	Montreal	Wm. Munro, agent
“	Toronto	J. H. Roper, manager	“	Royal Canad.	R. D. Freeman, agent
“	Royal Canad.	A. Storr, agent	Pembroke	Quebec	E. B. Crombie, agent
Cornwall	Montreal	Jas. Cox, acting agent	Peterborough	Toronto	Alex. Smith, manager
Elora	Montreal	W. P. Newman, agt	“	Montreal	R. Richardson, agent
Fergus	Montreal	G. D. Ferguson, agt	“	Ontario	D. S. Eastwood, mgr
“	Royal Canad.	J. Beattie, agent	“	Royal Canad.	Wm. Ogilvy, agent
Fredericton, NB.	Peoples'	S. W. Babbitt, cashier	Picton	Montreal	F. A. Despard, agent
Galt	Gore	John Davidson mangr	Pictou, N. S.	Nova Scotia	James Primrose, agt
“	Merchants'	Wm. Cooke, manager	Port Hope	Montreal	W. P. Crombie, agt
“	Royal Canad.	G. H. Patterson, agt	“	Ontario	J. Smart, manager
Gaspé Basin	La Nationale	John LeBoutillier, agt	“	Toronto	A. M. Cosby, agt
Goderich	Royal Canad.	A. M. Ross, agent	“	Royal Canad.	A. Campbell, agt
Guelph	Montreal	E. Brough, int. mangr	Port Perry	Royal Canad.	Jos. Bigelow, agt
“	Ontario	E. Morris, manager	Prescott	Merchants'	L. Gibson, agt
“	Ca. Commerce	G. W. Sandilands, mgr	Quebec	Quebec	J. Stevenson, cashier
Halifax, N. S	Halifax Bk Co.	S. H. Black, cashier	“	La Nationale	F. Vezina, cashier
“ “	Nova Scotia	J. Forman, cashier	“	Union	W. Dunn, cashier
“ “	B N America	Jas. Goldie, manager	“	B. N. Amer.	C. F. Smith, manager
“ “	Union, Halif.	W. S. Stirling, cashr	“	Montreal	P. P. Harris, manager
“ “	Merchants'	Geo. Maclean, cashier	“	City Bank	D. McGee, agt
“ “	Peoples'	Peter Jack, cashier	Sarnia	Montreal	Alex. Vidal, manager
“ “	Montreal	E. C. Jones, agent	Seaforth	Royal Canad.	J. D. M. Ridley, agt
Hamilton	Gore	Samuel Reid, manager	Sherbrooke	E. Townships	W. Farwell, jr., cash.
“	Ontario	R. Milloy, manager	“	City Bank	Wm. Addie, agent
“	B N America	W. N. Anderson, mgr	Simcoe	Gore	D. Campbell, manager
“	Montreal	W. J. Buchanan, mgr	“	Montreal	—. Buchanan, agt
“	Merchants'	J. Bancroft, manager	Stanstead	E. Townships	A. P. Ball, manager
“	Royal Canad.	Henry McKinstry, agt	St. Catharines	Niagara Dis.	C. M. Arnold, cashier
“	Ca. Commerce	C. R. Murray, mangr	“	Quebec	D. Reerekie, agt
Ingersoll	Merchants'	C. H. Sorley, Agent	“	Montreal	A. B. Buchanan, agt
“	Niagara Dist't	C. E. Chadwick, agt	“	Royal Canad.	J. A. Goodman, agt
Kingston	Merchants'	J. G. Macdonald, mgr	“	Ca. Commerce	H. C. Barwick, man.
“	B. N. America	James Riddell, mangr	St. John, N. B.	N. Brunswick	W. Girvan, cashier
“	Montreal	R. M. Moore, mangr	“ “	B. N. America	R. R. Grindley, man.
“	Royal Canad.	R. G. Fitzgerald, mgr	“ “	Montreal	A. Mccnider, agent
Lindsay	Ontario	G. H. G. McVity, mr	“ “	St. Stephens	S. J. Scovil, agent
“	Montreal	H. Dunsford, agent	St. Mary's	Montreal	R. Hillyard, agt
London	B. N. America	Hugh Simpson, mgr	St. Stephen, NB.	St. Stephen's	R. Watson, cashier.
“	Merchants'	W. F. Harper, mangr	St. Thomas	Merchants'	John McDonald, agt
“	Montreal	F. W. Thomas, mgr	Stratford	Merchants'	C. H. Ransom, agt
“	Ca. Commerce	H. S. Strathy, mgr	“	Montreal	James Hogg, agent
Montreal	Montreal	E. H. King, gen. mgr	“	Royal Canad.	James Young, agt
“	do. Branch	R. B. Angus, mangr	Strathroy	Ca. Commerce	Jos. S. Small, agt
“	City Bank	F. Macculloch, cashier	Sydney, C. B.	Nova Scotia	Hon. T. D. Archibald
“	Du Peuple	B. H. LeMoine, cashier	Three Rivers	Quebec	J. McDougall, agt
“	Molson's	W. Sache, cashier	Toronto	Upper Canad.	In liquidation
“	Jacq. Cartier	H. Cotté, cashier	“	Toronto	Geo. Hague, cashier
“	Mechanics'	A. Molson, man'g dir.	“	Royal Canad.	T. Woodside, cashier
“	Merchants'	Jackson Rae, cashier	“	Ca. Commerce	R. J. Dallas, cashier
“	B. N. America	Thos. Paton, gen. mr	“	B. N. Amer.	Samuel Taylor, man
“	do. Branch	A. C. Hooper, mangr	“	Merchants'	J. G. Harper, man.
“	Quebec	Wm. Rhind, manager	“	Montreal	G. W. Yarker, I. M.

BANKS IN CANADA—(*Continued.*)

PLACE.	BANK.	MANAGER OR AGENT.	PLACE.	BANK.	MANAGER OR AGENT.
"	City Bank.....	John Moat, manager	"	Royal Canad..	A. Richardson, agt
"	Quebec.........	R. H. Bethune, man.	Windsor, Ont....	Merchants.....	C. D. Grassett, agt
"	Ontario.........	Alex. Fisher, manager	Windsor, N.S....	Commercial...	D. H. Clarke, cashier
Walkerton........	Merchants'....	A. Sproat, Agent	Woodstock.	Gore	William Smith, man.
Waterloo, Q......	E. Townships.	W. G. Parmelee. M.	"	Royal Canad..	J. M. Burns, agent
" Ont...	Ontario.........	D. J. H. Crawford, man	Yarmouth, N.S..	Yarmouth.. ..	J. W. H. Rowley, cash.
Whitby...........	Ontario....... .	K. F. Lockhart, man.	" "	Nova Scotia...	J. Murray, jun., agt

FOREIGN AGENTS.

Bank of British North America—*London*, Head Office; *New York*, Walter Watson, C. M. Mylrea and A. McKinlay. *San Francisco*, J. G Shepherd & T. Menzies.

Bank of Montreal—*London*, The Union Bank; *Liverpool*, Bank of Liverpool; *Scotland*, British Linen Company; *New York*. R. Bell & F. Gundry, Bank of Commerce and Bank of New York; *Boston*, Merchant's Bank; *Chicago*, George C. Smith & Bros.

City Bank—*London*, Glyn, Mills, Currie & Co.; *Ireland*, National Bank; *New York*, Bank of the Republic; *Boston*, Kidder, Peabody & Co.

Bank of Toronto—*London*, City Bank; *New York* National Bank, Commerce & C. F. Smithers; *Oswego*, Lake Ontario, National Bank.

Quebec Bank—*London*, Union Bank of London; *Liverpool*, Bank of Liverpool; *New York*, Maitland, Phelps & Co.

Gore Bank—*London*, Glyn, Mills, Currie & Co.; *Edinburgh*, National Bank of Scotland; *Belfast*, Northern Banking Co., *New York*, Bell & Gundry; *Boston*, Merchant's National Bank; *Buffalo*, Third National Bank.

Ontario Bank—*London*, Glyn, Mills & Co.; *Liverpool*, Bank Liverpool; *New York*, City Bank; *Boston*, Tremont Bank.

Royal Canadian Bank—*London*, Union Bank; *New York*, National Park Bank; *Oswego*, Lake Ontario National Bank and City Bank; *Buffalo*, Farmers' and Mechanics' National Bank.

Molson's Bank—*London*, Glyn, Mills, Currie & Co.; *New York*, Mechanics' National Bank.

Niagara District Bank—*London*, Bosonquet, Salt & Co.; *New York*, Bank of Manhattan Co.

Canadian Bank of Commerce—*London*, London and County Bank; *New York*, C. Ashworth & National Bank of New York; *Boston*, Merchants' N. Bank; *Cleveland*, Merchants' N. Bank Cleveland; *St. Johns*, *Newfoundland*, Union Bank.

La Banque Jaques Cartier—*London*, Glyn, Mills & Co.; *Paris*, de Rothschild freres; *New York*, National Bank of Republic.

Union Bank of L. C.—*London*, London and County Bank; *New York*, C. Ashworth; and National Park Bank.

Merchants' Bank—*London*, London Joint Stock Bank; *New York*, National Bank of the Republic.

La Banque Nationale—*London*, National Bank of Scotland; *Paris*, F. S. Ballin & Co.; *New York*, National Bank Republic.

Merchants' Bank, Halifax—*Boston*, National Hide and Leather Bank; *New York*, Fulton National Bank; *Summerside*, *P. E. I.*, Summerside Bank; *Charlottetown*, *P. E. I.*, Union Bank of P. E. I.; *St. John's*, *Newfoundland*, Union Bank of Newfoundland.

People's Bank of Halifax—*London*, Union Bank; *Boston*, Williams & Hall; *New York*, Bank of New York.

Union Bank of Halifax—*London*, London and Westminster Bank; *Scotland*, Clydesdale Banking Co.; *Newfoundland*, Commercial Bank of Newfoundland; *New York*, National Bank of Republic; *Boston*, Merchants' National Bank.

Bank of New Brunswick—*London*, William Deacon & Co.; *New York*, Continental National Bank; *Boston*, Eliot National Bank; *Halifax*, Bank of Nova Scotia.

St. Stephen's Bank—*Boston*, Globe National Bank; *New York*, New York Bank and National Banking Association; *London*, Glyn, Mills, Currie & Co.

CANADIAN TARIFF OF CUSTOMS.

As in force on 1st October, 1868.

All Articles not hereafter enumerated as charged with an ad valorem duty, or charged with a specific duty, or declared free of duty, or chargeable with a duty of 15 per cent. on the value thereof.

	℘ c. *ad. val.*
Acid, Sulphuric............	⅛c. per lb.
Ascetic Acid.........................	15
Acids of every description, except Ascetic and Sulphuric Acid and Vinegar............	Free
Advertising Pamphlets..	15
Alabaster Ornaments...........	15
Alcohol, on every gallon of the strength of proof of Sykes' Hydrometer, and so in proportion for any greater strength and for every less quantity than a gallon,	80c. ℘ gall.
Ale, in casks, 10 per cent. and	5c. per gall.
Ale, in bottles (5 quarts or 10 pints to gallon) 10 per cent. and....................	...7c. per gall.
Alum....................................	Free
Anatomical Preparations	Free
Anchors	Free
Antimony	Free
Antiquities, cabinets of	Free
Argol.............	Free
Arms and Clothing for Army and Military Forces..........	Free
Articles for the public uses of the Dominion	Free
Articles imported by and for the use of the Governor General............................	Free
Articles for the use of the Foreign Consuls, General.........	Free
Ashes, Pot, Pearl and Soda......	Free
Atlases (not elsewhere mentioned)	15
Axes	15
Axles, Crank, Locomotive.....	Free
Axles, Railway Car..............	Free

℘ c. ad. val.

Bagatelle Boards.................. 15
Barilla or Kelp......................Free
Bark, Tanners' ....Free
Bark, used chiefly in dying......Free
Bark of the Corkwood Tree......Free
Bars, guide and slide for Locomotives ....Free
Bars, puddled iron, Blooms and Billets ....Free
Beer, in casks, 10 per cent. and 5c. per gall.
Beer, in bottles (5 quarts or 10 pints to a gallon), 10 per cent., and.............. 7c per gall.
Benzole ....15c. per gall.
Berries, used chiefly in dying..Free
Bibles, Testaments, Payer-B'ks and Devotional Books......... 5
Bichromate of Potash, when imported solely by room-paper manufacturers and stainers for manufacturing purposes only ....Free
Billiard Tables.......................... 15
Bill-Heads, &c.......................... 15
Bills, Printed, Lithographed, or Copper-plate 15
Biscuit, from Great Britain and the B. N. A. Provinces...Free
Bitters containing Spirit, Vermouth, and other Spirituous Liquors, of whatever strength not otherwise specified, on every gallon of the strength of proof of Sykes' Hydrometer, and so in proportion for any greater strength, and for every less quantity than a gallon .... 80c. per. gall.
Blacking 15
Bleaching Powders ....Free
Blue-black, when imported solely by room-paper manufacturers and stainers, for manufacturing purposes only.....Free
Blocks, Stereotype, for Printing purposes......... ....Free
Blue-Vitriol or Sulphate of Copper ....Free
Bolting Cloths... ....Free
Bonnets.................................. 15
Books, copyright reprints of... 12½
Books, which are copyrighted in Canada.......................... 15
Books----Printed Periodicals, Pamphlets and Newspapers, not being foreign reprints or British copyright works, nor Blank Account Books, Copy Books, nor Books to be written or drawn upon, nor School or other Books copy-righted in Canada, nor printed sheet Music.................................. 5
Bookbinders' Tools and Implements...... ....Free
Boots....................................... 15
Boot-felt ....Free
Borax ....Free
Bracelets 15
Brads...................................... 15
Braid, &c., made of hair........ 15

℘ c. ad. val.

Brandy (on every gallon of the strength of proof of Sykes' Hydrometer, and so in proportion for any greater strength, and for every less quantity than a gallon) 80c per gall.
Brass, in Bars, Rods, Sheets and Scraps .... Free
Brass or copper Wire Round or flat .... Free
Bread from Great Britain and the B. N. A. Provinces...... Free
Britannia Metal Ware............ 15
Brim Moulds for Gold Beaters. Free
Brimstone, in roll or flour...... Free
Bristles of all kinds............. Free
Bronze Ornaments.............. 15
Broom Corn........................ Free
Brooms and Brushes of all kinds 15
Bulbs and Roots.................. Free
Burrstones .... Free
Busts, natural size, not being casts, nor produced by any mere mechanical process...... Free
Butter........................4c. per lb.
Cabinet Ware or Furniture... 15
Cabinets of Coin.................Free
Cables—Iron Chain, Ships over ½ inch, shackled, swivelled or not................................Free
Cables—Hemp and Grass for ships only....................... 15
Cameos or Mosaics............ 15
Candles and Tapers of Tallow, Wax or any other material... 15
Candy Sugar Brown or White 1c. per lb....................... 25
Cane Juice . ...½c. per lb 25
Caoutchouc, unmanufactured.. Free
Caps 15
Carpets 15
Carriages not elsewhere specified 15
Carriages of Travellers and Carriages employed in carrying Merchandise (Hawkers and Circus Troupes excepted)... Free
Cassia, ground.................... 25
Cassia, unground................. 15
Casts, as models for the use of schools of design.............. Free
Cement, marine or hydraulic, unground .... Free
Cement, hydraulic, ground and calcined........................ 15
Chandeliers 15
Charts, not elsewhere mentioned 15
Cheese............. ....3c. per lb.
Chesnut and Cherry Plank...... Free
solely by room-paper manufacturers and stainers, for manufacturing purposes only Free
Chicory, or other Root or Vegetable used as Coffee, raw or green.... ....3 c. per lb.
Chicory, kiln-dried, roasted or ground.............. .....4c. per lb.
Chinese Blue, when imported
China Ware 15
Chocolate 15
Church Bells, when imported for churches only ....Free

℘ c. ad. val.

Cider 15
Cigars, value not over $10 per mille............................$3 per mille
Cigars, value over $10 and not over $20 ....$4 per mille
Cigars, value over $20 and not over $40...............$5 per mille
Cigars, value over $40..$6 per mille
Cinnamon, ground.............. 25
Cinnamon, unground........... 15
Clasps, Brass and Tin, for manufacture of Hoop Skirts......Free
Clays, in natural state.......... Free
Clocks 15
Cloth, Silver and Gold 15
Clothing or Wearing Apparel, made by hand or sewing machine 15
Clothing and Arms, for Army and Military Forces.......... Free
Clothing, donations of, for charitable Institutions............Free
Coach and Harness Furniture.. 15
Coal and Coke......................Free
Coal Oil, distilled, purified and refined ....15c. per gall
Cocoa.................................... 15
Cocoa Paste, from Great Britain and the B.N.A Provinces....Free
Cocoa, Bean and Shell............Free
Coffee, green ....3c. per lb.
Coffee roasted or ground 4c. per lb.
Coin and Bullion, except U. S. Silver Coin........................Free
Colors, not elsewhere specified, 15
Commissariat and Ordnance Stores...............................Free
Common Soap.........$1 per 100 lbs.
Communion Plate................Free
Composition Spikes and Nails Free
Confectionery ....1c. per lb. 25
Connecting Rods, Locomotive Free
Copper, in Pigs, Bars, Rods, Bolts. Shafts and Sheeting...Free
Copper Wire, round or flat .....Free
Cordage, for ships and vessels only...................................Free
Cordials.................$1.20 per gall.
Corks..................................... 15
Corkwood, Bark ....Free
Corn, Indian..........................Free
Cottons 15
Cotton, Candle Wick..............Free
Cotton Warp, Cotton Twist, and Cotton Yarn............. 15
Cotton Waste .. ..Free
Cotton Netting for India Rubber Shoes.............................Free
Cotton Wool..........................Free
Crank Axles, Locomotive.. ...Free
Crank Pins, Locomotive.........Free
Cranks, Locomotive...............Free
Cranks. Steamboat and Mill, forged in the rough............Free
Cream of Tartar, in Crystals...Free
Crinoline Thread, for covering Crinoline Wire..................Free
Crockery 15
Cutlery, polished, of all sorts... 15
Drawings, not in Oil.............Free
Diamonds and Precious Stones, not set ....Free

℘ c. ad. val.

Drain Tiles for Agricultural purposes .... Free
Dried Fruit 15
Drugs, not elsewhere specified. 15
Drugs, used chiefly in dyeing.. Free
Duck, for Belting and Hose ... Free
Earthenware....................... 15
Earths, Clays and Sand, natural state .... Free
Edge Tools 15
Eggs .... Free
Electrotype Blocks, for printing purposes .... Free
Embroideries, Silken, Woollen, Worsted and Cotton 15
Emery, Emery Paper, and Emery Cloth.............................. Free
Engravings 15
Essences, not elsewhere specified 15
Essential Oils of all kinds 15
Extract of Logwood .... Free
Fancy Goods and Millinery ... 15
Fancy Goods and Millinery—viz. : articles embroidered with Gold, Silver, or other Metals 15
Fancy and Ornamental Cases and Boxes........................ 15
Fans 15
Farming Utensils and Implements, when imported by Agricultural Societies for encouragement of agriculture.. Free
Feathers and Flowers............ 15
Felt for Hats and Boots......... Free
Fibre, Fibrillia, Mexican or Tampico, white and black, and other vegetable fibres for manufacturing .... Free
Firearms, of all kinds, from Great Britain only 15
Firebrick and Clay .... Free
Fire-engines, Steam, when imported by Municipal Corporations of Cities, Towns, or Villages, for their use...... ......Free
Firescreens.............. 15
Firewood .... Free
Fireworks.............. 15
Fish, fresh, not to include Oysters or Losbters in tins or kegs.............................. Free
Fish, preserved.. 15
Fish, salted and smoked. .1c. per lb
Fish Bait.......................... Free
Fishing Nets and Seines, Hooks, Lines, and Twines...Free
Flax, Hemp, & Tow, undressed Free
Flax Waste .... Free
Flour of Wheat and Rye. ...... Free
Flour and Meal of all other kinds......................... ...Free
Forks................................. 15
Fruits, green or dried............ 15
Furnishings, not elsewhere specified 15
Furniture or Cabinet Ware.. .. 15
Furs, and Skins, Pelts or Tails, undressed........................ Free
Gems and Cabinets of ....Free
Gas-fittings 15

℘ c. ad. val.

Gin (on every gallon of strength of proof of Sykes' Hydrometer, and so in proportion for any greater strength and for every less quantity than a gallon,
80c per gall.
Ginger, ground.................... 25
Ginger, unground... 15
Girandoles........................ 15
Glass and Glassware, Plate and Silvered, Stained, Painted or Coloured. 15
Glass Paper and Glass Cloth ...15
Gold and Silver Leaf, ana for Platers' use .... Free
Goldbeaters' Brim Moulds and Skins...................... ....Free
Grain of all kinds .... Free
Gravels .... Free
Grease and Scraps ... .Free
Greens, Paris and permanent, when imported by room paper manufrcturerers and stainers for manufacturing purposes only ....Free
Grindstones........................ 15
Gum, Copal ....Free
Gum, British, when imported solely by room paper manufacturers and stainers, for manufacturing purposes only. Free
Gunpowder 15
Guns, from Great Britain....... 15
Gutta Percha, manufactured ...Free
Gypsum, or Plaster of Paris, neither ground nor calcined . Free
Hair, Angola, Goat, Thibet, unmanufactured ....Free
Hair, Horse, Hog or Mohair, unmanufactured..... ....Free
Hair, Human ....Free
Hardware, not elsewhere specified.............................. 15
Harness and Harness Furniture 15
Hams...................... .....1c per lb.
Hat Felts .... Free
Hat Plush.......................... 15
Hats 15
Hay ....Free
Hemp, undressed ....Free
Hides and Horns ....Free
Hoes.................................. 15
Hops................................ Free
Hosiery 15
Horses........... ....$15 per head
Horned Cattle.........$10 per head
Imitation of Leather 15
Implements of Husbandry, (not merchandise) in actual use of persons coming to settle in the Dominion ....Free
India Rubber, unmanufactured, Free
Indigo ....Free
Inks of all kinds, except printing Inks 15
Indian Meal ....Free
Iron Castings 15
Iron of the description following, viz :
Iron Canada Plates and Tin
Iron, Sheet 5

℘ c. ad. val.

Plates........................... 5
Iron, Galvanized Spikes and Bolts ....Free
Iron Wire, Nail and Spike Rod round, square or flat......... 5
Iron, Bar, Rod or Hoop......... 5
Iron, Scrap, Galvanized or Pig 5
Iron, Hood or Tire, for Locomotive Wheels, bent and welded ....Free
Iron Boiler Plate.................. 5
Iron Railroad Bars, Frogs, Wrought Iron or Steel Chairs and Fish Plates...............Free
Rolled Plate......................... 5
Puddled Iron in Bars, Blooms and Billets ....Free
Jewellery 15
Junk ....Free
Japanned Tinware.............. 15
Kerosene Oil, distilled, purified and refined.......... ..15c. per gal.
Knees and Riders, Iron, for shipbuilding purposes ....Free
Kryolite..............................Free
Lakes, in pulp, scarlet & maroon, when importgd solely by room paper manufacturers and stainers, for manufactu. purposes only .... Free
Lard.. ....1c. per lb.
Lead, in Sheet or Pig............Free
Lead, Red and White, dry......Free
Leather, Sole & Upper Leather, and Cow Hides, split and kip, not elsewhere specified. 10
Leather, viz : Sheep, Calf, Goat and Chamois Skins, dressed, varnished or enamelled...... 15
Linen................................ 15
Linen Machine Thread ....Free
Linseed Cake ....Free
Litharge ....Free
Locomotive Engines 15
Locomotive Engine Frames ...Free
Locomotive and Passenger Baggage, and Freight Cars running upon any line of road crossing the frontier, so long as Canadian Locomotives and Cars are admitted free, under similar circumstances, in the United States ....Free
Lumber, Plank and Sawed, of Walnut, Rosewood, Cherry, Chesnut, Mahogany, & Pitch Pine ....Free
Mace 25
Macaroni 15
Machines, Mowing, Thrashing and Reaping............... 15
Machine Silk Twist... ....Free
Machine Linen Thread ....Free
Machinery, when used in the original construction of Mills and Factories, does not include Sewing Machines, Steam Engines, or parts thereof, Water Wheels, or Turbines ....Free
Manilla Grass, for Upholterers' purposes ....Free

Article	℘ c. ad. val.
Malt	40c. per bush.
Mantelpieces	15
Manufactures of Bone, Shell, Horn, Pearl and Ivory	15
Manufactures of Brass or Copper	15
Manufactures of Caoutchouc, India-rubber or Gutta-percha	15
Manufactures of Cashmere	15
Manufactures of Fur, or of which Fur is the principal part	15
Manufactures of Gold, Silver, Electroplate, Argentine, Albata, German Silver, and Plated and Gilded Ware of all kinds	15
Manufactures of Grass, Osier, Palm-leaf and Straw	15
Manufactures of Hair or Mohair	15
Manufactures of, or Imitations of, Marble, other than rough sawn Slabs or Blocks	15
Manufactures of Leather, including Boots and Shoes, Harness and Saddlery	15
Manufactures of Papier-mache.	15
Manufactures of Refined Sugar, including Succades and Confectionery ......1c. per lb.	25
Manufactures of Straw, except Plaits	15
Manufactures of Whalebone	15
Manufactures of Willow	15
Manufactures of Wood, not elsewhere specified	15
Manures	Free
Maps, not elsewhere mentioned	15
Marble, in Blocks, unwrought, or sawn on two sides only, or Slabs sawn from such Blocks, having at least two edges unwrought	Free
Marble Head and Foot Stones, squared or cut to order, or Columns, Shafts, or parts thereof	15
Meals of all kinds	Free
Meats, fresh, salted, or smoked	1c. per lb.
Meats, Preserved	15
Medals, Cabinets of	Free
Medicines—Proprietary Medicines commonly called Patent Medicines, or any Medicine or Preparation. of which the Recipe is kept secret, or the ingredients whereof are kept secret, recommended by advertisement, bill, or label, for the relief or cure of any disease or ailment	25
Medicinal Roots in their natural state	Free
Melado ......⅝c. per lb.	25
Menageries Horses, Cattle, Carriages, and Harness of	Free
Metalic Oxides, ground or unground, and washed or unwashed, dry, not calcined	Free
Military and Naval Stores	Free
Millinery	15
Models and Patterns of Invention	Free
Molasses, if used for the refining or the manufacture of sugar	73c per 100 lb.
Molasses, if not so used	25
Molasses, concentrated, or Syrup of ......⅝c per lb.	25
Moss, for upholsterers' purposes	Free
Mowing, Reaping and Threshings	15
Musical Boxes	15
Musical Instruments	15
Musical Instruments for Military Bands	Free
Mustard	15
Music, Sheet	15
Nails	15
Naptha	15c per gall.
Naval Stores	Free
Netting, Cotton and Woolen for India rubber shoes	Free
Newspapers, foreign, sent otherwise than through Post Office	15
Nitre or Saltpetre	Free
Nitrate of Soda	Free
Nuts, dried	15
Nuts, chiefly used in dyeing	Free
Nutmegs	25
Oakum	Free
Ochres, when Ground or calcined	15
Ochres, ground or unground, washed or unwashed, dry, not calcined	Free
Oil Cake	Free
Oil Cloths	15
Oil, Essential, of all kinds	Free
Oils, any way rectified, pumped racked, bleached, or pressed, not elsewhere specified	15
Oils, Coal and Kerosene, distilled, purified and refined.	15c. per gall.
Oils, Cocanut, Pine, and Palm, in their natural state	Free
Oils. Whale, in the casks from on ship-board, and in the condition in which it was first landed	Free
Opium	15
Ores of all kinds of Metals	Free
Ornaments of Bronze, Alabaster Terracotta, Composition	15
Osiers and Willow for Basketmakers' use	Free
Packages—Bottles, Jars, Demijohns, Brandy Casks, Barrels or other Packages in which Spirituous Liquors are contained, and carboys containing Sulphuric Acid	15
Packages of every description in which goods are usually imported, and cases covering casks of Wine or Brandy, in wood, and cases containing bottled Wines or bottled Spirits or other liquors	Free
Paints	15
Paper and Paper-hangings	15
Paintings in oil, by artists of well-known merit, or copies of old masters by such artists	Free
Paper, Book, Map or News Printing	15
Patent Medicines, commonly called Patent Medicines or any medicine or preparation of which the recipe is kept secret, or the ingredients of which are kept secret, recommended by advertisement bill or label, for the relief or cure of any disorder or ailment	25
Parasols	15
Pearl Ashes	Free
Pelts, undressed	Free
Pepper, ground	25
Pepper, unground	15
Perfumery, not elsewhere specified	25
Perfumed Spirits	$1 20 per gall.
Petroleum, crude	6c. per gall.
Petroleum, refined, purified, &c.	15c. per gall.
Philosophical Instruments and Apparatus, including Globes, when imported by and for the use of colleges, schools, and scientific and literary societies	Free
Phosphorus	Free
Pickles and Sauces	15
Pig Iron, Lead and Copper	Free
Pimento, ground	25
Pimento, unground	15
Pipeclay	Free
Pipes, Tobacco	15
Piston Rods for Locomotives	Free
Pitch	Free
Plaits—Straw, Tuscan or Grass Fancy	Free
Plants	Free
Plaster of Paris, neither ground nor calcined	Free
Plaster of Paris, ground and calcined	15
Plate, rolled iron	5
Plates, Boiler	5
Plates, Canada and Tin	5
Playing Cards	25
Plush for Hatters' use	Free
Porter, in casks ...5c. per gall.	10
Porter, in bottles (5 quarts or 10 pints to a gallon) 7c. per gall.	10
Portable Printing Presses	15
Pot Ashes	Free
Poultry, preserved	15
Precious Stones, not set	Free
Preserved Meats	15
Prints and Engravings	15
Printing Ink	Free
Printing Presses, except Portable Hand Printing Presses	Free
Products of Petroleum, Coal Shale and Lignite, not otherwise specified	10c. per gall.
Prunella	Free
Rags	Free
Railroad Bars	Free
Railroad Cars	15

℔ c. ad. val.

Rakes 15
Rattans, for caning chairs ......Free
Rosin ....Free
Rice 15
Rifles 15
Rod, Nail and Spike, round, square and flat Iron........... 5
Roots ....Free
Rosewood ....Free
Rugs, Hearth 15
Rum (on every gallon of strength of proof of Sykes' hydrometer, and so in proportion for every greater strength, and for every less quantity than a gallon.) 80c. per gall.
Saddlery 15
Sailcloth or Canvas, from No. 1 to No. 6, when imported by ship-builders or sailmakers for ship-building purposes ...Free
Sails, ready made 15
Sal-Ammoniac ....Free
Sal-Soda ....Free
Salt ....Free
Saltpetre ....Free
Sand ....Free
Sand-paper and Sand-cloth.....Free
Satins 15
Scrap Brass ....Free
Scythes 15
Sea Grass, for Upholsterers' purposes ....Free
Sewing Silk 15
Seeds, for Agricultural, Horticultural, and manufacturing purposes only ....Free
Shafts, steamboat and mill, forged in the rough...........Free
Shawls 15
Sheep.. ....$1 per head
Shellac 15
Ship's Binnacle Lamps.........Free
Ship's Blocks and Patent Bushes for Blocks.............. ....Free
Ship's Bunting ....Free
Ship's Compasses.................Free
Ship's Composition Spikes and Nails ....Free
Ship's Cordage, when used for ships only.........................Free
Ship's Dead Eyes and Dead Lights ....Free
Ship's Deck Plugs ....Free
Ship's Iron Knees and Riders..Free
Ship's Iron Masts or parts of Iron Masts.......................Free
Ship's Pumps and Pump Gear. Free
Ship's Sail Cloth or Canvas, from No. 1 to No. 6, when used for ships only ....Free
Ship's Shackles and Sheaves...Free
Ship's Sheathing Copper and Nails....... ....Free
Ship's Signal Lamps ....Free
Ship's Steering Apparatus......Free
Ship's Traveling Trucks] .....Free
Ship's Treenails and Wedges...Free
Ship's Wire Rigging.............Free
Ship's Yellow Metal, in bars or bolts..............................Free
Shoes............................... 15

℔ c. ad. val.

Ship's Yellow Metal for sheathing.................................Free
Shovels 15
Shrubs...................................Free
Silicate of Soda ....Free
Silk, Tram or Weaving, to make Elastic Webbing..............Free
Silks 15
Silk Twist and Silk and Mohair Twist............................. 15
Silk Twist, for Hats, boots and shoes ....Free
Silver Leaf............................Free
Skins, undressed ....Free
Slate ....Free
Slides and Spangles, and slotted Tapes, for hoop skirts.........Free
Small Wares........................ 15
Snaiths and Scythes 15
Snuff and Snuff Flour, dry damp, moist or pickled...15c per lb. 5
Soap, Fancy and Perfumed ... 25
Soap, common...............1c. per lb
Soda, Ash................. . ...Free
Soda, Caustic............ ....Free
Spades 15
Specimens of Natural History Mineralogy, and Botany... ..Free
Specimens of Sculpture.........Free
Spices, including Ginger, Pepper, Pimento, unground...... 15
Spices, including Ginger, Pepper, Pimento, ground...... .. 25
Spices, not elsewhere enumerated 15
Spirits, perfumed.......$1.20 per gal
Spirits of Turpentine 15
Spirits of Wine (on every gallon of strength of proof of Sykes' hydrometer, and so in proportion for any greater strength, and for every less quantity than a gallon) 80c ℔ gal
Sprigs 15
Starch ....2c. per lb
Stationery.......................... 15
Statues, of Bronze, Marble or Alabaster, natural size........ Free
Steel, wrought or cast, in bars or rods ....Free
Steel Plates, cut to any form, but not moulded ....Free
Steering Apparatus for Ships... Free
Stone, Lithographic ....Free
Stereotype Blocks for printing purposes ....Free
Stone, unwrought..................Free
Stoves 15
Straw, Tuscan and Grass, Fancy Plaits...............................Free
Succades.. .... 1c. per lb. 25
Sugar Candy, brown or white, 1c. per lb. 25
Sugar—all Sugar equal to or above No. 9, Dutch standard 1c. per lb. 25
Sugar—all Sugar equal to or below No. 9, Dutch standard
Satin, and fine washed White, for manufacturing purposes only...............................Free

℔ c. ad. val.

¾c. per lb. 25
Sugar of Lead, when imported solely by room-paper manufacturers and stainers, for manufacturing purposes only Free
Sulphur or Brimstone, in roll or flour ....Free
Syrup of Sugar or of Sugar Cane ¾c. per lb. 25
Swine.........................$2 per head
Tampico, white and black ... ..Free
Tacks.................................. 15
Tails, undressed ....Free
Tallow...........................1c. per lb.
Tabour work....................... 15
Tapers of Tallow, &c............ 15
Tapes, slotted for the manufacture of hoop skirts ....Free
Tar.......................................Free
Tea, Green and Japan, 7c. per lb. 15
Tea, Black............3½c. per lb. 15
Teazels.. ....Free
Thread, and other articles embroidered with gold, or for embroidery.. 15
Thread, Lace and Insertions... 15
Tinctures................63c. per gall.
Tin, granulated or bar............Free
Tin, blocks or pigs ....Free
Tire or Hoop for locomot. wheels bent and welded. ....Free
Tin, japanned, planished ware 15
Tobacco, manufactured, 15c. ℔lb 15
Tobacco, unmanufactured.......Free
Tobacco Pipes...................... 15
Toys.................................. 15
Tow, undressed ....Free
Travellers' Baggage..............Free
Treenails.. . ...Free
Trees, Plants and Shrubs.......Free
Tubes, Copper, Brass or Iron, and Piping when drawn .....Free
Turpentine, other than Spirits of Turpentine............. . ...Free
Type Metal, in blocks or pigs..Free
Type.................. 5
Ultramarine, when imported solely by room-paper manufacturers and stainers, for manufacturing purposes only, Free
Umber, raw, on same conditions Free
Umbrellas.......................... 15
Varnish, bright and black, when used for ships and vessels only Free
Varnish, other than bright or blk 15
Vegetables, preserved........... 15
Vegetables, culinary..............Free
Vegetables, chiefly used in dyeing.......... ....Free
Velvets 15
Veneering, of Wood or Ivory...Free
Vermicelli 15
Vinegar.............................. 15
Walnut, Plank ....Free
Watches 15
Wearing Apparel, made by hand or sewing machine... 15
Wearing Apparel of British subjects domiciled in Canada, dying abroad..............Free
Wearing Apparel, Settlers' and other personal effects in ac-

AMERICAN HOUSE,

MONTREAL,

C. S. BROWNE, PROPRIETOR.

THIS WELL KNOWN HOTEL HAS BEEN ENLARGED BY THE ADDITION OF THAT LARGE AND COMMODIOUS HOUSE KNOWN AS THE "EXCHANGE HOTEL."

The Whole has Undergone Thorough Repairs,

AND BEEN NEWLY FURNISHED.

The house fronts on Joseph Street, which is a continuation of Notre Dame, and is but 4 doors from McGill Street, is near Great St, James, St. Paul, and all the principal business streets, of the City. Being very centrally located, with regard to all places of interest about town, it cannot fail to commend itself to parties travelling either on business or for pleasure. In making the repairs, the Proprietor has taken great pains to provide

Every Comfort for his Guests,

And has fitted the House up with all the modern improvements and requirements, for A FIRST CLASS HOTEL, including Gas in every Room in the House, Hot and Cold Baths, etc., etc. And the Proprietor feels that he can offer to his guests accommodations that cannot fail to give satisfaction.

☞ Porters always in attendance at the Depot and Steamboat Landings with Omnibuses to the House.

TERMS, - - - $1.50 PER DAY.

℘ c. ad. val.

tual use, of persons coming to settle in the Dominion, including Household Furniture, Cattle, Horses, Harness, Waggons, &c., importer making oath that he intends becoming a *bona fide* settler within the Dominion.........Free

Whale Oils in the casks from on shipboard and in the condition in which it was first landed . ...Free

Wheat.................. .. ..Free

Whiskey (on every gallon of the strength of proof of Sykes' hydrometer, and so in proportion for any greater strength, and for every less quantity than a gall.) 80c. per gall

White, fine washed and satin, when imported solely by room-paper manufacturers & stainers, for manufacturing purposes only..................Free

Whiting or Whitening,.........Free

Wedges for ships ....Free

Willow for basket makers' use.Free

Wines of all kinds, including Ginger, Orange, Lemon, Gooseberry, Strawberry, Raspberry, Elderand Currant Wine (5 quarts and 10 pint bottles to contain a gall.) 10c. per gall.................... 20

Wire, of Brass or Copper, round or flat..............................Free

Wire Cloth, of Brass or Copper.Free

Wire, flat, for crinoline, covered 15

Wire Rigging, for ships..........Free

Wire, flat or round, uncovered, for crinoline......................Free

Wood, Cherry & Chestnut plank.Free

Wood, Cork.... . ...Free

Wood, Mahogany, plank........Free

Woods of all kinds, wholly unmanufactured.......................Free

Woods, used chiefly in dyeing..Free

Wool ....Free

Wollens. 15

Writing Desks...... 15

Wrought Iron or Steel Chairs, for railroads.......................Free

Yellow Metal, in bars or bolts..Free

Yellow Metal, Sheathing........Free

Zinc or Spelter, in sheet.........Free

Zinc or Spelter, in blocks or pigs...................................Free

Zinc, white, dry....................Free

RAILWAYS OF CANADA.

The asterisk (*) against a Station denotes that another line of Railway branches off therefrom.

GRAND TRUNK RAILWAY.

Stations.	Distances Between.	Total Distances.
Riviere du Loup.		
St. Alexandre	12	...
St. Helene	7	19
St. Paschal	6	25
River Ouelle	9	34
St. Anne	6	40
St. Roch	7	47
St. Jean, Port Joli	8	55
L'Islet	8	63
Cap St. Ignace	7	70
St. Thomas	7	77
Berthier	9	86
St. Michel	9	95
St. Charles	6	101
St. Henri	8	109
*Chaudierre Junction	9	118
Point Levi (opposite Quebec)	8	126
Point Levi (opposite Quebec)		
*Chaudiere Junction	8	...
Chaudiere	1	9
Craig's Road	6	15
Black River	5	20
Methot's Mills	9	29
Becancour	12	41
Somerset	8	49
Stanfold	6	55
Arthabaska	9	64
Warwick	8	72
Danville	12	84
**Richmond*	12	96
Arthabaska Junction		
Walker's Cutting	4	4
Bulstrode	7	11
Aston	7	18
St. Celestin	7	25
St. Gregoire	6	31
Doucet's Landing (opposite Three Rivers)	4	35

Stations.	Distances Between.	Total Distances.
**Portland*, U. S.	...	...
**Island Pond*, U. S.	...	149
**Island Pond.*		
Boundary Line (Stanhope)	17	...
Coaticook	8	25
Compton	8	33
Waterville	4	37
Lennoxville	7	44
Sherbrooke	3	47
Brompton Falls	6	53
Windsor Mills	8	61
**Richmond*	11	72
**Richmond.*		
South Durham	10	...
Acton Vale	12	22
Upton (St. Ephrem)	6	28
Britannia Mills	6	34
St. Hyacinthe	7	41
St. Hilaire	13	54
St. Lambert	15	69
**Montreal*	3	72
**Montreal.*		
*Lachine Junction	2	2
Pointe Claire	12½	14½
St. Anne	6½	21
Vaudreuil	3¼	24¼
Cedars	4¾	29
Riviere Rouge	5¼	34¼
Coteau Landing	8	37¼
River Beaudette	5¾	43¼
Lancaster	10½	53¾
Cornwall	13¾	67½
Moulinette	5	72½
Dickinson's Landing	4½	77
Aultsville	6¼	83¼
Williamsburg (Morrisburg)	8¾	92¼

GRAND TRUNK RAILWAY—(*Continued.*)

Stations.	Distances Between.	Total Distances.
Matilda (Iroquois)	6¾	99
Edwardsburg	5½	104½
*Prescott Junction	7½	112
Prescott	1½	113½
Maitland	6¾	120¼
*Brockville	5	125¼
Lyn	4¼	129½
Mallorytown	8¼	137¾
Lansdown	8½	146¼
Gananoque	8¾	155
Kingston Mills	13½	168½
Kingston	4	172½
Ernestown	15	187½
Bath Road	2¼	189¾
Napanee	8¾	198½
Tyendinaga	8	206½
Shannonville	6½	213
Belleville	7¼	220¼
Trenton	11½	231¾
Brighton	9½	241¼
Colborne	7½	248¾
Grafton	7¼	256
*Cobourg	7¾	263¾
*Port Hope	6¼	270
Newtonville (Clarke)	10	280
Newcastle	5¾	285¾
Bowmanville	4¼	290
Oshawa	9½	299½
Whitby	4	303½
Duffin's Creek (Pickering)	6½	310
Frenchman's Bay (Dunbarton)	2¼	312¼
Port Union	4¼	316½
Scarboro'	5½	322
Don	9¼	331¼
**Toronto*	1¾	333
**Toronto.*		
Carleton	5	5
Weston	3½	8½
Malton	6½	15
Brampton	6	21
Norval	7	27
Georgetown	2	29
Limehouse	3	32
Acton West	3½	35½
Rockwood	5½	41
*Guelph	7½	48½
Breslaw	9½	58
*Berlin	4½	62½
Petersburg	6¼	68¾

Stations.	Distances Between.	Total Distances.
Baden	3¾	72½
Hamburg	2¼	74¾
Shakspeare	7	81¾
*Stratford	6¼	88
*St. Marys	10½	98½
Lucan	15¼	113¾
Ailsa Craig	7	120¾
Swainby	7¾	128½
Widder	8¼	136¾
Forest	9¾	146½
Perch	12½	159
**Sarnia*	9¼	168¼
**Sarnia.*		
Port Huron, (U. S.) Ferry	1	1
**Detroit*, U.S.)	62¼	63¼
**St. Marys.*		
Thorndale	12	10
**London*	10¼	22¼
**Buffalo.*		
Fort Erie	2½	2½
Ridgeway	7	9½
Sherks	4	13½
Port Colborne	6	19½
Wainfleet	5¼	24¾
Boulton Ditch	6¼	30
Leeds	2¼	32¼
Dunville	5¾	38¼
Canfield	8¼	46½
Cooles	4¾	51¼
Caledonia (Seneca)	7½	58¾
Middleport	6½	65¼
Onondaga	2¼	67½
Cainsville	4½	72
Brantford	3¼	75¼
*Paris	8	83¼
Richwood	5¾	89
Drumbo	2¾	91¾
Plattsville	5¼	97
Ratho	3	100
Tavistock	7	107
*Stratford	8	115
Mitchell	12¼	127¼
Carronbrook	5¾	133
Seaforth	6¼	139¼
Harpurhay	1½	140¾
Clinton	6¾	147½
Goderich	12¾	160

TOTAL DISTANCES ON THE GRAND TRUNK RAILWAY.

Rivière du Loup and Chaudière Junction	...	118
Point Lévi and Richmond	...	96
Arthabaska and Doucet's Landing	...	35
Portland and Island Pond	...	149
Island Pond and Richmond	...	72
Richmond and Montreal	...	72
Montreal and Toronto	...	333
Toronto and Sarnia	...	168¼
Port Huron (opposite Sarnia) and Detroit	...	62¼
St. Mary's and London	...	22¼
Buffalo and Goderich	...	160¼
Total		1323

MONTREAL AND ROUSE'S POINT RAILWAY.

Stations.	Distances Between.	Total Distances.
**Montreal.*		
St. Lambert	1	1
Junction	10	11
L'Acadie	3	14
St. Johns	7	21
Grande Ligne	6	27
Stottsville	6	33
Lacolle	5	38
**Rouse's Point*	6	44

STANSTEAD, SHEFFORD AND CHAMBLY RAILWAY.

Stations.	Distances Between.	Total Distances.	Stations.	Distances Between.	Total Distances.
St. Johns.			Granby	8	29
Soixante (Versaille)	7	7	Holland's	7	36
St. Brigide	3	10	West Shefford	1	37
W. Farnham	4	14	*Waterloo*	6	43
St. George	7	21			

ST. JOHNS AND ST. ARMAND EN ROUTE TO ST. ALBANS.

Stations.	Distances Between.	Total Distances.	Stations.	Distances Between.	Total Distances.
St. Johns.			Stanbridge Station	3	18
St. Alexandre	8	8	Moor's "	4	22
Des Rivieres	7	15	**St. Armands* "	3	25

MONTREAL LACHINE AND PROVINCE LINE RAILWAY.

Stations.	Distances Between.	Total Distances.	Stations.	Distances Between.	Total Distances.
**Montreal.*			Lapigeonière	4	25
Lachine	8	8	Johnsons (Barrington)	7	32
Caughnawaga	2	10	Hemmingford	4	36
St. Isidore	5	15	**Province Line*	4	40
St. Remi	6	21			

ST. LAWRENCE AND OTTAWA RAILWAY.

Stations.	Distances Between.	Total Distances.	Stations.	Distances Between.	Total Distances.
Prescott.			Osgoode	8½	31
*Prescott Junction	2	2	Rossiters	6	37
Spencerville	7	9	Gloucester	6	43
Oxford	7½	16½	Billings	5	48
Kemptville	6	22½	*Ottawa*	6	54

BROCKVILLE AND OTTAWA RAILWAY.

Stations.	Distances Between.	Total Distances.	Stations.	Distances Between.	Total Distances.
Brockville.			Almonte	6	52
G. T. Junction	½	½	Smedden's	3¾	55¾
Fairfield	5	5½	Packenham	5¼	61
Clark's	1½	7	Arnprior	8	69
Bellamy's	3	10	*Sand Point*	5½	74½
Jelly's	2	12			
Bell's	1½	13½	*Smith's Falls.*		
Wolford	2½	16	Pike Falls	6	6
Irish Creek	5	21	Perth	6	12
Story's	4	25			
Smith's Falls	3	28	TOTAL DISTANCES.		
Ferguson's	5⅓	33⅓	Brockville and Sand Point		74½
Franktown	3⅔	37	Smith's Falls and Perth		12½
Beckwith	4	41			
Carlton Place	5	46	Total		86½

PORT HOPE, PETERBORO' AND LINDSAY RAILWAY.

Stations.	Distances Between.	Total Distances.	Stations.	Distances Between.	Total Distances.
**Port Hope.*			**Millbrook.*		
Quays	6	6	Frazerville (Springville)	7	7
Perrytown	2	8	*Peterboro'*	6	13
Campbells	2	10			
Summit	5	15			
*Millbrook	3	18			
Manvers (Bethany)	6	24	TOTAL DISTANCES.		
Brunswick	2	26	Port Hope and Lindsay	...	43
Lytles	2	28	Millbrook and Peterboro'	...	13
Omemee	5	33			
Kelleys	5	38	Total		56

NORTHERN RAILWAY.

Stations.	Distances Between.	Total Distances.	Stations.	Distances Between.	Total Distances.
Toronto.			Bell Ewart (Branch)	3	52
Davenport	5	5	Lefroy	1	53
Weston	3	8	Craigville	5½	58½
York	3¾	11¾	Barrie (Allandale)	5½	64
Thornhill	2¾	14½	Harrison's	5½	69½
Richmond Hill	4	18½	Essa	2½	72
King	4½	23	Angus	2½	74½
Aurora	7½	30½	New Lowell	5½	80
Newmarket	4¼	34¾	Sunnidale (Silvershoe)	1	81
Holland Landing	3¼	38	Warrington	5	86
Bradford	3¼	41¼	Stayner	1	87
Scanlans	2¾	44¼	*Collingwood*	8½	95½
Gilford	4¾	49			

COBOURG AND PETERBORO' RAILWAY.

Stations.	Distances Between.	Total Distances.	Stations.	Distances Between.	Total Distances.
**Cobourg.*			Indian Village	3	18
Baltimore	5	5	Keene	3	21
Bredin	5	10	*Peterboro.*	7	28
Harwood	5	15			

GREAT WESTERN RAILWAY.

Stations.	Distances Between.	Total Distances.	Stations.	Distances Between.	Total Distances.
Toronto.			Glencoe	5	149
Mimico	7	7	Newbury	6½	155½
Port Credit	6½	13½	Bothwell	4¼	159¾
Oakville	8	21½	Thamesville	8¾	168½
Bronte	4¼	25¾	Lewisville	6	174½
Wellington Square	6¼	32	Chatham	9	183½
Waterdown (Aldershott)	3	35	Baptiste Creek	14½	198
*Burlington Junction	2½	37½	Belle River	14	212
Hamilton	1½	39	**Windsor* (opposite Detroit)	17	229
**Clifton* (Suspension Bridge)					
Thorold	9¼	9¼	**Harrisburg.*		
St. Catherines	2	11¼	Branchton	6	6
Jordan	5¾	17	Galt	6	12
Beamsville	5	22	Preston	4	16
Grimsby	4¾	26¾	Hespeler	3½	19½
Ontario	5	31¾	**Guelph*	8	27½
Hamilton	11½	43¼			
*Burlington Junction	1¼	44½	**Komoka*		
Dundas	4	48½	Strathroy	10¼	
Flamboro'	3½	52	Kerrwood	6	16¼
Copetown	2¾	54¾	Watford	7¼	23½
Lynden	4¼	59	Wanstead	8¼	31¾
*Harrisburg	3½	62½	*Wyoming	2½	34¼
*Paris	9¾	72¼	Maudaumin	7	41¼
Princeton	7	79¼	**Sarnia*	9¾	51
Arnold's	2	81¼	**Wyoming*		
Eastwood	5¼	86½	*Petrolia*	5¼	5¼
Woodstock	4½	91			
Beachville	5	96	TOTAL DISTANCES GREAT WESTERN.		
Ingersoll	4¼	100¼	Toronto and Burlington Junction	...	37½
Dorchester	9½	109¾	Clifton and Windsor	...	229
*London	9½	119¼	Harrisburg and Guelph	...	27½
*Komoka	10¼	129½	Komoka and Sarnia	...	51
Mount Brydges	5	134½	Wyoming and Petrolia	...	5¼
Longwood	5	139½			
Appin	4½	144	Total	...	350¼

WELLAND RAILWAY.

Stations.	Distances Between.	Total Distances.	Stations.	Distances Between.	Total Distances.
Port Dalhousie:			Port Robinson	2	31
St. Catharines	3	3	Welland	4	17
*Thorold	4½	7½	**Port Colborne*	8	25
Allanburg	3½	11			

LONDON AND PORT STANLEY RAILWAY.

Stations.	Distances Between.	Total Distances.	Stations.	Distances Between.	Total Distances.
**London*			Yarmouth	3	12
Pond Mills	3	3	St. Thomas	3	15
Westminster North	3	6	White's	5	20
Westminster South	3	9	*Port Stanley*	4	24

ERIE AND NIAGARA LINE.

Stations.	Distances Between.	Total Distances.	Stations.	Distances Between.	Total Distances.
Fort Erie			Suspension Bridge	1½	18¾
*Black Creek	7		Queenston	5¾	24½
Chippewa	7	14	Niagara Town	6¼	30¾
The Falls (Clifton House)	3¼	17¼	Niagara Wharf	½	31¼

MASONIC.

THE GRAND LODGE OF ANCIENT FREE AND ACCEPTED MASONS OF CANADA.

List of Grand Officers for 1868-69.

M. W. Bro. A. A. Stevenson, Grand Master
R. W. Bro. James Seymour, Deputy Grand Master
" " John E. Brooke, D.D.G.M. London Dis.
" " David Curtis, D.D.G.M. Wilson "
" " Thos. Matheson, D.D.G.M. Huron "
" " John Parry, D.D.G.M., Hamilton "
" " M. H. Spencer, D.D.G.M., Toronto "
" " Wm. McCabe, D.D.G.M., Ontario "
" " H. W. Day, D.D.G.M., Prince Edw'd "
" " G. M. Wilkinson, D.D.G.M. St. Lawrence "
" " Wm. Mostyn, D.D.G.M., Ottawa "
" " Alex. Murray, D.D.G.M., Montreal "
" " Jno. H. Graham, D.D.G.M., Eastern Tp "
" " Alex. Walker, D.D.G.M., Quebec "
" " John W. Murton, Grand Senior Warden
" " Stevens Baker, Grand Junior Warden
" " Rev. Vincent Clementi, Grand Chaplain
" " Henry Groff, Grand Treasurer

R. W. Bro. Daniel Spry, Grand Registrar
" " Thomas B. Harris, Grand Secretary
V. W. Bro. John King, Grand Senior Deacon
" " Daniel Thomas, Grand Junior Deacon
" " A. T. Houel, Grand Superint'dt of Works
" " John Taylor, Grand Director of Ceremonies
" " Ed. Mitchell, Assistant Grand Secretary
" " E. C. Barber, Ast. Gd Direct. of Ceremonies
" " Frederick Mudge, Grand Sword Bearer
" " George E. Pearce, Grand Organist
" " A. E. Fife, Assistant Grand Organist
" " James Might, Grand Pursuivant
" " Robert Noxon, Grand Tyler
V. W. Bros. L. W. Decker, C. Cameron, W. B. Irving, Robt. Hendry, J. Quigg, G. Billington, S. J. J. Brown, John G. Gemmell, Allan McLean, H. T. Wood, I. B. Futvoye, C. Joncas, jr., Grand Stewards.

REPRESENTATIVES.—*In the Grand Lodge of Canada.*

R. W. Br. Sir John A. McDonald, K.C.B. from the U. G. L. of England
" " Kivas Tully, " G. L. of Ireland,
" " Thos. Drummond, " G. L. of Scotland,
M. W. Br. Wm. M. Wilson, " G. L. of Illinois,
" " " " " G. L. of St. Domingo,
" " A. Bernard, " G. L. of Vermont,
R. W. Br. Thomas B. Harris " G. L. of Kansas

R. W. Br. John H. Graham, from the G. L. of Maine
" " James A. Henderson " G. L. of N. York
M. W. Br. W. M. Wilson, " G. O. of Cuba
" " T. D. Harrington, " G. L. of N. Scotia
R. W. Br. Thomas B. Harris, " G. O. of Portugal
" " A. A. Stevenson, " G. O. of Brazil
" " Henry Macpherson, " G. O. of Uruguay
M. W. Br. A. Bernard, " G. O. of N. Gren'a

From the Grand Lodge of Canada.

R. W. Br. Rt. Hr Lord de Tabley in the U. G. L. of England
" " James V. Mackay, " G. L. of Ireland
" " Lindsay Mackersy, " G. L. of Scotland
" " ———— " G. L. of Vermont
" " Wm. Pitt Preble " G. L. of Maine
" " Henry W. Turner, " G. L. of New York
" " H. A. Johnson, " G. L. of Illinois
" " Jacinto de Castro " G. L. of St. Domigo
" " And. K. Mackinlay " G. L. of N. Scotia
" " E. T. Carr, " G. L. of Kansas

Ill. Br. G. M. C. Obed, at the G. O. of Cuba
" " Dr. F. De P. Romas, " G. O. of Brazil
" " J. M. Samper Augiano, " G. O. of N. Gren.
" " Antonio M. Mollejas, " G. O. of Venezula
" " L. Ximenez 33°, " G. O. of Uruguay
" " Joas C. D'Almeida, " G. O. of Portugal
" " Luis Goapil 33°, " G. O. of Mexico
" " Francesco De Luca " G. O. of Italy
" " A. M. Medina, " G. O. of Chili.

**The Fourteenth Annual Communication will be held at Montreal, the second Wednesday in July, A.L. 5869, A.D. 1869.

SUBORDINATE LODGES.

** *Lodges marked thus (*) hold their Installation of Officers on the Festival of St. John the Evangelist—all others on that of St. John the Baptist.*

NO.	LODGE.	WHERE HELD.	NIGHTS OF MEETING.		WORSHIPFUL MASTER.
—	*Antiquity Lodge.	Montreal	First Thursday	of every month.	W. Br. M. Gutman.
1	*Prevost	Dunham	Tuesday preceding full moon	"	" Stevens Baker.
2	Niagara	Niagara	Wednesday on or bef. full m.	"	" Henry J. Brown.
3	*St. John's.	Kingston	First Thursday	"	" G. M. Wilkinson.
4	*Dorchester	St. Johns.	First Tuesday	"	" R. Douglass.
5	*Sussex	Brockville	Wednesday on or prec. full m.	"	" T. Wilkinson.
6	Barton	Hamilton	Second Wednesday	"	" Wm. Edgar.
7	Union	Grimsby	Thursday on or bef. full moon	"	" Robert Kemp.
8	*Nelson.	Phillipsburg	Thursday on or bef. full moon	"	" L. W. Decker.
9	*Union	Napanee.	Friday before full moon	"	" F. Richardson.
10	*Norfolk	Simcoe	Tuesday on or bef, full moon	"	" John Clarke.
11	*Moira	Belleville	Wednesday on or pr. full moon	"	" N. B. Falkiner.
12	*Golden Rule	Stanstead	Tuesday on or before full moon	"	" T. Stevenson
14	*True Briton's	Perth	First Monday	"	" ————
15	St. George's	St. Catherines	Tuesday on or before full moon	"	" Lucius S. Oille
16	St. Andrew's	Toronto	Second Tuesday	"	" J. Adams, M.D.
17	St. John's	Cobourg	Monday on or before full moon	"	" W. I. Stanton

SUBORDINATE LODGES—(*Continued.*)

NO.	LODGE.	WHERE HELD.	NIGHTS OF MEETING.	WORSHIPFUL MASTERS.
18	*Prince Edward's.	Picton	Thursday on or pre. f. m. of ev. month	W. Br. Henry T. Wood
19	*St. George's	Montreal	Third Tuesday "	" C. E. Mortimer
20	*St. John's	London	Second Tuesday "	" James Moffatt
21	*Zetland	Montreal	Second Thursday "	" W. Armstrong
22	King Solomon's	Toronto	Second Thursday "	" Daniel Spry
23	Richmond	Richmond Hill	Thursday on or before full moon "	" A. L. Skeel
25	*Ionic	Toronto	First Tuesday "	" R. P. Stephens
26	*Ontario	Port Hope	Third Thursday "	" James Marshall
27	*Strict Observance	Hamilton	Third Tuesday "	" F. C. Bruce
28	*Mount Zion	Kemptville	Wednesday preceding full moon "	" Walter Kerr
29	*United	Brighton	Thursday before full moon "	" E. W. Edwards
30	*Composite	Whitby	First Thursday "	" R. J. Wilson
31	*Jerusalem	Bowmanville	Wednesday on or before full moon "	" B. Patterson
32	*Amity	Dunnville	Wednesday after full moon "	" L McCallum
34	*Thistle	Amherstburg	Tuesday before full moon "	" George Gott
35	St. John's	Cayuga	Thursdey on or after full moon "	" D. Cameron
36	Welland	Fonthill	Thursday on or before full moon "	" N. C. Holcomb
37	*King Hiram	Ingersoll	Tuesday on or before full moon "	" James Canfield
38	*Trent	Trenton	Tuesday before full moon "	" H. W. Day
39	*Mount Zion	Brooklyn	Tuesday on or preceeding full moon "	" J. P. Campbell
40	*St. John's	Hamilton	Third Thursday "	" George Walker
41	*St. George's	Kingsville	Thursday on or before full moon "	" J. B. Black
42	*St. George's	London	First Thursday "	" Thos. Beattie
43	King Solomon's	Woodstock	Tuesday on or before full moon "	" James S. Scarff
44	*St. Thomas	St. Thomas	First Thursday "	" John E. Smith
45	Brant	Brantford	Tuesday on or before full moon "	" F. Mudge
46	*Wellington	Chatham	Second Monday "	" John E. Brooke
47	*Great Western	Windsor	Thursday on or before full moon "	" A. J. Kennedy
48	*Madoc	Madoc	Tuesday on or before full moon "	" B. H. Maybee
49	*Harington	Quebec	Third Thursday	" John Tweddell
50	*Consecon	Consecon	Friday on or before full moon "	" S. B. Netherey
51	*Corinthian	Grahamville	Tuesday on or before full moon "	" Joseph Figg
53	*Shefford	Waterloo	First Monday "	" G. H. Allen
54	*Vaughan	Maple	Tuesday on or before full moon "	" P. Patterson
55	*Mirrickville	Mirickville	Tuesday after full moon	" Thomas Geer
56	Victoria	Sarnia	Tuesday before full moon	" Robert S. Gurd
57	*Harmony	Binbrook	Monday after full moon	" J. Brown, junr
58	*Doric	Ottawa	First Wednesday "	" J. G. Gemmell
59	*Corinthian	Ottawa	Third Thursday "	" E. C. Barber
60	*Hoyle	LaColle	Second Tuesday	" D. Galt
61	*Acacia	Hamilton	Fourth Friday "	" Edw. Mitchell
62	*St. Andrews	Caledonia	Wednesday on or before full moon "	" D. E. Broderick
64	*Kilwinning	London	Third Thursday "	" M. F. Morgan
66	*Durham	Newcastle	Friday on or before full moon "	" R. T. Wilkinson
67	*St. Francis	Richmond	First Thursday "	" Timothy Leet
68	St. John	Ingersoll	Thursday on or before full moon "	" Thomas Bowers
69	Stirling	Stirling	Thursday after full moon "	" George E. Bull
71	*Victoria	Sherbrooke	Second Tuesday "	" D. Thomas
72	Alma	Galt	Thursday on or before full moon "	" John Barbour
73	*St. James'	St. Mary's	First Monday "	" J. E. Harding.
74	*St. James'	Maitland	Monday nearest full moon "	" J. Suddaby.
75	St. Johns'	Toronto	First Monday "	" F. J. Menet.
76	*Oxford	Woodstock	Second Wednesday "	" Edward Burke.
77	*Faithful Brethr.	Lindsay	First Thursday "	" H. Gladman.
78	*King Hiram	Tilsonburg	Wednesday on or bef. full moon "	" Wm. Norris.
79	Simcoe	Bradford	Thursday after full moon "	" J. W. H. Wilson.
80	Albion	Newbury	First Tuesday "	" John Braken.
81	*St. John's	Mt. Brydges	Tuesday on or bef. full moon "	" G. Billington.
82	St. John's	Paris	First Tuesday "	" W. S. Martin.
83	*Beaver	Strathroy	Friday on or after full moon "	" J. Lenfesty, jun.
84	Clinton	Clinton	Wednesday on or after full m. "	" H. F. Sharpe.
85	Rising Sun	Farmersville	Thursday nearest full moon "	" A. Chamberlain.
86	*Wilson	Toronto	Third Tuesday "	" J. Segsworth.
87	Markham Union	Markham	Friday on or before full moon "	" D. McMurchy.
88	St. George's	Owen Sound	Wednesday on or bef. full moon "	" T. Gordon.
90	*Manito	Collingwood	Wednesday on or aft. full moon "	" John Nettleton
91	*Colborne	Colborne	Friday on or before full moon "	" C. R. Ford
92	*Cataraqui	Kingston	Second Wednesday "	" R. Henry, jun.
93	*Northern Light	Kincardine	Thursday after full moon "	" W. P. Brown

SUBORDINATE LODGES—(*Continued.*)

NO.	LODGE.	WHERE HELD.	NIGHTS OF MEETING.		WORSHIPFUL MASTERS.
94	*St. Mark's	Port Stanley	Second Tuesday	of every month	W. Br. N. S. McColl
95	Ridout	Otterville	Thursday on or before full moon	"	" John Wood
96	*Corinthian	Barrie	Thursday on or before full moon	"	" M. H. Spencer
97	*Sharon	Sharon	Tuesday on or before full moon	"	" A. Souter
98	True Blue	Albion	Friday on or before full moon	"	" Wm. Graham
99	*Tuscan	Newmarket	Second Wednesday	"	" James Sykes
100	Valley	Dundas	First Wednesday	"	" W. B. Irving
101	*Corinthian	Peterboro'	Wednesday preceding full moon	"	" Alexander Smith
103	*Maple Leaf	St. Catharines	Thursday on or after full moon	"	" Samuel Cole
104	St. John's	Norwichville	Wednesday after full moon	"	" Edwin Peake
105	St. Mark's	Drummondville	Tuesday on or before full moon	"	" Samuel Smith
106	*Burford	Burford	Wednesday before full moon	"	" F. Mudge
107	St. Paul's	Lambeth	Second Wednesday	"	" D. B. Burch
108	Blenheim	Drumbo	Wednesday on or before full moon	"	" John Hall
109	Albion	Harrowsmith	Tuesday after full moon	"	" N. F. Dupius
110	*Central	Prescott	First Tuesday	"	" George EnEarl
112	Maitland	Goderich	Second Tuesday	"	" J. Thompson
113	*Wilson	Waterford	Wednesday on or before full moon	"	" William Allan
114	*Hope	Port Hope	First Thursday	"	" A. T. Williams
115	*Ivy	Smithville	Tuesday on or after full moon	"	" James S. Bates
116	*Cassia	Widder	Monday on or before full moon	"	" John Dallas
117	*Stanbridge	Stanbridge	Wednesday on or before full moon	"	" M. R. Meigs
118	Union	Lloydtown	Monday on or before full moon	"	" J. T. Carson
119	*Maple Leaf	Bath	Monday before full moon	"	" B. C. Davy
120	Warren	Fingal	Second Thursday	"	" W. B. Burgess
121	*Doric	Brantford	Friday on or prec. full moon	"	" Samuel Hall
122	*Renfrew	Renfrew	Tuesday nearest full moon	"	" Charles Hudson
123	*The Belleville	Belleville	First Thursday	"	" L. H. Henderson
124	*Montreal Kilw	Montreal	Second Monday	"	" John B. Peavey
125	*Cornwall	Cornwall	Monday on or after full moon	"	" James Hawkes
126	*Golden Rule	Campbellford	Tuesday after full moon	"	" J. Dinwoodie, jr.
127	Franck	Frankford	Monday before full moon	"	" H. W. Delany
128	*Pembroke	Pembroke	Tuesday before full moon	"	" J. B. Coleman
129	The Rising Sun	Aurora	Friday on or before full moon	"	" T. W. Todd
130	*Yamaska	Granby	Wednesday before full moon	"	" J. H. Bartlett
131	*St. Lawrance	Southampton	Second Tuesday	"	" John McLean
133	*Lebanon Forest	Franceston	Monday on or before full moon	"	" Wm. Carick
134	*Shawenegan	Three Rivers	Second Wednesday	"	" John Broster
135	*St. Clair	Milton	Thursday on or before full moon	"	" ———
136	Richardson	Stouffville	Wednesday on or before full moon	"	" E. B. Armstrong
137	*Pythagoras	Meaford	Friday on or after full moon	"	" Alexander Mitchell
138	*Aylmer	Aylmer, P.Q	Second Tuesday	"	" C. H. Church
139	Lebanon	Oshawa	Second Tuesday	"	" John Boyd
140	*Malahide	Aylmer, O	Wednesday on or after full moon	"	" S. S. Clutton
141	*Tudor	Mitchell	Tuesday on or before full moon	"	" E. Hornibrook
142	*Excelsior	Morrisburgh	Thursday on or before full moon	"	" T. Chamberlain
143	*Friendly Broth's	Iroquois	Wednesday before full moon	"	" James Stephenson
144	*Tecumseh	Stratford	Thursday on or before full moon	"	" James P. Wood
145	*J. B. Hall	Millbrook	Second Thursday	"	" James Might
146	*Prince of Wales	Newburgh	Wednesday before full moon	"	" H. M. Wright
147	Mississippi	Almonte	Friday on or before full moon	"	" P. McDougall
148	*Civil Service	Seat of Gov't	Second Tuesday	"	" Thomas Monro
149	Erie	Port Dover	Monday on or before full moon	"	" Jesse V. Hoover
150	*Hastings	Hastings	Thursday on or before full moon	"	" Jas. C. Brown
151	The Grand River	Berlin	Tuesday on or before full moon	"	" Wm. Washburn
152	Clarenceville	Clarenceville	Third Thursday	"	" C. S. Rowe
153	*Burns	Wyoming	Thursday on or before full moon	"	" James McKay
154	*Irving	Lucan	Thursday on or before full moon	"	" J. O'Donohue
155	*Peterborough	Peterboro'	First Friday	"	" C. Cameron
156	*York	Eglington	Thursday on or before full moon	"	" A. L. Willson
157	Simpson	Delta	Tuesday on or after full moon	"	" R. H. Preston
158	*Alexandria	Oil Springs	Thursday on or after full moon	"	" Thomas Ellison
159	Goodwood	Richmond, O	First Tuesday	"	" Edward Reilly
160	*Quebec Garrison	Quebec	First Monday	"	" W. Wilkinson
161	*Percy	Warkworth	Wednesday before full moon	"	" I. Humphries
162	Forest	Wroxeter	Friday on or after full moon	"	" John Moffatt
163	*Browne	West Farnham	Friday on or before full moon	"	" C. P. Taber
164	*Star in the East	Wellington	Tuesday on or before full moon	"	" Ira Clinton
165	*Burlington	Wellington Sq	Wednesday on or before full moon	"	" Wm. Kerns

SUBORDINATE LODGES—(*Continued.*)

NO.	LODGE.	WHERE HELD.	NIGHTS OF MEETING.	WORSHIPFUL MASTERS.
166	*Wentworth	Stoney Creek	Monday on or before full mn. ev. month	W. Br. A. G. Jones
167	*Royal Albert	Montreal	First Wednesday "	" Frank Edgar
168	*Merritt	Welland	Monday on or before full moon "	" J. W. Schooley
169	*Macnab	Port Colborne	Tuesday on or before full moon "	" John C. Karr
170	*Britannia	Seaforth	Monday on or after full moon "	" A. Slimmon
171	*Prince of Wales.	Iona	Friday on or after full moon "	" J. Edgecombe
172	*Ayr	Ayr	Tuesday on or before full moon "	" F. Buckley
173	*Victoria	Montreal	First Monday "	" Alex. Murray
174	*Walsingham	Port Rowan	First Thursday after full moon "	" James Ryan
175	*St. John's	South Potton	Wednesday before full moon "	" R. Manson
176	Spartan	Sparta	Monday on or after full moon "	" W. T. Edge
177	The Builders	Ottawa	Friday on or before full moon "	" Thomas Painter
178	*Plattsville	Plattsville	Second Friday "	" George Risk
179	*Bothwell	Bothwell	Wednesday on or before full moon "	" H. F. Smith
180	*Speed	Guelph	Second Tuesday "	" Charles Sharpe
181	Oriental	Port Burwell	Tuesday on or before full moon "	" W. A. Glover
182	*Tus an	Levis	First Thursday "	" John Breakey
183	Prince Albert	Prince Albert	Friday on or before full moon "	" James Emaney
184	*Old Light	Lucknow	Thursday on or before full moon "	" James Somerville
185	*Enniskillen	York	Monday on or before full moon "	" J. B. Holden
186	*Plantagenet	Plantagenet	Monday on or before full moon "	" Henry Smith
187	*Royal Canadian	Sweetsburg	Second Wednesday "	" H. D. Pickel
188	*Ascot	Lennoxville	Monday on or before full moon "	" I. H. Stearns
189	*Filius Viduæ	Adolphustown	Wednesday on or before full moon "	" E. H. Smith
190	Belmont	Belmont	Friday on or before full moon "	" Francis Kunz
191	*Ashlar	Coaticook	First Wednesday "	" Geoorge Wood
192	*Orillia	Orillia	Friday on or after full moon "	" C. S. Elliot
193	*Scotland	Scotland	Monday on or before full moon "	" F. Mudge
194	*Petrolia	Petrolia	Second Wednesday "	" H. H. Hunt
195	The Tuscan	London	First Monday "	" T. Wilson
196	Madawaska	Arnprior	Thursday on or before full moon "	" Robert Meikle
197	Saugeen	Walkerton	Second Tuesday "	" H. B. O'Connor
198	White Oak	Oakville	Tuesday on or before full moon "	" G. K. Chisholm
199	Frelighsburgh	Frelighsburgh	Monday on or before full moon "	" G. R. Marvin
200	St. Alban's	Mount Forest	Friday on or before full moon "	" W. W. Winfield
201	Leeds	Gananoque	Tuesday on or before full moon "	" William Byers, jun.
202	Mount Royal	Montreal	Second Tuesday "	" Charles Stoter
203	Irvine	Elora	Third Friday "	" A. B. Petrie
204	Doric	Danville	Wednesday on or before full moon "	" Timothy Leef
205	New Dominion	New Hamburg	Monday on or after full moon "	" Louis Helmer

THE GRAND CHAPTER OF ROYAL ARCH MASONS OF CANADA.

OFFICERS OF THE GRAND CHAPTER, 1868–9.

M. E. Comp. T. D. Harington, Grand Z } G. Council
R. " " James Seymour, " H
" " " Isaac H. Stearns, " J
" " " Thomas B. Harris, " Scribe E
" " " Edward Willis, " " N
" " " Henry Robertson, " Prin. Sojourner
" " " John V. Noel, " Treasurer
" " " Henry J. Pratten, " Registrar
V. E. Comp. George EnEarl, " First Asst. Soj.
" " " W. G. Parmelee, " 2nd " "
" " " Wm. Johnson, " Sword Bearer
" " " Isaac F. Toms, " Standard Bearer
" " " E. P. Remon, " Dir. of Ceremonies
" " " Peter Begg, " Organist
" " " S. H. Blondheim, " Pursuivant
" " " F. C. Bruce, } Grand Stewards
" " " B. P. Patterson,

V. E. Comp. C. Stavely, } Grand Stewards
" " " John Taylor,
" Thomas Graham, " Janitor

GRAND SUPERINTENDENTS OF DISTRICTS.

R. E. Comp. Thos. F. McMullen...London District
" " Comp. Chas. L. Beard.........Wilson "
" " " Thos. Winter ....Huron "
" " " B. E. Charleon.........Hamilton "
" " " Wm. McCabe......Toronto & Ontario "
" " " H. W. DeLany.........Pr. Edward "
" " " M. J. May.............Central "
" " " Thomas Milton.........Montreal "
" " " W. A. Taylor.........East'n Tps. "
" " " Thomas Lambert......Quebec "
" " " Robert Marshall ......N. Brunswick

* The Twelfth Regular Convocation will be held at Kingston, on the 2nd Tuesday in August, A.I. 2399, A.D. 1869.

SUBORDINATE CHAPTERS.

NO.	CHAPTER.	WHERE HELD.	NIGHTS OF MEETING.	1ST PRINCIPAL.
1	Anc'nt Frontenac.	Kingston	Third Tuesday in Feb., May, Aug. and Nov	Samuel D. Fowler.
2	The Hiram	Hamilton	First Monday of every month	Wm. Reid.
4	St. Andrew's	Toronto	Third Wednesday in Jan. April, July and Oct	S. B. Harman.
5	St. George's	London	Fourth Friday in Feb., May, Aug. and Sept	T. F. McMullen.
6	St. John's	Hamilton	Second Thursday of every month	B. E. Charlton.
7	Moira	Belleville	First Tuesday of every month	A. A. Campbell.
8	King Solomon's	Toronto	First Thursday of every month	Thomas Sargant.
9	Golden Rule	Stanstead	Tuesday on or bef. f.m. in Mar. June, Sep. Dec.	H. J. Martin.
10	New Brunswick	St. John	Second Monday in every month	D. R. Munro.
12	Cataraqui	Kingston	Second Monday in Feb., May, Aug., and Nov	John V. Noel.
13	Stadacona	Quebec	Second Thursday in Jan., April, July and Oct.	Henry J. Pratten.
14	Bedford District	Dunham	First Thursday of every month	W. A. Taylor.
15	Wawanosh	Sarnia	Second Friday in Jan., April, July and Oct	Wm. M. Jamieson.
16	Carleton	Ottawa	Second Wednesday in Mar., June, Sep. and Dec.	M. J. May.
17	Dorchester	Waterloo	First Thursday of every mouth	Wm. G. Parmlee.
18	Oxford	Woodstock	First Friday of every month	Charles L. Beard.
19	Mount Moriah	St. Catharines	Friday on or bef. full m. of each month	Lucius S. Oille.
20	Mount Horeb	Brantford	First Wednesday of every month	J. W. Lethbridge.
21	Carnarvon	Montreal	Third Thursday in Feb., May, Aug. and Nov	J. H. Stearns.
22	Greenville	Prescott	First Wednesday in Jan., April, July and Oct	George EnEarl.
23	Ezra	Simcoe	Second Wednesday of every month	John Clarke.
24	Tecumseth	Stratford	Last Wednesday of every month	Thomas Winter.
25	Mount Horeb	Montreal	Second Wednesday in Mar., June, Sep. and Dec.	Thomas Milton.
26	St. Mark's	Trenton	Second Wednesday of every mouth	Peter Begg.
27	Manitou	Collingwood	First Friday of every month	John Nettleton.
28	Pentalpha	Oshawa	First Friday of every month	S. B. Fairbanks.
29	McCallum	Dunnville	Friday on or after full moon of every month	A. Brownson.
30	Huron	Goderich	First Wednesday of every month	Isaac F. Toms.
31	Prince Edward	Picton	Friday on or after full moon	Donald Ross.
32	Waterloo	Galt	Friday on or before full moon	A. T. H. Ball.

PROVINCIAL GRAND CONCLAVE OF CANADA.

Royal, Exalted, Religious & Military Order of Masonic Knights Templar, Malta, &c., under England & Wales.

V. E. Fra Col. W. J. B. McLeod Moore, Grand Prior for the Dominion of Canada.

V. E. Fr. T. D. Harington, Dep. G. Commander
E. " C. D. Macdonnell, Prov. G. Prior
" " J. Seymour, Dep. Sub-Prior
" Rev. J. A. Preston, Grand Prelate
" " J. Moffatt " First Captain
" " W. B. Colby, " Second Captain
" " " T. B. Harris, " Chancellor
" Thomas White, jun. " Vice-Chancellor
" F. C. Bruce " Registrar
" " L. H. Henderson " Treasurer
" R. Hunter " Chamberlain
" " H. Swales " Hospitaller

E. Fr. M. J. May Grand Expert
" " R. A. Smith " 1st Standard Bearer
" " A. R. Sowdon " 2nd " "
" " B. E. Charlton, " Almoner
" " Thomas Milton " 1st Aid-de-Camp
" " C. A. Birge " 2nd Aid-de-Camp
" " Alex. Servos " Dir. of Ceremonies
" " Robt. Gaskin " Captain of Lines
" " George P. Barnwell " 1st Herald
" " George P. Groves " 2nd Herald
" " Robert Town, " Sword Bearer
" " Thomas Graham " Equerry

The next Regular Assembly will be held at Kingston, on the 2nd Tuesday in August, A.M. 5873, A.D. 1869, A.O. 750.

SUBORDINATE ENCAMPMENT.

ENCAMPMENT.	WHERE HELD.	NIGHTS OF MEETING.	EMT. COMMANDER.
Hugh de Payens	Kingston	2nd Monday, Jan., April, July and Oct	H. E. Swales
Wm. de la More, the Martyr	Ottawa	2nd Monday, Feb., May, August and Nov.	T. D. Harrington
Geoffrey de St. Aldemar	Toronto	1st Friday, Feb., May, August and Nov	Not working
Godfrey de Bouillon	Hamilton	1st Friday in every month	Thomas B. Harris
Richard Cœur de Lion	London	2nd Friday in every month	Thomas McCraken
King Baldwin	Belleville	1st Monday, Jan., April, July and Oct	L. H. Henderson
Richard Cœur de Lion	Montreal	4th Thursday in each month	A. A. Stevenson
Plantagenet	St. Catharines	2nd Monday, Feb., April, July and Oct	Edwin Goodman
Sussex	Stanstead	Wednesd. next p.f.m. Mar., June, Sep. & Dec	W. B. Colby.

ADDRESS.

Sir W. J. B. McLeod Moore, Grand Prior, Laprairie, Province of Quebec, Canada.
" T. Douglas Harington, Dep. Grand Prior, Ottawa, " Ontario, "
" Thomas B. Harris, Prov. G. Chancellor, Hamilton, " " "

CANADIAN ORDER OF ODD FELLOWS, M. U.

Officers of the Order: George Bickell, Dundas, Grand Master; Daniel Evans, Hamilton, Dep. Grand Master; Thomas Tindall, Hamilton, Corresponding Secretary. Board of Directors: George H. Cozens, Andrew Dick, E. S. Thomas, William Black, John W. Norman, Samuel Harris (ex officio). Quarterly meetings of the Board, second Thursday in July, October, January and April. Trustees of Widows' and Orphans' Fund: J. G. Howard, Toronto; Joseph Hodgson, Toronto · F. H. Medcalf, Toronto.

INDEPENDENT ORDER OF ODD FELLOWS, B. U.

Grand Lodge of Ontario.—John Barr, M. W. Grand Master, Hamilton; Thomas Partridge, R. W. Deputy Grand Master, London; R. Kirkpatrick, R. W. Grand Warden, London; J. B. King, R. W. Grand Secretary and Treasurer, Brantford; James Woodcraft, R. W. Grand Rep. to G. L. U. S., Brantford; Henry McAfee, R. W. Grand Rep. to G. L. U. S., Windsor; George Wales, R. W. Grand Conductor, St. Catharines; William Mowatt, R. W. Grand Conductor, St. Catharines; William Mowatt, R. W. Grand Marshall, Stratford; John Noble, R.W. Grand Guardian, Brantford.

Toronto Lodges.—*Canada Lodge*, instituted Jan. 14, 1868, about 70 members—William Doran, Noble Grand; J. N. Langstaff, Vice Grand; John Fields, R. Secretary; W. R. Roberts, Past Grand. *Covenant Lodge*, instituted October 22, 1868, about 50 members—Hugh Blain, Noble Grand; M. E. Linder, Vice Grand; Joseph F. Elby, R. Secretary; John J. Ramsay, Past Grand.

LOYAL ORANGE INSTITUTION.

GRAND LODGE OF BRITISH NORTH AMERICA.

Hon John Hillyard Cameron, Toronto, Grand Master and Sovereign.
D'Arcy Boulton, Barrie, Deputy Grand Master.
M. Anderson, Mountain View, Grand Treasurer.
Andrew Fleming, Toronto, Grand Secretary.
J. Ross Robertson, Toronto, Grand Lecturer.

GRAND ORANGE LODGE OF WESTERN ONTARIO.—GRAND OFFICERS FOR 1869.

D'Alton McCarthy, Barrie, Grand Master.
W. W. Connor, J.P., Bayfield; J. Ross Robertson, *Daily Telegraph*, Toronto, Deputy Grand Masters.
Rev. Daniel Smyth, St. Marys, Grand Chaplain.
Thomas Keyes, St. Catharines, Grand Secretary.
James A. Bessey, St. Catharines, Grand Treasurer.
William Parkhill, King, Grand Lecturer.
Walter S. Fletcher, St. Catharines, Grand Director of Ceremonies.
Rev. Richard Cleary, Mono; Rev. A. H. R. Mulholland, R.D., Owen Sound; Rev. Henry Bartlett, Princeton; Rev. John Carry, B.D., Holland Landing; Rev. William Smith, St. Marys, Deputy Grand Chaplains.
Joseph Doupe, Angus, Deputy Grand Secretary.
Thomas Hopwood, Stratford; Robert Adair, Oshawa, Deputy Grand Lecturers.
John W. Hetherington, Toronto; James Bennett, Grand Auditors.

LOYAL BLACK INSTITUTION OF IRELAND.

Bro. Sir Knight J. Ross Robertson, Toronto, Right Worshipful Grand Master.
Bro. H. Griffith, Hamilton, Deputy Grand Master.
Bro. W. H. Scoles, Belleville, Grand Registrar.
Bro. John G. More, Belleville, Grand Treasurer.
Bro. Dawson, Mallorytown, Grand Chaplain.
Bro. J. F. Post, Belleville, Grand Pursuivant.

CANADIAN STAMP DUTIES.

ON BILLS OF EXCHANGE, DRAFTS AND PROMISSORY NOTES.

In computing the duty, it must be borne in mind that any interest payable at maturity, with the principal, is to be counted as part of the amount.

AMOUNT.	Singly.	Duplicate each part.	Triplicate each part.
$25 and under	$0 01	$0 01	$0 01
Over 25 and not exceeding $50	0 02	0 01	0 01
" 50 " " 100	0 03	0 02	0 01
" 100 " " 200	0 06	0 04	0 02
" 200 " " 300	0 09	0 06	0 03
" 300 " " 400	0 12	0 08	0 04
" 400 " " 500	0 15	0 10	0 05
" 500 " " 600	0 18	0 12	0 06

Example.—A Note for $2,637 73, if executed singly, would require to be stamped with 81 cents; i executed in duplicate, each part with 54 cents; if in more than two parts, each part with 27 cents.

Extract from Act of 1865.—"The person affixing such adhesive stamp, shall, at the time of affixing the same, write or stamp thereon the date at which it is affixed, and such stamp shall be held *prima facie* to have been affixed at the date stamped or written thereon; and if no date be so stamped or written thereon, such adhesive stamp shall be of no avail; any person wilfully writing or stamping a false date on any adhesive stamp shall incur a penalty of one hundred dollars for each offence."

CANADIAN STANDARD WEIGHT.

IN A BUSHEL OF GRAIN, SEED, AND VEGETABLES.

GRAIN.		SEEDS—(Continued.)	
Wheat	60 lbs.	Blue Grass Seeds	14 lbs.
Peas	60 lbs.	Hungarian Grass	48 lbs.
Beans	60 lbs.	Millet	48 lbs.
Indian Corn	56 lbs.	Red Top Grass	8 lbs.
Rye	56 lbs.	VEGETABLES.	
Barley	48 lbs.	Potatoes, Parsnips	60 lbs.
Buckwheat	48 lbs.	Carrots, Turnips	60 lbs.
Oats	34 lbs.	Beets and Onions	60 lbs.
SEEDS.		Salt	56 lbs.
Clover Seed	60 lbs.	Castor Beans	40 lbs.
Flax Seed	50 lbs.	Malt	36 lbs.
Timothy Seed	48 lbs.	Dried Peaches	33 lbs.
Hemp Seed	44 lbs.	Dried Apples	22 lbs.

TABLE SHOWING THE QUANTITY OF SEED USUALLY SOWN UPON AN ACRE.

Barley	bushels	1½	to	2	Grass (Timothy)	pounds	16	to	24
Beans	"	2	to	3	Hemp	bushels	1	to	1½
Beets	pounds	5	to	6	Indian Corn	"	1	to	2
Buckwheat	bushels	5	to	1¼	Oats	"	2	to	4
Carrots	pounds	4	to	5	Onions	pounds	4	to	6
Clover	"	8	to	12	Peas	bushels	2	to	3
Flax	"	1½	to	2	Turnips	pounds	1	to	2
Grass (Red Top)	"	6	to	8	Wheat	bushels	1	to	2

THE AREA OF THE DOMINION.

Ontario, (estimated)	120,260	square miles.
Quebec (do)	210,023	do
New Brunswick	27,104	do
Nova Scotia	18,560	do
Total	377,041	square miles.

Add to this the area of Prince Edward Island, 2,100 square miles; Newfoundland, 40,200 square miles; British Columbia, 220,000 square miles (including Vancouver's Island, 20,000); and Labrador, the Hudson's Bay and North-West Territories, say 2,750,000 square miles, we shall have a total for British America of 3,389,345 square miles.

WEIGHTS & MEASURES.

MEASURES OF LENGTH.

12 Inches	= 1 Foot	69 Miles	= 1 Degree	4 Inches	= 1 Hand
3 Feet	= 1 Yard	2¼ Inches	= 1 Nail	6 Feet	= 1 Fathom
5½ Yards	= 1 Pole	4 Nails	= 1 Quarter	7.92 Inches	= 1 Link
40 Poles	= 1 Furlong	4 Quarters	= 1 Yard	100 Links	= 1 Chain
8 Furlongs	= 1 Mile	5 Quarters	= 1 Ell		

MEASURES OF SURFACE.

144 Sq. Ins.	= 1 Sq. Foot	40 Perches	= 1 Rood	10 Sq. Chains	= 1 Acre
9 Sq. Feet	= 1 Sq. Yard	4 Roods	= 1 Acre	640 Acres	= 1 Sq. Mile
30¼ Sq. Yards	= 1 Perch				

MEASURES OF SOLIDITY AND CAPACITY.

1,728 Cubic Ins. = 1 Foot | 27 Cubic Feet = 1 Yard.

Imperial Measures of Capacity for Liquids and Dry Goods.

4 Gills	= 1 Pint	2 Gallons	= 1 Peck.	8 Bushels	= 1 Quarter.
2 Pints	= 1 Quart.	8 Gallons	= 1 Bushel.	5 Quarters	= 1 Load.
4 Quarts	= 1 Gallon.				

MEASURES OF WEIGHT.

AVOIRDUPOIS WEIGHT.

16 Drams	=1 Ounce.
16 Ounces	=1 Pound (lb.)
28 Pounds	=1 Quarter (qr.)
4 Quarters	=1 Hundred Weight (cwt.)
20 Cwts.	=1 Ton.

This weight is used in almost all commercial transactions and in the common dealings of life.

TROY WEIGHT.

24 Grains	=1 Pennyweight
20 Pennyweights	=1 Ounce
12 Ounces	=1 Pound (lb.)

APOTHECARIES' WEIGHT.

20 Grains	=1 Scruple.
3 Scruples	=1 Dram.
8 Drams	=1 Ounce
12 Ounces	=1 Pound. (lb.)

ANGULAR MEASURE, OR DIVISION OF THE CIRCLE.

60 Seconds	=1 Minute.	90 Degrees	=1 Quadrant.
60 Minutes	=1 Degree.	360 Degrees or	
30 Degrees	=1 Sign.	12 Signs	=1 Circumference.

WEIGHTS OF A CUBIC FOOT OF VARIOUS SUBSTANCES.

Loose Earth or Sand	95	Pounds	Clay and Stones	100	Pounds
Common Soil	134	"	Cork	15	"
Strong Soil	127	"	Tallow	59	"
Clay	135	"	Brick	125	"

TO FIND THE MEASUREMENT OF A BOX.

A Box	24	by	16	Inches square, and	22	deep, contains	1	Barrel.
"	24	"	16	"	11	"	½	"
"	16	"	16.8	"	8	"	1	Bushel.
"	12	"	11.2	"	8	"	½	"
"	8	"	8.4	"	8	"	¼	"
"	8	"	8	"	4.2	"	⅛	"
"	7	"	4	"	4.8	"	½	Gallon.
"	7	"	4	"	4.2	"	¼	"

INTEREST TABLE.

At Six per cent. in Dollars and Cents, from one Dollar to ten thousand.								At Seven per cent. in Dollars and Cents, from one Dollar to ten thousand.							
Dollars.	1 Day.	7 Days.	15 Days.	1 Month.	3 Months	6 Mons.	12 Mons.	Dollars.	1 Day.	7 Days.	15 Days.	1 Month.	3 Months	6 Months	12 Months.
	$ c.	$ c.	$ c.	$ c.	$ c.	$ c.	$ c.		$ c.	$ c.	$ c.	$ c.	$ c.	$ c.	$ c.
1	00	00	00¼	00½	01½	03	06	1	00	00	00½	00½	01¾	03½	07
3	00	00¼	00¾	01½	04½	09	18	3	00	00¼	00¾	01¾	05¼	10½	21
5	00	00½	01¼	02½	07½	15	30	5	00	00¾	01¼	03	08¾	17½	35
6	00	00¾	01½	03	09	18	36	6	00	00¾	01½	03½	10½	21	42
7	00	00¾	01¾	03½	10½	22	42	7	00	01	02	04	12¼	24½	49
8	00	01	02	04	12	24	48	8	00	01	02¼	04¾	14	28	56
9	00	01	02¼	04½	13½	27	54	9	00	01¼	02½	05¼	15¾	31½	63
10	00	01¼	02½	05	15	30	60	10	00¼	01¼	03	05¾	17½	35	70
20	00¼	02¼	05	10	30	60	1 20	20	00½	02¾	06	11¾	35	70	1 40
30	00½	03½	07½	15	45	90	1 80	30	00½	04	09	17½	52½	1 05	2 10
40	00¾	04½	10	20	60	1 20	2 40	40	00¾	05½	12	23½	70	1 40	2 80
50	01	06	12½	25	75	1 50	3 00	50	01	06¾	15	29¼	87½	1 75	3 50
100	01½	11¾	25	50	1 50	3 00	6 00	100	02	13½	29	58½	1 75	3 50	7 00
200	03	23½	50	1 00	3 00	6 00	12 00	200	04	27¼	58	1 16¾	3 50	7 00	14 00
300	05	35	75	1 50	4 50	9 00	18 00	300	06	40¾	87½	1 75	5 25	10 50	21 00
400	07	46½	1 00	2 00	6 00	12 00	24 00	400	08	54½	1 17	2 33⅓	7 00	14 00	28 00
500	08	58½	1 25	2 50	7 50	15 00	30 00	500	10	68	1 46	2 91⅔	8 75	17 50	35 00
1000	17	1 16½	2 50	5 00	15 00	30 00	60 00	1000	19½	1 36	2 92	5 83⅓	17 50	35 00	70 00
2000	33	2 33½	5 00	10 00	30 00	60 00	120 00	2000	39	2 72½	5 83	11 66⅔	35 00	70 00	140 00
3000	50	3 50	7 50	15 00	45 00	90 00	180 00	3000	58	4 08½	8 75	17 50	52 50	105 00	210 00
4000	67	4 66½	10 00	20 00	60 00	120 00	240 00	4000	78	5 44½	11 67	23 33⅓	70 00	140 00	280 00
5000	83	5 83½	12 50	25 00	85 00	150 00	300 00	5000	97	6 80½	14 58	29 16⅔	87 50	175 00	350 00
10000	1 67	11 66½	25 00	50 00	150 00	300 00	600 00	10000	1 94	13 61	29 17	58 33	175 00	350 00	700 00

PREMIUM AND DISCOUNT.

Showing the Premium on Gold and the corresponding value of a Gold Dollar in Greenbacks, also the corresponding Discount on Greenbacks, and value of the Greenback Dollar in Specie.

Premium on Gold.	Discn't on Green-backs.	Value of Gold Doll. in Green-backs.	Value of Green-b'ck Dol in Sp'ce.	Premium on Gold.	Disc'nt on Green-backs.	Value of Gold Doll. in Green-backs.	Value of Green-bc'k Dol in Sp'ce.	Premium on Gold.	Disc'nt on Green-backs.	Value of Gold Doll. in Green-backs.	Value of Green-bc'k Dol in Sp'ce.	Premium on Gold.	Disc'nt on Green-backs.	Value of G'ld Dol in Green backs.	Value of Green-b'ck Dol in Sp'ce.
		$ c.	c. 1/1000			$ c.	c. 1/1000			$ c.	c. 1/1000			$ c.	c. 1/10000
1	0.990	1 01	99,009	26	20.635	1 26	79,365	51	34.210	1 51	66,225	76	43.182	1 76	56,818
2	1.961	1 02	98,039	27	21.260	1 27	78,740	52	34.640	1 52	65,789	77	43.503	1 77	56,497
3	2.912	1 03	97,087	28	21.875	1 28	78,125	53	34.775	1 53	65,359	78	43.820	1 78	56,179
4	3.846	1 04	96,153	29	22.480	1 29	77,519	54	35.065	1 54	64,935	79	44.134	1 79	55,866
5	4.762	1 05	95,238	30	23.077	1 30	76,923	55	35.484	1 55	64,516	80	44.444	1 80	55,555
6	5.660	1 06	94,339	31	23.664	1 31	76,335	56	35.897	1 56	64,102	81	44.751	1 81	55,248
7	6.542	1 07	93,457	32	24.242	1 32	75,757	57	36.305	1 57	63,694	82	45.055	1 82	54,945
8	7.407	1 08	92,492	33	24.812	1 33	75,187	58	36.709	1 58	63,291	83	45.355	1 83	54,644
9	8.257	1 09	91,743	34	25.373	1 34	74,626	59	37.107	1 59	62,893	84	45.652	1 84	54,347
10	9.091	1 10	90,909	35	25.926	1 35	74,074	60	37.500	1 60	62,500	85	45.946	1 85	54,054
11	9.910	1 11	90,090	36	26.470	1 36	73,529	61	37.888	1 61	65,111	86	46.236	1 86	53,763
12	10.714	1 12	89,285	37	27.007	1 37	72,992	62	38.271	1 62	61,728	87	46.524	1 87	53,476
13	11.504	1 13	88,495	28	27.536	1 38	72,463	63	38.650	1 63	61,349	88	46.803	1 88	53,191
14	12.280	1 14	87,719	39	28.057	1 39	71,942	64	39.024	1 64	60,975	89	47.090	1 89	52,910
15	13.043	1 15	86,956	40	28.571	1 40	71,428	65	39.394	1 65	60,606	90	47,368	1 90	52,631
16	13.793	1 16	86,206	41	29.078	1 41	70,921	66	39.759	1 66	60,241	91	47.644	1 91	52,356
17	14.530	1 17	85,470	42	29.577	1 42	70,422	67	40.120	1 67	59,880	92	47.916	1 92	52,083
18	15.254	1 18	84,745	43	30.070	1 43	69,930	68	40.476	1 68	59,523	93	48.186	1 93	51,813
19	15 966	1 19	84,033	44	30.555	1 44	69,444	69	40.828	1 69	59,171	94	48.453	1 94	51,546
20	16.666	1 20	83,333	45	31.034	1 45	68,965	70	41.176	1 70	58,823	95	48.718	1 95	51,282
21	17.355	1 21	82,644	46	31.507	1 46	68,493	71	41.520	1 71	58,479	96	48.979	1 96	51,020
22	18 .033	1 22	81,967	47	31.972	1 47	68,027	72	41.860	1 72	58,139	97	49.233	1 97	50,761
23	18.700	1 23	81,300	48	32.432	1 48	67,567	73	42.193	1 73	57,803	98	49.495	1 98	50,505
24	19.355	1 25	80,645	49	32.856	1 49	67,114	74	42.528	1 74	57,471	99	49.748	1 99	50,251
25	20.000	1 24	80,000	50	33.333	1 50	66,666	75	42.856	1 75	57,143	1 00	50.000	2 00	50,000

EXPLANATION OF THE TABLE.—The first column gives the quoted Premium on Gold, and means that so many additional cents on the dollar or dollars on the hundred in Greenbacks are required to pay for one in specie. The second column shows the corresponding discount, or number of cents which must be taken off the Dollar Greenback to give its value in specie. The third column shows the specie value of the Dollar Greenback, corresponding to the quotations of either of the other columns. The fourth column shows the Greenback value of the specie dollar, corresponding to the quotations of either of the two first columns.

BANKING AND EQUATION TABLE.

Showing the number of days from any date in one month. EXAMPLE: How many days from the 2nd of February to the 2nd of August? Look for February at the left hand, and August at the top—in the angle is 181. In leap-year, add one day if February be included.

To	Jan.	Feb.	Mar.	April	May.	June.	July.	Aug.	Sept.	Oct.	Nov.	Dec.
January	365	31	59	90	120	151	181	212	243	273	304	334
February	334	365	28	59	89	120	150	181	212	242	273	303
March	306	337	365	31	61	92	122	143	184	214	245	275
April	275	306	334	365	30	61	91	122	153	183	214	244
May	245	276	304	335	365	31	61	92	123	153	184	214
June	214	245	273	304	334	365	30	61	92	122	153	183
July	184	215	243	274	304	335	365	31	62	92	123	153
August	153	184	212	243	274	304	334	365	31	61	92	122
September	122	153	181	212	242	273	303	334	365	30	61	91
October	92	123	151	182	212	243	273	304	335	365	31	61
November	61	92	120	151	181	212	242	273	304	334	365	30
December	31	62	90	121	151	182	212	243	274	304	335	365

TO REDUCE STERLING INTO CURRENCY.

To reduce Currency into dollars and cents.

Reduce the sum to sixpences, and add a cipher if there be no odd pence in the sum to be reduced; and if there be odd pence, add their equivalent in cents. The result will be the sum in cents.

Example.— Reduce £5 1s. 0d., to dollars and cents.

```
 £5: 1: 0
 20
 ———
 101
   2
 ———
 202 sixpences.
 10
 ———
2020 cents.
```

Answer, $20.20.

To reduce Sterling into dollars and cents.

If the value of the sterling money be reckoned at par of exchange, then substitute for every pound sterling £1 4s. 4d., and for every fraction of a pound sterling a similar fraction of £1 4s. 4d. The result in currency reduce by the *currency* table. If the value of the sterling money be calculated at the current rate of exchange, convert into currency as above reckoning the value of the pound sterling at the exchange rate, in lieu of £1 4s. 4d., and the fractions proportionately.

Example.—Reduce £1 15s. sterling to dollars and cents, calculating the pound sterling at par of exchange.

```
£1 stg. = £1:  4: 4 cy.
10s.    =  0: 12: 2
5s.     =  0:  6: 1
        ———— £2: 2: 7 : cy.,
```

which is by the first table, $8.51⅓.

TABLE FOR CALCULATING PERIODICAL PAYMENTS.

p. day.	p. week	p. mo.	p. ¼ yr.	p. ½ yr.	p. year.	p. day.	p. week	p. mo.	p. ¼ year.	p. ½ year.	p. year.
0 1	$0 7	$0 28	$0 91¼	$1 82½	$3 65	$0 60	$4 20	$16 80	$54 75	$109 50	$219 00
0 2	0 14	0 56	1 82½	3 65	7 30	0 70	4 90	19 60	63 87½	127 75	255 50
0 3	0 21	0 84	2 73¾	5 47½	10 95	0 75	5 25	21 00	68 43¾	136 87½	273 75
0 4	0 28	1 12	3 65	7 30	14 60	0 80	5 60	22 40	73 00	146 00	292 00
0 5	0 35	1 40	4 56¼	9 12½	18 25	0 90	6 30	25 20	82 12½	164 25	328 50
0 6	0 42	1 68	5 47½	10 95	21 90	1 00	7 00	28 00	91 25	182 50	365 00
0 7	0 49	1 96	6 38¾	12 77½	25 55	2 00	14 00	56 00	182 50	365 00	730 00
0 8	0 56	2 24	7 40	14 60	29 20	2 50	17 50	70 00	228 12½	456 25	912 50
0 9	0 63	2 52	8 21¼	16 42½	32 85	3 00	21 00	84 00	273 75	547 50	1095 00
0 10	0 70	2 80	9 12½	18 25	36 50	4 00	28 00	112 00	365 00	730 00	1460 00
0 12½	0 87½	3 50	11 40⅝	22 81¼	45 62½	5 00	35 42	140 00	456 25	912 50	1825 00
0 16⅔	1 16⅔	4 66⅔	15 20⅚	30 41⅔	60 83⅓	6 00	42 00	168 00	547 50	1095 00	2190 00
0 20	1 40	5 60	18 25	36 50	73 00	7 00	49 00	196 00	638 75	1277 50	2555 00
0 25	1 75	7 00	22 81¼	45 62½	91 25	7 50	52 50	210 00	684 37½	1368 75	2737 50
0 30	2 10	8 40	27 37½	54 75	109 50	8 00	56 00	224 00	730 00	1460 00	2920 00
0 40	2 80	11 20	36 50	73 00	146 00	9 00	63 00	252 00	821 25	1642 50	3285 00
0 50	3 50	14 00	45 62½	91 25	182 50	10 00	70 00	280 00	912 50	1825 00	3650 00

OFFICE OF THE SECRETARY OF STATE,

Ottawa, 14th May, 1868.

NOTICE is hereby given that parties requiring PASSPORTS, must apply until further notice, to this Department, transmitting at the same time a certificate of identity, accompanied in each case with a description of the applicant, signed by a Justice of the Peace, and also the fee of One Dollar.

HECTOR L. LANGEVIN,

Secretary of State.

DEPARTMENT OF THE SECRETARY OF STATE OF CANADA,

Ottawa, 23rd October, 1868.

PUBLIC NOTICE is hereby given that all communications relating to Indian Affairs and Lands, or to the Affairs of Ordnance Lands belonging to Canada, are in future to be addressed to "The Honorable the Secretary of State for Canada, Ottawa."

ETIENNE PARENT,

Under Secretary of State for Canada.

DOMINION OF CANADA.

EMIGRATION

TO THE

PROVINCE OF ONTARIO.

To Capitalists, Tenant Farmers, Agricultural Laborers, Day Laborers, and all parties desirous of improving their circumstances by Emigrating to a New Country.

Attention is invited to the great advantages presented by the Province of Ontario to various classes of new settlers. Persons living on the interest of their money can easily get 8 per cent on first class security in the Province of Ontario.

Tenant Farmers, with limited capital, can buy and stock a freehold estate in Ontario with the money needed to carry on a small farm in Britain. Good cleared land with a dwelling and barn on it, can be purchased in desirable localities at from 20 to 50 dollars, or £4 to £10 sterling., per acre. Farm hands can readily get work at good wages with their board found.

INDUCEMENTS TO INTENDING EMIGRANTS:

FREE GRANTS OF LAND TO ACTUAL SETTLERS.

LAND GIVEN AWAY TO ALL COMERS over 18 years of age.

A FAMILY OF SEVERAL PERSONS CAN SECURE A LARGE BLOCK OF LAND GRATIS.

The Government of Ontario offers as a Free Grant to any actual settler over 18 years of age, One Hundred Acres of Land in the Free Grant Districts.

THE FREE GRANT LANDS ARE EASY OF ACCESS.

There are Daily Mails between Toronto and the Free Grant Districts.

Parties desirous of fuller information concerning the Province of Ontario, will apply personally, or by letter, to WM. DIXON, Emigrant Agent, 11 Adam Street, Adelphi, London; or to any of the Imperial or Dominion Emigrant Agents in Europe; or to the GRAND TRUNK RAILWAY OFFICES, No. 21 Old Broad Street, London; or to the GREAT WESTERN, OF CANADA, RAILWAY OFFICE, 126 Gresham House, Old Broad Street, London, E. C.; or to the NORTHERN RAILWAY OFFICE, Messrs. CUTBILL, SON & DE LUNGO, No. 13 Gresham Street, London, E. C.; or to the CANADA COMPANY, No. 1 East India Avenue, Leadenhall Street, London; or to ALLAN, BROS. & CO., James Street, Liverpool; JAMES and ALEXANDER ALLAN, Great Clyde Street, Glasgow; ALLAN, BROS. & Co., Foyle Street, Londonderry; by whom Pamphlets, giving detailed information, maps, &c., will be supplied.

Emigrants bound for the Province of Ontario, will take vessel to Quebec, and proceed westward, either by Steamboat or Railway.

By reference to the Map, supplied by Government gratis, any desired point can be selected from which to look for a New Home.

JOHN CARLING,

Commissioner of Agriculture and Public Works for the Province of Ontario.

Printed in the USA
CPSIA information can be obtained
at www.ICGtesting.com
LVHW052133010324
773316LV00001B/5

9 781021 398000